KU-499-725

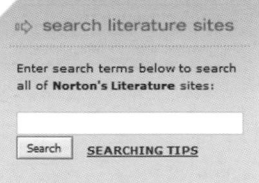

w w n o r t o n . c o m / l i t e r a t u r e
norton literature online

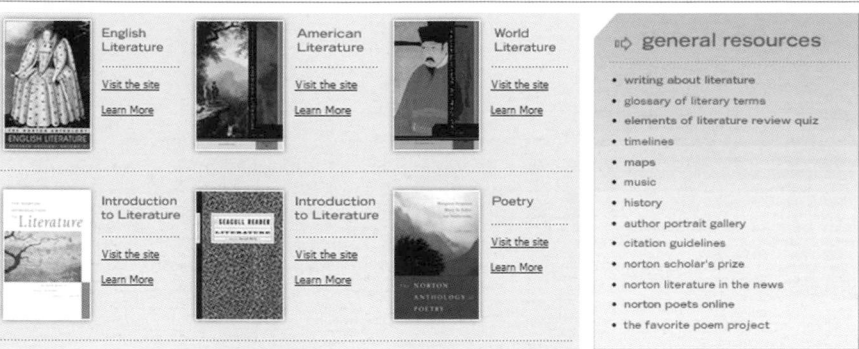

Welcome to Norton Literature Online, outstanding resources for students of literature

search literature sites

Enter search terms below to search all of Norton's Literature sites:

[Search] **SEARCHING TIPS**

English Literature
Visit the site
Learn More

American Literature
Visit the site
Learn More

World Literature
Visit the site
Learn More

Introduction to Literature
Visit the site
Learn More

Introduction to Literature
Visit the site
Learn More

Poetry
Visit the site
Learn More

general resources

- writing about literature
- glossary of literary terms
- elements of literature review quiz
- timelines
- maps
- music
- history
- author portrait gallery
- citation guidelines
- norton scholar's prize
- norton literature in the news
- norton poets online
- the favorite poem project

NORTON LITERATURE ONLINE

wwnorton.com/literature

Visit this exciting gateway to the outstanding online literature resources available from Norton.

Detach your registration card. On the front of the card you will find a registration code. This code offers free access to the site for twelve months. Once you register, you can change your password however you wish.

If the registration card has been removed from your textbook, visit wwnorton.com/literature for instructions regarding site access.

HOW TO ACCESS THIS WEB SITE:

STEP 1: Go to wwnorton.com/literature.

STEP 2: Click on "Access Norton Literature Online."

STEP 3: Click on "First-Time User? Register Here."

STEP 4: Fill out all fields and click "Submit." Your password is set instantly (and a confirmation will be emailed to you).

STEP 5: Click "Enter the Site." Wait for the Web site to load.

You're in!

Registration is good for 12 months from activation.

REGISTRATION CODE ➤

OSIZ-MEEF

The Norton Anthology
of Poetry

FIFTH EDITION

The Norton Anthology
of Poetry

FIFTH EDITION

Margaret Ferguson
UNIVERSITY OF CALIFORNIA, DAVIS

Mary Jo Salter
MOUNT HOLYOKE COLLEGE

Jon Stallworthy
OXFORD UNIVERSITY

W • W • NORTON & COMPANY • New York • London

W. W. Norton & Company has been independent since its founding in 1923, when William Warder Norton and Mary D. Herter Norton first published lectures delivered at the People's Institute, the adult education division of New York City's Cooper Union. The Nortons soon expanded their program beyond the Institute, publishing books by celebrated academics from America and abroad. By mid-century, the two major pillars of Norton's publishing program—trade books and college texts—were firmly established. In the 1950s, the Norton family transferred control of the company to its employees, and today—with a staff of four hundred and a comparable number of trade, college, and professional titles published each year—W. W. Norton & Company stands as the largest and oldest publishing house owned wholly by its employees.

The text of this book is composed in Fairfield Medium
with the display set in Bernhard Modern.
Composition by Binghamton Valley Composition.
Manufacturing by R. R. Donnelley & Sons, Inc.

Editor: Julia Reidhead
Developmental Editor: Kurt Wildermuth
Electronic Media and Ancillaries Editor: Eileen Connell
Assistant Editor: Erin Dye
Permissions Manager and Associate: Nancy Rodwan, Margaret Gorenstein
Book Designer: Antonina Krass
Production Manager: Diane O'Connor
Managing Editor, College: Marian Johnson

Library of Congress Cataloging-in-Publication Data
The Norton anthology of poetry / [edited by] Margaret Ferguson, Mary Jo Salter, Jon Stallworthy.—5th ed.
    p. cm.
Includes bibliographical references and index.

ISBN 0-393-97920-2 (pbk.)

1. English poetry. 2. American poetry. I. Ferguson, Margaret, W., 1948–   II. Salter, Mary Jo. III. Stallworthy, Jon.

PR1174.N6 2004b
821.008—dc22   2004058100

W. W. Norton & Company, Inc., 500 Fifth Avenue, New York, N.Y. 10110
www.wwnorton.com

W. W. Norton & Company Ltd., Castle House, 75/76 Wells Street, London W1T 3QT

7 8 9 0

Contents

Preface to the Fifth Edition

What is a poem? The definitions offered over the centuries are almost as numerous as the examples in this book. Although no two people may settle on the qualities all poems share, it might not be foolish to say that the best definition of poetry encompasses all definitions—even those that contradict each other. Poetry, after all, encourages us to embrace paradox and contradiction, the unexpected, the never-thought-of (and also, paradoxically, the universal, the shared, the familiar). Poetry began as song and continues as song; it is usually best appreciated when spoken or sung by a human voice. Since the advent of writing, however, the act of reading a poem on the page has added new dimensions to our experience. In these pages, we necessarily feature the written pleasures of poetry—even in those poems that were meant originally as song. What all these poems share, we hope, is something in the manner of their telling that cannot be achieved any better way. The best poems, too, make a claim on our memory. W. H. Auden wrote that "of the many definitions of poetry, the simplest is still the best: 'memorable speech.' " Many poems in this book have been part of English-speaking culture for centuries, while the newest poems here might well lodge in readers' memories in the future.

This Fifth Edition of *The Norton Anthology of Poetry* brings together more than eighteen hundred such records from "the round earth's imagined corners." We have set out to provide readers with a wide and deep sampling of the best poetry written in English. That previous editions have succeeded in this endeavor, within the limits of the pages available in a single volume, seems manifest in the acceptance of those editions by teachers and students alike. But as our friend and advisor M. H. Abrams has said in another context, "a vital literary culture is always on the move," both in the appearance of new works and in the altering response to existing texts: hence a Fifth Edition, which broadens and refines that cultural tradition. We believe that the vitality of our literary culture has been demonstrated by this collaboration.

In assembling the new edition, we have aimed to respond to the practical criticism and informed suggestions provided by teachers who have used the anthology. Our goal has been to make the anthology an even better teaching tool for their classes. In response to instructors' requests, a number of important works by major poets have been added to the Fifth Edition, among them a selection from *Beowulf,* in Seamus Heaney's prize-winning translation; Chaucer, "The Wife of Bath's Prologue and Tale"; Spenser, "The Shepheardes Calender: Aprill" and book 1, canto 2 of *The Faerie Queene*; Shakespeare, ten additional sonnets; Milton, from Book 4 of *Paradise Lost*; Wroth, seven additional sonnets; Swift, "Verses on the Death of Dr. Swift"; Keats, "Lamia"; Eliot, "Little Gidding" and "The Hollow Men." We have worked toward a balance between the older and the newer. Instructors committed to teaching the rich diversity—of forms and techniques as well as historical and geographic range—of English-language poetry in the twentieth century will welcome the Fifth Edition's increased attention to world poetry in English as well as the greater range of American voices. Among the seventeen poets newly included are Richard Wright, Weldon Kees, Robyn Sarah, Charles Bernstein, Anne Carson, Vikram Seth, and Simon Armitage. In addition to expanding representation, we have reconsidered, and in some instances reselected, the work of poets retained from earlier editions. Among the poets reselected are John Ashbery, Adrienne Rich, Derek Walcott, Seamus Heaney, Michael Ondaatje, Yusef Komunyakaa, Agha Shahid Ali, Jorie Graham, Carol Ann Duffy, and Li-Young Li.

The vernacular tradition, in which the poet "Anon" has spoken eloquently over the centuries, is brought forward from medieval lyrics and Elizabethan and Jacobean poems to African American spirituals and popular ballads of the twentieth century. Teachers can trace the history of the epic by comparing openings and selections from *Beowulf, The Faerie Queene, Paradise Lost,* Killigrew's (unfinished) *Alexandreis,* Pope's *Rape of the Lock,* and Wordsworth's *Prelude.* The tradition of light verse, too, can be traced from Lewis Carroll, W. S. Gilbert, and Edward Lear to Ogden Nash and Dorothy Parker to Wendy Cope, James Fenton, and John Updike.

We continue to expand opportunities for teaching intertextual "dialogues" among poets: the addition of Donne's "A Hymn to God the Father," for instance, allows that poem to be read with Jonson's hymn of the same name. Among the pairs entirely new to this edition: Elizabeth Bishop's "Casabianca" responds to Felicia Dorothea Hemans's poem of that title, which was, as Bishop knew, one of the most often taught and recited poems of the nineteenth century. Also new are Aphra Behn's "The Disappointment" and John Wilmot, earl of Rochester's "The Imperfect Enjoyment," which together form a dialogue about impotence. Other poetic dialogues present English-language responses to foreign sources, which may be secular—a Petrarchan sonnet, for instance, such as the one rendered in English by Wyatt ("Whoso List to Hunt") and by Spenser (*Amoretti* 67)—or biblical: we now include four versions of Psalms 58 and 114, ranging from Mary Sidney's to Christopher Smart's. Some poetic conversations present different perspectives on culturally fraught issues: a set of eighteenth-century poems on "spleen"—a malady strikingly like the one we call depression today—includes texts by Anne Finch, Alexander Pope, and Matthew Green; a newly augmented cluster of poems on the meaning of the color black includes Edward Herbert's "Sonnet of Black Beauty," Mary Wroth's sonnet 22 ("Like to the Indians)," Henry King's "The Boy's Answer to the Blackmoor," and Phillis Wheatley's "On Being Brought from Africa to America." We continue to emphasize call-and-response patterns that extend across periods: our selection from William Cowper's *The Task* includes the lines that inspired part of Coleridge's "Frost at Midnight"; and we invite readers to consider Marlowe's "The Passionate Shepherd to His Love" with Raleigh's "The Nymph's Reply to the Shepherd," then both of these poems with C. Day Lewis's elegiac, war-shocked "Two Songs," which reprises them as well as Jean Elliot's "The Flowers of the Forest." In turn, Elliot's and Lewis's poems may be set in dialogue with Pete Seeger's modern ballad "Where Have All the Flowers Gone?" To bring these potential dialogues to readers' attention, we have provided a number of cross-referencing annotations and expanded the discussion of intertextual pairs and groups in the Course Guide.

The Fifth Edition includes not merely the lyric and the epigrammatic but instead the entire range of poetic genres in English. Among the many longer poems are Aemilia Lanyer's "The Description of Cooke-ham" and Richard Howard's "Nikolaus Mardruz to his Master Ferdinand, Count of Tyrol, 1565," as well as teachable excerpts from John Skelton's "Phillip Sparow" and "Colin Clout," Charlotte Smith's "Beachy Head," Elizabeth Barrett Browning's *Aurora Leigh*, William Carlos Williams's "Asphodel, That Greeny Flower," and James Merrill's *The Changing Light at Sandover*. Although it is impossible to include all of *The Faerie Queene, Paradise Lost, The Prelude, Song of Myself,* or *The Dream Songs,* readers will find representative and self-sufficient selections from each of these works.

Three other features within the anthology facilitate its usefulness in the classroom. An indispensable aid in helping students become better readers and interpreters of poetry, Margaret Ferguson's new essay, "Poetic Syntax," addresses a perennial stumbling block—how to recognize, describe, analyze, and appreciate syntactic ambiguity in English poetry. Among the "types of ambiguity" (to borrow William Empson's phrase) discussed in the essay are those involving parts of speech, elisions, and punctuation, as well as the difficulties that the poet's traditional license to invert normal English word order can create for readers. Jon Stallworthy's essay, "Versification," has been selectively expanded to offer clearer explanations of rhyme, plus more attention to forms such as prose poetry, found poetry, and shaped poetry and to the metrics of Old and Middle English and Renaissance verse. In addition, the appendix of biographical sketches has been updated, streamlined, and cross-referenced to the individual poets.

Editorial Procedures

The order is chronological, poets appearing according to their dates of birth and their poems according to dates of publication in volume form (or estimated dates of composition in the case of Old and Middle English poets). The publication date is printed at the end of each poem, and to the right; when two dates are printed, they indicate published versions that differ in an important way. Dates on the left, when given, are those of composition. Many of our texts are modernized to help readers, but we continue an ongoing project of remarking editorial decisions in annotations, to let teachers and students consider issues pertaining to the materiality and complex histories of many poems in the anthology.

Annotation in the Fifth Edition has been thoroughly revised. In keeping with recent developments in editing, we have introduced notes that mention significant textual variants. These are intended to spark classroom discussion about poems whose multiple versions challenge the idea of textual "authority." We have added many notes that provide contextual information and clarify archaisms and allusions; however, as in previous editions, we minimize commentary that is interpretive rather than, in a limited sense, explanatory. As further help with teaching poetic syntax, we have added notes that discuss syntactical difficulties.

Marginal glosses for archaic, dialect, or unfamiliar words have been reconsidered and, for many poems, increased in number. For the convenience of the student, we have used square brackets to indicate titles supplied by the editors and have, whenever a portion of a text has been omitted, indicated that omission with three asterisks.

Instructors have long made inventive use of the rich intertextuality of *The Norton Anthology of Poetry*. Three supplemental resources—two in print and one online—expand the possibilities for teachers who wish to convey how poems speak to each other across time, place, and tradition through literal borrowings, form, theme, cultural concern, and conventions. *Teaching with* The Norton Anthology of Poetry: *A Guide for Instructors,* by Tyler Hoffman, makes available to teachers varied reading lists that help shape a course or courses along a number of lines—according to form, figurative language, traditions and countertraditions, and topics—and to establish relationships among poets and poems of different genres, periods, and concerns. Also for instructors, *Teaching Poetry: A Handbook of Exercises for Large and Small Classes,* by Allan J. Gedalof, offers innovative ideas and exercises for structuring a class centered on performance and discussion. Instructors should visit www.wwnorton.com for further information about obtaining these materials. For students, a new Web site, *The Norton Poetry Workshop Online* (www.wwnorton.com/nap), prepared by James F. Knapp (based on his innovative *Norton Poetry Workshop* CD-ROM), contains texts and recordings of thirty of the most-taught poems from the anthology, supported by a rich array of multimedia, exercises, and study aids.

We are indebted to our predecessors, the editors emeriti of *The Norton Anthology of Poetry,* whose presence on the title page signals their ongoing contribution, and to M. H. Abrams, advisor to the Norton English list, for his wise and ready counsel. We also thank the staff at Norton who helped this book come into being: Julia Reidhead used her remarkable resources of energy, intelligence, and good humor to keep the book on course; Diane O'Connor guided the book through production; Erin Dye gracefully facilitated communications and meetings; Nancy Rodwan and Margaret Gorenstein handled the massive task of securing permissions; and Eileen Connell capably oversaw the interrelated projects of the Web site and the Course Guide. Our development editor, Kurt Wildermuth, paid attention to (and in many cases perfected) the book's "minute particulars" in ways that William Blake would have admired. Kurt also kept a steady eye on the book's larger shape and primary goal: to bring English-language poems originating in different times and places to modern readers—who will, we hope, find pleasure within these covers.

MARGARET FERGUSON
MARY JO SALTER
JON STALLWORTHY

Acknowledgments

Among our many critics, advisors, and friends, the following were of special help in preparing the Fifth Edition. For assisting us in researching and preparing texts and other materials, thanks to John Barrell, Mike Bell, Steve Cassal, Alfred E. David, Ed Doughtie, Harriet Guest, S. Kristin Hall, Katie Kalpin, Laura Maestrelli, Andy Majeske, Frank Murphy, Marijane Osborn, and Beth Robertson. For preparing the biographical sketches, thanks to Sherri Vanden Akker and Jane Potter. Special thanks for their invaluable help goes to Andrea Bundy, Sandie Byrne, Sarita Cargas, Stephen L. Carr, Tony Edwards, Barry Goldensohn, Linda Gregerson, Marshall Grossman, Jenny Houlsby, Tim Kendall, Elizabeth Langland (dean of arts and letters at the University of California at Davis), David Simpson, Claire M. Waters, and Carolyn Williams.

We take pleasure in thanking those teachers who provided critiques and questionnaire responses: Paul F. Betz (Georgetown University), Michael Borich (Southwest Missouri State University), Suzannah Bowser (Humboldt State University), Joel J. Brattin (Worcester Polytechnic University), Seeta Chaganti (University of California, Davis), John Cobb (Wofford College), Rian Cooney (Santa Rosa Junior College), Martha Crowe (East Tennessee State University), Diana Cruz (Boston College), Jane Donawerth (University of Maryland), Sheila P. Donohue (Northwestern University), Beverly Friend (Oakton Community College), Julie Funderburk (University of North Carolina at Greensboro), Barry Goldensohn (Skidmore College), Marshall Grossman (University of Maryland), Brooke Haley (UC Irvine), Amy Hassinger (Iowa State University), Jeremy Hawthorn (Norweigan University of Science and Technology), Patrick Hicks (University of St. Thomas), Emily A. Bernhard Jackson (Brandeis University), Albert C. Labriola (Duquesne University), Mark Larabee (U.S. Naval Academy), Cynthia Lee Katona (Ohlone College), Eric Le May (Northwestern), Julia Levine, Tim Kendall (University of Bristol), Terry L. Kennedy (University of North Carolina at Greensboro), Millie M. Kidd (Mount St. Mary's College), Stephanie Kuduk (Wesleyan University), Herbert Lindenberger (Stanford University), Leon Litvack (University of Belfast), Debbie López (University of Texas at San Antonio), Christopher Lurasik (Boston University), Stacey Margolis (University of Utah), Patrick McGuire (University of Wisconsin at Parkside), Geoffrey Morley-Mower (James Madison University), Saundra Morris (Bucknell University), Micki Myers (University of Pittsburgh), Laura Orem (Villa Julie College), Kirk Nesset (Allegheny College), Larry Newman, Carol Percy (University of Toronto), Dwight Purdy (University of Minnesota, Morris), Elizabeth Robertson (University of Colorado at Boulder), Jeffrey Robinson (University of Colorado at Boulder), Catherine Robson (University of California, Davis), J. N. R. Saunders (University of Newcastle), Paul

Schlicke (University of Aberdeen), Mark Silverberg (Dalhousie University), Ellen M. Smith (University of Pittsburgh), David St. John (University of Southern California), Carol Simpson Stern (Northwestern University), John Thomas Stovall (National-Louis University), Herbert Tucker (University of Virginia), Anita Tully (Nicholls State University), Peter Van Egmond (University of Maryland), Claire Waters (University of California, Davis), Sallie P. Wolf (Anapahoe Community College).

CÆDMON'S HYMN[1]

Nu sculon *herigean*	*h*eofonrices Weard
Now we must praise	heaven-kingdom's Guardian,
*M*eotodes *m*eahte	and his *m*odgeþanc
the Measurer's might	and his mind-plans,
*w*eorc *W*uldor-Fæder	swa *h*e *w*undra gehwæs
the work of the Glory-Father,	when he of wonders of every one,
*e*ce Drihten	*or* onstealde
eternal Lord,	the beginning established.[2]

5
He ærest sceop	*i*elda[3] bearnum
He first created	for men's sons
*h*eofon to *h*rofe	*h*alig Scyppend
heaven as a roof,	holy Creator;
ða *m*iddangeard	*m*oncynnes Weard
then middle-earth	mankind's Guardian,
*e*ce Drihten	*æ*fter teode
eternal Lord,	afterwards made—
*f*irum *f*oldan	*Fr*ea *æ*lmihtig
for men earth,	Master almighty.

1. Cædmon's "Hymn" is probably the earliest extant Old English poem (composed sometime between 658 and 680). Old English texts have been preserved in copies of the Latin *Ecclesiastical History of the English People*, written by the great scholar Bede (ca. 673–735). Bede tells how Cædmon, an illiterate herdsman employed by the monastery of Whitby, miraculously received the gift of religious song, was received by the monks as a lay brother, and founded a school of Christian poetry. At feasts where the farmhands took turns singing and playing the harp, Cædmon would withdraw to his bed in the stable whenever the harp was passed his way. One night a man appeared to him in a dream and commanded, "Cædmon, sing me something." When Cædmon protested that he didn't know how to sing, the man insisted and told him to sing about the Creation. "At this, Cædmon immediately began to sing verses in praise of God the Creator, which he had never heard before." (After transcribing the hymn, Bede remarks that "this is the general sense but not the exact order of the words that [Cædmon] sang in his sleep; for it is impossible to make a literal translation, no matter how well written, of poetry into another language without losing some of the beauty and dignity." Bede refers here to his translation of the poem from Old English to Latin, but the poem also changes significantly from an oral to a written medium.) After Cædmon told the story to his foreman, the monks tested him to establish that the gift was from God, and he composed other religious poems based on biblical stories they told him. The Germanic tribes had oral poets (the *Beowulf* poet portrays such a bard, or "scop," performing in the mead hall), and Cædmon might have been trained as such a singer but concealed his knowledge of pagan poetry—what Bede calls "vain and idle songs." The "Hymn" is typical of Germanic verse: two half-lines, each containing two stressed and two or more unstressed syllables, linked by alliteration; interweaving of syntactically parallel formulaic expressions. For example, eight of the poem's half-lines consist of varying epithets for God: "Weard" (Guardian), "Meotod" (Measurer), "Wuldor-Fæderu" (Glory-Father), "Drihten" (Lord), "Scyppend" (Creator), and "Frea" (Master). The poem is given here in a West Saxon form with a literal interlinear translation by John Pope. In Old English spelling, æ (as in Cædmon's name and line 3) is a vowel symbol that has not survived; it represents the vowel of Modern English *cat*; Þ (line 2) and ð (line 7) both represent the sound *th*. The large space in the middle of the line indicates the caesura. The alliterating sounds that connect the half-lines have been italicized.

2. I.e., when he established the beginning of every wonder.

3. Later manuscript copies have "eorÞan" (earth) in place of "ælda" (West Saxon *ield*, meaning "men's").

FROM BEOWULF[1]

[Introduction: History and Praise of the Danes; Account of Grendel's Attacks on Heorot]

So. The Spear-Danes in days gone by
and the kings who ruled them had courage and greatness.
We have heard of those princes' heroic campaigns.
   There was Shield Sheafson,[2] scourge of many tribes,
5   a wrecker of mead-benches, rampaging among foes.
This terror of the hall-troops had come far.
A foundling to start with, he would flourish later on
as his powers waxed and his worth was proved.
In the end each clan on the outlying coasts
10   beyond the whale-road had to yield to him
and begin to pay tribute. That was one good king.
   Afterward a boy-child was born to Shield,
a cub in the yard, a comfort sent
by God to that nation. He knew what they had tholed,°   suffered
15   the long times and troubles they'd come through
without a leader; so the Lord of Life,
the glorious Almighty, made this man renowned.
Shield had fathered a famous son:
Beow's name was known through the north.
20   And a young prince must be prudent like that,
giving freely while his father lives
so that afterward in age when fighting starts
steadfast companions will stand by him
and hold the line. Behavior that's admired
25   is the path to power among people everywhere.
   Shield was still thriving when his time came
and he crossed over into the Lord's keeping.
His warrior band did what he bade them
when he laid down the law among the Danes:
30   they shouldered him out to the sea's flood,[3]
the chief they revered who had long ruled them.
A ring-whorled prow rode in the harbor,
ice-clad, outbound, a craft for a prince.
They stretched their beloved lord in his boat,
35   laid out by the mast, amidships,
the great ring-giver. Far-fetched treasures
were piled upon him, and precious gear.
I never heard before of a ship so well furbished

1. This epic poem was written in an Old English dialect sometime between the first part of the eighth century and the tenth century. Preserved in a late tenth-century manuscript, it was probably composed by a literate poet following the versification and style of Germanic oral poetry; the translation here is by the Irish poet Seamus Heaney (b. 1939; see pp. 1899–1910). The poem deals with the Germanic forebears of the English people, specifically the Danes, who inhabited the Danish island of Zealand, and the Geats of southern Sweden. In recounting the heroic feats of Beowulf of the Geats, the poem mixes elements of Christian tradition (the Germanic settlers in England had been converted to Christianity by the time the poem was written) with the heroic ideals of a non-Christian, warrior society.
2. A mythical king of the Scyldings (Danes), of divine origin and associated with agricultural fertility. Shield is the father of Beowulf the Dane, not Beowulf of the Geats.
3. Sea burials for chieftains, such as this one for Shield Sheafson, were probably more mythical than historical.

with battle-tackle, bladed weapons
40 and coats of mail. The massed treasure
was loaded on top of him: it would travel far
on out into the ocean's sway.
They decked his body no less bountifully
with offerings than those first ones did
45 who cast him away when he was a child
and launched him alone out over the waves.[4]
And they set a gold standard up
high above his head and let him drift
to wind and tide, bewailing him
50 and mourning their loss. No man can tell,
no wise man in hall or weathered veteran
knows for certain who salvaged that load.

    Then it fell to Beow to keep the forts.
He was well regarded and ruled the Danes
55 for a long time after his father took leave
of his life on earth. And then his heir,
the great Halfdane, held sway
for as long as he lived, their elder and warlord.
He was four times a father, this fighter prince:
60 one by one they entered the world,
Heorogar, Hrothgar, the good Halga,
and a daughter, I have heard, who was Onela's queen,
a balm in bed to the battle-scarred Swede.

    The fortunes of war favored Hrothgar.
65 Friends and kinsmen flocked to his ranks,
young followers, a force that grew
to be a mighty army. So his mind turned
to hall-building: he handed down orders
for men to work on a great mead-hall
70 meant to be a wonder of the world forever;
it would be his throne-room and there he would dispense
his God-given goods to young and old—
but not the common land or people's lives.
Far and wide through the world, I have heard,
75 orders for work to adorn that wallstead
were sent to many peoples. And soon it stood there
finished and ready, in full view,
the hall of halls. Heorot was the name
he had settled on it, whose utterance was law.
80 Nor did he renege, but doled out rings
and torques[5] at the table. The hall towered,
its gables wide and high and awaiting
a barbarous burning. That doom abided,
but in time it would come: the killer instinct
85 unleashed among in-laws, the blood-lust rampant.[6]

    Then a powerful demon, a prowler through the dark,

---

4. Shield appeared from the sea as a child, apparently on a divinely ordained mission.
5. Collars, necklaces, or bracelets. Early Germanic tribal kings, such as Hrothgar here, traditionally presented retainers with rings or other treasures to seal a mutual bond of loyalty between them.
6. An allusion to the future destruction of Heorot in a family feud.

nursed a hard grievance. It harrowed him
to hear the din of the loud banquet
every day in the hall, the harp being struck
90   and the clear song of a skilled poet
telling with mastery of man's beginnings,
how the Almighty had made the earth
a gleaming plain girdled with waters;
in His splendor He set the sun and the moon
95   to be earth's lamplight, lanterns for men,
and filled the broad lap of the world
with branches and leaves; and quickened life
in every other thing that moved.
     So times were pleasant for the people there
100   until finally one, a fiend out of hell,
began to work his evil in the world.
Grendel was the name of this grim demon
haunting the marches, marauding round the heath
and the desolate fens; he had dwelt for a time
105   in misery among the banished monsters,
Cain's clan, whom the Creator had outlawed
and condemned as outcasts.[7] For the killing of Abel
the Eternal Lord had exacted a price:
Cain got no good from committing that murder
110   because the Almighty made him anathema,
and out of the curse of his exile there sprang
ogres and elves and evil phantoms
and the giants too who strove with God
time and again until He gave them their reward.
115   So, after nightfall, Grendel set out
for the lofty house, to see how the Ring-Danes
were settling into it after their drink,
and there he came upon them, a company of the best
asleep from their feasting, insensible to pain
120   and human sorrow. Suddenly then
the God-cursed brute was creating havoc:
greedy and grim, he grabbed thirty men
from their resting places and rushed to his lair,
flushed up and inflamed from the raid,
125   blundering back with the butchered corpses.
     Then as dawn brightened and the day broke,
Grendel's powers of destruction were plain:
their wassail° was over, they wept to heaven   *revelry*
and mourned under morning. Their mighty prince,
130   the storied leader, sat stricken and helpless,
humiliated by the loss of his guard,
bewildered and stunned, staring aghast
at the demon's trail, in deep distress.
He was numb with grief, but got no respite
135   for one night later merciless Grendel

---

7. Grendel's descent is traced back to the biblical
Cain, son of Adam and Eve. For the crime of killing
his brother Abel, Cain was marked by God and sen-
tenced to roam the earth as an outcast (Genesis
4).

struck again with more gruesome murders.
Malignant by nature, he never showed remorse.
It was easy then to meet with a man
shifting himself to a safer distance
140 to bed in the bothies,[8] for who could be blind
to the evidence of his eyes, the obviousness
of the hall-watcher's hate? Whoever escaped
kept a weather-eye open and moved away.
    So Grendel ruled in defiance of right,
145 one against all, until the greatest house
in the world stood empty, a deserted wallstead.
For twelve winters, seasons of woe,
the lord of the Shieldings suffered under
his load of sorrow; and so, before long,
150 the news was known over the whole world.
Sad lays were sung about the beset king,
the vicious raids and ravages of Grendel,
his long and unrelenting feud,
nothing but war; how he would never
155 parley or make peace with any Dane
nor stop his death-dealing nor pay the death-price.[9]
No counselor could ever expect
fair reparation from those rabid hands.
All were endangered; young and old
160 were hunted down by that dark death-shadow
who lurked and swooped in the long nights
on the misty moors; nobody knows
where these reavers° from hell roam on their errands.   *marauders*
    So Grendel waged his lonely war,
165 inflicting constant cruelties on the people,
atrocious hurt. He took over Heorot,
haunted the glittering hall after dark,
but the throne itself, the treasure-seat,
he was kept from approaching; he was the Lord's outcast.
170   These were hard times, heartbreaking
for the prince of the Shieldings; powerful counselors,
the highest in the land, would lend advice,
plotting how best the bold defenders
might resist and beat off sudden attacks.
175 Sometimes at pagan shrines they vowed
offerings to idols, swore oaths
that the killer of souls[1] might come to their aid
and save the people. That was their way,
their heathenish hope; deep in their hearts
180 they remembered hell. The Almighty Judge
of good deeds and bad, the Lord God,
Head of the Heavens and High King of the World,
was unknown to them. Oh, cursed is he

---

8. "The Irish word *bothóg* means 'hut' or 'shanty,' often for unmarried workers on a farm. Grendel occupies Heorot, the seat of Danish culture, and ignores the outlying buildings" [Editor Daniel Donoghue's note, from *Beowulf: A Verse Transla-* *tion* (Norton Critical Edition)].
9. A Germanic law, called *wergild*, required compensatory payment by a criminal to the victim of a crime or to the victim's kin.
1. I.e., the Devil.

who in time of trouble has to thrust his soul
185   in the fire's embrace, forfeiting help;
he has nowhere to turn. But blessed is he
who after death can approach the Lord
and find friendship in the Father's embrace.
    So that troubled time continued, woe
190   that never stopped, steady affliction
for Halfdane's son, too hard an ordeal.
There was panic after dark, people endured
raids in the night, riven by the terror.

* * *

[The Fight with Grendel]

* * *

            Then out of the night
came the shadow-stalker, stealthy and swift.
The hall-guards were slack, asleep at their posts,
705   all except one; it was widely understood
that as long as God disallowed it,
the fiend could not bear them to his shadow-bourne.
One man,[2] however, was in fighting mood,
awake and on edge, spoiling for action.
710   In off the moors, down through the mist-bands
God-cursed Grendel came greedily loping.
The bane of the race of men roamed forth,
hunting for a prey in the high hall.
Under the cloud-murk he moved toward it
715   until it shone above him, a sheer keep
of fortified gold. Nor was that the first time
he had scouted the grounds of Hrothgar's dwelling—
although never in his life, before or since,
did he find harder fortune or hall-defenders.
720   Spurned and joyless, he journeyed on ahead
and arrived at the bawn.[3] The iron-braced door
turned on its hinge when his hands touched it.
Then his rage boiled over, he ripped open
the mouth of the building, maddening for blood,
725   pacing the length of the patterned floor
with his loathsome tread, while a baleful light,
flame more than light, flared from his eyes.
He saw many men in the mansion, sleeping,
a ranked company of kinsmen and warriors
730   quartered together. And his glee was demonic,
picturing the mayhem: before morning
he would rip life from limb and devour them,
feed on their flesh; but his fate that night
was due to change, his days of ravening

2. I.e., Beowulf.
3. "Fortified outwork of a court or castle" [from Heaney's note to line 523].

735 had come to an end.
                              Mighty and canny,
     Hygelac's kinsman was keenly watching
     for the first move the monster would make.
     Nor did the creature keep him waiting
     but struck suddenly and started in;
740 he grabbed and mauled a man on his bench,
     bit into his bone-lappings, bolted down his blood
     and gorged on him in lumps, leaving the body
     utterly lifeless, eaten up
     hand and foot. Venturing closer,
745 his talon was raised to attack Beowulf
     where he lay on the bed, he was bearing in
     with open claw when the alert hero's
     comeback and armlock forestalled him utterly.
     The captain of evil discovered himself
750 in a handgrip harder than anything
     he had ever encountered in any man
     on the face of the earth. Every bone in his body
     quailed and recoiled, but he could not escape.
     He was desperate to flee to his den and hide
755 with the devil's litter, for in all his days
     he had never been clamped or cornered like this.
     Then Hygelac's trusty retainer recalled
     his bedtime speech, sprang to his feet
     and got a firm hold. Fingers were bursting,
760 the monster back-tracking, the man overpowering.
     The dread of the land was desperate to escape,
     to take a roundabout road and flee
     to his lair in the fens. The latching power
     in his fingers weakened; it was the worst trip
765 the terror-monger had taken to Heorot.
     And now the timbers trembled and sang,
     a hall-session that harrowed every Dane
     inside the stockade: stumbling in fury,
     the two contenders crashed through the building.
770 The hall clattered and hammered, but somehow
     survived the onslaught and kept standing:
     it was handsomely structured, a sturdy frame
     braced with the best of blacksmith's work
     inside and out. The story goes
775 that as the pair struggled, mead-benches were smashed
     and sprung off the floor, gold fittings and all.
     Before then, no Shielding elder would believe
     there was any power or person upon earth
     capable of wrecking their horn-rigged hall
780 unless the burning embrace of a fire
     engulf it in flame. Then an extraordinary
     wail arose, and bewildering fear
     came over the Danes. Everyone felt it
     who heard that cry as it echoed off the wall,
785 a God-cursed scream and strain of catastrophe,

the howl of the loser, the lament of the hell-serf
keening his wound. He was overwhelmed,
manacled tight by the man who of all men
was foremost and strongest in the days of this life.

790   But the earl-troop's leader was not inclined
to allow his caller to depart alive:
he did not consider that life of much account
to anyone anywhere. Time and again,
Beowulf's warriors worked to defend
795 their lord's life, laying about them
as best they could, with their ancestral blades.
Stalwart in action, they kept striking out
on every side, seeking to cut
straight to the soul. When they joined the struggle
800 there was something they could not have known at the time,
that no blade on earth, no blacksmith's art
could ever damage their demon opponent.
He had conjured the harm from the cutting edge
of every weapon. But his going away
805 out of this world and the days of his life
would be agony to him, and his alien spirit
would travel far into fiends' keeping.
    Then he who had harrowed the hearts of men
with pain and affliction in former times
810 and had given offense also to God
found that his bodily powers failed him.
Hygelac's kinsman kept him helplessly
locked in a handgrip. As long as either lived,
he was hateful to the other. The monster's whole
815 body was in pain; a tremendous wound
appeared on his shoulder. Sinews split
and the bone-lappings burst. Beowulf was granted
the glory of winning; Grendel was driven
under the fen-banks, fatally hurt,
820 to his desolate lair. His days were numbered,
the end of his life was coming over him,
he knew it for certain; and one bloody clash
had fulfilled the dearest wishes of the Danes.
The man who had lately landed among them,
825 proud and sure, had purged the hall,
kept it from harm; he was happy with his nightwork
and the courage he had shown. The Geat captain
had boldly fulfilled his boast to the Danes:
he had healed and relieved a huge distress,
830 unremitting humiliations,
the hard fate they'd been forced to undergo,
no small affliction. Clear proof of this
could be seen in the hand the hero displayed
high up near the roof: the whole of Grendel's
835 shoulder and arm, his awesome grasp.

*   *   *

[The Last Survivor's Speech]

Death had come
and taken them all in times gone by
and the only one left to tell their tale,
the last of their line, could look forward to nothing
2240 but the same fate for himself: he foresaw that his joy
in the treasure would be brief.[4]

A newly constructed
barrow stood waiting, on a wide headland
close to the waves, its entryway secured.
Into it the keeper of the hoard had carried
2245 all the goods and golden ware
worth preserving. His words were few:
"Now, earth, hold what earls once held
and heroes can no more; it was mined from you first
by honorable men. My own people
2250 have been ruined in war; one by one
they went down to death, looked their last
on sweet life in the hall. I am left with nobody
to bear a sword or to burnish plated goblets,
put a sheen on the cup. The companies have departed.
2255 The hard helmet, hasped with gold,
will be stripped of its hoops; and the helmet-shiner
who should polish the metal of the war-mask sleeps;
the coat of mail that came through all fights,
through shield-collapse and cut of sword,
2260 decays with the warrior. Nor may webbed mail
range far and wide on the warlord's back
beside his mustered troops. No trembling harp,
no tuned timber, no tumbling hawk
swerving through the hall, no swift horse
2265 pawing the courtyard. Pillage and slaughter
have emptied the earth of entire peoples."
And so he mourned as he moved about the world,
deserted and alone, lamenting his unhappiness
day and night, until death's flood
brimmed up in his heart.

[The Last Survivor's Speech in Old English]

"Heald þu nu, hruse,   nu hæleð ne mostan,
eorla æhte!   Hwæt, hyt ær on ðe
gode begeaton.   Guþ-deað fornam,
2250 feorh-bealo frecne   fyra gehwylcne
leoda minra,   þara ðe þis lif ofgeaf,
gesawon sele-dreamas.   Nah hwa sweord wege

---

4. This passage comes near the end of the poem. Beowulf, now an old king who has ruled the Geats for fifty years, must fight a fierce flying dragon that guards a treasure hoard and terrorizes the region. These lines tell the history of the treasure: it is the accumulated wealth of a tribe of warriors, now per- ished. The "only one left to tell their tale" is the last survivor of the tribe. He carries the treasure to the barrow where his people are buried and speaks these words on the transience of earthly things. The Old English lines coincide with lines 2247– 66 of the translation.

   oððe feormie fæted wæge,
   drync-fæt deore; duguð ellor scoc.
2255 Sceal se hearda helm hyrsted golde
   fætum befeallen; feormynd swefað
   þa ðe beado-griman bywan sceoldon;
   ge swylce seo here-pad, sio æt hilde gebad
   ofer borda gebræc bite irena,
2260 brosnað æfter beorne; ne mæg byrnan hring
   æfter wig-fruman wide feran
   hæleðum be healfe. Næs hearpan wyn
   gomen gleo-beames, ne god hafoc
   geond sæl swingeð, ne se swifta mearh
2265 burh-stede beateð. Bealo-cwealm hafað
   fela feorh-cynna forð onsended!"

RIDDLES[1]

1

I am a lonely being, scarred by swords,
Wounded by iron, sated with battle-deeds,
Wearied by blades. Often I witness war,
Perilous fight, nor hope for consolation,
5 That any help may rescue me from strife
Before I perish among fighting men;
But hammered swords, hard edged and grimly sharp,
Batter me, and the handwork of the smith
Bites in the castles; I must ever wait
10 A contest yet more cruel. I could never
In any habitation find the sort
Of doctor who could heal my wounds with herbs;
But cuts from swords ever increase on me
Through deadly contest, both by day and night.

2

My dress is silent when I tread the ground
Or stay at home or stir upon the waters.
Sometimes my trappings and the lofty air
Raise me above the dwelling-place of men,
5 And then the power of clouds carries me far
Above the people; and my ornaments
Loudly resound, send forth a melody

---

1. The Old English riddles, like their counterparts in Latin poetic tradition (from which many of them are derived), are poems in which beings or objects from ordinary life are presented disguised in metaphoric terms. The riddles below, translated by Richard Hamer, are among those found in the Exeter Book, a tenth-century manuscript collection of Old English poetry. The "answers" appear in note 3 below.

And clearly sing, when I am not in touch
With earth or water, but a flying spirit.

3

A moth ate words; a marvellous event
I thought it when I heard about that wonder,
A worm had swallowed some man's lay,[2] a thief
In darkness had consumed the mighty saying
5   With its foundation firm. The thief was not
One whit the wiser when he ate those words.[3]

[Riddle 3 in Old English]

Moððe word fræt.   Me þæt þuhte
wrætlicu wyrd,   þa ic þæt wundor gefrægn,
þæt se wyrm forswealg   wera gied sumes,
þeof in þystro,   þrymfæstne cwide
5   ond þæs strangan staþol.   Stælgiest ne wæs
wihte þy gleawra,   þe he þam wordum swealg.

THE WIFE'S LAMENT[1]

I sing this song about myself, full sad,
My own distress, and tell what hardships I
Have had to suffer since I first grew up,
Present and past, but never more than now;
5   I ever suffered grief through banishment.
For since my lord departed from this people
Over the sea, each dawn have I had care
Wondering where my lord may be on land.
When I set off to join and serve my lord,
10   A friendless exile in my sorry plight,
My husband's kinsmen plotted secretly
How they might separate us from each other
That we might live in wretchedness apart
Most widely in the world: and my heart longed.
15   In the first place my lord had ordered me
To take up my abode here, though I had
Among these people few dear loyal friends;
Therefore my heart is sad. Then had I found

2. A short poem intended to be sung.
3. The solutions to these riddles are *shield, swan,* and *bookworm,* respectively.
1. This poem appears in the Exeter Book, a tenth-century manuscript collection of Old English poetry, immediately following a series of riddles. Different translations offer somewhat different interpretations of the poem; the one below, by Richard Hamer, suggests that the poem is a dramatic monologue spoken by a wife separated from her husband. Some critics have suggested that the poem may be an allegory in which the speaker represents either the soul or the children of Israel during the Babylonian captivity.

A fitting man, but one ill-starred, distressed,
20 Whose hiding heart was contemplating crime,
Though cheerful his demeanor. We had vowed
Full many a time that nought should come between us
But death alone, and nothing else at all.
All that has changed, and it is now as though
25 Our marriage and our love had never been,
And far or near forever I must suffer
The feud of my beloved husband dear.
So in this forest grove they made me dwell,
Under the oak-tree, in this earthy barrow.
30 Old is this earth-cave, all I do is yearn.
The dales are dark with high hills up above,
Sharp hedge surrounds it, overgrown with briars,
And joyless is the place. Full often here
The absence of my lord comes sharply to me.
35 Dear lovers in this world lie in their beds,
While I alone at crack of dawn must walk
Under the oak-tree round this earthy cave,
Where I must stay the length of summer days,
Where I may weep my banishment and all
40 My many hardships, for I never can
Contrive to set at rest my careworn heart,
Nor all the longing that this life has brought me.
A young man always must be serious,
And tough his character; likewise he should
45 Seem cheerful, even though his heart is sad
With multitude of cares. All earthly joy
Must come from his own self. Since my dear lord
Is outcast, far off in a distant land,
Frozen by storms beneath a stormy cliff
50 And dwelling in some desolate abode
Beside the sea, my weary-hearted lord
Must suffer pitiless anxiety.
And all too often he will call to mind
A happier dwelling. Grief must always be
55 For him who yearning longs for his beloved.

THE SEAFARER[1]

From the Anglo-Saxon

May I for my own self song's truth reckon,
Journey's jargon, how I in harsh days

---

1. This poem appears in the Exeter Book, a tenth-century manuscript collection of Old English poetry. This translation, by the American poet Ezra Pound (1885–1972; see pp. 1295–1310), was published in 1912; it ends at line 99. The end of the Old English poem, from Richard Hamer's translation, is provided in note 8 below. The poem realistically describes the hardships of a seafaring life, but some critics suggest that it is also a Christian allegory in which life is represented as a difficult journey over rough seas toward the harbor of heaven. Pound's translation plays down the Christian elements of the poem.

Hardship endured oft.
Bitter breast-cares have I abided,
5 Known on my keel[2] may a care's hold,
And dire sea-surge, and there I oft spent
Narrow nightwatch nigh the ship's head
While she tossed close to cliffs. Coldly afflicted,
My feet were by frost benumbed.
10 Chill its chains are; chafing sighs
Hew° my heart round and hunger begot   *strike*
Mere°-weary mood. Lest man know not   *sea*
That he on dry land loveliest liveth,
List how I, care-wretched, on ice-cold sea,
15 Weathered the winter, wretched outcast
Deprived of my kinsmen;
Hung with hard ice-flakes, where hail-scur° flew,   *hailstorms*
There I heard naught save the harsh sea
And ice-cold wave, at whiles the swan cries,
20 Did for my games the gannet's° clamor,   *large seabird's*
Sea-fowls' loudness was for me laughter,
The mews'° singing all my mead-drink.   *seagulls'*
Storms, on the stone-cliffs beaten, fell on the stern
In icy feathers; full oft the eagle screamed
25 With spray on his pinion.°   *wing*
                    Not any protector
May make merry man faring needy.
This he little believes, who aye in winsome° life   *pleasant*
Abides 'mid burghers° some heavy business,   *citizens*
Wealthy and wine-flushed, how I weary oft
30 Must bide above brine.[3]
Neareth nightshade, snoweth from north,
Frost froze the land, hail fell on earth then,
Corn of the coldest. Nathless[4] there knocketh now
The heart's thought that I on high streams
35 The salt-wavy tumult traverse alone.
Moaneth alway my mind's lust
That I fare forth, that I afar hence
Seek out a foreign° fastness.°   *remote / place*
For this there's no mood-lofty man over earth's midst,
40 Not though he be given his good, but will have in his youth greed;
Nor his deed to the daring, nor his king to the faithful
But shall have his sorrow for sea-fare
Whatever his lord will.
He hath not heart for harping, nor in ring-having
45 Nor winsomeness to wife, nor world's delight
Nor any whit else save the wave's slash,
Yet longing comes upon him to fare forth on the water.
Bosque° taketh blossom, cometh beauty of berries,   *grove*
Fields to fairness, land fares brisker,
50 All this admonisheth man eager of mood,

---

2. The timber of a ship or boat upon which the framework of the whole is built.
3. I.e., must live a life at sea.

4. Nevertheless. *Corn:* small, hard particles or grains.

The heart turns to travel so that he then thinks
On flood-ways to be far departing.
Cuckoo calleth with gloomy crying,
He singeth summerward, bodeth sorrow,
55   The bitter heart's blood. Burgher knows not—
He the prosperous man—what some perform
Where wandering them widest draweth
So that but now my heart burst from my breastlock,
My mood 'mid the mere-flood,
60   Over the whale's acre, would wander wide.[5]
On earth's shelter cometh oft to me,
Eager and ready, the crying lone-flyer,°   cuckoo
Whets for the whale-path the heart irresistibly,
O'er tracks of ocean; seeing that anyhow
65   My lord deems to me this dead life
On loan and on land,[6] I believe not
That any earth-weal eternal standeth
Save there be somewhat calamitous
That, ere a man's tide go, turn it to twain.
70   Disease or oldness or sword-hate
Beats out the breath from doom-gripped body.
And for this, every earl whatever, for those speaking after—
Laud of the living, boasteth some last word,
That he will work ere he pass onward,
75   Frame on the fair earth 'gainst foes his malice,
Daring° ado,° . . .   brave / deeds
So that all men shall honor him after
And his laud beyond them remain 'mid the English,[7]
Aye, for ever, a lasting life's-blast,
80   Delight 'mid the doughty.°   valiant
                    Days little durable,
And all arrogance of earthen riches,
There come now no kings nor Cæsars°   emperors
Nor gold-giving lords like those gone.
Howe'er in mirth most magnified
85   Who'er lived in life most lordliest,
Drear all this excellence, delights undurable!
Waneth the watch, but the world holdeth.
Tomb hideth trouble. The blade is layed low.
Earthly glory ageth and seareth.
90   No man at all going the earth's gait,
But age fares against him, his face paleth,
Gray-haired he groaneth, knows gone companions,
Lordly men, are to earth o'ergiven,
Nor may he then the flesh-cover, whose life ceaseth,
95   Nor eat the sweet nor feel the sorry,
Nor stir hand nor think in mid heart,
And though he strew the grave with gold,

---

5. Pound changes the original here by substituting "mood" for the O.E. term for "thoughts" and then by omitting a line describing the thoughts returning to the speaker "with greed and longing."

6. Behind Pound's phrase "on loan and on land" is an O.E. phrase meaning "briefly on Earth."

7. In the original, the sense is "with the angels," not "mid the English."

His born brothers, their buried bodies
Be an unlikely treasure hoard.[8]

[*The First Lines of "The Seafarer" in Old English*]

Mæg ic be me sylfum   soðgied wrecan,
siþas secgan,   hu ic geswincdagum
earfoðhwile   oft þrowade,
bitre breostceare   gebiden hæbbe,
5   gecunnad in ceole   cearselda fela,
atol yþa gewealc,   þær mec oft bigeat
nearo nihtwaco   æt nacan stefnan
þonne he be clifum cnossað . . .

ANONYMOUS LYRICS OF THE THIRTEENTH AND FOURTEENTH CENTURIES

Now Go'th Sun under Wood[1]

Nou goth sonne under wode—
Me reweth, Marie, thi faire rode.[2]
Nou goth sonne under tre—
Me reweth, Marie, thi sone and the.°   *thee*

The Cuckoo Song[3]

Sing, cuccu, nu.° Sing, cuccu.   *now*
Sing, cuccu. Sing, cuccu, nu.

8. Pound's translation omits the part of the original sentence that describes the gold buried with the brother's corpse as something that can "bring no help to the soul that's full of sins, / Against God's wrath, although he [the dead person] hide it here / Ready before his death while yet he lives." The ensuing lines, in Hamer's translation, go as follows:

Great is the might of God, by which earth moves;
For He established its foundations firm,
The land's expanses, and the sky above.
Foolish is he who does not fear his Lord,
For death will come upon him unprepared.
Blessed is he who humble lives; for grace
Shall come to him from heaven. The Creator
Shall make his spirit steadfast, for his faith
Is in God's might. Man must control himself
With strength of mind, and firmly hold to that,
True to his pledges, pure in all his ways.
With moderation should each man behave
In all his dealings with both friend and foe.
No man will wish the friend he's made to burn
In fires of hell, or on an earthly pyre,
Yet fate is mightier, the Lord's ordaining
More powerful than any man can know.
Let us think where we have our real home,
And then consider how we may come thither;

And let us labor also, so that we
May pass into eternal blessedness,
Where life belongs amid the love of God,
Hope in the heavens. The Holy One be thanked
That He has raised us up, the Prince of Glory,
Lord without end, to all eternity.
Amen.

1. This is one of the earliest Middle English lyrics presenting the Passion of Christ (his Crucifixion at Calvary), a subject that occurs frequently in Middle English lyrics. This poem, which was perhaps originally part of a longer one on the Passion, is notable for its wordplay: e.g., "sonne" means both "sun" and "son"; and the "wode" of line 1 refers both to the woods behind which the sun is setting and to Christ's wooden cross; "rode" (line 2) also plays on "cross" (the Old English *rood*), as does "tre" (line 3).
2. Face. According to John 19.25, Christ's mother, the Virgin Mary, witnessed the Crucifixion. *Me reweth:* I pity.
3. This song about summer or spring "coming in" is one of the earliest surviving Middle English lyrics. It is written, with music, in a manuscript that was owned by a religious house.

Sumer is i-cumen in—
　Lhude° sing, cuccu! — *loudly*
5　Groweth sed and bloweth° med° — *blooms / field*
　And springth° the wude° nu. — *buds / wood*
　Sing, cuccu!

　Awe° bleteth aftor lomb, — *ewe*
　Lhouth° after calve cu,° — *lows / cow*
10　Bulluc sterteth,° bucke verteth⁴— — *leaps*
　Murie° sing, cuccu! — *merrily*
　　Cuccu, cuccu.
　Wel singes thu,° cuccu. — *thou*
　Ne swik thu naver nu!⁵

Ubi Sunt Qui ante Nos Fuerunt?⁶

Were beth they biforen us weren,
Houndes ladden° and hauekes° beren° — *led / hawks / carried*
And hadden° feld and wode?° — *owned / wood*
　The riche levedies° in hoere° bour,° — *ladies / their / bower*
5　That wereden gold in hoere tressour,° — *headdress*
With hoere brightte rode,° — *face*

Eten and drounken and maden hem° glad; — *them*
Hoere lif was al with gamen° i-lad;° — *pleasure / led*
Men keneleden° hem biforen; — *knelt*
10　They beren hem wel swithe° heye°— — *very / haughtily*
And in a twincling of an eye
Hoere soules weren forloren.° — *completely lost*

Were is that lawing° and that song, — *laughing*
That trayling and that proude yong,⁷
15　Tho hauekes and tho houndes?
　Al that joye is went away;
That wele° is comen to welaway,° — *happiness / sadness*
To manie harde stoundes.° — *times*

Hoere paradis hy° nomen° here, — *they / took*
20 And nou they lien in helle i-fere°— — *together*
The fuir° hit brennes° hevere.° — *fire / burns / ever*
Long is ay° and long is ho,° — *ah / oh*
Long is wy° and long is wo°— — *alas / woe*
Thennes° ne cometh they nevere. — *thence*

---

4. Farts; thought to derive from the Old English *feortan*, although some commentators suggest a derivation from the Latin *vertere*, "to turn" or "to cavort."
5. Cease ("swik") thou never now, i.e., don't ever stop.
6. The first line translates the Latin title: "Where

are now those who lived before us?" This lyric is part of an extensive medieval tradition of *ubi sunt* poems lamenting the mutability of human life and institutions; for an Old English example, see "The Seafarer" (p. 12).
7. That trailing (of garments) and that proud gait.

25 Dreghy° here, man, thenne if thou wilt,   *suffer*
  A luitel pine,° that me the bit.[8]   *pain*
    Withdrau thine eyses ofte.
      They° thi pine be ounrede,°   *though / severe*
      And° thou thenke on thi mede,°   *if / reward*
30 Hit sal the thinken softe.[9]

  If that fend,[1] that foule thing,
  Thorou wikke roun,° thorou fals egging,°   *temptation / urging*
    Nethere° the haveth i-cast,   *down*
    Oup,° and be god chaunpioun!   *up*
35   Stond, ne fal° namore adoun   *fall*
    For a luytel blast.°   *puff of wind*

  Thou tak the rode to[2] thi staf
  And thenk on him that thereonne yaf°   *gave*
    His lif that wes so lef.°   *dear*
40   He hit yaf for the; thou yelde hit him.[3]
    Ayein° his fo that staf thou nim,°   *against / take*
    And wrek him of that thef.[4]

  Of rightte bileve[5] thou nim that sheld
  The wiles° that thou best° in that feld.   *while / are*
45   Thin hond to strenkthen fonde[6]
    And kep thy fo with staves ord[7]
    And do that traytre seien that word.[8]
    Biget° that murie londe   *gain*

  Thereinne is day withouten night,
50 Withouten ende strenkthe and might,
    And wreche° of° everich fo,   *vengeance / on*
    Mid° god himselwen eche° lif   *with / eternal*
    And pes and rest withoute strif,
    Wele° withouten wo.   *happiness*

55 Mayden moder, hevene quene,
  Thou might and const° and owest° to bene°   *can / ought / be*
    Oure sheld ayein° the fende.   *against*
    Help ous sunne for to flen[9]
    That we moten° thi sone i-seen   *might*
60   In joye withouten hende.°   *end*

  Amen.

8. That you are asked to bear. Literally, one ("me") that bids thee.
9. It shall seem soft to thee.
1. Fiend, or enemy (German *Feind*); i.e., Satan, whose name means "adversary" in Hebrew; cf. "fo" (line 41): foe.
2. Rod to be, with "rode" here also referring to Christ's cross (*rood*).
3. He gave it [his life] for thee; thou repay him for it. *Yelde:* yield.
4. Against his foe take thou that staff [the cross] and revenge him upon that thief [the Devil].
5. Right belief, or true faith.

6. Then try to strengthen your hand; an allusion to the "shield of faith" (Ephesians 6.16).
7. I.e., the point of your staff.
8. Make the traitor say the word (of surrender). Some editors place a comma after "word" and a period after "londe" in the next line. Our editorial decision about punctuating these difficult lines—a decision that breaks the pattern of syntactically self-contained stanzas—requires "thereinne" of line 49 to be interpreted as "wherein."
9. Help us to flee from sin—with a play on "sunne" (line 58) and "sone" (line 59).

Alison[1]

Bytwene Mersh° and Averil,	*March*
When spray° biginneth to springe,°	*twigs / open, leaf out*
The lutel° foul° hath hire° wyl	*little / bird / its*
On hyre lud° to synge,	*birdsong*
5 Ich° libbe° in love-longinge	*I / live*
For semlokest° of alle thinge—	*seemliest*
He° may me blisse bringe;	*she*
Ich am in hire baundoun°	*power*
An hendy hap ichabbe yhent[2]—	
10 Ichot° from hevene it is me sent:	*I know*
From alle wymmen mi love is lent°	*turned*
And lyht° on Alysoun.	*fallen*
On° heu° hire her° is fayr ynoh,°	*in / color / hair / enough*
Hire browe broune, hire eye blake—	
15 With lossum chere he on me loh[3]—	
With middel° smal and wel ymake.°	*waist / made*
Bote° he° me wolle to hire take,	*unless / she*
Forte buen hire owen make,[4]	
Longe to lyven ichulle° forsake	*I will*
20 And feye° fallen adoun	*dead, lifeless*
An hendy hap ichabbe yhent— . . .	
Nightes when I wende° and wake—	*turn*
Forthi° myn wonges° waxeth won°—	*therefore / cheeks / wan, pale*
Levedi,° al for thine sake	*lady*
25 Longinge is ylent me on.[5]	
In world nis non so wyter mon[6]	
That al hire bounte° telle con.	*excellence*
Hire swyre° is whittore then the swon,°	*neck / swan*
And feyrest may° in toune.	*maid*
30 An hendy hap ichabbe yhent— . . .	
Icham for wowyng al forwake,[7]	
Wery so water in wore,[8]	
Lest eny reve me my make[9]	
Ichabbe y-yerned yore.[1]	
35 Betere is tholien whyle sore[2]	
Then mournen evermore.	
Geynest under gore,[3]	

1. This lyric (like most Middle English poems, originally untitled) occurs in a famous anthology containing the so-called Harley Lyrics, written in the west of England in the early fourteenth century; the manuscript is now in the British Library (MS. Harley 2253).
2. A happy chance I have received.
3. I.e., with lovely face she laughed at ("loh" "on") me.
4. For to be her own mate.

5. I.e., come upon me.
6. I.e., in the world there is no man so wise.
7. I.e., I am entirely worn out from wooing.
8. I.e., like water in a weir, a pool made by damming up water.
9. I.e., lest anyone deprive me of my mate ("reve" being a form of the old verb *reave*, to rob).
1. I.e., [the mate] I have desired a long time.
2. I.e., better it is to suffer sorely for a while.
3. I.e., kindest of ladies (persons "under gown").

Herkne° to my roun.°   *listen / song*
    An hendy hap ichabbe yhent— . . .

Fowls in the Frith[4]

Fowles in the frith,
The fisshes in the flood,
And I mon° waxe° wood:°   *must / go / mad*
Much sorwe° I walke with   *sorrow*
5   For beste of boon[5] and blood.

I Am of Ireland[6]

Ich° am of Irlonde,   *I*
And of the holy londe
    Of Irlonde.

Goode sire, praye ich thee,
5   *For of° sainte° charitee,*   *sake of / holy*
Com and dance with me
    In Irlonde.

GEOFFREY CHAUCER
ca. 1343–1400

From The Canterbury Tales

The General Prologue

Whan that April with his° showres soote°   *its / fresh*
The droughte of March hath perced to the roote,
And bathed every veine in swich licour,[1]
Of which vertu[2] engendred is the flowr;
5   Whan Zephyrus° eek° with his sweete breeth   *the West Wind / also*
Inspired° hath in every holt° and heeth°   *breathed into / grove / field*
The tendre croppes,° and the yonge sonne   *shoots*
Hath in the Ram his halve cours yronne,[3]

---

4. This poem, with a musical accompaniment designed for two voices, appears on one side of a page in a manuscript comprised mainly of legal texts (it contains no other poems). The title means "Birds in the Woods."
5. Either "the best" or "beast" of bone. The ambiguity allows for both religious and erotic interpretations.
6. This lyric may be a fragment or an extract from a longer poem; it is written in prose in the manuscript. The first three lines are the burden, or refrain.
1. Such liquid. *Veine:* i.e., in plants.
2. By the power of which.
3. The sun is young because it has run only halfway through its course in Aries, the Ram—the first sign of the zodiac in the solar year.

And smale fowles° maken melodye   *birds*
10 That sleepen al the night with open yë°—   *eye*
So priketh hem° Nature in hir° corages°—   *them / their / hearts*
Thanne longen folk to goon° on pilgrimages,   *go*
And palmeres for to seeken straunge strondes
To ferne halwes,[4] couthe° in sondry° londes;   *known / various*
15 And specially from every shires ende
Of Engelond to Canterbury they wende,
The holy blisful martyr[5] for to seeke
That hem hath holpen° whan that they were seke.°   *helped / sick*
    Bifel° that in that seson on a day,   *it happened*
20 In Southwerk[6] at the Tabard as I lay,
Redy to wenden on my pilgrimage
To Canterbury with ful° devout corage,   *very*
At night was come into that hostelrye
Wel nine and twenty in a compaignye
25 Of sondry folk, by aventure° yfalle   *chance*
In felaweshipe, and pilgrimes were they alle
That toward Canterbury wolden° ride.   *would*
The chambres and the stables weren wide,
And wel we weren esed at the beste.[7]
30 And shortly, whan the sonne was to reste,[8]
So hadde I spoken with hem everichoon°   *every one*
That I was of hir felaweshipe anoon,°   *at once*
And made forward[9] erly for to rise,
To take oure way ther as I you devise.[1]
35   But nathelees,° whil I have time and space,[2]   *nevertheless*
Er° that I ferther in this tale pace,°   *before / proceed*
Me thinketh it accordant to resoun[3]
To telle you al the condicioun
Of eech of hem, so as it seemed me,
40 And whiche they were, and of what degree,°   *social rank*
And eek in what array that they were inne:
And at a knight thanne° wol I first biginne.   *then*
    A Knight ther was, and that a worthy man,
That fro the time that he first bigan
45 To riden out, he loved chivalrye,
Trouthe and honour, freedom and curteisye.[4]
Ful worthy was he in his lordes werre,°   *war*
And therto hadde he riden, no man ferre,°   *further*
As wel in Cristendom as hethenesse,°   *heathen lands*
50 And[5] evere honoured for his worthinesse.
    At Alisandre[6] he was whan it was wonne;

4. Far-off shrines. *Palmeres:* palmers, wide-ranging pilgrims—especially those who sought out the "straunge strondes" (foreign shores) of the Holy Land.
5. St. Thomas à Becket, murdered in Canterbury Cathedral (1170); his shrine was associated with healing.
6. Southwark, site of the Tabard Inn, was then a suburb of London, south of the Thames River.
7. Accommodated in the best possible way.
8. I.e., had set.
9. I.e., (we) made an agreement.

1. I.e., where I describe to you.
2. I.e., while I have the opportunity.
3. It seems to me according to reason.
4. Courtesy. *Trouthe:* integrity. *Freedom:* generosity of spirit.
5. I.e., and he was.
6. The Knight has taken part in campaigns fought against three groups who threatened Christian Europe during the fourteenth century: the Muslims in the Near East, from whom Alexandria was seized after a famous siege; the northern barbarians in Prussia, Lithuania, and Russia; and the

Ful ofte time he hadde the boord bigonne[7]
Aboven alle nacions in Pruce;
55   In Lettou had he reised,° and in Ruce,   *campaigned*
No Cristen man so ofte of his degree;
In Gernade° at the sege eek hadde he be   *Granada*
Of Algezir, and riden in Belmarye;
At Lyeis was he, and at Satalye,
Whan they were wonne; and in the Grete See°   *Mediterranean Sea*
60   At many a noble arivee° hadde he be.   *military landing*
      At mortal batailes[8] hadde he been fifteene,
And foughten for oure faith at Tramissene
In listes[9] thries,° and ay° slain his fo.   *thrice / always*
      This ilke° worthy Knight hadde been also   *same*
65   Somtime with the lord of Palatye[1]
Again° another hethen in Turkye;   *against*
And everemore he hadde a soverein pris.°   *reputation*
And though that he were worthy, he was wis,[2]
And of his port° as meeke as is a maide.   *demeanor*
70   He nevere yit no vilainye° ne saide   *rudeness*
In al his lif unto no manere wight:[3]
He was a verray,° parfit,° gentil° knight.   *true / perfect / noble*
But for to tellen you of his array,
His hors° were goode, but he was nat gay.[4]   *horses*
75   Of fustian he wered a gipoun[5]
Al bismotered with his haubergeoun,[6]
For he was late° come from his viage,°   *lately / expedition*
And wente for to doon his pilgrimage.
      With him ther was his sone, a yong Squier,[7]
80   A lovere and a lusty bacheler,
With lokkes crulle° as° they were laid in presse.   *curly / as if*
Of twenty yeer of age he was, I gesse.
Of his stature he was of evene° lengthe,   *moderate*
And wonderly delivere,° and of greet° strengthe.   *agile / great*
85   And he hadde been som time in chivachye[8]
In Flandres, in Artois, and Picardye,
And born him wel as of so litel space,[9]
In hope to stonden in his lady° grace.   *lady's*
      Embrouded° was he as it were a mede,°   *embroidered / mead, meadow*
90   Al ful of fresshe flowres, white and rede;°   *red*
Singing he was, or floiting,° al the day: *whistling*
He was as fressh as is the month of May.
Short was his gowne, with sleeves longe and wide.

Moors in North Africa. The place-names in the following lines refer to battlegrounds in these continuing wars.
7. Sat in the seat of honor at military feasts.
8. Tournaments fought to the death.
9. Lists, tournament grounds.
1. "The lord of Palatye" was a Muslim; alliances of convenience were often made during the Crusades between Christians and Muslims.
2. I.e., he was wise as well as bold.
3. Any sort of person. In Middle English, negatives are multiplied for emphasis, as in these two lines: "nevere," "no," "ne," "no."

4. I.e., gaily dressed.
5. I.e., he wore a tunic of thick cloth underneath the coat of mail.
6. All rust-stained from his hauberk (coat of mail).
7. The vague term "Squier" (Squire) here seems the equivalent of "bachelor," a young knight still in the service of an older one.
8. On cavalry expeditions. The places in the next line are sites of skirmishes in the constant warfare between the English and the French.
9. I.e., considering the little time he had been in service.

Wel coude he sitte on hors, and faire ride;
95 He coude songes make, and wel endite,°   compose verse
Juste and eek daunce,[1] and wel portraye° and write.   sketch
So hote° he loved that by° nightertale°   hotly / at / night
He slepte namore than dooth a nightingale.
Curteis he was, lowely,° and servisable,   humble
100 And carf biforn his fader at the table.[2]
        A Yeman hadde he[3] and servants namo°   no more
At that time, for him liste° ride so;   it pleased to
And he[4] was clad in cote and hood of greene.
A sheef of pecok arwes,° bright and keene,   arrows
105 Under his belt he bar° ful thriftily;°   bore / properly
Wel coude he dresse his takel yemanly:[5]
His arwes drouped nought with fetheres lowe.
And in his hand he bar a mighty bowe.
A not-heed° hadde he with a brown visage.   close-cut head
110 Of wodecraft wel coude° he al the usage.   knew
Upon his arm he bar a gay bracer,[6]
And by his side a swerd° and a bokeler,[7]   sword
And on that other side a gay daggere,
Harneised° wel and sharp as point of spere;   mounted
115 A Cristophre[8] on his brest of silver sheene;°   bright
An horn he bar, the baudrik[9] was of greene.
A forster° was he soothly,° as I gesse.   forester / truly
        Ther was also a Nonne, a Prioresse,[1]
That of hir smiling was ful simple° and coy.°   sincere / mild
120 Hir gretteste ooth was but by sainte Loy![2]
And she was cleped° Madame Eglantine.   named
Ful wel she soong° the service divine,   sang
Entuned in hir nose ful semely;[3]
And Frenssh she spak ful faire and fetisly,°   elegantly
125 After the scole of Stratford at the Bowe[4]—
For Frenssh of Paris was to hire unknowe.
At mete° wel ytaught was she withalle:°   meals / besides
She leet° no morsel from hir lippes falle,   let
Ne wette hir fingres in hir sauce deepe;
130 Wel coude she carye a morsel, and wel keepe°   take care
That no drope ne fille° upon hir brest.   should fall
In curteisye was set ful muchel hir lest.[5]
Hir over-lippe wiped she so clene
That in hir coppe° ther was no ferthing° seene   cup / bit
135 Of grece,° whan she dronken hadde hir draughte;   grease
Ful semely after hir mete she raughte.°   reached
And sikerly° she was of greet disport,[6]   certainly

1. Joust (fight in a tournament) and also dance.
2. It was a squire's duty to carve his lord's meat.
3. The Knight. *Yeman:* Yeoman; an independent commoner who acts as the Knight's military servant.
4. I.e., the Yeoman.
5. Tend to his gear in a workmanlike way.
6. Wristguard for archers.
7. Buckler (a small shield).
8. A medal of St. Christopher, patron saint of travelers.
9. Baldric (a supporting strap).

1. The Prioress is the mother superior of her nunnery.
2. Eloi, or Eligius, a saint associated with journeys and craftsmanship, was also famous for his personal beauty, courtesy, and refusal to swear.
3. I.e., chanted in a seemly manner.
4. The French learned in a convent school ("scole") in Stratford-at-the-Bow, a suburb of London, was evidently not up to the Parisian standard.
5. I.e., her chief delight lay in good manners.
6. Of great good cheer.

And ful plesant, and amiable of port,°   *mien*
And pained hire to countrefete cheere[7]
140   Of court, and to been statlich° of manere,   *dignified*
And to been holden digne[8] of reverence.
But, for to speken of hir conscience,
She was so charitable and so pitous°   *merciful*
She wolde weepe if that she saw a mous
145   Caught in a trappe, if it were deed° or bledde.   *dead*
Of[9] smale houndes hadde she that she fedde
With rosted flessh, or milk and wastelbreed;°   *fine white bread*
But sore wepte she if oon of hem were deed,
Or if men smoot it with a yerde smerte;[1]
150   And al was conscience and tendre herte.
Ful semely hir wimpel° pinched° was,   *headdress / pleated*
Hir nose tretis, hir yën greye[2] as glas,
Hir mouth ful smal, and therto° softe and reed,°   *moreover / red*
But sikerly she hadde a fair forheed:
155   It was almost a spanne brood, I trowe,[3]
For hardily,° she was nat undergrowe.   *assuredly*
Ful fetis° was hir cloke, as I was war;°   *becoming / aware*
Of smal° coral aboute hir arm she bar   *dainty*
A paire of bedes, gauded al with greene,[4]
160   And theron heeng° a brooch of gold ful sheene,°   *hung / bright*
On which ther was first writen a crowned A,[5]
And after, *Amor vincit omnia.*[6]
    Another Nonne with hire hadde she
That was hir chapelaine,° and preestes three.[7]   *secretary*
165   A Monk ther was, a fair for the maistrye,[8]
An outridere[9] that loved venerye,°   *hunting*
A manly man, to been an abbot able.°   *worthy*
Ful many a daintee° hors hadde he in stable,   *fine*
And whan he rood,° men mighte his bridel heere   *rode*
170   Ginglen° in a whistling wind as clere   *jingle*
And eek as loude as dooth the chapel belle
Ther as this lord was kepere of the celle.[1]
The rule of Saint Maure or of Saint Beneit,
By cause that it was old and somdeel strait[2]—
175   This ilke° Monk leet olde thinges pace,°   *same / pass away*
And heeld° after the newe world the space.[3]   *held*
He yaf nought of that text a pulled hen[4]
That saith that hunteres been° nought holy men,   *are*
Ne that a monk, whan he is recchelees,[5]
180   Is likned til° a fissh that is waterlees—   *to*

---

7. And took pains to imitate the behavior.
8. And to be considered worthy.
9. I.e., some.
1. If someone struck it with a rod sharply.
2. Her nose well-formed, her eyes gray (a conventional color for the eyes of heroines in romances).
3. A handsbreadth wide, I believe.
4. Provided with green beads to mark certain prayers. *Paire*: string (i.e., a rosary).
5. An *A* with an ornamental crown on it.
6. A Latin motto meaning "Love conquers all."
7. Later there is only one priest, who tells "The Nun's Priest's Tale."

8. I.e., a superlatively fine one.
9. A monk charged with supervising property distant from the monastery.
1. Prior of an outlying cell (branch) of the monastery.
2. Somewhat straight. *Saint Maure* and *Saint Beneit*: St. Maurus and St. Benedict, authors of monastic rules.
3. The course, or direction. I.e., he followed the new direction of things.
4. He didn't give a plucked hen for that text.
5. Reckless; careless of rule.

This is to sayn, a monk out of his cloistre;
But thilke° text heeld he nat worth an oystre.   *that same*
And I saide his opinion was good:
What° sholde he studye and make himselven wood°   *why / crazy*
185 Upon a book in cloistre alway to poure,°   *pore, read intently*
Or swinke° with his handes and laboure,   *work*
As Austin bit?[6] How shal the world be served?
Lat Austin have his swink to him reserved!
Therfore he was a prikasour° aright.   *hard rider*
190 Grehoundes he hadde as swift as fowl in flight.
Of priking° and of hunting for the hare   *riding*
Was al his lust,° for no cost wolde he spare.   *pleasure*
I sawgh his sleeves purfiled° at the hand   *fur-lined*
With gris,° and that the fineste of a land;   *gray fur*
195 And for to festne his hood under his chin
He hadde of gold wrought a ful curious[7] pin:
A love-knotte in the grettere° ende ther was.   *greater*
His heed was balled,° that shoon as any glas,   *bald*
And eek his face, as he hadde been anoint:
200 He was a lord ful fat and in good point;[8]
His yën steepe,° and rolling in his heed,   *protruding*
That stemed as a furnais of a leed,[9]
His bootes souple,° his hors in greet estat°—   *supple / condition*
Now certainly he was a fair prelat.[1]
205 He was nat pale as a forpined° gost: *wasted-away*
A fat swan loved he best of any rost.
His palfrey° was as brown as is a berye.   *saddle horse*
   A Frere[2] ther was, a wantoune° and a merye,   *jovial*
A limitour, a ful solempne° man.   *ceremonious*
210 In alle the ordres foure is noon that can°   *knows*
So muche of daliaunce° and fair langage: *sociability*
He hadde maad ful many a mariage
Of yonge wommen at his owene cost;
Unto his ordre he was a noble post.[3]
215 Ful wel biloved and familier was he
With frankelains over al[4] in his contree,
And with worthy wommen of the town—
For he hadde power of confessioun,
As saide himself, more than a curat,°   *parish priest*
220 For of° his ordre he was licenciat.[5]   *by*
Ful swetely herde he confessioun,
And plesant was his absolucioun.
He was an esy man to yive° penaunce   *give*
Ther as he wiste to have a good pitaunce[6]
225 For unto a poore ordre for to yive
Is signe that a man is wel yshrive;°   *shriven, absolved*

---

6. I.e., as St. Augustine bids. St. Augustine had
written that monks should perform manual labor.
7. Of careful workmanship.
8. In good shape, plump.
9. That glowed like a furnace with a pot in it.
1. Prelate (an important churchman).
2. The "Frere" (Friar) belongs to one of the four
religious orders whose members live by begging; as

a "limitour" (line 209) he has been granted exclu-
sive begging rights within a certain limited area.
3. I.e., pillar, a staunch supporter.
4. I.e., with franklins everywhere. Franklins were
well-to-do country men.
5. I.e., licensed to hear confessions.
6. Where he knew he would have a good donation.

For if he yaf, he dorste make avaunt
He wiste[7] that a man was repentaunt;
For many a man so hard is of his herte
230   He may nat weepe though him sore smerte:[8]
Therfore, in stede of weeping and prayeres,
Men mote° yive silver to the poore freres.[9]   *may*
      His tipet° was ay farsed° ful of knives   *scarf / packed*
And pinnes, for to yiven faire wives;
235   And certainly he hadde a merye note;
Wel coude he singe and playen on a rote;°   *fiddle*
Of yeddinges he bar outrely the pris.[1]
His nekke whit was as the flowr-de-lis;°   *lily*
Therto he strong was as a champioun.
240   He knew the tavernes wel in every town,
And every hostiler° and tappestere,°   *innkeeper / barmaid*
Bet than a lazar or a beggestere.[2]
For unto swich a worthy man as he
Accorded nat, as by his facultee,[3]
245   To have with sike° lazars aquaintaunce: *sick*
It is nat honeste,° it may nought avaunce,°   *dignified / profit*
For to delen with no swich poraile,[4]
But al with riche, and selleres of vitaile;°   *foodstuffs*
And over al ther as profit sholde arise,
250   Curteis he was, and lowely of servise.
Ther was no man nowher so vertuous:°   *effective*
He was the beste beggere in his hous.°   *friary*
And yaf a certain ferme for the graunt:[5]
Noon of his bretheren cam ther in his haunt.° *assigned territory*
255   For though a widwe° hadde nought a sho,°   *widow / shoe*
So plesant was his *In principio*[6]
Yit wolde he have a ferthing° er he wente;   *small coin*
His purchas was wel bettre than his rente.[7]
And rage he coude as it were right a whelpe,[8]
260   In love-dayes[9] ther coude he muchel° helpe,   *much*
For ther he was nat lik a cloisterer,
With a thredbare cope,° as is a poore scoler,   *cloak*
But he was lik a maister[1] or a pope.
Of double worstede was his semicope,°   *short cloak*
265   And rounded as a belle out of the presse.°   *bell mold*
Somwhat he lipsed for his wantounesse[2]
To make his Englissh sweete upon his tonge;

---

7. I.e., for if a man gave, the Friar would assert that he [the Friar] knew.
8. Though he is sorely grieved.
9. Before granting absolution, the confessor must be sure the sinner is contrite; moreover, the absolution is contingent upon the sinner's performance of an act of satisfaction. In the case of Chaucer's Friar, a liberal contribution served both as proof of contrition and as satisfaction.
1. He absolutely took the prize for ballads.
2. Better than a leper or a female beggar.
3. It was not suitable because of his position.
4. I.e., poor people. The oldest order of friars had been founded by St. Francis to administer to the spiritual needs of precisely those classes the Friar avoids.
5. And he paid a certain rent for the privilege of begging.
6. A friar's usual salutation: "In the beginning [was the Word]" (John 1.1).
7. I.e., the money he got through such activity was more than his regular income.
8. And he could flirt wantonly, as if he were a puppy.
9. Days appointed for the settlement of lawsuits out of court.
1. A man of recognized learning.
2. I.e., lisped in affectation.

And in his harping, whan he hadde songe,°   sung
His yën twinkled in his heed aright
270   As doon the sterres° in the frosty night.   stars
This worthy limitour was cleped Huberd.
   A Marchant was ther with a forked beerd,
In motelee,[3] and hye on hors he sat,
Upon his heed a Flandrissh° bevere hat,   Flemish
275   His bootes clasped faire and fetisly.°   elegantly
His resons° he spak ful solempnely,   opinions
Souning° alway th'encrees° of his winning.   sounding / increase
He wolde the see were kept for any thing[4]
Bitwixen Middelburgh and Orewelle.
280   Wel coude he in eschaunge sheeldes[5] selle.
This worthy man ful wel his wit bisette:°   employed
Ther wiste° no wight° that he was in dette,   knew / person
So statly° was he of his governaunce,[6]   dignified
With his bargaines,° and with his chevissaunce.° bargainings / borrowing
285   Forsoothe he was a worthy man withalle;
But, sooth to sayn, I noot° how men him calle.   don't know
   A Clerk[7] ther was of Oxenforde also
That unto logik hadde longe ygo.[8]
As lene was his hors as is a rake,
290   And he was nought right fat, I undertake,
But looked holwe,° and therto sobrely.   hollow
Ful thredbare was his overeste° courtepy,°   outer / cloak
For he hadde geten him yit no benefice,[9]
Ne was so worldly for to have office.°   secular employment
295   For him was levere[1] have at his beddes heed
Twenty bookes, clad in blak or reed,
Of Aristotle and his philosophye,
Than robes riche, or fithele,° or gay sautrye.[2]   fiddle
But al be that he was a philosophre[3]
300   Yit hadde he but litel gold in cofre;°   coffer
But al that he mighte of his freendes hente,°   take
On bookes and on lerning he it spente,
And bisily gan for the soules praye
Of hem that yaf him wherwith to scoleye.°   study
305   Of studye took he most cure° and most heede.   care
Nought oo° word spak he more than was neede,   one
And that was said in forme[4] and reverence,
And short and quik,° and ful of heigh sentence:[5]   lively
Souning° in moral vertu was his speeche,   resounding

3. Motley, a cloth of mixed color.
4. I.e., he wished the sea to be guarded at all costs. The sea route between Middleburgh (in the Netherlands) and Orwell (in Suffolk) was vital to the Merchant's export and import of wool—the basis of England's chief trade at the time.
5. Shields, *écus* (French coins), were units of transfer in international credit, which he exchanged at a profit.
6. The management of his affairs.
7. The Clerk is a student at Oxford; to become a student, he would have had to signify his intention of becoming a cleric, but he was not bound to proceed to a position of responsibility in the Church.
8. Who had long since matriculated in philosophy.
9. Ecclesiastical living, such as the income a parish priest receives.
1. He would rather.
2. Psaltery (a kind of harp).
3. The word may also mean "alchemist," someone who tries to turn base metals into gold. The Clerk's "philosophy" does not pay either way.
4. With decorum.
5. Elevated thought.

310   And gladly wolde he lerne, and gladly teche.
       A Sergeant of the Lawe, war and wis,[6]
    That often hadde been at the Parvis[7]
    Ther was also, ful riche of excellence.
    Discreet he was, and of greet reverence—
315   He seemed swich, his wordes weren so wise.
    Justice he was ful often in assise°   *circuit courts*
    By patente° and by plein° commissioun.   *royal warrant / full*
    For his science° and for his heigh renown   *knowledge*
    Of fees and robes hadde he many oon.
320   So greet a purchasour° was nowher noon;   *speculator in land*
    Al was fee simple[8] to him in effect—
    His purchasing mighte nat been infect.[9]
    Nowher so bisy a man as he ther nas;°   *was not*
    And yit he seemed bisier than he was.
325   In termes hadde he caas and doomes[1] alle
    That from the time of King William[2] were falle.
    Therto he coude endite and make a thing,[3]
    Ther coude no wight pinchen° at his writing;   *cavil*
    And every statut coude° he plein° by rote.° *knew / entire / heart*
330   He rood but hoomly° in a medlee cote,[4]   *unpretentiously*
    Girt with a ceint° of silk, with barres° smale. *belt / transverse stripes*
    Of his array telle I no lenger tale.
       A Frankelain[5] was in his compaignye:
    Whit was his beerd as is the dayesye;°   *daisy*
335   Of his complexion he was sanguin.[6]
    Wel loved he by the morwe a sop in win.[7]
    To liven in delit° was evere his wone,°   *pleasure / custom*
    For he was Epicurus[8] owene sone,
    That heeld opinion that plein° delit   *full*
340   Was verray felicitee parfit.[9]
    An housholdere and that a greet was he:
    Saint Julian[1] he was in his contree.
    His breed, his ale, was always after oon;[2]
    A bettre envined° man was nevere noon.   *wine-stocked*
345   Withouten bake mete was nevere his hous,
    Of fissh and flessh, and that so plentevous°   *plenteous*
    It snewed° in his hous of mete° and drinke, *snowed / food*
    Of alle daintees that men coude thinke.
    After° the sondry sesons of the yeer   *according to*
350   So chaunged he his mete° and his soper.° *dinner / supper*

6. Wary and wise; the Sergeant is not only a practicing lawyer but one of the high justices of the nation.
7. The "Paradise," the porch of St. Paul's Cathedral, a meeting place for lawyers and their clients.
8. Owned outright without legal impediments.
9. Invalidated on a legal technicality.
1. Probably, he had in Year Books ("termes") all the cases ("caas") and decisions ("doomes"). The Year Books were compiled from notes taken at trials.
2. I.e., the Conqueror (reigned 1066–87).
3. Compose and draw up a deed.
4. A coat of mixed color.
5. The "Frankelain" (Franklin) is a prosperous

country man, whose lower-class ancestry is no impediment to the importance he has attained in his county.
6. A reference to the fact that the Franklin's temperament is dominated by blood as well as to his red face (see note to line 423).
7. I.e., in the morning he was very fond of a piece of bread soaked in wine.
8. The ancient Greek philosopher whose teaching is popularly believed to make pleasure the chief goal of life.
9. I.e., was true perfect happiness.
1. The patron saint of hospitality.
2. Always of the same high quality.

Ful many a fat partrich hadde he in mewe,°   *cage*
And many a breem,° and many a luce° in stewe.°   *carp / pike / fishpond*
Wo was his cook but if his sauce were
Poinant° and sharp, and redy all his gere.   *pungent*
355   His table dormant in his halle alway
Stood redy covered all the longe day.[3]
At sessions ther was he lord and sire.
Ful ofte time he was Knight of the Shire.[4]
An anlaas° and a gipser° al of silk   *dagger / purse*
360   Heeng at his girdel,[5] whit as morne° milk.   *morning*
A shirreve° hadde he been, and countour.[6]   *sheriff*
Was nowher swich a worthy vavasour.[7]

    An Haberdasshere and a Carpenter,
A Webbe,° a Dyere, and a Tapicer°—   *weaver / tapestry maker*
365   And they were clothed alle in oo liveree[8]
Of a solempne and greet fraternitee.
Ful fresshe and newe hir gere apiked° was;   *trimmed*
Hir knives were chaped° nought with bras,   *mounted*
But al with silver; wrought ful clene and weel
370   Hir girdles and hir pouches everydeel.°   *altogether*
Wel seemed eech of hem a fair burgeis°   *burgher*
To sitten in a yeldehalle° on a dais.   *guildhall*
Everich, for the wisdom that he can,°   *was capable of*
Was shaply° for to been an alderman.   *suitable*
375   For catel° hadde they ynough and rente,°   *property / income*
And eek hir wives wolde it wel assente—
And elles certain were they to blame:
It is ful fair to been ycleped° "Madame,"   *called*
And goon to vigilies all bifore,[9]
380   And have a mantel royalliche ybore.[1]

    A Cook they hadde with hem for the nones,°   *occasion*
To boile the chiknes with the marybones,°   *marrowbones*
And powdre-marchant tart and galingale.[2]
Wel coude he knowe° a draughte of London ale.   *recognize*
385   He coude roste, and seethe,° and broile, and frye,   *boil*
Maken mortreux,° and wel bake a pie.   *stews*
But greet harm was it thoughte° me,   *seemed to*
That on his shine a mormal° hadde he.   *ulcer*
For blankmanger,[3] that made he with the beste.

390   A Shipman was ther, woning° fer by weste—   *dwelling*
For ought I woot,° he was of Dertemouthe.[4]   *know*
He rood upon a rouncy° as he couthe,[5]   *large nag*
In a gowne of falding° to the knee.   *heavy wool*
A daggere hanging on a laas° hadde he   *strap*

---

3. Tables were usually dismounted when not in use, but the Franklin kept his mounted and set ("covered"), hence "dormant."
4. County representative in Parliament. *Sessions:* i.e., sessions of the justices of the peace.
5. Hung at his belt.
6. Auditor of county finances.
7. Feudal landholder of lowest rank; a provincial gentleman.
8. In one livery, i.e., the uniform of their "frater-

nitee," or guild, a partly religious, partly social organization.
9. I.e., at the head of the procession. *Vigilies:* feasts held on the eve of saints' days.
1. A covering or cloak with a train, royally carried.
2. Like "powdre-marchant," a flavoring material.
3. A white stew or mousse, from the French *blanc* (white) + *manger* (to eat).
4. Dartmouth, a port in the southwest of England.
5. As best he could.

395 Aboute his nekke, under his arm adown.
     The hote somer hadde maad his hewe° al brown;   *color*
     And certainly he was a good felawe.
     Ful many a draughte° of win hadde he ydrawe   *drink*
     Fro Burdeuxward, whil that the chapman sleep:⁶
400 Of nice° conscience took he no keep°   *fastidious / heed*
     If that he faught and hadde the hyer hand,
     By water he sente hem hoom to every land.⁷
     But of his craft, to rekene wel his tides,
     His stremes° and his daungers° him bisides,⁸   *currents / hazards*
405 His herberwe° and his moone, his lodemenage,°   *anchorage / pilotage*
     There was noon swich from Hulle to Cartage.⁹
     Hardy he was and wis to undertake;
     With many a tempest hadde his beerd been shake;
     He knew alle the havenes° as they were   *harbors*
410 Fro Gotlond to the Cape of Finistere,¹
     And every crike° in Britaine° and in Spaine.   *inlet / Brittany*
     His barge ycleped was the Maudelaine.°   *Magdalene*
         With us ther was a Doctour of Physik:°   *medicine*
     In al this world ne was ther noon him lik
415 To speken of physik and of surgerye.
     For° he was grounded in astronomye,°   *because / astrology*
     He kepte° his pacient a ful greet deel²   *tended to*
     In houres by his magik naturel.³
     Wel coude he fortunen the ascendent
420 Of his images⁴ for his pacient.
     He knew the cause of every maladye,
     Were it of hoot or cold or moiste or drye,
     And where engendred and of what humour:⁵
     He was a verray parfit praktisour.⁶
425 The cause yknowe,° and of his° harm the roote,   *known / its*
     Anoon he yaf the sike man his boote.°   *remedy*
         Ful redy hadde he his apothecaries
     To senden him drogges° and his letuaries,°   *drugs / medicines*
     For eech of hem made other for to winne:
430 Hir frendshipe was nought newe to biginne.
     Wel knew he the olde Esculapius,⁷

6. I.e., drawn (stolen) wine from Bordeaux (the wine center of France), while the Merchant slept.
7. I.e., he drowned his prisoners.
8. Around him.
9. From Hull (in northern England) to Cartagena (in Spain).
1. From Gotland (an island in the Baltic) to Finisterre (the westernmost point in Spain).
2. I.e., closely.
3. Natural—as opposed to black—magic. *In houres:* i.e., the astrologically important hours (when conjunctions of the planets might help his recovery).
4. Assign the propitious time, according to the position of stars, for using talismanic images. Such images, representing either the patient or points in the zodiac, were thought to influence the course of the disease.
5. Diseases were thought to be caused by a disturbance of one or another of the four bodily

"humors," each of which, like the four elements, was a compound of two of the elementary qualities mentioned in line 422: the melancholy humor, seated in the black bile, was cold and dry (like earth); the sanguine, seated in the blood, hot and moist (like air); the choleric, seated in the yellow bile, hot and dry (like fire); the phlegmatic, seated in the phlegm, cold and moist (like water).
6. True perfect practitioner.
7. The Doctor is familiar with the treatises that the Middle Ages attributed to the "great names" of medical history, whom Chaucer lists in lines 431–36: the purely legendary Greek demigod Aesculapius; the Greeks Dioscorides, Rufus, Hippocrates, Galen, and Serapion; the Persians Hali and Rhazes; the Arabians Avicenna and Averroës; the early Christians John (?) of Damascus and Constantine Afer; the Scotsman Bernard Gordon; the Englishmen John of Gatesden and Gilbert, the former an early contemporary of Chaucer.

And Deiscorides and eek Rufus,
Olde Ipocras, Hali, and Galien,
Serapion, Razis, and Avicen,
435 Averrois, Damascien, and Constantin,
Bernard, and Gatesden, and Gilbertin.
Of his diete mesurable° was he,   *moderate*
For it was of no superfluitee,
But of greet norissing° and digestible.   *nourishment*
440 His studye was but litel on the Bible.
In sanguin° and in pers° he clad was al,   *blood red / blue*
Lined with taffata and with sendal;°   *silk*
And yit he was but esy of dispence;°   *expenditure*
He kepte that he wan in pestilence.[8]
445 For° gold in physik is a cordial,[9]   *because*
Therfore he loved gold in special.
    A good Wif was ther of biside Bathe,
But she was somdeel deef, and that was scathe.°   *a pity*
Of cloth-making she hadde swich an haunt,°   *practice*
450 She passed° hem of Ypres and of Gaunt.[1]   *surpassed*
In al the parissh wif ne was ther noon
That to the offring[2] bifore hire sholde goon,
And if ther dide, certain so wroth° was she   *angry*
That she was out of alle charitee.
455 Hir coverchiefs ful fine were of ground°—   *texture*
I dorste° swere they weyeden° ten pound   *dare / weighed*
That on a Sonday weren° upon hir heed.   *were*
Hir hosen weren of fin scarlet reed,°   *red*
Ful straite yteyd,[3] and shoes ful moiste° and newe.   *supple*
460 Bold was hir face and fair and reed of hewe.
She was a worthy womman al hir live:
Housbondes at chirche dore[4] she hadde five,
Withouten° other compaigny in youthe—   *not counting*
But therof needeth nought to speke as nouthe.°   *now*
465 And thries hadde she been at Jerusalem;
She hadde passed many a straunge° streem;   *foreign*
At Rome she hadde been, and at Boloigne,
In Galice at Saint Jame, and at Coloigne:[5]
She coude° muchel of wandring by the waye.   *knew*
470 Gat-toothed[6] was she, soothly for to saye.
Upon an amblere° esily she sat,   *horse with an easy gait*
Ywimpled° wel, and on hir heed an hat   *veiled*
As brood as is a bokeler or a targe,[7]
A foot-mantel° aboute hir hipes large,   *riding skirt*
475 And on hir feet a paire of spores° sharpe.   *spurs*

8. He saved the money he made during the plague time.
9. A stimulant. Gold was thought to have some medicinal properties.
1. Ypres and Ghent ("Gaunt") were Flemish cloth-making centers.
2. The offering in church, when the congregation brought its gifts forward.
3. Tightly laced.
4. In medieval times, weddings were often performed at the church door.
5. Rome, Boulogne (in France), St. James (of Compostella) in Galicia (Spain), Cologne (in Germany) were all sites of shrines much visited by pilgrims.
6. Gap-toothed; in medieval physiognomy, such teeth indicated an irreverent, luxurious, sexualized nature.
7. Like a "bokeler," a small shield.

In felaweshipe wel coude she laughe and carpe:°   *talk*
Of remedies of love she knew parchaunce,°   *as it happened*
For she coude of that art the olde daunce.[8]
    A good man was ther of religioun,
480 And was a poore Person° of a town,   *parson*
But riche he was of holy thought and werk.
He was also a lerned man, a clerk,
That Cristes gospel trewely° wolde preche;   *faithfully*
His parisshens° devoutly wolde he teche.   *parishioners*
485 Benigne he was, and wonder° diligent,   *wonderfully*
And in adversitee ful pacient,
And swich he was preved° ofte° sithes.°   *proved / often / times*
Ful loth were him to cursen for his tithes,[9]
But rather wolde he yiven, out of doute,[1]
490 Unto his poore parisshens aboute
Of his offring[2] and eek of his substaunce:°   *property*
He coude in litel thing have suffisaunce.°   *sufficiency*
Wid was his parissh, and houses fer asonder,
But he ne lafte° nought for rain ne thonder,   *neglected*
495 In siknesse nor in meschief,° to visite   *misfortune*
The ferreste° in his parissh, muche and lite,[3]   *farthest*
Upon his feet, and in his hand a staf.
This noble ensample° to his sheep he yaf   *example*
That first he wroughte,[4] and afterward he taughte.
500 Out of the Gospel he tho° wordes caughte,°   *those / took*
And this figure° he added eek therto: *metaphor*
That if gold ruste, what shal iren do?
For if a preest be foul, on whom we truste,
No wonder is a lewed° man to ruste.   *uneducated*
505 And shame it is, if a preest take keep,°   *heed*
A shiten° shepherde and a clene sheep.   *befouled*
Wel oughte a preest ensample for to yive
By his clennesse how that his sheep sholde live.
He sette nought his benefice to hire
510 And leet his sheep[5] encombred in the mire
And ran to London, unto Sainte° Poules,°   *St. / Paul's (Cathedral)*
To seeken him a chaunterye[6] for soules,
Or with a bretherhede to been withholde,[7]
But dwelte at hoom and kepte wel his folde,
515 So that the wolf ne made it nought miscarye:
He was a shepherde and nought a mercenarye.
And though he holy were and vertuous,
He was to sinful men nought despitous,°   *scornful*
Ne of his speeche daungerous° ne digne,°   *disdainful / haughty*
520 But in his teching discreet and benigne,

8. I.e., she knew all the tricks of that trade.
9. He would be most reluctant to invoke excommunication in order to collect his tithes.
1. Without doubt.
2. The offering made by the congregation of his church was at the Parson's disposal.
3. I.e., great and small.
4. I.e., he practiced what he preached.
5. I.e., he did not hire out his parish or leave his

sheep. A priest might rent his parish to another and take a more profitable position.
6. Chantry, i.e., a foundation that employed priests for the sole duty of saying Masses for the souls of certain persons. St. Paul's had many of them.
7. Or to be employed by a brotherhood; i.e., to take a lucrative and fairly easy position as chaplain with a parish guild.

To drawen folk to hevene by fairnesse
By good ensample—this was his bisinesse.
But it° were any persone obstinat,   *if there*
What so he were, of heigh or lowe estat,
525 Him wolde he snibben° sharply for the nones:[8]   *scold*
A bettre preest I trowe° ther nowher noon is.   *believe*
He waited after[9] no pompe and reverence,
Ne maked him a spiced conscience,[1]
But Cristes lore° and his Apostles twelve   *teaching*
530 He taughte, but first he folwed it himselve.
      With him ther was a Plowman, was his brother,
That hadde ylad° of dong° ful many a fother.°   *carried / dung / load*
A trewe swinkere° and a good was he,   *worker*
Living in pees° and parfit charitee.   *peace*
535 God loved he best with al his hoole° herte   *whole*
At alle times, though him gamed or smerte,[2]
And thanne his neighebor right as himselve.
He wolde thresshe, and therto dike° and delve,°   *make ditches / dig*
For Cristes sake, for every poore wight,
540 Withouten hire, if it laye in his might.
His tithes payed he ful faire and wel,
Bothe of his propre° swink° and his catel.°   *own / work / property*
In a tabard° he rood upon a mere.°   *workman's smock / mare*
      Ther was also a Reeve and a Millere,
545 A Somnour, and a Pardoner also,
A Manciple, and myself—ther were namo.[3]
      The Millere was a stout carl° for the nones.   *fellow*
Ful big he was of brawn° and eek of bones—   *muscle*
That preved[4] wel, for overal ther he cam
550 At wrastling he wolde have alway the ram.[5]
He was short-shuldred, brood,° a thikke° knarre.°   *broad / stout / fellow*
Ther was no dore that he nolde heve of harre,[6]
Or breke it at a renning° with his heed.°   *running / head*
His beerd as any sowe or fox was reed,°   *red*
555 And therto brood, as though it were a spade;
Upon the cop° right of his nose he hade   *tip*
A werte,° and theron stood a tuft of heres,   *wart*
Rede as the bristles of a sowes eres;°   *ears*
His nosethirles° blake were and wide.   *nostrils*
560 A swerd and a bokeler° bar° he by his side.   *shield / bore*
His mouth as greet was as a greet furnais.°   *furnace*
He was a janglere° and a Goliardais,[7]   *chatterer*
And that was most of sinne and harlotries.°   *obscenities*
Wel coude he stelen corn and tollen thries[8]—
565 And yit he hadde a thombe of gold, pardee.[9]

8. On any occasion.
9. I.e., expected.
1. Nor did he assume an overfastidious conscience.
2. Whether he was pleased or grieved.
3. No more. *Reeve:* estate manager. *Somnour:* Summoner, server of summonses to the ecclesiastical court. *Pardoner:* dispenser of papal pardons. *Manciple:* Steward. The Somnour appears at line

625; the Pardoner, at line 671.
4. Proved, i.e., was evident.
5. A ram was frequently offered as the prize in wrestling.
6. He would not heave off (its) hinge.
7. Goliard, teller of ribald stories.
8. Take toll thrice—i.e., deduct from the grain far more than the lawful percentage.
9. By heaven. *Thombe:* possibly an ironic refer-

A whit cote and a blew hood wered° he.   *wore*
A baggepipe wel coude he blowe and soune,°   *sound*
And therwithal° he broughte us out of towne.   *therewith*
    A gentil Manciple[1] was ther of a temple,
570 Of which achatours° mighte take exemple   *buyers of food*
For to been wise in bying of vitaile;°   *victuals*
For wheither that he paide or took by taile,[2]
Algate he waited so in his achat[3]
That he was ay biforn and in good stat.[1]
575   Now is nat that of God a ful fair grace
That swich a lewed° mannes wit shal pace°   *uneducated / surpass*
The wisdom of an heep of lerned men?
Of maistres° hadde he mo than thries ten   *masters*
That weren of lawe expert and curious,°   *cunning*
580 Of whiche ther were a dozeine in that hous
Worthy to been stiwardes of rente° and lond   *income*
Of any lord that is in Engelond,
To make him live by his propre° good°   *own / money*
In honour dettelees but if he were wood,[5]
585 Or live as scarsly as him list desire,[6]
And able for to helpen al a shire
In any caas° that mighte falle° or happe,   *event / befall*
And yit this Manciple sette hir aller cappe![7]
    The Reeve was a sclendre colerik[8] man;
590 His beerd was shave as neigh° as evere he can;   *close*
His heer was by his eres ful round yshorn;
His top was dokked[9] lik a preest biforn;
Ful longe were his legges and ful lene,
Ylik a staf, ther was no calf yseene.°   *visible*
595 Wel coude he keepe° a gerner° and a binne—   *guard / granary*
Ther was noon auditour coude on him winne.[1]
Wel wiste° he by the droughte and by the rain   *knew*
The yeelding of his seed and of his grain.
His lordes sheep, his neet,° his dayerye,°   *cattle / dairy herd*
600 His swin, his hors, his stoor,° and his pultrye   *stock*
Was hoolly° in this Reeves governinge,   *wholly*
And by his covenant yaf[2] the rekeninge,
Sin° that his lord was twenty-yeer of age.   *since*
There coude no man bringe him in arrerage.[3]
605 Ther nas baillif, hierde, nor other hine,
That he ne knew his sleighte and his covine[4]—
They were adrad° of him as of the deeth.°   *afraid / plague*
His woning° was ful faire upon an heeth;°   *dwelling / meadow*

---

ence to the proverb *An honest miller hath a golden thumb,* which apparently means "There are no honest millers."
1. The Manciple is the steward of a community of lawyers in London (a "temple").
2. By talley, i.e., on credit.
3. Always he was on the watch in his purchasing.
4. I.e., he was ahead of the game and in good financial condition.
5. Out of debt unless he were insane.
6. I.e., as economically as he would want.
7. This Manciple made fools of them all.

8. Slender choleric. "Colerik" (choleric) describes a person whose dominant humor is yellow bile (choler)—i.e., a hot-tempered person. The Reeve is the superintendent of a large farming estate.
9. Cut short; the clergy wore the head partially shaved.
1. I.e., find him in default.
2. And according to his contract he gave.
3. Convict him of being in arrears financially.
4. There was no bailiff (i.e., foreman), shepherd, nor other farm laborer whose craftiness and plots he didn't know.

With greene trees shadwed was his place.
610 He coude bettre than his lord purchace.°   *acquire goods*
Ful riche he was astored° prively.°   *stocked / secretly*
His lord wel coude he plesen subtilly,
To yive and lene° him of his owene good,°   *lend / property*
And have a thank, and yit a cote and hood.
615 In youthe he hadde lerned a good mister·°   *occupation*
He was a wel good wrighte, a carpenter.
This Reeve sat upon a ful good stot°   *stallion*
That was a pomely° grey and highte° Scot.   *dapple / was named*
A long surcote of pers upon he hade,[5]
620 And by his side he bar° a rusty blade.   *bore*
Of Northfolk was this Reeve of which I telle,
Biside a town men clepen Baldeswelle.°   *Bawdswell*
Tukked° he was as is a frere aboute,   *with clothing tucked up*
And evere he rood the hindreste of oure route.[6]
625   A Somnour[7] was ther with us in that place
That hadde a fir-reed cherubinnes[8] face,
For saucefleem° he was, with yën° narwe,°   *pimply / eyes / slitlike*
And hoot° he was, and lecherous as a sparwe,[9]   *hot*
With scaled° browes blake and piled[1] beerd: *scabby*
630 Of his visage children were aferd.°   *afraid*
Ther nas quiksilver, litarge, ne brimstoon,
Boras, ceruce, ne oile of tartre noon,[2]
Ne oinement that wolde clense and bite,
That him mighte helpen of his whelkes° white,   *pimples*
635 Nor of the knobbes° sitting on his cheekes.   *lumps*
Wel loved he garlek, oinons, and eek leekes,
And for to drinke strong win reed as blood.
Thanne wolde he speke and crye as he were wood;°   *insane*
And whan that he wel dronken hadde the win,
640 Thanne wolde he speke no word but Latin:
A fewe termes hadde he, two or three,
That he hadde lerned out of som decree;
No wonder is—he herde it al the day,
And eek ye knowe wel how that a jay°   *parrot*
645 Can clepen "Watte"[3] as wel as can the Pope—
But whoso coude in other thing him grope,°   *examine*
Thanne hadde he spent all his philosophye;[4]
Ay *Questio quid juris*[5] wolde he crye.
    He was a gentil harlot° and a kinde;   *rascal*
650 A bettre felawe sholde men nought finde:
He wolde suffre,° for a quart of win,   *permit*
A good felawe to have his concubin

---

5. I.e., he had on a long blue overcoat.
6. Hindmost of our group.
7. The "Somnour" (Summoner) is an employee of the ecclesiastical court, whose defined duty is to bring to court persons whom the archdeacon—the justice of the court—suspects of offenses against canon law. By this time, however, summoners had generally transformed themselves into corrupt detectives who spied out offenders and black-mailed them by threats of summonses.
8. Fire-red cherub's. Cherubs were often depicted in art with red faces.
9. The sparrow was traditionally associated with lechery.
1. Uneven; partly hairless.
2. These are all ointments for diseases affecting the skin, probably diseases of venereal origin.
3. Call out "Walter" (like modern parrots' "Polly").
4. I.e., learning.
5. "What point of law does this investigation involve?": a phrase frequently used in ecclesiastical courts.

A twelfmonth, and excusen him at the fulle;[6]
Ful prively° a finch eek coude he pulle.[7]   *secretly*
655   And if he foond° owher° a good felawe   *found / anywhere*
He wolde techen him to have noon awe
In swich caas of the Ercedekenes curs,[8]
But if[9] a mannes soule were in his purs,
For in his purs he sholde ypunisshed be.
660   "Purs is the Ercedekenes helle," saide he.
But wel I woot he lied right in deede:
Of cursing° oughte eech gilty man drede,   *excommunication*
For curs wol slee° right as assoiling° savith—   *slay / absolution*
And also war him of a *significavit*.[1]
665   In daunger[2] hadde he at his owene gise°   *disposal*
The yonge girles of the diocise,
And knew hir conseil,° and was al hir reed.[3]   *secrets*
A gerland hadde he set upon his heed
As greet as it were for an ale-stake;[4]
670   A bokeler hadde he maad him of a cake.
With him ther rood a gentil Pardoner[5]
Of Rouncival, his freend and his compeer,°   *comrade*
That straight was comen fro the Court of Rome.
Ful loude he soong,° "Com hider, love, to me."   *sang*
675   This Somnour bar to him a stif burdoun:[6]
Was nevere trompe° of half so greet a soun.   *trumpet*
This Pardoner hadde heer as yelow as wex,
But smoothe it heeng° as dooth a strike° of flex;°   *hung / hank / flax*
By ounces[7] heenge his lokkes that he hadde,
680   And therwith he his shuldres overspradde,°   *overspread*
But thinne it lay, by colpons,° oon by oon;   *strands*
But hood for jolitee° wered° he noon,   *attractiveness / wore*
For it was trussed up in his walet:°   *pack*
Him thoughte he rood al of the newe jet.°   *fashion*
685   Dischevelee° save his cappe he rood al bare.   *with hair down*
Swiche glaring yën hadde he as an hare.
A vernicle[8] hadde he sowed upon his cappe,
His walet biforn him in his lappe,
Bretful° of pardon, comen from Rome al hoot.°   *brimful / hot*
690   A vois he hadde as smal° as hath a goot;°   *fine / goat*
No beerd hadde he, ne nevere sholde have;
As smoothe it was as it were late yshave:
I trowe he were a gelding or a mare.[9]

6. Fully. Ecclesiastical courts had jurisdiction over many offenses that today would come under civil law, including sexual offenses.
7. I.e., "to pluck a finch": to swindle someone; also, an expression for sexual intercourse.
8. Archdeacon's sentence of excommunication.
9. *But if:* unless.
1. And also one should be careful of a *significavit* (the writ that transferred the guilty offender from the ecclesiastical to the civil arm for punishment).
2. Under his domination.
3. Was their chief source of advice.
4. A tavern was signalized by a pole ("alestake"), rather like a modern flagpole, projecting from its front wall; on this hung a garland, or "bush."

5. A Pardoner dispensed papal pardon for sins to those who contributed to the charitable institution that he was licensed to represent; this Pardoner purported to be collecting for the hospital of Roncesvalles ("Rouncival") in Spain, which had a London branch.
6. I.e., provided him with a strong bass accompaniment.
7. I.e., thin strands.
8. Portrait of Christ's face as it was said to have been impressed on St. Veronica's handkerchief, i.e., a souvenir reproduction of a famous relic in Rome.
9. I believe he was a castrated male horse or a female horse.

But of his craft, fro Berwik into Ware,[1]
695 Ne was ther swich another pardoner;
For in his male° he hadde a pilwe-beer°   bag / pillowcase
Which that he saide was Oure Lady veil;
He saide he hadde a gobet° of the sail   piece
That Sainte Peter hadde whan that he wente
700 Upon the see, til Jesu Crist him hente.°   seized
He hadde a crois° of laton,° ful of stones,   cross / brassy metal
And in a glas he hadde pigges bones,
But with thise relikes[2] whan that he foond°   found
A poore person dwelling upon lond,[3]
705 Upon° a day he gat° him more moneye   in / got
Than that the person gat in monthes twaye;°   two
And thus with feined° laterye and japes°   false / tricks
He made the person and the peple his apes.°   dupes
But trewely to tellen at the laste,
710 He was in chirche a noble ecclesiaste;
Wel coude he rede a lesson and a storye,°   liturgical narrative
But alderbest° he soong an offertorye,[4]   best of all
For wel he wiste° whan that song was songe,   knew
He moste° preche and wel affile° his tonge   must / sharpen
715 To winne silver, as he ful wel coude—
Therfore he soong the merierly° and loude.   more merrily
    Now have I told you soothly in a clause[5]
Th'estaat, th'array, the nombre, and eek the cause
Why that assembled was this compaignye
720 In Southwerk at this gentil hostelrye
That highte the Tabard, faste by the Belle;[6]
But now is time to you for to telle
How that we baren° us° that ilke° night   bore / ourselves / same
Whan we were in that hostelrye alight;
725 And after wol I telle of oure viage,°   trip
And al the remenant of oure pilgrimage.
But first I praye you of youre curteisye
That ye n'arette it nought my vilainye[7]
Though that I plainly speke in this matere
730 To telle you hir wordes and hir cheere,°   behavior
Ne though I speke hir wordes proprely;°   accurately
For this ye knowen also wel as I:
Who so shal telle a tale after a man
He moot° reherce,° as neigh as evere he can,   must / repeat
735 Everich a word, if it be in his charge,°   responsibility
Al° speke he nevere so rudeliche and large,°   although / broadly
Or elles he moot telle his tale untrewe,
Or feine° thing, or finde° wordes newe;   falsify / devise
He may nought spare[8] although he were his brother:
740 He moot as wel saye oo word as another.
Crist spake himself ful brode° in Holy Writ,   broadly

---

1. I.e., from one end of England to another.
2. Relics—i.e., the pigs' bones that the Pardoner
represented as saints' bones.
3. A poor parson living upcountry.
4. Part of the Mass sung before the offering of
alms.

5. I.e., in a few words.
6. Close by the Belle (another tavern in South-
wark, possibly a brothel).
7. That you do not charge it to my boorishness.
8. I.e., spare anyone.

And wel ye woot no vilainye° is it;   *rudeness*
Eek Plato saith, who so can him rede,
The wordes mote be cosin to the deede.
745   Also I praye you to foryive it me
Al° have I nat set folk in hir degree   *although*
Here in this tale as that they sholde stonde:
My wit is short, ye may wel understonde.
Greet cheere made oure Host⁹ us everichoon,
750   And to the soper sette he us anoon.°   *at once*
He served us with vitaile° at the beste.   *food*
Strong was the win, and wel to drinke us leste.°   *it pleased*
A semely man oure Hoste was withalle
For to been a marchal¹ in an halle;
755   A large man he was, with yën steepe,°   *prominent*
A fairer burgeis° was ther noon in Chepe²—   *townsman*
Bold of his speeche, and wis, and wel ytaught,
And of manhood him lakkede right naught.
Eek therto he was right a merye man,
760   And after soper playen he bigan,
And spak of mirthe amonges othere thinges—
Whan that we hadde maad° oure rekeninges°—   *paid / bills*
And saide thus, "Now, lordinges, trewely,
Ye been to me right welcome, hertely.°   *heartily*
765   For by my trouthe, if that I shal nat lie,
I sawgh nat this yeer so merye a compaignye
At ones in this herberwe° as is now.   *inn*
Fain° wolde I doon you mirthe, wiste I³ how.   *gladly*
And of a mirthe I am right now bithought,
770   To doon you ese, and it shal coste nought.
"Ye goon to Canterbury—God you speede;
The blisful martyr quite you youre meede.⁴
And wel I woot as ye goon by the waye
Ye shapen you⁵ to talen° and to playe,   *tell tales*
775   For trewely, confort ne mirthe is noon
To ride by the waye domb as stoon;°   *stone*
And therfore wol I maken you disport
As I saide erst,° and doon you som confort;   *before*
And if you liketh alle, by oon assent,
780   For to stonden at⁶ my juggement,
And for to werken as I shal you saye,
Tomorwe whan ye riden by the waye—
Now by my fader° soule that is deed,   *father's*
But° ye be merye I wol yive you myn heed!°   *unless / head*
785   Holde up youre handes withouten more speeche."
Oure counseil was nat longe for to seeche;°   *seek*
Us thoughte it was nat worth to make it wis,⁷
And graunted him withouten more avis,°   *deliberation*
And bade him saye his voirdit as him leste.⁸
790   "Lordinges," quod he, "now herkneth for the beste;

9. The Host is the landlord of the Tabard Inn.
1. Marshal, one who was in charge of feasts.
2. Cheapside, business center of London.
3. If I knew.
4. Pay you your reward.

5. *Ye shapen you:* you intend.
6. Abide by.
7. We didn't think it worthwhile to make an issue of it.
8. I.e., give his verdict as he pleased.

But taketh it nought, I praye you, in desdain.
This is the point, to speken short and plain,
That eech of you, to shorte° with oure waye   *shorten*
In this viage, shal tellen tales twaye°—   *two*
795   To Canterburyward, I mene it so,
And hoomward he shal tellen othere two,
Of aventures that whilom° have bifalle;   *once upon a time*
And which of you that bereth him best of alle—
That is to sayn, that telleth in this cas
800   Tales of best sentence° and most solas°—   *meaning / delight*
Shal have a soper at oure aller cost,⁹
Here in this place, sitting by this post,
Whan that we come again fro Canterbury.
And for to make you the more mury°   *merry*
805   I wol myself goodly° with you ride—   *kindly*
Right at myn owene cost—and be youre gide.
And who so wol my juggement withsaye°   *contradict*
Shal paye al that we spende by the waye.
And if ye vouche sauf that it be so,
810   Telle me anoon, withouten wordes mo,°   *more*
And I wol erly shape me¹ therfore."
      This thing was graunted and oure othes swore
With ful glad herte, and prayden² him also
That he wolde vouche sauf for to do so,
815   And that he wolde been oure governour,
And of oure tales juge and reportour,°   *accountant*
And sette a soper at a certain pris,°   *price*
And we wol ruled been at his devis,°   *wish, plan*
In heigh and lowe; and thus by oon assent
820   We been accorded to his juggement.
And therupon the win was fet° anoon;   *fetched*
We dronken and to reste wente eechoon
Withouten any lenger° taryinge.   *longer*
      Amorwe° whan that day bigan to springe   *in the morning*
825   Up roos oure Host and was oure aller cok,³
And gadred us togidres in a flok,
And forth we riden, a litel more than pas,°   *walking pace*
Unto the watering of Saint Thomas;⁴
And ther oure Host bigan his hors arreste,°   *to halt*
830   And saide, "Lordes, herkneth if you leste:°   *it please*
      Ye woot youre forward and it you recorde:⁵
If evensong and morwesong° accorde,°   *morningsong / agree*
Lat see now who shal telle the firste tale.
As evere mote° I drinken win or ale,   *may*
835   Who so be rebel to my juggement
Shal paye for al that by the way is spent.
Now draweth cut er that we ferre twinne:⁶
He which that hath the shorteste shal biginne.

---

9. I.e., at the expense of us all.
1. Will prepare myself.
2. I.e., we prayed.
3. I.e., was rooster for us all.

4. A watering place near Southwark.
5. You know your agreement and you recall it.
6. I.e., draw straws before we go farther.

"Sire Knight," quod he, "my maister and my lord,
840 Now draweth cut, for that is myn accord.°   *will*
Cometh neer," quod he, "my lady Prioresse,
And ye, sire Clerk, lat be youre shamefastnesse°—   *modesty*
Ne studieth nought. Lay hand to, every man!"
    Anoon to drawen every wight bigan,
845 And shortly for to tellen as it was,
Were it by aventure,° or sort°, or cas,°   *luck / fate / chance*
The soothe° is this, the cut fil° to the Knight;   *truth / fell*
Of which ful blithe and glad was every wight,
And telle he moste° his tale, as was resoun,   *must*
850 By forward° and by composicioun,°   *agreement / compact*
As ye han herd. What needeth wordes mo?
And whan this goode man sawgh that it was so,
As he that wis was and obedient
To keepe his forward by his free assent,
855 He saide, "Sin I shal biginne the game,
What, welcome be the cut, in Goddes name!
Now lat us ride, and herkneth what I saye."
And with that word we riden forth oure waye,
And he bigan with right a merye cheere°   *countenance*
860 His tale anoon, and saide as ye may heere.

The Wife of Bath's Prologue and Tale[1]

The Prologue

Experience, though noon auctoritee
Were in this world, is right ynough for me
To speke of wo that is in mariage:
For lordinges,° sith I twelf yeer was of age—   *gentlemen*
5 Thanked be God that is eterne on live—
Housbondes at chirche dore[2] I have had five
(If I so ofte mighte han wedded be),

1. The Wife of Bath's prologue and tale have no link to a preceding tale and together occupy different positions in the many manuscript versions of *The Canterbury Tales*. Most scholars agree, however, that the Wife's powerful voice begins a sequence of tales dealing with marriage. In her prologue, the Wife draws on and often comically questions classical and Christian traditions of antiwoman and antimarriage discourse in various genres. At once embodying and satirizing common stereotypes of women drawn from Christian and classical "authorities" (whom she sometimes comically misquotes), the Wife speaks from a position shaped, she claims, by her "experience," rather than by "auctoritee." In so doing, she reminds us that many fewer women than men had access to literacy—and its cultural prestige—during the Middle Ages than do today. This was, in part, because fewer girls than boys received formal education, but also because literacy was commonly defined as mastery of Latin, the language of the Church and the priesthood, which was often inaccessible or incomprehensible to women and to lay-

men. In creating a female character who uses a version of the English vernacular to engage in witty battle with generations of literate clerks and their writings about women, Chaucer engages in lively but also serious play in an arena of (ongoing) cultural debate.

The Wife's tale illustrates some of the claims she makes in her prologue about women's right to be "sovereign" (to rule) over men. While the Wife's prologue draws on contemporary history and her own life story, her tale transports us to a distant, largely fictional world of chivalric romance. Although the Wife at one point "interrupts" her fairy tale to continue the authority-citing debate of the prologue, her argument is mostly carried by a plot that combines elements from two traditional stories found in many European languages: that of a knight and a "loathly" lady and that of a man whose life depends on his being able to answer a certain question.

2. The actual wedding ceremony was performed at the church door.

And alle were worthy men in hir degree.
But me was told, certain, nat longe agoon is,
10 That sith that Crist ne wente nevere but ones[3]
To wedding in the Cane[4] of Galilee,
That by the same ensample° taughte he me   *example*
That I ne sholde wedded be but ones.
Herke eek, lo, which a sharp word for the nones,[5]
15 Biside a welle, Jesus, God and man,
Spak in repreve° of the Samaritan: *reproof*
"Thou hast yhad five housbondes," quod he,
"And that ilke° man that now hath thee   *same*
Is nat thyn housbonde." Thus saide he certain.
20 What that he mente therby I can nat sayn,
But that I axe° why the fifthe man   *ask*
Was noon housbonde to the Samaritan?[6]
How manye mighte she han in marriage?
Yit herde I nevere tellen in myn age
25 Upon this nombre diffinicioun.°   *definition*
Men may divine° and glosen° up and down,   *guess / interpret*
But wel I woot,° expres,° withouten lie,   *know / expressly*
God bad us for to wexe[7] and multiplye:
That gentil° text can I wel understonde.   *excellent, worthy*
30   Eek wel I woot° he saide that myn housbonde   *know*
Sholde lete° fader and moder and take to me,[8]   *leave*
But of no nombre mencion made he—
Of bigamye or of octogamye:[9]
Why sholde men thanne speke of it vilainye?
35   Lo, here the wise king daun° Salomon: *master*
I trowe° he hadde wives many oon,[1]   *believe*
As wolde God it leveful° were to me   *permissible*
To be refresshed half so ofte as he.
Which yifte° of God hadde he for alle his wives!   *gift*
40 No man hath swich° that in this world alive is.   *such*
God woot this noble king, as to my wit,°   *knowledge*
The firste night hadde many a merye fit°   *bout*
With eech of hem, so wel was him on live.[2]
Blessed be God that I have wedded five,
45 Of whiche I have piked out the beste,[3]
Bothe of hir nether purs and of hir cheste.[4]
Diverse scoles maken parfit° clerkes,   *perfect*
And diverse practikes in sondry werkes[5]

---

3. Once. *Ne . . . nevere:* in Middle English, double negatives reinforce each other rather than cancel each other out.
4. Cana, a town in Galilee where Christ attended a wedding and turned water into wine (see John 2.1).
5. Hark also, lo, what a sharp word to the purpose.
6. Christ was actually referring to a sixth man, with whom the Samaritan woman was living but to whom she was not married (cf. John 4.16–19).
7. I.e., increase (see Genesis 1.28).
8. Both the Hebrew and Christian Scriptures explain marriage as a union between husband and wife that requires the man to leave his parents to

become "one" with his wife; see Genesis 2.24 and Matthew 19.5.
9. I.e., of two or eight marriages. The Wife is referring to successive rather than simultaneous marriages.
1. Solomon had seven hundred wives and three hundred concubines (1 Kings 11.3).
2. I.e., so happy was he with life.
3. Whom I have cleaned out of everything worthwhile.
4. Of their lower purse (i.e., testicles) and their money box.
5. Practical experiences in various works.

Maken the werkman parfit sikerly:°   *certainly*
50 Of five housbondes scoleying° am I.   *learning*
Welcome the sixte whan that evere he shal![6]
For sith I wol nat kepe me chast in al,
Whan my housbonde is fro the world agoon,[7]
Som Cristen man shal wedde me anoon.°   *right away*
55 For thanne th'Apostle° saith that I am free   *St. Paul*
To wedde, a Goddes half, where it liketh me.[8]
He saide that to be wedded is no sinne:
Bet is to be wedded than to brinne.[9]
What rekketh me[1] though folk saye vilainye
60 Of shrewed Lamech[2] and his bigamye?
I woot wel Abraham was an holy man,
And Jacob eek, as fer as evere I can,°   *know*
And eech of hem hadde wives mo than two,
And many another holy man also.
65   Where can ye saye in any manere age
That hye God defended° mariage   *prohibited*
By expres word? I praye you, telleth me.
Or where comanded he virginitee?
I woot as wel as ye, it is no drede,°   *doubt*
70 Th'Apostle, whan he speketh of maidenhede,°   *virginity*
He saide that precept° therof hadde he noon: *command*
Men may conseile a womman to be oon,°   *single*
But conseiling nis° no comandement.   *is not*
He putte it in oure owene juggement.
75 For hadde God comanded maidenhede,
Thanne hadde he dampned wedding with the deede;[3]
And certes, if there were no seed ysowe,
Virginitee, thanne wherof sholde it growe?
Paul dorste nat comanden at the leeste
80 A thing of which his maister yaf° no heeste.°   *gave / command*
The dart[4] is set up for virginitee:
Cacche whoso may, who renneth° best lat see.   *runs*
But this word is nought take of every wight,[5]
But ther as[6] God list° yive it of his might.   *it pleases*
85 I woot wel that th'Apostle was a maide,°   *virgin*
But natheless, though that he wroot and saide
He wolde that every wight were swich° as he,   *such*
Al nis but conseil to virginitee;
And for to been a wif he yaf° me leve   *gave*
90 Of indulgence; so nis it no repreve°   *disgrace*
To wedde me[7] if that my make° die,   *mate*
Withouten excepcion of bigamye[8]—

6. Number six will be welcome when he comes along.
7. I.e., when my husband has passed away.
8. To wed, on God's behalf, as I please.
9. "It is better to marry than to burn" (1 Corinthians 7.9). Many of the Wife's citations of St. Paul are from this chapter.
1. What do I care.
2. The first man whom the Bible (Genesis 4.19–24) mentions as having two wives at once (bigamy). *Shrewed*: cursed.

3. I.e., then at the same time he condemned ("dampned") weddings.
4. I.e., prize in a race.
5. I.e., this word is not applicable to every person.
6. *There as*: where.
7. For me to marry.
8. I.e., as long as there is not a legal objection to the "bigamy," here understood as occurring when a widow remarries (in contrast to the meaning at line 60).

Al° were it good no womman for to touche⁹   *although*
(He mente as in his bed or in his couche,
95   For peril is bothe fir° and tow° t'assemble—   *fire / flax*
Ye knowe what this ensample may resemble).¹
This al and som,² he heeld virginitee
More parfit than wedding in freletee.°   *frailty*
(Freletee clepe I but if that³ he and she
100 Wolde leden al hir lif in chastitee.)
I graunte it wel, I have noon envye°   *hard feelings*
Though maidenhede preferre° bigamye.   *surpass*
It liketh hem to be clene in body and gost.°   *spirit*
Of myn estaat ne wol I make no boost;
105 For wel ye knowe, a lord in his houshold
Ne hath nat every vessel al of gold:
Some been of tree,° and doon hir lord servise.   *wood*
God clepeth° folk to him in sondry wise,   *calls*
And everich hath of God a propre⁴ yifte,
110 Som this, som that, as him liketh shifte:°   *ordain*
Virginitee is greet perfeccioun,
And continence eek with devocioun,⁵
But Crist, that of perfeccion is welle,°   *source*
Bad nat every wight he sholde go selle
115 Al that he hadde and yive it to the poore,
And in swich wise folwe him and his fore:⁶
He spak to hem that wolde live parfitly°—   *perfectly*
And lordinges, by youre leve, that am nat I.
I wol bistowe the flour of al myn age
120 In th'actes and in fruit of mariage.
        Telle me also, to what conclusioun°   *end*
Were membres maad of generacioun
And of so parfit wis a wrighte ywrought?⁷
        Trusteth right wel, they were nat maad for nought.
125 Glose° whoso wol, and saye bothe up and down   *interpret*
That they were maked for purgacioun
Of urine, and oure bothe thinges smale
Was eek° to knowe a femele from a male,   *also*
And for noon other cause—saye ye no?
130 Th'experience woot it is nought so.
So that the clerkes be nat with me wrothe,°   *angry*
I saye this, that they been maad for bothe—
That is to sayn, for office° and for ese°   *use / pleasure*
Of engendrure,° ther we nat God displese.   *procreation*
135 Why sholde men elles in hir bookes sette
That man shal yeelde° to his wif hir dette?°   *pay / (marital) debt*
Now wherwith sholde he make his payement
If he ne used his sely° instrument?   *innocent*

---

9. "It is good for a man not to touch a woman" (1
Corinthians 7.1).
1. I.e., what this metaphor may refer to.
2. This is all there is to it.
3. Frailty I call it unless.
4. I.e., his or her own.
5. The Wife distinguishes between "virginitee" for

unmarried persons and "continence" for husbands
and wives.
6. Footsteps. In Matthew 19.21, Christ tells a rich
man to give up his wealth if he wishes to gain
riches in heaven.
7. And made by so perfectly wise a maker.

Thanne were they maad upon a creature
140   To purge urine, and eek for engendrure.
     But I saye nought that every wight is holde,°   *bound*
That hath swich harneis° as I to you tolde,   *equipment*
To goon and usen hem in engendrure:
Thanne sholde men take of chastitee no cure.°   *heed*
145   Crist was a maide° and shapen as a man,   *virgin*
And many a saint sith that the world bigan,
Yit lived they evere in parfit chastitee.
I nil° envye no virginitee: *will not*
Lat hem be breed° of pured° whete seed,   *bread / refined*
150   And lat us wives hote° barly breed—   *be called*
And yit with barly breed, Mark telle can,
Oure Lord Jesu refresshed many a man.[8]
In swich estaat as God hath cleped° us   *called*
I wol persevere: I nam nat precious.°   *careful*
155   In wifhood wol I use myn instrument
As freely° as my Makere hath it sent.   *generously*
If I be daungerous,[9] God yive me sorwe:
Myn housbonde shal it han both eve and morwe,°   *morning*
     Whan that him list[1] come forth and paye his dette.
160   An housbonde wol I have, I wol nat lette,°   *leave off, stop*
Which shal be bothe my dettour° and my thral,°   *debtor / slave*
And have his tribulacion withal°   *as well*
Upon his flessh whil that I am his wif.
I have the power during al my lif
165   Upon his propre body, and nat he:[2]
Right thus th'Apostle tolde it unto me,
And bad oure housbondes for to love us weel.
Al this sentence° me liketh everydeel.°   *opinion / entirely*

[AN INTERLUDE]

     Up sterte° the Pardoner and that anoon: *started*
170   "Now dame," quod he, "by God and by Saint John,
Ye been a noble prechour in this cas.
I was aboute to wedde a wif: allas,
What° sholde I bye° it on my flessh so dere?   *why / purchase*
Yit hadde I levere° wedde no wif toyere,"°   *rather / this year*
175   "Abid," quod she, "my tale is nat bigonne.
Nay, thou shalt drinken of another tonne,°   *tun, barrel*
Er° that I go, shal savoure wors than ale.   *before*
And whan that I have told thee forth my tale
Of tribulacion in mariage,
180   Of which I am expert in al myn age—
This is to saye, myself hath been the whippe—
Thanne maistou chese° wheither thou wolt sippe   *choose*

---

8. In the descriptions of the miracle of the loaves and fishes, it is actually John, not Mark, who mentions barley bread (6.9).
9. In the vocabulary of romance, *dangerous* refers to the disdainfulness with which a highborn woman rejects a lover. The Wife means she will not withhold sexual favors, in emulation of God's generosity (line 156).
1. When he wishes her to.
2. I.e., as long as I am alive, he does not even control his body.

Of thilke° tonne that I shal abroche;°   *this same / open*
Be war of it, er thou too neigh° approche,   *near*
185   For I shal telle ensamples mo than ten.
'Whoso that nil° be war by othere men,   *will not*
By him shal othere men corrected be.'
This same wordes writeth Ptolomee:
Rede in his *Almageste* and take it there."[3]
190   "Dame, I wolde praye you if youre wil it were,"
Saide this Pardoner, "as ye bigan,
Telle forth youre tale; spareth for no man,
And teche us yonge men of youre practike."°   *mode of operation*
        "Gladly," quod she, "sith it may you like;°   *please*
195   But that I praye to al this compaignye,
If that I speke after my fantasye,[4]
As taketh nat agrief° of that I saye,   *amiss*
For myn entente nis but for to playe."

[THE WIFE CONTINUES]

Now sire, thanne wol I telle you forth my tale.
200   As evere mote I drinke win or ale,
I shal saye sooth: tho° housbondes that I hadde,   *those*
As three of hem were goode, and two were badde.
The three men were goode, and riche, and olde;
Unnethe° mighte they the statut holde   *scarcely*
205   In which they were bounden unto me—
Ye woot wel what I mene of this, pardee.°   *by God*
As help me God, I laughe whan I thinke
How pitously anight I made hem swinke°   *work*
And by my fay,° I tolde of it no stoor:[5]   *faith*
210   They hadde me yiven hir land and hir tresor;
Me needed nat do lenger diligence[6]
To winne hir love or doon hem reverence.
They loved me so wel, by God above,
That I ne tolde no daintee of[7] hir love.
215   A wis womman wol bisye hire evere in oon[8]
To gete hire love, ye, ther as she hath noon.
But sith I hadde hem hoolly in myn hand,
And sith that they hadde yiven me al hir land,
What° sholde I take keep° hem for to plese,   *why / care*
220   But it were for my profit and myn ese?
I sette hem so awerke,° by my fay,   *awork*
That many a night they songen° wailaway.   *sang*
The bacon was nat fet° for hem, I trowe,   *brought back*
That some men han in Essexe at Dunmowe.[9]
225   I governed hem so wel after° my lawe   *according to*

3. "He who will not be warned by the example of others shall become an example to others." The Wife wrongly attributes this proverb to the *Almagest*, an astronomical work by the second-century Greek astronomer and mathematician Ptolemy.
4. If I speak according to my fancy.
5. I set no store by it.
6. I.e., there was no need for me to make any fur-
ther effort.
7. Set no value on.
8. I.e., be busy constantly
9. At Dunmow, a side of bacon was awarded to the couple who after a year of marriage could claim no quarrels, no regrets, and the desire, if freed, to remarry one another.

That eech of hem ful blisful was and fawe°   *glad*
To bringe me gaye thinges fro the faire;
They were ful glade whan I spak hem faire,
For God it woot, I chidde° hem spitously.°   *chided / cruelly*
230   Now herkneth how I bar me[1] properly:
Ye wise wives, that conne understonde,
Thus sholde ye speke and bere him wrong on honde[2]—
For half so boldely can ther no man
Swere and lie as a woman can.
235   I saye nat this by wives that been wise,
But if it be whan they hem misavise,[3]
A wis wif, if that she can hir good,[4]
Shal bere him on hande the cow is wood,[5]
And take witnesse of hir owene maide
240   Of hir assent.[6] But herkneth how I saide:
"Sire olde cainard, is this thyn array?[7]
Why is my neighebores wif so gay?
She is honoured overal° ther she gooth: *wherever*
I sitte at hoom; I have no thrifty° cloth.   *decent*
245   What doostou at my neighebores hous?
Is she so fair? Artou so amorous?
What roune° ye with oure maide, benedicite?°   *whisper / bless ye*
Sire olde lechour, lat thy japes° be.   *tricks, intrigues*
And if I have a gossib° or a freend   *confidant*
250   Withouten gilt, ye chiden as a feend,
If that I walke or playe unto his hous.
Thou comest hoom as dronken as a mous,
And prechest on thy bench, with yvel preef.[8]
Thou saist to me, it is a greet meschief°   *misfortune*
255   To wedde a poore womman for costage.[9]
And if that she be riche, of heigh parage,°   *descent*
Thanne saistou that it is a tormentrye
To suffre hir pride and hir malencolye,°   *bad mood*
And if that she be fair, thou verray knave,
260   Thou saist that every holour° wol hire have: *lecher*
She may no while in chastitee abide
That is assailed upon eech a side.
"Thou saist som folk desiren us for richesse,
Som[1] for oure shap, and som for oure fairnesse,
265   And som for she can outher° singe or daunce,   *either*
And som for gentilesse and daliaunce,°   *flirtatiousness*
Som for hir handes and hir armes smale°—   *slender*
Thus gooth al to the devel by thy tale![2]
Thou saist men may nat keepe[3] a castel wal,
270   It may so longe assailed been overal.°   *everywhere*
And if that she be foul,° thou saist that she   *ugly*

1. *Bar me:* behaved.
2. I.e., accuse him falsely.
3. Unless it happens that they make a mistake.
4. If she knows what's good for her.
5. Shall persuade him the chough has gone crazy. The chough, a talking bird, was said to tell husbands of their wives' infidelity.
6. And call as a witness her maid, who is on her side.
7. I.e., sir old sluggard, is this how you behave?
8. I.e., (may you have) bad luck.
9. Because of the expense.
1. In this and the following lines, meaning "one."
2. I.e., according to your story.
3. I.e., keep safe.

Coveiteth° every man that she may see;   *desires*
For as a spaniel she wol on him lepe,
Til that she finde som man hire to chepe.°   *bargain for*
275   Ne noon so grey goos gooth ther in the lake,
As, saistou, wol be withoute make;°   *mate*
And saist it is an hard thing for to weelde°   *possess*
A thing that no man wol, his thankes, heelde.¹
Thus saistou, lorel,° whan thou goost to bedde,   *wretch*
280   And that no wis man needeth for to wedde,
Ne no man that entendeth° unto hevene—   *aims*
With wilde thonder-dint° and firy levene°   *thunderbolt / lightning*
Mote thy welked nekke be tobroke!⁵
Thou saist that dropping° houses and eek smoke   *leaking*
285   And chiding wives maken men to flee
Out of hir owene hous: a, benedicite,⁶
What aileth swich an old man for to chide?
Thou saist we wives wil oure vices hide
Til we be fast,⁷ and thanne we wol hem shewe—
290   Wel may that be a proverbe of a shrewe!⁸
Thou saist that oxen, asses, hors,° and houndes,   *horses*
They been assayed° at diverse stoundes°   *tried out / times*
Bacins, lavours,° er that men hem bye;°   *washbowls / buy*
Spoones, stooles, and al swich housbondrye,°   *household goods*
295   And so be° pottes, clothes, and array°—   *are / clothing*
But folk of wives maken noon assay
Til they be wedded—olde dotard shrewe!
And thanne, saistou, we wil oure vices shewe.
Thou saist also that it displeseth me
300   But if⁹ that thou wolt praise my beautee,
And but thou poure° alway upon my face,   *gaze*
And clepe me 'Faire Dame' in every place,
And but thou make a feeste on thilke day
That I was born, and make me fressh and gay,
305   And but thou do to my norice° honour,   *nurse*
And to my chamberere within my bowr,¹
And to my fadres folk, and his allies°—   *relatives by marriage*
Thus saistou, olde barel-ful of lies.
And yit of our apprentice Janekin,
310   For his crispe° heer, shining as gold so fin,   *curly*
And for° he squiereth me bothe up and down,   *because*
Yit hastou caught a fals suspecioun;
I wil° him nat though thou were deed° tomorwe.   *want / dead*
    "But tel me this, why hidestou with sorwe°   *sorrow*
315   The keyes of thy cheste° away fro me?   *money box*
It is my good° as wel as thyn, pardee.°   *property / by God*
What, weenestou° make an idiot of oure dame?²   *do you think to*
Now by that lord that called is Saint Jame,
Thou shalt nought bothe, though thou were wood,°   *furious*

---

4. No man would willingly hold.
5. May your withered neck be broken!
6. Oh, blessings upon you. The Wife appropriates
a Latin phrase used by priests in the Mass.
7. I.e., married.
8. The word initially meant "rascal" or "malignant

person" (see line 361), but by Chaucer's time it
could also signify a "scolding wife."
9. *But if:* unless.
1. And to my chambermaid within my bedroom.
2. I.e., me, the mistress of the house.

320 Be maister of my body and of my good:
That oon thou shalt forgo, maugree thine yën.[3]
"What helpeth it of me enquere° and spyen?   *inquire*
I trowe thou woldest loke° me in thy cheste.   *lock*
Thou sholdest saye, 'Wif, go wher thee leste.°   *it may please*
325 Taak youre disport.[4] I nil leve° no tales: *believe*
I knowe you for a trewe wif, dame Alis.'
We love no man that taketh keep° or charge°   *notice / interest*
Wher that we goon: we wol been at oure large.[5]
Of alle men yblessed mote he be
330 The wise astrologen° daun Ptolomee,   *astronomer*
That saith this proverbe in his *Almageste*:
'Of alle men his wisdom is the hyeste
That rekketh nat who hath the world in honde.[6]
By this proverbe thou shalt understonde,
335 Have thou[7] ynough, what thar° thee rekke or care   *need*
How merily that othere folkes fare?
For certes, olde dotard, by youre leve,
Ye shal han queinte[8] right ynough at eve:
He is too greet a nigard that wil werne°   *refuse*
340 A man to lighte a candle at his lanterne;
He shal han nevere the lasse° lighte, pardee.   *less*
Have thou ynough, thee thar nat plaine thee.[9]
"Thou saist also that if we make us gay
With clothing and with precious array,
345 That it is peril of oure chastitee,
And yit, with sorwe, thou moste enforce thee,[1]
And saye thise wordes in th'Apostles° name: *St. Paul's*
'In habit° maad with chastitee and shame   *clothing*
Ye wommen shal apparaile you,' quod he,
350 'And nat in tressed heer and gay perree,[2]
As perles, ne with gold ne clothes riche.[3]
After thy text, ne after thy rubriche,[4]
I wol nat werke as muchel as a gnat.
Thou saidest this, that I was lik a cat:
355 For whoso wolde senge° a cattes skin,   *singe*
Thanne wolde the cat wel dwellen in his in;°   *lodging*
And if the cattes skin be slik° and gay,   *sleek*
She wol nat dwelle in house half a day,
But forth she wol, er any day be° dawed,°   *has / dawned*
360 To shewe her skin and goon a-caterwawed.°   *caterwauling*
This is to saye, if I be gay, sire shrewe,
I wol renne° out, my borel° for to shewe.   *run / clothing*
Sir olde fool, what helpeth° thee t'espyen?   *does it help*
Though thou praye Argus with his hundred yën[5]

3. Despite your eyes, i.e., despite anything you can do about it.
4. Enjoy yourself.
5. I.e., liberty.
6. That cares not who rules the world.
7. If you have.
8. Elegant, pleasing thing (from the Old French adjective *coint*); also *cunt,* as Chaucer uses it in line 90 of the Miller's tale: "Prively he caught hir by the queynte."

9. I.e., you need not complain.
1. Strengthen your position.
2. I.e., not in elaborate hairdo and gay jewelry.
3. See St. Paul's prescriptions for modest female dress and behavior, in 1 Timothy 2.9.
4. Rubric, i.e., direction.
5. In Roman mythology, Argus was a monster sent by the goddess Juno to watch over one of Jupiter's (her husband's) mistresses. The god Mercury put all of Argus's hundred eyes to sleep and killed him.

365 To be my wardecors,° as he can best,   bodyguard
In faith, he shal nat keepe me but me lest:[6]
Yit coude I make his beerd,[7] so mote I thee.°   prosper
        "Thou saidest eek that ther been thinges three,
The whiche thinges troublen al this erthe,
370 And that no wight may endure the ferthe °   fourth
O leve° sire shrewe, Jesu shorte° thy lif!   dear / shorten
Yit prechestou and saist an hateful wif
Yrekened° is for oon of thise meschaunces.[8]   is counted
Been ther nat none othere resemblaunces
375 That ye may likne youre parables to,[9]
But if a sely[1] wif be oon of tho?
        "Thou liknest eek wommanes love to helle,
To bareine° land ther water may nat dwelle;   barren
Thou liknest it also to wilde fir—
380 The more it brenneth,° the more it hath desir   burns
To consumen every thing that brent° wol be;   burned
Thou saist right° as wormes shende° a tree,   just / destroy
Right so a wif destroyeth hir housbonde—
This knowen they that been to wives bonde."°   bound
385   Lordinges, right thus, as ye hand understonde,
Bar I stifly mine olde housbondes on honde[2]
That thus they saiden in hir dronkenesse—
And al was fals, but that I took witnesse
On Janekin and on my nece also.
390 O Lord, the paine I dide hem and the wo,
Ful giltelees, by Goddes sweete pine![3]
For as an hors I coude bite and whine;°   whinny
I coude plaine and I was in the gilt,[4]
Or elles often time I hadde been spilt.°   ruined
395 Whoso that first to mille comth first grint.°   grinds
I plained first: so was oure werre stint.[5]
They were ful glade to excusen hem ful blive°   quickly
Of thing of which they nevere agilte hir live.[6]
Of wenches wolde I beren hem on honde,[7]
400 Whan that for sik[8] they mighte unnethe° stonde,   scarcely
Yit tikled I his herte for that he
Wende° I hadde had of him so greet cheertee.°   thought / affection
I swoor that al my walking out by nighte
Was for to espye wenches that he dighte.°   had intercourse with
405 Under that colour[9] hadde I many a mirthe.
For al swich wit is yiven us in oure birthe:
Deceite, weeping, spinning God hath yive
To wommen kindely° whil they may live.   naturally
And thus of oo thing I avaunte me:[1]

6. Guard me unless I please.
7. I.e., yet could I deceive him.
8. For the other three misfortunes, see Proverbs 30.21–23.
9. Are there no other (appropriate) similitudes to which you might draw analogies.
1. But if a seely: unless an innocent.
2. I rigorously accused my husbands.
3. Christ's suffering ("pine") is called sweet because of the happiness that resulted from it.
4. I could complain if I was in the wrong.
5. So was our war ended.
6. Of which they were never guilty in their lives.
7. Falsely accuse them.
8. I.e., sickness.
9. I.e., pretense.
1. Avaunt me: boast.

410	At ende I hadde the bet° in eech degree,	*better*
	By sleighte or force, or by som manere thing,	
	As by continuel murmur° or grucching;°	*complaint / grumbling*
	Namely° abedde hadden they meschaunce:	*especially*
	Ther wolde I chide and do hem no plesaunce;²	
415	I wolde no lenger in the bed abide	
	If that I felte his arm over my side,	
	Til he hadde maad his raunson° unto me;	*ransom*
	Thanne wolde I suffre him do his nicetee.°	*foolishness (sex)*
	And therfore every man this tale I telle:	
420	Winne whoso may, for al is for to selle;	
	With empty hand men may no hawkes lure.	
	For winning° wolde I al his lust endure,	*profit*
	And make me a feined° appetit—	*pretended*
	And yit in bacon³ hadde I nevere delit.	
425	That made me that evere I wolde hem chide;	
	For though the Pope hadde seten° hem biside,	*sat*
	I wolde nought spare hem at hir owene boord.°	*table*
	For by my trouthe, I quitte° hem word for word.	*repaid*
	As help me verray God omnipotent,	
430	Though I right now sholde make my testament,	
	I ne owe hem nat a word that it nis quit.⁴	
	I broughte it so aboute by my wit	
	That they moste yive it up as for the beste,	
	Or elles hadde we nevere been in reste;	
435	For though he looked as a wood° leoun,°	*furious / lion*
	Yit sholde he faile of his conclusioun.°	*object*
	Thanne wolde I saye, "Goodelief, taak keep,⁵	
	How mekely looketh Wilekin,° oure sheep!	*Willie*
	Com neer my spouse, lat, me ba° thy cheeke—	*kiss*
440	Ye sholden be al pacient and meeke,	
	And han a sweete-spiced° conscience,	*mild*
	Sith ye so preche of Jobes pacience;	
	Suffreth alway, sin ye so wel can preche;	
	And but ye do, certain, we shal you teche	
445	That it is fair to han a wif in pees.°	*peace*
	Oon of us two moste bowen, doutelees,	
	And sith a man is more resonable	
	Than womman is, ye mosten been suffrable.°	*patient*
	What aileth you to grucche° thus and grone?	*grumble*
450	Is it for ye wolde have my queinte° allone?	*sexual organ*
	Why, taak it al—lo, have it everydeel.°	*all of it*
	Peter, I shrewe you but ye⁶ love it weel.	
	For if I wolde selle my bele chose,⁷	
	I coude walke as fressh as is a rose;	
455	But I wol keepe it for youre owene tooth.°	*taste*
	Ye be to blame. By God, I saye you sooth!"°	*the truth*
	Swiche manere° wordes hadde we on honde.	*kind of*

2. Give them no pleasure.
3. I.e., old meat.
4. I don't owe them (my husbands) one word that I haven't (re)paid; or, I gave as good as I got!
5. Good friend, take notice.
6. By St. Peter, I curse you if you don't.
7. Beautiful thing (French); a euphemism for female genitals.

Now wol I speke of my ferthe° housbonde.   *fourth*
　My ferthe housbonde was a revelour°   *reveler*
460 This is to sayn, he hadde a paramour°   *mistress*
And I was yong and ful of ragerye,°   *passion*
Stibourne° and strong and joly as a pie:°   *untamable / magpie*
How coude I daunce to an harpe smale,°   *gracefully*
And singe, ywis,° as any nightingale,   *Indeed*
465 Whan I hadde dronke a draughte of sweete win.
Metellius,[8] the foule cherl, the swin,
That with a staf birafte° his wif hir lif   *deprived*
For° she drank win, though I hadde been his wif, *because*
Ne sholde nat han daunted° me fro drinke,   *frightened*
470 And after win on Venus moste° I thinke,   *must*
For also siker° as cold engendreth hail,   *sure*
A likerous° mouth moste han a likerous° tail: *greedy / lecherous*
In womman vinolent° is no defence—   *who drinks*
This knowen lechours by experience.
475 　But Lord Crist, whan that it remembreth me[9]
Upon my youthe and on my jolitee,
It tikleth me aboute myn herte roote—
Unto this day it dooth myn herte boote°   *good*
That I have had my world as in my time.
480 But age, allas, that al wol envenime,°   *poison*
Hath me biraft my beautee and my pith[1]—
Lat go, farewel, the devel go therwith!
The flour is goon, ther is namore to telle:
The bren° as I best can now moste I selle;   *bran*
485 But yit to be right merye wol I fonde.°   *strive*
Now wol I tellen of my ferthe housbonde.
　I saye I hadde in herte greet despit
That he of any other hadde delit,
But he was quit,° by God and by Saint Joce: *paid back*
490 I made him of the same wode a croce[2]—
Nat of my body in no foul manere—
But, certainly, I made folk swich cheere[3]
That in his owene grece I made him frye,[4]
For angre and for verray jalousye.
495 By God, in erthe I was his purgatorye,
For which I hope his soule be in glorye.[5]
For God it woot, he sat ful ofte and soong°   *sang*
Whan that his sho ful bitterly him wroong.°   *pinched*
Ther was no wight save God and he that wiste°   *knew*
500 In many wise how sore I him twiste.
He deide whan I cam fro Jerusalem,
And lith ygrave under the roode-beem,[6]
Al° is his tombe nought so curious°   *although / carefully wrought*

8. Egnatius Metellius, a Roman whose story is told by the writer Valerius Maximus (ca. 20 B.C.E.–ca. 50 C.E.).
9. When I look back.
1. I.e., age has taken away from me ("biraft") my beauty and my vigor ("pith").
2. I made him a cross of the same wood. This proverb anticipates the one quoted in line 493.

3. I.e., pretended to be in love with others.
4. I.e., I made him stew in his own juice.
5. I.e., I provided so much suffering on Earth for my husband that his enjoyment of celestial bliss was assured.
6. I.e., and lies buried under the rood beam (the crucifix beam running between nave and chancel).

As was the sepulcre of him Darius,
505 Which that Apelles wroughte subtilly:[7]
It nis but wast to burye him preciously.°   *expensively*
Lat him fare wel, God yive his soule reste;
He is now in his grave and in his cheste.°   *coffin*
   Now of my fifthe housbonde wol I telle—
510 God lete his soule nevere come in helle—
And yit he was to me the moste° shrewe:°   *worst / rascal*
That feele I on my ribbes al° by° rewe,°   *in / a / row*
And evere shal unto myn ending day.
But in oure bed he was so fressh and gay,
515 And therwithal so wel coulde he me glose°   *flatter, coax*
Whan that he wolde han my bele chose,
That though he hadde me bet° on every boon,°   *beaten / bone*
He coude winne again my love anoon.°   *immediately*
I trowe I loved him best for that he
520 Was of his love daungerous to me.[8]
We wommen han, if that I shal nat lie,
In this matere a quainte° fantasye:°   *strange / fancy*
Waite what[9] thing we may nat lightly° have,   *easily*
Therafter wol we crye al day and crave;
525 Forbede us thing, and that desiren we;
Preesse on us faste, and thanne wol we flee.
With daunger oute we al oure chaffare:[1]
Greet prees° at market maketh dere° ware,   *crowd / expensive*
And too greet chepe is holden at litel pris.[2]
530 This knoweth every womman that is wis.
   My fifthe housbonde—God his soule blesse!—
Which that I took for love and no richesse,
He somtime was a clerk at Oxenforde,
And hadde laft° scole and wente at hoom to boorde   *left*
535 With my gossib,° dwelling in oure town   *confidante*
God have hir soule!—hir name was Alisoun;
She knew myn herte and eek my privetee°   *secrets*
Bet than oure parissh preest, as mote I thee.[3]
To hire biwrayed° I my conseil° al,   *disclosed / secrets*
540 For hadde myn housbonde pissed on a wal,
Or doon a thing that sholde han cost his lif,
To hire,° and to another worthy wif,   *her*
And to my nece which I loved weel,
I wolde han told his conseil everydeel;°   *entirely*
545 And so I dide ful often, God it woot,°   *knew*
That made his face often reed° and hoot°   *red / hot*
For verray shame, and blamed himself for he
Hadde told to me so greet a privetee.
   And so bifel that ones° in a Lente—   *once*
550 So often times I to my gossib wente,
For evere yit I loved to be gay,

---

7. According to medieval legend, the artist Apelles decorated the tomb of Darius, king of the Persians.
8. I.e., he played hard to get.
9. *Waite what:* whatever.
1. (Meeting) with reserve, we spread out our mer-

chandise.
2. Too good a bargain is held at little value.
3. The Wife's friend knew more of her secrets than did her official confessor. *Bet:* better. *As mote I thee:* as may I prosper (oath).

And for to walke in March, Averil, and May,
From hous to hous, to heere sondry tales—
That Janekin clerk and my gossib dame Alis
555   And I myself into the feeldes wente.
Myn housbonde was at London al that Lente:
I hadde the better leiser° for to playe,   leisure
And for to see, and eek for to be seye°   seen
Of lusty folk—what wiste I wher my grace[4]
560   Was shapen° for to be, or in what place?   destined
Therfore I made my visitaciouns
To vigilies[5] and to processiouns,
To preching eek, and to thise pilgrimages,
To playes of miracles[6] and to mariages,
565   And wered upon[7] my gaye scarlet gites°—   gowns
Thise wormes ne thise motthes ne thise mites,
Upon my peril, frete hem reveradeel:[8]
And woostou why? For they were used weel.
          Now wol I tellen forth what happed me.
570   I saye that in the feeldes walked we,
Til trewely we hadde swich daliaunce,°   flirtation
This clerk and I, that of my purveyaunce°   foresight
I spak to him and saide him how that he,
If I were widwe, sholde wedde me.
575   For certainly, I saye for no bobaunce,°   boast
Yit was I nevere withouten purveyaunce
Of mariage n'of othere thinges eek.
I holde a mouses herte nought worth a leek
That hath but oon hole for to sterte° to,   run
580   And if that faile thanne is al ydo.[9]
I bar him on hand[1] he hadde enchaunted me
(My dame° taughte me that subtiltee);   mother
And eek I saide I mette° of him al night;   dreamed
He wolde han slain me as I lay upright,°   on my back
585   And al my bed was ful of verray blood—
"But yit I hope that ye shul do me good;
For blood bitokeneth gold[2] as me was taught."
And al was fals, I dremed of it right naught,[3]
But as I folwed ay my dames° lore°   mother's / teaching
590   As wel of that as othere thinges more.
But now sire—lat me see, what shal I sayn?
Aha, by God, I have my tale again.
          Whan that my ferthe housbonde was on beere,°   funeral bier
I weep,° algate,° and made sory cheere,   wept / anyhow
595   As wives moten,° for it is usage,°   must / custom
And with my coverchief covered my visage;°   face

4. I.e., how would I know where my favor was des-
tined to be bestowed? *Grace:* luck.
5. Evening services before religious holidays.
6. Plays dealing with the lives of saints or martyrs
that were performed in various English towns.
7. *Wered upon:* wore.
8. I.e., when attending various religious events,
the Wife wore worldly (gay, scarlet) clothes that
neither worms, nor moths, nor mites devoured at

all (*freten:* to consume); so she swears, ironically
on her peril, i.e., at risk of being damned.
9. I.e., the game is up.
1. I pretended that.
2. Because both are red. Chaucer, like Shake-
speare, frequently relates the two through their
common color.
3. I never dreamed of it at all.

But for I was purveyed° of a make.°   *provided / mate*
I wepte but smale, and that I undertake.°   *guarantee*
  To chirche was myn housbonde born amorwe;[4]
600 With neighebores that for him maden sorwe,
And Janekin oure clerk was oon of tho.
As help me God, whan that I saw him go
After the beere, me thoughte he hadde a paire
Of legges and of feet so clene° and faire,   *neat*
605 That al myn herte I yaf unto his hold.°   *possession*
He was, I trowe,° twenty winter old,   *believe*
And I was fourty, if I shal saye sooth—
But yit I hadde alway a coltes tooth:[5]
Gat-toothed was I,[6] and that bicam me weel:
610 I hadde the prente of Sainte Venus seel.[7]
As help me God, I was a lusty oon,
And fair and riche and yong and wel-bigoon,°   *well-situated*
And trewely, as mine housbondes tolde me,
I hadde the beste quoniam[8] mighte be.
615 For certes I am al Venerien
In feeling, and myn herte is Marcien:[9]
Venus me yaf° my lust, my likerousnesse,°   *gave / amorousness*
And Mars yaf me my sturdy hardinesse,
Myn ascendent was Taur[1] and Mars therinne—
620 Allas, allas, that evere love was sinne![2]
I folwed ay° my inclinacioun   *ever*
By vertu of my constellacioun;[3]
That made me I coude nought withdrawe
My chambre of Venus from a good felawe.
625 Yit have I Martes° merk upon my face,   *Mars's*
And also in another privee place.[4]
For God so wis° be my savacioun,°   *surely / salvation*
I loved nevere by no discrecioun,°   *moderation*
But evere folwede myn appetit,
630 Al were he short or long or blak or whit;
I took no keep,° so that he liked° me,   *heed / pleased*
How poore he was, ne eek of what degree.
  What sholde I saye but at the monthes ende
This joly clerk Janekin that was so hende°   *courteous, nice*
635 Hath wedded me with greet solempnitee,°   *splendor*
And to him yaf I al the land and fee°   *property*
That evere was me yiven therbifore—
But afterward repented me ful sore:
He nolde suffre no thing of my list.[5]
640 By God, he smoot° me ones on the list°   *struck / ear*

---

4. Carried (on his bier) in the morning.
5. I.e., youthful appetites.
6. Gap-toothed women were thought to be lustful.
7. I.e., I was lascivious because I had the birthmark (*print*) of Venus's own mark (*seal*).
8. Because (Latin); another of the Wife's many terms for female genitals.
9. Influenced by Mars, Roman god of war; i.e., my heart is courageous. *Venerien:* influenced by Venus, Roman goddess of love and beauty.
1. My birth sign was the constellation Taurus, a

sign in which Venus is dominant.
2. I.e., alas that theologians and others view passionate love as sinful.
3. I.e., I always followed my desires because of my "nature," as determined (she claims) by astrology.
4. I.e., I have a reddish birthmark (thought to be a sign of Mars) on my face and also on my "private" parts.
5. He would not allow me anything of my own way.

For that I rente° out of his book a leef,   *tore*
That of the strook° myn ere weex° al deef.   *blow / grew*
Stibourne° I was as is a leonesse,   *stubborn*
And of my tonge a verray jangleresse,°   *chatterbox*
645   And walke I wolde, as I hadde doon biforn,
From hous to hous, although he hadde it[6] sworn;
For which he often times wolde preche,
And me of olde Romain geestes° teche,   *stories*
How he Simplicius Gallus lafte° his wif,   *left*
650   And hire forsook for terme of al his lif,
Nought but for open-heveded he hire sey[7]
Looking out at his dore upon a day.
     Another Romain tolde he me by name
That, for his wif was at a someres game[8]
655   Withouten his witing,° he forsook hire eke;   *knowlege*
And thanne wolde he upon his Bible seeke
That ilke proverbe of Ecclesiaste[9]
Where he comandeth and forbedeth faste°   *strictly*
Man shal nat suffre his wif go roule° aboute;   *roam*
660   Thanne wolde he saye right thus withouten doute:
"Whoso that buildeth his hous al of salwes,°   *willow sticks*
And priketh° his blinde hors over the falwes,°   *spurs / plowed land*
And suffreth° his wif to go seeken halwes,°   *allows / shrines*
Is worthy to be hanged on the galwes,"°   *gallows*
665   But al for nought—I sette nought an hawe[1]
Of his proverbes n'of his olde sawe;
N' I wolde nat of him corrected be:
I hate him that my vices telleth me,
And so doon mo, God woot, of us than I.[2]
670   This made him with me wood al outrely:°   *entirely*
I nolde nought forbere° him in no cas.   *submit to*
     Now wol I saye you sooth, by Saint Thomas,
Why that I rente° out of his book a leef,   *tore*
For which he smoot me so that I was deef.
675   He hadde a book that gladly night and day
For his disport° he wolde rede alway.   *entertainment*
He cleped it *Valerie and Theofraste,*[3]
At which book he lough° alway ful faste;   *laughed*
And eek ther was somtime a clerk at Rome,
680   A cardinal,[4] that highte Saint Jerome,
That made a book again Jovinian;[5]
In which book eek ther was Tertulan,
Crysippus, Trotula, and Helouis,
That was abbesse nat fer fro Paris;[6]

---

6. I.e., he had forbidden this.
7. Just because he saw her bareheaded. This story about Simplicius Gallus comes from the Roman writer Valerius Maximus, as does the story Jankyn told her about "another Roman" (lines 653 ff.).
8. Summer's game; i.e., sports, bonfires, and merrymaking, similar to events held in England on Midsummer's Eve.
9. Ecclesiasticus (25.25).
1. I did not rate at the value of a hawthorn berry.
2. I hate anyone who tells me my shortcomings—

and I'm not the only one, heaven knows.
3. I.e., Walter Map's *Letter of Valerius Concerning Not Marrying* and Theophrastus's *Book Concerning Marriage.* Medieval manuscripts often contained a number of different works, sometimes, as here, dealing with the same subject.
4. Until the late Middle Ages, a term applied to prominent priests in important churches.
5. St. Jerome's *Against Jovinian* denigrates women. *Again:* against.
6. *Tertulan:* Tertullian, author of treastises on sex-

685 And eek the Parables of Salomon
Ovides *Art*,[7] and bookes many oon—
And alle thise were bounden in oo volume.
And every night and day was his custume,
Whan he hadde leiser and vacacioun°   *free time*
690 From other worldly occupacioun,
To reden in this book of wikked wives.
He knew of hem mo legendes and lives
Than been of goode wives in the Bible.
For trusteth wel, it is an impossible°   *impossibility*
695 That any clerk wol speke good of wives,
But if it be of holy saintes lives,
N'of noon other womman nevere the mo—
Who painted the leon, tel me who?[8]
By God, if wommen hadden written stories,
700 As clerkes han within hir oratories,°   *chapels*
They wolde han writen of men more wikkednesse
Than al the merk° of Adam may redresse.   *mark, sex*
The children of Mercurye and Venus[9]
Been in hir werking° ful contrarious:°   *operation / opposed*
705 Mercurye loveth wisdom and science,
And Venus loveth riot° and dispence;°   *revelry / spending*
And for hir diverse disposicioun
Each falleth in otheres exaltacioun,[1]
And thus, God woot, Mercurye is desolat
710 In Pisces wher Venus is exaltat,[2]
And Venus falleth ther Mercurye is raised:
Therfore no womman of no clerk is praised.
The clerk, whan he is old and may nought do
Of Venus werkes worth his olde sho,°   *shoe*
715 Thanne sit° he down and writ° in his dotage   *sits / writes*
That wommen can nat keepe hir mariage.
    But now to purpose why I tolde thee
That I was beten for a book, pardee:
Upon a night Janekin, that was our° sire,°   *my / husband*
720 Redde on his book as he sat by the fire
Of Eva first, that for hir wikkednesse
Was al mankinde brought to wrecchednesse,
For which that Jesu Crist himself was slain
That boughte° us with his herte blood again—   *redeemed*
725 Lo, heer expres of wommen may ye finde
That womman was the los° of al mankinde.   *ruin*
    Tho° redde he me how Sampson loste his heres: *then*

---

ual modesty. *Crysippus*: mentioned by Jerome as a
writer who "ridiculed" women. *Trotula*: a female
doctor believed to have written a treatise on
women's diseases. *Helouis*: Heloise, who wrote
well-known letters to her lover, the great scholar
Abelard. The Wife draws on some of the anti-
female Latin texts in Jankyn's book, while resem-
bling Trotula and Heloise in being capable of
engaging in learned discourse with clerks.
7. *Art of Love*, by the Roman poet Ovid (43 B.C.E.–
?17 C.E.). *Parables of Salomon*: the biblical book of
Proverbs.

8. In one of Aesop's fables, the lion, shown a pic-
ture of a man killing a lion, asked who painted the
picture. The suggestion is that had the artist been
a lion, the roles would have been reversed.
9. I.e., clerks and women, astrologically ruled by
Mercury and Venus, respectively.
1. Because of their contrary positions (as planets),
each one descends (in the belt of the zodiac) as the
other rises; hence one loses its power as the other
becomes dominant.
2. I.e., Mercury is deprived of power in Pisces (the
sign of the fish), where Venus is most powerful.

	Sleeping his lemman° kitte° it with hir sheres,	*lover / cut*
	Thurgh which treson loste he both his yën.	
730	Tho redde he me, if that I shal nat lien,	
	Of Ercules and of his Dianire,	
	That caused him to sette himself afire.[3]	
	No thing forgat he the sorwe and wo	
	That Socrates hadde with his wives two—	
735	How Xantippa caste pisse upon his heed:[4]	
	This sely° man sat stille as he were deed;	*poor, hapless*
	He wiped his heed, namore dorste° he sayn	*dared*
	But "Er that thonder stinte,° comth a rain."	*stops*
	Of Pasipha[5] that was the queene of Crete—	
740	For shrewednesse° him thoughte the tale sweete—	*malice*
	Fy, speek namore, it is a grisly thing	
	Of hir horrible lust and hir liking.°	*pleasure*
	Of Clytermistra[6] for hir lecherye	
	That falsly made hir housbonde for to die,	
745	He redde it with ful good devocioun.	
	He tolde me eek for what occasioun	
	Amphiorax[7] at Thebes loste his lif:	
	Myn housbonde hadde a legende of his wif	
	Eriphylem, that for an ouche° of gold	*trinket*
750	Hath prively unto the Greekes told	
	Wher that hir housbonde hidde him in a place,	
	For which he hadde at Thebes sory grace.	
	Of Livia tolde he me and of Lucie:[8]	
	They bothe made hir housbondes for to die,	
755	That oon for love, that other was for hate;	
	Livia hir housbonde on an even° late	*evening*
	Empoisoned hath for that she was his fo;	
	Lucia likerous° loved hir housbonde so	*lecherous*
	That for[9] he sholde alway upon hire thinke,	
760	She yaf him swich a manere love-drinke	
	That he was deed er it were by the morwe.[1]	
	And thus algates° housbondes han sorwe.	*in every way*
	Thanne tolde he me how oon Latumius	
	Complained unto his felawe Arrius	
765	That in his garden growed swich a tree,	
	On which he saide how that his wives three	
	Hanged hemself for herte despitous.°	*spiteful*
	"O leve° brother," quod this Arrius,	*dear*
	"Yif me a plante of thilke blessed tree,	
770	And in my gardin planted shal it be."	
	Of latter date of wives hath he red	

3. In Greek mythology, Dejanira unwittingly gave Hercules a poisoned shirt, which hurt him so much that he committed suicide by fire.
4. From St. Jerome, the Wife borrows a story about the ancient Greek philosopher Socrates having two wives; many other sources relate the story of his patiently enduring the torments of his shrewish wife, Xantippa.
5. Pasiphaë, Greek mythological figure who had intercourse with a bull.
6. Clytemnestra, Greek mythological figure who,

with her lover, Aegisthus, slew her husband, Agamemnon.
7. Amphiaraus, betrayed by his wife, Eriphyle, and forced to go to the war against Thebes.
8. I.e., Lucilla, who was said to have poisoned her husband, the poet Lucretius, with a potion designed to keep him faithful. Livia murdered her husband on behalf of her lover, Sejanus.
9. In order that.
1. He was dead before it was near morning.

That some han slain hir housbondes in hir bed
And lete hir lechour dighte° hire al the night,   *have intercourse with*
Whan that the cors° lay in the floor upright;°   *corpse / on his back*
775 And some han driven nailes in hir brain
Whil that they sleepe, and thus they han hem slain;
Some han hem yiven poison in hir drinke.
He spak more hram than herte may bithinke,°   *imagine*
And therwithal he knew of mo proverbes
780 Than in this world ther growen gras or herbes:
"Bet° is," quod he, "thyn habitacioun   *better*
Be with a leon or a foul dragoun
Than with a womman using° for to chide."   *accustomed*
"Bet is," quod he, "hye in the roof abide
785 Than with an angry wif down in the hous:
They been so wikked° and contrarious,   *perverse*
They haten that hir housbondes loveth ay."
He saide, "A womman cast° hir shame away   *casts*
When she cast of hir smoke,"² and ferthermo,
790 "A fair womman, but° she be chast also,   *unless*
Is like a gold ring in a sowes nose."³
Who wolde weene,° or who wolde suppose   *think*
The wo that in myn herte was and pine?°   *suffering*
     And whan I sawgh he wolde nevere fine°   *end*
795 To reden on this cursed book al night,
Al sodeinly three leves have I plight°   *snatched*
Out of his book right as he redde, and eke
I with my fist so took⁴ him on the cheeke
That in oure fir he fil° bakward adown.   *fell*
800 And up he sterte as dooth a wood° leoun,   *raging*
And with his fist he smoot° me on the heed°   *hit / head*
That in the floor I lay as I were deed.°   *dead*
And whan he sawgh how stille that I lay,
He was agast, and wolde have fled his way,
805 Til atte laste out of my swough° I braide:°   *swoon / started*
"O hastou slain me, false thief?" I saide,
"And for my land thus hastou mordred° me?   *murdered*
Er I be deed yit wol I kisse thee."
And neer he cam and kneeled faire adown,
810 And saide, "Dere suster Alisoun,
As help me God, I shal thee nevere smite.
That I have doon, it is thyself to wite.°   *blame*
Foryif it me, and that I thee biseeke,"°   *beseech*
And yit eftsoones° I hitte him on the cheeke,   *another time*
815 And saide, "Thief, thus muchel am I wreke.°   *avenged*
Now wol I die: I may no lenger speke."
     But at the laste with muchel care and wo
We fille accorded by us selven two.⁵

2. Casts off her undergarment.
3. I.e., a fair woman who is not chaste is like a gold ring in a sow's nose. The Wife here makes a biblical proverb even more derogatory toward women than it is in the original (cf. Proverbs 11.22: "As a jewel of gold in a swine's snout, so is a fair woman without discretion").
4. I.e., hit.
5. I.e., but in the end, after great difficulty and complaint, we fell into accord, i.e., made it up between the two of us.

He yaf me al the bridel° in myn hand,   *bridle*
820 To han the governance of hous and land,
And of his tonge and his hand also;
And made him brenne° his book anoonright tho.   *burn*
And whan that I hadde geten unto me
By maistrye° al the sovereinetee,°   *skill / dominion*
825 And that he saide, "Myn owene trewe wIf,
Do as thee lust° the terme of al thy lif;   *it pleases*
Keep thyn honour, and keep eek myn estat,"
After that day we hadde nevere debat.
God help me so, I was to him as kinde
830 As any wif from Denmark unto Inde,°   *India*
And also trewe, and so was he to me.
I praye to God that sit° in majestee,   *sits*
So blesse his soule for his mercy dere.
Now wol I saye my tale if ye wol heere.

[ANOTHER INTERRUPTION]

835   The Frere lough° whan he hadde herd all this: *laughed*
"Now dame," quod he, "so have I joye or blis,
This is a long preamble of a tale."
And whan the Somnour⁶ herde the Frere gale,°   *exclaim*
"Lo," quod the Somnour, "Goddes armes two,
840 A frere wol entremette° him° evermo!   *intrude / himself*
Lo, goode men, a flye and eek a frere
Wol falle in every dissh and eek matere.⁷
What spekestou of preambulacioun?
What, amble or trotte or pisse or go sitte down!
845 Thou lettest° oure disport in this manere."   *hinder*
    "Ye, woltou so, sire Somnour?" quod the Frere.
"Now by my faith, I shal er that I go
Telle of a somnour swich a tale or two
That al the folk shal laughen in this place."
850   "Now elles, Frere, I wol bishrewe° thy face,"   *curse*
Quod this Somnour, "and I bishrewe me,
But if I telle tales two or three
Of freres, er I come to Sidingborne,⁸
That I shal make thyn herte for to moorne°—   *mourn*
855 For wel I woot thy pacience is goon."
    Oure Hoste cride, "Pees,° and that anoon!"   *peace*
And saide, "Lat the womman telle hir tale:
Ye fare as folk that dronken been of ale.
Do, dame, tel forth youre tale, and that is best."
860   "Al redy, sire," quod she, "right as you lest°—   *it pleases*
If I have licence of this worthy Frere."
"Yis, dame," quod he, "tel forth and I wol heere."

---

6. A secular servant of the ecclesiastical courts.
7. Just as a fly alights on every dish, so a friar inter-
feres in everyone else's affairs.
8. Sittingbourne, a town forty miles from London.

The Tale

In th'olde dayes of the King Arthour,
Of which that Britouns⁹ speken greet honour,
865 Al was this land fulfild of faïrye:¹
The elf-queene° with hir joly compaignye   *queen of the fairies*
Daunced ful ofte in many a greene mede°—   *meadow*
This was the olde opinion as I rede;°   *think*
I speke of many hundred yeres ago.
870 But now can no man see none elves mo,
For now the grete charitee and prayeres
Of limitours,² and othere holy freres,
That serchen every land and every streem,
As thikke as motes° in the sonne-beem,   *dust particles*
875 Blessing halles, chambres, kichenes, bowres,
Citees, burghes,° castels, hye towres,   *townships*
Thropes, bernes, shipnes,³ dayeries—
This maketh that ther been no faïries.
For ther as wont to walken was an elf
880 Ther walketh now the limitour himself,
In undermeles° and in morweninges,°   *afternoons / mornings*
And saith his Matins and his holy thinges,
As he gooth in his limitacioun.⁴
Wommen may go saufly° up and down: *safely*
885 In every bussh or under every tree
Ther is noon other incubus⁵ but he,
And he ne wol doon hem but dishonour.⁶
    And so bifel it that this King Arthour
Hadde in his hous a lusty bacheler,°   *young knight*
890 That on a day cam riding fro river,⁷
And happed° that, allone as he was born,   *it happened*
He sawgh a maide walking him biforn;
Of which maide anoon, maugree hir heed.⁸
By verray force he rafte hir maidenheed;⁹
895 For which oppression° was swich clamour,   *rape*
And swich pursuite° unto the King Arthour,   *petitioning*
That dampned was this knight for to be deed¹
By cours of lawe, and sholde han lost his heed—
Paraventure° swich was the statut tho—   *perchance*
900 But that the queene and othere ladies mo
So longe prayeden the king of grace,
Til he his lif him graunted in the place,
And yaf him to the queene, al at hir wille,
To chese wheither she wolde him save or spille²

---

9. I.e., Bretons. The stories of the Breton lais, or ballads, deal with the trials of lovers and often have supernatural elements.
1. I.e., filled full of supernatural creatures.
2. Friars licensed to beg in a certain territory.
3. Villages (*thorps*), barns, stables.
4. I.e., the friar's assigned area. His "holy thinges" are prayers.
5. An evil spirit that seduces mortal women.
6. I.e., the result of consorting with a friar would

be only loss of honor, while consorting with an incubus would result in conception.
7. Hawking, usually carried out on the banks of a stream.
8. Despite her head, i.e., despite anything she could do.
9. By force, he robbed her of her maidenhead.
1. This knight was condemned to death.
2. To choose whether to save or end his life.

905 The queene thanked the king with al hir might,
And after this thus spak she to the knight,
Whan that she saw hir time upon a day:
"Thou standest yit," quod she, "in swich array°   condition
That of thy lif yit hastou no suretee.°   guarantee
910 I graunte thee lif if thou canst tellen me
What thing it is that wommen most desiren:
Be war and keep thy nekke boon from iren.[3]
And if thou canst nat tellen me anoon,°   right away
Yit wol I yive thee leve for to goon
915 A twelfmonth and a day to seeche° and lere°   search / learn
An answere suffisant° in this matere,   satisfactory
And suretee wol I han er that thou pace,°   pass
Thy body for to yeelden in this place."
      Wo was this knight, and sorwefully he siketh.°   sighs
920 But what, he may nat doon al as him liketh,
And atte laste he chees° him for to wende,°   chose / go
And come again right at the yeres ende,
With swich answere as God wolde him purveye,°   provide
And taketh his leve and wendeth forth his waye.
925 He seeketh every hous and every place
Wher as he hopeth for to finde grace,
To lerne what thing wommen love most.
But he ne coude arriven in no coost[4]
Wher as he mighte finde in this matere
930 Two creatures according in fere.[5]
      Some saiden wommen loven best richesse;
Some saide honour, some saide jolinesse;°   pleasure
Some riche array, some saiden lust abedde,
And ofte time to be widwe and wedde.
935 Some saide that oure[6] herte is most esed
Whan that we been yflatered and yplesed—
He gooth ful neigh the soothe,° I wol nat lie: truth
A man shal winne us best with flaterye,
And with attendance° and with bisinesse°   attention / solicitude
940 Been we ylimed,° bothe more and lesse.   ensnared
      And some sayen that we loven best
For to be free, and do right as us lest,°   it pleases
And that no man repreve° us of oure vice,   reprove
But saye that we be wise and no thing nice.°   foolish
945 For trewely, ther is noon of us alle,
If any wight wol clawe° us on the galle,°   rub / sore spot
That we nil kike° for° he saith us sooth: kick / because
Assaye° and he shal finde it that so dooth.   try
For be we nevere so vicious withinne,
950 We wol be holden° wise and clene of sinne.   considered
      And some sayn that greet delit han we
For to be holden stable and eek secree,[7]

3. I.e., be very careful in choosing and save your-
self from execution. *Boon:* bone.
4. I.e., country.
5. Agreeing together.

6. The Wife speaks in her own person here and
does not return to her story for more than sixty
lines.
7. To be held reliable and also closemouthed.

	And in oo° purpos stedefastly to dwelle,	*one*
	And nat biwraye° thing that men us telle—	*disclose*
955	But that tale is nat worth a rake-stele.°	*rake handle*
	Pardee,° we wommen conne no thing hele:°	*by God / conceal*
	Witnesse on Mida.° Wol ye heere the tale?	*Midas*
	Ovide, amonges othere thinges smale,	
	Saide Mida hadde under his longe heres,	
960	Growing upon his heed, two asses eres,	
	The whiche vice° he hidde as he best mighte	*defect*
	Ful subtilly from every mannes sighte,	
	That save his wif ther wiste° of it namo.	*knew*
	He loved hire most and trusted hire also.	
965	He prayed hire that to no creature	
	She sholde tellen of his disfigure.°	*deformity*
	She swoor him nay, for al this world to winne,	
	She nolde do that vilainye or sinne	
	To make hir housbonde han so foul a name:	
970	She nolde nat telle it for hir owene shame.	
	But natheless, hir thoughte that she dyde°	*would die*
	That she so longe sholde a conseil° hide;	*secret*
	Hire thoughte it swal° so sore about hir herte	*swelled*
	That nedely som word hire moste asterte,[8]	
975	And sith she dorste nat telle it to no man,	
	Down to a mareis° faste° by she ran—	*marsh / close*
	Til she cam there hir herte was afire—	
	And as a bitore bombleth[9] in the mire,	
	She laide hir mouth unto the water down:	
980	"Biwray° me nat, thou water, with thy soun,"°	*betray / sound*
	Quod she. "To thee I telle it and namo:°	*to no one else*
	Myn housbonde hath longe asses eres two.	
	Now is myn herte al hool,[1] now is it oute.	
	I mighte no lenger keep it, out of doute."	
985	Here may ye see, though we a time abide,	
	Yit oute it moot:° we can no conseil hide.	*must*
	The remenant of the tale if ye wol heere,	
	Redeth Ovide, and ther ye may it lere.[2]	
	This knight of which my tale is specially,	
990	Whan that he sawgh he mighte nat come thereby—	
	This is to saye what wommen loven most—	
	Within his brest ful sorweful was his gost,°	*spirit*
	But hoom he gooth, he mighte nat sojourne:°	*delay*
	The day was come that hoomward moste° he turne.	*must*
995	And in his way it happed him to ride	
	In al this care under° a forest side,	*by*
	Wher as he sawgh upon a daunce go	
	Of ladies foure and twenty and yit mo;	
	Toward the whiche daunce he drow ful yerne,[3]	
1000	In hope that som wisdom sholde he lerne.	

8. Of necessity some word must escape her.
9. A bittern (type of heron) makes a booming noise.
1. I.e., sound, calm.

2. Learn. In Ovid's *Metamorphoses*, Midas's secret is betrayed not by his wife but by his barber.
3. Drew very quickly.

But certainly, er he cam fully there,
Vanisshed was this daunce, he niste° where.   knew not
No creature sawgh he that bar° lif,   bore
Save on the greene he sawgh sitting a wif°—   woman
1005   A fouler wight ther may no man devise.°   imagine
Again⁴ the knight this olde wif gan rise,
And saide, "Sire knight, heer forth lith° no way.°   lies / road
Telle me what ye seeken, by youre fay.°   faith
Paraventure it may the better be:
1010   Thise olde folk conne° muchel thing," quod she.   know
       "My leve moder,"° quod this knight, "certain,   mother
I nam but deed but if that I can sayn
What thing it is that wommen most desire.
Coude ye me wisse,° I wolde wel quite youre hire."⁵   teach
1015   "Plight° me thy trouthe here in myn hand," quod she, pledge
"The nexte thing that I requere° thee,   require of
Thou shalt it do, if it lie in thy might,
And I wol telle it you er it be night."
       "Have heer my trouthe," quod the knight. "I graunte."
1020   "Thanne," quod she, "I dar me wel avaunte°   boast
Thy lif is sauf,° for I wol stande therby.   safe
Upon my lif the queene wol saye as I.
Lat see which is the pruddeste° of hem alle   proudest
That wereth on⁶ a coverchief or a calle°   headdress
1025   That dar saye nay of that I shal thee teche.
Lat us go forth withouten lenger speeche."
Tho rouned° she a pistel° in his ere,   whispered / message
And bad° him to be glad and have no fere.   ordered
       Whan they be comen to the court, this knight
1030   Saide he hadde holde his day as he hadde hight,°   promised
And redy was his answere, as he saide.
Ful many a noble wif, and many a maide,
And many a widwe—for that they been wise—
The queene hirself sitting as justise,
1035   Assembled been this answere for to heere,
And afterward this knight was bode° appere.   bidden to
To every wight comanded was silence,
And that the knight sholde telle in audience°   open hearing
What thing that worldly wommen loven best.
1040   This knight ne stood nat stille as dooth a best,°   beast
But to his question anoon answerde
With manly vois that al the court it herde.
       "My lige° lady, generally," quod he,   liege
"Wommen desire to have sovereinetee°   dominion
1045   As wel over hir housbonde as hir love,⁷
And for to been in maistrye him above.
This is youre moste desir though ye me kille.
Dooth as you list:° I am here at youre wille."   please

---

4. I.e., to meet.
5. Repay your trouble.
6. That wears.
7. In the courtly love tradition, the lady's lightest

word was her lover's law. Here, the knight claims
that women want to exercise the same dominion
over their husbands.

In al the court ne was ther wif ne maide
1050 Ne widwe that contraried° that he saide,   *contradicted*
But saiden he was worthy han° his lif.   *to have*
    And with that word up sterte° that olde wif,   *started*
Which that the knight sawgh sitting on the greene;
"Mercy," quod she, "my soverein lady queene,
1055 Er that youre court departe, do me right.
I taughte this answere unto the knight,
For which he plighte me his trouthe there
The firste thing I wolde him requere°   *require*
He wolde it do, if it laye in his might.
1060 Bifore the court thanne praye I thee, sire knight,"
Quod she, "that thou me take unto thy wif,
For wel thou woost that I have kept° thy lif.   *saved*
If I saye fals, say nay, upon thy fay."
    This knight answerde, "Allas and wailaway,
1065 I woot right wel that swich was my biheeste.°   *promise*
For Goddes love, as chees° a newe requeste: *choose*
Taak al my good and lat my body go."
    "Nay thanne," quod she, "I shrewe° us bothe two.   *curse*
For though that I be foul and old and poore,
1070 I nolde for al the metal ne for ore
That under erthe is grave° or lith° above,   *buried / lies*
But if thy wif I were and eek thy love."
    "My love," quod he. "Nay, my dampnacioun!°   *damnation*
Allas, that any of my nacioun°   *family*
1075 Sholde evere so foule disparaged° be."   *degraded*
But al for nought, th'ende is this, that he
Constrained was: he needes moste hire wedde,
And taketh his olde wif and gooth to bedde.
    Now wolden some men saye, paraventure,
1080 That for my necligence I do no cure[8]
To tellen you the joye and al th'array
That at the feeste was that ilke day.
To which thing shortly answere I shal:
I saye ther nas no joye ne feeste at al;
1085 Ther nas but hevinesse and muche sorwe.
For prively he wedded hire on° morwe,°   *in / the morning*
And al day after hidde him as an owle,
So wo was him, his wif looked so foule.
    Greet was the wo the knight hadde in his thought:
1090 Whan he was with his wif abedde brought,
He walweth° and he turneth to and fro.   *tosses*
His olde wif lay smiling everemo,
And saide, "O dere housbonde, benedicite,°   *bless ye*
Fareth° every knight thus with his wif as ye?   *behaves*
1095 Is this the lawe of King Arthures hous?
Is every knight of his thus daungerous?°   *standoffish*
I am youre owene love and youre wif;
I am she which that saved hath youre lif;
And certes yit ne dide I you nevere unright.

8. I do not take the trouble.

1100 Why fare ye thus with me this firste night?
Ye faren like a man hadde lost his wit.
What is my gilt? For Goddes love, telle it,
And it shal been amended if I may."
"Amended!" quod this knight. "Allas, nay, nay,
1105 It wol nat been amended neveremo.
Thou art so lothly° and so old also,   hideous
And therto comen of so lowe a kinde,°   lineage
That litel wonder is though I walwe and winde.°   turn
So wolde God myn herte wolde breste!"°   break
1110 "Is this," quod she, "the cause of youre unreste?"
"Ye, certainly," quod he. "No wonder is."
"Now sire," quod she, "I coude amende al this,
If that me liste, er it were dayes three,
So° wel ye mighte bere you unto me.[9]   provided that
1115 "But for ye speken of swich gentilesse°   nobility
As is descended out of old richesse—
That therfore sholden ye be gentilmen—
Swich arrogance is nat worth an hen.
Looke who that is most vertuous alway,
1120 Privee and apert, and most entendeth ay[1]
To do the gentil deedes that he can,
Taak him for the gretteste° gentilman.   greatest
Crist wol° we claime of him oure gentilesse,   desires that
Nat of oure eldres for hir 'old richesse.'
1125 For though they yive us al hir heritage,
For which we claime to been of heigh parage,°   descent
Yit may they nat biquethe for no thing
To noon of us hir vertuous living,
That made hem gentilmen ycalled be,
1130 And bad° us folwen hem in swich degree.   ordered
"Wel can the wise poete of Florence,
That highte Dant,° speken in this sentence;°   Dante / topic
Lo, in swich manere rym is Dantes tale:
'Ful selde up riseth by his braunches smale
1135 Prowesse of man,[2] for God of his prowesse
Wol that of him we claime oure gentilesse.'
For of oure eldres may we no thing claime
But temporel thing that man may hurte and maime.[3]
Eek every wight woot this as wel as I,
1140 If gentilesse were planted natureelly
Unto a certain linage down the line,
Privee and apert, thanne wolde they nevere fine°   cease
To doon of gentilesse the faire office°—   function
They mighte do no vilainye or vice.
1145 "Taak fir and beer° it in the derkeste hous   bear
Bitwixe this and the Mount of Caucasus,
And lat men shette° the dores and go thenne,°   shut / thence

9. I.e., you might behave so satisfactorily toward me that I could change all this for the better—if I so desired—before three days had passed.
1. I.e., privately and publicly, and always tries.
2. I.e., seldom ("selde") does man's excellence ("prowesse") come through the branches of his

family tree. The Wife is quoting mainly from Dante, *Purgatorio* 7.121–23; she repeats this point against inherited nobility at line 1170.
3. "Man" is the object of the verbs "hurte" and "maime."

Yit wol the fir as faire lye° and brenne°   *blaze / burn*
As twenty thousand men mighte it biholde:
His° office natureel ay wol it holde,   *its*
Up° peril of my lif, til that it die.   *upon*
Heer may ye see wel how that genterye°   *gentility*
Is nat annexed to possessioun,[4]
Sith folk ne doon hir operacioun
Alway, as dooth the fir, lo, in his kinde.°   *nature*
For God it woot, men may wel often finde
A lordes sone do shame and vilainye;
And he that wol han pris of his gentrye,[5]
For he was boren° of a gentil° hous,   *born / noble*
And hadde his eldres noble and vertuous,
And nil himselven do no gentil deedes,
Ne folwen his gentil auncestre that deed° is,   *dead*
He nis nat gentil, be he duc° or erl—   *duke*
For vilaines sinful deedes maken a cherl.°   *lout*
Thy gentilesse nis but renomee[6]
Of thine auncestres for hir heigh bountee,°   *magnanimity*
Which is a straunge° thing for thy persone.   *external*
For gentilesse cometh fro God allone.[7]
Thanne comth oure verray gentilesse of grace.
It was no thing biquethe us with oure place.
Thenketh how noble, as saith Valerius,
Was thilke Tullius Hostilius[8]
That out of poverte° roos to heigh noblesse.   *poverty*
Redeth Senek and redeth eek Boece:[9]
Ther shul ye seen expres that no drede° is   *doubt*
That he is gentil that dooth gentil deedes.
And therfore, leve housbonde, I thus conclude:
Al° were it that mine auncestres weren rude,°   *although / lowborn*
Yit may the hye God—and so hope I—
Graunte me grace to liven vertuously.
Thanne am I gentil whan that I biginne
To liven vertuously and waive° sinne.   *avoid*
  "And ther as ye of poverte me repreve,°   *reprove*
The hye God, on whom that we bileve,
In wilful° poverte chees° to live his lif;   *voluntary / chose*
And certes every man, maiden, or wif
May understonde that Jesus, hevene king,
Ne wolde nat chese° a vicious living.   *choose*
Glad poverte is an honeste° thing, certain;   *honorable*
This wol Senek and othere clerkes sayn.
Whoso that halt him paid of[1] his poverte,
I holde him riche al hadde he nat a sherte.°   *shirt*
He that coveiteth[2] is a poore wight,
For he wolde han that is nat in his might;

1150
1155
1160
1165
1170
1175
1180
1185
1190

4. I.e., is not related to inheritable property.
5. Have credit for his noble birth.
6. I.e., the gentility you claim isn't just the renown.
7. I.e., nobility cannot be handed down from father to son, but is God's gift to the individual. See lines 1134–36.
8. The legendary third king of Rome.

9. I.e., the Roman philosopher Boethius (ca. 480–524); Chaucer translated Boethius's *Consolation of Philosophy* from Latin to English (as Boece). *Senek:* the Roman statesman, dramatist, and philosopher Seneca (4 B.C.E–65 C.E.).
1. Considers himself satisfied with.
2. Covets, desires what another person has.

1195 But he that nought hath, ne coveiteth° have,   *desires to*
        Is riche, although we holde him but a knave.
        Verray° poverte it singeth properly.°   *true / appropriately*
        Juvenal saith of poverte, 'Merily
        The poore man, whan he gooth by the waye,
1200 Biforn the theves he may singe and playe.'
        Poverte is hateful good, and as I gesse,
        A ful greet bringere out of bisinesse;[3]
        A greet amendere eek of sapience°   *wisdom*
        To him that taketh it in pacience;
1205 Poverte is thing, although it seeme elenge,°   *wretched*
        Possession that no wight wol chalenge;°   *claim as his property*
        Poverte ful often, whan a man is lowe,
        Maketh[4] his God and eek himself to knowe;
        Poverte a spectacle° is as thinketh me,   *pair of spectacles*
1210 Thurgh which he may his verray° freendes see.   *true*
        And therfore, sire, sin that I nought you greve,
        Of my poverte namore ye me repreve.°   *reproach*
           "Now sire, of elde° ye repreve me: *old age*
        And certes sire, though noon auctoritee
1215 Were in no book, ye gentils of honour
        Sayn that men sholde an old wight doon favour,
        And clepe him fader for youre gentilesse—
        And auctours[5] shal I finde, as I gesse.
           "Now ther ye saye that I am foul and old:
1220 Thanne drede you nought to been a cokewold,°   *cuckold*
        For filthe and elde, also mote I thee,[6]
        Been grete wardeins° upon chastitee.   *guardians*
        But nathelees, sin I knowe your delit,
        I shal fulfille youre worldly appetit.
1225   "Chees° now," quod she, "oon of thise thinges twaye: *choose*
        To han me foul and old til that I deye
        And be to you a trewe humble wif,
        And nevere you displese in al my lif,
        Or elles ye wol han me yong and fair,
1230 And take youre aventure of the repair[7]
        That shal be to youre hous by cause of me—
        Or in some other place, wel may be.
        Now chees youreselven wheither° that you liketh."   *whichever*
           This knight aviseth him[8] and sore siketh;°   *sighs*
1235 But atte laste he saide in this manere:
        "My lady and my love, and wif so dere,
        I putte me in youre wise governaunce:
        Cheseth° yourself which may be most plesaunce°   *choose / pleasure*
        And most honour to you and me also.
1240 I do no fors the wheither[9] of the two,
        For as you liketh it suffiseth° me."   *satisfies*
           "Thanne have I gete° of you maistrye," quod she,   *got*
        "Sin I may chese and governe as me lest?"°   *it pleases*

3. I.e., remover of cares.   7. I.e., your chances on the visits.
4. I.e., makes him.   8. Considers.
5. I.e., authorities.   9. I do not care whichever.
6. So may I prosper.

"Ye, certes, wif," quod he. "I holde it best."
1245 "Kisse me," quod she. "We be no lenger wrothe.
For by my trouthe, I wol be to you bothe—
This is to sayn, ye, bothe fair and good.
I praye to God that I mote sterven wood,[1]
But° I to you be al so good and trewe   unless
1250 As evere was wif sin that the world was newe.
And but I be tomorn° as fair to seene   tomorrow morning
As any lady, emperisse, or queene,
That is bitwixe the eest and eek the west,
Do with my lif and deeth right as you lest:
1255 Caste up the curtin, looke how that it is."[2]
        And whan the knight sawgh verraily° al this,   truly
That she so fair was and so yong therto,
For joye he hente° hire in his armes two;   took
His herte bathed° in a bath of blisse;   basked
1260 A thousand time arewe° he gan hire kisse,   in a row
And she obeyed him in every thing
That mighte do him plesance or liking.°   pleasure
And thus they live unto hir lives ende
In parfit° joye. And Jesu Crist us sende   perfect
1265 Housbondes meeke, yonge, and fresshe abedde—
And grace t'overbide° hem that we wedde.   outlive
And eek I praye Jesu shorte° hir lives   shorten
That nought wol be governed by hir wives.
And olde and angry nigardes of dispence°—   spending
1270 God sende hem soone a verray° pestilence!   veritable

FROM TROILUS AND CRISEIDE[1]

Cantus Troili[2]

400 "If no love is, O God, what feele I so?
And if love is, what thing and which is he?
If love be good, from whennes cometh my wo?
If it be wikke, a wonder thinketh me,
Whan every torment and adversitee
405 That cometh of him may to me savory° thinke,°   pleasant / seem
For ay thurste I, the more that ich° it drinke.   I

And if that at myn owene lust I brenne,°   burn
From whennes cometh my wailing and my plainte?°   lament
If harm agree me, wherto plaine I thenne?[3]—
410 I noot, ne why unwery that I fainte.[4]

1. Might die insane.
2. I.e., lift up the curtain around the bed and see how things are.
1. In this long poem, Chaucer tells the tragic story of the love between Troilus, the son of King Priam of Troy, and Criseide, the daughter of Calkas (a Trojan priest who defects to the Greek side during the Trojan War).
2. The song of Troilus (Latin). Troilus sings this song just after he has fallen in love with Criseide in book I. Prior to falling in love, Troilus had spurned love and mocked other lovers. These stanzas are adapted from the eighty-eighth sonnet of the Italian poet Petrarch (1304–1374).
3. I.e., if suffering is agreeable to me, why, then, do I lament?
4. I.e., I know not, nor why I faint even though I am not weary.

O quikke° deeth, O sweete harm so quainte,°   *living / strange*
How may° of thee in me swich quantitee,   *can there be*
But if° that I consente that it be?   *except*

And if that I consente, I wrongfully
415 Complaine: ywis,° thus possed° to and fro, *indeed / tossed*
Al stereless° within a boot am I   *rudderless*
Amidde the see, bitwixen windes two,
That in contrarye° stonden everemo.   *opposition*
Allas, what is this wonder maladye?
420 For hoot° of cold, for cold of hoot I die."[5]   *heat*

Lyrics and Occasional Verse

To Rosamond

Madame, ye been of alle beautee shrine
As fer as cercled is the mapemounde:[6]
For as the crystal glorious ye shine,
And like ruby been° youre cheekes rounde.   *are*
5 Therwith ye been so merye and so jocounde
That at a revel whan that I see you daunce
It is an oinement unto my wounde,
Though ye to me ne do no daliaunce.[7]

For though I weepe of teres ful a tine,°   *tub*
10 Yit may that wo myn herte nat confounde;
Youre semy° vois, that ye so smale outtwine,[8]   *small*
Maketh my thought in joye and blis habounde:° *abound*
So curteisly I go with love bounde
That to myself I saye in my penaunce,[9]
15 "Suffiseth me to love you, Rosemounde,
Though ye to me ne do no daliaunce."

Was nevere pik walwed in galauntine[1]
As I in love am walwed and ywounde,
For which ful ofte I of myself divine
20 That I am trewe Tristam[2] the secounde;
My love may not refreide° nor affounde;°   *cool / chill*
I brenne° ay in amorous plesaunce: *burn*
Do what you list, I wol youre thral° be founde, *slave*
Though ye to me ne do no daliaunce.

---

5. Such oxymorons were a convention of Petrar-
chan love poetry.
6. I.e., to the shrine of all beauty, to the farthest
circumference of the map of the world.
7. I.e., show me no encouragement.

8. That you so delicately spin out.
9. I.e., pangs of unrequited love.
1. Pike rolled in galantine sauce.
2. The famous lover of Isolt (Iseult, Isolde) in
medieval legend, renowned for his constancy.

Truth

Flee fro the prees and dwelle with soothfastnesse;[3]
Suffise unto thy thing,[4] though it be smal;
For hoord hath[5] hate, and climbing tikelnesse;°   *insecurity*
Prees hath envye, and wele° blent° overal.   *prosperity / blinds*
5 Savoure° no more than three bihoove shal;   *relish*
Rule wel thyself that other folk canst rede:°   *advise*
And Trouthe shal delivere,[6] it is no drede.°   *doubt*

Tempest thee nought al crooked to redresse[7]
In trust of hire that turneth as a bal;[8]
10 Muche wele stant in litel bisinesse;[9]
Be war therfore to spurne ayains an al.[1]
Strive nat as dooth the crokke° with the wal.[2]   *pot*
Daunte° thyself that dauntest otheres deede: *master*
And Trouthe shal delivere, it is no drede.°   *fear*

15 That thee is sent, receive in buxomnesse;°   *obedience*
The wrastling for the world axeth° a fal;   *asks for*
Here is noon hoom, here nis but wildernesse:[3]
Forth, pilgrim, forth! Forth, beest, out of thy stal!
Know thy countree, looke up, thank God of al.
20 Hold the heigh way and lat thy gost° thee lede: *spirit*
And Trouthe shal delivere, it is no drede.°   *fear*

Envoy

Therfore, thou Vache,[4] leve thyn olde wrecchednesse
Unto the world; leve[5] now to be thral.
Crye him mercy that of his heigh goodnesse
25 Made thee of nought, and in especial
Draw unto him, and pray in general,
For thee and eek for othere, hevenelich meede:°   *reward*
And Trouthe shal delivere, it is no drede.

Complaint to His Purse

To you, my purs, and to noon other wight,°   *person*
Complaine I, for ye be my lady dere.

---

3. Truthfulness. *Prees:* crowd; also, ambition. In some early manuscripts and printed editions, this poem is subtitled "Balade de Bon Conseyl" ("Ballad of Good Counsel").
4. Be content with your possessions.
5. Hoarding causes.
6. I.e., truth shall make you free; cf. John 8.32.
7. Do not struggle to correct all that's crooked.
8. I.e., do not trust in Fortune, who turns like a ball in that she is always presenting a different aspect to people.

9. I.e., much happiness will be found in little activity.
1. I.e., be careful therefore not to kick against an awl (a small, sharply pointed tool).
2. I.e., do not strive against impossible odds (as when a clay pot fights with a wall).
3. I.e., Here is no home, here is nothing but wilderness.
4. Probably Sir Philip de la Vache, with a pun on the French for "cow."
5. I.e., cease

I am so sory, now that ye be light,
For certes, but if[6] ye make me hevy cheere,
5   Me were as lief[7] be laid upon my beere;°   bier
For which unto youre mercy thus I crye:
Beeth hevy again, or elles moot° I die.   must

Now voucheth sauf this day er[8] it be night
That I of you the blisful soun may heere,
10   Or see youre colour, lik the sonne bright,
That of yelownesse hadde nevere peere.
Ye be my life, ye be myn hertes steere,°   rudder, guide
Queene of confort and of good compaignye:
Beeth hevy again, or elles moot I die.

15   Ye purs, that been to me my lives light
And saviour, as in this world down here,
Out of this towne[9] helpe me thurgh your might,
Sith that ye wol nat be my tresorere;°   treasurer
For I am shave as neigh as any frere.[1]
20   But yit I praye unto youre curteisye:
Beeth hevy again, or elles moot I die.

Envoy to Henry IV

O conquerour of Brutus Albioun,[2]
Which that by line and free eleccioun
Been verray king, this song to you I sende:
25   And ye, that mowen° alle oure harmes amende,   may
Have minde upon my supplicacioun.

To His Scribe[3] Adam

Adam scrivain,° if evere it thee bifalle   scribe
Boece or *Troilus*[4] for to written newe,
Under thy longe lokkes thou moste have the scalle,[5]
But after my making thou write more trewe,
5   So ofte a day I moot° thy werk renewe,   must
It to correcte, and eek° to rubbe and scrape:[6]   also
And al is thurgh thy necligence and rape.°   haste

---

6. *But if*: unless.
7. I'd just as soon.
8. Now grant this day before.
9. Probably Westminster, where Chaucer had rented a house.
1. Shaved as close as any (tonsured) friar, an expression for being broke.
2. Britain (Albion) was said to have been founded by Brutus, the grandson of Aeneas (the founder of Rome).
3. Copyist, responsible for making copies of the

poet's work.
4. Chaucer's long poem *Troilus and Criseide* (see p. 67). *Boece*: Chaucer's translation of the *Consolation of Philosophy*, by the Roman philosopher Boethius (ca. 480–524).
5. I.e., may you have scurf, a scaly or scabby disease of the scalp.
6. Corrections on parchment were made by scraping off the ink and rubbing the surface smooth again.

WILLIAM LANGLAND
ca. 1330–ca. 1400

Piers Plowman[1]

In a somer seson, whan softe was the sonne,°	sun
I shoop me into shroudes as I a sheep were,[2]	
In habite as an heremite unholy of werkes,[3]	
Wente wide in this world wondres to here.°	hear
5 Ac° on a May morwenynge[4] on Malverne Hilles	but; and
Me bifel a ferly, of Fairye me thoghte.[5]	
I was wery [of] wandred and wente me to reste	
Under a brood bank by a bournes° syde;	stream's
And as I lay and lenede and loked on the watres,	
10 I slombred into a slepyng, it sweyed so murye.°	merry
Thanne gan [me] to meten° a merveillous swevene°—	dream / dream
That I was in a wildernesse, wiste° I nevere where.	knew
As I biheeld into the eest an heigh to the sonne,[6]	
I seigh a tour° on a toft° trieliche ymaked,[7]	tower / knoll
15 A deep dale° bynethe, a dongeon° therinne,	valley / dungeon
With depe diches and derke and dredfulle of sighte.	
A fair feeld ful of folk fond[8] I ther bitwene—	
Of alle manere° of men, the meene° and the riche,	kinds / lowly
Werchynge° and wandrynge as the world asketh.°	working / requires
20 Somme putten hem° to the plough, pleiden° ful	themselves / playing
selde,°	seldom
In settynge° and sowynge swonken° ful harde,	planting / toiled
And wonnen that thise wastours with glotonye destroyeth[9]	
And somme putten hem° to pride, apparailed hem	themselves
therafter,	

---

1. Probably composed between 1360 and 1387, *The Vision of Piers Plowman* is a long religious, social, and political allegory. It is written in alliterative verse in a west-midlands dialect, which differs in many ways from that used by Chaucer in the nearly contemporaneous *Canterbury Tales*. *Piers* survives in several distinct versions, which scholars refer to as the A-, B-, C-, and Z-texts. The A-text (about twenty-four hundred lines) breaks off inconclusively; the B-text, which we follow here, is about four thousand lines longer. The C-text is poetically and doctrinally more conservative. Recently, scholars have focused on the Z-text as possibly being an earlier text than the other three. That a large number of manuscripts (and two sixteenth-century printed editions) survive suggests that the poem was quite popular during the early modern period.

The poem takes the form of a dream vision, a popular genre during the Middle Ages in which the author presents a story as the dream of the main character. The selection here from the poem's prologue introduces the dreamer's vision of the Field of Folk, which represents fourteenth-century English society and its failures to live in accordance with Christian principles.

2. I.e., I dressed in garments as if I were either a sheep or a shepherd.
3. Perhaps meaning one without holy works to his credit, but not necessarily one of sinful works. *In habite . . . heremite:* thus the simple clothes resemble those of a hermit.
4. Traveling forth on a May morning often initiated a dream vision in medieval poetry. As the setting of the vision, the "Malverne Hills," in the West Midlands, are generally thought to have been the site of Langland's early home (if such a person existed; see biographical sketch, p. 2107).
5. I.e., a marvel ("ferly") that seemed to be from fairyland.
6. I.e., looked toward the east on high, toward the sun. Both the east and the sun symbolize Christ.
7. This phrase has several possible meanings, including "well or wonderfully made" and "made like a tree," i.e., like the cross.
8. Found. The fair field of folk is commonly interpreted as a representation of the world, situated between heaven (the tower) and hell (the dungeon in the valley).
9. I.e., and won that which wasters destroyed with gluttony. An opposition between winners and wasters was a common idea during the period.

In contenaunce of clothynge comen disgised.[1]
25 In preieres° and penaunce putten hem manye, — *prayers*
Al for love of Oure Lord lyveden° ful streyte° — *living / strictly*
In hope to have heveneriche° blisse— — *heavenly*
As ancres and heremites that holden hem in hire selles,
Coveiten noght in contree to cairen aboute
30 For no likerous liflode hire likame to plese.[2]
And somme chosen chaffare;° they cheveden° the — *trade / succeeded*
bettre—
As it semeth to oure sight that swiche men thryveth;
And somme murthes° to make as mynstralles — *entertainments*
konne,° — *know how*
And geten gold with hire° glee°—synnelees,° I — *their / singing / guiltless*
leeve.° — *believe*
35 Ac japeres° and jangeleres, Judas children,[3] — *jesters*
Feynen hem fantasies, and fooles hem maketh,
And han wit at wille to werken if they sholde.[4]
That Poul[5] precheth of hem I wol nat preve° it here: — *prove*
Qui loquitur turpiloquium is Luciferes hyne.[6]
40 Bidderes° and beggeres faste aboute yede° — *beggars / went*
[Til] hire bely and hire bagge [were] bredful ycrammed;[7]
Faiteden° for hire foode, foughten at the ale.° — *begged falsely / alehouse*
In glotonye, God woot,° go thei to bedde, — *knows*
And risen with ribaudie,° tho Roberdes knaves;[8] — *obscenities*
45 Sleep and sory° sleuthe° seweth hem evere.° — *wretched / sloth / follow*
Pilgrymes and palmeres plighten hem togidere
To seken Seint Jame and seintes in Rome;[9]
Wenten forth in hire wey° with many wise tales,° — *way / speeches*
And hadden leve° to lyen° al hire lif after. — *leave / tell lies*
50 I seigh° somme that seiden° thei hadde ysought seintes: — *saw / said*
To ech a tale that thei tolde hire tonge was tempred° to lye — *tuned*
Moore than to seye sooth,° it semed bi hire speche. — *truth*
Heremytes on an heep° with hoked° staves — *crowd / crooked*
Wenten to Walsyngham[1]—and hire wenches after:
55 Grete lobies and longe that lothe were to swynke

---

1. I.e., and dressed themselves accordingly, disguised in an outward show of finery.
2. I.e., like anchorites and hermits who keep to their cells, instead of coveting to wander ("cairen") about the land ("contree") to indulge their bodies ("likame") with a luxurious way of life ("likerous liflode"). An anchorite (male) or anchoress (female) vowed to live a reclusive, religious life in a cell.
3. A proverbial term for sinners.
4. I.e., they devise fantasies and make fools of themselves even though they possess intelligence if they should choose to work.
5. Perhaps an allusion to St. Paul's words in 2 Thessalonians 3.10: "For even when we were with you, this we commanded you, that if any would not work, neither should he eat."
6. "He who utters foul speech" (Latin) is the Devil's servant; the quotation is not from St. Paul (nor does Langland say it is), but it bears some resemblance to his words in Ephesians 5.4 and Colossians 3.8.
7. I.e., until their bellies and their bags were crammed to the brimful; a bag was carried by beggars for receiving the food bestowed on them as alms.
8. A term for robbers; "roberdes" men were lawless vagabonds, notorious for their crimes during the period when *Piers Plowman* was written.
9. I.e., pilgrims and palmers pledged themselves to visit famous shrines of the day. Palmers were pilgrims who had gone to the Holy Land and carried a palm leaf or a badge in token of their journey. The shrine of St. James, or Santiago, was a famous place of pilgrimage in Spain, and one of the four pilgrimages assigned as penance for particularly grave sins. Rome was known for its many shrines.
1. The Walsingham shrine was the most famous shrine in England dedicated to the Virgin Mary.

Clothed hem in copes to ben knowen from othere,
And shopen hem heremytes hire ese to have.[2]
  I fond there freres, alle the foure ordres,[3]
Prechynge the peple for profit of [the] womb[e]:°   *belly*
60 Glosed the gospel as hem good liked;[4]
For coveitise of copes construwed it as thei wolde.
Manye of this maistres freres mowe clothen hem at likyng[5]
For hire moneie° and marchaundise marchen togideres.   *money*
For sith charite hath ben chapman and chief to shryve lordes[6]
65 Manye ferlies° han fallen in a fewe yeres.   *wondrous events*
But Holy Chirche and hii holde bettre togidres
The mooste meschief on molde is mountynge up faste.[7]
  Ther preched a pardoner as he a preest were:[8]
Broughte forth a bulle with bisshopes seles,
70 And seide that hymself myghte assoillen° hem alle   *absolve*
Of falshede° of fastynge, of avowes° ybroken.   *deceit / vows*
Lewed° men leved hym wel and liked hise wordes,   *unlearned*
Comen up knelynge to kissen hise bulles.
He bonched hem with his brevet and blered hire eighen,
75 And raughte with his rageman rynges and broches.[9]
Thus [ye] gyven [youre] gold glotons to helpe,
And leneth it losels that leccherie haunten![1]
Were the bisshop yblessed and worth bothe his eris,
His seel[2] sholde noght be sent to deceyve the peple.
80 Ac it is noght by the bisshop that the boy precheth[3]—
For the parisshe preest and the pardoner parten° the silver   *divide*
That the povere° [peple] of the parissche sholde have if they   *poor*
    ne were.
  Persons° and parisshe preestes pleyned° hem to   *rectors / complained*
    the bisshop
That hire parisshes weren povere sith the pestilence° tyme,   *plague*
85 To have a licence and leve° at London to dwelle,   *permission*

---

2. Lubbers ("lobies") or tall ("longe") idle louts, who are loath to work ("swynke"), disguised themselves as hermits to have their comfort. *Copes:* the special dress of friars or monks.

3. The four orders of friars: the Carmelites; Augustinians, or Jacobins; and Franciscans.

4. Complaints were frequently made in medieval literature that friars interpreted ("glosed") the Scriptures to serve their own purposes.

5. I.e., many of these masters can ("mowe") dress themselves as they like.

6. I.e., since Charity (or those who claim to work for it) has become a merchant and first ("chief") to hear the confessions ("shryve") of noblemen; alluding to money received by friars for hearing confessions.

7. I.e., unless Holy Church and they ("hii": i.e., the friars) hold together better, then great misfortune ("meschief") on Earth ("molde") is coming.

8. I.e., as if he were a priest. A pardoner was empowered by the pope to supply an indulgence for a sin, in return for some payment toward the Church. An indulgence granted remission of pun-

ishment by the Church for the sin, but not forgiveness from the guilt of the sin. While the payment was supposed to be a voluntary contribution to the works of the Church, the system was open to the kind of abuse shown in this pardoner. A papal bull was a formal statement of "indulgence," and the seals of bishops in whose diocese the pardoner was (ostensibly) licensed to preach were affixed to it.

9. I.e., he struck ("bonched") them with his document ("brevet"), and bleared their eyes, and thus got ("raughte") rings and brooches with his bull ("rageman": a long parchment with ragged edges), in payment for pardon.

1. I.e., thus you give your gold to help gluttons, and hand it ("leneth") to wretches ("losels") who indulge in lechery.

2. Seal of authorization. *Worth bothe his eris:* i.e., worthy to have his ears, being alert and vigilant.

3. I.e., it is not with the bishop's permission that the rogue preaches. Thus, the pardoner has illicitly obtained the bishop's seal; moreover, he has bribed the parish priest and divides the money with him.

And syngen ther for symonie[4] for silver is swete.
Bisshopes and bachelers, bothe maistres and doctours—
That han cure under Crist, and crownynge in tokene
And signe that thei sholden shryven hire parisshens,
90   Prechen and praye for hem, and the povere fede—
Liggen in Londoun in Lenten and ellis.[5]
Somme serven the King and his silver tellen,°   *keep account of*
In the Cheker and in the Chauncelrie chalangen hise dettes
Of wardes and of wardemotes, weyves and streyves.[6]
95   And somme serven as servaunts lordes and ladies,
And in stede° of stywardes sitten and demen.°   *position / judge*
Hire messe° and hire matyns° and many of   *Masses / morning prayers*
    hire houres°   *divine offices*
Arn doone undevoutliche;° drede is at the laste   *undevoutly*
Lest Crist in his Consistorie acorse[7] ful manye!
100   I parcevved° of the power that Peter hadde to kepe— *comprehended*
To bynden and to unbynden, as the Book telleth[8]—
How he it lefte with love as Oure Lorde highte°   *commanded*
Amonges foure vertues,[9] most vertuous of alle vertues,
That cardinals ben called and closynge yates[1]
105   There Crist is in kyngdom, to close and to shette,°   *shut*
And to opene it to hem and hevene blisse shewe.
Ac of the Cardinals at court that kaughte of that name
And power presumed in hem a Pope to make
To han the power that Peter hadde, impugnen I nelle[2]—
110   For in love and lettrure° the eleccion[3] bilongeth;   *learning*
Forthi° I kan and kan naught of court speke moore.   *therefore*

4. I.e., and sing Masses for payment; *simony:* the practice of buying or selling ecclesiastical preferment. After the plague caused depopulation and a loss of tithes and income, many priests went to London to make money by saying Masses for the souls of rich dead persons.
5. I.e., those who have responsibility under Christ, and clerical tonsure (or "crownynge": the part of a monk's or priest's head that has been shaved) as a symbol of their responsibility to hear the confessions of their parishioners, instead reside ("Liggen") in London during Lent (the busiest time of the Christian year) and at other times ("ellis").
6. In the courts, those serving the king claim dues arising to him from guardianship cases ("wardes"), meetings held in each ward ("wardemotes"), lost property ("weyves") and stray animals ("streyves"). The Exchequer ("Cheker") was the commission to receive revenue and the audit of accounts; the Chancery ("Chauncelrie") heard petitions addressed to the king.
7. Condemn. A consistory court was held by a bishop or his official to consider any case in which an ecclesiastic was involved.

8. In Matthew 16.15, Christ tells Peter: "And I will give unto thee the keys of the kingdom of heaven: and whatsoever thou shalt bind on earth shall be bound in heaven: and whatsoever thou shalt loose on earth shall be loosed in heaven."
9. The four cardinal virtues: prudence, temperance, fortitude, and justice.
1. Closing gates. A rough translation of Latin *cardinalis,* which is derived from *cardo,* or hinge; thus the power of the four cardinal virtues is made into the power of the hinges on the gates to heaven, where Christ rules. The word "cardinals" also plays on a double meaning, referring to the cardinals of the papal consistory.
2. I.e., but of the cardinals (or church officials) who grabbed ("kaughte") that name, and presumed to claim they have the power St. Peter had to name a pope, I will not find fault with them. Perhaps an allusion to the French cardinals who elected an antipope in 1378 (Clement VII, a Frenchman), thus creating the Great Schism.
3. Election of popes; also, a reference to salvation.

FROM PEARL[1]
1375–1400

I

1

Perle plesaunte to prynces paye	Pearl,[2] the precious prize of a king,
To clanly clos in golde so clere	Chastely set in cherished gold,
Oute of Oryent I hardyly saye	In all the East none equalling,
Ne proued I neuer her precios pere	No peer to her could I behold.
5 So rounde so reken in vche arave	So round, so rare, a radiant thing,
So smal so smoþe her sydeʒ were	So smooth she was, so small of mold,
Quere so euer I jugged gemmeʒ gaye	Wherever I judged gems glimmering
I sette hyr sengely in synglure	I set her apart, her price untold.
Allas I leste hyr in on erbere	Alas, I lost her in earth's green fold;
10 Þurʒ gresse to grounde hit fro me yot	Through grass to the ground, I searched in vain.
I dewyne fordolked of luf daungere	I languish alone; my heart grows cold
Of þat pryuy perle wythouten spot	For my precious pearl without a stain.[3]

2

Syþen in þat spote hit fro me sprange	Since in that spot it slipped from me,
Ofte haf I wayted wyschande þat wele	I lingered, longing for that delight
15 Þat wont watʒ whyle deuoyde my wrange	That from my sins once set me free
& heuen my happe & al my hele	And my happiness raised to the highest height.
Þat dotʒ bot þrych my hert þrange	Her going wounds me grievously;

1. *Pearl* was written in the latter half of the fourteenth century by an unknown author who probably lived in the northwest midlands of England. The one manuscript of the poem still extant also contains the poems *Sir Gawain and the Green Knight*, *Purity*, and *Patience*, all generally thought to be by the same author. *Pearl*, in the form of a dream vision, a popular convention of the time, is an elegy on the death of a child, perhaps the poet's daughter. Many scholars, however, read the poem as an allegory. In the poem's 101 stanzas, the dreamer carries on a dialogue with the Pearl maiden, who instructs him in Christian doctrine. The intricate pattern of the poem involves rhyme and repeated words and phrases that link the stanzas, forming, finally, a circular structure. The translation used here was done by Sara deFord and a group of her students at Goucher College. The translators chose to print their translation side by side with the original in Middle English (they modernized only the capitalization). They have attempted to remain true to the original form, retaining, where possible, the four-beat alliterative line, rhyme pattern, and repetition of words and phrases of the original. The first five stanzas of the poem, reproduced here, recount the narrator's grief at the loss of his Pearl, and the beginning of the "slumber" that will produce his dream vision of the maid. (The roman numeral *I* above our selection marks the first five-stanza section of the original text.)

2. In medieval tradition, the pearl symbolizes the pure and precious.

3. The translators note that the word "spot" is used in the first five stanzas, but because of the limited rhyme possibilities, they have substituted "stain" in the terminal position.

My breste in bale bot bolne &
 bele

It burns my breast both day and
 night.

3et þo3t me neuer so swete a
 sange

Yet I never imagined a melody

20 As stylle stounde let to me stele

So sweet as she, so brief, and
 slight.

For soþe þer fleten to me fele

But memory flowed through my
 mind's sight:

To þenke hir color so clad in clot

I thought how her color in clods[4]
 had lain

O moul þou marre3 a myry iuele

O dust that dims what once was
 bright,

My priuy perle wythouten spotte

My precious pearl without a stain.

3

25 Þat spot of spyse3 [mo] t nede3
 sprede

Rare spices on that spot must
 spread:

Þer such ryche3 to rot is runne

Such riches there to rot have run,

Blome3 blayke & blwe & rede

Blooms of yellow and blue and
 red,

Þer schyne3 ful schyr agayn þe
 sunne.

Their sheen a shimmer against
 the sun.

Flor & fryte may not be fede

Flower and fruit nor faded nor
 dead,

30 Þer hit doun drof in molde3
 dunne

Where the pearl dropped down in
 mouldering dun;[5]

For vch gresse mot grow of
 grayne3 dede

Each grass from a lifeless grain is
 bred,

No whete were elle3 to wone3
 wonne

Else to harvest no wheat were
 won:[6]

Of goud vche goude is ay bygonne

Always from good is good begun.

So semly a sede mo3t fayly not

So seemly[7] a seed could not die in
 vain,

35 Þat spryg ande spyce3 vp ne
 sponne

That sprig nor spice there would
 be none

Of þat precios perle wythouten
 spotte

Of that precious pearl without a
 stain.

4

To þat spot þat I in speche
 expoun

To the spot which I in speech
 portray,

I entred in þat erber grene

I entered in that arbor green,

In Augoste in a hy3 seysoun

In August on a holy day,

40 Quen corne is coruen wyth
 croke3 kene

When the corn is cut with sickles
 keen.

On huyle þer perle hit trendeled
 doun

On the little rise where my pearl
 rolled away,

---

4. I.e., clods of earth.
5. "Molde3 dunne" may be translated "dark clods of earth."
6. Christ uses this metaphor in reference to his own Crucifixion: "Verily, verily, I say unto you,

Except a corn of wheat fall into the ground and die, it abideth alone; but if it die, it bringeth forth much fruit" (John 12.24).
7. Beautiful.

Schadowed þis worteʒ ful schyre | The fairest flowers formed a
& schene | screen:
Gilofre gyngure & gromylyoun | Gillyflower, ginger, gromwell
 | spray,
& pyonys powdered ay bytwene | With peonies[8] powdered in
 | between.
45 ʒif hit watʒ semly on to sene | If they were seemly to be seen,
A fayr reflayr ʒet fro hit flot | Far sweeter the scents from that
 | domain,
Þer wonys þat worþyly I wot & | More worthy her dwelling, well I
wene | ween,[9]
My precious perle wythouten spot | My precious pearl without a stain.

5

Bifore þat spot my honde I | I mourned, hands clenched,
spenn[e]d | before that mound,
50 For care ful colde þat to me caʒt | For the piercing cold of grief had
 | caught
A deuely dele in my hert denned | Me in the doleful dread and
 | bound
Þaʒ resoun sette myseluen saʒt | My heart, though reason solace
 | sought.
I playned my perle þat þer watʒ | I longed for my pearl, locked in
spenned | the ground,
Wyth fyrte skylleʒ þat faste faʒt | While fierce contentions in me
 | fought.
55 Þaʒ kynde of Kryst me comfort | In Christ, though comfort could
kenned | be found,
My wreched wylle in wo ay | My wretched will was still
wraʒte | distraught.
I felle vpon þat floury flaʒt | I fell upon that flowery plot.
Suche odour to my herneʒ schot | Such odors eddied in my brain,
I slode vpon a slepyng-slaʒte | To sudden slumber I was brought
60 On þat prec[i]os perle wythouten | By that precious pearl without a
spot | stain.

CHARLES D'ORLÉANS
1391–1465

The Smiling Mouth[1]

The smiling mouth and laughing eyen° gray,   *eyes*
The breastes round and long small° armes twain,°   *slender / two*
    The handes smooth, the sides straight and plain,
    Your feetes lit°—what should I further say?   *little*

8. All these plants are types of spices; spices were precious plants valued for their rich scent.
9. Know.

1. This lyric is a rondel, with a refrain in lines 1 and 2, 7 and 8, and 13 and 14.

5   It is my craft° when ye are far away   *practice*
      To muse thereon in stinting° of my pain—   *soothing*
  The smiling mouth and laughing eyen gray,
      The breastes round and long small armes twain.
  So would I pray you, if I durst or may,
10   The sight to see as I have seen,
      Forwhy° that craft me is most fain,°   *because / pleasing*
  And will be to the hour in which I day°—   *die*
  The smiling mouth and laughing eyen gray,
      The breastes round and long small armes twain.

Oft in My Thought

Oft in my thought full busily have I sought,
  Against the beginning of this fresh new year,
What pretty thing that I best given ought
  To her that was mine hearte's lady dear;[2]
5   But all that thought bitane° is fro° me clear   *taken / from*
      Since death, alas, hath closed her under clay
     And hath this world fornaked° with her here— *stripped bare*
      God have her soul, I can no better say.

But for to keep in custom, lo, my thought,
10   And of my seely° service the manere,   *simple*
In showing als° that I forget her not   *also*
    Unto each wight,[3] I shall to my powere
    This dead her serve[4] with masses and prayere;
      For all too foul a shame were me, mafay,°   *by my faith*
15   Her to forget this time that nigheth° near—   *draws*
      God have her soul, I can no better say.

To her profit now nis° there to be bought   *is not*
  None other thing all° will I buy it dear;[5]   *although [I]*
Wherefore, thou Lord that lordest° all aloft,   *rules*
20   My deedes take, such as goodness steer,
    And crown her, Lord, within thine heavenly sphere
     As for most truest lady, may I say,
     Most good, most fair, and most benign of cheer°— *countenance*
      God have her soul, I can no better say.

25   When I her praise, or praising of her hear,
  Although it whilom° were to me pleasere,   *formerly*
    It fill enough it doth mine heart today,
    And doth° me wish I clothed had my bier[6]—   *makes*
      God have her soul, I can no better say.

2. The occasion of the poem is the approaching New Year; New Year's Day was the day for gift-giving during the Middle Ages. The speaker asks what gift he can give his love, who is dead. He can endow Masses, but the poem itself, a *ballade*, is a symbolic gift in memory of the lady.
3. Person; the speaker wants to show everyone that he does not forget his lady.
4. I.e., I will serve this dead woman ("her") to the best of my power.
5. I.e., if anything else could help her, I would pay any cost.
6. A movable stand on which a corpse is placed before burial; i.e., I wish that I had died.

ANONYMOUS LYRICS OF THE FIFTEENTH CENTURY[1]

Adam Lay I-bounden[2]

Adam lay i-bounden, bounden in a bond;
Foure thousand winter[3] thought he not too long.
And all was for an apple, an apple that he took,
As clerkes finden written in theire book.

5   Ne hadde the apple taken been,[4] the apple taken been,
Ne hadde never our Lady aye been heavene queen.
Blessed be the time that apple taken was,
Therefore we moun° singen, *"Deo gracias!"*[5]   *may*

I Sing of a Maiden[6]

I sing of a maiden
    That is makeles:[7]
King of alle kinges
    To° her sone she chees.°   *for / chose*

5   He cam also° stille°   *as / silently*
    Ther° his moder° was   *where / mother*
As dewe in Aprille
    That falleth on the gras.

He cam also stille
10   To his modres bowr[8]
As dewe in Aprille
    That falleth on the flowr.

1. The poems in this section do not appear in chronological order, since they cannot be dated with any certainty. Like the "Anonymous Lyrics of the Thirteenth and Fourteenth Centuries" (see pp. 15–19), these works often blend religious and secular themes; the line between sacred love and erotic love is particularly ambiguous in poems such as "I Have a Young Sister" and "The Corpus Christi Carol."

    English poems explicitly titled "carols" first appear in fifteenth-century manuscripts. In earlier centuries, the term usually denoted a ring-dance accompanied by singing that originated in France (the French *carole*) and was fashionable during Chaucer's lifetime. In the fifteenth and sixteenth centuries, carols were poems with uniform stanzas often rhyming *aaab* and linked by the last rhyme to a "burden," or refrain. The burden typically appears at the beginning of the carol and after each stanza. Carols initially treated many subjects, even celebrations of battle victories as in the "Carol of Agincourt" below. Gradually, however, they

became associated, as they are today, with the feast of Christmas.
2. This poem survives only in a fifteenth-century manuscript collection of carols. It explores the theological idea of the *felix culpa* (Latin, "happy fault"). The poet, in a kind of humorous, courtly gesture, identifies the happy event not as humankind's redemption but as the elevation of the Virgin Mary as queen of heaven. *I-bounden:* bound.
3. One tradition placed the Creation at about 4000 B.C.E.
4. I.e., if the apple had not been taken.
5. "Thanks be to God!" (Latin).
6. This poem celebrating the purity of Christ's mother and the mystery of Christ's birth from a virgin appears in a manuscript containing a variety of English ballads and carols as well as several songs in Latin.
7. A triple pun: mateless, matchless, and spotless.
8. A covert made of leafy branches; also, a bedchamber.

He cam also stille
Ther his moder lay
15 As dewe in Aprille
That falleth on the spray.°   *budding twig*

Moder and maiden°   *virgin*
Was nevere noon but she;
Well may swich° a lady   *such*
20 Godes moder be.

Out of Your Sleep Arise and Wake

Noel, noel, noel,[9]
Noel, noel, noel!

Out of your sleep[1] arise and wake,
For God mankind° now hath i-take,°   *human nature / taken*
5 All of° a maid without any make:°   *from / match, mate*
Of all women she beareth the bell.[2]

Noel, noel, noel . . .

And through a maide fair and wise
Now man is made of full great price;°   *worth*
10 Now angels kneel to man's servise,
And at this time all this befell.

Noel, noel, noel . . .

Now man is brighter than the sun;
Now man in heaven on high shall wone;°   *dwell*
15 Blessed be God this game[3] is begun,
And his mother empress of hell.[4]

Noel, noel, noel . . .

That° ever was thrall,° now is he free;   *who / captive*
That ever was small, now great is she;
20 Now shall God deem° both thee and me   *judge*
Unto his bliss if we do well.

Noel, noel, noel . . .

Now man may to heaven wend;°   *go*
Now heaven and earth to him they bend;

9. A word sung as an expression of joy, originally to commemorate Christ's birth; in this carol, included with music in two fifteenth-century manuscripts, the refrain celebrates both Christ and his virgin mother.
1. Figuratively, the repose of death; also, inactivity or sluggishness.

2. I.e., takes the prize; also, takes the foremost position; also, with a pun on bearing a child.
3. I.e., joy, delight.
4. According to medieval Catholic doctrine, Mary, as queen of heaven, had the power to intercede for those sent to hell.

25 He that was foe now is our friend.
    This is no nay that I you tell.[5]

    Noel, noel, noel . . .

    Now, blessèd brother, grant us grace
    At doomesday° to see thy face   *Judgment Day*
30 And in thy court to have a place,
    That we may there sing noel.

    Noel, noel, noel . . .

I Have a Young Sister

    I have a yong sister
        Fer° beyond the sea;   *far*
    Manye be the druries°   *love tokens*
        That she sente me.

5   She sente me the cherry
        Withouten any stone,
    And so she did the dove
        Withouten any bone.

    She sente me the brere°   *briar*
10   Withouten any rinde;°   *bark*
    She bade me love my lemman°   *sweetheart*
        Without longing.

    How should any cherry
        Be withoute stone?
15 And how should any dove
        Be withoute bone?

    How should any brere
        Be withoute rind?
    How should I love my lemman
20   Without longing?

    When the cherry was a flowr,
        Then hadde it no stone.
    When the dove was an ey,°   *egg*
        Then hadde it no bone.

25 When the briar was unbred,[6]
        Then hadde it no rinde.
    When the maiden hath that she loveth,
        She is without longinge.

---

5. I.e., what I tell you cannot be denied.   6. Unknown, i.e., still in the seed.

I Have a Gentle Cock

I have a gentle° cock,   *noble*
  Croweth me day;
He doth me risen[7] early
  My matins° for to say.   *morning prayers*

5 I have a gentle cock,
  Comen he is of great;°   *lofty lineage*
His comb is of red coral,
  His tail is of jet.°   *black*

I have a gentle cock,
10 Comen he is of kind;°   *good stock*
His comb is of red coral,
  His tail is of inde.°   *indigo*

His legges be of azure,
  So gentle and so small;°   *slender*
15 His spurres° are of silver white   *back claws*
  Into the wortewale.[8]

His eyen° are of crystal,   *eyes*
  Locked° all in amber;   *set*
And every night he percheth him
20 In my lady's chamber.

Timor Mortis[9]

In what estate[1] so ever I be
  Timor mortis conturbat me.

As I went on a merry morning,
I heard a bird both weep and sing.
5 This was the tenor° of her talking: *meaning*
  "Timor mortis conturbat me."

I asked that bird what she meant.
"I am a musket[2] both fair and gent;°   *gentle, noble*

7. Makes me rise. *Croweth me day:* crows at daybreak.
8. I.e., down to the base or imbedded portion of the spurs.
9. The title and refrain of this poem come from a prayer recited (in Latin) during the Catholic religious rite known as the Office of the Dead. "Since I have been sinning daily and repenting not," the prayer says, "the fear of death dismays me" (*timor mortis conturbat me*). A number of other medieval lyrics use the same line as their refrain, as does the

later poem by William Dunbar (see p. 86). This poem is unusual in combining the carol form with a narrative convention—that of the "unexpected encounter"—typical of the *chanson d'aventure* (French, "adventure song").
1. Condition; also, more specifically, an allusion to the medieval view of society as divided into three great "estates": the nobility, the clergy, and the workers.
2. Male sparrowhawk.

For dread of death I am all shent:°   *ruined*
10   *Timor mortis conturbat me.*

"When I shall die, I know no day;
What country or place I cannot say;
Wherefore this song sing I may:
      Timor mortis conturbat me.

15   "Jesu Christ, when he should die,
To his Father he gan° say,   *began [to]*
'Father,' he said, 'in Trinity,³
      Timor mortis conturbat me.'

"All Christian people, behold and see:
20   This world is but a vanity
And replete with necessity.
      Timor mortis conturbat me.

"Wake I or sleep, eate or drink,
When I on my last end° do think,   *death*
25   For greate fear my soul do shrink:
      Timor mortis conturbat me.

"God grant us grace him for to serve,
And be at our end when we sterve,°   *die*
And from the fiend° he us preserve.   *Devil*
30   *Timor mortis conturbat me."*

The Corpus Christi Carol⁴

Lully, lullay, lully, lullay,⁵
The falcon hath born my make° away.   *mate*

He bore him up, he bore him down,
He bore him into an orchard brown.

5   *Lully, lullay, lully, lullay, . . .*

In that orchard there was a hall
That was hanged with purple and pall.°   *black velvet*

3. The Christian doctrine that God the Father, God the Son, and God the Holy Ghost form one true, eternal God.
4. The title of this carol, Latin for "body of Christ," alludes both to the sacrament of the Holy Communion and to a feast of the Church in celebration of that sacrament. The appearance of the words on a stone in the poem's final line has led some critics to interpret the wounded knight as the crucified Christ and/or as the "Fisher King," a Christianized version of a hero in an ancient fertility myth.
   The version of the carol printed here first appears in a sixteenth-century manuscript anthol-

ogy, and some scholars believe that the poem dates from that century rather than from the fifteenth. The late dating has given rise to a historical-allegorical interpretation that takes the knight as a figure for King Henry VIII (1492–1547). He divorced his first wife, Katherine of Aragon, to marry Anne Boleyn, whose heraldic badge was a falcon.
5. This lullabylike refrain appears only in the version of the carol printed here, although several other versions have been recorded by folk-song collectors.

   Lully, lullay, lully, lullay, . . .

   And in that hall there was a bed,
10 It was hanged with gold so red.

   Lully, lullay, lully, lullay, . . .

   And in that bed there lieth a knight,
   His woundes bleeding day and night.

   Lully, lullay, lully, lullay, . . .

15 By that bed's side there kneeleth a may°   *maiden*
   And she weepeth both night and day.

   Lully, lullay, lully, lullay, . . .

   And by that bed's side there standeth a stone,
   Corpus Christi written thereon.

20   *Lully, lullay, lully, lullay, . . .*

Western Wind[6]

Westron wynde, when wylle thow blow,
 The smalle rayne down can rayne?
Cryst, yf my love were in my Armys°   *arms*
 And I yn my bed a gayne!

A Carol of Agincourt[7]

Deo gracias, Anglia,
Redde pro victoria.[8]

Oure kinge went forth to Normandy
With grace and might of chivalry.°   *men at arms*
5 Ther God for him wrought mervelusly:
Wherefore Englonde may calle and cry.

  Deo gracias . . .

6. This lyric survives, with music, in an early sixteenth-century manuscript. Although it seems to be a secular love song, several Tudor composers used it in settings of the Mass.
7. This is one of several poems in carol form celebrating the English victory over the French at Agincourt in 1415. This version is accompanied by music for solo voices and chorus. Contemporary accounts record a number of celebratory processions on Henry V's triumphant return to London at which such songs were sung. "Carol" is used here in the sense of a poem in short stanzas with a burden, or refrain, repeated after each stanza.
8. Return thanks to God, England, for victory (Latin).

He sette a sege, the sothe° for to say,   *truth*
To Harflu towne with ryal array:⁹
10 That towne he wan and made affray°   *terror*
That Fraunce shall riwe° till Domesday.° *rue / Judgment Day*

Deo gracias . . .

Than went oure kinge with alle his hoste°   *army*
Throwe Fraunce, for alle the Frenshe boste:¹
15 He spared, no drede, of lest ne moste,²
Till he come to Agincourt coste.°   *district*

Deo gracias . . .

Than, forsoth,° that knight comely° *truly / handsome*
In Agincourt feld° he faught manly.   *field*
20 Thorw grace of God most mighty
He had bothe the felde and the victory.

Deo gracias . . .

There dukis and erlis, lorde and barone,
Where take° and slaine, and that well sone,° *captured / quickly*
25 And summe were ladde° into Lundone° *led / London*
With joye and merthe and grete renone.°   *pomp*

Deo gracias . . .

Now gracious God he save oure kinge,³
His peple and alle his well-willinge:°   *friends*
30 Yef° him gode life and gode ending,   *give*
That we with merthe mowe° safely singe,   *may*

Deo gracias . . .

The Sacrament of the Altar⁴

It semes white and is red;
It is quike° and semes dede;°   *living / dead*
It is fleshe and semes bred;
It is on° and semes too;⁵   *one*
5 It is God body and no mo.°   *more*

9. Display of his military forces. Henry laid siege to and captured the French port of Harfleur shortly before the victory at Agincourt.
1. I.e., in spite of French boasts or threats.
2. I.e., he spared, no doubt, neither the great nor the humble. Some editors print this line without punctuation, in which case it may be read: he avoided no dangers, great or small.

3. I.e., may he save our king.
4. This poem, which dates from about 1450, examines the paradox of the sacrament of the bread used in the Communion service. According to the doctrine of transubstantiation, the bread becomes the living body of Christ.
5. Two, probably a reference to the bread and the wine of the Eucharist.

See! Here, My Heart[6]

O! Mankinde,
Have in thy minde
My Passion smert,°   *painful*
And thou shall finde
5 Me full kinde—
Lo! here my hert.

WILLIAM DUNBAR
ca. 1460–ca. 1525

Lament for the Makaris[1]

I that in heill° was and gladnes,   *health*
Am trublit now with gret seiknes,°   *sickness*
And feblit with infermite:
   Timor Mortis conturbat me.[2]

5 Our plesance heir is all vane glory
This fals warld is bot transitory,
The flesche is brukle,° the Fend is sle;°   *frail / sly*
   Timor Mortis conturbat me.

The state of man dois change and vary,
10 Now sound, now seik, now blith,° now sary,°   *happy / sorry*
Now dansand mery, now like to dee;[3]
   Timor Mortis conturbat me.

No stait in erd° heir standis sickir;°   *earth / securely*
As with the wynd wavis° the wickir,°   *waves / willow*
15 Wavis this warldis vanite;
   Timor Mortis conturbat me.

On to the ded gois all estatis,[4]
Princis, prelotis,° and potestatis,°   *prelates / potentates*
Baith riche and pur° of al degre;   *poor*
20 *Timor Mortis conturbat me.*

He takis the knychtis° in to feild,   *knights*
Anarmit° under helme and scheild;   *armed*

---

6. This poem is an early type of "emblem poem,"
a verse that interprets a symbolic picture. In a man-
uscript from the early 1500s, the poem appears to
the right of the face of a naked and wounded
Christ, who is offering a kneeling supplicant a large
and bleeding heart ("hert") with a wound in its
center.
1. Makers, poets.

2. The fear of death dismays me (Latin); a line
from the liturgical Office of the Dead. Cf. the
anonymous fifteenth-century poem with the same
refrain (p. 82).
3. I.e., now dance and be merry, now likely to die.
4. Estates. Society was said to be divided into
three estates, or groups: those who ruled, those
who prayed, and those who labored.

Victour he is at all mellie;°   *battles*
Timor Mortis conturbat me.

25 That strang° unmercifull tyrand   *strong*
Takis on the moderis° breist sowkand°   *mother's / sucking*
The bab, full of benignite;°   *gentleness*
Timor Mortis conturbat me.

He takis the campion° in the stour,°   *champion / battle*
30 The capitane closit in the tour,°   *tower*
The lady in bour° full of bewte;   *bower, chamber*
Timor Mortis conturbat me.

He sparis no lord for his piscense,°   *power*
Na clerk° for his intelligence;   *scholar*
35 His awful strak° may no man fle;   *stroke*
Timor Mortis conturbat me.

Art magicianis,[5] and astrologgis,°   *astrologers*
Rethoris,° logicianis, and theologgis,   *rhetoricians*
Thame helpis no conclusionis sle;[6]
40   *Timor Mortis conturbat me.*

In medicyne the most° practicianis,   *greatest*
Leichis,° surrigianis, and phisicianis,   *doctors*
Thame self fra ded° may not supple;°   *death / deliver*
Timor Mortis conturbat me.

45 I see that makaris amang the laif°   *remainder*
Playis heir ther pageant, syne° gois to grave;   *then*
Sparit° is nocht° ther faculte;   *spared / not*
Timor Mortis conturbat me.

He hes done petuously° devour   *piteously*
50 The noble Chaucer, of makaris flour,°   *flower*
The Monk of Bery, and Gower, all thre;[7]
Timor Mortis conturbat me.

The gude Syr Hew of Eglintoun,[8]
And eik° Heryot, and Wyntoun,   *also*
55 He hes tane out of this cuntre;
Timor Mortis conturbat me.

That scorpion fell hes done infeck'°   *infected*
Maister Johne Clerk and James Afflek,
Fra ballat making and tragidie;
60   *Timor Mortis conturbat me.*

---

5. Those practicing the art of magic.
6. I.e., no clever conclusions help them.
7. Three English poets. *The Monk of Bery:* John Lydgate (1370?–1451?) wrote a great variety of verse; he was considered second only to Chaucer during the sixteenth century. *Gower:* John Gower (1325?–1408), whose main poem is the *Confessio*

Amantis.
8. The first in a list of Scots poets, some well-known (e.g., Dunbar's contemporary Robert Henryson, line 82), some obscure; Dunbar presented Walter Kennedy (line 89) as his adversary in the poem *Flyting of Dunbar and Kennedie.*

Holland and Barbour he hes berevit;
Allace!° that he nocht with us levit   *alas*
Schir Mungo Lokert of the Le;°   *lea, meadow*
   Timor Mortis conturbat me.

65   Clerk of Tranent eik he hes tane,
       That maid the Anteris° of Gawane;   *adventures*
       Sir Gilbert Hay endit has he;[9]
          Timor Mortis conturbat me.

       He has Blind Hary, and Sandy Traill
70   Slaine with his schour° of mortal hail,   *shower*
       Quhilk° Patrick Johnestoun myght nocht   *which*
          flee;
          Timor Mortis conturbat me.

       He has reft Merseir his endite,[1]
       That did in luf so lifly write,
75   So schort, so quyk, of sentence hie;°   *lively*
          Timor Mortis conturbat me.

       He hes tane Roull of Aberdene,
       And gentill Roull of Corstorphin;
       Two bettir fallowis did no man se;
80   *Timor Mortis conturbat me.*

       In Dunfermelyne he has done° roune°   *made / a circuit*
       With Maister Robert Henrisoun;
       Schir Johne the Ros embrast hes he;
          Timor Mortis conturbat me.

85   And he hes now tane, last of aw,
       Gud gentill Stobo and Quintyne Schaw,[2]
       Of quham° all wichtis° has pete:°   *whom / creatures / pity*
          Timor Mortis conturbat me.

       Gud Maister Walter Kennedy
90   In poynt of dede lyis veraly,[3]
       Gret reuth° it wer that so suld° be;   *pity / should*
          Timor Mortis conturbat me.

       Sen he hes all my brether° tane,   *brothers*
       He will nocht lat me lif alane,
95   On forse I man his nyxt pray be;[4]
          Timor Mortis conturbat me.

---

9. The "clerkly" author is not known, but Arthurian romances focusing on the hero Gawain were popular in Scotland. Sir Gilbert Hay (d. 1456) translated from French the poem *The Buik* [i.e., *Book*] *of Alexander*.
1. I.e., Death has taken the practice of poetry from

Mercer.
2. A Scots poet. *Stobo*: a name for John Reid, priest and secretary to James II, III, and IV.
3. I.e., lies truly on the point of death.
4. Of necessity, I must be his next prey.

Sen for the deid remeid° is none,   *remedy*
Best is that we for dede dispone,°   *prepare*
Eftir our deid that lif may we;
100   *Timor Mortis conturbat me.*

1508

Done Is a Battle[5]

Done is a battle on° the dragon black,   *with*
Our campion[6] Christ confoundit has his force;
The yettis° of hell are broken with a crack,   *gates*
The sign triumphal raisit is of the cross,
5   The devillis trymmillis° with hiddous voce,   *tremble*
The saulis° are borrowit° and to the bliss can go,   *souls / ransomed*
Christ with his bloud our ransonis dois indoce:°   *endorse*
Surrexit Dominus de sepulchro.[7]

Dungan° is the deidly dragon Lucifer,   *beaten*
10   The cruewall serpent with the mortal stang;
The auld kene tiger, with his teith on char,[8]
Whilk° in a wait has lyen for us so lang,   *which*
Thinking to grip us in his clawis strang;
The merciful Lord wald° nocht° that it were so,   *would / not*
15   He made him for to failye° of that fang.°   *fail / prey*
Surrexit Dominus de sepulchro.

He for our saik that sufferit to be slane,
And lyk a lamb in sacrifice was dicht,°   *prepared*
Is lyk a lion rissen up agane,
20   And as a gyane° raxit° him on hicht;°   *giant / stretched / high*
Sprungen is Aurora[9] radious° and bricht,   *radiant*
On loft is gone the glorious Apollo,[1]
The blissful day departit° fro the nicht: *separated*
Surrexit Dominus de sepulchro.

25   The grit victour again is rissen on hicht,
That for our querrell to the deth was woundit;
The sun that wox° all pale now shynis bricht,   *waxed*
And, derkness clearit,° our faith is now refoundit;°   *cleared / reestablished*
The knell of mercy fra the heaven is soundit,
30   The Christin are deliverit of their wo,
The Jowis° and their errour are confoundit: *Jews*
Surrexit Dominus de sepulchro.

---

5. This Easter hymn depicts Christ's Resurrection as a battle with the Devil. Dunbar draws on the narrative of the harrowing of hell in the apocryphal Gospel of Nicodemus, in which Christ journeys to hell to free virtuous souls born before his coming.
6. Champion, i.e., one who fights on behalf of another.

7. The Lord is risen from the grave (Latin); the line echoes the opening of the Matins, or Easter-morning church service.
8. Ajar, i.e., with his mouth open.
9. Roman goddess of the dawn.
1. Greek and Roman god of sunlight, prophecy, music, and poetry.

The fo is chasit, the battle is done ceis,°   *ceased*
The presone broken, the jevellouris° fleit° and   *jailers / fled*
    flemit;°   *banished*
35 The weir° is gon, confermit is the peis,   *war*
The fetteris° lowsit° and the dungeon temit,°   *shackles / loosed / emptied*
The ransoun made, the prisoneris redeemit;
The field is won, owrecomen is the fo,
Dispuilit° of the treasure that he yemit:°   *despoiled / kept*
40 *Surrexit Dominus de sepulchro.*

ca. 1510

JOHN SKELTON
1460–1529

Mannerly Margery Milk and Ale[1]

Ay, beshrew° you! by my fay,°   *curse / faith*
These wanton clerks be nice[2] alway!
Avaunt,° avaunt, my popinjay![3]   *get out*
What, will ye do nothing but play?
5 Tilly vally, straw,[4] let be I say!
    Gup, Christian Clout, gup, Jack of the Vale![5]
    With Mannerly Margery Milk and Ale.

By God, ye be a pretty pode,°   *toad*
And I love you an whole cart-load.[6]
10 Straw, James Foder,[7] ye play the fode,°   *deceiver*
I am no hackney[8] for your rod:°   *riding*
Go watch a bull,[9] your back is broad!
    Gup, Christian Clout, gup, Jack of the Vale!
    With Mannerly Margery Milk and Ale.

15 Ywis° ye deal uncourteously;   *for certain*
What, would ye frumple° me? now fy!   *wrinkle, muss up*

1. Two copies of this poem survive, with considerable variation between them. Critics disagree about which lines belong to which speaker and about what "happens" between the third and fourth stanzas. The refrain could be divided between Margery and James, or it could be spoken by a third party, as is suggested by an early musical setting that makes the poem a song for three voices.
   The title is an epithet for a servant girl. *Mannerly*: well-mannered, with a possible ironic reflection on a serving girl's aspirations.
2. Variously meant foolish, finicky, or lascivious. "Clerk" originally denoted a member of the clergy (from Latin, *clericus*), but it became a general name for a scholar or student.
3. Parrot; a symbol of vanity.
4. Expressions of contemptuous rejection: fiddlesticks, poppycock, nonsense.
5. A contemptuous name. *Gup*: contracted (?) from *go up*; sometimes an exclamation of derision, remonstrance, or surprise, sometimes a command (get along, get out; get up; also, a command to a horse, giddy up). *Christian Clout*: an epithet for a rural fellow.
6. I.e., a large amount.
7. Jamesweed, ragwort, useless stuff. *Straw*: expression of contempt.
8. I.e., an ordinary riding horse (as distinct from a warhorse or a plowhorse); a prostitute.
9. I.e., go look after farm animals.

What, and ye shall be my pigesnye?[1]
By Christ, ye shall not, no hardely:°   *indeed*
I will not be japèd[2] bodily!
20   Gup, Christian Clout, gup, Jack of the Vale!
With Mannerly Margery Milk and Ale.

Walk forth your way, ye cost me nought;
Now have I found that I have sought:
The best cheap flesh that ever I bought.
25   Yet, for his love that all hath wrought,
Wed me, or else I die for thought.
     Gup, Christian Clout, your breath is stale!
     Go, Mannerly Margery Milk and Ale!
     Gup, Christian Clout, gup, Jack of the Vale!
30   With Mannerly Margery Milk and Ale.

ca. 1495   1523

To Mistress Margaret Hussey[3]

Merry Margaret,[4]
   As midsummer flower,
Gentle as falcon
Or hawk of the tower:[5]
5   With solace and gladness,
Much mirth and no madness,
All good and no badness;
   So joyously,
   So maidenly,
10   So womanly
   Her demeaning°   *demeanour*
In every thing,
Far, far passing
That I can indite,°   *compose*
15   Or suffice to write
Of Merry Margaret
   As midsummer flower,
Gentle as falcon
Or hawk of the tower.
20   As patient and still
And as full of good will
As fair Isaphill,[6]

1. Pet; also, a common flower.
2. Tricked, with a reference to sexual intercourse.
3. This poem is one of ten lyrics included in Skelton's *The Garland of Laurel*, in which the poet is crowned with a laurel wreath (the symbol of poetic achievement) by the countess of Surrey and her ladies; in return, he writes a poem in praise of each of them. "Margaret Hussey," while not identified with any certainty, was perhaps the daughter of Simon Blount of Mangotsfield and married to John

Hussey; she died in August 1492. *Mistress*: title for an upper-class married woman; a courteous form.
4. Meaning daisy, the flower.
5. A hawk bred and trained to fly high.
6. Hypsipyle, mythological daughter of Thaos, king of Lemnos, saved her father when the women of Lemnos killed the men of the island, bore twin sons to Jason, and was then deserted by him. She endured slavery while searching for her father and her sons.

Coriander,[7]
Sweet pomander,[8]
25   Good Cassander,[9]
Steadfast of thought,
Well made, well wrought,
Far may be sought
Ere that ye can find
30   So courteous, so kind
As Merry Margaret,
    This midsummer flower,
Gentle as falcon
Or hawk of the tower.

1492, 1522   1523

From Colin Clout[1]

HEREAFTER FOLLOWETH A LITTLE BOOK CALLED COLIN CLOUT,
COMPILED BY MASTER SKELTON, POET LAUREATE.[2]

Quis consurget mecum adversus malignantes? aut quis stabit mecum
adversus operantes iniquitatem? Nemo, Domine![3]

What can it avail[4]
To drive forth a snail,
Or to make a sail
Of an herring's tail;
5   To rhyme or to rail,
To write or to indict,
Either for delight
Or else for despight;
Or books to compile
10   Of divers manner of style,
Vice to revile
And sin to exile;

---

7. An aromatic herb, believed to soothe pain.
8. A mixture of perfumed or aromatic substances made into a ball.
9. Cassandra, mythological daughter of Priam, king of Troy; another figure of steadfastness. After she refused him as a lover, the god Apollo made her a prophet whom listeners would always disbelieve, as they did when she foretold the fall of Troy.
1. Colin, from the Latin *colonus* (farmer), was a stock name for a person of humble birth in the late medieval and Renaissance periods; "clout" has multiple meanings relevant to the poetic persona that Skelton creates and that Spenser significantly imitates in his *Shepheardes Calender* (see "Aprill," p. 159). Skelton plays on meanings not only of humble birth but also of satirical force: "clout" (variously spelled in this era) can signify a patch of cloth such as those worn by vagrant clerks, a clot or clod of earth (recalling Langland's persona Piers Plowman; see p. 71), a type of rough shoe, and also

a blow with the hand. In this poem of more than twelve hundred lines, Skelton uses his verse as a satirical weapon against bishops and archbishops of the English Church who placed worldly ambitions above their ecclesiastical duties. Skelton's prime opponent is Cardinal Thomas Wolsey (ca. 1475–1530), who rose to and fell from great power during Henry VIII's reign (1509–47), and who began the dissolution of monasteries—a process of alleged "reform" that Skelton abhorred.
2. In 1488, Skelton received the honorable title of "laureate" from Oxford University.
3. Who will rise up for me against the evil-doers? or who will stand up for me against the workers of iniquity? (Latin); from Psalm 94.14. No one, lord (Latin); from John 8.11.
4. I.e., what good can it do. The first four lines and many others in the poem are based on well-known proverbs.

To teach or to preach,
As reason will reach?
15 Say this, and say that,
His[5] head is so fat,
He wotteth° never what   *knows*
Nor whereof he speaketh;
He crieth and he creaketh,
20 He prieth and he peeketh,[6]
He chides and he chatters,
He prates and he patters,
He clitters° and he clatters,   *chatters*
He meddles and he smatters,
25 He gloses° and he flatters;   *interprets*
Or if he speak plain,
Then he lacketh brain,
He is but a fool;
Let him go to school,
30 On a three footed stool
That he may down sit,
For he lacketh wit;
And if that he hit
The nail on the head,
35 It standeth in no stead;
The devil, they say, is dead,
The devil is dead.[7]
    It may well so be,
Or else they would see
40 Otherwise, and flee
From worldly vanity,
And foul covetousness,
And other wretchedness,
Fickle falseness,
45 Variableness,
With unstableness.
    And if ye stand in doubt
Who brought this rhyme about,
My name is Colin Clout.
50 I purpose° to shake out   *aim*
All my connying bag,
Like a clerkly hag;[8]
For though my rhyme be ragged,
Tattered and jagged,
55 Rudely rain beaten,

---

5. Apparently refers to the poet as seen by his detractors, who scorn him whether he writes and prophesies through allegory or speaks "plainly" (line 26).
6. I.e., he pries into things and goads us (or, possibly, he pries and peeks into things).
7. Based on a proverbial saying, these lines evidently express the reaction of an imaginary audience that doesn't want to be bothered by Skelton's

critique of evil.
8. Wandering clerks (members of the clergy) typically carried pouches; although "hag" usually referred to an old woman, it was sometimes used as a general term of abuse. The image of the clerk's "connying" bag, to which the poet compares his own bag of poetic tricks, plays on the meanings of *cunning* both as "knowledge" and as "cheating," duping through cleverness.

Rusty and moth eaten,
If ye take well therewith,
It hath in it some pith.°   *meaning*

ca. 1521–22   ca. 1531

Phillip Sparow[9]

HEREAFTER FOLLOWETH [*SELECTIONS FROM*] THE BOOK OF
PHILLIP SPAROW, COMPILED BY MASTER SKELTON, POET LAUREATE.[1]

Pla ce bo,[2]
Who is there, who?
Di le xi,[3]
Dame Margery;
5   Fa, re, my, my,[4]
Wherefore and why, why?
For the soul of Phillip Sparow,
That was late slain at Carow,
Among the Nuns Black,[5]
10   For that sweet soul's sake,
And for all sparrows' souls,
Set in our bead-rolls,[6]
Pater noster qui,
With an *Ave Mari,*[7]
15   And with the corner of a creed,[8]
The more shall be your meed,°   *reward*
        Whan I remember again
How my Phillip was slain,
Never half the pain
20   Was between you twain,
Pyramus and Thisbe,[9]
As then befell° to me: *happened*

9. This poem of approximately 1,380 lines begins
with a long elegy (lines 1–884) for the pet sparrow
of a gentlewoman named Jane Scrope. (The sec-
ond part eulogizes Jane, and in the third part Skel-
ton defends himself against a detractor.) Imitating
classical elegies for dead birds by Catullus and
Ovid and perhaps also the description of how a fox
killed Chantekler's daughter in William Caxton's
early printed translation of the Dutch *Reynard the
Fox* (1481), Skelton's poem makes Jane the first-
person comic narrator of the first part, interweav-
ing her lamenting verse (in the running-rhyme
form known as "Skeltonic"; see "Versification,"
pp. 2046–47) with Latin phrases from the solemn
Catholic funeral service called the Office of the
Dead.
1. See note 2, p. 92.
2. I shall please [the Lord] (Latin); from Psalm
114.9. "Placebo," like all other citations of the
Psalms in this poem (cited according to their num-
bering in the Catholic Bible known as the Vulgate),
is used in the Vespers, or evening service of the
Office of the Dead. The spacing of the syllables
suggests the plainsong music of the Mass.

3. I love [the Lord, because he hath heard my
voice] (Latin); from Psalm 114.1.
4. Musical notes used at the close of the Office of
the Dead.
5. Refers to the black robes worn by members of
the Benedictine order. *Carow:* Carrow Abbey,
where Jane Scrope went to live after her mother was
widowed for the second time, in 1502. A senior nun
named Margery is mentioned in the records of this
abbey, which was founded by the Benedictines.
6. List of people for whom the nuns prayed with
the "beads" of their rosaries.
7. "Hail Mary"; the previous Latin phrase opens
the Lord's Prayer ("Our Father which . . .").
8. A prayer about Christian beliefs (from *credere,*
Latin for "to believe") that was typically printed,
along with the "Hail Mary" and "Our Father," on
the first page of elementary reading books (prim-
ers). Skelton probably refers to the "corner" of the
"creed" because only part of that prayer usually fit
on the first page of the primer.
9. Lovers tragically separated in a story told by
Ovid (*Metamorphoses*) and Chaucer (*Legend of
Good Women*), among others.

I wept and I wailèd,
The tears down hailèd;
25 But nothing it availèd[1]
To call Phillip again,
Whom Gib our cat hath slain.
    Gib, I say, our cat
Worrowed[2] her on that
30 Which I loved best:
It can not be expressed
My sorowful heaviness,
But all without redress;
For within that stound,°   moment
35 Half slumb'ring, in a sound°   faint
I fell down to the ground.
    Unneth° I cast mine eyes   scarcely
Toward the cloudy skies:
But when I did behold
40 My sparow dead and cold,
No creature but that would
Have rewed° upon me,   had pity
To behold and see
What heaviness did me pang;°   affect with pain
45 Wherewith my hands I wrang,
That my sinews cracked,
As though I had been racked,°   tortured
So painèd and so strainèd
That no life wellnigh remainèd.
50 I sighed and I sobbed,
For that I was robbed
Of my sparow's life.
O maiden, widow, and wife,
Of what estate ye be,
55 Of high or low degree,
Great sorow than° ye might see,   then
And learn to weep at° me!   from
Such pains did me fret,
That mine heart did beat,
60 My visage pale and dead,
Wan, and blue as lead;
The pangs of hateful death
Wellnigh had stopped my breath.

                    *   *   *

Though I have enrolled°   inscribed
750 A thousand new and old
Of these historious° tales,   historical
To fill bougets° and males°   bags / pouches
With books that I have read,
Yet I am nothing sped . . . [3]

---

1. I.e., it did no good.
2. Worried, i.e., bit. "Gib," short for Gilbert, was a standard name for a cat, as Phillip was for a pet sparrow.
3. I.e., I've gotten nowhere.

* * *

For, as I tofore° have said,   *before*
770   I am but a young maid,
And cannot in effect
My style as yet direct°   *control*
With English words elect.°   *well chosen*
Our natural tongue is rude,[4]
775   And hard to be ennewed°   *revived*
With polished terms lusty;
Our language is so rusty,
So cankered,° and so full   *infected*
Of frowards,° and so dull,   *badly formed words*
780   That if I would apply°   *try*
To write ornately,[5]
I wot° not where to find   *know*
Terms to serve my mind.

* * *

Wherefore hold me excused
If I have not well perused°   *studied carefully*
815   Mine English half abused;
Though it be refused,
In worth I shall it take,[6]
And fewer wordes make.
But, for my sparow's sake,
820   Yet as a woman may,
My wit I shall assay
An epitaph to write
In Latin plain and light,
Whereof the elegy
825   Followeth by and by:
Flos volucrum formose, vale![7]
Philippe, sub isto
Marmore jam recubas,
Qui mihi carus eras.
830   *Semper erunt nitido*
Radiantia sidera cælo;
Impressusque meo
Pectore semper eris.
Per me laurigerum
835   *Britonum Skeltonida vatem*
Hæc cecinisse licet

4. Uneducated, lacking in polish.
5. With rhetorical embellishment of the kind taught in the grammar schools, which focused during Skelton's era on Latin rather than English composition and which were generally closed to girls.
6. I.e., I'll take it in good part.
7. Although Jane claims to write the following lines, Skelton implicitly (and perhaps ironically) undermines her claim by switching to Latin; he explicitly asserts his own authorship of the entire first part of the poem in lines 827–44. Translated, lines 826–43 go as follows: "Farewell, flower of birds, beautiful one! Phillip, you lie now beneath this marble, you who were dear to me. So long as the stars shine in the sky, you will always be engraved in my heart. By me, Skelton, the laureate poet of Britain, these things could be sung under a feigned likeness. She whose bird you were is a maiden of surpassing beauty. Nias [presumably one of the classical water nymphs known as 'naiads'] was fair, but Jane is lovelier; Corinna was learned, but Jane is wiser." Corinna is the woman who laments her dead parrot in Ovid's *Amores*.

Ficta sub imagine texta.
Cujus eras volucris,
Præstanti corpore virgo:
840   Candida Nais erat,
Formosior ista Joanna est;
Docta Corinna fuit,
Sed magis ista sapit.
Bien m'en souvient.[8]

ca. 1505–07   ca. 1545

EARLY MODERN BALLADS[1]

The Douglas Tragedy[2]

1

"Rise up, rise up, now, Lord Douglas," she says,
   "And put on your armor so bright;
Let it never be said that a daughter of thine
   Was married to a lord under night.

2

5   "Rise up, rise up, my seven bold sons,
   And put on your armor so bright,
And take better care of your youngest sister,
   For your eldest's awa° the last night."   away

3

He's mounted her on a milk-white steed,
10   And himself on a dapple gray,
With a bugelet° horn hung down by his side,   small bugle
   And lightly they rode away.

4

Lord William looked o'er his left shoulder,
   To see what he could see,
15   And there he spied her seven brethren bold,
   Come riding over the lea.°   meadow

8. I remember it well (French); Skelton uses this phrase elsewhere in his poetry.
1. The following ballads exist in numerous versions, many of which are printed in the great collection of F. J. Child, *English and Scottish Popular Ballads* (five volumes, 1882–98). Child's different versions, designated by alphabetical letters here and in his edition, reveal different political and ethical interpretations of a given story. Ballads often contain topical allusions, and most popular ballads from the fourteenth through the seventeenth centuries, in contrast to later literary instances of the genre, were sung to well-known tunes. While some ballads originated as folk songs and were written down (and/or printed) much later (sometimes centuries later), other ballads were initially made to be read—and sold—as printed objects. Even manuscript or printed versions of ballads, among the latter being the "broadsides" printed cheaply on single sheets and sold at fairs and by peddlers along the road, might subsequently be orally transmitted, since they could be heard and memorized by the non- or partially literate person.
2. From Child, No. 7.B.

5

"Light down, light down, Lady Margret," he said,
　"And hold my steed in your hand,
Until that against your seven brethren bold,
20　　And your father, I mak a stand."

6

She held his steed in her milk-white hand,
　And never shed one tear,
Until that she saw her seven brethren fa',°　　　　　　　　　*fall*
　And her father hard fighting, who loved her so dear.

7

25　"O hold your hand, Lord William!" she said,
　"For your strokes they are wondrous sair;°　　　　　　　　*sore*
True lovers I can get many a ane,°　　　　　　　　　　　　*one*
　But a father I can never get mair."°　　　　　　　　　　*more*

8

O she's ta'en out her handkerchief,
30　It was o' the holland° sae° fine,　　　　　　　　　*linen / so*
And aye she dighted° her father's bloody wounds,　　　　　*dressed*
　That were redder than the wine.

9

"O choose, O choose, Lady Margret," he said,
　"O whether will ye gang° or bide?"　　　　　　　　　　*go*
35　"I'll gang, I'll gang, Lord William," she said,
　"For ye have left me no other guide."

10

He's lifted her on a milk-white steed,
　And himself on a dapple gray,
With a bugelet horn hung down by his side,
40　And slowly they baith rade away.

11

O they rade on, and on they rade,
　And a' by the light of the moon,
Until they came to yon wan° water,　　　　　　　　　　　*dark*
　And there they lighted down.

12

45　They lighted down to tak a drink
　Of the spring that ran sae clear,
And down the stream ran his good heart's blood,
　And sair she 'gan to fear.

13

"Hold up, hold up, Lord William," she says,
50   "For I fear that you are slain."
" 'Tis naething but the shadow of my scarlet cloak,
   That shines in the water sae plain."

14

O they rade on, and on they rade,
   And a' by the light of the moon,
55   Until they cam to his mother's ha'° door,   *hall*
   And there they lighted down.

15

"Get up, get up, lady mother," he says,
   "Get up, and let me in!
Get up, get up, lady mother," he says,
60   "For this night my fair lady I've win.

16

"O mak my bed, lady mother," he says,
   "O mak it braid° and deep,   *broad*
And lay Lady Margret close at my back,
   And the sounder I will sleep."

17

65 Lord William was dead lang° ere midnight,   *long*
   Lady Margret lang ere day,
And all true lovers that go thegither,°   *together*
   May they have mair luck than they!

18

Lord William was buried in St. Mary's kirk,°   *church*
70   Lady Margret in Mary's choir;
Out o' the lady's grave grew a bonny red rose,
   And out o' the knight's a briar.

19

And they twa met, and they twa plat,°   *plaited*
   And fain they wad° be near;   *would*
75 And a' the warld might ken° right weel   *know*
   They were twa lovers dear.

20

But by and rade the Black Douglas,
   And wow but he was rough!
For he pulled up the bonny briar,
80   And flang 't in St. Mary's Loch.°   *lake*

Lord Randal[3]

1

"O where ha' you been, Lord Randal, my son?
And where ha' you been, my handsome young man?"
"I ha' been at the greenwood; mother, mak my bed soon,
For I'm wearied wi' huntin', and fain wad° lie down."   *would*

2

5   "And wha° met ye there, Lord Randal, my son?   *who*
And wha met you there, my handsome young man?"
"O I met wi' my true-love; mother, mak my bed soon,
For I'm wearied wi' huntin', and fain wad lie down."

3

"And what did she give you, Lord Randal, my son?
10   And what did she give you, my handsome young man?"
"Eels fried in a pan; mother, mak my bed soon,
For I'm wearied wi' huntin', and fain wad lie down."

4

"And wha gat your leavin's, Lord Randal, my son?
And wha gat your leavin's, my handsome young man?"
15   "My hawks and my hounds; mother, mak my bed soon,
For I'm wearied wi' huntin', and fain wad lie down."

5

"And what becam of them, Lord Randal, my son?
And what becam of them, my handsome young man?"
"They stretched their legs out and died; mother, mak my bed soon,
20   For I'm wearied wi' huntin', and fain wad lie down."

6

"O I fear you are poisoned, Lord Randal, my son!
I fear you are poisoned, my handsome young man!"
"O yes, I am poisoned; mother, mak my bed soon,
For I'm sick at the heart, and I fain wad lie down."

7

25   "What d' ye leave to your mother, Lord Randal, my son?
What d'ye leave to your mother, my handsome young man?"
"Four and twenty milk kye°; mother, mak my bed soon,   *kine, cattle*
For I'm sick at the heart, and I fain wad lie down."

8

"What d' ye leave to your sister, Lord Randal, my son?
30   What d' ye leave to your sister, my handsome young man?"

3. Child, No. 12.A.

"My gold and my silver; mother, mak my bed soon,
For I'm sick at the heart, and I fain wad lie down."

9

"What d' ye leave to your brother, Lord Randal, my son?
What d' ye leave to your brother, my handsome young man?"
35 "My houses and my lands; mother, mak my bed soon,
For I'm sick at the heart, and I fain wad lie down."

10

"What d' ye leave to your true-love, Lord Randal, my son?
What d' ye leave to your true-love, my handsome young man?"
"I leave her hell and fire; mother, mak my bed soon,
40 For I'm sick at the heart, and I fain wad lie down."

The Three Ravens[4]

1

There were three ravens sat on a tree,
   Down a down, hay down, hay down.
There were three ravens sat on a tree,
   With a down,
5 There were three ravens sat on a tree,
They were as black as they might be.
   With a down derry, derry, derry, down, down.

2

The one of them said to his mate,
"Where shall we our breakfast take?"

3

10 "Down in yonder greene field,
There lies a knight slain under his shield.

4

"His hounds they lie down at his feet,
So well they can their master keep.

5

"His hawks they fly so eagerly,°   *fiercely*
15 There's no fowl dare him come nigh."

6

Down there comes a fallow[5] doe,
As great with young as she might go.

---

4. Child, No. 26; first printed in a songbook in 1611. All stanzas follow the pattern of the first, with the refrain in lines 2, 4, and 7, and the first line repeated in line 5.
5. A species of pale-brownish or reddish-yellow deer.

7

She lift up his bloody head
And kissed his wounds that were so red.

8

20 She got him up upon her back
And carried him to earthen lake.°   *ditch*

9

She buried him before the prime;[6]
She was dead herself ere even-song time.

10

God send every gentleman
25 Such hawks, such hounds, and such a leman.° *lover, sweetheart*

The Twa Corbies[7]

1

As I was walking all alane,
I heard twa corbies making a mane;°   *moan*
The tane° unto the t'other say,   *one*
"Where sall° we gang° and dine to-day?"   *shall / go*

2

5 "In behint you auld° fail° dyke,°   *old / turf / ditch*
I wot° there lies a new slain knight;   *know*
And naebody kens° that he lies there,   *knows*
But his hawk, his hound, and lady fair.

3

"His hound is to the hunting gane,°   *gone*
10 His hawk to fetch the wild-fowl hame,
His lady's ta'en another mate,
So we may mak our dinner sweet.

4

"Ye'll sit on his white hause-bane,°   *neck bone*
And I'll pike° out his bonny blue een°   *pick / eyes*
15 Wi' ae° lock o' his gowden° hair   *one / golden*
We'll theek° our nest when it grows bare.   *thatch*

5

"Mony° a one for him makes mane,   *many*
But nane° sall° ken° where he is gane;   *none / shall / know*
O'er his white banes,° when they are bare,   *bones*
20 The wind sall blaw for evermair."

---

6. According to Catholic Church ritual, the first
hour of the day, between 6 and 9 A.M.
7. The two ravens. First printed in Sir Walter

Scott's *Minstrelsy of the Scottish Border* (1802–03),
this ballad is a cynical version of "The Three Ravens," above.

Sir Patrick Spens[8]

1

The king sits in Dumferling town,
  Drinking the blude-reid° wine: *blood-red*
"O whar will I get guid° sailor,   *good*
  To sail this ship of mine?"

2

5   Up and spak° an eldern knicht,   *spoke*
  Sat at the king's richt knee:
"Sir Patrick Spens is the best sailor
  That sails upon the sea."

3

The king has written a braid[9] letter
10   And signed it wi' his hand,
And sent it to Sir Patrick Spens,
  Was walking on the sand.

4

The first line that Sir Patrick read,
  A loud lauch° lauched he;   *laugh*
15   The next line that Sir Patrick read,
  The tear blinded his ee.°   *eye*

5

"O wha is this has done this deed,
  This ill deed done to me,
To send me out this time o' the year,
20   To sail upon the sea?

6

"Mak haste, mak haste, my mirry men all,
  Our guid ship sails the morn."
"O say na sae,° my master dear,   *so*
  For I fear a deadly storm.

7

25   "Late, late yestre'en I saw the new moon
  Wi' the auld moon in hir arm,
And I fear, I fear, my dear master,
  That we will come to harm."

8. Child, No. 58.A. This ballad, first printed in 1765, tells a story that may be based on two voyages of thirteenth-century Scots noblemen to conduct princesses to royal marriages. Margaret, daughter of Alexander III, was married in 1281 to Eric of Norway, and many members of her escort were drowned on the voyage home. Her daughter, also named Margaret, was drowned with her escort on the way to a marriage in Scotland in 1290. In Child version H, Patrick is sent to Norway to bring the king's daughter home. In all versions, Patrick is sent to sea against his will.
9. Broad, i.e., long.

8

O our Scots nobles were richt laith°   *loath*
30 To weet° their cork-heeled shoon,°   *wet / shoes*
But lang or° a' the play were played   *before*
Their hats they swam aboon.[1]

9

O lang,° lang may their ladies sit,   *long*
Wi' their fans into their hand,
35 Or ere they see Sir Patrick Spens
Come sailing to the land.

IO

O lang, lang may the ladies stand
Wi' their gold kems° in their hair,   *combs*
Waiting for their ain dear lords,
40 For they'll see them na mair.

II

Half o'er, half o'er to Aberdour
It's fifty fadom deep,
And there lies guid Sir Patrick Spens
Wi' the Scots lords at his feet.

The Unquiet Grave[2]

1

"The wind doth blow today, my love,
And a few small drops of rain;
I never had but one true-love,
In cold grave she was lain.

2

5 "I'll do as much for my true-love
As any young man may;
I'll sit and mourn all at her grave
For a twelvemonth and a day."

3

The twelvemonth and a day being up,
10 The dead began to speak:
"Oh who sits weeping on my grave,
And will not let me sleep?"

4

" 'T is I, my love, sits on your grave,
And will not let you sleep;

---

1. I.e., their hats swam above (them).
2. Child, No. 78.A; from a nineteenth-century version collected in the journal *Folk Lore Record*.

15 For I crave one kiss of your clay-cold lips,
    And that is all I seek."

5

"You crave one kiss of my clay-cold lips,
    But my breath smells earthy strong;
If you have one kiss of my clay-cold lips,
20   Your time will not be long.

6

" 'T is down in yonder garden green,
    Love, where we used to walk,
The finest flower that e'er was seen
    Is withered to a stalk.

7

25 "The stalk is withered dry, my love,
    So will our hearts decay;
So make yourself content, my love,
    Till God calls you away."

The Wife of Usher's Well[3]

1

There lived a wife at Usher's Well,
    And a wealthy wife was she;
She had three stout and stalwart sons,
    And sent them o'er the sea.

2

5 They hadna been a week from her,
    A week but barely ane,°   *one*
Whan word came to the carlin° wife   *old*
    That her three sons were gane.

3

They hadna been a week from her,
10   A week but barely three,
Whan word came to the carlin wife
    That her sons she'd never see.

4

"I wish the wind may never cease,
    Nor fashes° in the flood,   *troubles*
15 Till my three sons come hame to me,
    In earthly flesh and blood."

---

3. Child, No. 79.A; from Sir Walter Scott's *Minstrelsy of the Scottish Border* (1802–03).

5

It fell about the Martinmass,[4]
   When nights are lang and mirk,°   *murky*
The carlin wife's three sons came hame,
20   And their hats were o' the birk.°   *birch*

6

It neither grew in syke° nor ditch,   *trench*
   Nor yet in any sheugh;°   *furrow*
But at the gates o' Paradise,
   That birk grew fair eneugh.

7

25 "Blow up the fire, my maidens,
   Bring water from the well;
For a' my house shall feast this night,
   Since my three sons are well."

8

And she has made to them a bed,
30   She's made it large and wide,
And she's ta'en her mantle° her about,   *cloak*
   Sat down at the bed-side.

9

Up then crew the red, red cock,
   And up and crew the gray;
35 The eldest to the youngest said,
   " 'T is time we were away."

10

The cock he hadna crawed but once,
   And clapped his wings at a',
When the youngest to the eldest said,
40   "Brother, we must awa'.

11

"The cock doth craw, the day doth daw,
   The channerin'° worm doth chide;   *fretting*
Gin° we be missed out o' our place,   *if*
   A sair° pain we maun° bide.   *sore / must*

12

45 "Fare ye weel, my mother dear!
   Fareweel to barn and byre!°   *cowhouse*
And fare ye weel, the bonny lass,
   That kindles my mother's fire!"

4. The feast of St. Martin (Pope Martin I, martyred 655 C.E.), November 11.

Bonny Barbara Allan[5]

1

It was in and about the Martinmas[6] time,
   When the green leaves were a falling,
That Sir John Græme, in the West Country,
   Fell in love with Barbara Allan.

2

5 He sent his man down through the town,
   To the place where she was dwelling:
"O haste and come to my master dear,
   Gin° ye be Barbara Allan."   *if*

3

O hooly,° hooly rose she up,   *slowly, gently*
10   To the place where he was lying,
And when she drew the curtain by:
   "Young man, I think you're dying."

4

"O it's I'm sick, and very, very sick,
   And 'tis a' for Barbara Allan."
15 "O the better for me ye s'° never be,   *shall*
   Though your heart's blood were a-spilling.

5

"O dinna° ye mind, young man," said she,   *don't*
   "When ye was in the tavern a drinking,
That ye made the healths gae° round and round,
20   And slighted Barbara Allan?"   *go*

6

He turned his face unto the wall,
   And death was with him dealing:
"Adieu, adieu, my dear friends all,
   And be kind to Barbara Allan."

7

25 And slowly, slowly raise she up,
   And slowly, slowly left him,
And sighing said, she could not stay,
   Since death of life had reft him.

8

She had not gane a mile but twa,
30   When she heard the dead-bell ringing,

---

5. Child, No. 84.A; from the *Tea Table Miscellany*   6. See note 4, p. 106.
(1763).

And every jow° that the dead-bell geid,°   *stroke / gave*
It cried, "Woe to Barbara Allan!"

9

"O mother, mother, make my bed!
O make it saft and narrow!
35 Since my love died for me to-day,
I'll die for him to-morrow."

Mary Hamilton[7]

1

Word's gane to the kitchen,
And word's gane to the ha',°   *hall*
That Marie Hamilton gangs° wi' bairn°   *goes / child*
To the hichest° Stewart of a'.   *highest*

2

5 He's courted her in the kitchen,
He's courted her in the ha',
He's courted her in the laigh cellar,[8]
And that was warst of a'.

3

She's tied it in her apron
10 And she's thrown it in the sea;
Says, "Sink ye, swim ye, bonny wee babe!
You'll ne'er get mair o' me."

4

Down then cam the auld queen,
Goud° tassels tying her hair: *gold*
15 "O Marie, where's the bonny wee babe
That I heard greet° sae° sair?"°   *cry / so / sorely*

5

"There was never a babe intill° my room,   *in*
As little designs to be;
It was but a touch o' my sair° side,   *sore*
20 Come o'er my fair body."

---

7. Child, No. 173.A. This ballad, first cited in 1790 and first printed in the early nineteenth century, is probably set at the court of Mary Stuart (1542–1587). According to the Calendar of State Papers, Mary, queen of Scotland, had four maids-in-waiting who bore her first name. The Protestant writer John Knox, hostile both to female rulers and to Catholics like Mary Stuart, denounced one of the maids-in-waiting for murdering a child she had conceived illicitly with the court apothecary (*History of the Reformation*). Most versions of the story in ballad form identify the baby's father as the king, probably alluding to Lord Darnley, Mary Stuart's frequently unfaithful second husband. Different versions of the ballad offer different views on Mary Hamilton's degree of guilt for the child's death. Child believes that this ballad alludes to events that occurred in the Russian court of Peter the Great (1672–1725) rather than in that of Mary Stuart.
8. Low cellar, basement.

6

"O Marie, put on your robes o' black,
    Or else your robes o' brown,
For ye maun° gang wi' me the night,   *must*
    To see fair Edinbro' town."

7

25 "I winna° put on my robes o' black,   *won't*
    Nor yet my robes o' brown;
But I'll put on my robes o' white,
    To shine through Edinbro' town."

8

When she gaed° up the Cannogate,⁹   *went*
30   She laughed loud laughters three;
But when she cam down the Cannogate
    The tear blinded her ee.°   *eye*

9

When she gaed up the Parliament stair,
    The heel cam aff her shee;
35 And lang or° she cam down again   *before*
    She was condemned to dee.

10

When she cam down the Cannogate,
    The Cannogate sae free,
Many a lady looked o'er her window,
40   Weeping for this lady.

11

"Ye need nae weep for me," she says,
    "Ye need nae weep for me;
For had I not slain mine own sweet babe,
    This death I wadna dee.

12

45 "Bring me a bottle of wine," she says,
    "The best that e'er ye ha'e,
That I may drink to my weil-wishers,
    And they may drink to me.

13

"Here's a health to the jolly sailors,
50   That sail upon the main;
Let them never let on to my father and mother
    But what I'm coming hame.

9. The Canongate is the Edinburgh street leading uphill from Holyrood House (where the queen and the "four Maries" of line 69 lived) to the Tolbooth, which was both jail and judicial chamber and, on occasion, the place where Parliament (line 33) sat.

14

"Here's a health to the jolly sailors,
That sail upon the sea;
55 Let them never let on to my father and mother
That I cam here to dee.

15

"Oh little did my mother think,
The day she cradled me,
What lands I was to travel through,
60 What death I was to dee.

16

"Oh little did my father think,
The day he held up me,
What lands I was to travel through,
What death I was to dee.

17

65 "Last night I washed the queen's feet,
And gently laid her down;
And a' the thanks I've gotten the night[1]
To be hanged in Edinbro' town!

18

"Last night there was four Maries,
70 The night there'll be but three;
There was Marie Seton, and Marie Beton,
And Marie Carmichael, and me."

Get Up and Bar the Door[2]

1

It fell about the Martinmas[3] time,
And a gay time it was then,
When our goodwife got puddings to make,
And she's boiled them in the pan.

2

5 The wind sae° cauld blew south and north,   *so*
And blew into the floor;
Quoth our goodman to our goodwife,
"Gae° out and bar the door."   *go*

3

"My hand is in my hussyfskap.°   *housewife's work*
10 Goodman, as ye may see;

---

1. I.e., tonight.
2. Child, No. 275.A; from David Herd, *The*
Ancient and Modern Scots Songs (1769).
3. See note 4, p. 106.

An° it should nae be barred this hundred year,   *if*
   It s'° no be barred for me."   *shall*

4

They made a paction° 'tween them twa,   *pact*
   They made it firm and sure,
15 That the first word whae'er should speak,
   Should rise and bar the door.

5

Then by there came two gentlemen,
   At twelve o'clock at night,
And they could neither see house nor hall,
20   Nor coal nor candle-light.

6

"Now whether is this a rich man's house,
   Or whether is it a poor?"
But ne'er a word wad° ane o' them speak,   *would*
   For barring of the door.

7

25 And first they ate the white puddings,
   And then they ate the black;
Though muckle° thought the goodwife to hersel,   *much, a lot*
   Yet ne'er a word she spak.

8

Then said the one unto the other,
30   "Here, man, tak ye my knife;
Do ye tak aff° the auld man's beard,   *off*
   And I'll kiss the goodwife."

9

"But there's nae water in the house,
   And what shall we do then?"
35 "What ails ye at[4] the pudding-broo,°   *-broth*
   That boils into the pan?"

10

O up then started our goodman,
   An angry man was he:
"Will ye kiss my wife before my een,°   *eyes*
40   And scad° me wi' pudding-bree?"°   *scald / -broth*

11

Then up and started our goodwife,
   Gied° three skips on the floor: *gave*

4. I.e., what's the matter with.

"Goodman, you've spoken the foremost word,
    Get up and bar the door."

The Bitter Withy[5]

1

As it fell out on a holy day,
    The drops of rain did fall, did fall,
Our Saviour asked leave of his mother Mary
    If he might go play at ball.

2

5   "To play at ball, my own dear son,
    It's time you was going or gone,
But be sure let me hear no complain of you,
    At night when you do come home."

3

It was upling scorn and downling scorn,[6]
10   Oh, there he met three jolly jerdins;°   *fellows*
Oh, there he asked the jolly jerdins
    If they would go play at ball.

4

"Oh, we are lords' and ladies' sons,
    Born in bower° or in hall,   *chamber*
15   And you are some poor maid's child
    Borned in an ox's stall."

5

"If you are lords' and ladies' sons,
    Borned in bower or in hall,
Then at last I'll make it appear
20   That I am above you all."

6

Our Saviour built a bridge with the beams of the sun,[7]
    And over it he gone, he gone he.
And after followed the three jolly jerdins,
    And drownded they were all three.

7

25   It was upling scorn and downling scorn,
    The mothers of them did whoop and call,

5. This ballad was first published in full in 1905, but is believed to be of much earlier origin. It describes an event found not in canonical Christian writings but rather in pseudo-evangelical chronicles of Christ's childhood. *Withy:* willow.

6. I.e., there was scorn everywhere ("upling," "downling").
7. The miracle of the bridge of sunbeams derives from a legend about Christ frequently found in medieval lives of the saints.

Crying out, "Mary mild, call home your child,
    For ours are drownded all."

8

Mary mild, Mary mild, called home her child,
30   And laid our Saviour across her knee,
And with a whole handful of bitter withy
    She gave him slashes three.

9

Then he says to his mother, "Oh! the withy, oh! the withy,
    The bitter withy that causes me to smart, to smart,
35   Oh! the withy, it shall be the very first tree
    That perishes at the heart."

The Knight and Shepherd's Daughter[8]

1

There was a shepherd's dochter
    Kept sheep on yonder hill;
Bye cam a knicht frae° the High College,[9]   *from*
    And he wad° hae° his will.   *would / have*

2

5   Whan he had got his wills o her,
    His will as he has taen:°   *taken*
"Wad ye be sae° gude° and kind   *so / good*
    As tell to me your name?"[1]

3

"Some ca's me Jock, some ca's me John,
10   Some disna° ken° my name,   *do not / know*
But whan I 'm into the king's court,
    Mitchcock[2] is my name."

4

"Mitchcock! hey!" the lady did say,
    And spelt it oure° again;   *over*
15 "If that 's your name in the Latin tongue,
    Earl Richard is your name!"

5

O jumpt he upon his horse,
    And said he wad go ride;

8. This Scottish ballad has several variants in which the identities of the knight and the shepherd's daughter differ but the events and outcome are similar. The version printed here, the C variant of Child Ballad No. 110, is from Kinloch's *Ancient Scottish Ballads*.
9. King's court.
1. The shepherd's daughter asks this question.
2. The knight gives the shepherd's daughter a false name (though she is not fooled).

Kilted° she her green claithing,   *tucked up*
20   And said she wad na° bide.°   *not / stay*

6

The knicht rade on, the lady ran,
   A live-lang simmer's° day,   *summer's*
Till they cam to a wan° water   *dark*
   Was calld the river Tay.[3]

7

25   "Jump on behind, ye weill-faurd° may,°   *well-favored / maid*
   Or do ye chuse to ride?"
"No, thank ye, sir," the lady said,
   "I rather chuse to wade";
And afore that he was mid-water,
30   She was at the ither side.

8

"Turn back, turn back, ye weill-faurd may,
   My heart will brak in three:"
"And sae did mine in yon bonny hill-side,
   Whan ye was [na] lat me be."

9

35   "Whare gat ye that gay° claithing   *fine*
   This day I see on thee?"
"My mither was a gude milk-nurse,
   And a gude nourice° was she;   *nurse*
She nursd the Earl of Stockford's daughter,
40   And gat aw this to me."

10

Whan she cam to the king's court,
   She rappit wi a ring;[4]
Sae ready as the king himsel
   Was to let the lady in!

11

45   "There is a knicht into your court
   This day has robbed me:"
"O has he taen your gowd,"° he says,   *gold*
   "Or has he taen your fee?"°   *wealth, possessions*

12

"He has na taen my gowd," she says,
50   "Nor yet has he my fee;
But he has taen my maiden-head,
   The flowr o° my fair bodie."   *of*

---

3. The longest river in Scotland.   4. I.e., rapped with the door knocker.

13

Then out bespak° the queen hersel,   *spoke*
 Wha sat by the king's knee:
55 There 's na a knicht in aw° our court   *all*
 Wad hae dune that to thee,
Unless it war my brither, Earl Richard,
 And forbid it it war he!⁵

14

Wad ye ken your love,
60 Amang a hunder° men?   *hundred*
"I wad," said the bonnie ladie,
 "Amang five hunder and ten."

15

The king made aw his merry men pass,
 By ane,° by twa, and three;   *one*
65 Earl Richard us'd to be the first man,
 But he was hinmost man that day.

16

He cam hauping° on ane foot,   *hopping*
 And winking with ae° ee;°   *one / eye*
But "Ha! ha!" said the bonnie ladie,
70 "That same young man are ye."

17

He 's taen° her up to a hie towr-head   *taken*
 And offerd her hunder punds in a glove:⁶
"Gin° ye be a courteous maid,   *if*
 Ye 'll choice° anither love."   *choose*

18

75 "What care I for your hunder pund?
 Na mair° than ye wad for mine;   *more*
What 's a hunder pund to me,
 To a marriage wi a king!"

19

Whan the marriage it was oure,
80 And ilk° ane took them horse,   *each*
"It never set a beggar's brat
 At nae knicht's back to be."⁷

---

5. I.e., God forbid (it)!
6. I.e., a hundred pounds tied up in a glove (which he offers in exchange for having to marry her).

7. I.e., it never suited a beggar's child to ride behind a lord.

20

The ladie met wi a beggar-wife,
    And gied her half o crown:
85   "Tell aw your neebours, whan ye gang hame,
    That Earl Richard's your gude-son."°   *son-in-law*

21

"O hold your tongue, ye beggar's brat,
    My heart will brak in three";
"And sae did mine on yon bonny hill-side,
90   Whan ye wad na let me be."

22

Whan she cam to yon nettle-dyke,°   *nettle-covered ditch*
. . . . .⁸
"An my auld° mither she was here,   *old*
    Sae weill as she wad ye pu.⁹

23

95   "She wad boil ye weill and butter ye weill,
    And sup till she war fu,¹
And lay her hed upon her dish-doup,²
    And sleep like onie° sow."   *any*

24

Whan she cam to Earl Richard's house,
100   The sheets war holland fine:³
"O haud° awa thae linen sheets,   *hold*
And bring to me the linsey clouts⁴
    I hae been best used° in."°   *accustomed / to*

25

["Awa, awa wi your siller° spoons,   *silver*
105   Haud them awa frae me;
It would set° me better to feed my flocks   *suit*
    Wi the brose-cap° on me knee: *oatmeal sack*
Sae bring to me the gude ram's horn,
    The spoons I've been used wi."]⁵

26

110   "Hold your tongue, ye beggar's brat,
    My heart will brak in three";
"And sae did mine on yon bonnie hillside,
    Whan ye wadna lat me be."

---

8. Line 92 is missing; like most folk ballads, this poem was transcribed from sung versions. Other printed versions suggest, however, that the line describes how the nettles were spread on the ground.
9. I.e., you would have to pull ("pu") the plough as well as she does.

1. I.e., and eat till she was full.
2. The bottom of her bowl.
3. A linen fabric made in Holland.
4. Woven patches of coarse wool and flax.
5. Child's brackets indicate that stanza 25 had been inserted in Kinloch's copy of *Ancient Scottish Ballads.*

27

"I wish I had drank the well-water
115   Whan first I drank the wine!
Never a shepherd's dochter
    Wad hae been a love o mine."

28

"O I wish I'd drank the well-water
    Whan first I drank the beer,
120   That ever a shepherd's dochter
    Shoud hae been my only dear!"

* * *6

29

"Ye 'll turn about, Earl Richard,
    And mak some mair° o me;   *more*
An ye mak me lady o ae puir plow,7
125   I can mak ye laird° o three."   *lord*

30

"If ye be the Earl of Stockford's dochter,
    As I 've taen some thouchts ye be,
Aft° hae I waited at your father's yett,°   *oft / gate*
    But your face I coud never see."8

ANONYMOUS ELIZABETHAN AND JACOBEAN POEMS

Love Me Little, Love Me Long1

Love me little, love me long,
    Is the burden° of my song.   *refrain*
Love that is too hot and strong
    Burneth soon to waste.
5   Still, I would not have thee cold,
Not too backward, nor too bold;
Love that lasteth till 'tis old
    Fadeth not in haste.
        Love me little, love me long,
10   *Is the burden of my song.*

---

6. Child's asterisks signal a gap in the story.
7. I.e., if you make me the lady of one poor plow (the area of land one plow will till in a year).
8. With the suggestion that she can make the knight lord of three plows, the story begins to reveal that the shepherd's daughter is high born. In some versions, however, her social status is mys-terious at the end; and in one text, the knight is revealed to be a blacksmith's son whereas the lady is a king's daughter.

1. This song was registered in 1569–70 with the Stationers' Company, which authorized all printed texts from 1557 onward. Our source is the *Extracts from the Stationers' Company* (1848).

If thou lovest me too much,
It will not prove as true as touch;[2]
Love me little, more than such,
   For I fear the end.
15 I am with little well content,
And a little from thee sent
Is enough, with true intent
   To be steadfast friend.
    Love me little, love me long,
20   *Is the burden of my song.*

Say thou lov'st me while thou live;
I to thee my love will give,
Never dreaming to deceive
   Whiles that life endures.
25 Nay, and after death, in sooth,
I to thee will keep my truth,
As now, when in my May of youth;
   This my love assures.
    Love me little, love me long,
30   *Is the burden of my song.*

Constant love is moderate ever,
And it will through life persever;
Give me that, with true endeavor
   I will it restore.
35 A suit of durance° let it be,   *durability*
For all weathers that for me,
For the land or for the sea,
   Lasting evermore.
    Love me little, love me long,
40   *Is the burden of my song.*

Winter's cold, or summer's heat,
Autumn's tempests on it beat,
It can never know defeat,
   Never can rebel.
45 Such the love that I would gain,
Such the love, I tell thee plain,
Thou must give, or woo in vain;
   So to thee, farewell!
    Love me little, love me long,
50   *Is the burden of my song.*

ca. 1570

---

2. Touchstone or basanite; gold or silver rubbed on touchstone produces a streak, the appearance of which was formerly used as a test for the purity of the metal.

Fine Knacks for Ladies[3]

Fine knacks for ladies, cheap, choice, brave and new!
Good pennyworths—but money cannot move:
I keep a fair but for the fair to view;
A beggar may be liberal of love.
5   Though all my wares be trash, the heart is true,
                    The heart is true.

Great gifts are guiles° and look for gifts again;   *deceits*
My trifles come as treasures from my mind.
It is a precious jewel to be plain;
10   Sometimes in shell the orient'st° pearls we find.   *most lustrous*
Of others take a sheaf, of me a grain!
                    Of me a grain!

Within this pack pins, points,[4] laces, and gloves,
And divers toys fitting a country fair;
15   But in my heart, where duty serves and loves,
Turtles and twins,[5] court's brood, a heavenly pair.
Happy the heart that thinks of no removes!
                    Of no removes!

                                                    1600

To His Love[6]

Come away! come, sweet love!
The golden morning breaks;
All the earth, all the air,
Of love and pleasure speaks.

5   Teach thine arms then to embrace,
And sweet rosy lips to kiss,
And mix our souls in mutual bliss.
Eyes were made for beauty's grace,
Viewing, rueing, love's long pain,
10   Procured by beauty's rude disdain.

Come away! come, sweet love!
The golden morning wastes,

---

3. This anonymous peddler's song was set for lute
accompaniment by John Dowland, a well-known
Elizabethan composer, and included in his *Second
Book of Songs or Airs* (1600).
4. Laces (such as shoelaces) with the ends tagged
or pointed for convenience in lacing.

5. Turtledoves ("turtles") and the "heavenly pair"
of twins, Castor and Pollux of the constellation
Gemini, were symbols of true love and constancy.
6. From *England's Helicon* (1600), an influential
anthology of verse.

While the sun from his sphere
His fiery arrows casts,
15 Making all the shadows fly,
Playing, staying in the grove,
To entertain the stealth of love.
Thither, sweet love, let us hie°   go
Flying, dying, in desire,
20 Wing'd with sweet hopes and heavenly fire.

Come away! come, sweet love!
Do not in vain adorn
Beauty's grace that should rise
Like to the naked morn.
25 Lilies on the river's side,
And fair Cyprian[7] flowers new-blown,
Desire no beauties but their own;
Ornament is nurse of pride.
Pleasure, measure love's delight.
30 Haste then, sweet love, our wishèd flight!

                                                                 1600

Weep You No More, Sad Fountains[8]

Weep you no more, sad fountains;
    What need you flow so fast?
Look how the snowy mountains
    Heaven's sun doth gently waste.
5   But my sun's heavenly eyes
        View not your weeping,
        That now lie sleeping
    Softly, now softly lies
        Sleeping.

10 Sleep is a reconciling,
    A rest that peace begets.
Doth not the sun rise smiling
    When fair at even° he sets?   evening
Rest you then, rest, sad eyes,
15   Melt not in weeping
        While she lies sleeping
    Softly, now softly lies
        Sleeping.

                                                                 1603

7. An allusion to Venus, Roman goddess of love and beauty; the center of her cult was the island of Cyprus.

8. From John Dowland's *Third Book of Songs or Airs* (1603).

There Is a Lady Sweet and Kind[9]

There is a lady sweet and kind,
Was never face so pleased my mind;
I did but see her passing by,
And yet I love her till I die.

5   Her gesture, motion and her smiles,
Her wit, her voice, my heart beguiles,
Beguiles my heart, I know not why,
And yet I love her till I die.

Her free behavior, winning looks,
10   Will make a lawyer burn his books.
I touched her not, alas, not I,
And yet I love her till I die.

Had I her fast betwixt mine arms,
Judge you that think such sports were harms,
15   Were't any harm? No, no, fie, fie!
For I will love her till I die.

Should I remain confinèd there,
So long as Phoebus[1] in his sphere,
I to request, she to deny,
20   Yet would I love her till I die.

Cupid[2] is wingèd and doth range;
Her country so my love doth change,
But change she earth, or change she sky,
Yet will I love her till I die.

1607

The Silver Swan[3]

The silver swan, who living had no note,
When death approached, unlocked her silent throat;
Leaning her breast against the reedy shore,
Thus sung her first and last, and sung no more:
5   "Farewell, all joys; Oh death, come close mine eyes;
More geese than swans now live, more fools than wise."

1612

---

9. From Thomas Ford's *Music of Sundry Kinds*
(1607).
1. Apollo, Greek and Roman god of the sun.
2. Roman god of erotic love.

3. From Orlando Gibbons's *First Set of Madrigals
and Motets* (1612). Gibbons, one of the last mad-
rigalists, may be implying an analogy between him-
self and the swan.

A Song Bewailing the Time of Christmas, So Much Decayed in England[4]

Christmas is my name, far have I gone, have I gone, have I gone,
have I gone without regard,
Whereas great men, by flocks they be flown, they be flown,
they be flown, they be flown to London ward,
5   Where they in pomp and pleasure do waste
that which Christmas had wont° to feast;   *been accustomed*
      Wellay day.
Houses where music was wonted° to ring,   *accustomed*
    Nothing but bats, and owls now do sing
10 Wellay day, wallay day, wallay day, where should I stay.

Christmas bread and beef is turned into stones, into stones, into
    stones,
Into stones and silken rags.
And lady money[5] it doth sleep, it doth sleep, it doth sleep,
It doth sleep in misers' bags.
15   Where many gallants once abound,
Nought but a dog and a shepherd is found,
      Wellay day.
Places where Christmas revels did keep,
Are now become habitations for sheep.
20 Wallay day, wallay day, wellay day, where should I stay.

Pan, the shepherd's god, doth deface, doth deface, doth deface,
doth deface, Lady Ceres' crown,[6]
And tilliges° doth decay, doth decay, doth decay,   *plowed land*
doth decay in every town.[7]
25   Landlords their rents so highly enhance,
That Peares the plowman[8] barefoot doth dance,
      Wellay day.

Farmers that Christmas would entertain,
hath scarsely withal them selves to maintain,
30 Wellay day, wellay day, wellay day, where should I stay.

---

4. This lament for Christmas festivities banned by Protestants after the Reformation (and for other social changes the speaker deplores) comes from a manuscript in the British Library (MS. Additional 38599); a longer version of the poem was printed around 1635.
5. Probably a reference to the money traditionally given out for charity on "Lady Days," dates in the Roman Catholic calendar devoted to celebrating events in the life of the Virgin Mary. One such celebration occurred (before the Reformation) on December 8, when the Virgin's immaculate conception was honored.
6. Ceres was the Roman goddess of grain and hence of the harvest; Pan, Greek god of shepherds and huntsmen, here symbolizes Protestant "iconolasts," who frequently "defaced" Catholic rituals and works of art, especially beheading or otherwise mutilating statues of religious figures in Catholic churches.
7. Probably a reference to the practice of "enclosure," whereby peasant farmers who were tenants of a manor lost their traditional access to "common" lands; during the sixteenth century, many wealthy landowners enclosed "tilled" land for the sake of the sheep being raised for England's expanding wool trade.
8. Peares is a traditional name for a plowman; cf. William Langland, "Piers Plowman" (p. 71).

Go to the Protestant, he'll protest, he'll protest, he'll protest,
he will protest and boldly boast,
  And to the Puritan, he is so hot, he is so hot, he is so hot,
he is so hot he will burn the roast,
35   The Catholic good deeds will not scorn,
nor will not see poor Christmas forlorn,
            Wellay day.
Since Holiness no good deeds will do,
  Protestants had best turn Papists too,
40   Wellay day, wellay day, wellay day, where should I stay.

    Pride and Luxury doth devour, doth devour, doth devour,
doth devour house keeping quite,°   *completely*
  And beggary doth beget, doth beget, doth beget,
doth beget in many a knight.
45   Madam for° sooth° in coach she must reel   *in / truth*
Although she wear her hose out at heel,
            Wellay day.
And on her back were that for her weed,
  that would both me, and many other feed,
50   Wellay day, wellay day, wellay day, where should I stay.

    Briefly for to end, here I find, here I find,
here I find such great vacation°   *emptying*
  That some great houses do seem to have, seem to have,
      seem to have,
for to have some great purgation,
55   With purging pills, such effects they have showed,
that out of doors, their owners they have spewed.[9]
            Wellay day.
And when Christmas goes by and calls,
  Nothing but solitude, and naked walls,
60   Wellay day, wellay day, wellay day, where should I stay.

    Philemel's cottages are turned into gold, into gold,
Into gold for harboring Jove.[1]
  And great mens' houses up for to hold, up for to hold,
up for to hold, make great men moan,
65   But in the city they say they do live,
Where gold by handfuls away they do give,
            Wellay day.
And therefor thither I purpose to pass,
  hoping at London to find the golden ass,
70   I'll away, I'll away, I'll away, I'll no longer stay.

ca. 1624   1635

9. Probably a reference to the widespread "disso-
lution" of ecclesiastical manors that began during
the reign of Henry VIII; the king (and his succes-
sors) raised money by dispossessing monasteries of
their lands and houses.

1. An allusion to the classical myth of Philemon,
a poor man who was visited by Jove and Mercury
in disguise. For entertaining the gods well, Phile-
mon and his wife, Baucis, were rewarded by having
their cottage transformed into a luxurious temple.

Tom o' Bedlam's Song[2]

From the hagg° and hungry goblin   *haggard*
That into rags would rend ye,
All the spirits that stand by the naked man
In the Book of Moons[3] defend ye
5   That of your five sound senses
You never be forsaken,
Nor wander from your selves with Tom
Abroad to beg your bacon.

     While I do sing "any food, any feeding,
10   *Feeding, drink or clothing,"*
     Come dame or maid, be not afraid,
     Poor Tom will injure nothing.

Of thirty bare years have I
Twice twenty been enragèd,°   *mad*
15   And of forty been three times fifteen
In durance° soundly cagèd.   *confinement, prison*
On the lordly lofts of Bedlam,
With stubble soft and dainty,
Brave bracelets strong, sweet whip's ding-dong,
20   With wholesome hunger plenty.

     And now I sing "any food, any feeding, . . .

With a thought I took for Maudlin[4]
And a cruse° of cockle° pottage,°   *pitcher / shellfish / soup*
With a thing thus tall, sky bless you all,
25   I befell into this dotage.
I slept not since the Conquest,[5]
Till then I never wakèd,
Till the roguish boy° of love where I lay   *Cupid*
Me found and stripped me naked.

30   *And now I sing "any food, any feeding, . . .*

When I short have shorn my sour face
And swigged my horny barrel,
In an oaken inn I pound my skin
As a suit of gilt apparel.
35   The moon's my constant Mistress,

---

2. This poem, like a number of other anonymous lyrics, purports to be sung by a madman, Tom, from "Bedlam," that is, the Hospital of St. Mary of Bethlehem, an asylum in London that housed the mentally ill from the fifteenth century on. The earliest known version of this poem is in a manuscript of songs and verses in the British Museum (MS. Additional 24665). Edgar in Shakespeare's *King Lear* assumes the persona of "Poor Tom," and this poem has been echoed by writers from Ben Jonson through Sir Walter Scott to Rudyard Kipling.
3. Probably an astrological book.
4. Tom's "lady" is frequently named Maudline (short for Magdalene and probably an allusion to the Christian Scripture character Mary Magdalene).
5. William of Normandy's conquest of England, in 1066.

And the lowly owl my marrow,
The flaming Drake° and the Nightcrow make   *male duck*
Me music to my sorrow.

While I do sing "any food, any feeding, . . .

40 The palsy plagues my pulses
    When I prigg° their pigs or pullen,°   *steal / chicken*
    Your culvers° take, or matchless make   *wood pigeons*
    Your Chanticleare,[6] or sullen.
    When I want provant,° with Humfry   *food*
45 I sup,[7] and when benighted,
    I repose in Paul's with waking souls,
    Yet never am affrighted.

But I do sing "any food, any feeding, . . .

    I know more than Apollo,[8]
50 For oft, when hee lies sleeping,
    I see the stars at bloody wars
    In the wounded welkin° weeping;   *sky*
    The moon embrace her shepherd,
    And the queen of Love her warrior,
55 While the first doth horn the star of morn,
    And the next the heavenly Farrier.[9]

While I do sing "any food, any feeding, . . .

    The Gipsy Snap and Pedro[1]
    Are none of Tom's comrados.
60 The punk I scorn and the cut purse sworn
    And the roaring boys bravado.
    The meek, the white, the gentle,
    Me handle, touch, and spare not,
    But those that cross Tom Rynosseros
65 Do what the panther dare not.

Although I sing "any food, any feeding, . . .

    With an host of furious fancies,
    Whereof I am commander,
    With a burning spear, and a horse of air,
70 To the wilderness I wander.
    By a knight of ghosts and shadows

6. I.e., take away your rooster's mate.
7. Refers to the legendary "Duke Humphrey's Walk," in front of St. Paul's Cathedral in London ("Paul's," line 46), where the poor congregated.
8. Greek and Roman god of poetry and the sun.
9. In Greek mythology, the Moon loved the shepherd Endymion, and Venus, the goddess of love, preferred Mars, the god of war, to her husband, Hephaestos, the god of metalworking and hence a

"heavenly Farrier," or horseshoer. The verb "horn," printed as "born" in some texts of the poem, suggests an image of the new moon "embracing" the morning star; in the second clause governed by this verb, there is a play on horn's figurative meaning as cuckold.
1. I.e., a gypsy rogue (with "Snap" probably connoting thievery) and a Spaniard.

I summoned am to tourney°   *take part in a tournament*
Ten leagues beyond the wide world's end.
Me thinks it is no journey.

75   *Yet will I sing "any food, any feeding, . . .*

Before 1615   1656

THOMAS WYATT*
1503–1542

The Long Love, That in My Thought Doth Harbor[1]

The long° love, that in my thought doth harbor,°   *enduring / lodge*
And in mine heart doth keep his residence,
Into my face presseth with bold pretense,
And therein campeth, spreading his banner.[2]
5   She that me learneth° to love and suffer,   *teaches*
And wills that my trust and lust's negligence
Be reined[3] by reason, shame and reverence,
With his hardiness° taketh displeasure.   *boldness*
Wherewithal, unto the heart's[4] forest he fleeth,
10   Leaving his enterprise with pain and cry;
And there him hideth, and not appeareth.
What may I do when my master feareth
But in the field with him to live and die?
For good is the life, ending faithfully.

                                           E. MS.

Whoso List[5] to Hunt

Whoso list to hunt, I know where is an hind,°   *female deer*
But as for me, alas, I may no more:
The vain travail hath wearied me so sore.

*Though Wyatt apparently meant to publish a collection of his poems, only a few of the poems were printed before his death (several appeared in *The Court of Venus*, a collection published between 1536 and 1540). Most of his works circulated in manuscript among aristocratic readers. After his death, however, the printer Richard Tottel published ninety-seven poems attributed to Wyatt—along with forty attributed to Henry Howard, earl of Surrey (ca. 1517–1547; see pp. 137–40) and Nicholas Grimald (1519?–1562?), respectively, and some by "Uncertain Authors"—in the book *Songs and Sonnets* (1557).

The Egerton manuscript (E. MS.) contains a number of poems in Wyatt's hand as well as his corrections of poems in other scribes' hands.

Whenever possible, we have used this manuscript's versions of Wyatt's poems. We also print poems from the Devonshire manuscript (D. MS.) and several others in which some of Wyatt's texts are preserved. Where modernization may obscure puns or affect Wyatt's meter, we give original spellings in the notes.
1. Translated from Petrarch, *Rime* 140. Cf. the translation by Henry Howard, earl of Surrey, "Love, That Doth Reign and Live within My Thought" (p. 137).
2. Raising the flag, i.e., taking up a position for battle and, figuratively, blushing.
3. Checked; with a probable pun on *reigned*.
4. With a pun on *heart* and *hart* (as deer).
5. Whoever likes.

I am of them that farthest cometh behind;
5   Yet may I by no means my wearied mind
        Draw from the deer: but as she fleeth afore,
    Fainting I follow. I leave off therefore,
        Since in a net I seek to hold the wind.
    Who list her hunt, I put him out of doubt,
10   As well as I may spend his time in vain:
        And, graven with diamonds, in letters plain
    There is written her fair neck round about:
        Noli me tangere,[6] for Caesar's I am;
    And wild for to hold, though I seem tame.

                        E. MS.

My Galley[7]

My galley charged° with forgetfulness   *loaded*
    Thorough° sharp seas in winter nights doth pass   *through*
    'Tween rock and rock; and eke° mine enemy, alas,   *also*
    That is my lord,[8] steereth with cruelness;
5   And every oar a thought in readiness,
    As though that death were light in such a case.
    An endless wind doth tear the sail apace
    Of forced sighs and trusty fearfulness.
    A rain of tears, a cloud of dark disdain,
10   Hath done the wearied cords[9] great hinderance;
    Wreathed with error and eke with ignorance.
The stars[1] be hid that led me to this pain;
    Drowned is reason that should me consort,°   *accompany*
    And I remain despairing of the port.

                        E. MS.

They Flee from Me

They flee from me that sometime did me seek
    With naked foot stalking in my chamber.
I have seen them gentle tame and meek
    That now are wild and do not remember

---

6. Touch me not (Latin). The phrase (in Italian in Petrarch) has roots both in Petrarch's sonnet *Rime* 190—Wyatt's main source—and in the Bible (see especially the Catholic Bible, the Vulgate: John 20.17 and Matthew 22.21). Renaissance commentators on Petrarch maintained that the deer in Caesar's royal forest wore collars bearing a similar inscription, to prevent anyone from hunting the animals. The allusion raises questions about Wyatt's relation to King Henry VIII ("Caesar," line 13). Wyatt was accused during his lifetime of having been the lover of Anne Boleyn, who became Henry VIII's second wife and a major cause of his break with the Roman Catholic Church.

7. It is difficult to say with certainty when Wyatt intended an *-ed* ending to be pronounced as a second syllable and when not. Hence no attempt has been made to mark syllabic endings with an accent in any of Wyatt's poems (although in this particular poem such endings may occur in lines 1, 8, 11, and 13). Wyatt's poem is based on Petrarch's *Rime* 189.

8. I.e., the god of love.

9. The worn lines of the sail, with a possible pun on the Latin for heart (*cor, cordis*).

1. I.e., the lady's eyes.

5　　That sometime they put themselves in danger
　　　To take bread at my hand; and now they range
　　　Busily seeking with a continual change.

　　　Thanked be fortune, it hath been otherwise
　　　Twenty times better;[2] but once in special
10　In thin array after a pleasant guise[3]
　　　When her loose gown from her shoulders did fall,
　　　And she me caught in her arms long and small;°　　　*slender*
　　　Therewithal sweetly did me kiss,
　　　And softly said *Dear heart,*[4] *how like you this?*

15　It was no dream: I lay broad waking.[5]
　　　But all is turned thorough° my gentleness　　　*through*
　　　Into a strange fashion of forsaking;
　　　And I have leave to go of her goodness[6]
　　　And she also to use newfangleness.
20　But since that I so kindly[7] am served,
　　　I would fain know what she hath deserved.

E. MS.

Patience, Though I Have Not

　　　Patience, though I have not
　　　　　The thing that I require,
　　　I must of force, God wot,°　　　*knows*
　　　　　Forbear my most desire;[8]
5　For no ways can I find
　　　　　To sail against the wind.

　　　Patience, do what they will
　　　　　To work me woe or spite,
　　　I shall content me still
10　　　To think both day and night,
　　　To think and hold my peace,
　　　　　Since there is no redress.

　　　Patience, withouten blame,[9]
　　　　　For I offended nought;
15　I know they know the same,
　　　　　Though they have changed their thought.
　　　Was ever thought so moved
　　　　　To hate that it hath loved?

2. I.e., better on twenty occasions or twenty times better.
3. In a thin gown made in a pleasing fashion.
4. With a pun on *heart* and *hart* (as deer); "sweetly" (line 13) is spelled "swetely" in Wyatt's original and perhaps was pronounced with three syllables.
5. I.e., wide awake.
6. Because of her goodness (ironic).

7. I.e., in the way typical of female nature, or "kind"; in a way that the narrator deserves (according to his "nature," or being repaid "in kind"); with kindness (ironic). Spelled "kyndely" in Wyatt's original and perhaps thus pronounced with three syllables. *Newfangleness:* a new fashion; novelty or inconstancy in her erotic relationships with men.
8. I.e., restrain or endure my strongest desire.
9. I.e., when one is without blame.

Patience of all my harm,[1]
20   For fortune is my foe;
Patience must be the charm
    To heal me of my woe:
Patience without offence
Is a painful patience.

E. MS.

My Lute Awake!

My lute awake! Perform the last
Labor that thou and I shall waste,
    And end that I have now begun;
For when this song is sung and past,
5   My lute be still, for I have done.

As to be heard where ear is none,
As lead to grave in marble stone,
    My song may pierce her heart as soon;[2]
Should we then sigh, or sing, or moan?
10   No, no, my lute, for I have done.

The rocks do not so cruelly
Repulse the waves continually
    As she my suit and affection.
So that I am past remedy:
15   Whereby my lute and I have done.

Proud of the spoil that thou hast got
Of simple hearts through love's shot,[3]
    By whom, unkind, thou hast them won,
Think not he hath his bow forgot,
20   Although my lute and I have done.

Vengeance shall fall on thy disdain,
That makest but game on earnest pain;[4]
    Think not alone under the sun
Unquit° to cause thy lovers plain,°   *unrequited / lamentation*
25   Although my lute and I have done.

Perchance thee lie withered and old,
The winter nights that are so cold,
    Plaining in vain unto the moon;
Thy wishes then dare not be told;
30   Care then who list,° for I have done.   *likes*

---

1. I.e., in all the harm I suffer.
2. I.e., it is as likely that sound will be heard with no ear to hear it, or soft lead will be able to engrave ("grave") hard marble, as it is that my song will move her. "Ear" is spelled "ere" in Wyatt's manuscript.

3. The arrow of Cupid (Roman god of erotic love). "Through" is spelled "thorough" in Wyatt's original, perhaps indicating a two-syllable pronunciation. The referent for "thou" is unclear.
4. Makes fun of or plays games with one in pain.

And then may chance thee to repent
The time that thou hast lost and spent
To cause thy lovers sigh and swoon;
Then shalt thou know beauty but lent,
35   And wish and want as I have done.

Now cease, my lute, this is the last
Labor that thou and I shall waste,
    And ended is that we begun;
Now is this song both sung and past:
40   My lute be still, for I have done.

E. MS.

Is It Possible

    Is it possible
    That so high debate,
So sharp, so sore, and of such rate,°   *pace; value*
Should end so soon and was begun so late?
5   Is it possible?

    Is it possible
    So cruel intent,
So hasty heat and so soon spent,
From love to hate, and thence for to relent?
10   Is it possible?

    Is it possible
    That any may find
Within one heart so diverse mind,
To change or turn as weather and wind?
15   Is it possible?

    Is it possible
    To spy it in an eye[5]
That turns as oft as chance on die?[6]
The troth° whereof can any try?   *truth, faith*
20   Is it possible?

    It is possible
    For to turn so oft,
To bring that lowest that was most aloft,
And to fall highest[7] yet to light soft?
25   It is possible.

---

5. I.e., to spy love; the eyes were often said to be where a person's true feelings could be seen.
6. I.e, as often as fortune changes in tosses of the dice. "Turns" is spelled "tornys" in Wyatt's original, perhaps indicating a two-syllable pronunciation.

7. From the highest place. The imagery here plays on the Renaissance figure of the wheel of life, the frequent turning of which causes people's fortunes to rise and fall unpredictably.

All is possible,
Whoso° list° believe;   *whoever / cares to*
Trust therefore first, and after preve:[8]
As men wed ladies by license and leave,
30   All is possible.

                                              D. MS.

Forget Not Yet

Forget not yet the tried intent
Of such a truth as I have meant,
My great travail so gladly spent
        Forget not yet.

5   Forget not yet when first began
The weary life ye know since whan,°   *when*
The suit, the service none tell[9] can.
        Forget not yet.

Forget not yet the great assays,°   *trials*
10 The cruel wrong, the scornful ways,
The painful patience in denays,°   *denials*
        Forget not yet.

Forget not yet, forget not this,
How long ago hath been and is
15 The mind that never meant amiss,
        Forget not yet.

Forget not then thine own approved,[1]
The which so long hath thee so loved,
Whose steadfast faith yet never moved,
20   Forget not this.

                                              D. MS.

Blame Not My Lute

Blame not my lute, for he must sound
Of this or that as liketh me;
For lack of wit the lute is bound
To give such tunes as pleaseth me;
5   Though my songs be somewhat strange
And speaks such words as touch thy change,[2]
        Blame not my lute.

8. I.e., learn by experience.
9. Give an account of, estimate. In courtly rheto-
ric, "service" often meant the actions of a male
lover.

1. I.e., the one of whom you approved.
2. I.e., the lute "speaks"—probably through a
change of musical key and/or rhythm—in a way
that reflects the lady's change of heart.

My lute, alas, doth not offend,
Though that perforce he must agree
To sound such tunes as I intend
To sing to them that heareth me;
Then though my songs be somewhat plain,
And toucheth some that use to fain,[3]
    Blame not my lute.

My lute and strings may not deny
But as I strike they must obey;
Break not them then so wrongfully,
But wreak° thyself some wiser way;   avenge
And though the songs which I endite°   compose
Do quit° thy change with rightful spite,   answer
    Blame not my lute.

Spite asketh spite and changing change,
And falsed° faith must needs be known,   betrayed
The fault so great, the case so strange,
Of right it must abroad be blown:
Then since that by thine own desert
My songs do tell how true thou art,
    Blame not my lute.

Blame but thy self that hast misdone
And well deserved to have blame;
Change thou thy way so evil begun
And then my lute shall sound that same;
But if till then my fingers play
By thy desart their wonted° way,   usual
    Blame not my lute.

Farewell, unknown, for though thou break
My strings in spite with great disdain
Yet have I found out for thy sake
Strings for to string my lute again;
And if perchance this foolish rhyme
Do make thee blush at any time
    Blame not my lute.

D. MS.

What Should I Say

What should I say
    Since faith is dead,
And truth away
    From you is fled?
        Should I be led

3. I.e., some who used to "feign," meaning both dissemble and desire.

With doubleness?
Nay, nay, Mistress![4]

I promised you
And you promised me,
10   To be as true
As I would be;
But since I see
Your double heart,
Farewell my part![5]

15   Though for to take
It is not my mind
But to forsake—
I am not blind—
And as I find
20   So will I trust.
Farewell, unjust!

Can ye say nay?
But you said
That I alway°   *always*
25   Should be obeyed;[6]
And thus betrayed
Or° that I wist°—   *before / knew*
Farewell, unkist!°   *unkissed*

D. MS.

Lucks, My Fair Falcon[7]

Lucks, my fair falcon, and your fellows all,
   How well pleasant it were your liberty!
Ye not forsake me that fair might ye befall.[8]
But they that sometime° liked my company: *formerly*
5   Like lice away from dead bodies they crawl.
Lo what a proof in light adversity!
But ye my birds, I swear by all your bells,[9]
Ye be my friends, and so be but few else.

Ad. Ms.

4. Title for an upper-class married woman; a courteous form.
5. Share in the relationship; spelled "perte" in Wyatt's original, suggesting a pun on the French word for loss (*perte*).
6. Some contemporary marriage services included a vow by the woman to obey the man; the point raises the possibility that the poem is addressed to the speaker's wife.
7. This poem appears in one manuscript (Additional MS. 36529) in the British Museum; it also appears in an early printed anthology (*Tottel's Miscellany*, 1557), with the title "Of Such as Had Forsaken Him." The speaker addresses a falcon whose

name evidently puns on *luck* and on the Latin word for light, *lux*. The first printed version of the poem gives the falcon's name as "Lux," whereas all the manuscripts give it as "luckes," possibly pronounced with two syllables. Scholars speculate that the poem was written shortly before Wyatt was imprisoned in 1541.
8. I.e., you do not forsake me so that fair fortune (good luck) will come to you. This line, with its compressed syntax, begins a contrast between the faithful falcon and unfaithful humans.
9. A bell was attached by a leather strap to each leg of a falcon.

Stand Whoso List[1]

Stand whoso list upon the slipper° top   *slippery*
  Of court's estates,[2] and let me here rejoice;
And use me quiet without let or stop,°   *hindrance*
  Unknown in court, that hath such brackish[3] joys:
5   In hidden place, so let my days forth pass,
  That when my years be done, withouten noise,
    I may die aged after the common trace.°   *way*
For him death gripeth right hard by the crope°   *throat*
  That is much known of other; and of himself alas,
10   Doth die unknown, dazed with dreadful[4] face.

Arundel Castle MS.

Mine Own John Poins[5]

Mine own John Poins, since ye delight to know
  The cause why that homeward I me draw,
  And flee the press of courts whereso they go,[6]
Rather than to live thrall, under the awe
5   Of lordly looks, wrapped within my cloak,
  To will and lust learning to set a law;[7]
It is not for because I scorn and mock
  The power of them, to whom fortune hath lent
  Charge over us, of right, to strike the stroke:[8]
10 But true it is that I have always meant
  Less to esteem them than the common sort,
  Of outward things that judge in their intent,
Without regard what doth inward resort.[9]
  I grant sometime that of glory the fire
15   Doth touch my heart: me° list° not to report   *I / care*
Blame by honor and honor to desire.[1]
  But how may I this honor now attain
  That cannot dye the color black a liar?[2]
My Poins, I cannot frame me tune to feign,[3]
20   To cloak the truth, for praise without desert,
  Of them that list all vice for to retain.[4]

1. This poem, a translation of Seneca's play *Thyestes*, lines 391–404, was printed in a quite different version by Tottel under the title "Of the Mean and Sure Estate." *Whoso list:* whoever likes.
2. Society was said to be divided into three groups: those who ruled, those who prayed, and those who labored.
3. Spoiled, like water that has gone bad.
4. Has a variety of possible meanings, including awful, terrified, and frightening.
5. Wyatt's friend; a member of Henry VIII's court. This verse epistle of informal satire is based on the tenth satire of the Italian poet Luigi Alamanni (1495–1556), but Wyatt Anglicizes it and adds personal details. It apparently was written during Wyatt's banishment from court in 1536.

6. In Renaissance England, the royal court frequently moved residence, sometimes through highly elaborate "progresses," or processions.
7. I.e., learning to set a law to (or keep in check) my passions. *Lust:* pleasure.
8. I.e., rightfully empowered to command and to punish us.
9. I.e., to have less esteem for them than do the common people (line 11), who base their judgment on what appears outwardly (lines 12–13).
1. I.e., I have no wish to represent faults as virtues or pleasure as honor.
2. A common proverb held that *black will take no other hue.*
3. I.e., shape my style falsely.
4. I.e., desire to keep vice in their service.

I cannot honor them that sets their part
    With Venus and Bacchus[5] all their life long;
    Nor hold my peace of them although I smart.
25 I cannot crouch nor kneel to do so great a wrong,
    To worship them, like God on earth alone,
    That are as wolves these sely° lambs among.   *innocent*
I cannot with my words complain and moan,
    And suffer naught; nor smart without complaint,
30   Nor turn the word that from my mouth is gone.
I cannot speak and look like a saint,
    Use wiles° for wit or make deceit a pleasure,   *cunning*
    And call craft° counsel, for profit still to paint;° *scheming / flatter*
I cannot wrest the law to fill the coffer
35   With innocent blood to feed myself fat,
    And do most hurt where most help I offer.
I am not he that can allow° the state   *accept*
    Of high Caesar and damn Cato to die,
    That with his death did 'scape out of the gate
40 From Caesar's hands (if Livy do not lie)[6]
    And would not live where liberty was lost:
    So did his heart the common weal apply.[7]
I am not he such eloquence to boast,
    To make the crow singing as the swan,[8]
45   Nor call the lion of coward beasts the most[9]
That cannot take a mouse as the cat can:
    And he that dieth for hunger of the gold
    Call him Alexander;[1] and say that Pan
Passeth Apollo in music manifold;[2]
50   Praise Sir Thopas for a noble tale,
    And scorn the story that the Knight told.[3]
Praise him for counsel that is drunk of ale;
    Grin when he laugheth that beareth all the sway,
    Frown when he frowneth and groan when he is pale;
55 On others' lust to hang both night and day:
    None of these points would ever frame in me;[4]
    My wit is naught—I cannot learn the way.
And much the less of things that greater be,
    That asken help of colors of device[5]
60   To join the mean° with each extremity,   *middle*
With the nearest virtue to cloak° alway the vice: *soften; cover*
    And as to purpose likewise it shall fall,
    To press° the virtue that it may not rise;[6]   *to press down*

---

5. Venus was the Roman goddess of love and beauty; Bacchus, the Roman god of wine.
6. The Roman historian Livy recounts the death of Cato the Younger, a statesman who committed suicide rather than submit to Julius Caesar's tyranny.
7. I.e., so did his heart practice the common good.
8. Swans supposedly sang beautifully just before dying.
9. Nor call a lion (a symbol of bravery) a coward.
1. Say that he is Alexander the Great, who was said to prefer glory and action to riches; i.e., he cannot say that one who is greedy for gold instead prefers glory.
2. The Greek god Pan played simple ditties on his pipe; the Greek and Roman god Apollo played divine melodies on his lyre.
3. Chaucer's tale of Sir Thopas (in *The Canterbury Tales*) is a deliberately dull parody that is cut off after a few stanzas by the Host. The Knight's tale, according to other pilgrims, is "a noble storie."
4. I.e., suit my character.
5. Artful language that "colors," or falsifies.
6. I.e., and intention will be subsumed by the deceit.

As drunkenness good fellowship to call;
65 The friendly foe with his double face
Say he is gentle and courteous therewithal;
And say that favel° hath a goodly grace   *flattery*
In eloquence; and cruelty to name
Zeal of justice and change in time and place;
70 And he that suff'reth offense without blame
Call him pitiful; and him true and plain
That raileth reckless[7] to every man's shame.
Say he is rude that cannot lie and feign;
The lecher a lover; and tyranny
75 To be the right of a prince's reign.
I cannot, I. No, no, it will not be.
This is the cause° that I could never yet   *reason*
Hang on their sleeves that weigh as thou mayst see
A chip° of chance more than a pound of wit.   *small amount*
80 This maketh me at home to hunt and hawk
And in foul weather at my book to sit.
In frost and snow then with my bow to stalk,
No man doth mark whereso I ride or go;
In lusty° leas° at liberty I walk,   *pleasant / meadows*
85 And of these news I feel nor weal° nor woe,   *happiness*
Save that a clog[8] doth hang yet at my heel:
No force° for that for it is ordered so,   *matter*
That I may leap both hedge and dike[9] full well.
I am not now in France to judge the wine,
90 With sav'ry sauce those delicates to feel;[1]
Nor yet in Spain where one must him incline
Rather than to be, outwardly to seem.
I meddle not with wits that be so fine,
Nor Flanders' cheer letteth not my sight to deem
95 Of black and white,[2] nor taketh my wit away
With beastliness, they beasts do so esteem;
Nor am I not where Christ is given in prey
For money, poison, and treason at Rome,[3]
A common practice used night and day:
100 But here I am in Kent and Christendom
Among the Muses[4] where I read and rhyme;
Where if thou list, my Poins, for to come,
Thou shalt be judge how I do spend my time.

                                                      E. MS.

---

7. Rants abusively.
8. Heavy object tied to a prisoner's foot to impede motion.
9. Ditch, used as a boundary.
1. To savor exquisite food.
2. I.e., to be able to tell the difference between black and white. *Flanders' cheer:* in the sixteenth century, the Flemings were notorious for drinking. *Letteth:* hinders.
3. In *Tottel's Miscellany,* an anthology published in 1557, during the reign of the Catholic Queen Mary, these lines read: "where truth is given prey / For money, poison and treason; of some."
4. In Greek mythology, nine sister goddesses who presided over song and poetry and the arts and sciences. Wyatt had extensive lands in Kent and could retire there when out of favor at court. He was elected to Parliament from Kent shortly before his death.

HENRY HOWARD, EARL OF SURREY
ca. 1517–1547

The Soote Season[1]

	The soote° season, that bud and bloom forth brings,	*sweet*
	With green hath clad the hill and eke° the vale;	*also*
	The nightingale with feathers new she sings;	
	The turtle° to her make° hath told her tale.	*turtledove / mate*
5	Summer is come, for every spray now springs;	
	The hart hath hung his old head on the pale;[2]	
	The buck in brake° his winter coat he flings,	*the bushes*
	The fishes float with new repairèd scale;	
	The adder all her slough away she slings,	
10	The swift swallow pursueth the flies small;	
	The busy bee her honey now she mings.°	*discharges*
	Winter is worn, that was the flowers' bale.°	*harm*
	And thus I see among these pleasant things,	
	Each care decays, and yet my sorrow springs.	

1557

Love, That Doth Reign and Live within My Thought[3]

	Love, that doth reign and live within my thought,	
	And built his seat within my captive breast,	
	Clad in the arms° wherein with me he fought,	*heraldic insignia*
	Oft in my face he doth his banner rest.	
5	But she that taught me love and suffer pain,	
	My doubtful hope and eke° my hot desire	*also*
	With shamefast° look to shadow and refrain,	*shamefaced*
	Her smiling grace converteth straight to ire.	
	And coward Love, then, to the heart apace°	*quickly*
10	Taketh his flight, where he doth lurk and plain,°	*complain*
	His purpose lost, and dare not show his face.	
	For my lord's guilt thus faultless bide° I pain,	*endure*
	Yet from my lord shall not my foot remove:[4]	
	Sweet is the death that taketh end by love.	

1557

---

1. Translated and adapted from Petrarch, *Rime* 310; first published, along with poems by Wyatt and others, in *Tottel's Miscellany* (1557), an early anthology.
2. I.e., has hung his antlers on the paling, or fence.
3. Translated from Petrarch, *Rime* 140. Compare the translation by Sir Thomas Wyatt, "The Long Love, That in My Thought Doth Harbor" (p. 126).
4. I.e., I will not leave his side.

Wyatt Resteth Here[5]

Wyatt resteth here, that quick° could never rest;   *living*
Whose heavenly gifts increasèd by disdain,[6]
And virtue sank the deeper in his breast;
Such profit he of envy could obtain.
5   A head where wisdom mysteries[7] did frame,
Whose hammers beat still in that lively brain
As on a stithy,° where some work of fame   *anvil*
Was daily wrought, to turn to Britain's gain.
A visage stern and mild, where both did grow,
10   Vice to contemn, in virtues to rejoice,
Amid great storms, whom grace assurèd so,
To live upright, and smile at fortune's choice.
A hand that taught what might be said in rhyme;
That reft° Chaucer the glory of his wit;   *bereft*
15   A mark, the which—unperfited,° for time—   *uncompleted*
Some may approach, but never none shall hit.
A tongue that served in foreign realms his king;
Whose courteous talk to virtue did enflame
Each noble heart; a worthy guide to bring
20   Our English youth, by travail, unto fame.
An eye whose judgment no affect° could blind,   *passion*
Friends to allure, and foes to reconcile;
Whose piercing look did represent a mind
With virtue fraught, reposèd, void of guile.
25   A heart where dread yet never so impressed
To hide the thought that might the truth advance;
In neither fortune lost, nor so repressed,
To swell in wealth, nor yield unto mischance.
A valiant corps,° where force and beauty met,   *body*
30   Happy, alas! too happy, but for foes,
Livèd, and ran the race that nature set;
Of manhood's shape, where she the mold did lose.
But to the heavens that simple soul is fled,
Which left with such as covet Christ to know[8]
35   Witness of faith that never shall be dead,
Sent for our health, but not receivèd so.
Thus, for our guilt, this jewel have we lost;
The earth his bones, the heavens possess his ghost.

1557

---

5. Surrey's epitaph on Thomas Wyatt (1503–   "envy").
1542; see pp. 126–36), published in 1542, soon   7. Hidden or subtle meanings.
after Wyatt's death.   8. I.e., Christians.
6. I.e., by others' disdain (as in line 4, of others'

So Cruel Prison[9]

So cruel prison how could betide,° alas,   *befall*
As proud Windsor?[1] Where I in lust° and joy   *pleasure*
With a king's son my childish° years did pass   *youthful*
In greater feast than Priam's[2] sons of Troy;
5 Where each sweet place returns a taste full sour:
The large green courts where we were wont to hove[3]
With eyes cast up unto the maidens' tower,
And easy sighs, such as folk draw in love;
The stately sales,° the ladies bright of hue,   *halls*
10 The dances short, long tales of great delight;
With words and looks that tigers could but rue,[4]
Where each of us did plead the other's right;
The palm play,° where, despoilèd° for the   *handball / disrobed*
    game,
With dazèd eyes oft we by gleams of love
15 Have missed the ball and got sight of our dame,
To bait[5] her eyes, which kept the leads above;
The graveled ground, with sleeves tied on the helm,[6]
On foaming horse, with swords and friendly hearts,
With cheer, as though the one should overwhelm;
20 Where we have fought, and chasèd oft with darts,
With silver drops the meads° yet spread for ruth,° *meadows / pity*
In active games of nimbleness and strength,
Where we did strain, trailed by swarms of youth,
Our tender limbs that yet shot up in length;
25 The secret groves which oft we made resound
Of pleasant plaint and of our ladies' praise,
Recording soft what grace each one had found,
What hope of speed, what dread of long delays;
The wild forest, the clothèd holt° with green,   *small wood*
30 With reins avaled,° and swift ybreathèd°   *slackened / exercised*
    horse,
With cry of hounds and merry blasts between,
Where we did chase the fearful hart aforce;°   *strenuously*
The void walls eke° that harbored us each night,   *also*
Wherewith, alas, revive within my breast
35 The sweet accord; such sleeps as yet delight,
The pleasant dreams, the quiet bed of rest;
The secret thoughts imparted with such trust,
The wanton talk, the divers change of play,
The friendship sworn, each promise kept so just,

---

9. As a boy and young man, Surrey had enjoyed the life at Windsor Palace as the close friend of Henry Fitzroy, an illegitimate son of Henry VIII. In 1537, a year after the death of his friend, Surrey was imprisoned temporarily at Windsor for striking another courtier.
1. I.e., how could proud Windsor (Castle) have become such a cruel prison?
2. Priam, king of Troy in Homer's *Iliad*.
3. Accustomed to linger.

4. The tiger conventionally symbolized unfeeling savagery.
5. To feed or to attract. The "leads" from which the lady watches may be either a leaded window or a flat, leaded roof.
6. A knight would customarily tie a favor received from a lady to his sleeve or helmet and wear it into a joust or a battle. *Graveled ground*: tiltyard, i.e., space strewn with gravel for jousting.

₄₀ Wherewith we passed the winter nights away.
And with this thought the blood forsakes my face,
The tears berain° my cheeks of deadly hue,   *wet*
The which as soon as sobbing sighs, alas,
Upsuppèd° have, thus I my plaint renew: *absorbed*
₄₅ O place of bliss, renewer of my woes,
Give me accompt[7]—where is my noble fere?°   *companion*
Whom in thy walls thou didst each night enclose,
To other lief,° but unto me most dear!   *beloved*
Echo, alas, that doth my sorrow rue,
₅₀ Returns thereto a hollow sound of plaint.
Thus I, alone, where all my freedom grew,
In prison pine with bondage and restraint;
And with remembrance of the greater grief
To banish the less, I find my chief relief.

1557

ANNE ASKEW
1521–1546

The Ballad Which Anne Askew Made and Sang When She Was in Newgate[1]

Like as the armèd knight
Appointed to the field,
With this world will I fight
And faith shall be my shield.[2]
₅ Faith is that weapon strong
Which will not fail at need;
My foes therefore among
Therewith will I proceed.
  As it is had in strength
₁₀ And force of Christ's way,
It will prevail at length
Though all the devils say nay.
  Faith in the father's old
Obtainèd rightwiseness°   *righteousness*
₁₅ Which make me very bold
To fear no world's distress.

---

7. I.e., tell me.
1. Askew was arrested and examined for heresy in June 1545. She was released, but was arrested again in June 1546, subjected to torture, and burned at the stake the next month. This ballad was included in the Protestant Bishop John Bale's two accounts of her examination and death,
printed in 1546 and 1547, respectively. *Newgate:* a London prison.
2. Ephesians 6.13–17 exhorts the Christian to put on "the whole armor of God," including "the shield of faith, with which ye shall be able to quench all the fiery darts of the wicked."

I now rejoice in heart
And hope bid me do so,
For Christ will take my part
20   And ease me of my woe.
     Thou sayst lord, who so kneck,[3]
To them wilt thou attend;
Undo therefore the lock
And thy strong power send.
25   More enemies now I have
Than hairs upon my head
Let them not me deprave,°   *villify*
But fight thou in my stead.
     On thee my care I cast
30   For all their cruel spite
I set not by their haste,[4]
For thou art my delight.
     I am not she that list°   *chooses*
My anchor to let fall
35   For every drizzling mist
My ship substantial.
     Not oft use I to write
In prose nor yet in rhyme,
Yet will I show one sight
40   That I saw in my time.
     I saw a royal throne
Where Justice should have sit,
But in her stead was one
Of modie° cruel wit.   *wrathful*
45   Absorbed° was rightwiseness   *swallowed up*
As of the raging flood;
Satan in his excess
Sucked up the guiltless blood.
     Then thought I, Jesus lord,
50   When thou shalt judge us all,
Hard is it to record
On these men what will fall.
     Yet lord I thee desire
For that° they do to me,   *what*
55   Let them not taste the hire°   *reward*
Of their iniquity.[5]

1546

---

3. Knocks. Matthew 7.7: "Ask, and it shall be given you; seek, and ye shall find; knock, and it shall be opened unto you."
4. I have no regard for their rashness.

5. Christ on the cross also asks mercy for his persecutors: "Father, forgive them; for they know not what they do" (Luke 23.34).

QUEEN ELIZABETH I
1533–1603

When I Was Fair and Young[1]

When I was fair and young, then favor graced me.
Of many was I sought their mistress° for to be,   *sweetheart*
But I did scorn them all and answered them therefore:
Go, go, go, seek some other where, importune me no more.

5   How many weeping eyes I made to pine in woe,
How many sighing hearts I have not skill to show,
But I the prouder grew and still this spake therefore:
Go, go, go, seek some other where, importune me no more.

Then spake fair Venus' son,[2] that proud victorious boy,
10   Saying: You dainty dame, for that you be so coy,
I will so pluck your plumes[3] as you shall say no more:
Go, go, go, seek some other where, importune me no more.

As soon as he had said, such change[4] grew in my breast
That neither night nor day I could take any rest.
15   Wherefore I did repent that I had said before:
Go, go, go, seek some other where, importune me no more.

ca. 1585?   1964

[The Doubt of Future Foes Exiles My Present Joy][5]

The doubt of future foes exiles my present joy,
And wit me warns to shun such snares as threaten mine annoy;[6]
For falsehood now doth flow, and subjects' faith doth ebb,
Which should not be if reason ruled or wisdom weaved the web.
5   But clouds of joys untried do cloak aspiring minds,
Which turn to rain of late repent by changed course of winds.

1. This poem is found with many variations in five manuscripts. We follow Leicester Bradner, *The Poems of Queen Elizabeth,* in using the British Museum's Harleian 7392 as the basis for our text. The Bodleian Library's Rawlinson manuscript, written between 1590 and 1600, also contains a version of the poem and states, furthermore, that it was written when Elizabeth "was suposed to be in love with mounsyre," that is, her French suitor, the duke of Alençon. Some modern scholars doubt that Elizabeth wrote the poem, but all accept it as an important cultural document about her.
2. Cupid, Roman god of erotic love, was the son of Venus, goddess of love and beauty.
3. I.e., remove your pride; a reference to the brightly colored plumes of the peacock, a traditional symbol of pride.
4. One manuscript, in the Folger Library, substitutes "care" for "change."
5. This poem is written in poulter's measure—

alternating lines of six and seven beats (see "Versification," p. 2047)—a popular form at this time (see Philip Sidney, "What Length of Verse?" p. 210). It appears to answer a sonnet written by Elizabeth's Catholic cousin Mary Stuart, queen of Scotland, in which Mary, who had fled to England from imprisonment in Scotland in 1568, asks to see Elizabeth. Until her execution in 1587, Mary was a constant threat, the impetus of many plots to depose Elizabeth and seat herself on the English throne. "The daughter of debate" in line 11 and the "foreign banished wight" in line 13 apparently refer to Mary.

    Versions of this poem appear in six manuscripts and two early printed texts, including George Puttenham's *Art of English Poesy* (1589). Our text follows that of Bodleian MS. Rawlinson, thought to have been compiled around 1570.
    Doubt: danger or thing to be dreaded.
6. I.e., cause me discomfort or trouble.

The top of hope supposed the root upreared shall be,[7]
And fruitless all their grafted guile,[8] as shortly ye shall see.
The dazzled eyes with pride, which great ambition blinds,
10 Shall be unsealed by worthy wights[9] whose foresight falsehood finds.
The daughter of debate that discord aye doth sow
Shall reap no gain where former rule still peace hath taught to know.
No foreign banished wight[1] shall anchor in this port;
Our realm brooks° not seditious sects, let them elsewhere resort.   *allows*
15 My rusty sword through rest shall first his edge employ
To poll their tops[2] that seek such change or gape° for future joy.   *long*

ca. 1570   1589

[Ah Silly Pug, Wert Thou So Sore Afraid][3]

Ah silly pug, wert thou so sore afraid,
Mourn not (my Wat[4]) nor be thou so dismayed,
It passeth fickle fortune's power and skill,
To force my heart to think thee any ill.
5   No fortune base thou sayest shall alter thee,
And may so blind a witch[5] so conquer me?
No no my pug, though fortune were not blind,
Assure thy self she could not rule my mind.
Fortune I know sometimes doth conquer kings
10   And rules & reigns on earth & earthly things,
But never think fortune can bear the sway,
If virtue watch & will not her obey.
Ne° chose I thee by fickle fortune's rede,°   *neither / advice*
Ne° she shall force me alter° with such speed   *nor / to change*
15   But if to try this mistress jest with thee,
. . . .[6]
Pull up thy heart, suppress thy brackish° tears,   *salty*
Torment thee not, but put away thy fears;
Dead to all joys & living unto woe,
Slain quite by her that ne're gave wiseman blow
20   Revive again & live without all dread,
The less afraid the better thou shalt speed.°   *succeed, prosper*

ca. 1578–88   1992

---

7. Variants on this line include: "The top of hope
suppressed the root upreared [i.e., exalted] shall
be" and "The top of hope supposed the root of ruth
[sorrow] will be."
8. The image of grafting, or inserting a shoot into
the root stock of another tree or plant, suggests
that conspirators have attempted to plant their
own seditious thoughts in the minds of others.
9. People. *Unsealed*: unsewn or unopened, as the
eyes of a hawk in the sport of hawking.
1. I.e., no person exiled to a foreign land.
2. I.e., cut off their heads.
3. This poem was written in answer to a poem by

Sir Walter Ralegh, probably "Fortune Hath Taken
Thee Away, My Love" (p. 158). *Silly*: deserving of
pity or compassion; also foolish, lacking in judg-
ment, helpless, defenseless, insignificant, or lowly.
Pug: a term of endearment.
4. A diminutive of Walter.
5. Fortune was often personified as a fickle
woman and sometimes depicted as blind or blind-
folded.
6. A line of the poem may be missing at this point;
alternatively, the queen may have written lines 13–
15 as a triplet of near-rhymes.

GEORGE GASCOIGNE*
ca. 1534–1577

And If I Did, What Then?

"And if I did, what then?
Are you aggrieved therefore?
The sea hath fish for every man,
And what would you have more?"

5   Thus did my mistress once
Amaze my mind with doubt,
And popped a question for the nonce¹
To beat my brains about.

Whereto I thus replied:
10   "Each fisherman can wish
That all the sea at every tide
Were his alone to fish.

And so did I, in vain;
But since it may not be,
15   Let such fish there as find the gain,
And leave the loss for me.

And with such luck and loss
I will content myself,
Till tides of turning time may toss
20   Such fishers on the shelf.

And when they stick on sands,
That every man may see,
Then will I laugh and clap my hands,
As they do now at me."

For That He Looked Not upon Her

You must not wonder, though you think it strange,
To see me hold my louring° head so low,   sullen
And that mine eyes take no delight to range
About the gleams which on your face do grow.
5   The mouse which once hath broken out of trap
Is seldom 'ticèd° with the trustless bait,   enticed
But lies aloof for fear of more mishap,
And feedeth still in doubt° of deep deceit.   suspicion
The scorchèd fly, which once hath 'scaped the flame,
10   Will hardly come to play again with fire,

---

*Gascoigne's poems were first published in *A Hundred Sundry Flowers* (1573), the source of our texts.
1. Expressly for the purpose of.

Whereby I learn that grievous is the game
Which follows fancy dazzled by desire:
So that I wink² or else hold down my head,
Because your blazing eyes my bale° have bred.   *anguish*

Gascoigne's Lullaby

Sing lullaby, as women do,
Wherewith they bring their babes to rest,
And lullaby can I sing too,
As womanly as can the best.
5   With lullaby they still the child,
And if I be not much beguiled,
Full many wanton babes have I,
Which must be stilled with lullaby.

First, lullaby, my youthful years,
10   It is now time to go to bed,
For crooked age and hoary hairs
Have won the haven within my head.
With lullaby then, youth, be still,
With lullaby content they will,
15   Since courage quails° and comes behind,   *shrinks*
Go sleep, and so beguile thy mind.

Next, lullaby, my gazing eyes,
Which wonted were³ to glance apace.°   *directly*
For every glass may now suffice
20   To show the furrows in my face.
With lullaby then wink⁴ awhile,
With lullaby your looks beguile.
Let no fair face nor beauty bright
Entice you eft° with vain delight.   *after*

25   And lullaby, my wanton will,
Let reason's rule now rein thy thought,
Since all too late I find by skill°   *experience*
How dear I have thy fancies bought.
With lullaby now take thine ease,
30   With lullaby thy doubts appease.
For trust to this, if thou be still,
My body shall obey thy will.

Eke° lullaby, my loving boy,   *also*
My little Robin,⁵ take thy rest.
35   Since age is cold and nothing coy,°   *lascivious*
Keep close thy coin,⁶ for so is best.

---

2. I.e., close my eyes; also, blink.
3. Which were accustomed.
4. I.e., shut your eyes.

5. I.e., a nickname for his penis.
6. I.e., don't expend your semen; with a play on
"coin" as money and as a sound in the poet's name.

With lullaby be thou content,
With lullaby thy lusts relent.
Let others pay which° hath mo° pence;   who / more
40   Thou art too poor for such expense.

Thus, lullaby, my youth, mine eyes,
My will, my ware, and all that was.
I can no mo delays devise,
But welcome pain, let pleasure pass.
45   With lullaby now take your leave,
With lullaby your dreams deceive,
And when you rise with waking eye,
Remember Gascoigne's lullaby.

1573

ISABELLA WHITNEY
fl. 1567–1573

From A Sweet Nosegay

A Communication Which the Author Had to London, Before She Made Her Will[1]

The time is come, I must depart
    from thee, ah famous city;
I never yet to rue my smart,°   pain
    did find that thou had'st pity.
5   Wherefore small cause there is, that I
    should grieve from thee to go;
But many women foolishly,
    like me, and other moe,°   more
Do such a fixèd fancy set,
10   on those which least deserve,
That long it is ere wit we get
    away from them to swerve.
But time with pity oft will tell
    to those that will her try,
15   Whether it best be more to mell,°   mix with
    or utterly defy.
And now hath time me put in mind
    of thy great cruelness,

---

1. This poem and the poetic testament that follows it conclude Whitney's *A Sweet Nosegay* (1573), a collection of poems that begins with 110 verse couplets of advice explicitly borrowed from Hugh Plat's *Flowers of Philosophy* (1572). While Plat's classicizing verses were aimed at an audience of university men and lawyers, Whitney's book seems designed for less privileged readers of both sexes. Her "will," occasioned not by impending death but rather by the poverty that compels her to leave London, plays on the fantasy that all of the city's riches are the author's to bequeath as she likes.

That never once a help would find,
20   to ease me in distress.
Thou never yet would'st credit give
     to board me for a year;
Nor with apparel me relieve,
     except thou payèd were.
25   No, no, thou never did'st me good,
     nor ever wilt, I know.
Yet am I in no angry mood,
     but will, or ere[2] I go,
In perfect love and charity,
30   my testament here write,
And leave to thee such treasury,
     as I in it recite.
Now stand aside and give me leave
     to write my latest will;
35   And see that none you do deceive
     of that I leave them till.[3]

From The Manner of Her Will, & What She Left to London, and to All Those in It, at Her Departing

I whole in body, and in mind,
     but very weak in purse,
Do make, and write my testament
     for fear it will be worse.
5   And first I wholly do commend
     my soul and body eke,°   *also*
To God the Father and the Son,
     so long as I can speak.
And after speech, my soul to him,
10   and body to the grave,
Till time that all shall rise again,
     their Judgement for to have.
And then I hope they both shall meet,
     to dwell for aye° in joy;   *ever*
15   Whereas° I trust to see my friends   *when*
     released from all annoy.
Thus have you heard touching my soul,
     and body what I mean:
I trust you all will witness bear,
20   I have a steadfast brain.
O God, now let me dispose such things,
     as I shall leave behind,
That those which shall receive the same,
     may know my willing mind.

2. In early modern English, "or" was often used with "ere" to mean "before."

3. I.e., of what I leave to them.

25 I first of all to London leave,
      because I there was bred,
    Brave buildings rare, of churches store,
      and Paul's to the head.[4]
    Between the same, fair treats there be,
30   and people goodly store;
    Because their keeping craveth° cost,   requires
      I yet will leave him° more.   them
    First for their food, I butchers leave,
      that every day shall kill;
35 By Thames° you shall have brewers' store,   river Thames
      and bakers at your will.
    And such as orders do observe,
      and eat fish thrice a week,[5]
    I leave two streets, full fraught therewith,[6]
40   they need not far to seek.
    Watling Street, and Canwick Street,
      I full of woolen° leave;
    And linen store in Friday Street,
      if they me not deceive.
45 And those which are of calling such,
      that costlier they require,
    I mercers° leave, with silk so rich,   textile merchants
      as any would desire.[7]
    In Cheap of them, they store shall find,
50   and likewise in that street,
    I goldsmiths leave, with jewels such,[8]
      as are for ladies meet.°   suitable

                    * * *

    Now when the folk are fed and clad
90   with such as I have named,
    For dainty mouths, and stomachs weak
      some junckets° must be framed.   sweet cakes
    Wherefore I potecaries leave,
      with banquets in their shop;[9]
95 Physicians also for the sick,
      Diseases for to stop.
    Some roysters° still must bide in thee,   revellers
      and such as cut it out;[1]

4. The greatest of the "store" (supply) of London's sixteenth-century churches was St. Paul's Cathedral.
5. Evidently playing on religious and secular meanings of "order," i.e., the clergy (those "in orders") and also anyone who obeyed the Act of 1563, which sought to stimulate the fishing trade by decreeing that fish was to be eaten three days a week rather than the two days stipulated in an Act of 1548.
6. Possibly Old Fish Street, London's original fish market, and New Fish Street, in a different part of the city. There were, however, other streets in which fish was sold.

7. Possibly an ironic allusion to the Sumptuary Laws that prevented persons below certain social ranks (or "callings," a Protestant term for vocations) from wearing luxurious fabrics.
8. I.e., she bequeathes to goldsmiths their own street, Goldsmith's Row, which was on the south side of Cheapside Market ("Cheap"); there, those who "require costlier" things may find many (a "store") of them.
9. Apothecaries carried not only drugs but also spices; hence one could supply "banquets" in their shops.
1. Show off.

That with the guiltless quarrel will,
100   to let their blood about.
For them I cunning surgeons² leave,
    some plasters to apply,
That ruffians may not still be hanged,
    nor quiet persons die.

*   *   *

To all the bookbinders by Paul's,
    because I like their art,
195   They every week shall money have,
    when they from books depart.
Among them all, my printer must
    have somewhat to his share;
I will my friends these books to buy
200   of him, with other ware.
For maidens poor, I widowers rich
    do leave, that oft shall dote:
And by that means shall marry them,
    to set the girls afloat.
205   And wealthy widows will I leave
    to help young gentlemen;
Which when you have, in any case,
    be courteous to them then:
And see their plate° and jewels eke°   *silverware / also*
210   may not be marred with rust;
Nor let their bags too long be full,
    for fear that they do burst.

*   *   *

225   And Bedlam³ must not be forgot,
    for that was oft my walk:
I people there too many leave,
    that out of tune do talk.

*   *   *

235   At th' Inns of Court, I lawyers leave
    to take their case in hand.
And also leave I at each Inn
    of Court, or Chancery,⁴
Of gentlemen, a youthful roote,°   *rout, throng*
240   full of activity,
For whom I store of books have left,
    at each bookbinder's stall:
And part of all that London hath,
    to furnish them withal.

2. Surgeons generally practiced "manual" arts of healing and operating in the early modern era and hence were often regarded as distinct from (and inferior to) physicians (see line 95).
3. The Hospital of St. Mary of Bethlehem, for the mentally ill; cf. "Tom o' Bedlam's Song" (p. 124).
4. The court of the lord chancellor of England, in which a number of young men lived and trained as clerks; the Inns of Court housed and trained students in the Common Law.

245 And when they are with study cloyed,°   *overfed*
        to recreate their mind,
Of tennis courts, of dancing schools,
        and fence° they store shall find.   *fencing*
And every Sunday at the least,
250   I leave to make them sport,
In divers places players,° that   *actors*
        of wonders shall report.
Now, London, have I (for thy sake)
        within thee, and without,[5]
255 As comes into my memory,
        dispersèd 'round about
Such needful things as they should have,
        here left now unto thee;
When I am gone, with conscience,
260   let them dispersèd be.
And though I nothing namèd have,
        to bury me withal,
Consider that above the ground,
        annoyance be I shall.
265 And let me have a shrouding sheet
        to cover me from shame,
And in oblivion bury me,
        and never more me name.
Ringings nor other ceremonies
270   use you not for cost,
Nor at my burial, make no feast,
        your money were but lost.

                    *   *   *

This xx of October, I,
        in ANNO° DOMINI,°   *year / of our Lord*
A thousand, v.° hundred seventy-three,   *five*
315   as almanacs descry,°   *show*
Did write this will with mine own hand,
        and it to London gave;
In witness of the standers-by,
        whose names, if you will have,
320 paper, pen and standish° were,   *writing stand*
        at that same present by,°   *nearby*
With Time, who promised to reveal
        so fast as she could buy
The same, lest of my nearer kin
325   for any thing should vary;[6]
So finally I make an end
        no longer can I tarry.

                                                            1573

---

5. A number of the places and institutions described, including the theaters, were outside the city proper, in suburbs called the "liberties."

6. I.e., lest anything should change for my close relatives, Time promised to reveal my bequests as fast as she could buy them.

CHIDIOCK TICHBORNE
d. 1586

[My Prime of Youth Is but a Frost of Cares][1]

My prime of youth is but a frost of cares,
My feast of joy is but a dish of pain,
My crop of corn is but a field of tares,°   *weeds*
And all my good is but vain hope of gain;
5   The day is past, and yet I saw no sun,
And now I live, and now my life is done.

My tale was heard and yet it was not told,
My fruit is fallen and yet my leaves are green,
My youth is spent and yet I am not old,
10   I saw the world and yet I was not seen;
My thread is cut and yet it is not spun,[2]
And now I live, and now my life is done.

I sought my death and found it in my womb,
I looked for life and saw it was a shade,
15   I trod the earth and knew it was my tomb,
And now I die, and now I was but made;
My glass° is full, and now my glass is run,   *hourglass*
And now I live, and now my life is done.

1586

SIR WALTER RALEGH
ca. 1552–1618

A Vision upon the Fairy Queen[1]

Methought I saw the grave where Laura[2] lay,
Within that temple where the vestal flame[3]
Was wont° to burn; and, passing by that way,   *accustomed*
To see that buried dust of living fame,
5   Whose tomb fair Love, and fairer Virtue kept:
All suddenly I saw the Fairy Queen;

1. This poem, first printed as "Tychborne's Lamentation," was preserved in more than thirty manuscripts written soon after Tichborne's execution on a charge of conspiring with other Catholics against Queen Elizabeth's life. Our text is from the Tanner MS. (in Oxford's Bodleian Library); the first owner of this manuscript noted that Tichborne had written the poem "with his own hande . . . not three days before his execution."
2. An allusion to the Fates, three goddesses in classical mythology; they spun the thread that determined the length of a person's life, cutting it when he or she was destined to die.

1. This poem appeared in both the 1590 and the 1596 editions of Edmund Spenser's epic poem *The Faerie Queene* (see p. 165).
2. The woman to whom the Italian poet Petrarch (1304–1374) addressed his sonnet sequence; with a pun on "laurel," a symbol of poetic achievement.
3. The sacred fire, guarded by virgin priestesses, in the temple of Vesta, Roman goddess of the hearth; thus an allusion to Laura's chastity and purity.

At whose approach the soul of Petrarch wept,
And, from thenceforth, those Graces[4] were not seen:
For they this queen attended; in whose stead
10   Oblivion laid him down on Laura's hearse:°   tomb
Hereat the hardest stones were seen to bleed,
And groans of buried ghosts the heavens did pierce:
Where Homer's spright[5] did tremble all for grief,
And cursed the access of that celestial thief!

1590

The Nymph's Reply to the Shepherd[6]

If all the world and love were young,
And truth in every shepherd's tongue,
These pretty pleasures might me move
To live with thee and be thy love.

5   Time drives the flocks from field to fold
When rivers rage and rocks grow cold,
And Philomel[7] becometh dumb;
The rest complains of cares to come.

The flowers do fade, and wanton fields[8]
10   To wayward winter reckoning yields;
A honey tongue, a heart of gall,°   bitterness
Is fancy's spring, but sorrow's fall.

Thy gowns, thy shoes, thy beds of roses,
Thy cap, thy kirtle,[9] and thy posies
15   Soon break, soon wither, soon forgotten—
In folly ripe, in reason rotten.

Thy belt of straw and ivy buds,
Thy coral clasps and amber studs,°   buttons
All these in me no means can move
20   To come to thee and be thy love.

But could youth last and love still breed,
Had joys no date[1] nor age no need,
Then these delights my mind might move
To live with thee and be thy love.

1600

4. I.e., Love and Virtue.
5. Ghost of the ancient Greek poet credited with composing the epic poems the *Iliad* and the *Odyssey.*
6. Written in reply to Christopher Marlowe's "The Passionate Shepherd to His Love" (p. 256).
7. In Greek mythology, Philomela was raped by her brother-in-law, Tereus, who then tore out her tongue so that she could not speak. She wove the story in a tapestry and sent it to her sister, who rescued her. Later changed into a nightingale while in flight from Tereus, she sings a mournful song in the springtime.
8. I.e., carelessly cultivated fields; also, fields with luxuriant summer growth.
9. A long dress, often worn under an outer garment.
1. I.e., terminal date.

The Passionate Man's Pilgrimage

Give me my scallop-shell[2] of quiet,
My staff of faith to walk upon,
My scrip[3] of joy, immortal diet,
My bottle of salvation,
5   My gown of glory, hope's true gage,°   pledge
And thus I'll take my pilgrimage.

Blood must be my body's balmer,°   embalmer
No other balm[4] will there be given,
Whilst my soul like a white palmer[5]
10   Travels to the land of heaven,
Over the silver mountains,
Where spring the nectar fountains;
And there I'll kiss
The bowl of bliss,
15   And drink my eternal fill
On every milken hill.
My soul will be a-dry° before,   dried out, thirsty
But after it will ne'er thirst more;[6]
And by the happy blissful way
20   More peaceful pilgrims I shall see
That have shook off their gowns of clay[7]
And go appareled fresh like me.
I'll bring them first
To slake° their thirst,   quench
25   And then to taste those nectar suckets,°   confections
At the clear wells
Where sweetness dwells,
Drawn up by saints in crystal buckets.

And when our bottles and all we
30   Are filled with immortality,
Then the holy paths we'll travel,
Strewed with rubies thick as gravel,
Ceilings of diamonds, sapphire floors,
High walls of coral, and pearl bowers,°   chambers
35   From thence to heaven's bribeless hall
Where no corrupted voices brawl,
No conscience molten into gold,
Nor forged accusers bought and sold,
No cause deferred, nor vain-spent journey,

---

2. A scallop shell or something resembling it was worn as the sign of a pilgrim.
3. Pilgrim's knapsack or bag.
4. Aromatic preparation for embalming the dead.
5. Person wearing a palm leaf as a sign that he or she had made a pilgrimage to the Holy Land.

6. Alludes to John 4.14: "But whosoever drinketh of the water that I shall give him shall never thirst. . . ." In line 16, "milken hill" alludes to the Promised Land as a land flowing in milk and honey (Joshua 5.6).
7. Earth, i.e., earthly bodies.

40 For there Christ is the king's attorney,
    Who pleads for all, without degrees,°   respect to rank
    And he hath angels,[8] but no fees.
    When the grand twelve million jury
    Of our sins and sinful fury,
45 'Gainst our souls black verdicts give,
    Christ pleads his death, and then we live
    Be thou my speaker, taintless pleader,
    Unblotted lawyer, true proceeder;
    Thou movest salvation even for alms,°   charitable deeds
50 Not with a bribed lawyer's palms.
    And this is my eternal plea
    To him that made heaven, earth, and sea,
    Seeing my flesh must die so soon,
    And want° a head to dine next noon,   need, lack
55 Just at the stroke when my veins start and spread,
    Set on my soul an everlasting head.
    Then am I ready, like a palmer fit,[9]
    To tread those blest paths which before I writ.

                                                            1604

The Lie

    Go, soul, the body's guest,
    Upon a thankless errand;
    Fear not to touch the best;
    The truth shall be thy warrant.°   guarantee, proof
5   Go, since I needs must die,
    And give the world the lie.[1]

    Say to the court, it glows
    And shines like rotten wood;
    Say to the church, it shows
10 What's good, and doth no good.
    If church and court reply,
    Then give them both the lie.

    Tell potentates,° they live   rulers
    Acting by others' action;
15 Not loved unless they give,
    Not strong but by a faction.
    If potentates reply,
    Give potentates the lie.

8. A punning reference to the gold coin of that name, ten shillings in value.
9. Outfitted (refers back to the first stanza); Ralegh is imagining his death by beheading, which occurred in 1618. When he wrote this poem, he was in prison, charged with treason.
1. To "give the lie" means to contradict, or to prove the falsity of something.

Tell men of high condition,
20   That manage the estate,[2]
Their purpose is ambition,
Their practice only hate.
And if they once reply,
Then give them all the lie.

25   Tell them that brave it most,[3]
They beg for more by spending,
Who, in their greatest cost,
Seek nothing but commending.
And if they make reply,
30   Then give them all the lie.

Tell zeal it wants° devotion;   *lacks*
Tell love it is but lust;
Tell time it is but motion;
Tell flesh it is but dust.
35   And wish them not reply,
For thou must give the lie.

Tell age it daily wasteth;
Tell honor how it alters;
Tell beauty how she blasteth;°   *withers*
40   Tell favor how it falters.
And as they shall reply,
Give every one the lie.

Tell wit how much it wrangles
In tickle° points of niceness;   *delicate, unreliable*
45   Tell wisdom she entangles
Herself in overwiseness.
And when they do reply,
Straight give them both the lie.

Tell physic° of her boldness;   *medicine*
50   Tell skill it is pretension;
Tell charity of coldness;
Tell law it is contention.
And as they do reply,
So give them still the lie.

55   Tell fortune of her blindness;
Tell nature of decay;
Tell friendship of unkindness;
Tell justice of delay.
And if they will reply,
60   Then give them all the lie.

2. Condition of human beings with respect to worldly prosperity; also, an implied analogy between England and a nobleman's estate or land.

3. I.e., show off the most; also, to dress extravagantly.

Tell arts they have no soundness,
But vary by esteeming;
Tell schools they want profoundness,
And stand too much on seeming.
65 If arts and schools reply,
Give arts and schools the lie.

Tell faith it's fled the city;
Tell how the country erreth;
Tell° manhood shakes off pity;   *say how*
70 Tell virtue least preferreth.⁴
And if they do reply,
Spare not to give the lie.

So when thou hast, as I
Commanded thee, done blabbing°—   *revealing secrets*
75 Although to give the lie
Deserves no less than stabbing—
Stab at thee he that will,
No stab the soul can kill.

1608

Nature, That Washed Her Hands in Milk

Nature, that washed her hands in milk,
And had forgot to dry them,
Instead of earth took snow and silk,
At love's request to try them,
5   If she a mistress could compose
To please love's fancy out of those.

Her eyes he would should be of light,
A violet breath, and lips of jelly;
Her hair not black, nor overbright,
10 And of the softest down her belly;
As for her inside he'd have it
Only of wantonness and wit.

At love's entreaty such a one
Nature made, but with her beauty
15 She hath framed a heart of stone;
So as love, by ill destiny,
Must die for her whom nature gave him,
Because her darling would not save him.

---

4. I.e., tell virtue that it succeeds least (less than vice does).

But time (which nature doth despise,
20 And rudely gives her love the lie,
Makes hope a fool, and sorrow wise)
His hands do neither wash nor dry;
But being made of steel and rust,
Turns snow and silk and milk to dust.

25 The light, the belly, lips, and breath,
He dims, discolors, and destroys;
With those he feeds but fills not death,
Which sometimes° were the food of joys.   *formerly*
Yea, time doth dull each lively wit,
30 And dries all wantonness with it.

Oh, cruel time! which takes in trust
Our youth, our joys, and all we have,
And pays us but with age and dust;
Who in the dark and silent grave
35 When we have wandered all our ways
Shuts up the story of our days.[5]

ca. 1610

If Cynthia Be a Queen, a Princess, and Supreme[6]

If Cynthia be a queen, a princess, and supreme,
Keep these among the rest,[7] or say it was a dream,
For those that like, expound, and those that loathe express
Meanings according as their minds are moved more or less;
5 For writing what thou art, or showing what thou were,
Adds to the one disdain, to the other but despair,
    Thy mind of neither needs, in both seeing it exceeds.

1589?   1870

5. Another version of this stanza, traditionally supposed to have been written by Ralegh on the night before his execution, was published in 1628. In it, the first three words are changed to "Even such is time," and the following couplet is added at the end: "And from which earth, and grave, and dust / The Lord shall raise me up, I trust." The poem as a whole existed only in manuscript until 1902.
6. This enigmatic poem probably was written at a time when Ralegh had fallen out of the queen's favor. It appears in a manuscript before a fragment of the longer poem "The Ocean to Cynthia." The "thou" of the poem may be the queen, Ralegh, or

a third party. *Cynthia:* also known as Diana, the virgin goddess of the moon, chastity, the hunt, and childbirth. The figure of Cynthia was often used for Queen Elizabeth I and was one she approved of. By referring to himself as the "Ocean," Ralegh suggests that the queen rules him as the moon rules the tides.
7. If Ralegh is addressing himself, "keep" may mean "don't send to her"; if the poet addresses the queen, he is telling her to keep his verses with the rest of the many poems of courtly love and praise she has received from him and other court poets.

[Fortune Hath Taken Thee Away, My Love][8]

Fortune hath taken thee away, my love,
My life's soul and my soul's heaven above;
Fortune hath taken thee away, my princess;
My only light and my true fancy's mistress.

5   Fortune hath taken all away from me,
Fortune hath taken all by taking thee.
Dead to all joy, I only live to woe,
So fortune now becomes my mortal foe.

In vain you eyes, you eyes do waste your tears,
10   In vain you sighs do smoke forth my despairs,
In vain you search the earth and heaven above,
In vain you search, for fortune rules in love.

Thus now I leave my love in fortune's hands,
Thus now I leave my love in fortune's bands,
15   And only love the sorrows due to me;
Sorrow henceforth it shall my princess be.

I joy in this, that fortune conquers kings;
Fortune that rules on earth and earthly things
Hath taken my love in spite of Cupid's[9] might;
20   So blind a dame[1] did never Cupid right.

With wisdom's eyes had but blind Cupid seen,
Then had my love my love for ever been;
But love farewell; though fortune conquer thee,
No fortune base shall ever alter me.

Before 1589   1992

8. This poem appears to have been written to Queen Elizabeth I, who replied to it with her poem "Ah Silly Pug, Wert Thou So Sore Afraid" (p. 143). Both poems are included in a manuscript of the 1620s in the Wiltshire record office, and both were written before 1589; George Puttenham quotes from both poems in his Art of English Poesy, pub-lished in that year.
9. Cupid, the Roman god of erotic love, is often depicted as a blind and winged boy.
1. Fortune was often personified as a fickle woman and sometimes depicted as blind or blind-folded. "Fortune My Foe" was a popular tune.

EDMUND SPENSER*
1552–1599

FROM THE SHEPHEARDES CALENDER[1]

Aprill

*Because Spenser adopted many archaisms to lend an antique appearance to his poetry, the English poet Ben Jonson (1572–1673; see pp. 323–45) said that Spenser "writ no language." For example, he imitated the archaic form of the participle common in Chaucer in which *y* represents a reduced form of the Old English prefix *ge*. Spenser was innovative as well: he coined many new words and played—often fancifully—with the native and foreign etymologies of English words. He thus participated in a project dear to the hearts of many educated Elizabethan writers—"enriching" the vernacular with borrowings from classical and modern languages and dialects to create a "kingdom of our own language," as Spenser called it in a letter to his friend the writer Gabriel Harvey (1550–1630).

Because Spenser's verbal wit depends in part on showing words' multiple meanings and various "roots," historical and imaginary, we have not modernized Spenser's texts except in minor ways. We regularize *i*'s, *j*'s, *u*'s, and *v*'s according to modern conventions, replace dipthongs with separate characters, and occasionally repunctuate lines when they seem particularly difficult for modern readers. We also print in roman type words italicized in the editions printed during Spenser's lifetime. (In general, we follow the first editions of his texts except in the case of *The Faerie Queene*, where we rely on the 1596 edition rather than the one of 1590.) Finally, to aid the reader in pronouncing and scanning Spenser's poetry, which often plays on correspondences and differences between the way words sound and the ways in which they appear on the page, we add some metrical accents.

1. Spenser's first independently published work, a series of twelve interlinked poems that draws on several literary genres including the classical eclogue, or short pastoral poem, the calendar-almanac, the romance, the beast fable, the satire, and the Petrarchan lyric (from the fourteenth-century Italian poet Petrarch). Spenser presents himself following a career path famously modeled by the ancient Roman poet Virgil: the young poet prepares for epic endeavor by writing pastoral poems. Each "aeglogue" (Spenser's deliberately old-fashioned English rendering) is named after a month and contains several parts. First comes a woodcut depicting the month's zodiacal sign and the poem's dramatic scenario. Then comes a brief prose "Argument," a synopsis of the poem's action. Following that are the verse text of the eclogue and then one or more verbal emblems, or "mottos," usually one for each of the poem's speakers. Finally, there are lengthy glosses on parts of the poem and on the emblems.

The glosses, and perhaps the "Arguments," are conspicuously attributed to someone designated only by the initials "E. K." This figure first appears as the author of the *Calender*'s dedicatory epistle to Gabriel Harvey (see preceding note) and has been identified both as Harvey and as Spenser, who would be adopting a scholarly, even pedantic persona to promote his reputation as an important poet. E. K.'s glosses, which include explications of difficult or archaic words as well as learned, and sometimes critical, discussions of Spenser's poetic texts, are usually published in full with the eclogues. Here, we incorporate those of E. K.'s glosses that seem especially useful to the modern reader; they too retain original spellings.

Aegloga Quarta[2]

ARGUMENT

This Aeglogue is purposely intended to the honor and prayse of our most gra-
cious sovereigne, Queene Elizabeth. The speakers herein be Hobbinoll and
Thenott, two shepheardes; the which Hobbinoll being before mentioned,
greatly to have loved Colin, is here set forth more largely, complayning him of
that boyes great misadventure in Love, whereby his mynd was alienate and with
drawen not onely from him, who moste loved him, but also from all former
delightes and studies, aswell in pleasaunt pyping, as conning[3] ryming and sing-
ing, and other his laudable exercises. Whereby he taketh occasion, for proofe
of his more excellencie and skill in poetrie, to recorde[4] a songe, which the sayd
Colin sometime made in honor of her Majestie, whom abruptely he termeth
Elysa.[5]

THENOT	HOBBINOLL

Tell me good Hobbinoll, what garres thee greete?[6]
What? hath some Wolfe thy tender Lambes ytorne?
Or is thy Bagpype broke, that soundes so sweete?
Or art thou of thy loved lasse forlorne?°   *forsaken*

5   Or bene thine eyes attempred to the yeare,[7]
Quenching the gasping furrowes thirst with rayne?
Like April shoure, so stremes the trickling teares
Adowne thy cheeke, to quenche thy thristye° payne.   *thirsty*

HOBBINOLL

Nor thys, nor that, so muche doeth make me mourne,
10   But for° the ladde, whome long I lovd so deare,   *that*
Nowe loves a lasse, that all his love doth scorne:
He plongd in payne, his tressed° locks dooth teare.   *curled*

Shepheards delights he dooth them all forsweare,
Hys pleasaunt Pipe, whych made us meriment,
15   He wylfully hath broke, and doth forbeare
His wonted songs, wherein he all outwent.[8]

2. I.e., Fourth Eclogue; "Aprill" thus alludes to
Virgil's Fourth Eclogue, which joyously predicts
the return of a "virgin" goddess and associates the
mythical Golden Age ruled by the goddess Astraea
with the era of Virgil's patron, Caesar Augustus.
Drawing not only on Virgil's poem but also on
medieval Christian texts that read it as foretelling
Christ's birth through the "vessel" of the Virgin
Mary, Spenser fashions his eclogue as a complex
compliment to England's Queen Elizabeth I
(1533–1604; see pp. 142–43).
    The woodcut for "Aprill" shows the shepherd
Colin Clout—Spenser's autobiographical persona
—piping a song in honor of Elizabeth ("Elysa," the
shepherd's queen). She is shown with her ladies of
the court; the shepherds Thenot and Hobbinol are
in the background, and the astrological sign for
April, Taurus the bull, is at the top.
3. I.e., learning.

4. Remember.
5. I.e., he called Elizabeth "Elysa" because it's
shorter. For Spenser's learned contemporaries, the
name would also have recalled "Elissa," the ancient
Carthaginian queen whom Virgil called "Dido" and
depicted falling fatally in love with the Trojan hero
Aeneas. In many non-Virgilian versions of this
queen's story, Dido is named "Elissa" and remains
a chaste widow; in that guise, she was often hon-
orifically linked to England's queen Elizabeth.
6. "Causeth thee [to] weepe and complain"
[E. K.].
7. "Agreeable to the season of the yeare, that is
Aprill, which moneth is most bent to shoures and
seasonable rayne: to quench . . . the drought"
[E. K.].
8. His usual songs, which surpassed those of all
others.

THENOT

What is he for a Ladde,[9] you so lament?
Ys love such pinching payne to them, that prove?°   *experience it*
And hath he skill to make[1] so excellent,
20   Yet hath so little skill to brydle love?

HOBBINOLL

Colin thou kenst,° the Southerne shepheardes boye:[2]   *knowest*
Him Love hath wounded with a deadly darte.
Whilome on him was all my care and joye,
Forcing° with gyfts to winne his wanton heart.   *striving*

25   But now from me hys madding° mynd is starte,°   *foolish / broken away*
And woes° the Widdowes daughter of the glenne:[3]   *woos*
So nowe fayre Rosalind hath bredde° hys smart,°   *caused / hurt*
So now his frend is chaunged for a frenne.°   *stranger*

THENOT

But if hys ditties bene so trimly dight,°   *adorned*
30   I pray thee Hobbinoll, recorde° some one: *sing*
The whiles our flockes doe graze about in sight,
And we close shrowded in thys shade alone.

HOBBINOL

Contented I: then will I singe his laye°   *song*
Of fayre Elisa, Queene of shepheardes all:[4]
35   Which once he made, as by a spring he laye,
And tuned it unto the Waters fall.

Ye dayntye Nymphs, that in this blessed Brooke
     doe bathe your brest,
For sake your watry bowres, and hether looke,
40   at my request:
And eke you Virgins, that on Parnasse dwell,
Whence floweth Helicon the learned well,[5]
     Helpe me to blaze[6]
     Her worthy praise,
45   Which in her sexe doth all excell.

---

9. "What maner of Ladde is he?" [E.K.].
1. "To rime and versifye" [E. K.]. The English word *poet* comes from the Greek word *poíein*, to make.
2. "Seemeth hereby that Colin perteyneth to some Southern noble man" [E. K.]. Spenser may be referring to the earl of Leicester, a courtier with whom Queen Elizabeth was romantically linked; more likely, the reference is to Bishop John Young, for whom Spenser served as secretary while composing the *Calender*.
3. "He calleth Rosalind the Widowes daughter of the glenne, that is, of a country hamlet or borough [the word may also mean "a wooded mountain valley"], which I thinke is rather sayde to concele the

person, then simply spoken. For it is well knowen . . . that shee is a Gentle woman of no meane house" [E. K.].
4. "In all this songe is not to be respected, what the worthinesse of her Majestie deserveth, nor what to the highnes of a Prince is agreeable, but what is moste comely for the meanesse of a shepheards witte, or to conceive, or to utter" [E. K.]
5. "The nine Muses . . . whose abode the Poets faine to be on Parnassus, a hill in Greece" [E. K.]. In Greek mythology, the Muses were nine sister goddesses who presided over song, poetry, and the arts and sciences.
6. A blazon was a poem cataloging and praising a lady's various physical features.

Of fayre Elisa be your silver song,
    that blessed wight:°   *person*
The flowre of Virgins, may shee florish long,
    In princely plight.°   *condition*
50 For shee is Syrinx daughter without spotte,
Which Pan the shepheards God of her begot:[7]
      So sprong her grace
      Of heavenly race,
No mortall blemishe may her blotte.

55 See, where she sits upon the grassie greene,
      (O seemely° sight)   *pleasing*
Yclad in Scarlot like a mayden Queene,
    And Ermines white.
Upon her head a Cremosin° coronet,   *crimson*
60 With Damaske roses and Daffadillies set:
      Bayleaves betweene,
      And Primroses greene
Embellish[8] the sweete Violet.

Tell me, have ye seene her angelick face,
65   Like Phoebe fayre?[9]
Her heavenly haveour,° her princely grace   *bearing*
    can you well compare?
The Redde rose medled with the White yfere,[1]
In either cheeke depeincten° lively chere.   *depict*
70   Her modest eye,
      Her Majestie,
Where have you seene the like, but there?

I sawe Phoebus thrust out his golden hedde,
    upon her to gaze:
75 But when he sawe, how broade her beames did spredde,[2]
    it did him amaze.
He blusht to see another Sunne belowe,
Ne durst againe his fyrye° face out showe: *fiery*
      Let him, if he dare,
80   His brightnesse compare
With hers, to have the overthrowe.[3]

Shewe thy selfe Cynthia[4] with thy silver rayes,
    and be not abasht:

---

7. In Greek mythology, "Syrinx is the name of a Nymphe of Arcadie, whom when Pan being in love pursued. . . . By Pan is here meant the most famous and victorious King, her highnesse Father, late of worthy memorye K. Henry the eyght" [E. K.]. "Without spotte" qualifies "Syrinx," not "daughter," thus covertly repudiating the scandals surrounding Anne Boleyn (1507?–1536), second wife of King Henry VIII (1491–1547) and mother of Elizabeth.
8. "Beautifye and set out" [E. K.], i.e., by contrast of colors.
9. In Greek mythology, "the Moone, whom the Poets faine to be sister unto Phoebus, that is the Sunne" [E. K.].
1. "Together" [E. K.]. *Medled:* mingled. Henry and Elizabeth were descended from the houses of Lancaster and York (symbolized, respectively, by the red rose and the white rose), whose conflicting claims to the throne caused the Wars of the Roses (1453–97).
2. The lady outshining the sun is a Petrarchan motif.
3. I.e., have the victory.
4. "The Moone" [E. K.]. A common epithet for Queen Elizabeth.

When shee the beames of her beauty displayes,
85   O how art thou dasht?
But I will not match her with Latonaes seede,
Such follic great sorow to Niobe did breede.[5]
        Now she is a stone,
        And makes dayly mone,
90   Warning all other to take heede.

Pan may be proud, that ever he begot
        such a Bellibone,[6]
And Syrinx rejoyse, that ever was her lot
        to beare such an one.
95   Soone as my younglings cryen for the dam,
To her will I offer a milkwhite Lamb:
        Shee is my goddesse plaine,°   *absolute*
        And I her shepherds swayne,°   *servant*
Albee forswonck and forswatt[7] I am.

100   I see Calliope° speede her to the place,   *Muse of epic poetry*
        where my Goddesse shines:
And after her the other Muses trace,°   *step*
        with their Violines.
Bene they not Bay braunches,[8] which they doe beare,
105   All for Elisa in her hand to weare?
        So sweetely they play,
        And sing all the way,
That it a heaven is to heare.

Lo how finely the graces[9] can it foote°   *dance*
110   to the Instrument.°   *shepherd's pipe*
They dauncen deffly,° and singen soote,°   *nimbly / sweetly*
        in their meriment.
Wants not a fourth grace, to make the daunce even?
Let that rowme° to my Lady be yeven.°   *place / given*
115   She shalbe a grace,
        To fyll the fourth place,
And reigne with the rest in heaven.

And whither rennes° this bevie° of Ladies bright,   *runs / company*
        raunged in a rowe?
120   They bene all Ladyes of the lake behight,[1]
        that unto her goe.
Chloris,[2] that is the chiefest Nymph of al,
Of Olive braunches beares a Coronall:°   *crown*

5. Niobe boasted that her seven sons and seven daughters made her superior to Latona, a goddess, whose two children, Apollo and Diana, then slew Niobe's entire progeny, after which her sorrow transformed her to stone. Cf. Ovid, *Metamorphoses* 6.148–312.
6. *Belle bonne:* "homely spoken for a fayre mayde or Bonilasse" [E. K.].
7. "Overlaboured and sunneburnt" [E. K.].
8. "Be the signe of honor and victory . . . and eke [also] of famous Poetes" [E. K.]; i.e., the garland or crown of laurel, given as a prize in ancient Greece.
9. "Be three sisters, the daughters of Jupiter, whose names are Aglaia, Thalia, Euphrosyne . . . whom the Poetes feyned to be Goddesses of al bountie and comelines" [E. K.].
1. Called. E. K. records the ancient view that every spring and fountain had a goddess, or water nymph, as its sovereign.
2. According to E. K., the nymph of flowers and green herbs; her name signifies greenness.

Olives bene for peace,
125   When wars doe surcease:
Such for a Princesse bene principall.[3]

Ye shepheards daughters, that dwell on the greene,
        hye° you there apace:°   *come / quickly*
Let none come there, but that Virgins bene,
130   to adorne her grace.
And when you come, whereas° shee is in place,   *where*
See, that your rudenesse doe not you disgrace:
        Binde your fillets° faste,   *hair ribbons*
        And gird in your waste,
135 For more finesse, with a tawdrie lace.[4]

Bring hether the Pincke and purple Cullambine,
        With Gelliflowres:[5]
Bring Coronations, and Sops in wine,
        worne of Paramoures.°   *lovers*
140 Strowe me the ground with Daffadowndillies,
And Cowslips, and Kingcups, and loved Lillies:
        The pretie Pawnce,
        And the Chevisaunce;
Shall match with the fayre flowre Delice.

145 Now ryse up Elisa,[6] decked as thou art,
        in royall aray:
And now ye daintie Damsells may depart
        echeone her way.
I feare, I have troubled your troupes to longe:
150 Let dame Eliza thanke you for her song.
        And if you come hether,
        When Damsines° I gether,   *damsons, plums*
I will part them all you among.[7]

THENOT

And was thilk° same song of Colins owne making?   *this*
155 Ah foolish boy, that is with love yblent:°   *blinded*
Great pittie is, he be in such taking,°   *plight*
For naught caren, that bene so lewdly bent.[8]

HOBBINOL

Sicker° I hold him, for a great fon,°   *surely / fool*
That loves the thing, he cannot purchase.
160 But let us homeward: for night draweth on,
And twincling starres the daylight hence chase.

---

3. Of prime importance. Elizabeth was celebrated in the 1570s for the continuous peace her reign had brought.
4. A band of lace or silk, sold during the fair of St. Audrey.
5. The following lines list flowers common in pastoral poetry: "Coronations" are carnations; "Sops in wine," clove pinks; "Daffadowndillies," daffodils; "Pawnce," pansies; "Chevisaunce," maybe a species of wallflower; "flowre Delice," fleur de lis, a kind of iris.
6. "Is the conclusion. For having so decked her prayses and comparisons, he returneth all the thanck of hys laboure to the excellencie of her Majestie" [E. K.].
7. Among you all.
8. I.e., for they that are so foolishly inclined are heedless of everything.

Thenots Embleme.

O quam te memorem virgo?

Hobbinols Embleme.

O dea certe.[9]

1579

FROM THE FAERIE QUEENE

The First Booke

*Contayning
The Legende of the
Knight of the Red Crosse,
or
Of Holinesse*[1]

I

Lo I the man, whose Muse[2] whilome° did maske,   *formerly*
As time her taught, in lowly Shepheards weeds,[3]
Am now enforst a far unfitter taske,
For trumpets sterne to chaunge mine Oaten reeds,[4]
5 And sing of Knights and Ladies gentle° deeds;   *noble*
Whose prayses having slept in silence long,
Me, all too meane, the sacred Muse areeds[5]
To blazon[6] broad emongst her learned throng:
Fierce warres and faithfull loves shall moralize my song.

---

9. These emblems are the words Aeneas speaks to his mother, Venus, disguised as a huntress: "What name shall I know you by, maiden? Surely a goddess" (*Aeneid* 1.327–28).
1. In a letter to the English poet Sir Walter Ralegh (ca. 1552–1618; see pp. 151–58) published with the first edition, Spenser declares that his principal intention in writing the poem is "to fashion a gentleman or noble person in virtuous and gentle discipline." Thus he sets forth a plan to write twelve books, each one having a hero distinguished for one of the private virtues; twelve books on the public virtues will follow. The six books that Spenser completed (the first three published in 1590, the remaining three published in 1596) present the virtues of Holiness, Temperance, Chastity, Friendship, Justice, and Courtesy. In addition, two cantos on Mutability (the principle of constant change in nature) were published in 1609 after Spenser's death, although no known authority exists for their division and numbering, or for the running title, "The Seventh Booke."

The title of the poem contains a dual reference to its character, Gloriana, the Fairy Queen, who bids the poem's heroes to set out on particular adventures, and to Queen Elizabeth I (1533–1603; see pp. 142–43), England's ruler from 1558 until 1603, or for almost all of Spenser's life; as an "Allegory, or darke conceit" (again, a claim that Spenser makes in the letter to Ralegh), the poem mirrors

Elizabeth not only in the figure of Gloriana but also in several other characters. In addition to various modes of allegory, the poem draws on many Renaissance genres, some of the most important being the courtesy book, the romance, and the epic.
2. One of nine Greek sister goddesses believed to be sources of inspiration for the arts.
3. Garments; i.e., the poet who before wrote humble pastoral poetry. Lines 1–4 imitate verses prefixed to Renaissance editions of the ancient Roman poet Virgil's epic poem the *Aeneid* and signal Spenser's imitation of Virgil, who began his poetic career with pastoral poetry and moved on to the epic, a move that Spenser copied (with the 1579 publication of *The Shepheardes Calender,* followed by the 1590 publication of *The Faerie Queene*). Spenser's organization of each book into twelve cantos also imitates the twelve books of Virgil's *Aeneid.*
4. Or pipes, a symbol of pastoral poetry. *Trumpets:* a symbol of epic poetry.
5. Commands and instructs. *Sacred Muse:* perhaps Clio, the Muse of history, often said to be the eldest of the nine Muses; or perhaps Calliope, the Muse of epic poetry; the "holy Virgin chiefe of nine" (line 10) also seems to refer to one of these two Muses.
6. To proclaim (from *blaze,* to announce by blowing a trumpet).

2

10   Helpe then, O holy Virgin chiefe of nine,
      Thy weaker° Novice to performe thy will,   *too weak*
      Lay forth out of thine everlasting scryne°   *coffer or shrine*
      The antique rolles, which there lye hidden still,
      Of Faerie knights and fairest Tanaquill,[7]
15   Whom that most noble Briton Prince° so long
      Sought through the world, and suffered so much ill,
      That I must rue his undeservèd wrong:
  O helpe thou my weake wit, and sharpen my dull tong.

3

  And thou most dreaded impe[9] of highest Jove,
20   Faire Venus sonne, that with thy cruell dart
      At that good knight so cunningly didst rove,°   *shoot*
      That glorious fire it kindled in his hart,°   *heart*
      Lay now thy deadly Heben° bow apart,   *ebony*
      And with thy mother milde come to mine ayde:
25   Come both, and with you bring triumphant Mart,°   *Mars*
      In loves and gentle jollities arrayd,
  After his murdrous spoiles and bloudy rage allayd.

4

  And with them eke,° O Goddesse heavenly bright,   *also*
      Mirrour of grace and Majestie divine,
30   Great Lady of the greatest Isle, whose light
      Like Phoebus lampe[1] throughout the world doth shine,
      Shed thy faire beames into my feeble eyne,
      And raise my thoughts too humble and too vile,
      To thinke of that true glorious type of thine,
35   The argument° of mine afflicted stile:[2]   *subject*
  The which to heare, vouchsafe, O dearest dred[3] a-while.

Canto 1

The Patron° of true Holinesse,   *sponsor or pattern*
Foule Errour doth defeate:
Hypocrisie him to entrappe,
Doth to his home entreate.

I

  A Gentle Knight was pricking° on the plaine,   *riding briskly*
  Ycladd in mightie armes and silver shielde,
  Wherein old dints of deepe wounds did remaine,

7. The wife of Tarquin, the first Etruscan king of Rome; noted for her chastity; i.e., a reference to Gloriana.
8. I.e., Arthur, first named in canto 9.
9. Offspring, i.e., Cupid, Roman god of love, whose arrows ("cruell dart," line 21) caused their victims to fall in love; he was the son of Venus, goddess of love and beauty. Mars, god of war and lover of Venus, was often said to be Cupid's father,
but Spenser stresses the line of descent from Jove, Venus's father and ruler of the gods.
1. The sun; Phoebus Apollo was the Roman god of the sun; Spenser is comparing Apollo to Queen Elizabeth, the "Goddesse" of line 28.
2. Humble pen; also, "stile" may refer to the poem itself.
3. Object of awe and fear. *Vouchsafe:* bestow (i.e., confer your ear upon my poem).

The cruell markes of many a bloudy fielde;
5   Yet armes till that time did he never wield:
His angry steede did chide his foming bitt,
As much disdayning to the curbe to yield:
Full jolly[4] knight he seemd, and faire did sitt,
As one for knightly giusts° and fierce encounters fitt.°   *jousts / suited*

2

10 But on his brest a bloudie Crosse he bore,
The deare remembrance of his dying Lord,
For whose sweete sake that glorious badge he wore,
And dead as living ever him ador'd:
Upon his shield the like was also scor'd,
15   For soveraine hope, which in his helpe he had:
Right faithfull true[5] he was in deede and word,
But of his cheere° did seeme too solemne sad;°   *face / grave*
Yet nothing did he dread, but ever was ydrad.°   *dreaded*

3

Upon a great adventure he was bond,°   *going; bound by a vow*
20   That greatest Gloriana to him gave,
That greatest Glorious Queene of Faerie lond,
To winne him worship,° and her grace to have,   *honor*
Which of all earthly things he most did crave;
And ever as he rode, his hart° did earne°   *heart / yearn*
25   To prove his puissance° in battell brave   *strength*
Upon his foe, and his new force to learne;
Upon his foe, a Dragon horrible and stearne.

4

A lovely Ladie rode him faire beside,
Upon a lowly Asse more white then° snow,   *than*
30   Yet she much whiter, but the same did hide
Under a vele, that wimpled° was full low,   *lying in folds*
And over all a blacke stole° she did throw,   *shawl*
As one that inly° mourned: so was she sad,   *inwardly*
And heavie sat upon her palfrey slow:
35   Seemèd in heart some hidden care she had,
And by her in a line a milke white lambe she lad.°   *led*

5

So pure an innocent, as that same lambe,
She was in life and every vertuous° lore,°   *moral / doctrine*
And by descent from Royall lynage came
40   Of ancient Kings and Queenes, that had of yore
Their scepters stretcht from East to Westerne shore,
And all the world in their subjection held;
Till that infernall feend with foule uprore°   *revolt*

4. The range of meanings includes gallant, hand-
some, amorous, brave, cheerful.
5. Echoes Revelation 19.11: "And I saw heaven
opened; and behold a white horse; and he that sat
upon him was called Faithful and True. . . ."

Forwasted° all their land, and them expeld: *laid waste*
45 Whom to avenge, she had this Knight from far compeld.°   *summoned*

6

Behind her farre away a Dwarfe did lag,
    That lasie seemd in being ever last,
    Or wearied with bearing of her bag
    Of needments at his backe. Thus as they past,
50   The day with cloudes was suddeine overcast,
    And angry Jove an hideous storme of raine
    Did poure into his Lemans[6] lap so fast,
    That every wight° to shrowd° it did constrain,   *creature / take cover*
And this faire couple eke° to shroud themselves were   *also*
    fain.°   *obliged*

7

55 Enforst to seeke some covert nigh at hand,
    A shadie grove not far away they spide,
    That promist ayde the tempest to withstand:
    Whose loftie trees yclad with sommers pride,
    Did spred so broad, that heavens light did hide,
60   Not perceable° with power of any starre: *penetrable*
    And all within were pathes and alleies wide,
    With footing worne, and leading inward farre:
Faire harbour that them seemes; so in they entred arre.

8

And foorth they passe, with pleasure forward led,
65   Joying to heare the birdes sweete harmony,
    Which therein shrouded from the tempest dred,°   *fearful*
    Seemd in their song to scorne the cruell sky.
    Much can° they prayse the trees so straight and hy,   *did*
    The sayling Pine,[7] the Cedar proud and tall,
70   The vine-prop Elme, the Poplar never dry,
    The builder Oake, sole king of forrests all,
The Aspine good for staves, the Cypresse funerall.

9

The Laurell, meed° of mightie Conquerours   *reward*
    And Poets sage, the Firre that weepeth still,
75   The Willow worne of forlorne Paramours,
    The Eugh obedient to the benders will,
    The Birch for shaftes, the Sallow for the mill,

6. His lover, i.e., the earth.
7. Spenser's catalog of trees imitates similar catalogs in Chaucer's *Parliament of Fowls,* Virgil's *Aeneid,* and Ovid's *Metamorphoses.* Ships or masts were made of "Sayling" pine; the "Poplar" grew by water; the "Oake" was used in building; the "Cypresse" was used to decorate graves. Garlands made from the "Laurell" were a sign of military or poetic achievement; the "Firre" continually exudes resin; the "Eugh" (yew) was traditionally used for bows; the "Sallow" (willow) was associated with stagnant water like that found at a millpond; the "Mirrhe" (myrrh), used as incense because of its sweet smell, was one of the gifts presented by the wise men to the infant Christ; the "Beech" was used to make the axle of the war chariot, according to Homer's *Iliad;* the "Platane" is perhaps listed as a classical contrast (as Socrates and his friends sat by a plane tree, in Plato's *Phaedrus* 230b) to the olive tree, with its Christian associations; the "Holme" (holly) was suitable for carving.

The Mirrhe sweete bleeding in the bitter wound,
The warlike Beech, the Ash for nothing ill,
80   The fruitful Olive, and the Platane round,
The carver Holme, the Maple seeldom inward sound.

10

Led with delight, they thus beguile° the way,   *wile away; charm*
Untill the blustring storme is overblowne;
When weening° to returne, whence they did stray,   *intending*
85   They cannot finde that path, which first was showne,
But wander too and fro in wayes unknowne,
Furthest from end then, when they neerest weene.[8]
That makes them doubt, their wits be not their owne:
So many pathes, so many turnings seene,
90   That which of them to take, in diverse° doubt they been.   *distracting*

11

At last resolving forward still to fare,
Till that some end they finde or in or out,
That path they take, that beaten seemd most bare,
And like to lead the labyrinth about;°   *out of*
95   Which when by tract° they hunted had throughout,   *track*
At length it brought them to a hollow cave,
Amid the thickest woods. The Champion stout°   *brave*
Eftsoones° dismounted from his courser brave,   *soon after*
And to the Dwarfe a while his needlesse spere[9] he gave.

12

100   Be well aware, quoth then that Ladie milde,
Least suddaine mischiefe° ye too rash provoke: *misfortune*
The danger hid, the place unknowne and wilde,
Breedes dreadfull doubts: Oft fire is without smoke,
And perill without show: therefore your stroke
105   Sir knight with-hold, till further triall made.
Ah Ladie (said he) shame were to revoke°   *draw back*
The forward footing for an hidden shade:
Vertue gives her selfe light, through darkenesse for to wade.

13

Yea but (quoth she) the perill of this place
110   I better wot° then° you, though now too late   *know / than*
To wish you backe returne with foule disgrace,
Yet wisedome warnes, whilest foot is in the gate,
To stay the steppe, ere forcèd to retrate.°   *retreat*
This is the wandring wood, this Errours den,
115   A monster vile, whom God and man does hate:
Therefore I read° beware. Fly fly (quoth then   *advise*
The fearefull Dwarfe:) this is no place for living men.

8. I.e., think to be nearest to it.
9. "Needlesse" because the spear is generally used only on horseback.

14

But full of fire and greedy hardiment,°   *boldness*
   The youthfull knight could not for ought° be staide,   *anything*
120 But forth unto the darksome hole he went,
   And lookèd in: his glistring° armor made   *shining*
   A litle glooming light, much like a shade,
   By which he saw the ugly monster plaine,
   Halfe like a serpent horribly displaide,
125   But th' other halfe did womans shape retaine,
Most lothsom, filthie, foule, and full of vile disdaine.°   *loathsomeness*

15

And as she lay upon the durtie ground,
   Her huge long taile her den all overspred,
   Yet was in knots and many boughtes° upwound,   *coils*
130 Pointed with mortall sting. Of her there bred
   A thousand yong ones, which she dayly fed,
   Sucking upon her poisonous dugs, eachone
   Of sundry shapes, yet all ill favorèd:
   Soone as that uncouth° light upon them shone,   *unfamiliar*
135 Into her mouth they crept, and suddain all were gone.

16

Their dam upstart, out of her den effraide,°   *alarmed*
   And rushèd forth, hurling her hideous taile
   About her cursèd head, whose folds displaid°   *extended*
   Were stretcht now forth at length without entraile.°   *winding*
140 She lookt about, and seeing one in mayle
   Armèd to point,[1] sought backe to turne againe;
   For light she hated as the deadly bale,°   *injury*
   Ay° wont° in desert darknesse to remaine,   *ever / accustomed*
Where plaine none might her see, nor she see any plaine.

17

145 Which when the valiant Elfe[2] perceiv'd, he lept
   As Lyon fierce upon the flying pray,
   And with his trenchand° blade her boldly kept   *sharp*
   From turning backe, and forcèd her to stay:
   Therewith enrag'd she loudly gan to bray,
150 And turning fierce, her speckled taile advaunst,
   Threatning her angry sting, him to dismay:°   *defeat*
   Who nough° aghast, his mightie hand enhaunst:°   *now / raised up*
The stroke down from her head unto her shoulder glaunst.

18

Much daunted with that dint,° her sence was dazd,   *blow*
155   Yet kindling rage, her selfe she gathered° round,   *coiled*
   And all attonce her beastly body raizd
   With doubled forces high above the ground:

---

1. Fully armed.
2. Literally, fairy; but Spenser often uses the term to designate a knight from his imagined Faerie Land rather than from Britain—as, here, Red-
crosse Knight, who is later described as "a Faeries sonne" (but who is ultimately revealed to be a changeling "of Saxon kings . . . in Britaine land" [1.10.64–65]).

Tho° wrapping up her wrethèd sterne arownd,   *then*
    Lept fierce upon his shield, and her huge traine°   *tail*
160 All suddenly about his body wound,
    That hand or foot to stirre he strove in vaine:
God helpe the man so wrapt in Errours endlesse traine.

19

His Lady sad to see his sore constraint,°   *fettered state*
    Cride out, Now now Sir knight, shew what ye bee,
165 Add faith unto your force, and be not faint:
    Strangle her, else she sure will strangle thee.
    That when he heard, in great perplexitie,
    His gall[3] did grate for griefe° and high disdaine,   *anger*
    And knitting all his force got one hand free,
170 Wherewith he grypt her gorge° with so great paine,   *throat*
That soone to loose her wicked bands did her constraine.

20

Therewith she spewd out of her filthy maw
    A floud of poyson horrible and blacke,
    Full of great lumpes of flesh and gobbets raw,[4]
175 Which stunck so vildly, that it forst him slacke
    His grasping hold, and from her turne him backe:
    Her vomit full of bookes and papers was,[5]
    With loathly frogs and toades, which eyes did lacke,
    And creeping sought way in the weedy gras:
180 Her filthy parbreake° all the place defilèd has.   *vomit*

21

As when old father Nilus[6] gins to swell
    With timely° pride above the Aegyptian vale,   *seasonal*
    His fattie° waves do fertile slime outwell,   *rich*
    And overflow each plaine and lowly dale:
185 But when his later spring gins to avale,°   *subside*
    Huge heapes of mudd he leaves, wherein there breed
    Ten thousand kindes of creatures, partly male
    And partly female of his fruitfull seed;
Such ugly monstrous shapes elswhere may no man reed.°   *see*

22

190 The same so sore annoyèd has the knight,
    That welnigh chokèd with the deadly stinke,
    His forces faile, ne can no longer fight.
    Whose corage when the feend perceived to shrinke,
    She pourèd forth out of her hellish sinke[7]
195 Her fruitfull cursèd spawne of serpents small,
    Deformèd monsters, fowle, and blacke as inke,

3. Gall bladder, considered the seat of anger.
4. Chunks of undigested food.
5. Among other meanings, the "bookes and papers" may include a reference to Catholic books and pamphlets that attacked the Protestant Queen Elizabeth, in which case Error may be, among other things, an allegorical representation of the Catholic Church.
6. The Nile River, which runs from East Africa to the Mediterranean Sea in Egypt, was commonly said to breed strange monsters.
7. I.e., her mouth.

Which swarming all about his legs did crall,
And him encombred sore, but could not hurt at all.

23

As gentle Shepheard in sweete even-tide,
200   When ruddy Phoebus gins to welke° in west,   *sink*
High on an hill, his flocke to vewen wide,
Markes° which do byte their hasty supper best;   *observes*
A cloud of combrous° gnattes do him molest,   *encumbering*
All striving to infixe their feeble stings,
205   That from their noyance he no where can rest,
But with his clownish° hands their tender wings   *rustic*
He brusheth oft, and oft doth mar their murmurings.

24

Thus ill bestedd,° and fearfull more of shame,   *situated*
Then of the certaine perill he stood in,
210   Halfe furious unto his foe he came,
Resolv'd in minde all suddenly to win,
Or soone to lose, before he once would lin;°   *cease*
And strooke at her with more then manly force,
That from her body full of filthie sin
215   He raft° her hatefull head without remorse;   *struck off*
A streame of cole black bloud forth gushèd from her corse.°   *corpse*

25

Her scattred brood, soone as their Parent deare
They saw so rudely° falling to the ground,   *violently*
Groning full deadly, all with troublous feare,
220   Gathred themselves about her body round,
Weening° their wonted entrance to have found   *thinking*
At her wide mouth: but being there withstood
They flockèd all about her bleeding wound,
And suckèd up their dying mothers blood,
225   Making her death their life, and eke° her hurt their good.   *also*

26

That detestable sight him much amazde,
To see th' unkindly° Impes° of heaven accurst,   *unnatural / offspring*
Devoure their dam; on whom while so he gazd,
Having all satisfide their bloudy thurst,
230   Their bellies swolne he saw with fulnesse burst,
And bowels gushing forth: well worthy end
Of such as drunke her life, the which them nurst;
Now needeth him no lenger labour spend,
His foes have slaine themselves, with whom he should contend.

27

235   His Ladie seeing all, that chaunst, from farre
Approcht in hast to greet° his victorie,   *congratulate*
And said, Faire knight, borne under happy° starre,   *auspicious*

Who see your vanquisht foes before you lye:
Well worthy be you of that Armorie,°   *armor*
240   Wherein ye have great glory wonne this day,
And proov'd your strength on a strong enimie,
Your first adventure: many such I pray,
And henceforth ever wish, that like succeed it may.

28

Then mounted he upon his Steede againe,
245   And with the Lady backward sought to wend;°   *go*
That path he kept, which beaten was most plaine,
Ne ever would to any by-way bend,
But still did follow one unto the end,
The which at last out of the wood them brought.
250   So forward on his way (with God to° frend)°   *as a / friend*
He passèd forth, and new adventure sought;
Long way he travellèd, before he heard of ought.

29

At length they chaunst to meet upon the way
An aged Sire, in long blacke weedes° yclad,°   *garments / dressed*
255   His feete all bare, his beard all hoarie° gray,   *ancient*
And by his belt his booke he hanging had;
Sober he seemde, and very sagely sad,°   *pensive*
And to the ground his eyes were lowly bent,
Simple in shew, and voyde of malice bad,
260   And all the way he prayèd, as he went,
And often knockt his brest, as one that did repent.

30

He faire the knight saluted, louting° low,   *bowing*
Who faire him quited,° as that courteous was: *answered*
And after askèd him, if he did know
265   Of straunge adventures, which abroad did pas.
Ah my deare Sonne (quoth he) how should, alas,
Silly° old man, that lives in hidden cell,   *simple*
Bidding his beades[8] all day for his trespas,
Tydings of warre and worldly trouble tell?
270   With holy father sits not with such things to mell.°   *meddle*

31

But if of daunger which hereby doth dwell,
And homebred evill ye desire to heare,
Of a straunge man I can you tidings tell,
That wasteth all this countrey farre and neare.
275   Of such (said he) I chiefly do inquere,
And shall you well reward to shew the place,
In which that wicked wight his dayes doth weare:°   *spend*
For to all knighthood it is foule disgrace,
That such a cursed creature lives so long a space.

---

8. Saying his prayers, i.e., counting rosary beads.

32

²⁸⁰ Far hence (quoth he) in wastfull° wildernesse   *desolate*
   His dwelling is, by which no living wight
   May ever passe, but thorough great distresse.
   Now (sayd the Lady) draweth toward night,
   And well I wote,° that of your later° fight   *know / recent*
²⁸⁵ Ye all forwearied be: for what so strong,
   But wanting rest will also want of might?
   The Sunne that measures heaven all day long,
At night doth baite° his steedes the Ocean waves emong.   *feed*

33

   Then with the Sunne take Sir, your timely rest,
²⁹⁰ And with new day new worke at once begin:
   Untroubled night they say gives counsell best.
   Right well Sir knight ye have advisèd bin,
   (Quoth then that aged man;) the way to win
   Is wisely to advise:° now day is spent;   *take thought*
²⁹⁵ Therefore with me ye may take up your In°   *lodging*
   For this same night. The knight was well content:
So with that godly father to his home they went.

34

   A little lowly Hermitage it was,
   Downe in a dale, hard by a forests side,
³⁰⁰ Far from resort of people, that did pas
   In travell to and froe: a little wyde°   *apart*
   There was an holy Chappell edifyde,°   *built*
   Wherein the Hermite dewly wont° to say   *was accustomed*
   His holy things° each morne and eventyde: *prayers*
³⁰⁵ Thereby a Christall streame did gently play,
Which from a sacred fountaine wellèd forth alway.

35

   Arrivèd there, the little house they fill,
   Ne looke for entertainement, where none was:
   Rest is their feast, and all things at their will;
³¹⁰ The noblest mind the best contentment has.
   With faire discourse the evening so they pas:
   For that old man of pleasing wordes had store,
   And well could file° his tongue as smooth as glas;   *polish*
   He told of Saintes and Popes, and evermore
³¹⁵ He strowd an Ave-Mary[9] after and before.

36

   The drouping Night thus creepeth on them fast,
   And the sad humour[1] loading their eye liddes,
   As messenger of Morpheus[2] on them cast
   Sweet slombring deaw, the which to sleepe them biddes.

9. Hail Mary (Latin); a Catholic prayer.   2. Greek god of sleep and of dreams.
1. Heavy moisture, the "deaw" (line 319) of sleep.

320   Unto their lodgings then his guestes he riddes:°   *dispatches*
        Where when all drownd in deadly° sleepe he findes,   *deathlike*
        He to his study goes, and there amiddes
        His Magick bookes and artes of sundry kindes,
    He seekes out mighty charmes, to trouble sleepy mindes.

37

325 Then choosing out few wordes most horrible,
        (Let none them read) thereof did verses frame,
        With which and other spelles like terrible,
        He bade awake blacke Plutoes griesly Dame,[3]
        And cursèd heaven, and spake reprochfull shame
330   Of highest God, the Lord of life and light;
        A bold bad man, that dared to call by name
        Great Gorgon,[4] Prince of darknesse and dead night,
    At which Cocytus quakes, and Styx is put to flight.

38

    And forth he cald out of deepe darknesse dred
335   Legions of Sprights, the which like little flyes[5]
        Fluttring about his ever damnèd hed,
        A-waite whereto their service he applyes,
        To aide his friends, or fray° his enimies: *frighten*
        Of those he chose out two, the falsest twoo,
340   And fittest for to forge true-seeming lyes;
        The one of them he gave a message too,
    The other by him selfe staide other worke to doo.

39

    He making speedy way through spersèd° ayre,   *dispersed*
        And through the world of waters wide and deepe,
345   To Morpheus house doth hastily repaire.
        Amid the bowels of the earth full steepe,
        And low, where dawning day doth never peepe,
        His dwelling is; there Tethys[6] his wet bed
        Doth ever wash, and Cynthia still[7] doth steepe
350   In silver deaw his ever-drouping hed,
    Whiles sad° Night over him her mantle black doth spred.   *sober*

40

    Whose double gates he findeth lockèd fast,
        The one faire fram'd of burnisht Yvory,
        The other all with silver overcast;
355   And wakefull dogges before them farre do lye,
        Watching to banish Care their enimy,
        Who oft is wont° to trouble gentle Sleepe.   *accustomed*
        By them the Sprite doth passe in quietly,

3. Persephone: Greek goddess of the underworld, wife of Pluto, and patron of witches.
4. Demogorgon, whose power is so great that the mention of his name causes hell's rivers (Cocytus and Styx) to quake.
5. The simile connects him to Beelzebub, lord of the flies.
6. Roman goddess of the sea; wife of Neptune.
7. Continually. *Cynthia:* Roman goddess of the moon.

And unto Morpheus comes, whom drownèd deepe
360 In drowsie fit he findes: of nothing he takes keepe.°   *notice*

41

And more, to lulle him in his slumber soft,
    A trickling streame from high rocke tumbling downe
    And ever drizling raine upon the loft,
    Mixt with a murmuring winde, much like the sowne°   *sound*
365   Of swarming Bees, did cast him in a swowne:°   *faint*
    No other noyse, nor peoples troublous cryes,
    As still° are wont t'annoy the wallèd towne,   *always*
    Might there be heard: but carelesse° Quiet lyes,   *free from care*
Wrapt in eternall silence farre from enemyes.

42

370 The messenger approching to him spake,
    But his wast° wordes returnd to him in vaine: *wasted*
    So sound he slept, that nought mought° him awake.   *might*
    Then rudely he him thrust, and pusht with paine,°   *effort*
    Whereat he gan to stretch: but he againe
375   Shooke him so hard, that forced him to speake.
    As one then in a dreame, whose dryer braine[8]
    Is tost with troubled sights and fancies° weake,   *fantasies*
He mumbled soft, but would not all° his silence breake.   *altogether*

43

The Sprite then gan more boldly him to wake,
380   And threatned unto him the dreaded name
    Of Hecate:[9] whereat he gan to quake,
    And lifting up his lumpish head, with blame
    Halfe angry askèd him, for what he came.
    Hither (quoth he) me Archimago[1] sent,
385   He that the stubborne Sprites can wisely tame,
    He bids thee to him send for his intent
A fit false dreame, that can delude the sleepers sent.°   *senses*

44

The God obayde, and calling forth straight way
    A diverse° dreame out of his prison darke,   *distracting*
390   Delivered it to him, and downe did lay
    His heavie head, devoide of carefull° carke,°   *anxious / concerns*
    Whose sences all were straight benumbd and starke.°   *paralyzed*
    He backe returning by the Yvorie dore,[2]
    Remounted up as light as chearefull Larke,
395   And on his litle winges the dreame he bore
In hast unto his Lord, where he him left afore.

---

8. Renaissance ideas of physiology held that being too "dry," or lacking a proper balance of bodily moisture, resulted in troubled dreams.
9. A Greek goddess of Hades; associated with witches, magic, and dreams.

1. Archmagician or chief deceiver, from the Latin *archi* (first) + *magus* (magician); also, the archimago, or chief image-maker.
2. According to Homer's *Odyssey* and Virgil's *Aeneid*, false dreams came through the ivory door.

45

Who all this while with charmes and hidden artes,
   Had made a Lady of that other Spright,
   And fram'd of liquid ayre her tender partes
400 So lively,° and so like in all mens sight,   *lifelike*
   That weaker° sence it could have ravisht quight: *too weak*
   The maker selfe for all his wondrous witt,
   Was nigh beguilèd with so goodly sight:
   Her all in white he clad, and over it
405 Cast a blacke stole, most like to seeme for Una³ fit.

46

Now when that ydle° dreame was to him brought, *unsubstantial*
   Unto that Elfin knight he bad him fly,
   Where he slept soundly void of evill thought,
   And with false shewes abuse his fantasy,°   *imagination*
410 In sort° as° he him schoolèd privily: *the way / that*
   And that new creature borne without her dew,⁴
   Full of the makers guile, with usage sly
   He taught to imitate that Lady trew,
   Whose semblance she did carrie under feignèd hew.° *form*

47

415 Thus well instructed, to their worke they hast
   And comming where the knight in slomber lay
   The one upon his hardy head him plast,°   *placed*
   And made him dreame of loves and lustfull play,
   That nigh his manly hart° did melt away,   *heart*
420 Bathèd in wanton blis and wicked joy:
   Then seemèd him his Lady by him lay,
   And to him playnd,° how that false wingèd boy,⁵ *complained*
Her chast hart had subdewd, to learne Dame pleasures toy.⁶

48

And she her selfe of beautie soveraigne Queene
425 Faire Venus seemde unto his bed to bring
   Her, whom he waking evermore did weene°   *think*
   To be the chastest flowre, that ay° did spring   *ever*
   On earthly braunch, the daughter of a king,
   Now a loose Leman° to vile service bound: *lover*
430 And eke the Graces seemèd all to sing,
   Hymen iô Hymen, dauncing all around,
Whilst freshest Flora⁷ her with Yvie girlond crownd.

49

In this great passion of unwonted° lust,   *unaccustomed*
   Or wonted feare of doing ought amis,

---

3. One, unity (Latin). Many Elizabethan readers
would have known the Latin phrase *Una Vera Fides*
(one true faith).
4. Unnaturally.
5. Cupid.

6. Lustful play. *Dame pleasures:* Venus.
7. Flower goddess; sometimes referred to as sex-
ually unchaste. *Graces:* handmaids of Venus; here,
they sing in praise of the marriage bed. *Hymen:*
Greek god of marriage.

435 He started up, as seeming to mistrust°   suspect
　　 Some secret ill, or hidden foe of his:
　　 Lo there before his face his Lady is,
　　 Under blake stole hyding her bayted hooke,
　　 And as halfe blushing offred him to kis,
440 With gentle blandishment° and lovely° looke,   flattering speech / loving
Most like that virgin true, which for her knight him took.

50

　　 All cleane dismayd to see so uncouth° sight,   strange
　　 And halfe enragèd at her shamelesse guise,
　　 He thought have slaine her in his fierce despight:°   indignation
445 But hasty heat tempring with sufferance wise,
　　 He stayde his hand, and gan himselfe advise
　　 To prove his sense, and tempt° her faignèd truth.   test
　　 Wringing her hands in wemens pitteous wise,
　　 Tho° can° she weepe, to stirre up gentle ruth,°   then / did / pity
450 Both for her noble bloud, and for her tender youth.

51

　　 And said, Ah Sir, my liege Lord and my love,
　　 Shall I accuse the hidden cruell fate,
　　 And mightie causes wrought in heaven above,
　　 Or the blind God, that doth me thus amate,°   dismay
455 For° hopèd love to winne me certaine hate?   instead of
　　 Yet thus perforce° he bids me do, or die.   forcibly
　　 Die is my dew:[8] yet rew° my wretched state   pity
　　 You, whom my hard avenging destinie
Hath made judge of my life or death indifferently.

52

460 Your owne deare sake forst me at first to leave
　　 My Fathers kingdome, There she stopt with teares;
　　 Her swollen hart° her speach seemd to bereave,   heart
　　 And then againe begun, My weaker yeares
　　 Captiv'd to fortune and frayle worldly feares,
465 Fly to your faith for succour and sure ayde:
　　 Let me not dye in languor° and long teares.   sorrow
　　 Why Dame (quoth he) what hath ye thus dismayd?
What frayes° ye, that were wont to comfort me affrayd?   frightens

53

　　 Love of your selfe, she said, and deare° constraint   dire
470 Lets me not sleepe, but wast the wearie night
　　 In secret anguish and unpittied plaint,
　　 Whiles you in carelesse sleepe are drownèd quight.
　　 Her doubtfull words made that redoubted[9] knight
　　 Suspect her truth: yet since no untruth he knew,
475 Her fawning love with foule disdainefull spight°   contempt

8. I.e., I deserve to die.
9. Dreaded; also, doubting again. *Doubtfull*: fearful; also, questionable.

He would not shend,° but said, Deare dame I rew,°   *reject / pity*
That for my sake unknowne such griefe unto you grew.

54

Assure your selfe, it fell not all to ground;
  For all so deare as life is to my hart,°   *heart*
480   I deeme your love, and hold me to you bound;
  Ne let vaine feares procure° your needlesse smart,°   *cause / harm*
  Where cause is none, but to your rest depart.
  Not all content, yet seemd she to appease°   *cease*
  Her mournefull plaintes, beguilèd° of her art,   *deprived*
485   And fed with words, that could not chuse but please,
So slyding softly forth, she turnd° as to her ease.   *returned*

55

Long after lay he musing at her mood,
  Much griev'd to thinke that gentle Dame so light,[1]
  For whose defence he was to shed his blood.
490   At last dull wearinesse of former fight
  Having yrockt a sleepe his irkesome spright,[2]
  That troublous dreame gan freshly tosse his braine,
  With bowres, and beds, and Ladies deare delight:
  But when he° saw his labour all was vaine,   *the dream*
495 With that misformèd spright he° backe returnd againe.   *the dream*

Canto 2

The guilefull great Enchaunter parts
The Redcrosse Knight from Truth:
Into whose stead faire falshood steps,
And workes him wofull ruth.°   *harm*

1

By this the Northerne wagoner had set
  His seven fold teame behind the stedfast starre,[1]
  That was in Ocean waves yet never wet,
  But firme is fixt, and sendeth light from farre
5   To all, that in the wide deepe wandring arre:
  And chearefull Chaunticlere with his note shrill
  Had warnèd once, that Phoebus fiery carre[2]
  In hast was climbing up the Easterne hill,
Full envious that night so long his roome did fill.

2

10 When those accursèd messengers of hell,
  That feigning dreame,[3] and that faire-forgèd Spright

---

1. I.e., so unchaste.
2. Tired or troublesome spirit (as mind or soul, but stressing the hero's similarity to the "misformed spright" of line 495, sent by Archimago).
1. I.e., by this time the "northerne Waggoner"— the constellation Boötes seen as the driver of the

"teame" of the seven bright stars in Ursa Major— had set behind the North Star.
2. The sun's chariot. *Chaunticlere:* a common name for a rooster.
3. I.e., the dream has caused the Knight to "feign" in the senses of "to desire" and "to imagine falsely":

Came to their wicked maister, and gan tell
Their bootelesse° paines, and ill succeeding night: *useless*
Who all in rage to see his skilfull might
15   Deluded so, gan threaten hellish paine
And sad Proserpines⁴ wrath, them to affright.
But when he saw his threatning was but vaine,
He cast about, and searcht his balefull° bookes againe.   *deadly*

3

Eftsoones° he tooke that miscreated faire,   *soon after*
20   And that false other Spright, on whom he spred
A seeming body of the subtile° aire,   *rarefied*
Like a young Squire, in loves and lusty-hed
His wanton dayes that ever loosely led,
Without regard of armes and dreaded fight:
25   Those two he tooke, and in a secret bed,
Covered with darknesse and misdeeming° night,   *misleading*
Them both together laid, to joy in vaine delight.

4

Forthwith he runnes with feignèd faithfull hast
Unto his guest, who after troublous sights
30   And dreames, gan now to take more sound repast,°   *rest*
Whom suddenly he wakes with fearefull frights,
As one aghast with feends or damnèd sprights,
And to him cals, "Rise rise unhappy Swaine,°   *rustic youth*
That here wex° old in sleepe, whiles wicked wights°   *grow / creatures*
35   Have knit themselves in Venus shamefull chaine;
Come see, where your false Lady doth her honour staine."

5

All in amaze he suddenly up start
With sword in hand, and with the old man went;
Who soone him brought into a secret part,
40   Where that false couple were full closely ment°   *mingled*
In wanton lust and lewd embracèment:
Which when he saw, he burnt with gealous fire,
The eye of reason was with rage yblent,°   *blinded*
And would have slaine them in his furious ire,
45   But hardly° was restreinèd of° that aged sire.   *with difficulty / by*

6

Returning to his bed in torment great,
And bitter anguish of his guiltie sight,
He could not rest, but did his stout heart eat,
And wast° his inward gall with deepe despight,°   *waste / malice*
50   Yrkesome° of life, and too long lingring night.   *tired*
At last faire Hesperus⁵ in highest skie

see canto 1, stanzas 46–47.
4. Roman name for Persephone, who in Greek
mythology was seized and held captive by Pluto,
god of the underworld.
5. The evening and morning star, i.e., the planet
Venus.

Had spent his lampe, and brought forth dawning light,
Then up he rose, and clad him hastily;
The Dwarfe him brought his steed: so both away do fly.

7

55 Now when the rosy-fingred Morning faire,
Weary of aged Tithones[6] saffron bed,
Had spred her purple robe through deawy aire,
And the high hils Titan° discoverèd,°   the sun / revealed
The royall virgin shooke off drowsy-hed,
60 And rising forth out of her baser° bowre,   too lowly
Lookt for her knight, who far away was fled,
And for her Dwarfe, that wont° to wait each houre: was accustomed
Then gan she waile and weepe, to see that woefull stowre.° affliction

8

And after him she rode with so much speede
65 As her slow beast could make; but all in vaine:
For him so far had borne his light-foot steede,
Prickèd with wrath and fiery fierce disdaine,°   indignation
That him to follow was but fruitless paine;
Yet she her weary limbes would never rest,
70 But every hill and dale, each wood and plaine
Did search, sore grievèd in her gentle brest,
He so ungently left her, whom she lovèd best.

9

But subtill° Archimago, when his guests   cunning
He saw divided into double parts,
75 And Una wandring in woods and forrests,
Th' end of his drift,° he praisd his divelish arts   plot
That had such might over true meaning harts;°   hearts
Yet rests not so, but other meanes doth make,
How he may worke unto her further smarts:°   harm
80 For her he hated as the hissing snake,
And in her many troubles did most pleasure take.

10

He then devisde himselfe how to disguise;
For by his mightie science° he could take   knowledge
As many formes and shapes in seeming wise,
85 As ever Proteus[7] to himselfe could make:
Sometime a fowle, sometime a fish in lake,
Now like a foxe, now like a dragon fell,°   fierce
That of himselfe he oft for feare would quake,
And oft would flie away. O who can tell
90 The hidden power of herbes, and might of Magicke spell?

---

6. Tithonus, in Roman mythology the husband of
Aurora, goddess of the dawn.
7. A Greek sea god who could change his shape at

will (*Odyssey* 4.398–424). *In seeming wise*: in
appearance.

11

But now seemde best, the person to put on
  Of that good knight, his late beguilèd⁸ guest:
  In mighty armes he was yclad anon,°   soon
  And silver shield: upon his coward brest
95 A bloudy crosse, and on his craven crest
  A bounch of haires discoloured° diversly.⁹   colored / variously
  Full jolly° knight he seemde, and well addrest,°   gallant / armed
  And when he sate upon his courser free,⁹
Saint George¹ himself ye would have deemèd him to be.

12

100 But he the knight, whose semblaunt° he did beare,   likeness
  The true Saint George was wandred far away,
  Still flying from° his thoughts and gealous feare;   because of
  Will was his guide,² and griefe led him astray.
  At last him chaunst to meete upon the way
105 A faithlesse Sarazin³ all armed to point,
  In whose great shield was writ with letters gay
  Sans° foy:° full large of limbe and every joint   without / faith
He was, and carèd not for God or man a° point.°   at / all

13

He had a faire companion of his way,
110 A goodly Lady clad in scarlot red,
  Purfled° with gold and pearle of rich assay,°   embroidered / value
  And like a Persian mitre° on her hed   headdress
  She wore, with crownes and owches° garnishèd,   brooches
  The which her lavish° lovers to her gave;⁴   extravagant
115 Her wanton° palfrey° all was overspred   unruly / lady's saddle horse
  With tinsell trappings, woven like a wave,
Whose bridle rung with golden bels and bosses°   ornaments
    brave.°   handsome

14

With faire disport° and courting dalliaunce°   diversion / talk
  She intertainde her lover all the way:
120 But when she saw the knight his speare advaunce,
  She soone left off her mirth and wanton play,
  And bad her knight addresse him to the fray:
His foe was nigh at hand. He prickt with pride

---

8. Deluded, deceived by guile; but contrast its use
at canto 1, line 82. *To put on:* to assume.
9. I.e., noble horse.
1. I.e., Archimago now assumes not only the Red-
crosse Knight's appearance but also the saintly
identity that the Knight will acquire after his
earthly adventures are over; the Knight will later
learn that he is to become England's dragon-
slaying patron, Saint George (10.61.8).
2. In Christian thought, the faculty of the will is
below and should be guided by the faculty of rea-
son, but the Knight's is "blinded" (see stanza 5, line
7) by passion.

3. I.e., Saracen, a name loosely and usually neg-
atively denoting non-Christians and, more specif-
ically, the Turkish or Arabic enemies of medieval
Christian "crusaders."
4. The lady's clothes associate her with the Whore
of Babylon (Revelation 17.3–4): "And I saw a
woman sit upon a scarlet colored beast, full of
names of blasphemy, having seven heads and ten
horns. And the woman was arrayed in purple and
scarlet color, and decked with gold and precious
stones and pearls." She represents false religion,
especially what Protestants saw as the pomp and
hypocrisy of Rome.

And hope to winne his Ladies heart that day,
125   Forth spurrèd fast: adowne his coursers side
The red bloud trickling staind the way, as he did ride.

15

The knight of the Redcrosse when him he spide,
    Spurring so hote with rage dispiteous,°   *cruel*
    Gan fairely couch° his speare, and towards ride: *lower*
130   Soone meete they both, both fell° and furious,   *fierce*
    That daunted° with their forces hideous,   *dazed*
    Their steeds do stagger, and amazèd stand,
    And eke° themselves too rudely rigorous,°   *also / violent*
    Astonied° with the stroke of their owne hand,   *stunned*
135 Do backe rebut,° and each to other yeeldeth land.   *recoil*

16

As when two rams stird with ambitious pride,
    Fight for the rule of the rich fleecèd flocke,
    Their hornèd fronts so fierce on either side
    Do meete, that with the terrour of the shocke
140   Astonied° both, stand sencelesse as a blocke,   *stunned, made stonelike*
    Forgetfull of the hanging° victory: *in the balance*
    So stood these twaine, unmovèd as a rocke,
    Both staring fierce, and holding idely
The broken reliques° of their former cruelty.   *remnants*

17

145 The Sarazin sore daunted with the buffe°   *blow*
    Snatcheth his sword, and fiercely to him flies;
    Who well it wards, and quyteth° cuff with cuff: *requites*
    Each others equall puissaunce° envies,   *strength*
    And through their iron sides with cruell spies°   *looks*
150   Does seeke to perce: repining° courage yields   *angry*
    No foote to foe. The flashing fier flies
    As from a forge out of their burning shields,
And streams of purple bloud new dies the verdant fields.

18

"Curse on that Crosse," quoth then the Sarazin,
155   "That keepes thy body from the bitter fit;[5]
    Dead long ygoe I wote° thou haddest bin,   *thought*
    Had not that charme from thee forwarnèd° it: *prevented*
    But yet I warne thee now assurèd° sitt,   *securely*
    And hide thy head." Therewith upon his crest
160   With rigour° so outrageous he smitt,   *violence; rigidity*
    That a large share° it hewd out of the rest,   *piece*
And glauncing downe his shield, from blame° him   *harm*
    fairely blest.°   *preserved*

5. Death pangs.

19

Who thereat wondrous wroth,° the sleeping spark   *angry*
    Of native vertue° gan eftsoones° revive,   *strength / soon after*
165   And at his haughtie helmet making mark,
    So hugely° stroke, that it the steele did rive,°   *mightily / tear apart*
    And cleft his head. He tumbling downe alive,
    With bloudy mouth his mother earth did kis
    Greeting his grave: his grudging° ghost did strive   *complaining*
170   With the fraile flesh; at last it flitted is,
Whither the soules do fly of men, that live amis.

20

The Lady when she saw her champion fall,
    Like the old ruines of a broken towre,
    Staid not to waile his woefull funerall,°   *death*
175   But from him fled away with all her powre;
    Who after her as hastily gan scowre,°   *scurry*
    Bidding the Dwarfe with him to bring away
    The Sarazins shield, signe of the conqueroure.
    Her soone he° overtooke, and bad to stay,   *Redcrosse*
180 For present cause was none of dread her to dismay.[6]

21

She turning backe with ruefull[7] countenaunce
    Cride, "Mercy mercy Sir vouchsafe to show
    On silly° Dame, subject to hard mischaunce,   *helpless*
    And to your mighty will." Her humblesse low
185   In so ritch weedes° and seeming glorious show   *clothes*
    Did much emmove his stout heroike heart,
    And said, "Deare dame, your sudden overthrow
    Much rueth° me; but now put feare apart,   *grieves*
And tell, both who ye be, and who that tooke your part."

22

190 Melting in teares, then gan she thus lament;
    "The wretched woman, whom unhappy howre
    Hath now made thrall° to your commandèment,   *slave*
    Before that angry heavens list to lowre,°   *frown*
    And fortune false betraide me to your powre
195   Was (O what now availeth that I was!)
    Borne the sole daughter of an Emperour,
    He that the wide West under his rule has,
And high hath set his throne, where Tiberis doth pas.[8]

23

    "He in the first flowre of my freshest age,
200   Betrothèd me unto the onely haire°   *heir*
    Of a most mighty king, most rich and sage;

---

6. There was no present cause for her to flee in fear.
7. Seeking to incite pity.

8. The Tiber River runs through Rome; hence the lady is associated with the Catholic Church.

Was never Prince so faithfull and so faire,
Was never Prince so meeke and debonaire;°   *gracious*
But ere my hopèd day of spousall shone,
205   My dearest Lord fell from high honours staire,
Into the hands of his accursèd fone,°   *foes*
And cruelly was slaine, that shall I ever mone.[9]

24

"His blessed body spoild of lively breath,
Was afterward, I know not how, convaid°   *carried away*
210   And fro me hid: of whose most innocent death
When tidings came to me unhappy maid,
O how great sorrow my sad soule assaid.°   *afflicted*
Then forth I went his woefull corse° to find,   *corpse*
And many yeares throughout the world I straid,°   *strayed*
215   A virgin widow, whose deepe wounded mind
With love, long time did languish as the striken hind.°   *deer*

25

"At last it chauncèd this proud Sarazin
To meete me wandring, who perforce° me led   *by violence*
With him away, but yet could never wih
220   The fort, that Ladies hold in soveraigne dread.
There lies he now with foule dishonour dead,
Who whiles he livde, was callèd proud Sans foy,
The eldest of three brethren, all three bred
Of one bad sire, whose youngest is Sans° joy,   *without*
225 And twixt them both was borne the bloudy bold Sans loy.[1]

26

"In this sad plight, friendless unfortunate,
Now miscrable I Fidessa° dwell,   *Faith*
Craving of you in pitty of my state,
To do none° ill, if please ye not do well."   *no*
230   He in great passion all this while did dwell,°   *continue*
More busying his quicke eyes, her face to view,
then his dull eares, to heare what she did tell;
And said, "Faire Lady hart of flint would rew°   *pity*
The undeservèd woes and sorrowes, which ye shew.

27

235 "Henceforth in safe assurance may ye rest,
Having both found a new friend you to aid,
And lost an old foe, that did you molest:
Better new friend than an old foe is° said."   *it is*
With chaunge of cheare the seeming simple maid

---

9. The lady claims to have been engaged to Christ, bridegroom of the Church, who was cruelly killed—which event the lady will forever lament.
1. Literally, without law. The names of Spenser's three "Sans" brothers hark back to St. Paul's Epistle to the Galatians 5.22–23: "But the fruit of the Spirit is love, joy . . . faith . . . temperance: against such there is no law."

240   Let fall her eyen, as° shamefast° to the earth,   *as if / modestly*
        And yeelding soft, in that she nought gain-said,
        So forth they rode, he feining° seemely merth,   *simulating*
        And she coy lookes: so dainty they say maketh derth.[2]

28

        Long time they thus together traveilèd,
245   Till weary of their way, they came at last,
        Where grew two goodly trees, that faire did spred
        Their armes abroad, with gray mosse overcast,
        And their greene leaves trembling with every blast,°   *breeze*
        Made a calme shadow far in compasse round:
250   The fearefull Shepheard often there aghast
        Under them never sat, ne wont° there sound   *was accustomed to*
        His mery oaten pipe, but shund th' unlucky ground.

29

        But this good knight soone as he them can° spie,   *did*
        For the coole shade him thither hastly got:
255   For golden Phoebus now ymounted hie,
        From fiery wheeles of his faire chariot
        Hurlèd his beame so scorching cruell hot,
        That living creature mote° it not abide;   *might*
        And his new Lady it endurèd not.
260   There they alight, in hope themselves to hide
        From the fierce heat, and rest their weary limbs a tide.°   *time*

30

        Faire seemely pleasaunce° each to other makes,   *courtesy*
        With goodly purposes there as they sit:
        And in his falsèd° fancy he her takes   *deceived*
265   To be the fairest wight° that livèd yit;   *creature*
        Which to expresse, he bends his gentle wit,
        And thinking of those braunches greene to frame
        A girlond° for her dainty forehead fit,   *garland*
        He pluckt a bough; out of whose rift there came
270   Small drops of gory bloud, that trickled downe the same.

31

        Therewith a piteous yelling voyce was heard,
        Crying, "O spare with guilty hands to teare
        My tender sides in this rough rynd embard,°   *imprisoned*
        But fly, ah fly far hence away, for feare
275   Least° to you hap, that happened to me heare,   *lest*
        And to this wretched Lady, my deare love,
        O too deare love, love bought with death too deare."
        Astond he stood,[3] and up his haire did hove°   *heave, raise*
        And with that sudden horror could no member move.

---

2. Proverbial: what's dear is rare; here, coyness   3. I.e., astonished, Redcrosse Knight stood up.
creates unsatisfied desire.

32

280 At last whenas the dreadful passiön
    Was overpast, and manhood well awake,
    Yet musing at the straunge occasiön
    And doubting much his sense, he thus bespake;
    "What voyce of damnèd Ghost from Limbo[4] lake,
285 Or guilefull spright wandring in empty aire,
    Both which fraile men do oftentimes mistake,°   *mislead*
    Sends to my doubtfull eares these speaches rare,
And ruefull plaints, me bidding guiltless bloud to spare?"

33

Then groning deepe, "Nor damned Ghost," quoth he,
290 "Nor guilefull sprite to thee these wordes doth speake,
    But once a man Fradubio,[5] now a tree,
    Wretched man, wretched tree; whose nature weake,
    A cruell witch her cursèd will to wreake,
    Hath thus transformed, and plast° in open plaines,   *placed*
295 Where Boreas° doth blow full bitter bleake,   *the north wind*
    And scorching Sunne does dry my secret vaines:
For though a tree I seeme, yet cold and heat me paines."

34

"Say on Fradubio then, or° man, or tree,"   *whether*
    Quoth then the knight, "by whose mischievous arts
300 Art thou misshapèd thus, as now I see?
    He oft finds med'cine, who his griefe imparts;
    But double griefs afflict concealing harts,°   *hearts*
    As raging flames who striveth to suppresse."
    "The author then," said he, "of all my smarts,°   *hurts*
305 Is one Duessa[6] a false sorceresse,
That many errant knights hath brought to wretchednesse.[7]

35

"In prime of youthly yeares, when corage hot
    The fire of love and joy of chevalree
    First kindled in my brest, it was my lot
310 To love this gentle Lady, whom ye see,
    Now not a Lady, but a seeming tree;
    With whom as once I rode accompanyde,
    Me chauncèd of a knight encountred bee,
    That had a like faire Lady by his syde,
315 Like a faire Lady, but did fowle Duessa hyde.

36

"Whose forgèd beauty he did take in hand,[8]
    All other Dames to have exceeded farre,

---

4. A region of hell and, traditionally, the place of the unbaptized.
5. *Fra* (Italian, "in" or "brother") + *dubbio* ("doubt"). Spenser borrows details from many previous epic depictions of a man imprisoned in a bleeding tree; among his sources are Virgil (*Aeneid* 3.27–42), Dante (*Inferno* 13.28–109), Ariosto (*Orlando Furioso* 6.26–53), and Tasso (*Gerusalemma Liberata* 13.38–46).
6. *Due* (Italian, "two," or double) + *esse* (Latin, "being").
7. I.e., Duessa has brought many wandering (with a pun on *erring*) knights to wretchedness.
8. He maintained.

I in defence of mine did likewise stand,
Mine, that did then shine as the Morning starre:
320   So both to battell fierce arraungèd arre,
In which his harder fortune was to fall
Under my speare: such is the dye° of warre: *hazard*
His Lady left as a prise° martiall,°   *spoil / of battle*
Did yield her comely person, to be at my call.

37
325   "So doubly loved of Ladies unlike° faire,   *differently*
Th' one seeming such, the other such indeede,
One day in doubt I cast° for° to compare,   *decided / to*
Whether° in beauties glorie did exceede;   *which one (of two)*
A Rosy girlond° was the victors meede:°   *garland / reward*
330   Both seemde to win, and both seemde won to bee,
So hard the discord was to be agreede.
Fraelissa[9] was as faire, as faire mote bee,
And ever false Duessa seemde as faire as shee.

38
"The wicked witch now seeing all this white
335   The doubtfull ballaunce equally to sway,
What not by right, she cast to win by guile,
And by her hellish science° raisd streight way   *knowledge*
A foggy mist, that overcast the day,
And a dull blast, that breathing on her face,
340   Dimmed her former beauties shining ray,
And with foule ugly forme did her disgrace
Then was she faire alone, when none was faire in place.[1]

39
"Then cride she out, 'Fye, fye, deformèd wight,
Whose borrowed beautie now appeareth plaine
345   To have before bewitchèd all mens sight;
O leave her soone, or let her soone be slaine.'
Her lothly visage viewing with disdaine.
Eftsoone° I thought her such, as she me told,   *before*
And would have kild her, but with faignèd paine,
350   The false witch did my wrathfull hand withhold;
So left her, where she now is turnd to treen° mould.° *a tree's / form*

40
"Thens forth I tooke Duessa for my Dame,
And in the witch unweeting° joyd long time,   *unknowingly*
Ne ever wist,° but that she was the same,   *knew*
355   Till on a day (that day is every Prime,[2]
When Witches wont° do penance for their crime) *are accustomed to*
I chaunst to see her in her proper° hew,°   *own / shape*
Bathing her selfe in origane and thyme:[3]

---

9. Frailty (in Italian, *Fralezza*).
1. When nobody else was fair. *She*: Duessa.
2. Spring; or the first appearance of the new
moon.
3. Oregano and thyme were used to cure scabs
and itching.

A filthy foule old woman I did vew,
360   That ever to have toucht her, I did deadly rew.°   *regret*

41

"Her neather partes misshapen, monstruous,
    Were hidd in water, that I could not see,
    But they did seeme more foule and hideous,
    Then womans shape man would beleeve to bee.
365   Thens forth from her most beastly companie
    I gan refraine, in minde to slip away,
    Soone as appeard safe opportunitie:
    For danger great, if not assured decay°   *destruction*
I saw before mine eyes, if I were knowne to stray.

42

370   "The divelish hag by chaunges of my cheare°   *countenance*
    Perceived my thought, and drownd in sleepie night,
    With wicked herbes and ointments did besmeare
    My bodie all, through charmes and magicke might,
    That all my senses were bereavèd quight:°   *quite*
375   Then brought she me into this desert waste,
    And by my wretched lovers side me pight,°   *planted*
    Where now enclosd in wooden wals full faste,⁴
Banisht from living wights,° our wearie dayes we waste."   *persons*

43

"But how long time," said then the Elfin knight,
380   "Are you in this misformèd house to dwell?"
    "We may not chaunge," quoth he, "this evil plight,
    Till we be bathèd in a living well;⁵
    That is the terme prescribèd by the spell."
    "O how," said he, "mote° I that well out find,   *might*
385   That may restore you to your wonted well?"°   *well-being*
    "Time and suffisèd fates to former kynd
Shall us restore,⁶ none else from hence may us unbynd."

44

The false Duessa, now Fidessa hight,°   *called*
    Heard how in vaine Fradubio did lament,
390   And knew well all was true. But the good knight
    Full of sad feare and ghastly dreriment,°   *gloom*
    When all this speech the living tree had spent,
    The bleeding bough did thrust into the ground,
    That from the bloud he might be innocent,
395   And with fresh clay did close the wooden wound:
Then turning to his Lady, dead with feare her found.

---

4. I.e., imprisoned within the trees.
5. Allusion to 1 John 4.14: "well of water, springing up into eternal life."

6. I.e., time and the satisfaction of the fates alone can restore us to our former human nature.

45

Her seeming dead he found with feignèd feare,
As all unweeting of that well she knew,[7]
And paynd himselfe with busie care to reare
400   Her out of carelesse° swowne. Her eylids blew   *unconscious*
And dimmèd sight with pale and deadly° hew°   *deathlike / appearance*
At last she up gan lift: with trembling cheare°   *demeanor*
Her up he tooke, too simple and too trew,
And oft her kist. At length all passèd feare,[8]
405   He set her on her steede, and forward forth did beare.

1590, 1596

FROM AMORETTI[1]

Sonnet 1

Happy ye leaves[2] when as those lilly hands,
Which hold my life in their dead doing might[3]
Shall handle you and hold in loves soft bands,
Lyke captives trembling at the victors sight.
5   And happy lines, on which with starry light,
Those lamping° eyes will deigne sometimes to look   *shining*
And reade the sorrowes of my dying spright,°   *spirit*
Written with teares in harts° close° bleeding book.   *heart's / secret*
And happy rymes bath'd in the sacred brooke,
10   Of Helicon[4] whence she derived is,
When ye behold that Angels blessed looke,
My soules long lacked foode, my heavens blis.
Leaves, lines, and rymes, seeke her to please alone,
Whom if ye please, I care for other none.

Sonnet 8

More then° most faire, full of the living fire,   *than*
Kindled above unto the maker neere:
No eies[5] but joyes, in which al powers conspire,
That to the world naught else be counted deare.

---

7. I.e., pretending ignorance of what she knew well.
8. I.e., having overcome all fear.
1. Little loves (Italian). This sequence of eighty-nine sonnets was published in 1595, together with *Epithalamion* (p. 195), a kind of poem written to celebrate a marriage. It is generally believed that these poems were written to Spenser's bride-to-be, Elizabeth Boyle. The Petrarchan sonnet cycle was popular at this time, but Spenser's sequence is unusual because the desire expressed is directed not at an unattainable mistress but toward the woman who became the poet's second wife. The rhyme scheme is *abab bcbc cdcd ee*, a difficult pattern in English because of the frequency of the repeating rhymes.
2. Pages; in line 13, the poet addresses his poems as "leaves, lines, and rymes."
3. Death-dealing power.
4. The Hippocrene Spring, on Mt. Helicon, was the haunt of the Muses, the nine Greek sister goddesses believed to be the source of inspiration for the arts.
5. The lover's eyes are imagined as the source of love, both erotic and spiritual (Platonic).

5   Thrugh your bright beams doth not the blinded guest[6]
     Shoot out his darts to base affections wound?
     But Angels come to lead fraile mindes to rest
     In chast desires on heavenly beauty bound.
     You frame my thoughts and fashion me within,
10   You stop my toung, and teach my hart° to speake,   *heart*
     You calme the storme that passion did begin,
     Strong thrugh your cause, but by your vertue weak.
     Dark is the world, where your light shined never;
     Well is he borne, that may behold you ever.

Sonnet 15[7]

     Ye tradefull[8] Merchants that with weary toyle,
     Do seeke most pretious things to make your gain:
     And both the Indias[9] of their treasures spoile,°   *despoil*
     What needeth you to seeke so farre in vaine?
5   For loe my love doth in her selfe containe
     All this worlds riches that may farre be found,
     If Saphyres, loe her eies be Saphyres plaine,°   *perfect*
     If Rubies, loe hir lips be Rubies sound:°   *free from defect*
     If Pearles, hir teeth be pearles both pure and round;
10   If Yvorie, her forhead yvory weene;[1]
     If Gold, her locks are finest gold on ground;°   *Earth*
     If silver, her faire hands are silver sheene;°   *bright*
     But that which fairest is, but few behold,
     Her mind adornd with vertues manifold.

Sonnet 23

     Penelope for her Ulisses sake,
     Deviz'd a Web her wooers to deceave:
     In which the worke that she all day did make
     The same at night she did again unreave:[2]
5   Such subtile° craft my Damzell doth conceave,°   *fine, clever / devise*
     Th' importune° suit of my desire to shonne:[3]   *importunate*
     For all that I in many dayes doo weave,
     In one short houre I find by her undonne.
     So when I thinke to end that° I begonne,   *that which*
10   I must begin and never bring to end:
     For with one looke she spils° that long I sponne,   *destroys*
     And with one word my whole years work doth rend.

6. I.e., Cupid, Roman god of erotic love.
7. This sonnet is a blazon, a series of comparisons or depictions cataloging the lady's parts.
8. Fully occupied with trading (this is the O.E.D.'s first recorded usage of the word).
9. The East and West Indies.
1. Beautiful; or, possibly, may be read as an imper-

ative, i.e., "think her forehead ivory."
2. During the long absence of her husband, Odysseus, Penelope warded off her suitors by saying she would choose one of them as soon as she finished weaving a shroud. Each night for three years she undid her day's work (Homer, *Odyssey* 2).
3. I.e., she shuns his desire's pleading.

Such labour like the Spyders web I fynd,
Whose fruitlesse worke is broken with least wynd.

Sonnet 54

Of this worlds Theatre in which we stay,
My love lyke the Spectàtor ydly sits
Beholding me that all the pageants° play,   *roles*
Disguysing diversly my troubled wits.
5 Sometimes I joy when glad occasion fits,
And mask[4] in myrth lyke to a Comedy:
Soone after when my joy to sorrow flits,
I waile and make my woes a Tragedy.
Yet she beholding me with constant eye,
10 Delights not in my merth nor rues° my smart:°   *pities / hurt*
But when I laugh she mocks, and when I cry
She laughes, and hardens evermore her hart.°   *heart*
What then can move her? if nor merth nor mone,°   *moan*
She is no woman, but a sencelesse stone.

Sonnet 67[5]

Lyke as a huntsman after weary chace,
Seeing the game from him escapt away,
Sits downe to rest him in some shady place,
With panting hounds beguilèd of their pray:
5 So after long pursuit and vaine assay,°   *attempt*
When I all weary had the chace forsooke,
The gentle deare[6] returnd the selfe-same way,
Thinking to quench her thirst at the next brooke.
There she beholding me with mylder looke,
10 Sought not to fly, but fearelesse still did bide:
Till I in hand her yet halfe trembling tooke,
And with her owne goodwill hir fyrmely tyde.
Strange thing me seemd[7] to see a beast so wyld,
So goodly wonne with her owne will beguyld.

Sonnet 68

Most glorious Lord of lyfe that on this day,[8]
Didst make thy triumph over death and sin:

---

4. Cover (or mask) his emotions; also, act in a masque, a short, allegorical drama.
5. An imitation of Petrarch's *Rime* 190, although with a dissimilar ending. Cf. Thomas Wyatt, "Whoso List to Hunt" (p. 126).
6. With a pun on *deer* and *dear* (beloved).
7. I.e., it seemed to me.
8. Easter.

And having harrowd hell[9] didst bring away
Captivity thence captive us to win:[1]
5   This joyous day, deare Lord, with joy begin,
And grant that we for whom thou diddest dye
Being with thy deare blood clene washt from sin,
May live for ever in felicity.
And that thy love we weighing worthily,
10   May likewise love thee for the same againe:[2]
And for thy sake that all lyke deare[3] didst buy,
With love may one another entertayne.
So let us love, deare love, lyke as we ought,
Love is the lesson which the Lord us taught.[4]

Sonnet 70

Fresh spring the herald of loves mighty king,
In whose cote° armour° richly are displayd   *coat / of arms*
All sorts of flowers the which on earth do spring
In goodly colours gloriously arrayd:
5   Goe to my love, where she is carelesse layd,
Yet in her winters bowre not well awake:
Tell her the joyous time wil not be staid°   *detained*
Unless she doe him by the forelock take.[5]
Bid her therefore her selfe soone ready make,
10   To wayt on love[6] amongst his lovely crew:
Where every one that misseth then her make,°   *mate*
Shall be by him amearst° with penance dew.   *punished*
Make hast therefore sweet love,[7] whilest it is prime,°   *spring*
For none can call againe the passèd time.

Sonnet 71

I joy to see how in your drawen work,[8]
Your selfe unto the Bee ye doe compare;
And me unto the Spyder that doth lurke,
In close° away° to catch her unaware.   *secret / ambush*
5   Right so your selfe were caught in cunning snare
Of a deare foe, and thralled° to his love: *enslaved*
In whose streight° bands ye now captived are   *tight*
So firmly, that ye never may remove.

9. A reference to the apocryphal account of Christ's descent into hell, after his Crucifixion, to rescue the captive souls of the just.
1. "When he ascended up on high, he led captivity captive" (Ephesians 4.8).
2. I.e., grant also that we, weighing thy love rightly, might love thee in the same way.
3. I.e., at the same cost.
4. "This is my commandment, That ye love one another, as I have loved you" (John 15.12).

5. "To take time by the forelock" is to act promptly.
6. I.e., to attend and serve Cupid.
7. The addressee of the poem changes here from Spring, as the herald of love, to the loved one herself.
8. Ornamental work done in textile fabrics by drawing out some of the threads so as to form patterns.

But as your worke is woven all about,
10   With woodbynd° flowers and fragrant   *honeysuckle*
       Enlantine:°   *sweetbriar*
    So sweet your prison you in time shall prove,°   *find*
    With many deare delights bedecked fyne.
    And all thensforth eternall peace shall see
    Betweene the Spyder and the gentle Bee

Sonnet 75

    One day I wrote her name upon the strand,°   *shore*
    But came the waves and washèd it away:
    Agayne I wrote it with° a second hand,°   *for / time*
    But came the tyde, and made my paynes his pray.°   *prey*
5   Vayne man, sayd she, that doest in vaine assay,°   *attempt*
    A mortall thing so to immortalize,
    For I my selve shall lyke to this decay,
    And eek° my name bee wypèd out lykewize.   *also*
    Not so, (quod° I) let baser things devize°   *quoth / plan*
10 To dy in dust, but you shall live by fame:
    My verse your vertues rare shall eternize,
    And in the hevens wryte your glorious name.
    Where whenas death shall all the world subdew,
    Our love shall live, and later life renew.

Sonnet 79

    Men call you fayre, and you doe credit° it,   *believe*
    For that your selfe ye dayly such doe see:
    But the trew fayre,° that is the gentle wit,   *beauty*
    And vertuous mind, is much more praysd of me.
5   For all the rest, how ever fayre it be,
    Shall turne to nought and loose that glorious hew:°   *form*
    But onely that is permanent and free
    From frayle corruption, that doth flesh ensew.°   *attend*
    That is true beautie: that doth argue you
10 To be divine and borne of heavenly seed:
    Deriv'd from that fayre Spirit,[9] from whom al true
    And perfect beauty did at first proceed.
    He onely fayre, and what he fayre hath made,
    All other fayre lyke flowres untymely fade.

Sonnet 81

    Fayre is my love, when her fayre golden heares,°   *hairs*
    With the loose wynd ye waving chance to marke:°   *notice*

9. I.e., God, the "he" of line 13.

Fayre when the rose in her red cheekes appeares,
Or in her eyes the fyre of love does sparke.
5   Fayre when her brest lyke a rich laden barke,
With pretious merchandize she forth doth lay:
Fayre when that cloud of pryde, which oft doth dark
Her goodly light with smiles she drives away.
But fayrest she, when so she doth display
10 The gate with pearles and rubyes richly dight:°   adorned
Throgh which her words so wise do make their way
To beare the message of her gentle spright.°   spirit
The rest be works of natures wonderment,
But this the worke of harts° astonishment.   heart's

Sonnet 89

Lyke as the Culver[1] on the barèd bough,
Sits mourning for the absence of her mate:
And in her songs sends many a wishfull vow,
For his returne that seemes to linger late,
5   So I alone now left disconsolate,
Mourne to my selfe the absence of my love:
And wandring here and there all desolate,
Seek with my playnts° to match that mournful   laments, complaints
        dove:
Ne joy of ought that under heaven doth hove,°   abide
10 Can comfort me, but her owne joyous sight:
Whose sweet aspèct both God and man can move,
In her unspotted pleasauns[2] to delight.
Dark is my day, whyles her fayre light I mis,
And dead my life that wants such lively blis.

                                                           1595

Epithalamion[1]

Ye learnèd sisters[2] which have oftentimes
Beene to me ayding, others to adorne:
Whom ye thought worthy of your gracefull[3] rymes,

1. Dove; a bird associated with fidelity, peace, and the Holy Spirit.
2. Charm or pleasing manners; also, a garden's pleasure area; cf. Song of Solomon 4.12, in which the bride is compared to an enclosed garden.
1. Meaning a wedding song or poem; its Greek name conveys that it was sung on the threshold of the bridal chamber. The genre, practiced by the Latin poets, characteristically includes the invocation to the Muses (the nine sister goddesses believed to be sources of inspiration for the arts), the bringing home of the bride, the singing and dancing at the wedding party, and the preparations for the wedding night.
  Published with the *Amoretti,* Spenser's *Epithalamion* has a uniquely complex structure. The cen-

tral section on the church ceremony (lines 185–222) is flanked by two symmetrical ten-stanza sections, each divided into units of three-four-three. The poem's structure reinforces the theme of time, with exactly 365 long lines, matching the number of days in the year, and twenty-four stanzas (including the envoy), matching the number of hours in one day. The first sixteen stanzas describe the day, making "night . . . come" (line 300) after sixteen and one-quarter stanzas: contemporary almanacs indicate sixteen and one-quarter hours of daylight in southern Ireland on June 11, 1594, the day Spenser was married.
2. The Muses.
3. Graceful; also, conferring grace.

That even the greatest did not greatly scorne
5   To heare theyr names sung in your simple layes,°   *songs*
But joyèd in theyr prayse.
And when ye list° your owne mishaps to mourne,   *desire*
Which death, or love, or fortunes wreck did rayse,
Your string could soone to sadder tenor° turne,   *mood*
10   And teach the woods and waters to lament
Your dolefull dreriment.°   *sadness*
Now lay those sorrowfull complaints aside,
And having all your heads with girland° crownd,   *garland*
Helpe me mine owne loves prayses to resound,
15   Ne let the same of° any be envìde: *by*
So Orpheus⁴ did for his owne bride,
So I unto my selfe alone will sing,
The woods shall to me answer and my Eccho ring.

Early before the worlds light giving lampe,⁵
20   His golden beame upon the hils doth spred,
Having disperst the nights unchearefull dampe,
Doe ye awake, and with fresh lusty hed,°   *cheerfulness*
Go to the bowre° of my belovèd love,   *bedchamber*
My truest turtle dove,
25   Bid her awake; for Hymen⁶ is awake,
And long since ready forth his maske to move,
With his bright Tead that flames with many a flake,°   *spark*
And many a bachelor to waite on him,
In theyr fresh garments trim.
30   Bid her awake therefore and soone her dight,°   *dress*
For lo the wishèd day is come at last,
That shall for al the paynes and sorrowes past,
Pay to her usury° of long delight: *interest*
And whylest she doth her dight,°   *dress*
35   Doe ye to her of joy and solace° sing,   *pleasure*
That all the woods may answer and your eccho ring.

Bring with you all the Nymphes that you can heare⁷
Both of the rivers and the forrests greene:
And of the sea that neighbours to her neare,
40   Al with gay girlands° goodly wel beseene.°   *garlands / beautified*
And let them also with them bring in hand
Another gay girland
For my fayre love of lillyes and of roses,
Bound truelove wize⁸ with a blew silke riband.
45   And let them make great store of bridale poses,°   *posies*
And let them eeke° bring store of other flowers   *also*
To deck the bridale bowers.

---

4. Son of the Muse Calliope, he was a figure of the poet in classical antiquity; his music was said to charm wild animals and to make stones and trees move. According to one tradition, he won his wife, Euridyce, with music. However, he failed to free her from the underworld after her death because he looked back at her on the journey out.
5. I.e., the sun.

6. The Greek god of the wedding feast, represented as a young man bearing a torch ("Tead," line 27) and leading a "maske" (line 26), or procession.
7. I.e., that can hear you. *Nymphes:* nymphs; mythological female spirits inhabiting a particular place, object, or natural phenomenon.
8. I.e., in the manner of true love.

And let the ground whereas° her foot shall tread, °*whereon*
For feare the stones her tender foot should wrong
50 Be strewed with fragrant flowers all along,
And diapred lyke the discolored mead.[9]
Which done, doe at her chamber dore awayt,
For she will waken strayt,° °*straightway*
The whiles doe ye this song unto her sing,
55 The woods shall to you answer and your Eccho ring.

Ye Nymphes of Mulla° which with carefull heed, °*an Irish river*
The silver scaly trouts doe tend full well,
And greedy pikes which use therein to feed,
(Those trouts and pikes all others doo excell)
60 And ye likewise which keepe the rushy lake,
Where none doo fishes take,
Bynd up the locks[1] the which hang scatterd light,
And in his waters which your mirror make,
Behold your faces as the christall bright,
65 That when you come whereas my love doth lie,
No blemish she may spie.
And eke° ye lightfoot mayds which keepe the deere, °*also*
That on the hoary mountayne use to towre,[2]
And the wylde wolves which seeke them to devoure,
70 With your steele darts doo chace from comming neer,
Be also present heere,
To helpe to decke her and to help to sing,
That all the woods may answer and your eccho ring.

Wake, now my love, awake; for it is time,
75 The Rosy Morne long since left Tithones bed,[3]
All ready to her silver coche° to clyme, °*coach*
And Phoebus[4] gins to shew his glorious hed.
Hark how the cheerefull birds do chaunt theyr laies° °*songs*
And carroll of loves praise.[5]
80 The merry Larke hir mattins° sings aloft, °*morning prayers*
The thrush replyes, the Mavis descant° playes, °*melodic counterpart*
The Ouzell shrills, the Ruddock warbles soft,
So goodly all agree with sweet consent,
To this dayes merriment.
85 Ah my deere love why doe ye sleepe thus long,
When meeter° were that ye should now awake, °*more appropriate*
T' awayt the comming of your joyous make,° °*mate*
And hearken to the birds lovelearnèd song,
The deawy leaves among.
90 For they of joy and pleasance to you sing,
That all the woods them answer and theyr eccho ring.

9. And variegated like the many-colored meadow.
1. I.e., the rushes.
2. A hawking term meaning "to climb high." *Light-foot mayds:* i.e., the nymphs.
3. The dawn, personified in mythology as the goddess Eos, or Aurora, was married to Tithonus, a mortal Trojan prince who aged while his wife stayed young.
4. Phoebus Apollo, the Greek sun god.
5. The birds' concert (following lines) is a convention of love poetry. The lark (a songbird) was associated with dawn. The mavis (song thrush), the ouzell (European blackbird), and the ruddock (robin) are all varieties of thrush.

My love is now awake out of her dreames,
And her fayre eyes like stars that dimmèd were
With darksome cloud, now shew theyr goodly beams
95 More bright then° Hesperus[6] his head doth rere.   *than*
Come now ye damzels, daughters of delight,
Helpe quickly her to dight,
But first come ye fayre houres[7] which were begot
In Joves sweet paradice, of Day and Night,
100 Which doe the seasons of the yeare allot,
And al that ever in this world is fayre
Doe make and still° repayre.   *continually*
And ye three handmayds of the Cyprian Queene,[8]
The which doe still adorne her beauties pride,
105 Helpe to addorne my beautifullest bride:
And as ye her array,° still throw betweene°   *dress / at intervals*
Some graces to be seene,
And as ye use to Venus, to her sing,[9]
The whiles the woods shal answer and your eccho ring.

110 Now is my love all ready forth to come,
Let all the virgins therefore well awayt,
And ye fresh boyes that tend upon her groome[1]
Prepare your selves; for he is comming strayt.°   *straightaway*
Set all your things in seemly good aray°   *order*
115 Fit for so joyfull day,
The joyfulst day that ever sunne did see.
Faire Sun, shew forth thy favourable ray,
And let thy lifull° heat not fervent be   *life-giving*
For feare of burning her sunshyny face,
120 Her beauty to disgrace.°   *spoil*
O fayrest Phoebus, father of the Muse,[2]
If ever I did honour thee aright,
Or sing the thing, that mote° thy mind delight,   *might*
Doe not thy servants simple boone° refuse,   *request*
125 But let this day let this one day be myne,
Let all the rest be thine.
Then I thy soverayne prayses loud wil sing,
That all the woods shal answer and theyr eccho ring.

Harke how the Minstrels gin to shrill aloud
130 Their merry Musick that resounds from far,
The pipe,° the tabor,° and the trembling Croud,[3]   *bagpipe / drum*
That well agree withouten breach or jar.°   *discord*
But most of all the Damzels doe delite,
When they their tymbrels° smyte,°   *tambourines / hit*
135 And thereunto doe daunce and carrol sweet,

6. The evening or morning star, sacred to Venus, Roman goddess of love and beauty.
7. The Horae, or Hours, were three daughters of Jove (ruler of the gods), commonly associated with the seasons and the principle of order.
8. Venus, whose handmaids were the three Graces: Aglaia, Thalia, and Euphrosyne. Their names mean "the brilliant one," "she who brings flowers," and "she who rejoices the heart."
9. I.e., as you are accustomed to sing to Venus, so sing to my bride.
1. Her bridegroom, i.e., the speaker of the poem.
2. Usually, Zeus (Jove) was considered father of the Muses; in contrast, Spenser names Phoebus as their father.
3. Primitive fiddle.

That all the sences they doe ravish quite,
The whyles the boyes run up and downe the street,
Crying aloud with strong confusèd noyce,
As if it were one voyce.
140   Hymen iô Hymen, Hymen[4] they do shout,
That even to the heavens theyr shouting shrill
Doth reach, and all the firmament doth fill,
To which the people standing all about,
As in approvance doe thereto applaud
145   And loud advaunce her laud,°   *praise*
And evermore they Hymen Hymen sing,
That al the woods them answer and theyr eccho ring.

Loe where she comes along with portly° pace,   *stately*
Lyke Phoebe[5] from her chamber of the East,
150   Arysing forth to run her mighty race,
Clad all in white, that seemes° a virgin best.   *befits*
So well it her beseemes that ye would weene°   *think*
Some angell she had beene.
Her long loose yellow locks lyke golden wyre,
155   Sprinckled with perle, and perling° flowres a tweene,   *winding*
Doe lyke a golden mantle her attyre,
And being crownèd with a girland° greene,   *garland*
Seeme lyke some mayden Queene.
Her modest eyes abashèd to behold
160   So many gazers, as on her do stare,
Upon the lowly ground affixèd are.
Ne dare lift up her countenance too bold,
But blush to heare her prayses sung so loud,
So farre from being proud.
165   Nathlesse° doe ye still loud her prayses sing,   *nevertheless*
That all the woods may answer and your eccho ring.

Tell me ye merchants daughters did ye see
So fayre a creature in your towne before?
So sweet, so lovely, and so mild as she,
170   Adornd with beautyes grace and vertues store,°   *wealth*
Her goodly eyes lyke Saphyres shining bright,
Her forehead yvory white,
Her cheekes lyke apples which the sun hath rudded,
Her lips lyke cherryes charming men to byte,
175   Her brest like to a bowle of creame uncrudded,°   *uncurdled*
Her paps lyke lyllies budded,
Her snowie necke lyke to a marble towre,
And all her body lyke a pallace fayre,
Ascending uppe with many a stately stayre,
180   To honors seat and chastities sweet bowre.[6]

4. Ritual exclamation at weddings in antiquity (see note 6, p. 196).
5. Another name for the virgin moon goddess, Diana, and thus an anticipation of night's coming. Phoebe was associated with chastity, a concept that Protestants defined as belonging not only to virgins but also to faithful wives.
6. The head, seat of reason. The catalog, or blazon, of the beloved's beauties harks back to the biblical Song of Solomon (4–8) and was a convention of love poetry.

Why stand ye still ye virgins in amaze,
Upon her so to gaze,
Whiles ye forget your former lay to sing,
To which the woods did answer and your eccho ring?

185 But if ye saw that which no eyes can see,
The inward beauty of her lively spright,°   *spirit*
Garnisht with heavenly guifts° of high degree,   *gifts*
Much more then would ye wonder at that sight,
And stand astonisht lyke to those which red°   *saw*
190 Medusaes mazeful hed.[7]
There dwels sweet love and constant chastity,
Unspotted fayth and comely womanhed,
Regard of honour and mild modesty,
There Vertue raynes as Queene in royal throne,
195 And giveth lawes alone.
The which the base° affections° doe obay,   *lowly / emotions*
And yeeld theyr services unto her will,
Ne thought of thing uncomely ever may
Thereto approch to tempt her mind to ill.
200 Had ye once seene these her celestial threasures,
And unrevealèd pleasures,
Then would ye wonder and her prayses sing,
That al the woods should answer and your echo ring.

Open the temple gates unto my love,
205 Open them wide that she may enter in,
And all the postes adorne as doth behove,[8]
And all the pillours deck with girlands° trim,   *garlands*
For to recyve this Saynt with honour dew,
That commeth in to you.
210 With trembling steps and humble reverence,
She commeth in, before th' almighties vew:
Of her ye virgins learne obedience,
When so ye come into those holy places,
To humble your proud faces;
215 Bring her up to th' high altar that she may,
The sacred ceremonies there partake,
The which do endlesse matrimony make,
And let the roring Organs loudly play
The praises of the Lord in lively notes,
220 The whiles with hollow throates
The Choristers the joyous Antheme sing,
That al the woods may answere and their eccho ring.

Behold whiles she before the altar stands
Hearing the holy priest that to her speakes
225 And blesseth her with his two happy hands,
How the red roses flush up in her cheekes,

7. In Greek mythology, the Gorgon Medusa had
serpents for hair; whoever looked upon her was
turned to stone. She was sometimes associated
with chastity.
8. I.e., as is fitting.

And the pure snow with goodly vermill° stayne,   *scarlet*
Like crimsin dyde in grayne,⁹
That even th' Angels which continually,
230   About the sacred Altare doe remaine,
Forget their service and about her fly,
Ofte peeping in her face that seemes more fayre,
The more they on it stare.
But her sad° eyes still fastened on the ground,   *sober*
235   Are governèd with goodly modesty,
That suffers not one looke to glaunce awry,
Which may let in a little thought unsownd.°   *unsound*
Why blush ye love to give to me your hand,
The pledge of all our band?°   *bond*
240   Sing ye sweet Angels, Alleluya sing,
That all the woods may answere and your eccho ring.

Now al is done; bring home the bride againe,
Bring home the triumph of our victory,
Bring home with you the glory of her gaine,¹
245   With joyance bring her and with jollity.
Never had man more joyfull day then this,
Whom heaven would heape with blis.
Make feast therefore now all this live long day,
This day for ever to me holy is,
250   Poure out the wine without restraint or stay,
Poure not by cups, but by the belly full,
Poure out to all that wull,°   *will*
And sprinkle all the postes and wals with wine,
That they may sweat, and drunken be withall.
255   Crowne ye God Bacchus² with a coronall,°   *garland*
And Hymen also crowne with wreathes of vine,
And let the Graces daunce unto the rest;
For they can doo it best:
The whiles the maydens doe theyr carroll sing,
260   To which the woods shal answer and theyr eccho ring.

Ring ye the bels, ye yong men of the towne,
And leave your wonted° labors for this day: *usual*
This day is holy; doe ye write it downe,
That ye for ever it remember may.
265   This day the sunne is in his chiefest hight,
With Barnaby the bright,³
From whence declining daily by degrees,
He somewhat loseth of his heat and light,
When once the Crab⁴ behind his back he sees.
270   But for this time it ill ordainèd was,
To chose the longest day in all the yeare,
And shortest night, when longest fitter weare:

9. I.e., dyed with colorfast dye.
1. I.e., of gaining her.
2. Roman god of wine and ecstasy.
3. St. Barnabas's Day (June 11) was also the day
of the summer solstice (the longest day of the year)
in the calendar used during Spenser's time.
4. Cancer the Crab, the fourth constellation in the
zodiac, through which the sun passes in July.

Yet never day so long, but late° would passe.   *finally*
Ring ye the bels, to make it weare away,
275 And bonefiers° make all day,   *bonfires*
And daunce about them, and about them sing:
That all the woods may answer, and your eccho ring.

Ah when will this long weary day have end,
And lende me leave to come unto my love?
280 How slowly do the houres theyr numbers spend?
How slowly does sad Time his feathers move?
Hast° thee O fayrest Planet to thy home[5]   *haste*
Within the Westerne fome:
Thy tyred steedes long since have need of rest.
285 Long though it be, at last I see it gloome,
And the bright evening star with golden creast°   *crest*
Appeare out of the East.
Fayre childe of beauty, glorious lampe of love
That all the host of heaven in rankes doost lead,
290 And guydest lovers through the nights dread,
How chearefully thou lookest from above,
And seemst to laugh atweene thy twinkling light
As joying in the sight
Of these glad many which for joy doe sing,
295 That all the woods them answer and their echo ring.

Now ceasse ye damsels[6] your delights forepast;
Enough is it, that all the day was youres:
Now day is doen, and night is nighing fast:
Now bring the Bryde into the brydall boures.°   *bowers, chambers*
300 Now night is come,[7] now soone her disaray,°   *undress*
And in her bed her lay;
Lay her in lillies and in violets,
And silken courteins° over her display,   *curtains*
And odourd° sheetes, and Arras[8] coverlets.   *perfumed*
305 Behold how goodly my faire love does ly
In proud humility;
Like unto Maia,[9] when as Jove her tooke,
In Tempe, lying on the flowry gras,
Twixt sleepe and wake, after she weary was,
310 With bathing in the Acidalian brooke.
Now it is night, ye damsels may be gon,
And leave my love alone,
And leave likewise your former lay to sing:
The woods no more shal answere, nor your echo ring.

---

5. The sun, drawn in its chariot (by "tyred stee-
des," line 284); in Ptolemaic astronomy, still often
accepted in Spenser's time, the sun was one of the
planets, which revolved about Earth.
6. I.e., all the aforementioned nymphs and spirits.
7. On the placement of this phrase, see the end of
note 1, p. 195.
8. A northeastern French city famous for its tap-
estries.

9. Said to be the most beautiful and modest of the
Pleiades, who were, in Greek mythology, the seven
daughters of Atlas and the Oceanid Pleione; Maia
was the mother of the god Hermes (and Jove was
his father, though Jove's encounter with Maia did
not traditionally take place in the Vale of Tempe,
in Thessaly). The "Acidalian brooke" (line 310) is
associated with Venus.

315   Now welcome night, thou night so long expected,°   *awaited*
      That long daies labour doest at last defray,°   *pay for*
      And all my cares, which cruell love collected,
      Hast sumd in one, and cancellèd for aye:
      Spread thy broad wing over my love and me,
320   That no man may us see,
      And in thy sable mantle us enwrap,
      From feare of perrill and foule horror free.
      Let no false treason seeke us to entrap,
      Nor any dread disquiet once annoy
325   The safety of our joy:
      But let the night be calme and quietsome,
      Without tempestuous storms or sad° afray:°   *dark / terror*
      Lyke as when Jove with fayre Alcmena[1] lay,
      When he begot the great Tirynthian groome:
330   Or lyke as when he with thy selfe did lie,
      And begot Majesty.[2]
      And let the mayds and yongmen cease to sing:
      Ne let the woods them answer, nor theyr eccho ring.

      Let no lamenting cryes, nor dolefull teares,
335   Be heard all night within nor yet without:
      Ne let false whispers breeding hidden feares,
      Breake gentle sleepe with misconceivèd dout.°   *fear*
      Let no deluding dreames, nor dreadful sights
      Make sudden sad affrights;
340   Ne let housefyres, nor lightnings helpelesse harmes,
      Ne let the Pouke,[3] nor other evill sprights,
      Ne let mischìvous witches with theyr charmes,
      Ne let hob Goblins, names whose sence we see not,
      Fray° us with things that be not.   *frighten*
345   Let not the shriech Oule, nor the Storke be heard:
      Nor the night Raven[4] that still° deadly yels,   *continually*
      Nor damnèd ghosts cald up with mighty spels,
      Nor griesly vultures make us once affeard:
      Ne let th' unpleasant Quyre of Frogs still croking
350   Make us to wish theyr choking.
      Let none of these theyr drery accents sing;
      Ne let the woods them answer, nor theyr eccho ring.

      But let stil Silence trew night watches keepe,
      That sacred peace may in assurance rayne,
355   And tymely sleep, when it is tyme to sleepe,
      May poure his limbs forth on your pleasant playne,°   *plain*
      The whiles an hundred little wingèd loves,°   *cupids (or amoretti)*

---

1. According to several versions of the story, Jove ordered the sun not to shine to make the night longer; the "Tirynthian groome" conceived by Alcmena was Heracles.
2. Spenser invents this myth of Night's creation. Ovid identifies Night's parents as Honor and Reverence (*Fasti* 5.23).

3. Puck, also called Hobgoblin; a small supernatural creature popular in English folklore and a character in Shakespeare's *A Midsummer Night's Dream*.
4. The night raven and the owl were birds of ill omen; the stork was sometimes figured as an avenger of adultery.

Like divers fethered doves,
Shall fly and flutter round about your bed,
360   And in the secret darke, that none reproves,
Their prety stealthes shal worke, and snares shal spread
To filch away sweet snatches of delight,
Conceald through covert night.
Ye sonnes of Venus, play your sports at will,
365   For greedy pleasure, carelesse of your toyes,°   *amorous sports*
Thinks more upon her paradise of joyes,
Then° what ye do, albe it good or ill.   *than*
All night therefore attend your merry play,
For it will soone be day:
370   Now none doth hinder you, that say or sing,
Ne will the woods now answer, nor your Eccho ring.

Who is the same, which at my window peepes?
Or whose is that faire face, that shines so bright,
Is it not Cinthia,[5] she that never sleepes,
375   But walkes about high heaven al the night?
O fayrest goddesse, do thou not envỳ
My love with me to spy:
For thou likewise didst love, though now unthought,[6]
And for a fleece of woll,° which privily,   *wool*
380   The Latmian shephard once unto thee brought,
His pleasures with thee wrought.
Therefore to us be favorable now;
And sith° of wemens labours thou hast charge,   *since*
And generation goodly dost enlarge,
385   Encline thy will t' effect our wishfull vow,
And the chast wombe informe with timely seed,
That may our comfort breed:
Till which we cease our hopefull° hap° to sing,   *hoped for / fate*
Ne let the woods us answere, nor our Eccho ring.

390   And thou great Juno,[7] which with awful° might   *awe-inspiring*
The lawes of wedlock still dost patronize,
And the religion° of the faith first plight   *sanctity*
With sacred rites hast taught to solemnize:[8]
And eeke for comfort often callèd art
395   Of women in their smart,°   *pains of childbirth*
Eternally bind thou this lovely° band,°   *loving / bond*
And all thy blessings unto us impart.
And thou glad Genius,[9] in whose gentle hand,
The bridale bowre and geniall° bed remaine,   *marriage*

5. Another name for Diana, the moon goddess, who was associated with chastity and also with Queen Elizabeth; see also "Phoebe," line 149 and note 5 there.
6. Not thought of. According to some versions of the story, Cynthia and Endymion, the "Latmian shephard" (line 380), made love on Mt. Latmos, after he brought her a fleece. In revenge, Zeus made Endymion sleep eternally.

7. Roman goddess of marriage and childbirth.
8. I.e., with the marriage vows.
9. A spirit presiding over generation. By invoking both Juno and Genius as patrons of the marriage bed, Spenser draws also on the belief that each individual is watched over from birth by a tutelary spirit called a "Juno" (for girls) or a "Genius" (for boys).

400 Without blemish or staine,
     And the sweet pleasures of theyr loves delight
     With secret ayde doest succour and supply,
     Till they bring forth the fruitfull progeny,
     Send us the timely fruit of this same night.
405 And thou fayre Hebe,[1] and thou Hymen free,
     Grant that it may so be.
     Til which we cease your further prayse to sing,
     Ne any woods shal answer, nor your Eccho ring.

     And ye high heavens, the temple of the gods,
410 In which a thousand torches flaming bright
     Doe burne, that to us wretched earthly clods,
     In dreadful darknesse lend desirèd light;
     And all ye powers which in the same remayne,
     More then we men can fayne,°   *imagine*
415 Poure out your blessing on us plentiously,
     And happy influence upon us raine,
     That we may raise a large posterity,
     Which from the earth, which they may long possesse,
     With lasting happinesse,
420 Up to your haughty pallaces may mount,
     And for the guerdon° of theyr glorious merit   *reward*
     May heavenly tabernacles there inherit,
     Of blessed Saints for to increase the count.
     So let us rest, sweet love, in hope of this,
425 And cease till then our tymely joyes to sing,
     The woods no more us answer, nor our eccho ring.

     Song made in lieu of many ornaments,[2]
     With which my love should duly have bene dect,°   *adorned*
     Which cutting off through hasty accidents,
430 Ye would not stay your dew time to expect,[3]
     But promist both to recompens,[4]
     Be unto her a goodly ornament,
     And for short time an endlesse moniment.

                                                                   1595

---

1. Daughter of Juno and goddess of youth.
2. These last seven lines are the poem's envoy, a traditional concluding verse paragraph in which the poet addresses and bids farewell to the work of art ("song") just completed. Spenser's envoy is full of puns and syntactical complexities expressing the poet's mingled attitudes of humility, impatience, and pride in his achievement of creating an "ornament" that is also a permanent monument for swiftly passing time.
3. Two possible readings: the thing being prematurely ended ("cut off") through sudden or rushed ("hasty") events or contingencies ("accidents") may be the poem itself, ended before it was really ready

to be born ("Ye would not stay" [remain] to "expect" [await] your due time); or these lines may describe the other ornaments or wedding gifts for which this poem is modestly said to substitute, i.e., those other gifts didn't arrive in time for the bride to deck herself out in them appropriately ("duly," line 428—but that adverb, like the adjective "dew," has multiple meanings).
4. For the fault of a premature "cutting off," the poet offers the "recompense" of the song; the referents of "both" are open to interpretation; possibly, the poet is seeking to fulfill a promise or repay a debt both to his bride and to time.

FULKE GREVILLE, LORD BROOKE
1554–1628

FROM CAELICA[1]

4

You little stars that live in skies
And glory in Apollo's[2] glory,
In whose aspècts conjoinèd lies
The heaven's will and nature's story,[3]
5   Joy to be likened to those eyes,[4]
Which eyes make all eyes glad or sorry;
   For when you force thoughts from above,
   These overrule your force by love.

And thou, O Love, which in these eyes
10   Hast married Reason with Affection,
And made them saints of Beauty's skies,
Where joys are shadows of perfection,
Lend me thy wings that I may rise
Up, not by worth, but thy election;[5]
15   For I have vowed in strangest fashion
   To love and never seek compassion.

ca. 1580   1633

39

The nurse-life° wheat within his green husk growing,   *life-fostering*
Flatters our hope, and tickles our desire,
Nature's true riches in sweet beauties showing,
Which set all hearts, with labor's love, on fire.

5   No less fair is the wheat when golden ear
Shows unto hope the joys of near enjoying;
Fair and sweet is the bud, more sweet and fair
The rose, which proves that time is not destroying.

Caelica, your youth, the morning of delight,
10   Enamel'd o'er with beauties white and red,
All sense and thoughts did to belief invite,

1. Heavenly (Latin). The title of Greville's poetic sequence refers to one of three ladies he addresses in the poems; the others are Cynthia and Myra. Heavily influenced by Sidney's *Astrophil and Stella* (see p. 213), the 110 poems in the first edition of *Caelica* treat religious and political themes as well as erotic ones.
2. Greek and Roman god of the sun; here, the sun itself.
3. As in astrology. The "aspect" of a star or planet was its position in the sky from an observation point on Earth. When two heavenly bodies occupied approximately the same position, their aspects were said to be "conjoined" or "in conjunction," a circumstance thought to exert a powerful influence ("the heaven's will") on mundane affairs ("nature's story").
4. I.e., the stars.
5. Calvinist theology held that salvation depended not on human merit but on "election" by God.

That love and glory there are brought to bed;
    And your ripe year's love-noon; he goes no higher,[6]
    Turns all the spirits of man into desire.

ca. 1580–1600   1633

JOHN LYLY
1554–1606

Cupid and My Campaspe[1]

Cupid and my Campaspe played
At cards for kisses; Cupid paid.
He stakes his quiver, bow, and arrows,
His mother's doves and team of sparrows,
5   Loses them too; then down he throws
The coral of his lip, the rose
Growing on 's cheek (but none knows how),
With these the crystal of his brow,
And then the dimple of his chin:
10   All these did my Campaspe win.
At last he set her both his eyes;
She won, and Cupid blind did rise.
    Oh Love! has she done this to thee?
    What shall (alas) become of me?

1632

Oh, For a Bowl of Fat Canary[2]

Oh, for a bowl of fat Canary,
Rich Palermo, sparkling Sherry,
Some nectar else, from Juno's dairy;[3]
Oh, these draughts would make us merry!

5   Oh, for a wench (I deal in faces,
And in other daintier things);
Tickled am I with her embraces,
Fine dancing in such fairy rings.[4]

6. I.e., your year or present age is love's noon; he (the morning sun) goes no higher.
1. This song appears in act 3, scene 5 of Lyly's play *Campaspe* (published in 1584), which tells the story of Alexander the Great's love for his Theban captive, Campaspe. Sung by Apelles, the painter who falls in love with Campaspe while painting her portrait, the song expresses his erotic frustration. *Cupid:* Roman god of erotic love; son of Venus, goddess of love and beauty.
2. Also from *Campaspe* (see note 1 above). In act 1, scene 2, three servant boys (Granichus, Psyllus, and Manes) sing this song as they prepare to feast at someone else's expense. Each boy sings one stanza, and all three sing the final verse. *Fat Canary:* well-bodied, light, sweet wine.
3. *Nectar:* the drink of the gods, hence coming from the "dairy" of Juno, queen of the gods in Roman mythology. *Palermo:* a wine from Palermo, in Sicily.
4. Circles of grass, differing in color from the surrounding grass; a phenomenon commonly supposed to be caused by dancing fairies.

Oh, for a plump fat leg of mutton,
10   Veal, lamb, capon, pig, and coney;[5]
None is happy but a glutton,
None an ass but who wants money.

Wines indeed and girls are good,
But brave victuals° feast the blood;   provisions, food
15   For wenches, wine, and lusty cheer,
Jove[6] would leap down to surfeit here.

1640

SIR PHILIP SIDNEY
1554–1586

Ye Goatherd Gods[1]

STREPHON.[2]   Ye goatherd gods, that love the grassy mountains,
Ye nymphs which haunt the springs in pleasant valleys,
Ye satyrs[3] joyed with free and quiet forests,
Vouchsafe your silent ears to plaining music,
5   Which to my woes gives still an early morning,
And draws the dolor on till weary evening.

KLAIUS.   O Mercury, foregoer to the evening,
O heavenly huntress[4] of the savage mountains,
O lovely star, entitled of the morning,
10   While that my voice doth fill these woeful valleys,
Vouchsafe your silent ears to plaining music,
Which oft hath Echo[5] tired in secret forests.

STREPHON.   I, that was once free burgess° of the forests,   citizen
Where shade from sun, and sport I sought in evening,
15   I, that was once esteemed for pleasant music,
Am banished now among the monstrous mountains
Of huge despair, and foul affliction's valleys,
Am grown a screech owl[6] to myself each morning.

5. Rabbit. *Capon:* a castrated rooster, especially one fattened for eating.
6. Or Jupiter, chief Roman god.
1. This poem is in the form of a double sestina, two sets of six six-line stanzas, with a triplet concluding the whole. The same six key words end the lines of each stanza; their order is always a permutation of the order in the stanza just preceding: the pattern is 6 1 5 2 4 3, i.e., the last word of line 1 of any stanza is always the same as the last word of line 6 in the preceding stanza. Line 2 ends like line 1 of the preceding stanza; line 3 like line 5; line 4 like line 2; line 5 like line 4; and line 6 like line 3. All six key words appear in the triplet in the same order as that of the first and seventh stanzas.
2. Strephon and Klaius are shepherds, both in love

with the absent Urania, in Sidney's heroic romance *Arcadia,* in which this poem appears.
3. In Greek mythology, woodland gods, usually having the head and torso of a man and the lower body of a goat; commonly associated with merriment and lust. *Nymphs:* minor nature goddesses.
4. The goddess Diana, the moon. *Mercury:* the evening star.
5. A nymph who was punished for her excessive talking by being deprived of her power of independent speech; when she fell in love with the youth Narcissus, she could express her (unrequited) feelings only by echoing his words.
6. Named for the sound of its voice and considered a bird of ill omen.

KLAIUS.   I, that was once delighted every morning,
20   Hunting the wild inhabiters of forests,
                       I, that was once the music of these valleys,
                       So darkened am that all my day is evening,
                       Heartbroken so, that molehills seem high mountains
                       And fill the vales with cries instead of music.

25 STREPHON.   Long since, alas, my deadly swannish[7] music
                       Hath made itself a crier of the morning,
                       And hath with wailing strength climbed highest
                                  mountains;
                       Long since my thoughts more desert be than forests,
                       Long since I see my joys come to their evening,
30   And state thrown down to overtrodden valleys.

KLAIUS.   Long since the happy dwellers of these valleys
                       Have prayed me leave my strange exclaiming music,
                       Which troubles their day's work and joys of evening;
                       Long since I hate the night, more hate the morning;
35   Long since my thoughts chase me like beasts in forests,
                       And make me wish myself laid under mountains.

STREPHON.   Meseems° I see the high and stately   *it seems to me*
                                  mountains
                       Transform themselves to low dejected valleys;
                       Meseems I hear in these ill-changèd forests
40   The nightingales do learn of owls their music;
                       Meseems I feel the comfort of the morning
                       Turned to the mortal serene[8] of an evening.

KLAIUS.   Meseems I see a filthy cloudy evening
                       As soon as sun begins to climb the mountains;
45   Meseems I feel a noisome° scent, the morning   *offensive*
                       When I do smell the flowers of these valleys;
                       Meseems I hear, when I do hear sweet music,
                       The dreadful cries of murdered men in forests.

STREPHON.   I wish to fire the trees of all these forests;
50   I give the sun a last farewell each evening;
                       I curse the fiddling finders-out of music;
                       With envy I do hate the lofty mountains,
                       And with despite despise the humble valleys;
                       I do detest night, evening, day, and morning.

55 KLAIUS.   Curse to myself my prayer is, the morning;
                       My fire is more than can be made with forests,
                       My state more base than are the basest valleys.
                       I wish no evenings more to see, each evening;
                       Shamèd, I hate myself in sight of mountains
60   And stop mine ears, lest I grow mad with music.

---

7. The swan was supposed to sing only just before
it died.

8. Damp evening air, thought to produce sickness
(*mortal:* deadly). The stress is on the first syllable.

STREPHON. For she whose parts maintained a perfect music,
Whose beauties shined more than the blushing
    morning,
Who much did pass[9] in state the stately mountains,
In straightness passed the cedars of the forests,
65   Hath cast me, wretch, into eternal evening
By taking her two suns[1] from these dark valleys.

KLAIUS. For she, with whom compared, the Alps are valleys,
She, whose least word brings from the spheres their
    music,[2]
At whose approach the sun rose in the evening,
70   Who where she went bare° in her forehead   bore
    morning,
Is gone, is gone, from these our spoilèd forests,
Turning to deserts our best pastured mountains.

STREPHON. These mountains witness shall, so shall these valleys,

KLAIUS. These forests eke,° made wretched by our music,   also
75   Our morning hymn this is, and song at evening.

1577–83   1593

What Length of Verse?[3]

What length of verse can serve brave° Mopsa's good to show,   splendid
Whose virtues strange, and beauties such, as no man them may
    know?
Thus shrewdly° burden, then, how can my Muse[4] escape?   severally
The gods must help, and precious things must serve to show her
    shape.

5   Like great god Saturn, fair, and like fair Venus, chaste;[5]
As smooth as Pan, as Juno mild, like goddess Iris fast.[6]

9. Surpass.
1. I.e., her eyes.
2. Music of the spheres: a popular theory during the period, based on the Pythagorean idea that the movement of the celestial bodies produced a musical harmony, inaudible to human ears.
3. This fourteen-line poem parodies the sonnet form and a number of conventions of pastoral love poetry. Written in poulter's measure (see "Versification," p. 2047), the poem occurs early in the first version of Sidney's pastoral romance, a version known now as the Old Arcadia. The poem is attributed to Alethes, whose name plays on a Greek word meaning "truth" or "sincerity"; in his verses, Alethes ironically praises "Mistress Mopsa," ugly daughter of boorish rural parents. Mopsa's qualities are associated with those of the verse itself. Although popular for much of the sixteenth century, poulter's measure is here defined as antiquated and "vulgar." For a different perspective on

the meter, see Queen Elizabeth I, "The Doubt of Future Foes Exiles My Present Joy" (p. 142).
4. Source of poetic inspiration.
5. This line initiates an inversion of classical gods' and goddesses' qualities: Saturn is ugly; Venus, unchaste; Cupid, blind; Vulcan, lame; and Momus, god of laughter and rebuke, censorious.
6. Iris is goddess of the rainbow, the ephemeral quality of which leads us to interpret the adjective spelled "faste" in several manuscripts as "fast"—meaning "steadfast"—rather than as "faced." William Ringler and several other modern editors choose "faced," and Ringler attempts to make this choice work by emending "Iris" (the reading of all manuscripts) to "Isis," an Egyptian goddess sometimes depicted as "cow-faced." But Ringler's reason for rejecting "Iris"—that she was "fast" in the sense of speedy, and hence the line so read would lose its irony—disappears if one reads "fast" as "steadfast."

With Cupid she foresees, and goes° god Vulcan's pace;   *walks with*
And for a taste of all these gifts, she borrows Momus' grace.

Her forehead jacinth-like, her cheeks of opal[7] hue,
10 Her twinkling eyes bedecked with pearl, her lips of sapphire blue,
Her hair pure crapall stone,[8] her mouth, O heavenly wide,
Her skin like burnished gold, her hands like silver ore untried.

As for those parts unknown, which hidden sure are best,
Happy be they which will believe, and never seek the rest.

ca. 1580   1593

The Nightingale[9]

The nightingale, as soon as April bringeth
Unto her rested sense a perfect waking,
While late° bare earth, proud of new clothing, springeth,   *recently*
Sings out her woes, a thorn her song-book making,
5 And mournfully bewailing,
Her throat in tunes expresseth
What grief her breast oppresseth
For Tereus' force on her chaste will prevailing.
O Philomela fair, O take some gladness,
10 That here is juster cause of plaintful sadness:
Thine earth now springs, mine fadeth;
Thy thorn without, my thorn my heart invadeth.

Alas, she hath no other cause of anguish
But Tereus' love, on her by strong hand wroken,[1]
15 Wherein she suffering, all her spirits languish;
Full womanlike complains her will was broken.
But I, who daily craving,
Cannot have to content me,
Have more cause to lament me,
20 Since wanting is more woe than too much having.
O Philomela fair, O take some gladness,
That here is juster cause of plaintful sadness:
Thine earth now springs, mine fadeth;
Thy thorn without, my thorn my heart invadeth.

ca. 1581   1598

7. Many-colored. *Jacinth-like:* yellow, reddish orange, or blue.

8. With a pun on *crap*, the line refers to *chelonitis*—according to bestiaries, a stone in the head of a frog. The stone was described as green or tortoise-shell colored.

9. Philomela, the nightingale, who sings a mournful song in the springtime. According to classical mythology, Philomela was raped by her brother-in-law, Tereus, who then tore out her tongue so that she could not reveal his crime. She wove the story in a tapestry and sent it to her sister, who rescued her. She was later changed into a nightingale while in flight from Tereus. Sidney follows the version in Ovid, *Metamorphoses* 6.424 ff.

1. Old past participle of *wreak*, "to urge or force upon."

Ring Out Your Bells

Ring out your bells, let mourning shows be spread,
For Love is dead.
All Love is dead, infected
With plague of deep disdain;
5   Worth as naught worth rejected,
And Faith fair scorn[2] doth gain.
From so ungrateful fancy,
From such a female franzy,°   *frenzy*
From them that use men thus,
10   *Good Lord, deliver us!*

Weep, neighbors, weep; do you not hear it said
That Love is dead?
His deathbed peacock's folly,[3]
His winding sheet[4] is shame,
15   His will false-seeming holy,
His sole exec'tor blame.
From so ungrateful fancy, . . .

Let dirge be sung and trentals[5] rightly read,
For Love is dead.
20   Sir Wrong his tomb ordaineth
My mistress, marble heart,
Which epitaph containeth,
"Her eyes were once his dart."
From so ungrateful fancy, . . .

25   Alas, I lie, rage hath this error bred;
Love is not dead.
Love is not dead, but sleepeth
In her unmatchèd mind,
Where she his counsel keepeth,
30   Till due desert° she find.   *reward*
Therefore from so vile fancy,
To call such wit a franzy,
Who Love can temper thus,
Good Lord, deliver us!

ca. 1581   1598

---

2. I.e., scorn from a fair lady.
3. I.e., ostentatious pride, as peacocks were a symbol of pride.
4. His shroud.

5. A series of thirty Masses for the dead, designed to mitigate the pains of purgatory; in Sidney's day, no longer accepted as a service by the Church of England.

FROM ASTROPHIL AND STELLA[6]

1

Loving in truth, and fain° in verse my love to show,   *eager*
That she dear she might take some pleasure of my pain,
Pleasure might cause her read, reading might make her know,
Knowledge might pity win, and pity grace obtain,
5   I sought fit words to paint the blackest face of woe:
Studying inventions[7] fine, her wits to entertain,
Oft turning others' leaves, to see if thence would flow
Some fresh and fruitful showers upon my sunburned brain.
But words came halting forth, wanting Invention's stay;°   *support*
10 Invention, Nature's child, fled stepdame Study's blows;
And others' feet[8] still seemed but strangers in my way.
Thus, great with child to speak, and helpless in my throes,[9]
Biting my truant pen, beating myself for spite:
"Fool," said my Muse[1] to me, "look in thy heart, and write."

14

Alas, have I not pain enough, my friend,
Upon whose breast a fiercer gripe° doth tire°   *vulture / tear*
Than did on him who first stale° down the fire,   *stole*
While Love[2] on me doth all his quiver spend,
5   But with your rhubarb° words you must contend   *cynical*
To grieve me worse, in saying that Desire
Doth plunge my well-formed soul even in the mire
Of sinful thoughts, which do in ruin end?
If that be sin which doth the manners frame,[3]
10 Well stayed° with truth in word and faith of deed,   *supported*
Ready of wit, and fearing naught but shame;
If that be sin which in fixed hearts doth breed
A loathing of all loose unchastity,
Then love is sin, and let me sinful be.

6. Starlover and Star (Latin). The first of the great Elizabethan sonnet cycles that relied heavily on the conventions developed by the Italian poet Petrarch (1304–1374), *Astrophil and Stella* has 108 sonnets and eleven songs. The sequence alludes to Sidney's ambiguous relationship with Penelope Devereux, who married Lord Robert Rich in 1581. It was circulated in manuscript form during Sidney's lifetime.
7. In art and literary composition, the devising of a subject or idea by the exercise of the intellect or imagination.
8. With a pun on the units of poetic measure (called *feet*).
9. I.e., birth-throes.
1. Source of poetic inspiration.
2. Cupid, Roman god of erotic love. *Him . . . fire:* In Greek mythology, Prometheus, for having stolen fire for man's benefit, was chained to a rock and preyed upon daily by a vulture that tore at his vitals.
3. Which builds character (*manners:* morals).

21[4]

Your words my friend (right healthful caustics[5]) blame
My young mind marred, whom Love doth windlass° so,   *ensnare*
That mine own writings like bad servants show
My wits, quick in vain thoughts, in virtue lame,
5   That Plato I read for nought, but if° he tame   *unless*
Such coltish gyres,[6] that to my birth I owe
Nobler desires, least° else that friendly foe,   *lest*
Great expectation,[7] wear a train of shame.
For since mad March great promise made of me,
10   If now the May of my years much decline,
What can be hoped my harvest time will be?
Sure you say well, your wisdom's golden mine
Dig deep with learning's spade, now tell me this,
Hath this world ought° so fair as Stella is?   *anything*

25

The wisest scholar of the wight° most wise   *creature*
By Phoebus' doom,[8] with sugared sentence says
That Virtue, if it once met with our eyes,
Strange flames of love it in our souls would raise;
5   But, for that man with pain this truth descries,[9]
While he each thing in sense's balance weighs,
And so nor will nor can behold those skies
Which inward sun to heroic mind displays,
Virtue of late, with virtuous care to stir
10   Love of herself, takes Stella's shape, that she[1]
To mortal eyes might sweetly shine in her.[2]
It is most true, for since I her did see,
Virtue's great beauty in that face I prove,°   *experience*
And find th'effect, for I do burn in love.

31

With how sad steps, Oh Moon, thou climb'st the skies,
How silently, and with how wan° a face!   *pale*
What may it be, that even in heav'nly place

4. One of several sonnets addressed to a friend—
perhaps the English poet Fulke Greville (1554–
1628; see pp. 206–07)—who takes a skeptical view
of the poet's love.
5. Medicines used for burning away diseased tis-
sue.
6. Youthful gyrations; cf. Plato, *Phaedrus* 254,
where the charioteer Reason reins in the horses of
Passion.
7. Hope of prestigious public employment and/or
recognition. *Birth*: position in society; Sidney was

the eldest son in a rich and powerful aristocratic
family.
8. Judgment. The "wight most wise" was Socrates,
so called by the oracle of Apollo (Phoebus) at Del-
phi. His "wisest scholar," or pupil, was Plato, who
(in *Phaedrus* 250D) provides the basis for lines 3–
8.
9. Discovers or perceives. *For that*: because.
1. I.e., Virtue.
2. I.e., Stella.

That busy archer[3] his sharp arrows tries?
5   Sure, if that long-with-love-acquainted eyes
Can judge of love, thou feel'st a lover's case;
I read it in thy looks: thy languished grace,
To me that feel the like, thy state descries.°   *reveals*
Then even of fellowship, Oh Moon, tell me,
10 Is constant love deemed there but want of wit?
Are beauties there as proud as here they be?
Do they above love to be loved, and yet
Those lovers scorn whom that love doth possess?
Do they call virtue there ungratefulness?[4]

39

Come sleep, Oh sleep, the certain knot of peace,
The baiting place[5] of wit, the balm of woe,
The poor man's wealth, the prisoner's release,
Th'indifferent° judge between the high and low;   *impartial*
5   With shield of proof[6] shield me from out the prease°   *press, multitude*
Of those fierce darts Despair at me doth throw;
Oh make in me[7] those civil wars to cease;
I will good tribute pay, if thou do so.
Take thou of me smooth pillows, sweetest bed,
10 A chamber deaf to noise and blind to light,
A rosy garland and a weary head;
And if these things, as being thine by right,
Move not thy heavy grace, thou shalt in me,
Livelier° than elsewhere, Stella's image see.   *more lifelike*

47

What, have I thus betrayed my liberty?
Can those black beams such burning marks[8] engrave
In my free side? or am I born a slave,
Whose neck becomes° such yoke of tyranny?   *befits*
5   Or want I sense to feel my misery?
Or sprite,° disdain of such disdain to have?   *spirit*
Who for long faith, though daily help I crave,
May get no alms but scorn of beggary.
Virtue, awake! Beauty but beauty is;
10 I may, I must, I can, I will, I do
Leave following that which it is gain to miss.
Let her go. Soft, but here she comes. Go to,
Unkind, I love you not! O me, that eye
Doth make my heart give to my tongue the lie!

3. I.e., Cupid.
4. I.e., do they give the name of virtue to ungrate-
fulness?
5. Resting place on a journey.

6. Of proven strength.
7. The speaker is offering these things to Sleep as
a tribute.
8. Brands; i.e., disdainful looks from his lover.

48

Soul's joy, bend not those morning stars° from me,   *Stella's eyes*
Where virtue is made strong by beauty's might,
Where love is chasteness, pain doth learn delight,
And humbleness grows one with majesty.
5 Whatever may ensue, O let me be
Co-partner of the riches of that sight;
Let not mine eyes be hell-driv'n° from that light;   *driven to hell*
O look, O shine, O let me die and see.
For though I oft my self of them bemoan,
10 That through my heart their beamy darts be gone,
Whose cureless wounds even now most freshly bleed,
Yet since my death wound is already got,
Dear⁹ killer, spare not thy sweet cruel shot;
A kind of grace it is to slay with speed.

49

I on my horse, and Love on me, doth try
Our horsemanships, while by strange work I prove
A horseman to my horse, a horse to Love,
And now man's wrongs in me, poor beast, descry.°   *discern*
5 The reins wherewith my rider doth me tie
Are humbled thoughts, which bit of reverence move,
Curbed¹ in with fear, but with gilt boss above
Of hope, which makes it seem fair to the eye.
The wand° is will; thou, fancy, saddle art,   *whip*
10 Girt fast by memory; and while I spur
My horse, he spurs with sharp desire my heart;
He sits me fast, however I do stir;
And now hath made me to his hand so right
That in the manage² myself takes delight.

52

A strife is grown between Virtue and Love,
While each pretends° that Stella must be his: *claims*
Her eyes, her lips, her all, saith Love, do this,
Since they do wear his badge,³ most firmly prove.
5 But Virtue thus that title doth disprove,
That Stella (O dear name) that Stella is
That virtuous soul, sure heir of heav'nly bliss;

9. With a pun on *dear* and *deer.*
1. The curb is a short chain or strap connecting
the upper branches of the bit and ornamented, in
this case, with a metal "boss" or decorative stud.

2. The schooling or handling of a horse.
3. Clothing or device worn to identify someone's
(here, Cupid's) servants.

Not this fair outside, which our hearts doth move.
And therefore, though her beauty and her grace
10　Be Love's indeed, in Stella's self he may
By no pretense claim any manner° place.　　　　　　　*kind of*
Well, Love, since this demur° our suit doth stay,°　*objection / detain*
Let Virtue have that Stella's self; yet thus,
That Virtue but that body grant to us.

63

O Grammar rules, ô now your virtues show;
So children still read you with awful° eyes,　　　　*awed*
As my young Dove may in your precepts wise
Her grant to me, by her own virtue know.
5　For late with heart most high, with eyes most low,
I crav'd the thing which ever she denies:
She lightning Love, displaying Venus' skies,[4]
Least once should not be heard, twice said, No, No.
Sing then my Muse, now Io Pean[5] sing,
10　Heav'ns envy not at my high triumphing:
But Grammar's force with sweet success confirme,
For Grammar sayes (ô this deare Stella weigh,)
For Grammar sayes (to Grammar who says nay)
That in one speech two Negatives affirm.[6]

71

Who will in fairest book of Nature know
How virtue may best lodged in beauty be,
Let him but learn of love to read in thee,
Stella, those fair lines which true goodness show.
5　There shall he find all vices' overthrow,
Not by rude force, but sweetest sovereignty
Of reason, from whose light those night birds fly,
That inward sun in thine eyes shineth so.
And, not content to be perfection's heir
10　Thyself, dost strive all minds that way to move,
Who mark in thee what is in thee most fair.
So while thy beauty draws the heart to love,
As fast thy virtue bends that love to good.
"But ah," Desire still cries, "give me some food."

4. Venus is the Roman goddess of love and beauty. Some editors modernize "lightning" as "lightening," a present participle parallel to "displaying," but one can also read the word as a noun comparing Stella to lightning that "displays" the night sky. 5. A hymn of thanksgiving for victory. Ovid uses this phrase in the opening of the second book of the *Ars Amatoria* to celebrate success with a long-pursued love. *Muse:* source of poetic inspiration. 6. In several of the preceding sonnets, Stella has engaged in scholastic disputation; the poet's reasoning here is sophistic, since the lady's double "no" is emphatic rather than a grammatical double negative signifying "yes"—as it did in Latin, but not in Elizabethan English.

72

Desire, though thou my old companion art,
And oft so clings to my pure Love that I
One from the other scarcely can descry,°   distinguish
While each doth blow the fire of my heart,
5   Now from thy fellowship I needs must part;
Venus is taught with Dian's[7] wings to fly;
I must no more in thy sweet passions lie;
Virtue's gold now must head my Cupid's dart.
Service and honor, wonder with delight,
10 Fear to offend, will worthy to appear,[8]
Care shining in mine eyes, faith in my sprite:°   spirit
These things are let me by my only dear;
But thou, Desire, because thou wouldst have all,
Now banished art. But yet alas how shall?

Fourth Song

Only joy, now here you are,
Fit to hear and ease my care;
Let my whispering voice obtain,
Sweet reward for sharpest pain;
5   Take me to thee, and thee to me.
No, no, no, no, my dear, let be.[9]

Night hath closed all in her cloak,
Twinkling stars love-thoughts provoke:
Danger hence good care doth keep,
10 Jealousy itself doth sleep;
Take me to thee, and thee to me.
No, no, no, no, my dear, let be.

Better place no wit can find,
Cupid's[1] yoke to loose or bind:
15 These sweet flowers on fine bed too,
Us in their best language woo;
Take me to thee, and thee to me.
No, no, no, no, my dear, let be.

This small light the moon bestows,
20 Serves thy beams but to disclose,
So to raise my hap° more high;   chances
Fear not else, none can us spy:
Take me to thee, and thee to me.
No, no, no, no, my dear, let be.

7. Diana, Roman goddess of the moon and patron of chastity. Venus, goddess of love and beauty; mother of Cupid, god of erotic love.
8. The phrase can mean alternately "the desire to appear worthy" or "desire that is worthy to appear (i.e., not shameful)."
9. Stella's "reply" to Astrophil occurs after each stanza and becomes the refrain.
1. Roman god of erotic love.

25   That° you heard was but a mouse,   *what*
       Dumb sleep holdeth all the house;
       Yet asleep, methinks they say,
       Young folks, take time while you may:[2]
       Take me to thee, and thee to me.
30   *No, no, no, no, my dear, let be.*

       Niggard° Time threats, if we miss   *miserly*
       This large offer of our bliss,
       Long stay° ere he grant the same;   *wait*
       Sweet then, while each thing doth frame,°   *serve*
35   Take me to thee, and thee to me.
       No, no, no, no, my dear, let be.

       Your fair mother is abed,
       Candles out, and curtains spread:
       She thinks you do letters write.
40   Write, but first let me indite:°   *dictate*
       Take me to thee and thee to me.
       No, no, no, no, my dear, let be.

       Sweet, alas, why strive you thus?
       Concord better fitteth us:
45   Leave to Mars[3] the force of hands,
       Your power in your beauty stands;
       Take me to thee, and thee to me.
       No, no, no, no, my dear, let be.

       Woe to me, and do you swear
50   Me to hate, but I forbear,
       Cursèd be my destines all
       That brought me so high to fall:
       Soon with my death I will please thee.
       No, no, no, no, my dear, let be.

Seventh Song

Whose senses in so evil consort,[4] their stepdame Nature lays,
That ravishing delight in them most sweet tunes do not raise;
Or if they do delight therein, yet are so cloyed° with wit,   *sated, burdened*
As with sententious° lips to set a title vain on it: *full of maxims*
5 O let them hear these sacred tunes, and learn in wonder's
     schools,
To be (in things past bounds of wit) fools, if they be not fools.[5]

Who have so leaden eyes, as not to see sweet beauty's show,
Or seeing, have so wooden° wits, as not that worth to know;   *dull*
Or knowing, have so muddy minds, as not to be in love;

2. An allusion to the traditional *carpe diem* (Latin, "seize the day") motif of seduction lyrics.
3. Roman god of war.
4. Company; accord, agreement.

5. I.e., the music will teach them (if they are not fools) that, in things that are beyond the limitations of reason and intellect ("wit"), they are deficient in understanding ("fools").

10 Or loving, have so frothy° thoughts, as eas'ly thence to   *shallow, trifling*
    move:
Or let them see these heavenly beams, and in fair letters read
A lesson fit, both sight and skill, love and firm love to breed.

Hear then, but then with wonder hear; see but adoring see,
No mortal gifts, no earthly fruits, now here descended be;
15 See, do you see this face? a face? nay, image of the skies,
Of which the two life-giving lights⁶ are figured in her eyes:
Hear you this soul-invading voice, and count it but a voice?
The very essence of their tunes, when Angels do rejoice.

90

Stella, think not that I by verse seek fame,
Who seek, who hope, who love, who live but thee;
Thine eyes my pride, thy lips my history;
If thou praise not, all other praise is shame.
5 Nor so ambitious am I, as to frame
A nest for my young praise in laurel tree:⁷
In truth I sweare, I wish not there should be
Graved in mine epitaph a Poet's name:
Nay if I would, could I just title make,
10 That any laud° to me thereof should grow,   *praise*
Without° my plumes from others' wings I take.   *unless*
For nothing from my wit or will doth flow,
Since all my words thy beauty doth endite,⁸
And love doth hold my hand, and makes me write.

107

Stella, since thou so right a princess art
Of all the powers which life bestows on me,
That ere by them aught° undertaken be   *anything*
They first resort unto that sovereign part;
5 Sweet, for a while give respite to my heart,
Which pants as though it still should leap to thee,
And on my thoughts give thy lieutenancy
To⁹ this great cause, which needs both use° and art,   *experience*
And as a queen, who from her presence sends
10 Whom she employs, dismiss from thee my wit,
Till it have wrought what thy own will attends.¹
On servants' shame oft master's blame doth sit.
Oh let not fools in me thy works reprove,
And scorning say, "See what it is to love."

ca. 1582   1591

6. I.e., the sun and the moon.
7. The laurel symbolized poetic achievement.
8. A variation of both *indict* (to proclaim) and *indite* (to inscribe or give literary form to).

9. I.e., delegate your authority to my thoughts so that they may pursue.
1. Is concerned about.

GEORGE PEELE
1557–1596

His Golden Locks Time Hath to Silver Turned[1]

His golden locks time hath to silver turned;
   Oh, time too swift, oh, swiftness never ceasing!
His youth 'gainst time and age hath ever spurned.°   *kicked*
   But spurned in vain; youth waneth by increasing.
5 Beauty, strength, youth, are flowers but fading seen;
Duty, faith, love, are roots, and ever green.

His helmet now shall make a hive for bees,
   And lover's sonnets turned to holy psalms,
A man-at-arms must now serve on his knees,
10   And feed on prayers, which are age his[2] alms;
But though from court to cottage he depart,
His saint[3] is sure of his unspotted heart.

And when he saddest sits in homely cell,
   He'll teach his swains° this carol for a song: *followers*
15 Blest be the hearts that wish my sovereign well,
   Cursed be the souls that think her any wrong!
Goddess, allow this aged man his right,
To be your beadsman[4] now, that was your knight.

                                   1590

Hot Sun, Cool Fire

Hot sun, cool fire, tempered with sweet air,
Black shade, fair nurse, shadow my white hair.
Shine, sun; burn, fire; breathe, air, and ease me;
Black shade, fair nurse, shroud me and please me.
5 Shadow, my sweet nurse, keep me from burning;
Make not my glad cause cause of mourning.
   Let not my beauty's fire
   Inflame unstaid desire,
   Nor pierce any bright eye
10   That wandereth lightly.

                                   1599

1. This poem refers to Sir Henry Lee, for years Queen Elizabeth I's champion in courtly jousts or contests of arms. At sixty, too old to take part in the queen's birthday tournament of 1590, he retired in favor of a younger man.

2. *Age his:* age's.
3. Seems to refer to Queen Elizabeth, as does "Goddess" in line 17.
4. One who offers prayers for the soul of another.

THOMAS LODGE
1558–1625

Rosalind's Madrigal[1]

Love in my bosom like a bee
  Doth suck his sweet;
Now with his wings he plays with me,
  Now with his feet.
5 Within mine eyes he makes his nest,
His bed amidst my tender breast;
My kisses are his daily feast,
And yet he robs me of my rest.
  Ah, wanton, will ye?

10 And if I sleep, then percheth he
  With pretty flight,
And makes his pillow of my knee
  The livelong night.
Strike I my lute, he tunes the string;
15 He music plays if so I sing;
He lends me every lovely thing;
Yet cruel he my heart doth sting.
  Whist,° wanton, still ye!   *be silent*

Else I with roses every day
20 Will whip you hence,
And bind you, when you long to play,
  For your offense.
I'll shut mine eyes to keep you in,
I'll make you fast it for your sin,
25 I'll count your power not worth a pin.
Alas! what hereby shall I win
  If he gainsay me?

What if I beat the wanton boy
  With many a rod?
30 He will repay me with annoy,
  Because a god.
Then sit thou safely on my knee,
And let thy bower° my bosom be;   *shelter*
Lurk in mine eyes, I like of thee.
35 O Cupid, so thou pity me,[2]
  Spare not, but play thee!

1590

---

1. *Madrigal:* a short lyrical poem, usually about love, suitable for a musical setting; a song.

2. I.e., as long as you show me some pity. *Cupid:* Roman god of erotic love.

ROBERT SOUTHWELL
ca. 1561–1595

The Burning Babe

As I in hoary winter's night stood shivering in the snow,
Surprised I was with sudden heat which made my heart to glow;
And lifting up a fearful eye to view what fire was near,
A pretty babe all burning bright did in the air appear;
5 Who, scorchèd with excessive heat, such floods of tears did shed
As though his floods should quench his flames which with his tears
      were fed.
"Alas," quoth he, "but newly born in fiery heats I fry,
Yet none approach to warm their hearts or feel my fire but I!
My faultless breast the furnace is, the fuel wounding thorns,
10 Love is the fire, and sighs the smoke, the ashes shame and scorns;
The fuel justice layeth on, and mercy blows the coals,
The metal in this furnace wrought are men's defilèd souls,
For which, as now on fire I am to work them to their good,
So will I melt into a bath to wash them in my blood."
15 With this he vanished out of sight and swiftly shrunk away,
And straight° I callèd unto mind that it was Christmas day.   *straightaway*

1602

New Heaven, New War

Come to your heaven, you heavenly choirs,
Earth hath the heaven of your desires.
Remove your dwelling to your God;
A stall° is now his best abode.   *stable*
5 Sith° men their homage do deny,   *since*
Come, angels, all their fault supply.

His chilling cold doth heat require;
Come, seraphs,[1] in lieu of fire.
This little ark no cover hath;
10 Let cherubs' wings his body swathe.°   *enwrap*
Come, Raphael,[2] this babe must eat;
Provide our little Toby meat.

1. Seraphs and cherubs (line 10) were generally understood to be orders among the angels, derived in Christian theology from Hebrew Scripture.
2. One of the seven archangels, the companion and protector of Tobias in the book of Tobit (one of the apocryphal books of the Hebrew Scriptures). Gabriel (line 13) and Michael (line 15) are also archangels.

Let Gabriel be now his groom,
That first took up his earthly room.
15 Let Michael stand in his defense,
Whom love hath linked to feeble sense.
Let graces rock when he doth cry,
And angels sing his lullaby.

The same you saw in heavenly seat
20 Is he that now sucks Mary's teat;
Agnize° your king a mortal wight,°   *acknowledge / person*
His borrowed weed° lets° not your sight.   *clothing / hinders*
Come, kiss the manger where he lies,
That is your bliss above the skies.

25 This little babe, so few days old,
Is come to rifle Satan's fold;
All hell doth at his presence quake,
Though he himself for cold do shake,
For in this weak unarmèd wise°   *manner*
30 The gates of hell he will surprise.

With tears he fights and wins the field;
His naked breast stands for a shield;
His battering shot are babish cries,
His arrows looks of weeping eyes,
35 His martial ensigns cold and need,
And feeble flesh his warrior's steed.

His camp is pitchèd in a stall,
His bulwark but a broken wall,
The crib his trench, hay stalks his stakes,
40 Of shepherds he his muster³ makes;
And thus, as sure his foe to wound,
The angels' trumps° alarum sound.   *trumpets*

My soul, with Christ join thou in fight;
Stick to the tents that he hath pight;°   *pitched*
45 Within his crib is surest ward,°   *protection*
This little babe will be thy guard.
If thou wilt foil thy foes with joy,
Then flit not from this heavenly boy.

1602

---

3. An assembly of troops for inspection.

MARY SIDNEY
1561–1621

Psalm 58: *Si Vere Utique*[1]

And call ye this to utter what is just,
    You that of justice hold the sov'reign throne?
And call ye this to yield, O sons of dust,
    To wronged brethren ev'ry man his own?
5 O no: it is your long malicious will
    Now to the world to make by practice known,
With whose oppression you the balance fill,
    Just to your selves, indiff'rent° else to none.[2]   *impartial*

But what could they, who ev'n in birth declined,[3]
10   From truth and right to lies and injuries?
To show the venom of their cankred° mind   *corrupt, malignant*
    The adder's image scarcely can suffice;
Nay scarce the aspic° may with them contend,   *asp*
    On whom the charmer all in vain applies
15 His skillfull'st spells: ay° missing of his end,   *always*
    While she self-deaf, and unaffected lies.[4]

Lord crack their teeth, Lord crush these lion's jaws,
    So let them sink as water in the sand:
When deadly bow their aiming fury draws,
20   Shiver° the shaft ere past the shooter's hand.   *shatter*
So make them melt as the dishoused snail
    Or as the embryo, whose vital band
Breaks ere it holds,[5] and formless eyes do fail
    To see the sun, though brought to lightful land.

25 O let their brood, a brood of springing thorns,
    Be by untimely rooting overthrown[6]
Ere bushes waxt,° they push with pricking horns,   *grew*
    As fruits yet green are oft by tempest blown.[7]
The good with gladness this revenge shall see,

1. If, indeed, it is true (Latin). Frequently the Latin titles for Psalms were taken from the Psalm's first line in the Vulgate version of the Bible. However, in this case the first line in the Vulgate is *Numquid vere* ("Is it true?"). Mary Sidney probably derived her title from one of the French or English Psalters she imitated. Cf. the versions of this Psalm and the next one from *The Massachusetts Bay Psalm Book* (pp. 391–93), by Isaac Watts (pp. 592–94), and by Christopher Smart (pp. 684–86).
2. I.e., now to make known to the world, through continual repetition, with whose oppression you fill the balance, being just to yourselves, but impartial to no one else.
3. I.e., but what else could they do, those who from birth turned aside?
4. The snake is "unaffected" by the snake charmer's music because she is "self-deaf," i.e.,

she stops her ears.
5. A reference to premature birth.
6. The Hebrew original here is problematic and hinges on the translation of an ambiguous word, *sir*, which can mean "pot" or "thorns." The verse has thus been rendered in a variety of ways, including: "Sooner than your poets can feel the heat of thorns, whether green or ablaze, may he sweep them away" (Revised Standard Version) and, "Before your thorns have ripened on the thorn-bush, a wrath will tear them out while they are still green" (Luther). Luther interpreted the "thorns" as the Jews.
7. I.e., before the bushes have fully grown, they [already] begin to grow thorns, and, as still unripe fruits, are often blown by the tempest. A further elaboration of the images of the thorns in the lines above.

30   And bathe his feet in blood of wicked one
       While all shall say: the just rewarded be,
       There is a God that carves to each his own.[8]

ca. 1588–99   1823

Psalm 114: *In Exitu Israel*[9]

At what time Jacob's race did leave of Egypt take,
     And Egypt's barbarous folk forsake:
Then, then our God, our king, elected Jacob's race
     His temple there and throne to place.
5   The sea beheld and fled: Jordan[1] with swift return
     To twinnèd spring his[2] streams did turn.
The mountains bounded so, as, fed in fruitful ground,
     The fleecèd rams do frisking bound.
The hillocks capreold[3] so, as wanton by their dams
10   We capreol see° the lusty lambs.   *to see*
O sea, why didst thou fly? Jordan, with swift return
     To twinnèd spring, what made thee turn?
Mountains, why bounded ye, as, fed in fruitful
     The fleecèd rams do frisking bound?
15   Hillocks why capreold ye, as wanton by their dams
     We capreol see the lusty lambs?
Nay you, and Earth with you, quake ever at the sight
     Of God Jehovah, Jacob's might,
Who in the hardest rocks makes standing waters grow
20   And purling° springs from flints to flow.   *rippling*

ca. 1588–99   1823

To the Thrice-Sacred Queen Elizabeth[4]

I

Even now that care,° which on thy crown attends   *burden*
And with thy happy° greatness daily grows,   *fortunate*
Tells me, thrice-sacred Queen, my muse[5] offends,
And of respect to thee the line out goes.[6]

8. I.e., the good person is glad to see the wicked overthrown in this manner, and bathes his feet in the blood of the wicked one, who has been destroyed before he has come to fruition. Seeing this, everyone will recognize that the just are rewarded and that God gives each person what he deserves.
9. A famous Psalm about the Israelites' departure from Egypt.
1. River in Palestine that empties into the Dead Sea.
2. I.e., the river Jordan's.
3. Capered, i.e., leaped or skipped.
4. This is a dedicatory poem originally prefixed to a translation of the Psalms of David, begun by Mary Sidney's brother Sir Philip Sidney (1554–1586; see pp. 208–20) and completed by Mary after Philip's death. The poem, preserved in a unique manuscript copy, was probably prepared for a presentation volume to be given to the queen (1553–1603; see pp. 142–43) when she visited the Sidney home in 1599. The expected visit did not occur. Sir Philip Sidney had been exiled from court after incurring Elizabeth's disfavor by counseling against a marriage with the duke of Anjou; furthermore, the Sidneys, devoted to the cause of Protestantism, felt that the queen should adopt a more aggressive policy in support of Protestant factions on the continent (especially the Netherlands). *Thrice*: to a high degree.
5. Source of poetic inspiration.
6. Ambiguous syntax; possibly: from respect to you (and the demands that your royal duties place on your time), my poetry ("the line") should be thrown out (as unworthy of your attention).

5   One instant will or willing can she lose[7]
      I say not reading, but receiving rhymes,
      On whom in chief dependeth to dispose°   *settle*
      What Europe acts in these most active times?

2

      Yet dare I so, as humbleness may dare,
10   Cherish some hope they° shall acceptance find;   *the poems*
      Not weighing less thy state, lighter thy care,
      But knowing more thy grace, abler thy mind.[8]
      What heavenly powers thee highest throne assigned,
      Assigned thee goodness suiting that degree,°   *position or rank*
15   And by thy strength thy burthen so defined,
      To others toil, is exercise to thee.[9]

3

      Cares, though still° great, cannot be greatest still,   *always*
      Business must ebb, though leisure never flow;
      Then these the posts[1] of duty and goodwill
20   Shall press° to offer what their senders owe,   *hurry*
      Which once in two, now in one subject go,[2]
      The poorer left, the richer reft° away,   *stolen*
      Who better might (O might, ah word of woe)
      Have given for me what I for him defray.°   *pay*

4

25   How can I name whom sighing signs extend,[3]
      And not unstop my tears' eternal spring?
      But he did warp, I weaved this web to end;[4]
      The stuff[5] not ours, our work no curious° thing,   *novel or ingenious*
      Wherein yet well we thought the Psalmist King[6]
30   Now English denizened, though Hebrew born,[7]
      Would to thy music undispleasèd sing,
      Oft having worse, without repining, worn;[8]

5

      And I the cloth° in both our names present,   *poems*
      A livery robe[9] to be bestowed by thee;

---

7. I.e., will she, or can she willingly, lose one instant?

8. I.e., not because I judge your status or responsibilities to be less than they are, but because I know how great is your grace and how able your mind.

9. I.e., your "burthen" is defined according to your strength, such that what would be burdensome labor to others is mere "exercise," i.e., customary practice, to you.

1. Postmen or letter carriers, here referring to the poems that convey the poet's "duty" and "goodwill" to the queen.

2. Sir Philip Sidney wrote the first forty-three translations (of 150 Psalms); the rest are Mary's. Philip died in 1586 fighting for the Protestant cause in the Netherlands.

3. I.e., how can I name him (Philip Sidney) whose memory is extended by "sighing signs" (i.e., the signs of grief)?

4. To completion. In clothmaking, the warp threads on a loom run lengthwise and are set first; the woof threads are then woven crosswise through them.

5. Raw material (i.e., the Hebrew Scriptures).

6. King David, the second king of Israel, believed to have written many of the Psalms of the Bible.

7. I.e., admitted to English citizenship, though born a Hebrew.

8. I.e., often having worn worse (than "thy music," i.e., the English language) without complaining ("repining"); "worse" probably refers to translations of the Psalms in other languages; these two lines might also refer to David's service, as a youth, to the tyrant Saul, whom David often soothed with his singing.

9. A suit of clothes bestowed by a noble upon his male retainers by which they may be recognized as his servants. Sidney seems to be saying that she presents the poems to Elizabeth, who will then give them a "livery robe" as a sign that they are her servants.

35 Small parcel of that undischargèd° rent,   *unpaid*
From which nor° pains nor payments can us free.   *neither*
And yet enough to cause our neighbors see
We will° our best, though scanted° in our will;   *attempt / limited*
And those nigh° fields where sown thy favors be   *nearby*
40 Unwealthy do, not else unworthy, till.[1]

6

For in our work what bring we but thine own?
What English is, by many names is thine,
There humble laurels[2] in thy shadows grown
To garland others would themselves repine.[3]
45 Thy breast the cabinet,° thy seat[4] the shrine,   *small room*
Where muses hang their vowèd° memories;   *consecrated*
Where wit, where art, where all that is divine
Conceivèd best, and best defended lies.

7

Which if men did not (as they do) confess,[5]
50 And wronging worlds would otherwise consent,
Yet here who minds so meet a patroness[6]
For authors' state° or writings' argument?°   *financial condition / subject*
A King should only to a Queen be sent;
God's lovèd choice unto his chosen love;
55 Devotion to devotion's president;[7]
What all applaud, to her whom none reprove.

8

And who sees ought,° but sees how justly square°   *anything / correspond*
His haughty° ditties° to thy glorious days?   *lofty / songs*
How well beseeming° thee his triumphs[8] are?   *resembling or matching*
60 His hope, his zeal, his prayer, plaint,° and praise,   *lamentation*
Needless thy person to their height to raise;
Less need to bend them down to thy degree;
These holy garments[9] each good soul assays,°   *tries on*
Some sorting all, all sort to none but thee.[1]

9

65 For even thy rule is painted in his reign;[2]
Both clear in right; both nigh by wrong oppressed;[3]

---

1. I.e., we till those nearby fields where your favors are sown without a show of wealth but not otherwise unworthily.
2. Leaves used to crown the heads of great poets; hence, the symbol of poetic achievement.
3. I.e., the laurels grown in your shadow would complain at being worn by others besides you.
4. Place of abode as well as Elizabeth's throne.
5. I.e., if people did not (as they do) agree that Elizabeth is the source of all English works.
6. I.e., who in England can remember so suitable ("meet") a supporter (as Elizabeth)?
7. One who presides over, perhaps referring to the fact that, as queen, Elizabeth was head of the Church of England. The first element in each of

lines 53 through 56 refers to King David, the second to Queen Elizabeth.
8. Both victories and triumphal songs.
9. I.e., the Psalms.
1. I.e., some fitting everyone, but all fitting no one but you.
2. I.e., is represented in David's reign.
3. Defeated (rather than its modern meaning); *nigh*: almost. David's succession to the throne of Israel was opposed by Saul, the first king of Israel, who tried to kill David. Elizabeth's succession to the crown of England was disputed (especially by Catholics who championed her cousin, Mary, queen of Scots) because of the questionable legality of Henry VIII's second marriage to Anne Bol-

And each at length (man crossing God in vain)
Possessed of place, and each in peace possessed.
Proud Philistines did interrupt his rest,
70 The foes of heaven no less have been thy foes;[4]
He with great conquest, thou with greater blessed;
Thou sure to win, and he secure to lose.[5]

10

Thus hand in hand with him thy glories walk;
But who can trace them[6] where alone they go?
75 Of thee two hemispheres on honor talk,[7]
And lands and seas thy trophies jointly show.
The very winds did on thy party blow,
And rocks in arms thy foemen eft[8] defy.
But soft, my muse, thy pitch[9] is earthly low;
80 Forbear° this heaven where only eagles fly.   *avoid*

11

Kings on a Queen enforced their states to lay;[1]
Mainlands for empire waiting on an isle;[2]
Men drawn by worth a woman to obey;
One moving all, herself unmoved[3] the while;
85 Truth's restitution, vanity exile,[4]
Wealth sprung of want, war held without annoy,°   *vexation*
Let subject be of some inspired style,
Till then the object of her subjects' joy.

12

Thy utmost can but offer to her sight
90 Her handmaid's task, which most her will endears,[5]
And pray unto thy pains life from that light
Which lively lightsome, court and kingdom cheers,[6]
What° wish she may (far past her living peers   *who*
And rival still to Judah's faithful king)

eyn, Elizabeth's mother. Despite opposition, both David and Elizabeth came to possess their respective thrones, although "each in peace possessed" (line 68) is a questionable claim. David continued to put down rebellions, including one by his own son, until late in his life. In 1587, Elizabeth had her cousin, Mary, beheaded, ending that particular claim to her throne.
4. Elizabeth and David both reigned in times of war; their enemies, the Spanish (who were Catholic) and the Philistines respectively, were perceived as enemies of the true religion.
5. Enigmatic phrasing; probably: secure (sure) against losing (so as not to contradict line 71).
6. I.e., who can follow or put down in writing thy glories.
7. I.e., about you, the whole world talks on the topic of honor.
8. Afterwards. The British defeated the Spanish Armada in 1588, aided by favorable winds; the remnant of the defeated Spanish fleet lost more ships when storms drove them onto the western coast of Ireland.
9. The height to which a falcon or other bird of

prey soars before swooping down on its prey, but also height in a figurative sense: degree, rank, status.
1. I.e., kings compelled to humble their greatness, splendor, power (all meanings of "state") to Elizabeth.
2. Continental countries, because of the greatness of Elizabeth's empire, serving England.
3. Perhaps a reference to Aristotle's idea of God as an "Unmoved Mover" (in *Nichomachean Ethics* 10 and *Metaphysics* 12).
4. Perhaps a reference to Elizabeth's restoration of the Protestant faith ("truth") in England after the reign of her half-sister, the Catholic Mary Tudor. The banishment of "vanity" would then refer to the banishment of the ornate rituals of the Catholic religion.
5. I.e., the most you can do is offer her the work of a handmaid, which most endears itself to her will. "Thy" seems to refer to Sidney's muse.
6. I.e., and pray to get life (a favorable response?) from that light, which, lively lightsome (luminous or bright), cheers the kingdom and court.

95 In more than he and more triumphant years,
Sing what God doth, and do what men may sing.[7]

1599   1962

SAMUEL DANIEL
1563–1619

From Delia[1]

1

Unto the boundless Ocean of thy beauty
Runs this poor river, charged with streams of zeal:
Returning thee the tribute of my duty,
Which here my love, my youth, my plaints reveal.
5   Here I unclasp the book of my charged soul,
Where I have cast th'accounts of all my care:
Here have I summed my sighs, here I enroll°   register
How they were spent for thee; look what they are.
Look on the dear expenses of my youth,
10   And see how just I reckon with thine eyes:
Examine well thy beauty with my truth,
And cross my cares ere greater sum arise.
Read it sweet maid, though it be done but slightly;
Who can show all his love, doth love but lightly.

2

Go wailing verse, the infants of my love,
Minerva[2]-like, brought forth without a Mother:
Present the image of the cares I prove,
Witness your Father's grief exceeds all other.
5   Sigh out a story of her cruel deeds,
With interrupted accents of despair:
A monument that whosoever reads,
May justly praise, and blame my loveless Fair.
Say her disdain hath dried up my blood,
10   And starved you, in succours° still denying: aid

7. I.e., who (members of her court and kingdom) wish that she (the queen) may sing what God does, and do (i.e., great things) that men may praise, (in a way that will be) far better than what other (contemporary) monarchs do, and equal, still, to (what was done by) Judah's king, David.
1. A sequence of fifty sonnets. The title, which recalls *Délie*, a collection by the French poet Maurice Scève (ca. 1500–ca. 1564), plays anagram-

matically on the lady's status as the poet's "Ideal." A dedicatory sonnet addressed to Mary Sidney (1561–1621; see pp. 225–30) appears in early editions of the sequence. The numbering of the sonnets varies by edition; we have followed the numbering and the text of the first edition.
2. In Roman mythology, the goddess of war, wisdom, arts, and justice; she sprang fully formed from the head of her father, Jove.

Press to her eyes, importune me some good;
Waken her sleeping pity with your crying.
Knock at that hard heart, beg till you have moved her;
And tell th'unkind, how dearly I have loved her.

6

Fair is my love, and cruel as she's fair:
Her brow shades frowns, although her eyes are sunny,
Her smiles are lightning, though her pride despair,
And her disdains are gall,° her favors honey.   *bitterness*
5   A modest maid, decked with a blush of honor,
Whose feet do tread green paths of youth and love;
The wonder of all eyes that look upon her,
Sacred on earth, designed a Saint above.
Chastity and Beauty, which were deadly foes,
10   Live reconcilèd friends within her brow;
And had she pity to conjoin with those,
Then who had heard the plaints I utter now?
Oh had she not been fair and thus unkind,
My Muse[3] had slept, and none had known my mind.

36

But love whilst that thou mayst be loved again,
Now whilst thy May hath filled thy lap with flowers,
Now whilst thy beauty bears without a stain,
Now use the summer smiles, ere winter lowers.
5   And whilst thou spread'st unto the rising sun
The fairest flower that ever saw the light,
Now joy thy time before thy sweet be done,
And, Delia, think thy morning must have night,
And that thy brightness sets at length to west,
10   When thou wilt close up that which now thou shew'st;
And think the same becomes thy fading best
Which then shall most inveil° and shadow most.   *cover*
Men do not weigh the stalk for what it was,
When once they find her flower, her glory, pass.

37

When men shall find thy flower, thy glory pass,
And thou, with careful brow sitting alone,
Receivèd hast this message from thy glass,°   *looking glass*

---

3. Source of poetic inspiration.

That tells thee truth, and says that all is gone,
5   Fresh shalt thou see in me the wounds thou madest,
Though spent thy flame, in me the heat remaining,
I that have loved thee thus before thou fadest,
My faith shall wax, when thou art in thy waning.
The world shall find this miracle in me,
10   That fire can burn when all the matter's spent;
Then what my faith hath been thyself shall see,
And that thou wast unkind thou mayst repent.
Thou mayst repent that thou hast scorned my tears,
When Winter snows upon thy golden hairs.

49

Care-charmer Sleep, son of the sable° Night,   *black*
Brother to Death, in silent darkness born.
Relieve my languish and restore the light;
With dark forgetting of my cares, return.
5   And let the day be time enough to mourn
The shipwreck of my ill-adventured youth;
Let waking eyes suffice to wail their scorn
Without the torment of the night's untruth.
Cease, dreams, th' imagery of our day desires,
10   To model forth⁴ the passions of the morrow;
Never let rising sun approve° you liars,   *prove*
To add more grief to aggravate my sorrow.
Still let me sleep, embracing clouds in vain,
And never wake to feel the day's disdain.

50

Let others sing of knights and paladins°   *chivalric heroes*
In agèd accents, and untimely° words;   *outdated*
Paint shadows in imaginary lines
Which well the reach of their high wits records;
5   But I must sing of thee, and those fair eyes
Authentic° shall my verse in time to come,   *authenticate*
When yet th' unborn shall say, "Lo where she lies,
Whose beauty made him speak that else was dumb."
These are the arks, the trophies I erect,
10   That fortify thy name against old age;
And these thy sacred virtues must protect
Against the dark and time's consuming rage.
Though th' error of my youth they shall discover,
Suffice, they show I lived and was thy lover.

---

4. To portray.

53

Unhappy pen and ill accepted papers,
That intimate in vain my chaste desires,
My chaste desires, the ever burning tapers,
Enkindled by her eyes' celestial fires.
5 Celestial fires and unrespecting powers,
That deign not view the glory of your might,[5]
In humble lines the work of careful hours,
The sacrifice I offer to her sight.
But since she scorns her own, this rests° for me,   *remains*
10 I'll moan my self, and hide the wrong I have:
And so content me that her frowns should be
To my infant style the cradle, and the grave.
What though my self no honor get thereby,[6]
Each bird sings t'herself, and so will I.

1592

Ulysses and the Siren[7]

SIREN. Come, worthy Greek, Ulysses, come,
Possess these shores with me;
The winds and seas are troublesome,
And here we may be free.
5 Here may we sit and view their toil
That travail in the deep,
And joy the day in mirth the while,
And spend the night in sleep.

ULYSSES. Fair nymph, if fame or honor were
10 To be attained with ease,
Then would I come and rest me there,
And leave such toils as these.
But here it dwells, and here must I
With danger seek it forth;
15 To spend the time luxuriously
Becomes not men of worth.

SIREN. Ulysses, Oh be not deceived
With that unreal name;
This honor is a thing conceived,
20 And rests on others' fame.

5. Now addressing the lady's eyes as "celestial fires" and as "powers" that refuse to "respect" his poem, the speaker defines his poem as that which glorifies the power of the lady's eyes.
6. I.e., although I'll get no respect for my attempt to be satisfied by her frowns alone.
7. In Greek mythology, the Sirens were beautiful but only partly human creatures who sang so sweetly that passing sailors would forget their work and homes and be lured to their destruction. When Ulysses (Odysseus), the hero of Homer's *Odyssey*, passed by, he had his sailors' ears filled with beeswax and had himself tied to the ship's mast so that he could listen without succumbing to their song.

Begotten only to molest
Our peace, and to beguile
The best thing of our life, our rest,
And give us up to toil.

25 ULYSSES. Delicious nymph, suppose there were
Nor honor nor report,
Yet manliness would scorn to wear
The time in idle sport.
For toil doth give a better touch,
30 To make us feel our joy;
And ease finds tediousness, as much
As labor yields annoy.

SIREN. Then pleasure likewise seems the shore
Whereto tends all your toil,
35 Which you forgo to make it more,
And perish oft the while.
Who may disport them diversly,
Find never tedious day,
And ease may have variety
40 As well as action may.

ULYSSES. But natures of the noblest frame
These toils and dangers please,
And they take comfort in the same
As much as you in ease,
45 And with the thoughts of actions past
Are recreated still;
When pleasure leaves a touch at last
To show that it was ill.

SIREN. That doth opinion only cause
50 That's out of custom bred,
Which makes us many other laws
Than ever nature did.
No widows wail for our delights,
Our sports are without blood;
55 The world, we see, by warlike wights°   *persons*
Receives more hurt than good.

ULYSSES. But yet the state of things require
These motions of unrest,
And these great spirits of high desire
60 Seem born to turn them best,
To purge the mischiefs that increase
And all good order mar;
For oft we see a wicked peace
To be well changed for war.

65 SIREN. Well, well, Ulysses, then I see
I shall not have thee here,

And therefore I will come to thee,
And take my fortunes there.
I must be won that cannot win,
70   Yet lost were I not won;
For beauty hath created been
T' undo, or be undone.

1605

Are They Shadows

Are they shadows that we see?
And can shadows pleasure give?
Pleasures only shadows be
Cast by bodies we conceive
5   And are made the things we deem
In those figures which they seem.

But these pleasures vanish fast
Which by shadows are expressed;
Pleasures are not, if they last;
10   In their passing is their best.
Glory is most bright and gay
In a flash, and so away.

Feed apace° then, greedy eyes,   *quickly*
On the wonder you behold;
15   Take it sudden as it flies,
Though you take it not to hold.
When your eyes have done their part,
Thought must length° it in the heart.   *lengthen*

1610

MICHAEL DRAYTON
1563–1631

A Roundelay between Two Shepherds[1]

1 Shep. Tell me, thou gentle shepherd swain,
          Who's yonder in the vale is set?

1. This roundelay, or simple song, was included in
the anthology *England's Helicon* (1600); it also
appeared (in a slightly different form) in the Ninth
Eclogue of Drayton's "Pastorals," published in his
collected *Poems* (1619). Pastoral poems, or
eclogues, a classical form practiced by the Roman
poet Virgil and others, are populated by shepherds
and nymphs, and usually portray a simple, happy
life of singing and dancing, rather than a life of
farm labor. The Ninth Eclogue describes a "Shep-
herd's Board," or feast, and contains several songs
by shepherds, or "swains," in praise of their lovers.

2 Shep.	Oh, it is she, whose sweets do stain The lily, rose, the violet!	
5 *1 Shep.*	Why doth the sun against his kind,° Fix° his bright chariot in the skies?²	*nature* *make motionless*
2 Shep.	Because the sun is stricken blind With looking on her heavenly eyes.	
1 Shep.	Why do thy flocks forbear their food,	
10	Which sometime° were thy chief delight?	*formerly*
2 Shep.	Because they need no other good That live in presence of her sight.	
1 Shep.	Why look these flowers so pale and ill, That once attired this goodly heath?	
15 *2 Shep.*	She hath robb'd Nature of her skill, And sweetens all things with her breath.	
1 Shep.	Why slide these brooks so slow away, Whose bubbling murmur pleased thine ear?	
2 Shep.	Oh, marvel not although they stay,°	*stand still*
20	When they her heavenly voice do hear!	
1 Shep.	From whence come all these shepherd swains, And lovely nymphs attired in green?	
2 Shep.	From gathering garlands on the plains, To crown our fair the shepherds' queen.	
25 *Both.*	The sun that lights this world below, Flocks, flowers, and brooks will witness bear: These nymphs and shepherds all do know, That it is she is only fair.	

1600

FROM IDEA³

To the Reader of these Sonnets

Into these loves who but for passion looks,
At this first sight here let him lay them by
And seek elsewhere, in turning other books,
Which better may his labor satisfy.
5 No far-fetched sigh shall ever wound my breast,
Love from mine eye a tear shall never wring,
Nor in *Ah me*'s my whining sonnets dressed,
A libertine,⁴ fantastically° I sing.   *capriciously*

2. In Greek mythology, the sun was a chariot driven daily across the sky by the god Apollo.
3. Drayton's fifty-nine sonnets addressed to "Idea" are concerned with the embodiment of the Platonic ideas of virtue and beauty: the sequence rep-resents his lifelong devotion (in the manner of a courtly lover) to Anne Goodyere, Lady Rainsford. His sequence first appeared as *Idea's Mirror* in 1594, and after revisions as *Idea* in 1619.
4. One not bound by conventional morality.

My verse is the true image of my mind,
10 Ever in motion, still° desiring change;   *ever*
And as thus to variety inclined,
So in all humors° sportively I range: *moods*
    My muse[5] is rightly of the English strain,
    That cannot long one fashion entertain.

6

How many paltry, foolish, painted things,
That now in coaches trouble every street,
Shall be forgotten, whom no poet sings,
Ere they be well wrapped in their winding-sheet?°   *shroud*
5 Where° I to thee eternity shall give,   *whereas*
When nothing else remaineth of these days,
And queens hereafter shall be glad to live
Upon the alms of thy superfluous praise.
Virgins and matrons reading these my rhymes
10 Shall be so much delighted with thy story
That they shall grieve they lived not in these times,
To have seen thee, their sex's only glory.
    So shalt thou fly above the vulgar throng,
    Still to survive in my immortal song.

14

If he from heaven that filched that living fire[6]
Condemned by Jove to endless torment be,
I greatly marvel how you still go free,
That far beyond Prometheus did aspire.
5 The fire he stole, although of heavenly kind,
Which from above he craftily did take,
Of liveless clods,° us living men to make,   *lumps of earth or clay*
He did bestow in temper of the mind.
But you broke into heaven's immortal store,
10 Where virtue, honor, wit, and beauty lay;
Which taking thence you have escaped away,
Yet stand as free as ere° you did before;   *ever*
    Yet old Prometheus punished for his rape.[7]
    Thus poor thieves suffer when the greater 'scape.° *escape*

---

5. Source of poetic inspiration.
6. Prometheus, a Greek mythological hero who stole fire from heaven and gave it to humans. He was chained to a rock by Jove (Zeus), the chief god, and preyed upon daily by a vulture that tore at his vitals. In some versions of the myth, Prometheus created humankind out of clay.
7. "Rape" referred not only to sexual assault but also to other acts of forceful appropriation such as Prometheus's theft of heavenly fire.

61

Since there's no help, come let us kiss and part;
Nay, I have done, you get no more of me,
And I am glad, yea glad with all my heart
That thus so cleanly I myself can free;
5   Shake hands forever, cancel all our vows,
And when we meet at any time again,
Be it not seen in either of our brows
That we one jot of former love retain.
Now at the last gasp of love's latest breath,
10   When, his pulse failing, Passion speechless lies,
When Faith is kneeling by his bed of death,
And Innocence is closing up his eyes,
       Now if thou wouldst, when all have given him over,
       From death to life thou mightst him yet recover.

1919

CHRISTOPHER MARLOWE
1564–1593

Hero and Leander

First Sestiad[1]

On Hellespont,[2] guilty of true love's blood,
In view and opposite, two cities stood
Sea-borderers, disjoined by Neptune's° might;   god of the sea
The one Abydos, the other Sestos hight.°   called
5   At Sestos Hero dwelt; Hero the fair,
Whom young Apollo° courted for her hair,   god of the sun
And offered as a dower° his burning throne,   wedding gift
Where she should sit for men to gaze upon.
The outside of her garments were of lawn,[3]
10   The lining purple silk, with gilt stars drawn;
Her wide sleeves green, and bordered with a grove
Where Venus in her naked glory strove
To please the careless and disdainful eyes
Of proud Adonis,[4] that before her lies;

---

1. A term for a book or canto (from Hero's city, Sestos). When the English playwright and translator George Chapman (1559?–1634) wrote a four-part continuation of Marlowe's work, he divided the entire poem into sestiads. The poem belongs to the genre of the minor epic, or *epyllion*, which flourished in the 1590s and showed the strong influence of the ancient Roman poet Ovid. Ovid told the story of Hero and Leander in two of his *Heroides* (fictional love letters) and in one of the *Elegies* Marlowe had translated.
2. The modern Dardanelles, a strait between the Aegean Sea and the Sea of Marmora, one mile wide at its narrowest point.
3. A sheer cotton or linen fabric.
4. Venus, goddess of love and beauty, passionately loved the young hunter Adonis, who was killed by a boar; in lines 91–93, Marlowe claims that the men of Sestos hold a festival in honor of Adonis every year.

15   Her kirtle° blue, whereon was many a stain,   *gown*
      Made with the blood of wretched lovers slain.
      Upon her head she ware a myrtle wreath,
      From whence her veil reached to the ground beneath.
      Her veil was artificial flowers and leaves,
20   Whose workmanship both man and beast deceives;
      Many would praise the sweet smell as she passed,
      When 'twas the odor which her breath forth cast;
      And there for honey, bees have sought in vain,
      And, beat from thence, have lighted there again.
25   About her neck hung chains of pebble-stone,
      Which, lightened° by her neck, like diamonds shone.   *illuminated*
      She ware no gloves, for neither sun nor wind
      Would burn or parch her hands, but to her mind[5]
      Or° warm or cool them, for they took delight   *either*
30   To play upon those hands, they were so white.
      Buskins° of shells all silvered, usèd she,   *high shoes, boots*
      And branchèd° with blushing coral to the knee,   *decorated*
      Where sparrows perched, of hollow pearl and gold,
      Such as the world would wonder to behold;
35   Those with sweet water oft her handmaid fills,
      Which, as she went, would chirrup through the° bills.   *their*
      Some say, for her the fairest Cupid[6] pined,
      And looking in her face, was strooken° blind.   *struck*
      But this is true: so like was one the other,
40   As he imagined Hero was his mother;
      And oftentimes into her bosom flew,
      About her naked neck his bare arms threw,
      And laid his childish head upon her breast,
      And with still panting rocked, there took his rest.
45   So lovely fair was Hero, Venus' nun,
      As Nature wept, thinking she was undone,
      Because she took more from her than she left
      And of such wondrous beauty her bereft;
      Therefore, in sign her treasure suffered wrack,
50   Since Hero's time hath half the world been black.[7]
      Amorous Leander, beautiful and young,
      (Whose tragedy divine Musaeus[8] sung)
      Dwelt at Abydos; since him dwelt there none
      For whom succeeding times make greater moan.
55   His dangling tresses that were never shorn,
      Had they been cut and unto Colchos[9] borne,
      Would have allured the vent'rous youth of Greece
      To hazard more than for the Golden Fleece.
      Fair Cynthia[1] wished his arms might be her sphere;°   *orbit*
60   Grief makes her pale, because she moves not there.

5. As she wished.
6. Venus's son, god of erotic love.
7. I.e., therefore, as a sign that her (Nature's) wealth had suffered a shipwreck (i.e., been harmed by Hero's beauty), Nature made half the world dark-haired or -complexioned.
8. A fifth-century Alexandrian whose poem on Hero and Leander served Marlowe as a source. Marlowe's term "divine" suggests that he may have identified him with an earlier, legendary Musaeus.
9. The country in Asia where Jason and his Argonauts found the Golden Fleece.
1. The moon. Leander is being compared to the moon's lover, Endymion.

His body was as straight as Circe's wand;[2]
Jove might have sipped out nectar from his hand.[3]
Even as delicious meat is to the taste,
So was his neck in touching, and surpassed
65   The white of Pelops' shoulder.[4] I could tell ye
How smooth his breast was, and how white his belly,
And whose immortal fingers did imprint
That heavenly path, with many a curious° dint,   *exquisite*
That runs along his back; but my rude pen
70   Can hardly blazon° forth the loves of men,   *show*
Much less of powerful gods; let it suffice
That my slack muse[5] sings of Leander's eyes,
Those orient cheeks and lips, exceeding his[6]
That leapt into the water for a kiss
75   Of his own shadow, and despising many,
Died ere he could enjoy the love of any.
Had wild Hippolytus[7] Leander seen,
Enamored of his beauty had he been;
His presence made the rudest peasant melt,
80   That in the vast uplandish° country dwelt;   *wild*
The barbarous Thracian soldier, moved with naught,
Was moved with him, and for his favor sought.
Some swore he was a maid in man's attire,
For in his looks were all that men desire:
85   A pleasant smiling cheek, a speaking° eye,   *expressive*
A brow for love to banquet royally;
And such as knew he was a man, would say,
"Leander, thou art made for amorous play;
Why art thou not in love, and loved of all?
90   Though thou be fair, yet be not thine own thrall."°   *captive*
    The men of wealthy Sestos every year,
For his sake whom their goddess held so dear,
Rose-cheeked Adonis, kept a solemn feast.
Thither resorted many a wandering guest
95   To meet their loves; such as had none at all
Came lovers home from this great festival;
For every street, like to a firmament,°   *sky*
Glistered with breathing stars, who, where they went,
Frighted the melancholy earth, which deemed
100   Eternal heaven to burn, for so it seemed
As if another Phaeton[8] had got
The guidance of the sun's rich chariot.
But, far above the loveliest, Hero shined,
And stole away the enchanted gazer's mind;
105   For like sea nymphs' inveigling° harmony,   *beguiling*

2. The enchantress Circe, in the *Odyssey*, possessed a magical wand capable of turning men into beasts.
3. Leander is being compared to Ganymede, the shepherd boy whom Jove "ravished" and made into his cupbearer.
4. Pelops's father, Tantalus, killed, cut up, cooked, and served his son at a dinner of the gods. The goddess Demeter ate his shoulder. Hermes later reconstituted Pelops, giving him a shoulder of ivory.
5. Source of poetic inspiration.
6. I.e., Narcissus's. *Orient*: glowing like eastern skies or gems.
7. A great hunter, contemptuous of love.
8. Son of the sun god, Apollo; Phaeton drove his father's chariot for one day, went too close to Earth, and was destroyed by Jove's thunderbolt.

So was her beauty to the standers by.
Nor that night-wandering pale and watery star⁹
(When yawning dragons draw her thirling¹ car
From Latmus' mount up to the gloomy sky,
110 Where, crowned with blazing light and majesty,
She proudly sits) more over-rules° the flood,   rules over
Than she the hearts of those that near her stood.
Even as when gaudy nymphs pursue the chase,
Wretched Ixion's shaggy-footed race,²
115 Incensed with savage heat, gallop amain
From steep pine-bearing mountains to the plain,
So ran the people forth to gaze upon her,
And all that viewed her were enamored on her.
And as in fury of a dreadful fight,
120 Their fellows being slain or put to flight,
Poor soldiers stand with fear of death dead-strooken,
So at her presence all, surprised and tooken,°   taken
Await the sentence of her scornful eyes;
He whom she favors lives, the other dies.
125 There might you see one sigh, another rage,
And some, their violent passions to assuage,°   ease
Compile sharp satires; but alas, too late,
For faithful love will never turn to hate.
And many, seeing great princes were denied,
130 Pined as they went, and thinking on her, died.
On this feast day, oh, cursed day and hour!
Went Hero thorough° Sestos, from her tower   through
To Venus' temple, where unhappily,
As after chanced, they did each other spy.
135 So fair a church as this had Venus none;
The walls were of discolored° jasper stone,   varicolored
Wherein was Proteus° carvèd, and o'erhead   a sea god
A lively° vine of green sea-agate spread,   lifelike
Where, by one hand, light-headed Bacchus° hung,   god of wine
140 And with the other, wine from grapes out-wrung.
Of crystal shining fair the pavement was;
The town of Sestos called it Venus' glass;
There might you see the gods in sundry shapes,
Committing heady° riots, incest, rapes;   violent; impetuous
145 For know that underneath this radiant floor
Was Danae's statue in a brazen tower;³
Jove slyly stealing from his sister's bed
To dally with Idalian Ganymed,

9. The moon.
1. Piercing, like a flying arrow; also, whirling. Latmus was the home of the shepherd Endymion, loved by Diana, the moon goddess.
2. The centaurs, half man and half horse, were the offspring of Ixion and a cloud. For loving Juno, Ixion was made "wretched" by being chained to a ceaselessly rolling wheel.
3. The next lines give specific examples of the "riots, incest, rapes." Jove frequently left Juno, his sister and wife, to pursue other women; whether his actions constituted seduction or rape often

depends on the particular account of a given myth, as well as on interpretation. Danaë was the daughter of the king of Argos, who imprisoned her because of a prophecy that a son born to her would kill him; Jove came to her in the form of a shower of gold, and as a result she gave birth to Perseus. Jove took the form of an eagle to abduct Ganymede (see note to line 62); the sexual nature of their relationship was a topic of great interest during the Renaissance. Jove took the form of a bull to rape Europa. The goddess of the rainbow (line 150) was Iris, a messenger of the gods.

And for his love Europa bellowing loud,
150 And tumbling with the rainbow in a cloud;
Blood-quaffing Mars heaving the iron net
Which limping Vulcan and his Cyclops set;[4]
Love kindling fire to burn such towns as Troy;
Silvanus weeping for the lovely boy
155 That now is turned into a cypress tree,[5]
Under whose shade the wood gods love to be.
And in the midst a silver altar stood;
There Hero sacrificing turtles'[6] blood,
Veiled° to the ground, veiling her eyelids close,   bowed, bent
160 And modestly they opened as she rose;
Thence flew love's arrow with the golden head,[7]
And thus Leander was enamorèd.
Stone still he stood, and evermore he gazed,
Till with the fire that from his countenance blazed,
165 Relenting Hero's gentle heart was strook;
Such force and virtue° hath an amorous look.   power, efficacy
  It lies not in our power to love or hate,
For will in us is over-ruled by fate.
When two are stripped,[8] long ere the course begin
170 We wish that one should lose, the other win;
And one especially do we affect°   prefer
Of two gold ingots, like in each respect.
The reason no man knows, let it suffice,
What we behold is censured° by our eyes.   judged
175 Where both deliberate, the love is slight;
Who ever loved, that loved not at first sight?
  He kneeled, but unto her devoutly prayed;
Chaste Hero to herself thus softly said:
"Were I the saint he worships, I would hear him";
180 And as she spake these words, came somewhat near him.
He started up; she blushed as one ashamed;
Wherewith Leander much more was inflamed.
He touched her hand; in touching it she trembled;
Love deeply grounded hardly° is dissembled.   with difficulty
185 These lovers parled° by the touch of hands;   spoke
True love is mute, and oft amazed stands.
Thus while dumb signs their yielding hearts entangled,
The air with sparks of living fire was spangled,°   speckled
And night, deep drenched in misty Acheron,[9]
190 Heaved up her head, and half the world upon
Breathed darkness forth (dark night is Cupid's day).
And now begins Leander to display
Love's holy fire with words, with sighs, and tears,
Which like sweet music entered Hero's ears;
195 And yet at every word she turned aside,

4. Vulcan and his helpers, the Cyclopes, trapped his wife, Venus, in bed with Mars, the god of war, and exposed them to the laughter of the other gods.
5. Cyparissus, changed by Apollo into a cypress tree, was mourned by the forest god, Sylvanus.
6. Turtledoves, which symbolized constancy in love.
7. According to Ovid, Cupid's arrows were tipped with gold or lead, the one producing love and the other loathing.
8. I.e., for a race.
9. The river of woe in the underworld.

And always cut him off as he replied.
At last, like to a bold sharp sophister,[1]
With cheerful hope thus he accosted her:
   "Fair creature, let me speak without offense;
200   I would my rude words had the influence
To lead thy thoughts as thy fair looks do mine!
Then shouldst thou be his prisoner who is thine.
Be not unkind and fair; misshapen stuff°   *persons*
Are of behavior boisterous and rough.
205   Oh, shun me not, but hear me ere you go,
God knows I cannot force love, as you do.
My words shall be as spotless as my youth,
Full of simplicity and naked truth.
This sacrifice, whose sweet perfume descending
210   From Venus' altar to your footsteps bending,
Doth testify that you exceed her far,
To whom you offer, and whose nun you are.
Why should you worship her? her you surpass
As much as sparkling diamonds flaring° glass.   *glaring, gaudy*
215   A diamond set in lead his worth retains;
A heavenly nymph,[2] beloved of human swains,°   *rustics*
Receives no blemish, but ofttimes more grace;
Which makes me hope, although I am but base,
Base in respect° of° thee, divine and pure,   *comparison / with*
220   Dutiful service may thy love procure,
And I in duty will excel all other,
As thou in beauty dost exceed Love's° mother.   *Cupid's*
Nor heaven, nor thou, were made to gaze upon;
As heaven preserves all things, so save thou one.
225   A stately builded ship, well rigged and tall,
The ocean maketh more majestical;
Why vowest thou then to live in Sestos here,
Who on love's seas more glorious wouldst appear?
Like untuned golden strings all women are,
230   Which long time lie untouched, will harshly jar.[3]
Vessels of brass, oft handled, brightly shine;
What difference betwixt the richest mine°   *ore*
And basest mold,° but use? for both, not used,   *earth*
Are of like worth. Then treasure is abused,
235   When misers keep it; being put to loan,
In time it will return us two for one.
Rich robes themselves and others do adorn;
Neither themselves nor others, if not worn.
Who builds a palace, and rams up the gate,
240   Shall see it ruinous and desolate.
Ah, simple Hero, learn thyself to cherish!
Lone women, like to empty houses, perish.
Less sins the poor rich man that starves himself
In heaping up a mass of drossy° pelf,°   *worthless / riches*

1. One who reasons adroitly rather than soundly;
also, a university student in his junior or senior
year.
2. Minor nature goddess.
3. I.e., unplayed musical instruments go out of
tune.

245 Than such as you; his golden earth remains,
Which, after his decease, some other gains;
But this fair gem, sweet in the loss alone,
When you fleet° hence, can be bequeathed to none.   *fly*
Or if it could, down from th' enameled° sky   *varicolored*
250 All heaven would come to claim this legacy,
And with intestine° broils° the world destroy,   *internal, civil / wars*
And quite confound nature's sweet harmony.
Well therefore by the gods decreed it is
We human creatures should enjoy that bliss.
255 One is no number;[4] maids are nothing, then,
Without the sweet society of men.
Wilt thou live single still? one shalt thou be
Though never-singling Hymen° couple thee.   *god of marriage*
Wild savages, that drink of running springs,
260 Think water far excels all earthly things,
But they that daily taste neat° wine, despise it;   *undiluted*
Virginity, albeit some highly prize it,
Compared with marriage, had you tried them both,
Differs as much as wine and water doth.
265 Base bullion for the stamp's[5] sake we allow;
Even so for men's impression do we you,
By which alone, our reverend fathers say,
Women receive perfection every way.
This idol which you term virginity
270 Is neither essence° subject to the eye,   *an existing thing*
No, nor to any one exterior sense,
Nor hath it any place of residence,
Nor is 't of earth or mold° celestial,   *form*
Or capable of any form at all.
275 Of that which hath no being, do not boast;
Things that are not at all, are never lost.
Men foolishly do call it virtuous;
What virtue is it, that is born with us?
Much less can honor be ascribed thereto;
280 Honor is purchased by the deeds we do.
Believe me, Hero, honor is not won
Until some honorable deed be done.
Seek you, for chastity, immortal fame,
And know that some have wronged Diana's name?[6]
285 Whose name is it, if she be false or not,
So she be fair, but some vile tongues will blot?
But you are fair, ay me, so wondrous fair,
So young, so gentle, and so debonair,°   *affable, courteous*
As Greece will think, if thus you live alone,
290 Some one or other keeps you as his own.
Then, Hero, hate me not, nor from me fly
To follow swiftly blasting infamy.

---

4. The theory that one is not a number appears in Aristotle's *Metaphysics* and was often discussed by later, Neoplatonic philosophers.
5. I.e., the impression that turns a mere piece of metal ("bullion") into a coin.
6. Diana was the goddess of chastity. Nevertheless, some stories attribute amorous relationships to her.

Perhaps thy sacred priesthood makes thee loath;
Tell me, to whom mad'st thou that heedless oath?"
295   "To Venus," answered she, and as she spake,
Forth from those two tralucent° cisterns brake   *translucent*
A stream of liquid pearl, which down her face
Made milk-white paths, whereon the gods might trace°   *go*
To Jove's high court. He thus replied: "The rites
300   In which love's beauteous empress most delights
Are banquets, Doric music,[7] midnight revel,
Plays, masques, and all that stern age counteth evil.
Thee as a holy idiot° doth she scorn,   *untutored person*
For thou, in vowing chastity, hast sworn
305   To rob her name and honor, and thereby
Commit'st a sin far worse than perjury,
Even sacrilege against her deity,
Through regular and formal purity.
To expiate which sin, kiss and shake hands;
310   Such sacrifice as this Venus demands."
        Thereat she smiled, and did deny him so
As, put° thereby, yet might he hope for mo.°   *put off / more*
Which makes him quickly reinforce his speech,
And her in humble manner thus beseech:
315   "Though neither gods nor men may thee deserve,
Yet for her sake whom you have vowed to serve,
Abandon fruitless cold virginity,
The gentle queen of love's sole enemy.
Then shall you most resemble Venus' nun,
320   When Venus' sweet rites are performed and done.
Flint-breasted Pallas[8] joys in single life,
But Pallas and your mistress are at strife.
Love, Hero, then, and be not tyrannous,
But heal the heart that thou hast wounded thus;
325   Nor stain thy youthful years with avarice;
Fair fools delight to be accounted nice.°   *coy*
The richest corn dies if it be not reaped;
Beauty alone° is lost, too warily kept."   *on its own*
        These arguments he used, and many more,
330   Wherewith she yielded, that was won before.
Hero's looks yielded, but her words made war;
Women are won when they begin to jar.°   *argue*
Thus having swallowed Cupid's golden hook,
The more she strived, the deeper was she strook;°   *love-struck*
335   Yet, evilly feigning anger, strove she still,
And would be thought to grant against her will.
So having paused awhile, at last she said:
"Who taught thee rhetoric to deceive a maid?
Ay me! such words as these should I abhor,
340   And yet I like them for the orator."
        With that Leander stooped to have embraced her,

---

7. Leander apparently confuses Doric music,   8. Pallas Athena, the virgin goddess of wisdom,
which was stirring and martial, with Lydian music, usually portrayed in armor.
which was soft and voluptuous.

But from his spreading arms away she cast her,
And thus bespake him: "Gentle youth, forbear
To touch the sacred garments which I wear.
345 Upon a rock, and underneath a hill,
Far from the town, where all is whist° and still   *silent*
Save that the sea playing on yellow sand
Sends forth a rattling murmur to the land,
Whose sound allures the golden Morpheus°   *god of sleep*
350 In silence of the night to visit us,
My turret stands; and there, God knows, I play
With Venus' swans and sparrows all the day.
A dwarfish beldame° bears me company,   *old woman*
That hops about the chamber where I lie,
355 And spends the night, that might be better spent,
In vain discourse and apish° merriment.   *silly*
Come thither." As she spake this, her tongue tripped,
For unawares, "Come thither," from her slipped;
And suddenly her former color changed,
360 And here and there her eyes, through anger, ranged.
And like a planet moving several ways⁹
At one self° instant, she, poor soul, assays,°   *and the same / tries*
Loving, not to love at all, and every part
Strove to resist the motions of her heart;
365 And hands so pure, so innocent, nay such
As might have made heaven stoop to have a touch,
Did she uphold to Venus, and again
Vowed spotless chastity, but all in vain.
Cupid beats down her prayers with his wings;
370 Her vows above the empty air he flings;
All deep enraged, his sinewy° bow he bent,   *strong*
And shot a shaft that burning from him went;
Wherewith she, strooken,° looked so dolefully,   *struck*
As made Love sigh to see his tyranny.
375 And as she wept, her tears to pearl he turned,
And wound them on his arm, and for her mourned.
Then towards the palace of the Destinies,¹
Laden with languishment and grief, he flies,
And to those stern nymphs° humbly made request,   *girls*
380 Both might enjoy each other, and be blest.
But with a ghastly dreadful countenance,
Threatening a thousand deaths at every glance,
They answered Love, nor would vouchsafe so much
As one poor word, their hate to him was such.
385 Hearken awhile, and I will tell you why:
Heaven's winged herald, Jove-born Mercury,°   *messenger god*
The selfsame day that he asleep had laid
Enchanted Argus,² spied a country maid,

9. As in Ptolemaic astronomy, where planets
moved both in their own orbits and through the
influence of other planets' motion. *Several*: differ-
ently.
1. The Fates, three sister goddesses who deter-
mined the course of human life by spinning and
cutting threads.
2. The watchman with a hundred eyes set by Juno
to guard Io, beloved of Jupiter. Mercury (also
called Hermes) lulled Argus asleep with his music,
then killed him, at Jove's command.

Whose careless hair, instead of pearl t' adorn it,
390 Glistered° with dew, as one that seemed to scorn it;³   *glistened*
Her breath as fragrant as the morning rose,
Her mind pure, and her tongue untaught to gloze;°   *flatter*
Yet proud she was, for lofty pride that dwells
In towered courts is oft in shepherds' cells,°   *huts*
395 And too too well the fair vermilion° knew,   *scarlet*
And silver tincture of her cheeks, that drew
The love of every swain.° On her this god   *rustic*
Enamored was, and with his snaky rod⁴
Did charm her nimble feet, and made her stay,
400 The while upon a hillock down he lay,
And sweetly on his pipe began to play,
And with smooth speech her fancy to assay;°   *try*
Till in his twining arms he locked her fast,
And then he wooed with kisses, and at last,
405 As shepherds do, her on the ground he laid,
And tumbling in the grass, he often strayed
Beyond the bounds of shame, in being bold
To eye those parts which no eye should behold.
And like an insolent commanding lover,
410 Boasting his parentage, would needs discover
The way to new Elysium;⁵ but she,
Whose only dower° was her chastity,   *dowry*
Having striv'n in vain, was now about to cry,
And crave the help of shepherds that were nigh.
415 Herewith he stayed his fury,° and began   *passion*
To give her leave to rise; away she ran;
After went Mercury, who used such cunning,
As she, to hear his tale, left off her running;
Maids are not won by brutish force and might,
420 But speeches full of pleasure and delight;
And knowing Hermes courted her, was glad
That she such loveliness and beauty had
As could provoke his liking, yet was mute,
And neither would deny nor grant his suit.
425 Still vowed he love, she wanting no excuse
To feed him with delays, as women use,°   *usually do*
Or thirsting after immortality—
All women are ambitious naturally—
Imposed upon her lover such a task
430 As he ought not perform, nor yet she ask.
A draught of flowing nectar she requested,
Wherewith the king of gods and men is feasted.
He, ready to accomplish what she willed,
Stole some from Hebe⁶ (Hebe Jove's cup filled)
435 And gave it to his simple rustic love;
Which being known (as° what is hid from Jove?)   *for*
He inly° stormed, and waxed more furious   *inwardly*

---

3. I.e., pearl or other jewelry.
4. The caduceus, Mercury's magic staff.
5. In Greek mythology, a place of ideal happiness

inhabited by the blessed dead.
6. Jove's cupbearer before Jove ravished Ganymede (see note to line 62).

Than for the fire filched by Prometheus,[7]
And thrusts him down from heaven; he wandering here
440 In mournful terms,° with sad and heavy cheer,°   *state / look*
Complained to Cupid. Cupid, for his° sake,   *Prometheus's*
To be revenged on Jove did undertake;
And those on whom heaven, earth, and hell relies,
I mean the adamantine° Destinies,   *unyielding*
445 He wounds with love, and forced them equally
To dote upon deceitful Mercury.
They offered him the deadly fatal knife
That shears the slender threads of human life;
At his fair-feathered feet the engines laid
450 Which th' earth from ugly Chaos' den upweighed;[8]
These he regarded not, but did entreat
That Jove, usurper of his father's seat,[9]
Might presently be banished into hell,
And aged Saturn in Olympus dwell.
455 They granted what he craved, and once again
Saturn and Ops° began their golden reign.   *Saturn's wife*
Murder, rape, war, lust, and treachery
Were with Jove closed in Stygian empery.[1]
But long this blessed time continued not;
460 As soon as he his wishèd purpose got,
He, reckless of his promise, did despise
The love of th' everlasting Destinies.
They seeing it, both Love and him abhorred,
And Jupiter unto his place restored.
465 And but that Learning,[2] in despite of Fate,
Will mount aloft, and enter heaven gate,
And to the seat of Jove itself advance,
Hermes had slept in hell with Ignorance;
Yet as a punishment they added this,
470 That he and Poverty should always kiss.
And to this day is every scholar poor;
Gross gold from them runs headlong to the boor.[3]
Likewise, the angry sisters thus deluded,
To venge themselves on Hermes, have concluded
475 That Midas'[4] brood shall sit in Honor's chair,
To which the Muses' sons[5] are only heir;
And fruitful wits that inaspiring° are   *not greedy*
Shall, discontent, run into regions far;
And few great lords in virtuous deeds shall joy,
480 But be surprised with every garish toy;[6]

---

7. Prometheus angered Jove by stealing fire from the gods for the benefit of humans.
8. The Fates also controlled the "beams" that "upweighed," or supported, Earth, since it was formed out of Chaos, the undifferentiated mass from which all things came.
9. I.e., that of Jove's father, Saturn, whose peaceful reign in heaven, before Jove dethroned him, was known as the Golden Age.
1. Dominion. Stygian: pertaining to the river Styx, in Hades.
2. Mercury, the god of learning. In the following

lines, Marlowe claims that Learning, because it is divine, naturally rises, but that the Fates, to punish Mercury for neglecting them, decreed that Learning went together with Poverty.
3. I.e., large amounts (a "gross") of gold go swiftly to the "boor," one who lacks refinement, rather than to the "scholar."
4. The king whose touch turned objects to gold.
5. I.e., people involved in music, poetry, and the arts and sciences, all of which were presided over by nine sister goddesses called the Muses.
6. I.e., be delighted with trivial things.

And still enrich the lofty° servile clown,   *proud*
Who with encroaching guile keeps learning down.
Then muse° not Cupid's suit no better sped,°   *marvel / succeeded*
Seeing in their loves the Fates were injurèd.

Second Sestiad

By° this, sad Hero, with love unacquainted,   *at*
Viewing Leander's face, fell down and fainted.
He kissed her and breathed life into her lips,
Wherewith, as one displeased, away she trips.
5   Yet as she went, full often looked behind,
And many poor excuses did she find
To linger by the way, and once she stayed
And would have turned again, but was afraid,
In offering parley,° to be counted light.°   *talk / wanton*
10 So on she goes, and in her idle flight,
Her painted fan of curlèd plumes let fall,
Thinking to train° Leander therewithal.   *entice*
He, being a novice, knew not what she meant,
But stayed, and after her a letter sent,
15 Which joyful Hero answered in such sort
As he had hoped to scale the beauteous fort
Wherein the liberal graces⁷ locked their wealth,
And therefore to her tower he got by stealth.
Wide open stood the door, he need not climb;
20 And she herself, before the 'pointed time,
Had spread the board, with roses strewed the room,
And oft looked out, and mused° he did not come.   *wondered why*
At last he came; Oh, who can tell the greeting
These greedy lovers had at their first meeting?
25 He asked, she gave, and nothing was denied;
Both to each other quickly were affied.°   *affianced*
Look how their hands, so were their hearts united,
And what he did she willingly requited.
(Sweet are the kisses, the embracements sweet,
30 When like desires and affections meet;
For from the earth to heaven is Cupid raised,
Where fancy is in equal balance peised.°)   *weighed*
Yet she this rashness suddenly repented,
And turned aside, and to herself lamented,
35 As if her name and honor had been wronged
By being possessed of him for whom she longed;
Aye, and she wished, albeit not from her heart,
That he would leave her turret and depart.
The mirthful god of amorous pleasure smiled
40 To see how he this captive nymph° beguiled;   *girl*
For hitherto he did but fan the fire,
And kept it down that it might mount the higher.
Now waxed she jealous° lest his love abated,   *fearful*

---

7. Charm and beauty (given by three sister goddesses called the Graces).

Fearing her own thoughts made her to be hated.
45 Therefore unto him hastily she goes,
And like light Salmacis,⁸ her body throws
Upon his bosom, where with yielding eyes
She offers up herself, a sacrifice
To slake° his anger if he were displeased.   *decrease*
50 Oh, what god would not therewith be appeased?
Like Aesop's cock,⁹ this jewel he enjoyed,
And as a brother with his sister toyed,
Supposing nothing else was to be done,
Now he her favor and good will had won.
55 But know you not that creatures wanting sense¹
By nature have a mutual appetence,°   *affinity*
And wanting organs to advance a step,
Moved by love's force, unto each other leap?
Much more in subjects having intellect,
60 Some hidden influence breeds like effect.
Albeit Leander, rude° in love and raw,   *untutored*
Long dallying with Hero, nothing saw
That might delight him more, yet he suspected
Some amorous rites or other were neglected.
65 Therefore unto his body hers he clung;°   *clasped*
She, fearing on the rushes² to be flung,
Strived with redoubled strength; the more she strived,
The more a gentle pleasing heat revived,
Which taught him all that elder lovers know;
70 And now the same gan so to scorch and glow,
As in plain terms, yet cunningly,° he craved it;   *skillfully*
Love always makes those eloquent that have it.
She, with a kind of granting, put him by it,³
And ever as he thought himself most nigh it,
75 Like to the tree of Tantalus⁴ she fled,
And, seeming lavish,° saved her maidenhead.   *immodest*
Ne'er king more sought to keep his diadem,°   *crown*
Than Hero this inestimable gem.
Above our life we love a steadfast friend,
80 Yet when a token of great worth we send,
We often kiss it, often look thereon,
And stay the messenger that would be gone;
No marvel then though Hero would not yield
So soon to part from that she dearly held;
85 Jewels being lost are found again, this never;
'Tis lost but once, and once lost, lost forever.
    Now had the morn espied her lover's steeds,⁵

8. A nymph (minor nature goddess) who became enamored of Hermaphroditus when she saw him bathing in her lake. Throwing herself upon him in spite of his resistance, she called on the gods to keep them together forever. In answer to her prayer, their two bodies united and became one, both male and female.
9. In one of Aesop's fables, a cock found a jewel in a dung heap, but had no notion of its value and traded it for a grain of corn.
1. I.e., that inanimate objects.
2. Reeds, used as floor mats in Elizabethan homes.
3. Deflected him.
4. For stealing nectar from the gods to give to humans, Jove punished Tantalus by placing him in a pool in Hades. Whenever Tantalus bent to drink, the water receded from his lips; when he reached for the fruit that dangled above his head, it rose out of his grasp.
5. The horses that pull the sun's chariot.

Whereat she starts, puts on her purple weeds,
And, red for anger that he stayed so long,
90　All headlong throws herself the clouds among.
And now Leander, fearing to be missed,
Embraced her suddenly, took leave, and kissed.
Long was he taking leave, and loath to go,
And kissed again, as lovers use to do.
95　Sad Hero wrung him by the hand and wept,
Saying, "Let your vows and promises be kept."
Then, standing at the door, she turned about,
As loath to see Leander going out.
And now the sun that through th' horizon peeps,
100　As pitying these lovers, downward creeps,
So that in silence of the cloudy night,
Though it was morning, did he take his flight.
But what the secret trusty night concealed,
Leander's amorous habit° soon revealed;　　　　　*clothing*
105　With Cupid's myrtle[6] was his bonnet crowned,
About his arms the purple riband° wound　　　　*ribbon*
Wherewith she wreathed her largely spreading hair;
Nor could the youth abstain, but he must wear
The sacred ring wherewith she was endowed,
110　When first religious chastity she vowed;
Which made his love through Sestos to be known,
And thence unto Abydos sooner blown
Than he could sail; for incorporeal Fame,
Whose weight consists in nothing but her name,
115　Is swifter than the wind, whose tardy plumes
Are reeking water and dull earthly fumes.[7]
Home, when he came, he seemed not to be there,
But like exilèd air thrust from his sphere,
Set in a foreign place;[8] and straight from thence,
120　Alcides° like, by mighty violence　　　　　*Hercules*
He would have chased away the swelling main°　*ocean*
That him from her unjustly did detain.
Like as the sun in a diameter[9]
Fires and inflames objects removèd far,
125　And heateth kindly, shining laterally,
So beauty sweetly quickens when 'tis nigh,
But being separated and removed,
Burns where it cherished, murders where it loved.
Therefore even as an index to a book,
130　So to his mind was young Leander's look.
Oh, none but gods have power their love to hide;
Affection by the countenance is descried.°　　*made known*
The light of hidden fire itself discovers,
And love that is concealed betrays poor lovers.
135　His secret flame apparently° was seen;　　　　*openly*
Leander's father knew where he had been,

6. Plant sacred to Cupid and Venus, symbolic of love.
7. I.e., are producing fog and mist.
8. I.e., air rushes to fill a vacuum.
9. Directly overhead, where it appears to be farther off than when low in the sky.

And for the same mildly rebuked his son,
Thinking to quench the sparkles new begun.
But love, resisted once, grows passionate,
140 And nothing more than counsel lovers hate;
For as a hot proud horse highly disdains
To have his head controlled, but breaks the reins,
Spits forth the ringled° bit, and with his hooves   ringed
Checks° the submissive ground, so he that loves,   stamps
145 The more he is restrained, the worse he fares.
What is it now but mad Leander dares?[1]
"Oh Hero, Hero!" thus he cried full oft,
And then he got him to a rock aloft,
Where having spied her tower, long stared he on 't,
150 And prayed the narrow toiling Hellespont
To part in twain, that he might come and go;
But still the rising billows answered "No."
With that he stripped him to the ivory skin,
And crying, "Love, I come!" leaped lively in.
155 Whereat the sapphire-visaged god grew proud,
And made his capering Triton[2] sound aloud,
Imagining that Ganymede,[3] displeased,
Had left the heavens; therefore on him he seized.
Leander strived; the waves about him wound,
160 And pulled him to the bottom, where the ground
Was strewed with pearl, and in low coral groves
Sweet singing mermaids sported with their loves
On heaps of heavy gold, and took great pleasure
To spurn in careless sort the shipwreck treasure.
165 For here the stately azure palace stood,
Where kingly Neptune and his train abode.
The lusty god embraced him, called him love,
And swore he never should return to Jove.
But when he knew it was not Ganymede,
170 For under water he was almost dead,
He heaved him up, and looking on his face,
Beat down the bold waves with his triple mace,[4]
Which mounted up, intending to have kissed him,
And fell in drops like tears, because they missed him.
175 Leander, being up, began to swim,
And looking back, saw Neptune follow him;
Whereat aghast, the poor soul gan to cry:
"Oh, let me visit Hero ere I die!"
The god put Helle's[5] bracelet on his arm,
180 And swore the sea should never do him harm.
He clapped his plump cheeks, with his tresses played,
And smiling wantonly, his love bewrayed.°   revealed
He watched his arms, and as they opened wide,

1. I.e., there is nothing now that mad Leander
wouldn't dare do.
2. The son and trumpeter of the "sapphire-
visaged" sea god, Neptune.
3. Jove's cupbearer (see note 3, p. 240).
4. The three-pronged fork carried by Neptune.

5. A Theban princess who, while fleeing from her
stepmother on the back of a winged, golden-
fleeced ram, fell into the strait that separates
Europe and Asia, named the Hellespont for her.
Marlowe seems to have invented the detail of the
bracelet.

At every stroke betwixt them would he slide,
185   And steal a kiss, and then run out and dance,
And as he turned, cast many a lustful glance,
And threw him gaudy toys to please his eye,
And dive into the water, and there pry
Upon his breast, his thighs, and every limb,
190   And up again, and close beside him swim,
And talk of love. Leander made reply:
"You are deceived, I am no woman, I."
Thereat smiled Neptune, and then told a tale
How that a shepherd, sitting in a vale,
195   Played with a boy so lovely, fair, and kind,
As for his love both earth and heaven pined;
That of the cooling river durst not drink
Lest water nymphs should pull him from the brink;
And when he sported in the fragrant lawns,
200   Goat-footed satyrs and up-staring fauns[6]
Would steal him thence. Ere half this tale was done,
"Ay me," Leander cried, "th' enamored sun,
That now should shine on Thetis' glassy bower,[7]
Descends upon my radiant Hero's tower.
205   Oh, that these tardy arms of mine were wings!"
And as he spake, upon the waves he springs.
Neptune was angry that he gave no ear,
And in his heart revenging malice bare;
He flung at him his mace, but as it went
210   He called it in, for love made him repent.
The mace returning back, his own hand hit,
As meaning to be venged for darting it.
When this fresh bleeding wound Leander viewed,
His color went and came, as if he rued
215   The grief which Neptune felt. In gentle breasts
Relenting thoughts, remorse, and pity rests;
And who have hard hearts and obdurate minds
But vicious, harebrained, and illiterate hinds?°   rustics
The god, seeing him with pity to be moved,
220   Thereon concluded that he was beloved.
(Love is too full of faith, too credulous,
With folly and false hope deluding us.)
Wherefore, Leander's fancy° to surprise,°   love / capture
To the rich ocean for gifts he flies.
225   'Tis wisdom to give much; a gift prevails
When deep persuading oratory fails.
       By this,° Leander, being near the land,   this time
Cast down his weary feet and felt the sand.
Breathless albeit he were, he rested not
230   Till to the solitary tower he got,
And knocked and called, at which celestial noise
The longing heart of Hero much more joys

6. Like satyrs, woodland deities; fauns prophesied   7. I.e., the sea. Thetis was a daughter of the sea
by looking to the heavens. *Nymphs:* minor nature   god Nereus.
goddesses.

Than nymphs or shepherds when the timbrel° rings,   *tambourine*
Or crooked° dolphin when the sailor sings;   *curving*
235 She stayed not for her robes, but straight arose,
And drunk with gladness, to the door she goes;
Where seeing a naked man, she screeched for fear,
(Such sights as this to tender maids are rare)
And ran into the dark herself to hide.
240 Rich jewels in the dark are soonest spied;
Unto her was he led, or rather drawn,
By those white limbs which sparkled through the lawn.[8]
The nearer that he came, the more she fled,
And seeking refuge, slipped into her bed.
245 Whereon Leander sitting, thus began,
Through numbing cold all feeble, faint, and wan:°   *pale*
"If not for love, yet, love, for pity sake,
Me in thy bed and maiden bosom take;
At least vouchsafe these arms some little room,
250 Who, hoping to embrace thee, cheerly° swum;   *gladly*
This head was beat with many a churlish billow,
And therefore let it rest upon thy pillow."
Herewith affrighted Hero shrunk away,
And in her lukewarm place Leander lay,
255 Whose lively heat like fire from heaven fet,°   *fetched*
Would animate gross clay, and higher set
The drooping thoughts of base declining souls,
Than dreary° Mars° carousing nectar bowls.   *bloody / god of war*
His hands he cast upon her like a snare;
260 She, overcome with shame and sallow° fear,   *pale, yellowish*
Like chaste Diana, when Actaeon spied her,[9]
Being suddenly betrayed, dived down to hide her;
And as her silver body downward went,
With both her hands she made the bed a tent,
265 And in her own mind thought herself secure,
O'ercast with dim and darksome coverture.
And now she lets him whisper in her ear,
Flatter, entreat, promise, protest, and swear;
Yet ever as he greedily assayed°   *tried*
270 To touch those dainties, she the harpy[1] played,
And every limb did, as a soldier stout,
Defend the fort and keep the foeman out;
For though the rising ivory mount he scaled,
Which is with azure circling lines empaled,
275 Much like a globe (a globe may I term this,
By which love sails to regions full of bliss)
Yet there with Sisyphus[2] he toiled in vain,
Till gentle parley° did the truce obtain.   *conference*
Wherein Leander on her quivering breast,
280 Breathless spoke something, and sighed out the rest;

8. A sheer cotton or linen fabric.
9. Actaeon, a hunter who saw the naked Diana
about to bathe in her favorite pool; as punishment,
he was turned into a stag and killed by hounds.
1. Harpies were often pictured as hideous crea-

tures, half woman and half bird; in Virgil's *Aeneid*,
several harpies seize the meal of an old prophet.
2. Who was condemned to Hades and made to roll
a stone uphill forever.

Which so prevailed, as he with small ado
Enclosed her in his arms and kissed her too.
And every kiss to her was as a charm,
And to Leander as a fresh alarm,°   *call to battle*
285 So that the truce was broke, and she, alas,
Poor silly° maiden, at his mercy was.   *innocent*
Love is not full of pity, as men say,
But deaf and cruel where he means to prey.
Even as a bird, which in our hands we wring,
290 Forth plungeth and oft flutters with her wing,
She trembling strove; this strife of hers, like that
Which made the world,³ another world begat
Of unknown joy. Treason was in her thought,
And cunningly to yield herself she sought.
295 Seeming not won, yet won she was at length;
In such wars women use but half their strength.
Leander now, like Theban Hercules,
Entered the orchard of th' Hesperides,⁴
Whose fruit none rightly can describe but he
300 That pulls or shakes it from the golden tree.
And now she wished this night were never done,
And sighed to think upon th' approaching sun;
For much it grieved her that the bright daylight
Should know the pleasure of this blessed night,
305 And them like Mars and Erycine⁵ display,
Both in each other's arms chained as they lay.
Again she knew not how to frame her look,
Or speak to him who in a moment took
That which so long, so charily she kept;
310 And fain by stealth away she would have crept,
And to some corner secretly have gone,
Leaving Leander in the bed alone.
But as her naked feet were whipping out,
He on the sudden clinged her so about,
315 That mermaid-like unto the floor she slid,
One half appeared, the other half was hid.
Thus near the bed she blushing stood upright,
And from her countenance behold ye might
A kind of twilight break, which through the hair,
320 As from an orient° cloud, glimpse here and there; *bright*
And round about the chamber this false morn
Brought forth the day before the day was born.
So Hero's ruddy cheek Hero betrayed,
And her all naked to his sight displayed;
325 Whence his admiring eyes more pleasure took
Than Dis⁶ on heaps of gold fixing his look.
By this, Apollo's golden harp began

---

3. According to the ancient Greek philosopher Empedocles, love and strife opposed each other and thus brought about creation.
4. Daughters of the Titan Atlas and custodians of a tree that bore golden apples. One of Hercules' superhuman labors was to steal the apples.
5. Venus; see note 4, p. 242.
6. Pluto, god of the underworld and god of wealth.

To sound forth music to the ocean;[7]
Which watchful Hesperus no sooner heard,
330 But he the day-bright-bearing car prepared,
And ran before, as harbinger of light,
And with his flaring beams mocked ugly night
Till she, o'ercome with anguish, shame, and rage,
Danged° down to hell her loathsome carriage.   *drove violently*

1598

The Passionate Shepherd to His Love[8]

Come live with me and be my love,
And we will all the pleasures prove°   *try*
That valleys, groves, hills, and fields,
Woods, or steepy mountain yields.

5   And we will sit upon the rocks,
Seeing the shepherds feed their flocks,
By shallow rivers to whose falls
Melodious birds sing madrigals.

And I will make thee beds of roses
10 And a thousand fragrant posies,
A cap of flowers, and a kirtle°   *gown*
Embroidered all with leaves of myrtle;

A gown made of the finest wool
Which from our pretty lambs we pull;
15 Fair lined slippers for the cold,
With buckles of the purest gold;

A belt of straw and ivy buds,
With coral clasps and amber studs:°   *buttons*
And if these pleasures may thee move,
20 Come live with me, and be my love.

The shepherds' swains° shall dance and sing   *followers*
For thy delight each May morning:
If these delights thy mind may move,
Then live with me and be my love.

1599, 1600

---

7. Presaging the rising of the sun. Hesperus is nor-
mally the evening star, but in the next line Marlowe
applies the name to the morning star, usually
called Phosphorus or Lucifer.

8. Cf. the response by Sir Walter Ralegh, "The
Nymph's Reply to the Shepherd" (p. 152); cf. also
C. Day Lewis's version of this poem (p. 1449).

WILLIAM SHAKESPEARE
1564–1616

FROM SONNETS

To the Only Begetter of
These Ensuing Sonnets
MR. W. H. All Happiness
and That Eternity
Promised
By
Our Ever-Living Poet
Wisheth
the Well-Wishing
Adventurer in
Setting Forth
T.T.[1]

1

From fairest creatures we desire increase,
That thereby beauty's rose might never die,
But as the riper should by time decease,
His tender° heir might bear his memory;   *young*
5   But thou, contracted[2] to thine own bright eyes,
Feed'st thy light's flame with self-substantial[3] fuel,
Making a famine where abundance lies,
Thyself thy foe, to thy sweet self too cruel.
Thou that art now the world's fresh ornament
10   And only° herald to the gaudy spring,   *principal; solitary*
Within thine own bud buriest thy content,[4]
And, tender churl,[5] mak'st waste in niggarding.°   *hoarding*
     Pity the world, or else this glutton be,
     To eat the world's due, by the grave and thee.

1. Much critical debate focuses on this dedication and its first set of initials (the second set refers to the publisher, Thomas Thorpe). "Mr. W. H." may be William Herbert, earl of Pembroke, or Henry Wriothesley, earl of Southampton; the former is a dedicatee of the volume of Shakespeare's plays known as the First Folio, while the latter is the dedicatee of Shakespeare's narrative poems *Venus and Adonis* and *Lucrece*. Patrons were often flatteringly depicted as "begetters" of poems, and it is therefore tempting to see an association between "Mr. W. H." and the beloved young man addressed in many of Shakespeare's sonnets, especially because the first seventeen poems in the sequence stress the young man's need to marry and beget heirs. No clear evidence, however, identifies a specific historical person either with the young man addressed in the sonnets or with the "Dark Lady" evoked as the third member of the erotic triangle Shakespeare dramatizes in these poems.

The sonnets evidently circulated in manuscript for some years before they were first published as a group in 1609 (a few appeared separately in anthologies). The ordering of the 154 poems in the 1609 Quarto may or may not reflect authorial design.

2. Betrothed; also implying withdrawn into, shrunken (not increased).
3. Of your own (unique) substance.
4. What contents you (marriage and fatherhood) and also what you contain (potential for fatherhood).
5. Gentle boor.

2

When forty winters shall besiege thy brow
And dig deep trenches in thy beauty's field,
Thy youth's proud° livery,° so gazed on now,   *splendid / clothing*
Will be a tottered° weed° of small worth held.   *tattered / garment*
5 Then being asked where all thy beauty lies—
Where all the treasure of thy lusty days—
To say within thine own deep-sunken eyes
Were an all-eating shame⁶ and thriftless praise.
How much more praise deserved thy beauty's use,⁷
10 If thou couldst answer, "This fair child of mine
Shall sum my count and make my old excuse"⁸—
Proving his beauty by succession thine.
   This were to be new made when thou art old,
   And see thy blood warm when thou feel'st it cold.

3

Look in thy glass° and tell the face thou viewest,   *mirror*
Now is the time that face should form another,
Whose fresh repair° if now thou not renewest,   *condition*
Thou dost beguile the world, unbless some mother.
5 For where is she so fair whose uneared⁹ womb
Disdains the tillage of thy husbandry?
Or who is he so fond° will be the tomb   *foolish*
Of his self-love, to stop posterity?
Thou art thy mother's glass, and she in thee
10 Calls back the lovely April of her prime;
So thou through windows of thine age shalt see,
Despite of wrinkles, this thy golden time.
   But if thou live rememb'red not to be,
   Die single, and thine image dies with thee.

12

When I do count the clock that tells the time,
And see the brave° day sunk in hideous night;   *resplendent*
When I behold the violet past prime,
And sable curls all silvered o'er with white;
5 When lofty trees I see barren of leaves,
Which erst° from heat did canopy the herd,   *formerly*
And summer's green all girded up in sheaves,
Borne on the bier¹ with white and bristly beard,

---

6. A total disgrace; also, an offense in which the beauty of youth has been devoured.
7. Investment for profit; also, sexual use.
8. Shall complete my account and justify me in my old age.
9. Immature; also, unplowed.
1. A frame for carrying harvested grain; also, a stand on which a corpse is carried to the grave.

Then of thy beauty do I question make,
10 That thou among the wastes of time must go,
Since sweets and beauties do themselves forsake
And die as fast as they see others grow;
    And nothing 'gainst Time's scythe can make defense
    Save breed,° to brave° him when he takes thee hence.   *progeny / defy*

15

When I consider everything that grows
Holds° in perfection but a little moment,   *remains*
That this huge stage presenteth nought but shows[2]
Whereon the stars in secret influence commént;[3]
5   When I perceive that men as plants increase,
Cheerèd and checked° ev'n by the selfsame sky,   *repressed*
Vaunt in their youthful sap,[4] at height decrease,
And wear their brave state out of memory,[5]
Then the conceit° of this inconstant stay   *conception, idea*
10 Sets you most rich in youth before my sight,
Where wasteful time debateth with[6] decay
To change your day of youth to sullied° night;   *soiled; darkened*
    And all in war with time for love of you,
    As he takes from you, I engraft you new.[7]

18

Shall I compare thee to a summer's day?
Thou art more lovely and more temperate:
Rough winds do shake the darling buds of May,
And summer's lease° hath all too short a date;   *alloted time*
5   Sometimes too hot the eye of heaven shines,
And often is his gold complexion dimmed;
And every fair° from fair sometimes declines,   *beauty*
By chance or nature's changing course untrimmed;[8]
But thy eternal summer shall not fade,
10 Nor lose possession of that fair thou ow'st;[9]
Nor shall death brag thou wand'rest in his shade,
When in eternal lines to Time thou grow'st:[1]
    So long as men can breathe, or eyes can see,
    So long lives this, and this gives life to thee.

2. This can be read as "presents only appearances of performances" with "shows" functioning as a noun, but "shows" also can operate as a verb and mean "reveals."
3. The stars secretly affect humankind's explanation of the world.
4. Exult in their youthful vigor; also, display themselves.
5. Wear out their splendid finery and are forgotten.
6. Fights with, fights against.
7. As time withers you, I renew you (with my poetry).
8. Divested of its beauty.
9. Own, with a play on *owe*.
1. I.e., when you are grafted to Time in this immortal poetry.

20

A woman's face, with nature's own hand painted,[2]
Hast thou, the master mistress of my passion—
A woman's gentle heart, but not acquainted
With shifting change, as is false° women's fashion;   *deceitful; artificial*
5 An eye more bright than theirs, less false in rolling,°   *roving*
Gilding the object whereupon it gazeth;
A man in hue all hues in his controlling,[3]
Which steals men's eyes and women's souls amazeth.
And for a woman wert thou first created,
10 Till nature as she wrought thee fell a-doting,°   *crazy; infatuated*
And by addition me of thee defeated,
By adding one thing to my purpose nothing.
    But since she pricked thee out for women's pleasure,
    Mine be thy love and thy love's use their treasure.[4]

29

When, in disgrace° with fortune and men's eyes,   *disfavor*
I all alone beweep my outcast state,
And trouble deaf heaven with my bootless° cries,   *futile*
And look upon myself, and curse my fate,
5 Wishing me like to one more rich in hope,
Featured° like him, like him[5] with friends   *formed; handsome*
    possessed,
Desiring this man's art° and that man's scope,[6]   *skill*
With what I most enjoy contented least;
Yet in these thoughts myself almost despising,
10 Haply I think on thee—and then my state,[7]
Like to the lark at break of day arising
From sullen earth, sings hymns at heaven's gate;
    For thy sweet love rememb'red such wealth brings
    That then I scorn to change my state with kings.

---

2. I.e., not made up with cosmetics.
3. "Controlling" works as a noun and as an adjective, depending on how one interprets "hue" (form, complexion, color, and apparition are the main possibilities). The line has been paraphrased in many ways, among them: "a man in form, all forms, i.e., all people, are subject to his power"; "a man in complexion, he has control over all other complexions, i.e., he causes people to grow pale or blush"; "a man in appearance, he can present any appearance he chooses."

4. Interest (as in usury), sexual enjoyment. Modern editors usually punctuate this line with a comma after "love," but some recent critics argue instead for a comma after "use"; we follow the 1609 Quarto in not punctuating the line internally, thereby allowing for more than one interpretation of the final couplet.
5. The "him"s here refer to two different men.
6. Freedom, range of ability.
7. Condition, state of mind (setting up the pun in line 14, where it also means chair of state, throne).

30

When to the sessions of sweet silent thought
I summon up[8] remembrance of things past,
I sigh the lack of many a thing I sought,
And with old woes new wail my dear time's waste:
5   Then can I drown an eye, unused to flow,
For precious friends hid in death's dateless° night,   *endless*
And weep afresh love's long since canceled woe,
And moan the expense° of many a vanished sight: *loss*
Then can I grieve at grievances foregone,°   *past*
10 And heavily from woe to woe tell° o'er   *count*
The sad account° of fore-bemoanèd moan,   *report; financial record*
Which I new pay as if not paid before.
      But if the while I think on thee, dear friend,
      All losses are restored and sorrows end.

33

Full many a glorious morning have I seen
Flatter the mountain-tops with sovereign eye,°   *sunlight*
Kissing with golden face the meadows green,
Gilding pale streams with heavenly alchemy,
5   Anon° permit the basest clouds to ride   *soon*
With ugly rack[9] on his celestial face,
And from the forlorn world his visage hide,
Stealing unseen to west with this disgrace:
Even so my sun one early morn did shine
10 With all-triumphant splendor on my brow;
But, out, alack!° he was but one hour mine,   *also*
The region cloud[1] hath masked him from me now.
      Yet him for this my love no whit disdaineth;
      Suns of the world may stain[2] when heaven's sun staineth.

35

No more be grieved at that which thou hast done:
Roses have thorns, and silver fountains mud,
Clouds and eclipses stain° both moon and sun,   *dim; defile*
And loathsome canker° lives in sweetest bud.   *rose worm*
5   All men make faults, and even I in this,
Authórizing° thy trespass with compare,   *justifying*
Myself corrupting salving thy amiss,[3]
Excusing thy sins more than thy sins are:

8. One may be "summoned" to the "sessions" (sit-   1. I.e., the clouds in the vicinity.
tings) of a court.   2. I.e., be stained.
9. A wind-driven mass of high, broken clouds.   3. Explaining, making acceptable or palliating

For to thy sensual fault I bring in sense°—   *reason*
10   Thy adverse party is thy advocate—
And 'gainst myself a lawful plea commence.
Such civil war is in my love and hate,
   That I an áccessary needs must be
   To that sweet thief which sourly robs from me.

55

Not marble, nor the gilded monuments
Of princes, shall outlive this powerful rhyme;
But you shall shine more bright in these contènts
Than unswept stone, besmeared with sluttish time.
5   When wasteful war shall statues overturn,
And broils° root out the work of masonry,[4]   *disturbances*
Nor Mars his[5] sword nor war's quick fire shall burn
The living record of your memory.
'Gainst death and all-oblivious enmity[6]
10   Shall you pace forth; your praise shall still find room
Even in the eyes of all posterity
That wear this world out to the ending doom.°   *Judgment Day*
   So, till the judgment that yourself arise,[7]
   You live in this, and dwell in lovers' eyes.

60

Like as the waves make towards the pebbled shore,
So do our minutes hasten to their end,
Each changing place with that which goes before,
In sequent toil[8] all forwards do contend.
5   Nativity, once in the main° of light,   *sea*
Crawls to maturity, wherewith being crowned,
Crookèd[9] eclipses 'gainst his glory fight,
And time that gave doth now his gift confound.
Time doth transfix the flourish set on youth,
10   And delves the parallels[1] in beauty's brow,
Feeds on the rarities of nature's truth,
And nothing stands but for[2] his scythe to mow.
   And yet to times in hope[3] my verse shall stand,
   Praising thy worth, despite his cruel hand.

---

your offense; also, smoothing and healing, as with
an ointment, your misdeed.
4. Products of the stonemason's work; work made
of stone.
5. I.e., neither Mars's.
6. The enmity of being forgotten.
7. I.e., until the Judgment Day when ("that") you
rise from the dead.
8. I.e., our minutes (like the waves) toil in contin-

uous succession, in unbroken series.
9. Malignant (in an astrological sense), but also
suggesting the crookedness of an old man bent by
age.
1. Digs the wrinkles ("parallels" are military
trenches). *Transfix the flourish*: destroy the beauty;
to "flourish" is also to blossom.
2. I.e., and stands for nothing except.
3. Future times.

65

Since brass, nor⁴ stone, nor earth, nor boundless sea
But sad mortality o'er-sways their power,
How with this rage° shall beauty hold a plea,   *destructive power*
Whose action is no stronger than a flower?
5   O, how shall summer's honey breath hold out
Against the wrackful° siege of batt'ring days,   *destructive*
When rocks impregnable are not so stout,
Nor gates of steel so strong, but time decays?
O fearful meditation! where, alack,°   *alas*
10 Shall time's best jewel from time's chest lie hid?
Or what strong hand can hold his swift foot back?
Or who his spoil of beauty⁵ can forbid?
      O, none, unless this miracle have might,
      That in black ink my love may still shine bright.

71

No longer mourn for me when I am dead
Than you shall hear the surly sullen bell⁶
Give warning to the world that I am fled
From this vile world, with vilest worms to dwell:
5   Nay, if you read this line, remember not
The hand that writ it; for I love you so,
That I in your sweet thoughts would be forgot,
If thinking on me then should make you woe.
Oh, if, I say, you look upon this verse
10 When I (perhaps) compounded am with clay,
Do not so much as my poor name rehearse,
But let your love even with my life decay;
      Lest the wise world should look into your moan,
      And mock you with me after I am gone.

73

That time of year thou mayst in me behold
When yellow leaves, or none, or few, do hang
Upon those boughs which shake against the cold,
Bare ruined choirs,⁷ where late the sweet birds sang.
5   In me thou see'st the twilight of such day
As after sunset fadeth in the west;
Which by and by black night doth take away,

---

4. I.e., since there is neither brass nor.
5. Ravaging of beauty; the Quarto has "or" for "of,"
and some modern editors follow that reading.
6. The bell rang to announce the death of a parish

member, one stroke for each year he or she had
lived.
7. Parts of churches occupied by singers or clergy.

Death's second self, that seals up all in rest.
In me thou see'st the glowing of such fire,
10 That on the ashes of his youth doth lie,
As the deathbed whereon it must expire,
Consumed with that which it was nourished by.
    This thou perceiv'st, which makes thy love more strong,
    To love that well which thou must leave ere long.

76

Why is my verse so barren of new pride,°   *adornment*
So far from variation or quick change?[8]
Why with the time do I not glance aside
To new-found methods, and to compounds[9] strange?
5 Why write I still all one, ever the same,
And keep invention in a noted° weed,°   *familiar / clothing*
That every word doth almost tell my name,
Showing their,° birth, and where they did proceed?   *the words'*
O know, sweet love, I always write of you,
10 And you and love are still my argument.°   *theme*
So all my best is dressing old words new,
Spending again what is already spent:
    For as the sun is daily new and old,
    So is my love still telling what is told.

87

Farewell, thou art too dear[1] for my possessing,
And like enough thou know'st thy estimate.°   *value*
The charter° of thy worth gives thee releasing;   *privilege; deed*
My bonds in thee are all determinate.°   *expired*
5 For how do I hold thee but by thy granting,
And for that riches where is my deserving?
The cause of this fair gift in me is wanting,
And so my patent° back again is swerving.   *title*
Thyself thou gav'st, thy own worth then not knowing,
10 Or me, to whom thou gav'st it, else mistaking;
So thy great gift, upon misprision° growing,   *error, oversight*
Comes home again, on better judgement making.[2]
    Thus have I had thee as a dream doth flatter:[3]
    In sleep a king, but waking no such matter.

8. Facile innovation; modishness.
9. Mixture, compound words, literary composi-
tions.

1. Precious (i.e., beloved), costly, grievous.
2. I.e., on your making a better judgment.
3. As in a flattering dream.

94

They that have power to hurt and will do none,
That do not do the thing they most do show,[4]
Who, moving others, are themselves as stone,
Unmovèd, cold, and to temptation slow;
5   They rightly do inherit heaven's graces,
And husband nature's riches from expense;[5]
They are the lords and owners of their faces,
Others but stewards° of their excellence.   *hired managers*
The summer's flower is to the summer sweet,
10   Though to itself it only live and die,
But if that flower with base infection meet,
The basest weed outbraves° his dignity: *surpasses*
    For sweetest things turn sourest by their deeds;
    Lilies that fester smell far worse than weeds.

97

How like a winter hath my absence been
From thee, the pleasure of the fleeting year!
What freezings have I felt, what dark days seen!
What old December's bareness everywhere!
5   And yet this time removed° was summer's time,   *of separation*
The teeming autumn big with rich increase,
Bearing the wanton burthen of the prime,[6]
Like widowed wombs after their lords' decease.
Yet this abundant issue seemed to me
10   But hope of orphans, and unfathered fruit;
For summer and his° pleasures wait on thee,   *its*
And thou away, the very birds are mute;
    Or if they sing, 'tis with so dull a cheer,[7]
    That leaves look pale, dreading the winter's near.

106

When in the chronicle of wasted° time   *past; destroyed*
I see descriptions of the fairest wights,°   *persons*
And beauty making beautiful old rhyme
In praise of ladies dead and lovely knights,
5   Then, in the blazon[8] of sweet beauty's best,
Of hand, of foot, of lip, of eye, of brow,

---

4. I.e., what their appearance indicates they will do.
5. I.e., guard against squandering nature's riches.
6. The children of wanton springtime, i.e., the crops planted at that time; also, the fruits of the

wantonness of one's sexual prime.
7. So gloomily; so downcast.
8. A catalog of attributes; a literary form characterized by a standardized description of the woman's body parts.

I see their antique pen would have expressed
Even such a beauty as you master now.
So all their praises are but prophecies
10 Of this our time, all you prefiguring;
And, for° they looked but° with divining eyes,   because / only
They had not skill enough your worth to sing·
    For we, which now behold these present days,
    Have eyes to wonder, but lack tongues to praise.

107

Not mine own fears, nor the prophetic soul
Of the wide world dreaming on things to come,
Can yet the lease of my true love control,
Supposed as forfeit to a cònfined doom.[9]
5   The mortal moon[1] hath her eclipse endured,
And the sad augurs mock their own presage;°   prediction
Incertainties now crown themselves assured,
And peace proclaims olives of endless age.
Now with the drops of this most balmy time
10 My love looks fresh, and death to me subscribes,°   submits
Since, spite of him, I'll live in this poor rhyme,
While he insults o'er dull and speechless tribes:
    And thou in this shalt find thy monument,
    When tyrants' crests and tombs of brass are spent.°   destroyed

116

Let me not to the marriage of true minds
Admit impediments. Love is not love
Which alters when it alteration finds,
Or bends with the remover to remove:
5   Oh, no! it is an ever-fixèd mark,
That looks on tempests and is never shaken;
It is the star to every wandering bark,°   ship
Whose worth's unknown, although his height be taken.[2]
Love's not Time's fool, though rosy lips and cheeks
10 Within his bending sickle's compass come;
Love alters not with his brief hours and weeks,
But bears it out even to the edge° of doom.°   brink / Judgment Day
    If this be error and upon me proved,
    I never writ, nor no man ever loved.

9. Playing on metaphors of real estate, the lines suggest that despite his fears, the poet's love has not yet suffered the fate of being limited ("confined") by death.
1. Queen Elizabeth I (1533–1603; see pp. 142–43), whose sixty-third year had been erroneously anticipated by astrologers ("augurs," line 6) as a time of disaster.
2. I.e., although the star's altitude may be measured.

126³

O thou, my lovely boy, who in thy pow'r
Dost hold time's fickle glass his sickle hour,⁴
Who hast by waning grown,⁵ and therein° show'st   *in contrast*
Thy lovers withering, as thy sweet self grow'st—
5   If nature, sovereign mistress over wrack,°   *destruction, ruin*
As thou goest onwards still will pluck thee back,
She keeps thee to this purpose, that her skill
May time disgrace, and wretched minute kill.
Yet fear her, O thou minion⁶ of her pleasure;
10   She may detain but not still° keep her treasure.   *always, forever*
Her audit,° though delayed, answered must be,   *final accounting*
And her quietus° is to render° thee.   *settlement / surrender*

129

Th' expense of spirit in a waste of shame
Is lust in action;⁷ and till action, lust
Is perjured, murderous, bloody, full of blame,
Savage, extreme, rude,° cruel, not to trust;   *brutal*
5   Enjoyed no sooner but despisèd straight:
Past reason hunted; and no sooner had,
Past reason hated, as a swallowed bait,
On purpose laid to make the taker mad:
Mad in pursuit, and in possession so;
10   Had, having, and in quest to have, extreme;
A bliss in proof,° and proved, a very woe;   *the experience*
Before, a joy proposed; behind, a dream.
    All this the world well knows; yet none knows well
    To shun the heaven that leads men to this hell.

130

My mistress' eyes are nothing like the sun;
Coral is far more red than her lips' red;
If snow be white, why then her breasts are dun;°   *dull grayish brown*
If hairs be wires, black wires grow on her head.
5   I have seen roses damasked,° red and white,   *variegated*
But no such roses see I in her cheeks;
And in some perfumes is there more delight

3. An envoy of six couplets, this "sonnet" ends the part of Shakespeare's sequence that seems addressed to a young man.
4. Hourglass. *Glass:* mirror, presumably in which the viewer can see time's ravaging of beauty. *Sickle:* scythe, here in adjectival sense, cutting.
5. Grown more beautiful over time.
6. Darling, favorite, plaything, servile follower.
7. I.e., lust, when put into action, is an expenditure of "spirit" (life, vigor, also semen) in a waste (desert, with a play on the crotch, or "waist," of shame).

Than in the breath that from my mistress reeks.
I love to hear her speak, yet well I know
10   That music hath a far more pleasing sound;
I grant I never saw a goddess go;°   walk
My mistress, when she walks, treads on the ground.
    And yet, by heaven, I think my love as rare
    As any she° belied with false compare.   woman

135

Whoever hath her wish, thou hast thy Will,[8]
And Will to boot, and Will in overplus;
More than enough am I that vex thee still,°   always
To thy sweet will making addition thus.
5   Wilt thou, whose will is large and spacious,
Not once vouchsafe° to hide my will in thine?   consent
Shall will in others seem right gracious,
And in° my will no fair acceptance shine?   in the case of
The sea, all water, yet receives rain still,
10   And in abundance addeth to his° store;°   its / reserves
So thou being rich in Will add to thy Will
One will of mine, to make thy large Will more.
    Let no unkind, no fair beseechers kill;[9]
    Think all but one, and me in that one Will.

138

When my love swears that she is made of truth,
I do believe her, though I know she lies,[1]
That° she might think me some untutored youth,   so that
Unlearnèd in the world's false subtleties.
5   Thus vainly thinking that she thinks me young,
Although she knows my days are past the best,[2]
Simply° I credit her false-speaking tongue: like a simpleton
On both sides thus is simple truth suppressed.
But wherefore says she not she is unjust?[3]
10   And wherefore say not I that I am old?
Oh, love's best habit° is in seeming trust,   clothes; custom
And age in love loves not to have years told.°   counted
    Therefore I lie with her and she with me,
    And in our faults by lies we flattered be.

---

8. Here, the word can refer to wishes, carnal
desire, male and female sexual organs, and a lover
named Will (Shakespeare?). Three, possibly four,
sonnets pun on "will"; we follow the 1609 Quarto's
way of printing the word.
9. Do not kill any of your suitors with unkindness.

1. Does not tell the truth, with a pun on "lies" with
men.
2. When this sonnet was first published, in the
anthology The Passionate Pilgrim (1599), Shake-
speare was thirty-five.
3. I.e., why does she not say that she is unfaithful?

144

Two loves I have of comfort and despair,[4]
Which like two spirits do suggest° me still°   *tempt / always*
The better angel is a man right fair,
The worser spirit a woman coloured ill.°   *dark*
5   To win me soon to hell, my female evil
Tempteth my better angel from my side,
And would corrupt my saint to be a devil,
Wooing his purity with her foul pride.°   *vanity; sexual wantonness*
And, whether that my angel be turn'd fiend,
10   Suspect I may, yet not directly tell,
But being both from° me both to each° friend,   *away from / each other*
I guess one angel in another's hell.[5]
   Yet this shall I ne'er know, but live in doubt,
   Till my bad angel fire my good one out.[6]

146

Poor soul, the center of my sinful earth,
Lord of[7] these rebel powers that thee array,°   *dress, deck out*
Why dost thou pine within and suffer dearth,
Painting thy outward walls so costly gay?
5   Why so large cost, having so short a lease,
Dost thou upon thy fading mansion spend?
Shall worms, inheritors of this excess,
Eat up thy charge?[8] Is this thy body's end?
Then, soul, live thou upon thy servant's loss,
10   And let that pine to aggravate thy store;[9]
Buy terms divine in selling hours of dross;[1]
Within be fed, without be rich no more.
   So shalt thou feed on death, that feeds on men,
   And death once dead, there's no more dying then.

1609

4. I have two beloveds; one brings me comfort, and the other despair.
5. Each is a punishment for the other; also, a double entendre.
6. The metaphor is from hunting: using fire and smoke to drive a fox from its hole. The line also alludes to the onset of venereal disease, to the Renaissance coin called an *angel,* and to various proverbial sayings including *One fire drives out another* and *Bad money drives out good.*
7. The 1609 Quarto repeats "My sinful earth,"

apparently a mistake, in place of "Lord of" (an editorial conjecture) at the beginning of this line. Other possibilities have been suggested, e.g., "Rebuke," "Thrall to," "Pressed by."
8. Your expenditure; your trust, i.e., your body; your burden.
9. I.e., let the body suffer ("pine") to increase your riches.
1. I.e., purchase ages of immortality through selling hours of mortal time. *Dross:* rubbish.

The Phoenix and the Turtle[2]

Let the bird of loudest lay,°   *song*
On the sole° Arabian tree,   *unique*
Herald sad° and trumpet be,   *solemn*
To whose sound chaste wings obey.

5   But thou shrieking harbinger,[3]
Foul precurrer of the fiend,[4]
Augur of the fever's end,[5]
To this troop come thou not near!

From this session interdict°   *forbid*
10   Every fowl of tyrant wing,[6]
Save the eagle, feathered king:
Keep the obsequy° so strict.   *funeral rites*

Let the priest in surplice° white,   *vestment*
That defunctive° music can,°   *funeral / knows*
15   Be the death-divining swan,[7]
Lest the requiem lack his° right.°   *its / due ceremony*

And thou treble-dated crow,[8]
That thy sable° gender mak'st   *black*
With the breath thou giv'st and tak'st,
20   'Mongst our mourners shalt thou go.

Here the anthem doth commence:
Love and constancy is dead,
Phoenix and the turtle fled
In a mutual flame from hence.

25   So they loved as° love in twain   *as if*
Had the essence but in one;
Two distincts, division none:
Number there in love was slain.[9]

Hearts remote, yet not asunder;
30   Distance, and no space was seen
'Twixt this turtle and his queen;
But in them it were a wonder.[1]

---

2. Turtledove, famous for steadfastness in love. The phoenix is a legendary bird, the only one of its kind. It is represented as living five hundred years in the Arabian desert before setting itself on fire, then rising anew from its own ashes. The identy of the bird in line 1 has been much debated; most critics agree that it is not the phoenix, which left "no posterity" (line 59).
3. I.e., the screech owl, harbinger of death.
4. I.e., forerunner of Satan.
5. I.e., presager of death.
6. I.e., every predatory bird.
7. Since the swan was said to sing only as its death drew near, it "divined" (knew) the time of its death.
8. The crow was supposed to live three times longer than humans and to conceive its young ("sable gender," line 18) through its beak.
9. Refers to the Aristotelian theory that "one is no number," as Marlowe puts it in *Hero and Leander*, line 255 (p. 244). The stanza depicts the lovers as paradoxically united but separate. Because they are neither one nor two, their "love" has "slain" the idea of "number."
1. I.e., in anyone except ("but") them, it would have been a wonder.

So° between them love did shine   *so much*
That the turtle saw his right°   *due; possession; nature*
35 Flaming in the phoenix' sight:°   *eyes*
Either was the other's mine.[2]

Property was thus appalled,
That the self was not the same;
Single nature's double name
40 Neither two nor one was called.

Reason, in itself confounded,°   *destroyed*
Saw division grow together,
To themselves yet either neither,
Simple were so well compounded;

45 That it cried, "How true° a twain   *faithful; truly*
Seemeth this concordant one!
Love hath reason, reason none,
If what parts can so remain."[3]

Whereupon it made this threne[4]
50 To the phoenix and the dove,
Co-supremes° and stars of love,   *joint rulers*
As chorus to their tragic scene.

Threnos

Beauty, truth,° and rarity,   *fidelity*
Grace in all simplicity,
55 Here enclosed in cinders lie.

Death is now the phoenix' nest;
And the turtle's loyal breast
To eternity doth rest,[5]

Leaving no posterity:
60 'Twas not their infirmity,°   *sterility*
It was married chastity.

Truth may seem, but cannot be;
Beauty brag, but 'tis not she:
Truth and Beauty buried be.

65 To this urn let those repair
That are either true or fair;
For these dead birds sigh a prayer.

1601

2. I.e., self; with a pun on source of (mineral) wealth.
3. I.e., if what is separate can remain joined, then reason yields to love as more reasonable.

4. Threnos or threnody (Greek), a lyrical lament over the dead.
5. Rests eternally; endures forever.

SONGS FROM THE PLAYS
When Daisies Pied[6]

Spring

When daisies pied° and violets blue   variegated
  And lady-smocks all silver-white
And cuckoo-buds of yellow hue[7]
  Do paint the meadows with delight,
5 The cuckoo then, on every tree,
Mocks married men;[8] for thus sings he,
      Cuckoo;
Cuckoo, cuckoo: Oh word of fear,
Unpleasing to a married ear!

10 When shepherds pipe on oaten° straws,°   reed / pipes
  And merry larks are plowmen's clocks,[9]
When turtles tread, and rooks, and daws,[1]
  And maidens bleach their summer smocks,
The cuckoo then, on every tree,
15 Mocks married men; for thus sings he,
      Cuckoo;
Cuckoo, cuckoo: Oh word of fear,
Unpleasing to a married ear!

Winter

When icicles hang by the wall
20 And Dick the shepherd blows his nail[2]
And Tom bears logs into the hall,
  And milk comes frozen home in pail.
When blood is nipped° and ways° be foul,   chilled / paths
Then nightly sings the staring owl,
25   Tu-who;
Tu-whit,[3] tu-who: a merry note,
While greasy Joan doth keel° the pot.   stir to cool

When all aloud the wind doth blow,
  And coughing drowns the parson's saw,°   wise saying
30 And birds sit brooding in the snow,
  And Marian's nose looks red and raw,
When roasted crabs° hiss in the bowl,°   crab apples / (of ale)
Then nightly sings the staring owl,
      Tu-who;
35 Tu-whit, tu-who: a merry note
While greasy Joan doth keel the pot.

1595?   1598

---

6. This song concludes *Love's Labour's Lost*. Announced as a "Dialogue . . . in praise of the Owl and the Cuckoo," it provides a lyric commentary on the bittersweet mood that pervades the play's final scene.
7. Modern commentators differ in identifying these flowers.
8. The cuckoo's song was often translated as *cuck-* old, meaning a husband whose wife is unfaithful.
9. Larks sing at sunrise.
1. Two kinds of crows. *When turtles tread*: i.e., when turtledoves mate.
2. I.e., breathes on his fingers to warm them; also, waits patiently while he has nothing to do.
3. Possibly "to woo; to it" (the latter a hunter's cry, here with sexual overtones).

Under the Greenwood Tree[4]

Under the greenwood tree
Who loves to lie with me,
And turn° his merry note   *attune*
Unto the sweet bird's throat,
5   Come hither, come hither, come hither:
         Here shall he see
         No enemy
But winter and rough weather.

         Who doth ambition shun
10   And loves to live i' the sun,
         Seeking the food he eats,
         And pleased with what he gets,
Come hither, come hither, come hither:
         Here shall he see
15   No enemy
But winter and rough weather.

1599?   1623

Blow, Blow, Thou Winter Wind[5]

Blow, blow, thou winter wind,
Thou art not so unkind
     As man's ingratitude;
Thy tooth is not so keen,
5   Because thou art not seen,
     Although thy breath be rude.°   *rough*
Heigh-ho! sing, heigh-ho! unto the green holly:[6]
Most friendship is feigning, most loving mere folly:
     Then, heigh-ho, the holly!
10   *This life is most jolly.*

Freeze, freeze, thou bitter sky,
That dost not bite so nigh
     As benefits forgot:
Though thou the waters warp,[7]
15   Thy sting is not so sharp
     As friend remembered not.
Heigh-ho! sing, heigh-ho! unto the green holly . . .

1599?   1623

---

4. From *As You Like It* (2.5). Sung by Amiens, a
lord attending the banished duke in the Forest of
Arden, the song addresses the play's concern with
the traditional opposition between pastoral and
courtly modes of life.
5. From *As You Like It* (2.7). Sung by Amiens, a
lord attending the banished duke in the Forest of
Arden, this lyric elaborates on the play's thematic
contrast between nature and human behavior.
6. An emblem of mirth.
7. I.e., freeze.

It Was a Lover and His Lass[8]

It was a lover and his lass,
    With a hey, and a ho, and a hey nonino,
That o'er the green corn° field did pass   *wheat*
    In springtime, the only pretty ring time,[9]
5 *When birds do sing, hey ding a ding, ding:*
    Sweet lovers love the spring.

Between the acres of the rye,[1]
    With a hey, and a ho, and a hey nonino,
These pretty country folks would lie,
10   *In springtime, the only pretty ring time . . .*

This carol° they began that hour,   *song*
    With a hey, and a ho, and a hey nonino,
How that a life was but a flower
    In springtime, the only pretty ring time . . .

15 And therefore take° the present time,   *seize*
    With a hey, and a ho, and a hey nonino;
For love is crownèd with the prime°   *springtime*
    In springtime, the only pretty ring time . . .

1599?   1623

Sigh No More[2]

Sigh no more, ladies, sigh no more.
    Men were deceivers ever,
One foot in sea, and one on shore,
    To one thing constant never.
5 Then sigh not so, but let them go,
    And be you blithe° and bonny,°   *cheerful / joyful*
Converting all your sounds of woe
    Into hey nonny, nonny.[3]

Sign no more ditties, sing no more
10   Of dumps° so dull and heavy.   *mournful songs or moods*
The fraud of men was ever so
    Since summer first was leafy.
Then sigh not so, but let them go,
    And be you blithe and bonny,

---

8. From *As You Like It* (5.3). Sung by two pages to the clown, Touchstone, and the "country wench," Audrey; in the next (and final) scene, this couple and three other couples will marry.
9. I.e., marriage season.

1. On unplowed ground between the planted fields.
2. Sung by Balthasar, attendant to the villainous Don Pedro, in *Much Ado About Nothing* (2.3).
3. (A nonsense refrain.)

15 Converting all your sounds of woe
    Into hey nonny, nonny.

1600   1623

Oh Mistress Mine[4]

Oh mistress mine! where are you roaming?
Oh! stay and hear; your true love's coming,
    That can sing both high and low.
Trip° no further, pretty sweeting;   go
5 Journeys end in lovers meeting,
    Every wise man's son[5] doth know.

What is love? 'tis not hereafter;
Present mirth hath present laughter;
    What's to come is still° unsure: always
10 In delay there lies no plenty;
    Then come kiss me, sweet and twenty,
    Youth's a stuff will not endure.

1602   1623

Come Away, Come Away, Death[6]

Come away, come away, death,
    And in sad cypress[7] let me be laid.
Fly away, fly away, breath;
    I am slain by a fair cruel maid.
5 My shroud of white, stuck all with yew,[8]
            O, prepare it!
My part of death, no one so true
            Did share it.

Not a flower, not a flower sweet,
10   On my black coffin let there be strown.
Not a friend, not a friend greet
    My poor corpse, where my bones shall be thrown.
A thousand thousand sighs to save,
            Lay me, O, where
15 Sad true lover never find my grave,
            To weep there!

1602   1623

4. From *Twelfth Night* (2.3). Sung by the clown, Feste, in response to a request by Sir Toby and Sir Andrew for a "love-song."
5. I.e., proverbially: every fool.
6. From *Twelfth Night* (2.4). Sung by the clown, Feste, in response to the lovesick duke's melan-

choly request for a song.
7. A coffin of cypress or a bier covered with cypress boughs. The tree symbolized mourning.
8. A tree symbolizing sadness, often planted in churchyards.

When That I Was and a Little Tiny Boy[9]

When that I was and a little tiny boy,
  With hey, ho, the wind and the rain,
A foolish thing was but a toy,[1]
  For the rain it raineth every day.

5 But when I came to man's estate,°   state, condition
  With hey, ho, the wind and the rain,
'Gainst knaves and thieves men shut their gate,
  For the rain it raineth every day.

But when I came, alas! to wive,
10   With hey, ho, the wind and the rain,
By swaggering° could I never thrive,   blustering
  For the rain it raineth every day.

But when I came unto my beds,
  With hey, ho, the wind and the rain,
15 With toss-pots° still had drunken heads,   drunkards
  For the rain it raineth every day.

A great while ago the world begun,
  With hey, ho, the wind and the rain,
But that's all one, our play is done,
20   And we'll strive to please you every day.

1602   1623

Fear No More the Heat o' the Sun[2]

Fear no more the heat o' the sun,
  Nor the furious winter's rages;
Thou thy worldly task hast done,
  Home art gone, and ta'en thy wages:
5 Golden lads and girls all must,
  As° chimney-sweepers, come to dust.   like

Fear no more the frown o' the great;
  Thou art past the tyrant's stroke;
Care no more to clothe and eat;
10   To thee the reed is as the oak:[3]
The scepter,° learning, physic,° must   royal power / medicine
  All follow this, and come to dust.

---

9. Sung by the clown, Feste, to conclude *Twelfth Night*.
1. Trifle. I.e., my mischief was not taken seriously.
2. From *Cymbeline* (4.2). A lament by two singers-

for Fidele, a "young boy" who is actually Imogen in disguise and is not actually dead.
3. I.e., to you, what is fragile ("the reed") is the same as what is enduring ("the oak").

Fear no more the lightning flash,
　　Nor the all-dreaded thunder stone;[4]
15　Fear not slander, censure rash;
　　Thou hast finished joy and moan:
All lovers young, all lovers must
Consign to thee,[5] and come to dust.

No exorciser harm thee!
20　Nor no witchcraft charm thee!
Ghost unlaid forbear thee!
Nothing ill come near thee!
Quiet consummation have;
And renownèd be thy grave!

1610?　　　　　　　　　　　　　　　　　　　　　　　1623

Full Fathom Five[6]

Full fathom five thy father lies;
　　Of his bones are coral made;
Those are pearls that were his eyes:
　　Nothing of him that doth fade,
5　But doth suffer a sea change
Into something rich and strange.
Sea nymphs[7] hourly ring his knell:
　　Ding-dong.
Hark! now I hear them—Ding-dong, bell.

1611　　　　　　　　　　　　　　　　　　　　　　　1623

Where the Bee Sucks, There Suck I[8]

Where the bee sucks, there suck I:
In a cowslip's° bell I lie;　　　　　　　　　　　*a wildflower's*
There I couch when owls do cry.
On the bat's back I do fly
5　After summer merrily.
Merrily, merrily shall I live now
Under the blossom that hangs on the bough.

1611　　　　　　　　　　　　　　　　　　　　　　　1623

---

4. Thunder was thought to be caused by meteorites falling from the sky.
5. I.e., accept the same terms that governed you.
6. From *The Tempest* (1.2). Ariel, the airy spirit of the enchanted isle, sings this song to lead the shipwrecked Ferdinand, prince of Naples, to Prospero.

7. In Greek mythology, minor goddesses who lived in water.
8. From *The Tempest* (5.1). Ariel, the airy spirit of the enchanted isle, sings this song in anticipation of his approaching freedom from servitude.

THOMAS CAMPION
1567–1620

My Sweetest Lesbia[1]

My sweetest Lesbia, let us live and love,
And though the sager sort our deeds reprove,
Let us not weigh° them. Heaven's great lamps do dive   *heed*
Into their west, and straight again revive,
5   But soon as once set is our little light,
Then must we sleep one ever-during night.

If all would lead their lives in love like me,
Then bloody swords and armor should not be;
No drum nor trumpet peaceful sleeps should move,
10 Unless alarm came from the camp of love.
But fools do live, and waste their little light,
And seek with pain their ever-during night.

When timely death my life and fortune ends,
Let not my hearse be vexed with mourning friends,
15 But let all lovers, rich in triumph, come
And with sweet pastimes grace my happy tomb;
And Lesbia, close up thou my little light,
And crown with love my ever-during night.

1601

I Care Not for These Ladies

I care not for these ladies,
That must be wooed and prayed:
Give me kind Amaryllis,
The wanton country[2] maid.
5 Nature art disdaineth,
Her beauty is her own.
    Her when we court and kiss,
    She cries, "Forsooth, let go!"
    But when we come where comfort is,
10   She never will say no.

If I love Amaryllis,
She gives me fruit and flowers:
But if we love these ladies,
We must give golden showers.[3]
15 Give them gold, that sell love,

---

1. The Roman poet Catullus (ca. 84–ca. 54 B.C.E.) sang the praises of his beloved Lesbia in a poem here imitated and partly translated by Campion.

2. With an obscene pun, as in line 9.
3. An allusion to the Greek myth in which Jove takes the form of a shower of gold to ravish Danaë.

Give me the nut-brown lass,
 Who, when we court and kiss,
 She cries, "Forsooth, let go!"
 But when we come where comfort is,
20 She never will say no.

These ladies must have pillows,
And beds by strangers wrought;
Give me a bower of willows,
Of moss and leaves unbought,
25 And fresh Amaryllis,
 With milk and honey fed;
  Who, when we court and kiss,
  She cries, "Forsooth, let go!"
  But when we come where comfort is,
30   She never will say no.

           1601

Follow Thy Fair Sun

Follow thy fair sun, unhappy shadow;[4]
Though thou be black as night,
And she made all of light,
Yet follow thy fair sun, unhappy shadow.

5 Follow her whose light thy light depriveth;
Though here thou liv'st disgraced,
And she in heaven is placed,
Yet follow her whose light the world reviveth!

Follow those pure beams whose beauty burneth,
10 That so have scorchèd thee,
As thou still black must be,[5]
Till her kind beams thy black to brightness turneth.

Follow her while yet her glory shineth;
There comes a luckless night,
15 That will dim all her light;
And this the black unhappy shade divineth.

Follow still since so thy fates ordained;
The sun must have his shade,
Till both at once do fade;
20 The sun still proved,° the shadow still disdained.   *approved*

           1601

---

4. Soul; also, a person imagined as dead (a *shade*, and lost to heaven's light).
5. In Renaissance England, dark skins were often held to be caused by the sun's burning; the line also plays on the idea of black as the color of sin (pointing toward an afterlife in hell) and as the sign of mourning.

When to Her Lute Corinna Sings

When to her lute Corinna sings,
Her voice revives the leaden strings,
And doth in highest notes appear
As any challenged° echo clear;   *aroused*
5   But when she doth of mourning speak,
Ev'n with her sighs the strings do break.

And as her lute doth live or die,
Led by her passion, so must I:
For when of pleasure she doth sing,
10   My thoughts enjoy a sudden spring,
But if she doth of sorrow speak,
Ev'n from my heart the strings do break.

1601

When Thou Must Home[6]

When thou must home to shades of underground,
And there arrived, a new admirèd guest,
The beauteous spirits do engirt° thee round,   *encircle*
White Iope, blithe Helen,[7] and the rest,
5   To hear the stories of thy finished love
From that smooth tongue whose music hell can move,[8]

Then wilt thou speak of banqueting delights,
Of masques[9] and revels which sweet youth did make,
Of tourneys and great challenges of knights,
10   And all these triumphs for thy beauty's sake;
When thou hast told these honors done to thee,
Then tell, Oh tell, how thou didst murther° me.   *murder*

1601

Rose-cheeked Laura[1]

Rose-cheeked Laura, come,
Sing thou smoothly with thy beauty's

6. This poem addresses a woman the speaker imagines as already dead, "home" in hell.
7. The Greek mythological figures Iope, or Cassiopeia, and Helen of Troy, the first renowned for beauty and vanity, the second for beauty and fickleness. *Blithe:* happy.
8. I.e., whose music can move hell. In Greek mythology, when Orpheus went to the underworld to reclaim his wife, Eurydice, his music moved, i.e., touched, the spirits of Hades.
9. Elaborate court entertainments in which aristocrats performed a dignified play, usually allegorical and mythological, that ended in a formal dance.
1. This poem exemplifies Campion's interest in quantitative verse (see "Versification," p. 2036).

Silent music, either° other   *each the*
    Sweetly gracing.

5 Lovely forms do flow
    From concent° divinely framed;   *sounds in harmony*
    Heav'n is music, and thy beauty's
        Birth is heavenly.

    These dull notes we sing
10 Discords need for helps to grace them;
    Only beauty purely loving
        Knows no discord,

    But still moves delight,
    Like clear springs renewed by flowing,
15 Ever perfect, ever in them-
        Selves eternal.

                                                    1602

Now Winter Nights Enlarge

Now winter nights enlarge
    The number of their hours;
And clouds their storms discharge
    Upon the airy towers.
5 Let now the chimneys blaze
    And cups o'erflow with wine,
Let well-tuned words amaze
    With harmony divine.
Now yellow waxen lights
10 Shall wait on honey love
While youthful revels, masques,² and courtly sights
    Sleep's leaden spells remove.

This time doth well dispense³
    With lovers' long discourse;
15 Much speech hath some defense,
    Though beauty no remorse.
All do not all things well;
    Some measures comely tread,⁴
Some knotted riddles tell,
20 Some poems smoothly read.
The summer hath his joys,
    And winter his delights;
Though love and all his pleasures are but toys,
    They shorten tedious nights.

                                                    1617

---

2. See note 9 above.   4. I.e., some dance (tread measures) in a beautiful
3. I.e., this time deals indulgently.   way.

There Is a Garden in Her Face

There is a garden in her face,
Where roses and white lilies grow,
A heavenly paradise is that place,
Wherein all pleasant fruits do flow.
5   There cherries grow, which none may buy
Till "Cherry ripe!"[5] themselves do cry.

Those cherries fairly do enclose
Of orient pearl a double row,
Which when her lovely laughter shows,
10   They look like rosebuds filled with snow.
Yet them nor° peer nor prince can buy,   *neither*
Till "Cherry ripe!" themselves do cry.

Her eyes like angels watch them still;
Her brows like bended bows do stand,
15   Threatening with piercing frowns to kill
All that attempt with eye or hand
Those sacred cherries to come nigh,
Till "Cherry ripe!" themselves do cry.

1617

THOMAS NASHE
1567–1601

FROM SUMMER'S LAST WILL

[Spring, the Sweet Spring][1]

Spring, the sweet spring, is the year's pleasant king,
Then blooms each thing, then maids dance in a ring,
Cold doth not sting, the pretty birds do sing:
    Cuckoo, jug-jug, pu-we, to-witta-woo![2]

5   The palm and may[3] make country houses gay,
Lambs frisk and play, the shepherds pipe all day,

---

5. A London street vendor's cry.
1. Sung by Ver (Latin for "spring") in Nashe's allegorical drama *Summer's Last Will and Testament*, first performed in 1592 in the palace of the archbishop of Canterbury.
2. Birdsongs of the cuckoo, nightingale, lapwing, owl.

3. Hawthorn blossoms. The palms may be left over from the religious celebration known as Palm Sunday, which occurs a week before Easter and commemorates Christ's entry into Jerusalem.

And we hear aye birds tune this merry lay:°   *song*
   Cuckoo, jug-jug, pu-we, to-witta-woo!

The fields breathe sweet, the daisies kiss our feet,
10 Young lovers meet, old wives a-sunning sit,
   In every street these tunes our ears do greet:
    Cuckoo, jug-jug, pu-we, to-witta-woo!
     Spring, the sweet spring!

[Adieu, Farewell, Earth's Bliss][4]

   Adieu, farewell, earth's bliss;
   This world uncertain is;
   Fond° are life's lustful joys;   *foolish*
   Death proves them all but toys;°   *trifles*
5 None from his darts can fly;
   I am sick, I must die.
    Lord, have mercy on us![5]

   Rich men, trust not in wealth,
   Gold cannot buy you health;
10 Physic° himself° must fade.   *medicine / itself*
   All things to end are made,
   The plague full swift goes by;
   I am sick, I must die.
    Lord, have mercy on us!

15 Beauty is but a flower
   Which wrinkles will devour;
   Brightness falls from the air;
   Queens have died young and fair;
   Dust hath closed Helen's[6] eye.
20 I am sick, I must die.
    Lord, have mercy on us!

   Strength stoops unto the grave,
   Worms feed on Hector[7] brave;

4. Often titled by editors "A Litany in Time of Plague," this lyric comes from Nashe's allegorical drama *Summer's Last Will and Testament*. First performed during the summer of 1592 in the palace of the archbishop of Canterbury, the play repeatedly alludes to the epidemic of plague that had driven the archbishop and his aristocratic guests from London. Summer, who enters the play already sick, requests a "doleful ditty" that will lament his "near-approaching death."

5. These recurring words—from the Litany, a standard prayer in Church of England services—were inscribed in red letters on plague-stricken houses.
6. Helen of Troy, who was renowned for her beauty, and whose abduction was said to be the cause of the Trojan War.
7. Renowned for his bravery, he was the son of Priam and leader of the Trojans against the Greeks.

Swords may not fight with fate,
25   Earth still holds ope her gate.
"Come, come!" the bells do cry.
I am sick, I must die.
        Lord, have mercy on us.

Wit with his wantonness
30   Tasteth death's bitterness;
Hell's executioner
Hath no ears for to hear
What vain art can reply.
I am sick, I must die.
35   Lord, have mercy on us.

Haste, therefore, each degree,°   rank; social station
To welcome destiny;
Heaven is our heritage,
Earth but a player's stage;
40   Mount we unto the sky.
I am sick, I must die.
        Lord, have mercy on us.

1592   1600

AEMILIA LANYER
1569–1645

From Salve Deus Rex Judaeorum[1]

Sith° Cynthia[2] is ascended to that rest   since
Of endless joy and true eternity,
That glorious place that cannot be expressed
By any wight° clad in mortality,   person
5   In her almighty love so highly blessed,
And crowned with everlasting sov'reignty;
    Where saints and angels do attend her throne,
    And she gives glory unto God alone.

---

1. Hail God, King of the Jews (Latin); a variant of the inscription on Christ's cross. Lanyer claimed that the title came to her in a dream. This long text is prefaced by a prose address ("To the Virtuous Reader") and by eight dedicatory poems to women patrons including Mary Sidney, countess of Pembroke (1561–1621; see pp. 225–30). The main part of Lanyer's poem begins and ends with praise of the poet Margaret Clifford, countess of Cumberland (1560–1616), Lanyer's friend and primary patron. The poem itself is divided into four parts:

"The Passion of Christ," "Eve's Apology in Defense of Women," "The Tears of the Daughters of Jerusalem," and "The Salutation and Sorrow of the Virgin Mary." The stanzas reprinted here are from the opening of the poem and from its second section.
2. A mythological name for the virgin goddess of the moon, frequently applied to Queen Elizabeth I (1533–1603; see pp. 142–43). As a powerful and much-revered queen, she is an appropriate "first muse," or source of inspiration, for Lanyer to invoke.

To thee great Countess[3] now I will apply
10   My pen, to write thy never dying fame;
      That when to heaven thy blessed soul shall fly,
      These lines on earth record thy reverend name:
      And to this task I mean my Muse to tie,
      Though wanting skill I shall but purchase blame:
15   Pardon (dear Lady) want of woman's wit
          To pen thy praise, when few can equal it.

* * *

745   Now Pontius Pilate is to judge the cause[4]
      Of faultless Jesus, who before him stands;
      Who neither hath offended prince, nor laws,
      Although he now be brought in woeful bands:
      O noble governor, make thou yet a pause,
750   Do not in innocent blood imbrue° thy hands;   stain
          But hear the words of thy most worthy wife,
          Who sends to thee, to beg her Savior's life.[5]

      Let barb'rous cruelty far depart from thee,
      And in true justice take affliction's part;
755   Open thine eyes, that thou the truth may'st see,
      Do not the thing that goes against thy heart,
      Condemn not him that must thy Savior be;
      But view his holy life, his good desert.
          Let not us women glory in men's fall,
760   Who had power given to over-rule us all.[6]

Eve's Apology

      Till now your indiscretion sets us free,
      And makes our former fault much less appear;[7]
      Our Mother Eve, who tasted of the Tree,
      Giving to Adam what she held most dear,
765   Was simply° good, and had no power to see,   ignorantly
      The after-coming harm did not appear;
      The subtle° serpent that our sex betrayed,   crafty
      Before our fall so sure a plot had laid.

      That undiscerning Ignorance[8] perceived
770   No guile, or craft that was by him° intended: the serpent

3. Margaret Clifford, countess of Cumberland (see note 1 above).
4. Case. Pilate was the Roman governor of Jerusalem from 26 to 36 C.E. For his condemnation of Christ, see Matthew 27.11–24.
5. In Matthew 27.19, Pontius Pilate's wife sends a message saying "Have thou nothing to do with that just man: for I have suffered many things this day in a dream because of him." Lanyer gives this minor biblical character a major narrative role, making her the dramatic advocate both of Christ and of Eve and hence a fulcrum linking the first and second parts of the poem; the "Apology" flows directly from Pontius Pilate's (unwise) refusal to heed his wife's words about her prophetic dream. Lanyer's speaker addresses Pilate, in an apostrophe, beginning in line 761.
6. According to Genesis 3.16, Eve was punished for the Fall by being made subject to her husband.
7. I.e., men "over-ruled" women until this (imagined) moment of Christ's judgment, when your error in condemning Christ (Pilate's error and by extension that of men in general) frees women by making Eve's sin seem much less by comparison.
8. I.e., Eve.

For, had she known of what we were bereaved,[9]
To his request she had not condescended.
But she (poor soul) by cunning was deceived[1]
No hurt therein her harmless heart intended:
775 For she alleged° God's word, which he° denies,   *asserted / the serpent*
That they should die, but even as gods, be wise.[2]

But surely Adam cannot be excused,
Her fault, though great, yet he was most to blame;
What weakness offered, strength might have refused,
780 Being lord of all, the greater was his shame:
Although the serpent's craft had her abused,
God's holy word ought all his actions frame:°   *shape*
For he was lord and king of all the earth,
Before poor Eve had either life or breath.

785 Who being framed by God's eternal hand,
The perfect'st man that ever breathed on earth,
And from God's mouth received that strait°   *strict, narrow*
    command,
The breach whereof he knew was present death:
Yea having power to rule both sea and land,
790 Yet with one apple won to lose that breath,
Which God hath breathèd in his beauteous face,
Bringing us all in danger and disgrace.

And then to lay the fault on Patience back,[3]
That we (poor women) must endure it all;
795 We know right well he did discretion lack,
Being not persuaded thereunto at all;
If Eve did err, it was for knowledge sake,
The fruit being fair persuaded him° to fall: *Adam*
No subtle serpent's falsehood did betray him,
800 If he would eat it, who had power to stay him?

Not Eve, whose fault was only too much love,
Which made her give this present to her dear,
That what she tasted, he likewise might prove,°   *experience*
Whereby his knowledge might become more clear;
805 He never sought her weakness to reprove,
With those sharp words, which he of God did hear;
Yet men will boast of knowledge, which he took
From Eve's fair hand, as from a learnèd book.

9. I.e., of eternal life. In Genesis 3, Eve is enticed by the serpent to eat the forbidden fruit, and Adam then eats when she offers it to him. God expels them from Eden, condemning Adam to hard work, Eve to pain in childbirth, and both to suffering and death.
1. Cf. 1 Timothy 2.14: "And Adam was not deceived but the woman being deceived was in the transgression."

2. Eve put forward God's "word" (that humans would die if they disobeyed), and the serpent denied that idea, arguing instead that humans would become "wise" as gods.
3. Eve is allegorized as Patience, with a glance at the literary tradition of the wronged but patient wife (e.g. the "patient Griselda" in Chaucer's "Clerk's Tale").

If any evil did in her remain,
810 Being made of him, he was the ground of all;[4]
If one of many worlds[5] could lay a stain
Upon our sex, and work so great a fall
To wretched man, by Satan's subtle train;[6]
What will so foul a fault amongst you all?
815 Her weakness did the serpent's words obey,
But you in malice God's dear Son betray.[7]

Whom, if unjustly you condemn to die,
Her° sin was small, to what you do commit;   *Eve's*
All mortal° sins that do for vengeance cry,   *punishable by damnation*
820 Are not to be comparèd unto it:
If many worlds would altogether try,
By all their sins the wrath of God to get;
This sin of yours, surmounts them all as far
As doth the sun, another little star.[8]

825 Then let us have our liberty again,
And challenge° to your selves no Sov'reignty;   *claim*
You came not in the world without our pain,°   *of childbirth*
Make that a bar against[9] your cruelty;
Your fault being greater, why should you disdain
830 Our being your equals, free from tyranny?
If one weak woman simply did offend,
This sin of yours hath no excuse, nor end.

To which (poor souls) we never gave consent,
Witness thy wife (O Pilate) speaks for all;
835 Who did but dream, and yet a message sent,
That thou should'st have nothing to do at all
With that just man; which, if thy heart relent,
Why wilt thou be a reprobate with Saul?[1]
To seek the death of him that is so good,
840 For thy soul's health to shed his dearest blood.

1611

4. With a pun on, in Hebrew, Adam's name (*hā'ādam*) and the word for ground (*hā'ādamā*). Eve was created from Adam's rib: "And the rib, which the Lord God had taken from man, made he a woman, and brought her unto the man" (Genesis 2.22).
5. Perhaps an allusion to the popular seventeenth-century belief in a plurality of inhabited globes in the universe, or at least in the solar system. Cf. Milton, *Paradise Lost* 3.565 ff. *One*: Adam.
6. Trickery. The identification of Satan with the serpent is traditional but not made in Genesis.
7. Here and in the preceding question, Pilate's wife addresses both men in general ("you all") and her husband, recalling the specific dramatic situation of Christ's trial.
8. In Ptolemaic astronomy, the sun was larger than the planets and fixed stars.
9. I.e., let that prevent.
1. I.e., morally unprincipled like Saul, the first king of Israel, who was rejected by God for disobedience, and who plotted to kill David, his successor (1 Samuel 22–23). (Or perhaps another Saul, who persecuted the first Christians, and who later converted to Christianity, changing his name to Paul [Acts 9.1–31].)

The Description of Cooke-ham[2]

Farewell (sweet Cooke-ham) where I first obtained
Grace from that grace where perfect grace[3] remained;
And where the muses[4] gave their full consent,
I should have power the virtuous to content;
5   Where princely palace willed me to indite,°   *compose, write*
The sacred story[5] of the soul's delight.
Farewell (sweet place) where virtue then did rest,
And all delights did harbor in her breast;
Never shall my sad eyes again behold
10   Those pleasures which my thoughts did then unfold.
Yet you (great Lady) Mistress of that place,
From whose desires did spring this work of grace;
Vouchsafe to think upon those pleasures past,
As fleeting worldly joys that could not last,
15   Or, as dim shadows of celestial[6] pleasures,
Which are desired above all earthly treasures.
Oh how (methought) against you thither came,[7]
Each part did seem some new delight to frame!
The house received all ornaments to grace it,
20   And would endure no foulness to deface it.
And walks put on their summer liveries,°   *uniforms*
And all things else did hold like similes.[8]
The trees with leaves, with fruits, with flowers clad,
Embraced each other, seeming to be glad,
25   Turning themselves to beauteous Canopies,
To shade the bright sun from your brighter eyes;
The crystal streams with silver spangles graced,
While by the glorious sun they were embraced;
The little birds in chirping notes did sing,
30   To entertain both you and that sweet spring.
And Philomela[9] with her sundry lays,
Both you and that delightful place did praise.
Oh how me thought each plant, each flower, each tree

2. The crown manor leased to William Russell, whose sister, Margaret Clifford, the countess of Cumberland (see note 1, p. 284), resided there periodically until 1605. The unhappiness alluded to in this poem refers to the countess's alienation from her husband, George Clifford, third earl of Cumberland, and her legal battles with his relatives after his death in 1605. The countess fought for the claims of her daughter, Cumberland's only heir, Anne Clifford, to his estates. King James and the court bureaucracy offered only a cash settlement—far less than the value of Cumberland's lands and titles—which the countess and her daughter refused to accept. This poem, which probably dates from 1609–10 and which followed the title poem in the first edition of Lanyer's *Salve Deus Rex Judaeorum*, is an early example of what would become the popular genre of the "country house" poem; cf. Ben Jonson's "To Penshurst" (p. 328).

3. Respectively (line 2): favor, noble person (i.e., Margaret Clifford, countess of Cumberland); God-given virtues.
4. The nine Greek sister goddesses believed to be sources of inspiration for the arts.
5. I.e., Christ's passion in *Salve Deus Rex Judaeorum*.
6. As reflections or images of heavenly.
7. I.e., when you went there.
8. Similarities; i.e., did the same.
9. The nightingale, whose various songs ("sundry lays") were said to express lovesickness and/or mourning; here, associated with the female poetic voice. In classical mythology, Philomela was raped by her brother-in-law, Tereus, who then tore out her tongue so that she could not speak. She wove the story in a tapestry and sent it to her sister, who rescued her. She was later changed into a nightingale while in flight from Tereus.

Set forth their beauties then to welcome thee!
35 The very hills right humbly did descend,
When you to tread on them did intend.
And as you set your feet, they still did rise,
Glad that they could receive so rich a prize.
The gentle winds did take delight to be
40 Among those woods that were so graced by thee,
And in sad murmur uttered pleasing sound,
That pleasure in that place might more abound.
The swelling banks delivered all their pride
When such a Phoenix¹ once they had espied.
45 Each arbor, bank, each seat, each stately tree,
Thought themselves honored in supporting thee.
The pretty birds would oft come to attend thee,
Yet fly away for fear they should offend thee;
The little creatures in the burrough° by   burrow
50 Would come abroad to sport them in your eye,
Yet fearful of the bow in your fair hand.²
Would run away when you did make a stand.
Now let me come unto that stately tree,
Wherein such goodly prospects you did see;
55 That oak that did in height his fellows pass,
As much as lofty trees, low growing grass,
Much like a comely cedar straight and tall,
Whose beauteous stature far exceeded all.
How often did you visit this fair tree,
60 Which seeming joyful in receiving thee,
Would like a palm tree spread his arms abroad,
Desirous that you there should make abode;
Whose fair green leaves much like a comely° veil,   attractive
Defended Phoebus³ when he would assail;
65 Whose pleasing boughs did yield a cool fresh air,
Joying° his happiness when you were there.   enjoying
Where being seated, you might plainly see
Hills, vales, and woods, as if on bended knee
They had appeared, your honor to salute,
70 Or to prefer° some strange unlooked-for suit;°   offer / request
All interlaced with brooks and crystal springs,
A prospect fit to please the eyes of kings.
And° thirteen shires appeared all in your sight,   if
Europe could not afford much more delight.
75 What was there then but gave you all content,
While you the time in meditation spent
Of their Creator's power, which there you saw,
In all his creatures held a perfect law;°   order
And in their beauties did you plain descry°   perceive
80 His beauty, wisdom, grace, love, majesty.

1. A legendary bird, the only one of its kind, rep-
resented as living five hundred years in the Arabian
desert before setting itself on fire, then rising anew
from its own ashes; here, also a reference to the
countess.

2. I.e., the countess is figured as Diana, the clas-
sical goddess of hunting, the moon, and chastity.
3. I.e., protected you from the sun; Phoebus
Apollo was the mythological god of the sun.

In these sweet woods how often did you walk,
With Christ and his Apostles there to talk;
Placing his holy Writ in some fair tree
To meditate what you therein did see.
85 With Moses[4] you did mount his holy hill
To know his pleasure, and perform his will.
With lowly David[5] you did often sing
His holy hymns to Heaven's eternal King.
And in sweet music did your soul delight
90 To sound his praises, morning, noon, and night.
With blessed Joseph[6] you did often feed
Your pinèd° brethren, when they stood in need.   *tired from hunger*
And that sweet Lady sprung from Clifford's race,[7]
Of noble Bedford's blood, fair stem of grace,
95 To honorable Dorset now espoused,
In whose fair breast true virtue then was housed,
Oh what delight did my weak spirits find
In those pure parts of her well framèd mind.
And yet it grieves me that I cannot be
100 Near unto her, whose virtues did agree
With those fair ornaments of outward beauty,
Which did enforce from all both love and duty.
Unconstant Fortune, thou art most to blame,
Who casts us down into so low a frame
105 Where our great friends we cannot daily see,
So great a difference is there in degree.
Many are placed in those orbs of state,[8]
Parters° in honor, so ordained by Fate,   *participants*
Nearer in show, yet farther off in love,
110 In which, the lowest always are above.[9]
But whither am I carried in conceit,°   *thought; pride*
My wit too weak to conster° of the great.   *consider, understand*
Why not? although we are but born of earth.
We may behold the heavens, despising death;
115 And loving heaven that is so far above,
May in the end vouchsafe us entire love.[1]
Therefore sweet memory do thou retain
Those pleasures past, which will not turn again:
Remember beauteous Dorset's° former sports,   *Anne Clifford's*
120 So far from being touched by ill reports,
Wherein myself did always bear a part,
While reverend love presented my true heart.
Those recreations let me bear in mind,

---

4. Who spoke with God on a mountaintop (Exodus 24.13–18).
5. The psalmist of the Bible; the second king of Judah and Israel.
6. Who was sold by his brothers into Egypt; after he became powerful, he fed his brothers during the great famine (Genesis 47.12).
7. Anne Clifford, countess of Dorset, the countess of Cumberland's daughter. Her father came from the Cliffords, earls of Cumberland; her mother came from the Russells, earls of Bedford. She mar-

ried into the Sackville family, earls of Dorset.
8. I.e., exalted social spheres.
9. I.e., while circumstance may place the high and the low near to each other, the lower-born are more devoted to the higher-born. In *Nichomachean Ethics*, Aristotle says that in friendship between unequals, "the better and more useful partner should receive more affection than he gives" (7.1158).
1. I.e., may bestow all love on us.

Which her sweet youth and noble thoughts did find,
125   Whereof deprived, I evermore must grieve,
Hating blind Fortune, careless to relieve.
And you sweet Cooke-ham, whom these ladies leave,
I now must tell the grief you did conceive
At their departure, when they went away,
130   How everything retained a sad dismay.
Nay long before, when once an inkling came,
Methought each thing did unto sorrow frame:
The trees that were so glorious in our view,
Forsook both flowers and fruit, when once they knew
135   Of your depart, their very leaves did wither,
Changing their colors as they grew together.
But when they saw this had no power to stay you,
They often wept, though, speechless, could not pray you,[2]
Letting their tears in your fair bosoms fall,
140   As if they said, Why will ye leave us all?
This being vain, they cast their leaves away
Hoping that pity would have made you stay:
Their frozen tops, like age's hoary° hairs,   *grayish white*
Shows their disasters, languishing in fears.
145   A swarthy° riveled° rind° all over spread,   *dark / rough / bark*
Their dying bodies half alive, half dead.
But your occasions called you so away
That nothing there had power to make you stay.
Yet did I see a noble grateful mind
150   Requiting° each according to their kind,   *rewarding*
Forgetting not to turn and take your leave
Of these sad creatures, powerless to receive
Your favor, when with grief you did depart,
Placing their former pleasures in your heart,
155   Giving great charge to noble memory
There to preserve their love continually.
But specially the love of that fair tree,
That first and last you did vouchsafe to see,
In which it pleased you oft to take the air
160   With noble Dorset, then a virgin fair,[3]
Where many a learned book was read and scanned,
To this fair tree, taking me by the hand,
You did repeat the pleasures which had passed,
Seeming to grieve they could no longer last.
165   And with a chaste, yet loving kiss took leave,
Of which sweet kiss I did it soon bereave,[4]
Scorning a senseless creature should possess
So rare a favor, so great happiness.
No other kiss it could receive from me,
170   For fear to give back what it took of thee,
So I ungrateful creature did deceive° it   *deprive*

2. I.e., beg you (to stay).
3. I.e., before marriage.
4. I.e., Lanyer claims to have kissed the tree after the countess did, and so deprived the tree of the countess's kiss.

Of that which you in love vouchsafed° to leave it.   *granted*
And though it oft had given me much content,
Yet this great wrong I never could repent;
175 But of the happiest made it most forlorn,
To show that nothing's free from Fortune's scorne,
While all the rest with this most beauteous tree
Made their sad consort[5] sorrow's harmony.
The flowers that on the banks and walks did grow,
180 Crept in the ground, the grass did weep for woe.
The winds and waters seemed to chide together
Because you went away they knew not whither;
And those sweet brooks that ran so fair and clear,
With grief and trouble wrinkled did appear.
185 Those pretty birds that wonted° were to sing,   *accustomed*
Now neither sing, nor chirp, nor use their wing,
But with their tender feet on some bare spray,
Warble forth sorrow, and their own dismay.
Fair Philomela leaves her mournful ditty,°   *song*
190 Drowned in deep sleep, yet can procure no pity.
Each arbor, bank, each seat, each stately tree
Looks bare and desolate now for want° of thee,   *lack*
Turning green tresses[6] into frosty gray,
While in cold grief they wither all away.
195 The sun grew weak, his beams no comfort gave,
While all green things did make the earth their grave.
Each brier, each bramble, when you went away
Caught fast your clothes, thinking to make you stay;
Delightful Echo wonted[7] to reply
200 To our last words, did now for sorrow die;
The house cast off each garment that might grace it,
Putting on dust and cobwebs to deface it.
All desolation then there did appear,
When you were going whom they held so dear.
205 This last farewell to Cooke-ham here I give,
When I am dead thy name in this may live,
Wherein I have performed her noble hest°   *bidding*
Whose virtues lodge in my unworthy breast,
And ever shall, so long as life remains,
210 Tying my life to her by those rich chains.

1611

---

5. Company, with a pun on "consort" as a musical "accord."
6. I.e., leaves.
7. Was accustomed to; with a pun on *wanted*, desired. In classical mythology, the nymph (minor nature goddess) Echo was punished for excessive speech by being allowed only to repeat the last words of others; scorned by her beloved, the youth Narcissus, she eventually lost her body and lived on as a sad voice. Lanyer revises this myth in line 200.

JOHN DONNE*
1572–1631

The Good-Morrow

I wonder, by my troth, what thou and I
Did, till we loved? were we not weaned till then?
But sucked on country[1] pleasures, childishly?
Or snorted° we in the Seven Sleepers' den?[2]   *snored*
5   'Twas so; but° this, all pleasures fancies be.   *except for*
If ever any beauty I did see,
Which I desired, and got, 'twas but a dream of thee.

And now good-morrow to our waking souls,
Which watch not one another out of fear;
10   For love, all love of other sights controls,
And makes one little room an everywhere.[3]
Let sea-discoverers to new worlds have gone,
Let maps[4] to others, worlds on worlds have shown,
Let us possess one[5] world, each hath one, and is one.

15   My face in thine eye, thine in mine appears,
And true plain hearts do in the faces rest;
Where can we find two better hemispheres,
Without sharp North, without declining West?
Whatever dies was not mixed equally;[6]
20   If our two loves be one, or, thou and I
Love so alike that none do slacken, none can die.

1633

*The Donne poems in this anthology up through "The Relic" are usually called *Songs and Sonnets,* a rubric applied to Donne's love poems in the second edition of his *Poems* (1635). There is no authorial warrant for that rubric, however, since even the first edition (1633) appeared after his death, and no copies of his poems in his own handwriting survive. Instead, the poems exist in posthumous printed editions as well as in a large number of manuscript copies, many of which circulated during Donne's lifetime; some manuscripts include musical settings for the poems. We cannot date most of Donne's love poems with any certainty, and the multiple copies, printed and in manuscript, show many variations in stanza forms, punctuation, spelling, and even diction and grammar. Like most modern editors, we base our texts on the 1633 *Poems*; significant variations are mentioned in the notes.

Donne's poems frequently have an apostrophe between words to indicate that the neighboring syllables are fused in pronunciation and counted as one metrically. Such contractions occur only under certain phonetic conditions (e.g., when one word ends, and the next begins, with a vowel).

1. Also with a sexual connotation.

2. Seven Christian youths, under the persecutions of the Roman Emperor Decius (who ruled 249–51), were said to have been sealed in a cave, where they slept for nearly two centuries. On awakening, they found Christianity established as a world religion.

3. The common Renaissance trope of the individual as a microcosm of the universe.

4. Terrestrial maps or sky charts.

5. In some manuscripts, "our."

6. In medieval and Renaissance medical theory, death was often considered the result of an imbalance in the body's elements. When elements were "not mixed equally," matter was mutable and mortal, but when they were mixed perfectly, it was changing and immortal.

Song

Go and catch a falling star,
  Get with child a mandrake root,[7]
Tell me where all past years are,
  Or who cleft the Devil's foot,
5   Teach me to hear mermaids[8] singing,
Or to keep off envy's stinging,
      And find
      What wind
Serves to advance an honest mind.

10 If thou beest born to strange sights,[9]
  Things invisible to see,
Ride ten thousand days and nights,
  Till age snow white hairs on thee,
Thou, when thou return'st, wilt tell me
15 All strange wonders that befell thee,
      And swear
      Nowhere
Lives a woman true, and fair.

If thou find'st one, let me know,
20   Such a pilgrimage were sweet;
Yet do not, I would not go,
  Though at next door we might meet;
Though she were true when you met her,
And last till you write your letter,
25   Yet she
      Will be
False, ere I come, to two, or three.

1633

Woman's Constancy

Now thou hast loved me one whole day,
Tomorrow when thou leav'st, what wilt thou say?
Wilt thou then antedate some new-made vow?[1]
    Or say that now
5   We are not just those persons which we were?
Or, that oaths made in reverential fear
Of Love, and his wrath, any may forswear?

---

7. The large, forked root of the mandrake roughly resembles a human body and was thought to be an aphrodisiac.
8. I.e., the Sirens (in Homer's *Odyssey*), whose seductive song only the cunning Odysseus successfully resisted.
9. I.e., if your nature inclines you to seek strange sights; alternatively, if you are carried ("borne," as the word is spelled in the 1633 text and most manuscript versions) to strange sights (cf. "return'st," line 14).
1. I.e., will you pretend that a new vow of love is older than that you have made to me? *Antedate*: affix an earlier date than the true date.

Or, as true° deaths, true marriages untie,   *real*
So lovers' contracts, images of those,[2]
10   Bind but till sleep, death's image, them unloose?
Or, your own end to justify,
For having purposed change, and falsehood, you
Can have no way but falsehood to be true?
Vain lunatic,[3] against these 'scapes° I could   *escapes, deceptions*
15   Dispute, and conquer, if I would,
Which I abstain to do,
For by tomorrow, I may think so too.

1633

The Apparition

When by thy scorn, O murd'ress, I am dead,
And that thou thinkst thee free
From all solicitation from me,
Then shall my ghost come to thy bed,
5   And thee, fained vestal,[4] in worse arms shall see;
Then thy sick taper° will begin to wink,°   *candle / flicker*
And he, whose thou art then, being tired before,
Will, if thou stir, or pinch to wake him, think
Thou call'st for more,
10   And in false sleep will from thee shrink,
And then, poor aspen wretch,[5] neglected thou
Bathed in a cold quicksilver sweat[6] wilt lie,
A verier° ghost than I;   *truer*
What I will say, I will not tell thee now,
15   Lest that preserve thee; and since my love is spent,
I had rather thou shouldst painfully repent,
Than by my threatnings rest still innocent.

1633

The Sun Rising

Busy old fool, unruly sun,
Why dost thou thus,
Through windows, and through curtains call on us?
Must to thy motions lovers' seasons run?
5   Saucy pedantic wretch, go chide
Late school boys and sour prentices,°   *apprentices*
Go tell court huntsmen[7] that the king will ride,

---

2. I.e., of true marriages.
3. The word has for Donne the additional meaning of "inconstant" or "fickle," since lunacy (from *luna*, moon) was supposed to be affected by the changing phases of the moon.
4. One of the virgins consecrated to the Roman goddess Vesta. *Fained*: counterfeit.

5. Aspen leaves flutter in the slightest breeze.
6. Sweating in terror; quicksilver (mercury) was a stock prescription for venereal disease, and sweating was part of the cure.
7. I.e., courtiers who hunt office by emulating King James's passion for hunting.

Call country ants to harvest offices;[8]
Love, all alike,[9] no season knows nor clime,
10   Nor hours, days, months, which are the rags° of time.   *fragments*

        Thy beams, so reverend and strong
        Why shouldst thou think?[1]
I could eclipse and cloud them with a wink,
But that I would not lose her sight so long;
15   If her eyes have not blinded thine,
        Look, and tomorrow late, tell me,
Whether both th' Indias of spice and mine[2]
Be where thou leftst them, or lie here with me.
Ask for those kings whom thou saw'st yesterday,
20   And thou shalt hear, All here in one bed lay.

        She's all states, and all princes, I,[3]
        Nothing else is.
Princes do but play us; compared to this,
All honor's mimic, all wealth alchemy.[4]
25   Thou, sun, art half as happy as we,[5]
        In that the world's contracted thus.
Thine age asks ease, and since thy duties be
To warm the world, that's done in warming us.
Shine here to us, and thou art everywhere;
30   This bed thy center is, these walls, thy sphere.[6]

                      1633

The Canonization[7]

For God's sake hold your tongue, and let me love,
    Or chide my palsy, or my gout,
My five gray hairs, or ruined fortune, flout,
    With wealth your state, your mind with arts improve,
5   Take you a course, get you a place,[8]
        Observe his honor, or his grace,[9]
Or the King's real, or his stampéd face[1]

---

8. "Harvest" may be read both as part of a noun phrase ("duties of the harvest," in which case "country ants" would refer to farm workers) and as a verb, in which case the "ants" would be provincial courtiers seeking to collect ("harvest") paid positions.
9. The same at all times.
1. I.e., what makes you think your light is so awesome?
2. India and the West Indies, whence came spices and gold (from mines) respectively.
3. One manuscript has "She is all princes, and all states, I, . . ."
4. A metallic composition imitating gold; i.e., a fraud.
5. The sun, being one thing, is half as happy as

two lovers.
6. I.e., the bedroom and the lovers are a microcosm of the solar system, with the bed (like Earth, in Ptolemaic astronomy) as the point around which the sun revolves.
7. The title refers to admission into the canon of Church saints, often attested by martyrdom. As part of the canonization process, a "devil's advocate" sought to ensure that the whole truth, including faults, emerged about a candidate.
8. An appointment, at court or elsewhere. *Take you a course*: begin a career.
9. Pay court to a lord or bishop.
1. I.e., on coins. The contrast is complicated by the fact that "real," spelled "royall" in several manuscripts, is also a term for a Spanish coin.

Contémplate; what you will, approve,°   *try*
So you will let me love.

10 Alas, alas, who's injured by my love?
What merchant's ships have my sighs drowned?
Who says my tears have overflowed his ground?
When did my colds a forward spring remove?[2]
When did the heats which my veins fill
15 Add one more to the plaguy bill?[3]
Soldiers find wars, and lawyers find out still
Litigious° men, which quarrels move,   *contentious*
Though she and I do love.

Call us what you will, we're made such by love;
20 Call her one, me another fly,
We're tapers too, and at our own cost die,[4]
And we in us find th' eagle and the dove.[5]
The phoenix riddle hath more wit°   *sense*
By us: we two being one, are it.
25 So, to one neutral thing both sexes fit.
We die and rise the same, and prove
Mysterious by this love.

We can die by it, if not live by love,
And if unfit for tombs and hearse
30 Our legend be, it will be fit for verse;
And if no piece of chronicle° we prove,[6]   *history*
We'll build in sonnets pretty rooms;[7]
As well a well-wrought urn becomes°   *befits*
The greatest ashes, as half-acre tombs;
35 And by these hymns,[8] all shall approve
Us canonized for love.

And thus invoke us: You whom reverend love
Made one another's hermitage;
You, to whom love was peace, that now is rage,°   *lust*
40 Who did the whole world's soul contract, and drove[9]
Into the glasses of your eyes
So made such mirrors, and such spies,

2. A common poetic conceit figured lovers as frozen by their mistresses' neglect; i.e., the speaker protests that his "colds" have not removed the warmth of an early ("forward") spring.
3. Weekly list of plague victims; many manuscripts have "man" instead of "more."
4. I.e., we're both "fly" (a moth or any winged insect) and "tapers," the self-consuming candles that attract winged insects. "Dying" was a popular metaphor for sexual climax in seventeenth-century English. "At our own cost" reflects the common supersitition that each orgasm shortened the man's life by a day.
5. A common symbol of peace and meekness; the "eagle" signifies strength. "Eagle" and "dove" are also alchemical terms for processes leading to the rise of "phoenix" (line 23), a stage in the transmutation of metals. The phoenix is a legendary bird; it was thought to be the only one of its kind, to contain both sexes, and to live five hundred years in the Arabian desert before setting itself on fire. Because a new phoenix supposedly arose from fire's ashes, the bird was often a symbol of the resurrected Christ.
6. One manuscript has "Chronicles." The biblical book of 1 Chronicles (1–9) lists the genealogies of the tribes of Israel. The speaker may be implying that if the "timeless" lovers leave no "progeny," they will leave poetry.
7. The "rooms" (punning on *stanza*, Italian for room) will hold the ashes, i.e., record their deeds.
8. I.e., the lover's poems.
9. Some manuscripts have "extract" for "contract" and "draw" for "drove."

That they did all to you epitomize,
    Countries, towns, courts:[1] Beg from above
45   A pattern of your love![2]

                                       1633

Song

Sweetest love, I do not go
    For weariness of thee,
Nor in hope the world can show
    A fitter love for me;
5   But since that I
Must die at last,'tis best
To use myself in jest,
        Thus by feigned deaths to die.[3]

Yesternight the sun went hence,
10   And yet is here today;
He hath no desire nor sense,
    Nor half so short a way:
        Then fear not me,
But believe that I shall make
15 Speedier journeys, since I take
    More wings and spurs than he.

O how feeble is man's power,
    That if good fortune fall,
Cannot add another hour,
20   Nor a lost hour recall!
        But come bad chance,
And we join to'it our strength,
And we teach it art and length,
        Itself o'er us to'advance.

25 When thou sigh'st, thou sigh'st not wind,
    But sigh'st my soul away;
When thou weep'st, unkindly[4] kind,
    My life's blood doth decay.
        It cannot be
30 That thou lov'st me, as thou say'st,
If in thine my life thou waste;
    Thou art the best of me.

---

1. I.e., you who contracted or distilled the whole world's soul and drove countries, towns, courts into such mirrors and "spies" (spyglasses, telescopes) that they epitomized (rendered in small but intense form) everything to you. Note that the direct object of "drove" comes in line 44.
2. Interpretations of this syntactically complex stanza turn, in part, on where one thinks that the direct address ends. Some editors put quotation markes before "You" (line 37) and after "love," and some manuscripts have "our" for "your."
3. Partings, and perhaps orgasms, as rehearsals for the final death of life. "Dying" was a popular metaphor for sexual climax in seventeenth-century English.
4. Can also mean "unnatural."

Let not thy divining° heart   *foreseeing*
 Forethink me any ill;
35 Destiny may take thy part,
 And may thy fears fulfill;
  But think that we
Are but turned aside to sleep;
They who one another keep
40 Alive, ne'er parted be.

             1633

The Anniversary

 All kings, and all their favorites,
 All glory'of honors, beauties, wits,
The sun itself, which makes times, as they pass,
Is elder by a year, now, than it was
5 When thou and I first one another saw:
All other things to their destruction draw,
  Only our love hath no decay;
This, no tomorrow hath, nor yesterday;
Running it never runs from us away,
10 But truly keeps his first, last, everlasting day.

 Two graves must hide thine and my corse;° *corpse*
 If one might, death were no divorce.
Alas, as well as other princes, we
(Who prince enough in one another be)
15 Must leave at last in death, these eyes, and ears,
Oft fed with true oaths, and with sweet salt tears;
  But souls where nothing dwells but love
(All other thoughts being inmates°) then shall *lodgers*
  prove°   *experience*
This, or a love increasèd there above,
20 When bodies to their graves, souls from their graves remove.

 And then we shall be throughly° blest, *thoroughly*
 But we no more than all the rest;[5]
Here upon earth, we're kings, and none but we
Can be such kings, nor of such subjects be;[6]
25 Who is so safe as we, where none can do
Treason to us, except one of us two?
  True and false fears let us refrain,
Let us love nobly,'and live, and add again
Years and years unto years, till we attain
30 To write threescore, this is the second of our reign.

             1633

5. Scholastic philosophers maintained that all souls are equally content in heaven but not equally blessed.

6. The conceit is that each lover is the other's king, and therefore each is also the other's only subject.

Love's Growth[7]

I scarce believe my love to be so pure
   As I had thought it was,
   Because it doth endure
Vicissitude,° and season, as the grass;   *change*
5 Methinks I lied all winter, when I swore
My love was infinite, if spring make'it more.

But if this medicine, love, which cures all sorrow
With more, not only be no quìntessence,[8]
But mixed of all stuffs paining soul or sense,
10 And of the sun his working vigor borrow,
Love's not so pure, and abstract, as they use
To say, which have no mistress but their muse,
But as all else, being elemented[9] too,
Love sometimes would contèmplate, sometimes do.

15 And yet no greater, but more eminent,°   *conspicuous, evident*
   Love by the spring is grown;
   As, in the firmament,
Stars by the sun are not enlarged, but shown,
Gentle love deeds, as blossoms on a bough,
20 From love's awakened root do bud out now.

If, as in water stirred more circles be
Produced by one, love such additions take,
Those, like so many spheres, but one heaven make,
For they are all concentric unto thee;[1]
25 And though each spring do add to love new heat,
As princes do in times of action get
New taxes, and remit them not in peace,
No winter shall abate the spring's increase.

                                      1633

A Valediction[2] of Weeping

Let me pour forth
My tears before thy face whilst I stay here,

---

7. In some manuscripts, titled "Spring." If "love's growth" refers to the swelling of pregnancy, then the irregular "growing" shape of the stanzas in the early editions and some manuscripts may be an instance of imitative form. The stanzas play on (by inverting) the Italian sonnet pattern of an octave followed by a sestet (see "Versification," p. 2042).
8. According to many ancient and medieval philosophers, there was a fifth, "quintessential" element, purer than the four elements of ordinary life (earth, air, fire, and water); the quintessence was thought to be a cure for all diseases. *This medicine*: in the early seventeenth century, cures were often sought according to a principle of likeness between medicine and illness.
9. Made up of a mixture of elements. *Muse*: source of inspiration.
1. Most astronomers in Donne's time conceived of nine concentric spheres, each of transparent crystal, turning around Earth. The various heavenly bodies were thought to be fixed in the surfaces of these spheres.
2. A departure speech or discourse; a bidding of farewell. Several manuscripts place a colon after "Valediction," but many, along with the 1633 edition, do not.

For thy face coins them, and thy stamp they bear,[3]
And by this mintage° they are something worth,   *coining a word*
5   For thus they be
            Pregnant of thee;
Fruits of much grief they are, emblems of more;
When a tear falls, that Thou falls which it bore,[4]
So thou and I are nothing then, when on a diverse° shore.   *separate*

10   On a round ball
A workman that hath copies by, can lay
An Europe, Afric, and an Asïa,
And quickly make that, which was nothing, all,[5]
            So doth each tear
15   Which thee doth wear,[6]
A globe, yea world, by that impression grow,
Till thy tears mixed with mine do overflow
This world; by waters sent from thee, my heaven dissolvèd so.

            O more than moon,
20 Draw not up seas to drown me in thy sphere;[7]
Weep me not dead,[8] in thine arms, but forbear
To teach the sea what it may do too soon.
            Let not the wind
            Example find
25 To do me more harm than it purposeth;
Since thou and I sigh one another's breath,
Whoe'er sighs most is cruelest, and hastes the other's death.

                      1633

A Valediction[9] of the Book

I'll tell thee now (dear Love) what thou shalt do
    To anger destiny, as she doth us,
      How I shall stay, though she esloygne° me thus   *remove far off*
And how posterity shall know it too;
5   How thine may out-endure
          Sybil's[1] glory, and obscure
          Her[2] who from Pindar could allure,

3. I.e., they reflect your face (among other meanings).
4. With a play on the image of pregnancy in the preceding lines. "That" is a demonstrative adjective modifying "Thou"; the tear of the speaker bears the impression of the lover.
5. I.e., an artist can paste maps of the continents on a blank globe. The "o" of the globe's shape is echoed in the word "nothing."
6. Can be read as either "which bears your impression" (i.e., the speaker's tears) or "which you weep" (i.e., bearing the speaker's impression).
7. I.e., heavenly body with greater power of attraction than the moon's, (when you affect the tides) don't pull the seas up to yourself.
8. I.e., do not weep me to death.
9. See note 2, p. 300.

1. The best-known "sibyl," or prophetess, was the Cumaean Sibyl, who (according to Virgil's *Aeneid*) lived for a thousand years. In a trancelike frenzy, she wrote inspired prophecies on leaves, which were scattered abroad by the wind. Her prophecies concerning the destiny of the Roman state were gathered into the Sibylline Books, which were preserved in the Roman temple of Capitoline Jupiter. These books were consulted during national emergencies and required interpretation by male priests.
2. According to tradition, Corinna the Boeotian (fl. ca. 500 B.C.E.?) taught writing to and competed successfully with the Greek lyric poet Pindar (ca. 522–ca. 438 B.C.E.). His poems are extant; Corinna's are not, except in fragments.

And her,[3] through whose help Lucan is not lame,
And her, whose book (they say) Homer did find, and name.[4]

10   Study our manuscripts, those myriads
     Of letters, which have past twixt thee and me,
     Thence write our annals, and in them will be
To all whom love's subliming fire invades,
       Rule and example found;
15   There, the faith of any ground[5]
       No schismatic[6] will dare to wound,
That sees, how Love this grace to us affords,
To make, to keep, to use, to be these his records.

  This book, as long-lived as the elements,
20   Or as the world's form, this all-graved tome[7]
     In cipher writ, or new made idiom;°   *language, dialect*
We for love's clergy only'are instruments,[8]
       When this book is made thus,
       Should again the ravenous
25   Vandals and the Goths[9] invade us,
     Learning were safe; in this our universe
Schools might learn sciences, spheres music, angels verse.[1]

  Here Love's divines° (since all divinity   *prophets, priests*
     Is love or wonder) may find all they seek,
30   Whether abstract spiritual love they like,
Their souls exhaled° with° what they do not see,   *drawn out / by*
       Or loth so to amuse
       Faith's[2] infirmity, they choose
       Something which they may see and use;
35   For, though mind be the heaven, where love doth sit,
Beauty'a convenient type[3] may be to figure° it.   *represent*

  Here more than in their books may lawyers find,
     Both by what titles[4] mistresses are ours,
     And how prerogative these states[5] devours,

3. Polla Argentaria, who helped her husband, the Roman poet Lucan (39–65 C.E.), write his historical epic, *Pharsalia*.
4. One tradition holds that Homer, the supposed author of the *Iliad* (and the *Odyssey*), took the subject of the siege of Troy from an epic poem on that event by Phantasia of Memphis. In another version of Donne's poem, the last three lines of this stanza read: "Her who from old allure, / And, through whose help Lucan is not lame, / And her, whose look (they say) Homer did find, and name." Note that this variant substitutes "look" for "book" and omits Corinna and Phantasia. The "her" of this last line refers to Helen of Troy, wife of the Greek king Menelaus, whose abduction (or seduction) by Paris, son of the king of Troy, began the Trojan War.
5. I.e., the trustworthiness of any fundamental doctrine.
6. One who promotes schism, or breach of unity in the Church; in this stanza and the next, the poet speaks of love as a sort of religion.
7. This indelibly written heavy book; one manuscript has "tomb" and another has "to me."

8. I.e., we are, in these letters, documents for love's initiates only; one variant has "are only" for "only'are."
9. Vandals and Goths were Germanic tribes that invaded Western Europe during the third, fourth, and fifth centuries; here, those who willfully and ignorantly destroy anything beautiful or worthy of preservation.
1. I.e., angelic hymns. *Schools:* scholastic philosophers. *Spheres music:* according to Pythagorean tradition, the motion of the planetary spheres created a music inaudible to human ears.
2. One variant has "doth" for "loth" and "faithless" for "Faith's."
3. A symbol or earthly reflection of the celestial original.
4. I.e., legal rights to the possession of property.
5. I.e., estates, presumably the "titles" mentioned in the above line. *Prerogative:* official right or privilege. Donne alludes here to the feudal practice by which a lord could demand from his vassals dues over and above those that were customary; also, at issue in the Parliament of 1601 was the prerogative of the monarch to levy special grants

40 Transferred from Love himself, to womankind.[6]
    Who though from heart, and eyes,
    They exact great subsidies,
    Forsake him who on them relies
And for the cause, honor, or conscience give,
45 Chimeras, vain as they, or their prerogative.[7]

Here statesmen (or of them, they which can read)
    May of their occupation find the grounds,°   *basic principles*
    Love and their art alike it deadly wounds,
If to consider what 'tis, one proceed,[8]
50   In both they do excel
    Who the present govern well,[9]
    Whose weakness none doth, or dares tell;[1]
In this thy book, such° will there nothing see,   *such people*
As in the Bible some can find out alchemy.[2]

55 Thus vent thy thoughts; abroad[3] I'll study thee,
    As he removes far off, that° great heights takes;[4]   *who*
    How great love is, presence best trial makes,
But absence tries how long this love will be;
    To take a latitude
60   Sun, or stars, are fitliest viewed
    At their brightest, but to conclude,
Of longitudes, what other way have we,
But to mark when, and where the dark eclipses be?[5]

1633

Love's Alchemy

Some that have deeper digged love's mine than I,
Say where his centric° happiness doth lie;   *central, essential*
    I've loved, and got, and told,[6]
But should I love, get, tell, till I were old,
5   I should not find that hidden mystery;

---

against noblemen's estates at time of need.

6. The "ours" of line 38 seems to refer to men. Thus the first four lines of this stanza might be paraphrased "Here, more than in their books, lawyers may discover both by what titles (legal rights to property, with, perhaps, a pun on *names*) mistresses belong to us (men), and how women's usurpation of the prerogative (privileges attendant on those legal rights), which rightfully belongs to Love, eats away at those rights ('states')."

7. I.e., and for their reason they plead conscience or honor, both illusions ("chimeras") as empty as themselves or their prerogative.

8. I.e., neither love nor politics can bear close scrutiny.

9. The suggestion of these lines seems to be that opportunists do well in both love and politics.

1. I.e., the weakness of lovers and politicians, about which "none doth, or dares tell" because they have been either deceived or intimidated.

2. The science applied to the pursuit of transmu-

tation of baser metals into gold and also to the search for a panacea or universal remedy. *Nothing:* worthlessness; one variant (printed in the 1633 edition) has "something" in place of "nothing." *Find out:* show the falsity of; or possibly, find support for (the Bible could be used to show the falsity of alchemy, but alchemists found support for their theories there).

3. I.e., while I'm away.

4. Measures. One variant has "shadows" for "great heights."

5. The latitude of a place may be measured by calculating its distance from the zenith of a star whose altitude (its distance from the equator) is known; longitude can be measured by noting the time at which an eclipse occurs at different points on Earth's surface. Donne here puns on "longitude," as it suggests (but does not mean) length or duration.

6. Tallied (counted) or estimated the quality of.

O, 'tis imposture all:
And as no chemic° yet th' elixir[7] got,   *alchemist*
  But glorifies his pregnant pot,[8]
  If by the way to him befall
10 Some odoriferous thing, or mèdicinal;
  So lovers dream a rich and long delight,
  But get a winter-seeming summer's night.

Our ease, our thrift, our honor, and our day,
  Shall we for this vain bubble's shadow pay?
15   Ends love in this, that my man°   *servant*
  Can be as happy as I can if he can
  Endure the short scorn of a bridegroom's play?
    That loving wretch that swears,
  'Tis not the bodies marry, but the minds,
20   Which he in her angelic finds,
    Would swear as justly that he hears,
  In that day's rude hoarse minstrelsy, the spheres.[9]
  Hope not for mind in women; at their best
  Sweetness and wit they're but mummy[1] possessed.

1633

A Nocturnal upon St. Lucy's Day,
Being the Shortest Day[2]

'Tis the year's midnight, and it is the day's,
Lucy's,[3] who scarce seven hours herself unmasks;
  The sun is spent, and now his flasks[4]
  Send forth light squibs, no constant rays;
5   The world's whole sap is sunk:[5]
  The general balm th' hydroptic[6] earth hath drunk,

7. A hypothetical substance, the goal of the alchemists' endeavors, supposedly capable of transmuting base metals into gold, curing all illnesses, and prolonging life indefinitely.
8. His fertile (also womb-shaped) retort; alchemists' quests to create the elixir of life were often compared to human reproduction.
9. I.e., the music of the spheres, or concentric transparent shells containing the heavenly bodies in Ptolemaic astronomy; they were thought to produce angelic music as they turned. Here, they are contrasted with the *charivari*, a raucous serenade using pots, pans, and trumpets, traditionally performed on the wedding night.
1. Lifeless flesh; also, a medication prepared from mummified remains. The poem is titled "Mummy" in some manuscripts.
  The syntax of the last two lines is obscure; the last line may be read with a comma after "wit," after "they're," after "but," and/or after "mummy." The final word may modify "mummy," to signify "mummy with a demon in it," or "they," to signify "women, once possessed by men" (i.e., married) or "women, after men possess them" (i.e., after marriage). Some manuscripts have a comma after

"best."
2. The "nocturns" of the Roman Catholic Church were night offices, or services; the title may also allude to an astronomical instrument used for telling time at night. According to the calendar in use during Donne's time, the winter solstice, or shortest day of the year, fell on December 12, the eve of St. Lucy's Day. St. Lucy was patron saint of the blind. Her festival is celebrated with lights and candles, and her name recalls the Latin word for light (*lux, lucis*). Lucy was the name of Donne's patron, the countess of Bedford, and some commentators have suggested that the poem was written on her death, in 1627. Others believe that the "she" of the poem is Donne's wife, Anne, who died in 1617. Donne's daughter, named Lucy after the countess of Bedford, also died in 1627.
3. In Latin, *lux, lucis* also means "day." "Lucy's" here is an appositive to "day's."
4. Powder flasks. I.e., the sun is compared to a gun shooting powder from powder flasks, but in "squibs" like small fireworks that spurt and fizzle as they burn.
5. Like that of trees and vegetation in winter.
6. Implies both saturation and insatiable thirst;

Whither, as to the bed's-feet, life is shrunk,
Dead and interred; yet all these seem to laugh,
Compared with me, who am their epitaph.[7]

10 Study me then, you who shall lovers be
   At the next world, that is, at the next spring:
     For I am every dead thing,
      In whom love wrought new alchemy.
       For his art did express°   *squeeze out*
15 A quintessence[8] even from nothingness,
   From dull privations, and lean emptiness:
   He ruined me, and I am re-begot
   Of absence, darkness, death; things which are not.

   All others, from all things, draw all that's good,
20 Life, soul, form, spirit, whence they being have;
     I, by love's limbeck,[9] am the grave
      Of all that's nothing. Oft a flood
       Have we two wept, and so
   Drowned the whole world, us two; oft did we grow
25 To be two chaoses,[1] when we did show
   Care to aught else;[2] and often absences
   Withdrew our souls, and made us carcasses.

   But I am by her death (which word wrongs her)
   Of the first nothing, the elixir grown;[3]
30   Were I a man, that I were one
     I needs must know; I should prefer,
      If I were any beast,
   Some ends, some means; yea plants, yea stones detest,
   And love;[4] all, all some properties invest;°   *put on*
35 If I an ordinary nothing were,
   As shadow,'a light and body must be here.

   But I am none; nor will my sun[5] renew.
   You lovers, for whose sake the lesser sun
     At this time to the Goat is run
40   To fetch new lust, and give it you,
      Enjoy your summer all;
   Since she enjoys her long night's festival,
   Let me prepare towards her, and let me call

---

i.e., insatiably thirsty. *General balm*: the *balsa-mum*, regarded as the vital, life-giving force in the branch of Renaissance medicine associated with Paracelsus.
7. Inscription on a tombstone.
8. A highly concentrated essence or extract, often identified with the "fifth essence" of ancient and medieval philosophy (see note 8, p. 300 and note 7, p. 304).
9. An alembic, an apparatus used in distillation, here associated with alchemy.
1. Includes a reference to the primordial empti-ness out of which all form arises.

2. I.e., when we turned our attention from each other.
3. He is now "grown" (become) the "elixir of the first nothing," i.e., the quintessence of the nothing that preceded creation of the world.
4. I.e., even plants and stones (like lodestones) have attractions and antipathies; even "beasts" have intentions.
5. I.e., the dead woman. The "lesser sun" (line 38) is the real sun, which is in the constellation of Cap-ricorn ("the Goat") during December. Goats were proverbial for their lustfulness.

This hour her vigil,[6] and her eve, since this
45   Both the year's, and the day's deep midnight is.

1633

A Valediction Forbidding Mourning[7]

As virtuous men pass mildly away,
    And whisper to their souls to go,
Whilst some of their sad friends do say
    The breath goes now, and some say, no;

5   So let us melt, and make no noise,
    No tear-floods, nor sigh-tempests move,
'Twere profanation of our joys
    To tell the laity[8] our love.

Moving of th' earth brings harms and fears,
10   Men reckon what it did and meant;
But trepidation of the spheres,[9]
    Though greater far, is innocent.

Dull sublunary[1] lovers' love
    (Whose soul is sense) cannot admit
15   Absence, because it doth remove
    Those things which elemented° it.   *composed*

But we by'a love so much refined
    That our selves know not what it is,
Inter-assurèd of the mind,
20   Care less,[2] eyes, lips, and hands to miss.

Our two souls therefore, which are one,
    Though I must go, endure not yet
A breach, but an expansion,
    Like gold to airy thinness beat.

25   If they be two, they are two so
    As stiff twin compasses[3] are two;
Thy soul, the fixed foot, makes no show
    To move, but doth, if th' other do.

6. The watch kept on the eve of a feast, with prayer.

7. Donne's friend Izaak Walton reported that this poem was written to Donne's wife when Donne went to the Continent in 1611. *Valediction:* see note 2, p. 300.

8. I.e., those who do not understand such love.

9. A trembling of the celestial spheres, hypothesized by Ptolemaic astronomers to account for unpredicted variations in the paths of the heavenly bodies.

1. Beneath the moon; earthly, hence changeable.

2. At least one manuscript and many editions from 1639 to 1654 give "carelesse" for "care lesse"; we choose the latter form because it allows for two interpretations of the lines.

3. I.e., the two legs of compasses used in drawing circles.

And though it in the center sit,
30   Yet when the other far doth roam,
It leans and hearkens after it,
        And grows erect, as that comes home.

Such wilt thou be to me, who must
        Like th' other foot, obliquely° run.   *diagonally, aslant*
35 Thy firmness makes my circle⁴ just,
        And makes me end where I begun.

                                                                        1633

The Ecstasy⁵

Where, like a pillow on a bed,
    A pregnant bank swelled up to rest
The violet's⁶ reclining head,
    Sat we two, one another's best.
5   Our hands were firmly cèmented
        With a fast balm,⁷ which thence did spring.
    Our eye-beams twisted, and did thread
        Our eyes upon one double string;
    So to'intergraft our hands, as yet
10   Was all the means to make us one,⁸
    And pictures° in our eyes to get°   *reflections / beget*
        Was all our propagation.⁹
    As 'twixt two equal armies, Fate
        Suspends uncertain victory,
15 Our souls (which to advance their state,
        Were gone out) hung 'twixt her and me.
    And whilst our souls negotiate there,
        We like sepulchral statues lay;
    All day the same our postures were,
20   And we said nothing all the day.
    If any, so by love refined
        That he soul's language understood,
    And by good love were grown all mind,
        Within convenient distance stood,
25 He (though he knew not which soul spake,
        Because both meant, both spake the same)
    Might thence a new concoction¹ take,
        And part far purer than he came.
    This ecstasy doth unperplex,

---

4. A symbol of perfection; with a dot in the middle, the alchemist's symbol for gold.
5. Literally, "a standing out" (from the Greek *ekstasis*); a term used by religious mystics to describe the experience in which the soul seemed to leave the body and rise superior to it in a state of heightened awareness.
6. An emblem of faithful love and truth.
7. I.e., perspiration; also, a moisture that pre-

serves them steadfast.
8. The lovers are joined "as yet" only by hands and eyes; "eye-beams" are invisible shafts of light, thought of as going out of the eyes and so enabling one to see.
9. Reflection of each person in the other's eyes; known also as "making babies."
1. Mixture of diverse elements refined (literally, cooked together) by heat; an alchemical term.

30   We said, and tell us what we love;
        We see by this it was not sex;
        We see we saw not what did move;[2]
        But as all several° souls contain   *separate*
        Mixture of things, they know not what,
35   Love these mixed souls doth mix again,
        And makes both one, each this and that.
        A single violet transplant,
        The strength, the color, and the size
        (All which before was poor, and scant)
40   Redoubles still, and multiplies.
        When love, with one another so
        Interinanimates two souls,
        That abler soul, which thence doth flow,[3]
        Defects of loneliness controls.
45   We then, who are this new soul, know,
        Of what we are composed, and made,
        For, th' atomies° of which we grow,   *atoms, components*
        Are souls, whom no change can invade.
        But O alas, so long, so far
50   Our bodies why do we forbear?
        They're ours, though they're not we; we are
        Th' intelligences, they the spheres.[4]
        We owe them thanks because they thus
        Did us to us at first convey,
55   Yielded their forces, sense, to us,
        Nor are dross to us, but allay.[5]
        On man heaven's influence works not so,
        But that it first imprints the air,[6]
        So soul into the soul may flow,
60   Though it to body first repair.°   *go*
        As our blood labors to beget
        Spirits[7] like souls as it can,
        Because such fingers need° to knit   *are needed*
        That subtle knot which makes us man:
65   So must pure lovers' souls descend
        To'affections,° and to faculties,[8]   *feelings*
        Which sense may reach and apprehend;
        Else a great Prince in prison lies.
        To'our bodies turn we then, that so
70   Weak men on love revealed may look;
        Love's mysteries in souls do grow,
        But yet the body is his book.
        And if some lover, such as we,
        Have heard this dialogue of one,

2. I.e., we see that we did not understand before what "did move" (motivated) us.
3. The "abler soul" derives from the union of the two lesser ones. *Interinanimates*: i.e., mutually breathes life into and mutually removes the consciousness of.
4. The nine orders of angels ("intelligences") were believed to govern the nine spheres of Ptolemaic astronomy.

5. Alloy, an impurity that strengthens metal. *Dross*: an impurity that weakens metal.
6. Astrological influences were conceived of as being transmitted through the medium of air; also, angels were thought to assume bodies of air in their dealings with humans.
7. Vapors believed to permeate the blood and to mediate between the body and the soul.
8. Dispositions; powers of the body.

75   Let him still mark us; he shall see
       Small change when we're to bodies gone.

1633

The Funeral

Whoever comes to shroud me, do not harm
    Nor question much
That subtle wreath of hair which crowns my arm;[9]
The mystery, the sign you must not touch,
5   For 'tis my outward soul,
Viceroy to that, which then to heaven being gone,
    Will leave this to control,
And keep these limbs, her[1] provinces, from dissolution.

For if the sinewy thread[2] my brain lets fall
10   Through every part
Can tie those parts and make me one of all;
These hairs, which upward grew, and strength and art
    Have from a better brain,
Can better do'it; except° she meant that I   *unless*
15   By this should know my pain,
As prisoners then are manacled, when they're condemned to die.

Whate'er she meant by 'it, bury it with me,
    For since I am
Love's martyr, it might breed idolatry,[3]
20   If into other's hands these relics came;
    As 'twas humility
To'afford to it all that a soul can do,
    So 'tis some bravery,
That since you would save none of me, I bury some of you.

1633

The Flea[4]

   Mark but this flea, and mark in this,
   How little that which thou deniest me is;
   It sucked me first, and now sucks thee,

---

9. I.e., a lock of hair that he had tied about his arm.
1. The soul's, but also the mistress's (cf. "she," line 14). *Viceroy*: one who acts in the name and by the authority of the supreme ruler.
2. One theory during the period maintained that the body is held in organic order by sinews or nerves emanating from the brain to every part.
3. A reference to the Roman Catholic practice of idolizing martyrs as saints and venerating objects

(relics) associated with them, such as bones or clothing.
4. The flea was a popular subject of Renaissance erotic poems in which, frequently, the narrator envies the flea for the liberties it takes with his lady and for its death at her hands (both *die* and *kill* were Renaissance slang terms for orgasm; the act of sexual intercourse was believed to reduce the man's life span). The narrator here addresses a woman who has scorned his advances.

And in this flea, our two bloods mingled be;
5   Thou know'st that this cannot be said
A sin, nor shame nor loss of maidenhead,[5]
    Yet this enjoys before it woo,[6]
    And pampered swells with one blood made of two,[7]
    And this, alas, is more then we would do.

10   Oh stay,[8] three lives in one flea spare,
Where we almost, yea more than married are.
This flea is you and I, and this
Our marriage bed, and marriage temple is;
Though parents grudge, and you, w'are met,
15   And cloistered in these living walls of jet.[9]
    Though use° make you apt to kill me,   *custom*
    Let not to that, self murder added be,
    And sacrilege,[1] three sins in killing three.

Cruel and sudden, hast thou since
20   Purpled thy nail, in blood of innocence?
Wherein could this flea guilty be,
Except in that drop which it sucked from thee?
Yet thou triumph'st, and say'st that thou
Find'st not thy self, nor me the weaker now;[2]
25   'Tis true, then learn how false, fears be;
    Just so much honor, when thou yield'st to me,
    Will waste, as this flea's death took life from thee.

1633

The Relic[3]

When my grave is broke up again
Some second guest to entertain[4]
(For graves have learned that woman-head°   *womanhood*
To be to more than one a bed),
5   And he that digs it, spies
A bracelet of bright hair about the bone,[5]
    Will he not let'us alone,
And think that there a loving couple lies,
Who thought that this device might be some way
10 To make their souls, at the last busy day,[6]
Meet at this grave, and make a little stay?

5. I.e., loss of virginity; the maidenhead is the hymen.
6. I.e., the flea enjoys this liberty without the effort of wooing the lady.
7. Renaissance medical theory held that blood was mingled during sexual intercourse, leading to conception; thus the image of swelling suggests pregnancy.
8. I.e., refrain from killing the flea.
9. Black marble; the "living walls of jet" here refer to the body of the flea.
1. Since the flea is a "marriage temple," killing it

would be sacrilege.
2. I.e., now that she has killed the flea.
3. See note 3, p. 309.
4. Reuse of a grave after an interval of several years was a common seventeenth-century practice (the bones of previous occupants were deposited in charnel houses).
5. See "The Funeral," line 3 and note 9 (p. 309).
6. Judgment Day, when all parts of the body would be reassembled and reunited with the soul in resurrection.

If this fall° in a time, or land,   *happen*
Where mis-devotion⁷ doth command,
Then he that digs us up, will bring
15   Us to the Bishop and the King,
To make us relics; then
Thou shalt be'a Mary Magdalen,⁸ and I
A something else thereby;
All women shall adore us, and some men;
20   And since at such time, miracles are sought,
I would have that age by this paper taught
What miracles we harmless lovers wrought.

First, we loved well and faithfully,
Yet knew not what we loved, nor why,
25   Difference of sex no more we knew,
Than our guardian angels do;
Coming and going, we
Perchance might kiss, but not between those meals;⁹
Our hands ne'er touched the seals,
30   Which nature, injured by late law,¹ sets free:
These miracles we did; but now, alas,
All measure and all language I should pass,
Should I tell what a miracle she was.

1633

Elegy VII²

Nature's lay idiot,³ I taught thee to love,
And in that sophistry,⁴ oh, thou dost prove
Too subtle: Fool, thou didst not understand
The mystic language of the eye nor hand:
5   Nor couldst thou judge the difference of the air
Of sighs, and say, this lies, this sounds° despair: *expresses*
Nor by the'eye's water call a malady
Desperately hot, or changing feverously.
I had not taught thee then, the alphabet
10   Of flowers, how they devicefully° being set   *ingeniously*
And bound up, might with speechless secrecy

---

7. False devotion; seems to refer to Catholicism.
8. The woman out of whom Christ had cast seven devils (Luke 8.2), traditionally identified with the repentant prostitute of Luke 7.37–50. Renaissance painters often depicted her with long, golden hair.
9. I.e., customary kisses of greeting and parting; kisses were thought to be food for the soul.
1. I.e., human law puts prohibitions ("seals," which may also here signify sexual organs) on that which nature originally set free.
2. Donne's "Elegies," heavily influenced by Ovid's *Amores,* are written in heroic couplets (rhyming iambic pentameter lines) that provide an apt English equivalent for the Latin elegiac meter of alternating dactyllic pentameter and hexameter lines. In Donne's time, elegies were reflective poems treating various topics including love and (increasingly often) death. Donne's elegies are thought to be early poems, mostly written in the 1590s. Five of the thirteen elegies designed for printing in the 1633 edition of the *Poems* were refused a licence by the official censors; the second edition of 1635 printed seventeen elegies, and others were added to later editions, such as the 1669. There is still no scholarly consensus on the canon of Donne's elegies, and the Roman numerals in the titles first appeared in twentieth-century editions.
3. I.e., one who is ignorant of the workings of nature, as a "layperson" is ignorant of religious mysteries.
4. Plausible but fallacious reasoning.

Deliver errands mutely, and mutually.
Remember since° all thy words used to be   *when*
To every suitor, "I,⁵ 'if my friends agree'";
15 Since, household charms,⁶ thy husband's name to teach,
Were all the love-tricks, that thy wit could reach;
And since, an hour's discourse could scarce have made
One answer in thee,⁷ and that ill arrayed
In broken proverbs, and torn sentences.
20 Thou art not by so many duties his,
That from the'world's common having severed thee,
Inlaid thee,⁸ neither to be seen, nor see,
As mine: who have with amorous delicacies
Refined thee'into a blissful paradise.
25 Thy graces and good words my creatures be;
I planted knowledge and life's tree⁹ in thee,
Which oh, shall strangers taste? Must I alas
Frame and enamel plate, and drink in glass?¹
Chafe° wax for others' seals? break a colt's force   *heat*
30 And leave him then, being made a ready horse?

1633

Elegy XIX. To His Mistress Going to Bed²

Come, madam, come, all rest my powers defy,
Until I labor, I in labor³ lie.
The foe oft-times having the foe in sight,
Is tired with standing though he never fight.
5 Off with that girdle, like heaven's zone⁴ glistering,
But a far fairer world encompassing.
Unpin that spangled breastplate⁵ which you wear,
That th' eyes of busy fools may be stopped there.
Unlace yourself, for that harmonious chime°   *chiming watch*
10 Tells me from you that now it is bed time.
Off with that happy busk,° which I envy,   *corset*
That still can be, and still can stand so nigh.
Your gown going off, such beauteous state reveals,

---

5. Some modern editions change "I"—the reading of all early editions and manuscripts—to "Ay."
6. Magic used to learn her future "husband's name."
7. I.e., could hardly have elicited a response from you.
8. I.e., laid thee in, set thee aside for his own use; with an allusion to the contested Renaissance practice of "enclosing" common agricultural lands for private uses.
9. The first paradise, Eden, included the tree of

the knowledge of good and evil and the tree of life (Genesis 2.9).
1. I.e., must I fashion and decorate a silver cup but drink from a glass one?
2. This poem was one of the five refused license for the 1633 edition (see note 2, p. 311).
3. Meaning "get to work" (sexually) in the first instance and "distress" (as of a woman in childbirth) in the second.
4. The belt of Orion.
5. Jeweled covering for the chest.

As when from flowry meads° th'hill's shadow steals.　　*meadows*
15　Off with that wiry coronet and show
　　The hairy diadem[6] which on you doth grow:
　　Now off with those shoes, and then safely[7] tread
　　In this love's hallowed temple, this soft bed.
　　In such white robes, heaven's angels used to be
20　Received by men; thou, Angel, bring'st with thee
　　A heaven like Mahomet's Paradise;[8] and though
　　Ill spirits walk in white, we easily know
　　By this these angels from an evil sprite:
　　Those set our hairs, but these our flesh upright.
25　　License my roving hands, and let them go
　　Before, behind, between, above, below.
　　O my America! my new-found-land,
　　My kingdom, safeliest when with one man manned,
　　My mine of precious stones, my empery,°　　*empire*
30　How blest am I in this discovering thee!
　　To enter in these bonds is to be free;
　　Then where my hand is set, my seal shall be.
　　　Full nakedness! All joys are due to thee,
　　As souls unbodied, bodies unclothed must be,
35　To taste whole joys. Gems which you women use
　　Are like Atlanta's balls,[9] cast in men's views,
　　That when a fool's eye lighteth on a gem,
　　His earthly soul may covet theirs, not them:
　　Like pictures, or like books' gay coverings made
40　For lay-men, are all women thus arrayed.
　　Themselves are mystic books,[1] which only we
　　(Whom their imputed grace will dignify)
　　Must see revealed. Then, since that I may know,
　　As liberally as to a midwife, show
45　Thyself: cast all, yea, this white linen hence,
　　There is no penance due to innocence:[2]
　　　To teach thee, I am naked first; why than,°　　*then*
　　What needst thou have more covering than a man?

　　　　　　　　　　　　　　　　　　　　　　　1669

6. A word for "crown," like the preceding line's "coronet"; but Donne leaves ambiguous the relation between figurative and literal crowns, and their bodily location.
7. Here and elsewhere in this poem, we substitute some manuscript variants for phrases in the 1669 edition, which has "softly" for "safely," "revealed to" (for "received by") in line 20, and "court" (for "covet") in line 38.
8. A heaven of sensual pleasures.
9. According to Greek mythology, Atalanta agreed to marry Hippomenes if he could defeat her in a foot race. As she was about to overtake him, he

cast in her path three golden apples (or "balls") given to him by Venus, the goddess of love and beauty. Distracted by their beauty, Atalanta stopped to retrieve them, and Hippomenes won the race.
1. A manuscript variant for "books" is "bodies."
2. Some manuscripts have "here is no penance much less innocence." White clothing was often considered penitential vestment; the speaker seems to be arguing that the women should cast off such clothing since innocence does not require penance.

Satire III[3]

Kind pity chokes my spleen;[4] brave scorn forbids
Those tears to issue which swell my eyelids;
I must not laugh,° nor weep° sins, and be wise,   *mock / lament*
Can railing then cure these worn maladies?
5 Is not our mistress fair Religion,
As worthy'of all our souls' devotion,
As virtue was to the first blinded age?[5]
Are not heaven's joys as valiant to assuage
Lusts, as earth's honor was to them?[6] Alas,
10 As we do them in means, shall they surpass
Us in the end, and shall thy father's spirit
Meet blind philosophers in heaven, whose merit
Of strict life may be'imputed faith,[7] and hear
Thee, whom he taught so easy ways and near
15 To follow, damned? O, if thou dar'st, fear this;
This fear great courage and high valor is.
Dar'st thou aid mutinous Dutch,[8] and dar'st thou lay
Thee in ships, wooden sepulchers, a prey
To leaders' rage, to storms, to shot, to dearth?°   *famine*
20 Dar'st thou dive seas and dungeons° of the earth?   *mines, caves*
Hast thou courageous fire to thaw the ice
Of frozen North discoveries? and thrice
Colder than salamanders, like divine
Children in the oven,[9] fires of Spain, and the line,°   *equator*
25 Whose countries limbecks to our bodies be,
Canst thou for gain bear?[1] And must every he
Which cries not, "Goddess!" to thy mistress, draw,[2]
Or eat thy poisonous words? Courage of straw!
O desperate coward, wilt thou seem bold, and

---

3. In this poem, Donne adapts techniques of classical Roman satirists (e.g., Horace, Juvenal, and Persius) to a contemporary problem: the proliferating divisions of belief among Christians in the period after the Protestant break with the Roman Catholic Church. Donne was raised Catholic and seems to have retained considerable sympathy for Catholic beliefs even after he abandoned them in the 1590s; still dubious about the "official" Church of England's doctrines, he refused to take Anglican orders in 1607 despite King James's wish that Donne pursue a career in the Church. Later, he became an Anglican minister, and in 1621 he was appointed dean of St. Paul's Cathedral. When "Satire III" was written, however—probably in the 1590s—Donne like many other English people was in a state of doubt about religious "truth."

 Donne's five satires are among the first formal experiments in the genre in English; they were initially refused a publication license, but the ban was later removed.
4. The seat of laughter and of melancholy (according to Renaissance physiology).
5. I.e., the age of paganism, "blinded" to Christianity but capable of a natural devotion to "virtue."
6. I.e., hope of heaven's "joys" should be as capable of calming our "lusts" as earthly "honor" was

able to appease the lusts of the pagans.
7. Donne reverses a reformed Protestant theological concept: instead of achieving Christians' salvation by imputing Christ's merits to them through faith, here virtuous pagans' salvation might be gained by imputing faith to them based on their moral lives.
8. In the last twenty years of the sixteenth century, the English aided the Protestant Dutch in their revolt against Spanish (and Catholic) rule. Donne had sailed in two raiding expeditions against the Spanish.
9. After alluding to expeditions to discover the Northwest Passage, Donne invokes the "divine children" Shadrach, Meshach, and Abednego, who are described in the Book of Daniel (3.20–30) as surviving a fiery furnace unharmed after refusing to worship a golden idol. Salamanders were thought to be so cold-blooded that they could endure fire.
1. The object of "bear" is "fires of Spain, and the line." "Fires of Spain" refers to the Inquisition, in which heretics were burned at the stake. Inquisitorial and equatorial heats burn people as chemists heat materials in "limbecks," apparatuses used for distilling liquids.
2. I.e., fight a duel.

30 To thy foes and his° (who made thee to stand   *God's*
    Sentinel in his world's garrison) thus yield,
    And for forbidden wars, leave th'appointed field?
    Know thy foes: The foul Devil he'is, whom thou
    Strivest to please: for hate, not love, would allow
35 Thee fain his whole realm to be quit;[3] and as
    The world's all parts wither away and pass,
    So the world's self, thy other loved foe, is
    In her decrepit wane, and thou, loving this,
    Dost love a withered and worn strumpet; last,
40 Flesh (itself's death) and joys which flesh can taste,
    Thou lovest; and thy fair goodly soul, which doth
    Give this flesh power to taste joy, thou dost loathe;
    Seek true religion. O, where? Mirreus,[4]
    Thinking her unhoused here, and fled from us,
45 Seeks her at Rome; there, because he doth know
    That she was there a thousand years ago.
    He loves her rags so, as we here obey
    The statecloth[5] where the Prince sat yesterday.
    Crantz to such brave loves will not be enthralled,
50 But loves her only, who'at Geneva'[6] is called
    Religion—plain, simple, sullen, young,
    Contemptuous, yet unhandsome; as among
    Lecherous humors,° there is one that judges   *dispositions*
    No wenches wholesome but coarse country drudges.
55 Graius[7] stays still at home here, and because
    Some preachers, vile ambitious bawds, and laws
    Still new, like fashions, bid him think that she
    Which dwells with us, is only° perfect, he   *solely*
    Embraceth her whom his Godfathers will
60 Tender to him, being tender, as wards still
    Take such wives as their guardians offer, or
    Pay values. Careless Phrygius[8] doth abhor
    All, because all cannot be good, as one
    Knowing some women whores, dares marry none.
65 Graccus[9] loves all as one, and thinks that so
    As women do in divers countries go
    In divers habits, yet are still one kind,
    So doth, so is religion; and this blind-
    ness too much light breeds;[1] but unmovèd thou
70 Of force° must one, and forced but one allow;   *necessity*

3. I.e., the devil would willingly ("fain")—but for hate, not love—give you his whole realm of hell to discharge a debt ("to be quit").

4. The fictional characters that follow represent different creeds. "Mirreus," from myrrh, a gum resin that gives incense its smell, is a Roman Catholic.

5. The royal canopy; a symbol of royal power.

6. The center of Calvinism; "Crantz" is a Geneva Presbyterian.

7. Probably an Erastian, i.e., one who believes that religious belief should be determined by the state; he could also be an Anglican, a follower of England's state religion after the Reformation.

8. Seems to be a skeptic, or one who rejects all creeds. "Values," or fines, had to be paid by young men (of "tender" years) who rejected the marriages arranged by their guardians; Catholics also had to pay fines if they refused to attend Anglican services.

9. A Universalist, or one who considers all creeds basically alike.

1. I.e., "too much light" grows for anyone to see the truth. Unlike Graccus, who finds the "light of truth" in every creed, the reader is advised to find the one "right" religion without being moved by other forces.

And the right; ask thy father which is she,
Let him ask his; though truth and falsehood be
Near twins, yet truth a little elder is;
Be busy to seek her, believe me this,
75   He's not of none, nor worst, that seeks the best.[2]
To'adore, or scorn an image, or protest,[3]
May all be bad; doubt wisely; in strange way
To stand inquiring right, is not to stray;
To sleep, or run wrong, is. On a huge hill,
80   Craggèd and steep, Truth stands, and he that will
Reach her, about° must, and about must go,   *around*
And what th'hill's suddenness° resists, win so;   *unexpected abruptness*
Yet strive so, that before age, death's twilight,
Thy soul rest, for none can work in that night.[4]
85   To will° implies delay, therefore now do.   *intend a future act*
Hard deeds, the body's pains; hard knowledge too
The mind's endeavors reach,[5] and mysteries
Are like the sun, dazzling, yet plain to'all eyes.
Keep the'truth which thou hast found; men do not stand
90   In so ill case that God hath with his hand
Signed kings' blank charters to kill whom they hate,
Nor are they vicars, but hangmen to fate.[6]
Fool and wretch, wilt thou let thy Soul be tied
To man's laws, by which she shall not be tried
95   At the last day? O, will it then boot° thee   *profit*
To say a Philip, or a Gregory,
A Harry, or a Martin[7] taught thee this?
Is not this excuse for mere° contraries   *absolute, complete*
Equally strong? Cannot both sides say so?
100   That thou mayest rightly'obey power, her° bounds know;   *power's*
Those passed, her nature'and name is changed; to be
Then humble to her is idolatry.
As streams are, power is; those blest flowers that dwell
At the rough stream's calm head, thrive and do well,
105   But having left their roots, and themselves given
To the stream's tyrannous rage, alas, are driven
Through mills, and rocks, and woods, and at last, almost
Consumed in going, in the sea are lost:
So perish souls, which more choose men's unjust
110   Power from God claimed, than God himself to trust.

1633

---

2. I.e., the person who seeks the true Church is not an unbeliever ("of none") nor the "worst" sort of believer.
3. "To'adore" alludes to Catholic worship, whereas to "scorn an image" and to "protest" are typical Protestant gestures.
4. Cf John 9.4: "I must work the work of him that sent me, while it is day. The night cometh, when no man can work."
5. I.e., just as the body's pains achieve ("reach") hard deeds, the mind's endeavors reach hard knowledge.

6. These syntactically and conceptually difficult lines seem to say that God has not given earthly rulers unconditional authority ("blank charters") to kill whomever they choose; when they do kill, they are serving not as God's "vicars" but rather as hangmen to "fate."
7. Martin Luther (1483–1546), German Reformation leader. *Philip:* Philip II (1527–1598) of Spain. *Gregory:* any one of several Pope Gregorys (VII, XIII, XIV). *Harry:* Henry VIII (1491–1547) of England.

Good Friday,[8] 1613. Riding Westward

Let man's soul be a sphere, and then, in this,
The'intelligence that moves, devotion is,[9]
And as the other spheres, by being grown
Subject to foreign motions, lose their own,
5   And being by others hurried every day,
Scarce in a year their natural form obey;
Pleasure or business, so, our souls admit
For their first mover, and are whirled by it.[1]
Hence is 't, that I am carried towards the West
10   This day, when my soul's form bends towards the East.
There I should see a Sun,[2] by rising, set,
And by that setting endless day beget;
But that° Christ on this cross did rise and fall,   *except that*
Sin had eternally benighted all.
15   Yet dare I'almost be glad I do not see
That spectacle, of too much weight for me.
Who sees God's face, that is self-life, must die;[3]
What a death were it then to see God die?
It made his own lieutenant, Nature, shrink;
20   It made his footstool crack, and the sun wink.[4]
Could I behold those hands which span the poles,
And tune[5] all spheres at once, pierced with those holes?
Could I behold that endless height which is
Zenith to us, and to'our antipodes,[6]
25   Humbled below us? Or that blood which is
The seat° of all our souls, if not of His,   *dwelling place*
Make dirt of dust, or that flesh which was worn
By God, for his apparel, ragg'd and torn?
If on these things I durst not look, durst I
30   Upon his miserable mother cast mine eye,
Who was God's partner here, and furnished thus
Half of that sacrifice which ransomed us?
Though these things, as I ride, be from° mine eye,   *away from*
They're present yet unto my memory,
35   For that looks towards them; and thou look'st towards me,
O Saviour, as thou hang'st upon the tree.
I turn my back to thee but to receive
Corrections, till thy mercies bid thee leave.°   *cease*

8. The Friday before Easter, observed as the anniversary of Christ's death.
9. I.e., just as an angel was believed to govern the movements of each of the nine concentric celestial spheres, so "devotion" is or should be the guiding principle for the movements of humans.
1. I.e., just as spheres are deflected from their true orbits by outside influences, so our souls are diverted by "pleasure or business." According to Ptolemaic astronomy, each sphere, in addition to its own motion, was influenced by the motions of those outside it ("foreign motions," line 4), the outermost being known as the *primum mobile*, or "first mover" (line 8).

2. With a pun on *Son*.
3. God told Moses: "Thou canst not see my face: for there shall no man see me and live" (Exodus 33.20).
4. A quaking of the earth (God's "footstool," according to Isaiah 66.1) and a solar eclipse marked Christ's Crucifixion (Matthew 27.45, 51).
5. The motion of the celestial spheres was believed to produce music; some manuscripts have "turn," which accords with the notion that God was the "first mover."
6. The zenith is that part of the heavens directly above any point on Earth; the antipodes are that part of Earth diametrically opposite such a point.

O think me worth thine anger; punish me;
40   Burn off my rusts and my deformity;
Restore thine image so much, by thy grace,
That thou may'st know me, and I'll turn my face.

1633

From Holy Sonnets[7]

1

Thou hast made me, and shall thy work decay?
Repair me now, for now mine end doth haste;
I run to death, and death meets me as fast,
And all my pleasures are like yesterday.
5   I dare not move my dim eyes any way,
Despair behind, and death before doth cast
Such terror, and my feeble flesh doth waste
By sin in it, which it towards hell doth weigh.
Only thou art above, and when towards thee
10 By thy leave I can look, I rise again;
But our old subtle foe° so tempteth me   *Satan*
That not one hour myself I can sustain.
Thy grace may wing° me to prevent° his art,   *give wings to / forestall*
And thou like adamant[8] draw mine iron° heart.   *obdurate*

1635

5

I am a little world[9] made cunningly
Of elements,° and an angelike sprite;°   *matter / spirit*
But black sin hath betrayed to endless night
My world's both parts, and O, both parts must die.
5   You which beyond that heaven which was most high
Have found new spheres, and of new lands can write,[1]
Pour new seas in mine eyes, that so I might
Drown my world with my weeping earnestly,
Or wash it if it must be drowned no more.[2]
10 But O, it must be burnt![3] Alas, the fire
Of lust and envy'have burnt it heretofore,

7. Donne's religious poetry is collectively known as the *Divine Poems*, of which the nineteen *Holy Sonnets* form the largest group. Although Donne probably began writing them around 1609, at least a decade after leaving the Catholic Church, the sonnets display an interest in the formal meditative exercise of the Jesuits. Our selections are numbered according to Sir Herbert Grierson's influential edition of 1912, which included several sonnets not published until the the nineteenth century. No one knows what ordering Donne might have intended for the *Holy Sonnets*.
8. Lodestone, a magnetic stone; or adamantine rock, a proverbially hard stone.

9. The individual as microcosm of the world was a common Renaissance notion.
1. Copernican astronomy (which placed the sun at the center of our system, unlike Ptolemaic astronomy, which placed Earth at the center) had changed people's ideas about the universe just as recent terrestrial exploration had changed people's ideas about the world.
2. God promised Noah that he would never again cover Earth with a flood (Genesis 9.11).
3. At the end of the world, "the elements shall melt with fervent heat, the earth also and the works that are therein shall be burned up" (2 Peter 3.10).

And made it fouler; let their flames retire,
And burn me, O Lord, with a fiery zeal
Of thee'and thy house, which doth in eating heal.[4]

1635

7

At the round earth's imagined corners, blow
Your trumpets, angels;[5] and arise, arise
From death, you numberless infinities
Of souls, and to your scattered bodies go;
5   All whom the flood did, and fire shall,[6] o'erthrow,
All whom war, dearth,° age, agues,° tyrannies,   *famine / fevers*
Despair, law, chance, hath slain, and you whose eyes
Shall behold God, and never taste death's woe.[7]
But let them sleep, Lord, and me mourn a space;
10 For, if above all these, my sins abound,
'Tis late to ask abundance of thy grace
When we are there. Here on this lowly ground,
Teach me how to repent; for that's as good
As if thou'hadst sealed my pardon with thy blood.

1633

9

If poisonous minerals, and if that tree
Whose fruit threw death on else° immortal us,   *otherwise*
If lecherous goats, if serpents envious
Cannot be damned,[8] alas, why should I be?
5   Why should intent or reason, born in me,
Make sins, else equal, in me more heinous?
And mercy being easy and glorious
To God, in his stern wrath why threatens he?
But who am I, that dare dispute with thee,
10 O God? Oh! of thine only worthy blood,
And my tears, make a heavenly Lethean[9] flood,
And drown in it my sins' black memory.
That thou remember them, some claim as debt;
I think it mercy if thou wilt forget.[1]

1633

4. "The zeal of thine house hath eaten me up" (Psalms 59.9); probably also a reference to the Christian rite of Communion, in which Christ's blood and body (his "house") are eaten.
5. The first eight lines of the poem recount the events of the end of the world and the Second Coming of Christ; Donne alludes specifically to Revelation 7.1: "I saw four angels standing on the four corners of the earth, holding the four winds of the earth."
6. See note 3, p. 318.
7. "But I tell you of a truth, there be some standing here, which shall not taste of death, till they see

the kingdom of God" (Christ's words to his disciples, Luke 9.27). According to 1 Thessalonians 4.17, believers who are alive at the time of Christ's Second Coming will not die but will be taken directly to heaven.
8. I.e., only creatures with the ability to reason can be damned. The tree is the tree of knowledge of good and evil, the fruit of which Adam and Eve were forbidden to eat or touch (Genesis 2).
9. Lethe was a river in the classical underworld; drinking its waters caused one to forget the past.
1. Cf. Jeremiah 31.34: "I will forgive their iniquity, and I will remember their sins no more."

10

Death, be not proud, though some have called thee
Mighty and dreadful, for thou are not so;
For those whom thou think'st thou dost overthrow
Die not, poor Death, nor yet canst thou kill me.
5 From rest and sleep, which but thy pictures be,
Much pleasure, then from thee much more must flow,
And soonest our best men with thee do go,
Rest of° their bones, and soul's delivery.   *for*
Thou'art slave to fate, chance, kings, and desperate men,
10 And dost with poison, war, and sickness dwell,
And poppy'or° charms can make us sleep as well   *opium or*
And better than thy stroke; why swell'st° thou then?   *puff with pride*
One short sleep past, we wake eternally,
And death shall be no more; Death, thou shalt die.[2]

                                1633

14

Batter my heart, three-personed God;[3] for You
As yet but knock, breathe, shine, and seek to mend;
That I may rise and stand, o'erthrow me,' and bend
Your force to break, blow, burn, and make me new.
5 I, like an usurped town, to'another due,
Labor to'admit You, but O, to no end;
Reason, Your viceroy[4] in me, me should defend,
But is captived, and proves weak or untrue.
Yet dearly'I love you,'and would be loved fain,°   *gladly*
10 But am betrothed unto your enemy.
Divorce me,'untie or break that knot again;
Take me to you, imprison me, for I,
Except you'enthrall[5] me, never shall be free,
Nor ever chaste, except you ravish me.

                                1633

18

Show me, dear Christ, thy spouse[6] so bright and clear.
What! is it she which on the other shore
Goes richly painted? or which, robbed and tore,
Laments and mourns in Germany and here?

---

2. Cf. Corinthians 15.26: "The last enemy that shall be destroyed is death."
3. The Trinity: Father, Son, and Holy Spirit.
4. One who acts in the name and by the authority of the supreme ruler.
5. Unless you make a prisoner of.
6. The true Church, "the bride of Christ" (cf. Song of Solomon 5.2: "Open to me, my sister, my love, my dove, my undefiled"). Lines 2–4 ask whether God's spouse is the Roman Catholic Church (in power in Continental countries such as France, Spain, and Italy, i.e., lands on the "other shore") or the Protestant Church "here," i.e., in England.

5 Sleeps she a thousand, then peeps up one year?
Is she self-truth, and errs? now new, now'outwore?
Doth she,'and did she, and shall she evermore
On one, on seven, or on no hill appear?[7]
Dwells she with us, or like adventuring knights

10 First travel[8] we to seek, and then make love?
Betray,° kind husband, thy spouse to our sights,   *reveal*
And let mine amorous soul court thy mild dove,[9]
Who is most true and pleasing to thee then
When she's embraced and open to most men.[1]

1615?   1894

A Hymn to God the Father[2]

Wilt thou forgive that sin where I begun,
    Which is my sin, though it were done before?[3]
Wilt thou forgive that sin through which I run,
    And do run still, though still I do deplore?
5   When thou hast done,[4] thou hast not done,
          For I have more.

Wilt thou forgive that sin by which I have won
    Others to sin? and made my sin their door?
Wilt thou forgive that sin which I did shun
10   A year or two, but wallowed in a score?
       When thou has done, thou hast not done,
          For I have more.

I have a sin of fear, that when I have spun
    My last thread, I shall perish on the shore;
15 Swear by thy self, that at my death thy Son
    Shall shine as he shines now and heretofore;
       And, having done that, thou hast done,
          I fear[5] no more.

1623?   1633

7. The church on "no hill" could be either the Presbyterian church of Geneva or the Episcopal Church of England, based in Canterbury. The church of "one" hill is an unclear reference, but perhaps it is Mt. Moriah (site of Solomon's temple). The church of "seven" hills is that of Rome.
8. Formerly, "labor" as well as "journey."
9. The dove was a symbol of the Holy Spirit.
1. I.e., universal, without division. An echo of the Song of Solomon (5.2), which was frequently interpreted as the song of love between Christ and the Church.

2. This hymn was sung by the entire congregation during the Anglican service. Donne wrote it during his illness of 1623, had it set to music, and liked to hear it performed by the choir of St. Paul's Cathedral.
3. I.e., he inherits the original sin of Adam and Eve.
4. Donne puns on his own name and may, in the next line, pun on his wife's maiden name, Ann More.
5. In some manuscripts, "have."

Hymn to God My God, in My Sickness

Since I am coming to that holy room
    Where, with thy choir of saints for evermore,
I shall be made thy music; as I come
    I tune the instrument here at the door,
5   And what I must do then, think here before.

Whilst my physicians by their love are grown
    Cosmographers,[6] and I their map, who lie
Flat on this bed, that by them may be shown
    That this is my southwest discovery
10   *Per fretum febris*,[7] by these straits to die,

I joy, that in these straits, I see my West;[8]
    For, though their currents yield return to none,
What shall my West hurt me? As West and East
    In all flat maps (and I am one) are one,[9]
15   So death doth touch the resurrection.

Is the Pacific Sea my home? Or are
    The Eastern riches? Is Jerusalem?
Anyan,° and Màgellan, and Gìbraltar,[1]   *Bering Straits*
    All straits, and none but straits, are ways to them,
20   Whether where Japhet dwelt, or Cham, or Shem.[2]

We think that Paradise and Calvary,
    Christ's cross, and Adam's tree, stood in one place;
Look, Lord, and find both Adams[3] met in me;
    As the first Adam's sweat surrounds my face,
25   May the last Adam's blood my soul embrace.

So, in his purple[4] wrapped, receive me, Lord;
    By these his thorns give me his other crown;
And, as to others' souls I preached Thy word,
    Be this my text, my sermon to mine own:
30   Therefore that he may raise the Lord throws down.[5]

1623?   1635

---

6. Ones who map the general features of the celestial and terrestrial worlds.

7. Through the straits of fever (Latin). Donne puns on the word "strait" as both a passageway between two bodies of water and a situation of distress. Cf. Christ's words in Matthew 7.4: "Because strait is the gate and narrow is the way, which leadeth unto life, and few there be that find it." Magellan had discovered the straits that bear his name in 1520. They lie at the southern tip of South America and are hence southwest from England.

8. Where the sun sets; hence, where life ends.

9. In one of his sermons (no. 55 in the collection *LXXX Sermons*), Donne noted that when a flat map is "pasted" on a round body, "then West and East are all one."

1. Behind these locations lie many ancient speculations about the location of paradise, which is analogous to heaven, as the various straits are to death.

2. The three sons of Noah (Genesis 10), who were thought to have settled in Europe, Africa, and Asia, respectively, after the Flood.

3. I.e., Adam and Christ. *Adam's tree:* the tree of the knowledge of good and evil in the Garden of Eden (Genesis 2). *In one place:* in the same region.

4. I.e., in the purple of Christ's blood or his purple robe (Mark 15.17).

5. Adapted from Psalms 146.8: "the Lord raiseth them that are bowed down."

BEN JONSON
1572–1637

To the Reader[1]

Pray thee, take care, that tak'st my book in hand,
To read it well: that is, to understand.

1616

On My First Daughter

Here lies, to each her parents' ruth,°   *sorrow*
Mary, the daughter of their youth;
Yet all heaven's gifts being heaven's due,
It makes the father less to rue.
5   At six months' end she parted hence
With safety of her innocence;
Whose soul heaven's queen, whose name she bears,
In comfort of her mother's tears,
Hath placed amongst her virgin-train:[2]
10   Where, while that severed doth remain,[3]
This grave partakes the fleshly birth;
Which cover lightly, gentle earth!

1616

On My First Son

Farewell, thou child of my right hand,[4] and joy;
My sin was too much hope of thee, loved boy:
Seven years thou'wert lent to me, and I thee pay,
Exacted by thy fate, on the just day.[5]
5   O could I lose all father now![6] for why
Will man lament the state he should envy,
To have so soon 'scaped world's and flesh's rage,
And, if no other misery, yet age?

1. From the book of epigrams that Jonson published along with a collection of poems called *The Forrest* in his *First Folio* of 1616. He seems initially to have planned another book of epigrams, but his later examples of the genre—in his collection of poems *The Underwood*—were not published until after his death, in the *Second Folio* of 1640. Modeled on poems by the Roman poet Martial (ca. 40–ca. 103), epigrams were terse and pointed, often ending with a witty turn of thought. Jonson's teacher, the historian William Camden, described them as "short and sweet poems, framed to praise or dispraise."
2. I.e., among those attending the Virgin Mary.
3. I.e., while her soul remains separate from her body (the soul and body will reunite at Resurrection).
4. A literal translation of the Hebrew *Benjamin*, the boy's name.
5. Jonson's son died on his seventh birthday, in 1603.
6. I.e., let go all fatherly thoughts and sorrow.

Rest in soft peace, and asked, say, "Here doth lie
10   Ben Jonson his best piece of poetry."
For whose sake henceforth all his[7] vows be such
As what he loves may never like too much.

1616

On Spies

Spies, you are lights in state,[8] but of base stuff,
Who, when you've burnt yourselves down to the snuff,°   candle end
Stink and are thrown away. End fair enough.

1616

To Fool or Knave

Thy praise or dispraise is to me alike:
One doth not stroke me, nor the other strike.

1616

To Sir Henry Cary[9]

That neither fame nor love might wanting be
To greatness, Cary, I sing that and thee;
Whose house,[1] if it no other honor had,
In only thee might be both great and glad;
5   Who, to upbraid° the sloth of this our time,   chastise
Durst valor make almost, but not, a crime;[2]
Which deed I know not, whether were more high,
Or thou more happy, it to justify
Against thy fortune: when no foe, that day,
10   Could conquer thee but chance, who did betray.
Love thy great loss, which a renown hath won,
To live when Broick not stands, nor Ruhr doth run.[3]
Love honors, which of best example be
When they cost dearest and are done most free;
15   Though every fortitude deserves applause,

---

7. I.e., Ben Jonson the father's.
8. Condition or form; with a likely pun on "state" as government.
9. Henry Cary (ca. 1576–1633) became Viscount Falkland in 1620 and was the father of Jonson's friend Lucius Cary (1609 or 1610–1643).
1. Family line, but also household, which in Cary's case was well known to include not "only" a husband but also a wife—Elizabeth Cary (ca. 1587–1639)—who aspired to public "honor" through her

writing.
2. In October 1605, Cary was with a group of English and Dutch soldiers who fled from a smaller Italian force—hence Cary, who tried to stop the rout and was captured, almost made "valor" a crime in English eyes.
3. "The castle and river near where he was taken" [Jonson's note]. Cary was captured near the confluence of the Rhur and the Rhine rivers.

It may be much or little in the cause.
He's valiant'st that dares fight, and not for pay;
That virtuous is, when the reward's away.

1616

On Playwright

Playwright, convict° of public wrongs to men,   *convicted*
Takes private beatings and begins again.
Two kinds of valor he doth show at once:
Active in 's° brain, and passive in his bones.   *his*

1616

To Elizabeth, Countess of Rutland[4]

That poets are far rarer births than kings
Your noblest father proved; like whom before,
Or then, or since, about our Muses' springs,
Came not that soul exhausted so their store.[5]
5   Hence was it that the destinies decreed
(Save that most masculine issue of his brain)[6]
No male unto him; who could so exceed
Nature, they thought, in all that he would fain.°   *make*
At which she, happily[7] displeased, made you,
10 On whom, if he were living now to look,
He should those rare and absolute numbers[8] view,
As he would burn or better far his book.

1616

On English Monsieur[9]

Would you believe, when you this monsieur see,
That his whole body should speak French, not he?
That so much scarf of France, and hat, and feather,
And shoe, and tie, and garter should come hether,°   *hither*
5   And land on one whose face durst never be
Toward the sea farther than Half-Way Tree?[1]

4. Daughter (1584–1612) of the poet Sir Philip
Sidney (1554–1586; see pp. 208–20), she married
Roger Manners, fifth earl of Rutland.
5. I.e., no one before or since Sidney has so well
used up the supply ("store") of poetic inspiration
symbolized by the "springs" of the "Muses" (nine
sister goddesses in Greek mythology).
6. I.e., his books.

7. I.e., by good fortune.
8. Metrical feet, hence lines or verses; perhaps
also, "proportions."
9. Sir, Mr. (French); pronounced *mes'-yer*, but
often spelled *monser* in Jonson's time, suggesting
an Anglicized pronunciation.
1. Perhaps a landmark between London and
Dover, where a traveler would embark for France.

That he, untraveled, should be French so much
As Frenchmen in his company should seem Dutch?
Or had his father, when he did him get,
10 The French disease,[2] with which he labors yet?
Or hung some monsieur's picture on the wall,
By which his dam conceived him, clothes and all?
Or is it some French statue? No: 'T° doth move,   *it*
And stoop, and cringe. O then, it needs must prove
15 The new French tailor's motion,° monthly made,   *puppet*
Daily to turn in Paul's,[3] and help the trade.

1616

To John Donne

Who shall doubt, Donne, where° I a poet be,   *whether*
When I dare send my epigrams[4] to thee?
That so alone canst judge, so'alone dost make;
And, in thy censures, evenly dost take
5 As free simplicity to disavow
As thou hast best authority t' allow.
Read all I send, and if I find but one
Marked by thy hand, and with the better stone,[5]
My title's sealed.[6] Those that for claps° do write,   *applause*
10 Let pui'nies',[7] porters', players'° praise delight,   *actors*
And, till they burst, their backs like asses load:[8]
A man should seek great glory, and not broad.°   *widespread, unrefined*

1616

Inviting a Friend to Supper[9]

Tonight, grave sir, both my poor house, and I
Do equally desire your company;
Not that we think us worthy such a guest,
But that your worth will dignify our feast
5 With those that come, whose grace may make that seem
Something, which else could hope for no esteem.
It is the fair acceptance, sir, creates
The entertainment perfect, not the cates.°   *food*

---

2. I.e., syphilis.
3. St. Paul's Cathedral, in London. In the seventeenth century, St. Paul's was a popular gathering place; merchants hired men to walk up and down in the yard advertising their wares.
4. On epigrams, see note 1, p. 323.
5. The allusion may be to the Thracian custom of recording the good or evil fortunes of each day by placing a stone counter of corresponding color in an urn. Jonson refers elsewhere to the description of this custom in Pliny's *Natural History* 7.40.

6. I.e., as a poet.
7. Puisnies (pronounced like *punies*), insignificant persons.
8. I.e., probably: let the praises made by insignificant persons load the backs of those who write for applause until their backs break ("burst"). *Asses:* beasts of burden, with a probable pun on "ass" as an ignorant person.
9. The versified invitation to share a meal was a popular type of classical and Renaissance verse epistle.

Yet shall you have, to rectify your palate,
10 An olive, capers, or some better salad
Ushering the mutton; with a short-legged hen,
If we can get her, full of eggs, and then
Lemons, and wine for sauce; to these a cony°   rabbit
Is not to be despaired of, for our money;
15 And, though fowl now be scarce, yet there are clerks,
The sky not falling, think we may have larks.[1]
I'll tell you of more, and lie, so you will come:
Of partridge, pheasant, woodcock, of which some
May yet be there, and godwit, if we can;
20 Knot, rail, and ruff too.[2] Howsoe'er, my man°   servant
Shall read a piece of Virgil, Tacitus,
Livy,[3] or of some better book to us,
Of which we'll speak our minds, amidst our meat;
And I'll profess° no verses to repeat.   promise
25 To° this, if aught appear which I not know of,   add to
That will the pastry, not my paper, show of.[4]
Digestive° cheese and fruit there sure will be;   aiding digestion
But that which most doth take my Muse[5] and me,
Is a pure cup of rich Canary wine,
30 Which is the Mermaid's[6] now, but shall be mine;
Of which had Horace, or Anacreon[7] tasted,
Their lives, as do their lines, till now had lasted.
Tobacco, nectar, or the Thespian spring,[8]
Are all but Luther's beer[9] to this I sing.
35 Of this we will sup free, but moderately,
And we will have no Pooley, or Parrot[1] by,
Nor shall our cups make any guilty men;
But, at our parting we will be as when
We innocently met. No simple word
40 That shall be uttered at our mirthful board,
Shall make us sad next morning or affright
The liberty that we'll enjoy tonight.

1616

1. Cf. the old proverb *When the sky falls we shall have larks. Clerks:* i.e., scholars (pronounced *clarks*).
2. The godwit, knot, rail, and ruff are all wading birds related to the curlew or sandpiper. They were formerly regarded as delicacies.
3. Roman historian (59 B.C.E.–17 C.E.). Virgil (70–19 B.C.E.), Roman poet. Cornelius Tacitus (ca. 56–ca. 120), Roman historian.
4. I.e., if papers appear, they will be only under pies ("pastry"; to keep them from sticking to the pans).
5. Source of inspiration. In Greek mythology, the Muses were nine sister goddesses who presided over poetry, song, and the arts and sciences.

6. London's Mermaid Tavern, a favorite haunt of Jonson's. Canary is a light, sweet wine.
7. The Greek poet Anacreon of Teos (ca. 582–ca. 485 B.C.E.) and the Roman poet Horace (65–68 B.C.E.) both wrote many poems praising wine.
8. Associated with the Muses. Smoking was often called "drinking tobacco." *Nectar:* the drink of the classical gods.
9. German beer, considered inferior.
1. Robert Pooly and (probably) Henry Parrot were government spies; Pooly was present when the poet Christopher Marlowe (1564–1593; see pp. 238–56) was killed, in a tavern brawl. With a pun on the chattering of parrots (Polly, a name for a parrot).

On Gut

Gut eats all day and lechers all the night;
So all his meat he tasteth[2] over twice;
And, striving so to double his delight,
He makes himself a thoroughfare of vice.
5   Thus in his belly can he change a sin:
Lust it comes out, that gluttony went in.

1616

Epitaph on Elizabeth, L. H.[3]

Wouldst thou hear what man can say
In a little? Reader, stay.
Underneath this stone doth lie
As much beauty as could die;
5   Which in life did harbor give
To more virtue than doth live.
If at all she had a fault,
Leave it buried in this vault.
One name was Elizabeth;
10 Th' other, let it sleep with death:
Fitter, where it died, to tell,
Than that it lived at all. Farewell.

1616

To Penshurst[4]

Thou art not, Penshurst, built to envious show,
Of touch[5] or marble; nor canst boast a row
Of polished pillars, or a roof of gold;
Thou hast no lantern,[6] whereof tales are told,
5   Or stair, or courts; but stand'st an ancient pile,
And, these grudged at, art reverenced the while.[7]
Thou joy'st in better marks, of soil, of air,
Of wood, of water; therein thou art fair.
Thou hast thy walks for health, as well as sport;
10 Thy mount,[8] to which the dryads° do resort,   wood nymphs
Where Pan and Bacchus[9] their high feasts have made,

---

2. Also meaning "to know carnally."
3. The subject of this epitaph (a poem written as if it were inscribed on a tombstone) has not been identified, although it is likely that the "L" stood for "Lady."
4. The country estate of the Sidney family, in Kent. An important early example of the "country house" poem in English, this poem was imitated by Jonson's contemporaries; cf. Aemilia Lanyer's "The Description of Cooke-ham" (p. 288).
5. Touchstone: a fine, black, costly variety of

basalt.
6. A glassed or open structure raised above the roof of a house.
7. I.e., while other buildings are envied, Penshurst is admired.
8. Some high ground on the estate.
9. Greek god of wine and revelry. *Pan:* Greek god of shepherds and hunters; half goat, half man, he was raised by Bacchus and was associated with lust and music.

Beneath the broad beech and the chestnut shade;
That taller tree, which of a nut was set
At his great birth where all the Muses[1] met.
15 There in the writhèd bark are cut the names
Of many a sylvan, taken with his flames;[2]
And thence the ruddy satyrs oft provoke
The lighter fauns to reach thy Lady's Oak.
Thy copse too, named of Gamage,[3] thou hast there,
20 That never fails to serve thee seasoned deer
When thou wouldst feast or exercise thy friends.
The lower land, that to the river bends,
Thy sheep, thy bullocks, kine,° and calves do feed;   *cows*
The middle grounds thy mares and horses breed.
25 Each bank doth yield thee conies;° and the tops,°   *rabbits / hills*
Fertile of wood, Ashore and Sidney's copse,[4]
To crown thy open table, doth provide
The purpled pheasant with the speckled side;
The painted partridge lies in every field,
30 And for thy mess° is willing to be killed.   *meal*
And if the high-swollen Medway° fail thy dish,   *local river*
Thou hast thy ponds, that pay thee tribute fish,
Fat aged carps that run into thy net,
And pikes, now weary their own kind to eat,
35 As loath the second draught[5] or cast to stay,°   *await*
Officiously° at first themselves betray;   *dutifully*
Bright eels that emulate them, and leap on land
Before the fisher, or into his hand.
Then hath thy orchard fruit, thy garden flowers,
40 Fresh as the air, and new as are the hours.
The early cherry, with the later plum,
Fig, grape, and quince, each in his time doth come;
The blushing apricot and woolly peach
Hang on thy walls, that every child may reach.
45 And though thy walls be of the country stone,
They're reared with no man's ruin, no man's groan;
There's none that dwell about them wish them down;
But all come in, the farmer and the clown,°   *countryman*
And no one empty-handed, to salute
50 Thy lord and lady, though they have no suit.°   *request to make*
Some bring a capon,[6] some a rural cake,
Some nuts, some apples; some that think they make
The better cheeses bring them, or else send
By their ripe daughters, whom they would commend

1. The nine Greek sister goddesses believed to be sources of inspiration for the arts. *At his great birth*: i.e., the poet Sir Philip Sidney's birth (on November 30, 1554; for his poetry, see pp. 208–20), when an oak was planted to commemorate the day.
2. I.e., the fires of love; perhaps the woodsman ("sylvan") is in love because of reading Sidney's poems. In the next lines, the "ruddy satyrs" (woodland gods associated with lust and drinking) challenge the "lighter fauns" (woodland gods described as less wild than the satyrs) to race to the tree named after a Lady Leicester, who is said to have entered into labor under its branches.
3. Barbara Gamage, wife of Sir Robert Sidney (Philip's younger brother and the current owner of Penshurst).
4. Two groves on the estate.
5. The drawing in of a net.
6. A castrated rooster, especially one fattened for eating.

55 This way to husbands, and whose baskets bear
An emblem of themselves in plum or pear.
But what can this (more than express their love)
Add to thy free provisions, far above
The need of such? whose liberal board° doth flow   *table*
60 With all that hospitality doth know;
Where comes no guest but is allowed to eat,
Without his fear, and of thy lord's own meat;
Where the same beer and bread, and selfsame wine,
That is his lordship's shall be also mine,
65 And I not fain° to sit (as some this day   *obliged*
At great men's tables), and yet dine away.[7]
Here no man tells° my cups; nor, standing by,   *counts*
A waiter doth my gluttony envy,
But gives me what I call, and lets me eat;
70 He knows below° he shall find plenty of meat.   *in servants' quarters*
Thy tables hoard not up for the next day;
Nor, when I take my lodging, need I pray
For fire, or lights, or livery;° all is there,   *provisions*
As if thou then wert mine, or I reigned here:
75 There's nothing I can wish, for which I stay.°   *wait*
That found King James when, hunting late this way
With his brave son, the prince,[8] they saw thy fires
Shine bright on every hearth, as the desires
Of thy Penates° had been set on flame   *Roman household gods*
80 To entertain them; or the country came
With all their zeal to warm their welcome here.
What (great I will not say, but) sudden cheer
Didst thou then make 'em! and what praise was heaped
On thy good lady then, who therein reaped
85 The just reward of her high housewifery;
To have her linen, plate, and all things nigh,
When she was far; and not a room but dressed
As if it had expected such a guest!
These, Penshurst, are thy praise, and yet not all.
90 Thy lady's noble, fruitful, chaste withal.
His children thy great lord may call his own,
A fortune in this age but rarely known.
They are, and have been, taught religion; thence
Their gentler spirits have sucked innocence.
95 Each morn and even they are taught to pray,
With the whole household, and may, every day,
Read in their virtuous parents' noble parts
The mysteries of manners, arms, and arts.
Now, Penshurst, they that will proportion° thee   *compare*
100 With other edifices, when they see
Those proud, ambitious heaps, and nothing else,
May say their lords have built, but thy lord dwells.

1616

7. I.e., to be insufficiently fed at "great men's tables," because the best food was reserved for the host, and so to dine elsewhere to finish.
8. Prince Henry (d. 1612), the heir apparent.

Song: To Celia (I)[9]

Come, my Celia, let us prove,°   *experience*
While we can, the sports of love;
Time will not be ours forever;
He at length our good will sever.
5 Spend not then his gifts in vain.
Suns that set may rise again;
But if once we lose this light,
'Tis with us perpetual night.
Why should we defer our joys?
10 Fame and rumor are but toys.
Cannot we delude the eyes
Of a few poor household spies,
Or his easier ears beguile,
So removèd by our wile?
15 'Tis no sin love's fruit to steal;
But the sweet thefts to reveal,
To be taken, to be seen,
These have crimes accounted been.

1606   1616

Song: To Celia (II)[1]

Drink to me only with thine eyes,
And I will pledge[2] with mine;
Or leave a kiss but in the cup,
And I'll not look for wine.
5 The thirst that from the soul doth rise,
Doth ask a drink divine:
But might I of Jove's nectar sup,
I would not change for thine.[3]
I sent thee late a rosy wreath,
10 Not so much honoring thee,
As giving it a hope, that there
It could not withered be.
But thou thereon did'st only breathe,
And sent'st it back to me;
15 Since when it grows and smells, I swear,
Not of itself, but thee.

1616

9. From Jonson's play *Volpone* 3.7 (1606). The lecherous Volpone attempts to seduce Celia, the virtuous wife of Corvino, whom Volpone has gotten out of the way by a stratagem (line 14). The poem draws on Catullus 5, translated by a number of English poets in this period. Cf. Thomas Campion, "My Sweetest Lesbia" (p. 278).
1. Based on five separate passages in the *Epistles* of the Greek rhetorician Philostratus (ca. 170–ca.

245).
2. Vow, with the added meaning "drink a toast."
3. Although the lines are ambiguous, the speaker seems to be saying that "even if I might taste ("sup") Jove's nectar (i.e., the drink of the gods of classical mythology—hence belonging to Jove, king of the gods), I would not take it in exchange for thine."

A Fit of Rhyme against Rhyme[4]

Rhyme, the rack° of finest wits,   *instrument of torture*
That expresseth but by fits
  True conceit,
Spoiling senses of their treasure,
5 Cozening judgment with a measure,
  But false weight;[5]
Wresting words from their true calling;
Propping verse for fear of falling
  To the ground;
10 Jointing syllabes,[6] drowning letters,
Fastening vowels, as with fetters
  They were bound!
Soon as lazy thou wert known,
All good poetry hence was flown,
15 And art banished:
For a thousand years together,[7]
All Parnassus'[8] green did wither,
  And wit vanish'd!
Pegasus[9] did fly away,
20 At the wells no Muse did stay,
  But bewailed,
So to see the fountain dry,
And Apollo's music die,
  All light failed!
25 Starveling rhymes did fill the stage,
Not a poet in an age
  Worthy crowning.
Not a work deserving bays,[1]
Nor a line deserving praise,
30 Pallas[2] frowning:
Greek was free from rhyme's infection,
Happy Greek, by this protection,
  Was not spoiled.

4. The issue of rhyme was hotly debated by many sixteenth- and seventeenth-century poets, including John Milton and John Dryden; some who denigrated rhyme in theory used it effectively in their poetic practice. In 1587, Christopher Marlowe attacked the "jigging veins of rhyming mother-wits" in the prologue to *Tamburlaine the Great*, part 1, and in 1602, Thomas Campion published a treatise arguing for the superiority of classical "quantitative meters" to English rhyming verse. In 1603, Samuel Daniel published his *Defense of Rhyme*; Jonson entered the fray with a witty poem he described to a friend as written "both against Campion and Daniel." "Fit" is an old term for a part of a poem, a canto; Jonson also plays (e.g., in line 2) on the term's meaning of "convulsion."
5. Punning on "measure" as a unit of poetical or musical rhythm and as a standard amount of a commodity, the line suggests that the rhyming poet cheats the buyer-reader by failing to "weigh" sounds properly, i.e., according to the system used in Latin prosody.

6. Syllables; i.e., making a rhyme by breaking a word on a syllabic unit (as Jonson does in some poems).
7. Classical Latin poetry did not use rhyme, but beginning in the third and fourth centuries C.E., Christian poets rhymed in Latin. Jonson's view that true poetry's "banishment" lasted a thousand years implies that the Italian humanists of the fourteenth century rescued poetry from the "wrongs" (line 35) of rhyme. One of those humanist scholars, Petrarch, used rhyme masterfully.
8. Mt. Parnassus, in central Greece, was considered sacred to the Muses, goddesses of the arts and sciences, and to Phoebus (Apollo), god of sunlight, prophecy, music, and poetry.
9. The winged horse Pegasus made the Hippocrene spring ("wells," line 20) for the Muses by striking his hoof on the ground.
1. I.e., the evergreen garland symbolizing a poet's superiority.
2. Pallas Athena, goddess of wisdom.

Whilst the Latin, queen of tongues,
35 Is not yet free from rhyme's wrongs,
  But rests foiled.
Scarce the hill again doth flourish,
Scarce the world a wit doth nourish,
  To restore
40 Phoebus to his crown again;
And the Muses to their brain;
  As before.
Vulgar³ languages that want
Words, and sweetness, and be scant
45   Of true measure,
Tyrant rhyme hath so abused,
That they long since have refused,
  Other cesure.°   *caesura*
He that first invented thee,
50 May his joints tormented be,
  Cramp'd for ever;
Still may syllabes jar with time,
Still may reason war with rhyme,
  Resting never!
55 May his sense when it would meet
The cold tumor in his feet,
  Grow unsounder;
And his title be long fool,⁴
That in rearing such a school
60   Was the founder!

1616?   1640–41

A Hymn to God the Father⁵

Hear me, O God!
A broken heart,
Is my best part;
Use still thy rod,⁶
5 That I may prove°   *experience*
Therein thy love.

If thou hadst not
Been stern to me,
But left me free,
10 I had forgot
Myself and thee.

For sin's so sweet,
As° minds ill bent   *that*

---

3. Vernacular, as opposed to Latin.
4. A play on the Latin saying *ars longa, vita brevis* (art is long, life short).

5. Cf. John Donne's poem with the same title (p. 321).
6. I.e., punishment.

Rarely repent,
15 Until they meet
Their punishment.

Who more can crave
Than thou hast done,
That gav'st a Son,[7]
20 To free a slave?
First made of naught,
With all since bought.[8]

Sin, Death, and Hell,
His glorious Name
25 Quite overcame,
Yet I rebel,
And slight the same.

But I'll come in
Before my loss
30 Me farther toss,
As sure to win
Under his Cross.

                                        1640–41

Her Triumph[9]

See the chariot at hand here of Love,
    Wherein my lady rideth!
Each that draws is a swan or a dove,[1]
    And well the care Love guideth.
5   As she goes, all hearts do duty
          Unto her beauty;
       And, enamored, do wish, so they might
          But enjoy such a sight,
That they still° were to run by her side,   *always*
10 Through[2] swords, through seas, whither° she would ride.   *wherever*

Do but look on her eyes; they do light
    All that Love's world compriseth!
Do but look on her hair; it is bright
    As Love's star[3] when it riseth!

---

7. I.e., who could crave more than what God ("thou") has already done, in giving his "Son" (Christ).
8. I.e., redeemed by Christ.
9. Published after Jonson's death, in "A Celebration of Charis in Ten Lyric Pieces"; although Jonson may have arranged these lyrics as they stand, they were (probably) not composed as a unit. The Greek word *charis* means "grace" or "loveliness"; the three Graces, sister goddesses in Greek mythology who gave charm and beauty, are *Char-* ites. "Charis" is also related to the Latin term for love, *caritas*, and is an obsolete form of "cherish." *Triumph:* following Petrarch, many Renaissance poets used the image of the triumphal procession to celebrate a person or concept (such as chastity, time, etc.).
1. Venus ("Love"), goddess of love and beauty, drove a chariot drawn by swans or doves.
2. Here pronounced as two syllables (often spelled "thorough").
3. I.e., Venus.

15 Do but mark, her forehead's smoother
        Than words that soothe her!
  And from her arched brows, such a grace
        Sheds itself through the face,
  As alone there triumphs to the life
20 All the gain, all the good, of the elements' strife.[4]

  Have you seen but a bright lily grow,
    Before rude hands have touched it?
  Ha' you marked but the fall o' the snow
    Before the soil hath smutched° it?   *smudged*
25 Ha' you felt the wool o' the beaver?
        Or swan's down ever?
  Or have smelt o' the bud o' the brier?
        Or the nard[5] in the fire?
  Or have tasted the bag° o' the bee?   *sack of honey*
30 O so white, O so soft, O so sweet is she!

1640–41

An Elegy[6]

  Though beauty be the mark of praise,
    And yours of whom I sing be such
    As not the world can praise too much,
  Yet is 't your virtue now I raise.

5 A virtue, like allay,° so gone   *alloy*
    Throughout your form, as, though that[7] move
    And draw and conquer all men's love,
  This[8] sùbjects you to love of one.

  Wherein you triumph yet; because
10   'Tis of yourself, and that you use
    The noblest freedom, not to choose
  Against or faith or honor's laws.

  But who should less expect from you,
    In whom alone Love[9] lives again?
15   By whom he is restored to men,
  And kept, and bred,[1] and brought up true.

  His falling temples you have reared,
    The withered garlands ta'en away;

4. The four elements (earth, water, air, and fire) were thought to be constantly at war; according to Platonic theory, heavenly harmony reconciles the skirmishing elements.
5. Spikenard, an aromatic plant used in preparing incense (as here) and perfumes.
6. Originally, the term meant a poem written in elegiac meter; in English tradition, an elegy dealt either with love or (increasingly from the seventeenth century on) with grief for a dead person.
7. I.e., your beauty.
8. I.e., your virtue.
9. I.e., Cupid, Roman god of erotic love.
1. Educated, or properly trained.

His altars kept from the decay
20   That envy wished, and nature feared;

And on them burn so chaste a flame,
    With so much loyalties' expense,
    As Love, t' acquit[2] such excellence,
Is gone himself into your name.[3]

25   And you are he; the deity
    To whom all lovers are designed
    That would their better objects find;
Among which faithful troop am I.

Who, as an offspring[4] at your shrine,
30   Have sung this hymn, and here entreat
    One spark of your diviner heat
To light upon a love of mine.

Which, if it kindle not, but scant
    Appear, and that to shortest view,
35   Yet give me leave t' adore in you
What I in her am grieved to want.

1640–41

An Ode to Himself[5]

Where dost thou careless lie
    Buried in ease and sloth?
Knowledge that sleeps doth die;
And this security,°   overconfidence
5   It is the common moth
That eats on wits and arts, and oft destroys them both.

Are all th' Aonian springs
    Dried up? Lies Thespia waste?[6]
Doth Clarius' harp[7] want strings,
10   That not a nymph[8] now sings;
    Or droop they as disgraced,
To see their seats and bowers by chattering pies[9] defaced?

If hence thy silence be,
    As 'tis too just a cause,
15   Let this thought quicken thee:

2. I.e., to reward.
3. I.e., the lady's name includes the letters of "love." Based on this hint, some scholars have suggested Lady Covell as the person addressed.
4. Possibly a misprint for *offering*.
5. A Horatian ode (see "Versification," p. 2048).
6. Aonia was the region in Greece near Mt. Helicon, home of the nine Muses, Greek sister goddesses believed to be sources of inspiration for the arts. Thespia, a town near Helicon, was the center of the cult of the Muses.
7. The lyre of Apollo, god of music and poetry (from his temple at Clarus, on the Ionian coast.)
8. A minor nature goddess.
9. The Muses changed the nine daughters of King Pierus into magpies for challenging their supremacy in poetry.

Minds that are great and free
 Should not on fortune pause;
'Tis crown enough to virtue still, her own applause.

What though the greedy fry[1]
20 Be taken with false baits
 Of worded balladry,
 And think it poesy?°   *poetry*
  They die with their conceits,
And only piteous scorn upon their folly waits.

25 Then take in hand thy lyre,
 Strike in thy proper strain,
 With Japhet's line,[2] aspire
 Sol's chariot[3] for new fire
  To give the world again;
30 Who aided him will thee, the issue of Jove's brain.[4]

And since our dainty age
 Cannot endure reproof,
 Make not thyself a page
 To that strumpet the stage,
35   But sing high and aloof,
Safe from the wolve's black jaw, and the dull ass's hoof.

                 1640

To the Immortal Memory and Friendship of That Noble Pair, Sir Lucius Cary and Sir Henry Morison[5]

The Turn[6]

Brave infant of Saguntum,[7] clear°   *explain or describe*
Thy coming forth in that great year,
When the prodigious Hannibal did crown
His rage with razing your immortal town.
5 Thou, looking then about,
 Ere thou wert half got out,

1. Youth, with a pun on "fry" as young fishes.
2. Prometheus, the son of Iapetus, stole fire from the gods for the benefit of humankind.
3. I.e., ascend to the sun (Sol being the Roman god of the sun).
4. Minerva (Greek Athena), goddess of wisdom, who was said to have sprung fully grown from the head of her father, Jove.
5. Morison (ca. 1608–1629) was knighted in 1627; he died of smallpox. His and Jonson's good friend Lucius Cary (1609 or 1610–1643), who married Morison's sister in 1630, was killed at the battle of Newbury in September 1643, fighting for the Royalist cause.
6. Unlike other "odes" by Jonson modeled on Horace's *Odes* (see, e.g., "An Ode to Himself," above), this one is modeled on a poetic structure used by the Greek poet Pindar (ca. 522–ca. 438 B.C.E).

Pindar's odes are typically arranged in groups of three stanzas (strophe, antistrophe, and epode) designed to be sung by a chorus; the chorus moved in one direction while chanting the strophe, reversed direction for the antistrophe, and stood still for the epode. Jonson's "turn," "counterturn," and "stand" (more or less translated from the Greek terms) imitate Pindar's pattern. As in Pindar, the metrical pattern of the turn is repeated in the counterturn, then varied in the stand. The pattern of these first three stanzas is then repeated exactly in the remaining sets of stanzas.
7. A town sacked by Hannibal in 219 B.C.E. The Roman naturalist Pliny the Elder (23–79 C.E.) records the story of a "brave infant," who returned to his mother's womb upon witnessing the city's destruction.

Wise child, didst hastily return,
And mad'st thy mother's womb thine urn.[8]
How summed a circle[9] didst thou leave mankind
10   Of deepest lore, could we the center find!

The Counterturn

Did wiser Nature draw thee back
From out the horror of that sack,
Where shame, faith, honor, and regard of right
Lay trampled on; the deeds of death and night
15   Urged, hurried forth, and hurled
Upon th' affrighted world;
Sword, fire, and famine, with fell fury met,
And all on utmost ruin set,
As, could they but life's miseries foresee,
20   No doubt all infants would return like thee?

The Stand

For what is life, if measured by the space,[1]
Not by the act?
Or maskèd man, if valued by his face
Above his fact?°   deed
25   Here's one outlived his peers
And told forth fourscore years;
He vexèd time and busied the whole state,
Troubled both foes and friends;
But ever to no ends:
30   What did this stirrer but die late?
How well at twenty had he fall'n or stood!
For three of his fourscore he did no good.

The Turn

He[2] entered well, by virtuous parts,
Got up and thrived with honest arts;
35   He purchased friends, and fame, and honors then,
And had his noble name advanced with men;
But weary of that flight
He stooped in all men's sight
To sordid flatteries, acts of strife,
40   And sunk in that dead sea of life
So deep, as he did then death's waters sup,°   taste
But that the cork of title buoyed him up.

The Counterturn

Alas, but Morison fell young;
He never fell, thou fall'st,[3] my tongue.

---

8. I.e., tomb.
9. Emblem of perfection. *Summed:* complete.
1. I.e., by the length of time.

2. I.e., another man, a separate example.
3. Slip, with a possible pun on the Latin *fallere* (to make a mistake).

45 He stood, a soldier to the last right end,
A perfect patriot, and a noble friend,
But most a virtuous son.
All offices° were done   *duties in life*
By him so ample, full, and round,
50 In weight, in measure, number, sound,
As, though his age imperfect° might appear,   *incomplete*
His life was of humanity the sphere.[4]

The Stand

Go now, and tell out days summed up with fears,
And make them years;
55 Produce thy mass of miseries on the stage
To swell thine age;
Repeat of things a throng,
To show thou hast been long,
Not lived; for life doth her great actions spell°   *tell over*
60 By what was done and wrought
In season, and so brought
To light: her measures are, how well
Each syllabe° answered, and was formed how fair;   *syllable*
These make the lines of life, and that's her air.[5]

The Turn

65 It is not growing like a tree
In bulk doth make man better be;
Or standing long an oak, three hundred year,
To fall a log at last, dry, bald, and sere:°   *withered*
A lily of a day
70 Is fairer far in May;
Although it fall and die that night,
It was the plant and flower of light.
In small proportions we just beauties see,
And in short measures life may perfect be.

The Counterturn

75 Call, noble Lucius, then for wine,
And let thy looks with gladness shine;
Accept this garland, plant it on thy head,
And think, nay know, thy Morison's not dead.
He leaped the present age,
80 Possessed with holy rage
To see that bright eternal day;
Of which we priests and poets say
Such truths as we expect for happy men,
And there he lives with memory, and Ben

---

4. I.e., the perfect model.
5. I.e., life's "measures" are its metrical patterns and the standards by which it is judged. *Air:* melody, song.

The Stand

85 Jonson! who sung this of him, ere he went
        Himself to rest,
    Or taste a part of that full joy he meant
        To have expressed
    In this bright asterism;°   constellation
90 Where it were friendship's schism
    (Were not his Lucius long with us to tarry)
        To separate these twi-
        Lights, the Dioscuri,[6]
    And keep the one half from his Harry.
95 But fate doth so altérnate the design,
    Whilst that in heaven, this light on earth must shine.

The Turn

    And shine as you exalted are,
    Two names of friendship, but one star:
    Of hearts the union. And those not by chance
100 Made, or indenture,° or leased out t'advance   contracted for
        The profits for a time.
    No pleasures vain did chime
    Of rimes, or riots, at your feasts,
    Orgies of drink, or feigned protests,°   protestations
105 But simple love of greatness and of good;
    That knits brave minds and manners more than blood.

The Counterturn

    This made you first to know the why
    You liked, then after to apply
    That liking, and approach so one the tother,°   other
110 Till either grew a portion of the other:
        Each styled by his end
        The copy of his friend.
    You lived to be the great surnames
    And titles by which all made claims
115 Unto the virtue. Nothing perfect done,
    But as a Cary, or a Morison.

The Stand

    And such a force the fair example had,
        As they that saw
    The good, and durst not practice it, were glad
120   That such a law
        Was left yet to mankind;

6. Or Castor and Pollux, in Greek mythology the twin sons of Zeus, famous for brotherly devotion. When Castor was killed, Zeus granted Pollux's prayer that he be allowed to share his life with his brother; henceforward each lived half the time on Earth and half in heaven. Their constellation is Gemini, the Twins.

Where they might read and find
Friendship, indeed, was written, not in words;
And with the heart, not pen,
125 Of two so early° men,   *young*
Whose lines her rolls were, and recòrds,
Who, ere the first down bloomèd on the chin,[7]
Had sowed these fruits, and got the harvest in.

1640

Still to Be Neat[8]

Still to be neat, still to be dressed,
As you were going to a feast;
Still to be powdered, still perfumed;
Lady, it is to be presumed,
5 Though art's hid causes are not found,
All is not sweet, all is not sound.

Give me a look, give me a face
That makes simplicity a grace;
Robes loosely flowing, hair as free;
10 Such sweet neglect more taketh me
Then all th' adulteries of art.
They strike mine eyes, but not my heart.

1609   1640–41

Though I Am Young and Cannot Tell[9]

Though I am young, and cannot tell
Either what Death or Love is well,
Yet I have heard they both bear darts,
And both do aim at human hearts.
5 And then again, I have been told
Love wounds with heat, as Death with cold;
So that I fear they do but bring
Extremes to touch, and mean one thing.

As in a ruin we it call
10 One thing to be blown up, or fall;
Or to our end like way may have
By a flash of lightning, or a wave;

---

7. I.e., before they had grown beards.
8. From Jonson's play *Epicoene, the Silent Woman* 1.1 (1609). Sung by a servant upon Clerimont's request; Clerimont is irritated with the Lady Haughty, who, he says, overdoes the art of makeup. The lyric perhaps derives from an anon-
ymous Latin poem in the *Anthologia latina* (sixteenth century).
9. From Jonson's play *The Sad Shepherd* 1.5 (1640). The monosyllables of the poem echo the pastoral simplicity of the character Karalin, who sings it.

So Love's inflaméd shaft or brand
    May kill as soon as Death's cold hand;
15 Except Love's fires the virtue have
    To fright the frost out of the grave.

1640–41

To the Memory of My Beloved, the Author Mr. William Shakespeare

And What He Hath Left Us[1]

To draw no envy, Shakespeare, on thy name,
Am I thus ample[2] to thy book and fame,
While I confess thy writings to be such
As neither man nor Muse[3] can praise too much.
5 'Tis true, and all men's suffrage.° But these ways   *consent*
Were not the paths I meant unto thy praise:
For silliest° ignorance on these may light,   *simplest*
Which, when it sounds at best, but echoes right;
Or blind affection,° which doth ne'er advance   *feeling*
10 The truth, but gropes, and urgeth all by chance;
Or crafty malice might pretend this praise,
And think to ruin where it seemed to raise.
These are as° some infamous bawd or whore   *as if*
Should praise a matron.[4] What could hurt her more?
15 But thou art proof against them, and, indeed,
Above th' ill fortune of them, or the need.
I therefore will begin. Soul of the age!
The applause! delight! the wonder of our stage!
My Shakespeare, rise; I will not lodge thee by
20 Chaucer or Spenser, or bid Beaumont lie[5]
A little further to make thee a room:
Thou art a monument without a tomb,
And art alive still while thy book doth live,
And we have wits to read and praise to give.
25 That I not mix thee so, my brain excuses,
I mean with great, but disproportioned Muses;[6]
For, if I thought my judgment were of years,[7]
I should commit° thee surely with thy peers,   *unite, connect*
And tell how far thou didst our Lyly outshine,
30 Or sporting Kyd, or Marlowe's mighty line.[8]
And though thou hadst small Latin and less Greek,[9]

---

1. Prefixed to the first collected edition—the First Folio—of Shakespeare's plays, 1623.
2. Copious, i.e., in this relatively long poem.
3. Source of inspiration.
4. A married woman with moral and social dignity.
5. All three authors—Geoffrey Chaucer (ca. 1340–1400), Edmund Spenser (ca. 1552–1599), Francis Beaumont (1584–1616)—are buried in Westminster Abbey, London. Shakespeare is buried in the Holy Trinity Church, Stratford-on-Avon (see "Avon," line 71).
6. I.e., that I do not place you with the other authors, whose poetry is "great" but still not comparable ("disproportioned") with your poetry.
7. I.e., over an extended period of time.
8. John Lyly (1554–1606), Thomas Kyd (1558–1594), and Christopher Marlowe (1564–1593), all Elizabethan dramatists; with "sporting" as "playing," activating the pun in Kyd's name (*kid*, baby goat).
9. By modern standards, Shakespeare had an adequate command of Latin (as well as French and Italian), but he lacked Jonson's knowledge of classical literature.

From thence to honor thee I would not seek°   *lack*
For names, but call forth thund'ring Aeschylus,
Euripides, and Sophocles to us,
35   Pacuvius, Accius, him of Cordova dead,[1]
To life again, to hear thy buskin[2] tread
And shake a stage; or, when thy socks were on,
Leave thee alone for the comparison
Of all that insolent Greece or haughty Rome
40   Sent forth, or since did from their ashes come.
Triumph, my Britain; thou hast one to show
To whom all scenes° of Europe homage owe.   *stages*
He was not of an age, but for all time!
And all the Muses still were in their prime
45   When like Apollo he came forth to warm
Our ears, or like a Mercury[3] to charm.
Nature herself was proud of his designs,
And joyed to wear the dressing of his lines,
Which were so richly spun, and woven so fit,
50   As, since, she will vouchsafe no other wit:
The merry Greek, tart Aristophanes,
Neat Terence, witty Plautus[4] now not please,
But antiquated and deserted lie,
As they were not of Nature's family.
55   Yet must I not give Nature all; thy Art,
My gentle Shakespeare, must enjoy a part.
For though the poet's matter Nature be,
His Art doth give the fashion;° and that he   *form, style*
Who casts° to write a living line must sweat   *undertakes*
60   (Such as thine are) and strike the second heat
Upon the Muses' anvil; turn the same,
And himself with it, that he thinks to frame,
Or for the laurel[5] he may gain a scorn;
For a good poet's made as well as born.
65   And such wert thou! Look how the father's face
Lives in his issue, even so the race
Of Shakespeare's mind and manners brightly shines
In his well-turnèd and true-filèd° lines,   *well-polished*
In each of which he seems to shake a lance,[6]
70   As brandished at the eyes of ignorance.
Sweet swan of Avon, what a sight it were
To see thee in our waters yet appear,
And make those flights upon the banks of Thames
That so did take Eliza and our James![7]
75   But stay; I see thee in the hemisphere
Advanced and made a constellation there!

---

1. I.e., Seneca, Roman tragedian of the first century C.E.; Marcus Pacuvius and Lucius Accius were Roman tragedians of the second century B.C.E. Aeschylus (525–456 B.C.E.), Euripides (ca. 484–406 B.C.E.), and Sophocles (ca. 496–406 B.C.E.) were all Greek dramatists.
2. The high-heeled boot worn by Greek tragic actors; the "sock" (line 37), or light shoe, was worn in comedies.
3. Roman god associated with good luck and enchantment. *Apollo*: the classical god of sunlight, prophecy, music, and poetry.
4. Aristophanes (Greek) and Terence and Plautus (Roman) were comic writers of the fourth to second centuries B.C.E.
5. As in the crowns of laurel that honored ancient Greek poets.
6. With a pun on *Shake-speare* (also see line 37).
7. I.e., to travel on the river banks as did Queen Elizabeth and King James.

Shine forth, thou star of poets, and with rage
Or influence[8] chide or cheer the drooping stage,
Which, since thy flight from hence, hath mourned like night,
80 And despairs day, but for thy volume's light.

1623   1640–41

A Sonnet to the Noble Lady, the Lady Mary Wroth[9]

I that have been a lover, and could show it,
    Though not in these,[1] in rithmes not wholly dumb,
    Since I exscribe° your sonnets, am become   copy out
A better lover, and much better poet.
5 Nor is my Muse[2] or I ashamed to owe it
    To those true numerous graces, whereof some
    But charm the senses, others overcome
Both brains and hearts; and mine now best do know it:
For in your verse all Cupid's[3] armory,
10   His flames, his shafts, his quiver, and his bow,
    His very eyes are yours to overthrow.
But then his mother's sweets you so apply,
    Her joys, her smiles, her loves, as readers take
For Venus' ceston° every line you make.   girdle

                                                    1640–41

Slow, Slow, Fresh Fount[4]

Slow, slow, fresh fount, keep time with my salt tears;
Yet slower, yet, O faintly, gentle springs!
List to the heavy part the music bears,
Woe weeps out her division,[5] when she sings.
5   Droop herbs and flowers;
    Fall grief in showers;
    Our beauties are not ours.
        O, I could still,
Like melting snow upon some craggy hill,
10   Drop, drop, drop, drop,
Since nature's pride is now a withered daffodil.

                                                    1600

---

8. "Rage" and "influence" describe a supposed emanation of power from the stars, affecting Earth's events. "Rage" also implies poetic inspiration.
9. English poet (1587?–1651?; see pp. 347–53), to whom Jonson dedicated his play *The Alchemist* (1610). As the niece of Sir Philip Sidney and of Mary Sidney, Wroth was a potential patron for Jonson, who also wrote a flattering poem to her husband, Sir Robert Wroth.
1. I.e., the sonnet form, typically used for love poetry but not by Jonson. (This is his only sonnet; by using the form here, he pays homage to Mary

Wroth's accomplishments in her sonnet sequence, *Pamphilia to Amphilanthus.*)
2. Source of poetic inspiration.
3. Roman god of erotic love; son of Venus, goddess of love and beauty.
4. From Jonson's play *Cynthia's Revels* 5.6 (1600). Inspired by classical mythology, the play deals satirically with the sin of self-love; this song is sung by Echo for Narcissus, who fell in love with his own reflection and was changed into the flower that bears his name. The daffodil (line 11) is a species of narcissus. *Fount:* spring.
5. Part in a song, as well as grief at parting.

Queen and Huntress[6]

Queen and huntress, chaste and fair,
Now the sun is laid to sleep,
Seated in thy silver chair,
State in wonted manner keep;
5   Hesperus entreats thy light,
Goddess excellently bright.

Earth, let not thy envious shade
Dare itself to interpose;[7]
Cynthia's shining orb was made
10 Heaven to clear, when day did close.
Bless us then with wishéd sight,
Goddess excellently bright.

Lay thy bow of pearl apart,
And thy crystal-shining quiver;
15 Give unto the flying hart[8]
Space to breathe, how short soever.
Thou that mak'st a day of night,
Goddess excellently bright.

1600

JOHN FLETCHER
1579–1625

Take, Oh, Take Those Lips Away[1]

Take, oh, take those lips away
That so sweetly were forsworn
And those eyes, like break of day,
Lights that do mislead the morn;
5   But my kisses bring again,
Seals of love, though sealed in vain.

Hide, oh, hide those hills of snow,
Which thy frozen bosom bears,
On whose tops the pinks that grow
10 Are of those that April wears;
But first set my poor heart free,
Bound in those icy chains by thee.

1639

---

6. From *Cynthia's Revels* 5.6 (1600). This lyric is sung by Hesperus, the evening star, to Cynthia (also known as Diana), goddess of the moon and of the hunt. Cynthia was often identified with Queen Elizabeth (1533–1603; see pp. 142–43) by poets of this period.

7. Eclipses were seen as evil portents.
8. A pun on "hart" (as deer) and *heart*.
1. The first stanza of this song appears as a complete poem in Shakespeare's play *Measure for Measure* (1604–05), from which Fletcher likely appropriated it.

EDWARD HERBERT
1582–1648

Sonnet of Black Beauty

Black beauty, which above that common light,
   Whose power can no colors here renew
   But those which darkness can again subdue,
Do'st still remain unvary'd to the sight,

5   And like an object equal to the view,
   Art neither chang'd with day, nor hid with night;
   When all these colors which the world call bright,
And which old poetry doth so persue,

Are with the night to perishéd and gone,
10   That of their being there remains no mark,
Thou still abidest so entirely one,
   That we may know thy blackness is a spark
Of light inaccessible, and alone
   Our darkness which can make us think it dark.[1]

1620   1665

Another Sonnet to Black Itself

Thou Black, wherein all colors are compos'd,
   And unto which they all at last return,
   Thou color of the sun where it doth burn,
And shadow, where it cools, in thee is clos'd
5   Whatever nature can, or hath dispos'd
   In any other hue: from thee do rise
Those tempers and complexions, which disclos'd,
   As parts of thee, do work as mysteries,
Of that thy hidden power; when thou dost reign
10   The characters of fate shine in the skies,
And tell us what the heavens do ordain,[2]
   But when earth's common light shines to our eyes,
Thou so retir'st thy self, that thy disdain
   All revelation unto man denies.[3]

1620   1665

---

1. I.e., it is only our moral blindness that can make us think things are dark.
2. I.e., the stars, "characters of fate," can be read to foretell the future.
3. I.e., in the bright light of day, the stars cannot be read, and the future is not revealed.

MARY WROTH
1587–1651?

From Pamphilia to Amphilanthus[1]

1

When night's black mantle could most darkness prove,
And sleep death's image did my senses hire°   *engage*
From knowledge of my self, then thoughts did move
Swifter than those most swiftness need require:

5 In sleep, a chariot drawn by wing'd desire
I saw: where sat bright Venus, queen of love,[2]
And at her feet her son,[3] still adding fire
To burning hearts which she did hold above;

But one heart flaming more than all the rest
10 The goddess held, and put it to my breast;
"Dear son, now shut,"[4] said she: "thus must we win";

He her obeyed, and martyred my poor heart;
I, waking, hoped as dreams it[5] would depart;
Yet since—O me—a lover I have been.

3

Yet is there hope: then Love° but play thy part;   *Cupid*
Remember well thy self, and think on me;
Shine in those eyes which conquered have my heart;
And see if mine be slack[6] to answer thee:

5 Lodge in that breast, and pity moving see,
For flames which in mine burn in truest smart,[7]
Exiling thoughts that touch inconstancy,
Or those which waste not in the constant art;[8]

1. Mary Wroth wrote the first work of prose fiction by an Englishwoman, her long but unfinished *The Countess of Montgomery's Urania.* Including a number of poems and modeled on her uncle Sir Philip Sidney's romance, *Arcadia* (ca. 1580), Wroth's text covertly alludes to various personages and scandals of the Jacobean court, and was met with a storm of criticism when part 1 was published in 1621. Appended to *Urania* is *Pamphilia to Amphilanthus,* a sonnet sequence (the only one by an Englishwoman of her time) consisting of eighty-three sonnets and twenty songs. Pamphilia (Latin, "All-loving") is the protagonist of *Urania;* Amphilanthus (Latin, "Lover of two") is her unfaithful beloved. Their names reflect the main theme of both the romance and the appended sonnet sequence—constancy in the face of unfaithfulness. *Pamphilia to Amphilanthus* is divided into several separately numbered series (the first of which includes forty-eight sonnets, with songs inserted after every sixth sonnet). We follow the ordering of the 1621 print version of the *Urania,* as reproduced and discussed in Josephine A. Roberts's edition of Wroth's poems.
2. Traditionally, Venus, Roman goddess of love and beauty, was represented in a chariot drawn by doves.
3. Cupid, god of erotic love.
4. I.e., enclose the flaming heart in Pamphilia's breast; by implication, her breast is also being cruelly opened, with a love wound like Amoret's in the climactic episode of Spenser's *Faerie Queene* 3.12.2–21.
5. I.e., the vision of Venus and Cupid.
6. Lacking in energy or diligence.
7. I.e., house yourself in my beloved's breast, and see him moved by pity for the flames that burn in my breast with truest pain.
8. I.e., exile [also] those thoughts that do not waste away in the art (discipline, pursuit) of constancy.

Watch but my sleep, if I take any rest
10   For thoughts of you, my spirit so distressed,
    As pale, and famished, I for mercy cry;

Will you your servant leave? Think but on this:
    Who wears love's crown,⁹ must not do so amiss,
    But seek their good, who on thy force do lie.°   *rely*

11

You endless torments that my rest oppress,
    How long will you delight in my sad pain?
    Will never love your favor more express?¹
    Shall I still live, and ever feel disdain?

5   Alas now stay,° and let my grief obtain   *refrain from acting*
    Some end; feed not my heart with sharp distress:
    Let me once see my cruel fortune's gain
    At least release, and long felt woes redress;

Let not the blame of cruelty disgrace
10   The honored title of your Godhead,° Love:°   *deity / Cupid*
    Give not just cause for me to say a place
    Is found for rage alone on me to move;²

O quickly end, and do not long debate
My needful aid, least° help do come too late.   *lest*

22

Like to the Indians, scorchèd with the sun,³
    The sun which they do as their God adore,
    So am I used by love, for ever more
    I worship him, less favors have I won;⁴

5   Better are they who thus to blackness run,
    And so can only whiteness' want deplore⁵
    Than I who pale, and white am with griefs' store,
    Nor can have hope, but to see hopes undone;⁶

---

9. The "crown" of love, a sign of Cupid's power as an absolute ruler, recurs in many later poems in Wroth's sequence and provides the key formal principle for the set of linked sonnets (the *corona*) with which *Pamphilia to Amphilanthus* closes.
1. Ambiguous syntax: "your" could refer to the initial addressee, "torments," i.e., will love not make you (endless torments) show more favor to me; alternatively, "your" could refer to "love," with the implied addressee shifting so that the poet is now asking a personified love to express his "favor" to the speaker more than he has in the past.
2. I.e., do not give me just cause to say either that

rage is the only emotion I can feel or that I am the only "place" where rage moves or acts.
3. Some early modern thinkers attributed Native Americans' and Africans' skin colors to the tanning power of the tropical sun.
4. I.e., as I worship love more, I receive less in terms of love's benefits.
5. I.e., can only deplore the lack of whiteness (though there may also be a sense, if "want" is taken to mean "desire" rather than "lack," that the desire for whiteness is being deplored).
6. I.e., I cannot have any hope except the (paradoxical) one of seeing my hopes undone.

Besides their sacrifice received's in sight
10   Of their chose° saint, mine hid as worthless rite;[7]   *chosen*
Grant me to see where I my off'rings give,

Then let me wear the mark of Cupid's might
  In heart as they in skin of Phoebus' light,[8]
Not ceasing off'rings to love while I live.

25

Poor eyes be blind, the light behold no more
  Since that is gone which is your dear delight,
  Ravished from you by greater pow'r, and might,
  Making your loss a gain to others' store;

5   O'erflow, and drown, till sight to you restore
  That blessed star,[9] and as in hateful spite
  Send forth your tears in floods, to kill all sight,
  And looks, that lost,[1] wherein you joyed before.

Bury these beams, which in some° kindled fires,   *some people*
10   And conquered have their love-burnt-hearts' desires,
  Losing, and yet no gain by you esteemed,

Till that bright star do once again appear
  Brighter than Mars when he doth shine most clear;
  See not: then by his might, be you redeemed.

37

Night, welcome art thou to my mind distressed
  Dark, heavy, sad, yet not more sad than I;
  Never could'st thou find fitter company
  For thine own humor than I thus oppressed.

5   If thou beest dark, my wrongs still unredressed°   *unremedied*
  Saw never light, nor smallest bliss can spy;
  If heavy, joy from me too fast doth hie°   *hurry away*
  And care outgoes my hope of quiet rest,

Then now in friendship join with hapless me,
10   Who am as sad, and dark as thou canst be
  Hating all pleasure, or delight of life;

---

7. I.e., besides, their sacrifice is received in sight of their chosen saint, whereas my sacrifice is hidden as a ritual (but also a "right") considered worthless.
8. The light of the sun (Phoebus being Apollo, the classical god of sunlight); the speaker prays to be allowed to see the object of her worship (as the Indians do) and to have the mark or sign of Cupid's power in her heart as the Indians have the sign of the sun's power on their skin.
9. Here and in line 12, the speaker refers to her beloved as a star and thus substitutes him for the planet Venus, traditionally linked to the planet Mars because Venus was the lover of the Roman god of war, Mars.
1. I.e., since that is lost (or, that being lost).

Silence, and grief, with thee I best do love
And from you three, I know I can not move,
Then let us live companions without strife.

39

If I were giv'n to mirth, 'twould° be more cross   *it would*
Thus to be robbed of my chiefest joy,
But silently I bear my greatest loss;
Who's used to sorrow, grief will not destroy;

5   Nor can I as° those pleasant wits enjoy   *like*
My own framed words, which I account the dross
Of purer thoughts, or reckon them as moss
While they (wit-sick) themselves to breath employ;

Alas, think I, your plenty shows your want,
10   For where most feeling is, words are more scant,
Yet pardon me, live, and your pleasure take,

Grudge not, if I, neglected, envy show;
'T is not to you² that I dislike do owe,
But crossed myself, wish some like me to make.

74

SONG

Love a child is ever crying,³
   Please him, and he straight is flying,
   Give him, he the more is craving⁴
   Never satisfied with having;

5   His desires have no measure,
   Endless folly is his treasure,
   What he promiseth he breaketh
   Trust not one word that he speaketh;

He vows nothing but false matter,
10   And to cozen you he'll flatter,⁵
   Let him gain the hand° he'll leave you,   *upper hand*
   And still glory to deceive you;

He will triumph in your wailing,
   And yet cause be of your failing,
15   These his virtues are, and slighter
   Are his gifts, his favors lighter,

2. I.e., the writer's own words (though possibly the person who inspired the poem).
3. Although depicting love as Cupid was a Renaissance commonplace, a "crying" Cupid is unusual; in this section of her sonnet sequence, Wroth uses

the image to explore Pamphilia's frustration in love.
4. I.e., the more he is given, the more he craves.
5. I.e., to deceive or cheat ("cozen") you, he'll flatter you.

Feathers are as firm in staying
Wolves no fiercer in their praying.
As a child then leave him crying
20   Nor seek him° so given to flying.°   *he who is / leaving*

From *A Crown of Sonnets Dedicated to Love*[6]

77

In this strange labyrinth how shall I turn?
    Ways° are on all sides, while the way I miss: *paths*
    If to the right hand, there in love I burn;
    Let me[7] go forward, therein danger is;

5   If to the left, suspicion hinders bliss,
    Let me turn back, shame cries I ought return,
    Nor faint,[8] though crosses° with my fortunes   *troubles, adversity*
       kiss;
    Stand still is harder, although sure to° mourn.   *to make me*

    Thus let me take the right, or left hand way,
10   Go forward, or stand still, or back retire:
    I must these doubts endure without allay°   *alleviation*
    Or help, but travail find for my best hire.[9]

    Yet that which most my troubled sense doth move,
    Is to leave all and take the thread of Love.[1]

78

Is to leave all and take the thread of Love,
    Which line straight leads unto the soul's content,
    Where choice delights with pleasure's wings do move,
    And idle fant'sy never room had lent.[2]

---

6. The "crown" is a complex poetic form, in which the last line of each poem serves as the first line of the next poem, until a circle is completed by the last line of the final poem, which is the same as the first line of the sequence. It was originally an Italian form that could be used to praise or condemn (and is often known by its Italian name, *corona*); various kinds of poems could be used for the sequence, with the number of poems ranging from seven to fourteen (as in Wroth's crown of fourteen sonnets).

    Sir Philip Sidney, Wroth's uncle, included one of the first examples of the crown in English in the first version of his prose romance, known as the *Old Arcadia*; her father, Sir Robert Sidney, wrote an incomplete crown thought to be in praise of a specific lady. Wroth, however, dedicates her crown more generally to "Love"; in a temporary recantation of the harsh judgment of love depicted in the preceding part of the *Pamphilia to Amphilanthus* sequence, Love is here portrayed as a monarch whose true service ennobles lovers. The crown includes sonnets 77–90 of the original sequence as numbered in the only manuscript in Wroth's hand, which is now in the Folger Shakespeare Library, Washington, D.C.

7. I.e., if I.

8. Lose heart; Wroth occasionally uses "nor" without including other negatives.

9. I.e., I find hard labor (or suffering) to be the reward for my best efforts. Instead of "traveile" (Folger Library manuscript), the 1621 edition prints "travell."

1. An allusion to the Greek myth in which Ariadne, defying her father, gave Theseus a thread to unwind behind him in the labyrinth at Crete. After killing the Minotaur, he was able to find his way out by following the thread; shortly thereafter, he abandoned Ariadne.

2. I.e., where room or space had never been loaned to idle fantasy.

5   When chaste thoughts guide us, then our minds are bent
      To take that good which ills from us remove:
      Light of true love brings fruit which none repent;
      But constant lovers seek and wish to prove.°   *try*

  Love is the shining star of blessing's light,
10   The fervent fire of zeal, the root of peace,
      The lasting lamp, fed with the oil of right,
      Image of faith, and womb for joy's increase.°   *children*

  Love is true virtue, and his end's delight,
  His flames are joys, his bands true lover's might.[3]

82

  He[4] may our prophet, and our tutor prove,
    In whom alone we do this power find,
    To join two hearts as in one frame to move;
    Two bodies, but one soul to rule the mind.[5]

5   Eyes which must care to one dear object bind,
    Ears to each others' speech as if above
    All else, they sweet, and learned were; this kind
    Content of lovers witnesseth true love.

  It doth enrich the wits, and make you see
10   That in your self which you knew not before,
    Forcing you to admire such gifts should be
    Hid from your knowledge, yet in you the store.

  Millions of these adorn the throne of Love,
  How blest are they then, who his favors prove.°   *experience*

85

  But where they may return with honor's grace
    Where° Venus' follies can no harbor win,   *there*
    But chasèd are as worthless of the face
    Or style of love who hath lascivious been.[6]

5   Our hearts are subject to her son; where sin
    Never did dwell, or rest one minute's space;[7]
    What faults he hath, in her, did still begin,
    And from her breast he sucked his fleeting pace;

---

3. I.e., Love's bands are the strength of true lovers, and not their shackles.
4. I.e., love personified.
5. Two hearts joined in one body, or two bodies joined in one soul; common Renaissance metaphors for true love.
6. In an extended analogy between sea voyaging and different kinds of love, this stanza contrasts those who love honorably with those who love lasciviously. The latter are "chasèd" from the safe harbor of virtue because they represent Venus's

"follies" (lusts); they are unworthy of the true "face" or "style" of love. In describing such lovers as "worthless," Wroth may pun on her name; in her play *Love's Victory*, an undesirable suitor, who resembles Wroth's historical husband, Robert Wroth, is repeatedly called "worthless."
7. Wroth follows a tradition of distinguishing between Venus as a figure for lust and her son, Cupid, as a figure for chaste love, but the sharp contrast begins to erode in lines 7–8.

If lust be counted love, 'tis falsely named
10   By wickedness, a fairer gloss to set
    Upon that vice,[8] which else makes men ashamed,
    In the° own phrase to warrant but beget   *its*

This child for love, who ought like monster born
Be from the court of Love, and reason torn.[9]

From Urania

Song[1]

Love what art thou? A vain thought
    In our minds by phant'sie° wrought,   *fancy*
    Idle smiles did thee beget
    While fond wishes made the net
5   Which so many fools have caught;

Love what art thou? light, and fair,
    Fresh as morning, clear as th'air,
    But too soon thy evening change
    Makes thy worth with coldness range;
10   Still thy joy is mixed with care.

Love what art thou? A sweet flow'r
    Once full blown, dead in an hour,
    Dust in wind as staid° remains   *steadfast*
    As thy pleasure, or our gains
15   If thy humor change to lour.°   *gloomy*

Love what art thou? childish, vain,
    Firm as bubbles made by rain;
    Wantonness thy greatest pride,
    These foul faults thy virtues hide,
20   But babes can no staidness gain.

Love what art thou? causeless curse,
    Yet alas these not the worst,
    Much more of thee may be said
    But thy law I once obeyed
25   Therefore say no more at first.

1621

---

8. I.e., wickedness falsely renames lust as love to put a "fairer gloss" on the vice.

9. The syntax of lines 11–14 is difficult, and we have not attempted to clarify it by supplying modern punctuation marks; the phrase "the own," often used to denote "its own" in early modern English, seems to refer to "that vice" of lust which attempts to legitimize ("warrant," legally name as its own) an illegitimate son who should rightfully be seen as monstrous and hence banished from the "court" of Love, and from that of reason too, if the latter is separate from love, as the comma between them suggests. (Wroth had two illegitimate sons with her cousin William Herbert, the historical inspiration for the character Amphilanthus in the *Urania*.)

1. Sung at the end of book 1 by a "delicate Mayd" with a sweet voice who seems to have "falne out with Love"; on Wroth's long prose romance, see note 1, p. 347.

ROBERT HERRICK
1591–1674

The Argument of His Book[1]

I sing of brooks, of blossoms, birds, and bowers,
Of April, May, of June, and July flowers.
I sing of Maypoles, hock carts, wassails, wakes,[2]
Of bridegrooms, brides, and of their bridal cakes.
5   I write of youth, of love, and have access
By these to sing of cleanly wantonness.
I sing of dews, of rains, and, piece by piece,
Of balm, of oil, of spice, and ambergris.[3]
I sing of times trans-shifting, and I write
10 How roses first came red and lilies white.
I write of groves, of twilights, and I sing
The court of Mab[4] and of the fairy king.
I write of hell; I sing (and ever shall)
Of heaven, and hope to have it after all.

The Vine

I dreamed this mortal part of mine
Was metamorphosed to a vine,
Which crawling one and every way
Enthralled° my dainty Lucia.[5]   *imprisoned*
5   Methought her long small° legs and thighs   *slender*
I with my tendrils did surprise;
Her belly, buttocks, and her waist
By my soft nervelets° were embraced.   *tendrils*
About her head I writhing hung,
10 And with rich clusters (hid among
The leaves) her temples I behung,
So that my Lucia seemed to me
Young Bacchus ravished by his tree.[6]
My curls about her neck did crawl,
15 And arms and hands they did enthrall,

1. The "argument" is the subject matter, and the "book" is a thick volume containing all of Herrick's poems—over fourteen hundred—divided into a religious set, titled *Noble Numbers*, and a secular set, titled *Hesperides*. In classical mythology, the Hesperides, daughters of Atlas and Hesperis (or, in another tradition, of Night), guarded a tree of golden apples in a far-western garden that Herrick often likens to his home in the western county of Devon.
  Since all of Herrick's poems were published in 1648, we do not repeat the date for each poem.

2. Vigils on the eves of festivals or of funerals. *Hock carts:* vehicles for carrying in the last load of the harvest. *Wassails:* drinking to the health of others.
3. A waxlike substance used in making perfumes, i.e., something rare and pleasing.
4. In English mythology, queen of the fairies.
5. For the sake of rhyme and meter, the name has three syllables here but two in line 12.
6. Bacchus was the Roman god of wine and revelry; his "tree" is the grapevine.

So that she could not freely stir
(All parts there made one prisoner).
But when I crept with leaves to hide
Those parts which maids keep unespied,
20   Such fleeting pleasures there I took
That with the fancy I awoke;
And found (ah me!) this flesh of mine
More like a stock° than like a vine.   *hardened stem*

To the Sour Reader

If thou dislik'st the piece thou light'st on first,
Think that of all that I have writ the worst;
But if thou read'st my book unto the end,
And still dost this and that verse reprehend,
5   O perverse man! If all disgustful be,
The extreme scab[7] take thee and thine, for me.

Delight in Disorder[8]

A sweet disorder in the dress
Kindles in clothes a wantonness.
A lawn° about the shoulders thrown   *fine linen scarf*
Into a fine distractiòn;
5   An erring lace, which here and there
Enthralls the crimson stomacher;[9]
A cuff neglectful, and thereby
Ribbons to flow confusedly;
A winning wave, deserving note,
10   In the tempestuous petticoat;
A careless shoestring, in whose tie
I see a wild civility;
Do more bewitch me than when art
Is too precise in every part.

---

7. The mange. "The extreme scab" is a borrowing from Horace's *Art of Poetry* (lines 416–18), in which an unpracticed dabbler in poetry is represented as saying, in the translation of Herrick's admired master, Ben Jonson (1572–1637; see pp. 323–44), "I make / An admirable verse: the great scab take / Him that is last, I scorn to come behind / Or, of the things that ne'er came in my mind, / Once say I'm ignorant. . . ."

8. Cf. Ben Jonson, "Still to Be Neat" (p. 341).

9. An ornamental piece worn under the open (and often laced) front of a bodice; the "erring" ("wandering," with an overtone of moral straying) lace thus "enthralls" (literally, makes a slave of) the stomacher.

Corinna's Going A-Maying

Get up! get up for shame! the blooming morn
Upon her wings presents the god unshorn.[1]
   See how Aurora[2] throws her fair
   Fresh-quilted colors through the air:
5   Get up, sweet slug-a-bed, and see
   The dew bespangling herb and tree.
Each flower has wept and bowèd toward the east
Above an hour since, yet you not dressed;
   Nay, not so much as out of bed?
10   When all the birds have matins° said,   *morning prayers*
   And sung their thankful hymns, 'tis sin,
   Nay, profanation to keep in,
Whenas a thousand virgins on this day
Spring, sooner than the lark, to fetch in May.[3]

15 Rise, and put on your foliage, and be seen
To come forth, like the springtime, fresh and green,
   And sweet as Flora.[4] Take no care
   For jewels for your gown or hair;
   Fear not; the leaves will strew
20   Gems in abundance upon you;
Besides, the childhood of the day has kept,
Against° you come, some orient pearls[5] unwept;   *until*
   Come and receive them while the light
   Hangs on the dew-locks of the night,
25   And Titan° on the eastern hill   *the sun*
   Retires himself, or else stands still
Till you come forth. Wash, dress, be brief in praying:
Few beads[6] are best when once we go a-Maying.

Come, my Corinna, come; and, coming mark
30 How each field turns° a street, each street a park   *turns into*
   Made green and trimmed with trees; see how
   Devotion gives each house a bough
   Or branch: each porch, each door ere this,
   An ark, a tabernacle is,[7]
35 Made up of whitethorn neatly interwove,
As if here were those cooler shades of love.
   Can such delights be in the street
   And open fields, and we not see 't?
   Come, we'll abroad; and let's obey

1. Apollo, the Greek and Roman sun god, whose hair (the rays of the sun) is never cut.
2. Roman goddess of the dawn, here tossing her blankets aside and spreading over Earth a newly made coverlet of light.
3. Boughs of white hawthorn, traditionally gathered to decorate streets and houses on May Day. Larks sing at sunrise.
4. Roman goddess of flowers.
5. I.e., lustrous and glowing ones; also, "Eastern," as pearls come from the "Orient."
6. I.e., prayers (with overtones of the rosary of Catholicism).
7. I.e., the doorways are like the Hebrew "ark" of the Covenant, or the sanctuary ("tabernacle") that housed it; i.e., May sprigs are the central mystery of the religion of nature.

40   The proclamation made for May,[8]
     And sin no more, as we have done, by staying;
     But, my Corinna, come, let's go a-Maying.

     There's not a budding boy or girl this day
     But is got up and gone to bring in May;
45   A deal of youth, ere this, is come
      Back, and with whitethorn laden home.
      Some have dispatched their cakes and cream
      Before that we have left to dream;
     And some have wept, and wooed, and plighted troth,
50   And chose their priest, ere we can cast off sloth.
      Many a green-gown has been given,[9]
      Many a kiss, both odd and even,[1]
      Many a glance, too, has been sent
      From out the eye, love's firmament;°   *sky*
55   Many a jest told of the keys betraying
     This night, and locks picked; yet we're not a-Maying.

     Come, let us go while we are in our prime,
     And take the harmless folly of the time.
      We shall grow old apace,° and die   *quickly*
60   Before we know our liberty.
      Our life is short, and our days run
      As fast away as does the sun;
     And, as a vapor or a drop of rain
     Once lost, can ne'er be found again;
65   So when or you or I are made
      A fable, song, or fleeting shade,
      All love, all liking, all delight
      Lies drowned with us in endless night.
     Then while time serves, and we are but decaying,
70   Come, my Corinna, come, let's go a-Maying.

To the Virgins, to Make Much of Time

     Gather ye rosebuds while ye may,
      Old time is still a-flying;
     And this same flower that smiles today
      Tomorrow will be dying.

5   The glorious lamp of heaven, the sun,
      The higher he's a-getting,
     The sooner will his race be run,
      And nearer he's to setting.

---

8. Probably refers to King James's declaration concerning lawful sports, published in 1618 and reissued by King Charles I in 1633.

9. I.e., by rolling in the grass.
1. Kisses are odd and even in kissing games.

That age is best which is the first,
10   When youth and blood are warmer;
But being spent, the worse, and worst
    Times still succeed the former.

Then be not coy, but use your time,
    And, while ye may, go marry;
15 For, having lost but once your prime,
    You may forever tarry.

Upon Julia's Breasts

Display thy breasts, my Julia, there let me
Behold that circummortal[2] purity;
Between whose glories, there my lips I'll lay,
Ravished in that fair *Via Lactea*.[3]

Upon a Child That Died

Here she lies, a pretty bud,
Lately made of flesh and blood,
Who as soon fell fast asleep
As her little eyes did peep.°   *open*
5 Give her strewings,[4] but not stir
The earth that lightly covers her.

His Prayer to Ben Jonson[5]

When I a verse shall make,
    Know I have prayed thee,
For old religion's sake,
    Saint Ben, to aid me.[6]

5 Make the way smooth for me,
    When I, thy Herrick,
Honoring thee, on my knee
    Offer my lyric.

2. A coinage by Herrick, literally "around or encompassing what is mortal"; therefore, perhaps, beyond or more than mortal.
3. Milky Way (Latin); with reference to the color white and to the constellation; also, figuratively, a way brilliant in appearance and leading to heaven.
4. I.e., flowers scattered on her grave.
5. Herrick's admired master (1572–1637; see pp. 323–44).
6. Herrick, who had been ordained in the Church of England, plays on the fact that Jonson was for a while a Catholic (of the "old religion"), as well as a saint in the mock religion of poetry. The Puritans (who came to power in the civil war, which began in 1642) were hostile to the invocation of saints and, especially, of secular "saints" such as Jonson; Herrick was dispossessed by the Puritans in 1647, shortly before his poems were published. "Religion" may also mean the sacredness of an oath, i.e., the vows of friendship.

Candles I'll give to thee,
10   And a new altar;
And thou, Saint Ben, shalt be
Writ in my psalter.[7]

The Night Piece, to Julia

Her eyes the glowworm lend thee;[8]
The shooting stars attend thee;
   And the elves also,
   Whose little eyes glow
5 Like the sparks of fire, befriend thee.

No will-o'-the-wisp[9] mislight thee;
Nor snake or slowworm° bite thee;   *adder*
   But on, on thy way,
   Not making a stay,
10 Since ghost there's none to affright thee.

Let not the dark thee cumber;°   *trouble*
What though the moon does slumber?
   The stars of the night
   Will lend thee their light,
15 Like tapers clear without number.

Then, Julia, let me woo thee,
Thus, thus to come unto me;
   And when I shall meet
   Thy silvery feet,
20 My soul I'll pour into thee.

Upon Julia's Clothes

Whenas in silks my Julia goes,
Then, then, methinks, how sweetly flows
That liquefaction° of her clothes.   *liquefying*

Next, when I cast mine eyes, and see
5 That brave° vibration, each way free,   *glorious, splendid*
O, how that glittering taketh me!

7. A collection of sacred poems called Psalms; also, the Book of Psalms, one of the books of the Hebrew Scriptures, composed of such poems.
8. I.e., may the glowworm (an insect, the female of which emits a shining green light from the abdo-
men) lend her eyes to thee.
9. The will-o'-the-wisp was said to draw travelers astray by holding a false light before them; the phenomenon of nocturnal light is caused by the combustion of marsh gas.

Upon Prue, His Maid

In this little urn is laid
Prudence Baldwin, once my maid,
From whose happy spark here let
Spring the purple violet.

Upon Ben Jonson[1]

Here lies Jonson with the rest
Of the poets; but the best.
Reader, would'st thou more have known?
Ask his story, not this stone.
5 That will speak what this can't tell
Of his glory. So farewell.

An Ode for Him

    Ah, Ben!
    Say how or when
    Shall we, thy guests,
Meet at those lyric feasts
5   Made at the Sun,
The Dog, the Triple Tun,[2]
Where we such clusters° had   *wine*
As made us nobly wild, not mad;
And yet each verse of thine
10 Outdid the meat, outdid the frolic wine.

    My Ben!
    Or come again,
    Or send to us
Thy wit's great overplus;
15   But teach us yet
Wisely to husband° it,   *manage thriftily, prudently*
Lest we that talent spend,
And having once brought to an end
That precious stock, the store
20 Of such a wit the world should have no more.

---

1. See note 5, p. 358.   2. The names of taverns.

The Pillar of Fame[3]

Fame's pillar here at last we set,
Out-during° marble, brass or jet;[4]   *outlasting*
Charmed and enchanted so
As to withstand the blow
5   O f o v e r t h r o w ;
Nor shall the seas,
O r   o u t r a g e s
Of storms, o'erbear
What we uprear;
10   Tho' kingdoms fall,
This pillar never shall
Decline or waste at all;
But stand for ever by his own
Firm and well-fixed foundation.

Neutrality Loathsome[5]

God will have all or none; serve Him, or fall
Down before Baal, Bel, or Belial.[6]
Either be hot or cold: God doth despise,
Abhor, and spew out all neutralities.[7]

To His Conscience

Can I not sin, but thou wilt be
My private protonotary?°   *law court's chief recorder*
Can I not woo thee to pass by
A short and sweet iniquity?
5 I'll cast a mist and cloud upon
My delicate transgression,
So utter dark, as that no eye
Shall see the hugged° impiety.   *cherished*
Gifts blind the wise,[8] and bribes do please,
10 And wind° all other witnesses;   *pervert*
And wilt not thou, with gold, be tied
To lay thy pen and ink aside?

---

3. This poem is "shaped" to resemble a pillar; cf. George Herbert, "The Altar" (p. 367).
4. Black marble or a hard form of lignite.
5. This and the following poems are from *Noble Numbers,* the collection of religious poems in Herrick's 1648 volume.
6. Baal (or Bel) and Belial were pagan divinities; hence false gods in general.
7. Cf. Revelation 3.16: ". . . because thou art lukewarm, and neither cold nor hot, I will spew thee out of my mouth."
8. Cf. Deuteronomy 16.19: ". . . a gift doth blind the eyes of the wise, and pervert the words of the righteous."

That in the murk° and tongueless night,   murky
Wanton I may, and thou not write?
15   It will not be; and therefore now,
For times to come, I'll make this vow:
From aberrations to live free;
So I'll not fear the judge[9] or thee.

To Find God[1]

Weigh me the fire; or canst thou find
A way to measure out the wind?
Distinguish° all those floods that are   separate
Mixed in that wat'ry theater,[2]
5   And taste thou them as saltless there,
As in their channel first they were.
Tell° me the people that do keep   count
Within the kingdoms of the deep;
Or fetch me back that cloud again,
10   Beshivered° into seeds of rain.   shattered
Tell me the motes, dust, sands, and spears
Of corn, when summer shakes his ears;
Show me that world of stars, and whence
They noiseless spill their influence.
15   This if thou canst;[3] then show me Him
That rides the glorious cherubim.[4]

The White Island, or Place of the Blest

In this world, the isle of dreams,
While we sit by sorrow's streams,
Tears and terrors are our themes
        Reciting:

5   But when once from hence we fly,
More and more approaching nigh
Unto young eternity,
        Uniting:

---

9. I.e., God on Judgment Day.
1. The "impossibility" theme was much used by seventeenth-century poets such as John Donne (see "Go and Catch a Falling Star," p. 294) and Andrew Marvell (see "To His Coy Mistress," p. 478); Herrick emphasizes the challenge issued by the concluding line: if you can do these things, then show me the supreme sight, a vision of God. This poem alludes to an Apocryphal book of the Bible, 2 Esdras: "Weigh me the weight of fire, or measure me the day that is past. . . . How many

dwellings are there in the heart of the sea, or how many streams at the source of the deep, or how many ways above the firmament . . ." (4.5–7).
2. I.e., the ocean.
3. Perhaps an echo of Ecclesiasticus 1.2–3: "The sand of the seas, and the drops of rain, and the days of eternity—who can count them? The height of the heavens, and the breadth of the earth, and the deep, and wisdom—who can track them out?"
4. One of the nine orders of angels; cf. Psalms 18.10: "he [the Lord] rode upon a cherub."

In that whiter island, where
10   Things are evermore sincere;
Candor° here and luster there   *whiteness, truthfulness*
       Delighting:

There no monstrous fancies shall
Out of hell an horror call,
15   To create, or cause at all,
       Affrighting.

There, in calm and cooling sleep
We our eyes shall never steep,
But eternal watch shall keep,
20   Attending

Pleasures, such as shall pursue
Me immortalized, and you;
And fresh joys, as never too
       Have ending.

                                              1648

HENRY KING
1592–1669

An Exequy to His Matchless, Never-to-Be-Forgotten Friend[1]

Accept, thou shrine of my dead saint,
Instead of dirges, this complaint;[2]
And for sweet flowers to crown thy hearse,
Receive a strew° of weeping verse   *scattering*
5   From thy grieved friend, whom thou might'st see
Quite melted into tears for thee,

Dear loss! since thy untimely fate
My task hath been to meditate
On thee, on thee; thou art the book,
10   The library whereon I look,
Though almost blind. For thee, loved clay,°   *mortal*
I languish out, not live, the day,
Using no other exercise
But what I practice with mine eyes;
15   By which wet glasses I find out
How lazily time creeps about

---

1. Written for his wife, Anne King, who died in 1623 (after eight years of marriage). *Exequy:* a funeral ceremony.
2. Instead of mourning songs, this plaintive poem.

To one that mourns: this, only this,
My exercise and business is.
So I compute the weary hours
20   With sighs dissolvèd into showers.

Nor wonder if my time go thus
Backward and most preposterous;[3]
Thou hast benighted me, thy set[4]
This eve of blackness did beget,
25   Who wast my day, though overcast
Before thou hadst thy noontide passed;
And I remember must in tears,
Thou scarce hadst seen so many years
As day tells° hours. By thy clear sun   counts
30   My love and fortune first did run;
But thou wilt never more appear
Folded within my hemisphere,
Since both thy light and motiòn
Like a fled star is fallen and gone;
35   And 'twixt me and my soul's dear wish
An earth now interposèd is,
Which such a strange eclipse doth make
As ne'er was read in almanac.

I could allow thee for a time
40   To darken me and my sad clime;°   climate, part of Earth
Were it a month, a year, or ten,
I would thy exile live till then,
And all that space my mirth adjourn,
So thou wouldst promise to return;
45   And putting off thy ashy shroud,
At length disperse this sorrow's cloud.

But woe is me! the longest° date   most distant
Too narrow° is to calculate   short
These empty hopes; never shall I
50   Be so much blest as to descry°   discern
A glimpse of thee, till that day come
Which shall the earth to cinders doom,
And a fierce fever must calcine°   reduce to dust by heat
The body of this world—like thine,
55   My little world! That fit of fire
Once off, our bodies shall aspire
To our souls' bliss; then we shall rise
And view ourselves with clearer eyes
In that calm region where no night
60   Can hide us from each other's sight.

---

3. In reverse order, monstrous, foolish.   4. I.e., placed me in darkness, thy setting (death).

Meantime, thou hast her, earth: much good
May my harm[5] do thee. Since it stood°   *agreed*
With heaven's will I might not call
Her longer mine, I give thee all
65 My short-lived right and interest
In her whom living I loved best;
With a most free and bounteous grief
I give thee what I could not keep.
Be kind to her, and prithee look
70 Thou write into thy doomsday° book   *Judgment Day*
Each parcel of this rarity
Which in thy casket shrined doth lie.
See that thou make thy reckoning straight,
And yield her back again by weight;
75 For thou must audit on thy trust
Each grain and atom of this dust,
As thou wilt answer him that lent,
Not gave thee, my dear monument.

So close the ground, and 'bout her shade
80 Black curtains draw; my bride is laid.

Sleep on, my love, in thy cold bed,
Never to be disquieted!
My last good-night! Thou wilt not wake
Till I thy fate shall overtake;
85 Till age, or grief, or sickness must
Marry my body to that dust
It so much loves; and fill the room
My heart keeps empty in thy tomb.
Stay for me there; I will not fail
90 To meet thee in that hollow vale.
And think not much of my delay;
I am already on the way,
And follow thee with all the speed
Desire can make, or sorrows breed.
95 Each minute is a short degree,
And every hour a step towards thee.
At night when I betake° to rest,   *go*
Next morn I rise nearer my west
Of life, almost by eight hours' sail,
100 Than when sleep breathed his drowsy gale.

Thus from the sun my bottom° steers,   *vessel*
And my day's compass° downward bears;   *limit*
Nor labor I to stem the tide
Through which to thee I swiftly glide.

5. I.e., her death that harms me so much.

105 'Tis true, with shame and grief I yield,
Thou like the van° first took'st the field,   *vanguard*
And gotten hast the victory
In thus adventuring to die
Before me, whose more years might crave
110 A just precèdence in the grave.
But hark! my pulse like a soft drum
Beats my approach, tells thee I come;
And slow howe'er my marches be,
I shall at last sit down by thee.

115 The thought of this bids me go on,
And wait my dissolutiòn.
With hope and comfort. Dear (forgive
The crime), I am content to live
Divided, with but half a heart,
120 Till we shall meet, and never part.

1657

The Boy's Answer to the Blackmoor[6]

Black maid, complain not that I fly,
When Fate commands antipathy:
Prodigious[7] might that union prove,
Where Night and Day together move,
5 And the conjunction of our lips
Not kisses make, but an eclipse,
In which the mixed black and white
Portends more terror than delight.
Yet if my shadow thou wilt be,
10 Enjoy thy dearest wish. But see
Thou take my shadow's property,
That hastes away when I come nigh.[8]
  Else stay till death hath blinded me,
And then I will bequeath myself to thee.

ca. 1612–24   1657

---

6. This poem replies to "A Blackmore Maid Wooing a Fair Boy," which King's friend Henry Rainolds had translated from a Latin poem by George Herbert (1593–1633; for Herbert's English poems, see pp. 367–85). That poem's speaker, modeled in part on the "black but comely" female speaker in the biblical Song of Solomon (1.5), argues that "Love does in dark shades delight." King's "boy," unlike the biblical lover, scorns the wooing maiden. The poem participates in a Renaissance tradition of debating the cause and value of blackness; cf. Thomas Campion, "Follow Thy Fair Sun" (p. 279); Mary Wroth's *Pamphilia to Amphilanthus* 22 (p. 348); Edward Herbert's sonnets about blackness (p. 346); and John Milton's "Il Penseroso," lines 17–20 (p. 406).
7. Causing wonder or amazement; but also, ominous or unnatural.
8. See [that] you adopt my shadow's characteristic of hastening away when I come near.

GEORGE HERBERT
1593–1633

FROM THE TEMPLE: SACRED POEMS AND PRIVATE EJACULATIONS[1]

The Altar[2]

A broken A L T A R , Lord, thy servant rears,
Made of a heart, and cemented with tears:
Whose parts are as thy hand did frame;
No workman's tool hath touched the same.[3]

5   A   H E A R T   alone
              Is   such   a   stone,
              As   nothing   but
              Thy power doth cut.
              Wherefore each part
10   Of my hard heart
              Meets in this frame,
              To praise thy Name:
That, if I chance to hold my peace,
These stones to praise thee may not cease.[4]
15 Oh let thy blessed S A C R I F I C E be mine,
And sanctify this A L T A R to be thine.

Redemption[5]

Having been tenant long to a rich lord,
    Not thriving, I resolvèd to be bold,
    And make a suit unto him, to afford°   *grant*
A new small-rented lease, and cancel th' old.[6]

1. Posthumously published in 1633, *The Temple* includes 160 poems, which Herbert carefully arranged to dramatize the central Christian concept of the believer's body as the "temple of the Holy Ghost" (Paul's First Epistle to the Corinthians, 6.19). Designed to illustrate the myriad links between the human "temple" and the Church of England that Herbert served—its doctrines, its rituals, even the physical construction of its churches—Herbert's book begins with the poem "The Church Porch" and proceeds to a long section called "The Church," from which the following poems are taken.
    Since all of Herbert's poems were published in 1633, we do not print the date for each one.
2. The first poem in the section of *The Temple* called "The Church," this poem, like "Easter Wings" below, is shaped to resemble the object evoked by its title. Its placement suggests that all of the following poems are offered as "sacrifices" on the symbolic altar constituted here.
3. A reference to the altar of uncut stone described in Exodus 20.25 and in Deuteronomy 27.5–8.
4. I.e., whether the poem is read or spoken, and whether its author is living or dead, he wants the words to praise God. Here, as so often in Herbert's poems, the "praise" involves echoing words of the Scriptures; see Luke 19.40: "I tell you that, if these should hold their peace, the stones would immediately cry out."
5. Literally, "buying back"; in Christian doctrine, Christ's death redeemed human beings from the consequences of their sin.
6. I.e., to ask for a new lease, with a smaller rent, and to cancel the old lease.

5   In heaven at his manor I him sought;
        They told me there that he was lately gone
        About some land, which he had dearly bought
    Long since on earth, to take possessiòn.

    I straight° returned, and knowing his great birth,   *straightaway*
10   Sought him accordingly in great resorts;°   *gatherings, crowds*
        In cities, theaters, gardens, parks, and courts;
    At length I heard a ragged noise and mirth

        Of thieves and murderers; there I him espied,
        Who straight, *Your suit is granted*, said, and died.

Easter Wings[7]

Lord, who createdst man in wealth and store,°   *abundance*
    Though foolishly he lost the same,[8]
      Decaying more and more
         Till   he   became
5   Most   poor:
          With   thee
        O let me rise
      As   larks,[9] harmoniously,
    And sing this day thy victories:
10 Then shall the fall further the flight in me.[1]

My tender age in sorrow did begin;
    And still with sicknesses and shame
      Thou didst so punish sin,
         That   I   became
15   Most   thin.
          With   thee
        Let me combine,
      And feel this day thy victory;
    For, if I imp[2] my wing on thine,
20 Affliction shall advance the flight in me.

7. The shape of this "pattern poem" represents some part of the subject. Following this version, we reproduce the poem almost as it was first published. The stanzas were printed on two pages and arranged to suggest two birds flying upward, wings outspread.
8. I.e., in the Fall from Eden.
9. Larks sing at sunrise.
1. I.e., paradoxically, the joy of Easter and redemption from sin (the "flight" to heaven) is greater because the Fall from Eden occurred.

The words "this day," which are superfluous in the metrical scheme of the poem, were perhaps included in the early editions to emphasize the occasion, Easter. They are omitted, however, in the only surviving manuscript book of Herbert's poems.
2. A term from falconry: additional feathers were "imped," or grafted, onto the wing of a hawk to improve its power of flight.

Easter Wings

Lord, who createdst man in wealth and store,
Though foolishly he lost the same,
Decaying more and more,
Till he became
Most poore:
With thee
O let me rise
As larks, harmoniously,
And sing this day thy victories:
Then shall the fall further the flight in me.

My tender age in sorrow did beginne:
And still with sicknesses and shame
Thou didst so punish sinne,
That I became
Most thinne.
With thee
Let me combine,
And feel this day thy victorie:
For, if I imp my wing on thine,
Affliction shall advance the flight in me.

Sin (I)[3]

Lord, with what care hast thou begirt° us round!   *girdled*
  Parents first season us: then schoolmasters
  Deliver us to laws; they send us bound
To rules of reason, holy messengers,
5   Pulpits and Sundays, sorrow dogging sin,
  Afflictions sorted, anguish of all sizes,
  Fine nets and stratagems to catch us in,
Bibles laid open, millions of surprises,
Blessings beforehand, ties of gratefulness,
10   The sound of glory ringing in our ears:
  Without, our shame; within, our consciences;
Angels and grace, eternal hopes and fears.
  Yet all these fences and their whole array
  One cunning bosom-sin[4] blows quite away.

Affliction (I)

When first thou didst entice to thee my heart,
  I thought the service brave:°   *splendid*
So many joys I writ down for my part,

---

3. Herbert frequently used the same title for several different poems; editors differentiate between them by adding numbers.
4. I.e., a sin within the heart.

Besides what I might have
5   Out of my stock of natural delights,
    Augmented with thy gracious benefits.

I lookèd on thy furniture so fine,
      And made it fine to me;
Thy glorious household stuff did me entwine,
10   And 'tice° me unto thee.   *entice*
Such stars I counted mine: both heaven and earth
Paid me my wages in a world of mirth.

What pleasures could I want,° whose king I served,   *lack*
      Where joys my fellows were?
15   Thus argued into hopes, my thoughts reserved
        No place for grief or fear;
Therefore my sudden soul caught at the place,
And made her youth and fierceness seek thy face:

At first thou gav'st me milk and sweetnesses;
20   I had my wish and way:
My days were strawed° with flowers and happiness;   *strewed*
      There was no month but May.
But with my years sorrow did twist and grow.
And made a party unawares for woe.

25   My flesh began unto my soul in pain,
        "Sicknesses cleave my bones;
Consuming agues° dwell in every vein,   *fevers*
      And tune my breath to groans."
Sorrow was all my soul; I scarce believed,
30   Till grief did tell me roundly,° that I lived.   *bluntly*

When I got health, thou took'st away my life,
      And more; for my friends die:
My mirth and edge was lost: a blunted knife
      Was of more use than I.
35   Thus thin and lean without a fence or friend,
I was blown through with ev'ry storm and wind.

Whereas my birth and spirit rather took
      The way that takes the town,[5]
Thou didst betray me to a lingering book,
40   And wrap me in a gown.°   *theology's garb*
I was entangled in the world of strife,
Before I had the power to change my life.

---

5. An allusion to the career at court that Herbert had sought until 1625; his hopes for advancement disappointed, he "betook himself to a Retreat from London" and resolved to "enter into *Sacred* Orders." Many poems of *The Temple* were composed after Herbert was ordained a deacon in 1626—a period during which he suffered from ill-health.

Yet, for I threatened oft the siege to raise,
    Not simpering all mine age,
45 Thou often didst with academic praise
    Melt and dissolve my rage.
I took thy sweetened pill, till I came where
I could not go away, nor persevere.

Yet lest perchance I should too happy be
50   In my unhappiness,
Turning my purge° to food, thou throwest me   *purgation*
    Into more sicknesses.
Thus doth thy power cross-bias⁶ me, not making
Thine own gift good, yet me from my ways taking.

55 Now I am here, what thou wilt do with me
    None of my books will show:
I read, and sigh, and wish I were a tree,
    For sure then I should grow
To fruit or shade; at least, some bird would trust
60 Her household to me, and I should be just.

Yet, though thou troublest me, I must be meek;
    In weakness must be stout:⁷
Well, I will change the service, and go seek
    Some other master out.
65 Ah, my dear God! though I am clean forgot,
Let me not love thee, if I love thee not.

Prayer (I)

Prayer, the church's banquet, angels' age,⁸
    God's breath in man returning to his birth,
    The soul in paraphrase, heart in pilgrimage,
The Christian plummet⁹ sounding heav'n and earth;

5 Engine against th' Almighty, sinner's tower,
    Reversèd thunder, Christ-side-piercing spear,
    The six-days' world transposing¹ in an hour,
A kind of tune, which all things hear and fear;

    Softness, and peace, and joy, and love, and bliss,
10   Exalted manna,² gladness of the best,

---

6. A term from the game of bowls: to alter the natural path of the ball. I.e., thy power frustrates.
7. Cf. Malachi 3.13: "Your words have been stout against me, saith the Lord."
8. Prayer acquaints humans with the timeless existence of the "angels' age" (in contrast to finite human life).
9. A plummet is a piece of metal attached to a line, used for sounding or measuring a vertical distance.

Paraphrase: usually a fuller, simpler version of a text.
1. A musical term: shifting pitch or key. The "six day's world" alludes to God's creation of the world in six days (Genesis 1).
2. Spiritual nourishment, or food divinely supplied. Manna was the substance miraculously supplied as food to the Israelites during their time in the wilderness (Exodus 16).

Heaven in ordinary,[3] man well dressed,
The Milky Way, the bird of Paradise,[4]

Church bells beyond the stars heard, the soul's blood,
The land of spices; something understood.

The Temper (I)

How should I praise thee, Lord! how should my rhymes
    Gladly engrave thy love in steel,
  If what my soul doth feel sometimes,
    My soul might ever° feel!   *always*

5 Although there were some forty heavens, or more,
    Sometimes I peer above them all;
  Sometimes I hardly reach a score;
    Sometimes to hell I fall.

O rack me not to such a vast extent;
10   Those distances belong to thee:
  The world's too little for thy tent,
    A grave too big for me.

Wilt thou meet arms with man, that thou dost stretch
    A crumb of dust from heaven to hell?
15   Will great God measure with a wretch?
    Shall he thy stature spell?

O let me, when thy roof my soul hath hid,
    O let me roost and nestle there;
  Then of a sinner thou art rid,
20   And I of hope and fear.

Yet take thy way; for, sure, thy way is best:
    Stretch or contract me, thy poor debtor:
  This is but tuning of my breast,
    To make the music better.

25 Whether I fly with angels, fall with dust,
    Thy hands made both, and I am there.
  Thy power and love, my love and trust,
    Make one place everywhere.

3. In the everyday course of things. More specifically, "ordinary" also meant a daily allowance of food or an established order or form, as of the divine service.

4. Perhaps chosen for its name, or for its brilliant coloring.

Jordan (I)[5]

Who says that fictions only and false hair
Become a verse? Is there in truth no beauty?
Is all good structure in a winding stair?
May no lines pass, except they do their duty
5   Not to a true, but painted chair?[6]

Is it no verse, except enchanted groves
And sudden arbors shadow coarse-spun lines?[7]
Must purling° streams refresh a lover's loves?   *swirling*
Must all be veiled while he that reads, divines,
10   Catching the sense at two removes?

Shepherds are honest people; let them sing:
Riddle who list,° for me, and pull for prime:[8]   *likes*
I envy no man's nightingale or spring;
Nor let them punish me with loss of rhyme,
15   Who plainly say, *My God, My King.*

The Windows

Lord, how can man preach thy eternal word?
    He is a brittle crazy° glass;   *flawed, distorting*
Yet in thy temple thou dost him afford
    This glorious and transcendent place,
5   To be a window, through thy grace.

But when thou dost anneal in glass[9] thy story,
    Making thy life to shine within
The holy preachers, then the light and glory
    More reverend grows, and more doth win;
10   Which else shows waterish, bleak, and thin.

Doctrine and life, colors and light, in one
    When they combine and mingle, bring
A strong regard and awe; but speech alone
    Doth vanish like a flaring thing,
15   And in the ear, not conscience, ring.[1]

5. The only river of ancient Palestine; the Israelites crossed it to enter the Promised Land, and Christ was baptized in it. The title may also allude to the many windings of the Jordan.
6. It was customary to bow or "do one's duty" to the king's chair of state even when unoccupied; also, alludes to the false imitation critiqued by Plato in *The Republic,* book 10.
7. I.e., is it not true poetry unless enchanted groves and suddenly appearing trees (effects sought by landscape architects) shade (but also overshadow) humble lines?

8. To draw a lucky card in the game of primero. Lines 11–12 have been variously interpreted; their ambiguity and syntactical density work to complicate the contrast Herbert seems to be drawing between a "plain" style (exemplified by the shepherds) and the artificial, worldly style described in line 12. *For me:* as far as I'm concerned.
9. Fix the colors in stained glass, after painting, by heating.
1. The last stanza seems to challenge the Puritan belief in the efficacy of the spoken word.

Denial

When my devotions could not pierce
        Thy silent ears,
Then was my heart broken, as was my verse;
      My breast was full of fears
5   And disorder.

My bent thoughts, like a brittle bow,
        Did fly asunder:
Each took his way; some would to pleasures go,
      Some to the wars and thunder
10   Of alarms.

"As good go anywhere," they say,
        "As to benumb
Both knees and heart, in crying night and day,
      Come, come, my God, O come!
15   But no hearing."

O that thou shouldst give dust a tongue
        To cry to thee,
And then not hear it crying! All day long
      My heart was in my knee,[2]
20   But no hearing.

Therefore my soul lay out of sight,
        Untuned, unstrung:
My feeble spirit, unable to look right,
      Like a nipped blossom, hung
25   Discontented.

O cheer and tune my heartless breast,
        Defer no time;
That so thy favors granting my request,
      They and my mind may chime,°   *ring together, agree*
30   And mend my rhyme.

Vanity (I)

The fleet astronomer can bore°   *pierce*
And thread the spheres[3] with his quick-piercing mind:
He views their stations, walks from door to door,
      Surveys, as if he had designed

---

2. I.e., my heart was bowed and bent in reverence, like my knee.
3. Concentric transparent shells containing the heavenly bodies, according to Ptolemaic astronomy; they were thought to produce angelic music as they turned.

5   To make a purchase there; he sees their dances,
     And knoweth long before
Both their full-eyed aspècts,[4] and secret glances.

    The nimble diver with his side[5]
Cuts through the working waves, that he may fetch
10 His dearly-earnèd pearl, which God did hide
     On purpose from the venturous wretch;
That he might save his life, and also hers
     Who with excessive pride
Her own destruction and his danger wears.

15   The subtle chymic° can divest   *chemist*
And strip the creature naked, till he find
The callow° principles within their nest: *bald, immature*
     There he imparts to them his mind,
Admitted to their bed-chamber,[6] before
20   They appear trim and dressed
To ordinary suitors at the door.

    What hath not man sought out and found,
But his dear God? who yet his glorious law
Embosoms in us, mellowing the ground
25   With showers and frosts, with love and awe,
So that we need not say, "Where's this command?"
     Poor man, thou searchest round
To find out death, but missest life at hand.

Virtue

Sweet day, so cool, so calm, so bright,
   The bridal of the earth and sky:
The dew shall weep thy fall tonight;
    For thou must die.

5 Sweet rose, whose hue, angry and brave,[7]
   Bids the rash gazer wipe his eye:
Thy root is ever in its grave,
    And thou must die.

Sweet spring, full of sweet days and roses,
10 A box where sweets° compacted lie;   *perfumes*
My music shows ye have your closes,[8]
    And all must die.

---

4. The relative positions of the heavenly bodies as they appear to an observer on Earth at a given time, and their supposed influence on earthly matters.
5. I.e., swimming on his side.
6. Herbert implies that the chemist examining creatures' inner natures in an overly intimate way is forming them according to his own intellect ("imparts to them his mind") rather than discovering their God-given reality.
7. Splendid. *Angry:* i.e., red, the color of anger.
8. A close is a cadence, the conclusion of a musical strain.

Only a sweet and virtuous soul,
Like seasoned timber, never gives;
15   But though the whole world turn to coal,[9]
Then chiefly lives.

Man

My God, I heard this day
That none doth build a stately habitation,
But he that means to dwell therein.
What house more stately hath there been,
5   Or can be, than is Man? to° whose creation   *compared to*
All things are in decay.

For Man is every thing,
And more: he is a tree, yet bears more fruit;[1]
A beast, yet is or should be more:
10   Reason and speech we only bring.
Parrots may thank us, if they are not mute,
They go upon the score.[2]

Man is all symmetry,
Full of proportions, one limb to another,
15   And all to all the world besides:[3]
Each part may call the furthest, brother;
For head with foot hath private amity,°   *friendship*
And both with moons and tides.[4]

Nothing hath got so far,
20   But man hath caught and kept it, as his prey.
His eyes dismount° the highest star: *bring down to Earth*
He is in little all the sphere.°   *universe*
Herbs gladly cure our flesh, because that they
Find their acquaintance there.

25   For us the winds do blow,
The earth doth rest, heaven move, and fountains flow.
Nothing we see but means our good,
As our delight or as our treasure:
The whole is either our cupboard of food,
30   Or cabinet of pleasure.

9. An allusion to Judgment Day, when the world
will end in a great fire (2 Peter 3.10).
1. This line presents a serious textual problem,
since all early printed versions of the poem have
"no" instead of "more" "fruit." We follow the read-
ing of the one surviving manuscript, which Herbert
saw, but the alternate reading has strong claims.
See, for instance, "Affliction (I)," lines 57–60
(p. 371), where Herbert contrasts the uncertainty
of human "fruitfulness"—dependent partly on

God's hidden will—with the tree's natural cycle of
growth.
2. "Man" is the only creature with "reason and
speech"; the parrot may seem to be an exception,
but it talks on credit ("upon the score"), i.e.,
because humans taught it how.
3. I.e., humanity is also symmetrical to—a micro-
cosm of—the world.
4. Refers to the notion that parts of the body are
affected by the motions of the moon and stars.

The stars have us to bed;
Night draws the curtain, which the sun withdraws;
  Music and light attend our head.
  All things unto our flesh are kind°   kin
35 In their descent and being; to our mind
    In their ascent and cause.

      Each thing is full of duty:[5]
  Waters united are our navigation;
    Distinguishèd, our habitation;
40   Below, our drink; above, our meat;
  Both are our cleanliness. Hath one such beauty?
    Then how are all things neat?[6]

      More servants wait on Man
  Than he'll take notice of: in every path
45 He treads down that which doth befriend him[7]
  When sickness makes him pale and wan.
  O mighty love! Man is one world, and hath
    Another to attend him.

      Since then, my God, thou hast
50 So brave a palace built, O dwell in it,
  That it may dwell with thee at last!
  Till then, afford us so much wit,
  That, as the world serves us, we may serve thee,
    And both thy servants be.

Life

  I made a posy,° while the day ran by: bouquet; poem
  "Here will I smell my remnant° out, and tie   remaining time
      My life within this band."
  But Time did beckon to the flowers, and they
5 By noon most cunningly did steal away,
      And withered in my hand.

  My hand was next to them, and then my heart;
  I took, without more thinking, in good part
      Time's gentle admonition;
10 Who did so sweetly death's sad taste convey,
  Making my mind to smell my fatal day,
      Yet sug'ring the suspicion.

5. I.e., all the elements serve God and humans.
Lines 38–40: oceans ("waters united") are valuable
for navigation; the dividing of the waters ("distin-
guished") during the Creation allowed humans to
live on Earth (Genesis 1.6). Water on Earth pro-
vides drink, while water from "above" (i.e., manna

or dew) is food.
6. I.e., if one element can serve so abundantly,
how wonderful ("neat") is the sum of all things.
7. I.e., he treads down the herb that cures ill-
nesses.

Farewell dear flowers, sweetly your time ye spent,
Fit, while ye lived, for smell or ornament,
15   And after death for cures.[8]
I follow straight without complaints or grief,
Since, if my scent be good, I care not if
          It be as short as yours.

Artillery

As I one evening sat before my cell,
Methought° a star did shoot into my lap.   *it seemed to me*
I rose and shook my clothes, as knowing well
That from small fires comes oft no small mishap;
5   When suddenly I heard one say,
        "Do as thou usest, disobey,
        Expel good motions from thy breast,
Which have the face of fire, but end in rest."[9]

I, who had heard of music in the spheres,[1]
10 But not of speech in stars, began to muse;
But turning to my God, whose ministers
The stars and all things are: "If I refuse,
        Dread Lord," said I, "so oft my good,
        Then I refuse not ev'n with blood
15   To wash away my stubborn thought;
For I will do or suffer what I ought.

"But I have also stars and shooters too,
Born where thy servants both artilleries use.
My tears and prayers night and day do woo
20 And work up to thee; yet thou dost refuse.
        Not but I am (I must say still)
        Much more obliged to do thy will
        Than thou to grant mine; but because
Thy promise now hath ev'n set thee thy laws.

25 "Then we are shooters both, and thou dost deign°   *condescend*
To enter combat with us, and contest
With thine own clay. But I would parley fain:[2]
Shun not my arrows, and behold my breast.
        Yet if thou shunnest, I am thine:
30   I must be so, if I am mine.
        There is no articling° with thee: *negotiating*
I am but finite, yet thine infinitely."

---

8. Flowers were sometimes used as an ingredient in medicines.
9. I.e., divine impulses, like falling stars, may have the appearance of dangerous fires, but ultimately end quietly.

1. The spheres of Ptolemaic astronomy, concentric transparent shells containing the heavenly bodies, were thought to produce angelic music as they turned.
2. Gladly speak. *Clay:* i.e., flesh.

The Collar[3]

I struck the board° and cried, "No more;   *table*
    I will abroad!
What? shall I ever sigh and pine?
My lines and life are free, free as the road,
5   Loose as the wind, as large as store.°   *abundance*
    Shall I be still in suit?[4]
Have I no harvest but a thorn
To let me blood, and not restore
What I have lost with cordial° fruit?   *life-giving*
10   Sure there was wine
Before my sighs did dry it; there was corn
    Before my tears did drown it.
Is the year only lost to me?
    Have I no bays[5] to crown it,
15   No flowers, no garlands gay? All blasted?
    All wasted?
Not so, my heart; but there is fruit,
    And thou hast hands.
Recover all thy sigh-blown age
20   On double pleasures: leave thy cold dispute
Of what is fit and not. Forsake thy cage,
    Thy rope of sands,[6]
Which petty thoughts have made, and made to thee
    Good cable, to enforce and draw,
25   And be thy law,
While thou didst wink° and wouldst not see.   *shut your eyes*
    Away! take heed;
    I will abroad.
Call in thy death's-head[7] there; tie up thy fears.
30   He that forbears
    To suit and serve his need,
    Deserves his load."
But as I raved and grew more fierce and wild
    At every word,
35   Methought I heard one calling, *Child!*
    And I replied, *My Lord.*

The Pulley[8]

When God at first made man,
Having a glass of blessings standing by,

3. A band of metal fixed round a prisoner's neck; also, something worn about the neck as a badge of servitude, as a priest wears a collar to show his service to God. Also, perhaps, a pun on *choler,* anger.
4. I.e., in attendance upon someone for a favor.
5. A laurel garland symbolizing poetic fame.
6. I.e., the restrictions on behavior, which the "petty thoughts" have made into "good" (or strong) cable.
7. A memento mori, or representation of a human skull intended to serve as a reminder that all humans must die.
8. A simple mechanical device, made of a rope, a wheel, and sometimes a block, used for changing the direction of a pulling force to lift weights.

"Let us," said he, "pour on him all we can.
Let the world's riches, which dispersèd lie,
5   Contract into a span."[9]

So strength first made a way;
Then beauty flowed, then wisdom, honor, pleasure.
When almost all was out, God made a stay,
Perceiving that, alone of all his treasure,
10   Rest° in the bottom lay.   *remainder; repose*

"For if I should," said he,
"Bestow this jewel also on my creature,
He would adore my gifts instead of me,
And rest in Nature, not the God of Nature;
15   So both should losers be.

"Yet let him keep the rest,
But keep them with repining restlessness.
Let him be rich and weary, that at least,
If goodness lead him not, yet weariness
20   May toss him to my breast."

The Flower

How fresh, oh Lord, how sweet and clean
Are thy returns! even as the flowers in spring;
To which, besides their own demean,[1]
The late-past frosts tributes of pleasure bring.
5   Grief melts away
          Like snow in May,
As if there were no such cold thing.

Who would have thought my shriveled heart
Could have recovered greenness? It was gone
10   Quite underground; as flowers depart
To see their mother-root, when they have blown,°   *bloomed*
          Where they together
          All the hard weather,
Dead to the world, keep house unknown.

15   These are thy wonders, Lord of power,
Killing and quickening,° bringing down to hell   *reviving*
          And up to heaven in an hour;
Making a chiming of a passing-bell.[2]
          We say amiss
20   This or that is:
Thy word is all, if we could spell.

9. A small space; the distance from the end of the thumb to the end of the little finger of a spread hand.
1. Demeanor or bearing; also *demesne*, estate, i.e.,
the estate of one's own beauty or pleasure.
2. A monotone bell tolled to announce a death; a chiming offers a pleasing variety.

Oh that I once past changing were,
Fast in thy Paradise, where no flower can wither!
Many a spring I shoot up fair,
Offering° at heaven, growing and groaning thither;   *aiming*
    Nor doth my flower
      Want° a spring shower,   *lack; desire*
My sins and I joining together.³

But while I grow in a straight line,
Still upwards bent, as if heaven were mine own,
Thy anger comes, and I decline:
What frost to that? what pole is not the zone
    Where all things burn,
      When thou dost turn,
And the least frown of thine is shown?⁴

And now in age I bud again,
After so many deaths I live and write;
I once more smell the dew and rain,
And relish versing. Oh, my only light,
    It cannot be
      That I am he
On whom thy tempests fell all night.

These are thy wonders, Lord of love,
To make us see we are but flowers that glide;°   *pass away silently*
    Which when we once can find and prove,°   *experience*
Thou hast a garden for us where to bide;
    Who would be more,
      Swelling through store,°   *possessions*
Forfeit their Paradise by their pride.

25 *(line 25)*
30 *(line 30)*
35 *(line 35)*
40 *(line 40)*
45 *(line 45)*

The Forerunners

The harbingers⁵ are come. See, see their mark:
White is their color, and behold my head.⁶
But must they have my brain? Must they dispark⁷
Those sparkling notions, which therein were bred?
    Must dullness turn me to a clod?
Yet have they left me, *Thou art still my God.*⁸

Good men ye be, to leave me my best room,
Ev'n all my heart, and what is lodgèd there:

5 *(line 5)*

---

3. I.e., the tears of contrition caused by the "join-ing" together of the poet's sins and his conscience.
4. I.e., what cold compares to God's anger? What chill would not seem like the heat of the equator, compared to God's wrath?
5. The advance agents of the king and his party on a royal progress, or tour. They marked with chalk the doors of those dwellings where the court would be accommodated.

6. I.e., the poet has been marked by the appear-ance of white hairs, a sign that all of his "sparkling notions" (line 4) must be dispossessed, to make room for his coming Lord.
7. I.e., *dis-park*, to turn out, as deer from a park; there may also be a play on *dis-spark*.
8. Echoes Psalm 31.14: "But I trusted in thee, O Lord: I said, Thou art my God." See also Christ's lament to God in Matthew 27.46 and Mark 15.34.

I pass not,[9] I, what of the rest become,
So *Thou art still my God* be out of fear.
     He will be pleasèd with that ditty;
And if I please him, I write fine and witty.

Farewell sweet phrases, lovely metaphors.
But will ye leave me thus? When ye before
Of stews and brothels only knew the doors,
Then did I wash you with my tears, and more,
     Brought you to church well dressed and clad:
My God must have my best, ev'n all I had.

Lovely enchanting language, sugar-cane,
Honey of roses, wither wilt thou fly?
Hath some fond lover 'ticed thee to thy bane?[1]
And wilt thou leave the church and love a sty?[2]
     Fie, thou wilt soil thy broidered coat,
And hurt thyself, and him that sings the note.

Let foolish lovers, if they will love dung,
With canvas, not with arras,[3] clothe their shame:
Let folly speak in her own native tongue.
True beauty dwells on high: ours is a flame
     But borrowed thence to light us thither.
Beauty and beauteous words should go together.

Yet if you go, I pass not; take your way:
For *Thou art still my God* is all that ye
Perhaps with more embellishment can say.
Go, birds of spring: let winter have his fee;
     Let a bleak paleness chalk the door,
So all within be livelier than before.

Discipline

Throw away thy rod,°   *punishment*
Throw away thy wrath:
     O my God,
Take the gentle path.

For my heart's desire
Unto thine is bent:
     I aspire
To a full consent.

Not a word or look
I affect to own,

9. I care not. I.e., all the other thoughts in the house (my mind, my soul) can be turned out of doors, as long as you leave my heart ("my best room") and its one inhabitant, the thought "Thou art still my God."
1. Destruction. *Ticed:* enticed.
2. Pigsty; also, a place of moral contamination.
3. I.e., with coarse cloth, not with tapestry.

But by book,
And thy book[4] alone.

Though I fail, I weep:
Though I halt in pace,
15   Yet I creep
To the throne of grace.

Then let wrath remove;
Love will do the deed:
           For with love
20   Stony hearts will bleed.

Love is swift of foot;
Love's a man of war,[5]
           And can shoot,
And can hit from far.

25   Who can 'scape his bow?
That which wrought on thee,
           Brought thee low,
Needs must work on me.

Throw away thy rod;
30   Though man frailties hath,
           Thou art God:
Throw away thy wrath.

The Elixir[6]

Teach me, my God and King,
In all things thee to see,
And what I do in anything,
To do it as for thee.

5   Not rudely, as a beast,
To run into an action;
But still to make thee prepossest,[7]
And give it his° perfection.   *its*

A man that looks on glass,
10   On it may stay his eye,
Or, if he pleaseth, through it pass,
And then the heaven espy.

---

4. I.e., the Bible. *By book*: i.e., as an actor follows a playbook.
5. A song by Moses in Exodus 15 calls the Lord a "man of war"; also, a possible reference to the classical image of the god Cupid and his arrow.
6. An elixir is a drug or essence supposed to pro-

long life indefinitely; here, it is identified with the "famous stone" (line 21) believed by the alchemists to turn other metals to gold. Figuratively, the quintessence or soul of a thing.
7. I.e., always to give thee a prior claim.

All may of thee partake:
        Nothing can be so mean
15 Which with his tincture (*for thy sake*)
        Will not grow bright and clean.[8]

A servant with this clause
        Makes drudgery divine:
Who sweeps a room as for thy laws,
20   Makes that and th' action fine.

This is the famous stone
        That turneth all to gold;
For that which God doth touch[9] and own
        Cannot for less be told.°   *measured*

Death

Death, thou wast once an uncouth hideous thing,
        Nothing but bones,
The sad effect of sadder groans:
Thy mouth was open, but thou couldst not sing.

5   For we considered thee as at some six
        Or ten years hence,
After the loss of life and sense,
Flesh being turned to dust, and bones to sticks.

We looked on this side of thee, shooting short;
10   Where we did find
The shells of fledge souls left behind,
Dry dust, which sheds no tears, but may extort.[1]

But since our Savior's death did put some blood
        Into thy face,
15   Thou art grown fair and full of grace,
Much in request, much sought for as a good.

For we do now behold thee gay and glad,
        As at Doomsday;°   *Judgment Day*
        When souls shall wear their new array,
20 And all thy bones with beauty shall be clad.

---

8. I.e., nothing is so insignificant ("mean") that it
can't grow bright and clean for thy sake by means
of its tincture (an immaterial principle that trans-
formed substances, according to alchemical the-
ory).
9. To test (gold) for purity by rubbing it with a
touchstone.
1. "Fledge souls" that have left the body and gone
to heaven are like fledgling chicks that have left
the shell behind. The shell (i.e., the corpse) can
draw ("extort") tears from survivors, although it
cannot shed them itself.

Therefore we can go die as sleep, and trust
　　　Half that we have
Unto an honest faithful grave;
Making our pillows either down, or dust.

Love (III)[2]

Love bade me welcome: yet my soul drew back,
　　　Guilty of dust and sin.
But quick-eyed Love, observing me grow slack[3]
　　　From my first entrance in,
5　Drew nearer to me, sweetly questioning
　　　If I lacked any thing.

"A guest," I answered, "worthy to be here":
　　　Love said, "You shall be he."
"I, the unkind, ungrateful? Ah, my dear,
10　　　I cannot look on thee."
Love took my hand, and smiling did reply,
　　　"Who made the eyes but I?"

"Truth, Lord; but I have marred them; let my shame
　　　Go where it doth deserve."
15　"And know you not," says Love, "who bore the blame?"[4]
　　　"My dear, then I will serve."
"You must sit down," says Love, "and taste my meat."[5]
　　　So I did sit and eat.

THOMAS CAREW
ca. 1595–1640

A Song

Ask me no more where Jove[1] bestows,
When June is past, the fading rose;
For in your beauty's orient deep,
These flowers, as in their causes,[2] sleep.

---

2. This is the last lyric in "The Church" both in the early Williams manuscript and in the 1633 edition of The Temple; some critics have therefore interpreted the poem as describing the soul's reception into heaven.
3. I.e., become hesitant because of misgivings.
4. I.e., Christ, who took on the "blame" for human beings' original sin.
5. A reference to the sacrament of Communion (according to Anglicans, the ritual taking of bread and wine in remembrance of Christ's body); also,

a reference to the final Communion in heaven, when God "shall gird himself, and make them to sit down to meat, and will come forth and serve them" (Luke 12.37).
1. The ruling god of Roman mythology.
2. Aristotelian philosophy regarded that from which a thing is made or comes into being as the "material cause" of the thing. The lady here is a summation of the previous summer and a cause of the next one. Orient: lustrous, but also "from the East."

5   Ask me no more whither doth stray
The golden atoms of the day;
For in pure love heaven did prepare
Those powders to enrich your hair.

Ask me no more whither doth haste
10   The nightingale when May is past;
For in your sweet dividing³ throat
She winters, and keeps warm her note.

Ask me no more where those stars light,
That downwards fall in dead of night;
15   For in your eyes they sit, and there
Fixèd become, as in their sphere.

Ask me no more if east or west
The phoenix⁴ builds her spicy nest;
For unto you at last she flies,
20   And in your fragrant bosom dies.

1640

The Spring

Now that the winter's gone, the earth hath lost
Her snow-white robes, and now no more the frost
Candies° the grass, or casts an icy cream   *ices*
Upon the silver lake or crystal stream;
5   But the warm sun thaws the benumbèd earth
And makes it tender, gives a sacred birth
To the dead swallow,⁵ wakes in hollow tree
The drowsy cuckoo and the humble bee.
Now do a choir of chirping minstrels bring
10   In triumph to the world the youthful spring.
The valleys, hills, and woods in rich array
Welcome the coming of the longed-for May.
Now all things smile: only my love doth lour,°   *frown*
Nor hath the scalding noonday sun the power
15   To melt that marble ice which still doth hold
Her heart congealed, and makes her pity cold.
The ox, which lately did for shelter fly
Into the stall, doth now securely lie
In open fields; and love no more is made
20   By the fireside, but in the cooler shade:
Amyntas now doth with his Chloris⁶ sleep

---

3. Harmonious (from *division*, an embellished
musical phrase).
4. A legendary bird, the only one of its kind, rep-
resented as living five hundred years in the Arabian
desert, being consumed in fire, then rising anew
from its own ashes. Also said to build its nest from

spicy shrubs.
5. Swallows were sacred to the Roman household
gods.
6. Conventional names for a shepherd and shep-
herdess.

Under a sycamore, and all things keep
Time with the season. Only she doth carry
June in her eyes, in her heart January.

1640

Mediocrity[7] in Love Rejected

Give me more love, or more disdain;
   The torrid or the frozen zone
Bring equal ease unto my pain;
   The temperate affords me none:
5   Either extreme, of love or hate,
   Is sweeter than a calm estate.°   *condition*

Give me a storm; if it be love,
   Like Danaë in that golden shower,[8]
I swim in pleasure; if it prove
10   Disdain, that torrent will devour
My vulture hopes; and he's possessed
Of heaven that's but from hell released.
   Then crown my joys, or cure my pain;
   Give me more love, or more disdain.

1640

Song. To My Inconstant Mistress

When thou, poor excommunicate
   From all the joys of love, shalt see
The full reward and glorious fate
   Which my strong faith shall purchase me,
5   Then curse thine own inconstancy.

A fairer hand than thine shall cure
   That heart which thy false oaths did wound,
And to my soul a soul more pure
   Than thine shall by Love's hand be bound,
10   And both with equal glory crowned.

Then shalt thou weep, entreat, complain
   To Love, as I did once to thee;
When all thy tears shall be as vain

---

7. Temperance, moderation.
8. Jove, the ruling god in Roman mythology, frequently left Juno, his sister and wife, to pursue other women; whether his actions constituted seduction or rape often depends on the particular account of a common myth, as well as on inter-pretation. Danaë was the daughter of the king of Argos, who imprisoned her because of a prophecy that a son born to her would kill him; Jove came to her in the form of a shower of gold, and as a result gave birth to Perseus.

As mine were then, for thou shalt be
15   Damned for thy false apostasy.[9]

1640

An Elegy upon the Death of the Dean of Paul's, Dr. John Donne[1]

Can we not force from widowed poetry,
Now thou art dead, great Donne, one elegy
To crown thy hearse? Why yet did we not trust,
Though with unkneaded dough-baked[2] prose, thy dust,
5   Such as the unscissored lect'rer[3] from the flower
Of fading rhetoric, short-lived as his hour,
Dry as the sand that measures it,[4] should lay
Upon the ashes on the funeral day?
Have we nor tune, nor voice? Didst thou dispense[5]
10   Through all our language both the words and sense?
'Tis a sad truth. The pulpit may her plain
And sober Christian precepts still retain;
Doctrines it may, and wholesome uses, frame,
Grave homilies° and lectures; but the flame   sermons
15   Of thy brave soul, that shot such heat and light
As burnt our earth and made our darkness bright,
Committed holy rapes[6] upon our will,
Did through the eye the melting heart distill,
And the deep knowledge of dark truths so teach
20   As sense might judge what fancy could not reach,[7]
Must be desired forever. So the fire
That fills with spirit and heat the Delphic choir,[8]
Which, kindled first by thy Promethean[9] breath,
Glowed here a while, lies quenched now in thy death.
25   The Muses'[1] garden, with pedantic weeds
O'erspread, was purged by thee; the lazy seeds
Of servile imitation thrown away,
And fresh invention planted; thou didst pay
The debts of our penurious° bankrupt age;   poverty-stricken
30   Licentious thefts, that make poetic rage
A mimic fury, when our souls must be

9. Abandonment of one's allegiance, often to a religious faith or god.
1. English poet (1572–1631; see pp. 293–322).
2. I.e., badly finished, flat.
3. I.e., lecturer with uncut hair; in the first edition, Carew wrote "church-man" instead of "lect'rer," and thus signalled an aim to distinguish this figure from Roman Catholic priests, whose hair was cut (tonsured) when they entered the Church. The line seems to have been altered to soften the critique of Protestant clergymen—implicit in the evocation of a "dry," inadequate elegy—on the occasion of Donne's official funeral. Although Donne was born a Catholic, he later became a famous Anglican preacher; he expressed doubts about various religious claims to truth in "Satire III" (p. 314) and other writings.
4. I.e., the sand in an hourglass.
5. Use up or lay out.
6. Forcible seizures. For Donne's use of the metaphor of a religious "rape," see Holy Sonnet 14 (p. 320).
7. I.e., so that things too intangible and elevated even to be imagined might be made plain to sense.
8. I.e., the choir of poets. Delphi was the site of an oracle of Apollo, the classical god of poetry.
9. In Greek mythology, Prometheus stole fire from the gods for the benefit of mortals.
1. In Greek mythology, nine sister goddesses who were sources of inspiration.

Possessed, or with Anacreon's ecstasy,
Or Pindar's,[2] not their own; the subtle cheat
Of sly exchanges, and the juggling feat
35   Of two-edged words, or whatsoever wrong
By ours was done the Greek or Latin tongue,
Thou hast redeemed, and opened us a mine
Of rich and pregnant fancy, drawn a line
Of masculine expression, which had good
40   Old Orpheus[3] seen, or all the ancient brood
Our superstitious fools admire, and hold
Their lead more precious than thy burnished gold,
Thou hadst been their exchequer,° and no more   *treasury*
They in each other's dung had searched for ore.
45   Thou shalt yield no precèdence, but of time
And the blind fate of language, whose tuned chime
More charms the outward sense; yet thou mayest claim
From so great disadvantage greater fame,
Since to the awe of thy imperious wit
50   Our troublesome language bends, made only fit
With her tough thick-ribbed hoops, to gird about
Thy giant fancy, which had proved too stout
For their soft melting phrases.[4] As in time
They had the start, so did they cull the prime
55   Buds of invention many a hundred year,
And left the rifled fields, besides the fear
To touch their harvest; yet from those bare lands
Of what is only thine, thy only hands
(And that their smallest work) have gleanèd more
60   Than all those times and tongues could reap before.
       But thou art gone, and thy strict laws will be
Too hard for libertines in poetry.
They will recall the goodly exiled train
Of gods and goddesses, which in thy just reign
65   Were banished° nobler poems; now with these   *banished from*
The silenced tales i' th' *Metamorphoses*[5]
Shall stuff their lines and swell the windy page,
Till verse, refined by thee in this last age,
Turn ballad-rhyme, or those old idols be
70   Adored again with new apostasy.[6]
       O pardon me, that break with untuned verse
The reverend silence that attends thy hearse,
Whose solemn awful° murmurs were to thee,   *awestruck*
More than these faint lines, a loud elegy,
75   That did proclaim in a dumb eloquence
The death of all the arts, whose influence,
Grown feeble, in these panting numbers lies
Gasping short-winded accents, and so dies:

---

2. Anacreon (ca. 582–ca. 485 B.C.E.) and Pindar (ca. 522–ca. 438 B.C.E.) were famous Greek poets.
3. In Greek mythology, the son of one of the Muses and the greatest of poets and musicians.
4. I.e., a metaphor describing Donne's wit as a barrel maker bending hoops of metal around the "wine" of his genius.
5. Earlier poets had drawn heavily on the stories in Ovid's *Metamorphoses* for the materials of their poetry.
6. Abandonment of one's allegiance, especially to a religious faith or a god.

So doth the swiftly turning wheel not stand
80 In th' instant we withdraw the moving hand,
But some small time retain a faint weak course
By virtue of the first impulsive force;
And so whilst I cast on thy funeral pile
Thy crown of bays,[7] oh, let it crack awhile
85 And spit disdain, till the devouring flashes
Suck all the moisture up; then turn to ashes.
    I will not draw thee envy to engross[8]
All thy perfections, or weep all the loss;
Those are too numerous for one elegy,
90 And this too great to be expressed by me.
Let others carve the rest; it shall suffice
I on thy grave this epitaph incise:

Here lies a king, that ruled as he thought fit
The universal monarchy of wit;
95 Here lie two flamens,° and both those the best: priests
Apollo's[9] first, at last the true God's priest.

1633, 1640

JAMES SHIRLEY
1596–1666

FROM AJAX

Dirge[1]

The glories of our blood and state
Are shadows, not substantial things;
There is no armor against fate;
Death lays his icy hand on kings.
5   Scepter and crown
       Must tumble down
And in the dust be equal made
With the poor crooked scythe and spade.

Some men with swords may reap the field
10 And plant fresh laurels[2] where they kill,
But their strong nerves at last must yield;
They tame but one another still.
       Early or late

---

7. A crown of bays, or laurel, was the traditional reward of the victor in a poetic competition.
8. Write, copy out, with a pun on the word's economic meanings: to buy up, monopolize.
9. I.e., the god of poetry's.
1. This poem concludes Shirley's play *The Con-*

tention of Ajax and Ulysses for the Armor of Achilles, which retells a story from Ovid's *Metamorphoses.*
2. The laurel's evergreen leaves, and also its flowers (cf. "garlands," line 17), symbolized military victory or success in poetic competitions.

They stoop to fate
15 And must give up their murmuring breath,
When they, pale captives, creep to death.

The garlands wither on your brow,
Then boast no more your mighty deeds;
Upon death's purple altar now
20 See where the victor-victim bleeds.
    Your heads must come
    To the cold tomb;
Only the actions of the just
Smell sweet and blossom in their dust.

1659

THE MASSACHUSETTS BAY PSALM BOOK*

Psalm 58[1]

1

Do ye, o congregation,
    indeed speak righteousness?
and o ye sons of earthly men,
    do ye judge unrightness?

2

5 Yea you in heart will working be
    injurious-wickedness;
and in the land you will weigh out
    your hands' violence.

3

The wicked are estranged from
10   the womb, they go astray
as soon as ever they are borne;
    uttering lies are they.

4

Their poison's like serpent's poison;
    they like deaf asp,° her ear   *small poisonous snake*
15 that stops. Though charmer wisely charm,
    his voice she will not hear.

*The first book published in the new colony of Massachusetts, compiled by twelve Puritan clergymen who sought (as John Cotton explained in his preface) a plainer, more literal rendering of the Hebrew than occurs in other Protestant translations of the Psalms. Often reprinted, in England and Scotland as well as in North America, this Psalter was one of the two most commonly owned books in New England (the other being *The New England Primer*).

1. Cf. the translations of this Psalm and the next one by Mary Sidney (pp. 225–26), Isaac Watts (pp. 592–94), and Christopher Smart (pp. 684–86).

5

Within their mouth do thou their teeth
   break out, O God most strong,
do thou Jehovah, the great teeth
20   break of the lion's young.

6

As waters let them melt away,
   that run continually:
and when he bends his shafts, let them
   as cut asunder be.

7

25 Like to a snail that melts, so let
   each of them pass away;
like to a woman's untimely birth
   see sun that never they may.

8

Before your pots can feel the thorns,
30   take them away shall he,
as with a whirlwind both living,
   and in his jealousy.

9

The righteous will rejoice when as
   the vengeance he doth see;
35 his feet wash shall he in the blood
   of them that wicked be.

10

So that a man shall say, surely
   for righteous, there is fruit:
sure there's a God that in the earth
40   judgement doth execute.

Psalm 114

When Israel did depart th'Egyptians from among,
   and Jacob's house from a people that were of a strange tongue,
Judah his holy place, Israel's dominion was.
The sea it saw and fled; Jordan[2] was forced back to pass.
5 The mountains they did leap upwards like unto rams;
   the little hills also they did leap up like unto lambs.
Thou sea what made thee fly? thou Jordan, back to go?
Ye mountains that ye skipped like rams, like lambs ye hills also?

---

2. River in Palestine that empties into the Dead Sea.

Earth at God's presence dread; at Jacob's God's presence;[3]
10   The rock who turns to waters lake, springs he from flint sends thence.[4]

1640

EDMUND WALLER
1606–1687

Song

Go, lovely rose!
Tell her that wastes her time and me
That now she knows,
When I resemble° her to thee,   *liken*
5   How sweet and fair she seems to be.

Tell her that's young,
And shuns to have her graces spied,
That hadst thou sprung
In deserts, where no men abide,
10   Thou must have uncommended died.

Small is the worth
Of beauty from the light retired;
Bid her come forth,
Suffer herself to be desired,
15   And not blush so to be admired.

Then die! that she
The common fate of all things rare
May read in thee;
How small a part of time they share
20   That are so wondrous sweet and fair!

1645

Of the Last Verses in the Book[1]

When we for age could neither read nor write,
The subject made us able to indite;°   *utter; dictate*
The soul, with nobler resolutions decked,
The body stooping, does herself erect.
5   No mortal parts are requisite to raise
Her that, unbodied, can her Maker praise.

---

3. I.e., Earth, dread God's presence, dread the
presence of Jacob's God.
4. I.e., he who turns the rock to standing water

and who sends springs from flint.
1. I.e., his book *Divine Poems*, first published in
1686.

The seas are quiet when the winds give o'er;
So calm are we when passions are no more!
For then we know how vain it was to boast
10 Of fleeting things, so certain to be lost.
Clouds of affection° from our younger eyes   *emotion*
Conceal that emptiness which age descries.°   *discerns*
    The soul's dark cottage, battered and decayed,
Lets in new light through chinks that time has made;
15 Stronger by weakness, wiser men become,
As they draw near to their eternal home.
Leaving the old, both worlds at once they view,
That stand upon the threshold of the new.
                        —*Miratur Limen Olympi*
                        Vergil[2]

                                              1686

JOHN MILTON*
1608–1674

On the Morning of Christ's Nativity[1]

I

This is the month, and this the happy morn,
Wherein the Son of Heaven's Eternal King,
Of wedded maid and virgin mother born,
Our great redemption from above did bring;
5 For so the holy sages[2] once did sing,
    That he our deadly forfeit[3] should release,
And with his Father work us a perpetual peace.

2

That glorious form, that light unsufferable,
And that far-beaming blaze of majesty,
10 Wherewith he wont° at Heaven's high council-table   *was accustomed*
To sit the midst of Trinal Unity,[4]
He laid aside, and, here with us to be,
    Forsook the courts of everlasting day,
And chose with us a darksome house of mortal clay.[5]

2. From a sentence in Virgil's Fifth Eclogue that reads, in translation, "Arrayed in dazzling white, he stands *enraptured at heaven's unfamiliar threshold.*" Through this Latin quotation, Waller gives the last words in his poem about his "divine poems" to a pagan author. Many Christian writers, most notably Dante, viewed Virgil as a precursor of Christianity, one who stood on its threshold without being able to enter.
*We have placed Milton's early works in the order of his *Poems* (1645), a carefully arranged collection that included poetry in English, Latin, and Italian and represented a key statement about his "career" to that point. For his later works, we follow the order of Milton's 1673 volume.

1. This poem celebrates Christ's birth and Milton's symbolic birth as a Christian poet bending classical forms such as the ode to new religious purposes. Milton portrays the triumph of the infant Christ over pagan gods, a theme of interest to both Catholics and Protestants of the early seventeenth century.
2. I.e., the Hebrew prophets.
3. The penalty of death, occasioned by the sin of Adam.
4. The Trinity: Father, Son, and Holy Ghost.
5. I.e., a human body.

3

15 Say, Heavenly Muse,[6] shall not thy sacred vein
Afford a present to the Infant God?
Hast thou no verse, no hymn, or solemn strain,
To welcome him to this his new abode,
Now while the heaven, by the Sun's team untrod,[7]
20   Hath took no print of the approaching light,
And all the spangled host[8] keep watch in squadrons bright?

4

See how from far upon the eastern road
The star-led wizards[9] haste with odors sweet!
Oh run, prevent° them with thy humble ode,[1]   go before
25 And lay it lowly at his blessèd feet;
Have thou the honor first thy Lord to greet,
    And join thy voice unto the angel choir
From out his secret altar touched with hallowed fire.[2]

The Hymn

1

    It was the winter wild,
30   While the heaven-born child
All meanly wrapt in the rude manger lies;
    Nature, in awe to him,
    Had doffed° her gaudy trim,   taken off
With her great Master so to sympathize:
35 It was no season then for her
To wanton with the Sun, her lusty paramour.°   beloved, lover

2

    Only with speeches fair
She woos the gentle air
To hide her guilty front with innocent snow,
40   And on her naked shame,
    Pollute with sinful blame,
The saintly veil of maiden white to throw;
Confounded, that her Maker's eyes
Should look so near upon her foul deformities.[3]

---

6. Perhaps a reference to Urania, the Muse of astronomy, later identified in Milton's epic poem *Paradise Lost* (line 6; see p. 421) with divine wisdom and treated by Milton as the source of creative inspiration. In Greek mythology, the Muses were nine sister goddesses believed to be sources of inspiration for the arts.
7. A reference to Apollo, Greek god of the sun, who drove the chariot of the sun behind mighty steeds (the "Sun's team").
8. An armed multitude (i.e., the angels).
9. The "wise men from the east" (Matthew 2.1), who brought gifts of gold, myrrh, and frankincense ("odors sweet").
1. A rhymed lyric, generally dignified or lofty in subject and style.
2. Cf. Isaiah 6.6–7, in which a seraph touches a prophet's lips with a burning coal from the altar.
3. Personifying Nature as a woman "polluted" by the Fall, Milton also portrays her as a hypocrite covering her foulness with a "saintly" white veil; he draws on Spenser's depiction of the witch Duessa stripped "naked" in "shame" (*Faerie Queene* 1.8.46–48) and on the Bible's whore of Babylon (Revelation 17.6). See also the portrait of "foul" sin in *Paradise Lost* 2.650–51.

3

45   But he, her fears to cease,
        Sent down the meek-eyed Peace:
She, crowned with olive green, came softly sliding
      Down through the turning sphere,[4]
      His ready harbinger,
50   With turtle[5] wing the amorous clouds dividing;
And, waving wide her myrtle wand,
She strikes a universal peace through sea and land.

4

No war, or battle's sound,
Was heard the world around;
55   The idle spear and shield were high uphung;
      The hookèd chariot[6] stood,
      Unstained with hostile blood;
The trumpet spake not to the armèd throng;
And kings sat still with awful eye,[7]
60   As if they surely knew their sovran Lord was by.

5

But peaceful was the night
Wherein the Prince of Light
His reign of peace upon the earth began.
The winds, with wonder whist,°   *hushed*
65   Smoothly the waters kissed,
Whispering new joys to the mild Ocean,
Who now hath quite forgot to rave,
While birds of calm[8] sit brooding on the charmèd wave.

6

The stars, with deep amaze,°   *amazement*
70   Stand fixed in steadfast gaze,
Bending one way their precious influence,[9]
      And will not take their flight,
      For all the morning light,
Or Lucifer[1] that often warned them thence;
75   But in their glimmering orbs[2] did glow,
Until their Lord himself bespake, and bid them go.

7

And, though the shady gloom
Had given day her room,

---

4. According to Ptolemaic astronomy, the heavenly spheres revolving around Earth.
5. Turtledove; an emblem of Venus, Roman goddess of love and beauty, as the olive crown is an emblem of Peace. *Harbinger:* one who prepares the way, or makes an announcement.
6. War chariots were sometimes armed with sicklelike hooks projecting from the hubs of the wheels.
7. I.e., with a look full of awe and reverence.
8. Halcyons, or kingfishers, which in ancient times were believed to build floating nests at sea

about the time of the winter solstice, and to calm the waves during the incubation of their young.
9. Medieval astrologers believed that stars emitted an ethereal liquid ("influence") that had the power to nourish or otherwise affect all things on Earth.
1. Light-bearer (Latin); a name for the morning star and also for Satan.
2. The concentric crystalline spheres of Ptolemaic astronomy; each sphere was supposed to contain one or more of the heavenly bodies in its surface and to revolve about Earth, creating beautiful music.

The Sun himself withheld his wonted° speed,   *usual*
80 And hid his head for shame,
   As° his inferior flame   *as if*
  The new-enlightened world no more should need:
  He saw a greater Sun appear
  Than his bright throne or burning axletree³ could bear.

8

85 The shepherds on the lawn,°   *meadow*
   Or ere the point of dawn,
  Sat simply chatting in a rustic row;
    Full little thought they than°   *then*
    That the mighty Pan⁴
90 Was kindly come to live with them below:
  Perhaps their loves, or else their sheep,
  Was all that did their silly° thoughts so busy keep. *simple*

9

   When such music sweet
   Their hearts and ears did greet
95 As never was by mortal finger strook,°   *struck*
    Divinely-warbled voice
    Answering the stringèd noise,
  As all their souls in blissful rapture took:
  The air, such pleasure loth to lose,
100 With thousand echoes still prolongs each heavenly close.° *cadence*

10

   Nature, that heard such sound
   Beneath the hollow round
  Of Cynthia's seat⁵ the airy region thrilling,
    Now was almost won
105   To think her part was done,
  And that her reign had here its last fulfilling:
  She knew such harmony alone
  Could hold all Heaven and Earth in happier uniòn.

11

   At last surrounds their sight
110   A globe of circular light,
  That with long beams the shamefaced Night arrayed;
    The helmèd cherubim
    And sworded seraphim⁶
  Are seen in glittering ranks with wings displayed,
115 Harping loud and solemn quire,°   *choir*
  With unexpressive° notes, to Heaven's new-born Heir. *inexpressible*

---

3. I.e., the sun's chariot. "Sun" includes the familiar *Son/sun* pun.
4. The Greek god of shepherds, whose name means "all," was often associated with Christ in Renaissance poetry.

5. I.e., beneath the sphere of the moon.
6. Seraphim and cherubim (both are plural forms) are the two highest of the nine orders of angels in the medieval classification.

12

Such music (as 'tis said)
Before was never made,
But when of old the sons of morning sung,[7]
120   While the Creator great
    His constellations set,
And the well-balanced world on hinges° hung,   *the two poles*
And cast the dark foundations deep,
And bid the weltering waves their oozy channel keep.

13

125   Ring out, ye crystal spheres,[8]
    Once bless our human ears,
If ye have power to touch our senses so;
    And let your silver chime
    Move in melodious time;
130   And let the bass of heaven's deep organ blow;
And with your ninefold harmony
Make up full consort° to th' angelic symphony.   *accord; mate*

14

    For, if such holy song
    Enwrap our fancy long,
135   Time will run back and fetch the age of gold;[9]
    And speckled vanity
    Will sicken soon and die;
And leprous sin will melt from earthly mold;[1]
And Hell itself will pass away,
140 And leave her dolorous mansions to the peering day.

15

    Yea, Truth and Justice then
    Will down return to men,
Orbed in a rainbow; and, like° glories wearing,   *similar*
    Mercy will sit between,
145   Throned in celestial sheen,[2]
With radiant feet the tissued[3] clouds down steering;
And Heaven, as at some festival,
Will open wide the gates of her high palace-hall.

---

7. Job speaks of the creation of the universe as the time "when the morning stars sang together, and all the sons of God shouted for joy" (Job 38.7).
8. A reference to the Pythagorean idea that the music of the spheres would be audible only to sinless humans (see note 2 above).
9. According to Roman mythology, Saturn, after his dethronement by Jupiter, fled to Italy and there brought in the Golden Age, a time of perfect peace and happiness. The idea of a "return" to the Golden Age, here and in line 142, alludes to the myth of Astraea, goddess of justice, who fled "unjust" Earth but came back as a virgin celebrated

by Virgil (*Eclogues* 4) in a passage many Christians read as an allegorical prophecy of Christ's birth from the Virgin Mary.
1. I.e., Earth; also, mortal humans. *Leprous sin:* i.e., sin that is like the loathsome disease leprosy.
2. This allegorical scene recalls Psalm 85.10–11 ("Mercy and Truth are met together; righteousness and peace have kissed each other"), which was part of the Christmas liturgy. Milton may also allude to depictions of the "four daughters of God" (among whom was Peace, who descends in lines 45–52) in morality plays, paintings, and masques.
3. I.e., like a cloth woven with silver and gold.

16

But wisest Fate says no,
150   This must not yet be so;
The Babe lies yet in smiling infancy
That on the bitter cross
Must redeem our loss,
So both himself and us to glorify:
155 Yet first, to those ychained in sleep,[4]
The wakeful° trump of doom must thunder through   *awakening*
    the deep,

17

With such a horrid clang
As on Mount Sinai rang,[5]
While the red fire and smoldering clouds outbrake:
160   The aged Earth, aghast,
With terror of that blast,
Shall from the surface to the center shake,
When, at the world's last sessiòn,
The dreadful Judge in middle air shall spread his throne.

18

165   And then at last our bliss
Full and perfect is,
But now begins; for from this happy day
Th' old Dragon° under ground,   *Satan*
In straiter limits bound,
170   Not half so far casts his usurpèd sway,
And, wroth to see his kingdom fail,
Swinges° the scaly horror of his folded tail.   *lashes*

19

The Oracles are dumb;[6]
No voice or hideous hum
175   Runs through the archèd roof in words deceiving.
Apollo from his shrine
Can no more divine,
With hollow shriek the steep of Delphos leaving.
No nightly trance, or breathèd spell,
180 Inspires the pale-eyed priest from the prophetic cell.

20

The lonely mountains o'er,
And the resounding shore,
A voice of weeping heard and loud lament;
From haunted spring, and dale
185   Edged with poplar pale,

4. I.e., death. *Ychained:* an archaic form recalling Chaucer and Spenser. Lines 155–64 allude to the Apocalypse as described in Revelation.
5. Moses received the Ten Commandments on Mount Sinai: "there were thunders and lightnings

. . . and the voice of the trumpet exceeding loud" (Exodus 19.16).
6. According to one ancient belief, pagan oracles ended with Christ's birth; according to another, the pagan gods became fallen angels.

The parting genius° is with sighing sent;   *local spirit*
With flower-inwoven tresses torn
The Nymphs[7] in twilight shade of tangled thickets mourn.

21

          In consecrated earth,
190   And on the holy hearth,
          The Lars and Lemures[8] moan with midnight plaint;
          In urns and altars round,
          A drear and dying sound
          Affrights the flamens° at their service quaint;°   *priests / elaborate*
195 And the chill marble seems to sweat,
      While each peculiar power forgoes his wonted° seat.   *usual*

22

          Peor[9] and Baalim
          Forsake their temples dim,
          With that twice-battered God of Palestine;[1]
200   And moonèd Ashtaroth,[2]
          Heaven's queen and mother both,
          Now sits not girt° with tapers'° holy shine: *encircled / candles'*
      The Libyc Hammon[3] shrinks his horn;
      In vain the Tyrian maids their wounded Thammuz mourn.[4]

23

205   And sullen Moloch,[5] fled,
          Hath left in shadows dread
          His burning idol all of blackest hue;
          In vain with cymbals' ring
          They call the grisly king,
210   In dismal dance about the furnace blue;
      The brutish gods of Nile as fast,
      Isis, and Orus, and the dog Anubis, haste.[6]

24

          Nor is Osiris seen
          In Memphian grove or green,
215   Trampling the unshowered grass[7] with lowings loud;
          Nor can he be at rest
          Within his sacred chest;
      Nought but profoundest Hell can be his shroud;

7. Mythological female spirits inhabiting a particular place, object, or natural phenomenon.
8. Hostile spirits of the unburied dead. *Lars:* tutelary gods or spirits of the ancient Romans, associated with particular places.
9. Baal, or Baal-Peor, the highest Canaanite god, whose shrine was at Mt. Peor. Baalim (the plural form) were lesser gods related to him.
1. Dagon, god of the Philistines, whose statue twice fell to the ground before the ark of the Lord (1 Samuel 5.1–4).
2. Astarte, a Phoenician fertility goddess identified with the moon.
3. The Egyptian god Ammon, represented as a horned ram. He had a famous temple and oracle

at an oasis in the Libyan desert.
4. The death of the god Thammuz, Ashtaroth's lover, symbolized the coming of winter. The Tyrian (Phoenician) women mourned for him in an annual ceremony.
5. A Phoenician fire god to whom children were sacrificed. Their cries were drowned out by the clang of cymbals.
6. The Egyptian goddess Isis was represented as a cow, the gods Orus and Anubis as a hawk and a dog (hence "brutish"). Osiris (line 213) the creator, who had a shrine at Memphis, was represented as a bull. *As fast:* i.e., hasten away as fast as Moloch fled.
7. I.e., the rainless Egyptian landscape.

In vain, with timbreled° anthems dark,   *tambourine-backed*
220 The sable-stolèd sorcerers bear his worshipped ark.

25

He feels from Juda's land
The dreaded Infant's hand;[8]
The rays of Bethlehem blind his dusky eyn;°   *eyes*
Nor all the gods beside
225 Longer dare abide,
Not Typhon[9] huge ending in snaky twine:
Our Babe, to show his Godhead true,
Can in his swaddling° bands control the damnèd crew.   *binding*

26

So, when the sun in bed,
230 Curtained with cloudy red,
Pillows his chin upon an orient° wave,   *Eastern; bright*
The flocking shadows pale
Troop to th' infernal[1] jail;
Each fettered ghost slips to his several° grave,   *separate*
235 And the yellow-skirted fays°   *fairies*
Fly after the night-steeds, leaving their moon-loved maze.[2]

27

But see! the Virgin blest
Hath laid her Babe to rest.
Time is our tedious song should here have ending:
240 Heaven's youngest-teemèd star[3]
Hath fixed her polished car,
Her sleeping Lord with handmaid lamp attending;
And all about the courtly stable
Bright-harnessed[4] angels sit in order serviceable.

1629   1645

On Shakespeare[5]

What needs my Shakespeare for his honored bones
The labor of an age in pilèd stones?
Or that his hallowed reliques should be hid
Under a star-ypointing[6] pyramid?
5 Dear son of Memory,[7] great heir of Fame,

8. I.e., the hand of Christ, who was descended from the tribe of Judah. Perhaps an allusion to Matthew 2.6, referring to Micah 5.2, on the power resident in Bethlehem, in the land of Judah.
9. In Greek mythology, a hundred-headed monster destroyed by Zeus.
1. Of the realm of the dead; i.e., hell(ish).
2. Labyrinth, i.e., the woods where the fairies dance.
3. I.e., newest-born star, the star that guided the wise men, now imagined as having halted its "car" or chariot over the manger.

4. I.e., clad in bright armor. *Courtly:* i.e., because it houses Christ, the king.
5. Milton's first published poem, printed in the Second Folio of Shakespeare's plays (1632) as "An Epitaph on the Admirable Dramatic Poet W. Shakespear."
6. An archaic form recalling Chaucer and Spenser.
7. In Greek mythology, Memory (Mnemosyne) was the mother of the Muses, the nine sister goddesses believed to be sources of inspiration for the arts.

What need'st thou such weak witness of thy name?
Thou in our wonder and astonishment
Hast built thyself a livelong monument.
For whilst, to th' shame of slow-endeavoring art,
10   Thy easy numbers° flow, and that each heart   *verses*
Hath from the leaves of thy unvalued° book   *invaluable*
Those Delphic[8] lines with deep impression took,
Then thou, our fancy of itself bereaving,
Dost make us marble with too much conceiving,
15   And so sepùlchred in such pomp dost lie
That kings for such a tomb would wish to die.

1630   1645

L'Allegro[9]

Hence loathèd Melancholy[1]
   Of Cerberus[2] and blackest midnight born,
In Stygian[3] cave forlorn
   'Mongst horrid shapes, and shrieks, and sights unholy,
5   Find out some uncouth[4] cell,
   Where brooding Darkness spreads his jealous wings,
And the night-raven sings;
   There under ebon° shades, and low-browed rocks,   *black*
As ragged as thy locks,
10   In dark Cimmerian[5] desert ever dwell.
But come thou goddess fair and free,
In Heaven yclept° Euphrosyne,[6]   *called*
And by men, heart-easing Mirth,
Whom lovely Venus° at a birth   *goddess of love and beauty*
15   With two sister Graces° more   *Aglaia and Thalia*
To ivy-crownèd Bacchus° bore;   *god of wine*
Or whether (as some sager sing)[7]
The frolic wind that breathes the spring,
Zephyr with Aurora playing,
20   As he met her once a-Maying,
There on beds of violets blue,
And fresh-blown° roses washed in dew,   *newly bloomed*
Filled her with thee a daughter fair,
So buxom,° blithe, and debonair.°   *merry / pleasant*

8. Pertaining to Apollo, god of poetry, who had an oracle at Delphi.
9. "L'Allegro" (Italian, "the happy man") is a companion poem to "Il Penseroso" ("the pensive man"). Probably written late in Milton's years at Cambridge, the poems influenced many later poets and were illustrated by William Blake (1757–1827).
1. Thought to arise from an excess of black bile, melancholy was a physiological condition that could lead to depression and madness. *Hence:* a command to depart.
2. In Greek mythology, the three-headed dog that guarded the gates of hell.
3. Pertaining to the Styx, one of the rivers of the classical underworld.
4. Unknown and dreadful.
5. According to Homer's *Odyssey*, the Cimmerians lived in a mysterious land somewhere across the ocean, where the sun never shone.
6. One of the three Graces, Greek sister goddesses believed to bring joy to humans. Her name means "mirth."
7. The following mythical account of Euphrosyne's birth seems to be Milton's invention. Zephyr is the west wind; Aurora, the dawn.

25   Haste thee nymph,° and bring with thee   *nature goddess*
     Jest and youthful Jollity,
     Quips and Cranks,° and wanton Wiles,   *jests*
     Nods, and Becks,° and wreathèd Smiles,   *beckonings*
     Such as hang on Hebe's[8] cheek,
30   And love to live in dimple sleek;
     Sport that wrinkled Care derides,
     And Laughter, holding both his sides.
     Come, and trip° it as ye go   *dance*
     On the light fantastic toe,
35   And in thy right hand lead with thee,
     The mountain nymph, sweet Liberty;
     And if I give thee honor due,
     Mirth, admit me of thy crew
     To live with her and live with thee,
40   In unreprovèd° pleasures free;   *unblamed*
     To hear the lark[9] begin his flight,
     And, singing, startle the dull night,
     From his watch-tower in the skies,
     Till the dappled dawn doth rise;
45   Then to come in spite° of sorrow,   *contempt*
     And at my window bid good morrow,
     Through the sweetbriar, or the vine,
     Or the twisted eglantine.[1]
     While the cock with lively din,
50   Scatters the rear of darkness thin,
     And to the stack, or the barn door,
     Stoutly struts his dames before;
     Oft listening how the hounds and horn
     Cheerly rouse the slumbering morn,
55   From the side of some hoar[2] hill,
     Through the high wood echoing shrill.
     Sometime walking not unseen
     By hedgerow elms, on hillocks green,
     Right against the eastern gate,
60   Where the great sun begins his state,°   *progress*
     Robed in flames, and amber light,
     The clouds in thousand liveries dight;°   *dressed*
     While the plowman near at hand,
     Whistles o'er the furrowed land,
65   And the milkmaid singeth blithe,
     And the mower whets his scythe,
     And every shepherd tells his tale,
     Under the hawthorn in the dale.
     Straight mine eye hath caught new pleasures
70   Whilst the landscape round it measures,
     Russet° lawns and fallows° gray,   *reddish brown / plowed land*
     Where the nibbling flocks do stray,
     Mountains on whose barren breast

---

8. Zeus's cupbearer and goddess of youth.
9. Larks sing at sunrise.
1. The sweetbriar, possibly used here to mean the honeysuckle.
2. Grayish white, perhaps because of a morning frost.

The laboring clouds do often rest;
75 Meadows trim with daisies pied,°   *variegated*
    Shallow brooks, and rivers wide.
    Towers and battlements it sees
    Bosomed high in tufted trees,
    Where perhaps some beauty lies,
80 The cynosure³ of neighboring eyes.
    Hard by, a cottage chimney smokes,
    From betwixt two aged oaks,
    Where Corydon and Thyrsis⁴ met,
    Are at their savory dinner set
85 Of herbs, and other country messes,°   *dishes*
    Which the neat-handed° Phyllis dresses;°   *dexterous / prepares*
    And then in haste her bower she leaves,
    With Thestylis to bind the sheaves;
    Or if the earlier season lead
90 To the tanned haycock in the mead.⁵
    Sometimes with secure° delight   *carefree*
    The upland hamlets will invite,
    When the merry bells ring round
    And the jocund° rebecks⁶ sound   *merry*
95 To many a youth and many a maid,
    Dancing in the checkered shade;
    And young and old come forth to play
    On a sunshine holiday,
    Till the livelong daylight fail;
100 Then to the spicy nut-brown ale,
    With stories told of many a feat,
    How fairy Mab the junkets eat;⁷
    She was pinched and pulled, she said,
    And he, by Friar's lantern⁸ led,
105 Tells how the drudging goblin⁹ sweat
    To earn his cream-bowl, duly set,
    When in one night, ere glimpse of morn,
    His shadowy flail hath threshed the corn
    That ten day-laborers could not end;
110 Then lies him down the lubber° fiend,   *loutish*
    And, stretched out all the chimney's° length,   *fireplace's*
    Basks at the fire his hairy strength;
    And crop-full out of doors he flings
    Ere the first cock his matin° rings.   *morning*
115 Thus done the tales, to bed they creep,
    By whispering winds soon lulled asleep.
    Towered cities please us then,
    And the busy hum of men,

3. The North Star, or anything that attracts attention.
4. Conventional male names in pastoral poetry, like Thestylis (line 88); Phyllis (line 86) is a conventional female pastoral name.
5. I.e., the sun-dried, conical heap of hay in the field.
6. Small, three-stringed fiddles.
7. I.e., Mab, queen of the fairies, ate the delicacies ("junkets"). The behavior attributed to fairies here and in the following lines reflects traditional rustic lore.
8. The will-o'-the-wisp, which was said to draw travelers astray by holding a false light before them; the phenomenon of nocturnal light is caused by the combustion of marsh gas.
9. A hobgoblin, also known as Robin Goodfellow or Puck, was a small supernatural creature popular in northern-European folk traditions. He is an important character in Shakespeare's *A Midsummer Night's Dream*, a play that "L'Allegro" frequently echoes.

Where throngs of knights and barons bold,
120 In weeds° of peace high triumphs° hold,   *garments / pageants*
With store° of ladies, whose bright eyes   *plenty*
Rain influence,¹ and judge the prize
Of wit, or arms, while both contend
To win her grace, whom all commend.
125 There let Hymen° oft appear   *god of marriage*
In saffron° robe, with taper° clear,   *orange-yellow / torch*
And pomp, and feast, and revelry,
With masque, and antique² pageantry;
Such sights as youthful poets dream
130 On summer eves by haunted stream.
Then to the well-trod stage anon,
If Jonson's learnèd sock³ be on,
Or sweetest Shakespeare, fancy's child,
Warble his native wood-notes wild.
135 And ever against eating cares
Lap me in soft Lydian airs⁴
Married to immortal verse
Such as the meeting soul may pierce
In notes, with many a winding bout°   *turn*
140 Of linkèd sweetness long drawn out,
With wanton heed, and giddy cunning,
The melting voice through mazes running;
Untwisting all the chains that tie
The hidden soul of harmony;
145 That Orpheus' self⁵ may heave his head
From golden slumber on a bed
Of heaped Elysian° flowers, and hear   *glorious*
Such strains as would have won the ear
Of Pluto, to have quite set free
150 His half-regained Eurydice.
These delights if thou canst give,
Mirth, with thee I mean to live.⁶

ca. 1631   1645

Il Penseroso⁷

Hence⁸ vain deluding Joys,
The brood of Folly without father bred.

1. The ladies' eyes are compared to stars, alluding to the medieval idea that the stars emitted an ethereal liquid ("influence") that could powerfully affect human lives.
2. Ancient; also, antic. *Masque*: an elaborate form of court entertainment, in which aristocrats performed in a dignified play, usually allegorical and mythological, that ended in a formal dance.
3. The light shoe worn by Greek comic actors, here standing for the comedies of Ben Jonson (1572–1637).
4. Lydian music was noted for its voluptuous sweetness.
5. The great poet and musician of classical

mythology, whose wife, Eurydice, died on their wedding day. He won permission from Pluto, god of the underworld, to lead her back to the land of the living, but only on the condition that he not look to see if she was following him. Unable to resist a backward glance, he lost her forever.
6. Lines 151–52 echo Christopher Marlowe, "The Passionate Shepherd to His Love," lines 23–24 (see p. 256).
7. See "L'Allegro," note 9 (p. 402). Here, the Pensive Man celebrates a melancholy that produces not depression and madness but the scholarly temperament, ruled by the Roman god Saturn.
8. A command to depart.

How little you bestead,°   *profit*
   Or fill the fixèd mind with all your toys;°   *trifles*
5 Dwell in some idle brain,
   And fancies fond° with gaudy shapes possess,   *foolish*
As thick and numberless
   As the gay motes° that people the sunbeams,   *specks*
Or likest hovering dreams,
10   The fickle pensioners° of Morpheus'⁹ train.   *attendants*
But hail thou Goddess, sage and holy,
Hail, divinest Melancholy,
Whose saintly visage is too bright
To hit° the sense of human sight;   *affect*
15 And therefore to our weaker view,
O'erlaid with black, staid Wisdom's hue.
Black, but such as in esteem,
Prince Memnon's sister¹ might beseem,
Or that starred Ethiope queen² that strove
20 To set her beauty's praise above
The sea nymphs, and their powers offended.
Yet thou art higher far descended;
Thee bright-haired Vesta long of yore
To solitary Saturn bore;³
25 His daughter she (in Saturn's reign
Such mixture was not held a stain).
Oft in glimmering bowers and glades
He met her, and in secret shades
Of woody Ida's inmost grove,
30 While yet there was no fear of Jove.⁴
Come pensive nun, devout and pure,
Sober, steadfast, and demure,
All in a robe of darkest grain,°   *color*
Flowing with majestic train,
35 And sable° stole of cypress lawn⁵   *black*
Over thy decent shoulders drawn.
Come, but keep thy wonted° state,   *usual; wanted*
With even step and musing gait,
And looks commercing with the skies,
40 Thy rapt soul sitting in thine eyes:
There held in holy passion still,
Forget thyself to marble, till
With a sad° leaden downward cast,   *serious*
Thou fix them on the earth as fast.
45 And join with thee calm Peace and Quiet,
Spare Fast, that oft with gods doth diet,
And hears the Muses⁶ in a ring

9. Greek god of sleep.
1. Memnon, an Ethiopian prince, was called the handsomest of men (Homer's *Odyssey*, book 11). His sister was Hemera, whose name means "day."
2. Cassiopeia, who boasted that her beauty (or her daughter's, in some accounts) surpassed that of the daughters of the sea god Nereus. "Starred" refers to the fact that a constellation bears her name.
3. The parentage here attributed to Melancholy is Milton's invention. Saturn, who ruled on Mt. Ida before being overthrown by his son Jove, was asso-
ciated with melancholy because of the supposedly "saturnine" influence of the planet that bears his name. His daughter Vesta was the goddess of purity.
4. The most powerful god of Roman mythology.
5. A gauzy, crepelike material, usually dyed black and used for mourning garments; *cypress:* Cyprus, where the material was originally made.
6. The nine sister goddesses believed to be sources of inspiration for the arts; at the foot of Mt. Helicon, they danced about the altar of Jove.

Aye° round about Jove's altar sing.   *continually*
And add to these retired Leisure,
50   That in trim gardens takes his pleasure;
But first, and chiefest, with thee bring,
Him that yon soars on golden wing,
Guiding the fiery-wheelèd throne,
The cherub Contemplation;[7]
55   And the mute Silence hist° along   *beckon*
'Less Philomel[8] will deign a song,
In her sweetest, saddest plight,
Smoothing the rugged brow of night,
While Cynthia[9] checks her dragon yoke
60   Gently o'er th' accustomed oak;
Sweet bird that shunn'st the noise of folly,
Most musical, most melancholy!
Thee chantress oft the woods among,
I woo to hear thy evensong;[1]
65   And missing thee, I walk unseen
On the dry smooth-shaven green,
To behold the wandering moon,
Riding near her highest noon,
Like one that had been led astray
70   Through the Heaven's wide pathless way;
And oft as if her head she bowed,
Stooping through a fleecy cloud.
Oft on a plat° of rising ground,   *plot*
I hear the far-off curfew sound,[2]
75   Over some wide-watered shore,
Swinging slow with sullen roar;
Or if the air will not permit,
Some still removèd place will fit,
Where glowing embers through the room
80   Teach light to counterfeit a gloom
Far from all resort of mirth,
Save the cricket on the hearth,
Or the bellman's° drowsy charm,   *night watchman's*
To bless the doors from nightly harm;
85   Or let my lamp at midnight hour
Be seen in some high lonely tower,
Where I may oft outwatch the Bear,[3]
With thrice great Hermes, or unsphere[4]

7. A reference to the vision of the four cherubim (a high order of angels) stationed beside four wheels of fire under the throne of the Lord (Ezekiel 1 and 10).
8. I.e., or else Philomel will condescend to sing a song. Philomel, the nightingale, who sings a mournful song in the springtime: according to Ovid's version of this popular myth, Philomela was raped by her brother-in-law, Tereus, who then tore out her tongue so that she could not speak. She wove the story in a tapestry and sent it to her sister, who rescued her. She was later changed into a nightingale while in flight from Tereus.
9. Goddess of the moon, sometimes represented as driving a team of dragons.
1. The evening liturgy traditionally sung by clois-

tered monks and nuns (here, a "chantress"). Cf. "L'Allegro," line 114, where a cock announces "matins," the morning liturgy.
2. The customary ringing of a bell at a fixed hour in the evening.
3. The Great Bear, or Big Dipper, which in northern latitudes never sets.
4. To call Plato back, by magic, from whatever sphere of the universe he inhabits now, or, in practical terms, to read his books. "Thrice great Hermes" refers to an ancient Egyptian philosopher (Hermes Trismegistus) often identified with Thoth, Egyptian god of wisdom, and alleged to have written many books on astrological, alchemical, and other subjects.

The spirit of Plato to unfold
90 What worlds, or what vast regions hold
The immortal mind that hath forsook
Her mansion in this fleshly nook;
And of those demons⁵ that are found
In fire, air, flood, or underground,
95 Whose power hath a true consent°   *correspondence*
With planet, or with element.
Some time let gorgeous Tragedy
In sceptered° pall° come sweeping by,   *royal / robe*
Presenting Thebes, or Pelops' line,
100 Or the tale of Troy divine.⁶
Or what (though rare) of later age
Ennobled hath the buskined stage.⁷
But, O sad virgin, that thy power
Might raise Musaeus⁸ from his bower,
105 Or bid the soul of Orpheus sing
Such notes as, warbled to the string,
Drew iron tears down Pluto's cheek,
And made Hell grant what Love did seek.
Or call up him⁹ that left half told
110 The story of Cambuscan bold,
Of Camball, and of Algarsife,
And who had Canacee to wife,
That owned the virtuous° ring and glass,°   *potent / mirror*
And of the wondrous horse of brass,
115 On which the Tartar king did ride;
And if aught else great bards beside
In sage and solemn tunes have sung,
Of tourneys and of trophies hung,
Of forests and enchantments drear,
120 Where more is meant than meets the ear.
Thus, Night, oft see me in thy pale career,
Till civil-suited morn¹ appear,
Not tricked° and frounced° as she was   *adorned / curled*
     wont,°   *accustomed to be*
With the Attic boy to hunt,
125 But kerchiefed in a comely cloudly
While rocking winds are piping loud,
Or ushered with a shower still,°   *gentle; yet*
When the gust hath blown his fill,
Ending on the rustling leaves,
130 With minute-drops from off the eaves.

---

5. Supernatural beings inhabiting each of the four "elements": fire, air, water, and earth.
6. The city of Thebes, the descendants of Pelops, and the Trojan War afforded the subjects of most Greek tragedies.
7. The buskin was the high boot worn by Greek tragic actors.
8. A legendary Greek poet, contemporary of Orpheus (line 105); for the story of Orpheus, see "L'Allegro," note 5 (p. 405).

9. Chaucer, whose "Squire's Tale" leaves unfinished the story of the Tartar king Cambuscan, his two sons, Camball and Algarsife, and his daughter, Canacee. At a banquet celebrating Cambuscan's reign, a mysterious guest offered several magical gifts to the king.
1. Aurora, goddess of the dawn, soberly dressed ("civil-suited"); she loved Cephalus ("the Attic boy," line 124).

And when the sun begins to fling
His flaring beams, me, Goddess, bring
To archèd walks of twilight groves,
And shadows brown that Sylvan² loves

135 Of pine or monumental oak,
Where the rude ax with heavèd stroke,
Was never heard the nymphs³ to daunt,
Or fright them from their hallowed haunt.
There in close covert° by some brook,   *hidden place*

140 Where no profaner eye may look,
Hide me from day's garish eye,
While the bee with honeyed thigh,
That at her flowery work doth sing,
And the waters murmuring

145 With such consort° as they keep,   *harmony*
Entice the dewy-feathered sleep;
And let some strange mysterious dream,
Wave at his wings in airy stream,
Of lively portraiture displayed,

150 Softly on my eyelids laid.
And as I wake, sweet music breathe
Above, about, or underneath,
Sent by some spirit to mortals good,
Or th' unseen genius° of the wood.   *indwelling spirit*

155 But let my due feet never fail
To walk the studious cloister's pale,°   *enclosure*
And love the high embowèd roof,
With antic° pillars massy proof,   *fancifully decorated; antique*
And storied windows⁴ richly dight,°   *dressed*

160 Casting a dim religious light.
There let the pealing organ blow,
To the full-voiced choir below,
In service high, and anthems clear,
As may with sweetness, through mine ear,

165 Dissolve me into ecstasies,
And bring all heaven before mine eyes.
And may at last my weary age
Find out the peaceful hermitage,
The hairy gown and mossy cell,

170 Where I may sit and rightly spell°   *speculate*
Of every star that Heaven doth show,
And every herb that sips the dew
Till old experience do attain
To something like prophetic strain.

175 These pleasures, Melancholy, give,
And I with thee will choose to live.⁵

ca. 1631   1645

---

2. Sylvanus, Roman god of forests.
3. Mythological female spirits inhabiting a particular place, object, or natural phenomenon.
4. Stained-glass windows depicting biblical sto-

ries. *Massy proof:* massive solidity.
5. Cf. "L'Allegro," lines 151–52 and note 6 (p. 405).

How Soon Hath Time[6]

How soon hath Time, the subtle thief of youth,
  Stoln on his wing my three and twentieth year!
  My hasting days fly on with full career,
  But my late spring no bud or blossom shew'th.°   *showeth*
5 Perhaps my semblance° might deceive the truth,   *appearance*
  That I to manhood am arrivèd so near,
  And inward ripeness doth much less appear,
  That some more timely-happy spirits endu'th.°   *endoweth*
  Yet be it° less or more, or soon or slow,   *inner "ripeness"*
10 It shall be still in strictest measure even°   *equal; adequate*
  To that same lot, however mean or high,
  Toward which Time leads me, and the will of Heaven;
  All is, if I have grace to use it so,
  As ever in my great Taskmaster's eye.[7]

1631   1645

Lycidas

In This Monody the Author Bewails a Learned Friend,[8] Unfortunately Drowned in His Passage from Chester on the Irish Seas, 1637. And by Occasion Foretells the Ruin of Our Corrupted Clergy, Then in Their Height.

Yet once more, O ye laurels[9] and once more
  Ye myrtles brown,° with ivy never sere,°   *dark / withered*
  I come to pluck your berries harsh and crude,°   *unripe*
  And with forced fingers rude,°   *unskilled*
5 Shatter your leaves before the mellowing year.
  Bitter constraint, and sad occasion dear,°   *heartfelt, dire*
  Compels me to disturb your season due;
  For Lycidas is dead, dead ere his prime,
  Young Lycidas, and hath not left his peer.
10 Who would not sing for Lycidas? He knew
  Himself to sing, and build the lofty rhyme.
  He must not float upon his watery bier[1]
  Unwept, and welter° to the parching wind,   *roll about*
  Without the meed° of some melodious tear.°   *tribute / elegy*
15 Begin then, sisters of the sacred well

6. Milton's twenty-third birthday was on December 9, 1631. He enclosed a copy of this poem in a letter to a friend who, according to Milton, had accused him of dreaming away his "years in the arms of a studious retirement."
7. The metaphor of God as Taskmaster alludes to two parables in which God appears to be harsh to his servants: the parable of the talents (Matthew 25.14–30) and the parable of the vineyard (Matthew 20.1–10).
8. Edward King, a young scholar, poet, and clergyman at Cambridge with Milton. This poem, which draws heavily on pastoral traditions, was first published with some elegies by King's friends at Cambridge in 1638 after King's ship mysteriously foundered on a clear day in August 1637. His body was not recovered. Milton added this headnote when he published the elegy in his 1645 *Poems*. *Monody*: an elegy or dirge sung by a single voice.
9. Laurel, myrtle, and ivy were all traditional materials for garlands bestowed on poets.
1. A stand on which a corpse is carried to the grave.

That from beneath the seat of Jove doth spring,
Begin, and somewhat loudly sweep the string.[2]
Hence with denial vain, and coy excuse;
So may some gentle° Muse°   *kindly / poet*
20 With lucky words favor my destined urn,[3]
And as he passes turn,
And bid fair peace be to my sable° shroud.   *black*
For we were nursed upon the selfsame hill,
Fed the same flock, by fountain, shade, and rill.°   *brook*
25   Together both, ere the high lawns° appeared   *pastures*
Under the opening eyelids of the morn,
We drove afield, and both together heard
What time the grayfly winds her sultry horn,[4]
Battening° our flocks with the fresh dews of night,   *fattening*
30 Oft till the star that rose at evening bright[5]
Toward Heaven's descent had sloped his westering wheel.
Meanwhile the rural ditties were not mute,
Tempered to th' oaten flute,[6]
Rough satyrs danced, and fauns with cloven heel[7]
35 From the glad sound would not be absent long,
And old Damoetas[8] loved to hear our song.
    But O the heavy change, now thou art gone,
Now thou art gone, and never must return!
Thee, shepherd,[9] thee the woods and desert caves,
40 With wild thyme and the gadding° vine o'ergrown,   *wandering*
And all their echoes mourn.
The willows and the hazel copses° green   *groves*
Shall now no more be seen,
Fanning their joyous leaves to thy soft lays.°   *songs*
45 As killing as the canker° to the rose,   *cankerworm*
Or taint-worm to the weanling herds that graze,
Or frost to flowers that their gay wardrobe wear,
When first the white thorn blows;°   *blooms*
Such, Lycidas, thy loss to shepherd's ear.
50   Where were ye, nymphs,[1] when the remorseless deep
Closed o'er the head of your loved Lycidas?
For neither were ye playing on the steep,
Where your old Bards, the famous Druids lie,
Nor on the shaggy top of Mona high,
55 Nor yet where Deva spreads her wizard stream:[2]
Ay me! I fondly° dream—   *foolishly*

2. I.e., play your music. *Sisters of the sacred well:* the Muses, nine Greek sister goddesses believed to be sources of inspiration for the arts and goddesses of song; the well sacred to them was Aganippe, at the foot of Mt. Helicon, where they danced about the altar of Jove (Greek Zeus), the supreme god.
3. I.e., place of burial.
4. I.e., the insect hum of midday, as the grayfly blows ("winds") her horn in the ("sultry") heat of day.
5. I.e., Hesperus, the evening star.
6. Panpipes, traditionally played by shepherds in pastoral.
7. In Roman mythology, the half-goat, half-man woodland gods associated with lust and drinking

(although the fauns were sometimes described as less wild than the satyrs).
8. A conventional pastoral name, here perhaps referring to one of the tutors at Cambridge.
9. I.e., Lycidas.
1. Mythological female spirits inhabiting a particular place, object, or natural phenomenon.
2. The "steep" is probably the mountain Kerig-y-Druidion, a burial ground in northern Wales for the Druids, priestly poet-kings of Celtic Britain. Mona is the Isle of Anglesey, Deva the river Dee, called "wizard" because its changes of course were supposed to foretell the country's fortune. All three places are just south of that part of the Irish Sea where King drowned.

Had ye been there—for what could that have done?
What could the Muse[3] herself that Orpheus bore,
The Muse herself, for her inchanting son
60   Whom universal Nature did lament,
When by the rout that made the hideous roar,
His gory visage° down the stream was sent,   *face*
Down the swift Hebrus to the Lesbian shore?
Alas! What boots° it with uncessant care   *profits*
65   To tend the homely slighted shepherd's trade,
And strictly meditate the thankless Muse?[4]
Were it not better done as others use,
To sport with Amaryllis[5] in the shade,
Or with the tangles of Neaera's hair?
70   Fame is the spur that the clear spirit doth raise
(That last infirmity of noble mind)
To scorn delights, and live laborious days;[6]
But the fair guerdon° when we hope to find,   *reward*
And think to burst out into sudden blaze,
75   Comes the blind Fury[7] with th' abhorrèd shears,
And slits the thin spun life. "But not the praise,"
Phoebus[8] replied, and touched my trembling ears;
"Fame is no plant that grows on mortal soil,
Nor in the glistering foil[9]
80   Set off to th' world, nor in broad rumor lies,
But lives and spreads aloft by those pure eyes,
And perfect witness of all-judging Jove;
As he pronounces lastly on each deed,
Of so much fame in Heaven expect thy meed."°   *reward*
85   O fountain Arethuse,[1] and thou honored flood,
Smooth-sliding Mincius, crowned with vocal reeds,
That strain I heard was of a higher mood.
But now my oat° proceeds,   *oaten pipe; song*
And listens to the herald of the sea
90   That came in Neptune's plea.[2]
He asked the waves, and asked the felon° winds,   *savage*
"What hard mishap hath doomed this gentle swain?"°   *rustic fellow*
And questioned every gust of rugged° wings   *stormy*
That blows from off each beakèd promontory;
95   They knew not of his story,
And sage Hippotades[3] their answer brings,
That not a blast was from his dungeon strayed,

3. Calliope, the Muse of epic poetry. Her son, Orpheus, the greatest of all poets and musicians, was torn limb from limb by a band of Thracian Maenads, who flung his head into the river Hebrus, whence it drifted across the Aegean to the island of Lesbos.
4. I.e., do a poet's work.
5. A conventional pastoral name for a woman, like Neaera in the next line.
6. I.e., fame is an incentive to virtue and hard work.
7. Atropos, the third of the three classical goddesses called the Fates; she cut the thread of a person's life after it had been spun and measured by her sisters.
8. Phoebus Apollo, god of poetic inspiration, who plucked Virgil's ears as a warning against impatient ambition (see Virgil's *Eclogues* 6.3–4).
9. The setting for a gem, especially one that enhances the appearance of an inferior or false stone.
1. A fountain in Sicily, associated with the pastoral poems of the Greek poet Theocritus (ca. 310–250 B.C.E.). The Mincius (next line) is a river in Italy described in one of Virgil's pastorals.
2. The merman Triton comes to plead that his master, Neptune, is innocent of Lycidas's death.
3. Aeolus, son of Hippotas and god of the winds.

The air was calm, and on the level brine,[4]
Sleek Panope[5] with all her sisters played.
100 It was that fatal and perfidious bark[6]
Built in th' eclipse, and rigged with curses dark,[7]
That sunk so low that sacred head of thine.
Next Camus,[8] reverend sire, went footing slow,
His mantle hairy, and his bonnet sedge,
105 Inwrought with figures dim, and on the edge
Like to that sanguine flower inscribed with woe.
"Ah! who hath reft," quoth he, "my dearest pledge?"[0]   *child*
Last came and last did go
The pilot of the Galilean lake,[9]
110 Two massy keys he bore of metals twain°   *two*
(The golden opes,° the iron shuts amain).°   *opens / vehemently*
He shook his mitered locks, and stern bespake:
"How[1] well could I have spared° for thee, young swain,   *given up*
Enow° of such as for their bellies' sake,   *enough*
115 Creep and intrude, and climb into the fold!
Of other care they little reckoning make,
Than how to scramble at the shearers' feast,
And shove away the worthy bidden guest.
Blind mouths! That scarce themselves know how to hold
120 A sheep-hook, or have learned aught else the least
That to the faithful herdsman's art belongs!
What recks it them?[2] What need they? They are sped;[3]
And when they list,° their lean and flashy° songs   *choose / insipid*
Grate on their scrannel° pipes of wretched straw.   *meager*
125 The hungry sheep look up, and are not fed,
But swoln with wind, and the rank mist they draw,°   *inhale*
Rot inwardly, and foul contagion spread,
Besides what the grim wolf with privy paw[4]
Daily devours apace,° and nothing said.   *quickly*
130 But that two-handed engine at the door
Stands ready to smite once, and smite no more."[5]
Return, Alpheus,[6] the dread voice is past,
That shrunk thy streams; return, Sicilian muse,
And call the vales, and bid them hither cast

4. I.e., the surface; *brine:* saltwater.
5. One of the Nereids, daughters of Nereus, the Old Man of the Sea.
6. I.e., the ship.
7. Eclipses were considered evil omens.
8. The god of the river Cam, representing Cambridge University, personified as wearing an academic robe ("mantle" and "bonnet") with colors like the dark reeds ("sedge") on its banks, but relieved by the crimson hyacinth ("sanguine flower"). Certain markings on the hyacinth—created by Apollo from the blood of the youth Hyacinthus, whom he had killed by accident with a discus—are supposed to be the letters AIAI ("Alas, alas!"), inscribed by Apollo.
9. St. Peter, the Galilean fisherman, to whom Christ promised the keys of the kingdom of heaven (Matthew 16.19). He wears the bishop's miter (line 112) as the first head of Christ's Church.
1. Here begins the speech condemning the "corrupted clergy" and foretelling their "ruin" as

described in the argument. Camus uses the common metaphor of the shepherd as the pastor (*pastor* is Latin for shepherd) and the sheep as the congregation.
2. I.e., what does it matter to them?
3. I.e., they have prospered.
4. I.e., anti-Protestant forces, either Roman Catholic or Anglican; *privy:* furtive, sly.
5. A satisfactory explanation of these two lines has yet to be made, although many have been attempted. Most have taken the "two-handed engine" as an instrument of retribution against those clergy who neglect their responsibilities; possibilities include the ax of reformation, the two-handed sword of the archangel Michael, the two houses of Parliament, or death and damnation.
6. A river god who fell in love with the nymph Arethusa. When she fled to Sicily, he pursued her by diving under the sea and emerging on the island. There she was turned into a fountain (see line 85), and their waters mingled.

135 Their bells and flowerets of a thousand hues.
Ye valleys low where the mild whispers use,°   *frequent*
Of shades° and wanton winds, and gushing brooks,   *shadows*
On whose fresh lap the swart star⁷ sparely looks,
Throw hither all your quaint enameled eyes,
140 That on the green turf suck the honeyed showers,
And purple all the ground with vernal° flowers.⁸   *springtime*
Bring the rathe° primrose that forsaken dies,   *early*
The tufted crow-toe, and pale jessamine,⁹
The white pink, and the pansy freaked° with jet,   *mottled*
145 The glowing violet,
The musk-rose, and the well attired woodbine.°   *honeysuckle*
With cowslips wan° that hang the pensive head,   *pale*
And every flower that sad embroidery wears:
Bid amaranthus¹ all his beauty shed,
150 And daffadillies fill their cups with tears,
To strew the laureate° hearse° where Lycid lies.   *laurel-decked / bier*
For so to interpose a little ease,
Let our frail thoughts dally with false surmise.°   *conjecture*
Ay me! Whilst thee the shores and sounding seas
155 Wash far away, where'er thy bones are hurled,
Whether beyond the stormy Hebrides,²
Where thou perhaps under the whelming° tide   *overwhelming*
Visit'st the bottom of the monstrous° world;   *monster-filled; huge*
Or whether thou, to our moist vows³ denied,
160 Sleep'st by the fable of Bellerus old,⁴
Where the great vision of the guarded mount
Looks toward Namancos and Bayona's hold;
Look homeward angel now, and melt with ruth:°   *pity*
And, O ye dolphins, waft° the hapless youth.⁵   *transport*
165   Weep no more, woeful shepherds, weep no more,
For Lycidas your sorrow is not dead,
Sunk though he be beneath the watery floor,
So sinks the day-star° in the ocean bed,   *sun*
And yet anon° repairs his drooping head,   *soon*
170 And tricks° his beams, and with new-spangled ore,°   *dresses / gold*
Flames in the forehead of the morning sky:
So Lycidas sunk low, but mounted high,
Through the dear might of him that walked the waves,⁶
Where other groves, and other streams along,
175 With nectar pure his oozy° locks he laves,°   *slimy / bathes*
And hears the unexpressive° nuptial song,⁷   *inexpressible*
In the blest kingdoms meek of joy and love.

7. Sirius, the Dog Star, thought to have a swart, or malignant, influence (perhaps because this star is in the zenith in late summer, when vegetation often withers).
8. Here begins a catalog of flowers, a traditional element of pastoral elegy.
9. Jasmine, fragrant white flowers. *Crow-toe:* a name for various plants, either wild hyacinth or buttercups.
1. A legendary flower, supposed never to fade.
2. The islands that lie west of Scotland's coast.
3. I.e., tearful prayers.
4. A legendary figure supposedly buried at Land's End, in Cornwall. The "mount" of the next line is St. Michael's Mount, at the tip of Land's End, "guarded" by the archangel Michael, who gazes southward toward Nemancos and the stronghold of Bayona, in northwestern Spain.
5. According to Greek mythology, Palaemon, a boy, drowned near Corinth; a dolphin carried his body to shore, and a temple was built to commemorate him. Milton may also be alluding to the myths of Arion and of Icadius, youths saved by dolphins from drowning.
6. I.e., Christ (Matthew 14.26).
7. Perhaps a reference to the "marriage supper of the lamb" (i.e., Christ), as described by St. John in the Apocalypse (Revelation 19.9).

There entertain him all the saints above,
In solemn troops and sweet societies
180 That sing, and singing in their glory move,
And wipe the tears forever from his eyes.
Now, Lycidas, the shepherds weep no more;
Henceforth thou art the genius of the shore,[8]
In thy large recompense, and shalt be good
185 To all that wander in that perilous flood.

    Thus sang the uncouth° swain to th' oaks and rills,   *unlettered*
While the still morn went out with sandals gray;
He touched the tender stops of various quills,[9]
With eager thought warbling his Doric[1] lay:
190 And now the sun had stretched out all the hills,
And now was dropped into the western bay;
At last he rose, and twitched his mantle° blue: *cloak*
Tomorrow to fresh woods, and pastures new.

1637   1645

From Comus[2]

Song[3]

Sweet Echo, sweetest nymph, that liv'st unseen
    Within thy airy shell,[4]
By slow Meander's margent green,[5]
And in the violet-embroider'd vale,
5   Where the love-lorn nightingale[6]
Nightly to thee her sad song mourneth well;

Canst thou not tell me of a gentle pair
    That likest thy Narcissus are?
      O, if thou have
10   Hid them in some flowery cave,
      Tell me but where,

8. The local divinity who protects navigators on the Irish Sea ("flood").
9. The individual reeds in a set of panpipes.
1. Pastoral, because Doric was the dialect of the ancient Greek pastoral writers Theocritus, Bion, and Moschus.
2. The last English work in Milton's 1645 *Poems*, the poetic drama commonly called *Comus* was originally titled simply "A Mask Presented at Ludlow Castle." It was produced in collaboration with the English composer Henry Lawes (1569–1662), who wrote music for these songs. Masques, popular in the seventeenth century, were court entertainments that included dance, song, drama, and spectacle; they usually celebrated an occasion—in this case, the earl of Bridgewater's assuming the presidency of Wales and the Marches. In the action of this masque, the Lady (played by the earl's daughter, Alice) is separated from her two younger brothers in a wood and accosted by Comus (a classical god of feast and revelry) and his band of revelers. Comus attempts to persuade the chaste and virtuous Lady to join their revelry, but she resists and is rescued by her brothers with help from the river nymph, Sabrina.
3. Lost in the forest, the Lady calls on the nymph Echo for assistance.
4. The sphere of air around Earth; Echo, in love with the handsome youth Narcissus, who spurned her love, pined away until only her voice remained (see Ovid, *Metamorphosis* 3.359–401).
5. Meander is a river in Phrygia with a very winding (thus "slow") course. *Margent*: margin, i.e., bank.
6. The nightingale is known for its sweet, nocturnal song; there are many classical myths about this bird. The Ovidian story of Philomela seems a likely subtext for the Lady's song because Philomela, like Echo, loses her full powers of speech. Philomela, however, was "love-lorn" only in the ironic sense of being victimized by another's passion; she was raped by her brother-in-law, Tereus, who then tore out her tongue so that she could not speak. She wove the story into a tapestry and sent it to her sister, who rescued her. She was later changed into a nightingale while in flight from Tereus.

Sweet queen of parley,° daughter of the sphere!⁷   *speech*
So mayst thou be translated to the skies,
And give resounding grace to all heav'n's harmonies.⁸

Song⁹

    Sabrina fair,
      Listen where thou art sitting
    Under the glassy, cool, translucent wave,
    In twisted braids of lilies knitting
5   The loose train of thy amber-dropping hair;¹
      Listen for dear honor's sake,
      Goddess of the silver lake,
        Listen and save.

Sabrina rises, attended by water-nymphs, and sings.

    By the rushy-fringèd bank,
10   Where grows the willow and the osier² dank,
      My sliding chariot stays,°   *halts*
    Thick set with agate, and the azure sheen³
    Of turkis° blue, and emerald green,   *turquoise*
      That in the channel strays;
15   Whilst from off the waters fleet,
    Thus I set my printless feet
    O'er the cowslip's° velvet head,   *a wildflower's*
      That bends not as I tread;
    Gentle Swain,⁴ at thy request
20   I am here.

1634   1645

To Mr. H. Lawes, On His Airs⁵

Harry, whose tuneful and well-measured song
    First taught our English music how to span°   *measure*
    Words with just note and accent, not to scan

7. Echo was, according to some accounts, the daughter of Air and Earth. Before her encounter with Narcissus, she distracted Hera, queen of the gods, by chattering while Hera's husband, Zeus, consorted with other nymphs and mortal women. Hera punished Echo by depriving her of the ability to speak, except to repeat the words of others.

8. In myth, a traditional method of bestowing immortality is transformation into a star or constellation; thus "translated to the skies," Echo will provide, with her echoes, a resonance to "heav'n's harmonies," perhaps the songs of the angels or the music of the spheres—a music, according to Pythagorean tradition, caused by the motion of the planetary spheres.

9. The attendant Spirit, who has aided the brothers' search for the Lady, calls on Sabrina for help. Sabrina was the goddess of the Severn; according to a story retold by Spenser, among others, she was a mortal girl thrown into the river by her vengeful

stepmother, who was angry at the illicit liaison that resulted in Sabrina's birth. Milton adds to the legend Sabrina's magical powers and her special concern for virgins. In the text of the masque that Milton published in 1645, the Spirit speaks twenty-one lines of poetry between the first and second segments of this song.

1. Amber may refer to the color of her hair, i.e., blonde, through which water drips; or perhaps her hair is wet with amber-colored water; or amber is a perfume (from ambergris, a product of the whale), and thus her hair is shedding perfume.

2. A species of willow.

3. Deep blue luster. *Agate:* a precious stone.

4. Shepherd; the attendant Spirit is dressed as a shepherd.

5. Melodies. The composer Henry Lawes (see note 2, p. 415) had written the music for Milton's masque *Comus* (and printed the masque without Milton's name in 1637).

With Midas' ears,[6] committing° short and long,   *misjoining*
5 Thy worth and skill exempts thee from the throng,
   With praise enough for Envy to look wan;°   *pale*
   To after-age thou shalt be writ the man
   That with smooth air couldst humor best our tongue.
   Thou honor'st Verse, and Verse must lend her wing
10   To honor thee, the priest of Phœbus' choir,
   That tun'st their happiest lines in hymn or story.[7]
Dante shall give Fame leave to set thee higher
   Than his Casella,[8] whom he wooed to sing,
   Met in the milder shades of Purgatory.

1645   1648

I Did but Prompt the Age

I did but prompt the age to quit their clogs[9]
   By the known rules of ancient liberty,
   When straight a barbarous noise environs me
   Of owls and cuckoos, asses, apes, and dogs;[1]
5 As when those hinds that were transformed to frogs
   Railed at Latona's twin-born progeny,[2]
   Which after held the sun and moon in fee.°   *possession*
But this is got by casting pearl to hogs,[3]
   That bawl for freedom in their senseless mood,
10   And still revolt when truth would set them free.[4]
   License they mean when they cry liberty;
For who loves that must first be wise and good:
   But from that mark how far they rove we see,
   For all this waste of wealth and loss of blood.

1645/6   1673

To the Lord General Cromwell[5]

Cromwell, our chief of men, who through a cloud,
   Not of war only, but detractions rude,
   Guided by faith and matchless fortitude,

6. In Greek mythology, King Midas was given ass's ears for preferring the music of Pan, god of pastures, flocks, and shepherds, to that of Phoebus Apollo, god of music and poetry.
7. Perhaps a reference to "The Story," a poem by William Cartwright (1611–1643) that Lawes set to music.
8. In *The Divine Comedy,* Dante represents himself, on the threshold of Purgatory, as meeting the shade of his musician friend Casella, who sings a ballad to him.
9. Heavy objects tied to prisoners' feet to impede motion.
1. Milton had been attacked for advocating liberalized divorce laws. "Known rules of ancient liberty" (line 2) refers to the law of divorce set forth in Deuteronomy 24.1 and also to the natural law of reason.

2. Apollo and Diana, afterwards deities of the sun and moon, respectively. Their mother, Latona, was refused a drink by Lycian peasants ("hinds"), whom she then transformed into frogs.
3. I.e., I receive this response because I gave something valuable to those who could not appreciate its value. Cf. Matthew 7.6: "Give not that which is holy unto the dogs, neither cast your pearls before swine, lest they trample them under their feet, and turn again and rend you."
4. Cf. John 8.32: "And ye shall know the truth and the truth shall make you free."
5. Oliver Cromwell (1599–1655), successor to Sir Thomas Fairfax as commander in chief of the Parliamentary armies. Because of its subject, this poem could not be published in Milton's 1673 *Poems.*

To peace and truth thy glorious way hast ploughed,[6]
5   And on the neck[7] of crownèd Fortune proud
Hast reared God's trophies, and His work pursued,
While Darwen stream, with blood of Scots imbrued,°   *stained*
And Dunbar field, resounds thy praises loud,
And Worcester's laureate wreath:[8] yet much remains
10   To conquer still; peace hath her victories
No less renowned than war: new foes arise,
Threatening to bind our souls with secular chains.[9]
Help us to save free conscience from the paw
Of hireling wolves, whose gospel is their maw.[1]

1652   1694

When I Consider How My Light Is Spent[2]

When I consider how my light is spent
Ere half my days, in this dark world and wide,
And that one talent which is death to hide[3]
Lodged with me useless,[4] though my soul more bent
5   To serve therewith my Maker, and present
My true account, lest he returning chide;
"Doth God exact day-labor, light denied?"[5]
I fondly° ask; but Patience to prevent   *foolishly*
That murmur, soon replies, "God doth not need
10   Either man's work or his own gifts; who best
Bear his mild yoke, they serve him best. His state
Is kingly. Thousands at his bidding speed
And post o'er land and ocean without rest:
They also serve who only stand and wait."

ca. 1652   1673

On the Late Massacre in Piedmont[6]

Avenge, O Lord, thy slaughtered saints, whose bones
Lie scattered on the Alpine mountains cold,
Even them who kept thy truth so pure of old

6. In 1651, Parliament issued a coin bearing the words "Truth and Peace," to express confidence in the results of Cromwell's victories over the Scots at Preston on the banks of the Darwen (line 7) and at Dunbar (line 8) and Worcester (line 9).
7. King Charles I was beheaded in 1649.
8. I.e., as in the garlands of laurels bestowed on victors in ancient Greece.
9. A possible reference to the clergy who in 1652 asked Parliament to establish the English Church on broad Protestant principles but with a State-salaried and State-controlled ministry.
1. Indicating a voracious appetite; see Christ's warning to "beware of false prophets, which come to you in sheep's clothing, but inwardly they are ravening wolves" (Matthew 7.15).
2. Milton had become totally blind in 1652.

3. An allusion to the parable of the talents, in which the servant who buried the single talent his lord had given him, instead of investing it, was deprived of all he had and cast "into outer darkness" at the lord's return (Matthew 25.14–30).
4. With a pun on *usury*, or interest.
5. Alludes to the parable of the vineyard (Matthew 20.1–10) and to John 9.4, Jesus' statement before curing a blind man: "I must work the works of him that sent me, while it is day: the night cometh, when no man can work."
6. Some seventeen hundred members of the Protestant Waldensian sect in the Piedmont in northwestern Italy died as a result of a treacherous attack by the duke of Savoy's forces on Easter Day, 1655.

When all our fathers worshipped stocks and stones,[7]
5   Forget not: in thy book record their groans
Who were thy sheep and in their ancient fold
Slain by the bloody Piedmontese that rolled
Mother with infant down the rocks. Their moans
The vales redoubled to the hills, and they
10   To Heaven. Their martyred blood and ashes sow
O'er all th' Italian fields where still doth sway
The triple tyrant:[8] that from these may grow
A hundredfold, who having learnt thy way
Early may fly the Babylonian woe.[9]

1655   1673

Cyriack,[1] Whose Grandsire

Cyriack, whose grandsire on the royal bench
Of British Themis,[2] with no mean applause,
Pronounced, and in his volumes taught, our laws,
Which others at their bar so often wrench,
5   Today deep thoughts resolve with me to drench
In mirth that after no repenting draws;
Let Euclid rest, and Archimedes pause,[3]
And what the Swede intend, and what the French.[4]
To measure life learn thou betimes,° and know   *early*
10   Toward solid good what leads the nearest way;
For other things mild Heaven a time ordains,
And disapproves that care, though wise in show,
That with superfluous burden loads the day,
And, when God sends a cheerful hour, refrains.

ca. 1655   1673

Methought I Saw

Methought I saw my late espousèd saint[5]
Brought to me like Alcestis[6] from the grave,

7. In Milton's time, Protestants thought the Waldensian sect dated from early Christian times rather than (as historians now think) from the twelfth century. "Stocks and stones" echoes the prophet Jeremiah's denunciation of the Israelites' worship of idols made of wood and stone (Jeremiah 3.9); Milton's phrase could encompass both pagan and Catholic forms of idolatry, and is appropriate in a lament for members of a heretical sect known for rejecting materialist tendencies in the Catholic Church.
8. The pope, whose tiara has three crowns.
9. Babylon, as a city of luxury and vice, was often linked with the Papal Court by Protestants, who took the destruction of the city described in Revelation 18 as an allegory of the fate in store for the Roman Church.
1. Cyriack Skinner, a pupil of Milton and grandson of Sir Edward Coke, the great jurist who had been chief justice of the King's Bench under

James I.
2. The Greek goddess of justice.
3. Euclid and Archimedes (both third century B.C.E.), Greek mathematicians; Skinner's interest in Greek mathematics may have begun when he was a pupil in Milton's school on Aldersgate Street.
4. In 1655, King Charles X of Sweden was leading military campaigns against the Poles; Cardinal Mazarin was leading French policy.
5. The "saint," or soul in heaven, is probably Milton's second wife, Katherine Woodcock, to whom he had been married less than two years (hence "late espousèd") when she died, in 1658; since Milton had become blind in 1652, he almost certainly had never seen his wife. However, critics do not agree on the identity of the "saint." It is possibly a reference to Mary Powell, Milton's first wife, who died in childbirth in 1652.
6. The wife brought back from the dead to her husband, Admetus, by the hero Hercules ("Jove's

Whom Jove's great son to her glad husband gave,
Rescued from Death by force, though pale and faint.
5   Mine, as whom° washed from spot of child-bed taint   one whom
Purification in the Old Law did save,[7]
And such, as yet once more I trust to have
Full sight of her in heaven without restraint,
Came vested all in white, pure as her mind.
10   Her face was veiled; yet to my fancied sight
Love, sweetness, goodness, in her person shined
So clear as in no face with more delight.
But O, as to embrace me she inclined,
I waked, she fled, and day brought back my night.

ca. 1658   1673

FROM PARADISE LOST[1]

The Verse[2]

The measure is English heroic verse without rhyme, as that of Homer in
Greek, and of Virgil in Latin;[3] rhyme being no necessary adjunct or true

great son,") in Euripides' *Alcestis*. She is veiled and must remain silent until ritually cleansed.

7. Hebrew law (Leviticus 12) prescribed certain sacrificial rituals for the purification of women after childbirth.

1. Milton wrote this epic poem to "justify the ways of God to men," as he asserts in the opening of Book 1. Although he eschews the traditional subject matter of epic poetry—"fabled knights / In battles feigned" (9.30–31)—he follows many conventions of the epic form, including the beginning *in medias res* ("in the middle of things"), the invocation of a muse (a request for divine aid in the writing of the poem), the division of the poem into twelve books, the use of epic similes (extended and elaborately detailed comparisons that temporarily draw the reader's attention from the subject at hand), and the epic catalog (as of ships in Homer's *Iliad* and fallen angels in *Paradise Lost*). While Milton establishes that his poem is part of an epic tradition that includes Homer's *Iliad* and *Odyssey* and Virgil's *Aeneid*, he questions some assumptions of that tradition (he introduces, for example, a different concept of heroism) and incorporates other generic elements such as pastoral and drama.

The poem begins in hell, where Satan and his fallen angels plot their revenge against God through the destruction of his newest creation, the human race (Books 1 and 2). In Book 3, the scene shifts to heaven, where God predicts the disobedience of Adam and Eve, and Christ volunteers to undertake their redemption. In Book 4, Satan enters Eden and attempts to enter Eve's mind in a dream. God sends the angel Raphael to warn Adam and Eve of Satan's intentions. In Books 5 and 6, Raphael narrates to Adam the story of the war in heaven between Satan and his followers, and God, Christ, and the angels loyal to God. Raphael goes on to relate the creation of the world and its inhabitants by God (Book 7). Adam, in Book 8, tells Raphael what he remembers of his own creation and of Eve's. Book 9 chronicles the temptation and fall of Adam and Eve. Christ descends from heaven

to the garden to pronounce punishment upon the humans, and Sin and Death create a broad highway between hell and Earth (Book 10). Finally, God sends the angel Michael to expel Adam and Eve from the garden, but first Michael shows Adam the history of the world up through the coming of Christ, relating God's promise to redeem the human race through the sacrifice of his Son (Books 11 and 12). Adam and Eve, heartened by this promise, depart the garden "hand in hand with wand'ring steps and slow" (12.648). Although Milton draws on biblical accounts of the events he narrates, he both embellishes these accounts and adds entire events of his own devising (such as the war in heaven, modeled on classical stories of battles among gods).

While there are many ways of approaching this poem, any approach will benefit from a careful consideration of Milton's language and the formal features of his poetry. Milton is a master of prosody, and he frequently varies the meter of his blank verse in ways that enhance or complicate the meaning of the words. His wordplay and the ambiguous syntax of his long, complexly subordinated sentences allow the reader the experience, in small, of the freedom to choose within a predetermined structure, an experience not unlike that of the characters in his poem.

2. This note first appeared in a 1668 reissue of the first edition of *Paradise Lost*, following a note in which the printer, S. Simmons, claimed that he had "procured" the note to satisfy many readers curious about why "the poem rhymes not." Milton's decision to add the note may have been influenced by a debate between the poet John Dryden (1631–1700) and the dramatist Sir Robert Howard (1626–1698). Dryden's *Essay on Dramatic Verse* (1668) records the controversy, in which Dryden argues the merits of rhyme and Howard champions blank verse.

3. English heroic verse was the iambic line of five feet, or ten syllables; heroic verse in Greek and Latin poetry was the hexameter.

ornament of poem or good verse, in longer works especially, but the invention of a barbarous age, to set off wretched matter and lame meter; graced indeed since by the use of some famous modern poets, carried away by custom, but much to their own vexation, hindrance, and constraint, to express many things otherwise, and for the most part worse, than else they would have expressed them. Not without cause, therefore, some both Italian and Spanish poets of prime note have rejected rhyme both in longer and shorter works, as have also, long since, our best English tragedies, as a thing of itself, to all judicious ears, trivial and of no true musical delight; which consists only in apt numbers, fit quantity of syllables, and the sense variously drawn out from one verse into another, not in the jingling sound of like endings, a fault avoided by the learned ancients both in poetry and all good oratory. This neglect then of rhyme, so little is to be taken for a defect, though it may seem so perhaps to vulgar readers, that it rather is to be esteemed an example set, the first in English, of ancient liberty recovered to heroic poem from the troublesome and modern bondage of rhyming.

Book 1

[*The Invocation*]⁴

    Of man's first disobedience, and the fruit
Of that forbidden tree⁵ whose mortal° taste   *deadly*
Brought death into the world, and all our woe,
With loss of Eden, till one greater Man⁶
5   Restore us, and regain the blissful seat,
Sing, Heavenly Muse,⁷ that, on the secret top
Of Oreb, or of Sinai, didst inspire
That shepherd who first taught the chosen seed
In the beginning how the Heavens and Earth
10   Rose out of Chaos: or, if Sion hill
Delight thee more, and Siloa's brook that flowed
Fast by the oracle of God, I thence
Invoke thy aid to my adventurous song,
That with no middle flight intends to soar
15   Above th' Aonian mount, while it pursues
Things unattempted yet in prose or rhyme.⁸
And chiefly thou, O Spirit, that dost prefer

4. In these opening lines, Milton follows long-established epic tradition by stating his subject and invoking divine aid in the treatment of it.
5. In Genesis 2.17, God commands that Adam and Eve not eat from the fruit of one tree.
6. Christ, the second Adam.
7. The invocation of the muse is an epic convention. In the invocation to Book 7, Milton specifically calls upon Urania, the patroness of astronomy and one of the nine Muses of Greek tradition, to assist him in telling the story of Creation. But he insists that it is the "meaning, not the Name I call" (7.5), suggesting that the non-Christian name is inadequate to his true intentions.
   Here, the muse seems to represent the Spirit of God, the same Spirit that spoke to Moses ("That shepherd," line 8) out of the burning bush on Mt.

Horeb (also called Sinai) and commanded him to lead Israel ("the chosen seed") out of Egypt. God's Spirit might also be found at Jerusalem in the Temple of Mount Sion ("the oracle of God," line 12) overlooking the stream Siloam, here contrasted with such haunts of the pagan Muses as "th' Aonian mount" (Helicon, in Greece, line 15). Milton asks this Spirit not only for inspiration but for instruction, since God alone was present "from the first" (line 19) and knows the whole truth of the events Milton is about to relate.
8. Ironically, Milton's claim of originality in this line translates a boast made by Ariosto in his *Orlando Furioso* (1.2). In *Paradise Lost*, Book 9, lines 27–47 (see p. 426), Milton criticizes the kind of chivalric epic written by Ariosto and by Edmund Spenser.

Before all temples th' upright heart and pure,
Instruct me, for thou know'st; thou from the first
20 Wast present, and, with mighty wings outspread,
Dovelike sat'st brooding on the vast abyss,
And mad'st it pregnant: what in me is dark
Illumine; what is low, raise and support;
That, to the height of this great argument,°   theme
25 I may assert Eternal Providence,
And justify the ways of God to men.

From Book 4[9]

O for that warning voice, which he who saw
Th' Apocalypse, heard cry in heaven aloud,
Then when the Dragon, put to second rout,°   defeat
Came furious down to be revenged on men,
5 "Woe to the inhabitants on earth!"[1] that now,
While time was,[2] our first parents had been warned
The coming of their secret foe, and scaped°   escaped
Haply so scaped his mortal snare;[3] for now
Satan, now first inflamed with rage, came down,
10 The tempter ere° th' accuser of mankind,   before being
To wreck° on innocent frail man his loss[4]   avenge, wreak
Of that first battle, and his flight to Hell:
Yet not rejoicing in his speed, though bold,
Far off and fearless, nor with cause to boast,
15 Begins his dire attempt, which nigh the birth
Now rolling,° boils in his tumultuous breast,   moving on
And like a devilish engine[5] back recoils
Upon himself; horror and doubt distract
His troubled thoughts, and from the bottom stir
20 The Hell within him, for within him Hell
He brings, and round about him, nor from Hell
One step no more than from himself can fly
By change of place: now conscience wakes despair
That slumbered, wakes the bitter memory
25 Of what he was, what is, and what must be

9. Book 4 opens on the newly created Earth, and specifically in the garden of Eden, which Satan is approaching as the "foe" of "our first parents" (lines 7–8), Adam and Eve. Satan is a "secret" enemy because Adam and Eve do not yet know of his fall and vengeful decision to continue his battle against God by attacking God's new, human creatures. The narrator opens the book by expressing a desire to warn Adam and Eve of the danger they face "now" (line 8), in the epic's re-creation of a paradisal present time. Before seeing Eden, the reader sees and "hears" Satan, speaking in soliloquy. This speech was, according to Milton's nephew Edward Phillips, the first part of the epic Milton wrote, when he was still contemplating treating the Genesis story as a drama (to be called *Adam Unparadized*). Satan's hostile address to the sun (with a punning allusion to the Son of God, who, we later learn, has driven Satan from heaven) recalls the opening soliloquy of Shakespeare's *Richard III*, in which Richard, in the "winter of our discontent," also depicts his rival as a son/sun.
1. John of Patmos, in Revelation 12.7–12, hears such a cry during a second war in heaven between the dragon and the angels, at the end of time.
2. While there was still time.
3. His deadly (and, in this case, death-creating) trap. *Haply:* i.e., perhaps; also, with a play on *happily*.
4. I.e., Satan's, for which he seeks to "wreck"— take revenge—on "man" as a substitute for God and Christ.
5. I.e., the cannon that Satan invents in Book 6; but also a play on *engine* as "plot."

Worse; of worse deeds worse sufferings must ensue.
Sometimes towards Eden which now in his view
Lay pleasant, his grieved look he fixes sad,
Sometimes towards Heav'n and the full-blazing sun,
30 Which now sat high in his meridian tow'r:[6]
Then much revolving,° thus in sighs began.   *pondering*
   "O thou that with surpassing glory crowned,
Look'st from thy sole dominion like the god
Of this new world: at whose sight all the stars
35 Hide their diminished heads; to thee I call,
But with no friendly voice, and add thy name
O sun, to tell thee how I hate thy beams
That bring to my remembrance from what state
I fell, how glorious once above thy sphere;
40 Till pride and worse ambition threw me down
Warring in Heav'n against Heav'n's matchless King:
Ah wherefore! he deserved no such return
From me, whom he created what I was
In that bright eminence, and with his good
45 Upbraided none,[7] nor was his service hard.
What could be less than to afford him praise,
The easiest recompense, and pay him thanks,
How due! yet all his good proved ill in me,
And wrought but malice; lifted up so high
50 I 'sdained° subjection, and thought one step higher   *disdained*
Would set me highest, and in a moment quit°   *repay*
The debt immense of endless gratitude,
So burthensome still° paying, still to owe;   *always*
Forgetful what from him I still received,
55 And understood not that a grateful mind
By owing owes not, but still pays, at once
Indebted and discharged; what burden then?
O had his powerful destiny ordained
Me some inferior angel, I had stood
60 Then happy; no unbounded hope had raised
Ambition. Yet why not? some other Power°   *angel*
As great might have aspired, and me though mean°   *inferior, low*
Drawn to his part; but other Powers as great
Fell not, but stand unshaken, from within
65 Or from without, to all temptations armed.
Hadst thou[8] the same free will and power to stand?
Thou hadst: whom hast thou then or what to accuse,
But Heav'n's free love dealt equally to all?
Be then his love accursed, since love or hate,
70 To me alike, it deals eternal woe.
Nay cursed be thou; since against his thy will
Chose freely what it now so justly rues.°   *regrets*
Me miserable![9] which way shall I fly

6. Midday, the height of noon.
7. Demanded no return for his benefits. Cf. James
1.5: "If any of you lack wisdom, let him ask of God
. . . and upbraideth not. . . ."

8. Satan addresses himself.
9. This phrase recalls the common Latin construction describing the self as an object, in the "accusative" case: *me miserum!*

Infinite wrath, and infinite despair?[1]
75 Which way I fly is Hell; myself am Hell;
And in the lowest deep a lower deep
Still threat'ning to devour me opens wide,
To which the Hell I suffer seems a Heav'n.
O then at last relent! is there no place
80 Left for repentance, none for pardon left?
None left but by submission; and that word
Disdain forbids me, and my dread of shame
Among the Spirits beneath, whom I seduced
With other promises and other vaunts°   boasts
85 Than to submit, boasting I could subdue
Th' Omnipotent. Ay me, they little know
How dearly I abide° that boast so vain,   pay the penalty for
Under what torments inwardly I groan:
While they adore me on the throne of Hell,
90 With diadem° and scepter high advanced   crown
The lower still I fall, only supreme
In misery; such joy ambition finds.
But say I could repent and could obtain
By act of grace[2] my former state; how soon
95 Would hight recall high thoughts, how soon unsay
What feigned submission swore: ease would recant[3]
Vows made in pain, as violent° and void.   forced
For never can true reconcilement grow
Where wounds of deadly hate have pierced so deep:
100 Which would but lead me to a worse relapse,
And heavier fall: so should I purchase dear
Short intermission bought with double smart.°   sting
This knows my punisher; therefore as far
From granting he, as I from begging peace:
105 All hope excluded thus, behold instead
Of us outcast, exiled, his new delight,
Mankind created, and for him this world.
So farewell hope, and with hope farewell fear,
Farewell remorse: all good to me is lost;
110 Evil be thou my good; by thee at least
Divided empire with Heav'n's King I hold
By thee, and more than half perhaps will reign;[4]
As man ere long, and this new world shall know."

*   *   *

1. Compressed syntax: whichever way I fly, I shall find. . . .
2. By a favor, not a right; the term was often used in political contexts to describe a formal pardon.
3. Literally, sing again; the verb was often used to describe formal renunciations of religious views that the state deemed erroneous (e.g., Catholics might "recant" their views when arrested and inter-

rogated by official authorities). Satan is ironically suggesting that a condition of "ease" acquired through submission would lead him to change the vows of "repentance" made in his present condition of pain.
4. Spelled raign in the original text, the verb is transitive and means "rule over."

Book 9

The Argument[5]

Satan, having compassed the Earth, with meditated guile returns as a mist by night into Paradise; enters into the Serpent sleeping. Adam and Eve in the morning go forth to their labors, which Eve proposes to divide in several places, each laboring apart: Adam consents not, alleging the danger lest that enemy of whom they were forewarned should attempt her found alone. Eve, loth to be thought not circumspect or firm enough, urges her going apart, the rather desirous to make trial of her strength; Adam at last yields. The Serpent finds her alone: his subtle approach, first gazing, then speaking, with much flattery extolling Eve above all other creatures. Eve, wondering to hear the Serpent speak, asks how he attained to human speech and such understanding not till now; the Serpent answers that by tasting of a certain tree in the Garden he attained both to speech and reason, till then void of both. Eve requires him to bring her to that tree, and finds it to be the Tree of Knowledge forbidden; the Serpent, now grown bolder, with many wiles and arguments induces her at length to eat. She, pleased with the taste, deliberates a while whether to impart thereof to Adam or not; at last brings him of the fruit; relates what persuaded her to eat thereof. Adam, at first amazed, but perceiving her lost, resolves, through vehemence of love, to perish with her, and, extenuating the trespass, eats also of the fruit. The effects thereof in them both; they seek to cover their nakedness; then fall to variance and accusation of one another.

No more of talk where God or angel guest[6]
With man, as with his friend, familiar used
To sit indulgent, and with him partake
Rural repast, permitting him the while
5   Venial° discourse unblamed. I now must change   *allowable*
Those notes to tragic—foul distrust, and breach
Disloyal, on the part of man, revolt
And disobedience; on the part of Heaven,
Now alienated, distance and distaste,
10 Anger and just rebuke, and judgment given,
That brought into this world a world of woe,
Sin and her shadow Death, and Misery,
Death's harbinger. Sad task, yet argument
Not less but more heroic than the wrath
15 Of stern Achilles on his foe pursued
Thrice fugitive about Troy wall; or rage
Of Turnus for Lavinia disespoused;
Or Neptune's ire, or Juno's, that so long
Perplexed the Greek, and Cytherea's son:[7]

---

5. The Argument is a prose summary of the action of the book. *Paradise Lost* was originally published without Arguments, but the printer asked Milton to provide them because many readers found the poem difficult. They first appeared, with the note on the verse, in a 1668 reissue of the first edition.
6. Adam has just concluded a conversation with the angel Raphael (at the end of Book 8).
7. Important moments in important epics. Achilles, whose "wrath" is the epic subject announced

20 If answerable° style I can obtain   *suitable, fitting*
Of my celestial Patroness,[8] who deigns°   *condescends to grant*
Her nightly visitation unimplored,
And dictates to me slumbering, or inspires
Easy my unpremeditated verse,
25 Since first this subject for heroic song
Pleased me, long choosing and beginning late,
Not sedulous° by nature to indite°   *diligent / write about*
Wars, hitherto the only argument°   *subject*
Heroic deemed, chief mastery to dissect
30 With long and tedious havoc fabled knights
In battles feigned (the better fortitude
Of patience and heroic martyrdom
Unsung), or to describe races and games,
Or tilting furniture,[9] emblazoned shields,
35 Impreses quaint, caparisons and steeds,
Bases and tinsel trappings, gorgeous knights
At joust and tournament; then marshaled feast
Served up in hall with sewers° and seneschals:°   *waiters / stewards*
The skill of artifice° or office mean;°   *applied art / low*
40 Not that which justly gives heroic name
To person or to poem. Me, of these
Nor° skilled nor studious, higher argument   *neither*
Remains,[1] sufficient of itself to raise
That name,[2] unless an age too late, or cold
45 Climate, or years, damp my intended wing
Depressed; and much they may if all be mine,
Not hers who brings it nightly to my ear.[3]
    The sun was sunk, and after him the star
Of Hesperus,° whose office is to bring   *the evening star*
50 Twilight upon the Earth, short arbiter
'Twixt day and night, and now from end to end
Night's hemisphere had veiled the horizon round,
When Satan, who late fled before the threats
Of Gabriel out of Eden, now improved°   *made worse*
55 In meditated fraud and malice, bent
On man's destruction, maugre° what might hap°   *despite / happen*
Of heavier[4] on himself, fearless returned.
By night he fled, and at midnight returned
From compassing the Earth—cautious of day

---

in the first line of the *Iliad*, pursued Hector three times around the walls of Troy before slaying him. Turnus (in the *Aeneid*) fought with Aeneas for the hand of Lavinia. Neptune hindered Odysseus ("the Greek") in his attempts to return home after the Trojan War, and Juno, hostile to Venus ("Cytherea"), made difficulties for Venus's son Aeneas.
8. Urania, the "Heavenly Muse" whose aid Milton had invoked in Book 1, line 6 (but see also note 7, p. 421).
9. The equipment used in a tilt, or tournament, examples of which follow. *Impreses:* heraldic emblems displayed on shields. *Caparisons:* orna-

mented coverings spread over the saddles or harnesses of horses. *Bases:* skirtlike coverings, sometimes of armor, intended to decorate and protect warhorses.
1. I.e., to me, not skilled or learned in these things, remains a more important subject.
2. I.e., "heroic name" (from line 40).
3. I.e., these things, "an age too late" (the age of the world), "cold Climate," or "years" (the poet's age), might indeed "damp" or benumb his intent if the effort of writing the poem were all his instead of "hers," i.e., that of his "celestial Patroness."
4. *Of heavier:* worse.

60 Since Uriel, regent of the sun, descried
His entrance, and forewarned the Cherubim[5]
That kept their watch. Thence, full of anguish, driven,
The space of seven continued nights he rode
With darkness; thrice the equinoctial line
65 He circled, four times crossed the car of Night
From pole to pole, traversing each colure;[6]
On the eighth returned, and on the coast° averse°   *side / turned away*
From entrance or cherubic watch by stealth
Found unsuspected way. There was a place
70 (Now not, though Sin, not Time, first wrought the change)
Where Tigris, at the foot of Paradise,
Into a gulf shot under ground, till part
Rose up a fountain by the Tree of Life.
In with the river sunk and with it rose
75 Satan, involved in rising mist; then sought
Where to lie hid. Sea he had searched and land,
From Eden over Pontus,[7] and the pool
Maeotis, up beyond the river Ob;
Downward as far antarctic; and, in length,
80 West from Orontes to the ocean barred
At Darien, thence to the land where flows
Ganges and Indus. Thus the orb he roamed
With narrow search, and with inspection deep
Considered every creature, which of all
85 Most opportune might serve his wiles, and found
The serpent subtlest beast of all the field.[8]
Him, after long debate, irresolute
Of thoughts revolved, his final sentence° chose   *judgment*
Fit vessel, fittest imp° of fraud, in whom   *offshoot, child*
90 To enter, and his dark suggestions hide
From sharpest sight; for in the wily snake
Whatever sleights° none would suspicious mark,   *artifices*
As from his wit and native subtlety
Proceeding, which, in other beasts observed,
95 Doubt° might beget of diabolic power   *suspicion*
Active within beyond the sense of brute.
Thus he resolved, but first from inward grief
His bursting passion into plaints thus poured:
    "O Earth, how like to Heaven, if not preferred
100 More justly, seat worthier of Gods, as built

5. An order of angels. In medieval astronomy, each of the concentric crystalline spheres containing one of the heavenly bodies was supposed to be inhabited by an angel, its "intelligence," who governed its motion; Uriel is one of the four great archangels of the Jewish tradition, along with Raphael, Gabriel, and Michael.
6. The "equinoctial line" is the equator. The "car of Night" is Earth's shadow, depicted as the chariot of the goddess Night. The colures are two of the great circles that pass through the celestial poles, one intersecting the ecliptic at the equinoxes, the other at the solstices. Satan circles Earth for the

space of seven days, first along the equator and then over the poles, always timing his flight so as to remain hidden on the dark side.
7. In lines 77–82, Satan's search extends from the Black Sea (Pontus) to the connecting Sea of Azov (the pool Maeotis) and northward beyond the river Ob in Siberia: southward to the antarctic; and westward from the Orontes River in Syria to the isthmus of Panama (Darien) and on around the world to India.
8. Milton here follows Genesis 3.1: "Now the serpent was more subtle than any beast of the field which the Lord God had made."

With second thoughts, reforming what was old!
For what God, after better, worse would build?
Terrestrial Heaven, danced round by other Heavens,
That shine, yet bear their bright officious° lamps,   helpful
105 Light above light, for thee alone, as seems,
In thee concentring all their precious beams
Of sacred influence!⁹ As God in Heaven
Is center, yet extends to all, so thou
Centring receiv'st from all those orbs; in thee,
110 Not in themselves, all their known virtue appears,
Productive in herb, plant, and nobler birth
Of creatures animate with gradual life
Of growth, sense, reason, all summed up in man.¹
With what delight could I have walked thee round,
115 If I could joy in aught; sweet interchange
Of hill and valley, rivers, woods, and plains,
Now land, now sea, and shores with forest crowned,
Rocks, dens, and caves! But I in none of these
Find place or refuge; and, the more I see
120 Pleasures about me, so much more I feel
Torment within me, as from the hateful siege
Of contraries; all good to me becomes
Bane,° and in Heaven much worse would be my state.   poison, evil
But neither here seek I, no, nor in Heaven,
125 To dwell, unless by mastering Heaven's Supreme;
Nor hope to be myself less miserable
By what I seek, but others to make such
As I, though thereby worse to me redound.°   return
For only in destroying I find ease
130 To my relentless thoughts; and him° destroyed,   Adam
Or won to what may work his utter loss,
For whom all this was made, all this² will soon
Follow, as to him linked in weal° or woe: happiness
In woe then, that destruction wide may range!
135 To me shall be the glory sole among
The infernal Powers, in one day to have marred
What he, Almighty styled, six nights and days
Continued making, and who knows how long
Before had been contriving; though perhaps
140 Not longer than since I in one night freed
From servitude inglorious well nigh half
The angelic name,³ and thinner left the throng
Of his adorers. He, to be avenged,
And to repair his numbers thus impaired—
145 Whether such virtue,° spent of old, now failed   power, energy
More angels to create (if they at least
Are his created),⁴ or to spite us more—

9. Satan seems to describe here a Ptolemaic sys-
tem of the universe, in which Earth is the center
around which many heavenly bodies turn.
1. Earth is populated with forms of life on a grad-
uated scale ranging from plants, which merely
grow; to animals, which both grow and feel; to
humans, who grow, feel, and think.
2. I.e., Earth (and specifically Eden), which is

harmed, as Satan predicts, at 9.782–84 (p. 442).
3. I.e., half the angels. Satan alludes to the revolt
he led against God, the consequence of which was
that he and his supporters (whose number he exag-
gerates here) were cast out of heaven into hell.
4. Only once (at the beginning of Book 4, line 43)
does Satan speak of the angels as created by God,
instead of self-created (as he implies here).

Determined to advance into our room
A creature formed of earth,[5] and him endow,
150   Exalted from so base original,
With Heavenly spoils, our spoils. What he decreed
He effected; Man he made, and for him built
Magnificent this World, and Earth his seat,
Him Lord pronounced, and, O indignity!
155   Subjected to his service angel-wings
And flaming ministers, to watch and tend
Their earthy charge. Of these the vigilance
I dread, and to elude, thus wrapped in mist
Of midnight vapor, glide obscure, and pry
160   In every bush and brake, where hap° may find   *luck*
The serpent sleeping, in whose mazy folds
To hide me, and the dark intent I bring.
O foul descent! that I, who erst contended
With Gods to sit the highest, am now constrained
165   Into a beast, and, mixed with bestial slime,
This essence to incarnate and imbrute,[6]
That to the height of deity aspired!
But what will not ambition and revenge
Descend to? Who aspires must down as low
170   As high he soared, obnoxious,° first or last,   *exposed*
To basest things. Revenge, at first though sweet,
Bitter ere long back on itself recoils.
Let it; I reck° not, so it light well aimed,   *care*
Since higher I fall short, on him who next
175   Provokes my envy, this new favorite
Of Heaven, this man of clay, son of despite,°   *spite, scorn*
Whom, us the more to spite, his Maker raised
From dust: spite then with spite is best repaid."
    So saying, through each thicket, dank or dry,
180   Like a black mist low-creeping, he held on
His midnight search, where soonest he might find
The serpent. Him fast sleeping soon he found,
In labyrinth of many a round self-rolled,
His head the midst, well stored with subtle wiles:
185   Not yet in horrid shade or dismal den,
Nor nocent° yet, but on the grassy herb,   *harmful*
Fearless, unfeared, he slept. In at his mouth
The Devil entered, and his brutal° sense,   *animal*
In heart or head, possessing soon inspired
190   With act intelligential; but his sleep
Disturbed not, waiting close° the approach of morn.   *hidden*
    Now, whenas sacred light began to dawn
In Eden on the humid flowers, that breathed
Their morning incense, when all things that breathe
195   From th' Earth's great altar send up silent praise
To the Creator, and his nostrils fill

---

5. Milton explains in Book 7 (lines 524–26) that Adam is made from earth: "he form'd thee, Adam, thee O man / Dust of the ground, and in thy nostrils breath'd / The breath of Life," following Genesis 2.7: "And the Lord God formed man of the dust of the ground, and breathed into his nostrils the breath of life."
6. Satan's incarnation in the body of the serpent is a grotesque parody of Christ's incarnation in human form.

With grateful smell, forth came the human pair,
And joined their vocal worship to the choir
Of creatures wanting° voice; that done, partake   lacking
200 The season, prime° for sweetest scents and airs;   best
Then cómmune how that day they best may ply
Their growing work; for much their work outgrew
The hands' dispatch of two gardening so wide:
And Eve first to her husband thus began:
205   "Adam, well may we labor still° to dress   continually
This garden, still to tend plant, herb, and flower,
Our pleasant task enjoined; but, till more hands
Aid us, the work under our labor grows,
Luxurious° by restraint: what we by day   luxuriant
210 Lop overgrown, or prune, or prop, or bind,
One night or two with wanton growth derides,
Tending to wild. Thou, therefore, now advise,
Or hear what to my mind first thoughts present.
Let us divide our labors; thou where choice
215 Leads thee, or where most needs, whether to wind
The woodbine⁷ round this arbor, or direct
The clasping ivy where to climb; while I
In yonder spring° of roses intermixed   growth
With myrtle⁸ find what to redress° till noon.   set upright
220 For, while so near each other thus all day
Our task we choose, what wonder if so near
Looks intervene and smiles, or object new
Casual discourse draw on, which intermits
Our day's work, brought to little, though begun
225 Early, and the hour of supper comes unearned!"
        To whom mild answer Adam thus returned:
"Sole Eve, associate sole,⁹ to me beyond
Compare above all living creatures dear!
Well hast thou motioned,° well thy thoughts employed   suggested
230 How we might best fulfil the work which here
God hath assigned us, nor of me shalt pass
Unpraised; for nothing lovelier can be found
In woman than to study household good,
And good works in her husband to promote.
235 Yet not so strictly hath our Lord imposed
Labor as to debar us when we need
Refreshment, whether food, or talk between,
Food of the mind, or this sweet intercourse
Of looks and smiles; for smiles from reason flow,
240 To brute denied, and are of love the food;
Love, not the lowest end of human life.
For not to irksome toil, but to delight,
He made us, and delight to reason joined.
These paths and bowers° doubt not but our joint hands   arbors
245 Will keep from wilderness with ease, as wide
As we need walk, till younger hands ere long

7. A name for various climbing plants.   Venus, and thus an emblem of love.
8. The myrtle tree, having shiny green leaves and   9. With a pun: "unrivaled" and "only."
white flowers; associated with the Roman goddess

Assist us. But, if much converse perhaps
Thee satiate, to short absence I could yield;
For solitude sometimes is best society,
250 And short retirement urges sweet return.
But other doubt possesses me, lest harm
Befall thee, severed from me; for thou know'st
What hath been warned us—what malicious foe,
Envying our happiness, and of his own
255 Despairing, seeks to work us woe and shame
By sly assault, and somewhere nigh at hand
Watches, no doubt, with greedy hope to find
His wish and best advantage, us asunder,
Hopeless to circumvent° us joined, where each   outwit
260 To other speedy aid might lend at need.
Whether his first design be to withdraw
Our fealty from God, or to disturb
Conjugal love—than which perhaps no bliss
Enjoyed by us excites his envy more—
265 Or° this, or worse, leave not the faithful side   whether
That gave thee being,¹ still shades thee and protects.
The wife, where danger or dishonor lurks,
Safest and seemliest by her husband stays,
Who guards her, or with her the worst endures."
270   To whom the virgin° majesty of Eve,   innocent
As one who loves, and some unkindness meets,
With sweet austere composure thus replied:
"Offspring of Heaven and Earth, and all Earth's lord!
That such an enemy we have, who seeks
275 Our ruin, both by thee informed I learn,
And from the parting angel overheard,
As in a shady nook I stood behind,
Just then returned at shut of evening flowers.
But that thou shouldst my firmness therefore doubt
280 To God or thee, because we have a foe
May tempt it, I expected not to hear.
His violence thou fear'st not, being such
As we, not capable of death or pain,
Can either not receive, or can repel.
285 His fraud is, then, thy fear; which plain infers
Thy equal fear that my firm faith and love
Can by his fraud be shaken or seduced:
Thoughts, which how found they harbor in thy breast,
Adam, misthought of° her to thee so dear?"   about
290   To whom, with healing words, Adam replied:
"Daughter of God and Man, immortal Eve!
For such thou art, from sin and blame entire°   wholly free
Not diffident° of thee do I dissuade   mistrustful
Thy absence from my sight, but to avoid
295 Th' attempt itself, intended by our foe.
For he who tempts, though in vain, at least asperses²

1. In Book 8 (lines 465–71), Adam describes
God's creation of Eve out of a rib taken from his
side, following Genesis 2.22: "And the rib, which
the Lord God had taken from man, made he a
woman, and brought her unto the man."
2. Maligns (literally, sprinkles).

The tempted with dishonor foul, supposed
Not incorruptible of faith, not proof
Against temptation. Thou thyself with scorn
300　And anger wouldst resent the offered wrong,
Though ineffectual found; misdeem not, then,
If such affront I labor to avert
From thee alone, which on us both at once
The enemy, though bold, will hardly dare;
305　Or, daring, first on me th' assault shall light.
Nor thou his malice and false guile contemn°—　　*regard scornfully*
Subtle he needs must be who could seduce
Angels—nor think superfluous others' aid.
I from the influence of thy looks receive
310　Access° in every virtue—in thy sight　　*increase*
More wise, more watchful, stronger, if need were
Of outward strength; while shame, thou looking on,
Shame to be overcome or overreached,°　　*outwitted*
Would utmost vigor raise, and raised unite.
315　Why shouldst not thou like sense within thee feel
When I am present, and thy trial choose
With me, best witness of thy virtue tried?"
　　So spake domestic Adam in his care
And matrimonial love; but Eve, who thought
320　Less° attributed to her faith sincere,　　*too little*
Thus her reply with accent sweet renewed:
　　"If this be our condition, thus to dwell
In narrow circuit straitened° by a foe,　　*constrained, limited*
Subtle or violent, we not endued°　　*endowed*
325　Single with like defense wherever met,
How are we happy, still° in fear of harm?　　*continually*
But harm precedes not sin: only our foe
Tempting affronts us with his foul esteem
Of our integrity: his foul esteem
330　Sticks no dishonor on our front,° but turns　　*brow*
Foul on himself; then wherefore shunned or feared
By us, who rather double honor gain
From his surmise proved false, find peace within,
Favor from Heaven, our witness, from the event?°　　*outcome*
335　And what is faith, love, virtue, unassayed°　　*untested*
Alone, without exterior help sustained?
Let us not then suspect our happy state
Left so imperfect by the Maker wise
As not secure to single or combined.
340　Frail is our happiness, if this be so;
And Eden were no Eden, thus exposed."
　　To whom thus Adam fervently replied:
"O woman, best are all things as the will
Of God ordained them; his creating hand
345　Nothing imperfect or deficient left
Of all that he created, much less man,
Or aught that might his happy state secure,
Secure from outward force. Within himself

The danger lies, yet lies within his power;
350   Against his will he can receive no harm.
But God left free the will; for what obeys
Reason is free; and reason he made right,
But bid her³ well beware, and still erect,°   *alert*
Lest, by some fair appearing good surprised,
355   She dictate false, and misinform the will
To do what God expressly hath forbid.
Not then mistrust, but tender love, enjoins
That I should mind° thee oft; and mind thou me.   *remind; pay heed to*
Firm we subsist,° yet possible to swerve,   *stand; exist*
360   Since reason not impossibly may meet
Some specious° object by the foe suborned,⁴   *fair-appearing*
And fall into deception unaware,
Not keeping strictest watch, as she was warned.
Seek not temptation, then, which to avoid
365   Were better, and most likely if from me
Thou sever not: trial will come unsought.
Wouldst thou approve° thy constancy, approve   *prove*
First thy obedience; the other who can know,
Not seeing thee attempted, who attest?
370   But, if thou think trial unsought may find
Us both securer⁵ than thus warned thou seem'st,
Go; for thy stay, not free, absents thee more.
Go in thy native innocence; rely
On what thou hast of virtue; summon all;
375   For God towards thee hath done his part: do thine."
        So spake the patriarch of mankind; but Eve
Persisted; yet submiss,° though last, replied: *submissive*
"With thy permission, then, and thus forewarned,
Chiefly by what thy own last reasoning words
380   Touched only, that our trial, when least sought,
May find us both perhaps far less prepared,
The willinger I go, nor much expect
A foe so proud will first the weaker seek;
So bent, the more shall shame him his repulse."
385   Thus saying, from her husband's hand her hand
Soft she withdrew, and like a wood nymph light,
Oread or dryad, or of Delia's train,⁶
Betook her to the groves, but Delia's self
In gait surpassed and goddesslike deport,
390   Though not as she with bow and quiver armed,
But with such gardening tools as art yet rude,°   *primitive*
Guiltless of fire had formed,⁷ or angels brought.
To Pales, or Pomona, thus adorned,

3. I.e., Reason. Right reason, originally a classical concept, is the God-given ability to recognize truth and moral law.
4. Procured by corrupt means and with a sinister motive.
5. Milton may be playing on both senses of the Latin word *securus*, which means both "safe" or "free from care" and "careless" or "negligent."
6. Band of nymphs (minor nature divinities) who

accompanied Delia, or Diana (born at Delos), goddess of the hunt. *Oread or dryad:* mountain nymph or wood nymph; neither class of nymphs was immortal; the dryads died with their trees.
7. There was no need of fire in Eden; the association of guilt with fire suggests the myth of Prometheus, who stole fire from the gods to give to humans.

Likest she seemed, Pomona when she fled
395   Vertumnus, or to Ceres in her prime,
Yet virgin of Proserpina from Jove.[8]
Her long with ardent look his eye pursued
Delighted, but desiring more her stay.
Oft he to her his charge of quick return
400   Repeated; she to him as oft engaged
To be returned by noon amid the bower,
And all things in best order to invite
Noontide repast, or afternoon's repose.
O much deceived, much failing, hapless Eve,
405   Of thy presumed return! Event perverse!
Thou never from that hour in Paradise
Found'st either sweet repast, or sound repose;
Such ambush hid among sweet flowers and shades
Waited with hellish rancor imminent
410   To intercept thy way, or send thee back
Despoiled of innocence, of faith, of bliss.
For now, and since first break of dawn, the fiend,
Mere serpent in appearance, forth was come,
And on his quest, where likeliest he might find
415   The only two of mankind, but in them
The whole included race, his purposed prey.
In bower and field he sought, where any tuft
Of grove or garden-plot more pleasant lay,
Their tendance° or plantation for delight;   object of care
420   By fountain or by shady rivulet
He sought them both, but wished his hap° might find   luck
Eve separate; he wished, but not with hope
Of what so seldom chanced; when to his wish,
Beyond his hope, Eve separate he spies,
425   Veiled in a cloud of fragrance, where she stood,
Half spied, so thick the roses bushing round
About her glowed, oft stooping to support
Each flower of slender stalk, whose head though gay
Carnation, purple, azure, or specked with gold,
430   Hung drooping unsustained, them she upstays
Gently with myrtle band, mindless° the while   heedless
Herself, though fairest unsupported flower,
From her best prop so far, and storm so nigh.
Nearer he drew, and many a walk traversed
435   Of stateliest covert, cedar, pine, or palm;
Then voluble° and bold, now hid, now seen   undulating
Among thick-woven arborets° and flowers   shrubs
Embordered on each bank, the hand° of Eve: handiwork
Spot more delicious than those gardens feigned[9]

8. In Roman mythology, the supreme god, who impregnated Ceres, the supreme agricultural goddess, with Proserpina. Pales was the goddess of flocks and pastures. Pomona, goddess of fruit trees, was long pursued by Vertumnus, god of the seasons; disguised as a reaper, he awakened "answering passion" in Pomona, according to Ovid's *Metamorphoses*.
9. Mythical or legendary gardens. In the first (below), the youth Adonis was nursed by Venus after having been killed by a boar, then revived; the second was visited by Odysseus ("Laertes' son"), who found springtime and harvest time both continuous there. The third garden mentioned—the garden of Solomon ("the sapient king") and his bride, the pharaoh's daughter—Milton regards as historical, not "mystic," or mythical.

440 Or of revived Adonis, or renowned
    Alcinous, host of old Laertes' son,
    Or that, not mystic, where the sapient king
    Held dalliance with his fair Egyptian spouse.
    Much he° the place admired, the person more.   *Satan*
445 As one who long in populous city pent,
    Where houses thick and sewers annoy° the air,   *pollute*
    Forth issuing on a summer's morn to breathe
    Among the pleasant villages and farms
    Adjoined, from each thing met conceives delight,
450 The smell of grain, or tedded[1] grass, or kine,°   *cattle*
    Or dairy, each rural sight, each rural sound:
    If chance with nymphlike step fair virgin pass,
    What pleasing seemed, for° her now pleases more,   *because of*
    She most, and in her look sums all delight.
455 Such pleasure took the serpent to behold
    This flowery plat,° the sweet recess° of Eve   *plot / retreat*
    Thus early, thus alone; her heavenly form
    Angelic, but more soft, and feminine,
    Her graceful innocence, her every air°   *manner*
460 Of gesture or least action overawed
    His malice, and with rapine[2] sweet bereaved
    His fierceness of the fierce intent it brought:
    That space the evil one abstracted° stood   *withdrawn*
    From his own evil, and for the time remained
465 Stupidly good, of enmity disarmed,
    Of guile, of hate, of envy, of revenge.[3]
    But the hot Hell that always in him burns,
    Though in mid Heaven, soon ended his delight,
    And tortures him now more, the more he sees
470 Of pleasure not for him ordained: then soon
    Fierce hate he recollects, and all his thoughts
    Of mischief, gratulating,° thus excites: *exulting*
      "Thoughts, whither have ye led me? with what sweet
    Compulsion thus transported to forget
475 What hither brought us? hate, not love, nor hope
    Of Paradise for Hell, hope here to taste
    Of pleasure, but all pleasure to destroy,
    Save what is in destroying; other joy
    To me is lost. Then let me not let pass
480 Occasion which now smiles; behold alone
    The woman, opportune° to all attempts,   *open*
    Her husband, for I view far round, not nigh,
    Whose higher intellectual° more I shun,   *intellect*
    And strength, of courage haughty, and of limb
485 Heroic built, though of terrestrial° mold;°   *earthly / composition*
    Foe not informidable, exempt from wound,
    I not; so much hath Hell debased, and pain
    Enfeebled me, to what I was in Heaven.

---

1. Spread out to dry to make hay.
2. Robbery; from *rapere*, Latin for "to seize," the root of both *rape* and *rapture*. Here, the ravisher is temporarily ravished.

3. Amazed by Eve's beauty, Satan is momentarily stunned into inaction and, while thus incapacitated, is insensibly good.

She fair, divinely fair, fit love for gods,
490 Not terrible,° though terror be in love   *exciting fear*
     And beauty, not° approached by stronger hate,   *unless*
     Hate stronger, under show of love well feigned,
     The way which to her ruin now I tend."
         So spake the enemy of mankind, enclosed
495 In serpent, inmate bad, and toward Eve
     Addressed his way, not with indented° wave,   *zigzag*
     Prone on the ground, as since, but on his rear,
     Circular base of rising folds, that towered
     Fold above fold a surging maze; his head
500 Crested aloft, and carbuncle° his eyes;   *ruby-colored*
     With burnished neck of verdant gold, erect
     Amidst his circling spires,° that on the grass   *coils*
     Floated redundant.° Pleasing was his shape,   *waving; excessive*
     And lovely; never since of serpent kind
505 Lovelier, not those that in Illyria changed
     Hermione and Cadmus, or the god
     In Epidaurus; nor to which transformed
     Ammonian Jove, or Capitoline was seen,
     He with Olympias, this with her who bore
510 Scipio, the height of Rome.⁴ With tract° oblique   *course*
     At first, as one who sought access, but feared
     To interrupt, sidelong he works his way.
     As when a ship by skillful steersman wrought
     Nigh river's mouth or foreland, where the wind
515 Veers oft, as oft so steers, and shifts her sail:
     So varied he, and of his tortuous train
     Curled many a wanton° wreath in sight of Eve,   *unrestrained; lewd*
     To lure her eye: she busied heard the sound
     Of rustling leaves, but minded not, as used
520 To such disport before her through the field,
     From every beast, more duteous at her call,
     Than at Circean call the herd disguised.⁵
     He bolder now, uncalled before her stood:
     But as in gaze admiring; oft he bowed
525 His turret crest, and sleek enameled° neck,   *multicolored*
     Fawning, and licked the ground whereon she trod.
     His gentle dumb expression turned at length
     The eye of Eve to mark his play: he, glad
     Of her attention gained, with serpent tongue
530 Organic, or impulse of vocal air,⁶
     His fraudulent temptation thus began.
         "Wonder not, sovereign mistress, if perhaps
     Thou canst, who art sole wonder; much less arm

4. Cadmus, king of Thebes, and his wife, Har-
monia ("Hermione"), were transformed into ser-
pents after their retirement to Illyria. The "god in
Epidaurus" is Aesculapius, god of healing, whose
art included the use of serpents and who some-
times appeared in the form of a serpent at his tem-
ple in Epidaurus. Jove (here called Ammonian and
Capitoline after temples associated with him) was
said to have coupled with Olympias and Sempronia
in the form of a serpent. Alexander the Great was
born of the first union, and the Roman leader
Scipio Africanus was born of the second.
5. In the *Odyssey*, book 10, the enchantress Circe
changes men into swine, who then dutifully follow
her about.
6. I.e., Satan speaks through the serpent either
using the serpent's own tongue or by directly
impelling the air to make it seem voicelike; there
is a pun on "impulse," which means both "motion"
and "strong suggestion from a spirit."

Thy looks, the heaven of mildness, with disdain,
535 Displeased that I approach thee thus, and gaze
Insatiate, I thus single, nor have feared
Thy awful° brow, more awful thus retired.   *awe-inspiring*
Fairest resemblance of thy Maker fair,
Thee all things living gaze on, all things thine
540 By gift, and thy celestial beauty adore
With ravishment° beheld, there best beheld   *rapture, ecstasy*
Where universally admired: but here
In this enclosure wild, these beasts among,
Beholders rude, and shallow to discern
545 Half what in thee is fair, one man except,
Who sees thee? (and what is one?) who shouldst be seen
A goddess among gods, adored and served
By angels numberless, thy daily train."
    So glozed° the tempter, and his proem° tuned;   *flattered / prelude*
550 Into the heart of Eve his words made way,
Though at the voice much marveling: at length,
Not unamazed, she thus in answer spake.
"What may this mean? Language of man pronounced
By tongue of brute, and human sense expressed?
555 The first at least of these I thought denied
To beasts, whom God on their creation-day
Created mute to all articulate sound;
The latter I demur,° for in their looks   *hesitate about*
Much reason, and in their actions oft appears.
560 Thee, serpent, subtlest beast of all the field
I knew, but not with human voice endued:°   *endowed*
Redouble then this miracle, and say,
How cam'st thou speakable° of mute, and how   *able to speak*
To me so friendly grown above the rest
565 Of brutal kind, that daily are in sight?
Say, for such wonder claims attention due."
    To whom the guileful tempter thus replied:
"Empress of this fair world, resplendent Eve!
Easy to me it is to tell thee all
570 What thou command'st and right thou shouldst be obeyed:
I was at first as other beasts that graze
The trodden herb, of abject thoughts and low,
As was my food, nor aught but food discerned
Or sex, and apprehended nothing high:
575 Till on a day, roving the field, I chanced
A goodly tree far distant to behold
Loaden with fruit of fairest colors mixed,
Ruddy and gold; I nearer drew to gaze;
When from the boughs a savory odor blown,
580 Grateful to appetite, more pleased my sense
Than smell of sweetest fennel, or the teats
Of ewe or goat dropping with milk at even,
Unsucked of lamb or kid,[7] that tend their play.

---

7. It was popularly believed that snakes were especially fond of the herb fennel and that they stole milk from sheep and goats.

To satisfy the sharp desire I had
585 Of tasting those fair apples, I resolved
Not to defer: hunger and thirst at once,
Powerful persuaders, quickened at the scent
Of that alluring fruit, urged me so keen.
About the mossy trunk I wound me soon,
590 For, high from ground, the branches would require
Thy utmost reach, or Adam's, round the tree
All other beasts that saw, with like desire
Longing and envying stood, but could not reach.
Amid the tree now got, where plenty hung
595 Tempting so nigh, to pluck and eat my fill
I spared not; for such pleasure till that hour
At feed or fountain never had I found.
Sated at length, ere long I might perceive
Strange alteration in me, to degree
600 Of reason in my inward powers, and speech
Wanted° not long, though to this shape retained.   *lacked*
Thenceforth to speculations high or deep
I turned my thoughts, and with capacious° mind   *wide, spacious*
Considered all things visible in Heaven,
605 Or Earth, or middle,° all things fair and good: *regions between*
But all that fair and good in thy divine
Semblance, and in thy beauty's heavenly ray
United I beheld: no fair° to° thine   *beauty / compared to*
Equivalent or second, which compelled
610 Me thus, though importune° perhaps, to come   *inopportunely*
And gaze, and worship thee of right declared
Sovereign of creatures, universal dame."
    So talked the spirited° sly snake: and Eve   *spirit-possessed*
Yet more amazed, unwary thus replied:
615   "Serpent, thy overpraising leaves in doubt
The virtue° of that fruit, in thee first proved.°   *power / experienced*
But say, where grows the tree, from hence how far?
For many are the trees of God that grow
In Paradise, and various, yet unknown
620 To us; in such abundance lies our choice,
As leaves a greater store of fruit untouched,
Still hanging incorruptible, till men
Grow up to their provision, and more hands
Help to disburden Nature of her birth."[8]
625   To whom the wily adder, blithe and glad:
"Empress, the way is ready, and not long,
Beyond a row of myrtles, on a flat,°   *plot*
Fast by a fountain, one small thicket past
Of blowing° myrrh and balm: if thou accept   *blooming*
630 My conduct,° I can bring thee thither soon."   *guidance*

---

8. I.e., what Nature bears. *Till men . . . provision:* i.e., until enough humans exist to eat all the food on
Earth.

"Lead then," said Eve. He leading swiftly rolled
In tangles, and made intricate seem straight,
To mischief swift. Hope elevates, and joy
Brightens his crest; as when a wandering fire
635 Compact of unctuous vapor,[9] which the night
Condenses, and the cold environs round,
Kindled through agitation to a flame
(Which oft, they say, some evil spirit attends),
Hovering and blazing with delusive light,
640 Misleads th' amazed night-wanderer from his way
To bogs and mires, and oft through pond or pool,
There swallowed up and lost, from succor° far: help
So glistered the dire snake, and into fraud
Led Eve our credulous mother, to the tree
645 Of prohibition,[1] root of all our woe:
Which when she saw, thus to her guide she spake:
     "Serpent, we might have spared our coming hither,
Fruitless to me, though fruit be here to excess,
The credit of whose virtue rest with thee;[2]
650 Wondrous indeed, if cause of such effects!
But of this tree we may not taste nor touch:
God so commanded, and left that command
Sole daughter of his voice; the rest,[3] we live
Law to ourselves; our reason is our law."
655   To whom the Tempter guilefully replied:
"Indeed? Hath God then said that of the fruit
Of all these garden trees ye shall not eat,
Yet lords declared of all in Earth or air?"
     To whom thus Eve, yet sinless: "Of the fruit
660 Of each tree in the garden we may eat,
But of the fruit of this fair tree amidst
The garden, God hath said, 'Ye shall not eat
Thereof, nor shall ye touch it, lest ye die.'"
     She scarce had said, though brief, when now more bold,
665 The tempter, but with show of zeal and love
To man, and indignation at his wrong,
New part puts on, and as° to passion moved,   as if
Fluctuates disturbed, yet comely,° and in act°   attractive / bearing
Raised, as of some great matter to begin.
670 As when of old some orator renowned
In Athens or free Rome, where eloquence
Flourished, since mute, to some great cause addressed,
Stood in himself collected, while each part,
Motion, each act, won audience ere the tongue,
675 Sometimes in height began, as no delay
Of preface brooking, through his zeal of right.[4]

9. Composed of oily vapor. The allusion is to the will-o'-the-wisp (*ignis fatuus*), which was said to draw travelers astray by holding a false light before them; the phenomenon of nocturnal light is caused by the combustion of marsh gas.
1. I.e., the prohibited tree.

2. I.e., my belief in the effects of the fruit must continue to depend solely on your testimony.
3. I.e., in everything else.
4. I.e., the orator, convinced of the rightness of his cause, bursts directly into his argument, impatient of the "delay" of an introduction.

So standing, moving, or to height upgrown
The tempter all impassioned thus began:
    "O sacred, wise, and wisdom-giving plant,
680 Mother of science!° now I feel thy power   *knowledge*
Within me clear, not only to discern
Things in their causes, but to trace the ways
Of highest agents, deemed however wise.
Queen of this universe! do not believe
685 Those rigid threats of death. Ye shall not die;
How should ye? By the fruit? it gives you life
To° knowledge; by the Threatener? look on me,   *in addition to*
Me who have touched and tasted, yet both live,
And life more perfect have attained than Fate
690 Meant me, by venturing higher than my lot.
Shall that be shut to man, which to the beast
Is open? Or will God incense his ire
For such a petty trespass, and not praise
Rather your dauntless virtue,° whom the pain   *courage*
695 Of death denounced,° whatever thing death be,   *threatened*
Deterred not from achieving what might lead
To happier life, knowledge of good and evil?
Of good, how just!⁵ Of evil, if what is evil
Be real, why not known, since easier shunned?
700 God therefore cannot hurt ye, and be just;
Not just, not God; not feared then, nor obeyed:
Your fear itself of death removes the fear.
Why then was this forbid? Why but to awe,
Why but to keep ye low and ignorant,
705 His worshippers? He knows that in the day
Ye eat thereof, your eyes that seem so clear,
Yet are but dim, shall perfectly be then
Opened and cleared, and ye shall be as gods,
Knowing both good and evil, as they know.
710 That ye should be as gods, since I as man,
Internal° man, is but proportion meet,   *internally*
I, of brute, human; ye, of human, gods.
So ye shall die perhaps, by putting off
Human, to put on gods: death to be wished,
715 Though threatened, which no worse than this can bring.
And what are gods that man may not become
As they, participating° godlike food?   *sharing*
The gods are first, and that advantage use
On our belief, that all from them proceeds.
720 I question it; for this fair Earth I see,
Warmed by the sun, producing every kind,
Them nothing: If they all things,⁶ who enclosed
Knowledge of good and evil in this tree,
That whoso eats thereof forthwith attains
725 Wisdom without their leave? And wherein lies

5. I.e., how just, to deny the knowledge of good!   6. The verb here, "produce," is understood.
(Satan is being ironic.)

Th' offense, that man should thus attain to know?
What can your knowledge hurt him, or this tree
Impart against his will if all be his?
Or is it envy, and can envy dwell
730 In heavenly breasts? These, these, and many more
Causes import° your need of this fair fruit.   imply, indicate
Goddess humane,[7] reach then, and freely taste!"
      He ended, and his words, replete with guile,
Into her heart too easy entrance won:
735 Fixed on the fruit she gazed, which to behold
Might tempt alone, and in her ears the sound
Yet rung of his persuasive words, impregned°   impregnated
With reason, to her seeming, and with truth;
Meanwhile the hour of noon drew on, and waked
740 An eager appetite, raised by the smell
So savory of that fruit, which with desire,
Inclinable now grown to touch or taste,
Solicited her longing eye;[8] yet first
Pausing a while, thus to herself she mused:
745   "Great are thy virtues,° doubtless, best of fruits,   powers
Though kept from man, and worthy to be admired,
Whose taste, too long forborn, at first essay°   testing
Gave elocution to the mute, and taught
The tongue not made for speech to speak thy praise:
750 Thy praise he also who forbids thy use,
Conceals not from us, naming thee the Tree
Of Knowledge, knowledge both of good and evil;
Forbids us then to taste; but his forbidding
Commends thee more, while it infers the good
755 By thee communicated, and our want:°   lack
For good unknown, sure is not had, or had
And yet unknown, is as not had at all.
In plain° then, what forbids he but to know?   plain words
Forbids us good, forbids us to be wise!
760 Such prohibitions bind not. But if Death
Bind us with after-bands, what profits then
Our inward freedom? In the day we eat
Of this fair fruit, our doom is, we shall die.
How dies the serpent? He hath eaten and lives,
765 And knows, and speaks, and reasons, and discerns,
Irrational till then. For us alone
Was death invented? Or to us denied
This intellectual food, for beasts reserved?
For beasts it seems: yet that one beast which first
770 Hath tasted, envies not, but brings with joy
The good befallen him, author unsuspect,[9]
Friendly to man, far from deceit or guile.
What fear I then, rather what know to fear

---

7. "Humane" probably means "kindly" or "gracious," but also suggests the oxymoron "human Goddess," expressing Satan's prediction of what Eve will become if she eats the fruit.

8. All five of Eve's senses—sight, hearing, smell, taste, and touch—are involved in her temptation.
9. I.e., authority whose testimony does not arouse suspicion.

Under this ignorance of good and evil,
775 Of God or death, of law or penalty?
Here grows the cure of all, this fruit divine,
Fair to the eye, inviting to the taste,
Of virtue° to make wise: what hinders then   *power*
To reach, and feed at once both body and mind?"
780   So saying, her rash hand in evil hour,
Forth reaching to the fruit, she plucked, she eat.°   *ate*
Earth felt the wound, and Nature from her seat
Sighing through all her works gave signs of woe,
That all was lost. Back to the thicket slunk
785 The guilty serpent, and well might, for Eve
Intent now wholly on her taste, naught else
Regarded; such delight till then, as seemed,
In fruit she never tasted, whether true
Or fancied so, through expectation high
790 Of knowledge; nor was godhead from her thought.[1]
Greedily she engorged without restraint,
And knew not eating death:[2] satiate at length,
And heightened as with wine, jocund and boon,°   *jovial*
Thus to herself she pleasingly began:
795   "O sovereign, virtuous, precious of all trees
In Paradise! of operation blest
To sapience,[3] hitherto obscured, infamed,°   *defamed*
And thy fair fruit let hang, as to no end
Created; but henceforth my early care,
800 Not without song each morning, and due praise
Shall tend thee, and the fertile burden ease
Of thy full branches offered free to all;
Till dieted by thee I grow mature
In knowledge, as the gods who all things know;
805 Though others[4] envy what they cannot give:
For had the gift been theirs, it had not here
Thus grown. Experience, next to thee I owe,
Best guide; not following thee I had remained
In ignorance; thou open'st Wisdom's way,
810 And giv'st access, though secret° she retire.   *hidden*
And I perhaps am secret;° Heaven is high,   *unseen*
High and remote to see from thence distinct
Each thing on Earth; and other care perhaps
May have diverted from continual watch
815 Our great Forbidder, safe with all his spies
About him. But to Adam in what sort°   *guise*
Shall I appear? Shall I to him make known
As yet my change, and give him to partake
Full happiness with me, or rather not,
820 But keep the odds of knowledge in my power

1. I.e., she also expected to achieve godhead.
2. I.e., she was eating death and did not know it; also, she was unaware while she ate death.
3. Wisdom, of the wise and those with good taste;

from the Latin *sapere*, "to be wise," which has its roots in the verb "to taste."
4. I.e., the other gods; Eve here echoes the lesson taught her by the serpent.

Without copartner? so to add what wants°   *lacks*
In female sex, the more to draw his love,
And render me more equal, and perhaps,
A thing not undesirable, sometime
825 Superior: for, inferior, who is free?
This may be well: but what if God have seen
And death ensue? Then I shall be no more,
And Adam, wedded to another Eve,
Shall live with her enjoying, I extinct;
830 A death to think. Confirmed then I resolve,
Adam shall share with me in bliss or woe:
So dear I love him, that with him all deaths
I could endure, without him live no life."
       So saying, from the tree her step she turned,
835 But first low reverence done, as to the power
That dwelt within, whose presence had infused
Into the plant sciental° sap, derived   *knowledge-giving*
From nectar, drink of gods. Adam the while
Waiting desirous her return, had wove
840 Of choicest flowers a garland to adorn
Her tresses, and her rural labors crown,
As reapers oft are wont° their harvest queen.   *accustomed to do [to]*
Great joy he promised to his thoughts, and new
Solace in her return, so long delayed:
845 Yet oft his heart, divine° of something ill,   *apprehensive*
Misgave him; he the faltering measure[5] felt;
And forth to meet her went, the way she took
That morn when first they parted. By the Tree
Of Knowledge he must pass; there he her met,
850 Scarce from the tree returning; in her hand
A bough of fairest fruit that downy smiled,
New gathered, and ambrosial smell diffused.
To him she hastened, in her face excuse
Came prologue, and apology to prompt,[6]
855 Which with bland° words at will she thus addressed: *mild; coaxing*
       "Hast thou not wondered, Adam, at my stay?
Thee I have missed, and thought it long, deprived
Thy presence, agony of love till now
Not felt, nor shall be twice; for never more
860 Mean I to try, what rash untried I sought,
The pain of absence from thy sight. But strange
Hath been the cause, and wonderful to hear:
This tree is not as we are told, a tree
Of danger tasted,° nor to evil unknown   *if tasted*
865 Opening the way, but of divine effect
To open eyes, and make them gods who taste;
And hath been tasted such. The serpent wise,
Or° not restrained as we, or not obeying,   *either*

5. I.e., the irregular beat (of his heart).
6. Her excuse, apparent in her expression, is a pro-   logue to her "apology," or formal defense of her
                                                        actions.

Hath eaten of the fruit, and is become,
870 Not dead, as we are threatened, but thenceforth
Endued with human voice and human sense,
Reasoning to° admiration, and with me   *so as to produce*
Persuasively hath so prevailed, that I
Have also tasted, and have also found
875 Th' effects to correspond—opener mine eyes,
Dim erst,° dilated spirits, ampler heart,   *previously*
And growing up to godhead; which for thee
Chiefly I sought, without thee can despise.
For bliss, as thou hast part, to me is bliss,
880 Tedious, unshared with thee, and odious soon.
Thou therefore also taste, that equal lot
May join us, equal joy, as equal love;
Lest, thou not tasting, different degree[7]
Disjoin us, and I then too late renounce
885 Deity for thee, when Fate will not permit."
      Thus Eve with countenance blithe her story told;
But in her cheek distemper° flushing glowed.   *intoxicated*
On th' other side, Adam, soon as he heard
The fatal trespass done by Eve, amazed,
890 Astonied[8] stood and blank, while horror chill
Ran through his veins, and all his joints relaxed;
From his slack hand the garland wreathed for Eve
Down dropped, and all the faded roses shed.
Speechless he stood and pale, till thus at length
895 First to himself he inward silence broke:
      "O fairest of creation, last and best
Of all God's works, creature in whom excelled
Whatever can to sight or thought be formed,
Holy, divine, good, amiable, or sweet!
900 How art thou lost, how on a sudden lost,
Defaced, deflowered, and now to death devote?°   *doomed*
Rather how hast thou yielded to transgress
The strict forbiddance, how to violate
The sacred fruit forbidden! Some cursèd fraud
905 Of enemy hath beguiled thee, yet unknown,
And me with thee hath ruined, for with thee
Certain my resolution is to die.
How can I live without thee, how forgo
Thy sweet converse and love so dearly joined,
910 To live again in these wild woods forlorn?
Should God create another Eve, and I
Another rib afford, yet loss of thee
Would never from my heart; no, no! I feel
The link of nature draw me: flesh of flesh,
915 Bone of my bone thou art, and from thy state
Mine never shall be parted, bliss or woe."
      So having said, as one from sad dismay

---

7. I.e., different rank, since she, as she believes,
has grown "up to godhead" while he has not.

8. Stunned, with a likely pun: turned to stone.

Recomforted, and after thoughts disturbed
Submitting to what seemed remediless,
920   Thus in calm mood his words to Eve he turned:
    "Bold deed thou hast presumed, adventurous Eve
And peril great provoked, who thus hast dared
Had it been only coveting to eye
That sacred fruit, sacred° to abstinence,   *dedicated*
925   Much more to taste it, under ban to touch.
But past who can recall, or done undo?
Not God omnipotent, nor Fate! Yet so
Perhaps thou shalt not die, perhaps the fact°   *deed*
Is not so heinous now, foretasted fruit,
930   Profaned first by the serpent, by him first
Made common and unhallowed ere our taste,
Nor yet on him found deadly; he yet lives,
Lives, as thou saidst, and gains to live as man
Higher degree of life: inducement strong
935   To us, as likely, tasting, to attain
Proportional ascent, which cannot be
But to be gods, or angels, demigods.
Nor can I think that God, Creator wise,
Though threatening, will in earnest so destroy
940   Us his prime creatures, dignified so high,
Set over all his works, which in our fall,
For us created, needs with us must fail,
Dependent made; so God shall uncreate,
Be frustrate, do, undo, and labor lose;
945   Not well conceived of God, who, though his power
Creation could repeat, yet would be loath
Us to abolish, lest the adversary
Triumph and say: 'Fickle their state whom God
Most favors; who can please him long? Me first
950   He ruined, now mankind; whom will he next?'
Matter of scorn, not to be given the foe.
However, I with thee have fixed my lot,
Certain° to undergo like doom: if death   *resolved*
Consort° with thee, death is to me as life;   *keep company*
955   So forcible within my heart I feel
The bond of nature draw me to my own,
My own in thee, for what thou art is mine;
Our state cannot be severed; we are one,
One flesh; to lose thee were to lose myself."
960   So Adam, and thus Eve to him replied:
"O glorious trial of exceeding love,
Illustrious evidence, example high!
Engaging me to emulate; but short
Of thy perfection, how shall I attain,
965   Adam? from whose dear side I boast me sprung,
And gladly of our union hear thee speak,
One heart, one soul in both; whereof good proof
This day affords, declaring thee resolved,
Rather than death or aught than death more dread

970　Shall separate us, linked in love so dear,
　　To undergo with me one guilt, one crime,
　　If any be, of tasting this fair fruit;
　　Whose virtue (for of good still good proceeds,
　　Direct, or by occasion°) hath presented　　　　　　　　　*indirection*
975　This happy trial of thy love, which else
　　So eminently never had been known.
　　Were it I thought death menaced would ensue
　　This my attempt, I would sustain alone
　　The worst, and not persuade thee, rather die
980　Deserted, than oblige° thee with a fact°　　　*involve in guilt / deed*
　　Pernicious to thy peace, chiefly assured
　　Remarkably so late of thy so true,
　　So faithful love unequaled; but I feel
　　Far otherwise th' event°—not death, but life　　　　*outcome*
985　Augmented, opened eyes, new hopes, new joys,
　　Taste so divine, that what of sweet before
　　Hath touched my sense, flat seems to this, and harsh.
　　On my experience, Adam, freely taste,
　　And fear of death deliver to the winds."
990　　So saying, she embraced him, and for joy
　　Tenderly wept, much won that he his love
　　Had so ennobled, as of choice to incur
　　Divine displeasure for her sake, or death.
　　In recompense (for such compliance bad
995　Such recompense best merits), from the bough
　　She gave him of that fair enticing fruit
　　With liberal hand; he scrupled not to eat,
　　Against his better knowledge, not deceived,[9]
　　But fondly° overcome with female charm.　　　　　　*foolishly*
1000　Earth trembled from her entrails, as again
　　In pangs, and Nature gave a second groan,
　　Sky lowered, and muttering thunder, some sad drops
　　Wept at completing of the mortal sin
　　Original; while Adam took no thought,
1005　Eating his fill, nor Eve to iterate
　　Her former trespass feared, the more to soothe
　　Him with her loved society; that now
　　As with new wine intoxicated both,
　　They swim in mirth, and fancy that they feel
1010　Divinity within them breeding wings
　　Wherewith to scorn the Earth. But that false fruit
　　Far other operation first displayed,
　　Carnal desire inflaming; he on Eve
　　Began to cast lascivious eyes, she him
1015　As wantonly repaid; in lust they burn,
　　Till Adam thus 'gan Eve to dalliance move:
　　　"Eve, now I see thou art exact° of taste,　　　*discriminating*
　　And elegant, of sapience[1] no small part,

9. Cf. 1 Timothy 2.14: "And Adam was not　　transgression."
deceived, but the woman being deceived was in the　　1. See note 3, p. 442.

Since to each meaning savor we apply,
1020 And palate call judicious. I the praise
Yield thee, so well this day thou hast purveyed.° *provisioned us*
Much pleasure we have lost, while we abstained
From this delightful fruit, nor known till now
True relish, tasting; if such pleasure be
1025 In things to us forbidden, it might be wished,
For this one tree had been forbidden ten.
But come; so well refreshed, now let us play,
As meet° is, after such delicious fare; *appropriate*
For never did thy beauty, since the day
1030 I saw thee first and wedded thee, adorned
With all perfections, so enflame my sense
With ardor to enjoy thee, fairer now
Than ever, bounty of this virtuous tree."
      So said he, and forbore not glance or toy° *caress*
1035 Of amorous intent, well understood
Of° Eve, whose eye darted contagious fire. *by*
Her hand he seized, and to a shady bank,
Thick overhead with verdant roof embowered
He led her, nothing loath; flowers were the couch,
1040 Pansies, and violets, and asphodel,[2]
And hyacinth—Earth's freshest, softest lap.
There they their fill of love and love's disport
Took largely, of their mutual guilt the seal,
The solace of their sin, till dewy sleep
1045 Oppressed them, wearied with their amorous play.
      Soon as the force of that fallacious fruit,
That with exhilarating vapor bland° *pleasing*
About their spirits had played, and inmost powers
Made err, was now exhaled, and grosser sleep
1050 Bred of unkindly° fumes,° with conscious dreams *unnatural / vapors*
Encumbered, now had left them, up they rose
As from unrest, and each the other viewing,
Soon found their eyes how opened, and their minds
How darkened. Innocence, that as a veil
1055 Had shadowed them from knowing ill, was gone;
Just confidence, and native righteousness,
And honor from about them, naked left
To guilty Shame; he° covered,° but his robe *Shame / [them]*
Uncovered more. So rose the Danite strong,
1060 Herculean Samson, from the harlot-lap
Of Philistean Dalilah, and waked
Shorn of his strength;[3] they destitute and bare
Of all their virtue. Silent, and in face
Confounded, long they sat, as strucken mute;
1065 Till Adam, though not less than Eve abashed,
At length gave utterance to these words constrained:

2. A flower conventionally held to be immortal and said to cover the Elysian meadows.
3. The Philistine Dalilah betrayed her husband, Samson (of the tribe of Dan), by cutting off his hair, the source of his strength, while he slept. Their story is told in Judges 16 and retold in Milton's "Samson Agonistes."

"O Eve, in evil[4] hour thou didst give ear
To that false worm,° of whomsoever taught   *serpent*
To counterfeit man's voice, true in our fall,
1070   False in our promised rising; since our eyes
Opened we find indeed, and find we know
Both good and evil, good lost, and evil got:
Bad fruit of knowledge, if this be to know,
Which leaves us naked thus, of honor void,
1075   Of innocence, of faith, of purity,
Our wonted° ornaments now soiled and stained,   *customary*
And in our faces evident the signs
Of foul concupiscence;° whence evil store,   *lust*
Even shame, the last of evils; of the first
1080   Be sure then. How shall I behold the face
Henceforth of God or angel, erst with joy
And rapture so oft beheld? Those heavenly shapes
Will dazzle now this earthly° with their blaze   *earthly nature*
Insufferably bright. O might I here
1085   In solitude live savage, in some glade
Obscured, where highest woods, impenetrable
To star or sunlight, spread their umbrage° broad,   *shade*
And brown as evening! Cover me, ye pines,
Ye cedars, with innumerable boughs
1090   Hide me, where I may never see them more!
But let us now, as in bad plight, devise
What best may for the present serve to hide
The parts of each from other, that seem most
To shame obnoxious,° and unseemliest seen;   *liable*
1095   Some tree whose broad smooth leaves together sewed,
And girded on our loins, may cover round
Those middle parts, that this newcomer, Shame,
There sit not, and reproach us as unclean."
      So counseled he, and both together went
1100   Into the thickest wood; there soon they chose
The figtree, not that kind for fruit renowned,
But such as at this day, to Indians known,
In Malabar or Deccan[5] spreads her arms
Branching so broad and long, that in the ground
1105   The bended twigs take root, and daughters grow
About the mother tree, a pillared shade
High overarched, and echoing walks between;
There oft the Indian herdsman, shunning heat,
Shelters in cool, and tends his pasturing herds
1110   At loopholes cut through thickest shade. Those leaves
They gathered, broad as Amazonian targe,[6]
And with what skill they had, together sewed,
To gird their waist; vain covering, if to hide

---

4. Here punning bitterly on Eve's name, Adam will reaffirm its etymology—from *hava*, Hebrew for "life"—in 11.159–61.

5. Sections of southern India.
6. The Amazons, mythical female warriors, carried large, crescent-shaped shields called "targes."

Their guilt and dreaded shame! O how unlike
1115　To that first naked glory! Such of late
Columbus found th' American, so girt
With feathered cincture,° naked else and wild　　　　　*belt*
Among the trees on isles and woody shores.
Thus fenced, and, as they thought, their shame in part
1120　Covered, but not at rest or ease of mind,
They sat them down to weep; nor only tears
Rained at their eyes, but high winds worse within
Began to rise, high passions, anger, hate,
Mistrust, suspicion, discord, and shook sore
1125　Their inward state of mind, calm region once
And full of peace, now tossed and turbulent:
For Understanding ruled not, and the Will
Heard not her lore, both in subjection now
To sensual Appetite, who, from beneath
1130　Usurping over sovereign Reason, claimed
Superior sway.[7] From thus distempered breast,
Adam, estranged in look and altered style,
Speech intermitted thus to Eve renewed:
　　"Would thou hadst hearkened to my words, and stayed
1135　With me, as I besought thee, when that strange
Desire of wandering, this unhappy morn,
I know not whence possessed thee! we had then
Remained still happy, not as now, despoiled
Of all our good, shamed, naked, miserable.
1140　Let none henceforth seek needless cause to approve°　　*prove*
The faith they owe;° when earnestly they seek　　　　　*own*
Such proof, conclude, they then begin to fail."
　　　To whom, soon moved with touch of blame, thus Eve:
"What words have passed thy lips, Adam severe?
1145　Imput'st thou that to my default, or will
Of wandering, as thou call'st it, which who knows
But might as ill have happened, thou being by,
Or to thyself perhaps? Hadst thou been there,
Or here th' attempt, thou couldst not have discerned
1150　Fraud in the serpent, speaking as he spake;
No ground of enmity between us known,
Why he should mean me ill, or seek to harm?
Was I to have never parted from thy side?
As good have grown there still a lifeless rib.
1155　Being as I am, why didst not thou, the head,[8]
Command me absolutely not to go,
Going into such danger, as thou saidst?
Too facile° then, thou didst not much gainsay,　　　　　*easy, mild*
Nay, didst permit, approve, and fair dismiss.

---

7. As a result of the Fall, the higher faculties, reason and understanding, are subjected to appetite and the physical senses.

8. Cf. Corinthians 11.3: "the head of the woman is the man."

1160 Hadst thou been firm and fixed in thy dissent,
Neither had I transgressed, nor thou with me."
    To whom, then first incensed, Adam replied:
"Is this the love, is this the recompense
Of mine to thee, ingrateful Eve, expressed°   *revealed*
1165 Immutable when thou were lost, not I,
Who might have lived and joyed immortal bliss,
Yet willingly chose rather death with thee?
And am I now upbraided as the cause
Of thy transgressing? not enough severe,
1170 It seems, in thy restraint! What could I more?
I warned thee, I admonished thee, foretold
The danger, and the lurking enemy
That lay in wait: beyond this had been force,
And force upon free will hath here no place.
1175 But confidence then bore thee on, secure
Either to meet no danger, or to find
Matter of glorious trial; and perhaps
I also erred in overmuch admiring
What seemed in thee so perfect, that I thought
1180 No evil durst attempt thee! but I rue
That error now, which is become my crime,
And thou th' accuser. Thus it shall befall
Him who, to worth in women overtrusting,
Lets her will rule; restraint she will not brook,°   *tolerate*
1185 And, left to herself, if evil thence ensue,
She first his weak indulgence will accuse."
    Thus they in mutual accusation spent
The fruitless hours, but neither self-condemning;
And of their vain contèst appeared no end.

1660–65   1667, 1674

From Samson Agonistes[9]

60 But peace, I must not quarrel with the will
Of highest dispensation,[1] which herein
Haply° had ends above my reach to know: *perhaps*
Suffices that to me strength is my bane,[2]
And proves the source of all my miseries,
65 So many, and so huge, that each apart,
Would ask° a life to wail; but chief of all,   *need*

9. This dramatic poem tells the story of the bibli-
cal Samson (Judges 13–16) from the time of his
captivity to his death. Samson was given great
strength by God to deliver his people from their
longtime enemies, the Philistines. The source of
his strength was his long hair. His Philistine wife,
Dalila, badgered him into revealing the secret of
his strength, then cut his hair and betrayed him to

the Philistines, who blinded him and set him to
work as a slave. In these lines, Samson laments his
fate.
1. I.e., God; dispensation refers to the ordering of
events by divine providence.
2. I.e., it is sufficient that (I know?) my strength
is the cause of my downfall.

O loss of sight, of thee I most complain!
Blind among enemies, O worse than chains,
Dungeon, or beggary, or decrepit age!
70 Light the prime work of God to me is extinct,
And all her various objects of delight
Annull'd, which might in part my grief have eased,
Inferior to the vilest now become
Of man or worm; the vilest here excel me,
75 They creep, yet see; I dark in light exposed
To daily fraud, contempt, abuse, and wrong.
Within doors, or without, still° as a fool   *always*
In power of others, never in my own;
Scarce half I seem to live, dead more than half.
80 O dark, dark, dark, amid the blaze of noon,
Irrecoverably dark, total eclipse
Without all hope of day!
O first created beam, and thou great word,
Let there be light, and light was over all;[3]
85 Why am I thus bereaved° thy prime decree?   *robbed of*
The sun to me is dark
And silent as the moon,
When she deserts the night
Hid in her vacant interlunar cave.[4]
90 Since light so necessary is to life,
And almost life itself, if it be true
That light is in the soul,
She[5] all in every part; why was the sight
To such a tender ball as th' eye confined,
95 So obvious° and so easy to be quench'd,   *exposed*
And not, as feeling, through all parts diffused,
That she might look at will through every pore?
Then had I not been thus exiled from light,
As in the land of darkness yet in light,
100 To live a life half dead, a living death,
And buried; but O yet more miserable!
Myself my sepulchre, a moving grave,
Buried, yet not exempt
By privilege of death and burial
105 From worst of other evils, pains, and wrongs,
But made hereby obnoxious° more   *exposed*
To all the miseries of life,
Life in captivity
Among inhuman foes.

1647–70?   1671

---

3. Genesis 1.3: "And God said, Let there be light: and there was light"; this is God's "prime work" (line 70) and his "prime decree" (line 85) because it was his first (and perhaps most important) creation.
4. The Romans called the moon, when it was in conjunction with the sun, *silentiis lunae*; thus "silent" means "not shining." This phase of the

moon was called the interlunar time (*interlunii*); during this time, according to myth, the moon retired to a cave somewhere beneath the earth; "vacant," from the Latin *vacare*, to be at leisure, i.e., resting.
5. I.e., the soul; according to Augustine (*De Trinitate* 5.6), the soul is whole in every part of the body.

SIR JOHN SUCKLING
1609–1642

Song[1]

Why so pale and wan, fond° lover?   *foolish*
  Prithee,° why so pale?   *pray thee*
Will, when looking well can't move her,
  Looking ill prevail?
5   Prithee, why so pale?

Why so dull and mute, young sinner?
  Prithee, why so mute?
Will, when speaking well can't win her,
  Saying nothing do 't?
10   Prithee, why so mute?

Quit, quit, for shame; this will not move,°   *persuade*
  This cannot take her.
If of herself she will not love,
  Nothing can make her:
15   The devil take her!

                           1638

Sonnet II[2]

Of thee, kind boy, I ask no red and white,[3]
  To make up my delight;
    No odd becoming graces,
Black eyes, or little know-not-whats in faces;
5 Make me but mad enough, give me good store
  Of love for her I count;
    I ask no more,
'Tis love in love that makes the sport.

There's no such thing as that we beauty call,
10   It is mere cozenage° all;   *fraud*
    For though some, long ago,
Liked certain colors[4] mingled so and so,
That doth not tie me now from choosing new;
  If I a fancy take
15   To black and blue,
That fancy doth it beauty make.

1. First printed in Suckling's play *Aglaura* 4.2 (1638). Orsames, a friend to the prince (Thersames), sings it upon request, and then claims it is "a little foolish counsell (Madam) I gave a friend of mine foure or five yeares agoe." It was evidently popular, occurring in at least five musical settings, with the first probably written by Henry Lawes for the first performance of the play, in 1637.
2. The term "sonnet" was formerly applied to any short love lyric.
3. The colors conventionally used to depict female beauty in love poetry (in the Petrarchan tradition). *Kind boy*: Cupid, as god of love.
4. I.e., the "red and white" of line 1.

'Tis not the meat, but 'tis the appetite
   Makes eating a delight;
   And if I like one dish
20 More than another, that a pheasant is;
What in our watches, that in us is found:
So to the height and nick°   *critical point*
   We up be wound,
No matter by what hand or trick.

1646

Upon My Lady Carlisle's Walking in Hampton Court Garden

DIALOGUE[5]

T.C.   J.S.

Thom.

Didst thou not find the place inspired,
And flowers, as if they had desired
No other sun, start from their beds,
And for a sight steal out their heads?
5 Heardst thou not music when she talked?
And didst not find that as she walked
She threw rare perfumes all about,
Such as bean-blossoms newly out,
Or chafèd° spices give?—   *warmed*

J.S.

10 I must confess those perfumes, Tom,
I did not smell; nor found that from
Her passing by ought sprung up new.
The flowers had all their birth from you;
For I passed o'er the self-same walk
15 And did not find one single stalk
Of anything that was to bring
This unknown after-after-spring.

Thom.

Dull and insensible, couldst see
A thing so near a deity
20 Move up and down, and feel no change?

---

5. Lucy Hay, countess of Carlisle (1599–1660), was a patron of many poets. The "T.C." or "Thom." of this dialogue is the poet Thomas Carew (ca. 1595–1640; see pp. 385–90), who wrote two poems to Hay; "J.S." is John Suckling.

J.S.

None, and so great, were alike strange;
I had my thoughts, but not your way.
All are not born, sir, to the bay.[6]
Alas! Tom, I am flesh and blood,
25   And was consulting how I could
In spite of masks and hoods descry°   reveal
The parts defiled unto the eye.
I was undoing all she wore,
And had she walked but one turn more,
30   Eve in her first state had not been
More naked or more plainly seen.

Thom.

'Twas well for thee she left the place;
There is great danger in that face.
But hadst thou viewed her leg and thigh,
35   And upon that discovery
Searched after parts that are more dear
(As fancy seldom stops so near),
No time or age had ever seen
So lost a thing as thou hadst been.

1646

A Ballad upon a Wedding[7]

I tell thee, Dick,[8] where I have been,
Where I the rarest things have seen,
    Oh, things without compare!
Such sights again cannot be found
5   In any place on English ground,
    Be it at wake° or fair.   parish festival

At Charing Cross,[9] hard by the way
Where we (thou know'st) do sell our hay,
    There is a house with stairs;
10   And there did I see coming down

---

6. A crown of bay (or laurel) leaves was the traditional recognition of poetic achievement.
7. This poem parodies the epithalamion, a poem written to celebrate a marriage, the Greek name of which conveys that it was sung on the threshold of the bridal chamber. The genre, as practiced by the Latin poets, characteristically includes the invocation to the Muses (sources of artistic inspiration), the bringing home of the bride, the singing and dancing at the wedding party, and the preparations for the wedding night. The first English example was written by Sir Philip Sidney (1554–

1586) in about 1580, and Edmund Spenser (ca. 1552–1599) published perhaps the most well-known instance of the form in 1595 (see p. 195).
8. As a short form of the name Richard, a generic name for a man. The names used below (in lines 22–24) are all conventional or type names for men. "Bridget" and "Nell" (both line 132) are conventional peasant names for women.
9. A busy center in London located near the Haymarket; originally the site of a stone cross erected by King Edward I (1239–1307) in memory of his queen, Eleanor.

Such folk as are not in our town,
    Forty, at least, in pairs.

        Amongst the rest, one pest'lent° fine   *exceptionally*
        (His beard no bigger, though, than thine)
15   Walked on before the rest.
        Our landlord looks like nothing to him;
        The king (God bless him!), 'twould undo him
          Should he go still° so dressed.   *always*

        At course-a-park,[1] without all doubt,
20   He should have first been taken out
          By all the maids i' th' town,
        Though lusty Roger there had been,
        Or little George upon the Green,
          Or Vincent of the Crown.

25   But wot° you what? the youth was going   *know*
        To make an end of all his wooing;
          The parson for him stayed.
        Yet by his leave, for all his haste,
        He did not so much wish all past,
30   Perchance, as did the maid.

        The maid (and thereby hangs a tale),
        For such a maid no Whitsun-ale[2]
          Could ever yet produce;
        No grape, that's kindly ripe,[3] could be
35   So round, so plump, so soft as she,
          Nor half so full of juice.

        Her finger was so small the ring
        Would not stay on, which they did bring;
          It was too wide a peck:[4]
40   And to say truth (for out it must),
        It looked like the great collar (just)
          About our young colt's neck.

        Her feet beneath her petticoat,
        Like little mice, stole in and out,
45   As if they feared the light;
        But oh, she dances such a way,
        No sun upon an Easter day
          Is half so fine a sight!

        He would have kissed her once or twice,
50   But she would not, she was so nice,°   *demure*
          She would not do 't in sight;

1. A rural game in which a girl chooses a boy to chase her.
2. A church festival, or "ale," at which much ale was drunk; held at Whitsuntide (or Pentecost, seventh Sunday after Easter).
3. Naturally ripe; i.e., vine-ripened.
4. A measure of capacity; i.e., much too large.

And then she looked as who should say,
"I will do what I list° today;   *desire*
   And you shall do 't at night."

55   Her cheeks so rare a white was on,
No daisy makes comparison
   (Who sees them is undone),
For streaks of red were mingled there,
Such as are on a Catherine pear[5]
60   (The side that's next the sun).

Her lips were red, and one was thin
Compared to that was next her chin
   (Some bee had stung it newly);
But, Dick, her eyes so guard her face
65   I durst no more upon them gaze
   Than on the sun in Jùly.

Her mouth so small, when she does speak,
Thou 'dst swear her teeth her words did break,
   That they might passage get;
70   But she so handled still the matter,
They came as good as ours, or better,
   And are not spent° a° whit.°   *used up / one / bit*

If wishing should be any sin,
The parson himself had guilty been
75   (She looked that day so purely);
And did the youth so oft the feat
At night, as some did in conceit,°   *imagination*
   It would have spoiled him, surely.

Passion o' me, how I run on![6]
80   There's that that would be thought upon,
   I trow,° besides the bride.   *suppose*
The business of the kitchen's great,
For it is fit that man should eat,
   Nor was it there denied.

85   Just in the nick the cook knocked thrice,
And all the waiters in a trice
   His summons did obey;
Each serving-man, with dish in hand,
Marched boldly up, like our trained band,°   *militia*
90   Presented, and away.

When all the meat was on the table,
What man of knife or teeth was able

---

5. A small variety of pear.
6. In the 1646 edition of Suckling's collection *Fragmenta Aurea*, this stanza, with the first three lines following the last three, appears after line 96. The order here is that of the 1648 and subsequent editions.

To stay to be entreated?[7]
And this the very reason was,
95 Before the parson could say grace,
     The company was seated.

Now hats fly off, and youths carouse;
Healths° first go round, and then the house;   *toasts*
     The bride's came thick and thick:
100 And when 'twas named another's health,
Perhaps he made it hers by stealth;
     And who could help it, Dick?

O' th' sudden up they rise and dance;
Then sit again and sigh and glance;
105   Then dance again and kiss.
Thus several ways the time did pass,
Till every woman wished her place,
     And every man wished his!

By this time all were stolen aside
110 To counsel and undress the bride,
     But that he must not know;
But yet 'twas thought he guessed her mind,
And did not mean to stay behind
     Above an hour or so.

115 When in he came, Dick, there she lay
Like new-fallen snow melting away
     ('Twas time, I trow,° to part);   *believe*
Kisses were now the only stay,
Which soon she gave, as who would say,
120 "God b' w' ye,[8] with all my heart."

But just as heaven would have, to cross it,
In came the bridesmaids with the posset.[9]
     The bridegroom ate in spite,
For had he left the women to 't,
125 It would have cost two hours to do 't,
     Which were too much that night.

At length the candle's out, and now
All that they had not done, they do.
     What that is, who can tell?
130 But I believe it was no more
Than thou and I have done before
     With Bridget and with Nell.

ca. 1641   1646

---

7. I.e., what man able to eat could wait to be asked to sit down?
8. A contraction for *God be with ye,* pronounced in two syllables.

9. A hot drink of spiced milk curdled with ale or wine, traditionally given to a groom on his wedding night.

Out upon It!

Out upon it! I have loved
    Three whole days together;
And am like to love three more,
    If it prove fair weather.

5   Time shall molt away his wings,
        Ere he shall discover
In the whole wide world again
        Such a constant lover.

But the spite on 't is, no praise
10   Is due at all to me;
Love with me had made no stays[1]
        Had it any been but she.

Had it any been but she,
        And that very face,[2]
15 There had been at least ere this
        A dozen dozen in her place.

                                                    1659

ANNE BRADSTREET
ca. 1612–1672

In Honor of that High and Mighty Princess, Queen Elizabeth, of Most Happy Memory[1]

The Proem[2]

Although, great Queen, thou now in silence lie,
Yet thy loud herald° fame doth to the sky   *royal crier*
Thy wondrous worth proclaim in every clime,°   *climate, region*
And so has vowed, whilst there is world, or time;
5   So great's thy glory, and thine excellence,
The sound thereof raps° every humane sense;   *enraptures*
That men account it no impiety,
To say, thou wert a fleshly° deity.°   *earthly / goddess*
Thousands bring off'rings, (though out of date)
10 Thy world of honors to accumulate,
'Mongst hundred hecatombs of roaring[3] verse,

---

1. I.e., found no support.
2. In other versions, this line reads "That very very face."
1. Queen Elizabeth I (1533–1603; see pp. 142–43), who ruled England for forty-four years.

2. Brief introductory verse.
3. Loud. *Hecatombs*: a great number of things presented as an offering (originally from the Greek, the sacrifice of one hundred oxen).

Mine bleating[4] stands before thy royal hearse:°   *grave*
Thou never didst, nor canst thou now disdain,
T' accept the tribute of a loyal brain;
15 Thy clemency did yerst° esteem as much   *formerly*
The acclamations of the poor, as rich;
Which makes me deem,° my rudeness is no wrong,   *think*
Though I resound thy greatness 'mongst the throng.

The Poem

No° phoenix pen, nor Spenser's poetry,   *neither*
20 No Speed's, nor Camden's learned history,[5]
Eliza's° works, wars, praise, can e're   *Elizabeth's*
    compact,°   *summarize*
The world's the theater where she did act;
No memories, nor volumes can contain,
The nine Olimp'ades[6] of her happy reign,
25 Who was so good, so just, so learned, so wise,
From all the kings on earth she won the prize;
Nor say I more than duly is her due,
Millions will testify that this is true;
She hath wiped off th' aspersion of her sex,
30 That women wisdom lack to play the Rex;°   *King*
Spain's monarch says not so; nor yet his host,°   *followers*
She taught them better manners to their cost.[7]
The Salique law[8] had not in force now been,
If France had ever hoped for such a Queen;
35 But can you Doctors[9] now this point dispute,
She's argument enough to make you mute;
Since first the sun did run, his ne'er° runned° race,   *never / finished*
And earth had twice a year, a new-old face;[1]
Since time was time, and man unmanly man,[2]
40 Come show me such a phoenix[3] if you can;
Was ever people better ruled than hers?
Was ever land more happy, freed from stirs?°   *public disturbances*

4. Crying of a sheep, goat, or calf, used contemptuously for a human utterance.
5. William Camden (1551–1623) wrote *Annals or The History of the Most Renowned and Victorious Princess Elizabeth* (translated from the Latin by R. Norton, 1630). The phoenix is a legendary bird, the only one of its kind. It is represented as living five hundred years in the Arabian desert before setting itself on fire, then rising anew from its own ashes; the "phoenix" here refers to Sir Philip Sidney (1554–1586; see pp. 208–20). Edmund Spenser (1552–1599; see pp. 159–205) wrote *The Faerie Queene* (1590, 1596), the title of which refers to Queen Elizabeth. John Speed (1552–1629) wrote *History of Great Britain under the Conquests of the Romans, Saxons, Danes and Normans from Julius Caesar to Our Most Gracious Sovereign King James* (1611).
6. Olympiads: periods of four years reckoned from one celebration of the Olympics to the next, by which the ancient Greeks computed time. The version of this poem published in 1678 has " 'leven" in place of "nine"; eleven corresponds to Eliza-

beth's forty-four-year reign, while the meaning of nine is unclear.
7. Spain's monarch was Philip II (1527–1598); his great naval fleet, the Spanish Armada, was defeated by the British naval forces in 1588.
8. A much-debated law excluding females from succession to the French crown.
9. Learned men or, more specifically, men proficient in the knowledge of law.
1. A reference to the seasonal changes of spring and fall, at which times Earth dons a "new" face, though "old" because recurring annually.
2. Time became measurable with the creation of day and night, and distinct from eternity when God made humans mortal as punishment for the sin of Adam and Eve; as a result of the Fall, Adam lost his true manly nature, thus becoming "unmanly man."
3. The Phoenix was an emblem used to represent Queen Elizabeth (who was often called the "Virgin Queen") because of its associations with the Virgin Mary (the bird is both virginal and unique).

Did ever wealth in England so abound?
Her victories in foreign coasts resound?
45 Ships more invincible than Spain's, her foe
She racked, she sacked, she sunk his Armadoe;°   *Armada*
Her stately troops advanced to Lisbon's wall,
Don Anthony in's right for to install;[4]
She frankly helped Franks' (brave) distressèd King,[5]
50 The states united now her fame do sing;[6]
She their protectrix was, they well do know,
Unto our dread virago,[7] what they owe;
Her nobles sacrificed their noble blood,
Nor men, nor coin she spared, to do them good;
55 The rude untamed Irish she did quell,
And Tiron[8] bound, before her picture fell.
Had ever Prince such counsellors as she?
Her self Minerva,[9] caused them so to be;
Such soldiers, and such captains never seen,
60 As were the subjects of our (Pallas) Queen;
Her sea-men through all straights[1] the world did round,
Terra incognitae[2] might know her sound;
Her Drake came laded home with Spanish gold,[3]
Her Essex took Cades, their Herculean hold.[4]
65 But time would fail me, so my wit would too,
To tell of half she did, or she could do;
Semiramis[5] to her is but obscure,
More infamy than fame she did procure;
She placed her glory but on Babel's walls,
70 World's wonder for a time, but yet it falls;
Fierce Tomris[6] (Cyrus' heads-man, Sythians' Queen)
Had put her harness off, had she but seen
Our Amazon i'th' camp at Tilberry:[7]

4. Don Antonio of Crato (1531–1595), a claimant to the throne of Portugal, was used by Elizabeth to cause trouble for Philip II. In 1589, he went to coastal Portugal and Spain with Sir Francis Drake (1546–1596) and Sir John Norris (1547–1597), their intention being to provoke rebellion in Portugal against the rule of Philip. Their expedition was a failure.
5. From 1589 to 1590, Elizabeth sent troops and £300,000 to Henry IV, the Huguenot king of France (the "Franks"), first against the Catholic League, which raised a puppet king against him, and later against Spain.
6. A reference to the provinces of the Low Countries (the representative assembly of the Netherlands was called the States General). Elizabeth aided the Protestant Netherlands in their wars against Spain.
7. A vigorous, heroic woman; a female warrior.
8. Hugh O'Neill (ca. 1540–1616), second earl of Tyrone and an Irish chieftain, intrigued with both the Spanish and the Scots against England. He was defeated by Lord Mountjoy and the English forces in 1601.
9. The Roman goddess of war, wisdom, chastity, the arts, and justice; also called Pallas Athena (Greek).
1. Straits: narrow waterways connecting two large bodies of water; may also mean difficulties.

2. Unknown lands (Latin).
3. In his expedition of 1577–80, Sir Francis Drake (1540 or 1543–1596) plundered spoils of immense value from Spanish settlements along the coast of Chile and Peru.
4. Robert Devereux (1566–1601), second earl of Essex, captured Cádiz, a Spanish port, in 1596. Hercules was a mythological hero with superhuman strength; thus "Herculean" suggests the port was very strong or well fortified.
5. Late ninth-century queen of Assyria famed for her beauty, military prowess, and promiscuity; she ruled after the death of her husband Ninus (in whose murder she may have had a hand); she reputedly built Babylon.
6. First-century queen of the Massagetae, a Scythian tribe, defeated Cyrus the Great of Persia; she had his head cut off and thrown into a pot of blood, because, she said, he thirsted for it.
7. A fortification on the north bank of the river Thames, near London. In August 1588, the English army was assembled there, in readiness to repulse an expected Spanish invasion. Queen Elizabeth reviewed the troops and gave a celebrated address, reportedly wearing a silver breastplate over her white dress and carrying a truncheon. The Amazons were a legendary tribe of women warriors.

(Judging all valor, and all majesty)
75   Within that Princess to have residence,
And prostrate yielded to her excellence:
Dido[8] first foundress of proud Carthage walls,
(Who living consummates her funerals)
A great Eliza,[9] but compared with ours,
80   How vanisheth her glory, wealth, and powers;
Proud profuse Cleopatra,[1] whose wrong name,
Instead of glory proved her country's shame:
Of her what worth in story's to be seen,
But that she was a rich Egyptian Queen;
85   Zenobia,[2] potent empress of the East,
And of all these without compare the best;
(Whom none but great Aurelius could quell)
Yet for our Queen is no fit parallel:
She was a phoenix Queen, so shall she be,
90   Her ashes not revived more phoenix she;
Her personal perfections, who would tell,
Must dip his pen i'th' Heliconian well;[3]
Which I may not, my pride doth but aspire,
To read what others write, and then admire.
95   Now say, have women worth, or have they none?
Or had they some, but with our Queen is't gone?
Nay Masculines, you have thus taxed° us long,   *accused*
But she though dead, will vindicate our wrong.
Let such, as say our sex is void of reason,
100 Know 'tis a slander now, but once was treason.
But happy England, which had such a Queen,
O happy, happy, had those days still been,
But happiness lies in a higher sphere;
Then wonder not, Eliza moves not here.
105 Full fraught with honor, riches, and with days,
She set, she set, like Titan° in his rays.   *the sun*
No more shall rise or set such glorious sun
Until the heavens' great revolution:[4]
If then new things, their old form must retain,
110 Eliza shall rule Albion° once again.   *England*

<hr>

8. Legendary founder and queen of Carthage, who burned herself on a funeral pyre, either to escape marriage to Iarbas, a local king, or, according to Virgil, because she had been abandoned by Aeneas, who left her before founding Rome.
9. According to some authors, Dido's true name was Elyssa; when depicted as a chaste queen, she was an appropriate figure for England's "Eliza," though less great, Bradstreet insists.
1. First-century Egyptian queen and mistress of Julius Caesar, she married Marc Antony and the two were defeated by Octavius at the battle of Actium; she killed herself rather than be paraded in triumph by Octavius. Her story is told in Shakespeare's tragedy *Antony and Cleopatra*. "Cleopatra" means "glory to the father" in Greek; Bradstreet

evidently takes Cleopatra's name as referring by metaphorical extension to her "fatherland."
2. Queen of Palmyra, a city-state in ancient Syria. After the death of her husband, Odaenathus, whom she may have murdered, she embarked on wars of expansion and called herself "Augusta" and the "Empress of the East"; she distinguished herself in warfare but was finally defeated by the Roman emperor Aurelian in 273.
3. The Hippocrene Spring, on Mt. Helicon, was the haunt of the Muses, the nine Greek sister goddesses believed to be the sources of inspiration for the arts.
4. A reference to the Apocalypse, after which a "new heaven and a new earth" (Revelation 21.1), eternal and idyllic, will be established.

Her Epitaph

Here sleeps the Queen, this is the royal bed.
O'th' damask Rose, sprung from the white and red,[5]
Whose sweet perfume fills the all-filling air,
This Rose is withered, once so lovely fair,
115　On neither tree did grow such Rose before,
The greater was our gain, our loss the more.

Another

Here lies the pride of Queens, pattern of Kings,
So blaze° it fame, here's feathers for thy wings,　　　　　*announce*
Here lies the envied, yet unparalleled Prince
120　Whose living virtues speak (though dead long since)
If many worlds, as that fantastic framed,[6]
In every one, be her great glory famed.

1643　　　　　　　　　　　　　　　　　　　　　　　　1650

The Prologue[7]

I

To sing of wars, of captains, and of kings,
Of cities founded, common-wealths begun,
For my mean° pen, are too superior things,　　　　　*inferior*
And how they all, or each, their dates have run
5　Let poets, and historians set these forth,
My obscure verse shall not so dim their worth.

2

But when my wond'ring eyes, and envious heart,
Great Bartas'[8] sugared lines do but read o'er,
Fool, I do grudge the Muses[9] did not part°　　　　　*divide*
10　'Twixt him and me that over-fluent store;
A Bartas can do what a Bartas will,
But simple I, according to my skill.

---

5. Queen Elizabeth I was the daughter of Henry VIII, whose father was Henry VII, of the House of Lancaster, and whose mother was Elizabeth, daughter of Edward IV, of the house of York. These two houses, whose symbols were the red rose and the white rose respectively, warred upon each other for many years. The "Damask Rose," a pink or variegated red-and-white rose, is here used to represent the merging of the two houses in the person of Elizabeth.
6. I.e., if there are many worlds, as that visionary or fantastical person surmised; in fact, a number of Bradstreet's contemporaries, influenced by Copernicus's revolutionary theory of a heliocentric universe, had speculated about the possible existence of "other worlds"; see, e.g., Margaret Cavendish, "Of Many Worlds in This World" (p. 500).
7. This poem appeared at the beginning of Bradstreet's first volume of poetry, *The Tenth Muse Lately Sprung Up in America* (1650), which was evidently published without Bradstreet's knowledge.
8. Guillaume du Bartas (1544–1590), French poet and author of *La Semaine* (1578), an epic poem on Christian history; his works greatly influenced Bradstreet.
9. The nine Greek sister goddesses believed to be the source of inspiration for the arts.

3

From school-boys tongue, no rhetoric[1] we expect,
Nor yet a sweet consort,° from broken strings,   *concert, harmony*
15 Nor perfect beauty, where's a main defect;
My foolish, broken, blemished Muse so sings;
And this to mend, alas, no art is able,
'Cause nature made it so irreparable.

4

Nor can I, like that fluent sweet-tongued Greek
20 Who lisped at first,[2] speak afterwards more plain.
By art, he gladly found what he did seek,
A full requital of his striving pain:
Art can do much, but this maxim's most sure.
A weak or wounded brain admits no cure.

5

25 I am obnoxious° to each carping tongue,   *vulnerable*
Who says my hand a needle better fits;
A poet's pen all scorn I should thus wrong;
For such despite° they cast on female wits: *scorn*
If what I do prove well, it won't advance,°   *be recognized*
30 They'll say it's stolen, or else it was by chance.

6

But sure the antick[3] Greeks were far more mild,
Else of our sex, why feignèd° they those nine,[4]   *invented*
And poesy made Calliope's owne child?[5]
So 'mongst the rest, they placed the arts divine:
35 But this weak knot[6] they will full soon untie,
The Greeks did nought, but play the fool and lie.

7

Let Greeks be Greeks, and women what they are,
Men have precedency,[7] and still excel;
It is but vain, unjustly to wage war;
40 Men can do best, and women know it well;
Preeminence in each and all is yours,
Yet grant some small acknowledgement of ours.

---

1. Skill in using eloquent and persuasive language.
2. The Greek orator Demosthenes (384–322 B.C.E.), was said to have overcome a speech defect.
3. Ancient; but also absurd, bizarre.
4. I.e., the nine Muses.
5. Calliope was the Muse of heroic poetry.
6. I.e., this argument for women's right to compose poetry; "they" refers to those who disapprove of women writing poetry; the last line of the stanza is what "they" might say to refute the argument made by the speaker in the first four lines of the stanza.
7. Superiority in rank or estimation; also, priority in time or succession.

8

And oh, ye high flown quills[8] that soar the skies,
And ever with your prey, still catch your praise,
45 If e'er you deign° these lowly lines your eyes,   *think fit for*
Give wholesome parsley wreath, I ask no bays:[9]
This mean and unrefinèd stuff of mine,
Will make your glistering gold but more to shine.

1650

Before the Birth of One of Her Children

All things within this fading world hath end,
Adversity doth still our joys attend;
No ties so strong, no friends so dear and sweet,
But with death's parting blow is sure to meet.
5 The sentence past is most irrevocable,[1]
A common thing, yet oh inevitable;
How soon, my dear,[2] death may my steps attend,
How soon't may be thy lot to lose thy friend;
We both are ignorant, yet love bids me
10 These farewell lines to recommend to thee,
That when that knot's untied[3] that made us one,
I may seem thine, who in effect am none.
And if I see not half my days that's due,[4]
What nature would, God grant to yours and you;
15 The many faults that well you know I have,
Let be interr'd in my oblivion's[5] grave;
If any worth or virtue were in me,
Let that live freshly in thy memory,
And when thou feel'st no grief, as I no harms,
20 Yet love thy dead, who long lay in thine arms:
And when thy loss shall be repaid with gains,
Look to my little babes, my dear remains.
And if thou love thy self, or loved'st me,
These O protect from step-dame's injury.
25 And if chance to thine eyes shall bring this verse,
With some sad sighs honor my absent Hearse;°   *corpse*
And kiss this paper for thy love's dear sake,
Who with salt tears this last farewell did take.

1678

8. Feathers, poetic for wings; also, pens.
9. Leaves of the bay tree, woven into a wreath to reward a poet; hence the fame or repute gained by poetic achievement.
1. The sin of Adam and Eve brought the "sentence" of death to humans.
2. The poet addresses her husband; death due to

complications in childbirth was common at this time.
3. I.e., the "knot" of marriage, "untied" by death.
4. I.e., she fears she may die before age thirty-five, half of the seventy years traditionally seen as humankind's allotment.
5. Some editors emend to "oblivious."

To My Dear and Loving Husband

If ever two were one, then surely we.
If ever man were loved by wife, then thee;
If ever wife was happy in a man,
Compare with me ye women if you can.
5   I prize thy love more than whole mines of gold,
Or all the riches that the East doth hold.
My love is such that rivers cannot quench,
Nor ought but love from thee give recompense.
Thy love is such I can no way repay;
10   The heavens reward thee manifold, I pray.
Then while we live, in love let's so persever,
That when we live no more we may live ever.

1678

The Author to Her Book[6]

Thou ill-formed offspring of my feeble brain,
Who after birth didst by my side remain,
Till snatched from thence by friends, less wise than true,
Who thee abroad, exposed to public view,
5   Made thee in rags, halting to th' press to trudge,
Where errors were not lessened (all may judge).
At thy return my blushing was not small,
My rambling brat (in print) should mother call,
I cast thee by as one unfit for light,
10   The visage was so irksome in my sight;
Yet being mine own, at length affection would
Thy blemishes amend, if so I could.
I washed thy face, but more defects I saw,
And rubbing off a spot still made a flaw.
15   I stretched thy joints to make thee even feet,[7]
Yet still thou run'st more hobbling than is meet;°   *appropriate*
In better dress to trim thee was my mind,
But nought save homespun cloth i' th' house I find.
In this array 'mongst vulgars° may'st thou roam.   *common people*
20   In critic's hands beware thou dost not come,
And take thy way where yet thou art not known;
If for thy father asked, say thou hadst none;
And for thy mother, she alas is poor,
Which caused her thus to send thee out of door.

1678

---

6. Bradstreet is thought to have written this poem in 1666, when a second edition of *The Tenth Muse* (see note 7, p. 462) was contemplated.

7. I.e., metrical feet; to smooth out the lines.

A Letter to Her Husband, Absent upon
Public Employment[8]

My head, my heart, mine eyes, my life, nay, more,
My joy, my magazine° of earthly store,   *storehouse*
If two be one, as surely thou and I,
How stayest thou there, whilst I at Ipswich[9] lie?
5 So many steps, head[1] from the heart to sever,
If but a neck, soon should we be together.
I, like the Earth this season, mourn in black,
My Sun is gone so far in's zodiac,
Whom whilst I 'joyed, nor storms, nor frost I felt,
10 His warmth such frigid colds did cause to melt.
My chillèd limbs now numbèd lie forlorn;
Return; return, sweet Sol, from Capricorn;[2]
In this dead time, alas, what can I more
Than view those fruits which through thy heat I bore?
15 Which sweet contentment yield me for a space,
True living pictures of their father's face.
O strange effect! now thou art southward gone,
I weary grow the tedious day so long;
But when thou northward to me shalt return,
20 I wish my Sun may never set, but burn
Within the Cancer[3] of my glowing breast,
The welcome house of him my dearest guest.
Where ever, ever stay, and go not thence,
Till nature's sad decree shall call thee hence;
25 Flesh of thy flesh, bone of thy bone,[4]
I here, thou there, yet both but one.

1678

Here Follows Some Verses upon the Burning
of Our House July 10th, 1666

Copied Out of a Loose Paper

In silent night when rest I took
For sorrow near I did not look
I wakened was with thund'ring noise
And piteous shrieks of dreadful voice.
5 That fearful sound of "Fire!" and "Fire!"
Let no man know is my desire.[5]

8. Simon Bradstreet was in Boston as a member of the General Court, which was working to combine several individual colonies into the United Colonies of New England.
9. Town in Massachusetts, north of Boston.
1. Perhaps including an allusion to the biblical idea that "the head of the woman is the man" (1 Corinthians 11.3).

2. Tenth sign of the zodiac; represents winter. *Sol*: sun.
3. Fourth sign of the zodiac; represents summer.
4. After God created Eve from Adam's rib, Adam said, "This is now bone of my bones, and flesh of my flesh" (Genesis 2.23).
5. I.e., I desire that no man know that "fearful sound."

I, starting up, the light did spy,
And to my God my heart did cry
To strengthen me in my distress
10 And not to leave me succorless.°   *without aid*
Then, coming out, beheld a° space°   *for a / time*
The flame consume my dwelling place.
And when I could no longer look,
I blest His name that gave and took,[6]
15 That laid my goods now in the dust.
Yea, so it was, and so 'twas just.
It was His own, it was not mine,
Far be it that I should repine;°   *complain*
He might of all justly bereft
20 But yet sufficient for us left.
When by the ruins oft I past
My sorrowing eyes aside did cast,
And here and there the places spy
Where oft I sat and long did lie:
25 Here stood that trunk, and there that chest,
There lay that store I counted best.
My pleasant things in ashes lie,
And them behold no more shall I.
Under thy roof no guest shall sit,
30 Nor at thy table eat a bit.
No pleasant tale shall e'er be told,
Nor things recounted done of old.
No candle e'er shall shine in thee,
Nor bridegroom's voice e'er heard shall be.
35 In silence ever shall thou lie,
Adieu, Adieu, all's vanity.°   *empty, worthless*
Then straight I 'gin my heart to chide,
And did thy wealth on earth abide?
Didst fix thy hope on mold'ring dust?
40 The arm of flesh didst make thy trust?
Raise up thy thoughts above the sky
That dunghill mists away may fly.
Thou hast an house on high erect,
Framed by that mighty Architect,
45 With glory richly furnished,
Stands permanent though this be fled.
It's purchasèd and paid for too
By Him[7] who hath enough to do.
A price so vast as is unknown
50 Yet by His gift is made thine own;
There's wealth enough, I need no more,
Farewell, my pelf,[8] farewell my store.
The world no longer let me love,
My hope and treasure lies above.

1867

6. "The Lord gave, and the Lord hath taken away; blessed be the name of the Lord" (Job 1.21).
7. I.e., Christ, whose death is said to pay for the sins of Adam and Eve.
8. Possessions, usually falsely gained.

RICHARD CRASHAW
1613–1649

On the Baptized Ethiopian[1]

Let it no longer be a forlorn hope
      To wash[2] an Ethiope;
He's washed, his gloomy skin a peaceful shade
      For his white soul is made,
5   And now, I doubt not, the Eternal Dove[3]
      A black-faced house will love.

                                         1646

To the Infant Martyrs[4]

Go, smiling souls, your new-built cages[5] break,
In heaven you'll learn to sing, ere here to speak,[6]
Nor let the milky fonts[7] that bathe your thirst
      Be your delay;
5   The place that calls you hence is, at the worst,
      Milk all the way.[8]

                                         1646

Upon the Infant Martyrs

To see both blended in one flood,
The mothers' milk, the children's blood,
Make me doubt° if heaven will gather   *wonder*
Roses hence, or lilies rather.

                                         1646

The Tear

    What bright soft thing is this?
    Sweet Mary, thy fair eyes' expense?[9]

1. Acts 8.26–39 tells how an Ethiopian eunuch of great authority under Queen Candace was converted and baptized by Philip the Evangelist.
2. I.e., baptize. An allusion to the phrase *washing an Ethiope white,* used as an expression for an impossible task.
3. I.e., the Holy Spirit; the spirit of God descends "like a dove" during Christ's baptism (Matthew 3.16).
4. The Holy Innocents, all the children of Bethlehem of two years and under, who were slain by Herod in an effort to destroy the one who, according to prophecy, would become the ruler of Israel, i.e., Jesus (Matthew 2.16).
5. I.e., their bodies, which confined them to an earthly existence.
6. "Infant" derives from *infans,* Latin for "unable to speak."
7. "Fonts" are receptacles used in the sacrament of baptism; i.e., a reference both to baptism and to mother's milk.
8. I.e., at worst, the Milky Way will replace their mothers' milk; at best, they will be even higher in the heavens.
9. I.e., is this the product of your fair eyes, Mary?

A moist spark it is,
A wat'ry diamond; from whence
5   The very term, I think, was found
The water[1] of a diamond.

O 'tis not a tear,
'Tis a star about to drop
From thine eye its sphere;
10 The sun will stoop and take it up.
Proud will his sister[2] be to wear
This thine eyes' jewel in her ear.

O 'tis a tear
Too true a tear; for no sad eyne,°   eyes
15 How sad so e're,°   ever
Rain so true a teare as thine;
Each drop leaving a place so dear,
Weeps for itself, is its own tear.

Such a pearl as this is,
20 (Slipped from Aurora's° dewy breast)   the dawn's
The rose bud's sweet lip kisses;
And such the rose itself, when vexed
With ungentle flames, does shed,
Sweating in too warm a bed.

25 Such the maiden gem,
By the wanton spring put on,
Peeps from her parent stem,
And blushes on the manly sun:
This wat'ry blossom of thy eyne,
30 Ripe, will make the richer wine.

Faire drop, why quak'st thou so?
'Cause thou straight° must lay thy head   immediately
In the dust? o no;
The dust shall never be thy bed:
35 A pillow for thee will I bring,
Stuffed with down of angels' wing.

Thus carried up on high,
(For to Heaven thou must go)
Sweetly shalt thou lie
40 And in soft slumbers bathe thy woe;
Till the singing orbs[3] awake thee,
And one of their bright chorus make thee.

There thy self shalt be
An eye, but not a weeping one,

1. The term for the transparency and luster of a diamond.
2. The moon.
3. In Ptolemaic astronomy, the concentric crys- talline spheres that contained one or more of the heavenly bodies and revolved about Earth, creating beautiful music.

45   Yet I doubt of thee,
            Whether th'hadst rather there have shone
        An eye of Heaven; or still shine here,
        In th'Heaven of Mary's eye, a tear.

                                                        1646

ABRAHAM COWLEY
1618–1667

The Wish

        Well then; I now do plainly see,
    This busy world and I shall ne'er agree;
    The very honey of all earthly joy
        Does of all meats the soonest cloy;[1]
5   And they, methinks, deserve my pity
    Who for it can endure the stings,
    The crowd, and buzz, and murmurings
        Of this great hive, the city.

        Ah, yet, ere I descend to the grave
10   May I a small house and large garden have!
    And a few friends, and many books, both true,
        Both wise, and both delightful too!
        And since love ne'er will from me flee,
    A mistress moderately fair,
15 And good as guardian angels are,
        Only beloved, and loving me!

        O fountains, when in you shall I
    Myself, eased of unpeaceful thoughts, espy?
    O fields! O woods! when, when shall I be made
20   The happy tenant of your shade?
        Here's the spring-head of pleasure's flood,
    Here's wealthy Nature's treasury,
    Where all the riches lie that she
        Has coined and stamped for good.

25   Pride and ambition here
    Only in farfetched metaphors appear;
    Here naught but winds can hurtful murmurs scatter,
        And naught but Echo[2] flatter.
        The gods, when they descended, hither
30 From heaven did always choose their way;
    And therefore we may boldly say
        That 'tis the way, too, thither.[3]

1. Overfeed to the point of loathing.
2. In Greek mythology, a nymph, who misused her power of speech and was therefore condemned to repeat others' words.

3. I.e., since the gods always come here when they descend from heaven, we can say that the way to heaven ("thither") is from here.

How happy here should I
And one dear she live and, embracing, die!
35   She who is all the world, and can exclude
      In deserts, solitude.
      I should have then this only fear,
Lest men, when they my pleasures see,
Should hither throng to live like me,
40   And so make a city here.

                                                    1647

Platonic Love[4]

1

      Indeed I must confess,
      When souls mix 'tis an happiness,
But not complete till bodies too do join,
And both our wholes into one whole combine;
5   But half of heaven the souls in glory taste
      Till by love in heaven at last
      Their bodies too are placed.

2

      In thy immortal part
      Man, as well as I, thou art.[5]
10   But something 'tis that differs° thee and me,   *distinguishes*
And we must one even in that difference be.
I thee both as a man and woman prize,[6]
      For a perfect love implies
      Love in all capacities.

3

15   Can that for true love pass
      When a fair woman courts her glass?°   *mirror*
Something unlike must in love's likeness be:
His° wonder is one and variety.   *love's*
For he whose soul nought but a soul can move
20   Does a new Narcissus prove,[7]
      And his own image love.

4

      That souls do beauty know
      'Tis to the body's help they owe;
If when they know't they straight abuse that trust
25   And shut the body from't, 'tis as unjust

---

4. Based on the ideas of the ancient Greek philosopher Plato, the concept of Platonic love (as it was expressed by many Renaissance writers) held that physical beauty is the outer sign of a moral and spiritual beauty of the soul; the proper Platonic lover adores the beloved's physical beauty only as a manifestation of spirit.

5. I.e., in your soul, you are equal to man.
6. I.e., I value you both as my equal (as a "man") and as a lover (as a "woman").
7. I.e., prove to be a new Narcissus: in Greek mythology, a youth who fell in love with his own reflection in a pool of water, then drowned in an attempt to embrace the reflection.

As if I brought my dearest friend to see
My mistress and at th' instant he
Should steal her quite from me.

1656

RICHARD LOVELACE*
1618–1658

To Althea, from Prison

When Love with unconfinèd wings[1]
Hovers within my gates,
And my divine Althea brings
To whisper at the grates;
5   When I lie tangled in her hair
And fettered to her eye,
The gods[2] that wanton in the air
Know no such liberty.

When flowing cups run swiftly round,
10   With no allaying Thames,[3]
Our careless heads with roses bound,
Our hearts with loyal flames;
When thirsty grief in wine we steep,
When healths° and draughts go free,   toasts
15   Fishes, that tipple° in the deep,   drink
Know no such liberty.

When, like committed° linnets,° I   caged / finches
With shriller throat shall sing
The sweetness, mercy, majesty,
20   And glories of my King;
When I shall voice aloud how good
He is, how great should be,
Enlargèd winds, that curl the flood,
Know no such liberty.

25   Stone walls do not a prison make,
Nor iron bars a cage;
Minds innocent and quiet take
That for an hermitage.
If I have freedom in my love,

*Since all the poems here are from Lovelace's volume *Lucasta* (1649), we do not repeat the publication date for each.
1. I.e., Cupid, the winged god of erotic love in Roman mythology.

2. Some seventeenth-century versions read "birds."
3. I.e., with no mixture of water in the wine (the river Thames flows through London).

30 And in my soul am free,
  Angels alone, that soar above,
   Enjoy such liberty.

To Lucasta, Going to the Wars

 Tell me not, sweet, I am unkind,
  That from the nunnery
 Of thy chaste breast and quiet mind,
  To war and arms I fly.

5 True, a new mistress now I chase,
  The first foe in the field;
 And with a stronger faith embrace
  A sword, a horse, a shield.

 Yet this inconstancy is such
10 As you too shall adore;
 I could not love thee, dear, so much,
  Loved I not honor more.

To Amarantha, That She Would Dishevel Her Hair

  Amarantha sweet and fair,
  Ah, braid no more that shining hair!
   As my curious hand or eye,
  Hovering round thee, let it fly.

5 Let it fly as unconfined
  As its calm ravisher, the wind,
   Who hath left his darling, th' East,
  To wanton o'er that spicy nest.

  Every tress must be confessed[4]
10 But neatly tangled at the best,
   Like a clue° of golden thread,   *ball*
  Most excellently raveled.

  Do not then wind up that light
  In ribands,° and o'ercloud in night;   *ribbons*
15 Like the sun in's early ray,
  But shake your head and scatter day.

  See, 'tis broke![5] Within this grove,
  The bower and the walks of love,

---

4. I.e., said to be.
5. I.e., the morning has broken, or started (a continuation of the previous stanza, in which the speaker compares Amarantha's hair to the sun, and encourages her to shake it free, as the sun scatters its light and begins day).

Weary lie we down and rest
20   And fan each other's panting breast.

Here we'll strip and cool our fire
In cream below, in milk-baths higher;
And when all wells are drawn dry,
I'll drink a tear out of thine eye.

25   Which our very joys shall leave,
That sorrows thus we can deceive;
Or our very sorrows weep,
That joys so ripe so little keep.

The Grasshopper[6]

To My Noble Friend, Mr. Charles Cotton[7]

O thou that swing'st upon the waving hair
Of some well-fillèd oaten beard,[8]
Drunk every night with a delicious tear°   *dew, water*
Dropped thee from heaven, where now th'° art reared;   *you*

5   The joys of earth and air are thine entire,
That with thy feet and wings dost hop and fly;
And, when thy poppy° works, thou dost retire   *sleeping potion*
To thy carved acorn-bed to lie.

Up with the day, the sun thou welcom'st then,
10   Sport'st in the gilt-plats° of his beams,   *golden braids*
And all these merry days mak'st merry men,
Thyself, and melancholy streams.[9]

But ah, the sickle! Golden ears are cropped;
Ceres and Bacchus[1] bid good night;
15   Sharp, frosty fingers all your flowers have topped,
And what scythes spared, winds shave off quite.

Poor verdant° fool, and now green ice! thy joys,   *green*
Large and as lasting as thy perch of grass,
Bid us lay in[2] 'gainst winter rain, and poise°   *balance*
20   Their floods with an o'erflowing glass.

Thou best of men and friends! we will create
A genuine summer in each other's breast,

6. This poem, a translation of an ancient Greek lyric thought to be by Anacreon, embellishes the traditional ant and grasshopper fable, in which the ant dutifully prepares for the coming winter, while the grasshopper plays instead of working. The circumstances are evidently those of the Interregnum, a winter of Puritanism for Royalists such as Lovelace.
7. A poet and fellow Royalist.

8. I.e., grain.
9. "Men," "thyself" and "melancholy streams" are all possible objects of "mak'st merry."
1. The grain and the grape, from Ceres, Roman goddess of the harvest, and Bacchus, Roman god of wine.
2. Prepare for by storing food and drink ("o'erflowing glass," line 20). *Now green ice:* i.e., the grasshopper has frozen.

And spite of this cold time and frozen fate,
    Thaw us a warm seat to our rest.

25 Our sacred hearths shall burn eternally,
        As vestal flames;[3] the North Wind, he
    Shall strike his frost-stretched wings, dissolve, and fly
        This Etna in epitome.[4]

    Dropping December shall come weeping in,
30   Bewail th' usurping of his reign:
    But when in showers of old Greek we begin,
        Shall cry he hath his crown again![5]

    Night, as clear Hesper,[6] shall our tapers whip
        From the light casements where we play,
35 And the dark hag from her black mantle strip,[7]
        And stick there everlasting day.

    Thus richer than untempted kings[8] are we,
        That, asking nothing, nothing need:
    Though lord of all what seas embrace, yet he
40   That wants himself is poor indeed.[9]

                                                    1649

ANDREW MARVELL*
1621–1678

The Coronet[1]

When for the thorns with which I long, too long,
    With many a piercing wound,
    My Savior's head have crowned,
I seek with garlands[2] to redress that wrong;
5   Through every garden, every mead,°   meadow
    I gather flowers (my fruits are only flowers)
        Dismantling all the fragrant towers°   high headdresses
    That once adorned my shepherdess's head.

3. The vestal virgins, consecrated to Vesta, Roman goddess of the hearth, kept a sacred fire burning perpetually on her altar.
4. I.e., Boreas, the north wind, strikes (or folds up) his wings and flees from the underground warmth of Etna, a Sicilian volcano, whose flame serves as an emblem (or "epitome") of the flame of friendship.
5. Greek wine was favored in the classical world, and drinkers often wore festive crowns; December "crowns" or terminates the year; also, may allude to the crown worn by "King Christmas" at festivities banned by Puritans and to the crown Cavaliers hoped Charles II would regain.
6. Hesperus, the evening star.

7. I.e., by keeping our lights ("tapers") burning all night, we will strip her black garment ("mantle") from Hecate ("the dark hag"), a Greek goddess associated with night.
8. I.e., kings who have everything.
9. I.e., even one who is lord of all and can embrace the seas is poor, if he "wants" himself (does not have self-knowledge).
*Since all of Marvell's poems were first published (posthumously) in 1681, we do not print the date for each selection.
1. A wreath of flowers; also, a small crown; here, the devotional poem itself. See also note 5 above.
2. Wreaths; also, since garlands were a symbol of poetic achievement, poems of praise.

And now when I have summed up all my store,
10   Thinking (so I myself deceive)
        So rich a chaplet° thence to weave   *garland*
As never yet the king of glory[3] wore;
        Alas I find the serpent old[4]
        That, twining in his speckled breast,
15   About the flowers disguised does fold,
        With wreaths° of fame and interest.[5]   *coils*
Ah, foolish man, that wouldst debase with them,
And mortal glory, heaven's diadem!°   *crown*
        But Thou[6] who only couldst the serpent tame,
20   Either his slippery knots at once untie,
And disentangle all his winding snare;
Or shatter too with him my curious° frame,°   *elaborate / structure*
And let these° wither, so that he may die,   *poetic flowers*
Though set with skill and chosen out with care,
25   That they, while Thou on both their spoils dost tread,
May crown Thy feet, that could not crown Thy head.[7]

Bermudas

        Where the remote Bermudas ride,°   *float*
        In th' ocean's bosom unespied,
        From a small boat that rowed along,
        The listening winds received this song:
5   "What should we do but sing His praise,
        That led us through the watery maze
        Unto an isle so long unknown,
        And yet far kinder than our own?
        Where He the huge sea monsters wracks,°   *casts ashore*
10   That lift the deep upon their backs;
        He lands us on a grassy stage,
        Safe from the storms, and prelate's rage.[8]
        He gave us this eternal spring
        Which here enamels everything,
15   And sends the fowls to us in care,
        On daily visits through the air;
        He hangs in shades the orange bright,
        Like golden lamps in a green night,
        And does in the pomegranates close
20   Jewels more rich than Ormus[9] shows;
        He makes the figs our mouths to meet,
        And throws the melons at our feet;
        But apples° plants of such a price,   *pineapples*

3. I.e., Christ.
4. A reference to the serpent who tempted Eve and thus brought about humanity's Fall from paradise (Genesis 3).
5. I.e., self-glorification and self-advancement.
6. I.e., Christ.
7. Cf. God's curse on Satan, from Genesis 3.15:

"And I will put enmity between thee and the woman, and between thy seed and her seed; it shall bruise thy head, and thou shalt bruise his heel."
8. Storms at sea are here associated with bishops (thus indicating a Puritan stance by Marvell).
9. Hormuz, a Persian Gulf island from which gems were exported.

No tree could ever bear them twice;
25 With cedars, chosen by His hand,
From Lebanon,[1] He stores the land;
And makes the hollow seas, that roar,
Proclaim the ambergris[2] on shore;
He cast (of which we rather° boast)   *more properly*
30 The Gospel's pearl upon our coast,[3]
And in these rocks for us did frame
A temple, where to sound His name.
O! let our voice His praise exalt,
Till it arrive at heaven's vault,
35 Which, thence (perhaps) rebounding, may
Echo beyond the Mexique Bay."[4]
    Thus sung they in the English boat,
An holy and a cheerful note;
And all the way, to guide their chime,
40 With falling oars they kept the time.

A Dialogue between the Soul and Body[5]

Soul

Oh, who shall from this dungeon raise
A soul enslaved so many ways?[6]
With bolts of bones that fettered stands
In feet, and manacled in hands;
5   Here blinded with an eye, and there
Deaf with the drumming of an ear;
A soul hung up, as 'twere, in chains
Of nerves and arteries and veins;
Tortured, besides each other part,
10 In a vain head and double° heart.   *deceitful*

Body

Oh, who shall me deliver whole
From bonds of this tyrannic soul?
Which stretched upright, impales me so
That mine own precipice[7] I go,
15 And warms and moves this needless frame[8]—
A fever could but do the same—
And, wanting where[9] its spite to try,

---

1. The tree called the cedar of Lebanon from its most famous early locality.
2. The roaring seas announce ("proclaim") their bounty. *Ambergris*: a soapy secretion of the sperm whale, gathered on beaches and used in perfumes.
3. In Matthew 13.45–46, the kingdom of heaven is compared to a "pearl of great price."
4. I.e., the Gulf of Mexico.
5. Deriving from the medieval "débat," a literary form wherein two speakers dispute a topic.

6. Cf. St. Paul's Epistle to the Romans, 7.24: "O wretched man that I am! who shall deliver me from the body of this death?"
7. Humans walk "upright" instead of prowling like animals because they possess souls; however, possession of a soul is also the reason they can fall and be damned, so the soul is an internal "precipice."
8. I.e., this frame, which does not need the soul.
9. I.e., lacking an object.

Has made me live to let me die:
A body that could never rest,
20   Since this ill spirit it possessed.

Soul

What magic could me thus confine
Within another's grief to pine?
Where whatsoever it complain,
I feel, that cannot feel,[1] the pain,
25   And all my care itself employs,
That to preserve which me destroys,
Constrained not only to endure
Diseases, but, what's worse, the cure;
And ready oft the port[2] to gain,
30   And shipwrecked into health again.

Body

But physic° yet could never reach   *medicine*
The maladies thou me dost teach:
Whom first the cramp of hope does tear,
And then the palsy shakes of fear;
35   The pestilence of love does heat,
Or hatred's hidden ulcer eat;
Joy's cheerful madness does perplex,
Or sorrow's other madness vex;
Which knowledge forces me to know,
40   And memory will not forgo.
What but a soul could have the wit
To build me up for sin so fit?
So architects do square and hew
Green trees that in the forest grew.

To His Coy[3] Mistress

Had we but world enough, and time,
This coyness, lady, were no crime.
We would sit down, and think which way
To walk, and pass our long love's day.
5   Thou by the Indian Ganges'° side   *Ganges River*
Shoudst rubies[4] find; I by the tide
Of Humber would complain.[5] I would

---

1. I.e., the soul can sympathize even though it has
no power of physical sensation.
2. I.e., death.
3. In the seventeenth century, "coy" could mean
"shy" or "quiet" as well as "coquettish," the com-
mon modern meaning.

4. Rubies were thought to help preserve virginity.
5. The Humber River flows through Marvell's
native town of Hull (i.e., on the other side of the
world from the Ganges); "complain" implies plain-
tive lyrics of unavailing love.

Love you ten years before the flood,
And you should, if you please, refuse
10   Till the conversion of the Jews.[6]
My vegetable[7] love should grow
Vaster than empires and more slow;
An hundred years should go to praise
Thine eyes, and on thy forehead gaze;
15   Two hundred to adore each breast,
But thirty thousand to the rest;
An age at least to every part,
And the last age should show your heart.
For, lady, you deserve this state,°   *dignity*
20   Nor would I love at lower rate.[8]
    But at my back I always hear
Time's wingèd chariot hurrying near;
And yonder all before us lie
Deserts of vast eternity.
25   Thy beauty shall no more be found;
Nor, in thy marble vault, shall sound
My echoing song; then worms shall try
That long-preserved virginity,
And your quaint[9] honor turn to dust,
30   And into ashes all my lust:
The grave's a fine and private place,
But none, I think, do there embrace.
    Now therefore, while the youthful hue
Sits on thy skin like morning dew,[1]
35   And while thy willing soul transpires°   *breathes out*
At every pore with instant fires,
Now let us sport us while we may,
And now, like amorous birds of prey,
Rather at once our time devour
40   Than languish in his slow-chapped° power.   *slowly devouring*
Let us roll all our strength and all
Our sweetness up into one ball,
And tear our pleasures with rough strife
Through the iron gates[2] of life:
45   Thus, though we cannot make our sun
Stand still,[3] yet we will make him run.

6. To occur, as Christian tradition had it, at the end of recorded history.
7. I.e., characterized by growth; in context, increasing without conscious nurturing.
8. I.e., at any smaller amounts of time ("lower rate") than what I've just mentioned.
9. Has several meanings, including fine, elegant, fastidious, oversubtle, and out of date; also, with a pun on the Middle English noun *queynte,* or female genitals.
1. In the 1681 text, line 34 ends with the word "glew," rhyming with *hew.* Some modern editors emend to "glow" rather than "dew." One recent

scholar argues for retaining "glew" on the grounds that the term had a specific meaning in alchemical processes of distillation and that Marvell was deeply interested in alchemy.
2. The obscure "iron gates" suggests that the "ball" of line 42 has become a missile from a siege gun, battering its way into a citadel. One manuscript has "iron grates."
3. An allusion to the power of Zeus, the chief Greek god, who, to prolong his night with the mortal Alcmena, ordered the sun not to shine; also, see Joshua 10.12–13.

The Fair Singer[4]

To make a final conquest of all me,
Love did compose so sweet an enemy,
In whom both beauties to my death agree,
Joining themselves in fatal harmony;
5 That while she with her eyes my heart does bind,
She with her voice might captivate my mind.

I could have fled from one but singly fair:
My disentangled soul itself might save,
Breaking the curlèd trammels° of her hair.   *fine nets; braids*
10 But how should I avoid to be her slave,
Whose subtle art invisibly can wreathe
My fetters of the very air I breathe?

It had been easy fighting in some plain,
Where victory might hang in equal choice,
15 But all resistance against her is vain,
Who has th' advantage both of eyes and voice,
And all my forces needs must be undone,
She having gainèd both the wind and sun.[5]

The Definition of Love[6]

My Love is of a birth as rare
As 'tis, for object, strange and high;[7]
It was begotten by Despair
Upon Impossibility.

5 Magnanimous Despair alone
Could show me so divine a thing,
Where feeble Hope could ne'er have flown
But vainly flapped its tinsel[8] wing.

And yet I quickly might arrive
10 Where my extended soul is fixed;[9]
But Fate does iron wedges drive,
And always crowds itself betwixt.

For Fate with jealous eye does see
Two perfect loves, nor lets them close;°   *unite*

---

4. A poem in the genre of the courtly compliment paid to a lady to commend her skill in music or dancing.
5. In earlier warfare (especially at sea), the force with the wind and sun behind it had distinct advantages.
6. This poem plays upon a Platonic definition of love as an unfulfilled longing. Cf. Abraham Cow-

ley, "Platonic Love" (p. 471).
7. I.e., my love's lineage is as rare as my love itself is strange and high.
8. Glittering; also, flashy, with little or no intrinsic worth.
9. The speaker describes his soul as having gone out of his body ("extended") and attached ("fixed") itself to his mistress.

15   Their union would her ruin be,
     And her tyrannic power depose.[1]

     And therefore her decrees of steel
     Us as the distant poles have placed
     (Though Love's whole world on us doth wheel),[2]
20   Not by themselves to be embraced,

     Unless the giddy heaven fall,
     And earth some new convulsion tear,
     And, us to join, the world should all
     Be cramped into a planisphere.[3]

25   As lines, so loves oblique may well
     Themselves in every angle greet;[4]
     But ours, so truly parallel,
     Though infinite, can never meet.

     Therefore the love which us doth bind,
30   But Fate so enviously debars,
     Is the conjunction of the mind,
     And opposition of the stars.[5]

The Picture of Little T. C. in a Prospect[6] of Flowers

     See with what simplicity
     This nymph[7] begins her golden days!
     In the green grass she loves to lie,
     And there with her fair aspect tames
5   The wilder flowers, and gives them names;
     But only with the roses plays,
         And them does tell
     What color best becomes them, and what smell.

     Who can foretell for what high cause
10   This darling of the gods was born?
     Yet this is she whose chaster laws
     The wanton Love[8] shall one day fear,

1. A reference to the idea that an even mixture of pure elements formed an altogether stable compound, able to withstand any sudden change, and hence, in context, defying fate.
2. Though by decree of fate the lovers are as far apart as Earth's two poles, the relationship (literally, the line) between them forms the axis on which love's world turns.
3. A chart formed by the projection of a sphere on a plane; the two poles could come together only if the charted world were collapsed.
4. I.e., the lines may converge at any angle. "Oblique" lovers, in one sense, might deviate from accepted behavior or thought.
5. In this astronomical image, the minds of the lovers are in accord (literally in "conjunction," or occupying the same celestial longitude), but the stars determining their destinies are entirely hostile (literally in "opposition," or 180 degrees apart).
6. A background scene, or representation of a view. T. C.: a little girl; possibly Theophila Cornewall, who was baptized on September 26, 1644, the second daughter of that name in the family. The first Theophila had died two days after birth.
7. A young, beautiful female; in Greek mythology, nymphs inhabited a particular place or natural phenomenon.
8. I.e., Cupid, Roman god of erotic love. The speaker predicts that "T. C." will follow "chaster laws," with a likely allusion to those laws followed by Diana, the mythological goddess of chastity and hunting.

And, under her command severe,
See his bow broke and ensigns torn.
15   Happy who can
Appease this virtuous enemy of man![9]

O then let me in time compound°   *bargain*
And parley[1] with those conquering eyes,
Ere they have tried their force to wound;
20   Ere with their glancing wheels they drive
In triumph over hearts that strive,
And them that yield but more despise:
         Let me be laid
Where I may see thy glories from some shade.

25   Meantime, whilst every verdant° thing   *green*
Itself does at thy beauty charm,[2]
Reform the errors of the spring;
Make that the tulips may have share
Of sweetness, seeing they are fair;
30   And roses of their thorns disarm;
         But most procure
That violets may a longer age endure.

But, O young beauty of the woods,
Whom nature courts with fruits and flowers,
35   Gather the flowers, but spare the buds,
Lest Flora, angry at thy crime
To kill her infants[3] in their prime,
Do quickly make the example yours;
         And ere we see,
40   Nip in the blossom all our hopes and thee.

The Mower against Gardens[4]

Luxurious man, to bring his vice in use,[5]
    Did after him the world seduce,
And from the fields the flowers and plants allure,
    Where Nature was most plain and pure.
5   He first enclosed within the gardens square
    A dead and standing pool of air,
And a more luscious earth for them did knead,
    Which stupefied them while it fed.
The pink grew then as double as his mind;[6]
10   The nutriment did change the kind.

9. By doing battle with Cupid, breaking his bow and tearing his flags ("ensigns"), she ("T. C.") will be a "virtuous enemy" to man (i.e., one whose chaste virtue causes her to be the foe of love).
1. Speak; also, hold a conference with the enemy.
2. Enchants itself at thy beauty.
3. I.e., the buds. *Flora:* Roman goddess of flowers.
4. One of four "mower" poems that examine dif-

ferent aspects of rural life. *Mower:* one who cuts grass with a scythe.
5. I.e., to establish his vice as custom. *Luxurious:* lustful; voluptuous.
6. The double pink carnation is produced by a hypocritical ("double") mind, i.e., one who counterfeits the natural color.

With strange perfumes he did the roses taint;
    And flowers themselves were taught to paint.
The tulip white did for complexion seek,
    And learned to interline its cheek;
15 Its onion root they then so high did hold,
    That one was for a meadow sold:[7]
Another world was searched through oceans new,
    To find the Marvel of Peru;[8]
And yet these rarities might be allowed
20   To man, that sovereign thing and proud,
Had he not dealt between the bark and tree,[9]
    Forbidden mixtures there to see.
No plant now knew the stock from which it came;
    He grafts upon the wild the tame,
25 That the uncertain and adulterate° fruit   *counterfeit*
    Might put the palate in dispute.[1]
His green seraglio has its eunuchs too,
    Lest any tyrant him outdo;[2]
And in the cherry he does Nature vex,
30   To procreate without a sex.[3]
'Tis all enforced, the fountain and the grot,[4]
    While the sweet fields do lie forgot,
Where willing Nature does to all dispense
    A wild and fragrant innocence;
35 And fauns[5] and fairies do the meadows till
    More by their presence than their skill.
Their statues polished by some ancient hand,
    May to adorn the gardens stand;
But, howsoe'er the figures do excel,
40   The Gods themselves with us do dwell.

The Mower to the Glowworms[6]

Ye living lamps, by whose dear light
The nightingale does sit so late,
And studying all the summer night,
Her matchless songs does meditate;[7]

7. A tulip fad in the 1630s brought extremely high prices for rare varieties. *Onion root:* bulb.
8. A tuliplike flower (*mirabilis jalapa*) that opens late in the afternoon.
9. I.e., by grafting; proverbial for interfering.
1. I.e., the result of which grafting confuses the palate as to what it tastes.
2. *Seraglio:* harem in a sultan's palace, hence a place of confinement. I.e., his garden ("green seraglio") has its castrated slaves ("eunuchs"; here, the grafted plants, some of which could not reproduce) just like any tyrant.
3. Cherries are often propagated by budding on the stocks of sturdier but less productive varieties.
4. Grotto, a picturesque structure made to imitate a cave, serving as a cool retreat.
5. In classical mythology, half-goat, half-man

woodland gods associated with lust and drinking (often described as less wild than satyrs).
6. Insects, the females of which emit a shining green light from the abdomen. *Mower:* see note 4, p. 482.
7. The nightingale is known for its sweet and sad song, which has perhaps given rise to one tradition that the bird's song laments the tragic result of wrongful love. Another tale of the nightingale, as told by Ovid, has the mournful song refer to the violence committed on Philomela, who was raped by her brother-in-law, Tereus, who then tore out her tongue so that she could not speak. She wove the story in a tapestry and sent it to her sister, who rescued her. She was later changed into a nightingale while in flight from Tereus, after seeking revenge on him.

5   Ye country comets, that portend
    No war nor prince's funeral,[8]
    Shining unto no higher end
    Than to presage° the grass's fall;   *foretell*

    Ye glowworms, whose officious° flame   *dutiful*
10 To wandering mowers shows the way,
    That in the night have lost their aim,
    And after foolish fires[9] do stray;

    Your courteous lights in vain you waste,
    Since Juliana here is come,
15 For she my mind hath so displaced
    That I shall never find my home.

The Garden

    How vainly men themselves amaze°   *perplex*
    To win the palm, the oak, or bays,[1]
    And their incessant° labors see   *unceasing*
    Crowned from some single herb, or tree,
5 Whose short and narrow-vergèd[2] shade
    Does prudently their toils upbraid;
    While all flowers and all trees do close°   *join*
    To weave the garlands of repose!

    Fair Quiet, have I found thee here,
10 And Innocence, thy sister dear?
    Mistaken long, I sought you then
    In busy companies of men.
    Your sacred plants,° if here below,   *cuttings*
    Only among the plants will grow;
15 Society is all but° rude°   *merely / barbarous*
    To° this delicious solitude.   *compared to*

    No white nor red[3] was ever seen
    So amorous as this lovely green.
    Fond° lovers, cruel as their flame,   *foolish*
20 Cut in these trees their mistress' name:[4]
    Little, alas, they know or heed
    How far these beauties hers exceed!
    Fair trees, wheresoe'er your barks I wound,
    No name shall but your own be found.

8. Comets were sometimes believed to be portents of approaching disasters.

9. *Ignis fatuus* (Latin), also known as the will-o'-the-wisp; said to draw travelers astray by holding a false light before them; the phenomenon of nocturnal light is caused by the combustion of marsh gas.

1. The wreaths awarded, respectively, for military, civic, and poetic accomplishments.

2. Confined, not spreading luxuriantly like the living branch.

3. The colors conventionally used to depict female beauty in love poetry (in the Petrarchan tradition).

4. According to a poetic tradition, a lover carved his beloved's name in a tree (as Petrarch did with Laura's).

25   When we have run our passion's heat,°   *course*
    Love hither makes his best retreat.
    The gods, that mortal beauty chase,
    Still in a tree did end their race:[5]
    Apollo hunted Daphne so,
30   Only that she might laurel grow;
    And Pan did after Syrinx speed,
    Not as a nymph, but for a reed.

      What wondrous life is this I lead!
    Ripe apples drop about my head;
35   The luscious clusters of the vine
    Upon my mouth do crush their wine;
    The nectarine and curious° peach   *exquisite*
    Into my hands themselves do reach;
    Stumbling on melons,[6] as I pass,
40   Insnared with flowers, I fall on grass.

      Meanwhile the mind, from pleasure less,[7]
    Withdraws into its happiness;
    The mind, that ocean where each kind
    Does straight° its own resemblance find;[8]   *immediately*
45   Yet it creates, transcending these,
    Far other worlds and other seas,
    Annihilating all that's made
    To a green thought in a green shade.

      Here at the fountain's sliding foot,
50   Or at some fruit tree's mossy root,
    Casting the body's vest[9] aside,
    My soul into the boughs does glide:
    There, like a bird, it sits and sings,
    Then whets° and combs its silver wings,   *preens*
55   And, till prepared for longer flight,
    Waves in its plumes the various° light.   *iridescent*

      Such was that happy garden-state,
    While man there walked without a mate:
    After a place so pure and sweet,
60   What other help could yet be meet![1]
    But 'twas beyond a mortal's share
    To wander solitary there:
    Two paradises 'twere in one
    To live in paradise alone.[2]

5. I.e., even the gods who chase after their desired nymphs (events described in the following lines) succeed only in achieving a garden prize. According to Ovid's versions of these two myths, the nymphs (Daphne and Syrinx) both elude the unwanted sexual advances of their pursuers (Apollo and Pan, respectively) by being metamorphosed into a laurel tree (Daphne) and reeds (Syrinx) through the intervention of sympathetic deities.
6. "Melon" has an etymological root in the Greek word for apple; perhaps an allusion to the apple that led to the Fall (or "stumbling") of humankind.
7. "Less" may modify either "pleasure" or "mind."
8. As every land creature was thought to have its counterpart sea creature, so also in the ocean of the mind (in Neoplatonic philosophy).
9. Garment; i.e., the body itself.
1. Fit, suitable; also, God created Eve because "for Adam there was not found an help meet for him" (Genesis 2.20).
2. I.e., it would be twice as wonderful to be alone in paradise (i.e., before Eve).

65 How well the skillful gardener drew
    Of flowers and herbs this dial[3] new,
        Where, from above, the milder sun
        Does through a fragrant zodiac run;
    And as it works, th' industrious bee
70 Computes its time[4] as well as we!
    How could such sweet and wholesome hours
    Be reckoned but with herbs and flowers?

An Horatian Ode[5]

Upon Cromwell's Return from Ireland[6]

The forward° youth that would appear   *eager, ambitious*
Must now forsake his Muses[7] dear,
    Nor in the shadows sing
    His numbers° languishing: *poems*

5   'Tis time to leave the books in dust,
    And oil the unusèd armor's rust,
        Removing from the wall
        The corslet of the hall.[8]

So restless Cromwell could not cease°   *rest*
10 In the inglorious arts of peace,
        But through adventurous war
        Urgèd his active star;

And like the three-forked lightning, first
Breaking the clouds where it was nursed,
15   Did thorough° his own side   *through*
        His fiery way divide.[9]

For 'tis all one to courage high,
The emulous[1] or enemy;
    And with such to inclose
20   Is more than to oppose.[2]

3. Flowers planted to form a dial face, through which the sun follows its course; it is "milder" because its intense rays are tempered by the flowers through which they filter.
4. With a pun on *thyme*.
5. Originally a classical form, an ode is a serious lyric poem, dignified by its theme, occasion, or subject. In contrast to the odes of the Greek poet Pindar (ca. 522–ca. 438 B.C.E.), which typically praised or glorified someone, a Horatian ode, derived from the work of the Roman poet Horace (65–8 B.C.E.), promises a poem of cool and balanced judgment. Balanced judgments of Oliver Cromwell (see note 6 below) were not politic in the Restoration, and the poem was canceled from all but two known copies of the 1681 edition of *Miscellaneous Poems*.
6. Oliver Cromwell (1599–1658), English general and statesman, lord protector of England, returned from conquering Ireland in May 1650, about eighteen months after the execution of King Charles I. His victory over the Irish was sometimes taken as a sign that God approved of Charles's beheading.
7. The nine Greek sister goddesses believed to be sources of inspiration for the arts.
8. The suit of armor belonging to the household.
9. Cromwell had begun as a Presbyterian, but became the leader of the more radical group known as the Independents, or the Rump. The comparison to the "three-forked lightning" links him to Zeus, the chief classical god, whose daughter Athena sprang fully formed from Zeus's head.
1. One who is greedy for praise or power; also, one who imitates or rivals.
2. Possible paraphrase of stanza: It challenges high courage as much to deal with competitors as to deal with the enemy; and to make common cause with men like the sectarians of the Parlia-

Then burning through the air he went,
And palaces and temples rent;°   *tore*
    And Caesar's head at last
    Did through his laurels blast.[3]

25 'Tis madness to resist or blame
The force of angry heaven's flame;[4]
    And if we would speak true,
    Much to the man is due,

Who, from his private gardens, where
30 He lived reservèd and austere
    (As if his highest plot
    To plant the bergamot),[5]

Could by industrious valor climb
To ruin the great work of time,
35   And cast the kingdom old
    Into another mold;[6]

Though Justice against Fate complain,
And plead the ancient rights in vain;
    But those do hold or break,
40   As men are strong or weak.

Nature, that hateth emptiness,
Allows of penetration less,[7]
    And therefore must make room
    Where greater spirits come.

45 What field of all the civil wars,
Where his were not the deepest scars?
    And Hampton shows what part
    He had of wiser art;[8]

Where, twining subtle fears with hope,
50 He wove a net of such a scope
    That Charles himself might chase
    To Carisbrooke's narrow case,[9]

---

mentary Party is more of an accomplishment than effectually to oppose them. (Marvell's obscurities may be deliberate and politic.)

3. I.e., like lightning, Cromwell beheaded Charles I ("Caesar"). Laurels were used for classical crowns because they were supposed to protect from lightning, which represented the gods' jealousy.

4. The lightning hurled by Zeus represents divine judgment.

5. A variety of pear; its etymology (from the Turkish, "prince's pear") may hold the insinuation that Cromwell had been plotting for power even in his early days of private life.

6. I.e., a reference to the change from monarchy to republic.

7. I.e., Nature, which abhors a vacuum, is even less willing to let two bodies occupy the same space.

8. Cromwell purportedly let Charles escape from Hampton Court to Carisbrooke Castle, on the Isle of Wight, to convince Parliament that the king could not be trusted and must be executed.

9. "Case" may mean either "plight" or "prison."

That thence the royal actor borne
The tragic scaffold might adorn;
55   While round the armèd bands
Did clap their bloody hands.

He[1] nothing common did or mean
Upon that memorable scene,
     But with his keener eye
60   The axe's edge did try;°   *test*

Nor called the gods with vulgar spite
To vindicate his helpless right;
     But bowed his comely head
     Down, as upon a bed.

65 This was that memorable hour
Which first assured the forcèd power:
     So, when they did design
     The Capitol's first line,

A bleeding head, where they begun,
70 Did fright the architects to run;
     And yet in that the state
     Foresaw its happy fate.[2]

And now the Irish are ashamed
To see themselves in one year tamed;
75   So much one man can do
     That does both act and know.

They can affirm his praises best,
And have, though overcome, confessed
     How good he is, how just,
80   And fit for highest trust.

Nor yet grown stiffer with command,
But still in the republic's hand—
     How fit he is to sway
     That can so well obey!

85 He to the Commons' feet presents
A kingdom for his first year's rents;
     And, what he may, forbears
     His fame to make it theirs;

---

1. I.e., Charles.
2. When foundations were being dug for Jupiter's temple in Rome (according to Livy and Pliny), a bloody head was uncovered. The workers at first thought it was an ill omen, but then were per-suaded to believe it meant that Rome would be "head" of an empire. The temple and the hill on which it stood were thereafter called Capitoline or the Capitol (from the Latin *caput,* head).

And has his sword and spoils ungirt,
90 To lay them at the public's skirt:[3]
        So when the falcon high
        Falls heavy from the sky,

She, having killed, no more does search
But on the next green bough to perch;
95   Where, when he first does lure,
        The falconer[4] has her sure.

What may not, then, our isle presume,
While victory his crest[5] does plume?
        What may not others fear,
100   If thus he crown each year?

A Caesar he, ere long, to Gaul
To Italy an Hannibal,[6]
        And to all states not free
        Shall climactèric[7] be.

105 The Pict no shelter now shall find
Within his parti-colored mind,[8]
        But from this valor sad°   steadfast
        Shrink underneath the plaid;°   tartan kilts

Happy if in the tufted brake°   bushes
110 The English hunter him mistake,
        Nor lay his hounds in near
        The Caledonian° deer.[9]   Scottish

But thou, the war's and fortune's son,
March indefatigably on!
115   And for the last effect,
        Still keep thy sword erect;

Besides the force it has to fright
The spirits of the shady night,[1]
        The same arts that did gain
120   A power must it maintain.

1681

3. I.e., at the feet of the Republic, conceived as a Roman senator wearing a toga.
4. I.e., when the falconer casts out his lure—a bunch of feathers attached to a cord and baited with meat.
5. Of the falcon; also, the plumed helmet of the warrior.
6. The Roman general Gaius Julius Caesar (100–44 B.C.E.) conquered Gaul; the Carthaginian general Hannibal (247–183 B.C.E.) conquered Italy. Cromwell was expected to take action against European Catholic States.
7. I.e., ushering in a new epoch.
8. The Scots, called *Picti* ("painted men") by the Romans because they painted their bodies for battle, are stigmatized as factious (with a pun on *party* and "parti-colored"). They were in fact torn between their Calvinism and their loyalty to the Catholic or Anglo-Catholic Stuart kings.
9. I.e., the "Pict" shall be happy if the English hunter mistakenly misses him and fails to send his hounds in after him.
1. Swords held upright to suggest a cross were believed to ward off evil spirits.

HENRY VAUGHAN*
1621–1695

Regeneration

A ward, and still in bonds,[1] one day
    I stole abroad;
It was high spring, and all the way
    Primrosed and hung with shade;
5   Yet was it frost within,
      And surly winds
Blasted my infant buds, and sin
    Like clouds eclipsed my mind.

Stormed thus, I straight perceived my spring
10   Mere stage and show,
My walk a monstrous,° mountained thing,   *strange, unnatural*
    Roughcast with rocks and snow;
And as a pilgrim's eye,
    Far from relief,
15 Measures the melancholy sky,
    Then drops and rains for grief,

So sighed I upwards still;[2] at last
    'Twixt steps and falls
I reached the pinnacle,° where placed   *summit*
20   I found a pair of scales;
    I took them up and laid
In th' one, late pains;
The other smoke and pleasures weighed,
    But proved the heavier grains.[3]

25 With that some cried, "Away!" Straight° I   *immediately*
      Obeyed, and led
Full east,[4] a fair, fresh field could spy;
    Some called it Jacob's bed,[5]
    A virgin soil which no
30   Rude feet ere trod,
Where, since he stepped there, only go
    Prophets and friends of God.

*The poems printed here are from Vaughan's book *Silex Scintillans* (Latin for "sparkling, or fiery, flint"). First published in 1650 and reissued with additional poems in 1655, the volume dramatizes Vaughan's experience of religious conversion. Its title alludes to the poet's "stony" heart, from which God strikes divine, purifying sparks. In the 1650 edition, the subtitle on the engraved title page acknowledges Vaughan's indebtedness to George Herbert (1593–1633; see pp. 367–85), who had used the same subtitle for *The Temple* (1633): "Sacred Poems and Private Ejaculations."

1. Literally, the constraints of being below legal age; metaphorically, the bondage of sin; the line has been variously interpreted. "Ward" may mean "prisoner" or "young person under the guardianship of another," here, perhaps, God.

2. I.e., as a pilgrim still far from relief looks up at the dark sky—but also, albeit perhaps unknowingly, up toward God—then cries, so did I keep sighing as I climbed.

3. I.e., his sins ("smoke and pleasures"), being compared to grains of corn or other seed, weigh more than his recent penance ("late pains").

4. I.e., toward the place of rebirth.

5. Sleeping in a field, Jacob saw a ladder reaching from Earth to heaven, with angels ascending and descending on it (Genesis 28.10–12).

Here I reposed; but scarce° well set,°   scarcely / settled
   A grove descried°   saw
35 Of stately height, whose branches met
   And mixed on every side;
      I entered, and once in,
         Amazed to see 't,
   Found all was changed, and a new spring
40   Did all my senses greet.

   The unthrift° sun shot vital gold,   spendthrift
      A thousand pieces,
   And heaven its azure did unfold,
      Checkered with snowy fleeces;
45   The air was all in spice,
         And every bush
   A garland wore; thus fed my eyes,
      But all the ear lay hush.°   quiet

   Only a little fountain[6] lent
50   Some use for ears,
   And on the dumb shades language spent°   expended
      The music of her tears;
      I drew her near, and found
         The cistern full
55 Of divers stones, some bright and round,
      Others ill-shaped and dull.[7]

   The first, pray mark, as quick as light
      Danced through the flood,[8]
   But the last, more heavy than the night,
60   Nailed to the center stood;[9]
      I wondered much, but tired
         At last with thought,
   My restless eye that still desired
      As strange an object brought.[1]

65 It was a bank of flowers, where I descried
      Though 'twas midday,
   Some fast asleep, others broad-eyed
      And taking in the ray;[2]
      Here, musing long, I heard
70   A rushing wind
   Which still increased, but whence it stirred
      No where I could not find.

---

6. Perhaps alluding to a baptismal font, or, per-
haps, to the traditional allegory of Christ as a foun-
tain.
7. Critics have proposed various interpretations of
the stones, e.g., ideas, images, and souls.
8. The water. *Pray mark*: i.e., take note.
9. Probably the "heaviest stone" is the idea of
Christ's Crucifixion, with the cross as the "center"

of Christian theology. Other interpretations of
"center" include Earth and hell.
1. I.e., his eye, still desiring to see something,
brought to his sight an object as strange as the one
just described.
2. God and Christ were often symbolized by the
sun. *Fast asleep*: i.e., spiritually sluggish.

I turned me round, and to each shade
        Dispatched an eye
75 To see if any leaf had made
        Least motion or reply,
    But while I listening sought
        My mind to ease
    By knowing where 'twas, or where not,
80   It whispered, "Where I please."[3]

"Lord," then said I, "on me one breath,[4]
And let me die before my death!"

Cant. chap. 5. ver. 17[5]

*Arise O North, and come thou South-wind and blow upon my garden, that
the spices thereof may flow out.*

1650

The Retreat

    Happy those early days! when I
    Shined in my angel infancy.
    Before I understood this place
    Appointed for my second race,[6]
5   Or taught my soul to fancy aught
    But a white, celestial thought;
    When yet I had not walked above
    A mile or two from my first love,[7]
    And looking back, at that short space,
10 Could see a glimpse of His bright face;
    When on some gilded cloud or flower
    My gazing soul would dwell an hour,
    And in those weaker glories spy
    Some shadows of eternity;
15 Before I taught my tongue to wound
    My conscience with a sinful sound,
    Or had the black art to dispense
    A several° sin to every sense,   separate
    But felt through all this fleshly dress[8]
20 Bright shoots of everlastingness.
        O, how I long to travel back,
        And tread again that ancient track!

---

3. "The wind bloweth where it listeth, and thou hearest the sound thereof, but canst not tell whence it cometh, and whither it goeth: so is every one that is born of the Spirit" (John 3.8).
4. I.e., blow one of your life-giving (and perhaps also poetry-inspiring) breaths on me.
5. The poem ends by merging its voice, imaged as breath, with that of the biblical Song of Solomon (though from 4.16, not 5.17).

6. "Race" is a traditional Christian metaphor for "life"; by "second" race Vaughan evidently alludes to a belief in the soul's heavenly existence prior to its human life. Such a belief was held by some Christian Neoplatonists and Hermetic authors; it reappears in Wordsworth's "Ode: Intimations of Immortality" (see p. 796).
7. I.e., Christ; see Revelation 2.4.
8. I.e., the mortal body.

That I might once more reach that plain
Where first I left my glorious train,[9]
25 From whence th' enlightened spirit sees
That shady city of palm trees.[1]
But, ah! my soul with too much stay°   delay
Is drunk, and staggers in the way.
Some men a forward motion love;
30 But I by backward steps would move,
And when this dust falls to the urn,[2]
In that state I came, return.

1650

The World

I saw eternity the other night,
Like a great ring of pure and endless light,
    All calm as it was bright;
And round beneath it, Time, in hours, days, years,
5   Driven by the spheres[3]
Like a vast shadow moved, in which the world
    And all her train were hurled.
The doting lover in his quaintest° strain   most ingenious
    Did there complain;
10 Near him, his lute, his fancy, and his flights,
    Wit's sour delights,
With gloves and knots,° the silly snares of pleasure,   love knots
    Yet his dear treasure,
All scattered lay, while he his eyes did pour
15   Upon a flower.

The darksome statesman hung with weights and woe
Like a thick midnight fog moved there so slow
    He did nor° stay nor go;   neither
Condemning thoughts, like sad eclipses, scowl
20   Upon his soul,
And clouds of crying witnesses without°   all around
    Pursued him with one shout.
Yet digged the mole,[4] and, lest his ways be found,
    Worked underground,
25 Where he did clutch his prey. But one did see
    That policy:°   strategy
Churches and altars fed him; perjuries
    Were gnats and flies;
It rained about him blood and tears; but he
30   Drank them as free.[5]

---

9. I.e., my previous mode of existence, or, possibly, my place in God's angelic entourage.
1. Heaven or the Promised Land, as shown to Moses (Deuteronomy 34.1–4); for its identification with Jericho, see Deuteronomy 34.3.

2. Tomb. *This dust*: my body.
3. The concentric crystalline spheres of Ptolemaic astronomy.
4. I.e., the "darksome statesman" of line 16.
5. I.e., as freely as they rained.

The fearful miser on a heap of rust
  Sat pining all his life there, did scarce° trust   *scarcely*
    His own hands with the dust;
  Yet would not place° one piece above, but lives   *invest*
35   In fear of thieves.
Thousands there were as frantic as himself,
    And hugged each one his pelf:°   *money, riches*
The downright epicure[6] placed heaven in sense,
    And scorned pretense;
40 While others, slipped into a wide excess,
    Said little less;
The weaker sort slight, trivial wares enslave,
    Who think them brave°   *fine, showy*
  And poor, despised Truth sat counting by[7]
45   Their victory.

Yet some, who all this while did weep and sing,
And sing and weep, soared up into the ring;
    But most would use no wing.
"O fools!" said I, "thus to prefer dark night
50   Before true light!
To live in grots° and caves, and hate the day   *caverns*
    Because it shows the way,
The way which from this dead and dark abode
    Leads up to God,
55 A way where you might tread the sun and be
    More bright than he!"
But as I did their madness so discuss,
    One whispered thus:
"This ring the bridegroom did for none provide,
60   But for his bride."[8]

John Chap. 2. ver. 16, 17

All that is in the world, the lust of the flesh, the lust of the eyes, and the pride of life, is not of the father, but is of the world.

And the world passeth away, and the lusts thereof, but he that doth the will of God abideth forever.

1650

They Are All Gone into the World of Light!

They are all gone into the world of light!
  And I alone sit lingering here;
Their very memory is fair and bright,
  And my sad thoughts doth clear.

---

6. One who delights in the experience of the senses.
7. *Counting by*: recording.

8. See Revelation 19.7–9 and 21 for the marriage of the Lamb and the bride (Christ and his Church).

5 It° glows and glitters in my cloudy breast   *the memory*
    Like stars upon some gloomy grove,
Or those faint beams in which this hill is dressed
    After the sun's remove.

I see them walking in an air of glory,
10   Whose light doth trample on my days;
My days, which are at best but dull and hoary,°   *gray, ancient*
    Mere glimmering and decays.

O holy hope! and high humility,
    High as the heavens above!
15 These are your walks, and you have showed them me
    To kindle my cold love.

Dear, beauteous death! the jewel of the just,
    Shining nowhere but in the dark;
What mysteries do lie beyond thy dust,
20   Could man outlook that mark!°   *boundary*

He that hath found some fledged bird's nest may know[9]
    At first sight if the bird be flown;
But what fair well° or grove he sings in now,   *spring*
    That is to him° unknown.   *the seeker*

25 And yet, as angels in some brighter dreams
    Call to the soul when man doth sleep,
So some strange thoughts transcend our wonted themes,[1]
    And into glory peep.

If a star were confined into a tomb,[2]
30   Her captive flames must needs burn there;
But when the hand that locked her up gives room,
    She'll shine through all the sphere.

O Father of eternal life, and all
    Created glories under Thee!
35 Resume° Thy spirit from this world of thrall°   *take back / slavery*
    Into true liberty!

Either disperse these mists, which blot and fill
    My perspective[3] still as they pass;
Or else remove me hence unto that hill
40   Where I shall need no glass.[4]

1655

9. The bird often symbolizes the human soul; cf. George Herbert, "Easter Wings" (p. 368). *Fledged:* fit to fly.
1. I.e., accustomed ideas.
2. Probably a metaphor for the body, with the "star" as the soul.
3. Literally, telescope; more generally, ability to see into the distance.

4. Vaughan superimposes the modern image of the magnifying telescope onto the traditional Christian and Platonic image of life as an experience of distorted vision or darkness; "for now we see through a glass, darkly; but then face to face" (1 Corinthians 13.12). *Hill:* Sion hill; figuratively, heaven.

The Waterfall

With what deep murmurs through time's silent stealth
Doth thy transparent, cool, and watery wealth
    Here flowing fall,
    And chide, and call,
5 As if his liquid, loose retìnue[5] stayed
Lingering, and were of this steep place afraid,
    The common pass
    Where, clear as glass,
    All must descend—
10   Not to an end,
But quickened by this deep and rocky grave,
Rise to a longer course more bright and brave.[6]

    Dear stream! dear bank, where often I
    Have sat and pleased my pensive eye,
15   Why, since each drop of thy quick° store   *living*
    Runs thither whence it flowed before,[7]
    Should poor souls fear a shade or night,
    Who came, sure, from a sea of light?[8]
    Or since those drops are all sent back
20   So sure to thee, that none doth lack,
    Why should frail flesh doubt any more
    That what God takes He'll not restore?

    O useful element and clear!
    My sacred wash and cleanser here,
25   My first consignor[9] unto those
    Fountains of life where the Lamb goes!
    What sublime truths and wholesome themes
    Lodge in thy mystical deep streams!
    Such as dull man can never find
30   Unless that Spirit lead his mind
    Which first upon thy face did move,[1]
    And hatched all with His quickening love.
    As this loud brook's incessant fall
    In streaming rings restagnates° all,   *becomes stagnant*
35   Which reach by course the bank, and then
    Are no more seen, just so pass men.

5. Those in service; i.e., the water that has not yet flowed over the edge is likened to time's ("his") followers or "retainers," with a probable bilingual pun on *retenu*, French for "held back."

6. I.e., elaborating on the central Christian paradox of resurrection, Vaughan imagines death as a quickening in the grave (a movement like that of a child in the womb) followed by a rising that defies the waterfall's apparently natural downward "course." *Brave:* splendid; cf. George Herbert, "Virtue," line 5 (p. 375).

7. A reference to the cyclical movement of water (from river to sea to clouds to rain or snow to rivers again), often held to be a sign of God's ordering of the universe.

8. A Hermetic concept; see "The Retreat," line 4 (p. 492).

9. One who dispatches goods to another, i.e., the baptismal water ("cleanser here") delivers the speaker to eternal life ("where the Lamb goes"). Cf. Revelation 7.17: "For the Lamb which is in the midst of the throne shall feed them, and shall lead them unto living fountains of waters: and God shall wipe away all tears from their eyes."

1. Describes the beginning of Creation (thus "hatched all," line 31): "And the Spirit of God moved upon the face of the waters" (Genesis 1.2).

O my invisible estate,°　　　　　　　　*condition*
My glorious liberty, still late!²
Thou art the channel my soul seeks,
40　　Not this with cataracts° and creeks.　　*waterfalls*

1655

The Night

John 3.2

Through that pure virgin shrine,³
That sacred veil drawn o'er Thy glorious noon,⁴
That men might look and live, as glowworms⁵ shine,
　　And face the moon,
5　　Wise Nicodemus saw such light
As made him know his God by night.⁶

　　Most blest believer he!
Who in that land of darkness and blind eyes
Thy long-expected healing wings⁷ could see,
10　　When Thou didst rise!
And, what can never more be done,
Did at midnight speak with the Sun!⁸

　　O who will tell me where
He found Thee at that dead and silent hour?
15 What hallowed solitary ground did bear
　　So rare a flower,
Within whose sacred leaves did lie
The fulness of the Deity?

　　No mercy-seat of gold,
20 No dead and dusty cherub, nor carved stone,
But His own living works did my Lord hold
　　And lodge alone;⁹

2. I.e., not yet arrived (i.e., the liberty of eternal life after death); cf. Romans 8.21: "Because the creature itself also shall be delivered from the bondage of corruption into the glorious liberty of the children of God."
3. Refers both to Christ's mortal body and to the night sky; indeed, the "virgin shrine" condenses allusions not only to Christ but also to his mother, Mary, and probably to Diana, virgin and goddess of the moon (according to classical myth).
4. Christ was often figured as the sun. *Sacred veil*: Paul writes of "a new and living way which he [Christ] hath consecrated for us, through the veil, that is to say, his flesh" (Hebrews 10.20).
5. An insect, (the female of) which emits a shining green light from the abdomen; i.e., perhaps, as the glowworms shine by reflecting the moon's light, so humans spiritually shine by reflecting Christ's light.

6. Nicodemus, coming to Christ at night, addressed him as "come from God"; in the same account, Christ speaks of his coming as "the light" (John 3.1–21).
7. A prophecy of Christ's coming: "But unto you that fear my Name shall the Sun of righteousness arise with healing in his wings" (Malachi 4.2).
8. A reference back to Nicodemus, who spoke with Christ at midnight in a miracle the speaker thinks (perhaps erroneously) can never recur.
9. God instructed Moses on how to make the ark of the Covenant: "And thou shalt make a mercy seat of pure gold. . . . And thou shalt make two cherubims of gold, of beaten work shalt thou make them, in the two ends of the mercy seat" (Exodus 25.17–18). Vaughan contrasts the physical temples of the Old Testament with the "living works" in which Christ lodges.

Where trees and herbs did watch and peep
And wonder, while the Jews did sleep.[1]

25   Dear night! this world's defeat;
The stop to busy fools; care's check and curb;
The day of spirits; my soul's calm retreat
      Which none disturb!
Christ's progress, and His prayer time;[2]
30   The hours to which high heaven doth chime;

      God's silent, searching flight;
When my Lord's head is filled with dew, and all
His locks are wet with the clear drops of night;
      His still, soft call;
35   His knocking time;[3] the soul's dumb watch,
When spirits their fair kindred catch.

      Were all my loud, evil days
Calm and unhaunted as is thy dark tent,
Whose peace but by some angel's wing or voice
40   Is seldom rent,°   torn
Then I in heaven all the long year
Would keep, and never wander here.

      But living where the sun
Doth all things wake, and where all mix and tire
45 Themselves and others, I consent and run
      To every mire,
And by this world's ill-guiding light,[4]
Err more than I can do by night.

      There is in God, some say,
50 A deep but dazzling darkness, as men here
Say it is late and dusky, because they
      See not all clear.
O for that night! where I in Him
Might live invisible and dim!

                                                                        1655

---

1. Vaughan imputes to plants an eagerness for Christ's coming lacking in the Jews. Their spiritual lethargy ("sleep") prevents them from recognizing Christ's divinity.
2. "Mark, chap. i.35. Luke, chap. xxi.37" [Vaughan's note]. The cited passages mention Christ's praying at night.
3. "I sleep, but my heart waketh: it is the voice of my beloved that knocketh, saying, Open to me, my sister, my love, my dove, my undefiled: for my head is filled with dew, and my locks with the drops of the night" (Song of Solomon 5.2).
4. The speaker's own "consent" to error, along with the "ill-guiding light" of the world, cause him to run into a spiritual swamp ("mire"). The "ill-guiding light" may allude to the will-o'-the-wisp, which was said to draw travelers astray into bogs by holding a false light before them; the phenomenon of nocturnal light is caused by the combustion of marsh gas.

MARGARET CAVENDISH
1623–1673

An Apology for Writing So Much upon This Book[1]

Condemn me not, I make so much ado
About this book; it is my child, you know.
Just like a bird, when her young are in nest,
Goes in, and out, and hops, and takes no rest:
5   But when their young are fledg'd, their heads out-peep,
Lord! What a chirping does the old one keep!
So I, for fear my strengthless child should fall
Against a door, or stool, aloud I call;
Bid have a care of such a dangerous place:
10   Thus write I much, to hinder all disgrace.

The Sea Similized to Meadows and Pastures: the Mariners, to Shepherds: the Mast, to a May-Pole:[2] the Fish, to Beasts

The waves, like ridges of plow'd land, are high;
Whereat the ship oft stumbling, down doth lie.
But, in a calm, the sea's like meadows seen
Level; its saltness makes it look as green.
5   When ships thereon a slow soft pace do walk;
Then mariners, as shepherds, sing and talk:
Some whistle, and some on their pipes do play;
And thus, with mirth, they pass their time away.
And every mast is like a May-pole high,
10   Round which they dance, though not so merrily
As shepherds do, when they their lasses bring
Garlands, to May-poles tied with a silk string.
Instead of garlands, they hang on their mast
Huge sails and ropes, to tie these garlands fast.
15   Instead of lasses, they do dance with Death;
And for their music, they have Boreas[3] breath.
Instead of wine and wassails,[4] drink salt tears;
And for their meat, they feed on nought but fears.
For flocks of sheep, great schools of herrings swim;
20   The whales, as ravenous wolves, do feed on them.
As sportful kids skip over hillocks green,
So dancing dolphins, on the waves are seen.
The porpoise, like their watchful dog espies,
And gives them warning when great winds will rise.

1. This poem appeared in slightly different versions at the beginning of all three editions of Margaret Cavendish's poems published during her lifetime (in 1653, 1664, and 1668; our selections follow the 1668 text). For the metaphor of the book or poem as child, see Sir Philip Sidney, *Astrophil and Stella*, sonnet 1 (p. 213) and Anne Bradstreet, "The Author to Her Book" (p. 465).
2. A high pole, painted with spiral stripes of different colors, decked with flowers, set up on a green for revelers to dance around at a May Day festival. *Similized:* compared.
3. The north wind's.
4. The liquor with which healths were drunk.

25   Instead of barking, he his head doth show
       Above the waters, when they roughly flow:
       And, like as men, in time of show'ring rain
       And wind, do not in open fields remain;
       But quickly run for shelter to a tree:
30   So ships at anchor lie upon the sea.

Of Many Worlds in This World

    Just like as in a nest of boxes[5] round,
    Degrees of sizes in each box are found:
    So, in this world, may many others be
    Thinner and less, and less still by degree:
5   Although they are not subject to our sense,
    A world may be no bigger than two-pence.[6]
    Nature is curious,° and such works may shape,   *ingenious, skillful*
    Which our dull senses easily escape:
    For creatures, small as atoms,[7] may be there,
10   If every one a creature's figure bear.
    If atoms four, a world can make,[8] then see
    What several worlds might in an ear-ring be:
    For, millions of those atoms may be in
    The head of one small, little, single pin.
15   And if thus small, then ladies may well wear
    A world of worlds, as pendents in each ear.

                                 1668

JOHN DRYDEN
1631–1700

Song from *The Indian Emperor*[1]

    Ah, fading joy, how quickly art thou past!
       Yet we thy ruin haste.
    As if the cares of human life were few,
       We seek out new:
5   And follow fate, which would too fast pursue.[2]

5. A set of boxes of graduated sizes packed inside one another.
6. An English silver coin having the value of two pennies; a very small amount.
7. Very minute or microscopic objects.
8. In another poem, Cavendish declares that the four elements—earth, water, air, and fire—are made of four different kinds of atoms: "square flat," "round," "long straight," and "sharpest," respectively.
1. This play, first performed by the King's Company in the spring of 1665, focuses on the conquest of Mexico by the Spanish conquistador Hernán Cortés (1485–1547). The song is sung by an Indian woman to a group of Spaniards reclining by a fountain (4.3); immediately after the song's end, they are captured by Indian forces.
2. I.e., which, even if we did not conspire with it, would hurry us too quickly to our end. Dryden, in response to criticism of this metaphor, explained that it was borrowed from a line in Virgil's *Aeneid* (11.695).

See how on every bough the birds express
    In their sweet notes their happiness.
    They all enjoy and nothing spare;
    But on their mother nature lay their care.
10 Why then should man, the lord of all below,
    Such troubles choose to know
    As none of all his subjects undergo?

    Hark, hark, the waters fall, fall, fall,
    And with a murmuring sound
15 Dash, dash upon the ground,
    To gentle slumbers call.

                                        1667

Song from *Troilus and Cressida*[3]

1

    Can life be a blessing,
    Or worth the possessing,
Can life be a blessing, if love were away?
Ah, no! though our love all night keep us waking,
5 And though he[4] torment us with cares all the day,
    Yet he sweetens, he sweetens our pains in the taking;
There's an hour at the last, there's an hour to repay.

2

    In every possessing
    The ravishing blessing,
10 In every possessing the fruit of our pain,
    Poor lovers forget long ages of anguish,
Whate'er they have suffered and done to obtain;
    'Tis a pleasure, a pleasure to sigh and to languish,
When we hope, when we hope to be happy again.

                                        1679

From Absalom and Achitophel: A Poem[5]

    In pious times, ere priestcraft did begin,
    Before polygamy was made a sin;

3. *Troilus and Cressida, or Truth Found Too Late* is Dryden's third and last adaptation of a Shakespeare play; the Homeric story of two lovers, Troilus and Cressida, separated during the siege of Troy, had also been told by Chaucer (see p. 67). Dryden alters Shakespeare's play considerably; unlike Shakespeare, Dryden has both title characters die, for instance. In both versions, Cressida's uncle, Pandarus, is a voyeuristic, lewd character who schemes to bring about the physical consummation of the lovers' desires, but only in Dryden's text does Pandarus use a song to serenade the lovers. In this scene (3.2), Pandarus listens outside the lovers' door the morning after they have consummated their love, and then instructs a group of musicians to sing this song.
4. Love is commonly personified as the young boy, Cupid.
5. The title names refer the reader to 2 Samuel 13–18. Absalom there rebels against his father, King David; Achitophel advises Absalom to destroy David at once. Like many other texts from this period, Dryden's poem uses this biblical story as an analogue for the religious and political crisis of 1678 that came to be known as the "Popish Plot," and its aftermath of bitter political struggle

When man on many multiplied his kind,
Ere one to one was cursedly confined;
5   When nature prompted and no law denied
Promiscuous use of concubine and bride;
Then Israel's monarch after Heaven's own heart,[6]
His vigorous warmth did variously impart
To wives and slaves; and, wide as his command,
10   Scattered his Maker's image through the land.
Michal,[7] of royal blood, the crown did wear,
A soil ungrateful to the tiller's care:
Not so the rest; for several mothers bore
To godlike David several sons before.
15   But since like slaves his bed they did ascend,
No true succession could their seed attend.
Of all this numerous progeny was none
So beautiful, so brave, as Absalom:
Whether, inspired by some diviner lust,
20   His father got° him with a greater gust,°   begot / enjoyment
Or that° his conscious destiny made way,   whether
By manly beauty, to imperial sway.[8]
Early in foreign fields he won renown,
With kings and states allied to Israel's crown:
25   In peace the thoughts of war he could remove,
And seemed as° he were only born for love.   as if
Whate'er he did, was done with so much ease,
In him alone 'twas natural to please:
His motions all accompanied with grace;
30   And paradise was opened in his face.
With secret joy indulgent David viewed
His youthful image in his son renewed:
To all his wishes nothing he denied;
And made the charming Annabel his bride.
35   What faults he had (for who from faults is free?)
His father could not, or he would not see.
Some warm excesses which the law forbore,
Were cònstrued youth that purged by boiling o'er:

---

between King Charles II and the earl of Shaftesbury: David stands for Charles II and Absalom for the duke of Monmouth, Charles's illegitimate son. Achitophel represents the earl of Shaftesbury, who urged Monmouth to seek the succession to the throne in an attempt to displace Charles's brother James, the duke of York, an openly practicing Catholic. In 1678, Titus Oates offered sworn testimony of the existence of a Jesuit plot to assassinate the king, burn London, massacre Protestants, and restore the Catholic Church; this testimony, combined with the discovery of the murder of a London justice of the peace, Sir Edmund Berry Godfrey, who had received a copy of the oath for safekeeping, prompted fear of a Catholic uprising; Protestant leaders took advantage of the panic to try to exclude James from the succession. To what extent (if any) such a plot really existed is a matter of historical debate. Charles managed to retain his brother's position as heir and charged Shaftesbury with high treason. Dryden anonymously published the first part of "Absalom and Achitophel" in 1681

while the earl was under arrest, apparently as an attempt to stir public opinion against him; however, the grand jury soon set the earl free (he died two years later). A second part appeared in 1682, although much of this work is attributed to Nahum Tate. After Charles II died in 1685 and James II succeeded to the throne, Dryden (and his two sons) converted to Catholicism in 1686; he remained a Catholic for the rest of his life.
6. God calls David "a man after mine own heart" in Acts 13.22.
7. David's childless wife. She stands for Charles's childless queen, Catherine of Portugal.
8. Although the lines are ambiguous, Dryden seems to be asking whether Absalom gained imperial power (sway) by heredity or by deliberate use of his "manly beauty." Dryden alludes here to Monmouth's personal attractiveness and, in the following lines, to his prowess in wars against the Dutch and later the French, and to his marriage (arranged by the king) to the Scottish heiress Anne Scott.

And Amnon's murder,[9] by a specious name,
40   Was called a just revenge for injured fame.
Thus praised and loved the noble youth remained,
While David, undisturbed, in Sion[1] reigned.
But life can never be sincerely° blest;   *wholly*
Heaven punishes the bad, and proves° the best.   *tries*
45   The Jews,[2] a headstrong, moody, murmuring race,
As ever tried the extent and stretch of grace;
God's pampered people, whom, debauched with ease,
No king could govern, nor no God could please
(Gods they had tried of every shape and size
50   That god-smiths could produce, or priests devise);[3]
These Adam-wits,[4] too fortunately free,
Began to dream they wanted° liberty;   *lacked*
And when no rule, no precedent was found,
Of men by laws less circumscribed and bound,
55   They led their wild desires to woods and caves,[5]
And thought that all but savages were slaves.
They who, when Saul was dead, without a blow,
Made foolish Ishbosheth the crown forego;[6]
Who banished David did from Hebron[7] bring,
60   And with a general shout proclaimed him king:
Those very Jews, who, at their very best,
Their humor° more than loyalty expressed,   *caprice*
Now wondered why so long they had obeyed
An idol monarch,[8] which their hands had made;
65   Thought they might ruin him they could create,
Or melt him to that golden calf, a state.[9]
But these were random bolts;° no formed design   *shots*
Nor interest made the factious crowd to join:
The sober part of Israel, free from stain,
70   Well knew the value of a peaceful reign;
And, looking backward with a wise affright,°   *fear*
Saw seams of wounds, dishonest° to the sight: *dishonorable*
In contemplation of whose ugly scars
They cursed the memory of civil wars.[1]

9. Absalom killed his half-brother Amnon, who had raped Absalom's half-sister, Tamar (2 Samuel 13.28–29). The parallel with Monmouth is vague, although he had a reputation for violence in his youth, and his troopers had recently attacked an abusive Parliamentarian, Sir John Coventry. Cònstrued: interpreted as the result of.
1. I.e., London.
2. I.e., the English.
3. Perhaps a reference to the novelties in Church doctrine and practice that had issued in the disestablishment of the Anglican Church under the Commonwealth; more generally, the recent political and religious controversies that had divided England. The Israelites (God's chosen people) were frequently converted to the worship of the pagan gods of the tribes and peoples with whom they fought and traded.
4. The word calls attention to the supposedly untutored quality of the dissenters from the Anglican Communion, and also to the biblical Adam's rebellion against the single restraint imposed on

him (see Genesis 2.16–17).
5. Dissenters from the Church of England were sometimes forced to worship in hiding.
6. Saul stands for Oliver Cromwell (1599–1658), English general and statesman, lord protector of England; Ishbosheth, Saul's son who briefly ruled Israel, here represents Richard Cromwell (1626–1712), who had succeeded his father as lord protector before being forced to abdicate in 1659.
7. David was first crowned king of the tribe of Judah, in Hebron, before becoming king of Israel (2 Samuel 1–5); Charles II was first crowned king in Scotland, before being restored to the throne in England in 1660.
8. I.e., Oliver Cromwell. Jews were not allowed to worship idols (Exodus 20.4).
9. I.e., that idol, a republic or commonwealth. The biblical reference is to the image of a calf, made of melted golden earrings, which the Israelites worshiped while Moses was on Mt. Sinai (Exodus 32.1–4).
1. I.e., such as the religious and political turmoil

75 The moderate sort of men, thus qualified,°   *mollified*
Inclined the balance to the better side;
And David's mildness managed it so well,
The bad found no occasion to rebel.
But when to sin our biased nature leans,[2]
80 The careful° Devil is still at hand with means;   *watchful*
And providently pimps for ill desires:[3]
The Good Old Cause[4] revived, a plot requires.
Plots, true or false, are necessary things,
To raise up commonwealths and ruin kings.
85   The inhabitants of old Jerusalem
Were Jebusites;[5] the town so called from them;
And theirs the native right.
But when the chosen people[6] grew more strong,
The rightful cause at length became the wrong;
90 And every loss the men of Jebus bore,
They still were thought God's enemies the more.
Thus worn and weakened, well or ill content,
Submit they must to David's government:
Impoverished and deprived of all command,
95 Their taxes doubled as they lost their land;
And, what was harder yet to flesh and blood,
Their gods disgraced, and burnt like common wood.
This set the heathen priesthood[7] in a flame;
For priests of all religions are the same:
100 Of whatsoe'er descent their godhead be,
Stock,[8] stone, or other homely pedigree,
In his defense his servants are as bold,
As if he had been born of beaten gold.
The Jewish rabbins, though their enemies,
105 In this conclude them honest men and wise:[9]
For 'twas their duty, all the learned think,
To espouse his cause, by whom they eat and drink.[1]
From hence began that Plot,[2] the nation's curse,
Bad in itself, but represented worse;
110 Raised in extremes, and in extremes decried;
With oaths affirmed, with dying vows denied;
Not weighed or winnowed by the multitude;[3]

---

that had led to the beheading of Charles II's father, Charles I, in 1649.

2. *Biased*: prejudiced, or inclined in some direction (the *O.E.D.* cites Dryden's line); i.e., when our human inclination to sin takes over.

3. I.e., the devil prudently provides the means ("pimps") for sinful desires.

4. A popular phrase referring to the Commonwealth.

5. The Jebusites (Judges 1.21) represent Roman Catholics; Jerusalem stands for London.

6. The Protestants, some of whom claimed for England a divinely appointed destiny like that of the Hebrews.

7. The Catholic clergy, suffering from the recent flare-up of prejudice as well as from the long history of restrictions to which Dryden has just alluded; in particular, many oppressive laws against Catholics were established under the forty-five-year reign of Queen Elizabeth I (1533–1603;

see pp. 142–43).

8. Block of wood, i.e., of humble descent.

9. I.e., even though the Anglican divines ("Jewish rabbins") are "enemies" to Catholics, they consider Catholics wise in the "bold" defense of their God.

1. I.e., Christ, whose body Catholics "eat and drink" in Communion; according to the Catholic doctrine of transubstantiation, the bread and wine actually become the body of Christ during Communion (whereas Protestant doctrine holds that the bread and wine symbolize or represent his body).

2. I.e., the Catholic plot described in note 5, p. 501.

3. According to this simile, in which the reports of a plot are compared to grain, the populace has not carefully "weighed" and "winnowed" (separated the good from the bad) the grain, but has swallowed it whole.

But swallowed in the mass, unchewed and crude.
Some truth there was, but dashed° and brewed with lies,   *mixed*
115 To please the fools, and puzzle all the wise.
Succeeding times did equal folly call,
Believing nothing, or believing all.
The Egyptian[4] rites the Jebusites embraced,
Where gods were recommended by their taste.
120 Such savory deities must needs be good,
As served at once for worship and for food.
By force they could not introduce these gods,
For ten to one in former days was odds;[5]
So fraud was used (the sacrificer's trade):[6]
125 Fools are more hard to conquer than persuade.
Their busy teachers mingled with the Jews,
And raked for converts even the court and stews:°   *brothels*
Which Hebrew priests the more unkindly took,
Because the fleece accompanies the flock.[7]
130 Some thought they God's anointed[8] meant to slay
By guns, invented since full many a day:
Our author swears it not; but who can know
How far the Devil and Jebusites may go?
This Plot, which failed for want of common sense,
135 Had yet a deep and dangerous consequence:
For, as when raging fevers boil the blood,
The standing lake soon floats into a flood,
And every hostile humor, which before
Slept quiet in its channels, bubbles o'er;
140 So several factions from this first ferment
Work up to foam, and threat the government.
Some by their friends, more by themselves thought wise,
Opposed the power to which they could not rise.
Some had in courts been great, and thrown from thence,
145 Like fiends were hardened in impenitence;°   *unrepentance*
Some, by their monarch's fatal mercy, grown
From pardoned rebels kinsmen to the throne,
Were raised in power and public office high;
Strong bands, if bands ungrateful men could tie.
150   Of these the false Achitophel[9] was first;
A name to all succeeding ages cursed:
For close° designs, and crooked counsels fit;   *secret*
Sagacious, bold, and turbulent of wit;°   *imagination*
Restless, unfixed in principles and place;
155 In power unpleased, impatient of disgrace:
A fiery soul, which, working out its way, ⎫
Fretted the pygmy° body to decay,   ⎬   *overly small*
And o'er-informed the tenement of clay.[1] ⎭

4. I.e., the French; hence Roman Catholics. The allusion is to the Mass, incorporating the doctrine of transubstantiation.
5. I.e., because Protestants outnumbered Catholics (although the difference in numbers was probably much smaller than Dryden indicates).
6. I.e., those who use fraud sacrifice innocent people.
7. Dryden implies that the Anglican clergy ("Hebrew priests") resented any loss of tithes ("fleece") paid to the established Church; such loss was caused by Catholic conversions.
8. The king.
9. Shaftesbury had been a member of Cromwell's council of state; later, he had helped bring back Charles II and was made a member of the Cabal, a powerful committee of the Privy Council.
1. I.e., overanimated his body.

A daring pilot in extremity;
160   Pleased with the danger, when the waves went high,
He sought the storms; but, for a calm unfit,
Would steer too nigh the sands, to boast his wit.
Great wits° are sure to madness near allied,   *geniuses*
And thin partitions do their bounds divide;
165   Else why should he, with wealth and honor blest,
Refuse his age the needful hours of rest?
Punish a body which he could not please,
Bankrupt of life, yet prodigal of ease?
And all to leave what with his toil he won,
170   To that unfeathered two-legged thing,[2] a son;
Got,° while his soul did huddled° notions try;   *begotten / confused*
And born a shapeless lump, like anarchy.
In friendship false, implacable in hate,
Resolved to ruin or to rule the state.
175   To compass° this the triple bond he broke,[3]   *accomplish*
The pillars of the public safety shook,
And fitted Israel for a foreign yoke;
Then seized with fear, yet still affecting fame,
Usurped a patriot's all-atoning name.[4]
180   So easy still it proves in factious times,
With public zeal to cancel private crimes.
How safe is treason, and how sacred ill,
Where none can sin against the people's will!
Where crowds can wink, and no offense be known,
185   Since in another's guilt they find their own!
Yet fame deserved, no enemy can grudge;
The statesman we abhor, but praise the judge.
In Israel's courts ne'er sat an Abbethdin[5]
With more discerning eyes, or hands more clean;
190   Unbribed, unsought, the wretched to redress;
Swift of dispatch, and easy of access.
Oh, had he been content to serve the crown,
With virtues only proper to the gown;°   *judiciary*
Or had the rankness of the soil been freed
195   From cockle,° that oppressed the noble seed;   *weedlike plant*
David for him his tuneful harp had strung,
And Heaven had wanted one immortal song.[6]
But wild Ambition loves to slide, not stand,
And Fortune's ice prefers to Virtue's land.
200   Achitophel, grown weary to possess
A lawful fame, and lazy happiness,
Disdained the golden fruit to gather free,

2. Plato's definition of cloddish man.
3. Shaftesbury helped bring about the war against Holland, with France as an ally, in 1672. *Triple bond:* an alliance (1668) between England, Sweden, and the Dutch Republic against France, which was thought to pose the threat of an invasion (line 177).
4. The name of "patriot" was "affected" (put on), then and thereafter, by the party out of power.
5. A rabbinical term for a justice. Shaftesbury pre-sided over the Court of Chancery from 1672 to 1673.
6. I.e., heaven would have lacked one Psalm of David. Many interpretations exist for this difficult couplet: perhaps it is a reference to Psalm 3, written, as tradition would have it, when David fled from Absalom; other suggestions include Psalm 4 and Psalm 109. The application to Charles II is unclear; some have suggested that it refers to Dryden's poem.

And lent the crowd his arm to shake the tree.
Now, manifest° of° crimes contrived long since,   *detected / in*
205 He stood at bold defiance with his prince;
Held up the buckler° of the people's cause   *protector*
Against the crown, and skulked behind the laws.
The wished occasion of the Plot he takes;
Some circumstances finds, but more he makes.
210 By buzzing emissaries fills the ears
Of listening crowds with jealousies° and fears   *suspicions*
Of arbitrary counsels brought to light,
And proves the king himself a Jebusite.
Weak arguments! which yet he knew full well
215 Were strong with people easy to rebel.
For, governed by the moon, the giddy Jews
Tread the same track when she the prime renews;
And once in twenty years, their scribes record,[7]
By natural instinct they change their lord.
220 Achitophel still wants a chief, and none
Was found so fit as warlike Absalom:
Not that he wished his greatness to create
(For politicians neither love nor hate),
But, for he knew his title not allowed,
225 Would keep him still depending on the crowd,
That kingly power, thus ebbing out, might be
Drawn to the dregs of a democracy.[8]
Him he attempts with studied arts to please,
And sheds his venom in such words as these:
230   "Auspicious prince, at whose nativity
Some royal planet[9] ruled the southern sky;
Thy longing country's darling and desire;
Their cloudy pillar and their guardian fire:
Their second Moses,[1] whose extended wand
235 Divides the seas, and shows the promised land;
Whose dawning day in every distant age
Has exercised the sacred prophet's rage:
The people's prayer, the glad diviners' theme,
The young men's vision, and the old men's dream![2]
240 Thee, savior, thee, the nation's vows confess,
And, never satisfied with seeing, bless:
Swift unbespoken° pomps° thy steps proclaim,   *voluntary / celebrations*
And stammering babes are taught to lisp thy name.
How long wilt thou the general joy detain,

7. The phases of the moon fall on the same day of
the calendar year at roughly twenty-year intervals.
Crises in English politics occurred in 1640 (the
rebellion against Charles I), 1660 (the restoration
of Charles II), and the time of the poem.
8. I.e., mob rule.
9. A planet whose influence determines that he
(Absalom) should be king.
1. I.e., their guide; after their exodus from Egypt
under the leadership of Moses, who separated the
waters of the Red Sea long enough to allow them
to escape, the Israelites were led in their forty-year
wandering by a pillar of clouds by day and a pillar
of fire by night (Exodus 13–14). In reference to
Christ, Moses said, "A Prophet shall the Lord your
God raise up unto you of your brethren, like unto
me": Christ is sometimes referred to as "the second
Moses" (see Acts 7.37). Here, Achitophel tells
Absalom that he is meant to be a second Moses.
2. Cf. the prophecy delivered to Joel: "And it shall
come to pass afterward, that I will pour out my
spirit upon all flesh; and your sons and your daugh-
ters shall prophesy, your old men shall dream
dreams, your young men shall see visions" (Joel
2.28).

245 Starve and defraud the people of thy reign?
     Content ingloriously to pass thy days
     Like one of Virtue's fools that feeds on praise;
     Till thy fresh glories, which now shine so bright,
     Grow stale and tarnish with our daily sight.
250 Believe me, royal youth, thy fruit must be
     Or° gathered ripe, or rot upon the tree.   *either*
     Heaven has to all allotted, soon or late,
     Some lucky revolution of their fate;
     Whose motions if we watch and guide with skill
255 (For human good depends on human will),
     Our Fortune rolls as from a smooth descent,[3]
     And from the first impression takes the bent;
     But, if unseized, she glides away like wind,
     And leaves repenting Folly far behind.
260 Now, now she meets you with a glorious prize,
     And spreads her locks before her as she flies.
     Had thus Old David, from whose loins you spring,
     Not dared, when Fortune called him, to be king,
     At Gath[4] an exile he might still remain,
265 And heaven's anointing oil[5] had been in vain.
     Let his successful youth your hopes engage;
     But shun the example of declining age;
     Behold him setting in his western skies,
     The shadows lengthening as the vapors rise.[6]
270 He is not now, as when on Jordan's sand[7]
     The joyful people thronged to see him land,
     Covering the beach, and blackening all the strand;°   *shore*
     But, like the Prince of Angels,[8] from his height
     Comes tumbling downward with diminished light,
275 Betrayed by one poor plot to public scorn
     (Our only blessing since his cursed return),[9]
     Those heaps of people which one sheaf did bind,
     Blown off and scattered by a puff of wind.[1]
     What strength can he to your designs oppose,
280 Naked of friends, and round beset with foes?
     If Pharaoh's[2] doubtful succor he should use,
     A foreign aid would more incense the Jews:
     Proud Egypt would dissembled friendship bring;
     Foment° the war, but not support the king: *heat, rouse*
285 Nor would the royal party e'er unite
     With Pharaoh's arms to assist the Jebusite;
     Or if they should, their interest soon would break,
     And with such odious aid make David weak.

3. Achitophel stresses the workings of Fortune, or what emblem books called "Occasion," rather than divine Providence. He uses traditional images of Fortune standing on a ball and having to be seized by a forelock as she approaches, the back of her head being bald.
4. David escaped Saul by fleeing to Gath (1 Samuel 27.1–4); here, a reference to Brussels, where Charles spent much of his exile.
5. God sent Samuel to anoint David as a token that he would finally come to the throne (1 Samuel 16.1–13).
6. The vapors or humors associated with night.
7. I.e., at Dover, where Charles II landed at the time of the Restoration.
8. I.e., Lucifer; cf. Luke 10.18: "I beheld Satan as lightning fall from heaven."
9. I.e., the crisis of 1678 was the only favorable opportunity for the conspirators since the Restoration.
1. I.e., the unity and loyalty of the people who had supported the king are easily dispersed.
2. I.e., King Louis XIV of France.

All sorts of men by my successful arts,
290   Abhorring kings, estrange their altered hearts
From David's rule: and 'tis the general cry,
'Religion, commonwealth, and liberty.'
If you, as champion of the public good,
Add to their arms a chief of royal blood,
295   What may not Israel hope, and what applause
Might such a general gain by such a cause?
Not barren praise alone, that gaudy flower
Fair only to the sight, but solid power;
And nobler is a limited command,
300   Given by the love of all your native land,
Than a successive title, long and dark,
Drawn from the moldy rolls of Noah's ark."[3]
    What cannot praise effect in mighty minds,
When flattery soothes, and when ambition blinds!
305   Desire of power, on earth a vicious weed,
Yet, sprung from high, is of celestial seed:
In God 'tis glory; and when men aspire,
'Tis but a spark too much of heavenly fire.[4]
The ambitious youth, too covetous of fame,
310   Too full of angel's metal[5] in his frame,
Unwarily was led from virtue's ways,
Made drunk with honor, and debauched with praise.
Half loath, and half consenting to the ill
(For loyal blood within him struggled still),
315   He thus replied: "And what pretense have I
To take up arms for public liberty?
My father governs with unquestioned right;
The faith's defender, and mankind's delight,
Good, gracious, just, observant of the laws:
320   And heaven by wonders has espoused his cause.
Whom has he wronged in all his peaceful reign?
Who sues for justice to his throne in vain?
What millions has he pardoned of his foes,
Whom just revenge did to his wrath expose?
325   Mild, easy, humble, studious of our good,
Inclined to mercy, and averse from blood;
If mildness ill with stubborn Israel suit,
His crime is God's belovèd attribute.
What could he gain, his people to betray,
330   Or change his right for arbitrary sway?
Let haughty Pharaoh curse with such a reign
His fruitful Nile, and yoke a servile train.[6]
If David's rule Jerusalem displease,
The Dog Star[7] heats their brains to this disease.

---

3. Achitophel (Shaftesbury) espouses constitutional monarchy ("a limited command") and parliamentary as opposed to hereditary determination of the succession.
4. Perhaps including a reference to Prometheus, who angered the gods by stealing fire for the benefit of mortals.
5. A double pun: the gold of which the coin ("angel") is made, and the spirit ("mettle") of the

rebellious angels led by Satan.
6. I.e., if King Louis XIV of France were to help Charles II remain in power, he would only be cursing his own country. In Exodus, the Pharaoh's refusal to release the enslaved Israelites caused God to visit a series of plagues on the Egyptian people.
7. Sirius, the morning and evening star of late summer, associated with crazing heat.

335   Why then should I, encouraging the bad,
        Turn rebel and run popularly mad?
        Were he a tyrant, who, by lawless might
        Oppressed the Jews, and raised the Jebusite,
        Well might I mourn; but nature's holy bands
340   Would curb my spirits and restrain my hands:
        The people might assert their liberty,
        But what was right in them were crime in me.
        His favor leaves me nothing to require,
        Prevents my wishes, and outruns desire.
345   What more can I expect while David lives?
        All but his kingly diadem° he gives: *crown*
        And that"—But there he paused; then sighing, said—
        "Is justly destined for a worthier head.
        For when my father from his toils shall rest
350   And late augment the number of the blest,[8]
        His lawful issue shall the throne ascend,
        Or the collateral° line, where that shall end.   *brother's*
        His brother,[9] though oppressed with vulgar spite,
        Yet dauntless, and secure of native right,
355   Of every royal virtue stands possessed;
        Still dear to all the bravest and the best.
        His courage foes,[1] his friends his truth proclaim;
        His loyalty the king, the world his fame.
        His mercy even the offending crowd will find,
360   For sure he comes of a forgiving kind.°   *family*
        Why should I then repine° at heaven's decree,   *complain*
        Which gives me no pretense to royalty?
        Yet O that fate, propitiously° inclined,   *favorably*
        Had raised my birth, or had debased my mind;
365   To my large soul not all her treasure lent,
        And then betrayed it to a mean° descent!   *low*
        I find, I find my mounting spirits bold,
        And David's part disdains my mother's mold.
        Why am I scanted by a niggard[2] birth?
370   My soul disclaims the kindred of her earth;[3]
        And, made for empire, whispers me within,
        'Desire of greatness is a godlike sin.' "
          Him staggering so when hell's dire agent[4] found,
        While fainting Virtue scarce maintained her ground,
375   He pours fresh forces in, and thus replies:
          "The eternal God, supremely good and wise,
        Imparts not these prodigious gifts in vain:
        What wonders are reserved to bless your reign!
        Against your will, your arguments have shown,
380   Such virtue's only given to guide a throne.

---

8. I.e., increase the number of souls in heaven.
9. Although Monmouth and the duke of York were able to get along for many years, by 1679 they were opposed to each other, and so it is unlikely that Monmouth would have felt the emotions for his uncle that Dryden here has him express.
1. I.e., his foes proclaim his courage.
2. Ungenerous; the birth of a king's son should

confer succession to the throne.
3. I.e., her body.
4. I.e., as Absalom (Monmouth) wavers, tempted by the sin of pride to attempt the throne despite his own arguments against it, Achitophel (Shaftesbury), acting as "hell's agent," again tries to persuade him to rebel.

Not that your father's mildness I contemn,
But manly force becomes the diadem.
'Tis true he grants the people all they crave;
And more, perhaps, than subjects ought to have:
385   For lavish grants suppose a monarch tame,
And more his goodness than his wit° proclaim.   *intelligence*
But when should people strive their bonds to break,
If not when kings are negligent or weak?
Let him give on till he can give no more,
390   The thrifty Sanhedrin[5] shall keep him poor;
And every shekel which he can receive,
Shall cost a limb of his prerogative.[6]
To ply him with new plots shall be my care;
Or plunge him deep in some expensive war;
395   Which when his treasure can no more supply,
He must, with the remains of kingship, buy.
His faithful friends our jealousies and fears
Call Jebusites, and Pharaoh's pensioners;
Whom when our fury from his aid has torn,
400   He shall be naked left to public scorn.
The next successor, whom I fear and hate,
My arts have made obnoxious to the state;
Turned all his virtues to his overthrow,
And gained our elders[7] to pronounce a foe.
405   His right, for sums of necessary gold,
Shall first be pawned, and afterward be sold;
Till time shall ever-wanting David draw,
To pass your doubtful title into law:
If not, the people have a right supreme
410   To make their kings; for kings are made for them.
All empire is no more than power in trust,
Which, when resumed, can be no longer just.
Succession, for the general good designed,
In its own wrong a nation cannot bind;
415   If altering that the people can relieve,
Better one suffer than a nation grieve.
The Jews well know their power: ere Saul they chose,
God was their king, and God they durst depose.[8]
Urge now your piety,° your filial name,   *dutifulness*
420   A father's right, and fear of future fame;
The public good, that universal call,
To which even heaven submitted, answers all.
Nor let his love enchant your generous mind;
'Tis Nature's trick to propagate her kind.

5. The high council of the Jews; here, the Parliament, which provided the crown with its monies. The Whigs hoped to limit the powers of the crown by refusing to vote money to Charles, but he lived on French subsidies and refused to summon Parliament for the duration of the crisis.
6. A term used with particular reference to a sovereign's rights (in theory, subject to no restrictions).
7. In the Bible, the Jewish magistrates; in the poem, the Parliamentarians who voted to exclude James from the succession.
8. The Israelites' demand that a secular king (Saul, as it happened) replace the theocratic Judges was condemned as impious: "And the Lord said . . . , they have rejected me, that I should not reign over them" (1 Samuel 8.7). As Saul replaced the Judges, so, in the poem, Oliver Cromwell took over authority from the theocrats of the Commonwealth.

425   Our fond begetters, who would never die,
        Love but themselves in their posterity.
        Or let his kindness by the effects be tried,
        Or let him lay his vain pretense aside.
        God said he loved your father; could he bring
430   A better proof than to anoint him king?
        It surely showed he loved the shepherd⁹ well,
        Who gave so fair a flock as Israel.
        Would David have you thought his darling son?
        What means he then, to alienate¹ the crown?
435   The name of godly he may blush to bear:
        'Tis after God's own heart to cheat his heir.²
        He to his brother gives supreme command;
        To you a legacy of barren land,³
        Perhaps the old harp, on which he thrums his lays,°   *songs*
440   Or some dull Hebrew ballad in your praise.
        Then the next heir, a prince severe and wise,
        Already looks on you with jealous eyes;
        Sees through the thin disguises of your arts,
        And marks your progress in the people's hearts.
445   Though now his mighty soul its grief contains,
        He meditates revenge who least complains;
        And, like a lion, slumbering in the way,
        Or sleep dissembling, while he waits his prey,
        His fearless foes within his distance draws,
450   Constrains his roaring, and contracts his paws;
        Till at the last, his time for fury found,
        He shoots with sudden vengeance from the ground;
        The prostrate vulgar° passes o'er and spares,   *populace*
        But with a lordly rage his hunters tears.
455   Your case no tame expedients will afford:
        Resolve on death, or conquest by the sword,
        Which for no less a stake than life you draw;
        And self-defense is nature's eldest law.
        Leave the warm⁴ people no considering time;
460   For then rebellion may be thought a crime.
        Prevail° yourself of what occasion gives,   *avail*
        But try your title while your father lives;
        And that your arms may have a fair pretense,°   *pretext*
        Proclaim you take them in the king's defense;
465   Whose sacred life each minute would expose
        To plots, from seeming friends, and secret foes.
        And who can sound the depth of David's soul?
        Perhaps his fear his kindness may control.⁵
        He fears his brother, though he loves his son,
470   For plighted vows too late to be undone.
        If so, by force he wishes to be gained,

---

9. As a youth, David tended sheep for his father.
1. I.e., transfer title to another (a legal term).
2. A reference to the story of Jacob and Esau
(Genesis 27–28). Esau, the older twin, was entitled
to the birthright and blessing of his father, but God
chose Jacob to continue the covenant he had made
with Abraham. Jacob tricked Esau out of his birth-
right and blessing, apparently with God's approval;

see also line 981. Conflicting interpretations exist
for how these lines apply to Charles II.
3. James had been titled generalissimo (the
supreme commander of combined forces) in 1678;
Monmouth had been exiled the following year.
4. I.e., recently heated or roused in anger.
5. I.e., perhaps his fear of James keeps Charles II
from being kind to you.

Like women's lechery, to seem constrained.°   *forced*
Doubt not; but when he most affects the frown,
Commit a pleasing rape° upon the crown.   *seizure*
475 Secure his person to secure your cause:
They who possess the prince, possess the laws."
      He said, and this advice above the rest
With Absalom's mild nature suited best:
Unblamed of life (ambition set aside),[6]
480 Not stained with cruelty, nor puffed with pride,
How happy had he been, if destiny
Had higher placed his birth, or not so high!
His kingly virtues might have claimed a throne,
And blest all other countries but his own.
485 But charming greatness since so few refuse,
'Tis juster to lament him than accuse.
Strong were his hopes a rival to remove,
With blandishments to gain the public love;
To head the faction while their zeal was hot,
490 And popularly prosecute the Plot.
To further this, Achitophel unites
The malcontents of all the Israelites;[7]
Whose differing parties he could wisely join,
For several ends, to serve the same design:
495 The best (and of the princes some were such),
Who thought the power of monarchy too much;
Mistaken men, and patriots in their hearts;
Not wicked, but seduced by impious arts.
By these the springs of property were bent,
500 And wound so high, they cracked the government.
The next[8] for interest sought to embroil the state,
To sell their duty at a dearer rate;
And make their Jewish markets of the throne,
Pretending public good, to serve their own.
505 Others thought kings an useless heavy load,
Who cost too much, and did too little good.
These were for laying honest David by,
On principles of pure good husbandry.°   *economy*
With them joined all the haranguers of the throng,
510 That thought to get preferment by the tongue.
Who follow next, a double danger bring,
Not only hating David, but the king:
The Solymaean rout,[9] well-versed of old
In godly faction, and in treason bold;
515 Cowering and quaking at a conqueror's sword,
But lofty to a lawful prince restored;
Saw with disdain an ethnic[1] plot begun,
And scorned by Jebusites to be outdone.
Hot Levites[2] headed these; who, pulled before

6. I.e., not guilty except perhaps for ambition.
7. Lines 492–543 describe the various groups that
Shaftesbury sought to unite against Charles II.
8. I.e., those primarily concerned with economic
gain, namely London merchants.
9. The London populace. Solyma was a name for

Jerusalem.
1. In the biblical context, gentile; in the historical,
Catholic.
2. Men of the tribe of Levi conveyed the ark of the
Covenant when Israel moved camp (Numbers
4.15); the Presbyterian clergy administered the

520 From the ark, which in the Judges' days they bore,
    Resumed their cant, and with a zealous cry
    Pursued their old beloved theocracy:
    Where Sanhedrin and priest enslaved the nation,
    And justified their spoils by inspiration:
525 For who so fit for reign as Aaron's race,[3]
    If once dominion they could found in grace?
    These led the pack, though not of surest scent,
    Yet deepest-mouthed° against the government.   *baying loudest*
    A numerous host of dreaming saints[4] succeed,
530 Of the true old enthusiastic° breed: *fanatic*
    'Gainst form and order they their power employ,
    Nothing to build, and all things to destroy.
    But far more numerous was the herd of such,
    Who think too little, and who talk too much.
535 These out of mere instinct, they knew not why,
    Adored their fathers' God and property;
    And, by the same blind benefit of fate,
    The Devil and the Jebusite did hate:
    Born to be saved, even in their own despite,
540 Because they could not help believing right.[5]
    Such were the tools; but a whole Hydra[6] more
    Remains, of sprouting heads too long to score.°   *record*
    Some of their chiefs were princes of the land:
    In the first rank of these did Zimri[7] stand;
545 A man so various, that he seemed to be
    Not one, but all mankind's epitome:
    Stiff in opinions, always in the wrong;
    Was everything by starts, and nothing long;
    But, in the course of one revolving moon,
550 Was chemist, fiddler, statesman, and buffoon:
    Then all for women, painting, rhyming, drinking,
    Besides ten thousand freaks° that died in thinking.   *whims*
    Blest madman, who could every hour employ,
    With something new to wish, or to enjoy!
555 Railing and praising were his usual themes;
    And both (to show his judgment) in extremes:
    So over-violent, or over-civil,
    That every man, with him, was God or Devil.
    In squandering wealth with his peculiar art:
560 Nothing went unrewarded but desert.°   *worth*
    Beggared by fools, whom still° he found too late,   *always*
    He had his jest, and they had his estate.
    He laughed himself from court; then sought relief
    By forming parties, but could ne'er be chief;
565 For, spite of him, the weight of business fell

---

state religion under the Commonwealth ("in the Judges' days").
3. The priestly family; (derisively) the theocratically disposed dissenters.
4. A term used by some dissenters for those elected to salvation.
5. Dryden calls attention to the Calvinist doctrines of predestination and election, and (in line 536) to the commercial origins of many dissenters.
6. Mythical beast with nine heads, each of which was replaced by two heads when it was cut off.
7. An Israelite executed for whoredom (Numbers 25); a second Zimri was a traitor and regicide (1 Kings 26.8–20). Dryden gives the name to George Villiers, duke of Buckingham, a latecomer to Monmouth's cause (described in lines 492–543).

On Absalom and wise Achitophel:
Thus, wicked but in will, of means bereft,
He left not faction, but of that was left.[8]

* * *

With all these loads of injuries oppressed,
And long revolving in his careful breast
935 The event° of things, at last, his patience tired,   outcome
Thus from his royal throne, by Heaven inspired,
The godlike David spoke: with awful fear
His train their Maker in their master hear.
  "Thus long have I, by native mercy swayed,
940 My wrongs dissembled, my revenge delayed:
So willing to forgive the offending age,
So much the father did the king assuage.
But now so far my clemency they slight,
The offenders question my forgiving right.[9]
945 That one was made for many, they contend;
But 'tis to rule; for that's a monarch's end.
They call my tenderness of blood my fear;
Though manly tempers can the longest bear.
Yet, since they will divert my native course,
950 'Tis time to show I am not good by force.
Those heaped affronts that haughty subjects bring,
Are burdens for a camel, not a king:
Kings are the public pillars of the State,
Born to sustain and prop the nation's weight:
955 If my young Samson will pretend a call
To shake the column, let him share the fall:[1]
But, oh, that yet he would repent and live!
How easy 'tis for parents to forgive!
With how few tears a pardon might be won
960 From nature, pleading for a darling son!
Poor pitied youth, by my paternal care
Raised up to all the height his frame could bear:
Had God ordained his fate for empire born,
He would have given his soul another turn:

8. The passage here omitted has five parts. (1) Lines 569–681: A further roll of the rebels or dissenters, including briefly "The well-hung Balaam and cold Caleb," "canting Nadab" and "bull-faced Jonas," and, extensively, Shimei (Slingsby Bethel, a sheriff of London), "whose youth did early promise bring / Of zeal to God and hatred to his king," and Corah (Titus Oates), whose "zeal to heaven made him his prince despise." (2) Lines 682–752: Absalom's courting of the people and the development of the plot against David. (3) Lines 753–810: Dryden's analysis of the issues involved in conflicts between the people (divinely obligated to obedience) and their monarchs (divinely obligated to just stewardship), culminating thus: "Yet, grant our lords the people kings can make, / What prudent men a settled throne would shake? / For whatsoe'er their sufferings were before, / That change they covet makes them suffer more. . . . If ancient fabrics nod, and threat to fall, / To patch the flaws, and buttress up the wall, / Thus far 'tis duty; but here fix the mark; / For all beyond it is to touch the ark" (lines 795–804; to touch the ark of the Covenant, which contained the Ten Commandments, is to commit sacrilege). (4) Lines 811–913: A short roll of David's supporters, including at length Barzillai (the duke of Ormond)—"The court he practiced, not the courtier's art: / Large was his wealth, but larger was his heart"—and, briefly, Zadoc, Adriel, Jotham, Hushai, and Amiel. (5) Lines 914–932: A brief reprise of number 2, Absalom's courting of the people, and an indication of the mounting danger of open revolt.

9. The right of the king to pardon, questioned by some members of the opposition.

1. Samson, pulling down the supporting columns of a Philistine temple, was destroyed in the ruin (Judges 16.29–30).

965 Gulled° with a patriot's name, whose modern sense   *deceived*
Is one that would by law supplant his prince:
The people's brave,[2] the politician's tool;
Never was patriot yet, but was a fool.
Whence comes it that religion and the laws
970 Should more be Absalom's than David's cause?
His old instructor, ere he lost his place,[3]
Was never thought Indued° with so much grace   *endowed*
Good heavens, how faction can a patriot paint!
My rebel ever proves my people's saint:
975 Would *they* impose an heir upon the throne?
Let Sanhedrins be taught to give their own.
A king's at least a part of government,
And mine as requisite as their consent;
Without my leave a future king to choose,
980 Infers a right the present to depose:
True, they petition me to approve their choice;
But Esau's hands suit ill with Jacob's voice.[4]
My pious subjects for my safety pray,
Which to secure, they take my power away.
985 From plots and treasons Heaven preserve my years,
But save me most from my petitioners.[5]
Unsatiate as the barren womb or grave;
God cannot grant so much as they can crave.
What then is left but with a jealous eye
990 To guard the small remains of royalty?
The law shall still direct my peaceful sway,
And the same law teach rebels to obey:
Votes shall no more established power control—
Such votes as make a part exceed the whole:
995 No groundless clamors shall my friends remove,
Nor crowds have power to punish ere they prove:
For gods and godlike kings their care express,
Still to defend their servants in distress.
O that my power to saving were confined:
1000 Why am I forced, like Heaven, against my mind, ⎫
To make examples of another kind? ⎬
Must I at length the sword of justice draw? ⎭
O curst effects of necessary law!
How ill my fear they by my mercy scan![6]
1005 Beware the fury of a patient man.
Law they require, let Law then show her face;
They could not be content to look on Grace,
Her hinder parts, but with a daring eye
To tempt the terror of her front and die.[7]
1010 By their own arts, 'tis righteously decreed,

2. I.e., hero (derisive); show-off.
3. Shaftesbury had been dismissed as chancellor in 1673 and as lord president of the Council in 1679.
4. Jacob deceived his old, blind father by making his hands hairy (like Esau's) with animal fur; but he could not mask his voice (Genesis 27).
5. Shaftesbury (and others) made use of petitions

in attempts to force the king to meet the demands of the Parliament in 1681.
6. I.e., how wrong they are to estimate my fear (determine that I am afraid) by the mercy I show.
7. Moses, on Mt. Sinai, was forbidden on pain of death to look upon God's face, but he was able to see God's back after God had passed by (Exodus 33.20–23).

Those dire artificers of death shall bleed.
Against themselves their witnesses will swear,
Till viper-like their mother Plot they tear:
And suck for nutriment that bloody gore,[8]
1015   Which was their principle of life before.
Their Belial with their Belzebub[9] will fight;
Thus on my foes, my foes shall do me right:
Nor doubt the event,° for factious crowds engage,   outcome
In their first onset, all their brutal rage.
1020   Then let 'em take an unresisted course,
Retire and traverse, and delude their force:
But when they stand all breathless, urge the fight,
And rise upon 'em with redoubled might:
For lawful power is still superior found,
1025   When long driven back, at length it stands the ground."
He said. The Almighty, nodding, gave consent;
And peals of thunder shook the firmament.°   heavens
Henceforth a series of new time began,
The mighty years in long procession ran:
1030   Once more the godlike David was restored,
And willing nations knew their lawful lord.

1681

Mac Flecknoe[1]

All human things are subject to decay,
And when fate summons, monarchs must obey.
This Flecknoe found, who, like Augustus, young
Was called to empire, and had governed long;[2]
5   In prose and verse, was owned, without dispute,
Through all the realms of Nonsense, absolute.
This agèd prince, now flourishing in peace,
And blest with issue of a large increase,[3]
Worn out with business, did at length debate
10   To settle the succession of the state;[4]

8. The simile is based on a common idea that vipers eat their own mothers.
9. I.e., their principal leaders; in Milton's *Paradise Lost,* Belial and Beelzebub, leaders of Satan's host, disagree about their course of action (Book 2).
1. Or Thomas Shadwell (1640–1692), a comic playwright who considered himself the dramatic heir of Ben Jonson and the champion of the type of comedy that Jonson had written, the "comedy of humors." Such plays allude to the medical theory that said a healthy human body was composed of four humors, kept in careful balance. Characters without such a balance have a predominant humor portrayed as a comic eccentricity. Dryden and Shadwell conducted a public argument for years on the merits of Jonson's plays. Dryden names Shadwell "Mac" (Gaelic for "son of") Flecknoe, making him heir not of Jonson but of the recently dead Irish priest Richard Flecknoe, a poet Dryden considered not only prolific but tiresome.
   "Mac Flecknoe" was probably circulated in man-

uscript for a few years before being printed in a pirated edition in 1682 by an obscure publisher. A subtitle, "Or a Satire Upon the True-Blue Protestant Poet, T. S.," evoked contemporary political controversies by referring to Shadwell's membership in the Whig party, the political haven of dissenting Protestants. This subtitle, presumably added when the poem was published to stimulate sales, was removed in the 1684 edition and all others that Dryden oversaw.
2. Augustus (Octavian) became the first Roman emperor at thirty-six and reigned from 27 B.C.E. to 14 C.E.
3. Figuratively, children; also, perhaps, a more specific reference to Flecknoe's practice of collecting pieces from his earlier publications and publishing them again with a new title. "Increase" was stressed on the second syllable.
4. Comic allusion to the serious question of who would succeed King Charles II. *Business:* with a play on sexual intercourse.

And, pondering which of all his sons was fit
To reign, and wage immortal war with wit,[5]
Cried: " 'Tis resolved; for Nature pleads that he
Should only rule, who most resembles me.
15 Sh——[6] alone my perfect image bears,
Mature in dullness from his tender years:
Sh—— alone, of all my sons, is he
Who stands confirmed in full stupidity.
The rest to some faint meaning make pretense,
20 But Sh—— never deviates into sense.
Some beams of wit on other souls may fall,
Strike through, and make a lucid interval;[7]
But Sh——'s genuine night admits no ray,
His rising fogs prevail upon the day.
25 Besides, his goodly fabric[8] fills the eye,
And seems designed for thoughtless majesty:
Thoughtless as monarch oaks that shade the plain,
And, spread in solemn state, supinely reign.
Heywood and Shirley[9] were but types° of thee,   precursors
30 Thou last great prophet of tautology.[1]
Even I, a dunce of more renown than they,
Was sent before but to prepare thy way;
And, coarsely clad in Norwich drugget,[2] came
To teach the nations in thy greater name.
35 My warbling lute, the lute I whilom° strung,   formerly
When to King John of Portugal I sung,[3]
Was but the prelude to that glorious day,
When thou on silver Thames didst cut thy way,[4]
With well-timed oars before the royal barge,
40 Swelled with the pride of thy celestial charge;
And big with hymn, commander of a host,
The like was ne'er in Epsom blankets tossed.[5]
Methinks I see the new Arion[6] sail,
The lute still trembling underneath thy nail.°   fingernail
45 At thy well-sharpened thumb from shore to shore
The treble squeaks for fear, the basses roar;
Echoes from Pissing Alley Sh—— call,
And Sh—— they resound from A—— Hall.[7]
About thy boat the little fishes throng,

5. "Wit," here as in other poems of the time, variously denotes the intellect, the poetic imagination, and a general sprightliness of mind.
6. A transparent pretense of anonymity for Shadwell. The use of dashes is a common device of the period's satire. Also, a scatological suggestion. The name is spelled out in some manuscripts.
7. A bright period; also, a medical term referring to periods of sanity between attacks of lunacy.
8. His body; Shadwell was corpulent.
9. Thomas Heywood (1574?–1641) and James Shirley (1596–1666), prolific playwrights of an earlier time, now out of fashion. Dryden suggests that they prefigure Shadwell as the Hebrew Scripture prophets and (in lines 31–34) John the Baptist prefigured Christ.
1. A repetition of the same point in different words.

2. A coarse cloth.
3. Flecknoe, a Catholic priest, visited the king of Portugal and claimed him as a patron.
4. Dryden alludes here to the royal pageants performed on the river Thames, which flows through London.
5. A simultaneous reference to two of Shadwell's plays: The Virtuoso (1676), in which a character who thinks himself a "wit" is tossed in a blanket in a farcical scene, and Epsom Wells (1673).
6. When the semilegendary Greek poet Arion was cast into the sea, a dolphin, charmed by his singing, bore him ashore. Shadwell was proud of his own musical accomplishments.
7. This scatologically named hall, written out as "Aston" in the 1682 edition, has not been located. Pissing Alley ran between the Strand and the Thames.

50 As at the morning toast[8] that floats along.
Sometimes, as prince of thy harmonious band,
Thou wield'st thy papers in thy threshing hand.[9]
St. André's feet[1] ne'er kept more equal time,
Not ev'n the feet of thy own *Psyche's* rhyme,

55 Though they in number° as in sense excel: *meter*
So just, so like tautology, they° fell,   *the papers*
That, pale with envy, Singleton forswore
The lute and sword, which he in triumph bore,
And vowed he ne'er would act Villerius[2] more."

60 Here stopped the good old sire, and wept for joy
In silent raptures of the hopeful boy.[3]
All arguments, but most his plays, persuade,
That for anointed dullness[4] he was made.
       Close to the walls which fair Augusta[5] bind

65 (The fair Augusta much to fears inclined),
An ancient fabric° raised to inform the sight   *building*
There stood of yore, and Barbican it hight:°   *was called*
A watchtower once; but now, so fate ordains,
Of all the pile an empty name remains.

70 From its old ruins brothel houses rise,
Scenes of lewd loves, and of polluted joys,
Where their vast courts the mother-strumpets keep,
And, undisturbed by watch, in silence sleep.
Near these a Nursery[6] erects its head,

75 Where queens are formed, and future heroes bred;
Where unfledged actors learn to laugh and cry,
Where infant punks° their tender voices try,   *prostitutes*
And little Maximins[7] the gods defy.
Great Fletcher never treads in buskins here,

80 Nor greater Jonson dares in socks appear;[8]
But gentle Simkin[9] just reception finds
Amidst this monument of vanished minds:
Pure clinches° the suburbian Muse[1] affords,   *puns*
And Panton° waging harmless war with words.   *a punster*

85 Here Flecknoe, as a place to fame well known,

8. A comic metaphor for sewage.
9. I.e., his hand beats or strikes as with a flail, with a pun on the violence of his "beating," or writing, and the accents or beats in measured verse. In the following lines, Dryden continues to make fun of the mechanical metrics of the songs in Shadwell's opera *Psyche* (1675). Shadwell had apologized for his use of rhyme in the preface to the printed text.
1. With a pun on dancing and metrical feet. *St. André:* a French dancing master, choreographer of Shadwell's *Psyche.*
2. A role in Sir William Davenant's *The Siege of Rhodes* (1656), the first English opera. *Singleton:* John Singleton (d. 1686), a musician of the Theatre Royal. Dryden seems to be suggesting (sarcastically) that Shadwell's art is so skilled that it evokes the admiration of an undistinguished performer.
3. I.e., Mac Flecknoe, or Shadwell (who was in his mid thirties). *Good old sire:* i.e., Flecknoe.
4. The expected phrase is *anointed majesty,* since English kings are anointed with oil at their coro-

nations; i.e., all arguments favor Mac Flecknoe's ascent to the throne of dullness, but most of all his plays.
5. I.e., London; an allusion to contemporary fears of a Catholic plot to burn down the city (see "*From Absalom and Achitophel: A Poem,*" note 5, p. 501).
6. The name of a training school for young actors built in the Barbican in 1671, against the wishes of many residents.
7. The bombastic Roman emperor in Dryden's *Tyrannic Love* (1669).
8. "Buskins," the high-soled boots worn in Athenian tragedy, are opposed to "socks," the low shoes worn in comedy (thus the reference to Ben Jonson). *Fletcher:* John Fletcher (1579–1625), a playwright.
9. A clown; a popular character in farces.
1. The nine Muses were Greek sister goddesses believed to be sources of inspiration for the arts; this Muse, unlike the classical ones, is associated with the licentious suburbs of London, where brothels and theaters were located.

Ambitiously designed his Sh——'s throne;
For ancient Dekker[2] prophesied long since,
That in this pile would reign a mighty prince,
Born for a scourge of wit, and flail of sense;[3]
90 To whom true dullness should some *Psyches* owe,
But worlds of *Misers* from his pen should flow;[4]
Humorists and *Hypocrites* it should produce,
Whole Raymond families, and tribes of Bruce.
    Now Empress Fame had published the renown
95 Of Sh——'s coronation through the town.
Roused by report of Fame, the nations meet,
From near Bunhill, and distant Watling Street.[5]
No Persian carpets spread the imperial way,
But scattered limbs of mangled poets lay;
100 From dusty shops neglected authors come,
Martyrs of pies, and relics of the bum.[6]
Much Heywood, Shirley, Ogilby[7] there lay,
But loads of Sh—— almost choked the way.
Bilked stationers[8] for yeomen stood prepared,
105 And H—— was captain of the guard.
The hoary° prince in majesty appeared,   *gray, aged*
High on a throne of his own labors reared.
At his right hand our young Ascanius[9] sate,
Rome's other hope, and pillar of the state.
110 His brows thick fogs, instead of glories, grace,
And lambent dullness played around his face.
As Hannibal did to the altars come,
Sworn by his sire a mortal foe to Rome,[1]
So Sh—— swore, nor should his vow be vain,
115 That he till death true dullness would maintain;
And, in his father's right, and realm's defense,
Ne'er to have peace with wit, nor truce with sense.
The king himself the sacred unction° made,   *ointment*
As king by office, and as priest by trade.
120 In his sinister hand, instead of ball,[2]
He placed a mighty mug of potent ale;

2. Thomas Dekker (ca. 1572–1632), a playwright satirized by Ben Jonson in *The Poetaster* (1602). He probably figures in the line of poets leading up to Shadwell because he was a city poet and a proponent of a dramatic realism that Dryden deplored.
3. I.e., born to be one who punishes wit and whips sense.
4. In these lines, Dryden names plays of (and characters in plays by) Shadwell.
5. Victims of the plague (1665–66) were buried in Bunhill. Because these locations are both within a half-mile of the scene of the supposed coronation ("the Nursery"), Mac Flecknoe's fame is narrowly circumscribed; furthermore, his subjects live in the unfashionable commercial center of the city, regarded as a place of bad taste and vulgarity.
6. I.e., unsold books, the paper of which was used in bakers' shops and in privies (toilets).
7. John Ogilby (1600–1676), a translator of Virgil and Homer and a dramatic entrepreneur derided

by Dryden (and later by Pope); Thomas Heywood and James Shirley (see note 9, p. 518).
8. Booksellers, impoverished because they had stocked the works of Shadwell and others, stood guard to protect what remained of their interests. Their "captain," Henry Herringman, however, referred to in line 105, had been Dryden's publisher as well as Shadwell's.
9. Aeneas's son; hence, like Shadwell, the destined heir. Virgil referred to him as *"spes altera Romae"* ("Rome's other hope," *Aeneid* 12.168); as Troy fell, his favor with the gods was marked by a flickering ("lambent") flame that played around his head (*Aeneid* 2.680–84).
1. Hannibal (247–183 B.C.E.), the Carthaginian general who invaded Italy, and whose father ("sire") had dedicated Hannibal to the conquering of Rome.
2. In British coronations, the monarch holds in his or her left ("sinister") hand a globe surmounted by a cross.

*Love's Kingdom*³ to his right he did convey,
At once his scepter, and his rule of sway;
Whose righteous lore the prince had practiced young,

125 And from whose loins recorded *Psyche* sprung.
His temples, last, with poppies⁴ were o'erspread,
That nodding seemed to consecrate his head.
Just at that point of time, if fame not lie,
On his left hand twelve reverend owls⁵ did fly.

130 So Romulus, 'tis sung, by Tiber's brook,
Presage of sway from twice six vultures took.⁶
The admiring throng loud acclamations make,
And omens of his future empire take.
The sire then shook the honors⁷ of his head,

135 And from his brows damps° of oblivion shed   vapors
Full on the filial dullness: long he stood,
Repelling from his breast the raging god;
At length burst out in this prophetic mood:
     "Heavens bless my son, from Ireland let him reign

140 To far Barbadoes on the western main;⁸
Of his dominion may no end be known,
And greater than his father's be his throne;
Beyond *Love's Kingdom* let him stretch his pen!"
He paused, and all the people cried, "Amen."

145 Then thus continued he: "My son, advance
Still in new imprudence, new ignorance.
Success let others teach, learn thou from me
Pangs without birth, and fruitless industry.
Let *Virtuosos* in five years be writ;

150 Yet not one thought accuse thy toil of wit.⁹
Let gentle George¹ in triumph tread the stage,
Make Dorimant betray, and Loveit rage;
Let Cully, Cockwood, Fopling, charm the pit,
And in their folly show the writer's wit.

155 Yet still thy fools shall stand in thy defense,
And justify their author's want of sense.
Let 'em be all by thy own model made
Of dullness, and desire no foreign aid;
That they to future ages may be known,

160 Not copies drawn, but issue of thy own.
Nay, let thy men of wit too be the same,
All full of thee, and differing but in name.

3. A pastoral tragicomedy by Flecknoe, apparently visualized by Dryden as a rolled-up manuscript held like a scepter. Shadwell's *Psyche*, a pastoral opera, could be described as the child ("from whose loins") of *Love's Kingdom* (1644).
4. Connoting both intellectual heaviness and Shadwell's addiction to opiates; a parody of the laurel wreath with which a poet was traditionally crowned as a sign of poetic achievement.
5. Symbols of dullness.
6. When the site ("Tiber's brook") that Romulus had chosen for Rome was visited by twelve vultures, or twice as many as had visited the site picked by his brother Remus, the kingship ("sway")

of Romulus was presaged.
7. Locks; in Virgil's *Aeneid*, Jove, ruler of the gods, shakes his locks. Here and in the following lines, Dryden parodies two epic motifs: the father influencing his son and the Sybil receiving the "raging God" who speaks through her (see *Aeneid* 6.46–51).
8. I.e., a realm of empty ocean.
9. I.e., even if Shadwell spent five years writing a comedy, it would still lack wit.
1. Sir George Etherege (ca. 1635–1691), playwright who set the tone for stylish Restoration comedy; Dryden proceeds to name five of his characters.

But let no alien S—dl—y[2] interpose,
To lard with wit[3] thy hungry *Epsom* prose.
165 And when false flowers of rhetoric thou wouldst cull,
Trust nature, do not labor to be dull;
But write thy best, and top; and, in each line,
Sir Formal's[4] oratory will be thine:
Sir Formal, though unsought, attends thy quill,
170 And does thy northern dedications[5] fill
Nor let false friends seduce thy mind to fame,
By arrogating Jonson's hostile name.
Let father Flecknoe fire thy mind with praise,
And uncle Ogilby thy envy raise.
175 Thou art my blood, where Jonson has no part:
What share have we in nature, or in art?
Where did his wit on learning fix a brand,
And rail at arts he did not understand?[6]
Where made he love in Prince Nicander's vein,
180 Or swept the dust in *Psyche's* humble strain?[7]
Where sold he bargains,[8] 'whip-stitch, kiss my arse,'
Promised a play and dwindled to a farce?
When did his Muse from Fletcher scenes purloin,°   steal
As thou whole Eth'rege dost transfuse to thine?
185 But so transfused, as oil on water's flow,
His always floats above, thine sinks below.
This is thy province, this thy wondrous way,
New humors to invent for each new play:
This is that boasted bias[9] of thy mind,
190 By which one way, to dullness, 'tis inclined;
Which makes thy writings lean on one side still,
And, in all changes, that way bends thy will.
Nor let thy mountain-belly make pretense
Of likeness; thine's a tympany[1] of sense.
195 A tun° of man in thy large bulk is writ,   big cask
But sure thou'rt but a kilderkin° of wit.   little cask
Like mine, thy gentle numbers° feebly creep;   verses
Thy tragic Muse gives smiles, thy comic sleep.
With whate'er gall thou sett'st thyself to write,
200 Thy inoffensive satires never bite.
In thy felonious heart though venom lies,
It does but touch thy Irish pen, and dies.
Thy genius[2] calls thee not to purchase fame

---

2. Sir Charles Sedley (ca. 1639–1701), Restoration wit who had contributed a prologue and (Dryden suggests in line 184) a part of the text to Shadwell's *Epsom Wells*.
3. The phrase recalls a sentence in *Anatomy of Melancholy* (1621), by the English clergyman and scholar Robert Burton (1577–1640): "They lard their lean books with the fat of others' works."
4. Sir Formal Trifle was an inflated orator in *The Virtuoso*.
5. I.e., to Shadwell's patron the duke of Newcastle, whose seat was in northern England.
6. Perhaps an allusion to the satire on experimental science in *The Virtuoso*.

7. Nicander pays court to the title character, Psyche, in Shadwell's opera.
8. A "bargain" is a gross rejoinder to an innocent question. The rest of the line, a kind of bargain, echoes a farcical character in *The Virtuoso*.
9. In bowling, the spin a player puts on the ball to make it swerve. *Humors*: parodying Shadwell's dedication to *The Virtuoso*, in which he claims that "four of the humours are entirely new."
1. A swelling caused by air.
2. The tutelary spirit allotted to every person at birth to govern his or her fortunes and determine the individual's character. Dryden terms Shadwell Irish as an insult.

In keen iambics,[3] but mild anagram.[4]
205 Leave writing plays, and choose for thy command
Some peaceful province in acrostic land.
There thou may'st wings display and altars raise,
And torture one poor word ten thousand ways.
Or, if thou wouldst thy different talent suit,
210 Set thy own songs, and sing them to thy lute."
    He said: but his last words were scarcely heard }
For Bruce and Longville had a trap prepared, }
And down they sent the yet declaiming bard.[5] }
Sinking he left his drugget° robe behind,   coarse
215 Borne upwards by a subterranean wind.
The mantle fell to the young prophet's part,[6]
With double portion of his father's art.

ca. 1676   1682, 1684

To the Memory of Mr. Oldham[7]

Farewell, too little, and too lately known,
Whom I began to think and call my own:
For sure our souls were near allied, and thine
Cast in the same poetic mold with mine.[8]
5 One common note on either lyre did strike,
And knaves and fools we both abhorred alike.
To the same goal did both our studies° drive;   endeavors
The last set out the soonest did arrive.
Thus Nisus[9] fell upon the slippery place,
10 While his young friend performed° and won the race.   completed
O early ripe! to thy abundant store
What could advancing age have added more?
It might (what nature never gives the young)
Have taught the numbers° of thy native tongue.   metrics
15 But satire needs not those, and wit will shine
Through the harsh cadence of a rugged line:
A noble error, and but seldom made,
When poets are by too much force betrayed.

---

3. The meter of (Greek) satire; hence satire itself.
4. The transposition of letters in a word so as to make a new word; *mild*: tame, feeble. Dryden scorns this form of ingenuity, and the others that follow, as trivial. An "acrostic" (line 206) is a poem in which the first letter of each line, read downward, makes up the name of the person or thing that is the subject of the poem. "Wings" and "altars" (line 207) refer to poems in the shape of their subjects, such as George Herbert's "The Altar" (p. 367) and "Easter Wings" (p. 368).
5. These characters in *The Virtuoso* so trap Sir Formal Trifle.
6. When the prophet Elijah was carried to heaven in a chariot of fire borne on a whirlwind, his mantle fell on Elisha, his successor (2 Kings 2.8–14).

Flecknoe's "subterranean wind" is a fart, and an allusion to the moment in *Paradise Lost* where Satan lands on ground seemingly destroyed by "the force / Of subterranean wind" (1.231).
7. John Oldham (1653–1683), author of *Satires Upon the Jesuits* (1681), was a promising young poet, harsh (partly by calculation) in metrics and manner, but earnest and vigorous. He died of smallpox.
8. Dryden cast horoscopes and had the same birthday as Oldham.
9. A footracer in Virgil's *Aeneid*, he slipped in a pool of blood. His young friend Euryalus came from behind to reach the goal before him (5.315 ff.).

Thy generous fruits, though gathered ere their prime,
20   Still showed a quickness,° and maturing time   *sharpness*
But mellows what we write to the dull sweets of rhyme.
Once more, hail and farewell; farewell, thou young,
But ah too short, Marcellus[1] of our tongue;
Thy brows with ivy, and with laurels bound;
25   But fate and gloomy night encompass thee around.[2]

1684

A Song for St. Cecilia's Day[3]

1

From harmony, from heavenly harmony
    This universal frame[4] began:
    When Nature[5] underneath a heap
      Of jarring atoms lay,
5   And could not heave her head,
The tuneful voice was heard from high:
    "Arise, ye more than dead."
Then cold, and hot, and moist, and dry,[6]
    In order to their stations leap,
10   And Music's power obey.
From harmony, from heavenly harmony
    This universal frame began:
    From harmony to harmony
Through all the compass° of the notes it ran,   *full range*
15 The diapason[7] closing full in man.

2

What passion cannot Music raise and quell!
    When Jubal[8] struck the corded shell,
    His listening brethren stood around,
    And, wondering, on their faces fell
20   To worship that celestial sound.
Less than a god they thought there could not dwell

1. Roman Emperor Augustus Caesar's nephew, who died at twenty after a meteoric military career.
2. The Roman elegiac phrase *Hail and farewell!* (line 22); the mention of Marcellus (line 23) and of the classical poet's wreath, a symbol of poetic achievement (line 24); and the echo of Virgil's lament for Marcellus (see *Aeneid* 6.866) work to Romanize Oldham.
3. St. Cecilia, a Roman martyr of the second or third century, was patron saint of music, customarily represented at the organ (cf. line 52). Celebrations of her festival day (November 22) in England were usually devoted to music, and from about 1683 to 1703 the Musical Society in London annually commemorated it with a religious service and a public concert. Dryden's ode was set to music (by the Italian composer Giovanni Battista Draghi) for this occasion in 1687. In 1739, the

British (German-born) composer George Frideric Handel composed a new musical setting for the poem.
4. The physical universe.
5. Created nature as distinguished from chaos.
6. The four elements: earth, fire, water, and air.
7. The entire range or scale of tones; representing the perfection of God's harmony in his final creation, humankind. The just gradation of notes in a scale is analogous to the equally just gradation in the ascending scale of created beings according to the idea of the Chain of Being (in which the Creation is ordered from inanimate nature up to humans, God's best and final work).
8. "Father of all such as handle the harp and organ" (Genesis 4.21). The "corded" or stringed tortoise "shell" is a harp or lyre.

Within the hollow of that shell
That spoke so sweetly and so well.
What passion cannot Music raise and quell!

3

25   The trumpet's loud clangor
       Excites us to arms,
With shrill notes of anger,
       And mortal alarms.
The double double double beat
30   Of the thundering drum
Cries: "Hark! the foes come;
Charge, charge, 'tis too late to retreat."

4

The soft complaining flute
In dying notes discovers
35   The woes of hopeless lovers,
Whose dirge is whispered by the warbling lute.

5

Sharp violins[9] proclaim
Their jealous pangs, and desperation,
Fury, frantic indignation,
40   Depth of pains, and height of passion,
For the fair, disdainful dame.

6

But O! what art can teach,
What human voice can reach,
The sacred organ's praise?
45   Notes inspiring holy love,
Notes that wing their heavenly ways
To mend the choirs above.[1]

7

Orpheus could lead the savage race;
And trees unrooted left their place,
50   Sequacious of[2] the lyre;
But bright Cecilia raised the wonder higher:
When to her organ vocal breath[3] was given,
An angel heard, and straight appeared,
Mistaking earth for heaven.

9. A reference to the bright tone of the violin, recently introduced into England. The tone of the old-fashioned viol is much duller.
1. I.e., to improve the music of the angels.
2. Following. According to Greek mythology, Orpheus, son of the Muse Calliope, played so wonderfully on the lyre that wild beasts ("the savage race") grew tame and followed him, as did even rocks and trees.
3. I.e., its ability to sustain notes as the human voice does. According to the legend, however, Cecilia's piety, not her music, made an angel appear.

Grand Chorus

55   As from the power of sacred lays
       The spheres began to move,
       And sung the great Creator's praise[4]
       To all the blest above;
       So, when the last and dreadful hour
60   This crumbling pageant[5] shall devour,
       The trumpet[6] shall be heard on high,
       The dead shall live,[7] the living die,
       And Music shall untune the sky.

1687

KATHERINE PHILIPS
1632–1664

Epitaph

On Her Son H. P. at St. Syth's Church Where Her Body Also Lies Interred

What on Earth deserves our trust?
Youth and beauty both are dust.
Long we gathering are with pain,
What one moment calls again.
5   Seven years childless marriage past,
A son, a son is born at last;
So exactly limbed[1] and fair,
Full of good spirits, mien, and air,[2]
As a long life promisèd,
10   Yet, in less than six weeks dead.
Too promising, too great a mind
In so small room to be confined:
Therefore, fit in Heaven to dwell,
He quickly broke the prison shell.
15   So the subtle alchimist,[3]
Can't with Hermes' seal[4] resist
The powerful spirit's subtler flight,

---

4. As it was harmony that ordered the universe, so it was angelic song ("sacred lays") that put the celestial bodies ("spheres") in motion. The harmonious chord that results from the music of the spheres (in Ptolemaic astronomy, angelic music produced by the turning of the spheres, concentric transparent shells containing the heavenly bodies) is a hymn of "praise" sung by created nature to its "Creator."
5. The universe, the stage on which the drama of human salvation has been acted out. *The last and dreadful hour*: Judgment Day.
6. The sounding of the last trumpet announces the Resurrection (in which the "dead shall live") and the Last Judgement (1 Corinthians 15.52).
7. I.e., the sounding of the last trumpet will end the harmony of the spheres.
1. I.e., having perfect limbs.
2. Apparent character or disposition. *Mien*: appearance or expression.
3. Alchemy was the science aiming to achieve the transmutation of baser metals into gold and also to find a panacea or universal remedy.
4. Hermetic seal, the airtight closure of a container, named after Hermes, the Greek messenger god.

But t'will bid him long good night.
So the Sun if it arise
20   Half so glorious as his eyes,
Like this infant, takes a shroud,
Buried in a morning cloud.

1655   1667

To Mr. Henry Lawes[5]

Nature, which is the vast creation's soul,
That steady curious agent[6] in the whole,
The art of Heaven, the order of this frame,
Is only number[7] in another name.
5   For as some king conqu'ring what was his own,
Hath choice of several titles to his crown;
So harmony on this score now, that then,
Yet still is all that takes and governs men.[8]
Beauty is but composure, and we find
10   Content° is but the concord of the mind,   *contentment*
Friendship the unison of well-tuned hearts,
Honor the chorus of the noblest parts,[9]
And all the world on which we can reflect
Music to th'ear, or to the intellect.
15   If then each man a little world must be,[1]
How many worlds are copied out in thee,
Who art so richly formed, so complete
T'epitomize all that is good and great;
Whose stars[2] this brave advantage did impart,
20   Thy nature's as harmonious as thy art?
Thou dost above the poets' praises live,
Who fetch from thee th'eternity they give.

5. A friend of Philips, and a well-known musician and composer, he set to music the words of some of the most prominent poets of his day, including Jonson, Davenant, Waller, Herrick, Carew, Lovelace, Cartwright, and Milton (see "To Mr. H. Lawes, On His Airs," p. 416).
6. The material cause whereby effects are produced. In the *Timaeus*, Plato gives an account of the generation of the soul of the world in terms of the Pythagorean generation of the consonant intervals in music; in the *Somnium Scipionis*, Cicero describes the musical creation of the universe in terms of proportional intervals and tones. Many early Christian writers also explained the creation of the world in Pythagorean terms.
7. Music; drawing on Pythagorean ideas, many classical and Neoplatonic writers believed that to understand God, the universe, or humankind, one had to understand numbers and their relationships. Music, based on numerical relationships, spatial measurements of intervals, and metrical measurements of time, afforded one access to the measurements of those things that were intangible or invisible.

8. I.e., just as a king, who has conquered lands that are by rights his, may be called by the title of any of those lands, so harmony, by natural right, may be credited with being both the force that initiates and preserves the order of the natural world ("that then" refers to this topic, mentioned in the first four lines) and that which "takes and governs" the world of human society (as Philips demonstrates in the next four lines, thus "on this score now").
9. In these lines, Philips plays on the musical meanings of words. *Composure*: collectedness, but also referring to a musical composition. *Concord*: agreement, but also referring to a combination of notes that is pleasing to the ear. *Unison*: a sound or note of the same pitch as another. *Chorus*: both a choir and the song sung by the choir.
1. Perhaps a reference to the Platonic idea that the soul of humankind and the soul of the universe are similarly harmonious, and therefore music may reveal to the human being ("a little world") the divine harmony of the universe, or larger world, in which his or her soul shares.
2. Destiny as determined by astrology.

And as true reason triumphs over sense,
Yet is subjected to intelligence:[3]
25 So poets on the lower world look down,
But Lawes on them; his height is all his own.
For, like Divinity it self, his lyre
Rewards the wit it did at first inspire.[4]
And thus by double right poets allow
30 His and their laurel should adorn his brow.[5]
Live then, great soul of nature, to assuage
The savage dulness of this sullen age.
Charm us to sense; for though experience fail
And reason too,[6] thy numbers° may prevail.   *songs*
35 Then, like those ancients, strike, and so command
All nature to obey thy gen'rous hand.[7]
None will resist but such who needs will be
More stupid° than a stone, a fish, a tree.   *senseless*
Be it thy care our age to new-create:
40 What built a world may sure repair a state.[8]

1667

On the Welsh Language[9]

If honor to an ancient name be due,
Or riches challenge it for one that's new,
The British language[1] claims in either sense
Both for its age, and for its opulence.°   *wealth*
5 But all great things must be from us removed,
To be with higher reverence beloved.
So landskips° which in prospects distant lie,   *landscapes*
With greater wonder draw the pleasèd eye.
Is not great Troy to one dark ruin hurled?
10 Once the fam'd scene of all the fighting world.[2]

3. According to Aristotle, reason governs the lesser faculties of the soul—the physical senses and the appetites they generate. Both reason and sense are subject to intelligence, which Aristotle believed to be the divine element in humans.
4. I.e., his songs "reward" (by setting to music) the poetry originally inspired by his art.
5. The laurel was a symbol of poetic achievement.
6. According to Aristotle, sense experience gives knowledge of the concrete, while reason acts on that knowledge to arrive at an understanding of universal or first principles.
7. Perhaps a reference to Orpheus, famed for singing and playing the lyre, and said to have charmed birds, animals, rocks, and trees with his music. Other "ancients" that Philips may have had in mind: Amphion, who with his music caused stones to build the walls of Thebes, and Arion, whose singing won him the love of dolphins. *Strike:* here, to play a stringed instrument.
8. Philips is thought to have had Royalist sympathies; therefore this line, along with the reference to "this sullen age" in line 32, may refer to her dissatisfaction with the British government during the Interregnum (1649–60).

9. The Welsh language appears here to mean that language spoken by the earliest settlers of Britain, namely the Britons, or Celts. That language was thought to have survived in Wales, which was a stronghold of resistance against the Romans in the first century and against the Anglo-Saxons in the fourth and fifth centuries. After the defeat of Wales by King Edward I, in the thirteenth century, Welsh cultural identity began to erode, and in 1636, when Wales was officially incorporated into England, Welshmen holding positions in Henry VIII's regime were required to speak English. In the seventeenth century, however, some interest developed among the Welsh in preserving their language. Philips moved with her husband to Cardigan, Wales, when she was seventeen years old, and lived there for twelve years.
1. The language spoken by the ancient Britons.
2. Troy was the site of the legendary Trojan War, in which the Greeks fought with the Trojans to possess Helen. Helen, married to Menelaus, a Greek king, was carried off by Paris, a son of the king of Troy. At the end of the ten-year war, the Greeks defeated the Trojans and destroyed the city.

Where's Athens now, to whom Rome learning owes,
And the safe laurels that adorned her brows?[3]
A strange reverse of fate she did endure,
Never once greater, than she's now obscure.
15 Even Rome her self can but some footsteps show
Of Scipio's times, or those of Cicero.[4]
And as the Roman and the Grecian state,
The British fell,[5] the spoil of time and fate.
But though the language hath the beauty lost,
20 Yet she has still some great remains to boast.
For 'twas in that,[6] the sacred bards of old,
In deathless numbers° did their thoughts unfold.   *poetry*
In groves, by rivers, and on fertile plains,
They civilized and taught the listening swains;°   *rustics*
25 Whilst with high raptures, and as great success,
Virtue they clothed in music's charming dress.
This Merlin spoke, who in his gloomy cave,
Even Destiny her self seemed to enslave.
For to his sight the future time was known,
30 Much better than to others is their own;
And with such state, predictions from him fell,
As if he did decree, and not foretell.
This spoke King Arthur,[7] who, if fame be true,
Could have compelled mankind to speak it too.
35 In this once Boadicca[8] valor taught,
And spoke more nobly than her soldiers fought:
Tell me what hero could be more than she,
Who fell at once for fame and liberty?
Nor could a greater sacrifice belong,
40 Or° to her children's, or her country's wrong.   *either*
This spoke Caractacus,[9] who was so brave,
That to the Roman fortune check he gave:
And when their yoke he could decline no more,
He it so decently and nobly wore,
45 That Rome her self with blushes did believe,
A Britain° would the law of honor[1] give;   *a Briton, British person*

3. Athens was the Greek city that became the cultural, military, and economic center of an extensive empire (during the sixth and fifth centuries B.C.E.) In 86 B.C.E., the city was taken over by the Romans, who adopted and imitated Greek culture and learning. Laurel wreaths, sometimes worn on the head, were symbols of both poetic and military achievement.
4. Marcus Tullius Cicero (106–43 B.C.E.), a Roman statesman and orator who was executed on the order of Marc Antony after the assassination of Julius Caesar. There were two "Scipios": Scipio the Great, or Publius Cornelius Scipio (236–184 or 183 B.C.E.), a Roman general and statesman who distinguished himself in the Punic Wars; and Aemilianus Numantinus (185 or 184–129 B.C.E.), who was represented by Cicero as the ideal of wise statesmanship.
5. A reference to the Roman conquest of the British Isles. By 78 C.E., Wales had been brought under Roman control, but its language survived.
6. I.e., the Welsh language, also the referent of "this" in lines 27, 33, 35, and 41.

7. A legendary king of Britain, who, according to Geoffrey of Monmouth's *Historia Regum Britanniae*, defeated a Roman army but was mortally wounded in battle during a rebellion at home by his nephew, Mordred. Chrétien de Troyes added to the legend of King Arthur in the late twelfth century, as did Thomas Malory in his *Le Morte Darthur*, written in the fifteenth century. Merlin, a magician who could foresee the future, served both Arthur and his father, Uther Pendragon.
8. A British queen who led a revolt against the Romans but was finally defeated in 61 C.E.
9. A king of Silures, in the west of Britain, during the reign of Claudius, Caractacus (or Caraduc) was defeated by the Romans and taken as a prisoner to Rome in 51 C.E. The Roman emperor was so impressed by his noble spirit that he pardoned and released him.
1. Perhaps a reference to the agreement between the Roman emperor and Caractacus that the latter, if pardoned, would not engage in armed resistance against the Romans.

And hastily his chains away she threw,
Lest her own captive else should her subdue.

1667

To My Excellent Lucasia, on Our Friendship[2]

I did not live until this time
    Crowned my felicity,
When I could say without a crime,[3]
    I am not thine, but thee.

5 This carcass breathed, and walked, and slept,
    So that the world believed
There was a soul the motions kept;[4]
    But they were all deceived.

For as a watch by art[5] is wound
10   To motion, such was mine:
But never had Orinda[6] found
    A soul till she found thine;

Which now inspires, cures and supplies,
    And guides my darkened breast:
15 For thou art all that I can prize,
    My joy, my life, my rest.

No bridegroom's nor crown-conqueror's mirth
    To mine compared can be:
They have but pieces of the earth,
20   I've all the world in thee.

Then let our flames still light and shine,
    And no false fear control,
As innocent as our design,
    Immortal as our soul.

1667

2. In her poems on the theme of friendship, Philips frequently employs the terminology and imagery of love poems. The addressee of this poem is Mrs. Anne Owens, whom Philips calls "Lucasia," a name taken from William Cartwright's play *The Lady Errant* (1636).
3. This line recalls a famous and disputed phrase in line 19 of Ovid's *Heroides* 15, a verse letter in which Ovid imagines the Greek poet Sappho addressing a male beloved, Phaon, and mentioning the many women she previously loved "without crime" (*sine crimine*). Some Renaissance editors emended Ovid's line to "not without crime." Same-sex love was a legally and culturally debated topic in the seventeenth century.
4. I.e., that guided the body's movements.
5. I.e., by artificial means.
6. Philips's name for herself.

THOMAS TRAHERNE*
1637–1674

The Salutation

These little limbs,
These eyes and hands which here I find,
These rosy cheeks wherewith my life begins,
Where have ye been? behind
5   What curtain were ye from me hid so long?
Where was, in what abyss, my speaking tongue?

When silent I
So many thousand, thousand years
Beneath the dust did in a chaos lie,
10   How could I smiles or tears,
Or lips or hands or eyes or ears perceive?
Welcome ye treasures which I now receive.

I that so long
Was nothing from eternity,
15   Did little think such joys as ear or tongue
To celebrate or see:
Such sounds to hear, such hands to feel, such feet,
Beneath the skies on such a ground to meet.

New burnished joys,
20   Which yellow gold and pearls excel!
Such sacred treasures are the limbs in boys,
In which a soul doth dwell;
Their organizèd joints and azure veins
More wealth include than all the world contains.

25   From dust I rise,
And out of nothing now awake;
These brighter regions which salute mine eyes,
A gift from God I take.
The earth, the seas, the light, the day, the skies,
30   The sun and stars are mine if those I prize.

Long time before
I in my mother's womb was born,
A God, preparing, did this glorious store,
The world, for me adorn.
35   Into this Eden so divine and fair,
So wide and bright, I come His son and heir.

---

*Traherne's poems were discovered in 1903 by the scholar Bertram Dobell, who found an anonymous manuscript and attributed it to Traherne after comparing it with the one work that Traherne published in his lifetime, an anti-Catholic prose tract called *Roman Forgeries* (1673). Traherne's poems do not appear to have circulated widely (if at all) during his lifetime.

A stranger here
Strange things doth meet, strange glories see;
Strange treasures lodged in this fair world appear,
40   Strange all and new to me;
But that they mine should be, who nothing was,
That strangest is of all, yet brought to pass.

ca. 1665   1903

Wonder

How like an angel came I down!
How bright are all things here!
When first among his works I did appear
Oh, how their glory me did crown!
5   The world resembled his eternity,
In which my soul did walk;
And everything that I did see
Did with me talk.

The skies in their magnificence,
10   The lively, lovely air,
Oh, how divine, how soft, how sweet, how fair!
The stars did entertain my sense,
And all the works of God, so bright and pure,
So rich and great did seem,
15   As if they ever must endure
In my esteem.

A native health and innocence
Within my bones did grow;
And while my God did all his glories show,
20   I felt a vigor in my sense
That was all Spirit. I within did flow
With seas of life, like wine;
I nothing in the world did know
But° 'twas divine.   except that

25   Harsh ragged objects were concealed;
Oppressions, tears, and cries,
Sins, griefs, complaints, dissensions, weeping eyes
Were hid, and only things revealed
Which heavenly spirits and the angels prize.
30   The state of innocence
And bliss, not trades° and poverties,   goods
Did fill my sense.

The streets were paved with golden stones,
The boys and girls were mine,
35 Oh, how did all their lovely faces shine!

The sons of men were holy ones,
In joy and beauty they appeared to me,
And everything I found,
While like an angel I did see,
40   Adorned the ground.

Rich diamond and pearl and gold
In every place was seen;
Rare splendors, yellow, blue, red, white, and green,
Mine eyes did everywhere behold.
45 Great wonders clothed with glory did appear,
Amazement was my bliss,
That and my wealth met everywhere;
          No joy to° this!   compared to

Cursed and devised proprieties,[1]
50   With envy, avarice,
And fraud, those fiends that spoil even paradise,
Flew from the splendor of mine eyes;
And so did hedges, ditches, limits, bounds:
I dreamed not aught of those,
55 But wandered over all men's grounds,
          And found repose.

Proprieties themselves were mine,
And hedges ornaments;
Walls, boxes, coffers, and their rich contents
60 To make me rich combine.
Clothes, ribbons, jewels, laces, I esteemed
My joys by others worn:
For me they all to wear them seemed
          When I was born.

ca. 1665   1903

To the Same Purpose

To the same purpose: he, not long before
Brought home from nurse, going to the door
To do some little thing
He must not do within,
5   With wonder cries,
          As in the skies
He saw the moon, "O yonder is the moon,
Newly come after me to town,
That shined at Lugwardin[2] but yesternight,
10   Where I enjoyed the self-same sight."

---

1. Properties, including both private property and the self.

2. A town in south-central England on the Lugg River.

As if it had ev'n twenty thousand faces,
　It shines at once in many places;
　　To all the earth so wide
　　God doth the stars divide,
15　　　　With so much art
　　　The moon impart,
They serve us all; serve wholly every one
　As if they servèd him alone.
While every single person hath such store,
20　'Tis want of sense that makes us poor.

ca. 1665　　　　　　　　　　　　　　　　　　　　　　1910

Shadows in the Water

In unexperienced° infancy　　　　　　　　　　　*inexperienced*
Many a sweet mistake doth lie:
Mistake though false, intending° true;　　　　　*directing to*
A seeming somewhat more than view;[3]
5　　That doth instruct the mind
　　In things that lie behind,
And many secrets to us show
Which afterwards we come to know.

Thus did I by the water's brink
10　Another world beneath me think;
And while the lofty spacious skies
Reversèd there, abused mine eyes,
　　I fancied other feet
　　Came mine to touch or meet;
15　As by some puddle I did play
Another world within it lay.

Beneath the water people drowned,
Yet with another heaven crowned,
In spacious regions seemed to go
20　As freely moving to and fro:
　　In bright and open space
　　I saw their very face;
Eyes, hands, and feet they had like mine;
Another sun did with them shine.

25　'Twas strange that people there should walk,
And yet I could not hear them talk:
That through a little watery chink,
Which one dry ox or horse might drink,
　　We other worlds should see,
30　　Yet not admitted be;

---

3. I.e., an outward appearance ("seeming") that suggests more than what is visible to the eye.

And other confines there behold
Of light and darkness, heat and cold.

I called them oft, but called in vain;
No speeches we could entertain:
35   Yet did I there expect to find
Some other world, to please my mind.
    I plainly saw by these
    A new antipodes,[4]
Whom, though they were so plainly seen,
40   A film kept off that stood between.

By walking men's reversèd feet
I chanced another world to meet;
Though it did not to view exceed
A phantom, 'tis a world indeed,
45   Where skies beneath us shine,
    And earth by art divine
Another face presents below,
Where people's feet against ours go.

Within the regions of the air,
50   Compassed about with heavens fair,
Great tracts of land there may be found
Enriched with fields and fertile ground;
    Where many numerous hosts
    In those far distant coasts,
55   For other great and glorious ends
Inhabit, my yet unknown friends.

O ye that stand upon the brink,
Whom I so near me through the chink
With wonder see: what faces there,
60   Whose feet, whose bodies, do ye wear?
    I my companions see
    In you, another me.
They seemèd others, but are we;
Our second selves these shadows be.

65   Look how far off those lower skies
Extend themselves! scarce with mine eyes
I can them reach. O ye my friends,
What secret borders on those ends?
    Are lofty heavens hurled
70   'Bout your inferior world?
Are yet the representatives
Of other peoples' distant lives?

Of all the playmates which I knew
That here I do the image view
75   In other selves, what can it mean?

---

4. People living at a diametrically opposite point on the globe (literally, "with the feet opposite").

But that below the purling° stream   *swirling; murmuring*
    Some unknown joys there be
    Laid up in store for me;
To which I shall, when that thin skin
80   Is broken, be admitted in.

ca. 1665   1910

EDWARD TAYLOR
ca. 1642–1729

Meditation 8[1]

I kenning[2] through astronomy divine
    The world's bright battlement,° wherein I spy   *heavens*
A golden path my pencil cannot line,
    From that bright throne unto my threshold lie.
5   And while my puzzled thoughts about it pore
    I find the bread of life in it at my door.

When that this bird of paradise[3] put in
    This wicker cage (my corpse)[4] to tweedle° praise   *sing*
Had pecked the fruit forbad,[5] and so did fling
10   Away its food, and lost its golden days,
    It fell into celestial famine sore,
    And never could attain a morsel more.

Alas! alas! Poor bird, what wilt thou do?
    The creatures' field no food for souls e'er gave.
15 And if thou knock at angels' doors they show
    An empty barrel; they no soul bread have.
    Alas! Poor bird, the world's white loaf[6] is done,
    And cannot yield thee here the smallest crumb.

In this sad state, God's tender bowels[7] run
20 Out streams of grace; and he to end all strife
The purest wheat in heaven, his dear, dear son
    Grinds, and kneads up into this bread of life.
    Which bread of life from heaven down came and stands
    Dished on my table up by angels' hands.

1. Based on the words of Christ in John 6.51: "I am the living bread that came down from heaven; if any man eat of this bread, he shall live forever; and the bread that I will give is my flesh, which I will give for the life of the world."
2. Here, an adjective describing the speaker as "learning," through divine astronomy, how the universe is constructed; as a noun, "kenning" signifies the distance bounding the range of ordinary vision. A kenning-glass is a small telescope.
3. I.e., the soul.
4. In this context, the living body, with an emphasis on its mortality.
5. A reference to the sin of Adam and Eve, who ate the fruit that God had forbidden them (Genesis 2.17).
6. A reference to God's gift to the Israelites, the manna "like coriander seed, white" (Exodus 16.31).
7. I.e., God's powers of mercy and compassion.

25   Did God mould up this bread in heaven, and bake,
      Which from his table came, and to thine goeth?
   Doth he bespeak thee thus: This soul bread take;
      Come eat thy fill of this thy God's white loaf?
   It's food too fine for angels, yet come, take
30   And eat thy fill: it's heaven's sugar cake.

   What grace is this knead° in this loaf? This thing   *kneaded*
      Souls are but petty things it to admire.
   Ye angels, help. This fill would to the brim
      Heaven's whelmed-down[8] crystal meal bowl, yea and higher,
35   This bread of life dropped in thy mouth, doth cry:
      Eat, eat me, soul, and thou shalt never die.

1684   1937

Upon Wedlock, and Death of Children[9]

   A curious knot[1] God made in paradise,
      And drew it out enameled° neatly fresh.   *variously colored*
   It was the truelove knot, more sweet than spice
      And set with all the flowers of grace's dress.
5   Its wedding knot, that ne'er can be untied;
      No Alexander's sword can it divide.[2]

   The slips° here planted, gay and glorious grow,   *sprigs*
      Unless an hellish breath do singe their plumes.
   Here primrose, cowslips, roses, lilies blow°   *bloom*
10   With violets and pinks that void° perfumes: *give off, exude*
      Whose beauteous leaves o'er laid with honey-dew,
      And chanting birds chirp out sweet music true.

   When in this knot I planted was, my stock[3]
      Soon knotted, and a manly flower out brake.
15   And after it my branch again did knot;
      Brought out another flower its sweet breathed mate.
      One knot gave one t'other the t'other's place;
      Whence chuckling smiles fought in each other's face.

   But oh! a glorious hand from glory came
20   Guarded with angels, soon did crop this flower
      Which almost tore the root up of the same

8. Turned over upon something so as to cover it.
9. Taylor had fourteen children; this poem appears to allude to his first four children: two daughters who died in childhood and two sons who lived to maturity.
1. In this poem, Taylor plays on several meanings of the word "knot," including the marriage bond; an intricately laid out flower bed; the base of a woody branch enclosed in the stem from which it arises; figuratively, something intricate, involved, or difficult to trace out or explain; as a verb, of plants: to bud, to begin to develop fruit.
2. In Greek mythology, Gordius, king of Phrygia, devised a complicated knot to be undone only by the person who was to rule Asia; Alexander the Great cut the knot with a blow of his sword. Jesus said, concerning marriage, "what, therefore, God hath joined together, let not man put asunder" (Matthew 19.6).
3. Stem, as in cuttings used for grafting; but also genealogical tree.

At that unlooked for, dolesome, darksome hour,
In prayer to Christ perfumed it did ascend,
And angels bright did it to heaven tend.

25 But pausing on't, this sweet[4] perfumed my thought,
Christ would in glory have a flower, choice, prime,
And having choice, chose this my branch forth brought.
Lord take't. I thank thee, thou takest aught° of mine,   nothing
It is my pledge in glory; part of me
30 Is now in it, Lord, glorified with thee.

But praying o'er my branch, my branch did sprout
And bore another manly flower, and gay;
And after that another, sweet, brake out,
The which the former hand soon got° away.   took
35 But oh! the tortures, vomit, screechings, groans,
And six weeks fever would pierce hearts like stones.

Grief o'er doth flow, and nature fault would find
Were not thy will, my spell charm, joy, and gem;
That as I said, I say, take, Lord, they're thine.
40 I piecemeal pass to glory bright in them.
I joy, may I sweet flowers for glory breed,
Whether thou getst them green, or let them seed.

ca. 1682   1937

Upon a Spider Catching a Fly

Thou sorrow, venom elf:
    Is this thy ploy,
To spin a web out of thyself
    To catch a fly?
5   For why?

I saw a pettish° wasp   peevish, petulant
    Fall foul therein,
Whom yet thy whorl-pins[5] did not clasp
    Lest he should fling
10   His sting.

But as afraid, remote
    Didst stand hereat
And with thy little fingers stroke
    And gently tap
15   His back.

4. I.e., this sweet thought or idea.
5. Technically, the pin that attaches the spindle of a spinning wheel to the whorl, the flywheel on the spindle that regulates speed. Here, the spider's legs.

Thus gently him didst treat
  Lest he should pet,°   *take offense*
And in a froppish,° waspish heat   *fretful*
  Should greatly fret
20   Thy net.

Whereas the silly fly,
  Caught by its leg
Thou by the throat tookst hastily
  And hind° the head   *behind*
25   Bite dead.

This goes to pot, that not[;]°
  Nature doth call.
Strive not above what strength hath got
  Lest in the brawl
30   Thou fall.

This fray seems thus to us.
  Hell's spider gets
His entrails spun to whip-cords[7] thus,
  And wove to nets
35   And sets.

To tangle Adam's race
  In's° strategems   *in his*
To their destructions, spoiled, made base
  By venom things,
40   Damned sins.

But mighty, gracious Lord
  Communicate
Thy grace to break the cord, afford
  Us glory's gate
45   And state.

We'll nightingale sing like
  When perched on high
In glory's cage, thy glory, bright,
  And thankfully,
50   For joy.

ca. 1680–82   1939

6. An enigmatic statement, especially because the manuscript supplies no punctuation between "not" and "Nature." If punctuation is supplied editorially, one can paraphrase, "This (i.e., the fly) deteriorates, that (i.e., the spider) does not, according to the law ('call') of nature." Another possible meaning: "this goes to show ('pot' as an old form of 'put,' as in put forward for consideration) that what is 'not nature' (i.e., the hellish spider) compels or calls."
7. Strong cord or binding, like that made of hemp or catgut.

Housewifery

Make me, O Lord, thy spinning wheel complete.[8]
Thy holy word my distaff make for me.
Make mine affections thy swift flyers neat,
And make my soul thy holy spool to be.
My conversation make to be thy reel,
And reel the yarn thereon spun on thy wheel.

Make me thy loom then, knit therein this twine;
And make thy holy spirit, Lord, wind quills.[9]
Then weave the web thyself. The yarn is fine.
Thine ordinances make my fulling mills.[1]
Then dye the same in heavenly colors choice,
All pinked° with varnished° flowers of   ornamented / luminous
    paradise.

Then clothe therewith mine understanding, will,
Affections, judgment, conscience, memory,
My words, and actions, that their shine may fill
My ways with glory and thee glorify.
Then mine apparel shall display before ye
That I am clothed in holy robes for glory.

1682–83   1939

APHRA BEHN
1640?–1689

Song

Love Armed[1]

Love in fantastic triumph[2] sat,
Whilst bleeding hearts a round him flowed,
For whom fresh pains he did create,
And strange tyrannic power he showed;

8. In the first stanza, parts of the spinning wheel specified are: the "distaff," which holds the material to be spun; "flyers," which twist the thread as it conducts it to and winds it upon the bobbin; "spool," on which the thread is wound as it is spun; "reel," which receives the finished thread.
9. "Quills" are the spools of a looming machine.
1. In the "fulling mills," the cloth is "fulled," or milled, by being pressed between rollers and cleansed with soap or fuller's earth.
1. This lyric, one of Behn's most popular, was first published at the beginning of her play *Abdelazar, or the Moor's Revenge.* The song arouses the heroic villain Abdelazar to action and seems initially to describe the emotional condition of the queen who illicitly loves him—and whom he secretly scorns.

The song ironically foreshadows the Moor's own fate of suffering from unrequited love.
2. A formal celebration of conquest in which the defeated party in a war was, according to Roman tradition, paraded through the streets as a trophy of victory; a popular Renaissance masque (a court entertainment that included dancing, song, drama, and spectacle) was the Triumph of Cupid, in which the Roman god of erotic love displays his spoils; the scene in this poem is reminiscent of the masque of Cupid depicted in Edmund Spenser's *The Faerie Queene,* in which Amoret appears carrying her own heart, steeped in blood, "in silver basin layd, / Quite through transfixèd with a deadly dart" (3.12.21.2–3). Cf. also Mary Wroth, *Pamphilia to Amphilanthus,* sonnet 1 (p. 347).

5 From thy bright eyes he took his fire,
      Which round about, in sport he hurled;
      But 'twas from mine he took desire,
      Enough to undo the amorous world.

      From me he took his sighs and tears,
10 From thee his pride and cruelty;
      From me his languishments and fears,
      And every killing dart from thee;
      Thus thou and I, the God have armed,
      And set him up a deity;
15 But my poor heart alone is harmed,
      Whilst thine the victor is, and free.

      1677

The Disappointment[3]

I

One day the amorous Lysander,[4]
By an impatient passion swayed,
Surprised fair Cloris,[5] that lovèd maid,
Who could defend her self no longer.
5 All things did with his love conspire;
      The gilded planet of the day,[6]
      In his gay chariot drawn by fire,
      Was now descending to the sea,
      And left no light to guide the world,
10 But what from Cloris' brighter eyes was hurled.

II

In a lone thicket made for love,
Silent as yielding maids' consent,
She with a charming languishment,
Permits his force, yet gently strove;°   *struggled*
15 Her hands his bosom softly meet,
      But not to put him back designed,
      Rather to draw 'em on inclined;
      Whilst he lay trembling at her feet,
      Resistance 'tis in vain to show;
20 She wants° the power to say—*Ah! What d'ye do?*[7]   *lacks*

3. A free translation of parts of a French poem about impotence by Jean Benech de Cantenac (ca. 1630–1714), Behn's poem, like others on this topic, harks back to Ovid's *Amores* 3.7. Her poem was originally attributed to John Wilmot, earl of Rochester, but her speaker adopts a distinctly different perspective on impotence than Rochester's speaker does in "The Imperfect Enjoyment" (p. 551).

4. A conventional name for a male lover in pastoral poetry.
5. A conventional name for a young woman in pastoral poetry.
6. I.e., the sun; according to myth, the god Apollo drove his chariot, the sun, across the sky daily.
7. The question of whether an alleged victim of rape had "shown resistance" by crying out was important in English trials for rape.

III

Her bright eyes sweet, and yet severe,
Where love and shame confusedly strive,
Fresh vigor to Lysander give;
And breathing faintly in his ear,
25   She cried—*Cease, cease—your vain desire,*
Or I'll call out—What would you do?
My dearer honor ev'n to you
I cannot, must not give—retire,
Or take this life, whose chiefest part
30   *I gave you with the conquest of my heart.*

IV

But he as much unused to fear,
As he was capable of love,
The blessèd minutes to improve,°   *employ to advantage*
Kisses her mouth, her neck, her hair;
35   Each touch her new desire alarms,
His burning trembling hand he prest
Upon her swelling snowy brest,
While she lay panting in his arms.
All her unguarded beauties lie
40   The spoils and trophies of the enemy.

V

And now without respect or fear,
He seeks the object of his vows,
(His love no modesty allows)
By swift degrees advancing—where
45   His daring hand that altar seized,
Where gods of love do sacrifice:
That awful[8] throne, that paradise
Where rage is calmed, and anger pleased;
That fountain where delight still flows,
50   And gives the universal world repose.

VI

Her balmy lips encount'ring his,
Their bodies, as their souls, are joined;
Where both in transports unconfined
Extend themselves upon the moss.
55   Cloris half dead and breathless lay;
Her soft eyes cast a humid light,
Such as divides the day and night;
Or falling stars, whose fires decay:
And now no signs of life she shows,
60   But what in short-breathed sighs returns and goes.

---

8. Awe-inspiring; the word has the sense both of "causing dread" and of "commanding profound respect or reverential fear."

VII

He saw how at her length she lay;
He saw her rising bosom bare;
Her loose thin robes, through which appear
A shape designed for love and play;
65 Abandoned by her pride and shame,
She does her softest joys dispense,
Off'ring her virgin-innocence
A victim to love's sacred flame;
While the o'er-ravished shepherd lies
70 Unable to perform the sacrifice.

VIII

Ready to taste a thousand joys,
The too transported hapless swain°   rustic fellow
Found the vast pleasure turned to pain;
Pleasure which too much love destroys:
75 The willing garments by he laid,
And heaven all opened to his view,
Mad to possess, himself he threw
On the defenseless lovely maid.
But Oh what envying gods conspire
80 To snatch his power, yet leave him the desire!

IX

Nature's support, (without whose aid
She can no human being give)[9]
It self now wants° the art° to live;   lacks / capacity
Faintness its slackened nerves invade:
85 In vain th' enragèd youth essayed°   tried
To call its fleeting vigor back,
No motion 'twill from motion take;
Excess of love his love betrayed;
In vain he toils, in vain commands;
90 The insensible[1] fell weeping in his hand.

X

In this so amorous cruel strife,
Where love and fate were too severe,
The poor Lysander in despair
Renounced his reason with his life:
95 Now all the brisk and active fire
That should the nobler part inflame,
Served to increase his rage and shame,
And left no spark for new desire:
Not all her naked charms could move
100 Or calm that rage that had debauched his love.

9. I.e., the aid of "Nature's support," without
which Nature ("she") cannot give life ("being") to

any human.
1. Lacking feeling; also, too small to be noticed.

XI

Cloris returning from the trance
Which love and soft desire had bred,
Her timorous hand she gently laid
(Or° guided by design or chance)   *whether*
105 Upon that fabulous Priapus,²
That potent god, as poets feign;
But never did young shepherdess,
Gath'ring of fern upon the plain,
More nimbly draw her fingers back,
110 Finding beneath the verdant leaves a snake;

XII

Than Cloris her fair hand withdrew,
Finding that god of her desires
Disarmed of all his awful fires,
And cold as flowers bathed in the morning dew.
115 Who can the Nymph's confusion guess?
The blood forsook the hinder place,
And strewed with blushes all her face,
Which both disdain and shame expressed:
And from Lysander's arms she fled,
120 Leaving him fainting on the gloomy bed.

XIII

Like lightning through the grove she hies,
Or Daphne from the Delphic God,³
No print upon the grassy road
She leaves, t' instruct pursuing eyes.
125 The wind that wantoned in her hair,
And with her ruffled garments played,
Discovered in the flying maid
All that the gods e'er made, if fair.
So Venus, when her love was slain,
130 With fear and haste flew o'er the fatal plain.⁴

XIV

The Nymph's resentments none but I
Can well imagine or condole:
But none can guess Lysander's soul,
But° those who swayed his destiny.   *except*
135 His silent griefs swell up to storms,
And not one god his fury spares;

2. A god of fertility often represented with grotesquely enlarged genitals; here, a euphemism for penis.
3. The nymph Daphne spurned the advances of Apollo ("the Delphic God"), whose oracle was at Delphi. Fleeing from him, she begged assistance from her father, a river god, and was turned into a laurel.
4. Adonis, the beloved of Venus, goddess of love, was killed by a wild boar during a hunt. Venus rushed to his side, but was unable to save him.

He cursed his birth, his fate, his stars;
But more the shepherdess's charms,
Whose soft bewitching influence
140   Had damn'd him to the hell of impotence.

1680

Song

On Her Loving Two Equally[5]

SET BY CAPTAIN PACK[6]

I

How strongly does my passion flow,
Divided equally 'twixt two?
Damon had ne'er subdu'd my heart,
Had not Alexis took his part;
5   Nor cou'd Alexis pow'rful prove,
Without my Damon's aid, to gain my love.

II

When my Alexis present is,
Then I for Damon sigh and mourn;
But when Alexis I do miss,
10   Damon gains nothing but my scorn.
But if it chance they both are by,
For both alike I languish, sigh, and die.

III

Cure then, thou mighty winged god,[7]
This restless fever in my blood;
15   One golden-pointed dart take back:
But which, O Cupid, wilt thou take?
If Damon's, all my hopes are crost;
Or that of my Alexis, I am lost.

1684

5. This poem first appeared as "How Strangely
Does My Passion Grow" in Behn's play *The False
Count* (1682). This version of the poem was first
printed in Behn's volume *Poems on Several Occa-
sions* (1684).

6. Simon Pack (1654–1701), an amateur musi-
cian who achieved some fame as a composer of
songs for plays.
7. Cupid, Roman god of erotic love.

On the Death of the Late Earl of Rochester[8]

Mourn, mourn, ye Muses,[9] all your loss deplore,
The young, the noble Strephon[1] is no more.
Yes, yes, he fled quick as departing light,
And ne'er shall rise from Death's eternal night,
5   So rich a prize the Stygian[2] gods ne'er bore,
Such wit, such beauty, never graced their shore.
He was but lent this duller world t' improve
In all the charms of poetry, and love;
Both were his gift, which freely he bestowed,
10   And like a god, dealt to the wond'ring crowd.
Scorning the little vanity of fame,
Spight° of himself attained a glorious name.   *in spite*
But oh! in vain was all his peevish[3] pride,
The sun as soon might his vast luster hide,
15   As piercing, pointed, and more lasting bright,
As suffering no vicissitudes[4] of night.
       Mourn, mourn, ye Muses, all your loss deplore,
       The young, the noble Strephon is no more.
Now uninspired upon your banks[5] we lie,
20   Unless when we would mourn his elegy;[6]
His name's a genius[7] that would wit dispense,
And give the theme a soul, the words a sense.
But all fine thought that ravisht° when it spoke,   *enraptured*
With the soft youth eternal leave has took;
25   Uncommon wit that did the soul o'ercome,
Is buried all in Strephon's worshipped tomb;
Satire has lost its art, its sting is gone,
The Fop and Cully[8] now may be undone;
That dear instructing rage is now allayed,°   *laid down*
30   And no sharp pen dares tell 'em how they've strayed;
Bold as a god was ev'ry lash he took,
But kind and gentle the chastizing stroke.
       Mourn, mourn, ye youths, whom fortune has betrayed,
       The last reproacher of your vice is dead.

---

8. This poem eulogizes John Wilmot, the second earl of Rochester (1647–1680; see pp. 549–53), a lyric poet, satirist, and leading member of the "wits" at the court of King Charles II. Rochester lived a fashionable life in London, reputedly had several mistresses, and, according to Samuel Johnson, "blazed out his youth and health in lavish voluptuousness."
9. The nine Greek sister goddesses believed to be the sources of inspiration for the arts.
1. A conventional name for a pastoral lover.
2. Infernal; Styx was one of the rivers of the underworld, over which Charon ferried the shades of the dead.
3. Obstinate; "peevish" can also be an epithet of

disparagement expressing the speaker's feeling toward, rather than a quality of, the object referred to.
4. Changes, mutations; particularly an alternation of opposite or contrasting things or conditions.
5. According to mythology, the Muses sang on the banks of the Hippocrene spring, on Mt. Helicon.
6. A funeral song or lament; here, a sorrowful utterance.
7. A spirit with the capacity to influence or inspire the character, conduct, or fortunes of a person.
8. The fool and dupe (one easily taken in); these types were frequent objects of satire in Restoration literature.

35   Mourn, all ye beauties, put your Cyprus[9] on,
     The truest swain[1] that e're adored you's gone;
     Think how he loved, and writ, and sighed, and spoke,
     Recall his mien,° his fashion, and his look.   bearing, manner
     By what dear arts the soul he did surprise,
40   Soft as his voice, and charming as his eyes.
     Bring garlands all of never-dying flowers,
     Bedewed with everlasting falling showers;
     Fix your fair eyes upon your victimed slave,
     Sent gay and young to his untimely grave.
45   See where the noble swain extended lies,
     Too sad a triumph of your victories;[2]
     Adorned with all the graces Heaven e'er lent, ⎫
     All that was great, soft, lovely, excellent   ⎬
     You've laid into his early monument.   ⎭
50   Mourn, mourn, ye beauties, your sad loss deplore,
       The young, the charming Strephon is no more.

     Mourn, all ye little gods of love,[3] whose darts
     Have lost their wonted° power of piercing hearts;   usual
     Lay by the gilded quiver and the bow,
55   The useless toys can do no mischief now,
     Those eyes that all your arrows' points inspired,
     Those lights[4] that gave ye fire are now retired,
     Cold as his tomb, pale as your mother's doves;[5]
     Bewail him then oh all ye little loves,
60   For you the humblest votary° have lost   devoted worshiper
     That ever your divinities could boast;
     Upon your hands your weeping heads decline,
     And let your wings encompass round his shrine;
     In stead of flowers your broken arrows strow,°   scatter about
65   And at his feet lay the neglected bow.
       Mourn, all ye little gods, your loss deplore,
       The soft, the charming Strephon is no more.

     Large was his fame, but short his glorious race,
     Like young Lucretius[6] lived and died apace.°   quickly
70   So early roses fade, so over all
     They cast their fragrant scents, then softly fall,
     While all the scattered perfumed leaves declare,
     How lovely 'twas when whole, how sweet, how fair.
     Had he been to the Roman Empire known,

9. A light, transparent material like lawn or crepe, originally from Cyprus; but also, perhaps, with reference to a branch of the cypress tree, regarded as a symbol of mourning.
1. Lover; but also, shepherd, in keeping with the pastoral references in the poem.
2. Triumph here refers to the defeated party in a war, who was, according to Roman tradition, paraded through the streets as a trophy of victory.
3. Figures of Eros, or Cupid, the god of erotic love, who was often portrayed as a winged child or boy armed with a quiver and bow. His gold-tipped arrows incited his victims to love.
4. I.e., eyes.
5. Venus, Cupid's mother and the goddess of love and beauty, was often depicted attended by doves.
6. A Roman poet of the early first century B.C.E., author of *De Rerum Natura* ("On the Nature of Things"), the themes of which included the mortality of the soul and the pointlessness of the fear of death; he was said to have committed suicide.

75 When great Augustus[7] filled the peaceful throne;
Had he the noble wond'rous poet seen,[8]
And known his genius, and surveyed his mien,
(When wits, and heroes graced divine abodes),
He had increased the number of their gods;
80 The royal judge[9] had temples rear'd to's° name,　　　　　*to his*
And made him as immortal as his fame;
In love, and verse his Ovid he'ad[1] out-done,
And all his laurels, and his Julia[2] won.
　Mourn, mourn, unhappy world, his loss deplore,
85 　The great, the charming Strephon is no more.

　　　　　　　　　　　　　　　　　　　　　　　1685

To the Fair Clarinda, Who Made Love to Me, Imagined More Than Woman[3]

　Fair lovely maid, or if that title be
　Too weak, too feminine for nobler thee,
　Permit a name that more approaches truth:
　And let me call thee, lovely charming youth.[4]
5　This last will justify my soft complaint,[5]
　While that may serve to lessen my constraint;
　And without blushes I the youth pursue,
　When so much beauteous woman is in view.
　Against thy charms we struggle but in vain ⎫
10　With thy deluding form thou giv'st us pain, ⎬
　While the bright nymph betrays us to the swain.[6] ⎭
　In pity to our sex sure thou wert sent,
　That we might love, and yet be innocent:
　For sure no crime with thee we can commit;
15　Or if we should—thy form excuses it.
　For who, that gathers fairest flowers believes
　A snake lies hid beneath the fragrant leaves.

　　Thou beauteous wonder of a different kind,
　　Soft Cloris with the dear Alexis joined;[7]

7. The first Roman emperor, Augustus ruled from 27 B.C.E. until his death in 14 C.E., a period marked by relative peace, cultural achievement, and civil improvements. Virgil, Horace, and Ovid were among the writers of this period.
8. I.e., if "he," Augustus, had seen Rochester, "the noble wond'rous poet"; this line begins an "if . . . then" construction: if Augustus had known Rochester, then he (Augustus) would have added the English poet to the ranks of the Roman gods, built temples in his honor, and made him immortal.
9. I.e., Augustus.
1. He had, i.e., he would have. Ovid is famous for, among other things, his love poems, including the *Amores*, purportedly based on his own experiences. Ovid was popular during the Restoration for his wit and sensuality.
2. The daughter of Augustus, thought to have

been Ovid's mistress and one cause of his being banished from Rome by Augustus; "his laurels" refers to Ovid's poetic achievement.
3. This final phrase can modify either "Clarinda" or "me," the speaker. Clarinda is a conventional pastoral name.
4. Young man; although "youth" can denote simply a young person, it is used here in opposition to the title of "maid," i.e., young woman, in line 1.
5. A lyric poem in which the speaker bewails the misery caused by his or her absent or unresponsive beloved.
6. The nymph and the swain are conventional characters of pastoral poetry. The nymph is a young, beautiful woman; the swain is a young, male shepherd or rustic.
7. I.e., she combines features of stock male and female pastoral figures.

20 When e'er the manly part of thee, would plead
    Thou tempts us with the image of the maid,
    While we the noblest passions do extend
    The love to Hermes, Aphrodite[8] the friend.

                                                            1688

A Thousand Martyrs[9]

A thousand martyrs I have made,
    All sacrificed to my desire;
A thousand beauties have betrayed,
    That languish in resistless fire.
5   The untamed heart to hand I brought,
And fixed the wild and wandering thought.

I never vowed nor sighed in vain
    But both, though false, were well received.
The fair are pleased to give us pain,
10   And what they wish is soon believed.
And though I talked of wounds and smart,
Love's pleasures only touched my heart.

Alone the glory and the spoil
    I always laughing bore away;
15 The triumphs, without pain or toil,
    Without the hell, the heav'n of joy.
And while I thus at random rove
Despise the fools that whine for love.

                                                            1688

JOHN WILMOT, EARL OF ROCHESTER
1647–1680

The Disabled Debauchee

As some brave admiral, in former war
    Deprived of force, but pressed with courage still,
Two rival fleets appearing from afar,
    Crawls to the top of an adjacent hill;

---

8. Hermaphroditus was the son of Hermes (Mercury), the messenger god, and Aphrodite (Venus). Bathing in the fountain of the nymph Salmacis, whose love he spurned, he merged with her and became male and female in one body. Behn was described by a contemporary, Daniel Kendricks, as belonging to a "third" sex: "ah, more than woman, more than man she is," he wrote in 1688.

9. This lyric is from Behn's *Lycidus: Or the Lover in Fashion*, a prose work with verse interspersed that translates *Le Second Voyage de l'Isle d'Amour* (1664), by the Abbé Paul Tallemant. This song is introduced by the narrator with the line "Take then the history of my heart, which I assure, boasts itself of the conquests it has made."

5 From whence, with thoughts full of concern, he views
      The wise and daring conduct of the fight,
  Whilst each bold action to his mind renews
      His present glory and his past delight;

  From his fierce eyes flashes of fire he throws,
10   As from black clouds when lightning breaks away;
  Transported, thinks himself amidst the foes,
      And absent, yet enjoys the bloody day;

  So, when my days of impotence approach,
      And I'm by pox[1] and wine's unlucky chance
15 Forced from the pleasing billows of debauch
      On the dull shore of lazy temperance,

  My pains at least some respite shall afford
      While I behold the battles you maintain
  When fleets of glasses sail about the board,°   *table*
20   From whose broadsides[2] volleys of wit shall rain.

  Nor let the sight of honorable scars,
      Which my too forward valor did procure,
  Frighten new-listed° soldiers from the wars: *newly enlisted*
      Past joys have more than paid what I endure.

25 Should any youth (worth being drunk) prove nice,° *reluctant, fastidious*
      And from his fair inviter meanly shrink,
  'Twill please the ghost of my departed vice
      If, at my counsel, he repent and drink.

  Or should some cold-complexioned sot° forbid,   *fool*
30   With his dull morals, our bold night-alarms,
  I'll fire his blood by telling what I did
      When I was strong and able to bear arms.

  I'll tell of whores attacked, their lords at home;
      Bawds' quarters beaten up,[3] and fortress won;
35 Windows demolished, watches° overcome;   *watchmen*
      And handsome ills by my contrivance done.

  Nor shall our love-fits, Chloris,[4] be forgot,
      When each the well-looked linkboy[5] strove t' enjoy,
  And the best kiss was the deciding lot
40   Whether the boy fucked you, or I the boy.

  With tales like these I will such thoughts inspire
      As to important mischief shall incline:

---

1. Venereal disease often left extensive scarring.
2. The table's sides; ship's artillery; sheets on which satirical verses were printed.
3. Madams' "houses" aroused, disturbed.
4. A conventional poetic name for a young woman.
5. A boy employed to carry a torch to light the way for people in the streets.

I'll make him long some ancient church to fire,
    And fear no lewdness he's called to by wine.

45 Thus, statesmanlike, I'll saucily impose,
    And safe from action, valiantly advise;
  Sheltered in impotence, urge you to blows,
    And being good for nothing else, be wise.

1680

The Imperfect Enjoyment[6]

Naked she lay, clasped in my longing arms,
I filled with love, and she all over charms;
Both equally inspired with eager fire,
Melting through kindness, flaming in desire.
5 With arms, legs, lips close clinging to embrace,
She clips° me to her breast, and sucks me to her face.   *hugs*
Her nimble tongue, love's lesser lightning, played
Within my mouth, and to my thoughts conveyed
Swift orders that I should prepare to throw
10 The all-dissolving thunderbolt below.
My fluttering soul, sprung with the pointed kiss,
Hangs hovering o'er her balmy brinks of bliss.
But whilst her busy hand would guide that part
Which should convey my soul up to her heart,
15 In liquid raptures I dissolve all o'er,
Melt into sperm, and spend at every pore.
A touch from any part of her had done 't:
Her hand, her foot, her very look's a cunt.
    Smiling, she chides in a kind murmuring noise,
20 And from her body wipes the clammy joys,
When, with a thousand kisses wandering o'er
My panting bosom, "Is there then no more?"
She cries. "All this to love and rapture's due;
Must we not pay a debt to pleasure too?"
25   But I, the most forlorn, lost man alive,
To show my wished obedience vainly strive:
I sigh, alas! and kiss, but cannot swive.°   *screw*
Eager desires confound my first intent,
Succeeding shame does more success prevent,
30 And rage at last confirms me impotent.
Ev'n her fair hand, which might bid heat return
To frozen age, and make cold hermits burn,
Applied to my dead cinder,[7] warms no more
Than fire to ashes could past flames restore.
35 Trembling, confused, despairing, limber,° dry,   *slack, limp*

---

6. Like Ovid (*Amores* 3.7) and several seventeenth-century poets, both French and English, Rochester here explores a scene of erotic failure from the man's point of view. For a similar scenario that includes a "nymph's" point of view, see Aphra Behn, "The Disappointment" (p. 541).
7. Partly burned coal that, unlike ashes, could be reignited and reused a number of times.

A wishing, weak, unmoving lump I lie.
This dart of love, whose piercing point, oft tried,
With virgin blood ten thousand maids has dyed,
Which nature still directed with such art
40   That it through every cunt reached every heart—
Stiffly resolved, 'twould carelessly invade
Woman or man, nor ought° its fury stayed:°   *anything / kept back*
Where'er it pierced, a cunt it found or made—
Now languid lies in this unhappy hour,
45   Shrunk up and sapless like a withered flower.
     Thou treacherous, base deserter of my flame,
False to my passion, fatal to my fame,
Through what mistaken magic dost thou prove
So true to lewdness, so untrue to love?
50   What oyster-cinder-beggar-common whore[8]
Didst thou e'er fail in all thy life before?
When vice, disease, and scandal lead the way,
With what officious haste doest thou obey!
Like a rude,° roaring hector° in the streets   *blustery / bully*
55   Who scuffles, cuffs, and justles all he meets,
But if his king or country claim his aid,
The rakehell villain shrinks and hides his head;
Ev'n so thy brutal valor is displayed,
Breaks every strew,[9] does each small whore invade,
60   But when great Love the onset does command,
Base recreant to thy prince, thou dar'st not stand.
Worst part of me, and henceforth hated most,
Through all the town a common fucking post,
On whom each whore relieves her tingling cunt
65   As hogs on gates do rub themselves and grunt,
Mayst thou to ravenous chancres° be a prey,   *venereal ulcers*
Or in consuming weepings waste away;
May strangury and stone[1] they days attend;
May'st thou never piss, who didst refuse to spend
70   When all my joys did on false thee depend.
     And may ten thousand abler pricks agree
To do the wronged Corinna right for thee.

1680

The Mock Song[2]

I swive° as well as others do,   *screw*
   I'm young, not yet deformed,
My tender heart, sincere, and true,
   Deserves not to be scorned.

---

8. I.e., what oyster-woman, cinder-woman, beggar-woman, or common whore?
9. Enters forcefully every brothel.
1. Usually fatal diseases in men that rendered uri-nation difficult. *Weepings*: the flow or discharge of humors from the body.
2. This poem is a burlesque of a song probably composed by Rochester's enemy Sir Carr Scroope.

5 Why Phyllis then, why will you swive,
    With forty lovers more?
  Can I (said she) with Nature strive,
    Alas I am, alas I am a whore.

  Were all my body larded[3] o'er,
10   With darts of love, so thick,
  That you might find in ev'ry pore,
    A well stuck standing prick;
  Whilst yet my eyes alone were free,
    My heart, would never doubt,
15 In am'rous rage, and ecstasy,
    To wish those eyes, to wish those eyes fucked out.

1680

A Song of a Young Lady to Her Ancient Lover

  Ancient person, for whom I
  All the flattering youth defy,
  Long be it ere thou grow old,
  Aching, shaking, crazy, cold;
5   But still continue as thou art,
    Ancient person of my heart.

  On thy withered lips and dry,
  Which like barren furrows lie,
  Brooding kisses I will pour
10 Shall thy youthful [heat][4] restore
  (Such kind showers in autumn fall,
  And a second spring recall);
    Nor from thee will ever part,
    Ancient person of my heart.

15 Thy nobler part, which but to name
  In our sex would be counted shame,
  By age's frozen grasp possessed,
  From [his] ice shall be released,
  And soothed by my reviving hand,
20 In former warmth and vigor stand.
  All a lover's wish can reach
  For thy joy my love shall teach,
  And for they pleasure shall improve
  All that art can add to love.
25   Yet still I love thee without art,
    Ancient person of my heart.

1691

3. Smeared with lard, greased.
4. Modern editorial conjecture; the posthumously printed text reads "heart."

ANNE KILLIGREW
1660–1685

Alexandreis[1]

I sing the man that never equal knew,
Whose mighty arms all Asia did subdue,[2]
Whose conquests through the spacious world do ring,
That city-raser,[3] king-destroying king,
5 Who o'er the warlike Macedons did reign,
And worthily the name of Great did gain.
This is the prince (if fame you will believe,
To ancient story any credit give.)
Who when the globe of Earth he had subdued,
10 With tears the easy victory pursued;
Because that no more worlds there were to win,
No further scene to act his glories in.

    Ah that some pitying Muse[4] would now inspire
My frozen style with a poetic fire,
15 And raptures worthy of his matchless fame,
Whose deeds I sing, whose never fading name
Long as the world shall fresh and deathless last,
No less to future ages, then° the past.   *than*
Great my presumption is, I must confess,
20 But if I thrive, my glory's ne'er the less;
Nor will it from his conquests derogate°   *detract*
A female pen his acts did celebrate.
If thou O Muse wilt thy assistance give,
Such as made Naso and great Maro[5] live,
25 With him whom Melas'[6] fertile banks did bear,
Live, though their bodies dust and ashes are;
Whose laurels[7] were not fresher, than their fame
Is now, and will for ever be the same.
If the like favor thou wilt grant to me,
30 O Queen of Verse,[8] I'll not ungrateful be,
My choicest hours to thee I'll dedicate,
'Tis thou shalt rule, 'tis thou shalt be my fate.

1. This unfinished poem was an early work of the young poet, who apparently (according to the note, reprinted here, at the end of the poem in the volume of collected works published after her death) felt herself unequal to the task of completing an epic poem about Alexander the Great. Alexander (356–323 B.C.E.), considered one of the greatest military leaders of all time, became king of Macedon in 336 B.C.E. and succeeded during his short life in conquering Egypt and most of Southeast Asia.
2. Cf. the beginning of Virgil's great epic, the *Aeneid*: "Of arms and the man I sing . . ."
3. One who razes, or obliterates, cities. In 335 B.C.E., Thebes, a Greek state, revolted. Alexander put down the revolt and destroyed the city. In the course of his conquests (of Phoenicia, Egypt, Tyre, Asia Minor, Persia, and the Punjab), Alexander destroyed many kings.
4. The Muses were nine Greek sister goddesses believed to be the sources of inspiration for the arts. The invocation of the Muse, requesting divine aid in the writing of the poem, is an epic convention.
5. Publius Vergilius Maro (70–19 B.C.E.) is the full name of the Roman poet Virgil; Publius Ovidius Naso (43 B.C.E.–17? C.E.) is the full name of the Roman poet Ovid, author of the *Metamorphoses*.
6. The ancient Greek poet Homer, author of the *Iliad* and the *Odyssey*, was said to have been born and lived by the Melas River.
7. The laurel was a symbol of poetic achievement.
8. I.e., the Muse of epic poetry, Calliope.

But if coy goddess thou shalt this deny,
And from my humble suit disdaining fly,
35 I'll stoop and beg no more, since I know this,
Writing of him, I cannot write amiss:
His lofty deeds will raise each feeble line,
And god-like acts will make my verse divine.
  'Twas at the time the golden sun doth rise,
40 And with his beams enlights the azure skies,
When lo a troop in silver arms drew near,
The glorious sun did nere° so bright appear;   *never*
Dire⁹ scarlet plumes adorned their haughty crests,°   *helmets*
And crescent shields did shade their shining breasts;
45 Down from their shoulders hung a panther's hide,
A bow and quiver rattled by their side;
Their hands a knotty well tried spear did bear,
Jocund° they seemed, and quite devoid of fear.   *merry*
These warlike virgins were, that do reside
50 Near Thermodon's smooth banks¹ and verdant° side,   *green*
The plains of Themiscyre² their birth do boast,
Thalestris³ now did head the beauteous host;
She emulating that illustrious dame,
Who to the aid of Troy and Priam came,⁴
55 And her who the Retulian prince did aid,⁵
Though dearly both for their assistance paid.
But fear she scorned, nor the like fate did dread,
Her host she often to the field had led,
As oft in triumph had returned again,
60 Glory she only sought for all her pain.
  This martial queen⁶ had heard how loudly fame,
Echoed our conqueror's redoubted° name,   *respected; dreaded*
Her soul his conduct and his courage fired,
To see the hero she so much admired;
65 And to Hyrcania for this cause she went,
Where Alexander (wholly then intent
On triumphs⁷ and such military sport)
At truce with war held both his camp and court.
And while before the town she did attend°   *await*
70 Her messengers return, she saw ascend
A cloud of dust, that covered all the sky,
And still at every pause there stroke° her eye.   *struck*
The interrupted beams of burnished gold,

9. Terrible, in the sense of inspiring terror or fear in an onlooker.
1. The Amazons were a tribe of warrior women believed to live on the plain of the Thermodon River, which sprang from the Amazonian Mountains and emptied into the Black Sea.
2. The capital city of the Amazons.
3. A queen of the Amazons who desired to have a daughter sired by Alexander. Legend has it that she consorted with him for thirteen days at Hyrcania, but died shortly after returning to her own country.
4. Penthesilea, an earlier queen of the Amazons, fought in the Trojan War against the Greeks. In most versions of her story, she arrives in Troy after the death of the Trojan hero Hector, with the Trojans all but defeated. She and a small band of Amazons fight valiantly against the Greeks, killing many Greek heroes, before she is killed by Achilles, who is so impressed by her beauty and valor that he laments her death and prevents the Greeks from desecrating her body. Priam was the king of Troy.
5. In the *Aeneid*, Virgil records the bravery of the warrior queen Camilla, who fought with Turnus, prince of the Rutulians, against Aeneas and the Trojans. She is killed in the battle.
6. I.e., Thalestris.
7. Formal celebrations of conquests.

As dust the splendor hid, or did unfold;
75   Loud neighings of the steeds, and trumpets' sound
Filled all the air, and echoed from the ground:
The gallant Greeks with a brisk march drew near,
And their great chief did at their head appear.
And now come up to th'Amazonian band,
80   They made a halt and a respectful stand:
And both the troops (with like amazement strook°)   *struck*
Did each on other with deep silence look.
Th'heroic queen (whose high pretence° to war   *aspiration*
Cancelled the bashful laws and nicer bar
85   Of modesty,[8] which did her sex restrain)
First boldly did advance before her train,
And thus she spake. All but a god in name,
And that a debt time owes unto thy fame.

> *This was the first essay° of this young lady in*   *attempt*
> *poetry, but finding the task she had undertaken*
> *hard, she laid it by till practice and more time*
> *should make her equal to so great a work.*

1686

ANNE FINCH, COUNTESS OF WINCHILSEA
1661–1720

The Introduction[1]

Did I, my lines intend for public view,
How many censures, would their faults pursue,
Some would, because such words they do affect,
Cry they're insipid, empty, uncorrect.
5   And many have attained, dull and untaught,
The name of wit only by finding fault.
True judges might condemn their want° of wit,   *lack*
And all might say, they're by a woman writ.
Alas! a woman that attempts the pen,
10   Such an intruder on the rights of men,
Such a presumptuous creature, is esteemed,
The fault can by no virtue be redeemed.
They tell us we mistake our sex and way;
Good breeding, fashion, dancing, dressing, play
15   Are the accomplishments we should desire;

---

8. I.e., the queen's martial aims cancel (or super-cede) the laws that usually "restrain" women by requiring them to be bashful and to adhere to the stricter limits ("nicer bar") of modesty.
1. Most critics think this poem was written early in Finch's poetic career, probably as a preface to an imagined book of poems. For reasons explained in the text, Finch did not publish this poem;

indeed, many of her works remained in manuscript at her death, or were first printed anonymously. She did, however, allow a collection of poems to be published in 1713. With the exception of "The Introduction," our ordering follows dates of first printing and, for poems first printed in her 1713 book, the order given there.

To write, or read, or think, or to inquire
Would cloud our beauty, and exhaust our time,
And interrupt the conquests of our prime;
Whilst the dull manage of a servile house

20   Is held by some our outmost° art, and use.   *utmost*
    Sure 'twas not ever thus, nor are we told
Fables, of women that excelled of old;
To whom, by the diffusive hand of Heaven
Some share of wit, and poetry was given.

25   On that glad day, on which the Ark returned,[2]
The holy pledge, for which the land had mourned,
The joyful tribes, attend it on the way,
The Levites do the sacred charge convey,
Whilst various instruments, before it play;

30   Here, holy virgins in the concert join
The louder notes, to soften, and refine,
And with alternate verse[3] complete the hymn divine.
Lo! the young Poet,[4] after God's own heart,
By Him inspired, and taught the Muses'[5] art,

35   Returned from conquest, a bright chorus meets,
That sing his slain ten thousand in the streets.
In such loud numbers[6] they his acts declare,
Proclaim the wonders of his early war,
That Saul upon the vast applause does frown,

40   And feels its mighty thunder shake the crown.
What, can the threatened judgment now prolong?
Half of the kingdom is already gone;
The fairest half, whose influence guides the rest,
Have David's empire o'er their hearts confessed.

45   A woman[7] here, leads fainting Israel on,
She fights, she wins, she triumphs with a song,
Devout, majestic, for the subject fit,
And far above her arms,[8] exalts her wit;
Then, to the peaceful, shady palm withdraws,

50   And rules the rescued nation, with her laws.
How are we fall'n, fall'n by mistaken rules?
And education's, more than nature's fools,
Debarred from all improvements of the mind,

2. The ark of the Covenant was captured by the Philistines, but God forced them to return it by smiting them with pestilence. However, God did not allow the ark to be returned to Jerusalem, because of the transgressions of the Israelites, and during its absence "all the house of Israel lamented after the Lord" (1 Samuel 7.2). The ark was returned to Jerusalem twenty years later, during the reign of David. The Levites (the tribe of priests) were assigned to convey it to the city, and it was accompanied by a procession with much singing and music (1 Chronicles 15.25–28).
3. A series of couplets. The choir of virgins (Finch's invention) chants every other line, in response, as in some of the Psalms.
4. I.e., David, second king of Israel, who wrote many of the Psalms. Before he became king, during the reign of Saul, David won a great battle over the Philistines. Upon returning to Jerusalem, the women of the city sang and said, "Saul hath slain his thousands, and David his ten thousands" (1 Samuel 18.7). The prophet Samuel had earlier predicted Saul's downfall and replacement by "a neighbor of thine, who is better than thou" (1 Samuel 15.28), and the women's praise initiated Saul's jealous rage against David.
5. The nine Greek sister goddesses believed to be sources of inspiration for the arts.
6. Measures of music and verse.
7. Deborah, the fourth judge of Israel (before Israel had kings, judges administered the laws given by God; see Judges 4.5). When the Israelites were enslaved by the Canaanites, Deborah urged her fellow judge, Barak, to wage war against the enslavers and accompanied him to the site of the battle. After their victory, Deborah and Barak wrote a song of praise (Judges 5).
8. I.e., her military feats.

And to be dull, expected and designed;°   *appointed, intended*
55 And if some one would soar above the rest,
With warmer fancy, and ambition pressed,
So strong th' opposing faction still appears,
The hopes to thrive can ne'er outweigh the fears,
Be cautioned then my Muse, and still⁹ retired;
60 Nor be despised, aiming to be admired;
Conscious of wants, still with contracted wing,
To some few friends, and to thy sorrows sing;
For groves of laurel¹ thou wert never meant;
Be dark enough thy shades, and be thou there content.

1689?   1903

The Spleen²

A Pindaric Poem³

What art thou, Spleen, which ev'ry thing dost ape?
  Thou Proteus⁴ to abused mankind,
  Who never yet thy real cause could find,
Or fix thee to remain in one continued shape.
5   Still varying thy perplexing form,
    Now a Dead Sea⁵ thou'lt represent,
    A calm of stupid° discontent,   *unfeeling, unreasoning*
Then, dashing on the rocks wilt rage into a storm.
    Trembling sometimes thou dost appear,
10   Dissolved into a panic fear;
    On sleep intruding dost thy shadows spread,
    Thy gloomy terrors round the silent bed,
And crowd with boding° dreams the melancholy head;   *forboding*
    Or, when the midnight hour is told,
15   And drooping lids thou still dost waking hold,
    Thy fond delusions cheat° the eyes,   *deceive*
    Before them antic° spectres dance,   *antique; bizarre*
    Unusual fires their pointed heads advance,
    And airy phantoms rise.
20   Such was the monstrous vision seen,
  When Brutus⁶ (now beneath his cares opprest,

9. Here and in line 61, may mean both "always" and "motionless."
1. The laurel was a symbol of poetic achievement.
2. A mysterious illness, believed to be connected with the organ of the same name, the effects of which seemed to be depression, hypochondria, ill-temper, melancholy, and a variety of other nervous disorders. Although considered largely a disease of women, it sometimes afflicted men. It often affected lovers and poets, and other eighteenth-century poets examined it, notably Alexander Pope, in *The Rape of the Lock* (see p. 604), and Matthew Green, in *The Spleen* (see p. 645). In this poem, Finch distinguishes between those who pretend to be affected by the disorder and those who really do suffer from it. Finch suffered from "spleen" and was praised by at least one contemporary physician for this accurate portrayal of the symptoms of the disease.
3. The Greek poet Pindar (ca. 522–ca. 438 B.C.E.) was an early practitioner of the ode form. An ode is a lyric poem, usually with a serious subject and a dignified style.
4. In Greek mythology, a shape-changing sea god.
5. The Dead Sea, located on the border between Israel and Jordan, is a salt lake, called "dead" because it contains no visible plant or animal life.
6. Before the Battle of Philippi (42 B.C.E.), the Roman politician Brutus saw the ghost of Caesar, whom he had assassinated. Brutus was defeated at Philippi by Marc Anthony and Octavius, Caesar's nephew and eventual successor.

And all Rome's fortunes rolling in his breast,
   Before Philippi's latest field,
Before his fate did to Octavius lead)
25   Was vanquished by the Spleen.

   Falsely, the mortal part we blame
   Of our depressed, and pond'rous° frame,   *heavy, unwieldy*
   Which, till the first degrading sin
   Let thee,° its dull attendant, in,   *spleen*
30   Still with the other did comply,[7]
Nor clogged the active soul, disposed to fly,
And range the mansions of its native sky.
   Nor, whilst in his own heaven he dwelt,
   Whilst Man his paradise possessed,
35 His fertile Garden in the fragrant East,
   And all united odors smelled,
   No armèd sweets,[8] until thy reign,
   Could shock the sense, or in the face
   A flushed, unhandsome color place.
40 Now the jonquil° o'ercomes the feeble brain;   *daffodil*
We faint beneath the aromatic pain,
Till some offensive scent thy pow'rs appease,
And pleasure we resign° for short and nauseous ease.   *give up*

   In ev'ry one thou dost possess,
45   New are thy motions,° and thy dress: *effects*
   Now in some grove a list'ning friend
   Thy false suggestions must attend,
Thy whispered griefs, thy fancied sorrows hear,
Breathed in a sigh, and witnessed° by a tear;   *confirmed*
50   Whilst in the light and vulgar crowd,[9]
   Thy slaves, more clamorous and loud,
By laughters unprovoked, thy influence too confess.
   In the imperious wife thou vapors[1] art,
   Which from o'erheated passions rise
55   In clouds to the attractive[2] brain,
   Until descending thence again,
   Through the o'er-cast and show'ring eyes,
   Upon her husband's softened heart,
   He the disputed point must yield,
60 Something resign of the contested field;
Till lordly Man, born to imperial sway,
Compounds° for peace, to make that right away,   *bargains*
And Woman, arm'd with Spleen, does servilely obey.

7. I.e., before Adam and Eve's original sin let spleen into the human body, it (our "frame," denoting the uncorrupted, immortal body) complied with the soul ("the other"). Finch here revises traditional stories that see the mortal body as a clog (hindrance) to the soul.
8. Finch seems to imply that sweet odors bring on the disorder and that foul odors can "appease" or lessen the symptoms.
9. A description of those (the frivolous and pretentious or uncultivated) who counterfeit the

symptoms of "spleen," such as the two examples that follow: the "imperious wife" of line 53 and the "fool" of line 64.
1. A disorder associated with "spleen" and supposed to be caused by exhalations within the organs of the body and characterized by depression, hypochondria, hysteria, and other nervous disorders.
2. In the medical sense of drawing something (the "passions," in this case) to itself.

The fool, to imitate the wits,
65   Complains of thy pretended fits,
And dullness, born with him, would lay
Upon[3] thy accidental sway;
Because, sometimes, thou dost presume
Into the ablest heads to come:
70   That, often, men of thoughts refined,
Impatient of unequal sense,
Such slow returns, where they so much dispense,
Retiring from the crowd, are to thy shades inclined.[4]
O'er me alas! thou dost too much prevail:
75   I feel thy force, whilst I against thee rail;
I feel my verse decay, and my cramped numbers° fail.   *verses, poetry*
Through thy black jaundice I all objects see,
As dark and terrible as thee,
My lines decried, and my employment thought
80   An useless folly, or presumptuous fault:
Whilst in the Muses'[5] paths I stray,
Whilst in their groves, and by their secret springs
My hand delights to trace° unusual things,   *write*
And deviates from the known and common way;
85   Nor will in fading silks compose
Faintly th' inimitable rose,
Fill up an ill-drawn bird, or paint on glass[6]
The sov'reign's blurred and undistinguished face,
The threat'ning angel, and the speaking ass.[7]

90   Patron thou art to ev'ry gross° abuse,   *flagrant*
The sullen husband's feigned excuse,
When the ill humor with his wife he spends,°   *exhausts*
And bears recruited° wit, and spirits° to his   *strengthened / cheerfulness*
    friends.
The son of Bacchus[8] pleads thy pow'r,
95   As to the glass he still° repairs,°   *continually / returns to*
Pretends but to remove thy cares,
Snatch from thy shades one gay and smiling hour,
And drown thy kingdom in a purple show'r.[9]
When the Coquette,[1] whom ev'ry fool admires,
100   Would in variety be fair,

3. I.e., would blame.
4. According to Robert Burton's *Anatomy of Melancholy* (1621), love of learning could be a cause of "spleen."
5. The nine Greek sister goddesses believed to be sources of inspiration for the arts. Originally they were nymphs of wells or springs, which inspired those who drank from them and near which they were worshipped.
6. Acceptable artistic pursuits for women were embroidery, painting, and tapestry making. *Inimitable:* surpassing or defying imitation.
7. The subjects of such art (see previous note): the "sov'reign" at this time would have been William of Orange (1650–1702); line 89 refers to the bib-

lical story of the prophet Balaam and his ass. Intent on cursing the Israelites, Balaam ignores the commands of God until he is rebuked by his ass and threatened by an angel of the Lord (Numbers 22.21–25).
8. Bacchus is the Roman god of wine, sometimes called the "drunken god"; thus "Son of Bacchus" is one who indulges or overindulges in drink.
9. I.e., in wine or drink.
1. A flirtatious woman who uses arts to gain the admiration and affection of men for the gratification of vanity or desire for conquest. A type much commented on and satirized during the Restoration.

And, changing hastily the scene,
　　From light, impertinent, and vain,
Assumes a soft, a melancholy air,
And of her eyes rebates° the wand'ring fires,   *diminishes*
105　The careless posture, and the head reclined,
　　The thoughtful, and composèd face,
Proclaiming the withdrawn, the absent mind,
　　Allows the Fop[2] more liberty to gaze,
Who gently for the tender cause inquires;
110　The cause, indeed, is a defect in sense,
Yet is the Spleen alleged,° and still the dull pretence.   *blamed*
　　　But these are thy fantastic° harms,   *imaginary*
　　　The tricks of thy pernicious stage,
　　　Which do the weaker sort engage;
115　Worse are the dire effects of thy more pow'rful charms.
　　　By thee Religion, all we know,
　　　That should enlighten here below,
　　　Is veiled in darkness, and perplexed
With anxious doubts, with endless scruples° vexed,   *uncertainties*
120　And some restraint implied from each perverted text.[3]
　　　Whilst touch not, taste not, what is freely giv'n,
Is but thy niggard° voice, disgracing bounteous heav'n.[4]   *miserly*
　　From speech restrained, by thy deceits abused,
　　To deserts banished, or in cells reclused,
125　Mistaken vot'ries° to the pow'rs divine,   *devout worshipers*
　　Whilst they a purer sacrifice design,
Do but the Spleen obey, and worship at thy shrine.
　　　In vain to chase thee ev'ry art we try,
　　　In vain all remedies apply,
130　　In vain the Indian leaf° infuse,   *tea*
　　　Or the parched Eastern berry° bruise;   *coffee*
Some pass, in vain, those bounds, and nobler liquors use.
　　　Now harmony, in vain, we bring,
　　　Inspire the flute, and touch the string.
135　　From harmony no help is had;
Music but soothes thee, if too sweetly sad,
And if too light, but turns thee gaily mad.
　　　Though the physicians greatest gains,
　　　Although his growing wealth he sees
140　　Daily increased by ladies' fees,
Yet dost thou baffle all his studious pains.
　　　Not skillful Lower[5] thy source could find,
　　　Or through the well-dissected body trace
　　　The secret, the mysterious ways,
145　By which thou dost surprise, and prey upon the mind.

---

2. A fool or dandy; one who is foolishly attentive to his attentions and manners; another type satirized during the Restoration.
3. I.e, some prohibition ("restraint") inferred from misreadings of biblical texts.
4. Puritan zeal was considered another manifes-

tation of "spleen." The Puritans were seen as harshly repressive.
5. Richard Lower (1631–1691), an English physician noted for his research in anatomy and physiology; author of *Treatise on the Heart* (1669).

Though in the search, too deep for humane thought,
   With unsuccessful toil he wrought,°   *worked*
'Till thinking thee to've catched, himself by thee was caught,
   Retained thy pris'ner, thy acknowledged slave,
150   And sunk beneath thy chain to a lamented grave.

1701, 1713

Adam Posed[6]

Could our first father, at his toilsome plow,
Thorns in his path, and labor on his brow,
Clothed only in a rude, unpolished skin,
Could he a vain fantastic nymph[7] have seen,
5   In all her airs, in all her antic° graces,   *bizarre*
Her various fashions, and more various faces;
How had it posed that skill, which late assigned
Just appellations to each several kind![8]
A right idea of the sight to frame;
10   T'have guessed from what new element[9] she came;
T'have hit the wav'ring form,[1] or giv'n this thing a name.

1709, 1713

To Death

O King of terrors, whose unbounded sway
All that have life must certainly obey;
The King, the Priest, the Prophet, all are thine,
Nor would ev'n God (in flesh) thy stroke decline.[2]
5   My name is on thy roll, and sure I must
Increase thy gloomy kingdom in the dust.
My soul at this no apprehension feels,
But trembles at thy swords, thy racks, thy wheels;[3]
Thy scorching fevers, which distract the sense,
10   And snatch us raving, unprepared, from hence;
At thy contagious darts, that wound the heads
Of weeping friends, who wait at dying beds.
Spare these, and let thy time be when it will;

---

6. Perplexed.

7. "Fantastic" may mean "capricious" or "foppish in attire," but may also have the sense of "imaginary" or "unreal." "Nymph" is a conventional pastoral word for a young woman. The character is a coquette, or flirtatious young woman, a type much commented on and satirized during the Restoration. Attacks on artificiality and the use of cosmetics were common during the Renaissance and still popular during the Restoration.

8. According to Genesis 2.19, Adam named ("assign'd / just appellations to") all the animals.

9. I.e., she is not created from one of the four elements—earth, air, water, and fire—out of which all things were believed to be composed.

1. I.e., to have accurately identified the nature of her changing form.

2. I.e., Christ (God in his human incarnation) suffered death on the cross.

3. Like "racks," instruments of torture.

My bus'ness is to die, and thine to kill.
15 Gently thy fatal scepter on me lay,
And take to thy cold arms, insensibly, thy prey.

1713

Friendship between Ephelia and Ardelia[4]

Eph. What Friendship is, Ardelia show.
Ard. 'Tis to love, as I love you.
Eph. This account, so short (tho' kind)
Suits not my inquiring mind.
5   Therefore farther now repeat:
What is Friendship when complete?
Ard. 'Tis to share all joy and grief;
'Tis to lend all due relief
From the tongue, the heart, the hand;
10   'Tis to mortgage house and land;
For a friend be sold a slave;
'Tis to die upon a grave,
If a friend therein do lie.
Eph. This indeed, tho' carried high,[5]
15   This, tho' more than e'er was done
Underneath the rolling sun,
This has all been said before.
Can Ardelia say no more?
Ard. Words indeed no more can show:
20   *But 'tis to love, as I love you.*

1713

A Nocturnal Reverie

In such a night,[6] when every louder wind
Is to its distant cavern safe confined;
And only gentle Zephyr[7] fans his wings,
And lonely Philomel, still waking,[8] sings;
5 Or from some tree, famed for the owl's delight,
She, hollowing° clear, directs the wand'rer right: *crying out*
In such a night, when passing clouds give place,
Or thinly veil the heav'ns' mysterious face;

4. Ardelia is a conventional poetic name that Finch sometimes used to refer to herself.
5. I.e., expressed loudly or in high style; or, perhaps, highly esteemed.
6. This phrase, repeated twice below, recalls the same repeated phrase in the night scene that opens act 5 of Shakespeare's *Merchant of Venice*. Finch also echoes many words from Milton's "Il Penseroso" (see p. 405).

7. According to myth, Zephyr, the west wind, is warm and mild. The four winds resided in caves.
8. I.e., ever wakeful; according to myth, Philomela was raped by her brother-in-law, Tereus, who then tore out her tongue so that she could not speak. She wove the story into a tapestry and sent it to her sister, who rescued her. She was later changed into a nightingale while in flight from Tereus.

When in some river, overhung with green,
10   The waving moon and trembling leaves are seen;
        When freshened grass now bears itself upright,
        And makes cool banks to pleasing rest invite,
        Whence springs the woodbind,° and the bramble-rose,   honeysuckle
        And where the sleepy cowslip sheltered grows;
15   Whilst now a paler hue the foxglove takes,
        Yet checkers still with red the dusky brakes[9]
        When scatter'd glow-worms,[1] but in twilight fine,
        Shew trivial beauties, watch their hour to shine;[2]
        Whilst Salisb'ry stands the test of every light,
20   In perfect charms, and perfect virtue bright:
        When odors, which declined repelling day,[3]
        Through temp'rate air uninterrupted stray;
        When darkened groves their softest shadows wear,
        And falling waters we distinctly hear;
25   When through the gloom more venerable[4] shows
        Some ancient fabric, awful[5] in repose,
        While sunburnt hills their swarthy looks conceal,
        And swelling haycocks[6] thicken up the vale:°   valley
        When the loosed horse now, as his pasture leads,
30   Comes slowly grazing through th' adjoining meads,°   meadows
        Whose stealing pace, and lengthened shade we fear,
        Till torn-up forage in his teeth we hear:
        When nibbling sheep at large pursue their food,
        And unmolested kine° rechew the cud;   cattle
35   When curlews[7] cry beneath the village walls,
        And to her straggling brood the partridge calls;
        Their shortlived jubilee the creatures keep,
        Which but endures, whilst tyrant man does sleep;
        When a sedate content the spirit feels,
40   And no fierce light disturbs, whilst it reveals;
        But silent musings urge the mind to seek
        Something, too high for syllables to speak;
        Till the free soul to a composedness charmed,
        Finding the elements of rage disarmed,
45   O'er all below a solemn quiet grown,
        Joys in th' inferior world, and thinks it like her own:
        In such a night let me abroad remain,
        Till morning breaks, and all's confused again;
        Our cares, our toils, our clamors are renewed,
50   Or pleasures, seldom reached, again pursued.

1713

---

9. Thickets; tall ferns or bracken. English cowslips
(line 13) have droopy yellow petals.
1. Insects, (the females of) which emit a shining
green light from the abdomen.
2. I.e., show lesser beauties and—unlike the
countess of Salisbury, Anne Tufton, of the follow-
ing line—make the most of their limited opportu-
nities to shine.

3. I.e., when the aromas ("odors") of field and
wood, which refused to come forth ("declined")
under the hot, "repelling" rays of the sun ("day").
4. Impressive or worthy of religious reverence.
5. May mean both awe-inspiring and causing fear
or dread. *Fabric:* structure, i.e., building.
6. Conical piles of hay.
7. A kind of shore bird, similar to a sandpiper.

The Answer[8]

(To Pope's Impromptu)

Disarmed with so genteel an air,
    The contest I give o'er;
Yet, Alexander, have a care,
    And shock the sex no more.
5 We rule the world our life's whole race,
    Men but assume that right;
First slaves to ev'ry tempting face,
    Then martyrs to our spite.
You of one Orpheus[9] sure have read,
10 Who would like you have writ
Had he in London town been bred,
    And polished too his wit;
But he poor soul thought all was well,
    And great should be his fame,
15 When he had left his wife in hell,
    And birds and beasts could tame.
Yet venturing then with scoffing rhymes
    The women to incense,
Resenting heroines of those times
20 Soon punished his offense.
And as the Hebrus rolled his skull,
    And harp besmeared with blood,
They clashing as the waves grew full,
    Still harmonized the flood.
25 But you our follies gently treat,
    And spin so fine the thread,
You need not fear his awkward fate,
    The lock[1] won't cost the head.
Our admiration you command
30 For all that's gone before;
What next we look for at your hand
    Can only raise it more.
Yet sooth° the ladies I advise   *truly*
    (As me too pride has wrought)
35 We're born to wit, but to be wise
    By admonitions taught.

1717

8. Finch and Alexander Pope engaged in a dispute over some lines in his *Rape of the Lock* that deprecated female wits (see 4.59–62 [p. 616]). He responded to her complaint in a short poem, "Impromptu," subtitled "To Lady Winchelsea" (see p. 637), in which he complimented her poetic talent while slighting the talent of earlier women poets. This poem is her response.
9. According to Greek mythology, Orpheus, famed for singing and playing the lyre, was able to charm birds and animals with his music. When his wife, Eurydice, died, he traveled to the underworld, charmed the infernal gods with his singing, and was granted permission to lead Eurydice out of hell on condition that he not look back to see her following. When they were nearly out of hell, he glanced over his shoulder and she returned to the ranks of the dead. Inconsolable, Orpheus never again took pleasure in women, but continued to sing, enchanting even the stones and trees. The Maenads, frenzied devotees of the god Dionysus, hated Orpheus (perhaps because of his lack of interest in them), and one day they tore him to pieces, casting his head and lyre into the river Hebros. The severed head continued to sing as it floated down the river.
1. I.e., *The Rape of the Lock*; see note 8 above.

On Myself

Good Heav'n, I thank thee, since it was designed
I should be framed, but of the weaker kind,
That yet, my Soul, is rescued from the love
Of all those trifles which their passions move.
5 Pleasures and praise and plenty have with me
But° their just value. If allowed they be,   *only*
Freely, and thankfully as much I taste,
As will not reason or religion waste.
If they're denied, I on my self can live,
10 And slight° those aids unequal chance does give.   *disdain*
When in the sun, my wings can be displayed,
And, in retirement, I can bless the shade.

1903

MATTHEW PRIOR
1664–1721

A Fable

In Æsop's tales an honest wretch we find,
Whose years and comforts equally declined;
He in two wives had two domestic ills,
For different age they had, and different wills;
5 One plucked his black hairs out, and one his gray,
The man for quietness did both obey,
Till all his parish saw his head quite bare,
And thought he wanted brains as well as hair.

The Moral

The parties, henpecked William,[1] are thy wives,
10 The hairs they pluck are thy prerogatives;[2]
Tories thy person hate, the Whigs thy power,[3]
Though much thou yieldest, still they tug for more,
Till this poor man and thou alike are shown,
He without hair, and thou without a crown.

1703

---

1. King William III (1650–1702), who ruled
England from 1689 until his death.
2. The rights of the king, previously not subject to
parliamentary restriction.

3. The Tories and Whigs were the two main polit-
ical parties in seventeenth- and eighteenth-century
England.

To a Lady: She Refusing to Continue a Dispute with Me, and Leaving Me in the Argument

1

Spare, gen'rous victor, spare the slave,
   Who did unequal war pursue;
That more than triumph he might have,
   In being overcome by you.

2

5   In the dispute whate'er I said,
   My heart was by my tongue belied;
And in my looks you might have read,
   How much I argued on your side.

3

You, far from danger as from fear,
10   Might have sustained an open fight:
For seldom your opinions err;
   Your eyes are always in the right.

4

Why, fair one, would you not rely
   On reason's force with beauty's joined?
15   Could I their prevalence deny;
   I must at once be deaf and blind.

5

Alas! not hoping to subdue,
   I only to the fight aspired:
To keep the beauteous foe in view
20   Was all the glory I desired.

6

But she, howe'er of vict'ry sure,
   Contemns the wreath[4] too long delayed;
And, armed with more immediate pow'r,
   Calls cruel silence to her aid.

7

25   Deeper to wound, she shuns the fight:
   She drops her arms, to gain the field:
Secures her conquest by her flight;
   And triumphs, when she seems to yield.

8

So when the Parthian[5] turned his steed,
30   And from the hostile camp withdrew;

4. A wreath of laurel or other leaves was a symbol of victory.

5. A people of western Asia, whose cavalry fought in the manner Prior describes.

With cruel skill the backward reed°   *arrow*
He sent; and as he fled, he slew.

               1718

An Ode

The merchant, to secure his treasure,
 Conveys it in a borrowed name;
Euphelia serves to grace my measure,[6]
 But Cloe is my real flame.

5 My softest verse, my darling lyre,
 Upon Euphelia's toilet° lay;   *dressing table*
When Cloe noted her desire
 That I should sing, that I should play.

My lyre I tune, my voice I raise,
10 But with my numbers° mix my sighs;   *songs*
And whilst I sing Euphelia's praise,
 I fix my soul on Cloe's eyes.

Fair Cloe blushed; Euphelia frowned;
 I sung and gazed; I played and trembled;
15 And Venus to the Loves around[7]
 Remarked how ill we all dissembled.

               1718

JONATHAN SWIFT
1667–1745

A Description of the Morning

Now hardly here and there a hackney-coach[1]
Appearing, showed the ruddy morn's approach.
Now Betty from her master's bed had flown,
And softly stole to discompose her own;
5 The slip-shod 'prentice from his master's door
Had pared the dirt and sprinkled round the floor.
Now Moll[2] had whirled her mop with dext'rous airs,
Prepared to scrub the entry and the stairs.
The youth with broomy stumps began to trace

---

6. I.e., Euphelia adorns or adds grace to my poetry, or is the name used in my poetry.
7. Venus is the Greek goddess of love and beauty. Her attendant "Loves" are, in mythology, the Graces, givers of charm and beauty; in the social context, attractive young women.
1. A horse-drawn carriage, for hire.
2. A diminuitive form of Mary; a common name for a servant.

10   The kennel-edge,[3] where wheels had worn the place.
     The small-coal man[4] was heard with cadence deep,
     Till drowned in shriller notes of chimney-sweep:
     Duns° at his lordship's gate began to meet;   *bill collectors*
     And brickdust Moll[5] had screamed through half the street.
15   The turnkey° now his flock returning sees,   *jailer*
     Duly let out a-nights to steal for fees:[6]
     The watchful bailiffs[7] take their silent stands,
     And schoolboys lag with satchels in their hands.

                                             1709

A Description of a City Shower

    Careful observers may foretell the hour
    (By sure prognostics) when to dread a shower:
    While rain depends,° the pensive cat gives o'er   *impends*
    Her frolics, and pursues her tail no more.
5   Returning home at night, you'll find the sink°   *sewer*
    Strike your offended sense with double stink.
    If you be wise, then go not far to dine;
    You'll spend in coach hire more than save in wine.
    A coming shower your shooting corns presage,
10   Old achès throb, your hollow tooth will rage.
    Sauntering in coffeehouse is Dulman° seen;   *dull man*
    He damns the climate and complains of spleen.°   *melancholy*
      Meanwhile the South,° rising with dabbled° wings,   *a wind* / *spattered*
    A sable cloud athwart the welkin° flings,   *sky*
15   That swilled more liquor than it could contain,
    And, like a drunkard, gives it up again.
    Brisk Susan whips her linen from the rope,
    While the first drizzling shower is borne aslope:°   *slanting*
    Such is that sprinkling which some careless quean°   *wench*
20   Flirts° on you from her mop, but not so clean: *flicks*
    You fly, invoke the gods; then turning, stop
    To rail; she singing, still whirls on her mop.
    Not yet the dust had shunned the unequal strife,
    But, aided by the wind, fought still for life,
25   And wafted with its foe by violent gust,
    'Twas doubtful which was rain and which was dust.
    Ah! where must needy poet seek for aid,
    When dust and rain at once his coat invade?
    Sole coat, where dust cemented by the rain
30   Erects the nap,[8] and leaves a mingled stain.
      Now in contiguous drops the flood comes down,
    Threatening with deluge this devoted° town.   *doomed*

3. Curb of the road.
4. Seller of charcoal.
5. A woman selling powdered brick (used for cleaning knives).
6. Prisoners were allowed out to get money to pay their jailers, who could charge fees for allowing certain privileges, such as better accommodations.
7. I.e., sheriff's deputies.
8. I.e., makes the fibers on the surface of the fabric stand up stiffly.

To shops in crowds the daggled° females fly,   *mud-spattered*
Pretend to cheapen° goods, but nothing buy.   *bargain for*
35 The Templar spruce,[9] while every spout's abroach,°   *running*
Stays till 'tis fair, yet seems to call a coach.
The tucked-up sempstress° walks with hasty strides,   *seamstress*
While streams run down her oiled umbrella's sides.
Here various kinds, by various fortunes led,
40 Commence acquaintance underneath a shed.
Triumphant Tories and desponding Whigs[1]
Forget their feuds, and join to save their wigs.
Boxed in a chair° the beau impatient sits,   *sedan chair*
While spouts run clattering o'er the roof by fits,
45 And ever and anon with frightful din
The leather[2] sounds; he trembles from within.
So when Troy chairmen bore the wooden steed,
Pregnant with Greeks impatient to be freed
(Those bully Greeks, who, as the moderns do,
50 Instead of paying chairmen, run them through),
Laocoön struck the outside with his spear,
And each imprisoned hero quaked for fear.[3]
     Now from all parts the swelling kennels° flow,   *gutters*
And bear their trophies with them as they go:
55 Filth of all hues and odors seem to tell
What street they sailed from, by their sight and smell.
They, as each torrent drives with rapid force,
From Smithfield or St. Pulchre's shape their course,
And in huge confluence joined at Snow Hill ridge,
60 Fall from the conduit prone° to Holborn Bridge.[4]   *downward*
Sweepings from butchers' stalls, dung, guts, and blood,   ⎫
Drowned puppies, stinking sprats,° all drenched in mud,   ⎬ *herring*
Dead cats, and turnip tops, come tumbling down the flood. ⎭

1710

Stella's Birthday

March 13, 1727[5]

This day, whate'er the fates decree,
Shall still° be kept with joy by me: *always*
This day then, let us not be told
That you are sick, and I grown old,
5   Nor think on our approaching ills,
And talk of spectacles and pills;
Tomorrow will be time enough

---

9. The dapper law student.
1. The Tories and Whigs were the two main political parties in seventeenth- and eighteenth-century England; the Tories (Swift's party) had recently assumed power.
2. Leather roof of the sedan chair.
3. In Virgil's *Aeneid* 2, Laocoön so struck the side of the Trojan horse, frightening the Greeks within.

4. The offal from the Smithfield cattle market would be swept toward the Fleet Ditch, spanned by Holborn Bridge, where it would merge with garbage floating down the Snow Hill stream. *St. Pulchre's*: St. Sepulchre's Church, in Holborn.
5. The forty-sixth birthday of Swift's devoted companion and protégée, Esther Johnson.

To hear such mortifying° stuff.   *depressing*
Yet since from reason may be brought
10 A better and more pleasing thought,
Which can in spite of all decays
Support a few remaining days:
From not the gravest of divines,
Accept for once some serious lines.
15   Although we now can form no more
Long schemes of life, as heretofore;
Yet you, while time is running fast,
Can look with joy on what is past.
        Were future happiness and pain
20 A mere contrivance of the brain,
As atheists argue, to entice
And fit their proselytes° for vice   *converts*
(The only comfort they propose,
To have companions in their woes),
25 Grant this the case, yet sure 'tis hard
That virtue, styled its own reward,
And by all sages understood
To be the chief of human good,
Should acting, die, nor leave behind
30 Some lasting pleasure in the mind,
Which, by remembrance, will assuage
Grief, sickness, poverty, and age;
And strongly shoot a radiant dart,
To shine through life's declining part.
35   Say, Stella, feel you no content,
Reflecting on a life well spent?
Your skillful hand employed to save
Despairing wretches from the grave;
And then supporting from your store
40 Those whom you dragged from death before
(So Providence on mortals waits,
Preserving what it first creates);
Your generous boldness to defend
An innocent and absent friend;
45 That courage which can make you just,
To merit humbled in the dust:
The detestation you express
For vice in all its glittering dress:
That patience under torturing pain,
50 Where stubborn stoics[6] would complain.
        Must these like empty shadows pass,
Or forms reflected from a glass?
Or mere chimeras° in the mind,   *wild fancies*
That fly and leave no marks behind?
55 Does not the body thrive and grow
By food of twenty years ago?
And, had it not been still supplied,
It must a thousand times have died.

6. Those who practice repression of emotion, indifference to pleasure and pain, and patient endurance.

Then who with reason can maintain
60 That no effects of food remain?
And is not virtue in mankind
The nutriment that feeds the mind?
Upheld by each good action past,
And still continued by the last:
65 Then who with reason can pretend
That all effects of virtue end?
　　Believe me, Stella, when you show
That true contempt for things below,
Nor prize your life for other ends
70 Than merely to oblige your friends,
Your former actions claim their part,
And join to fortify your heart.
For virtue in her daily race,
Like Janus,[7] bears a double face,
75 Looks back with joy where she has gone,
And therefore goes with courage on.
She at your sickly couch will wait,
And guide you to some better state.
　　O then, whatever Heaven intends,
80 Take pity on your pitying friends;
Nor let your ills affect your mind,
To fancy they can be unkind.
Me, surely me, you ought to spare,
Who gladly would your sufferings share;
85 Or give my scrap of life to you,
And think it far beneath your due;
You, to whose care so oft I owe
That I'm alive to tell you so.

1727

The Lady's Dressing Room

Five hours, (and who can do it less in?)
By haughty Celia[8] spent in dressing;
The goddess from her chamber issues,
Arrayed in lace, brocades and tissues.[9]
5 　　Strephon, who found the room was void,
And Betty otherwise employed,
Stole in, and took a strict survey,
Of all the litter as it lay;
Whereof, to make the matter clear,
10 An inventory follows here.
　　And first a dirty smock appeared,
Beneath the armpits well besmeared.

7. The Roman god of doors, with opposed faces, one looking forward, the other back.
8. Celia and Strephon (line 5) are conventional poetic names often used in pastoral poetry.
9. Fine, lightweight fabric. *Brocades:* a rich silk fabric with raised patterns in gold and silver.

Strephon, the rogue, displayed it wide,
And turned it round on every side.
On such a point few words are best,
And Strephon bids us guess the rest,
But swears how damnably the men lie,
In calling Celia sweet and cleanly.
Now listen while he next produces
The various combs for various uses,
Filled up with dirt so closely fixt,
No brush could force a way betwixt.
A paste of composition rare,
Sweat, dandruff, powder, lead¹ and hair;
A forehead cloth with oil upon't
To smooth the wrinkles on her front;°   brow
Here alum flower to stop the steams,²
Exhaled from sour unsavory streams,
There night-gloves made of Tripsy's hide,
Bequeathed by Tripsy when she died,
With puppy water,³ beauty's help
Distilled from Tripsy's darling whelp;
Here gallypots⁴ and vials placed,
Some filled with washes, some with paste,
Some with pomatum, paints and slops,
And ointments good for scabby chops.⁵
Hard by a filthy basin stands,
Fouled with the scouring of her hands;
The basin takes whatever comes
The scrapings of her teeth and gums,
A nasty compound of all hues,
For here she spits, and here she spews.
But oh! it turned poor Strephon's bowels,
When he beheld and smelled the towels,
Begummed, bemattered, and beslimed
With dirt, and sweat, and earwax grimed.
No object Strephon's eye escapes,
Here petticoats in frowzy° heaps;   ill-smelling, unkempt
Nor be the handkerchiefs forgot
All varnished o'er with snuff⁶ and snot.
The stockings why should I expose,
Stained with the marks of stinking toes;
Or greasy coifs and pinners⁷ reeking,
Which Celia slept at least a week in?
A pair of tweezers next he found
To pluck her brows in arches round,
Or hairs that sink the forehead low,
Or on her chin like bristles grow.

Line numbers: 15, 20, 25, 30, 35, 40, 45, 50, 55

1. Then used to make hair glossy.
2. Vapors or exhalations produced as an excretion of the body, e.g., hot breath, perspiration, or the infectious effluvium of a disease. *Alum flower:* powdered mineral salt used in medicine.
3. The urine of a puppy, used as a cosmetic.
4. Small ceramic pots, often containers for medicine.

5. Painful fissures or cracks in the skin. *Washes:* liquid cosmetic for the complexion. *Paste:* either medicinal or cosmetic compound. *Pomatum:* scented ointment for application to the skin. *Paints:* rouges. *Slops:* refuse liquid.
6. Powdered tobacco inhaled through the nostrils.
7. *Coifs and pinners:* types of headwear.

The virtues we must not let pass,
60 Of Celia's magnifying glass.
When frighted Strephon cast his eye on't
It showed visage° of a giant.   face
A glass that can to sight disclose,
The smallest worm in Celia's nose,
65 And faithfully direct her nail
To squeeze it out from head to tail;
For catch it nicely by the head,
It must come out alive or dead.
    Why Strephon will you tell the rest?
70 And must you needs describe the chest?°   commode
That careless wench! no creature warn her
To move it out from yonder corner;
But leave it standing full in sight
For you to exercise your spite.
75 In vain the workman showed his wit
With rings and hinges counterfeit
To make it seem in this disguise
A cabinet to vulgar eyes;
For Strephon ventured to look in,
80 Resolved to go through thick and thin;
He lifts the lid, there needs no more,
He smelled it all the time before.
As from within Pandora's box,
When Epimetheus[8] op'd the locks,
85 A sudden universal crew
Of human evils upwards flew;
He still was comforted to find
That Hope at last remained behind;
So Strephon lifting up the lid,
90 To view what in the chest was hid.
The vapors flew from out the vent,
But Strephon cautious never meant
The bottom of the pan° to grope,   vessel
And foul his hands in search of Hope.
95 O never may such vile machine
Be once in Celia's chamber seen!
O may she better learn to keep
Those "secrets of the hoary deep!"[9]
    As mutton cutlets, prime of meat,
100 Which though with art you salt and beat
As laws of cookery require,
And toast them at the clearest fire;
If from adown the hopeful chops
The fat upon a cinder drops,
105 To stinking smoke it turns the flame
Pois'ning the flesh from whence it came,

8. In Greek mythology, brother of Prometheus and husband of Pandora. Created by the gods as the first human woman, Pandora brought with her to Earth a box containing all human ills, which, when it was opened, were released into the world, leaving only Hope behind.

9. From Milton's *Paradise Lost* (2.891), a poetic reference to the ocean; Swift puns on "hoary," which means ancient but may also mean corrupt, and perhaps also on *whore* and on the homonym, *hory,* meaning filthy.

And up exhales a greasy stench,
For which you curse the careless wench;
So things, which must not be expressed,
110   When plumped° into the reeking chest,   *dropped*
Send up an excremental smell
To taint the parts from whence they fell.
The petticoats and gown perfume,
Which waft a stink round every room.
115   Thus finishing his grand survey,
Disgusted Strephon stole away
Repeating in his amorous fits,
Oh! Celia, Celia, Celia shits!
      But Vengeance, goddess never sleeping
120   Soon punished Strephon for his peeping;
His foul imagination links
Each Dame he sees with all her stinks:
And, if unsavory odors fly,
Conceives a lady standing by:
125   All women his description fits,
And both ideas jump like wits:[1]
By vicious fancy coupled fast,
And still appearing in contrast.
I pity wretched Strephon blind
130   To all the charms of female kind;
Should I the queen of love[2] refuse,
Because she rose from stinking ooze?
To him that looks behind the scene,
Satira's but some pocky queen.[3]
135   When Celia in her glory shows,
If Strephon would but stop his nose
(Who now so impiously blasphemes
Her ointments, daubs, and paints and creams,
Her washes, slops, and every clout,°   *rag*
140   With which he makes so foul a rout°)   *fuss*
He soon would learn to think like me,
And bless his ravished sight to see
Such order from confusion sprung,
Such gaudy tulips raised from dung.

1730

A Beautiful Young Nymph Going to Bed

Corinna, pride of Drury-Lane[4]
For whom no shepherd sighs in vain;
Never did Covent Garden[5] boast

1. *Jump*: match; from the proverbial phrase *good wits jump*, i.e., great minds think alike.
2. Aphrodite, or Venus, the classical goddess often depicted as rising out of the sea.
3. Whore, here infected with pox (usually syphilis), or marked with pocks or pustules. *Satira*: prob-

ably Statira, one of the wives of Alexander the Great in Nathaniel Lee's tragedy *Rival Queens* (1677).
4. A London street notorious for prostitutes.
5. A flashy, vulgar district in London.

So bright a battered, strolling toast;
  5 No drunken rake to pick her up,
No cellar where on tick° to sup;   *credit*
Returning at the midnight hour;
Four stories climbing to her bow'r;°   *room*
Then, seated on a three-legged chair,[6]
  10 Takes off her artificial hair.
Now, picking out a crystal eye,
She wipes it clean, and lays it by.
Her eye-brows from a mouse's hide,
Stuck on with art on either side,
  15 Pulls off with care, and first displays 'em,
Then in a play-book smoothly lays 'em.
Now dextrously her plumpers[7] draws,
That serve to fill her hollow jaws.
Untwists a wire; and from her gums
  20 A set of teeth completely comes.
Pulls out the rags contrived to prop
Her flabby dugs° and down they drop.   *breasts*
Proceeding on, the lovely goddess
Unlaces next her steel-ribbed bodice;
  25 Which by the operator's skill,
Press down the lumps, the hollows fill,
Up goes her hand, and off she slips
The bolsters that supply her hips.
With gentlest touch, she next explores
  30 Her shankers,[8] issues, running sores,
Effects of many a sad disaster;
And then to each applies a plaister.°   *plaster for face*
But must, before she goes to bed,
Rub off the dawbs of white and red;
  35 And smooth the furrows in her front°   *forehead*
With greasy paper stuck upon't.
She takes a bolus[9] ere she sleeps;
And then between two blankets creeps.
With pains of love tormented lies;
  40 Or if she chance to close her eyes,
Of Bridewell and the Compter[1] dreams,
And feels the lash, and faintly screams;
Or, by a faithless bully° drawn,   *pimp*
At some hedge-tavern° lies in pawn;   *poor, squalid inn*
  45 Or to Jamaica seems transported,[2]
Alone, and by no planter courted;
Or, near Fleet-Ditch's[3] oozy brinks,
Surrounded with a hundred stinks,
Belated, seems on watch to lie,
  50 And snap some cully° passing by;   *simpleton*

6. I.e., one missing a leg.
7. Small, light balls sometimes carried in the mouth for filling out hollow cheeks.
8. Chancres: ulcers resulting from venereal disease.
9. A larger than ordinary pill.

1. Pronounced *counter;* a city prison. Bridewell was a prison for vagrant women and prostitutes.
2. Some convicts were shipped to Jamaica and other West Indian sites, although the majority were transported to the North American colonies.
3. An open sewer in London.

Or, struck with fear, her fancy runs
On watchmen, constables and duns,°   *debt collectors*
From whom she meets with frequent rubs;°   *unpleasant encounters*
But, never from religious clubs;[4]
55 Whose favor she is sure to find,
Because she pays 'em all in kind.
    Corinna wakes. A dreadful sight!
Behold the ruins of the night!
A wicked rat her plaster stole,
60 Half eat, and dragged it to his hole.
The crystal eye, alas, was missed;
And puss had on her plumpers pissed.
A pigeon picked her issue-peas;
And Shock[5] her tresses° filled with fleas.   *artificial hair*
65 The nymph, tho' in this mangled plight,
Must ev'ry morn her limbs unite.
But how shall I describe her arts
To recollect the scattered parts?
Or shew the anguish, toil, and pain,
70 Of gath'ring up herself again?
The bashful muse° will never bear   *source of inspiration*
In such a scene to interfere.
Corinna in the morning dizened,°   *dressed up*
Who sees, will spew; who smells, be poison'd.

1731

Verses on the Death of Dr. Swift, D.S.P.D.[6]

Occasioned by Reading a Maxim in Rochefoucauld[7]

*Dans l'adversité de nos meilleurs amis nous trouvons toujours
quelque chose, qui ne nous déplaît pas.*
    "In the adversity of our best friends, we find something that does
not displease us."

    As Rochefoucauld his maxims drew
From nature, I believe 'em true:
They argue° no corrupted mind   *suggest*

4. Groups of religious dissenters or enthusiasts who were often suspected of hypocrisy.
5. Shough, the name for a kind of lapdog, became "Shock" in Alexander Pope's *Rape of the Lock* 1.115 (see p. 607). *Issue-peas:* peas or other small, globular bodies placed in surgical incisions to continue the irritation that made a discharge.
6. The initials signify "Dean of St. Patrick's, Dublin." Evidently intending this poem to be published only after his death, Swift allowed some of his friends to see the (changing) text in manuscript; he completed explanatory notes for it in 1732. We have included most of these notes below. They were omitted, along with over 150 lines deemed potentially offensive, in the version of the poem that one of Swift's friends, Dr. William King, arranged to have printed in London in 1739. Editing the poem with the help of other English friends

of Swift, most notably Alexander Pope, King managed to offend the author while thinking to do him a favor. "Much dissatisfied" with the censored version, Swift arranged for the poem and notes to be printed in Dublin; this version, although much longer, still had many blanks in lieu of proper names. Swift correctly foresaw that the poem would prove controversial, both in its attacks on Queen Caroline and her prime minister, Robert Walpole, and in its praise of leading political opponents of Walpole such as William Pulteney and Henry St. John, Lord Viscount Bolingbroke, to whom Pope had written his "Essay on Man" (see p. 623) and whom Swift praises in his note to line 196.
7. François de la Rochefoucauld (1613–1680), writer of witty, cynical maxims.

In him; the fault is in mankind.

5 This maxim more than all the rest
Is thought too base for human breast:
"In all distresses of our friends
We first consult our private ends,
While Nature, kindly bent to ease us,

10 Points out some circumstance to please us."
  If this perhaps your patience move,
Let reason and experience prove.[8]
  We all behold with envious eyes
Our equal raised above our size.

15 Who would not at a crowded show
Stand high himself, keep others low?
I love my friend as well as you,
But why should he obstruct my view?
Then let me have the higher post;

20 Suppose it but an inch at most.
  If in a battle you should find
One, whom you love of all mankind,
Had some heroic action done,
A champion killed, or trophy won;

25 Rather than thus be overtopped°   *outdone*
Would you not wish his laurels[9] cropped?
  Dear honest Ned is in the gout,[1]
Lies racked with pain, and you without:
How patiently you hear him groan!

30 How glad the case is not your own!
  What poet would not grieve to see
His brethren write as well as he?
But rather than they should excel,
He'd wish his rivals all in hell.

35 Her end when emulation° misses,   *imitation*
She turns to envy, stings, and hisses:
The strongest friendship yields to pride,
Unless the odds be on our side.
  Vain humankind! fantastic race!

40 Thy various follies who can trace?
Self-love, ambition, envy, pride,
Their empire in our hearts divide.
Give others riches, power, and station;
'Tis all on me an usurpation;

45 I have no title to aspire,[2]
Yet, when you sink, I seem the higher.
In Pope I cannot read a line,
But with a sigh I wish it mine:
When he can in one couplet fix

---

8. I.e., if this perhaps strains your patience, let reason and experience prove its truth. Rochefoucauld evidently thought this maxim would tax some readers' patience, because he omitted it from all editions of his *Reflexions . . . et maximes* after the first edition of 1665.
9. Laurels were traditionally worn by poets, ath-

letes, and warriors as a sign of victory or distinction.
1. A disease characterized by painful inflammation of the joints. Ned is a generic name for the type of "friend" Rochefoucauld had described.
2. I.e., I don't aim for a title of noble rank; or, I have no title to announce.

50 More sense than I can do in six,
It gives me such a jealous fit,
I cry, "Pox take him and his wit!"
    I grieve to be outdone by Gay[3]
In my own humorous biting way.
55 Arbuthnot[4] is no more my friend,
Who dares to irony pretend,
Which I was born to introduce,
Refined it first, and showed its use.
St. John, as well as Pulteney,[5] knows
60 That I had some repute for prose;
And, till they drove me out of date,
Could maul a minister of state.
If they have mortified my pride,
And made me throw my pen aside;
65 If with such talents Heaven hath blessed 'em,
Have I not reason to detest 'em?
    To all my foes, dear Fortune, send
Thy gifts, but never to my friend:
I tamely can endure the first,
70 But this with envy makes me burst.
    Thus much may serve by way of proem;°   *preface*
Proceed we therefore to our poem.
    The time is not remote, when I
Must by the course of nature die;
75 When, I foresee, my special friends
Will try to find their private ends:°   *benefits*
Though it is hardly° understood°   *hard to / understand*
Which way my death can do them good;
Yet thus methinks I hear 'em speak:
80 "See how the Dean begins to break!°   *weaken*
Poor gentleman! he droops apace!°   *quickly*
You plainly find it in his face.
That old vertigo° in his head   *dizziness*
Will never leave him till he's dead.
85 Besides, his memory decays;
He recollects not what he says;
He cannot call his friends to mind;
Forgets the place where last he dined;
Plies you with stories o'er and o'er;
90 He told them fifty times before.
How does he fancy we can sit
To hear his out-of-fashion wit?
But he takes up with younger folks,
Who for his wine will bear his jokes.
95 Faith, he must make his stories shorter,
Or change his comrades once a quarter;

---

3. John Gay (1685–1732; see pp. 594–96), poet, playwright, author of the *Beggar's Opera* (1728), and intimate friend of Swift and Pope.
4. Dr. John Arbuthnot (1667–1735), physician and wit, friend of Swift, Gay, and Pope. See the latter's "Epistle to Dr. Arbuthnot" (p. 626).
5. For these two politicians, both opposed to Prime Minister Walpole, see note 6 above and Swift's notes to lines 194 and 196.

In half the time he talks them round,[6]
There must another set be found.
    "For poetry, he's past his prime;
100 He takes an hour to find a rhyme;
His fire is out, his wit decayed,
His fancy sunk, his Muse a jade.[7]
I'd have him throw away his pen—
But there's no talking to some men."
105   And then their tenderness appears
By adding largely to my years:
"He's older than he would be reckoned,
And well remembers Charles the Second.[8]
He hardly drinks a pint of wine;
110 And that, I doubt,° is no good sign.   suspect
His stomach,° too, begins to fail;   appetite
Last year we thought him strong and hale;°   healthy
But now he's quite another thing;
I wish he may hold out till spring."
115 They hug themselves, and reason thus:
"It is not yet so bad with us."
    In such a case they talk in tropes,°   figures of speech
And by their fears express their hopes.
Some great misfortune to portend°   predict
120 No enemy can match a friend.
With all the kindness they profess,
The merit of a lucky guess
(When daily how-d'ye's come of course,[9]
And servants answer, "Worse and worse!")
125 Would please 'em better, than to tell
That God be praised the Dean is well.
Then he who prophesied the best,
Approves his foresight to the rest:
"You know I always feared the worst,
130 And often told you so at first."
He'd rather choose that I should die,
Than his prediction prove a lie.
Not one foretells I shall recover,
But all agree to give me over.
135   Yet, should some neighbor feel a pain
Just in the parts where I complain,
How many a message would he send!
What hearty prayers that I should mend!
Inquire what regimen I kept;
140 What gave me ease, and how I slept,
And more lament, when I was dead,
Then all the snivelers round my bed.
    My good companions, never fear;
For though you may mistake a year,

6. I.e., he tells all his stories once, then starts   8. King of England who died in 1685, when Swift
again.   was eighteen.
7. His Muse, source of inspiration personified as   9. I.e., when it's routinely asked, "How is he?"
a female, is a worn-out horse or a whore.

145 Though your prognostics run too fast,
They must be verified at last.
   Behold the fatal day arrive!
"How is the Dean?"—"He's just alive."
Now the departing prayer is read.
150 "He hardly breathes"—"The Dean is dead."
Before the passing° bell begun,°   *death / begun to ring*
The news through half the town has run.
"Oh! may we all for death prepare!
What has he left? and who's his heir?"
155 "I know no more than what the news is;
'Tis all bequeathed to public uses."[1]
"To public use! a perfect whim!
What had the public done for him?
Mere envy, avarice, and pride.
160 He gave it all—but first he died.
And had the Dean in all the nation
No worthy friend, no poor relation?
So ready to do strangers good,
Forgetting his own flesh and blood?"
165 Now Grub Street[2] wits are all employed;
With elegies the town is cloyed;°   *overfilled*
Some paragraph in every paper
To curse the Dean, or bless the Drapier.[3]
   The doctors, tender° of their fame,   *careful*
170 Wisely on me lay all the blame.
"We must confess his case was nice,[4]
But he would never take advice.
Had he been ruled, for aught appears,
He might have lived these twenty years:
175 For, when we opened him, we found,
That all his vital parts were sound."
   From Dublin soon to London spread,
'Tis told at court, "The Dean is dead."
Kind Lady Suffolk,[5] in the spleen,
180 Runs laughing up to tell the Queen.
The Queen, so gracious, mild and good,
Cries, "Is he gone? 'tis time he should.
He's dead, you say; why, let him rot:
I'm glad the medals were forgot.[6]

1. I.e., the inheritance is all left to charity.
2. Originally a street in London inhabited largely by hack writers; later, a term applied to all writers paid to produce (often scandalous) stories for London publishers.
3. "The author imagines, that the scribblers of the prevailing [political] party, which he always opposed, will libel him after his death; but that others will remember him with gratitude, who consider the service he had done to Ireland, under the name of M.B. Drapier." [Swift's note refers to the character that Swift constructed in his *Drapier's Letters* (1724–25) to encourage Irish resistance to the imposition of a new coin, called "Wood's halfpence." He believed that this coin would hurt the Irish economy. See lines 407–08.]

4. Delicate; thus demanding careful diagnosis and treatment.
5. Mrs. Howard, later the countess of Suffolk, was the mistress of the Prince of Wales (later crowned as George II) and the lady of the bed-chamber for the Princess of Wales (who became Queen Caroline in 1727). She "professed much friendship for the Dean" [Swift's note]. *In the spleen*: in low spirits (ironic, as "laughing" in the next line indicates).
6. According to Swift, the princess commanded him "a dozen times" to visit her; he finally did so on "the advice of friends," and then, in return, he "taxed" (asked) the princess for a present worth ten pounds. She promised him some medals, but they were not ready when he returned to Ireland, and later, "she forgot them, or thought them too dear"

185 I promised him, I own; but when?
  I only was the Princess then;
  But now, as consort of the King,
  You know, 'tis quite a different thing."
   Now Chartres,[7] at Sir Robert's levee,
190 Tells with a sneer the tidings heavy:
  "Why, is he dead without his shoes?"[8]
  Cries Bob,[9] "I'm sorry for the news:
  Oh, were the wretch but living still,
  And in his place my good friend Will![1]
195 Or had a miter° on his head,   *bishop's hat*
  Provided Bolingbroke[2] were dead!"
   Now Curll his shop from rubbish drains.[3]
  Three genuine tomes of Swift's remains!
  And then, to make them pass° the glibber,° *sell / better*
200 Revised by Tibbalds, Moore, and Cibber.[4]
  He'll treat me as he does my betters,
  Publish my will, my life, my letters;
  Revive the libels born to die,
  Which Pope must bear, as well as I.
205 Here shift the scene, to represent
  How those I love my death lament.
  Poor Pope will grieve a month, and Gay
  A week, and Arbuthnot a day.
   St. John himself will scarce forbear°   *refrain*
210 To bite his pen, and drop a tear.
  The rest will give a shrug, and cry,
  "I'm sorry—but we all must die!"
   Indifference clad in wisdom's guise
  All fortitude of mind supplies:

(expensive). Swift's note continues: "The Dean, being in Ireland, sent Mrs. Howard a piece of Indian plaid made in that kingdom [Ireland]: which the Queen [on] seeing[,] took from her, and wore it herself and sent to the Dean for as much as would clothe herself and her children, desiring he would send charge of it. He did the former. It cost thirty-five pounds, but he said he would have nothing except the medals. He was the summer following in England, was treated as usual, and she being then Queen, the Dean was promised a settlement in England, but returned as he went, and, instead of favor or medals, hath been ever since under her Majesty's displeasure."
7. Francis Charteris was "a most infamous, vile scoundrel, grown from a foot-boy, or worse, to a prodigious fortune" [Swift's note]. Charteris was convicted of rape and then pardoned by Robert Walpole in 1730 after "sacrificing a great part of his fortune," according to Swift. A "levee," or rising, is a morning audience held in an important person's bedroom.
8. I.e., did he die in his bed rather than in the violent fashion that Swift imagines Walpole preferring?
9. "Sir Robert Walpole, Chief Minister of State, treated the Dean, in 1726, with great distinction, invited him to dinner . . . with the Dean's friends chosen on purpose; appointed an hour to talk with him of Ireland, to which kingdom and people the Dean found him no great friend. . . . The Dean

would see him no more [and Walpole, in turn] would never see him again" [Swift's note].
1. "Mr. William Pulteney, from being Mr. Walpole's intimate friend, detesting his Administration, opposed his measures, and joined with my Lord Bolingbroke, to represent his [Walpole's] conduct in an excellent paper, called *Craftsman*, which is still continued" [Swift's note].
2. "Henry St. John, Lord Viscount Bolingbroke, Secretary of State to Queen Anne of blessed memory [i.e., Anne Stuart, who reigned before George I]. He is reckoned the most universal genius in Europe; Walpole dreading his abilities, treated him most injuriously, working with King George, who forgot his promise of restoring the said Lord, upon the restless importunity [pleading] of Walpole" [Swift's note].
3. "Edmund Curll hath been the most infamous bookseller of any age or country: his character in part may be found in Mr. Pope's *Dunciad*. He [Curll] published three volumes all charged on [attributed to] the Dean, who never writ three pages of them: he hath used many of the Dean's friends in almost as vile a manner" [Swift's note].
4. "Three stupid verse writers in London, the last to the shame of the court, and the highest disgrace to wit and learning, was made Laureate" [Swift's note]. Lewis Theobald (1688–1744), James Moore Smythe (1702–1734), and Colley Cibber (1671–1757) were all men of letters satirized in Pope's *Dunciad*.

215   For how can stony bowels melt
     In those who never pity felt?[5]
     When *we* are lashed, *they* kiss the rod,[6]
     Resigning to the will of God.
       The fools, my juniors by a year,
220   Are tortured with suspense and fear;
     Who wisely thought my age a screen,
     When death approached, to stand between:
     The screen removed, their hearts are trembling;
     They mourn for me without dissembling.
225   My female friends, whose tender hearts
     Have better learned to act their parts,
     Receive the news in doleful dumps:
     "The Dean is dead (and what is trumps?)
     Then, Lord have mercy on his soul!
230   (Ladies, I'll venture for the vole.)[7]
     Six deans, they say, must bear the pall.
     (I wish I knew what king to call.)
     Madam, your husband will attend
     The funeral of so good a friend?"
235   "No, madam, 'tis a shocking sight;
     And he's engaged tomorrow night:
     My Lady Club would take it ill,
     If he should fail her at quadrille.
     He loved the Dean—(I lead a heart)
240   But dearest friends; they say, must part.
     His time was come; he ran his race;
     We hope he's in a better place."
       Why do we grieve that friends should die?
     No loss more easy to supply.
245   One year is past; a different scene!
     No further mention of the Dean,
     Who now, alas! no more is missed,
     Than if he never did exist.
     Where's now this favorite of Apollo?[8]
250   Departed—and his works must follow,
     Must undergo the common fate;
     His kind of wit is out of date.
       Some country squire to Lintot[9] goes,
     Inquires for Swift in verse and prose.
255   Says Lintot, "I have heard the name;
     He died a year ago."—"The same."
     He searches all the shop in vain.
     "Sir, you may find them in Duck Lane.[1]
     I sent them, with a load of books,
260   Last Monday to the pastry-cook's[2]

---

5. I.e., how can hard-heartedness dissolve in persons who have never felt pity?
6. Humbly accept chastisement; kissing a monarch's scepter was a gesture of submission to authority.
7. I.e., the female speaker will bid for all the tricks in the popular card game quadrille.

8. Greek and Roman sun god and patron of poets.
9. Bernard Lintot, the London publisher of some of Pope's and Gay's works.
1. "A place in London where old [i.e., secondhand and remaindered] books are sold" [Swift's note].
2. I.e., to be used as wastepaper for wrapping parcels and lining baking dishes.

To fancy they could live a year!
I find you're but a stranger here.
The Dean was famous in his time,
And had a kind of knack at rhyme.
265 His way of writing now is past:
The town has got a better taste.
I keep no antiquated stuff;
But spick and span I have enough.
Pray do but give me leave to show 'em:
270 Here's Colley Cibber's birthday poem.[3]
This ode you never yet have seen.
By Stephen Duck[4] upon the Queen.
Then here's a letter finely penned.
Against the *Craftsman*[5] and his friend;
275 It clearly shows that all reflection
On ministers is disaffection.
Next, here's Sir Robert's vindication,[6]
And Mr. Henley's last oration.[7]
The hawkers° have not got them yet: street sellers
280 Your honor please to buy a set?
        "Here's Woolston's tracts,[8] the twelfth edition;
'Tis read by every politician:
The country members,° when in town,   members of Parliament
To all their boroughs° send them down;   districts
285 You never met a thing so smart;
The courtiers have them all by heart,
Those maids of honor (who can read)
Are taught to use them for their creed
The reverend author's good intention
290 Has been rewarded with a pension.
He does an honor to his gown,
By brayely running priestcraft down;
He shows, as sure as God's in Gloucester,[9]
That Jesus was a grand impostor;
295 That all his miracles were cheats,
Performed as jugglers do their feats:
The Church had never such a writer;
A shame he has not got a miter!"°   bishop's hat
        Suppose me dead; and then suppose

3. Cibber, appointed poet laureate in 1730 for political rather than artistic reasons, fulfilled the laureate's duty of writing a poem every year for the monarch's birthday.
4. Agricultural laborer (1705–1756), known as the "thresher poet"; his poetry brought him the notice and patronage of Queen Caroline. Swift mocked him in On Stephen Duck, the Thresher, and Favorite Poet, A Quibbling Epigram (1730).
5. A periodical written in opposition to Walpole from 1726 onwards; the title defines Walpole as a man of "craft" in the sense of "deception"; see Swift's note to line 194.
6. "Walpole hires a set of party scribblers, who do nothing else but write in his defense" [Swift's note].
7. The Rev. John Henley (1692–1756), "lacking both merit and luck to get preferment [advance-

ment] in the established Church" of England, set up a pulpit, or "oratory," of his own, where, "at set times, he delivereth strange speeches, compiled by himself and his associates. . . . He is an absolute dunce, but generally reputed crazy" [Swift's note].
8. "Woolston was a clergyman, but for want of bread, hath in several treatises, in the most blasphemous manner, attempted to turn our Savior and his miracles into ridicule. He is much caressed by many great courtiers, and by all the infidels, and his books read generally by the Court ladies" [Swift's note]. Swift is probably referring to Thomas Woolston (1670–1733), a freethinker who gained notoriety with his Discourses on the Miracles of our Savior.
9. Before the Reformation, Gloucestershire had been rich in monasteries, and hence was proverbially God's home.

300   A club assembled at the Rose;[1]
        Where, from discourse of this and that
        I grow the subject of their chat.
        And while they toss my name about,
        With favor some, and some without,
305   One, quite indifferent in the cause,
        My character impartial° draws: *impartially, without bias*
        "The Dean, if we believe report,
        Was never ill received at court.
        As for his works in verse and prose,
310   I own myself no judge of those;
        Nor can I tell what critics thought 'em,
        But this I know, all people bought 'em,
        As with a moral view designed
        To cure the vices of mankind.
315   "His vein, ironically grave,
        Exposed the fool and lashed the knave,
        To steal a hint was never known,
        But what he writ was all his own.[2]
        "He never thought an honor done him,
320   Because a duke was proud to own him,
        Would rather slip aside and choose
        To talk with wits in dirty shoes;
        Despised the fools with stars and garters,[3]
        So often seen caressing Chartres.[4]
325   He never courted men in station,
        Nor persons held in admiration;
        Of no man's greatness was afraid,
        Because he sought for no man's aid.
        Though trusted long in great affairs,
330   He gave himself no haughty airs;
        Without regarding private ends,
        Spent all his credit for his friends;
        And only chose the wise and, good;
        No flatterers, no allies in blood;
335   But succored° virtue in distress,   *aided*
        And seldom failed of good success;
        As numbers in their hearts must own°   *acknowledge*
        Who, but for him, had been unknown.
        "With princes kept a due decorum,
340   But never stood in awe before 'em.[5]
        He followed David's lesson just:
        In princes never put thy trust:[6]

1. A fashionable tavern popular with playgoers because it was near the Drury Lane Theater.
2. An ironic line, since Swift praises his own originality with a line stolen from Sir John Denham's elegy for another poet, Abraham Cowley (1618–1667; see pp. 470–72): "To him no author was unknown / Yet what he wrote was all his own."
3. Stars and garters were symbols of knighthood and other high honor. Garters were worn by the members of the chivalric order called the Knights of the Garter, membership in which allowed a man to put *Sir* before his name.

4. See the note to line 189.
5. Two early copies of Swift's poem insert the following lines after line 340, presumably from manuscripts containing some of Swift's corrections to the much revised text (see note 6, p. 577): "And to her majesty, God bless her, / Would speak as free as to her dresser, / She thought it his peculiar whim, / Nor took it ill as come from him." The reference is to Queen Caroline and Lady Suffolk, her "dresser."
6. Cf. Psalm 146.3. David, the second king of Israel, is the biblical Psalmist.

And would you make him truly sour,
Provoke him with a slave in power.
345 The Irish senate if you named,
With what impatience he declaimed!
Fair Liberty was all his cry.
For her he stood prepared to die;
For her he boldly stood alone;
350 For her he oft exposed his own.
Two kingdoms, just as faction led,
Had set a price upon his head,
But not a traitor could be found,
To sell him for six hundred pound.[7]
355   "Had he but spared his tongue and pen,
He might have rose like other men;
But power was never in his thought,
And wealth he valued not a groat:[8]
Ingratitude he often found,
360 And pitied those who meant the wound;
But kept the tenor° of his mind,   usual course
To merit well of human kind:
Nor made a sacrifice of those
Who still° were true, to please his foes.   always
365 He labored many a fruitless hour,
To reconcile his friends in power;
Saw mischief by a faction brewing,
While they pursued each other's ruin.
But finding vain was all his care,
370 He left the court in mere° despair.[9]   complete
    "And, oh! how short are human schemes!
Here ended all our golden dreams.
What St. John's skill in state affairs,
What Ormonde's[1] valor, Oxford's cares,
375 To save their sinking country lent,
Was all destroyed by one event.[2]
Too soon that precious life was ended,
On which alone our weal° depended   well-being
When up a dangerous faction starts,[3]

7. Two "proclamations," one from the queen in 1713, one from Lord Carteret, a member of the queen's party, in 1724, offered rewards of £300 to anyone who could "discover the author" of, respectively, *The Public Spirit of the Whigs* and *The Drapier's Fourth Letter* [for the latter, see note to line 168]; in neither case "was the Dean discovered" [Swift's note].
8. English coin from 1351 until 1662; the equivalent of four pence.
9. In the last months of Queen Anne's life, her Tory "Ministry fell to variance [into dispute]. . . . [Simon] Harcourt the Chancellor, and Lord Bolingbroke the Secretary, were discontented with the Treasurer [Robert Harley, earl of] Oxford, for his too much mildness to the Whig Party. . . . The Dean, who was the only person who endeavored to reconcile them, found it impossible, and

thereupon returned to his Deanery in Dublin, where for many years he was worried by the new people in power" [Swift's note].
1. James Butler, duke of Ormonde, who succeeded to the command of the English armies on the Continent when the duke of Marlborough was stripped of his offices by Anne, in 1711. He went into exile in 1714 and was active in Jacobite political intrigues, i.e., efforts to return the Stuart monarchy to the throne. For Bolingbroke and Oxford, see previous note.
2. "In the height of the quarrel between the ministers, the Queen [Anne] died" [Swift's note].
3. After Anne's death, the opposing party, the Whigs, came to power, "which they exercised with the utmost rage and revenge" [Swift's note]. Swift feared for his own safety and considered emigrating to one of the Channel Islands.

380   With wrath and vengeance in their hearts;
       By solemn League and Covenant bound,[4]
       To ruin, slaughter, and confound;
       To turn religion to a fable,
       And make the government a Babel;
385   Pervert the laws, disgrace the gown,
       Corrupt the senate, rob the crown;
       To sacrifice old England's glory,
       And make her infamous in story:
       When such a tempest shook the land,
390   How could unguarded Virtue stand?
       With horror, grief, despair, the Dean
       Beheld the dire destructive scene:
       His friends in exile, or the Tower,[5]
       Himself within the frown of power,
395   Pursued by base envenomed pens,[6]
       Far to the land of slaves and fens;[7]
       A servile race in folly nursed,
       Who truckle° most, when treated worst.   *cringe obsequiously*
       "By innocence and resolution,
400   He bore continual persecution;
       While numbers to preferment rose,
       Whose merits were to be his foes;
       When even his own familiar friends,
       Intent upon their private ends,
405   Like renegadoes now he feels,
       Against him lifting up their heels.[8]
       "The Dean did, by his pen, defeat
       An infamous destructive cheat;[9]
       Taught fools their interest how to know,
410   And gave them arms to ward° the blow.   *ward off*
       Envy has owned it was his doing,
       To save that hapless land from ruin;
       While they who at the steerage[1] stood,
       And reaped the profit, sought his blood.
415   "To save them from their evil fate,
       In him was held a crime of state.
       A wicked monster on the bench,[2]
       Whose fury blood could never quench;
       As vile and profligate a villain,

4. A reference to the establishment of Scottish Presbyterianism, in 1643; as an Anglican, Swift deplored this development.
5. Bolingbroke was in exile; the Whigs sent Oxford to the Tower of London, where suspected traitors were imprisoned.
6. "Upon the Queen's death, the Dean returned to live in Dublin. . . . Numberless libels were writ against him England, as a Jacobite; he was insulted in the street" [Swift's note].
7. Ireland; *fens:* wetlands.
8. Cf. Psalm 41.9: "Yea, mine own familiar friend, in whom I trusted, which did eat of my bread, hath lifted up his heel against me."
9. A reference to the scheme to introduce Wood's

copper halfpence into Ireland in 1723–24. See note to line 168.
1. The helm for steering a ship or, metaphorically, public affairs in Ireland.
2. William Whitshed, lord chief justice of the King's Bench of Ireland. In 1720, when the jury refused to find Swift's anonymous pamphlet *Proposal for the Universal Use of Irish Manufacture* wicked and seditious, Whitshed sent them back nine times hoping to force them to another verdict. Swift further notes that Whitshed "sat as a Judge afterwards on the trial of the printer of the Drapier's Fourth Letter [by Swift; see note to line 168] but the Jury, against all he could say or swear, threw out the bill."

420 As modern Scroggs, or old Tresilian;[3]
Who long all justice had discarded,
Nor feared he God, nor man regarded;[4]
Vowed on the Dean his rage to vent,
And make him of his zeal repent:
425 But Heaven his innocence defends,
The grateful people stand his friends;
Not strains of law, nor judge's frown,
Nor topics° brought to please the crown,   *charges*
Nor witness hired, nor jury picked,
430 Prevail to bring him in convict.
    "In exile,[5] with a steady heart,
He spent his life's declining part;
Where folly, pride, and faction sway,
Remote from St. John, Pope, and Gay.
435 "His friendships there, to few confined,
Were always of the middling kind;[6]
No fools of rank, a mongrel breed,
Who fain would pass for lords indeed:
Where titles give no right or power,
440 And peerage is a withered flower;[7]
He would have held it a disgrace,
If such a wretch had known his face.
On rural squires, that kingdom's bane,
He vented oft his wrath in vain;
445 Biennial squires[8] to market brought:
Who sell their souls, and votes for naught;
The nation stripped, go joyful back,
To rob the church, their tenants rack,°   *torture by excessive rent*
Go snacks with rogues and rapparees;[9]
450 And keep the peace[1] to pick up fees;
In every job to have a share,
A jail or barrack to repair;
And turn the tax for public roads,
Commodious to their own abodes.[2]
455   "Perhaps I may allow the Dean
Had too much satire in his vein;
And seemed determined not to starve it,

3. Sir William "Scroggs was Chief Justice under King Charles the Second: his judgment always varied in State trials, according to directions from the [royal] Court." Scroggs was impeached for his misdemeanors in office in 1680. Sir Robert "Tresilian was a wicked Judge, hanged above three hundred years ago [impeached in 1381 and hanged in 1387]" [Swift's note].
4. Cf. Luke 18.2: "There was in a city a judge, which feared not God, neither regarded man."
5. "In Ireland, which he had reason to call a place of exile; to which country nothing could have driven him, but the Queen's death, who had determined to fix him to England" [Swift's note].
6. "The Dean was not acquainted with one single Lord spiritual or temporal. He only conversed with private gentlemen of the clergy or laity, and but a small number of either" [Swift's note; not entirely true].

7. "The peers of Ireland lost a great part of their jurisdiction by one single Act [of 1720] and tamely submitted to this infamous mark of slavery without the least resentment, or remonstrance" [Swift's note].
8. "The Parliament . . . in Ireland meet but once in two years; and after giving five times more than they can afford, return home to reimburse themselves by all country jobs and oppression, of which some few only are here mentioned" [Swift's note].
9. "The highwaymen in Ireland are . . . usually called rapparees, which was a name given to those Irish soldiers who in small parties used . . . to plunder the Protestants" [Swift's note].
1. Act as magistrates.
2. Make the new public turnpike roads more convenient for themselves by having them cross near their homes.

Because no age could more deserve it.
Yet malice never was his aim;
460   He lashed the vice, but spared the name;[3]
No individual could resent,
Where thousands equally were meant;
His satire points at no defect,
But what all mortals may correct;
465   For he abhorred that senseless tribe
Who call it humor when they gibe:
He spared a hump, or crooked nose,
Whose owners set not up for beaux.
True genuine dullness moved his pity,
470   Unless it offered to be witty.
Those who their ignorance confessed,
He ne'er offended with a jest;
But laughed to hear an idiot quote
A verse from Horace[4] learned by rote.
475   "He knew an hundred pleasant stories,
With all the turns of Whigs and Tories:
Was cheerful to his dying day;
And friends would let him have his way.
   "He gave the little wealth he had
480   To build a house for fools and mad;[5]
And showed by one satiric touch,
No nation wanted it so much.
That kingdom he hath left his debtor,
I wish it soon may have a better."

1731–32   1739

ISAAC WATTS
1674–1748

The Day of Judgment

An Ode Attempted in English Sapphic[1]

When the fierce north wind with his airy forces
Rears up the Baltic to a foaming fury,
And the red lightning with a storm of hail comes
          Rushing amain° down,   *violently*

5   How the poor sailors stand amazed and tremble,
While the hoarse thunder, like a bloody trumpet,

---

3. An ironic disclaimer, as this poem shows.
4. Roman poet and satirist (65–8 B.C.E.).
5. Swift's will left a substantial sum for the construction of a mental hospital, the first in Ireland, which was opened in 1757 as St. Patrick's

Hospital.
1. A poetic form consisting of quatrains utilizing a meter derived from the ancient Greek poet Sappho.

Roars a loud onset° to the gaping waters,   *assault*
        Quick to devour them!

   Such shall the noise be and the wild disorder,
10 (If things eternal may be like these earthly)
   Such the dire terror, when the great Archangel
        Shakes the creation,

   Tears the strong pillars of the vault of heaven,
   Breaks up old marble, the repose of princes;
15 See the graves open, and the bones arising,
        Flames all around 'em!

   Hark, the shrill outcries of the guilty wretches!
   Lively bright horror and amazing anguish
   Stare through their eyelids, while the living worm lies[2]
20   Gnawing within them.

   Thoughts like old vultures prey upon their heart-strings,
   And the smart° twinges,° when the eye beholds the   *sharp / pains*
   Lofty Judge frowning, and a flood of vengeance
        Rolling afore him.

25 Hopeless immortals! how they scream and shiver,
   While devils push them to the pit wide-yawning
   Hideous and gloomy, to receive them headlong
        Down to the center.[3]

   Stop here, my fancy: (all away ye horrid
30 Doleful° ideas); come, arise to Jesus;   *gloomy*
   How He sits God-like! and the saints around him
        Throned, yet adoring!

   Oh may I sit there when he comes triumphant
   Dooming the nations! then ascend to glory
35 While our hosannas[4] all along the passage
        Shout the Redeemer.

                                                            1706

A Prospect of Heaven Makes Death Easy

   There is a land of pure delight
      Where saints immortal reign;
   Infinite day excludes the night,
      And pleasures banish pain.

---

2. In Mark 9.44, Christ describes hell as a place "where their worm dieth not."
3. At the Last Judgment, Christ will judge "all the nations," separating the believers from the unbe-
lievers, casting the unbelievers into hell ("the pit"), and inviting believers to inherit the kingdom of heaven (Matthew 25.31–41).
4. Expressions of great praise.

5 There everlasting spring abides,
  And never-withering flowers;
 Death like a narrow sea divides
  This heavenly land from ours.

 Sweet fields beyond the swelling flood
10 Stand dressed in living green:
 So to the Jews old Canaan stood,
  While Jordan rolled between.[5]

 But timorous° mortals start° and shrink   *fearful / recoil*
  To cross this narrow sea,
15 And linger shivering on the brink,
  And fear to launch away.

 Oh could we make our doubts remove,°   *withdraw*
  These gloomy doubts that rise,
 And see the Canaan that we love,
20 With unbeclouded eyes;

 Could we but climb where Moses stood
  And view the landscape o'er,[6]
 Not Jordan's stream, nor death's cold flood,
  Should fright us from the shore.

1707

Our God, Our Help[7]

 Our God, our help in ages past,
  Our hope for years to come,
 Our shelter from the stormy blast,
  And our eternal home:

5 Under the shadow of thy throne
  Thy saints have dwelt secure;
 Sufficient is thine arm alone,
  And our defense is sure.

 Before the hills in order stood
10 Or earth received her frame,°   *shape, structure*
 From everlasting thou art God,
  To endless years the same.

 Thy word commands our flesh to dust,
  "Return, ye sons of men";[8]

5. Canaan was the land, "flowing with milk and honey" (Joshua 5.6), promised to the Israelites after their forty years of wandering in the wilderness. To reach it they had to cross the Jordan River.
6. Moses was allowed to ascend Mt. Nebo to see the promised land, but was not allowed to enter Canaan because of his sins (Deuteronomy 34.1–4).

7. Originally titled "Man Frail and God Eternal," this hymn derives from Psalm 90.
8. From Psalm 90.3; God's curse after the sin of Adam and Eve: "In the sweat of thy face shalt thou eat bread, till thou return unto the ground; for out of it was thou taken: for dust thou art, and unto dust shalt thou return" (Genesis 3.19).

15   All nations rose from earth at first,
      And turn to earth again.

    A thousand ages in thy sight
      Are like an evening gone;
    Short as the watch[9] that ends the night
20   Before the rising sun.

    The busy tribes of flesh and blood,
      With all their lives and cares,
    Are carried downwards by thy flood,
      And lost in following years.

25   Time, like an ever-rolling stream,
      Bears all its sons away;
    They fly forgotten, as a dream
      Dies at the opening day.

    Like flowery fields the nations stand,
30   Pleased with the morning light;
    The flowers beneath the mower's hand
      Lie withering e'er 'tis night.

    Our God, our help in ages past,
      Our hope for years to come,
35   Be thou our guard while troubles last,
      And our eternal home.

                               1719

Psalm 58

Warning to Magistrates[1]

Judges, who rule the world by laws,
Will ye despise the righteous cause,
    When th'injur'd poor before you stands?
Dare ye condemn the righteous poor,
5   And let rich sinners 'scape secure,
    While gold and greatness bribe your hands?

Have ye forgot or never knew
That God will judge the judges too?
    High in the Heavens his justice reigns;
10   Yet you invade the rights of God,
And send your bold decrees abroad
    To bind the conscience in your chains.

---

9. One of the three, four, or five periods into which the night was divided.

1. Cf. the versions of this Psalm and the next one by Mary Sidney (pp. 225–26), from *The Massachu-* setts *Bay Psalm Book* (pp. 391–93), and by Christopher Smart (pp. 684–86). All of Watts's versions of the Psalms have short, italicized narrative titles.

A poisoned arrow is your tongue,
The arrow sharp, the poison strong,
15   And death attends where e'er it wounds:
You hear no counsels, cries or tears;
So the deaf adder stops her ears
      Against the power of charming sounds.

Break out their teeth, eternal God,
20   Those teeth of lions dyed in blood;
      And crush the serpents in the dust:
As empty chaff,[2] when whirlwinds rise,
Before the sweeping tempest flies,
      So let their hopes and names be lost.

25   Th'Almighty thunders from the sky,
Their grandeur melts, their titles die,
      As hills of snow dissolve and run,
Or snails that perish in their slime,
Or births that come before their time,
30   Vain births, that never see the sun.

Thus shall the vengeance of the Lord
Safety and joy to saints afford;
      And all that hear shall join and say,
"Sure there's a God that rules on high,
35   "A God that hears his children cry,
      "And will their sufferings well repay."

1719

Psalm 114

Miracles Attending Israel's Journey

When Isr'el, freed from Pharaoh's hand,
Left the proud tyrant and his land,[3]
The tribes with cheerful homage own°   *acknowledge*
Their king; and Judah was his throne.[4]

5   Across the deep their journey lay;
The deep° divides to make them way.   *Red Sea*
Jordan[5] beheld their march, and led,
With backward current, to his head.

The mountains shook like frighted sheep,
10   Like lambs the little hillocks leap;

2. The husks of the grain separated by threshing or winnowing.
3. I.e., Egypt.
4. Originally (Genesis 29) the name of the fourth son of Jacob and Leah, Judah (which comes from the Hebrew word for praise) came to designate the southern portion of the Israelites' land.
5. River in Palestine that empties into the Dead Sea. For the river's miraculous turning back, see Joshua 3; for the Red Sea's splitting, see Exodus 14.

Not Sinai[6] on her base could stand,
Conscious of sov'reign pow'r at hand.

What pow'r could make the deep divide?
Make Jordan backward roll his tide?
15   Why did ye leap, ye little hills?
And whence the fright that Sinai feels?

Let ev'ry mountain, ev'ry flood,
Retire and know th' approaching God,
The King of Isr'el: see him here!
20   Tremble, thou earth, adore and fear.

He thunders, and all nature mourns;
The rock to standing pools he turns,
Flints spring with fountains at his word,
And fires and seas confess the Lord.

1719

JOHN GAY
1685–1732

Songs from *The Beggar's Opera*[1]

Act I, Scene viii, Air X—"*Thomas, I Cannot*,"[2] etc.

Polly.	I like a ship in storms was tossed,
	Yet afraid to put into land,
	For seized in the port the vessel's lost
	Whose treasure is contraband.° *smuggled goods*
5	The waves are laid,
	My duty's° paid; *tax on imports*
	O joy beyond expression!
	Thus safe ashore
	I ask no more;
10	My all is in my possession.

6. Mt. Sinai, the mountain in a desert region south and west of modern-day Israel from which God, according to Exodus 20.1–20, gave the Ten Commandments to Moses. For the miraculous events associated with Sinai during the Israelites' journey out of Egypt, see Exodus 19.16–20.

1. *The Beggar's Opera* (1728) was the first ballad opera, a type of play in which the action, usually comic, is conveyed in prose interspersed with songs set to traditional or contemporary melodies (each set of lyrics here is sung to a preexisting tune). This opera is a satire of corrupt government, and its comic but realistic characters are the underclass of London. Polly, the daughter of Peacham (an informer and receiver of stolen goods),

marries the handsome highwayman, Macheath. Peacham informs against Macheath (both to collect the reward and to rid himself of an unwanted son-in-law). Lucy Lockit, the prison warder's daughter, whom Macheath had previously seduced and promised to marry, effects his escape. Macheath is recaptured and sentenced to hang, but through an absurd twist the play ends happily.

Because all the songs from *The Beggar's Opera* were published in 1728, we do not print the date for each.

2. A popular song, the tune to which these words are sung; Polly, having secretly married Macheath, has been first violently chided, then forgiven, by her parents.

Act I, Scene ix, Air XI—"A Soldier and a Sailor"[3]

A fox may steal your hens, sir,
A whore your health and pence,° sir,   *money*
Your daughter rob your chest, sir,
Your wife may steal your rest, sir,
5 A thief your goods and plate.
But this is all for picking,° *pilfering, petty thievery*
With rest, pence, chest and chicken;
It ever was decreed, sir,
If lawyer's hand is fee'd, sir,
10 He steals your whole estate.

Act I, Scene xiii, Air XVI—"Over the Hills, and Far Away"[4]

Mac. Were I laid on Greenland's coast,
    And in my arms embraced my lass,
    Warm amidst eternal frost,
    Too soon the half-year's night would pass.
5 Polly. Were I sold on Indian soil,
    Soon as the burning day was closed,
    I could mock the sultry toil
    When on my charmer's breast reposed.
Mac. And I would love you all the day,
10 Polly. Every night would kiss and play,
Mac. If with me you'd fondly stray
Polly. Over the hills, and far away.

Act II, Scene iv, Air IV—Cotillion[5]

Youth's the season made for joys,
  Love is then our duty:
She alone who that employs,
  Well deserves her beauty.
5   Let's be gay
   While we may,
Beauty's a flower despised in decay.

Chorus. Youth's the season, etc.

Let us drink and sport to-day,
10 Ours is not to-morrow:
Love with youth flies swift away,
  Age is naught but sorrow.
   Dance and sing,
   Time's on the wing,
15 Life never knows the return of spring.

Chorus. Let us drink, etc.

---

3. Sung by Polly's father, Peacham; Polly's parents worry that Macheath may have several wives, so that if he were to die, her inheritance of his property would come into dispute.
4. Polly fears that Macheath will be deported to a penal settlement; here, they sing about their desire not to be separated.
5. A dance of French origin; Macheath dances and sports with a group of women in a tavern.

Act II, Scene xv, Air XXII—"The Lass of Patie's Mill"[6]

Lucy.   I like the fox shall grieve,
            Whose mate hath left her side;
            Whom hounds, from morn to eve,
            Chase o'er the country wide.

5   Where can my lover hide?
            Where cheat the wary pack?
            If love be not his guide,
            He never will come back.

Act III, Scene xiii, Air XXVII—"Green Sleeves"[7]

Since laws were made, for every degree,
To curb vice in others, as well as me,
I wonder we han't better company
            Upon Tyburn tree.[8]
5   But gold from law can take out the sting;
And if rich men, like us, were to swing,
'Twould thin the land, such numbers to string
            Upon Tyburn tree.

1728

ALEXANDER POPE
1688–1744

From An Essay on Criticism

Part II

Of all the causes which conspire to blind
Man's erring judgment, and misguide the mind,
What the weak head with strongest bias rules,
Is pride, the never-failing vice of fools.
205 Whatever Nature has in worth denied,
She gives in large recruits° of needful pride;   supplies
For as in bodies, thus in souls, we find
What wants° in blood and spirits swelled with wind: lacks
Pride, where wit fails, steps in to our defense,
210 And fills up all the mighty void of sense.
If once right reason drives that cloud away,
Truth breaks upon us with resistless day.
Trust not yourself: but your defects to know,
Make use of every friend—and every foe.

---

6. Lucy has agreed to help Macheath escape, and he has promised to send for her when it is safe.
7. Macheath, recaptured and condemned to hang, sits in his jail cell, drinking and singing.
8. The gallows; Tyburn was a place of public execution in Middlesex until 1783.

215   A little learning is a dangerous thing;
Drink deep, or taste not the Pierian spring.[1]
There shallow draughts intoxicate the brain,
And drinking largely sobers us again.
Fired at first sight with what the Muse imparts,
220   In fearless youth we tempt° the heights of arts,   *attempt*
While from the bounded level of our mind
Short views we take, nor see the lengths behind;
But more advanced, behold with strange surprise
New distant scenes of endless science rise!
225   So pleased at first the towering Alps we try,
Mount o'er the vales,° and seem to tread the sky,   *valleys*
The eternal snows appear already past,
And the first clouds and mountains seem the last;
But, those attained, we tremble to survey
230   The growing labors of the lengthened way,
The increasing prospect tires our wandering eyes,
Hills peep o'er hills, and Alps on Alps arise!
      A perfect judge will read each work of wit
With the same spirit that its author writ:
235   Survey the whole, nor seek slight faults to find
Where Nature moves, and rapture warms the mind;
Nor lose, for that malignant dull delight,
The generous pleasure to be charmed with wit.
But in such lays as neither ebb nor flow,
240   Correctly cold, and regularly low,
That, shunning faults, one quiet tenor keep,
We cannot blame indeed—but we may sleep.
In wit, as nature, what affects our hearts
Is not the exactness of peculiar° parts;   *particular*
245   'Tis not a lip, or eye, we beauty call,
But the joint force and full result of all.
Thus when we view some well-proportioned dome
(The world's just wonder, and even thine, O Rome![2]),
No single parts unequally surprise,
250   All comes united to the admiring eyes:
No monstrous height, or breadth, or length appear;
The whole at once is bold and regular.
      Whoever thinks a faultless piece to see,
Thinks what ne'er was, nor is, nor e'er shall be.
255   In every work regard the writer's end,
Since none can compass more than they intend;
And if the means be just, the conduct true,
Applause, in spite of trivial faults, is due.
As men of breeding, sometimes men of wit,
260   To avoid great errors must the less commit,
Neglect the rules each verbal critic lays,
For not to know some trifles is a praise.

1. The spring in Pieria on Mt. Olympus, sacred to the Muses (in Greek mythology, nine sister goddesses who inspired song, poetry, and the arts and sciences).

2. Refers either to the dome of St. Peter's, i.e., the wonder *in* (Catholic) Rome; or to the dome of St. Paul's, in London, i.e., a wonder *to* Rome.

Most critics, fond of some subservient art,
Still make the whole depend upon a part:
265   They talk of principles, but notions prize,
And all to one loved folly sacrifice.
      Once on a time La Mancha's knight,[3] they say,
A certain bard encountering on the way,
Discoursed in terms as just, with looks as sage,
270   As e'er could Dennis,[4] of the Grecian stage;
Concluding all were desperate sots and fools
Who durst depart from Aristotle's rules.[5]
Our author, happy in a judge so nice,°   *overrefined*
Produced his play, and begged the knight's advice;
275   Made him observe the subject and the plot,
The manners, passions, unities; what not?
All which exact to rule were brought about,
Were but a combat in the lists° left out.   *arena*
"What! leave the combat out?" exclaims the knight.
280   "Yes, or we must renounce the Stagirite."[6]
"Not so, by Heaven!" he answers in a rage,
"Knights, squires, and steeds must enter on the stage."
"So vast a throng the stage can ne'er contain."
"Then build a new, or act it in a plain."
285   Thus critics of less judgment than caprice,
Curious,° not knowing, not exact, but nice,   *laboriously careful*
Form short ideas, and offend in arts
(As most in manners), by a love to parts.
      Some to conceit[7] alone their taste confine,
290   And glittering thoughts struck out at every line;
Pleased with a work where nothing's just or fit,
One glaring chaos and wild heap of wit.
Poets, like painters, thus unskilled to trace
The naked nature and the living grace,
295   With gold and jewels cover every part,
And hide with ornaments their want of art.
      True wit is Nature to advantage dressed,
What oft was thought, but ne'er so well expressed;
Something whose truth convinced at sight we find,
300   That gives us back the image of our mind.
As shades more sweetly recommend the light,
So modest plainness sets off sprightly wit;
For works may have more wit than does them good,
As bodies perish through excess of blood.
305   Others for language all their care express,
And value books, as women men, for dress.
Their praise is still°—the style is excellent;   *continually*
The sense they humbly take upon content.°   *mere acquiescence*

3. Don Quixote, hero of Cervantes's novel; but
this story comes from a spurious sequel to it, by
Don Alonzo Fernandez de Avellaneda.
4. John Dennis (1657–1734), an English critic.
5. Refers to the description of the purpose and
forms of tragic drama contained in Aristotle's
Poetics.

6. I.e., Aristotle, a native of Stagira. One of his
principles was that tragic drama should maintain
unity of time and place.
7. Pointed wit, ingenuity and extravagance, or
affectation in the use of figures, especially similes
and metaphors.

Words are like leaves; and where they most abound,
310   Much fruit of sense beneath is rarely found.
False eloquence, like the prismatic glass,
Its gaudy colors spreads on every place;
The face of Nature we no more survey,
All glares alike, without distinction gay.
315   But true expression, like the unchanging sun,
Clears and improves whate'er it shines upon;
It gilds all objects, but it alters none.
Expression is the dress of thought, and still
Appears more decent as more suitable.
320   A vile conceit in pompous words expressed
Is like a clown° in regal purple dressed: *peasant*
For different styles with different subjects sort,
As several garbs with country, town, and court.
Some by old words to fame have made pretense,
325   Ancients in phrase, mere moderns in their sense.
Such labored nothings, in so strange a style,
Amaze the unlearned, and make the learned smile;
Unlucky as Fungoso[8] in the play,
These sparks with awkward vanity display
330   What the fine gentleman wore yesterday;
And but so mimic ancient wits at best,
As apes our grandsires in their doublets[9] dressed.
In words as fashions the same rule will hold,
Alike fantastic if too new or old:
335   Be not the first by whom the new are tried,
Nor yet the last to lay the old aside.
     But most by numbers° judge a poet's song,   *versification*
And smooth or rough with them is right or wrong.
In the bright Muse though thousand charms conspire,
340   Her voice is all these tuneful fools admire,
Who haunt Parnassus[1] but to please their ear,
Not mend their minds; as some to church repair,
Not for the doctrine, but the music there.
These equal syllables alone require,
345   Though oft the ear the open vowels tire,
While expletives[2] their feeble aid do join,
And ten low words oft creep in one dull line:
While they ring round the same unvaried chimes,
With sure returns of still expected rhymes;
350   Where'er you find "the cooling western breeze,"
In the next line, it "whispers through the trees";
If crystal streams "with pleasing murmurs creep,"
The reader's threatened (not in vain) with "sleep";
Then, at the last and only couplet fraught
355   With some unmeaning thing they call a thought,
A needless Alexandrine[3] ends the song
That, like a wounded snake, drags its slow length along.

8. A character in Ben Jonson's comedy *Every Man out of His Humor* (1599).
9. Jackets in a style popular in the sixteenth and seventeenth centuries.
1. The mountain in Greece sacred to the Muses.

2. Words added to fill out lines—for example, "do" in this line.
3. A line in iambic hexameter—for example, the next line.

Leave such to tune their own dull rhymes, and know
What's roundly smooth or languishingly slow;
360 And praise the easy vigor of a line
Where Denham's strength and Waller's sweetness join.⁴
True ease in writing comes from art, not chance,
As those move easiest who have learned to dance.
'Tis not enough no harshness gives offense,
365 The sound must seem an echo to the sense.
Soft is the strain when Zephyr° gently blows,   *the west wind*
And the smooth stream in smoother numbers flows;
But when loud surges lash the sounding shore,
The hoarse, rough verse should like the torrent roar.
370 When Ajax⁵ strives some rock's vast weight to throw,
The line too labors, and the words move slow;
Not so when swift Camilla scours the plain,
Flies o'er the unbending corn, and skims along the main.
Hear how Timotheus'⁶ varied lays surprise,
375 And bid alternate passions fall and rise!
While at each change the son of Libyan Jove⁷
Now burns with glory, and then melts with love;
Now his fierce eyes with sparkling fury glow,
Now sighs steal out, and tears begin to flow:
380 Persians and Greeks like turns of nature⁸ found
And the world's victor stood subdued by sound!
The power of music all our hearts allow,
And what Timotheus was is Dryden now.
    Avoid extremes; and shun the fault of such
385 Who still are pleased too little or too much.
At every trifle scorn to take offense:
That always shows great pride, or little sense.
Those heads, as stomachs, are not sure the best,
Which nauseate° all, and nothing can digest.   *vomit*
390 Yet let not each gay turn thy rapture move;
For fools admire,° but men of sense approve:⁹   *wonder*
As things seem large which we through mists descry,°   *perceive*
Dullness is ever apt to magnify.
    Some foreign writers, some our own despise;
395 The ancients only, or the moderns prize.
Thus wit, like faith, by each man is applied
To one small sect, and all are damned beside.
Meanly they seek the blessing to confine,
And force that sun but on a part to shine,
400 Which not alone the southern wit sublimes,°   *raises, purifies*
But ripens spirits in cold northern climes;
Which from the first has shone on ages past,
Enlights the present, and shall warm the last;

4. John Dryden (1631–1700; see pp. 500–526),
whom Pope echoes here, considered Sir John Den-
ham (1615–1669) and Edmund Waller (1606–
1687; see pp. 393–94) the principal shapers of the
closed pentameter couplet. He distinguished
between Denham's "strength" and Waller's "sweet-
ness."
5. The strongest, though not the most intelligent,

of the Greek warriors in the war with Troy. He is
contrasted with Camilla, a swift-footed messenger
of the moon goddess, Diana.
6. The musician in Dryden's "Alexander's Feast."
7. *The . . . Jove:* Alexander the Great.
8. Comparable alternations of feelings.
9. I.e., only after due deliberation.

Though each may feel increases and decays,
405 And see now clearer and now darker days.
Regard not then if wit be old or new,
But blame the false and value still the true.
　　Some ne'er advance a judgment of their own,
But catch the spreading notion of the town;
410 They reason and conclude by precedent,
And own° stale nonsense which they ne'er invent.　　　　*claim as theirs*
Some judge of authors' names, not works, and then
Nor praise nor blame the writings, but the men.
Of all this servile herd the worst is he
415 That in proud dullness joins with quality,
A constant critic at the great man's board,°　　　　　　*table*
To fetch and carry nonsense for my lord.
What woeful stuff this madrigal would be
In some starved hackney° sonneteer or me!　　　　　*for-hire*
420 But let a lord once own° the happy lines,　　　*acknowledge as his*
How the wit brightens! how the style refines!
Before his sacred name flies every fault,
And each exalted stanza teems with thought!
　　The vulgar thus through imitation err;
425 As oft the learn'd by being singular;°　　　　　　　*peculiar*
So much they scorn the crowd, that if the throng
By chance go right, they purposely go wrong.
So schìsmatics¹ the plain believers quit,
And are but damned for having too much wit.
430 Some praise at morning what they blame at night,
But always think the last opinion right.
A Muse by these is like a mistress used,
This hour she's idolized, the next abused;
While their weak heads like towns unfortified,
435 'Twixt sense and nonsense daily change their side.
Ask them the cause; they're wiser still, they say;
And still tomorrow's wiser than today.
We think our fathers fools, so wise we grow;
Our wiser sons, no doubt, will think us so.
440 Once school divines² this zealous isle o'erspread;
Who knew most sentences³ was deepest read.
Faith, Gospel, all seemed made to be disputed,
And none had sense enough to be confuted.
Scotists and Thomists now in peace remain
445 Amidst their kindred cobwebs in Duck Lane.⁴
If faith itself has different dresses worn,
What wonder modes in wit should take their turn?
Oft, leaving what is natural and fit,
The current folly proves the ready wit;
450 And authors think their reputation safe,
Which lives as long as fools are pleased to laugh.

1. Those who divide the church on points of
theology.
2. Scholastic philosophers such as the Scotists
and Thomists (followers of the medieval theologi-
ans Duns Scotus and St. Thomas Aquinas) men-
tioned below.
3. Alludes to Peter Lombard's *Book of Sentences,*
a twelfth-century theological work.
4. A place in London where secondhand and
remaindered books were sold.

Some valuing those of their own side or mind,
Still make themselves the measure of mankind:
Fondly° we think we honor merit then,   foolishly
455 When we but praise ourselves in other men.
Parties in wit attend on those of state,
And public faction doubles private hate.
Pride, Malice, Folly against Dryden rose,
In various shapes of parsons, critics, beaux;
460 But sense survived, when merry jests were past;
For rising merit will buoy up at last.
Might he return and bless once more our eyes,
New Blackmores and new Milbourns must arise.[5]
Nay, should great Homer lift his awful head,
465 Zoilus[6] again would start up from the dead.
Envy will merit, as its shade,° pursue,   ghost
But like a shadow, proves the substance true;
For envied wit, like Sol° eclipsed, makes known   the sun
The opposing body's grossness, not its own.
470 When first that sun too powerful beams displays,
It draws up vapors which obscure its rays;
But even those clouds at last adorn its way,
Reflect new glories, and augment the day.
Be thou the first true merit to befriend;
475 His praise is lost who stays till all commend.
Short is the date, alas! of modern rhymes,
And 'tis but just to let them live betimes.°   early
No longer now that golden age appears,
When patriarch wits survived a thousand years:
480 Now length of fame (our second life) is lost,
And bare threescore is all even that can boast;
Our sons their fathers' failing language see,
And such as Chaucer is shall Dryden be.
So when the faithful pencil has designed
485 Some bright idea of the master's mind,
Where a new world leaps out at his command,
And ready Nature waits upon his hand;
When the ripe colors soften and unite,
And sweetly melt into just shade and light;
490 When mellowing years their full perfection give,
And each bold figure just begins to live,
The treacherous colors the fair art betray,
And all the bright creation fades away!
Unhappy wit, like most mistaken° things,   misunderstood
495 Atones not for that envy which it brings.
In youth alone its empty praise we boast,
But soon the short-lived vanity is lost;
Like some fair flower the early spring supplies,
That gaily blooms, but even in blooming dies,
500 What is this wit, which must our cares employ?

5. Sir Richard Blackmore (1650–1729), physician
and poet, had attacked Dryden for the immorality
of his plays; the Rev. Luke Milbourne (1649–
1720) had attacked his translation of Virgil.
6. A Greek critic of the fourth century B.C.E., who
wrote a book of carping criticism of Homer.

The owner's wife, that other men enjoy;
Then most our trouble still when most admired,
And still the more we give, the more required;
Whose fame with pains we guard, but lose with ease,
505   Sure some to vex, but never all to please;
'Tis what the vicious fear, the virtuous shun,
By fools 'tis hated, and by knaves undone!
    If wit so much from ignorance undergo,
Ah, let not learning too commence its foe!
510   Of old those met rewards who could excel,
And such were praised who but endeavored well;
Though triumphs were to generals only due,
Crowns were reserved to grace the soldiers too.
Now they who reach Parnassus' lofty crown
515   Employ their pains to spurn some others down;
And while self-love each jealous writer rules,
Contending wits become the sport of fools;
But still the worst with most regret commend,
For each ill author is as bad a friend.
520   To what base ends, and by what abject ways,
Are morals urged through sacred° lust of praise!   *accursed*
Ah, ne'er so dire a thirst of glory boast,
Nor in the critic let the man be lost!
Good nature and good sense must ever join;
525   To err is human, to forgive divine.
    But if in the noble minds some dregs remain
Nor yet purged off, spleen and sour disdain,
Discharge that rage on more provoking crimes,
Nor fear a dearth in these flagitious° times.   *shameful, wicked*
530   No pardon vile obscenity should find,
Though wit and art conspire to move your mind;
But dullness with obscenity must prove
As shameful sure as impotence in love.
In the fat age of pleasure, wealth, and ease
535   Sprung the rank weed, and thrived with large increase:
When love was all an easy monarch's[7] care,
Seldom at council, never in a war;
Jilts° ruled the state, and statesmen farces writ;   *king's mistresses*
Nay, wits had pensions, and young lords had wit;
540   The fair sat panting at a courtier's play,
And not a mask[8] went unimproved away;
The modest fan was lifted up no more,
And virgins smiled at what they blushed before.
The following license of a foreign reign[9]
545   Did all the dregs of bold Socinus[1] drain;
Then unbelieving priests reformed the nation,
And taught more pleasant methods of salvation;
Where Heaven's free subjects might their rights dispute,

---

7. Charles II, king of England from 1660 to 1685. The following lines describe the corruption of morals and letters under this recently dead monarch.
8. A woman in a mask, as at a masquerade.

9. That of William III, king of England from 1689 to 1702. He was born in Holland.
1. The name of two sixteenth-century Italian theologians who denied the divinity of Jesus.

Lest God himself should seem too absolute;
550 Pulpits their sacred satire learned to spare,
And Vice admired to find a flatterer there!
Encouraged thus, wit's Titans[2] braved the skies,
And the press groaned with licensed blasphemies.
These monsters, critics! with your darts engage,
555 Here point your thunder, and exhaust your rage!
Yet shun their fault, who, scandalously nice,°   overrefined
Will needs mistake[3] an author into vice;
All seems infected that the infected spy,
As all looks yellow to the jaundiced eye.

1709   1711

The Rape of the Lock

An Heroi-Comical Poem in Five Cantos[4]

*Nolueram, Belinda, tuos violare capillos; sed juvat hoc precibus me
tribuisse tuis.*[5]

—MARTIAL

CANTO I

What dire offense from amorous causes springs,
What mighty contests rise from trivial things,
I sing—This verse to Caryll, Muse! is due:
This, even Belinda may vouchsafe to view:
5 Slight is the subject, but not so the praise,
If she inspire, and he approve my lays.°   songs
     Say what strange motive, Goddess! could compel
A well-bred lord to assault a gentle belle?
Oh, say what stranger cause, yet unexplored,
10 Could make a gentle belle reject a lord?
In tasks so bold can little men engage,
And in soft bosoms dwells such mighty rage?
     Sol° through white curtains shot a timorous ray,   the sun
And oped those eyes that must eclipse the day.[6]
15 Now lapdogs give themselves the rousing shake,
And sleepless lovers just at twelve awake:
Thrice rung the bell, the slipper knocked the ground,[7]

2. Primordial giants, whose rule over Earth was
broken by the Olympian gods.
3. I.e., give a wrong meaning to (an author's writ-
ings).
4. Based on an actual incident. A young man,
Lord Petre, had sportively cut off a lock of a Miss
Arabella Fermor's hair. She and her family were
angered by the prank, and Pope's friend John
Caryll (line 3), a relative of Lord Petre's, asked the
poet to turn the incident into jest, so that good
relations (and possibly negotiations toward a mar-
riage between the principals) might be resumed.
Pope responded by treating the incident in a mock
epic, or "heroi-comical poem." The epic conven-
tions first encountered are the immediate state-

ment of the topic, which the poet says he will
"sing" as if in oral recitation, and the request to the
Muse (line 7) to grant him the necessary insight.
In Greek mythology, the Muses were nine sister
goddesses who presided over poetry, song, and the
arts and sciences.
5. I did not want, Belinda, to violate your locks,
but it pleases me to have paid this tribute to your
prayers (Latin); from the ancient Roman poet Mar-
cus Valerius Martialis. Miss Fermor did not in fact
request the poem.
6. The eyes of lovely young women—though
Belinda is still asleep.
7. These are two ways of summoning servants.

And the pressed watch returned a silver sound.[8]
Belinda still her downy pillow pressed,
20 Her guardian Sylph[9] prolonged the balmy rest:
'Twas he had summoned to her silent bed
The morning dream that hovered o'er her head.
A youth more glittering than a birthnight beau[1]
(That even in slumber caused her cheek to glow)
25 Seemed to her ear his winning lips to lay,
And thus in whispers said, or seemed to say:
    "Fairest of mortals, thou distinguished care°   object of care
Of thousand bright inhabitants of air!
If e'er one vision touched thy infant thought,
30 Of all the nurse and all the priest have taught,
Of airy elves by moonlight shadows seen,
The silver token, and the circled green,[2]
Or virgins visited by angel powers,
With golden crowns and wreaths of heavenly flowers,
35 Hear and believe! thy own importance know,
Nor bound thy narrow views to things below.
Some secret truths, from learned pride concealed,
To maids alone and children are revealed:
What though no credit doubting wits may give?
40 The fair and innocent shall still believe.
Know, then, unnumbered spirits round thee fly,
The light militia of the lower sky:
These, though unseen, are ever on the wing,
Hang o'er the box, and hover round the Ring.[3]
45 Think what an equipage thou hast in air,
And view with scorn two pages and a chair.°   sedan chair
As now your own, our beings were of old,
And once enclosed in woman's beauteous mold;
Thence, by a soft transition, we repair
50 From earthly vehicles[4] to these of air.
Think not, when woman's transient breath is fled,
That all her vanities at once are dead:
Succeeding vanities she still regards,
And though she plays no more, o'erlooks the cards.
55 Her joy in gilded chariots,° when alive,   carriages
And love of ombre,[5] after death survive.
For when the Fair in all their pride expire,
To their first elements their souls retire:[6]

8. In a darkened bed, one discovered the approximate time by a watch that chimed the hour and quarter-hour when the stem was pressed.
9. Air spirit. He accounts for himself in the lines below.
1. Courtier dressed for a royal birthday celebration.
2. The silver token is the coin left by a fairy or elf, and the circled green is a ring of bright green grass, supposed dancing circle of fairies.
3. The box is a theater box; the Ring, the circular carriage course in Hyde Park.
4. Mediums of existence, with a side glance at the fondness of young women for riding in carriages.
5. A popular card game, pronounced *omber*. See

note 9, p. 611.
6. Namely, to fire, water, earth, and air, the four elements of the old cosmology and the several habitats (in the Rosicrucian myths upon which Pope embroiders) of four different kinds of "spirit." Envisaging these spirits as the transmigrated souls of different kinds of women, Pope causes termagants (scolds) to become fire spirits, or Salamanders (line 60); irresolute women to become water spirits, or Nymphs (line 62); prudes, or women who delight in rejection and negation, to become earth spirits, or Gnomes (line 63); and coquettes to become air spirits, or Sylphs (line 65). Since "nymph" could designate either a water spirit or (in literary usage) a young lady, Pope permits his water

The sprites of fiery termagants in flame
60   Mount up, and take a Salamander's name.
Soft yielding minds to water glide away,
And sip, with Nymphs, their elemental tea.
The graver prude sinks downward to a Gnome,
In search of mischief still on earth to roam.
65   The light coquettes in Sylphs aloft repair,
And sport and flutter in the fields of air.
    "Know further yet; whoever fair and chaste
Rejects mankind, is by some Sylph embraced:
For spirits, freed from mortal laws, with ease
70   Assume what sexes and what shapes they please.[7]
What guards the purity of melting maids,
In courtly balls, and midnight masquerades,
Safe from the treacherous friend, the daring spark,
The glance by day, the whisper in the dark,
75   When kind occasion prompts their warm desires,
When music softens, and when dancing fires?
'Tis but their Sylph, the wise Celestials know,
Though Honor is the word with men below.
    "Some nymphs there are, too conscious of their face,
80   For life predestined to the Gnomes' embrace.
These swell their prospects and exalt their pride,
When offers are disdained, and love denied:
Then gay ideas crowd the vacant brain,
While peers, and dukes, and all their sweeping train,
85   And garters, stars, and coronets[8] appear,
And in soft sounds, 'your Grace' salutes their ear.
'Tis these that early taint the female soul,
Instruct the eyes of young coquettes to roll,
Teach infant cheeks a bidden blush to know,
90   And little hearts to flutter at a beau.
    "Oft, when the world° imagine women stray,   *fashionable people*
The Sylphs through mystic mazes guide their way,
Through all the giddy circle they pursue,
And old impertinence° expel by new.   *trifle*
95   What tender maid but must a victim fall
To one man's treat, but for another's ball?
When Florio speaks what virgin could withstand,
If gentle Damon[9] did not squeeze her hand?
With varying vanities, from every part,
100   They shift the moving toyshop of their heart;
Where wigs with wigs, with sword-knots sword-knots strive,[1]
Beaux banish beaux, and coaches coaches drive.
This erring mortals levity may call;
Oh, blind to truth! the Sylphs contrive it all.
105   "Of these am I, who thy protection claim,
A watchful sprite, and Ariel is my name.
Late, as I ranged the crystal wilds of air,

---

spirits to claim tea (pronounced *tay*) as their native
element (line 62) and to keep their former com-
pany at tea parties.
7. Like Milton's angels (*Paradise Lost* 1.423 ff.).
8. Insignia of rank and court status.

9. Like Florio, a conventional poetic name.
1. Sword knots are ribbons tied to hilts. The verbal
repetition and the tangled syntax recall descrip-
tions of the throng and press of battle appearing in
English translations of classical epic.

In the clear mirror of thy ruling star
I saw, alas! some dread event impend,
110 Ere to the main² this morning sun descend,
But Heaven reveals not what, or how, or where:
Warned by the Sylph, O pious maid, beware!
This to disclose is all thy guardian can:
Beware of all, but most beware of Man!"
115 He said; when Shock,³ who thought she slept too long,
Leaped up, and waked his mistress with his tongue.
'Twas then, Belinda, if report say true,
Thy eyes first opened on a billet-doux;⁴
Wounds, charms, and ardors were no sooner read,
120 But all the vision vanished from thy head.
 And now, unveiled, the toilet stands displayed,
Each silver vase in mystic order laid.
First, robed in white, the nymph intent adores,
With head uncovered, the cosmetic powers.
125 A heavenly image in the glass⁵ appears;
To that she bends, to that her eyes she rears.
The inferior priestess, at her altar's side,
Trembling begins the sacred rites of pride.
Unnumbered treasures ope at once, and here
130 The various offerings of the world appear;
From each she nicely culls with curious toil,
And decks the goddess with the glittering spoil.
This casket India's glowing gems unlocks,
And all Arabia⁶ breathes from yonder box.
135 The tortoise here and elephant unite,
Transformed to combs, the speckled and the white.
Here files of pins extend their shining rows,
Puffs, powders, patches, Bibles, billet-doux.
Now awful° Beauty put on all its arms;   *awe-inspiring*
140 The fair each moment rises in her charms,
Repairs her smiles, awakens every grace,
And calls forth all the wonders of her face;
Sees by degrees a purer blush arise,
And keener lightnings quicken in her eyes.
145 The busy Sylphs surround their darling care,
These set the head, and those divide the hair,
Some fold the sleeve, whilst others plait the gown;
And Betty's praised for labors not her own.

CANTO II

 Not with more glories, in the ethereal plain,°   *sky*
The sun first rises o'er the purpled main,°   *sea*
Than, issuing forth, the rival of his beams⁷
Launched on the bosom of the silver Thames.

2. Broad expanse of land or sea.
3. A name for lapdogs (like "Poll" for parrots; see 4.164 [p. 618]); they looked like little "shocks" of hair.
4. A love letter. The affected language of the fashionable love letter is exhibited in the next line.
5. The mirror. Her image is the object of venera-

tion, the "goddess" named later. Belinda presides over the appropriate rites. Betty, her maid, is the "inferior priestess."
6. (Source of) perfumes.
7. I.e., Belinda. She is en route to Hampton Court, a royal palace some twelve miles up the river Thames from London.

5 Fair nymphs and well-dressed youths around her shone,
   But every eye was fixed on her alone.
   On her white breast a sparkling cross she wore,
   Which Jews might kiss, and infidels adore.
   Her lively looks a sprightly mind disclose,
10 Quick as her eyes, and as unfixed as those:
   Favors to none, to all she smiles extends;
   Oft she rejects, but never once offends.
   Bright as the sun, her eyes the gazers strike,
   And, like the sun, they shine on all alike.
15 Yet graceful ease, and sweetness void of pride,
   Might hide her faults, if belles had faults to hide:
   If to her share some female errors fall,
   Look on her face, and you'll forget 'em all.
       This nymph, to the destruction of mankind,
20 Nourished two locks which graceful hung behind
   In equal curls, and well conspired to deck
   With shining ringlets the smooth ivory neck.
   Love in these labyrinths his slaves detains,
   And mighty hearts are held in slender chains.
25 With hairy springes° we the birds betray,   snares
   Slight lines of hair surprise the finny prey,
   Fair tresses man's imperial race ensnare,
   And beauty draws us with a single hair.
       The adventurous Baron the bright locks admired,
30 He saw, he wished, and to the prize aspired.
   Resolved to win, he meditates the way,
   By force to ravish, or by fraud betray;
   For when success a lover's toil attends,
   Few ask if fraud or force attained his ends.
35   For this, ere Phoebus[8] rose, he had implored
   Propitious Heaven, and every power adored,
   But chiefly Love—to Love an altar built,
   Of twelve vast French romances, neatly gilt.
   There lay three garters, half a pair of gloves,
40 And all the trophies of his former loves.
   With tender billet-doux he lights the pyre,
   And breathes three amorous sighs to raise the fire.
   Then prostrate falls, and begs with ardent eyes
   Soon to obtain, and long possess the prize:
45 The powers gave ear, and granted half his prayer,
   The rest the winds dispersed in empty air.
       But now secure the painted vessel glides,
   The sunbeams trembling on the floating tides,
   While melting music steals upon the sky,
50 And softened sounds along the waters die.
   Smooth flow the waves, the zephyrs° gently play,   west winds
   Belinda smiled, and all the world was gay.
   All but the Sylph—with careful thoughts oppressed,
   The impending woe sat heavy on his breast.
55 He summons straight his denizens° of air;   inhabitants

8. Apollo, Greek and Roman god of the sun.

The lucid squadrons round the sails repair:°   *assemble*
Soft o'er the shrouds aërial whispers breathe
That seemed but zephyrs to the train beneath.
Some to the sun their insect-wings unfold,
60   Waft on the breeze, or sink in clouds of gold.
Transparent forms too fine for mortal sight,
Their fluid bodies half dissolved in light,
Loose to the wind their airy garments flew,
Thin glittering textures of the filmy dew,⁹
65   Dipped in the richest tincture of the skies,
Where light disports in ever-mingling dyes,
While every beam new transient colors flings,
Colors that change whene'er they wave their wings.
Amid the circle, on the gilded mast,
70   Superior by the head was Ariel placed;
His purple pinions opening to the sun,
He raised his azure wand, and thus begun:
    "Ye Sylphs and Sylphids, to your chief give ear!
Fays, Fairies, Genii, Elves, and Daemons, hear!
75   Ye know the spheres and various tasks assigned
By laws eternal to the aërial kind.
Some in the fields of purest ether play,
And bask and whiten in the blaze of day.
Some guide the course of wandering orbs on high,
80   Or roll the planets through the boundless sky.
Some less refined, beneath the moon's pale light
Pursue the stars that shoot athwart the night,
Or suck the mists in grosser air below,
Or dip their pinions in the painted bow,°   *rainbow*
85   Or brew fierce tempests on the wintry main,
Or o'er the glebe° distill the kindly rain.   *farmland*
Others on earth o'er human race preside,
Watch all their ways, and all their actions guide:
Of these the chief the care of nations own,
90   And guard with arms divine the British Throne.
    "Our humbler province is to tend the Fair,
Not a less pleasing, though less glorious care:
To save the powder from too rude a gale,
Nor let the imprisoned essences exhale;
95   To draw fresh colors from the vernal flowers;
To steal from rainbows e'er they drop in showers
A brighter wash;° to curl their waving hairs,   *cosmetic lotion*
Assist their blushes, and inspire their airs;
Nay oft, in dreams invention we bestow,
100   To change a flounce, or add a furbelow.°   *ornamental pleat*
    "This day black omens threat the brightest fair,
That e'er deserved a watchful spirit's care;
Some dire disaster, or° by force or slight,   *whether*
But what, or where, the Fates have wrapped in night:
105   Whether the nymph shall break Diana's law,¹
Or some frail china jar receive a flaw,

---

9. The supposed material of spider webs.   1. Diana was the goddess of chastity.

Or stain her honor or her new brocade,
Forget her prayers, or miss a masquerade,
Or lose her heart, or necklace, at a ball;
110 Or whether Heaven has doomed that Shock² must fall.
Haste, then, ye spirits! to your charge repair:
The fluttering fan be Zephyretta's care,
The drops° to thee, Brillante, we consign;   *earrings*
And, Momentilla, let the watch be thine;
115 Do thou, Crispissa,³ tend her favorite Lock;
Ariel himself shall be the guard of Shock.
     "To fifty chosen Sylphs, of special note,
We trust the important charge, the petticoat;
Oft have we known that sevenfold fence to fail,
120 Though stiff with hoops, and armed with ribs of whale.
Form a strong line about the silver bound,
And guard the wide circumference around.
     "Whatever spirit, careless of his charge,
His post neglects, or leaves the fair at large,
125 Shall feel sharp vengeance soon o'ertake his sins,
Be stopped in vials, or transfixed with pins,
Or plunged in lakes of bitter washes lie,
Or wedged whole ages in a bodkin's° eye;   *large needle's*
Gums and pomatums⁴ shall his flight restrain,
130 While clogged he beats his silken wings in vain,
Or alum styptics with contracting power
Shrink his thin essence like a riveled° flower: *shriveled*
Or, as Ixion⁵ fixed, the wretch shall feel
The giddy motion of the whirling mill,°   *cocoa mill*
135 In fumes of burning chocolate shall glow,
And tremble at the sea that froths below!"
     He spoke; the spirits from the sails descend;
Some, orb in orb, around the nymph extend;
Some thread the mazy ringlets of her hair;
140 Some hang upon the pendants of her ear:
With beating hearts the dire event they wait,
Anxious, and trembling for the birth of Fate.

CANTO III

Close by those meads,° forever crowned with flowers,   *meadows*
Where Thames with pride surveys his rising towers,
There stands a structure of majestic frame,⁶
Which from the neighboring Hampton takes its name.
5 Here Britain's statesmen oft the fall foredoom
Of foreign tyrants and of nymphs at home;
Here thou, great Anna!⁷ whom three realms obey,
Dost sometimes counsel take—and sometimes tea.
     Hither the heroes and the nymphs resort,
10 To taste awhile the pleasures of a court;

---

2. See note to 1.115 (p. 607).
3. To "crisp" is to curl (hair).
4. Scented, apple-based ointments applied to the
face and hair.

5. In Greek mythology, a king punished by being
bound eternally to a turning wheel.
6. Hampton Court (see note 7, p. 607).
7. Anne, then queen of England.

In various talk the instructive hours they passed,
Who gave the ball, or paid the visit last;
One speaks the glory of the British Queen,
And one describes a charming Indian screen;
15   A third interprets motions, looks, and eyes;
At every word a reputation dies.
Snuff,[8] or the fan, supply each pause of chat,
With singing, laughing, ogling, and all that.
      Meanwhile, declining from the noon of day,
20   The sun obliquely shoots his burning ray;
The hungry judges soon the sentence sign,
And wretches hang that jurymen may dine;
The merchant from the Exchange° returns in peace,   stock market
And the long labors of the toilet cease.
25   Belinda now, whom thirst of fame invites,
Burns to encounter two adventurous knights,
At ombre[9] singly to decide their doom,
And swells her breast with conquests yet to come.
Straight the three bands prepare in arms° to join,   combat
30   Each band the number of the sacred nine.
Soon as she spreads her hand, the aërial guard
Descend, and sit on each important card:
First Ariel perched upon a Matadore,
Then each according to the rank they bore;
35   For Sylphs, yet mindful of their ancient race,
Are, as when women, wondrous fond of place.
      Behold, four Kings in majesty revered,
With hoary° whiskers and a forky beard;   gray or white
And four fair Queens whose hands sustain a flower,
40   The expressive emblem of their softer power;
Four Knaves in garbs succinct,[1] a trusty band,
Caps on their heads, and halberts[2] in their hand;
And parti°-colored troops, a shining train,   variously
Draw forth to combat on the velvet plain.
45   The skillful nymph reviews her force with care;
"Let Spades be trumps!" she said, and trumps they were
      Now move to war her sable° Matadores,   black
In show like leaders of the swarthy Moors.
Spadillio first, unconquerable lord!

8. Pulverized tobacco to be inhaled through the nostrils, chewed, or placed against the gums.
9. This game is like three-handed bridge with some features of poker added. From a deck lacking 8s, 9s, and 10s, nine cards are dealt to each player (line 30) and the rest put in a central pool on the green velvet cloth (line 44) that provides the playing surface. A declarer, called the Ombre (*hombre*, Spanish for man), commits himself to taking more tricks than either of his opponents individually; hence Belinda's encountering two knights "singly." The declarer, followed by the other players, then selects discards and replenishes his hand with cards drawn sight unseen from the pool (line 45). He proceeds to name his trumps (line 46). The three principal trumps, called Matadors (line 47), always include the black aces. When spades are declared, the Matadors are, in order of value, the ace of spades (Spadille, line 49), the deuce of spades (Manille, line 51), and the ace of clubs (Basto, line 53). The remaining spades fill out the trump suit. In the game here described, Belinda leads out her high trumps (lines 49–56), but the suit breaks badly (line 54); the Baron retains the queen (line 67), with which he presently trumps her king of clubs (line 69). He then leads high diamonds until she is on the verge of a set (Codille, line 92). But she makes her bid at the last trick (line 94), taking his ace of hearts with her king (line 95), this being, in ombre, the highest card in the heart suit.
1. Hemmed up short, not flowing.
2. Weapons combining pike and ax on a single shaft.

50 Led off two captive trumps, and swept the board.
As many more Manillio forced to yield,
And marched a victor from the verdant° field.   *green*
Him Basto followed, but his fate more hard
Gained but one trump and one plebeian card.
55 With his broad saber next, a chief in years,
The hoary Majesty of Spades appears,
Puts forth one manly leg, to sight revealed,
The rest his many-colored robe concealed.
The rebel Knave,° who dares his prince engage,   *jack*
60 Proves the just victim of his royal rage.
Even mighty Pam,³ that kings and queens o'erthrew
And mowed down armies in the fights of loo,
Sad chance of war! now destitute of aid,
Falls undistinguished by the victor Spade.
65   Thus far both armies to Belinda yield;
Now to the Baron fate inclines the field.
His warlike amazon her host invades,
The imperial consort of the crown of Spades.
The Club's black tyrant first her victim died,
70 Spite of his haughty mien° and barbarous pride.   *expression*
What boots the regal circle on his head,
His giant limbs, in state unwieldy spread?
That long behind he trails his pompous robe.
And of all monarchs only grasps the globe?
75   The Baron now his Diamonds pours apace;
The embroidered King who shows but half his face,
And his refulgent Queen, with powers combined
Of broken troops an easy conquest find.
Clubs, Diamonds, Hearts, in wild disorder seen,
80 With throngs promiscuous strew the level green.
Thus when dispersed a routed army runs,
Of Asia's troops, and Afric's sable sons,
With like confusion different nations fly,
Of various habit,° and of various dye,°   *dress / color*
85 The pierced battalions disunited fall
In heaps on heaps; one fate o'erwhelms them all.
    The Knave of Diamonds tries his wily arts,
And wins (oh, shameful chance!) the Queen of Hearts.
At this, the blood the virgin's cheek forsook,
90 A livid paleness spreads o'er all her look;
She sees, and trembles at the approaching ill,
Just in the jaws of ruin, and Codille,
And now (as oft in some distempered state)
On one nice° trick depends the general fate.   *subtle; particular*
95 An Ace of Hearts steps forth: the King unseen
Lurked in her hand, and mourned his captive Queen.
He springs to vengeance with an eager pace,
And falls like thunder on the prostrate Ace.
The nymph exulting fills with shouts the sky,
100 The walls, the woods, and long canals⁴ reply.

3. The jack of clubs, paramount trump in the   4. Passages between avenues of trees.
game of loo.

O thoughtless mortals! ever blind to fate,
Too soon dejected, and too soon elate:
Sudden these honors shall be snatched away,
And cursed forever this victorious day.
105   For lo! the board° with cups and spoons is crowned,   *table*
The berries crackle, and the mill turns round;[5]
On shining altars of Japan[6] they raise
The silver lamp; the fiery spirits blaze:
From silver spouts the grateful liquors glide,
110 While China's earth[7] receives the smoking tide.
At once they gratify their scent and taste,
And frequent cups prolong the rich repast.
Straight hover round the fair her airy band;
Some, as she sipped, the fuming liquor fanned,
115 Some o'er her lap their careful plumes displayed,
Trembling, and conscious of the rich brocade.
Coffee (which makes the politician wise,
And see through all things with his half-shut eyes)
Sent up in vapors to the Baron's brain
120 New stratagems, the radiant Lock to gain.
Ah, cease, rash youth! desist ere 'tis too late,
Fear the just Gods, and think of Scylla's fate![8]
Changed to a bird, and sent to flit in air,
She dearly pays for Nisus' injured hair!
125   But when to mischief mortals bend their will,
How soon they find fit instruments of ill!
Just then, Clarissa drew with tempting grace
A two-edged weapon from her shining case:
So ladies in romance assist their knight,
130 Present the spear, and arm him for the fight.
He takes the gift with reverence, and extends
The little engine on his fingers' ends;
This just behind Belinda's neck he spread,
As o'er the fragrant steams she bends her head.
135 Swift to the Lock a thousand sprites° repair,   *spirits*
A thousand wings, by turns, blow back the hair,
And thrice they twitched the diamond in her ear,
Thrice she looked back, and thrice the foe drew near.
Just in that instant, anxious Ariel sought
140 The close recesses of the virgin's thought;
As on the nosegay° in her breast reclined,   *posy*
He watched the ideas rising in her mind,
Sudden he viewed, in spite of all her art,
An earthly lover lurking at her heart.
145 Amazed, confused, he found his power expired,[9]
Resigned to fate, and with a sigh retired.
    The Peer now spreads the glittering forfex° wide,   *scissors*
To enclose the Lock; now joins it, to divide.

5. As coffee beans are roasted and ground.
6. Lacquered tables.
7. Ceramic cups.
8. In Greek mythology, Scylla cut from the head of her father, Nisus, the lock of hair on which his life depended and gave it to her lover, Minos of Crete, who was besieging Nisus's city. For this she was turned into a seabird relentlessly pursued by an eagle.
9. Belinda, being strongly attracted to the baron (line 144), can no longer merely flirt. She hence passes beyond Ariel's control.

Even then, before the fatal engine closed,
150 A wretched Sylph too fondly interposed;
Fate urged the shears, and cut the Sylph in twain
(But airy substance soon unites again):[1]
The meeting points the sacred hair dissever
From the fair head, forever, and forever!
155   Then flashed the living lightning from her eyes,
And screams of horror rend the affrighted skies.
Not louder shrieks to pitying heaven are cast,
When husbands, or when lapdogs breathe their last;
Or when rich china vessels fallen from high,
160 In glittering dust and painted fragments lie!
"Let wreaths of triumph now my temples twine,"
The victor cried, "the glorious prize is mine!
While fish in streams, or birds delight in air,
Or in a coach and six the British Fair,
165 As long as *Atalantis*[2] shall be read,
Or the small pillow grace a lady's bed,
While visits shall be paid on solemn days,
When numerous wax-lights in bright order blaze,[3]
While nymphs take treats, or assignations give,
170 So long my honor, name, and praise shall live!
What Time would spare, from Steel receives its date,°   termination
And monuments, like men, submit to fate!
Steel could the labor of the Gods destroy,
And strike to dust the imperial towers of Troy;[4]
175 Steel could the works of mortal pride confound,
And hew triumphal arches to the ground.
What wonder then, fair nymph! thy hairs should feel,
The conquering force of unresisted Steel?"

CANTO IV

But anxious cares the pensive nymph oppressed,
And secret passions labored in her breast.
Not youthful kings in battle seized alive,
Not scornful virgins who their charms survive,
5   Not ardent lovers robbed of all their bliss,
Not ancient ladies when refused a kiss,
Not tyrants fierce that unrepenting die,
Not Cynthia when her manteau's° pinned awry,   robe is
E'er felt such rage, resentment, and despair,
10 As thou, sad virgin! for thy ravished hair.
For, that sad moment, when the Sylphs withdrew
And Ariel weeping from Belinda flew,
Umbriel,[5] a dusky, melancholy sprite°   spirit

1. Like Milton's angels (*Paradise Lost* 6.329–31);
cf. 1.70 (p. 606).
2. Delarivière Manley's *New Atalantis* (1709), a
set of memoirs that, under thin disguise, recounted
actual scandals.
3. I.e., attending the formal evening visits of the
previous line.
4. Ancient city-state that, according to Greek

mythology, was built by the gods Apollo and Posei-
don and destroyed by the Greeks at the end of the
Trojan War.
5. Suggesting *umbra*, shadow; and *umber*, brown.
The final *el* of this name is a further reminiscence
of Milton's angels: Gabriel, Abdiel, Zophiel. (Cf.
1.70 [p. 606] and 3.152 [above].)

As ever sullied the fair face of light,
15 Down to the central earth, his proper scene,
Repaired to search the gloomy Cave of Spleen.[6]
    Swift on his sooty pinions flits the Gnome,
And in a vapor reached the dismal dome.
No cheerful breeze this sullen region knows,
20 The dreaded east is all the wind that blows.
Here in a grotto, sheltered close from air,
And screened in shades from day's detested glare,
She sighs forever on her pensive bed,
Pain at her side, and Megrim° at her head.   migraine
25   Two handmaids wait° the throne: alike in place,   attend
But differing far in figure and in face.
Here stood Ill-Nature like an ancient maid,
Her wrinkled form in black and white arrayed;
With store of prayers for mornings, nights, and noons,
30 Her hand is filled; her bosom with lampoons.°   slanders
    There Affectation, with a sickly mien,°   appearance
Shows in her cheek the roses of eighteen,
Practiced to lisp, and hang the head aside,
Faints into airs, and languishes with pride,
35 On the rich quilt sinks with becoming woe,
Wrapped in a gown, for sickness and for show.
The fair ones feel such maladies as these,
When each new nightdress gives a new disease.
    A constant vapor o'er the palace flies,
40 Strange phantoms rising as the mists arise;
Dreadful as hermit's dreams in haunted shades,
Or bright as visions of expiring maids.
Now glaring fiends, and snakes on rolling spires,°   coils
Pale specters, gaping tombs, and purple fires;
45 Now lakes of liquid gold, Elysian scenes,
And crystal domes, and angels in machines.[7]
    Unnumbered throngs on every side are seen
Of bodies changed to various forms by Spleen.
Here living teapots stand, one arm held out,
50 One bent; the handle this, and that the spout:
A pipkin[8] there, like Homer's tripod, walks;
Here sighs a jar, and there a goose pie talks;
Men prove with child, as powerful fancy works,
And maids, turned bottles, call aloud for corks.
55   Safe passed the Gnome through this fantastic band,
A branch of healing spleenwort[9] in his hand.
Then thus addressed the Power: "Hail, wayward Queen!

6. This journey is formally equivalent to Odysseus's and Aeneas's visits to the underworld. "Spleen" refers to the human organ, the supposed seat of melancholy; hence to melancholy itself. Believed to be induced by misty weather such as the east wind brings (lines 18–20), the condition was also called the "vapors." In its severer manifestations, it tended toward madness; in its milder forms, it issued in peevishness and suspicion. See the poems on "spleen" in this anthology by Anne Finch (p. 558) and Matthew Green (p. 645).

7. These images are 1) the hallucinations of insane melancholy and 2) parodies of stage properties and effects.

8. An earthen pot; it walks like the three-legged stools that Vulcan made for the gods in *Iliad* 18.

9. A kind of fern, purgative of spleen; suggesting the golden bough that Aeneas bore as a passport to Hades in *Aeneid* 6.

Who rule the sex to fifty from fifteen:
Parent of vapors and of female wit,
60 Who give the hysteric or poetic fit,
On various tempers act by various ways,
Make some take physic,° others scribble plays;   *medicine*
Who cause the proud their visits to delay,
And send the godly in a pet° to pray.   *fit of anger*
65 A nymph there is that all thy power disdains,
And thousands more in equal mirth maintains.
But oh! if e'er thy Gnome could spoil a grace,
Or raise a pimple on a beauteous face,
Like citron-waters° matrons' cheeks inflame,   *lemon brandy*
70 Or change complexions at a losing game;
If e'er with airy horns I planted heads,[1]
Or rumpled petticoats, or tumbled beds,
Or caused suspicion when no soul was rude,
Or discomposed the headdress of a prude,
75 Or e'er to costive° lapdog gave disease,   *constipated*
Which not the tears of brightest eyes could ease,
Hear me, and touch Belinda with chagrin:°   *annoyance*
That single act gives half the world the spleen."
       The Goddess with a discontented air
80 Seems to reject him though she grants his prayer.
A wondrous bag with both her hands she binds,
Like that where once Ulysses held the winds;[2]
There she collects the force of female lungs,
Sighs, sobs, and passions, and the war of tongues.
85 A vial next she fills with fainting fears,
Soft sorrows, melting griefs, and flowing tears.
The Gnome rejoicing bears her gifts away,
Spreads his black wings, and slowly mounts to day.
       Sunk in Thalestris'[3] arms the nymph he found,
90 Her eyes dejected and her hair unbound.
Full o'er their heads the swelling bag he rent,
And all the Furies issued at the vent.
Belinda burns with more than mortal ire,
And fierce Thalestris fans the rising fire.
95 "O wretched maid!" she spreads her hands, and cried
(While Hampton's[4] echoes, "Wretched maid!" replied),
"Was it for this you took such constant care
The bodkin,° comb, and essence° to prepare?   *hairpin / perfume*
For this your locks in paper durance bound,
100 For this with torturing irons wreathed around?
For this with fillets° strained your tender head,   *bands*
And bravely bore the double loads of lead?[5]
Gods! shall the ravisher display your hair,
While the fops envy, and the ladies stare!
105 Honor forbid! at whose unrivaled shrine

1. I.e., made men imagine they were being cuck-
olded.
2. Aeolus, the wind god, enabled Odysseus (Ulys-
ses) so to contain all adverse winds in *Odyssey* 10.
3. The name of an Amazon; hence a fierce, com-

bative woman.
4. Hampton Court's (see note 7, p. 607).
5. The means by which Belinda's locks were fash-
ioned into a ringlet: lead strips held her curl papers
in place.

Ease, pleasure, virtue, all, our sex resign.
Methinks already I your tears survey,
Already hear the horrid things they say,
Already see you a degraded toast,
110 And all your honor in a whisper lost!
How shall I, then, your helpless fame defend?
'Twill then be infamy to seem your friend!
And shall this prize, the inestimable prize,
Exposed through crystal to the gazing eyes,
115 And heightened by the diamond's circling rays,
On that rapacious hand forever blaze?
Sooner shall grass in Hyde Park Circus⁶ grow,
And wits take lodgings in the sound of Bow;⁷
Sooner let earth, air, sea, to chaos fall,
120 Men, monkeys, lapdogs, parrots, perish all!"
    She said; then raging to Sir Plume repairs,
And bids her beau demand the precious hairs
(Sir Plume of amber snuffbox justly vain,
And the nice° conduct° of a clouded cane).   *precise / handling*
125 With earnest eyes, and round unthinking face,
He first the snuffbox⁸ opened, then the case,
And thus broke out—"My Lord, why, what the devil!
Zounds!° damn the lock! 'fore Gad, you must be civil!   *God's wounds*
Plague on't! 'tis past a jest—nay prithee, pox!
130 Give her the hair"—he spoke, and rapped his box.
    "It grieves me much," replied the Peer again,
"Who speaks so well should ever speak in vain.
But by this Lock, this sacred Lock I swear
(Which never more shall join its parted hair;
135 Which never more its honors shall renew,
Clipped from the lovely head where late it grew),
That while my nostrils draw the vital air,
This hand, which won it, shall forever wear."
He spoke, and speaking, in proud triumph spread
140 The long-contended honors° of her head.   *ornaments*
    But Umbriel, hateful Gnome, forbears not so;
He breaks the vial whence the sorrows flow.
Then see! the nymph in beauteous grief appears,
Her eyes half languishing, half drowned in tears;
145 On her heaved bosom hung her drooping head,
Which with a sigh she raised, and thus she said:
    "Forever cursed be this detested day,
Which snatched my best, my favorite curl away!
Happy! ah, ten times happy had I been,
150 If Hampton Court these eyes had never seen!
Yet am not I the first mistaken maid,
By love of courts to numerous ills betrayed.
Oh, had I rather unadmired remained
In some lone isle, or distant northern land;

---

6. The fashionable carriage course (the "Ring" of 1.44).
7. I.e., the sound of the church bells of St. Mary

Le Bow, in the unfashionable commercial section of London.
8. See note 8, p. 611.

155 Where the gilt chariot never marks the way,
    Where none learn ombre, none e'er taste bohea!°   *fine tea*
    There kept my charms concealed from mortal eye,
    Like roses that in deserts bloom and die.
    What moved my mind with youthful lords to roam?
160 Oh, had I stayed, and said my prayers at home!
    'Twas this the morning omens seemed to tell,
    Thrice from my trembling hand the patch box⁹ fell;
    The tottering china shook without a wind,
    Nay, Poll sat mute, and Shock was most unkind!
165 A Sylph too warned me of the threats of fate,
    In mystic visions, now believed too late!
    See the poor remnants of these slighted hairs!
    My hands shall rend what e'en thy rapine spares.
    These in two sable ringlets taught to break,
170 Once gave new beauties to the snowy neck;
    The sister lock now sits uncouth, alone,
    And in its fellow's fate foresees its own;
    Uncurled it hands, the fatal shears demands,
    And tempts once more thy sacrilegious hands.
175 Oh, hadst thou, cruel! been content to seize
    Hairs less in sight, or any hairs but these!"

CANTO V

    She said: the pitying audience melt in tears.
    But Fate and Jove° had stopped the Baron's ears.   *chief Roman god*
    In vain Thalestris with reproach assails,
    For who can move when fair Belinda fails?
5   Not half so fixed the Trojan could remain,
    While Anna begged and Dido raged in vain.¹
    Then grave Clarissa graceful waved her fan;
    Silence ensued, and thus the nymph began:
        "Say why are beauties praised and honored most,
10 The wise man's passion, and the vain man's toast?
    Why decked with all that land and sea afford,
    Why angels called, and angel-like adored?
    Why round our coaches crowd the white-gloved beaux,
    Why bows the side box² from its inmost rows?
15 How vain are all these glories, all our pains,
    Unless good sense preserve what beauty gains;
    That men may say when we the front box grace,
    'Behold the first in virtue as in face!'
    Oh! if to dance all night, and dress all day,
20 Charmed the smallpox, or chased old age away,
    Who would not scorn what housewife's cares produce,
    Or who would learn one earthly thing of use?
    To patch, nay ogle, might become a saint,
    Nor could it sure be such a sin to paint.°   *apply cosmetics*
25 But since, alas! frail beauty must decay,

9. A box for ornamental patches of court plaster worn to accent the face.
1. Aeneas was determined to leave Carthage for Italy, though the enamored queen Dido raved and her sister Anna pleaded with him to stay.
2. I.e., at the theater.

Curled or uncurled, since locks will turn to gray;
Since painted, or not painted, all shall fade,
And she who scorns a man must die a maid;
What then remains but well our power to use,
30 And keep good humor still whate'er we lose?
And trust me, dear, good humor can prevail
When airs, and flights, and screams, and scolding fail.
Beauties in vain their pretty eyes may roll;
Charms strike the sight, but merit wins the soul."[3]
35   So spoke the dame, but no applause ensued;
Belinda frowned, Thalestris called her prude.
"To arms, to arms!" the fierce virago cries,
And swift as lightning to the combat flies.
All side in parties, and begin the attack;
40 Fans clap, silks rustle, and tough whalebones crack;
Heroes' and heroines' shouts confusedly rise,
And bass and treble voices strike the skies.
No common weapons in their hands are found,
Like Gods they fight, nor dread a mortal wound.
45   So when bold Homer makes the Gods engage,
And heavenly breasts with human passions rage;
'Gainst Pallas, Mars; Latona, Hermes arms;[4]
And all Olympus rings with loud alarms:
Jove's thunder roars, heaven trembles all around,
50 Blue Neptune[5] storms, the bellowing deeps resound:
Earth shakes her nodding towers, the ground gives way,
And the pale ghosts start at the flash of day!
    Triumphant Umbriel on a sconce's° height   *mounted candlestick*
Clapped his glad wings, and sat to view the fight:
55 Propped on the bodkin spears, the sprites° survey   *spirits*
The growing combat, or assist the fray.
    While through the press enraged Thalestris flies,
And scatters death around from both her eyes,
A beau and witling° perished in the throng,   *one of little wit*
60 One died in metaphor, and one in song.
"O cruel nymph! a living death I bear,"
Cried Dapperwit, and sunk beside his chair.
A mournful glance Sir Fopling upwards cast,
"Those eyes are made so killing"—was his last.
65 Thus on Maeander's[6] flowery margin lies
The expiring swan, and as he sings he dies.[7]
    When bold Sir Plume had drawn Clarissa down,
Chloe stepped in, and killed him with a frown;
She smiled to see the doughty hero slain,
70 But, at her smile, the beau revived again.
    Now Jove suspends his golden scales in air,[8]

---

3. Clarissa's address parallels—indeed, closely parodies Pope's 1709 translation of—a speech in *Iliad* 12, wherein Sarpedon tells Glaucus that, as leaders of the army, they must justify their privilege by extraordinary prowess.
4. Mars arms against Pallas, and Hermes against Latona, in *Iliad* 20. The tangled syntax is supposed to mirror the press of battle.
5. Neptune is the Roman god of the sea.
6. A river in Asia Minor noted for its wandering course.
7. The swan was said to sing only before its death.
8. He so weighs the fortunes of war in classical epic.

Weighs the men's wits against the lady's hair;
The doubtful beam long nods from side to side;
At length the wits mount up, the hairs subside.
75   See, fierce Belinda on the Baron flies,
With more than usual lightning in her eyes;
Nor feared the chief the unequal fight to try,
Who sought no more than on his foe to die.[9]
But this bold lord with manly strength endued,
80   She with one finger and a thumb subdued:
Just where the breath of life his nostrils drew,
A charge of snuff the wily virgin threw;
The Gnomes direct, to every atom just,
The pungent grains of titillating dust.
85   Sudden, with starting tears each eye o'erflows,
And the high dome re-echoes to his nose.
"Now meet thy fate," incensed Belinda cried,
And drew a deadly bodkin[1] from her side.
(The same, his ancient personage to deck,
90   Her great-great-grandsire wore about his neck,
In three seal rings; which after, melted down,
Formed a vast buckle for his widow's gown:
Her infant grandame's whistle next it grew,
The bells she jingled, and the whistle blew;
95   Then in a bodkin graced her mother's hairs,
Which long she wore, and now Belinda wears.)
"Boast not my fall," he cried, "insulting foe!
Thou by some other shalt be laid as low.
Nor think to die dejects my lofty mind:
100   All that I dread is leaving you behind!
Rather than so, ah, let me still survive,
And burn in Cupid's flames—but burn alive."
"Restore the Lock!" she cries; and all around
"Restore the Lock!" the vaulted roofs rebound.
105   Not fierce Othello in so loud a strain
Roared for the handkerchief that caused his pain.[2]
But see how oft ambitious aims are crossed,
And chiefs contend till all the prize is lost!
The lock, obtained with guilt, and kept with pain,
110   In every place is sought, but sought in vain:
With such a prize no mortal must be blessed,
So Heaven decrees! with Heaven who can contest?
Some thought it mounted to the lunar sphere,
Since all things lost on earth are treasured there.
115   There heroes' wits are kept in ponderous vases,
And beaux' in snuffboxes and tweezer cases.
There broken vows and deathbed alms are found,
And lovers' hearts with ends of riband bound,
The courtier's promises, and sick man's prayers,
120   The smiles of harlots, and the tears of heirs,

---

9. I.e., to experience sexual bliss.
1. Here an ornamental hairpin. Its history suggests that of Agamemnon's scepter in *Iliad* 2. "Seal rings" (line 91) are for impressing seals on letters and legal documents.
2. In *Othello* 3.4.

Cages for gnats, and chains to yoke a flea,
Dried butterflies, and tomes of casuistry.[3]
    But trust the Muse—she saw it upward rise,
Though marked by none but quick, poetic eyes
125 (So Rome's great founder to the heavens withdrew,
To Proculus alone confessed in view);[4]
A sudden star, it shot through liquid° air,   *clear*
And drew behind a radiant trail of hair.
Not Berenice's locks first rose so bright,[5]
130 The heavens bespangling with disheveled light.
The Sylphs behold it kindling as it flies,
And pleased pursue its progress through the skies.
    This the beau monde shall from the Mall[6] survey,
And hail with music its propitious ray.
135 This the blest lover shall for Venus[7] take,
And send up vows from Rosamonda's Lake.
This Partridge soon shall view in cloudless skies,
When next he looks through Galileo's eyes;[8]
And hence the egregious wizard shall foredoom
140 The fate of Louis, and the fall of Rome.
    Then cease, bright nymph! to mourn thy ravished hair,
Which adds new glory to the shining sphere!
Not all the tresses that fair head can boast,
Shall draw such envy as the Lock you lost.
145 For, after all the murders of your eye,
When, after millions slain, yourself shall die:
When those fair suns shall set, as set they must,
And all those tresses shall be laid in dust,
This Lock the Muse shall consecrate to fame,
150 And 'midst the stars inscribe Belinda's name.

1712   1714

Epistle to Miss Blount[9]

On Her Leaving the Town, after the Coronation

    As some fond virgin, whom her mother's care
Drags from the town to wholesome country air,
Just when she learns to roll a melting eye,
And hear a spark,° yet think no danger nigh;   *beau, gallant*
5 From the dear man unwilling she must sever,
Yet takes one kiss before she parts forever:

3. Books of seemingly solid but false reasoning.
4. According to Livy's *Early History of Rome*, the empire's "founder" and first king, Romulus, vanished in a storm cloud. A senator, Proculus, calmed the citizenry by claiming that Romulus descended from heaven, assured him of Rome's invincibility, then reascended.
5. The locks that the ancient Egyptian queen Berenice dedicated to her husband's safe return were turned into a constellation.
6. A fashionable walk that, like Rosamonda's Lake

(line 136), was in St. James's Park.
7. Greek goddess of love and beauty.
8. *Galileo's eyes:* the telescope. *Partridge:* John Partridge, a London astrologer who predicted calamities for the enemies of England and Protestantism. Some of Pope's contemporaries had satirized Partridge's annually published predictions in 1708.
9. Teresa Blount, sister of Pope's lifelong friend Martha Blount. The "coronation" was that of George I (1714).

Thus from the world fair Zephalinda[1] flew,
Saw others happy, and with sighs withdrew;
Not that their pleasures caused her discontent;

10   She sighed not that they stayed, but that she went.
   She went to plain-work,° and to purling[2] brooks,   *needlework*
Old-fashioned halls, dull aunts, and croaking rooks:[3]
She went from opera, park, assembly, play,
To morning walks, and prayers three hours a day;

15   To part her time 'twixt reading and bohea,°   *fine tea*
To muse, and spill her solitary tea,
Or o'er cold coffee trifle with the spoon,
Count the slow clock, and dine exact at noon;[4]
Divert her eyes with pictures in the fire,

20   Hum half a tune, tell stories to the squire;
Up to her godly garret after seven,
There starve and pray, for that's the way to heaven.
   Some squire, perhaps, you take delight to rack,°   *torture*
Whose game is whist, whose treat a toast in sack;°   *wine, sherry*

25   Who visits with a gun, presents you birds,
Then gives a smacking buss,° and cries—"No words!"   *kiss*
Or with his hounds comes hollowing from the stable,
Makes love with nods and knees beneath a table;
Whose laughs are hearty, though his jests are coarse,

30   And loves you best of all things—but his horse.
   In some fair evening, on your elbow laid,
You dream of triumphs in the rural shade;
In pensive thought recall the fancied scene,
See coronations rise on every green:

35   Before you pass the imaginary sights
Of lords and earls and dukes and gartered knights,
While the spread fan o'ershades your closing eyes;
Then gives one flirt,[5] and all the vision flies.
Thus vanish scepters, coronets, and balls,

40   And leave you in lone woods, or empty walls!
   So when your slave,[6] at some dear idle time
(Not plagued with headaches or the want of rhyme)
Stands in the streets, abstracted from the crew,
And while he seems to study, thinks of you;

45   Just when his fancy points[7] your sprightly eyes,
Or sees the blush of soft Parthenia[8] rise,
Gay[9] pats my shoulder, and you vanish quite;
Streets, chairs,° and coxcombs[1] rush upon my sight;   *sedan chairs*
Vexed to be still in town, I knit my brow,

50   Look sour, and hum a tune—as you may now.

1717

---

1. A fanciful name adopted by Miss Blount.
2. Gently rippling.
3. Crowlike birds.
4. While fashionable Londoners dined at three or four o'clock, the old-fashioned and rustic might have dined at noon.
5. I.e., suddenly opens and closes her fan.

6. I.e., the speaker, Pope.
7. Focuses or zeroes in on.
8. Martha Blount.
9. The poet John Gay (1685–1732; see pp. 594–96), Pope's friend.
1. Dandies, fops.

From An Essay on Man, in Four Epistles[2]

TO HENRY ST. JOHN, LORD BOLINGBROKE[3]

From *Epistle 1. Of the Nature and State of Man, with Respect to the Universe*

Awake, my St. John! leave all meaner things
To low ambition, and the pride of kings.
Let us (since life can little more supply
Than just to look about us and to die)
5   Expatiate° free o'er all this scene of man;   *range; expound*
A mighty maze! but not without a plan;
A wild, where weeds and flowers promiscuous shoot,
Or garden, tempting with forbidden fruit.
Together let us beat this ample field,
10   Try what the open, what the covert yield;
The latent° tracts,° the giddy heights, explore   *hidden / areas*
Of all who blindly creep, or sightless soar;
Eye Nature's walks, shoot folly as it flies,
And catch the manners living as they rise;
15   Laugh where we must, be candid° where we can;   *kindly, frank*
But vindicate the ways of God to man.

1. Say first, of God above, or man below,
What can we reason, but from what we know?
Of man, what see we but his station here,
20   From which to reason, or to which refer?
Through worlds unnumbered though the God be known,
'Tis ours to trace him only in our own.
He, who through vast immensity can pierce,
See worlds on worlds compose one universe,
25   Observe how system into system runs,
What other planets circle other suns,
What varied being peoples every star,
May tell why Heaven has made us as we are.
But of this frame the bearings, and the ties,
30   The strong connections, nice dependencies,
Gradations just, has thy pervading soul
Looked through? or can a part contain the whole?

2. In this ambitious poem (from which we include the first four parts of epistle 1), Pope employs what he calls an "epistolary way of writing" to describe humanity's place in the "universal system." Explicitly taking up (and revising) Milton's ambition to "justify the ways of God to men" (*Paradise Lost* 1.26; see p. 422), Pope states in a prefatory address to the reader that he will initially consider "man in the abstract, his Nature and his State, since, to prove any moral duty, to enforce any moral precept, or to examine the perfection or imperfection of any creature whatsoever, it is necessary first to know what condition and relation it is placed in, and what is the proper end and purpose of its being." Pope tells the reader that he chooses verse over prose because verse comes naturally to him and is more striking and memorable than prose.
3. English statesman (1678–1751), secretary of state in the Tory ministry of 1710–14; now out of political office. He became close friends with Pope after settling near him at Dawley farm. St. John was pronounced *sín-jun*—a fact important for scanning the poem's first line.

Is the great chain, that draws all to agree,
And drawn supports, upheld by God, or thee?[4]

35   2. Presumptuous man! the reason wouldst thou find,
Why formed so weak, so little, and so blind?
First, if thou canst, the harder reason guess,
Why formed no weaker, blinder, and no less!
Ask of thy mother earth, why oaks are made
40 Taller or stronger than the weeds they shade?
Or ask of yonder argent° fields above,   silvery
Why Jove's satellites[5] are less than Jove?
    Of systems possible, if 'tis confessed
That Wisdom Infinite must form the best,
45 Where all must full or not coherent be,
And all that rises, rise in due degree;
Then, in the scale of reasoning life, 'tis plain,
There must be, somewhere, such a rank as man:
And all the question (wrangle e'er so long)
50 Is only this, if God has placed him wrong?
    Respecting man, whatever wrong we call,
May, must be right, as relative to all.[6]
In human works, though labored on with pain,
A thousand movements scarce one purpose gain;
55 In God's, one single can its end produce;
Yet serves to second too some other use.
So man, who here seems principal alone,
Perhaps acts second to some sphere unknown,
Touches some wheel, or verges to some goal;
60 'Tis but a part we see, and not a whole.
    When the proud steed shall know why man restrains
His fiery course, or drives him o'er the plains;
When the dull ox, why now he breaks the clod,°   earth
Is now a victim, and now Egypt's god:
65 Then shall man's pride and dullness comprehend
His actions', passions', being's use and end;
Why doing, suffering, checked, impelled; and why
This hour a slave, the next a deity.
    Then say not man's imperfect, Heaven in fault;
70 Say rather, man's as perfect as he ought;°   ought to be
His knowledge measured to his state and place,
His time a moment, and a point his space.
If to be perfect in a certain sphere,
What matter, soon or late, or here or there?[7]
75 The blest today is as completely so,
As who° began a thousand years ago.   whoever

---

4. The Great Chain of Being is a visual metaphor for a divinely inspired hierarchy that ranks all forms of life from highest to lowest.
5. The planets. Jove (Jupiter) was the chief god of Roman mythology.
6. I.e., what seems wrong in relation to humankind may, indeed must, be right relative to the

other parts of the Chain of Being.
7. Lines 73–74 are compressed in syntax and in thought. A possible paraphrase: If perfection is defined as a condition of completeness measured by specific time and place, then variations of time and place do not affect this ideal.

3. Heaven from all creatures hides the book of Fate,
All but the page prescribed, their present state:
From brutes what men, from men what spirits know:
80   Or who could suffer being here below?
The lamb thy riot dooms to bleed today,
Had he thy reason, would he skip and play?
Pleased to the last, he crops the flowery food,
And licks the hand just raised to shed his blood.
85   O blindness to the future! kindly given,
That each may fill the circle marked by Heaven:
Who sees with equal eye, as God of all,
A hero perish, or a sparrow fall,
Atoms or systems° into ruin hurled.   *solar systems*
90   And now a bubble burst, and now a world.
    Hope humbly then; with trembling pinions soar;
Wait the great teacher Death, and God adore!
What future bliss, he gives not thee to know,
But gives that hope to be thy blessing now.
95   Hope springs eternal in the human breast:
Man never is, but always to be blest:
The soul, uneasy and confined from home,
Rests and expatiates in a life to come.
    Lo! the poor Indian, whose untutored mind
100   Sees God in clouds, or hears him in the wind;
His soul proud Science never taught to stray
Far as the solar walk, or milky way;
Yet simple Nature to his hope has given,
Behind the cloud-topped hill, an humbler heaven;
105   Some safer world in depth of woods embraced,
Some happier island in the watery waste,
Where slaves once more their native land behold,
No fiends torment, no Christians thirst for gold!
To be, contents his natural desire,
110   He asks no angel's wing, no seraph's° fire;   *high-ranking angel's*
But thinks, admitted to that equal sky,
His faithful dog shall bear him company.

    4. Go, wiser thou! and, in thy scale of sense,
Weigh thy opinion against Providence;
115   Call imperfection what thou fancy'st such,
Say, here he gives too little, there too much;
Destroy all creatures for thy sport or gust,°   *taste*
Yet cry, if man's unhappy, God's unjust;
If man alone engross not Heav'n's high care,
120   Alone made perfect here, immortal there:
Snatch from his hand the balance and the rod,
Rejudge his justice, be the God of God!
In pride, in reasoning pride, our error lies;
All quit their sphere, and rush into the skies.
125   Pride still is aiming at the blest abodes,
Men would be angels, angels would be gods.
Aspiring to be gods, if angels fell,

Aspiring to be angels, men rebel:
And who but wishes to invert the laws
130 Of order, sins against the Eternal Cause.

* * *

1733

Epistle to Dr. Arbuthnot[8]

P. Shut, shut the door, good John![9] (fatigued, I said),
Tie up the knocker, say I'm sick, I'm dead.
The Dog Star[1] rages! nay 'tis past a doubt
All Bedlam, or Parnassus,[2] is let out:
5 Fire in each eye, and papers in each hand,
They rave, recite, and madden round the land.
    What walls can guard me, or what shades can hide?
They pierce my thickets, through my grot[3] they glide,
By land, by water, they renew the charge,
10 They stop the chariot,° and they board the barge.[4]   carriage
No place is sacred, not the church is free;
Even Sunday shines no Sabbath day to me:
Then from the Mint[5] walks forth the man of rhyme,
Happy to catch me just at dinner time.
15   Is there a parson, much bemused in beer,
A maudlin poetess, a rhyming peer,
A clerk foredoomed his father's soul to cross,
Who pens a stanza when he should engross?[6]
Is there who,° locked from ink and paper, scrawls   one who
20 With desperate charcoal round his darkened walls?
All fly to Twit'nam,° and in humble strain   Twickenham
Apply to me to keep them mad or vain.
Arthur,[7] whose giddy son neglects the laws,
Imputes to me and my damned works the cause:
25 Poor Cornus[8] sees his frantic wife elope,
And curses wit, and poetry, and Pope.
    Friend to my life (which did not you prolong,
The world had wanted many an idle song)
What drop or nostrum° can this plague remove?   drug

8. John Arbuthnot (1667–1735), former physician to Queen Anne, was Pope's physician, and friend and literary collaborator of Pope, Swift, and Gay. (See Swift's "Verses on the Death of Dr. Swift, D.S.P.D.," esp. lines 53–58 [p. 579].) He had asked Pope to moderate his attacks on his personal and literary enemies and was hence a logical person to whom to address an apology for writing satire.
9. John Serle, Pope's servant.
1. The summer star Sirius, attendant upon crazing heat. In ancient Rome, late summer was a season for public recitations of poetry.
2. Mt. Parnassus, the haunt of the Muses (in Greek mythology, nine sister goddesses who pre-

sided over poetry, song, and the arts and sciences).
Bedlam: London's Bethlehem Hospital for the insane.
3. Pope's "grotto," one entrance to the grounds of his villa at Twickenham.
4. Pope often traveled from Twickenham to London by water.
5. A sanctuary for debtors. They emerged on Sunday, being everywhere immune from arrest on that day.
6. Prepare legal documents.
7. Arthur Moore, whose son, the playwright James Moore Smythe, had plagiarized some lines from Pope.
8. From cornu, Latin for horn; hence a cuckold.

30　Or which must end me, a fool's wrath or love?
　　A dire dilemma! either way I'm sped,°　　　　　　　　　*ruined*
　　If foes, they write, if friends, they read me dead.
　　Seized and tied down to judge, how wretched I!
　　Who can't be silent, and who will not lie.
35　To laugh were want° of goodness and of grace,　　　　*a lack*
　　And to be grave exceeds all power of face.
　　I sit with sad° civility, I read　　　　　　　　　　　*sober*
　　With honest anguish and an aching head,
　　And drop at last, but in unwilling ears,
40　This saving counsel, "Keep your piece nine years."[9]
　　　　"Nine years!" cries he, who high in Drury Lane,[1]
　　Lulled by soft zephyrs° through the broken pane,　　　*winds*
　　Rhymes ere he wakes, and prints before term° ends, *the publishing season*
　　Obliged by hunger and request of friends:
45　"The piece, you think, is incorrect? why, take it,
　　I'm all submission, what you'd have it, make it."
　　　　Three things another's modest wishes bound,
　　My friendship, and a prologue, and ten pound.
　　　　Pitholeon[2] sends to me: "You know his Grace,
50　I want a patron; ask him for a place."
　　Pitholeon libeled me—"but here's a letter
　　Informs you, sir, 'twas when he knew no better.
　　Dare you refuse him? Curll[3] invites to dine,
　　He'll write a *Journal*, or he'll turn divine."[4]
55　Bless me! a packet.—" 'Tis a stranger sues,
　　A virgin tragedy, an orphan Muse."
　　If I dislike it, "Furies, death, and rage!"
　　If I approve, "Commend it to the stage."
　　There (thank my stars) my whole commission ends,
60　The players and I are, luckily, no friends.
　　Fired that the house° reject him, " 'Sdeath, I'll print it,　*playhouse*
　　And shame the fools—Your interest, sir, with Lintot!"[5]
　　Lintot, dull rogue, will think your price too much.
　　"Not, sir, if you revise it, and retouch."
65　All my demurs but double his attacks;
　　At last he whispers, "Do; and we go snacks."°　　　　　*shares*
　　Glad of a quarrel, straight I clap the door,
　　"Sir, let me see your works and you no more."
　　　　'Tis sung, when Midas' ears began to spring
70　(Midas, a sacred person and a king),
　　His very minister who spied them first
　　(Some say his queen) was forced to speak, or burst.[6]

9. Horace, *Ars Poetica* (lines 386–89).
1. The theater district, where the speaker lives in a garret.
2. "A foolish poet of Rhodes, who pretended much to Greek" [Pope's note]. He stands for Leonard Welsted, translator of Longinus and an enemy of Pope's.
3. Edmund Curll, an unscrupulous publisher, derided in Pope's *Dunciad*.
4. Referring to attacks on Pope in *The London Journal* and (perhaps) to Welsted's theological

writing.
5. Bernard Lintot, an early publisher of Pope.
6. According to Greek mythology, King Midas, preferring Pan's music to Apollo's, was given ass's ears by the affronted god. His barber (in Chaucer's version of the tale, his wife) discovered the ears and, fairly bursting with the secret, whispered it into a hole in the ground. Here, Pope suggests that Prime Minister Walpole and Queen Caroline know that George II is an ass.

And is not mine, my friend, a sorer case,
When every coxcomb perks them in my face?
75   A. Good friend, forbear! you deal in dangerous things.
I'd never name queens, ministers, or kings;
Keep close to ears, and those let asses prick;
'Tis nothing—— P. Nothing? if they bite and kick?
Out with it, *Dunciad!* let the secret pass,
80 That secret to each fool, that he's an ass:
The truth once told (and wherefore should we lie?)
The queen of Midas slept, and so may I.
    You think this cruel? take it for a rule,
No creature smarts° so little as a fool.   *hurts*
85 Let peals of laughter, Codrus![7] round thee break,
Thou unconcerned canst hear the mighty crack.
Pit, box, and gallery in convulsions hurled,
Thou stand'st unshook amidst a bursting world.
Who shames a scribbler? break one cobweb through,
90 He spins the slight, self-pleasing thread anew:
Destroy his fib or sophistry,[8] in vain;
The creature's at his dirty work again,
Throned in the center of his thin designs,
Proud of a vast extent of flimsy lines.
95 Whom have I hurt? has poet yet or peer
Lost the arched eyebrow or Parnassian[9] sneer?
And has not Colley[1] still his lord and whore?
His butchers Henley? his freemasons Moore?[2]
Does not one table Bavius still admit?
100 Still to one bishop Philips seem a wit?
Still Sappho—— A. Hold! for God's sake—you'll offend.
No names—be calm—learn prudence of a friend.
I too could write, and I am twice as tall;
But foes like these!—— P. One flatterer's worse than all.
105 Of all mad creatures, if the learn'd are right,
It is the slaver° kills, and not the bite.   *spittle*
A fool quite angry is quite innocent:
Alas! 'tis ten times worse when they repent.
    One dedicates in high heroic prose,
110 And ridicules beyond a hundred foes;
One from all Grub Street[3] will my fame defend,
And, more abusive, calls himself my friend.
This prints my letters,[4] that expects a bribe,
And others roar aloud, "Subscribe, subscribe!"[5]
115   There are, who to my person pay their court:
I cough like Horace, and, though lean, am short;

---

7. Ancient Roman poet ridiculed by Virgil and Juvenal.
8. Seemingly solid but flawed reasoning.
9. Pertaining to poetry and the Muses.
1. Colley Cibber, poet laureate.
2. John Henley (known as "Orator" Henley) was an independent preacher with a mass following. James Moore Smythe was a member of the Masonic order. Bavius (line 99) was a bad poet

referred to by Virgil. The bishop of Armagh employed Ambrose Philips (line 100; called "Namby-Pamby" by the wits) as his secretary. "Sappho" (line 101) is the poet Lady Mary Wortley Montagu (1689–1762; see pp. 639–45).
3. The traditional haunt of hack writers.
4. As Curll had done without permission.
5. Pay for copies in advance of publication.

Ammon's great son[6] one shoulder had too high,
Such Ovid's nose, and "Sir! you have an eye—"
Go on, obliging creatures, make me see
120 All that disgraced my betters met in me.
Say for my comfort, languishing in bed,
"Just so immortal Maro° held his head":   *Virgil*
And when I die, be sure you let me know
Great Homer died three thousand years ago.
125   Why did I write? what sin to me unknown
Dipped me in ink, my parents', or my own?
As yet a child, nor yet a fool to fame,
I lisped in numbers,° for the numbers came.   *verses*
I left no calling for this idle trade,
130 No duty broke, no father disobeyed.
The Muse but served to ease some friend, not wife,
To help me through this long disease, my life,
To second, Arbuthnot! thy art and care,
And teach the being° you preserved, to bear.°   *life / endure*
135   A. But why then publish? P. Granville the polite,[7]
And knowing Walsh, would tell me I could write;
Well-natured Garth inflamed with early praise,
And Congreve loved, and Swift endured my lays;
The courtly Talbot, Somers, Sheffield, read;
140 Even mitered Rochester[8] would nod the head,
And St. John's[9] self (great Dryden's friends before)
With open arms received one poet more.
Happy my studies, when by these approved!
Happier their author, when by these beloved!
145 From these the world will judge of men and books,
Not from the Bùrnets, Òldmixons, and Cookes.[1]
    Soft were my numbers; who could take offense
While pure description held the place of sense?
Like gentle Fanny's[2] was my flowery theme,
150 A painted mistress, or a purling° stream.   *murmuring*
Yet then did Gildon[3] draw his venal quill;
I wished the man a dinner, and sat still.
Yet then did Dennis[4] rave in furious fret;
I never answered, I was not in debt.
155 If want° provoked, or madness made them print,   *lack*
I waged no war with Bedlam or the Mint.[5]
    Did some more sober critic come abroad?
If wrong, I smiled; if right, I kissed° the rod.°   *accepted / punishment*
Pains, reading, study are their just pretense,

<hr>

6. Alexander the Great was called the son, or descendant, of the supreme Libyan god, Ammon.
7. There follow the names of poets and men of letters, Pope's early friends. They were literary elder statesmen, chiefly, who had befriended John Dryden (1631–1700; see pp. 500–526) in his later years.
8. The bishop of Rochester (the miter being a bishop's hat).
9. Pronounced *sín-jín's.*

1. Thomas Burnet, John Oldmixon, and Arthur Cooke had all attacked Pope or his works.
2. Lord Hervey, satirized as Sporus in lines 305 ff.
3. Charles Gildon, a critic who had, as Pope believed, written against him "venally," to curry favor with the essayist and poet Joseph Addison.
4. John Dennis, who wrote a furious condemnation of Pope's *Essay on Criticism.*
5. See note 2 to line 4 and note 5 to line 13 above.

160　And all they want is spirit, taste, and sense.
　　　Commas and points they set exactly right,
　　　And 'twere a sin to rob them of their mite.°　　　　　　*small coin*
　　　Yet ne'er one sprig of laurel graced these ribalds,
　　　From slashing Bentley down to piddling Tibbalds.[6]
165　Each wight° who reads not, and but scans and spells,　　　　*man*
　　　Each word-catcher that lives on syllables,
　　　Even such small critics some regard may claim,
　　　Preserved in Milton's or in Shakespeare's name.
　　　Pretty! in amber to observe the forms
170　Of hairs, or straws, or dirt, or grubs, or worms!
　　　The things, we know, are neither rich nor rare,
　　　But wonder how the devil they got there.
　　　　　Were others angry? I excused them too;
　　　Well might they rage; I gave them but their due.
175　A man's true merit 'tis not hard to find;
　　　But each man's secret standard in his mind,
　　　That casting weight[7] pride adds to emptiness,
　　　This, who can gratify? for who can guess?
　　　The bard whom pilfered pastorals renown,
180　Who turns a Persian tale for half a crown,[8]
　　　Just writes to make his barrenness appear,
　　　And strains from hard-bound brains eight lines a year:
　　　He, who still wanting, though he lives on theft,
　　　Steals much, spends little, yet has nothing left;
185　And he who now to sense, now nonsense leaning,
　　　Means not, but blunders round about a meaning:
　　　And he whose fustian's° so sublimely bad,　　　　　*pretentious writing's*
　　　It is not poetry, but prose run mad:
　　　All these, my modest satire bade translate,
190　And owned that nine such poets made a Tate.[9]
　　　How did they fume, and stamp, and roar, and chafe!
　　　And swear, not Addison[1] himself was safe.
　　　　　Peace to all such! but were there one whose fires
　　　True Genius kindles, and fair Fame inspires;
195　Blessed with each talent and each art to please,
　　　And born to write, converse, and live with ease:
　　　Should such a man, too fond to rule alone,
　　　Bear, like the Turk, no brother near the throne;[2]
　　　View him with scornful, yet with jealous eyes,
200　And hate for arts that caused himself to rise;
　　　Damn with faint praise, assent with civil leer,
　　　And without sneering, teach the rest to sneer;
　　　Willing to wound, and yet afraid to strike,

6. Richard Bentley, a classical scholar, had edited
Paradise Lost with undue license on the grounds
that Milton was blind and never saw his text. Lewis
Theobald, no wit but a closer scholar than Pope,
had exposed the faults of Pope's edition of Shake-
speare in a subsequent edition of his own. *Laurel:*
classical symbol of poetic achievement *Ribalds:*
rascals.
7. Weight tipping the scales.
8. Ambrose Philips (named in line 100), who had

competed with the youthful Pope as a pastoral
poet; author of *Persian Tales.*
9. Nahum Tate, successor to Dryden as poet lau-
reate. This line adapts the adage that it takes nine
tailors to make a man.
1. Joseph Addison, coauthor of *The Tatler* and *The
Spectator,* and arbiter of polite taste.
2. The Ottoman emperors, Europeans believed,
regularly killed their principal kinsmen upon
ascending the throne.

Just hint a fault, and hesitate dislike;
205   Alike reserved to blame or to commend,
A timorous foe, and a suspicious friend;
Dreading even fools; by flatterers besieged,
And so obliging that he ne'er obliged;
Like Cato, give his little senate laws,[3]
210   And sit attentive to his own applause;
While wits and Templars° every sentence raise,   law students
And wonder with a foolish face of praise—
Who but must laugh, if such a man there be?
Who would not weep, if Atticus[4] were he?
215   What though my name stood rubric° on the walls?   in red letters
Or plastered posts, with claps,° in capitals?   posters
Or smoking forth, a hundred hawkers' load,
On wings of winds came flying all abroad?
I sought no homage from the race that write;
220   I kept, like Asian monarchs, from their sight:
Poems I heeded (now berhymed so long)
No more than thou, great George![5] a birthday song.
I ne'er with wits or witlings° passed my days   ones of little wit
To spread about the itch of verse and praise;
225   Nor like a puppy daggled° through the town   dragged about
To fetch and carry sing-song up and down;
Nor at rehearsals sweat, and mouthed, and cried,
With handkerchief and orange at my side;
But sick of fops, and poetry, and prate,
230   To Bufo left the whole Castalian state.[6]
      Proud as Apollo on his forkèd hill,[7]
Sat full-blown Bufo, puffed by every quill;
Fed with soft dedication all day long,
Horace and he went hand in hand in song.
235   His library (where busts of poets dead
And a true Pindar[8] stood without a head)
Received of wits an undistinguished race,
Who first his judgment asked, and then a place:
Much they extolled his pictures, much his seat,°   estate
240   And flattered every day, and some days eat:°   ate
Till grown more frugal in his riper days,
He paid some bards with port, and some with praise;
To some a dry° rehearsal was assigned,   without performance
And others (harder still) he paid in kind.[9]
245   Dryden alone (what wonder?) came not nigh;
Dryden alone escaped this judging eye:
But still the great have kindness in reserve;

3. Addison, author of the immensely popular trag-
edy *Cato* (1713), presided over an admiring com-
pany of political and literary partisans at Button's
Coffee House. Pope's prologue to Cato includes
the line "While Cato gives his little senate laws."
4. A wealthy, wise man of letters (109–32 B.C.E.)
and a friend of Cicero; here, a pseudonym for Addi-
son.
5. George II.
6. Pope leaves Bufo the whole republic of letters,
named from the spring Castalia, which was sacred
to Apollo (Greek and Roman god of poetry) and
the Muses. Bufo (Latin for toad), perhaps a com-
posite of Lord Halifax and "Bubo," Bubb Doding-
ton, represents a type of tasteless patron of the arts.
7. The twin peaks of Parnassus, one sacred to
Apollo and the other sacred to Dionysus (Greek
god of wine).
8. Ancient Greek poet famous for his odes and
lyrics.
9. I.e., he read them his poetry in turn.

He helped to bury whom he helped to starve.
    May some choice patron bless each gray goose quill!°   *quill pen*
250 May every Bavius have his Bufo still![1]
So when a statesman wants a day's defense,
Or Envy holds a whole week's war with Sense,
Or simple Pride for flattery makes demands,
May dunce by dunce be whistled off my hands!
255 Blessed be the great! for those they take away,
And those they left me—for they left me Gay;[2]
Left me to see neglected genius bloom,
Neglected die, and tell it on his tomb;
Of all thy blameless life the sole return
260 My verse, and Queensberry weeping o'er thy urn!
Oh, let me live my own, and die so too!
("To live and die is all I have to do")[3]
Maintain a poet's dignity and ease,
And see what friends, and read what books I please;
265 Above a patron, though I condescend
Some times to call a minister my friend.
I was not born for courts or great affairs;
I pay my debts, believe, and say my prayers,
Can sleep without a poem in my head,
270 Nor know if Dennis be alive or dead.
    Why am I asked what next shall see the light?
Heavens! was I born for nothing but to write?
Has life no joys for me? or (to be grave)
Have I no friend to serve, no soul to save?
275 "I found him close with Swift"—"Indeed? no doubt,"
Cries prating Balbus, "something will come out."
'Tis all in vain, deny it as I will.
"No, such a genius never can lie still,"
And then for mine obligingly mistakes
280 The first lampoon Sir Will or Bubo[4] makes.
Poor guiltless I! and can I choose but smile,
When every coxcomb knows me by my style?
    Cursed be the verse, how well soe'er it flow,
That tends to make one worthy man my foe,
285 Give Virtue scandal, Innocence a fear,
Or from the soft-eyed virgin steal a tear!
But he who hurts a harmless neighbor's peace,
Insults fallen worth, or Beauty in distress,
Who loves a lie, lame Slander helps about,
290 Who writes a libel, or who copies out:
That fop whose pride affects a patron's name,
Yet absent, wounds an author's honest fame;
Who can your merit selfishly approve,

---

1. For Bavius, see note 2 to line 98; for Bufo, note 6 to line 230.
2. John Gay (1685–1732; see pp. 594–96), author of *The Beggar's Opera*, associate of Pope and Swift; befriended (line 260) by the duke and duchess of Queensberry.
3. Quotation from Denham's poem "Of Prudence."
4. Sir William Yonge or Bubb Dodington. Both were Pope's political adversaries as well as, in some degree, silly men.

And show the sense of it without the love;
295 Who has the vanity to call you friend,
Yet wants the honor, injured, to defend;
Who tells whate'er you think, whate'er you say,
And, if he lie not, must at least betray:
Who to the dean and silver bell can swear,
300 And sees at Cannons what was never there:[5]
Who reads but with a lust to misapply,
Make satire a lampoon, and fiction, lie:
A lash like mine no honest man shall dread,
But all such babbling blockheads in his stead.
305   Let Sporus[6] tremble—— A. What? that thing of silk,
Sporus, that mere white curd of ass's milk?
Satire or sense, alas! can Sporus feel?
Who breaks a butterfly upon a wheel?
        P. Yet let me flap this bug with gilded wings,
310 This painted child of dirt, that stinks and stings;
Whose buzz the witty and the fair annoys,
Yet wit ne'er tastes, and beauty ne'er enjoys;
So well-bred spaniels civilly delight
In mumbling of the game they dare not bite.
315 Eternal smiles his emptiness betray,
As shallow streams run dimpling all the way.
Whether in florid impotence he speaks,
And, as the prompter breathes, the puppet squeaks;
Or at the ear of Eve,[7] familiar toad,
320 Half froth, half venom, spits himself abroad,
In puns, or politics, or tales, or lies,
Or spite, or smut, or rhymes, or blasphemies.
His wit all seesaw between *that* and *this*,
Now high, now low, now master up, now miss,
325 And he himself one vile antithesis.
Amphibious thing! that acting either part,
The trifling head or the corrupted heart,
Fop at the toilet, flatterer at the board,
Now trips° a lady, and now struts a lord.   *walks like*
330 Eve's tempter thus the rabbins° have expressed,   *Hebrew scholars*
A cherub's face, a reptile all the rest;
Beauty that shocks you, parts° that none will trust,   *talents*
Wit that can creep, and pride that licks the dust.
        Not Fortune's worshiper, nor Fashion's fool,
335 Not Lucre's° madman, nor Ambition's tool,   *Money's*
Not proud, nor servile, be one poet's praise,
That if he pleased, he pleased by manly ways:
That flattery, even to kings, he held a shame,
And thought a lie in verse or prose the same:

---

5. In his *Epistle to Burlington*, Pope satirized "Timon's Villa," an estate where a silver bell and an obsequious dean invite worshipers to an over-stuffed chapel. Mischief-makers had unjustly identified this estate with Cannons, the ostentatious home of Pope's well-wisher the duke of Chandos.
6. Roman eunuch, object of Nero's sexual desires;

in the poem, Lord Hervey, a foppish and effeminate courtier who was Pope's personal, political, and literary enemy. He attested his frailty by drinking ass's milk as a tonic.
7. Like Satan in Eden (*Paradise Lost* 4.790 ff.). Hervey was Queen Caroline's confidant; the word "familiar" suggests a demonic ministrant.

340   That not in fancy's maze he wandered long,
        But stooped[8] to truth, and moralized his song:
        That not for fame, but Virtue's better end,
        He stood the furious foe, the timid friend,
        The damning critic, half approving wit,
345   The coxcomb hit, or fearing to be hit;
        Laughed at the loss of friends he never had,
        The dull, the proud, the wicked, and the mad;
        The distant threats of vengeance on his head,
        The blow unfelt, the tear he never shed;
350   The tale revived, the lie so oft o'erthrown,
        The imputed trash, and dullness not his own;
        The morals blackened when the writings 'scape,
        The libeled person, and the pictured shape;[9]
        Abuse on all he loved, or loved him, spread,
355   A friend in exile, or a father dead;
        The whisper,[1] that to greatness still too near,
        Perhaps yet vibrates on his sovereign's ear—
        Welcome for thee, fair Virtue! all the past!
        For thee, fair Virtue! welcome even the last!
360   A. But why insult the poor, affront the great?
        P. A knave's a knave to me in every state:
        Alike my scorn, if he succeed or fail,
        Sporus at court, or Japhet[2] in a jail,
        A hireling scribbler, or a hireling peer,
365   Knight of the post[3] corrupt, or of the shire,
        If on a pillory, or near a throne,
        He gain his prince's ear, or lose his own.
          Yet soft by nature, more a dupe than wit,
        Sappho can tell you how this man was bit:°   *deceived*
370   This dreaded satirist Dennis will confess
        Foe to his pride, but friend to his distress:[4]
        So humble, he has knocked at Tibbald's door,
        Has drunk with Cibber, nay, has rhymed for Moore.
        Full ten years slandered, did he once reply?
375   Three thousand suns went down on Welsted's lie.[5]
        To please a mistress one[6] aspersed° his life;   *maligned*
        He lashed him not, but let her be his wife.
        Let Budgell charge low Grub Street on his quill,
        And write whate'er he pleased, except his will;[7]
380   Let the two Curlls, of town and court,[8] abuse
        His father, mother, body, soul, and muse.
        Yet why? that father held it for a rule,
        It was a sin to call our neighbor fool;
        That harmless mother thought no wife a whore:

8. Swooped down, perceiving prey (a term from falconry).
9. Cartoons were drawn of Pope's hunched posture.
1. Hervey's whisper to Queen Caroline.
2. Japhet Crook, a forger; his ears were cropped for his crime (line 367). For Sporus, see note 6 to line 305.
3. *Knight of the post*: professional witness.

4. Pope contributed to a benefit performance for the aging Dennis.
5. Welsted had accused Pope of causing the death of a female admirer.
6. The statesman William Windham.
7. Eustace Budgell (perhaps falsely) attributed to Pope a squib in the *Grub-Street Journal* charging that Budgell had forged a will.
8. The publisher Edmund Curll and Lord Hervey.

385 Hear this, and spare his family, James Moore![9]
Unspotted names, and memorable long,
If there be force in virtue, or in song.
    Of gentle blood (part shed in honor's cause,
    While yet in Britain honor had applause)
390 Each parent sprung——— A. What fortune, pray?——— P. Their own,
And better got than Bestia's[1] from the throne.
Born to no pride, inheriting no strife,
Nor marrying discord in a noble wife,
Stranger to civil and religious rage,
395 The good man walked innoxious° through his age.   *harmless*
No courts he saw, no suits would ever try,
Nor dared an oath, nor hazarded a lie.[2]
Unlearned, he knew no schoolman's subtle art,
No language but the language of the heart.
400 By nature honest, by experience wise,
Healthy by temperance, and by exercise;
His life, though long, to sickness passed unknown,
His death was instant, and without a groan.
Oh, grant me thus to live, and thus to die!
405 Who sprung from kings shall know less joy than I.
    O friend! may each domestic bliss be thine!
Be no unpleasing melancholy mine:
Me, let the tender office long engage,
To rock the cradle of reposing Age,
410 With lenient arts extend a mother's breath,[3]
Make Languor smile, and smooth the bed of Death,
Explore the thought, explain the asking eye,
And keep a while one parent from the sky!
On cares like these if length of days attend,
415 May Heaven, to bless those days, preserve my friend,
Preserve him social, cheerful, and serene,
And just as rich as when he served a Queen![4]
A. Whether that blessing be denied or given,
Thus far was right—the rest belongs to Heaven.

1735

The Universal Prayer

Father of all! in every age,
    In every clime adored,
By saint, by savage, and by sage,
    Jehovah, Jove, or Lord!

---

9. See lines 23 and 373.
1. A Roman consul who was bribed to arrange a dishonorable peace; here, probably, the duke of Marlborough.
2. He did not take the special oath required of Catholics wanting to enter public life or the professions, nor did he evade by falsehood the restric-

tions on Catholics.
3. Pope was nursing his sick mother when, in 1731, he wrote these lines (she died in 1733).
4. Arbuthnot, who had sought no professional profit as physician to Queen Anne, continued to earn the same income after her death.

5   Thou Great First Cause,[5] least understood:
      Who all my sense confined
    To know but this—that thou art good,
      And that myself am blind:

    Yet gave me, in this dark estate,
10   To see the good from ill;
    And binding Nature fast in fate,
      Left free the human will.

    What conscience dictates to be done,
      Or warns me not to do,
15   This, teach me more than Hell to shun,
      That, more than Heaven pursue.[6]

    What blessings thy free bounty gives,
      Let me not cast away;
    For God is paid when man receives,
20   To enjoy is to obey.

    Yet not to earth's contracted span,
      Thy goodness let me bound,
    Or think thee Lord alone of man,
      When thousand worlds are round:

25   Let not this weak, unknowing hand
      Presume thy bolts[7] to throw,
    And deal damnation round the land,
      On each I judge thy foe.

    If I am right, thy grace impart,
30   Still in the right to stay;
    If I am wrong, oh teach my heart
      To find that better way.

    Save me alike from foolish pride,
      Or impious discontent,
35   At aught thy wisdom has denied,
      Or aught thy goodness lent.

    Teach me to feel another's woe,
      To hide the fault I see;
    That mercy I to others show,
40   That mercy show to me.

---

5. God considered as the first principle, creator of all creatures, cause of all truth and goodness.
6. I.e., teach me to refine my conscience here on Earth instead of concerning myself overmuch with the afterlife.
7. The weapons, thunderbolts, of Zeus, chief Greek god.

Mean though I am, not wholly so
 Since quickened by thy breath;
Oh lead me wheresoe'er I go,
 Through this day's life or death.

45 This day, be bread and peace[8] my lot:
 All else beneath the sun,
Thou know'st if best bestowed or not,
 And let thy will be done.

To thee, whose temple is all space,
50 Whose altar, earth, sea, skies!
One chorus let all being raise!
 All Nature's incense rise!

ca. 1715   1738

Impromptu

To Lady Winchelsea,
Occasioned by four Satirical Verses on Women Wits,
In The Rape of the Lock[9]

In vain you boast poetic names of yore,
And cite those Sapphos we admire no more:[1]
Fate doomed the fall of every female wit;
But doomed it then, when first Ardelia[2] writ.
5 Of all examples by the world confessed,
I knew Ardelia could not quote the best;
Who, like her mistress on Britannia's throne,
Fights and subdues in quarrels not her own.[3]
To write their praise you but in vain essay;
10 Even while you write, you take that praise away.
Light to the stars the sun does thus restore,
But shines himself till they are seen no more.

ca. 1715   1741

8. Perhaps an allusion to the Lord's Prayer: "Give us this day our daily bread . . ."
9. Ostensibly written casually, without premeditation ("impromptu"), this poem to Anne Finch, countess of Winchilsea (1661–1720), replies to some verses she had sent Pope in response to *The Rape of the Lock* 4.59–62 (see p. 616). Since these lines, from the "Cave of Spleen" episode, are directed specifically against female poets, and Anne Finch wrote a poem titled "The Spleen" (p. 558), she was probably right in reading Pope's verses as containing a comic slur directed at her. Her initial response to Pope has not survived, but her witty "Answer" to this "Impromptu" was printed in 1717 (p. 565). In a letter to a male friend written in 1713, Pope complained that the experience of hearing Lady Winchilsea read her poetry at a dinner party gave him a headache—an ailment that in the *Rape* he associates only with women. For another view of spleen—an ailment similar to depression—see the selection from Matthew Green's poem on that subject (p. 645).
1. Applies to all female poets the name of the ancient Greek poet.
2. The name under which Anne Finch sometimes wrote.
3. An allusion to Queen Anne (reigned 1702–14), who involved England in wars (of the Spanish Succession) that Pope viewed as irrelevant to the national interest.

From The Dunciad

[The Triumph of Dulness][4]

In vain, in vain,—the all-composing hour
Resistless° falls: the Muse obeys the power.   *irresistibly*
She[5] comes! she comes! the sable° throne behold   *black*
630   Of Night primeval, and of Chaos old![6]
Before her, Fancy's gilded clouds decay,
And all its varying rainbows die away.
Wit shoots in vain its momentary fires,
The meteor drops, and in a flash expires.
635   As one by one, at dread Medea's strain,
The sickening stars fade off the ethereal plain;[7]
As Argus' eyes by Hermes' wand oppressed,
Closed one by one to everlasting rest;[8]
Thus at her felt approach, and secret might,
640   Art after Art goes out, and all is night.
See skulking Truth to her old cavern fled,[9]
Mountains of casuistry[1] heaped o'er her head!
Philosophy, that leaned on Heaven before,
Shrinks to her second cause,[2] and is no more.
645   Physic° of Metaphysic begs defense,   *natural science*
And Metaphysic calls for aid on Sense!
See Mystery° to Mathematics fly!   *mystical knowledge*
In vain! they gaze, turn giddy, rave, and die.
Religion blushing veils her sacred fires,
650   And unawares *Morality* expires.
Nor public flame, nor private, dares to shine;
Nor human spark is left, nor glimpse divine!
Lo! thy dread empire, Chaos is restored;
Light dies before thy uncreating word:[3]
655   Thy hand, great Anarch! lets the curtain fall;
And universal darkness buries all.

1721–25   1747

4. *Dunciad* (B) 4.627–56.
5. Dulness, the center of a mock-apocalyptic vision in which the light of the arts and sciences is extinguished.
6. Milton, in *Paradise Lost* 1.543, describes the elements separating heaven and hell as "Chaos and old Night," or disorder and darkness, the first materials of the cosmos.
7. In Seneca's *Medea*, the stars obey the curse of Medea, a magician and avenger.
8. Hermes, the Greek gods' messenger, charmed the hundred-eyed watchman, Argus, to sleep and then killed him.
9. "Alluding to the saying of Democritus, that Truth lay at the bottom of a deep well" [Pope's note].
1. Discourse about "cases of conscience"; also, overly complex reasoning.
2. In classical philosophy, God is defined as the first cause of all things. Under the sway of Dulness, a materialistic explanation (or "second cause") is substituted.
3. As opposed to God's first creating words in Genesis, "Let there be light."

LADY MARY WORTLEY MONTAGU
1689–1762

Saturday

The Small-Pox

FLAVIA[1]

The wretched Flavia, on her couch reclined,
Thus breathed the anguish of a wounded mind.
A glass° reversed in her right hand she bore,   *mirror*
For now she shunned the face she sought before.
5   "How am I changed! alas! how am I grown
A frightful spectre, to myself unknown!
Where's my complexion? where the radiant bloom,
That promised happiness for years to come?
Then,° with what pleasure I this face surveyed!   *in the past*
10   To look once more, my visits oft delayed!
Charmed with the view, a fresher red would rise,
And a new life shot sparkling from my eyes!
Ah! faithless glass, my wonted° bloom restore!   *accustomed*
Alas! I rave, that bloom is now no more!
15   "The greatest good the gods on men bestow,
Ev'n youth itself, to me is useless now.
There was a time (oh! that I could forget!)
When opera-tickets poured before my feet;
And at the Ring[2] where brightest beauties shine,
20   The earliest cherries of the spring were mine.
Witness, O Lillie, and thou, Motteux, tell,
How much japan[3] these eyes have made you sell.
With what contempt ye saw me oft despise
The humble offer of the raffled prize;
25   For at each raffle still the prize I bore,
With scorn rejected, or with triumph wore.
Now beauty's fled, and presents are no more.
     "For me the patriot has the House[4] forsook,
And left debates to catch a passing look;
30   For me the soldier has soft verses writ;
For me the beau° has aimed to be a wit.   *suitor*
For me the wit to nonsense was betrayed;
The gamester has for me his dun° delayed   *demand for payment*

1. Eclogues are traditionally sophisticated, medium-length pastoral poems; see, e.g., Edmund Spenser's "Aprill" (p. 159). In this poem, as in her other five "town" eclogues, Montagu revises the genre, satirizing Londoners' manners and morals through characters given classical (Greek and Roman) names. Here, focusing on "Flavia," Montagu examines a disease that had killed her brother and ten-year-old nephew; she had suffered from it in 1715, but without being badly scarred. She later had her son inoculated for smallpox in Turkey and became a vocal advocate of inoculation when she returned to England in 1718. She wrote various letters and an essay attacking physicians who opposed inoculation and the "fools" who believed in them.
2. A fashionable area in Hyde Park.
3. Japanese work with painted and varnished design; Charles Lillie and Peter Motteux were men of letters who also dealt in Asian goods.
4. I.e., the House of Commons, the lower house of the English Parliament.

And overseen° the card I would have paid.[5]   overlooked
35 The bold and haughty by success made vain,
Awed by my eyes, has trembled to complain:
The bashful squire, touched with a wish unknown,
Has dared to speak with spirit not his own:
Fired by one wish, all did alike adore;
40 Now beauty's fled, and lovers are no more.
    "As round the room I turn my weeping eyes,
New unaffected scenes of sorrow rise.
Far from my sight that killing picture bear,
The face disfigure, or the canvas tear![6]
45 That picture, which with pride I used to show,
The lost resemblance but upbraids me now.
And thou, my toilette, where I oft have sat,
While hours unheeded passed in deep debate,
How curls should fall, or where a patch[7] to place;
50 If blue or scarlet best became my face;
Now on some happier nymph° your aid bestow;   girl
On fairer heads, ye useless jewels, glow!
No borrowed lustre can my charms restore,
Beauty is fled, and dress is now no more.
55   "Ye meaner beauties, I permit you shine;
Go, triumph in the hearts that once were mine;
But, midst your triumphs with confusion know,
'Tis to my ruin all your charms ye owe.
Would pitying heaven restore my wonted° mien,°   usual / appearance
60 Ye still might move unthought of and unseen:
But oh, how vain, how wretched is the boast
Of beauty faded, and of empire lost!
What now is left but weeping to deplore
My beauty fled, and empire now no more?
65   "Ye cruel chemists,° what withheld your aid?   druggists
Could no pomatums[8] save a trembling maid?
How false and trifling is that art you boast;
No art can give me back my beauty lost!
In tears, surrounded by my friends I lay,
70 Masked o'er, and trembling at the light of day;
Mirmillo[9] came my fortune to deplore
(A golden-headed cane well carved he bore):
Cordials, he cried, my spirits must restore!
Beauty is fled, and spirit is no more!
75 Galen the grave, officious Squirt was there,
With fruitless grief and unavailing care:
Machaon too, the great Machaon, known
By his red cloak and his superior frown;
And why, he cried, this grief and this despair?

5. I.e., underwritten her next bet.
6. The painting is "killing" to her present sense of
self because it shows her face as it used to be,
unblemished; in anger, she wishes to "disfigure"
the painting as the disease has disfigured her.
7. A small piece of silk or court plaster worn on
the face to heighten the complexion and attract
attention.

8. Scented, apple-based ointments applied to the
face and hair.
9. A "Mirmillo," or mermillo, was a type of Roman
gladiator typically represented in statues as armed
with helmet, oval shield, and a short sword held in
front of him. This name, like "Galen," "Squirt," and
"Machaon" in the next lines, is a mock-heroic allu-
sion to a contemporary medical expert.

80   You shall again be well, again be fair;
       Believe my oath (with that an oath he swore);
       False was his oath! my beauty is no more.
            "Cease, hapless maid, no more thy tale pursue,
       Forsake mankind, and bid the world adieu.
85   Monarchs and beauties rule with equal sway,
       All strive to serve, and glory to obey:
       Alike unpitied when deposed they grow,
       Men mock the idol of their former vow.
            "Adieu, ye parks—in some obscure recess,
90   Where gentle streams will weep at my distress,
       Where no false friend will in my grief take part,
       And mourn my ruin with a joyful heart;
       There let me live in some deserted place,
       There hide in shades this lost inglorious face.
95   Plays, operas, circles,° I no more must view!   *tiers of theater seats*
       My toilette, patches, all the world, adieu!"

1716   1747

The Lover: A Ballad

       At length, by so much importunity pressed,
       Take, Molly,[1] at once, the inside of my breast;
       This stupid indifference so often you blame
       Is not owing to nature, to fear, or to shame;
5   I am not as cold as a Virgin in lead,[2]
       Nor is Sunday's sermon so strong in my head;
       I know but too well how time flies along,
       That we live but few years and yet fewer are young.

       But I hate to be cheated, and never will buy
10   Long years of repentance for moments of joy.
       Oh was there a man (but where shall I find
       Good sense and good nature so equally joined?)
       Would value his pleasure, contribute to mine,
       Not meanly would boast, nor would lewdly design,°   *plot*
15   Not over severe, yet not stupidly vain,
       For I would have the power though not give the pain;

       No pedant yet learnèd, not rakehelly° gay   *like a libertine*
       Or laughing because he has nothing to say,
       To all my whole sex obliging and free,
20   Yet never be fond of any but me;
       In public preserve the decorum that's just,
       And show in his eyes he is true to his trust,

---

1. Molly Skerrett, a friend of Montagu, was the mistress of the English statesman Sir Robert Walpole.

2. I.e., an image of the Virgin Mary, either as a leaden statue or as a stained-glass window framed in lead.

Then rarely approach, and respectfully bow,
Yet not fulsomely pert, nor yet foppishly low.

25   But when the long hours of public are past
And we meet with champagne and a chicken at last,
May every fond pleasure that hour endear,
Be banished afar both discretion and fear,
Forgetting or scorning the airs of the crowd
30   He may cease to be formal, and I to be proud,
Till lost in the joy we confess that we live,
And he may be rude, and yet I may forgive.

And that my delight may be solidly fixed,
Let the friend and the lover be handsomely mixed,
35   In whose tender bosom my soul might confide,
Whose kindness can sooth me, whose counsel could guide.
From such a dear lover as here I describe
No danger should fright me, no millions should bribe;
But till this astonishing creature I know,
40   As I long have lived chaste, I will keep myself so.

I never will share with the wanton coquette,
Or be caught by a vain affectation of wit.
The toasters and songsters may try all their art
But never shall enter the pass of my heart.
45   I loathe the lewd rake, the dressed fopling despise;
Before such pursuers the nice° virgin flies;   *fastidious*
And as Ovid has sweetly in parables told
We harden like trees, and like rivers are cold.[3]

ca. 1721–25   1747

A Receipt to Cure the Vapors[4]

I

Why will Delia thus retire,
    And idly languish life away?
While the sighing crowd admire,
    'Tis too soon for hartshorn tea:[5]

II

5   All those dismal looks and fretting
    Cannot Damon's life restore;

3. In Ovid's *Metamorphoses,* two nymphs (minor
nature goddesses) escape from gods: Daphne, flee-
ing from Apollo, is turned into a laurel; Arethusa,
fleeing from Alpheus, becomes a fountain.
4. This poem was apparently written to Lady Anne
Irwin, widowed eight or nine years previously and
addressed here under the stereotypical name
Delia. (Damon, line 6, is also a conventional poetic

name.) *Receipt:* formula of a remedy for a disease.
Vapors: a disorder supposed to be caused by exha-
lations within the organs of the body and charac-
terized by depression, hypochondria, hysteria, and
other nervous disorders. Synonymous with the
malaise of "spleen," analyzed by Anne Finch (see
p. 558) and Matthew Green (p. 645).
5. A medicinal tea made from ammonia.

Long ago the worms have eat him,
    You can never see him more.

III

Once again consult your toilette,[6]
10   In the glass° your face review: *mirror*
So much weeping soon will spoil it,
    And no spring your charms renew.

IV

I, like you, was born a woman,
    Well I know what vapors mean:
15   The disease, alas! is common;
    Single, we have all the spleen.[7]

V

All the morals that they tell us,
    Never cured the sorrow yet:
Chuse, among the pretty fellows,
20   One of honor, youth, and wit.

VI

Prithee hear him every morning
    At the least an hour or two;
Once again at night returning—
    I believe the dose will do.

ca. 1730   1748

Epistle from Mrs. Yonge to Her Husband[8]

Think not this paper comes with vain pretense
To move your pity, or to mourn th' offense.
Too well I know that hard obdurate heart;
No softening mercy there will take my part,
5   Nor can a woman's arguments prevail,

6. I.e., consider your manner of dressing.
7. I.e., we alone (i.e., women only) are affected by vapors; or, alternatively, women are affected by vapors when they are "single" (i.e., without the company of a man).
8. In 1724, the notorious libertine William Yonge, separated from his wife, Mary, discovered that she (like him) had committed adultery. He sued her lover, Colonel Norton, for damages and collected £1,500. Later that year, according to the law of the time, he petitioned the Houses of Parliament for a divorce. The case was tried in public, Mrs. Yonge's love letters were read aloud, and two men testified that they had found her and Norton "together in naked bed." Yonge was granted the divorce, his wife's dowry, and the greater part of her fortune.
    Though the "Epistle" is obviously based on this

sensational affair, it is also a work of imagination. Like Alexander Pope's "Eloisa to Abelard"—to which Pope called Montagu's attention—it takes the form of a heroic epistle, the passionate outcry of an abandoned woman. The poet, entering into the feelings of Mrs. Yonge, justifies her conduct with reasons of both the heart and the head. The objects of her attack include the institution of marriage, which binds wives in "eternal chains"; the double standard of morality, which requires chastity from women but not men; the hypocrisy of society, which condemns the very behavior it secretly lusts after; and the craven greed and cruelty of the husband. But eighteenth-century women seldom dared speak like this in public, and the "Epistle" was not published until the 1970s.

When even your patron's wise example fails.[9]
But this last privilege I still retain;
Th' oppressed and injured always may complain.
    Too, too severely laws of honor bind
10 The weak submissive sex of womankind.
If sighs have gained or force compelled our hand,
Deceived by art, or urged by stern command,
Whatever motive binds the fatal tie,
The judging world expects our constancy.
15   Just heaven! (for sure in heaven does justice reign,
Though tricks below that sacred name profane)
To you appealing I submit my cause,
Nor fear a judgment from impartial laws.
All bargains but° conditional° are made;   *only / conditionally*
20 The purchase void, the creditor unpaid;
Defrauded servants are from service free;
A wounded slave regains his liberty.
For wives ill used no remedy remains,
To daily racks condemned, and to eternal chains.
25   From whence is this unjust distinction grown?
Are we not formed with passions like your own?
Nature with equal fire our souls endued,
Our minds as haughty, and as warm our blood;
O'er the wide world your pleasures you pursue,
30 The change is justified by something new;
But we must sigh in silence—and be true.
Our sex's weakness you expose and blame
(Of every prattling fop the common theme),
Yet from this weakness you suppose is due
35 Sublimer virtue than your Cato[1] knew.
Had heaven designed us trials so severe,
It would have formed our tempers then to bear.
    And I have borne (oh what have I not borne!)
The pang of jealousy, the insults of scorn.
40 Wearied at length, I from your sight remove,
And place my future hopes in secret love.
In the gay bloom of glowing youth retired,
I quit the woman's joy to be admired,
With that small pension your hard heart allows,
45 Renounce your fortune, and release your vows.
To custom (though unjust) so much is due;
I hide my frailty from the public view.
My conscience clear, yet sensible of shame,
My life I hazard, to preserve my fame.
50 And I prefer this low inglorious state   ⎫
To vile dependence on the thing I hate—   ⎬
But you pursue me to this last retreat.   ⎭
Dragged into light, my tender crime is shown
And every circumstance of fondness known.
55 Beneath the shelter of the law you stand,

9. Sir Robert Walpole, Yonge's friend at court, was rumored to tolerate his own wife's infidelities.
1. The asceticism and self-discipline of the ancient Roman statesman Cato had been emphasized in Addison's famous tragedy *Cato* (1713).

And urge my ruin with a cruel hand,
While to my fault thus rigidly severe,
Tamely submissive to the man you fear.[2]
 This wretched outcast, this abandoned wife,
60 Has yet this joy to sweeten shameful life:
By your mean° conduct, infamously loose,   *vulgar*
You are at once my accuser and excuse.
Let me be damned by the censorious prude
(Stupidly dull, or spiritually lewd),
65 My hapless case will surely pity find
From every just and reasonable mind.
When to the final sentence I submit,
The lips condemn me, but their souls acquit.
 No more my husband, to your pleasures go,
70 The sweets of your recovered freedom know.
Go: court the brittle friendship of the great,
Smile at his board,° or at his levee[3] wait;   *dining table*
And when dismissed, to madam's toilet fly,[4]
More than her chambermaids, or glasses,° lie,   *mirrors*
75 Tell her how young she looks, how heavenly fair,
Admire the lilies and the roses there.
Your high ambition may be gratified,
Some cousin of her own be made your bride,
And you the father of a glorious race
80 Endowed with Ch——l's strength and Low——r's face.[5]

1724   1972

MATTHEW GREEN
1696–1737

From The Spleen[1]

An Epistle to Mr. Cuthbert Jackson

This motley piece to you I send,
Who always were a faithful friend;
Who, if disputes should happen hence,
Can best explain the author's sense;
5 And, anxious for the public weal,
Do, what I sing, so often feel.[2]

2. I.e., Walpole. Montagu suggests that the whole political establishment of England takes sides against Mrs. Yonge.
3. Morning reception of visitors.
4. It was fashionable for women like Lady Walpole to receive visitors during the last stages of dressing (their "toilet").
5. General Churchill was rumored to have had an affair with Lady Walpole; Anthony Lowther was a notorious gallant. The author implies that Yonge's next wife may be as untrue as his first. Mrs. Yonge remarried immediately after her divorce; five years later, Yonge (whose divorce had made him rich) married the daughter of a baron.

1. The effects of "the spleen" were believed to be depression, hypochondria, ill-temper, melancholy, and a variety of other nervous disorders. Green wrote this poem supposedly in reply to a friend who asked him how he coped with this malady. Although he cites causes and treatments for the disorder, Green uses the subject to write a satire on religion, politics, and contemporary social practices. Cf. Anne Finch, "The Spleen" (p. 558).
2. Green claims to suffer from "what I sing," i.e., "spleen," as a result of his concern for the "public weal," i.e., the public welfare, a reference to his

The want of method pray excuse,
Allowing for a vapored Muse;[3]
Nor to a narrow path confined,
10   Hedge in by rules a roving mind.

The child is genuine, you may trace
Throughout the sire's transmitted° face,   *inherited*
Nothing is stolen: my Muse, though mean,°   *lowly, poor*
Draws from the spring she finds within;
15   Nor vainly° buys what Gildon[4] sells,   *in vain*
Poetic buckets for dry wells.

School-helps I want,[5] to climb on high,
Where all the ancient treasures lie,
And there unseen commit a theft
20   On wealth in Greek exchequers° left.   *treasuries*
Then where? from whom? what can I steal,
Who only with the moderns deal?
This were attempting to put on
Raiment from naked bodies won:[6]
25   They safely sing before a thief,
They cannot give who want relief;
Some few excepted, names well known,
And justly laureled[7] with renown,
Whose stamp of genius marks their ware,
30   And theft detects: of theft beware;
From More so lashed,[8] example fit,
Shun petty larceny in wit.

First know, my friend, I do not mean
To write a treatise on the spleen;
35   Nor to prescribe when nerves convulse;
Nor mend th' alarum watch, your pulse.
If I am right, your question lay,
What course I take to drive away
The day-mare[9] Spleen, by whose false pleas
40   Men prove mere suicides in ease;[1]
And how I do myself demean°   *manage*
In stormy world to live serene.

When by its magic lantern[2] Spleen
With frightful figures spreads life's scene,

---

job as a clerk in a Custom House (the office responsible for levying taxes on imported and exported goods) in London.
3. The Muses were the nine Greek sister goddesses supposed to be the sources of inspiration for the arts. *Vapored*: i.e., afflicted with the vapors, a disorder supposed to be caused by exhalations within the organs of the body and characterized by symptoms similar to those of spleen.
4. Charles Gildon (1665–1724), author of *The Complete Art of English Poetry*.
5. Lack; Green claims to not have a classical education, a claim somewhat belied by the many learned allusions in the poem.
6. Perhaps a reference to two lines from Edward

Howard's epic poem *British Princes* (1669): "A painted vest Prince Vortiger had on, / Which from a naked Pict his grandsire won."
7. The laurel was a symbol of poetic achievement.
8. In *The Dunciad* 2.50, Alexander Pope (1688–1744) "lashed," i.e., castigated, the playwright James Moore Smythe (1702–1734) for having plagiarized.
9. Similar to a nightmare, but occurring during wakefulness; a term coined by Green.
1. Without hesitation; or, at leisure. *Mere*: unassisted (legal).
2. An optical instrument by means of which a magnified image of a picture on glass is thrown upon a white screen or wall in a darkened room.

45   And threat'ning prospects° urged my fears,   *expectations*
       A stranger to the luck of heirs;[3]
       Reason, some quiet to restore,
       Showed part was substance, shadow more;
       With Spleen's dead weight though heavy grown,
50   In life's rough tide I sunk not down,
       But swam, 'till Fortune threw a rope,
       Buoyant on bladders[4] fill'd with hope.

       I always choose the plainest food
       To mend viscidity° of blood.   *glutinousness*
55   Hail! water-gruel,° healing power,   *thin porridge*
       Of easy access to the poor;
       Thy help love's confessors implore,
       And doctors secretly adore;
       To thee, I fly, by thee dilute—
60   Through veins my blood doth quicker shoot,[5]
       And by swift current throws off clean
       Prolific particles of Spleen.

       I never sick by drinking grow,
       Nor keep myself a cup too low,°   *sad, gloomy*
65   And seldom Cloe's lodgings haunt,
       Thrifty of spirits, which I want.[6]

       Hunting I reckon very good
       To brace the nerves, and stir the blood:
       But after no field-honors° itch,   *honors won in the hunt*
70   Achieved by leaping hedge and ditch,
       While Spleen lies soft relaxed in bed,
       Or o'er coal fires inclines the head,
       Hygeia's sons[7] with hound and horn,
       And jovial cry awake the morn.

       *   *   *

       To cure the mind's wrong bias, Spleen,
90   Some recommend the bowling-green;[8]
       Some, hilly walks; all, exercise;
       Fling but a stone, the giant dies;[9]
       Laugh and be well. Monkeys have been
       Extreme good doctors for the Spleen;
95   And kitten, if the humor hit,[1]
       Has harlequinned° away the fit.   *conjured away*

       *   *   *

---

3. I.e., he has no hope of an inheritance.
4. Animals' bladders, inflated and used as flotation devices.
5. "Blood" is the noun acted on by the past participle, "dilute": i.e., "blood," diluted by the gruel, "doth quicker shoot" through the veins.
6. I.e., economical of liveliness or energy, which I lack. C[h]loe: a conventional poetic name for a young woman.

7. Healthy men (Hygeia being the Greek goddess of health).
8. The lawn on which bowls, a popular English game, is played.
9. The metaphor alludes to 1 Samuel 17, in which a young David kills the Philistine giant, Goliath, with a stone from his sling.
1. I.e., if it affects the disposition.

125 If spleen-fogs rise at close of day,
I clear my evening with a play,
Or to some concert take my way.
The company, the shine of lights,
The scenes of humor, music's flights,
130 Adjust and set the soul to rights.

Life's moving pictures, well-wrought plays,
To others' grief attention raise:
Here, while the tragic fictions glow,
We borrow joy by pitying woe;
135 There gaily comic scenes delight,
And hold true mirrors to our sight.
Virtue, in charming dress arrayed,
Calling the passions to her aid,
When moral scenes just actions join,
140 Takes shape, and shows her face divine.

* * *

Sometimes I dress, with women sit,
And chat away the gloomy fit;
Quit the stiff garb of serious sense,
185 And wear a gay impertinence,°   *indifference*
Nor think nor speak with any pains,
But lay on fancy's neck the reins;
Talk of unusual swell of waist
In maid of honor[2] loosely laced,
190 And beauty borr'wing Spanish red,[3]
And loving pair with sep'rate bed,
And jewels pawned for loss of game,
And then redeemed by loss of fame;
Of Kitty (aunt left in the lurch
195 By grave pretence to go to church)
Perceived in hack° with lover fine,   *rented carriage*
Like Will and Mary on the coin:[4]
And thus in modish° manner we,   *fashionable*
In aid of sugar, sweeten tea.

200   Permit, ye fair,° your idol form,   *beautiful woman*
Which e'en the coldest heart can warm,
May with its beauties grace my line,
While I bow down before its shrine,
And your thronged altars with my lays°   *songs*
205 Perfume, and get by giving praise.
With speech so sweet, so sweet a mien,°   *appearance*
You excommunicate the Spleen.

* * *

1737

---

2. An unmarried woman, usually of noble birth, who attends upon a queen or princess.
3. A cosmetic that added reddish color to the cheeks.

4. William and Mary were joint rulers of England from 1689 until her death, in 1694. During their reign, coins were minted that bore the likenesses of their two heads in profile.

JAMES THOMSON
1700–1748

From The Seasons

From *Winter*

    The keener tempests come: and, fuming dun°   *dark; murky*
From all the livid east or piercing north,
225 Thick clouds ascend, in whose capacious womb
A vapory deluge lies, to snow congealed.
Heavy they roll their fleecy world along,
And the sky saddens with the gathered storm.
Through the hushed air the whitening shower descends,
230 At first thin-wavering; till at last the flakes
Fall broad and wide and fast, dimming the day
With a continual flow. The cherished fields
Put on their winter robe of purest white.
'Tis brightness all; save where the new snow melts
235 Along the mazy current. Low the woods
Bow their hoar° head; and, ere the languid sun   *frozen, icy*
Faint from the west emits his evening ray,
Earth's universal face, deep-hid and chill,
Is one wild dazzling waste that buries wide
240 The works of man. Drooping, the laborer-ox
Stands covered o'er with snow, and then demands
The fruit of all his toil. The fowls of heaven,
Tamed by the cruel season, crowd around
The winnowing store,[1] and claim the little boon
245 Which Providence assigns them. One alone,
The redbreast, sacred to the household gods,
Wisely regardful of the embroiling sky,
In joyless fields and thorny thickets leaves
His shivering mates, and pays to trusted man
250 His annual visit. Half afraid, he first
Against the window beats; then brisk alights
On the warm hearth; then, hopping o'er the floor,
Eyes all the smiling family askance,
And pecks, and starts, and wonders where he is—
255 Till, more familiar grown, the table crumbs
Attract his slender feet. The foodless wilds
Pour forth their brown inhabitants. The hare,
Though timorous of heart, and hard beset
By death in various forms, dark snares, and dogs,
260 And more unpitying men, the garden seeks,
Urged on by fearless want. The bleating kind[2]
Eye the bleak heaven, and next the glistening earth,
With looks of dumb despair; then, sad-dispersed,
Dig for the withered herb through heaps of snow.

---

1. Place where the harvest has been threshed.   2. Sheep.

265   Now, shepherds, to your helpless charge be kind;
        Baffle the raging year, and fill their pens
        With food at will; lodge them below the storm,
        And watch them strict, for, from the bellowing east,
        In this dire season, oft the whirlwind's wing
270   Sweeps up the burden of whole wintry plains
        In one wide weft,° and o'er the hapless flocks,   *web*
        Hid in the hollow of two neighboring hills,
        The billowy tempest whelms,° till, upward urged,   *pours*
        The valley to a shining mountain swells,
275   Tipped with a wreath high-curling in the sky.
            As thus the snows arise, and, foul and fierce,
        All Winter drives along the darkened air,
        In his own loose-revolving° fields the swain°   *giddily turning / rustic*
        Disastered stands; sees other hills ascend,
280   Of unknown joyless brow, and other scenes,
        Of horrid prospect, shag° the trackless plain;   *make shaggy*
        Nor finds the river nor the forest, hid
        Beneath the formless wild, but wanders on
        From hill to dale, still more and more astray,
285   Impatient flouncing through the drifted heaps,
        Stung with the thoughts of home—the thoughts of home
        Rush on his nerves and call their vigor forth
        In many a vain attempt. How sinks his soul!
        What black despair, what horror fills his heart,
290   When, for the dusky spot which fancy feigned
        His tufted° cottage rising through the snow,   *tree-surrounded*
        He meets the roughness of the middle waste,
        Far from the track and blest abode of man,
        While round him night resistless closes fast,
295   And every tempest, howling o'er his head,
        Renders the savage wilderness more wild.
        Then throng the busy shapes into his mind
        Of covered pits, unfathomably deep,
        A dire descent! beyond the power of frost;
300   Of faithless bogs; of precipices huge,
        Smoothed up with snow; and (what is land unknown,
        What water) of the still unfrozen spring,
        In the loose marsh or solitary lake,
        Where the fresh fountain from the bottom boils.
305   These check his fearful steps; and down he sinks
        Beneath the shelter of the shapeless drift,
        Thinking o'er all the bitterness of death,
        Mixed with the tender anguish nature shoots
        Through the wrung bosom of the dying man—
310   His wife, his children, and his friends unseen.
        In vain for him the officious° wife prepares   *dutiful*
        The fire fair-blazing and the vestment warm;
        In vain his little children, peeping out
        Into the mingling storm, demand their sire
315   With tears of artless innocence. Alas!
        Nor wife nor children more shall he behold,

Nor friends, nor sacred home. On every nerve
The deadly winter seizes, shuts up sense,
And, o'er his inmost vitals creeping cold,
320   Lays him along the snows a stiffened corse,°   *corpse*
Stretched out and bleaching in the northern blast.
    Ah! little think the gay licentious proud,
Whom pleasure, power, and affluence surround—
They who their thoughtless hours in giddy mirth,
325   And wanton, often cruel, riot° waste—   *revelry*
Ah! little think they, while they dance along,
How many feel, this very moment, death
And all the sad variety of pain;
How many sink in the devouring flood,
330   Or more devouring flame; how many bleed,
By shameful variance° betwixt man and man;   *quarreling*
How many pine in want,° and dungeon glooms,   *lack*
Shut from the common air and common use
Of their own limbs; how many drink the cup
335   Of baleful grief, or eat the bitter bread
Of misery; sore pierced by wintry winds,
How many shrink into the sordid hut
Of cheerless poverty; how many shake
With all the fiercer tortures of the mind,
340   Unbounded passion, madness, guilt, remorse—
Whence, tumbled headlong from the height of life,
They furnish matter for the Tragic Muse;[3]
Even in the vale,° where wisdom loves to dwell,   *valley*
With friendship, peace, and contemplation joined,
345   How many, racked with honest passions, droop
In deep retired distress; how many stand
Around the death-bed of their dearest friends,
And point° the parting anguish! Thought fond man   *accentuate*
Of these, and all the thousand nameless ills
350   That one incessant struggle render life,[4]
One scene of toil, of suffering, and of fate,
Vice in his high career would stand appalled,
And heedless rambling Impulse learn to think;
The conscious° heart of Charity would warm,   *sympathetic*
355   And her wide wish Benevolence dilate°   *diffuse*
The social tear would rise, the social sigh;
And into clear perfection, gradual° bliss,   *progressive*
Refining still, the social passions work.

1726

3. Melpomene, Muse of tragedy, one of the nine sister goddesses in Greek mythology who inspired the arts.

4. I.e., if foolish human beings thought of these, and of all the thousand nameless ills that render life one incessant struggle.

CHARLES WESLEY
1707–1788

HYMNS[1]

[My God! I Know, I Feel Thee Mine[2]]

1

My God! I know, I feel thee mine,
    And will not quit my claim
Till all I have is lost in thine,
    And all renewed I am.

2

5   I hold thee with a trembling hand,
        But will not let thee go
    Till steadfastly by faith I stand,
        And all thy goodness know.

3

    When shall I see the welcome hour
10   That plants my God in me!
    Spirit of health, and life, and power,
        And perfect liberty!

4

    Jesu, thine all-victorious love
        Shed in my heart abroad!
15 Then shall my feet no longer rove,
        Rooted and fixed in God.

5

    Love only can the conquest win,
        The strength of sin subdue
    (Mine own unconquerable sin),
20   And form my soul anew.

6

    Love can bow down the stubborn neck,
        The stone to flesh convert;

---

1. Many tenets of the Methodist movement, founded by John Wesley (1703–1791) in 1739, are expressed by the hymns of his brother, Charles. Some Methodists believed in the assurance of salvation (rejecting the Calvinist doctrine of predestination) and acquired their name by advocating methodical study and devotion as a means of attaining Christian perfection. Charles Wesley wrote more than six thousand hymns and helped popularize hymn singing in English at worship services. The hymns selected below were first printed in different editions of the Wesleys' *Hymns and Sacred Prayers;* we follow the text of the 1780 *Hymnbook.*
2. The subtext for this hymn is Romans 4.13: "For the promise that he should be the heir of the world was not to Abraham, or to his seed, through the law, but through the righteousness of faith."

Soften, and melt, and pierce, and break
   An adamantine° heart.   *unyielding, hard*

7

25 Oh, that in me the sacred fire
   Might now begin to glow,
Burn up the dross of base desire,
   And make the mountains flow!

8

Oh, that it now from heaven might fall,
30   And all my sins consume!
Come, Holy Ghost, for thee I call,
   Spirit of burning, come!

9

Refining fire, go through my heart,
   Illuminate my soul;
35 Scatter thy life through every part,
   And sanctify the whole.

10

Sorrow and sin shall then expire,
   While, entered into rest,
I only live my God t'admire—
40   My God forever blest.

11

No longer then my heart shall mourn,
   While purified by grace
I only for his glory burn,
   And always see his face.

12

45 My steadfast soul, from falling free,
   Shall then no longer move;
But Christ be all the world to me,
   And all my heart be love.

                                 1740

[Come on, My Partners in Distress]

1

Come on, my partners in distress,
My comrades through the wilderness,[3]
   Who still your bodies feel;

---

3. Where the Israelites wandered for forty years; also, the place where Christ was tempted, thus a place of suffering, testing, wandering, used here as a metaphor for earthly life.

Awhile forget your griefs and fears,
5   And look beyond this vale of tears
To that celestial hill.[4]

2

Beyond the bounds of time and space
Look forward to that heavenly place,
The saints' secure abode;
10   On faith's strong eagle pinions rise,
And force your passage to the skies,
And scale the mount of God.

3

Who suffer with our Master[5] here,
We shall before his face appear,
15   And by his side sit down;
To patient faith the prize is sure,
And all that to the end endure
The cross, shall wear the crown.[6]

4

Thrice blessed bliss-inspiring hope!
20   It lifts the fainting spirits up,
It brings to life the dead;
Our conflicts here shall soon be past,
And you and I ascend at last
Triumphant with our head.[7]

5

25   That great mysterious Deity
We soon with open face shall see;
The beatific sight[8]
Shall fill heaven's sounding courts with praise,
And wide diffuse the golden blaze
30   Of everlasting light.

6

The Father shining on his throne,
The glorious, co-eternal Son,
The Spirit, one and seven,[9]
Conspire our rapture to complete,
35   And lo! we fall before his feet,
And silence heightens heaven.

---

4. The heavenly Jerusalem is thought to be located on a hill, Mt. Sion. *Vale of tears*: this world, regarded as a place of trouble, sorrow, misery, or weeping.
5. I.e., Christ.
6. The New Testament promises a "crown of life" to the faithful Christian (James 1.12).

7. I.e., Christ; "the head of every man is Christ" (1 Corinthians 11.3).
8. A sight of the glories of heaven, especially that first granted to a disembodied spirit.
9. The "seven spirits of God" are referred to in Revelation 1.4, 3.1, 4.5, 5.6.

7

In hope of that ecstatic pause,
Jesu, we now sustain the cross,
    And at thy footstool fall,
40 Till thou our hidden life reveal,
Till thou our ravished spirits fill,
    And God is all in all.

1749

SAMUEL JOHNSON
1709–1784

Prologue Spoken by Mr. Garrick[1]

At the Opening of the Theater Royal, Drury Lane, 1747

When Learning's triumph o'er her barbarous foes
First reared the stage, immortal Shakespeare rose;
Each change of many-colored life he drew,
Exhausted worlds, and then imagined new:
5 Existence saw him spurn her bounded reign,
And panting Time toiled after him in vain.
His powerful strokes presiding Truth impressed,
And unresisted Passion stormed the breast.
    Then Jonson[2] came, instructed from the school
10 To please in method and invent by rule;
His studious patience and laborious art
By regular approach essayed the heart;
Cold Approbation gave the lingering bays,[3]
For those who durst not censure, scarce could praise.
15 A mortal born, he met the general doom,
But left, like Egypt's kings, a lasting tomb.
    The wits of Charles[4] found easier ways to fame,
Nor wished for Jonson's art, or Shakespeare's flame;
Themselves they studied; as they felt, they writ;
20 Intrigue was plot, obscenity was wit.
Vice always found a sympathetic friend;
They pleased their age, and did not aim to mend.°   amend it
Yet bards like these aspired to lasting praise,
And proudly hoped to pimp° in future days.   bid for reward
25 Their cause was general, their supports were strong,
Their slaves were willing, and their reign was long:
Till Shame regained the post that Sense betrayed,
And Virtue called Oblivion to her aid.
    Then, crushed by rules, and weakened as refined,
30 For years the power of Tragedy declined;

1. David Garrick (1717–1779), English actor and theater manager.
2. Ben Jonson (1572–1637), poet and playwright.
3. Laurel, given in recognition of poetic achievement.
4. The comic playwrights of the Restoration.

From bard to bard the frigid caution crept,
Till Declamation roared while Passion slept;
Yet still did Virtue deign the stage to tread;
Philosophy remained though Nature fled;
35   But forced at length her ancient reign to quit,
She saw great Faustus[5] lay the ghost of Wit;
Exulting Folly hailed the joyous day,
And Pantomime and Song confirmed her sway.
    But who the coming changes can presage,
40   And mark the future periods of the stage?
Perhaps if skill could distant times explore,
New Behns, new Durfeys,[6] yet remain in store;
Perhaps where Lear has raved, and Hamlet died,
On flying cars new sorcerers may ride;
45   Perhaps (for who can guess the effects of chance?)
Here Hunt may box, or Mahomet may dance.[7]
    Hard is his lot that, here by fortune placed,
Must watch the wild vicissitudes of taste;
With every meteor of caprice must play,
50   And chase the new-blown bubbles of the day.
Ah! let not censure term our fate our choice,
The stage but echoes back the public voice;
The drama's laws, the drama's patrons give,
For we that live to please, must please to live.
55   Then prompt no more the follies you decry,
As tyrants doom their tools of guilt to die;
'Tis yours this night to bid the reign commence
Of rescued Nature and reviving Sense;
To chase the charms of Sound, the pomp of Show,
60   For useful Mirth and salutary Woe;
Bid scenic Virtue form the rising age,
And Truth diffuse her radiance from the stage.

                          1747

The Vanity of Human Wishes

In Imitation of the Tenth Satire of Juvenal[8]

    Let Observation, with extensive view,
Survey mankind, from China to Peru;
Remark each anxious toil, each eager strife,
And watch the busy scenes of crowded life;
5   Then say how hope and fear, desire and hate
O'erspread with snares the clouded maze of fate,
Where wavering man, betrayed by venturous pride
To tread the dreary paths without a guide,

5. Magician of German legend, here as treated in current farce and pantomime.
6. Playwrights like Aphra Behn (1640?–1689), admired by some but also attacked for her racy plays, and Thomas D'Urfey (1653–1723), play-wright and poetaster who was a standing joke among the wits.
7. Referring to two then-popular figures, a pugilist and a tightrope dancer.
8. Ancient Roman poet and satirist.

As treacherous phantoms in the mist delude,
10 Shuns fancied ills, or chases airy good;
How rarely Reason guides the stubborn choice,
Rules the bold hand, or prompts the suppliant voice;
How nations sink, by darling schemes oppressed,
When Vengeance listens to the fool's request.[9]
15 Fate wings with every wish the afflictive dart,
Each gift of nature, and each grace of art;[1]
With fatal heat impetuous courage glows,
With fatal sweetness elocution flows,
Impeachment stops the speaker's powerful breath,
20 And restless fire precipitates on death.[2]
    But scarce observed, the knowing and the bold
Fall in the general massacre of gold;
Wide-wasting pest! that rages unconfined,
And crowds with crimes the records of mankind;
25 For gold his sword the hireling ruffian draws,
For gold the hireling judge distorts the laws;
Wealth heaped on wealth, nor truth nor safety buys,
The dangers gather as the treasures rise.
    Let History tell where rival kings command,
30 And dubious title shakes the madded land,
When statutes glean the refuse of the sword,
How much more safe the vassal than the lord,
Low skulks the hind° beneath the rage of power,   *peasant*
And leaves the wealthy traitor in the Tower,[3]
35 Untouched his cottage, and his slumbers sound,
Though Confiscation's vultures hover round.
    The needy traveler, serene and gay,
Walks the wild heath, and sings his toil away.
Does envy seize thee? crush the upbraiding joy,
40 Increase his riches and his peace destroy;
New fears in dire vicissitude invade,
The rustling brake° alarms, and quivering shade,   *thicket*
Nor light nor darkness bring his pain relief,
One shows the plunder, and one hides the thief.
45   Yet still one general cry the skies assails,
And gain and grandeur load the tainted gales;
Few know the toiling statesman's fear or care,
The insidious rival and the gaping heir.
    Once more, Democritus,[4] arise on earth,
50 With cheerful wisdom and instructive mirth,
See motley life in modern trappings dressed,
And feed with varied fools the eternal jest:
Thou who couldst laugh where Want enchained Caprice,
Toil crushed Conceit, and man was of a piece;
55 Where Wealth unloved without a mourner died;

---

9. I.e., when vengeance hangs over a nation, ready to descend on it if the proposals of political fools prevail.
1. The sense of this couplet is that men can be hurried toward misery by their desires and even by their talents and accomplishments.

2. Perhaps, i.e., impetuous energy hastens men to their death.
3. Tower of London (a prison).
4. Greek philosopher of the late fifth century B.C.E., a fatalist who exalted cheerfulness and derided all immoderate pretensions.

And scarce a sycophant was fed by Pride;
Where ne'er was known the form of mock debate,
Or seen a new-made mayor's unwieldy state;°   *pomp*
Where change of favorites made no change of laws,
60   And senates heard before they judged a cause;
How wouldst thou shake at Britain's modish tribe,
Dart the quick taunt, and edge the piercing gibe?
Attentive truth and nature to descry,
And pierce each scene with philosophic eye,
65   To thee were solemn toys or empty show
The robes of pleasures and the veils of woe:
All aid the farce, and all thy mirth maintain,
Whose joys are causeless, or whose griefs are vain.
     Such was the scorn that filled the sage's mind,
70   Renewed at every glance on human kind;
How just that scorn ere yet thy voice declare,
Search every state, and canvass every prayer.
     Unnumbered suppliants crowd Preferment's gate,
Athirst for wealth, and burning to be great;
75   Delusive Fortune hears the incessant call,
They mount, they shine, evaporate, and fall.
On every stage the foes of peace attend,
Hate dogs their flight, and Insult mocks their end.
Love ends with hope, the sinking statesman's door
80   Pours in the morning worshiper no more;[5]
For growing names the weekly scribbler lies,
To growing wealth the dedicator flies;
From every room descends the painted face,
That hung the bright palladium[6] of the place;
85   And smoked in kitchens, or in auctions sold,
To better features yields the frame of gold;
For now no more we trace in every line
Heroic worth, benevolence divine:
The form distorted justifies the fall,
90   And Detestation rids the indignant wall.
     But will not Britain hear the last appeal,
Sign her foes' doom, or guard her favorites' zeal?
Through Freedom's sons no more remonstrance rings,
Degrading nobles and controlling kings;
95   Our supple tribes repress their patriot throats,
And ask no questions but the price of votes,
With weekly libels and septennial ale.[7]
Their wish is full° to riot and to rail.   *satisfied*
     In full-blown dignity, see Wolsey[8] stand,
100   Law in his voice, and fortune in his hand:
To him the church, the realm, their powers consign,
Through him the rays of regal bounty shine;

5. Important personages received petitions and official calls in the morning.
6. An image of Pallas (Athena, Greek goddess of wisdom) that supposedly preserved Troy from capture as long as it remained in the city; hence a safeguard.
7. I.e., public attacks in the weekly press and ale distributed at the parliamentary elections held every seventh year.
8. Thomas Cardinal Wolsey (ca. 1475–1530), lord chancellor under Henry VIII.

Turned by his nod the stream of honor flows,
His smile alone security bestows:
105 Still to new heights his restless wishes tower,
Claim leads to claim, and power advances power;
Till conquest unresisted ceased to please,
And rights submitted, left him none to seize.
At length his sovereign frowns—the train of state[9]
110 Mark the keen glance, and watch the sign to hate.
Where'er he turns, he meets a stranger's eye,
His suppliants scorn him, and his followers fly;
At once is lost the pride of awful state,
The golden canopy, the glittering plate,
115 The regal palace, the luxurious board,°   table
The liveried army, and the menial lord.
With age, with cares, with maladies oppressed,
He seeks the refuge of monastic rest.
Grief aids disease, remembered folly stings,
120 And his last sighs reproach the faith of kings.
    Speak thou, whose thoughts at humble peace repine,°   complain
Shall Wolsey's wealth, with Wolsey's end be thine?
Or liv'st thou now, with safer pride content,
The wisest justice on the banks of Trent?[1]
125 For why did Wolsey, near the steeps of fate,
On weak foundations raise the enormous weight?
Why but to sink beneath misfortune's blow,
With louder ruin to the gulfs below?
    What gave great Villiers[2] to the assassin's knife,
130 And fixed disease on Harley's closing life?
What murdered Wentworth, and what exiled Hyde,
By kings protected and to kings allied?
What but their wish indulged in courts to shine,
And power too great to keep or to resign?
135   When first the college rolls receive his name,
The young enthusiast quits his ease for fame;
Resistless burns the fever of renown
Caught from the strong contagion of the gown:[3]
O'er Bodley's dome his future labors spread,
140 And Bacon's mansion trembles o'er his head.[4]
Are these thy views? proceed, illustrious youth,
And Virtue guard thee to the throne of Truth!
Yet should thy soul indulge the generous heat,
Till captive Science yields her last retreat;

9. I.e., followers of the king.
1. A river flowing through the English Midlands.
2. George Villiers, duke of Buckingham, court favorite of James I and Charles I; assassinated in 1628. Robert Harley (line 130), earl of Oxford, a member of the Tory ministry under Queen Anne, was subsequently imprisoned and suffered a decline. Thomas Wentworth (line 131), earl of Strafford, advisor to Charles I, was executed in 1641, under the Long Parliament. Edward Hyde (line 131), earl of Clarendon, who was Charles II's lord chancellor and whose daughter married into the royal family, was impeached and exiled in

1667.
3. Academic gown, put on upon entering the university, with allusion to the shirt of Nessus, the flaming robe that clung to the mythical Greek hero Hercules and drove him to his death.
4. "There is a tradition, that the study of friar Bacon [i.e., the thirteenth-century scientist and philosopher Roger Bacon], built on an arch over the bridge, will fall, when a man greater than Bacon shall pass under it" [Johnson's note]. Bodley's dome: the Bodleian Library, Oxford (Latin for domus, house).

145   Should Reason guide thee with her brightest ray,
       And pour on misty Doubt resistless day;
       Should no false kindness lure to loose delight,
       Nor praise relax, nor difficulty fright;
       Should tempting Novelty thy cell refrain,°   *pass by, avoid*
150   And Sloth effuse her opiate fumes in vain;
       Should Beauty blunt on fops her fatal dart,
       Nor claim the triumph of a lettered heart,
       Should no disease thy torpid veins invade,
       Nor Melancholy's phantoms haunt thy shade;
155   Yet hope not life from grief or danger free,
       Nor think the doom of man reversed for thee:
       Deign on the passing world to turn thine eyes,
       And pause a while from letters, to be wise;
       There mark what ills the scholar's life assail,
160   Toil, envy, want, the patron, and the jail.
       See nations slowly wise, and meanly just,
       To buried merit raise the tardy bust.
       If dreams yet flatter, once again attend,
       Hear Lydiat's life, and Galileo's end.[5]
165   Nor deem, when Learning her last prize bestows,
       The glittering eminence exempt from foes;
       See when the vulgar 'scapes, despised or awed,
       Rebellion's vengeful talons seize on Laud.[6]
       From meaner minds though smaller fines content,
170   The plundered palace, or sequestered[7] rent;
       Marked out by dangerous parts he meets the shock,
       And fatal Learning leads him to the block:
       Around his tomb let Art and Genius weep,
       But hear his death, ye blockheads, hear and sleep.[8]
175   The festal blazes, the triumphal show,
       The ravished standard, and the captive foe,
       The senate's thanks, the gazette's[9] pompous tale,
       With force resistless o'er the brave prevail.
       Such bribes the rapid Greek[1] o'er Asia whirled,
180   For such the steady Romans shook the world;
       For such in distant lands the Britons shine,
       And stain with blood the Danube or the Rhine;
       This power has praise that virtue scarce can warm,[2]
       Till fame supplies the universal charm.
185   Yet Reason frowns on War's unequal game,
       Where wasted nations raise a single name,
       And mortgaged states their grandsires' wreaths regret
       From age to age in everlasting debt;
       Wreaths which at last the dear-bought right convey

---

5. Galileo (1564–1642), the Italian astronomer, was imprisoned for heresy by the Inquisition; he died blind. Thomas Lydiat (1572–1646), the Oxford mathematician and don, endured lifelong poverty because of his Royalist sympathies.
6. William Laud (1573–1645), archbishop of Canterbury under Charles I; executed in 1645, under the Long Parliament, for his devotion to episcopacy.

7. Confiscated by the state.
8. Rest secure, i.e., since you lack Laud's learning and gifts.
9. Newspaper's or official report's.
1. I.e., Alexander the Great.
2. I.e., praise has a power (to activate the brave) that an abstract love of virtue can scarcely begin to kindle.

190　To rust on medals, or on stones decay.
　　　　On what foundation stands the warrior's pride,
　　　How just his hopes, let Swedish Charles[3] decide;
　　　A frame of adamant, a soul of fire,
　　　No dangers fright him, and no labors tire;
195　O'er love, o'er fear, extends his wide domain,
　　　Unconquered lord of pleasure and of pain;
　　　No joys to him pacific scepters yield,
　　　War sounds the trump, he rushes to the field;
　　　Behold surrounding kings their powers combine,
200　And one capitulate, and one resign;[4]
　　　Peace courts his hand, but spreads her charms in vain;
　　　"Think nothing gained," he cries, "till naught remain,
　　　On Moscow's walls till Gothic° standards fly,　　　　　　*Teutonic*
　　　And all be mine beneath the polar sky."
205　The march begins in military state,
　　　And nations on his eye suspended wait;
　　　Stern Famine guards the solitary coast,
　　　And Winter barricades the realms of Frost;
　　　He comes, nor want nor cold his course delay—
210　Hide, blushing Glory, hide Pultowa's day:
　　　The vanquished hero leaves his broken bands,
　　　And shows his miseries in distant lands;
　　　Condemned a needy supplicant to wait,
　　　While ladies interpose, and slaves debate.
215　But did not Chance at length her error mend?
　　　Did no subverted empire mark his end?
　　　Did rival monarchs give the fatal wound?
　　　Or hostile millions press him to the ground?
　　　His fall was destined to a barren strand,
220　A petty fortress, and a dubious hand;
　　　He left the name at which the world grew pale,
　　　To point a moral, or adorn a tale.
　　　　　　All times their scenes of pompous woes afford,
　　　From Persia's tyrant to Bavaria's lord.[5]
225　In gay hostility, and barbarous pride,
　　　With half mankind embattled at his side,
　　　Great Xerxes comes to seize the certain prey,
　　　And starves exhausted regions in his way;
　　　Attendant Flattery counts his myriads o'er,
230　Till counted myriads soothe his pride no more;
　　　Fresh praise is tried till madness fires his mind,
　　　The waves he lashes, and enchains the wind;
　　　New powers are claimed, new powers are still bestowed,
　　　Till rude resistance lops the spreading god;
235　The daring Greeks deride the martial show,

3. King Charles XII (1682–1718) of Sweden. Defeated by the Russians at Pultowa in 1709, and escaping as "a needy supplicant" (line 213), he sought an alliance with the Turkish Sultan. He was killed in an attack on "a petty fortress" (line 220), Fredrikshald, in Norway.
4. Frederick IV of Denmark capitulated to Charles in 1700, and Augustus II of Poland resigned his throne to Charles in 1704.
5. Charles Albert, elector of Bavaria, who successfully aspired to the crown of the Holy Roman Empire but was deposed in a few years through the political skill of Maria Theresa ("fair Austria," line 245). *Persia's tyrant:* Xerxes, emperor whose forces the Greeks defeated by sea at Salamis in 480 B.C.E. and later, on land, at Plataea.

And heap their valleys with the gaudy foe;
The insulted sea with humbler thought he gains,
A single skiff to speed his flight remains;
The encumbered oar scarce leaves the dreaded coast
240 Through purple° billows and a floating host.   blood-stained
    The bold Bavarian, in a luckless hour,
Tries the dread summits of Caesarean° power,   imperial
With unexpected legions bursts away,
And sees defenseless realms receive his sway;
245 Short sway! fair Austria spreads her mournful charms,
The queen, the beauty, sets the world in arms;
From hill to hill the beacon's rousing blaze
Spreads wide the hope of plunder and of praise;
The fierce Croatian, and the wild Hussar,[6]
250 With all the sons of ravage crowd the war;
The baffled prince, in honor's flattering bloom,
Of hasty greatness finds the fatal doom;
His foes' derision, and his subjects' blame,
And steals to death from anguish and from shame.
255   Enlarge my life with multitude of days!
In health, in sickness, thus the suppliant prays;
Hides from himself his state, and shuns to know,
That life protracted is protracted woe.
Time hovers o'er, impatient to destroy,
260 And shuts up all the passages of joy;
In vain their gifts the bounteous seasons pour,
The fruit autumnal, and the vernal flower;
With listless eyes the dotard views the store,
He views, and wonders that they please no more;
265 Now pall the tasteless meats, and joyless wines,
And Luxury with sighs her slave resigns.
Approach, ye minstrels, try the soothing strain,
Diffuse the tuneful lenitives° of pain: relievers
No sounds, alas! would touch the impervious ear,
270 Though dancing mountains witnessed Orpheus[7] near;
Nor lute nor lyre his feeble powers attend,
Nor sweeter music of a virtuous friend,
But everlasting dictates crowd his tongue,
Perversely grave, or positively wrong.
275 The still returning tale, and lingering jest,
Perplex the fawning niece and pampered guest,
While growing hopes scarce awe the gathering sneer,
And scarce a legacy can bribe to hear;
The watchful guests still hint the last offense;
280 The daughter's petulance, the son's expense,
Improve° his heady rage with treacherous skill,   play upon
And mold his passions till they make his will.
    Unnumbered maladies his joints invade,
Lay siege to life and press the dire blockade;
285 But unextinguished avarice still remains,

6. Hungarian cavalryman.
7. In Greek mythology, a poet and musician whose playing could move even trees and hills.

And dreaded losses aggravate his pains;
He turns, with anxious heart and crippled hands,
His bonds of debt, and mortgages of lands;
Or views his coffers with suspicious eyes,
290   Unlocks his gold, and counts it till he dies.
    But grant, the virtues of a temperate prime
Bless with an age exempt from scorn or crime;
An age that melts with unperceived decay,
And glides in modest innocence away;
295   Whose peaceful day Benevolence endears,
Whose night congratulating Conscience cheers;
The general favorite as the general friend:
Such age there is, and who shall wish its end?
    Yet even on this her load Misfortune flings,
300   To press the weary minutes' flagging wings;
New sorrow rises as the day returns,
A sister sickens, or a daughter mourns.
Now kindred Merit fills the sable° bier,   *black*
Now lacerated Friendship claims a tear;
305   Year chases year, decay pursues decay,
Still drops some joy from withering life away;
New forms arise, and different views engage,
Superfluous lags the veteran[8] on the stage,
Till pitying Nature signs the last release,
310   And bids afflicted Worth retire to peace.
    But few there are whom hours like these await,
Who set unclouded in the gulfs of Fate.
From Lydia's monarch[9] should the search descend,
By Solon cautioned to regard his end,
315   In life's last scene what prodigies surprise,
Fears of the brave, and follies of the wise!
From Marlborough's eyes the streams of dotage flow,
And Swift expires a driveler and a show.[1]
    The teeming mother, anxious for her race,
320   Begs for each birth the fortune of a face:
Yet Vane could tell what ills from beauty spring;
And Sedley[2] cursed the form that pleased a king.
Ye nymphs of rosy lips and radiant eyes,
Whom Pleasure keeps too busy to be wise,
325   Whom Joys with soft varieties invite,
By day the frolic, and the dance by night;
Who frown with vanity, who smile with art,
And ask the latest fashion of the heart;
What care, what rules your heedless charms shall save,
330   Each nymph your rival, and each youth your slave?
Against your fame with Fondness Hate combines,
The rival batters, and the lover mines.°   *undermines*

8. I.e., an aged person.
9. Croesus (d. ca. 549 B.C.E.), a very rich king who boasted of his happiness, and who was advised by the Athenian lawmaker Solon to regard no man as securely happy. He was later deposed.
1. Both the military hero John Churchill, duke of Marlborough, and the writer Jonathan Swift (1667–1745; see pp. 568–89) declined into senility.
2. Catherine Sedley, mistress of James II. Anne Vane, mistress of Frederick, prince of Wales, died at thirty-one.

With distant voice neglected Virtue calls,
Less heard and less, the faint remonstrance falls;
335 Tired with contempt, she quits the slippery reign,
And Pride and Prudence take her seat in vain.
In crowd at once, where none the pass defend,
The harmless freedom, and the private friend.
The guardians yield, by force superior plied:
340 To Interest, Prudence; and to Flattery, Pride.
Now Beauty falls betrayed, despised, distressed,
And hissing Infamy proclaims the rest.
     Where then shall Hope and Fear their objects find?
Must dull Suspense corrupt the stagnant mind?
345 Must helpless man, in ignorance sedate,
Roll darkling down the torrent of his fate?
Must no dislike alarm, no wishes rise,
No cries invoke the mercies of the skies?
Inquirer, cease; petitions yet remain,
350 Which Heaven may hear, nor deem religion vain.
Still raise for good the supplicating voice,
But leave to Heaven the measure and the choice.
Safe in His power, whose eyes discern afar
The secret ambush of a specious prayer.
355 Implore His aid, in His decisions rest,
Secure, whate'er He gives, He gives the best.
Yet when the sense of sacred presence fires,
And strong devotion to the skies aspires,
Pour forth thy fervors for a healthful mind,
360 Obedient passions, and a will resigned;
For love, which scarce collective man can fill;
For patience sovereign o'er transmuted ill;[3]
For faith, that panting for a happier seat,
Counts death kind Nature's signal of retreat:
365 These goods for man the laws of Heaven ordain,
These goods He grants, who grants the power to gain;
With these celestial Wisdom calms the mind,
And makes the happiness she does not find.

1749

On the Death of Dr. Robert Levet[4]

Condemned to Hope's delusive mine,
     As on we toil from day to day,
By sudden blasts, or slow decline,
     Our social comforts drop away.

---

3. I.e., a capacity for love such that all humankind together can hardly engage it fully; and for patience, which, by asserting sovereignty over ills, changes their nature.

4. An unlicensed physician, who practiced among the poor and who had long lived in Johnson's house. He was uncouth in appearance and stiff in manner.

5   Well tried through many a varying year,
        See Levet to the grave descend;
    Officious,° innocent, sincere,   *dutiful*
        Of every friendless name the friend.

    Yet still he fills Affection's eye,
10   Obscurely wise, and coarsely kind;
    Nor, lettered Arrogance, deny
        Thy praise to merit unrefined.

    When fainting Nature called for aid,
        And hovering Death prepared the blow,
15   His vigorous remedy displayed
        The power of art without the show.

    In Misery's darkest cavern known,
        His useful care was ever nigh,
    Where hopeless Anguish poured his groan,
20   And lonely Want retired to die.

    No summons mocked by chill delay,
        No petty gain disdained by pride,
    The modest wants of every day
        The toil of every day supplied.

25   His virtues walked their narrow round,
        Nor made a pause, nor left a void;
    And sure the Eternal Master found
        The single talent[5] well employed.

    The busy day, the peaceful night,
30   Unfelt, uncounted, glided by;
    His frame was firm, his powers were bright,
        Though now his eightieth year was nigh.

    Then with no throbbing fiery pain,
        No cold gradations of decay,
35   Death broke at once the vital chain,
        And freed his soul the nearest way.

                                                                1783

---

5. An allusion to the parable of the talents, in which Christ suggests that salvation will be granted to those who use well their abilities, however small (Matthew 25.14–30).

THOMAS GRAY
1716–1771

Ode on a Distant Prospect of Eton College

Ἄνθρωπος· ἱκανὴ πρόφασις εἰς τὸ δνστυχεῖν.[1]
—MENANDER

Ye distant spires, ye antique towers,
  That crown the watery glade,
Where grateful Science° still adores   *learning*
  Her Henry's holy shade;[2]
5 And ye, that from the stately brow
Of Windsor's heights[3] the expanse below
  Of grove, of lawn, of mead° survey,   *meadow*
Whose turf, whose shade, whose flowers among
Wanders the hoary° Thames along   *aged*
10   His silver-winding way.

Ah happy hills, ah pleasing shade,
  Ah fields beloved in vain,
Where once my careless childhood strayed,
  A stranger yet to pain!
15 I feel the gales, that from ye blow,
A momentary bliss bestow,
  As waving fresh their gladsome wing,
My weary soul they seem to soothe,
And, redolent of joy and youth,
20   To breathe a second spring.

Say, Father Thames, for thou hast seen
  Full many a sprightly race
Disporting on thy margent° green   *marginal*
  The paths of pleasure trace,
25 Who foremost now delight to cleave
With pliant arm thy glassy wave?
  The captive linnet which enthrall?°   *imprison*
What idle progeny succeed[4]
To chase the rolling circle's° speed,   *hoop's*
30   Or urge the flying ball?

While some on earnest business bent
  Their murmuring labors ply
'Gainst graver hours, that bring constraint
  To sweeten liberty:
35 Some bold adventurers disdain
The limits of their little reign,
  And unknown regions dare descry:°   *discover*

1. I am a man, and that is reason enough for being miserable (Greek); from the dramatist Menander (342–292 B.C.E.).
2. Henry VI, founder of Eton.
3. On the opposite side of the river Thames from Eton; most of the "height" belongs to the castle.
4. Follow the example of the preceding generation.

Still as they run they look behind,
They hear a voice in every wind,
40   And snatch a fearful joy.

Gay hope is theirs by fancy fed,
   Less pleasing when possessed;
The tear forgot as soon as shed,
   The sunshine of the breast:
45   Theirs buxom° health of rosy hue,   *zestful, jolly*
Wild wit, invention ever new,
   And lively cheer of vigor born;
The thoughtless day, the easy night,
The spirits pure, the slumbers light,
50   That fly the approach of morn.

Alas, regardless of their doom,
   The little victims play!
No sense have they of ills to come,
   Nor care beyond today.
55   Yet see how all around 'em wait
The ministers of human fate,
   And black Misfortune's baleful train!
Ah, show them where in ambush stand
To seize their prey the murderous band!
60   Ah, tell them they are men!

These shall the fury Passions tear,
   The vultures of the mind,
Disdainful Anger, pallid Fear,
   And Shame that skulks behind;
65   Or pining Love shall waste their youth,
Or Jealousy with rankling tooth,
   That inly gnaws the secret heart,
And Envy wan, and faded Care,
Grim-visaged comfortless Despair,
70   And Sorrow's piercing dart.

Ambition this[5] shall tempt to rise,
   Then whirl the wretch from high,
To bitter Scorn a sacrifice,
   And grinning Infamy.
75   The stings of Falsehood those[6] shall try,
And hard Unkindness' altered eye,
   That mocks the tear it forced to flow;
And keen Remorse with blood defiled,
And moody Madness laughing wild
80   Amid severest woe.

Lo, in the vale of years beneath[7]
   A grisly troop are seen,

5. I.e., one of them.   7. A pointed variation on the common description
6. I.e., others.   of life as a "vale of tears."

The painful family of Death,
  More hideous than their queen:
85 This racks the joints, this fires the veins,
That every laboring sinew strains,
  Those in the deeper vitals rage:
Lo, Poverty, to fill the band,
That numbs the soul with icy hand,
90   And slow-consuming Age.

To each his sufferings: all are men,
  Condemned alike to groan;
The tender for another's pain,
  The unfeeling for his own.
95 Yet ah! why should they know their fate?
Since sorrow never comes too late,
  And happiness too swiftly flies.
Thought would destroy their paradise.
No more; where ignorance is bliss,
100   'Tis folly to be wise.

1742   1747

Ode

On the Death of a Favorite Cat, Drowned in a Tub of Goldfishes

'Twas on a lofty vase's side,
Where China's gayest art had dyed
  The azure flowers that blow;°   *bloom*
Demurest of the tabby kind,
5 The pensive Selima reclined,
  Gazed on the lake below.

Her conscious tail her joy declared;
The fair round face, the snowy beard,
  The velvet of her paws,
10 Her coat, that with the tortoise vies,
Her ears of jet,° and emerald eyes,   *black*
  She saw; and purred applause.

Still had she gazed; but 'midst the tide
Two angel forms were seen to glide,
15   The genii° of the stream: *guardian spirits*
Their scaly armor's Tyrian hue
Through richest purple to the view
  Betrayed a golden gleam.[8]

The hapless nymph with wonder saw:
20 A whisker first and then a claw,

8. "Tyrian" and (in classical reference) "purple" cover a considerable spectrum, including crimson. The fish are seen, through red highlights, as golden.

With many an ardent wish,
  She stretched in vain to reach the prize.
What female heart can gold despise?
  What cat's averse to fish?

25 Presumptuous maid! with looks intent
  Again she stretched, again she bent,
    Nor knew the gulf between.
(Malignant Fate sat by and smiled)
The slippery verge her feet beguiled,
30   She tumbled headlong in.

Eight times emerging from the flood
She mewed to every watery god,
  Some speedy aid to send.
No dolphin came, no Nereid stirred;
35 Nor cruel Tom, nor Susan heard;[9]
  A favorite has no friend!

From hence, ye beauties, undeceived,
Know, one false step is ne'er retrieved,
  And be with caution bold.
40 Not all that tempts your wandering eyes
And heedless hearts, is lawful prize;
  Nor all that glisters, gold.

1747   1748

Elegy Written in a Country Churchyard

The curfew° tolls the knell of parting day,   *evening bell*
  The lowing herd wind slowly o'er the lea,
The plowman homeward plods his weary way,
  And leaves the world to darkness and to me.

5 Now fades the glimmering landscape on the sight,
  And all the air a solemn stillness holds,
Save where the beetle wheels his droning flight,
  And drowsy tinklings lull the distant folds;

Save that from yonder ivy-mantled tower
10   The moping owl does to the moon complain
Of such, as wandering near her secret bower,
  Molest her ancient solitary reign.

Beneath those rugged elms, that yew tree's shade,
  Where heaves the turf in many a moldering heap,

9. In Greek mythology, a dolphin saved the singer Arion when he was cast overboard. A Nereid is a sea nymph; both meanings of "nymph," water spirit and maiden, are at play in line 19, where the "nymph" is the personified cat. Tom and Susan are conventional names for servants.

15   Each in his narrow cell forever laid,
      The rude° forefathers of the hamlet sleep.   *rustic*

The breezy call of incense-breathing morn,
    The swallow twittering from the straw-built shed,
The cock's shrill clarion, or the echoing horn,°   *hunting horn*
20   No more shall rouse them from their lowly bed.

For them no more the blazing hearth shall burn,
    Or busy housewife ply her evening care;
No children run to lisp their sire's return,
    Or climb his knees the envied kiss to share.

25   Oft did the harvest to their sickle yield,
     Their furrow oft the stubborn glebe° has broke;   *soil*
How jocund did they drive their team afield!
    How bowed the woods beneath their sturdy stroke!

Let not Ambition mock their useful toil,
30   Their homely joys, and destiny obscure;
Nor Grandeur hear with a disdainful smile
    The short and simple annals of the poor.

The boast of heraldry,[1] the pomp of power,
    And all that beauty, all that wealth e'er gave,
35   Awaits alike the inevitable hour.
    The paths of glory lead but to the grave.

Nor you, ye proud, impute to these the fault,
    If Memory o'er their tomb no trophies[2] raise,
Where through the long-drawn aisle and fretted° vault   *ornamented*
40   The pealing anthem swells the note of praise.

Can storied urn[3] or animated° bust   *lifelike*
    Back to its mansion call the fleeting breath?
Can Honor's voice provoke° the silent dust,   *call forth*
    Or Flattery soothe the dull cold ear of Death?

45   Perhaps in this neglected spot is laid
     Some heart once pregnant with celestial fire;
Hands that the rod of empire might have swayed,
    Or waked to ecstasy the living lyre.

But Knowledge to their eyes her ample page
50   Rich with the spoils of time did ne'er unroll;
Chill Penury repressed their noble rage,
    And froze the genial current of the soul.

Full many a gem of purest ray serene,
    The dark unfathomed caves of ocean bear:

1. I.e., noble family.
2. Memorials to military heroes; typically, statuary   representations of arms captured in battle.
    3. Funeral urn with descriptive epitaph.

55   Full many a flower is born to blush unseen,
        And waste its sweetness on the desert air.

    Some village Hampden,[4] that with dauntless breast
        The little tyrant of his fields withstood;
    Some mute inglorious Milton here may rest,
60   Some Cromwell[5] guiltless of his country's blood.

    The applause of listening senates to command,
        The threats of pain and ruin to despise,
    To scatter plenty o'er a smiling land,
        And read their history in a nation's eyes,

65   Their lot forbade: nor circumscribed alone
        Their growing virtues, but their crimes confined;
    Forbade to wade through slaughter to a throne,
        And shut the gates of mercy on mankind,

    The struggling pangs of conscious truth to hide,
70   To quench the blushes of ingenuous shame,
    Or heap the shrine of Luxury and Pride
        With incense kindled at the Muse's[6] flame.

    Far from the madding[7] crowd's ignoble strife,
        Their sober wishes never learned to stray;
75   Along the cool sequestered vale of life
        They kept the noiseless tenor of their way.

    Yet even these bones from insult to protect
        Some frail memorial still erected nigh,
    With uncouth rhymes and shapeless sculpture decked,
80   Implores the passing tribute of a sigh.

    Their name, their years, spelt by the unlettered Muse,
        The place of fame and elegy supply:
    And many a holy text around she strews,
        That teach the rustic moralist to die.

85   For who to dumb Forgetfulness a prey,
        This pleasing anxious being e'er resigned,
    Left the warm precincts of the cheerful day,
        Nor cast one longing lingering look behind?

    On some fond breast the parting soul relies,
90   Some pious drops the closing eye requires;
    Even from the tomb the voice of Nature cries,
        Even in our ashes live their wonted° fires.   *usual*

---

4. John Hampden (1594–1643), leader of the opposition to Charles I in the controversy over ship money; killed in battle in the civil wars.
5. Oliver Cromwell (1599–1658), general and statesman; lord protector of England 1653–58.
6. One of the nine Greek sister goddesses who inspired the arts.
7. I.e., either maddening or acting madly.

For thee, who mindful of the unhonored dead
    Dost in these lines their artless tale relate;
95 If chance, by lonely contemplation led,
    Some kindred spirit shall inquire thy fate,

Haply some hoary°-headed swain° may say,   *gray or white / rustic*
    "Oft have we seen him at the peep of dawn
Brushing with hasty steps the dews away
100   To meet the sun upon the upland lawn.

"There at the foot of yonder nodding beech
    That wreathes its old fantastic roots so high,
His listless length at noontide would he stretch,
    And pore upon the brook that babbles by.

105 "Hard by yon wood, now smiling as in scorn,
    Muttering his wayward fancies he would rove,
Now drooping, woeful wan, like one forlorn,
    Or crazed with care, or crossed in hopeless love.

"One morn I missed him on the customed hill,
110   Along the heath and near his favorite tree;
Another came; nor yet beside the rill,
    Nor up the lawn, nor at the wood was he;

"The next with dirges due in sad array
    Slow through the churchway path we saw him borne.
115 Approach and read (for thou canst read) the lay,°   *song*
    Graved on the stone beneath yon aged thorn."

The Epitaph

Here rests his head upon the lap of Earth
    A youth to Fortune and to Fame unknown.
Fair Science° frowned not on his humble birth,   *learning*
120   *And Melancholy marked him for her own.*

Large was his bounty, and his soul sincere,
    Heaven did a recompense as largely send:
He gave to Misery all he had, a tear,
    He gained from Heaven ('twas all he wished) a friend.

125 *No farther seek his merits to disclose,*
    Or draw his frailties from their dread abode
(There they alike in trembling hope repose),
    The bosom of his Father and his God.

ca. 1742–50   1751

Sonnet

On the Death of Mr. Richard West[8]

In vain to me the smiling mornings shine,
  And reddening Phoebus° lifts his golden fire;   the sun
The birds in vain their amorous descant join,°   harmonize
  Or cheerful fields resume their green attire;
5 These ears, alas! for other notes repine,
  A different object do these eyes require;°   ask for
My lonely anguish melts no heart but mine,
  And in my breast the imperfect joys expire.
Yet morning smiles the busy race to cheer,
10 And newborn pleasure brings to happier men;
The fields to all their wonted° tribute bear;   usual
  To warm their little loves the birds complain:[9]
I fruitless mourn to him that cannot hear,
  And weep the more, because I weep in vain.

1742   1775

WILLIAM COLLINS
1721–1759

Ode Written in the Beginning of the Year 1746[1]

How sleep the brave who sink to rest
By all their country's wishes blest!
When Spring, with dewy fingers cold,
Returns to deck their hallowed mold,°   earth
5 She there shall dress a sweeter sod
Than Fancy's feet have ever trod.

By fairy hands their knell is rung,
By forms unseen their dirge is sung;
There Honor comes, a pilgrim gray,
10 To bless the turf that wraps their clay,
And Freedom shall awhile repair,
To dwell a weeping hermit there!

1746

---

8. A friend of Gray since preparatory school, who died at twenty-six.
9. I.e., sing of their unfulfilled desire. "Little loves" puns on its Italian translation, *amoretti*, the title of Edmund Spenser's sonnet sequence (see

p. 190).
1. This poem celebrates Englishmen who fell resisting the pretender to the throne (Bonnie Prince Charlie, the grandson of James II) in 1745.

Ode on the Poetical Character

Strophe[2]

As once, if not with light regard,
I read aright that gifted bard
(Him whose school above the rest
His loveliest Elfin Queen has blest).[3]
5   One, only one, unrivaled fair,
Might hope the magic girdle[4] wear,
At solemn tourney° hung on high,   *tournament*
The wish of each love-darting eye;
Lo! to each other nymph in turn applied,
10   As if, in air unseen, some hovering hand,
Some chaste and angel-friend to virgin-fame,
   With whispered spell had burst the starting band,
It left unblest her loathed dishonored side;
   Happier, hopeless fair, if never
15   Her baffled hand with vain endeavor
Had touched that fatal zone to her denied!
Young Fancy thus, to me divinest name,
   To whom, prepared and bathed in Heaven
   The cest of amplest power is given;
20   To few the godlike gift assigns,
   To gird their blest, prophetic loins,
And gaze her visions wild, and feel unmixed her flame!

Epode

The band, as fairy legends say,
Was wove on that creating day,
25   When He, who called with thought to birth
Yon tented sky, this laughing earth,
And dressed with springs, and forests tall,
And poured the main° engirting all,   *sea*
Long by the loved Enthusiast[5] wooed,
30   Himself in some diviner mood,
Retiring, sate with her alone,
And placed her on his sapphire throne;
The whiles, the vaulted shrine around,
Seraphic° wires were heard to sound,   *angelic*
35   Now sublimest triumph° swelling,   *trumpet*
Now on love and mercy dwelling;
And she, from out the veiling cloud,
Breathed her magic notes aloud:
And thou, thou rich-haired Youth of Morn,[6]

2. Initial segment of the Greek choral ode, delivered with the chorus in motion; normally followed by the antistrophe, with the chorus in reverse motion, and then by the epode, with the chorus standing still.
3. Edmund Spenser (1552–1599; see pp. 159–205), whose followers ("school") have exalted his *Faerie Queene* above his other poems.

4. A belt, "band" (line 12), "zone" (line 16), or "cest" (line 19) described in *Faerie Queene* 4.5: it "gave the virtue of chaste love and wifehood to all that did it bear." "Peerless was she thought" that wore it.
5. Literally, one inspired by God; i.e., Fancy.
6. Apollo, the sun, Greek and Roman god of poetry.

40   And all thy subject life was born!
      The dangerous Passions kept aloof,
      Far from the sainted growing woof;[7]
      But near it sate ecstatic Wonder,
      Listening the deep applauding thunder;
45   And Truth, in sunny vest arrayed,
      By whose the tarsel's° eyes were made;   *male falcon's*
      All the shadowy tribes of Mind,
      In braided dance their murmurs joined,
      And all the bright uncounted Powers
50   Who feed on Heaven's ambrosial flowers.
      Where is the bard, whose soul can now
      Its high presuming hopes avow?
      Where he who thinks, with rapture blind,
      This hallow'd work for him designed?

Antistrophe

55   High on some cliff, to Heaven up-piled,
      Of rude access, of prospect wild,
      Where, tangled round the jealous steep,
      Strange shades o'erbrow the valleys deep,
      And holy Genii° guard the rock,   *guardian spirits*
60   Its glooms embrown, its springs unlock,
      While on its rich ambitious head,
      An Eden, like his° own, lies spread;   *Milton's*
      I view that oak, the fancied glades among,
      By which as Milton lay, his evening ear,
65   From many a cloud that dropped ethereal dew,
      Nigh sphered in Heaven its native strains could hear;
      On which that ancient trump[8] he reached was hung;
          Thither oft, his glory greeting,
          From Waller's[9] myrtle shades retreating,
70   With many a vow from Hope's aspiring tongue,
      My trembling feet his guiding steps pursue;
          In vain—such bliss to one alone,
          Of all the sons of soul was known,
          And Heaven, and Fancy, kindred powers,
75   Have now o'erturned the inspiring bowers,[1]
      Or curtained close such scene from every future view.

                        1746

Ode to Evening

    If aught of oaten stop,[2] or pastoral song,
      May hope, chaste Eve, to soothe thy modest ear,

---

7. The fabric of the girdle (line 6).
8. Milton's epic or sublime trumpet. The line echoes "Il Penseroso," lines 59–60 ("While Cynthia checks her Dragon yoke, / Gently o'er th'accustomed Oke"), and "Ode on the Morning of Christ's Nativity," line 156 ("The wakefull trump").

9. Edmund Waller (1606–1687; see pp. 393–94). The myrtle, sacred to Venus, Roman goddess of love and beauty, is an emblem of love.
1. Leafy coverts or arbors; also, poetically, idealized abodes.
2. I.e., if any modulation of a (shepherd's) reed.

Like thy own solemn springs,
Thy springs and dying gales,
5   O nymph° reserved, while now the bright-haired sun   *maiden*
Sits in yon western tent, whose cloudy skirts,
With brede° ethereal wove,   *braid*
O'erhang his wavy bed:
Now air is hushed, save where the weak-eyed bat,
10 With short shrill shriek flits by on leathern wing,
Or where the beetle winds
His small but sullen horn,
As oft he rises 'midst the twilight path,
Against the pilgrim° borne in heedless hum: *wayfarer*
15   Now teach me, maid composed,
To breathe some softened strain,
Whose numbers, stealing through thy darkening vale,[3]
May not unseemly with its stillness suit,
As, musing slow, I hail
20   Thy genial loved return!
For when thy folding-star[4] arising shows
His paly° circlet, at his warning lamp   *pale*
The fragrant Hours, and elves
Who slept in flowers the day,
25 And many a nymph who wreaths her brows with sedge,
And sheds the freshening dew, and, lovelier still,
The pensive Pleasures sweet,
Prepare thy shadowy car.°   *carriage*
Then lead, calm votaress,° where some sheety lake   *devotee*
30 Cheers the lone heath, or some time-hallowed pile
Or upland fallows[5] gray
Reflect its last cool gleam.
But when chill blustering winds, or driving rain,
Forbid my willing feet, be mine the hut
35   That from the mountain's side
Views wilds, and swelling floods,
And hamlets° brown, and dim-discovered spires,   *villages*
And hears their simple bell, and marks o'er all
Thy dewy fingers draw
40   The gradual dusky veil.
While Spring shall pour his showers, as oft he wont,°   *is accustomed*
And bathe thy breathing tresses, meekest Eve;
While Summer loves to sport
Beneath thy lingering light;
45 While sallow Autumn fills thy lap with leaves;
Or Winter, yelling through the troublous air,
Affrights thy shrinking train,
And rudely rends thy robes;
So long, sure-found beneath the sylvan shed,[6]
50 Shall Fancy, Friendship, Science, rose-lipped Health,

3. Valley. *Numbers:* measures.
4. The evening star, which, when it becomes visible, tells the shepherd to drive his flock to the sheepfold.
5. I.e., ploughed land. Cf. Milton, "L'Allegro," line 71 (p. 403).
6. I.e., secure beneath the shelter of the forest.

Thy gentlest influence own,
And hymn thy favorite name!

1746, 1748

JEAN ELLIOT
1727–1805

The Flowers of the Forest[1]

I've heard the lilting[2] at our yowe°-milking,   *ewe*
Lasses a-lilting before the dawn o' day;
But now they are moaning on ilka° green loaning:[3] *each*
"The Flowers of the Forest are a' wede away."[4]

5 At buchts,° in the morning, nae° blythe lads are *sheepfolds / no*
   scorning;°   *teasing*
 The lasses are lonely, and dowie,° and wae;° *sad / wretched*
 Nae daffin',° nae gabbin', but sighing and   *foolish playing*
   sabbing:°   *sobbing*
 Ilk° ane° lifts her leglen,° and hies her away. *each / one / milk pail*

 In hairst,° at the shearing, nae youths now are jeering, *harvest*
10 The bandsters[5] are lyart,° and runkled° and gray; *silvery / rumpled*
 At fair or at preaching, nae wooing, nae fleeching:° *flattering*
 The Flowers of the Forest are a' wede away.

 At e'en, in the gloaming,° nae swankies[6] are roaming *twilight*
 'Bout stacks[7] wi' the lasses at bogle° to play, *hide-and-seek*
15 But ilk ane sits drearie, lamenting her dearie:
 The Flowers of the Forest are a' wede away.

 Dule° and wae° for the order sent our lads to the Border; *grief / woe*
 The English, for ance,° by guile wan° the day; *once / won*
 The Flowers of the Forest, that foucht aye the foremost,
20 The prime o' our land, are cauld° in the clay. *cold*

 We'll hear nae mair° lilting at our yowe-milking, *more*
 Women and bairns° are heartless and wae; *children*
 Sighing and moaning on ilka green loaning:
 "The Flowers of the Forest are a' wede away."

1769

1. This poem is a ballad on the battle of Flodden, an English victory over the Scots in 1513. James IV of Scotland, in alliance with France, had invaded the north of England. At Flodden, in Northumberland, James's army occupied a strong position and outnumbered the English troops, but James proved an incompetent, though brave, general. More than ten thousand Scots were killed at Flodden, James among them. Elliot set the words of the ballad to an old Scottish air, from which she takes her first and fourth lines; cf. Pete Seeger, "Where Have All the Flowers Gone?" (p. 1853).
2. Sweet and cheerful singing.
3. Uncultivated ground used for milking.
4. Carried off, especially by death.
5. Those who bind sheaves behind the reaper.
6. Strapping young men.
7. Large piles of dried peat erected outdoors as a fuel store.

CHRISTOPHER SMART
1722–1771

From Jubilate Agno[1]

For I will consider my Cat Jeoffry.
For he is the servant of the Living God, duly and daily serving him.
For at the first glance of the glory of God in the East he worships in
    his way.
700 For is this done by wreathing his body seven times round with
    elegant quickness.
For then he leaps up to catch the musk,[2] which is the blessing of
    God upon his prayer.
For he rolls upon prank[3] to work it in.
For having done duty and received blessing he begins to consider
    himself.
For this he performs in ten degrees.
705 For first he looks upon his forepaws to see if they are clean.
For secondly he kicks up behind to clear away there.
For thirdly he works it upon stretch with the forepaws extended.
For fourthly he sharpens his paws by wood.
For fifthly he washes himself.
710 For sixthly he rolls upon wash.
For seventhly he fleas himself, that he may not be interrupted upon
    the beat.[4]
For eighthly he rubs himself against a post.
For ninthly he looks up for his instructions.
For tenthly he goes in quest of food.
715 For having considered God and himself he will consider his neighbor.
For if he meets another cat he will kiss her in kindness.
For when he takes his prey he plays with it to give it a chance.
For one mouse in seven escapes by his dallying.
For when his day's work is done his business more properly begins.
720 For he keeps the Lord's watch in the night against the adversary.
For he counteracts the powers of darkness by his electrical skin and
    glaring eyes.
For he counteracts the Devil, who is death, by brisking about the
    life.
For in his morning orisons he loves the sun and the sun loves him.
For he is of the tribe of Tiger.
725 For the Cherub Cat is a term of the Angel Tiger.[5]
For he has the subtlety and hissing of a serpent, which in goodness
    he suppresses.
For he will not do destruction if he is well-fed, neither will he spit
    without provocation.

1. Rejoice in the Lamb (Latin); i.e., in Jesus, the Lamb of God. Smart wrote this poem while confined for insanity. Its form derives from the biblical Psalms.
2. His own or another animal's scent, or perhaps a plant odor.
3. I.e., in display or jest.
4. Upon his daily round, possibly of hunting.
5. Smart apparently thinks of Jeoffry as an immature or diminutive phase of a larger creature—cherubs being by artistic convention small and childlike angels.

For he purrs in thankfulness when God tells him he's a good Cat.
For he is an instrument for the children to learn benevolence upon.
730 For every house is incomplete without him, and a blessing is lacking in the spirit.
For the Lord commanded Moses concerning the cats at the departure of the Children of Israel from Egypt.
For every family had one cat at least in the bag.[6]
For the English Cats are the best in Europe.
For he is the cleanest in the use of his forepaws of any quadruped.
735 For the dexterity of his defense is an instance of the love of God to him exceedingly.
For he is the quickest to his mark of any creature.
For he is tenacious of his point.
For he is a mixture of gravity and waggery.
For he knows that God is his Saviour.
740 For there is nothing sweeter than his peace when at rest.
For there is nothing brisker than his life when in motion.
For he is of the Lord's poor, and so indeed is he called by benevolence perpetually—Poor Jeoffry! poor Jeoffry! the rat has bit thy throat.
For I bless the name of the Lord Jesus that Jeoffry is better.
For the divine spirit comes about his body to sustain it in complete cat.
745 For his tongue is exceeding pure so that it has in purity what it wants in music.
For he is docile and can learn certain things.
For he can sit up with gravity, which is patience upon approbation.
For he can fetch and carry, which is patience in employment.
For he can jump over a stick, which is patience upon proof positive.
750 For he can spraggle upon waggle[7] at the word of command.
For he can jump from an eminence into his master's bosom.
For he can catch the cork and toss it again.
For he is hated by the hypocrite and miser.
For the former is afraid of detection.
755 For the latter refuses the charge.
For he camels his back to bear the first notion of business.
For he is good to think on, if a man would express himself neatly.
For he made a great figure in Egypt for his signal services.
For he killed the Icneumon rat, very pernicious by land.[8]
760 For his ears are so acute that they sting again.
For from this proceeds the passing quickness of his attention.
For by stroking of him I have found out electricity.
For I perceived God's light about him both wax and fire.
For the electrical fire is the spiritual substance which God sends from heaven to sustain the bodies both of man and beast.
765 For God has blessed him in the variety of his movements.
For, though he cannot fly, he is an excellent clamberer.
For his motions upon the face of the earth are more than any other quadruped.

6. The Israelites took with them silver and gold ornaments and raiment, as well as flocks and herds (Exodus 11.2 and 12.32, 35). Smart adds the cats.

7. He can sprawl at the waggle of a finger.
8. The Ichneumon resembles a weasel; the ancient Egyptians venerated and domesticated it.

For he can tread to all the measures⁹ upon the music.
For he can swim for life.
770 For he can creep.

1759–63   1939

From A Song to David¹

David the son of Jesse said, and the man who was raised up on
high, the anointed of the God of Jacob, and the sweet psalmist of
Israel, said, "The Spirit of the Lord spake by me, and His Word was
in my tongue."

—*2 Samuel* 23.1, 2

1

O Thou, that sit'st upon a throne,   [*Invocation*]²
With harp of high majestic tone,
    To praise the King of kings;
And voice of heav'n-ascending swell,
5   Which, while its deeper notes excel,
        Clear, as a clarion,° rings: trumpet

2

To bless each valley, grove and coast,
And charm the cherubs³ to the post
    Of gratitude in throngs;
10   To keep the days on Zion's mount,⁴
And send the year to his account,
    With dances and with songs:⁵

3

O Servant of God's holiest charge,
The minister of praise at large,
15   Which thou may'st now receive;⁶
From thy blessed mansion hail and hear,
From topmost eminence appear
    To this the wreath I weave.⁷

---

9. He can dance in a rhythmic or stately manner.
1. The second king of Israel. In an advertisement
for the first edition (printed in *Poems on Several
Occasions*, 1763), Smart called this work "A Poem
composed in a Spirit of affection and thankfulness
to the great Author of the Book of Gratitude, which
is the Psalms of David the King." Smart's main
sources for the poem were the Bible and Patrick
Delaney's *An Historical Account of the Life and
Reign of David King of Israel* (1740).
2. In the first edition, Smart prefaced the poem
with a summary, here reprinted as a series of mar-
ginal glosses. The invocation is a poetic convention
in which the poet requests divine inspiration and
assistance to write his poem. Smart here calls on
David.

3. One of the nine orders of angels.
4. Mt. Zion, one of the hills of Jerusalem; here,
perhaps, the Israelites, the Christian Church, the
heavenly Jerusalem, or a place of worship.
5. David's task, to "keep the days," is both to
observe the religious rites and festivals and to rec-
ord the Israelites' history, to "send the year to his
[God's] account," i.e., to his reckoning, for his
sake, or to his credit. (One of Smart's own projects
was to compose a complete cycle of hymns for the
major occasions in the calendar of the Anglican
Church.)
6. I.e., David, whose responsibility is praise of
God, will now receive the praise of the poet.
7. Smart compares his poem to a wreath; the lau-
rel wreath was a symbol of poetic achievement.

4

Great, valiant, pious, good, and clean,   [*The excellence and luster*
20   Sublime, contemplative, serene,   *of David's character in*
        Strong, constant, pleasant, wise![8]   *twelve points of view*]
    Bright effluence° of exceeding grace;   *outflowing*
    Best man!—the swiftness and the race,
        The peril, and the prize!

5

25   Great—from the luster of his crown,   [*proved from the*
    From Samuel's horn[9] and God's renown,   *history of his life*]
        Which is the people's voice;
    From all the host° from rear to van,°   *Israelites / front*
    Applauded and embraced the man—
30   The man of God's own choice.

6

Valiant—the word, and up he rose—
    The fight—he triumphed o'er the foes,
        Whom God's just laws abhor;°   *hate*
    And armed in gallant faith he took
35   Against the boaster,[1] from the brook
        The weapons of the war,

7

Pious—magnificent and grand;
    'Twas he the famous temple planned:
        (The seraph in his soul)[2]
40   Foremost to give the Lord his dues,
    Foremost to bless the welcome news,
        And foremost to condole.

8

Good—from Jehudah's genuine vein,
    From God's best nature good in grain,[3]
45   His aspect and his heart;
    To pity, to forgive, to save,
    Witness En-gedi's conscious cave,[4]
        And Shimei's blunted dart.[5]

---

8. The next twelve stanzas will give an example from David's life of each of these twelve virtues. (In "Jubilate Agno," Smart associates these virtues with the twelve tribes of Israel.)

9. God sent Samuel to Bethlehem to choose David, a then-unknown shepherd-boy, to be the next king of Israel: "Then Samuel took the horn of oil, and anointed him in the midst of his brethren: and the spirit of the Lord came upon David from that day forward" (1 Samuel 16.13).

1. The Philistine giant, Goliath, whom David killed using his sling and a stone from a brook.

2. David received the "pattern," or plan, for the temple "by the Spirit" (1 Chronicles 28.12); the "seraph" seems to be Delaney's invention. David wanted to build the temple himself, but the prophet Nathan said that God would not allow him to do so and that David's son, Solomon, would do it. "Welcome news" (line 41) is the Davidic Covenant, God's promise that David's line would be established kings of Israel.

3. In background and substance; David came from the tribe of Judah (of which Jehudah is a variation).

4. Before David became king of Israel, Saul, the reigning king, pursued him with an army in an attempt to kill him. One day, in the wilderness of Engedi, Saul wandered alone into a cave where David and his men were hiding. Although his men urged him to kill Saul, David refused (1 Samuel 24).

5. Shimei, a relative of Saul, cursed and threw stones at David, but David refused to kill him (2 Samuel 16, 19).

9

Clean—if perpetual prayer be pure,
50 And love, which could itself inure°   *accustom*
        To fasting and to fear—
Clean in his gestures, hands, and feet,
To smite the lyre, the dance complete,
        To play the sword and spear.

10

55 Sublime—invention ever young,
Of vast conception, towering tongue,
        To God the external theme;
Notes from yon exaltations caught,
Unrivaled royalty of thought,
60   O'er meaner strains supreme.

11

Contemplative—on God to fix
His musings, and above the six
        The sabbath-day he blessed;
'Twas then his thoughts self-conquest pruned,
65 And heavenly melancholy tuned,
        To bless and bear the rest.

12

Serene—to sow the seeds of peace,
Remembering, when he watched the fleece,
        How sweetly Kidron⁶ purled°—   *murmured*
70 To further knowledge, silence vice,
And plant perpetual paradise
        When God had calmed the world.

13

Strong—in the Lord, who could defy
Satan, and all his powers that lie
75   In sempiternal° night;   *everlasting*
And hell, and horror, and despair
Were as the lion and the bear⁷
        To his undaunted might.

14

Constant—in love to God The Truth,
80 Age, manhood, infancy, and youth—
        To Jonathan his friend

---

6. A brook that borders the district of Jerusalem. As a youth, David tended his father's flocks near this brook.

7. In 1 Samuel 17, David credits God with helping him kill a lion and a bear that were ravaging his flock.

Constant, beyond the verge of death;
And Ziba, and Mephibosheth
   His endless fame attend.[8]

15

85 Pleasant—and various as the year;
Man, soul, and angel, without peer,
   Priest, champion, sage and boy;
In armor, or in ephod° clad,   *priestly vestment*
His pomp, his piety was glad;
90   Majestic was his joy.

16

Wise—in recovery from his fall,[9]
Whence rose his eminence o'er all,
   Of all the most reviled;
The light of Israel in his ways,
95 Wise are his precepts, prayer and praise,
   And counsel to his child.[1]

17

His muse,[2] bright angel of his verse,   *[He consecrates his*
Gives balm for all the thorns that pierce, *genius for consolation*
   For all the pangs that rage   *and edification]*
100 Blessed light, still gaining on the gloom,
The more than Michal of his bloom,
   The Abishag of his age.[3]

18

He sung of god—the mighty source   *[The subjects he*
Of all things—the stupendous force   *made choice of—*
105   Of which all strength depends;   *the Supreme Being;]*
From whose right arm, beneath whose eyes,
All period,[4] power, and enterprise
   Commences, reigns, and ends.

1763   1763

---

8. During the time that Saul was trying to kill him, David became fast friends with Saul's son Jonathan. David made a covenant with Jonathan, promising to extend his kindness to Jonathan's house, even after Jonathan's death (1 Samuel 20.15). David honored this covenant many years later when he restored Saul's land to Jonathan's son, Mephibosheth, and invited him to eat at David's own table (2 Samuel 9). The stewardship of the land was awarded to Ziba (a servant of Saul) and his family.

9. David's "fall" resulted from his lust for Bathsheba and his arranging to have her husband, Uriah, killed in battle. David repented of his sin and asked God's forgiveness (Psalm 51). Delaney emphasizes David's repentance and insists that his greatness rose out of his recovery from sin.

1. According to 1 Kings 2 and 1 Chronicles 22, just before his death David gave advice to Solomon, his son and successor, counseling him to keep the commandments of God and to build the temple. Delaney notes that David left precepts for his son in the Psalms and Proverbs.

2. Source of inspiration.

3. Michal was David's first wife; Abishag, a young woman who nursed him in his old age.

4. Possibly meaning accomplishments, achievements; or, set amount of time (during which one has power).

Psalm 58[5]

Ye congregation of the tribes,[6]
    On justice do you set your mind;
And are ye free from guile and bribes
    Ye judges of mankind?

5   Nay, ye of frail and mortal mould
    Imagine mischief in your heart;
Your suffrages[7] and selves are sold
    Unto the general mart.

Men of unrighteous seed betray
10   Perverseness from their mother's womb;[8]
As soon as they can run astray,
    Against the truth presume.

They are with foul infection stained,
    Ev'n with the serpent's taint impure;
15   Their ears to blest persuasion chained,
    And locked against her lure.[9]

Though Christ himself the pipe should tune,
    They will not to the measure tread,[1]
Nor will they with his grief commune°   *sympathize*
20   Though tears of blood he shed.

Lord, humanize their scoff and scorn,
    And their malevolence defeat;
Of water and the spirit born[2]
    Let grace their change complete.

25   Let them with pious ardor burn,
    And make thy holy church their choice;
To thee with all their passions turn,
    And in thy light rejoice.

As quick as lightning to its mark,
30   So let thy gracious angel speed;

5. Cf. the versions of this Psalm and the next one by Mary Sidney (pp. 225–26), from *The Massachusetts Bay Psalm Book* (pp. 391–93), and by Isaac Watts (pp. 592–94).
6. "Congregation," a common Protestant term for members of a church, here refers to the collective body of the Israelites; there were twelve tribes of Israel.
7. Intercessory prayers; petitions to god; supplications; also, in the Church of England, various versicles and their responses in morning and evening prayer and in the Litany.
8. The doctrine of original sin holds that children are born sinful, but Smart seems here to allude to the Calvinist idea that some people are predestined to damnation.

9. Cf. the King James Bible's image (in Psalm 58) of an adder that "stoppeth up her ear" so that the charmer cannot charm her.
1. "To tread a measure" is to dance in a rhythmic or stately manner.
2. Jesus uses these terms in the Christian Scriptures: "Except a man be born of water and of the Spirit, he cannot enter the kingdom of God" (John 3.5); but in the Hebrew Scriptures, God, in forming a new covenant with the people of Israel, says, "Then will I sprinkle clean water upon you, and ye shall be clean; from all your filthiness, and from all your idols, will I cleanse you. A new heart also will I give you, and a new spirit will I put within you" (Ezekiel 36.25–26).

And take their spirits in thine ark[3]
    To their eternal mead.°   *reward*

The righteous shall exult the more
    As he such powerful mercy sees,
35 Such wrecks and ruins safe on shore,
    Such tortured souls at ease.

So that a man shall say, no doubt,
    The penitent has his reward;
There is a God to bear him out,
40   And he is Christ our Lord.

1763   1765

Psalm 114

When Israel came from Egypt's coast,
    And Goshen's[4] marshy plains,
And Jacob with his joyful host
    From servitude and chains;

5 Then was it seen how much the Jews
    Were holy in his sight,
And God did Israel's kingdom choose
    To manifest his might.

The sea beheld it, and with dread
10   Retreated to make way;
And Jordan° to his fountain head   *river in Palestine*
    Ran backwards in dismay.

The mountains, like the rams that bound,
    Exulted on their base;
15 Like lambs the little hills around
    Skipt lightly from their place.

What is the cause, thou mighty sea,
    That thou thyself should shun;
And Jordan, what is come to thee,
20   That thou should backward run?

Ye mountains that ye leaped so high
    From off the solid rock,
Ye hills that ye should gambols° try,   *leaps, dances*
    Like firstlings of the flock?

---

3. The ark of the Covenant contained "the two tables of stone, which Moses put there at Horeb, when the Lord made a covenant with the children of Israel, when they came out of the land of Egypt" (1 Kings 8.9); thus it symbolizes God's promise to guide and protect the Israelites.
4. The Hebrew word refers to the fertile land allotted to the Israelites during their exile in Egypt; metaphorically, Goshen is a place of plenty and light.

25 Earth, from the center to the sod
        His fearful presence hail
    The presence of Jeshurun's[5] God,
        In whom our arms prevail.

    Who beds of rocks in pools to stand
30   Can by his word compel,
    And from the veiny flint command
        The fountain and the well.

                                                    1765

OLIVER GOLDSMITH
ca. 1730–1774

When Lovely Woman Stoops to Folly

    When lovely woman stoops to folly,
        And finds too late that men betray,
    What charm can soothe her melancholy,
        What art can wash her guilt away?

5   The only art her guilt to cover,
        To hide her shame from every eye,
    To give repentance to her love,
        And wring his bosom—is to die.

                                                    1766

The Deserted Village

    Sweet Auburn![1] loveliest village of the plain,
    Where health and plenty cheered the laboring swain,°   rustic
    Where smiling spring its earliest visit paid,
    And parting summer's lingering blooms delayed:
5   Dear lovely bowers[2] of innocence and ease,
    Seats of my youth, when every sport could please,
    How often have I loitered o'er thy green,
    Where humble happiness endeared each scene;
    How often have I paused on every charm,
10 The sheltered cot,° the cultivated farm,   cottage
    The never-failing brook, the busy mill,
    The decent church that topped the neighboring hill,
    The hawthorn bush, with seats beneath the shade,

---

5. A poetic title for Israel, meaning "the dear upright people."
1. Apparently a fictional, ideal village; there is much debate about its exact prototype.
2. Leafy coverts or arbors; also, poetically, idealized abodes.

For talking age and whispering lovers made;
15 How often have I blessed the coming day,°   *holiday*
When toil remitting lent its turn to play,
And all the village train, from labor free,
Led up their sports beneath the spreading tree,
While many a pastime circled in the shade,
20 The young contending as the old surveyed;
And many a gambol frolicked o'er the ground,
And sleights of art and feats of strength went round;
And still as each repeated pleasure tired,
Succeeding sports the mirthful band inspired;
25 The dancing pair that simply sought renown,
By holding out to tire each other down;
The swain mistrustless of his smutted face,
While secret laughter tittered round the place;
The bashful virgin's sidelong looks of love,
30 The matron's glance that would those looks reprove:
These were thy charms, sweet village! sports like these,
With sweet succession, taught even toil to please;
These round thy bowers their cheerful influence shed,
These were thy charms—But all these charms are fled.
35   Sweet smiling village, loveliest of the lawn,
Thy sports are fled, and all thy charms withdrawn;
Amidst thy bowers the tyrant's hand is seen,
And desolation saddens all thy green:
One only master grasps the whole domain,
40 And half a tillage³ stints thy smiling plain;
No more thy glassy brook reflects the day,
But choked with sedges, works its weedy way;
Along thy glades, a solitary guest,
The hollow-sounding bittern⁴ guards its nest;
45 Amidst thy desert walks the lapwing flies,
And tires their echoes with unvaried cries.
Sunk are thy bowers, in shapeless ruin all,
And the long grass o'ertops the moldering wall,
And, trembling, shrinking from the spoiler's hand,
50 Far, far away thy children leave the land.
    Ill fares the land, to hastening ills a prey,
Where wealth accumulates, and men decay;⁵
Princes and lords may flourish, or may fade;
A breath can make them, as a breath has made;
55 But a bold peasantry, their country's pride,
When once destroyed, can never be supplied.
    A time there was, ere England's griefs began,
When every rood⁶ of ground maintained its man;
For him light labor spread her wholesome store,
60 Just gave what life required, but gave no more:

---

3. I.e., only half the land is cultivated under the new monopoly; or, the land was being plowed and was left unfinished when ownership changed. The significant landowners were displacing less prosperous freeholders and at the same time appropriating land formerly held in common.
4. Marsh bird with a booming call.

5. In the opening dedication to the English painter Sir Joshua Reynolds (1723–1792), Goldsmith writes, "I . . . continue to think those luxuries prejudicial to states, by which so many vices are introduced, and so many kingdoms have been undone."
6. A measure of land, varying by locality.

His best companions, innocence and health;
And his best riches, ignorance of wealth.
    But times are altered; Trade's unfeeling train
Usurp the land and dispossess the swain;
65 Along the lawn, where scattered hamlets rose,
Unwieldy wealth, and cumbrous pomp repose;
And every want to opulence allied,
And every pang that folly pays to pride.
These gentle hours that plenty bade to bloom,
70 Those calm desires that asked but little room,
Those healthful sports that graced the peaceful scene,
Lived in each look, and brightened all the green;
These far departing seek a kinder shore,
And rural mirth and manners are no more.
75   Sweet Auburn! parent of the blissful hour,
Thy glades forlorn confess the tyrant's power.
Here, as I take my solitary rounds,
Amidst thy tangling walks, and ruined grounds,
And, many a year elapsed, return to view
80 Where once the cottage stood, the hawthorn grew,
Remembrance wakes with all her busy train,
Swells at my breast, and turns the past to pain.
    In all my wanderings round this world of care,
In all my griefs—and God has given my share—
85 I still had hopes my latest hours to crown,
Amidst these humble bowers to lay me down;
To husband out life's taper° at the close,   *candle*
And keep the flame from wasting by repose.
I still had hopes, for pride attends us still,
90 Amidst the swains to show my book-learned skill,
Around my fire an evening group to draw,
And tell of all I felt, and all I saw;
And, as an hare whom hounds and horns pursue,
Pants to the place from whence at first she flew,
95 I still had hopes, my long vexations past,
Here to return—and die at home at last.
    O blest retirement, friend to life's decline,
Retreats from care that never must be mine,
How happy he who crowns in shades like these
100 A youth of labor with an age of ease;
Who quits a world where strong temptations try,
And, since 'tis hard to combat, learns to fly!
For him no wretches, born to work and weep,
Explore the mine, or tempt the dangerous deep;
105 No surly porter stands in guilty state
To spurn imploring famine from the gate;
But on he moves to meet his latter end,
Angels around befriending virtue's friend;
Bends to the grave with unperceived decay,
110 While Resignation gently slopes the way;
And, all his prospects brightening to the last,
His Heaven commences ere the world be passed!

Sweet was the sound when oft at evening's close,
Up yonder hill the village murmur rose;
115   There, as I passed with careless steps and slow,
The mingling notes came softened from below;
The swain responsive as the milkmaid sung,
The sober herd that lowed to meet their young,
The noisy geese that gabbled o'er the pool,
120   The playful children just let loose from school;
The watchdog's voice that bayed the whispering wind,
And the loud laugh that spoke the vacant° mind;   *carefree*
These all in sweet confusion sought the shade,
And filled each pause the nightingale had made.
125   But now the sounds of population fail,
No cheerful murmurs fluctuate in the gale,
No busy steps the grass-grown footway tread,
For all the bloomy flush of life is fled.
All but yon widowed, solitary thing
130   That feebly bends beside the plashy° spring;   *marshy*
She, wretched matron, forced, in age, for bread,
To strip the brook with mantling° cresses spread,   *covering*
To pick her wintry faggot° from the thorn,   *firewood*
To seek her nightly shed, and weep till morn;
135   She only left of all the harmless train,
The sad historian of the pensive plain.
     Near yonder copse,° where once the garden smiled,   *grove*
And still where many a garden flower grows wild,
There, where a few torn shrubs the place disclose,
140   The village preacher's modest mansion[7] rose.
A man he was, to all the country dear,
And passing rich with forty pounds a year;
Remote from towns he ran his godly race,
Nor e'er had changed, nor wished to change his place;
145   Unpracticed he to fawn, or seek for power,
By doctrines fashioned to the varying hour;
Far other aims his heart had learned to prize,
More skilled to raise the wretched than to rise.
His house was known to all the vagrant train,
150   He chid their wanderings, but relieved their pain;
The long-remembered beggar was his guest,
Whose beard descending swept his aged breast;
The ruined spendthrift, now no longer proud,
Claimed kindred there, and had his claims allowed;
155   The broken soldier, kindly bade to stay,
Sate by his fire, and talked the night away;
Wept o'er his wounds, or tales of sorrow done,
Shouldered his crutch, and showed how fields were won.
Pleased with his guests, the good man learned to glow,
160   And quite forgot their vices in their woe;
Careless their merits, or their faults to scan,
His pity gave ere charity began.

7. There seem to have been no conventional mansions in Goldsmith's village; see lines 195 and 238, and cf. George Crabbe, "The Parish Register," line 19 (p. 724).

Thus to relieve the wretched was his pride,
And even his failings leaned to Virtue's side;
165 But in his duty prompt at every call,
He watched and wept, he prayed and felt, for all.
And, as a bird each fond endearment tries,
To tempt its new-fledged offspring to the skies,
He tried each art, reproved each dull delay,
170 Allured to brighter worlds, and led the way.
    Beside the bed where parting life was laid,
And sorrow, guilt, and pain, by turns dismayed,
The reverend champion stood. At his control,
Despair and anguish fled the struggling soul;
175 Comfort came down the trembling wretch to raise,
And his last faltering accents whispered praise.
    At church, with meek and unaffected grace,
His looks adorned the venerable place;
Truth from his lips prevailed with double sway,
180 And fools, who came to scoff, remained to pray.
The service past, around the pious man,
With steady zeal each honest rustic ran;
Even children followed with endearing wile,
And plucked his gown, to share the good man's smile.
185 His ready smile a parent's warmth expressed,
Their welfare pleased him, and their cares distressed;
To them his heart, his love, his griefs were given,
But all his serious thoughts had rest in Heaven.
As some tall cliff that lifts its awful form,
190 Swells from the vale,° and midway leaves the storm,   *valley*
Though round its breast the rolling clouds are spread,
Eternal sunshine settles on its head.
    Beside yon straggling fence that skirts the way,
With blossomed furze° unprofitably gay,   *a wild shrub*
195 There, in his noisy mansion, skilled to rule,
The village master taught his little school;
A man severe he was, and stern to view,
I knew him well, and every truant knew;
Well had the boding° tremblers learned to trace   *anxious*
200 The day's disasters in his morning face;
Full well they laughed with counterfeited glee,
At all his jokes, for many a joke had he;
Full well the busy whisper circling round,
Conveyed the dismal tidings when he frowned;
205 Yet he was kind, or if severe in aught,
The love he bore to learning was in fault;[8]
The village all declared how much he knew;
'Twas certain he could write, and cipher too;
Lands he could measure, terms and tides presage,[9]
210 And even the story ran that he could gauge.

---

8. Pronounced like *fought*.
9. He could calculate (for example) when rents were due, the dates of feasts and seasons in the church year, and the sea tides. "Tides" here literally means "times." To "gauge" (line 210) is to calculate the fluid content of casks and other vessels.

In arguing too, the parson owned his skill,[1]
For even though vanquished, he could argue still;
While words of learned length, and thundering sound,
Amazed the gazing rustics ranged around;
215   And still they gazed, and still the wonder grew,
That one small head could carry all he knew.
    But past is all his fame. The very spot
Where many a time he triumphed, is forgot.
Near yonder thorn, that lifts its head on high,
220   Where once the signpost caught the passing eye,
Low lies that house where nut-brown draughts inspired,[2]
Where graybeard Mirth and smiling Toil retired,
Where village statesmen talked with looks profound,
And news much older than their ale went round.
225   Imagination fondly stoops to trace
The parlor splendors of that festive place:
The whitewashed wall, the nicely sanded floor,
The varnished clock that clicked behind the door;
The chest contrived a double debt to pay,
230   A bed by night, a chest of drawers by day;
The pictures placed for ornament and use,
The twelve good rules, the royal game of goose;°   *a board game*
The hearth, except when winter chilled the day,
With aspen boughs, and flowers, and fennel gay,
235   While broken teacups, wisely kept for show,
Ranged o'er the chimney, glistened in a row.
    Vain transitory splendors! Could not all
Reprieve the tottering mansion from its fall!
Obscure it sinks, nor shall it more impart
240   An hour's importance to the poor man's heart;
Thither no more the peasant shall repair
To sweet oblivion of his daily care;
No more the farmer's news, the barber's tale,
No more the woodman's ballad shall prevail;
245   No more the smith his dusky brow shall clear,
Relax his ponderous strength, and lean to hear;
The host himself no longer shall be found
Careful to see the mantling bliss[3] go round;
Nor the coy maid, half willing to be pressed,
250   Shall kiss the cup to pass it to the rest.
    Yes! let the rich deride, the proud disdain,
These simple blessings of the lowly train,
To me more dear, congenial to my heart,
One native charm, than all the gloss of art;
255   Spontaneous joys, where nature has its play,
The soul adopts, and owns their first-born sway;
Lightly they frolic o'er the vacant mind,

1. I.e., admitted his (the schoolmaster's) skill.
2. I.e., the public house where ale inspired the customers. Cf. Crabbe's "The Parish Register," which transfers Goldsmith's "twelve good rules" (line 232), rules of conduct often posted in taverns, to the cottage of the "industrious swain," and which describes the pub as a place of crime and corruption.
3. The ale covering itself with foam.

Unenvied, unmolested, unconfined.
But the long pomp, the midnight masquerade,
260   With all the freaks of wanton wealth arrayed,
In these, ere triflers half their wish obtain,
The toiling pleasure sickens into pain;
And, even while fashion's brightest arts decoy,
The heart distrusting asks if this be joy.
265   Ye friends to truth, ye statesmen, who survey
The rich man's joys increase, the poor's decay,
'Tis yours to judge how wide the limits stand
Between a splendid and an happy land.
Proud swells the tide with loads of freighted ore,
270   And shouting Folly hails them from her shore;
Hoards, even beyond the miser's wish abound,
And rich men flock from all the world around.
Yet count our gains. This wealth is but a name
That leaves our useful products still the same.
275   Not so the loss. The man of wealth and pride,
Takes up a space that many poor supplied;
Space for his lake, his park's extended bounds,
Space for his horses, equipage, and hounds;
The robe that wraps his limbs in silken sloth
280   Has robbed the neighboring fields of half their growth;
His seat, where solitary sports are seen,
Indignant spurns the cottage from the green;
Around the world each needful product flies,
For all the luxuries the world supplies:
285   While thus the land adorned for pleasure, all
In barren splendor feebly waits the fall.
        As some fair female unadorned and plain,
Secure to please while youth confirms her reign,
Slights every borrowed charm that dress supplies,
290   Nor shares with art the triumph of her eyes;
But when those charms are past, for charms are frail,
When time advances, and when lovers fail,
She then shines forth, solicitous to bless,
In all the glaring impotence of dress:
295   Thus fares the land, by luxury betrayed;
In nature's simplest charms at first arrayed;
But verging to decline, its splendors rise,
Its vistas strike, its palaces surprise;
While scourged by famine from the smiling land,
300   The mournful peasant leads his humble band;
And while he sinks without one arm to save,
The country blooms—a garden, and a grave.
        Where then, ah where, shall Poverty reside,
To 'scape the pressure of contiguous Pride?
305   If to some common's fenceless limits strayed,
He drives his flock to pick the scanty blade,
Those fenceless fields the sons of wealth divide,
And even the bare-worn common is denied.[4]

4. Refers to the enclosure and appropriation of common land.

If to the city sped—What waits him there?
310 To see profusion that he must not share;
To see ten thousand baneful arts combined
To pamper luxury, and thin mankind;
To see those joys the sons of pleasure know,
Extorted from his fellow creature's woe.
315 Here, while the courtier glitters in brocade,
There the pale artist° plies the sickly trade;   *artisan*
Here, while the proud their long-drawn pomps display,
There the black gibbet° glooms beside the way.   *gallows*
The dome where Pleasure holds her midnight reign,
320 Here, richly decked, admits the gorgeous train;
Tumultuous grandeur crowds the blazing square,
The rattling chariots clash, the torches glare.
Sure scenes like these no troubles e'er annoy!
Sure these denote one universal joy!
325 Are these thy serious thoughts?—Ah, turn thine eyes
Where the poor houseless shivering female lies.
She once, perhaps, in village plenty blest,
Has wept at tales of innocence distressed;
Her modest looks the cottage might adorn,
330 Sweet as the primrose peeps beneath the thorn;
Now lost to all; her friends, her virtue fled,
Near her betrayer's door she lays her head,
And pinched with cold, and shrinking from the shower,
With heavy heart deplores that luckless hour,
335 When idly first, ambitious of the town,
She left her wheel and robes of country brown.
    Do thine, sweet Auburn, thine, the loveliest train,
Do thy fair tribes participate her pain?
Even now, perhaps, by cold and hunger led,
340 At proud men's doors they ask a little bread!
    Ah, no. To distant climes, a dreary scene,
Where half the convex world intrudes between,
Through torrid tracts with fainting steps they go,
Where wild Altama⁵ murmurs to their woe.
345 Far different there from all that charmed before,
The various terrors of that horrid shore;
Those blazing suns that dart a downward ray,
And fiercely shed intolerable day;
Those matted woods where birds forget to sing,
350 But silent bats in drowsy clusters cling,
Those poisonous fields with rank luxuriance crowned,
Where the dark scorpion gathers death around;
Where at each step the stranger fears to wake
The rattling terrors of the vengeful snake;
355 Where crouching tigers° wait their hapless prey,   *pumas*
And savage men, more murderous still than they;
While oft in whirls the mad tornado flies,
Mingling the ravaged landscape with the skies.
Far different these from every former scene,

5. Altamaha, a river in Georgia (North America).

360　The cooling brook, the grassy-vested green,
　　　The breezy covert of the warbling grove,
　　　That only sheltered thefts of harmless love.
　　　　Good Heaven! what sorrows gloomed that parting day,
　　　That called them from their native walks away;
365　When the poor exiles, every pleasure past,
　　　Hung round their bowers, and fondly looked their last,
　　　And took a long farewell, and wished in vain
　　　For seats like these beyond the western main;
　　　And shuddering still to face the distant deep,
370　Returned and wept, and still returned to weep.
　　　The good old sire the first prepared to go
　　　To new-found worlds, and wept for other's woe;
　　　But for himself, in conscious virtue brave,
　　　He only wished for worlds beyond the grave.
375　His lovely daughter, lovelier in her tears,
　　　The fond companion of his helpless years,
　　　Silent went next, neglectful of her charms,
　　　And left a lover's for a father's arms.
　　　With louder plaints° the mother spoke her woes,　　　　　*lamentations*
380　And blessed the cot where every pleasure rose;
　　　And kissed her thoughtless babes with many a tear,
　　　And clasped them close in sorrow doubly dear;
　　　Whilst her fond husband strove to lend relief
　　　In all the silent manliness of grief.
385　　O luxury! Thou cursed by Heaven's decree,
　　　How ill exchanged are things like these for thee!
　　　How do thy potions, with insidious joy,
　　　Diffuse their pleasures only to destroy!
　　　Kingdoms, by thee, to sickly greatness grown,
390　Boast of a florid vigor not their own.
　　　At every draught more large and large they grow,
　　　A bloated mass of rank unwieldy woe;
　　　Till sapped their strength, and every part unsound,
　　　Down, down they sink, and spread a ruin round.
395　　Even now the devastation is begun,
　　　And half the business of destruction done;
　　　Even now, methinks, as pondering here I stand,
　　　I see the rural Virtues leave the land.
　　　Down where yon anchoring vessel spreads the sail,
400　That idly waiting flaps with every gale,
　　　Downward they move, a melancholy band,
　　　Pass from the shore, and darken all the strand.
　　　Contented Toil, and hospitable Care,
　　　And kind connubial Tenderness are there;
405　And Piety, with wishes placed above,
　　　And steady Loyalty, and faithful Love:
　　　And thou, sweet Poetry, thou loveliest maid,
　　　Still first to fly where sensual joys invade;
　　　Unfit in these degenerate times of shame,
410　To catch the heart, or strike for honest fame;
　　　Dear charming Nymph, neglected and decried,

My shame in crowds, my solitary pride;
Thou source of all my bliss, and all my woe,
That found'st me poor at first, and keep'st me so;
415   Thou guide by which the nobler arts excel,
Thou nurse of every virtue, fare thee well.
Farewell, and O! where'er thy voice be tried,
On Torno's cliffs, or Pambamarca's side,[6]
Whether where equinoctial° fervors glow,   *tropical*
420   Or winter wraps the polar world in snow,
Still let thy voice, prevailing over time,
Redress the rigors of the inclement clime;
Aid slighted truth, with thy persuasive strain
Teach erring man to spurn the rage of gain;
425   Teach him that states of native strength possessed,
Though very poor, may still be very blest;
That Trade's proud empire hastes to swift decay,
As ocean sweeps the labored mole° away;   *breakwater*
While self-dependent power can time defy,
430   As rocks resist the billows and the sky.[7]

1770

WILLIAM COWPER
1731–1800

From Olney Hymns[1]

Light Shining out of Darkness

God moves in a mysterious way,
   His wonders to perform;
He plants his footsteps in the sea,
   And rides upon the storm.

5   Deep in unfathomable mines
   Of never failing skill,
He treasures up his bright designs,
   And works his sovereign will.

Ye fearful saints, fresh courage take,
10   The clouds ye so much dread
Are big with mercy, and shall break
   In blessings on your head.

Judge not the Lord by feeble sense,
   But trust him for his grace;

6. I.e., on the cliffs overlooking the river Torne, in Sweden, or the side of Mt. Pambamarca, in Ecuador.
7. The last four lines are by Samuel Johnson

(1709–1784; see pp. 655–65).
1. Cowper lived in Olney, Buckinghamshire, from 1767 until 1786.

15   Behind a frowning providence,
        He hides a smiling face.

    His purposes will ripen fast,
        Unfolding every hour;
    The bud may have a bitter taste,
20   But sweet will be the flower.

    Blind unbelief is sure to err,
        And scan his work in vain;
    God is his own interpreter,
        And he will make it plain.

                                                1779

Epitaph on a Hare

    Here lies, whom hound did ne'er pursue,
        Nor swifter greyhound follow,
    Whose foot ne'er tainted° morning dew,   *left a scent on*
        Nor ear heard huntsman's hallo',

5   Old Tiney, surliest of his kind,
        Who, nursed with tender care,
    And to domestic bounds confined,
        Was still a wild jack-hare.

    Though duly from my hand he took
10   His pittance every night,
    He did it with a jealous look,
        And, when he could, would bite.

    His diet was of wheaten bread,
        And milk, and oats, and straw,
15 Thistles, or lettuces instead,
        With sand to scour his maw.

    On twigs of hawthorn he regaled,°   *feasted*
        On pippins'° russet peel;   *apples'*
    And, when his juicy salads failed,
20   Sliced carrot pleased him well.

    A Turkey carpet was his lawn,[2]
        Whereon he loved to bound,
    To skip and gambol like a fawn,
        And swing his rump around.

25 His frisking was at evening hours,
        For then he lost his fear;

2. Cowper exercised his hares on his parlor carpet of Turkey red.

But most before approaching showers,
  Or when a storm drew near.

Eight years and five round-rolling moons
30 He thus saw steal away,
Dozing out all his idle noons,
  And every night at play.

I kept him for his humor's sake,
  For he would oft beguile
35 My heart of thoughts that made it ache,
  And force me to a smile.

But now, beneath this walnut-shade
  He finds his long, last home,
And waits in snug concealment laid,
40 Till gentler Puss shall come.

He,[3] still more agèd, feels the shocks
  From which no care can save,
And, partner once of Tiney's box,
  Must soon partake his grave.

1783   1784

From The Task[4]

From *Book IV: The Winter Evening*

* * *

  Just when our drawing-rooms begin to blaze
With lights, by clear reflection multiplied
From many a mirror, in which he of Gath,
270 Goliath,[5] might have seen his giant bulk
Whole without stooping, towering crest and all,
My pleasures too begin. But me perhaps
The glowing hearth may satisfy awhile
With faint illumination, that uplifts
275 The shadow to the ceiling, there by fits
Dancing uncouthly to the quivering flame.
Not undelightful is an hour to me
So spent in parlour twilight; such a gloom
Suits well the thoughtful or unthinking mind,
280 The mind contemplative, with some new theme
Pregnant, or indisposed alike to all.
Laugh ye, who boast your more mercurial powers
That never feel a stupor, know no pause,

3. Puss, the longest-lived of Cowper's three hares.
4. So called because, when he complained of the lack of a poetic topic, a friend, Lady Austen, set him the task of writing about the parlor sofa. The completed work ran to six books and ranged over diverse subjects.
5. The giant slain by David (1 Samuel 17.19–51).

Nor need one; I am conscious,° and confess,   *conscious of*

285 Fearless, a soul that does not always think.

Me oft has fancy ludicrous and wild

Soothed with a waking dream of houses, towers,

Trees, churches, and stranger visages expressed

In the red cinders, while with poring eye

290 I gazed, myself creating what I saw.[6]

Nor less amused have I quiescent watched

The sooty films that play upon the bars°   *fireplace grate*

Pendulous, and foreboding in the view

Of superstition, prophesying still,

295 Though still deceived, some stranger's near approach

'Tis thus the understanding takes repose

In indolent vacuity of thought,

And sleeps and is refreshed. Meanwhile the face

Conceals the mood lethargic with a mask

300 Of deep deliberation, as° the man   *as if*

Were tasked to his full strength, absorbed and lost.

Thus oft reclined at ease, I lose an hour

At evening, till at length the freezing blast

That sweeps the bolted shutter, summons home

305 The recollected powers, and, snapping short

The glassy threads with which the fancy weaves

Her brittle toys, restores me to myself.

How calm is my recess! and how the frost

Raging abroad, and the rough wind, endear

310 The silence and the warmth enjoyed within!

I saw the woods and fields at close of day

A variegated show; the meadows green

Though faded, and the lands, where lately waved

The golden harvest, of a mellow brown,

315 Upturned so lately by the forceful share;°   *plough*

I saw far off the weedy fallows° smile   *dormant land*

With verdure not unprofitable, grazed

By flocks fast feeding, and selecting each

His favorite herb; while all the leafless groves

320 That skirt th' horizon wore a sable° hue,   *black*

Scarce noticed in the kindred dusk of eve.

Tomorrow brings a change, a total change,

Which even now, though silently perform'd

And slowly, and by most unfelt, the face

325 Of universal nature undergoes.

Fast falls a fleecy shower; the downy flakes,

Descending and with never-ceasing lapse°   *gentle downward glide*

Softly alighting upon all below,

Assimilate all objects. Earth receives

330 Gladly the thickening mantle, and the green

And tender blade that feared the chilling blast,

Escapes unhurt beneath so warm a veil.

*　　*　　*

6. Cf. lines 291–310 with Coleridge, "Frost at Midnight" (p. 810).

From *Book VI: The Winter Walk at Noon*

* * *

The groans of nature in this nether world,
730 Which Heaven has heard for ages, have an end.
Foretold by prophets, and by poets sung,
Whose fire was kindled at the prophets' lamp,
The time of rest, the promised Sabbath, comes.[7]
Six thousand years[8] of sorrow have well-nigh
735 Fulfilled their tardy and disastrous course
Over a sinful world; and what remains
Of this tempestuous state of human things
Is merely as the working of a sea
Before a calm, that rocks itself to rest:
740 For He, whose car° the winds are, and the clouds   chariot
The dust that waits upon his sultry march,
When sin hath moved him, and his wrath is hot,
Shall visit earth in mercy; shall descend,
Propitious, in his chariot paved with love;
745 And what his storms have blasted and defaced
For man's revolt shall with a smile repair.
    Sweet is the harp of prophecy; too sweet
Not to be wronged by a mere mortal touch:
Nor can the wonders it records be sung
750 To meaner music, and not suffer loss.
But, when a poet, or when one like me,
Happy to rove among poetic flowers,
Though poor in skill to rear them, lights at last
On some fair theme, some theme divinely fair,
755 Such is the impulse and the spur he feels
To give it praise proportioned to its worth,
That not t' attempt it, arduous as he deems
The labor, were a task more arduous still.
    Oh scenes surpassing fable, and yet true,
760 Scenes of accomplished bliss! which who can see,
Though but in distant prospect, and not feel
His soul refreshed with foretaste of the joy?
Rivers of gladness water all the earth,
And clothe all climes with beauty; the reproach
765 Of barrenness is past. The fruitful field
Laughs with abundance; and the land, once lean,
Or fertile only in its own disgrace,
Exults to see its thistly curse repealed.
The various seasons woven into one,
770 And that one season an eternal spring,
The garden fears no blight, and needs no fence,
For there is none to covet, all are full.
The lion, and the libbard,° and the bear   leopard

7. An allusion to the end of the world and the second coming of Christ, when God will make "a new heaven and a new earth" (Revelation 21.1). Lines 759–817 are Cowper's visionary description of this "promised Sabbath."
8. The creation of the world was traditionally believed to have taken place four thousand years before the birth of Christ.

Graze with the fearless flocks; all bask at noon
775   Together, or all gambol in the shade
Of the same grove, and drink one common stream.
Antipathies are none. No foe to man
Lurks in the serpent now: the mother sees,
And smiles to see, her infant's playful hand
780   Stretched forth to dally with the crested worm,°   *serpent*
To stroke his azure neck, or to receive
The lambent° homage of his arrowy tongue.   *flickering*
All creatures worship man, and all mankind
One Lord, one Father. Error has no place:
785   That creeping pestilence is driven away;
The breath of heaven has chased it. In the heart
No passion touches a discordant string,
But all is harmony and love. Disease
Is not: the pure and uncontaminate blood
790   Holds its due course, nor fears the frost of age.
One song employs all nations; and all cry,
"Worthy the Lamb, for he was slain for us!"
The dwellers in the vales° and on the rocks   *valleys*
Shout to each other, and the mountain tops
795   From distant mountains catch the flying joy;
Till, nation after nation taught the strain,
Earth rolls the rapturous hosanna[9] round.
Behold the measure of the promise filled;
See Salem[1] built, the labor of a God!
800   Bright as a sun the sacred city shines;
All kingdoms and all princes of the earth
Flock to that light; the glory of all lands
Flows into her; unbounded is her joy,
And endless her increase. Thy rams are there,
805   Nebaioth, and the flocks of Kedar there;[2]
The looms of Ormus, and the mines of Ind,
And Saba's spicy groves, pay tribute there.[3]
Praise is in all her gates: upon her walls,
And in her streets, and in her spacious courts,
810   Is heard salvation. Eastern Java there
Kneels with the native of the farthest west;
And Ethiopia spreads abroad the hand,
And worships. Her report has traveled forth
Into all lands. From every clime they come
815   To see thy beauty and to share thy joy,
O Sion![4] an assembly such as earth
Saw never, such as heaven stoops down to see.

9. Expression of great praise.
1. Jerusalem; not only the terrestrial city but the New Jerusalem or Holy City, God's perfect and eternal order of the future. See Revelation 31.2: "And I John saw the holy city, new Jerusalem, coming down from God out of heaven."
2. "Nebaioth and Kedar, the sons of Ishmael and progenitors of the Arabs, in the prophetic Scripture here alluded to may be reasonably considered as representatives of the Gentiles at large" [Cowper's note]. By "the prophetic Scripture here alluded to" Cowper means Isaiah 60.3–7, in which God promises a blessed future to Jerusalem: "And the Gentiles shall come to thy light. . . . All the flocks of Keder shall be gathered together unto thee, the rams of Nebaioth shall minister unto thee."
3. Ormus (or Hormuz, an island in the Persian Gulf), India, and Saba (Sheba, a country in Arabia) were renowned for their wealth.
4. Often, as here, equivalent to Jerusalem.

Thus heaven-ward all things tend. For all were once
Perfect, and all must be at length restored.
820 So God has greatly purposed; who would else
In his dishonored works himself endure
Dishonor, and be wronged without redress.
Haste, then, and wheel away a shattered world,
Ye slow-revolving seasons! we would see
825 (A sight to which our eyes are strangers yet)
A world that does not dread and hate his laws,
And suffer for its crime; would learn how fair
The creature is that God pronounces good,
How pleasant in itself what pleases him.
830 Here every drop of honey hides a sting,
Worms wind themselves into our sweetest flowers;
And even the joy that haply° some poor heart   *luckily*
Derives from heaven, pure as the fountain is,
Is sullied in the stream, taking a taint
835 From touch of human lips, at best impure.
Oh for a world in principle as chaste
As this is gross and selfish! over which
Custom and prejudice shall bear no sway,
That govern all things here, shouldering aside
840 The meek and modest truth, and forcing her
To seek a refuge from the tongue of strife
In nooks obscure, far from the ways of men;
Where violence shall never lift the sword,
Nor cunning justify the proud man's wrong,
845 Leaving the poor no remedy but tears;
Where he that fills an office shall esteem
Th' occasion it presents of doing good
More than the perquisite;° where law shall speak   *profits*
Seldom, and never but as wisdom prompts
850 And equity; not jealous more to guard
A worthless form, than to decide aright;
Where fashion shall not sanctify abuse,
Nor smooth good breeding (supplemental grace)
With lean performance ape the work of love!
855   Come then, and, added to thy many crowns,
Receive yet one, the crown of all the earth,
Thou who alone art worthy! It was thine
By ancient covenant, ere nature's birth;
And thou hast made it thine by purchase since,
860 And overpaid its value with thy blood.
Thy saints proclaim thee king; and in their hearts
Thy title is engraven with a pen
Dipped in the fountain of eternal love.
Thy saints proclaim thee king; and thy delay
865 Gives courage to their foes, who, could they see
The dawn of thy last advent, long desired,
Would creep into the bowels of the hills,
And flee for safety to the falling rocks.
The very spirit of the world is tired

870 Of its own taunting question, asked so long,
  "Where is the promise of your Lord's approach?"
  The infidel has shot his bolts° away,   *arrows*
  Till, his exhausted quiver yielding none,
  He gleans the blunted shafts that have recoiled,
875 And aims them at the shield of truth again.
  The veil is rent, rent too by priestly hands,
  That hides divinity from mortal eyes;[5]
  And all the mysteries to faith proposed,
  Insulted and traduced, are cast aside,
880 As useless, to the moles and to the bats.
  They now are deemed the faithful, and are praised,
  Who, constant only in rejecting thee,
  Deny thy Godhead with a martyr's zeal,
  And quit their office for their error's sake.
885 Blind, and in love with darkness! yet even these
  Worthy, compared with sycophants, who knee
  Thy name adoring, and then preach thee man!
  So fares thy church. But how thy church may fare
  The world takes little thought. Who will may preach,
890 And what they will. All pastors are alike
  To wandering sheep, resolved to follow none.
  Two gods divide them all—Pleasure and Gain:
  For these they live, they sacrifice to these,
  And in their service wage perpetual war
895 With conscience and with thee. Lust in their hearts,
  And mischief in their hands, they roam the earth
  To prey upon each other: stubborn, fierce,
  High-minded, foaming out their own disgrace.
  Thy prophets speak of such; and, noting down
900 The features of the last degenerate times,
  Exhibit every lineament of these.
  Come then, and, added to thy many crowns,
  Receive yet one, as radiant as the rest,
  Due to thy last and most effectual work,
905 Thy word fulfilled, the conquest of a world!

                    *   *   *

                                                    1785

The Castaway

  Obscurest night involved° the sky,   *engulfed*
    The Atlantic billows roared,
  When such a destined wretch as I,
    Washed headlong from on board,

---

5. The veil of the Temple in Jerusalem divided the inner sanctuary from the rest of the Temple. For Christians, rending of the veil represented gaining direct access to God, notably through Christ's death. "And Jesus cried with a loud voice, and gave up the ghost. And the veil of the temple was rent in twain from the top to the bottom" (Mark 15.37–8).

5   Of friends, of hope, of all bereft,
    His floating home forever left.

    No braver chief could Albion boast
       Than he with whom he went,[6]
    Nor ever ship left Albion's coast,
10   With warmer wishes sent.
    He loved them both, but both in vain,
    Nor him beheld, nor her again.

    Not long beneath the whelming brine,
       Expert to swim, he lay;
15   Nor soon he felt his strength decline,
       Or courage die away;
    But waged with death a lasting strife,
    Supported by despair of life.

    He shouted; nor his friends had failed
20   To check the vessel's course,
    But so the furious blast prevailed,
       That, pitiless perforce,
    They left their outcast mate behind,
    And scudded still before the wind.

25   Some succor yet they could afford;
       And, such as storms allow,
    The cask, the coop, the floated cord,
       Delayed not to bestow.
    But he (they knew) nor ship, nor shore,
30   Whate'er they gave, should visit more.

    Nor, cruel as it seemed, could he
       Their haste himself condemn,
    Aware that flight, in such a sea,
       Alone could rescue them;
35   Yet bitter felt it still to die
    Deserted, and his friends so nigh.

    He long survives, who lives an hour
       In ocean, self-upheld;
    And so long he, with unspent power,
40   His destiny repelled;
    And ever, as the minutes flew,
    Entreated help, or cried, "Adieu!"

    At length, his transient respite past,
       His comrades, who before
45   Had heard his voice in every blast,
       Could catch the sound no more.

6. Namely, George, Lord Anson (1697–1762), who told the castaway's story in his memoir, *Voyage Round the World* (1748).

For then, by toil subdued, he drank
The stifling wave, and then he sank.

No poet wept him; but the page
50   Of narrative sincere,
That tells his name, his worth, his age,
    Is wet with Anson's tear.
And tears by bards or heroes shed
Alike immortalize the dead.

55 I therefore purpose not, or dream,
    Descanting° on his fate,   *singing*
To give the melancholy theme
    A more enduring date:
But misery still delights to trace
60 Its semblance in another's case.

No voice divine the storm allayed,
    No light propitious shone,
When, snatched from all effectual aid,
    We perished, each alone;
65 But I beneath a rougher sea,
And whelmed in deeper gulfs than he.

1799   1803

Lines Written during a Period of Insanity

Hatred and vengeance, my eternal portion,
Scarce can endure delay of execution,
Wait, with impatient readiness, to seize my
                Soul in a moment.

5 Damned below Judas:[7] more abhorred than he was,
Who for a few pence sold his holy Master.
Twice betrayed Jesus me, the last delinquent,
                Deems the profanest.[8]

Man disavows, and Deity disowns me:
10 Hell might afford my miseries a shelter;
Therefore hell keeps her ever hungry mouths all
                Bolted against me.

Hard lot! encompassed with a thousand dangers;
Weary, faint, trembling with a thousand terrors;
15 I'm called, if vanquished, to receive a sentence
                Worse than Abiram's.[9]

7. Judas betrayed Jesus to the chief priests for money (Matthew 26.14–16).
8. I.e., Jesus, betrayed by me as well as by Judas, deems me the most profane.
9. Abirim, rebelling against the authority of Moses and Aaron, was swallowed up with his fellow dissidents in a cleft of the earth. They "went down alive into the pit, and the earth closed upon them" (Numbers 16.33).

Him the vindictive rod of angry justice
Sent quick and howling to the center headlong;
I, fed with judgment, in a fleshly tomb, am
20   Buried above ground.

ca. 1774   1816

ANNA LAETITIA BARBAULD
1743–1825

The Rights of Woman[1]

Yes, injured Woman! rise, assert thy right!
Woman! too long degraded, scorned, oppressed;
O born to rule in partial° Law's despite,°   *biased / contempt*
Resume thy native empire o'er the breast!

5   Go forth arrayed in panoply[2] divine;
That angel pureness which admits no stain;
Go, bid proud Man his boasted rule resign,
And kiss the golden scepter of thy reign.

Go, gird thyself with grace; collect thy store
10   Of bright artillery glancing° from afar;   *gleaming*
Soft melting tones thy thundering cannon's roar,
Blushes and fears thy magazine[3] of war.

Thy rights are empire: urge no meaner° claim,—   *humbler*
Felt, not defined, and if debated, lost;
15   Like sacred mysteries, which withheld from fame,
Shunning discussion, are revered the most.

Try all that wit and art suggest to bend
Of thy imperial foe the stubborn knee;
Make treacherous Man thy subject, not thy friend;
20   Thou mayst command, but never canst be free.

Awe the licentious, and restrain the rude;
Soften the sullen, clear the cloudy brow:
Be, more than princes' gifts, thy favors sued;°—   *sought*
She hazards all, who will the least allow.

25   But hope not, courted idol of mankind,
On this proud eminence secure to stay;
Subduing and subdued, thou soon shalt find
Thy coldness soften, and thy pride give way.

---

1. Until the last two stanzas, a seemingly positive response to Mary Wollstonecraft's *A Vindication of the Rights of Woman* (1792), a radical look at the place of women in society.

2. Complete armor; Ephesians 6.11: "Put on the whole armor of God, that ye may be able to stand against the wiles of the devil."
3. Storage place for weapons or ammunition.

Then, then, abandon each ambitious thought,
30   Conquest or rule thy heart shall feebly move,
In Nature's school, by her soft maxims taught,
That separate rights are lost in mutual love.

ca. 1795   1825

To the Poor

Child of distress, who meet'st the bitter scorn
Of fellow-men to happier prospects born,
Doomed Art and Nature's various stores to see
Flow in full cups of joy—and not for thee;
5   Who seest the rich, to heaven and fate resigned,
Bear *thy* afflictions with a patient mind;
Whose bursting heart disdains unjust control,
Who feel'st oppression's iron in thy soul,
Who dragg'st the load of faint and feeble years,
10   Whose bread is anguish, and whose water tears;
Bear, bear thy wrongs—fulfill thy destined hour,
Bend thy meek neck beneath the foot of Power;
But when thou feel'st the great deliverer nigh,
And thy freed spirit mounting seeks the sky,
15   Let no vain fears thy parting hour molest,
No whispered terrors shake thy quiet breast:
Think not their threats can work thy future woe,
Nor deem the Lord above like lords below;—
Safe in the bosom of that love repose
20   By whom the sun gives light, the ocean flows;
Prepare to meet a Father undismayed,
Nor fear the God whom priests and kings have made.

1795   1825

Life

Animula, vagula, blandula.[4]

Life! I know not what thou art,
But know that thou and I must part;
And when, or how, or where we met,
I own° to me's a secret yet.   *acknowledge*
5   But this I know, when thou art fled,
Where'er they lay these limbs, this head,
No clod so valueless shall be,
As all that then remains of me.

4. Charming little soul, hastening away (Latin); the first line of a poem supposedly composed by the Roman emperor Hadrian (76–138 c.e.) on his deathbed, quoted from Aelius Spartianus, *Life of Hadrian* 25.

O whither, whither dost thou fly,
10   Where bend unseen thy trackless course,
        And in this strange divorce,
Ah tell where I must seek this compound I?

To the vast ocean of empyreal° flame,   *celestial*
        From whence thy essence came,
15   Dost thou thy flight pursue, when freed
From matter's base encumbering weed?
        Or dost thou, hid from sight,
        Wait, like some spell-bound knight,
Through blank oblivious years th' appointed hour,
20   To break thy trance and reassume thy power?
Yet canst thou without thought or feeling be?
O say what art thou, when no more thou 'rt thee?

        Life! we've been long together,
        Through pleasant and through cloudy weather;
25   'Tis hard to part when friends are dear;
        Perhaps 't will cost a sigh, a tear;
        Then steal away, give little warning,
            Choose thine own time;
        Say not Good night, but in some brighter clime
30   Bid me Good morning.

                                                1825

HANNAH MORE
1745–1833

Inscription in a Beautiful Retreat Called Fairy Bower[1]

        Airy spirits, you who love
        Cooling bower, or shady grove;
        Streams that murmur as they flow,
        Zephyrs[2] bland that softly blow;

5   Babbling echo,[3] or the tale
        Of the lovelorn Nightingale;[4]

---

1. A leafy covert or arbor; also, poetically, an idealized abode.
2. Gentle breezes from the west.
3. In Greek mythology, Echo was a nymph whose chatter distracted Hera, the queen of the gods, while Zeus, Hera's husband, consorted with other nymphs and mortal women. Hera punished her by depriving her of speech, save to repeat the words of others. Later, Echo pined for the youth Narcissus, who spurned her love, until nothing was left of her but her voice.

4. The nightingale is known for its sweet, nocturnal song; there are several classical myths about nightingales. Ovid tells the story of Philomela: she was raped by her brother-in-law, Tereus, who then tore out her tongue so that she could not speak. She wove the story into a tapestry and sent it to her sister, who rescued her. She was later changed into a nightingale while in flight from Tereus; Philomela was "lovelorn" only in the ironic sense of being victimized by another's passion.

Hither, airy spirits, come,
This is your peculiar° home.   *own*

    If you love a verdant° glade,   *green*
10 If you love a noon-tide shade,
Hither, Sylphs⁵ and Fairies, fly,
Unobserved of earthly eye.

    Come, and wander every night,
By the moonbeam's glimmering light;
15 And again at early day
Brush the silver dews away.

    Mark where first the daisies blow,°   *bloom*
Where the bluest violets grow;
Where the sweetest linnet° sings,   *a songbird*
20 Where the earliest cowslip° springs;   *a wildflower*

    Where the largest acorn lies,
Precious in a Fairy's eyes:
Sylphs, though unconfined to place,
Love to fill an acorn's space.

25   Come, and mark within what bush
Builds the blackbird or the thrush;
Great his joy who first espies,
Greater his who spares the prize.

    Come, and watch the hallowed bower,
30 Chase the insect from the flower;
Little offices like these,
Gentle souls and Fairies please.

    Mortals! formed of grosser clay,
From our haunts keep far away;
35 Or, if you should dare appear,
See that you from vice are clear.

    Folly's minion,° Fashion's fool,   *darling*
Mad ambition's restless tool!
Slave of passion, slave of power,
40 Fly, ah fly! this tranquil bower!

    Son of avarice,° soul of frost,   *greed*
Wretch! of Heaven abhorred the most,
Learn to pity others' wants,°   *needs*
Or avoid these hallowed haunts.

5. Spirits supposed to inhabit the air.

45   Eye, unconscious of a tear,
      When affliction's train appear;
      Heart that never heaved a sigh,
      For another, come not nigh.

      But, ye darling sons of Heaven,
50   Giving freely what was given,
      You, whose liberal hands dispense
      The blessings of benevolence:

      You, who wipe the tearful eye,
      You, who stop the rising sigh;
55   You, whose souls have understood
      The luxury of doing good,

      Come, ye happy virtuous few,
      Open is my bower to you;
      You, these mossy banks may press;
60   You, each guardian Fay° shall bless.   *fairy*

                                                              1774

From The Slave Trade

                          *   *   *

      Strange power of song![6] the strain that warms the heart
      Seems the same inspiration to impart;
      Touched by the extrinsic° energy alone,   *external*
      We think the flame which melts us is our own;
5   Deceived, for genius we mistake delight,
      Charmed as we read, we fancy we can write.[7]
          Though not to me, sweet Bard, thy powers belong,
      The cause I plead shall sanctify my song.
      The Muse[8] awakes no artificial fire,
10   For Truth rejects what Fancy would inspire:
      Here Art would weave her gayest flowers in vain,
      The bright invention Nature would disdain.
      For no fictitious ills these numbers° flow,   *verses*
      But living anguish, and substantial woe;
15   No individual griefs my bosom melt,
      For millions feel what Oronoko felt:
      Fired by no single wrongs, the countless host
      I mourn, by rapine° dragged from Afric's coast.   *seizure*
          Perish the illiberal[9] thought which would debase

6. The "song" refers to Thomas Southerne's *Oroonoko: A Tragedy* (1696), a stage adaptation of Aphra Behn's *Oroonoko, or the Royal Slave,* (1688). Both the novel and the play critiqued some aspects of the slave trade. The title character is an African prince, sold into slavery in Surinam, who leads a slave revolt and is eventually executed. Southerne is the "sweet Bard" referred to in line 7 below.

7. I.e., we mistake the pleasure we receive from reading for genius of our own, leading us to think we can write.
8. One of the nine Greek sister goddesses believed to be the source of inspiration for the arts.
9. Not generous in respect of the rights or liberties of others, narrow-minded or bigoted.

20   The native genius of the sable° race!   *dark-complexioned*
     Perish the proud philosophy, which sought
     To rob them of the powers of equal thought![1]
     Does then the immortal principle within
     Change with the casual color of a skin?
25   Does matter° govern spirit? or is mind   *body*
     Degraded by the form to which 'tis joined?
       No; they have heads to think, and hearts to feel,
     And souls to act, with firm, though erring zeal;[2]
     For they have keen affections, kind desires,
30   Love strong as death, and active patriot fires;
     All the rude energy, the fervid flame,
     Of high-souled passion, and ingenuous[3] shame:
     Strong, but luxuriant virtues boldly shoot
     From the wild vigor of a savage root.
35   Nor weak their sense of honor's proud control,
     For pride is virtue in a Pagan soul;
     A sense of worth, a conscience° of desert,°   *consciousness / worth*
     A high, unbroken haughtiness of heart;
     That self-same stuff which erst° proud empires swayed,   *formerly*
40   Of which the conquerors of the world were made.
     Capricious fate of men! that very pride
     In Afric scourged, in Rome was deified.
       No Muse, O Qua-shi![4] shall thy deeds relate,
     No statue snatch thee from oblivious fate!
45   For thou wast born where never gentle Muse
     On Valor's grave the flowers of Genius strews;
     And thou wast born where no recording page
     Plucks the fair deed from Time's devouring rage.
     Had Fortune placed thee on some happier coast,
50   Where *polished*[5] Pagans' souls heroic boast,
     To thee, who soughtest a voluntary grave,
     The uninjured honors of thy name to save,
     Whose generous arm thy barbarous Master spared,[6]
     Altars had smoked, and temples had been reared.
55   Whenever to Afric's shores I turn my eyes,
     Horrors of deepest, deadliest guilt arise;
     I see, by more than Fancy's mirror[7] shewn,
     The burning village, and the blazing town:
     See the dire victim torn from social life,
60   The shrieking babe, the agonizing wife!
     She, wretch forlorn! is dragged by hostile hands,
     To distant tyrants sold, in distant lands!
     Transmitted[8] miseries, and successive chains,

1. Perhaps an allusion to Aristotle's theory (in the *Politics* 1.5) that some are "naturally" born as slaves or inferior persons.
2. Erring because not Christian.
3. Noble, freeborn. The slaves feel shame because they are "ingenuous."
4. A slave in Bermuda who killed himself rather than undergo punishment by the master with whom he had been brought up as a playfellow.
5. Made more refined or elegant by the stories told about them.
6. When his master tried to punish him, Quashi resisted. In the ensuing struggle, Quashi gained the upper hand and drew a knife, but used it to kill himself rather than the master.
7. Fictions generated by imagination; perhaps referring to Southerne's play or other theatrical or literary works.
8. Passed by inheritance.

The sole sad heritage her child obtains!
65 Even this last wretched boon° their foes deny,   *request*
To weep together, or together die.
By felon hands, by one relentless stroke,
See the fond links of feeling Nature broke!
The fibers twisting round a parent's heart,
70 Torn from their grasp, and bleeding as they part.

1788

CHARLOTTE SMITH
1749–1806

Written in the Church Yard at Middleton in Sussex

Pressed by the moon, mute arbitress of tides,
    While the loud equinox its power combines,
    The sea no more its swelling surge confines,
But o'er the shrinking land sublimely rides.
5 The wild blast, rising from the western cave,
    Drives the huge billows from their heaving bed,
    Tears from their grassy tombs the village dead,
And breaks the silent sabbath of the grave!
With shells and sea-weed mingled, on the shore
10   Lo! their bones whiten in the frequent wave;
    But vain to them the winds and waters rave;
They hear the warring elements no more:
While I am doomed—by life's long storm oppressed,
To gaze with envy on their gloomy rest.

1789

To the Shade of Burns[1]

Mute is thy wild harp, now, O Bard sublime!
    Who, amid Scotia's° mountain solitude,   *Scotland's*
Great Nature taught to "build the lofty rhyme,"[2]
    And even beneath the daily pressure, rude,°   *harsh*
5 Of laboring Poverty,[3] thy generous blood,
Fired with the love of freedom—Not subdued
    Wert thou by thy low fortune: But a time
    Like this we live in, when the abject chime
Of echoing Parasite is best approved,[4]

1. This sonnet was written upon the death of the Scottish poet Robert Burns (1759–1796; see pp. 747–60).
2. Cf. Milton, "Lycidas," line 11 (p. 410).
3. Burns was the son of an unsuccessful farmer; his own health was broken by efforts to earn a living at farming.
4. I.e., in our time (unlike Burns's), public taste favors "low," unoriginal (parasitical) poetry.

10   Was not for thee—Indignantly is fled
        Thy noble Spirit; and no longer moved
            By all the ills o'er which thine heart has bled,
            Associate worthy of the illustrious dead,
        Enjoys with them "the Liberty it loved."⁵

1796   1797

Written near a Port on a Dark Evening

        Huge vapors brood above the clifted shore,
            Night on the Ocean settles, dark and mute,
        Save where is heard the repercussive roar
            Of drowsy billows,° on the rugged foot   waves
5   Of rocks remote; or still more distant tone
            Of seamen in the anchored bark° that tell   ship
        The watch relieved; or one deep voice alone
            Singing the hour, and bidding "Strike the bell."
        All is black shadow, but the lucid line
10   Marked by the light surf on the level sand,
        Or where afar the ship-lights faintly shine
            Like wandering fairy fires,⁶ that oft on land
        Mislead the Pilgrim—Such the dubious ray
        That wavering Reason lends, in life's long darkling way.

                                                            1797

Written in October

        The blasts of Autumn as they scatter round
            The faded foliage of another year,
        And muttering many a sad and solemn sound,
            Drive the pale fragments o'er the stubble sere,°   dry; withered
5   Are well attuned to my dejected mood;
            (Ah! better far than airs that breathe of Spring!)
            While the high rooks, that hoarsely clamoring
        Seek in black phalanx⁷ the half-leafless wood,
            I rather hear, than that enraptured lay°   song
10   Harmonious, and of Love and Pleasure born,
            Which from the golden furze,⁸ or flowering thorn
                Awakes the Shepherd in the ides° of May;   fifteenth
        Nature delights *me* most when most she mourns,
        For never more to me the Spring of Hope returns!

                                                            1797

---

5. Cf. Alexander Pope, "Epitaph on Sir William Trumbull," lines 11–12: "Such this man was, who now, from earth remov'd, / At length enjoys that Liberty he lov'd."
6. The will-o'-the-wisp was said to draw travelers astray by holding a false light before them; the phe-nomenon of nocturnal light is caused by the com-bustion of marsh gas.
7. A flock of rooks (a species of crow that nests in a colony and hence looks like a phalanx).
8. A spiny evergreen shrub with yellow flowers.

Nepenthe[9]

Oh! for imperial Polydamna's art,
   Which to bright Helen was in Egypt taught,
To mix with magic power the oblivious draught[1]
Of force to staunch the bleeding of the heart,
5   And to Care's wan and hollow cheek impart
   The smile of happy youth, uncursed with thought.
Potent indeed the charm that could appease
   Affection's ceaseless anguish, doomed to weep
O'er the cold grave; or yield even transient ease
10   By soothing busy Memory to sleep!
—Around me those who surely must have tried
   Some charm of equal power, I daily see,
But still to *me* Oblivion is denied,
   There's no Nepenthe, now, on earth for me.

1797

Stanzas

Ah! think'st thou, Laura,[2] then, that wealth
Should make me thus my youth, and health,
   And freedom and repose resign?—
Ah, no!—I toil to gain by stealth
5   One look, one tender glance of thine.

Born where huge hills on hills are piled,
In Caledonia's[3] distant wild,
   Unbounded Liberty was mine:
But thou upon my hopes hast smiled,
10   And bade me be a slave of thine!

Amid these gloomy haunts of gain,
Of weary hours I not complain,
   While Hope forbids me to repine,°   *complain*
And whispering tells me I obtain
15   Pity from that soft heart of thine.

---

9. A drink or drug supposed to bring forgetfulness of trouble or grief, used by Helen (in Homer, *Odyssey* 4.219–32) to quell the lament over the apparently lost Odysseus. In a note to this poem, Smith cites lines from Alexander Pope's "Odyssey," which describes Helen's mixing the potion and her acquisition of the drug from "Thone's imperial wife," i.e., Polydamna, the Egyptian woman from whom she learned the art of herbs.
1. A potion or drink producing forgetfulness.
2. This poem originally appeared in Smith's *The Young Philosopher: A Novel* (1798), in which it is written by the character Glenmorris to Laura, his future wife.
3. Caledonia is the Roman name for the northern part of Britain; hence, used poetically for Scotland.

Tho' far capricious Fortune flies,
Yet Love will bless the sacrifice,
    And all his purer joys combine;
    While I my little world comprise
20   In that fair form, and fairer soul of thine.

1798

Ode to Death

Friend of the wretched! wherefore° should the eye   *why*
    Of blank Despair, whence tears have ceased to flow,
Be turned from thee?—Ah! wherefore fears to die
    He, who compelled each poignant grief to know,
5   Drains to its lowest dregs the cup of woe?

Would Cowardice postpone thy calm embrace,
    To linger out long years in torturing pain?
Or not prefer thee to the ills that chase
    Him, who too much impoverished to obtain
10   From British Themis[4] *right*, implores her aid in vain!

Sharp goading Indigence° who would not fly,   *poverty*
    That urges toil the exhausted strength above?
Or shun the *once* fond friend's averted eye?
    Or who to *thy* asylum not remove,
15   To lose the wasting pain of unrequited love?

Can then the wounded wretch who must deplore
    What most she loved, to thy cold arms consigned,
Who hears the voice that soothed her soul no more,[5]
    Fear *thee*, O Death!—Or hug the chains that bind
20   To joyless, cheerless life, her sick, reluctant mind?

Oh! Misery's Cure; who e'er in pale dismay
    Has watched the angel form they could not save,
And seen their dearest blessing tore away,
    May well the terrors of *thy* triumph brave,
25   Nor pause in fearful dread before the opening grave!

1797, 1800

---

4. The British judicial system. Smith spent many years embroiled in the legal system, trying to settle her father-in-law's will in order to allow her children to claim their shares in his estate.

5. Smith refers to the death of her daughter, Anna Augusta de Foville, who died while giving birth in 1795.

From Beachy Head[6]

On thy stupendous summit, rock sublime!
That o'er the channel reared, half way at sea
The mariner at early morning hails,[7]
I would recline; while Fancy should go forth,
5   And represent the strange and awful hour
Of vast concussion;[8] when the Omnipotent
Stretched forth his arm, and rent the solid hills,
Bidding the impetuous main flood rush between
The rifted shores, and from the continent
10   Eternally divided this green isle.
Imperial lord of the high southern coast!
From thy projecting head-land I would mark
Far in the east the shades of night disperse,
Melting and thinned, as from the dark blue wave
15   Emerging, brilliant rays of arrowy light
Dart from the horizon; when the glorious sun
Just lifts above it his resplendent orb.
Advances now, with feathery silver touched,
The rippling tide of flood; glisten the sands,
20   While, inmates of the chalky clefts that scar
Thy sides precipitous, with shrill harsh cry,
Their white wings glancing in the level beam,
The terns, and gulls, and tarrocks, seek their food,[9]
And thy rough hollows echo to the voice
25   Of the gray choughs,[1] and ever restless daws,
With clamor, not unlike the chiding hounds,
While the lone shepherd, and his baying dog,
Drive to thy turfy crest his bleating flock.

The high meridian of the day is past,
30   And Ocean now, reflecting the calm Heaven,
Is of cerulean hue; and murmurs low
The tide of ebb, upon the level sands.
The sloop, her angular canvas shifting still,
Catches the light and variable airs
35   That but a little crisp the summer sea,
Dimpling its tranquil surface.

*   *   *

1807

6. This long poem (732 lines) appeared in Smith's last volume of poetry, *Beachy Head and Other Poems,* published after her death. The notes below are Smith's, printed originally as endnotes.
7. "In crossing the Channel from the coast of France, Beachy-Head is the first land made."
8. "Alluding to an idea that this Island was once joined to the continent of Europe, and torn from it by some convulsion of Nature. I confess I never could trace the resemblance between the two countries. Yet the cliffs about Dieppe, resemble the chalk cliffs on the southern coast. But Normandy has no likeness whatever to the part of England opposite to it."
9. "Terns. *Sterna hirundo,* or Sea Swallow. Gulls. *Larus canus.* Tarrocks. *Larus tridactylus.*"
1. "Gray choughs. *Corvus Graculus,* Cornish Choughs, or, as these birds are called by the Sussex people, Saddle-backed Crows, build in great numbers on this coast."

PHILIP FRENEAU
1752–1832

The Indian Burying Ground

In spite of all the learned have said,
　　I still my opinion keep;
The posture, that we give the dead,
　　Points out the soul's eternal sleep.

5　Not so the ancients of these lands—
　　The Indian, when from life released,
Again is seated[1] with his friends,
　　And shares again the joyous feast.

His imaged birds, and painted bowl,
10　　And venison, for a journey dressed,[2]
Bespeak the nature of the soul,
　　Activity, that knows no rest.

His bow, for action ready bent,
　　And arrows, with a head of stone,
15　Can only mean that life is spent,
　　And not the old ideas gone.

Thou, stranger, that shalt come this way,
　　No fraud upon the dead commit—
Observe the swelling turf, and say
20　　They do not lie, but here they sit.

Here still a lofty rock remains,
　　On which the curious eye may trace
(Now wasted, half, by wearing rains)
　　The fancies of a ruder race.

25　Here still an aged elm aspires,
　　Beneath whose far-projecting shade
(And which the shepherd still admires)
　　The children of the forest played!

There oft a restless Indian queen
30　　(Pale Shebah,[3] with her braided hair)
And many a barbarous form is seen
　　To chide the man that lingers there.

1. "The North American Indians bury their dead in a sitting posture; decorating the corpse with wampum, the images of birds, quadrupeds, etc.: And (if that of a warrior) with bows, arrows, tomahawks and other military weapons" [Freneau's note].
2. Pun on "dress": to prepare for cooking as well as to clothe.
3. Sheba, the queen who visited Solomon to judge his wisdom (1 Kings 10.1–13).

By midnight moons, o'er moistening dews;
In habit for the chase arrayed,
35 The hunter still the deer pursues,
The hunter and the deer, a shade!°   soul

And long shall timorous fancy see
The painted chief, and pointed spear,
And Reason's self shall bow the knee
40 To shadows and delusions here.

1787   1788

To Sir Toby[4]

A Sugar Planter in the Interior Parts of Jamaica, Near the City of San Jago De La Vega (Spanish Town), 1784

"The motions of his spirit are black as night,
And his affections dark as Erebus."
—SHAKESPEARE[5]

If there exists a hell—the case is clear—
Sir Toby's slaves enjoy that portion here:
Here are no blazing brimstone lakes—'tis true;
But kindled rum too often burns as blue;
5   In which some fiend, whom nature must detest,
Steeps Toby's brand, and marks poor Cudjoe's breast.[6]
Here whips on whips excite perpetual fears,
And mingled howlings vibrate on my ears:
Here nature's plagues abound, to fret and tease,
10 Snakes, scorpions, despots, lizards, centipedes—
No art, no care escapes the busy lash;
All have their dues—and all are paid in cash—
The eternal driver keeps a steady eye
On a black herd, who would his vengeance fly,
15 But chained, imprisoned, on a burning soil,
For the mean avarice of a tyrant toil![7]
The lengthy cart-whip guards this monster's reign—
And cracks, like pistols, from the fields of cane.
Ye powers! who formed these wretched tribes, relate,
20 What had they done, to merit such a fate!
Why were they brought from Eboe's[8] sultry waste,
To see that plenty which they must not taste—

4. First published in the *Daily Advertiser*, February 1, 1791, titled "The Island Field Negro." We print the 1809 text.
5. *The Merchant of Venice* 5.1. Freneau has substituted "black" for *dull Erebus*: darkness; in Greek mythology, part of the underworld through which the dead passed before entering Hades.
6. Cudge or Cudjoe was a common name for a

slave. "This passage has a reference to the West Indian custom (sanctioned by law) of branding a newly imported slave on the breast, with a red hot iron, as evidence of the purchaser's property" [Freneau's note].
7. Lines 13–16 were added in 1809.
8. "A small Negro kingdom near the river Senegal" [Freneau's note].

Food, which they cannot buy, and dare not steal;
Yams and potatoes—many a scanty meal!—
25 One, with a gibbet° wakes his negro's fears,   *gallows*
One to the windmill nails him by the ears;
One keeps his slave in darkened dens, unfed,
One puts the wretch in pickle⁹ ere he's dead:
This, from a tree suspends him by the thumbs,
30 That, from his table grudges even the crumbs!
O'er yond' rough hills a tribe of females go,
Each with her gourd,° her infant, and her hoe;   *water cup*
Scorched by a sun that has no mercy here,
Driven by a devil, whom men call overseer—
35 In chains, twelve wretches to their labors haste;
Twice twelve I saw, with iron collars graced!—
Are such the fruits that spring from vast domains?
Is wealth, thus got, Sir Toby, worth your pains!—
Who would your wealth on terms, like these, possess,
40 Where all we see is pregnant with distress—
Angola's¹ natives scourged by ruffian hands,
And toil's hard product shipped to foreign lands.
Talk not of blossoms, and your endless spring;
What joy, what smile, can scenes of misery bring?—
45 Though Nature, here, has every blessing spread,
Poor is the laborer—and how meanly fed!—
Here Stygian² paintings light and shade renew,
Pictures of hell, that Virgil's³ pencil drew:
Here, surly Charons make their annual trip,
50 And ghosts arrive in every Guinea ship,⁴
To find what beasts these western isles afford,
Plutonian⁵ scourges, and despotic lords:—
Here, they, of stuff determined to be free,
Must climb the rude cliffs of the Liguanee;⁶
55 Beyond the clouds, in sculking haste repair,
And hardly safe from brother traitors⁷ there.—

1784   1791, 1809

9. I.e., rubs salt or salt and vinegar on the slave's back after a flogging.
1. West African Portuguese colony's.
2. Hellish; alluding to the river Styx, which, in Greek mythology, souls must cross to enter Hades. They were ferried across to the underworld by Charon.
3. "See *Aeneid*, Book 6th.—and Fenelon's Telemachus, Book 18" [Freneau's note]. The Trojan hero Aeneas descends to the underworld in the sixth book of the epic by the Latin poet Virgil (70–19 B.C.E.). The French theologian François de Salignac de la Mothe-Fénelon (1651–1715) wrote *Télémaque* (1699), a didactic romance concerning the son of the hero Ulysses as he searches for his father.
4. Slave ships from West Africa.
5. Hellish; Pluto was the Roman name for the god of the underworld.
6. "The mountains northward of the kingdom" [Freneau's note].
7. "Alluding to the *Independent* negroes in the blue mountains, who, for a stipulated reward, deliver up every fugitive that falls into their hands, to the English Government" [Freneau's note].

PHILLIS WHEATLEY
ca. 1753–1784

A Farewell to America. To Mrs. S. W.[1]

I

Adieu, New-England's smiling meads,°   *meadows*
  Adieu, the flow'ry plain:
I leave thine op'ning charms, O spring,
  And tempt the roaring main.°   *sea*

II

5 In vain for me the flow'rets rise,
  And boast their gaudy pride,
While here beneath the northern skies
  I mourn for health denied.[2]

III

Celestial maid of rosy hue,[3]
10   O let me feel thy reign!°   *influence, dominion*
I languish till thy face I view,
  Thy vanished joys regain.

IV

Susannah mourns, nor can I bear
  To see the crystal show'r,
15 Or mark the tender falling tear
  At sad departure's hour;

V

Not unregarding can I see
  Her soul with grief opprest;
But let no sighs, no groans for me,
20   Steal from her pensive breast.

VI

In vain the feathered warblers sing,
  In vain the garden blooms,
And on the bosom of the spring
  Breathes out her sweet perfumes,

VII

25 While for Britannia's distant shore
  We sweep the liquid plain,
And with astonished eyes explore
  The wide-extended main.

1. Susanna Wheatley (1709–1774), Wheatley's owner and mistress, who had afforded her an excellent education and had encouraged her writing. Wheatley departed Boston for London in May 1773.

2. Wheatley was frail and sickly for much of her life, and she went to England partly to improve her health.

3. I.e., New England (or America?).

VIII

Lo! Health appears! celestial dame!
30   Complacent and serene,
With Hebe's[4] mantle o'er her frame,
    With soul-delighting mien.°   *appearance, expression*

IX

To mark the vale° where London lies   *valley*
    With misty vapors crowned,
35 Which cloud Aurora's[5] thousand dyes,
    And veil her charms around,

X

Why, Phoebus,[6] moves thy car so slow?
    So slow thy rising ray?
Give us the famous town to view,
40   Thou glorious king of day!

XI

For thee, Britannia, I resign
    New England's smiling fields;
To view again her charms divine,
    What joy the prospect yields!

XII

45 But thou! Temptation hence away,
    With all thy fatal train
Nor once seduce my soul away,
    By thine enchanting strain.

XIII

Thrice happy they, whose heav'nly shield
50   Secures their souls from harms,
And fell° Temptation on the field   *destructive*
    Of all its pow'r disarms!

Boston, May 7, 1773

On Being Brought from Africa to America[7]

'Twas mercy brought me from my pagan land,
Taught my benighted[8] soul to understand
That there's a God, that there's a Savior too:

---

4. Hebe, the Greek goddess of youth, performed small services for the gods, including cupbearing (until replaced by Ganymede); she was considered the personification of youthful beauty. "Health" in this stanza may refer to Hygieia, the Greek goddess of health.
5. The Greek and Roman goddess of the dawn.
6. Apollo, the Greek and Roman god of the sun, who daily drove his chariot ("car"), the sun, across the sky.
7. Wheatley was brought from West Africa to Boston in July 1761, as a child of eight.
8. Overtaken by darkness; also, figuratively, involved in intellectual or moral darkness, involved in obscurity.

Once I redemption neither sought nor knew.
5   Some view our sable° race with scornful eye,   *black*
"Their color is a diabolic dye."
Remember, Christians, Negros, black as Cain,⁹
May be refined, and join th' angelic train.

1773

To S. M.,¹ a Young African Painter, on Seeing His Works

To show the lab'ring bosom's deep intent,
And thought in living characters to paint,
When first thy pencil did those beauties give,
And breathing figures learnt from thee to live,
5   How did those prospects give my soul delight,
A new creation rushing on my sight?
Still,° wond'rous youth! each noble path pursue,   *always*
On deathless glories fix thine ardent view:
Still may the painter's and the poet's fire
10   To aid thy pencil, and thy verse conspire!
And may the charms of each seraphic² theme
Conduct thy footsteps to immortal fame!
High to the blissful wonders of the skies
Elate thy soul, and raise thy wishful eyes.
15   Thrice happy, when exalted to survey
That splendid city, crowned with endless day,
Whose twice six gates on radiant hinges ring:
Celestial Salem³ blooms in endless spring.
        Calm and serene thy moments glide along,
20   And may the muse⁴ inspire each future song!
Still, with the sweets of contemplation blessed,
May peace with balmy wings your soul invest!
But when these shades⁵ of time are chased away,
And darkness ends in everlasting day,
25   On what seraphic pinions⁶ shall we move,
And view the landscapes in the realms above?
There shall thy tongue in heav'nly murmurs flow,
And there my muse with heav'nly transport glow:
No more to tell of Damon's⁷ tender sighs,
30   Or rising radiance of Aurora's⁸ eyes,

9. The son of Adam and Eve, Cain killed his brother, Abel, and God punished him with this curse: "When thou tillest the ground, it shall not henceforth yield unto thee its strength; a fugitive and a vagabond shalt thou be in the earth" (Genesis 4.12).
1. Scipio Moorhead, the slave of a Boston clergyman, John Moorhead.
2. Resembling a seraph (a member of one of the nine orders of angels) either in beauty or in fervor of exalted devotion.
3. The heavenly Jerusalem.
4. Imagined source of poetic power.

5. Souls of the dead in the classical underworld.
6. Wings; from the Latin, *pennae*, feathers, and therefore with a pun on the associated meaning, pens (originally made from quills).
7. According to one version of the Greek legend, Damon was a friend of Pythias, who had been condemned to death by the tyrant Dionysius. Damon stood pledge for Pythias as the latter left to settle his affairs. When Pythias returned, Dionysius was so impressed by the actions of both men that he pardoned Pythias.
8. The Greek and Roman goddess of the dawn's.

For nobler themes demand a nobler strain,
And purer language on th' ethereal plain.
Cease, gentle muse! the solemn gloom of night
Now seals the fair creation from my sight.

1773

On Imagination

Thy various works, imperial queen, we see,
How bright their forms! how deck'd with pomp by thee!
Thy wond'rous acts in beauteous order stand,
And all attest how potent is thine hand.

5   From Helicon's⁹ refulgent° heights attend,   *bright, shining*
Ye sacred choir, and my attempts befriend:
To tell her glories with a faithful tongue,
Ye blooming Graces,¹ triumph in my song.

Now here, now there, the roving Fancy flies,
10 Till some loved object strikes her wand'ring eyes,
Whose silken fetters° all the senses bind,   *shackles*
And soft captivity involves the mind.

Imagination! who can sing thy force?
Or who describe the swiftness of thy course?
15 Soaring through air to find the bright abode,
Th' empyreal° place of the thund'ring God,   *heavenly*
We on thy pinions² can surpass the wind,
And leave the rolling universe behind:
From star to star the mental optics rove,
20 Measure the skies, and range the realms above.
There in one view we grasp the mighty whole,
Or with new worlds amaze th' unbounded soul.

Though Winter frowns to Fancy's raptured eyes
The fields may flourish, and gay scenes arise;
25 The frozen deeps may break their iron bands,
And bid their waters murmur o'er the sands.
Fair Flora³ may resume her fragrant reign,
And with her flow'ry riches deck the plain;
Sylvanus⁴ may diffuse his honors round,
30 And all the forest may with leaves be crowned:
Show'rs may descend, and dews their gems disclose,
And nectar sparkle on the blooming rose.

---

9. A mountain in Greece that was sacred to the
Muses (nine sister goddesses who presided over
poetry, song, and the arts and sciences) and thus
figures poetic inspiration.
1. In Greek mythology, three sister goddesses who
gave charm and beauty. *Her:* i.e., imagination's.

2. Wings; from the Latin, *pennae*, feathers, and
therefore with a pun on the associated meaning,
pens (originally made from quills).
3. Roman goddess of flowers.
4. Roman god of the woods.

Such is thy pow'r, nor are thine orders vain,
O thou the leader of the mental train:
35 In full perfection all thy works are wrought,
And thine the sceptre o'er the realms of thought.
Before thy throne the subject-passions bow,
Of subject-passions sov'reign ruler Thou,
At thy command joy rushes on the heart,
40 And through the glowing veins the spirits dart.

Fancy might now her silken pinions try
To rise from earth, and sweep th' expanse on high;
From Tithon's bed now might Aurora[5] rise,
Her cheeks all glowing with celestial dies,°   *colors*
45 While a pure stream of light o'erflows the skies.
The monarch of the day° I might behold,   *sun*
And all the mountains tipt with radiant gold,
But I reluctant leave the pleasing views,
Which Fancy dresses to delight the Muse;
50 Winter austere forbids me to aspire,
And northern tempests damp the rising fire;[6]
They chill the tides of Fancy's flowing sea,
Cease then, my song, cease the unequal lay.[7]

1784

GEORGE CRABBE
1754–1832

From The Parish Register[1]

Part I

BAPTISMS

Tum porro puer (ut sævis projectus ab undis,
Navita) nudus humi jacet infans indigus omni
Vitali auxilio, . . .
Vagituque locum lugubri complet, ut æquum est,
Cui tantum in vitâ restat transire malorum.[2]

5. Greek and Roman goddess of the dawn, represented as rising with rosy fingers from the bed of her aged lover, Tithonus.
6. Wheatley here alludes to and revises Milton's famous lines to his Muse (his source of inspiration) expressing his fear that he is too old, or was born in a time and place too inhospitable to poetry, to accomplish his poetic aims; without the Muse's help, "an age too late" or a climate too northern or "cold" may "damp" (depress) his "intended wing" (*Paradise Lost* 9.44–45; see p. 426).
7. A "lay" is a short narrative or lyric poem, but the term harks back, specifically, to the late medieval lais—tales of magic and romance—written in England and Northern France. Wheatley's adjective "unequal" is ambiguous, referring perhaps (with ironic modesty?) to her short poem's inability

to compete with Milton's epic. She has, however, echoed Milton's acknowledgment of his inability to write without the help of a power greater than (unequal to) his own.
1. Crabbe's poem is modeled on the parish registers in which baptisms, marriages, and deaths are recorded. The following section, although titled "Baptisms," serves as an introduction to the whole poem.
2. From Lucretius, *De Rerum Natura* (Latin, *On the Nature of Things*) 5.222–24, 225–27: "Then the child, like a sailor thrown forth by the cruel waves, lies naked on the ground, speechless, needing all kinds of vital support . . . and he fills the surrounding air with sad cries—as is appropriate, given that so much trouble awaits in life."

The year revolves, and I again explore
The simple Annals of my Parish poor;
What Infant-members in my flock appear,
What Pairs I blessed in the departed year;
5 And who, of Old or Young, or Nymphs or Swains,[3]
Are lost to Life, its pleasures and its pains.
    No Muse I ask, before my view to bring
The humble actions of the swains I sing.—
How passed the youthful, how the old their days;
10 Who sank in sloth, and who aspired to praise;
Their tempers, manners, morals, customs, arts,
What parts they had, and how they employed their parts;
By what elated, soothed, seduced, depressed,
Full well I know—these Records give the rest.
15   Is there a place, save one the poet sees,
A land of love, of liberty and ease;
Where labor wearies not, nor cares suppress
Th' eternal flow of rustic happiness;
Where no proud mansion frowns in awful state,
20 Or keeps the sunshine from the cottage-gate;
Where young and old, intent on pleasure, throng,
And half man's life is holiday and song?
Vain search for scenes like these! no view appears;
By sighs unruffled or unstained by tears;
25 Since vice the world subdued and waters drowned,
Auburn[4] and Eden can no more be found.
    Hence good and evil mixed, but man has skill
And power to part them, when he feels the will!
Toil, care, and patience bless th' abstemious° few,   *not self-indulgent*
30 Fear, shame, and want the thoughtless herd pursue.
    Behold the Cot!° where thrives th' industrious swain,   *cottage*
Source of his pride, his pleasure, and his gain;
Screened from the winter's wind, the sun's last ray
Smiles on the window and prolongs the day;
35 Projecting thatch the woodbine's branches stop,
And turn their blossoms to the casement's top:
All need requires is in that cot contained,
And much that taste untaught and unrestrained
Surveys delighted; there she loves to trace,
40 In one gay picture, all the royal race;
Around the walls are heroes, lovers, kings;
The print that shows them and the verse that sings.
    Here the last Lewis on his throne is seen,
And there he stands imprisoned, and his Queen;[5]
45 To these the mother takes her child, and shows
What grateful duty to his God he owes;
Who gives to him a happy home, where he
Lives and enjoys his freedom with the free;

3. Poetic diction for "or beautiful young women
or young men."
4. The fictive village invoked by Oliver Goldsmith
in "The Deserted Village" (see p. 686). The open-
ing section of Crabbe's poem argues explicitly
against Goldsmith's views of village life.
5. Louis XVI and Marie Antoinette of France, who
were guillotined in 1793.

When kings and queens, dethroned, insulted, tried,
50 Are all these blessings of the poor denied.
     There is King Charles, and all his Golden Rules,[6]
Who proved Misfortune's was the best of schools:
And there his Son,[7] who, tried by years of pain,
Proved that misfortunes may be sent in vain.
55   The Magic-mill that grinds the gran'nams young,[8]
Close at the side of kind Godiva hung;[9]
She, of her favorite place the pride and joy,
Of charms at once most lavish and most coy,
By wanton act the purest fame could raise,
60 And give the boldest deed the chastest praise.
     There stands the stoutest Ox in England fed;[1]
There fights the boldest Jew, Whitechapel bred;[2]
And here Saint Monday's worthy votaries live,
In all the joys that ale and skittles[3] give.
65   Now lo! on Egypt's coast that hostile fleet,
By nations dreaded and by NELSON beat;[4]
And here shall soon another triumph come,
A deed of glory in a day of gloom;
Distressing glory! grievous boon of fate!
70 The proudest conquest, at the dearest rate.[5]
     On shelf of deal° beside the cuckoo-clock,   pine or fir wood
Of cottage-reading rests the chosen stock;
Learning we lack, not books, but have a kind
For all our wants, a meat for every mind:
75 The tale for wonder and the joke for whim,
The half-sung sermon and the half-groaned hymn.
     No need of classing; each within its place,
The feeling finger in the dark can trace;
"First from the corner, farthest from the wall,"
80 Such all the rules, and they suffice for all.
     There pious works for Sunday's use are found;
Companions for that Bible newly bound;
That Bible, bought by sixpence weekly saved,
Has choicest prints by famous hands engraved;
85 Has choicest notes by many a famous head,
Such as to doubt, have rustic readers led;
Have made them stop to reason *why?* and *how?*
And, where they once agreed, to cavil now.
Oh! rather give me commentators plain,
90 Who with no deep researches vex the brain;
Who from the dark and doubtful love to run,
And hold their glimmering tapers to the sun;

6. British King Charles I was thought to have authored twelve popular maxims shortly before he was executed, in 1649.
7. Charles II (reigned 1660–85).
8. A popular contemporary print depicting the Guildford Mill, comically imagined to grind old women into young ones.
9. An eleventh-century noblewoman reputed to have ridden naked through the streets of Coventry to dissuade her husband from imposing heavy taxes on the citizens.
1. A Lancashire ox famous for its size.
2. The boxer Daniel Mendoza.
3. An English bowling game. "Saint Monday's . . . votaries" are working people devoted to taking Monday (as well as Sunday) as "holy days."
4. At the Battle of the Nile (1798).
5. I.e., the Battle of Trafalgar (1805), in which Admiral Horatio Nelson died.

Who simple truth with nine-fold reasons back,
And guard the point no enemies attack.
95   Bunyan's famed Pilgrim rests that shelf upon,
A genius rare but rude was honest John;[6]
Not one who, early by the Muse beguiled,
Drank from her well the waters undefiled;[7]
Not one who slowly gained the hill sublime,[8]
100   Then often sipped and little at a time;
But one who dabbled in the sacred springs,
And drank them muddy, mixed with baser things.
        Here to interpret dreams we read the rules,
Science our own! and never taught in schools;
105   In moles and specks we Fortune's gifts discern,
And Fate's fixed will from Nature's wanderings learn.
        Of Hermit Quarll we read, in island rare,[9]
Far from mankind and seeming far from care;
Safe from all want, and sound in every limb;
110   Yes! there was he, and there was care with him.
        Unbound and heaped, these valued tomes beside,
Lay humbler works, the pedlar's pack supplied;
Yet these, long since, have all acquired a name;
The Wandering Jew[1] has found his way to fame;
115   And fame, denied to many a labored song,
Crowns Thumb the Great, and Hickathrift the strong.
        There too is he, by wizard-power upheld,
Jack,[2] by whose arm the giant-brood were quelled:
His shoes of swiftness on his feet he placed;
120   His coat of darkness on his loins he braced;
His sword of sharpness in his hand he took,
And off the heads of doughty° giants stroke: mighty
Their glaring eyes beheld no mortal near;
No sound of feet alarmed the drowsy ear;
125   No English blood their pagan sense could smell,
But heads dropt headlong, wondering why they fell.
        These are the peasant's joy, when placed at ease,
Half his delighted offspring mount his knees.
        To every cot° the lord's indulgent mind   cottage
130   Has a small space for garden-ground assigned;
Here—till return of morn dismissed the farm—
The careful peasant plies the sinewy arm,
Warmed as he works, and casts his look around
On every foot of that improving ground:

6. John Bunyan (1628–1688), English preacher
and author of *Pilgrim's Progress* (1678).
7. A phrase applied by Spenser (*Faerie Queene*
5.2.32) to Chaucer, and by Samuel Johnson (in the
preface to his *Dictionary*) to Spenser and others.
8. Perhaps Milton, who contrasted his "slow-
endeavoring art" to Shakespeare's "easy numbers"
("On Shakespeare") and who stressed the idea of
temperance throughout *Paradise Lost*.
9. Attributed to Edward Dorrington, *The Hermit*,

or *Unparalleled Sufferings and Surprising Adven-
tures of Philip Quarll* tells the story of a Robinson
Crusoe–like hero. First published in 1727, it was
often adapted for children.
1. A proverbial figure condemned to a life of eter-
nal wandering as punishment for his cruelty to
Christ.
2. Jack the Giant Killer; like Tom Thumb and Tom
Hickathrift, a folk hero.

135   It is his own he sees; his master's eye
     Peers not about, some secret fault to spy;
     Nor voice severe is there, nor censure known;—
     Hope, profit, pleasure,—they are all his own.
     Here grow the humble cives,° and, hard by them,   *chives*
140   The leek with crown globose° and reedy stem;   *globular*
     High climb his pulse° in many an even row,   *peas, beans*
     Deep strike the ponderous roots in soil below;
     And herbs of potent smell and pungent taste,
     Give a warm relish to the night's repast.
145   Apples and cherries grafted by his hand,
     And clustered nuts for neighboring market stand.
       Nor thus concludes his labor; near the cot,
     The reed-fence rises round some favorite spot;
     Where rich carnations, pinks with purple eyes,
150   Proud hyacinths, the least some florist's prize,
     Tulips tall-stemmed and pounced auriculas° rise.   *primroses*
       Here on a Sunday-eve, when service ends,
     Meet and rejoice a family of friends;
     All speak aloud, are happy and are free,
155   And glad they seem, and gaily they agree.
       What, though fastidious ears may shun the speech,
     Where all are talkers, and where none can teach;
     Where still the welcome and the words are old,
     And the same stories are for ever told;
160   Yet theirs is joy that, bursting from the heart,
     Prompts the glad tongue these nothings to impart;
     That forms these tones of gladness we despise,
     That lifts their steps, that sparkles in their eyes;
     That talks or laughs or runs or shouts or plays,
165   And speaks in all their looks and all their ways.
       Fair scenes of peace! ye might detain us long,
     But vice and misery now demand the song;
     And turn our view from dwellings simply neat,
     To this infected row, we term our Street.
170   Here, in cabal,° a disputatious crew   *illegal assembly*
     Each evening meet; the sot, the cheat, the shrew:
     Riots are nightly heard:—the curse, the cries
     Of beaten wife, perverse in her replies;
     While shrieking children hold each threatening hand,
175   And sometimes life, and sometimes food demand:
     Boys, in their first-stolen rags, to swear begin,
     And girls, who heed not dress, are skilled in gin:
     Snarers° and smugglers here their gains divide;   *poachers*
     Ensnaring females here their victims hide;
180   And here is one, the Sibyl[3] of the Row,
     Who knows all secrets, or affects to know.
     Seeking their fate, to her the simple run,
     To her the guilty, theirs awhile to shun;

3. Name given by the Greeks and Romans to certain women who prophesied and claimed divine inspiration.

Mistress of worthless arts, depraved in will,
185 Her care unblest and unrepaid her skill,
Slave to the tribe, to whose command she stoops,
And poorer than the poorest maid she dupes.
    Between the road-way and the walls, offence
Invades all eyes and strikes on every sense:
190 There lie, obscene, at every open door,
Heaps from the hearth and sweepings from the floor,
And day by day the mingled masses grow,
As sinks are disembogued° and kennels flow.   *drained*
    There hungry dogs from hungry children steal;
195 There pigs and chickens quarrel for a meal;
There dropsied infants wail without redress,
And all is want and wo and wretchedness:
Yet should these boys, with bodies bronzed and bare,
High-swollen and hard, outlive that lack of care—
200 Forced on some farm, the unexerted strength,
Though loth to action, is compelled at length,
When warmed by health, as serpents in the spring,
Aside their slough of indolence they fling.
    Yet, ere they go, a greater evil comes—
205 See! crowded beds in those contiguous rooms;
Beds but ill parted, by a paltry screen
Of papered lath or curtain dropt between;
Daughters and sons to yon compartments creep,
And parents here beside their children sleep:
210 Ye who have power, these thoughtless people part,
Nor let the ear be first to taint the heart.
    Come! search within, nor sight nor smell regard;
The true physician walks the foulest ward.
See! on the floor, what frousy° patches rest!   *dirty, messy*
215 What nauseous fragments on yon fractured chest!
What downy dust beneath yon window-seat!
And round these posts that serve this bed for feet;
This bed where all those tattered garments lie,
Worn by each sex, and now perforce thrown by!
220 See! as we gaze, an infant lifts its head,
Left by neglect and burrowed in that bed;
The Mother-gossip has the love suppressed
An infant's cry once wakened in her breast;
And daily prattles, as her round she takes,
225 (With strong resentment) of the want she makes.
    Whence all these woes?—From want of virtuous will,
Of honest shame, of time-improving skill;
From want of care t' employ the vacant hour,
And want of ev'ry kind but want of power.
230 Here are no wheels for either wool or flax,
But packs of cards—made up of sundry packs;
Here is no clock, nor will they turn the glass,
And see how swift th' important moments pass;
Here are no books, but ballads on the wall,

235   Are some abusive, and indecent all;
       Pistols are here, unpaired; with nets and hooks,
       Of every kind, for rivers, ponds, and brooks;
       An ample flask, that nightly rovers fill
       With recent poison from the Dutchman's still;[4]
240   A box of tools, with wires of various size,
       Frocks, wigs, and hats, for night or day disguise,
       And bludgeons stout to gain or guard a prize.
         To every house belongs a space of ground,
       Of equal size, once fenced with paling° round;   *pointed stakes*
245   That paling now by slothful waste destroyed,
       Dead gorse and stumps of elder[5] fill the void;
       Save in the center-spot, whose walls of clay
       Hide sots and striplings at their drink or play:
       Within, a board,[6] beneath a tiled retreat,
250   Allures the bubble° and maintains the cheat;   *dupe*
       Where heavy ale in spots like varnish shows,
       Where chalky tallies yet remain in rows;
       Black pipes and broken jugs the seats defile,
       The walls and windows, rhymes and reck'nings vile;
255   Prints of the meanest kind disgrace the door,
       And cards, in curses torn, lie fragments on the floor.
         Here his poor bird th' inhuman Cocker[7] brings,
       Arms his hard heel and clips his golden wings;
       With spicy food th' impatient spirit feeds,
260   And shouts and curses as the battle bleeds.
       Struck through the brain, deprived of both his eyes,
       The vanquished bird must combat till he dies;
       Must faintly peck at his victorious foe,
       And reel and stagger at each feeble blow:
265   When fallen, the savage grasps his dabbled plumes,
       His blood-stained arms, for other deaths assumes;
       And damns the craven-fowl, that lost his stake,
       And only bled and perished for his sake.
         Such are our Peasants, those to whom we yield
270   Praise with relief,° the fathers of the field;   *welfare*
       And these who take from our reluctant hands,
       What Burn[8] advises or the Bench° commands.   *judiciary*
         Our Farmers round, well pleased with constant gain,
       Like other farmers, flourish and complain.—
275   These are our groups; our Portraits next appear,
       And close our Exhibition for the year.

                                     1807

---

4. I.e., with illegally imported alcohol.
5. Elderberry; like gorse, a shrub.
6. Probably a gambling table.
7. The owner of fighting cocks.

8. Richard Burn (1709–1795), English legal scholar who wrote *Justice of the Peace* and *Ecclesiastical Law.*

From The Borough

From *Letter XXII, The Poor of The Borough: Peter Grimes*

* * *

165   Alas! for Peter, not a helping hand,
So was he hated, could he now command.[9]
Alone he rowed his boat, alone he cast
His nets beside, or made his anchor fast;
To hold a rope or hear a curse was none—
170   He toiled and railed, he groaned and swore alone.
    Thus by himself compelled to live each day,
To wait for certain hours the tide's delay;
At the same times the same dull views to see,
The bounding marsh-bank and the blighted tree;
175   The water only, when the tides were high,
When low, the mud half-covered and half-dry;
The sun-burnt tar that blisters on the planks,
And bank-side stakes in their uneven ranks;
Heaps of entangled weeds that slowly float,
180   As the tide rolls by the impeded boat.
    When tides were neap° and, in the sultry day,   *low*
Through the tall bounding mud-banks made their way,
Which on each side rose swelling, and below
The dark warm flood ran silently and slow;
185   There anchoring, Peter chose from man to hide,
There hang his head, and view the lazy tide
In its hot slimy channel slowly glide;
Where the small eels that left the deeper way
For the warm shore within the shallows play;
190   Where gaping mussels, left upon the mud,
Slope their slow passage to the fallen flood.
Here dull and hopeless he'd lie down and trace
How sidelong crabs had scrawled their crooked race,
Or sadly listen to the tuneless cry
195   Of fishing gull or clanging golden-eye;°   *species of wild duck*
What time the sea-birds to the marsh would come,
And the loud bittern,[1] from the bulrush° home,   *cattail*
Gave from the salt-ditch side the bellowing boom.
He nursed the feelings these dull scenes produce,
200   And loved to stop beside the opening sluice;
Where the small stream, confined in narrow bound,
Ran with a dull, unvaried, saddening sound;
Where all, presented to the eye or ear,
Oppressed the soul with misery, grief, and fear.
205   Besides these objects, there were places three,
Which Peter seemed with certain dread to see;
When he drew near them he would turn from each,

---

9. Grimes has fatally exploited three boys provided by the workhouses as child laborers and has been forbidden to employ any more.
1. Marsh bird with a booming call.

And loudly whistle till he passed the reach.[2]
    A change of scene to him brought no relief;
210 In town, 'twas plain, men took him for a thief.
The sailors' wives would stop him in the street,
And say, "Now, Peter, thou'st no boy to beat!"
Infants at play, when they perceived him, ran,
Warning each other—"That's the wicked man!"
215 He growled an oath, and in an angry tone
Cursed the whole place and wished to be alone.
    Alone he was, the same dull scenes in view,
And still more gloomy in his sight they grew;
Though man he hated, yet employed alone
220 At bootless labor, he would swear and groan,
Cursing the shoals° that glided by the spot,   *schools of fish*
And gulls that caught them when his arts could not.
    Cold nervous tremblings shook his sturdy frame,
And strange disease—he couldn't say the name;
225 Wild were his dreams, and oft he rose in fright,
Waked by his view of horrors in the night—
Horrors that would the sternest minds amaze,
Horrors that demons might be proud to raise;
And though he felt forsaken, grieved at heart
230 To think he lived from all mankind apart,
Yet, if a man approached, in terrors he would start.
    A winter passed since Peter saw the town,
And summer lodgers were again come down.
These, idly curious, with their glasses° spied   *telescopes*
235 The ships in bay as anchored for the tide—
The river's craft—the bustle of the quay—
And sea-port views, which landmen love to see.
    One, up the river, had a man and boat
Seen day by day, now anchored, now afloat;
240 Fisher he seemed, yet used no net nor hook,
Of sea-fowl swimming by no heed he took,
But on the gliding waves still fixed his lazy look.
At certain stations he would view the stream,
As if he stood bewildered in a dream,
245 Or that° some power had chained him for a time,   *as if*
To feel a curse or meditate on crime.
    This known, some curious, some in pity went,
And others questioned—"Wretch, dost thou repent?"
He heard, he trembled, and in fear resigned
250 His boat; new terror filled his restless mind;
Furious he grew, and up on the country ran,
And there they seized him—a distempered man.
Him we received, and to a parish-bed,[3]
Followed and cursed, the groaning man was led.

             *   *   *

1810

2. A "reach" is the distance between two points on a river or along its banks. The places correspond to the three dead boys.
3. A bed in the charity hospital.

WILLIAM BLAKE
1757–1827

From POETICAL SKETCHES

To the Muses[1]

Whether on Ida's[2] shady brow,
    Or in the chambers of the East,
The chambers of the sun, that now
    From ancient melody have ceas'd;

5 Whether in Heav'n ye wander fair,
    Or the green corners of the earth,
Or the blue regions of the air,
    Where the melodious winds have birth;

Whether on chrystal rocks ye rove,
10   Beneath the bosom of the sea
Wand'ring in many a coral grove,
    Fair Nine, forsaking Poetry!

How have you left the ancient love
    That bards of old enjoy'd in you!
15 The languid strings do scarcely move!
    The sound is forc'd, the notes are few!

                         1783

Song

How sweet I roam'd from field to field,
    And tasted all the summer's pride,
'Till I the prince of love beheld,
    Who in the sunny beams did glide!

5 He shew'd me lilies for my hair,
    And blushing roses for my brow;
He led me through his gardens fair,
    Where all his golden pleasures grow.

With sweet May dews my wings were wet,
10   And Phoebus fir'd my vocal rage;[3]
He caught me in his silken net,
    And shut me in his golden cage.

1. In Greek mythology, nine sister goddesses who presided over the arts and sciences, especially poetry.
2. Mountain in Asia Minor, distant from Helicon and Parnassus, mountains in Greece sacred to the Muses.
3. Impassioned song. Phoebus is Apollo, Greek and Roman god of poetic inspiration.

He loves to sit and hear me sing,
   Then, laughing, sports and plays with me;
15 Then stretches out my golden wing,
   And mocks my loss of liberty.

1783

To the Evening Star[4]

Thou fair-hair'd angel of the evening,
Now, while the sun rests on the mountains, light
Thy bright torch of love; thy radiant crown
Put on, and smile upon our evening bed!
5 Smile on our loves; and, while thou drawest the
Blue curtains of the sky, scatter thy silver dew
On every flower that shuts its sweet eyes
In timely sleep. Let thy west wind sleep on
The lake; speak silence with thy glimmering eyes,
10 And wash the dusk with silver. Soon, full soon,
Dost thou withdraw; then the wolf rages wide,
And the lion glares thro' the dun forest:
The fleeces of our flocks are cover'd with
Thy sacred dew: protect them with thine influence.[5]

1783

FROM SONGS OF INNOCENCE

Introduction

Piping down the valleys wild
Piping songs of pleasant glee
On a cloud I saw a child,
And he laughing said to me,

5 "Pipe a song about a Lamb";
So I piped with merry cheer.
"Piper pipe that song again"—
So I piped, he wept to hear.

"Drop thy pipe thy happy pipe
10 Sing thy songs of happy cheer";
So I sung the same again
While he wept with joy to hear.

---

4. Venus, Roman goddess of love and beauty.
5. In astrology, the effect that heavenly bodies exert on earthly things and creatures.

"Piper sit thee down and write
In a book that all may read"—
15 So he vanish'd from my sight.
And I pluck'd a hollow reed,

And I made a rural pen,
And I stain'd the water clear,
And I wrote my happy songs
20 Every child may joy to hear.

1789

The Lamb

Little Lamb, who made thee?
Dost thou know who made thee?
Gave thee life & bid thee feed,
By the stream & o'er the mead;
5 Gave thee clothing of delight,
Softest clothing wooly bright;
Gave thee such a tender voice,
Making all the vales rejoice!
Little Lamb who made thee?
10 Dost thou know who made thee?

Little Lamb I'll tell thee,
Little Lamb I'll tell thee!
He° is calléd by thy name,   *Christ*
For he calls himself a Lamb:
15 He is meek & he is mild,
He became a little child:
I a child & thou a lamb,
We are calléd by his name.
Little Lamb God bless thee.
20 Little Lamb God bless thee.

1789

Holy Thursday [I.]

'Twas on a Holy Thursday,[6] their innocent faces clean,
The children[7] walking two & two, in red & blue & green,
Gray headed beadles[8] walkd before with wands as white as snow,
Till into the high dome of Paul's they like Thames'[9] waters flow.

---

6. Probably Ascension Day (the Thursday forty days after Easter).
7. The children of charity schools, here depicted in St. Paul's Cathedral, London.
8. Ushers charged with keeping order.
9. The river Thames.

5 O what a multitude they seemd, these flowers of London town!
Seated in companies they sit with radiance all their own.
The hum of multitudes was there, but multitudes of lambs,
Thousands of little boys & girls raising their innocent hands.

Now like a mighty wind they raise to heaven the voice of song,
10 Or like harmonious thunderings the seats of heaven among.
Beneath them sit the aged men, wise guardians of the poor;
Then cherish pity, lest you drive an angel from your door.

1789

The Divine Image

To Mercy, Pity, Peace, and Love,
All pray in their distress:
And to these virtues of delight
Return their thankfulness.

5 For Mercy, Pity, Peace, and Love,
Is God, our father dear:
And Mercy, Pity, Peace, and Love,
Is Man, his child and care.

For Mercy has a human heart,
10 Pity, a human face:
And Love, the human form divine,
And Peace, the human dress.

Then every man of every clime,
That prays in his distress,
15 Prays to the human form divine,
Love, Mercy, Pity, Peace.

And all must love the human form,
In heathen, Turk, or Jew.
Where Mercy, Love, & Pity dwell,
20 There God is dwelling too.

1789

The Little Black Boy

My mother bore me in the southern wild,
And I am black, but O! my soul is white;
White as an angel is the English child:
But I am black as if bereav'd of light.

5 My mother taught me underneath a tree,
And sitting down before the heat of day,
She took me on her lap and kissèd me,
And pointing to the east, began to say:

"Look on the rising sun: there God does live,
10 And gives his light, and gives his heat away;
And flowers and trees and beasts and men receive
Comfort in morning, joy in the noon day.

"And we are put on earth a little space,
That we may learn to bear the beams of love,
15 And these black bodies and this sun-burnt face
Is but a cloud, and like a shady grove.

"For when our souls have learn'd the heat to bear,
The cloud will vanish; we shall hear his voice,
Saying: 'Come out from the grove, my love & care,
20 And round my golden tent like lambs rejoice.' "

Thus did my mother say, and kissèd me;
And thus I say to little English boy:
When I from black and he from white cloud free,
And round the tent of God like lambs we joy,

25 I'll shade him from the heat till he can bear
To lean in joy upon our father's knee;
And then I'll stand and stroke his silver hair,
And be like him, and he will then love me.

1789

The Little Boy Lost

"Father, father, where are you going?
O do not walk so fast.
Speak, father, speak to your little boy
Or else I shall be lost."

5 The night was dark, no father was there,
The child was wet with dew.
The mire was deep, & the child did weep,
And away the vapor flew.

1789

The Little Boy Found

The little boy lost in the lonely fen,
Led by the wand'ring light,[1]
Began to cry, but God ever nigh
Appeard like his father in white.

5   He kissed the child & by the hand led
And to his mother brought,
Who in sorrow pale, thro' the lonely dale,
Her little boy weeping sought.

1789

THE BOOK OF THEL[2]

Thel's Motto

Does the Eagle know what is in the pit?
Or wilt thou go ask the Mole?
Can Wisdom be put in a silver rod?
Or Love in a golden bowl?

1

5   The daughters of Mne Seraphim[3] led round their sunny flocks,
All but the youngest; she in paleness sought the secret air,
To fade away like morning beauty from her mortal day;
Down by the river of Adona[4] her soft voice is heard,
And thus her gentle lamentation falls like morning dew:

10   "O life of this our spring! why fades the lotus of the water?
Why fade these children of the spring? born but to smile & fall.
Ah! Thel is like a watry bow, and like a parting cloud,
Like a reflection in a glass, like shadows in the water,
Like dreams of infants, like a smile upon an infant's face,
15   Like the dove's voice, like transient day, like music in the air.
Ah! gentle may I lay me down, and gentle rest my head,
And gentle sleep the sleep of death and gentle hear the voice
Of him that walketh in the garden in the evening time."

The Lilly of the valley, breathing in the humble grass,
20   Answer'd the lovely maid and said: "I am a watry weed,
And I am very small, and love to dwell in lowly vales;[5]
So weak, the gilded butterfly scarce perches on my head;

---

1. A will-o'-the-wisp, said to draw travelers astray by holding a false light before them; the phenomenon of nocturnal light is caused by the combustion of marsh gas.
2. "Thel," like the other proper names in the poem, is Blake's invention, and its meaning can only be inferred.

3. Angels who guard Jehovah's throne. *Mne*: possibly a misprint for "the."
4. Probably the river Adonis in Milton's *Paradise Lost* 1.540–42, associated with rituals of fertility and of death and rebirth.
5. Valleys.

Yet I am visited from heaven, and he that smiles on all
Walks in the valley and each morn over me spreads his hand,
25   Saying: 'Rejoice, thou humble grass, thou new-born lilly flower,
Thou gentle maid of silent valleys and of modest brooks;
For thou shalt be clothed in light, and fed with morning manna,[6]
Till summer's heat melts thee beside the fountains and the springs
To flourish in eternal vales.' Then why should Thel complain?

30   Why should the mistress of the vales of Har utter a sigh?"

She ceasd & smild in tears, then sat down in her silver shrine.

Thel answerd: "O thou little virgin of the peaceful valley,
Giving to those that cannot crave, the voiceless, the o'ertired;
Thy breath doth nourish the innocent lamb, he smells thy milky
        garments,
35   He crops thy flowers, while thou sittest smiling in his face,
Wiping his mild and meekin mouth[7] from all contagious taints.
Thy wine doth purify the golden honey; thy perfume,
Which thou dost scatter on every little blade of grass that springs,
Revives the milkèd w, & tames the fire-breathing steed.
40   But Thel is like a faint cloud kindled at the rising sun:
I vanish from my pearly throne, and who shall find my place?"
"Queen of the vales," the Lilly answered, "ask the tender cloud,
And it shall tell thee why it glitters in the morning sky,
And why it scatters its bright beauty thro' the humid air.
45   Descend, O little cloud, & hover before the eyes of Thel."

The Cloud descended, and the Lilly bowd her modest head,
And went to mind her numerous charge among the verdant grass.

2

"Oh little Cloud," the virgin said, "I charge thee tell to me,
Why thou complainest not when in one hour thou fade away:
50   Then we shall seek thee but not find; ah, Thel is like to Thee.
I pass away, yet I complain, and no one hears my voice."

The Cloud then shew'd his golden head & his bright form emerg'd,
Hovering and glittering on the air before the face of Thel.

"O virgin, know'st thou not our steeds drink of the golden springs
55   Where Luvah[8] doth renew his horses? Look'st thou on my youth,
And fearest thou, because I vanish and am seen no more,
Nothing remains? O maid, I tell thee, when I pass away,
It is to tenfold life, to love, to peace, and raptures holy:
Unseen descending, weigh my light wings upon balmy flowers,
60   And court the fair eyed dew, to take me to her shining tent;
The weeping virgin trembling kneels before the risen sun,

---

6. Food (from heaven).
7. Perhaps describing a lamb's delicately wrin-
kling mouth.

8. In Blake's mythology, a sun god of Love (Love,
Lover, Luvah).

Till we arise link'd in a golden band, and never part,
But walk united, bearing food to all our tender flowers."

"Dost thou, O little Cloud? I fear that I am not like thee;
65 For I walk through the vales of Har and smell the sweetest flowers,
But I feed not the little flowers; I hear the warbling birds,
But I feed not the warbling birds; they fly and seek their food;
But Thel delights in these no more, because I fade away,
And all shall say, 'Without a use this shining woman liv'd,
70 Or did she only live to be at death the food of worms?' "

The Cloud reclind upon his airy throne and answer'd thus:

"Then if thou are the food of worms, O virgin of the skies,
How great thy use, how great thy blessing! Every thing that lives
Lives not alone, nor for self; fear not, and I will call
75 The weak worm from its lowly bed, and thou shalt hear its voice.
Come forth, worm of the silent valley, to thy pensive queen."
The helpless worm arose, and sat upon the Lilly's leaf,
And the bright Cloud saild on, to find his partner in the vale.

3

Then Thel astonish'd view'd the Worm upon its dewy bed.

80 "Art thou a Worm? Image of weakness, art thou but a Worm?
I see thee like an infant wrapped in the Lilly's leaf;
Ah, weep not, little voice, thou can'st not speak, but thou can'st
    weep.
Is this a Worm? I see thee lay helpless & naked, weeping,
And none to answer, none to cherish thee with mother's smiles."

85 The Clod of Clay heard the Worm's voice, & raisd her pitying head;
She bow'd over the weeping infant, and her life exhal'd
In milky fondness; then on Thel she fix'd her humble eyes.

"O beauty of the vales of Har! we live not for ourselves;
Thou seest me the meanest thing, and so I am indeed.
90 My bosom of itself is cold, and of itself is dark;

But he that loves the lowly, pours his oil upon my head,
And kisses me, and binds his nuptial bands around my breast,
And says: 'Thou mother of my children, I have lovèd thee,
And I have given thee a crown that none can take away.'
95 But how this is, sweet maid, I know not, and I cannot know;
I ponder, and I cannot ponder; yet I live and love."

The daughter of beauty wip'd her pitying tears with her white veil,
And said: "Alas! I knew not this, and therefore did I weep.
That God would love a Worm, I knew, and punish the evil foot
100 That, wilful, bruis'd its helpless form; but that he cherish'd it
With milk and oil I never knew; and therefore did I weep,

And I complaind in the mild air, because I fade away,
And lay me down in thy cold bed, and leave my shining lot."

"Queen of the vales," the matron Clay answerd, "I heard thy sighs,
105 And all thy moans flew o'er my roof, but I have call'd them down.
Wilt thou, O Queen, enter my house? 'Tis given thee to enter
And to return; fear nothing, enter thy virgin feet."

4

The eternal gates' terrific porter lifted the northern bar:[9]
Thel enter'd in & saw the secrets of the land unknown.
110 She saw the couches of the dead, & where the fibrous roots
Of every heart on earth infixes deep its restless twists:
A land of sorrows & of tears where never smile was seen.

She wanderd in the land of clouds thro' valleys dark, listning
Dolors & lamentations; waiting oft beside a dewy grave,
115 She stood in silence, listning to the voices of the ground,
Till to her own grave plot she came, & there she sat down,
And heard this voice of sorrow breathèd from the hollow pit:

"Why cannot the Ear be closed to its own destruction?
Or the glistning Eye to the poison of a smile?
120 Why are Eyelids stord with arrows ready drawn,
Where a thousand fighting men in ambush lie?
Or an Eye of gifts & graces, show'ring fruits & coinèd gold?
Why a Tongue impress'd with honey from every wind?
Why an Ear, a whirlpool fierce to draw creations in?
125 Why a Nostril wide inhaling terror, trembling, & affright?
Why a tender curb upon the youthful burning boy?
Why a little curtain of flesh on the bed of our desire?"

The Virgin started from her seat, & with a shriek
Fled back unhinderd till she came into the vales of Har.

THE END

1789–91

From SONGS OF EXPERIENCE

Introduction

Hear the voice of the Bard!
Who Present, Past, & Future sees,
Whose ears have heard

---

9. Possibly the gate through which a soul or spirit enters the world of earthly life and death.

The Holy Word
5 That walk'd among the ancient trees;[1]

Calling the lapsèd Soul
And weeping in the evening dew;
That might controll
The starry pole,
10 And fallen fallen light renew!

"O Earth O Earth return!
Arise from out the dewy grass;
Night is worn,
And the morn
15 Rises from the slumberous mass.

"Turn away no more:
Why wilt thou turn away?
The starry floor
The watry shore
20 Is giv'n thee till the break of day."

1794

A Divine Image

Cruelty has a Human heart
And Jealousy a Human Face,
Terror, the Human Form Divine,
And Secrecy, the Human Dress.

5 The Human Dress is forgèd Iron,
The Human Form, a fiery Forge,
The Human Face, a Furnace seal'd,
The Human Heart, its hungry Gorge.°   *throat*

1790–91   1921

Holy Thursday [II.]

Is this a holy thing to see,
In a rich and fruitful land,
Babes reducd to misery,
Fed with cold and usurous hand?

5 Is that trembling cry a song?
Can it be a song of joy?

1. "And Adam and Eve heard the voice of the Lord God walking in the garden in the cool of the day" (Genesis 3.8).

And so many children poor?
It is a land of poverty!

And their sun does never shine,
10   And their fields are bleak & bare,
And their ways are fill'd with thorns;
It is eternal winter there.

For where-e'er the sun does shine,
And where-e'er the rain does fall,
15   Babe can never hunger there,
Nor poverty the mind appall.

1794

The Clod & the Pebble

"Love seeketh not Itself to please,
Nor for itself hath any care;
But for another gives its ease,
And builds a Heaven in Hell's despair."

5   So sang a little Clod of Clay,
Trodden with the cattle's feet;
But a Pebble of the brook,
Warbled out these meters meet:°   *appropriate*

"Love seeketh only Self to please,
10   To bind another to its delight,
Joys in another's loss of ease,
And builds a Hell in Heaven's despite."

1794

The Sick Rose

O Rose, thou art sick.
The invisible worm
That flies in the night
In the howling storm

5   Has found out thy bed
Of crimson joy,
And his dark secret love
Does thy life destroy.

1794

A Poison Tree

I was angry with my friend:
I told my wrath, my wrath did end.
I was angry with my foe:
I told it not, my wrath did grow.

5 And I waterd it in fears,
Night & morning with my tears;
And I sunnèd it with smiles,
And with soft deceitful wiles.

And it grew both day and night,
10 Till it bore an apple bright.
And my foe beheld it shine,
And he knew that it was mine,

And into my garden stole,
When the night had veild the pole;
15 In the morning glad I see
My foe outstretchd beneath the tree.

1794

The Tyger

Tyger! Tyger! burning bright
In the forests of the night,
What immortal hand or eye
Could frame thy fearful symmetry?

5 In what distant deeps or skies
Burnt the fire of thine eyes?
On what wings dare he aspire?
What the hand dare seize the fire?

And what shoulder, & what art,
10 Could twist the sinews of thy heart?
And when thy heart began to beat,
What dread hand? & what dread feet?

What the hammer? what the chain?
In what furnace was thy brain?
15 What the anvil? what dread grasp
Dare its deadly terrors clasp?

When the stars threw down their spears,
And water'd heaven with their tears,
Did he smile his work to see?
20 Did he who made the Lamb make thee?

Tyger! Tyger! burning bright
In the forests of the night,
What immortal hand or eye
Dare frame thy fearful symmetry?

1794

Ah Sun-flower

Ah Sun-flower! weary of time,
Who countest the steps of the Sun,
Seeking after that sweet golden clime
Where the traveller's journey is done;

5   Where the Youth pined away with desire,
And the pale Virgin shrouded in snow,
Arise from their graves and aspire,
Where my Sun-flower wishes to go.

1794

The Garden of Love

I went to the Garden of Love,
And saw what I never had seen:
A Chapel was built in the midst,
Where I used to play on the green.

5   And the gates of this Chapel were shut,
And "Thou shalt not" writ over the door;
So I turn'd to the Garden of Love,
That so many sweet flowers bore,

And I saw it was filled with graves,
10   And tomb-stones where flowers should be:
And Priests in black gowns were walking their rounds,
And binding with briars my joys & desires.

1794

London

I wander thro' each charter'd² street,
Near where the charter'd Thames does flow,
And mark in every face I meet
Marks of weakness, marks of woe.

2. Mapped out, legally defined, constricted.

5 In every cry of every man,
   In every Infant's cry of fear,
   In every voice, in every ban,[3]
   The mind-forg'd manacles I hear.

   How the Chimney-sweeper's cry
10 Every blackning Church appalls;°   horrifies; casts a pall over
   And the hapless Soldier's sigh
   Runs in blood down Palace walls.

   But most thro' midnight streets I hear
   How the youthful Harlot's curse
15 Blasts the new-born Infant's tear,
   And blights with plagues the Marriage hearse.

                                                    1794

FROM SONGS AND BALLADS

I Askèd a Thief

   I askèd a thief to steal me a peach,
   He turned up his eyes;
   I ask'd a lithe lady to lie her down,
   Holy & meek she cries.

5 As soon as I went
   An angel came.
   He wink'd at the thief
   And smild at the dame—

   And without one word said
10 Had a peach from the tree
   And still as a maid
   Enjoy'd the lady.

1796   1863

Mock on, Mock on, Voltaire, Rousseau

   Mock on, Mock on, Voltaire, Rousseau;[4]
   Mock on, Mock on, 'tis all in vain.
   You throw the sand against the wind,
   And the wind blows it back again.

---

3. A law or notice commanding or forbidding; a published penalty.
4. Leaders of the pre-Revolutionary French

"Enlightenment"; critics of the established order, here representing thinkers who destroy without creating.

5 And every sand becomes a Gem
Reflected in the beams divine;
Blown back, they blind the mocking Eye,
But still in Israel's paths they shine.

The Atoms of Democritus
10 And Newton's Particles of light[5]
Are sands upon the Red sea shore,[6]
Where Israel's tents do shine so bright.

1800–08   1863

Eternity

He who binds to himself a joy
Does the wingèd life destroy
But he who kisses the joy as it flies
Lives in eternity's sun rise.

1800–08   1863

A Question Answered

What is it men in women do require?
The lineaments of Gratified Desire.
What is it women do in men require?
The lineaments of Gratified Desire.

1800–08   1863

FROM MILTON

And Did Those Feet

And did those feet in ancient time
Walk upon England's mountains green?
And was the holy Lamb of God
On England's pleasant pastures seen?

5 And did the Countenance Divine
Shine forth upon our clouded hills?
And was Jerusalem builded here,
Among these dark Satanic Mills?[7]

5. The Greek philosopher Democritus (fifth century B.C.E) and the English physicist Sir Isaac Newton (1642–1727) are represented as nonsensically reducing nature to inanimate matter.
6. Where God delivered the Israelites from the Egyptians (Exodus 14).
7. The primary meaning is "millstone"—two heavy cylindrical stones that grind grain into meal between them; "factory" is an extended meaning.

Bring me my Bow of burning gold:
10   Bring me my Arrows of desire:
Bring me my Spear: O clouds unfold!
Bring me my Chariot of fire!

I will not cease from Mental Fight,
Nor shall my Sword sleep in my hand,
15   Till we have built Jerusalem
In England's green & pleasant Land.

1804–10   1804–10

FROM JERUSALEM

England! Awake! Awake! Awake!

England! awake! awake! awake!
    Jerusalem thy Sister calls!
Why wilt thou sleep the sleep of death?
    And close her from thy ancient walls.

5   Thy hills & valleys felt her feet
                     Gently upon their bosoms move:
                     Thy gates beheld sweet Zion's ways;
                     Then was a time of joy and love.

And now the time returns again:
10   Our souls exult & London's towers,
Receive the Lamb of God to dwell
    In England's green & pleasant bowers.

1804–09   1818

ROBERT BURNS
1759–1796

Green Grow the Rashes

Green grow the rashes,° O;   tall grasses or rushes
    Green grow the rashes, O;
The sweetest hours that e'er I spend,
    Are spent amang the lasses, O!

5   There's nought but care on ev'ry han',
    In ev'ry hour that passes, O:
What signifies the life o' man,
    An'° 'twere na for the lasses, O.   if

Green grow the rashes, O; . . .

10   The warly° race may riches chase,   *worldly*
        An' riches still may fly them, O;
    An' though at last they catch them fast,
        Their hearts can ne'er enjoy them, O.

Green grow the rashes, O; . . .

15   But gie me a canny° hour at e'en,   *pleasant*
        My arms about my Dearie, O;
    An' warly cares, an' warly men,
        May a' gae tapsalteerie,° O!   *topsy-turvy*

Green grow the rashes, O; . . .

20   For you sae douce,° ye sneer at this,   *prudent*
        Ye're nought but senseless asses, O:
    The wisest man[1] the warl' saw,
        He dearly loved the lasses, O.

Green grow the rashes, O; . . .

25   Auld Nature swears, the lovely Dears
        Her noblest work she classes, O:
    Her prentice han' she tried on man,
        An' then she made the lasses, O.

Green grow the rashes, O; . . .

1784   1787

To a Mouse

On Turning Her up in Her Nest with the Plough, November, 1785

    Wee, sleeket,° cow'rin, tim'rous beastie,   *sleek*
    O, what a panic's in thy breastie!
    Thou need na start awa sae hasty,
            Wi' bickering° brattle!°   *hurried / scamper*
5   I wad be laith° to rin an' chase thee,   *loath*
            Wi' murd'ring pattle!°   *plowstaff ("paddle")*

    I'm truly sorry Man's dominion
    Has broken Nature's social union,
    An' justifies that ill opinion,
10   Which makes thee startle,

---

1. Solomon, king of Israel (tenth century B.C.E.), who had many wives and was proverbial for his wisdom.

At me, thy poor, earth-born companion,
　　　　An' fellow-mortal!

I doubt na, whiles,° but thou may thieve;   *sometimes*
What then? poor beastie, thou maun° live!   *must*
15　A daimen-icker in a thrave[2]
　　　　'S a sma' request:
I'll get a blessin wi' the lave,°   *rest*
　　　　An' never miss't!

Thy wee bit housie, too, in ruin!
20　Its silly° wa's the win's are strewin!   *frail*
An' naething, now, to big° a new ane,   *build*
　　　　O' foggage° green!   *mosses*
An' bleak December's winds ensuin,
　　　　Baith snell° an' keen!   *bitter*

25　Thou saw the fields laid bare and wast,°   *waste*
An' weary winter comin fast,
An' cozie here, beneath the blast,
　　　　Thou thought to dwell,
Till crash! the cruel coulter° past   *plowshare*
30　　　　Out thro' thy cell.

That wee bit heap o' leaves an' stibble°   *stubble*
Has cost thee mony a weary nibble!
Now thou's turned out, for a' thy trouble,
　　　　But° house or hald,°   *without / home ("hold")*
35　To thole° the winter's sleety dribble,   *endure*
　　　　An' cranreuch° cauld!   *hoarfrost*

But, Mousie, thou art no thy-lane,[3]
In proving foresight may be vain:
The best laid schemes o' mice an' men
40　　　　Gang° aft a-gley.°   *go / astray*
An' lea'e us nought but grief an' pain,
　　　　For promised joy!

Still, thou art blest, compared wi' me!
The present only toucheth thee:
45　But och! I backward cast my e'e,
　　　　On prospects drear!
An' forward, tho' I canna see,
　　　　I guess an' fear!

1785   1786

---

2. A rare ear of corn in a stook/stack of (generally twelve) sheaves.

3. *No thy-lane:* not alone.

Holy Willie's[4] Prayer

O Thou that in the heavens does dwell!
Wha, as it pleases best thysel,
Sends ane to heaven and ten to hell,
    A' for thy glory!
5 And no for ony guid or ill
      They've done before thee.

I bless and praise thy matchless might,
Whan thousands thou has left in night,
That I am here before thy sight,
10   For gifts and grace
A burning an' a shining light
      To a' this place.

What was I, or my generation,
That I should get such exaltation?
15 I, wha deserv'd most just damnation,
      For broken laws
Sax thousand years ere my creation,
      Thro' Adam's cause!

When from my mother's womb I fell,
20 Thou might hae plunged me deep in hell,
To gnash my gooms, and weep and wail,
      In burning lakes,
Where damnèd devils roar and yell
      Chained to their stakes.

25 Yet I am here, a chosen sample,
To show thy grace is great and ample:
I'm here, a pillar o' thy temple,
      Strong as a rock,
A guide, a ruler, and example
30   To a' thy flock.

O Lord thou kens what zeal I bear,
When drinkers drink, and swearers swear,
And singin' there, and dancin' here,
      Wi' great an' sma';
35 For I am keepet by thy fear,
      Free frae them a'.

But yet—O Lord—confess I must—
At times I'm fashed° wi' fleshy lust;   *troubled*

4. William Fisher, an elder in the church at Mauchline, the seat of Burns's farm. He habitually censured other men's behavior and doctrine, but was himself rebuked for drunkenness and was suspected of stealing church funds.

And sometimes too, in warldly trust
40   Vile Self gets in;
But thou remembers we are dust,
          Defiled wi' sin.

O Lord—yestreen—° thou kens—wi' Meg—   *last night*
Thy pardon I sincerely beg!
45 O may't ne'er be a living plague,
          To my dishonor!
And I'll ne'er lift a lawless leg
          Again upon her.

Besides, I farther maun° allow,   *must*
50 Wi' Lizzie's lass, three times—I trow°—   *believe*
But Lord, that Friday I was fou°   *full (of liquor)*
          When I cam near her;
Or else, thou kens, thy servant true
          Wad never steer° her.   *touch ("stir")*

55 Maybe thou lets this fleshly thorn
Buffet thy servant e'en and morn,
Lest he o'er high and proud should turn,
          That he's sae gifted;
If sae, thy hand maun e'en be borne
60   Until thou lift it.

Lord bless thy Chosen in this place,
For here thou hast a chosen race;
But God, confound their stubborn face,
          And blast their name,
65 Wha bring thy elders to disgrace
          And open shame.

Lord mind Gaun Hamilton's⁵ deserts!
He drinks, and swears, and plays at cartes,
Yet has sae mony taking arts
70   Wi' Great an' Sma',
Frae God's ain priest the people's hearts
          He steals awa'.

An when we chastened him therefore,
Thou kens how he bred sic a splore°   *row*
75 As set the warld in a roar
          O' laughin at us;
Curse thou his basket and his store,
          Kail° and potatoes.   *cabbage*

---

5. Gavin Hamilton, a convivial lawyer friend of Burns. Accused of Sabbath-breaking and other offenses by the elders of Mauchline Church, he was cleared by the Presbytery of Ayr (line 80) with the help of his counsel, Robert Aiken (line 85).

Lord hear my earnest cry and prayer
80 Against that Presbytery of Ayr!
Thy strong right hand, Lord, make it bare
    Upon their heads!
Lord visit them, and dinna spare,
    For their misdeeds!

85 O Lord my God, that glib-tongued Aiken!
My very heart and flesh are quaking
To think how I sat, sweating, shaking,
    And pissed wi' dread,
While Auld, wi' hingin° lips gaed sneaking   *hanging*
90   And hid his head!

Lord, in thy day o' vengeance try him!
Lord visit him that did employ him!
And pass not in thy mercy by them,
    Nor hear their prayer;
95 But for thy people's sake destroy them,
    And dinna spare!

But Lord, remember me and mine
Wi' mercies temporal and divine!
That I for grace and gear° may shine   *wealth*
100   Excelled by nane!
And a' the glory shall be thine!
    AMEN, AMEN!

1785   1808

Of A' the Airts[6]

Of a' the airts the wind can blaw,
    I dearly like the west,
For there the bonie lassie lives,
    The lassie I lo'e best:
5 There's wild woods grow, and rivers row,°   *flow*
    And mony a hill between;
But day and night my fancy's flight
    Is ever wi' my Jean.

I see her in the dewy flowers,
10   I see her sweet and fair;
I hear her in the tunefu' birds,
    I hear her charm the air:
There's not a bonie flower that springs
    By fountain, shaw,° or green,   *wood*

6. Written from Dumfriesshire to Burns's wife, Jean Armour, in Ayrshire, the county to the west. *Airts*: quarters.

15   There's not a bonie bird that sings,
        But minds me o' my Jean.

1788   1790

Auld Lang Syne[7]

Should auld acquaintance be forgot
    And never brought to mind?
Should auld acquaintance be forgot,
    And auld lang syne!

5   *For auld lang syne, my jo,°*   joy
    For auld lang syne,
    We'll tak a cup o' kindness yet
    For auld lang syne.

And surely ye'll be° your pint stowp!°   pay for / pint cup
10   And surely I'll be mine!
    And we'll tak a cup o' kindness yet,
        For auld lang syne.

        For auld lang syne, my jo, . . .

We twa hae run about the braes°   slopes
15   And pou'd the gowans° fine;   daisies
    But we've wander'd many a weary fitt,
        Sin auld lang syne.

        For auld lang syne, my jo, . . .

We twa hae paidl'd in the burn°   stream
20   Frae morning sun till dine;°   dinner, noon
    But seas between us braid° hae roar'd,   broad
        Sin auld lang syne.

        For auld lang syne, my jo, . . .

And there's a hand, my trusty fiere!°   friend
25   And gie's a hand o' thine!
    And we'll tak a right gude-willie-waught,[8]
        For auld lang syne

        For auld lang syne, my jo, . . .

1788   1796

---

7. Old long since (Scottish), the days of long ago.   8. Good-will swig.

John Anderson My Jo

John Anderson my jo,° John,   joy
   When we were first acquent;
Your locks were like the raven;
   Your bonie brow was brent;[9]
5 But now your brow is beld, John,
   Your locks are like the snow;
But blessings on your frosty pow,°   head
   John Anderson my jo.

John Anderson my jo, John,
10 We clamb° the hill thegither;   climbed
And mony a canty° day, John,   merry
   We've had wi' ane anither:
Now we maun totter down, John,
   And hand in hand we'll go,
15 And sleep thegither at the foot,
   John Anderson my jo.

1789   1790

Tam O'Shanter

Of Brownyis and of Bogillis full is this Buke.[1]
           —Gavin Douglas

When chapman° billies° leave the street,   *peddler / fellows*
And drouthy° neebors neebors meet,   *thirsty*
As market-days are wearing late,
An' folk begin to tak the gate;°   *road*
5 While we sit bousing at the nappy,°   *ale*
An' getting fou° and unco° happy,   *full / very*
We think na on the lang Scots miles,
The mosses,° waters, slaps,° and styles,   *bogs / gaps in walls*
That lie between us and our hame,
10 Where sits our sulky sullen dame,
Gathering her brows like gathering storm,
Nursing her wrath to keep it warm.
   This truth fand° honest Tam o' Shanter,   *found*
As he frae Ayr ae night did canter,
15 (Auld Ayr, wham ne'er a town surpasses
For honest men and bonie lasses).
   O Tam! hadst thou but been sae wise,
As ta'en thy ain wife Kate's advice!
She tauld thee weel thou was a skellum,°   *good-for-nothing*
20 A blethering,° blustering, drunken blellum,°   *babbling / windbag*

9. Straight, steep; not rounding off into a bald
pate.
1. From the prologue to the sixth book of Virgil's

Aeneid, translated into Scots dialect by Gavin
Douglas (1474–1522). Brownies are friendly gob-
lins; bogles, unfriendly.

That frae November till October,
Ae market-day thou was nae sober;
That ilka° melder,° wi' the miller   *every / meal-grinding*
Thou sat as lang as thou had siller;°   *silver*
25 That every naig° was ca'd° a shoe on,   *horse / driven*
The smith and thee gat roaring fou on;
That at the Lord's house, even on Sunday,
Thou drank wi' Kirkton Jean¹ till Monday.
She prophesied that, late or soon,
30 Thou would be found deep drowned in Doon;
Or catched wi' warlocks° in the mirk,°   *wizards / dark*
By Alloway's auld haunted kirk.²
       Ah, gentle dames! it gars° me greet°   *makes / weep*
To think how mony counsels sweet,
35 How mony lengthened sage advices,
The husband frae the wife despises!
       But to our tale: Ae market night,
Tam had got planted unco right;
Fast by an ingle,° bleezing° finely,   *fireplace / blazing*
40 Wi' reaming° swats,° that drank divinely;   *foaming / ale*
And at his elbow, Souter° Johnny,   *cobbler*
His ancient, trusty, drouthy crony;
Tam lo'ed him like a vera brither;
They had been fou for weeks thegither.
45 The night drave on wi' sangs and clatter;°   *talk*
And aye the ale was growing better:
The landlady and Tam grew gracious,
Wi' favors, secret, sweet, and precious:
The souter tauld his queerest stories;
50 The landlord's laugh was ready chorus:
The storm without might rair° and rustle,   *roar*
Tam did na mind the storm a whistle.
     Care, mad to see a man sae happy,
E'en drowned himsel amang the nappy;
55 As bees flee hame wi' lades° o' treasure,   *loads*
The minutes winged their way wi' pleasure;
Kings may be blest, but Tam was glorious,
O'er a' the ills o' life victorious!
       But pleasures are like poppies spread,
60 You seize the flow'r, its bloom is shed;
Or like the snow falls in the river,
A moment white—then melts for ever;
Or like the borealis race,
That flit ere you can point their place;
65 Or like the rainbow's lovely form
Evanishing amid the storm—
Nae man can tether time nor tide;
The hour approaches Tam maun° ride;   *must*
That hour, o' night's black arch the key-stane,°   *keystone*
70 That dreary hour, he mounts his beast in;

---

1. Mistress of a tavern.
2. The ruins of a church near Burns's home, the object of much superstitious dread.

And sic a night he taks the road in,
As ne'er poor sinner was abroad in.
    The wind blew as 'twad° blawn its last;   *it would have*
The rattling show'rs rose on the blast;
75 The speedy gleams the darkness swallowed;
Loud, deep, and lang, the thunder bellowed:
That night, a child might understand,
The Deil° had business on his hand.   *Devil*
    Weel mounted on his gray mare, Meg,
80 A better never lifted leg,
Tam skelpit° on thro' dub° and mire,   *hurried / puddle*
Despising wind, and rain, and fire;
Whiles° holding fast his guid blue bonnet;   *sometimes*
Whiles crooning° o'er some auld Scots sonnet;° *humming / song*
85 Whiles glow'ring° round wi' prudent cares,   *staring*
Lest bogles catch him unawares.
Kirk-Alloway was drawing nigh,
Whare ghaists° and houlets° nightly cry.   *ghosts / owls*
    By this time he was cross the ford,
90 Where in the snaw the chapman smoored;°   *smothered*
And past the birks° and meikle° stane,° *birches / great / stone*
Where drunken Charlie brak's neck-bane;
And thro' the whins,° and by the cairn,   *furze*
Where hunters fand the murdered bairn;°   *child*
95 And near the thorn, aboon° the well,   *above*
Where Mungo's mither hanged hersel.
Before him Doon pours all his floods;
The doubling storm roars thro' the woods;
The lightnings flash from pole to pole;
100 Near and more near the thunders roll:
When, glimmering thro' the groaning trees,
Kirk-Alloway seemed in a bleeze;°   *blaze*
Thro' ilka° bore° the beams were glancing, *every / chink*
And loud resounded mirth and dancing.
105   Inspiring bold John Barleycorn!
What dangers thou canst make us scorn!
Wi' tippenny,° we fear nae evil;   *twopenny ale*
Wi' usquebae° we'll face the devil!   *whisky*
The swats° sae reamed° in Tammie's noddle, *ale / foamed*
110 Fair play, he cared na deils a boddle.°   *farthing*
But Maggie stood right sair° astonished,   *sorely*
Till, by the heel and hand admonished,
She ventured forward on the light;
And, vow! Tam saw an unco sight!
115 Warlocks and witches in a dance;
Nae cotillon° brent° new frae France,   *dance / brand*
But hornpipes, jigs, strathspeys,° and reels, *Highland dances*
Put life and mettle in their heels.
A winnock-bunker° in the east,   *window seat*
120 There sat auld Nick, in shape o' beast;
A towzie° tyke,° black, grim, and large!   *tousled / dog*
To gie them music was his charge:

	He screwed the pipes and gart° them skirl,°	*made / shrill*
	Till roof and rafters a' did dirl.°	*ring*
125	Coffins stood round like open presses,°	*closets*
	That shawed the dead in their last dresses;	
	And by some devilish cantraip° slight°	*weird / trick*
	Each in its cauld hand held a light,	
	By which heroic Tam was able	
130	To note upon the haly table	
	A murderer's banes in gibbet-airns;°	*-irons*
	Twa span-lang,[3] wee, unchristened bairns;°	*children*
	A thief new-cutted frae a rape,°	*rope*
	Wi' his last gasp his gab° did gape;	*mouth*
135	Five tomahawks, wi' blude red-rusted;	
	Five scymitars, wi' murder crusted;	
	A garter, which a babe had strangled;	
	A knife, a father's throat had mangled,	
	Whom his ain son o' life bereft,	
140	The gray hairs yet stack to the heft;	
	Wi' mair of horrible and awfu',	
	Which even to name wad be unlawfu'.	
	As Tammie glowred,° amazed, and curious,	*stared*
	The mirth and fun grew fast and furious:	
145	The piper loud and louder blew;	
	The dancers quick and quicker flew;	
	They reeled, they set, they crossed, they	
	cleekit,°	*joined hands*
	Till ilka carlin° swat° and reekit,°	*old woman / sweated / steamed*
	And coost° her duddies° to the wark,	*cast off / dress*
150	And linkit° at it in her sark!°	*tripped nimbly / shift*
	Now Tam, O Tam! had thae been queans,°	*girls*
	A' plump and strapping in their teens;	
	Their sarks, instead o' creeshie° flannen,°	*greasy / flannel*
	Been snaw-white seventeen hunder linen![4]	
155	Thir° breeks o' mine, my only pair,	*these*
	That ance were plush, o' gude blue hair,	
	I wad hae gi'en them off my hurdies,°	*buttocks*
	For ae blink o' the bonie burdies!°	*maidens*
	But wither'd beldams,° auld and droll,	*old women*
160	Rigwoodie° hags wad spean° a foal,	*scrawny / wean*
	Louping° and flinging on a crummock,°	*leaping / staff*
	I wonder didna turn thy stomach.	
	But Tam kend what was what fu' brawlie,°	*well*
	There was ae winsome wench and wawlie°	*buxom*
165	That night enlisted in the core,°	*company*
	(Lang after kent° on Carrick shore	*known*
	For mony a beast to dead she shot,	
	And perished mony a bonie boat,	
	And shook baith meikle° corn and bear,°	*much / barley*
170	And kept the country-side in fear).	
	Her cutty° sark, o' Paisley harn,°	*short / coarse cloth*

3. Two spans long (a span is the distance from outstretched thumb to pinkie).

4. Fine linen, with seventeen hundred threads to a width.

That while a lassie she had worn,
In longitude tho' sorely scanty,
It was her best, and she was vauntie.°   proud
175 Ah! little kend thy reverend grannie
That sark she coft° for her wee Nannie   bought
Wi' twa pund Scots ('twas a' her riches)
Wad ever graced a dance of witches!
    But here my Muse her wing maun cour;°   stoop
180 Sic flights are far beyond her pow'r—
To sing how Nannie lap° and flang,   leaped
(A souple jade she was, and strang),
And how Tam stood, like ane bewitched,
And thought his very een° enriched;   eyes
185 Even Satan glowr'd, and fidged° fu' fain,°   wriggled / happy
And hotched° and blew wi' might and main: hitched (himself)
Till first ae caper, syne° anither,   then
Tam tint° his reason a' thegither,   lost
And roars out, "Weel done, Cutty-sark!"
190 And in an instant all was dark!
And scarcely had he Maggie rallied,
When out the hellish legion sallied.
    As bees bizz out wi' angry fyke,°   fuss
When plundering herds° assail their byke;°   shepherds / hive
195 As open° pussie's° mortal foes,   bay / the hare's
When pop! she starts before their nose;
As eager runs the market-crowd,
When "Catch the thief!" resounds aloud;
So Maggie runs; the witches follow,
200 Wi' mony an eldritch° skriech and hollow.   unearthly
    Ah, Tam! ah, Tam! thou'll get thy fairin!° punishment
In hell they'll roast thee like a herrin!
In vain thy Kate awaits thy comin!
Kate soon will be a woefu' woman!
205 Now do thy speedy utmost, Meg,
And win the key-stane o' the brig;°   bridge
There at them thou thy tail may toss,
A running stream they dare na cross.
But ere the key-stane she could make,
210 The fient a tail she had to shake!⁵
For Nannie, far before the rest,
Hard upon noble Maggie prest,
And flew at Tam wi' furious ettle;°   purpose
But little wist she Maggie's mettle.
215 Ae spring brought off her master hale,°   whole
But left behind her ain gray tail:
The carlin claught° her by the rump,   clutched
And left poor Maggie scarce a stump.
    Now, wha this tale o' truth shall read,
220 Each man and mother's son, take heed:
Whene'er to drink you are inclined,
Or cutty-sarks run in your mind,

5. I.e., she had no tail left. *Fient a:* devil-a.

Think! ye may buy the joys o'er dear;
Remember Tam o' Shanter's mare.

1790   1791

The Banks o' Doon

Ye flowery banks o' bonie Doon,
  How can ye blume sae fair;
How can ye chant, ye little birds,
  And I sae fu' o' care!

5 Thou'll break my heart, thou bonie bird
  That sings upon the bough;
Thou minds me o' the happy days
  When my fause° luve was true.   *false*

Thou'll break my heart, thou bonie bird,
10   That sings beside thy mate;
For sae I sat, and sae I sang,
  And wist° na o' my fate.   *knew*

Aft hae I rov'd by bonie Doon
  To see the wood-bine twine,
15 And ilka° bird sang o' its love,   *every*
  And sae did I o' mine.

Wi' lightsome heart I pu'd a rose
  Frae aff its thorny tree,
And my fause luver staw° the rose,   *stole*
20   But left the thorn wi' me.

Wi' lightsome heart I pu'd a rose,
  Upon a morn in June:
And sae I flourish'd on the morn,
  And sae was pu'd or noon!

1791   1792

A Red Red Rose

O my luve's like a red, red rose,
  That's newly sprung in June;
O my luve's like the melodie
  That's sweetly played in tune.

5 As fair art thou, my bonie lass,
  So deep in luve am I;

And I will luve thee still, my dear,
   Till a' the seas gang dry.

Till a' the seas gang dry, my dear,
10   And the rocks melt wi' the sun:
O I will love thee still, my dear,
   While the sands o' life shall run.

And fare thee weel, my only luve!
   And fare thee weel a while!
15 And I will come again, my luve,
   Tho' it were ten thousand mile!

1796

Oh Wert Thou in the Cauld Blast

Oh wert thou in the cauld blast,
   On yonder lea, on yonder lea;
My plaidie to the angry airt,°   *quarter (of the wind)*
   I'd shelter thee, I'd shelter thee:
5 Or did misfortune's bitter storms
   Around thee blaw, around thee blaw,
Thy bield° should be my bosom,   *shelter*
   To share it a', to share it a'.

Or were I in the wildest waste,
10 Sae black and bare, sae black and bare,
The desart were a paradise,
   If thou wert there, if thou wert there.
Or were I monarch o' the globe,
   Wi' thee to reign, wi' thee to reign;
15 The brightest jewel in my crown,
   Wad be my queen, wad be my queen.

1796   1800

JOANNA BAILLIE
1762–1851

A Mother to Her Waking Infant

Now in thy dazzling° half-oped eye,   *dazed*
Thy curled nose and lip awry,
Thy up-hoist arms and noddling° head,   *nodding*
And little chin with crystal spread,
5 Poor helpless thing! what do I see,
   That I should sing of thee?

From thy poor tongue no accents come,
Which can but rub thy toothless gum;
Small understanding boasts thy face,
10   Thy shapeless limbs nor step nor grace;
A few short words thy feats may tell,
   And yet I love thee well.

When sudden wakes the bitter shriek,
And redder swells thy little cheek;
15   When rattled keys thy woes beguile,
And through the wet eye gleams the smile,
Still for thy weakly self is spent
   Thy little silly plaint.

But when thy friends are in distress,
20   Thou'lt laugh and chuckle ne'er the less;
Nor e'en with sympathy be smitten,
Though all are sad but thee and kitten;
Yet little varlet° that thou art,   *rascal*
   Thou twitchest at the heart.

25   Thy rosy cheek so soft and warm;
Thy pinky hand and dimpled arm;
Thy silken locks that scantly peep,
With gold-tipped ends, where circles deep
Around thy neck in harmless grace
30   So soft and sleekly hold their place,
Might harder hearts with kindness fill,
   And gain our right good will.

Each passing clown bestows his blessing,
Thy mouth is worn with old wives' kissing:
35   E'en lighter looks the gloomy eye
Of surly sense, when thou art by;
And yet I think whoe'er they be,
   They love thee not like me.

Perhaps when time shall add a few
40   Short years to thee, thou'lt love me too.
Then wilt thou through life's weary way
Become my sure and cheering stay:
Wilt care for me, and be my hold,
   When I am weak and old.

45   Thou'lt listen to my lengthened tale,
And pity me when I am frail—
But see, the sweepy spinning fly
Upon the window takes thine eye.
Go to thy little senseless play—
50   Thou dost not heed my lay.°   *song*

1790

Song: Woo'd and Married and A'

The bride she is winsome and bonny,
    Her hair it is snooded° sae sleek,   *bound up with a ribbon*
And faithfu' and kind is her Johnny,
    Yet fast fa' the tears on her cheek.
5 New pearlins° are cause of her sorrow,   *lace trimmings*
    New pearlins and plenishing° too,   *furnishings*
The bride that has a' to borrow,
    Has e'en right mickle° ado,   *much*
        Woo'd and married and a'!
10   Woo'd and married and a'!
Is na' she very weel aff
    To be woo'd and married at a'?

Her mither then hastily spak,
    "The lassie is glaikit° wi' pride;   *foolish*
15 In my pouch I had never a plack°   *farthing*
    On the day when I was a bride.
E'en tak' to your wheel, and be clever,
    And draw out your thread in the sun;
The gear° that is gifted,° it never   *goods, wealth / given*
20   Will last like the gear that is won.°   *earned*
        Woo'd and married and a'!
        Wi' havins° and toucher° sae sma',   *possessions / dowry*
    I think ye are very weel aff,
    To be woo'd and married at a'!"

25 "Toot, toot!" quo' her gray-headed faither,
    "She's less o' a bride than a bairn;°   *child*
She's ta'en like a cout° frae the heather,   *colt*
    Wi' sense and discretion to learn.
Half husband, I trow, and half daddy,
30   As humor inconstantly leans,
The chiel° maun° be patient and steady,   *man / must*
    That yokes wi' a mate in her teens.
        A kerchief sae douce° and sae neat,   *sedate; respectable*
        O'er her locks that the winds used to blaw!
35 I'm baith like to laugh and to greet,°   *weep*
    When I think o' her married at a'!"

Then out spak' the wily bridegroom;
    Weel waled° were his wordies, I ween—   *chosen*
"I'm rich, though my coffer be toom,°   *empty*
40   Wi' the blinks o' your bonny blue een.°   *eyes*
I'm prouder o' thee by my side,
    Though thy ruffles or ribbons be few,
Than if Kate o' the Croft were my bride,
    Wi' purfles° and pearlins enow.   *embroidered trimmings*
45   Dear and dearest of ony!

Ye're woo'd and buikit[1] and a'!"
And do ye think scorn o' your Johnny,
   And grieve to be married at a'?"

She turn'd, and she blush'd, and she smiled,
50   And she looket sae bashfully down;
The pride o' her heart was beguiled,
   And she played wi' the sleeves o' her gown;
She twirled the tag o' her lace,
   And she nippet her boddice sae blue,
55 Syne° blinket sae sweet in his face,   *then*
   And aff like a maukin° she flew.   *hare*
     Woo'd and married and a'!
       Wi' Johnny to roose° her and a'!   *praise*
   She thinks hersel very weel aff,
60 To be woo'd and married at a'!

                          1822

WILLIAM WORDSWORTH
1770–1850

Expostulation and Reply[1]

"Why, William, on that old gray stone,
Thus for the length of half a day,
Why, William, sit you thus alone,
And dream your time away?

5 "Where are your books?—that light bequeathed
To Beings else forlorn and blind!
Up! up! and drink the spirit breathed
From dead men to their kind.

"You look round on your Mother Earth,
10 As if she for no purpose bore you;
As if you were her first-born birth,
And none had lived before you!"

One morning thus, by Esthwaite lake,
When life was sweet, I knew not why,
15 To me my good friend Matthew spake,
And thus I made reply.

---

1. "Booked," i.e., officially registered as engaged in the book of the session clerk.
1. With the following, companion poem, "Expostulation and Reply" forms a dialogue between two friends, who advance somewhat exaggerated arguments about the relative merits of nature and of books.

"The eye—it cannot choose but see;
We cannot bid the ear be still;
Our bodies feel, where'er they be,
20 Against or with our will.

"Nor less I deem that there are Powers
Which of themselves our minds impress;
That we can feed this mind of ours
In a wise passiveness.

25 "Think you, 'mid all this mighty sum
Of things for ever speaking,
That nothing of itself will come,
But we must still be seeking?

"—Then ask not wherefore, here, alone,
30 Conversing² as I may,
I sit upon this old gray stone,
And dream my time away."

Spring 1798   1798

The Tables Turned

An Evening Scene on the Same Subject

Up! up! my Friend, and quit your books;
Or surely you'll grow double:
Up! up! my Friend, and clear your looks;
Why all this toil and trouble?

5   The sun, above the mountain's head,
A freshening lustre mellow
Through all the long green fields has spread,
His first sweet evening yellow.

Books! 'tis a dull and endless strife:
10 Come, hear the woodland linnet,°   a songbird
How sweet his music! on my life,
There's more of wisdom in it.

And hark! how blithe the throstle° sings!   song thrush
He, too, is no mean preacher:
15 Come forth into the light of things,
Let Nature be your Teacher.

She has a world of ready wealth,
Our minds and hearts to bless—
Spontaneous wisdom breathed by health,
20 Truth breathed by cheerfulness.

2. I.e., communing (with the "things for ever speaking").

One impulse from a vernal wood
May teach you more of man,
Of moral evil and of good,
Than all the sages can.

25   Sweet is the lore which Nature brings;
Our meddling intellect
Mis-shapes the beauteous forms of things:—
We murder to dissect.

Enough of Science and of Art;
30   Close up those barren leaves;
Come forth, and bring with you a heart
That watches and receives.

1798   1798

Lines

Composed a Few Miles above Tintern Abbey on Revisiting the Banks of the Wye during a Tour.[3] July 13, 1798

Five years have passed; five summers, with the length
Of five long winters! and again I hear
These waters, rolling from their mountain-springs
With a soft inland murmur. Once again
5   Do I behold these steep and lofty cliffs,
That on a wild secluded scene impress
Thoughts of more deep seclusion; and connect
The landscape with the quiet of the sky.
The day is come when I again repose
10   Here, under this dark sycamore, and view
These plots of cottage ground, these orchard tufts,
Which at this season, with their unripe fruits,
Are clad in one green hue, and lose themselves
'Mid groves and copses.° Once again I see   *small woods*
15   These hedgerows, hardly hedgerows, little lines
Of sportive wood run wild; these pastoral farms,
Green to the very door; and wreaths of smoke
Sent up, in silence, from among the trees!
With some uncertain notice, as might seem
20   Of vagrant dwellers in the houseless woods,
Or of some Hermit's cave, where by his fire
The Hermit sits alone.

                                    These beauteous forms,
Through a long absence, have not been to me
As is a landscape to a blind man's eye;
25   But oft, in lonely rooms, and 'mid the din

---

3. I.e., a walking trip (with his sister, Dorothy) through the Wye valley in Monmouthshire, the location of the ruins of a medieval abbey, noted for its scenery.

Of towns and cities, I have owed to them,
In hours of weariness, sensations sweet,
Felt in the blood, and felt along the heart;
And passing even into my purer mind,
30 With tranquil restoration—feelings too
Of unremembered pleasure; such, perhaps,
As have no slight or trivial influence
On that best portion of a good man's life,
His little, nameless, unremembered, acts
35 Of kindness and of love. Nor less, I trust,
To them I may have owed another gift,
Of aspect more sublime; that blessed mood,
In which the burthen° of the mystery,   *burden*
In which the heavy and the weary weight
40 Of all this unintelligible world,
Is lightened—that serene and blessed mood,
In which the affections gently lead us on—
Until, the breath of this corporeal frame
And even the motion of our human blood
45 Almost suspended, we are laid asleep
In body, and become a living soul;
While with an eye made quiet by the power
Of harmony, and the deep power of joy,
We see into the life of things.

                                        If this
50 Be but a vain belief, yet, oh! how oft—
In darkness and amid the many shapes
Of joyless daylight; when the fretful stir
Unprofitable, and the fever of the world,
Have hung upon the beatings of my heart—
55 How oft, in spirit, have I turned to thee,
O sylvan° Wye! thou wanderer through the woods,   *wooded*
How often has my spirit turned to thee!

     And now, with gleams of half-extinguished thought,
With many recognitions dim and faint,
60 And somewhat of a sad perplexity,
The picture of the mind revives again;
While here I stand, not only with the sense
Of present pleasure, but with pleasing thoughts
That in this moment there is life and food
65 For future years. And so I dare to hope,
Though changed, no doubt, from what I was when first
I came among these hills; when like a roe
I bounded o'er the mountains, by the sides
Of the deep rivers, and the lonely streams,
70 Wherever nature led—more like a man
Flying from something that he dreads than one
Who sought the thing he loved. For nature then
(The coarser⁴ pleasures of my boyish days,

4. I.e., primarily physical.

And their glad animal movements all gone by)
75 To me was all in all.—I cannot paint
What then I was. The sounding cataract°   *waterfall*
Haunted me like a passion; the tall rock,
The mountain, and the deep and gloomy wood,
Their colors and their forms, were then to me
80 An appetite; a feeling and a love,
That had no need of a remoter charm,
By thought supplied, nor any interest
Unborrowed from the eye.—That time is past,
And all its aching joys are now no more,
85 And all its dizzy raptures. Not for this
Faint° I, nor mourn nor murmur; other gifts   *become discouraged*
Have followed; for such loss, I would believe,
Abundant recompense. For I have learned
To look on nature, not as in the hour
90 Of thoughtless youth; but hearing oftentimes
The still, sad music of humanity,
Nor harsh nor grating, though of ample power
To chasten and subdue. And I have felt
A presence that disturbs me with the joy
95 Of elevated thoughts; a sense sublime
Of something far more deeply interfused,
Whose dwelling is the light of setting suns,
And the round ocean and the living air,
And the blue sky, and in the mind of man:
100 A motion and a spirit, that impels
All thinking things, all objects of all thought,
And rolls through all things. Therefore am I still
A lover of the meadows and the woods,
And mountains; and of all that we behold
105 From this green earth; of all the mighty world
Of eye, and ear—both what they half create,
And what perceive; well pleased to recognize
In nature and the language of the sense
The anchor of my purest thoughts, the nurse,
110 The guide, the guardian of my heart, and soul
Of all my moral being.

                    Nor perchance,
If I were not thus taught, should I the more
Suffer my genial° spirits° to decay: *creative / powers*
For thou art with me here upon the banks
115 Of this fair river; thou my dearest Friend,[5]
My dear, dear Friend; and in thy voice I catch
The language of my former heart, and read
My former pleasures in the shooting lights
Of thy wild eyes. Oh! yet a little while
120 May I behold in thee what I was once,
My dear, dear Sister! and this prayer I make,
Knowing that Nature never did betray

5. His sister, Dorothy.

The heart that loved her; 'tis her privilege,
Through all the years of this our life, to lead
125 From joy to joy: for she can so inform
The mind that is within us, so impress
With quietness and beauty, and so feed
With lofty thoughts, that neither evil tongues,
Rash judgments, nor the sneers of selfish men,
130 Nor greetings where no kindness is, nor all
The dreary intercourse of daily life,
Shall e'er prevail against us, or disturb
Our cheerful faith, that all which we behold
Is full of blessings. Therefore let the moon
135 Shine on thee in thy solitary walk;
And let the misty mountain winds be free
To blow against thee: and, in after years,
When these wild ecstasies shall be matured
Into a sober pleasure; when thy mind
140 Shall be a mansion for all lovely forms,
Thy memory be as a dwelling place
For all sweet sounds and harmonies; oh! then,
If solitude, or fear, or pain, or grief
Should be thy portion, with what healing thoughts
145 Of tender joy wilt thou remember me,
And these my exhortations! Nor, perchance—
If I should be where I no more can hear
Thy voice, nor catch from thy wild eyes these gleams
Of past existence—wilt thou then forget
150 That on the banks of this delightful stream
We stood together; and that I, so long
A worshiper of Nature, hither came
Unwearied in that service; rather say
With warmer love—oh! with far deeper zeal
155 Of holier love. Nor wilt thou then forget,
That after many wanderings, many years
Of absence, these steep woods and lofty cliffs,
And this green pastoral landscape, were to me
More dear, both for themselves and for thy sake!

1798

The Ruined Cottage[6]

First Part

'Twas Summer and the sun was mounted high.
Along the south the uplands feebly glared
Through a pale steam, and all the northern downs,
In clearer air ascending, showed far off
5 Their surfaces with shadows dappled o'er
Of deep embattled clouds. Far as the sight

---

6. A shorter version of a narrative that comprised the first book of *The Excursion* (1814). First published by Jonathan Wordsworth in *The Music of Humanity* (1969).

Could reach those many shadows lay in spots
Determined° and unmoved, with steady beams   *exactly fixed*
Of clear and pleasant sunshine interposed—
10   Pleasant to him who on the soft cool grass
Extends his careless limbs beside the root
Of some huge oak whose agèd branches make
A twilight of their own, a dewy shade
Where the wren warbles while the dreaming man,
15   Half conscious of that soothing melody,
With sidelong eye looks out upon the scene,
By those impending branches made more soft,
More soft and distant.

                    Other lot was mine.
Across a bare wide Common I had toiled
20   With languid feet which by the slippery ground
Were baffled still, and when I stretched myself
On the brown earth my limbs from very heat
Could find no rest, nor my weak arm disperse
The insect host which gathered round my face
25   And joined their murmurs to the tedious noise
Of seeds of bursting gorse that crackled round.
I rose and turned towards a group of trees
Which midway in that level stood alone;
And thither come at length, beneath a shade
30   Of clustering elms that sprang from the same root
I found a ruined house, four naked walls
That stared upon each other. I looked round
And near the door I saw an agèd Man,
Alone and stretched upon the cottage bench,
35   An iron-pointed staff lay at his side.
With instantaneous joy I recognized
That pride of nature and of lowly life,
The venerable Armytage, a friend
As dear to me as is the setting sun.

40   Two days before
We had been fellow travelers. I knew
That he was in this neighborhood, and now
Delighted found him here in the cool shade.
He lay, his pack of rustic merchandise
45   Pillowing his head. I guess he had no thought
Of his way-wandering life. His eyes were shut,
The shadows of the breezy elms above
Dappled his face. With thirsty heat oppressed
At length I hailed him, glad to see his hat
50   Bedewed with waterdrops, as if the brim
Had newly scooped a running stream. He rose
And pointing to a sunflower, bade me climb
The [   ]⁷ wall where that same gaudy flower
Looked out upon the road.

---

7. Blank space in the manuscript.

It was a plot
55 Of garden ground now wild, its matted weeds
Marked with the steps of those whom as they passed,
The gooseberry trees that shot in long lank slips,
Or currants hanging from their leafless stems
In scanty strings, had tempted to o'erleap
60 The broken wall. Within that cheerless spot,
Where two tall hedgerows of thick alder boughs
Joined in a damp cold nook, I found a well
Half covered up with willow flowers and grass.
I slaked my thirst and to the shady bench
65 Returned, and while I stood unbonneted
To catch the motion of the cooler air,
The old Man said, "I see around me here
Things which you cannot see. We die, my Friend,
Nor we alone, but that which each man loved
70 And prized in his peculiar nook of earth
Dies with him, or is changed, and very soon
Even of the good is no memorial left.
The Poets, in their elegies and songs
Lamenting the departed, call the groves,
75 They call upon the hills and streams to mourn,
And senseless rocks—nor idly, for they speak
In these their invocations with a voice
Obedient to the strong creative power
Of human passion. Sympathies there are
80 More tranquil, yet perhaps of kindred birth,
That steal upon the meditative mind
And grow with thought. Beside yon spring I stood,
And eyed its waters till we seemed to feel
One sadness, they and I. For them a bond
85 Of brotherhood is broken; time has been
When every day the touch of human hand
Disturbed their stillness, and they ministered
To human comfort. When I stopped to drink
A spider's web hung to the water's edge,
90 And on the wet and slimy footstone lay
The useless fragment of a wooden bowl.
It moved my very heart.

"The day has been
When I could never pass this road but she
Who lived within these walls, when I appeared,
95 A daughter's welcome gave me, and I loved her
As my own child. Oh Sir, the good die first,
And they whose hearts are dry as summer dust
Burn to the socket. Many a passenger
Has blessed poor Margaret for her gentle looks
100 When she upheld the cool refreshment drawn
From that forsaken spring, and no one came
But he was welcome, no one went away
But that it seemed she loved him. She is dead,

The worm is on her cheek, and this poor hut,
105 Stripped of its outward garb of household flowers,
Of rose and sweetbriar, offers to the wind
A cold bare wall whose earthy top is tricked
With weeds and the rank spear grass. She is dead,
And nettles rot and adders sun themselves
110 Where we have sate together while she nursed
Her infant at her breast. The unshod colt,
The wandring heifer and the Potter's ass,
Find shelter now within the chimney wall
Where I have seen her evening hearthstone blaze
115 And through the window spread upon the road
Its cheerful light. You will forgive me, sir,
But often on this cottage do I muse
As on a picture, till my wiser mind
Sinks, yielding to the foolishness of grief.

120 "She had a husband, an industrious man,
Sober and steady. I have heard her say
That he was up and busy at his loom
In summer ere the mower's scythe had swept
The dewy grass, and in the early spring
125 Ere the last star had vanished. They who passed
At evening, from behind the garden fence
Might hear his busy spade, which he would ply
After his daily work till the daylight
Was gone, and every leaf and flower were lost
130 In the dark hedges. So they passed their days
In peace and comfort, and two pretty babes
Were their best hope next to the God in Heaven.

"You may remember, now some ten years gone,
Two blighting seasons when the fields were left
135 With half a harvest. It pleased heaven to add
A worse affliction in the plague of war,
A happy land was stricken to the heart,
'Twas a sad time of sorrow and distress.
A wanderer among the cottages,
140 I with my pack of winter raiment saw
The hardships of that season. Many rich
Sunk down as in a dream among the poor,
And of the poor did many cease to be,
And their place knew them not. Meanwhile, abridged
145 Of daily comforts, gladly reconciled
To numerous self-denials, Margaret
Went struggling on through those calamitous years
With cheerful hope. But ere the second autumn
A fever seized her husband. In disease
150 He lingered long, and when his strength returned
He found the little he had stored to meet
The hour of accident, or crippling age,
Was all consumed. As I have said, 'twas now

A time of trouble: shoals of artisans
155   Were from their daily labor turned away
To hang for bread on parish charity,
They and their wives and children, happier far
Could they have lived as do the little birds
That peck along the hedges, or the kite
160   That makes her dwelling in the mountain rocks.

"Ill fared it now with Robert, he who dwelt
In this poor cottage. At his door he stood
And whistled many a snatch of merry tunes
That had no mirth in them, or with his knife
165   Carved uncouth figures on the heads of sticks.
Then idly sought about through every nook
Of house or garden any casual task
Of use or ornament, and with a strange
Amusing but uneasy novelty
170   He blended where he might the various tasks
Of summer, autumn, winter, and of spring.
But this endured not, his good humor soon
Became a weight in which no pleasure was,
And poverty brought on a petted° mood   *irritable*
175   And a sore temper. Day by day he drooped.
And he would leave his home, and to the town
Without an errand would he turn his steps,
Or wander here and there among the fields.
One while he would speak lightly of his babes
180   And with a cruel tongue, at other times
He played with them wild freaks of merriment.
And 'twas a piteous thing to see the looks
Of the poor innocent children. 'Every smile,'
Said Margaret to me here beneath these trees,
'Made my heart bleed.' "

185   At this the old Man paused
And looking up to those enormous elms
He said, " 'Tis now the hour of deepest noon.
At this still season of repose and peace,
This hour when all things which are not at rest
190   Are cheerful, while this multitude of flies
Fills all the air with happy melody,
Why should a tear be in an old man's eye?
Why should we thus with an untoward mind,
And in the weakness of humanity,
195   From natural wisdom turn our hearts away.
To natural comfort shut our eyes and ears.
And, feeding on disquiet, thus disturb
The calm of Nature with our restless thoughts?"

END OF THE FIRST PART

Second Part

He spake with somewhat of a solemn tone,
200 But when he ended there was in his face
Such easy cheerfulness, a look so mild,
That for a little time it stole away
All recollection, and that simple tale
Passed from my mind like a forgotten sound.
205 A while on trivial things we held discourse
To me soon tasteless. In my own despite
I thought of that poor woman as of one
Whom I had known and loved. He had rehearsed
Her homely tale with such familiar power,
210 With such an active countenance, an eye
So busy, that the things of which he spake
Seemed present, and, attention now relaxed,
There was a heartfelt chillness in my veins.
I rose, and turning from that breezy shade
215 Went out into the open air, and stood
To drink the comfort of the warmer sun.
Long time I had not stayed ere, looking round
Upon that tranquil ruin, I returned
And begged of the old man that for my sake
He would resume his story.

220   He replied,
"It were a wantonness, and would demand
Severe reproof, if we were men whose hearts
Could hold vain dalliance with the misery
Even of the dead, contented thence to draw
225 A momentary pleasure, never marked
By reason, barren of all future good.
But we have known that there is often found
In mournful thoughts, and always might be found,
A power to virtue friendly; were't not so
230 I am a dreamer among men, indeed
An idle dreamer. 'Tis a common tale
By moving accidents[8] uncharactered,
A tale of silent suffering, hardly clothed
In bodily form, and to the grosser sense
235 But ill adapted, scarcely palpable
To him who does not think. But at your bidding
I will proceed.

                    "While thus it fared with them
To whom this cottage till that hapless year
Had been a blessed home, it was my chance
240 To travel in a country far remote;
And glad I was when, halting by yon gate
That leads from the green lane, again I saw

---

8. High adventures. Shakespeare's Othello speaks "of moving accidents by flood and field" (1.3.134).

These lofty elm trees. Long I did not rest:
With many pleasant thoughts I cheered my way
245   O'er the flat common. At the door arrived,
I knocked, and when I entered, with the hope
Of usual greeting, Margaret looked at me
A little while, then turned her head away
Speechless, and sitting down upon a chair
250   Wept bitterly. I wist not what to do,
Or how to speak to her. Poor wretch, at last
She rose from off her seat, and then, oh Sir,
I cannot tell how she pronounced my name.
With fervent love, and with a face of grief
255   Unutterably helpless, and a look
That seemed to cling upon me, she enquired
If I had seen her husband. As she spake
A strange surprise and fear came to my heart,
Nor had I power to answer ere she told
260   That he had disappeared—just two months gone.
He left his house: two wretched days had passed,
And on the third by the first break of light,
Within her casement full in view she saw
A purse of gold.[9] 'I trembled at the sight,'
265   Said Margaret, 'for I knew it was his hand
That placed it there. And on that very day
By one, a stranger, from my husband sent,
The tidings came that he had joined a troop
Of soldiers going to a distant land.
270   He left me thus. Poor Man, he had not heart
To take farewell of me, and he feared
That I should follow with my babes, and sink
Beneath the misery of a soldier's life.'

"This tale did Margaret tell with many tears,
275   And when she ended I had little power
To give her comfort, and was glad to take
Such words of hope from her own mouth as served
To cheer us both. But long we had not talked
Ere we built up a pile of better thoughts,
280   And with a brighter eye she looked around,
As if she had been shedding tears of joy.
We parted. It was then the early spring:
I left her busy with her garden tools,
And well remember, o'er that fence she looked,
285   And, while I paced along the footway path,
Called out and sent a blessing after me,
With tender cheerfulness, and with a voice
That seemed the very sound of happy thoughts.

"I roved o'er many a hill and many a dale
290   With this my weary load, in heat and cold,
Through many a wood and many an open ground,

9. The payment her husband had received for enlisting.

In sunshine or in shade, in wet or fair,
Now blithe, now drooping, as it might befall;
My best companions now the driving winds
295 And now the 'trotting brooks'[1] and whispering trees,
And now the music of my own sad steps,
With many a short-lived thought that passed between
And disappeared.

                    "I came this way again
Towards the wane of summer, when the wheat
300 Was yellow, and the soft and bladed grass
Sprang up afresh and o'er the hay field spread
Its tender green. When I had reached the door
I found that she was absent. In the shade,
Where we now sit, I waited her return.
305 Her cottage in its outward look appeared
As cheerful as before, in any show
Of neatness little changed, but that I thought
The honeysuckle crowded round the door,
And from the wall hung down in heavier tufts,
310 And knots of worthless stonecrop started out
Along the window's edge, and grew like weeds
Against the lower panes. I turned aside
And strolled into her garden. It was changed.
The unprofitable bindweed spread his bells
315 From side to side, and with unwieldy wreaths
Had dragged the rose from its sustaining wall
And bent it down to earth. The border tufts,
Daisy, and thrift, and lowly camomile,
And thyme, had straggled out into the paths
Which they were used to deck.

320   "Ere this an hour
Was wasted. Back I turned my restless steps,
And as I walked before the door it chanced
A stranger passed, and guessing whom I sought,
He said that she was used to ramble far.
325 The sun was sinking in the west, and now
I sate with sad impatience. From within
Her solitary infant cried aloud.
The spot though fair seemed very desolate,
The longer I remained more desolate;
330 And looking round I saw the cornerstones,
Till then unmarked, on either side the door
With dull red stains discolored, and stuck o'er
With tufts and hairs of wool, as if the sheep
That feed upon the commons thither came
335 Familiarly, and found a couching place
Even at her threshold.

---

1. Slightly misquoted ("trotting burns") from Robert Burns's "Epistle to William Simpson," a poem in praise of natural feelings.

"The house clock struck eight:
I turned and saw her distant a few steps.
Her face was pale and thin, her figure too
Was changed. As she unlocked the door she said,
340 'It grieves me you have waited here so long,
But in good truth I've wandered much of late,
And sometimes, to my shame I speak, have need
Of my best prayers to bring me back again.'
While on the board she spread our evening meal,
345 She told me she had lost her elder child,
That he for months had been a serving boy,
Apprenticed by the parish. 'I perceive
You look at me, and you have cause. Today
I have been traveling far, and many days
350 About the fields I wander, knowing this
Only, that what I seek I cannot find.
And so I waste my time: for I am changed,
And to myself,' she said, 'have done much wrong,
And to this helpless infant. I have slept
355 Weeping, and weeping I have waked. My tears
Have flowed as if my body were not such
As others are, and I could never die.
But I am now in mind and in my heart
More easy, and I hope,' she said, 'that heaven
360 Will give me patience to endure the things
Which I behold at home.'

                                  "It would have grieved
Your very soul to see her. Sir, I feel
The story linger in my heart. I fear
'Tis long and tedious, but my spirit clings
365 To that poor woman. So familiarly
Do I perceive her manner and her look
And presence, and so deeply do I feel
Her goodness, that not seldom in my walks
A momentary trance comes over me,
370 And to myself I seem to muse on one
By sorrow laid asleep or borne away,
A human being destined to awake
To human life, or something very near
To human life, when he shall come again
375 For whom she suffered. Sir, it would have grieved
Your very soul to see her: evermore
Her eyelids drooped, her eyes were downward cast,
And when she at her table gave me food
She did not look at me. Her voice was low,
380 Her body was subdued. In every act
Pertaining to her house affairs appeared
The careless stillness which a thinking mind
Gives to an idle matter. Still she sighed,
But yet no motion of the breast was seen,
385 No heaving of the heart. While by the fire

We sate together, sighs came on my ear,
I knew not how, and hardly whence they came.
I took my staff, and when I kissed her babe
The tears stood in her eyes. I left her then
390 With the best hope and comfort I could give:
She thanked me for my will, but for my hope
It seemed she did not thank me.

        "I returned
And took my rounds along this road again
Ere on its sunny bank the primrose flower
395 Had chronicled the earliest day of spring.
I found her sad and drooping. She had learned
No tidings of her husband; if he lived,
She knew not that he lived; if he were dead,
She knew not he was dead. She seemed the same
400 In person or appearance, but her house
Bespoke a sleepy hand of negligence.
The floor was neither dry nor neat, the hearth
Was comfortless,
The windows too were dim, and her few books,
405 Which one upon the other heretofore
Had been piled up against the corner panes
In seemly order, now with straggling leaves
Lay scattered here and there, open or shut,
As they had chanced to fall. Her infant babe
410 Had from its mother caught the trick of grief,
And sighed among its playthings. Once again
I turned towards the garden gate, and saw
More plainly still that poverty and grief
Were now come nearer to her. The earth was hard,
415 With weeds defaced and knots of withered grass;
No ridges there appeared of clear black mold,
No winter greenness. Of her herbs and flowers
It seemed the better part were gnawed away
Or trampled on the earth. A chain of straw,
420 Which had been twisted round the tender stem
Of a young apple tree, lay at its root;
The bark was nibbled round by truant sheep.
Margaret stood near, her infant in her arms,
And, seeing that my eye was on the tree,
425 She said, 'I fear it will be dead and gone
Ere Robert come again.'

        "Towards the house
Together we returned, and she enquired
If I had any hope. But for her Babe,
And for her little friendless Boy, she said,
430 She had no wish to live—that she must die
Of sorrow. Yet I saw the idle loom
Still in its place. His Sunday garments hung
Upon the selfsame nail, his very staff

Stood undisturbed behind the door. And when
435   I passed this way beaten by Autumn winds,
She told me that her little babe was dead,
And she was left alone. That very time,
I yet remember, through the miry lane
She walked with me a mile, when the bare trees
440   Trickled with foggy damps, and in such sort
That any heart had ached to hear her, begged
That wheresoe'r I went I still would ask
For him whom she had lost. We parted then,
Our final parting; for from that time forth
445   Did many seasons pass ere I returned
Into this tract again.

               "Five tedious years
She lingered in unquiet widowhood,
A wife and widow. Needs must it have been
A sore heart-wasting. I have heard, my friend,
450   That in that broken arbor she would sit
The idle length of half a sabbath day;
There, where you see the toadstool's lazy head;
And when a dog passed by she still would quit
The shade and look abroad. On this old Bench
455   For hours she sate, and evermore her eye
Was busy in the distance, shaping things
Which made her heart beat quick. Seest thou that path?
The green sward° now has broken its gray line—   *grassy land*
There to and fro she paced through many a day
460   Of the warm summer, from a belt of flax
That girt her waist, spinning the long-drawn thread
With backward steps. Yet ever as there passed
A man whose garments showed the Soldier's red,
Or crippled Mendicant in Sailor's garb,
465   The little child who sate to turn the wheel
Ceased from his toil, and she, with faltering voice,
Expecting still to hear her husband's fate,
Made many a fond enquiry; and when they
Whose presence gave no comfort, were gone by,
470   Her heart was still more sad. And by yon gate,
Which bars the traveler's road, she often stood,
And when a stranger horseman came, the latch
Would lift, and in his face look wistfully,
Most happy if from aught discovered there
475   Of tender feeling she might dare repeat
The same sad question.

               "Meanwhile her poor hut
Sunk to decay; for he was gone, whose hand
At the first nippings of October frost
Closed up each chink, and with fresh bands of straw
480   Chequered the green-grown thatch. And so she lived
Through the long winter, reckless° and alone,   *not caring for herself*

Till this reft° house, by frost, and thaw, and rain,   *emptied*
Was sapped; and when she slept, the nightly damps
Did chill her breast, and in the stormy day
485   Her tattered clothes were ruffled by the wind
Even at the side of her own fire. Yet still
She loved this wretched spot, nor would for worlds
Have parted hence; and still that length of road,
And this rude° bench, one torturing hope endeared,   *roughly made*
490   Fast rooted at her heart. And here, my friend,
In sickness she remained; and here she died,
Last human tenant of these ruined walls."

The old Man ceased: he saw that I was moved.
From that low bench rising instinctively,
495   I turned aside in weakness, nor had power
To thank him for the tale which he had told.
I stood, and leaning o'er the garden gate
Reviewed that Woman's sufferings; and it seemed
To comfort me while with a brother's love
500   I blessed her in the impotence of grief.
At length towards the cottage I returned
Fondly, and traced with milder interest,
That secret spirit of humanity
Which, 'mid the calm oblivious tendencies
505   Of nature, 'mid her plants, her weeds and flowers,
And silent overgrowings, still survived.
The old man seeing this resumed, and said,
"My friend, enough to sorrow have you given,
The purposes of Wisdom ask no more:
510   Be wise and cheerful, and no longer read
The forms of things with an unworthy eye.
She sleeps in the calm earth, and peace is here.
I well remember that those very plumes,
Those weeds, and the high spear grass on that wall,
515   By mist and silent raindrops silvered o'er,
As once I passed, did to my mind convey
So still an image of tranquility,
So calm and still, and looked so beautiful
Amid the uneasy thoughts which filled my mind,
520   That what we feel of sorrow and despair
From ruin and from change, and all the grief
The passing shows of being leave behind,
Appeared an idle dream that could not live
Where meditation was. I turned away,
525   And walked along my road in happiness."

He ceased. By this the sun declining shot
A slant and mellow radiance, which began
To fall upon us where beneath the trees
We sate on that low bench. And now we felt,
530   Admonished thus, the sweet hour coming on:
A linnet warbled from those lofty elms,

A thrush sang loud, and other melodies
At distance heard, peopled the milder air.
The old man rose and hoisted up his load.
535 Together casting then a farewell look
Upon those silent walls, we left the shade;
And, ere the stars were visible, attained
A rustic inn, our evening resting place.

THE END

1797–98   1969

Anecdote for Fathers

"Retine vim istam, falsa enim dicam, si coges."
EUSEBIUS.[2]

I have a boy of five years old;
His face is fair and fresh to see;
His limbs are cast in beauty's mold,
And dearly he loves me.

5   One morn we strolled on our dry walk,
Our quiet home all full in view,
And held such intermitted talk
As we are wont to do.

My thoughts on former pleasures ran;
10   I thought of Kilve's[3] delightful shore,
Our pleasant home when spring began,
A long, long year before.

A day it was when I could bear
Some fond regrets to entertain;
15   With so much happiness to spare,
I could not feel a pain.

The green earth echoed to the feet
Of lambs that bounded through the glade,
From shade to sunshine, and as fleet
20   From sunshine back to shade.

Birds warbled round me—and each trace
Of inward sadness had its charm;
Kilve, thought I, was a favored place,
And so is Liswyn farm.

25   My boy beside me tripped, so slim
And graceful in his rustic dress!

2. Latin translation by Eusebius (*Preparatio Evangelica* 6.5) of a Greek line from Porphyro that purports to be the warning of Apollo (Greek and Roman god of sunlight, prophecy, music, and poetry) to any who would try to coerce the oracle: "Restrain your violence, for I shall lie if you force me."
3. Village on the Bristol Channel.

And, as we talked, I questioned him,
In very idleness.

"Now tell me, had you rather be,"
30   I said, and took him by the arm,
"On Kilve's smooth shore, by the green sea,
Or here at Liswyn farm?"

In careless mood he looked at me,
While still I held him by the arm,
35   And said, "At Kilve I'd rather be
Than here at Liswyn farm."

"Now, little Edward, say why so:
My little Edward, tell me why."—
"I cannot tell, I do not know."—
40   "Why, this is strange," said I;

"For, here are woods, hills smooth and warm:
There surely must some reason be
Why you would change sweet Liswyn farm
For Kilve by the green sea."

45   At this, my boy hung down his head,
He blushed with shame, nor made reply;
And three times to the child I said,
"Why, Edward, tell me why?"

His head he raised—there was in sight,
50   It caught his eye, he saw it plain—
Upon the house-top, glittering bright,
A broad and gilded vane.

Then did the boy his tongue unlock,
And eased his mind with this reply:
55   "At Kilve there was no weather-cock;
And that's the reason why."

O dearest, dearest boy! my heart
For better lore would seldom yearn,
Could I but teach the hundredth part
60   Of what from thee I learn.

1798   1798

From The Prelude

From Book I

Fair seedtime had my soul, and I grew up
Fostered alike by beauty and by fear:
Much favored in my birthplace,[4] and no less

4. Cockermouth, a town in the northern part of the English Lake District.

In that belovèd Vale[5] to which erelong
305 We were transplanted—there were we let loose
For sports of wider range. Ere I had told
Ten birthdays, when among the mountain slopes
Frost, and the breath of frosty wind, had snapped
The last autumnal crocus, 'twas my joy
510 With store of springes° o'er my shoulder hung   snares
To range the open heights where woodcocks run
Along the smooth green turf. Through half the night,
Scudding away from snare to snare, I plied
That anxious visitation—moon and stars
315 Were shining o'er my head. I was alone,
And seemed to be a trouble to the peace
That dwelt among them. Sometimes it befell
In these night wanderings, that a strong desire
O'erpowered my better reason, and the bird
320 Which was the captive of another's toil
Became my prey; and when the deed was done
I heard among the solitary hills
Low breathings coming after me, and sounds
Of undistinguishable motion, steps
325 Almost as silent as the turf they trod.

    Nor less, when spring had warmed the cultured° Vale, *cultivated*
Moved we as plunderers where the mother bird
Had in high places built her lodge; though mean
Our object and inglorious, yet the end
330 Was not ignoble. Oh! when I have hung
Above the raven's nest, by knots of grass
And half-inch fissures in the slippery rock
But ill sustained, and almost (so it seemed)
Suspended by the blast that blew amain,°   *at full speed*
335 Shouldering the naked crag, oh, at that time
While on the perilous ridge I hung alone,
With what strange utterance did the loud dry wind
Blow through my ear! the sky seemed not a sky
Of earth—and with what motion moved the clouds!

340   Dust as we are, the immortal spirit grows
Like harmony in music; there is a dark
Inscrutable workmanship that reconciles
Discordant elements, makes them cling together
In one society. How strange that all
345 The terrors, pains, and early miseries,
Regrets, vexations, lassitudes interfused
Within my mind, should e'er have borne a part,
And that a needful part, in making up
The calm existence that is mine when I
350 Am worthy of myself! Praise to the end!
Thanks to the means which Nature deigned to employ;
Whether her fearless visitings, or those

5. Esthwaite, also in the Lakes.

That came with soft alarm, like hurtless light
Opening the peaceful clouds; or she may use
355   Severer interventions, ministry
More palpable, as best might suit her aim.

    One summer evening (led by her) I found
A little boat tied to a willow tree
Within a rocky cave, its usual home.
360   Straight I unloosed her chain, and stepping in
Pushed from the shore. It was an act of stealth
And troubled pleasure, nor without the voice
Of mountain echoes did my boat move on;
Leaving behind her still, on either side,
365   Small circles glittering idly in the moon,
Until they melted all into one track
Of sparkling light. But now, like one who rows,
Proud of his skill, to reach a chosen point
With an unswerving line, I fixed my view
370   Upon the summit of a craggy ridge,
The horizon's utmost boundary; for above
Was nothing but the stars and the gray sky.
She was an elfin pinnace;° lustily   *small boat*
I dipped my oars into the silent lake,
375   And, as I rose upon the stroke, my boat
Went heaving through the water like a swan;
When, from behind that craggy steep till then
The horizon's bound, a huge peak, black and huge,
As if with voluntary power instinct,
380   Upreared its head. I struck and struck again,
And growing still in stature the grim shape
Towered up between me and the stars, and still,
For so it seemed, with purpose of its own
And measured motion like a living thing,
385   Strode after me. With trembling oars I turned,
And through the silent water stole my way
Back to the covert of the willow tree;
There in her mooring place I left my bark,
And through the meadows homeward went, in grave
390   And serious mood; but after I had seen
That spectacle, for many days, my brain
Worked with a dim and undetermined sense
Of unknown modes of being; o'er my thoughts
There hung a darkness, call it solitude
395   Or blank desertion. No familiar shapes
Remained, no pleasant images of trees,
Of sea or sky, no colors of green fields;
But huge and mighty forms, that do not live
Like living men, moved slowly through the mind
400   By day, and were a trouble to my dreams.

    Wisdom and Spirit of the universe!
Thou Soul that art the eternity of thought,

That givest to forms and images a breath
And everlasting motion, not in vain
405   By day or starlight thus from my first dawn
Of childhood didst thou intertwine for me
The passions that build up our human soul;
Not with the mean and vulgar° works of man,   *commonplace*
But with high objects, with enduring things—
410   With life and nature—purifying thus
The elements of feeling and of thought,
And sanctifying, by such discipline,
Both pain and fear, until we recognize
A grandeur in the beating of the heart.
415   Nor was this fellowship vouchsafed to me
With stinted kindness. In November days,
When vapors rolling down the valley made
A lonely scene more lonesome, among woods,
At noon and 'mid the calm of summer nights,
420   When, by the margin of the trembling lake,
Beneath the gloomy hills homeward I went
In solitude, such intercourse was mine;
Mine was it in the fields both day and night,
And by the waters, all the summer long.

425   And in the frosty season, when the sun
Was set, and visible for many a mile
The cottage windows blazed through twilight gloom,
I heeded not their summons: happy time
It was indeed for all of us—for me
430   It was a time of rapture! Clear and loud
The village clock tolled six—I wheeled about,
Proud and exulting like an untired horse
That cares not for his home. All shod with steel,
We hissed along the polished ice in games
435   Confederate, imitative of the chase
And woodland pleasures—the resounding horn,
The pack loud chiming, and the hunted hare.
So through the darkness and the cold we flew,
And not a voice was idle; with the din
440   Smitten, the precipices rang aloud;
The leafless trees and every icy crag
Tinkled like iron; while far distant hills
Into the tumult sent an alien sound
Of melancholy not unnoticed, while the stars
445   Eastward were sparkling clear, and in the west
The orange sky of evening died away.
Not seldom from the uproar I retired
Into a silent bay, or sportively
Glanced sideway, leaving the tumultuous throng,
450   To cut across the reflex° of a star   *reflection*
That fled, and, flying still before me, gleamed
Upon the glassy plain; and oftentimes,
When we had given our bodies to the wind,

And all the shadowy banks on either side
455 Came sweeping through the darkness, spinning still
The rapid line of motion, then at once
Have I, reclining back upon my heels,
Stopped short; yet still the solitary cliffs
Wheeled by me—even as if the earth had rolled
460 With visible motion her diurnal° round!   *daily*
Behind me did they stretch in solemn train,°   *succession*
Feebler and feebler, and I stood and watched
Till all was tranquil as a dreamless sleep.

Ye Presences of Nature in the sky
465 And on the earth! Ye Visions of the hills!
And Souls of lonely places! can I think
A vulgar hope was yours when ye employed
Such ministry, when ye, through many a year
Haunting me thus among my boyish sports,
470 On caves and trees, upon the woods and hills,
Impressed upon all forms the characters°   *signs*
Of danger or desire; and thus did make
The surface of the universal earth
With triumph and delight, with hope and fear,
475 Work° like a sea?   *seethe*
                    Not uselessly employed,
Might I pursue this theme through every change
Of exercise and play, to which the year
Did summon us in his delightful round.

We were a noisy crew; the sun in heaven
480 Beheld not vales more beautiful than ours;
Nor saw a band in happiness and joy
Richer, or worthier of the ground they trod.
I could record with no reluctant voice
The woods of autumn, and their hazel bowers
485 With milk-white clusters hung; the rod and line,
True symbol of hope's foolishness, whose strong
And unreproved enchantment led us on
By rocks and pools shut out from every star,
All the green summer, to forlorn cascades
490 Among the windings hid of mountain brooks.
—Unfading recollections! at this hour
The heart is almost mine with which I felt,
From some hill-top on sunny afternoons,
The paper kite high among fleecy clouds
495 Pull at her rein like an impetuous courser;
Or, from the meadows sent on gusty days,
Beheld her breast the wind, then suddenly
Dashed headlong, and rejected by the storm.

Ye lowly cottages wherein we dwelt,
500 A ministration of your own was yours;
Can I forget you, being as you were

So beautiful among the pleasant fields
In which ye stood? or can I here forget
The plain and seemly countenance with which
505 Ye dealt out your plain comforts? Yet had ye
Delights and exultations of your own.
Eager and never weary we pursued
Our home-amusements by the warm peat-fire
At evening, when with pencil, and smooth slate
510 In square divisions parceled out and all
With crosses and with cyphers scribbled o'er,
We schemed and puzzled, head opposed to head
In strife too humble to be named in verse:
Or round the naked table, snow-white deal,°   *pine board*
515 Cherry or maple, sate in close array,
And to the combat, Loo or Whist,[6] led on
A thick-ribbed army; not, as in the world,
Neglected and ungratefully thrown by
Even for the very service they had wrought,
520 But husbanded through many a long campaign.
Uncouth assemblage was it, where no few
Had changed their functions; some, plebeian cards
Which Fate, beyond the promise of their birth,
Had dignified, and called to represent
525 The persons of departed potentates.
Oh, with what echoes on the board they fell!
Ironic diamonds,—clubs, hearts, diamonds, spades,
A congregation piteously akin!
Cheap matter offered they to boyish wit,
530 Those sooty knaves, precipitated down
With scoffs and taunts, like Vulcan[7] out of heaven:
The paramount ace, a moon in her eclipse,
Queens gleaming through their splendor's last decay,
And monarchs surly at the wrongs sustained
535 By royal visages. Meanwhile abroad
Incessant rain was falling, or the frost
Raged bitterly, with keen and silent tooth;
And, interrupting oft that eager game,
From under Esthwaite's splitting fields of ice
540 The pent-up air, struggling to free itself,
Gave out to meadow grounds and hills a loud
Protracted yelling, like the noise of wolves
Howling in troops along the Bothnic main.[8]

Nor, sedulous° as I have been to trace   *diligent*
545 How Nature by extrinsic° passion first   *unrelated*
Peopled the mind with forms sublime or fair,
And made me love them, may I here omit
How other pleasures have been mine, and joys

---

6. Card games resembling poker and bridge; the pack of cards described in lines 516–35 through long use has been damaged and repaired, with low ("plebeian," line 522) cards made into high ("potentates," line 525) and others partially defaced.

7. In Roman mythology, the god of fire, or the smith of the gods (hence "sooty," line 530); his father, Jove, once hurled him out of heaven.

8. A northern gulf of the Baltic Sea.

Of subtler origin; how I have felt,
550 Not seldom even in that tempestuous time,
Those hallowed and pure motions of the sense
Which seem, in their simplicity, to own
An intellectual° charm; that calm delight   *spiritual*
Which, if I err not, surely must belong
555 To those first-born° affinities that fit   *innate*
Our new existence to existing things,
And, in our dawn of being, constitute
The bond of union between life and joy.

Yes, I remember when the changeful earth,
560 And twice five summers on my mind had stamped
The faces of the moving year, even then
I held unconscious intercourse with beauty
Old as creation, drinking in a pure
Organic pleasure from the silver wreaths
565 Of curling mist, or from the level plain
Of waters colored by impending° clouds.   *overhanging*

The sands of Westmoreland, the creeks and bays
Of Cumbria's rocky limits,[9] they can tell
How, when the Sea threw off his evening shade,
570 And to the shepherd's hut on distant hills
Sent welcome notice of the rising moon,
How I have stood, to fancies such as these
A stranger, linking with the spectacle
No conscious memory of a kindred sight,
575 And bringing with me no peculiar sense
Of quietness or peace; yet have I stood,
Even while mine eye hath moved o'er many a league
Of shining water, gathering as it seemed,
Through every hairbreadth in that field of light,
580 New pleasure like a bee among the flowers.
    Thus oft amid those fits of vulgar joy
Which, through all seasons, on a child's pursuits
Are prompt attendants, 'mid that giddy bliss
Which, like a tempest, works along the blood
585 And is forgotten; even then I felt
Gleams like the flashing of a shield—the earth
And common face of Nature spake to me
Rememberable things; sometimes, 'tis true,
By chance collisions and quaint accidents
590 (Like those ill-sorted unions, work supposed
Of evil-minded fairies), yet not vain
Nor profitless, if haply they impressed
Collateral objects and appearances,
Albeit lifeless then, and doomed to sleep
595 Until maturer seasons called them forth
To impregnate and to elevate the mind.
—And if the vulgar joy by its own weight

9. Coastline areas of the Lake District.

Wearied itself out of the memory,
The scenes which were a witness of that joy
600 Remained in their substantial lineaments
Depicted on the brain, and to the eye
Were visible, a daily sight; and thus
By the impressive discipline of fear,
By pleasure and repeated happiness,
605 So frequently repeated, and by force
Of obscure feelings representative
Of things forgotten, these same scenes so bright,
So beautiful, so majestic in themselves,
Though yet the day was distant, did become
610 Habitually dear, and all their forms
And changeful colors by invisible links
Were fastened to the affections.°   *feelings*
                    I began
My story early—not misled, I trust,
By an infirmity of love for days
615 Disowned by memory—fancying flowers where none,
Not even the sweetest, do or can survive
For him at least whose dawning day they cheered.
Nor will it seem to thee, O Friend![1] so prompt
In sympathy, that I have lengthened out
620 With fond and feeble tongue a tedious tale.
Meanwhile, my hope has been, that I might fetch
Invigorating thoughts from former years;
Might fix the wavering balance of my mind,
And haply meet reproaches too, whose power
625 May spur me on, in manhood now mature,
To honorable toil. Yet should these hopes
Prove vain, and thus should neither I be taught
To understand myself, nor thou to know
With better knowledge how the heart was framed
630 Of him thou lovest; need I dread from thee
Harsh judgments, if the song be loth to quit
Those recollected hours that have the charm
Of visionary things, those lovely forms
And sweet sensations that throw back our life,
635 And almost make remotest infancy
A visible scene, on which the sun is shining?

    One end at least hath been attained; my mind
Hath been revived, and if this genial° mood   *creative*
Desert me not, forthwith shall be brought down
640 Through later years the story of my life.
The road lies plain before me—'tis a theme
Single and of determined bounds; and hence
I choose it rather at this time, than work
Of ampler or more varied argument,
645 Where I might be discomfited and lost:

---

1. Samuel Taylor Coleridge (1772–1834; see pp. 805–31), the poet and philosopher to whom *The Prelude* was addressed; Wordsworth's particular friend and collaborator.

And certain hopes are with me, that to thee
This labor will be welcome, honored Friend!

1798–1800   1850

She Dwelt among the Untrodden Ways

> She dwelt among the untrodden ways
>   Beside the springs of Dove.[2]
> A Maid whom there were none to praise
>   And very few to love;
>
> 5   A violet by a mossy stone
>   Half hidden from the eye!
> —Fair as a star, when only one
>   Is shining in the sky.
>
> She lived unknown, and few could know
> 10   When Lucy ceased to be;
> But she is in her grave, and, oh,
>   The difference to me!

1799   1800

Three Years She Grew

> Three years she grew in sun and shower,
> Then Nature said, "A lovelier flower
> On earth was never sown;
> This Child I to myself will take;
> 5   She shall be mine, and I will make
> A Lady of my own.
>
> "Myself will to my darling be
> Both law and impulse: and with me
> The Girl, in rock and plain,
> 10 In earth and heaven, in glade and bower,
> Shall feel an overseeing power
> To kindle or restrain.
>
> "She shall be sportive as the fawn
> That wild with glee across the lawn
> 15 Or up the mountain springs;
> And hers shall be the breathing balm,
> And hers the silence and the calm
> Of mute insensate things.

2. Several rivers in England are named Dove.

"The floating clouds their state shall lend
20 To her; for her the willow bend;
Nor shall she fail to see
Even in the motions of the Storm
Grace that shall mold the Maiden's form
By silent sympathy.

25 "The stars of midnight shall be dear
To her; and she shall lean her ear
In many a secret place
Where rivulets dance their wayward round,
And beauty born of murmuring sound
30 Shall pass into her face.

"And vital feelings of delight
Shall rear her form to stately height,
Her virgin bosom swell;
Such thoughts to Lucy I will give
35 While she and I together live
Here in this happy dell."

Thus Nature spake—the work was done—
How soon my Lucy's race was run!
She died, and left to me
40 This health, this calm, and quiet scene;
The memory of what has been,
And never more will be.

1799   1800

A Slumber Did My Spirit Seal

A slumber did my spirit seal;
    I had no human fears:
She seemed a thing that could not feel
    The touch of earthly years.

5   No motion has she now, no force;
    She neither hears nor sees;
Rolled round in earth's diurnal° course,   *daily*
    With rocks, and stones, and trees.

1799   1800

Resolution and Independence

I

There was a roaring in the wind all night;
The rain came heavily and fell in floods;

But now the sun is rising calm and bright;
The birds are singing in the distant woods;
5 Over his own sweet voice the Stock-dove broods;
The Jay makes answer as the Magpie chatters;
And all the air is filled with pleasant noise of waters.

2

All things that love the sun are out of doors;
The sky rejoices in the morning's birth;
10 The grass is bright with rain-drops;—on the moors
The hare is running races in her mirth;
And with her feet she from the plashy earth
Raises a mist; that, glittering in the sun,
Runs with her all the way, wherever she doth run.

3

15 I was a Traveler then upon the moor;
I saw the hare that raced about with joy;
I heard the woods and distant waters roar;
Or heard them not, as happy as a boy:
The pleasant season did my heart employ:
20 My old remembrances went from me wholly;
And all the ways of men, so vain and melancholy.

4

But, as it sometimes chanceth, from the might
Of joy in minds that can no further go,
As high as we have mounted in delight
25 In our dejection do we sink as low;
To me that morning did it happen so;
And fears and fancies thick upon me came;
Dim sadness—and blind thoughts, I knew not, nor could name.

5

I heard the sky-lark warbling in the sky;
30 And I bethought me of the playful hare:
Even such a happy Child of earth am I;
Even as these blissful creatures do I fare;
Far from the world I walk, and from all care;
But there may come another day to me—
35 Solitude, pain of heart, distress, and poverty.

6

My whole life I have lived in pleasant thought,
As if life's business were a summer mood;
As if all needful things would come unsought
To genial faith, still rich in genial good;
40 But how can He expect that others should
Build for him, sow for him, and at his call
Love him, who for himself will take no heed at all?

7

I thought of Chatterton,[3] the marvelous Boy,
The sleepless Soul that perished in his pride;
45 Of Him[4] who walked in glory and in joy
Following his plow, along the mountain-side:
By our own spirits are we deified:
We Poets in our youth begin in gladness;
But thereof come in the end despondency and madness.

8

50 Now, whether it were by peculiar grace,
A leading from above, a something given,
Yet it befell, that, in this lonely place,
When I with these untoward thoughts had striven,
Beside a pool bare to the eye of heaven
55 I saw a Man before me unawares:
The oldest man he seemed that ever wore gray hairs.

9

As a huge stone is sometimes seen to lie
Couched on the bald top of an eminence;
Wonder to all who do the same espy,
60 By what means it could thither come, and whence;
So that it seems a thing endued with sense:
Like a sea-beast crawled forth, that on a shelf
Of rock or sand reposeth, there to sun itself;

10

Such seemed this Man, not all alive nor dead,
65 Nor all asleep—in his extreme old age:
His body was bent double, feet and head
Coming together in life's pilgrimage;
As if some dire constraint of pain, or rage
Of sickness felt by him in times long past,
70 A more than human weight upon his frame had cast.

11

Himself he propped, limbs, body, and pale face,
Upon a long gray staff of shaven wood:
And, still as I drew near with gentle pace,
Upon the margin of that moorish flood
75 Motionless as a cloud the old Man stood,
That heareth not the loud winds when they call;
And moveth all together, if it move at all.

12

At length, himself unsettling, he the pond
Stirred with his staff, and fixedly did look
80 Upon the muddy water, which he conned,°   *studied*

---

3. Thomas Chatterton (1752–1770), a gifted
young English poet who committed suicide.

4. Robert Burns (1759–1796; see pp. 747–60),
who died before achieving his later great renown.

As if he had been reading in a book:
And now a stranger's privilege I took;
And, drawing to his side, to him did say,
"This morning gives us promise of a glorious day."

13

85 A gentle answer did the old Man make,
In courteous speech which forth he slowly drew:
And him with further words I thus bespake,
"What occupation do you there pursue?
This is a lonesome place for one like you."
90 Ere he replied, a flash of mild surprise
Broke from the sable orbs of his yet-vivid eyes.

14

His words came feebly, from a feeble chest,
But each in solemn order followed each,
With something of a lofty utterance drest—
95 Choice word and measured phrase, above the reach
Of ordinary men; a stately speech;
Such as grave Livers[5] do in Scotland use,
Religious men, who give to God and man their dues.

15

He told, that to these waters he had come
100 To gather leeches,[6] being old and poor:
Employment hazardous and wearisome!
And he had many hardships to endure:
From pond to pond he roamed, from moor to moor;
Housing, with God's good help, by choice or chance;
105 And in this way he gained an honest maintenance.

16

The old Man still stood talking by my side;
But now his voice to me was like a stream
Scarce heard; nor word from word could I divide;
And the whole body of the Man did seem
110 Like one whom I had met with in a dream;
Or like a man from some far region sent,
To give me human strength, by apt admonishment.

17

My former thoughts returned: the fear that kills;
And hope that is unwilling to be fed;
115 Cold, pain, and labor, and all fleshly ills;

---

5. Those who live austerely and gravely. See
Wordsworth's "The Excursion," 1.113–17; the reference is to a Scottish family:

> Pure livers were they all, austere and grave,
> And fearing God; the very children taught
> Stern self-respect, a reverence for God's word,

And an habitual piety, maintained
With strictness scarcely known on English
ground.

6. Aquatic bloodsuckers, once widely used for
medicinal bloodletting.

And mighty Poets in their misery dead.
—Perplexed, and longing to be comforted,
My question eagerly did I renew,
"How is it that you live, and what is it you do?"

18

120 He with a smile did then his words repeat;
And said, that, gathering leeches, far and wide
He traveled; stirring thus about his feet
The waters of the pools where they abide.
"Once I could meet with them on every side;
125 But they have dwindled long by slow decay;
Yet still I persevere, and find them where I may."

19

While he was talking thus, the lonely place,
The old Man's shape, and speech—all troubled me:
In my mind's eye I seemed to see him pace
130 About the weary moors continually,
Wandering about alone and silently.
While I these thoughts within myself pursued,
He, having made a pause, the same discourse renewed.

20

And soon with this he other matter blended,
135 Cheerfully uttered, with demeanor kind,
But stately in the main; and when he ended,
I could have laughed myself to scorn to find
In that decrepit Man so firm a mind.
"God," said I, "be my help and stay° secure;   support (noun)
140 I'll think of the Leech-gatherer on the lonely moor!"

1802   1807

It Is a Beauteous Evening[7]

It is a beauteous evening, calm and free,
The holy time is quiet as a Nun
Breathless with adoration; the broad sun
Is sinking down in its tranquility;
5   The gentleness of heaven broods o'er the Sea:
Listen! the mighty Being is awake,
And doth with his eternal motion make
A sound like thunder—everlastingly.
Dear Child! dear Girl! that walkest with me here,
10   If thou appear untouched by solemn thought,
Thy nature is not therefore less divine:

---

7. The "Dear Child" was Caroline (then ten years old), his daughter by Annette Vallon.

Thou liest in Abraham's bosom[8] all the year,
And worship'st at the Temple's inner shrine,[9]
God being with thee when we know it not.

1802   1807

London, 1802

Milton! thou shouldst be living at this hour:
England hath need of thee: she is a fen
Of stagnant waters: altar, sword, and pen,
Fireside, the heroic wealth of hall and bower,
5   Have forfeited their ancient English dower
Of inward happiness. We are selfish men;
Oh! raise us up, return to us again;
And give us manners, virtue, freedom, power.
Thy soul was like a Star, and dwelt apart;
10   Thou hadst a voice whose sound was like the sea:
Pure as the naked heavens, majestic, free,
So didst thou travel on life's common way,
In cheerful godliness; and yet thy heart
The lowliest duties on herself did lay.

1802   1807

Composed upon Westminster Bridge, September 3, 1802

Earth has not anything to show more fair:
Dull would he be of soul who could pass by
A sight so touching in its majesty;
This City now doth, like a garment, wear
5   The beauty of the morning; silent, bare,
Ships, towers, domes, theaters, and temples lie
Open unto the fields, and to the sky;
All bright and glittering in the smokeless air.
Never did sun more beautifully steep
10   In his first splendor, valley, rock, or hill;
Ne'er saw I, never felt, a calm so deep!
The river glideth at his own sweet will:
Dear God! the very houses seem asleep;
And all that mighty heart is lying still!

1802   1807

8. Where souls in heaven rest (as in Luke 16.22).
9. The holy of holies (as in the ancient temple in Jerusalem); where God is present.

Nuns Fret Not at Their Convent's Narrow Room

Nuns fret not at their convent's narrow room;
And hermits are contented with their cells;
And students with their pensive citadels;
Maids at the wheel, the weaver at his loom,
5 Sit blithe and happy; bees that soar for bloom,
High as the highest Peak of Furness-fells,[1]
Will murmur by the hour in foxglove bells:
In truth the prison, into which we doom
Ourselves, no prison is: and hence for me,
10 In sundry moods, 'twas pastime to be bound
Within the Sonnet's scanty plot of ground;
Pleased if some Souls (for such there needs must be)
Who have felt the weight of too much liberty,
Should find brief solace there, as I have found.

1802   1807

My Heart Leaps Up

My heart leaps up when I behold
   A rainbow in the sky:
So was it when my life began;
So is it now I am a man;
5 So be it when I shall grow old,
   Or let me die!
The Child is father of the Man;
And I could wish my days to be
Bound each to each by natural piety.

1802   1807

Ode

Intimations of Immortality from Recollections of Early Childhood

The Child is father of the Man;
And I could wish my days to be
Bound each to each by natural piety.[2]

I

There was a time when meadow, grove, and stream,
The earth, and every common sight,
      To me did seem
   Appareled in celestial light,

---

1. Mountains in the English Lake District.
2. Final lines of Wordsworth's "My Heart Leaps Up" (above).

5   The glory and the freshness of a dream.
It is not now as it hath been of yore—
       Turn whereso'er I may,
         By night or day,
The things which I have seen I now can see no more.

2

10   The Rainbow comes and goes,
       And lovely is the Rose,
       The Moon doth with delight
Look round her when the heavens are bare,
       Waters on a starry night
15   Are beautiful and fair;
    The sunshine is a glorious birth;
    But yet I know, where'er I go,
That there hath passed away a glory from the earth.

3

Now, while the birds thus sing a joyous song,
20   And while the young lambs bound
       As to the tabor's° sound,   *small drum's*
To me alone there came a thought of grief:
A timely utterance gave that thought relief,
       And I again am strong:
25 The cataracts blow their trumpets from the steep;
No more shall grief of mine the season wrong;
I hear the Echoes through the mountains throng,
The Winds come to me from the fields of sleep,
       And all the earth is gay;
30   Land and sea
       Give themselves up to jollity,
        And with the heart of May
       Doth every Beast keep holiday—
        Thou Child of Joy,
35 Shout round me, let me hear thy shouts, thou happy Shepherd-boy!

4

Ye blessèd Creatures, I have heard the call
    Ye to each other make; I see
The heavens laugh with you in your jubilee;
    My heart is at your festival,
40   My head hath its coronal,°   *circlet of wildflowers*
The fullness of your bliss, I feel—I feel it all.
       Oh, evil day! if I were sullen
       While Earth herself is adorning,
       This sweet May morning,
45   And the Children are culling
        On every side,
       In a thousand valleys far and wide,
       Fresh flowers; while the sun shines warm,
And the Babe leaps up on his Mother's arm—

50   I hear, I hear, with joy I hear!
              —But there's a Tree, of many, one,
        A single Field which I have looked upon,
        Both of them speak of something that is gone:
                  The Pansy at my feet
55   Doth the same tale repeat:
        Whither is fled the visionary gleam?
        Where is it now, the glory and the dream?

                            5
        Our birth is but a sleep and a forgetting:
        The Soul that rises with us, our life's Star,
60   Hath had elsewhere its setting,
                  And cometh from afar:
                  Not in entire forgetfulness,
                  And not in utter nakedness,
        But trailing clouds of glory do we come
65   From God, who is our home:
        Heaven lies about us in our infancy!
        Shades of the prison-house begin to close
                  Upon the growing Boy
                  But he
70   Beholds the light, and whence it flows,
                  He sees it in his joy;
        The Youth, who daily farther from the east
                  Must travel, still is Nature's Priest,
                  And by the vision splendid
75   Is on his way attended;
        At length the Man perceives it die away,
        And fade into the light of common day.

                            6
        Earth fills her lap with pleasures of her own;
        Yearnings she hath in her own natural kind,
80   And, even with something of a Mother's mind,
                  And no unworthy aim,
                  The homely° Nurse doth all she can   simple; kindly
        To make her foster child, her Inmate Man,
                  Forget the glories he hath known,
85   And that imperial palace whence he came.

                            7
        Behold the Child among his newborn blisses,
        A six-years' Darling of a pygmy size!
        See, where 'mid work of his own hand he lies,
        Fretted° by sallies of his mother's kisses,   vexed
90   With light upon him from his father's eyes!
        See, at his feet, some little plan or chart,
        Some fragment from his dream of human life,
        Shaped by himself with newly-learnèd art;
                  A wedding or a festival,

95   A mourning or a funeral;
              And this hath now his heart,
              And unto this he frames his song;
              Then will he fit his tongue
         To dialogues of business, love, or strife;
100   But it will not be long
              Ere this be thrown aside,
              And with new joy and pride
         The little Actor cons° another part;   *commits to memory*
         Filling from time to time his "humorous stage"[3]
105   With all the Persons,° down to palsied Age,   *dramatis personae*
         That Life brings with her in her equipage;°   *group of servants*
              As if his whole vocation
              Were endless imitation.

8

         Thou, whose exterior semblance doth belie
110   Thy Soul's immensity;
         Thou best Philosopher, who yet dost keep
         Thy heritage, thou Eye among the blind,
         That, deaf and silent, read'st the eternal deep,
         Haunted forever by the eternal mind—
115   Mighty Prophet! Seer blest!
              On whom those truths do rest,
         Which we are toiling all our lives to find,
         In darkness lost, the darkness of the grave;
         Thou, over whom thy Immortality
120   Broods like the Day, a Master o'er a Slave,
         A Presence which is not to be put by;
         Thou little Child, yet glorious in the might
         Of heaven-born freedom on thy being's height,
         Why with such earnest pains dost thou provoke
125   The years to bring the inevitable yoke,
         Thus blindly with thy blessedness at strife?
         Full soon thy Soul shall have her earthly freight,
         And custom lie upon thee with a weight,
         Heavy as frost, and deep almost as life!

9

130   O joy! that in our embers
              Is something that doth live,
              That nature yet remembers
              What was so fugitive!
         The thought of our past years in me doth breed
135   Perpetual benediction: not indeed
         For that which is most worthy to be blest;
         Delight and liberty, the simple creed
         Of Childhood, whether busy or at rest,
         With new-fledged hope still fluttering in his breast—

---

3. I.e., playing the parts of characters with various temperaments, called "humors" by Elizabethan poets and playwrights. "Humorous stage" is a quotation from line 1 of a sonnet by Samuel Daniel (ca. 1562–1619; for some of his sonnets and other poems, see pp. 230–35).

140   Not for these I raise
        The song of thanks and praise;
But for those obstinate questionings
Of sense and outward things,
Fallings from us, vanishings;
145   Blank misgivings of a Creature
Moving about in worlds not realized,°   *seeming real*
High instincts before which our mortal Nature
Did tremble like a guilty Thing surprised;
        But for those first affections,
150   Those shadowy recollections,
        Which, be they what they may,
Are yet the fountain light of all our day,
Are yet a master light of all our seeing;
        Uphold us, cherish, and have power to make
155 Our noisy years seem moments in the being
Of the eternal Silence: truths that wake,
           To perish never;
Which neither listlessness, nor mad endeavor,
           Nor Man nor Boy,
160 Nor all that is at enmity with joy,
Can utterly abolish or destroy!
        Hence in a season of calm weather
        Though inland far we be,
Our Souls have sight of that immortal sea
165   Which brought us hither,
        Can in a moment travel thither,
And see the Children sport upon the shore,
And hear the mighty waters rolling evermore.

           10

Then sing, ye Birds, sing, sing a joyous song!
170   And let the young Lambs bound
        As to the tabor's sound!
We in thought will join your throng,
        Ye that pipe and ye that play,
        Ye that through your hearts today
175   Feel the gladness of the May!
What though the radiance which was once so bright
Be now forever taken from my sight,
        Though nothing can bring back the hour
Of splendor in the grass, of glory in the flower;
180   We will grieve not, rather find
        Strength in what remains behind;
        In the primal sympathy
        Which having been must ever be;
        In the soothing thoughts that spring
185   Out of human suffering;
        In the faith that looks through death,
In years that bring the philosophic mind.

11

And O, ye Fountains, Meadows, Hills, and Groves,
Forebode not any severing of our loves!
190   Yet in my heart of hearts I feel your might;
I only have relinquished one delight
To live beneath your more habitual sway.
I love the Brooks which down their channels fret,
Even more than when I tripped lightly as they;
195   The innocent brightness of a newborn Day
        Is lovely yet;
The clouds that gather round the setting sun
Do take a sober coloring from an eye
That hath kept watch o'er man's mortality;
200   Another race hath been, and other palms° are won.   *symbols of victory*
Thanks to the human heart by which we live,
Thanks to its tenderness, its joys, and fears,
To me the meanest° flower that blows° can give   *most ordinary / blooms*
Thoughts that do often lie too deep for tears.

1802–04   1807

I Wandered Lonely as a Cloud

I wandered lonely as a cloud
That floats on high o'er vales and hills,
When all at once I saw a crowd,
A host, of golden daffodils;
5   Beside the lake, beneath the trees,
Fluttering and dancing in the breeze.

Continuous as the stars that shine
And twinkle on the milky way,
They stretched in never-ending line
10   Along the margin of a bay:
Ten thousand saw I at a glance,
Tossing their heads in sprightly dance.

The waves beside them danced; but they
Outdid the sparkling waves in glee;
15   A poet could not but be gay,
In such a jocund° company;   *cheerful*
I gazed—and gazed—but little thought
What wealth the show to me had brought:

For oft, when on my couch I lie
20   In vacant or in pensive mood,
They flash upon that inward eye
Which is the bliss of solitude;
And then my heart with pleasure fills,
And dances with the daffodils.

1804   1807

She Was a Phantom of Delight

    She was a Phantom° of delight   *vivid image*
    When first she gleamed upon my sight;
    A lovely Apparition, sent
    To be a moment's ornament;
5   Her eyes as stars of Twilight fair,
    Like Twilight's, too, her dusky hair;
    But all things else about her drawn
    From May-time and the cheerful Dawn;
    A dancing Shape, an Image gay,
10 To haunt, to startle, and way-lay.

    I saw her upon nearer view,
    A Spirit, yet a Woman too!
    Her household motions light and free,
    And steps of virgin-liberty;
15 A countenance in which did meet
    Sweet records, promises as sweet;
    A Creature not too bright or good
    For human nature's daily food;
    For transient sorrows, simple wiles,
20 Praise, blame, love, kisses, tears, and smiles.

    And now I see with eye serene
    The very pulse of the machine;°   *organism*
    A Being breathing thoughtful breath,
    A Traveler between life and death;
25 The reason firm, the temperate will,
    Endurance, foresight, strength, and skill;
    A perfect Woman, nobly planned,
    To warn, to comfort, and command;
    And yet a Spirit still, and bright
30 With something of angelic light.

1804   1807

The World Is Too Much with Us

    The world is too much with us; late and soon,
    Getting and spending, we lay waste our powers;
    Little we see in Nature that is ours;
    We have given our hearts away, a sordid boon!°   *gift*
5 This Sea that bares her bosom to the moon,
    The winds that will be howling at all hours,
    And are up-gathered now like sleeping flowers,
    For this, for everything, we are out of tune;
    It moves us not.—Great God! I'd rather be
10 A Pagan suckled in a creed outworn;

So might I, standing on this pleasant lea,°   *open meadow*
Have glimpses that would make me less forlorn;
Have sight of Proteus rising from the sea;
Or hear old Triton blow his wreathèd horn.[4]

1802–04   1807

The Solitary Reaper

Behold her, single in the field,
Yon solitary Highland Lass!
Reaping and singing by herself;
Stop here, or gently pass!
5   Alone she cuts and binds the grain,
And sings a melancholy strain;
O listen! for the Vale° profound   *valley*
Is overflowing with the sound.

No Nightingale did ever chaunt
10   More welcome notes to weary bands
Of travelers in some shady haunt,
Among Arabian sands;
A voice so thrilling ne'er was heard
In springtime from the Cuckoo bird,
15   Breaking the silence of the seas
Among the farthest Hebrides.

Will no one tell me what she sings?—
Perhaps the plaintive numbers flow
For old, unhappy, far-off things,
20   And battles long ago;
Or is it some more humble lay,
Familiar matter of today?
Some natural sorrow, loss, or pain,
That has been, and may be again?

25   Whate'er the theme, the Maiden sang
As if her song could have no ending;
I saw her singing at her work,
And o'er the sickle bending—
I listened, motionless and still;
30   And, as I mounted up the hill,
The music in my heart I bore,
Long after it was heard no more.

1805   1807

4. In Greek mythology, Proteus, the "Old Man of the Sea," rises from the sea at midday and can be forced to read the future by anyone who holds him while he takes many frightening shapes. Triton is the son of the sea god, Neptune; the sound of his conch-shell horn calms the waves.

Surprised by Joy

Surprised by Joy—impatient as the Wind
I turned to share the transport—Oh! with whom
But thee,[5] deep buried in the silent tomb,
That spot which no vicissitude can find?
5   Love, faithful love, recalled thee to my mind—
But how could I forget thee? Through what power,
Even for the least division of an hour,
Have I been so beguiled as to be blind
To my most grievous loss!—That thought's return
10   Was the worst pang that sorrow ever bore,
Save one, one only, when I stood forlorn,
Knowing my heart's best treasure was no more;
That neither present time, nor years unborn
Could to my sight that heavenly face restore.

1813–14   1815

Mutability

From low to high doth dissolution climb,
And sink from high to low, along a scale
Of awful notes, whose concord shall not fail;
A musical but melancholy chime,
5   Which they can hear who meddle not with crime,
Nor avarice, nor over-anxious care.
Truth fails not; but her outward forms that bear
The longest date do melt like frosty rime,°   *thin coating*
That in the morning whitened hill and plain
10   And is no more; drop like the tower sublime
Of yesterday, which royally did wear
His crown of weeds, but could not even sustain
Some casual shout that broke the silent air,
Or the unimaginable touch of Time.

1821   1822

Scorn Not the Sonnet

Scorn not the sonnet; critic, you have frowned,
Mindless of its just honors; with this key
Shakespeare unlocked his heart; the melody
Of this small lute gave ease to Petrarch's[6] wound;

5. The poet's daughter Catharine, who died in   his unconsummated love for a woman he called
1812, at age four.   "Laura."
6. Italian poet (1304–1374), whose "wound" was

5 A thousand times this pipe did Tasso[7] sound;
With it Camöens soothed an exile's grief;[8]
The sonnet glittered a gay myrtle leaf
Amid the cypress with which Dante crowned
His visionary brow; a glow-worm lamp,
10 It cheered mild Spenser, called from Faeryland
To struggle through dark ways; and, when a damp°   dark mist
Fell round the path of Milton, in his hand
The thing became a trumpet; whence he blew
Soul-animating strains—alas, too few!

1827   1827

SAMUEL TAYLOR COLERIDGE
1772–1834

The Aeolian Harp[1]

Composed at Clevedon, Somersetshire

My pensive Sara![2] thy soft cheek reclined
Thus on mine arm, most soothing sweet it is
To sit beside our Cot,° our Cot o'ergrown   cottage
With white-flowered Jasmin, and the broad-leaved Myrtle,
5 (Meet° emblems they of Innocence and Love!)   appropriate
And watch the clouds, that late were rich with light,
Slow saddening round, and mark the star of eve
Serenely brilliant (such should Wisdom be)
Shine opposite! How exquisite the scents
10 Snatched from yon bean-field! and the world so hushed!
The stilly murmur of the distant Sea
Tells us of silence.

           And that simplest Lute,
Placed length-ways in the clasping casement, hark!
How by the desultory breeze caressed,
15 Like some coy maid half yielding to her lover,
It pours such sweet upbraiding, as must needs
Tempt to repeat the wrong! And now, its strings
Boldlier swept, the long sequacious° notes   uninterruptedly flowing
Over delicious surges sink and rise,
20 Such a soft floating witchery of sound
As twilight Elfins make, when they at eve
Voyage on gentle gales from Fairy-Land,
Where Melodies round honey-dropping flowers,

7. Italian poet (1544–1595).
8. Camöens (1524?–1580), Portuguese poet, was banished from the royal court.
1. The wind harp (named after Aeolus, Greek god of the winds) has a sounding board equipped with a set of strings that vibrate in response to air currents. German and English Romantic writers often presented it as a symbol of the mind.
2. Sara Fricker, whom Coleridge married in 1795. He wrote this poem during their honeymoon.

Footless and wild, like birds of Paradise,[3]
25   Nor pause, nor perch, hovering on untamed wing!
O! the one Life within us and abroad,
Which meets all motion and becomes its soul,
A light in sound, a sound-like power in light,
Rhythm in all thought, and joyance everywhere—
30   Methinks, It should have been impossible
Not to love all things in a world so filled;
Where the breeze warbles, and the mute still air
Is Music slumbering on her instrument.

And thus, my Love! as on the midway slope
35   Of yonder hill I stretch my limbs at noon,
Whilst through my half-closed eyelids I behold
The sunbeams dance, like diamonds, on the main,
And tranquil muse upon tranquility:
Full many a thought uncalled and undetained,
40   And many idle flitting phantasies,
Traverse my indolent and passive brain,
As wild and various as the random gales
That swell and flutter on this subject Lute!

And what if all of animated nature
45   Be but organic Harps diversely framed,
That tremble into thought, as o'er them sweeps
Plastic and vast, one intellectual breeze,
At once the Soul of each, and God of all?

But thy more serious eye a mild reproof
50   Darts, O belovèd Woman! nor such thoughts
Dim and unhallowed dost thou not reject,
And biddest me walk humbly with my God.
Meek Daughter in the family of Christ!
Well hast thou said and holily dispraised
55   These shapings of the unregenerate mind;
Bubbles that glitter as they rise and break
On vain Philosophy's aye-babbling spring.
For never guiltless may I speak of him,
The Incomprehensible! save when with awe
60   I praise him, and with Faith that inly *feels*;
Who with his saving mercies healèd me,
A sinful and most miserable man,
Wildered and dark, and gave me to possess
Peace, and this Cot, and thee, heart-honored Maid!

1795   1796, 1817

---

3. Bright-plumaged birds of New Guinea and nearby islands; mistakenly supposed to have no feet and to spend their lives on the wing.

This Lime-Tree Bower My Prison

In the June of 1797, some long-expected Friends paid a visit to the author's cottage and on the morning of their arrival, he met with an accident, which disabled him from walking during the whole time of their stay. One evening, when they had left him for a few hours he composed the following lines in the garden bower.[4]

Well, they are gone, and here must I remain,
This lime-tree bower my prison! I have lost
Beauties and feelings, such as would have been
Most sweet to my remembrance even when age
5   Had dimmed mine eyes to blindness! They, meanwhile,
Friends, whom I never more may meet again,
On springy[5] heath, along the hill-top edge,
Wander in gladness, and wind down, perchance,
To that still roaring dell, of which I told;
10 The roaring dell, o'erwooded, narrow deep,
And only speckled by the mid-day sun;
Where its slim trunk the ash from rock to rock
Flings arching like a bridge;—that branchless ash,
Unsunned and damp, whose few poor yellow leaves
15 Ne'er tremble in the gale, yet tremble still,
Fanned by the water-fall! and there my friends
Behold the dark green file of long lank weeds,
That all at once (a most fantastic sight!)
Still nod and drip beneath the dripping edge
20 Of the blue clay-stone.

                  Now, my friends emerge
Beneath the wide wide Heaven—and view again
The many-steepled tract magnificent
Of hilly fields and meadows, and the sea,
With some fair bark, perhaps, whose sails light up
25 The slip of smooth clear blue betwixt two Isles
Of purple shadow! Yes! they wander on
In gladness all; but thou, methinks, most glad,
My gentle-hearted Charles! for thou hast pined
And hungered after Nature,[6] many a year,
30 In the great City pent, winning thy way
With sad yet patient soul, through evil and pain
And strange calamity![7] Ah! slowly sink
Behind the western ridge, thou glorious sun!
Shine in the slant beams of the sinking orb,

---

4. In fact, in July 1797, Coleridge's wife, Sara, accidentally spilled boiling milk on his foot during a visit from the poet William Wordsworth (1770–1850; see pp. 763–805); Wordsworth's sister, Dorothy; and the essayist and critic Charles Lamb, to whom the earliest printed text of this poem was "Addressed."

5. "*Elastic*, I mean" [Coleridge's note].
6. In fact, Lamb, a devoted Londoner, considered nature "dead."
7. About ten months earlier, Lamb's sister, Mary, in a fit of insanity, had stabbed their mother to death.

35   Ye purple heath-flowers! richlier burn, ye clouds!
     Live in the yellow light, ye distant groves!
     And kindle, thou blue ocean! So my Friend
     Struck with deep joy may stand, as I have stood,
     Silent with swimming sense; yea, gazing round
40   On the wide landscape, gaze till all doth seem
     Less gross than bodily; and of such hues
     As veil the Almighty Spirit, when yet he makes
     Spirits perceive his presence.

                                        A delight
     Comes sudden on my heart, and I am glad
45   As I myself were there! Nor in this bower,
     This little lime-tree bower, have I not marked
     Much that has soothed me. Pale beneath the blaze
     Hung the transparent foliage; and I watched
     Some broad and sunny leaf, and loved to see
50   The shadow of the leaf and stem above
     Dappling its sunshine! And that walnut-tree
     Was richly tinged, and a deep radiance lay
     Full on the ancient ivy, which usurps
     Those fronting elms, and now, with blackest mass
55   Makes their dark branches gleam a lighter hue
     Through the late twilight: and though now the bat
     Wheels silent by, and not a swallow twitters,
     Yet still the solitary humble bee
     Sings in the bean-flower! Henceforth, I shall know
60   That Nature ne'er deserts the wise and pure;
     No plot so narrow, be but Nature there,
     No waste so vacant, but may well employ
     Each faculty of sense, and keep the heart
     Awake to Love and Beauty! and sometimes
65   'Tis well to be bereft of promised good,
     That we may lift the Soul, and contemplate
     With lively joy the joys we cannot share.
     My gentle-hearted Charles! when the last rook
     Beat its straight path along the dusky air
70   Homewards, I blessed it! deeming its black wing
     (Now a dim speck, now vanishing in light)
     Had crossed the mighty orb's dilated glory,
     While thou stood'st gazing; or when all was still,
     Flew creeking o'er thy head, and had a charm
75   For thee, my gentle-hearted Charles, to whom
     No sound is dissonant which tells of Life.

1797   1800

Kubla Khan[8]

Or a Vision in a Dream. A Fragment

In Xanadu did Kubla Khan
A stately pleasure dome decree:
Where Alph, the sacred river, ran
Through caverns measureless to man
5   Down to a sunless sea.
So twice five miles of fertile ground
With walls and towers were girdled round:
And there were gardens bright with sinuous° rills,°   *curving / streams*
Where blossomed many an incense-bearing tree;
10 And here were forests ancient as the hills,
Enfolding sunny spots of greenery.

But oh! that deep romantic chasm which slanted
Down the green hill athwart a cedarn cover!
A savage place! as holy and enchanted
15 As e'er beneath a waning moon was haunted
By woman wailing for her demon lover!
And from this chasm, with ceaseless turmoil seething,
As if this earth in fast thick pants were breathing,
A mighty fountain momently was forced:
20 Amid whose swift half-intermitted burst
Huge fragments vaulted like rebounding hail,
Or chaffy grain beneath the thresher's flail:
And 'mid these dancing rocks at once and ever
It flung up momently the sacred river.
25 Five miles meandering with a mazy motion
Through wood and dale the sacred river ran,
Then reached the caverns measureless to man,
And sank in tumult to a lifeless ocean:
And 'mid this tumult Kubla heard from far
30 Ancestral voices prophesying war!

8. The first *khan*, or ruler, of the Mongol dynasty, in thirteenth-century China. The topography and place-names are fictitious. In a prefatory note to the poem, Coleridge gave the following background: "In the summer of the year 1797, the author, then in ill health, had retired to a lonely farmhouse between Porlock and Linton, on the Exmoor confines of Somerset and Devonshire. In consequence of a slight indisposition, an anodyne had been prescribed, from the effects of which he fell asleep in his chair at the moment that he was reading the following sentence, or words of the same substance, in *Purchas's Pilgrimage*: 'Here the Khan Kubla commanded a palace to be built, and a stately garden thereunto. And thus ten miles of fertile ground were inclosed with a wall.' The author continued for about three hours in a profound sleep, at least of the external sense, during which time he has the most vivid confidence that he could not have composed less than from two to three hundred lines; if that indeed can be called composition in which all the images rose up before him as *things*, with a parallel production of the correspondent expressions, without any sensation or consciousness of effort. On awaking he appeared to himself to have a distinct recollection of the whole, and taking his pen, ink, and paper, instantly and eagerly wrote down the lines that are here preserved. At this moment he was unfortunately called out by a person on business from Porlock, and detained by him above an hour, and on his return to his room, found, to his no small surprise and mortification, that though he still retained some vague and dim recollection of the general purport of the vision, yet, with the exception of some eight or ten scattered lines and images, all the rest had passed away like the images on the surface of a stream into which a stone has been cast, but, alas! without the after restoration of the latter!"

The shadow of the dome of pleasure
Floated midway on the waves;
Where was heard the mingled measure
From the fountain and the caves.
35 It was a miracle of rare device,
A sunny pleasure dome with caves of ice!

A damsel with a dulcimer[9]
In a vision once I saw:
It was an Abyssinian maid,
40 And on her dulcimer she played,
Singing of Mount Abora.
Could I revive within me
Her symphony and song,
To such a deep delight 'twould win me,
45 That with music loud and long,
I would build that dome in air,
That sunny dome! those caves of ice!
And all who heard should see them there,
And all should cry, Beware! Beware!
50 His flashing eyes, his floating hair!
Weave a circle round him thrice,
And close your eyes with holy dread,
For he on honey-dew hath fed,
And drunk the milk of Paradise.

1797–98   1816

Frost at Midnight

The Frost performs its secret ministry,
Unhelped by any wind. The owlet's cry
Came loud—and hark, again! loud as before.
The inmates of my cottage, all at rest,
5 Have left me to that solitude, which suits
Abstruser musings: save that at my side
My cradled infant[1] slumbers peacefully.
'Tis calm indeed! so calm, that it disturbs
And vexes meditation with its strange
10 And extreme silentness. Sea, hill, and wood,
This populous village! Sea, and hill, and wood,
With all the numberless goings-on of life,
Inaudible as dreams! the thin blue flame
Lies on my low-burnt fire, and quivers not;
15 Only that film,[2] which fluttered on the grate,
Still flutters there, the sole unquiet thing.
Methinks its motion in this hush of nature

9. A harplike instrument.
1. Coleridge's eldest son, Hartley.
2. Bits of soot fluttering in a fireplace; in folklore,

said to foretell the arrival of an unexpected guest,
and hence called "strangers" (lines 26, 41).

Gives it dim sympathies with me who live,
Making it a companionable form,
20   Whose puny flaps and freaks the idling Spirit
By its own moods interprets, everywhere
Echo or mirror seeking of itself,
And makes a toy of Thought.

                        But O! how oft,
How oft, at school, with most believing mind,
25   Presageful,° have I gazed upon the bars,   *foretelling*
To watch that fluttering *stranger!* and as oft
With unclosed lids, already had I dreamt
Of my sweet birthplace, and the old church tower,
Whose bells, the poor man's only music, rang
30   From morn to evening, all the hot Fair-day,[3]
So sweetly, that they stirred and haunted me
With a wild pleasure, falling on mine ear
Most like articulate sounds of things to come!
So gazed I, till the soothing things, I dreamt,
35   Lulled me to sleep, and sleep prolonged my dreams!
And so I brooded all the following morn,
Awed by the stern preceptor's° face, mine eye   *schoolmaster's*
Fixed with mock study on my swimming book:[4]
Save if the door half opened, and I snatched
40   A hasty glance, and still my heart leaped up,
For still I hoped to see the *stranger's* face,
Townsman, or aunt, or sister more beloved,
My playmate when we both were clothed alike![5]

    Dear Babe, that sleepest cradled by my side,
45   Whose gentle breathings, heard in this deep calm,
Fill up the interspersèd vacancies
And momentary pauses of the thought!
My babe so beautiful! it thrills my heart
With tender gladness, thus to look at thee,
50   And think that thou shalt learn far other lore,
And in far other scenes! For I was reared
In the great city, pent 'mid cloisters dim,
And saw nought lovely but the sky and stars.
But *thou,* my babe! shalt wander like a breeze
55   By lakes and sandy shores, beneath the crags
Of ancient mountain, and beneath the clouds,
Which image in their bulk both lakes and shores
And mountain crags: so shalt thou see and hear
The lovely shapes and sounds intelligible
60   Of that eternal language, which thy God
Utters, who from eternity doth teach
Himself in all, and all things in himself.
Great universal Teacher! he shall mold
Thy spirit, and by giving make it ask.

3. Market day, often a time of festivities.   5. In early childhood, when boys and girls wore
4. I.e., seen unclearly because of emotion.   the same kind of infants' clothing.

65 Therefore all seasons shall be sweet to thee,
    Whether the summer clothe the general° earth   *generative, vernal*
    With greenness, or the redbreast sit and sing
    Betwixt the tufts of snow on the bare branch
    Of mossy apple tree, while the nigh thatch
70 Smokes in the sun-thaw; whether the eave-drops fall
    Heard only in the trances of the blast,
    Or if the secret ministry of frost
    Shall hang them up in silent icicles,
    Quietly shining to the quiet Moon.

1798   1798

The Rime of the Ancient Mariner

IN SEVEN PARTS

> *Facile credo, plures esse Naturas invisibiles quam visibiles in rerum*
> *universitate. Sed horum [sic] omnium familiam quis nobis enarrabit?*
> *et gradus et cognationes et discrimina et singulorum munera? Quid*
> *agunt? quae loca habitant? Harum rerum notitiam semper ambivit*
> *ingenium humanum, nunquam attigit. Juvat, interea, non diffiteor,*
> *quandoque in animo, in tabulâ, majoris et melioris mundi imaginem*
> *contemplari: ne mens assuefacta hodiernae vitae minutiis se contra-*
> *hat nimis, et tota subsidat in pusillas cogitationes. Sed veritati interea*
> *invigilandum est, modusque servandus, ut certa ab incertis, diem a*
> *nocte, distinguamus.*

—T. BURNET[6]

Part I

An ancient Mariner   It is an ancient Mariner
meeteth three Gal-   And he stoppeth one of three.
lants bidden to a   —"By thy long gray beard and glittering eye,
wedding feast, and   Now wherefore stopp'st thou me?
detaineth one.

                        The Bridegroom's doors are opened wide,   5
                        And I am next of kin;
                        The guests are met, the feast is set:
                        May'st hear the merry din."

                        He holds him with his skinny hand,
                        "There was a ship," quoth he.   10
                        "Hold off! unhand me, graybeard loon!"
                        Eftsoons° his hand dropped he.   *straightway*

6. Thomas Burnet, seventeenth-century English theologian, from his *Archaeologiae Philosophiae:* "I can easily believe that there are more invisible than visible beings in the universe. But of their families, degrees, connections, distinctions, and functions, who shall tell us? How do they act? Where are they found? About such matters the human mind has always circled without attaining knowledge. Yet I do not doubt that sometimes it is well for the soul to contemplate as in a picture the image of a larger and better world, lest the mind, habituated to the small concerns of daily life, limit itself too much and sink entirely into trivial thinking. But meanwhile we must be on watch for the truth, avoiding extremes, so that we may distinguish certain from uncertain, day from night."

The Wedding Guest
is spellbound by the
eye of the old seafar-
ing man, and con-
strained to hear his
tale.

He holds him with his glittering eye—
The Wedding Guest stood still,
And listens like a three years' child:
The Mariner hath his will.   15

The Wedding Guest sat on a stone:
He cannot choose but hear;
And thus spake on that ancient man,
The bright-eyed Mariner.   20

"The ship was cheered, the harbor cleared,
Merrily did we drop
Below the kirk,° below the hill,   church
Below the lighthouse top.

The Mariner tells
how the ship sailed
southward with a
good wind and fair
weather, till it
reached the line.

The Sun came up upon the left,   25
Out of the sea came he!
And he shone bright, and on the right
Went down into the sea.

Higher and higher every day,
Till over the mast at noon—"   30
The Wedding Guest here beat his breast,
For he heard the loud bassoon.

The Wedding Guest
heareth the bridal
music; but the Mari-
ner continueth his
tale.

The bride hath paced into the hall,
Red as a rose is she;
Nodding their heads before her goes   35
The merry minstrelsy.

The Wedding Guest he beat his breast,
Yet he cannot choose but hear;
And thus spake on that ancient man,
The bright-eyed Mariner.   40

The ship driven by a
storm toward the
South Pole.

"And now the STORM-BLAST came, and he
Was tyrannous and strong;
He struck with his o'ertaking wings,
And chased us south along.

With sloping masts and dipping prow,   45
As who pursued with yell and blow
Still treads the shadow of his foe,
And forward bends his head,
The ship drove fast, loud roared the blast,
And southward aye we fled.   50

And now there came both mist and snow,
And it grew wondrous cold:
And ice, mast-high, came floating by,
As green as emerald.

The land of ice, and
of fearful sounds
where no living thing
was to be seen.
And through the drifts the snowy clifts°   *cliffs*   55
Did send a dismal sheen:
Nor shapes of men nor beasts we ken—
The ice was all between.

The ice was here, the ice was there,
The ice was all around;   60
It cracked and growled, and roared and howled,
Like noises in a swound!°   *swoon*

Till a great sea bird,
called the Albatross,
came through the
snow-fog, and was
received with great
joy and hospitality.
At length did cross an Albatross,
Thorough the fog it came;
As if it had been a Christian soul,   65
We hailed it in God's name.

It ate the food it ne'er had eat,
And round and round it flew.
The ice did split with a thunder-fit;
The helmsman steered us through!   70

And lo! the Albatross
proveth a bird of good
omen, and followeth
the ship as it returned
northward through
fog and floating ice.
And a good south wind sprung up behind;
The Albatross did follow,
And every day, for food or play,
Came to the mariners' hollo!

In mist or cloud, on mast or shroud,[7]   75
It perched for vespers° nine;   *evenings*
Whiles all the night, through fog-smoke white,
Glimmered the white Moon-shine."

The ancient Mariner
inhospitably killeth
the pious bird of good
omen.
"God save thee, ancient Mariner!
From the fiends, that plague thee thus!—   80
Why look'st thou so?"—With my crossbow
I shot the ALBATROSS.

Part II

The Sun now rose upon the right:
Out of the sea came he,
Still hid in mist, and on the left   85
Went down into the sea.

And the good south wind still blew behind,
But no sweet bird did follow,
Nor any day for food or play
Came to the mariners' hollo!   90

7. Rope supporting a mast.

His shipmates cry out against the ancient Mariner, for killing the bird of good luck.

And I had done a hellish thing,
And it would work 'em woe:
For all averred, I had killed the bird
That made the breeze to blow.
Ah wretch! said they, the bird to slay,   95
That made the breeze to blow!

But when the fog cleared off, they justify the same, and thus make themselves accomplices in the crime.

Nor dim nor red, like God's own head,
The glorious Sun uprist:°   *arose*
Then all averred, I had killed the bird
That brought the fog and mist.   100
'Twas right, said they, such birds to slay,
That bring the fog and mist.

The fair breeze continues; the ship enters the Pacific Ocean, and sails northward, even till it reaches the Line.°

The fair breeze blew, the white foam flew,
The furrow followed free;
We were the first that ever burst   105
Into that silent sea.   *equator*

The ship hath been suddenly becalmed.

Down dropped the breeze, the sails dropped down,
'Twas sad as sad could be;
And we did speak only to break
The silence of the sea!   110

All in a hot and copper sky,
The bloody Sun, at noon,
Right up above the mast did stand,
No bigger than the Moon.

Day after day, day after day,   115
We stuck, nor breath nor motion;
As idle as a painted ship
Upon a painted ocean.

And the Albatross begins to be avenged.

Water, water, everywhere,
And all the boards did shrink;   120
Water, water, everywhere,
Nor any drop to drink.

The very deep did rot: O Christ!
That ever this should be!
Yea, slimy things did crawl with legs   125
Upon the slimy sea.

About, about, in reel and rout
The death-fires[8] danced at night;
The water, like a witch's oils,
Burnt green, and blue and white.   130

---

8. Either St. Elmo's fire—light from atmospheric electricity on a ship's rigging (regarded as a portent of disaster)—or *ignis fatuus,* "foolish fire" (Latin) caused by the decomposition of putrescent matter in the ocean.

And some in dreams assurèd were

A Spirit had followed them; one of the invisible inhabitants of this planet, neither departed souls nor angels; concerning whom the learned Jew, Josephus, and the Platonic Constantinopolitan, Michael Psellus, may be consulted. They are very numerous, and there is no climate or element without one or more.

Of the Spirit that plagued us so;
Nine fathom deep he had followed us
From the land of mist and snow.

And every tongue, through utter drought,   135
Was withered at the root;
We could not speak, no more than if
We had been choked with soot.

The shipmates, in their sore distress, would fain throw the whole guilt on the ancient Mariner: in sign whereof they hang the dead sea bird round his neck.

Ah! well-a-day! what evil looks
Had I from old and young!   140
Instead of the cross, the Albatross
About my neck was hung.

Part III

There passed a weary time. Each throat
Was parched, and glazed each eye.
A weary time! a weary time!   145
How glazed each weary eye,

The ancient Mariner beholdeth a sign in the element afar off.

When looking westward, I beheld
A something in the sky.

At first it seemed a little speck,
And then it seemed a mist;   150
It moved and moved, and took at last
A certain shape, I wist.°   *knew*

A speck, a mist, a shape, I wist!
And still it neared and neared:
As if it dodged a water sprite,   155
It plunged and tacked and veered.

At its nearer approach, it seemeth him to be a ship; and at a dear ransom he freeth his speech from the bonds of thirst.

With throats unslaked, with black lips baked,
We could nor laugh nor wail;
Through utter drought all dumb we stood!
I bit my arm, I sucked the blood,   160
And cried, A sail! a sail!

With throats unslaked, with black lips baked,
Agape they heard me call:

A flash of joy;

Gramercy!° they for joy did grin,   *thank heavens!*
And all at once their breath drew in,   165
As they were drinking all.

And horror follows. For can it be a ship that comes onward without wind or tide?

See! see! (I cried) she tacks no more!
Hither to work us weal;°   *benefit*
Without a breeze, without a tide,
She steadies with upright keel!   170

The western wave was all aflame.
The day was well nigh done!
Almost upon the western wave
Rested the broad bright Sun;
When that strange shape drove suddenly   175
Betwixt us and the Sun.

It seemeth him but the skeleton of a ship.

And straight the Sun was flecked with bars,
(Heaven's Mother send us grace!)
As if through a dungeon grate he peered
With broad and burning face.   180

And its ribs are seen as bars on the face of the setting Sun.

Alas! (thought I, and my heart beat loud)
How fast she nears and nears!
Are those *her* sails that glance in the Sun,
Like restless gossameres?°   *cobwebs*

The Specter-Woman and her Deathmate, and no other on board the skeleton ship.

Are those *her* ribs through which the Sun   185
Did peer, as through a grate?
And is that Woman all her crew?
Is that a DEATH? and are there two?
Is DEATH that woman's mate?

Like vessel, like crew!

Her lips were red, *her* looks were free,   190
Her locks were yellow as gold:
Her skin was as white as leprosy,
The Nightmare LIFE-IN-DEATH was she,
Who thicks man's blood with cold.

Death and Life-in-Death have diced for the ship's crew and she (the latter) winneth the ancient Mariner.

The naked hulk alongside came,   195
And the twain were casting dice;
"The game is done! I've won! I've won!"
Quoth she, and whistles thrice.

No twilight within the courts of the Sun.

The Sun's rim dips; the stars rush out:
At one stride comes the dark;   200
With far-heard whisper, o'er the sea,
Off shot the specter-bark.

At the rising of the Moon,

We listened and looked sideways up!
Fear at my heart, as at a cup,
My lifeblood seemed to sip!   205
The stars were dim, and thick the night,
The steersman's face by his lamp gleamed white;
From the sails the dew did drip—
Till clomb° above the eastern bar   *climbed*
The hornèd Moon, with one bright star   210
Within the nether tip.

One after another,

One after one, by the star-dogged Moon,
Too quick for groan or sigh,

Each turned his face with ghastly pang,
And cursed me with his eye. 215

*His shipmates drop
down dead.*

Four times fifty living men,
(And I heard nor sigh nor groan)
With heavy thump, a lifeless lump,
They dropped down one by one.

*But Life-in-Death
begins her work on
the ancient Mariner.*

The souls did from their bodies fly— 220
They fled to bliss or woe!
And every soul, it passed me by,
Like the whizz of my cross-bow!

Part IV

*The Wedding Guest
feareth that a Spirit is
talking to him;*

"I fear thee, ancient Mariner!
I fear thy skinny hand! 225
And thou art long, and lank, and brown,
As is the ribbed sea-sand.

I fear thee and thy glittering eye,
And thy skinny hand, so brown."—

*But the ancient Mar-
iner assureth him of
his bodily life, and
proceedeth to relate
his horrible penance.*

Fear not, fear not, thou Wedding Guest! 230
This body dropped not down.

Alone, alone, all, all alone,
Alone on a wide wide sea!
And never a saint took pity on
My soul in agony. 235

*He despiseth the
creatures of the calm,*

The many men, so beautiful!
And they all dead did lie:
And a thousand thousand slimy things
Lived on; and so did I.

*And envieth that they
should live, and so
many lie dead.*

I looked upon the rotting sea, 240
And drew my eyes away;
I looked upon the rotting deck,
And there the dead men lay.

I looked to heaven, and tried to pray;
But or ever a prayer had gushed, 245
A wicked whisper came, and made
My heart as dry as dust.

I closed my lids, and kept them close,
And the balls like pulses beat,
For the sky and the sea, and the sea and the sky 250
Lay like a load on my weary eye,
And the dead were at my feet.

But the curse liveth for him in the eye of the dead men.

The cold sweat melted from their limbs,
Nor rot nor reek did they:
The look with which they looked on me   255
Had never passed away.

An orphan's curse would drag to hell
A spirit from on high;
But oh! more horrible than that
Is the curse in a dead man's eye!   260
Seven days, seven nights, I saw that curse,
And yet I could not die.

The moving Moon went up the sky,
And nowhere did abide:

In his loneliness and fixedness he yearneth towards the journeying Moon, and the stars that still sojourn, yet still move onward; and everywhere the blue sky belongs to them, and is their appointed rest, and their native country and their own natural homes, which they enter unannounced, as lords that are certainly expected and yet there is a silent joy at their arrival.

Softly she was going up,   265
And a star or two beside—

Her beams bemocked the sultry main,
Like April hoar-frost spread;
But where the ship's huge shadow lay,
The charmèd water burnt alway   270
A still and awful red.

By the light of the Moon he beholdeth God's creatures of the great calm.

Beyond the shadow of the ship,
I watched the water snakes:
They moved in tracks of shining white,
And when they reared, the elfish light   275
Fell off in hoary° flakes.   ° *gray or white*

Within the shadow of the ship
I watched their rich attire:
Blue, glossy green, and velvet black,
They coiled and swam; and every track   280
Was a flash of golden fire.

Their beauty and their happiness.

O happy living things! no tongue
Their beauty might declare:

He blesseth them in his heart.

A spring of love gushed from my heart,
And I blessed them unaware: 285
Sure my kind saint took pity on me,
And I blessed them unaware.

The spell begins to break.

The self-same moment I could pray;
And from my neck so free
The Albatross fell off, and sank   290
Like lead into the sea.

Part V

Oh sleep! it is a gentle thing,
Beloved from pole to pole!

To Mary Queen the praise be given!
She sent the gentle sleep from Heaven,   295
That slid into my soul.

*By grace of the holy
Mother, the ancient
Mariner is refreshed
with rain.*

The silly° buckets on the deck,   *lowly; harmless*
That had so long remained,
I dreamt that they were filled with dew;
And when I awoke, it rained.   300

My lips were wet, my throat was cold,
My garments all were dank;
Sure I had drunken in my dreams,
And still my body drank.

I moved, and could not feel my limbs: 305
I was so light—almost
I thought that I had died in sleep,
And was a blessèd ghost.

*He heareth sounds
and seeth strange
sights and commo-
tions in the sky and
the element.*

And soon I heard a roaring wind:
It did not come anear;   310
But with its sound it shook the sails,
That were so thin and sere.°   *dry; withered*

The upper air burst into life!
And a hundred fire-flags sheen,[9]
To and fro they were hurried about!   315
And to and fro, and in and out,
The wan stars danced between.

And the coming wind did roar more loud,
And the sails did sigh like sedge;[1]
And the rain poured down from one black cloud;   320
The Moon was at its edge.

The thick black cloud was cleft, and still
The Moon was at its side:
Like waters shot from some high crag,
The lightning fell with never a jag,   325
A river steep and wide.

*The bodies of the
ship's crew are
inspirited, and the
ship moves on;*

The loud wind never reached the ship,
Yet now the ship moved on!
Beneath the lightning and the Moon
The dead men gave a groan.   330

They groaned, they stirred, they all uprose,
Nor spake, nor moved their eyes;

---

9. Shone. The "fire-flags" may be St. Elmo's fire   ning.
(see note 8, p. 815), the Southern Lights, or light-   1. Rushlike plants bordering streams and lakes.

It had been strange, even in a dream,
To have seen those dead men rise.

The helmsman steered, the ship moved on;   335
Yet never a breeze up-blew;
The mariners all 'gan work the ropes,
Where they were wont to do;
They raised their limbs like lifeless tools—
We were a ghastly crew.   340

The body of my brother's son
Stood by me, knee to knee:
The body and I pulled at one rope,
But he said nought to me.

But not by the souls
of the men, nor by
demons of earth or
middle air, but by a
blessèd troop of
angelic spirits, sent
down by the invoca-
tion of the guardian
saint.

"I fear thee, ancient Mariner!"   345
Be calm, thou Wedding Guest!
'Twas not those souls that fled in pain,
Which to their corses° came again,   *corpses*
But a troop of spirits blest:

For when it dawned—they dropped their arms,   350
And clustered round the mast;
Sweet sounds rose slowly through their mouths,
And from their bodies passed.

Around, around, flew each sweet sound,
Then darted to the Sun;   355
Slowly the sounds came back again,
Now mixed, now one by one.

Sometimes a-dropping from the sky
I heard the sky-lark sing;
Sometimes all little birds that are,   360
How they seemed to fill the sea and air
With their sweet jargoning!°   *warbling*

And now 'twas like all instruments,
Now like a lonely flute;
And now it is an angel's song,   365
That makes the heavens be mute.

It ceased; yet still the sails made on
A pleasant noise till noon,
A noise like of a hidden brook
In the leafy month of June,   370
That to the sleeping woods all night
Singeth a quiet tune.

Till noon we quietly sailed on,
Yet never a breeze did breathe:

Slowly and smoothly went the ship,   375
Moved onward from beneath.

The lonesome Spirit Under the keel nine fathom deep,
from the South Pole From the land of mist and snow,
carries on the ship as The spirit slid: and it was he
far as the Line, in That made the ship to go.   380
obedience to the The sails at noon left off their tune,
angelic troop, but
still requireth And the ship stood still also.
vengeance.

The Sun, right up above the mast,
Had fixed her to the ocean:
But in a minute she 'gan stir,   385
With a short uneasy motion—
Backwards and forwards half her length
With a short uneasy motion.

Then like a pawing horse let go,
She made a sudden bound: 390
It flung the blood into my head,
And I fell down in a swound.

The Polar Spirit's fel- How long in that same fit I lay,
low demons, the I have not² to declare;
invisible inhabitants
of the element, take But ere my living life returned,   395
part in his wrong; I heard and in my soul discerned
and two of them Two voices in the air.
relate, one to the
other, that penance
long and heavy for "Is it he?" quoth one, "Is this the man?
the ancient Mariner By him who died on cross,
hath been accorded With his cruel bow he laid full low   400
to the Polar Spirit, The harmless Albatross.
who returneth south-
ward.
The spirit who bideth by himself
In the land of mist and snow,
He loved the bird that loved the man
Who shot him with his bow."   405

The other was a softer voice,
As soft as honey-dew:
Quoth he, "The man hath penance done,
And penance more will do."

Part VI

FIRST VOICE

"But tell me, tell me! speak again,   410
Thy soft response renewing—
What makes that ship drive on so fast?
What is the ocean doing?"

2. I.e., have not the knowledge.

SECOND VOICE

"Still as a slave before his lord,
The ocean hath no blast;   415
His great bright eye most silently
Up to the Moon is cast—

If he may know which way to go;
For she guides him smooth or grim.
See, brother, see! how graciously   420
She looketh down on him."

FIRST VOICE

The Mariner hath   "But why drives on that ship so fast,
been cast into a   Without or wave or wind?"
trance; for the angelic
power causeth the
vessel to drive north-
ward faster than
human life could
endure.

SECOND VOICE

"The air is cut away before,
And closes from behind.   425

Fly, brother, fly! more high, more high!
Or we shall be belated:
For slow and slow that ship will go,
When the Mariner's trance is abated."

The supernatural   I woke, and we were sailing on   430
motion is retarded;   As in a gentle weather:
the Mariner awakes,   'Twas night, calm night, the moon was high;
and his penance   The dead men stood together.
begins anew.

All stood together on the deck,
For a charnel-dungeon fitter: 435
All fixed on me their stony eyes,
That in the Moon did glitter.

The pang, the curse, with which they died,
Had never passed away:
I could not draw my eyes from theirs,   440
Nor turn them up to pray.

The curse is finally   And now this spell was snapped: once more
expiated.   I viewed the ocean green,
And looked far forth, yet little saw
Of what had else been seen—   445

Like one, that on a lonesome road
Doth walk in fear and dread,
And having once turned round walks on,
And turns no more his head;
Because he knows, a frightful fiend   450
Doth close behind him tread.

But soon there breathed a wind on me,
Nor sound nor motion made:
Its path was not upon the sea,
In ripple or in shade.   455

It raised my hair, it fanned my cheek
Like a meadow-gale of spring—
It mingled strangely with my fears,
Yet it felt like a welcoming.

Swiftly, swiftly flew the ship,   460
Yet she sailed softly too:
Sweetly, sweetly blew the breeze—
On me alone it blew.

And the ancient Mar-
iner beholdeth his
native country.

Oh! dream of joy! is this indeed
The lighthouse top I see?   465
Is this the hill? is this the kirk?
Is this mine own countree?

We drifted o'er the harbor-bar,
And I with sobs did pray—
O let me be awake, my God   470
Or let me sleep alway.

The harbor-bay was clear as glass,
So smoothly it was strewn!
And on the bay the moonlight lay,
And the shadow of the Moon.   475

The rock shone bright, the kirk no less,
That stands above the rock:
The moonlight steeped in silentness
The steady weathercock.

And the bay was white with silent light,   480
Till rising from the same,

The angelic spirits
leave the dead bodies,

Full many shapes, that shadows were,
In crimson colors came.

A little distance from the prow
Those crimson shadows were: 485

And appear in their
own forms of light.

I turned my eyes upon the deck—
Oh, Christ! what saw I there!

Each corse lay flat, lifeless and flat,
And, by the holy rood!°   *cross of Christ*
A man all light, a seraph°-man,   *angel-like* 490
On every corse there stood.

This seraph-band, each waved his hand:
It was a heavenly sight!

They stood as signals to the land,
Each one a lovely light;   495

This seraph-band, each waved his hand,
No voice did they impart—
No voice; but oh! the silence sank
Like music on my heart.

But soon I heard the dash of oars,   500
I heard the Pilot's cheer;
My head was turned perforce away
And I saw a boat appear.

The Pilot and the Pilot's boy,
I heard them coming fast: 505
Dear Lord in Heaven! it was a joy
The dead men could not blast.

I saw a third—I heard his voice:
It is the Hermit good!
He singeth loud his godly hymns   510
That he makes in the wood.
He'll shrieve[3] my soul, he'll wash away
The Albatross's blood.

Part VII

The Hermit of the Wood.

This Hermit good lives in that wood
Which slopes down to the sea.   515
How loudly his sweet voice he rears!
He loves to talk with marineres
That come from a far countree.

He kneels at morn, and noon, and eve—
He hath a cushion plump: 520
It is the moss that wholly hides
The rotted old oak stump.

The skiff-boat neared: I heard them talk,
"Why, this is strange, I trow!
Where are those lights so many and fair,   525
That signal made but now?"

Approacheth the ship with wonder.

"Strange, by my faith!" the Hermit said—
"And they answered not our cheer!
The planks looked warped! and see those sails,
How thin they are and sere!   530

3. Set free from sin.

I never saw aught like to them,
Unless perchance it were

Brown skeletons of leaves that lag
My forest-brook along;
When the ivy tod° is heavy with snow,   *bushy clump*   535
And the owlet whoops to the wolf below,
That eats the she-wolf's young."

"Dear Lord! it hath a fiendish look,"
The Pilot made reply,
"I am a-feared"—"Push on, push on!"   540
Said the Hermit cheerily.

The boat came closer to the ship,
But I nor spake nor stirred;
The boat came close beneath the ship,
And straight a sound was heard.   545

The ship suddenly sinketh.

Under the water it rumbled on,
Still louder and more dread:
It reached the ship, it split the bay;
The ship went down like lead.

The ancient Mariner is saved in the Pilot's boat.

Stunned by that loud and dreadful sound,   550
Which sky and ocean smote,
Like one that hath been seven days drowned
My body lay afloat;
But swift as dreams, myself I found
Within the Pilot's boat.   555

Upon the whirl, where sank the ship,
The boat spun round and round;
And all was still, save that the hill
Was telling of the sound.

I moved my lips—the Pilot shrieked   560
And fell down in a fit;
The holy Hermit raised his eyes,
And prayed where he did sit.

I took the oars: the Pilot's boy,
Who now doth crazy go,   565
Laughed loud and long, and all the while
His eyes went to and fro.
"Ha! ha!" quoth he, "full plain I see,
The Devil knows how to row."

And now, all in my own countree,   570
I stood on the firm land!
The Hermit stepped forth from the boat,
And scarcely he could stand.

*The ancient Mariner
earnestly entreateth
the Hermit to shrieve
him; and the penance
of life falls on him.*

"O shrieve me, shrieve me, holy man!"
The Hermit crossed[4] his brow.   575
"Say quick," quoth he, "I bid thee say—
What manner of man art thou?"

Forthwith this frame of mine was wrenched
With a woeful agony,
Which forced me to begin my tale;   580
And then it left me free.

*And ever and anon
throughout his future
life an agony con-
straineth him to
travel from land to
land;*

Since then, at an uncertain hour,
That agony returns:
And till my ghastly tale is told,
This heart within me burns.   585

I pass, like night, from land to land;
I have strange power of speech;
That moment that his face I see,
I know the man that must hear me:
To him my tale I teach.   590

What loud uproar bursts from that door!
The wedding guests are there:
But in the garden-bower the bride
And bridemaids singing are:
And hark the little vesper bell,   595
Which biddeth me to prayer!

O Wedding Guest! this soul hath been
Alone on a wide wide sea:
So lonely 'twas, that God himself
Scarce seeméd there to be.   600

O sweeter than the marriage feast,
'Tis sweeter far to me,
To walk together to the kirk
With a goodly company!

To walk together to the kirk,   605
And all together pray,
While each to his great Father bends,
Old men, and babes, and loving friends
And youths and maidens gay!

*And to teach, by his
own example, love
and reverence to all
things that God made
and loveth.*

Farewell, farewell! but this I tell   610
To thee, thou Wedding Guest!
He prayeth well, who loveth well
Both man and bird and beast.

He prayeth best, who loveth best
All things both great and small;   615

4. Made the sign of the cross upon.

For the dear God who loveth us,
He made and loveth all.

The Mariner, whose eye is bright,
Whose beard with age is hoar,
Is gone: and now the Wedding Guest   620
Turned from the bridegroom's door.

He went like one that hath been stunned,
And is of sense forlorn:°   *forsaken*
A sadder and a wiser man,
He rose the morrow morn.   625

1797–98   1817

Dejection: An Ode

Late, late yestreen I saw the new Moon,
With the old Moon in her arms;
And I fear, I fear, my master dear!
We shall have a deadly storm.
        Ballad of Sir Patrick Spence[5]

1

Well! If the bard was weather-wise, who made
    The grand old ballad of Sir Patrick Spence,
    This night, so tranquil now, will not go hence
Unroused by winds, that ply a busier trade
5   Than those which mold yon cloud in lazy flakes,
Or the dull sobbing draft, that moans and rakes
Upon the strings of this Aeolian lute,[6]
        Which better far were mute.
    For lo! the New-moon winter-bright!
10   And overspread with phantom light,
        (With swimming phantom light o'erspread
        But rimmed and circled by a silver thread)
    I see the old Moon in her lap, foretelling
    The coming-on of rain and squally blast.
15 And oh! that even now the gust were swelling,
        And the slant night shower driving loud and fast!
    Those sounds which oft have raised me, whilst they awed,
        And sent my soul abroad,
    Might now perhaps their wonted° impulse give,   *usual*
20 Might startle this dull pain, and make it move and live!

2

    A grief without a pang, void, dark, and drear,
        A stifled, drowsy, unimpassioned grief,

---

5. An early modern ballad (see p. 103).
6. The wind harp (named after Aeolus, Greek god of the winds) has a sounding board equipped with

a set of strings that vibrate in response to air currents.

Which finds no natural outlet, no relief,
   In word, or sigh, or tear—
25 O Lady! in this wan and heartless mood,
To other thoughts by yonder throstle° wooed,   *song thrush*
   All this long eve, so balmy and serene,
Have I been gazing on the western sky,
   And its peculiar tint of yellow green:
30 And still I gaze—and with how blank an eye!
And those thin clouds above, in flakes and bars,
That give away their motion to the stars;
Those stars, that glide behind them or between,
Now sparkling, now bedimmed, but always seen:
35 Yon crescent Moon, as fixed as if it grew
In its own cloudless, starless lake of blue;
I see them all so excellently fair,
I see, not feel, how beautiful they are!

3

   My genial° spirits° fail;   *creative / energies*
40   And what can these avail
To lift the smothering weight from off my breast?
   It were a vain endeavor,
      Though I should gaze forever
On that green light that lingers in the west:
45 I may not hope from outward forms to win
The passion and the life, whose fountains are within.

4

O Lady! we receive but what we give,
And in our life alone does Nature live:
Ours is her wedding garment, ours her shroud!
50   And would we aught behold, of higher worth,
Than that inanimate cold world allowed
To the poor loveless ever-anxious crowd,
   Ah! from the soul itself must issue forth
A light, a glory, a fair luminous cloud
55   Enveloping the Earth—
And from the soul itself must there be sent
   A sweet and potent voice, of its own birth,
Of all sweet sounds the life and element!

5

O pure of heart! thou need'st not ask of me
60 What this strong music in the soul may be!
What, and wherein it doth exist,
This light, this glory, this fair luminous mist,
This beautiful and beauty-making power.
   Joy, virtuous Lady! Joy that ne'er was given,
65 Save to the pure, and in their purest hour,
Life, and Life's effluence, cloud at once and shower,
Joy, Lady! is the spirit and the power,

Which wedding Nature to us gives in dower
  A new Earth and new Heaven,
70 Undreamt of by the sensual and the proud—
Joy is the sweet voice, Joy the luminous cloud—
    We in ourselves rejoice!
And thence flows all that charms or ear or sight,
  All melodies the echoes of that voice,
75 All colors a suffusion from that light.

6

There was a time when, though my path was rough,
  This joy within me dallied with distress,
And all misfortunes were but as the stuff
  Whence Fancy made me dreams of happiness:
80 For hope grew round me, like the twining vine,
And fruits, and foliage, not my own, seemed mine.
But now afflictions bow me down to earth:
Nor care I that they rob me of my mirth;
    But oh! each visitation
85 Suspends what nature gave me at my birth,
  My shaping spirit of Imagination.

For not to think of what I needs must feel,
  But to be still and patient, all I can;
And happly by abstruse research to steal
90   From my own nature all the natural man—
  This was my sole resource, my only plan:
Till that which suits a part infects the whole,
And now is almost grown the habit of my soul.

7

Hence, viper thoughts, that coil around my mind,
95   Reality's dark dream!
I turn from you, and listen to the wind,
  Which long has raved unnoticed. What a scream
Of agony by torture lengthened out
That lute sent forth! Thou Wind, that rav'st without,
100   Bare crag, or mountain tairn,° or blasted tree,   *pool*
Or pine grove whither woodman never clomb,
Or lonely house, long held—the witches' home,
  Methinks were fitter instruments for thee,
Mad lutanist! who in this month of showers,
105 Of dark-brown gardens, and of peeping flowers,
Mak'st devils' yule,[7] with worse than wintry song,
The blossoms, buds, and timorous° leaves among.   *timid*
  Thou actor, perfect in all tragic sounds!
Thou mighty poet, e'en to frenzy bold!
110   What tell'st thou now about?
    'Tis of the rushing of an host in rout,
  With groans, of trampled men, with smarting wounds—
At once they groan with pain, and shudder with the cold!

---

7. A winter storm in spring; hence an unnatural or "devils' " Christmas.

But hush! there is a pause of deepest silence!
115   And all that noise, as of a rushing crowd,
With groans, and tremulous shudderings—all is over—
   It tells another tale, with sounds less deep and loud!
     A tale of less affright,
     And tempered with delight,
120 As Otway's[8] self had framed the tender lay—
     'Tis of a little child
     Upon a lonesome wild,
Not far from home, but she hath lost her way:
And now moans low in bitter grief and fear,
125 And now screams loud, and hopes to make her mother hear.

8

'Tis midnight, but small thoughts have I of sleep:
Full seldom may my friend such vigils keep!
Visit her, gentle Sleep! with wings of healing,
   And may this storm be but a mountain birth,
130 May all the stars hang bright above her dwelling,
   Silent as though they watched the sleeping Earth!
     With light heart may she rise,
     Gay fancy, cheerful eyes,
   Joy lift her spirit, joy attune her voice;
135 To her may all things live, from pole to pole,
Their life the eddying of her living soul!
   O simple spirit, guided from above,
Dear Lady! friend devoutest of my choice,
Thus mayest thou ever, evermore rejoice.

1802   1802

WALTER SAVAGE LANDOR
1775–1864

Rose Aylmer[1]

Ah what avails the sceptered race,
   Ah what the form divine!
What every virtue, every grace!
   Rose Aylmer, all were thine.
5 Rose Aylmer, whom these wakeful eyes
     May weep, but never see,
A night of memories and of sighs
   I consecrate to thee.

1806, 1831, 1846

8. Thomas Otway (1652–1685), poet and drama-
tist, author of "The Poet's Complaint of His Muse"
(1680), a work thought to have influenced Cole-
ridge.

1. The Honorable Rose Whitworth Aylmer (1779–
1800), whom Landor had known in Wales, died
suddenly, in Calcutta.

Past Ruined Ilion Helen[2] Lives

Past ruined Ilion Helen lives,
    Alcestis[3] rises from the shades;
Verse calls them forth; 'tis verse that gives
    Immortal youth to mortal maids.

5 Soon shall Oblivion's deepening veil
    Hide all the peopled hills you see,
The gay, the proud, while lovers hail
    In distant ages you and me.

The tear for fading beauty check,
10   For passing glory cease to sigh;
One form shall rise above the wreck,
    One name, Ianthe,[4] shall not die.

1831

Dirce[5]

Stand close around, ye Stygian set,[6]
    With Dirce in one boat conveyed!
Or Charon, seeing may forget
    That he is old and she a shade.

1831, 1846

To Robert Browning[7]

There is delight in singing, though none hear
Beside the singer; and there is delight
In praising, though the praiser sit alone
And see the praised far off him, far above.
5 Shakspeare is not *our* poet, but the world's,
Therefore on him no speech; and short for thee,
Browning! Since Chaucer was alive and hale,
No man hath walked along our roads with step
So active, so inquiring eye, or tongue
10 So varied in discourse. But warmer climes
Give brighter plumage, stronger wing; the breeze

2. Helen of Troy ("Ilion"), whose abduction brought about the Trojan War.
3. In Greek mythology, Alcestis sacrificed her life for her husband, who was stricken with a mortal illness. She was then brought back from the underworld by Hercules.
4. The name given by Landor to Sophia Jane Swift, an Irishwoman who eventually became Countess de Morlandé and with whom he conducted a long-term affair.
5. In Greek mythology, the wife of King Lycus, killed by being tied to a bull's horns.
6. The shades of the dead who were ferried by Charon over the river Styx to Hades.
7. English poet (1812–1889; see pp. 1009–41).

Of Alpine heights thou playest with, borne on
Beyond Sorrento and Amalfi, where
The Siren waits thee, singing song for song.[8]

1845

Dying Speech of an Old Philosopher

I strove with none, for none was worth my strife:
Nature I loved, and, next to Nature, Art:
I warmed both hands before the fire of Life;
It sinks; and I am ready to depart.

1849

GEORGE GORDON, LORD BYRON
1788–1824

Written after Swimming from Sestos to Abydos[1]

1

If, in the month of dark December,
    Leander, who was nightly wont°   *accustomed*
(What maid will not the tale remember?)
    To cross thy stream, broad Hellespont!

2

5 If, when the wintry tempest roared,
    He sped to Hero, nothing loath,
And thus of old thy current poured,
    Fair Venus! how I pity both!

3

For *me*, degenerate modern wretch,
10   Though in the genial month of May,
My dripping limbs I faintly stretch,
    And think I've done a feat today.

4

But since he crossed the rapid tide,
    According to the doubtful story,

---

8. In Greek mythology, the Sirens drowned them-
selves in despair when Odysseus escaped the lure
of their song. *Sorrento and Amalfi:* towns near
Naples that Browning visited on his second trip to
Italy in 1844 and that figure in some of his early
poems.

1. The Hellespont, or Dardanelles, is the strait
separating Europe from Asia Minor, between Aby-
dos on the Greek shore and Sestos on the Asian.
In Greek mythology, Leander used to swim from
Abydos to visit his sweetheart, Hero, at Sestos.

15   To woo—and—Lord knows what beside,
          And swam for Love, as I for Glory;

5

'Twere hard to say who fared the best:
          Sad mortals! thus the gods still plague you!
He lost his labor, I my jest;
20   For he was drowned, and I've the ague.°   chills and fever

1810   1812

She Walks in Beauty

1

She walks in beauty, like the night
          Of cloudless climes and starry skies;
And all that's best of dark and bright
          Meet in her aspect and her eyes:
5   Thus mellowed to that tender light
          Which heaven to gaudy day denies.

2

One shade the more, one ray the less,
          Had half impaired the nameless grace
Which waves in every raven tress,
10   Or softly lightens o'er her face;
Where thoughts serenely sweet express
          How pure, how dear their dwelling place.

3

And on that cheek, and o'er that brow,
          So soft, so calm, yet eloquent,
15   The smiles that win, the tints that glow,
          But tell of days in goodness spent,
A mind at peace with all below,
          A heart whose love is innocent!

1814   1815

The Destruction of Sennacherib[2]

1

The Assyrian came down like the wolf on the fold,
And his cohorts were gleaming in purple and gold;
And the sheen of their spears was like stars on the sea,
When the blue wave rolls nightly on deep Galilee.

---

2. Assyrian king, whose armies, while besieging Jerusalem (701 B.C.E.), were attacked by a violent plague
(2 Kings 19.35).

2

5   Like the leaves of the forest when summer is green,
That host with their banners at sunset were seen:
Like the leaves of the forest when autumn hath blown,
That host on the morrow lay withered and strown.

3

For the Angel of Death spread his wings on the blast,
10 And breathed in the face of the foe as he passed;
And the eyes of the sleepers waxed deadly and chill,
And their hearts but once heaved, and forever grew still!

4

And there lay the steed with his nostril all wide,
But through it there rolled not the breath of his pride;
15 And the foam of his gasping lay white on the turf,
And cold as the spray of the rock-beating surf.

5

And there lay the rider distorted and pale,
With the dew on his brow, and the rust on his mail:
And the tents were all silent, the banners alone,
20 The lances unlifted, the trumpet unblown.

6

And the widows of Ashur° are loud in their wail,   Assyria
And the idols are broke in the temple of Baal;[3]
And the might of the Gentile,[4] unsmote by the sword,
Hath melted like snow in the glance of the Lord!

1815   1815

When We Two Parted

1

When we two parted
   In silence and tears,
Half broken-hearted
   To sever for years,
5   Pale grew thy cheek and cold,
   Colder thy kiss;
Truly that hour foretold
   Sorrow to this.

2

The dew of the morning
10 Sunk chill on my brow—
It felt like the warning

3. Deity of the Assyrians.   4. A non-Jewish person; here, Sennacherib.

Of what I feel now.
Thy vows are all broken,
    And light is thy fame;
15 I hear thy name spoken,
    And share in its shame.

3

They name thee before me,
    A knell to mine ear;
A shudder comes o'er me—
20 Why wert thou so dear?
They know not I knew thee,
    Who knew thee too well—
Long, long shall I rue thee,
    Too deeply to tell.

4

25 In secret we met—
    In silence I grieve,
That thy heart could forget,
    Thy spirit deceive.
If I should meet thee
30 After long years,
How should I greet thee?—
    With silence and tears.

1815   1815

So We'll Go No More A-Roving

1

So we'll go no more a-roving
    So late into the night,
Though the heart be still as loving,
    And the moon be still as bright.

2

5   For the sword outwears its sheath,
    And the soul wears out the breast,
And the heart must pause to breathe,
    And Love itself have rest.

3

Though the night was made for loving,
10   And the day returns too soon,
Yet we'll go no more a-roving
    By the light of the moon.

1817   1830

From Don Juan[5]

Fragment on the Back of the Ms. of Canto I

I would to Heaven that I were so much clay,
  As I am blood, bone, marrow, passion, feeling—
Because at least the past were passed away,
  And for the future—(but I write this reeling,
5 Having got drunk exceedingly to-day,
  So that I seem to stand upon the ceiling)
I say—the future is a serious matter—
And so—for God's sake—hock[6] and soda-water!

From *Canto the First*

1

I want° a hero: an uncommon want,   lack
  When every year and month sends forth a new one,
Till, after cloying the gazettes[7] with cant,
  The age discovers he is not the true one;
5 Of such as these I should not care to vaunt,
  I'll therefore take our ancient friend Don Juan—
We all have seen him, in the pantomime,[8]
Sent to the Devil somewhat ere his time.

2

Vernon, the butcher Cumberland, Wolfe, Hawke,
10 Prince Ferdinand, Granby, Burgoyne, Keppel, Howe,[9]
Evil and good, have had their tithe° of talk,   due tribute
  And filled their sign-posts then, like Wellesley now;
Each in their turn like Banquo's monarchs stalk,
  Followers of Fame, "nine farrow" of that sow:[1]
15 France, too, had Buonaparté and Dumourier
Recorded in the *Moniteur* and *Courier*.[2]

3

Barnave, Brissot, Condorcet, Mirabeau,
  Petion, Clootz, Danton, Marat, La Fayette[3]
Were French, and famous people, as we know;

---

5. Pronounced in the English fashion, *Don Joóun*. The hero is a legendary Spanish nobleman, a notorious seducer of women; in most versions, but not Byron's satire, finally carried off to hell. Canto I comprises 222 stanzas; stanzas 1–119, given here, conclude with the beginning of the romance between Don Juan and Donna Julia.
6. Rhine wine, a supposed remedy for the hangover.
7. Official notices or newspapers.
8. I.e., on the stage, in one or another of many adaptations.
9. British military leaders of the eighteenth century, their fame extinguished by more recent

"heroes," such as Wellesley (line 12), the duke of Wellington, who defeated Napoleon at Waterloo.
1. Cf. Shakespeare's *Macbeth* 4.1, lines 80–81 ("Pour in sow's blood that hath eaten / Her nine farrow") and 118–19 ("shall Banquo's issue ever / Reign in this kingdom?"). The sow, Fame, eats her offspring—i.e., the heroes just listed.
2. "Buonaparté" is Napoleon, and Dumourier a French general, both of whose victories and defeats were chronicled in the French newspapers *Gazette Nationale; ou le Moniteur Universel* and *le Courier Republicain*.
3. French generals and politicians connected with the French Revolution, many of them guillotined.

20   And there were others, scarce forgotten yet,
Joubert, Hoche, Marceau, Lannes, Desaix, Moreau,[4]
    With many of the military set,
Exceedingly remarkable at times,
But not at all adapted to my rhymes.

4

25   Nelson[5] was once Britannia's god of War,
    And still should be so, but the tide is turned;
There's no more to be said of Trafalgar,
    'Tis with our hero quietly inurned;
Because the army's grown more popular,
30   At which the naval people are concerned;
Besides, the Prince is all for the land-service,
Forgetting Duncan, Nelson, Howe, and Jervis.[6]

5

Brave men were living before Agamemnon[7]
    And since, exceeding valorous and sage,
35   A good deal like him too, though quite the same none;
    But then they shone not on the poet's page,
And so have been forgotten:—I condemn none,
    But can't find any in the present age
Fit for my poem (that is, for my new one);
40   So, as I said, I'll take my friend Don Juan.

6

Most epic poets plunge *"in medias res"*[8]
    (Horace makes this the heroic turnpike road),
And then your hero tells, when'er you please,
    What went before—by way of episode,
45   While seated after dinner at his ease,
    Beside his mistress in some soft abode,
Palace, or garden, paradise, or cavern,
Which serves the happy couple for a tavern.

7

That is the usual method, but not mine—
50   My way is to begin with the beginning;
The regularity of my design
    Forbids all wandering as the worst of sinning,
And therefore I shall open with a line
    (Although it cost me half an hour in spinning),
55   Narrating somewhat of Don Juan's father,
And also of his mother, if you'd rather.

---

4. Other French military men; most of these died in battle.
5. British naval hero, fatally wounded at the Battle of Trafalgar (1805).
6. British naval commanders. *The Prince:* the prince of Wales.

7. Commander of the Greeks at the siege of Troy.
8. In *Ars Poetica* 148–49, the Roman poet and satirist Horace (65–8 B.C.E.) asserted that the writer of an epic should rush his readers "into the middle of the story."

8

In Seville was he born, a pleasant city,
  Famous for oranges and women—he
Who has not seen it will be much to pity,
60   So says the proverb—and I quite agree;
Of all the Spanish towns is none more pretty,
  Cadiz perhaps—but that you soon may see;
Don Juan's parents lived beside the river,
A noble stream, and called the Guadalquivir.

9

65 His father's name was Jóse[9]—*Don,* of course,—
  A true Hidalgo,[1] free from every stain
Of Moor or Hebrew blood, he traced his source
  Through the most Gothic gentlemen of Spain;[2]
A better cavalier ne'er mounted horse,
70   Or, being mounted, e'er got down again,
Than José, who begot our hero, who
Begot—but that's to come—Well, to renew:

10

His mother was a learnèd lady, famed
  For every branch of every science known—
75 In every Christian language ever named,
  With virtues equaled by her wit alone:
She made the cleverest people quite ashamed,
  And even the good with inward envy groan,
Finding themselves so very much exceeded,
80 In their own way, by all the things that she did.

11

Her memory was a mine: she knew by heart
  All Calderon and greater part of Lopé,[3]
So, that if any actor missed his part,
  She could have served him for the prompter's copy;
85 For her Feinagle's[4] were an useless art,
  And he himself obliged to shut up shop—he
Could never make a memory so fine as
That which adorned the brain of Donna Inez.

12

Her favorite science was the mathematical,
90   Her noblest virtue was her magnanimity,
Her wit (she sometimes tried at wit) was Attic[5] all,
  Her serious sayings darkened to sublimity;

---

9. The Spanish spelling is *José,* but Byron's meter requires *Jóse.*
1. Spanish noble of minor degree.
2. Descended from the Visigoths, who conquered Spain in the fifth century.
3. Calderón de la Barca (1600–1681) and Lope

de Vega (1562–1635), preeminent Spanish dramatists.
4. Gregor von Feinagle (1765–1819), originator of mnemonics, a method of memorization. He lectured in England in 1811.
5. Athenian; i.e., refined, learned.

In short, in all things she was fairly what I call
   A prodigy—her morning dress was dimity,
95 Her evening silk, or, in the summer, muslin,
   And other stuffs, with which I won't stay puzzling.

13

She knew the Latin—that is, "the Lord's prayer,"
   And Greek—the alphabet—I'm nearly sure;
She read some French romances here and there,
100   Although her mode of speaking was not pure;
For native Spanish she had no great care,
   At least her conversation was obscure;
Her thoughts were theorems, her words a problem,
As if she deemed that mystery would ennoble 'em.

14

105 She liked the English and the Hebrew tongue,
   And said there was analogy between 'em;
She proved it somehow out of sacred song,
   But I must leave the proofs of those who've seen 'em;
But this I heard her say, and can't be wrong,
110   And all may think which way their judgments lean 'em,
" 'Tis strange—the Hebrew noun which means 'I am,'[6]
The English always use to govern d——n."[7]

15

Some women use their tongues—she *looked* a lecture,
   Each eye a sermon, and her brow a homily,
115 An all-in-all sufficient self-director,
   Like the lamented late Sir Samuel Romilly,[8]
The Law's expounder, and the State's corrector,
   Whose suicide was almost an anomaly—
One sad example more, that "All is vanity"[9]—
120 (The jury brought their verdict in "Insanity!")

16

In short, she was a walking calculation,
   Miss Edgeworth's novels stepping from their covers,
Or Mrs. Trimmer's books on education,
   Or "Coelebs' Wife"[1] set out in quest of lovers,
125 Morality's prim personifation,
   In which not Envy's self a flaw discovers;
To others' share let "female errors fall,"[2]
For she had not even one—the worst of all.

---

6. The name of God, "I am that I am" (Exodus 3.14).
7. English gentlemen traveling on the European continent were sometimes known as "Goddams," from their habitual profanity.
8. Lawyer for Byron's wife in a suit for separation.
9. Cf. Ecclesiastes 1.2.

1. A novel by Hannah More (1745–1833; see pp. 707–11), who like Maria Edgeworth (line 122) and Sarah Trimmer (line 123) was a writer Byron could not take seriously.
2. Quoted from Alexander Pope, *The Rape of the Lock* 2.17. *Errors*: frailties or foibles.

17

Oh! she was perfect past all parallel—
130   Of any modern female saint's comparison;
So far above the cunning powers of Hell,
    Her Guardian Angel had given up his garrison;
Even her minutest motions went as well
    As those of the best time-piece made by Harrison;[3]
135 In virtues nothing earthly could surpass her,
Save thine "incomparable oil," Macassar![4]

18

Perfect she was, but as perfection is
    Insipid in this naughty world of ours,
Where our first parents[5] never learned to kiss
140   Till they were exiled from their earlier bowers,
Where all was peace, and innocence, and bliss,
    (I wonder how they got through the twelve hours),
Don Jóse, like a lineal son of Eve,
Went plucking various fruit without her leave.

19

145 He was a mortal of the careless kind,
    With no great love for learning, or the learned,
Who chose to go where'er he had a mind,
    And never dreamed his lady was concerned;
The world, as usual, wickedly inclined
150   To see a kingdom or a house o'erturned,
Whispered he had a mistress, some said *two*.
But for domestic quarrels *one* will do.

20

Now Donna Inez had, with all her merit,
    A great opinion of her own good qualities;
155 Neglect, indeed, requires a saint to bear it,
    And such, indeed, she was in her moralities;°   *moralizing*
But then she had a devil of a spirit,
    And sometimes mixed up fancies with realities,
And let few opportunities escape
160 Of getting her liege lord into a scrape.

21

This was an easy matter with a man
    Oft in the wrong, and never on his guard;
And even the wisest, do the best they can,
    Have moments, hours, and days, so unprepared,
165 That you might "brain them with their lady's fan";[6]
    And sometimes ladies hit exceeding hard,

---

3. John Harrison (1693–1776) improved the
accuracy of watches and chronometers.
4. A much-advertised hairdressing.

5. I.e., Adam and Eve; see Genesis.
6. Modified quotation from Shakespeare, *1 Henry
IV* 2.4.19.

And fans turn into falchions° in fair hands,   *swords*
And why and wherefore no one understands.

22

'Tis pity learnèd virgins ever wed
170   With persons of no sort of education,
Or gentlemen, who, though well born and bred,
     Grow tired of scientific conversation:
I don't choose to say much upon this head,
     I'm a plain man, and in a single station,
175 But—Oh! ye lords of ladies intellectual,
Inform us truly, have they not hen-pecked you all?

23

Don Jóse and his lady quarrelled—*why*,
     Not any of the many could divine,
Though several thousand people chose to try,
180   'Twas surely no concern of theirs nor mine;
I loath that low vice—curiosity;
     But if there's anything in which I shine,
'Tis in arranging all my friends' affairs,
Not having, of my own, domestic cares.

24

185 And so I interfered, and with the best
     Intentions, but their treatment was not kind;
I think the foolish people were possessed,
     For neither of them could I ever find,
Although their porter afterwards confessed—
190   But that's no matter, and the worst's behind,
For little Juan o'er me threw, down stairs,
A pail of housemaid's water unawares.

25

A little curly-headed, good-for-nothing,
     And mischief-making monkey from his birth;
195 His parents ne'er agreed except in doting
     Upon the most unquiet imp on earth;
Instead of quarrelling, had they been but both in
     Their senses, they'd have sent young master forth
To school, or had him soundly whipped at home,
200 To teach him manners for the time to come.

26

Don Jóse and the Donna Inez led
     For some time an unhappy sort of life,
Wishing each other, not divorced, but dead;
     They lived respectably as man and wife,
205 Their conduct was exceedingly well-bred,
     And gave no outward signs of inward strife,

Until at length the smothered fire broke out,
And put the business past all kind of doubt.

27

For Inez called some druggists and physicians,
210   And tried to prove her loving lord was *mad,*
But as he had some lucid intermissions,
    She next decided he was only *bad;*
Yet when they asked her for her depositions,
    No sort of explanation could be had,
215 Save that her duty both to man and God
Required this conduct—which seemed very odd.

28

She kept a journal, where his faults were noted,
    And opened certain trunks of books and letters,
All which might, if occasion served, be quoted;
220   And then she had all Seville for abettors,
Besides her good old grandmother (who doted);
    The hearers of her case became repeaters,
Then advocates, inquisitors, and judges,
Some for amusement, others for old grudges.

29

225 And then this best and meekest woman bore
    With such serenity her husband's woes,
Just as the Spartan ladies did of yore,
    Who saw their spouses killed, and nobly chose
Never to say a word about them more—
230   Calmly she heard each calumny that rose,
And saw *his* agonies with such sublimity,
That all the world exclaimed, "What magnanimity!"

30

No doubt this patience, when the world is damning us,
    Is philosophic in our former friends;
235 'Tis also pleasant to be deemed magnanimous,
    The more so in obtaining our own ends;
And what the lawyers call a *"malus animus"*[7]
    Conduct like this by no means comprehends:
Revenge in person's certainly no virtue,
240 But then 'tis not *my* fault, if *others* hurt you.

31

And if our quarrels should rip up old stories,
    And help them with a lie or two additional,
I'm not to blame, as you well know—no more is
    Any one else—they were become traditional;
245 Besides, their resurrection aids our glories
    By contrast, which is what we just were wishing all:

---

7. Malicious intent (Latin).

And Science profits by this resurrection—
Dead scandals form good subjects for dissection.

32

250   Their friends had tried at reconciliation,
      Then their relations, who made matters worse.
    ('Twere hard to tell upon a like occasion
      To whom it may be best to have recourse—
    I can't say much for friend or yet relation):
      The lawyers did their utmost for divorce,
255   But scarce a fee was paid on either side
    Before, unluckily, Don Jóse died.

33

    He died: and most unluckily, because,
      According to all hints I could collect
    From Counsel learnéd in those kinds of laws,
260   (Although their talk's obscure and circumspect)
    His death contrived to spoil a charming cause;°   *legal case*
      A thousand pities also with respect
    To public feeling, which on this occasion
    Was manifested in a great sensation.

34

265   But ah! he died; and buried with him lay
      The public feeling and the lawyers' fees:
    His house was sold, his servants sent away,
      A Jew took one of his two mistresses,
    A priest the other—at least so they say:
270   I asked the doctors after his disease—
    He died of the slow fever called the tertian,[8]
    And left his widow to her own aversion.

35

    Yet Jóse was an honorable man,
      That I must say, who knew him very well;
275   Therefore his frailties I'll no further scan,
      Indeed there were not many more to tell:
    And if his passions now and then outran
      Discretion, and were not so peaceable
    As Numa's (who was also named Pompilius),[9]
280   He had been ill brought up, and was born bilious.°   *bad tempered*

36

    Whate'er might be his worthlessness or worth,
      Poor fellow! he had many things to wound him.
    Let's own—since it can do no good on earth—
      It was a trying moment that which found him
285   Standing alone beside his desolate hearth,

8. A form of malaria.
9. Ancient Roman king, famed for the comparative peace of his forty-three-year reign.

Where all his household gods lay shivered° round him: *broken*
No choice was left his feelings or his pride,
Save Death or Doctor's Commons° so he died.   *divorce courts*

37

Dying intestate,° Juan was sole heir   *leaving no will*
290   To a chancery suit,[1] and messuages,° and lands,   *household lands*
Which, with a long minority[2] and care,
    Promised to turn out well in proper hands:
Inez became sole guardian, which was fair,
    And answered but to Nature's just demands;
295   An only son left with an only mother
Is brought up much more wisely than another.

38

Sagest of women, even of widows, she
    Resolved that Juan should be quite a paragon,
And worthy of the noblest pedigree,
300   (His Sire was of Castile, his Dam from Aragon):
Then, for accomplishments of chivalry,
    In case our Lord the King should go to war again,
He learned the arts of riding, fencing, gunnery,
And how to scale a fortress—or a nunnery.

39

305   But that which Donna Inez most desired,
    And saw into herself each day before all
The learnéd tutors whom for him she hired,
    Was, that his breeding should be strictly moral:
Much into all his studies she inquired,
310   And so they were submitted first to her, all,
Arts, sciences—no branch was made a mystery
To Juan's eyes, excepting natural history.

40

The languages, especially the dead,
    The sciences, and most of all the abstruse,
315   The arts, at least all such as could be said
    To be the most remote from common use,
In all these he was much and deeply read:
    But not a page of anything that's loose,
Or hints continuation of the species,
320   Was ever suffered, lest he should grow vicious.

41

His classic studies made a little puzzle,
    Because of filthy loves of gods and goddesses,
Who in the earlier ages raised a bustle,
    But never put on pantaloons or bodices;

---

1. Drawn-out legal proceedings over inheritance of property.   2. Before he should come of age.

325 His reverend tutors had at times a tussle,
    And for their Aeneids, Iliads, and Odysseys,
Were forced to make an odd sort of apology,
For Donna Inez dreaded the Mythology.

42

Ovid's a rake, as half his verses show him,
330   Anacreon's morals are a still worse sample,
Catullus scarcely has a decent poem,
    I don't think Sappho's Ode a good example,[3]
Although Longinus[4] tells us there is no hymn
    Where the Sublime soars forth on wings more ample;
335 But Virgil's songs are pure, except that horrid one
Beginning with *"Formosum Pastor Corydon."*[5]

43

Lucretius' irreligion is too strong
    For early stomachs, to prove wholesome food;
I can't help thinking Juvenal was wrong,
340   Although no doubt his real intent was good,
For speaking out so plainly in his song,
    So much indeed as to be downright rude;
And then what proper person can be partial
To all those nauseous epigrams of Martial?[6]

44

345 Juan was taught from out the best edition,
    Expurgated by learnèd men, who place,
Judiciously, from out the schoolboy's vision,
    The grosser parts; but, fearful to deface
Too much their modest bard by this omission,
350   And pitying sore his mutilated case,
They only add them all in an appendix,[7]
Which saves, in fact, the trouble of an index;

45

For there we have them all "at one fell swoop,"[8]
    Instead of being scattered through the pages;
355 They stand forth marshaled in a handsome troop,
    To meet the ingenuous youth of future ages,
Till some less rigid editor shall stoop
    To call them back into their separate cages,
Instead of standing staring all together,
360 Like garden gods[9]—and not so decent either.

---

3. These lines name Greek and Roman classic and erotic poets.
4. The presumed author (first century C.E.) of a treatise on "the sublime" in literature.
5. "Handsome Shepherd Corydon": opening words of Virgil's Second Eclogue (a pastoral poem), concerned with love between young men.
6. Like Lucretius (line 337) and Juvenal (line 339), a Roman poet. Lucretius was a philosophic atheist; Juvenal and Martial were severe and some-times obscene satirists.
7. "Fact! There is, or was, such an edition, with all the obnoxious epigrams of Martial placed by themselves at the end" [Byron's note].
8. Allusion to Macduff's reaction upon learning of the death of his family: "What! All my pretty chickens and their dam / At one fell swoop?" (Shakespeare, *Macbeth* 4.3.219–20).
9. Statues of fertility deities, often phallic.

46

The Missal too (it was the family Missal)
   Was ornamented in a sort of way
Which ancient mass-books often are, and this all
   Kinds of grotesques illumined; and how they,
365 Who saw those figures on the margin kiss all,
   Could turn their optics to the text and pray,
Is more than I know—But Don Juan's mother
Kept this herself, and gave her son another.

47

Sermons he read, and lectures he endured,
370   And homilies, and lives of all the saints;
To Jerome and to Chrysostom[1] inured,
   He did not take such studies for restraints;
But how Faith is acquired, and then insured,
   So well not one of the aforesaid paints
375 As Saint Augustine[2] in his fine Confessions,
Which make the reader envy his transgressions.

48

This, too, was a sealed book to little Juan—
   I can't but say that his mamma was right,
If such an education was the true one.
380   She scarcely trusted him from out her sight;
Her maids were old, and if she took a new one,
   You might be sure she was a perfect fright;
She did this during even her husband's life—
I recommend as much to every wife.

49

385 Young Juan waxed in goodliness and grace;
   At six a charming child, and at eleven
With all the promise of as fine a face
   As e'er to man's maturer growth was given:
He studied steadily, and grew apace,
390   And seemed, at least, in the right road to Heaven,
For half his days were passed at church, the other
Between his tutors, confessor,° and mother.   *private chaplain*

50

At six, I said, he was a charming child,
   At twelve he was a fine, but quiet boy;
395 Although in infancy a little wild,
   They tamed him down amongst them: to destroy
His natural spirit not in vain they toiled,
   At least it seemed so; and his mother's joy
Was to declare how sage, and still, and steady,
400 Her young philosopher was grown already.

---

1. Saints and teachers of the early Church.
2. Another early father of the Church; his auto-biography candidly describes his worldy life before conversion.

51

I had my doubts, perhaps I have them still,
    But what I say is neither here nor there:
I knew his father well, and have some skill
    In character—but it would not be fair
405 From sire to son to augur good or ill:
    He and his wife were an ill-sorted pair—
But scandal's my aversion—I protest
Against all evil speaking, even in jest.

52

For my part I say nothing—nothing—but
410   *This* I will say—my reasons are my own—
That if I had an only son to put
    To school (as God be praised that I have none),
'Tis not with Donna Inez I would shut
    Him up to learn his catechism[3] alone,
415 No—no—I'd send him out betimes to college,
For there it was I picked up my own knowledge.

53

For there one learns—'tis not for me to boast,
    Though I acquired—but I pass over *that*,
As well as all the Greek I since have lost:
420   I say that there's the place—but *"Verbum sat,"*[4]
I think I picked up too, as well as most,
    Knowledge of matters—but no matter *what*—
I never married—but, I think, I know
That sons should not be educated so.

54

425 Young Juan now was sixteen years of age,
    Tall, handsome, slender, but well knit: he seemed
Active, though not so sprightly, as a page;
    And everybody but his mother deemed
Him almost man; but she flew in a rage
430   And bit her lips (for else she might have screamed)
If any said so—for to be precocious
Was in her eyes a thing the most atrocious.

55

Amongst her numerous acquaintance, all
    Selected for discretion and devotion,
435 There was the Donna Julia, whom to call
    Pretty were but to give a feeble notion
Of many charms in her as natural
    As sweetness to the flower, or salt to Ocean,

---

3. A brief summary of Christian teaching.   4. A word to the wise suffices (Latin).

Her zone to Venus,[5] or his bow to Cupid,
440   (But this last simile is trite and stupid.)

56

The darkness of her Oriental eye
    Accorded with her Moorish origin;
(Her blood was not all Spanish; by the by,
    In Spain, you know, this is a sort of sin;)
445 When proud Granada fell, and, forced to fly,
    Boabdil[6] wept: of Donna Julia's kin
Some went to Africa, some stayed in Spain—
Her great great grandmamma chose to remain.

57

She married (I forget the pedigree)
450   With an Hidalgo, who transmitted down
His blood less noble than such blood should be;
    At such alliances his sires would frown,
In that point so precise in each degree
    That they bred *in and in,* as might be shown,
455 Marrying their cousins—nay, their aunts, and nieces,
Which always spoils the breed, if it increases.

58

This heathenish cross restored the breed again,
    Ruined its blood,[7] but much improved its flesh;
For from a root the ugliest in Old Spain
460   Sprung up a branch as beautiful as fresh;
The sons no more were short, the daughters plain:
    But there's a rumor which I fain would hush,
'Tis said that Donna Julia's grandmamma
Produced her Don more heirs at love than law.

59

465 However this might be, the race went on
    Improving still through every generation,
Until it centered in an only son,
    Who left an only daughter; my narration
May have suggested that this single one
470   Could be but Julia (whom on this occasion
I shall have much to speak about), and she
Was married, charming, chaste, and twenty-three.

60

Her eye (I'm very fond of handsome eyes)
    Was large and dark, suppressing half its fire
475 Until she spoke, then through its soft disguise
    Flashed an expression more of pride than ire,

---

5. The magical girdle ("zone") of Venus, Roman goddess of love and beauty, made its wearer sexually attractive.

6. The last Moorish king of Granada, a province of Spain.
7. Bloodline, i.e., pure lineage.

And love than either; and there would arise
A something in them which was not desire,
But would have been, perhaps, but for the soul
480 Which struggled through and chastened down the whole.

61

Her glossy hair was clustered o'er a brow
    Bright with intelligence, and fair, and smooth;
Her eyebrow's shape was like the aërial bow,°   rainbow
    Her cheek all purple° with the beam of youth,   rosy
485 Mounting, at times, to a transparent glow,
    As if her veins ran lightning; she, in sooth,
Possessed an air and grace by no means common:
Her stature tall—I hate a dumpy woman.

62

Wedded she was some years, and to a man
490   Of fifty, and such husbands are in plenty;
And yet, I think, instead of such a ONE
    'Twere better to have TWO of five-and-twenty,
Especially in countries near the sun:
    And now I think on't, "mi vien in mente,"[8]
495 Ladies even of the most uneasy virtue
Prefer a spouse whose age is short of thirty.

63

'Tis a sad thing, I cannot choose but say,
    And all the fault of that indecent sun,
Who cannot leave alone our helpless clay,
500   But will keep baking, broiling, burning on,
That howsoever people fast and pray,
    The flesh is frail, and so the soul undone:
What men call gallantry, and gods adultery,
Is much more common where the climate's sultry.

64

505 Happy the nations of the moral North!
    Where all is virtue, and the winter season
Sends sin, without a rag on, shivering forth
    ('Twas snow that brought St. Anthony to reason);[9]
Where juries cast up what a wife is worth,
510   By laying whate'er sum, in mulct,[1] they please on
The lover, who must pay a handsome price,
Because it is a marketable vice.

65

Alfonso was the name of Julia's lord,
    A man well looking for his years, and who
515 Was neither much beloved nor yet abhorred:

8. It comes to my mind (Italian).
9. St. Anthony recommended the application of
snow as a remedy for lust.
1. As a fine.

They lived together as most people do,
  Suffering each other's foibles by accord,
    And not exactly either *one* or *two*;
  Yet he was jealous, though he did not show it,
520 For Jealousy dislikes the world to know it.

66

Julia was—yet I never could see why—
  With Donna Inez quite a favorite friend;
Between their tastes there was small sympathy,
  For not a line had Julia ever penned:
525 Some people whisper (but, no doubt, they lie,
  For Malice still imputes some private end)
That Inez had, ere Don Alfonso's marriage,
Forgot with him her very prudent carriage;°   behavior

67

And that still keeping up the old connection,
530 Which Time had lately rendered much more chaste,
She took his lady also in affection,
  And certainly this course was much the best:
She flattered Julia with her sage protection,
  And complimented Don Alfonso's taste;
535 And if she could not (who can?) silence scandal,
At least she left it a more slender handle.

68

I can't tell whether Julia saw the affair
  With other people's eyes, or if her own
Discoveries made, but none could be aware
540 Of this, at least no symptom e'er was shown;
Perhaps she did not know, or did not care,
  Indifferent from the first, or callous grown:
I'm really puzzled what to think or say,
She kept her counsel in so close a way.

69

545 Juan she saw, and, as a pretty child,
  Caressed him often—such a thing might be
Quite innocently done, and harmless styled,
  When she had twenty years, and thirteen he;
But I am not so sure I should have smiled
550 When he was sixteen, Julia twenty-three;
These few short years make wondrous alterations,
Particularly amongst sun-burnt nations.

70

Whate'er the cause might be, they had become
  Changed; for the dame grew distant, the youth shy,
555 Their looks cast down, their greetings almost dumb,
  And much embarrassment in either eye;

There surely will be little doubt with some
    That Donna Julia knew the reason why,
But as for Juan, he had no more notion
560   Than he who never saw the sea of Ocean.

71

Yet Julia's very coldness still was kind,
    And tremulously gentle her small hand
Withdrew itself from his, but left behind
    A little pressure, thrilling, and so bland
565   And slight, so very slight, that to the mind
    'Twas but a doubt; but ne'er magician's wand
Wrought change with all Armida's[2] fairy art
Like what this light touch left on Juan's heart.

72

And if she met him, though she smiled no more,
570   She looked a sadness sweeter than her smile,
As if her heart had deeper thoughts in store
    She must not own, but cherished more the while
For that compression in its burning core;
    Even Innocence itself has many a wile,
575   And will not dare to trust itself with truth,
And Love is taught hypocrisy from youth.

73

But Passion most dissembles, yet betrays
    Even by its darkness; as the blackest sky
Foretells the heaviest tempest, it displays
580   Its workings through the vainly guarded eye,
And in whatever aspect it arrays
    Itself, 'tis still the same hypocrisy;
Coldness or Anger, even Disdain or Hate,
Are masks it often wears, and still too late.

74

585   Then there were sighs, the deeper for suppression,
    And stolen glances, sweeter for the theft,
And burning blushes, though for no transgression,
    Tremblings when met, and restlessness when left;
All these are little preludes to possession,
590   Of which young Passion cannot be bereft,
And merely tend to show how greatly Love is
Embarrassed at first starting with a novice.

75

Poor Julia's heart was in an awkward state;
    She felt it going, and resolved to make
595   The noblest efforts for herself and mate,

---

2. An enchantress who seduces Christian knights in Tasso's epic poem *Jerusalem Delivered* (sixteenth century).

For Honor's, Pride's, Religion's, Virtue's sake:
  Her resolutions were most truly great,
    And almost might have made a Tarquin[3] quake:
  She prayed the Virgin Mary for her grace,
600 As being the best judge of a lady's case.

76

She vowed she never would see Juan more,
  And next day paid a visit to his mother,
    And looked extremely at the opening door,
  Which, by the Virgin's grace, let in another;
605 Grateful she was, and yet a little sore—
  Again it opens, it can be no other,
'Tis surely Juan now—No! I'm afraid
That night the Virgin was no further prayed.

77

She now determined that a virtuous woman
610   Should rather face and overcome temptation,
That flight was base and dastardly, and no man
  Should ever give her heart the least sensation,
That is to say, a thought beyond the common
  Preference, that we must feel, upon occasion,
615 For people who are pleasanter than others,
But then they only seem so many brothers.

78

And even if by chance—and who can tell?
  The Devil's so very sly—she should discover
That all within was not so very well,
620   And, if still free,[4] that such or such a lover
Might please perhaps, a virtuous wife can quell
  Such thoughts, and be the better when they're over;
And if the man should ask, 'tis but denial:
I recommend young ladies to make trial.

79

625 And, then, there are such things as Love divine,
  Bright and immaculate, unmixed and pure,
Such as the angels think so very fine,
  And matrons, who would be no less secure,
Platonic, perfect, "just such love as mine;"
630   Thus Julia said—and thought so, to be sure;
And so I'd have her think, were I the man
On whom her reveries celestial ran.

80

Such love is innocent, and may exist
  Between young persons without any danger.

---

3. In Shakespeare's *Rape of Lucrece* (based on Roman legend), the rapist of a Roman noble-woman renowned for her chastity.
4. I.e., if she were not already married.

635 A hand may first, and then a lip be kissed;
　　For my part, to such doings I'm a stranger,
　　But *hear* these freedoms form the utmost list
　　　Of all o'er which such love may be a ranger:
　　If people go beyond, 'tis quite a crime,
640 But not my fault—I tell them all in time.

81

Love, then, but Love within its proper limits,
　　Was Julia's innocent determination
In young Don Juan's favor, and to him its
　　Exertion might be useful on occasion;
645 And, lighted at too pure a shrine to dim its
　　Ethereal luster, with what sweet persuasion
He might be taught, by Love and her together—
I really don't know what, nor Julia either.

82

Fraught with this fine intention, and well fenced
650　In mail of proof—her purity of soul—
She, for the future, of her strength convinced,
　　And that her honor was a rock, or mole,°　　　　　　*breakwater*
Exceeding sagely from that hour dispensed
　　With any kind of troublesome control;
655 But whether Julia to the task was equal
Is that which must be mentioned in the sequel.

83

Her plan she deemed both innocent and feasible,
　　And, surely, with a stripling of sixteen
Not Scandal's fangs could fix on much that's seizable,
660　Or if they did so, satisfied to mean
Nothing but what was good, her breast was peaceable—
　　A quiet conscience makes one so serene!
Christians have burnt each other, quite persuaded
That all the Apostles would have done as they did.

84

665 And if in the mean time her husband died,
　　But Heaven forbid that such a thought should cross
Her brain, though in a dream! (and then she sighed)
　　Never could she survive that common loss;
But just suppose that moment should betide,
670　I only say suppose it—*inter nos:*[5]
(This should be *entre nous,* for Julia thought
In French, but then the rhyme would go for nought.)

85

I only say, suppose this supposition:
　　Juan being then grown up to man's estate

5. Just between ourselves (Latin).

675   Would fully suit a widow of condition,
     Even seven years hence it would not be too late;
   And in the interim (to pursue this vision)
     The mischief, after all, could not be great,
   For he would learn the rudiments of Love,
680   I mean the *seraph*° way of those above.   *angelic, pure*

86

   So much for Julia! Now we'll turn to Juan.
     Poor little fellow! he had no idea
   Of his own case, and never hit the true one;
     In feelings quick as Ovid's Miss Medea,[6]
685   He puzzled over what he found a new one,
     But not as yet imagined it could be a
   Thing quite in course, and not at all alarming,
   Which, with a little patience, might grow charming.

87

   Silent and pensive, idle, restless, slow,
690   His home deserted for the lonely wood,
   Tormented with a wound he could not know,
     His, like all deep grief, plunged in solitude:
   I'm fond myself of solitude or so,
     But then, I beg it may be understood,
695   By solitude I mean a Sultan's (not
   A Hermit's), with a harem for a grot.°   *grotto*

88

   "Oh Love! in such a wilderness as this,
     Where Transport and Security entwine,
   Here is the Empire of thy perfect bliss,
700   And here thou art a God indeed divine."
   The bard[7] I quote from does not sing amiss,
     With the exception of the second line,
   For that same twining "Transport and Security"
   Are twisted to a phrase of some obscurity.

89

705   The Poet meant, no doubt, and thus appeals
     To the good sense and senses of mankind,
   The very thing which everybody feels,
     As all have found on trial, or may find,
   That no one likes to be disturbed at meals
710   Or love—I won't say more about "entwined"
   Or "Transport," as we knew all that before,
   But beg "Security" will bolt the door.

---

6. In Ovid's *Metamorphoses,* the young Medea finds herself irresistibly infatuated with the hero Jason.

7. Byron's contemporary, Thomas Campbell, whose *Gertrude of Wyoming* is here paraphrased.

90

Young Juan wandered by the glassy brooks,
 Thinking unutterable things; he threw
715 Himself at length within the leafy nooks
 Where the wild branch of the cork forest grew;
There poets find materials for their books,
 And every now and then we read them through,
So that their plan and prosody are eligible,
720 Unless, like Wordsworth,[8] they prove unintelligible.

91

He, Juan (and not Wordsworth), so pursued
 His self-communion with his own high soul,
Until his mighty heart, in its great mood,
 Had mitigated part, though not the whole
725 Of its disease; he did the best he could
 With things not very subject to control,
And turned, without perceiving his condition,
Like Coleridge,[9] into a metaphysician.

92

He thought about himself, and the whole earth,
730 Of man the wonderful, and of the stars,
And how the deuce they ever could have birth;
 And then he thought of earthquakes, and of wars,
How many miles the moon might have in girth,
 Of air-balloons, and of the many bars
735 To perfect knowledge of the boundless skies;—
And then he thought of Donna Julia's eyes.

93

In thoughts like these true Wisdom may discern
 Longings sublime, and aspirations high,
Which some are born with, but the most part learn
740 To plague themselves withal, they know not why:
'Twas strange that one so young should thus concern
 His brain about the action of the sky;
If *you* think 'twas Philosophy that this did,
I can't help thinking puberty assisted.

94

745 He pored upon the leaves, and on the flowers,
 And heard a voice in all the winds; and then
He thought of wood-nymphs and immortal bowers,
 And how the goddesses came down to men:
He missed the pathway, he forgot the hours,
750 And when he looked upon his watch again,
He found how much old Time had been a winner—
He also found that he had lost his dinner.

8. William Wordsworth (1770–1850; see
pp. 763–805).

9. Samuel Taylor Coleridge (1772–1834; see
pp. 805–31).

95

Sometimes he turned to gaze upon his book,
    Boscan, or Garcilasso;[1]—by the wind
755 Even as the page is rustled while we look,
    So by the poesy of his own mind
Over the mystic leaf his soul was shook,
    As if 'twere one whereon magicians bind
Their spells, and give them to the passing gale,
760 According to some good old woman's tale.

96

Thus would he while his lonely hours away
    Dissatisfied, not knowing what he wanted;
Nor glowing reverie, nor poet's lay,
    Could yield his spirit that for which it panted,
765 A bosom whereon he his head might lay,
    And hear the heart beat with the love it granted,
With—several other things, which I forget,
Or which, at least, I need not mention yet.

97

Those lonely walks, and lengthening reveries,
770 Could not escape the gentle Julia's eyes;
She saw that Juan was not at his ease;
    But that which chiefly may, and must surprise,
Is, that the Donna Inez did not tease
    Her only son with question or surmise;
775 Whether it was she did not see, or would not,
Or, like all very clever people, could not.

98

This may seem strange, but yet 'tis very common;
    For instance—gentlemen, whose ladies take
Leave to o'erstep the written rights of Woman,
780 And break the—Which commandment is't they break?
    (I have forgot the number, and think no man
    Should rashly quote, for fear of a mistake;)
I say, when these same gentlemen are jealous,
They make some blunder, which their ladies tell us.

99

785 A real husband always is suspicious,
    But still no less suspects in the wrong place,
Jealous of some one who had no such wishes,
    Or pandering blindly to his own disgrace,
By harboring some dear friend extremely vicious;
790 The last indeed's infallibly the case:
And when the spouse and friend are gone off wholly,
He wonders at their vice, and not his folly.

1. Spanish poets of the early sixteenth century.

100

Thus parents also are at times short-sighted:
　　Though watchful as the lynx, they ne'er discover,
795　The while the wicked world beholds delighted,
　　Young Hopeful's mistress, or Miss Fanny's lover,
Till some confounded escapade has blighted
　　The plan of twenty years, and all is over;
And then the mother cries, the father swears,
800　And wonders why the devil he got heirs.

101

But Inez was so anxious, and so clear
　　Of sight, that I must think, on this occasion,
She had some other motive much more near
　　For leaving Juan to this new temptation,
805　But what that motive was, I shan't say here;
　　Perhaps to finish Juan's education,
Perhaps to open Don Alfonso's eyes,
In case he thought his wife too great a prize.

102

It was upon a day, a summer's day—
810　Summer's indeed a very dangerous season,
And so is spring about the end of May;
　　The sun, no doubt, is the prevailing reason;
But whatsoe'er the cause is, one may say,
　　And stand convicted of more truth than treason,
815　That there are months which nature grows more merry in,—
　March has its hares, and May must have its heroine.

103

'Twas on a summer's day—the sixth of June:
　　I like to be particular in dates,
Not only of the age, and year, but moon;
820　They are a sort of post-house, where the Fates
Change horses, making History change its tune,
　　Then spur away o'er empires and o'er states,
Leaving at last not much besides chronology,
Excepting the post-obits[2] of theology.

104

825　'Twas on the sixth of June, about the hour
　　Of half-past six—perhaps still nearer seven—
When Julia sate within as pretty a bower
　　As e'er held houri[3] in that heathenish heaven
Described by Mahomet, and Anacreon Moore,[4]
830　　To whom the lyre and laurels have been given,

---

2. Postobit bonds: loans repaid from the estate of
a person after his or her death; probably referring
to rewards or punishments in the afterlife.
3. A beautiful maiden said to entertain faithful
Muslims in paradise.

4. Byron's friend, Thomas Moore, author of
Oriental tales in his long poem *Lalla Rookh* and
translator of love poems by the ancient Greek poet
Anacreon.

With all the trophies of triumphant song—
He won them well, and may he wear them long!

105

She sate, but not alone; I know not well
    How this same interview had taken place,
835 And even if I knew, I should not tell—
    People should hold their tongues in any case;
No matter how or why the thing befell,
    But there were she and Juan, face to face—
When two such faces are so, 'twould be wise,
840 But very difficult, to shut their eyes.

106

How beautiful she looked! her conscious heart[5]
    Glowed in her cheek, and yet she felt no wrong:
Oh Love! how perfect is thy mystic art,
    Strengthening the weak, and trampling on the strong!
845 How self-deceitful is the sagest part
    Of mortals whom thy lure hath led along!
The precipice she stood on was immense,
So was her creed° in her own innocence.   *trust*

107

She thought of her own strength, and Juan's youth,
850   And of the folly of all prudish fears,
Victorious Virtue, and domestic Truth,
    And then of Don Alfonso's fifty years:
I wish these last had not occurred, in sooth,
    Because that number rarely much endears,
855 And through all climes, the snowy and the sunny,
Sounds ill in love, whate'er it may in money.

108

When people say, "I've told you *fifty* times,"
    They mean to scold, and very often do;
When poets say, "I've written *fifty* rhymes,"
860   They make you dread that they'll recite them too;
In gangs of *fifty*, thieves commit their crimes;
    At *fifty* love for love is rare, 'tis true,
But then, no doubt, it equally as true is,
A good deal may be bought for *fifty* Louis.[6]

109

865 Julia had honor, virtue, truth, and love
    For Don Alfonso; and she inly swore,
By all the vows below to Powers above,
    She never would disgrace the ring she wore,
Nor leave a wish which wisdom might reprove;
870   And while she pondered this, besides much more,

---

5. Her deep emotion.   6. French gold coins.

One hand on Juan's carelessly was thrown,
Quite by mistake—she thought it was her own;

110

Unconsciously she leaned upon the other,
    Which played within the tangles of her hair;
875 And to contend with thoughts she could not smother
    She seemed by the distraction of her air.
'Twas surely very wrong in Juan's mother
    To leave together this imprudent pair,
She who for many years had watched her son so—
880 I'm very certain *mine* would not have done so.

111

The hand which still held Juan's, by degrees
    Gently, but palpably confirmed its grasp,
As if it said, "Detain me, if you please";
    Yet there's no doubt she only meant to clasp
885 His fingers with a pure Platonic squeeze;
    She would have shrunk as from a toad, or asp,
Had she imagined such a thing could rouse
A feeling dangerous to a prudent spouse.

112

I cannot know what Juan thought of this,
890   But what he did, is much what you would do;
His young lip thanked it with a grateful kiss,
    And then, abashed at its own joy, withdrew
In deep despair, lest he had done amiss—
    Love is so very timid when 'tis new:
895 She blushed, and frowned not, but she strove to speak,
And held her tongue, her voice was grown so weak.

113

The sun set, and up rose the yellow moon:
    The Devil's in the moon for mischief; they
Who called her CHASTE, methinks, began too soon
900   Their nomenclature; there is not a day,
The longest, not the twenty-first of June,
    Sees half the business in a wicked way,
On which three single hours of moonshine smile—
And then she looks so modest all the while!

114

905 There is a dangerous silence in that hour,
    A stillness, which leaves room for the full soul
To open all itself, without the power
    Of calling wholly back its self-control;
The silver light which, hallowing tree and tower,
910   Sheds beauty and deep softness o'er the whole,

Breathes also to the heart, and o'er it throws
A loving languor, which is not repose.

115

And Julia sate with Juan, half embraced
    And half retiring from the glowing arm,
915 Which trembled like the bosom where 'twas placed;
    Yet still she must have thought there was no harm,
Or else 'twere easy to withdraw her waist;
    But then the situation had its charm,
And then—God knows what next—I can't go on;
920 I'm almost sorry that I e'er begun.

116

Oh Plato! Plato! you have paved the way,
    With your confounded fantasies, to more
Immoral conduct by the fancied sway
    Your system feigns o'er the controlless core
925 Of human hearts, than all the long array
    Of poets and romancers:—You're a bore,
A charlatan, a coxcomb—and have been,
At best, no better than a go-between.

117

And Julia's voice was lost, except in sighs,
930   Until too late for useful conversation;
The tears were gushing from her gentle eyes,
    I wish, indeed, they had not had occasion;
But who, alas! can love, and then be wise?
    Not that Remorse did not oppose Temptation;
935 A little still she strove, and much repented,
And whispering "I will ne'er consent"—consented.

118

'Tis said that Xerxes[7] offered a reward
    To those who could invent him a new pleasure:
Methinks the requisition's rather hard,
940   And must have cost his Majesty a treasure:
For my part, I'm a moderate-minded bard,
    Fond of a little love (which I call leisure);
I care not for new pleasures, as the old
Are quite enough for me, so they but hold.

119

945 Oh Pleasure! you're indeed a pleasant thing,
    Although one must be damned for you, no doubt:
I make a resolution every spring
    Of reformation, ere the year run out,
But somehow, this my vestal vow takes wing,
950   Yet still, I trust, it may be kept throughout:

---

7. King of Persia, fifth century B.C.E.

I'm very sorry, very much ashamed,
And mean, next winter, to be quite reclaimed.

1818   1819

Stanzas

When a Man Hath No Freedom to Fight for at Home

When a man hath no freedom to fight for at home,
   Let him combat for that of his neighbors;
Let him think of the glories of Greece and of Rome,
   And get knocked on his head for his labors.

5 To do good to mankind is the chivalrous plan,
   And is always as nobly requited;
Then battle for freedom wherever you can,
   And, if not shot or hanged, you'll get knighted.

1820   1830

On This Day I Complete My Thirty-sixth Year

Missolonghi,[8] January 22, 1824

'Tis time this heart should be unmoved,
   Since others it hath ceased to move:
Yet, though I cannot be beloved,
     Still let me love!

5 My days are in the yellow leaf;
   The flowers and fruits of love are gone;
The worm, the canker,° and the grief   *deep infection*
     Are mine alone!

The fire that on my bosom preys
10 Is lone as some volcanic isle;
No torch is kindled at its blaze—
     A funeral pile.

The hope, the fear, the jealous care,
   The exalted portion of the pain
15 And power of love, I cannot share,
     But wear the chain.

But 'tis not *thus*—and 'tis not *here*—
   Such thoughts should shake my soul, nor *now*,

---

8. A town in Greece, where Byron had gone to support the Greek war for independence from Turkey, and where he died, April 19, 1824.

Where glory decks the hero's bier,
20   Or binds his brow.

The sword, the banner, and the field,
    Glory and Greece, around me see!
The Spartan, borne upon his shield,
        Was not more free.

25 Awake! (not Greece—she *is* awake!)
    Awake, my spirit! Think through *whom*
Thy life-blood tracks its parent lake,
        And then strike home!

Tread those reviving passions down,
30   Unworthy manhood!—unto thee
Indifferent should the smile or frown
        Of beauty be.

If thou regrett'st thy youth, *why live?*
    The land of honorable death
35 Is here:—up to the field, and give
        Away thy breath!

Seek out—less often sought than found—
    A soldier's grave, for thee the best;
Then look around, and choose thy ground,
40   And take thy rest.

1824   1824

PERCY BYSSHE SHELLEY
1792–1822

To Wordsworth[1]

Poet of Nature, thou hast wept to know
    That things depart which never may return;
    Childhood and youth, friendship and love's first glow,
    Have fled like sweet dreams, leaving thee to mourn.
5   These common woes I feel. One loss is mine,
    Which thou too feel'st, yet I alone deplore;
    Thou wert as a lone star whose light did shine
    On some frail bark in winter's midnight roar;
Thou hast like to a rock-built refuge stood
10   Above the blind and battling multitude;
    In honored poverty thy voice did weave
Songs consecrate to truth and liberty;—

---

1. William Wordsworth (1770–1850; see pp. 763–805), who had ceased to champion the liberal and revolutionary ideas of his youth and, in Shelley's view, had compromised himself.

Deserting these, thou leavest me to grieve,
Thus having been, that thou shouldst cease to be.

1816

Mutability

1

The flower that smiles today
    Tomorrow dies;
All that we wish to stay,
    Tempts and then flies.
5 What is this world's delight?
Lightning that mocks the night,
  Brief even as bright.

2

Virtue, how frail it is!
    Friendship how rare!
10 Love, how it sells poor bliss
    For proud despair!
But we, though soon they fall,
Survive their joy and all
  Which ours we call.

3

15 Whilst skies are blue and bright,
    Whilst flowers are gay,
Whilst eyes that change ere night
    Make glad the day,
Whilst yet the calm hours creep,
20 Dream thou—and from thy sleep
  Then wake to weep.

1815–16   1824

Hymn to Intellectual Beauty[2]

1

The awful shadow of some unseen Power
  Floats though unseen among us—visiting
  This various world with as inconstant wing
As summer winds that creep from flower to flower—
5 Like moonbeams that behind some piny mountain shower,[3]
    It visits with inconstant glance
    Each human heart and countenance;
  Like hues and harmonies of evening—

---

2. Beauty perceived not by the senses but by spir-   3. Used as a verb.
itual illumination.

Like clouds in starlight widely spread—
10   Like memory of music fled—
Like aught that for its grace may be
Dear, and yet dearer for its mystery.

2

Spirit of BEAUTY, that dost consecrate
With thine own hues all thou dost shine upon
15   Of human thought or form—where art thou gone?
Why dost thou pass away and leave our state,
This dim vast vale of tears, vacant and desolate?
        Ask why the sunlight not forever
        Weaves rainbows o'er yon mountain river,
20 Why aught should fail and fade that once is shown,
        Why fear and dream and death and birth
        Cast on the daylight of this earth
        Such gloom—why man has such a scope
For love and hate, despondency and hope?

3

25 No voice from some sublimer world hath ever
        To sage or poet these responses given—
        Therefore the names of Daemon, Ghost, and Heaven,
Remain the records of their vain endeavor,
Frail spells—whose uttered charm might not avail to sever,
30   From all we hear and all we see,
        Doubt, chance, and mutability.
Thy light alone—like mist o'er mountains driven,
        Or music by the night wind sent
        Through strings of some still instrument,°   *wind harp*
35   Or moonlight on a midnight stream,
Gives grace and truth to life's unquiet dream.

4

Love, Hope, and Self-esteem, like clouds depart
        And come, for some uncertain moments lent.
        Man were immortal, and omnipotent,
40 Didst thou, unknown and awful as thou art,
Keep with thy glorious train° firm state within his heart.   *company*
        Thou messenger of sympathies,
        That wax and wane in lovers' eyes—
Thou—that to human thought art nourishment,
45   Like darkness to a dying flame!
        Depart not as thy shadow came,
        Depart not—lest the grave should be,
Like life and fear, a dark reality.

5

While yet a boy I sought for ghosts, and sped
50   Through many a listening chamber, cave and ruin,
        And starlight wood, with fearful steps pursuing

Hopes of high talk with the departed dead.
I called on poisonous names[4] with which our youth is fed;
   I was not heard—I saw them not—
55   When musing deeply on the lot
Of life, at that sweet time when winds are wooing
    All vital things that wake to bring
    News of birds and blossoming—
   Sudden, thy shadow fell on me;
60   I shrieked, and clasped my hands in ecstasy!

6

I vowed that I would dedicate my powers
   To thee and thine—have I not kept the vow?
   With beating heart and streaming eyes, even now
I call the phantoms of a thousand hours
65   Each from his voiceless grave: they have in visioned bowers
    Of studious zeal or love's delight
    Outwatched with me the envious night—
They know that never joy illumed my brow
    Unlinked with hope that thou wouldst free
70   This world from its dark slavery,
    That thou—O awful LOVELINESS,
Wouldst give whate'er these words cannot express.

7

The day becomes more solemn and serene
   When noon is past—there is a harmony
75   In autumn, and a luster in its sky,
Which through the summer is not heard or seen,
As if it could not be, as if it had not been!
    Thus let thy power, which like the truth
    Of nature on my passive youth
80   Descended, to my onward life supply
    Its calm—to one who worships thee,
    And every form containing thee,
    Whom, SPIRIT fair, thy spells did bind
To fear[5] himself, and love all human kind.

1816   1817

Mont Blanc[6]

Lines Written in the Vale of Chamouni[7]

I

The everlasting universe of things
Flows through the mind, and rolls its rapid waves,

4. Possibly alluding to attempts to summon spirits of the dead by means of magic rites.
5. Perhaps in the old sense of "regard with reverence and awe."
6. The highest of the Alps.

7. Through the Chamouni valley flows the river Arve, which originates in a glacier on the mountain and empties into the river Rhone, which in due course reaches the Mediterranean.

Now dark—now glittering—now reflecting gloom—
Now lending splendor, where from secret springs
5 The source of human thought its tribute brings
Of waters,—with a sound but half its own,
Such as a feeble brook will oft assume
In the wild woods, among the mountains lone,
Where waterfalls around it leap for ever,
10 Where woods and winds contend, and a vast river
Over its rocks ceaselessly bursts and raves.

2

Thus thou, Ravine of Arve—dark, deep Ravine—
Thou many-colored, many voicèd vale,
Over whose pines, and crags, and caverns sail
15 Fast cloud-shadows and sunbeams: awful° scene,   *awesome*
Where Power in likeness of the Arve comes down
From the ice-gulfs that gird his secret throne,
Bursting through these dark mountains like the flame
Of lightning through the tempest;—thou dost lie,
20 Thy giant brood of pines around thee clinging,
Children of elder time, in whose devotion
The chainless winds still come and ever came
To drink their odors, and their mighty swinging
To hear—an old and solemn harmony;
25 Thine earthly rainbows stretched across the sweep
Of the ethereal waterfall, whose veil
Robes some unsculptured image; the strange sleep
Which when the voices of the desert fail
Wraps all in its own deep eternity;—
30 Thy caverns echoing to the Arve's commotion,
A loud, lone sound no other sound can tame;
Thou art pervaded with that ceaseless motion,
Thou art the path of that unresting sound—
Dizzy Ravine! and when I gaze on thee
35 I seem as in a trance sublime and strange
To muse on my own separate fantasy,
My own, my human mind, which passively
Now renders and receives fast influencings,
Holding an unremitting interchange
40 With the clear universe of things around;
One legion of wild thoughts, whose wandering wings
Now float above thy darkness, and now rest
Where that or thou art no unbidden guest,
In the still cave of the witch Poesy,[8]
45 Seeking among the shadows that pass by
Ghosts of all things that are, some shade of thee,
Some phantom, some faint image; till the breast
From which they fled recalls them, thou art there!

_____
8. The power of the imagination.

3

Some say that gleams of a remoter world
50 Visit the soul in sleep,—that death is slumber,
And that its shapes the busy thoughts outnumber
Of those who wake and live.—I look on high;
Has some unknown omnipotence unfurled
The veil of life and death? or do I lie
55 In dream, and does the mightier world of sleep
Spread far around and inaccessibly
Its circles? For the very spirit fails,
Driven like a homeless cloud from steep to steep
That vanishes among the viewless° gales!   invisible
60 Far, far above, piercing the infinite sky,
Mont Blanc appears,—still, snowy, and serene—
Its subject mountains their unearthly forms
Pile around it, ice and rock; broad vales° between   valleys
Of frozen floods, unfathomable deeps,
65 Blue as the overhanging heaven, that spread
And wind among the accumulated steeps;
A desert peopled by the storms alone,
Save when the eagle brings some hunter's bone,
And the wolf tracks her there—how hideously
70 Its shapes are heaped around! rude, bare, and high,
Ghastly, and scarred, and riven.—Is this the scene
Where the old Earthquake-demon[9] taught her young
Ruin? Were these their toys? or did a sea
Of fire envelop once this silent snow?
75 None can reply—all seems eternal now.
The wilderness has a mysterious tongue
Which teaches awful° doubt, or faith so mild,   profoundly disturbing
So solemn, so serene, that man may be,
But for such faith, with nature reconciled;[1]
80 Thou hast a voice, great Mountain, to repeal
Large codes of fraud and woe; not understood
By all, but which the wise, and great, and good
Interpret, or make felt, or deeply feel.

4

The fields, the lakes, the forests, and the streams,
85 Ocean, and all the living things that dwell
Within the daedal[2] earth; lightning, and rain,
Earthquake, and fiery flood, and hurricane,
The torpor of the year when feeble dreams
Visit the hidden buds, or dreamless sleep
90 Holds every future leaf and flower;—the bound
With which from that detested trance they leap;
The works and ways of man, their death and birth,
And that of him and all that his may be;

9. Personification of geologic forces.
1. A debated passage; perhaps to be paraphrased
as: the "tongue" may teach either that the cosmos
and the human mind are deeply at odds, or that we
may have "faith" that they are in harmony.
2. Intricately made, as by Daedalus, the legendary
Greek craftsman.

All things that move and breathe with toil and sound
95   Are born and die; revolve, subside, and swell.
Power dwells apart in its tranquility,
Remote, serene, and inaccessible:
And *this*, the naked countenance of earth,
On which I gaze, even these primeval mountains
100   Teach the adverting mind. The glaciers creep
Like snakes that watch their prey, from their far fountains,
Slow rolling on; there, many a precipice,
Frost and the Sun in scorn of mortal power
Have piled: dome, pyramid, and pinnacle,
105   A city of death, distinct with many a tower
And wall impregnable of beaming ice.
Yet not a city, but a flood of ruin
Is there, that from the boundaries of the sky
Rolls its perpetual stream; vast pines are strewing
110   Its destined path, or in the mangled soil
Branchless and shattered stand; the rocks, drawn down
From yon remotest waste, have overthrown
The limits of the dead and living world,
Never to be reclaimed. The dwelling-place
115   Of insects, beasts, and birds, becomes its spoil
Their food and their retreat for ever gone,
So much of life and joy is lost. The race
Of man flies far in dread; his work and dwelling
Vanish, like smoke before the tempest's stream,
120   And their place is not known. Below, vast caves
Shine in the rushing torrents' restless gleam,
Which from those secret chasms in tumult welling
Meet in the vale, and one majestic River,
The breath and blood of distant lands, for ever
125   Rolls its loud waters to the ocean-waves,
Breathes its swift vapors to the circling air.[3]

5

Mont Blanc yet gleams on high:—the power is there,
The still and solemn power of many sights,
And many sounds, and much of life and death.
130   In the calm darkness of the moonless nights,
In the lone glare of day, the snows descend
Upon that Mountain; none beholds them there,
Nor when the flakes burn in the sinking sun,
Or the star-beams dart through them:—Winds contend
135   Silently there, and heap the snow with breath
Rapid and strong, but silently! Its home
The voiceless lightning in these solitudes
Keeps innocently, and like vapor broods
Over the snow. The secret Strength of things
140   Which governs thought, and to the infinite dome
Of Heaven is as a law, inhabits thee![4]

3. Cf. Coleridge, "Kubla Khan," lines 12–24   4. I.e., Mont Blanc.
(p. 809).

And what were thou, and earth, and stars, and sea,
If to the human mind's imaginings
Silence and solitude were vacancy?

July 23, 1816   1817

Ozymandias[5]

I met a traveler from an antique land
Who said: Two vast and trunkless legs of stone
Stand in the desert . . . Near them, on the sand,
Half sunk, a shattered visage lies, whose frown,
5   And wrinkled lip, and sneer of cold command,
Tell that its sculptor well those passions read
Which yet survive, stamped on these lifeless things,
The hand that mocked them, and the heart that fed:
And on the pedestal these words appear:
10   "My name is Ozymandias, king of kings:
Look on my works, ye Mighty, and despair!"
Nothing beside remains. Round the decay
Of that colossal wreck, boundless and bare
The lone and level sands stretch far away.

1817   1818

Stanzas Written in Dejection, Near Naples

1

The sun is warm, the sky is clear,
     The waves are dancing fast and bright,
Blue isles and snowy mountains wear
     The purple noon's transparent might,
5   The breath of the moist earth is light,
Around its unexpanded buds;
     Like many a voice of one delight,
The winds, the birds, the ocean floods,
The City's voice itself is soft like Solitude's.

2

10   I see the Deep's untrampled floor
     With green and purple seaweeds strown;
I see the waves upon the shore,
     Like light dissolved in star-showers, thrown:
     I sit upon the sands alone—
15   The lightning of the noontide ocean

---

5. Greek name for the Egyptian monarch Ramses II (thirteenth century B.C.E.), who is said to have erected
a huge statue of himself.

Is flashing round me, and a tone
Arises from its measured motion;
How sweet! did any heart now share in my emotion.

3

Alas! I have nor hope nor health,
20   Nor peace within nor calm around,
Nor that content surpassing wealth
    The sage in meditation found,
    And walked with inward glory crowned—
Nor fame, nor power, nor love, nor leisure.
25   Others I see whom these surround—
Smiling they live, and call life pleasure;
To me that cup has been dealt in another measure.

4

Yet now despair itself is mild,
    Even as the winds and waters are;
30   I could lie down like a tired child,
    And weep away the life of care
    Which I have borne and yet must bear,
Till death like sleep might steal on me,
    And I might feel in the warm air
35   My cheek grow cold, and hear the sea
Breathe o'er my dying brain its last monotony.

5

Some might lament that I were cold,
    As I, when this sweet day is gone,
Which my lost heart, too soon grown old,
40   Insults with this untimely moan;
    They might lament—for I am one
Whom men love not—and yet regret,
    Unlike this day, which, when the sun
    Shall on its stainless glory set,
45 Will linger, though enjoyed, like joy in memory yet.

1818   1824

England in 1819

An old, mad, blind, despised, and dying king[6]—
Princes, the dregs of their dull race,[7] who flow
Through public scorn—mud from a muddy spring;
Rulers who neither see, nor feel, nor know,
5 But leechlike to their fainting country cling,
Till they drop, blind in blood, without a blow;

6. George III (1738–1820), who lived for years in a state of advanced senility. The "Princes" of line 2 are George III's sons, including the prince-regent, later George IV, whom Shelley detested.
7. The "Hanoverian" line of English monarchs, beginning in 1714 with George I.

A people starved and stabbed in the untilled field—
An army, which liberticide[8] and prey
Makes as a two-edged sword to all who wield;
10 Golden and sanguine laws[9] which tempt and slay;
Religion Christless, Godless—a book sealed;
A Senate—Time's worst statute[1] unrepealed—
Are graves, from which a glorious Phantom[2] may
Burst, to illumine our tempestuous day.

1819   1839

Ode to the West Wind[3]

I

O wild West Wind, thou breath of Autumn's being,
Thou, from whose unseen presence the leaves dead
Are driven, like ghosts from an enchanter fleeing,

Yellow, and black, and pale, and hectic red,
5 Pestilence-stricken multitudes: O thou,
Who chariotest to their dark wintry bed

The wingèd seeds, where they lie cold and low,
Each like a corpse within its grave, until
Thine azure sister of the Spring shall blow

10 Her clarion[4] o'er the dreaming earth, and fill
(Driving sweet buds like flocks to feed in air)
With living hues and odors plain and hill:

Wild Spirit, which art moving everywhere;
Destroyer and preserver; hear, oh, hear!

2

15 Thou on whose stream, mid the steep sky's commotion,
Loose clouds like earth's decaying leaves are shed,
Shook from the tangled boughs of Heaven and Ocean,

Angels[5] of rain and lightning: there are spread
On the blue surface of thine aëry surge,
20 Like the bright hair uplifted from the head

8. Destruction of liberty. An allusion to the Peterloo Massacre. On August 16, 1819, a cavalry troop attacked a crowd at a peaceful political rally in St. Peter's Field, near Manchester. *Peterloo* ironically conflates *St. Peter* with the Battle of *Waterloo*.
9. Laws bought with gold and causing bloodshed.
1. Probably the Act of Union (1801), uniting Ireland to England and excluding Roman Catholics from exercising full citizenship.
2. I.e., the spirit of liberty.
3. "This poem was conceived and chiefly written in a wood that skirts the Arno, near Florence, and

on a day when that tempestuous wind, whose temperature is at once mild and animating, was collecting the vapours which pour down the autumnal rains" [Shelley's note]. Florence was the home of Dante, the fourteenth-century poet whose masterpiece, *The Divine Comedy*, originated *terza rima*, the verse form of Shelley's poem (see "Versification," pp. 2040–41).
4. Trumpet-call.
5. In Greek derivation, messengers or divine messengers.

Of some fierce Maenad,[6] even from the dim verge
Of the horizon to the zenith's height,
The locks of the approaching storm. Thou dirge

Of the dying year, to which this closing night
25 Will be the dome of a vast sepulcher,
Vaulted with all thy congregated might

Of vapors,° from whose solid atmosphere   clouds
Black rain, and fire, and hail will burst: oh, hear!

3

Thou who didst waken from his summer dreams
30 The blue Mediterranean, where he lay,
Lulled by the coil of his crystàlline streams,

Beside a pumice isle in Baiae's bay,[7]
And saw in sleep old palaces and towers
Quivering within the wave's intenser day,

35 All overgrown with azure moss and flowers
So sweet, the sense faints picturing them! Thou
For whose path the Atlantic's level powers

Cleave themselves into chasms, while far below
The sea-blooms and the oozy woods which wear
40 The sapless foliage of the ocean, know

Thy voice, and suddenly grow gray with fear,
And tremble and despoil themselves: oh, hear![8]

4

If I were a dead leaf thou mightest bear;
If I were a swift cloud to fly with thee;
45 A wave to pant beneath thy power, and share

The impulse of thy strength, only less free
Than thou, O uncontrollable! If even
I were as in my boyhood, and could be

The comrade of thy wanderings over Heaven,
50 As then, when to outstrip thy skyey speed
Scarce seemed a vision; I would ne'er have striven

As thus with thee in prayer in my sore need.
Oh, lift me as a wave, a leaf, a cloud!
I fall upon the thorns of life! I bleed!

6. Frenzied dancer, worshiper of Dionysus (Greek god of wine and fertility).
7. Near Naples, Italy.

8. "The vegetation at the bottom of the sea . . . sympathizes with that of the land in the change of seasons" [Shelley's note].

55   A heavy weight of hours has chained and bowed
      One too like thee: tameless, and swift, and proud.

5

      Make me thy lyre, even as the forest is:
      What if my leaves are falling like its own!
      The tumult of thy mighty harmonies

60   Will take from both a deep, autumnal tone,
      Sweet though in sadness. Be thou, Spirit fierce,
      My spirit! Be thou me, impetuous one!

      Drive my dead thoughts over the universe
      Like withered leaves to quicken a new birth!
65   And, by the incantation of this verse,

      Scatter, as from an unextinguished hearth
      Ashes and sparks, my words among mankind!
      Be through my lips to unawakened earth

      The trumpet of a prophecy! O Wind,
70   If Winter comes, can Spring be far behind?

1819   1820

The Cloud

      I bring fresh showers for the thirsting flowers,
          From the seas and the streams;
      I bear light shade for the leaves when laid
          In their noonday dreams.
5   From my wings are shaken the dews that waken
          The sweet buds every one,
      When rocked to rest on their mother's breast,
          As she dances about the sun.
      I wield the flail of the lashing hail,
10   And whiten the green plains under,
      And then again I dissolve it in rain,
          And laugh as I pass in thunder.

      I sift the snow on the mountains below,
          And their great pines groan aghast;
15   And all the night 'tis my pillow white,
          While I sleep in the arms of the blast.
      Sublime on the towers of my skyey bowers,
          Lightning my pilot[9] sits;
      In a cavern under is fettered the thunder,
20   It struggles and howls at fits;°   *intervals*

9. Electrical energy, here represented as directing the cloud in response to the attraction of opposite charges ("genii," line 23) under the sea.

Over earth and ocean, with gentle motion,
    This pilot is guiding me,
Lured by the love of the genii that move
    In the depths of the purple sea;
25 Over the rills, and the crags, and the hills,
    Over the lakes and the plains,
Wherever he dream, under mountain or stream,
    The Spirit he loves remains;
And I all the while bask in Heaven's blue smile,
30   Whilst he is dissolving in rains.

The sanguine Sunrise, with his meteor eyes,
    And his burning plumes outspread,
Leaps on the back of my sailing rack,[1]
    When the morning star shines dead;
35 As on the jag of a mountain crag,
    Which an earthquake rocks and swings,
An eagle alit one moment may sit
    In the light of its golden wings.
And when Sunset may breathe, from the lit sea beneath,
40   Its ardors of rest and of love,
And the crimson pall of eve may fall
    From the depth of Heaven above,
With wings folded I rest, on mine aëry nest,
    As still as a brooding dove.

45 That orbèd maiden with white fire laden,
    Whom mortals call the Moon,
Glides glimmering o'er my fleecelike floor,
    By the midnight breezes strewn;
And wherever the beat of her unseen feet,
50   Which only the angels hear,
May have broken the woof° of my tent's thin roof,   *fabric*
    The stars peep behind her and peer;
And I laugh to see them whirl and flee,
    Like a swarm of golden bees,
55 When I widen the rent in my wind-built tent,
    Till the calm rivers, lakes, and seas,
Like strips of the sky fallen through me on high,
    Are each paved with the moon and these.

I bind the Sun's throne with a burning zone,°   *belt*
60   And the Moon's with a girdle of pearl;
The volcanoes are dim, and the stars reel and swim,
    When the whirlwinds my banner unfurl.
From cape to cape, with a bridgelike shape,
    Over a torrent sea,
65 Sunbeam-proof, I hang like a roof—
    The mountains its columns be.
The triumphal arch through which I march
    With hurricane, fire, and snow,

---

1. Wind-driven clouds.

When the Powers of the air are chained to my chair,
70   Is the million-colored bow;
The sphere-fire above its soft colors wove,
      While the moist Earth was laughing below.

I am the daughter of Earth and Water,
      And the nursling of the Sky;
75   I pass through the pores of the ocean and shores;
      I change, but I cannot die.
For after the rain when with never a stain
      The pavilion of Heaven is bare,
And the winds and sunbeams with their convex° gleams   *upward-arching*
80   Build up the blue dome of air,
I silently laugh at my own cenotaph,[2]
      And out of the caverns of rain,
Like a child from the womb, like a ghost from the tomb,
      I arise and unbuild it again.

1820   1820

To a Skylark

Hail to thee, blithe Spirit!
      Bird thou never wert,
That from Heaven, or near it,
      Pourest thy full heart
5   In profuse strains of unpremeditated art.

Higher still and higher
      From the earth thou springest
Like a cloud of fire;
      The blue deep thou wingest,
10 And singing still dost soar, and soaring ever singest.

In the golden lightning
      Of the sunken sun,
O'er which clouds are bright'ning,
      Thou dost float and run;
15 Like an unbodied joy whose race is just begun.

The pale purple even
      Melts around thy flight;
Like a star of Heaven,
      In the broad daylight
20 Thou art unseen, but yet I hear thy shrill delight,

Keen as are the arrows
      Of that silver sphere,°   *star*

2. Monument honoring a person who is buried elsewhere.

      Whose intense lamp narrows
        In the white dawn clear
25 Until we hardly see—we feel that it is there.

      All the earth and air
        With thy voice is loud,
      As, when night is bare,
        From one lonely cloud
30 The moon rains out her beams, and Heaven is overflowed.

      What thou art we know not;
        What is most like thee?
      From rainbow clouds there flow not
        Drops so bright to see
35 As from thy presence showers a rain of melody.

      Like a Poet hidden
        In the light of thought,
      Singing hymns unbidden,
        Till the world is wrought
40 To sympathy with hopes and fears it heeded not:

      Like a high-born maiden
        In a palace tower,
      Soothing her love-laden
        Soul in secret hour
45 With music sweet as love, which overflows her bower:

      Like a glowworm golden
        In a dell of dew,
      Scattering unbeholden
        Its aërial hue
50 Among the flowers and grass, which screen it from the view!

      Like a rose embowered
        In its own green leaves,
      By warm winds deflowered,
        Till the scent it gives
55 Makes faint with too much sweet those heavy-wingèd thieves:

      Sound of vernal showers
        On the twinkling grass,
      Rain-awakened flowers,
        All that ever was
60 Joyous, and clear, and fresh, thy music doth surpass:

      Teach us, Sprite° or Bird,   *spirit*
        What sweet thoughts are thine:
      I have never heard
        Praise of love or wine
65 That panted forth a flood of rapture so divine.

Chorus Hymeneal,[3]
  Or triumphal chant,
Matched with thine would be all
  But an empty vaunt,
70 A thing wherein we feel there is some hidden want.

What objects are the fountains
  Of thy happy strain?
What fields, or waves, or mountains?
  What shapes of sky or plain?
75 What love of thine own kind? what ignorance of pain?

With thy clear keen joyance
  Languor cannot be:
Shadow of annoyance
  Never came near thee:
80 Thou lovest—but ne'er knew love's sad satiety.

Waking or asleep,
  Thou of death must deem
Things more true and deep
  Than we mortals dream,
85 Or how could thy notes flow in such a crystal stream?

We look before and after,
  And pine for what is not:
Our sincerest laughter
  With some pain is fraught;
90 Our sweetest songs are those that tell of saddest thought.

Yet if we could scorn
  Hate, and pride, and fear;
If we were things born
  Not to shed a tear,
95 I know not how thy joy we ever should come near.

Better than all measures
  Of delightful sound,
Better than all treasures
  That in books are found,
100 Thy skill to poet were, thou scorner of the ground!

Teach me half the gladness
  That thy brain must know,
Such harmonious madness
  From my lips would flow
105 The world should listen then—as I am listening now.

1820   1820

3. As for a wedding (from Hymen, Greek god of marriage).

Adonais[4]

An Elegy on the Death of John Keats, Author of Endymion, Hyperion, etc.[5]

ἀστὴρ πρὶν μὲν ἔλαμπες ἐνὶ ζωοῖσιν ἑῷος,
νῦν δὲ θανὼν λάμπεις ἕσπερος ἐν φθιμένοις.[6]
—PLATO

1

I weep for Adonais—he is dead!
Oh, weep for Adonais! though our tears
Thaw not the frost which binds so dear a head!
And thou, sad Hour, selected from all years
5 To mourn our loss, rouse thy obscure compeers,°   *equals*
And teach them thine own sorrow, say: with me
Died Adonais; till the Future dares
Forget the Past, his fate and fame shall be
An echo and a light unto eternity!

2

10 Where wert thou mighty Mother,[7] when he lay,
When thy Son lay, pierced by the shaft which flies
In darkness? where was lorn° Urania   *abandoned*
When Adonais died? With veilèd eyes,
'Mid listening Echoes, in her Paradise
15 She sate, while one, with soft enamored breath,
Rekindled all the fading melodies,
With which, like flowers that mock the corse° beneath,   *corpse*
He had adorned and hid the coming bulk of death.

3

Oh, weep for Adonais—he is dead!
20 Wake, melancholy Mother, wake and weep!
Yet wherefore? Quench within their burning bed
Thy fiery tears, and let thy loud heart keep
Like his, a mute and uncomplaining sleep;
For he is gone, where all things wise and fair
25 Descend:—oh, dream not that the amorous Deep
Will yet restore him to the vital air;
Death feeds on his mute voice, and laughs at our despair.

---

4. A name derived from *Adonis*, in Greek mythology a young hunter beloved of Aphrodite and killed by a wild boar. The root meaning of his name, *Adon*, is "the lord," and in the form *Adonai* appears in Hebrew scriptures as a synonym for *God*.
5. Keats died, in Rome, on February 23, 1821; for his poetry, see pp. 905–41.
6. "Thou wert the morning star among the living, / Ere thy fair light had fled— / Now, having died, thou art as Hesperus, giving / New splendor to the dead" [Shelley's translation]. Venus is both Hesperus (also Vesper), the evening star, and Lucifer, the morning star.
7. Urania, "heavenly one," Venus invoked as the Muse (divine inspirer) of noble poetry. Adonais is represented as her son.

4

Most musical of mourners, weep again!
Lament anew, Urania!—He[8] died,
30 Who was the Sire of an immortal strain,
    Blind, old, and lonely, when his country's pride,
    The priest, the slave, and the liberticide,°   destroyer of liberty
    Trampled and mocked with many a loathèd rite
    Of lust and blood; he went, unterrified,
35 Into the gulf of death; but his clear Sprite°   spirit
  Yet reigns o'er earth; the third among the sons of light.[9]

5

Most musical of mourners, weep anew!
Not all to that bright station dared to climb;
And happier they their happiness who knew,
40 Whose tapers yet burn through that night of time
    In which suns perished; others more sublime,
    Struck by the envious wrath of man or God,
    Have sunk, extinct in their refulgent° prime;   shining
    And some yet live, treading the thorny road,
45 Which leads, through toil and hate, to Fame's serene abode.

6

But now, thy youngest, dearest one, has perished,
The nursling of thy widowhood, who grew,
Like a pale flower by some sad maiden cherished,
And fed with true-love tears, instead of dew;
50 Most musical of mourners, weep anew!
    Thy extreme° hope, the loveliest and the last,   highest, latest
    The bloom, whose petals nipped before they blew
    Died on the promise of the fruit, is waste;
  The broken lily lies—the storm is overpast.

7

55 To that high Capital,° where kingly Death   Rome
    Keeps his pale court in beauty and decay,
    He came; and bought, with price of purest breath,
    A grave among the eternal.—Come away!
    Haste, while the vault of blue Italian day
60 Is yet his fitting charnel-roof! while still
    He lies, as if in dewy sleep he lay;
    Awake him not! surely he takes his fill
  Of deep and liquid rest, forgetful of all ill.

8

He will awake no more, oh, never more!—
65 Within the twilight chamber spreads apace
    The shadow of white Death, and at the door
    Invisible Corruption waits to trace

---

8. Milton, who also invoked the aid of Urania (see *Paradise Lost* 1.6–16, p. 421 above).

9. Rivaled as a poet by only two predecessors, Homer and Dante.

His extreme way to her dim dwelling-place;
The eternal Hunger sits, but pity and awe
70   Soothe her pale rage, nor dares she to deface
So fair a prey, till darkness and the law
Of change, shall o'er his sleep the mortal curtain draw.

9

Oh, weep for Adonais!—The quick° Dreams,   *living*
The passion-wingèd Ministers of thought,
75   Who were his flocks, whom near the living streams
Of his young spirit he fed, and whom he taught
The love which was its music, wander not—
Wander no more, from kindling brain to brain,
But droop there, whence they sprung; and mourn their lot
80   Round the cold heart, where, after their sweet pain,
They ne'er will gather strength, or find a home again.

10

And one with trembling hand clasps his cold head,
And fans him with her moonlight wings, and cries,
"Our love, our hope, our sorrow, is not dead;
85   See, on the silken fringe of his faint eyes,
Like dew upon a sleeping flower, there lies
A tear some Dream has loosened from his brain."
Lost Angel of a ruined Paradise!
She knew not 'twas her own; as with no stain
90   She faded, like a cloud which had outwept its rain.

11

One from a lucid° urn of starry dew   *luminous*
Washed his light limbs as if embalming them;
Another clipped her profuse locks, and threw
The wreath upon him, like an anadem,°   *garland*
95   Which frozen tears instead of pearls begem;
Another in her willful grief would break
Her bow and wingèd reeds, as if to stem
A greater loss with one which was more weak;
And dull the barbèd fire against his frozen cheek.

12

100   Another Splendor on his mouth alit,
That mouth, whence it was wont to draw the breath
Which gave it strength to pierce the guarded wit,[1]
And pass into the panting heart beneath
With lightning and with music: the damp death
105   Quenched its caress upon its icy lips;
And, as a dying meteor stains a wreath
Of moonlight vapor, which the cold night clips,°   *envelops*
It flushed through his pale limbs, and passed to its eclipse.

---

1. The defensive analytical mind.

13

And others came . . . Desires and Adorations,
110 Wingèd Persuasions and veiled Destinies,
Splendors, and Glooms, and glimmering Incarnations
Of hopes and fears, and twilight Phantasies;
And Sorrow, with her family of Sighs,
And Pleasure, blind with tears, led by the gleam
115 Of her own dying smile instead of eyes,
Came in slow pomp;—the moving pomp might seem
Like pageantry of mist on an autumnal stream.

14

All he had loved, and molded into thought
From shape, and hue, and odor, and sweet sound,
120 Lamented Adonais. Morning sought
Her eastern watch-tower, and her hair unbound,
Wet with the tears which should adorn the ground,
Dimmed the aërial eyes that kindle day;
Afar the melancholy thunder moaned,
125 Pale Ocean in unquiet slumber lay,
And the wild Winds flew round, sobbing in their dismay.

15

Lost Echo[2] sits amid the voiceless mountains,
And feeds her grief with his remembered lay,
And will no more reply to winds or fountains,
130 Or amorous birds perched on the young green spray,
Or herdsman's horn, or bell at closing day;
Since she can mimic not his lips, more dear
Than those for whose disdain she pined away
Into a shadow of all sounds:—a drear
135 Murmur, between their songs, is all the woodmen hear.

16

Grief made the young Spring wild, and she threw down
Her kindling buds, as if she Autumn were,
Or they dead leaves; since her delight is flown
For whom should she have waked the sullen year?
140 To Phoebus was not Hyacinth[3] so dear,
Nor to himself Narcissus, as to both
Thou, Adonais; wan they stand and sere°   dry; withered
Amid the faint companions of their youth,
With dew all turned to tears; odor, to sighing ruth.°   pity

17

145 Thy spirit's sister, the lorn° nightingale,   lost, abandoned
Mourns not her mate with such melodious pain;

---

2. In Greek mythology, a nymph, or minor nature goddess, who loved Narcissus and who pined away into a mere voice when that youth fell in love with his own reflection in a pool.

3. Youth loved by Apollo ("Phoebus," Greek and Roman god of sunlight, prophecy, music, and poetry), who killed him by accident.

Not so the eagle, who like thee could scale
Heaven, and could nourish in the sun's domain
Her mighty youth,[4] with morning, doth complain,
150   Soaring and screaming round her empty nest,
As Albion° wails for thee: the curse of Cain[5]   England
Light on his head[6] who pierced thy innocent breast,
And scared the angel soul that was its earthly guest!

18

Ah, woe is me! Winter is come and gone,
155   But grief returns with the revolving year;
The airs and streams renew their joyous tone;
The ants, the bees, the swallows reappear;
Fresh leaves and flowers deck the dead Seasons' bier;
The amorous birds now pair in every brake,°   thicket
160   And build their mossy homes in field and brere;°   briar
And the green lizard, and the golden snake,
Like unimprisoned flames, out of their trance awake.

19

Through wood and stream and field and hill and Ocean,
A quickening life from the Earth's heart has burst
165   As it has ever done, with change and motion,
From the great morning of the world when first
God dawned on Chaos; in its stream immersed
The lamps of Heaven flash with a softer light;
All baser things pant with life's sacred thirst;
170   Diffuse themselves; and spend in love's delight,
The beauty and the joy of their renewèd might.

20

The leprous corpse touched by this spirit tender
Exhales itself in flowers of gentle breath;
Like incarnations of the stars, when splendor
175   Is changed to fragrance, they illumine death
And mock the merry worm that wakes beneath;
Nought we know, dies. Shall that alone which knows
Be as a sword consumed before the sheath
By sightless lightning?—the intense atom[7] glows
180   A moment, then is quenched in a most cold repose.

21

Alas! that all we loved of him should be,
But for our grief, as if it had not been.
And grief itself be mortal! Woe is me!
Whence are we, and why are we? of what scene

4. In folklore, an eagle could recapture its youth
by soaring close to the sun.
5. God's curse upon Cain for having slain his
brother Abel was that nothing should grow for him
and that he should be homeless (Genesis 3.11–
12).

6. The anonymous critic whose venomous review
of Keats's "Endymion" had hastened, Shelley
believed, Keats's death.
7. Indivisible and indestructible unit of anything
that exists. *Sightless:* unseeing and unseen.

185   The actors or spectators? Great and mean
    Meet massed in death, who lends what life must borrow.
    As long as skies are blue, and fields are green,
    Evening must usher night, night urge the morrow,
Month follow month with woe, and year wake year to sorrow.

22

190   *He* will awake no more, oh, never more!
    "Wake thou," cried Misery, "childless Mother, rise
    Out of thy sleep, and slake, in thy heart's core,
    A wound more fierce than his with tears and sighs."
    And all the Dreams that watched Urania's eyes,
195   And all the Echoes whom their sister's song[8]
    Had held in holy silence, cried, "Arise!"
    Swift as a Thought by the snake Memory stung,
From her ambrosial° rest the fading Splendor°   *immortal / Urania*
    sprung.

23

    She rose like an autumnal Night, that springs
200   Out of the East, and follows wild and drear
    The golden Day, which, on eternal wings,
    Even as a ghost abandoning a bier,
    Has left the Earth a corpse. Sorrow and fear
    So struck, so roused, so rapt Urania;
205   So saddened round her like an atmosphere
    Of stormy mist; so swept her on her way
Even to the mournful place where Adonais lay.

24

    Out of her secret Paradise she sped,
    Through camps and cities rough with stone, and steel,
210   And human hearts, which to her aery tread
    Yielding not, wounded the invisible
    Palms of her tender feet where'er they fell:
    And barbéd tongues, and thoughts more sharp than they,
    Rent the soft Form they never could repel,
215   Whose sacred blood, like the young tears of May,
Paved with eternal flowers that undeserving way.

25

    In the death-chamber for a moment Death,
    Shamed by the presence of that living Might,
    Blushed to annihilation, and the breath
220   Revisited those lips, and life's pale light
    Flashed through those limbs, so late her dear delight.
    "Leave me not wild and drear and comfortless,
    As silent lightning leaves the starless night!
    Leave me not!" cried Urania: her distress
225 Roused Death: Death rose and smiled, and met her vain caress.

8. The Echo in line 127.

26

"Stay yet awhile! speak to me once again;
Kiss me, so long but as a kiss may live;
And in my heartless breast and burning brain
That word, that kiss, shall all thoughts else survive,
230 With food of saddest memory kept alive,
Now thou art dead, as if it were a part
Of thee, my Adonais! I would give
All that I am to be as thou now art,
But I am chained to Time, and cannot thence depart!

27

235 "O gentle child, beautiful as thou wert,
Why didst thou leave the trodden paths of men
Too soon, and with weak hands though mighty heart
Dare the unpastured dragon in his den?
Defenseless as thou wert, oh! where was then
240 Wisdom the mirrored shield, or scorn the spear?[9]
Or hadst thou waited the full cycle, when
Thy spirit should have filled its crescent sphere,
The monsters of life's waste had fled from thee like deer.

28

"The herded wolves, bold only to pursue;
245 The obscene ravens, clamorous o'er the dead;
The vultures, to the conqueror's banner true,
Who feed where Desolation first has fed,
And whose wings rain contagion;—how they[1] fled,
When like Apollo, from his golden bow,
250 The Pythian of the age[2] one arrow sped
And smiled!—The spoilers tempt no second blow,
They fawn on the proud feet that spurn them lying low.

29

"The sun comes forth, and many reptiles spawn;
He sets, and each ephemeral insect then
255 Is gathered into death without a dawn,
And the immortal stars awake again;
So is it in the world of living men:
A godlike mind soars forth, in its delight
Making earth bare and veiling heaven, and when
260 It sinks, the swarms that dimmed or shared its light
Leave to its kindred lamps the spirit's awful night."

30

Thus ceased she: and the mountain shepherds came
Their garlands sere, their magic mantles rent;

---

9. An allusion to the Greek hero Perseus, who killed the monster Medusa, evading her gaze, which could turn him into stone, by using his shield as a mirror.
1. Critics, here characterized as beasts and birds of prey.

2. Byron (1788–1824; see pp. 833–63), Shelley's friend, who attacked the critics in *English Bards and Scotch Reviewers* (1809); here compared to Apollo the Pythian, who slew the monster Python near Delphi.

The Pilgrim of Eternity,[3] whose fame
265   Over his living head like Heaven is bent,
An early but enduring monument,
Came, veiling all the lightnings of his song
In sorrow; from her wilds Ierne° sent   *Ireland*
The sweetest lyrist of her saddest wrong,[4]
270   And love taught grief to fall like music from his tongue.

31

Midst others of less note, came one frail Form,[5]
A phantom among men; companionless
As the last cloud of an expiring storm,
Whose thunder is its knell; he, as I guess,
275   Had gazed on Nature's naked loveliness,
Actaeon-like,[6] and now he fled astray
With feeble steps o'er the world's wilderness,
And his own thoughts, along that rugged way,
Pursued, like raging hounds, their father and their prey.

32

280   A pardlike[7] Spirit beautiful and swift—
A Love in desolation masked;—a Power
Girt round with weakness;—it can scarce uplift
The weight of the superincumbent° hour;   *heavily resting*
It is a dying lamp, a falling shower,
285   A breaking billow;—even whilst we speak
Is it not broken? On the withering flower
The killing sun smiles brightly: on a cheek
The life can burn in blood, even while the heart may break.

33

His head was bound with pansies overblown,
290   And faded violets, white, and pied,° and blue;   *multicolored*
And a light spear topped with a cypress cone,
Round whose rude shaft dark ivy-tresses grew
Yet dripping with the forest's noonday dew,
Vibrated, as the ever-beating heart
295   Shook the weak hand that grasped it; of that crew
He came the last, neglected and apart;
A herd-abandoned deer, struck by the hunter's dart.

34

All stood aloof, and at his partial moan[8]
Smiled through their tears; well knew that gentle band
300   Who in another's fate now wept his own;

---

3. Byron, as author of *Childe Harold's Pilgrimage*.
4. Thomas Moore (1779–1852), poet, author of *Irish Melodies*.
5. Shelley, as poet-mourner, here wearing emblems of Dionysus, Greek god of wine.
6. Actaeon, a young hunter, offended Diana, goddess of the forest, by discovering her while she was bathing. She transformed him into a stag, and he was torn to pieces by his hounds.
7. Leopardlike; the leopard was sacred to Dionysus.
8. Expressing a bond of sympathy (partiality) toward Adonais.

As in the accents of an unknown land,
He sung new sorrow; sad Urania scanned
The Stranger's mien,° and murmured: "Who art thou?"   *expressions*
He answered not, but with a sudden hand
305   Made bare his branded and ensanguined brow,
Which was like Cain's or Christ's—oh! that it should be so!

35

What softer voice is hushed over the dead?
Athwart what brow is that dark mantle thrown?
What form leans sadly o'er the white death-bed,
310   In mockery° of monumental stone,   *imitation*
The heavy heart heaving without a moan?
If it be He,⁹ who, gentlest of the wise,
Taught, soothed, loved, honored the departed one;
Let me not vex, with inharmonious sighs,
315   The silence of that heart's accepted sacrifice.

36

Our Adonais has drunk poison—oh!
What deaf and viperous murderer could crown
Life's early cup with such a draught of woe?
The nameless worm¹ would now itself disown:
320   It felt, yet could escape the magic tone
Whose prelude held° all envy, hate and wrong,   *held off*
But what was howling in one breast alone,
Silent with expectation of the song,
Whose master's hand is cold, whose silver lyre unstrung.

37

325   Live thou, whose infamy is not thy fame!
Live! fear no heavier chastisement from me,
Thou noteless blot on a remembered name!
But be thyself, and know thyself to be!
And ever at thy season be thou free
330   To spill the venom when thy fangs o'erflow:
Remorse and Self-contempt shall cling to thee;
Hot Shame shall burn upon thy secret brow,
And like a beaten hound tremble thou shalt—as now.

38

Nor let us weep that our delight is fled
335   Far from these carrion° kites° that scream below;   *scavenger / hawks*
He wakes or sleeps with the enduring dead;
Thou canst not soar where he is sitting now.
Dust to the dust! but the pure spirit shall flow
Back to the burning fountain whence it came,

9. Leigh Hunt (1784–1859), poet and critic, friend of Keats and Shelley.

1. Serpent; the anonymous reviewer (see line 152).

340   A portion of the Eternal, which must glow
        Through time and change, unquenchably the same,
   Whilst thy² cold embers choke the sordid hearth of shame.

39

        Peace, peace! he is not dead, he doth not sleep—
        He hath awakened from the dream of life—
345   'Tis we, who lost in stormy visions, keep
        With phantoms an unprofitable strife,
        And in mad trance strike with our spirit's knife
        Invulnerable nothings.—*We* decay
        Like corpses in a charnel; fear and grief
350   Convulse us and consume us day by day,
   And cold hopes swarm like worms within our living clay.

40

        He has outsoared the shadow of our night;
        Envy and calumny and hate and pain,
        And that unrest which men miscall delight,
355   Can touch him not and torture not again;
        From the contagion of the world's slow stain
        He is secure, and now can never mourn
        A heart grown cold, a head grown gray in vain;
        Nor, when the spirit's self has ceased to burn,
360 With sparkless ashes load an unlamented urn.

41

        He lives, he wakes—'tis Death is dead, not he;
        Mourn not for Adonais.—Thou young Dawn,
        Turn all thy dew to splendor, for from thee
        The spirit thou lamentest is not gone;
365   Ye caverns and ye forests, cease to moan!
        Cease ye faint flowers and fountains, and thou Air,
        Which like a morning veil thy scarf hadst thrown
        O'er the abandoned Earth, now leave it bare
   Even to the joyous stars which smile on its despair!

42

370   He is made one with Nature: there is heard
        His voice in all her music, from the moan
        Of thunder, to the song of night's sweet bird;³
        He is a presence to be felt and known
        In darkness and in light, from herb and stone,
375   Spreading itself where'er that Power may move
        Which has withdrawn his being to its own;
        Which wields the world with never wearied love,
   Sustains it from beneath, and kindles it above.

---

2. The reviewer's.
3. Nightingale; an allusion to Keats's "Ode to a Nightingale" (see p. 935).

43

He is a portion of the loveliness
380   Which once he made more lovely: he doth bear
His part, while the one Spirit's plastic° stress   *formative*
Sweeps through the dull dense world, compelling there
All new successions to the forms they wear;
Torturing the unwilling dross° that checks its flight   *coarse matter*
385   To its own likeness, as each mass may bear;
And bursting in its beauty and its might
From trees and beasts and men into the Heaven's light.

44

The splendors of the firmament of time
May be eclipsed, but are extinguished not;
390   Like stars to their appointed height they climb,
And death is a low mist which cannot blot
The brightness it may veil. When lofty thought
Lifts a young heart above its mortal lair,
And love and life contend in it, for what
395   Shall be its earthly doom, the dead live there
And move like winds of light on dark and stormy air.

45

The inheritors of unfulfilled renown
Rose from their thrones, built beyond mortal thought,
Far in the Unapparent. Chatterton[4]
400   Rose pale, his solemn agony had not
Yet faded from him; Sidney,[5] as he fought
And as he fell and as he lived and loved
Sublimely mild, a Spirit without spot,
Arose; and Lucan,[6] by his death approved:°   *vindicated*
405   Oblivion as they rose shrank like a thing reproved

46

And many more, whose names on Earth are dark
But whose transmitted effluence cannot die
So long as fire outlives the parent spark,
Rose, robed in dazzling immortality.
410   "Thou art become as one of us," they cry,
"It was for thee yon kingless sphere has long
Swung blind in unascended majesty,
Silent alone amid an Heaven of Song.
Assume thy wingéd throne, thou Vesper of our throng!"

---

4. Thomas Chatterton (1752–1770), a gifted young poet who committed suicide.
5. Sir Philip Sidney (1554–1586; see pp. 208–20), a poet, critic, courtier, and soldier, fatally wounded in battle.

6. A young Roman poet (39–65 c.e.), who took his own life rather than die under sentence of the notorious emperor Nero, against whom he had conspired.

47

415 Who mourns for Adonais? Oh, come forth,
Fond wretch! and know thyself and him aright.
Clasp with thy panting soul the pendulous[7] Earth;
As from a center, dart thy spirit's light
Beyond all worlds, until its spacious might
420 Satiate the void circumference: then shrink
Even to a point within our day and night;
And keep thy heart light lest it make thee sink
When hope has kindled hope, and lured thee to the brink.

48

Or go to Rome, which is the sepulcher,
425 Oh, not of him, but of our joy: 'tis nought
That ages, empires, and religions there
Lie buried in the ravage they have wrought;
For such as he can lend—they borrow not
Glory from those who made the world their prey;
430 And he is gathered to the kings of thought
Who waged contention with their time's decay,
And of the past are all that cannot pass away.

49

Go thou to Rome,—at once the Paradise,
The grave, the city, and the wilderness;
435 And where its wrecks like shattered mountains rise,
And flowering weeds, and fragrant copses° dress   *small woods*
The bones of Desolation's nakedness
Pass, till the Spirit of the spot shall lead
Thy footsteps to a slope of green access
440 Where, like an infant's smile, over the dead
A light of laughing flowers along the grass is spread,

50

And gray walls moulder round, on which dull Time
Feeds, like slow fire upon a hoary brand;°   *burning log*
And one keen pyramid[8] with wedge sublime,
445 Pavilioning the dust of him who planned
This refuge for his memory, doth stand
Like flame transformed to marble; and beneath,
A field is spread, on which a newer band
Have pitched in Heaven's smile their camp of death,
450 Welcoming him we lose with scarce extinguished breath.

51

Here pause: these graves are all too young as yet
To have outgrown the sorrow which consigned
Its charge to each; and if the seal is set,

---

7. Floating poised in space.
8. Tomb of Gaius Cestius, an officer of ancient

Rome, beside the Protestant cemetery where Keats
and Shelley are buried.

Here, on one fountain of a mourning mind,
455   Break it not thou! too surely shalt thou find
Thine own well full, if thou returnest home,
Of tears and gall. From the world's bitter wind
Seek shelter in the shadow of the tomb.
What Adonais is, why fear we to become?

52

460   The One remains, the many change and pass;
Heaven's light forever shines, Earth's shadows fly;
Life, like a dome of many-colored glass,
Stains the white radiance of Eternity,
Until Death tramples it to fragments.—Die,
465   If thou wouldst be with that which thou dost seek!
Follow where all is fled!—Rome's azure sky,
Flowers, ruins, statues, music, words, are weak
The glory they transfuse with fitting truth to speak.

53

Why linger, why turn back, why shrink, my Heart?
470   Thy hopes are gone before: from all things here
They have departed; thou shouldst now depart!
A light is past from the revolving year,
And man, and woman; and what still is dear
Attracts to crush, repels to make thee wither.
475   The soft sky smiles,—the low wind whispers near:
'Tis Adonais calls! oh, hasten thither,
No more let life divide what Death can join together.

54

That Light whose smile kindles the Universe,
That Beauty in which all things work and move,
480   That Benediction which the eclipsing Curse
Of birth can quench not, that sustaining Love
Which through the web of being blindly wove
By man and beast and earth and air and sea,
Burns bright or dim, as each are mirrors of
485   The fire for which all thirst; now beams on me,
Consuming the last clouds of cold mortality.

55

The breath whose might I have invoked in song
Descends on me; my spirit's bark° is driven,   *small ship*
Far from the shore, far from the trembling throng
490   Whose sails were never to the tempest given;
The massy earth and spherèd skies are riven!
I am borne darkly, fearfully, afar;
Whilst burning through the inmost veil of Heaven,
The soul of Adonais, like a star,
495 Beacons from the abode where the Eternal are.

1821   1821

FROM HELLAS[9]

The World's Great Age

The world's great age begins anew,
   The golden years return,
The earth doth like a snake[1] renew
   Her winter weeds[2] outworn:
5 Heaven smiles, and faiths and empires gleam,
Like wrecks of a dissolving dream.

A brighter Hellas rears its mountains
   From waves serener far;
A new Peneus[3] rolls his fountains
10   Against the morning star.
Where fairer Tempes[4] bloom, there sleep
Young Cyclads[5] on a sunnier deep.

A loftier Argo[6] cleaves the main,
   Fraught with a later prize;
15 Another Orpheus[7] sings again,
   And loves, and weeps, and dies.
A new Ulysses leaves once more
Calypso[8] for his native shore.

Oh, write no more the tale of Troy,
20   If earth Death's scroll must be!
Nor mix with Laian rage[9] the joy
   Which dawns upon the free:
Although a subtler Sphinx renew
Riddles of death Thebes never knew.

25 Another Athens shall arise,
   And to remoter time
Bequeath, like sunset to the skies,
   The splendor of its prime;
And leave, if nought so bright may live,
30 All earth can take or Heaven can give.

Saturn and Love their long repose
   Shall burst, more bright and good

---

9. *Hellas*, an ancient name for Greece, is the title of a drama in which Shelley celebrates the contemporary Greek struggle for independence, which he saw as heralding the return of the legendary "Age of Saturn" or "Age of Gold," the first, best period of human history.
1. Shedding its skin after hibernation, a symbol of regeneration.
2. Clothes, especially mourning garments.
3. Greek river of legendary beauty.
4. Valley of the Peneus.
5. Or Cyclades, islands in the Aegean Sea.
6. In Greek mythology, the first seagoing vessel, on which Jason sailed to gain the "prize" (line 14) of the Golden Fleece.

7. Mythological Greek poet and musician of magical genius, whose playing on the lyre caused his wife, Eurydice, to be released from the realm of the dead on condition that he would not look at her until they had reached the upper world. Breaking his pledge at the last moment, he lost her forever.
8. Island nymph with whom Ulysses (Odysseus) lived for seven years during his return to Ithaca from the Trojan War.
9. Ignorant of his own identity, Oedipus in a rage killed King Laius of Thebes (in fact his father). Oedipus then delivered Thebes from the power of a sphinx by answering her riddles and won Jocasta (in fact his mother) as his wife and queen.

Than all who fell, than One who rose,
　　Than many unsubdued:[1]
35　Not gold, not blood, their altar dowers,
But votive tears and symbol flowers.

Oh, cease! must hate and death return?
　　Cease! must men kill and die?
Cease! drain not to its dregs the urn
40　　Of bitter prophecy.
The world is weary of the past,
Oh, might it die or rest at last!

1821   1822

JOHN CLARE
1793–1864

Badger

When midnight comes a host of dogs and men
Go out and track the badger to his den,
And put a sack within the hole, and lie
Till the old grunting badger passes by.
5　He comes and hears—they let the strongest loose.
The old fox hears the noise and drops the goose.
The poacher shoots and hurries from the cry,
And the old hare half wounded buzzes by.
They get a forkéd stick to bear him down
10　And clap the dogs and take him to the town,
And bait him all the day with many dogs,
And laugh and shout and fright the scampering hogs.
He runs along and bites at all he meets:
They shout and hollo down the noisy streets.

15　He turns about to face the loud uproar
And drives the rebels to their very door.
The frequent stone is hurled where'er they go;
When badgers fight, then everyone's a foe.
The dogs are clapped and urged to join the fray;
20　The badger turns and drives them all away.
Though scarcely half as big, demure and small,
He fights with dogs for hours and beats them all.
The heavy mastiff, savage in the fray,
Lies down and licks his feet and turns away.
25　The bulldog knows his match and waxes cold,

---

1. Saturn and Love are the restored deities of the "world's great age"; "all who fell" are the deities who "fell" when Christ arose from the dead; the "many unsubdued" are idols still worshiped throughout the world.

The badger grins and never leaves his hold.
He drives the crowd and follows at their heels
And bites them through—the drunkard swears and reels.

The frighted women take the boys away,
30   The blackguard laughs and hurries on the fray.
He tries to reach the woods, an awkward race,
But sticks and cudgels quickly stop the chase.
He turns again and drives the noisy crowd
And beats the many dogs in noises loud.
35   He drives away and beats them every one,
And then they loose them all and set them on.
He falls as dead and kicked by boys and men,
Then starts and grins and drives the crowd again;
Till kicked and torn and beaten out he lies
40   And leaves his hold and crackles, groans, and dies.

1835–37   1920

Gypsies

The snow falls deep; the forest lies alone;
The boy goes hasty for his load of brakes,°   brushwood
Then thinks upon the fire and hurries back;
The gypsy knocks his hands and tucks them up,
5   And seeks his squalid camp, half hid in snow,
Beneath the oak which breaks away the wind,
And bushes close in snow like hovel warm;
There tainted mutton wastes upon the coals,
And the half-wasted dog squats close and rubs,
10   Then feels the heat too strong, and goes aloof;
He watches well, but none a bit can spare,
And vainly waits the morsel thrown away.
'Tis thus they live—a picture to the place,
A quiet, pilfering, unprotected race.

1837–41   1920

Song: Love Lives beyond the Tomb

Love lives beyond
The tomb, the earth, which fades like dew—
I love the fond,
The faithful, and the true.

5   Love lives in sleep,
'Tis happiness of healthy dreams,
Eve's dews may weep,
But love delightful seems.

'Tis seen in flowers,
10 And in the even's pearly dew
On earth's green hours,
And in the heaven's eternal blue.

'Tis heard in spring
When light and sunbeams, warm and kind,
15   On angel's wing
Brings love and music to the wind.

And where's the voice
So young, so beautiful, and sweet
As nature's choice,
20 Where spring and lovers meet?

Love lives beyond
The tomb, the earth, the flowers, and dew.
I love the fond,
The faithful, young, and true.

1842–64   1873

First Love

I ne'er was struck before that hour
With love so sudden and so sweet,
Her face it bloomed like a sweet flower
And stole my heart away complete.
5 My face turned pale as deadly pale.
My legs refused to walk away,
And when she looked, what could I ail?
My life and all seemed turned to clay.

And then my blood rushed to my face
10   And took my eyesight quite away,
The trees and bushes round the place
Seemed midnight at noonday.
I could not see a single thing,
Words from my eyes did start—
15 They spoke as chords do from the string,
And blood burnt round my heart.

Are flowers the winter's choice?
Is love's bed always snow?
She seemed to hear my silent voice,
20   Not love's appeals to know.
I never saw so sweet a face
As that I stood before.
My heart has left its dwelling-place
And can return no more.

1842–64   1920

Farewell

Farewell to the bushy clump close to the river
And the flags where the butter-bump[1] hides in forever;
Farewell to the weedy nook, hemmed in by waters;
Farewell to the miller's brook and his three bonny daughters;
5 Farewell to them all while in prison I lie—
In the prison a thrall° sees naught but the sky.   *servant slave*

Shut out are the green fields and birds in the bushes;
In the prison yard nothing builds, blackbirds or thrushes.
Farewell to the old mill and dash of the waters,
10 To the miller and, dearer still, to his three bonny daughters.

In the nook, the larger burdock[2] grows near the green willow;
In the flood, round the moor-cock dashes under the billow;[3]
To the old mill farewell, to the lock, pens, and waters,
To the miller himsel', and his three bonny daughters.

1842–64   1920

I Am

I am: yet what I am none cares or knows
    My friends forsake me like a memory lost,
I am the self-consumer of my woes—
    They rise and vanish in oblivious host,
5 Like shadows in love's frenzied, stifled throes—
And yet I am, and live—like vapors tossed

Into the nothingness of scorn and noise,
    Into the living sea of waking dreams,
Where there is neither sense of life or joys,
10   But the vast shipwreck of my life's esteems;
Even the dearest, that I love the best,
Are strange—nay, rather stranger than the rest.

I long for scenes, where man hath never trod,
    A place where woman never smiled or wept—
15 There to abide with my Creator, God,
    And sleep as I in childhood sweetly slept,
Untroubling, and untroubled where I lie,
The grass below—above the vaulted sky.

1842–64   1865

---

1. Bittern, a marsh bird with a booming call. *Flags:*
irises (tall plants).

2. Type of coarse weed.
3. Wave, water. *Moor-cock:* type of waterfowl.

FELICIA DOROTHEA HEMANS
1793–1835

England's Dead

Son of the ocean isle!
Where sleep your mighty dead?
Show me what high and stately pile
Is reared o'er Glory's bed.

5   Go, stranger! track the deep,
Free, free the white sail spread!
Wave may not foam, nor wild wind sweep,
Where rest not England's dead.

On Egypt's burning plains,
10   By the pyramid o'erswayed,
With fearful power the noonday reigns,
And the palm trees yield no shade.[1]

But let the angry sun
From heaven look fiercely red,
15   Unfelt by those whose task is done!—
There slumber England's dead.

The hurricane hath might
Along the Indian shore,
And far by Ganges' banks at night,
20   Is heard the tiger's roar.

But let the sound roll on!
It hath no tone of dread,
For those that from their toils are gone;—
There slumber England's dead.

25   Loud rush the torrent floods
The western wilds among,
And free, in green Columbia's woods,
The hunter's bow is strung.

But let the floods rush on!
30   Let the arrow's flight be sped!
Why should *they* reck° whose task is done?—   *care*
There slumber England's dead!

The mountain storms rise high
In the snowy Pyrenees,

---

1. This specific reference—to the defeat of French forces by the British at Alexandria in the spring of 1801—is followed by more general military references: to eighteenth-century and early nineteenth-century battles in India (lines 17–24), America (lines 25–32), Spain (lines 33–40), and on the sea (lines 41–48).

35 And toss the pine boughs through the sky,
       Like rose leaves on the breeze.

    But let the storm rage on!
    Let the fresh wreaths be shed!
    For the Roncesvalles' field[2] is won,—
40   *There* slumber England's dead.

    On the frozen deep's repose
    'Tis a dark and dreadful hour,
    When round the ship the ice-fields close,
    And the northern night clouds lower.°   *look threatening*

45   But let the ice drift on!
    Let the cold-blue desert spread!
    Their course with mast and flag is done,—
       Even there sleep England's dead.

    The warlike of the isles,
50   The men of field and wave!
    Are not the rocks their funeral piles,
       The seas and shores their grave?

    Go, stranger! track the deep,
    Free, free the white sail spread!
55 Wave may not foam, nor wild wind sweep,
       Where rest not England's dead.

                                             1822

The Landing of the Pilgrim Fathers in New England

> Look now abroad—another race has fill'd
>   Those populous borders—wide the wood recedes,
> And towns shoot up, and fertile realms are till'd;
>   The land is full of harvests and green meads.
>   —BRYANT[3]

    The breaking waves dashed high
       On a stern and rock-bound coast,
    And the woods against a stormy sky
       Their giant branches tossed;

5   And the heavy night hung dark,
       The hills and waters o'er,
    When a band of exiles moored their bark°   *ship*
       On the wild New England shore.

---

2. During the Peninsular War (1808–14) between France and Great Britain, fighting occurred in Roncesvalles, a pass in the Pyrenees (mountains separating France and Spain).
3. William Cullen Bryant (1794–1878; see pp. 902–05), *The Ages*, lines 280–83.

Not as the conqueror comes,
10   They, the true-hearted, came;
Not with the roll of the stirring drums,
    And the trumpet that sings of fame;

Not as the flying come,
    In silence and in fear;—
15 They shook the depths of the desert gloom
    With their hymns of lofty cheer.

Amidst the storm they sang,
    And the stars heard and the sea;
And the sounding aisles of the dim woods rang
20   To the anthem of the free!

The ocean eagle soared
    From his nest by the white wave's foam;
And the rocking pines of the forest roared—
    This was their welcome home!

25 There were men with hoary hair
    Amidst that pilgrim band;—
Why had *they* come to wither there,
    Away from their childhood's land?

There was woman's fearless eye,
30   Lit by her deep love's truth;
There was manhood's brow serenely high,
    And the fiery heart of youth.

What sought they thus afar?
    Bright jewels of the mine?
35 The wealth of seas, the spoils of war?—
    They sought a faith's pure shrine!

Aye, call it holy ground,
    The soil where first they trod.
They have left unstained what there they found—
40   Freedom to worship God.

                                        1826

Casabianca[4]

The boy stood on the burning deck
    Whence all but he had fled;

---

4. "Young Casabianca, a boy about thirteen years
old, son to the Admiral of the *Orient*, remained at
his post (in the Battle of the Nile) after the ship
had taken fire, and all the guns had been aban-
doned; and perished in the explosion of the vessel,
when the flames had reached the powder"
[Hemans's note]. In the Battle of the Nile (August
1, 1798), British admiral Horatio Nelson captured
and destroyed the French fleet in Aboukir Bay. Cf.
Elizabeth Bishop, "Casabianca" (p. 1515).

The flame that lit the battle's wreck
   Shone round him o'er the dead.

5 Yet beautiful and bright he stood,
   As born to rule the storm;
A creature of heroic blood,
   A proud, though childlike form.

The flames roll'd on—he would not go
10 Without his father's word;
That father, faint in death below,
   His voice no longer heard.

He call'd aloud:—"Say, Father, say
   If yet my task is done?"
15 He knew not that the chieftain lay
   Unconscious of his son.

"Speak, Father!" once again he cried,
   "If I may yet be gone!"
And but the booming shots replied,
20 And fast the flames roll'd on.

Upon his brow he felt their breath,
   And in his waving hair,
And look'd from that lone post of death
   In still, yet brave despair.

25 And shouted but once more aloud,
   "My Father! must I stay?"
While o'er him fast, through sail and shroud,
   The wreathing fires made way.

They wrapt the ship in splendor wild,
30 They caught the flag on high,
And stream'd above the gallant child,
   Like banners in the sky.

There came a burst of thunder sound—
   The boy—oh! where was he?
35 Ask of the winds that far around
   With fragments strew'd the sea!—

With mast, and helm, and pennon° fair,   *long narrow flag*
   That well had borne their part,
But the noblest thing which perish'd there
40 Was that young faithful heart!

1826

Indian Woman's Death-Song[5]

An Indian woman, driven to despair by her husband's desertion of her for another wife, entered a canoe with her children, and rowed it down the Mississippi towards a cataract.[6] Her voice was heard from the shore singing a mournful death-song, until overpowered by the sound of the waters in which she perished. The tale is related in Long's "Expedition to the Source of St. Peter's River."

"Non, je ne puis vivre avec un coeur brisé. Il faut que je retrouve la joie, et que je m'unisse aux esprits libres de l'air."
—*Bride of Messina*—Translated by MADAME DE STAEL[7]

"Let not my child be a girl, for very sad is the life of a woman."
The Prairie[8]

Down a broad river of the western wilds,
Piercing thick forest-glooms, a light canoe
Swept with the current: fearful was the speed
Of the frail bark, as by a tempest's wing
5   Borne leaf-like on to where the mist of spray
Rose with the cataract's thunder. Yet within,
Proudly, and dauntlessly, and all alone,
Save that a babe lay sleeping at her breast,
A woman stood! Upon her Indian brow
10   Sat a strange gladness, and her dark hair waved
As if triumphantly. She pressed her child,
In its bright slumber, to her beating heart,
And lifted her sweet voice, that rose awhile
Above the sound of waters, high and clear,
15   Wafting a wild proud strain—a song of death.

"Roll swiftly to the spirit's land, thou mighty stream and free!
Father of ancient waters, roll! and bear our lives with thee!
The weary bird that storms have tossed would seek the sunshine's
    calm,
And the deer that hath the arrow's hurt flies to the woods of balm.

20   "Roll on!—my warrior's eye hath looked upon another's face,
And mine hath faded from his soul, as fades a moonbeam's trace:
My shadow comes not o'er his path, my whisper to his dream,
He flings away the broken reed. Roll swifter yet, thou stream!

"The voice that spoke of other days is hushed within *his* breast,
25   But *mine* its lonely music haunts, and will not let me rest;
It sings a low and mournful song of gladness that is gone—
I cannot live without that light. Father of waves! roll on!

5. From Hemans's *Records of Women* (1828).
6. Waterfall.
7. No, I can't live with a broken heart. I must retrieve my happiness, and be reunited with the spirits of the air (French). From *The Bride of Messina* (1803), a play by the German poet and dramatist Friedrich von Schiller (1759–1805), translated by the French writer Madame Anne-Louise-Germaine de Staël (1766–1817).
8. An 1827 novel by the American writer James Fenimore Cooper (1789–1851).

"Will he not miss the bounding step that met him from the chase?
The heart of love that made his home an ever-sunny place?
30 The hand that spread the hunter's board, and decked his couch of
      yore?
He will not! Roll, dark foaming stream, on to the better shore!

"Some blessèd fount amidst the woods of that bright land must flow,
Whose waters from my soul may lave the memory of this woe;
Some gentle wind must whisper there, whose breath may waft away
35 The burden of the heavy night, the sadness of the day.

"And thou, my babe! though born, like me, for woman's weary lot,
Smile!—to that wasting of the heart, my own! I leave thee not;
Too bright a thing art *thou* to pine in aching love away—
Thy mother bears thee far, young fawn! from sorrow and decay.

40 "She bears thee to the glorious bowers where none are heard to
      weep,
And where the unkind one hath no power again to trouble sleep;
And where the soul shall find its youth, as wakening from a dream:
One moment, and that realm is ours. On, on, dark rolling stream!"

1828

WILLIAM CULLEN BRYANT
1794–1878

To a Waterfowl

    Whither, 'midst falling dew,
While glow the heavens with the last steps of day,
Far, through their rosy depths, dost thou pursue
    Thy solitary way?

5   Vainly the fowler's° eye   *bird hunter's*
Might mark thy distant flight, to do thee wrong,
As, darkly seen against the crimson sky,
    Thy figure floats along.

    Seek'st thou the plashy° brink   *splashy*
10 Of weedy lake, or marge° of river wide,   *margin, bank*
Or where the rocking billows rise and sink
    On the chaféd ocean side?

    There is a Power, whose care
Teaches thy way along that pathless coast,—
15 The desert and illimitable air,
    Lone wandering, but not lost,

All day thy wings have fanned,
At that far height, the cold thin atmosphere;
Yet stoop not, weary, to the welcome land,
20   Though the dark night is near.

And soon that toil shall end,
Soon shalt thou find a summer home, and rest,
And scream among thy fellows; reeds shall bend,
      Soon, o'er thy sheltered nest.

25   Thou'rt gone, the abyss of heaven
Hath swallowed up thy form, yet, on my heart
Deeply hath sunk the lesson thou hast given,
      And shall not soon depart.

He, who, from zone to zone,
30   Guides through the boundless sky thy certain flight,
In the long way that I must trace alone,
      Will lead my steps aright.

1815   1818, 1821

Thanatopsis[1]

To him who in the love of Nature holds
Communion with her visible forms, she speaks
A various language; for his gayer hours
She has a voice of gladness, and a smile
5 And eloquence of beauty, and she glides
Into his darker musings, with a mild
And healing sympathy, that steals away
Their sharpness ere he is aware. When thoughts
Of the last bitter hour come like a blight
10 Over thy spirit, and sad images
Of the stern agony, and shroud, and pall,
And breathless darkness, and the narrow house,
Make thee to shudder, and grow sick at heart;—
Go forth, under the open sky, and list
15 To Nature's teachings, while from all around—
Earth and her waters, and the depths of air,—
Comes a still voice—Yet a few days, and thee
The all-beholding sun shall see no more
In all his course; nor yet in the cold ground,
20 Where thy pale form was laid, with many tears.
Nor in the embrace of ocean, shall exist
Thy image. Earth, that nourished thee, shall claim
Thy growth, to be resolved to earth again,
And, lost each human trace, surrendering up
25 Thine individual being, shalt thou go

---

1. Meditation on death (Greek).

To mix for ever with the elements,
To be a brother to the insensible rock
And to the sluggish clod,° which the rude swain°   soil / farmer
Turns with his share,° and treads upon. The oak   plowshare
30   Shall send his roots abroad, and pierce thy mold.

         Yet not to thine eternal resting-place
      Shall thou retire alone,—nor couldst thou wish
      Couch° more magnificent. Thou shalt lie down   bed
      With patriarchs of the infant° world—with kings,   early
35   The powerful of the earth—the wise, the good,
      Fair forms, and hoary seers of ages past,
      All in one mighty sepulchre. The hills
      Rock-ribbed and ancient as the sun; the vales°   valleys
      Stretching in pensive quietness between;
40   The venerable woods; rivers that move
      In majesty, and the complaining brooks
      That make the meadows green; and, poured round all,
      Old ocean's gray and melancholy waste,—
      Are but the solemn decorations all
45   Of the great tomb of man. The golden sun,
      The planets, all the infinite host of heaven,
      Are shining on the sad abodes of death,
      Through the still lapse of ages. All that tread
      The globe are but a handful to the tribes
50   That slumber in its bosom.—Take the wings
      Of morning,[2] traverse Barca's[3] desert sands,
      Or lose thyself in the continuous woods
      Where rolls the Oregan,[4] and hears no sound,
      Save his own dashings—yet—the dead are there:
55   And millions in those solitudes, since first
      The flight of years began, have laid them down
      In their last sleep—the dead reign there alone.
      So shalt thou rest, and what if thou withdraw
      In silence from the living, and no friend
60   Take note of thy departure? All that breathe
      Will share thy destiny. The gay will laugh
      When thou art gone, the solemn brood of care
      Plod on, and each one as before will chase
      His favorite phantom; yet all these shall leave
65   Their mirth and their employments, and shall come,
      And make their bed with thee. As the long train
      Of ages glide away, the sons of men,
      The youth in life's green spring, and he who goes
      In the full strength of years, matron, and maid,
70   And the sweet babe, and the gray-headed man,—
      Shall one by one be gathered to thy side,
      By those, who in their turn shall follow them.

2. Cf. Psalm 139.9–10: "If I take the wings of   3. Desert in northeast Libya.
morning, and dwell in the uttermost parts of the   4. Initial name of the Columbia River in Oregon.
sea; even there shall thy hand lead me . . ."

So live, that when thy summons comes to join
The innumerable caravan, which moves
75 To that mysterious realm, where each shall take
His chamber in the silent halls of death,
Thou go not, like the quarry-slave at night,
Scourged to his dungeon, but, sustained and soothed
By an unfaltering trust, approach thy grave
80 Like one who wraps the drapery of his couch[5]
About him, and lies down to pleasant dreams.

ca. 1814   1821

JOHN KEATS
1795–1821

On First Looking into Chapman's Homer[1]

Much have I traveled in the realms of gold,
   And many goodly states and kingdoms seen;
   Round many western islands have I been
Which bards in fealty° to Apollo[2] hold.   *allegiance*
5 Oft of one wide expanse had I been told
   That deep-browed Homer ruled as his demesne;°   *domain*
   Yet did I never breathe its pure serene°   *atmosphere*
Till I heard Chapman speak out loud and bold:
Then felt I like some watcher of the skies
10   When a new planet swims into his ken;
Or like stout Cortez[3] when with eagle eyes
   He stared at the Pacific—and all his men
Looked at each other with a wild surmise—
   Silent, upon a peak in Darien.

1816   1816

On Sitting Down to Read *King Lear* Once Again

O golden-tongued Romance with serene lute!
   Fair plumèd Siren!° Queen of far away!   *enchantress*
   Leave melodizing on this wintry day,
Shut up thine olden pages, and be mute:
5 Adieu! for once again the fierce dispute
   Betwixt damnation and impassioned clay
   Must I burn through; once more humbly assay°   *test*
The bitter-sweet of this Shakespearean fruit.
Chief Poet! and ye clouds of Albion,[4]

---

5. I.e., wraps his bedclothes.
1. Translations from Homer's *Odyssey*, in particular book 5, by George Chapman, a contemporary of Shakespeare.
2. Greek and Roman god of poetic inspiration.

3. Spanish conqueror of Mexico; in fact, Balboa, not Cortez, was the first European to see the Pacific, from Darien, in Panama.
4. Ancient name for England, especially referring to pre-Roman Britain, the era of King Lear.

10   Begetters of our deep eternal theme,
When through the old oak forest I am gone,
    Let me not wander in a barren dream,
But when I am consumèd in the fire,
Give me new Phoenix[5] wings to fly at my desire.

1818   1838

When I Have Fears

When I have fears that I may cease to be
    Before my pen has gleaned my teeming brain,
Before high-pilèd books, in charact'ry,°   *written symbols*
    Hold like rich garners the full-ripened grain;
5 When I behold, upon the night's starred face,
    Huge cloudy symbols of a high romance,
And think that I may never live to trace
    Their shadows, with the magic hand of chance;
And when I feel, fair creature of an hour,
10   That I shall never look upon thee more,
Never have relish in the faery° power   *magical*
    Of unreflecting love!—then on the shore
Of the wide world I stand alone, and think
Till Love and Fame to nothingness do sink.

1818   1848

To Homer[6]

Standing aloof in giant ignorance,[7]
    Of thee I hear and of the Cyclades,[8]
As one who sits ashore and longs perchance
    To visit dolphin-coral in deep seas.
5 So thou wast blind!—but then the veil was rent;
    For Jove[9] uncurtain'd Heaven to let thee live,
And Neptune made for thee a spumy tent,
    And Pan made sing for thee his forest-hive;
Aye, on the shores of darkness there is light,
10   And precipices show untrodden green;
There is a budding morrow in midnight;
    There is a triple sight in blindness keen;
Such seeing hadst thou, as it once befel
To Dian,[1] Queen of Earth, and Heaven, and Hell.

1818?   1848

5. Fabled Arabian bird that, after living for centuries, consumes itself in fire and is reborn.
6. By tradition, blind; here, a symbol of poetic illumination.
7. Keats could not read Homer's Greek.

8. Islands near the Greek coast.
9. Jove, Neptune (line 7), and Pan (line 8): Homer's gods of heaven, sea, and land.
1. The "three-formed" goddess presiding in the moon, forests, and the underworld.

The Eve of St. Agnes[2]

1

St. Agnes' Eve—Ah, bitter chill it was!
The owl, for all his feathers, was a-cold;
The hare limped trembling through the frozen grass,
And silent was the flock in woolly fold:
5   Numb were the Beadsman's fingers, while he told
His rosary,[3] and while his frosted breath,
Like pious incense from a censer old,
Seemed taking flight for heaven, without a death,
Past the sweet Virgin's picture, while his prayer he saith.

2

10   His prayer he saith, this patient, holy man;
Then takes his lamp, and riseth from his knees,
And back returneth, meager, barefoot, wan,
Along the chapel aisle by slow degrees:
The sculptured dead, on each side, seem to freeze,
15   Imprisoned in black, purgatorial rails:
Knights, ladies, praying in dumb° orat'ries,°   *silent / chapels*
He passeth by; and his weak spirit fails
To think[4] how they may ache in icy hoods and mails.

3

Northward he turneth through a little door,
20   And scarce three steps, ere Music's golden tongue
Flattered° to tears this agèd man and poor;   *beguiled*
But no—already had his deathbell rung:
The joys of all his life were said and sung:
His was harsh penance on St. Agnes' Eve:
25   Another way he went, and soon among
Rough ashes sat he for his soul's reprieve,
And all night kept awake, for sinner's sake to grieve.

4

That ancient Beadsman heard the prelude soft;
And so it chanced, for many a door was wide,
30   From hurry to and fro. Soon, up aloft,
The silver, snarling trumpets 'gan to chide:
The level chambers, ready with their pride,°   *ostentation*
Were glowing to receive a thousand guests:
The carvèd angels, ever eager-eyed,
35   Stared, where upon their heads the cornice rests,
With hair blown back, and wings put crosswise on their breasts.

---

2. January 20, proverbially the coldest winter night. St. Agnes, martyred in the fourth century at age thirteen, is patroness of virgins. Traditionally, a maiden who observes the ritual of St. Agnes's Eve will see a vision of her husband-to-be.

3. A string of beads on which a series of short prayers are counted ("told"). *Beadsman:* from Middle English *bede,* prayer; a needy dependent, paid a small stipend to pray regularly for his benefactor.
4. I.e., when he thinks.

5

At length burst in the argent° revelry,°   *brightly dressed / revelers*
With plume, tiara, and all rich array,
Numerous as shadows haunting faerily
40   The brain, new stuffed, in youth, with triumphs gay
Of old romance. These let us wish away,
And turn, sole-thoughted, to one Lady there,
Whose heart had brooded, all that wintry day,
On love, and winged St. Agnes' saintly care,
45   As she had heard old dames full many times declare.

6

They told her how, upon St. Agnes' Eve,
Young virgins might have visions of delight,
And soft adorings from their loves receive
Upon the honeyed middle of the night,
50   If ceremonies due they did aright;
As, supperless to bed they must retire,
And couch supine their beauties, lily white;
Nor look behind, nor sideways, but require
Of Heaven with upward eyes for all that they desire.

7

55   Full of this whim was thoughtful Madeline:
The music, yearning like a God in pain,
She scarcely heard: her maiden eyes divine,
Fixed on the floor, saw many a sweeping train
Pass by—she heeded not at all: in vain
60   Came many a tiptoe, amorous cavalier,
And back retired; not cooled by high disdain;
But she saw not: her heart was otherwhere:
She sighed for Agnes' dreams, the sweetest of the year.

8

She danced along with vague, regardless eyes,
65   Anxious her lips, her breathing quick and short:
The hallowed hour was near at hand: she sighs
Amid the timbrels,° and the thronged resort   *hand drums*
Of whisperers in anger, or in sport;
'Mid looks of love, defiance, hate, and scorn,
70   Hoodwinked with faery fancy; all amort,[5]
Save to St. Agnes and her lambs unshorn,[6]
And all the bliss to be before tomorrow morn.

9

So, purposing each moment to retire,
She lingered still. Meantime, across the moors,
75   Had come young Porphyro, with heart on fire

---

5. Dead; i.e., oblivious.
6. Symbolically associated with St. Agnes; new wool offered at the Mass commemorating the saint

was later spun and woven by the nuns (lines 115–17).

For Madeline. Beside the portal doors,
Buttressed from moonlight,[7] stands he, and implores
All saints to give him sight of Madeline,
But for one moment in the tedious hours,
80   That he might gaze and worship all unseen;
Perchance speak, kneel, touch, kiss—in sooth such things have been.

10

He ventures in: let no buzzed whisper tell:
All eyes be muffled, or a hundred swords
Will storm his heart, Love's fev'rous citadel:
85   For him, those chambers held barbarian hordes,
Hyena foemen, and hot-blooded lords,
Whose very dogs would execrations howl
Against his lineage: not one breast affords
Him any mercy, in that mansion foul,
90   Save one old beldame,° weak in body and in soul.   old woman

11

Ah, happy chance! the agèd creature came,
Shuffling along with ivory-headed wand,
To where he stood, hid from the torch's flame,
Behind a broad hall-pillar, far beyond
95   The sound of merriment and chorus bland:°   soft
He startled her; but soon she knew his face,
And grasped his fingers in her palsied hand,
Saying, "Mercy, Porphyro! hie thee from this place;
They are all here tonight, the whole bloodthirsty race!

12

100   "Get hence! get hence! there's dwarfish Hildebrand;
He had a fever late, and in the fit
He cursèd thee and thine, both house and land:
Then there's that old Lord Maurice, not a whit
More tame for his gray hairs—Alas me! flit!
105   Flit like a ghost away."—"Ah, Gossip[8] dear,
We're safe enough; here in this armchair sit,
And tell me how"—"Good Saints! not here, not here;
Follow me, child, or else these stones will be thy bier."

13

He followed through a lowly archèd way,
110   Brushing the cobwebs with his lofty plume,
And as she muttered "Well-a—well-a-day!"
He found him in a little moonlight room,
Pale, latticed, chill, and silent as a tomb.
"Now tell me where is Madeline," said he,
115   "O tell me, Angela, by the holy loom
Which none but secret sisterhood may see,
When they St. Agnes' wool are weaving piously."

7. I.e., concealed in dark shadows.   8. Old kinswoman or household retainer.

14

"St. Agnes! Ah! it is St. Agnes' Eve—
Yet men will murder upon holy days:
120   Thou must hold water in a witch's sieve,
And be liege lord of all the Elves and Fays,[9]
To venture so: it fills me with amaze
To see thee, Porphyro!—St. Agnes' Eve!
God's help! my lady fair the conjuror plays[1]
125   This very night: good angels her deceive!
But let me laugh awhile, I've mickle° time to grieve."   *much*

15

Feebly she laugheth in the languid moon,
While Porphyro upon her face doth look,
Like puzzled urchin on an agèd crone
130   Who keepeth closed a wondrous riddle-book,
As spectacled she sits in chimney nook.
But soon his eyes grew brilliant, when she told
His lady's purpose; and he scarce could brook°   *check*
Tears, at the thought of those enchantments cold,
135 And Madeline asleep in lap of legends old.

16

Sudden a thought came like a full-blown rose,
Flushing his brow, and in his painèd heart
Made purple riot: then doth he propose
A stratagem, that makes the beldame start:
140   "A cruel man and impious thou art:
Sweet lady, let her pray, and sleep, and dream
Alone with her good angels, far apart
From wicked men like thee. Go, go!—I deem
Thou canst not surely be the same that thou didst seem."

17

145   "I will not harm her, by all saints I swear,"
Quoth Porphyro: "O may I ne'er find grace
When my weak voice shall whisper its last prayer,
If one of her soft ringlets I displace,
Or look with ruffian passion in her face:
150   Good Angela, believe me by these tears;
Or I will, even in a moment's space,
Awake, with horrid shout, my foemen's ears,
And beard° them, though they be more fanged than wolves   *confront*
    and bears."

18

"Ah! why wilt thou affright a feeble soul?
155   A poor, weak, palsy-stricken, churchyard thing,[2]
Whose passing bell[3] may ere the midnight toll;

---

9. I.e., to hold water in a sieve and to command
elves and fairies ("Fays"), Porphyro would have to
be a magician.

1. I.e., is trying magic spells.
2. I.e., soon to die.
3. Tolled when a person died ("passed away").

Whose prayers for thee, each morn and evening,
Were never missed."—Thus plaining,° doth she bring   *complaining*
A gentler speech from burning Porphyro;
160   So woeful and of such deep sorrowing,
That Angela gives promise she will do
Whatever he shall wish, betide her weal or woe.

19

Which was, to lead him, in close secrecy,
Even to Madeline's chamber, and there hide
165   Him in a closet, of such privacy
That he might see her beauty unespied,
And win perhaps that night a peerless bride,
While legioned faeries paced the coverlet,
And pale enchantment held her sleepy-eyed.
170   Never on such a night have lovers met,
Since Merlin paid his Demon all the monstrous debt.[4]

20

"It shall be as thou wishest," said the Dame:
"All cates° and dainties shall be storèd there   *delicacies*
Quickly on this feast[5] night: by the tambour frame[6]
175   Her own lute thou wilt see: no time to spare,
For I am slow and feeble, and scarce dare
On such a catering trust my dizzy head.
Wait here, my child, with patience; kneel in prayer
The while: Ah! thou must needs the lady wed,
180   Or may I never leave my grave among the dead."

21

So saying, she hobbled off with busy fear.
The lover's endless minutes slowly passed:
The dame returned, and whispered in his ear
To follow her; with aged eyes aghast
185   From fright of dim espial. Safe at last,
Through many a dusky gallery, they gain
The maiden's chamber, silken, hushed, and chaste;
Where Porphyro took covert, pleased amain.°   *greatly*
His poor guide hurried back with agues° in her brain.   *fevers*

22

190   Her falt'ring hand upon the balustrade,
Old Angela was feeling for the stair,
When Madeline, St. Agnes' charmèd maid,
Rose, like a missioned spirit, unaware:
With silver taper's light, and pious care,
195   She turned, and down the agèd gossip led
To a safe level matting. Now prepare,

---

4. Possibly alluding to the tale in the Arthurian legends in which Merlin, a great wizard, lies bound for ages by a spell he gave to an evil woman to buy her love.
5. The festival, or Mass, honoring St. Agnes.
6. A circular embroidery frame.

Young Porphyro, for gazing on that bed;
She comes, she comes again, like ringdove frayed° and fled. / *frightened*

23

Out went the taper as she hurried in;
200   Its little smoke, in pallid moonshine, died:
She closed the door, she panted, all akin
To spirits of the air, and visions wide.
No uttered syllable, or, woe betide!
But to her heart, her heart was voluble,
205   Paining with eloquence her balmy side;
As though a tongueless nightingale should swell
Her throat in vain, and die, heart-stifled, in her dell.

24

A casement high and triple-arched there was,
All garlanded with carven imag'ries
210   Of fruits, and flowers, and bunches of knot-grass,
And diamonded with panes of quaint device,
Innumerable of stains and splendid dyes,
As are the tiger-moth's deep-damasked wings;
And in the midst,'mong thousand heraldries,
215   And twilight saints, and dim emblazonings,
A shielded scutcheon blushed with blood of queens and kings.[7]

25

Full on this casement shone the wintry moon,
And threw warm gules[8] on Madeline's fair breast,
As down she knelt for heaven's grace and boon;°   *gift*
220   Rose-bloom fell on her hands, together pressed,
And on her silver cross soft amethyst,
And on her hair a glory,° like a saint: *halo*
She seemed a splendid angel, newly dressed,
Save wings, for heaven—Porphyro grew faint:
225 She knelt, so pure a thing, so free from mortal taint.

26

Anon his heart revives: her vespers done,
Of all its wreathèd pearls her hair she frees;
Unclasps her warmèd jewels one by one;
Loosens her fragrant bodice; by degrees
230   Her rich attire creeps rustling to her knees:
Half-hidden, like a mermaid in sea-weed,
Pensive awhile she dreams awake, and sees,
In fancy, fair St. Agnes in her bed,
But dares not look behind, or all the charm is fled.

---

7. A shield representing a coat of arms ("scutch-
eon") showed the red pigments ("blushed") indi-
cating royal ancestry.
8. Heraldic red; here, in stained glass.

27

235 Soon, trembling in her soft and chilly nest,
In sort of wakeful swoon, perplexed she lay,
Until the poppied warmth of sleep oppressed
Her soothèd limbs, and soul fatigued away;
Flown, like a thought, until the morrow-day;
240 Blissfully havened both from joy and pain;
Clasped like a missal where swart Paynims[9] pray;
Blinded alike from sunshine and from rain,
As though a rose should shut, and be a bud again.

28

Stol'n to this paradise, and so entranced,
245 Porphyro gazed upon her empty dress,
And listened to her breathing, if it chanced
To wake into a slumberous tenderness;
Which when he heard, that minute did he bless,
And breathed himself: then from the closet crept,
250 Noiseless as fear in a wide wilderness,
And over the hushed carpet, silent, stepped,
And 'tween the curtains peeped, where, lo!—how fast she slept.

29

Then by the bedside, where the faded moon
Made a dim, silver twilight, soft he set
255 A table, and, half anguished, threw thereon
A cloth of woven crimson, gold, and jet—
O for some drowsy Morphean amulet![1]
The boisterous, midnight, festive clarion,°   high-pitched trumpet
The kettledrum, and far-heard clarinet,
260 Affray his ears, though but in dying tone—
The hall door shuts again, and all the noise is gone.

30

And still she slept an azure-lidded sleep,
In blanchèd linen, smooth, and lavendered,
While he from forth the closet brought a heap
265 Of candied apple, quince, and plum, and gourd;
With jellies soother than the creamy curd,
And lucent° syrups, tinct° with cinnamon;   clear / tinctured
Manna and dates, in argosy transferred
From Fez;° and spicèd dainties, every one,   Morocco
270 From silken Samarcand to cedared Lebanon.[2]

31

These delicates he heaped with glowing hand
On golden dishes and in baskets bright
Of wreathèd silver: sumptuous they stand

9. Dark pagans. *Missal*: Christian prayer book.
1. An object, such as an engraved stone, exerting
the power of Morpheus, Greek god of dreams.
2. Places associated with ancient luxury and
wealth.

In the retirèd quiet of the night,
275   Filling the chilly room with perfume light.—
"And now, my love, my seraph° fair, awake!   *angel*
Thou art my heaven, and I thine eremite:°   *hermit; devotee*
Open thine eyes, for meek St. Agnes' sake,
Or I shall drowse beside thee, so my soul doth ache."

32

280   Thus whispering, his warm, unnervèd arm
Sank in her pillow. Shaded was her dream
By the dusk curtains: 'twas a midnight charm
Impossible to melt as icèd stream:
The lustrous salvers° in the moonlight gleam;   *serving dishes*
285   Broad golden fringe upon the carpet lies:
It seemed he never, never could redeem
From such a steadfast spell his lady's eyes;
So mused awhile, entoiled in woofèd° fantasies.   *enwoven*

33

Awakening up, he took her hollow lute—
290   Tumultuous—and, in chords that tenderest be,
He played an ancient ditty, long since mute,
In Provence called *"La belle dame sans merci"*[3]
Close to her ear touching the melody;
Wherewith disturbed, she uttered a soft moan:
295   He ceased—she panted quick—and suddenly
Her blue affrayèd eyes wide open shone:
Upon his knees he sank, pale as smooth-sculptured stone.

34

Her eyes were open, but she still beheld,
Now wide awake, the vision of her sleep:
300   There was a painful change, that nigh expelled
The blisses of her dream so pure and deep,
At which fair Madeline began to weep,
And moan forth witless words with many a sigh;
While still her gaze on Porphyro would keep,
305   Who knelt, with joinèd hands and piteous eye,
Fearing to move or speak, she looked so dreamingly.

35

"Ah, Porphyro!" said she, "but even now
Thy voice was at sweet tremble in mine ear,
Made tunable with every sweetest vow;
310   And those sad eyes were spiritual and clear:
How changed thou art! how pallid, chill, and drear!
Give me that voice again, my Porphyro,
Those looks immortal, those complainings dear!
Oh leave me not in this eternal woe,
315   For if thou diest, my Love, I know not where to go."

3. The lovely but merciless lady (French). Keats adopted this title, of a poem by Alain Chartier (1380/90–ca. 1430), for one of his own (see p. 917).

36

Beyond a mortal man impassioned far
At these voluptuous accents, he arose,
Ethereal, flushed, and like a throbbing star
Seen mid the sapphire heaven's deep repose;
320　Into her dream he melted, as the rose
Blendeth its odor with the violet—
Solution sweet: meantime the frost-wind blows
Like Love's alarum° pattering the sharp sleet　　　　signal, call to arms
Against the windowpanes; St. Agnes' moon hath set.

37

325　'Tis dark: quick pattereth the flaw-blown° sleet:　　　　gust-blown
"This is no dream, my bride, my Madeline!"
'Tis dark: the icèd gusts still rave and beat:
"No dream, alas! alas! and woe is mine!
Porphyro will leave me here to fade and pine.—
330　Cruel! what traitor could thee hither bring?
I curse not, for my heart is lost in thine,
Though thou forsakest a deceivèd thing—
A dove forlorn and lost with sick unprunèd⁴ wing."

38

"My Madeline! sweet dreamer! lovely bride!
335　Say, may I be for aye thy vassal blest?
Thy beauty's shield, heart-shaped and vermeil° dyed?　　　　vermilion
Ah, silver shrine, here will I take my rest
After so many hours of toil and quest,
A famished pilgrim—saved by miracle.
340　Though I have found, I will not rob thy nest
Saving of thy sweet self; if thou think'st well
To trust, fair Madeline, to no rude infidel.

39

"Hark! 'tis an elfin-storm from faery land,
Of haggard° seeming, but a boon indeed:　　　　wild, ugly
345　Arise—arise! the morning is at hand—
The bloated wassaillers° will never heed—　　　　drunken revelers
Let us away, my love, with happy speed;
There are no ears to hear, or eyes to see—
Drowned all in Rhenish and the sleepy mead:⁵
350　Awake! arise! my love, and fearless be,
For o'er the southern moors I have a home for thee."

40

She hurried at his words, beset with fears,
For there were sleeping dragons all around,
At glaring watch, perhaps, with ready spears—
355　Down the wide stairs a darkling way⁶ they found.—
In all the house was heard no human sound.

---

4. Unpreened; i.e., disarranged, rumpled.
5. Rhine wine and a sleep-inducing drink made of　fermented honey and water.
　　6. A way in the dark.

A chain-dropped lamp was flickering by each door;
The arras, rich with horseman, hawk, and hound,
Fluttered in the besieging wind's uproar;
360 And the long carpets rose along the gusty floor.

41

They glide, like phantoms, into the wide hall;
Like phantoms, to the iron porch, they glide;
Where lay the Porter, in uneasy sprawl,
With a huge empty flagon by his side:
365 The wakeful bloodhound rose, and shook his hide,
But his sagacious eye an inmate owns:°   recognizes
By one, and one, the bolts full easy slide:
The chains lie silent on the footworn stones;
The key turns, and the door upon its hinges groans.

42

370 And they are gone: aye, ages long ago
These lovers fled away into the storm.
That night the Baron dreamt of many a woe,
And all his warrior-guests, with shade and form
Of witch, and demon, and large coffin-worm,
375 Were long be-nightmared. Angela the old
Died palsy-twitched, with meager face deform;
The Beadsman, after thousand aves[7] told,
For aye° unsought for slept among his ashes cold.   ever

1819   1820

On the Sonnet

If by dull rhymes our English must be chained,
    And, like Andromeda,[8] the Sonnet sweet
Fettered, in spite of painèd loveliness;
Let us find out, if we must be constrained,
5   Sandals more interwoven and complete
To fit the naked foot of poesy;
Let us inspect the lyre, and weigh the stress
Of every chord, and see what may be gained
    By ear industrious, and attention meet;
10   Misers of sound and syllable, no less
Than Midas[9] of his coinage, let us be
    Jealous° of dead leaves in the bay-wreath crown;[1]   intolerant

---

7. As in *Ave Maria* ("Hail Mary"), a salutation to the Virgin.
8. In Greek mythology, a beautiful princess chained naked to a rock as a sacrifice to a sea monster, but rescued by the hero Perseus.

9. According to legend, a fabulously wealthy king who wished to turn all that he touched into gold; granted his wish by the gods, he quickly repented it.
1. Awarded as prize to a true poet.

So, if we may not let the Muse[2] be free,
  She will be bound with garlands of her own.

1819   1848

La Belle Dame sans Merci[3]

O what can ail thee, Knight at arms,
  Alone and palely loitering?
The sedge has withered from the Lake
  And no birds sing!

5 O what can ail thee, Knight at arms,
  So haggard, and so woebegone?
The squirrel's granary is full
  And the harvest's done.

I see a lily on thy brow
10 With anguish moist and fever dew,
And on thy cheeks a fading rose
  Fast withereth too.

"I met a Lady in the Meads,°   *meadows*
  Full beautiful, a faery's child,
15 Her hair was long, her foot was light
  And her eyes were wild.

"I made a Garland for her head,
  And bracelets too, and fragrant Zone;°   *girdle*
She looked at me as she did love
20 And made sweet moan.

"I set her on my pacing steed
  And nothing else saw all day long,
For sidelong would she bend and sing
  A faery's song.

25 "She found me roots of relish sweet,
  And honey wild, and manna° dew,   *food (from heaven)*
And sure in language strange she said
  'I love thee true.'

"She took me to her elfin grot°   *grotto*
30 And there she wept and sighed full sore,
And there I shut her wild wild eyes
  With kisses four.

2. Source of poetic inspiration.
3. The lovely but merciless lady (French). This is an earlier (and widely preferred) version of a poem first published in 1820.

"And there she lullèd me asleep,
    And there I dreamed, Ah Woe betide!
35 The latest° dream I ever dreamt   *last*
    On the cold hill side.

"I saw pale Kings, and Princes too,
    Pale warriors, death-pale were they all;
They cried, 'La belle dame sans merci
40   Hath thee in thrall!'

"I saw their starved lips in the gloam
    With horrid warning gapèd wide,
And I awoke, and found me here
    On the cold hill's side.

45 "And this is why I sojourn here,
    Alone and palely loitering;
Though the sedge is withered from the Lake
    And no birds sing."

April 1819   1888

Lamia[4]

Part 1

Upon a time, before the faery broods
Drove Nymph and Satyr[5] from the prosperous woods,
Before King Oberon's bright diadem,[6]
Sceptre, and mantle, clasp'd with dewy gem,
5 Frighted away the Dryads and the Fauns
From rushes green, and brakes, and cowslip'd[7] lawns,
The ever-smitten Hermes[8] empty left
His golden throne, bent warm on amorous theft:
From high Olympus had he stolen light,
10 On this side of Jove's clouds, to escape the sight
Of his great summoner, and made retreat
Into a forest on the shores of Crete.
For somewhere in that sacred island dwelt
A nymph, to whom all hoofèd Satyrs knelt;
15 At whose white feet the languid Tritons[9] poured
Pearls, while on land they wither'd and adored.
Fast by the springs where she to bathe was wont,°   *accustomed*
And in those meads° where sometime she might haunt,   *meadows*
Were strewn rich gifts, unknown to any Muse,[1]

4. In Greek mythology, a female demon who preyed on humans.
5. Like dryads and fauns (line 5), nymphs and satyrs were minor classical deities.
6. Crown of Oberon, king of the fairies (post-classical supernatural beings).
7. Covered with cowslips (a species of wildflower).

Brakes: thickets.
8. Or Mercury, the gods' messenger, especially at the service of Jove (or Jupiter, Zeus), the chief god.
9. Minor sea gods.
1. One of the nine sister goddesses who presided over song, poetry, and the arts and sciences.

20 Though Fancy's casket were unlock'd to choose.
    Ah, what a world of love was at her feet!
    So Hermes thought, and a celestial heat
    Burnt from his wingèd heels to either ear,
    That from a whiteness, as the lily clear,
25 Blush'd into roses 'mid his golden hair,
    Fallen in jealous curls about his shoulders bare.

        From vale° to vale, from wood to wood, he flew,   *valley*
    Breathing upon the flowers his passion new,
    And wound with many a river to its head,
30 To find where this sweet nymph prepar'd her secret bed:
    In vain; the sweet nymph might nowhere be found,
    And so he rested on the lonely ground,
    Pensive, and full of painful jealousies
    Of the Wood-Gods, and even the very trees.
35 There as he stood, he heard a mournful voice,
    Such as once heard, in gentle heart, destroys
    All pain but pity: thus the lone voice spake:
    "When from this wreathèd tomb shall I awake!
    When move in a sweet body fit for life,
40 And love, and pleasure, and the ruddy strife
    Of hearts and lips! Ah, miserable me!"
    The God, dove-footed,[2] glided silently
    Round bush and tree, soft-brushing, in his speed,
    The taller grasses and full-flowering weed,
45 Until he found a palpitating snake,
    Bright, and cirque-couchant[3] in a dusky brake.

        She was a gordian[4] shape of dazzling hue,
    Vermilion-spotted, golden, green, and blue;
    Striped like a zebra, freckled like a pard,°   *leopard*
50 Eyed like a peacock,[5] and all crimson barr'd;
    And full of silver moons, that, as she breathed,
    Dissolv'd, or brighter shone, or interwreathed,
    Their lustres with the gloomier tapestries—
    So rainbow-sided, touch'd with miseries,
55 She seem'd, at once, some penanced lady elf,
    Some demon's mistress, or the demon's self.
    Upon her crest she wore a wannish° fire   *dark*
    Sprinkled with stars, like Ariadne's tiar:[6]
    Her head was serpent, but ah, bitter-sweet!
60 She had a woman's mouth with all its pearls[7] complete:
    And for her eyes: what could such eyes do there
    But weep, and weep, that they were born so fair?
    As Proserpine still weeps for her Sicilian air.[8]

2. I.e., gently as a dove.
3. Lying in a circular coil.
4. Intricately twisted, seemingly impossible to undo, like the knot tied by Gordius, legendary Phrygian king.
5. With multicolored spots (like the "eyes" in a peacock's tail).
6. Tiara. In a painting by the Italian Renaissance artist Titian, Ariadne, a Greek mythological figure who was transformed into a constellation, wears a crown of stars.
7. A common Elizabethan metaphor for teeth.
8. The goddess Proserpina (Persephone) was taken from the field of Enna, in Sicily, to Hades by the god Pluto.

Her throat was serpent, but the words she spake
65 Came, as through bubbling honey, for Love's sake,
And thus; while Hermes on his pinions° lay,   *wings*
Like a stoop'd° falcon ere he takes his prey.   *plunging*

"Fair Hermes, crown'd with feathers, fluttering light,
I had a splendid dream of thee last night:
70 I saw thee sitting, on a throne of gold,
Among the Gods, upon Olympus old,
The only sad one; for thou didst not hear
The soft, lute-finger'd Muses chaunting clear,
Nor even Apollo⁹ when he sang alone,
75 Deaf to his throbbing throat's long, long melodious moan.
I dreamt I saw thee, robed in purple flakes,
Break amorous through the clouds, as morning breaks,
And, swiftly as a bright Phœbean dart,°   *ray*
Strike for the Cretan isle; and here thou art!
80 Too gentle Hermes, hast thou found the maid?"
Whereat the star of Lethe¹ not delay'd
His rosy eloquence, and thus inquired:
"Thou smooth-lipp'd serpent, surely high inspired!
Thou beauteous wreath, with melancholy eyes,
85 Possess whatever bliss thou canst devise,
Telling me only where my nymph is fled,—
Where she doth breathe!" "Bright planet, thou hast said,"
Return'd the snake, "but seal with oaths, fair God!"
"I swear," said Hermes, "by my serpent rod,
90 And by thine eyes, and by thy starry crown!"
Light flew his earnest words, among the blossoms blown.
Then thus again the brilliance feminine:
"Too frail of heart! for this lost nymph of thine,
Free as the air, invisibly, she strays
95 About these thornless wilds; her pleasant days
She tastes unseen; unseen her nimble feet
Leave traces in the grass and flowers sweet;
From weary tendrils, and bow'd branches green,
She plucks the fruit unseen, she bathes unseen:
100 And by my power is her beauty veil'd
To keep it unaffronted, unassail'd
By the love-glances of unlovely eyes,
Of Satyrs, Fauns, and blear'd Silenus'² sighs.
Pale grew her immortality, for woe
105 Of all these lovers, and she grievèd so
I took compassion on her, bade her steep
Her hair in weïrd° syrops,° that would keep   *magical / potions*
Her loveliness invisible, yet free
To wander as she loves, in liberty.
110 Thou shalt behold her, Hermes, thou alone,
If thou wilt, as thou swearest, grant my boon!"

9. Phoebus Apollo, the sun god.
1. Hermes, who appeared like a star on the dark banks of the river Lethe, in Hades.

2. Satyr, tutor of Bacchus (Dionysus, god of wine). *Blear'd*: drunk.

Then, once-again, the charmèd God began
An oath, and through the serpent's ears it ran
Warm, tremulous, devout, psalterian.[3]
115 Ravish'd, she lifted her Circean head,
Blush'd a live damask,[4] and swift-lisping said,
"I was a woman, let me have once more
A woman's shape, and charming as before.
I love a youth of Corinth—O the bliss!
120 Give me my woman's form, and place me where he is.
Stoop, Hermes, let me breathe upon thy brow,
And thou shalt see thy sweet nymph even now."
The God on half-shut feathers sank serene,
She breath'd upon his eyes, and swift was seen
125 Of both the guarded nymph near-smiling on the green.
It was no dream; or say a dream it was,
Real are the dreams of Gods, and smoothly pass
Their pleasures in a long immortal dream.
One warm, flush'd moment, hovering, it might seem
130 Dash'd by the wood-nymph's beauty, so he burn'd;
Then, lighting on the printless verdure, turn'd
To the swoon'd serpent, and with languid arm,
Delicate, put to proof the lythe Caducean charm.[5]
So done, upon the nymph his eyes he bent
135 Full of adoring tears and blandishment,
And towards her stept: she, like a moon in wane,
Faded before him, cower'd, nor could restrain
Her fearful sobs, self-folding like a flower
That faints into itself at evening hour:
140 But the God fostering her chillèd hand,   softly
She felt the warmth, her eyelids open'd bland,°
And, like new flowers at morning song of bees,
Bloom'd, and gave up her honey to the lees.°   dregs
Into the green-recessed woods they flew;
145 Nor grew they pale, as mortal lovers do.

        Left to herself, the serpent now began
To change; her elfin blood in madness ran,
Her mouth foam'd, and the grass, therewith besprent,°   sprinkled
Wither'd at dew so sweet and virulent;
150 Her eyes in torture fix'd, and anguish drear,
Hot, glaz'd, and wide, with lid-lashes all sear,
Flash'd phosphor and sharp sparks, without one cooling tear.
The colors all inflam'd throughout her train,
She writh'd about, convuls'd with scarlet pain:
155 A deep volcanian yellow took the place
Of all her milder-moonèd body's grace;[6]
And, as the lava ravishes the mead,
Spoilt all her silver mail, and golden brede;°   embroidery

---

3. Like a psalm or like the sound of a psaltery (an ancient stringed instrument).
4. Turned the pink color of a damask rose. *Circean:* resembling Circe, enchantress in the *Odyssey.*

5. I.e., tested the magic of Hermes' flexible staff (called Caduceus).
6. I.e., sulfurous yellow (as though from a volcanic eruption) replaced her silvery moon color.

Made gloom of all her frecklings, streaks and bars,
160 Eclips'd her crescents, and lick'd up her stars:
So that, in moments few, she was undrest
Of all her sapphires, greens, and amethyst,
And rubious-argent:° of all these bereft,   *silvery red*
Nothing but pain and ugliness were left.
165 Still shone her crown; that vanish'd, also she
Melted and disappear'd as suddenly;
And in the air, her new voice luting soft,
Cried, "Lycius! gentle Lycius!"—Borne aloft
With the bright mists about the mountains hoar°   *gray with age*
170 These words dissolv'd: Crete's forests heard no more.

Whither fled Lamia, now a lady bright,
A full-born beauty new and exquisite?
She fled into that valley they pass o'er
Who go to Corinth from Cenchreas' shore;[7]
175 And rested at the foot of those wild hills,
The rugged founts of the Peæran rills,[8]
And of that other ridge whose barren back
Stretches, with all its mist and cloudy rack,
South-westward to Cleone. There she stood
180 About a young bird's flutter from a wood,
Fair, on a sloping green of mossy tread,
By a clear pool, wherein she passionèd[9]
To see herself escap'd from so sore ills,
While her robes flaunted with the daffodils.

185 Ah, happy Lycius!—for she was a maid
More beautiful than ever twisted braid,
Or sigh'd, or blush'd, or on spring-flowered lea°   *meadow*
Spread a green kirtle° to the minstrelsy: *gown*
A virgin purest lipp'd yet in the lore
190 Of love deep learned to the red heart's core:
Not one hour old, yet of sciential° brain   *knowledgeable*
To unperplex° bliss from its neighbor pain;   *disentangle*
Define their pettish° limits, and estrange   *quarreled-over*
Their points of contact, and swift counterchange;[1]
195 Intrigue with the specious chaos,[2] and dispart
Its most ambiguous atoms with sure art;
As though in Cupid's college she had spent
Sweet days a lovely graduate, still unshent,°   *unspoiled*
And kept his rosy terms[3] in idle languishment.

200 Why this fair creature chose so fairily
By the wayside to linger, we shall see;
But first 'tis fit to tell how she could muse
And dream, when in the serpent prison-house,

7. I.e., Cenchrea, a Corinthian harbor, in southern Greece.
8. Streams flowing from the Pierian Spring (on Mt. Olympus, in Greece), sacred to the Muses.
9. Felt intense excitement.

1. Change of condition into its opposite. *Estrange:* separate out.
2. I.e., use the illusory ("specious") chaos.
3. Terms spent "in Cupid's college."

Of all she list,° strange or magnificent: *wished*
205 How, ever, where she will'd, her spirit went;
Whether to faint Elysium, or where
Down through tress-lifting waves the Nereids fair
Wind into Thetis'⁴ bower by many a pearly stair;
Or where God Bacchus drains his cups divine,
210 Stretch'd out, at ease, beneath a glutinous° pine;   *gummy*
Or where in Pluto's gardens palatine°   *palatial*
Mulciber's columns gleam in far piazzian line.⁵
And sometimes into cities she would send
Her dream, with feast and rioting to blend;
215 And once, while among mortals dreaming thus,
She saw the young Corinthian Lycius
Charioting foremost in the envious race,
Like a young Jove with calm uneager face,
And fell into a swooning love of him.
220 Now on the moth-time of that evening dim
He would return that way, as well she knew,
To Corinth from the shore; for freshly blew
The eastern soft wind, and his galley now
Grated the quaystones with her brazen prow
225 In port Cenchreas, from Egina isle
Fresh anchor'd; whither he had been awhile
To sacrifice to Jove, whose temple there
Waits with high marble doors for blood and incense rare.
Jove heard his vows, and better'd his desire;
230 For by some freakful chance he made retire
From his companions, and set forth to walk,
Perhaps grown wearied of their Corinth talk:
Over the solitary hills he fared,
Thoughtless at first, but ere eve's star appeared
235 His phantasy was lost, where reason fades,
In the calm'd twilight of Platonic shades.⁶
Lamia beheld him coming, near, more near—
Close to her passing, in indifference drear,
His silent sandals swept the mossy green;
240 So neighbour'd to him, and yet so unseen
She stood: he pass'd, shut up in mysteries,
His mind wrapp'd like his mantle, while her eyes
Follow'd his steps, and her neck regal white
Turn'd—syllabling thus, "Ah, Lycius bright,
245 And will you leave me on the hills alone?
Lycius, look back! and be some pity shown."
He did; not with cold wonder fearingly,
But Orpheus-like at an Eurydice;⁷
For so delicious were the words she sung,
250 It seem'd he had lov'd them a whole summer long:
And soon his eyes had drunk her beauty up,

4. One of the Nereids, or sea nymphs.
5. In long lines around piazzas, or open courts.
Mulciber: or Vulcan, god of fire and metalworking.
6. I.e., while he pondered difficult questions
raised by Plato's philosophy.

7. Pluto allowed Orpheus to lead Eurydice,
Orpheus's wife, back to Earth from Hades on the
condition that Orpheus not look back at her. When
he could not resist looking, he lost her.

Leaving no drop in the bewildering cup,
And still the cup was full,—while he, afraid
Lest she should vanish ere his lip had paid
255   Due adoration, thus began to adore;
Her soft look growing coy, she saw his chain so sure:
"Leave thee alone! Look back! Ah, Goddess, see
Whether my eyes can ever turn from thee!
For pity do not this sad heart belie°—   *be false to*
260   Even as thou vanishest so I shall die.
Stay! though a Naiad of the rivers, stay!
To thy far wishes will thy streams obey:
Stay! though the greenest woods be thy domain,
Alone they can drink up the morning rain:
265   Though a descended Pleiad,[8] will not one
Of thine harmonious sisters keep in tune
Thy spheres, and as thy silver proxy shine?
So sweetly to these ravish'd ears of mine
Came thy sweet greeting, that if thou shouldst fade
270   Thy memory will waste me to a shade:—
For pity do not melt!"—"If I should stay,"
Said Lamia, "here, upon this floor of clay,
And pain my steps upon these flowers too rough,
What canst thou say or do of charm enough
275   To dull the nice[9] remembrance of my home?
Thou canst not ask me with thee here too roam
Over these hills and vales, where no joy is,—
Empty of immortality and bliss!
Thou art a scholar, Lycius, and must know
280   That finer spirits cannot breathe below
In human climes, and live: Alas! poor youth,
What taste of purer air hast thou to soothe
My essence? What serener palaces,
Where I may all my many senses please,
285   And by mysterious sleights a hundred thirsts appease?
It cannot be—Adieu!" So said, she rose
Tiptoe with white arms spread. He, sick to lose
The amorous promise of her lone complain,
Swoon'd, murmuring of love, and pale with pain.
290   The cruel lady, without any show
Of sorrow for her tender favorite's woe,
But rather, if her eyes could brighter be,
With brighter eyes and slow amenity,
Put her new lips to his, and gave afresh
295   The life she had so tangled in her mesh:
And as he from one trance was wakening
Into another, she began to sing,
Happy in beauty, life, and love, and every thing,
A song of love, too sweet for earthly lyres,
300   While, like held breath, the stars drew in their panting fires.
And then she whisper'd in such trembling tone,

8. One of the seven sisters that form the constel-   9. Detailed, minutely accurate.
lation Pleiades.

As those who, safe together met alone
For the first time through many anguish'd days,
Use other speech than looks; bidding him raise
His drooping head, and clear his soul of doubt,   305
For that she was a woman, and without
Any more subtle fluid in her veins
Than throbbing blood, and that the self-same pains
Inhabited her frail-strung heart as his.
And next she wonder'd how his eyes could miss   310
Her face so long in Corinth, where, she said,
She dwelt but half retir'd, and there had led
Days happy as the gold coin could invent
Without the aid of love; yet in content
Till she saw him, as once she pass'd him by,   315
Where 'gainst a column he leant thoughtfully
At Venus' temple porch, 'mid baskets heap'd
Of amorous herbs and flowers, newly reap'd
Late on that eve, as 'twas the night before
The Adonian feast;[1] whereof she saw no more,   320
But wept alone those days, for why should she adore?
Lycius from death awoke into amaze,
To see her still, and singing so sweet lays;°   *songs*
Then from amaze into delight he fell
To hear her whisper woman's lore so well;   325
And every word she spake entic'd him on
To unperplex'd delight[2] and pleasure known.
Let the mad poets say whate'er they please
Of the sweets of Fairies, Peris,[3] Goddesses,
There is not such a treat among them all,   330
Haunters of cavern, lake, and waterfall,
As a real woman, lineal indeed
From Pyrrha's pebbles[4] or old Adam's seed.
Thus gentle Lamia judg'd, and judg'd aright,
That Lycius could not love in half a fright,   335
So threw the goddess off, and won his heart
More pleasantly by playing woman's part,
With no more awe than what her beauty gave,
That, while it smote, still guaranteed to save.
Lycius to all made eloquent reply,   340
Marrying to every word a twinborn sigh;
And last, pointing to Corinth, ask'd her sweet,
If 'twas too far that night for her soft feet.
The way was short, for Lamia's eagerness
Made, by a spell, the triple league decrease   345
To a few paces; not at all surmised
By blinded Lycius, so in her comprized.°   *bound up, absorbed*
They pass'd the city gates, he knew not how,
So noiseless, and he never thought to know.

1. Feast of Adonis, a youth loved by Venus (Aphrodite), goddess of love.
2. I.e., unmixed with its neighbor, pain; cf. line 192.
3. Fairylike creatures in Persian mythology.
4. Descended from the pebbles with which, in Greek mythology, Pyrrha and Deucalion repopulated Earth after a great flood.

350   As men talk in a dream, so Corinth all,
Throughout her palaces imperial,
And all her populous streets and temples lewd,⁵
Mutter'd, like tempest in the distance brew'd,
To the wide-spreaded night above her towers.
355 Men, women, rich and poor, in the cool hours,
Shuffled their sandals o'er the pavement white,
Companion'd or alone; while many a light
Flared, here and there, from wealthy festivals,
And threw their moving shadows on the walls,
360 Or found them cluster'd in the corniced shade
Of some arch'd temple door, or dusky colonnade.

    Muffling his face, of greeting friends in fear,
Her fingers he press'd hard, as one came near
With curl'd gray beard, sharp eyes, and smooth bald crown,
365 Slow-stepp'd, and robed in philosophic gown:
Lycius shrank closer, as they met and past,
Into his mantle, adding wings to haste,
While hurried Lamia trembled: "Ah," said he,
"Why do you shudder, love, so ruefully?
370 Why does your tender palm dissolve in dew?"—
"I'm wearied," said fair Lamia: "tell me who
Is that old man? I cannot bring to mind
His features:—Lycius! wherefore did you blind
Yourself from his quick eyes?" Lycius replied,
375 " 'Tis Apollonius sage, my trusty guide
And good instructor; but to-night he seems
The ghost of folly haunting my sweet dreams."

    While yet he spake they had arrived before
A pillar'd porch, with lofty portal door,
380 Where hung a silver lamp, whose phosphor glow
Reflected in the slabbèd steps below,
Mild as a star in water; for so new,
And so unsullied was the marble hue,
So through the crystal polish, liquid fine,
385 Ran the dark veins, that none but feet divine
Could e'er have touch'd there. Sounds Æolian⁶
Breath'd from the hinges, as the ample span
Of the wide doors disclos'd a place unknown
Some time to any, but those two alone,
390 And a few Persian mutes, who that same year
Were seen about the markets: none knew where
They could inhabit; the most curious
Were foil'd, who watch'd to trace them to their house:
And but the flitter-wingèd verse must tell,
395 For truth's sake, what woe afterwards befel,

---

5. Temples of Venus, whose worship sometimes involved sexual activity.
6. Sounds like those of the wind harp (named after Aeolus, god of winds), a stringed instrument that responds to air currents.

'Twould humor many a heart to leave them thus,
Shut from the busy world of more incredulous.

Part 2

Love in a hut, with water and a crust,
Is—Love, forgive us!—cinders, ashes, dust;
Love in a palace is perhaps at last
More grievous torment than a hermit's fast:—
5   That is a doubtful tale from faery land,
Hard for the non-elect to understand.
Had Lycius liv'd to hand his story down,
He might have given the moral a fresh frown,
Or clench'd it quite: but too short was their bliss
10   To breed distrust and hate, that make the soft voice hiss.
Besides, there, nightly, with terrific glare,
Love, jealous grown of so complete a pair,
Hover'd and buzz'd his wings, with fearful roar,
Above the lintel of their chamber door,
15   And down the passage cast a glow upon the floor.

     For all this came a ruin: side by side
They were enthroned, in the even tide,
Upon a couch, near to a curtaining
Whose airy texture, from a golden string,
20   Floated into the room, and let appear
Unveil'd the summer heaven, blue and clear,
Betwixt two marble shafts:—there they reposed,
Where use had made it sweet, with eyelids closed,
Saving a tythe[7] which love still open kept,
25   That they might see each other while they almost slept;
When from the slope side of a suburb hill,
Deafening the swallow's twitter, came a thrill
Of trumpets—Lycius started—the sounds fled,
But left a thought, a buzzing in his head.
30   For the first time, since first he harbor'd in
That purple-linèd palace of sweet sin,
His spirit pass'd beyond its golden bourn
Into the noisy world almost forsworn.
The lady, ever watchful, penetrant,
35   Saw this with pain, so arguing a want°   *lack*
Of something more, more than her empery°   *empire*
Of joys; and she began to moan and sigh
Because he mused beyond her, knowing well
That but a moment's thought is passion's passing° bell.°   *death / knell*
40   "Why do you sigh, fair creature?" whisper'd he:
"Why do you think?" return'd she tenderly:
"You have deserted me;—where am I now?
Not in your heart while care weighs on your brow:
No, no, you have dismiss'd me; and I go

---

7. Except for a slit. *Tythe* (more commonly *tithe*): a small—literally, a tenth—part.

45   From your breast houseless: ay, it must be so."
      He answer'd, bending to her open eyes,
      Where he was mirror'd small in paradise,
      "My silver planet, both of eve and morn![8]
      Why will you plead yourself so sad forlorn,
50   While I am striving how to fill my heart
      With deeper crimson, and a double smart?°   *pain*
      How to entangle, trammel up[9] and snare
      Your soul in mine, and labyrinth you there
      Like the hid scent in an unbudded rose?
55   Ay, a sweet kiss—you see your mighty woes.[1]
      My thoughts! shall I unveil them? Listen then!
      What mortal hath a prize, that other men
      May be confounded and abash'd withal,
      But lets it sometimes pace abroad majestical,
60   And triumph, as in thee I should rejoice
      Amid the hoarse alarm of Corinth's voice.
      Let my foes choke, and my friends shout afar,
      While through the thronged streets your bridal car°   *chariot*
      Wheels round its dazzling spokes."—The lady's cheek
65   Trembled; she nothing said, but, pale and meek,
      Arose and knelt before him, wept a rain
      Of sorrows at his words; at last with pain
      Beseeching him, the while his hand she wrung,
      To change his purpose. He thereat was stung,
70   Perverse, with stronger fancy to reclaim
      Her wild and timid nature to his aim:
      Besides, for all his love, in self despite,
      Against his better self, he took delight
      Luxurious in her sorrows, soft and new.
75   His passion, cruel grown, took on a hue
      Fierce and sanguineous° as 'twas possible   *bloodred*
      In one whose brow had no dark veins to swell.
      Fine was the mitigated fury, like
      Apollo's presence when in act to strike
80   The serpent—Ha, the serpent! certes,° she   *certainly*
      Was none. She burnt, she lov'd the tyranny,
      And, all subdued, consented to the hour
      When to the bridal he should lead his paramour.
      Whispering in midnight silence, said the youth,
85   "Sure some sweet name thou hast, though, by my truth,
      I have not ask'd it, ever thinking thee
      Not mortal, but of heavenly progeny,
      As still I do. Hast any mortal name,
      Fit appellation for this dazzling frame?
90   Or friends or kinsfolk on the citied earth,
      To share our marriage feast and nuptial mirth?
      "I have no friends," said Lamia, "no, not one;
      My presence in wide Corinth hardly known:

---

8. The planet Venus is both the morning star and the evening star.
9. Catch in a net.

1. I.e., she teases him about exaggerating his troubles.

My parents' bones are in their dusty urns
95 Sepulchred, where no kindled incense burns,
Seeing all their luckless race are dead, save me,
And I neglect the holy rite for thee.
Even as you list invite your many guests;
But if, as now it seems, your vision rests
100 With any pleasure on me, do not bid
Old Apollonius—from him keep me hid."
Lycius, perplex'd at words so blind and blank,
Made close inquiry; from whose touch she shrank,
Feigning a sleep; and he to the dull shade
105 Of deep sleep in a moment was betray'd.

It was the custom then to bring away,
The bride from home at blushing shut of day,
Veil'd, in a chariot, heralded along
By strewn flowers, torches, and a marriage song,
110 With other pageants: but this fair unknown
Had not a friend. So being left alone,
(Lycius was gone to summon all his kin)
And knowing surely she could never win
His foolish heart from its mad pompousness,
115 She set herself, high-thoughted, how to dress
The misery in fit magnificence.
She did so, but 'tis doubtful how and whence
Came, and who were her subtle servitors.°   *male servants*
About the halls, and to and from the doors,
120 There was a noise of wings, till in short space
The glowing banquet-room shone with wide-arched grace.
A haunting music, sole perhaps and lone
Supportress of the faery-roof, made moan
Throughout, as fearful the whole charm might fade.
125 Fresh carvèd cedar, mimicking a glade
Of palm and plantain, met from either side,
High in the midst, in honor of the bride:
Two palms and then two plantains, and so on,
From either side their stems branch'd one to one
130 All down the aislèd place; and beneath all
There ran a stream of lamps straight on from wall to wall.
So canopied, lay an untasted feast
Teeming with odors. Lamia, regal drest,
Silently paced about, and as she went,
135 In pale contented sort of discontent,
Mission'd her viewless servants to enrich
The fretted² splendor of each nook and niche.
Between the tree-stems, marbled plain at first,
Came jasper pannels; then, anon, there burst
140 Forth creeping imagery of slighter trees,
And with the larger wove in small intricacies.
Approving all, she faded at self-will,
And shut the chamber up, close, hush'd and still,

2. Decorated with fretwork.

Complete and ready for the revels rude,°   *uncouth*
145 When dreadful° guests would come to spoil her solitude.   *terrifying*

    The day appear'd, and all the gossip rout.
  O senseless Lycius! Madman! wherefore flout
  The silent-blessing fate, warm cloister'd hours,
  And show to common eyes these secret bowers?
150 The herd approach'd; each guest, with busy brain,
  Arriving at the portal, gaz'd amain,°   *intently*
  And enter'd marveling: for they knew the street,
  Remember'd it from childhood all complete
  Without a gap, yet ne'er before had seen
155 That royal porch, that high-built fair demesne;°   *estate*
  So in they hurried all, maz'd, curious and keen:
  Save one, who look'd thereon with eye severe,
  And with calm-planted steps walk'd in austere;
  'Twas Apollonius: something too he laugh'd,
160 As though some knotty problem, that had daft°   *baffled*
  His patient thought, had now begun to thaw,
  And solve and melt:—'twas just as he foresaw.

    He met within the murmurous vestibule
  His young disciple. " 'Tis no common rule,
165 Lycius," said he, "for uninvited guest
  To force himself upon you, and infest
  With an unbidden presence the bright throng
  Of younger friends; yet must I do this wrong,
  And you forgive me." Lycius blush'd, and led
170 The old man through the inner doors broad-spread;
  With reconciling words and courteous mien°   *demeanor*
  Turning into sweet milk the sophist's spleen.³

    Of wealthy lustre was the banquet-room,
  Fill'd with pervading brilliance and perfume:
175 Before each lucid pannel fuming stood
  A censer fed with myrrh and spicèd wood,
  Each by a sacred tripod held aloft,
  Whose slender feet wide-swerv'd upon the soft
  Wool-woofed° carpets: fifty wreaths of smoke   *-woven*
180 From fifty censers their light voyage took
  To the high roof, still mimick'd as they rose
  Along the mirror'd walls by twin-clouds odorous.
  Twelve sphered tables, by silk seats insphered,°   *encircled*
  High as the level of a man's breast rear'd
185 On libbard's° paws, upheld the heavy gold   *leopard's*
  Of cups and goblets, and the store° thrice told   *story*
  Of Ceres' horn,⁴ and, in huge vessels, wine
  Come from the gloomy tun° with merry shine.   *cask*
  Thus loaded with a feast the tables stood,
190 Each shrining in the midst the image of a God.

3. Here, the melancholy of one whose reasoning seems solid but is flawed.

4. Horn of plenty, filled with grain (Ceres is the goddess of grain).

When in an antichamber every guest
Had felt the cold full sponge to pleasure press'd,
By minist'ring slaves, upon his hands and feet,
And fragrant oils with ceremony meet
195 Pour'd on his hair, they all mov'd to the feast
In white robes, and themselves in order placed
Around the silken couches, wondering
Whence all this mighty cost and blaze of wealth could spring.

Soft went the music the soft air along,
200 While fluent Greek a vowel'd undersong
Kept up among the guests, discoursing low
At first, for scarcely was the wine at flow;
But when the happy vintage touch'd their brains,
Louder they talk, and louder come the strains
205 Of powerful instruments:—the gorgeous dyes,
The space, the splendor of the draperies,
The roof of awful richness, nectarous cheer,
Beautiful slaves, and Lamia's self, appear,
Now, when the wine has done its rosy deed,
210 And every soul from human trammels freed,
No more so strange; for merry wine, sweet wine,
Will make Elysian shades⁵ not too fair, too divine.

Soon was God Bacchus at meridian° height;   *full*
Flush'd were their cheeks, and bright eyes double bright:
215 Garlands of every green, and every scent
From vales° deflower'd, or forest-trees branch-rent,   *valleys*
In baskets of bright osier'd⁶ gold were brought
High as the handles heap'd, to suit the thought
Of every guest; that each, as he did please,
220 Might fancy-fit his brows, silk-pillow'd at his ease.

What wreath for Lamia? What for Lycius?
What for the sage, old Apollonius?
Upon her aching forehead be there hung
The leaves of willow and of adder's tongue;⁷
225 And for the youth, quick, let us strip for him
The thyrsus,⁸ that his watching eyes may swim
Into forgetfulness; and, for the sage,
Let spear-grass and the spiteful thistle wage
War on his temples. Do not all charms fly
230 At the mere touch of cold philosophy?⁹
There was an awful° rainbow once in heaven: *awe-inspiring*
We know her woof, her texture; she is given
In the dull catalogue of common things.
Philosophy will clip an Angel's wings,
235 Conquer all mysteries by rule and line,

5. Spirits in Elysium, abode of the blessed after death.
6. Plaited, as with the strips of willow used to weave baskets.
7. Fern with spikes that resemble serpents' tongues.
8. Bacchus's vine-covered staff, used to signal drunkenness.
9. Natural philosophy, i.e., science.

Empty the haunted air, and gnomèd° mine—   *gnome-guarded*
Unweave a rainbow, as it erewhile made
The tender-person'd Lamia melt into a shade.

    By her glad Lycius sitting, in chief place,
240   Scarce saw in all the room another face,
Till, checking his love trance, a cup he took
Full brimm'd, and opposite sent forth a look
'Cross the broad table, to beseech a glance
From his old teacher's wrinkled countenance,
245   And pledge° him. The bald-head philosopher   *drink a toast to*
Had fix'd his eye, without a twinkle or stir
Full on the alarmèd beauty of the bride,
Brow-beating her fair form, and troubling her sweet pride.
Lycius then press'd her hand, with devout touch,
250   As pale it lay upon the rosy couch:
'Twas icy, and the cold ran through his veins;
Then sudden it grew hot, and all the pains
Of an unnatural heat shot to his heart.
"Lamia, what means this? Wherefore dost thou start?
255   Know'st thou that man?" Poor Lamia answer'd not.
He gaz'd into her eyes, and not a jot
Own'd° they the lovelorn piteous appeal: *acknowledged*
More, more he gaz'd: his human senses reel:
Some hungry spell that loveliness absorbs;
260   There was no recognition in those orbs.
"Lamia!" he cried—and no soft-toned reply.
The many heard, and the loud revelry
Grew hush; the stately music no more breathes;
The myrtle[1] sicken'd in a thousand wreaths.
265   By faint degrees, voice, lute, and pleasure ceased;
A deadly silence step by step increased,
Until it seem'd a horrid presence there,
And not a man but felt the terror in his hair.
"Lamia!" he shriek'd; and nothing but the shriek
270   With its sad echo did the silence break.
"Begone, foul dream!" he cried, gazing again
In the bride's face, where now no azure vein
Wander'd on fair-spaced temples; no soft bloom
Misted the cheek; no passion to illume
275   The deep-recessèd vision:—all was blight;
Lamia, no longer fair, there sat a deadly white.
"Shut, shut those juggling[2] eyes, thou ruthless man!
Turn them aside, wretch! or the righteous ban
Of all the Gods, whose dreadful images
280   Here represent their shadowy presences,
May pierce them on the sudden with the thorn
Of painful blindness; leaving thee forlorn,
In trembling dotage to the feeblest fright
Of conscience, for their long offended might,
285   For all thine impious proud-heart sophistries,

1. An emblem of love, because sacred to Venus.   2. Deceiving.

Unlawful magic, and enticing lies.
Corinthians! look upon that gray-beard wretch!
Mark how, possess'd, his lashless eyelids stretch
Around his demon eyes! Corinthians, see!
290 My sweet bride withers at their potency."
"Fool!" said the sophist, in an under-tone
Gruff with contempt; which a death-nighing moan
From Lycius answer'd, as heart-struck and lost,
He sank supine beside the aching ghost.
295 "Fool! Fool!" repeated he, while his eyes still
Relented not, nor mov'd; "from every ill
Of life have I preserv'd thee to this day,
And shall I see thee made a serpent's prey?"
Then Lamia breath'd death breath; the sophist's eye,
300 Like a sharp spear, went through her utterly,
Keen, cruel, perceant,° stinging: she, as well   *piercing*
As her weak hand could any meaning tell,
Motion'd him to be silent; vainly so,
He look'd and look'd again a level—No!
305 "A Serpent!" echoed he; no sooner said,
Than with a frightful scream she vanishèd:
And Lycius' arms were empty of delight,
As were his limbs of life, from that same night.
On the high couch he lay!—his friends came round—
310 Supported him—no pulse, or breath they found,
And, in its marriage robe, the heavy body wound.

July–August 1819   1820

Ode to Psyche[3]

O Goddess! hear these tuneless numbers,° wrung   *verses*
    By sweet enforcement and remembrance dear,
And pardon that thy secrets should be sung
    Even into thine own soft-conchèd° ear;   *shell-like*
5   Surely I dreamt today, or did I see
    The wingèd Psyche with awakened eyes?
I wandered in a forest thoughtlessly,
    And, on the sudden, fainting with surprise,
Saw two fair creatures, couchèd side by side
10   In deepest grass, beneath the whisp'ring roof
    Of leaves and trembled blossoms, where there ran
        A brooklet, scarce espied:
    'Mid hushed, cool-rooted flowers, fragrant-eyed,
        Blue, silver-white, and budded Tyrian,[4]
15 They lay calm-breathing on the bedded grass;
    Their arms embracèd, and their pinions° too;   *wings*

3. In Greek mythology, Psyche (a mortal woman, whose name means "soul") was loved in secret and in darkness by Cupid, the "wingèd" son of the goddess Venus. After many trials, Psyche was united with Cupid in immortality.
4. Purple or red, as in the "royal" dye made in ancient Tyre.

Their lips touched not, but had not bade adieu,
As if disjoinèd by soft-handed slumber,
And ready still past kisses to outnumber
20 At tender eye-dawn of aurorean° love: *dawning*
     The wingèd boy I knew;
But who wast thou, O happy, happy dove?
     His Psyche true!

O latest born and loveliest vision far
25   Of all Olympus' faded hierarchy![5]
Fairer than Phoebe's° sapphire-regioned star,   *the moon's*
     Or Vesper;° amorous glowworm[6] of the sky;   *the evening star*
Fairer than these, though temple thou hast none,
     Nor altar heaped with flowers;
30 Nor virgin choir to make delicious moan
     Upon the midnight hours;
No voice, no lute, no pipe, no incense sweet
     From chain-swung censer teeming;
No shrine, no grove, no oracle, no heat
35   Of pale-mouthed prophet dreaming.

O brightest! though too late for antique vows,
     Too, too late for the fond believing lyre,
When holy were the haunted forest boughs,
     Holy the air, the water, and the fire;
40 Yet even in these days so far retired
     From happy pieties, thy lucent fans,°   *wings*
     Fluttering among the faint Olympians,
I see, and sing, by my own eyes inspired.
So let me be thy choir, and make a moan
45   Upon the midnight hours;
Thy voice, thy lute, thy pipe, thy incense sweet
     From swingèd censer teeming;
Thy shrine, thy grove, thy oracle, thy heat
     Of pale-mouthed prophet dreaming.

50 Yes, I will be thy priest, and build a fane°   *temple*
     In some untrodden region of my mind,
Where branchèd thoughts, new grown with pleasant pain,
     Instead of pines shall murmur in the wind:
Far, far around shall those dark-clustered trees
55   Fledge the wild-ridgèd mountains steep by steep;
And there by zephyrs,° streams, and birds, and bees,   *breezes*
     The moss-lain Dryads° shall be lulled to sleep;   *tree nymphs*
And in the midst of this wide quietness
     A rosy sanctuary will I dress
60 With the wreathed trellis of a working brain,
     With buds, and bells, and stars without a name,
With all the gardener Fancy e'er could feign,
     Who breeding flowers, will never breed the same:

5. Lines 24–25: last of the deities to be added to   6. Wingless, female firefly that emits light from
the company of the Greek Olympian gods.   the abdomen.

And there shall be for thee all soft delight
65   That shadowy thought can win,
A bright torch, and a casement ope at night,
    To let the warm Love[7] in!

1819   1820

Ode to a Nightingale

1

My heart aches, and a drowsy numbness pains
    My sense, as though of hemlock[8] I had drunk,
Or emptied some dull opiate to the drains
    One minute past, and Lethe-wards[9] had sunk:
5   'Tis not through envy of thy happy lot,
    But being too happy in thine happiness—
        That thou, light-wingèd Dryad° of the trees,   *nymph*
            In some melodious plot
Of beechen green, and shadows numberless,
10   Singest of summer in full-throated ease.

2

O, for a draught of vintage! that hath been
    Cooled a long age in the deep-delvèd earth,
Tasting of Flora[1] and the country green,
    Dance, and Provençal song,[2] and sunburnt mirth!
15   O for a beaker full of the warm South,
    Full of the true, the blushful Hippocrene,[3]
        With beaded bubbles winking at the brim,
            And purple-stainèd mouth;
    That I might drink, and leave the world unseen,
20   And with thee fade away into the forest dim:

3

Fade far away, dissolve, and quite forget
    What thou among the leaves hast never known,
The weariness, the fever, and the fret
    Here, where men sit and hear each other groan;
25   Where palsy shakes a few, sad, last gray hairs,
    Where youth grows pale, and specter-thin, and dies,
        Where but to think is to be full of sorrow
            And leaden-eyed despairs,
    Where Beauty cannot keep her lustrous eyes,
30   Or new Love pine at them beyond tomorrow.

---

7. I.e., Cupid.
8. Opiate made from a poisonous herb.
9. Towards the river Lethe, whose waters in Hades bring the dead forgetfulness.
1. Roman goddess of springtime and flowers.

2. Of the late medieval troubadours of Provence, in southern France.
3. The fountain of the Muses (goddesses of poetry and the arts) on Mt. Helicon, in Greece; its waters induce poetic inspiration.

4

Away! away! for I will fly to thee,
   Not charioted by Bacchus and his pards,[4]
But on the viewless° wings of Poesy,   *invisible*
   Though the dull brain perplexes and retards:
35 Already with thee! tender is the night,
     And haply the Queen-Moon is on her throne,
       Clustered around by all her starry Fays;°   *fairies*
        But here there is no light,
     Save what from heaven is with the breezes blown
40   Through verdurous° glooms and winding mossy ways.   *green-leaved*

5

I cannot see what flowers are at my feet,
   Nor what soft incense hangs upon the boughs,
But, in embalmèd° darkness, guess each sweet   *perfumed*
   Wherewith the seasonable month endows
45 The grass, the thicket, and the fruit tree wild;
     White hawthorn, and the pastoral eglantine;[5]
       Fast fading violets covered up in leaves;
        And mid-May's eldest child,
     The coming musk-rose, full of dewy wine,
50   The murmurous haunt of flies on summer eves.

6

Darkling° I listen; and for many a time   *in darkness*
   I have been half in love with easeful Death,
Called him soft names in many a musèd rhyme,
   To take into the air my quiet breath;
55 Now more than ever seems it rich to die,
     To cease upon the midnight with no pain,
       While thou art pouring forth thy soul abroad
        In such an ecstasy!
     Still wouldst thou sing, and I have ears in vain—
60   To thy high requiem become a sod.

7

Thou wast not born for death, immortal Bird!
   No hungry generations tread thee down;
The voice I hear this passing night was heard
   In ancient days by emperor and clown:
65 Perhaps the selfsame song that found a path
     Through the sad heart of Ruth,[6] when, sick for home,
       She stood in tears amid the alien corn;
        The same that ofttimes hath
     Charmed magic casements, opening on the foam
70   Of perilous seas, in faery lands forlorn.

---

4. Leopards, drawing the chariot of Bacchus, god of wine.
5. Sweetbrier; wood roses.
6. In the Hebrew Scriptures, a woman of great loy-alty and modesty who, as a stranger in Judah, won a husband while gleaning in the barley fields ("the alien corn," line 67).

8

Forlorn! the very word is like a bell
 To toll me back from thee to my sole self!
Adieu! the fancy cannot cheat so well
 As she is famed to do, deceiving elf.
75 Adieu! adieu! thy plaintive anthem fades
 Past the near meadows, over the still stream,
  Up the hill side; and now 'tis buried deep
   In the next valley-glades:
 Was it a vision, or a waking dream?
80 Fled is that music:—Do I wake or sleep?

May 1819   1820

Ode on Melancholy

1

No, no, go not to Lethe,[7] neither twist
 Wolfsbane, tight-rooted, for its poisonous wine;
Nor suffer thy pale forehead to be kissed
 By nightshade, ruby grape of Proserpine;[8]
5 Make not your rosary of yew-berries,[9]
 Nor let the beetle, nor the death-moth be
  Your mournful Psyche, nor the downy owl[1]
A partner in your sorrow's mysteries;
 For shade to shade will come too drowsily,
10 And drown the wakeful anguish of the soul.

2

But when the melancholy fit shall fall
 Sudden from heaven like a weeping cloud,
That fosters the droop-headed flowers all,
 And hides the green hill in an April shroud;
15 Then glut thy sorrow on a morning rose,
 Or on the rainbow of the salt sand-wave,
  Or on the wealth of globèd peonies;
Or if thy mistress some rich anger shows,
 Imprison her soft hand, and let her rave,
20 And feed deep, deep upon her peerless eyes.

3

She[2] dwells with Beauty—Beauty that must die;
 And Joy, whose hand is ever at his lips
Bidding adieu; and aching Pleasure nigh,

7. River in Hades, the waters of which bring forgetfulness to the dead.
8. Queen of Hades. "Nightshade" and "wolfsbane" (line 2) are poisonous herbs from which sedatives and opiates were extracted.
9. Symbols of mourning; often growing in cemeteries.

1. Beetles, moths, and owls traditionally have been associated with darkness, death, and burial; Psyche (the soul) sometimes has been symbolized by a moth that escapes the mouth in sleep or at death.
2. The goddess Melancholy.

Turning to Poison while the bee-mouth sips:
25 Aye, in the very temple of Delight
      Veiled Melancholy has her sov'reign shrine,
         Though seen of none save him whose strenuous tongue
      Can burst Joy's grape against his palate fine;°   *sensitive*
His soul shall taste the sadness of her might,
30   And be among her cloudy trophies[3] hung.

May 1819   1820

Ode on a Grecian Urn

1

Thou still unravished bride of quietness,
   Thou foster child of silence and slow time,
Sylvan° historian, who canst thus express   *rustic*
   A flowery tale more sweetly than our rhyme:
5 What leaf-fringed legend haunts about thy shape
      Of deities or mortals, or of both,
         In Tempe or the dales of Arcady?[4]
      What men or gods are these? What maidens loath?
What mad pursuit? What struggle to escape?
10   What pipes and timbrels? What wild ecstasy?

2

Heard melodies are sweet, but those unheard
   Are sweeter; therefore, ye soft pipes, play on;
Not to the sensual ear, but, more endeared,
   Pipe to the spirit ditties of no tone:
15 Fair youth, beneath the trees, thou canst not leave
      Thy song, nor ever can those trees be bare;
         Bold Lover, never, never canst thou kiss,
      Though winning near the goal—yet, do not grieve;
         She cannot fade, though thou hast not thy bliss,
20   Forever wilt thou love, and she be fair!

3

Ah, happy, happy boughs! that cannot shed
   Your leaves, nor ever bid the Spring adieu;
And, happy melodist, unwearièd,
   Forever piping songs forever new;
25 More happy love! more happy, happy love!
      Forever warm and still to be enjoyed,
         Forever panting, and forever young;
      All breathing human passion far above,
         That leaves a heart high-sorrowful and cloyed,
30   A burning forehead, and a parching tongue.

---

3. Symbols of victory, such as banners, hung in religious shrines.

4. Tempe and Arcady (or Arcadia), in Greece, are traditional symbols of perfect pastoral landscapes.

4

Who are these coming to the sacrifice?
　　To what green altar, O mysterious priest,
Lead'st thou that heifer lowing at the skies,
　　And all her silken flanks with garlands dressed?
35　What little town by river or sea shore,
　　Or mountain-built with peaceful citadel,
　　　　Is emptied of this folk, this pious morn?
And, little town, thy streets forevermore
　　Will silent be; and not a soul to tell
40　　　Why thou art desolate, can e'er return.

5

O Attic⁵ shape! Fair attitude! with brede°   *woven pattern*
　　Of marble men and maidens overwrought,
With forest branches and the trodden weed;
　　Thou, silent form, dost tease us out of thought
45　As doth eternity: Cold Pastoral!
　　When old age shall this generation waste,
　　　　Thou shalt remain, in midst of other woe
Than ours, a friend to man, to whom thou say'st,
　　"Beauty is truth, truth beauty,"⁶—that is all
50　　　Ye know on earth, and all ye need to know.

May 1819   1820

To Autumn

1

Season of mists and mellow fruitfulness,
　　Close bosom-friend of the maturing sun;
Conspiring with him how to load and bless
　　With fruit the vines that round the thatch-eaves run;
5　To bend with apples the mossed cottage-trees,
　　And fill all fruit with ripeness to the core;
　　　　To swell the gourd, and plump the hazel shells
With a sweet kernel; to set budding more,
And still more, later flowers for the bees,
10　Until they think warm days will never cease,
　　　　For Summer has o'er-brimmed their clammy cells.

2

Who hath not seen thee oft amid thy store?
　　Sometimes whoever seeks abroad may find
Thee sitting careless on a granary floor,
15　　Thy hair soft-lifted by the winnowing⁷ wind;

---

5. Greek, especially Athenian.
6. The quotation marks around this phrase are absent from some other versions also having good authority. This discrepancy has led some readers to ascribe only this phrase to the voice of the urn; others ascribe to the urn the whole of the two concluding lines.
7. Blowing the grain clear of the lighter chaff.

Or on a half-reaped furrow sound asleep,
　　Drowsed with the fume of poppies, while thy hook[8]
　　Spares the next swath and all its twinèd flowers:
And sometimes like a gleaner[9] thou dost keep
20　　Steady thy laden head across a brook;
　　Or by a cider-press, with patient look,
　　　Thou watchest the last oozings hours by hours.

3

Where are the songs of Spring? Aye, where are they?
　　Think not of them, thou hast thy music too—
25　While barrèd clouds bloom the soft-dying day,
　　And touch the stubble-plains with rosy hue;
Then in a wailful choir the small gnats mourn
　　Among the river sallows,° borne aloft　　　*low-growing willows*
　　　Or sinking as the light wind lives or dies;
30　And full-grown lambs loud bleat from hilly bourn;°　　*field*
　　Hedge crickets sing; and now with treble soft
The redbreast whistles from a garden-croft;[1]
　　And gathering swallows twitter in the skies.

September 19, 1819　　　　　　　　　　　　　　　　　1820

Bright Star

Bright star, would I were steadfast as thou art—
　　Not in lone splendor hung aloft the night
And watching, with eternal lids apart,
　　Like nature's patient, sleepless Eremite,°　　*hermit; devotee*
5　The moving waters at their priestlike task
　　Of pure ablution[2] round earth's human shores,
Or gazing on the new soft fallen mask
　　Of snow upon the mountains and the moors—
No—yet still steadfast, still unchangeable,
10　Pillowed upon my fair love's ripening breast,
To feel forever its soft fall and swell,
　　Awake forever in a sweet unrest,
Still, still to hear her tender-taken breath,
And so live ever—or else swoon to death.

1819　　　　　　　　　　　　　　　　　　　　　　1838

This Living Hand[3]

This living hand, now warm and capable
Of earnest grasping, would, if it were cold

---

8. Small, curved blade for cutting grain; sickle.
9. Someone who gathers up ears of corn after reapers have passed.
1. Small field, as for a vegetable garden, near a house.
2. Washing as part of a religious ritual.
3. Written on a manuscript page of Keats's unfinished poem, "The Cap and Bells."

And in the icy silence of the tomb,
So haunt thy days and chill thy dreaming nights
5   That thou wouldst wish thine own heart dry of blood
So in my veins red life might stream again,
And thou be conscience-calmed—see here it is—
I hold it towards you.

1819?   1898

RALPH WALDO EMERSON
1803–1882

Concord Hymn

Sung at the Completion of the Battle Monument,[1] *July 4, 1837*

By the rude° bridge that arched the flood,   roughly made
    Their flag to April's breeze unfurled,
Here once the embattled farmers stood
    And fired the shot heard round the world.

5   The foe long since in silence slept;
    Alike the conqueror silent sleeps;
And Time the ruined bridge has swept
    Down the dark stream which seaward creeps.

On this green bank, by this soft stream,
10   We set to-day a votive° stone;   offered in gratitude
That memory may their deed redeem,
    When, like our sires, our sons are gone.

Spirit, that made those heroes dare
    To die, and leave their children free,
15   Bid Time and Nature gently spare
    The shaft we raise to them and thee.

1837, 1876

The Rhodora[2]

On Being Asked, Whence Is the Flower?

In May, when sea-winds pierced our solitudes,
I found the fresh Rhodora in the woods,
Spreading its leafless blooms in a damp nook,
To please the desert and the sluggish brook.
5   The purple petals, fallen in the pool,
Made the black water with their beauty gay;

1. Commemorating the battles of Lexington and   2. An azalea native to the northeastern United
Concord, April 19, 1775.   States.

Here might the red-bird come his plumes to cool,
And court the flower that cheapens his array.
Rhodora! if the sages ask thee why
10 This charm is wasted on the earth and sky,
Tell them, dear, that if eyes were made for seeing,
Then Beauty is its own excuse for being:
Why thou wert there, O rival of the rose!
I never thought to ask, I never knew,
15 But, in my simple ignorance, suppose
The self-same Power that brought me there brought you.

1834   1839, 1847

The Snow-Storm

Announced by all the trumpets of the sky,
Arrives the snow, and, driving o'er the fields,
Seems nowhere to alight: the whited air
Hides hills and woods, the river, and the heaven,
5 And veils the farmhouse at the garden's end.
The sled and traveler stopped, the courier's feet
Delayed, all friends shut out, the housemates sit
Around the radiant fireplace, enclosed
In a tumultuous privacy of storm.

10   Come see the north wind's masonry.
Out of an unseen quarry evermore
Furnished with tile, the fierce artificer
Curves his white bastions with projected roof
Round every windward stake, or tree, or door.
15 Speeding, the myriad-handed, his wild work
So fanciful, so savage, nought cares he
For number or proportion. Mockingly,
On coop or kennel he hangs Parian[3] wreaths;
A swan-like form invests the hidden thorn;
20 Fills up the farmer's lane from wall to wall,
Maugre° the farmer's sighs; and, at the gate,   *in spite of*
A tapering turret overtops the work.
And when his hours are numbered, and the world
Is all his own, retiring, as he were not,
25 Leaves, when the sun appears, astonished Art
To mimic in slow structures, stone by stone,
Built in an age, the mad wind's night-work,
The frolic architecture of the snow.

1841, 1847

---

3. I.e., like the fine white marble from the Greek island of Paros.

Ode

Inscribed to W. H. Channing[4]

Though loath to grieve
The evil time's sole patriot,
I cannot leave
My honied thought
5   For the priest's cant,
Or statesman's rant.

If I refuse
My study for their politique,
Which at the best is trick,
10   The angry Muse°   *source of inspiration*
Puts confusion in my brain.

But who is he that prates
Of the culture of mankind,
Of better arts and life?
15   Go, blindworm, go,
Behold the famous States
Harrying Mexico
With rifle and with knife![5]

Or who, with accent bolder,
20   Dare praise the freedom-loving mountaineer?
I found by thee, O rushing Contoocook![6]
And in thy valleys, Agiochook![7]
The jackals of the negro-holder.

The God who made New Hampshire
25   Taunted the lofty land
With little men;—
Small bat and wren
House in the oak:—
If earth-fire cleave
30   The upheaved land, and bury the folk,
The southern crocodile would grieve.
Virtue palters;° Right is hence;   *hesitates, equivocates*
Freedom praised, but hid;
Funeral eloquence
35   Rattles the coffin-lid.

---

4. William Henry Channing (1810–1884), American clergyman and abolitionist, who urged Emerson to involve himself more actively in the antislavery movement.
5. A reference to the war between the United States and Mexico (1846–48), chiefly over the question of the boundaries of Texas. Emerson was among those Americans who believed the United States was engaged in an immoral, imperialist enterprise that would extend slaveholding territory.
6. Part of the Merrimack River in New Hampshire.
7. The White Mountains of New Hampshire.

What boots° thy zeal,   *profits*
O glowing friend,
That would indignant rend
The northland from the south?
40   Wherefore? to what good end?
Boston Bay and Bunker Hill[8]
Would serve things still;—
Things are of the snake.

The horseman serves the horse,
45   The neatherd° serves the neat,°   *cowherd / cow*
The merchant serves the purse,
The eater serves his meat;
'Tis the day of the chattel,
Web to weave, and corn to grind;
50   Things are in the saddle,
And ride mankind.

There are two laws discrete,
Not reconciled,—
Law for man, and law for things;
55   The last builds town and fleet,
But it runs wild,
And doth the man unking.

'Tis fit the forest fall,
The steep be graded,
60   The mountain tunnelled,
The sand shaded,
The orchard planted,
The glebe° tilled,   *plot of land*
The prairie granted,
65   The steamer built.

Let man serve law for man;
Live for friendship, live for love,
For truth's and harmony's behoof;°   *benefit*
The state may follow how it can,
70   As Olympus follows Jove.[9]

    Yet do not I implore
The wrinkled shopman to my surrounding woods,
Nor bid the unwilling senator
Ask votes of thrushes in the solitudes.
75   Every one to his chosen work;—
Foolish hands may mix and mar;

---

8. Hill in Charlestown, Massachusetts, site of the
first major battle of the American Revolutionary
War, on June 17, 1775. *Boston Bay:* site of the Bos-
ton Tea Party, on December 16, 1773, an incident
that helped provoke the Revolutionary War.
9. Or Jupiter, chief of the Roman gods (Greek
Zeus), who lived on Mt. Olympus.

Wise and sure the issues are.
Round they roll till dark is light,
Sex to sex, and even to odd;—
80 The over-god
Who marries Right to Might,
Who peoples, unpeoples,—
He who exterminates
Races by stronger races,
85 Black by white faces,—
Knows to bring honey
Out of the lion;[1]
Grafts gentlest scion
On pirate and Turk.

90 The Cossack eats Poland,[2]
Like stolen fruit;
Her last noble is ruined,
Her last poet mute:
Straight, into double band
95 The victors divide;
Half for freedom strike and stand;—
The astonished Muse finds thousands at her side.

1847

Intellect[3]

Rule which by obeying grows
Knowledge not its fountain knows
Wave removing whom it bears
From the shores which he compares
5 Adding wings thro° things to range   *through*
Makes him to his own blood strange

1851   1903

Brahma[4]

If the red slayer think he slays,
Or if the slain think he is slain,
They know not well the subtle ways
I keep, and pass, and turn again.

---

1. Lines 83–87 allude to Samson, who killed a lion and returned later to find the carcass filled with honey (Judges 14.5–10).
2. Russian military despotism, established in Poland after the popular insurrections of 1830–31, was challenged by a new Polish uprising (lines 94–96) in 1846.
3. An untitled notebook entry of Emerson's; the title was added posthumously in 1903.
4. The supreme god of Hindu mythology; in later theological developments, the divine reality, once thought to comprehend the entire universe.

5 Far or forgot to me is near;
    Shadow and sunlight are the same;
The vanished gods to me appear;
    And one to me are shame and fame.

They reckon ill who leave me out;
10   When me they fly, I am the wings;
I am the doubter and the doubt,
    And I the hymn the Brahmin sings.

The strong gods pine for my abode,
    And pine in vain the sacred Seven,[5]
15 But thou, meek lover of the good!
    Find me, and turn thy back on heaven.

1856   1857, 1867

Days

Daughters of Time, the hypocritic Days,
Muffled and dumb like barefoot dervishes,°   *whirling dancers*
And marching single in an endless file,
Bring diadems and fagots[6] in their hands.
5 To each they offer gifts after his will,
Bread, kingdom, stars, and sky that holds them all.
I, in my pleachéd[7] garden, watched the pomp,
Forgot my morning wishes, hastily
Took a few herbs and apples, and the Day
10 Turned and departed silent. I, too late,
Under her solemn fillet° saw the scorn.   *hair band*

                                                              1857, 1867

Fate

Her planted eye to-day controls,
Is in the morrow most at home,
And sternly calls to being souls
That curse her when they come.

                                                              1867

5. Perhaps the seven saints high in the Brahman   6. Bundles of sticks. *Diadems:* crowns.
hierarchy but lesser than Brahma.   7. Entwined or plaited.

ELIZABETH BARRETT BROWNING
1806–1861

From Sonnets from the Portuguese[1]

1

I thought once how Theocritus had sung[2]
  Of the sweet years, the dear and wished-for years,
  Who each one in a gracious hand appears
To bear a gift for mortals, old or young:
5 And, as I mused it in his antique tongue,
  I saw, in gradual vision through my tears,
  The sweet, sad years, the melancholy years,
Those of my own life, who by turns had flung
A shadow across me. Straightway I was 'ware,
10 So weeping, how a mystic Shape did move
Behind me, and drew me backward by the hair;[3]
  And a voice said in mastery, while I strove,—
"Guess now who holds thee?"—"Death," I said. But, there,
The silver answer rang,—"Not Death, but Love."

43

How do I love thee? Let me count the ways.
I love thee to the depth and breadth and height
My soul can reach, when feeling out of sight
For the ends of Being and ideal Grace.
5 I love thee to the level of everyday's
Most quiet need, by sun and candle-light.
I love thee freely, as men strive for Right;
I love thee purely, as they turn from Praise.
I love thee with the passion put to use
10 In my old griefs, and with my childhood's faith.
I love thee with a love I seemed to lose
With my lost saints—I love thee with the breath,
Smiles, tears, of all my life!—and, if God choose,
I shall but love thee better after death.

1845–46   1850

1. The "Sonnets from the Portuguese" were written between 1845, when Elizabeth Barrett met Robert Browning (1812–1889; see pp. 1009–41), and 1846, when they were married. An earlier poem, "Catrina to Camoëns," in which Barrett had assumed the persona of the girl who was loved by the sixteenth-century Portuguese poet Camoëns, suggested the lightly disguising title when the sonnets were published in 1850.
2. In Idyll 15 of Theocritus, the Greek pastoral poet of the third century B.C.E., a singer describes the Hours, who have brought Adonis back from the underworld, as "the dear soft-footed Hours, slowest of all the Blessed Ones; but their coming is always longed for, and they bring something for all men."
3. In book 1 of the *Iliad*, just as Achilles is drawing his sword to raise it against his leader, Agamemnon, the goddess Athena, standing behind him and hence invisible to the others, catches him by his hair to warn him.

From Aurora Leigh

From *Book* 5

[POETS AND THE PRESENT AGE]

*   *   *

      The critics say that epics have died out
140   With Agamemnon and the goat-nursed gods;[4]
      I'll not believe it. I could never deem,
      As Payne Knight[5] did (the mythic mountaineer
      Who travelled higher than he was born to live,
      And showed sometimes the goitre[6] in his throat
145   Discoursing of an image seen through fog),
      That Homer's heroes measured twelve feet high.
      They were but men:—his Helen's[7] hair turned gray
      Like any plain Miss Smith's who wears a front;[8]
      And Hector's infant whimpered at a plume[9]
150   As yours last Friday at a turkey-cock.
      All actual heroes are essential men,
      And all men possible heroes: every age,
      Heroic in proportions, double-faced,
      Looks backward and before, expects a morn
155   And claims an epos.°   *epic poem*
                   Ay, but every age
      Appears to souls who live in 't (ask Carlyle)[1]
      Most unheroic. Ours, for instance, ours:
      The thinkers scout it, and the poets abound
      Who scorn to touch it with a finger-tip:
160   A pewter age,[2]—mixed metal, silver-washed;
      An age of scum, spooned off the richer past,
      An age of patches for old gabardines,[3]
      An age of mere transition,[4] meaning nought
      Except that what succeeds must shame it quite
165   If God please. That's wrong thinking, to my mind,
      And wrong thoughts make poor poems.
                        Every age,
      Through being beheld too close, is ill-discerned
      By those who have not lived past it. We'll suppose

4. References to Greek mythological figures: Zeus, king of the gods, had been nursed by a goat; Agamemnon, a chieftain, returned from the Trojan War and was murdered by his wife, Clytemnestra.
5. Richard Payne Knight (1750–1824), a classical philologist, argued that not all of the Elgin Marbles—sculptures and architectural details brought to England from the Parthenon by Lord Elgin— were Greek.
6. An enlargement of the thyroid gland, symptomatic of a disease often caught in mountainous regions and due to a lack of iodine in the water supply.
7. Helen of Troy, the legendary beauty whose abduction led to the Trojan War.
8. A hairpiece worn by women over the forehead.
9. In book 6 of the *Iliad*, when the warrior Hector attempts to hold his infant son, the boy is so fright-

ened by the crest on his father's helmet that he clings to his nurse and cries.
1. In *On Heroes, Hero-Worship, and the Heroic in History* (1841), the Scottish historian and essayist Thomas Carlyle (1795–1881) called for a renewed interest in heroism.
2. I.e., a debased time; refers to the practice, initiated by the Greek poet Hesiod (first century B.C.E.), of assigning the names of increasingly less valuable metals to increasingly less elevated periods in history, such as the Golden Age, the Silver Age, and the Bronze Age.
3. Coats or other garments made of gabardine; also, the smocks of English laborers.
4. "An age of transition" is a quotation from *The Spirit of the Age* (1831), by the English philosopher and economist John Stuart Mill (1806–1873).

Mount Athos carved, as Alexander schemed,
170　　To some colossal statue of a man.[5]
　　　The peasants, gathering brushwood in his ear,
　　　Had guessed as little as the browsing goats
　　　Of form or feature of humanity
　　　Up there,—in fact, had traveled five miles off
175　　Or ere the giant image broke on them,
　　　Full human profile, nose and chin distinct,
　　　Mouth, muttering rhythms of silence up the sky
　　　And fed at evening with the blood of suns;
　　　Grand torso,—hand, that flung perpetually
180　　The largesse° of a silver river down　　　　　　　　　　*bounty*
　　　To all the country pastures. 'Tis even thus
　　　With times we live in,—evermore too great
　　　To be apprehended near.
　　　　　　　　　　　　　But poets should
　　　Exert a double vision; should have eyes
185　　To see near things as comprehensively
　　　As if afar they took their point of sight,
　　　And distant things as intimately deep
　　　As if they touched them. Let us strive for this.
　　　I do distrust the poet who discerns
190　　No character or glory in his times,
　　　And trundles back his soul five hundred years,
　　　Past moat and drawbridge, into a castle-court,
　　　To sing—oh, not of lizard or of toad
　　　Alive i' the ditch there,—'twere excusable,
195　　But of some black chief, half knight, half sheep-lifter,
　　　Some beauteous dame, half chattel and half queen,
　　　As dead as must be, for the greater part,
　　　The poems made on their chivalric bones;
　　　And that's no wonder: death inherits death.

200　　Nay, if there's room for poets in this world
　　　A little overgrown (I think there is),
　　　Their sole work is to represent the age,
　　　Their age, not Charlemagne's,[6]—this live, throbbing age,
　　　That brawls, cheats, maddens, calculates, aspires,
205　　And spends more passion, more heroic heat,
　　　Betwixt the mirrors of its drawing-rooms,
　　　Than Roland[7] with his knights at Roncesvalles.
　　　To flinch from modern varnish, coat or flounce,
　　　Cry out for togas and the picturesque,
210　　Is fatal,—foolish too. King Arthur's self
　　　Was commonplace to Lady Guenever;
　　　And Camelot to minstrels seemed as flat
　　　As Fleet Street[8] to our poets.

5. According to legend, Alexander the Great considered a proposal by the sculptor Dionocrates to carve Mt. Athos into the statue of a conqueror. In his left hand this massive figure would have held a city, while in his right hand he would have held a basin to catch the waters of the region and to irrigate the pastures below.

6. Charles the Great, or Charles I (742–814), a Frankish king and the ruler of a European empire.
7. Hero of the medieval French epic *Chanson de Roland*.
8. Street in London, center of the London newspaper- and book-publishing district.

Never flinch,
But still, unscrupulously epic, catch
215 Upon the burning lava of a song
The full-veined, heaving, double-breasted Age:
That, when the next shall come, the men of that
May touch the impress with reverent hand, and say
"Behold,—behold the paps° we all have sucked!   *breasts*
220 This bosom seems to beat still, or at least
It sets ours beating: this is living art,
Which thus presents and thus records true life."

*   *   *

1853–56   1857

A Musical Instrument

What was he doing, the great god Pan,[9]
    Down in the reeds by the river?
Spreading ruin and scattering ban,°   *baleful influence*
Splashing and paddling with hoofs of a goat,
5 And breaking the golden lilies afloat
    With the dragonfly on the river.

He tore out a reed, the great god Pan,
    From the deep cool bed of the river;
The limpid water turbidly ran,
10 And the broken lilies a-dying lay,
And the dragonfly had fled away,
    Ere he brought it out of the river.

High on the shore sat the great god Pan
    While turbidly flowed the river;
15 And hacked and hewed as a great god can,
With his hard bleak steel at the patient reed,
Till there was not a sign of the leaf indeed
    To prove it fresh from the river.

He cut it short, did the great god Pan
20   (How tall it stood in the river!),
Then drew the pith, like the heart of a man,
Steadily from the outside ring,
And notched the poor dry empty thing
    In holes, as he sat by the river.

---

9. In Greek mythology, god of pastures, flocks, and shepherds, in shape half goat and half human. He played the reed flute, and later pastoral poets made him the patron of their art. One of his loves was the nymph, or minor nature goddess, Syrinx, who tried to escape him and sought help from the river nymphs. They turned her into a reed bed, and from a reed Pan made his flute.

25 "This is the way," laughed the great god Pan
        (Laughed while he sat by the river),
    "The only way, since gods began
    To make sweet music, they could succeed."
    Then, dropping his mouth to a hole in the reed,
30   He blew in power by the river.

    Sweet, sweet, sweet, O Pan!
        Piercing sweet by the river!
    Blinding sweet, O great god Pan!
    The sun on the hill forgot to die,
35 And the lilies revived, and the dragonfly
        Came back to dream on the river.

    Yet half a beast is the great god Pan,
        To laugh as he sits by the river,
    Making a poet out of a man;
40 The true gods sigh for the cost and pain—
    For the reed which grows nevermore again
        As a reed with the reeds in the river.

1860   1862

HENRY WADSWORTH LONGFELLOW
1807–1882

From Evangeline[1]

This is the forest primeval. The murmuring pines and the hemlocks,
Bearded with moss, and in garments green, indistinct in the twilight,
Stand like Druids of eld,[2] with voices sad and prophetic,
Stand like harpers hoar,[3] with beards that rest on their bosoms.
5 Loud from its rocky caverns, the deep-voiced neighbouring ocean
Speaks, and in accents disconsolate answers the wail of the forest.

    This is the forest primeval; but where are the hearts that beneath it
Leaped like the roe, when he hears in the woodland the voice of the
        huntsman?
Where is the thatch-roofed village, the home of Acadian farmers,—
10 Men whose lives glided on like rivers that water the woodlands,

---

1. Some introductory verses to a long poem, a tale of divided lovers, based on a true story told to the American writer Nathaniel Hawthorne (1804–1864), and by him to Longfellow. The poem opens in Nova Scotia, Canada (where Longfellow never visited), a region often called Acadia or Acadie, which France ceded to Great Britain in 1713. When the French and Indian War broke out, the French inhabitants who refused to take an oath of allegiance were shipped off; about three thousand were deported in 1755, like those of the village of Grand Pré. The poem is credited with having provoked a wider interest in English hexameter.
2. Old. *Druids:* members of a prophetic priesthood in ancient Gaul, Britain, and Ireland.
3. Ancient harpists.

Darkened by shadows of earth, but reflecting an image of heaven?
Waste are those pleasant farms, and the farmers forever departed!
Scattered like dust and leaves, when the mighty blasts of October
Seize them, and whirl them aloft, and sprinkle them far o'er the
    ocean.
15   Naught but tradition remains of the beautiful village of Grand-Pré.

1847

The Jewish Cemetery at Newport[4]

How strange it seems! These Hebrews in their graves,
    Close by the street of this fair seaport town,
Silent beside the never-silent waves,
    At rest in all this moving up and down!

5   The trees are white with dust, that o'er their sleep
    Wave their broad curtains in the southwind's breath,
While underneath these leafy tents they keep
    The long, mysterious Exodus[5] of Death.

And these sepulchral stones, so old and brown,
10   That pave with level flags their burial-place,
Seem like the tablets of the Law, thrown down
    And broken by Moses at the mountain's base.[6]

The very names recorded here are strange,
    Of foreign accent, and of different climes;
15   Alvares and Rivera[7] interchange
    With Abraham and Jacob of old times.

"Blessed be God! for he created Death!"
    The mourners said, "and Death is rest and peace;"
Then added, in the certainty of faith,
20   "And giveth Life that nevermore shall cease."

Closed are the portals of their Synagogue,
    No Psalms of David now the silence break,
No Rabbi reads the ancient Decalogue°   *Ten Commandments*
    In the grand dialect the Prophets spake.

25   Gone are the living, but the dead remain,
    And not neglected; for a hand unseen,
Scattering its bounty, like a summer rain,
    Still keeps their graves and their remembrance green.

4. The oldest synagogue in the United States is in
Newport, Rhode Island.
5. The flight of Moses and the Israelites from
Egypt.
6. Moses, angered by the disobedience of the Isra-
elites, broke the tablets of the law that God had
given them (see Exodus 32.19).
7. Many of the early Jewish families in New
England were from Spain and Portugal.

How came they here? What burst of Christian hate,
30   What persecution, merciless and blind,
Drove o'er the sea—that desert desolate—
    These Ishmaels and Hagars of mankind?[8]

They lived in narrow streets and lanes obscure,
    Ghetto and Judenstrass,[9] in mirk and mire;
35   Taught in the school of patience to endure
    The life of anguish and the death of fire.

All their lives long, with the unleavened bread
    And bitter herbs of exile and its fears,
The wasting famine of the heart they fed,
40   And slaked its thirst with marah[1] of their tears.

Anathema maranatha![2] was the cry
    That rang from town to town, from street to street;
At every gate the accursed Mordecai[3]
    Was mocked and jeered, and spurned by Christian feet.

45   Pride and humiliation hand in hand
    Walked with them through the world where'er they went;
Trampled and beaten were they as the sand,
    And yet unshaken as the continent.

For in the background figures vague and vast
50   Of patriarchs and of prophets rose sublime,
And all the great traditions of the Past
    They saw reflected in the coming time.

And thus forever with reverted look
    The mystic volume of the world they read,
55   Spelling it backward, like a Hebrew book,[4]
    Till life became a Legend of the Dead.

But ah! what once has been shall be no more!
    The groaning earth in travail and in pain
Brings forth its races, but does not restore,
60   And the dead nations never rise again.

1852   1854, 1858

8. Hagar, concubine of Abraham, wandered in the desert with Ishmael, her son by Abraham, after she was sent away by Abraham and Sarah (see Genesis 21.9–21). In many countries, Jews faced legal restrictions as well as prejudice.
9. Street of Jews (German). Ghetto: originally, the section of a city in which Jews were forced to live.
1. The Hebrew word for "bitter" or "bitterness," and the name of a bitter spring the fleeing Israelites found (Exodus 15.23). Salt water (symbolizing tears), unleavened bread, and bitter herbs are all part of the Passover meal, which commemorates the Exodus.
2. A Greek-Aramaic phrase signifying a terrible curse, applied to those who "love not the Lord Jesus Christ" (1 Corinthians 16.22), and later specifically to the Jews.
3. When Haman, the favored advisor of Ahasuerus (Xerxes), king of Persia, sought to destroy Mordecai and the rest of the Jews, Mordecai stood at the king's gate crying out against the persecution (see Esther 3–4).
4. Hebrew is read from right to left.

From The Song of Hiawatha[5]

From III. Hiawatha's Childhood

By the shores of Gitche Gumee,[6]
65 By the shining Big-Sea-Water,
Stood the wigwam of Nokomis,[7]
Daughter of the Moon, Nokomis.
Dark behind it rose the forest,
Rose the black and gloomy pine-trees,
70 Rose the firs with cones upon them;
Bright before it beat the water,
Beat the clear and sunny water,
Beat the shining Big-Sea-Water.
        There the wrinkled old Nokomis
75 Nursed the little Hiawatha,
Rocked him in his linden cradle,
Bedded soft in moss and rushes,
Safely bound with reindeer sinews;
Stilled his fretful wail by saying,
80 "Hush! the Naked Bear[8] will hear thee!"
Lulled him into slumber, singing,
"Ewa-yea!° my little owlet!   lullaby
Who is this, that lights the wigwam?
With his great eyes lights the wigwam?
85 Ewa-yea! my little owlet!"
        Many things Nokomis taught him
Of the stars that shine in heaven;
Showed him Ishkoodah,° the comet,   fire
Ishkoodah, with fiery tresses;
90 Showed the Death-Dance of the spirits,
Warriors with their plumes and war-clubs,
Flaring far away to northward
In the frosty nights of Winter;
Showed the broad white road in heaven,
95 Pathway of the ghosts, the shadows,
Running straight across the heavens,
Crowded with the ghosts, the shadows.
        At the door on summer evenings
Sat the little Hiawatha;
100 Heard the whispering of the pine-trees,
Heard the lapping of the waters,
Sounds of music, words of wonder;
"Minne-wawa!" said the pine-trees,
"Mudway-aushka!" said the water.

5. He Makes Rivers (Ojibwa); a Native American cultural hero (fl. ca. 1440 or ca. 1550), perhaps a chief of the Mohawk tribe or the Onondaga tribe; he might also be a composite of several people. Longfellow added to the confusion about Hiawatha's identity by giving the name to the title character of this long poem, which actually recounts the legend of the Algonquian mythic hero Nanabozho. Phenomenally popular during Longfellow's lifetime, *Hiawatha* employs the trochaic tetrameter of the Finnish epic *Kalevala*.
6. Big Sea Water (Ojibwa); Lake Superior.
7. Hiawatha's grandmother, who raises him upon the death of his mother, Wenonah.
8. In Native American legend, equivalent to the bogeyman (or boogeyman).

105   Saw the fire-fly, Wah-wah-taysee,
Flitting through the dusk of evening,
With the twinkle of its candle
Lighting up the brakes and bushes,
And he sang the song of children,
110 Sang the song Nokomis taught him:
"Wah-wah-taysee, little fire-fly,
Little, flitting, white-fire insect,
Little, dancing, white-fire creature,
Light me with your little candle,
115 Ere upon my bed I lay me,
Ere in sleep I close my eyelids!"
    Saw the moon rise from the water
Rippling, rounding from the water,
Saw the flecks and shadows on it,
120 Whispered, "What is that, Nokomis?"
And the good Nokomis answered:
"Once a warrior, very angry,
Seized his grandmother, and threw her
Up into the sky at midnight;
125 Right against the moon he threw her;
'Tis her body that you see there."
    Saw the rainbow in the heaven,
In the eastern sky, the rainbow,
Whispered, "What is that, Nokomis?"
130 And the good Nokomis answered:
" 'T is the heaven of flowers you see there
All the wild-flowers of the forest,
All the lilies of the prairie,
When on earth they fade and perish,
135 Blossom in that heaven above us."
    When he heard the owls at midnight,
Hooting, laughing in the forest,
"What is that?" he cried in terror,
"What is that," he said, "Nokomis?"
140 And the good Nokomis answered:
"That is but the owl and owlet,
Talking in their native language,
Talking, scolding at each other."
    Then the little Hiawatha
145 Learned of every bird its language,
Learned their names and all their secrets
How they built their nests in Summer,
Where they hid themselves in Winter,
Talked with them whene'er he met them,
150 Called them "Hiawatha's Chickens."
    Of all beasts he learned the language,
Learned their names and all their secrets,
How the beavers built their lodges,
Where the squirrels hid their acorns,
155 How the reindeer ran so swiftly,
Why the rabbit was so timid,

Talked with them whene'er he met them,
Called them "Hiawatha's Brothers."

* * *

1855

Snow-Flakes

Out of the bosom of the Air,
   Out of the cloud-folds of her garments shaken,
Over the woodlands brown and bare,
   Over the harvest-fields forsaken,
5   Silent, and soft, and slow
     Descends the snow.

Even as our cloudy fancies take
   Suddenly shape in some divine expression,
Even as the troubled heart doth make
10   In the white countenance confession,
     The troubled sky reveals
     The grief it feels.

This is the poem of the air,
   Slowly in silent syllables recorded;
15 This is the secret of despair,
   Long in its cloudy bosom hoarded,
     Now whispered and revealed
     To wood and field.

1863

The Cross of Snow[9]

In the long, sleepless watches of the night,
  A gentle face—the face of one long dead—
  Looks at me from the wall, where round its head
  The night-lamp casts a halo of pale light.
5 Here in this room she died; and soul more white
  Never through martyrdom of fire was led
  To its repose; nor can in books be read
  The legend of a life more benedight.°   *blessed*
There is a mountain in the distant West
10   That, sun-defying, in its deep ravines
  Displays a cross of snow upon its side.
Such is the cross I wear upon my breast

---

9. Longfellow's second wife, Fanny, died in 1861 when her dress caught fire; he too was burned trying to save her. The poem was found in his portfolio after his death.

These eighteen years, through all the changing scenes
And seasons, changeless since the day she died.

1879   1886

JOHN GREENLEAF WHITTIER
1807–1892

Telling the Bees[1]

Here is the place; right over the hill
    Runs the path I took;
You can see the gap in the old wall still,
    And the stepping-stones in the shallow brook.

5   There is the house, with the gate red-barred,
    And the poplars tall;
And the barn's brown length, and the cattle-yard,
    And the white horns tossing above the wall.

There are the beehives ranged in the sun;
10   And down by the brink
Of the brook are her poor flowers, weed-o'errun,
    Pansy and daffodil, rose and pink.

A year has gone, as the tortoise goes,
    Heavy and slow;
15   And the same rose blows, and the same sun glows,
    And the same brook sings of a year ago.

There's the same sweet clover-smell in the breeze;
    And the June sun warm
Tangles his wings of fire in the trees,
20   Setting, as then, over Fernside farm.

I mind me how with a lover's care
    From my Sunday coat
I brushed off the burrs, and smoothed my hair,
    And cooled at the brookside my brow and throat.

25   Since we parted, a month had passed,—
    To love, a year;
Down through the beeches I looked at last
    On the little red gate and the well-sweep near.

---

1. Whittier's note explains the former custom in rural New England of informing the bees of the death of a family member and dressing their hives in mourning to prevent them from leaving the hives for a new home.

I can see it all now,—the slantwise rain
30   Of light through the leaves,
The sundown's blaze on her window-pane,
    The bloom of her roses under the eaves.

Just the same as a month before,—
    The house and the trees,
35   The barn's brown gable, the vine by the door,—
    Nothing changed but the hives of bees.

Before them, under the garden wall,
    Forward and back,
Went drearily singing the chore-girl small,
40   Draping each hive with a shred of black.

Trembling, I listened: the summer sun
    Had the chill of snow;
For I knew she was telling the bees of one
    Gone on the journey we all must go!

45   Then I said to myself, "My Mary weeps
    For the dead to-day:
Haply her blind old grandsire sleeps
    The fret and the pain of his age away."

But her dog whined low; on the doorway sill,
50   With his cane to his chin,
The old man sat; and the chore-girl still
    Sang to the bees stealing out and in.

And the song she was singing ever since
    In my ear sounds on:—
55   "Stay at home, pretty bees, fly not hence!
    Mistress Mary is dead and gone!"

1858

From Snowbound: A Winter Idyl

155   Shut in from all the world without
    We sat the clean-winged hearth about,
    Content to let the north-wind roar
    In baffled rage at pane and door,
    While the red logs before us beat
160   The frost-line back with tropic heat;
    And ever, when a louder blast
    Shook beam and rafter as it passed,
    The merrier up its roaring draught
    The great throat of the chimney laughed,
165   The house-dog on his paws outspread

Laid to the fire his drowsy head,
The cat's dark silhouette on the wall
A couchant² tiger's seemed to fall;
And, for the winter fireside meet,

170 Between the andirons' straddling feet,
The mug of cider simmered slow,
The apples sputtered in a row,
And, close at hand, the basket stood
With nuts from brown October's wood.

175 What matter how the night behaved?
What matter how the north-wind raved?
Blow high, blow low, not all its snow
Could quench our hearth-fire's ruddy glow.
O Time and Change!—with hair as gray

180 As was my sire's that winter day,
How strange it seems, with so much gone
Of life and love, to still live on!
Ah, brother! only I and thou
Are left of all that circle now,—

185 The dear home faces whereupon
That fitful firelight paled and shone.
Henceforward, listen as we will,
The voices of that hearth are still;
Look where we may, the wide earth o'er,

190 Those lighted faces smile no more.
We tread the paths their feet have worn,
   We sit beneath their orchard trees,
   We hear, like them, the hum of bees
And rustle of the bladed corn;

195 We turn the pages that they read,
   Their written words we linger o'er,
But in the sun they cast no shade,
No voice is heard, no sign is made,
   No step is on the conscious floor!

200 Yet Love will dream, and faith will trust,
(Since He who knows our need is just,)
That somehow, somewhere, meet we must.
Alas for him who never sees
The stars shine through his cypress-trees!

205 Who, hopeless, lays his dead away,
Nor looks to see the breaking day
Across the mournful marbles° play!   *gravestones*
Who hath not learned, in hours of faith,
   The truth to flesh and sense unknown,

210 That Life is ever lord of Death,
   And Love can never lose its own!
We sped the time with stories old,
Wrought puzzles out, and riddles told,
Or stammered from our school-book lore

---

2. Lying down (term from heraldry).

215   "The Chief of Gambia's golden shore."[3]
How often since, when all the land
Was clay in Slavery's shaping hand,
As if a trumpet called, I've heard
Dame Mercy Warren's rousing word:
220   *"Does not the voice of reason cry,*
    Claim the first right which Nature gave,
From the red scourge of bondage fly,
    Nor deign to live a burdened slave!"
Our father rode again his ride
225   On Memphremagog's[4] wooded side;
Sat down again to moose and samp°   *mush*
In trapper's hut and Indian camp;
Lived o'er the old idyllic ease
Beneath St. François'[5] hemlock-trees;
230   Again for him the moonlight shone
On Norman cap and bodiced zone;[6]
Again he heard the violin play
Which led the village dance away,
And mingled in its merry whirl
235   The grandam and the laughing girl.
Or, nearer home, our steps he led
Where Salisbury's[7] level marshes spread
    Mile-wide as flies the laden bee;
Where merry mowers, hale and strong,
240   Swept, scythe on scythe, their swaths along
    The low green prairies of the sea.
We shared the fishing off Boar's Head,
    And round the rocky Isles of Shoals[8]
    The hake-broil on the drift-wood coals;
245   The chowder on the sand-beach made,
Dipped by the hungry, steaming hot,
With spoons of clam-shell from the pot.
We heard the tales of witchcraft old,
And dream and sign and marvel told
250   To sleepy listeners as they lay
Stretched idly on the salted hay,
Adrift along the winding shores,
When favoring breezes deigned to blow
The square sail of the gundelow°   *flat-bottomed boat*
255   And idle lay the useless oars.

*   *   *

1866

---

3. From the poem "The African Chief," by the American abolitionist Sarah Wentworth Morton (1759–1846). Whittier mistakenly attributes the poem to the American historian Mercy Otis Warren (1728–1814).
4. Lake between Vermont and Quebec.
5. Rural municipality north of Lake Memphre-

magog.
6. I.e., the clothes of women in French Canadian settlements: caps like those worn in Normandy and bodices that draw in the waist, or "zone."
7. Town in northeastern Massachusetts.
8. Like Boar's Head, off the New Hampshire coast.

EDWARD FITZGERALD
1809–1883

The Rubáiyát of Omar Khayyám of Naishápúr[1]

I

Wake! For the Sun, who scattered into flight
The Stars before him from the Field of Night,
   Drives Night along with them from Heav'n, and strikes
The Sultán's Turret with a Shaft of Light.

2

5   Before the phantom of False morning[2] died,
Methought a Voice within the Tavern cried,
   "When all the Temple is prepared within,
"Why nods the drowsy Worshipper outside?"

3

And, as the Cock crew, those who stood before
10   The Tavern shouted—"Open then the Door!
   "You know how little while we have to stay,
"And, once departed, may return no more."

4

Now the New Year[3] reviving old Desires,
The thoughtful Soul to Solitude retires,
15   Where the WHITE HAND OF MOSES on the Bough
Puts out, and Jesus from the Ground suspires.[4]

5

Irám[5] indeed is gone with all his Rose,
And Jamshýd's Sev'n-ringed Cup[6] where no one knows;
   But still a Ruby kindles in the Vine,
20   And many a Garden by the Water blows.

6

And David's lips are lockt; but in divine
High-piping Pehleví,[7] with "Wine! Wine! Wine!

---

1. Omar Khayyám (ca. 1050–1132?), Persian poet, mathematician, and astronomer, lived at Nishapur, in the province of Khurasan. FitzGerald translated his epigrammatic quatrains (Rubáiyát, plural of ruba'i, quatrain), which he first published in 1859; in three subsequent editions (the fourth edition is printed here), FitzGerald made many alterations of detail, arrangement, and number of stanzas.
2. "A transient Light on the Horizon about an hour before the . . . True Dawn" [FitzGerald's note].
3. "Beginning with the Vernal Equinox [i.e., spring], it must be remembered" [FitzGerald's note].
4. The blossoming of trees is compared to the whiteness of Moses' hand as it is described in Exodus 4.6, and the sweetness of flowers to the healing sweetness of Jesus' breath.
5. "A royal Garden now sunk somewhere in the Sands of Arabia" [FitzGerald's note].
6. In Persian mythology, Jamshýd was a king of the peris (celestial beings), who, because he had boasted of his immortality, was compelled to live on Earth in human form for seven hundred years, becoming one of the kings of Persia. His cup, the invention of Kai-Kosru (line 38), another Persian king, great-grandson of Kai-Kobad (line 36), was decorated with signs enabling its possessor to foretell the future.
7. The ancient literary language of Persia.

"Red Wine!"—the Nightingale cries to the Rose
That sallow cheek of hers to incarnadine.°   redden

7

25   Come, fill the Cup, and in the fire of Spring
Your Winter-garment of Repentance fling:
    The Bird of Time has but a little way
To flutter—and the Bird is on the Wing.

8

Whether at Naishápúr or Babylon,
30   Whether the Cup with sweet or bitter run,
    The Wine of Life keeps oozing drop by drop,
The Leaves of Life keep falling one by one.

9

Each Morn a thousand Roses brings, you say;
Yes, but where leaves the Rose of Yesterday?
35   And this first Summer month that brings the Rose
Shall take Jamshýd and Kaikobád away.

10

Well, let it take them! What have we to do
With Kaikobád the Great, or Kaikhosrú?
    Let Zál and Rustum[8] bluster as they will,
40   Or Hátim[9] call to Supper—heed not you.

11

With me along the strip of Herbage strown
That just divides the desert from the sown,
    Where name of Slave and Sultán is forgot—
And Peace to Mahmúd[1] on his golden Throne!

12

45   A Book of Verses underneath the Bough,
A Jug of Wine, a Loaf of Bread—and Thou
    Beside me singing in the Wilderness—
Oh, Wilderness were Paradise enow!

13

Some for the Glories of This World; and some
50   Sigh for the Prophet's[2] Paradise to come;
    Ah, take the Cash, and let the Credit go,
Nor heed the rumble of a distant Drum!

14

Look to the blowing Rose about us—"Lo,
"Laughing," she says, "into the world I blow,

8. "The 'Hercules' of Persia, and Zál his Father"
[FitzGerald's note].
9. Hátim Tai: a Persian chieftain and an archetype
of Eastern hospitality.

1. Sultan Máhmúd (971–1031) of Ghazni, in
Afghanistan, renowned both as ruler and as the
conqueror of India.
2. I.e., Mohammed's.

55   "At once the silken tassel of my Purse
"Tear, and its Treasure on the Garden throw."

15

And those who husbanded the Golden grain,
And those who flung it to the winds like Rain,
   Alike to no such aureate° Earth are turned   *brilliant*
60 As, buried once, Men want dug up again.

16

The Worldly Hope men set their Hearts upon
Turns Ashes—or it prospers; and anon,
   Like Snow upon the Desert's dusty Face,
Lighting a little hour or two—is gone.

17

65 Think, in this battered Caravanserai°   *inn*
Whose Portals are alternate Night and Day,
   How Sultán after Sultán with his Pomp
Abode his destined Hour, and went his way.

18

They say the Lion and the Lizard keep
70 The Courts where Jamshýd gloried and drank deep:
   And Bahrám,[3] that great Hunter—the Wild Ass
Stamps o'er his Head, but cannot break his Sleep.

19

I sometimes think that never blows so red
The Rose as where some buried Caesar bled;
75   That every Hyacinth the Garden wears
Dropt in her Lap from some once lovely Head.

20

And this reviving Herb whose tender Green
Fledges the river-lip on which we lean—
   Ah, lean upon it lightly! for who knows
80 From what once lovely Lip it springs unseen!

21

Ah, my Belovèd, fill the Cup that clears
TODAY of past Regrets and future Fears:
   Tomorrow!—Why, Tomorrow I may be
Myself with Yesterday's Sev'n thousand Years.

22

85 For some we loved, the loveliest and the best
That from his Vintage rolling Time hath prest,
   Have drunk their Cup a Round or two before,
And one by one crept silently to rest.

---

3. A Sassanian king who, according to legend, met his death while hunting a wild ass.

23

And we, that make merry in the Room
90　They left, and Summer dresses in new bloom,
　　　Ourselves must we beneath the Couch of Earth
Descend—ourselves to make a Couch—for whom?

24

Ah, make the most of what we yet may spend,
Before we too into the Dust descend;
95　　Dust into Dust, and under Dust to lie,
Sans Wine, sans Song, sans Singer, and sans End!

25

Alike for those who for TODAY prepare,
And those that after some TOMORROW stare,
　　　A Muezzín[4] from the Tower of Darkness cries,
100　"Fools! your Reward is neither Here nor There."

26

Why, all the Saints and Sages who discussed
Of the Two Worlds so wisely—they are thrust
　　　Like foolish Prophets forth; their Words to Scorn
Are scattered, and their Mouths are stopt with Dust.

27

105　Myself when young did eagerly frequent
Doctor and Saint, and heard great argument
　　　About it and about: but evermore
Came out by the same door where in I went.

28

With them the seed of Wisdom did I sow,
110　And with mine own hand wrought to make it grow;
　　　And this was all the Harvest that I reaped—
"I came like Water, and like Wind I go."

29

Into this Universe, and Why not knowing
Nor Whence, like Water willy-nilly flowing;
115　　And out of it, as Wind along the Waste,
I know not Whither, willy-nilly blowing.

30

What, without asking, hither hurried Whence?
And, without asking, Whither hurried hence!
　　　Oh, many a Cup of this forbidden Wine[5]
120　Must drown the memory of that insolence!

---

4. The crier who calls the hours of prayer from the　　5. Alcohol is forbidden to strict Muslims.
tower of a mosque.

31

Up from Earth's Center through the Seventh Gate
I rose, and on the Throne of Saturn[6] sate,
   And many a Knot unraveled by the Road;
But not the Master-knot of Human Fate.

32

125 There was the Door to which I found no Key;
There was the Veil through which I might not see:
   Some little talk awhile of ME and THEE
There was—and then no more of THEE and ME.

33

Earth could not answer; nor the Seas that mourn
130 In flowing Purple, of their Lord forlorn;
   Nor rolling Heaven, with all his Signs revealed
And hidden by the sleeve of Night and Morn.

34

Then of the THEE IN ME who works behind
The Veil, I lifted up my hands to find
135   A lamp amid the Darkness; and I heard,
As from Without—"THE ME WITHIN THEE BLIND!"

35

Then to the Lip of this poor earthen Urn
I leaned, the Secret of my Life to learn:
   And Lip to Lip it murmured—"While you live,
140 "Drink! for, once dead, you never shall return."

36

I think the Vessel, that with fugitive
Articulation answered, once did live,
   And drink; and Ah! the passive Lip I kissed,
How many Kisses might it take—and give!

37

145 For I remember stopping by the way
To watch a Potter thumping his wet Clay:
   And with its all-obliterated Tongue
It murmured—"Gently, Brother, gently, pray!"

38

And has not such a Story from of Old
150 Down Man's successive generations rolled
   Of such a clod of saturated Earth
Cast by the Maker into Human mold?

---

6. "Lord of the Seventh Heaven" [FitzGerald's note]. In ancient astronomy, Saturn was the most remote of the seven known planets; hence Omar had reached the bounds of astronomical knowledge.

39

And not a drop that from our Cups we throw
For Earth to drink of, but may steal below
   To quench the fire of Anguish in some Eye
There hidden—far beneath, and long ago.

40

As then the Tulip for her morning sup
Of Heav'nly Vintage from the soil looks up,
   Do you devoutly do the like, till Heav'n
To Earth invert you—like an empty Cup.

41

Perplext no more with Human or Divine,
Tomorrow's tangle to the winds resign,
   And lose your fingers in the tresses of
The Cypress-slender Minister of Wine.[7]

42

And if the Wine you drink, the Lip you press,
End in what All begins and ends in—Yes;
   Think then you are TODAY what YESTERDAY
You were—TOMORROW you shall not be less.

43

So when that Angel of the darker Drink
At last shall find you by the river-brink,
   And, offering his Cup, invite your Soul
Forth to your Lips to quaff—you shall not shrink.

44

Why, if the Soul can fling the Dust aside,
And naked on the Air of Heaven ride,
   Were't not a Shame—were't not a Shame for him
In this clay carcase crippled to abide?

45

'Tis but a Tent where takes his one day's rest
A Sultán to the realm of Death addrest;
   The Sultán rises, and the dark Ferrásh[8]
Strikes, and prepares it for another Guest.

46

And fear not lest Existence closing your
Account, and mine, should know the like no more;
   The Eternal Sákí° from that Bowl has poured   *cupbearer*
Millions of Bubbles like us, and will pour.

---

7. The maidservant who pours the wine.
8. The servant charged with setting up and striking the tent.

47

185 When You and I behind the Veil are past,
Oh, but the long, long while the World shall last,
    Which of our Coming and Departure heeds
As the Sea's self should heed a pebble-cast.

48

A Moment's Halt—a momentary taste
190 Of Being from the Well amid the Waste—
    And Lo!—the phantom Caravan has reached
The Nothing it set out from—Oh, make haste!

49

Would you that spangle of Existence spend
About the secret—quick about it, Friend!
195   A Hair perhaps divides the False and True—
And upon what, prithee, may life depend?

50

A Hair perhaps divides the False and True;
Yes; and a single Alif⁹ were the clue—
    Could you but find it—to the Treasure-house,
200 And peradventure to The Master too;

51

Whose secret Presence, through Creation's veins
Running Quicksilver-like eludes your pains;
    Taking all shapes from Máh to Máhi;¹ and
They change and perish all—but He remains;

52

205 A moment guessed—then back behind the Fold
Immerst of Darkness round the Drama rolled
    Which, for the Pastime of Eternity,
He doth Himself contrive, enact, behold.

53

But if in vain, down on the stubborn floor
210 Of Earth, and up to Heav'n's unopening Door,
    You gaze Today, while You are You—how then
Tomorrow, You when shall be You no more?

54

Waste not your Hour, nor in the vain pursuit
Of This and That endeavor and dispute;
215   Better be jocund° with the fruitful Grape   mirthful
Than sadden after none, or bitter, Fruit.

---

9. First letter of the Arabic alphabet, consisting of   1. From lowest to highest.
a single vertical stroke.

55

You know, my Friends, with what a brave Carouse
I made a Second Marriage in my house;
   Divorced old barren Reason from my Bed,
220 And took the Daughter of the Vine to Spouse.

56

For "Is" and "Is-not" though with Rule and Line
And "Up-and-down" by Logic I define,
   Of all that one should care to fathom, I
Was never deep in anything but—Wine.

57

225 Ah, but my Computations, People say,
Reduced the Year to better reckoning?[2]—Nay,
   'Twas only striking from the Calendar
Unborn Tomorrow, and dead Yesterday.

58

And lately, by the Tavern Door agape,
230 Came shining through the Dusk an Angel Shape
   Bearing a Vessel on his Shoulder; and
He bid me taste of it; and 'twas—the Grape!

59

The Grape that can with Logic absolute
The Two-and-Seventy jarring Sects[3] confute:
235   The sovereign Alchemist that in a trice
Life's leaden metal into Gold transmute:

60

The mighty Mahmúd, Allah-breathing Lord,[4]
That all the misbelieving and black Horde
   Of Fears and Sorrows that infest the Soul
240 Scatters before him with his whirlwind Sword.

61

Why, be this Juice the growth of God, who dare
Blaspheme the twisted tendril as a Snare?
   A Blessing, we should use it, should we not?
And if a Curse—why, then, Who set it there?

62

245 I must abjure the Balm of Life, I must,
Scared by some After-reckoning ta'en on trust,
   Or lured with Hope of some Diviner Drink,
To fill the Cup—when crumbled into Dust!

2. Omar was one of the learned men who had been charged with reforming the calendar.
3. "The 72 sects into which Islamism so soon split" [FitzGerald's note].
4. "This alludes to Máhmúd's Conquest of India and its swarthy Idolators" [FitzGerald's note].

63

Oh threats of Hell and Hopes of Paradise!
250   One thing at least is certain—*This* Life flies;
      One thing is certain and the rest is Lies;
    The Flower that once has blown for ever dies.

64

Strange, is it not? that of the myriads who
Before us passed the door of Darkness through,
255   Not one returns to tell us of the Road,
    Which to discover we must travel too.

65

The Revelations of Devout and Learned
Who rose before us, and as Prophets burned,[5]
      Are all but Stories, which, awoke from Sleep
260   They told their comrades, and to Sleep returned.

66

I sent my Soul through the Invisible,
Some letter of that Afterlife to spell:
      And by and by my Soul returned to me,
    And answered "I Myself am Heav'n and Hell:"

67

265   Heav'n but the Vision of fulfilled Desire,
And Hell the Shadow from a Soul on fire,
      Cast on the Darkness into which Ourselves,
    So late emerged from, shall so soon expire.

68

We are no other than a moving row
270   Of Magic Shadow-shapes that come and go
      Round with the Sun-illumined Lantern held
    In Midnight by the Master of the Show;

69

But helpless Pieces of the Game He plays
Upon his Checkerboard of Nights and Days;
275   Hither and thither moves, and checks, and slays,
    And one by one back in the Closet lays.

70

The Ball no question makes of Ayes and Noes,
But Here or There as strikes the Player° goes;   *polo player*
      And He that tossed you down into the Field,
280   *He* knows about it all—HE knows—HE knows!

---

5. I.e., felt inspired to spread their prophecies.

71

The Moving Finger writes; and, having writ,
Moves on: nor all your Piety nor Wit
   Shall lure it back to cancel half a Line,
Nor all your Tears wash out a Word of it.

72

285 And that inverted Bowl they call the Sky,
Whereunder crawling cooped we live and die,
   Lift not your hands to *It* for help—for It
As impotently moves as you or I.

73

With Earth's first Clay They did the Last Man knead,
290 And there of the Last Harvest sowed the Seed:
   And the first Morning of Creation wrote
What the Last Dawn of Reckoning shall read.

74

YESTERDAY *This* Day's Madness did prepare;
TOMORROW'S Silence, Triumph, or Despair:
295   Drink! for you know not whence you came, nor why:
Drink! for you know not why you go, nor where.

75

I tell you this—When, started from the Goal,
Over the flaming shoulders of the Foal[6]
   Of Heav'n, Parwín and Mushtarí they flung,
300 In my predestined Plot of Dust and Soul.[7]

76

The Vine had struck a fiber: which about
If clings my Being—let the Dervish[8] flout;
   Of my Base metal may be filed a Key,
That shall unlock the Door he howls without.

77

305 And this I know: whether the one True Light
Kindle to Love, or Wrath consume me quite,
   One Flash of It within the Tavern caught
Better than in the Temple lost outright.

78

What! out of senseless Nothing to provoke
310 A conscious Something to resent the yoke
   Of unpermitted Pleasure, under pain
Of Everlasting Penalties, if broke!

6. The constellation known as the Colt (*Equuleus*) or Foal.
7. Omar ascribes his fate to the position of the stars and planets at the time of his birth. *Parwín* and *Mushtarí*: "The Pleiads and Jupiter" [FitzGerald's note].
8. Member of any of several Muslim orders taking vows of austerity and poverty.

79

What! from his helpless Creature be repaid
Pure Gold for what he lent him dross-allayed—
    Sue for a Debt he never did contract,
And cannot answer—Oh the sorry trade!

315

80

Oh Thou, who didst with pitfall and with gin°   trap
Beset the Road I was to wander in,
    Thou wilt not with Predestined Evil round
Enmesh, and then impute my Fall to Sin!

320

81

Oh Thou, who Man of baser Earth didst make,
And ev'n with Paradise devise the Snake:
    For all the Sin wherewith the Face of Man
Is blackened—Man's forgiveness give—and take!

———————

82

As under cover of departing Day
Slunk hunger-stricken Ramazán⁹ away,
    Once more within the Potter's house alone
I stood, surrounded by the Shapes of Clay.

325

83

Shapes of all Sorts and Sizes, great and small,
That stood along the floor and by the wall;
    And some loquacious Vessels were; and some
Listened perhaps, but never talked at all.

330

84

Said one among them—"Surely not in vain
"My substance of the common Earth was ta'en
    "And to this Figure molded, to be broke,
"Or trampled back to shapeless Earth again."

335

85

Then said a Second—"Ne'er a peevish Boy
"Would break the Bowl from which he drank in joy;
    "And He that with his hand the Vessel made
"Will surely not in after Wrath destroy."

340

86

After a momentary silence spake
Some Vessel of a more ungainly Make;
    "They sneer at me for leaning all awry:
"What! did the Hand then of the Potter shake?"

———————

9. Muslims' annual thirty-day fast, during which no food is eaten from dawn to sunset.

87

345 Whereat some one of the loquacious Lot—
I think a Súfi° pipkin°—waxing hot—   *mystic / small pot*
    "All this of Pot and Potter—Tell me then,
    "Who is the Potter, pray, and who the Pot?"

88

"Why," said another, "Some there are who tell
350 "Of one who threatens he will toss to Hell
    "The luckless Pots he marred in making—Pish!
"He's a Good Fellow, and 'twill all be well."

89

"Well," murmured one, "Let whoso make or buy,
"My Clay with long Oblivion is gone dry:
355   "But fill me with the old familiar Juice,
"Methinks I might recover by and by."

90

So while the Vessels one by one were speaking,
The little Moon[1] looked in that all were seeking:
    And then they jogged each other, "Brother! Brother!
360 "Now for the Porter's shoulder-knot[2] a-creaking!"

91

Ah, with the Grape my fading Life provide,
And wash the Body whence the Life has died,
    And lay men shrouded in the living Leaf,
By some not unfrequented Garden-side.

92

365 That ev'n my buried Ashes such a snare
Of Vintage shall fling up into the Air
    As not a True-believer passing by
But shall be overtaken unaware.

93

Indeed the Idols I have loved so long
370 Have done my credit in this World much wrong:
    Have drowned my Glory in a shallow Cup,
And sold my Reputation for a Song.

94

Indeed, indeed, Repentance oft before
I swore—but was I sober when I swore?
375   And then and then came Spring, and Rose-in-hand
My threadbare Penitence apieces tore.

---

1. The new moon, which signaled the end of Ramazán.

2. The knot on the porter's shoulder strap from which the wine jars were hung.

95

And much as Wine has played the Infidel,
And robbed me of my Robe of Honor—Well,
    I wonder often what the Vintners buy
380 One half so precious as the stuff they sell.

96

Yet Ah, that Spring should vanish with the Rose!
That Youth's sweet-scented manuscript should close!
    The Nightingale that in the branches sang,
Ah whence, and whither flown again, who knows!

97

385 Would but the Desert of the Fountain yield
One glimpse—if dimly, yet indeed, revealed,
    To which the fainting Traveler might spring,
As springs the trampled herbage of the field!

98

Would but some wingèd Angel ere too late
390 Arrest the yet unfolded Roll of Fate,
    And make the stern Recorder otherwise
Enregister, or quite obliterate!

99

Ah Love! could you and I with Him conspire
To grasp this sorry Scheme of Things entire,
395   Would not we shatter it to bits—and then
Remold it nearer to the Heart's Desire!

100

Yon rising Moon that looks for us again—
How oft hereafter will she wax and wane;
    How oft hereafter rising look for us
400 Through this same Garden—and for *one* in vain!

101

And when like her, oh Sákí, you shall pass
Among the Guests Star-scattered on the Grass,
    And in your joyous errand reach the spot
Where I made One—turn down an empty Glass!

TAMÁM[3]

1857   1859, 1879

_____

3. It is ended (Persian).

OLIVER WENDELL HOLMES
1809–1894

The Chambered Nautilus[1]

This is the ship of pearl, which, poets feign,
    Sails the unshadowed main,°   *sea*
    The venturous bark that flings
On the sweet summer wind its purpled wings
5 In gulfs enchanted, where the Siren[2] sings,
    And coral reefs lie bare,
Where the cold sea-maids rise to sun their streaming hair.

Its webs of living gauze no more unfurl;
    Wrecked is the ship of pearl!
10   And every chambered cell,
Where its dim dreaming life was wont° to dwell,   *accustomed*
As the frail tenant shaped his growing shell,
    Before thee lies revealed,
Its irised° ceiling rent, its sunless crypt unsealed!   *iridescent*

15 Year after year beheld the silent toil
    That spread his lustrous coil;
    Still, as the spiral grew,
He left the past year's dwelling for the new,
Stole with soft step its shining archway through,
20   Built up its idle door,
Stretched in his last-found home, and knew the old no more.

Thanks for the heavenly message brought by thee,
    Child of the wandering sea,
    Cast from her lap, forlorn!
25 From thy dead lips a clearer note is born
Than ever Triton[3] blew from wreathéd horn!
    While on mine ear it rings,
Through the deep caves of thought I hear a voice that sings:

Build thee more stately mansions,[4] O my soul,
30   As the swift seasons roll!
    Leave thy low-vaulted past!
Let each new temple, nobler than the last,
Shut thee from heaven with a dome more vast,
    Till thou at length art free,
35 Leaving thine outgrown shell by life's unresting sea!

1858

1. A small mollusk with an external spiral shell, pearly on the inside (lines 1, 9), that grows as chambers are added; the webbed membranes on its back were once thought to function as sails.
2. In Greek mythology, a female creature whose magically sweet song drew sailors to their deaths on the reef of her island.
3. Greek demigod of the ocean, who blew on a sea conch. Cf. William Wordsworth, "The World Is Too Much with Us," line 14 (p. 802).
4. Cf. John 14.2: "In my Father's house are many mansions."

EDGAR ALLAN POE
1809–1849

Sonnet—To Science

Science! true daughter of Old Time thou art!
  Who alterest all things with thy peering eyes.
Why preyest thou thus upon the poet's heart,
  Vulture, whose wings are dull realities?
5 How should he love thee? or how deem thee wise?
  Who wouldst not leave him in his wandering
To seek for treasure in the jeweled skies,
  Albeit he soared with an undaunted wing?
Hast thou not dragged Diana[1] from her car?
10 And driven the Hamadryad[2] from the wood
To seek a shelter in some happier star?
  Hast thou not torn the Naiad° from her flood,   *nymph*
The Elfin from the green grass, and from me
The summer dream beneath the tamarind tree?[3]

1829   1829, 1845

To Helen[4]

Helen, thy beauty is to me
  Like those Nicéan barks[5] of yore,
That gently, o'er a perfumed sea,
  The weary, way-worn wanderer bore
5   To his own native shore.

On desperate seas long wont° to roam,   *accustomed*
  Thy hyacinth hair,[6] thy classic face,
Thy Naiad° airs have brought me home   *nymphlike*
  To the glory that was Greece
10 And the grandeur that was Rome.

Lo! in yon brilliant window-niche
  How statue-like I see thee stand,
  The agate lamp within thy hand!

1. Roman goddess of the hunt, revered for her chastity; her "car" is the moon.
2. Wood nymph in Greek and Roman mythology, said to live and die with the tree she inhabits.
3. An Asian tree, the fruit of which is used for medicine and for food.
4. Helen of Troy, whose beauty was renowned and whose abduction led to the Trojan War.

5. Boats, perhaps from some Mediterranean location; variously interpreted by Poe scholars.
6. In his story "Ligeia" (1838), Poe calls "the raven-black, the glossy, the luxuriant and naturally curling tresses . . . 'hyacinthine.' " In Greek mythology, the blood of the slain youth Hyacinthus, whom the god Apollo loved, was changed into a purple flower.

Ah! Psyche,[7] from the regions which
15   Are Holy Land!

1823   1831, 1845

The City in the Sea

Lo! Death has reared himself a throne
In a strange city lying alone
Far down within the dim West,[8]
Where the good and the bad and the worst and the best
5   Have gone to their eternal rest.
There shrines and palaces and towers
(Time-eaten towers that tremble not!)
Resemble nothing that is ours.
Around, by lifting winds forgot,
10   Resignedly beneath the sky
The melancholy waters lie.

No rays from the holy heaven come down
On the long night-time of that town;
But light from out the lurid sea
15   Streams up the turrets silently—
Gleams up the pinnacles far and free—
Up domes—up spires—up kingly halls—
Up fanes°—up Babylon-like[9] walls—   temples, churches
Up shadowy long-forgotten bowers
20   Of sculptured ivy and stone flowers—
Up many and many a marvelous shrine
Whose wreathéd friezes intertwine
The viol, the violet, and the vine.

Resignedly beneath the sky
25   The melancholy waters lie.
So blend the turrets and shadows there
That all seem pendulous in air,
While from a proud tower in the town
Death looks gigantically down.

30   There open fanes and gaping graves
Yawn level with the luminous waves;
But not the riches there that lie
In each idol's diamond eye—

7. In classical mythology, a beautiful princess, whose name means "soul" in Greek. Having lost her lover, Cupid, (Roman) god of erotic love, because she disobeyed his order not to look at him (he awakened when a drop of hot oil from her lamp fell on him), Psyche appealed for help to his mother, Venus, goddess of love and beauty. One punitive task set by Venus was that Psyche bring her a portion of the beauty of Proserpina, queen of the underworld.
8. To "go west" is to die.
9. Babylon traditionally symbolizes the wicked city doomed (see, e.g., Isaiah 14.4–23 and Revelation 16.18–19).

Not the gaily-jeweled dead
35   Tempt the waters from their bed;
For no ripples curl, alas!
Along that wilderness of glass—
No swellings tell that winds may be
Upon some far-off happier sea—
40   No heavings hint that winds have been
On seas less hideously serene.

But lo, a stir is in the air!
The wave—there is a movement there!
As if the towers had thrust aside,
45   In slightly sinking, the dull tide—
As if their tops had feebly given
A void within the filmy Heaven.
The waves have now a redder glow—
The hours are breathing faint and low—
50   And when, amid no earthly moans,
Down, down that town shall settle hence,
Hell, rising from a thousand thrones,
Shall do it reverence.

1831, 1845

The Raven[1]

Once upon a midnight dreary, while I pondered, weak and weary,
Over many a quaint and curious volume of forgotten lore—
While I nodded, nearly napping, suddenly there came a tapping,
As of some one gently rapping, rapping at my chamber door.
5   " 'Tis some visiter," I muttered, "tapping at my chamber door—
                Only this and nothing more."

Ah, distinctly I remember it was in the bleak December;
And each separate dying ember wrought its ghost upon the floor.
Eagerly I wished the morrow;—vainly I had sought to borrow
10   From my books surcease of sorrow—sorrow for the lost Lenore—
For the rare and radiant maiden whom the angels name Lenore—
                Nameless *here* for evermore.

And the silken, sad, uncertain rustling of each purple curtain
Thrilled me—filled me with fantastic terrors never felt before;
15   So that now, to still the beating of my heart, I stood repeating
" 'Tis some visiter entreating entrance at my chamber door—
Some late visiter entreating entrance at my chamber door;—
                This it is and nothing more."

---

1. Many slightly different texts of this poem exist; reprinted here is the version published in *The Raven and Other Poems*.

Presently my soul grew stronger; hesitating then no longer,
20   "Sir," said I, "or Madam, truly your forgiveness I implore;
But the fact is I was napping, and so gently you came rapping,
And so faintly you came tapping, tapping at my chamber door,
That I scarce was sure I heard you"—here I opened wide the door;—
                              Darkness there and nothing more.

25   Deep into that darkness peering, long I stood there wondering, fearing,
Doubting, dreaming dreams no mortal ever dared to dream before;
But the silence was unbroken, and the stillness gave no token,
And the only word there spoken was the whispered word, "Lenore?"
This I whispered, and an echo murmured back the word, "Lenore!"
30   Merely this and nothing more.

Back into the chamber turning, all my soul within me burning,
Soon again I heard a tapping somewhat louder than before.
"Surely," said I, "surely that is something at my window lattice;
Let me see, then, what thereat is, and this mystery explore—
35   Let my heart be still a moment and this mystery explore;—
                              'Tis the wind and nothing more!"

Open here I flung the shutter, when, with many a flirt and flutter,
In there stepped a stately Raven of the saintly days of yore;
Not the least obeisance made he; not a minute stopped or stayed he;
40   But, with mien of lord or lady, perched above my chamber door—
Perched upon a bust of Pallas[2] just above my chamber door—
                              Perched, and sat, and nothing more.

Then this ebony bird beguiling my sad fancy into smiling,
By the grave and stern decorum of the countenance it wore,
45   "Though thy crest be shorn and shaven, thou," I said, "art sure no
        craven,
Ghastly grim and ancient Raven wandering from the Nightly shore—
Tell me what thy lordly name is on the Night's Plutonian[3] shore!"
                              Quoth the Raven "Nevermore."

Much I marvelled this ungainly fowl to hear discourse so plainly,
50   Though its answer little meaning—little relevancy bore;
For we cannot help agreeing that no living human being
Ever yet was blessed with seeing bird above his chamber door—
Bird or beast upon the sculptured bust above his chamber door,
                              With such name as "Nevermore."

55   But the Raven, sitting lonely on the placid bust, spoke only
That one word, as if his soul in that one word he did outpour.
Nothing farther then he uttered—not a feather then he fluttered—
Till I scarcely more than muttered "Other friends have flown before—
On the morrow *he* will leave me, as my Hopes have flown before."
60   Then the bird said "Nevermore."

2. Athena, Greek goddess of wisdom and the arts.
3. Black; Pluto was the Greek god of the underworld.

Startled at the stillness broken by reply so aptly spoken,
"Doubtless," said I, "what it utters is its only stock and store
Caught from some unhappy master whom unmerciful Disaster
Followed fast and followed faster till his songs one burden bore—
65 Till the dirges of his Hope that melancholy burden bore
                       Of 'Never—nevermore.' "

But the Raven still beguiling my sad fancy into smiling,
Straight I wheeled a cushioned seat in front of bird, and bust and
    door;
Then, upon the velvet sinking, I betook myself to linking
70 Fancy unto fancy, thinking what this ominous bird of yore—
What this grim, ungainly, ghastly, gaunt, and ominous bird of yore
                 Meant in croaking "Nevermore."

This I sat engaged in guessing, but no syllable expressing
To the fowl whose fiery eyes now burned into my bosom's core;
75 This and more I sat divining, with my head at ease reclining
On the cushion's velvet lining that the lamp-light gloated o'er,
But whose velvet-violet lining with the lamp-light gloating o'er,
                She shall press, ah, nevermore!

Then, methought, the air grew denser, perfumed from an unseen
    censer
80 Swung by seraphim[4] whose foot-falls tinkled on the tufted floor.
"Wretch," I cried, "thy God hath lent thee—by these angels he hath
    sent thee
Respite—respite and nepenthe[5] from thy memories of Lenore;
Quaff, oh quaff this kind nepenthe and forget this lost Lenore!"
                 Quoth the Raven "Nevermore."

85 "Prophet!" said I, "thing of evil!—prophet still, if bird or devil!—
Whether Tempter sent, or whether tempest tossed thee here ashore,
Desolate yet all undaunted, on this desert land enchanted—
On this home by Horror haunted—tell me truly, I implore—
Is there—*is* there balm in Gilead?[6]—tell me—tell me, I implore!"
90   Quoth the Raven "Nevermore."

"Prophet!" said I, "thing of evil!—prophet still, if bird or devil!
By that Heaven that bends above us—by that God we both adore—
Tell this soul with sorrow laden if, within the distant Aidenn,[7]
It shall clasp a sainted maiden whom the angels name Lenore—
95 Clasp a rare and radiant maiden whom the angels name Lenore."
                 Quoth the Raven "Nevermore."

---

4. Angels of the highest order.
5. Oblivion-inducing drug.
6. As in Jeremiah 8.22: "Is there no balm in Gilead; is there no physician there?" Evergreens grow-ing in Gilead, a mountainous area east of the Jordan River, were tapped for medicinal resins.
7. Invented place-name, suggestive of Eden.

"Be that word our sign of parting, bird or fiend!" I shrieked, upstarting—
"Get thee back into the tempest and the Night's Plutonian shore!
Leave no black plume as a token of that lie thy soul hath spoken!
100 Leave my loneliness unbroken!—quit the bust above my door!
Take thy beak from out my heart, and take thy form from off my door!"
                                        Quoth the Raven "Nevermore."

And the Raven, never flitting, still is sitting, *still* is sitting
On the pallid bust of Pallas just above my chamber door;
105 And his eyes have all the seeming of a demon's that is dreaming,
And the lamp-light o'er him streaming throws his shadow on the floor;
And my soul from out that shadow that lies floating on the floor
                                        Shall be lifted—nevermore!

                                                    1845

Eldorado[8]

                   Gaily bedight,°   *equipped*
                   A gallant knight,
                   In sunshine and in shadow,
                   Had journeyed long,
          5   Singing a song,
                   In search of Eldorado.

                   But he grew old—
                   This knight so bold—
                   And o'er his heart a shadow
          10   Fell as he found
                   No spot of ground
                   That looked like Eldorado.

                   And, as his strength
                   Failed him at length,
          15   He met a pilgrim shadow—
                   "Shadow," said he,
                   "Where can it be—
                   This land of Eldorado?"

                   "Over the Mountains
          20   Of the Moon,
                   Down the Valley of the Shadow,
                   Ride, boldly ride,"
                   The shade replied,—
                   "If you seek for Eldorado!"

                                                    1849

8. The gilded one (Spanish). The name of a mythical South American land of gold and vast wealth, sought by European explorers beginning in the sixteenth century; more generally, any such place.

Annabel Lee

It was many and many a year ago,
    In a kingdom by the sea,
That a maiden there lived whom you may know
    By the name of Annabel Lee;
5   And this maiden she lived with no other thought
    Than to love and be loved by me.

She was a child and *I* was a child,
    In this kingdom by the sea,
But we loved with a love that was more than love—
10   I and my Annabel Lee—
With a love that the wingéd seraphs[9] of Heaven
    Coveted her and me.

And this was the reason that, long ago,
    In this kingdom by the sea,
15 A wind blew out of a cloud by night
    Chilling my Annabel Lee;
So that her highborn kinsmen came
    And bore her away from me,
To shut her up in a sepulchre
20   In this kingdom by the sea.

The angels, not half so happy in Heaven,
    Went envying her and me:
Yes! that was the reason (as all men know,
    In this kingdom by the sea)
25 That the wind came out of the cloud, chilling
    And killing my Annabel Lee.

But our love it was stronger by far than the love
    Of those who were older than we—
    Of many far wiser than we—
30 And neither the angels in Heaven above
    Nor the demons down under the sea,
Can ever dissever my soul from the soul
    Of the beautiful Annabel Lee:

For the moon never beams without bringing me dreams
35   Of the beautiful Annabel Lee;
And the stars never rise but I see the bright eyes
    Of the beautiful Annabel Lee;
And so, all the night-tide, I lie down by the side
Of my darling, my darling, my life and my bride,
40   In her sepulchre there by the sea—
    In her tomb by the side of the sea.

1849, 1850

9. Angels of the highest order.

ALFRED, LORD TENNYSON
1809–1892

Mariana

"Mariana in the moated grange."
—*Measure for Measure*[1]

With blackest moss the flower-plots
   Were thickly crusted, one and all;
The rusted nails fell from the knots
   That held the pear to the gable-wall.
5 The broken sheds looked sad and strange:
   Unlifted was the clinking latch;
   Weeded and worn the ancient thatch
Upon the lonely moated grange.
     She only said, "My life is dreary,
10   He cometh not," she said;
     She said, "I am aweary, aweary,
       I would that I were dead!"

Her tears fell with the dews at even;
   Her tears fell ere the dews were dried;
15 She could not look on the sweet heaven,
   Either at morn or eventide.
After the flitting of the bats,
   When thickest dark did trance the sky,
   She drew her casement-curtain by,
20 And glanced athwart the glooming flats.
     She only said, "The night is dreary,
       He cometh not," she said;
     She said, "I am aweary, aweary,
       I would that I were dead!"

25 Upon the middle of the night,
   Waking she heard the night-fowl crow;
The cock sung out an hour ere light;
   From the dark fen the oxen's low
Came to her: without hope of change,
30   In sleep she seemed to walk forlorn,
   Till cold winds woke the gray-eyed morn
About the lonely moated grange.
     She only said, "The day is dreary,
       He cometh not," she said;
35   She said, "I am aweary, aweary,
       I would that I were dead!"

About a stone-cast from the wall
   A sluice with blackened waters slept,

---

1. Cf. Shakespeare, *Measure for Measure* 3.1.254, where the duke notes that Mariana waits in a grange, or country house, for the lover who has rejected her.

And o'er it many, round and small,
40   The clustered marish°-mosses crept.   marsh-
Hard by a poplar shook alway,
    All silver-green with gnarlèd bark:
    For leagues no other tree did mark
The level waste, the rounding gray.
45   She only said, "My life is dreary,
                He cometh not," she said;
            She said, "I am aweary, aweary,
                I would that I were dead!"

And ever when the moon was low,
50   And the shrill winds were up and away,
In the white curtain, to and fro,
    She saw the gusty shadow sway.
But when the moon was very low,
    And wild winds bound within their cell,[2]
55   The shadow of the poplar fell
Upon her bed, across her brow.
            She only said, "The night is dreary,
                He cometh not," she said;
            She said, "I am aweary, aweary,
60   I would that I were dead!"

All day within the dreamy house,
    The doors upon their hinges creaked;
The blue fly sung in the pane; the mouse
    Behind the moldering wainscot shrieked,
65   Or from the crevice peered about.
        Old faces glimmered through the doors,
        Old footsteps trod the upper floors,
    Old voices called her from without.
            She only said, "My life is dreary,
70   He cometh not," she said;
            She said, "I am aweary, aweary,
                I would that I were dead!"

The sparrow's chirrup on the roof,
    The slow clock ticking, and the sound
75 Which to the wooing wind aloof
        The poplar made, did all confound
Her sense; but most she loathed the hour
    When the thick-moted sunbeam lay
    Athwart the chambers, and the day
80 Was sloping toward his western bower.
            Then, said she, "I am very dreary,
                He will not come," she said;
            She wept, "I am aweary, aweary,
                Oh God, that I were dead!"

1830

---

2. Virgil relates that Aeolus, god of winds, kept them in a cave (*Aeneid* 1.50–59).

The Kraken[3]

Below the thunders of the upper deep;
Far, far beneath in the abysmal sea,
His ancient, dreamless, uninvaded sleep
The Kraken sleepeth: faintest sunlights flee
5   About his shadowy sides: above him swell
Huge sponges of millennial growth and height;
And far away into the sickly light,
From many a wondrous grot and secret cell
Unnumbered and enormous polypi[4]
10   Winnow with giant fins the slumbering green.
There hath he lain for ages and will lie
Battening upon huge seaworms in his sleep,
Until the latter fire shall heat the deep;[5]
Then once by men and angels to be seen,
15   In roaring he shall rise and on the surface die.

1830

The Lady of Shalott

Part I

On either side the river lie
Long fields of barley and of rye,
That clothe the wold° and meet the sky;   *rolling plain*
And through the field the road runs by
5   To many towered Camelot;[6]
And up and down the people go,
Gazing where the lilies blow°   *bloom*
Round an island there below,
     The island of Shalott.

10   Willows whiten, aspens quiver,
Little breezes dusk and shiver
Through the wave that runs for ever
By the island in the river
     Flowing down to Camelot.
15   Four gray walls, and four gray towers,
Overlook a space of flowers,
And the silent isle imbowers
     The Lady of Shalott.

---

3. A mythical sea monster, called in an eighteenth-century *Natural History of Norway* "the largest and most surprising of all the animal creation" (*O.E.D.*).
4. Octopuslike creatures.
5. At the end of the world, "the elements shall melt with fervent heat, the earth also and the works that are therein shall be burned up" (2 Peter 3.10). See also Revelation 8.8–9: "And the second angel sounded, and as it were a great mountain burning with fire was cast into the sea: and the third part of the sea became blood: and there died the third part of the creatures which were in the sea." 6. The legendary King Arthur's castle.

By the margin, willow-veiled,
20   Slide the heavy barges trailed
By slow horses; and unhailed
The shallop° flitteth silken-sailed   *light open boat*
    Skimming down to Camelot:
But who hath seen her wave her hand?
25   Or at the casement seen her stand?
Or is she known in all the land,
    The Lady of Shalott?

Only reapers, reaping early
In among the bearded barley,
30   Hear a song that echoes cheerly
From the river winding clearly,
    Down to towered Camelot:
And by the moon the reaper weary,
Piling sheaves in uplands airy,
35   Listening, whispers " 'Tis the fairy
    Lady of Shalott."

Part II

There she weaves by night and day
A magic web with colors gay.
She has heard a whisper say,
40   A curse is on her if she stay
    To look down to Camelot.
She knows not what the curse may be,
And so she weaveth steadily,
And little other care hath she,
45   The Lady of Shalott.

And moving through a mirror clear[7]
That hangs before her all the year,
Shadows of the world appear.
There she sees the highway near
50   Winding down to Camelot:
There the river eddy whirls,
And there the surly village-churls,
And the red cloaks of market girls,
    Pass onward from Shalott.

55   Sometimes a troop of damsels glad,
An abbot on an ambling pad,°   *easy-paced horse*
Sometimes a curly shepherd-lad,
Or long-haired page in crimson clad,
    Goes by to towered Camelot;
60   And sometimes through the mirror blue
The knights come riding two and two:

---

7. Weavers placed mirrors facing their looms to see the progress of their work.

She hath no loyal knight and true,
　　The Lady of Shalott.

But in her web she still delights
65　To weave the mirror's magic sights,
For often through the silent nights
A funeral, with plumes and lights
　　And music, went to Camelot:
Or when the moon was overhead.
70　Came two young lovers lately wed;
"I am half sick of shadows," said
　　The Lady of Shalott.

Part III

A bow-shot from her bower-eaves,
He rode between the barley-sheaves,
75　The sun came dazzling through the leaves,
And flamed upon the brazen greaves[8]
　　Of bold Sir Lancelot.
A red-cross knight for ever kneeled[9]
To a lady in his shield,
80　That sparkled on the yellow field,
　　Beside remote Shalott.

The gemmy bridle glittered free,
Like to some branch of stars we see
Hung in the golden Galaxy.
85　The bridle bells rang merrily
　　As he rode down to Camelot:
And from his blazoned baldric° slung　　　　　　　*shoulder belt*
A mighty silver bugle hung,
And as he rode his armor rung,
90　　Beside remote Shalott.

All in the blue unclouded weather
Thick-jewelled shone the saddle-leather,
The helmet and the helmet-feather
Burned like one burning flame together,
95　　As he rode down to Camelot.
As often through the purple night,
Below the starry clusters bright,
Some bearded meteor, trailing light,
　　Moves over still Shalott.

100　His broad clear brow in sunlight glowed;
On burnished hooves his war-horse trode;
From underneath his helmet flowed
His coal-black curls as on he rode,
　　As he rode down to Camelot.

8. Armor for the shins.
9. Cf. Edmund Spenser, *The Faerie Queene* 1 and 3.2.17–25.

105 From the bank and from the river
He flashed into the crystal mirror,
"Tirra lirra," by the river
        Sang Sir Lancelot.

She left the web, she left the loom,
110 She made three paces through the room,
She saw the water-lily bloom,
She saw the helmet and the plume,
        She looked down to Camelot.
Out flew the web and floated wide;
115 The mirror cracked from side to side;
"The curse is come upon me," cried
        The Lady of Shalott.

                Part IV

In the stormy east-wind straining,
The pale yellow woods were waning,
120 The broad stream in his banks complaining.
Heavily the low sky raining
        Over towered Camelot;
Down she came and found a boat
Beneath a willow left afloat,
125 And round about the prow she wrote
        The Lady of Shalott.

And down the river's dim expanse
Like some bold seër in a trance,
Seeing all his own mischance—
130 With a glassy countenance
        Did she look to Camelot.
And at the closing of the day
She loosed the chain, and down she lay;
The broad stream bore her far away,
135   The Lady of Shalott.

Lying, robed in snowy white
That loosely flew to left and right—
The leaves upon her falling light—
Through the noises of the night
140   She floated down to Camelot:
And as the boat-head wound along
The willowy hills and fields among,
They heard her singing her last song,
        The Lady of Shalott.

145 Heard a carol, mournful, holy,
Chanted loudly, chanted lowly,
Till her blood was frozen slowly,
And her eyes were darkened wholly,
        Turned to towered Camelot.

150 For ere she reached upon the tide
    The first house by the water-side,
    Singing in her song she died,
        The Lady of Shalott.

    Under tower and balcony,
155 By garden-wall and gallery,
    A gleaming shape she floated by,
    Dead-pale between the houses high,
        Silent into Camelot.
    Out upon the wharfs they came,
160 Knight and burgher, lord and dame,
    And round the prow they read her name,
        The Lady of Shalott.

    Who is this? and what is here?
    And in the lighted palace near
165 Died the sound of royal cheer;
    And they crossed themselves for fear,
        All the knights at Camelot:
    But Lancelot mused a little space;
    He said, "She has a lovely face;
170 God in his mercy lend her grace,
        The Lady of Shalott."

1831–32   1832, 1842

The Lotos-Eaters[1]

"Courage!" he said, and pointed toward the land,
"This mounting wave will roll us shoreward soon."
In the afternoon they came unto a land
In which it seemèd always afternoon.
5 All round the coast the languid air did swoon,
Breathing like one that hath a weary dream.
Full-faced above the valley stood the moon;
And, like a downward smoke, the slender stream
Along the cliff to fall and pause and fall did seem.

10 A land of streams! some, like a downward smoke,
Slow-dropping veils of thinnest lawn,[2] did go;
And some through wavering lights and shadows broke,
Rolling a slumbrous sheet of foam below.
They saw the gleaming river seaward flow
15 From the inner land: far off three mountain-tops,
Three silent pinnacles of agèd snow,
Stood sunset-flushed; and, dewed with showery drops,
Up-clomb the shadowy pine above the woven copse.°   *forest*

---

1. In Greek mythology, a people who ate the fruit of the lotos, the effect of which was to induce drowsy languor and forgetfulness. Homer de- scribes the visit of Odysseus ("he," line 1) and his men to their island in the *Odyssey* 9.82–97.
2. Sheer cotton fabric.

The charmèd sunset lingered low adown
20 In the red West; through mountain clefts the dale
Was seen far inland, and the yellow down
Bordered with palm, and many a winding vale
And meadow, set with slender galingale;[3]
A land where all things always seemed the same!
25 And round about the keel with faces pale,
Dark faces pale against that rosy flame,
The mild-eyed melancholy Lotos-eaters came.

Branches they bore of that enchanted stem,
Laden with flower and fruit, whereof they gave
30 To each, but whoso did receive of them
And taste, to him the gushing of the wave
Far far away did seem to mourn and rave
On alien shores; and if his fellow spake,
His voice was thin, as voices from the grave;
35 And deep-asleep he seemed, yet all awake,
And music in his ears his beating heart did make.

They sat them down upon the yellow sand,
Between the sun and moon upon the shore;
And sweet it was to dream of Fatherland,
40 Of child, and wife, and slave; but evermore
Most weary seemed the sea, weary the oar,
Weary the wandering fields of barren foam.
Then some one said, "We will return no more;"
And all at once they sang, "Our island home
45 Is far beyond the wave; we will no longer roam."

Choric Song

1

There is sweet music here that softer falls
Than petals from blown roses on the grass,
Or night-dews on still waters between walls
Of shadowy granite, in a gleaming pass;
50 Music that gentlier on the spirit lies,
Than tired eyelids upon tired eyes;
Music that brings sweet sleep down from the blissful skies.
Here are cool mosses deep,
And through the moss the ivies creep,
55 And in the stream the long-leaved flowers weep,
And from the craggy ledge the poppy hangs in sleep.

2

Why are we weighed upon with heaviness,
And utterly consumed with sharp distress,
While all things else have rest from weariness?
60 All things have rest: why should we toil alone,
We only toil, who are the first of things,

---

3. A reedlike plant, a species of marsh grass.

And make perpetual moan,
Still from one sorrow to another thrown;
Nor ever fold our wings,
65 And cease from wanderings,
Nor steep our brows in slumber's holy balm;
Nor harken what the inner spirit sings,
"There is no joy but calm!"
Why should we only toil, the roof and crown of things?

3

70 Lo! in the middle of the wood,
The folded leaf is wooed from out the bud
With winds upon the branch, and there
Grows green and broad, and takes no care,
Sun-steeped at noon, and in the moon
75 Nightly dew-fed; and turning yellow
Falls, and floats adown the air.
Lo! sweetened with the summer light,
The full-juiced apple, waxing over-mellow,
Drops in a silent autumn night.
80 All its allotted length of days,
The flower ripens in its place,
Ripens and fades, and falls, and hath no toil,
Fast-rooted in the fruitful soil.

4

Hateful is the dark-blue sky,
85 Vaulted o'er the dark-blue sea.
Death is the end of life; ah, why
Should life all labor be?
Let us alone. Time driveth onward fast
And in a little while our lips are dumb.
90 Let us alone. What is it that will last?
All things are taken from us, and become
Portions and parcels of the dreadful Past.
Let us alone. What pleasure can we have
To war with evil? Is there any peace
95 In ever climbing up the climbing wave?
All things have rest, and ripen toward the grave
In silence; ripen, fall, and cease:
Give us long rest or death, dark death, or dreamful ease.

5

How sweet it were, hearing the downward stream,
100 With half-shut eyes ever to seem
Falling asleep in a half-dream!
To dream and dream, like yonder amber light,
Which will not leave the myrrh-bush on the height;
To hear each other's whispered speech;
105 Eating the Lotos day by day,
To watch the crisping° ripples on the beach,   *curling*

And tender curving lines of creamy spray;
To lend our hearts and spirits wholly
To the influence of mild-minded melancholy;
110 To muse and brood and live again in memory,
With those old faces of our infancy
Heaped over with a mound of grass,
Two handfuls of white dust, shut in an urn of brass!

6

Dear is the memory of our wedded lives,
115 And dear the last embraces of our wives
And their warm tears: but all hath suffered change:
For surely now our household hearths are cold:
Our sons inherit us: our looks are strange:
And we should come like ghosts to trouble joy.
120 Or else the island princes[4] over-bold
Have eat our substance, and the minstrel sings
Before them of the ten years' war in Troy,
And our great deeds, as half-forgotten things.
Is there confusion in the little isle?
125 Let what is broken so remain.
The Gods are hard to reconcile:
'Tis hard to settle order once again.
There *is* confusion worse than death,
Trouble on trouble, pain on pain,
130 Long labor unto agèd breath,
Sore tasks to hearts worn out by many wars
And eyes grown dim with gazing on the pilot-stars.

7

But, propt on beds of amaranth and moly,[5]
How sweet (while warm airs lull us, blowing lowly)
135 With half-dropt eyelid still,
Beneath a heaven dark and holy,
To watch the long bright river drawing slowly
His waters from the purple hill—
To hear the dewy echoes calling
140 From cave to cave through the thick-twinèd vine—
To watch the emerald-colored water falling
Through many a woven acanthus-wreath divine!
Only to hear and see the far-off sparkling brine,
Only to hear were sweet, stretched out beneath the pine.

8

145 The Lotos blooms below the barren peak,
The Lotos blows by every winding creek;
All day the wind breathes low with mellower tone;
Through every hollow cave and alley lone
Round and round the spicy downs the yellow Lotos-dust is blown.

4. The princes who had remained behind in Ith-
aca ("the little isle," line 124) while Odysseus was
at Troy.

5. An herb with magical properties. *Amaranth:* a
legendary flower, reputed not to fade.

150 We have had enough of action, and of motion we,
Rolled to starboard, rolled to larboard, when the surge was seething
free,
Where the wallowing monster spouted his foam-fountains in the sea.
Let us swear an oath, and keep it with an equal mind,
In the hollow Lotos-land to live and lie reclined
155 On the hills like Gods together, careless of mankind.
For they lie beside their nectar, and the bolts are hurled
Far below them in the valleys, and the clouds are lightly curled
Round their golden houses, girdled with the gleaming world:
Where they smile in secret, looking over wasted lands,
160 Blight and famine, plague and earthquake, roaring deeps and fiery
sands,
Clanging fights, and flaming towns, and sinking ships, and praying
hands.
But they smile, they find a music centered in a doleful song
Steaming up, a lamentation and an ancient tale of wrong,
Like a tale of little meaning though the words are strong;
165 Chanted from an ill-used race of men that cleave the soil,
Sow the seed, and reap the harvest with enduring toil,
Storing yearly little dues of wheat, and wine and oil;
Till they perish and they suffer—some,'tis whispered—down in hell
Suffer endless anguish, others in Elysian valleys dwell,
170 Resting weary limbs at last on beds of asphodel.[6]
Surely, surely, slumber is more sweet than toil, the shore
Than labor in the deep mid-ocean, wind and wave and oar;
O, rest ye, brother mariners, we will not wander more.

1832, 1842

Ulysses[7]

It little profits that an idle king,
By this still hearth, among these barren crags,
Matched with an agèd wife, I mete and dole
Unequal laws unto a savage race,
5 That hoard, and sleep, and feed, and know not me.

I cannot rest from travel: I will drink
Life to the lees: all times I have enjoyed
Greatly, have suffered greatly, both with those
That loved me, and alone; on shore, and when
10 Through scudding drifts the rainy Hyades[8]
Vext the dim sea: I am become a name;
For always roaming with a hungry heart

6. A plant of the lily family supposed to grow in
the Elysian valleys.
7. Tennyson's Ulysses (Odysseus), restless after
his return to Ithaca, eager to renew the life of great
deeds he had known during the Trojan War and
the adventures of his ten-year journey home,
resembles the figure of Ulysses presented by Dante
(*Inferno* 26).
8. A group of stars in the constellation Taurus,
believed to foretell the coming of rain when they
rose with the sun.

Much have I seen and known; cities of men
And manners, climates, councils, governments,
15   Myself not least, but honored of them all;
And drunk delight of battle with my peers,
Far on the ringing plains of windy Troy.
I am a part of all that I have met;
Yet all experience is an arch wherethrough
20   Gleams that untraveled world whose margin fades
For ever and for ever when I move.
How dull it is to pause, to make an end,
To rust unburnished, not to shine in use!
As though to breathe were life! Life piled on life
25   Were all too little, and of one to me
Little remains: but every hour is saved
From that eternal silence, something more,
A bringer of new things; and vile it were
For some three suns to store and hoard myself,
30   And this gray spirit yearning in desire
To follow knowledge like a sinking star,
Beyond the utmost bound of human thought.

This is my son, mine own Telemachus,
To whom I leave the scepter and the isle—
35   Well-loved of me, discerning to fulfill
This labor, by slow prudence to make mild
A rugged people, and through soft degrees
Subdue them to the useful and the good.
Most blameless is he, centered in the sphere
40   Of common duties, decent not to fail
In offices of tenderness, and pay
Meet adoration to my household gods,
When I am gone. He works his work, I mine.

There lies the port; the vessel puffs her sail:
45   There gloom the dark, broad seas. My mariners,
Souls that have toiled, and wrought, and thought with me—
That ever with a frolic welcome took
The thunder and the sunshine, and opposed
Free hearts, free foreheads—you and I are old;
50   Old age hath yet his honor and his toil;
Death closes all: but something ere the end,
Some work of noble note, may yet be done,
Not unbecoming men that strove with Gods.
The lights begin to twinkle from the rocks:
55   The long day wanes: the slow moon climbs: the deep
Moans round with many voices. Come, my friends,
'Tis not too late to seek a newer world.
Push off, and sitting well in order smite
The sounding furrows; for my purpose holds
60   To sail beyond the sunset, and the baths
Of all the western stars, until I die.
It may be that the gulfs will wash us down:

It may be we shall touch the Happy Isles,[9]
And see the great Achilles, whom we knew.
65 Though much is taken, much abides; and though
We are not now that strength which in old days
Moved earth and heaven; that which we are, we are,
One equal temper of heroic hearts,
Made weak by time and fate, but strong in will
70 To strive, to seek, to find, and not to yield.

1833   1842

Break, Break, Break

Break, break, break,
  On thy cold gray stones, O Sea!
And I would that my tongue could utter
  The thoughts that arise in me.

5 O well for the fisherman's boy,
  That he shouts with his sister at play!
O well for the sailor lad,
  That he sings in his boat on the bay!

And the stately ships go on
10   To their haven under the hill;
But O for the touch of a vanished hand,
  And the sound of a voice that is still!

Break, break, break,
  At the foot of thy crags, O Sea!
15 But the tender grace of a day that is dead
  Will never come back to me.

1834   1842

Songs from The Princess[1]

The Splendor Falls

The splendor falls on castle walls
  And snowy summits old in story:
The long light shakes across the lakes,
  And the wild cataract° leaps in glory.   waterfall
5 Blow, bugle, blow, set the wild echoes flying,
  Blow, bugle; answer, echoes, dying, dying, dying.

---

9. The Islands of the Blessed, or Elysium, the abode after death of those favored by the gods, especially heroes and patriots; supposed, in earlier myth, to be located beyond the western limits of the known world.
1. A long narrative poem in blank verse, except for songs such as those printed here.

O hark, O hear! how thin and clear,
　And thinner, clearer, farther going!
O sweet and far from cliff and scar[2]
10　　The horns of Elfland faintly blowing!
Blow, let us hear the purple glens replying:
Blow, bugle; answer, echoes, dying, dying, dying.

O love, they die in yon rich sky,
　They faint on hill or field or river:
15　Our echoes roll from soul to soul,
　And grow for ever and for ever.
Blow, bugle, blow, set the wild echoes flying,
And answer, echoes, answer, dying, dying, dying.

1850

Tears, Idle Tears

Tears, idle tears, I know not what they mean,
Tears from the depth of some divine despair
Rise in the heart, and gather to the eyes,
In looking on the happy Autumn-fields,
5　And thinking of the days that are no more.

Fresh as the first beam glittering on a sail,
That brings our friends up from the underworld,
Sad as the last which reddens over one
That sinks with all we love below the verge;
10　So sad, so fresh, the days that are no more.

Ah, sad and strange as in dark summer dawns
The earliest pipe of half-awakened birds
To dying ears, when unto dying eyes
The casement slowly grows a glimmering square;
15　So sad, so strange, the days that are no more.

Dear as remembered kisses after death,
And sweet as those by hopeless fancy feigned
On lips that are for others; deep as love,
Deep as first love, and wild with all regret;
20　O Death in Life, the days that are no more!

1847

Now Sleeps the Crimson Petal

Now sleeps the crimson petal, now the white;
Nor waves the cypress in the palace walk;
Nor winks the gold fin in the porphyry font:[3]
The firefly wakens: waken thou with me.

---

2. Isolated rock, or rocky height.　　　　3. Basin. Porphyry is a type of hard rock.

5   Now droops the milkwhite peacock like a ghost,
       And like a ghost she glimmers on to me.

       Now lies the Earth all Danaë⁴ to the stars,
       And all thy heart lies open unto me.

       Now slides the silent meteor on, and leaves
10   A shining furrow, as thy thoughts in me.

       Now folds the lily all her sweetness up,
       And slips into the bosom of the lake:
       So fold thyself, my dearest, thou, and slip
       Into my bosom and be lost in me.

                                                      1847

From In Memoriam A.H.H.⁵

OBIIT. MDCCCXXXIII⁶

1

       I held it truth, with him who sings
           To one clear harp in divers tones,⁷
           That men may rise on stepping-stones
       Of their dead selves to higher things.

5   But who shall so forecast the years
           And find in loss a gain to match?
           Or reach a hand through time to catch
       The far-off interest of tears?

       Let Love clasp Grief lest both be drowned,
10   Let darkness keep her raven gloss:
           Ah, sweeter to be drunk with loss,
       To dance with death, to beat the ground,

       Than that the victor Hours should scorn
           The long result of love, and boast,
15   "Behold the man that loved and lost,
       But all he was is overworn."

---

4. A princess in ancient Greece whose father, warned by an oracle that she would bear a son who would kill him, shut her up in a bronze chamber, where she was visited by Zeus, the supreme god, in a shower of gold.
5. Arthur Henry Hallam (1811–1833) had been Tennyson's close friend at Cambridge, they had traveled together in France and Germany, and Hallam had been engaged to the poet's sister. To his associates at Cambridge, Hallam had seemed to give the most brilliant promise of greatness. In the summer of 1833, when he had been traveling on the Continent with his father, Hallam died, of a stroke, in Vienna.
6. Died 1833.
7. According to Tennyson, the German poet Johann Wolfgang von Goethe (1749–1832).

2

Old Yew, which graspest at the stones
    That name the under-lying dead,
    Thy fibers net the dreamless head,
Thy roots are wrapt about the bones.

5   The seasons bring the flowers again,
    And bring the firstling to the flock;
    And in the dusk of thee, the clock
Beats out the little lives of men.

O not for thee the glow, the bloom,
10   Who changest not in any gale,
    Nor branding summer suns avail
To touch thy thousand years of gloom:

And gazing on thee, sullen tree,
    Sick for thy stubborn hardihood,
15   I seem to fail from out my blood
And grow incorporate into thee.

7

Dark house, by which once more I stand
    Here in the long unlovely street,[8]
    Doors, where my heart was used to beat
So quickly, waiting for a hand,

5   A hand that can be clasped no more—
    Behold me, for I cannot sleep,
    And like a guilty thing I creep
At earliest morning to the door.

He is not here; but far away
10   The noise of life begins again,
    And ghastly through the drizzling rain
On the bald street breaks the blank day.

11

Calm is the morn without a sound,
    Calm as to suit a calmer grief,
    And only through the faded leaf
The chestnut pattering to the ground:

5   Calm and deep peace on this high wold,°   upland plain
    And on these dews that drench the furze,°   a shrub
    And all the silvery gossamers
That twinkle into green and gold:

8. I.e., Wimpole St., where Hallam had been living after he left Cambridge.

Calm and still light on yon great plain
10   That sweeps with all its autumn bowers,
       And crowded farms and lessening towers,
To mingle with the bounding main:

Calm and deep peace in this wide air,
       These leaves that redden to the fall,
15   And in my heart, if calm at all,
If any calm, a calm despair:

Calm on the seas, and silver sleep,
       And waves that sway themselves in rest,
       And dead calm in the noble breast
20 Which heaves but with the heaving deep.

19

The Danube to the Severn gave
       The darkened heart that beat no more;[9]
       They laid him by the pleasant shore,
And in the hearing of the wave.

5   There twice a day the Severn fills;
       The salt sea-water passes by,
       And hushes half the babbling Wye,[1]
And makes a silence in the hills.

The Wye is hushed nor moved along,
10   And hushed my deepest grief of all,
       When filled with tears that cannot fall,
I brim with sorrow drowning song.

The tide flows down, the wave again
       Is vocal in its wooded walls;
15   My deeper anguish also falls,
And I can speak a little then.

50

Be near me when my light is low,
       When the blood creeps, and the nerves prick
       And tingle; and the heart is sick,
And all the wheels of Being slow.

5   Be near me when the sensuous frame
       Is racked with pangs that conquer trust;
       And Time, a maniac scattering dust,
And Life, a Fury slinging flame.

9. Vienna, where Hallam died, is on the Danube; the Severn empties into the Bristol Channel near Clevedon, Somersetshire, Hallam's burial place.
1. The Wye, a tributary of the Severn, also runs into the Bristol Channel; the incoming tide deepens the river and makes it quiet, but as the tide ebbs the Wye once more becomes "vocal" (line 14).

Be near me when my faith is dry,
10   And men the flies of latter spring,
        That lay their eggs, and sting and sing
And weave their petty cells and die.

Be near me when I fade away,
        To point the term of human strife,
15   And on the low dark verge of life
The twilight of eternal day.

54

Oh yet we trust that somehow good
        Will be the final goal of ill,
        To pangs of nature, sins of will,
Defects of doubt, and taints of blood;

5   That nothing walks with aimless feet;
        That not one life shall be destroyed,
        Or cast as rubbish to the void,
When God hath made the pile complete;

That not a worm is cloven in vain;
10   That not a moth with vain desire
        Is shriveled in a fruitless fire,
Or but subserves another's gain.

Behold, we know not anything;
        I can but trust that good shall fall
15   At last—far off—at last, to all,
And every winter change to spring.

So runs my dream: but what am I?
        An infant crying in the night:
        An infant crying for the light:
20   And with no language but a cry.

55

The wish, that of the living whole
        No life may fail beyond the grave,
        Derives it not from what we have
The likest God within the soul?

5   Are God and Nature then at strife,
        That Nature lends such evil dreams?
        So careful of the type° she seems,   *species*
So careless of the single life;

That I, considering everywhere
10   Her secret meaning in her deeds,

And finding that of fifty seeds
She often brings but one to bear,

I falter where I firmly trod,
And falling with my weight of cares
15   Upon the great world's altar-stairs
That slope through darkness up to God,

I stretch lame hands of faith, and grope,
And gather dust and chaff, and call
To what I feel is Lord of all,
20   And faintly trust the larger hope.

56

"So careful of the type?" but no.
   From scarpèd[2] cliff and quarried stone
   She[3] cries, "A thousand types are gone;
I care for nothing, all shall go.

5 "Thou makest thine appeal to me:
   I bring to life, I bring to death:
   The spirit does but mean the breath:
I know no more." And he, shall he,

Man, her last work, who seemed so fair,
10   Such splendid purpose in his eyes,
   Who rolled the psalm to wintry skies,
Who built him fanes° of fruitless prayer,   *temples, churches*

Who trusted God was love indeed
   And love Creation's final law—
15   Though Nature, red in tooth and claw
With ravine,° shrieked against his creed—   *seizing prey*

Who loved, who suffered countless ills,
   Who battled for the True, the Just,
   Be blown about the desert dust,
20   Or sealed within the iron hills?

No more? A monster then, a dream,
   A discord. Dragons of the prime,
   That tare° each other in their slime,   *tore (archaic)*
Were mellow music matched with him.

25   O life as futile, then, as frail!
   O for thy voice to soothe and bless!
   What hope of answer, or redress?
Behind the veil, behind the veil.

---

2. Cut down vertically, thus displaying the strata   3. I.e., Nature.
of geologic growth and the fossils they contain.

67

When on my bed the moonlight falls,
    I know that in thy place of rest
    By that broad water of the west
There comes a glory on the walls;[4]

Thy marble bright in dark appears,
    As slowly steals a silver flame
    Along the letters of thy name,
And o'er the number of thy years.

The mystic glory swims away;
    From off my bed the moonlight dies;
    And closing eaves of wearied eyes
I sleep till dusk is dipt in gray:

And then I know the mist is drawn
    A lucid veil from coast to coast,
    And in the dark church like a ghost
Thy tablet glimmers to the dawn.

88

Wild bird, whose warble, liquid sweet,
    Rings Eden through the budded quicks,[5]
    O tell me where the senses mix,
O tell me where the passions meet,

Whence radiate: fierce extremes employ
    Thy spirits in the darkening leaf,
    And in the midmost heart of grief
Thy passion clasps a secret joy:

And I—my harp would prelude woe—
    I cannot all command the strings;
    The glory of the sum of things
Will flash along the chords and go.

95

By night we lingered on the lawn,
    For underfoot the herb was dry;
    And genial warmth; and o'er the sky
The silvery haze of summer drawn;

And calm that let the tapers burn
    Unwavering: not a cricket chirred;

4. Hallam's tomb is inside Clevedon Church, just south of Clevedon, Somersetshire, on a hill overlooking the Bristol Channel.
5. Hawthorn hedges.

The brook alone far-off was heard,
And on the board the fluttering urn:[6]

And bats went round in fragrant skies,
10   And wheeled or lit the filmy shapes[7]
        That haunt the dusk, with ermine capes
And woolly breasts and beaded eyes;

While now we sang old songs that pealed
        From knoll to knoll, where, couched at ease,
15   The white kine° glimmered, and the trees   *cattle*
Laid their dark arms about the field.

But when those others, one by one,
        Withdrew themselves from me and night,
        And in the house light after light
20 Went out, and I was all alone,

A hunger seized my heart; I read
        Of that glad year which once had been,
        In those fallen leaves which kept their green,
The noble letters of the dead:

25 And strangely on the silence broke
        The silent-speaking words, and strange
        Was love's dumb cry defying change
To test his worth; and strangely spoke

The faith, the vigor, bold to dwell
30   On doubts that drive the coward back,
        And keen through wordy snares to track
Suggestion to her inmost cell.

So word by word, and line by line,
        The dead man touched me from the past,
35   And all at once it seemed at last
The living soul was flashed on mine,

And mine in this was wound, and whirled
        About empyreal heights of thought,
        And came on that which is, and caught
40 The deep pulsations of the world,

Æonian music[8] measuring out
        The steps of Time—the shocks of Chance—
        The blows of Death. At length my trance
Was cancelled, stricken through with doubt.

---

6. I.e., on the table an urn for making tea or cof-
fee, heated by a fluttering flame beneath.
7. White-winged night moths called ermine

moths.
8. I.e., the rhythm of the universe; it has persisted
for eons.

45 Vague words! but ah, how hard to frame
        In matter-molded forms of speech,
        Or even for intellect to reach
    Through memory that which I became:

    Till now the doubtful dusk revealed
50   The knolls once more where, couched at ease,
        The white kine glimmered, and the trees
    Laid their dark arms about the field:

    And sucked from out the distant gloom
        A breeze began to tremble o'er
55   The large leaves of the sycamore,
    And fluctuate all the still perfume,

    And gathering freshlier overhead,
        Rocked the full-foliaged elms, and swung
        The heavy-folded rose, and flung
60 The lilies to and fro, and said

    "The dawn, the dawn," and died away;
        And East and West, without a breath,
        Mixt their dim lights, like life and death,
    To broaden into boundless day.

119

    Doors, where my heart was used to beat
        So quickly, not as one that weeps
        I come once more; the city sleeps;
    I smell the meadow in the street;

5   I hear a chirp of birds; I see
        Betwixt the black fronts long-withdrawn
        A light-blue lane of early dawn,
    And think of early days and thee,

    And bless thee, for thy lips are bland,
10   And bright the friendship of thine eye;
        And in my thoughts with scarce a sigh
    I take the pressure of thine hand.

121

    Sad Hesper° o'er the buried sun   *evening star*
        And ready, thou, to die with him,
        Thou watchest all things ever dim
    And dimmer, and a glory done:

5   The team is loosened from the wain,°   *wagon*
        The boat is drawn upon the shore;

Thou listenest to the closing door,
And life is darkened in the brain.

Bright Phosphor,° fresher for the night,   *morning star*
10   By thee the world's great work is heard
Beginning, and the wakeful bird;
Behind thee comes the greater light:

The market boat is on the stream,
And voices hail it from the brink;
15   Thou hear'st the village hammer clink,
And see'st the moving of the team.

Sweet Hesper-Phosphor, double name[9]
For what is one, the first, the last,
Thou, like my present and my past,
20   Thy place is changed; thou art the same.

130

Thy voice is on the rolling air;
I hear thee where the waters run;
Thou standest in the rising sun,
And in the setting thou art fair.

5   What are thou then? I cannot guess;
But though I seem in star and flower
To feel thee some diffusive power,
I do not therefore love thee less:

My love involves the love before;
10   My love is vaster passion now;
Though mixed with God and Nature thou,
I seem to love thee more and more.

Far off thou art, but ever nigh;
I have thee still, and I rejoice;
15   I prosper, circled with thy voice;
I shall not lose thee though I die.

1833–50   1850

The Eagle

Fragment

He clasps the crag with crooked hands;
Close to the sun in lonely lands,
Ringed with the azure world, he stands.

---

9. Hesper and Phosphor are both the planet Venus.

The wrinkled sea beneath him crawls;
5   He watches from his mountain walls,
And like a thunderbolt he falls.

1851

The Charge of the Light Brigade[1]

1

Half a league, half a league,
  Half a league onward,
All in the valley of Death
  Rode the six hundred.
5   "Forward, the Light Brigade!
Charge for the guns!" he said:
Into the valley of Death
  Rode the six hundred.

2

  "Forward, the Light Brigade!"
10   Was there a man dismayed?
Not though the soldier knew
  Some one had blundered:
Theirs not to make reply,
Theirs not to reason why,
15   Theirs but to do and die:
Into the valley of Death
  Rode the six hundred.

3

Cannon to right of them,
Cannon to left of them,
20   Cannon in front of them
  Volleyed and thundered;
Stormed at with shot and shell,
Boldly they rode and well,
Into the jaws of Death,
25   Into the mouth of Hell
  Rode the six hundred.

4

Flashed all their sabers° bare,   *curved swords*
Flashed as they turned in air
Sabring the gunners there,
30   Charging an army, while
  All the world wondered:
Plunged in the battery-smoke

1. Written after Tennyson had read an account in the London *Times* of an incident in the Crimean War when, due to confused orders, three-quarters of a British cavalry unit were cut down by a battery of Russian artillery they had charged with reckless courage.

Right through the line they broke;
Cossack and Russian
35 Reeled from the saber-stroke
Shattered and sundered.
Then they rode back, but not
Not the six hundred.

5

Cannon to right of them,
40 Cannon to left of them,
Cannon behind them
Volleyed and thundered;
Stormed at with shot and shell,
While horse and hero fell,
45 They that had fought so well
Came through the jaws of Death,
Back from the mouth of Hell,
All that was left of them,
Left of six hundred.

6

50 When can their glory fade?
O the wild charge they made!
All the world wondered.
Honor the charge they made!
Honor the Light Brigade,
55 Noble six hundred!

1854   1855

Tithonus[2]

The woods decay, the woods decay and fall,
The vapors weep their burthen to the ground,
Man comes and tills the field and lies beneath,
And after many a summer dies the swan.
5 Me only cruel immortality
Consumes: I wither slowly in thine arms,
Here at the quiet limit of the world,
A white-haired shadow roaming like a dream
The ever-silent spaces of the East,
10 Far-folded mists, and gleaming halls of morn.

Alas! for this gray shadow, once a man—
So glorious in his beauty and thy choice,
Who madest him thy chosen, that he seemed
To his great heart none other than a God!
15 I asked thee, "Give me immortality."
Then didst thou grant mine asking with a smile,

2. A Trojan prince beloved by Aurora, Roman goddess of the dawn, who took him as her spouse. She begged Jupiter, the supreme god, to grant him eternal life, but forgot to ask also for the gift of eternal youth.

Like wealthy men who care not how they give.
But thy strong Hours indignant worked their wills,
And beat me down and marred and wasted me,
20 And though they could not end me, left me maimed
To dwell in presence of immortal youth.
Immortal age beside immortal youth,
And all I was, in ashes. Can thy love,
Thy beauty, make amends, though even now,
25 Close over us, the silver star,[3] thy guide,
Shines in those tremulous eyes that fill with tears
To hear me? Let me go: take back thy gift:
Why should a man desire in any way
To vary from the kindly race of men,
30 Or pass beyond the goal of ordinance[4]
Where all should pause, as is most meet for all?

    A soft air fans the cloud apart; there comes
A glimpse of that dark world where I was born.
Once more the old mysterious glimmer steals
35 From thy pure brows, and from thy shoulders pure,
And bosom beating with a heart renewed.
Thy cheek begins to redden through the gloom,
Thy sweet eyes brighten slowly close to mine,
Ere yet they blind the stars, and the wild team[5]
40 Which love thee, yearning for thy yoke, arise,
And shake the darkness from their loosened manes,
And beat the twilight into flakes of fire.
    Lo! ever thus thou growest beautiful
In silence, then before thine answer given
45 Departest, and thy tears are on my cheek.

    Why wilt thou ever scare me with thy tears,
And make me tremble lest a saying learnt,
In days far-off, on that dark earth, be true?
"The Gods themselves cannot recall their gifts."
50   Ay me! ay me! with what another heart
In days far-off, and with what other eyes
I used to watch—if I be he that watched—
The lucid outline forming round thee; saw
The dim curls kindle into sunny rings;
55 Changed with thy mystic change, and felt my blood
Glow with the glow that slowly crimsoned all
Thy presence and thy portals, while I lay,
Mouth, forehead, eyelids, growing dewy-warm
With kisses balmier than half-opening buds
60 Of April, and could hear the lips that kissed
Whispering I knew not what of wild and sweet,
Like that strange song I heard Apollo° sing,   *god of music*
While Ilion like a mist rose into towers.[6]

---

3. I.e., the morning star.
4. What is ordained as human destiny.
5. The horses that draw Aurora's chariot into the sky at dawn.

6. According to legend, the walls and towers of Ilion (Troy) were raised by the sound of Apollo's song, as related by Ovid, *Heroides* 16.179.

Yet hold me not for ever in thine East:
65 How can my nature longer mix with thine?
Coldly thy rosy shadows bathe me, cold
Are all thy lights, and cold my wrinkled feet
Upon thy glimmering thresholds, when the steam
Floats up from those dim fields about the homes
70 Of happy men that have the power to die,
And grassy barrows° of the happier dead.   grave mounds
Release me, and restore me to the ground;
Thou seëst all things, thou wilt see my grave:
Thou wilt renew thy beauty morn by morn;
75 I earth in earth forget these empty courts,
And thee returning on thy silver wheels.

1833, 1859   1860

"Frater Ave atque Vale"[7]

Row us out from Desenzano, to your Sirmione row!
So they rowed, and there we landed—"O venusta Sirmio!"[8]
There to me through all the groves of olive in the summer glow,
There beneath the Roman ruin where the purple flowers grow,
5 Came that "Ave atque Vale" of the Poet's hopeless woe,
Tenderest of Roman poets nineteen-hundred years ago,
"Frater Ave atque Vale"—as we wandered to and fro
Gazing at the Lydian laughter of the Garda Lake below[9]
Sweet Catullus's all-but-island, olive-silvery Sirmio!

1880   1885

Crossing the Bar

Sunset and evening star,
    And one clear call for me!
And may there be no moaning of the bar,[1]
    When I put out to sea,

5 But such a tide as moving seems asleep,
    Too full for sound and foam,
When that which drew from out the boundless deep
    Turns again home.

---

7. The title (Latin: "Brother, hail and farewell") is the concluding phrase of Catullus's poem number 101, in which the poet records the journey to visit his brother's tomb, in Asia Minor. Tennyson's poem, written on a visit to the little peninsula of Sirmio (on Lake Garda, in northern Italy), shortly after his own brother had died, echoes phrases from poem 31, in which Catullus describes his pleasure in returning to Sirmio after a long absence.
8. O lovely Sirmio (Latin).
9. Catullus's line "And rejoice, O Lydian waves of the lake" (31.13) alludes to the old belief that the Etruscans of the Garda region had originated in Lydia, in Asia Minor.
1. Mournful sound of waves beating on a sandbar.

Twilight and evening bell,
10   And after that the dark!
And may there be no sadness of farewell,
    When I embark;

For though from out our bourne° of Time and Place   boundary
    The flood may bear me far,
15 I hope to see my Pilot face to face
    When I have crost the bar.

1889   1889

ROBERT BROWNING
1812–1889

Porphyria's Lover[1]

The rain set early in tonight,
    The sullen wind was soon awake,
It tore the elm-tops down for spite,
    And did its worst to vex the lake:
5   I listened with heart fit to break.
When glided in Porphyria; straight
    She shut the cold out and the storm,
And kneeled and made the cheerless grate
    Blaze up, and all the cottage warm;
10   Which done, she rose, and from her form
Withdrew the dripping cloak and shawl,
    And laid her soiled gloves by, untied
Her hat and let the damp hair fall,
    And, last, she sat down by my side
15   And called me. When no voice replied,
She put my arm about her waist,
    And made her smooth white shoulder bare,
And all her yellow hair displaced,
    And, stooping, made my cheek lie there,
20   And spread, o'er all, her yellow hair,
Murmuring how she loved me—she
    Too weak, for all her heart's endeavor,
To set its struggling passion free
    From pride, and vainer ties dissever,
25   And give herself to me forever.
But passion sometimes would prevail,
    Nor could tonight's gay feast restrain
A sudden thought of one so pale
    For love of her, and all in vain:
30   So, she was come through wind and rain.

---

1. Originally published with another monologue under the title *Madhouse Cells*, which indicated the speaker's abnormal state of mind.

Be sure I looked up at her eyes
    Happy and proud; at last I knew
Porphyria worshiped me: surprise
    Made my heart swell, and still it grew
35   While I debated what to do.
That moment she was mine, mine, fair,
    Perfectly pure and good: I found
A thing to do, and all her hair
    In one long yellow string I wound
40   Three times her little throat around,
And strangled her. No pain felt she;
    I am quite sure she felt no pain.
As a shut bud that holds a bee,
    I warily oped her lids: again
45   Laughed the blue eyes without a stain.
And I untightened next the tress
    About her neck; her cheek once more
Blushed bright beneath my burning kiss:
    I propped her head up as before,
50   Only, this time my shoulder bore
Her head, which droops upon it still:
    The smiling rosy little head,
So glad it has its utmost will,
    That all it scorned at once is fled,
55   And I, its love, am gained instead!
Porphyria's love: she guessed not how
    Her darling one wish would be heard.
And thus we sit together now,
    And all night long we have not stirred,
60   And yet God has not said a word!

1834   1836, 1842

Soliloquy of the Spanish Cloister

1

Gr-r-r—there go, my heart's abhorrence!
    Water your damned flower-pots, do!
If hate killed men, Brother Lawrence,
    God's blood, would not mine kill you!
5   What? your myrtle-bush wants trimming?
    Oh, that rose has prior claims—
Needs its leaden vase filled brimming?
    Hell dry you up with its flames!

2

At the meal we sit together:
10   *Salve tibi!*[2] I must hear
Wise talk of the kind of weather,
    Sort of season, time of year:

2. Hail to thee! (Latin).

Not a plenteous cork-crop: scarcely
  Dare we hope oak-galls,[3] I doubt:
15 What's the Latin name for "parsley"?
  What's the Greek name for Swine's Snout?[4]

3

Whew! We'll have our platter burnished,
  Laid with care on our own shelf!
With a fire-new spoon we're furnished,
20   And a goblet for ourself,
Rinsed like something sacrificial
  Ere 'tis fit to touch our chaps—
Marked with L for our initial!
  (He-he! There his lily snaps!)

4

25 Saint, forsooth! While brown Dolores
  Squats outside the Convent bank
With Sanchicha, telling stories,
  Steeping tresses in the tank,
Blue-black, lustrous, thick like horsehairs,
30   —Can't I see his dead eye glow,
Bright as 'twere a Barbary corsair's?[5]
  (That is, if he'd let it show!)

5

When he finishes refection,°   dinner
  Knife and fork he never lays
35 Cross-wise, to my recollection,
  As do I, in Jesu's praise.
I the Trinity illustrate,
  Drinking watered orange-pulp—
In three sips the Arian[6] frustrate;
40   While he drains his at one gulp.

6

Oh, those melons? If he's able
  We're to have a feast! so nice!
One goes to the Abbot's table,
  All of us get each a slice.
45 How go on your flowers? None double?
  Not one fruit-sort can you spy?
Strange! And I, too, at such trouble,
  Keep them close-nipped on the sly!

7

There's a great text in Galatians,[7]
50   Once you trip on it, entails

3. Growths produced on oak leaves by gallflies.
4. Nineteenth-century name for dandelion.
5. *Barbary corsair*: pirate from the Berber countries on the north coast of Africa.
6. Follower of Arius, a fourth-century Alexandrian heretic who denied the doctrine of the Trinity.
7. The line has sometimes been taken as referring to Galatians 3.10; but see Galatians 5.14–15, with its ironic applicability to the spirit of the monologue, and also 5.16–24.

Twenty-nine distinct damnations,
   One sure, if another fails:
If I trip him just a-dying,
   Sure of heaven as sure can be,
55 Spin him around and send him flying
   Off to hell, a Manichee?[8]

8

Or, my scrofulous° French novel   *morally corrupt*
   On gray paper with blunt type!
Simply glance at it, you grovel
60   Hand and foot in Belial's[9] gripe:
If I double down its pages
   At the woeful sixteenth print,
When he gathers his greengages,°   *greenish plums*
   Ope a sieve and slip it in't?

9

65 Or, there's Satan! one might venture
   Pledge one's soul to him, yet leave
Such a flaw in the indenture
   As he'd miss till, past retrieve,
Blasted lay that rose-acacia
70   We're so proud of![1] *Hy, Zy, Hine*[2] . . .
'St, there's vespers! *Plena gratiâ*
   Ave, Virgo![3] Gr-r-r—you swine!

ca. 1839   1842

My Last Duchess[4]

Ferrara

That's my last duchess painted on the wall,
Looking as if she were alive. I call
That piece a wonder, now: Frà Pandolf's hands
Worked busily a day, and there she stands.
5 Will't please you sit and look at her? I said
"Frà Pandolf" by design, for never read

---

8. The Manichean heresy, which the speaker hopes to lure Brother Lawrence into accepting, claimed that the world was divided between forces of good and forces of evil.
9. Hebrew personification of lawlessness, hence one of the names for the Devil.
1. The speaker seems to say that, if all else fails, he might secure Brother Lawrence's damnation by pledging his own soul to the Devil in return—but being careful to leave a flaw in the contract that would invalidate it.
2. Possibly an incantation used in calling up the Devil.
3. Full of grace, Hail, Virgin! (Latin). The speaker

mixes up the opening words of the *Ave Maria:* "Ave, Maria, gratia plena."
4. The events of Browning's poem parallel historical events, but its emphasis is rather on truth to Renaissance attitudes than on historic specificity. Alfonso II d'Este, duke of Ferrara (born 1533), in Northern Italy, had married his first wife, daughter of Cosimo I de' Medici, duke of Florence, in 1558, when she was fourteen; she died on April 21, 1561, under suspicious circumstances, and soon after he opened negotiations for the hand of the niece of the count of Tyrol, the seat of whose court was at Innsbruck, in Austria. "Frà Pandolf" and "Claus of Innsbruck" are types rather than specific artists.

Strangers like you that pictured countenance,
The depth and passion of its earnest glance,
But to myself they turned (since none puts by
10 The curtain I have drawn for you, but I)
And seemed as they would ask me, if they durst,
How such a glance came there; so, not the first
Are you to turn and ask thus. Sir, 'twas not
Her husband's presence only, called that spot
15 Of joy into the Duchess' cheek: perhaps
Frà Pandolf chanced to say "Her mantle laps
Over my lady's wrist too much," or "Paint
Must never hope to reproduce the faint
Half-flush that dies along her throat": such stuff
20 Was courtesy, she thought, and cause enough
For calling up that spot of joy. She had
A heart—how shall I say?—too soon made glad,
Too easily impressed; she liked whate'er
She looked on, and her looks went everywhere.
25 Sir, 'twas all one! My favor at her breast,
The dropping of the daylight in the West,
The bough of cherries some officious fool
Broke in the orchard for her, the white mule
She rode with round the terrace—all and each
30 Would draw from her alike the approving speech,
Or blush, at least. She thanked men—good! but thanked
Somehow—I know not how—as if she ranked
My gift of a nine-hundred-years-old name
With anybody's gift. Who'd stoop to blame
35 This sort of trifling? Even had you skill
In speech—which I have not—to make your will
Quite clear to such an one, and say, "Just this
Or that in you disgusts me; here you miss,
Or there exceed the mark"—and if she let
40 Herself be lessoned so, nor plainly set
Her wits to yours, forsooth, and made excuse,
—E'en then would be some stooping; and I choose
Never to stoop. Oh sir, she smiled, no doubt,
Whene'er I passed her; but who passed without
45 Much the same smile? This grew; I gave commands;
Then all smiles stopped together. There she stands
As if alive. Will 't please you rise? We'll meet
The company below, then. I repeat,
The Count your master's known munificence
50 Is ample warrant that no just pretense
Of mine for dowry will be disallowed;
Though his fair daughter's self, as I avowed
At starting, is my object. Nay, we'll go
Together down, sir. Notice Neptune, though,
55 Taming a sea-horse, thought a rarity,
Which Claus of Innsbruck cast in bronze for me!

1842   1842

The Bishop Orders His Tomb at Saint Praxed's Church[5]

Rome, 15—

Vanity, saith the preacher, vanity![6]
Draw round my bed: is Anselm keeping back?
Nephews—sons mine   ah God, I know not! Well—
She, men would have to be your mother once,
5   Old Gandolf envied me, so fair she was!
What's done is done, and she is dead beside,
Dead long ago, and I am Bishop since,
And as she died so must we die ourselves,
And thence ye may perceive the world's a dream.
10   Life, how and what is it? As here I lie
In this state-chamber, dying by degrees,
Hours and long hours in the dead night, I ask
"Do I live, am I dead?" Peace, peace seems all.
Saint Praxed's ever was the church for peace;
15   And so, about this tomb of mine. I fought
With tooth and nail to save my niche, ye know:
—Old Gandolf cozened° me, despite my care;   *cheated*
Shrewd was that snatch from out the corner south
He graced his carrion with, God curse the same!
20   Yet still my niche is not so cramped but thence
One sees the pulpit o' the epistle-side,[7]
And somewhat of the choir, those silent seats,
And up into the aery dome where live
The angels, and a sunbeam's sure to lurk:
25   And I shall fill my slab of basalt there,
And 'neath my tabernacle[8] take my rest,
With those nine columns round me, two and two,
The odd one at my feet where Anselm stands:
Peach-blossom marble all, the rare, the ripe
30   As fresh-poured red wine of a mighty pulse.
—Old Gandolf with his paltry onion-stone,
Put me where I may look at him! True peach,
Rosy and flawless: how I earned the prize!
Draw close: that conflagration of my church
35   —What then? So much was saved if aught were missed!
My sons, ye would not be my death? Go dig
The white-grape vineyard where the oil-press stood,
Drop water gently till the surface sink,
And if ye find . . . Ah God, I know not, I! . . .
40   Bedded in store of rotten fig-leaves soft,
And corded up in a tight olive-frail,°   *olive basket*

---

5. The church of Santa Prassede, in Rome, dedicated to a Roman virgin, dates from the fifth century but was rebuilt early in the ninth and restored at later times. The sixteenth-century bishop who speaks here is a fictional figure, as is his predecessor, Gandolf.

6. An echo of Ecclesiastes 1.2: "Vanity of vanities, saith the Preacher, vanity of vanities; all is vanity."
7. The right-hand side as one faces the altar, the side from which the Epistles of the New Testament were read.
8. Canopy over his tomb.

Some lump, ah God, of *lapis lazuli*,[9]
Big as a Jew's head cut off at the nape,
Blue as a vein o'er the Madonna's breast . . .
45   Sons, all have I bequeathed you, villas, all,
That brave Frascati[1] villa with its bath,
So, let the blue lump poise between my knees,
Like God the Father's globe on both his hands
Ye worship in the Jesu Church[2] so gay,
50   For Gandolf shall not choose but see and burst!
Swift as a weaver's shuttle fleet our years:[3]
Man goeth to the grave, and where is he?
Did I say basalt for my slab, sons? Black—
'Twas ever antique-black I meant! How else
55   Shall ye contrast my frieze to come beneath?
The bas-relief in bronze ye promised me,
Those Pans and Nymphs ye wot of, and perchance
Some tripod, thyrsus,[4] with a vase or so,
The Saviour at his sermon on the mount,
60   Saint Praxed in a glory,[5] and one Pan
Ready to twitch the Nymph's last garment off,
And Moses with the tables° . . . but I know   tablets
Ye mark me not! What do they whisper thee,
Child of my bowels, Anselm? Ah, ye hope
65   To revel down my villas while I gasp
Bricked o'er with beggar's moldy travertine[6]
Which Gandolf from his tomb-top chuckles at!
Nay, boys, ye love me—all of jasper,[7] then!
'T is jasper ye stand pledged to, lest I grieve
70   My bath must needs be left behind, alas!
One block, pure green as a pistachio-nut,
There's plenty jasper somewhere in the world—
And have I not Saint Praxed's ear to pray
Horses for ye, and brown Greek manuscripts,
75   And mistresses with great smooth marbly limbs?
—That's if ye carve my epitaph aright,
Choice Latin, picked phrase, Tully's[8] every word,
No gaudy ware like Gandolf's second line—
Tully, my masters? Ulpian[9] serves his need!
80   And then how I shall lie through centuries,
And hear the blessed mutter of the mass,
And see God made and eaten all day long,[1]
And feel the steady candle-flame, and taste
Good strong thick stupefying incense-smoke!

9. A vivid blue stone, one of the so-called hard stones, used for ornament.
1. A resort town in the mountains.
2. The baroque Jesuit church Il Gesù, in Rome. The sculptured group of the Trinity includes a terrestrial globe carved from the largest known block of lapis lazuli.
3. See Job 7.6: "My days are swifter than a weaver's shuttle, and are spent without hope."
4. A staff ornamented with ivy or vine leaves, carried by followers of Bacchus, Roman god of wine and revelry.
5. Rays of gold, signifying sanctity, around the head or body of the saint portrayed.
6. Ordinary limestone used in building.
7. A variety of quartz.
8. Familiar name for Cicero (Marcus Tullius Cicero).
9. His Latin would be stylistically inferior to that of Cicero.
1. Refers to the doctrine of transubstantiation.

85 For as I lie here, hours of the dead night,
  Dying in state and by such slow degrees,
  I fold my arms as if they clasped a crook,[2]
  And stretch my feet forth straight as stone can point,
  And let the bedclothes, for a mortcloth,[3] drop
90 Into great laps and folds of sculptor's-work:
  And as yon tapers dwindle, and strange thoughts
  Grow, with a certain humming in my ears,
  About the life before I lived this life,
  And this life too, popes, cardinals and priests,
95 Saint Praxed at his sermon on the mount,[4]
  Your tall pale mother with her talking eyes,
  And new-found agate urns as fresh as day,
  And marble's language, Latin pure, discreet,
  —Aha, ELUCESCEBAT[5] quoth our friend?
100 No Tully, said I, Ulpian at the best!
  Evil and brief hath been my pilgrimage.
  All *lapis*, all, son! Else I give the Pope
  My villas! Will ye ever eat my heart?
  Ever your eyes were as a lizard's quick,
105 They glitter like your mother's for my soul,
  Or ye would heighten my impoverished frieze,
  Piece out its starved design, and fill my vase
  With grapes, and add a vizor and a Term,[6]
  And to the tripod ye would tie a lynx
110 That in his struggle throws the thyrsus down,
  To comfort me on my entablature
  Whereon I am to lie till I must ask
  "Do I live, am I dead?" There, leave me, there!
  For ye have stabbed me with ingratitude
115 To death—ye wish it—God, ye wish it! Stone—
  Gritstone, a-crumble! Clammy squares which sweat
  As if the corpse they keep were oozing through—
  And no more *lapis* to delight the world!
  Well, go! I bless ye. Fewer tapers there,
120 But in a row: and, going, turn your backs
  —Ay, like departing altar-ministrants,
  And leave me in my church, the church for peace,
  That I may watch at leisure if he leers—
  Old Gandolf, at me, from his onion-stone,
125 As still he envied me, so fair she was!

1844   1845, 1849

2. I.e., the bishop's crozier, with its emblematic resemblance to a shepherd's crook.
3. The pall with which a coffin is draped.
4. As the bishop's mind wanders, he attributes Christ's Sermon on the Mount to Santa Prassede.
5. A word from Gandolf's epitaph (a form of the Latin verb meaning "to shine forth"); the bishop claims that this form is inferior to *elucebat*, which Cicero would have used.
6. A pillar adorned with a bust of Terminus, Roman god of boundaries. *Vizor*: face mask on a helmet. Both are motifs of classical sculpture imitated by the Renaissance.

Home-Thoughts, from Abroad

1

Oh, to be in England
Now that April's there,
And whoever wakes in England
Sees, some morning, unaware,
5   That the lowest boughs and the brushwood sheaf
Round the elm-tree bole are in tiny leaf,
While the chaffinch sings on the orchard bough
In England—now!

2

And after April, when May follows,
10   And the whitethroat builds, and all the swallows!
Hark, where my blossomed pear-tree in the hedge
Leans to the field and scatters on the clover
Blossoms and dewdrops—at the bent spray's edge—
That's the wise thrush; he sings each song twice over,
15   Lest you should think he never could recapture
The first fine careless rapture!
And though the fields look rough with hoary dew
All will be gay when noontide wakes anew
The buttercups, the little children's dower
20   —Far brighter than this gaudy melon-flower!

ca. 1845   1845

A Toccata of Galuppi's[7]

1

Oh Galuppi, Baldassare, this is very sad to find!
I can hardly misconceive you; it would prove me deaf and blind;
But although I take your meaning, 'tis with such a heavy mind!

2

Here you come with your old music, and here's all the good it brings.
5   What, they lived once thus at Venice where the merchants were the
      kings,
Where Saint Mark's is, where the Doges used to wed the sea with
      rings?[8]

---

7. This poem presents the reflections of a nineteenth-century Englishman as he plays a toccata by the eighteenth-century Venetian composer Baldassare Galuppi. (A toccata is a "touch-piece," the word derived from the Italian verb *toccare*, "to touch": "a composition intended to exhibit the touch and execution of the performer," and hence often having the character of "showy improvisation" [*Grove's Dictionary of Music and Musicians*].
8. Each year the doge, chief magistrate of the Venetian republic, threw a ring into the sea with the ceremonial words "We wed thee, O sea, in sign of true and everlasting dominion."

3

Ay, because the sea's the street there; and 'tis arched by . . . what you
    call
. . . Shylock's bridge⁹ with houses on it, where they kept the carnival:
I was never out of England—it's as if I saw it all.

4

10   Did young people take their pleasure when the sea was warm in May?
Balls and masks¹ begun at midnight, burning ever to mid-day,
When they made up fresh adventures for the morrow, do you say?

5

Was a lady such a lady, cheeks so round and lips so red—
On her neck the small face buoyant, like a bellflower on its bed,
15   O'er the breast's superb abundance where a man might base his head?

6

Well, and it was graceful of them—they'd break talk off and afford
—She, to bite her mask's black velvet—he, to finger on his sword,
While you sat and played Toccatas, stately at the clavichord?²

7

What? Those lesser thirds so plaintive, sixths diminished, sigh on sigh,
20   Told them something? Those suspensions, those solutions—"Must we
    die?"
Those commiserating sevenths³—"Life might last! we can but try!"

8

"Were you happy?" "Yes." "And are you still as happy?" "Yes. And you?"
"Then, more kisses!" "Did *I* stop them, when a million seemed so few?"
Hark, the dominant's persistence till it must be answered to!

9

25   So, an octave struck the answer. Oh, they praised you, I dare say!
"Brave Galuppi! that was music! good alike at grave and gay!
"I can always leave off talking when I hear a master play!"

10

Then they left you for their pleasure: till in due time, one by one,
Some with lives that came to nothing, some with deeds as well
    undone,
30   Death stepped tacitly and took them where they never see the sun.

---

9. The Rialto, a bridge over the Grand Canal.
1. Masquerades.
2. A keyboard instrument, similar to a piano but
sounding more like a harpsichord. In stanzas 7–9,
the quoted words represent the thoughts, feelings,
or casual remarks of Galuppi's Venetian audience,
now dispersed by death.

3. This term and others in these lines refer to the
technical devices Galuppi used to produce alter-
nating moods in his music, conflict in each case
being resolved into harmony. Thus the "dominant"
(the fifth note of the scale), after being persistently
sounded, is answered by a resolving chord (lines
24–25).

11

But when I sit down to reason, think to take my stand nor swerve,
While I triumph o'er a secret wrung from nature's close reserve,
In you come with your cold music[4] till I creep through every nerve.

12

Yes, you, like a ghostly cricket, creaking where a house was burned:
35 "Dust and ashes, dead and done with, Venice spent what Venice
earned.
"The soul, doubtless, is immortal—where a soul can be discerned.

13

"Yours for instance: you know physics, something of geology,
"Mathematics are your pastime; souls shall rise in their degree;
"Butterflies may dread extinction—you'll not die, it cannot be!

14

40 "As for Venice and her people, merely born to bloom and drop,
"Here on earth they bore their fruitage, mirth and folly were the crop:
"What of soul was left, I wonder, when the kissing had to stop?

15

"Dust and ashes!" So you creak it, and I want° the heart to scold.   *lack*
Dear dead women, with such hair, too—what's become of all the
gold
45 Used to hang and brush their bosoms? I feel chilly and grown old.

ca. 1847   1855

Memorabilia[5]

1

Ah, did you once see Shelley plain,
    And did he stop and speak to you
And did you speak to him again?
    How strange it seems and new!

2

5   But you were living before that,
        And also you are living after;
    And the memory I started at—
        My starting moves your laughter.

3

    I crossed a moor, with a name of its own
10   And a certain use in the world no doubt,

---

4. In stanzas 12–15, the quoted words are what
the speaker imagines Galuppi is saying to him.
5. Memorable things. Line 1 refers to the English

poet Percy Bysshe Shelley (1792–1822; see pp.
863–93).

Yet a hand's-breadth of it shines alone
  'Mid the blank miles round about:

4

For there I picked up on the heather
  And there I put inside my breast
15 A moulted feather, an eagle-feather!
  Well, I forget the rest.

ca. 1851   1855

"Childe Roland to the Dark Tower Came"

(See Edgar's Song in "Lear")[6]

I

My first thought was, he lied in every word,
  That hoary cripple, with malicious eye
  Askance° to watch the working of his lie   *squinting sideways*
On mine, and mouth scarce able to afford
5 Suppression of the glee, that pursed and scored
  Its edge, at one more victim gained thereby.

2

What else should he be set for, with his staff?
  What, save to waylay with his lies, ensnare
  All travelers who might find him posted there,
10 And ask the road? I guessed what skull-like laugh
  Would break, what crutch 'gin write my epitaph
  For pastime in the dusty thoroughfare,

3

If at his counsel I should turn aside
  Into that ominous tract which, all agree,
15 Hides the Dark Tower. Yet acquiescingly
  I did turn as he pointed: neither pride
  Nor hope rekindling at the end descried,
  So much as gladness that some end might be.

4

For, what with my whole world-wide wandering,
20 What with my search drawn out through years, my hope
  Dwindled into a ghost not fit to cope
With that obstreperous° joy success would bring,—   *unruly*
  I hardly tried now to rebuke the spring
  My heart made, finding failure in its scope.

---

6. In Shakespeare's *King Lear* 6.4, Edgar, Gloucester's son, disguised as a madman, meets Lear in the midst of a storm; at the end of the scene, Edgar sings: "Child Rowland to the dark tower came, / His word was still—Fie, foh, and fum, / I smell the blood of a British man.' " *Childe:* medieval title applied to a youth awaiting knighthood.

5

25 As when a sick man very near to death
    Seems dead indeed, and feels begin and end
    The tears, and takes the farewell of each friend,
And hears one bid the other go, draw breath
Freelier outside, ("since all is o'er," he saith,
30   "And the blow fallen no grieving can amend;")

6

While some discuss if near the other graves
    Be room enough for this, and when a day
    Suits best for carrying the corpse away,
With care about the banners, scarves and staves:
35 And still the man hears all, and only craves
    He may not shame such tender love and stay.

7

Thus, I had so long suffered in this quest,
    Heard failure prophesied so oft, been writ
    So many times among "The Band"—to wit,
40 The knights who to the Dark Tower's search addressed
    Their steps—that just to fail as they, seemed best,
    And all the doubt was now—should I be fit?

8

So, quiet as despair, I turned from him,
    That hateful cripple, out of his highway
45   Into the path he pointed. All the day
Had been a dreary one at best, and dim
Was settling to its close, yet shot one grim
    Red leer to see the plain catch its estray.[7]

9

For mark! no sooner was I fairly found
50   Pledged to the plain, after a pace or two,
    Than, pausing to throw backward a last view
O'er the safe road, 'twas gone; gray plain all round:
Nothing but plain to the horizon's bound.
    I might go on; naught else remained to do.

10

55 So, on I went. I think I never saw
    Such starved ignoble nature; nothing throve:
    For flowers—as well expect a cedar grove!
But cockle, spurge,[8] according to their law
Might propagate their kind, with none to awe,
60   You'd think: a burr had been a treasure trove.

---

7. A stray or unclaimed domestic animal.
8. Cockle is a weed that bears burrs (line 60), prickly seed-heads; spurge, a bitter-tasting weed.

11

No! penury, inertness and grimace,
    In some strange sort, were the land's portion. "See
    Or shut your eyes," said Nature peevishly,
"It nothing skills:⁹ I cannot help my case:
65   'Tis the Last Judgment's fire must cure this place,
    Calcine° its clods and set my prisoners free."   *burn to powder*

12

If there pushed any ragged thistle-stalk
    Above its mates, the head was chopped; the bents°   *reeds, rushes*
    Were jealous else. What made those holes and rents
70 In the dock's¹ harsh swarth° leaves, bruised as to balk   *dark*
All hope of greenness? 'tis a brute must walk
    Pashing° their life out, with a brute's intents.   *crushing*

13

As for the grass, it grew as scant as hair
    In leprosy; thin dry blades pricked the mud
75   Which underneath looked kneaded up with blood.
One stiff blind horse, his every bone a-stare,
Stood stupefied, however he came there:
    Thrust out past service from the devil's stud!

14

Alive? he might be dead for aught I know,
80   With that red gaunt colloped° neck a-strain,   *chafed, ridged*
    And shut eyes underneath the rusty mane;
Seldom went such grotesqueness with such woe;
I never saw a brute I hated so;
    He must be wicked to deserve such pain.

15

85 I shut my eyes and turned them on my heart.
    As a man calls for wine before he fights,
    I asked one draught of earlier, happier sights,
Ere fitly I could hope to play my part.
Think first, fight afterwards—the soldier's art:
90   One taste of the old time sets all to rights.

16

Not it! I fancied Cuthbert's reddening face
    Beneath its garniture° of curly gold,   *trimming*
    Dear fellow, till I almost felt him fold
An arm in mine to fix me to the place,
95   That way he used. Alas, one night's disgrace!
    Out went my heart's new fire and left it cold.

9. I.e., it is useless.   1. Coarse, weedy plant's.

17

Giles then, the soul of honor—there he stands
    Frank as ten years ago when knighted first.
    What honest man should dare (he said) he durst.
100 Good—but the scene shifts—faugh! what hangman hands
Pin to his breast a parchment? His own bands
    Read it. Poor traitor, spit upon and curst!

18

Better this present than a past like that;
    Back therefore to my darkening path again!
105   No sound, no sight as far as eye could strain.
Will the night send a howlet° or a bat?   *owl*
I asked: when something on the dismal flat
    Came to arrest my thoughts and change their train.

19

A sudden little river crossed my path
110   As unexpected as a serpent comes.
    No sluggish tide congenial to the glooms;
This, as it frothed by, might have been a bath
For the fiend's glowing hoof—to see the wrath
    Of its black eddy bespate° with flakes and spumes.   *spattered*

20

115 So petty yet so spiteful! All along,
    Low scrubby alders kneeled down over it;
    Drenched willows flung them headlong in a fit
Of mute despair, a suicidal throng:
The river which had done them all the wrong,
120   Whate'er that was, rolled by, deterred no whit.

21

Which, while I forded,—good saints, how I feared
    To set my foot upon a dead man's cheek,
    Each step, or feel the spear I thrust to seek
For hollows, tangled in his hair or beard!
125 —It may have been a water-rat I speared,
    But, ugh! it sounded like a baby's shriek.

22

Glad was I when I reached the other bank.
    Now for a better country. Vain presage!
    Who were the strugglers, what war did they wage,
130 Whose savage trample thus could pad the dank
Soil to a plash?° Toads in a poisoned tank,   *puddle*
    Or wild cats in a red-hot iron cage—

23

The fight must so have seemed in that fell cirque.[2]
    What penned them there, with all the plain to choose?

2. Dreadful hollow encircled by heights.

135 No footprint leading to that horrid mews,°   *stabling area*
 None out of it. Mad brewage set to work
 Their brains, no doubt, like galley-slaves the Turk
  Pits for his pastime, Christians against Jews.

24

 And more than that—a furlong on—why, there!
140 What bad use was that engine° for, that wheel,   *mechanism*
  Or brake,³ not wheel—that harrow fit to reel
 Men's bodies out like silk? with all the air
  Of Tophet's° tool, on earth left unaware,   *Hell's*
  Or brought to sharpen its rusty teeth of steel.

25

145 Then came a bit of stubbed ground, once a wood,
  Next a marsh, it would seem, and now mere earth
  Desperate and done with; (so a fool finds mirth,
 Makes a thing and then mars it, till his mood
 Changes and off he goes!) within a rood⁴—
150 Bog, clay and rubble, sand and stark black dearth.

26

 Now blotches rankling,° colored gay and grim,   *festering*
  Now patches where some leanness of the soil's
  Broke into moss or substances like boils;
 Then came some palsied oak, a cleft in him
155 Like a distorted mouth that splits its rim
  Gaping at death, and dies while it recoils.

27

 And just as far as ever from the end!
  Nought in the distance but the evening, nought
  To point my footstep further! At the thought,
160 A great black bird, Apollyon's⁵ bosom-friend,
 Sailed past, nor beat his wide wing dragon-penned⁶
  That brushed my cap—perchance the guide I sought.

28

 For, looking up, aware I somehow grew,
  'Spite of the dusk, the plain had given place
165 All round to mountains—with such name to grace
 Mere ugly heights and heaps now stolen in view.
 How thus they had surprised me,—solve it, you!
  How to get from them was no clearer case.

---

3. A toothed machine for breaking up flax or hemp, to separate the fiber; here, an instrument of torture.
4. Quarter acre of land.

5. "The angel of the bottomless pit, whose name in the Hebrew tongue is Abaddon, but in the Greek tongue . . . Apollyon" (Revelation 9.11).
6. With pinions, wings, like a dragon's.

29

Yet half I seemed to recognize some trick
170 Of mischief happened to me, God knows when—
In a bad dream perhaps. Here ended, then,
Progress this way. When, in the very nick
Of giving up, one time more, came a click
As when a trap shuts—you're inside the den!

30

175 Burningly it came on me all at once,
This was the place! those two hills on the right,
Crouched like two bulls locked horn in horn in fight;
While to the left, a tall scalped mountain . . . . Dunce,
Dotard, a-dozing at the very nonce,°   moment
180 After a life spent training for the sight!

31

What in the midst lay but the Tower itself?
The round squat turret, blind as the fool's heart,
Built of brown stone, without a counterpart
In the whole world. The tempest's mocking elf
185 Points to the shipman thus the unseen shelf
He strikes on, only when the timbers start.

32

Not see? because of night perhaps?—why, day
Came back again for that! before it left,
The dying sunset kindled through a cleft:
190 The hills, like giants at a hunting, lay,
Chin upon hand, to see the game at bay,—
"Now stab and end the creature—to the heft!"[7]

33

Not hear? when noise was everywhere! it tolled
Increasing like a bell. Names in my ears
195 Of all the lost adventurers my peers,—
How such a one was strong, and such was bold,
And such was fortunate, yet each of old
Lost, lost! one moment knelled the woe of years.

34

There they stood, ranged along the hillsides, met
200 To view the last of me, a living frame
For one more picture! in a sheet of flame
I saw them and I knew them all. And yet
Dauntless the slug-horn[8] to my lips I set,
And blew. *"Childe Roland to the Dark Tower came."*

1852   1855

7. Handle of a dagger or sword.
8. Here, a kind of trumpet. Literally, a Scottish term for a clan's war cry.

Fra Lippo Lippi[9]

I am poor brother Lippo, by your leave!
You need not clap your torches to my face.
Zooks,[1] what's to blame? you think you see a monk!
What, 'tis past midnight, and you go the rounds,
5   And here you catch me at an alley's end
Where sportive ladies leave their doors ajar?
The Carmine's my cloister:[2] hunt it up,
Do—harry out, if you must show your zeal,
Whatever rat, there, haps on his wrong hole,
10   And nip each softling of a wee white mouse,
Weke, weke, that's crept to keep him company!
Aha, you know your betters! Then, you'll take
Your hand away that's fiddling on my throat,
And please to know me likewise. Who am I?
15   Why, one, sir, who is lodging with a friend
Three streets off—he's a certain . . . how d'ye call?
Master—a . . . Cosimo of the Medici,[3]
I' the house that caps the corner. Boh! you were best!
Remember and tell me, the day you're hanged,
20   How you affected such a gullet's-gripe![4]
But you, sir, it concerns you that your knaves
Pick up a manner nor discredit you:
Zooks, are we pilchards,° that they sweep the streets   *fish*
And count fair prize what comes into their net?
25   He's Judas to a tittle, that man is![5]
Just such a face! Why, sir, you make amends.
Lord, I'm not angry! Bid your hangdogs go
Drink out this quarter-florin to the health
Of the munificent House that harbors me
30   (And many more beside, lads! more beside!)
And all's come square again. I'd like his face—
His, elbowing on his comrade in the door
With the pike and lantern—for the slave that holds
John Baptist's head a-dangle by the hair
35   With one hand ("Look you, now," as who should say)
And his weapon in the other, yet unwiped!
It's not your chance to have a bit of chalk,
A wood-coal or the like? or you should see!
Yes, I'm the painter, since you style me so.
40   What, brother Lippo's doings, up and down,
You know them and they take you? like enough!
I saw the proper twinkle in your eye—

9. Florentine painter (ca. 1406–1469), whose life
Browning knew from Giorgio Vasari's *Lives of the
Most Eminent Painters, Sculptors, and Architects*
and from other sources, and whose paintings he
had studied during his years in Florence.
1. Short for *Gadzooks,* a mild oath (perhaps orig-
inally *God's truth*).
2. Fra Lippo had entered the Carmelite cloister
Santa Maria del Carmine while still a boy. He gave

up monastic vows in 1421, but was clothed by the
monastery until 1431 and was called "Fra Filippo"
in documents until his death.
3. Cosimo de' Medici (1389–1464), Fra Lippo's
wealthy patron and an important political power in
Florence.
4. I.e., grip on my throat.
5. He says one of the watchmen who have arrested
him looks exactly like Judas.

'Tell you, I liked your looks at very first.
Let's sit and set things straight now, hip to haunch.
45 Here's spring come, and the nights one makes up bands
To roam the town and sing out carnival,
And I've been three weeks shut within my mew,[6]
A-painting for the great man, saints and saints
And saints again. I could not paint all night—
50 Ouf! I leaned out of window for fresh air.
There came a hurry of feet and little feet,
A sweep of lute-strings, laughs, and whiffs of song—
Flower o' the broom,
Take away love, and our earth is a tomb!
55 *Flower o' the quince,*
I let Lisa go, and what good in life since?
Flower o' the thyme—and so on. Round they went.
Scarce had they turned the corner when a titter
Like the skipping of rabbits by moonlight—three slim shapes,
60 And a face that looked up . . . zooks, sir, flesh and blood,
That's all I'm made of! Into shreds it went,
Curtain and counterpane and coverlet,
All the bed-furniture—a dozen knots,
There was a ladder! Down I let myself,
65 Hands and feet, scrambling somehow, and so dropped,
And after them. I came up with the fun
Hard by Saint Laurence,[7] hail fellow, well met—
Flower o' the rose,
If I've been merry, what matter who knows?
70 And so as I was stealing back again
To get to bed and have a bit of sleep
Ere I rise up to-morrow and go work
On Jerome knocking at his poor old breast[8]
With his great round stone to subdue the flesh,
75 You snap me of the sudden. Ah, I see!
Though your eye twinkles still, you shake your head—
Mine's shaved—a monk, you say—the sting's in that!
If Master Cosimo announced himself,
Mum's the word naturally; but a monk!
80 Come, what am I a beast for? tell us, now!
I was a baby when my mother died
And father died and left me in the street.
I starved there, God knows how, a year or two
On fig-skins, melon-parings, rinds and shucks,
85 Refuse and rubbish. One fine frosty day,
My stomach being empty as your hat,
The wind doubled me up and down I went.
Old Aunt Lapaccia trussed me with one hand,
(Its fellow was a stinger as I knew)
90 And so along the wall, over the bridge,
By the straight cut to the convent. Six words there,

6. I.e., within the confines of my quarters (in the Medici palace).
7. The church of San Lorenzo, not far from the Medici palace.
8. I.e., on a painting of St. Jerome in the Desert.

While I stood munching my first bread that month:
"So, boy, you're minded," quoth the good fat father
Wiping his own mouth, 't was refection-time°—   mealtime
95   "To quit this very miserable world?
"Will you renounce" . . . "the mouthful of bread?" thought I;
By no means! Brief, they made a monk of me;
I did renounce the world, its pride and greed,
Palace, farm, villa, shop and banking-house,
100   Trash, such as these poor devils of Medici
Have given their hearts to—all at eight years old.
Well, sir, I found in time, you may be sure,
'T was not for nothing—the good bellyful,
The warm serge and the rope that goes all round,
105   And day-long blessed idleness beside!
"Let's see what the urchin's fit for"—that came next.
Not overmuch their way, I must confess.
Such a to-do! They tried me with their books:
Lord, they'd have taught me Latin in pure waste!
110   *Flower o' the clove,*
All the Latin I construe is, "amo" I love!
But, mind you, when a boy starves in the streets
Eight years together, as my fortune was,
Watching folk's faces to know who will fling
115   The bit of half-stripped grape-bunch he desires,
And who will curse or kick him for his pains—
Which gentleman processional and fine,
Holding a candle to the Sacrament,
Will wink and let him lift a plate and catch
120   The droppings of the wax to sell again,
Or holla for the Eight[9] and have him whipped—
How say I? nay, which dog bites, which lets drop
His bone from the heap of offal in the street—
Why, soul and sense of him grow sharp alike,
125   He learns the look of things, and none the less
For admonition from the hunger-pinch.
I had a store of such remarks, be sure,
Which, after I found leisure, turned to use.
I drew men's faces on my copy-books,
130   Scrawled them within the antiphonary's[1] marge,
Joined legs and arms to the long music-notes,
Found eyes and nose and chin for A's and B's,
And made a string of pictures of the world
Betwixt the ins and outs of verb and noun,
135   On the wall, the bench, the door. The monks looked black.
"Nay," quoth the Prior, "turn him out, d'ye say?
"In no wise. Lose a crow and catch a lark.
"What if at last we get our man of parts,
"We Carmelites, like those Camaldolese
140   "And Preaching Friars,[2] to do our church up fine

9. The Florentine magistrates.
1. The book containing the antiphons, or re-
sponses chanted in the liturgy.

2. I.e., members of a Dominican religious order.
Camaldolese: members of a Benedictine religious
order at Camaldoli, in the Apennines.

"And put the front on it that ought to be!"
And hereupon he bade me daub away.
Thank you! my head being crammed, the walls a blank,
Never was such prompt disemburdening.
145 First, every sort of monk, the black and white,
I drew them, fat and lean: then, folk at church,
From good old gossips waiting to confess
Their cribs° of barrel-droppings, candle-ends—   minor thefts
To the breathless fellow at the altar-foot,
150 Fresh from his murder, safe and sitting there
With the little children round him in a row
Of admiration, half for his beard and half
For that white anger of his victim's son
Shaking a fist at him with one fierce arm,
155 Signing³ himself with the other because of Christ
(Whose sad face on the cross sees only this
After the passion° of a thousand years)   suffering
Till some poor girl, her apron o'er her head,
(Which the intense eyes looked through) came at eve
160 On tiptoe, said a word, dropped in a loaf,
Her pair of earrings and a bunch of flowers
(The brute took growling), prayed, and so was gone.
I painted all, then cried " 'Tis ask and have;
"Choose, for more's ready!"—laid the ladder flat,
165 And showed my covered bit of cloister-wall.
The monks closed in a circle and praised loud
Till checked, taught what to see and not to see,
Being simple bodies—"That's the very man!
"Look at the boy who stoops to pat the dog!
170 "That woman's like the Prior's niece who comes
"To care about his asthma: it's the life!"
But there my triumph's straw-fire flared and funked;⁴
Their betters took their turn to see and say:
The Prior and the learned pulled a face
175 And stopped all that in no time. "How? what's here?
"Quite from the mark of painting, bless us all!
"Faces, arms, legs and bodies like the true
"As much as pea and pea! it's devil's-game!
"Your business is not to catch men with show,
180 "With homage to the perishable clay,
"But lift them over it, ignore it all,
"Make them forget there's such a thing as flesh.
"Your business is to paint the souls of men—
"Man's soul, and it's a fire, smoke . . . no, it's not . . .
185 "It's vapor done up like a new-born babe—
"(In that shape when you die it leaves your mouth)
"It's . . . well, what matters talking, it's the soul!
"Give us no more of body than shows soul!
"Here's Giotto,⁵ with his Saint a-praising God,

3. Making the sign of the cross with one hand,
because of the image of Christ on the altar.
4. Expired in smoke.

5. The great Florentine painter Giotto di Bondone
(1267–1337).

190   "That sets us praising—why not stop with him?
      "Why put all thoughts of praise out of our head
      "With wonder at lines, colors, and what not?
      "Paint the soul, never mind the legs and arms!
      "Rub all out, try at it a second time.
195   "Oh, that white smallish female with the breasts,
      "She's just my niece . . . Herodias,[6] I would say—
      "Who went and danced and got men's heads cut off!
      "Have it all out!" Now, is this sense, I ask?
      A fine way to paint soul, by painting body
200   So ill, the eye can't stop there, must go further
      And can't fare worse! Thus, yellow does for white
      When what you put for yellow's simply black,
      And any sort of meaning looks intense
      When all beside itself means and looks nought.
205   Why can't a painter lift each foot in turn,
      Left foot and right foot, go a double step,
      Make his flesh liker and his soul more like,
      Both in their order? Take the prettiest face,
      The Prior's niece . . . patron-saint—is it so pretty
210   You can't discover if it means hope, fear,
      Sorrow or joy? won't beauty go with these?
      Suppose I've made her eyes all right and blue,
      Can't I take breath and try to add life's flash,
      And then add soul and heighten them threefold?
215   Or say there's beauty with no soul at all—
      (I never saw it—put the case the same—)
      If you get simple beauty and nought else,
      You get about the best thing God invents:
      That's somewhat: and you'll find the soul you have missed,
220   Within yourself, when you return him thanks.
      "Rub all out!" Well, well, there's my life, in short,
      And so the thing has gone on ever since.
      I'm grown a man no doubt, I've broken bounds:
      You should not take a fellow eight years old
225   And make him swear to never kiss the girls.
      I'm my own master, paint now as I please—
      Having a friend, you see, in the Corner-house![7]
      Lord, it's fast holding by the rings in front—
      Those great rings serve more purposes than just
230   To plant a flag in, or tie up a horse!
      And yet the old schooling sticks, the old grave eyes
      Are peeping o'er my shoulder as I work,
      The heads shake still—"It's art's decline, my son!
      "You're not of the true painters, great and old;
235   "Brother Angelico's the man, you'll find;
      "Brother Lorenzo[8] stands his single peer:

6. Also called Salomé; her mother (whose name was Herodias as well), sister-in-law of the tetrarch Herod, had demanded that John the Baptist be imprisoned. When Salomé so pleased the king with her dancing that he promised her anything she asked, Herodias instructed her to ask for the head of John the Baptist on a platter (Matthew 14.1–12).
7. I.e., the Medici palace.
8. Fra Angelico (1387–1455) and Fra Lorenzo Monaco (1370–1425).

"Fag° on at flesh, you'll never make the third!"   toil
    Flower o' the pine,
    You keep your mistr . . . . manners, and I'll stick to mine!
240 I'm not the third, then: bless us, they must know!
     Don't you think they're the likeliest to know,
     They with their Latin? So, I swallow my rage,
     Clench my teeth, suck my lips in tight, and paint
     To please them—sometimes do and sometimes don't;
245 For, doing most, there's pretty sure to come
     A turn, some warm eve finds me at my saints—
     A laugh, a cry, the business of the world—
     (*Flower o' the peach,*
     Death for us all, and his own life for each!)
250 And my whole soul revolves, the cup runs over,
     The world and life's too big to pass for a dream,
     And I do these wild things in sheer despite,
     And play the fooleries you catch me at,
     In pure rage! The old mill-horse, out at grass
255 After hard years, throws up his stiff heels so,
     Although the miller does not preach to him
     The only good of grass is to make chaff.
     What would men have? Do they like grass or no—
     May they or mayn't they? all I want's the thing
260 Settled for ever one way. As it is,
     You tell too many lies and hurt yourself:
     You don't like what you only like too much,
     You do like what, if given you at your word,
     You find abundantly detestable.
265 For me, I think I speak as I was taught;
     I always see the garden and God there
     A-making man's wife: and, my lesson learned,
     The value and significance of flesh,
     I can't unlearn ten minutes afterwards.

270   You understand me: I'm a beast, I know.
     But see, now—why, I see as certainly
     As that the morning-star's about to shine,
     What will hap some day. We've a youngster here
     Comes to our convent, studies what do,
275 Slouches and stares and lets no atom drop:
     His name is Guidi—he'll not mind the monks—
     They call him Hulking Tom,[9] he lets them talk—
     He picks my practice up—he'll paint apace,
     I hope so—though I never live so long,
280 I know what's sure to follow. You be judge!
     You speak no Latin more than I, belike;
     However, you're my man, you've seen the world
     —The beauty and the wonder and the power,

9. The painter Tommaso Guidi (1401–1428), known as Masaccio (from *Tomasaccio,* meaning "Big Tom" or "Hulking Tom"). The series of frescoes that he painted in Santa Maria del Carmine, of key importance in the history of Florentine painting, was completed by Fra Lippo's son, Filippino Lippi, and it is in fact more likely that Fra Lippo learned from Masaccio than that he saw him as a promising newcomer.

The shapes of things, their colors, lights and shades,
285   Changes, surprises—and God made it all!
—For what? Do you feel thankful, ay or no,
For this fair town's face, yonder river's line,
The mountain round it and the sky above,
Much more the figures of man, woman, child,
290   These are the frame to? What's it all about?
To be passed over, despised? or dwelt upon,
Wondered at? oh, this last of course!—you say.
But why not do as well as say, paint these
Just as they are, careless what comes of it?
295   God's works—paint anyone, and count it crime
To let a truth slip. Don't object, "His works
"Are here already; nature is complete:
"Suppose you reproduce her (which you can't)
"There's no advantage! you must beat her, then."
300   For, don't you mark? we're made so that we love
First when we see them painted, things we have passed
Perhaps a hundred times nor cared to see;
And so they are better, painted—better to us,
Which is the same thing. Art was given for that;
305   God uses us to help each other so,
Lending our minds out. Have you noticed, now,
Your cullion's° hanging face? A bit of chalk,   *rascal's*
And trust me but you should, though! How much more,
If I drew higher things with the same truth!
310   That were to take the Prior's pulpit-place,
Interpret God to all of you! Oh, oh,
It makes me mad to see what men shall do
And we in our graves! This world's no blot for us,
Nor blank; it means intensely, and means good:
315   To find its meaning is my meat and drink.
"Ay, but you don't so instigate to prayer!"
Strikes in the Prior: "when your meaning's plain
"It does not say to folk—remember matins,°   *morning prayers*
"Or, mind you fast next Friday!" Why, for this
320   What need of art at all? A skull and bones,
Two bits of stick nailed crosswise, or, what's best,
A bell to chime the hour with, does as well.
I painted a Saint Laurence six months since
At Prato,[1] splashed the fresco in fine style:
325   "How looks my painting, now the scaffold's down?"
I ask a brother: "Hugely," he returns—
"Already not one phiz° of your three slaves   *face*
"Who turn the Deacon off his toasted side,[2]
"But's scratched and prodded to our heart's content,
330   "The pious people have so eased their own
"With coming to say prayers there in a rage:
"We get on fast to see the bricks beneath.

---

1. Smaller town near Florence, where Fra Lippo painted some of his most important pictures.
2. Saint Lawrence was martyred by being roasted on a gridiron; according to legend, he urged his executioners to turn him over, saying that he was done on one side.

"Expect another job this time next year,
"For pity and religion grow i' the crowd—
335 "Your painting serves its purpose!" Hang the fools!

       —That is—you'll not mistake an idle word
Spoke in a huff by a poor monk, God wot,°   knows
Tasting the air this spicy night which turns
The unaccustomed head like Chianti wine!
340 Oh, the church knows! don't misreport me, now!
It's natural a poor monk out of bounds
Should have his apt word to excuse himself:
And hearken how I plot to make amends.
I have bethought me: I shall paint a piece
345 . . . There's for you! Give me six months, then go, see
Something in Sant' Ambrogio's!³ Bless the nuns!
They want a cast° o' my office.° I shall paint   sample / work
God in the midst, Madonna and her babe,
Ringed by a bowery flowery angel-brood,
350 Lilies and vestments and white faces, sweet
As puff on puff of grated orris-root⁴
When ladies crowd to Church at midsummer.
And then i' the front, of course a saint or two—
Saint John, because he saves the Florentines,⁵
355 Saint Ambrose, who puts down in black and white
The convent's friends and gives them a long day,
And Job, I must have him there past mistake,
The man of Uz (and Us without the z,
Painters who need his patience). Well, all these
360 Secured at their devotion, up shall come
Out of a corner when you least expect,
As one by a dark stair into a great light,
Music and talking, who but Lippo! I!
Mazed, motionless and moonstruck—I'm the man!
365 Back I shrink—what is this I see and hear?
I, caught up with my monk's-things by mistake,
My old serge gown and rope that goes all round,
I, in this presence, this pure company!
Where's a hole, where's a corner for escape?
370 Then steps a sweet angelic slip of a thing
Forward, puts out a soft palm—"Not so fast!"
—Addresses the celestial presence, "nay—
"He made you and devised you, after all,
"Though he's none of you! Could Saint John there draw—
375 "His camel-hair⁶ make up a painting-brush?
"We come to brother Lippo for all that,
"Iste perfecit opus!"⁷ So, all smile—

3. Fra Lippo painted the *Coronation of the Virgin*,
here described, for the high altar of Sant' Ambrogio
in 1447.
4. Talcumlike powder made from flower roots.
5. San Giovanni is the patron saint of Florence.
6. John the Baptist is often portrayed wearing
a rough robe of camel's hair, in accord with

Mark 1.6.
7. This man made the work! (Latin); possibly a ref-
erence to the commissioning of the painting. The
figure that Browning took to be that of the painter
may be that of the patron, the Very Reverend Fran-
cesco Marenghi, who ordered the painting in
1441.

I shuffle sideways with my blushing face
Under the cover of a hundred wings
380   Thrown like a spread of kirtles[8] when you're gay°   *cheerful*
And play hot cockles,[9] all the doors being shut,
Till, wholly unexpected, in there pops
The hothead husband! Thus I scuttle off
To some safe bench behind, not letting go
385   The palm of her, the little lily thing
That spoke the good word for me in the nick,
Like the Prior's niece . . . Saint Lucy, I would say.
And so all's saved for me, and for the church
A pretty picture gained. Go, six months hence!
390   Your hand, sir, and good-bye: no lights, no lights!
The street's hushed, and I know my own way back,
Don't fear me! there's the gray beginning. Zooks!

ca. 1853   1855

Andrea del Sarto[1]

Called "The Faultless Painter"

But do not let us quarrel any more,
No, my Lucrezia; bear with me for once:
Sit down and all shall happen as you wish.
You turn your face, but does it bring your heart?
5   I'll work then for your friend's friend, never fear,
Treat his own subject after his own way,
Fix his own time, accept too his own price,
And shut the money into this small hand
When next it takes mine. Will it? tenderly?
10   Oh, I'll content him—but tomorrow, Love!
I often am much wearier than you think,
This evening more than usual, and it seems
As if—forgive now—should you let me sit
Here by the window with your hand in mine
15   And look a half-hour forth on Fiesole,[2]
Both of one mind, as married people use,
Quietly, quietly the evening through
I might get up tomorrow to my work
Cheerful and fresh as ever. Let us try.
20   Tomorrow, how you shall be glad for this!
Your soft hand is a woman of itself,

---

8. Women's gowns or skirts.
9. A game in which a blindfolded player must guess who has struck him or her.
1. The Florentine painter Andrea del Sarto (1486–1530) spent his entire life in Florence except for a year's sojourn at the court of the French king, Francis I, at Fontainebleau, 1518–19. He had been married since 1517 to Lucrezia del Fede, a widow, and in response to her pleading he left Fontainebleau, with the understanding that he would soon return to complete work for which

he had been paid. But he did not return, and he spent money that the king had given him to purchase works of art in Italy on a house in Florence for him and Lucrezia. These and other facts Browning derived from Giorgio Vasari's *Lives of the Most Eminent Painters, Sculptors, and Architects.* But the poem also depends on Browning's own response to Andrea's art.
2. A small town on the crown of a hill above Florence.

And mine the man's bared breast she curls inside.
Don't count the time lost, neither; you must serve
For each of the five pictures we require:
25   It saves a model. So! keep looking so—
My serpenting beauty, rounds on rounds![3]
—How could you ever prick those perfect ears,
Even to put the pearl there! oh, so sweet—
My face, my moon, my everybody's moon,
30   Which everybody looks on and calls his,
And, I suppose, is looked on by in turn,
While she looks—no one's: very dear, no less.[4]
You smile? why, there's my picture ready made,
There's what we painters call our harmony!
35   A common grayness silvers everything,
All in a twilight, you and I alike
—You, at the point of your first pride in me
(That's gone you know)—but I, at every point;
My youth, my hope, my art, being all toned down
40   To yonder sober pleasant Fiesole.
There's the bell clinking from the chapel-top;
That length of convent-wall across the way
Holds the trees safer, huddled more inside;
The last monk leaves the garden; days decrease,
45   And autumn grows, autumn in everything.
Eh? the whole seems to fall into a shape
As if I saw alike my work and self
And all that I was born to be and do,
A twilight-piece. Love, we are in God's hand.
50   How strange now, looks the life he makes us lead;
So free we seem, so fettered fast we are!
I feel he laid the fetter: let it lie!
This chamber for example—turn your head—
All that's behind us! You don't understand
55   Nor care to understand about my art,
But you can hear at least when people speak:
And that cartoon,[5] the second from the door
—It is the thing, Love! so such things should be—
Behold Madonna! I am bold to say.
60   I can do with my pencil what I know,
What I see, what at bottom of my heart
I wish for, if I ever wish so deep—
Do easily, too—when I say, perfectly,
I do not boast, perhaps: yourself are judge,
65   Who listened to the Legate's[6] talk last week,
And just as much they used to say in France.
At any rate 'tis easy, all of it!
No sketches first, no studies, that's long past:
I do what many dream of, all their lives,

3. Coils of hair like a serpent's coils.
4. Her affections are focused on no one person, not even on her husband, yet she is very dear to him.

5. A preparatory drawing, on heavy paper, of the same size as the painting to be executed from it in oil or fresco.
6. The pope's representative's.

70   —Dream? strive to do, and agonize to do,
      And fail in doing. I could count twenty such
      On twice your fingers, and not leave this town,
      Who strive—you don't know how the others strive
      To paint a little thing like that you smeared
75   Carelessly passing with your robes afloat—
      Yet do much less, so much less, Someone says,
      (I know his name, no matter)—so much less!
      Well, less is more, Lucrezia: I am judged.
      There burns a truer light of God in them,
80   In their vexed beating stuffed and stopped-up brain,
      Heart, or whate'er else, than goes on to prompt
      This low-pulsed forthright craftsman's hand of mine.
      Their works drop groundward, but themselves, I know,
      Reach many a time a heaven that's shut to me,
85   Enter and take their place there sure enough,
      Though they come back and cannot tell the world.
      My works are nearer heaven, but I sit here.
      The sudden blood of these men! at a word—
      Praise them, it boils, or blame them, it boils too.
90   I, painting from myself and to myself,
      Know what I do, am unmoved by men's blame
      Or their praise either. Somebody remarks
      Morello's[7] outline there is wrongly traced,
      His hue mistaken; what of that? or else,
95   Rightly traced and well ordered; what of that?
      Speak as they please, what does the mountain care?
      Ah, but a man's reach should exceed his grasp,
      Or what's a heaven for? All is silver-gray
      Placid and perfect with my art: the worse!
100   I know both what I want and what might gain,
      And yet how profitless to know, to sigh
      "Had I been two, another and myself,
      Our head would have o'erlooked the world!" No doubt.
      Yonder's a work now, of that famous youth
105   The Urbinate[8] who died five years ago.
      ('Tis copied, George Vasari[9] sent it me.)
      Well, I can fancy how he did it all,
      Pouring his soul, with kings and popes to see,
      Reaching, that heaven might so replenish him,
110   Above and through his art—for it gives way;
      That arm is wrongly put—and there again—
      A fault to pardon in the drawing's lines,
      Its body, so to speak: its soul is right,
      He means right—that, a child may understand.
115   Still, what an arm! and I could alter it:
      But all the play, the insight and the stretch—
      Out of me, out of me! And wherefore out?
      Had you enjoined them on me, given me soul,
      We might have risen to Rafael, I and you!

---

7. Monte Morello is a mountain lying a little to the northwest of Florence in the Apennines.
8. The painter Raphael (1483–1520), so called

because he was born at Urbino.
9. Giorgio Vasari, the biographer, was a painter and an architect and had been Andrea's pupil.

120   Nay, Love, you did give all I asked, I think—
     More than I merit, yes, by many times.
     But had you—oh, with the same perfect brow,
     And perfect eyes, and more than perfect mouth,
     And the low voice my soul hears, as a bird
125   The fowler's° pipe, and follows to the snare—   *bird-catcher's*
     Had you, with these the same, but brought a mind!
     Some women do so. Had the mouth there urged
     "God and the glory! never care for gain.
     The present by the future, what is that?
130   Live for fame, side by side with Agnolo![1]
     "Rafael is waiting: up to God, all three!"
     I might have done it for you. So it seems:
     Perhaps not. All is as God over-rules.
     Beside, incentives come from the soul's self;
135   The rest avail not. Why do I need you?
     What wife had Rafael, or has Agnolo?
     In this world, who can do a thing, will not;
     And who would do it, cannot, I perceive:
     Yet the will's somewhat—somewhat, too, the power—
140   And thus we half-men struggle. At the end,
     God, I conclude, compensates, punishes.
     'Tis safer for me, if the award be strict,
     That I am something underrated here,
     Poor this long while, despised, to speak the truth.
145   I dared not, do you know, leave home all day,
     For fear of chancing on the Paris lords.
     The best is when they pass and look aside;
     But they speak sometimes; I must bear it all.
     Well may they speak! That Francis, that first time,
150   And that long festal year at Fontainebleau![2]
     I surely then could sometimes leave the ground,
     Put on the glory, Rafael's daily wear,
     In that humane great monarch's golden look—
     One finger in his beard or twisted curl
155   Over his mouth's good mark that made the smile,
     One arm about my shoulder, round my neck,
     The jingle of his gold chain in my ear,
     I painting proudly with his breath on me,
     All his court round him, seeing with his eyes,
160   Such frank French eyes, and such a fire of souls
     Profuse, my hand kept plying by those hearts—
     And, best of all, this, this, this face beyond,
     This in the background, waiting on my work,
     To crown the issue with a last reward!
165   A good time, was it not, my kingly days?
     And had you not grown restless . . . but I know—
     'Tis done and past; 'twas right, my instinct said;
     Too live the life grew, golden and not gray,
     And I'm the weak-eyed bat no sun should tempt

1. I.e., Michelangelo (1475–1564).
2. The village southwest of Paris where Francis I built the royal palace.

170   Out of the grange° whose four walls make his world.   *country house*
How could it end in any other way?
You called me, and I came home to your heart.
The triumph was—to reach and stay there; since
I reached it ere the triumph, what is lost?
175   Let my hands frame your face in your hair's gold,
You beautiful Lucrezia that are mine!
"Rafael did this, Andrea painted that;
"The Roman's[3] is the better when you pray,
"But still the other's Virgin was his wife—"
180   Men will excuse me. I am glad to judge
Both pictures in your presence; clearer grows
My better fortune, I resolve to think.
For, do you know, Lucrezia, as God lives,
Said one day Agnolo, his very self,
185   To Rafael . . . I have known it all these years . . .
(When the young man was flaming out his thoughts
Upon a palace-wall for Rome to see,
Too lifted up in heart because of it)
"Friend, there's a certain sorry little scrub
190   Goes up and down our Florence, none cares how,
Who, were he set to plan and execute
As you are, pricked on by your popes and kings,
Would bring the sweat into that brow of yours!"
To Rafael's! And indeed the arm is wrong.
195   I hardly dare . . . yet, only you to see,
Give the chalk here—quick, thus the line should go!
Ay, but the soul! he's Rafael! rub it out!
Still, all I care for, if he spoke the truth,
(What he? why, who but Michel Agnolo?
200   Do you forget already words like those?)
If really there was such a chance, so lost,
Is, whether you're—not grateful—but more pleased.
Well, let me think so. And you smile indeed!
This hour has been an hour! Another smile?
205   If you would sit thus by me every night
I should work better, do you comprehend?
I mean that I should earn more, give you more.
See, it is settled dusk now; there's a star;
Morello's gone, the watch-lights show the wall,
210   The cue-owls[4] speak the name we call them by.
Come from the window, love—come in, at last,
Inside the melancholy little house
We built to be so gay with. God is just.
King Francis may forgive me: oft at nights
215   When I look up from painting, eyes tired out,
The walls become illumined, brick from brick
Distinct, instead of mortar, fierce bright gold,
That gold of his I did cement them with!
Let us but love each other. Must you go?
220   That Cousin here again? he waits outside?

3. Refers to Raphael, who worked in Rome for the last twelve years of his life.   4. A Mediterranean owl whose name derives from its cry, *ki-ou.*

Must see you—you, and not with me? Those loans?
More gaming debts to pay? you smiled for that?
Well, let smiles buy me! have you more to spend?
While hand and eye and something of a heart
225   Are left me, work's my ware, and what's it worth?
I'll pay my fancy. Only let me sit
The gray remainder of the evening out,
Idle, you call it, and muse perfectly
How I could paint, were I but back in France,
230   One picture, just one more—the Virgin's face,
Not yours this time! I want you at my side
To hear them—that is, Michel Agnolo—
Judge all I do and tell you of its worth.
Will you? Tomorrow, satisfy your friend.
235   I take the subjects for his corridor,
Finish the portrait out of hand—there, there,
And throw him in another thing or two
If he demurs; the whole should prove enough
To pay for this same Cousin's freak. Beside,
240   What's better and what's all I care about,
Get you the thirteen scudi[5] for the ruff!
Love, does that please you? Ah, but what does he,
The Cousin! what does he to please you more?

     I am grown peaceful as old age tonight.
245   I regret little, I would change still less.
Since there my past life lies, why alter it?
The very wrong to Francis! it is true
I took his coin, was tempted and complied,
And built this house and sinned, and all is said.
250   My father and my mother died of want.
Well, had I riches of my own? you see
How one gets rich! Let each one bear his lot.
They were born poor, lived poor, and poor they died:
And I have labored somewhat in my time
255   And not been paid profusely. Some good son
Paint my two hundred pictures—let him try!
No doubt, there's something strikes a balance. Yes,
You loved me quite enough, it seems tonight.
This must suffice me here. What would one have?
260   In heaven, perhaps, new chances, one more chance—
Four great walls in the New Jerusalem,[6]
Meted on each side by the angel's reed,
For Leonard,[7] Rafael, Agnolo and me
To cover—the three first without a wife,
265   While I have mine! So—still they overcome
Because there's still Lucrezia—as I choose.

     Again the Cousin's whistle! Go, my Love.

ca. 1853   1855

5. Shields (Italian); silver coins bearing a shield.   7. I.e., Leonardo da Vinci (1452–1519).
6. Cf. Revelation 21.10–21.

Two in the Campagna[8]

1

I wonder do you feel today
    As I have felt since, hand in hand,
We sat down on the grass, to stray
    In spirit better through the land,
5 This morn of Rome and May?

2

For me, I touched a thought, I know,
    Has tantalized me many times,
(Like turns of thread the spiders throw
    Mocking across our path) for rhymes
10 To catch at and let go.

3

Help me to hold it! First it left
    The yellowing fennel,[9] run to seed
There, branching from the brickwork's cleft,
    Some old tomb's ruin: yonder weed
15 Took up the floating weft,°   *spider web*

4

Where one small orange cup amassed
    Five beetles—blind and green they grope
Among the honey-meal: and last,
    Everywhere on the grassy slope
20 I traced it. Hold it fast!

5

The champaign[1] with its endless fleece
    Of feathery grasses everywhere!
Silence and passion, joy and peace,
    An everlasting wash of air—
25 Rome's ghost since her decease.

6

Such life here, through such lengths of hours,
    Such miracles performed in play,
Such primal naked forms of flowers,
    Such letting nature have her way
30 While heaven looks from its towers!

7

How say you? Let us, O my dove,
    Let us be unashamed of soul,

8. The grassy, rolling countryside around Rome.
9. A yellow-flowered plant, whose aromatic seeds
are used as a condiment.
1. I.e., grassland—here, the Campagna.

As earth lies bare to heaven above!
   How is it under our control
35 To love or not to love?

8

I would that you were all to me,
   You that are just so much, no more.
Nor yours nor mine, nor slave nor free!
   Where does the fault lie? What the core
40 O' the wound, since wound must be?

9

I would I could adopt your will,
   See with your eyes, and set my heart
Beating by yours, and drink my fill
   At your soul's springs—your part my part
45 In life, for good and ill.

10

No. I yearn upward, touch you close,
   Then stand away. I kiss your cheek,
Catch your soul's warmth—I pluck the rose
   And love it more than tongue can speak—
50 Then the good minute goes.

11

Already how am I so far
   Out of that minute? Must I go
Still like the thistle-ball, no bar,
   Onward, whenever light winds blow,
55 Fixed by no friendly star?

12

Just when I seemed about to learn!
   Where is the thread now? Off again!
The old trick! Only I discern—
   Infinite passion, and the pain
60 Of finite hearts that yearn.

1854   1855

EDWARD LEAR

1812–1888

There Was an Old Man with a Beard

There was an Old Man with a beard,
Who said, "It is just as I feared!—

Two Owls and a Hen, four Larks and a Wren,
Have all built their nests in my beard!"

1846

There Was an Old Man In a Tree

There was an Old Man in a tree,
Who was horribly bored by a Bee;
When they said, "Does it buzz?" he replied, "Yes, it does!"
"It's a regular brute of a Bee!"

1846

There Was an Old Man Who Supposed

There was an Old Man who supposed,
That the street door was partially closed;
But some very large rats, ate his coats and his hats,
While that futile old gentleman dozed.

1846

The Owl and the Pussy-Cat

1

The Owl and the Pussy-cat went to sea
    In a beautiful pea-green boat,
They took some honey, and plenty of money,
    Wrapped up in a five-pound note.
5   The Owl looked up to the stars above,
        And sang to a small guitar,
"O lovely Pussy! O Pussy, my love,
    What a beautiful Pussy you are,
            You are,
10   You are!
    What a beautiful Pussy you are!"

2

Pussy said to the Owl, "You elegant fowl!
    How charmingly sweet you sing!
O let us be married! too long we have tarried:
15   But what shall we do for a ring?"
They sailed away, for a year and a day,
    To the land where the Bong-tree grows
And there in a wood a Piggy-wig stood
    With a ring at the end of his nose,

20   His nose,
          His nose,
    With a ring at the end of his nose.

                          3
    "Dear Pig, are you willing to sell for one shilling
      Your ring?" Said the Piggy, "I will."
25 So they took it away, and were married next day
      By the Turkey who lives on the hill.
    They dined on mince, and slices of quince,
      Which they ate with a runcible spoon;[1]
    And hand in hand, on the edge of the sand,
30   They danced by the light of the moon,
          The moon,
          The moon,
    They danced by the light of the moon.

                                        1871

How Pleasant to Know Mr. Lear

    How pleasant to know Mr. Lear!
      Who has written such volumes of stuff!
    Some think him ill-tempered and queer,
      But a few think him pleasant enough.

5   His mind is concrete and fastidious,
      His nose is remarkably big;
    His visage is more or less hideous,
      His beard it resembles a wig.

    He has ears, and two eyes, and ten fingers,
10   Leastways if you reckon two thumbs;
    Long ago he was one of the singers,
      But now he is one of the dumbs.

    He sits in a beautiful parlor,
      With hundreds of books on the wall;
15 He drinks a great deal of Marsala,[2]
      But never gets tipsy at all.

    He has many friends, laymen and clerical;
      Old Foss is the name of his cat;
    His body is perfectly spherical,
20   He weareth a runcible hat.[3]

---

1. Fork with three broad, curved prongs and sharpened edge. Lear coined the word "runcible" and used it often in his nonsense verse.

2. A dark, sweet Spanish wine.
3. On "runcible," see note 1 above.

When he walks in a waterproof° white,   *raincoat*
   The children run after him so!
Calling out, "He's come out in his night-
   Gown, that crazy old Englishman, oh!"

25 He weeps by the side of the ocean,
   He weeps on the top of the hill;
He purchases pancakes and lotion,
   And chocolate shrimps from the mill.

He reads but he cannot speak Spanish,
30   He cannot abide ginger-beer:
Ere the days of his pilgrimage vanish,
   How pleasant to know Mr. Lear!

                                       1871

JONES VERY
1813–1880

The Dead[1]

I see them crowd on crowd they walk the earth
Dry, leafless trees no Autumn wind laid bare;
And in their nakedness find cause for mirth,
And all unclad would winter's rudeness° dare;   *harshness*
5 No sap doth through their clattering branches flow,
Whence springing leaves and blossoms bright appear;
Their hearts the living God have ceased to know,
Who gives the spring time to th' expectant year;
They mimic life, as if from him to steal
10 His glow of health to paint the livid° cheek;   *pale*
They borrow words for thoughts they cannot feel,
That with a seeming heart their tongue may speak;
And in their show of life more dead they live
Than those that to the earth with many tears they give.

1838   1839

The Lost

The fairest day that ever yet has shone,
   Will be when thou the day within shalt see;
The fairest rose that ever yet has blown,

1. In September 1838, Very, a tutor of Greek at Harvard, had a mystical experience; he told his students that the Holy Spirit was speaking through him and that the end of the world was at hand. His employment at Harvard was terminated, and he was sent briefly to an asylum, though many considered him sane. Both of these poems date from his visionary period.

When thou the flower thou lookest on shalt be.
5   But thou art far away among Time's toys;
Thyself the day thou lookest for in them,
Thyself the flower that now thine eye enjoys,
But wilted now thou hang'st upon thy stem.
The bird thou hearest on the budding tree,
10 Thou hast made sing with thy forgotten voice;
But when it swells again to melody,
The song is thine in which thou wilt rejoice;
And thou new risen 'midst these wonders live,
That now to them dost all thy substance give.

1838–40   1883

HENRY DAVID THOREAU
1817–1862

I Am a Parcel of Vain Strivings Tied

I am a parcel of vain strivings tied
        By a chance bond together,
    Dangling this way and that, their links
        Were made so loose and wide,
5   Methinks,
            For milder weather.

A bunch of violets without their roots,
        And sorrel intermixed,
    Encircled by a wisp of straw
10   Once coiled about their shoots,
            The law
        By which I'm fixed.

A nosegay which Time clutched from out
        Those fair Elysian fields,[1]
15 With weeds and broken stems, in haste,
        Doth make the rabble rout
            That waste
        The day he yields.

And here I bloom for a short hour unseen,
20   Drinking my juices up,
    With no root in the land
        To keep my branches green,
            But stand
        In a bare cup.

                                                          1841

---

1. In Greek and Roman mythology, the home of the blessed in the afterlife.

Smoke

Light-winged Smoke, Icarian bird,[2]
Melting thy pinions in thy upward flight;
Lark without song, and messenger of dawn,
Circling above the hamlets as thy nest;
5   Or else, departing dream, and shadowy form
Of midnight vision, gathering up thy skirts;
By night star-veiling, and by day
Darkening the light and blotting out the sun;
Go thou my incense upward from this hearth,
10 And ask the gods to pardon this clear flame.

1843, 1854

EMILY BRONTË
1818–1848

[Long Neglect Has Worn Away]

Long neglect has worn away
Half the sweet enchanting smile;
Time has turned the bloom to gray;
Mold and damp the face defile.

5   But that lock of silky hair,
Still beneath the picture twined,
Tells what once those features were,
Paints their image on the mind.

Fair the hand that traced that line,
10 "Dearest, ever deem me true";
Swiftly flew the fingers fine
When the pen that motto drew.

1837   1923

Hope

Hope was but a timid friend—
She sat without° my grated den   *outside*
Watching how my fate would tend
Even as selfish-hearted men.

---

2. According to Greek mythology, Icarus and his father, Daedalus, escaped from Crete by flying with wings of wax and feathers. When Icarus flew too near the sun, his wings melted.

5 She was cruel in her fear.
Through the bars, one dreary day,
I looked out to see her there
And she turned her face away!

Like a false guard false watch keeping
10 Still in strife she whispered peace;
She would sing while I was weeping,
If I listened, she would cease.

False she was, and unrelenting.
When my last joys strewed the ground
15 Even Sorrow saw repenting
Those sad relics scattered round;

Hope—whose whisper would have given
Balm to all that frenzied pain—
Stretched her wings and soared to heaven;
20 Went—and ne'er returned again!

1843   1843

Remembrance[1]

Cold in the earth—and the deep snow piled above thee,
Far, far removed, cold in the dreary grave!
Have I forgot, my only Love, to love thee,
Severed at last by Time's all-severing wave?

5 Now, when alone, do my thoughts no longer hover
Over the mountains, on that northern shore,
Resting their wings where heath and fern leaves cover
Thy noble heart forever, ever more?

Cold in the earth—and fifteen wild Decembers,
10 From those brown hills, have melted into spring;
Faithful, indeed, is the spirit that remembers
After such years of change and suffering!

Sweet Love of youth, forgive, if I forget thee,
While the world's tide is bearing me along;
15 Other desires and other hopes beset me,
Hopes which obscure, but cannot do thee wrong!

No later light has lightened up my heaven,
No second morn has ever shone for me;

1. One of the Gondal poems. As children, Emily and Anne Brontë had written poems and stories about the inhabitants of Gondal, an imaginary island in the North Pacific, and Emily, at least, continued to write Gondal poems throughout her life.

All my life's bliss from thy dear life was given,
20   All my life's bliss is in the grave with thee.

But, when the days of golden dreams had perished,
And even Despair was powerless to destroy,
Then did I learn how existence could be cherished,
Strengthened, and fed without the aid of joy.

25   Then did I check the tears of useless passion—
Weaned my young soul from yearning after thine;
Sternly denied its burning wish to hasten
Down to that tomb already more than mine.

And, even yet, I dare not let it languish,
30   Dare not indulge in memory's rapturous pain;
Once drinking deep of that divinest anguish,
How could I seek the empty world again?

1845   1846

The Prisoner. A Fragment[2]

In the dungeon-crypts, idly did I stray,
Reckless of the lives wasting there away;
"Draw the ponderous bars! open, Warder stern!"
He dared not say me nay—the hinges harshly turn.

5   "Our guests are darkly lodged," I whisper'd, gazing through
The vault, whose grated eye showed heaven more gray than blue;
(This was when glad spring laughed in awaking pride;)
"Aye, darkly lodged enough!" returned my sullen guide.

Then, God forgive my youth; forgive my careless tongue;
10   I scoffed, as the chill chains on the damp flag-stones rung:
"Confined in triple walls, art thou so much to fear,
That we must bind thee down and clench thy fetters here?"

The captive raised her face, it was as soft and mild
As sculptured marble saint, or slumbering unwean'd child;
15   It was so soft and mild, it was so sweet and fair,
Pain could not trace a line, nor grief a shadow there!

The captive raised her hand and pressed it to her brow;
"I have been struck," she said, "and I am suffering now;
Yet these are little worth, your bolts and irons strong,
20   And, were they forged in steel, they could not hold me long."

---

2. Taken from a poem in the Brontë sisters' Gondal manuscript (see note 1 above), *Julian M. and A.G. Rochelle*, this excerpt describes an episode not found in the story. The speaker is visiting a dungeon in his father's castle.

Hoarse laughed the jailor grim: "Shall I be won to hear;
Dost think, fond, dreaming wretch, that *I* shall grant thy prayer?
Or, better still, wilt melt my master's heart with groans?
Ah! sooner might the sun thaw down these granite stones.

25 "My master's voice is low, his aspect bland and kind,
But hard as hardest flint, the soul that lurks behind;
And I am rough and rude, yet not more rough to see
Than is the hidden ghost that has its home in me."

About her lips there played a smile of almost scorn,
30 "My friend," she gently said, "you have not heard me mourn;
When you my kindred's lives, *my* lost life, can restore,
Then may I weep and sue,—but never, friend, before!

Still, let my tyrants know, I am not doomed to wear
Year after year in gloom, and desolate despair;
35 A messenger of Hope, comes every night to me,
And offers for short life, eternal liberty.

He comes with western winds, with evening's wandering airs,
With that clear dusk of heaven that brings the thickest stars.
Winds take a pensive tone, and stars a tender fire,
40 And visions rise, and change, that kill me with desire.

Desire for nothing known in my maturer years,
When Joy grew mad with awe, at counting future tears.
When, if my spirit's sky was full of flashes warm,
I knew not whence they came, from sun, or thunder storm.

45 But, first, a hush of peace—a soundless calm descends;
The struggle of distress, and fierce impatience ends.
Mute music soothes my breast, unuttered harmony,
That I could never dream, till Earth was lost to me.

Then dawns the Invisible; the Unseen its truth reveals;
50 My outward sense is gone, my inward essence feels:
Its wings are almost free—its home, its harbor found,
Measuring the gulph, it stoops, and dares the final bound.

Oh, dreadful is the check—intense the agony—
When the ear begins to hear, and the eye begins to see;
55 When the pulse begins to throb, the brain to think again,
The soul to feel the flesh, and the flesh to feel the chain.

Yet I would lose no sting, would wish no torture less,
The more that anguish racks, the earlier it will bless;
And robed in fires of hell, or bright with heavenly shine,
60 If it but herald death, the vision is divine!"[3]

---

3. Cf. the dying words of Catherine in Emily's
Wuthering Heights (1847): "The thing that irks me
most is this shattered prison [my body]. . . . I'm
tired, tired of being enclosed here. I'm wearying to
escape into that glorious world, and to be always
there. . . . I shall be incomparably beyond and
above you all."

She ceased to speak, and we, unanswering, turned to go—
We had no further power to work the captive woe:
Her cheek, her gleaming eye, declared that man had given
A sentence, unapproved, and overruled by Heaven.

1845   1846

No Coward Soul Is Mine

No coward soul is mine,
No trembler in the world's storm-troubled sphere!
I see Heaven's glories shine,
And Faith shines equal, arming me from Fear.

5   O God within my breast,
Almighty ever-present Deity!
Life, that in me hast rest
As I, undying Life, have power in thee!

Vain are the thousand creeds
10 That move men's hearts, unutterably vain;
Worthless as withered weeds,
Or idlest froth, amid the boundless main

To waken doubt in one
Holding so fast by thy infinity,
15 So surely anchored on
The steadfast rock of Immortality.

With wide-embracing love
Thy spirit animates eternal years,
Pervades and broods above,
20 Changes, sustains, dissolves, creates and rears.

Though earth and moon were gone,
And suns and universes ceased to be,
And thou were left alone,
Every Existence would exist in thee.

25 There is not room for Death,
Nor atom that his might could render void
Since thou art Being and Breath,
And what thou art may never be destroyed.

1846   1850

ARTHUR HUGH CLOUGH
1819–1861

From Amours de Voyage

From *Canto I*

Over the great windy waters, and over the clear crested summits,
    Unto the sun and the sky, and unto the perfecter earth,
Come, let us go,—to a land wherein gods of the old time wandered,
    Where every breath even now changes to ether¹ divine.
5   *Come, let us go; though withal a voice whisper, "The world that we live in,*
    Whithersoever we turn, still is the same narrow crib;
'Tis but to prove limitation, and measure a cord, that we travel;
    Let who would 'scape and be free go to his chamber and think;
'Tis but to change idle fancies for memories wilfully falser;
10   *'Tis but to go and have been."—Come, little bark!°*   small boat
    let us go.

I. CLAUDE TO EUSTACE

Dear Eustatio, I write that you may write me an answer,
Or at the least to put us again en rapport² with each other.
Rome disappoints me much,—St. Peter's, perhaps, in especial;
Only the Arch of Titus and view from the Lateran please me:
15 This, however, perhaps, is the weather, which truly is horrid.
Greece must be better, surely; and yet I am feeling so spiteful,
That I could travel to Athens, to Delphi, and Troy, and Mount Sinai,
Though but to see with my eyes that these are vanity also.
    Rome disappoints me much; I hardly as yet understand, but
20 *Rubbishy* seems the word that most exactly would suit it.
All the foolish destructions, and all the sillier savings,
All the incongruous things of past incompatible ages,
Seem to be treasured up here to make fools of present and future.
Would to Heaven the old Goths³ had made a cleaner sweep of it!
25 Would to Heaven some new ones would come and destroy these
    churches!
However, one can live in Rome as also in London.
Rome is better than London, because it is other than London.
It is a blessing, no doubt, to be rid, at least for a time, of
All one's friends and relations,—yourself (forgive me!) included,—
30 All the *assujettissement*⁴ of having been what one has been,
What one thinks one is, or thinks that others suppose one;
Yet, in despite of all, we turn like fools to the English.
Vernon has been my fate; who is here the same that you knew him,—
Making the tour, it seems, with friends of the name of Trevellyn.

---

1. The clear upper air, or a heavenly material not matter.
2. In sympathy (French).
3. One of the barbarian tribes that sacked ancient Rome.
4. Constraint (French).

II. CLAUDE TO EUSTACE

35   Rome disappoints me still; but I shrink and adapt myself to it.
    Somehow a tyrannous sense of a superincumbent° oppression   *overlying*
    Still, wherever I go, accompanies ever, and makes me
    Feel like a tree (shall I say?) buried under a ruin of brickwork.
    Rome, believe me, my friend, is like its own Monte Testaceo,
40   Merely a marvellous mass of broken and castaway wine-pots.
    Ye gods! what do I want with this rubbish of ages departed,
    Things that Nature abhors, the experiments that she has failed in?
    What do I find in the Forum? An archway and two or three pillars.
    Well, but St. Peter's? Alas, Bernini[5] has filled it with sculpture!
45   No one can cavil, I grant, at the size of the great Coliseum.
    Doubtless the notion of grand and capacious and massive amusement,
    This the old Romans had; but tell me, is this an idea?
    Yet of solidity much, but of splendor little is extant:
    "Brickwork I found thee, and marble I left thee!" their Emperor
        vaunted;
50   "Marble I thought thee, and brickwork I find thee!" the Tourist may
    answer.

III. GEORGINA TREVELLYN TO LOUISA

    At last, dearest Louisa, I take up my pen to address you.
    Here we are, you see, with the seven-and-seventy boxes,
    Courier, Papa and Mamma, the children, and Mary and Susan:
    Here we all are at Rome, and delighted of course with St. Peter's,
55   And very pleasantly lodged in the famous Piazza di Spagna.
    Rome is a wonderful place, but Mary shall tell you about it;
    Not very gay, however; the English are mostly at Naples;
    There are the A.s, we hear, and most of the W. party.
    George, however, is come; did I tell you about his mustachios?
60   Dear, I must really stop, for the carriage, they tell me, is waiting.
    Mary will finish; and Susan is writing, they say, to Sophia.
    Adieu, dearest Louise,—evermore your faithful Georgina.
    Who can a Mr. Claude be whom George has taken to be with?
    Very stupid, I think, but George says so *very* clever.

           *   *   *

1858

The Latest Decalogue[6]

    Thou shalt have one God only; who
    Would be at the expense of two?
    No graven images may be
    Worshipped, except the currency:

---

5. Giovanni Lorenzo Bernini (1598–1680), Italian sculptor.

6. The Latest Ten Commandments.

5   Swear not at all; for for thy curse
    Thine enemy is none the worse:
    At church on Sunday to attend
    Will serve to keep the world thy friend:
    Honor thy parents; that is, all
10 From whom advancement may befall:
    Thou shalt not kill; but needst not strive
    Officiously to keep alive:
    Do not adultery commit;
    Advantage rarely comes of it:
15 Thou shalt not steal; an empty feat,
    When it's so lucrative to cheat:
    Bear not false witness; let the lie
    Have time on its own wings to fly:
    Thou shalt not covet; but tradition
20 Approves all forms of competition.

    The sum of all is, thou shalt love,
    If any body, God above:
    At any rate shall never labor
    More than thyself to love thy neighbor.

1862

Say Not the Struggle Nought Availeth

Say not the struggle nought availeth,
    The labor and the wounds are vain,
The enemy faints not, nor faileth,
    And as things have been, things remain.

5   If hopes were dupes, fears may be liars;
    It may be, in yon smoke concealed,
Your comrades chase e'en now the fliers,
    And, but for you, possess the field.

For while the tired waves, vainly breaking,
10   Seem here no painful inch to gain,
Far back through creeks and inlets making
    Came, silent, flooding in, the main,°   sea

And not by eastern windows only,
    When daylight comes, comes in the light,
15 In front the sun climbs slow, how slowly,
    But westward, look, the land is bright.

1849   1862

JULIA WARD HOWE
1819–1910

Battle-Hymn of the Republic[1]

Mine eyes have seen the glory of the coming of the Lord:
He is trampling out the vintage where the grapes of wrath are stored;
He hath loosed the fateful lightning of his terrible swift sword:
    His truth is marching on.

5   I have seen Him in the watch-fires of a hundred circling camps;
They have builded Him an altar in the evening dews and damps;
I can read His righteous sentence by the dim and flaring lamps.
    His day is marching on.

I have read a fiery gospel, writ in burnished rows of steel:
10 "As ye deal with my contemners, so with you my grace shall deal;
Let the Hero, born of woman, crush the serpent with his heel,
    Since God is marching on."

He has sounded forth the trumpet that shall never call retreat;
He is sifting out the hearts of men before his judgment-seat:
15 Oh! be swift, my soul, to answer Him! be jubilant, my feet!
    Our God is marching on.

In the beauty of the lilies Christ was born across the sea,
With a glory in his bosom that transfigures you and me:
As he died to make men holy, let us die to make men free,
20   While God is marching on.

1861   1866

HERMAN MELVILLE
1819–1891

The Portent

Hanging from the beam,
    Slowly swaying (such the law),
Gaunt the shadow on your green,
    Shenandoah![1]
5   The cut is on the crown

---

1. When Howe saw Union troops camped along the roadside in Washington, D.C., she joined friends in singing the popular Civil War song that begins "John Brown's body lies a-mouldering in the grave." That night, she responded to someone's suggestion that she write new verses to the same tune. Howe here compares the reckoning that will come at the end of the war with the Day of Jehovah; see especially Isaiah 63.

1. Valley in northern Virginia; the scene of famous Civil War battles between 1862 and 1864.

(Lo, John Brown),[2]
And the stabs shall heal no more.

Hidden in the cap
  Is the anguish none can draw;
10 So your future veils its face,
    Shenandoah!
But the streaming beard is shown
  (Weird John Brown),
The meteor of the war.

1859   1866

Shiloh[3]

A Requiem (April 1862)

Skimming lightly, wheeling still,
  The swallows fly low
Over the field in clouded days,
  The forest-field of Shiloh—
5 Over the field where April rain
Solaced the parched one stretched in pain
  Through the pause of night
  That followed the Sunday fight
  Around the church of Shiloh—
10 The church so lone, the log-built one,
That echoed to many a parting groan
    And natural prayer
  Of dying foemen mingled there—
Foemen at morn, but friends at eve—
15   Fame or country least their care:
(What like a bullet can undeceive!)
    But now they lie low,
While over them the swallows skim,
  And all is hushed at Shiloh.

1866

The Maldive[4] Shark

About the Shark, phlegmatical one,
Pale sot° of the Maldive sea,   *drinker*
The sleek little pilot-fish, azure and slim,
How alert in attendance be.
5 From his saw-pit of mouth, from his charnel of maw,

2. American abolitionist (1800–1859), who was hanged for leading a raid on the United States armory at Harpers Ferry, West Virginia, near the Shenandoah Valley.
3. The battle at Shiloh Church, in Tennessee, on April 6 and 7, 1862, was one of the bloodiest of the Civil War; close to twenty-four thousand men died.
4. I.e., of the area around the Maldives, a group of islands in the Indian Ocean.

They have nothing of harm to dread,
But liquidly glide on his ghastly flank
Or before his Gorgonian[5] head;
Or lurk in the port of serrated teeth
10   In white triple tiers of glittering gates,
And there find a haven when peril's abroad,
An asylum in jaws of the Fates!

They are friends; and friendly they guide him to prey,
Yet never partake of the treat—
15   Eyes and brains to the dotard lethargic and dull,
Pale ravener of horrible meat.

                                                                        1888

The Berg

A Dream

I saw a Ship of martial build
(Her standards set, her brave apparel on)
Directed as by madness mere
Against a stolid iceberg steer,
5   Nor budge it, though the infatuate° Ship went down.   *foolish*
The impact made huge ice-cubes fall
Sullen, in tons that crashed the deck;
But that one avalanche was all—
No other movement save the foundering wreck.

10   Along the spurs of ridges pale,
Not any slenderest shaft and frail,
A prism over glass-green gorges lone,
Toppled; nor lace of traceries fine,
Nor pendant drops in grot or mine
15   Were jarred, when the stunned Ship went down.

Nor sole the gulls in cloud that wheeled
Circling one snow-flanked peak afar,
But nearer fowl the floes that skimmed
And crystal beaches, felt no jar.
20   No thrill transmitted stirred the lock
Of jack-straw needle-ice at base;
Towers undermined by waves—the block
Atilt impending—kept their place.
Seals, dozing sleek on sliddery ledges
25   Slipt never, when by loftier edges,
Through very inertia overthrown,
The impetuous ship in bafflement went down.

---

5. In Greek mythology, the Gorgons were three sisters with terrifying faces and serpent hair; whoever looked at them turned to stone.

Hard Berg (methought), so cold, so vast,
With mortal damps self-overcast;
30   Exhaling still thy dankish breath—
Adrift dissolving, bound for death;
Though lumpish thou, a lumbering one—
A lumbering lubbard loitering slow,
Impingers rue thee and go down,
35   Sounding thy precipice below,
Nor stir the slimy slug that sprawls
Along thy dead indifference of walls.[6]

1888

Monody[7]

To have known him, to have loved him
    After loneness long;
And then to be estranged in life,
    And neither in the wrong;
5   And now for death to set his seal—
    Ease me, a little ease, my song!

By wintry hills his hermit-mound
    The sheeted snow-drifts drape,
And houseless there the snow-bird flits
10   Beneath the fir-trees' crape:
Glazed now with ice the cloistral vine
    That hid the shyest grape.

1891

SPIRITUALS

Go Down, Moses[1]

Go down, Moses,
Way down in Egyptland
Tell old Pharaoh
To let my people go.

---

6. Manuscript version of Melville's final line. In his first published edition of the poem, the final line reads "Along thy dense stolidity of walls."
7. Lament; originally, a Greek ode sung by a single voice, as in a tragedy. Some critics have surmised that Melville may have been writing about a cooled friendship with the American writer Nathaniel Hawthorne (1804–1864).

1. Hebrew lawgiver; according to the Hebrew Scriptures, he led his people out of bondage in Egypt to the edge of Canaan. Cf. Exodus 5: "Afterward Moses . . . went to Pharaoh and said, 'Thus says the Lord, the God of Israel, "Let my people go, that they may hold a feast to me in the wilderness." '"

5   When Israel was in Egyptland
Let my people go
Oppressed so hard they could not stand
Let my people go.

Go down, Moses,
10   Way down in Egyptland
Tell old Pharaoh
"Let my people go."

"Thus saith the Lord," bold Moses said,
"Let my people go;
15   If not I'll smite your first-born dead[2]
Let my people go.

"No more shall they in bondage toil,
Let my people go;
Let them come out with Egypt's spoil,
20   Let my people go."

The Lord told Moses what to do
Let my people go;
To lead the children of Israel through,
Let my people go.

25   Go down, Moses,
Way down in Egyptland,
Tell old Pharaoh,
"Let my people go!"

Steal Away to Jesus

Steal away, steal away, steal away to Jesus,
Steal away, steal away home,
I ain't got long to stay here.

My Lord, He calls me,
5   He calls me by the thunder,
The trumpet sounds within-a my soul,
I ain't got long to stay here.

Steal away, steal away, steal away to Jesus,
Steal away, steal away home,
10   I ain't got long to stay here.

Green trees a-bending,
Po' sinner stands a-trembling,

---

2. After Pharaoh refused to free the Israelites, God sent a series of miracles, plagues, and punishments. Cf. Exodus 11: "And Moses said, 'Thus says the Lord: About midnight I will go forth in the midst of Egypt; and all the first-born in the land of Egypt shall die.' "

The trumpet sounds within-a my soul,
I ain't got long to stay here.

15   Steal away, steal away, steal away to Jesus,
Steal away, steal away home,
I ain't got long to stay here.

Ezekiel Saw the Wheel[3]

Ezek'el saw the wheel
'Way up in the middle o' the air,
Ezek'el saw the wheel
'Way up in the middle o' the air.

5   The big wheel moved by Faith,
The little wheel moved by the Grace of God,
A wheel in a wheel,
'Way up in the middle o' the air.

Jes' let me tell you what a hypocrite'll do,
10   'Way up in the middle o' the air,
He'll talk about me an' he'll talk about you!
'Way up in the middle o' the air.

Ezek'el saw the wheel
'Way up in the middle o' the air,
15   Ezek'el saw the wheel
'Way up in the middle o' the air.

The big wheel moved by Faith,
The little wheel moved by the Grace of God,
A wheel in a wheel,
20   'Way up in the middle o' the air.

Watch out my sister how you walk on the cross,
'Way up in the middle o' the air,
Your foot might slip and your soul get lost!
'Way up in the middle o' the air.

25   Ezek'el saw the wheel
'Way up in the middle o' the air,
Ezek'el saw the wheel
'Way up in the middle o' the air.

3. Hebrew Scripture prophecy. Cf. Ezekiel 15: "Now as I looked at the living creatures, I saw a wheel upon the earth beside the living creatures, one for each of the four of them . . . their construction being as it were a wheel within a wheel. . . . And when the living creatures went, the wheels went beside them; and when the living creatures rose from the earth, the wheels rose. Wherever the spirit would go, they went, and the wheels rose along with them; for the spirit of the living creatures was in the wheels."

The big wheel moved by Faith,
30 The little wheel moved by the Grace of God,
A wheel in a wheel,
'Way up in the middle o' the air.

You say the Lord has set you free,
'Way up in the middle o' the air,
35 Why don't you let your neighbors be!
'Way up in the middle o' the air.

Ezek'el saw the wheel
'Way up in the middle o' the air,
Ezek'el saw the wheel
40 'Way up in the middle o' the air.

The big wheel moved by Faith,
The little wheel moved by the Grace of God,
A wheel in a wheel,
'Way up in the middle o' the air.

WALT WHITMAN
1819–1892

From Song of Myself[1]

1

I celebrate myself, and sing myself,
And what I assume you shall assume,
For every atom belonging to me as good belongs to you.

I loafe and invite my soul,
5 I lean and loafe at my ease observing a spear of summer grass.

My tongue, every atom of my blood, form'd from this soil, this air,
Born here of parents born here from parents the same, and their
    parents the same,
I, now thirty-seven years old in perfect health begin,
Hoping to cease not till death.

10 Creeds and schools in abeyance,
Retiring back a while sufficed at what they are, but never forgotten,
I harbor for good or bad, I permit to speak at every hazard,
Nature without check with original energy.

---

1. The title Whitman gave in 1881 to the poem that constituted more than half of *Leaves of Grass*, originally published in 1855. The book, radical in both form and content (particularly in its explicit treatment of sexual themes), was years in the making and underwent many, though often slight, revisions.

"Song of Myself" was both untitled and unsectioned in its first appearance. This version is based on the 2002 Norton Critical Edition by Michael Moon, itself based on the Blodgett and Bradley 1973 Norton Critical Edition of *Leaves of Grass*, which was based on Whitman's 1891–92 text.

5

I believe in you my soul, the other I am must not abase itself to you,
And you must not be abased to the other.

Loafe with me on the grass, loose the stop from your throat,
85   Not words, not music or rhyme I want, not custom or lecture, not
      even the best,
Only the lull I like, the hum of your valvèd voice.

I mind how once we lay such a transparent summer morning,
How you settled your head athwart my hips and gently turn'd over
      upon me,
And parted the shirt from my bosom-bone, and plunged your tongue
      to my bare-stript heart,
90   And reach'd till you felt my beard, and reach'd till you held my feet.
Swiftly arose and spread around me the peace and knowledge that
      pass all the argument of the earth,
And I know that the hand of God is the promise of my own,
And I know that the spirit of God is the brother of my own,
And that all the men ever born are also my brothers, and the women
      my sisters and lovers,
95   And that a kelson[2] of the creation is love,
And limitless are leaves stiff or drooping in the fields,
And brown ants in the little wells beneath them,
And mossy scabs of the worm fence, heap'd stones, elder, mullein
      and poke-weed.[3]

6

A child said *What is the grass?* fetching it to me with full hands;
100   How could I answer the child? I do not know what it is any more
      than he.

I guess it must be the flag of my disposition, out of hopeful green
      stuff woven.

Or I guess it is the handkerchief of the Lord,
A scented gift and remembrancer designedly dropt,
Bearing the owner's name someway in the corners, that we may see
      and remark, and say *Whose?*

105   Or I guess the grass is itself a child, the produced babe of the
      vegetation.

Or I guess it is a uniform hieroglyphic,
And it means, Sprouting alike in broad zones and narrow zones,
Growing among black folks as among white,
Kanuck, Tuckahoe, Congressman, Cuff,[4] I give them the same, I
      receive them the same.

---

2. Line of timber inside a ship that joins the bottom structure (keel) and the floorboards; i.e., a source of stability.
3. A shrub, an herb, and a weed, respectively.

4. Slang for an African American. *Kanuck:* a French Canadian. *Tuckahoe:* an inhabitant of the lowlands of Virginia.

110   And now it seems to me the beautiful uncut hair of graves.

Tenderly will I use you curling grass,
It may be you transpire from the breasts of young men,
It may be if I had known them I would have loved them,
It may be you are from old people, or from offspring taken soon out
    of their mothers' laps,
115   And here you are the mothers' laps.

This grass is very dark to be from the white heads of old mothers,
Darker than the colorless beards of old men,
Dark to come from under the faint red roofs of mouths.

O I perceive after all so many uttering tongues,
120   And I perceive they do not come from the roofs of mouths for
    nothing.

I wish I could translate the hints about the dead young men and
    women,
And the hints about old men and mothers, and the offspring taken
    soon out of their laps.

What do you think has become of the young and old men?
And what do you think has become of the women and children?

125   They are alive and well somewhere,
The smallest sprout shows there is really no death,
And if ever there was it led forward life, and does not wait at the
    end to arrest it,
And ceas'd the moment life appear'd.

All goes onward and outward, nothing collapses,
130   And to die is different from what any one supposed, and luckier.

11

Twenty-eight young men bathe by the shore,
200   Twenty-eight young men and all so friendly;
Twenty-eight years of womanly life and all so lonesome.

She owns the fine house by the rise of the bank,
She hides handsome and richly drest aft the blinds of the window.

Which of the young men does she like the best?
205   Ah the homeliest of them is beautiful to her.

Where are you off to, lady? for I see you,
You splash in the water there, yet stay stock still in your room.

Dancing and laughing along the beach came the twenty-ninth
    bather,
The rest did not see her, but she saw them and loved them.

210   The beards of the young men glisten'd with wet, it ran from their
      long hair,
     Little streams, pass'd all over their bodies.

     An unseen hand also pass'd over their bodies,
     It descended tremblingly from their temples and ribs.

     The young men float on their backs, their white bellies bulge to the
      sun, they do not ask who seizes fast to them,
215   They do not know who puffs and declines with pendant and bending
      arch,
     They do not think whom they souse with spray.

13

225   The negro holds firmly the reins of his four horses, the block swags
      underneath on its tied-over chain,
     The negro that drives the long dray of the stone-yard, steady and tall
      he stands pois'd on one leg on the string-piece,[5]
     His blue shirt exposes his ample neck and breast and loosens over
      his hip-band,
     His glance is calm and commanding, he tosses the slouch of his hat
      away from his forehead,
     The sun falls on his crispy hair and mustache, falls on the black of
      his polish'd and perfect limbs.

230   I behold the picturesque giant and love him, and I do not stop there,
     I go with the team also.

     In me the caresser of life wherever moving, backward as well as
      forward sluing,°   *turning*
     To niches aside and junior° bending, not a person or object   *smaller*
      missing,
     Absorbing all to myself and for this song.

235   Oxen that rattle the yoke and chain or halt in the leafy shade, what
      is that you express in your eyes?
     It seems to me more than all the print I have read in my life.

     My tread scares the wood-drake and wood-duck on my distant and
      day-long ramble,
     They rise together, they slowly circle around.
     I believe in those wing'd purposes,
240   And acknowledge red, yellow, white, playing within me,
     And consider green and violet and the tufted crown intentional,
     And do not call the tortoise unworthy because she is not something
      else,
     And the jay in the woods never studied the gamut,° yet   *musical scale*
      trills pretty well to me,
     And the look of the bay mare shames silliness out of me.

---

5. Long, heavy, squared timber used to secure a load, a pier, or some construction.

24

Walt Whitman, a kosmos, of Manhattan the son,
Turbulent, fleshy, sensual, eating, drinking and breeding,
No sentimentalist, no stander above men and women or apart from
    them,
500 No more modest than immodest.

Unscrew the locks from the doors!
Unscrew the doors themselves from their jambs!

Whoever degrades another degrades me,
And whatever is done or said returns at last to me.

505 Through me the afflatus° surging and surging, through   *inspiration*
    me the current and index.

I speak the pass-word primeval, I give the sign of democracy,
By God! I will accept nothing which all cannot have their
    counterpart of on the same terms.

Through me many long dumb voices,
Voices of the interminable generations of prisoners and slaves,
510 Voices of the diseas'd and despairing and of thieves and dwarfs,
Voices of cycles of preparation and accretion,
And of the threads that connect the stars, and of wombs and of the
    father-stuff,
And of the rights of them the others are down upon,
Of the deform'd, trivial, flat, foolish, despised,
515 Fog in the air, beetles rolling balls of dung.

Through me forbidden voices,
Voices of sexes and lusts, voices veil'd and I remove the veil,
Voices indecent by me clarified and transfigur'd.

I do not press my fingers across my mouth,
520 I keep as delicate around the bowels as around the head and heart,
Copulation is no more rank to me than death is.

I believe in the flesh and the appetites,
Seeing, hearing, feeling, are miracles, and each part and tag of me is
    a miracle.

Divine am I inside and out, and I make holy whatever I touch or am
    touch'd from,
525 The scent of these arm-pits aroma finer than prayer,
This head more than churches, bibles, and all the creeds.

If I worship one thing more than another it shall be the spread of
    my own body, or any part of it,
Translucent mould of me it shall be you!
Shaded ledges and rests it shall be you!

530 Firm masculine colter[6] it shall be you!
Whatever goes to the tilth[7] of me it shall be you!
You my rich blood! your milky stream pale strippings of my life!
Breast that presses against other breasts it shall be you!
My brain it shall be your occult convolutions!
535 Root of wash'd sweet-flag! timorous pond-snipe! nest of guarded
        duplicate eggs! it shall be you!
Mix'd tussled hay of head, beard, brawn, it shall be you!
Trickling sap of maple, fibre of manly wheat, it shall be you!
Sun so generous it shall be you!
Vapors lighting and shading my face it shall be you!
540 You sweaty brooks and dews it shall be you!
Winds whose soft-tickling genitals rub against me it shall be you!
Broad muscular fields, branches of live oak, loving lounger in my
        winding paths, it shall be you!
Hands I have taken, face I have kiss'd, mortal I have ever touch'd, it
        shall be you.

I dote on myself, there is that lot of me and all so luscious,
545 Each moment and whatever happens thrills me with joy,
I cannot tell how my ankles bend, nor whence the cause of my
        faintest wish,
Nor the cause of the friendship I emit, nor the cause of the
        friendship I take again.

That I walk up my stoop, I pause to consider if it really be,
A morning-glory at my window satisfies me more than the
        metaphysics of books.

550 To behold the day-break!
The little light fades the immense and diaphanous shadows,
The air tastes good to my palate.

Hefts of the moving world at innocent gambols silently rising,
        freshly exuding,
Scooting obliquely high and low.

555 Something I cannot see puts upward libidinous prongs,
Seas of bright juice suffuse heaven.

The earth by the sky staid with, the daily close of their junction,
The heav'd challenge from the east that moment over my head,
The mocking taunt, See then whether you shall be master!

52

The spotted hawk swoops by and accuses me, he complains of my
        gab and my loitering.

6. A cutting edge fastened to a plow ahead of the   7. Land under cultivation; also, the act of culti-
plowshare.   vating soil.

I too am not a bit tamed, I too am untranslatable,
I sound my barbaric yawp over the roofs of the world.

The last scud[8] of day holds back for me,
1335 It flings my likeness after the rest and true as any on the shadow'd
wilds,
It coaxes me to the vapor and the dusk.

I depart as air, I shake my white locks at the runaway sun,
I effuse my flesh in eddies, and drift it in lacy jags.

I bequeath myself to the dirt to grow from the grass I love,
1340 If you want me again look for me under your boot-soles.

You will hardly know who I am or what I mean,
But I shall be good health to you nevertheless,
And filter and fibre your blood.

Failing to fetch me at first keep encouraged,
1345 Missing me one place search another,
I stop somewhere waiting for you.

1855, 1881

Crossing Brooklyn Ferry

1

Flood-tide below me! I see you face to face!
Clouds of the west—sun there half an hour high—I see you also
face to face.

Crowds of men and women attired in the usual costumes, how
curious you are to me!
On the ferry-boats the hundreds and hundreds that cross, returning
home, are more curious to me than you suppose,
5 And you that shall cross from shore to shore years hence are more
to me, and more in my meditations, than you might suppose.

2

The impalpable sustenance of me from all things at all hours of the
day,
The simple, compact, well-join'd scheme, myself disintegrated, every
one disintegrated yet part of the scheme,
The similitudes of the past and those of the future,
The glories strung like beads on my smallest sights and hearings, on
the walk in the street and the passage over the river,
10 The current rushing so swiftly and swimming with me far away,
The others that are to follow me, the ties between me and them,
The certainty of others, the life, love, sight, hearing of others.

8. Wind-driven clouds.

Others will enter the gates of the ferry and cross from shore to
    shore,
Others will watch the run of the flood-tide,
15 Others will see the shipping of Manhattan north and west, and the
    heights of Brooklyn to the south and east,
Others will see the islands large and small;
Fifty years hence, others will see them as they cross, the sun half an
    hour high,
A hundred years hence, or ever so many hundred years hence, oth-
    ers will see them,
Will enjoy the sunset, the pouring-in of the flood-tide, the falling-
    back to the sea of the ebb-tide.

3

20 It avails not, time nor place—distance avails not,
I am with you, you men and women of a generation, or ever so many
    generations hence,
Just as you feel when you look on the river and sky, so I felt,
Just as any of you is one of a living crowd, I was one of a crowd,
Just as you are refresh'd by the gladness of the river and the bright
    flow, I was refresh'd,
25 Just as you stand and lean on the rail, yet hurry with the swift
    current, I stood yet was hurried,
Just as you look on the numberless masts of ships and the
    thick-stemm'd pipes of steamboats, I look'd.

I too many and many a time cross'd the river of old,
Watched the Twelfth-month° sea-gulls, saw them high in   *December*
    the air floating with motionless wings, oscillating their
    bodies,
Saw how the glistening yellow lit up parts of their bodies and left
    the rest in strong shadow,
30 Saw the slow-wheeling circles and the gradual edging toward the
    south,
Saw the reflection of the summer sky in the water,
Had my eyes dazzled by the shimmering track of beams,
Look'd at the fine centrifugal spokes of light round the shape of my
    head in the sunlit water,
Look'd on the haze on the hills southward and south-westward,
35 Look'd on the vapor as it flew in fleeces tinged with violet,
Look'd toward the lower bay to notice the vessels arriving,
Saw their approach, saw aboard those that were near me,
Saw the white sails of schooners and sloops, saw the ships at
    anchor,
The sailors at work in the rigging or out astride the spars,
40 The round masts, the swinging motion of the hulls, the slender
    serpentine pennants,
The large and small steamers in motion, the pilots in their pilot-
    houses,
The white wake left by the passage, the quick tremulous whirl of the
    wheels,
The flags of all nations, the falling of them at sunset,

The scallop-edged waves in the twilight, the ladled cups, the frolic-
    some crests and glistening,
45 The stretch afar growing dimmer and dimmer, the gray walls of the
    granite storehouses by the docks,
On the river the shadowy group, the big steam-tug closely flank'd on
    each side by the barges, the hay-boat, the belated lighter,[9]
On the neighboring shore the fires from the foundry chimneys
    burning high and glaringly into the night,
Casting their flicker of black contrasted with wild red and yellow
    light over the tops of houses, and down into the clefts of
    streets.

4

These and all else were to me the same as they are to you,
50 I loved well those cities, loved well the stately and rapid river,
The men and women I saw were all near to me,
Others the same—others who look back on me because I look'd
    forward to them,
(The time will come, though I stop° here to-day and to-night.)   *stay*

5

What is it then between us?
55 What is the count of the scores or hundreds of years between us?

Whatever it is, it avails not—distance avails not, and place avails
    not,
I too lived, Brooklyn of ample hills was mine,
I too walk'd the streets of Manhattan island, and bathed in the
    waters around it,
I too felt the curious abrupt questionings stir within me,
60 In the day among crowds of people sometimes they came upon me,
In my walks home late at night or as I lay in my bed they came upon
    me,
I too had been struck from the float forever held in solution,
I too had receiv'd identity by my body,
That I was I knew was of my body, and what I should be I knew I
    should be of my body.

6

65 It is not upon you alone the dark patches fall,
The dark threw its patches down upon me also,
The best I had done seem'd to me blank and suspicious,
My great thoughts as I supposed them, were they not in reality
    meagre?
Nor is it you alone who know what it is to be evil,
70 I am he who knew what it was to be evil,
I too knitted the old knot of contrariety,

9. Barge used for loading and unloading ships.

Blabb'd, blush'd, resented, lied, stole, grudg'd,
Had guile, anger, lust, hot wishes I dared not speak,
Was wayward, vain, greedy, shallow, sly, cowardly, malignant,
75 The wolf, the snake, the hog, not wanting in me,
The cheating look, the frivolous word, the adulterous wish, not
    wanting,
Refusals, hates, postponements, meanness, laziness, none of these
    wanting,
Was one with the rest, the days and haps[1] of the rest,
Was call'd by my nighest name by clear loud voices of young men as
    they saw me approaching or passing,
80 Felt their arms on my neck as I stood, or the negligent leaning of
    their flesh against me as I sat,
Saw many I loved in the street or ferry-boat or public assembly, yet
    never told them a word,
Lived the same life with the rest, the same old laughing, gnawing,
    sleeping,
Play'd the part that still looks back on the actor or actress,
The same old role, the role that is what we make it, as great as we
    like,
85 Or as small as we like, or both great and small.

7

Closer yet I approach you,
What thought you have of me now, I had as much of you—I laid in
    my stores in advance,
I consider'd long and seriously of you before you were born.

Who was to know what should come home to me?
90 Who knows but I am enjoying this?
Who knows, for all the distance, but I am as good as looking at you
    now, for all you cannot see me?

8

Ah, what can ever be more stately and admirable to me than mast-
    hemm'd Manhattan?
River and sunset and scallop-edg'd waves of flood-tide?
The sea-gulls oscillating their bodies, the hay-boat in the twilight,
    and the belated lighter?
95 What gods can exceed these that clasp me by the hand, and with
    voices I love call me promptly and loudly by my nighest name
    as I approach?
What is more subtle than this which ties me to the woman or man
    that looks in my face?
Which fuses me into you now, and pours my meaning into you?

We understand then do we not?
What I promis'd without mentioning it, have you not accepted?

1. Chance occurrences.

100   What the study could not teach—what the preaching could not
           accomplish is accomplish'd, is it not?

9

Flow on, river! flow with the flood-tide, and ebb with the ebb-tide!
Frolic on, crested and scallop edg'd waves!
Gorgeous clouds of the sunset! drench with your splendor me, or
    the men and women generations after me!
Cross from shore to shore, countless crowds of passengers!
105   Stand up, tall masts of Mannahatta![2] stand up, beautiful hills of
           Brooklyn!
Throb, baffled and curious brain! throw out questions and answers!
Suspend here and everywhere, eternal float of solution!
Gaze, loving and thirsting eyes, in the house or street or public
    assembly!
Sound out, voices of young men! loudly and musically call me by my
    nighest name!
110   Live, old life! play the part that looks back on the actor or actress!
Play the old role, the role that is great or small according as one
    makes it!
Consider, you who peruse me, whether I may not in unknown ways
    be looking upon you;
Be firm, rail over the river, to support those who lean idly, yet haste
    with the hasting current;
Fly on, sea birds! fly sideways, or wheel in large circles high in the
    air;
115   Receive the summer sky, you water, and faithfully hold it till all
    downcast eyes have time to take it from you!
Diverge, fine spokes of light, from the shape of my head, or any
    one's head, in the sunlit water!
Come on, ships from the lower bay! pass up or down, white-sail'd
    schooners, sloops, lighters!
Flaunt away, flags of all nations! be duly lower'd at sunset!
Burn high your fires, foundry chimneys! cast black shadows at
    nightfall! cast red and yellow light over the tops of the houses!
120   Appearances, now or henceforth, indicate what you are,
You necessary film, continue to envelop the soul,
About my body for me, and your body for you, be hung our divinest
    aromas,
Thrive, cities—bring your freight, bring your shows, ample and
    sufficient rivers,
Expand, being than which none else is perhaps more spiritual,
125   Keep your places, objects than which none else is more lasting.

You have waited, you always wait, you dumb, beautiful ministers,
We receive you with free sense at last, and are insatiate[3]
    henceforward,
Not you any more shall be able to foil us, or withhold yourselves
    from us,

2. Variant for the Native American word normally   3. Insatiable.
spelled Manhattan.

We use you, and do not cast you aside—we plant you permanently
    within us,
130 We fathom you not—we love you—there is perfection in you also,
    You furnish your parts toward eternity,
    Great or small, you furnish your parts toward the soul.

1856   1881

When I Heard the Learn'd Astronomer

When I heard the learn'd astronomer,
When the proofs, the figures, were ranged in columns before me,
When I was shown the charts and diagrams, to add, divide, and
    measure them,
When I sitting heard the astronomer where he lectured with much
    applause in the lecture-room,
5 How soon unaccountable I became tired and sick,
Till rising and gliding out I wander'd off by myself,
In the mystical moist night-air, and from time to time,
Look'd up in perfect silence at the stars.

1865   1865

Vigil Strange I Kept on the Field One Night

Vigil strange I kept on the field one night;
When you my son and my comrade dropt at my side that day,
One look I but gave which your dear eyes return'd with a look I shall
    never forget,
One touch of your hand to mine O boy, reach'd up as you lay on the
    ground,
5 Then onward I sped in the battle, the even-contested battle,
Till late in the night reliev'd to the place at last again I made my
    way,
Found you in death so cold dear comrade, found your body son of
    responding kisses, (never again on earth responding,)
Bared your face in the starlight, curious the scene, cool blew the
    moderate night-wind,
Long there and then in vigil I stood, dimly around me the
    battle-field spreading,
10 Vigil wondrous and vigil sweet there in the fragrant silent night,
But not a tear fell, not even a long-drawn sigh, long I gazed,
Then on the earth partially reclining sat by your side leaning my
    chin in my hands,
Passing sweet hours, immortal and mystic hours with you dearest
    comrade—not a tear, not a word,
Vigil of silence, love and death, vigil for you my son and my soldier,
15 As onward silently stars aloft, eastward new ones upward stole,

Vigil final for you brave boy, (I could not save you, swift was your
  death,
I faithfully loved you and cared for you living, I think we shall surely
  meet again,)
Till at latest lingering of the night, indeed just as the dawn appear'd,
My comrade I wrapt in his blanket, envelop'd well his form,
20 Folded the blanket well, tucking it carefully over head and carefully
  under feet,
And there and then and bathed by the rising sun, my son in his
  grave, in his rude-dug grave I deposited,
Ending my vigil strange with that, vigil of night and battle-field dim,
Vigil for boy of responding kisses, (never again on earth responding,)
Vigil for comrade swiftly slain, vigil I never forget, how as day
  brighten'd,
25 I rose from the chill ground and folded my soldier well in his blanket,
And buried him where he fell.

1865   1867

Beat! Beat! Drums!

Beat! beat! drums!—blow! bugles! blow!
Through the windows—through doors—burst like a ruthless force,
Into the solemn church, and scatter the congregation,
Into the school where the scholar is studying;
5 Leave not the bridegroom quiet—no happiness must he have now
  with his bride,
Nor the peaceful farmer any peace, ploughing his field or gathering
  his grain,
So fierce you whirr and pound you drums—so shrill you bugles
  blow.

Beat! beat! drums!—blow! bugles! blow!
Over the traffic of cities—over the rumble of wheels in the streets;
10 Are beds prepared for sleepers at night in the houses? no sleepers
  must sleep in those beds,
No bargainers' bargains by day—no brokers or speculators—would
  they continue?
Would the talkers be talking? would the singer attempt to sing?
Would the lawyer rise in the court to state his case before the judge?
Then rattle quicker, heavier drums—you bugles wilder blow.

15 Beat! beat! drums!—blow! bugles! blow!
Make no parley[4]—stop for no expostulation,
Mind not the timid—mind not the weeper or prayer,
Mind not the old man beseeching the young man,
Let not the child's voice be heard, nor the mother's entreaties,

4. Conference with an enemy.

20   Make even the trestles to shake the dead where they lie awaiting the
       hearses,
    So strong you thump O terrible drums—so loud you bugles blow.

1861   1867

Cavalry Crossing a Ford

A line in long array where they wind betwixt green islands,
They take a serpentine course, their arms flash in the sun—hark to
    the musical clank,
Behold the silvery river, in it the splashing horses loitering stop to
    drink,
Behold the brown-faced men, each group, each person a picture, the
    negligent rest on the saddles,
5   Some emerge on the opposite bank, others are just entering the ford—
      while,
Scarlet and blue and snowy white,
The guidon[5] flags flutter gayly in the wind.

1865   1871

Out of the Cradle Endlessly Rocking

Out of the cradle endlessly rocking,
Out of the mocking-bird's throat, the musical shuttle,
Out of the Ninth-month[6] midnight,
Over the sterile sands and the fields beyond, where the child leaving
    his bed wander'd alone, bareheaded, barefoot,
5   Down from the shower'd halo,
Up from the mystic play of shadows twining and twisting as if they
    were alive,
Out from the patches of briers and blackberries,
From the memories of the bird that chanted to me,
From your memories sad brother, from the fitful risings and fallings
    I heard,
10   From under that yellow half-moon late-risen and swollen as if with
      tears,
From those beginning notes of yearning and love there in the mist,
From the thousand responses of my heart never to cease,
From the myriad thence-arous'd words,
From the word stronger and more delicious than any,
15   From such as now they start the scene revisiting,
As a flock, twittering, rising, or overhead passing,
Borne hither, ere all eludes me, hurriedly,
A man, yet by these tears a little boy again,

5. Small flag or banner used by a military unit as
a signal or guide.
6. The Quaker designation for September may

here also suggest the human cycle of fertility and
birth, in contrast with "sterile sands" in the next
line.

Throwing myself on the sand, confronting the waves,
20   I, chanter of pains and joys, uniter of here and hereafter,
Taking all hints to use them, but swiftly leaping beyond them,
A reminiscence sing.

Once Paumanok,[7]
When the lilac-scent was in the air and Fifth-month grass was
    growing,
25   Up this seashore in some briers,
Two feather'd guests from Alabama, two together,
And their nest, and four light-green eggs spotted with brown,
And every day the he-bird to and fro near at hand,
And every day the she-bird crouch'd on her nest, silent, with bright
    eyes,
30   And every day I, a curious boy, never too close, never disturbing
    them,
Cautiously peering, absorbing, translating.

Shine! shine! shine!
Pour down your warmth, great sun!
While we bask, we two together.

35   *Two together!*
Winds blow south, or winds blow north,
Day come white, or night come black,
Home, or rivers and mountains from home,
Singing all time, minding no time,
40   *While we two keep together.*

Till of a sudden,
May-be kill'd, unknown to her mate,
One forenoon the she-bird crouch'd not on the nest,
Nor return'd that afternoon, nor the next,
45   Nor ever appear'd again.

And thenceforward all summer in the sound of the sea,
And at night under the full of the moon in calmer weather,
Over the hoarse surging of the sea,
Or flitting from brier to brier by day,
50   I saw, I heard at intervals the remaining one, the he-bird,
The solitary guest from Alabama.

Blow! blow! blow!
Blow up sea-winds along Paumanok's shore;
I wait and I wait till you blow my mate to me.

55   Yes, when the stars glisten'd,
All night long on the prong of a moss-scallop'd stake,
Down almost amid the slapping waves,
Sat the lone singer wonderful causing tears.

7. The Native American name for Long Island.

He call'd on his mate,
60 He pour'd forth the meanings which I of all men know.

Yes my brother I know,
The rest might not, but I have treasur'd every note,
For more than once dimly down to the beach gliding,
Silent, avoiding the moonbeams, blending myself with the shadows,
65 Recalling now the obscure shapes, the echoes, the sounds and sights
    after their sorts,
The white arms out in the breakers tirelessly tossing,
I, with bare feet, a child, the wind wafting my hair,
Listen'd long and long.

Listen'd to keep, to sing, now translating the notes,
70 Following you my brother.

    Soothe! soothe! soothe!
Close on its wave soothes the wave behind,
And again another behind embracing and lapping, every one close,
But my love soothes not me, not me.

75 *Low hangs the moon, it rose late,*
It is lagging—O I think it is heavy with love, with love.

O madly the sea pushes upon the land,
With love, with love.

O night! do I not see my love fluttering out among the breakers?
80 *What is that little black thing I see there in the white?*

Loud! loud! loud!
Loud I call to you, my love!
High and clear I shoot my voice over the waves,
Surely you must know who is here, is here,
85 *You must know who I am, my love.*

Low-hanging moon!
What is that dusky spot in your brown yellow?
O it is the shape, the shape of my mate!
O moon do not keep her from me any longer.

90 *Land! land! O land!*
Whichever way I turn, O I think you could give me my mate back
    again if you only would,
For I am almost sure I see her dimly whichever way I look.

O rising stars!
Perhaps the one I want so much will rise, will rise with some of you.

95 *O throat! O trembling throat!*
Sound clearer through the atmosphere!

Pierce the woods, the earth,
Somewhere listening to catch you must be the one I want.

Shake out carols!
100   *Solitary here, the night's carols!*
Carols of lonesome love! death's carols!
Carols under that lagging, yellow, waning moon!
O under that moon where she droops almost down into the sea!
O reckless despairing carols.

105   *But soft! sink low!*
Soft! let me just murmur,
And do you wait a moment you husky-nois'd sea,
For somewhere I believe I heard my mate responding to me,
So faint, I must be still, be still to listen,
110   *But not altogether still, for then she might not come immediately to*
    me.

Hither my love!
Here I am! here!
With this just-sustain'd note I announce myself to you,
This gentle call is for you my love, for you.

115   *Do not be decoy'd elsewhere,*
That is the whistle of the wind, it is not my voice,
That is the fluttering, the fluttering of the spray,
Those are the shadows of leaves.

O darkness! O in vain!
120   *O I am very sick and sorrowful.*

O brown halo in the sky near the moon, drooping upon the sea!
O troubled reflection in the sea!
O throat! O throbbing heart!
And I singing uselessly, uselessly all the night.

125   *O past! O happy life! O songs of joy!*
In the air, in the woods, over fields,
Loved! loved! loved! loved! loved!
But my mate no more, no more with me!
We two together no more.

130   The aria sinking,
All else continuing, the stars shining,
The winds blowing, the notes of the bird continuous echoing,
With angry moans the fierce old mother incessantly moaning,
On the sands of Paumanok's shore gray and rustling,
135   The yellow half-moon enlarged, sagging down, drooping, the face of
    the sea almost touching,
The boy ecstatic, with his bare feet the waves, with his hair the
    atmosphere dallying,

The love in the heart long pent, now loose, now at last tumultuously
    bursting,
The aria's meaning, the ears, the soul, swiftly depositing,
The strange tears down the cheeks coursing,
140 The colloquy° there, the trio, each uttering,   *conference*
The undertone, the savage old mother incessantly crying,
To the boy's soul's questions sullenly timing, some drown'd secret
    hissing,
To the outsetting bard.

Demon or bird! (said the boy's soul,)
145 Is it indeed toward your mate you sing? or is it really to me?
For I, that was a child, my tongue's use sleeping, now I have heard
    you,
Now in a moment I know what I am for, I awake,
And already a thousand singers, a thousand songs, clearer, louder
    and more sorrowful than yours,
A thousand warbling echoes have started to life within me, never to
    die.

150 O you singer solitary, singing by yourself, projecting me,
O solitary me listening, never more shall I cease perpetuating you,
Never more shall I escape, never more the reverberations,
Never more the cries of unsatisfied love be absent from me,
Never again leave me to be the peaceful child I was before what
    there in the night,
155 By the sea under the yellow and sagging moon,
The messenger there arous'd, the fire, the sweet hell within,
The unknown want, the destiny of me.

O give me the clew! (it lurks in the night here somewhere,)
O if I am to have so much, let me have more!

160 A word then, (for I will conquer it,)
The word final, superior to all,
Subtle, sent up—what is it?—I listen;
Are you whispering it, and have been all the time, you sea-waves?
Is that it from your liquid rims and wet sands?

165 Whereto answering, the sea,
Delaying not, hurrying not,
Whisper'd me through the night, and very plainly before daybreak,
Lisp'd to me the low and delicious word death,
And again death, death, death, death,
170 Hissing melodious, neither like the bird nor like my arous'd child's
    heart,
But edging near as privately for me rustling at my feet,
Creeping thence steadily up to my ears and laving me softly all over,
Death, death, death, death, death.

Which I do not forget,
175 But fuse the song of my dusky demon and brother,

That he sang to me in the moonlight on Paumanok's gray beach,
With the thousand responsive songs at random,
My own songs awaked from that hour,
And with them the key, the word up from the waves,
180 The word of the sweetest song and all songs,
That strong and delicious word which, creeping to my feet,
(Or like some old crone rocking the cradle, swathed in sweet
    garments, bending aside,)
The sea whisper'd me.

1859   1881

The Dalliance of the Eagles

Skirting the river road, (my forenoon walk, my rest,)
Skyward in air a sudden muffled sound, the dalliance of the eagles,
The rushing amorous contact high in space together,
The clinching interlocking claws, a living, fierce, gyrating wheel,
5 Four beating wings, two beaks, a swirling mass tight grappling,
In tumbling turning clustering loops, straight downward falling,
Till o'er the river pois'd, the twain yet one, a moment's lull,
A motionless still balance in the air, then parting, talons loosing,
Upward again on slow-firm pinions slanting, their separate diverse
    flight,
10 She hers, he his, pursuing.

1880   1881

Reconciliation

Word over all, beautiful as the sky,
Beautiful that war and all its deeds of carnage must in time be
    utterly lost,
That the hands of the sisters Death and Night incessantly softly
    wash again, and ever again, this soil'd world;
For my enemy is dead, a man divine as myself is dead,
5 I look where he lies white-faced and still in the coffin—I draw near,
Bend down and touch lightly with my lips the white face in the coffin.

1865–66   1881

When Lilacs Last in the Dooryard Bloom'd[8]

1

When lilacs last in the dooryard bloom'd,
And the great star early droop'd in the western sky in the night,
I mourn'd, and yet shall mourn with ever-returning spring.

8. Composed immediately after the assassination of President Abraham Lincoln, April 14, 1865. Venus
("the great star," line 2), low in the western sky at this time, becomes associated with Lincoln.

Ever-returning spring, trinity sure to me you bring,
5   Lilac blooming perennial and drooping star in the west,
And thought of him I love.

2

O powerful western fallen star!
O shades of night—O moody, tearful night!
O great star disappear'd—O the black murk that hides the star!
10   O cruel hands that hold me powerless—O helpless soul of me!
O harsh surrounding cloud that will not free my soul.

3

In the dooryard fronting an old farm-house near the white-wash'd
    palings,
Stands the lilac-bush tall-growing with heart-shaped leaves of rich
    green,
With many a pointed blossom rising delicate, with the perfume strong
    I love,
15   With every leaf a miracle—and from this bush in the dooryard,
With delicate-color'd blossoms and heart-shaped leaves of rich green,
A sprig with its flower I break.

4

In the swamp in secluded recesses,
A shy and hidden bird is warbling a song.

20   Solitary the thrush,
The hermit withdrawn to himself, avoiding the settlements,
Sings by himself a song.

Song of the bleeding throat,
Death's outlet song of life, (for well dear brother I know,
25   If thou wast not granted to sing thou would'st surely die.)

5

Over the breast of the spring, the land, amid cities,
Amid lanes and through old woods, where lately the violets peep'd
    from the ground, spotting the gray debris,
Amid the grass in the fields each side of the lanes, passing the
    endless grass,
Passing the yellow-spear'd wheat, every grain from its shroud in the
    dark-brown fields uprisen,
30   Passing the apple-tree blows of white and pink in the orchards,
Carrying a corpse to where it shall rest in the grave,
Night and day journeys a coffin.

6

Coffin that passes through lanes and streets,[9]
Through day and night with the great cloud darkening the land,
35 With the pomp of the inloop'd flags with the cities draped in black,
With the show of the States themselves as of crape-veil'd women
standing,
With processions long and winding and the flambeaus° of the   *torches*
night,
With the countless torches lit, with the silent sea of faces and the
unbared heads,
With the waiting depot, the arriving coffin, and the sombre faces,
40 With dirges through the night, with the thousand voices rising strong
and solemn,
With all the mournful voices of the dirges pour'd around the coffin,
The dim-lit churches and the shuddering organs—where amid these
you journey,
With the tolling tolling bells' perpetual clang,
Here, coffin that slowly passes,
45 I give you my sprig of lilac.

7

(Nor for you, for one alone,
Blossoms and branches green to coffins all I bring,
For fresh as the morning, thus would I chant a song for you O sane
and sacred death.

All over bouquets of roses,
50 O death, I cover you over with roses and early lilies,
But mostly and now the lilac that blooms the first,
Copious I break, I break the sprigs from the bushes,
With loaded arms I come, pouring for you,
For you and the coffins all of you O death.)

8

55 O western orb sailing the heaven,
Now I know what you must have meant as a month since I walk'd,
As I walk'd in silence the transparent shadowy night,
As I saw you had something to tell as you bent to me night after
night,
As you droop'd from the sky low down as if to my side, (while the
other stars all look'd on,)
60 As we wander'd together the solemn night, (for something I know not
what kept me from sleep,)
As the night advanced, and I saw on the rim of the west how full you
were of woe,
As I stood on the rising ground in the breeze in the cool transparent
night,

9. Lincoln's funeral procession traveled from Washington, D.C., to Springfield, Illinois, stopping at cities
and towns all along the way for the people to honor the murdered president.

As I watch'd where you pass'd and was lost in the netherward black of
    the night,
As my soul in its trouble dissatisfied sank, as where you sad orb,
65 Concluded, dropt in the night, and was gone.

9

Sing on there in the swamp,
O singer bashful and tender, I hear your notes, I hear your call,
I hear, I come presently, I understand you,
But a moment I linger, for the lustrous star has detain'd me,
70 The star my departing comrade holds and detains me.

10

O how shall I warble myself for the dead one there I loved?
And how shall I deck my song for the large sweet soul that has gone?
And what shall my perfume be for the grave of him I love?

Sea-winds blown from east and west,
75 Blown from the Eastern sea and blown from the Western sea, till
    there on the prairies meeting,
These and with these and the breath of my chant,
I'll perfume the grave of him I love.

11

O what shall I hang on the chamber walls?
And what shall the pictures be that I hang on the walls,
80 To adorn the burial-house of him I love?

Pictures of growing spring and farms and homes,
With the Fourth-month° eve at sundown, and the gray smoke   *April*
    lucid and bright,
With floods of the yellow gold of the gorgeous, indolent, sinking sun,
    burning, expanding the air,
With the fresh sweet herbage under foot, and the pale green leaves of
    the trees prolific,
85 In the distance the flowing glaze, the breast of the river, with a wind-
    dapple here and there,
With ranging hills on the banks, with many a line against the sky, and
    shadows,
And the city at hand with dwellings so dense, and stacks of chimneys,
And all the scenes of life and the workshops, and the workmen home-
    ward returning.

12

Lo, body and soul—this land,
90 My own Manhattan with spires, and the sparkling and hurrying tides,
    and the ships,

The varied and ample land, the South and the North in the light,
    Ohio's shores and flashing Missouri,
And ever the far-spreading prairies cover'd with grass and corn.

Lo, the most excellent sun so calm and haughty,
The violet and purple morn with just-felt breezes,
95   The gentle soft-born measureless light,
The miracle spreading bathing all, the fulfill'd noon,
The coming eve delicious, the welcome night and the stars,
Over my cities shining all, enveloping man and land.

13

Sing on, sing on you gray-brown bird,
100   Sing from the swamps, the recesses, pour your chant from the
    bushes,
Limitless out of the dusk, out of the cedars and pines.

Sing on dearest brother, warble your reedy song,
Loud human song, with voice of uttermost woe.

O liquid and free and tender!
105   O wild and loose to my soul—O wondrous singer!
You only I hear—yet the star holds me, (but will soon depart,)
Yet the lilac with mastering odor holds me.

14

Now while I sat in the day and look'd forth,
In the close of the day with its light and the fields of spring, and the
    farmers preparing their crops,
110   In the large unconscious scenery of my land with its lakes and
    forests,
In the heavenly aerial beauty, (after the perturb'd winds and the
    storms,)
Under the arching heavens of the afternoon swift passing, and the
    voices of children and women,
The many-moving sea-tides, and I saw the ships how they sail'd,
And the summer approaching with richness, and the fields all busy
    with labor,
115   And the infinite separate houses, how they all went on, each with its
    meals and minutia of daily usages,
And the streets how their throbbings throbb'd, and the cities pent—
    lo, then and there,
Falling upon them all and among them all, enveloping me with the
    rest,
Appear'd the cloud, appear'd the long black trail,
And I knew death, its thought, and the sacred knowledge of death.

120   Then with the knowledge of death as walking one side of me,
And the thought of death close-walking the other side of me,

And I in the middle as with companions, and as holding the hands of
    companions,
I fled forth to the hiding receiving night that talks not,
Down to the shores of the water, the path by the swamp in the
    dimness,
125 To the solemn shadowy cedars and ghostly pines so still.

And the singer so shy to the rest receiv'd me,
The gray-brown bird I know receiv'd us comrades three,
And he sang the carol of death, and a verse for him I love.

From deep secluded recesses,
130 From the fragrant cedars and the ghostly pines so still,
Came the carol of the bird.

And the charm of the carol rapt me,
As I held as if by their hands my comrades in the night,
And the voice of my spirit tallied the song of the bird.

135 *Come lovely and soothing death,*
Undulate round the world, serenely arriving, arriving,
In the day, in the night, to all, to each,
Sooner or later delicate death.

Prais'd be the fathomless universe,
140 *For life and joy, and for objects and knowledge curious,*
And for love, sweet love—but praise! praise! praise!
For the sure-enwinding arms of cool-enfolding death.

Dark mother always gliding near with soft feet,
Have none chanted for thee a chant of fullest welcome?
145 *Then I chant it for thee, I glorify thee above all,*
I bring thee a song that when thou must indeed come, come
    unfalteringly.

Approach strong deliveress,
When it is so, when thou hast taken them I joyously sing the dead,
Lost in the loving floating ocean of thee,
150 *Laved in the flood of thy bliss O death.*

From me to thee glad serenades,
Dances for thee I propose saluting thee, adornments and feastings for
    thee,
And the sights of the open landscape and the high-spread sky are
    fitting,
And life and the fields, and the huge and thoughtful night.

155 *The night in silence under many a star,*
The ocean shore and the husky whispering wave whose voice I know,
And the soul turning to thee O vast and well-veil'd death,
And the body gratefully nestling close to thee.

Over the tree-tops I float thee a song,
160 *Over the rising and sinking waves, over the myriad fields and the*
    prairies wide,
Over the dense-pack'd cities all and the teeming wharves and ways,
I float this carol with joy, with joy to thee O death.

15

To the tally of my soul,
Loud and strong kept up the gray-brown bird,
165 With pure deliberate notes spreading filling the night.

Loud in the pines and cedars dim,
Clear in the freshness moist and the swamp-perfume,
And I with my comrades there in the night.

While my sight that was bound in my eyes unclosed,
170 As to long panoramas of visions.

And I saw askant the armies,
I saw as in noiseless dreams hundreds of battle-flags,
Borne through the smoke of the battles and pierc'd with missiles I
    saw them,
And carried hither and yon through the smoke, and torn and bloody,
175 And at last but a few shreds left on the staffs, (and all in silence,)
And the staffs all splinter'd and broken.

I saw battle-corpses, myriads of them,
And the white skeletons of young men, I saw them,
I saw the debris and debris of all the slain soldiers of the war,
180 But I saw they were not as was thought,
They themselves were fully at rest, they suffer'd not,
The living remain'd and suffer'd, the mother suffer'd,
And the wife and the child and the musing comrade suffer'd,
And the armies that remain'd suffer'd.

16

185 Passing the visions, passing the night,
Passing, unloosing the hold of my comrades' hands,
Passing the song of the hermit bird and the tallying song of my soul,
Victorious song, death's outlet song, yet varying ever-altering song,
As low and wailing, yet clear the notes, rising and falling, flooding the
    night,
190 Sadly sinking and fainting, as warning and warning, and yet again
    bursting with joy,
Covering the earth and filling the spread of the heaven,
As that powerful psalm in the night I heard from recesses,
Passing, I leave thee lilac with heart-shaped leaves,
I leave thee there in the door-yard, blooming, returning with spring.

195 I cease from my song for thee,
From my gaze on thee in the west, fronting the west, communing
  with thee,
O comrade lustrous with silver face in the night.

Yet each to keep and all, retrievements out of the night,
The song, the wondrous chant of the gray-brown bird,
200 And the tallying chant, the echo arous'd in my soul,
With the lustrous and drooping star with the countenance full of
  woe,
With the holders holding my hand nearing the call of the bird,
Comrades mine and I in the midst, and their memory ever to keep,
  for the dead I loved so well,
For the sweetest, wisest soul of all my days and lands—and this for
  his dear sake,
205 Lilac and star and bird twined with the chant of my soul,
There in the fragrant pines and the cedars dusk and dim.

1865–66   1881

A Noiseless Patient Spider

A noiseless patient spider,
I mark'd where on a little promontory it stood isolated,
Mark'd how to explore the vacant vast surrounding,
It launch'd forth filament, filament, filament, out of itself,
5 Ever unreeling them, ever tirelessly speeding them.

And you O my soul where you stand,
Surrounded, detached, in measureless oceans of space,
Ceaselessly musing, venturing, throwing, seeking the spheres to
  connect them,
Till the bridge you will need be form'd, till the ductile anchor hold,
10 Till the gossamer thread you fling catch somewhere, O my soul.

1868   1881

To a Locomotive in Winter

Thee for my recitative,
Thee in the driving storm even as now, the snow, the winter-day
  declining,
Thee in thy panoply,[1] thy measur'd dual throbbing and thy beat
  convulsive,
Thy black cylindric body, golden brass and silvery steel,
5 Thy ponderous side-bars, parallel and connecting rods, gyrating,
  shuttling at thy sides,

---

1. Protective covering or magnificent display.

Thy metrical, now swelling pant and roar, now tapering in the
    distance,
Thy great protruding head-light fix'd in front,
Thy long, pale, floating vapor-pennants, tinged with delicate purple,
The dense and murky clouds out-belching from thy smoke-stack,
10   Thy knitted frame, thy springs and valves, the tremulous twinkle of
    thy wheels,
Thy train of cars behind, obedient, merrily following,
Through gale or calm, now swift, now slack, yet steadily careering;
Type of the modern—emblem of motion and power—pulse of the
    continent,
For once come serve the Muse[2] and merge in verse, even as here I
    see thee,
15   With storm and buffeting gusts of wind and falling snow,
By day thy warning ringing bell to sound its notes,
By night thy silent signal lamps to swing.

Fierce-throated beauty!
Roll through my chant with all thy lawless music, thy swinging
    lamps at night,
20   Thy madly-whistled laughter, echoing, rumbling like an earthquake,
    rousing all,
Law of thyself complete, thine own track firmly holding,
(No sweetness debonair of tearful harp or glib piano thine,)
Thy trills of shrieks by rocks and hills return'd,
Launch'd o'er the prairies wide, across the lakes,
25   To the free skies unpent and glad and strong.

1876   1881

FREDERICK GODDARD TUCKERMAN
1821–1873

From Sonnets, Third Series[1]

IV

Thin little leaves of wood fern, ribbed and toothed,
Long curved sail needles of the green pitch pine,
With common sandgrass, skirt the horizon line,
And over these the incorruptible blue!
5   Here let me gently lie and softly view
All world asperities,° lightly touched and smoothed   *roughnesses*
As by his gracious hand, the great Bestower.
What though the year be late? some colors run
Yet through the dry, some links of melody.
10   Still let me be, by such, assuaged and soothed
And happier made, as when, our schoolday done,

2. Source of poetic inspiration.
1. Tuckerman wrote five series of sonnets; some, including the third, were published posthumously.

We hunted on from flower to frosty flower,
Tattered and dim, the last red butterfly,
Or the old grasshopper molasses-mouthed.

V

How well do I recall that walk in state
Across the Common, by the paths we knew:
Myself in silver badge and riband° blue,   *ribbon*
My little sister with her book and slate;
5   The elm tree by the Pond, the fence of wood,
The burial place that at the corner stood
Where once we crossed, through the forbidden grate,
The stones that grudg'd us way, the graveside weed,
The ominous wind that turned us half about.
10 Smit° by the flying drops, at what a speed   *hit*
Across the paths, unblessed and unforgiven
We hurried homeward when the day was late
And heard, with awe that left no place for doubt,
God's anger mutter in the darkened heaven.

VI

I looked across the rollers of the deep,
Long land-swells, ropes of weed, and riding foam,
With bitter angry heart: did I not roam
Ever like these? And what availeth sleep?
5   Or wakefulness? or pain? And still the sea
Rustled and sang, "Alike! and one to me!"
Ay! once I trod these shores too happily,
Murmuring my gladness to the rocks and ground
And, while the wave broke loud on ledge and reef,
10 Whispered it in the pause, like one who tells
His heart's dream and delight! And still the sea
Went back and forth upon its bar of shells,
Washed and withdrew, with a soft shaling sound,
As though the wet were dry and joy were grief.

1860–72   1931

MATTHEW ARNOLD
1822–1888

Shakespeare

Others abide our question. Thou art free.
We ask and ask—Thou smilest and art still,
Out-topping knowledge. For the loftiest hill,
Who to the stars uncrowns his majesty,

5 Planting his steadfast footsteps in the sea,
Making the heaven of heavens his dwelling-place,
Spares but the cloudy border of his base
To the foiled searching of mortality;

And thou, who didst the stars and sunbeams know,
10 Self-schooled, self-scanned, self-honored, self-secure,
Didst tread on earth unguessed at—better so!

All pains the immortal spirit must endure,
All weakness which impairs, all griefs which bow,
Find their sole speech in that victorious brow.

1849

To Marguerite

Yes! in the sea of life enisled,
With echoing straits between us thrown,
Dotting the shoreless watery wild,
We mortal millions live *alone*.
5 The islands feel the enclasping flow,
And then their endless bounds they know.

But when the moon their hollows lights,
And they are swept by balms of spring,
And in their glens, on starry nights,
10 The nightingales divinely sing;
And lovely notes, from shore to shore,
Across the sounds and channels pour—

Oh! then a longing like despair
Is to their farthest caverns sent;
15 For surely once, they feel, we were
Parts of a single continent!
Now round us spreads the watery plain—
Oh might our marges° meet again!   margins

Who ordered, that their longing's fire
20 Should be, as soon as kindled, cooled?
Who renders vain their deep desire?—
A God, a God their severance ruled!
And bade betwixt their shores to be
The unplumbed, salt, estranging sea.

1852

The Scholar-Gypsy[1]

Go, for they call you, shepherd, from the hill;
  Go, shepherd, and untie the wattled cotes![2]
  No longer leave thy wistful flock unfed,
  Nor let thy bawling fellows rack their throats,
5   Nor the cropped herbage shoot another head.
    But when the fields are still,
  And the tired men and dogs all gone to rest,
  And only the white sheep are sometimes seen
  Cross and recross the strips of moon-blanched green,
10 Come, shepherd, and again begin the quest!

Here, where the reaper was at work of late—
  In this high field's dark corner, where he leaves
  His coat, his basket, and his earthen cruse,°   *vessel*
  And in the sun all morning binds the sheaves,
15   Then here, at noon, comes back his stores to use—
    Here will I sit and wait,
  While to my ear from uplands far away
  The bleating of the folded° flocks is borne,   *penned up*
  With distant cries of reapers in the corn°—   *grain*
20 All the live murmur of a summer's day.

Screened is this nook o'er the high, half-reaped field,
  And here till sundown, shepherd! will I be.
  Through the thick corn the scarlet poppies peep,
  And round green roots and yellowing stalks I see
25   Pale pink convolvulus in tendrils creep;
    And air-swept lindens yield
  Their scent, and rustle down their perfumed showers
  Of bloom on the bent grass where I am laid,
  And bower me from the August sun with shade;
30 And the eye travels down to Oxford's towers.

And near me on the grass lies Glanvil's book—
  Come, let me read the oft-read tale again!
  The story of the Oxford scholar poor,
  Of pregnant parts[3] and quick inventive brain,
35   Who, tired of knocking at preferment's door,
    One summer-morn forsook

1. " 'There was very lately a lad in the University of Oxford, who was by his poverty forced to leave his studies there; and at last to join himself to a company of vagabond gypsies. Among these extravagant people, by the insinuating subtlety of his carriage, he quickly got so much of their love and esteem as that they discovered to him their mystery. After he had been a pretty while well exercised in the trade, there chanced to ride by a couple of scholars, who had formerly been of his acquaintance. They quickly spied out their old friend among the gypsies; and he gave them an account of the necessity which drove him to that kind of life, and told them that the people he went with were not such impostors as they were taken for, but that they had a traditional kind of learning among them, and could do wonders by the power of imagination, their fancy binding that of others: that himself had learned much of their art, and when he had compassed the whole secret, he intended, he said, to leave their company, and give the world an account of what he had learned.'— Glanvil's *Vanity of Dogmatizing,* 1661" [Arnold's note].
2. Sheepfolds made of woven boughs (wattles).
3. I.e., of intellectual abilities.

His friends, and went to learn the gypsy-lore,
    And roamed the world with that wild brotherhood,
    And came, as most men deemed, to little good,
40 But came to Oxford and his friends no more.

But once, years after, in the country-lanes,
    Two scholars, whom at college erst he knew,
    Met him, and of his way of life enquired;
    Whereat he answered, that the gypsy-crew,
45   His mates, had arts to rule as they desired
        The workings of men's brains,
    And they can bind them to what thoughts they will.
    "And I," he said, "the secret of their art,
    When fully learned, will to the world impart;
50 But it needs heaven-sent moments for this skill."

This said, he left them, and returned no more.—
    But rumors hung about the country-side,
    That the lost Scholar long was seen to stray,
    Seen by rare glimpses, pensive and tongue-tied,
55   In hat of antique shape, and cloak of gray.
        The same the gypsies wore.
    Shepherds had met him on the Hurst⁴ in spring;
    At some lone alehouse in the Berkshire moors,
    On the warm ingle°-bench, the smock-frocked   *fireside*
        boors°   *rustics*
60 Had found him seated at their entering,

But, 'mid their drink and clatter, he would fly.
    And I myself seem half to know thy looks,
    And put the shepherds, wanderer! on thy trace;
    And boys who in lone wheatfields scare the rooks⁵
65   I ask if thou hast passed their quiet place;
        Or in my boat I lie
    Moored to the cool bank in the summer-heats,
    'Mid wide grass meadows which the sunshine fills,
    And watch the warm, green-muffled Cumner hills,
70 And wonder if thou haunt'st their shy retreats.

For most, I know, thou lov'st retirèd ground!
    Thee at the ferry Oxford riders blithe,
    Returning home on summer-nights, have met
    Crossing the stripling Thames⁶ at Bab-lock-hithe,
75   Trailing in the cool stream thy fingers wet,
        As the punt's rope chops round;⁷
    And leaning backward in a pensive dream,
    And fostering in thy lap a heap of flowers

---

4. A hill near Oxford. (All place-names in the poem, with the obvious exception of the Mediterranean localities of the last two stanzas, refer to the countryside around Oxford.)
5. The boys have been hired to frighten crows away from eating wheat grains.
6. The narrow upper reaches of the river before it broadens out to its full width.
7. I.e., as the rope tying the small boat to the bank shifts around.

Plucked in shy fields and distant Wychwood bowers,
80 And thine eyes resting on the moonlit stream.

And then they land, and thou art seen no more!
Maidens, who from the distant hamlets come
To dance around the Fyfield elm in May,
Oft through the darkening fields have seen thee roam,
85 Or cross a stile into the public way.
Oft thou hast given them store
Of flowers—the frail-leafed, white anemone,
Dark bluebells drenched with dews of summer eves,
And purple orchises with spotted leaves—
90 But none hath words she can report of thee.

And, above Godstow Bridge, when hay-time's here
In June, and many a scythe in sunshine flames,
Men who through those wide fields of breezy grass
Where black-winged swallows haunt the glittering Thames,
95 To bathe in the abandoned lasher[8] pass,
Have often passed thee near
Sitting upon the river bank o'ergrown;
Marked thine outlandish garb, thy figure spare,
Thy dark vague eyes, and soft abstracted air—
100 But, when they came from bathing, thou wast gone!

At some lone homestead in the Cumner hills,
Where at her open door the housewife darns,
Thou hast been seen, or hanging on a gate
To watch the threshers in the mossy barns.
105 Children, who early range these slopes and late
For cresses from the rills,°   streams
Have known thee eying, all an April-day,
The springing pastures and the feeding kine;°   cattle
And marked thee, when the stars come out and shine,
110 Through the long dewy grass move slow away.

In autumn, on the skirts of Bagley Wood—
Where most the gypsies by the turf-edged way
Pitch their smoked tents, and every bush you see
With scarlet patches tagged and shreds of gray,
115 Above the forest-ground called Thessaly—
The blackbird, picking food,
Sees thee, nor stops his meal, nor fears at all;
So often has he known thee past him stray,
Rapt, twirling in thy hand a withered spray,
120 And waiting for the spark from heaven to fall.

And once, in winter, on the causeway chill
Where home through flooded fields foot-travelers go,
Have I not passed thee on the wooden bridge,

8. Slack water above a weir, or dam.

Wrapt in thy cloak and battling with the snow,
125   Thy face tow'rd Hinksey and its wintry ridge?
            And thou hast climbed the hill,
      And gained the white brow of the Cumner range;
            Turned once to watch, while thick the snowflakes fall,
            The line of festal light in Christ Church hall—
130   Then sought thy straw in some sequestered grange.[9]

      But what—I dream! Two hundred years are flown
            Since first thy story ran through Oxford halls,
                  And the grave Glanvil did the tale inscribe
            That thou wert wandered from the studious walls
135   To learn strange arts, and join a gypsy-tribe;
                  And thou from earth art gone
            Long since, and in some quiet churchyard laid—
                  Some country-nook, where o'er thy unknown grave
                  Tall grasses and white flowering nettles wave,
140   Under a dark, red-fruited yew-tree's shade.

      —No, no, thou hast not felt the lapse of hours!
            For what wears out the life of mortal men?
                  'Tis that from change to change their being rolls;
                  'Tis that repeated shocks, again, again,
145   Exhaust the energy of strongest souls
                  And numb the elastic powers.
            Till having used our nerves with bliss and teen,°   vexation
                  And tired upon a thousand schemes our wit,
                  To the just-pausing Genius[1] we remit
150   Our worn-out life, and are—what we have been.

      Thou hast not lived, why should'st thou perish, so?
            Thou hadst *one* aim, *one* business, *one* desire;
                  Else wert thou long since numbered with the dead!
            Else hadst thou spent, like other men, thy fire!
155   The generations of thy peers are fled.
                  And we ourselves shall go;
            But thou possessest an immortal lot,
                  And we imagine thee exempt from age
                  And living as thou liv'st on Glanvil's page,
160   Because thou hadst—what we, alas! have not.

      For early didst thou leave the world, with powers
            Fresh, undiverted to the world without,
                  Firm to their mark, not spent on other things;
            Free from the sick fatigue, the languid doubt,
165   Which much to have tried, in much been baffled, brings.
                  O life unlike to ours!
            Who fluctuate idly without term or scope,

9. Country house. *Christ Church hall*: dining hall   assigned to each being to see it through the world
of an Oxford college.   and finally to usher it out.
1. In classical mythology, the protecting spirit

Of whom each strives, nor knows for what he strives,
And each half[2] lives a hundred different lives;
170 Who wait like thee, but not, like thee, in hope.

Thou waitest for the spark from heaven! and we,
Light half-believers of our casual creeds,
Who never deeply felt, nor clearly willed,
Whose insight never has borne fruit in deeds,
175 Whose vague resolves never have been fulfilled;
For whom each year we see
Breeds new beginnings, disappointments new;
Who hesitate and falter life away,
And lose tomorrow the ground won today—
180 Ah! do not we, wanderer! await it too?

Yes, we await it! but it still delays,
And then we suffer! and amongst us one,[3]
Who most has suffered, takes dejectedly
His seat upon the intellectual throne;
185 And all his store of sad experience he
Lays bare of wretched days;
Tells us his misery's birth and growth and signs,
And how the dying spark of hope was fed,
And how the breast was soothed, and how the head,
190 And all his hourly varied anodynes.

This for our wisest! and we others pine,
And wish the long unhappy dream would end,
And waive all claim to bliss, and try to bear;
With close-lipped patience for our only friend,
195 Sad patience, too near neighbor to despair—
But none has hope like thine!
Thou through the fields and through the woods dost stray,
Roaming the countryside, a truant boy,
Nursing thy project in unclouded joy,
200 And every doubt long blown by time away.

O born in days when wits were fresh and clear,
And life ran gaily as the sparkling Thames;
Before this strange disease of modern life,
With its sick hurry, its divided aims,
205 Its head o'ertaxed, its palsied hearts, was rife—
Fly hence, our contact fear!
Still fly, plunge deeper in the bowering wood!
Averse, as Dido did with gesture stern
From her false friend's approach in Hades turn,[4]
210 Wave us away, and keep thy solitude!

2. I.e., half-heartedly.
3. Possibly the German poet Johann Wolfgang von Goethe (1749–1832) or the English poet Alfred, Lord Tennyson (1809–1892; see pp. 982–1009).
4. According to Virgil's Aeneid, Dido, queen of Carthage, had been deserted by Aeneas after giving her love to him. Aeneas later encountered her in the underworld, among the shades of those who had died of unhappy love, but when he greeted her she turned her back on him.

Still nursing the unconquerable hope,
   Still clutching the inviolable shade,
      With a free, onward impulse brushing through,
   By night, the silvered branches of the glade—
215   Far on the forest-skirts, where none pursue,
         On some mild pastoral slope
   Emerge, and resting on the moonlit pales°   *fences*
   Freshen thy flowers as in former years
   With dew, or listen with enchanted ears,
220   From the dark dingles,° to the nightingales!   *valleys*

   But fly our paths, our feverish contact fly!
   For strong the infection of our mental strife,
      Which, though it gives no bliss, yet spoils for rest;
   And we should win thee from thy own fair life,
225   Like us distracted, and like us unblest.
         Soon, soon thy cheer would die,
   Thy hopes grow timorous, and unfixed thy powers,
      And thy clear aims be cross and shifting made;
      And then thy glad perennial youth would fade,
230   Fade, and grow old at last, and die like ours.

   Then fly our greetings, fly our speech and smiles!
   —As some grave Tyrian[5] trader, from the sea,
      Descried at sunrise an emerging prow
   Lifting the cool-haired creepers stealthily,
235   The fringes of a southward-facing brow
         Among the Aegean isles;
   And saw the merry Grecian coaster come,
      Freighted with amber grapes, and Chian[6] wine,
      Green, bursting figs, and tunnies° steeped in brine—   *tuna*
240   And knew the intruders on his ancient home,

   The young light-hearted masters of the waves—
      And snatched his rudder, he shook out more sail;
      And day and night held on indignantly
   O'er the blue Midland waters with the gale,
245   Betwixt the Syrtes[7] and soft Sicily,
         To where the Atlantic raves
   Outside the western straits;[8] and unbent sails
      There, where down cloudy cliffs, through sheets of foam,
      Shy traffickers, the dark Iberians[9] come;
250   And on the beach undid his corded bales.

                                                          1853

---

5. A native of the ancient Phoenician city of Tyre, in the eastern Mediterranean.
6. From the island of Chios, famous for its wine.
7. Two gulfs on the North African coast, one off Cyrenaica, the other off Tunisia.
8. I.e., the Straits of Gibraltar.
9. Ancient name for the inhabitants of Spain.

Thyrsis

A Monody, to Commemorate the Author's Friend, Arthur Hugh Clough, Who Died at Florence, 1861[1]

How changed is here each spot man makes or fills!
  In the two Hinkseys[2] nothing keeps the same;
    The village street its haunted mansion lacks,
  And from the sign is gone Sibylla's name,[3]
5   And from the roofs the twisted chimney-stacks—
      Are ye too changed, ye hills?
See, 'tis no foot of unfamiliar men
    Tonight from Oxford up your pathway strays!
    Here came I often, often, in old days—
10 Thyrsis and I; we still had Thyrsis then.

Runs it not here, the track by Childsworth Farm,
  Past the high wood, to where the elm-tree crowns
    The hill behind whose ridge the sunset flames?
  The signal-elm, that looks on Ilsley Downs,
15   The Vale, the three lone weirs,° the youthful Thames?   *dams*
      This winter-eve is warm,
Humid the air! leafless, yet soft as spring,
    The tender purple spray on copse° and briers!   *small wood*
    And that sweet city with her dreaming spires,
20 She needs not June for beauty's heightening,

Lovely all times she lies, lovely tonight!
  Only, methinks, some loss of habit's power
    Befalls me wandering through this upland dim.
  Once passed I blindfold here, at any hour;
25   Now seldom come I, since I came with him.
      That single elm-tree bright
Against the west—I miss it! is it gone?
    We prized it dearly; while it stood, we said,
    Our friend, the Gypsy-Scholar, was not dead;
30 While the tree lived, he in these fields lived on.

Too rare, too rare, grow now my visits here,
  But once I knew each field, each flower, each stick;
    And with the country-folk acquaintance made

---

1. The friendship between Arnold and the English poet Clough (1819–1861; see pp. 1051–53) had been at its closest while they were at Oxford, and Arnold chooses as the framework for this poem a visit to Oxford—at least in reminiscence—and more specifically to a hill above the town crowned by the "signal-elm." They connected the tree with the continuing symbolic presence in the countryside of the Scholar-Gypsy and his lonely faithfulness to an ideal of truth-seeking. (See Arnold's poem "The Scholar-Gypsy" and his note to it,

above.) As in his use of the names Thyrsis (for Clough) and Corydon (line 80, for himself), both traditional designations for shepherd-poets, Arnold is adopting the conventions of the Greek and Latin pastoral elegy for his monody, or poem in which a single mourner laments.
2. North and South Hinksey, two villages near Oxford.
3. Sibylla Kerr, a tavern keeper when Arnold and Clough were students.

By barn in threshing-time, by new-built rick.
35   Here, too, our shepherd-pipes we first assayed.
        Ah me! this many a year
My pipe is lost, my shepherd's holiday!
        Needs must I lose them, needs with heavy heart
        Into the world and wave of men depart;
10   But Thyrsis of his own will went away.[4]

It irked him to be here, he could not rest.
He loved each simple joy the country yields,
        He loved his mates; but yet he could not keep,°   stay
For that a shadow loured on the fields,
45   Here with the shepherds and the silly° sheep.   innocent
        Some life of men unblest
He knew, which made him droop; and filled his head.
        He went; his piping took a troubled sound
        Of storms[5] that rage outside our happy ground;
50   He could not wait their passing, he is dead.

So, some tempestuous morn in early June,
When the year's primal burst of bloom is o'er,
        Before the roses and the longest day—
When garden-walks and all the grassy floor
55   With blossoms red and white of fallen May
        And chestnut-flowers are strewn—
So have I heard the cuckoo's parting cry,
        From the wet field, through the vext garden-trees,
        Come with the volleying rain and tossing breeze:
60   *The bloom is gone, and with the bloom go I!*

Too quick despairer, wherefore wilt thou go?
Soon will the high Midsummer pomps come on,
        Soon will the musk carnations break and swell,
Soon shall we have gold-dusted snapdragon,
65   Sweet-William with his homely cottage-smell,
        And stocks in fragrant blow;
Roses that down the alleys shine afar,
        And open, jasmine-muffled lattices,
        And groups under the dreaming garden-trees,
70   And the full moon, and the white evening-star.

He hearkens not! light comer, he is flown!
What matters it? next year he will return,
        And we shall have him in the sweet spring-days,
With whitening hedges, and uncrumpling fern,
75   And bluebells trembling by the forest-ways,
        And scent of hay new-mown.
But Thyrsis never more we swains shall see;
        See him come back, and cut a smoother reed,

---

4. Arnold left Oxford in 1847 to earn a living, first as a minor diplomat, then as inspector of schools. Clough resigned his Oxford fellowship in 1848, rather than subscribe to the Thirty-nine Articles of the Anglican Church.
5. Religious and political controversies.

And blow a strain the world at last shall heed—
80 For Time, not Corydon, hath conquered thee!

Alack, for Corydon no rival now!
   But when Sicilian shepherds lost a mate,
      Some good survivor with his flute would go,
   Piping a ditty sad for Bion's fate;[6]
85   And cross the unpermitted ferry's flow,[7]
         And relax Pluto's brow,
   And make leap up with joy the beauteous head
      Of Proserpine, among whose crownèd hair
      Are flowers first opened on Sicilian air,
90 And flute his friend, like Orpheus,[8] from the dead.

O easy access to the hearer's grace
   When Dorian[9] shepherds sang to Proserpine!
      For she herself had trod Sicilian fields,
   She knew the Dorian water's gush divine,
95   She knew each lily white which Enna yields,
         Each rose with blushing face;
   She loved the Dorian pipe, the Dorian strain.
      But ah, of our poor Thames she never heard!
      Her foot the Cumner cowslips° never stirred;   *wildflowers*
100 And we should tease her with our plaint in vain!

Well! wind-dispersed and vain the words will be,
   Yet, Thyrsis, let me give my grief its hour
      In the old haunt, and find our tree-topped hill!
   Who, if not I, for questing here hath power?
105   I know the wood which hides the daffodil,
         I know the Fyfield tree,
   I know what white, what purple fritillaries[1]
      The grassy harvest of the river-fields,
      Above by Ensham, down by Sandford, yields,
110 And what sedged brooks are Thames's tributaries;

I know these slopes; who knows them if not I?
   But many a dingle° on the loved hillside,   *valley*
      With thorns once studded, old, white-blossomed trees,
   Where thick the cowslips grew, and far descried
115   High towered the spikes of purple orchises,
         Hath since our day put by
   The coronals of that forgotten time;[2]
      Down each green bank hath gone the ploughboy's team,

6. Refers to a Greek pastoral poet of the first century B.C.E. who lived in Sicily and was mourned in "Lament for Bion," sometimes ascribed to his pupil Moschus.
7. The ferry across the river Styx to Hades, ruled over by Pluto and his queen, Proserpine, whom he had abducted while she was gathering flowers in the fields near Enna, in Sicily. She spent half of each year in the underworld and half on Earth.
8. Who, because of the power and charm of his music, had been permitted to attempt to lead his wife, Eurydice, back from the dead.
9. One of the ancient Greek lyrical modes, characterized by simplicity and nobility.
1. Flowers commonly found in moist meadows.
2. I.e., the flowers that once crowned them.

And only in the hidden brookside gleam
120   Primroses, orphans of the flowery prime.

Where is the girl, who by the boatman's door,
        Above the locks, above the boating throng,
          Unmoored our skiff when through the Wytham flats,
        Red loosestrife and blond meadow-sweet[3] among
125   And darting swallows and light water-gnats,
            We tracked the shy Thames shore?
        Where are the mowers, who, as the tiny swell
          Of our boat passing heaved the river-grass,
          Stood with suspended scythe to see us pass?
130   They all are gone, and thou art gone as well!

Yes, thou art gone! and round me too the night
        In ever-nearing circle weaves her shade.
          I see her veil draw soft across the day,
        I feel her slowly chilling breath invade
135   The cheek grown thin, the brown hair sprent° with gray;   *sprinkled*
            I feel her finger light
        Laid pausefully upon life's headlong train;
          The foot less prompt to meet the morning dew,
          The heart less bounding at emotion new,
140   And hope, once crushed, less quick to spring again.

And long the way appears, which seemed so short
        To the less practiced eye of sanguine° youth;   *confident*
          And high the mountain-tops, in cloudy air,
        The mountain-tops where is the throne of Truth,
145   Tops in life's morning-sun so bright and bare!
            Unbreachable the fort
        Of the long-battered world uplifts its wall;
          And strange and vain the earthly turmoil grows,
          And near and real the charm of thy repose,
150   And night as welcome as a friend would fall.

But hush! the upland hath a sudden loss
        Of quiet!—Look, adown the dusk hillside,
          A troop of Oxford hunters going home,
        As in old days, jovial and talking, ride!
155   From hunting with the Berkshire hounds they come.
            Quick! let me fly, and cross
        Into yon farther field!—'Tis done; and see,
          Backed by the sunset, which doth glorify
          The orange and pale violet evening-sky,
160   Bare on its lonely ridge, the Tree! the Tree!

I take the omen! Eve lets down her veil,
        The white fog creeps from bush to bush about,
          The west unflushes, the high stars grow bright,
        And in the scattered farms the lights come out.

---

3. Like loosestrife, flowers that grow in moist meadows and near streams.

165   I cannot reach the signal-tree to-night,
            Yet, happy omen, hail!
        Hear it from thy broad lucent Arno-vale[4]
            (For there thine earth-forgetting eyelids keep
            The morningless and unawakening sleep
170   Under the flowery oleanders pale),

        Hear it, O Thyrsis, still our tree is there!
            Ah, vain! These English fields, this upland dim,
            These brambles pale with mist engarlanded,
            That lone, sky-pointing tree, are not for him;
175   To a boon southern country he is fled,
                And now in happier air,
            Wandering with the great Mother's train divine[5]
            (And purer or more subtle soul than thee,
            I trow, the mighty Mother doth not see)
180   Within a folding of the Apennine,[6]

        Thou hearest the immortal chants[7] of old!
            Putting his sickle to the perilous grain
            In the hot cornfield of the Phrygian king,
            For thee the Lityerses-song again
185   Young Daphnis with his silver voice doth sing;[8]
                Sings his Sicilian fold,
            His sheep, his hapless love, his blinded eyes—
            And how a call celestial round him rang,
            And heavenward from the fountain-brink he sprang,
190   And all the marvel of the golden skies.

        There thou art gone, and me thou leavest here
            Sole in these fields! yet will I not despair.
                Despair I will not, while I yet descry
            Neath the mild canopy of English air
195   That lonely tree against the western sky.
                Still, still these slopes, 'tis clear,
            Our Gypsy-Scholar haunts, outliving thee!
                Fields where soft sheep from cages pull the hay,
                Woods with anemonies in flower till May,
200   Know him a wanderer still; then why not me?

4. Clough is buried in the Protestant cemetery in Florence, which is situated in the valley of the Arno River.
5. Devotees of Demeter (whose name may mean Earth Mother), goddess of agriculture.
6. The Apennines are a mountain range in Italy.
7. Sung in Demeter's honor.
8. "Daphnis, the ideal Sicilian shepherd of Greek pastoral poetry, was said to have followed into Phrygia his mistress Piplea, who had been carried off by robbers, and to have found her in the power of the king of Phrygia, Lityerses. Lityerses used to make strangers try a contest with him in reaping corn, and to put them to death if he overcame them. Hercules arrived in time to save Daphnis, took upon himself the reaping-contest with Lityerses, overcame him, and slew him. The Lityerses-song connected with this tradition was, like the Linus-song, one of the early plaintive strains of Greek popular poetry, and used to be sung by corn-reapers. Other traditions represented Daphnis as beloved by a nymph who exacted from him an oath to love no one else. He fell in love with a princess, and was struck blind by the jealous nymph. Mercury, who was his father, raised him to heaven, and made a fountain spring up in the place from which he ascended. At this fountain the Sicilians offered yearly sacrifices.—See Servius, Comment. in Virgil. Bucol., v.20 and viii.68" [Arnold's note].

A fugitive and gracious light he seeks,
　　Shy to illumine; and I seek it too.
　　　This does not come with houses or with gold,
　　　With place, with honor, and a flattering crew;
205　　　'Tis not in the world's market bought and sold—
　　　　But the smooth-slipping weeks
　　Drop by, and leave its seeker still untired;
　　　Out of the heed of mortals he is gone,
　　　He wends unfollowed, he must house alone;
210　　Yet on he fares, by his own heart inspired.

　　Thou too, O Thyrsis, on like quest wast bound;
　　　Thou wanderest with me for a little hour!
　　　　Men gave thee nothing; but this happy quest,
　　　If men esteemed thee feeble, gave thee power,
215　　　If men procured thee trouble, gave thee rest.
　　　　And this rude Cumner ground,
　　Its fir-topped Hurst,° its farms, its quiet fields,　　　　*a hill*
　　　Here cam'st thou in thy jocund youthful time,
　　　Here was thine height of strength, thy golden prime!
220　　And still the haunt beloved a virtue yields.

　　What though the music of thy rustic flute
　　　Kept not for long its happy, country tone;
　　　　Lost it too soon, and learnt a stormy note
　　　Of men contention-tost, of men who groan,
225　　　Which tasked thy pipe too sore, and tired thy throat—
　　　　It failed, and thou wast mute!
　　Yet hadst thou alway visions of our light,
　　　And long with men of care thou couldst not stay,
　　　And soon thy foot resumed its wandering way,
230　　Left human haunt, and on alone till night.

　　Too rare, too rare, grow now my visits here!
　　　'Mid city-noise, not, as with thee of yore,
　　　　Thyrsis! in reach of sheep-bells is my home.
　　　—Then through the great town's harsh, heart-wearying roar,
235　　　Let in thy voice a whisper often come,
　　　　To chase fatigue and fear:
　　Why faintest thou? I wandered till I died.
　　　Roam on! The light we sought is shining still.
　　　Dost thou ask proof? Our tree yet crowns the hill,
240　　*Our Scholar travels yet the loved hillside.*

1866

Dover Beach

The sea is calm tonight.
The tide is full, the moon lies fair
Upon the straits; on the French coast the light
Gleams and is gone; the cliffs of England stand,
5   Glimmering and vast, out in the tranquil bay.
Come to the window, sweet is the night-air!
Only, from the long line of spray
Where the sea meets the moon-blanched land,
Listen! you hear the grating roar
10   Of pebbles which the waves draw back, and fling,
At their return, up the high strand,
Begin, and cease, and then again begin,
With tremulous cadence slow, and bring
The eternal note of sadness in.

15   Sophocles long ago
Heard it on the Aegean, and it brought
Into his mind the turbid ebb and flow
Of human misery;[9] we
Find also in the sound a thought,
20   Hearing it by this distant northern sea.

The Sea of Faith
Was once, too, at the full, and round earth's shore
Lay like the folds of a bright girdle furled.
But now I only hear
25   Its melancholy, long withdrawing roar,
Retreating, to the breath
Of the night-wind, down the vast edges drear
And naked shingles[1] of the world.

Ah, love, let us be true
30   To one another! for the world, which seems
To lie before us like a land of dreams,
So various, so beautiful, so new,
Hath really neither joy, nor love, nor light,
Nor certitude, nor peace, nor help for pain;
35   And we are here as on a darkling plain
Swept with confused alarms of struggle and flight,
Where ignorant armies clash by night.

1867

9. A reference to a chorus in Sophocles' play *Antigone,* lines 583–92: "Happy are they whose life has not tasted evils. But for those whose house has been shaken by God, no mass of ruin fails to creep upon their families. It is like the sea-swell . . . when an undersea darkness drives upon it with gusts of Thracian wind; it rolls the dark sand from the depths, and the beaches, beaten by the waves and wind, groan and roar."
1. Beaches covered with water-worn small stones and pebbles.

DANTE GABRIEL ROSSETTI
1828–1882

The Blessed Damozel[1]

The blessed damozel leaned out
    From the gold bar of Heaven;
Her eyes were deeper than the depth
    Of waters stilled at even;
5 She had three lilies in her hand,
    And the stars in her hair were seven.

Her robe, ungirt from clasp to hem,
    No wrought flowers did adorn,
But a white rose of Mary's gift,
10   For service meetly° worn;   *properly*
Her hair that lay along her back
    Was yellow like ripe corn.°   *wheat, grain*

Herseemed° she scarce had been a day   *it seemed to her*
    One of God's choristers;
15 The wonder was not yet quite gone
    From that still look of hers;
Albeit, to them she left, her day
    Had counted as ten years.

(To one, it is ten years of years.
20   . . . Yet now, and in this place,
Surely she leaned o'er me—her hair
    Fell all about my face. . . .
Nothing: the autumn fall of leaves.
    The whole year sets apace.)

25 It was the rampart of God's house
    That she was standing on;
By God built over the sheer depth
    The which is Space begun;
So high, that looking downward thence
30   She scarce could see the sun.

It lies in Heaven, across the flood
    Of ether, as a bridge.
Beneath, the tides of day and night
    With flame and darkness ridge
35 The void, as low as where this earth
    Spins like a fretful midge.°   *gnatlike insect*

Around her, lovers, newly met
    In joy no sorrow claims,

---

1. Older form of *damsel*, meaning "young unmarried lady," preferred by Romantic and later writers because
it avoids the simpler, homelier associations of *damsel*.

Spoke evermore among themselves
40   Their rapturous new names;
And the souls mounting up to God
      Went by her like thin flames.

And still she bowed herself and stooped
      Out of the circling charm;
45 Until her bosom must have made
      The bar she leaned on warm,
And the lilies lay as if asleep
      Along her bended arm.

From the fixed place of Heaven she saw
50   Time like a pulse shake fierce
Through all the worlds. Her gaze still strove
      Within the gulf to pierce
Its path; and now she spoke as when
      The stars sang in their spheres.

55 The sun was gone now; the curled moon
      Was like a little feather
Fluttering far down the gulf; and now
      She spoke through the still weather.
Her voice was like the voice the stars
60   Had when they sang together.

(Ah sweet! Even now, in that bird's song,
      Strove not her accents there,
Fain to be hearkened? When those bells
      Possessed the midday air,
65 Strove not her steps to reach my side
      Down all the echoing stair?)

"I wish that he were come to me,
      For he will come," she said.
"Have I not prayed in Heaven?—on earth,
70   Lord, Lord, has he not prayed?
Are not two prayers a perfect strength?
      And shall I feel afraid?

"When round his head the aureole° clings,   *radiant light*
      And he is clothed in white,
75 I'll take his hand and go with him
      To the deep wells of light;
We will step down as to a stream,
      And bathe there in God's sight.

"We two will stand beside that shrine,
80   Occult, withheld, untrod,
Whose lamps are stirred continually
      With prayer sent up to God;
And see our old prayers, granted, melt
      Each like a little cloud.

85   "We two will lie i' the shadow of
      That living mystic tree
  Within whose secret growth the Dove
      Is sometimes felt to be,
  While every leaf that His plumes touch
90   Saith His Name audibly.

  "And I myself will teach to him,
      I myself, lying so,
  The songs I sing here; which his voice
      Shall pause in, hushed and slow,
95   And find some knowledge at each pause,
      Of some new thing to know."

  (Alas! We two, we two, thou say'st!
      Yea, one wast thou with me
  That once of old. But shall God lift
100   To endless unity
  The soul whose likeness with thy soul
      Was but its love for thee?)

  "We two," she said, "will seek the groves
      Where the lady Mary is,
105   With her five handmaidens, whose names
      Are five sweet symphonies,
  Cecily, Gertrude, Magdalen,
      Margaret and Rosalys.

  "Circlewise sit they, with bound locks
110   And foreheads garlanded;
  Into the fine cloth white like flame
      Weaving the golden thread,
  To fashion the birth-robes for them
      Who are just born, being dead.

115   "He shall fear, haply, and be dumb:
      Then will I lay my cheek
  To his, and tell about our love,
      Not once abashed or weak:
  And the dear Mother will approve
120   My pride, and let me speak.

  "Herself shall bring us, hand in hand,
      To Him round whom all souls
  Kneel, the clear-ranged unnumbered heads
      Bowed with their aureoles:
125   And angels meeting us shall sing
      To their citherns and citoles.[2]

---

2. The cithern is a seventeenth-century guitarlike instrument with wire strings; the citole, a stringed instrument dating from the thirteenth to the fifteenth century.

"There will I ask of Christ the Lord
    Thus much for him and me:—
Only to live as once on earth
130   With Love—only to be,
As then awhile, forever now
    Together, I and he."

She gazed and listened and then said,
    Less sad of speech than mild,
135 "All this is when he comes." She ceased.
    The light thrilled towards her, filled
With angels in strong level flight.
    Her eyes prayed, and she smiled.

(I saw her smile.) But soon their path
140   Was vague in distant spheres:
And then she cast her arms along
    The golden barriers,
And laid her face between her hands,
    And wept. (I heard her tears.)

1846   1850

Sudden Light

I have been here before,
    But when or how I cannot tell:
I know the grass beyond the door,
    The sweet keen smell,
5 The sighing sound, the lights around the shore.

You have been mine before,
    How long ago I may not know:
But just when at that swallow's soar
    Your neck turned so,
10 Some veil did fall—I knew it all of yore.

Has this been thus before?
    And shall not thus time's eddying flight
Still with our lives our love restore
    In death's despite,
15 And day and night yield one delight once more?

1854   1863

The Woodspurge

The wind flapped loose, the wind was still,
Shaken out dead from tree and hill:

I had walked on at the wind's will—
I sat now, for the wind was still.

5   Between my knees my forehead was—
My lips, drawn in, said not Alas!
My hair was over in the grass,
My naked ears heard the day pass.

My eyes, wide open, had the run
10   Of some ten weeds to fix upon;
Among those few, out of the sun,
The woodspurge flowered, three cups in one.

From perfect grief there need not be
Wisdom or even memory:
15   One thing then learnt remains to me—
The woodspurge has a cup of three.

1856   1870

From The House of Life

A Sonnet

A Sonnet is a moment's monument,—
  Memorial from the Soul's eternity
  To one dead deathless hour. Look that it be,
Whether for lustral° rite or dire portent,   *purificatory*
5   Of its own arduous fullness reverent:
    Carve it in ivory or in ebony,
    As Day or Night may rule; and let Time see
Its flowering crest impearled and orient.

A Sonnet is a coin: its face reveals
10   The soul—its converse, to what Power 'tis due:
Whether for tribute to the august appeals
    Of Life, or dower in Love's high retinue,
It serve; or, 'mid the dark wharf's cavernous breath,
In Charon's[3] palm it pay the toll to Death.

19. Silent Noon

Your hands lie open in the long fresh grass—
  The finger-points look through like rosy blooms:
  Your eyes smile peace. The pasture gleams and glooms
'Neath billowing skies that scatter and amass.
5   All round our nest, far as the eye can pass,
    Are golden kingcup-fields with silver edge
    Where the cow-parsley skirts the hawthorn-hedge.
'Tis visible silence, still as the hour-glass.

---

3. In Greek mythology, Charon received a coin, an *obolus*, for ferrying the shades of the newly dead across the river Styx to Hades.

Deep in the sun-searched growths the dragonfly
10   Hangs like a blue thread loosened from the sky:
      So this winged hour is dropt to us from above.
Oh! clasp we to our hearts, for deathless dower,°   *gift*
This close-companioned inarticulate hour
      When twofold silence was the song of love.

70. *The Hill Summit*

This feast-day of the sun, his altar there
      In the broad west has blazed for vesper°-song;   *evening*
      And I have loitered in the vale° too long   *valley*
And gaze now a belated worshipper.
5   Yet may I not forget that I was 'ware,°   *aware*
      So journeying, of his face at intervals
      Transfigured where the fringed horizon falls,
A fiery bush with coruscating° hair.   *glittering*

And now that I have climbed and won this height,
10   I must tread downward through the sloping shade
And travel the bewildered tracks till night.
      Yet for this hour I still may here be stayed
      And see the gold air and the silver fade
And the last bird fly into the last light.

1847–80   1870, 1881

GEORGE MEREDITH
1828–1909

From Modern Love[1]

1

By this he knew she wept with waking eyes:
That, at his hand's light quiver by her head,
The strange low sobs that shook their common bed
Were called into her with a sharp surprise,
5   And strangled mute, like little gaping snakes,
Dreadfully venomous to him. She lay
Stone-still, and the long darkness flowed away
With muffled pulses. Then, as midnight makes
Her giant heart of Memory and Tears
10   Drink the pale drug of silence, and so beat
Sleep's heavy measure, they from head to feet
Were moveless, looking through their dead black years,
By vain regret scrawled over the blank wall.
Like sculptured effigies they might be seen

1. A sequence of fifty sixteen-line sonnets, a kind of novel in verse about the breakup of a marriage. For most of the sequence the husband is the speaker, but the opening and closing sections are told in the third person.

15 Upon their marriage-tomb,[2] the sword between;
    Each wishing for the sword that severs all.

17

    At dinner, she is hostess, I am host.
    Went the feast ever cheerfuller? She keeps
    The Topic over intellectual deeps
    In buoyancy afloat. They see no ghost.
5   With sparkling surface-eyes we ply the ball:
    It is in truth a most contagious game:
    HIDING THE SKELETON, shall be its name.
    Such play as this the devils might appall!
    But here's the greater wonder; in that we,
10 Enamored of an acting naught can tire,
    Each other, like true hypocrites, admire;
    Warm-lighted looks, Love's ephemerioe,°   *short-lived creatures*
    Shoot gaily o'er the dishes and the wine.
    We waken envy of our happy lot.
15 Fast, sweet, and golden, shows the marriage-knot.
    Dear guests, you now have seen Love's corpse-light[3] shine.

30

    What are we first? First, animals; and next
    Intelligences at a leap; on whom
    Pale lies the distant shadow of the tomb,
    And all that draweth on the tomb for text.
5   Into which state comes Love, the crowning sun:
    Beneath whose light the shadow loses form.
    We are the lords of life, and life is warm.
    Intelligence and instinct now are one.
    But nature says: "My children most they seem
10 When they least know me: therefore I decree
    That they shall suffer." Swift doth young Love flee,
    And we stand wakened, shivering from our dream.
    Then if we study Nature we are wise.
    Thus do the few who live but with the day:
15 The scientific animals are they—
    Lady, this is my sonnet to your eyes.[4]

48

    Their sense is with their senses all mixed in,
    Destroyed by subtleties these women are![5]
    More brain, O Lord, more brain! or we shall mar
    Utterly this fair garden we might win.

2. I.e., as motionless as sculptured stone statues on a tomb. In medieval legend, a naked sword between lovers symbolized chastity.
3. Flame seen in a churchyard and believed to be an omen of death.
4. A poetic convention of love sonnets was the praise of one of the lady's features, such as her eyes. Meredith uses it as an ironic close to a state-ment of his theory of evolution.
5. Earlier, the couple had at last talked together about the wife's affair with another man and had become reconciled. But when the husband tells her of his own recent passing affair with his "lost Lady" (line 9), she resolves to give him up to his mistress. Her resolve is a noble one but, in his view, without "sense" or "brain."

5   Behold! I looked for peace, and thought it near.
    Our inmost hearts had opened, each to each.
    We drank the pure daylight of honest speech.
    Alas! that was the fatal draught, I fear.
    For when of my lost Lady came the word,
10 This woman, O this agony of flesh!
    Jealous devotion bade her break the mesh,
    That I might seek that other like a bird.
    I do adore the nobleness! despise
    The act! She has gone forth, I know not where.
15 Will the hard world my sentience of her share?
    I feel the truth; so let the world surmise.

49

    He found her by the ocean's moaning verge,
    Nor any wicked change in her discerned;
    And she believed his old love had returned,
    Which was her exultation, and her scourge.
5   She took his hand, and walked with him, and seemed
    The wife he sought, though shadow-like and dry.
    She had one terror, lest her heart should sigh,
    And tell her loudly she no longer dreamed.
    She dared not say, "This is my breast: look in."
10 But there's a strength to help the desperate weak.
    That night he learned how silence best can speak
    The awful things when Pity pleads for Sin.
    About the middle of the night her call
    Was heard, and he came wondering to the bed.
15 "Now kiss me, dear! it may be, now!" she said.
    Lethe[6] had passed those lips, and he knew all.

50

    Thus piteously Love closed what he begat:
    The union of this ever-diverse pair!
    These two were rapid falcons in a snare,
    Condemned to do the flitting of the bat.
5   Lovers beneath the singing sky of May,
    They wandered once; clear as the dew on flowers:
    But they fed not on the advancing hours:
    Their hearts held cravings for the buried day.
    Then each applied to each that fatal knife,
10 Deep questioning, which probes to endless dole.°   sorrow
    Ah, what a dusty answer gets the soul
    When hot for certainties in this our life!—
    In tragic hints here see what evermore
    Moves dark as yonder midnight ocean's force,
15 Thundering like ramping° hosts of warrior horse,   rearing
    To throw that faint thin line upon the shore!

                                                             1862

---

6. River of forgetfulness in Hades, the mythological Greek underworld.

Lucifer in Starlight

On a starred night Prince Lucifer uprose.
Tired of his dark dominion, swung the fiend
Above the rolling ball, in cloud part screened,
Where sinners hugged their specter of repose.
5 Poor prey to his hot fit of pride were those.
And now upon his western wing he leaned,
Now his huge bulk o'er Afric's sands careened,
Now the black planet shadowed Arctic snows.
Soaring through wider zones that pricked his scars
10 With memory of the old revolt from Awe,[7]
He reached a middle height, and at the stars,
Which are the brain of heaven, he looked, and sank.
Around the ancient track marched, rank on rank,
The army of unalterable law.

1883

EMILY DICKINSON*
1830–1886

39 (49)

I never lost as much but twice -
And that was in the sod.
Twice have I stood a beggar
Before the door of God!

5 Angels - twice descending
Reimbursed my store -
Burglar! Banker - Father!
I am poor once more!

1858   1890

68 (89)

Some things that fly there be -
Birds - Hours - the Bumblebee -
Of these no Elegy.

---

7. I.e., God. Satan is reminded of the wounds he suffered when his revolt against God was crushed and he was hurled from heaven into hell.

*R. W. Franklin's 1998 edition of Emily Dickinson's poems built on and has now supplanted the editions by Thomas Johnson (1955 and following) with which most contemporary readers are familiar. Phrasing, spelling, punctuation, and other features in Franklin, often differing from Johnson, reflect as closely as possible Dickinson's choices.

(She often misused the apostrophe, especially in the possessive of *it*, which she wrote as *it's*, and she also commonly misspelled words, such as *opon* for *upon*.) Franklin has also renumbered the poems after considering their likely chronology. Date on left, often approximate, refers to first known manuscript; date on right, to first book publication. Each poem here is identified by Franklin number, then by Johnson number in parentheses.

Some things that stay there be -
5   Grief - Hills - Eternity -
Nor this behooveth me.[1]

There are that resting, rise.
Can I expound the skies?
How still the Riddle lies!

1859   1890

112 (67)

Success is counted sweetest
By those who ne'er succeed.
To comprehend a nectar
Requires sorest need.

5   Not one of all the purple Host°   *army*
Who took the Flag today
Can tell the definition
So clear of Victory

As he defeated - dying -
10 On whose forbidden ear
The distant strains of triumph
Burst agonized and clear!

1859   1890

124 (216), first version[2]

Safe in their Alabaster[3] Chambers -
Untouched by morning
And untouched by noon -
Sleep the meek members of the Resurrection -
5   Rafter of satin,
And Roof of stone.

Light laughs the breeze
In her Castle above them -
Babbles the Bee in a stolid Ear,
10 Pipe the sweet Birds in ignorant cadence -
Ah, what sagacity perished here!

1859   1862

1. I.e., nor do I need to write about these.
2. This poem is one of many that exist in varying versions and illustrate wholesale revision. Dickinson sent the 1859 version to her sister-in-law, Sue Dickinson, whose suggestions prompted substantial changes. The first version here, the earliest extant, was one of the few poems Dickinson published (in a magazine). In correspondence in 1862 with Thomas W. Higginson, the literary critic who would help publish her poems posthumously, Dickinson sent a modified version, the basis of the second version here.
3. Translucent white material.

124 (216), second version

Safe in their Alabaster Chambers -
Untouched by Morning -
And untouched by noon -
Sleep the meek members of the Resurrection,
5   Rafter of Satin and Roof of Stone -

Grand go the Years,
In the Crescent above them -
Worlds scoop their Arcs -
And Firmaments - row -
10 Diadems° - drop -   *crowns*
And Doges[4] - surrender -
Soundless as Dots,
On a Disc of Snow.

1862   1890

145 (59)

A little East of Jordan,
Evangelists record,[5]
A Gymnast and an Angel
Did wrestle long and hard -

5   Till morning touching mountain
And Jacob, waxing strong,
The Angel begged permission
To Breakfast - to return!

Not so, said cunning Jacob!
10 "I will not let thee go
Except thou bless me" - Stranger!
The which acceded to -

Light swung the silver fleeces[6]
"Peniel" Hills beyond,
15 And the bewildered Gymnast
Found he had worsted God!

1860   1914

---

4. Chief magistrates in the republics of Venice and Genoa from the eleventh through the sixteenth centuries.
5. The story actually occurs in Genesis 32.24–30. Jacob wrestled with the angel for a blessing; having succeeded, "Jacob called the place Peniel: for I have seen God face to face, and my life is preserved."
6. Clouds; also, a possible allusion to the Golden Fleece that, in Greek mythology, Jason long traveled to find.

202 (185)

"Faith" is a fine invention
For Gentlemen who *see!*
But Microscopes are prudent
In an Emergency!

1861   1891

259 (287)

A Clock stopped -
Not the Mantel's -
Geneva's farthest skill[7]
Cant put the puppet bowing -
5   That just now dangled still -

An awe came on the Trinket!
The Figures hunched - with pain -
Then quivered out of Decimals -
Into Degreeless noon -

10   It will not stir for Doctor's -
This Pendulum of snow -
The Shopman importunes it -
While cool- concernless No -

Nods from the Gilded pointers -
15   Nods from the Seconds slim -
Decades of Arrogance between
The Dial life -
And Him -

1861   1896

260 (288)

I'm Nobody! Who are you?
Are you - Nobody - too?
Then there's a pair of us!
Dont tell! they'd advertise - you know!

5   How dreary - to be - Somebody!
How public - like a Frog -
To tell one's name - the livelong June -
To an admiring Bog!

1861   1891

7. Geneva, Switzerland, is famous for clock- and watchmaking.

269 (249)

Wild nights - Wild nights!
Were I with thee
Wild nights should be
Our luxury!

5   Futile - the winds -
To a Heart in port -
Done with the Compass -
Done with the Chart!

Rowing in Eden -
10   Ah - the Sea!
Might I but moor - tonight -
In thee!

1861   1891

314 (254)

"Hope" is the thing with feathers -
That perches in the soul -
And sings the tune without the words -
And never stops - at all -

5   And sweetest - in the Gale - is heard -
And sore must be the storm -
That could abash the little Bird
That kept so many warm -

I've heard it in the chillest land -
10   And on the strangest Sea -
Yet - never - in Extremity,
It asked a crumb - of me.

1862   1891

320 (258)

There's a certain Slant of light,
Winter Afternoons -
That oppresses, like the Heft
Of Cathedral Tunes -

5   Heavenly Hurt, it gives us -
We can find no scar,

But internal difference -
Where the Meanings, are -

None may teach it - Any -
10   'Tis the Seal Despair -
An imperial affliction
Sent us of the Air -

When it comes, the Landscape listens -
Shadows - hold their breath -
15   When it goes, 'tis like the Distance
On the look of Death -

1862   1890

339 (241)

I like a look of Agony,
Because I know it's true -
Men do not sham Convulsion,
Nor simulate, a Throe -

5   The eyes glaze once - and that is Death -
Impossible to feign
The Beads opon the Forehead
By homely Anguish strung.

1862   1890

340 (280)

I felt a Funeral, in my Brain,
And Mourners to and fro
Kept treading - treading - till it seemed
That Sense was breaking through -

5   And when they all were seated,
A Service, like a Drum -
Kept beating - beating - till I thought
My mind was going numb -

And then I heard them lift a Box
10   And creak across my Soul
With those same Boots of Lead, again,
Then Space - began to toll,

As all the Heavens were a Bell,
And Being, but an Ear,

15 And I, and Silence, some strange Race
   Wrecked, solitary, here -

   And then a Plank in Reason, broke,
   And I dropped down, and down -
   And hit a World, at every plunge,
20 And Finished knowing - then -

1862   1896

348 (505)

   I would not paint - a picture -
   I'd rather be the One
   It's bright impossibility
   To dwell - delicious - on -
5 And wonder how the fingers feel
   Whose rare - celestial - stir -
   Evokes so sweet a torment -
   Such sumptuous - Despair -

   I would not talk, like Cornets -
10 I'd rather be the One
   Raised softly to the Ceilings -
   And out, and easy on -
   Through Villages of Ether -
   Myself endued° Balloon   endowed
15 By but a lip of Metal -
   The pier to my Pontoon° -   boat

   Nor would I be a Poet -
   It's finer - Own the Ear -
   Enamored - impotent - content -
20 The License to revere,
   A privilege so awful°   awesome
   What would the Dower° be,   dowry, gift
   Had I the Art to stun myself
   With Bolts - of Melody!

1862   1945

359 (328)

A Bird, came down the Walk -
He did not know I saw -
He bit an Angle Worm in halves
And ate the fellow, raw,

5   And then, he drank a Dew
From a convenient Grass -
And then hopped sidewise to the Wall
To let a Beetle pass -

He glanced with rapid eyes,
10 That hurried all abroad -
They looked like frightened Beads, I thought,
He stirred his Velvet Head. -

Like one in danger, Cautious,
I offered him a Crumb,
15 And he unrolled his feathers,
And rowed him softer Home -

Than Oars divide the Ocean,
Too silver for a seam,
Or Butterflies, off Banks of Noon,
20 Leap, plashless° as they swim.   *splashless*

1862   1891

372 (341)

After great pain, a formal feeling comes -
The Nerves sit ceremonious, like Tombs -
The stiff Heart questions "was it He, that bore,
And "Yesterday, or Centuries before"?

5 The Feet, mechanical, go round -
A Wooden way
Of Ground, or Air, or Ought° -   *nothing, anything*
Regardless grown,
A Quartz contentment, like a stone -

10 This is the Hour of Lead -
Remembered, if outlived,
As Freezing persons, recollect the Snow -
First - Chill - then Stupor - then the letting go -

1862   1929

383 (585)

I like to see it lap the Miles -
And lick the Valleys up -
And stop to feed itself at Tanks -
And then - prodigious step

5   Around a Pile of Mountains -
And supercilious peer
In Shanties - by the sides of Roads -
And then a Quarry pare

To fit it's sides
10   And crawl between
Complaining all the while
In horrid - hooting stanza -
Then chase itself down Hill -

And neigh like Boanerges[8] -
15   Then - prompter than a Star
Stop - docile and omnipotent
At it's own stable door -

1862   1891

409 (303)

The Soul selects her own Society -
Then - shuts the Door -
To her divine Majority -
Present no more -

5   Unmoved - she notes the Chariots - pausing -
At her low Gate -
Unmoved - an Emperor be kneeling
Opon her Mat -

I've known her - from an ample nation -
10   Choose One -
Then - close the Valves of her attention -
Like Stone -

1862   1890

411 (528)

Mine - by the Right of the White Election!
Mine - by the Royal Seal!
Mine - by the sign in the Scarlet prison -
Bars - cannot conceal!

5   Mine - here - in Vision - and in Veto!
Mine - by the Grave's Repeal -

---

8. Like thunder. Cf. Mark 3.17: "And James the son of Zebedee, and John the brother of James; and he surnamed them Boanerges, which is, The sons of thunder."

Titled - Confirmed -
Delirious Charter!
Mine - long as Ages steal!

1862   1890

445 (613)

They shut me up in Prose -
As when a little Girl
They put me in the Closet -
Because they liked me "still" -

5   Still! Could themself have peeped -
And seen my Brain - go round -
They might as wise have lodged a Bird
For Treason - in the Pound -

Himself has but to will
10 And easy as a Star
Look down opon Captivity -
And laugh - No more have I -

1862   1935

479 (712)

Because I could not stop for Death -
He kindly stopped for me -
The Carriage held but just Ourselves -
And Immortality.

5   We slowly drove - He knew no haste
And I had put away
My labor and my leisure too,
For His Civility -

We passed the School, where Children strove
10 At Recess - in the Ring -
We passed the Fields of Gazing Grain -
We passed the Setting Sun -

Or rather - He passed Us -
The Dews drew quivering and Chill -
15 For only Gossamer, my Gown -
My Tippet - only Tulle[9] -

---

9. Sheer silk net. *Tippet*: shoulder cape.

We paused before a House that seemed
A Swelling of the Ground -
The Roof was scarcely visible -
20   The Cornice° - in the Ground -   *crowning point*

Since then - 'tis Centuries - and yet
Feels shorter than the Day
I first surmised the Horses' Heads
Were toward Eternity -

1862   1890

533 (569)

I reckon - When I count at all -
First - Poets - Then the Sun -
Then Summer - Then the Heaven of God -
And then - the List is done -

5   But, looking back - the First so seems
To Comprehend the Whole -
The Others look a needless Show -
So I write - Poets - All -

Their Summer - lasts a solid Year -
10 They can afford a Sun
The East - would deem extravagant -
And if the Further Heaven -

Be Beautiful as they prepare
For Those who worship Them -
15 It is too difficult a Grace -
To Justify the Dream -

1863   1929

588 (536)

The Heart asks Pleasure - first -
And then - excuse from Pain -
And then - those little Anodynes
That deaden suffering -

5 And then - to go to sleep -
And then - if it should be
The will of it's Inquisitor
The privilege to die -

1863   1890

591 (465)

I heard a Fly buzz - when I died -
The Stillness in the Room
Was like the Stillness in the Air -
Between the Heaves of Storm -

5 The Eyes around - had wrung them dry -
And Breaths were gathering firm
For that last Onset - when the King
Be witnessed - in the Room -

I willed my Keepsakes - Signed away
10 What portion of me be
Assignable - and then it was
There interposed a Fly -

With Blue - uncertain - stumbling Buzz -
Between the light - and me -
15 And then the Windows failed - and then
I could not see to see -

1863   1896

620 (435)

Much Madness is divinest Sense -
To a discerning Eye -
Much Sense - the starkest Madness -
'Tis the Majority
5 In this, as all, prevail -
Assent - and you are sane -
Demur - you're straightway dangerous -
And handled with a Chain -

1863   1890

740 (789)

On a Columnar Self -
How ample to rely
In Tumult - or Extremity -
How good the Certainty

5 That Lever cannot pry -
And Wedge cannot divide
Conviction - That Granitic Base -
Though none be on our side -

Suffice Us - for a Crowd -
10   Ourself - and Rectitude -
And that Assembly - not far off
From furthest Spirit - God -

1863   1929

764 (754)

My Life had stood - a Loaded Gun -
In Corners - till a Day
The Owner passed - identified -
And carried Me away -

5   And now We roam in Sovreign Woods -
And now We hunt the Doe -
And every time I speak for Him
The Mountains straight reply -

And do I smile, such cordial light
10   Opon the Valley glow -
It is as a Vesuvian[1] face
Had let it's pleasure through -

And when at Night - Our good Day done -
I guard My Master's Head -
15   'Tis better than the Eider Duck's
Deep Pillow[2] - to have shared -

To foe of His - I'm deadly foe -
None stir the second time -
On whom I lay a Yellow Eye -
20   Or an emphatic Thumb -

Thought I than He - may longer live
He longer must - than I -
For I have but the power to kill,
Without - the power to die -

1863   1929

781 (744)

Remorse - is Memory - awake -
Her Parties all astir -
A Presence of Departed Acts -
At window - and at Door -

---

1. Capable of erupting, like Mt. Vesuvius, the vol-   2. I.e., pillow stuffed with feathers or down.
cano near Naples.

5   It's Past - set down before the Soul
And lighted with a match -
Perusal - to facilitate -
And help Belief to stretch -

Remorse is cureless - the Disease
10 Not even God - can heal -
For 'tis His institution - and
The Adequate of Hell -

1863   1891

782 (745)

Renunciation - is a piercing Virtue -
The letting go
A Presence - for an Expectation -
Not now -
5   The putting out of Eyes -
Just Sunrise -
Lest Day -
Day's Great Progenitor -
Outvie
10 Renunciation - is the Choosing
Against itself -
Itself to justify
Unto itself -
When larger function -
15 Make that appear -
Smaller - that Covered Vision - Here -

1863   1929

788 (709)

Publication - is the Auction
Of the Mind of Man -
Poverty - be justifying
For so foul a thing

5   Possibly - but We - would rather
From Our Garret go
White - unto the White Creator -
Than invest - Our snow -

Thought belong to Him who gave it -
10 Then - to Him Who bear
It's Corporeal illustration - sell
The Royal Air -

In the Parcel - Be the Merchant
Of the Heavenly Grace -
15 But reduce no Human Spirit
To Disgrace of Price -

1863   1929

895 (1068)

Further in Summer than the Birds -
Pathetic from the Grass -
A minor Nation[3] celebrates
It's unobtrusive Mass.

5 No Ordinance° be seen -   *prescribed usage*
So gradual the Grace
A gentle Custom it becomes -
Enlarging Loneliness -

Antiquest felt at Noon -
10 When August burning low
Arise this spectral Canticle°   *liturgical song*
Repose to typify -

Remit as yet no Grace -
No furrow on the Glow,
15 But a Druidic[4] Difference
Enhances Nature now -

1865, 1883   1891

905 (861)

Split the Lark - and you'll find the Music -
Bulb after Bulb, in Silver rolled -
Scantily dealt to the Summer Morning
Saved for your Ear, when Lutes be old -

5 Loose the Flood - you shall find it patent° -   *open*
Gush after Gush, reserved for you -
Scarlet Experiment! Sceptic Thomas![5]
Now, do you doubt that your Bird was true?

1865   1896

---

3. I.e., insects.
4. Pertaining to the ancient sacred lore of the Celtic priest-magicians.
5. Doubting Thomas, who would not believe Christ's divinity until he had seen the print of the nails in Jesus' hands and thrust a hand into Jesus' side (John 20.25).

935 (1540)

As imperceptibly as Grief
The Summer lapsed away -
Too imperceptible at last
To seem like Perfidy° -   *treachery*
5   A Quietness distilled
As Twilight long begun,
Or Nature spending with herself
Sequestered Afternoon -
The Dusk drew earlier in -
10 The Morning foreign shone -
A courteous, yet harrowing Grace,
As Guest, that would be gone -
And thus, without a Wing
Or service of a Keel
15 Our Summer made her light escape
Into the Beautiful -

1865   1891

1096 (986)

A narrow Fellow in the Grass
Occasionally rides -
You may have met him? Did you not
His notice instant is -

5   The Grass divides as with a Comb -
A spotted Shaft is seen,
And then it closes at your Feet
And opens further on -

He likes a Boggy Acre -
10 A Floor too cool for Corn -
But when a Boy and Barefoot
I more than once at Noon

Have passed I thought a Whip Lash
Unbraiding in the Sun
15 When stooping to secure it
It wrinkled And was gone -

Several of Nature's People
I know and they know me
I feel for them a transport
20 Of Cordiality

But never met this Fellow
Attended or alone
Without a tighter Breathing
And Zero at the Bone.

1865   1891

1108 (1078)

The Bustle in a House
The Morning after Death
Is solemnest of industries
Enacted opon Earth -

5   The Sweeping up the Heart
And putting Love away
We shall not want to use again
Until Eternity -

1865   1890

1263 (1129)

Tell all the truth but tell it slant -
Success in Circuit lies
Too bright for our infirm Delight
The Truth's superb surprise
5   As Lightning to the Children eased
With explanation kind
The Truth must dazzle gradually
Or every man be blind -

1872   1945

1489 (1463)

A Route of Evanescence,
With a revolving Wheel -
A Resonance of Emerald
A Rush of Cochineal° -   *red dye*
5   And every Blossom on the Bush
Adjusts it's tumbled Head -
The Mail from Tunis⁶ - probably,
An easy Morning's Ride -

1879   1891

6. City on the northern coast of Africa.

1577 (1545)

The Bible is an antique Volume -
Written by faded Men
At the suggestion of Holy Spectres -
Subjects - Bethlehem -
5   Eden - the ancient Homestead -
Satan - the Brigadier -
Judas - the Great Defaulter -
David - the Troubadour -
Sin - a distinguished Precipice
10   Others must resist -
Boys that "believe" are very lonesome -
Other Boys are "lost" -
Had but the Tale a warbling Teller -
All the Boys would come -
15   Orpheu's[7] Sermon captivated -
It did not condemn -

1882   1924

1793 (1732)

My life closed twice before it's close;
It yet remains to see
If Immortality unveil
A third event to me,

5   So huge, so hopeless to conceive
As these that twice befell.
Parting is all we know of heaven,
And all we need of hell.

1896

1788 (1763)

Fame is a bee.
It has a song -
It has a sting -
Ah, too, it has a wing.

1955

---

7. *Orpheu's:* i.e., that of Orpheus, the Greek mythological figure whose music attracted and controlled beasts, rocks, and trees.

CHRISTINA ROSSETTI
1830–1894

Song

When I am dead, my dearest,
  Sing no sad songs for me;
Plant thou no roses at my head,
  Nor shady cypress tree:
5 Be the green grass above me
  With showers and dewdrops wet;
And if thou wilt, remember,
  And if thou wilt, forget.

I shall not see the shadows,
10 I shall not feel the rain;
I shall not hear the nightingale
  Sing on, as if in pain:
And dreaming through the twilight
  That doth not rise nor set,
15 Haply I may remember,
  And haply may forget.

1848   1862

Remember

Remember me when I am gone away,
  Gone far away into the silent land;
  When you can no more hold me by the hand,
Nor I half turn to go yet turning stay.
5 Remember me when no more day by day
  You tell me of our future that you planned:
  Only remember me; you understand
It will be late to counsel then or pray.
Yet if you should forget me for a while
10 And afterwards remember, do not grieve:
  For if the darkness and corruption leave
  A vestige of the thoughts that once I had,
Better by far you should forget and smile
  Than that you should remember and be sad.

1849   1862

Echo

Come to me in the silence of the night;
  Come in the speaking silence of a dream;

Come with soft rounded cheeks and eyes as bright
   As sunlight on a stream;
5   Come back in tears,
O memory, hope, love of finished years.

Oh dream how sweet, too sweet, too bitter sweet,
   Whose wakening should have been in Paradise,
Where souls brimful of love abide and meet;
10   Where thirsting longing eyes
      Watch the slow door
That opening, letting in, lets out no more.

Yet come to me in dreams, that I may live
   My very life again tho' cold in death:
15 Come back to me in dreams, that I may give
   Pulse for pulse, breath for breath:
     Speak low, lean low,
As long ago, my love, how long ago.

1854   1862

In an Artist's Studio

One face looks out from all his canvases,
   One selfsame figure sits or walks or leans:
   We found her hidden just behind those screens,
That mirror gave back all her loveliness.
5 A queen in opal or in ruby dress,
    A nameless girl in freshest summer-greens,
    A saint, an angel—every canvas means
The same one meaning, neither more nor less.
He feeds upon her face by day and night,
10   And she with true kind eyes looks back on him,
Fair as the moon and joyful as the light:
   Not wan with waiting, not with sorrow dim;
Not as she is, but was when hope shone bright;
   Not as she is, but as she fills his dream.

1856   1896

Up-Hill

Does the road wind up-hill all the way?
   Yes, to the very end.
Will the day's journey take the whole long day?
   From morn to night, my friend.

5   But is there for the night a resting-place?
          A roof for when the slow dark hours begin.
       May not the darkness hide it from my face?
          You cannot miss that inn.

       Shall I meet other wayfarers at night?
10   Those who have gone before.
       Then must I knock, or call when just in sight?
          They will not keep you standing at that door.

       Shall I find comfort, travel-sore and weak?
          Of labor you shall find the sum.
15   Will there be beds for me and all who seek?
          Yea, beds for all who come.

1858   1862

The Convent Threshold

       There's blood between us, love, my love,
       There's father's blood, there's brother's blood;
       And blood's a bar I cannot pass:
       I choose the stairs that mount above,
5   Stair after golden skyward stair,
       To city and to sea of glass.
       My lily feet are soiled with mud,
       With scarlet mud which tells a tale
       Of hope that was, of guilt that was,
10   Of love that shall not yet avail;
       Alas, my heart, if I could bare
       My heart, this selfsame stain is there:
       I seek the sea of glass and fire
       To wash the spot, to burn the snare;
15   Lo, stairs are meant to lift us higher:
       Mount with me, mount the kindled stair.

       Your eyes look earthward, mine look up.
       I see the far-off city grand,
       Beyond the hills a watered land,
20   Beyond the gulf a gleaming strand
       Of mansions where the righteous sup;
       Who sleep at ease among their trees,
       Or wake to sing a cadenced hymn
       With Cherubim and Seraphim;[1]
25   They bore the Cross, they drained the cup,
       Racked, roasted, crushed, wrenched limb from limb,
       They the offscouring[2] of the world:

---

1. Plurals (Hebrew, biblical) of, respectively, *cherub* and *seraph*; seraphim are the highest order of angels, just above the cherubim.

2. What is "scoured off," hence refuse, that which is rejected.

The heaven of starry heavens unfurled,
The sun before their face is dim.

30 You looking earthward, what see you?
Milk-white, wine-flushed among the vines,
Up and down leaping, to and fro,
Most glad, most full, made strong with wines,
Blooming as peaches pearled with dew,
35 Their golden windy hair afloat,
Love-music warbling in their throat,
Young men and women come and go.

You linger, yet the time is short:
Flee for your life, gird up your strength
40 To flee; the shadows stretched at length
Show that day wanes, that night draws nigh;
Flee to the mountain, tarry not.
Is this a time for smile and sigh,
For songs among the secret trees
45 Where sudden blue birds nest and sport?
The time is short and yet you stay:
Today while it is called today
Kneel, wrestle, knock, do violence, pray;
Today is short, tomorrow nigh:
50 Why will you die? why will you die?

You sinned with me a pleasant sin:
Repent with me, for I repent.
Woe's me the lore I must unlearn!
Woe's me that easy way we went,
55 So rugged when I would return!
How long until my sleep begin,
How long shall stretch these nights and days?
Surely, clean Angels cry, she prays;
She laves her soul with tedious tears:
60 How long must stretch these years and years?

I turn from you my cheeks and eyes,
My hair which you shall see no more—
Alas for joy that went before,
For joy that dies, for love that dies.
65 Only my lips still turn to you,
My livid lips that cry, Repent.
Oh weary life, Oh weary Lent,[3]
Oh weary time whose stars are few.

How should I rest in Paradise,
70 Or sit on steps of heaven alone?
If Saints and Angels spoke of love
Should I not answer from my throne:

3. Period in the Christian calendar from Ash Wednesday to Easter Eve, devoted to fasting and penitence in commemoration of Christ's fasting in the wilderness.

Have pity upon me, ye my friends,
For I have heard the sound thereof:
75   Should I not turn with yearning eyes,
Turn earthwards with a pitiful pang?
Oh save me from a pang in heaven.
By all the gifts we took and gave,
Repent, repent, and be forgiven·
80   This life is long, but yet it ends;
Repent and purge your soul and save:
No gladder song the morning stars
Upon their birthday morning sang
Than Angels sing when one repents.

85   I tell you what I dreamed last night:
A spirit with transfigured face
Fire-footed clomb° an infinite space.   *climbed*
I heard his hundred pinions° clang,   *feathered wings*
Heaven-bells rejoicing rang and rang,
90   Heaven-air was thrilled with subtle scents,
Worlds spun upon their rushing cars:
He mounted shrieking: "Give me light."
Still light was poured on him, more light;
Angels, Archangels he outstripped
95   Exultant in exceeding might,
And trod the skirts of Cherubim.
Still "Give me light," he shrieked; and dipped
His thirsty face, and drank a sea,
Athirst with thirst it could not slake.
100   I saw him, drunk with knowledge, take
From aching brows the aureole crown⁴—
His locks writhed like a cloven snake—
He left his throne to grovel down
And lick the dust of Seraphs' feet:
105   For what is knowledge duly weighed?
Knowledge is strong, but love is sweet;
Yea all the progress he had made
Was but to learn that all is small
Save love, for love is all in all.

110   I tell you what I dreamed last night:
It was not dark, it was not light,
Cold dews had drenched my plenteous hair
Thro' clay; you came to seek me there.
And "Do you dream of me?" you said.
115   My heart was dust that used to leap
To you; I answered half asleep:
"My pillow is damp, my sheets are red,
There's a leaden tester° to my bed: *canopy*
Find you a warmer playfellow,
120   A warmer pillow for your head,
A kinder love to love than mine."

4. Golden crown or halo.

You wrung your hands; while I like lead
Crushed downwards thro' the sodden earth:
You smote your hands but not in mirth,
125   And reeled but were not drunk with wine.

For all night long I dreamed of you:
I woke and prayed against my will,
Then slept to dream of you again.
At length I rose and knelt and prayed:
130   I cannot write the words I said,
My words were slow, my tears were few;
But thro' the dark my silence spoke
Like thunder. When this morning broke,
My face was pinched, my hair was gray,
135   And frozen blood was on the sill
Where stifling in my struggle I lay.

If now you saw me you would say:
Where is the face I used to love?
And I would answer: Gone before;
140   It tarries veiled in paradise.
When once the morning star shall rise,
When earth with shadow flees away
And we stand safe within the door,
Then you shall lift the veil thereof.
145   Look up, rise up: for far above
Our palms are grown, our place is set;
There we shall meet as once we met
And love with old familiar love.

1858   1862

Passing Away, Saith the World, Passing Away

Passing away, saith the World, passing away:
Chances, beauty and youth sapped day by day:
Thy life never continueth in one stay.
Is the eye waxen dim, is the dark hair changing to gray
5   That hath won neither laurel nor bay?[5]
I shall clothe myself in Spring and bud in May:
Thou, root-stricken, shalt not rebuild thy decay
On my bosom for aye.
Then I answered: Yea.

10   Passing away, saith my Soul, passing away:
With its burden of fear and hope, of labor and play;
Hearken what the past doth witness and say:

5. In ancient Greece, victors in the Pythian games were crowned with a wreath made from the leaves of the laurel, and later such wreaths were bestowed on the winners of academic or poetic honors. "Bay" is synonymous with laurel.

Rust in thy gold, a moth is in thine array,
A canker is in thy bud, thy leaf must decay.
15 At midnight, at cockcrow, at morning, one certain day
Lo the bridegroom shall come and shall not delay:
Watch thou and pray.
Then I answered: Yea.

Passing away, saith my God, passing away:
20 Winter passeth after the long delay:
New grapes on the vine, new figs on the tender spray,
Turtle calleth turtle in Heaven's May.
Tho' I tarry, wait for Me, trust Me, watch and pray.
Arise, come away, night is past and lo it is day,
25 My love, My sister, My spouse, thou shalt hear Me say.
Then I answered: Yea.

1860   1862

Amor Mundi[6]

"Oh where are you going with your love-locks flowing
On the west wind blowing along this valley track?"
"The downhill path is easy, come with me an° it please ye,   *if*
We shall escape the uphill by never turning back."

5 So they two went together in glowing August weather,
The honey-breathing heather lay to their left and right;
And dear she was to dote on, her swift feet seemed to float on
The air like soft twin pigeons too sportive to alight.

"Oh what is that in heaven where gray cloud-flakes are seven,
10 Where blackest clouds hang riven just at the rainy skirt?"
Oh that's a meteor sent us, a message dumb, portentous,
An undeciphered solemn signal of help or hurt."

"Oh what is that glides quickly where velvet flowers grow thickly,
Their scent comes rich and sickly?"—"A scaled and hooded
worm."
15 "Oh what's that in the hollow, so pale I quake to follow?"
"Oh that's a thin dead body which waits the eternal term."

"Turn again, O my sweetest,—turn again, false and fleetest:
This beaten way thou beatest I fear is hell's own track."
"Nay, too steep for hill-mounting; nay, too late for cost-counting:
20 This downhill path is easy, but there's no turning back."

1865   1875

6. Love of the world (Latin).

LEWIS CARROLL
(CHARLES LUTWIDGE DODGSON)
1832–1898

Jabberwocky[1]

There was a book lying near Alice on the table, and while she sat watching the White King (for she was still a little anxious about him, and had the ink all ready to throw over him, in case he fainted again), she turned over the leaves, to find some part that she could read, "—for it's all in some language I don't know," she said to herself. It was like this:

Jabberwocky

'Twas brillig, and the slithy toves
Did gyre and gimble in the wabe:
All mimsy were the borogoves,
And the mome raths outgrabe.

She puzzled over this for some time, but at last a bright thought struck her. "Why, it's a Looking-glass book, of course! And, if I hold it up to a glass, the words will all go the right way again."

This was the poem that Alice read:

Jabberwocky

'Twas brillig, and the slithy toves
    Did gyre and gimble in the wabe:
All mimsy were the borogoves,
    And the mome raths outgrabe.

5 "Beware the Jabberwock, my son!
    The jaws that bite, the claws that catch!
Beware the Jubjub bird, and shun
    The frumious Bandersnatch!"

He took his vorpal sword in hand:
10   Long time the manxome foe he sought—
So rested he by the Tumtum tree,
    And stood awhile in thought.

And, as in uffish thought he stood,
    The Jabberwock, with eyes of flame,
15 Came whiffling through the tulgey wood,
    And burbled as it came!

1. From *Through the Looking-Glass*, chapter 1.

One, two! One, two! And through and through
    The vorpal blade went snicker-snack!
He left it dead, and with its head
20   He went galumphing back.

"And hast thou slain the Jabberwock?
    Come to my arms, my beamish boy!
O frabjous day! Callooh! Callay!"
    He chortled in his joy.

25   'Twas brillig, and the slithy toves
    Did gyre and gimble in the wabe:
All mimsy were the borogoves,
    And the mome raths outgrabe.

[Humpty Dumpty's Explication of *Jabberwocky*][2]

"You seem very clever at explaining words, Sir," said Alice. "Would you kindly tell me the meaning of the poem *Jabberwocky*?"

"Let's hear it," said Humpty Dumpty. "I can explain all the poems that ever were invented—and a good many that haven't been invented just yet."

This sounded very hopeful, so Alice repeated the first verse:

" 'Twas brillig, and the slithy toves
    Did gyre and gimble in the wabe;
All mimsy were the borogoves,
    And the mome raths outgrabe."

"That's enough to begin with," Humpty Dumpty interrupted: "there are plenty of hard words there. 'Brillig' means four o'clock in the afternoon—the time when you begin *broiling* things for dinner."

"That'll do very well," said Alice: "and 'slithy'?"[3]

"Well, 'slithy' means 'lithe and slimy.' 'Lithe' is the same as 'active.' You see it's like a portmanteau—there are two meanings packed up into one word."

"I see it now," Alice remarked thoughtfully: "and what are 'toves'?"

"Well, 'toves' are something like badgers—they're something like lizards—and they're something like corkscrews."

"They must be very curious creatures."

"They are that," said Humpty Dumpty: "also they make their nests under sundials—also they live on cheese."

"And what's to 'gyre' and to 'gimble'?"

"To 'gyre' is to go round and round like a gyroscope. To 'gimble' is to make holes like a gimlet."

"And the 'wabe' is the grass plot round a sundial, I suppose?" said Alice, surprised at her own ingenuity.

---

2. From *Through the Looking-Glass*, chapter 6.
3. Concerning the pronunciation of these words, Carroll later said: "The 'i' in 'slithy' is long, as in 'writhe'; and 'toves' is pronounced so as to rhyme with 'groves.' Again, the first 'o' in 'borogoves' is pronounced like the 'o' in 'borrow.' I have heard people try to give it the sound of the 'o' in 'worry.' Such is Human Perversity."

"Of course it is. It's called 'wabe,' you know, because it goes a long way before it, and a long way behind it—"

"And a long way beyond it on each side," Alice added.

"Exactly so. Well then, 'mimsy' is 'flimsy and miserable' (there's another portmanteau for you). And a 'borogove' is a thin shabby-looking bird with its feathers sticking out all round—something like a live mop."

"And then 'mome raths'?" said Alice. "If I'm not giving you too much trouble."

"Well, a 'rath' is a sort of green pig: but 'mome' I'm not certain about. I think it's short for 'from home'—meaning that they'd lost their way, you know."

"And what does 'outgrabe' mean?"

"Well, 'outgribing' is something between bellowing and whistling, with a kind of sneeze in the middle: however, you'll hear it done, maybe—down in the wood yonder—and when you've once heard it you'll be *quite* content. Who's been repeating all that hard stuff to you?"

"I read it in a book," said Alice.

1871

The White Knight's Song[4]

Haddock's Eyes or *The Aged Aged Man* or
Ways and Means or *A-Sitting on a Gate*

> I'll tell thee everything I can;
>   There's little to relate.
> I saw an aged, aged man,
>   A-sitting on a gate.
> 5 "Who are you, aged man?" I said.
>   "And how is it you live?"
> And his answer trickled through my head
>   Like water through a sieve.
>
> He said "I look for butterflies
> 10   That sleep among the wheat;
> I make them into mutton-pies,
>   And sell them in the street.
> I sell them unto men," he said,
>   "Who sail on stormy seas;
> 15 And that's the way I get my bread—
>   A trifle, if you please."
>
> But I was thinking of a plan
>   To dye one's whiskers green,
> And always use so large a fan
> 20   That it could not be seen.
> So, having no reply to give

---

4. From *Through the Looking-Glass,* chapter 8; the song is in part a parody of Wordsworth's "Resolution and Independence" (see p. 790).

To what the old man said,
I cried, "Come, tell me how you live!"
And thumped him on the head.

25 His accents mild took up the tale;
He said, "I go my ways,
And when I find a mountain-rill,°   -stream
I set it in a blaze;
And thence they make a stuff they call
30 Rowland's Macassar Oil[5]—
Yet twopence-halfpenny is all
They give me for my toil."

But I was thinking of a way
To feed oneself on batter,
35 And so go on from day to day
Getting a little fatter.
I shook him well from side to side,
Until his face was blue;
"Come, tell me how you live," I cried
40 "And what it is you do!"

He said, "I hunt for haddocks' eyes
Among the heather bright,
And work them into waistcoat-buttons
In the silent night.
45 And these I do not sell for gold
Or coin of silvery shine,
But for a copper halfpenny,
And that will purchase nine.

"I sometimes dig for buttered rolls,
50 Or set limed twigs for crabs;
I sometimes search the grassy knolls
For wheels of hansom-cabs.
And that's the way" (he gave a wink)
"By which I get my wealth—
55 And very gladly will I drink
Your Honor's noble health."

I heard him then, for I had just
Completed my design
To keep the Menai bridge[6] from rust
60 By boiling it in wine.
I thanked him much for telling me
The way he got his wealth,
But chiefly for his wish that he
Might drink my noble health.

65 And now, if e'er by chance I put
My fingers into glue,

---

5. A patented hairdressing.   6. Railway bridge in Wales.

Or madly squeeze a right-hand foot
  Into a left-hand shoe,
Or if I drop upon my toe
70   A very heavy weight,
I weep, for it reminds me so
Of that old man I used to know—
Whose look was mild, whose speech was slow,
Whose hair was whiter than the snow,
75 Whose face was very like a crow,
With eyes, like cinders, all aglow,
Who seemed distracted with his woe,
Who rocked his body to and fro,
And muttered mumblingly and low,
80 As if his mouth were full of dough,
Who snorted like a buffalo—
That summer evening long ago
  A-sitting on a gate.

1871

WILLIAM MORRIS
1834–1896

The Haystack in the Floods[1]

Had she come all the way for this,
To part at last without a kiss?
Yea, had she borne the dirt and rain
That her own eyes might see him slain
5 Beside the haystack in the floods?

Along the dripping leafless woods,
The stirrup touching either shoe,
She rode astride as troopers do;
With kirtle° kilted to her knee,   *long skirt*
10 To which the mud splashed wretchedly;
And the wet dripped from every tree
Upon her head and heavy hair,
And on her eyelids broad and fair;
The tears and rain ran down her face.
15 By fits and starts they rode apace,
And very often was his place
Far off from her; he had to ride
Ahead, to see what might betide
When the roads crossed; and sometimes, when
20 There rose a murmuring from his men,

1. The events of the poem take place immediately after the Battle of Poitiers (1356), in which the English defeated the French. An English knight, Sir Robert de Marny, and his mistress, Jehane, are attempting to escape the French by reaching Gascony, held by the English.

Had to turn back with promises;
Ah me! she had but little ease;
And often for pure doubt and dread
She sobbed, made giddy in the head
25 By the swift riding; while, for cold,
Her slender fingers scarce could hold
The wet reins; yea, and scarcely, too,
She felt the foot within her shoe
Against the stirrup: all for this,
30 To part at last without a kiss
Beside the haystack in the floods.

For when they neared that old soaked hay,
They saw across the only way
That Judas, Godmar, and the three
35 Red running lions dismally
Grinned from his pennon,° under which,   banner
In one straight line along the ditch,
They counted thirty heads.

So then,
While Robert turned round to his men,
40 She saw at once the wretched end,
And, stooping down, tried hard to rend
Her coif the wrong way from her head,
And hid her eyes; while Robert said:
"Nay, love, 'tis scarcely two to one,
45 At Poitiers where we made them run
So fast—why, sweet my love, good cheer.
The Gascon frontier is so near,
Nought after this."

But, "O," she said,
"My God! my God! I have to tread
50 The long way back without you; then
The court at Paris; those six men;[2]
The gratings of the Chatelet;
The swift Seine[3] on some rainy day
Like this, and people standing by,
55 And laughing, while my weak hands try
To recollect how strong men swim,[4]
All this, or else a life with him,
For which I should be damned at last,
Would God that this next hour were past!"

60 He answered not, but cried his cry,
"St. George for Marny!" cheerily;
And laid his hand upon her rein.

2. I.e., the judges.
3. The river that runs through Paris. Le Châtelet
is a prison in the city.
4. When captured, she will have to undergo trial
by water to determine whether she is a witch: if
she sinks, she will be presumed innocent and will
be rescued, but if she swims, this will be assumed
to be by virtue of her powers as a witch, and she
will be burned at the stake.

Alas! no man of all his train°   *following*
Gave back that cheery cry again;
65 And, while for rage his thumb beat fast
Upon his sword-hilts, someone cast
About his neck a kerchief long,
And bound him.

    Then they went along
To Godmar; who said: "Now, Jehane,
70 Your lover's life is on the wane
So fast, that, if this very hour
You yield not as my paramour,
He will not see the rain leave off—
Nay, keep your tongue from gibe and scoff,
75 Sir Robert, or I slay you now."

She laid her hand upon her brow,
Then gazed upon the palm, as though
She thought her forehead bled, and—"No,"
She said, and turned her head away,
80 As there were nothing else to say,
And everything were settled: red
Grew Godmar's face from chin to head:
"Jehane, on yonder hill there stands
My castle, guarding well my lands:
85 What hinders me from taking you,
And doing that I list to do
To your fair willful body, while
Your knight lies dead?"
     A wicked smile
Wrinkled her face, her lips grew thin,
90 A long way out she thrust her chin:
"You know that I should strangle you
While you were sleeping; or bite through
Your throat, by God's help—ah!" she said,
"Lord Jesus, pity your poor maid!
95 For in such wise they hem me in,
I cannot choose but sin and sin,
Whatever happens: yet I think
They could not make me eat or drink,
And so should I just reach my rest."
100 "Nay, if you do not my behest,
O Jehane! though I love you well,"
Said Godmar, "would I fail to tell
All that I know." "Foul lies," she said.
"Eh? lies my Jehane? by God's head,
105 At Paris folks would deem them true!
Do you know, Jehane, they cry for you,
'Jehane the brown! Jehane the brown!
Give us Jehane to burn or drown!'—
Eh—gag me Robert!—sweet my friend,
110 This were indeed a piteous end

For those long fingers, and long feet,
And long neck, and smooth shoulders sweet;
An end that few men would forget
That saw it—so, an hour yet:
115 Consider, Jehane, which to take
Of life or death!"

         So, scarce awake,
Dismounting, did she leave that place,
And totter some yards: with her face
Turned upward to the sky she lay,
120 Her head on a wet heap of hay,
And fell asleep: and while she slept,
And did not dream, the minutes crept
Round to the twelve again; but she,
Being waked at last, sighed quietly,
125 And strangely childlike came, and said:
"I will not." Straightway Godmar's head,
As though it hung on strong wires, turned
Most sharply round, and his face burned.

For Robert—both his eyes were dry,
130 He could not weep, but gloomily
He seemed to watch the rain; yea, too,
His lips were firm; he tried once more
To touch her lips; she reached out, sore
And vain desire so tortured them,
135 The poor gray lips, and now the hem
Of his sleeve brushed them.
           With a start
Up Godmar rose, thrust them apart;
From Robert's throat he loosed the bands
Of silk and mail; with empty hands
140 Held out, she stood and gazed, and saw,
The long bright blade without a flaw
Glide out from Godmar's sheath, his hand
In Robert's hair; she saw him bend
Back Robert's head; she saw him send
145 The thin steel down; the blow told well,
Right backward the knight Robert fell,
And moaned as dogs do, being half dead,
Unwitting, as I deem: so then
Godmar turned grinning to his men,
150 Who ran, some five or six, and beat
His head to pieces at their feet.

Then Godmar turned again, and said:
"So, Jehane, the first fitte⁵ is read!
Take note, my lady, that your way
155 Lies backward to the Chatelet!"
She shook her head and gazed awhile

5. Division of a song, poem, or tale.

At her cold hands with a rueful smile,
As though this thing had made her mad.

This was the parting that they had
160   Beside the haystack in the floods.

1858

The Earthly Paradise[6]

Of heaven or hell I have no power to sing,
I cannot ease the burden of your fears,
Or make quick-coming death a little thing,
Or bring again the pleasure of past years,
5   Nor for my words shall ye forget your tears,
Or hope again for aught that I can say,
The idle singer of an empty day.

But rather, when, aweary of your mirth,
From full hearts still unsatisfied ye sigh,
10   And, feeling kindly unto all the earth,
Grudge every minute as it passes by,
Made the more mindful that the sweet days die—
Remember me a little then I pray,
The idle singer of an empty day.

15   The heavy trouble, the bewildering care
That weighs us down who live and earn our bread,
These idle verses have no power to bear;
So let me sing of names rememberéd,
Because they, living not, can ne'er be dead,
20   Or long time take their memory quite away
From us poor singers of an empty day.

Dreamer of dreams, born out of my due time,
Why should I strive to set the crooked straight?
Let it suffice me that my murmuring rhyme
25   Beats with light wing against the ivory gate,[7]
Telling a tale not too importunate
To those who in the sleepy region stay,
Lulled by the singer of an empty day.

Folk say, a wizard to a northern king
30   At Christmas-tide such wondrous things did show,
That through one window men beheld the spring,
And through another saw the summer glow,
And through a third the fruited vines a-row,

6. The dedicatory stanzas to Morris's poem *The Earthly Paradise* (1868–70), consisting of a prologue and twenty-four tales on classical and medieval—especially Norse—subjects.

7. In Homer, dreams came through one or the other of two gates: through the gates of ivory, those that were untrue; through the gates of horn, those that were true.

While still, unheard, but in its wonted° way,   *usual*
35   Piped the drear wind of that December day.

So with this Earthly Paradise it is,
If ye will read aright, and pardon me,
Who strive to build a shadowy isle of bliss
Midmost the heating of the steely sea,
40   Where tossed about all hearts of men must be;
Whose ravening monsters mighty men shall slay,
Not the poor singer of an empty day.

1868–70

W. S. GILBERT
1836–1911

I Am the Very Model of a Modern Major-General[1]

I am the very model of a modern Major-General,
I've information vegetable, animal, and mineral,
I know the kings of England, and I quote the fights historical,
From Marathon to Waterloo, in order categorical;[2]
5   I'm very well acquainted too with matters mathematical,
I understand equations, both the simple and quadratical,
About binomial theorem I'm teeming with a lot o' news—
With many cheerful facts about the square of the hypotenuse.[3]

ALL   With many cheerful facts, etc.

10   GEN.   I'm very good at integral and differential calculus,
I know the scientific names of beings animalculous;[4]
In short, in matters vegetable, animal, and mineral,
I am the very model of a modern Major-General.

ALL   In short, in matters vegetable, animal, and mineral,
15   He is the very model of a modern Major-General.

GEN.   I know our mythic history, King Arthur's and Sir Caradoc's,
I answer hard acrostics, I've a pretty taste for paradox,
I quote in elegiacs all the crimes of Heliogabalus,
In conics I can floor peculiarities parabolous.[5]

1. Sung by the Major-General on his entrance in act 1 of *The Pirates of Penzance*.
2. The Greeks defeated the Persians in a famous battle at Marathon in 490 B.C.E.; the duke of Wellington won his decisive victory over Napoleon at Waterloo in 1815.
3. All these are mathematical terms.
4. Microscopic organisms.
5. More examples of the Major-General's abstruse bits of knowledge: Sir Caradoc was a legendary figure in British history, supposedly one of King Arthur's knights; acrostics are word puzzles (forerunners of crossword puzzles); elegiacs were a classical verse form of praise, quite unsuitable to describe the life of the most depraved Roman emperor; conics is the study of three-dimensional figures, of which the parabola is one.

20   I can tell undoubted Raphaels from Gerard Dows and
          Zoffanies,
      I know the croaking chorus from the *Frogs* of Aristophanes,
      Then I can hum a fugue of which I've heard the music's
          dinafore,
      And whistle all the airs from that infernal nonsense *Pinafore*.[6]

ALL   And whistle all the airs, etc.

25 GEN. Then I can write a washing bill in Babylonic cuneiform,
      And tell you every detail of Caractacus's uniform;[7]
      In short, in matters vegetable, animal, and mineral,
      I am the very model of a modern Major-General.

ALL   In short, in matters vegetable, animal, and mineral,
30   He is the very model of a modern Major-General.

GEN. In fact, when I know what is meant by "mamelon" and "ravelin,"
      When I can tell at sight a chassepôt rifle from a javelin,
      When such affairs as sorties and surprises I'm more wary at,
      And when I know precisely what is meant by "commissariat,"
35   When I have learnt what progress has been made in modern
          gunnery,
      When I know more of tactics than a novice in a nunnery:
      In short, when I've a smattering of elemental strategy,
      You'll say a better Major-General has never *sat* a gee—[8]

ALL   You'll say a better, etc.

40 GEN. For my military knowledge, though I'm plucky and adventury,
      Has only been brought down to the beginning of the century;
      But still in matters vegetable, animal, and mineral,
      I am the very model of a modern Major-General.

ALL   But still in matters vegetable, animal, and mineral,
45   He is the very model of a modern Major-General.

                                                        1879

6. Raphael was one of the great painters of the early Italian Renaissance, as opposed to Gerhard Dou and Johann Zoffany, undistinguished seventeenth- and eighteenth-century painters; in *The Frogs*, by Aristophanes, the great classical comic playwright, a chorus of frogs chants "Brekke-ko-ax, ko-ax, ko-ax"; a fugue is a learned (and, incidentally, multivoiced) musical composition; the last line of the verse is Gilbert's sly dig at the immense popularity of the previous Gilbert and Sullivan operetta, *H.M.S. Pinafore* (1878).
7. Cuneiform was a form of writing (made by pressing a stick into clay) practiced in ancient Babylonia; Caractacus is an alternate form of *Caradoc*.
8. Horse (usually a work horse). The Major-General has just listed his "smattering" of military terms: a mamelon is a fortified mound, while a ravelin is a detached outwork also used in fortification; the chassepôt rifle was a bolt-action, breech-loading rifle, very recently invented in Gilbert's time, while a javelin is a light spear that has been used in warfare for centuries; sorties and surprises are sudden military attacks; a commissariat is the system for supplying an army with food.

Titwillow[9]

On a tree by a river a little tom-tit
    Sang "Willow, titwillow, titwillow!"
And I said to him, "Dicky-bird, why do you sit
    Singing 'Willow, titwillow, titwillow'?"
5 "Is it weakness of intellect, birdie?" I cried,
"Or a rather tough worm in your little inside?"
With a shake of his poor little head, he replied,
    "Oh, willow, titwillow, titwillow!"

He slapped at his chest, as he sat on that bough,
10   Singing "Willow, titwillow, titwillow!"
And a cold perspiration bespangled his brow,
    Oh, willow, titwillow, titwillow!
He sobbed and he sighed, and a gurgle he gave,
Then he plunged himself into the billowy wave,
15 And an echo arose from the suicide's grave—
    "Oh, willow, titwillow, titwillow!"

Now I feel just as sure as I'm sure that my name
    Isn't Willow, titwillow, titwillow,
That 'twas blighted affection that made him exclaim
20   "Oh, willow, titwillow, titwillow!"
And if you remain callous and obdurate, I
Shall perish as he did, and you will know why,
Though I probably shall not exclaim as I die,
    "Oh, willow, titwillow, titwillow!"

1885

ALGERNON CHARLES SWINBURNE
1837–1909

Chorus from *Atalanta in Calydon*

When the Hounds of Spring Are on Winter's Traces

When the hounds of spring are on winter's traces,
    The mother of months[1] in meadow or plain
Fills the shadows and windy places
    With lisp of leaves and ripple of rain;
5   And the brown bright nightingale amorous

---

9. Sung by Ko-Ko in act 2 of *The Mikado*.
1. This chorus, with which Swinburne's tragedy
begins, is addressed to Artemis, called "mother of

months" because in Greek mythology she is the
moon goddess.

Is half assuaged for Itylus,[2]
For the Thracian ships and the foreign faces,
    The tongueless vigil, and all the pain.

Come with bows bent and with emptying of quivers,
10   Maiden most perfect, lady of light,
With a noise of winds and many rivers,
    With a clamor of waters, and with might;
Bind on thy sandals, O thou most fleet,
Over the splendor and speed of thy feet;
15   For the faint east quickens, the wan west shivers,
    Round the feet of the day and the feet of the night.

Where shall we find her, how shall we sing to her,
    Fold our hands round her knees, and cling?
O that man's heart were as fire and could spring to her,
20   Fire, or the strength of the streams that spring!
For the stars and the winds are unto her
As raiment, as songs of the harp-player;
For the risen stars and the fallen cling to her,
    And the southwest wind and the west wind sing.

25   For winter's rains and ruins are over,
    And all the season of snows and sins;
The days dividing lover and lover,
    The light that loses, the night that wins;
And time remembered is grief forgotten,
30   And frosts are slain and flowers begotten,
And in green underwood and cover
    Blossom by blossom the spring begins.

The full streams feed on flower of rushes,
    Ripe grasses trammel a traveling foot,
35   The faint fresh flame of the young year flushes
    From leaf to flower and flower to fruit;
And fruit and leaf are as gold and fire,
And the oat° is heard above the lyre,   *musical pipe*
And the hoofèd heel of a satyr[3] crushes
40   The chestnut-husk at the chestnut-root.

And Pan by noon and Bacchus by night,[4]
    Fleeter of foot than the fleet-foot kid,
Follows with dancing and fills with delight
    The Maenad and the Bassarid;
45   And soft as lips that laugh and hide
The laughing leaves of the trees divide,

2. Tereus, king of Thrace, raped his sister-in-law, Philomela, and cut out her tongue to ensure her silence. But Philomela wove the story of his deed into a tapestry, and in revenge her sister, Procne, served up to her husband the cooked flesh of their son Itys (or Itylus), at a banquet. The sisters, fleeing from Tereus, were changed into birds before he could overtake them, Procne into a swallow, Philomela into a nightingale.
3. A woodland god, half man, half beast.
4. Pan was the Greek god of flocks and shepherds; Bacchus, or Dionysus, god of wine, was accompanied in his revels (Bacchanalia) by a train of devotees that included Maenads and Bassarids (line 44).

And screen from seeing and leave in sight
    The god pursuing, the maiden hid.

The ivy falls with the Bacchanal's hair
50   Over her eyebrows hiding her eyes;
The wild vine slipping down leaves bare
    Her bright breast shortening into sighs;
The wild vine slips with the weight of its leaves,
But the berried ivy catches and cleaves
55   To the limbs that glitter, the feet that scare
    The wolf that follows, the fawn that flies.

1865

The Garden of Proserpine[5]

    Here, where the world is quiet;
      Here, where all trouble seems
    Dead winds' and spent waves' riot
      In doubtful dreams of dreams;
5   I watch the green field growing
    For reaping folk and sowing,
    For harvest-time and mowing,
      A sleepy world of streams.

    I am tired of tears and laughter,
10   And men that laugh and weep;
    Of what may come hereafter
      For men that sow to reap:
    I am weary of days and hours,
    Blown buds of barren flowers,
15   Desires and dreams and powers
      And everything but sleep.

    Here life has death for neighbor,
      And far from eye or ear
    Wan waves and wet winds labor,
20   Weak ships and spirits steer;
    They drive adrift, and whither
    They wot° not who make thither;   *know*
    But no such winds blow hither,
      And no such things grow here.

25   No growth of moor or coppice,°   *forest*
      No heather-flower or vine,
    But bloomless buds of poppies,
      Green grapes of Proserpine,

5. Persephone, in Roman mythology Proserpine, the daughter of Zeus and Demeter, had been abducted by Hades (the Roman Pluto), god of the underworld (over which she ruled with him thereafter as his queen and as goddess of death and eternal sleep).

Pale beds of blowing rushes
30 Where no leaf blooms or blushes
Save this whereout she crushes
For dead men deadly wine.

Pale, without name or number,
In fruitless fields of corn,°   *wheat*
35 They bow themselves and slumber
All night till light is born;
And like a soul belated,
In hell and heaven unmated,
By cloud and mist abated
40 Comes out of darkness morn.

Though one were strong as seven,
He too with death shall dwell,
Nor wake with wings in heaven,
Nor weep for pains in hell;
45 Though one were fair as roses,
His beauty clouds and closes;
And well though love reposes,
In the end it is not well.

Pale, beyond porch and portal,
50 Crowned with calm leaves, she stands
Who gathers all things mortal
With cold immortal hands;
Her languid lips are sweeter
Than love's who fears to greet her
55 To men that mix and meet her
From many times and lands.

She waits for each and other,
She waits for all men born;
Forgets the earth her mother,
60 The life of fruits and corn;
And spring and seed and swallow
Take wing for her and follow
Where summer song rings hollow
And flowers are put to scorn.

65 There go the loves that wither,
The old loves with wearier wings;
And all dead years draw thither,
And all disastrous things;
Dead dreams of days forsaken,
70 Blind buds that snows have shaken,
Wild leaves that winds have taken,
Red strays of ruined springs.

We are not sure of sorrow,
And joy was never sure;

75   Today will die tomorrow;
      Time stoops to no man's lure;[6]
    And love, grown faint and fretful,
    With lips but half regretful
    Sighs, and with eyes forgetful
80   Weeps that no love endure.

    From too much love of living,
      From hope and fear set free,
    We thank with brief thanksgiving
      Whatever gods may be
85   That no life lives for ever;
    That dead men rise up never;
    That even the weariest river
      Winds somewhere safe to sea.

    Then star nor sun shall waken,
90   Nor any change of light:
    Nor sound of waters shaken,
      Nor any sound or sight:
    Nor wintry leaves nor vernal,°   *of spring*
    Nor days nor things diurnal;°   *daily*
95   Only the sleep eternal
      In an eternal night.

1866

A Forsaken Garden

In a coign° of the cliff between lowland and highland,   *corner*
    At the sea-down's edge between windward and lee,
Walled round with rocks as an inland island,
    The ghost of a garden fronts the sea.
5   A girdle of brushwood and thorn encloses
    The steep square slope of the blossomless bed
Where the weeds that grew green from the graves of its roses
    Now lie dead.

    The fields fall southward, abrupt and broken,
10   To the low last edge of the long lone land.
If a step should sound or a word be spoken,
    Would a ghost not rise at the strange guest's hand?
So long have the grey bare walks lain guestless,
    Through branches and briars if a man make way,
15   He shall find no life but the sea-wind's, restless
      Night and day.

6. In falconry, a device used to recall the hawk to the falconer's wrist.

The dense hard passage is blind and stifled
    That crawls by a track none turn to climb
To the strait waste place that the years have rifled
20   Of all but the thorns that are touched not of time.
The thorns he spares when the rose is taken;
    The rocks are left when he wastes the plain.
The wind that wanders, the weeds wind-shaken,
        These remain.

25 Not a flower to be pressed of the foot that falls not;
    As the heart of a dead man the seed-plots are dry;
From the thicket of thorns whence the nightingale calls not,
    Could she call, there were never a rose to reply.
Over the meadows that blossom and wither
30   Rings but the note of a sea-bird's song;
Only the sun and the rain come hither
        All year long.

The sun burns sere° and the rain dishevels   *dry*
    One gaunt bleak blossom of scentless breath.
35 Only the wind here hovers and revels
    In a round where life seems barren as death.
Here there was laughing of old, there was weeping,
    Haply, of lovers none ever will know,
Whose eyes went seaward a hundred sleeping
40   Years ago.

Heart handfast in heart as they stood, "Look thither,"
    Did he whisper? "look forth from the flowers to the sea,
For the foam-flowers endure when the rose-blossoms wither,
    And men that love lightly may die—but we?"
45 And the same wind sang and the same waves whitened,
    And or ever the garden's last petals were shed,
In the lips that had whispered, the eyes that had lightened,
        Love was dead.

Or they loved their life through, and then went whither?
50   And were one to the end—but what end who knows?
Love deep as the sea as a rose must wither,
    As the rose-red seaweed that mocks the rose.
Shall the dead take thought for the dead to love them?
    What love was ever as deep as a grave?
55 They are loveless now as the grass above them
        Or the wave.

All are at one now, roses and lovers,
    Not known of the cliffs and the fields and the sea.
Not a breath of the time that has been hovers
60   In the air now soft with a summer to be.
Not a breath shall there sweeten the seasons hereafter
    Of the flowers or the lovers that laugh now or weep,
When as they that are free now of weeping and laughter
        We shall sleep.

₆₅   Here death may deal not again for ever;
      Here change may come not till all change end.
    From the graves they have made they shall rise up never,
      Who have left nought living to ravage and rend.
    Earth, stones, and thorns of the wild ground growing,
₇₀   While the sun and the rain live, these shall be;
    Till a last wind's breath upon all these blowing
          Roll the sea.

    Till the slow sea rise and the sheer cliff crumble,
      Till terrace and meadow the deep gulfs drink,
₇₅ Till the strength of the waves of the high tides humble
      The fields that lessen, the rocks that shrink,
    Here now in his triumph where all things falter,
      Stretched out on the spoils that his own hand spread,
    As a god self-slain on his own strange altar,
₈₀   Death lies dead.

1876   1878

THOMAS HARDY
1840–1928

Hap[1]

    If but some vengeful god would call to me
    From up the sky, and laugh: "Thou suffering thing,
    Know that thy sorrow is my ecstasy,
    That thy love's loss is my hate's profiting!"

₅   Then would I bear it, clench myself, and die,
    Steeled by the sense of ire unmerited;
    Half-eased in that a Powerfuller than I
    Had willed and meted me the tears I shed.

    But not so. How arrives it joy lies slain,
₁₀ And why unblooms the best hope ever sown?
    —Crass Casualty obstructs the sun and rain,
    And dicing Time for gladness casts a moan. . . .
    These purblind Doomsters had as readily strown
    Blisses about my pilgrimage as pain.

1866   1898

---

1. I.e., chance (as also "Casualty," line 11).

Neutral Tones

We stood by a pond that winter day,
And the sun was white, as though chidden° of° God,   *rebuked / by*
And a few leaves lay on the starving sod;°   *turf*
    —They had fallen from an ash, and were grey.

5 Your eyes on me were as eyes that rove
Over tedious riddles of years ago;
And some words played between us to and fro
    On which lost the more by our love.

The smile on your mouth was the deadest thing
10 Alive enough to have strength to die;
And a grin of bitterness swept thereby
    Like an ominous bird a-wing . . .

Since then, keen lessons that love deceives,
And wrings with wrong, have shaped to me
15 Your face, and the God-curst sun, and a tree,
    And a pond edged with greyish leaves.

1867   1898

I Look into My Glass[2]

I look into my glass,
And view my wasting skin,
And say, "Would God it came to pass
My heart had shrunk as thin!"

5 For then, I, undistrest
By hearts grown cold to me,
Could lonely wait my endless rest
With equanimity.

But Time, to make me grieve,
10 Part steals, lets part abide;
And shakes this fragile frame at eve
With throbbings of noontide.

                                                        1898

2. Mirror.

Drummer Hodge[3]

1

They throw in Drummer Hodge, to rest
    Uncoffined—just as found:
His landmark is a kopje-crest[4]
    That breaks the veldt around;
5   And foreign constellations west[5]
    Each night above his mound.

2

Young Hodge the Drummer never knew—
    Fresh from his Wessex home—
The meaning of the broad Karoo,
10   The Bush,[6] the dusty loam,
And why uprose to nightly view
    Strange stars amid the gloam.

3

Yet portion of that unknown plain
    Will Hodge forever be;
15 His homely Northern breast and brain
    Grow to some Southern tree,
And strange-eyed constellations reign
    His stars eternally.

1899   1902

A Broken Appointment

You did not come,
And marching Time drew on, and wore me numb.
Yet less for loss of your dear presence there
Than that I thus found lacking in your make
5   That high compassion which can overbear
Reluctance for pure lovingkindness' sake
Grieved I, when, as the hope-hour stroked its sum,
    You did not come.

    You love not me,
10 And love alone can lend you loyalty;
    —I know and knew it. But, unto the store
    Of human deeds divine in all but name,

3. The poem presents an incident from the Boer War (1899–1902) and when first published bore this note: "One of the Drummers killed was a native of a village near Casterbridge," i.e., Dorchester, the principal city of the region of southern England to which, in his novels and poems, Hardy gave its medieval name, Wessex.

4. Crest of a small hill (South African Dutch). The veldt (line 4) is open country, unenclosed pasture land; the Karoo (line 9), barren tracts of plateau-land.
5. Set. *Foreign:* i.e., to an English soldier.
6. Uncleared area of land (British colonial word).

Was it not worth a little hour or more
To add yet this: Once you, a woman, came
15   To soothe a time-torn man; even though it be
          You love not me?

                                                                          1902

The Darkling Thrush

I leant upon a coppice gate[7]
     When Frost was spectre-grey,
And Winter's dregs made desolate
     The weakening eye of day.
5   The tangled bine-stems[8] scored the sky
     Like strings of broken lyres,
And all mankind that haunted nigh
     Had sought their household fires.

The land's sharp features seemed to be
10   The Century's corpse outleant,[9]
His crypt the cloudy canopy,
     The wind his death-lament.
The ancient pulse of germ and birth
     Was shrunken hard and dry,
15   And every spirit upon earth
     Seemed fervourless as I.

At once a voice arose among
     The bleak twigs overhead
In a full-hearted evensong
20   Of joy illimited;
An aged thrush, frail, gaunt, and small,
     In blast-beruffled plume,
Had chosen thus to fling his soul
     Upon the growing gloom.

25   So little cause for carolings
     Of such ecstatic sound
Was written on terrestrial things
     Afar or nigh around,
That I could think there trembled through
30   His happy good-night air
Some blessed Hope, whereof he knew
     And I was unaware.

December 31, 1900   1902

---

7. Gate leading to a small wood.
8. Shoots or stems of a climbing plant.

9. Leaning out (i.e., of its coffin); note the poem's
composition date.

The Ruined Maid

"O'Melia, my dear, this does everything crown!
Who could have supposed I should meet you in Town?
And whence such fair garments, such prosperi-ty?"
"O didn't you know I'd been ruined?" said she.

5   "You left us in tatters, without shoes or socks,
Tired of digging potatoes, and spudding up docks;[1]
And now you've gay bracelets and bright feathers three!"
"Yes: that's how we dress when we're ruined," said she.

"At home in the barton° you said 'thee' and 'thou,'   *farm*
10   And 'thik oon,' and 'theäs oon,' and 't'other'; but now
Your talking quite fits 'ee for high compa-ny!"
"Some polish is gained with one's ruin," said she.

"Your hands were like paws then, your face blue and bleak
But now I'm bewitched by your delicate cheek,
15   And your little gloves fit as on any la-dy!"
"We never do work when we're ruined," said she.

"You used to call home-life a hag-ridden dream,
And you'd sigh, and you'd sock;° but at present you seem   *sigh*
To know not of megrims° or melancho-ly!"   *low spirits*
20   "True. One's pretty lively when ruined," said she.

"I wish I had feathers, a fine sweeping gown,
And a delicate face, and could strut about Town!"
"My dear—a raw country girl, such as you be,
Cannot quite expect that. You ain't ruined," said she.

1866   1902

The Convergence of the Twain

Lines on the Loss of the Titanic[2]

I

In a solitude of the sea
Deep from human vanity,
And the Pride of Life that planned her, stilly couches she.

2

Steel chambers, late the pyres
5   Of her salamandrine fires,[3]
Cold currents thrid,° and turn to rhythmic tidal lyres.   *thread*

1. Digging up weedy herbs.
2. The White Star liner R.M.S. *Titanic* was sunk, with great loss of life, as the result of collision with an iceberg on its maiden voyage from Southampton to New York on April 15, 1912. *Twain:* two.

3. The ship's fires, which burn though immersed in water, are compared to the salamander, a lizard-like creature that according to fable could live in the midst of fire.

3

Over the mirrors meant
To glass the opulent
The sea-worm crawls—grotesque, slimed, dumb, indifferent.

4

10   Jewels in joy designed
To ravish the sensuous mind
Lie lightless, all their sparkles bleared and black and blind.

5

Dim moon-eyed fishes near
Gaze at the gilded gear
15   And query: "What does this vaingloriousness down here?"

6

Well: while was fashioning
This creature of cleaving wing,
The Immanent Will[4] that stirs and urges everything

7

Prepared a sinister mate
20   For her—so gaily great—
A Shape of Ice, for the time far and dissociate.

8

And as the smart ship grew
In stature, grace, and hue,
In shadowy silent distance grew the Iceberg too.

9

25   Alien they seemed to be:
No mortal eye could see
The intimate welding of their later history,

10

Or sign that they were bent
By paths coincident
30   On being anon° twin halves of one august° event,   *soon / important*

11

Till the Spinner of the Years
Said "Now!" And each one hears,
And consummation comes, and jars two hemispheres.

1912

Channel Firing[5]

That night your great guns, unawares,
Shook all our coffins as we lay,

---

4. The blind force (in Hardy's belief system, not
identified with any deity) that drives the world.
5. I.e., gunnery practice in the English Channel.

Four months after Hardy wrote this poem, World
War I began.

And broke the chancel[6] window-squares,
We thought it was the Judgment-day

5   And sat upright. While drearisome
Arose the howl of wakened hounds:
The mouse let fall the altar-crumb,
The worms drew back into the mounds,

The glebe cow[7] drooled. Till God called, "No;
10   It's gunnery practice out at sea
Just as before you went below;
The world is as it used to be:

"All nations striving strong to make
Red war yet redder. Mad as hatters
15   They do no more for Christés sake
Than you who are helpless in such matters.

"That this is not the judgment-hour
For some of them's a blessed thing,
For if it were they'd have to scour
20   Hell's floor for so much threatening. . . .

"Ha, ha. It will be warmer when
I blow the trumpet (if indeed
I ever do; for you are men,
And rest eternal sorely need)."

25   So down we lay again. "I wonder,
Will the world ever saner be,"
Said one, "than when He sent us under
In our indifferent century!"

And many a skeleton shook his head.
30   "Instead of preaching forty year,"
My neighbour Parson Thirdly said,
"I wish I had stuck to pipes and beer."

Again the guns disturbed the hour,
Roaring their readiness to avenge,
35   As far inland as Stourton Tower,
And Camelot, and starlit Stonehenge.[8]

April 1914   1914

6. Part of a church nearest the altar.
7. Cow pastured on the glebe, a piece of land attached to a vicarage or rectory.
8. Stourton Tower, built in 1772, and locally known as "Alfred's Tower," stands on the highest point of the estate of Stourhead, in Wiltshire, close to the Somersetshire border. Camelot, the seat of the legendary King Arthur's court, has been variously associated with Winchester and with certain places in Somersetshire. Stonehenge is a circular grouping of megalithic monuments on Salisbury Plain, Wiltshire, dating back to the late Neolithic or early Bronze Age.

Under the Waterfall

"Whenever I plunge my arm, like this,
In a basin of water, I never miss
The sweet sharp sense of a fugitive day
Fetched back from its thickening shroud of grey.
5   Hence the only prime
              And real love-rhyme
              That I know by heart,
              And that leaves no smart,
Is the purl[9] of a little valley fall
10 About three spans wide and two spans tall
Over a table of solid rock
And into a scoop of the self-same block;
The purl of a runlet that never ceases
In stir of kingdoms, in wars, in peaces;
15 With a hollow boiling voice it speaks
And has spoken since hills were turfless peaks."

"And why gives this the only prime
Idea to you of a real love-rhyme?
And why does plunging your arm in a bowl
20 Full of spring water, bring throbs to your soul?"

"Well, under the fall, in a crease of the stone,
Though where precisely none ever has known,
Jammed darkly, nothing to show how prized,
And by now with its smoothness opalized,
25   Is a drinking-glass:
              For, down that pass
              My lover and I
              Walked under a sky
Of blue with a leaf-wove awning of green,
30 In the burn of August, to paint the scene,
And we placed our basket of fruit and wine
By the runlet's rim, where we sat to dine;
And when we had drunk from the glass together,
Arched by the oak-copse° from the weather,   *-thicket*
35 I held the vessel to rinse in the fall,
Where it slipped, and sank, and was past recall,
Though we stooped and plumbed the little abyss
With long bared arms. There the glass still is.
And, as said, if I thrust my arm below
40 Cold water in basin or bowl, a throe°   *violent pang*
From the past awakens a sense of that time,
And the glass we used, and the cascade's rhyme.
The basin seems the pool, and its edge
The hard smooth face of the brook-side ledge,

9. Flow with a murmuring sound.

45   And the leafy pattern of china-ware
The hanging plants that were bathing there.

"By night, by day, when it shines or lours,°   *darkens*
There lies intact that chalice of ours,
And its presence adds to the rhyme of love
50   Persistently sung by the fall above.
No lip has touched it since his and mine
In turns therefrom sipped lovers' wine."

1914

The Voice

Woman much missed, how you call to me, call to me,
Saying that now you are not as you were
When you had changed from the one who was all to me,
But as at first, when our day was fair.

5   Can it be you that I hear? Let me view you, then,
Standing as when I drew near to the town
Where you would wait for me: yes, as I knew you then,
Even to the original air-blue gown!

Or is it only the breeze, in its listlessness
10 Travelling across the wet mead° to me here,   *meadow*
You being ever dissolved to wan wistlessness,° *heedlessness*
Heard no more again far or near?

Thus I; faltering forward,
Leaves around me falling,
15 Wind oozing thin through the thorn from norward,°   *northward*
And the woman calling.

December 1912   1914

During Wind and Rain

They sing their dearest songs—
He, she, all of them—yea,
Treble and tenor and bass,
And one to play;
5   With the candles mooning° each face. . . .   *lighting*
Ah, no; the years O!
How the sick leaves reel down in throngs!

They clear the creeping moss—
Elders and juniors—aye,

10   Making the pathways neat
      And the garden gay;
    And they build a shady seat. . . .
      Ah, no; the years, the years;
See, the white storm-birds wing across.

15   They are blithely° breakfasting all—   *cheerfully*
    Men and maidens—yea,
    Under the summer tree,
      With a glimpse of the bay,
      While pet fowl come to the knee. . . .
20   Ah, no; the years O!
And the rotten rose is ript from the wall.

    They change to a high new house,
    He, she, all of them—aye,
    Clocks and carpets and chairs
25   On the lawn all day,
    And brightest things that are theirs. . . .
      Ah, no; the years, the years
Down their carved names the rain-drop ploughs.

1917

In Time of "The Breaking of Nations"[1]

1

Only a man harrowing° clods°   *cultivating / earth*
    In a slow silent walk
With an old horse that stumbles and nods
    Half asleep as they stalk.

2

5   Only thin smoke without flame
      From the heaps of couch-grass;
Yet this will go onward the same
      Though Dynasties pass.

3

Yonder a maid and her wight°   *man*
10   Come whispering by:
War's annals will cloud into night
      Ere their story die.

1915   1916

---

1. Cf. Jeremiah 51.20: "Thou art my battle ax and weapons of war: for with thee will I break in pieces the nations, and with thee will I destroy kingdoms."

Afterwards

When the Present has latched its postern° behind my   *back gate*
    tremulous stay
  And the May month flaps its glad green leaves like wings,
Delicate-filmed as new-spun silk, will the neighbours say,
  "He was a man who used to notice such things"?

5 If it be in the dusk when, like an eyelid's soundless blink,
  The dewfall-hawk comes crossing the shades to alight
Upon the wind-warped upland thorn, a gazer may think,
  "To him this must have been a familiar sight."

If I pass during some nocturnal blackness, mothy and warm,
10 When the hedgehog travels furtively over the lawn,
One may say, "He strove that such innocent creatures should come to
    no harm,
  But he could do little for them; and now he is gone."

If, when hearing that I have been stilled at last, they stand at the door,
  Watching the full-starred heavens that winter sees,
15 Will this thought rise on those who will meet my face no more,
  "He was one who had an eye for such mysteries"?

And will any say when my bell of quittance is heard in the gloom,
  And a crossing breeze cuts a pause in its outrollings,
  Till they rise again, as they were a new bell's boom,
20 "He hears it not now, but used to notice such things"?

                                          1917

SIDNEY LANIER
1842–1881

From the Flats[1]

    What heartache—ne'er a hill!
  Inexorable, vapid, vague, and chill
  The drear sand-levels drain my spirit low.
  With one poor word they tell me all they know;
5 Whereat their stupid tongues, to tease my pain,
  Do drawl it o'er again and o'er again.
  They hurt my heart with griefs I cannot name:
    Always the same, the same.

---

1. Written in Tampa, Florida; Lanier was from Georgia.

> Nature hath no surprise,
> 10   No ambuscade° of beauty 'gainst mine eyes   *ambush*
> From brake or lurking dell or deep defile;°   *narrow pass*
> No humors, frolic forms—this mile, that mile;
> No rich reserves or happy-valley hopes
> Beyond the bends of roads, the distant slopes.
> 15   Her fancy fails, her wild is all run tame:
> Ever the same, the same.
>
> Oh, might I through these tears
> But glimpse some hill my Georgia high uprears,
> Where white the quartz and pink the pebble shine,
> 20   The hickory heavenward strives, the muscadine°   *grapevine*
> Swings o'er the slope, the oak's far-falling shade
> Darkens the dogwood in the bottom glade,
> And down the hollow from a ferny nook
> Bright leaps a living brook!

1877

The Marshes of Glynn[2]

> Glooms of the live-oaks,[3] beautiful-braided and woven
> With intricate shades of the vines that myriad-cloven
>   Clamber the forks of the multiform boughs,—
>   Emerald twilights,—
> 5   Virginal shy lights,
> Wrought of the leaves to allure to the whisper of vows,
> When lovers pace timidly down through the green colonnades
>   Of the dim sweet woods, of the dear dark woods,
>   Of the heavenly woods and glades,
> 10   That run to the radiant marginal sand-beach within
>   The wide sea-marshes of Glynn;—
>
> Beautiful glooms, soft dusks in the noon-day fire,—
> Wildwood privacies, closets of lone desire,
> Chamber from chamber parted with wavering arras° of   *tapestry*
>   leaves,—
> 15 Cells for the passionate pleasure of prayer to the soul that grieves,
>   Pure with a sense of the passing of saints through the wood,
>   Cool for the dutiful weighing of ill with good;—
>
> O braided dusks of the oak and woven shades of the vine,
> While the riotous noon-day sun of the June-day long did shine,
> 20 Ye held me fast in your heart and I held you fast in mine;
>   But now when the noon is no more, and riot is rest,
>   And the sun is a-wait at the ponderous gate of the West,
>   And the slant yellow beam down the wood-aisle doth seem

2. Glynn County, Georgia.
3. Evergreen oaks, indigenous to the American South.

Like a lane into heaven that leads from a dream,—
25   Ay, now, when my soul all day hath drunken the soul of the oak,
And my heart is at ease from men, and the wearisome sound of the
        stroke
Of the scythe of time and the trowel of trade is low,
And belief overmasters doubt, and I know that I know,
And my spirit is grown to a lordly great compass within,
30   That the length and the breadth and the sweep of the marshes of
        Glynn
Will work me no fear like the fear they have wrought me of yore
When length was fatigue, and when breadth was but bitterness
        sore,
And when terror and shrinking and dreary unnamable pain
Drew over me out of the merciless miles of the plain,—
35   Oh, now, unafraid, I am fain[4] to face
           The vast sweet visage of space.
        To the edge of the wood I am drawn, I am drawn,
Where the gray beach glimmering runs, as a belt of the dawn,
        For a mete° and a mark   *measure*
40   To the forest-dark:—
           So:
Affable live-oak, leaning low,—
Thus—with your favor—soft, with a reverent hand,
(Not lightly touching your person, Lord of the land!)
45   Bending your beauty aside, with a step I stand
        On the firm-packed sand,
          Free
By a world of marsh that borders a world of sea.
Sinuous southward and sinuous northward the shimmering band
50   Of the sand-beach fastens the fringe of the marsh to the folds of the
        land.
Inward and outward to northward and southward the beachlines linger
        and curl
As a silver-wrought garment that clings to and follows the firm sweet
        limbs of a girl.
Vanishing, swerving, evermore curving again into sight,
Softly the sand-beach wavers away to a dim gray looping of light.
55   And what if behind me to westward the wall of the woods stands
        high?
The world lies east: how ample, the marsh and the sea and the
        sky!
A league[5] and a league of marsh-grass, waist-high, broad in the
        blade,
Green, and all of a height, and unflecked with a light or a shade,
        Stretch leisurely off, in a pleasant plain,
60   To the terminal blue of the main.°   *sea*

        Oh, what is abroad in the marsh and the terminal sea?
          Somehow my soul seems suddenly free
From the weighing of fate and the sad discussion of sin,
By the length and the breadth and the sweep of the marshes of
        Glynn.

---

4. I would like.   5. An English unit of about three miles.

65 Ye marshes, how candid and simple and nothing-withholding and free
    Ye publish yourselves to the sky and offer yourselves to the sea!
    Tolerant plains, that suffer the sea and the rains and the sun,
    Ye spread and span like the catholic[6] man who hath mightily won
        God out of knowledge and good out of infinite pain
70   And sight out of blindness and purity out of a stain.

      As the marsh-hen secretly builds on the watery sod,
      Behold I will build me a nest on the greatness of God:
      I will fly in the greatness of God as the marsh-hen flies
      In the freedom that fills all the space 'twixt the marsh and the
        skies:
75   By so many roots as the marsh-grass sends in the sod
      I will heartily lay me a-hold on the greatness of God:
      Oh, like to the greatness of God is the greatness within
      The range of the marshes, the liberal marshes of Glynn.

    And the sea lends large, as the marsh: lo, out of his plenty the sea
80   Pours fast: full soon the time of the flood-tide must be:
       Look how the grace of the sea doth go
    About and about through the intricate channels that flow
          Here and there,
          Everywhere,
85 Till his waters have flooded the uttermost creeks and the low-lying
      lanes,
      And the marsh is meshed with a million veins,
    That like as with rosy and silvery essences flow
      In the rose-and-silver evening glow.
        Farewell, my lord Sun!
90   The creeks overflow: a thousand rivulets run
    'Twixt the roots of the sod; the blades of the marsh-grass stir;
    Passeth a hurrying sound of wings that westward whirr;
    Passeth, and all is still; and the currents cease to run;
       And the sea and the marsh are one.

95   How still the plains of the waters be!
       The tide is in his ecstasy.
       The tide is at his highest height:
         And it is night.

    And now from the Vast of the Lord will the waters of sleep
100   Roll in on the souls of men,
      But who will reveal to our waking ken°   *range of vision*
      The forms that swim and the shapes that creep
        Under the waters of sleep?
    And I would I could know what swimmeth below when the tide
      comes in
105 On the length and the breadth of the marvellous marshes of
      Glynn.

                         1878

---

6. Broad-minded.

GERARD MANLEY HOPKINS
1844–1889

God's Grandeur

The world is charged with the grandeur of God.
    It will flame out, like shining from shook foil;[1]
    It gathers to a greatness, like the ooze of oil
Crushed.[2] Why do men then now not reck his rod?
5 Generations have trod, have trod, have trod;
    And all is seared with trade; bleared, smeared with toil;
    And wears man's smudge and shares man's smell: the soil
Is bare now, nor can foot feel, being shod.

And for° all this, nature is never spent;   *despite*
10   There lives the dearest freshness deep down things;
And though the last lights off the black West went
    Oh, morning, at the brown brink eastward, springs—
Because the Holy Ghost over the bent
    World broods with warm breast and with ah! bright wings.

1877   1895

The Windhover[3]

To Christ Our Lord

I caught this morning morning's minion,° king-   *darling, favorite*
    dom of daylight's dauphin,[4] dapple-dawn-drawn Falcon, in his riding
    Of the rolling level underneath him steady air, and striding
High there, how he rung upon[5] the rein of a wimpling° wing   *rippling*
5 In his ecstasy! then off, off forth on swing,
    As a skate's heel sweeps smooth on a bow-bend: the hurl and gliding
    Rebuffed the big wind. My heart in hiding
Stirred for a bird,—the achieve of, the mastery of the thing!

Brute beauty and valour and act, oh, air, pride, plume, here
10   Buckle![6] AND the fire that breaks from thee then, a billion
Times told lovelier, more dangerous, O my chevalier![7]

1. In a letter of 1883, Hopkins writes: "I mean foil in its sense of leaf or tinsel, and no other word whatever will give the effect I want. Shaken gold-foil gives off broad glares like sheet lightning and also, and this is true of nothing else, owing to its zigzag dints and crossings and network of small many cornered facets, a sort of fork lightning too."
2. I.e., as when olives are crushed for their oil.
3. The kestrel, a small hawk, that hovers with its head to the wind.
4. The eldest son of the king of France was called the *dauphin:* hence the word here means "heir to a splendid, kingly condition."
5. Circled at the end of.
6. "Buckle" brings to a focus the elements of line 9, both in their literal sense, as descriptive of a single, sudden movement of the airborne bird, and in their symbolic sense as descriptive of Christ and with further reference to the poet and the lesson he draws from his observation. It may be read as either indicative or imperative, and in one or another of its possible meanings: "to fasten," "to join closely," "to equip for battle," "to grapple with, engage," but also "to cause to bend, give way, crumple."
7. Knight, nobleman, champion.

No wonder of it: shéer plód makes plough down sillion[8]
Shine, and blue-bleak embers, ah my dear,
Fall, gall° themselves, and gash gold-vermilion.   *break the surface of*

1877   1918

Pied[9] Beauty

Glory be to God for dappled things—
    For skies of couple-colour as a brinded° cow;   *brindled*
      For rose-moles all in stipple upon trout that swim;
Fresh-firecoal chestnut-falls;[1] finches' wings;
5   Landscape plotted and pieced—fold, fallow, and plough;[2]
      And áll trádes, their gear and tackle and trim.°   *equipment*
All things counter,° original, spare,° strange;   *contrary / rare*
    Whatever is fickle, freckled (who knows how?)
      With swift, slow; sweet, sour; adazzle, dim;
10 He fathers-forth whose beauty is past change:
                        Praise him.

1877   1918

[As Kingfishers Catch Fire, Dragonflies Draw Flame][3]

As kingfishers catch fire, dragonflies draw flame;
    As tumbled over rim in roundy wells
    Stones ring; like each tucked° string tells, each hung   *touched, plucked*
      bell's
Bow swung finds tongue to fling out broad its name;
5 Each mortal thing does one thing and the same:
    Deals out that being indoors each one dwells;[4]
    Selves[5]—goes itself; *myself* it speaks and spells,
Crying *What I do is me: for that I came.*

I say more: the just man justices;
10   Keeps gráce: thát keeps all his goings graces;
Acts in God's eye what in God's eye he is—
    Chríst. For Christ plays in ten thousand places,
Lovely in limbs, and lovely in eyes not his
    To the Father through the features of men's faces.

1877   1918

---

8. Ridge between two furrows of a plowed field.
9. Having two or more colors, in patches or blotches.
1. In his *Journals*, Hopkins writes of "chestnuts as bright as coals or spots of vermilion."
2. The land makes a pattern of varicolored patches by reason of its several uses, as for pasture, or being left fallow for a season, or being plowed and sown.
3. I.e., as their bright colors flash in the light.
4. I.e., gives utterance to the essential nature that dwells within ("indoors") each individual being.
5. I.e., gives being to its own individuality.

Felix Randal

Felix Randal the farrier,° O is he dead then? my duty all   *blacksmith*
    ended,
Who have watched his mould of man, big-boned and hardy-handsome
Pining, pining, till time when reason rambled in it and some
Fatal four disorders, fleshed there, all contended?

5   Sickness broke him. Impatient, he cursed at first, but mended
Being anointed[6] and all; though a heavenlier heart began some
Months earlier, since I had our sweet reprieve and ransom
Tendered to him.[7] Ah well, God rest him all road ever he offended![8]

This seeing the sick endears them to us, us too it endears.
10 My tongue had taught thee comfort, touch had quenched thy tears,
Thy tears that touched my heart, child, Felix, poor Felix Randal;

How far from then forethought of, all thy more boisterous years,
When thou at the random[9] grim forge, powerful amidst peers,
Didst fettle[1] for the great grey drayhorse his bright and battering sandal!

1880   1918

Spring and Fall

To a Young Child

Márgarét, áre you gríeving
Over Goldengrove unleaving?
Leáves, líke the things of man, you
With your fresh thoughts care for, can you?
5   Áh! ás the heart grows older
It will come to such sights colder
By and by, nor spare a sigh
Though worlds of wanwood leafmeal[2] lie;
And yet you *will* weep and know why.
10 Now no matter, child, the name:
Sórrow's spríngs áre the same.
Nor mouth had, no nor mind, expressed
What heart heard of, ghost° guessed: *spirit, soul*
It ís the blight man was born for,
15 It is Margaret you mourn for.

1880   1893

---

6. Having received the sacrament for the dying.
7. I.e., since I had a priest visit him to hear his
confession and give absolution.
8. I.e., for any way in which he may have offended.
9. Ramshackle, as applied to the forge itself; but
also meaning that the man's life as a blacksmith
was merely one casual earthly life as opposed to
the sure way of Christian salvation.

1. To prepare (the horse's shoe).
2. Coined by Hopkins by analogy with *piecemeal*
and meaning "leaf by leaf" or "leaf mold"—in the
first sense, the foliage lies about the grove, having
fallen leaf by leaf; in the second, foliage gradually
decays to leaf mold. *Wanwood:* "pale" or "dim"—
the groves are pale because of their light-colored
autumn foliage, or dim because of the filtered light.

[Carrion Comfort]

Not, I'll not, carrion³ comfort, Despair, not feast on thee;
Not untwist—slack they may be—these last strands of man
In me ór, most weary, cry *I can no more*. I can;
Can something, hope, wish day come, not choose not to be.
5   But ah, but O thou terrible, why wouldst thou rude° on me   *roughly*
Thy wring-world right foot⁴ rock? lay a lionlimb against me? scan
With darksome devouring eyes my bruisèd bones? and fan,
O in turns of tempest, me heaped there; me frantic to avoid thee
    and flee?

Why? That my chaff might fly; my grain lie, sheer and clear.
10   Nay in all that toil, that coil,° since (seems) I kissed the rod,   *tumult*
Hand⁵ rather, my heart lo! lapped strength, stole joy, would
    laugh, chéer.
Cheer whom though? The hero whose heaven-handling flung me,
    fóot tród
Me? or me that fought him? O which one? is it each one? That
    night, that year
Of now done darkness I wretch lay wrestling with (my God!) my God.

1885   1918

[No Worst, There Is None. Pitched Past Pitch of Grief]

No worst, there is none. Pitched past pitch of grief,
More pangs will, schooled at forepangs, wilder wring.
Comforter, where, where is your comforting?
Mary, mother of us, where is your relief?

5   My cries heave, herds-long; huddle in a main, a chief-
woe, world-sorrow; on an age-old anvil wince and sing—
Then lull, then leave off. Fury had shrieked "No ling-
ering! Let me be fell:° force° I must be brief".   *fierce / perforce*

O the mind, mind has mountains; cliffs of fall
10   Frightful, sheer, no-man-fathomed. Hold them cheap
May who ne'er hung there. Nor does long our small
Durance° deal with that steep or deep. Here! creep,   *endurance*
Wretch, under a comfort serves in a whirlwind: all
Life death does end and each day dies with sleep.

1885   1918

---

3. Dead and putrefying flesh.
4. I.e., the foot capable of causing the world to writhe or twist.
5. I.e., the hand that wields the rod.

[I Wake and Feel the Fell of Dark, Not Day]

I wake and feel the fell[6] of dark, not day.
What hours, O what black hoürs we have spent
This night! what sights you, heart, saw; ways you went!
And more must, in yet longer light's delay.

5   With witness I speak this. But where I say
Hours I mean years, mean life. And my lament
Is cries countless, cries like dead° letters sent   *undelivered*
To dearest him that lives alas! away.

I am gall, I am heartburn. God's most deep decree
10   Bitter would have me taste: my taste was me;
Bones built in me, flesh filled, blood brimmed the curse.

Selfyeast of spirit a dull dough sours. I see
The lost are like this, and their scourge to be
As I am mine, their sweating selves, but worse.

1885   1918

[My Own Heart Let Me More Have Pity On]

My own heart let me more have pity on; let
Me live to my sad self hereafter kind,
Charitable; not live this tormented mind
With this tormented mind tormenting yet.

5   I cast for comfort I can no more get
By groping round my comfortless, than blind
Eyes in their dark can day or thirst can find
Thirst's all-in-all in all a world of wet.[7]

Soul, self; come, poor Jackself,[8] I do advise
10   You, jaded, let be; call off thoughts awhile
Elsewhere; leave comfort root-room;[9] let joy size°   *grow*

---

6. Can be read in a number of senses: as "the hide or hairy skin of a beast," or, in an obsolete or rare sense, as "gall, bitterness; hence, animosity, rancor" [O.E.D.], or possibly as the adjective *fell*— fierce, savage, cruel—used as a noun.
7. I.e., as shipwrecked persons adrift without drinking water cannot quench their thirst, even though they are surrounded by "wet." "World" is common to all three instances: the speaker's "comfortless" world, the blind eyes' "dark" world, the "world of wet" in which the shipwrecked are adrift.
8. The humble self—"Jack" used in a pitying, deprecating sense (as in "jack-of-all-trades").
9. Room for its roots to grow.

At God knows when to God knows what;[1] whose smile
's not wrung,[2] see you; unforeseen times rather—as skies
Betweenpie mountains[3]—lights a lovely mile.

1885   1918

That Nature is a Heraclitean Fire[4] and
of the comfort of the Resurrection

Cloud-puffball, torn tuffs, tossed pillows | flaunt forth, then
    chevy° on an air-   *race, scamper*
built thoroughfare: heaven-roysterers, in gay-gangs[5] | they throng;
    they glitter in marches.
Down roughcast,[6] down dazzling whitewash, | wherever an elm arches,
Shivelights and shadowtackle[7] in long | lashes lace, lance, and pair.
5   Delightfully the bright wind boisterous | ropes, wrestles, beats earth bare
Of yestertempest's creases; | in pool and rutpeel parches[8]
Squandering ooze to squeezed | dough, crust, dust; stanches, starches
Squadroned masks and manmarks | treadmire toil there
Footfretted in it. Million-fuelèd, | nature's bonfire burns on.
10 But quench her bonniest, dearest | to her, her clearest-selvèd spark
Man, how fast his firedint,[9] | his mark on mind, is gone!
Both are in an unfathomable, all is in an enormous dark
Drowned. O pity and indig | nation! Manshape, that shone
Sheer off, disseveral,° a star, | death blots black out;   *separate*
    nor mark
15   Is any of him at all so stark
But vastness blurs and time | beats level. Enough! the Resurrection,
A heart's-clarion!° Away grief's gasping, | joyless days,   *-trumpet*
    dejection.
      Across my foundering deck shone
A beacon, an eternal beam. | Flesh fade, and mortal trash
20 Fall to the residuary worm; | world's wildfire, leave but ash:
      In a flash, at a trumpet crash,
I am at once what Christ is, | since he was what I am, and
This Jack,[1] joke, poor potsherd, | patch, matchwood, immortal
    diamond,
      Is immortal diamond.

1888   1918

1. I.e., at unpredictable times until it reaches an unpredictable condition.
2. Cannot be forced, but must come as it will.
3. The brightness of skies, seen between mountains, makes a variegated patterning of light and dark. *Betweenpie:* verb coined by Hopkins based on the adjective *pied* (see "Pied Beauty," above).
4. Heraclitus (ca. 540–ca. 480 B.C.E.), founder of an important school of pre-Socratic philosophy, taught that all is in flux and that the world had its origin in fire and will end in fire.
5. Sky-swaggerers, in carefree groups.

6. A mixture of lime and gravel used to coat walls.
7. Shadows in complicated shapes, as of ship's ropes, tackle, gear. *Shivelights:* light in splinters, fragments.
8. I.e., in pool and rutpeel [ruts described as peeled places] the bright wind parches.
9. Hopkins's compound, meaning the mark made by the flame of humanity's spirit, the spirit's power to make its mark.
1. Common mortal (like "poor Jackself" in "My Own Heart Let Me More Have Pity On," above).

[Thou Art Indeed Just, Lord . . .]

Justus quidem tu es, Domine, si disputem tecum: verumtamen
justa loquar ad te: Quare via impiorum prosperatur? & c.²

Thou art indeed just, Lord, if I contend
With thee; but, sir, so what I plead is just.
Why do sinners' ways prosper? and why must
Disappointment all I endeavour end?
 5   Wert thou my enemy, O thou my friend,
How wouldst thou worse, I wonder, than thou dost
Defeat, thwart me? Oh, the sots and thralls of lust
Do in spare hours more thrive than I that spend,
Sir, life upon thy cause. See, banks and brakes°   *thickets*
 10 Now, leavèd how thick! lacèd they are again
With fretty chervil,³ look, and fresh wind shakes
Them; birds build—but not I build; no, but strain,
Time's eunuch, and not breed one work that wakes.
Mine, O thou lord of life, send my roots rain.

1889   1893

EMMA LAZARUS
1849–1887

The New Colossus¹

Not like the brazen giant of Greek fame,
With conquering limbs astride from land to land;
Here at our sea-washed, sunset gates shall stand
A mighty woman with a torch, whose flame
 5 Is the imprisoned lightning, and her name
Mother of Exiles. From her beacon-hand
Glows world-wide welcome; her mild eyes command
The air-bridged harbor that twin cities frame.
"Keep, ancient lands, your storied pomp!"² cries she
 10 With silent lips. "Give me your tired, your poor,
Your huddled masses yearning to breathe free,
The wretched refuse of your teeming shore.

---

2. The Latin epigraph, Hopkins's original title, is from the Vulgate version of Jeremiah 12.1; the first three lines of the poem translate it. The "& c" indicates that the whole of Jeremiah 12 is relevant to the poem, which, while it does not continue to translate it directly, parallels it frequently.
3. An herb of the carrot or parsley family, with curled leaves.
1. Written as part of a fundraising campaign for the Statue of Liberty, in New York harbor. The poem was recited in 1866 at the statue's dedica-

tion; later its final lines were engraved on the pedestal. Lazarus contrasts the Statue of Liberty with the Colossus of Rhodes, one of the Seven Wonders of the World, a statue to the sun god, Helios, that stood in the harbor at Rhodes, Greece. Contrary to legend that dates from the Middle Ages, the statue could not have straddled the harbor entrance (line 2).
2. The splendors of your history. *Twin cities*: New York City and Jersey City, New Jersey.

Send these, the homeless, tempest-tost° to me,   *-tossed*
I lift my lamp beside the golden door!"

1883   1888

A. E. HOUSMAN
1859–1936

Loveliest of Trees, the Cherry Now

Loveliest of trees, the cherry now
Is hung with bloom along the bough,
And stands about the woodland ride
Wearing white for Eastertide.

5   Now, of my threescore years and ten,
Twenty will not come again,
And take from seventy springs a score,
It only leaves me fifty more.

And since to look at things in bloom
10   Fifty springs are little room,
About the woodlands I will go
To see the cherry hung with snow.

1896

Reveille

Wake: the silver dusk returning
   Up the beach of darkness brims,
And the ship of sunrise burning
   Strands upon the eastern rims.

5   Wake: the vaulted shadow shatters,
   Trampled to the floor it spanned,
And the tent of night in tatters
   Straws° the sky-pavilioned land.   *strews*

Up, lad, up, 'tis late for lying:
10   Hear the drums of morning play;
Hark, the empty highways crying
   "Who'll beyond the hills away?"

Towns and countries woo together,
   Forelands beacon, belfries call;

15 Never lad that trod on leather
    Lived to feast his heart with all.

Up, lad; thews° that lie and cumber   *limbs*
    Sunlit pallets never thrive;
Morns abed and daylight slumber
20   Were not meant for man alive.

Clay lies still, but blood's a rover;
    Breath's a ware that will not keep.
Up, lad: when the journey's over
    There'll be time enough to sleep.

1896

When I Watch the Living Meet

When I watch the living meet,
    And the moving pageant file
Warm and breathing through the street
    Where I lodge a little while,

5 If the heats of hate and lust
    In the house of flesh are strong,
Let me mind the house of dust
    Where my sojourn shall be long.

In the nation that is not
10   Nothing stands that stood before;
There revenges are forgot,
    And the hater hates no more;

Lovers lying two and two
    Ask not whom they sleep beside,
15 And the bridegroom all night through
    Never turns him to the bride.

1896

To an Athlete Dying Young

The time you won your town the race
We chaired you through the market-place;
Man and boy stood cheering by,
And home we brought you shoulder-high.

5 Today, the road all runners come,
Shoulder-high we bring you home,

And set you at your threshold down,
Townsman of a stiller town.

Smart lad, to slip betimes away
10 From fields where glory does not stay
And early though the laurel grows
It withers quicker than the rose.

Eyes the shady night has shut
Cannot see the record cut,°   broken
15 And silence sounds no worse than cheers
After earth has stopped the ears:

Now you will not swell the rout°   crowd
Of lads that wore their honours out,
Runners whom renown outran
20 And the name died before the man.

So set, before its echoes fade,
The fleet foot on the sill of shade,
And hold to the low lintel up
The still-defended challenge-cup.

25 And round that early-laurelled[1] head
Will flock to gaze the strengthless dead,
And find unwithered on its curls
The garland briefer than a girl's.

                                                   1896

Is My Team Ploughing

"Is my team ploughing,
    That I was used to drive
And hear the harness jingle
    When I was man alive?"

5   Ay, the horses trample,
    The harness jingles now;
No change though you lie under
    The land you used to plough.

"Is football playing
10   Along the river shore,
With lads to chase the leather,
    Now I stand up no more?"

Ay, the ball is flying,
    The lads play heart and soul;

---

1. In ancient Greece and Rome, victorious athletes wore laurel wreaths as crowns.

15   The goal stands up, the keeper
            Stands up to keep the goal.

        "Is my girl happy,
            That I thought hard to leave,
        And has she tired of weeping
20   As she lies down at eve?"

        Ay, she lies down lightly,
            She lies not down to weep:
        Your girl is well contented.
            Be still, my lad, and sleep.

25   "Is my friend hearty,
            Now I am thin and pine,
        And has he found to sleep in
            A better bed than mine?"

        Yes, lad, I lie easy,
30   I lie as lads would choose;
        I cheer a dead man's sweetheart,
            Never ask me whose.

                                        1896

On Wenlock Edge[2] the Wood's in Trouble

        On Wenlock Edge the wood's in trouble;
            His forest fleece the Wrekin[3] heaves;
        The gale, it plies the saplings double,
            And thick on Severn[4] snow the leaves.

5   'Twould blow like this through holt and hanger[5]
            When Uricon[6] the city stood:
        'Tis the old wind in the old anger,
            But then it threshed another wood.

        Then, 'twas before my time, the Roman
10   At yonder heaving hill would stare:
        The blood that warms an English yeoman,
            The thoughts that hurt him, they were there.

        There, like the wind through woods in riot,
            Through him the gale of life blew high;
15   The tree of man was never quiet:
            Then 'twas the Roman, now 'tis I.

---

2. A range of hills in Shropshire.
3. A prominent, isolated hill in Shropshire.
4. The Severn River, which flows past the Wrekin and into Wales.

5. A holt is a wood or wooded hill; a hanger is a steep wooded slope.
6. The Roman town Uriconium, on the site of the modern town of Wroxeter, Shropshire.

The gale, it plies the saplings double,
   It blows so hard, 'twill soon be gone:
To-day the Roman and his trouble
20   Are ashes under Uricon.

1896

From Far, from Eve and Morning

From far, from eve and morning
   And yon twelve-winded sky,[7]
The stuff of life to knit me
   Blew hither: here am I.

5   Now—for a breath I tarry
   Nor yet disperse apart—
Take my hand quick and tell me,
   What have you in your heart.

Speak now, and I will answer;
10   How shall I help you, say;
Ere to the wind's twelve quarters
   I take my endless way.

1896

With Rue My Heart Is Laden

With rue my heart is laden
   For golden friends I had,
For many a rose-lipt maiden
   And many a lightfoot lad.

5   By brooks too broad for leaping
   The lightfoot boys are laid;
The rose-lipt girls are sleeping
   In fields where roses fade.

1896

"Terence,[8] This Is Stupid Stuff . . ."

"Terence, this is stupid stuff:
   You eat your victuals fast enough;

7. I.e., winds blowing from the twelve compass points.
8. Housman had at first planned to call the volume in which this poem appeared *The Poems of Terence Hearsay*.

There can't be much amiss, 'tis clear,
To see the rate you drink your beer.
5   But oh, good Lord, the verse you make,
It gives a chap the belly-ache.
The cow, the old cow, she is dead;
It sleeps well, the hornèd head:
We poor lads, 'tis our turn now
10   To hear such tunes as killed the cow.
Pretty friendship 'tis to rhyme
Your friends to death before their time
Moping melancholy mad:
Come, pipe a tune to dance to, lad."

15   Why, if 'tis dancing you would be,
There's brisker pipes than poetry.
Say, for what were hop-yards meant,
Or why was Burton built on Trent?[9]
Oh many a peer of England brews
20   Livelier liquor than the Muse,[1]
And malt does more than Milton can
To justify God's ways to man.[2]
Ale, man, ale's the stuff to drink
For fellows whom it hurts to think:
25   Look into the pewter pot
To see the world as the world's not.
And faith, 'tis pleasant till 'tis past:
The mischief is that 'twill not last.
Oh I have been to Ludlow[3] fair
30   And left my necktie God knows where,
And carried halfway home, or near,
Pints and quarts of Ludlow beer:
Then the world seemed none so bad,
And I myself a sterling lad;
35   And down in lovely muck I've lain,
Happy till I woke again.
Then I saw the morning sky:
Heigho, the tale was all a lie;
The world, it was the old world yet,
40   I was I, my things were wet,
And nothing now remained to do
But begin the game anew.

Therefore, since the world has still
Much good, but much less good than ill,
45   And while the sun and moon endure
Luck's a chance, but trouble's sure,
I'd face it as a wise man would,

9. The principal industry of Burton-on-Trent, a town in Staffordshire, is the brewing of ale. Some of the town's nineteenth-century brewery magnates were raised to the peerage.
1. In Greek mythology, Calliope, one of the nine sister goddesses known as the Muses, presided

over (inspired) epic poetry.
2. An echo of Milton's epic, *Paradise Lost* (1.25–26): "I may assert Eternal Providence, / And justify the ways of God to men."
3. A market town in Shropshire.

And train for ill and not for good.
'Tis true, the stuff I bring for sale
50 Is not so brisk a brew as ale:
Out of a stem that scored° the hand   *cut*
I wrung it in a weary land.
But take it: if the smack is sour,
The better for the embittered hour;
55 It should do good to heart and head
When your soul is in my soul's stead;
And I will friend you, if I may,
In the dark and cloudy day.

There was a king reigned in the East:
60 There, when kings will sit to feast,
They get their fill before they think
With poisoned meat and poisoned drink.
He gathered all that springs to birth
From the many-venomed earth;
65 First a little, thence to more,
He sampled all her killing store;
And easy, smiling, seasoned sound,
Sate the king when healths went round.
They put arsenic in his meat
70 And stared aghast to watch him eat;
They poured strychnine in his cup
And shook to see him drink it up:
They shook, they stared as white's their shirt:
Them it was their poison hurt.
75 —I tell the tale that I heard told.
Mithridates, he died old.[4]

1896

Astronomy

The Wain[5] upon the northern steep
    Descends and lifts away.
Oh I will sit me down and weep
    For bones in Africa.[6]

5   For pay and medals, name and rank,
    Things that he has not found,
He hove the Cross[7] to heaven and sank
    The pole-star underground.

And now he does not even see
10   Signs of the nadir° roll   *lowest point*

4. Mithridates VI, king of Pontus (in Asia Minor) in the first century B.C.E., made himself immune to certain poisons by taking small, gradual doses.
5. The constellation Ursa Minor.

6. Housman's brother Herbert died fighting in the Boer War in 1901.
7. The Southern Cross, a constellation visible from the southern hemisphere.

At night over the ground where he
Is buried with the pole.

1922

Epitaph on an Army of Mercenaries[8]

These, in the day when heaven was falling,
　The hour when earth's foundations fled,
Followed their mercenary calling
　And took their wages and are dead.

5　Their shoulders held the sky suspended;
　They stood, and earth's foundations stay;
What God abandoned, these defended,
　And saved the sum of things for pay.

1915   1922

Crossing Alone the Nighted Ferry

Crossing alone the nighted ferry
　With the one coin for fee,[9]
Whom, on the wharf of Lethe waiting,
　Count you to find? Not me.

5　The brisk fond lackey to fetch and carry,
　The true, sick-hearted slave,
Expect him not in the just city
　And free land of the grave.

1936

Here Dead Lie We Because We Did Not Choose

Here dead lie we because we did not choose
　To live and shame the land from which we sprung.
Life, to be sure, is nothing much to lose;
　But young men think it is, and we were young.

1936

8. This poem honors the professional soldiers of
the British regular army who fought in the First
Battle of Ypres (1914), toward the beginning of
World War I. For the Scottish poet Hugh Mac-
Diarmid's reply, "Another Epitaph on an Army of
Mercenaries," see p. 1379.

9. In Greek mythology, the souls of the dead paid
Charon an obolus (a coin) to ferry them over the
river Styx to Hades. Souls about to be reincarnated
forgot their previous existences by drinking water
from Lethe (line 3), another river in the under-
world.

RUDYARD KIPLING
1865–1936

Tommy[1]

I went into a public-'ouse° to get a pint o'beer,   *bar*
The publican° 'e up an' sez, "We serve no red-coats here."   *barkeep*
The girls be'ind the bar they laughed an' giggled fit to die,
I outs into the street again an' to myself sez I:
5   O it's Tommy this, an' Tommy that, an' "Tommy, go away";
     But it's "Thank you, Mister Atkins," when the band begins to play—
     The band begins to play, my boys, the band begins to play,
     O it's "Thank you, Mister Atkins," when the band begins to play.

I went into a theatre as sober as could be,
10 They gave a drunk civilian room, but 'adn't none for me;
They sent me to the gallery or round the music-'alls,[2]
But when it comes to fightin', Lord! they'll shove me in the stalls!
     For it's Tommy this, an' Tommy that, an' "Tommy, wait outside";
     But its "Special train for Atkins" when the trooper's on the tide—
15   The troopship's on the tide, my boys, the troopship's on the tide,
     O it's "Special train for Atkins" when the trooper's on the tide.

Yes, makin' mock o' uniforms that guard you while you sleep
Is cheaper than them uniforms, an' they're starvation cheap;
An' hustlin' drunken soldiers when they're goin' large a bit
20 Is five times better business than paradin' in full kit.°   *equipment*
     Then it's Tommy this, an' Tommy that, an' "Tommy, 'ow's yer soul?"
     But it's "Thin red line of 'eroes"[3] when the drums begin to roll—
     The drums begin to roll, my boys, the drums begin to roll,
     O it's "Thin red line of 'eroes" when the drums begin to roll.

25 We aren't no thin red 'eroes, nor we aren't no blackguards° too, *criminals*
But single men in barricks, most remarkable like you;
An' if sometimes our conduck isn't all your fancy paints,
Why, single men in barricks don't grow into plaster saints;
     While it's Tommy this, an' Tommy that, an' "Tommy, fall be'ind,"
30   But it's "Please to walk in front, sir," when there's trouble in the
       wind—
     There's trouble in the wind, my boys, there's trouble in the wind,
     O it's "Please to walk in front, sir," when there's trouble in the
       wind.

You talk o' better food for us, an' schools, an' fires, an' all:
We'll wait for extry rations if you treat us rational.
35 Don't mess about the cook-room slops, but prove it to our face
The Widow's Uniform[4] is not the soldier-man's disgrace.

1. The typical soldier (British usage, derived from "Thomas Atkins," name used as a model in official army forms).
2. Cheaper seats in a theater, in the balcony; the best seats, in the orchestra, are the stalls (line 12).
3. W. H. Russell, a London *Times* correspondent, had used the phrase "thin red line tipped with steel" to describe the 93rd Highlanders infantry regiment as they stood to meet the advancing Russian cavalry at Balaclava (1854), in the Crimean War.
4. I.e., the queen's uniform. In his poems and sto-

For it's Tommy this, an' Tommy that, an' "Chuck him out, the
    brute!"
But it's "Saviour of 'is country" when the guns begin to shoot;
An' it's Tommy this, an' Tommy that, an' anything you please;
40   An' Tommy ain't a bloomin' fool—you bet that Tommy sees!

1890

Recessional[5]

1897[6]

God of our fathers, known of old,
    Lord of our far-flung battle-line,
Beneath whose awful Hand we hold
    Dominion over palm and pine—
5 Lord God of Hosts, be with us yet,
    Lest we forget—lest we forget!

The tumult and the shouting dies;
    The Captains and the Kings depart:
Still stands Thine ancient sacrifice,
10   An humble and a contrite heart.[7]
Lord God of Hosts, be with us yet,
    Lest we forget—lest we forget!

Far-called, our navies melt away;
    On dune and headland sinks the fire:[8]
15 Lo, all our pomp of yesterday
    Is one with Nineveh and Tyre![9]
Judge of the Nations, spare us yet,
    Lest we forget—lest we forget!

If, drunk with sight of power, we loose
20   Wild tongues that have not Thee in awe,
Such boastings as the Gentiles use,
    Or lesser breeds without the Law—[1]
Lord God of Hosts, be with us yet,
    Lest we forget—lest we forget!

25 For heathen heart that puts her trust
    In reeking tube and iron shard,

---

ries, Kipling occasionally referred to Queen Vic-
toria as "The Widow at Windsor."
5. A piece of music or a hymn to be played or sung
at the close of a religious service.
6. The year of Queen Victoria's Diamond Jubilee,
celebrating the sixtieth year of her reign, the occa-
sion serving also to celebrate the great extent,
power, and prosperity of the British Empire.

7. Cf. Psalms 51.17.
8. On the night of the anniversary of Victoria's
accession to the throne, bonfires were lit on high
points throughout Great Britain.
9. Nineveh, ancient capital of Assyria, and Tyre,
capital of Phoenicia, were once great cities, but
dwindled to ruins and a small town, respectively.
1. Cf. Romans 2.14.

All valiant dust that builds on dust,
　　And guarding, calls not Thee to guard,
　　For frantic boast and foolish word—
30　Thy mercy on Thy People, Lord!

1897　　　　　　　　　　　　　　　　　　　　　　　　　1899

Epitaphs of the War

1914–18

"Equality of Sacrifice"

A. "I was a Have." B. "I was a 'have-not.' "
　(*Together.*) "What hast thou given which I gave not?"

A Servant

We were together since the war began.
He was my servant—and the better man.

A Son

My son was killed while laughing at some jest. I would I knew
What it was, and it might serve me in a time when jests are few.

An Only Son

I have slain none except my mother. She
(Blessing her slayer) died of grief for me.

Ex-clerk

Pity not! The army gave
Freedom to a timid slave:
In which freedom did he find
Strength of body, will, and mind:
5　By which strength he came to prove
Mirth, companionship, and love:
For which love to death he went:
In which death he lies content.

The Wonder

Body and spirit I surrendered whole
To harsh instructors—and received a soul . . .
If mortal man could change me through and through
From all I was—what may the God not do?

Hindu Sepoy[2] in France

This man in his own country prayed we know not to what powers.
We pray them to reward him for his bravery in ours.

The Coward

I could not look on death, which being known,
Men led me to him, blindfold and alone.

Shock

My name, my speech, my self I had forgot.
My wife and children came—I knew them not.
I died. My mother followed. At her call
And on her bosom I remembered all.

A Grave Near Cairo

Gods of the Nile, should this stout fellow here
Get out—get out! He knows not shame nor fear.

Pelicans in the Wilderness

(A GRAVE NEAR HALFA)[3]

The blown sand heaps on me, that none may learn
Where I am laid for whom my children grieve. . . .
O wings that beat at dawning, ye return
Out of the desert to your young at eve!

Two Canadian Memorials

I

We giving all gained all.
Neither lament us nor praise.
Only in all things recall,
It is fear, not death that slays.

2

From little towns in a far land we came,
To save our honour and a world aflame.
By little towns in a far land we sleep;
And trust that world we won for you to keep.

The Favour

Death favoured me from the first, well knowing I could not endure
To wait on him day by day. He quitted my betters and came

---

2. Native of India employed as soldier under Euro-
pean (especially British) discipline.
3. In the Sudan.

Whistling over the fields, and, when he had made all sure,
  "Thy line is at end," he said, "but at least I have saved its
    name."

The Beginner

On the first hour of my first day
  In the front trench I fell.
(Children in boxes at a play
  Stand up to watch it well.)

R.A.F.[4] (Aged Eighteen)

Laughing through clouds, his milk-teeth still unshed,
Cities and men he smote from overhead.
His deaths delivered, he returned to play
Childlike, with childish things now put away.

The Refined Man

I was of delicate mind. I stepped aside for my needs,
  Disdaining the common office. I was seen from afar and killed. . . .
How is this matter for mirth? Let each man be judged by his deeds.
  I have paid my price to live with myself on the terms that I willed.

Native Water-Carrier (M.E.F.)

Prometheus[5] brought down fire to men.
  This brought up water.
The Gods are jealous—now, as then,
  Giving no quarter.

Bombed in London

On land and sea I strove with anxious care
To escape conscription. It was in the air!

The Sleepy Sentinel

Faithless the watch that I kept: now I have none to keep.
I was slain because I slept: now I am slain I sleep.
Let no man reproach me again, whatever watch is unkept—
I sleep because I am slain. They slew me because I slept.

Batteries Out of Ammunition

If any mourn us in the workshop, say
We died because the shift kept holiday.

---

4. Royal Air Force.
5. In Greek mythology, a Titan who gave fire to   humanity and was punished by the gods. *M.E.F.*: Mediterranean Expeditionary Force.

Common Form

If any question why we died,
Tell them, because our fathers lied.

A Dead Statesman

I could not dig: I dared not rob:
Therefore I lied to please the mob.
Now all my lies are proved untrue
And I must face the men I slew.
5   What tale shall serve me here among
Mine angry and defrauded young?

The Rebel

If I had clamoured at Thy gate
    For gift of life on earth,
And, thrusting through the souls that wait,
    Flung headlong into birth—
5   Even then, even then, for gin and snare
    About my pathway spread,
Lord, I had mocked Thy thoughtful care
    Before I joined the dead!
But now? . . . I was beneath Thy hand
10   Ere yet the planets came.
And now—though planets pass, I stand
    The witness to Thy shame!

The Obedient

Daily, though no ears attended,
    Did my prayers arise.
Daily, though no fire descended,
    Did I sacrifice.
5   Though my darkness did not lift,
    Though I faced no lighter odds,
Though the Gods bestowed no gift,
    Nonetheless,
    Nonetheless, I served the Gods!

A Drifter Off Tarentum⁶

He from the wind-bitten North with ship and companions descended,
    Searching for eggs of death spawned by invisible hulls.
Many he found and drew forth. Of a sudden the fishery ended
    In flame and a clamorous breath known to the eye-pecking gulls.

---

6. Roman name for Taranto, just under the heel of the Italian peninsula.

Destroyers in Collision

For fog and fate no charm is found
  To lighten or amend.
I, hurrying to my bride, was drowned—
  Cut down by my best friend.

Convoy Escort

I was a shepherd to fools
  Causelessly bold or afraid.
They would not abide by my rules.
  Yet they escaped. For I stayed.

Unknown Female Corpse

Headless, lacking foot and hand,
Horrible I come to land.
I beseech all women's sons
Know I was a mother once.

Raped and Revenged

One used and butchered me: another spied
Me broken—for which thing an hundred died.
So it was learned among the heathen hosts
How much a freeborn woman's favour costs.

Salonikan[7] Grave

I have watched a thousand days
Push out and crawl into night
Slowly as tortoises.
Now I, too, follow these.
5   It is fever, and not the fight—
Time, not battle,—that slays.

The Bridegroom

Call me not false, beloved,
  If, from thy scarce-known breast
So little time removed,
  In other arms I rest.

5   For this more ancient bride,
  Whom coldly I embrace,
Was constant at my side
  Before I saw thy face.

---

7. Of Thessalonica (or Salonika), the second largest city in Greece, destroyed by fire in 1917.

Our marriage, often set—
10   By miracle delayed—
At last is consummate,
And cannot be unmade.

Live, then, whom life shall cure,
15   Almost, of memory,
And leave us to endure
Its immortality.

V.A.D.[8] (Mediterranean)

Ah, would swift ships had never been, for then we ne'er had found,
These harsh Aegean[9] rocks between, this little virgin drowned,
Whom neither spouse nor child shall mourn, but men she nursed through
    pain
And—certain keels for whose return the heathen look in vain.

Actors

ON A MEMORIAL TABLET IN HOLY TRINITY CHURCH, STRATFORD-ON-AVON[1]

We counterfeited once for your disport
    Men's joy and sorrow: but our day has passed.
We pray you pardon all where we fell short—
    Seeing we were your servants to this last.

Journalists

ON A PANEL IN THE HALL OF THE INSTITUTE OF JOURNALISTS

We have served our day.

1919, 1940

WILLIAM BUTLER YEATS*
1865–1939

The Stolen Child

Where dips the rocky highland
Of Sleuth Wood[1] in the lake,
There lies a leafy island
Where flapping herons wake

---

8. Voluntary Aid Detachment.
9. Aegean Sea, part of the Mediterranean Sea.
1. Town in central England where Shakespeare was born, lived part of his life, and died.
*Yeats's poems are arranged here in the order in which they appear in The Collected Poems of Wil-

liam Butler Yeats (1940).
1. Place-names throughout the poem refer to the area near Sligo, in the west of Ireland: Rosses Point on Sligo Bay, and Glen-Car, a small lake near Sligo.

5 The drowsy water-rats;
There we've hid our faery vats,
Full of berries
And of reddest stolen cherries.
Come away, O human child!
10 *To the waters and the wild*
With a faery, hand in hand,
For the world's more full of weeping than you can understand.

Where the wave of moonlight glosses
The dim grey sands with light,
15 Far off by furthest Rosses
We foot it all the night,
Weaving olden dances,
Mingling hands and mingling glances
Till the moon has taken flight;
20 To and fro we leap
And chase the frothy bubbles,
While the world is full of troubles
And is anxious in its sleep.
Come away, O human child!
25 *To the waters and the wild*
With a faery, hand in hand,
For the world's more full of weeping than you can understand.

Where the wandering water gushes
From the hills above Glen-Car,
30 In pools among the rushes
That scarce could bathe a star,
We seek for slumbering trout
And whispering in their ears
Give them unquiet dreams;
35 Leaning softly out
From ferns that drop their tears
Over the young streams.
Come away, O human child!
To the waters and the wild
40 *With a faery, hand in hand,*
For the world's more full of weeping than you can understand.

Away with us he's going,
The solemn-eyed:
He'll hear no more the lowing
45 Of the calves on the warm hillside
Or the kettle on the hob
Sing peace into his breast,
Or see the brown mice bob
Round and round the oatmeal-chest.
50 *For he comes, the human child!*
To the waters and the wild
With a faery, hand in hand,
From a world more full of weeping than he can understand.

1889

The Lake Isle of Innisfree[2]

I will arise and go now, and go to Innisfree,
And a small cabin build there, of clay and wattles[3] made:
Nine bean-rows will I have there, a hive for the honey-bee,
And live alone in the bee-loud glade.

5   And I shall have some peace there, for peace comes dropping slow,
Dropping from the veils of the morning to where the cricket sings;
There midnight's all a glimmer, and noon a purple glow,
And evening full of the linnet's° wings.   *a songbird's*

I will arise and go now, for always night and day
10 I hear lake water lapping with low sounds by the shore;
While I stand on the roadway, or on the pavements grey,
I hear it in the deep heart's core.

1890   1892

When You Are Old[4]

When you are old and grey and full of sleep,
And nodding by the fire, take down this book,
And slowly read, and dream of the soft look
Your eyes had once, and of their shadows deep;

5   How many loved your moments of glad grace,
And loved your beauty with love false or true,
But one man loved the pilgrim soul in you,
And loved the sorrows of your changing face;

And bending down beside the glowing bars,
10 Murmur, a little sadly, how Love fled
And paced upon the mountains overhead
And hid his face amid a crowd of stars.

1891   1893

Adam's Curse[5]

We sat together at one summer's end,
That beautiful mild woman, your close friend,[6]
And you and I, and talked of poetry.

2. Island in Lough Gill, County Sligo.
3. Rods interwoven with twigs or branches to form a framework for walls or roof.
4. This poem derives from a sonnet by the French poet Pierre de Ronsard (1524–1585) that begins *"Quand vous serez bien vieille, au soir à la chandelle"* ("When you are very old, in the evening, by

candlelight"), but is a free adaptation rather than a translation.
5. After the Fall, God cursed Adam to work the ground for his food (Genesis 3.17–19).
6. The two women who figure in the poem are the Irish nationalist Maud Gonne (whom Yeats loved unrequitedly) and, rather than a friend, her

I said, "A line will take us hours maybe;
5   Yet if it does not seem a moment's thought,
Our stitching and unstitching has been naught.
Better go down upon your marrow-bones
And scrub a kitchen pavement, or break stones
Like an old pauper, in all kinds of weather;
10   For to articulate sweet sounds together
Is to work harder than all these, and yet
Be thought an idler by the noisy set
Of bankers, schoolmasters, and clergymen
The martyrs call the world."

                  And thereupon
15   That beautiful mild woman for whose sake
There's many a one shall find out all heartache
On finding that her voice is sweet and low
Replied, "To be born woman is to know—
Although they do not talk of it at school—
20   That we must labour to be beautiful."

I said, "It's certain there is no fine thing
Since Adam's fall but needs much labouring.
There have been lovers who thought love should be
So much compounded of high courtesy
25   That they would sigh and quote with learned looks
Precedents out of beautiful old books;
Yet now it seems an idle trade enough."

We sat grown quiet at the name of love;
We saw the last embers of daylight die,
30   And in the trembling blue-green of the sky
A moon, worn as if it had been a shell
Washed by time's waters as they rose and fell
About the stars and broke in days and years.

I had a thought for no one's but your ears:
35   That you were beautiful, and that I strove
To love you in the old high way of love;
That it had all seemed happy, and yet we'd grown
As weary-hearted as that hollow moon.

November 1902   1904

No Second Troy[7]

Why should I blame her[8] that she filled my days
With misery, or that she would of late
Have taught to ignorant men most violent ways,

---

sister, Kathleen Pilcher.
7. According to legend, Helen of Troy (see note 8, p. 1197) caused the Trojan War and hence the destruction of the first city of Troy, on the east side of the Aegean entrance to the Dardanelles.
8. Maud Gonne (see note 6 above).

Or hurled the little streets upon the great,
5   Had they but courage equal to desire?
What could have made her peaceful with a mind
That nobleness made simple as a fire,
With beauty like a tightened bow, a kind
That is not natural in an age like this,
10 Being high and solitary and most stern?
Why, what could she have done, being what she is?
Was there another Troy for her to burn?

December 1908   1910

The Wild Swans at Coole[9]

The trees are in their autumn beauty,
The woodland paths are dry,
Under the October twilight the water
Mirrors a still sky;
5   Upon the brimming water among the stones
Are nine-and-fifty swans.

The nineteenth autumn has come upon me
Since I first made my count;[1]
I saw, before I had well finished,
10 All suddenly mount
And scatter wheeling in great broken rings
Upon their clamorous wings.

I have looked upon those brilliant creatures,
And now my heart is sore.
15 All's changed since I, hearing at twilight,
The first time on this shore,
The bell-beat of their wings above my head,
Trod with a lighter tread.

Unwearied still, lover by lover,
20 They paddle in the cold
Companionable streams or climb the air;
Their hearts have not grown old;
Passion or conquest, wander where they will,
Attend upon them still.

25 But now they drift on the still water,
Mysterious, beautiful;
Among what rushes will they build,
By what lake's edge or pool

---

9. Coole Park, the estate in western Ireland of Lady Augusta Gregory, Yeats's patroness and friend.

1. Yeats had first visited Coole Park nineteen years earlier.

Delight men's eyes when I awake some day
30   To find they have flown away?

October 1916   1917

An Irish Airman Foresees His Death[2]

I know that I shall meet my fate
Somewhere among the clouds above;
Those that I fight I do not hate,
Those that I guard I do not love;
5   My country is Kiltartan Cross,[3]
My countrymen Kiltartan's poor,
No likely end could bring them loss
Or leave them happier than before.
Nor law, nor duty bade me fight,
10 Nor public men, nor cheering crowds,
A lonely impulse of delight
Drove to this tumult in the clouds;
I balanced all, brought all to mind,
The years to come seemed waste of breath,
15 A waste of breath the years behind
In balance with this life, this death.

                                                               1919

The Scholars

Bald heads forgetful of their sins,
Old, learned, respectable bald heads
Edit and annotate the lines
That young men, tossing on their beds,
5   Rhymed out in love's despair
To flatter beauty's ignorant ear.

All shuffle there; all cough in ink;
All wear the carpet with their shoes;
All think what other people think;
10 All know the man their neighbour knows.
Lord, what would they say
Did their Catullus[4] walk that way?

                                                               1917

2. The airman, killed in action in Italy in January 1918, is Major Robert Gregory, son of Yeats's friend and patron Lady Augusta Gregory.
3. A village near the Gregory estate, Coole Park, in County Galway, western Ireland.
4. Gaius Valerius Catullus (ca. 84–ca. 54 B.C.E.), Roman poet famous for his erotic verse.

Easter 1916[5]

I have met them at close of day
Coming with vivid faces
From counter or desk among grey
Eighteenth-century houses.
5   I have passed with a nod of the head
Or polite meaningless words,
Or have lingered awhile and said
Polite meaningless words,
And thought before I had done
10 Of a mocking tale or a gibe
To please a companion
Around the fire at the club,
Being certain that they and I
But lived where motley[6] is worn:
15 All changed, changed utterly:
A terrible beauty is born.

That woman's days were spent
In ignorant good will,
Her nights in argument
20 Until her voice grew shrill.
What voice more sweet than hers
When, young and beautiful,
She rode to harriers?[7]
This man had kept a school
25 And rode our wingéd horse;[8]
This other his helper and friend
Was coming into his force;
He might have won fame in the end,
So sensitive his nature seemed,
30 So daring and sweet his thought.
This other man I had dreamed
A drunken, vainglorious lout.[9]
He had done most bitter wrong
To some who are near my heart,
35 Yet I number him in the song;
He, too, has resigned his part

---

5. This title, echoing Yeats's "September 1913," suggests the poem is a palinode (one in which the author retracts something said in a previous poem). On Easter Monday of 1916, Irish nationalists launched a heroic but unsuccessful revolt against the British government; the week of street fighting that followed is known as the Easter Rising. As a result, a number of the nationalists were executed; Britain, at war with Germany, was in no mood to tolerate Irish agitation for independence—which was supported, for obvious reasons, by Germany. Yeats knew the chief rebels personally.
6. Jester's multicolored costume.

7. Countess Constance Georgina Markiewicz, née Gore-Booth, an Irish aristocrat and nationalist.
8. Pádraic Pearse, a schoolmaster and prolific writer of poems, plays, stories, and essays on Irish politics and Gaelic literature. The mythological winged horse, Pegasus, is here used as a symbol of poetic inspiration. "This other" (line 26) was Thomas MacDonough, a schoolteacher.
9. Major John MacBride, who had married Maud Gonne (the Irish nationalist with whom Yeats had for years been hopelessly in love) in 1903 and separated from her in 1905.

In the casual comedy;
He, too, has been changed in his turn,
Transformed utterly:
40   A terrible beauty is born.

Hearts with one purpose alone
Through summer and winter seem
Enchanted to a stone
To trouble the living stream.
45   The horse that comes from the road,
The rider, the birds that range
From cloud to tumbling cloud,
Minute by minute they change;
A shadow of cloud on the stream
50   Changes minute by minute;
A horse-hoof slides on the brim,
And a horse plashes within it;
The long-legged moor-hens dive,
And hens to moor-cocks call;
55   Minute by minute they live:
The stone's in the midst of all.

Too long a sacrifice
Can make a stone of the heart.
O when may it suffice?
60   That is Heaven's part, our part
To murmur name upon name,
As a mother names her child
When sleep at last has come
On limbs that had run wild.
65   What is it but nightfall?
No, no, not night but death;
Was it needless death after all?
For England may keep faith
For all that is done and said.
70   We know their dream; enough
To know they dreamed and are dead;
And what if excess of love
Bewildered them till they died?
I write it out in a verse—
75   MacDonagh and MacBride
And Connolly and Pearse
Now and in time to be,
Wherever green is worn,
Are changed, changed utterly.
80   A terrible beauty is born.

September 25, 1916   1916

The Second Coming

Turning and turning in the widening gyre
The falcon cannot hear the falconer;[1]
Things fall apart; the centre cannot hold;
Mere anarchy is loosed upon the world,
5   The blood-dimmed tide is loosed, and everywhere
The ceremony of innocence is drowned;
The best lack all conviction, while the worst
Are full of passionate intensity.

Surely some revelation is at hand;
10   Surely the Second Coming is at hand:
The Second Coming! Hardly are those words out
When a vast image out of *Spiritus Mundi*[2]
Troubles my sight: somewhere in sands of the desert
A shape with lion body and the head of a man,[3]
15   A gaze blank and pitiless as the sun,
Is moving its slow thighs, while all about it
Reel shadows of the indignant desert birds.
The darkness drops again; but now I know
That twenty centuries of stony sleep
20   Were vexed to nightmare by a rocking cradle,[4]
And what rough beast, its hour come round at last,
Slouches towards Bethlehem[5] to be born?

January 1919   1921

A Prayer for My Daughter[6]

Once more the storm is howling, and half hid
Under this cradle-hood and coverlid
My child sleeps on. There is no obstacle
But Gregory's wood[7] and one bare hill
5   Whereby the haystack- and roof-levelling wind,
Bred on the Atlantic, can be stayed;

---

1. The gyre (Yeats's term, pronounced with a hard g) is a conical shape based on the geometrical figure of interpenetrating cones; here, it is traced in the falcon's sweep upward and out in widening circles from the falconer. Yeats used this "fundamental symbol" to diagram his cyclical view of history, as in "The Great Wheel" (*A Vision*, 1937). He saw the cycle of Greco-Roman civilization as having been brought to a close by the advent of Christianity, and in the violence of his own times—"the growing murderousness of the world"—he saw signs that the two-thousand-year cycle of Christianity was about to end and be replaced by a system antithetical to it.
2. Or *Anima Mundi*, the Great Memory (Latin); according to Yeats, "a great memory passing on from generation to generation. . . . Our daily thought was certainly but the line of foam at the shallow edge of a vast luminous sea."
3. In the introduction to his play *The Resurrection* (in *Wheels and Butterflies*, 1935), Yeats describes the way in which the sphinx image had first manifested itself to him: "Our civilisation was about to reverse itself, or some new civilisation about to be born from all that our age had rejected . . . ; because we had worshipped a single god it would worship many. . . . I associated [the 'brazen winged beast'] with laughing, ecstatic destruction."
4. That of the infant Christ.
5. Christ's birthplace.
6. Yeats's daughter, Anne Butler Yeats, was born on February 26, 1919.
7. Part of the Gregory estate—about which, and about Yeats's tower (line 10), which he called Thoor Ballylee, see note to the next poem.

And for an hour I have walked and prayed
Because of the great gloom that is in my mind.

I have walked and prayed for this young child an hour
10 And heard the sea-wind scream upon the tower,
And under the arches of the bridge, and scream
In the elms above the flooded stream;
Imagining in excited reverie
That the future years had come,
15 Dancing to a frenzied drum,
Out of the murderous innocence of the sea.

May she be granted beauty and yet not
Beauty to make a stranger's eye distraught,
Or hers before a looking glass, for such,
20 Being made beautiful overmuch,
Consider beauty a sufficient end,
Lose natural kindness and maybe
The heart-revealing intimacy
That chooses right, and never find a friend.

25 Helen[8] being chosen found life flat and dull
And later had much trouble from a fool,
While that great Queen,[9] that rose out of the spray,
Being fatherless could have her way
Yet chose a bandy-leggèd smith for man.
30 It's certain that fine women eat
A crazy salad with their meat,
Whereby the Horn of Plenty is undone.

In courtesy I'd have her chiefly learned;
Hearts are not had as a gift but hearts are earned
35 By those that are not entirely beautiful;
Yet many, that have played the fool
For beauty's very self, has charm made wise,
And many a poor man that has roved,
Loved and thought himself beloved,
40 From a glad kindness cannot take his eyes.

May she become a flourishing hidden tree
That all her thoughts may like the linnet° be,   *a songbird*
And have no business but dispensing round
Their magnanimities of sound,
45 Nor but in merriment begin a chase,
Nor but in merriment a quarrel.
Oh, may she live like some green laurel
Rooted in one dear perpetual place.

8. Helen of Troy, whose beauty was legendary. The daughter of Zeus (the supreme god) and Leda (a mortal), she married Menelaus, brother of the Greek leader, Agamemnon. She was abducted by Paris, son of the king of Troy; the Greeks undertook an expedition to Troy to bring her back, besieged the city for ten years, and finally took it. Helen was reunited with Menelaus.
9. Aphrodite, Greek goddess of love. "Fatherless" (line 28) in the sense that, in Hesiod's version of the myth, she sprang from sea foam. She was married to Hephaestus, the blacksmith, lame from birth, who forged thunderbolts for the gods.

My mind, because the minds that I have loved,
50 The sort of beauty that I have approved,
    Prosper but little, has dried up of late,
    Yet knows that to be choked with hate
    May well be of all evil chances chief.
    If there's no hatred in a mind
55 Assault and battery of the wind
    Can never tear the linnet from the leaf.

    An intellectual hatred is the worst,
    So let her think opinions are accursed.
    Have I not seen the loveliest woman born[1]
60 Out of the mouth of Plenty's horn,
    Because of her opinionated mind
    Barter that horn and every good
    By quiet natures understood
    For an old bellows full of angry wind?

65 Considering that, all hatred driven hence,
    The soul recovers radical innocence
    And learns at last that it is self-delighting,
    Self-appeasing, self-affrighting,
    And that its own sweet will is Heaven's will;
70 She can, though every face should scowl
    And every windy quarter howl
    Or every bellows burst, be happy still.

    And may her bridegroom bring her to a house
    Where all's accustomed, ceremonious;
75 For arrogance and hatred are the wares
    Peddled in the thoroughfares.
    How but in custom and in ceremony
    Are innocence and beauty born?
    Ceremony's a name for the rich horn,
80 And custom for the spreading laurel tree.

February–June 1919   1921

To Be Carved on a Stone at Thoor Ballylee[2]

I, the poet William Yeats,
With old mill boards and sea-green slates,
And smithy work from the Gort forge,
Restored this tower for my wife George;

1. Doubtless Maud Gonne, whom Yeats had loved hopelessly since meeting her in 1889, and who had married Major John MacBride in 1903; often to Yeats's dismay, she was a very daring activist in the cause of Irish liberation.
2. In June 1917, Yeats had purchased a small plot of land and the buildings on it, including a ruined Norman tower, Thoor (Gaelic for "tower") Ballylee, part of the Gregory estate, Coole Park, in Kiltartan, near the village of Gort, County Galway. After marrying Georgie (changed by Yeats to George) Hyde-Lees in October 1917, he made the tower and two cottages suitable for habitation.

5   And may these characters remain
     When all is ruin once again.

1918   1921

Sailing to Byzantium[3]

1

That is no country for old men. The young
In one another's arms, birds in the trees
—Those dying generations—at their song,
The salmon-falls, the mackerel-crowded seas,
5 Fish, flesh, or fowl, commend all summer long
Whatever is begotten, born, and dies.
Caught in that sensual music all neglect
Monuments of unaging intellect.

2

An aged man is but a paltry thing,
10 A tattered coat upon a stick, unless
Soul clap its hands and sing, and louder sing
For every tatter in its mortal dress,
Nor is there singing school but studying
Monuments of its own magnificence;
15 And therefore I have sailed the seas and come
To the holy city of Byzantium.

3

O sages standing in God's holy fire
As in the gold mosaic of a wall,
Come from the holy fire, perne in a gyre,[4]
20 And be the singing-masters of my soul.
Consume my heart away; sick with desire

3. Of the ancient city of Byzantium—on the site of modern Istanbul, capital of the Eastern Roman Empire, and the center, especially in the fifth and sixth centuries, of highly developed and characteristic forms of art and architecture—Yeats made a many-faceted symbol, which, since it is a symbol, should not be brought within the limits of too narrowly specific interpretation. Byzantine painting and the mosaics that decorated its churches (Yeats had seen later derivatives of these mosaics in Italy, at Ravenna and elsewhere) were stylized and formal, making no attempt at the full naturalistic rendering of human forms, so that the city and its art can appropriately symbolize a way of life in which art is frankly accepted and proclaimed as artifice. As artifice, as a work of the intellect, this art is not subject to the decay and death that overtake the life of "natural things." But while such an opposition of artifice and nature is central to the poem, there are references to Byzantium in Yeats's prose that suggest the wider range of meaning that the city held for him. In A Vision (1937), particularly, he makes of it an exemplar of a civilization that had achieved "Unity of Being": "I think if I could be given a month of Antiquity and leave to spend it where I chose, I would spend it in Byzantium a little before Justinian [who ruled at Byzantium from 527 to 565] opened St. Sophia and closed the Academy of Plato [i.e., circa 535]. . . . I think that in early Byzantium, maybe never before or since in recorded history, religious, aesthetic and practical life were one, that architect and artificers . . . spoke to the multitude and the few alike. The painter, the mosaic worker, the worker in gold and silver, the illuminator of sacred books, were almost impersonal, almost perhaps without the consciousness of individual design, absorbed in their subject-matter and that the vision of a whole people."
4. Out of the noun *pern* (usually *pirn*), a weaver's bobbin, spool, or reel, Yeats makes a verb meaning to move in the spiral pattern taken by thread being unwound from a bobbin or being wound upon it. Here the speaker entreats the sages to descend to him in this manner, to come down into the gyres of history, the cycles of created life, out of their eternity. On "gyre," see note 1, p. 1196.

And fastened to a dying animal
It knows not what it is; and gather me
Into the artifice of eternity.

4

25 Once out of nature I shall never take
My bodily form from any natural thing,
But such a form as Grecian goldsmiths make
Of hammered gold and gold enamelling
To keep a drowsy Emperor awake;
30 Or set upon a golden bough to sing
To lords and ladies of Byzantium
Of what is past, or passing, or to come.

September 1926   1927

Leda and the Swan[5]

A sudden blow: the great wings beating still
Above the staggering girl, her thighs caressed
By the dark webs, her nape caught in his bill,
He holds her helpless breast upon his breast.

5 How can those terrified vague fingers push
The feathered glory from her loosening thighs?
And how can body, laid in that white rush,
But feel the strange heart beating where it lies?

A shudder in the loins engenders there
10 The broken wall, the burning roof and tower
And Agamemnon dead.
                              Being so caught up,
So mastered by the brute blood of the air,
Did she put on his knowledge with his power
Before the indifferent beak could let her drop?

September 1923   1924

Among School Children

I

I walk through the long schoolroom questioning;
A kind old nun in a white hood replies;
The children learn to cipher and to sing,

5. In Greek mythology, Leda, raped by Zeus, the supreme god, in the guise of a swan, gave birth to Helen of Troy and the twins Castor and Pollux. Helen's abduction by Paris from her husband, Menelaus, caused the Trojan War. Leda was also the mother of Clytemnestra, who murdered her own husband, Agamemnon, on his return from the war. Yeats saw Leda as the recipient of an annunciation that would found Greek civilization, as the Annunciation to Mary would found Christianity.

To study reading-books and histories,
5   To cut and sew, be neat in everything
In the best modern way—the children's eyes
In momentary wonder stare upon
A sixty-year-old smiling public man.

2

I dream of a Ledaean body,[6] bent
10 Above a sinking fire, a tale that she
Told of a harsh reproof, or trivial event
That changed some childish day to tragedy—
Told, and it seemed that our two natures blent
Into a sphere from youthful sympathy,
15 Or else, to alter Plato's parable,
Into the yolk and white of the one shell.[7]

3

And thinking of that fit of grief or rage
I look upon one child or t'other there
And wonder if she stood so at that age—
20 For even daughters of the swan can share
Something of every paddler's heritage—
And had that colour upon cheek or hair,
And thereupon my heart is driven wild:
She stands before me as a living child.

4

25 Her present image floats into the mind—
Did Quattrocento finger[8] fashion it
Hollow of cheek as though it drank the wind
And took a mess of shadows for its meat?
And I though never of Ledaean kind
30 Had pretty plumage once—enough of that,
Better to smile on all that smile, and show
There is a comfortable kind of old scarecrow.

5

What youthful mother, a shape upon her lap
Honey of generation had betrayed,
35 And that must sleep, shriek, struggle to escape
As recollection or the drug decide,[9]

---

6. I.e., the body of a woman he has known and loved and who has seemed to him as beautiful as Leda or her daughter, Helen of Troy—about both of whom, see note to the previous poem.
7. In Plato's *Symposium*, one of the speakers, to explain the origin of human love, recounts the legend according to which human beings were originally double their present form until Zeus, the supreme god, fearing their power, cut them in two, which he did "as men cut sorbapples in two when they are preparing them for pickling, or as they cut eggs in two with a hair." Since then, "each of us is . . . but the half of a human being, . . . each is forever seeking his missing half."

8. I.e., the hand of an Italian artist of the fifteenth century.
9. "I have taken the 'honey of generation' from Porphyry's essay on 'The Cave of the Nymphs' but find no warrant in Porphyry for considering it the 'drug' that destroys the 'recollection' of pre-natal freedom" [Yeats's note]. In the essay, which explains the symbolism of a passage from book 13 of the *Odyssey*, the Neoplatonic philosopher Porphyry (ca. 232–305) makes such statements as that "the sweetness of honey signifies . . . the same thing as the pleasure arising from copulation," the pleasure "which draws souls downward to generation."

Would think her son, did she but see that shape
With sixty or more winters on its head,
A compensation for the pang of his birth,
40   Or the uncertainty of his setting forth?

6

Plato thought nature but a spume that plays
Upon a ghostly paradigm of things;[1]
Solider Aristotle played the taws
Upon the bottom of a king of kings;[2]
45   World-famous golden-thighed Pythagoras[3]
Fingered upon a fiddle-stick or strings
What a star sang and careless Muses[4] heard:
Old clothes upon old sticks to scare a bird.

7

Both nuns and mothers worship images,
50   But those the candles light are not as those
That animate a mother's reveries,
But keep a marble or a bronze repose.
And yet they too break hearts—O Presences
That passion, piety or affection knows,
55   And that all heavenly glory symbolize—
O self-born mockers of man's enterprise;

8

Labour is blossoming or dancing where
The body is not bruised to pleasure soul,
Nor beauty born out of its own despair,
60   Nor blear-eyed wisdom out of midnight oil.
O chestnut-tree, great-rooted blossomer,
Are you the leaf, the blossom or the bole?°   *trunk*
O body swayed to music, O brightening glance,
How can we know the dancer from the dance?

June 1926   1927

Byzantium[5]

The unpurged images of day recede;
The Emperor's drunken soldiery are abed;

---

1. In Plato's philosophy, the world of nature, of
appearances, that we know is but the copy of a
world of ideal, permanently enduring prototypes.
2. Aristotle's philosophy differed most markedly
from Plato's in that it emphasized the systematic
investigation of verifiable phenomena. Aristotle
was tutor to the son of King Philip of Macedo-
nia, later Alexander the Great. *Played the taws*:
whipped.
3. Greek philosopher (ca. 580–ca. 500 B.C.E.),
about whom many legends clustered even in his
own lifetime, as that he was the incarnation of the
god Apollo, that he had a golden hipbone or thigh-
bone, and so on. Central to the Pythagorean school

of philosophy (along with the doctrine of the trans-
migration of souls) was the premise that the uni-
verse is mathematically regular, an idea based on
the Pythagoreans' observations of the exact math-
ematical relationships underlying musical har-
mony.
4. In Greek mythology, nine sister goddesses who
presided over song, poetry, and the arts and sci-
ences.
5. Under the heading "Subject for a Poem, April
30th," Yeats wrote in his *1930 Diary:* "Describe
Byzantium as it is in the system [that is, his system
in *A Vision*] towards the end of the first Christian
millennium. A walking mummy. Flames at the

Night resonance recedes, night-walkers' song
After great cathedral gong;
5   A starlit or a moonlit dome disdains[6]
All that man is,
All mere complexities,
The fury and the mire of human veins.

Before me floats an image, man or shade,
10   Shade more than man, more image than a shade;
For Hades' bobbin bound in mummy-cloth
May unwind the winding path;[7]
A mouth that has no moisture and no breath
Breathless mouths may summon;[8]
15   I hail the superhuman;
I call it death-in-life and life-in-death.

Miracle, bird or golden handiwork,
More miracle than bird or handiwork,
Planted on the starlit golden bough,
20   Can like the cocks of Hades crow,[9]
Or, by the moon embittered, scorn aloud
In glory of changeless metal
Common bird or petal
And all complexities of mire or blood.

25   At midnight on the Emperor's pavement flit
Flames that no faggot[1] feeds, nor steel has lit,
Nor storm disturbs, flames begotten of flame,
Where blood-begotten spirits come
And all complexities of fury leave,
30   Dying into a dance,
An agony of trance,
An agony of flame that cannot singe a sleeve.

---

street corners where the soul is purified, birds of hammered gold singing in the golden trees, in the harbor [dolphins], offering their backs to the wailing dead that they may carry them to Paradise."

6. If the dome is "starlit" at the dark of the moon and "moonlit" at the full, then these terms may refer to Phase 1 and Phase 15, respectively, of the twenty-eight phases of the moon in the system of *A Vision*. As Yeats's character Michael Robartes says in "The Phases of the Moon," "There's no human life at the full or the dark," these being "the superhuman phases," opposite to one another on the Wheel of Being. Phase 1 is the phase of complete objectivity, the soul being "completely absorbed by its supernatural environment," waiting to be formed, in a state of "complete plasticity." Phase 15 is the state of complete subjectivity, when the soul is completely absorbed in an achieved state, "a phase of complete beauty." Thus the world of "mere complexities," the world in which humanity is in a state of becoming, is banished from the poem at the beginning, as the "unpurged images of day" have been banished.

7. Hades was the Greek god of the underworld, the realm of the dead. The comparison of a dead body or soul to a bobbin (spool) is at first visual, to describe the figure, wrapped in a winding-sheet or mummy-cloth, but it also conveys the idea that the soul may unwind the thread of its fate by retracing its path, returning to the world to serve as guide, instructor, inspiration.

8. The two lines have been read in two different ways, depending on which of the two phrases ("a mouth" or "breathless mouths") is seen as subject and which as object of "may summon." Taking "breathless mouths" as subject: mouths of the living, breathless with the intensity of the act of invocation, may call up the mouths of the dead to instruct them.

9. A symbol of rebirth and resurrection. In a book on Roman sculpture that Yeats is believed to have known, *Apotheosis and After Life* (1915), Eugenia Strong writes: "The great vogue of the cock on later Roman tombstones is due . . . to the fact that as herald of the sun he becomes by an easy transition the herald of rebirth and resurrection." In the next sentence, she mentions a visual symbol that figures in the poem's last stanza: "The dolphins and marine monsters, another frequent decoration, form a mystic escort of the dead to the Islands of the Blest."

1. Bundle of sticks.

Astraddle on the dolphin's mire and blood,
Spirit after spirit! The smithies break the flood.
35 The golden smithies of the Emperor!
Marbles of the dancing floor
Break bitter furies of complexity,
Those images that yet
Fresh images beget,
40 That dolphin-torn, that gong-tormented sea.

September 1930   1932

Crazy Jane[2] Talks with the Bishop

I met the Bishop on the road
And much said he and I.
"Those breasts are flat and fallen now,
Those veins must soon be dry;
5   Live in a heavenly mansion,
Not in some foul sty."

"Fair and foul are near of kin,
And fair needs foul," I cried.[3]
"My friends are gone, but that's a truth
10   Nor grave nor bed denied,
Learned in bodily lowliness
And in the heart's pride.

"A woman can be proud and stiff
When on love intent;
15   But Love has pitched his mansion in
The place of excrement;
For nothing can be sole or whole
That has not been rent."

November 1931   1932

Lapis Lazuli[4]

(For Harry Clifton)

I have heard that hysterical women say
They are sick of the palette and fiddle-bow,
Of poets that are always gay,

2. In a series of poems, Yeats presents her as a source of wisdom.
3. Cf. *Macbeth* 1.1.10: "Fair is foul, and foul is fair."
4. A deep-blue semiprecious stone. In a letter dated July 6, 1935, Yeats wrote, "Someone [i.e., the English writer Harry Clifton (1908–1978)] has sent me a present of a great piece [of lapis lazuli]

carved by some Chinese sculptor into the semblance of a mountain with temple, trees, paths and an ascetic and pupil about to climb the mountain. Ascetic, pupil, hard stone, eternal theme of the sensual east. The heroic cry in the midst of despair. But no, I am wrong, the east has its solutions always and therefore knows nothing of tragedy. It is we, not the east, that must raise the heroic cry."

For everybody knows or else should know
5 That if nothing drastic is done
Aeroplane and Zeppelin⁵ will come out,
Pitch like King Billy⁶ bomb-balls in
Until the town lie beaten flat.

All perform their tragic play,
10 There struts Hamlet, there is Lear,
That's Ophelia, that Cordelia;
Yet they, should the last scene be there,
The great stage curtain about to drop,
If worthy their prominent part in the play,
15 Do not break up their lines to weep.
They know that Hamlet and Lear are gay;
Gaiety transfiguring all that dread.
All men have aimed at, found and lost;
Black out; Heaven blazing into the head:
20 Tragedy wrought to its uttermost.
Though Hamlet rambles and Lear rages,
And all the drop-scenes drop at once
Upon a hundred thousand stages,
It cannot grow by an inch or an ounce.

25 On their own feet they came, or on shipboard,
Camelback, horseback, ass-back, mule-back,
Old civilizations put to the sword.
Then they and their wisdom went to rack:
No handiwork of Callimachus,⁷
30 Who handled marble as if it were bronze,
Made draperies that seemed to rise
When sea-wind swept the corner, stands;
His long lamp-chimney shaped like the stem
Of a slender palm, stood but a day;
35 All things fall and are built again,
And those that build them again are gay.

Two Chinamen, behind them a third,
Are carved in lapis lazuli,
Over them flies a long-legged bird,
40 A symbol of longevity;
The third, doubtless a serving-man,
Carries a musical instrument.

Every discolouration of the stone,
Every accidental crack or dent,
45 Seems a water-course or an avalanche,
Or lofty slope where it still snows
Though doubtless plum or cherry-branch

---

5. Cylindrical airship.
6. At the Battle of the Boyne on July 1, 1690, William III, king of England since 1689, had defeated the forces of the deposed king, James II.
7. Greek sculptor of the fifth century B.C.E. In A *Vision*, Yeats says that only one example of his work remains, a marble chair, and goes on to mention "that bronze lamp [in the Erechtheum, a temple of the guardian deities of Athens] shaped like a palm, known to us by a description in Pausanias."

Sweetens the little half-way house
Those Chinamen climb towards, and I
50 Delight to imagine them seated there;
There, on the mountain and the sky,
On all the tragic scene they stare.
One asks for mournful melodies;
Accomplished fingers begin to play.
55 Their eyes mid many wrinkles, their eyes,
Their ancient, glittering eyes, are gay.

July 1936   1938

Long-Legged Fly

That civilisation may not sink,
Its great battle lost,
Quiet the dog, tether the pony
To a distant post;
5 Our master Caesar is in the tent
Where the maps are spread,
His eyes fixed upon nothing,
A hand under his head.
Like a long-legged fly upon the stream
10 *His mind moves upon silence.*

That the topless towers be burnt
And men recall that face,[8]
Move most gently if move you must
In this lonely place.
15 She thinks, part woman, three parts a child,
That nobody looks; her feet
Practice a tinker shuffle
Picked up on a street.
Like a long-legged fly upon the stream
20 *Her mind moves upon silence.*

That girls at puberty may find
The first Adam in their thought,
Shut the door of the Pope's chapel,[9]
Keep those children out.
25 There on that scaffolding reclines
Michael Angelo.
With no more sound than the mice make
His hand moves to and fro.
Like a long-legged fly upon the stream
30 *His mind moves upon silence.*

November 1937   1939

8. Helen, legendary beauty whose abduction caused the Trojan War and hence the fall of Troy. An echo of Christopher Marlowe's play *Dr. Faustus:* "Was this the face that launched a thousand ships, / And burnt the topless towers of Ilium?"

9. On the ceiling of the Sistine Chapel, so called because it was built under Pope Sixtus IV, Michelangelo (1475–1564) painted a series of biblical scenes, including the creation of Adam.

The Circus Animals' Desertion

1

I sought a theme and sought for it in vain,
I sought it daily for six weeks or so.
Maybe at last, being but a broken man,
I must be satisfied with my heart, although
5 Winter and summer till old age began
My circus animals were all on show,
Those stilted boys, that burnished chariot,[1]
Lion and woman and the Lord knows what.

2

What can I but enumerate old themes?
10 First that sea-rider Oisin[2] led by the nose
Through three enchanted islands, allegorical dreams,
Vain gaiety, vain battle, vain repose,
Themes of the embittered heart, or so it seems,
That might adorn old songs or courtly shows;
15 But what cared I that set him on to ride,
I, starved for the bosom of his faery bride?

And then a counter-truth filled out its play,
The Countess Cathleen[3] was the name I gave it;
She, pity-crazed, had given her soul away,
20 But masterful Heaven had intervened to save it.
I thought my dear[4] must her own soul destroy,
So did fanaticism and hate enslave it,
And this brought forth a dream and soon enough
This dream itself had all my thought and love.

25 And when the Fool and Blind Man stole the bread
Cuchulain fought the ungovernable sea;[5]
Heart-mysteries there, and yet when all is said
It was the dream itself enchanted me:
Character isolated by a deed
30 To engross the present and dominate memory.
Players and painted stage took all my love,
And not those things that they were emblems of.

---

1. The images of lines 7–8 may refer to motifs
from earlier works by Yeats (in his play *The Uni-
corn from the Stars,* for instance, a gilded state
coach, adorned with lion and unicorn, is being
built on stage), or they may be generalized images,
in line with the title and argument of the poem, of
the people and things to be encountered in the
heightened, unreal world of a circus.
2. The hero of Yeats's allegorical (and symbolic)
long poem, *The Wanderings of Oisin* (pronounced
Ushēēn), 1889, is led by the fairy Niamh (pro-
nounced *Nee-ave*) in succession to the three
Islands of, respectively, Dancing (changeless joy),
Victories (also called "Of Many Fears"), and For-
getfulness.
3. Yeats's first play, 1892. In it, the people, in a
time of famine, are selling their souls to emissaries
of the Devil. To save their souls, the Countess
Cathleen sells hers "for a great price." She dies,
but an angel announces that she is "passing to the
floor of peace."
4. Maud Gonne, whom Yeats had loved since first
meeting her in 1889, and who had married John
MacBride in 1903; she was a daring, even violent,
activist in the cause of Irish liberation.
5. In another early play, *On Baile's Strand*, 1904,
Cuchulain (pronounced *Cuhoolin*) unwittingly
kills his own son; maddened, he rushes out to fight
the waves. As the people run to the shore to watch,
the fool and the blind man hurry off to steal the
bread from their ovens.

3

Those masterful images because complete
Grew in pure mind, but out of what began?
35 A mound of refuse or the sweeping of a street,
Old kettles, old bottles, and a broken can,
Old iron, old bones, old rags, that raving slut
Who keeps the till. Now that my ladder's gone,
I must lie down where all the ladders start,
40 In the foul rag-and-bone shop of the heart.

1939

Under Ben Bulben[6]

1

Swear by what the sages spoke
Round the Mareotic Lake[7]
That the Witch of Atlas knew,
Spoke and set the cocks a-crow.[8]

5 Swear by those horsemen, by those women
Complexion and form prove superhuman,[9]
That pale, long-visaged company
That air in immortality
Completeness of their passions won;
10 Now they ride the wintry dawn
Where Ben Bulben sets the scene.[1]

Here's the gist of what they mean.

2

Many times man lives and dies
Between his two eternities,
15 That of race and that of soul,
And ancient Ireland knew it all.

6. A mountain in County Sligo, in the west of Ireland, that overlooks Drumcliff Churchyard, where Yeats is buried. The last three lines of the poem are carved on his tombstone.
7. Lake Mareotis, a salt lake in northern Egypt, near which the Christian monks and nuns of the Thebaid, among them St. Anthony (ca. 251–356), had withdrawn to contemplation. In his *1930 Diary*, Yeats wrote that "men went on pilgrimage to Saint Anthony that they might learn about their spiritual states, what was about to happen and why it happened, and Saint Anthony would reply neither out of traditional casuistry or common sense but from spiritual powers."
8. In the poem "The Witch of Atlas," by Percy Bysshe Shelley (1792–1822; for his poetry, see pp. 863–93), the protagonist, a spirit of love,

beauty, and freedom, visits Egypt and the Mareotic Lake in the course of her magic journeyings. The knowledge and belief that Yeats describes as common to her and to the sages "set the cocks a-crow" in the sense that, like "the cocks of Hades" and the golden bird in Yeats's "Byzantium" (see p. 1202), they summon to a spiritual rebirth.
9. Fairies called the Sidhe (pronounced *shee*) were believed to ride through the countryside near Ben Bulben.
1. In another late poem, "Alternative Song for the Severed Head in 'The King of the Great Clock Tower,'" Yeats reintroduces some of the Irish mythological or legendary heroes and heroines who figure in his early poems—Cuchulain, Niamh and others—with whom the supernatural riders of these lines may be identified.

Whether man die in his bed
Or the rifle knocks him dead,
A brief parting from those dear
20   Is the worst man has to fear.
Though gravediggers' toil is long,
Sharp their spades, their muscles strong,
They but thrust their buried men
Back in the human mind again.

3

25   You that Mitchel's prayer have heard,
"Send war in our time, O Lord!"[2]
Know that when all words are said
And a man is fighting mad,
Something drops from eyes long blind,
30   He completes his partial mind,
For an instant stands at ease,
Laughs aloud, his heart at peace.
Even the wisest man grows tense
With some sort of violence
35   Before he can accomplish fate,
Know his work or choose his mate.

4

Poet and sculptor, do the work,
Nor let the modish painter shirk
What his great forefathers did,
40   Bring the soul of man to God,
Make him fill the cradles right.

Measurement began our might:[3]
Forms a stark Egyptian thought,
Forms that gentler Phidias wrought.
45   Michael Angelo left a proof
On the Sistine Chapel roof,[4]
Where but half-awakened Adam
Can disturb globe-trotting Madam
Till her bowels are in heat,
50   Proof that there's a purpose set
Before the secret working mind:
Profane perfection of mankind.
Quattrocento[5] put in paint
On backgrounds for a God or Saint

2. John Mitchel (1815–1875), Irish nationalist, wrote in his *Jail Journal, or Five Years in British Prisons* (1854): "Czar, I bless thee, I kiss the hem of thy garment. I drink to thy health and longevity. Give us war in our time, O Lord."
3. The achievements of Western civilization (now, according to the poem, being challenged or destroyed) began with the exact mathematical rules that the Egyptians followed in working out the proportions of their sculptured figures—rules that Phidias (line 44), the great Greek sculptor of the fifth century B.C.E., used, and that have been implicit in the greatest Western art up to the present, when "confusion [falls] upon our thought" (line 67).
4. See note 9, p. 1206.
5. The Italian fifteenth century.

55   Gardens where a soul's at ease;
Where everything that meets the eye,
Flowers and grass and cloudless sky,
Resemble forms that are or seem
When sleepers wake and yet still dream,
60   And when it's vanished still declare,
With only bed and bedstead there,
That heavens had opened.
                      Gyres[6] run on;
When that greater dream had gone
Calvert and Wilson, Blake and Claude,
65   Prepared a rest for the people of God,
Palmer's phrase,[7] but after that
Confusion fell upon our thought.

5

Irish poets, learn your trade,
Sing whatever is well made,
70   Scorn the sort now growing up
All out of shape from toe to top,
Their unremembering hearts and heads
Base-born products of base beds.
Sing the peasantry, and then
75   Hard-riding country gentlemen,
The holiness of monks, and after
Porter°-drinkers' randy laughter;   *dark brown beer*
Sing the lords and ladies gay
That were beaten into the clay
80   Through seven heroic centuries;
Cast your mind on other days
That we in coming days may be
Still the indomitable Irishry.

6

Under bare Ben Bulben's head
85   In Drumcliff churchyard Yeats is laid.
An ancestor was rector there[8]
Long years ago, a church stands near,
By the road an ancient cross.
No marble, no conventional phrase;
90   On limestone quarried near the spot
By his command these words are cut:

6. I.e., the cycles of history. See note 1, p. 1196.
7. Lines 64–66 name five artists who had provided Yeats with images and with ideals of what art should be. Claude Lorrain (1600–1682), French landscape painter, was a central standard for landscape painters up to the early nineteenth century, including the English artists mentioned here, especially Richard Wilson (1714–1782). Edward Cal-

vert (1799–1883) and Samuel Palmer (1805–1881), visionaries, landscape painters, and engravers, had found inspiration in the life and work of William Blake (1757–1827; see pp. 732–47).
8. Yeats's great-grandfather, the Reverend John Yeats (1774–1847), was rector of Drumcliff from 1805.

Cast a cold eye
On life, on death.
Horseman, pass by!

September 4, 1938   1939

ERNEST DOWSON
1867–1900

Vitae summa brevis spem nos vetat incohare longam[1]

They are not long, the weeping and the laughter,
    Love and desire and hate:
I think they have no portion in us after
    We pass the gate.

5   They are not long, the days of wine and roses:
        Out of a misty dream
    Our path emerges for a while, then closes
        Within a dream.

1891   1896

Non sum qualis eram bonae sub regno Cynarae[2]

Last night, ah, yesternight, betwixt her lips and mine
There fell thy shadow, Cynara! thy breath was shed
Upon my soul between the kisses and the wine;
And I was desolate and sick of an old passion,
5   Yea, I was desolate and bowed my head:
I have been faithful to thee, Cynara! in my fashion.

All night upon mine heart I felt her warm heart beat,
Night-long within mine arms in love and sleep she lay;
Surely the kisses of her bought red mouth were sweet;
10 But I was desolate and sick of an old passion,
    When I awoke and found the dawn was grey:
I have been faithful to thee, Cynara! in my fashion.

I have forgot much, Cynara! gone with the wind,
Flung roses, roses riotously with the throng,
15 Dancing, to put thy pale, lost lilies out of mind;
But I was desolate and sick of an old passion,

---

1. The brevity of life forbids us to entertain hopes of long duration (Latin); Horace, *Odes* 1.4.15.
2. I am not as I was under the reign of the good Cynara (Latin); Horace, *Odes* 4.1.3–4: the poet urges Venus, Roman goddess of love and beauty, to spare him new efforts in her service, because he is no longer up to the task.

Yea, all the time, because the dance was long:
I have been faithful to thee, Cynara! in my fashion.

I cried for madder music and for stronger wine,
20   But when the feast is finished and the lamps expire,
Then falls thy shadow, Cynara! the night is thine;
And I am desolate and sick of an old passion,
    Yea hungry for the lips of my desire:
I have been faithful to thee, Cynara! in my fashion.

1891   1896

EDWIN ARLINGTON ROBINSON
1869–1935

Richard Cory

Whenever Richard Cory went down town,
We people on the pavement looked at him:
He was a gentleman from sole to crown,
Clean favored, and imperially slim.

5   And he was always quietly arrayed,
And he was always human when he talked;
But still he fluttered pulses when he said,
"Good-morning," and he glittered when he walked.

And he was rich—yes, richer than a king—
10   And admirably schooled in every grace:
In fine, we thought that he was everything
To make us wish that we were in his place.

So on we worked, and waited for the light,
And went without the meat, and cursed the bread;
15   And Richard Cory, one calm summer night,
Went home and put a bullet through his head.

1869

George Crabbe[1]

Give him the darkest inch your shelf allows,
Hide him in lonely garrets, if you will,
But his hard, human pulse is throbbing still
With the sure strength that fearless truth endows.

---

1. English poet, physician, and curate (1754–1832; see pp. 723–31), known for his realistic narrative
poems.

₅ In spite of all fine science disavows,
Of his plain excellence and stubborn skill
There yet remains what fashion cannot kill,
Though years have thinned the laurel[2] from his brows.

Whether or not we read him, we can feel
₁₀ From time to time the vigor of his name
Against us like a finger for the shame
And emptiness of what our souls reveal
In books that are as altars where we kneel
To consecrate the flicker, not the flame.

1897

Reuben Bright

Because he was a butcher and thereby
Did earn an honest living (and did right),
I would not have you think that Reuben Bright
Was any more a brute than you or I;

₅ For when they told him that his wife must die,
He stared at them, and shook with grief and fright,
And cried like a great baby half that night,
And made the women cry to see him cry.

And after she was dead, and he had paid
₁₀ The singers and the sexton and the rest,
He packed a lot of things that she had made
Most mournfully away in an old chest
Of hers, and put some chopped-up cedar boughs
In with them, and tore down the slaughter-house.

1897

Miniver Cheevy

Miniver Cheevy, child of scorn,
    Grew lean while he assailed the seasons;
He wept that he was ever born,
    And he had reasons.

₅ Miniver loved the days of old
    When swords were bright and steeds were prancing;
The vision of a warrior bold
    Would set him dancing.

2. In classical Greece, laurel was associated with prophecy and poetry; laurel wreaths crowned poets as well as the victors in athletic contests.

Miniver sighed for what was not,
10 And dreamed, and rested from his labors;
He dreamed of Thebes and Camelot,
    And Priam's[3] neighbors.

Miniver mourned the ripe renown
    That made so many a name so fragrant;
15 He mourned Romance, now on the town,
    And Art, a vagrant.

Miniver loved the Medici,[4]
    Albeit he had never seen one;
He would have sinned incessantly
20 Could he have been one.

Miniver cursed the commonplace
    And eyed a khaki suit with loathing;
He missed the medieval grace
    Of iron clothing.

25 Miniver scorned the gold he sought,
    But sore annoyed was he without it;
Miniver thought, and thought, and thought,
    And thought about it.

Miniver Cheevy, born too late,
30 Scratched his head and kept on thinking;
Miniver coughed, and called it fate,
    And kept on drinking.

                                        1910

The Mill

The miller's wife had waited long,
    The tea was cold, the fire was dead;
And there might yet be nothing wrong
    In how he went and what he said:
5 "There are no millers any more,"
    Was all that she had heard him say;
And he had lingered at the door
    So long that it seemed yesterday.

Sick with a fear that had no form
10 She knew that she was there at last;
And in the mill there was a warm
    And mealy fragrance of the past.

---

3. King of Troy during the Trojan War, immortal-
ized in Homer's *Iliad*. *Thebes*: Ancient Greek city,
famous in history and legend. *Camelot*: according
to English legend, the site of King Arthur's court.

4. Merchant-princes of Renaissance Florence,
known both for cruelty and for their support of
learning and art.

What else there was would only seem
    To say again what he had meant;
15 And what was hanging from a beam
    Would not have heeded where she went.

And if she thought it followed her,
    She may have reasoned in the dark
That one way of the few there were
20   Would hide her and would leave no mark:
Black water, smooth above the weir°   *milldam*
    Like starry velvet in the night,
Though ruffled once, would soon appear
    The same as ever to the sight.

1920

Mr. Flood's Party

Old Eben Flood, climbing alone one night
Over the hill between the town below
And the forsaken upland hermitage
That held as much as he should ever know
5 On earth again of home, paused warily.
The road was his with not a native near;
And Eben, having leisure, said aloud,
For no man else in Tilbury Town to hear:

"Well, Mr. Flood, we have the harvest moon
10 Again, and we may not have many more;
The bird is on the wing, the poet says,[5]
And you and I have said it here before.
Drink to the bird." He raised up to the light
The jug that he had gone so far to fill,
15 And answered huskily: "Well, Mr. Flood,
Since you propose it, I believe I will."

Alone, as if enduring to the end
A valiant armor of scarred hopes outworn,
He stood there in the middle of the road
20 Like Roland's ghost winding a silent horn.[6]
Below him, in the town among the trees,
Where friends of other days had honored him,
A phantom salutation of the dead
Rang thinly till old Eben's eyes were dim.

5. A paraphrase of the seventh stanza of *The Rubáiyát of Omar Khayyám* as translated in 1859 by the English poet Edward FitzGerald (1809–1883; see pp. 961–73).

6. The hero of the French poem *The Song of Roland* (ca. 1000) had an enchanted horn; in battle at Roncevalles (778), he sounded his horn for help just before dying.

25 Then, as a mother lays her sleeping child
Down tenderly, fearing it may awake,
He set the jug down slowly at his feet
With trembling care, knowing that most things break;
And only when assured that on firm earth
30 It stood, as the uncertain lives of men
Assuredly did not, he paced away,
And with his hand extended paused again:

"Well, Mr. Flood, we have not met like this
In a long time; and many a change has come
35 To both of us, I fear, since last it was
We had a drop together. Welcome home!"
Convivially returning with himself,
Again he raised the jug up to the light;
And with an acquiescent quaver said:
40 "Well, Mr. Flood, if you insist, I might.

"Only a very little, Mr. Flood—
For auld lang syne.[7] No more, sir; that will do."
So, for the time, apparently it did,
And Eben evidently thought so too;
45 For soon amid the silver loneliness
Of night he lifted up his voice and sang,
Secure, with only two moons listening,
Until the whole harmonious landscape rang—

"For auld lang syne." The weary throat gave out,
50 The last word wavered; and the song being done,
He raised again the jug regretfully
And shook his head, and was again alone.
There was not much that was ahead of him,
And there was nothing in the town below—
55 Where strangers would have shut the many doors
That many friends had opened long ago.

1920

CHARLOTTE MEW
1869–1928

The Farmer's Bride

Three Summers since I chose a maid,
Too young maybe—but more's to do
At harvest-time than bide and woo.
    When us was wed she turned afraid

---

7. Old long since (Scottish), the days of long ago; title and refrain of a famous song by the eighteenth-century Scottish poet Robert Burns (see p. 753).

5   Of love and me and all things human;
       Like the shut of a winter's day.
       Her smile went out, and 'twasn't a woman—
           More like a little frightened fay.°   *fairy*
               One night, in the Fall, she runned away.

10   "Out 'mong the sheep, her be," they said,
       'Should properly have been abed;
       But sure enough she wasn't there
       Lying awake with her wide brown stare.
   So over seven-acre field and up-along across the down°   *upland pasture*
15   We chased her, flying like a hare
       Before our lanterns. To Church-Town
           All in a shiver and a scare
       We caught her, fetched her home at last
           And turned the key upon her, fast.

20   She does the work about the house
       As well as most, but like a mouse:
           Happy enough to chat and play
           With birds and rabbits and such as they,
           So long as men-folk keep away.
25   "Not near, not near!" her eyes beseech
       When one of us comes within reach.
           The women say that beasts in stall
           Look round like children at her call.
           I've hardly heard her speak at all.

30   Shy as a leveret,° swift as he,   *young hare*
       Straight and slight as a young larch tree,
       Sweet as the first wild violets, she,
       To her wild self. But what to me?

       The short days shorten and the oaks are brown,
35   The blue smoke rises to the low grey sky,
       One leaf in the still air falls slowly down,
           A magpie's spotted feathers lie
       On the black earth spread white with rime,°   *frozen dew*
       The berries redden up to Christmas-time.
40   What's Christmas-time without there be
           Some other in the house than we!

           She sleeps up in the attic there
           Alone, poor maid. 'Tis but a stair
       Betwixt us. Oh! my God! the down,°   *light, soft body hair*
45   The soft young down of her, the brown,
   The brown of her—her eyes, her hair, her hair!

1912   1916

In Nunhead Cemetery

It is the clay that makes the earth stick to his spade;
　　He fills in holes like this year after year;
The others have gone; they were tired, and half afraid
　　But I would rather be standing here;

5　There is nowhere else to go. I have seen this place
　　From the windows of the train that's going past
Against the sky. This is rain on my face—
　　It was raining here when I saw it last.

There is something horrible about a flower;
10　This, broken in my hand, is one of those
He threw in just now: it will not live another hour;
　　There are thousands more: you do not miss a rose.

One of the children hanging about
　　Pointed at the whole dreadful heap and smiled
15　This morning, after THAT was carried out;
　　There is something terrible about a child.

We were like children, last week, in the Strand;[1]
　　That was the day you laughed at me
Because I tried to make you understand
20　The cheap, stale chap I used to be
　　Before I saw the things you made me see.

This is not a real place; perhaps by-and-by
　　I shall wake—I am getting drenched with all this rain:
To-morrow I will tell you about the eyes of the Crystal Palace[2] train
25　Looking down on us, and you will laugh and I shall see what you
　　　see again.

　　　Not here, not now. We said "Not yet
　　　Across our low stone parapet
　　Will the quick shadows of the sparrows fall."

　　　But still it was a lovely thing
30　　Through the grey months to wait for Spring
　　　With the birds that go a-gypsying
　　In the parks till the blue seas call.
　　　And next to these, you used to care
　　　For the lions in Trafalgar Square,[3]
35　Who'll stand and speak for London when her bell of Judgment tolls—
　　　And the gulls at Westminster that were
　　　The old sea-captains' souls.

---

1. Street in central London.
2. Large building made of glass and iron, erected in London's Great Exhibition of 1851.
3. Grand plaza in the Westminster borough of London, wherein four bronze lions stand at the base of a commemorative column. Gulls gather in the fountains of Trafalgar, as in areas surrounding the nearby river Thames.

To-day again the brown tide splashes, step by step, the river stair,
    And the gulls are there!

40 By a month we have missed our Day:
    The children would have hung about
Round the carriage and over the way
    As you and I came out.

We should have stood on the gulls' black cliffs and heard the sea
45   And seen the moon's white track,
I would have called, you would have come to me
    And kissed me back.

You have never done that: I do not know
    Why I stood staring at your bed
50 And heard you, though you spoke so low,
    But could not reach your hands, your little head.
There was nothing we could not do, you said,
    And you went, and I let you go!

Now I will burn you back, I will burn you through,
55   Though I am damned for it we two will lie
And burn, here where the starlings fly
    To these white stones from the wet sky—;
Dear, you will say this is not I—
    It would not be you, it would not be you!

60 If for only a little while
    You will think of it you will understand,
    If you will touch my sleeve and smile
    As you did that morning in the Strand
    I can wait quietly with you
65   Or go away if you want me to—
    God! What is God? but your face has gone and your hand!
    Let me stay here too.

    When I was quite a little lad
    At Christmas-time we went half mad
70   For joy of all the toys we had,
And then we used to sing about the sheep
    The shepherds watched by night;
We used to pray to Christ to keep
    Our small souls safe till morning light—;
75 I am scared, I am staying with you to-night—
        Put me to sleep.

I shall stay here: here you can see the sky;
The houses in the streets are much too high;
    There is no one left to speak to there;
80   Here they are everywhere,
And just above them fields and fields of roses lie—
If he would dig it all up again they would not die.

                1916

STEPHEN CRANE
1871–1900

From The Black Riders and Other Lines[1]

I

BLACK RIDERS CAME FROM THE SEA.
THERE WAS CLANG AND CLANG OF SPEAR AND SHIELD,
AND CLASH AND CLASH OF HOOF AND HEEL,
WILD SHOUTS AND THE WAVE OF HAIR
5   IN THE RUSH UPON THE WIND:
THUS THE RIDE OF SIN.

III

IN THE DESERT
I SAW A CREATURE, NAKED, BESTIAL,
WHO, SQUATTING UPON THE GROUND,
HELD HIS HEART IN HIS HANDS,
5   AND ATE OF IT.
I SAID, "IS IT GOOD, FRIEND?"
"IT IS BITTER—BITTER," HE ANSWERED;
"BUT I LIKE IT
"BECAUSE IT IS BITTER,
10   "AND BECAUSE IT IS MY HEART."

XXV

BEHOLD, THE GRAVE OF A WICKED MAN,
AND NEAR IT, A STERN SPIRIT.

THERE CAME A DROOPING MAID WITH VIOLETS,
BUT THE SPIRIT GRASPED HER ARM.
5   "NO FLOWERS FOR HIM," HE SAID.
THE MAID WEPT:
"AH, I LOVED HIM."
BUT THE SPIRIT, GRIM AND FROWNING:
"NO FLOWERS FOR HIM."

10   NOW, THIS IS IT——
IF THE SPIRIT WAS JUST,
WHY DID THE MAID WEEP?

1. The stylish Boston publishers of Crane's first poetry collection, *The Black Riders and Other Lines,* proposed what they called a "severely classic" design, printing the poems in capitals only—which greatly pleased Crane. Modern editors have reproduced the poems in standard typography; here the original look of the "lines" ("I never call them poems," Crane said) is more closely approximated.

LVI

A MAN FEARED THAT HE MIGHT FIND AN ASSASSIN;
ANOTHER THAT HE MIGHT FIND A VICTIM.
ONE WAS MORE WISE THAN THE OTHER.

1895

From War is Kind[2]

Do not weep, maiden, for war is kind.
Because your lover threw wild hands toward the sky
And the affrighted steed ran on alone,
Do not weep.
5   War is kind.

     Hoarse, booming drums of the regiment
     Little souls who thirst for fight,
     These men were born to drill and die
     The unexplained glory flies above them
10   Great is the battle-god, great, and his kingdom——
     A field where a thousand corpses lie.

Do not weep, babe, for war is kind.
Because your father tumbled in the yellow trenches,
Raged at his breast, gulped and died,
15   Do not weep.
War is kind.

     Swift, blazing flag of the regiment
     Eagle with crest of red and gold,
     These men were born to drill and die
20   Point for them the virtue of slaughter
     Make plain to them the excellence of killing
     And a field where a thousand corpses lie.

Mother whose heart hung humble as a button
On the bright splendid shroud of your son,
25   Do not weep.
War is kind.

1899

[A Man Adrift on a Slim Spar]

A man adrift on a slim spar
A horizon smaller than the rim of a bottle

2. The poems in Crane's second and final collection of verse were printed conventionally, with upper- and lowercase letters.

Tented waves rearing lashy dark points
The near whine of froth in circles.
5   God is cold.

The incessant raise and swing of the sea
And growl after growl of crest
The sinkings, green, seething, endless
The upheaval half-completed.
10   God is cold.

The seas are in the hollow of The Hand;
Oceans may be turned to a spray
Raining down through the stars
Because of a gesture of pity toward a babe.
15 Oceans may become grey ashes,
Die with a long moan and a roar
Amid the tumult of the fishes
And the cries of the ships,
Because The Hand beckons the mice.

20 A horizon smaller than a doomed assassin's cap,
Inky, surging tumults
A reeling, drunken sky and no sky
A pale hand sliding from a polished spar.
                                          God is cold.

25 The puff of a coat imprisoning air.
A face kissing the water-death
A weary slow sway of a lost hand
And the sea, the moving sea, the sea.
                                          God is cold.

ca. 1897   1929

PAUL LAURENCE DUNBAR
1872–1906

A Summer's Night

The night is dewy as a maiden's mouth,
   The skies are bright as are a maiden's eyes,
   Soft as a maiden's breath, the wind that flies
Up from the perfumed bosom of the South.
5 Like sentinels, the pines stand in the park;
   And hither hastening like rakes that roam,
   With lamps to light their wayward footsteps home,
The fire-flies come stagg'ring down the dark.

                                                                                      1895

We Wear the Mask

We wear the mask that grins and lies,
It hides our cheeks and shades our eyes—
This debt we pay to human guile;
With torn and bleeding hearts we smile,
5 And mouth with myriad subtleties.

Why should the world be over-wise,
In counting all our tears and sighs?
Nay, let them only see us, while
    We wear the mask.

10 We smile, but, O great Christ, our cries
To thee from tortured souls arise.
We sing, but oh the clay is vile
Beneath our feet, and long the mile;
But let the world dream otherwise,
15   We wear the mask!

1896

Little Brown Baby

Little brown baby wif spa'klin' eyes,
  Come to yo' pappy an' set on his knee.
What you been doin', suh-makin' san' pies?
  Look at dat bib—you's ez du'ty ez me.
5 Look at dat mouf—dat's merlasses, I bet;
  Come hyeah, Maria, an' wipe off his han's.
Bees gwine to ketch you an' eat you up yit,
  Bein' so sticky an sweet—goodness lan's!°   *lands!*

Little brown baby wif spa'klin' eyes,
10 Who's pappy's darlin' an' who's pappy's chile?
Who is it all de day nevah once tries
  Fu' to be cross, er once loses dat smile?
Whah did you git dem teef? My, you's a scamp!
  Whah did dat dimple come f'om in yo' chin?
15 Pappy do' know you—I b'lieves you's a tramp;
  Mammy, dis hyeah's some ol' straggler got in!

Let's th'ow him outen de do' in de san',
  We do' want stragglers a-layin' 'roun' hyeah;
Let's gin him 'way to de big buggah-man;
20 I know he's hidin' erroun' hyeah right neah.
Buggah-man, buggah-man, come in de do',
Hyeah's a bad boy you kin have fu' to eat.

Mammy an' pappy do' want him no mo',
   Swaller him down f'om his haid to his feet!

25   Dah, now, I t'ought dat you'd hug me up close.
    Go back, ol' buggah, you sha'n't have dis boy.
   He ain't no tramp, ner no straggler, of co'se;
    Ho'o pappy's pa'dner an' playmate an' joy.
   Come to you' pallet now—go to yo' res';
30   Wisht you could allus know ease an' cleah skies;
   Wisht you could stay jes' a chile on my breas'—
    Little brown baby wif spa'klin' eyes!

1899?

Sympathy

I know what the caged bird feels, alas!
   When the sun is bright on the upland slopes;
When the wind stirs soft through the springing grass,
And the river flows like a stream of glass;
5   When the first bird sings and the first bud opes,°   *opens*
And the faint perfume from its chalice steals—
I know what the caged bird feels!

I know why the caged bird beats his wing
   Till its blood is red on the cruel bars;
10 For he must fly back to his perch and cling
When he fain would be[1] on the bough a-swing;
   And a pain still throbs in the old, old scars
And they pulse again with a keener sting—
I know why he beats his wing!

15 I know why the caged bird sings, ah me,
   When his wing is bruised and his bosom sore,—
When he beats his bars and he would be free;
It is not a carol of joy or glee,
   But a prayer that he sends from his heart's deep core,
20 But a plea, that upward to Heaven he flings—
I know why the caged bird sings!

1899

1. He would like to be.

JOHN McCRAE
1872–1918

In Flanders Fields[1]

In Flanders fields the poppies blow
Between the crosses, row on row,
  That mark our place; and in the sky
  The larks, still bravely singing, fly
5 Scarce heard amid the guns below.

We are the Dead. Short days ago
We lived, felt dawn, saw sunset glow,
  Loved and were loved, and now we lie,
    In Flanders fields.

10 Take up our quarrel with the foe:
To you from failing hands we throw
  The torch; be yours to hold it high.
  If ye break faith with us who die
We shall not sleep, though poppies grow
15   In Flanders fields.

1915   1919

WALTER DE LA MARE
1873–1956

The Listeners

"Is there anybody there?" said the Traveller,
  Knocking on the moonlit door;
And his horse in the silence champed the grasses
  Of the forest's ferny floor:
5 And a bird flew up out of the turret,
  Above the Traveller's head:
And he smote upon the door again a second time;
  "Is there anybody there?" he said.
But no one descended to the Traveller;
10 No head from the leaf-fringed sill
Leaned over and looked into his grey eyes,

1. Written in April 1915 during the Second Battle of Ypres, France, in the region (once the country) called Flanders, which encompasses parts of modern France, Belgium, and the Netherlands. McCrae, a Canadian soldier and physician, survived massive German shelling in one of the bloodiest chapters in World War I. Major-General E. W. B. Morrison, who commanded McCrae's brigade, wrote: "During periods in the battle men who were shot actually rolled down the bank [of the Ypres Canal] into his dressing station. . . . [H]e and I watched [men] burying their dead whenever there was a lull. Thus the crosses, row on row, grew into a good-sized cemetery." The poem, first published in the December 1915 issue of *Punch* magazine, achieved instant international fame and was memorized by soldiers.

Where he stood perplexed and still.
But only a host of phantom listeners
    That dwelt in the lone house then
15 Stood listening in the quiet of the moonlight
    To that voice from the world of men:
Stood thronging the faint moonbeams on the dark stair,
    That goes down to the empty hall,
Hearkening in an air stirred and shaken
20   By the lonely Traveller's call.
And he felt in his heart their strangeness,
    Their stillness answering his cry,
While his horse moved, cropping the dark turf,
    'Neath the starred and leafy sky;
25 For he suddenly smote on the door, even
    Louder, and lifted his head:—
"Tell them I came, and no one answered,
    That I kept my word," he said.
Never the least stir made the listeners,
30   Though every word he spake
Fell echoing through the shadowiness of the still house
    From the one man left awake:
Ay, they heard his foot upon the stirrup,
    And the sound of iron on stone,
35 And how the silence surged softly backward,
    When the plunging hoofs were gone.

                                        1912

Fare Well

When I lie where shades of darkness
    Shall no more assail mine eyes,
Nor the rain make lamentation
    When the wind sighs;
5   How will fare the world whose wonder
    Was the very proof of me?
Memory fades, must the remembered
    Perishing be?

Oh, when this my dust surrenders
10 Hand, foot, lip, to dust again,
May these loved and loving faces
    Please other men!
May the rusting harvest hedgerow
    Still the Traveller's Joy[1] entwine,
15 And as happy children gather
    Posies once mine.

---

1. Wild climbing plant also known as Virgin's Bower or Old Man's Beard.

Look thy last on all things lovely,
Every hour. Let no night
Seal thy sense in deathly slumber
20   Till to delight
Thou have paid thy utmost blessing;
Since that all things thou wouldst praise
Beauty took from those who loved them
    In other days.

1918

ROBERT FROST
1874–1963

Mending Wall

Something there is that doesn't love a wall,
That sends the frozen-ground-swell under it,
And spills the upper boulders in the sun;
And makes gaps even two can pass abreast.
5 The work of hunters is another thing:
I have come after them and made repair
Where they have left not one stone on a stone,
But they would have the rabbit out of hiding,
To please the yelping dogs. The gaps I mean,
10 No one has seen them made or heard them made,
But at spring mending-time we find them there.
I let my neighbor know beyond the hill;
And on a day we meet to walk the line
And set the wall between us once again.
15 We keep the wall between us as we go.
To each the boulders that have fallen to each.
And some are loaves and some so nearly balls
We have to use a spell to make them balance:
"Stay where you are until our backs are turned!"
20 We wear our fingers rough with handling them.
Oh, just another kind of outdoor game,
One on a side. It comes to little more:
There where it is we do not need the wall:
He is all pine and I am apple orchard.
25 My apple trees will never get across
And eat the cones under his pines, I tell him.
He only says, "Good fences make good neighbors."
Spring is the mischief in me, and I wonder
If I could put a notion in his head:
30 "*Why* do they make good neighbors? Isn't it
Where there are cows? But here there are no cows.
Before I built a wall I'd ask to know

What I was walling in or walling out,
And to whom I was like to give offense.
35 Something there is that doesn't love a wall,
That wants it down." I could say "Elves" to him,
But it's not elves exactly, and I'd rather
He said it for himself. I see him there
Bringing a stone grasped firmly by the top
40 In each hand, like an old-stone savage armed.
He moves in darkness as it seems to me,
Not of woods only and the shade of trees.
He will not go behind his father's saying,
And he likes having thought of it so well
45 He says again, "Good fences make good neighbors."

1914

Home Burial

He saw her from the bottom of the stairs
Before she saw him. She was starting down,
Looking back over her shoulder at some fear.
She took a doubtful step and then undid it
5 To raise herself and look again. He spoke
Advancing toward her. "What is it you see
From up there always—for I want to know."
She turned and sank upon her skirts at that,
And her face changed from terrified to dull.
10 He said to gain time: "What is it you see,"
Mounting until she cowered under him.
"I will find out now—you must tell me, dear."
She, in her place, refused him any help
With the least stiffening of her neck and silence.
15 She let him look, sure that he wouldn't see,
Blind creature; and awhile he didn't see.
But at last he murmured, "Oh," and again, "Oh."

"What is it—what?" she said.

                              "Just that I see."

20 "You don't," she challenged. "Tell me what it is."

"The wonder is I didn't see at once.
I never noticed it from here before.
I must be wonted° to it—that's the reason.   accustomed
The little graveyard where my people are!
25 So small the window frames the whole of it.
Not so much larger than a bedroom, is it?
There are three stones of slate and one of marble,

Broad-shouldered little slabs there in the sunlight
On the sidehill. We haven't to mind *those*.
30 But I understand: it is not the stones,
But the child's mound—"

                              "Don't, don't, don't, don't," she cried.

She withdrew shrinking from beneath his arm
That rested on the bannister, and slid downstairs;
35 And turned on him with such a daunting look,
He said twice over before he knew himself:
"Can't a man speak of his own child he's lost?"

"Not you! Oh, where's my hat? Oh, I don't need it!
I must get out of here. I must get air.
40 I don't know rightly whether any man can."

"Amy! Don't go to someone else this time.
Listen to me. I won't come down the stairs."
He sat and fixed his chin between his fists.
"There's something I should like to ask you, dear."

45 "You don't know how to ask it."

                              "Help me, then."

Her fingers moved the latch for all reply.

"My words are nearly always an offense.
I don't know how to speak of anything
50 So as to please you. But I might be taught
I should suppose. I can't say I see how.
A man must partly give up being a man
With women-folk. We could have some arrangement
By which I'd bind myself to keep hands off
55 Anything special you're a-mind to name.
Though I don't like such things 'twixt those that love.
Two that don't love can't live together without them.
But two that do can't live together with them."
She moved the latch a little. "Don't—don't go.
60 Don't carry it to someone else this time.
Tell me about it if it's something human.
Let me into your grief. I'm not so much
Unlike other folks as your standing there
Apart would make me out. Give me my chance.
65 I do think, though, you overdo it a little.
What was it brought you up to think it the thing
To take your mother-loss of a first child
So inconsolably—in the face of love.
You'd think his memory might be satisfied—"

70 "There you go sneering now!"

"I'm not, I'm not!
You make me angry. I'll come down to you.
God, what a woman! And it's come to this,
A man can't speak of his own child that's dead."

75   "You can't because you don't know how to speak.
If you had any feelings, you that dug
With your own hand—how could you?—his little grave;
I saw you from that very window there,
Making the gravel leap and leap in air,
80   Leap up, like that, like that, and land so lightly
And roll back down the mound beside the hole.
I thought, Who is that man? I didn't know you.
And I crept down the stairs and up the stairs
To look again, and still your spade kept lifting.
85   Then you came in. I heard your rumbling voice
Out in the kitchen, and I don't know why,
But I went near to see with my own eyes.
You could sit there with the stains on your shoes
Of the fresh earth from your own baby's grave
90   And talk about your everyday concerns.
You had stood the spade up against the wall
Outside there in the entry, for I saw it."

"I shall laugh the worst laugh I ever laughed.
I'm cursed. God, if I don't believe I'm cursed."

95   "I can repeat the very words you were saying.
Three foggy mornings and one rainy day
Will rot the best birch fence a man can build.
Think of it, talk like that at such a time!
What had how long it takes a birch to rot
100   To do with what was in the darkened parlor.
You *couldn't* care! The nearest friends can go
With anyone to death, comes so far short
They might as well not try to go at all.
No, from the time when one is sick to death,
105   One is alone, and he dies more alone.
Friends make pretense of following to the grave,
But before one is in it, their minds are turned
And making the best of their way back to life
And living people, and things they understand.
110   But the world's evil. I won't have grief so
If I can change it. Oh, I won't, I won't!"

"There, you have said it all and you feel better.
You won't go now. You're crying. Close the door.
The heart's gone out of it: why keep it up.
115   Amy! There's someone coming down the road!"

"*You*—oh, you think the talk is all. I must go—
Somewhere out of this house. How can I make you—"

"If—you—do!" She was opening the door wider.
"Where do you mean to go? First tell me that.
120   I'll follow and bring you back by force. I *will!*—"

                    1914

After Apple-Picking

My long two-pointed ladder's sticking through a tree
Toward heaven still,
And there's a barrel that I didn't fill
Beside it, and there may be two or three
5   Apples I didn't pick upon some bough.
But I am done with apple-picking now.
Essence of winter sleep is on the night,
The scent of apples: I am drowsing off.
I cannot rub the strangeness from my sight
10   I got from looking through a pane of glass
I skimmed this morning from the drinking trough
And held against the world of hoary grass.
It melted, and I let it fall and break.
But I was well
15   Upon my way to sleep before it fell,
And I could tell
What form my dreaming was about to take.
Magnified apples appear and disappear,
Stem end and blossom end,
20   And every fleck of russet showing clear.
My instep arch not only keeps the ache,
It keeps the pressure of a ladder-round.
I feel the ladder sway as the boughs bend.
And I keep hearing from the cellar bin
25   The rumbling sound
Of load on load of apples coming in.
For I have had too much
Of apple-picking: I am overtired
Of the great harvest I myself desired.
30   There were ten thousand thousand fruit to touch,
Cherish in hand, lift down, and not let fall.
For all
That struck the earth,
No matter if not bruised or spiked with stubble,
35   Went surely to the cider-apple heap
As of no worth.
One can see what will trouble
This sleep of mine, whatever sleep it is.
Were he not gone,
40   The woodchuck could say whether it's like his
Long sleep, as I describe its coming on,
Or just some human sleep.

                    1914

The Wood-Pile

Out walking in the frozen swamp one gray day,
I paused and said, "I will turn back from here.
No, I will go on farther—and we shall see."
The hard snow held me, save where now and then
5   One foot went through. The view was all in lines
Straight up and down of tall slim trees
Too much alike to mark or name a place by
So as to say for certain I was here
Or somewhere else: I was just far from home.
10 A small bird flew before me. He was careful
To put a tree between us when he lighted,
And say no word to tell me who he was
Who was so foolish as to think what *he* thought.
He thought that I was after him for a feather—
15 The white one in his tail; like one who takes
Everything said as personal to himself.
One flight out sideways would have undeceived him.
And then there was a pile of wood for which
I forgot him and let his little fear
20 Carry him off the way I might have gone,
Without so much as wishing him good-night.
He went behind it to make his last stand.
It was a cord of maple, cut and split
And piled—and measured, four by four by eight.
25 And not another like it could I see.
No runner tracks in this year's snow looped near it.
And it was older sure than this year's cutting,
Or even last year's or the year's before.
The wood was gray and the bark warping off it
30 And the pile somewhat sunken. Clematis
Had wound strings round and round it like a bundle.
What held it though on one side was a tree
Still growing, and on one a stake and prop,
These latter about to fall. I thought that only
35 Someone who lived in turning to fresh tasks
Could so forget his handiwork on which
He spent himself, the labor of his ax,
And leave it there far from a useful fireplace
To warm the frozen swamp as best it could
40 With the slow smokeless burning of decay.

1914

The Road Not Taken

Two roads diverged in a yellow wood,
And sorry I could not travel both

And be one traveler, long I stood
And looked down one as far as I could
5   To where it bent in the undergrowth;

Then took the other, as just as fair,
And having perhaps the better claim,
Because it was grassy and wanted wear;
Though as for that the passing there
10 Had worn them really about the same,

And both that morning equally lay
In leaves no step had trodden black.
Oh, I kept the first for another day!
Yet knowing how way leads on to way,
15 I doubted if I should ever come back.

I shall be telling this with a sigh
Somewhere ages and ages hence:
Two roads diverged in a wood, and I—
I took the one less traveled by,
20 And that has made all the difference.

1916

The Oven Bird

There is a singer everyone has heard,
Loud, a mid-summer and a mid-wood bird,
Who makes the solid tree trunks sound again.
He says that leaves are old and that for flowers
5 Mid-summer is to spring as one to ten.
He says the early petal-fall is past
When pear and cherry bloom went down in showers
On sunny days a moment overcast;
And comes that other fall we name the fall.
10 He says the highway dust is over all.
The bird would cease and be as other birds
But that he knows in singing not to sing.
The question that he frames in all but words
Is what to make of a diminished thing.

1916

Birches

When I see birches bend to left and right
Across the lines of straighter darker trees,
I like to think some boy's been swinging them.

But swinging doesn't bend them down to stay
5　　As ice-storms do. Often you must have seen them
Loaded with ice a sunny winter morning
After a rain. They click upon themselves
As the breeze rises, and turn many-colored
As the stir cracks and crazes their enamel.
10　　Soon the sun's warmth makes them shed crystal shells
Shattering and avalanching on the snow-crust—
Such heaps of broken glass to sweep away
You'd think the inner dome of heaven had fallen.
They are dragged to the withered bracken° by the load,　　　　*ferns*
15　　And they seem not to break; though once they are bowed
So low for long, they never right themselves:
You may see their trunks arching in the woods
Years afterwards, trailing their leaves on the ground
Like girls on hands and knees that throw their hair
20　　Before them over their heads to dry in the sun.
But I was going to say when Truth broke in
With all her matter-of-fact about the ice-storm
I should prefer to have some boy bend them
As he went out and in to fetch the cows—
25　　Some boy too far from town to learn baseball,
Whose only play was what he found himself,
Summer or winter, and could play alone.
One by one he subdued his father's trees
By riding them down over and over again
30　　Until he took the stiffness out of them,
And not one but hung limp, not one was left
For him to conquer. He learned all there was
To learn about not launching out too soon
And so not carrying the tree away
35　　Clear to the ground. He always kept his poise
To the top branches, climbing carefully
With the same pains you use to fill a cup
Up to the brim, and even above the brim.
Then he flung outward, feet first, with a swish,
40　　Kicking his way down through the air to the ground.
So was I once myself a swinger of birches.
And so I dream of going back to be.
It's when I'm weary of considerations,
And life is too much like a pathless wood
45　　Where your face burns and tickles with the cobwebs
Broken across it, and one eye is weeping
From a twig's having lashed across it open.
I'd like to get away from earth awhile
And then come back to it and begin over.
50　　May no fate willfully misunderstand me
And half grant what I wish and snatch me away
Not to return. Earth's the right place for love:
I don't know where it's likely to go better.
I'd like to go by climbing a birch tree,
55　　And climb black branches up a snow-white trunk

Toward heaven, till the tree could bear no more,
But dipped its top and set me down again.
That would be good both going and coming back.
One could do worse than be a swinger of birches.

1916

The Hill Wife

Loneliness

HER WORD

One ought not to have to care
    So much as you and I
Care when the birds come round the house
    To seem to say good-by;

5 Or care so much when they come back
    With whatever it is they sing;
The truth being we are as much
    Too glad for the one thing

As we are too sad for the other here—
10   With birds that fill their breasts
But with each other and themselves
    And their built or driven nests.

House Fear

Always—I tell you this they learned—
Always at night when they returned
To the lonely house from far away
To lamps unlighted and fire gone gray,
5 They learned to rattle the lock and key
To give whatever might chance to be
Warning and time to be off in flight:
And preferring the out- to the in-door night,
They learned to leave the house-door wide
10 Until they had lit the lamp inside.

The Smile

HER WORD

I didn't like the way he went away.
That smile! It never came of being gay.
Still he smiled—did you see him?—I was sure!
Perhaps because we gave him only bread
5 And the wretch knew from that that we were poor.
Perhaps because he let us give instead

Of seizing from us as he might have seized.
Perhaps he mocked at us for being wed,
Or being very young (and he was pleased
10   To have a vision of us old and dead).
I wonder how far down the road he's got.
He's watching from the woods as like as not.

The Oft-Repeated Dream

She had no saying dark enough
    For the dark pine that kept
Forever trying the window-latch
    Of the room where they slept.

5   The tireless but ineffectual hands
    That with every futile pass
Made the great tree seem as a little bird
    Before the mystery of glass!

It never had been inside the room,
10   And only one of the two
Was afraid in an oft-repeated dream
    Of what the tree might do.

The Impulse

It was too lonely for her there,
    And too wild,
And since there were but two of them,
    And no child,

5   And work was little in the house,
    She was free,
And followed where he furrowed field,
    Or felled tree.

She rested on a log and tossed
10   The fresh chips,
With a song only to herself
    On her lips.

And once she went to break a bough
    Of black alder.
15   She strayed so far she scarcely heard
    When he called her—

And didn't answer—didn't speak—
    Or return.
She stood, and then she ran and hid
20   In the fern.

He never found her, though he looked
    Everywhere,

And he asked at her mother's house
  Was she there.

25 Sudden and swift and light as that
  The ties gave,
  And he learned of finalities
  Besides the grave.

1916

Stopping by Woods on a Snowy Evening

Whose woods these are I think I know.
His house is in the village though;
He will not see me stopping here
To watch his woods fill up with snow.

5 My little horse must think it queer
To stop without a farmhouse near
Between the woods and frozen lake
The darkest evening of the year.

He gives his harness bells a shake
10 To ask if there is some mistake.
The only other sound's the sweep
Of easy wind and downy flake.

The woods are lovely, dark and deep,
But I have promises to keep,
15 And miles to go before I sleep,
And miles to go before I sleep.

1923

Acquainted with the Night

I have been one acquainted with the night.
I have walked out in rain—and back in rain.
I have outwalked the furthest city light.

I have looked down the saddest city lane.
5 I have passed by the watchman on his beat
And dropped my eyes, unwilling to explain.

I have stood still and stopped the sound of feet
When far away an interrupted cry
Came over houses from another street,

10   But not to call me back or say good-by;
      And further still at an unearthly height,
      One luminary clock against the sky

      Proclaimed the time was neither wrong nor right.
      I have been one acquainted with the night.

                                                    1928

West-Running Brook

"Fred, where is north?"

                    "North? North is there, my love.
The brook runs west."

                              "West-running Brook then call it."
5   (West-running Brook men call it to this day.)
     "What does it think it's doing running west
     When all the other country brooks flow east
     To reach the ocean? It must be the brook
     Can trust itself to go by contraries
10   The way I can with you—and you with me—
     Because we're—we're—I don't know what we are.
     What are we?"

                    "Young or new?"

                                   "We must be something.
15   We've said we two. Let's change that to we three.
     As you and I are married to each other,
     We'll both be married to the brook. We'll build
     Our bridge across it, and the bridge shall be
     Our arm thrown over it asleep beside it.
20   Look, look, it's waving to us with a wave
     To let us know it hears me."

                              "Why, my dear,
     That wave's been standing off this jut of shore—"
     (The black stream, catching on a sunken rock,
25   Flung backward on itself in one white wave,
     And the white water rode the black forever,
     Not gaining but not losing, like a bird
     White feathers from the struggle of whose breast
     Flecked the dark stream and flecked the darker pool
30   Below the point, and were at last driven wrinkled
     In a white scarf against the far shore alders.)
     "That wave's been standing off this jut of shore
     Ever since rivers, I was going to say,
     Were made in heaven. It wasn't waved to us."

35 "It wasn't, yet it was. If not to you
    It was to me—in an annunciation."

    "Oh, if you take it off to lady-land,
    As't were the country of the Amazons[1]
    We men must see you to the confines of
40 And leave you there, ourselves forbid to enter,—
    It is your brook! I have no more to say."

    "Yes, you have, too. Go on. You thought of something."

    "Speaking of contraries, see how the brook
    In that white wave runs counter to itself.
45 It is from that in water we were from
    Long, long before we were from any creature.
    Here we, in our impatience of the steps,
    Get back to the beginning of beginnings,
    The stream of everything that runs away.
50 Some say existence like a Pirouot
    And Pirouette,[2] forever in one place,
    Stands still and dances, but it runs away,
    It seriously, sadly, runs away
    To fill the abyss' void with emptiness.
55 It flows beside us in this water brook,
    But it flows over us. It flows between us
    To separate us for a panic moment.
    It flows between us, over us, and *with* us.
    And it is time, strength, tone, light, life, and love—
60 And even substance lapsing unsubstantial;
    The universal cataract of death
    That spends to nothingness—and unresisted,
    Save by some strange resistance in itself,
    Not just a swerving, but a throwing back,
65 As if regret were in it and were sacred.
    It has this throwing backward on itself
    So that the fall of most of it is always
    Raising a little, sending up a little.
    Our life runs down in sending up the clock.
70 The brook runs down in sending up our life.
    The sun runs down in sending up the brook.
    And there is something sending up the sun.
    It is this backward motion toward the source,
    Against the stream, that most we see ourselves in,
75 The tribute of the current to the source.
    It is from this in nature we are from.
    It is most us."

                "Today will be the day
        You said so."

1. Legendary female warriors who inhabited a   2. Traditional characters in French pantomime.
country without men.

80   "No, today will be the day
You said the brook was called West-running Brook."

"Today will be the day of what we both said."

1928

Neither Out Far Nor In Deep

The people along the sand
All turn and look one way.
They turn their back on the land.
They look at the sea all day.

5   As long as it takes to pass
A ship keeps raising its hull;
The wetter ground like glass
Reflects a standing gull.

The land may vary more;
10 But wherever the truth may be—
The water comes ashore,
And the people look at the sea.

They cannot look out far.
They cannot look in deep.
15 But when was that ever a bar
To any watch they keep?

1936

Design

I found a dimpled spider, fat and white,
On a white heal-all,[3] holding up a moth
Like a white piece of rigid satin cloth—
Assorted characters of death and blight
5 Mixed ready to begin the morning right,
Like the ingredients of a witches' broth—
A snow-drop spider, a flower like a froth,
And dead wings carried like a paper kite.

What had that flower to do with being white,
10 The wayside blue and innocent heal-all?
What brought the kindred spider to that height,
Then steered the white moth thither in the night?

---

3. One of a variety of plants in the mint family; the flowers are usually violet-blue.

What but design of darkness to appall?—
If design govern in a thing so small.

1936

Provide, Provide

The witch that came (the withered hag)
To wash the steps with pail and rag,
Was once the beauty Abishag,[4]

The picture pride of Hollywood.
5 Too many fall from great and good
For you to doubt the likelihood.

Die early and avoid the fate.
Or if predestined to die late,
Make up your mind to die in state.

10 Make the whole stock exchange your own!
If need be occupy a throne,
Where nobody can call *you* crone.

Some have relied on what they knew;
Others on being simply true.
15 What worked for them might work for you.

No memory of having starred
Atones for later disregard,
Or keeps the end from being hard.

Better to go down dignified
20 With boughten friendship at your side
Than none at all. Provide, provide!

1934
1936

The Silken Tent

She is as in a field a silken tent
At midday when a sunny summer breeze
Has dried the dew and all its ropes relent,
So that in guys[5] it gently sways at ease,
5 And its supporting central cedar pole,
That is its pinnacle to heavenward
And signifies the sureness of the soul,

---

4. A beautiful maiden brought to warm King
David in his old age (1 Kings 1.2–4).

5. Ropes or cables used to steady an object.

Seems to owe naught to any single cord,
But strictly held by none, is loosely bound
10 By countless silken ties of love and thought
To everything on earth the compass round,
And only by one's going slightly taut
In the capriciousness of summer air
Is of the slightest bondage made aware.

1942

Come In

As I came to the edge of the woods,
Thrush music—hark!
Now if it was dusk outside,
Inside it was dark.

5 Too dark in the woods for a bird
By sleight of wing
To better its perch for the night,
Though it still could sing.

The last of the light of the sun
10 That had died in the west
Still lived for one song more
In a thrush's breast.

Far in the pillared dark
Thrush music went—
15 Almost like a call to come in
To the dark and lament.

But no, I was out for stars:
I would not come in.
I meant not even if asked,
20 And I hadn't been.

1942

Never Again Would Birds' Song Be the Same[6]

He would declare and could himself believe
That the birds there in all the garden round
From having heard the daylong voice of Eve
Had added to their own an oversound,
5 Her tone of meaning but without the words.
Admittedly an eloquence so soft

---

6. Cf. Genesis 2.18 ff., God's creation of Eve for Adam.

Could only have had an influence on birds
When call or laughter carried it aloft.
Be that as may be, she was in their song.
10 Moreover her voice upon their voices crossed
Had now persisted in the woods so long
That probably it never would be lost.
Never again would birds' song be the same.
And to do that to birds was why she came.

1942

The Most of It

He thought he kept the universe alone;
For all the voice in answer he could wake
Was but the mocking echo of his own
From some tree-hidden cliff across the lake.
5 Some morning from the boulder-broken beach
He would cry out on life, that what it wants
Is not its own love back in copy speech,
But counter-love, original response.
And nothing ever came of what he cried
10 Unless it was the embodiment that crashed
In the cliff's talus[7] on the other side,
And then in the far distant water splashed,
But after a time allowed for it to swim,
Instead of proving human when it neared
15 And someone else additional to him,
As a great buck it powerfully appeared,
Pushing the crumpled water up ahead,
And landed pouring like a waterfall,
And stumbled through the rocks with horny tread,
20 And forced the underbrush—and that was all.

1942

The Gift Outright

The land was ours before we were the land's.
She was our land more than a hundred years
Before we were her people. She was ours
In Massachusetts, in Virginia,
5 But we were England's, still colonials,
Possessing what we still were unpossessed by,
Possessed by what we now no more possessed.
Something we were withholding made us weak
Until we found it was ourselves

---

7. Sloping rock debris.

10 We were withholding from our land of living,
    And forthwith found salvation in surrender.
    Such as we were we gave ourselves outright
    (The deed of gift was many deeds of war)
    To the land vaguely realizing westward,
15 But still unstoried, artless, unenhanced,
    Such as she was, such as she would become.

1942

Directive

    Back out of all this now too much for us,
    Back in a time made simple by the loss
    Of detail, burned, dissolved, and broken off
    Like graveyard marble sculpture in the weather,
5   There is a house that is no more a house
    Upon a farm that is no more a farm
    And in a town that is no more a town.
    The road there, if you'll let a guide direct you
    Who only has at heart your getting lost,
10 May seem as if it should have been a quarry—
    Great monolithic knees the former town
    Long since gave up pretense of keeping covered.
    And there's a story in a book about it:
    Besides the wear of iron wagon wheels
15 The ledges show lines ruled southeast northwest,
    The chisel work of an enormous Glacier
    That braced his feet against the Arctic Pole.
    You must not mind a certain coolness from him
    Still said to haunt this side of Panther Mountain.
20 Nor need you mind the serial ordeal
    Of being watched from forty cellar holes
    As if by eye pairs out of forty firkins.°   small wooden tubs
    As for the woods' excitement over you
    That sends light rustle rushes to their leaves,
25 Charge that to upstart inexperience.
    Where were they all not twenty years ago?
    They think too much of having shaded out
    A few old pecker-fretted[8] apple trees.
    Make yourself up a cheering song of how
30 Someone's road home from work this once was,
    Who may be just ahead of you on foot
    Or creaking with a buggy load of grain.
    The height of the adventure is the height
    Of country where two village cultures faded
35 Into each other. Both of them are lost.
    And if you're lost enough to find yourself
    By now, pull in your ladder road behind you
    And put a sign up CLOSED to all but me.

8. I.e., marked by woodpeckers.

Then make yourself at home. The only field
40 Now left's no bigger than a harness gall.[9]
First there's the children's house of make believe,
Some shattered dishes underneath a pine,
The playthings in the playhouse of the children.
Weep for what little things could make them glad.
45 Then for the house that is no more a house,
But only a belilaced cellar hole,
Now slowly closing like a dent in dough.
This was no playhouse but a house in earnest.
Your destination and your destiny's
50 A brook that was the water of the house,
Cold as a spring as yet so near its source,
Too lofty and original to rage.
(We know the valley streams that when aroused
Will leave their tatters hung on barb and thorn.)
55 I have kept hidden in the instep arch
Of an old cedar at the waterside
A broken drinking goblet like the Grail
Under a spell so the wrong ones can't find it,
So can't get saved, as Saint Mark says they mustn't.[1]
60 (I stole the goblet from the children's playhouse.)
Here are your waters and your watering place.
Drink and be whole again beyond confusion.

1947

AMY LOWELL
1874–1925

Patterns

I walk down the garden paths,
And all the daffodils
Are blowing, and the bright blue squills.[1]
I walk down the patterned garden-paths
5 In my stiff, brocaded gown.
With my powdered hair and jewelled fan,
I too am a rare
Pattern. As I wander down
The garden paths.

10 My dress is richly figured,
And the train
Makes a pink and silver stain

9. A sore caused by chafing against a harness.
1. Cf. Mark 16.16: "He that believeth and is baptized shall be saved; but he that believeth not shall be damned." *The Grail:* the cup used by Jesus at the Last Supper, the object of many quests in medieval and Arthurian romance.
1. Plants of the lily family.

On the gravel, and the thrift
Of the borders.
15　Just a plate of current fashion,
Tripping by in high-heeled, ribboned shoes.
Not a softness anywhere about me,
Only whalebone and brocade.
And I sink on a seat in the shade
20　Of a lime tree. For my passion
Wars against the stiff brocade.
The daffodils and squills
Flutter in the breeze
As they please.
25　And I weep;
For the lime-tree is in blossom
And one small flower has dropped upon my bosom.

And the plashing° of waterdrops　　　　　　　　　　*splashing*
In the marble fountain
30　Comes down the garden-paths.
The dripping never stops.
Underneath my stiffened gown
Is the softness of a woman bathing in a marble basin,
A basin in the midst of hedges grown
35　So thick, she cannot see her lover hiding,
But she guesses he is near,
And the sliding of the water
Seems the stroking of a dear
Hand upon her.
40　What is Summer in a fine brocaded gown!
I should like to see it lying in a heap upon the ground.
All the pink and silver crumpled up on the ground.

I would be the pink and silver as I ran along the paths,
And he would stumble after,
45　Bewildered by my laughter.
I should see the sun flashing from his sword-hilt and the buckles on
　　his shoes.
I would choose
To lead him in a maze along the patterned paths,
A bright and laughing maze for my heavy-booted lover.
50　Till he caught me in the shade,
And the buttons of his waistcoat bruised my body as he clasped me,
Aching, melting, unafraid.
With the shadows of the leaves and the sundrops,
And the plopping of the waterdrops,
55　All about us in the open afternoon—
I am very like to swoon
With the weight of this brocade,
For the sun sifts through the shade.

Underneath the fallen blossom
60　In my bosom,
Is a letter I have hid.

It was brought to me this morning by a rider from the Duke.
"Madam, we regret to inform you that Lord Hartwell
Died in action Thursday se'nnight."°   *a week ago*
65 As I read it in the white, morning sunlight,
The letters squirmed like snakes.
"Any answer, Madam," said my footman.
"No," I told him.
"See that the messenger takes some refreshment.
70 No, no answer."
And I walked into the garden,
Up and down the patterned paths,
In my stiff, correct brocade.
The blue and yellow flowers stood up proudly in the sun,
75 Each one.
I stood upright too,
Held rigid to the pattern
By the stiffness of my gown.
Up and down I walked,
80 Up and down.

In a month he would have been my husband.
In a month, here, underneath this lime,
We would have broke the pattern;
He for me, and I for him,
85 He as Colonel, I as Lady,
On this shady seat.
He had a whim
That sunlight carried blessing.
And I answered, "It shall be as you have said."
90 Now he is dead.

In Summer and in Winter I shall walk
Up and down
The patterned garden-paths
In my stiff, brocaded gown.
95 The squills and daffodils
Will give place to pillared roses, and to asters, and to snow.
I shall go
Up and down,
In my gown.
100 Gorgeously arrayed,
Boned and stayed.
And the softness of my body will be guarded from embrace
By each button, hook, and lace.
For the man who should loose me is dead,
105 Fighting with the Duke in Flanders,²
In a pattern called a war.
Christ! What are patterns for?

1916

2. A medieval country; later the term for a region comprised of parts of France, Belgium, and the Netherlands. The poem was written during World War I, when Flanders was also a famous site of battle.

The Weather-Cock Points South

I put your leaves aside,
One by one:
The stiff, broad outer leaves;
The smaller ones,
5   Pleasant to touch, veined with purple;
The glazed inner leaves.
One by one
I parted you from your leaves,
Until you stood up like a white flower
10   Swaying slightly in the evening wind.

White flower,
Flower of wax, of jade, of unstreaked agate;
Flower with surfaces of ice,
With shadows faintly crimson.
15   Where in all the garden is there such a flower?
The stars crowd through the lilac leaves
To look at you.
The low moon brightens you with silver.

The bud is more than the calyx.[3]
20   There is nothing to equal a white bud,
Of no colour, and of all,
Burnished by moonlight,
Thrust upon by a softly-swinging wind.

1919

GERTRUDE STEIN
1874–1946

From Stanzas in Meditation[1]

Part I

STANZA XIII

She may count three little daisies very well
By multiplying to either six nine or fourteen
Or she can be well mentioned as twelve
Which they may like which they can like soon

---

3. Outermost group of the parts of a flower.
1. Written in the same year as Stein's hugely popular *Autobiography of Alice B. Toklas*, *Stanzas in Meditation* is a long-neglected five-part poem with autobiographical elements, but which resists straightforward interpretation. "These austere 'stanzas' are made up almost entirely of colorless connecting words such as 'where,' 'which,' 'there,' 'of,' 'not,' 'have,' 'about,' and so on, though now and then Miss Stein throws in an orange, a lilac, or an Albert to remind us that it really is the world, our world, that she has been talking about" [American poet John Ashbery (b. 1927; see pp. 1736–40)]. In the *Autobiography*, Stein calls the *Stanzas* "her real achievement of the commonplace."

5 Or more than ever which they wish as a button
Just as much as they arrange which they wish
Or they can attire where they need as which say
Can they call a hat or a hat a day
Made merry because it is so.

Part III

STANZA II

I think very well of Susan but I do not know her name
I think very well of Ellen but which is not the same
I think very well of Paul I tell him not to do so
I think very well of Francis Charles but do I do so
5 I think very well of Thomas but I do not not do so
I think very well of not very well of William
I think very well of any very well of him
I think very well of him.
It is remarkable how quickly they learn
10 But if they learn and it is very remarkable how quickly they learn
It makes not only but by and by
And they can not only be not here
But not there
Which after all makes no difference
15 After all this does not make any does not make any difference
I add added it to it.
I could rather be rather be here.

STANZA V

It is not a range of a mountain
Of average of a range of a average mountain
Nor can they of which of which of arrange
To have been not which they which
5 Can add a mountain to this.
Upper an add it then maintain
That if they were busy so to speak
Add it to and
It not only why they could not add ask
10 Or when just when more each other
There is no each other as they like
They add why then emerge an add in
It is of absolutely no importance how often they add it.

Part V

STANZA XXXVIII

Which I wish to say is this
There is no beginning to an end
But there is a beginning and an end
To beginning.
5 Why yes of course.

Any one can learn that north of course
Is not only north but north as north
Why were they worried.
What I wish to say is this.
10   Yes of course

STANZA LXIII

I wish that I had spoken only of it all.

1932   1956

TRUMBULL STICKNEY
1874–1904

[And, the Last Day Being Come, Man Stood Alone]

And, the last day being come,[1] Man stood alone
Ere sunrise on the world's dismantled verge,°   edge
Awaiting how from everywhere should urge
The Coming of the Lord. And, behold, none

5   Did come,—but indistinct from every realm
Of earth and air and water, growing more
And louder, shriller, heavier, a roar
Up the dun° atmosphere did overwhelm   dark

His ears; and as he looked affrighted round
10   Every manner of beast innumerable
All thro' the shadows crying grew, until
The wailing was like grass upon the ground.

Asudden then within his human side
Their anguish, since the goad[2] he wielded first,
15   And, since he gave them not to drink, their thirst,
Darted compressed and vital.—As he died,

Low in the East now lighting gorgeously
He saw the last sea-serpent iris-mailed[3]
Which, with a spear transfixèd, yet availed
20   To pluck the sun down into the dead sea.

1905

---

1. Stickney's apocalyptic vision of the Lord's coming partakes of imagery in Revelation and other books of the Bible, but is essentially original.

2. A pointed stick for driving cattle and other animals.

3. In rainbow-colored armor.

An Athenian Garden

The burned and dusty garden said:
"My leaves are echoes, and thy earth
Is packed with footsteps of the dead.

"The strength of spring-time brought to birth
5   Some needles on the crooked fir,—
A rose, a laurel[4]—little worth.

"Come here, ye dreaming souls that err
Among the immortals of the grave:[5]
My summer is your sepulchre.

10   "On earth what darker voices rave
Than now this sea-breeze, driving dust
And whirling radiance wave on wave,

"With lulls so fearful thro' the gust
That on the shapeless flower-bed
15   Like timber splits the yellow crust.

"O thirsty, thirsty are the dead,[6]
Still thirsty, ever unallayed.
Where is no water, bring no bread."

I then had almost answer made,
20   When round the path in pleasure drew
Three golden children to the shade.

They stirred the dust with pail and hoe.
Then did the littlest from his fears
Come up and with his eyes of blue

25   Give me some berries seriously.
And as he turned to his brother, I
Looked after him thro' happy tears.

1903   1905

---

4. The laurel is a symbol of glory; the fir, of time; the rose, of love.
5. Stickney, a devotee of the ancient Greek philosopher Plato, may be referring to Plato's Myth of Er, according to which immortal souls are given lots that allow them to choose, wisely or unwisely, from an assortment of next lives (*Republic* 10).
6. In Greek mythology, the dead are often represented as thirsty.

From Fragments

IX[7]

I hear a river thro' the valley wander
Whose water runs, the song alone remaining.
A rainbow stands and summer passes under.

1905

CARL SANDBURG
1878–1967

Chicago

Hog Butcher for the World,
Tool Maker, Stacker of Wheat,
Player with Railroads and the Nation's Freight Handler;
Stormy, husky, brawling,
5   City of the Big Shoulders:

They tell me you are wicked and I believe them, for I have seen your
    painted women under the gas lamps luring the farm boys.
And they tell me you are crooked and I answer: Yes, it is true I have
    seen the gunman kill and go free to kill again.
And they tell me you are brutal and my reply is: On the faces of
    women and children I have seen the marks of wanton hunger.
And having answered so I turn once more to those who sneer at this
    my city, and I give them back the sneer and say to them:
10   Come and show me another city with lifted head singing so proud to
    be alive and coarse and strong and cunning.
Flinging magnetic curses amid the toil of piling job on job, here is a
    tall bold slugger set vivid against the little soft cities;
Fierce as a dog with tongue lapping for action, cunning as a savage
    pitted against the wilderness,
      Bareheaded,
      Shoveling,
15   Wrecking,
      Planning,
      Building, breaking, rebuilding,
Under the smoke, dust all over his mouth, laughing with white
    teeth,
Under the terrible burden of destiny laughing as a young man
    laughs,
20   Laughing even as an ignorant fighter laughs who has never lost a
    battle,

---

7. Cf. John Hollander's homage to this poem, "Variations on a Fragment by Trumbull Stickney" (p. 1777).

Bragging and laughing that under his wrist is the pulse, and under
    his ribs the heart of the people,
                Laughing!
Laughing the stormy, husky, brawling laughter of Youth, half-naked,
    sweating, proud to be Hog Butcher, Tool Maker, Stacker of
    Wheat, Player with Railroads and Freight Handler to the
    Nation.

1916

Grass

Pile the bodies high at Austerlitz[1] and Waterloo.
Shovel them under and let me work—
        I am the grass; I cover all.

And pile them high at Gettysburg
5 And pile them high at Ypres and Verdun.
Shovel them under and let me work.
Two years, ten years, and passengers ask the conductor:
        What place is this?
        Where are we now?

10   I am the grass.
        Let me work.

1918

EDWARD THOMAS
1878–1917

Adlestrop[1]

Yes, I remember Adlestrop—
The name, because one afternoon
Of heat the express-train drew up there
Unwontedly. It was late June.

5 The steam hissed. Someone cleared his throat.
No one left and no one came
On the bare platform. What I saw
Was Adlestrop—only the name

---

1. The places listed here are sites of major, bloody battles in the Napoleonic Wars, the Civil War, and World War I.

1. Village in Gloucestershire, southwest-central England.

And willows, willow-herb, and grass,
10 And meadowsweet, and haycocks dry,
No whit less still and lonely fair
Than the high cloudlets in the sky.

And for that minute a blackbird sang
Close by, and round him, mistier,
15 Farther and farther, all the birds
Of Oxfordshire and Gloucestershire.

1915   1917

The Owl

Downhill I came, hungry, and yet not starved;
Cold, yet had heat within me that was proof
Against the North wind; tired, yet so that rest
Had seemed the sweetest thing under a roof.

5   Then at the inn I had food, fire, and rest,
Knowing how hungry, cold, and tired was I.
All of the night was quite barred out except
An owl's cry, a most melancholy cry

Shaken out long and clear upon the hill,
10 No merry note, nor cause of merriment,
But one telling me plain what I escaped
And others could not, that night, as in I went.

And salted was my food, and my repose,
Salted and sobered, too, by the bird's voice
15 Speaking for all who lay under the stars,
Soldiers and poor, unable to rejoice.

1917

In Memoriam [Easter 1915]

The flowers left thick at nightfall in the wood
This Eastertide call into mind the men,
Now far from home, who, with their sweethearts, should
Have gathered them and will do never again.

1915   1917

Rain

Rain, midnight rain, nothing but the wild rain
On this bleak hut, and solitude, and me
Remembering again that I shall die
And neither hear the rain nor give it thanks
5 For washing me cleaner than I have been
Since I was born into this solitude.
Blessed are the dead that the rain rains upon:
But here I pray that none whom once I loved
Is dying tonight or lying still awake
10 Solitary, listening to the rain,
Either in pain or thus in sympathy
Helpless among the living and the dead,
Like a cold water among broken reeds,
Myriads of broken reeds all still and stiff,
15 Like me who have no love which this wild rain
Has not dissolved except the love of death,
If love it be towards what is perfect and
Cannot, the tempest tells me, disappoint.

1916   1917

As the team's head brass[2]

As the team's head brass flashed out on the turn
The lovers disappeared into the wood.
I sat among the boughs of the fallen elm
That strewed an angle of the fallow,[3] and
5 Watched the plough narrowing a yellow square
Of charlock.[4] Every time the horses turned
Instead of treading me down, the ploughman leaned
Upon the handles to say or ask a word,
About the weather, next about the war.
10 Scraping the share he faced towards the wood,
And screwed along the furrow till the brass flashed
Once more.
                    The blizzard felled the elm whose crest
I sat in, by a woodpecker's round hole,
15 The ploughman said. "When will they take it away?"
"When the war's over." So the talk began—
One minute and an interval of ten,
A minute more and the same interval.
"Have you been out?" "No." "And don't want to, perhaps?"
20 "If I could only come back again, I should.
I could spare an arm. I shouldn't want to lose

---

2. A team of horses pulling a plow, the head brass being the ornamental brass plaque attached to their bridle.

3. Cultivated land left unplanted during the growing season.

4. Wild mustard, a common, yellow field weed.

A leg. If I should lose my head, why, so,
I should want nothing more. . . . Have many gone
From here?" "Yes." "Many lost?" "Yes, a good few.
25 Only two teams work on the farm this year.
One of my mates is dead. The second day
In France they killed him. It was back in March,
The very night of the blizzard, too. Now if
He had stayed here we should have moved the tree."
30 "And I should not have sat here. Everything
Would have been different. For it would have been
Another world." "Ay, and a better, though
If we could see all all might seem good." Then
The lovers came out of the wood again:
35 The horses started and for the last time
I watched the clods crumble and topple over
After the ploughshare and the stumbling team.

1916   1917

WALLACE STEVENS
1879–1955

The Snow Man

One must have a mind of winter
To regard the frost and the boughs
Of the pine-trees crusted with snow;

And have been cold a long time
5   To behold the junipers shagged° with ice,   *shaggy*
The spruces rough in the distant glitter

Of the January sun; and not to think
Of any misery in the sound of the wind,
In the sound of a few leaves,

10 Which is the sound of the land
Full of the same wind
That is blowing in the same bare place

For the listener, who listens in the snow,
And, nothing himself, beholds
15 Nothing that is not there and the nothing that is.

1923

The Emperor of Ice-Cream

Call the roller of big cigars,
The muscular one, and bid him whip

In kitchen cups concupiscent curds.
Let the wenches dawdle in such dress
5 As they are used to wear, and let the boys
Bring flowers in last month's newspapers.
Let be be finale of seem.
The only emperor is the emperor of ice-cream.

Take from the dresser of deal.°   *pine or firwood*
10 Lacking the three glass knobs, that sheet
On which she embroidered fantails° once   *fantail pigeons*
And spread it so as to cover her face.
If her horny feet protrude, they come
To show how cold she is, and dumb.
15 Let the lamp affix its beam.
The only emperor is the emperor of ice-cream.

1923

Sunday Morning

1

Complacencies of the peignoir,° and late   *negligée*
Coffee and oranges in a sunny chair,
And the green freedom of a cockatoo
Upon a rug mingle to dissipate
5 The holy hush of ancient sacrifice.
She dreams a little, and she feels the dark
Encroachment of that old catastrophe,
As a calm darkens among water-lights.
The pungent oranges and bright, green wings
10 Seem things in some procession of the dead,
Winding across wide water, without sound.
The day is like wide water, without sound,
Stilled for the passing of her dreaming feet
Over the seas, to silent Palestine,
15 Dominion of the blood and sepulchre.[1]

2

Why should she give her bounty to the dead?
What is divinity if it can come
Only in silent shadows and in dreams?
Shall she not find in comforts of the sun,
20 In pungent fruit and bright, green wings, or else
In any balm or beauty of the earth,
Things to be cherished like the thought of heaven?
Divinity must live within herself:
Passions of rain, or moods in falling snow;
25 Grievings in loneliness, or unsubdued
Elations when the forest blooms; gusty

---

1. I.e., the holy sepulcher, the cave in Jerusalem where Jesus was entombed; at the Last Supper, Jesus referred to his blood as sealing "the covenant between God and his people" (Matthew 26.28).

Emotions on wet roads on autumn nights;
All pleasures and all pains, remembering
The bough of summer and the winter branch.
30   These are the measures destined for her soul.

3

Jove[2] in the clouds had his inhuman birth.
No mother suckled him, no sweet land gave
Large-mannered motions to his mythy mind
He moved among us, as a muttering king,
35   Magnificent, would move among his hinds,[3]
Until our blood, commingling, virginal,
With heaven, brought such requital to desire
The very hinds discerned it, in a star.
Shall our blood fail? Or shall it come to be
40   The blood of paradise? And shall the earth
Seem all of paradise that we shall know?
The sky will be much friendlier then than now,
A part of labor and a part of pain,
And next in glory to enduring love,
45   Not this dividing and indifferent blue.

4

She says, "I am content when wakened birds,
Before they fly, test the reality
Of misty fields, by their sweet questionings;
But when the birds are gone, and their warm fields
50   Return no more, where, then, is paradise?"
There is not any haunt of prophecy,
Nor any old chimera[4] of the grave,
Neither the golden underground, nor isle
Melodious, where spirits gat them home,
55   Nor visionary south, nor cloudy palm
Remote on heaven's hill, that has endured
As April's green endures; or will endure
Like her remembrance of awakened birds,
Or her desire for June and evening, tipped
60   By the consummation of the swallow's wings.

5

She says, "But in contentment I still feel
The need of some imperishable bliss."
Death is the mother of beauty; hence from her,
Alone, shall come fulfilment to our dreams
65   And our desires. Although she strews the leaves
Of sure obliteration on our paths,
The path sick sorrow took, the many paths

2. Or Jupiter (meaning "sky father"), supreme
Roman god. His Greek counterpart, Zeus, was
suckled by a goat in his childhood.
3. Farmhands, rustics; alludes to the shepherds
who saw the Star of Bethlehem, which signaled

Jesus' birth.
4. In Greek mythology, a monster with a lion's
head, goat's body, and serpent's tail. Also, an illu-
sion or fabrication of the mind.

Where triumph rang its brassy phrase, or love
Whispered a little out of tenderness,
70 She makes the willow shiver in the sun
For maidens who were wont° to sit and gaze   *accustomed*
Upon the grass, relinquished to their feet.
She causes boys to pile new plums and pears
On disregarded plate.⁵ The maidens taste
75 And stray impassioned in the littering leaves.

6

Is there no change of death in paradise?
Does ripe fruit never fall? Or do the boughs
Hang always heavy in that perfect sky,
Unchanging, yet so like our perishing earth,
80 With rivers like our own that seek for seas
They never find, the same receding shores
That never touch with inarticulate pang?
Why set the pear upon those river-banks
Or spice the shores with odors of the plum?
85 Alas, that they should wear our colors there,
The silken weavings of our afternoons,
And pick the strings of our insipid lutes!
Death is the mother of beauty, mystical,
Within whose burning bosom we devise
90 Our earthly mothers waiting, sleeplessly.

7

Supple and turbulent, a ring of men
Shall chant in orgy on a summer morn
Their boisterous devotion to the sun,
Not as a god, but as a god might be,
95 Naked among them, like a savage source.
Their chant shall be a chant of paradise,
Out of their blood, returning to the sky;
And in their chant shall enter, voice by voice,
The windy lake wherein their lord delights,
100 The trees, like serafin,⁶ and echoing hills,
That choir among themselves long afterward.
They shall know well the heavenly fellowship
Of men that perish and of summer morn.
And whence they came and whither they shall go
105 The dew upon their feet shall manifest.

8

She hears, upon that water without sound,
A voice that cries, "The tomb in Palestine
Is not the porch of spirits lingering.
It is the grave of Jesus, where he lay."
110 We live in an old chaos of the sun,

5. "Plate is used in the sense of so-called family plate. Disregarded refers to the disuse into which things fall that have been possessed for a long time. I mean, therefore, that death releases and renews" [*Letters of Wallace Stevens*, 1966, 183–84].
6. I.e., seraphim, the highest order of angels.

Or old dependency of day and night,
Or island solitude, unsponsored, free,
Of that wide water, inescapable.
Deer walk upon our mountains, and the quail
115 Whistle about us their spontaneous cries;
Sweet berries ripen in the wilderness;
And, in the isolation of the sky,
At evening, casual flocks of pigeons make
Ambiguous undulations as they sink,
120 Downward to darkness, on extended wings.

1915   1923

Anecdote of the Jar

I placed a jar in Tennessee,
And round it was, upon a hill.
It made the slovenly wilderness
Surround that hill.

5 The wilderness rose up to it,
And sprawled around, no longer wild.
The jar was round upon the ground
And tall and of a port in air.

It took dominion everywhere.
10 The jar was gray and bare.
It did not give of bird or bush,
Like nothing else in Tennessee.

1923

Thirteen Ways of Looking at a Blackbird

I

Among twenty snowy mountains,
The only moving thing
Was the eye of the blackbird.

II

I was of three minds,
5 Like a tree
In which there are three blackbirds.

III

The blackbird whirled in the autumn winds.
It was a small part of the pantomime.

IV

A man and a woman
10 Are one.
A man and a woman and a blackbird
Are one.

V

I do not know which to prefer,
The beauty of inflections
15 Or the beauty of innuendoes,
The blackbird whistling
Or just after.

VI

Icicles filled the long window
With barbaric glass.
20 The shadow of the blackbird
Crossed it to and fro.
The mood
Traced in the shadow
An indecipherable cause.

VII

25 O thin men of Haddam,[7]
Why do you imagine golden birds?
Do you not see how the blackbird
Walks around the feet
Of the women about you?

VIII

30 I know noble accents
And lucid, inescapable rhythms;
But I know, too,
That the blackbird is involved
In what I know.

IX

35 When the blackbird flew out of sight,
It marked the edge
Of one of many circles.

---

7. A town in Connecticut. Stevens explains: "The thin men of Haddam are entirely fictitious. . . . I just like the name. . . . It has a completely Yankee sound" [*Letters*, 340].

X

At the sight of blackbirds
Flying in a green light,
40   Even the bawds of euphony[8]
Would cry out sharply.

XI

He rode over Connecticut
In a glass coach.
Once, a fear pierced him
45   In that he mistook
The shadow of his equipage°   coach
For blackbirds.

XII

The river is moving.
The blackbird must be flying.

XIII

50   It was evening all afternoon.
It was snowing
And it was going to snow.
The blackbird sat
In the cedar-limbs.

1923

Peter Quince at the Clavier[9]

I

Just as my fingers on these keys
Make music, so the selfsame sounds
On my spirit make a music, too.

Music is feeling, then, not sound;
5   And thus it is that what I feel,
Here in this room, desiring you,

Thinking of your blue-shadowed silk,
Is music. It is like the strain
Waked in the elders by Susanna.[1]

---

8. I.e., madams or prostitutes of sweet sound.
9. Early keyboard instrument. *Peter Quince*: the stage manager of the rustic actors who clumsily perform a "tragedy" within Shakespeare's comedy *A Midsummer Night's Dream*. Also, an allusion to the poem "Quince to Lilac: to G. H.," from Bliss Carmen and Richard Hovey's once-popular book

More Songs from Vagabondia (1895).
1. In Daniel 13, a chapter in the Apocrypha, Susanna refuses seduction by two Hebrew elders, or tribal councilors, who then falsely accuse her of a liaison with a young man. Daniel protects her from being punished.

10 Of a green evening, clear and warm,
   She bathed in her still garden, while
   The red-eyed elders watching, felt

   The basses of their beings throb
   In witching chords, and their thin blood
15 Pulse pizzicati of Hosanna.[2]

II

   In the green water, clear and warm,
   Susanna lay.
   She searched
   The touch of springs,
20 And found
   Concealed imaginings.
   She sighed,
   For so much melody.

   Upon the bank, she stood
25 In the cool
   Of spent emotions.
   She felt, among the leaves,
   The dew
   Of old devotions.

30 She walked upon the grass,
   Still quavering.
   The winds were like her maids,
   On timid feet,
   Fetching her woven scarves,
35 Yet wavering.

   A breath upon her hand
   Muted the night.
   She turned—
   A cymbal crashed,
40 And roaring horns.

III

   Soon, with a noise like tambourines,
   Came her attendant Byzantines.[3]

   They wondered why Susanna cried
   Against the elders by her side;

45 And as they whispered, the refrain
   Was like a willow swept by rain.

2. Great praise. *Pizzicati:* musical passages in which strings are plucked.
3. People of the Byzantine Empire (fourth through the fifteenth centuries); an anachronism, as they postdated Susanna.

Anon, their lamps' uplifted flame
Revealed Susanna and her shame.

And then, the simpering Byzantines
50 Fled, with a noise like tambourines.

IV

Beauty is momentary in the mind—
The fitful tracing of a portal;
But in the flesh it is immortal.

The body dies; the body's beauty lives.
55 So evenings die, in their green going,
A wave, interminably flowing.
So gardens die, their meek breath scenting
The cowl of winter, done repenting.
So maidens die, to the auroral
60 Celebration of a maiden's choral.

Susanna's music touched the bawdy strings
Of those white elders; but, escaping,
Left only Death's ironic scraping.
Now, in its immortality, it plays
65 On the clear viol of her memory,
And makes a constant sacrament of praise.

1923   1931

The Idea of Order at Key West[4]

She sang beyond the genius[5] of the sea.
The water never formed to mind or voice,
Like a body wholly body, fluttering
Its empty sleeves; and yet its mimic motion
5 Made constant cry, caused constantly a cry,
That was not ours although we understood,
Inhuman, of the veritable ocean.
The sea was not a mask. No more was she.
The song and water were not medleyed sound
10 Even if what she sang was what she heard,
Since what she sang was uttered word by word.
It may be that in all her phrases stirred
The grinding water and the gasping wind;
But it was she and not the sea we heard.
15 For she was the maker of the song she sang.
The ever-hooded, tragic-gestured sea
Was merely a place by which she walked to sing.
Whose spirit is this? we said, because we knew

4. One of the coral islands off the south coast of
Florida.

5. The pervading and guardian spirit of a place.

It was the spirit that we sought and knew
20   That we should ask this often as she sang.

If it was only the dark voice of the sea
That rose, or even colored by many waves;
If it was only the outer voice of sky
And cloud, of the sunken coral water-walled,
25   However clear, it would have been deep air,
The heaving speech of air, a summer sound
Repeated in a summer without end
And sound alone. But it was more than that,
More even than her voice, and ours, among
30   The meaningless plungings of water and the wind,
Theatrical distances, bronze shadows heaped
On high horizons, mountainous atmospheres
Of sky and sea.
                         It was her voice that made
35   The sky acutest at its vanishing.
She measured to the hour its solitude.
She was the single artificer of the world
In which she sang. And when she sang, the sea,
Whatever self it had, became the self
40   That was her song, for she was the maker. Then we,
As we beheld her striding there alone,
Knew that there never was a world for her
Except the one she sang and, singing, made.

Ramon Fernandez,[6] tell me, if you know,
45   Why, when the singing ended and we turned
Toward the town, tell why the glassy lights,
The lights in the fishing boats at anchor there,
As the night descended, tilting in the air,
Mastered the night and portioned out the sea,
50   Fixing emblazoned zones and fiery poles,
Arranging, deepening, enchanting night.

Oh! Blessed rage for order, pale Ramon,
The maker's rage to order words of the sea,
Words of the fragrant portals, dimly-starred,
55   And of ourselves and of our origins,
In ghostlier demarcations, keener sounds.

1936

Waving Adieu, Adieu, Adieu[7]

That would be waving and that would be crying,
Crying and shouting and meaning farewell,

6. Stevens claimed (*Letters*, 798) that he had sim-
ply combined two common Spanish names at ran-
dom, without conscious reference to the French
literary critic and essayist Ramon Fernandez

(1894–1944).
7. Cf. Mark Strand's homage to this poem in *Dark
Harbor*, XVI (p. 1864).

Farewell in the eyes and farewell at the centre,
Just to stand still without moving a hand.

5   In a world without heaven to follow, the stops
Would be endings, more poignant than partings, profounder,
And that would be saying farewell, repeating farewell,
Just to be there and just to behold.

To be one's singular self, to despise
10 The being that yielded so little, acquired
So little, too little to care, to turn
To the ever-jubilant weather, to sip

One's cup and never to say a word,
Or to sleep or just to lie there still,
15 Just to be there, just to be beheld,
That would be bidding farewell, be bidding farewell.

One likes to practice the thing. They practice,
Enough, for heaven. Ever-jubilant,
What is there here but weather, what spirit
20 Have I except it comes from the sun?

                                                          1936

The Poems of Our Climate

I

Clear water in a brilliant bowl,
Pink and white carnations. The light
In the room more like a snowy air,
Reflecting snow. A newly-fallen snow
5   At the end of winter when afternoons return.
Pink and white carnations—one desires
So much more than that. The day itself
Is simplified: a bowl of white,
Cold, a cold porcelain, low and round,
10 With nothing more than the carnations there.

II

Say even that this complete simplicity
Stripped one of all one's torments, concealed
The evilly compounded, vital I
And made it fresh in a world of white,
15 A world of clear water, brilliant-edged,
Still one would want more, one would need more,
More than a world of white and snowy scents.

III

There would still remain the never-resting mind,
So that one would want to escape, come back
20   To what had been so long composed.
The imperfect is our paradise.
Note that, in this bitterness, delight,
Since the imperfect is so hot in us,
Lies in flawed words and stubborn sounds.

1942

The House Was Quiet and the World Was Calm

The house was quiet and the world was calm.
The reader became the book; and summer night

Was like the conscious being of the book.
The house was quiet and the world was calm.

5   The words were spoken as if there was no book,
Except that the reader leaned above the page,

Wanted to lean, wanted much most to be
The scholar to whom his book is true, to whom

The summer night is like a perfection of thought.
10   The house was quiet because it had to be.

The quiet was part of the meaning, part of the mind:
The access of perfection to the page.

And the world was calm. The truth in a calm world,
In which there is no other meaning, itself

15   Is calm, itself is summer and night, itself
Is the reader leaning late and reading there.

1947

Table Talk

Granted, we die for good.
Life, then, is largely a thing
Of happens to like, not should.

And that, too, granted, why
5   Do I happen to like red bush,
Gray grass and green-gray sky?

What else remains? But red,
Gray, green, why those of all?
That is not what I said:

10   Not those of all. But those.
One likes what one happens to like.
One likes the way red grows.

It cannot matter at all.
Happens to like is one
15   Of the ways things happen to fall.

ca. 1935   1957

A Room on a Garden

O stagnant east-wind, palsied mare,
Giddap! The ruby roses' hair
Must blow.

Behold how order is the end
5   Of everything. The roses bend
As one.

Order, the law of hoes and rakes,
May be perceived in windy quakes
And squalls.

10   The gardener searches earth and sky
The truth in nature to espy
In vain.

He well might find that eager balm
In lilies' stately-statued calm;
15   But then

He well might find it in this fret
Of lilies rusted, rotting, wet
With rain.

ca. 1935   1957

Of Mere Being

The palm at the end of the mind,
Beyond the last thought, rises
In the bronze decor,[8]

8. In the first published version of this poem, the 1957 *Opus Posthumous* incorrectly gave "decor" as "distance." The 1989 edition provided a correction.

A gold-feathered bird
5 Sings in the palm, without human meaning,
Without human feeling, a foreign song.

You know then that it is not the reason
That makes us happy or unhappy.
The bird sings. Its feathers shine.

10 The palm stands on the edge of space.
The wind moves slowly in the branches.
The bird's fire-fangled feathers dangle down.

1955?   1957, 1989

WITTER BYNNER
1881–1968

Haskell[1]

Here in Kansas is a school
Made of square stones and windows,
Where Indian boys are taught to use a tool,
A printing-press, a book,
5   And Indian girls
To read, to dress, to cook.
And as I watch today
The orderly industrious classes,
Only their color and silence and the way
10 The hair lies flat and black on their heads proclaims them Sioux,
Comanche, Choctaw, Cherokee,
Creek, Chippewa, Paiute[2]—and the red and blue
Of the girls' long sweaters and the purple and yellow,
And the tawny slant of the machine-made shirts . . .

15 Noon—and out they come. And one tall fellow,
Breaking from the others with a glittering yell and crouching slim,
Gives a leap like the leap of Mordkin,[3]
And the sun carves under him
A canyon of glory . . .
20 And then it shadows, and he darts,
With head hung, to the dormitory.

1920

---

1. Town in Kansas.
2. Names of Native American tribes.

3. Mikhail Mordkin (1881–1944), Russian ballet dancer.

From Chinese Drawings

A Philosopher

What though they conquer us?
The tea has come.
In at most nine hundred years,
Someone will conquer them.

1920

The Wintry Mind

Winter uncovers distances, I find;
And so the cold and so the wintry mind
Takes leaves away, till there is left behind
A wide cold world. And so the heart grows blind
5   To the earth's green motions lying warm below
Field upon field, field upon field, of snow.

1940

More Lovely than Antiquity

There comes a moment in her veins
Not of the earth, not of the rains,
Something not of stalks and stems
But of dim crowns and diadems,°   *royal headbands*
5   Something commanding her to be
More ancient than antiquity
And to soothe her head on a pike above
The vacant circumstance of love.

1947

E. J. PRATT
1883–1964

Come Not the Seasons Here

Comes not the springtime here,
   Though the snowdrop came,
And the time of the cowslip° is near,   *a wildflower*
   For a yellow flame
5   Was found in a tuft of green;

And the joyous shout
Of a child rang out
That a cuckoo's eggs were seen.

Comes not the summer here,
10   Though the cowslip be gone,
Though the wild rose blow as the year
    Draws faithfully on;
Though the face of the poppy be red
    In the morning light,
15   And the ground be white
With the bloom of the locust shed.

Comes not the autumn here,
    Though someone said
He found a leaf in the sere°   *withered state*
20   By an aster dead;
And knew that the summer was done,
    For a herdsman cried
That his pastures were brown in the sun,
    And his wells were dried.

25 Nor shall the winter come,
    Though the elm be bare,
And every voice be dumb
    On the frozen air;
But the flap of a waterfowl
30   In the marsh alone,
Or the hoot of a horned owl
    On a glacial stone.

1923

From Stone to Steel

From stone to bronze, from bronze to steel
Along the road-dust of the sun
Two revolutions of the wheel
From Java to Geneva run.[1]

5   The snarl Neanderthal is worn
Close to the smiling Aryan[2] lips,
The civil polish of the horn
Gleams from our praying finger tips.

The evolution of desire
10 Has but matured a toxic wine,

1. Java, now part of Indonesia, was the site of fossil excavations where the bones of an early type of prehistoric human ("Neanderthal," line 5) were found. Geneva, in Switzerland, was the headquarters of the League of Nations from 1919 until the outbreak of World War II.
2. According to Nazi racial theory, the Aryan "race" was superior to all others.

Drunk long before its heady fire
Reddened Euphrates or the Rhine.[3]

Between the temple and the cave
The boundary lies tissue-thin:
15 The yearlings still the altars crave
As satisfaction for a sin.

The road goes up, the road goes down—
Let Java or Geneva be—
But whether to the cross or crown,
20 The path lies through Gethsemane.[4]

1932

WILLIAM CARLOS WILLIAMS
1883–1963

Danse Russe[1]

If when my wife is sleeping
and the baby and Kathleen
are sleeping
and the sun is a flame-white disc
5   in silken mists
above shining trees,—
if I in my north room
dance naked, grotesquely
before my mirror
10   waving my shirt round my head
and singing softly to myself:
"I am lonely, lonely.
I was born to be lonely,
I am best so!"
15   If I admire my arms, my face,
my shoulders, flanks, buttocks
against the yellow drawn shades,—

Who shall say I am not
the happy genius[2] of my household?

1917

---

3. The Euphrates was one of the two great river valleys of ancient Mesopotamian civilization. The river Rhine flows through western Germany and the Netherlands.
4. The garden where Christ prayed while his disciples slept, and where Judas betrayed him (Matthew 26.36–56).

1. Russian dance (French). Just before writing this poem, Williams had seen a performance in New York City by the Ballet Russes, a company led by the producer and critic Sergey Pavlovich Diaghilev (1872–1929).
2. The pervading and guardian spirit of a place.

Portrait of a Lady[3]

Your thighs are appletrees
whose blossoms touch the sky.
Which sky? The sky
where Watteau hung a lady's
5   slipper.[4] Your knees
are a southern breeze—or
a gust of snow. Agh! what
sort of man was Fragonard?
—as if that answered
10   anything. Ah, yes—below
the knees, since the tune
drops that way, it is
one of those white summer days,
the tall grass of your ankles
15   flickers upon the shore—
Which shore?—
the sand clings to my lips—
Which shore?
Agh, petals maybe. How
20   should I know?
Which shore? Which shore?
I said petals from an appletree.

1920, 1934

Queen-Anne's-Lace[5]

Her body is not so white as
anemone petals nor so smooth—nor
so remote a thing. It is a field
of the wild carrot taking
5   the field by force; the grass
does not raise above it.
Here is no question of whiteness,
white as can be, with a purple mole
at the center of each flower.
10   Each flower is a hand's span
of her whiteness. Wherever
his hand has lain there is
a tiny purple blemish. Each part
is a blossom under his touch

3. The title recalls those of works by the English (American-born) novelist Henry James (1843–1916), the English (American-born) poet T. S. Eliot (1888–1965; see pp. 1340–66), and the American poet Ezra Pound (1885–1972; see pp. 1295–1310). Cf. Pound's poem "Portrait d'une Femme" (p. 1295).

4. Williams seems to be conflating the French painter Jean-Antoine Watteau (1684–1721) with the French artist Jean-Honoré Fragonard (1732–1806). In Fragonard's famous painting *The Swing*, a girl on a swing has kicked off her slipper, which remains suspended in air.
5. A common field flower.

15   to which the fibres of her being
stem one by one, each to its end,
until the whole field is a
white desire, empty, a single stem,
a cluster, flower by flower,
20   a pious wish to whiteness gone over—
or nothing

1921

The Red Wheelbarrow

so much depends
upon

a red wheel
barrow

5   glazed with rain
water

beside the white
chickens.

1923

This Is Just to Say[6]

I have eaten
the plums
that were in
the icebox

5   and which
you were probably
saving
for breakfast

Forgive me
10   they were delicious
so sweet
and so cold

1934

6. Cf. Kenneth Koch's parody of this poem, "Variations on a Theme by William Carlos Williams" (p. 1693).

Poem

As the cat
climbed over
the top of

the jamcloset
5 first the right
forefoot

carefully
then the hind
stepped down

10 into the pit of
the empty
flowerpot

1934

The Yachts

contend in a sea which the land partly encloses
shielding them from the too-heavy blows
of an ungoverned ocean which when it chooses

tortures the biggest hulls, the best man knows
5 to pit against its beatings, and sinks them pitilessly.
Mothlike in mists, scintillant in the minute

brilliance of cloudless days, with broad bellying sails
they glide to the wind tossing green water
from their sharp prows while over them the crew crawls

10 ant-like, solicitously grooming them, releasing,
making fast as they turn, lean far over and having
caught the wind again, side by side, head for the mark.

In a well guarded arena of open water surrounded by
lesser and greater craft which, sycophant, lumbering
15 and flittering follow them, they appear youthful, rare

as the light of a happy eye, live with the grace
of all that in the mind is fleckless, free and
naturally to be desired. Now the sea which holds them

is moody, lapping their glossy sides, as if feeling
20 for some slightest flaw but fails completely.
Today no race. Then the wind comes again. The yachts

move, jockeying for a start, the signal is set and they
are off. Now the waves strike at them but they are too
well made, they slip through, though they take in canvas.

25 Arms with hands grasping seek to clutch at the prows.
Bodies thrown recklessly in the way are cut aside,
It is a sea of faces about them in agony, in despair

until the horror of the race dawns staggering the mind,
the whole sea become an entanglement of watery bodies
30 lost to the world bearing what they cannot hold. Broken,

beaten, desolate, reaching from the dead to be taken up
they cry out, failing, failing! their cries rising
in waves still as the skillful yachts pass over.

1935

A Sort of a Song

Let the snake wait under
his weed
and the writing
be of words, slow and quick, sharp
5 to strike, quiet to wait,
sleepless.

—through metaphor to reconcile
the people and the stones.
Compose. (No ideas
10 but in things) Invent!
Saxifrage[7] is my flower that splits
the rocks.

1944

From Asphodel, That Greeny Flower[8]

Book I

Of asphodel, that greeny flower,
        like a buttercup

---

7. Breaking rocks (Latin); a perennial herb.
8. A tripartite love poem, with coda, for the poet's wife. The green asphodel first impressed Williams as a child in Switzerland, and it appears in his early work *Kora in Hell: Improvisations* (1920). (Kora— or *Kore*, Greek for girl or young woman—is another name for the mythological figure Persephone. The daughter of Demeter, she was carried to the underworld by its ruler, Hades. In the under-

world of Homer's *Odyssey*, a grove of poplars sacred to Persephone stood at the entrance of *asphodel limona*, fields of asphodel inhabited by the souls of the dead.) The opening lines were originally published in the October 1952 issue of *Poetry* magazine, as "Paterson, Book V: The River of Heaven," but were later removed from Williams's epic, *Paterson*.

```
                        upon its branching stem—
        save that it's green and wooden—
 5              I come, my sweet,
                        to sing to you.
        We lived long together
                a life filled,
                        if you will,
10      with flowers. So that
                I was cheered
                        when I came first to know
        that there were flowers also
                        in hell.
15                      Today
        I'm filled with the fading memory of those flowers
                that we both loved,
                        even to this poor
        colorless thing—
20              I saw it
                        when I was a child—
        little prized among the living
                but the dead see,
                        asking among themselves:
25      What do I remember
                that was shaped
                        as this thing is shaped?
        while our eyes fill
                with tears.
30                      Of love, abiding love
        it will be telling
                though too weak a wash of crimson
                        colors it
        to make it wholly credible.
35              There is something
                        something urgent
        I have to say to you
                and you alone
                        but it must wait
40      while I drink in
                the joy of your approach,
                        perhaps for the last time.
        And so
                with fear in my heart
45                      I drag it out
        and keep on talking
                for I dare not stop.
                        Listen while I talk on
        against time.
50              It will not be
                        for long.
        I have forgot
                and yet I see clearly enough
                        something
```

55   central to the sky
                which ranges round it.
                        An odor
       springs from it!
                A sweetest odor!
60   Honeysuckle! And now
       there comes the buzzing of a bee!
                and a whole flood
                        of sister memories!
       Only give me time,
65   time to recall them
                        before I shall speak out.
       Give me time,
                time.
       When I was a boy
70   I kept a book
                        to which, from time
       to time,
                I added pressed flowers
                        until, after a time,
75   I had a good collection.
                The asphodel,
                        forebodingly,
       among them.
                I bring you,
80   reawakened,
       a memory of those flowers.
                They were sweet
                        when I pressed them
       and retained
85   something of their sweetness
                        a long time.
       It is a curious odor,
                a moral odor,
                        that brings me
90   near to you.
                The color
                        was the first to go.
       There had come to me
                a challenge,
95   your dear self,
       mortal as I was,
                the lily's throat
                        to the hummingbird!
       Endless wealth,
100   I thought,
                        held out its arms to me.
       A thousand tropics
                in an apple blossom.
                        The generous earth itself
105   gave us lief.[9]
                The whole world

9. Leave, or permission. An obsolete form of *leaf* and *life*, "lief" also connotes gladness.

became my garden!
But the sea
which no one tends
110 is also a garden
when the sun strikes it
and the waves
are wakened.
I have seen it
115 and so have you
when it puts all flowers
to shame.
Too, there are the starfish
stiffened by the sun
120 and other sea wrack
and weeds. We knew that
along with the rest of it
for we were born by the sea,
knew its rose hedges
125 to the very water's brink.
There the pink mallow grows
and in their season
strawberries
and there, later,
130 we went to gather
the wild plum.
I cannot say
that I have gone to hell
for your love
135 but often
found myself there
in your pursuit.
I do not like it
and wanted to be
140 in heaven. Hear me out.
Do not turn away.
I have learned much in my life
from books
and out of them
145 about love.
Death
is not the end of it.
There is a hierarchy
which can be attained,
150 I think,
in its service.
Its guerdon°   reward
is a fairy flower;
a cat of twenty lives.
155 If no one came to try it
the world
would be the loser.
It has been
for you and me

160   as one who watches a storm
           come in over the water.
                 We have stood
    from year to year
           before the spectacle of our lives
165   with joined hands.
    The storm unfolds.
          Lightning
                plays about the edges of the clouds.
    The sky to the north
170   is placid,
                blue in the afterglow
    as the storm piles up.
          It is a flower
              that will soon reach
175   the apex of its bloom.
          We danced,
             in our minds,
    and read a book together.
          You remember?
180   It was a serious book.
    And so books
          entered our lives.
    The sea! The sea!
          Always
185   when I think of the sea
    there comes to mind
          the *Iliad*
             and Helen's public fault
    that bred it.[1]
190   Were it not for that
             there would have been
    no poem but the world
          if we had remembered,
            those crimson petals
195   spilled among the stones,
          would have called it simply
             murder.
    The sexual orchid that bloomed then
          sending so many
200   disinterested
    men to their graves
          has left its memory
            to a race of fools
    or heroes
205   if silence is a virtue.
          The sea alone
    with its multiplicity
          holds any hope.
          The storm

1. In Greek mythology, the beautiful Helen (daughter of the god Zeus and the mortal Leda; wife of the Spartan King Menelaus) was abducted by Paris (son of the Trojan king, Priam). The dispute that followed was a cause of the Trojan War.

210 has proven abortive
                    but we remain
                                after the thoughts it roused
to
                    re-cement our lives.
215   It is the mind
the mind
                    that must be cured
                                short of death's
intervention,
220   and the will becomes again
                                a garden. The poem
is complex and the place made
                    in our lives
                                for the poem.
225 Silence can be complex too,
                    but you do not get far
                                with silence.
Begin again.
                    It is like Homer's
230   catalogue of ships:[2]
it fills up the time.
                    I speak in figures,
                                well enough, the dresses
you wear are figures also,
235   we could not meet
                                otherwise. When I speak
of flowers
                    it is to recall
                                that at one time
240 we were young.
                    All women are not Helen,
                                I know that,
but have Helen in their hearts.
                    My sweet,
245   you have it also, therefore
I love you
                    and could not love you otherwise.
                                Imagine you saw
a field made up of women
250   all silver-white.
                                What should you do
but love them?
                    The storm bursts
                                or fades! it is not
255 the end of the world.
                    Love is something else,
                                or so I thought it,
a garden which expands,
                    though I knew you as a woman
260   and never thought otherwise,
until the whole sea

2. Cf. *Iliad* 2.484–785, where the Greek ships that sailed to Troy are listed.

          has been taken up
             and all its gardens.
It was the love of love,
265   the love that swallows up all else,
             a grateful love,
a love of nature, of people,
          animals,
             a love engendering
270 gentleness and goodness
          that moved me
             and *that* I saw in you.
I should have known,
          though I did not,
275   that the lily-of-the-valley
is a flower makes many ill
          who whiff it.
             We had our children,
rivals in the general onslaught.
280   I put them aside
             though I cared for them
as well as any man
          could care for his children
             according to my lights.
285 You understand
          I had to meet you
             after the event
and have still to meet you.
          Love
290   to which you too shall bow
along with me—
          a flower
             a weakest flower
shall be our trust
295   and not because
             we are too feeble
to do otherwise
          but because
             at the height of my power
300 I risked what I had to do,
          therefore to prove
             that we love each other
while my very bones sweated
          that I could not cry to you
305   in the act.
Of asphodel, that greeny flower,
          I come, my sweet,
             to sing to you!
My heart rouses
310   thinking to bring you news
             of something
that concerns you
          and concerns many men. Look at
             what passes for the new.

315 You will not find it there but in
          despised poems.
                    It is difficult
to get the news from poems
          yet men die miserably every day
320   for lack
of what is found there.
          Hear me out
                    for I too am concerned
and every man
325   who wants to die at peace in his bed
                    besides.

1955

From Pictures from Brueghel[3]

II Landscape with the Fall of Icarus[4]

          According to Brueghel
          when Icarus fell
          it was spring

          a farmer was ploughing
5   his field
          the whole pageantry

          of the year was
          awake tingling
          near

10   the edge of the sea
          concerned
          with itself

          sweating in the sun
          that melted
15   the wings' wax

          unsignificantly
          off the coast
          there was

          a splash quite unnoticed
20   this was
          Icarus drowning

1962

---

3. Peter Brueghel (or Breughel) the Elder (1521?–1569), Flemish painter; this poem, taking its title from one of Brueghel's paintings, is one of ten in a series.
4. In Greek mythology, Icarus and his father, Daedalus, sought to escape Crete on wings Daedalus made of feathers and wax. Icarus flew too close to the sun and fell into the sea when his wings melted. Cf. W. H. Auden, "Musée des Beaux Arts" (p. 1471), which like Williams's poem notes Brueghel's marginal treatment of Icarus's legs in the sea.

D. H. LAWRENCE
1885–1930

Love on the Farm[1]

What large, dark hands are those at the window
Grasping in the golden light
Which weaves its way through the evening wind
    At my heart's delight?

5 Ah, only the leaves! But in the west
I see a redness suddenly come
Into the evening's anxious breast—
    'Tis the wound of love goes home!

The woodbine° creeps abroad   *honeysuckle*
10 Calling low to her lover:
    The sun-lit flirt who all the day
    Has poised above her lips in play
    And stolen kisses, shallow and gay
    Of pollen, now has gone away—
15   She woos the moth with her sweet, low word:
And when above her his moth-wings hover
Then her bright breast she will uncover
And yield her honey-drop to her lover.

Into the yellow, evening glow
20 Saunters a man from the farm below;
Leans, and looks in at the low-built shed
Where the swallow has hung her marriage bed.
    The bird lies warm against the wall.
    She glances quick her startled eyes
25   Towards him, then she turns away
    Her small head, making warm display
    Of red upon the throat. Her terrors sway
    Her out of the nest's warm, busy ball,
    Whose plaintive cry is heard as she flies
30   In one blue stoop from out the sties°   *pens for animals*
    Into the twilight's empty hall.
Oh, water-hen, beside the rushes
Hide your quaintly scarlet blushes,
Still your quick tail, lie still as dead,
35 Till the distance folds over his ominous tread!

The rabbit presses back her ears,
Turns back her liquid, anguished eyes
And crouches low; then with wild spring
Spurts from the terror of *his* oncoming;
40 To be choked back, the wire ring
Her frantic effort throttling:

1. Originally published as "Cruelty and Love," but retitled for the *Collected Poems* (1928).

Piteous brown ball of quivering fears!
Ah, soon in his large, hard hands she dies,
And swings all loose from the swing of his walk!
45 Yet calm and kindly are his eyes
And ready to open in brown surprise
Should I not answer to his talk
Or should he my tears surmise.

I hear his hand on the latch, and rise from my chair
50 Watching the door open; he flashes bare
His strong teeth in a smile, and flashes his eyes
In a smile like triumph upon me; then careless-wise
He flings the rabbit soft on the table board
And comes towards me: ah! the uplifted sword
55 Of his hand against my bosom! and oh, the broad
Blade of his glance that asks me to applaud
His coming! With his hand he turns my face to him
And caresses me with his fingers that still smell grim
Of the rabbit's fur! God, I am caught in a snare!°   *wire trap*
60 I know not what fine wire is round my throat;
I only know I let him finger there
My pulse of life, and let him nose like a stoat[2]
Who sniffs with joy before he drinks the blood.

And down his mouth comes to my mouth! and down
65 His bright dark eyes come over me, like a hood
Upon my mind! his lips meet mine, and a flood
Of sweet fire sweeps across me, so I drown
Against him, die, and find death good.

1913

Piano

Softly, in the dusk, a woman is singing to me;
Taking me back down the vista of years, till I see
A child sitting under the piano, in the boom of the tingling strings
And pressing the small, poised feet of a mother who smiles as she sings.

5 In spite of myself, the insidious mastery of song
Betrays me back, till the heart of me weeps to belong
To the old Sunday evenings at home, with winter outside
And hymns in the cosy parlour, the tinkling piano our guide.

So now it is vain for the singer to burst into clamour
10 With the great black piano appassionato. The glamour
Of childish days is upon me, my manhood is cast
Down in the flood of remembrance, I weep like a child for the past.

1918

2. Small, carnivorous animal of the weasel family.

Snake

A snake came to my water-trough
On a hot, hot day, and I in pyjamas for the heat,
To drink there.

In the deep, strange-scented shade of the great dark carob-tree
5   I came down the steps with my pitcher
And must wait, must stand and wait, for there he was at the trough
        before me.

He reached down from a fissure in the earth-wall in the gloom
And trailed his yellow-brown slackness soft-bellied down, over the
        edge of the stone trough
And rested his throat upon the stone bottom,
10 And where the water had dripped from the tap, in a small clearness,
He sipped with his straight mouth,
Softly drank through his straight gums, into his slack long body,
Silently.

Someone was before me at my water-trough,
15 And I, like a second comer, waiting.

He lifted his head from his drinking, as cattle do,
And looked at me vaguely, as drinking cattle do,
And flickered his two-forked tongue from his lips, and mused a
        moment,
And stooped and drank a little more,
20 Being earth-brown, earth-golden from the burning bowels of the
        earth
On the day of Sicilian July, with Etna[3] smoking.
The voice of my education said to me
He must be killed,
For in Sicily the black, black snakes are innocent, the gold are
        venomous.

25 And voices in me said, If you were a man
You would take a stick and break him now, and finish him off.

But must I confess how I liked him,
How glad I was he had come like a guest in quiet, to drink at my
        water-trough

And depart peaceful, pacified, and thankless,
30 Into the burning bowels of this earth?

Was it cowardice, that I dared not kill him?
Was it perversity, that I longed to talk to him?

---

3. Mt. Etna, a volcano.

Was it humility, to feel so honoured?
I felt so honoured.

35 And yet those voices:
If you were not afraid, you would kill him!

And truly I was afraid, I was most afraid,
But even so, honoured still more
That he should seek my hospitality
40 From out the dark door of the secret earth.

He drank enough
And lifted his head, dreamily, as one who has drunken,
And flickered his tongue like a forked night on the air, so black,
Seeming to lick his lips,
45 And looked around like a god, unseeing, into the air,
And slowly turned his head,
And slowly, very slowly, as if thrice adream,
Proceeded to draw his slow length curving round
And climb again the broken bank of my wall-face.

50 And as he put his head into that dreadful hole,
And as he slowly drew up, snake-easing his shoulders, and entered
        farther,
A sort of horror, a sort of protest against his withdrawing into that
        horrid black hole,
Deliberately going into the blackness, and slowly drawing himself
        after,
Overcame me now his back was turned.

55 I looked round, I put down my pitcher,
I picked up a clumsy log
And threw it at the water-trough with a clatter.

I think it did not hit him,
But suddenly that part of him that was left behind convulsed in
        undignified haste.
60 Writhed like lightning, and was gone
Into the black hole, the earth-lipped fissure in the wall-front,
At which, in the intense still noon, I stared with fascination.

And immediately I regretted it.
I thought how paltry, how vulgar, what a mean act!
65 I despised myself and the voices of my accursed human education.

And I thought of the albatross[4]
And I wished he would come back, my snake.

For he seemed to me again like a king,
Like a king in exile, uncrowned in the underworld,
70 Now due to be crowned again.

4. In Samuel Taylor Coleridge's "Rime of the Ancient Mariner" (see p. 812).

And so, I missed my chance with one of the lords
Of life.[5]
And I have something to expiate;
A pettiness.

Taormina.
1923

Elemental

Why don't people leave off being lovable
Or thinking they are lovable, or wanting to be lovable,
And be a bit elemental instead?

Since man is made up of the elements
5   Fire, and rain, and air, and live loam
And none of these is lovable
But elemental,
Man is lop-sided on the side of the angels.

I wish men would get back their balance among the elements
10 And be a bit more fiery, as incapable of telling lies
As fire is.
I wish they'd be true to their own variation, as water is,
Which goes through all the stages of steam and stream and ice
Without losing its head.

15 I am sick of lovable people,
Somehow they are a lie.

1929

Self-Protection

When science starts to be interpretive
It is more unscientific even than mysticism.

To make self-preservation and self-protection the first law of existence
Is about as scientific as making suicide the first law of existence,
5   And amounts to very much the same thing.

A nightingale singing at the top of his voice
Is neither hiding himself nor preserving himself nor propagating his
    species;
He is giving himself away in every sense of the word;
And obviously, it is the culminating point of his existence.

---

5. Cf. George Meredith, "Modern Love," 30, line 7 (p. 1108).

10 A tiger is striped and golden for his own glory.
He would certainly be much more invisible if he were grey-green.
And I don't suppose the ichthyosaurus sparkled like the
      humming-bird,
No doubt he was khaki-colored with muddy protective colouration,
So why didn't he survive?

15 As a matter of fact, the only creatures that seem to survive
Are those that give themselves away in flash and sparkle
And gay flicker of joyful life;
Those that go glittering abroad
With a bit of splendour.

20 Even mice play quite beautifully at shadows,
And some of them are brilliantly piebald.°   *of different colors*

I expect the dodo looked like a clod,
A drab and dingy bird.

1929

Trees in the Garden

Ah in the thunder air
How still the trees are!

And the lime-tree, lovely and tall, every leaf silent
Hardly looses even a last breath of perfume.

5 And the ghostly, creamy coloured little tree of leaves
White, ivory white among the rambling greens
How evanescent, variegated elder, she hesitates on the green grass
As if, in another moment, she would disappear
With all her grace of foam!

10 And the larch that is only a column, it goes up too tall to see:
And the balsam-pines that are blue with the grey-blue blueness of
      things from the sea,
And the young copper beech, its leaves red-rosy at the ends
How still they are together, they stand so still
In the thunder air, all strangers to one another
15 As the green grass glows upwards, strangers in the garden.

Lichtental.[6]

1932

---

6. A village near Baden-Baden, in south Germany, where Lawrence wrote the poem.

The English Are So Nice!

The English are so nice
So awfully nice
They are the nicest people in the world.

And what's more, they're very nice about being nice
5   About your being nice as well!
If you're not nice they soon make you feel it.

Americans and French and Germans and so on
They're all very well
But they're not *really* nice, you know.
10 They're not nice in *our* sense of the word, are they now?

That's why one doesn't have to take them seriously.
We must be nice to them, of course,
Of course, naturally.
But it doesn't really matter what you say to them,
15 They don't really understand
You can just say anything to them:
Be nice, you know, just nice
But you must never take them seriously, they wouldn't understand,
Just be nice, you know! oh, fairly nice,
20 Not too nice of course, they take advantage
But nice enough, just nice enough
To let them feel they're not quite as nice as they might be.

1932

Andraitx⁷—Pomegranate Flowers

It is June, it is June
The pomegranates are in flower,
The peasants are bending cutting the bearded wheat.

The pomegranates are in flower
5   Beside the high road, past the deathly dust,
And even the sea is silent in the sun.

Short gasps of flame in the green of night, way off
The pomegranates are in flower,
Small sharp red fires in the night of leaves.

10 And noon is suddenly dark, is lustrous, is silent and dark
Men are unseen, beneath the shading hats;
Only, from out the foliage of the secret loins

---

7. A town on the island of Majorca, Spain.

Red flamelets here and there reveal
A man, a woman there.

1932

Bavarian Gentians[8]

Not every man has gentians in his house
in Soft September, at slow, sad Michaelmas.[9]

Bavarian gentians, big and dark, only dark
darkening the daytime, torch-like with the smoking blueness of
    Pluto's gloom,[1]
5 ribbed and torch-like, with their blaze of darkness spread blue
down flattening into points, flattened under the sweep of white day
torch-flower of the blue-smoking darkness, Pluto's dark-blue daze,
black lamps from the halls of Dis, burning dark blue,
giving off darkness, blue darkness, as Demeter's pale lamps give off
    light,
10 lead me then, lead the way.

Reach me a gentian, give me a torch!
let me guide myself with the blue, forked torch of this flower
down the darker and darker stairs, where blue is darkened on
    blueness
even where Persephone goes, just now, from the frosted September
15 to the sightless realm where darkness is awake upon the dark
and Persephone herself is but a voice
or a darkness invisible enfolded in the deeper dark
of the arms Plutonic, and pierced with the passion of dense gloom,
among the splendour of torches of darkness, shedding darkness on
    the lost bride and her groom.

1932

The Ship of Death[2]

1

Now it is autumn and the falling fruit
and the long journey towards oblivion.

---

8. Herbs with striking blue flowers.
9. September 29, the feast day celebrating St.
Michael the Archangel.
1. Pluto (Greek Hades), also known as Dis (line
8), was the Roman god of the underworld. He
abducted Persephone (Roman Proserpine), the
daughter of Demeter (Roman Ceres), goddess of
growing vegetation and living nature. Persephone
ruled with him as queen of the underworld, but
returned to spend six months of each year with her
mother in the world above.
2. In *Etruscan Places* (1932), the book that
describes his visit to the Etruscan painted tombs
in central Italy in the spring of 1927, Lawrence
mentions that originally, before the tombs were pil-
laged, there would be found in the last chamber
among "the sacred treasures of the dead, the little
bronze ship that should bear [the soul of the dead]
over to the other world." He had in mind his own
imminent death.

The apples falling like great drops of dew
to bruise themselves an exit from themselves.

5 And it is time to go, to bid farewell
to one's own self, and find an exit
from the fallen self.

2

Have you built your ship of death, O have you?
O build your ship of death, for you will need it.

10 The grim frost is at hand, when the apples will fall
thick, almost thundrous, on the hardened earth.

And death is on the air like a smell of ashes!
Ah! can't you smell it?

And in the bruised body, the frightened soul
15 finds itself shrinking, wincing from the cold
that blows upon it through the orifices.

3

And can a man his own quietus° make   release from life
with a bare bodkin?[3]

With daggers, bodkins, bullets, man can make
20 a bruise or break of exit for his life;
but is that a quietus, O tell me, is it quietus?

Surely not so! for how could murder, even self-murder
ever a quietus make?

4

O let us talk of quiet that we know,
25 that we can know, the deep and lovely quiet
of a strong heart at peace!

How can we this, our own quietus, make?

5

Build then the ship of death, for you must take
the longest journey, to oblivion.

---

3. I.e., his death bring about with an unsheathed dagger? Cf. *Hamlet* 3.1.77–78.

30 And die the death, the long and painful death
     that lies between the old self and the new.

     Already our bodies are fallen, bruised, badly bruised,
     already our souls are oozing through the exit
     of the cruel bruise.

35 Already the dark and endless ocean of the end
     is washing in through the breaches of our wounds,
     already the flood is upon us.

     Oh build your ship of death, your little ark
     and furnish it with food, with little cakes, and wine
40 for the dark flight down oblivion.

6

     Piecemeal the body dies, and the timid soul
     has her footing washed away, as the dark flood rises.

     We are dying, we are dying, we are all of us dying
     and nothing will stay the death-flood rising within us
45 and soon it will rise on the world, on the outside world.

     We are dying, we are dying, piecemeal our bodies are dying
     and our strength leaves us,
     and our soul cowers naked in the dark rain over the flood,
     cowering in the last branches of the tree of our life.

7

50 We are dying, we are dying, so all we can do
     is now to be willing to die, and to build the ship
     of death to carry the soul on the longest journey.

     A little ship, with oars and food
     and little dishes, and all accoutrements
55 fitting and ready for the departing soul.

     Now launch the small ship, now as the body dies
     and life departs, launch out, the fragile soul
     in the fragile ship of courage, the ark of faith
     with its store of food and little cooking pans
60 and change of clothes,
     upon the flood's black waste
     upon the waters of the end
     upon the sea of death, where still we sail
     darkly, for we cannot steer, and have no port.

65 There is no port, there is nowhere to go
     only the deepening blackness darkening still
     blacker upon the soundless, ungurgling flood

darkness at one with darkness, up and down
and sideways utterly dark, so there is no direction any more.
70 and the little ship is there; yet she is gone.
She is not seen, for there is nothing to see her by.
She is gone! gone! and yet
somewhere she is there.
Nowhere!

8

75 And everything is gone, the body is gone
completely under, gone, entirely gone.
The upper darkness is heavy as the lower,
between them the little ship
is gone
80 she is gone.

It is the end, it is oblivion.

9

And yet out of eternity, a thread
separates itself on the blackness,
a horizontal thread
85 that fumes a little with pallor upon the dark.

Is it illusion? or does the pallor fume
A little higher?
Ah wait, wait, for there's the dawn,
the cruel dawn of coming back to life
90 out of oblivion.

Wait, wait, the little ship
drifting, beneath the deathly ashy grey
of a flood-dawn.

Wait, wait! even so, a flush of yellow
95 and strangely, O chilled wan soul, a flush of rose.

A flush of rose, and the whole thing starts again.

10

The flood subsides, and the body, like a worn sea-shell
emerges strange and lovely.
And the little ship wings home, faltering and lapsing
100 on the pink flood,
and the frail soul steps out, into her house again
filling the heart with peace.

Swings the heart renewed with peace
even of oblivion.

105   Oh build your ship of death, oh build it!
       for you will need it.
       For the voyage of oblivion awaits you.

1929–30   1932

EZRA POUND
1885–1972

Portrait d'une Femme[1]

    Your mind and you are our Sargasso Sea,[2]
    London has swept about you this score years
    And bright ships left you this or that in fee:
    Ideas, old gossip, oddments of all things,
5   Strange spars of knowledge and dimmed wares of price.
    Great minds have sought you—lacking someone else.
    You have been second always. Tragical?
    No. You preferred it to the usual thing:
    One dull man, dulling and uxorious,
10   One average mind—with one thought less, each year.
    Oh, you are patient, I have seen you sit
    Hours, where something might have floated up.
    And now you pay one. Yes, you richly pay.
    You are a person of some interest, one comes to you
15   And takes strange gain away:
    Trophies fished up; some curious suggestion;
    Fact that leads nowhere; and a tale or two,
    Pregnant with mandrakes,[3] or with something else
    That might prove useful and yet never proves,
20   That never fits a corner or shows use,
    Or finds its hour upon the loom of days:
    The tarnished, gaudy, wonderful old work;
    Idols and ambergris[4] and rare inlays,
    These are your riches, your great store; and yet
25   For all this sea-hoard of deciduous things,
    Strange woods half sodden, and new brighter stuff:
    In the slow float of differing light and deep,
    No! there is nothing! In the whole and all,
    Nothing that's quite your own.
30   Yet this is you.

                                                  1912

1. Portrait of a lady (French). Cf. William Carlos Williams, "Portrait of a Lady" (p. 1273)
2. A relatively calm part of the North Atlantic, named for an abundance of floating gulfweed.
3. Plants, the root of which, shaped roughly like a human body, traditionally was believed to promote female fertility.
4. Waxlike substance produced by sperm whales, used in making perfume.

The Garden

En robe de parade.[5]
—SAMAIN

Like a skein of loose silk blown against a wall
She walks by the railing of a path in Kensington Gardens,[6]
And she is dying piecemeal
    of a sort of emotional anemia.

5   And round about there is a rabble
Of the filthy, sturdy, unkillable infants of the very poor.
They shall inherit the earth.[7]

In her is the end of breeding.
Her boredom is exquisite and excessive.
10 She would like some one to speak to her,
And is almost afraid that I
    will commit that indiscretion.

1913, 1916

A Pact

I make a pact with you, Walt Whitman[8]—
I have detested you long enough.
I come to you as a grown child
Who has had a pig-headed father;
5   I am old enough now to make friends.
It was you that broke the new wood,
Now is a time for carving.
We have one sap and one root—
Let there be commerce between us.

1913, 1916

Ts'ai Chi'h[9]

The petals fall in the fountain,
   the orange-colored rose-leaves,
Their ochre clings to the stone.

1913, 1916

---

5. Dressed as for a state occasion; from "The Infanta," a poem by the French poet Albert Samain (1858–1900).
6. Extensive public gardens in a residential district of London.
7. Cf. Psalm 37.11: "But the meek shall inherit the earth; and shall delight themselves in the abundance of peace."
8. American poet (1819–1892; see pp. 1060–86).
9. More usually Ts'ao Chih, a Chinese poet (192–232) who wrote five-character poems.

In a Station of the Metro[1]

The apparition of these faces in the crowd;
Petals on a wet, black bough.

1913, 1916

The River-Merchant's Wife: a Letter[2]

While my hair was still cut straight across my forehead
I played about the front gate, pulling flowers.
You came by on bamboo stilts, playing horse,
You walked about my seat, playing with blue plums.
5 And we went on living in the village of Chokan:[3]
Two small people, without dislike or suspicion.
At fourteen I married My Lord you.
I never laughed, being bashful.
Lowering my head, I looked at the wall.
10 Called to, a thousand times, I never looked back.

At fifteen I stopped scowling,
I desired my dust to be mingled with yours
Forever and forever and forever.
Why should I climb the look out?

15 At sixteen you departed,
You went into far Ku-to-yen,[4] by the river of swirling eddies,
And you have been gone five months.
The monkeys make sorrowful noise overhead.

You dragged your feet when you went out.
20 By the gate now, the moss is grown, the different mosses,
Too deep to clear them away!
The leaves fall early this autumn, in wind.
The paired butterflies are already yellow with August
Over the grass in the West garden;
25 They hurt me. I grow older.
If you are coming down through the narrows of the river Kiang,
Please let me know beforehand,

1. Pound writes in *Gaudier-Brzeska: A Memoir* (1916) of having suddenly seen a succession of beautiful faces one day on the Paris Métro (subway), after which he tried all day to find words "as worthy, or as lovely as that sudden emotion. And that evening . . . I was still trying and I found, suddenly, the expression. I do not mean that I found words, but there came an equation . . . not in speech, but in little splotches of color. . . . The 'one-image poem' is a form of super-position, that is to say, it is one idea set on top of another. I found it useful in getting out of the impasse in which I

had been left by my metro emotion. I wrote a thirty-line poem, and destroyed it. . . . Six months later I made the following *hokku*-like sentence."
2. Adaptation from the Chinese of Li Po (701–762), named Rihaku in Japanese. Pound's work is based on notes by the American scholar Ernest Fenellosa, themselves based on interpretations by Japanese scholars.
3. Ch'ang-Kan, a suburb of Nanking.
4. Ch'üt'ang, a Chinese river called Kiang in Japanese (line 26), here treated as a place.

And I will come out to meet you
  As far as Cho-fu-Sa.[5]

By Rihaku
1915

Hugh Selwyn Mauberley

LIFE AND CONTACTS[6]

E. P. Ode pour l'election de Son Sépulchre[7]

For three years, out of key with his time,
He strove to resuscitate the dead art
Of poetry; to maintain "the sublime"
In the old sense. Wrong from the start—

5   No, hardly, but seeing he had been born
In a half savage country,[8] out of date;
Bent resolutely on wringing lilies from the acorn;
Capaneus;[9] trout for factitious° bait;   *false, artificial*

Ἴδμεν γάρ τοι πάνθ’ ὅσ’ ἐνὶ Τροίη[1]
10   Caught in the unstopped ear;
Giving the rocks small lee-way
The chopped seas held him, therefore, that year.

His true Penelope was Flaubert,[2]
He fished by obstinate isles;
15   Observed the elegance of Circe's[3] hair
Rather than the mottoes on sundials.

Unaffected by "the march of events,"
He passed from men's memory in *l'an trentiesme
De son eage;*[4] the case presents
20   No adjunct to the Muses' diadem.[5]

---

5. Chang-feng Sha, a beach several hundred miles up the river from Nanking.

6. *Hugh Selwyn Mauberley* comprises two sets of poems: the thirteen poems reprinted here ("Life and Contacts," or "Contacts and Life," as Pound subtitled a 1957 edition) and five poems that follow, headed "Mauberley (1920)." The entire volume bore an epigraph from the fourth Eclogue of the third-century Carthaginian poet Nemesianus: *Vocat aestus in umbram* (Latin, "The heat calls us into the shade").

7. Cf. Pierre de Ronsard (1524–1585), *Odes* 4.5, *"De l'élection de son sépulchre"* [French, "Concerning the choice of his tomb"], in which the poet describes the kind of burial place and the kind of fame he would like to have.

8. I.e., the United States.

9. In Aeschylus's tragedy *The Seven against Thebes* (467 B.C.E.), Capaneus swore he would sack that city despite the god Zeus and was struck dead with a thunderbolt.

1. For we know all the things that [were suffered] in Troy (Greek); Homer, *Odyssey* 12.189. From the song of the Sirens, which was meant to lure Odysseus's ship onto the rocks. Odysseus plugged his companions' ears with wax, and he alone, bound to the mast, heard the song with "unstopped ear" (line 10).

2. Gustave Flaubert (1821–1880), French realist novelist and meticulous craftsman. Penelope, the paradigmatic faithful wife, fended off suitors while Odysseus spent ten years at the siege of Troy and another ten years returning home.

3. Beautiful enchantress who seduced Odysseus; he stayed on her island for over a year.

4. In the thirty-first year of his age (French); Pound's age when his book *Lustra* was published. Adapted from the beginning of *Le Grand Testament*, by the fifteenth-century French poet François Villon: "In the thirtieth year of my age."

5. Crown. In Greek mythology, the Muses were nine sister goddesses who presided over song, poetry, and the arts and sciences.

II

The age demanded an image
Of its accelerated grimace,
Something for the modern stage,
Not, at any rate, an Attic[6] grace;

5 Not, not certainly, the obscure reveries
Of the inward gaze;
Better mendacities
Than the classics in paraphrase!

The "age demanded" chiefly a mold in plaster,
10 Made with no loss of time,
A prose kinema,[7] not, not assuredly, alabaster
Or the "sculpture" of rhyme.

III

The tea-rose tea-gown, etc.
Supplants the mousseline of Cos,[8]
The pianola° "replaces"   *player piano*
Sappho's barbitos.[9]

5 Christ follows Dionysus,[1]
Phallic and ambrosial
Made way for macerations;°   *fastings, wastings*
Caliban casts out Ariel.[2]

All things are a flowing,
10 Sage Heracleitus[3] says;
But a tawdry cheapness
Shall outlast our days.

Even the Christian beauty
Defects—after Samothrace;[4]
15 We see τὸ καλόν[5]
Decreed in the market place.

Faun's flesh is not to us,
Nor the saint's vision.
We have the press for wafer;
20 Franchise for circumcision.

---

6. Athenian; i.e., simple, pure, classical.
7. Motion (Greek); and an early spelling of *cinema* (motion pictures).
8. Greek island. *Mousseline:* fine cloth (muslin).
9. Lyrelike instrument played by the Greek lyric poet Sappho (fl. ca. 610–ca. 580 B.C.E.).
1. Greek god of fertility, wine, and poetic inspiration, whose worship included ecstatic frenzies, sexual rites, and dramatic festivals.

2. In Shakespeare's *Tempest*, Caliban is earthbound and coarse, Ariel a beautiful and imaginative spirit.
3. Greek philosopher (ca. 540–ca. 480 B.C.E.), whose teaching emphasized flux ("all things flow").
4. Greek island where a mystery cult was centered and where the famous statue *Winged Victory* was found.
5. The beautiful (Greek).

All men, in law, are equals.
Free of Pisistratus,[6]
We choose a knave or an eunuch
To rule over us.

25 O bright Apollo,
τίν᾽ ἄνδρα, τίν᾽ ἥρωα, τίνα θεόν,[7]
What god, man, or hero
Shall I place a tin wreath upon!

IV

These fought in any case,
and some believing,
                    pro domo,[8] in any case . . .

Some quick to arm,
5 some for adventure,
some from fear of weakness,
some from fear of censure,
some for love of slaughter, in imagination,
learning later . . .
10 some in fear, learning love of slaughter;

Died some, pro patria,
                    non "dulce" non "et decor" . . . [9]
walked eye-deep in hell
believing in old men's lies, then unbelieving
15 came home, home to a lie,
home to many deceits,
home to old lies and new infamy;
usury age-old and age-thick
and liars in public places.

20 Daring as never before, wastage as never before.
Young blood and high blood,
fair cheeks, and fine bodies;
fortitude as never before

frankness as never before,
25 disillusions as never told in the old days,
hysterias, trench confessions,
laughter out of dead bellies.

V

There died a myriad,
And of the best, among them,

---

6. Three times the absolute ruler of Athens (d. 527 B.C.E.), he made the city the foremost power in Ionia and supported the arts.
7. What man, what hero, what god (Greek); cf. the Greek poet Pindar's Olympian Ode 2.2: "What god, what hero, what man shall we loudly praise?"
8. For home (Latin).
9. For one's native land, not sweetly, not gloriously (Latin); cf. the Roman poet Horace's Odes 3.2.13: "Sweet and fitting it is to die for one's country."

For an old bitch gone in the teeth,
For a botched civilization,

5   Charm, smiling at the good mouth,
Quick eyes gone under earth's lid,

For two gross of broken statues,
For a few thousand battered books.

Yeux Glauques[1]

Gladstone[2] was still respected,
When John Ruskin produced
"King's Treasuries";[3] Swinburne
And Rossetti still abused.[4]

5   Fetid Buchanan lifted up his voice
When that faun's head of hers
Became a pastime for
Painters and adulterers.

The Burne-Jones cartons[5]
10 Have preserved her eyes;
Still, at the Tate, they teach
Cophetua to rhapsodize;

Thin like brook water,
With a vacant gaze.
15 The English Rubaiyat was stillborn[6]
In those days.

The thin, clear gaze, the same
Still darts out faunlike from the half-ruined face,
Questing and passive. . . .
20 "Ah, poor Jenny's case"[7] . . .

Bewildered that a world
Shows no surprise
At her last maquero's[8]
Adulteries.

1. Sea-green eyes (French). Pound's poem focuses on the eyes of Elizabeth Siddal (d. 1862), wife of the English poet and painter Dante Gabriel Rossetti (1828–1882) and the model used for many of his paintings as well as for those of other Pre-Raphaelite painters, including Edward Burne-Jones (1833–1898), in whose painting *King Cophetua and the Beggar Maid* (1884; now in the Tate Gallery, London; see the third stanza below) she appears as the beggar maid.
2. William Ewart Gladstone (1809–1898), active in British politics for over sixty years, was four times prime minister.
3. "Sesame. Of King's Treasuries" is the first lecture in *Sesame and Lilies* (1865), in which the English critic John Ruskin (1819–1900) accuses the English of having "despised literature . . . . science . . . Art! . . . Nature . . . compassion."
4. Rossetti and the English poet Algernon Swinburne (1837–1909) were abused by the Scottish writer Robert W. Buchanan (1841–1901) in "The Fleshly School of Poetry" (1871).
5. Cartoons (French); preliminary sketches.
6. Edward FitzGerald's translation of *The Rubáiyát of Omar Khayyám* (see p. 961), first published in 1859, became popular only when the Pre-Raphaelites "discovered" it.
7. Buchanan had particularly attacked Rossetti's "Jenny," a sympathetic portrayal of a prostitute.
8. Perhaps a pun, suggesting both one who lacquers pictures (from the Spanish verb *maquear*) and a pimp (from the French noun *maquereau*).

"*Siena Mi Fe'; Disfecemi Maremma*"[9]

Among the pickled fetuses and bottled bones,
Engaged in perfecting the catalogue,
I found the last scion of the
Senatorial families of Strasbourg, Monsieur Verog.[1]

5   For two hours he talked of Gallifet;[2]
Of Dowson; of the Rhymers' Club;[3]
Told me how Johnson (Lionel) died[4]
By falling from a high stool in a pub . . .

But showed no trace of alcohol
10   At the autopsy, privately performed—
Tissue preserved—the pure mind
Arose toward Newman[5] as the whiskey warmed.

Dowson found harlots cheaper than hotels;
Headlam for uplift; Image[6] impartially imbued
15   With raptures for Bacchus, Terpsichore[7] and the Church.
So spoke the author of "The Dorian Mood,"

M. Verog, out of step with the decade,
Detached from his contemporaries,
Neglected by the young,
20   Because of these reveries.

Brennbaum[8]

The skylike limpid eyes,
The circular infant's face,
The stiffness from spats to collar
Never relaxing into grace;

5   The heavy memories of Horeb, Sinai and the forty years[9]
Showed only when the daylight fell

9. Siena made me; the Maremma undid me (Italian; *Purgatorio* 5.134). Words spoken to Dante by the spirit of Pia de' Tolomei, encountered in Purgatory among those who died by violence and without absolution. She was murdered by her husband. The line carries with it the idea of exile from one's native place; the subject of Pound's poem had been born in Alsace.
1. Pound's model for Verog was the poet and librarian of the Royal College of Surgeons Victor Gustav Plarr (1863–1929), author of the poem "In the Dorian-Mood" (line 16). His friends included the poets Ernest Dowson (1867–1900; see pp. 1211–12) and Lionel Johnson (1867–1902). He, like them, was a member of the Rhymers' Club (see line 6, note 2); he published a memoir of Dowson. Pound edited Johnson's *Poetical Works* (1915).
2. Marquis de Galliffet (1830–1909), a French general who led a cavalry charge at the Battle of Sedan (1870), in the Franco-Prussian War.
3. London literary club founded in 1891 by the Irish poet William Butler Yeats (1865–1939; see pp. 1188–1211) and his friends.
4. I.e., from a fall in the street.
5. John Henry Newman (1801–1890), the most famous Victorian convert to Roman Catholicism (and eventually a cardinal). Johnson was also an ardent convert.
6 Selwyn Image (1849–1930), artist, poet, and clergyman; the Reverend Stewart Headlam (1847–1924), liberal clergyman who was for many years a vicar in the East End of London, writer on social and religious questions. Both members of the Rhymers' Club, they founded the Church and Stage Guild.
7. Greek Muse of the dance. *Bacchus:* Roman god of wine.
8. Often identified as Max Beerbohm (1872–1956), English critic and caricaturist, who was known as "the Incomparable Max." Pound mistakenly thought he was Jewish.
9. After the Exodus from Egypt, the Israelites, led by Moses, spent forty years in the wilderness. At

Level across the face
Of Brennbaum "The Impeccable."

Mr. Nixon[1]

In the cream gilded cabin of his steam yacht
Mr. Nixon advised me kindly, to advance with fewer
Dangers of delay. "Consider
               Carefully the reviewer.

5   "I was as poor as you are;
"When I began I got, of course,
"Advance on royalties, fifty at first," said Mr. Nixon,
"Follow me, and take a column,
"Even if you have to work free.

10 "Butter reviewers. From fifty to three hundred
"I rose in eighteen months;
"The hardest nut I had to crack
"Was Dr. Dundas.

"I never mentioned a man but with the view
15 "Of selling my own works.
"The tip's a good one, as for literature
"It gives no man a sinecure.

"And no one knows, at sight, a masterpiece.
"And give up verse, my boy,
20 "There's nothing in it."

. . . .

Likewise a friend of Bloughram's[2] once advised me:
Don't kick against the pricks,[3]
Accept opinion. The "Nineties"° tried your game   *1890s*
And died, there's nothing in it.

X

Beneath the sagging roof
The stylist[4] has taken shelter,
Unpaid, uncelebrated,
At last from the world's welter

5 Nature receives him;
With a placid and uneducated mistress

Horeb, God spoke to Moses from a burning bush
(Exodus 3.1–4); on Mt. Sinai, Moses received the
Ten Commandments (Exodus 19–20).
1. Pound wrote that Nixon "is a fictitious name for
a real person"—perhaps the English novelist
Arnold Bennett (1867–1931), who owned a yacht.
2. The speaker in "Bishop Blougram's Apology"
(1855), by the English poet Robert Browning

(1812–1889; see pp. 1009–41), is more practical
than devotional in his beliefs.
3. Cf. Jesus' words to Saul: "It is hard for thee to
kick against the pricks" (Acts 9.5).
4. Probably based on the English writer Ford
Madox Ford (1873–1939), a friend of Pound and
an influence on his writing style.

He exercises his talents
And the soil meets his distress.

The haven from sophistications and contentions
10 Leaks through its thatch;
He offers succulent cooking;
The door has a creaking latch.

XI

"Conservatrix of Milésien"[5]
Habits of mind and feeling,
Possibly. But in Ealing[6]
With the most bank-clerkly of Englishmen?

5 No, "Milésian" is an exaggeration.
No instinct has survived in her
Older than those her grandmother
Told her would fit her station.

XII

"Daphne with her thighs in bark
Stretches toward me her leafy hands,"[7]—
Subjectively. In the stuffed-satin drawing room
I await The Lady Valentine's commands,

5 Knowing my coat has never been
Of precisely the fashion
To stimulate, in her,
A durable passion;

Doubtful, somewhat, of the value
10 Of well-gowned approbation
Of literary effort,
But never of The Lady Valentine's vocation:

Poetry, her border of ideas,
The edge, uncertain, but a means of blending
15 With other strata
Where the lower and higher have ending;

A hook to catch the Lady Jane's attention,
A modulation toward the theatre,
Also, in the case of revolution,

5. I.e., preserver of Milesian tradition; cf. the phrase "Women, conservers of Milesian traditions," from the short story "Stratages," by the French writer Rémy de Gourmont (1858–1915). The Greek city Miletus, a center of literature and philosophy, was also associated with the erotic stories of Aristides' *Milesian Tales* (second century B.C.E.), which have not survived and so cannot be conserved.

6. Staid, middle-class London suburb.
7. A translation of two lines from "Le Château de Souvenir," by the French poet Théophile Gautier (1811–1872). In Greek mythology, Daphne, pursued by the god Apollo, was turned into a laurel to enable her to escape.

20   A possible friend and comforter.

. . . .

Conduct, on the other hand, the soul
"Which the highest cultures have nourished"[8]
To Fleet St. where
Dr. Johnson[9] flourished;

25   Beside this thoroughfare
The sale of half-hose has
Long since superseded the cultivation
Of Pierian[1] roses.

Envoi (1919)

Go, dumb-born book,[2]
Tell her that sang me once that song of Lawes:
Hadst thou but song
As thou hast subjects known,
5   *Then were there cause in thee that should condone*
Even my faults that heavy upon me lie,
And build her glories their longevity.

Tell her that sheds
Such treasure in the air,
10   *Recking naught else but that her graces give*
Life to the moment,
I would bid them live
As roses might, in magic amber laid,
Red overwrought with orange and all made
15   *One substance and one color*
Braving time.

Tell her that goes
With song upon her lips
But sings not out the song, nor knows
20   *The maker of it, some other mouth,*
May be as fair as hers,
Might, in new ages, gain her worshipers,
When our two dusts with Waller's shall be laid,
Siftings on siftings in oblivion,
25   *Till change hath broken down*
All things save Beauty alone.

1920

8. A translation of two lines from "Complainte de
Pianos," by the French poet Jules Laforgue (1860–
1887).
9. Samuel Johnson (1709–1784), poet, journalist,
critic, essayist, lexicographer, and the dominant
English man of letters of the mid-eighteenth cen-
tury. *Fleet Street*: the center of London newspaper
publishing.
1. Pieria is a region of northern Greece associated

with the Muses, nine sister goddesses in Greek
mythology who presided over song, poetry, and the
arts and sciences.
2. Here and throughout this poem, Pound echoes
Edmund Waller's "Song" (see p. 393), which
begins "Go, lovely rose!" and which was set to
music by the English composer Henry Lawes
(1596–1662).

Medallion[3]

Luini[4] in porcelain!
The grand piano
Utters a profane
Protest with her clear soprano.

5   The sleek head emerges
From the gold-yellow frock
As Anadyomene[5] in the opening
Pages of Reinach.

Honey-red, closing the face-oval,
10   A basket-work of braids which seem as if they were
Spun in King Minos'[6] hall
From metal, or intractable amber;

The face-oval beneath the glaze,
Bright in its suave bounding-line, as,
15   Beneath half-watt rays,
The eyes turn topaz.

1920

FROM THE CANTOS

I[7]

And then went down to the ship,
Set keel to breakers, forth on the godly sea, and
We set up mast and sail on that swart ship,
Bore sheep aboard her, and our bodies also
5   Heavy with weeping, and winds from sternward
Bore us out onward with bellying canvas,
Circe's this craft, the trim-coifed goddess.[8]
Then sat we amidships, wind jamming the tiller,

---

3. This poem was originally an "Envoi (1919)"–like (see above) final section of Pound's "1920 (Mauberley)," itself an extension of and comment on "Hugh Selwyn Mauberley: Life and Contacts."
4. Bernardino Luini (ca. 1480–1532), Italian painter.
5. Rising [from the sea] (Greek); *Aphroditē anaduomenē* was a famous painting by Apelles (fourth century B.C.E.), and similar depictions of the goddess in sculpture are illustrated in Salomon Reinach's *Apollo: An Illustrated History of Art throughout the Ages* (1904).
6. In Greek mythology, king of Crete.
7. The opening of Pound's *Cantos*, the complex

poem of epic proportions on which he worked for over fifty years, is taken up, through line 67, with Pound's translation of the beginning of book 11 of Homer's *Odyssey*, not directly from the Greek but from the sixteenth-century Latin translation of Andreas Divus (see line 68 and note 3). Book 11 describes Odysseus's trip to the underworld to consult the spirit of Tiresias, the blind Theban prophet, who will give him instructions for the final stages of his return to his home island, Ithaca.
8. Circe was the enchantress with whom Odysseus lived for over a year and who told him to seek Tiresias's advice.

Thus with stretched sail, we went over sea till day's end.
10 Sun to his slumber, shadows o'er all the ocean,
Came we then to the bounds of deepest water,
To the Kimmerian lands,⁹ and peopled cities
Covered with close-webbed mist, unpierced ever
With glitter of sun-rays
15 Nor with stars stretched, nor looking back from heaven
Swartest night stretched over wretched men there.
The ocean flowing backward, came we then to the place
Aforesaid by Circe.
Here did they rites, Perimedes and Eurylochus,¹
20 And drawing sword from my hip
I dug the ell-square pitkin;²
Poured we libations unto each the dead,
First mead³ and then sweet wine, water mixed with white flour.
Then prayed I many a prayer to the sickly death's-heads;
25 As set in Ithaca, sterile bulls of the best
For sacrifice, heaping the pyre with goods,
A sheep to Tiresias only, black and a bell-sheep.⁴
Dark blood flowed in the fosse,°   trench, ditch
Souls out of Erebus,⁵ cadaverous dead, of brides
30 Of youths and of the old who had borne much;
Souls stained with recent tears, girls tender,
Men many, mauled with bronze lance heads,
Battle spoil, bearing yet dreory⁶ arms,
These many crowded about me; with shouting,
35 Pallor upon me, cried to my men for more beasts;
Slaughtered the herds, sheep slain of bronze;
Poured ointment, cried to the gods,
To Pluto the strong, and praised Proserpine;⁷
Unsheathed the narrow sword,
40 I sat to keep off the impetuous impotent dead,
Till I should hear Tiresias.
But first Elpenor⁸ came, our friend Elpenor,
Unburied, cast on the wide earth,
Limbs that we left in the house of Circe,
45 Unwept, unwrapped in sepulchre, since toils urged other.
Pitiful spirit. And I cried in hurried speech:
"Elpenor, how art thou come to this dark coast?
"Cam'st thou afoot, outstripping seamen?"
          And he in heavy speech:

9. The Cimmerians were a mythical people living in darkness and mist on the farthest borders of the known world.
1. Two of Odysseus's men.
2. Small, square pit, one ell (forty-five inches) on each side.
3. Alcoholic drink made from fermented honey.
4. The sheep that leads the herd, here likened to Tiresias.
5. A dark place in the underworld, on the way to Hades.
6. Bloody (from the Old English *dreorig*).
7. Roman name for Persephone, goddess of regeneration and wife of Pluto (Roman Dis), god of the underworld.
8. The youngest of Odysseus's men, he had drunkenly fallen asleep on a loft on the eve of their departure from her island and fell to his death when he tried to climb down a ladder.

50   "Ill fate and abundant wine. I slept in Circe's ingle.°   *nook, corner*
    "Going down the long ladder unguarded,
    "I fell against the buttress,
    "Shattered the nape-nerve, the soul sought Avernus.[9]
    "But thou, O King, I bid remember me, unwept, unburied,
55   "Heap up mine arms, be° tomb by sea-bord, and inscribed: *make my*
    "*A man of no fortune, and with a name to come.*
    "And set my oar up, that I swung mid fellows."

    And Anticlea[1] came, whom I beat off, and then Tiresias Theban,
    Holding his golden wand, knew me, and spoke first:
60   "A second time?[2] why? man of ill star,
    "Facing the sunless dead and this joyless region?
    "Stand from the fosse, leave me my bloody bever°   *drink*
    "For soothsay."
          And I stepped back,
65 And he strong with the blood, said then: "Odysseus
    "Shalt return through spiteful Neptune, over dark seas,
    "Lose all companions." And then Anticlea came.
    Lie quiet Divus. I mean, that is Andreas Divus,[3]
    In officina Wecheli, 1538, out of Homer.
70 And he sailed, by Sirens and thence outward and away
    And unto Circe.[4]
          Venerandam,[5]
    In the Cretan's phrase, with the golden crown, Aphrodite,
    Cypri munimenta sortita est, mirthful, oricalchi,[6] with golden
75 Girdles and breast bands, thou with dark eyelids
    Bearing the golden bough of Argicida. So that:[7]

1921   1930

---

9. A lake near Naples believed by the ancients to be the entrance to the underworld.
1. Odysseus's mother; according to the *Odyssey*, Odysseus wept at seeing her, but obeyed Circe's instruction to speak to no one until he had heard Tiresias.
2. They first saw each other on Earth.
3. The sixteenth-century Italian whose translation of the *Odyssey* had been published "in officina Wecheli," at the printing shop of Chrétien Wechel, Paris, in 1538.
4. After this visit to the underworld, Odysseus returned to Circe and then, forewarned by her, successfully sailed past the Sirens.
5. Worthy of worship (Latin); applied to Aphrodite, Greek goddess of love and beauty. This, like the Latin words and phrases in the next lines, derives from a Latin translation of two Hymns to Aphrodite (among the so-called Homeric Hymns, dating from the eighth to the sixth century B.C.E). This translation by Georgius Dartona Cretensis ("the Cretan," line 73) was contained in the volume in which Pound had found Divus's translation of the *Odyssey*. One hymn begins with the words

that figure, in Latin or in English, in the closing lines of the Canto: "Reverend golden-crowned beautiful Aphrodite I shall sing, who has received as her lot the citadels of all sea-girt Cyprus. . . ."
6. Of copper. I.e., Aphrodite has received earrings, flower-shaped, of copper and gold.
7. The Canto ends on the colon, going immediately into Canto II, which begins with the words "Hang it all, Robert Browning, / There can be but one 'Sordello.' " *Argicida:* an epithet for Hermes, the gods' messenger and "slayer of Argos" (the many-eyed herdsman set to watch Io); from the other Homeric Hymn, which recounts the union of Aphrodite and Anchises, a union that led to the birth of the Trojan leader Aeneas. Aphrodite, deceiving Anchises at first, says that she is a mortal maiden, that the "slayer of Argos, with wand of gold" has brought her to be his wife. Before descending to the underworld, Aeneas offered the golden bough to Proserpine; it is sacred to the goddess Diana, though Pound seems to associate it with Aphrodite, "slayer of Argi" (Greeks) during the Trojan War.

XLV

With *Usura*[8]

With usura hath no man a house of good stone
each block cut smooth and well fitting
that design might cover their face,
with usura
5   hath no man a painted paradise on his church wall
harpes et luthes[9]
or where virgin receiveth message
and halo projects from incision,
with usura
10   seeth no man Gonzaga his heirs and his concubines[1]
no picture is made to endure nor to live with
but it is made to sell and sell quickly
with usura, sin against nature,
is thy bread ever more of stale rags
15   is thy bread dry as paper,
with no mountain wheat, no strong flour
with usura the line grows thick
with usura is no clear demarcation
and no man can find site for his dwelling.
20   Stone cutter is kept from his stone
weaver is kept from his loom
WITH USURA
wool comes not to market
sheep bringeth no gain with usura
25   Usura is a murrain,° usura   plague
blunteth the needle in the maid's hand
and stoppeth the spinner's cunning. Pietro Lombardo[2]
came not by usura
Duccio[3] came not by usura
30   nor Pier della Francesca; Zuan Bellin' not by usura
nor was "La Calunnia"[4] painted.
Came not by usura Angelico; came not Ambrogio Praedis,
Came no church of cut stone signed: *Adamo me fecit.*[5]
Not by usura St Trophime
35   Not by usura Saint Hilaire,[6]
Usura rusteth the chisel

8. Usury (Latin). "N.B. Usury: a charge for the use of purchasing power, levied without regard to production; often without regard to the possibilities of production. (Hence the failure of the Medici bank)" [Pound's note]. *Medici bank:* operated 1397–1494 by the Medici family of Florence. Pound felt that the legalizing of usury during the Reformation had profound, negative effects on society.
9. Allusion to a poem of the *Grand Testament*, by the French poet François Villon (1431–1463?): "Painted paradise where there are harps and lutes."
1. *Gonzaga, His Heirs and Concubines* is a painting of a powerful patron of Mantua, Francesco Gonzaga (1444–1483), by the Italian painter Andrea Mantegna (1431–1506).

2. Italian architect and sculptor (1435–1515). He and other artists in the poem were supported by patrons.
3. Agostino di Duccio (1418?–1481), Italian sculptor.
4. Calumny (Italian); title of painting by Sandro Botticelli (1444–1510). Piero della Francesca (ca. 1420–1492) and Giovanni Bellini (ca. 1430–1516), Italian painters.
5. Adam made me (Latin); a sculptor's inscription in the Church of San Zeno, Verona, Italy. Fra Angelico (ca. 1400–1455) and Ambrogio Praedis (1455?–1508), Italian painters.
6. Church in Poitiers, France. *St Trophime:* church in Arles, France.

It rusteth the craft and the craftsman
It gnaweth the thread in the loom
None learneth to weave gold in her pattern;
40   Azure hath a canker by usura; cramoisi[7] is unbroidered
Emerald findeth no Memling[8]
Usura slayeth the child in the womb
It stayeth the young man's courting
It hath brought palsey to bed, lyeth
45   between the young bride and her bridegroom
                    CONTRA NATURAM[9]
They have brought whores for Eleusis[1]
Corpses are set to banquet
at behest of usura.

                                                                1937

ELINOR WYLIE
1885–1928

Full Moon

My bands of silk and miniver°   *white fur*
Momently grew heavier;
The black gauze was beggarly thin;
The ermine muffled mouth and chin;
5   I could not suck the moonlight in.

Harlequin in lozenges[1]
Of love and hate, I walked in these
Striped and ragged rigmaroles;[2]
Along the pavement my footsoles
10   Trod warily on living coals.

Shouldering the thoughts I loathed,
In their corrupt disguises clothed,
Mortality I could not tear
From my ribs, to leave them bare
15   Ivory in silver air.

There I walked, and there I raged;
The spiritual savage caged
Within my skeleton, raged afresh
To feel, behind a carnal mesh,
20   The clean bones crying in the flesh.

                                                                1923

7. Crimson cloth (French).
8. Hans Memling (1430?–1495), Flemish painter.
9. Against nature (Latin); phrase used in Aristotle's *Politics* to describe usury.
1. Town in ancient Greece known for spring fertility rites (involving priestesses—Pound substitutes "whores").

1. Diamond shapes. *Harlequin:* a buffoon, a character in the Italian *commedia dell'arte,* or one dressed in fabric of certain variegated patterns.
2. Literally, confused or meaningless statements.

Doomsday

The end of everything approaches;
I hear it coming
Loud as the wheels of painted coaches
On turnpikes drumming;
5   Loud as the pomp of plumy hearses,
Or pennoned charges;[3]
Loud as when every oar reverses
Venetian barges;
Loud as the caves of covered bridges
10   Fulfilled with rumble
Of hooves; and loud as cloudy ridges
When glaciers tumble;
Like creeping thunder this continues
Diffused and distant,
15   Loud in our ears and in our sinews,
Insane, insistent;
Loud as a lion scorning carrion
Further and further;
Loud as the ultimate loud clarion
20   Or the first murther.°   murder

1932

H. D. (HILDA DOOLITTLE)
1886–1961

Sea Rose

Rose, harsh rose,
marred and with stint of petals,
meager flower, thin,
sparse of leaf,

5   more precious
than a wet rose
single on a stem—
you are caught in the drift.

Stunted, with small leaf,
10   you are flung on the sand,
you are lifted
in the crisp sand
that drives in the wind.

---

3. Military charges with streaming banners.

Can the spice-rose
15   drip such acrid fragrance
hardened in a leaf?

1916

Sea Violet

The white violet
is scented on its stalk,
the sea-violet
fragile as agate,
5   lies fronting all the wind
among the torn shells
on the sand-bank.

The greater blue violets
flutter on the hill,
10   but who would change for these
who would change for these
one root of the white sort?

Violet
your grasp is frail
15   on the edge of the sand-hill,
but you catch the light—
frost, a star edges with its fire.

1916

Helen[1]

All Greece hates
the still eyes in the white face,
the luster as of olives
where she stands,
5   And the white hands.

All Greece reviles
the wan face when she smiles,
hating it deeper still
when it grows wan and white,
10   remembering past enchantments
and past ills.

---

1. In Greek mythology, the beautiful wife of the Greek leader Menelaus; abducted by the Trojan prince Paris, she was blamed for the Trojan War, waged to regain her.

Greece sees unmoved,
God's daughter, born of love,[2]
the beauty of cool feet
15 and slenderest knees,
could love indeed the maid,
only if she were laid,
white ash amid funereal cypresses.

1924

Wine Bowl

I will rise
from my troth
with the dead,
I will sweeten my cup
5 and my bread
with a gift;
I will chisel a bowl for the wine,
for the white wine
and red;
10 I will summon a Satyr to dance,[3]
a Centaur,
a Nymph
and a Faun;
I will picture
15 a warrior King,
a Giant,
a Naiad,
a Monster;
I will cut round the rim of the crater,[4]
20 some simple
familiar thing,
vine leaves
or the sea-swallow's wing;
I will work at each separate part
25 till my mind is worn out
and my heart:
in my skull,
where the vision had birth,
will come wine,
30 would pour song
of the hot earth,
of the flower and the sweet

2. Helen was said to be the daughter of Zeus, ruler of the gods, and Leda, a mortal woman, whom Zeus raped in the guise of a swan.
3. Lines 10–18 evoke figures from classical mythology. Nymphs were minor nature goddesses; those who lived in springs, fountains, rivers, and lakes were called naiads. In Greek mythology, satyrs were woodland spirits in the form of men with the legs of goats and with pointed ears or horns. The Romans identified satyrs with their own woodland spirits, the fauns. Centaurs had the faces and chests of men and the bodies of horses. Satyrs are usually associated with lechery; centaurs, with savagery.
4. I.e., a *kratēr,* the usual Greek term for a drinking bowl.

of the hill,
thyme,
35   meadow-plant,
grass-blade and sorrel;
in my skull,
from which vision took flight,
will come wine
40   will pour song
of the cool night,
of the silver and blade of the moon,
of the star,
of the sun's kiss at midnoon;
45   I will challenge the reed-pipe
and stringed lyre,[5]
to sing sweeter,
pipe wilder,
praise louder
50   the fragrance and sweet
of the wine jar,
till each lover
must summon another,
to proffer a rose
55   where all flowers are,
in the depths of the exquisite crater;
flower will fall upon flower
till the red shower
inflame all
60   with intimate fervor;
till:
men who travel afar
will look up,
sensing grape
65   and hill-slope
in the cup;
men who sleep by the wood
will arise,
hearing ripple and fall
70   of the tide,
being drawn by the spell of the sea;
the bowl will ensnare and enchant
men who crouch by the hearth
till they want
75   but the riot of stars in the night;
those who dwell far inland
will seek ships;
the deep-sea fisher,
plying his nets,
80   will forsake them
for wheat-sheaves and loam;
men who wander

---

5. The pipe was the instrument of Pan, Greek god of forests, pastures, flocks, and herds; the lyre was the instrument of Apollo, Greek and Roman god of sunlight, prophecy, music, and poetry.

will yearn for their home,
men at home
85　will depart.

I will rise
from my troth with the dead,
I will sweeten my cup
and my bread
90　*with a gift;*
I will chisel a bowl for the wine,
for the white wine
and red.

1931

From The Walls Do Not Fall[6]

[1]

An incident here and there,
and rails gone (for guns)
from your (and my) old town square:

mist and mist-grey, no colour,
5　still the Luxor[7] bee, chick and hare
pursue unalterable purpose

in green, rose-red, lapis;
they continue to prophesy
from the stone papyrus:

10　there, as here, ruin opens
the tomb, the temple; enter,
there as here, there are no doors:

the shrine lies open to the sky,
the rain falls, here, there
15　sand drifts; eternity endures:

ruin everywhere, yet as the fallen roof
leaves the sealed room
open to the air,

6. The first of three book-length poems (the other two being *Tribute to the Angels* and *The Flowering of the Rod*) that would be known as H. D.'s war trilogy. "The parallel between ancient Egypt and 'ancient' London is obvious. In I (*The Walls Do Not Fall*) the 'fallen roof leaves the sealed room open to the air' is of course true of our own house of life—outer violence touching the deepest hidden subconscious terrors, etc. and we see so much of our past 'on show,' as it were 'another sliced wall where poor utensils show like rare objects in a museum' " (H. D., in a letter to her eventual literary executor, the American scholar Norman Holmes Pearson).
7. An Egyptian town on the Nile, near the ruins of ancient Thebes. Representations of the bee, chick, and hare appear on the Temple of Karnak, in Thebes.

so, through our desolation,
20   thoughts stir, inspiration stalks us
through gloom:

unaware, Spirit announces the Presence;
shivering overtakes us,
as of old, Samuel:[8]

25   trembling at a known street-corner,
we know not nor are known;
the Pythian[9] pronounces—we pass on

to another cellar, to another sliced wall
where poor utensils show
30   like rare objects in a museum;

Pompeii[1] has nothing to teach us,
we know crack of volcanic fissure,
slow flow of terrible lava,

pressure on heart, lungs, the brain
35   about to burst its brittle case
(what the skull can endure!):

over us, Apocryphal[2] fire,
under us, the earth sway, dip of a floor,
slope of a pavement

40   where men roll, drunk
with a new bewilderment,
sorcery, bedevilment:

the bone-frame was made for
no such shock knit within terror,
45   yet the skeleton stood up to it:

the flesh? it was melted away,
the heart burnt out, dead ember,
tendons, muscles shattered, outer husk dismembered,

yet the frame held:
50   we passed the flame: we wonder
what saved us? what for?

1944

8. Cf. 1 Samuel 28.15, where the prophet Samuel is disturbed at being raised from the dead, and 1 Samuel 28.3: "When Saul saw the army of the Philistines, he was afraid, and his heart trembled greatly."
9. In Greek mythology, high priestess of the oracle at Delphi.
1. Ancient city on the bay of Naples, buried by an eruption of Mt. Vesuvius in 79 C.E.
2. Or perhaps "apocalyptic," meaning the fiery judgments of the Apocalypse prophesied in the Christian Scriptures. Cf. 1 Corinthians 3.15: "If any man's work shall be burned, he shall suffer loss: but he himself shall be saved; yet so as by fire." The Apocrypha are books rejected from the Bible because of dubious authenticity.

SIEGFRIED SASSOON
1886–1967

Christ and the Soldier

I

The straggled soldier halted—stared at Him—
Then clumsily dumped down upon his knees,
Gasping, "O blessed crucifix, I'm beat!"
And Christ, still sentried by the seraphim,[1]
5   Near the front-line, between two splintered trees,
Spoke him: "My son, behold these hands and feet."

The soldier eyed Him upward, limb by limb,
Paused at the Face; then muttered, "Wounds like these
Would shift a bloke to Blighty[2] just a treat!"
10   Christ, gazing downward, grieving and ungrim,
Whispered, "I made for you the mysteries,
Beyond all battles moves the Paraclete."[3]

II

The soldier chucked his rifle in the dust,
And slipped his pack, and wiped his neck, and said—
15   "O Christ Almighty, stop this bleeding fight!"
Above that hill the sky was stained like rust
With smoke. In sullen daybreak flaring red
The guns were thundering bombardment's blight.

The soldier cried, "I was born full of lust,
20   With hunger, thirst, and wishfulness to wed.
Who cares today if I done wrong or right?"
Christ asked all pitying, "Can you put no trust
In my known word that shrives each faithful head?
Am I not resurrection, life and light?"

III

25   Machine-guns rattled from below the hill;
High bullets flicked and whistled through the leaves;
And smoke came drifting from exploding shells.
Christ said, "Believe; and I can cleanse your ill.
I have not died in vain between two thieves;
30   Nor made a fruitless gift of miracles."

1. Angels of the highest of nine orders. In the Bible (Isaiah 6), six-winged celestial beings.
2. Slang for Britain.
3. Advocate or counselor; sometimes, as here, applied to the Holy Ghost.

The soldier answered, "Heal me if you will,
Maybe there's comfort when a soul believes
In mercy, and we need it in these hells.
But be you for both sides? I'm paid to kill
35 And if I shoot a man his mother grieves.
Does that come into what your teaching tells?"

A bird lit on the Christ and twittered gay;
Then a breeze passed and shook the ripening corn.
A Red Cross waggon bumped along the track.
40 Forsaken Jesus dreamed in the desolate day—
Uplifted Jesus, Prince of Peace forsworn—
An observation post for the attack.

"Lord Jesus, ain't you got no more to say?"
Bowed hung that head below the crown of thorns.
45 The soldier shifted, and picked up his pack,
And slung his gun, and stumbled on his way.
"O God," he groaned, "why ever was I born?" . . .
The battle boomed, and no reply came back.

1916   1973

"They"

The Bishop tells us: "When the boys come back
They will not be the same; for they'll have fought
In a just cause: they lead the last attack
On Anti-Christ; their comrades' blood has bought
5 New right to breed an honourable race,
They have challenged Death and dared him face to face."

"We're none of us the same!" the boys reply.
"For George lost both his legs; and Bill's stone blind;
Poor Jim's shot through the lungs and like to die;
10 And Bert's gone syphilitic: you'll not find
A chap who's served that hasn't found *some* change."
And the Bishop said: "The ways of God are strange!"

1916   1917

The General

"Good-morning, good-morning!" the General said
When we met him last week on our way to the line.
Now the soldiers he smiled at are most of 'em dead,
And we're cursing his staff for incompetent swine.

5   "He's a cheery old card," grunted Harry to Jack
     As they slogged up to Arras[4] with rifle and pack.

                            . . .

     But he did for them both by his plan of attack.

1917   1918

Glory of Women

     You love us when we're heroes, home on leave,
     Or wounded in a mentionable place.
     You worship decorations; you believe
     That chivalry redeems the war's disgrace.
5   You make us shells. You listen with delight,
     By tales of dirt and danger fondly thrilled.
     You crown our distant ardours while we fight,
     And mourn our laurelled memories when we're killed.
     You can't believe that British troops "retire"
10   When hell's last horror breaks them, and they run,
     Trampling the terrible corpses—blind with blood.
       O German mother dreaming by the fire,
     While you are knitting socks to send your son
     His face is trodden deeper in the mud.

1917   1918

Everyone Sang

     Everyone suddenly burst out singing;
     And I was filled with such delight
     As prisoned birds must find in freedom,
     Winging wildly across the white
5   Orchards and dark-green fields; on—on—and out of sight.

     Everyone's voice was suddenly lifted;
     And beauty came like the setting sun:
     My heart was shaken with tears; and horror
     Drifted away . . . O, but Everyone
10   Was a bird; and the song was wordless; the singing will never be done.

1919   1919

---

4. A city in northern France, in the front line throughout much of World War I. The British assault on the Western Front that began on April 9, 1917, was known as the Battle of Arras. The British suffered casualties of eighty-four thousand troops, inflicted casualties of seventy-five thousand on the Germans, and took thirteen thousand prisoners.

On Passing the New Menin Gate[5]

Who will remember, passing through this Gate,
The unheroic Dead who fed the guns?
Who shall absolve the foulness of their fate,—
Those doomed, conscripted, unvictorious ones?
5   Crudely renewed, the Salient[6] holds its own.
Paid are its dim defenders by this pomp;
Paid, with a pile of peace-complacent stone,
The armies who endured that sullen swamp.

Here was the world's worst wound. And here with pride
10   "Their name liveth for ever," the Gateway claims.
Was ever an immolation so belied
As these intolerably nameless names?
Well might the Dead who struggled in the slime
Rise and deride this sepulchre of crime.

1927–28   1928

ROBINSON JEFFERS
1887–1962

Shine, Perishing Republic

While this America settles in the mold of its vulgarity, heavily
  thickening to empire,
And protest, only a bubble in the molten mass, pops and sighs out,
  and the mass hardens,

I sadly smiling remember that the flower fades to make fruit, the fruit
  rots to make earth.
Out of the mother; and through the spring exultances, ripeness and
  decadence; and home to the mother.

5 You making haste haste on decay: not blameworthy; life is good, be it
    stubbornly long or suddenly
A mortal splendor: meteors are not needed less than mountains:
  shine, perishing republic.

But for my children, I would have them keep their distance from the
  thickening center; corruption
Never has been compulsory, when the cities lie at the monster's feet
  there are left the mountains.

---

5. The names of 54,889 men killed in World War I are engraved on the gate, a war memorial in Belgium.

6. Projecting part of a line of defensive trenches, open to attack from the front and both sides.

And boys, be in nothing so moderate as in love of man, a clever
  servant, insufferable master.
10 There is the trap that catches noblest spirits, that caught—they say—
  God, when he walked on earth.

1924

Boats in a Fog

Sports and gallantries, the stage, the arts, the antics of dancers,
The exuberant voices of music,
Have charm for children but lack nobility; it is bitter earnestness
That makes beauty; the mind
5 Knows, grown adult.
                A sudden fog-drift muffled the ocean,
A throbbing of engines moved in it,
At length, a stone's throw out, between the rocks and the vapor,
One by one moved shadows
10 Out of the mystery, shadows, fishing-boats, trailing each other,
Following the cliff for guidance,
Holding a difficult path between the peril of the sea-fog
And the foam on the shore granite.
One by one, trailing their leader, six crept by me,
15 Out of the vapor and into it,
The throb of their engines subdued by the fog, patient and cautious,
Coasting all round the peninsula
Back to the buoys in Monterey harbor.[1] A flight of pelicans
Is nothing lovelier to look at;
20 The flight of the planets is nothing nobler; all the arts lose virtue
Against the essential reality
Of creatures going about their business among the equally
Earnest elements of nature.

1924

Hurt Hawks

1

The broken pillar of the wing jags from the clotted shoulder,
The wing trails like a banner in defeat,
No more to use the sky forever but live with famine
And pain a few days: cat nor coyote
5 Will shorten the week of waiting for death, there is game without
  talons.
He stands under the oak-bush and waits
The lame feet of salvation; at night he remembers freedom
And flies in a dream, the dawns ruin it.

1. Part of Monterey Bay, a Pacific inlet in California.

He is strong and pain is worse to the strong, incapacity is worse.
10 The curs of the day come and torment him
At distance, no one but death the redeemer will humble that head,
The intrepid readiness, the terrible eyes.
The wild God of the world is sometimes merciful to those
That ask mercy, not often to the arrogant.
15 You do not know him, you communal people, or you have forgotten
him;
Intemperate and savage, the hawk remembers him;
Beautiful and wild, the hawks, and men that are dying, remember
him.

2

I'd sooner, except the penalties, kill a man than a hawk;
but the great redtail°   red-tailed hawk
Had nothing left but unable misery
20 From the bone too shattered for mending, the wing that trailed under
his talons when he moved.
We had fed him six weeks, I gave him freedom,
He wandered over the foreland hill and returned in the evening,
asking for death,
Not like a beggar, still eyed with the old
Implacable arrogance. I gave him the lead gift in the twilight. What
fell was relaxed,
25 Owl-downy, soft feminine feathers; but what
Soared: the fierce rush: the night-herons by the flooded river cried
fear at its rising
Before it was quite unsheathed from reality.

1928

The Purse-Seine²

Our sardine fishermen work at night in the dark of the moon; daylight
or moonlight
They could not tell where to spread the net, unable to see the
phosphorescence of the shoals° of fish.   schools
They work northward from Monterey, coasting Santa Cruz; off
New Year's Point or off Pigeon Point³
The look-out man will see some lakes of milk-color light on the sea's
night-purple; he points, and the helmsman
5 Turns the dark prow, the motorboat circles the gleaming shoal and
drifts out her seine-net. They close the circle
And purse the bottom of the net, then with great labor haul it in.

I cannot tell you
How beautiful the scene is, and a little terrible, then, when the
crowded fish

2. Large fishing net with a closeable bottom.
3. These are all places in the Monterey Bay area of western California.

Know they are caught, and wildly beat from one wall to the other of
    their closing destiny the phosphorescent
10 Water to a pool of flame, each beautiful slender body sheeted with
    flame, like a live rocket
A comet's tail wake of clear yellow flame; while outside the narrowing
Floats and cordage of the net great sea-lions come up to watch, sigh-
    ing in the dark; the vast walls of night
Stand erect to the stars.

                   Lately I was looking from a night mountain-top
15 On a wide city, the colored splendor, galaxies of light: how could I
    help but recall the seine-net
Gathering the luminous fish? I cannot tell you how beautiful the city
    appeared, and a little terrible.
I thought, We have geared the machines and locked all together into
    interdependence; we have built the great cities; now
There is no escape. We have gathered vast populations incapable of
    free survival, insulated
From the strong earth, each person in himself helpless, on all depend-
    ent. The circle is closed, and the net
20 Is being hauled in. They hardly feel the cords drawing, yet they shine
    already. The inevitable mass-disasters
Will not come in our time nor in our children's, but we and our
    children
Must watch the net draw narrower, government take all powers—or
    revolution, and the new government
Take more than all, add to kept bodies kept souls—or anarchy, the
    mass-disasters.

                These things are Progress;
25 Do you marvel our verse is troubled or frowning, while it keeps its
    reason? Or it lets go, lets the mood flow
In the manner of the recent young men into mere hysteria, splintered
    gleams, crackled laughter. But they are quite wrong.
There is no reason for amazement: surely one always knew that
    cultures decay, and life's end is death.

                                   1937

Birds and Fishes

Every October millions of little fish come along the shore,
Coasting this granite edge of the continent
On their lawful occasions: but what a festival for the sea-fowl.
What a witches' sabbath[4] of wings
5 Hides the dark water. The heavy pelicans shout "Haw!" like Job's
    friend's warhorse[5]
And dive from the high air, the cormorants[6]

4. Midnight meeting of witches and wizards, believed to be devil worshipers, to celebrate the witchcraft cult.
5. In Job 39.19–25, God describes the strength of the horse, who "saith among the trumpets Ha, ha; and he smelleth the battle afar off, the thunder of the captains and the shouting."
6. Aquatic birds with dark plumage.

Slip their long black bodies under the water and hunt like wolves
Through the green half-light. Screaming, the gulls watch,
Wild with envy and malice, cursing and snatching. What hysterical
    greed!
10   What a filling of pouches! the mob
Hysteria is nearly human—these decent birds!—as if they were finding
Gold in the street. It is better than gold,
It can be eaten: and which one in all this fury of wild-fowl pities the
    fish?
No one certainly. Justice and mercy
15   Are human dreams, they do not concern the birds nor the fish nor
    eternal God.
However—look again before you go.
The wings and wild hungers, the wave-worn skerries,°   *reefs*
    the bright quick minnows
Living in terror to die in torment—
Man's fate and theirs—and the island rocks and immense ocean
    beyond, and Lobos[7]
20   Darkening above the bay: they are beautiful?
That is their quality: not mercy, not mind, not goodness, but the
    beauty of God.[8]

                                          1963

RUPERT BROOKE
1887–1915

Sonnet

Oh! Death will find me, long before I tire
    Of watching you; and swing me suddenly
Into the shade and loneliness and mire°   *mud*
    Of the last land! There, waiting patiently,

5   One day, I think, I'll feel a cool wind blowing,
    See a slow light across the Stygian[1] tide,
And hear the Dead about me stir, unknowing,
    And tremble. And *I* shall know that you have died,

And watch you, a broad-browed and smiling dream,
10   Pass, light as ever, through the lightless host,
Quietly ponder, start, and sway, and gleam—
    Most individual and bewildering ghost!—

7. Point Lobos, a promontory on the Pacific in California.
8. Cf. Shakespeare, *The Merchant of Venice* 4.1.179–81: "The quality of mercy is not strained. / It droppeth as the gentle rain from heaven / Upon the place beneath."

1. Of Styx, one of the mythological rivers of Hades, across which the ferryman Charon rowed the souls of the dead.

And turn, and toss your brown delightful head
Amusedly, among the ancient Dead.

April 1909   1911

From The Old Vicarage, Grantchester[2]

(*Café des Westens, Berlin, May 1912*)

Just now the lilac is in bloom,
All before my little room;
And in my flower-beds, I think,
Smile the carnation and the pink;
5   And down the borders, well I know,
The poppy and the pansy blow . . .
Oh! there the chestnuts, summer through,
Beside the river make for you
A tunnel of green gloom, and sleep
10   Deeply above; and green and deep
The stream mysterious glides beneath,
Green as a dream and deep as death.
—Oh, damn! I know it! and I know
How the May fields all golden show,
15   And when the day is young and sweet,
Gild gloriously the bare feet
That run to bathe . . .
                              Du lieber Gott![3]

Here am I, sweating, sick, and hot,
20   And there the shadowed waters fresh
Lean up to embrace the naked flesh.
Temperamentvoll[4] German Jews
Drink beer around;—and *there* the dews
Are soft beneath a morn of gold.
25   Here tulips bloom as they are told;
Unkempt about those hedges blows
An English unofficial rose;
And there the unregulated sun
Slopes down to rest when day is done,
30   And wakes a vague unpunctual star,
A slippered Hesper;° and there are   *evening star (Venus)*
Meads° towards Haslingfield and Coton   *meadows*
Where *das Betreten*'s not *verboten*.[5]

εἴθε γενοίμην[6] . . . would I were
35   In Grantchester, in Grantchester!—

---

2. Like Haslingfield and Coton (both line 32) and
Madingley (line 129), a village near Cambridge,
England. The Old Vicarage was Brooke's house.
3. [You] dear God! (German).
4. Temperamental (German).
5. Forbidden (German). *Das Betreten:* walking on
the grass (German).
6. Would I were (Greek).

Some, it may be, can get in touch
With Nature there, or Earth, or such.
And clever modern men have seen
A Faun a-peeping through the green,
40 And felt the Classics were not dead,
To glimpse a Naiad's reedy head,
Or hear the Goat-foot[7] piping low: . . .
But these are things I do not know.
I only know that you may lie
45 Day-long and watch the Cambridge sky,
And, flower-lulled in sleepy grass,
Hear the cool lapse of hours pass,
Until the centuries blend and blur
In Grantchester, in Grantchester. . . .
50 Still in the dawnlit waters cool
His ghostly Lordship swims his pool,[8]
And tries the strokes, essays the tricks,
Long learnt on Hellespont, or Styx.[9]
Dan Chaucer[1] hears his river still
55 Chatter beneath a phantom mill.
Tennyson[2] notes, with studious eye,
How Cambridge waters hurry by . . .
And in that garden, black and white,
Creep whispers through the grass all night;
60 And spectral dance, before the dawn,
A hundred Vicars down the lawn;
Curates,[3] long dust, will come and go
On lissom,° clerical, printless toe;   *lithe, nimble*
And oft between the boughs is seen
65 The sly shade of a Rural Dean[4] . . .
Till, at a shiver in the skies,
Vanishing with Satanic cries,
The prim ecclesiastic rout
Leaves but a startled sleeper-out,
70 Grey heavens, the first bird's drowsy calls,
The falling house that never falls.

* * *

116 Ah God! to see the branches stir
Across the moon at Grantchester!

7. I.e., Pan, Greek god of pastures, flocks, and shepherds; half man and half goat, he played the reed flute. *Faun:* Roman mythological figure (Greek satyr), also half man and half goat, associated with nature. *Naiad:* a nymph (i.e., Greek mythological figure, female counterpart to the satyr) associated with lakes, rivers, springs, and fountains.
8. "Byron's Pool," a favorite bathing place in the river Cam, named for the English poet (then Cambridge student) George Gordon, Lord Byron (1788–1824; see pp. 833–63).
9. One of the mythological rivers of Hades over which Charon ferried the souls of the dead. *Hellespont:* the "Sea of Helle"—now known as the Dardanelles—between Bulgaria and Turkey; straits across which Byron once swam.
1. Geoffrey Chaucer (ca. 1343–1400; see pp. 19–70), who set "The Reeve's Tale" at the border of Cambridge and Grantchester, near a mill. *Dan:* master, sir (archaic).
2. Alfred, Lord Tennyson (1809–1892; see pp. 982–1009).
3. Junior clergyman in the Church of England.
4. Clergyman in the Church of England with responsibility for certain country parishes.

To smell the thrilling-sweet and rotten
Unforgettable, unforgotten
120 River-smell, and hear the breeze
Sobbing in the little trees.
Say, do the elm-clumps greatly stand
Still guardians of that holy land?
The chestnuts shade, in reverend dream,
125 The yet unacademic stream?
Is dawn a secret shy and cold
Anadyomene,[5] silver-gold?
And sunset still a golden sea
From Haslingfield to Madingley?
130 And after, ere the night is born,
Do hares come out about the corn?
Oh, is the water sweet and cool,
Gentle and brown, above the pool?
And laughs the immortal river still
135 Under the mill, under the mill?
Say, is there Beauty yet to find?
And Certainty? and Quiet kind?
Deep meadows yet, for to forget
The lies, and truths, and pain? . . . Oh! yet
140 Stands the Church clock at ten to three?
And is there honey still for tea?

1912   1914

The Soldier

If I should die, think only this of me:
    That there's some corner of a foreign field
That is for ever England. There shall be
    In that rich earth a richer dust concealed;
5 A dust whom England bore, shaped, made aware,
    Gave, once, her flowers to love, her ways to roam,
A body of England's, breathing English air,
    Washed by the rivers, blest by suns of home.

And think, this heart, all evil shed away,
10   A pulse in the eternal mind, no less
        Gives somewhere back the thoughts by England given;
Her sights and sounds; dreams happy as her day;
    And laughter, learnt of friends; and gentleness,
        In hearts at peace, under an English heaven.

November–December 1914   1914

---

5. Rising (Greek); name given to the goddess Aphrodite, who rose (at her birth) from the sea.

MARIANNE MOORE
1887–1972

To a Steam Roller

The illustration
is nothing to you without the application.
   You lack half wit. You crush all the particles down
     into close conformity, and then walk back and forth on them.

5   Sparkling chips of rock
are crushed down to the level of the parent block.
   Were not "impersonal judgment in aesthetic
     matters, a metaphysical impossibility,"[1] you

might fairly achieve
10 it. As for butterflies, I can hardly conceive
   of one's attending upon you, but to question
     the congruence of the complement is vain, if it exists.

1915   1921

To a Chameleon[2]

Hid by the august foliage and fruit of the grape-vine
   twine
     your anatomy
       round the pruned and polished stem,
5   Chameleon.
         Fire laid upon
       an emerald as long as
     the Dark King's massy
   one,
10 could not snap the spectrum up for food as you have done.

1916   1921

The Fish

wade
through black jade.
   Of the crow-blue mussel-shells, one keeps
   adjusting the ash-heaps;
5   opening and shutting itself like

---

1. Quotation, slightly changed, from an article by the American music critic Lawrence Gilman (1878–1939) in the April 1915 *New American Review*.

2. Originally published with the title "You are Like the Realistic Product of an Idealistic Search for Gold at the Foot of the Rainbow."

an
injured fan.
The barnacles which encrust the side
of the wave, cannot hide

10   there for the submerged shafts of the

sun,
split like spun
glass, move themselves with spotlight swiftness
into the crevices—

15   in and out, illuminating

the
turquoise sea
of bodies. The water drives a wedge
of iron through the iron edge

20   of the cliff; whereupon the stars,

pink
rice-grains, ink-
bespattered jelly-fish, crabs like green
lilies, and submarine

25   toadstools, slide each on the other.

All
external
marks of abuse are present on this
defiant edifice—

30   all the physical features of

ac-
cident—lack
of cornice, dynamite grooves, burns, and
hatchet strokes, these things stand

35   out on it; the chasm-side is

dead.
Repeated
evidence has proved that it can live
on what can not revive

40   its youth. The sea grows old in it.

1918   1921, 1935

Poetry[3]

I, too, dislike it: there are things that are important beyond all this
     fiddle.
     Reading it, however, with a perfect contempt for it, one discovers in

3. Moore later cut this poem to the first three lines.

it after all, a place for the genuine.
    Hands that can grasp, eyes
5   that can dilate, hair that can rise
            if it must, these things are important not because a

high-sounding interpretation can be put upon them but because they are
    useful. When they become so derivative as to become unintelligible,
    the same thing may be said for all of us, that we
10   do not admire what
            we cannot understand: the bat
                holding on upside down or in quest of something to

eat, elephants pushing, a wild horse taking a roll, a tireless wolf under
    a tree, the immovable critic twitching his skin like a horse that feels
        a flea, the base-
15   ball fan, the statistician—
            nor is it valid
                to discriminate against "business documents and

school-books";[4] all these phenomena are important. One must make a
        distinction
    however: when dragged into prominence by half poets, the result is
            not poetry,
20   nor till the poets among us can be
        "literalists of
        the imagination"[5]—above
            insolence and triviality and can present
for inspection, "imaginary gardens with real toads in them", shall we
25   have it. In the meantime, if you demand on the one hand,
        the raw material of poetry in
            all its rawness and
            that which is on the other hand
                genuine, you are interested in poetry.

1919   1921

A Grave

Man looking into the sea,
taking the view from those who have as much right to it as you have
        to it yourself,
it is human nature to stand in the middle of a thing,
but you cannot stand in the middle of this;

---

4. "*Diary of Tolstoy* (Dutton), p. 84. 'Where the boundary between prose and poetry lies, I shall never be able to understand. The question is raised in manuals of style, yet the answer to it lies beyond me. Poetry is verse: prose is not verse. Or else poetry is everything with the exception of business documents and school books' " [Moore's note]. Leo Tolstoy (1828–1910), Russian novelist, philosopher, and mystic.
5. "Yeats: *Ideas of Good and Evil* (A. H. Bullen), p. 182. 'The limitation of [Blake's] view was from the very intensity of his vision; he was a too literal realist of imagination, as others are of nature; and because he believed that the figures seen by the mind's eye, when exalted by inspiration, were "eternal existences," symbols of divine essences, he hated every grace of style that might obscure their lineaments' " [Moore's note]. William Butler Yeats (1865–1939; see pp. 1188–1211), Irish poet and dramatist.

5   the sea has nothing to give but a well excavated grave.
The firs stand in a procession, each with an emerald turkey-foot at the
        top,
reserved as their contours, saying nothing;
repression, however, is not the most obvious characteristic of the sea;
the sea is a collector, quick to return a rapacious look.
10 There are others besides you who have worn that look—
whose expression is no longer a protest; the fish no longer investigate
        them
for their bones have not lasted:
men lower nets, unconscious of the fact that they are desecrating a
        grave,
and row quickly away—the blades of the oars
15 moving together like the feet of water-spiders as if there were no such
        thing as death.
The wrinkles progress among themselves in a phalanx[6]—beautiful
        under networks of foam,
and fade breathlessly while the sea rustles in and out of the seaweed;
the birds swim through the air at top speed, emitting cat-calls as
        heretofore—
the tortoise-shell scourges about the feet of the cliffs, in motion
        beneath them;
20 and the ocean, under the pulsation of lighthouses and noise of
        bell-buoys,
advances as usual, looking as if it were not that ocean in which
        dropped things are bound to sink—
in which if they turn and twist, it is neither with volition nor
        consciousness.

1921   1924, 1935

The Steeple-Jack

Revised, 1961

Dürer[7] would have seen a reason for living
        in a town like this, with eight stranded whales
to look at; with the sweet sea air coming into your house
on a fine day, from water etched
5   with waves as formal as the scales
on a fish.

One by one in two's and three's, the seagulls keep
        flying back and forth over the town clock,
or sailing around the lighthouse without moving their wings—
10 rising steadily with a slight
        quiver of the body—or flock
mewing where

a sea the purple of the peacock's neck is
        paled to greenish azure as Dürer changed

6. Compact body of troops.   and engraver particularly gifted in rendering
7. Albrecht Dürer (1471–1528), German painter   closely and meticulously observed detail.

15   the pine green of the Tyrol[8] to peacock blue and guinea
        gray.[9] You can see a twenty-five-
            pound lobster; and fishnets arranged
        to dry. The

        whirlwind fife-and-drum of the storm bends the salt
20   marsh grass, disturbs stars in the sky and the
        star on the steeple; it is a privilege to see so
        much confusion. Disguised by what
            might seem the opposite, the sea-
        side flowers and

25   trees are favored by the fog so that you have
            the tropics at first hand: the trumpet-vine,
        fox-glove, giant snap-dragon, a salpiglossis[1] that has
        spots and stripes; morning-glories, gourds,
            or moon-vines trained on fishing-twine
30   at the back

        door; cat-tails, flags, blueberries and spiderwort,
            striped grass, lichens, sunflowers, asters, daisies—
        yellow and crab-claw ragged sailors with green bracts[2]—toad-plant,
        petunias, ferns; pink lilies, blue
35   ones, tigers; poppies; black sweet-peas.
        The climate

        is not right for the banyan, frangipani, or
            jack-fruit trees;[3] or an exotic serpent
        life. Ring lizard and snake-skin for the foot, if you see fit;
40   but here they've cats, not cobras, to
            keep down the rats. The diffident
        little newt

        with white pin-dots on black horizontal spaced
            out bands lives here; yet there is nothing that
45   ambition can buy or take away. The college student
        named Ambrose sits on the hillside
            with his not-native books and hat
        and sees boats

        at sea progress white and rigid as if in
50   a groove. Liking an elegance of which
        the source is not bravado, he knows by heart the antique
        sugar-bowl shaped summer-house of
            interlacing slats, and the pitch
        of the church

8. The mountainous western area of Austria.
9. The slate gray, speckled with white, of the guinea fowl.
1. An herb with large, varicolored flowers that often have striking markings.
2. Flowerlike leaves on some plants (e.g., flower-

ing dogwood).
3. The banyan is an East Indian tree, some of whose branches send out trunks that grow downward; frangipani is a tropical American shrub (red jasmine is a species); the jackfruit is a large East Indian tree with large edible fruit.

55   spire, not true,[4] from which a man in scarlet lets
       down a rope as a spider spins a thread;
he might be part of a novel, but on the sidewalk a
sign says C. J. Poole, Steeple Jack,
       in black and white; and one in red
60   and white says

Danger. The church portico has four fluted
       columns, each a single piece of stone, made
modester by white-wash. This would be a fit haven for
waifs, children, animals, prisoners,
65   and presidents who have repaid
sin-driven

senators by not thinking about them. The
       place has a school-house, a post-office in a
store, fish-houses, hen-houses, a three-masted
70   schooner on
the stocks. The hero, the student,
       the steeple-jack, each in his way,
is at home.

It could not be dangerous to be living
75   in a town like this, of simple people,
who have a steeple-jack placing danger-signs by the church
while he is gilding the solid-
       pointed star, which on a steeple
stands for hope.

1932   1935, 1961

No Swan So Fine

"No water so still as the
       dead fountains of Versailles."[5] No swan,
with swart blind look askancc
and gondoliering legs,[6] so fine
5   as the chintz china one with fawn-
brown eyes and toothed gold
collar on to show whose bird it was.

Lodged in the Louis Fifteenth
       candelabrum-tree[7] of cockscomb-
10   tinted buttons, dahlias,
       sea-urchins, and everlastings,[8]
       it perches on the branching foam

4. Not placed or fitted accurately.
5. "Percy Phillip, *New York Times Magazine,* May 10, 1931" [Moore's note]. Famed palace of French kings, including Louis XV, in the late seventeenth and early eighteenth centuries; now a museum.
6. Italian gondoliers paddle from the stern to propel their gondolas.

7. "A pair of Louis XV candelabra with Dresden figures of swans belonging to Lord Balfour" [Moore's note].
8. Plants with flowers that may be dried without losing their form or color; also, the flowers from such plants.

of polished sculptured
flowers—at ease and tall. The king is dead.

1932   1935, 1951

What Are Years?

What is our innocence,
what is our guilt? All are
    naked, none is safe. And whence
is courage: the unanswered question,
5   the resolute doubt,—
    dumbly calling, deafly listening—that
in misfortune, even death,
        encourages others
        and in its defeat, stirs

10   the soul to be strong? He
sees deep and is glad, who
    accedes to mortality
and in his imprisonment rises
upon himself as
15 the sea in a chasm, struggling to be
free and unable to be,
        in its surrendering
        finds its continuing.

So he who strongly feels,
20 behaves. The very bird,
    grown taller as he sings, steels
his form straight up. Though he is captive,
his mighty singing
says, satisfaction is a lowly
25 thing, how pure a thing is joy.
        This is mortality,
        this is eternity.

1931–39   1941

Nevertheless

you've seen a strawberry
        that's had a struggle; yet
        was, where the fragments met,

a hedgehog or a star-
5   fish for the multitude
        of seeds. What better food

than apple-seeds—the fruit
    within the fruit—locked in
    like counter-curved twin

10 hazel-nuts? Frost that kills
    the little rubber-plant-
    leaves of *kok-saghyz*-stalks,[9] can't

harm the roots; they still grow
    in frozen ground. Once where
15   there was a prickly-pear-

leaf clinging to barbed wire,
    a root shot down to grow
    in earth two feet below;

as carrots form mandrakes[1]
20   or a ram's-horn root some-
    times. Victory won't come

to me unless I go
    to it; a grape-tendril
    ties a knot in knots till

25 knotted thirty times,—so
    the bound twig that's under-
    gone and over-gone, can't stir.

The weak overcomes its
    menace, the strong over-
30   comes itself. What is there

like fortitude! What sap
    went through that little thread
    to make the cherry red!

1944

The Mind Is an Enchanting Thing

is an enchanted thing
    like the glaze on a
katydid-wing
      subdivided by sun
5   till the nettings are legion.
Like Gieseking playing Scarlatti;[2]

9. Russian dandelions.
1. Medicinal plants with forked roots.
2. Walter Wilhelm Gieseking (1895–1956),

German (French-born) pianist, was famous for his renditions of the music of the Italian composer Domenico Scarlatti (1685–1757).

like the apteryx-awl[3]
as a beak, or the
kiwi's rain-shawl
10   of haired feathers, the mind
           feeling its way as though blind,
walks along with its eyes on the ground.

It has memory's ear
     that can hear without
15 having to hear.
           Like the gyroscope's fall,
                truly unequivocal
because trued° by regnant° certainty,   *balanced / authoritative*

it is a power of
20   strong enchantment. It
is like the dove-
           neck animated by
                sun; it is memory's eye;
it's conscientious inconsistency.

25 It tears off the veil; tears
           the temptation, the
mist the heart wears,
           from its eyes—if the heart
                has a face; it takes apart
30 dejection. It's fire in the dove-neck's

iridescence; in the
     inconsistencies
of Scarlatti.
           Unconfusion submits
35   its confusion to proof; it's
not a Herod's oath[4] that cannot change.

                                        1944

EDWIN MUIR
1887–1959

Childhood

Long time he lay upon the sunny hill,
     To his father's house below securely bound.
Far off the silent, changing sound was still,
     With the black islands lying thick around.

---

3. New Zealand bird, related to the kiwi, with an awl-shaped beak.
4. Herod, ruler of Judea under the Romans, ful-

filled an oath to Salome by having John the Baptist beheaded. Cf. Mark 6.22–27.

⁵ He saw each separate height, each vaguer hue,
      Where the massed islands rolled in mist away,
And though all ran together in his view
      He knew that unseen straits between them lay.

Often he wondered what new shores were there.
¹⁰   In thought he saw the still light on the sand,
The shallow water clear in tranquil air,
      And walked through it in joy from strand to strand.

Over the sound a ship so slow would pass
      That in the black hill's gloom it seemed to lie.
¹⁵ The evening sound was smooth like sunken glass,
      And time seemed finished ere the ship passed by.

Grey tiny rocks slept round him where he lay,
      Moveless as they, more still as evening came,
The grasses threw straight shadows far away,
²⁰   And from the house his mother called his name.

                                                        1925

The Return of the Greeks

      The veteran Greeks came home
      Sleepwandering from the war.[1]
      We saw the galleys come
      Blundering over the bar.
⁵   Each soldier with his scar
      In rags and tatters came home.

      Reading the wall of Troy
      Ten years without a change
      Was such intense employ
¹⁰   (Just out of the arrows' range),
      All the world was strange
      After ten years of Troy.

      Their eyes knew every stone
      In the huge heartbreaking wall
¹⁵   Year after year grown
      Till there was nothing at all
      But an alley steep and small,
      Tramped earth and towering stone.

      Now even the hills seemed low
²⁰   In the boundless sea and land,
      Weakened by distance so.

1. The Trojan War, during which the Greeks besieged the city of Troy for ten years (as described in Homer's *Iliad*).

How could they understand
Space empty on every hand
And the hillocks squat and low?

25   And when they arrived at last
They found a childish scene
Embosomed in the past,
And the war lying between—
A child's preoccupied scene
30   When they came home at last.

But everything trite and strange,
The peace, the parcelled ground,
The vinerows—never a change!
The past and the present bound
35   In one oblivious round
Past thinking trite and strange.

But for their grey-haired wives
And their sons grown shy and tall
They would have given their lives
40   To raise the battered wall
Again, if this was all
In spite of their sons and wives.

Penelope[2] in her tower
Looked down upon the show
45   And saw within an hour
Each man to his wife go,
Hesitant, sure and slow:
She, alone in her tower.

1946

Adam's Dream

They say the first dream Adam our father had
After his agelong daydream in the Garden[3]
When heaven and sun woke in his wakening mind,
The earth with all its hills and woods and waters,
5   The friendly tribes of trees and animals,
And earth's last wonder Eve (the first great dream
Which is the ground of every dream since then)—
They say he dreamt lying on the naked ground,
The gates shut fast behind him as he lay
10   Fallen in Eve's fallen arms, his terror drowned
In her engulfing terror, in the abyss

---

2. Wife of Odysseus, a Greek leader who took another ten years to return home (as described in the *Odyssey*).
3. I.e., after the Fall. According to Genesis 2–3,

Adam and Eve were expelled from the Garden of Eden because they ate the fruit of the one tree forbidden to them by God (the tree of the knowledge of good and evil).

Whence there's no further fall, and comfort is—
That he was standing on a rocky ledge
High on the mountainside, bare crag behind,
15 In front a plain as far as eye could reach,
And on the plain a few small figures running
That were like men and women, yet were so far away
He could not see their faces. On they ran,
And fell, and rose again, and ran, and fell,
20 And rising were the same yet not the same,
Identical or interchangeable,
Different in indifference. As he looked
Still there were more of them, the plain was filling
As by an alien arithmetical magic
25 Unknown in Eden, a mechanical
Addition without meaning, joining only
Number to number in no mode or order,
Weaving no pattern. For these creatures moved
Towards no fixed mark even when in growing bands
30 They clashed against each other and clashing fell
In mounds of bodies. For they rose again,
Identical or interchangeable,
And went their way that was not like a way;
Some back and forward, back and forward, some
35 In a closed circle, wide or narrow, others
In zigzags on the sand. Yet all were busy,
And tense with purpose as they cut the air
Which seemed to press them back. Sometimes they paused
While one stopped one—fortuitous assignations
40 In the disorder, whereafter two by two
They ran awhile,
Then parted and again were single. Some
Ran straight against the frontier of the plain
Till the horizon drove them back. A few
45 Stood still and never moved. Then Adam cried
Out of his dream, "What are you doing there?"
And the crag answered "Are you doing there?"
"What are you doing there?"—"you doing there?"
The animals had withdrawn and from the caves
50 And woods stared out in fear or condemnation,
Like outlaws or like judges. All at once
Dreaming or half-remembering, "This is time,"
Thought Adam in his dream, and time was strange
To one lately in Eden. "I must see,"
55 He cried, "the faces. Where are the faces? Who
Are you all out there?" Then in his changing dream
He was a little nearer, and he saw
They were about some business strange to him
That had a form and sequence past their knowledge;
60 And that was why they ran so frenziedly.
Yet all, it seemed, made up a story, illustrated
By these the living, the unknowing, cast
Each singly for his part. But Adam longed

For more, not this mere moving pattern, not
65 This illustrated storybook of mankind
Always a-making, improvised on nothing.
At that he was among them, and saw each face
Was like his face, so that he would have hailed them
As sons of God but that something restrained him.
70 And he remembered all, Eden, the Fall,
The Promise, and his place, and took their hands
That were his hands, his and his children's hands,
Cried out and was at peace, and turned again
In love and grief in Eve's encircling arms.

1950, 1952

T. S. ELIOT
1888–1965

The Love Song of J. Alfred Prufrock

*S'io credesse che mia risposta fosse
A persona che mai tornasse al mondo,
Questa fiamma staria senza piu scosse.
Ma perciocche giammai di questo fondo
Non torno vivo alcun, s'i'odo il vero,
Senza tema d'infamia ti rispondo.*[1]

Let us go then, you and I,
When the evening is spread out against the sky
Like a patient etherised upon a table;
Let us go, through certain half-deserted streets,
5 The muttering retreats
Of restless nights in one-night cheap hotels
And sawdust restaurants with oyster-shells:
Streets that follow like a tedious argument
Of insidious intent
10 To lead you to an overwhelming question . . .
Oh, do not ask, "What is it?"
Let us go and make our visit.

    In the room the women come and go
    Talking of Michelangelo.

15   The yellow fog that rubs its back upon the window-panes,
The yellow smoke that rubs its muzzle on the window-panes
Licked its tongue into the corners of the evening,
Lingered upon the pools that stand in drains,

---

1. Dante, *Inferno* 27.61–66. These words are spoken by Guido da Montefeltro, whom Dante has encountered among the false counselors (each spirit is concealed within a flame): "If I thought my answer were given / to anyone who would ever return to the world, / this flame would stand still without moving any further. / But since never from this abyss / has anyone ever returned alive, if what I hear is true, / without fear of infamy I answer you."

Let fall upon its back the soot that falls from chimneys,
20 Slipped by the terrace, made a sudden leap,
And seeing that it was a soft October night,
Curled once about the house, and fell asleep.

And indeed there will be time²
For the yellow smoke that slides along the street,
25 Rubbing its back upon the window-panes;
There will be time, there will be time
To prepare a face to meet the faces that you meet;
There will be time to murder and create,
And time for all the works and days³ of hands
30 That lift and drop a question on your plate;
Time for you and time for me,
And time yet for a hundred indecisions,
And for a hundred visions and revisions,
Before the taking of a toast and tea.

35 In the room the women come and go
Talking of Michelangelo.

And indeed there will be time
To wonder, "Do I dare?" and, "Do I dare?"
Time to turn back and descend the stair,
40 With a bald spot in the middle of my hair—
[They will say: "How his hair is growing thin!"]
My morning coat, my collar mounting firmly to the chin,
My necktie rich and modest, but asserted by a simple pin—
[They will say: "But how his arms and legs are thin!"]
45 Do I dare
Disturb the universe?
In a minute there is time
For decisions and revisions which a minute will reverse.

For I have known them all already, known them all—
50 Have known the evenings, mornings, afternoons,
I have measured out my life with coffee spoons;
I know the voices dying with a dying fall⁴
Beneath the music from a farther room.
  So how should I presume?

55 And I have known the eyes already, known them all—
The eyes that fix you in a formulated phrase,
And when I am formulated, sprawling on a pin,
When I am pinned and wriggling on the wall,
Then how should I begin
60 To spit out all the butt-ends of my days and ways?
  And how should I presume?

2. Cf. Andrew Marvell, "To His Coy Mistress," line 1 (p. 478).
3. *Works and Days*, by the Greek poet Hesiod (eighth century B.C.E.), is a didactic poem about farming and family life.
4. Cf. Shakespeare, *Twelfth Night* 1.1.1–4: "If music be the food of love, play on. . . . That strain again, it had a dying fall."

And I have known the arms already, known them all—
Arms that are braceleted and white and bare
[But in the lamplight, downed with light brown hair!]
65 Is it perfume from a dress
That makes me so digress?
Arms that lie along a table, or wrap about a shawl.
    And should I then presume?
    And how should I begin?

           . . . .

70 Shall I say, I have gone at dusk through narrow streets
And watched the smoke that rises from the pipes
Of lonely men in shirt-sleeves, leaning out of windows? . . .

    I should have been a pair of ragged claws
Scuttling across the floors of silent seas.

           . . . .

75 And the afternoon, the evening, sleeps so peacefully!
Smoothed by long fingers,
Asleep . . . tired . . . or it malingers,
Stretched on the floor, here beside you and me.
Should I, after tea and cakes and ices,
80 Have the strength to force the moment to its crisis?
But though I have wept and fasted, wept and prayed,
Though I have seen my head [grown slightly bald] brought in upon a
    platter,[5]
I am no prophet—and here's no great matter;
I have seen the moment of my greatness flicker,
85 And I have seen the eternal Footman hold my coat, and snicker,
And in short, I was afraid.

    And would it have been worth it, after all,
After the cups, the marmalade, the tea,
Among the porcelain, among some talk of you and me,
90 Would it have been worth while,
To have bitten off the matter with a smile,
To have squeezed the universe into a ball[6]
To roll it toward some overwhelming question,
To say: "I am Lazarus,[7] come from the dead,
95 Come back to tell you all, I shall tell you all"—
If one, settling a pillow by her head,
    Should say: "That is not what I meant at all.
    That is not it, at all."

---

5. The head of John the Baptist was presented to
Salome on a plate at her request (Mark 6.17–20,
Matthew 14.3–11).

6. Cf. "To His Coy Mistress," lines 41–44.
7. On the resurrection of Lazarus, see John 11.1–
44, Luke 16.19–31.

And would it have been worth it, after all,
100 Would it have been worth while,
After the sunsets and the dooryards and the sprinkled streets,
After the novels, after the teacups, after the skirts that trail along the
    floor—
And this, and so much more?—
It is impossible to say just what I mean!
105 But as if a magic lantern threw the nerves in patterns on a screen:
Would it have been worth while
If one, settling a pillow or throwing off a shawl,
And turning toward the window, should say:
    "That is not it at all,
110   That is not what I meant, at all."
           . . . .

No! I am not Prince Hamlet, nor was meant to be;
Am an attendant lord, one that will do
To swell a progress,[8] start a scene or two,
Advise the prince; no doubt, an easy tool,
115 Deferential, glad to be of use,
Politic, cautious, and meticulous;
Full of high sentence,° but a bit obtuse;   *sententiousness*
At times, indeed, almost ridiculous—
Almost, at times, the Fool.

120   I grow old . . . I grow old . . .
I shall wear the bottoms of my trousers rolled.

    Shall I part my hair behind? Do I dare to eat a peach?
I shall wear white flannel trousers, and walk upon the beach.
I have heard the mermaids singing, each to each.

125   I do not think that they will sing to me.

    I have seen them riding seaward on the waves
Combing the white hair of the waves blown back
When the wind blows the water white and black.

    We have lingered in the chambers of the sea
130 By sea-girls wreathed with seaweed red and brown
Till human voices wake us, and we drown.

1910–11   1915, 1917

8. Journey made by a royal court, often depicted in Elizabethan drama, in which the Fool (line 119) was
also a fixture.

The Waste Land[9]

"Nam Sibyllam quidem Cumis ego ipse oculis meis vidi in ampulla
pendere, et cum illi pueri dicerent: Σίβυλλα τί θέλεις respondebat-
illa: ἀποθαυειν θέλω."[1]

FOR EZRA POUND

IL MIGLIOR FABBRO.[2]

I The Burial of the Dead[3]

April is the cruellest month, breeding[4]
Lilacs out of the dead land, mixing
Memory and desire, stirring
Dull roots with spring rain.
5 Winter kept us warm, covering
Earth in forgetful snow, feeding
A little life with dried tubers.
Summer surprised us, coming over the Starnbergersee[5]
With a shower of rain; we stopped in the colonnade,
10 And went on in sunlight, into the Hofgarten,
And drank coffee, and talked for an hour.
Bin gar keine Russin, stamm' aus Litauen, echt deutsch.[6]
And when we were children, staying at the arch-duke's,
My cousin's, he took me out on a sled,
15 And I was frightened. He said, Marie,
Marie, hold on tight. And down we went.
In the mountains, there you feel free.
I read, much of the night, and go south in the winter.

What are the roots that clutch, what branches grow
20 Out of this stony rubbish? Son of man,[7]
You cannot say, or guess, for you know only
A heap of broken images, where the sun beats,
And the dead tree gives no shelter, the cricket no relief,[8]
And the dry stone no sound of water. Only

9. On its publication in book form, T. S. Eliot provided *The Waste Land* with many (and perhaps sometimes parodic) notes. They begin: "Not only the title, but the plan and a good deal of the incidental symbolism of the poem were suggested by Miss Jessie L. Weston's book on the Grail legend: *From Ritual to Romance* (Cambridge, [1902]). Indeed, so deeply am I indebted, Miss Weston's book will elucidate the difficulties of the poem much better than my notes can do; and I recommend it (apart from the great interest of the book itself) to any who think such elucidation of the poem worth the trouble. To another work of anthropology I am indebted in general, one which has influenced our generation profoundly; I mean *The Golden Bough* [by Sir James Frazer; 12 volumes, 1890–1915]. I have used especially the two volumes *Adonis, Attis, Osiris.* Anyone who is acquainted with these works will immediately recognize in the poem certain references to vegetation ceremonies [i.e., fertility rites]."
1. "For indeed I myself have seen, with my own eyes, the Sibyl hanging in a bottle at Cumae, and when those boys would say to her: 'Sibyl, what do you want?' she replied, 'I want to die.'" From Petronius (d. 66), *Satyricon*, chapter 48. The Sibyl of Cumae, a prophetess of the god Apollo, was immortal but not eternally young.
2. The better craftsman (Italian). So the poet Guido Guinizelli characterizes the Provençal poet Arnaut Daniel in Dante's *Purgatorio* 26.117.
3. The burial service of the Anglican Church.
4. Perhaps an echo of Chaucer, "General Prologue" to *The Canterbury Tales*, line 1 (p. 19).
5. Lake a few miles south of Munich. The Hofgarten (line 10) is a public garden in Munich, partly surrounded by a colonnaded walk.
6. I am certainly no Russian, I come from Lithuania, a true German (German).
7. "Cf. Ezekiel II, i" [Eliot's note], where God addresses Ezekiel: "Son of man, stand upon thy feet, and I will speak unto thee."
8. "Cf. Ecclesiastes XII, v" [Eliot's note], a description of times of fear and death, when "the grasshopper shall be a burden, and desire shall fail." The passage continues, "Then shall the dust return to the earth as it was" (12.7); cf. line 30 below.

25 There is shadow under this red rock,
(Come in under the shadow of this red rock),⁹
And I will show you something different from either
Your shadow at morning striding behind you
Or your shadow at evening rising to meet you;
30 I will show you fear in a handful of dust.
            Frisch weht der Wind
            Der Heimat zu
            Mein Irisch Kind,
            *Wo weilest du?*¹
35 "You gave me hyacinths first a year ago;
"They called me the hyacinth girl."
—Yet when we came back, late, from the Hyacinth garden,
Your arms full, and your hair wet, I could not
Speak, and my eyes failed, I was neither
40 Living nor dead, and I knew nothing,
Looking into the heart of light, the silence.
*Oed' und leer das Meer.*²

      Madame Sosostris,³ famous clairvoyante,
      Had a bad cold, nevertheless
45 Is known to be the wisest woman in Europe,
With a wicked pack of cards.⁴ Here, said she,
Is your card, the drowned Phoenician Sailor,
(Those are pearls that were his eyes.⁵ Look!)
Here is Belladonna, the Lady of the Rocks,
50 The lady of situations.
Here is the man with three staves, and here the Wheel,
And here is the one-eyed merchant, and this card,
Which is blank, is something he carries on his back,
Which I am forbidden to see. I do not find
55 The Hanged Man. Fear death by water.
I see crowds of people, walking round in a ring.
Thank you. If you see dear Mrs. Equitone,
Tell her I bring the horoscope myself:
One must be so careful these days.

60   Unreal City,⁶
      Under the brown fog of a winter dawn,

---

9. Cf. Isaiah's prophecy of a Messiah who will be "as rivers of water in a dry place, as the shadow of a great rock in a weary land" (Isaiah 32.2).
1. "V. *Tristan und Isolde,* I, verses 5–8" [Eliot's note]. The sailor's song from an opera by the German composer Richard Wagner (1813–1883): "Fresh blows the wind / Toward home. / My Irish child, / Where are you waiting?"
2. "Id. III, verse 24" [Eliot's note]. Empty and waste the sea (German); i.e., the ship bringing Isolde back to the dying Tristan is nowhere in sight.
3. A pseudo-Egyptian name assumed by a fortune-teller in the English writer Aldous Huxley's novel *Chrome Yellow* (1921).
4. "I am not familiar with the exact constitution of the Tarot pack of cards, from which I have obviously departed to suit my own convenience. The Hanged Man, a member of the traditional pack,

fits my purpose in two ways: because he is associated in my mind with the Hanged God of Frazer, and because I associate him with the hooded figure in the passage of the disciples to Emmaus in Part V. The Phoenician Sailor and the Merchant appear later; also the 'crowds of people' and Death by Water is executed in Part IV. The Man with Three Staves (an authentic member of the Tarot pack) I associate, quite arbitrarily, with the Fisher King himself" [Eliot's note]. The tarot cards are used in fortune-telling; some of the figures named in the following lines come from tarot decks.
5. From Ariel's song in Shakespeare, *Tempest* 1.2: "Full fathom five thy father lies." *Phoenician Sailor:* the Phoenicians were seagoing merchants (cf. "Mr. Eugenides," line 209, and "Phlebas the Phoenician," line 312).
6. "Cf. Baudelaire: 'Fourmillante cité, cité pleine de rêves, / Où le spectre en plein jour raccroche le

A crowd flowed over London Bridge, so many,
I had not thought death had undone so many.[7]
Sighs, short and infrequent, were exhaled,[8]
65 And each man fixed his eyes before his feet.
Flowed up the hill and down King William Street,
To where Saint Mary Woolnoth kept the hours
With a dead sound on the final stroke of nine.[9]
There I saw one I knew, and stopped him, crying: "Stetson!
70 "You who were with me in the ships at Mylae![1]
"That corpse you planted last year in your garden,
"Has it begun to sprout? Will it bloom this year?
"Or has the sudden frost disturbed its bed?
"Oh keep the Dog far hence, that's friend to men,
75 "Or with his nails he'll dig it up again![2]
"You! hypocrite lecteur!—mon semblable,—mon frère!"[3]

II. A Game of Chess[4]

The Chair she sat in, like a burnished throne,[5]
Glowed on the marble, where the glass
Held up by standards wrought with fruited vines
80 From which a golden Cupidon peeped out
(Another hid his eyes behind his wing)
Doubled the flames of sevenbranched candelabra[6]
Reflecting light upon the table as
The glitter of her jewels rose to meet it,
85 From satin cases poured in rich profusion;
In vials of ivory and coloured glass
Unstoppered, lurked her strange synthetic perfumes,
Unguent,° powdered, or liquid—troubled, confused   ointment
And drowned the sense in odours; stirred by the air
90 That freshened from the window, these ascended
In fattening the prolonged candle-flames,

---

passant' " [Eliot's note]. Swarming city, city filled
with dreams, / Where the specter in broad daylight
accosts the passerby (French); from one of the
poems in the French poet Charles Baudelaire's Les
Fleurs du mal (1857).
7. "Cf. Inferno III, 55–57: 'si lunga tratta / di
gente, ch' io non avrei mai creduto / che morte
tanta n'avesse disfatta' " [Eliot's note]. On his arri-
val in the Inferno, Dante sees the vast crowd, "such
a long procession of people, that I would never
have believed that death had undone so many"
(Italian).
8. "Cf. Inferno IV, 25–27: 'Quivi, secondo che per
ascoltare, / non avea pianto, ma' che di sospiri, /
che l'aura eterna facevan tremare' " [Eliot's note].
Dante descends into the first circle of Hell, filled
with virtuous pagans condemned to Limbo
because they had lived before Christianity: "Here,
if one trusted to hearing, there was no weeping but
so many sighs as caused the everlasting air to trem-
ble" (Italian).
9. "A phenomenon which I have often noticed"
[Eliot's note]. The church and the other London
sites are in the City, London's financial and busi-
ness center.
1. Sicilian seaport; at the battle of Mylae (260

B.C.E.), the Romans defeated the Carthaginians.
2. "Cf. the Dirge in Webster's White Devil [1612]"
[Eliot's note]. In the English dramatist John Web-
ster's play, the song is sung by a crazed mother,
who has witnessed one son murder another, and
ends, "But keep the wolf far thence, that's foe to
men; / For with his nails he'll dig them up again"
(5.4.97–98).
3. "V. Baudelaire, Preface to Fleurs du mal"
[Eliot's note]. Hypocrite reader!—my likeness,—
my brother! (French); last line of the prefatory
poem, "Au lecteur" ("To the Reader").
4. The title alludes to two plays by the English
dramatist Thomas Middleton, A Game of Chess
(1627) and Women Beware Women (1657), both
of which involve sexual intrigue. In the second, a
game of chess is used to mark a seduction, the
moves in the game paralleling its steps.
5. "Cf. Antony and Cleopatra, II, ii, 1[ine] 190"
[Eliot's note]. Eliot's language recalls the passage
in Shakespeare that describes Cleopatra's first
meeting with Antony, which begins: "The barge
she sat in, like a burnished throne / Burned on the
water."
6. The Menorah, used in Jewish worship.

Flung their smoke into the laquearia,[7]
Stirring the pattern on the coffered° ceiling.   *with recessed panels*
Huge sea-wood fed with copper
95   Burned green and orange, framed by the coloured stone,
In which sad light a carvéd dolphin swam.
Above the antique mantel was displayed
As though a window gave upon the sylvan scene[8]
The change of Philomel, by the barbarous king[9]
100   So rudely forced; yet there the nightingale[1]
Filled all the desert with inviolable voice
And still she cried, and still the world pursues,
"Jug Jug"[2] to dirty ears.
And other withered stumps of time
105   Were told upon the walls; staring forms
Leaned out, leaning, hushing the room enclosed.
Footsteps shuffled on the stair.
Under the firelight, under the brush, her hair
Spread out in fiery points
110   Glowed into words, then would be savagely still.

    "My nerves are bad to-night. Yes, bad. Stay with me.
"Speak to me. Why do you never speak. Speak.
    "What are you thinking of? What thinking? What?
"I never know what you are thinking. Think."

115   I think we are in rats' alley[3]
Where the dead men lost their bones.

    "What is that noise?"
                 The wind under the door.[4]
"What is that noise now? What is the wind doing?"
120   Nothing again nothing.
                            "Do
"You know nothing? Do you see nothing? Do you remember
"Nothing?"

       I remember
125   Those are pearls that were his eyes.[5]
"Are you alive, or not? Is there nothing in your head?"

                                   But
O O O O that Shakespeherian Rag—
It's so elegant

7. "Laquearia. V. *Aeneid*, I, 726: dependent lychni laquearibus aureis / Incensi, et noctem flammis funalia vincunt" [Eliot's note]. Lighted lamps hang from the golden paneled ceiling [*laquearia*], and the torches conquer the night with their flames (Latin); description of the banquet hall where Dido welcomes Aeneas to Carthage (her passion for the visitor, like Cleopatra's, ended in suicide).
8. "Sylvan scene. V. Milton, *Paradise Lost*, IV, 140" [Eliot's note]. The phrase occurs in the description of Eden as first seen by Satan.
9. "V. Ovid, *Metamorphoses*, VI, Philomela" [Eliot's note]. Ovid describes how Tereus raped his sister-in-law, Philomela, and cut out her tongue.

To avenge her, his wife, Procne, murdered her son and fed him to Tereus. All three were changed into birds: the sisters into the nightingale and swallow, Tereus into the hoopoe pursuing them.
1. "Cf. Part III, l[ine] 204" [Eliot's note].
2. In Elizabethan poetry, the conventional rendering of the nightingale's song.
3. "Cf. Part III, l[ine] 195" [Eliot's note].
4. "Cf. Webster: 'Is the wind in that door still?'" [Eliot's note], referring to John Webster's play *The Devil's Law Case* (1623) 3.2.162. In context, the speaker is asking if someone is still alive.
5. "Cf. Part I, ll. 37, 48" [Eliot's note]. See note 5, p. 1345.

130   So intelligent[6]
    "What shall I do now? What shall I do?"
    "I shall rush out as I am, and walk the street
    "With my hair down, so. What shall we do tomorrow?
    "What shall we ever do?"
135   The hot water at ten.
    And if it rains, a closed car at four.
    And we shall play a game of chess,
    Pressing lidless eyes and waiting for a knock upon the door.[7]

       When Lil's husband got demobbed,[8] I said—
140   I didn't mince my words, I said to her myself,
    HURRY UP PLEASE ITS TIME[9]
    Now Albert's coming back, make yourself a bit smart.
    He'll want to know what you done with that money he gave you
    To get yourself some teeth. He did, I was there.
145   You have them all out, Lil, and get a nice set,
    He said, I swear, I can't bear to look at you.
    And no more can't I, I said, and think of poor Albert,
    He's been in the army four years, he wants a good time,
    And if you don't give it him, there's others will, I said.
150   Oh is there, she said. Something o' that, I said.
    Then I'll know who to thank, she said, and give me a straight look.
    HURRY UP PLEASE ITS TIME
    If you don't like it you can get on with it, I said.
    Others can pick and choose if you can't.
155   But if Albert makes off, it won't be for lack of telling.
    You ought to be ashamed, I said, to look so antique.
    (And her only thirty-one.)
    I can't help it, she said, pulling a long face,
    It's them pills I took, to bring it off,[1] she said.
160   (She's had five already, and nearly died of young George.)
    The chemist° said it would be all right, but I've never been   *druggist*
       the same.
    You *are* a proper fool, I said.
    Well, if Albert won't leave you alone, there it is, I said,
    What you get married for if you don't want children?
165   HURRY UP PLEASE ITS TIME
    Well, that Sunday Albert was home, they had a hot
       gammon,°   *smoked ham*
    And they asked me in to dinner, to get the beauty of it hot—
    HURRY UP PLEASE ITS TIME
    HURRY UP PLEASE ITS TIME
170   Goonight Bill. Goonight Lou. Goonight May. Goonight.
    Ta ta. Goonight. Goonight.
    Good night, ladies, good night, sweet ladies, good night, good night.[2]

---

6. Cf. the chorus to "The Shakespearian Rag," a popular song from 1912: "That Shakespearian Rag, most intelligent, very elegant."
7. "Cf. the game of chess in Middleton's *Women Beware Women*" [Eliot's note].
8. Demobilized (discharged from military service) after World War I.

9. Typical call of a British bartender to clear the bar at closing time.
1. To cause an abortion.
2. Cf. Ophelia's farewell before drowning (*Hamlet* 4.5.69–70) and the popular song lyric "Good night ladies, we're going to leave you now."

III. The Fire Sermon[3]

The river's tent is broken: the last fingers of leaf
Clutch and sink into the wet bank. The wind
175 Crosses the brown land, unheard. The nymphs are departed
Sweet Thames, run softly, till I end my song.[4]
The river bears no empty bottles, sandwich papers,
Silk handkerchiefs, cardboard boxes, cigarette ends
Or other testimony of summer nights. The nymphs are departed.
180 And their friends, the loitering heirs of city directors;
Departed, have left no addresses.
By the waters of Leman I sat down and wept[5] . . .
Sweet Thames, run softly till I end my song,
Sweet Thames, run softly, for I speak not loud or long.
185 But at my back in a cold blast I hear[6]
The rattle of the bones, and chuckle spread from ear to ear.
A rat crept softly through the vegetation
Dragging its slimy belly on the bank
While I was fishing in the dull canal
190 On a winter evening round behind the gashouse
Musing upon the king my brother's wreck[7]
And on the king my father's death before him.
White bodies naked on the low damp ground
And bones cast in a little low dry garret,
195 Rattled by the rat's foot only, year to year.
But at my back from time to time I hear[8]
The sound of horns and motors, which shall bring
Sweeney to Mrs. Porter in the spring.[9]
O the moon shone bright on Mrs. Porter
200 And on her daughter
They wash their feet in soda water[1]
Et O ces voix d'enfants, chantant dans la coupole![2]

3. I.e., Buddha's Fire Sermon; see Eliot's note to line 309.
4. "V. Spenser, *Prothalamion*" [Eliot's note]. The line is the refrain of the marriage song by Edmund Spenser (1552–1599; see pp. 159–205), a pastoral celebration of a wedding near the Thames, the river that flows through London.
5. An echo of the exiled Jews mourning for their homeland (Psalm 137): "By the rivers of Babylon, there we sat down, yea, we wept, when we remembered Zion." Lac Léman is the French name for Lake Geneva, and much of *The Waste Land* was written at Lausanne, on its shore. *Leman* is also an archaic word for lover or mistress.
6. Cf. Andrew Marvell, "To His Coy Mistress," lines 21–22 (p. 479).
7. "Cf. *The Tempest*, I, ii" [Eliot's note]. Just before Ariel sings "Full fathom five thy father lies" (see line 48), Ferdinand describes himself as "sitting on a bank, / Weeping again the King my father's wreck. / This music crept by me upon the waters."
8. "Cf. Marvell, *To His Coy Mistress*" [Eliot's note]. See line 185.
9. "Cf. Day, *Parliament of Bees*: "When of the sudden, listening, you shall hear, / A noise of horns and hunting, which shall bring / Actaeon to Diana in the spring' " [Eliot's note]. In Greek mythology, Actaeon saw Diana, chaste goddess of the hunt, naked as she bathed; the goddess changed him into a stag, and his own hounds killed him. *The Parliament of Bees* is the best-known work of the Elizabethan dramatist John Day.
1. "I do not know the origin of the ballad from which these lines are taken: it was reported to me from Sydney, Australia" [Eliot's note]. The bawdy song was popular with Australian soldiers in World War I. Sweeney (line 198) is the figure of vulgar, thoughtless sexual enterprise who figures in Eliot's "Sweeney Among the Nightingales" and "Sweeney Agonistes."
2. "V. Verlaine, *Parsifal*" [Eliot's note]. And O those children's voices singing in the dome! (French); last line of a sonnet by the French poet Paul Verlaine (1844–1896) that treats ironically the conquering of fleshly temptation. In Wagner's opera *Parsifal*, the feet of the title character, a questing knight, are washed before he enters the sanctuary of the Grail.

Twit twit twit
Jug jug jug jug jug jug
205 So rudely forc'd.
Tereu³

Unreal City
Under the brown fog of a winter noon
Mr. Eugenides, the Smyrna° merchant   *port in West Turkey*
210 Unshaven, with a pocket full of currants
C.i.f. London: documents at sight,⁴
Asked me in demotic⁵ French
To luncheon at the Cannon Street Hotel
Followed by a weekend at the Metropole.⁶

215   At the violet hour, when the eyes and back
Turn upward from the desk, when the human engine waits
Like a taxi throbbing waiting,
I Tiresias,⁷ though blind, throbbing between two lives,
Old man with wrinkled female breasts, can see
220 At the violet hour, the evening hour that strives
Homeward, and brings the sailor home from sea,⁸
The typist home at teatime, clears her breakfast, lights
Her stove, and lays out food in tins.
Out of the window perilously spread
225 Her drying combinations° touched by the sun's last rays,   *underwear*
On the divan are piled (at night her bed)
Stockings, slippers, camisoles, and stays.°   *corset*
I Tiresias, old man with wrinkled dugs°   *breasts*
Perceived the scene, and foretold the rest—
230 I too awaited the expected guest.
He, the young man carbuncular,° arrives,   *with pimples*
A small house agent's clerk, with one bold stare,

3. Another conventional Elizabethan rendering of the nightingale's song, as well as a form of the name Tereus (see lines 99–103).
4. "The currants were quoted at a price 'carriage and insurance free to London'; and the Bill of Lading etc. were to be handled to the buyer upon payment of the sight draft" [Eliot's note]. "C.i.f." can also mean "cost, insurance, and freight."
5. I.e., vulgar or simplified.
6. A large hotel at Brighton, a seaside town on England's south coast. *Cannon Street Hotel:* a very large hotel in London's commercial district.
7. "Tiresias, although a mere spectator and not indeed a 'character,' is yet the most important personage in the poem, uniting all the rest. Just as the one-eyed merchant, seller of currants, melts into the Phoenician sailor, and the latter is not wholly distinct from Ferdinand Prince of Naples, so all the women are one woman, and the two sexes meet in Tiresias. What Tiresias *sees,* in fact, is the substance of the poem. The whole passage from Ovid is of great anthropological interest" [Eliot's note]. Eliot then cites in Latin Ovid's version of why Tiresias was blinded, then granted a seer's power (*Metamorphoses* 3.320–38): "Jove [the supreme god, here very drunk] said jokingly to Juno [his wife]: 'You women have greater pleasure in love than that enjoyed by men.' She denied it. So they decided to refer the question to wise Tiresias who knew love from both points of view. For once, with a blow of his staff, he had separated two huge snakes who were copulating in the forest, and miraculously was changed instantly from a man into a woman and remained so for seven years. In the eighth year he saw the snakes again and said: 'If a blow against you is so powerful that it changes the sex of the author of it, now I shall strike you again.' With these words he struck them, and his former shape and masculinity were restored. As referee in the sportive quarrel, he supported Jove's claim. Juno, overly upset by the decision, condemned the arbitrator to eternal blindness. But the all-powerful father (inasmuch as no god can undo what has been done by another god) gave him the power of prophecy, with this honor compensating him for the loss of sight."
8. "This may not appear as exact as Sappho's lines, but I had in mind the 'longshore' or 'dory' fisherman, who returns at nightfall" [Eliot's note]. Fragment 149 of the Greek poet Sappho (fl. ca. 610–ca. 580 B.C.E.): "Evening, bringing all that light-giving dawn has scattered, you bring the sheep, you bring the goat, you bring the child to its mother." But cf. "Requiem," by the Scottish poet Robert Louis Stevenson (1850–1894): "Home is the sailor, home from the sea."

One of the low on whom assurance sits
As a silk hat on a Bradford[9] millionaire.
235   The time is now propitious, as he guesses,
The meal is ended, she is bored and tired,
Endeavours to engage her in caresses
Which still are unreproved, if undesired.
Flushed and decided, he assaults at once;
240   Exploring hands encounter no defence;
His vanity requires no response,
And makes a welcome of indifference.
(And I Tiresias have foresuffered all
Enacted on this same divan or bed;
245   I who have sat by Thebes below the wall[1]
And walked among the lowest of the dead.)
Bestows one final patronizing kiss,
And gropes his way, finding the stairs unlit . . .

    She turns and looks a moment in the glass,
250   Hardly aware of her departed lover;
Her brain allows one half-formed thought to pass:
"Well now that's done: and I'm glad it's over."
When lovely woman stoops to folly and
Paces about her room again, alone,
255   She smoothes her hair with automatic hand,
And puts a record on the gramophone.[2]

    "This music crept by me upon the waters"[3]
And along the Strand, up Queen Victoria Street.
O City city, I can sometimes hear
260   Beside a public bar in Lower Thames Street,
The pleasant whining of a mandoline
And a clatter and a chatter from within
Where fishmen lounge at noon: where the walls
Of Magnus Martyr[4] hold
265   Inexplicable splendour of Ionian white and gold.

       The river sweats[5]
       Oil and tar
       The barges drift
       With the turning tide
270   Red sails
       Wide
       To leeward, swing on the heavy spar.
       The barges wash

9. A manufacturing town in Yorkshire, England, that enjoyed an industrial boom during World War I.
1. Tiresias prophesied in the marketplace by the wall of Thebes, foretold the fall of the Theban kings Oedipus and Creon, and continued to prophesy in the underworld.
2. "V. Goldsmith, the song in *The Vicar of Wakefield*" [Eliot's note]. Cf. Oliver Goldsmith, "When Lovely Woman Stoops to Folly" (p. 686).
3. "V. *The Tempest*, as above" [Eliot's note]. See note to line 191, p. 1349.
4. "The interior of [London's] St. Magnus Martyr is to my mind one of the finest among [Christopher] Wren's interiors" [Eliot's note].
5. "The song of the (three) Thames-daughters begins here. From line 292 to 306 inclusive they speak in turn. V. *Götterdämmerung*, III, i: the Rhine-daughters" [Eliot's note]. Lines 277–78 and 290–91 repeat the refrain of the Rhine maidens lamenting the lost beauty of their river in Wagner's opera.

Drifting logs
275   Down Greenwich reach
Past the Isle of Dogs.[6]
       Weialala leia
       Wallala leialala

Elizabeth and Leicester[7]
280   Beating oars
The stern was formed
A gilded shell
Red and gold
The brisk swell
285   Rippled both shores
Southwest wind
Carried down stream
The peal of bells
White towers
290   Weialala leia
           Wallala leialala

"Trams and dusty trees.
Highbury bore me. Richmond and Kew
Undid me.[8] By Richmond I raised my knees
295   Supine on the floor of a narrow canoe."

"My feet are at Moorgate,[9] and my heart
Under my feet. After the event
He wept. He promised 'a new start.'
I made no comment. What should I resent?"

300   "On Margate Sands.[1]
I can connect
Nothing with nothing.
The broken fingernails of dirty hands.
My people humble people who expect
305   Nothing."
        la la

To Carthage then I came[2]

---

6. A peninsula extending into the Thames opposite Greenwich, a borough of London and Queen Elizabeth I's birthplace.

7. "V. Froude, [*Reign of*] Elizabeth, Vol. I, ch. iv, letter of [Bishop] De Quadra [the ambassador] to Philip of Spain: 'In the afternoon we were in a barge, watching the games on the river. (The queen) was alone with the Lord Robert and myself on the poop, when they began to talk nonsense, and went so far that Lord Robert at last said, as I was on the spot there was no reason why they should not be married if the queen pleased'" [Eliot's note]. Sir Robert Dudley (1532?–1588), earl of Leicester, was romantically involved with the queen.

8. "Cf. Purgatorio, V, 133" [Eliot's note], referring to Dante's "Remember me, who am la Pia; Sien made me, the Maremma undid me"; also quoted by Ezra Pound in "Hugh Selwyn Mauberley" (see note 9, p. 1302). Highbury is a residential suburb in North London; Richmond and Kew are up the river from London.

9. A slum in East London.

1. A beach resort in Kent—popular with London residents—where the Thames broadens into the Channel.

2. "V. St. Augustine's *Confessions*: 'to Carthage then I came, where a cauldron of unholy loves sang all about mine ears'" [Eliot's note]. Augustine is recounting his licentious youth.

Burning burning burning burning[3]
O Lord Thou pluckest me out[4]
310   O Lord Thou pluckest

burning

IV. Death by Water

Phlebas the Phoenician, a fortnight dead,
Forgot the cry of gulls, and the deep sea swell
And the profit and loss.
315   A current under sea
Picked his bones in whispers. As he rose and fell
He passed the stages of his age and youth
Entering the whirlpool.
                         Gentile or Jew
320   O you who turn the wheel and look to windward,
Consider Phlebas, who was once handsome and tall as you.

V. What the Thunder Said[5]

After the torchlight red on sweaty faces
After the frosty silence in the gardens
After the agony in stony places
325   The shouting and the crying
Prison and palace and reverberation
Of thunder of spring over distant mountains
He who was living is now dead
We who were living are now dying
330   With a little patience

Here is no water but only rock
Rock and no water and the sandy road
The road winding above among the mountains
Which are mountains of rock without water
335   If there were water we should stop and drink
Amongst the rock one cannot stop or think
Sweat is dry and feet are in the sand
If there were only water amongst the rock
Dead mountain mouth of carious° teeth that cannot spit   decayed
340   Here one can neither stand nor lie nor sit
There is not even silence in the mountains
But dry sterile thunder without rain
There is not even solitude in the mountains

3. Taken from "the complete text of the Buddha's Fire Sermon (which corresponds in importance to the Sermon on the Mount)" [Eliot's note].
4. "From St. Augustine's *Confessions* again. The collocation of these two representatives of eastern and western asceticism, as the culmination of this part of the poem, is not an accident" [Eliot's note]. Cf. Zechariah 3.2, where the Lord (i.e., God) calls Joshua "a brand plucked out of the fire."
5. "In the first part of Part V three themes are

employed: the journey to Emmaus, the approach to the Chapel Perilous (see Miss Weston's book) and the present decay of eastern Europe" [Eliot's note]. On the third day after his Crucifixion, Jesus appeared to two of his disciples as they walked to the village of Emmaus, but they knew him only when he vanished (Luke 24.13–34). The Chapel Perilous is connected with the quest for the Holy Grail, in which only those of perfect purity can succeed.

But red sullen faces sneer and snarl
345 From doors of mudcracked houses
                           If there were water
   And no rock
   If there were rock
   And also water
350 And water
   A spring
   A pool among the rock
   If there were the sound of water only
   Not the cicada[6]
355 And dry grass singing
   But sound of water over a rock
   Where the hermit-thrush[7] sings in the pine trees
   Drip drop drip drop drop drop drop
   But there is no water

360 Who is the third who walks always beside you?[8]
   When I count, there are only you and I together
   But when I look ahead up the white road
   There is always another one walking beside you
   Gliding wrapt in a brown mantle, hooded
365 I do not know whether a man or a woman
   —But who is that on the other side of you?

   What is that sound high in the air[9]
   Murmur of maternal lamentation
   Who are those hooded hordes swarming
370 Over endless plains, stumbling in cracked earth
   Ringed by the flat horizon only
   What is the city over the mountains
   Cracks and reforms and bursts in the violet air
   Falling towers
375 Jerusalem Athens Alexandria
   Vienna London
   Unreal

   A woman drew her long black hair out tight
   And fiddled whisper music on those strings
380 And bats with baby faces in the violet light
   Whistled, and beat their wings
   And crawled head downward down a blackened wall

6. Grasshopper. Cf. line 23 and note 8, p. 1344.
7. "This is . . . the hermit-thrush which I have heard in Quebec Province. . . . Its 'water-dripping song' is justly celebrated" [Eliot's note].
8. "The following lines were stimulated by the account of one of the Antarctic expeditions (I forget which, but I think one of Shackleton's): it was related that the party of explorers, at the extremity of their strength, had the constant delusion that there was *one more member* than could actually be counted" [Eliot's note]. These lines also recall the journey to Emmaus; see note 2 directly above.
9. Eliot's note to lines 367–77 quotes a passage from the nonfiction book *Blick ins Chaos* (*A Glimpse into Chaos*), by the German writer Herman Hesse (1877–1962), that may be translated as follows: "Already half Europe, already at least half of Eastern Europe, is on the road to Chaos, drives drunken in holy madness along the abyss and sings the while, sings drunk and hymnlike as Dmitri Karamazov sang [in the novel *The Brothers Karamazov*, by the Russian writer Fyodor Dostoyevsky (1821–1881)]. The bourgeois laughs, offended, at these songs, the saint and the prophet hear them with tears."

And upside down in air were towers
Tolling reminiscent bells, that kept the hours
385 And voices singing out of empty cisterns and exhausted wells.

      In this decayed hole among the mountains
In the faint moonlight, the grass is singing
Over the tumbled graves, about the chapel
There is the empty chapel, only the wind's home.
390 It has no windows, and the door swings,
Dry bones can harm no one.
Only a cock stood on the rooftree
Co co rico co co rico[1]
In a flash of lightning. Then a damp gust
395 Bringing rain

      Ganga[2] was sunken, and the limp leaves
Waited for rain, while the black clouds
Gathered far distant, over Himavant.°   *Himalayan peak*
The jungle crouched, humped in silence.
400 Then spoke the thunder
Da[3]
Datta: what have we given?
My friend, blood shaking my heart
The awful daring of a moment's surrender
405 Which an age of prudence can never retract
By this, and this only, we have existed
Which is not to be found in our obituaries
Or in memories draped by the beneficent spider[4]
Or under seals broken by the lean solicitor°   *lawyer*
410 In our empty rooms
Da
Dayadhvam: I have heard the key[5]
Turn in the door once and turn once only
We think of the key, each in his prison
415 Thinking of the key, each confirms a prison
Only at nightfall, ethereal rumours
Revive for a moment a broken Coriolanus[6]

1. When Peter denied Jesus, "immediately the cock crew," as Jesus had predicted (Matthew 26.34, 74–75). Also, in folklore a cock's crow signals the departure of ghosts.
2. The Sanskrit name of the Indian river Ganges.
3. " 'Datta, dayadhvam, damyata' (Give, sympathize, control). The fable of the meaning of the Thunder is found in the *Brihadaranyaka—Upanishad*, 5, 1" [Eliot's note]. In the Hindu fable (found within the ancient, sacred Sanskrit dialogues known as the Upanishads), the supreme deity, Prajapati, gives instruction in the form of the syllable *Da*, which the gods understand as "be restrained" (*damyata*), humans as "give alms" (*datta*), and demons as "have compassion" (*dayadhvam*). All are correct, and a divine voice repeats the syllable with the force of thunder.
4. "Cf. Webster, *The White Devil*, V. vi: ' . . . they'll remarry / Ere the worm pierce your winding-sheet, ere the spider / Make a thin curtain for your epitaphs' " [Eliot's note].
5. "Cf. *Inferno*, XXXIII, 46" [Eliot's note], where Ugolino recalls his imprisonment with his sons in the tower where they starved to death: "And I heard below the door of the horrible tower being locked up." Eliot also cites F. H. Bradley, *Appearance and Reality* (1893), p. 346: "My external sensations are no less private to myself than are my thoughts or my feelings. In either case my experience falls within my own circle, a circle closed on the outside; and, with all its elements alike, every sphere is opaque to the others which surround it. . . . In brief, regarded as an existence which appears in a soul, the whole world for each is peculiar and private to that soul."
6. Legendary Roman patrician, the protagonist of Shakespeare's tragedy *Coriolanus*, who joined forces with the enemy he had once defeated when the leaders of the Roman populace opposed him.

DA
Damyata: The boat responded
420 Gaily, to the hand expert with sail and oar
The sea was calm, your heart would have responded
Gaily, when invited, beating obedient
To controlling hands

                              I sat upon the shore
425 Fishing,[7] with the arid plain behind me
Shall I at least set my lands in order?[8]
London Bridge is falling down falling down falling down[9]
Poi s'ascose nel foco che gli affina[1]
Quando fiam uti chelidon[2]—O swallow swallow[3]
430 *Le Prince d'Aquitaine à la tour abolie*[4]
These fragments I have shored against my ruins
Why then Ile fit you. Hieronymo's mad againe.[5]
Datta. Dayadhvam. Damyata.
                  Shantih   shantih   shantih[6]

                                                        1922

The Hollow Men

Mistah Kurtz—he dead.[7]

A penny for the Old Guy[8]

I

We are the hollow men
We are the stuffed men

---

7. "V. Weston: *From Ritual to Romance;* chapter on the Fisher King" [Eliot's note].
8. Cf. Isaiah 38.1: "Thus saith the Lord, Set thine house in order: for thou shalt die, and not live."
9. One of the later lines of this nursery rhyme is "Take the key and lock her up, my fair lady."
1. "V. *Purgatorio,* XXVI, 148" [Eliot's note]. Eliot here quotes the final lines of Dante's encounter with the late twelfth-century poet Arnaut Daniel, encountered among the lustful in Purgatory: " 'And so I pray you, by that Virtue which guides you to the top of the stair, be reminded in time of my pain.' Then he hid himself in the fire that purifies them" (Italian). This last sentence translates line 428 of *The Waste Land.*
2. "V. *Pervigilium Veneris.* Cf. Philomela in Parts I and II" [Eliot's note]. *The Vigil of Venus,* an anonymous Latin poem (ca. second century C.E.) celebrating the spring festival of the goddess Venus, ends with an allusion to the Procne-Philomela-Tereus myth. The quoted line means "When shall I become like the swallow"; the Latin continues, "that I may cease to be silent."
3. Cf. "Itylus," by Algernon Charles Swinburne (1837–1909; see pp. 1146–52), which begins: "Swallow, my sister, O sister Swallow." Cf. also the song in *The Princess,* by Alfred, Lord Tennyson (1809–1892; see pp. 982–1009), that begins: "O

Swallow, Swallow, flying, flying south."
4. "V. [French writer] Gérard de Nerval [1808–1855], Sonnet *El Desdichado*" [Eliot's note]. The line reads: "The prince of Aquitania in the ruined tower" (French).
5. "V. Kyd's *Spanish Tragedy*" [Eliot's note]. The subtitle of *The Spanish Tragedy,* by the English playwright Thomas Kyd (1558–1594), is *Hieronymo's Mad Againe.* Hieronymo, driven mad by his son's death, "fits" the parts in a court masque so that in the course of it he kills his son's murderers before himself committing suicide.
6. "Shantih. Repeated as here, a formal ending to an Upanishad. 'The Peace which passeth understanding' is our nearest equivalent to this word" [Eliot's note].
7. From the novella *Heart of Darkness,* by the Polish English (Ukrainian-born) novelist Joseph Conrad (1857–1924). The dying words of Mr. Kurtz, the official of a trading company, who has entered the African jungle and descended into evil, are "The horror! The horror!"
8. I.e., money to buy fireworks to burn Guy Fawkes in effigy. Said by begging children in England on November 5, Guy Fawkes Day, a commemoration of Fawkes's failed conspiracy, for which he was executed, to blow up the House of Commons in 1605.

Leaning together
Headpiece filled with straw. Alas!
5   Our dried voices, when
We whisper together
Are quiet and meaningless
As wind in dry grass
Or rats' feet over broken glass
10 In our dry cellar

Shape without form, shade without colour,
Paralysed force, gesture without motion;

Those who have crossed
With direct eyes, to death's other Kingdom
15 Remember us—if at all—not as lost
Violent souls, but only
As the hollow men
The stuffed men.

II

Eyes I dare not meet in dreams
20 In death's dream kingdom
These do not appear:
There, the eyes are
Sunlight on a broken column
There, is a tree swinging
25 And voices are
In the wind's singing
More distant and more solemn
Than a fading star.

Let me be no nearer
30 In death's dream kingdom
Let me also wear
Such deliberate disguises
Rat's coat, crowskin, crossed staves
In a field
35 Behaving as the wind behaves
No nearer—

Not that final meeting
In the twilight kingdom

III

This is the dead land
40 This is cactus land
Here the stone images
Are raised, here they receive
The supplication of a dead man's hand
Under the twinkle of a fading star.

45 Is it like this
In death's other kingdom
Waking alone
At the hour when we are
Trembling with tenderness
50 Lips that would kiss
Form prayers to broken stone.

IV

The eyes are not here
There are no eyes here
In this valley of dying stars
55 In this hollow valley
This broken jaw of our lost kingdoms

In this last of meeting places
We grope together
And avoid speech
60 Gathered on this beach of the tumid river

Sightless, unless
The eyes reappear
As the perpetual star
Multifoliate rose[9]
65 Of death's twilight kingdom
The hope only
Of empty men.

V

Here we go round the prickly pear
Prickly pear prickly pear
70 *Here we go round the prickly pear*
At five o'clock in the morning.[1]

Between the idea
And the reality
Between the motion
75 And the act
Falls the Shadow
                    For Thine is the Kingdom[2]
Between the conception
And the creation
80 Between the emotion
And the response
Falls the Shadow
                    Life is very long

---

9. Reference to the vision of saved souls surrounding God in *Paradiso*, the third part of Dante's *Divine Comedy*.
1. An ironic variation on the children's chant "Here we go round the mulberry bush."
2. Fragment from the end of the Lord's Prayer: "For Thine is the Kingdom, and the power, and the glory, forever and ever, Amen."

Between the desire
85 And the spasm
Between the potency
And the existence
Between the essence
And the descent
90 Falls the Shadow
      For Thine is the Kingdom

For Thine is
Life is
For Thine is the

95 *This is the way the world ends*
    This is the way the world ends
    This is the way the world ends
    Not with a bang but a whimper.

                                                          1925

Journey of the Magi[3]

    "A cold coming we had of it,[4]
    Just the worst time of the year
    For a journey, and such a long journey:
    The ways deep and the weather sharp,
5   The very dead of winter."
    And the camels galled, sore-footed, refractory,
    Lying down in the melting snow.
    There were times we regretted
    The summer palaces on slopes, the terraces,
10 And the silken girls bringing sherbet.
    Then the camel men cursing and grumbling
    And running away, and wanting their liquor and women,
    And the night-fires going out, and the lack of shelters,
    And the cities hostile and the towns unfriendly
15 And the villages dirty and charging high prices:
    A hard time we had of it.
    At the end we preferred to travel all night,
    Sleeping in snatches,
    With the voices singing in our ears, saying
20 That this was all folly.

    Then at dawn we came down to a temperate valley,
    Wet, below the snow line, smelling of vegetation;
    With a running stream and a water-mill beating the darkness,

---

3. The poem re-creates the recollections of one of the wise men, or Magi, who followed the star to Bethlehem bearing gifts for the newly born Jesus (Matthew 2.1–12).

4. The first five lines are adapted from the sermon preached at Christmas, 1622, by Bishop Lancelot Andrewes.

And three trees on the low sky,[5]
25 And an old white horse galloped away in the meadow.
Then we came to a tavern with vine-leaves over the lintel,
Six hands at an open door dicing for pieces of silver,
And feet kicking the empty wine-skins.
But there was no information, and so we continued
30 And arrived at evening, not a moment too soon
Finding the place; it was (you may say) satisfactory.

All this was a long time ago, I remember,
And I would do it again, but set down
This set down
35 This: were we led all that way for
Birth or Death? There was a Birth, certainly,
We had evidence and no doubt. I had seen birth and death,
But had thought they were different; this Birth was
Hard and bitter agony for us, like Death, our death.
40 We returned to our places, these Kingdoms,
But no longer at ease here, in the old dispensation,
With an alien people clutching their gods.
I should be glad of another death.

1927

FROM FOUR QUARTETS

Little Gidding[6]

I

Midwinter spring is its own season
Sempiternal° though sodden towards sundown,   *everlasting*
Suspended in time, between pole and tropic.
When the short day is brightest, with frost and fire,
5 The brief sun flames the ice, on pond and ditches,
In windless cold that is the heart's heat,
Reflecting in a watery mirror
A glare that is blindness in the early afternoon.
And glow more intense than blaze of branch, or brazier,
10 Stirs the dumb spirit: no wind, but pentecostal fire[7]

---

5. The image prefigures the three crosses of the Crucifixion (Luke 23.32), as line 27 suggests the Roman soldiers casting lots for Jesus' robe (John 19.23–24), as well as the pieces of silver paid to Judas for betraying him (Matthew 26.14–15).
6. The final and, in Eliot's opinion, the best poem of *Four Quartets*, each of which is divided into five parts. This quartet, like the others, addresses one of the four elements; in "Little Gidding" it is fire. The imagery is reminiscent of the "Fire Sermon" section of *The Waste Land* (p. 1349), in which fire suggests both torment and salvation. Little

Gidding, an Anglican religious community, was founded by Nicholas Ferrar in 1625. The community was dispersed after the Puritans' victory in the English Civil War, but in the nineteenth century its chapel was rebuilt.
7. See Acts 2.2–4, where Jesus' disciples are assembled on the feast of Pentecost: "And suddenly there came a sound from heaven, as of a rushing mighty wind. . . . And there appeared unto them cloven tongues, like as of fire. . . . And they were all filled with the Holy Ghost."

In the dark time of the year. Between melting and freezing
The soul's sap quivers. There is no earth smell
Or smell of living thing. This is the spring time
But not in time's covenant. Now the hedgerow
15   Is blanched for an hour with transitory blossom
Of snow, a bloom more sudden
Than that of summer, neither budding nor fading,
Not in the scheme of generation.
Where is the summer, the unimaginable
20   Zero summer?

                    If you came this way,
Taking the route you would be likely to take
From the place you would be likely to come from,
If you came this way in may time, you would find the hedges
25   White again, in May, with voluptuary sweetness.
It would be the same at the end of the journey,
If you came at night like a broken king,[8]
If you came by day not knowing what you came for,
It would be the same, when you leave the rough road
30   And turn behind the pig-sty to the dull façade
And the tombstone. And what you thought you came for
Is only a shell, a husk of meaning
From which the purpose breaks only when it is fulfilled
If at all. Either you had no purpose
35   Or the purpose is beyond the end you figured
And is altered in fulfilment. There are other places
Which also are the world's end, some at the sea jaws,
Or over a dark lake, in a desert or a city—
But this is the nearest, in place and time,
40   Now and in England.

                    If you came this way,
Taking any route, starting from anywhere,
At any time or at any season,
It would always be the same: you would have to put off
45   Sense and notion. You are not here to verify,
Instruct yourself, or inform curiosity
Or carry report. You are here to kneel
Where prayer has been valid. And prayer is more
Than an order of words, the conscious occupation
50   Of the praying mind, or the sound of the voice praying.
And what the dead had no speech for, when living,
They can tell you, being dead: the communication
Of the dead is tongued with fire beyond the language of the living.
Here, the intersection of the timeless moment
55   Is England and nowhere. Never and always.

---

8. King Charles I (1600–1649), who went to Little Gidding after his defeat in the civil war.

II

Ash on an old man's sleeve
Is all the ash the burnt roses leave.
Dust in the air suspended
Marks the place where a story ended.
60 Dust inbreathed was a house—
The wall, the wainscot and the mouse.
The death of hope and despair,
        This is the death of air.[9]
    There are flood and drouth
65   Over the eyes and in the mouth,
Dead water and dead sand
Contending for the upper hand.
The parched eviscerate soil
Gapes at the vanity of toil,
70 Laughs without mirth.
        This is the death of earth.

        Water and fire succeed
The town, the pasture and the weed.
Water and fire deride
75 The sacrifice that we denied.
Water and fire shall rot
The marred foundations we forgot,
Of sanctuary and choir.
        This is the death of water and fire.

80   In the uncertain hour before the morning[1]
        Near the ending of interminable night
        At the recurrent end of the unending
After the dark dove with the flickering tongue[2]
        Had passed below the horizon of his homing
85   While the dead leaves still rattled on like tin
Over the asphalt where no other sound was
        Between three districts whence the smoke arose
        I met one walking, loitering and hurried
As if blown towards me like the metal leaves
90   Before the urban dawn wind unresisting.
        And as I fixed upon the down-turned face
That pointed scrutiny with which we challenge
        The first-met stranger in the waning dusk
        I caught the sudden look of some dead master
95 Whom I had known, forgotten, half recalled
        Both one and many; in the brown baked features
        The eyes of a familiar compound ghost[3]
Both intimate and unidentifiable.

9. The Greek philosopher Heraclitus (ca. 540–ca. 480 B.C.E.) theorized about the conflict among the elements: "Fire lives in the death of air."
1. The terza rima stanza pattern used by Dante in his *Divine Comedy* is roughly suggested by Eliot's form in this final section of part II. The speaker here patrols the streets as Eliot had done as an air-raid warden in London during World War II.
2. The Nazi dive bomber.
3. I.e., compounding the ghosts of two Irish-Anglo poets, William Butler Yeats (1865–1939; see pp. 1188–1211) and Jonathan Swift (1667–1745; see pp. 568–89).

So I assumed a double part, and cried
100   And heard another's voice cry: "What! are *you* here?"[4]
Although we were not. I was still the same,
    Knowing myself yet being someone other—
    And he a face still forming; yet the words sufficed
To compel the recognition they preceded.
105   And so, compliant to the common wind,
    Too strange to each other for misunderstanding,
In concord at this intersection time
    Of meeting nowhere, no before and after,
    We trod the pavement in a dead patrol.
110 I said: "The wonder that I feel is easy,
    Yet ease is cause of wonder. Therefore speak:
    I may not comprehend, may not remember."
And he: "I am not eager to rehearse
    My thought and theory which you have forgotten.
115   These things have served their purpose: let them be.
So with your own, and pray they be forgiven
    By others, as I pray you to forgive
    Both bad and good. Last season's fruit is eaten
And the fullfed beast shall kick the empty pail.
120   For last year's words belong to last year's language
    And next year's words await another voice.
But, as the passage now presents no hindrance
    To the spirit unappeased and peregrine°   *wandering*
    Between two worlds become much like each other,
125 So I find words I never thought to speak
    In streets I never thought I should revisit
    When I left my body on a distant shore.
Since our concern was speech, and speech impelled us
    To purify the dialect of the tribe[5]
130   And urge the mind to aftersight and foresight,
Let me disclose the gifts reserved for age
    To set a crown upon your lifetime's effort.
    First, the cold friction of expiring sense
Without enchantment, offering no promise
135   But bitter tastelessness of shadow fruit
    As body and soul begin to fall asunder.
Second, the conscious impotence of rage[6]
    At human folly, and the laceration
    Of laughter at what ceases to amuse.[7]
140 And last, the rending pain of re-enactment
    Of all that you have done, and been; the shame
    Of motives late revealed, and the awareness

4. Dante's words when he recognizes his mentor, Brunetto Latini, in *Inferno* 15.30.
5. From the poem "Le Tombeau d'Edgar Poe," by the French poet Stéphane Mallarmé (1842–1898): "Donner un sens plus pur aux mots de la tribu."
6. Cf. W. B. Yeats, "The Spur," lines 1–2: "You think it horrible that lust and rage / Should dance attendance upon my old age."
7. Allusion to Swift's Latin epitaph for himself, as translated by Yeats: "Savage indignation now / Cannot lacerate his breast."

Of things ill done and done to others' harm
Which once you took for exercise of virtue.[8]
145   Then fools' approval stings, and honour stains.
From wrong to wrong the exasperated spirit
Proceeds, unless restored by that refining fire[9]
Where you must move in measure, like a dancer."[1]
The day was breaking. In the disfigured street
150   He left me, with a kind of valediction,
And faded on the blowing of the horn.[2]

III

There are three conditions which often look alike
Yet differ completely, flourish in the same hedgerow:
Attachment to self and to things and to persons, detachment
155   From self and from things and from persons; and, growing between
        them, indifference
Which resembles the others as death resembles life,
Being between two lives—unflowering, between
The live and the dead nettle. This is the use of memory:
For liberation—not less of love but expanding
160   Of love beyond desire, and so liberation
From the future as well as the past. Thus, love of a country
Begins as attachment to our own field of action
And comes to find that action of little importance
Though never indifferent. History may be servitude,
165   History may be freedom. See, now they vanish,
The faces and places, with the self which, as it could, loved them,
To become renewed, transfigured, in another pattern.

    Sin is Behovely,[3] but
All shall be well, and
170   All manner of thing shall be well.
If I think, again, of this place,
And of people, not wholly commendable,
Of no immediate kin or kindness,
But some of peculiar genius,
175   All touched by a common genius,
United in the strife which divided them;
If I think of a king at nightfall,
Of three men, and more, on the scaffold[4]
And a few who died forgotten
180   In other places, here and abroad,

8. Cf. Yeats, "Vacillation," esp. lines 51–56: "Things said or done long years ago, / Or things I did not do or say / But thought that I might say or do, / Weigh me down . . ."
9. As in the "Fire Sermon" section of *The Waste Land,* which alludes to Buddha's counseling his followers to turn away from the fires of passion and to attain freedom from earthly things.
1. Allusion to the images of humankind as dancers in Yeats, "Among School Children" and "Nineteen Hundred and Nineteen."

2. Eliot's description of the "All clear" siren fading after the air raid is phrased to recall the disappearance of Hamlet's father's ghost in *Hamlet* 1.1.138: "It faded on the crowing of the cock."
3. Necessary in God's eye. The fourteenth-century mystic Julian of Norwich wrote, "Sin is behovable but all shall be well . . . and all manner of things shall be well."
4. King Charles I and, earlier, his aides Thomas Wentworth and Archbishop Laud were executed on the scaffold.

And a few who died blind and quiet,[5]
Why should we celebrate
These dead men more than the dying?
It is not to ring the bell backward
185 Nor is it an incantation
To summon the spectre of a Rose.[6]
We cannot revive old factions
We cannot restore old policies
Or follow an antique drum.
190 These men, and those who opposed them
And those whom they opposed
Accept the constitution of silence
And are folded in a single party.
Whatever we inherit from the fortunate
195 We have taken from the defeated
What they had to leave us—a symbol:
A symbol perfected in death.
And all shall be well and
All manner of thing shall be well
200 By the purification of the motive
In the ground of our beseeching.[7]

IV

The dove[8] descending breaks the air
With flame of incandescent terror
Of which the tongues declare
205 The one discharge from sin and error.
The only hope, or else despair
    Lies in the choice of pyre or pyre—
    To be redeemed from fire by fire.

Who then devised the torment? Love.
210 Love is the unfamiliar Name
Behind the hands that wove
The intolerable shirt of flame
Which human power cannot remove.[9]
    We only live, only suspire°   breathe
215 Consumed by either fire or fire.

V

What we call the beginning is often the end
And to make an end is to make a beginning.

1942, 1943

5. I.e., Milton, who sided against Charles during
the civil war.
6. Allusions here to the title of a ballet in which a
girl dreams of a rose she wore to a ball, and to the
Wars of the Roses, in which the house of Lancaster
was the white rose and the house of York the red.
7. According to Julian of Norwich, "the ground of

our beseeching" is love.
8. Here, symbolizing the Holy Ghost, with its
tongues of fire, and the dive bomber.
9. In Greek mythology, the shirt that Hercules'
wife gave Nessus because she believed it would win
his love; it clung to his skin so painfully that he
immolated himself on a pyre.

The end is where we start from. And every phrase
And sentence that is right (where every word is at home,
220 Taking its place to support the others,
The word neither diffident nor ostentatious,
An easy commerce of the old and the new,
The common word exact without vulgarity,
The formal word precise but not pedantic,
225 The complete consort dancing together)
Every phrase and every sentence is an end and a beginning,
Every poem an epitaph. And any action
Is a step to the block, to the fire, down the sea's throat
Or to an illegible stone: and that is where we start.
230 We die with the dying:
See, they depart, and we go with them.
We are born with the dead:
See, they depart, and we go with them.
The moment of the rose and the moment of the yew-tree[1]
235 Are of equal duration. A people without history
Is not redeemed from time, for history is a pattern
Of timeless moments. So, while the light fails
On a winter's afternoon, in a secluded chapel
History is now and England.
240 With the drawing of this Love and the voice of this Calling[2]

     We shall not cease from exploration
And the end of all our exploring
Will be to arrive where we started
And know the place for the first time.
245 Through the unknown, remembered gate
When the last of earth left to discover
Is that which was the beginning;
At the source of the longest river
The voice of the hidden waterfall
250 And the children in the apple-tree
Not known, because not looked for
But heard, half-heard, in the stillness
Between two waves of the sea.
Quick now, here, now, always—[3]
255 A condition of complete simplicity
(Costing not less than everything)
And all shall be well and
All manner of thing shall be well
When the tongues of flame are in-folded
260 Into the crowned knot[4] of fire
And the fire and the rose are one.

                            1942, 1943

---

1. Symbolizing death and grief, in contrast with the rose.
2. Quotation from the anonymous fourteenth-century religious work *The Cloud of Unknowing*.
3. Eliot comes full circle, to an image from *Four*

Quartets's first poem, "Burnt Norton": "There rises the hidden laughter / Of children in the foliage / Quick now, here, always."
4. A nautical knot, tied to prevent untwisting.

JOHN CROWE RANSOM
1888–1974

Bells for John Whiteside's Daughter

There was such speed in her little body,
And such lightness in her footfall,
It is no wonder her brown study
Astonishes us all.

5 Her wars were bruited° in our high window.   *loudly voiced*
We looked among orchard trees and beyond
Where she took arms against her shadow,
Or harried unto the pond

The lazy geese, like a snow cloud
10 Dripping their snow on the green grass,
Tricking and stopping, sleepy and proud,
Who cried in goose, Alas,

For the tireless heart within the little
Lady with rod that made them rise
15 From their noon apple-dreams and scuttle
Goose-fashion under the skies!

But now go the bells, and we are ready,
In one house we are sternly stopped
To say we are vexed at her brown study,
20 Lying so primly propped.

1924

Piazza Piece[1]

—I am a gentleman in a dustcoat trying
To make you hear. Your ears are soft and small
And listen to an old man not at all,
They want the young men's whispering and sighing.
5 But see the roses on your trellis dying
And hear the spectral singing of the moon;
For I must have my lovely lady soon,
I am a gentleman in a dustcoat trying.

—I am a lady young in beauty waiting
10 Until my truelove comes, and then we kiss.
But what gray man among the vines is this
Whose words are dry and faint as in a dream?

1. This sonnet plays upon the old folktale of Death and the Maiden. *Piazza*: porch.

Back from my trellis, Sir, before I scream!
I am a lady young in beauty waiting.

1925   1927

Blue Girls

Twirling your blue skirts, travelling the sward°   *grass*
Under the towers of your seminary,
Go listen to your teachers old and contrary
Without believing a word.

5   Tie the white fillets° then about your hair   *ribbons*
And think no more of what will come to pass
Than bluebirds that go walking on the grass
And chattering on the air.

Practise your beauty, blue girls, before it fail;
10   And I will cry with my loud lips and publish
Beauty which all our power shall never establish,
It is so frail.

For I could tell you a story which is true;
I know a woman with a terrible tongue,
15   Blear° eyes fallen from blue,   *bleary*
All her perfections tarnished—yet it is not long
Since she was lovelier than any of you.

1927

Parting, without a Sequel

She has finished and sealed the letter
At last, which he so richly has deserved,
With characters venomous and hatefully curved,
And nothing could be better.

5   But even as she gave it
Saying to the blue-capped functioner of doom,
"Into his hands," she hoped the leering groom
Might somewhere lose and leave it.

Then all the blood
10   Forsook the face. She was too pale for tears,
Observing the ruin of her younger years.
She went and stood

Under her father's vaunting oak
Who kept his peace in wind and sun, and glistened
15   Stoical in the rain; to whom she listened
If he spoke.

And now the agitation of the rain
Rasped his sere leaves, and he talked low and gentle
Reproaching the wan daughter by the lintel;
20   Ceasing and beginning again.

Away went the messenger's bicycle,
His serpent's track went up the hill forever,
And all the time she stood there hot as fever
And cold as any icicle.

                                  1927

Lady Lost

This morning, flew up the lane
A timid lady bird to our birdbath
And eyed her image dolefully as death;
This afternoon, knocked on our windowpane
5   To be let in from the rain.

And when I caught her eye
She looked aside, but at the clapping thunder
And sight of the whole world blazing up like tinder
Looked in on us again so miserably
10   It was as if she would cry.

So I will go out into the park and say,
"Who has lost a delicate brown-eyed lady
In the West End section? Or has anybody
Injured some fine woman in some dark way
15   Last night, or yesterday?

"Let the owner come and claim possession,
No questions will be asked. But stroke her gently
With loving words, and she will evidently
Return to her full soft-haired white-breasted fashion
20   And her right home and her right passion."

                                  1927

CONRAD AIKEN
1889–1973

From Senlin:[1] A Biography

II. His Futile Preoccupations

2[2]

It is morning, Senlin says, and in the morning
When the light drips through the shutters like the dew,
I arise, I face the sunrise,
And do the things my fathers learned to do.
5   Stars in the purple dusk above the rooftops
Pale in a saffron mist and seem to die,
And I myself on a swiftly tilting planet
Stand before a glass and tie my tie.

Vine leaves tap my window,
10   Dew-drops sing to the garden stones,
The robin chirps in the chinaberry tree
Repeating three clear tones.

It is morning. I stand by the mirror
And tie my tie once more.
15   While waves far off in a pale rose twilight
Crash on a coral shore.
I stand by a mirror and comb my hair:
How small and white my face!—
The green earth tilts through a sphere of air
20   And bathes in a flame of space.

There are houses hanging above the stars
And stars hung under a sea.
And a sun far off in a shell of silence
Dapples my walls for me.

25   It is morning, Senlin says, and in the morning
Should I not pause in the light to remember god?
Upright and firm I stand on a star unstable,
He is immense and lonely as a cloud.[3]
I will dedicate this moment before my mirror
30   To him alone, for him I will comb my hair.
Accept these humble offerings, cloud of silence!
I will think of you as I descend the stair.

Vine leaves tap my window,
The snail-track shines on the stones,

---

1. An invented name that, according to Aiken's preface to *The Divine Pilgrim* (1949), "means literally the 'little old man' that each of us must become"; the poem poses "the basic and possibly unanswerable question, *who and what am I,* how is it that I am I, Senlin, and not someone else?"
2. This section has also been published separately as "Morning Song."
3. An allusion to William Wordsworth, "I Wandered Lonely as a Cloud" (p. 801).

35 Dew-drops flash from the chinaberry tree
    Repeating two clear tones.

    It is morning, I awake from a bed of silence,
    Shining I rise from the starless waters of sleep.
    The walls are about me still as in the evening,
40 I am the same, and the same name still I keep.
    The earth revolves with me, yet makes no motion,
    The stars pale silently in a coral sky.
    In a whistling void I stand before my mirror,
    Unconcerned, and tie my tie.

45 There are horses neighing on far-off hills
    Tossing their long white manes,
    And mountains flash in the rose-white dusk,
    Their shoulders black with rains.
    It is morning. I stand by the mirror
50 And surprise my soul once more;
    The blue air rushes above my ceiling,
    There are suns beneath my floor.

    . . . It is morning, Senlin says, I ascend from darkness
    And depart on the winds of space for I know not where,
55 My watch is wound, a key is in my pocket,
    And the sky is darkened as I descend the stair.
    There are shadows across the windows, clouds in heaven,
    And a god among the stars; and I will go
    Thinking of him as I might think of daybreak
60 And humming a tune I know.

    Vine leaves tap at the window,
    Dewdrops sing to the garden stones,
    The robin chirps in the chinaberry tree
    Repeating three clear tones.

                                                    1918

IVOR GURNEY
1890–1937

To His Love

    He's gone, and all our plans
        Are useless indeed.
    We'll walk no more on Cotswold[1]
        Where the sheep feed
5   Quietly and take no heed.

---

1. Range of hills in Gloucestershire, in southwest-central England.

His body that was so quick
　　Is not as you
Knew it, on Severn river[2]
　　Under the blue
10　　Driving our small boat through.

You would not know him now . . .
　　But still he died
Nobly, so cover him over
　　With violets of pride
15　　Purple from Severn side.

Cover him, cover him soon!
　　And with thick-set
Masses of memoried flowers—
　　Hide that red wet
20　　Thing I must somehow forget.

1919

The Silent One

Who died on the wires,[3] and hung there, one of two—
Who for his hours of life had chattered through
Infinite lovely chatter of Bucks[4] accent:
Yet faced unbroken wires; stepped over, and went
5　A noble fool, faithful to his stripes—and ended.
But I weak, hungry, and willing only for the chance
Of line—to fight in the line, lay down under unbroken
Wires, and saw the flashes and kept unshaken,
Till the politest voice—a finicking accent, said:
10　"Do you think you might crawl through there: there's a hole."
Darkness, shot at: I smiled, as politely replied—
"I'm afraid not, Sir." There was no hole no way to be seen
Nothing but chance of death, after tearing of clothes.
Kept flat, and watched the darkness, hearing bullets whizzing—
15　And thought of music—and swore deep heart's deep oaths
(Polite to God) and retreated and came on again,
Again retreated—and a second time faced the screen.

1954

First Time In

After the dread tales and red yarns of the Line
Anything might have come to us; but the divine

---

2. Which flows west of the Cotswolds.
3. The barbed wire protecting the front from
infantry attack.
4. Buckinghamshire, in southern England.

Afterglow brought us up to a Welsh colony
Hiding in sandbag ditches, whispering consolatory
5   Soft foreign things. Then we were taken in
To low huts candle-lit, shaded close by slitten°   *slit*
Oilsheets, and there the boys gave us kind welcome,
So that we looked out as from the edge of home,
Sang us Welsh things, and changed all former notions
10   To human hopeful things. And the next day's guns
Nor any line-pangs ever quite could blot out
That strangely beautiful entry to war's rout;
Candles they gave us, precious and shared over-rations—
Ulysses[5] found little more in his wanderings without doubt.
15   "David of the White Rock", the "Slumber Song" so soft, and that
Beautiful tune to which roguish words by Welsh pit boys
Are sung—but never more beautiful than there under the guns'
    noise.

1919–20   1982

ISAAC ROSENBERG
1890–1918

Break of Day in the Trenches

The darkness crumbles away.
It is the same old druid[1] Time as ever,
Only a live thing leaps my hand,
A queer sardonic rat,
5   As I pull the parapet's[2] poppy
To stick behind my ear.
Droll rat, they would shoot you if they knew
Your cosmopolitan sympathies.
Now you have touched this English hand
10   You will do the same to a German
Soon, no doubt, if it be your pleasure
To cross the sleeping green between.
It seems you inwardly grin as you pass
Strong eyes, fine limbs, haughty athletes,
15   Less chanced than you for life,
Bonds to the whims of murder,
Sprawled in the bowels of the earth,
The torn fields of France.
What do you see in our eyes
20   At the shrieking iron and flame
Hurled through still heavens?
What quaver—what heart aghast?

5. Or Odysseus, the hero of Homer's *Odyssey*, who
spent ten years wandering on his way home after
the Trojan War.

1. Member of an ancient Celtic order of priest-
magicians.
2. Wall protecting a trench in World War I.

Poppies whose roots are in man's veins
Drop, and are ever dropping;
25   But mine in my ear is safe—
Just a little white with the dust.

June 1916   1922

Louse Hunting

Nudes—stark and glistening,
Yelling in lurid glee. Grinning faces
And raging limbs
Whirl over the floor one fire.
5   For a shirt verminously busy
Yon soldier tore from his throat, with oaths
Godhead might shrink at, but not the lice.
And soon the shirt was aflare
Over the candle he'd lit while we lay.

10   Then we all sprang up and stript
To hunt the verminous brood.
Soon like a demons' pantomime
The place was raging.
See the silhouettes agape,
15   See the gibbering shadows
Mixed with the battled arms on the wall.
See gargantuan hooked fingers
Pluck in supreme flesh
To smutch supreme littleness.
20   See the merry limbs in hot Highland fling[3]
Because some wizard vermin
Charmed from the quiet this revel
When our ears were half lulled
By the dark music
25   Blown from Sleep's trumpet.

1917   1922

Dead Man's Dump

The plunging limbers[4] over the shattered track
Racketed with their rusty freight,
Struck out like many crowns of thorns,
And the rusty stakes like sceptres old
5   To stay the flood of brutish men
Upon our brothers dear.

---

3. Scottish dance.
4. Two-wheeled vehicles for pulling guns or caissons (ammunition wagons).

The wheels lurched over sprawled dead
But pained them not, though their bones crunched,
Their shut mouths made no moan.
10 They lie there huddled, friend and foeman,
Man born of man, and born of woman,
And shells go crying over them
From night till night and now.

Earth has waited for them
15 All the time of their growth
Fretting for their decay:
Now she has them at last!
In the strength of their strength
Suspended—stopped and held.

20 What fierce imaginings their dark souls lit
Earth! have they gone into you?
Somewhere they must have gone,
And flung on your hard back
Is their souls' sack,
25 Emptied of God-ancestralled essences.
Who hurled them out? Who hurled?

None saw their spirits' shadow shake the grass,
Or stood aside for the half-used life to pass
Out of those doomed nostrils and the doomed mouth,
30 When the swift iron burning bee
Drained the wild honey of their youth.

What of us, who flung on the shrieking pyre,
Walk, our usual thoughts untouched,
Our lucky limbs as on ichor[5] fed,
35 Immortal seeming ever?
Perhaps when the flames beat loud on us,
A fear may choke in our veins
And the startled blood may stop.

The air is loud with death,
40 The dark air spurts with fire
The explosions ceaseless are.
Timelessly now, some minutes past,
These dead strode time with vigorous life,
Till the shrapnel called "an end!"
45 But not to all. In bleeding pangs
Some borne on stretchers dreamed of home,
Dear things, war-blotted from their hearts.

A man's brains splattered on
A stretcher-bearer's face;
50 His shook shoulders slipped their load,
But when they bent to look again

5. In Greek mythology, the ethereal fluid flowing through the veins of the gods.

The drowning soul was sunk too deep
For human tenderness.

They left this dead with the older dead,
55 Stretched at the cross roads.

Burnt black by strange decay,
Their sinister faces lie
The lid over each eye,
The grass and coloured clay
60 More motion have than they,
Joined to the great sunk silences.

Here is one not long dead;
His dark hearing caught our far wheels,
And the choked soul stretched weak hands
65 To reach the living word the far wheels said,
The blood-dazed intelligence beating for light,
Crying through the suspense of the far torturing wheels
Swift for the end to break,
Or the wheels to break,
70 Cried as the tide of the world broke over his sight.

Will they come? Will they ever come?
Even as the mixed hoofs of the mules,
The quivering-bellied mules,
And the rushing wheels all mixed
75 With his tortured upturned sight,
So we crashed round the bend,
We heard his weak scream,
We heard his very last sound,
And our wheels grazed his dead face.

1917   1922

HUGH MacDIARMID
(CHRISTOPHER MURRAY GRIEVE)
1892–1978

From Lament for the Great Music

Yet there is no great problem in the world to-day
Except disease and death men cannot end
If no man tries to dominate another.
The struggle for material existence is over. It has been won.
5 The need for repressions and disciplines has passed.
The struggle for truth and that indescribable necessity,
Beauty, begins now, hampered by none of the lower needs.

No one now needs live less or be less than his utmost.
And in the slow and devious development that has brought men to
    this stage
10 Scottish genius has played a foremost role. Yet I turn to you,
For unselfish intellect rises like a perfume
Above the faults and follies of the world of will.
But for the excellence of the typical swift life no nation
Deserves to be remembered more than the sands of the sea.

15 I am only that Job[1] in feathers, a heron myself,
Gaunt and unsubstantial—yet immune to the vicissitudes
Other birds accept as a matter of course; impervious to the effects
Of even the wildest weather, no mean consideration in a country
    like this;
And my appetite is not restricted to any particular fare.
20 Hence I am encountered in places far removed from one another
And widely different in an intimately topographical sense
—Spearing a rat at the mouth of a culvert at midnight
And bolting an eel on the seashore in the halflight of dawn—
Communal dweller yet lone hunter, lumbering yet swift and
    sustained flier,
25 The usual steely expression of my eyes does not flatter me;
Few birds perhaps have so successfully solved
The problem of existence as my grey lanky self
That in light or darkness, wet or shine, subsists
By a combination of alertness, patience, and passivity.
30 A kind of Caolite mac Ronain[2] too; but it takes
    All my wits in Scotland to-day.

This is the darkness where you have been; and have left
I think forever. It is the darkness from which nothing is cast out,
No loss, no wanton pain, no disease, no insanity,
35 None of the unripe intelligence of so-called dead nature,
Abortive attempts of nature to reflect itself.
All the unintelligible burden that alone leads to the height
Where it seems that extremes meet and I could reach you
i bh-fogus do dhul ar neamh-nidh, with a leim eanamhail.[3]
40 In this depth that I dare not leave
I who am no dilettante of chaos and find
No bitter gratification in the contemplation of ultimate Incoherence
Know that the world is at any given moment anything it may be
    called
And even more difficult to group round any central character,
45 Yet it is out of this aimless dispersion, all these zig-zagging efforts,
All this disorderly growth, that the ideal of an epoch ends
By disentangling itself. Myriads of human activities
Are scattered in all directions by the indifferent forces

1. Biblical character who has come to represent
patience in adversity.
2. "The grey spare swift runner, he who saved
Fionn once by that wonderful feat of gathering
couples of all the wild beasts and birds of Ireland
(a ram and a crimson sheep from Inis, two water-
birds from the Erne, two cormorants from the
Cliannth, two foxes from Slieve Gullion, and the
rest)" [MacDiarmid's note].
3. Birdlike leap (Gaelic). I bh-fogus do dhul ar
neamh-nidh: on the confines of vanishing (Gaelic).

Of self-interest, passion, crime, madness—but out of their number
50 Some few of these activities are endowed with a little constancy
By the pure in heart, for reasons which seem to respond
To the most elementary designs of the spirit.
Civilisation, culture, all the good in the world
Depends ultimately on the existence of a few men of good will.
55 The perspective will converge upon them yet.
I dare not leave this dark and distracted scene.
I believe in the necessary and unavoidable responsibility of man
And in the ineluctable certainty of the resurrection
And know that the mind of man creates no ideas
60 Though it is ideas alone that create.
Mind is the organ through which the Universe reaches
Such consciousness of itself as is possible now, and I must not
        brood
On the intermittence of genius, the way consciousness varies
Or declines, as in Scotland here, till it seems
65 Heaven itself may be only the best that is feasible
For most people, but a sad declension from music like yours.
Yes, I am prepared to see the Heavens open
And find the celestial music poor by comparison.
Yet my duty is here. It is now the duty of the Scottish genius
70 Which has provided the economic freedom for it
To lead in the abandonment of creeds and moral compromises
Of every sort and to commence to express the unity of life
By confounding the curse of short-circuited thought
Circumscribing consciousness, for that is the thought
75 Of compromise, the medium of the time-server.
This must be done to lead men to cosmic consciousness
And as it cannot be quick, except on occasion
And *that* the creative instant, the moment of divine realisation,
When the self is lit up by its own inner light
80 Caused in the self by its intensity of thought
Possibly over a long period, it must be thought of as a craft
In which the consummation of the idea, not in analysis but in
        synthesis,
Must be the subject of the object—life.
Wherefore I cannot take the bird-like leap to you
85 Though well I know that: "He that can endure
To follow with allegiance a fallen lord
Does conquer him that did his master conquer."[4]

I dare not leap to you now. But after all since I cannot believe
You will ever be really for everyone or even for many
90 And are likely to pursue in the hereafter
A separate destiny from theirs—or simply because
I long to hear the great pipers play their great music themselves.
And they all dead (save one) centuries before I was born,
And have one glimpse of my beloved Scotland yet
95 As the land I have dreamt of where the supreme values
Which the people recognise are states of mind

4. Shakespeare, *Antony and Cleopatra* 3.13.42–44.

Their ruling passion the attainment of higher consciousness,
And their actual rulers those in whom they find,
Or think they do, the requisite knowledge for such attainments
100 And where one is not required to believe anything
But even warned of the dangers of doing so
Except with infinite qualifications and care,
My duty done, I will try to follow you on the last day of the world,
And pray I may see you all standing shoulder to shoulder
105 With Patrick Mor MacCrimmon and Duncan Ban MacCrimmon in
    the centre
In the hollow[5] at Boreraig or in front of Dunvegan Castle
Or on the lip of the broken graves in Kilmuir Kirkyard[6]
While, the living stricken ghastly in the eternal light
And the rest of the dead all risen blue-faced from their graves
110 (Though, the pipes to your hand, you will be once more
Perfectly at ease, and as you were in your prime)
All ever born crowd the islands and the West Coast of Scotland
Which has standing room for them all, and the air curdled with
    angels,
And everywhere that feeling seldom felt on the earth before
115 Save in the hearts of parents or in youth untouched by tragedy
That in its very search for personal experience often found
A like impersonality and self-forgetfulness,
And you playing: "Farewell to Scotland, and the rest of the Earth,"
The only fit music there can be for that day
120 —And I will leap then and hide behind one of you,
Us Caismeachd phiob-mora bras shroiceadh am puirt.[7]

Look! Is that only the setting sun again?
Or a piper coming from far away?

1934

Another Epitaph on an Army of Mercenaries[8]

It is a God-damned lie to say that these
Saved, or knew, anything worth any man's pride.
They were professional murderers and they took
Their blood money and impious risks and died.
5 In spite of all their kind some elements of worth
With difficulty persist here and there on earth.

1935

---

5. I.e., the pipers' hollow where the students at the college of the MacCrimmons (1500–1800) practiced. Ten generations of MacCrimmons were the hereditary pipers of MacLeod, whose seat is at Dunvegan Castle in the Isle of Skye. Boreraig was where the MacCrimmons lived.
6. Near Dunvegan.

7. While the notes of the great pipes shrilly sounded out their cries (Gaelic); from "Charles Son of James," by the Scottish poet Alasdair MacMhaighstir Alasdair (1695–1770).
8. "In reply to A. E. Housman's" [MacDiarmid's note]. See A. E. Housman's poem "Epitaph on an Army of Mercenaries" (p. 1180).

From In Memoriam James Joyce

We Must Look at the Harebell[9]

We must look at the harebell as if
We had never seen it before.
Remembrance gives an accumulation of satisfaction
Yet the desire for change is very strong in us
5   And change is in itself a recreation.
To those who take any pleasure
In flowers, plants, birds, and the rest
An ecological change is recreative.
(Come. Climb with me. Even the sheep are different
10   And of new importance.
The coarse-fleeced, hardy Herdwick,
The Hampshire Down, artificially fed almost from birth,
And butcher-fat from the day it is weaned,
The Lincoln-Longwool, the biggest breed in England,
15   With the longest fleece, and the Southdown
Almost the smallest—and between them thirty other breeds,
Some whitefaced, some black,
Some with horns and some without,
Some long-wooled, some short-wooled,
20   In England where the men, and women too,
Are almost as interesting as the sheep.)
Everything is different, everything changes,
Except for the white bedstraw which climbs all the way
Up from the valleys to the tops of the high passes
25   The flowers are all different and more precious
Demanding more search and particularity of vision.
Look! Here and there a pinguicula[1] eloquent of the Alps
Still keeps a purple-blue flower
On the top of its straight and slender stem.
30   Bog-asphodel, deep-gold, and comely in form,
The queer, almost diabolical, sundew,
And when you leave the bog for the stag moors and the rocks
The parsley fern—a lovelier plant
Than even the proud Osmunda Regalis[2]—
35   Flourishes in abundance
Showing off oddly contrasted fronds
From the cracks of the lichened stones.
It is pleasant to find the books
Describing it as "very local."
40   Here is a change indeed!
The universal *is* the particular.

1955

---

9. A blue flower, with bell-shaped blossom, that grows wild in Scotland.
1. The butterwort, a small herb that secretes a sticky liquid to catch insects.
2. The flowering, or "royal," fern.

ARCHIBALD MacLEISH
1892–1982

Ars Poetica[1]

A poem should be palpable and mute
As a globed fruit,

Dumb
As old medallions to the thumb,

5   Silent as the sleeve-worn stone
Of casement ledges where the moss has grown—

A poem should be wordless
As the flight of birds.

*

A poem should be motionless in time
10   As the moon climbs,

Leaving, as the moon releases
Twig by twig the night-entangled trees,

Leaving, as the moon behind the winter leaves,
Memory by memory the mind—

15   A poem should be motionless in time
As the moon climbs.

*

A poem should be equal to:
Not true.

For all the history of grief
20   An empty doorway and a maple leaf.

For love
The leaning grasses and two lights above the sea—

A poem should not mean
But be.

1926

---

1. The art of poetry (Latin); title of a treatise on poetics by the Roman poet Horace (65–8 B.C.E.).

The Snowflake Which Is Now and Hence Forever

Will it last? he says.
Is it a masterpiece?
Will generation after generation
Turn with reverence to the page?

5 Birdseye scholar of the frozen fish,
What would he make of the sole, clean, clear
Leap of the salmon that has disappeared?

To *be*, yes!—whether they like it or not!
But not to last when leap and water are forgotten,
10 A plank of standard pinkness in the dish.

They also live
Who swerve and vanish in the river.[2]

1952

EDNA ST. VINCENT MILLAY
1892–1950

First Fig[1]

My candle burns at both ends;
    It will not last the night;
But ah, my foes, and oh, my friends—
    It gives a lovely light!

1920

Second Fig[2]

Safe upon the solid rock the ugly houses stand:
Come and see my shining palace built upon the sand!

1920

---

2. An allusion to Milton, "When I Consider How My Light Is Spent" (p. 418), a sonnet that concludes, "They also serve who only stand and wait."
1. From *A Few Figs from Thistles*, a title derived from Matthew 7.16: "Do men gather grapes of thorns, or figs of thistles?"
2. See the preceding note and Matthew 7.26–27, referring to "a foolish man, which built his house upon the sand."

Euclid Alone Has Looked on Beauty Bare

Euclid[3] alone has looked on Beauty bare.
Let all who prate of Beauty hold their peace,
And lay them prone upon the earth and cease
To ponder on themselves, the while they stare
5   At nothing, intricately drawn nowhere
In shapes of shifting lineage; let geese
Gabble and hiss, but heroes seek release
From dusty bondage into luminous air.
O blinding hour, O holy, terrible day,
10   When first the shaft into his vision shone
Of light anatomized! Euclid alone
Has looked on Beauty bare. Fortunate they
Who, though once only and then but far away,
Have heard her massive sandal set on stone.

1920

Spring

To what purpose, April, do you return again?
Beauty is not enough.
You can no longer quiet me with the redness
Of little leaves opening stickily.
5   I know what I know.
The sun is hot on my neck as I observe
The spikes of the crocus.
The smell of the earth is good.
It is apparent that there is no death.
10   But what does that signify?
Not only under ground are the brains of men
Eaten by maggots.
Life in itself
Is nothing,
15   An empty cup, a flight of uncarpeted stairs.
It is not enough that yearly, down this hill,
April
Comes like an idiot, babbling and strewing flowers.

1921

[I, Being Born a Woman and Distressed]

I, being born a woman and distressed
By all the needs and notions of my kind,

---

3. Greek mathematician (ca. 300 B.C.E.), best-known for his treatise on geometry.

Am urged by your propinquity° to find   *nearness*
Your person fair, and feel a certain zest
5 To bear your body's weight upon my breast:
So subtly is the fume of life designed,
To clarify the pulse and cloud the mind,
And leave me once again undone, possessed.
Think not for this, however, the poor treason
10 Of my stout blood against my staggering brain,
I shall remember you with love, or season
My scorn with pity,—let me make it plain:
I find this frenzy insufficient reason
For conversation when we meet again.

                                       1923

The Buck in the Snow

White sky, over the hemlocks bowed with snow,
Saw you not at the beginning of evening the antlered buck and his
    doe
Standing in the apple-orchard? I saw them. I saw them suddenly go,
Tails up, with long leaps lovely and slow,
5 Over the stone-wall into the wood of hemlocks bowed with snow.

Now lies he here, his wild blood scalding the snow.

How strange a thing is death, bringing to his knees, bringing to his
    antlers
The buck in the snow.
How strange a thing,—a mile away by now, it may be,
10 Under the heavy hemlocks that as the moments pass
Shift their loads a little, letting fall a feather of snow—
Life, looking out attentive from the eyes of the doe.

                                         1928

I Dreamed I Moved among the Elysian Fields[4]

I dreamed I moved among the Elysian fields,
In converse with sweet women long since dead;
And out of blossoms which that meadow yields
I wove a garland for your living head.
5 Danae,[5] that was the vessel for a day
Of golden Jove, I saw, and at her side,
Whom Jove the Bull desired and bore away,
Europa[6] stood, and the Swan's featherless bride.[7]
All these were mortal women, yet all these

---

4. The abode of the happy dead in the Greek mythological underworld.
5. Whom Jove (Zeus), the supreme god, seduced by descending upon her as a shower of gold.
6. Carried away by Jove in the form of a bull.
7. Leda, raped by Jove in the form of a swan.

10   Above the ground had had a god for guest;
     Freely I walked beside them and at ease,
     Addressing them, by them again addressed,
     And marveled nothing, for remembering you,
     Wherefore I was among them well I knew.

1930

Ragged Island

    There, there where those black spruces crowd
    To the edge of the precipitous cliff,
    Above your boat, under the eastern wall of the island;
    And no wave breaks; as if
5   All had been done, and long ago, that needed
    Doing; and the cold tide, unimpeded
    By shoal or shelving ledge, moves up and down,
    Instead of in and out;
    And there is no driftwood there, because there is no beach;
10 Clean cliff going down as deep as clear water can reach;

    No driftwood, such as abounds on the roaring shingle,[8]
    To be hefted home, for fires in the kitchen stove;
    Barrels, banged ashore about the boiling outer harbor;
    Lobster-buoys, on the eel-grass of the sheltered cove:

15 There, thought unbraids itself, and the mind becomes single.
    There you row with tranquil oars, and the ocean
    Shows no scar from the cutting of your placid keel;
    Care becomes senseless there; pride and promotion
    Remote; you only look; you scarcely feel.

20 Even adventure, with its vital uses,
    Is aimless ardour now; and thrift is waste.

    Oh, to be there, under the silent spruces,
    Where the wide, quiet evening darkens without haste
    Over a sea with death acquainted, yet forever chaste.

1954

Armenonville[9]

    By the lake at Armenonville in the Bois de Boulogne
    Small begonias had been set in the embankment, both pink and red;
    With polished leaf and brittle, juicy stem;
    They covered the embankment; there were wagon-loads of them,
5 Charming and neat, gay colours in the warm shade.

8. Stones on a seashore.
9. Pavilion in the park of the Bois de Boulogne, in Paris.

We had preferred a table near the lake, half out of view,
Well out of hearing, for a voice not raised above
A low, impassioned question and its low reply.
We both leaned forward with our elbows on the table, and you
10   Watched my mouth while I answered, and it made me shy.
I looked about, but the waiters knew we were in love,
And matter-of-factly left us blissfully alone.

There swam across the lake, as I looked aside, avoiding
Your eyes for a moment, there swam from under the pink and red
    begonias
15   A small creature; I thought it was a water-rat; it swam very well,
In complete silence, and making no ripples at all
Hardly; and when suddenly I turned again to you,
Aware that you were speaking, and perhaps had been speaking for
    some time,
I was aghast at my absence, for truly I did not know
20   Whether you had been asking or telling.

                                              1954

WILFRED OWEN
1893–1918

Anthem for Doomed Youth

What passing-bells for these who die as cattle?[1]
    —Only the monstrous anger of the guns.
    Only the stuttering rifles' rapid rattle
Can patter out their hasty orisons.°   *prayers*
5   No mockeries now for them; no prayers nor bells;
    Nor any voice of mourning save the choirs,—
The shrill, demented choirs of wailing shells;
    And bugles calling for them from sad shires.°   *counties*

What candles may be held to speed them all?
10   Not in the hands of boys but in their eyes
Shall shine the holy glimmers of goodbyes.
    The pallor of girls' brows shall be their pall;
Their flowers the tenderness of patient minds,
And each slow dusk a drawing-down of blinds.

September–October 1917   1920

1. Owen was probably responding to the anonymous prefatory note to *Poems of Today* (1916), of which he possessed a copy: "This book has been compiled in order that boys and girls, already perhaps familiar with the great classics of the English speech, may also know something of the newer poetry of their own day. Most of the writers are living, and the rest are still vivid memories among us, while one of the youngest, almost as these words are written, has gone singing to lay down his life for his country's cause. . . . There is no arbitrary isolation of one theme from another; they mingle and interpenetrate throughout, to the music of Pan's flute, and of Love's viol, and the bugle-call of Endeavour, and the passing-bells of Death."

Dulce Et Decorum Est[2]

Bent double, like old beggars under sacks,
Knock-kneed, coughing like hags, we cursed through sludge,
Till on the haunting flares we turned our backs
And towards our distant rest began to trudge.
5   Men marched asleep. Many had lost their boots
But limped on, blood-shod. All went lame; all blind;
Drunk with fatigue; deaf even to the hoots
Of tired, outstripped Five-Nines[3] that dropped behind.

Gas! Gas! Quick, boys!—An ecstasy of fumbling,
10   Fitting the clumsy helmets just in time;
But someone still was yelling out and stumbling,
And flound'ring like a man in fire or lime . . .
Dim, through the misty panes[4] and thick green light,
As under a green sea, I saw him drowning.

15   In all my dreams, before my helpless sight,
He plunges at me, guttering, choking, drowning.

If in some smothering dreams you too could pace
Behind the wagon that we flung him in,
And watch the white eyes writhing in his face,
20   His hanging face, like a devil's sick of sin;
If you could hear, at every jolt, the blood
Come gargling from the froth-corrupted lungs,
Obscene as cancer, bitter as the cud
Of vile, incurable sores on innocent tongues,—
25   My friend,[5] you would not tell with such high zest
To children ardent for some desperate glory,
The old Lie: Dulce et decorum est
Pro patria mori.

October 1917–March 1918   1920

Insensibility

1

Happy are men who yet before they are killed
Can let their veins run cold.
Whom no compassion fleers°   *mocks*
Or makes their feet

---

2. "The famous Latin tag [from Horace, *Odes* 3.2.13] means, of course, *It is sweet and meet to die for one's country. Sweet! And decorous!*" [Owen's letter to his mother, October 16, 1917].
3. I.e., 5.9-caliber shells.

4. Of the gas mask's celluloid window.
5. Jessie Pope, to whom the poem was originally to have been dedicated, was the author of numerous prewar children's books as well as *Jessie Pope's War Poems* (1915).

5   Sore on the alleys cobbled[6] with their brothers.
The front line withers.
But they are troops who fade, not flowers,
For poets' tearful fooling:
Men, gaps for filling:
10 Losses, who might have fought
Longer; but no one bothers.

2

And some cease feeling
Even themselves or for themselves.
Dullness best solves
15 The tease and doubt of shelling,
And Chance's strange arithmetic
Comes simpler than the reckoning of their shilling.[7]
They keep no check on armies' decimation.

3

Happy are these who lose imagination:
20 They have enough to carry with ammunition.
Their spirit drags no pack.
Their old wounds, save with cold, can not more ache.
Having seen all things red,
Their eyes are rid
25 Of the hurt of the colour of blood for ever.
And terror's first constriction over,
Their hearts remain small-drawn.
Their senses in some scorching cautery of battle
Now long since ironed,
30 Can laugh among the dying, unconcerned.

4

Happy the soldier home, with not a notion
How somewhere, every dawn, some men attack,
And many sighs are drained.
Happy the lad whose mind was never trained:
35 His days are worth forgetting more than not.
He sings along the march
Which we march taciturn, because of dusk,
The long, forlorn, relentless trend
From larger day to huger night.

---

6. "They are dying again at Beaumont Hamel, which already in 1916 was cobbled with skulls" [Owen's letter to his sister, March 1918].

7. A "King's shilling" was traditionally given to the newly established soldier by the recruiting officer.

5

40 We wise,[8] who with a thought besmirch
     Blood over all our soul,
     How should we see our task
     But through his blunt and lashless eyes?
     Alive, he is not vital overmuch;
45 Dying, not mortal overmuch;
     Nor sad, nor proud,
     Nor curious at all.
     He cannot tell
     Old men's placidity from his.

6

50 But cursed are dullards whom no cannon stuns,
     That they should be as stones.
     Wretched are they, and mean
     With paucity that never was simplicity.
     By choice they made themselves immune
55 To pity and whatever moans in man
     Before the last sea and the hapless stars;
     Whatever mourns when many leave these shores;
     Whatever shares
     The eternal reciprocity of tears.

1917–18   1920

Strange Meeting[9]

     It seemed that out of battle I escaped
     Down some profound dull tunnel, long since scooped
     Through granites which titanic wars had groined.°   grooved

     Yet also there encumbered sleepers groaned,
5   Too fast in thought or death to be bestirred.
     Then, as I probed them, one sprang up, and stared
     With piteous recognition in fixed eyes,
     Lifting distressful hands, as if to bless.
     And by his smile, I knew that sullen hall,—
10 By his dead smile I knew we stood in Hell.

     With a thousand pains that vision's face was grained;
     Yet no blood reached there from the upper ground,
     And no guns thumped, or down the flues made moan.

---

8. I.e., poets.
9. Cf. Shelley, *The Revolt of Islam*, lines 1828–32:

And one whose spear had pierced me, leaned beside,
  With quivering lips and humid eyes;—and all

Seemed like some brothers on a journey wide
  Gone forth, whom now strange meeting did befall
In a strange land.

The speaker of Owen's poem imagines his victim a German poet.

"Strange friend," I said, "here is no cause to mourn."
15 "None," said that other, "save the undone years,
The hopelessness. Whatever hope is yours,
Was my life also; I went hunting wild
After the wildest beauty in the world,
Which lies not calm in eyes, or braided hair,
20 But mocks the steady running of the hour,
And if it grieves, grieves richlier than here.
For by my glee might many men have laughed.
And of my weeping something had been left,
Which must die now. I mean the truth untold,
25 The pity of war, the pity war distilled.[1]
Now men will go content with what we spoiled,
Or, discontent, boil bloody, and be spilled.
They will be swift with swiftness of the tigress.
None will break ranks, though nations trek from progress.
30 Courage was mine, and I had mystery,
Wisdom was mine, and I had mastery:
To miss the march of this retreating world
Into vain citadels that are not walled.
Then, when much blood had clogged their chariot-wheels,
35 I would go up and wash them from sweet wells,
Even with truths that lie too deep for taint.
I would have poured my spirit without stint
But not through wounds; not on the cess[2] of war.
Foreheads of men have bled where no wounds were.

40 "I am the enemy you killed, my friend.
I knew you in this dark: for so you frowned
Yesterday through me as you jabbed and killed.
I parried; but my hands were loath and cold.
Let us sleep now. . . ."

January–March 1918   1920

Futility

Move him into the sun—
Gently its touch awoke him once,
At home, whispering of fields half-sown.
Always it woke him, even in France,
5 Until this morning and this snow.
If anything might rouse him now
The kind old sun will know.

Think how it wakes the seeds—
Woke once the clays of a cold star.

---

1. "My subject is War, and the pity of War. The Poetry is in the pity" [Owen's draft preface to his poems].

2. Luck, as in the phrase *bad cess to you* (may evil befall you); also muck or excrement, as in the word *cesspool*.

10 Are limbs, so dear achieved, are sides
    Full-nerved, still warm, too hard to stir?
    Was it for this the clay grew tall?
    —O what made fatuous sunbeams toil
    To break earth's sleep at all?

May 1918   1920

DOROTHY PARKER
1893–1967

Unfortunate Coincidence

By the time you swear you're his,
    Shivering and sighing,
And he vows his passion is
    Infinite, undying—
5   Lady, make a note of this:
    One of you is lying.

                                                           1926

Résumé

Razors pain you;
Rivers are damp;
Acids stain you;
And drugs cause cramp.
5   Guns aren't lawful;
Nooses give;
Gas smells awful;
You might as well live.

                                                           1926

One Perfect Rose

A single flow'r he sent me, since we met.
    All tenderly his messenger he chose;
Deep-hearted, pure, with scented dew still wet—
    One perfect rose.

5   I knew the language of the floweret;
    "My fragile leaves," it said, "his heart enclose."
Love long has taken for his amulet
    One perfect rose.

Why is it no one ever sent me yet
10   One perfect limousine, do you suppose?
Ah no, it's always just my luck to get
One perfect rose.

1926

E. E. CUMMINGS
1894–1962

All in green went my love riding

All in green went my love riding
on a great horse of gold
into the silver dawn.

four lean hounds crouched low and smiling
5   the merry deer ran before.

Fleeter be they than dappled dreams
the swift sweet deer
the red rare deer.

Four red roebuck at a white water
10   the cruel bugle sang before.

Horn at hip went my love riding
riding the echo down
into the silver dawn.

four lean hounds crouched low and smiling
15   the level meadows ran before.

Softer be they than slippered sleep
the lean lithe deer
the fleet flown deer.

Four fleet does at a gold valley
20   the famished arrow sang before.

Bow at belt went my love riding
riding the mountain down
into the silver dawn.

four lean hounds crouched low and smiling
25   the sheer peaks ran before.

Paler be they than daunting death
the sleek slim deer
the tall tense deer.

Four tall stags at a green mountain
30   the lucky hunter sang before.

All in green went my love riding
on a great horse of gold
into the silver dawn.

four lean hounds crouched low and smiling
35   my heart fell dead before.

                                                    1923

the Cambridge ladies who live in furnished souls

the Cambridge ladies who live in furnished souls
are unbeautiful and have comfortable minds
(also, with the church's protestant blessings
daughters, unscented shapeless spirited)
5   they believe in Christ and Longfellow,[1] both dead,
are invariably interested in so many things—
at the present writing one still finds
delighted fingers knitting for the is it Poles?
perhaps. While permanent faces coyly bandy
10   scandal of Mrs. N and Professor D
. . . . the Cambridge ladies do not care,above
Cambridge if sometimes in its box of
sky lavender and cornerless,the
moon rattles like a fragment of angry candy

                                                    1923

Spring is like a perhaps hand

Spring is like a perhaps hand
(which comes carefully
out of Nowhere)arranging
a window,into which people look(while
5   people stare
arranging and changing placing
carefully there a strange
thing and a known thing here)and

changing everything carefully

10   spring is like a perhaps
Hand in a window
(carefully to

---

1. For most of his life, the American poet Henry Wadsworth Longfellow (1807–1882; see pp. 951–57) lived in Cambridge, Massachusetts, where for two decades he taught modern languages at Harvard University.

and fro moving New and
Old things,while
15   people stare carefully
moving a perhaps
fraction of flower here placing
an inch of air there)and

without breaking anything.

1925

"next to of course god america i

"next to of course god america i
love you land of the pilgrims' and so forth oh
say can you see by the dawn's early my
country 'tis of centuries come and go
5   and are no more what of it we should worry
in every language even deafanddumb
thy sons acclaim your glorious name by gorry
by jingo[2] by gee by gosh by gum
why talk of beauty what could be more beaut-
10   iful than these heroic happy dead
who rushed like lions to the roaring slaughter
they did not stop to think they died instead
then shall the voice of liberty be mute?"

He spoke. And drank rapidly a glass of water

1926

since feeling is first

since feeling is first
who pays any attention
to the syntax of things
will never wholly kiss you;

5   wholly to be a fool
while Spring is in the world

my blood approves,
and kisses are a better fate
than wisdom
10   lady i swear by all flowers. Don't cry
—the best gesture of my brain is less than
your eyelids' flutter which says

2. "Jingo" is both part of a mild oath and a reference to jingoism: extreme nationalism, especially as demonstrated in a belligerent foreign policy.

we are for each other:then
laugh,leaning back in my arms
15   for life's not a paragraph

And death i think is no parenthesis

1926

somewhere i have never travelled,gladly beyond

somewhere i have never travelled,gladly beyond
any experience,your eyes have their silence:
in your most frail gesture are things which enclose me,
or which i cannot touch because they are too near

5   your slightest look easily will unclose me
though i have closed myself as fingers,
you open always petal by petal myself as Spring opens
(touching skilfully,mysteriously)her first rose

or if your wish be to close me,i and
10   my life will shut very beautifully,suddenly,
as when the heart of this flower imagines
the snow carefully everywhere descending;

nothing which we are to perceive in this world equals
the power of your intense fragility:whose texture
15   compels me with the colour of its countries,
rendering death and forever with each breathing

(i do not know what it is about you that closes
and opens;only something in me understands
the voice of your eyes is deeper than all roses)
20   nobody,not even the rain,has such small hands

1931

may i feel said he

may i feel said he
(i'll squeal said she
just once said he)
it's fun said she

5   (may i touch said he
how much said she
a lot said he)
why not said she

(let's go said he
10 not too far said she
what's too far said he
where you are said she)

may i stay said he
(which way said she
15 like this said he
if you kiss said she

may i move said he
is it love said she)
if you're willing said he
20 (but you're killing said she

but it's life said he
but your wife said she
now said he)
ow said she

25 (tiptop said he
don't stop said she
oh no said he)
go slow said she

(cccome?said he
30 ummm said she)
you're divine!said he
(you are Mine said she)

1935

anyone lived in a pretty how town

anyone lived in a pretty how town
(with up so floating many bells down)
spring summer autumn winter
he sang his didn't he danced his did.

5 Women and men(both little and small)
cared for anyone not at all
they sowed their isn't they reaped their same
sun moon stars rain

children guessed(but only a few
10 and down they forgot as up they grew
autumn winter spring summer)
that noone loved him more by more

when by now and tree by leaf
she laughed his joy she cried his grief

15 bird by snow and stir by still
anyone's any was all to her

someones married their everyones
laughed their cryings and did their dance
(sleep wake hope and then)they
20 said their nevers they slept their dream

stars rain sun moon
(and only the snow can begin to explain
how children are apt to forget to remember
with up so floating many bells down)

25 one day anyone died i guess
(and noone stooped to kiss his face)
busy folk buried them side by side
little by little and was by was

all by all and deep by deep
30 and more by more they dream their sleep
noone and anyone earth by april
wish by spirit and if by yes.

Women and men(both dong and ding)
summer autumn winter spring
35 reaped their sowing and went their came
sun moon stars rain

1940

who are you,little i

who are you,little i

(five or six years old)
peering from some high

window;at the gold

5 of november sunset

(and feeling:that if day
has to become night

this is a beautiful way)

1963

JEAN TOOMER
1894–1967

FROM CANE[1]

Reapers

Black reapers with the sound of steel on stones
Are sharpening scythes. I see them place the hones
In their hip-pockets as a thing that's done,
And start their silent swinging, one by one.
Black horses drive a mower through the weeds,
And there, a field rat, startled, squealing bleeds,
His belly close to ground. I see the blade,
Blood-stained, continue cutting weeds and shade.

5

Face

Hair—
silver-gray,
like streams of stars,
Brows—
recurved canoes
quivered by the ripples blown by pain,
Her eyes—
mist of tears
condensing on the flesh below
And her channeled muscles
are cluster grapes of sorrow
purple in the evening sun
nearly ripe for worms.

5

10

Georgia Dusk

The sky, lazily disdaining to pursue
    The setting sun, too indolent to hold
    A lengthened tournament for flashing gold,
Passively darkens for night's barbecue,

5   A feast of moon and men and barking hounds,
    An orgy for some genius of the South
    With blood-hot eyes and cane-lipped scented mouth,
Surprised in making folksongs from soul sounds.

1. A collection—of fiction, drama, and poetry— that Toomer saw as a unified book not to be excerpted. Set in Georgia and in Washington, D.C., it was partly inspired by the period in which the urban Toomer, of black and white ancestry, worked in a school in Sparta, Georgia.

The sawmill blows its whistle, buzz-saws stop,
10   And silence breaks the bud of knoll and hill,
        Soft settling pollen where plowed lands fulfill
Their early promise of a bumper crop.

Smoke from the pyramidal sawdust pile
        Curls up, blue ghosts of trees, tarrying low
15   Where only chips and stumps are left to show
The solid proof of former domicile.

Meanwhile, the men, with vestiges of pomp,
        Race memories of king and caravan,
        High-priests, an ostrich, and a juju-man,[2]
20   Go singing through the footpaths of the swamp.

Their voices rise . . the pine trees are guitars,
        Strumming, pine-needles fall like sheets of rain . .
        Their voices rise . . the chorus of the cane
Is caroling a vesper to the stars . .

25   O singers, resinous and soft your songs
        Above the sacred whisper of the pines,
        Give virgin lips to cornfield concubines,
Bring dreams of Christ to dusky cane-lipped throngs.

Portrait in Georgia

Hair—braided chestnut,
    coiled like a lyncher's rope,
Eyes—fagots,°   *bundles of sticks*
Lips—old scars, or the first red blisters,
5   Breath—the last sweet scent of cane,
And her slim body, white as the ash
    of black flesh after flame.

Harvest Song

I am a reaper whose muscles set at sundown. All my oats are cradled.
But I am too chilled, and too fatigued to bind them. And I hunger.

I crack a grain between my teeth. I do not taste it.
I have been in the fields all day. My throat is dry. I hunger.

5   My eyes are caked with dust of oatfields at harvest-time.
    I am a blind man who stares across the hills, seeking stacked fields of
        other harvesters.

2. One who controls the magic associated with jujus, the fetishes or charms of West African peoples.

It would be good to see them . . crook'd, split, and iron-ringed handles
   of the scythes. It would be good to see them, dust-caked and
   blind. I hunger.

(Dusk is a strange feared sheath their blades are dulled in.)
My throat is dry. And should I call, a cracked grain like the oats . . .
   eoho—

10   I fear to call. What should they hear me, and offer me their grain,
   oats, or wheat, or corn? I have been in the fields all day. I fear I
   could not taste it. I fear knowledge of my hunger.

My ears are caked with dust of oatfields at harvest-time.
I am a deaf man who strains to hear the calls of other harvesters
   whose throats are also dry.

It would be good to hear their songs . . reapers of the sweet-stalked
   cane, cutters of the corn . . even though their throats cracked and
   the strangeness of their voices deafened me.

I hunger. My throat is dry. Now that the sun has set and I am chilled,
   I fear to call. (Eoho, my brothers!)

15   I am a reaper. (Eoho!) All my oats are cradled. But I am too fatigued
   to bind them. And I hunger. I crack a grain. It has no taste to it.
   My throat is dry . . .

O my brothers, I beat my palms, still soft, against the stubble of my
   harvesting. (You beat your soft palms, too.) My pain is sweet.
   Sweeter than the oats or wheat or corn. It will not bring me
   knowledge of my hunger.

                                                              1923

ROBERT GRAVES
1895–1985

Love Without Hope

Love without hope, as when the young bird-catcher
Swept off his tall hat to the Squire's own daughter,
So let the imprisoned larks escape and fly
Singing about her head, as she rode by.

                                                              1925

In Broken Images

He is quick, thinking in clear images;
I am slow, thinking in broken images.

He becomes dull, trusting to his clear images;
I become sharp, mistrusting my broken images.

5   Trusting his images, he assumes their relevance;
Mistrusting my images, I question their relevance.

Assuming their relevance, he assumes the fact;
Questioning their relevance, I question the fact.

When the fact fails him, he questions his senses;
10   When the fact fails me, I approve my senses.

He continues quick and dull in his clear images;
I continue slow and sharp in my broken images.

He in a new confusion of his understanding;
I in a new understanding of my confusion.

1929

Warning to Children

Children, if you dare to think
Of the greatness, rareness, muchness,
Fewness of this precious only
Endless world in which you say
5   You live, you think of things like this:
Blocks of slate enclosing dappled
Red and green, enclosing tawny
Yellow nets, enclosing white
And black acres of dominoes,
10   Where a neat brown paper parcel
Tempts you to untie the string.
In the parcel a small island,
On the island a large tree,
On the tree a husky fruit.
15   Strip the husk and pare the rind off:
In the kernel you will see
Blocks of slate enclosed by dappled
Red and green, enclosed by tawny
Yellow nets, enclosed by white
20   And black acres of dominoes,
Where the same brown paper parcel—
Children, leave the string alone!
For who dares undo the parcel
Finds himself at once inside it,
25   On the island, in the fruit,
Blocks of slate about his head,
Finds himself enclosed by dappled
Green and red, enclosed by yellow
Tawny nets, enclosed by black

30   And white acres of dominoes,
       With the same brown paper parcel
       Still unopened on his knee.
       And, if he then should dare to think
       Of the fewness, muchness, rareness,
35   Greatness of this endless only
       Precious world in which he says
       He lives—he then unties the string.

1929

The Persian Version

Truth-loving Persians do not dwell upon
The trivial skirmish fought near Marathon.[1]
As for the Greek theatrical tradition
Which represents that summer's expedition
5 Not as a mere reconnaissance in force
By three brigades of foot and one of horse
(Their left flank covered by some obsolete
Light craft detached from the main Persian fleet)
But as a grandiose, ill-starred attempt
10 To conquer Greece—they treat it with contempt;
And only incidentally refute
Major Greek claims, by stressing what repute
The Persian monarch and the Persian nation
Won by this salutary demonstration:
15 Despite a strong defence and adverse weather
All arms combined magnificently together.

1945

To Juan at the Winter Solstice[2]

There is one story and one story only
That will prove worth your telling,
Whether as learned bard or gifted child;[3]
To it all lines or lesser gauds[4] belong
5 That startle with their shining
Such common stories as they stray into.

Is it of trees you tell, their months and virtues,[5]
Or strange beasts that beset you,

---

1. The Battle of Marathon (490 B.C.E.) was a deci-
sive Greek victory over the Persians.
2. Graves's "grammar of poetic myth," *The White
Goddess* (1948), finds the only theme for true
poetry in the story of the life cycle of the Sun God,
or Sun Hero, his marriage with the Goddess, and
his inevitable death at her hands or by her com-
mand. The poet's son Juan was born on December
21, 1945, one day before the winter solstice, which
(being the time when the sun gives least heat and

light to the north) is in many religions the birthday
of the Sun Hero.
3. The ancient Celtic bard Taliesin, as a "gifted
child," outmatched twenty-four experienced court
poets.
4. The larger beads placed between the decades
of "aves" in a Roman Catholic rosary (i.e., every
eleventh bead).
5. Graves cites, in addition to Taliesin's poem
"The Battle of the Trees," an ancient Druidic "tree-

Of birds that croak at you the Triple will?[6]
10 Or of the Zodiac and how slow it turns
Below the Boreal Crown,[7]
Prison of all true kings that ever reigned?

Water to water, ark again to ark,
From woman back to woman:
15 So each new victim treads unfalteringly
The never altered circuit of his fate,
Bringing twelve peers[8] as witness
Both to his starry rise and starry fall.[9]

Or is it of the Virgin's silver beauty,
20 All fish below the thighs?
She in her left hand bears a leafy quince;[1]
When with her right she crooks a finger, smiling,
How may the King hold back?
Royally then he barters life for love.

25 Or of the undying snake from chaos hatched,
Whose coils contain the ocean,
Into whose chops with naked sword he springs,
Then in black water, tangled by the reeds,
Battles three days and nights,
30 To be spewed up beside her scalloped shore?[2]

Much snow is falling, winds roar hollowly,
The owl hoots from the elder,
Fear in your heart cries to the loving-cup:
Sorrow to sorrow as the sparks fly upward.
35 The log groans and confesses:[3]
There is one story and one story only.

Dwell on her graciousness, dwell on her smiling,
Do not forget what flowers
The great boar trampled down in ivy time.[4]
40 Her brow was creamy as the crested wave,
Her sea-grey eyes were wild[5]
But nothing promised that is not performed.

1945

---

calendar" that describes the natural and magic properties of different trees and associates each with a different month or season.
6. The Goddess sometimes speaks through such "prophetic" birds as the owl and eagle and has been called the Triple Goddess because of her threefold aspect as Goddess of the Underworld, Earth, and Sky.
7. "*Corona Borealis*, . . . which in Thracian-Libyan mythology carried to Bronze Age Britain, was the purgatory where Solar Heroes went after death" [Graves's note]. The twelve signs of the turning zodiac correspond to the twelve months.
8. Perhaps the twelve knights of King Arthur's round table, Christ's twelve apostles, or the twelve signs of the zodiac.
9. The king (or Solar Hero), reincarnated, reappears at the winter solstice floating in an ark on the water.

the water.
1. Two forms of the Goddess are Aphrodite, Greek goddess of love, whose emblem is the quince, and Rahab, the Hebraic sea goddess, who was depicted with a fish's tail.
2. The snake, Ophion, was created by the Goddess and mated with her. From their egg, the world was hatched by the sun's rays. The king (or Solar Hero) must kill the snake to win the Goddess, but in October the snake (perhaps reincarnated as the boar of line 39) must kill the king.
3. Cf. Job 5.7: "Man is born unto trouble, as the sparks fly upward." "The log is the Yule [or Christmas] log, burned at the year's end" [Graves's note].
4. Aphrodite's lover, Adonis, was killed by a boar.
5. Cf. Keats, "La Belle Dame sans Merci," line 16: "And her eyes were wild" (p. 917).

The White Goddess[6]

All saints revile her, and all sober men
Ruled by the God Apollo's golden mean[7]—
In scorn of which we sailed to find her
In distant regions likeliest to hold her
5   Whom we desired above all things to know,
Sister of the mirage and echo.

It was a virtue not to stay,
To go our headstrong and heroic way
Seeking her out at the volcano's head,
10   Among pack ice, or where the track had faded
Beyond the cavern of the seven sleepers:[8]
Whose broad high brow was white as any leper's,
Whose eyes were blue, with rowan-berry lips,
With hair curled honey-coloured to white hips.

15   Green sap of Spring in the young wood a-stir
Will celebrate the Mountain Mother,
And every song-bird shout awhile for her;
But we are gifted, even in November
Rawest of seasons, with so huge a sense
20   Of her nakedly worn magnificence
We forget cruelty and past betrayal,
Heedless of where the next bright bolt may fall.

1953

EDMUND BLUNDEN
1896–1974

Forefathers

Here they went with smock and crook,
    Toiled in the sun, lolled in the shade,
Here they mudded out the brook
    And here their hatchet cleared the glade:
5   Harvest-supper woke their wit,
    Huntsman's moon their wooings lit.

From this church they led their brides,
    From this church themselves were led
Shoulder-high; on these waysides
10   Sat to take their beer and bread.

---

6. See note 2, p. 1402.
7. The middle way, moderation. Apollo's motto was "Nothing in Excess."

8. Cf. Donne, "The Good Morrow," line 4 (p. 293): "Or snorted we in the Seven Sleepers' den?"

Names are gone—what men they were
These their cottages declare.

Names are vanished, save the few
    In the old brown Bible scrawled;
15   These were men of pith and thew,[1]
    Whom the city never called;
Scarce could read or hold a quill,
Built the barn, the forge, the mill.

On the green they watched their sons
20   Playing till too dark to see,
As their fathers watched them once,
    As my father once watched me;
While the bat and beetle flew
On the warm air webbed with dew.

25 Unrecorded, unrenowned,
    Men from whom my ways begin,
Here I know you by your ground
    But I know you not within—
There is silence, there survives
30 Not a moment of your lives.

Like the bee that now is blown
    Honey-heavy on my hand,
From his toppling tansy[2]-throne
    In the green tempestuous land—
35 I'm in clover now, nor know
Who made honey long ago.

                                                1922

1916 seen from 1921

Tired with dull grief, grown old before my day,
I sit in solitude and only hear
Long silent laughters, murmurings of dismay,
The lost intensities of hope and fear;
5   In those old marshes yet the rifles lie,
On the thin breastwork flutter the grey rags,
The very books I read are there—and I
Dead as the men I loved, wait while life drags

Its wounded length from those sad streets of war
10 Into green places here, that were my own;
But now what once was mine is mine no more,
I seek such neighbours here and I find none.

---

1. Strong muscle. *Of pith:* i.e., forcible and terse.   2. Tall, yellow-flowered plant.

With such strong gentleness and tireless will
Those ruined houses seared themselves in me,
15 Passionate I look for their dumb story still,
And the charred stub outspeaks the living tree.

I rise up at the singing of a bird
And scarcely knowing slink along the lane,
I dare not give a soul a look or word
20 Where all have homes and none's at home in vain:
Deep red the rose burned in the grim redoubt,[3]
The self-sown wheat around was like a flood,
In the hot path the lizard lolled time out,
The saints in broken shrines were bright as blood.

25 Sweet Mary's shrine between the sycamores!
There we would go, my friend of friends and I,
And snatch long moments from the grudging wars,
Whose dark made light intense to see them by.
Shrewd bit the morning fog, the whining shots
30 Spun from the wrangling wire;[4] then in warm swoon
The sun hushed all but the cool orchard plots,
We crept in the tall grass and slept till noon.

1922   1930

LOUISE BOGAN
1897–1970

Medusa[1]

I had come to the house, in a cave of trees,
Facing a sheer sky.
Everything moved,—a bell hung ready to strike,
Sun and reflection wheeled by.

5 When the bare eyes were before me
And the hissing hair,
Held up at a window, seen through a door.
The stiff bald eyes, the serpents on the forehead
Formed in the air.

10 This is a dead scene forever now.
Nothing will ever stir.
The end will never brighten it more than this,
Nor the rain blur.

3. Earthwork defensive position enclosed on all sides.
4. Barbed wire.
1. One of the Gorgons, Greek mythological sisters with monstrous faces and snakes for hair, the sight of whom was so terrible it turned people to stone. Perseus killed Medusa by cutting off her head, which retained the power to petrify (in both senses) its viewers.

The water will always fall, and will not fall,
15 And the tipped bell make no sound.
The grass will always be growing for hay
Deep on the ground.

And I shall stand here like a shadow
Under the great balanced day,
20 My eyes on the yellow dust, that was lifting in the wind,
And does not drift away.

1923

Juan's Song

When beauty breaks and falls asunder
I feel no grief for it, but wonder.
When love, like a frail shell, lies broken,
I keep no chip of it for token.
5 I never had a man for friend
Who did not know that love must end.
I never had a girl for lover
Who could discern when love was over.
What the wise doubt, the fool believes—
10 Who is it, then, that love deceives?

1923

Man Alone

It is yourself you seek
In a long rage,
Scanning through light and darkness
Mirrors, the page,

5 Where should reflected be
Those eyes and that thick hair,
That passionate look, that laughter.
You should appear

Within the book, or doubled,
10 Freed, in the silvered glass;
Into all other bodies
Yourself should pass.

The glass does not dissolve;
Like walls the mirrors stand;
15 The printed page gives back
Words by another hand.

And your infatuate eye
Meets not itself below:
Strangers lie in your arms
20   As I lie now.

1937

Roman Fountain

Up from the bronze, I saw
Water without a flaw
Rush to its rest in air,
Reach to its rest, and fall.

5   Bronze of the blackest shade,
An element man-made,
Shaping upright the bare
Clear gouts of water in air.

O, as with arm and hammer,
10   Still it is good to strive
To beat out the image whole,
To echo the shout and stammer
When full-gushed waters, alive,
Strike on the fountain's bowl
15   After the air of summer.

1937

Song for the Last Act

Now that I have your face by heart, I look
Less at its features than its darkening frame
Where quince and melon, yellow as young flame,
Lie with quilled dahlias and the shepherd's crook.
5   Beyond, a garden. There, in insolent ease
The lead and marble figures watch the show
Of yet another summer loath to go
Although the scythes hang in the apple trees.

Now that I have your face by heart, I look.

10   Now that I have your voice by heart, I read
In the black chords upon a dulling page
Music that is not meant for music's cage,
Whose emblems mix with words that shake and bleed.
The staves[2] are shuttled over with a stark

2. Horizontal lines on which music is written.

15 Unprinted silence. In a double dream
I must spell out the storm, the running stream.
The beat's too swift. The notes shift in the dark.

Now that I have your voice by heart, I read.

Now that I have your heart by heart, I see
20 The wharves with their great ships and architraves;[3]
The rigging and the cargo and the slaves
On a strange beach under a broken sky.
O not departure, but a voyage done!
The bales stand on the stone; the anchor weeps
25 Its red rust downward, and the long vine creeps
Beside the salt herb, in the lengthening sun.

Now that I have your heart by heart, I see.

1954

Night

The cold remote islands
And the blue estuaries
Where what breathes, breathes
The restless wind of the inlets,
5 And what drinks, drinks
The incoming tide;

Where shell and weed
Wait upon the salt wash of the sea,
And the clear nights of stars
10 Swing their lights westward
To set behind the land;

Where the pulse clinging to the rocks
Renews itself forever;
Where, again on cloudless nights,
15 The water reflects
The firmament's partial setting;

—O remember
In your narrowing dark hours
That more things move
20 Than blood in the heart.

1968

---

3. Beams on columns.

HART CRANE
1899–1932

My Grandmother's Love Letters

There are no stars to-night
But those of memory.
Yet how much room for memory there is
In the loose girdle of soft rain.

5   There is even room enough
For the letters of my mother's mother,
Elizabeth,
That have been pressed so long
Into a corner of the roof
10   That they are brown and soft,
And liable to melt as snow.

Over the greatness of such space
Steps must be gentle.
It is all hung by an invisible white hair.
15   It trembles as birch limbs webbing the air.

And I ask myself:

"Are your fingers long enough to play
Old keys that are but echoes:
Is the silence strong enough
20   To carry back the music to its source
And back to you again
As though to her?"
Yet I would lead my grandmother by the hand
Through much of what she would not understand;
25   And so I stumble. And the rain continues on the roof
With such a sound of gently pitying laughter.

1926

At Melville's[1] Tomb

Often beneath the wave, wide from this ledge
The dice[2] of drowned men's bones he saw bequeath
An embassy. Their numbers as he watched,
Beat on the dusty shore and were obscured.

5   And wrecks passed without sound of bells,
The calyx[3] of death's bounty giving back

---

1. The American poet and novelist Herman Melville (1819–1891; see pp. 1054–57), best-known for his works dealing with the sea.
2. Small, broken pieces. "Dice as a symbol of chance and circumstance is also implied" [Crane's note to editor Harriet Monroe].
3. Literally, the outer whorl of a flower, formed by modified leaves. "This calyx refers in a double ironic sense both to a cornucopia (cone-shaped receptacle) and the vortex made by a sinking ves-

A scattered chapter, livid hieroglyph,
The portent wound in corridors of shells.

Then in the circuit calm of one vast coil,
10   Its lashings charmed and malice reconciled,
Frosted eyes there were that lifted altars;
And silent answers crept across the stars.

Compass, quadrant and sextant[4] contrive
No farther tides . . . High in the azure steeps
15   Monody[5] shall not wake the mariner.
This fabulous shadow only the sea keeps.

1926

Voyages

1

Above the fresh ruffles of the surf
Bright striped urchins flay each other with sand.
They have contrived a conquest for shell shucks,
And their fingers crumble fragments of baked weed
5   Gaily digging and scattering.

And in answer to their treble interjections
The sun beats lightning on the waves,
The waves fold thunder on the sand;
And could they hear me I would tell them:

10   O brilliant kids, frisk with your dog,
Fondle your shells and sticks, bleached
By time and the elements; but there is a line
You must not cross nor ever trust beyond it
Spry cordage° of your bodies to caresses   *ropes in ship's rigging*
15   Too lichen-faithful from too wide a breast.
The bottom of the sea is cruel.

2

—And yet this great wink of eternity,
Of rimless floods, unfettered leewardings,
Samite[6] sheeted and processioned where
Her undinal[7] vast belly moonward bends,
5   Laughing the wrapt inflections of our love;

---

sel" [Crane's note to Monroe].
4. Instruments used in navigation: the compass determines geographic directions; the quadrant and sextant measure angles and reckon altitudes. Crane's note to Monroe suggests that they "have inadvertently so extended the concepts of the entity they were invented to measure . . . that they may metaphorically be said to have extended the original boundaries of the entity measured."
5. Elegy or dirge sung by one person.
6. A rich, silky fabric interwoven with gold or silver. *Leewardings:* ship's movements away from the wind.
7. The adjective suggests both waves and undines, or water spirits.

Take this Sea, whose diapason° knells   *burst of sound*
On scrolls of silver snowy sentences,
The sceptered terror of whose sessions rends
As her demeanors motion well or ill.
10   All but the pieties of lovers' hands.

And onward, as bells off San Salvador[8]
Salute the crocus lusters of the stars,
In these poinsettia[9] meadows of her tides—
Adagios of islands, O my Prodigal,[1]
15   Complete the dark confessions her veins spell.

Mark how her turning shoulders wind the hours,
And hasten while her penniless rich palms
Pass superscription of bent foam and wave—
Hasten, while they are true—sleep, death, desire,
20   Close round one instant in one floating flower.

Bind us in time, O Seasons clear, and awe.
O minstrel galleons of Carib[2] fire,
Bequeath us to no earthly shore until
Is answered in the vortex of our grave
25   The seal's wide spindrift gaze toward paradise.

3

Infinite consanguinity° it bears—   *blood relationship*
This tendered theme of you that light
Retrieves from sea plains where the sky
Resigns a breast that every wave enthrones;
5   While ribboned water lanes I wind
Are laved and scattered with no stroke
Wide from your side, whereto this hour
The sea lifts, also, reliquary hands.[3]

And so, admitted through black swollen gates
10   That must arrest all distance otherwise,
Past whirling pillars and lithe pediments,
Light wrestling there incessantly with light,
Star kissing star through wave on wave unto
Your body rocking!
15   and where death, if shed,
Presumes no carnage, but this single change,
Upon the steep floor flung from dawn to dawn
The silken skilled transmemberment[4] of song;

Permit me voyage, love, into your hands . . .

---

8. An island of the Bahamas group, Columbus's first landfall on the first voyage.
9. Showy plant native to Central America.
1. Wasteful, lavish one; cf. the Prodigal Son in Luke 15. *Adagios:* divisions of a composition that

are musically slow and graceful.
2. Some of the West Indian islands, or the sea surrounding them.
3. I.e., hands holding sacred relics.
4. Exchange or transformation of parts.

4

Whose counted smile of hours and days, suppose
I know as spectrum of the sea and pledge
Vastly now parting gulf on gulf of wings
Whose circles bridge, I know, (from palms to the severe
5 Chilled albatross's[5] white immutability)
No stream of greater love advancing now
Than, singing, this mortality alone
Through clay aflow immortally to you.

All fragrance irrefragibly,[6] and claim
10 Madly meeting logically in this hour
And region that is ours to wreathe again,
Portending eyes and lips and making told
The chancel[7] port and portion of our June—

Shall they not stem and close in our own steps
15 Bright staves of flowers and quills to-day as I
Must first be lost in fatal tides to tell?

In signature of the incarnate word
The harbor shoulders to resign in mingling
Mutual blood, transpiring as foreknown
20 And widening noon within your breast for gathering
All bright insinuations that my years have caught
For islands where must lead inviolably
Blue latitudes and levels of your eyes—

In this expectant, still exclaim receive
25 The secret oar and petals of all love.

5

Meticulous, past midnight in clear rime,°   *frost*
Infrangible° and lonely, smooth as though cast   *inviolable*
Together in one merciless white blade—
The bay estuaries fleck the hard sky limits.

5 —As if too brittle or too clear to touch!
The cables of our sleep so swiftly filed,
Already hang, shred ends from remembered stars.
One frozen trackless smile . . . What words
Can strangle this deaf moonlight? For we

10 Are overtaken. Now no cry, no sword
Can fasten or deflect this tidal wedge,
Slow tyranny of moonlight, moonlight loved
And changed . . . "There's

5. That of a large seabird capable of long, sustained flights away from land, believed to sleep in the air without moving its wings.

6. Undeniably; unalterably.
7. The part of a church that contains the altar and seats for the clergy and choir.

Nothing like this in the world," you say,
15   Knowing I cannot touch your hand and look
Too, into that godless cleft of sky
Where nothing turns but dead sands flashing.

"—And never to quite understand!" No,
In all the argosy[8] of your bright hair I dreamed
20   Nothing so flagless as this piracy.

                                        But now
Draw in your head, alone and too tall here.
Your eyes already in the slant of drifting foam;
Your breath sealed by the ghosts I do not know:
25   Draw in your head and sleep the long way home.

6

Where icy and bright dungeons lift
Of swimmers their lost morning eyes,
And ocean rivers, churning, shift
Green borders under stranger skies,

5   Steadily as a shell secretes
Its beating leagues of monotone,
Or as many waters trough the sun's
Red kelson[9] past the cape's wet stone;

O rivers mingling toward the sky
10   And harbor of the phoenix'[1] breast—
My eyes pressed black against the prow,
—Thy derelict and blinded guest

Waiting, afire, what name, unspoke,
I cannot claim: let thy waves rear
15   More savage than the death of kings,
Some splintered garland for the seer.

Beyond siroccos[2] harvesting
The solstice thunders, crept away,
Like a cliff swinging or a sail
20   Flung into April's inmost day—

Creation's blithe and petaled word
To the lounged goddess when she rose
Conceding dialogue with eyes
That smile unsearchable repose—

8. A rich supply; also, a large ship or a fleet of ships.
9. A beam laid parallel to the keel of a ship to hold together the flooring and the keel.
1. A mythological bird said to end its very long life by burning itself; from its ashes arises a new phoenix. The phoenix is also a symbol of the Resurrection.
2. Hot, moist winds, usually those from North African deserts.

25 Still fervid covenant, Belle Isle,[3]
    —Unfolded floating dais before
    Which rainbows twine continual hair—
    Belle Isle, white echo of the oar!

    The imaged Word, it is, that holds
30 Hushed willows anchored in its glow.
    It is the unbetrayable reply
    Whose accent no farewell can know.

1926

From The Bridge

Proem: To Brooklyn Bridge

    How many dawns, chill from his rippling rest
    The seagull's wings shall dip and pivot him,
    Shedding white rings of tumult, building high
    Over the chained bay waters Liberty—

5 Then, with inviolate curve, forsake our eyes
    As apparitional as sails that cross
    Some page of figures to be filed away;
    —Till elevators drop us from our day . . .

    I think of cinemas, panoramic sleights
10 With multitudes bent toward some flashing scene
    Never disclosed, but hastened to again,
    Foretold to other eyes on the same screen;

    And Thee,[4] across the harbor, silver-paced
    As though the sun took step of thee, yet left
15 Some motion ever unspent in thy stride—
    Implicitly thy freedom staying thee!

    Out of some subway scuttle, cell or loft
    A bedlamite° speeds to thy parapets,   *madman*
    Tilting there momently, shrill shirt ballooning,
20 A jest falls from the speechless caravan.

    Down Wall,[5] from girder into street noon leaks,
    A rip-tooth of the sky's acetylene,
    All afternoon the cloud-flown derricks turn . . .
    Thy cables breathe the North Atlantic still.

25 And obscure as that heaven of the Jews,[6]
    Thy guerdon° . . . Accolade thou dost bestow   *reward*

3. Tiny island near Newfoundland that is the first land seen by boats coming from Europe.
4. I.e., Brooklyn Bridge.
5. Wall Street is less than half a mile south of the bridge's Manhattan end.
6. I.e., heaven is a vaguer notion in the Jewish tradition than in the Christian.

Of anonymity time cannot raise:
Vibrant reprieve and pardon thou dost show.

O harp and altar, of the fury fused,
30 (How could mere toil align thy choiring strings!)[7]
Terrific threshold of the prophet's pledge,
Prayer of pariah, and the lover's cry—

Again the traffic lights that skim thy swift
Unfractioned idiom, immaculate sigh of stars,
35 Beading thy path—condense eternity:
And we have seen night lifted in thine arms.

Under thy shadow by the piers I waited;
Only in darkness is thy shadow clear.
The City's fiery parcels all undone,
40 Already snow submerges an iron year . . .

O Sleepless as the river under thee,
Vaulting the sea, the prairies' dreaming sod,
Unto us lowliest sometime sweep, descend
And of the curveship lend a myth to God.

1930

To Emily Dickinson[8]

You who desired so much—in vain to ask—
Yet fed your hunger like an endless task,
Dared dignify the labor, bless the quest—
Achieved that stillness ultimately best,

5 Being, of all, least sought for: Emily, hear!
O sweet, dead Silencer, most suddenly clear
When singing that Eternity possessed
And plundered momently in every breast;

—Truly no flower yet withers in your hand,
10 The harvest you descried and understand
Needs more than wit to gather, love to bind.
Some reconcilement of remotest mind—

Leaves Ormus rubyless, and Ophir chill.[9]
Else tears heap all within one clay-cold hill.

1933

7. The suspension bridge has cables formed from parallel steel wires that were spun in place.
8. American poet (1830–1886; see pp. 1110–27).
9. Ormus (or Hormuz), ancient city on the Persian Gulf; in 1 Kings 10.11, Solomon receives rich gifts, including gold and precious stones, from a region called Ophir.

ALLEN TATE
1899–1979

Ode to the Confederate Dead

Row after row with strict impunity
The headstones yield their names to the element,
The wind whirrs without recollection;
In the riven troughs the splayed leaves
5   Pile up, of nature the casual sacrament
To the seasonal eternity of death;
Then driven by the fierce scrutiny
Of heaven to their election in the vast breath,
They sough° the rumor of mortality.   *moan*

10   Autumn is desolation in the plot
Of a thousand acres where these memories grow
From the inexhaustible bodies that are not
Dead, but feed the grass row after rich row.
Think of the autumns that have come and gone!
15   Ambitious November with the humors of the year,
With a particular zeal for every slab,
Staining the uncomfortable angels that rot
On the slabs, a wing chipped here, an arm there:
The brute curiosity of an angel's stare
20   Turns you, like them, to stone,
Transforms the heaving air
Till plunged to a heavier world below
You shift your sea-space blindly
Heaving, turning like the blind crab.

25   Dazed by the wind, only the wind
         The leaves flying, plunge

You know who have waited by the wall
The twilight certainty of an animal,
Those midnight restitutions of the blood
30   You know—the immitigable[1] pines, the smoky frieze
Of the sky, the sudden call: you know the rage,
The cold pool left by the mounting flood,
Of muted Zeno and Parmenides.[2]
You who have waited for the angry resolution
35   Of those desires that should be yours tomorrow,
You know the unimportant shrift of death
And praise the vision
And praise the arrogant circumstance
Of those who fall
40   Rank upon rank, hurried beyond decision—
Here by the sagging gate, stopped by the wall.

---

1. Unable to become less harsh.
2. Greek philosophers (fifth century B.C.E.) of the Eleatic school. They held that what is various and changeable, all "development," is illusory, for reality is one and changeless.

Seeing, seeing only the leaves
Flying, plunge and expire

Turn your eyes to the immoderate past,
45 Turn to the inscrutable infantry rising
Demons out of the earth—they will not last.
Stonewall, Stonewall, and the sunken fields of hemp,
Shiloh, Antietam, Malvern Hill, Bull Run.[3]
Lost in that orient of the thick and fast
50 You will curse the setting sun.

Cursing only the leaves crying
Like an old man in a storm

You hear the shout, the crazy hemlocks point
With troubled fingers to the silence which
55 Smothers you, a mummy, in time.

The hound bitch
Toothless and dying, in a musty cellar
Hears the wind only.

Now that the salt of their blood
60 Stiffens the saltier oblivion of the sea,
Seals the malignant purity of the flood,
What shall we who count our days and bow
Our heads with a commemorial woe
In the ribboned coats of grim felicity,
65 What shall we say of the bones, unclean,
Whose verdurous[4] anonymity will grow?

The ragged arms, the ragged heads and eyes
Lost in these acres of the insane green?
The gray lean spiders come, they come and go;
70 In a tangle of willows without light
The singular screech-owl's tight
Invisible lyric seeds the mind
With the furious murmur of their chivalry.

We shall say only the leaves
75 Flying, plunge and expire

We shall say only the leaves whispering
In the improbable mist of nightfall
That flies on multiple wing:
Night is the beginning and the end
80 And in between the ends of distraction
Waits mute speculation, the patient curse
That stones the eyes, or like the jaguar leaps
For his own image in a jungle pool, his victim.

---

3. Names of important Civil War battles. *Stonewall*: Thomas "Stonewall" Jackson (1824–1863), Confederate general, earned his nickname at the first battle of Bull Run (1861); fatally wounded by his men at Chancellorsville.
4. Green (i.e., vigorous) as growing vegetation.

What shall we say who have knowledge
85   Carried to the heart? Shall we take the act
To the grave? Shall we, more hopeful, set up the grave
In the house? The ravenous grave?

        Leave now
The shut gate and the decomposing wall:
90   The gentle serpent, green in the mulberry bush,
Riots with his tongue through the hush—
Sentinel of the grave who counts us all!

                                   1928

The Swimmers

SCENE: *Montgomery County,*
Kentucky, July 1911

Kentucky water, clear springs: a boy fleeing
    To water under the dry Kentucky sun,
    His four little friends in tandem with him, seeing

Long shadows of grapevine wriggle and run
5   Over the green swirl; mullein under the ear
    Soft as Nausicaä's[5] palm; sullen fun

Savage as childhood's thin harmonious tear:
    O fountain, bosom source undying-dead
    Replenish me the spring of love and fear

10   And give me back the eye that looked and fled
    When a thrush idling in the tulip tree
    Unwound the cold dream of the copperhead.

—Along the creek the road was winding; we
    Felt the quicksilver sky. I see again
15   The shrill companions of that odyssey:

Bill Eaton, Charlie Watson, "Nigger" Layne
    The doctor's son, Harry Duèsler who played
    The flute; and Tate, with water on the brain.

Dog-days:[6] the dusty leaves where rain delayed
20   Hung low on poison-oak and scuppernong,[7]
    And we were following the active shade

Of water, that bells and bickers all night long.
    "No more'n a mile," Layne said. All five stood still.
    Listening, I heard what seemed at first a song;

5. The king's daughter who welcomes Odysseus in book 6 of the *Odyssey. Mullein:* wooly-leaved herb.

6. The hottest days of the year.

7. Kind of grapevine.

25 Peering, I heard the hooves come down the hill.
   The posse passed, twelve horse; the leader's face
   Was worn as limestone on an ancient sill.

Then, as sleepwalkers shift from a hard place
   In bed, and rising to keep a formal pledge
30   Descend a ladder into empty space,

We scuttled down the bank below a ledge
   And marched stiff-legged in our common fright
   Along a hog-track by the riffle's[8] edge.

Into a world where sound shaded the sight
35   Dropped the dull hooves again; the horsemen came
   Again, all but the leader: it was night

Momently and I feared: eleven same
   Jesus-Christers unmembered and unmade,
   Whose Corpse had died again in dirty shame.

40 The bank then levelling in a speckled glade,
   We stopped to breathe above the swimming-hole;
   I gazed at its reticulated° shade   *netlike*

Recoiling in blue fear, and felt it roll
   Over my ears and eyes and lift my hair
45   Like seaweed tossing on a sunk atoll.

I rose again. Borne on the copper air
   A distant voice green as a funeral wreath
   Against a grave: "That dead nigger there."

The melancholy sheriff slouched beneath
50   A giant sycamore; shaking his head
   He plucked a sassafras twig and picked his teeth:

"We come too late." He spoke to the tired dead
   Whose ragged shirt soaked up the viscous flow
   Of blood in which It lay discomfited.

55 A butting horse-fly gave one ear a blow
   And glanced off, as the sheriff kicked the rope
   Loose from the neck and hooked it with his toe

Away from the blood.—I looked back down the slope:
   The friends were gone that I had hoped to greet.—
60   A single horseman came at a slow lope

And pulled up at the hanged man's horny feet;
   The sheriff noosed the feet, the other end
   The stranger tied to his pommel in a neat

8. Shallow part of a stream.

Slip-knot. I saw the Negro's body bend
65 And straighten, as a fish-line cast transverse
Yields to the current that it must subtend.

The sheriff's Goddamn was a murmured curse
Not for the dead but for the blinding dust
That boxed the cortège[9] in a cloudy hearse

70 And dragged it towards our town. I knew I must
Not stay till twilight in that silent road;
Sliding my bare feet into the warm crust,

I hopped the stonecrop like a panting toad
Mouth open, following the heaving cloud
75 That floated to the court-house square its load

Of limber corpse that took the sun for shroud.
There were three figures in the dying sun
Whose light were company where three was crowd.

My breath crackled the dead air like a shotgun
80 As, sheriff and the stranger disappearing,
The faceless head lay still. I could not run

Or walk, but stood. Alone in the public clearing
This private thing was owned by all the town,
Though never claimed by us within my hearing.

1953

BASIL BUNTING
1900–1985

From Briggflatts[1]

From I

Brag, sweet tenor bull,
descant on Rawthey's madrigal,[2]
each pebble its part
for the fells'[3] late spring.
5 Dance tiptoe, bull,
black against may.[4]
Ridiculous and lovely
chase hurdling shadows
morning into noon.

---

9. Funeral procession.
1. In an interview, Bunting remarked, "My autobiography is Briggflatts." His poem's title is the name of a small village, straddling the river Rawthey, in the Lake District of northern England.

2. Part-song for three or more voices. *Descant:* sing the upper part of a part-song.
3. Hills or stretches of high moorland.
4. Flowers, pink or white, of the hawthorn tree.

10 May on the bull's hide
and through the dale
furrows fill with may,
paving the slowworm's[5] way.

A mason times his mallet
15 to a lark's twitter,
listening while the marble rests,
lays his rule
at a letter's edge,
fingertips checking,
20 till the stone spells a name
naming none,
a man abolished.
Painful lark, labouring to rise!
the solemn mallet says:
25 In the grave's slot
he lies. We rot.

Decay thrusts the blade,
Wheat stands in excrement
trembling. Rawthey trembles.
30 Tongue stumbles, ears err
for fear of spring.
Rub the stone with sand,
wet sandstone rending
roughness away. Fingers
35 ache on the rubbing stone.
The mason says: Rocks
happen by chance.
No one here bolts the door,
love is so sore.

40 Stone smooth as skin,
cold as the dead they load
on a low lorry° by night.   truck
The moon sits on the fell
but it will rain.
45 Under sacks on the stone
two children lie,
hear the horse stale,°   urinate
the mason whistle,
harness mutter to shaft,
50 felloe° to axle squeak,   exterior rim of a wheel
rut thud the rim,
crushed grit.

Stocking to stocking, jersey° to jersey,   sweater
head to a hard arm,
55 they kiss under the rain,
bruised by their marble bed.

5. Or blind worm, a small, burrowing, limbless lizard.

In Garsdale, dawn;
at Hawes, tea from the can.[6]
Rain stops, sacks
60   steam in the sun, they sit up.
Copper-wire moustache,
sea-reflecting eyes
and Baltic plainsong speech
declare: By such rocks
65   men killed Bloodaxe.[7]

Fierce blood throbs in his tongue,
lean words.
Skulls cropped for steel caps
huddle round Stainmore.[8]
70   Their becks ring on limestone,
whisper to peat.[9]
The clogged cart pushes the horse downhill.
In such soft air
they trudge and sing,
75   laying the tune frankly on the air.
All sounds fall still,
fellside bleat,
hide-and-seek peewit.[1]

Her pulse their pace,
80   palm countering palm,
till a trench is filled,
stone white as cheese
jeers at the dale.
Knotty wood, hard to rive,°   *split*
85   smoulders to ash;
smell of October apples.
The road again,
at a trot.
Wetter, warmed, they watch
90   the mason meditate
on name and date.

Rain rinses the road,
the bull streams and laments.
Sour rye porridge from the hob[2]
95   with cream and black tea,
meat, crust and crumb.
Her parents in bed
the children dry their clothes.
He has untied the tape

6. Metal container with handle and cover (not, i.e., a modern sealed can). Garsdale and Hawes are small country towns in northern England.
7. Eric Bloodaxe, ruler of the Viking kingdom of Northumbria, was overthrown and killed by the English in 954. "Baltic plainsong" refers to the Vikings' rough yet rhythmic speech.
8. Desolate forest in the north of England. *Steel*

caps: helmets.
9. "Beck" is a dialect word for a mattock, an agricultural instrument; it would "ring" on hard limestone, but "whisper" cutting into soft "peat," or decayed vegetable tissue in the earth.
1. Bird noted for its shrill, wailing cry.
2. Shelf in a fireplace, where a kettle can be kept warm.

100   of her striped flannel drawers
before the range. Naked
on the pricked rag mat[3]
his fingers comb
thatch of his manhood's home.

105   Gentle generous voices weave
over bare night
words to confirm and delight
till bird dawn.
Rainwater from the butt
110   she fetches and flannel
to wash him inch by inch,
kissing the pebbles.
Shining slowworm part of the marvel.
The mason stirs:
115   Words!
Pens are too light.
Take a chisel to write.

Every birth a crime,
every sentence life.
120   Wiped of mould and mites
would the ball run true?
No hope of going back.
Hounds falter and stray,
Shame deflects the pen.
125   Love murdered neither bleeds nor stifles
but jogs the draftsman's elbow.
what can he, changed, tell
her, changed, perhaps dead?
Delight dwindles. Blame
130   stays the same.

Brief words are hard to find,
shapes to carve and discard:
Bloodaxe, king of York,
king of Dublin, king of Orkney.[4]
135   Take no notice of tears;
letter the stone to stand
over love laid aside lest
insufferable happiness impede
flight to Stainmore,
140   to trace
lark, mallet,
becks, flocks
and axe knocks.

Dung will not soil the slowworm's
145   mosaic. Breathless lark

3. Rug made from strips of rag hooked through a sacking base.
4. Islands off the northeast coast of Scotland;

"king" here is in the sense of an early tribal chieftain.

drops to nest in sodden trash;
Rawthey truculent, dingy.
Drudge at the mallet, the may is down,
fog on fells. Guilty of spring
150 and spring's ending
amputated years ache after
the bull is beef, love a convenience.
It is easier to die than to remember.
Name and date
155 split in soft slate
a few months obliterate.

*   *   *

1965   1966

LAURA (RIDING) JACKSON
1901–1991

The Wind Suffers

The wind suffers of blowing,
The sea suffers of water,
And fire suffers of burning,
And I of a living name.

5   As stone suffers of stoniness,
As light of its shiningness,
As birds of their wingedness,
So I of my whoness.

And what the cure of all this?
10   What the not and not suffering?
What the better and later of this?
What the more me of me?

How for the pain-world to be
More world and no pain?
15   How for the old rain to fall
More wet and more dry?

How for the wilful blood to run
More salt-red and sweet-white?
And how for me in my actualness
20   To more shriek and more smile?

By no other miracles,
By the same knowing poison,
By an improved anguish,
By my further dying.

1930

Ding-Donging

With old hours all belfry heads
Are filled, as with thoughts.
With old hours ring the new hours
Between their bells.
5 And this hour-long ding-donging
So much employs the hour-long silences
That bells hang thinking when not striking,
When striking think of nothing.

Chimes of forgotten hours
10 More and more are played
While bells stare into space,
And more and more space wears
A look of having heard
But hearing not:
15 Forgotten hours chime louder
In the meantime, as if always,
And spread ding-donging back
More and more to yesterdays.

1930

STERLING A. BROWN
1901–1989

Slim in Atlanta[1]

Down in Atlanta,
    De whitefolks got laws
For to keep all de niggers
    From laughin' outdoors.

5   Hope to Gawd I may die
            If I ain't speakin' truth
        Make de niggers do deir laughin'
            In a telefoam booth.

        Slim Greer hit de town
10   An' de rebs[2] got him told,—
        "Dontcha laugh on de street,
            If you want to die old."

---

1. One of a series of poems about the fictional
character Slim Greer.
2. Abbreviation for rebels, or members of the Con-
federacy in the Civil War; here, a general term for
southerners.

Den dey showed him de booth,
An' a hundred shines°   *black people*
15   In front of it, waitin'
In double lines.

Slim thought his sides
Would bust in two,
Yelled, "Lookout, everybody,
20   I'm coming through!"

Pulled de other man out,
An' bust in de box,
An' laughed four hours
By de Georgia clocks.

25   Den he peeked through de door,
An' what did he see?
Three hundred niggers there
In misery.—

Some holdin' deir sides,
30   Some holdin' deir jaws,
To keep from breakin'
De Georgia laws.

An' Slim gave a holler,
An' started again;
35   An' from three hundred throats
Come a moan of pain.

An' everytime Slim
Saw what was outside,
Got to whoopin' again
40   Till he nearly died.

An' while de poor critters
Was waitin' deir chance,
Slim laughed till dey sent
Fo' de ambulance.

45   De state paid de railroad
To take him away;
Den, things was as usural
In Atlanta, Gee A.[3]

1932

---

3. GA; abbreviation for the state of Georgia.

Chillen Get Shoes

Hush little Lily,
　　Don't you cry;
You'll get your silver slippers
　　Bye and bye.[4]

5　Moll wears silver slippers
　　With red heels,
And men come to see her
　　In automobiles.

Lily walks wretched,
10　　Dragging her doll,
Worshipping stealthily
　　Good-time Moll;

Envying bitterly
　　Moll's fine clothes,
15　And her plump legs clad
　　In openwork hose.

Don't worry, Lily,
　　Don't you cry;
You'll be like Moll, too,
20　　Bye and bye.

　　　　　　　　　　　　　　　　　　　　　　　1932

Bitter Fruit of the Tree

They said to my grandmother: "Please do not be bitter,"
When they sold her first-born and let the second die,
When they drove her husband till he took to the swamplands,
And brought him home bloody and beaten at last.
5　They told her, "It is better you should not be bitter,
Some must work and suffer so that we, who must, can live,
Forgiving is noble, you must not be heathen bitter;
These are your orders: you *are* not to be bitter."
And they left her shack for their porticoed house.

10　They said to my father: "Please do not be bitter,"
When he ploughed and planted a crop not his,
When he weatherstripped a house that he could not enter,
And stored away a harvest he could not enjoy.
They answered his questions: "It does not concern you,

---

4. Cf. the lullaby "Hush Little Baby."

15   It is not for you to know, it is past your understanding,[5]
All you need know is: you must not be bitter."

1939   1980

Conjured

"She done put huh little hands
On the back uh my head;
I cain't git away from her
Twill I'm dead.

5   "She done laid her little body
Beneaf my breast,
And I won't never
Git no rest.

"She done been in my arms
10   Twill the break of day
Won't never
Git away. . . .

"She done put her little shoes
Underneaf my bed
15   Never git away from her
Twill I'm dead.

"Won't want to leave her
Then," he said.
"Oh, baby, gotta lay
20   So long
Alone. . . ."

1930s   1980

LANGSTON HUGHES
1902–1967

The Weary Blues

Droning a drowsy syncopated tune,
Rocking back and forth to a mellow croon,
I heard a Negro play.
Down on Lenox Avenue[1] the other night

---

5. Ironic echo of Phillipians 4, esp. 4.7: "And the peace of God, which passeth all understanding, shall keep your hearts and minds through Christ Jesus."

1. A main thoroughfare in New York City, in the heart of Harlem; now called Malcolm X Blvd.

5   By the pale dull pallor of an old gas light
        He did a lazy sway. . . .
        He did a lazy sway. . . .
  To the tune o' those Weary Blues.
  With his ebony hands on each ivory key
10   He made that poor piano moan with melody.
        O Blues!
  Swaying to and fro on his rickety stool
  He played that sad raggy tune like a musical fool.
        Sweet Blues!
15   Coming from a black man's soul.
        O Blues!
  In a deep song voice with a melancholy tone
  I heard that Negro sing, that old piano moan—
        "Ain't got nobody in all this world,
20   Ain't got nobody but ma self.
        I's gwine to quit ma frownin'
        And put ma troubles on the shelf."
  Thump, thump, thump, went his foot on the floor.
  He played a few chords then he sang some more—

25   "I got the Weary Blues
        And I can't be satisfied.
        Got the Weary Blues
        And can't be satisfied—
        I ain't happy no mo'
30   And I wish that I had died."
  And far into the night he crooned that tune.
  The stars went out and so did the moon.
  The singer stopped playing and went to bed
  While the Weary Blues echoed through his head.
35   He slept like a rock or a man that's dead.

1926

The Negro Speaks of Rivers

(To W.E.B. Du Bois)[2]

I've known rivers:
I've known rivers ancient as the world and older than the flow of
    human blood in human veins.
My soul has grown deep like the rivers.

  I bathed in the Euphrates when dawns were young.
5   I built my hut near the Congo and it lulled me to sleep.
  I looked upon the Nile and raised the pyramids above it.
  I heard the singing of the Mississippi when Abe Lincoln went down
    to New Orleans,[3] and I've seen its muddy bosom turn all golden
    in the sunset.

2. American historian, educator, and activist (1868–1963); he was one of the founders of the NAACP (National Association for the Advancement of Colored People), and in later life became increasingly interested in Pan-Africanism.
3. President Lincoln's decision to end slavery was partly inspired by this trip.

I've known rivers:
Ancient, dusky rivers.

10   My soul has grown deep like the rivers.

1926

Dream Variations

To fling my arms wide
In some place of the sun,
To whirl and to dance
Till the white day is done.
5   Then rest at cool evening
Beneath a tall tree
While night comes on gently,
    Dark like me—
That is my dream!

10   To fling my arms wide
In the face of the sun,
Dance! Whirl! Whirl!
Till the quick day is done.
Rest at pale evening . . .
15   A tall, slim tree . . .
Night coming tenderly
    Black like me.

1926

Cross

My old man's a white old man
And my old mother's black.
If ever I cursed my white old man
I take my curses back.

5   If ever I cursed my black old mother
And wished she were in hell,
I'm sorry for that evil wish
And now I wish her well.

My old man died in a fine big house.
10   My ma died in a shack.
I wonder where I'm gonna die,
Being neither white nor black?

1926

Bad Luck Card

Cause you don't love me
Is awful, awful hard.
Gypsy done showed me
My bad luck card.

5 There ain't no good left
In this world for me.
Gypsy done tole me—
Unlucky as can be.

I don't know what
10 Po' weary me can do.
Gypsy says I'd kill my self
If I was you.

1927

Song for a Dark Girl

Way Down South in Dixie
    (Break the heart of me)
They hung my black young lover
    To a cross roads tree.

5 Way Down South in Dixie
    (Bruised body high in air)
I asked the white Lord Jesus
    What was the use of prayer.

Way Down South in Dixie
10   (Break the heart of me)
Love is a naked shadow
    On a gnarled and naked tree.

1927

Harlem Sweeties

Have you dug the spill
Of Sugar Hill?[4]
Cast your gims°   eyes
On this sepia° thrill: brown
5 Brown sugar lassie,
Caramel treat,

4. In the early part of the twentieth century, the most fashionable residential area of Harlem.

Honey-gold baby
Sweet enough to eat.
Peach-skinned girlie,
10   Coffee and cream,
Chocolate darling
Out of a dream.
Walnut tinted
Or cocoa brown,
15   Pomegranate-lipped
Pride of the town.
Rich cream-colored
To plum-tinted black,
Feminine sweetness
20   In Harlem's no lack.
Glow of the quince
To blush of the rose.
Persimmon bronze
To cinnamon toes.
25   Blackberry cordial,
Virginia Dare[5] wine—
All those sweet colors
Flavor Harlem of mine!
Walnut or cocoa,
30   Let me repeat:
Caramel, brown sugar,
A chocolate treat.
Molasses taffy,
Coffee and cream,
35   Licorice, clove, cinnamon
To a honey-brown dream.
Ginger, wine-gold,
Persimmon, blackberry,
All through the spectrum
40   Harlem girls vary—
So if you want to know beauty's
Rainbow-sweet thrill,
Stroll down luscious,
Delicious, *fine* Sugar Hill.

1942

Harlem

What happens to a dream deferred?

Does it dry up
like a raisin in the sun?
Or fester like a sore—
5   And then run?

5. A brand of wine.

Does it stink like rotten meat?
Or crust and sugar over—
like a syrupy sweet?

Maybe it just sags
10   like a heavy load.

Or does it explode?

1951

Theme for English B

The instructor said,

Go home and write
a page tonight.
And let that page come out of you—
5   *Then, it will be true.*

I wonder if it's that simple?
I am twenty-two, colored, born in Winston-Salem.
I went to school there, then Durham,[6] then here
to this college[7] on the hill above Harlem.
10   I am the only colored student in my class.
The steps from the hill lead down into Harlem,
through a park, then I cross St. Nicholas,
Eighth Avenue, Seventh, and I come to the Y,
the Harlem Branch Y, where I take the elevator
15   up to my room, sit down, and write this page:

It's not easy to know what is true for you or me
at twenty-two, my age. But I guess I'm what
I feel and see and hear, Harlem, I hear you:
hear you, hear me—we two—you, me, talk on this page.
20   (I hear New York, too.) Me—who?
Well, I like to eat, sleep, drink, and be in love.
I like to work, read, learn, and understand life.
I like a pipe for a Christmas present,
or records—Bessie,[8] bop, or Bach.
25   I guess being colored doesn't make me *not* like
the same things other folks like who are other races.
So will my page be colored that I write?
Being me, it will not be white.

6. Like Winston-Salem, a city in North Carolina.   8. Bessie Smith (1894 or 1898–1937), American
7. City College of the City University of New York   blues singer.
(CCNY).

But it will be
30   a part of you, instructor.
You are white—
yet a part of me, as I am a part of you.
That's American.
Sometimes perhaps you don't want to be a part of me.
35   Nor do I often want to be a part of you.
But we are, that's true!
I guess you learn from me—
although you're older—and white—
and somewhat more free.

40   This is my page for English B.

                                                            1951

Dinner Guest: Me

I know I am
The Negro Problem[9]
Being wined and dined,
Answering the usual questions
5   That come to white mind
Which seeks demurely
To probe in polite way
The why and wherewithal
Of darkness U.S.A.—
10   Wondering how things got this way
In current democratic night,
Murmuring gently
Over *fraises du bois*,[1]
"I'm so ashamed of being white."

15   The lobster is delicious,
The wine divine,
And center of attention
At the damask table, mine.
To be a Problem on
20   Park Avenue at eight
Is not so bad.
Solutions to the Problem,
Of course, wait.

                                                            1967

9. Allusion to the controversial 1963 essay "My Negro Problem—and Ours," by the American writer Norman Podhoretz (b. 1930).

1. Wild strawberries (French); ironic allusion to W. E. B. Du Bois (see note 2, p. 1430).

ROY CAMPBELL
1902–1957

The Zulu Girl

To F. C. Slater

When in the sun the hot red acres smoulder,
Down where the sweating gang its labour plies,
A girl flings down her hoe, and from her shoulder
Unslings her child tormented by the flies.

5   She takes him to a ring of shadow pooled
By thorn-trees: purpled with the blood of ticks,
While her sharp nails, in slow caresses ruled,
Prowl through his hair with sharp electric clicks,

His sleepy mouth, plugged by the heavy nipple,
10   Tugs like a puppy, grunting as he feeds:
Through his frail nerves her own deep languors ripple
Like a broad river sighing through its reeds.

Yet in that drowsy stream his flesh imbibes
An old unquenched unsmotherable heat—
15   The curbed ferocity of beaten tribes,
The sullen dignity of their defeat.

Her body looms above him like a hill
Within whose shade a village lies at rest,
Or the first cloud so terrible and still
20   That bears the coming harvest in its breast.

1926   1930

The Sisters

After hot loveless nights, when cold winds stream
Sprinkling the frost and dew, before the light,
Bored with the foolish things that girls must dream
Because their beds are empty of delight,

5   Two sisters rise and strip. Out from the night
Their horses run to their low-whistled pleas—
Vast phantom shapes with eyeballs rolling white
That sneeze a fiery steam about their knees:

Through the crisp manes their stealthy prowling hands,
10   Stronger than curbs, in slow caresses rove,
They gallop down across the milk-white sands
And wade far out into the sleeping cove:

The frost stings sweetly with a burning kiss
As intimate as love, as cold as death:
15   Their lips, whereon delicious tremors hiss,
Fume with the ghostly pollen of their breath.

Far out on the grey silence of the flood
They watch the dawn in smouldering gyres° expand   *spiral turnings*
Beyond them: and the day burns through their blood
20   Like a white candle through a shuttered hand.

1926   1930

OGDEN NASH
1902–1971

The Cow

The cow is of the bovine ilk;
One end is moo, the other, milk.

1931

Reflections on Ice-breaking

Candy
Is dandy
But liquor
Is quicker.

1931

Requiem

There was a young belle of old Natchez[1]
Whose garments were always in patchez.
When comment arose
On the state of her clothes,
5   She drawled, When Ah itchez, Ah scratchez!

1935

1. Town in Mississippi.

Columbus

Once upon a time there was an Italian,
And some people thought he was a rapscallion,
But he wasn't offended,
Because other people thought he was splendid,
5 And he said the world was round,
And everybody made an uncomplimentary sound,
But he went and tried to borrow some money from Ferdinand
But Ferdinand said America was a bird in the bush and he'd rather
    have a berdinand,
But Columbus' brain was fertile, it wasn't arid,
10 And he remembered that Ferdinand was married,
And he thought, there is no wife like a misunderstood one,
Because if her husband thinks something is a terrible idea she is
    bound to think it a good one,
So he perfumed his handkerchief with bay rum and citronella,
And he went to see Isabella,
15 And he looked wonderful but he had never felt sillier,
And she said, I can't place the face but the aroma is familiar,
And Columbus didn't say a word,
All he said was, I am Columbus, the fifteenth-century Admiral Byrd,[2]
And, just as he thought, her disposition was very malleable,
20 And she said, Here are my jewels, and she wasn't penurious like
    Cornelia the mother of the Gracchi,[3] she wasn't referring to her
    children, no, she was referring to her jewels, which were very
    very valuable,
So Columbus said, Somebody show me the sunset and somebody
    did and he set sail for it,
And he discovered America and they put him in jail for it,
And the fetters gave him welts,
And they named America after somebody else,[4]
25 So the sad fate of Columbus ought to be pointed out to every child
    and every voter,
Because it has a very important moral, which is, Don't be a discoverer,
    be a promoter.

1935

The Turtle

The turtle lives 'twixt plated decks
Which practically conceal its sex.
I think it clever of the turtle
In such a fix to be so fertile.

1940

2. Richard Evelyn Byrd (1888–1957), American explorer of the North and South Poles.
3. Cornelia (second century B.C.E.) was the Roman model of matronly virtue. Though hardly penurious, she famously responded to a request to show her jewels by producing her two sons (famous men in their own right).
4. Amerigo Vespucci (1454–1512), Italian navigator and explorer, who first sailed across the Atlantic in 1497.

STEVIE SMITH
1902–1971

No Categories!

I cry I cry
To God who created me
Not to you Angels who frustrated me
Let me fly, let me die,
5   Let me come to Him.

Not to you Angels on the wing,
With your severe faces,
And your scholarly grimaces,
And your do this and that,
10   And your exasperating pit-pat
Of appropriate admonishment.

That is not what the Creator meant.
In the day of his gusty creation
He made this and that
15   And laughed to see them grow fat.

Plod on, you Angels say, do better aspire higher
And one day you may be like us, or those next below us,
Or nearer the lowest,
Or lowest,
20   Doing their best.

Oh no no, you Angels, I say,
No hierarchies I pray.

Oh God, laugh not too much aside
Say not, it is a small matter.
25   See what your Angels do; scatter
Their pride; laugh them away.

Oh no categories I pray.

1950

Mr. Over

Mr. Over is dead
He died fighting and true
And on his tombstone they wrote
Over to You.

5   And who pray is this You
To whom Mr. Over is gone?

Oh if we only knew that
We should not do wrong.

But who is this beautiful You
10 We all of us long for so much
Is he not our friend and our brother
Our father and such?

Yes he is this and much more
This is but a portion
15 A sea-drop in a bucket
Taken from the ocean

So the voices spake
Softly above my head
And a voice in my heart cried: Follow
20 Where he has led

And a devil's voice cried: Happy
Happy the dead.

                                                                    1950

The Death Sentence

Cold as No Plea,
Yet wild with all negation,
Weeping I come
To my heart's destination,
5 To my last bed
Between th' unhallowed boards—
The Law allows it
And the Court awards.

                                                                    1950

Not Waving but Drowning

Nobody heard him, the dead man,
But still he lay moaning:
I was much further out than you thought
And not waving but drowning.

5 Poor chap, he always loved larking
And now he's dead
It must have been too cold for him his heart gave way,
They said.

Oh, no no no, it was too cold always
10 (Still the dead one lay moaning)
I was much too far out all my life
And not waving but drowning.

1957

The Celts

I think of the Celts[1] as rather a whining lady
Who was beautiful once but is not so much so now
She is not very loving, but there is one thing she loves
It is her grievance which she hugs and takes out walking.
5 The Celtic lady likes fighting very much for freedom
But when she has got it she is a proper tyrant
Nobody likes her much when she is governing.

The Celtic lady is not very widely popular
But the English love her oh they love her very much
10 Especially when the Celtic lady is Irish they love her
Which is odd as she hates them then more than anyone else,
When she's Welsh the English stupidly associate her chiefly
With national hats, eisteddfods[2] and Old Age Pensions.
(They don't think of her at all when she is Scotch, it is rather a
    problem.)

15 Oh the Celtic lady when she's Irish is the one for me
Oh she is so witty and wild, my word witty,
And flashing and spiteful this Celtic lady we love
All the same she is not so beautiful as she was.

1957

Thoughts about the Person from Porlock[3]

Coleridge received the Person from Porlock
And ever after called him a curse,
Then why did he hurry to let him in?
He could have hid in the house.

5 It was not right of Coleridge in fact it was wrong
(But often we all do wrong)

---

1. Peoples speaking languages related to those of
the ancient Gauls, including Bretons, Cornish,
Welsh, Irish, etc.
2. Traditional Welsh congresses of bards, min-
strels, and poets, at which contests of minstrelsy,
singing, or oratory are conducted.
3. See Samuel Taylor Coleridge's poem "Kubla

Khan" and, especially, note 8 (p. 809). Coleridge
attributed his leaving "Kubla Khan" unfinished to
an interruption, while he was writing it, by "a per-
son on business from Porlock." Having been
"detained by him for above an hour," Coleridge
proved unable to recapture the vision that was the
substance of the poem.

As the truth is I think he was already stuck
With Kubla Khan.

He was weeping and wailing: I am finished, finished,
10   I shall never write another word of it,
When along comes the Person from Porlock
And takes the blame for it.

It was not right, it was wrong,
But often we all do wrong.

15   May we enquire the name of the Person from Porlock?
Why, Porson, didn't you know?
He lived at the bottom of Porlock Hill
So had a long way to go,

He wasn't much in the social sense
20   Though his grandmother was a Warlock,
One of the Rutlandshire ones I fancy
And nothing to do with Porlock,

And he lived at the bottom of the hill as I said
And had a cat named Flo,
25   And had a cat named Flo.

I long for the Person from Porlock
To bring my thoughts to an end,
I am becoming impatient to see him
I think of him as a friend,

30   Often I look out the window
Often I run to the gate
I think, He will come this evening,
I think it is rather late.

I am hungry to be interrupted
35   For ever and ever amen
O Person from Porlock come quickly
And bring my thoughts to an end.

I felicitate the people who have a Person from Porlock
To break up everything and throw it away
40   Because then there will be nothing to keep them
And they need not stay.

Why do they grumble so much?
He comes like a benison°   blessing
They should be glad he has not forgotten them
45   They might have had to go on.

These thoughts are depressing I know. They are depressing,
I wish I was more cheerful, it is more pleasant,

Also it is a duty, we should smile as well as submitting
To the purpose of One Above who is experimenting
50   With various mixtures of human character which goes best,
All is interesting for him it is exciting, but not for us.
There I go again. Smile, smile, and get some work to do
Then you will be practically unconscious without positively
        having to go.

                                                    1962

COUNTEE CULLEN
1903–1946

Heritage

For Harold Jackman

What is Africa to me:
Copper sun or scarlet sea,
Jungle star or jungle track,
Strong bronzed men, or regal black
5   Women from whose loins I sprang
When the birds of Eden sang?
One three centuries removed
From the scenes his fathers loved,
Spicy grove, cinnamon tree,
10   *What is Africa to me?*

So I lie, who all day long
Want no sound except the song
Sung by wild barbaric birds
Goading massive jungle herds,
15   Juggernauts[1] of flesh that pass
Trampling tall defiant grass
Where young forest lovers lie,
Plighting troth beneath the sky.
So I lie, who always hear,
20   Though I cram against my ear
Both my thumbs, and keep them there,
Great drums throbbing through the air.
So I lie, whose fount of pride,
Dear distress, and joy allied,
25   Is my somber flesh and skin,
With the dark blood dammed within
Like great pulsing tides of wine
That, I fear, must burst the fine
Channels of the chafing net
30   Where they surge and foam and fret.

---

1. Great forces or massive objects that crush everything in their path.

Africa? A book one thumbs
Listlessly, till slumber comes.
Unremembered are her bats
Circling through the night, her cats
35   Crouching in the river reeds,
Stalking gentle flesh that feeds
By the river brink; no more
Does the bugle-throated roar
Cry that monarch claws have leapt
40   From the scabbards where they slept.
Silver snakes that once a year
Doff the lovely coats you wear,
Seek no covert in your fear
Lest a mortal eye should see;
45   What's your nakedness to me?
Here no leprous flowers rear
Fierce corollas° in the air;   petals
Here no bodies sleek and wet,
Dripping mingled rain and sweat,
50   Tread the savage measures of
Jungle boys and girls in love.
What is last year's snow to me,[2]
Last year's anything? The tree
Budding yearly must forget
55   How its past arose or set—
Bough and blossom, flower, fruit,
Even what shy bird with mute
Wonder at her travail there,
Meekly labored in its hair.
60   *One three centuries removed*
From the scenes his fathers loved,
Spicy grove, cinnamon tree,
What is Africa to me?

So I lie, who find no peace
65   Night or day, no slight release
From the unremittent beat
Made by cruel padded feet
Walking through my body's street.
Up and down they go, and back,
70   Treading out a jungle track.
So I lie, who never quite
Safely sleep from rain at night—
I can never rest at all
When the rain begins to fall;
75   Like a soul gone mad with pain
I must match its weird refrain;
Ever must I twist and squirm,
Writhing like a baited worm,

---

2. Cf. the refrain of "Ballad of the Ladies of Bygone Time," by the French poet François Villon (1431–
1463?): "Where are the snows of yesteryear?"

While its primal measures drip
80 Through my body, crying, "Strip!
Doff this new exuberance.
Come and dance the Lover's Dance!"
In an old remembered way
Rain works on me night and day.

85 Quaint, outlandish heathen gods
Black men fashion out of rods,
Clay, and brittle bits of stone,
In a likeness like their own,
My conversion came high-priced;
90 I belong to Jesus Christ,
Preacher of Humility;
Heathen gods are naught to me.

Father, Son, and Holy Ghost,
So I make an idle boast;
95 Jesus of the twice-turned cheek,[3]
Lamb of God, although I speak
With my mouth thus, in my heart
Do I play a double part.
Ever at Thy glowing altar
100 Must my heart grow sick and falter,
Wishing He I served were black,
Thinking then it would not lack
Precedent of pain to guide it,
Let who would or might deride it;
105 Surely then this flesh would know
Yours had borne a kindred woe.
Lord, I fashion dark gods, too,
Daring even to give You
Dark despairing features where,
110 Crowned with dark rebellious hair,
Patience wavers just so much as
Mortal grief compels, while touches
Quick and hot, of anger, rise
To smitten cheek and weary eyes.
115 Lord, forgive me if my need
Sometimes shapes a human creed.
All day long and all night through,
One thing only must I do:
Quench my pride and cool my blood,
120 *Lest I perish in the flood,*
Lest a hidden ember set
Timber that I thought was wet
Burning like the dryest flax,
Melting like the merest wax,

---

3. Cf. Matthew 5.39: "I say unto you, that ye resist not evil: but whosoever shall smite thee on the right cheek, turn to him the other also."

125   *Lest the grave restore its dead.*
Not yet has my heart or head
In the least way realized
They and I are civilized.

1925

Incident

Once riding in old Baltimore,
Heart-filled, head-filled with glee,
I saw a Baltimorean
Keep looking straight at me.

5   Now I was eight and very small,
And he was no whit bigger,
And so I smiled, but he poked out
His tongue, and called me, "Nigger."

I saw the whole of Baltimore
10   From May until December;
Of all the things that happened there
That's all that I remember.

1925

Yet Do I Marvel

I doubt not God is good, well-meaning, kind,
And did He stoop to quibble could tell why
The little buried mole continues blind,
Why flesh that mirrors Him must some day die,
5   Make plain the reason tortured Tantalus[4]
Is baited by the fickle fruit, declare
If merely brute caprice dooms Sisyphus[5]
To struggle up a never-ending stair.
Inscrutable His ways are, and immune
10   To catechism by a mind too strewn
With petty cares to slightly understand
What awful brain compels His awful hand.
Yet do I marvel at this curious thing:
To make a poet black, and bid him sing!

1925

---

4. Figure in Greek mythology who was offered food and water only to have it taken away.

5. Figure in Greek mythology who perpetually rolled a stone uphill only to see it roll down again.

EARLE BIRNEY
1904–1991

Bushed

He invented a rainbow but lightning struck it
shattered it into the lake-lap of a mountain
so big his mind slowed when he looked at it

Yet he built a shack on the shore
5 learned to roast porcupine belly and
wore the quills on his hatband

At first he was out with the dawn
whether it yellowed bright as wood-columbine
or was only a fuzzed moth in a flannel of storm
10 But he found the mountain was clearly alive
sent messages whizzing down every hot morning
boomed proclamations at noon and spread out
a white guard of goat
before falling asleep on its feet at sundown

15 When he tried his eyes on the lake   ospreys[1]
would fall like valkyries[2]
choosing the cut-throat
He took then to waiting
till the night smoke rose from the boil of the sunset

20 But the moon carved unknown totems
out of the lakeshore
owls in the beardusky woods derided him
moosehorned cedars circled his swamps and tossed
their antlers up to the stars
25 Then he knew   though the mountain slept   the winds
were shaping its peak to an arrowhead
poised

And now he could only
bar himself in and wait
30 for the great flint to come singing into his heart

1952

The Bear on the Delhi Road[3]

Unreal   tall as a myth
by the road the Himalayan bear

---

1. Large, fish-eating hawks.
2. In Norse mythology, the warrior-maidens of Odin; they selected the heroes who were to die in battle and afterwards carried them to Valhalla, the hall of the heroic slain.
3. In India.

is beating the brilliant air
with his crooked arms
5   About him two men   bare
spindly as locusts   leap
One pulls on a ring
in the great soft nose   His mate
flicks   flicks with a stick
10   up at the rolling eyes

They have not led him here
down from the fabulous hills
to this bald alien plain
and the clamorous world   to kill
15   but simply to teach him to dance

They are peaceful both   these spare
men of Kashmir[4]   and the bear
alive is their living   too
If   far on the Delhi way
20   around him galvanic[5] they dance
it is merely to wear   wear
from his shaggy body the tranced
wish forever to stay
only an ambling bear
25   four-footed in berries

It is no more joyous for them
in this hot dust to prance
out of reach of the praying claws
sharpened to paw for ants
30   in the shadows of deodars°   *East Indian cedars*
It is not easy to free
myth from reality
or rear this fellow up
to lurch   lurch with them
35   in the tranced dancing of men

1962   1975

C. DAY LEWIS
1904–1972

Two Songs

I've heard them lilting at loom and belting,[1]
Lasses lilting before dawn of day:

---

4. Mountainous region of northern India.
5. I.e., exciting him as if with electric shock.

1. Cf. Jean Elliot, "The Flowers of the Forest" (p. 677).

But now they are silent, not gamesome and gallant—
The flowers of the town are rotting away.

5   There was laughter and loving in the lanes at evening;
Handsome were the boys then, and girls were gay.
But lost in Flanders[2] by medalled commanders
The lads of the village are vanished away.

Cursed be the promise that takes our men from us—
10   All will be champion if you choose to obey:
They fight against hunger but still it is stronger—
The prime of our land grows cold as the clay.

The women are weary, once lilted so merry,
Waiting to marry for a year and a day:
15   From wooing and winning, from owning or earning
The flowers of the town are all turned away.

Come, live with me and be my love,[3]
And we will all the pleasures prove
Of peace and plenty, bed and board,
20   That chance employment may afford.

I'll handle dainties° on the docks   *delicacies*
And thou shalt read of summer frocks:
At evening by the sour canals
We'll hope to hear some madrigals.

25   Care on thy maiden brow shall put
A wreath of wrinkles, and thy foot
Be shod with pain: not silken dress
But toil shall tire thy loveliness.

Hunger shall make thy modest zone°   *belt*
30   And cheat fond death of all but bone—
If these delights thy mind may move,
Then live with me and be my love.

1935

Where are the War Poets?

They who in folly or mere greed
Enslaved religion, markets, laws,
Borrow our language now and bid
Us to speak up in freedom's cause.

Shepherd to His Love" (p. 256) and Sir Walter
Ralegh, "The Nymph's Reply to the Shepherd"
(p. 152).

5 It is the logic of our times,
No subject for immortal verse—
That we who lived by honest dreams
Defend the bad against the worse.

1943

RICHARD EBERHART
b. 1904

The Fury of Aerial Bombardment

You would think the fury of aerial bombardment
Would rouse God to relent; the infinite spaces
Are still silent. He looks on shock-pried faces.
History, even, does not know what is meant.

5 You would feel that after so many centuries
God would give man to repent; yet he can kill
As Cain[1] could, but with multitudinous will,
No farther advanced than in his ancient furies.

Was man made stupid to see his own stupidity?
10 Is God by definition indifferent, beyond us all?
Is the eternal truth man's fighting soul
Wherein the Beast ravens in its own avidity?

Of Van Wettering I speak, and Averill,
Names on a list, whose faces I do not recall
15 But they are gone to early death, who late° in school   *recently*
Distinguished the belt feed lever from the belt holding pawl.[2]

1947

PATRICK KAVANAGH
1904–1967

Sanctity

To be a poet and not know the trade,
To be a lover and repel all women;
Twin ironies by which great saints are made,
The agonising pincer-jaws of Heaven.

1936

---

1. The firstborn son of Adam and Eve, he murdered his brother Abel (Genesis 4.8).
2. Parts of the .50-caliber Browning machine gun, mounted in American aircraft during World War II. Eberhart was an aerial gunnery instructor during the summer of 1944.

From The Great Hunger[1]

I

Clay is the word and clay is the flesh
Where the potato-gatherers like mechanised scarecrows move
Along the side-fall of the hill—Maguire and his men.
If we watch them an hour is there anything we can prove
5 Of life as it is broken-backed over the Book
Of Death? Here crows gabble over worms and frogs
And the gulls like old newspapers are blown clear of the hedges,
    luckily.
Is there some light of imagination in these wet clods?
Or why do we stand here shivering?
10   Which of these men
Loved the light and the queen
Too long virgin? Yesterday was summer. Who was it promised
    marriage to himself
Before apples were hung from the ceilings for Hallowe'en?
We will wait and watch the tragedy to the last curtain,
15 Till the last soul passively like a bag of wet clay
Rolls down the side of the hill, diverted by the angles
Where the plough missed or a spade stands, straitening the way.

A dog lying on a torn jacket under a heeled-up cart,
A horse nosing along the posied headland, trailing
20 A rusty plough. Three heads hanging between wide-apart
Legs. October playing a symphony on a slack wire paling.
Maguire watches the drills flattened out
And the flints that lit a candle for him on a June altar
Flameless. The drills slipped by and the days slipped by
25 And he trembled his head away and ran free from the world's halter,
And thought himself wiser than any man in the townland[2]
When he laughed over pints of porter°   *strong, dark ale*
Of how he came free from every net spread
In the gaps of experience. He shook a knowing head
30 And pretended to his soul
That children are tedious in hurrying fields of April
Where men are spanging° across wide furrows.   *leaping*
Lost in the passion that never needs a wife—
The pricks that pricked were the pointed pins of harrows.
35 Children scream so loud that the crows could bring
The seed of an acre away with crow-rude jeers.
Patrick Maguire, he called his dog and he flung a stone in the air
And hallooed the birds away that were the birds of the years.

---

1. Kavanagh's most famous work is his long poem in fourteen sections, *The Great Hunger* (1942). Named for a severe famine that decimated the Irish population during the 1840s, the poem focuses on the spiritual and sexual hunger of the Irish peasantry among whom Kavanagh grew up. The central figure is a potato farmer named Patrick Maguire, who is bound to the soil by the need not to leave his aged mother, and whose Church-induced sense of sin is so strong that he dies a bachelor and perhaps a virgin.
2. In Ireland, an area of land comparable to a township.

Turn over the weedy clods and tease out the tangled skeins.
40 What is he looking for there?
He thinks it is a potato, but we know better
Than his mud-gloved fingers probe in this insensitive hair.

"Move forward the basket and balance it steady
In this hollow. Pull down the shafts of that cart, Joe,
45 And straddle the horse," Maguire calls.
"The wind's over Brannagan's, now that means rain.
Graip° up some withered stalks and see that no potato falls   *fork*
Over the tail-board going down the ruckety pass—
And *that's* a job we'll have to do in December,
50 Gravel it and build a kerb on the bog-side. Is that Cassidy's ass
Out in my clover? Curse o' God—
Where is that dog?
Never where he's wanted." Maguire grunts and spits
Through a clay-wattled moustache and stares about him from the
          height.
55 His dream changes again like the cloud-swung wind
And he is not so sure now if his mother was right
When she praised the man who made a field his bride.

Watch him, watch him, that man on a hill whose spirit
Is a wet sack flapping about the knees of time.
60 He lives that his little fields may stay fertile when his own body
Is spread in the bottom of a ditch under two coulters³ crossed in
          Christ's Name.

He was suspicious in his youth as a rat near strange bread,
When girls laughed; when they screamed he knew that meant
The cry of fillies in season. He could not walk
65 The easy road to his destiny. He dreamt
The innocense of young brambles to hooked treachery.
O the grip, O the grip of irregular fields! No man escapes.
It could not be that back of the hills love was free
And ditches straight.
70 No monster hand lifted up children and put down apes
As here
                              "O God if I had been wiser!"
That was his sigh like the brown breeze in the thistles.
He looks towards his house and haggard.° "O God if I had been wiser!"   *yard*
75 But now a crumpled leaf from the whitethorn bushes
Darts like a frightened robin, and the fence
Shows the green of after-grass through a little window,
And he knows that his own heart is calling his mother a liar.
God's truth is life—even the grotesque shapes of its foulest fire.

80 The horse lifts its head and cranes
Through the whins° and stones   *masses of gorse shrub*
To lip late passion in the crawling clover.

---

3. Iron blades in ploughs.

In the gap there's a bush weighted with boulders like morality,
The fools of life bleed if they climb over.

85 The wind leans from Brady's, and the coltsfoot leaves are holed with
 rust,
Rain fills the cart-tracks and the sole-plate grooves;
A yellow sun reflects in Donaghmoyne[4]
The poignant light in puddles shaped by hooves.

Come with me, Imagination, into this iron house
90 And we will watch from the doorway the years run back,
And we will know what a peasant's left hand wrote on the page.
Be easy, October. No cackle hen, horse neigh, tree sough, duck quack.

1942

Epic

I have lived in important places, times
When great events were decided, who owned
That half a rood° of rock, a no-man's land   *quarter acre*
Surrounded by our pitchfork-armed claims.
5 I heard the Duffys shouting "Damn your soul"
And old McCabe stripped to the waist, seen
Step the plot defying blue cast-steel—
"Here is the march along these iron stones"
That was the year of the Munich bother.[5] Which
10 Was more important? I inclined
To lose my faith in Ballyrush and Gortin[6]
Till Homer's ghost came whispering to my mind
He said: I made the Iliad[7] from such
A local row. Gods make their own importance.

1951

Canal Bank Walk[8]

Leafy-with-love banks and the green waters of the canal
Pouring redemption for me, that I do
The will of God, wallow in the habitual, the banal,
Grow with nature again as before I grew.
5 The bright stick trapped, the breeze adding a third
Party to the couple kissing on an old seat,
And a bird gathering materials for the nest for the Word
Eloquently new and abandoned to its delirious beat.

4. A stream in County Monaghan.
5. Diplomatic crisis of September 1939 (involving
Britain, Czechoslovakia, France, and Germany)
that precipitated World War II.

6. Small townships, near Kavanagh's home, in
County Monaghan.
7. Homer's epic poem about the Trojan War.
8. Along Dublin's Grand Canal.

O unworn world enrapture me, encapture me in a web
10   Of fabulous grass and eternal voices by a beech,
Feed the gaping need of my senses, give me ad lib
To pray unselfconsciously with overflowing speech
For this soul needs to be honoured with a new dress woven
From green and blue things and arguments that cannot be proven.

1960

STANLEY KUNITZ
b. 1905

He[1]

He runs before the wise men: he
Is moving on the hills like snow.
No gifts, no tears, no company
He brings, but wind-rise and water-flow.

5   In meadows of descended day
His motion leans, dividing air:
He takes the unforgiving way
Beneath the apostolic star.[2]

She who has known him calls him stranger.
10   Parting the night's long hair, he steals
Within the heart, that humble manger
Where the white, astonished spirit kneels.

His vertical inflicting pride,
Whose shadow cuts the nib of space,
15   Bends to this virtue fructified.[3]
But though he kiss the little face

Like rapture breaking on the mind,
The necessary fierce details
Implacably he has designed.
20   Redemption hangs upon the nails.

1928, 1958   1930, 1958

Robin Redbreast

It was the dingiest bird
you ever saw, all the color

---

1. Kunitz's preferred version of a poem he wrote
at twenty-three, inspired by Luke's account, in the
Christian Scriptures, of the Annunciation and

Incarnation.
2. The star of Bethlehem.
3. Made fruitful, productive. *Nib*: point of a pen.

washed from him, as if
he had been standing in the rain,
5   friendless and stiff and cold,
since Eden went wrong.
In the house marked For Sale,
where nobody made a sound,
in the room where I lived
10 with an empty page, I had heard
the squawking of the jays
under the wild persimmons
tormenting him.
So I scooped him up
15 after they knocked him down,
in league with that ounce of heart
pounding in my palm,
that dumb beak gaping.
Poor thing! Poor foolish life!
20 without sense enough to stop
running in desperate circles,
needing my lucky help
to toss him back into his element.
But when I held him high,
25 fear clutched my hand,
for through the hole in his head,
cut whistle-clean . . .
through the old dried wound
between his eyes
30 where the hunter's brand
had tunneled out his wits . . .
I caught the cold flash of the blue
unappeasable sky.

1971

Touch Me

Summer is late, my heart.
Words plucked out of the air
some forty years ago
when I was wild with love
5 and torn almost in two
scatter like leaves this night
of whistling wind and rain.
It is my heart that's late,
it is my song that's flown.
10 Outdoors all afternoon
under a gun-metal sky
staking my garden down,
I kneeled to the crickets trilling
underfoot as if about

15 to burst from their crusty shells;
and like a child again
marveled to hear so clear
and brave a music pour
from such a small machine.
20 What makes the engine go?
Desire, desire, desire.
The longing for the dance
stirs in the buried life.
One season only,
25   and it's done.
So let the battered old willow
thrash against the windowpanes
and the house timbers creak.
Darling, do you remember
30 the man you married? Touch me,
remind me who I am.

1995

ROBERT PENN WARREN
1905–1989

Bearded Oaks

The oaks, how subtle and marine,
Bearded, and all the layered light
Above them swims; and thus the scene,
Recessed, awaits the positive night.

5   So, waiting, we in the grass now lie
Beneath the languorous tread of light:
The grasses, kelp-like, satisfy
The nameless motions of the air.

Upon the floor of light, and time,
10 Unmurmuring, of polyp made,
We rest; we are, as light withdraws,
Twin atolls on a shelf of shade.

Ages to our construction went,
Dim architecture, hour by hour:
15 And violence, forgot now, lent
The present stillness all its power.

The storm of noon above us rolled,
Of light the fury, furious gold,
The long drag troubling us, the depth:
20 Dark is unrocking, unrippling, still.

Passion and slaughter, ruth, decay
Descend, minutely whispering down,
Silted down swaying streams, to lay
Foundation for our voicelessness.

25 All our debate is voiceless here,
As all our rage, the rage of stone;
If hope is hopeless, then fearless is fear,
And history is thus undone.

Our feet once wrought the hollow street
30 With echo when the lamps were dead
At windows, once our headlight glare
Disturbed the doe that, leaping, fled.

I do not love you less that now
The caged heart makes iron stroke,
35 Or less that all that light once gave
The graduate° dark should now revoke.   *increasing*

We live in time so little time
And we learn all so painfully,
That we may spare this hour's term
40 To practice for eternity.

1944

Masts at Dawn

Past second cock-crow yacht masts in the harbor go slowly white.

No light in the east yet, but the stars show a certain fatigue.
They withdraw into a new distance, have discovered our unworthiness.
    It is long since

The owl, in the dark eucalyptus, dire and melodious, last called, and

5 Long since the moon sank and the English
Finished fornicating in their ketches.[1] In the evening there was a
    strong swell.

Red died the sun, but at dark wind rose easterly, white sea nagged the
    black harbor headland.

When there is a strong swell, you may, if you surrender to it,
    experience
A sense, in the act, of mystic unity with that rhythm. Your peace is the
    sea's will.

10 But now no motion, the bay-face is glossy in darkness, like

1. Sailing vessels.

An old window pane flat on black ground by the wall, near the ash
    heap. It neither
Receives nor gives light. Now is the hour when the sea

Sinks into meditation. It doubts its own mission. The drowned cat
That on the evening swell had kept nudging the piles of the pier and
    had seemed

15   To want to climb out and lick itself dry, now floats free. On that
    surface a slight convexity only, it is like

An eyelid, in darkness, closed. You must learn to accept the kiss of
    fate, for

The masts go white slow, as light, like dew, from darkness
Condensed on them, on oiled wood, on metal. Dew whitens in
    darkness.

I lie in my bed and think how, in darkness, the masts go white.

20   The sound of the engine of the first fishing dory dies seaward. Soon
In the inland glen wakes the dawn-dove. We must try

To love so well the world that we may believe, in the end, in God.

                                            1968

There's a Grandfather's Clock in the Hall

There's a grandfather's clock in the hall, watch it closely. The minute
    hand stands still, then it jumps, and in between jumps there is no-
    Time,
And you are a child again watching the reflection of early morning
    sunlight on the ceiling above your bed,

Or perhaps you are fifteen feet under water and holding your breath
    as you struggle with a rock-snagged anchor, or holding your
    breath just long enough for one more long, slow thrust to make
    the orgasm really intolerable,
Or you are wondering why you really do not give a damn, as they
    trundle you off to the operating room,

5   Or your mother is standing up to get married and is very pretty, and
    excited and is a virgin, and your heart overflows, and you watch
    her with tears in your eyes, or
She is the one in the hospital room and she is really dying.

They have taken out her false teeth, which are now in a tumbler on
    the bedside table, and you know that only the undertaker will
    ever put them back in.
You stand there and wonder if you will ever have to wear false teeth.

She is lying on her back, and God, is she ugly, and
10   With gum-flabby lips and each word a special problem, she is asking if
          it is a new suit that you are wearing.

You say yes, and hate her uremic[2] guts, for she has no right to make
          you hurt the way that question hurts.
You do not know why that question makes your heart hurt like a kick
          in the scrotum,

For you do not yet know that the question, in its murderous triviality, is
          the last thing she will ever say to you,
Nor know what baptism is occurring in a sod-roofed hut or hole on
          the night-swept steppes of Asia, and a million mouths, like ruined
          stars in darkness, make a rejoicing that howls like wind, or
          wolves,

15   Nor do you know the truth, which is: *Seize the nettle of innocence in*
          both your hands, for this is the only way, and every
Ulcer in love's lazaret[3] may, like a dawn-stung gem, sing—or even burst
into whoops of, perhaps, holiness.

But, in any case, watch the clock closely. Hold your breath and wait.
Nothing happens, nothing happens, then suddenly, quick as a wink,
          and slick as a mink's prick, Time thrusts through the time of no-
          Time.

                                                                              1974

Evening Hawk

From plane of light to plane, wings dipping through
Geometries and orchids that the sunset builds,
Out of the peak's black angularity of shadow, riding
The last tumultuous avalanche of
5   Light above pines and the guttural gorge,
The hawk comes.

                    His wing
Scythes down another day, his motion
Is that of the honed steel-edge, we hear
10   The crashless fall of stalks of Time.

The head of each stalk is heavy with the gold of our error.

Look! Look! he is climbing the last light
Who knows neither Time nor error, and under
Whose eye, unforgiving, the world, unforgiven, swings
15   Into shadow.

2. Characterized by a toxic condition associated   3. Storeroom; also (*lazaretto*), quarters for quar-
with kidney disease.   antine or contagious hospital.

Long now,
The last thrush is still, the last bat
Now cruises in his sharp hieroglyphics. His wisdom
Is ancient, too, and immense. The star
20 Is steady, like Plato,[4] over the mountain.

If there were no wind we might, we think, hear
The earth grind on its axis, or history
Drip in darkness like a leaking pipe in the cellar.

1975

JOHN BETJEMAN
1906–1984

Death in Leamington[1]

She died in the upstairs bedroom
By the light of the evening star
That shone through the plate glass window
From over Leamington Spa.

5 Beside her the lonely crochet
Lay patiently and unstirred,
But the fingers that would have worked it
Were dead as the spoken word.

And Nurse came in with the tea-things
10   Breast high 'mid the stands and chairs—
But Nurse was alone with her own little soul,
And the things were alone with theirs.

She bolted the big round window,
She let the blinds unroll,
15 She set a match to the mantle,[2]
She covered the fire with coal.

And "Tea!" she said in a tiny voice
"Wake up! It's nearly *five*."
Oh! Chintzy,[3] chintzy cheeriness,
20   Half dead and half alive!

Do you know that the stucco is peeling?
Do you know that the heart will stop?
From those yellow Italianate arches
Do you hear the plaster drop?

4. Here, a symbol of the "steady" because he characterized physical objects as impermanent representations of unchanging ideas.
1. Leamington Spa is a health resort in Warwickshire, England, with medicinal springs and baths.

2. The incandescent cloth hood of a gaslight jet.
3. Not in the slang sense of gaudy or cheap, but meaning that the room's hangings and furniture coverings are of the flower-patterned, glazed-cotton fabric called chintz.

25   Nurse looked at the silent bedstead,
       At the grey, decaying face,
    As the calm of a Leamington evening
       Drifted into the place.

    She moved the table of bottles
30   Away from the bed to the wall;
    And tiptoeing gently over the stairs
       Turned down the gas in the hall.

1932

The Arrest of Oscar Wilde at the Cadogan Hotel[4]

    He sipped at a weak hock[5] and seltzer
       As he gazed at the London skies
    Through the Nottingham lace of the curtains
       Or was it his bees-winged[6] eyes?

5   To the right and before him Pont Street
       Did tower in her new built red,
    As hard as the morning gaslight
       That shone on his unmade bed,

    "I want some more hock in my seltzer,
10   And Robbie,[7] please give me your hand—
    Is this the end or beginning?
       How can I understand?

    "So you've brought me the latest *Yellow Book*:[8]
       And Buchan[9] has got in it now:
15   Approval of what is approved of
       Is as false as a well-kept vow.

    "More hock, Robbie—where is the seltzer?
       Dear boy, pull again at the bell!
    They are all little better than *cretins*,
20   Though this *is* the Cadogan Hotel.

    "One astrakhan coat is at Willis's—
       Another one's at the Savoy:
    Do fetch my morocco portmanteau,
       And bring them on later, dear boy."

---

4. On May 27, 1895, the Irish writer Oscar Wilde (1856–1900) was convicted of "indecencies between grown men, in public or private" (i.e., of homosexuality) and was sentenced to two years hard labor.
5. Generic term for German white wine.
6. Filmed over (from *beeswing*: a film that forms on old wines).
7. Robert Ross, a friend who remained loyal to Wilde after the latter's downfall.
8. An elaborately illustrated hardcover periodical, which appeared quarterly from 1894 to 1897, and in which many writers associated with the Aesthetic movement were published.
9. John Buchan, later Lord Tweedsmuir (1875–1940), author of several popular novels, contributed two stories to *The Yellow Book* in 1896.

25   A thump, and a murmur of voices—
        ("Oh why must they make such a din?")
      As the door of the bedroom swung open
        And TWO PLAIN CLOTHES POLICEMEN came in:

      "Mr. Woilde, we'ave come for tew take yew
30   Where felons and criminals dwell:
      We must ask yew tew leave with us quoietly
        For this *is* the Cadogan Hotel."

      He rose, and he put down *The Yellow Book.*
        He staggered—and, terrible-eyed,
35   He brushed past the palms on the staircase
        And was helped to a hansom outside.

                                                        1937

East Anglian Bathe[1]

      Oh when the early morning at the seaside
        Took us with hurrying steps from Horsey Mere
      To see the whistling bent-grass on the leeside
        And then the tumbled breaker-line appear,
5   On high, the clouds with mighty adumbration°   *shadows*
        Sailed over us to seaward fast and clear
      And jellyfish in quivering isolation
        Lay silted in the dry sand of the breeze
      And we, along the tableland of beach blown
10   Went gooseflesh from our shoulders to our knees
      And ran to catch the football, each to each thrown,
        In the soft and swirling music of the seas.

      There splashed about our ankles as we waded
        Those intersecting wavelets morning-cold,
15   And sudden dark a patch of sea was shaded,
        And sudden light, another patch would hold
      The warmth of whirling atoms in a sun-shot
        And underwater sandstorm green and gold.
      So in we dived and louder than a gunshot
20   Sea water broke in fountains down the ear.
      How cold the bathe, how chattering cold the drying,
        How welcoming the inland reeds appear,
      The wood smoke and the breakfast and the frying,
        And your warm freshwater ripples, Horsey Mere.

                                                        1945

1. East Anglia comprises the English counties of Norfolk and Suffolk; Horsey Mere ("Mere," deriving from Latin *mare*, the sea, indicating the resort area of the town of Horsey) is on the coast of Norfolk, north of Great Yarmouth.

False Security

I remember the dread with which I at a quarter past four
Let go with a bang behind me our house front door
And, clutching a present for my dear little hostess tight,
Sailed out for the children's party into the night
5 Or rather the gathering night. For still some boys
In the near municipal acres were making a noise
Shuffling in fallen leaves and shouting and whistling
And running past hedges of hawthorn, spikey and bristling.
And black in the oncoming darkness stood out the trees
10 And pink shone the ponds in the sunset ready to freeze
And all was still and ominous waiting for dark
And the keeper was ringing his closing bell in the park
And the arc lights started to fizzle and burst into mauve
As I climbed West Hill to the great big house in The Grove,
15 Where the children's party was and the dear little hostess.
But halfway up stood the empty house where the ghost is
I crossed to the other side and under the arc
Made a rush for the next kind lamppost out of the dark
And so to the next and the next till I reached the top
20 Where the Grove branched off to the left. Then ready to drop
I ran to the ironwork gateway of number seven
Secure at last on the lamplit fringe of Heaven.
Oh who can say how subtle and safe one feels
Shod in one's children's sandals from Daniel Neal's,
25 Clad in one's party clothes made of stuff from Heal's?[2]
And who can still one's thrill at the candle shine
On cakes and ices and jelly and blackcurrant wine,
And the warm little feel of my hostess's hand in mine?
Can I forget my delight at the conjuring show?
30 And wasn't I proud that I was the last to go?
Too overexcited and pleased with myself to know
That the words I heard my hostess's mother employ
To a guest departing, would ever diminish my joy,
I WONDER WHERE JULIA FOUND THAT STRANGE, RATHER COMMON LITTLE
BOY?

1958

WILLIAM EMPSON
1906–1984

Legal Fiction[1]

Law makes long spokes of the short stakes of men.
Your well fenced out real estate of mind

---

2. English interior-design chain. *Daniel Neal's:*
famous English shoe store.

1. Something assumed to be true for the purpose
of legal argument, whether or not it is true.

No high flat of the nomad citizen
Looks over, or train leaves behind.

5 Your rights extend under and above your claim
Without bound; you own land in heaven and hell;
Your part of earth's surface and mass the same,
Of all cosmos' volume, and all stars as well.

Your rights reach down where all owners meet, in hell's
10 Pointed exclusive conclave, at earth's centre
(Your spun farm's root still on that axis dwells),
And up, through galaxies, a growing sector.

You are nomad yet; the lighthouse beam you own
Flashes, like Lucifer,² through the firmament.
15 Earth's axis varies; your dark central cone
Wavers a candle's shadow, at the end.

                                              1935

Missing Dates

Slowly the poison the whole blood stream fills.
It is not the effort nor the failure tires.
The waste remains, the waste remains and kills.

It is not your system or clear sight that mills
5 Down small to the consequence a life requires;
Slowly the poison the whole blood stream fills.

They bled an old dog dry yet the exchange rills°   streams
Of young dog blood gave but a month's desires;
The waste remains, the waste remains and kills.

10 It is the Chinese tombs and the slag hills
Usurp the soil, and not the soil retires.³
Slowly the poison the whole blood stream fills.

Not to have fire is to be a skin that shrills.
The complete fire is death. From partial fires
15 The waste remains, the waste remains and kills.

It is the poems you have lost, the ills
From missing dates, at which the heart expires.
Slowly the poison the whole blood stream fills.
The waste remains, the waste remains and kills.

                                              1940

2. The morning star (Venus); also, a name of Satan (meaning "light-bearer") before he was cast out of heaven.
3. "It is true about the old dog, at least I saw it reported somewhere, but the legend that a fifth or some such part of the soil of China is given up to ancestral tombs is (by the way) not true" [Empson's note].

W. H. AUDEN
1907–1973

Lullaby

Lay your sleeping head, my love,
Human on my faithless arm;
Time and fevers burn away
Individual beauty from
5   Thoughtful children, and the grave
Proves the child ephemeral:
But in my arms till break of day
Let the living creature lie,
Mortal, guilty, but to me
10   The entirely beautiful.

Soul and body have no bounds:
To lovers as they lie upon
Her tolerant enchanted slope
In their ordinary swoon,
15   Grave the vision Venus[1] sends
Of supernatural sympathy,
Universal love and hope;
While an abstract insight wakes
Among the glaciers and the rocks
20   The hermit's carnal ecstasy.

Certainty, fidelity
On the stroke of midnight pass
Like vibrations of a bell
And fashionable madmen raise
25   Their pedantic boring cry:
Every farthing[2] of the cost,
All the dreaded cards foretell,
Shall be paid, but from this night
Not a whisper, not a thought,
30   Not a kiss nor look be lost.

Beauty, midnight, vision dies:
Let the winds of dawn that blow
Softly round your dreaming head
Such a day of welcome show
35   Eye and knocking heart may bless,
Find our mortal world enough;
Noons of dryness find you fed
By the involuntary powers,
Nights of insult let you pass
40   Watched by every human love.

January 1937   1940

1. Roman goddess of love and beauty.   2. Old British coin worth one fourth of a penny.

Spain 1937[3]

Yesterday all the past. The language of size
Spreading to China along the trade-routes; the diffusion
      Of the counting-frame and the cromlech;[4]
Yesterday the shadow-reckoning in the sunny climates.

5   Yesterday the assessment of insurance by cards,
The divination of water; yesterday the invention
      Of cart-wheels and clocks, the taming of
Horses; yesterday the bustling world of the navigators.

Yesterday the abolition of fairies and giants;
10   The fortress like a motionless eagle eyeing the valley,
      The chapel built in the forest;
Yesterday the carving of angels and of frightening gargoyles;

The trial of heretics among the columns of stone;
Yesterday the theological feuds in the taverns
15   And the miraculous cure at the fountain;
Yesterday the Sabbath of Witches.[5] But to-day the struggle.

Yesterday the installation of dynamos and turbines;
The construction of railways in the colonial desert;
      Yesterday the classic lecture
20   On the origin of Mankind. But to-day the struggle.

Yesterday the belief in the absolute value of Greek;
The fall of the curtain upon the death of a hero;
      Yesterday the prayer to the sunset,
And the adoration of madmen. But to-day the struggle.

25   As the poet whispers, startled among the pines
Or, where the loose waterfall sings, compact, or upright
      On the crag by the leaning tower:
"O my vision. O send me the luck of the sailor."

And the investigator peers through his instruments
30   At the inhuman provinces, the virile bacillus
      Or enormous Jupiter finished:
"But the lives of my friends. I inquire, I inquire."

And the poor in their fireless lodgings dropping the sheets
Of the evening paper: "Our day is our loss. O show us
35   History the operator, the
Organiser, Time the refreshing river."

3. Auden traveled to Spain in January 1936, saying he was going to drive an ambulance for the left-wing Republican forces then engaged in a civil war with the Fascist Nationalists, but returned shortly, without having done so, horrified by what he had seen.
4. Ancient stone monument.
5. Ceremonial gathering of witches in parody of Christian service.

And the nations combine each cry, invoking the life
That shapes the individual belly and orders
      The private nocturnal terror:
40   "Did you not found once the city state of the sponge,

"Raise the vast military empires of the shark
And the tiger, establish the robin's plucky canton?°   *district*
      Intervene. O descend as a dove[6] or
A furious papa or a mild engineer:[7] but descend."

45   And the life, if it answers at all, replies from the heart
And the eyes and the lungs, from the shops and squares of the city:
      "O no, I am not the Mover,
Not to-day, not to you. To you I'm the

"Yes-man, the bar-companion, the easily-duped:
50   I am whatever you do; I am your vow to be
      Good, your humorous story;
I am your business voice; I am your marriage.

"What's your proposal? To build the Just City?[8] I will.
I agree. Or is it the suicide pact, the romantic
55   Death? Very well, I accept, for
I am your choice, your decision: yes, I am Spain."

Many have heard it on remote peninsulas,
On sleepy plains, in the aberrant fishermen's islands,
      In the corrupt heart of the city;
60   Have heard and migrated like gulls or the seeds of a flower.

They clung like burrs to the long expresses that lurch
Through the unjust lands, through the night, through the alpine tunnel;
      They floated over the oceans;
They walked the passes: they came to present their lives.

65   On that arid square, that fragment nipped off from hot
Africa, soldered so crudely to inventive Europe,
      On that tableland scored by rivers,
Our fever's menacing shapes are precise and alive.

To-morrow, perhaps, the future: the research on fatigue
70   And the movements of packers; the gradual exploring of all the
      Octaves of radiation;
To-morrow the enlarging of consciousness by diet and breathing.

To-morrow the rediscovery of romantic love;
The photographing of ravens; all the fun under
75   Liberty's masterful shadow;
To-morrow the hour of the pageant-master and the musician.

---

6. In the Bible and Christian iconography, the Holy Ghost often takes the form of a dove descending to Earth.
7. Refers to a *deus ex machina* (Latin translation of the Greek for "god from the machinery"), the device by which in Greek theater the gods were shown in the air.
8. A topic discussed by Plato in his *Republic*.

To-morrow for the young the poets exploding like bombs,
The walks by the lake, the winter of perfect communion;
    To-morrow the bicycle races
80 Through the suburbs on summer evenings: but to-day the struggle.

To-day the inevitable increase in the chances of death;
The conscious acceptance of guilt in the fact of murder;[9]
    To-day the expending of powers
On the flat ephemeral pamphlet and the boring meeting.

85 To-day the makeshift consolations; the shared cigarette;
The cards in the candle-lit barn and the scraping concert,
    The masculine jokes; to-day the
Fumbled and unsatisfactory embrace before hurting.

The stars are dead; the animals will not look:
90 We are left alone with our day, and the time is short and
    History to the defeated
May say Alas but cannot help or pardon.

April 1937   1937, 1940

As I Walked Out One Evening

As I walked out one evening,
  Walking down Bristol Street,
The crowds upon the pavement
  Were fields of harvest wheat.

5 And down by the brimming river
  I heard a lover sing
Under an arch of the railway:
  "Love has no ending.

"I'll love you, dear, I'll love you
10   Till China and Africa meet,
And the river jumps over the mountain
  And the salmon sing in the street,

"I'll love you till the ocean
  Is folded and hung up to dry
15 And the seven stars go squawking
  Like geese about the sky.

"The years shall run like rabbits,
  For in my arms I hold
The Flower of the Ages,
20   And the first love of the world."

---

9. At its first printing, this line read: "The conscious acceptance of guilt in the necessary murder." Auden later suppressed the poem, largely because of its seeming support for murder.

But all the clocks in the city
   Began to whirr and chime:
"O let not Time deceive you,
   You cannot conquer Time.

25   "In the burrows of the Nightmare
     Where Justice naked is,
Time watches from the shadow
   And coughs when you would kiss.

"In headaches and in worry
30   Vaguely life leaks away,
And Time will have his fancy
   Tomorrow or today.

"Into many a green valley
   Drifts the appalling snow;
35   Time breaks the threaded dances
   And the diver's brilliant bow.

"O plunge your hands in water,
   Plunge them in up to the wrist;
Stare, stare in the basin
40   And wonder what you've missed.

"The glacier knocks in the cupboard,
   The desert sighs in the bed,
And the crack in the teacup opens
   A lane to the land of the dead.

45   "Where the beggars raffle the banknotes
    And the Giant is enchanting to Jack,
And the Lily-white Boy is a Roarer,
   And Jill goes down on her back.

"O look, look in the mirror,
50   O look in your distress;
Life remains a blessing
   Although you cannot bless.

"O stand, stand at the window
   As the tears scald and start;
55   You shall love your crooked neighbour
   With your crooked heart."

It was late, late in the evening,
   The lovers they were gone;
The clocks had ceased their chiming,
60   And the deep river ran on.

November 1937   1940

From Twelve Songs

IX. [*Funeral Blues*]

Stop all the clocks, cut off the telephone,
Prevent the dog from barking with a juicy bone,
Silence the pianos and with muffled drum
Bring out the coffin, let the mourners come.

5   Let aeroplanes circle moaning overhead
Scribbling on the sky the message He Is Dead,
Put crêpe bows round the white necks of the public doves,
Let the traffic policemen wear black cotton gloves.

He was my North, my South, my East and West,
10   My working week and my Sunday rest,
My noon, my midnight, my talk, my song;
I thought that love would last for ever: I was wrong.

The stars are not wanted now: put out every one;
Pack up the moon and dismantle the sun;
15   Pour away the ocean and sweep up the wood;
For nothing now can ever come to any good.

1936?   1940

XII. [*Tell Me the Truth About Love*]

Some say that love's a little boy,
   And some say it's a bird,
Some say it makes the world go round,
   And some say that's absurd,
5   And when I asked the man next-door,
     Who looked as if he knew,
His wife got very cross indeed,
   And said it wouldn't do.

     Does it look like a pair of pyjamas,
10   Or the ham in a temperance hotel?[1]
     Does its odour remind one of llamas,[2]
      Or has it a comforting smell?
     Is it prickly to touch as a hedge is,
      Or soft as eiderdown fluff?[3]
15   Is it sharp or quite smooth at the edges?
     O tell me the truth about love.

     Our history books refer to it
      In cryptic little notes,
     It's quite a common topic on
20   The Transatlantic boats;

---

1. A hotel where no alcohol is available.   3. Fluffy duck feathers.
2. South American camel-like animals.

I've found the subject mentioned in
 Accounts of suicides,
And even seen it scribbled on
 The backs of railway-guides.

25 Does it howl like a hungry Alsatian,
  Or boom like a military band?
 Could one give a first-rate imitation
  On a saw or a Steinway Grand?[4]
 Is its singing at parties a riot?
30 Does it only like Classical stuff?
 Will it stop when one wants to be quiet?
  O tell me the truth about love.

I looked inside the summer-house;
 It wasn't ever there:
35 I tried the Thames at Maidenhead,
  And Brighton's[5] bracing air.
I don't know what the blackbird sang,
 Or what the tulip said;
But it wasn't in the chicken-run,
40 Or underneath the bed.

Can it pull extraordinary faces?
 Is it usually sick on a swing?
Does it spend all its time at the races,
 Or fiddling with pieces of string?
45 Has it views of its own about money?
  Does it think Patriotism enough?
 Are its stories vulgar but funny?
  O tell me the truth about love.

When it comes, will it come without warning
50 Just as I'm picking my nose?
Will it knock on my door in the morning,
 Or tread in the bus on my toes?
Will it come like a change in the weather?
 Will its greeting be courteous or rough?
55 Will it alter my life altogether?
  O tell me the truth about love.

January 1938   1940

Musée des Beaux Arts[6]

About suffering they were never wrong,
The Old Masters: how well they understood

4. Brand of grand piano.
5. Resort town on the English Channel. *Thames at Maidenhead*: the river Thames, as it runs
through a town west of London.
6. Museum of Fine Arts (French).

Its human position; how it takes place
While someone else is eating or opening a window or just walking
    dully along;
5 How, when the aged are reverently, passionately waiting
For the miraculous birth, there always must be
Children who did not specially want it to happen, skating
On a pond at the edge of the wood:
They never forgot
10 That even the dreadful martyrdom must run its course
Anyhow in a corner, some untidy spot
Where the dogs go on with their doggy life and the torturer's horse
Scratches its innocent behind on a tree.

In Brueghel's *Icarus*,[7] for instance: how everything turns away
15 Quite leisurely from the disaster; the ploughman may
Have heard the splash, the forsaken cry,
But for him it was not an important failure; the sun shone
As it had to on the white legs disappearing into the green
Water; and the expensive delicate ship that must have seen
20 Something amazing, a boy falling out of the sky,
Had somewhere to get to and sailed calmly on.

December 1938   1940

In Memory of W. B. Yeats[8]

(d. Jan. 1939)

I

He disappeared in the dead of winter:
The brooks were frozen, the airports almost deserted,
And snow disfigured the public statues;
The mercury sank in the mouth of the dying day.
5 What instruments we have agree
The day of his death was a dark cold day.

Far from his illness
The wolves ran on through the evergreen forests,
The peasant river was untempted by the fashionable quays;
10 By mourning tongues
The death of the poet was kept from his poems.

---

7. *The Fall of Icarus,* by the Flemish artist Pieter Brueghel (ca. 1525–1569), the painting described here, is in the Musée d'Art Ancien, a section of the Musées Royaux des Beaux Arts, in Brussels. Daedalus, the legendary Athenian craftsman, constructed a labyrinth for Minos, king of Crete, but was then imprisoned in it with his son, Icarus. Daedalus made wings of feathers and wax, with which they flew away, but Icarus flew too near the sun, the wax melted, and he fell into the sea.

The poem also alludes to the Nativity scene in Brueghel's *Numbering at Bethlehem,* skaters in his *Winter Landscape with Skaters and a Bird Trap,* and a horse scratching its behind in his *Massacre of the Innocents.*
Cf. William Carlos Williams, "Pictures from Brueghel" (p. 1283).
8. The Irish poet and dramatist William Butler Yeats (b. 1865; see pp. 1188–1211), died in Roquebrune (southern France) on January 29, 1939.

But for him it was his last afternoon as himself,
An afternoon of nurses and rumours;
The provinces of his body revolted,
15   The squares of his mind were empty,
Silence invaded the suburbs,
The current of his feeling failed; he became his admirers.

Now he is scattered among a hundred cities
And wholly given over to unfamiliar affections.
20   To find his happiness in another kind of wood[9]
And be punished under a foreign code of conscience.[1]
The words of a dead man
Are modified in the guts of the living.

But in the importance and noise of to-morrow
25   When the brokers are roaring like beasts on the floor of the Bourse,[2]
And the poor have the sufferings to which they are fairly accustomed,
And each in the cell of himself is almost convinced of his freedom,
A few thousand will think of this day
As one thinks of a day when one did something slightly unusual.

30   What instruments we have agree
The day of his death was a dark cold day.

II

You were silly like us;[3] your gift survived it all:
The parish of rich women,[4] physical decay,
Yourself. Mad Ireland hurt you into poetry.
35   Now Ireland has her madness and her weather still,
For poetry makes nothing happen: it survives
In the valley of its making where executives
Would never want to tamper, flows on south
From ranches of isolation and the busy griefs,
40   Raw towns that we believe and die in; it survives,
A way of happening, a mouth.

III

Earth, receive an honoured guest:
William Yeats is laid to rest.
Let the Irish vessel lie
45   Emptied of its poetry.[5]

9. At the beginning of the *Inferno* (1.1–3), middle-aged Dante finds himself in a metaphorical "dark wood."
1. Yeats, as represented by his work, must endure the judgment of the living; a veiled reference to his Irish nationalism.
2. The French stock exchange.
3. In his prose pieces, Auden objects to aspects of Yeats's thought, particularly to his interest in the supernatural.
4. Lady Augusta Gregory (1852–1932), Irish dramatist, was one of several wealthy women who provided financial help to Yeats.
5. This section's stanza pattern echoes the meter

and rhyme of Yeats's late poem "Under Ben Bulben" (see p. 1208). In *Collected Shorter Poems* (1966) and thereafter, Auden omitted the three stanzas that originally followed:

Time that is intolerant
Of the brave and innocent,
And indifferent in a week
To a beautiful physique,

Worships language and forgives
Everyone by whom it lives;
Pardons cowardice, conceit
Lays its honours at their feet,

In the nightmare of the dark
All the dogs of Europe bark.[6]
And the living nations wait,
Each sequestered in its hate;

50   Intellectual disgrace
Stares from every human face,
And the seas of pity lie
Locked and frozen in each eye.

Follow, poet, follow right
55   To the bottom of the night,
With your unconstraining voice
Still persuade us to rejoice;

With the farming of a verse
Make a vineyard of the curse,
60   Sing of human unsuccess
In a rapture of distress;

In the deserts of the heart
Let the healing fountain start,
In the prison of his days
65   Teach the free man how to praise.

February 1939   1940

September 1, 1939[7]

I sit in one of the dives
On Fifty-Second Street[8]
Uncertain and afraid
As the clever hopes expire
5   Of a low dishonest decade:
Waves of anger and fear
Circulate over the bright
And darkened lands of the earth,
Obsessing our private lives;
10   The unmentionable odour of death
Offends the September night.

Accurate scholarship can
Unearth the whole offence

Time that with this strange excuse
Pardoned Kipling and his views,
And will pardon Paul Claudel,
Pardons him for writing well.

The English writer Rudyard Kipling (1865–1936; see pp. 1181–88) was imperialistic and jingoistic. The French poet, dramatist, and diplomat Paul Claudel (1868–1955) was extremely right-wing.

Yeats was at times antidemocratic and appeared to favor dictatorship.
6. A reference to World War II, which began in September 1939.
7. The date of Hitler's invasion of Poland, which started World War II.
8. Perhaps the Dizzy Club, a bar on West 52nd Street, New York City.

From Luther[9] until now
15   That has driven a culture mad,
Find what occurred at Linz,[1]
What huge imago[2] made
A psychopathic god:
I and the public know
20   What all schoolchildren learn,
Those to whom evil is done
Do evil in return.

Exiled Thucydides[3] knew
All that a speech can say
25   About Democracy,
And what dictators do,
The elderly rubbish they talk
To an apathetic grave;
Analysed all in his book,
30   The enlightenment driven away,
The habit-forming pain,
Mismanagement and grief:
We must suffer them all again.

Into this neutral air
35   Where blind skyscrapers use
Their full height to proclaim
The strength of Collective Man,
Each language pours its vain
Competitive excuse:
40   But who can live for long
In an euphoric dream;
Out of the mirror they stare,
Imperialism's face
And the international wrong.

45   Faces along the bar
Cling to their average day:
The lights must never go out,
The music must always play,
All the conventions conspire
50   To make this fort assume
The furniture of home;
Lest we should see where we are,
Lost in a haunted wood,
Children afraid of the night
55   Who have never been happy or good.

The windiest militant trash
Important Persons shout

9. Martin Luther (1483–1546), biblical scholar and founder of the Protestant Reformation.
1. Hitler spent his boyhood in the Austrian city of Linz.
2. Psychoanalytic term for the subconscious image that influences a person's attitudes and behavior.
3. Greek general (460–400 B.C.E.), whose *History of the Peloponnesian War* Auden read in the summer of 1939.

Is not so crude as our wish:
What mad Nijinsky wrote
60   About Diaghilev[4]
Is true of the normal heart;
For the error bred in the bone
Of each woman and each man
Craves what it cannot have,
65   Not universal love
But to be loved alone.[5]

From the conservative dark
Into the ethical life
The dense commuters come,
70   Repeating their morning vow,
"I *will* be true to the wife,
I'll concentrate more on my work",
And helpless governors wake
To resume their compulsory game:
75   Who can release them now,
Who can reach the deaf,
Who can speak for the dumb?

All I have is a voice
To undo the folded lie,
80   The romantic lie in the brain
Of the sensual man-in-the-street
And the lie of Authority
Whose buildings grope the sky:
There is no such thing as the State
85   And no one exists alone;
Hunger allows no choice
To the citizen or the police;
We must love one another or die.[6]

Defenceless under the night
90   Our world in stupor lies;
Yet, dotted everywhere,
Ironic points of light
Flash out wherever the Just
Exchange their messages:
95   May I, composed like them
Of Eros[7] and of dust,

4. Vaslav Nijinsky (1890–1950), dancer and choreographer, was a star of the Russian Ballet, directed by the impresario Sergey Diaghilev (1872–1929).

5. Auden borrowed lines 65–66 from *The Diary of Vaslav Nijinsky* (1937): "Some politicians are hypocrites like Diaghilev, who does not want universal love, but to be loved alone. I want universal love."

6. In his foreword to the first edition of B. C. Bloomfield's *W. H. Auden: A Bibliography* (1964), Auden writes:

  Rereading a poem of mine, *1st September, 1939*, after it had been published, I came to the line "We must love one another or die" and said to myself: "That's a damned lie! We must die anyway." So, in the next edition, I altered it to "We must love one another and die." This didn't seem to do either, so I cut the stanza. Still no good. The whole poem, I realized, was infected with an incurable dishonesty—and must be scrapped.

The popularity of the poem persuaded Auden to restore it in later editions of his work.

7. Greek god of erotic love; hence, here, sexual love.

Beleaguered by the same
Negation and despair,
Show an affirming flame.

September 1939   1939

In Praise of Limestone

If it form the one landscape that we, the inconstant ones,
    Are consistently homesick for, this is chiefly
Because it dissolves in water. Mark these rounded slopes
    With their surface fragrance of thyme and, beneath,
5 A secret system of caves and conduits; hear the springs
    That spurt out everywhere with a chuckle,
Each filling a private pool for its fish and carving
    Its own little ravine whose cliffs entertain
The butterfly and the lizard; examine this region
10   Of short distances and definite places:
What could be more like Mother or a fitter background
    For her son, the flirtatious male who lounges
Against a rock in the sunlight, never doubting
    That for all his faults he is loved; whose works are but
15 Extensions of his power to charm? From weathered outcrop
    To hilltop temple, from appearing waters to
Conspicuous fountains, from a wild to a formal vineyard,
    Are ingenious but short steps that a child's wish
To receive more attention than his brothers, whether
20   By pleasing or teasing, can easily take.

Watch, then, the band of rivals as they climb up and down
    Their steep stone gennels° in twos and threes, at times   *channels*
Arm in arm, but never, thank God, in step; or engaged
    On the shady side of a square at midday in
25 Voluble discourse, knowing each other too well to think
    There are any important secrets, unable
To conceive a god whose temper tantrums are moral
    And not to be pacified by a clever line
Or a good lay: for, accustomed to a stone that responds,
30   They have never had to veil their faces in awe
Of a crater whose blazing fury could not be fixed;
    Adjusted to the local needs of valleys
Where everything can be touched or reached by walking,
    Their eyes have never looked into infinite space
35 Through the latticework of a nomad's comb; born lucky,
    Their legs have never encountered the fungi
And insects of the jungle, the monstrous forms and lives
    With which we have nothing, we like to hope, in common.
So, when one of them goes to the bad, the way his mind works
40   Remains comprehensible: to become a pimp

Or deal in fake jewelry or ruin a fine tenor voice
　　For effects that bring down the house, could happen to all
But the best and the worst of us . . .
　　　　　　　　　　　　　　　　That is why, I suppose,
　　The best and worst never stayed here long but sought
45　Immoderate soils where the beauty was not so external,
　　　The light less public and the meaning of life
Something more than a mad camp. "Come!" cried the granite wastes,
　　"How evasive is your humour, how accidental
Your kindest kiss, how permanent is death." (Saints-to-be
50　Slipped away sighing.) "Come!" purred the clays and gravels.
"On our plains there is room for armies to drill; rivers
　　Wait to be tamed and slaves to construct you a tomb
In the grand manner: soft as the earth is mankind and both
　　Need to be altered." (Intendant Caesars[8] rose and
55　Left, slamming the door.) But the really reckless were fetched
　　By an older colder voice, the oceanic whisper:
"I am the solitude that asks and promises nothing;
　　That is how I shall set you free. There is no love;
There are only the various envies, all of them sad."
60　They were right, my dear, all those voices were right
And still are; this land is not the sweet home that it looks,
　　Nor its peace the historical calm of a site
Where something was settled once and for all: A backward
　　And dilapidated province, connected
65　To the big busy world by a tunnel, with a certain
　　Seedy appeal, is that all it is now? Not quite:
It has a worldly duty which in spite of itself
　　It does not neglect, but calls into question
All the Great Powers assume; it disturbs our rights. The poet,
70　Admired for his earnest habit of calling
The sun the sun, his mind Puzzle, is made uneasy
　　By these marble statues which so obviously doubt
His antimythological myth; and these gamins,° 　　　　　　*street urchins*
　　Pursuing the scientist down the tiled colonnade
75　With such lively offers, rebuke his concern for Nature's
　　Remotest aspects: I, too, am reproached, for what
And how much you know. Not to lose time, not to get caught,
　　Not to be left behind, not, please! to resemble
The beasts who repeat themselves, or a thing like water
80　Or stone whose conduct can be predicted, these
Are our Common Prayer, whose greatest comfort is music
　　Which can be made anywhere, is invisible,
And does not smell. In so far as we have to look forward
　　To death as a fact, no doubt we are right: But if
85　Sins can be forgiven, if bodies rise from the dead,
　　These modifications of matter into
Innocent athletes and gesticulating fountains,
　　Made solely for pleasure, make a further point:
The blessed will not care what angle they are regarded from,
90　Having nothing to hide. Dear, I know nothing of

---

8. I.e., administrative emperors.

Either, but when I try to imagine a faultless love
  Or the life to come, what I hear is the murmur
  Of underground streams, what I see is a limestone landscape.

May 1948   1951

Their Lonely Betters

As I listened from a beach-chair in the shade
To all the noises that my garden made,
It seemed to me only proper that words
Should be withheld from vegetables and birds.

5   A robin with no Christian name ran through
The Robin-Anthem which was all it knew,
And rustling flowers for some third party waited
To say which pairs, if any, should get mated.

Not one of them was capable of lying,
10 There was not one which knew that it was dying
Or could have with a rhythm or a rhyme
Assumed responsibility for time.

Let them leave language to their lonely betters
Who count some days and long for certain letters;
15 We, too, make noises when we laugh or weep:
Words are for those with promises to keep.

1950   1951

The Shield of Achilles[9]

She looked over his shoulder
  For vines and olive trees,
Marble well-governed cities
  And ships upon untamed seas,
5   But there on the shining metal
  His hands had put instead
An artificial wilderness
  And a sky like lead.

---

9. In books 16–17 of Homer's *Iliad*, Achilles, the chief Greek hero in the Trojan War, loses his armor when his great friend Patroclus, wearing it, is slain by Hector. While Achilles mourns his friend, his mother, the goddess Thetis, goes to Mt. Olympus to entreat Hephaestos to make new armor for Achilles, whom both she and Hephaestos pity because he is fated to die soon and his life has not been happy. The splendid shield, incorporating gold and silver as well as less precious metals, is described at length in *Iliad* 18.478–608, the scenes depicted on it constituting an epitome of the universe and human life. Hephaestos portrays on it the earth, the heavens, the sea, and the planets; a city in peace (with a wedding and a trial) and a city at war; country life (including a harvest feast and a grape-gathering), animal life, and the joyful life of young men and women. Around all these scenes, closing them in as the outer border, flows the ocean.

A plain without a feature, bare and brown,
10   No blade of grass, no sign of neighbourhood,
Nothing to eat and nowhere to sit down,
        Yet, congregated on its blankness, stood
        An unintelligible multitude,
        A million eyes, a million boots in line,
15 Without expression, waiting for a sign.

Out of the air a voice without a face
        Proved by statistics that some cause was just
In tones as dry and level as the place:
        No one was cheered and nothing was discussed;
20   Column by column in a cloud of dust
They marched away enduring a belief
Whose logic brought them, somewhere else, to grief.

                She looked over his shoulder
                        For ritual pieties,
25   White flower-garlanded heifers,
                        Libation and sacrifice,[1]
                But there on the shining metal
                        Where the altar should have been,
                She saw by his flickering forge-light
30   Quite another scene.

Barbed wire enclosed an arbitrary spot
        Where bored officials lounged (one cracked a joke)
And sentries sweated for the day was hot:
        A crowd of ordinary decent folk
35   Watched from without and neither moved nor spoke
As three pale figures were led forth and bound
To three posts driven upright in the ground.

The mass and majesty of this world, all
        That carries weight and always weighs the same
40 Lay in the hands of others; they were small
        And could not hope for help and no help came:
        What their foes liked to do was done, their shame
Was all the worst could wish; they lost their pride
And died as men before their bodies died.

45   She looked over his shoulder
                        For athletes at their games,
                Men and women in a dance
                        Moving their sweet limbs
                        Quick, quick, to music,
50   But there on the shining shield
                His hands had set no dancing-floor
                        But a weed-choked field.

---

1. Lines 23–26: cf. John Keats, "Ode on a Grecian Urn," lines 31–34 (p. 939). *Libation:* sacrifice involving wine or other liquid.

A ragged urchin, aimless and alone,
   Loitered about that vacancy, a bird
55 Flew up to safety from his well-aimed stone:
   That girls are raped, that two boys knife a third,
   Were axioms to him, who'd never heard
Of any world where promises were kept,
Or one could weep because another wept.

60   The thin-lipped armourer,
       Hephaestos hobbled away,
     Thetis of the shining breasts
       Cried out in dismay
     At what the god had wrought
65   To please her son, the strong
     Iron-hearted man-slaying Achilles
     Who would not live long.

1952   1955

A. D. HOPE
1907–2000

Australia

A Nation of trees, drab green and desolate grey
In the field uniform of modern wars,
Darkens her hills, those endless, outstretched paws
Of Sphinx[1] demolished or stone lion worn away.

5 They call her a young country, but they lie:
She is the last of lands, the emptiest,
A woman beyond her change of life,[2] a breast
Still tender but within the womb is dry.

Without songs, architecture, history:
10 The emotions and superstitions of younger lands,
Her rivers of water drown among inland sands,
The river of her immense stupidity

Floods her monotonous tribes from Cairns to Perth.[3]
In them at last the ultimate men arrive
15 Whose boast is not: "we live" but "we survive."
A type who will inhabit the dying earth.

1. A reference to the monumental stone sphinx of
Egypt.
2. Menopause; i.e., she is past her childbearing
years.

3. I.e., from one end of the continent to the other.
Cairns is at the far northeast of Australia, Perth at
the southwest.

And her five cities, like five teeming sores,
Each drains her: a vast parasite robber-state
Where second-hand Europeans pullulate°   *breed*
20 Timidly on the edge of alien shores.

Yet there are some like me turn gladly home
From the lush jungle of modern thought, to find
The Arabian desert of the human mind,
Hoping, if still from the deserts the prophets come,

25 Such savage and scarlet as no green hills dare
Springs in that waste, some spirit which escapes
The learned doubt, the chatter of cultured apes
Which is called civilization over there.

1939

Imperial[4] Adam

Imperial Adam, naked in the dew,
Felt his brown flanks and found the rib was gone.
Puzzled he turned and saw where, two and two,
The mighty spoor of Jahweh° marked the lawn.   *Jehovah, God*

5   Then he remembered through mysterious sleep
The surgeon fingers probing at the bone,
The voice so far away, so rich and deep:
"It is not good for him to live alone."[5]

Turning once more he found Man's counterpart
10 In tender parody breathing at his side.
He knew her at first sight, he knew by heart
Her allegory of sense unsatisfied.

The pawpaw[6] drooped its golden breasts above
Less generous than the honey of her flesh;
15 The innocent sunlight showed the place of love;
The dew on its dark hairs winked crisp and fresh.

This plump gourd severed from his virile root,
She promised on the turf of Paradise
Delicious pulp of the forbidden fruit;
20 Sly as the snake she loosed her sinuous thighs,

And waking, smiled up at him from the grass;
Her breasts rose softly and he heard her sigh—
From all the beasts whose pleasant task it was
In Eden to increase and multiply

---

4. I.e., emperor.
5. Genesis 2.18: "And the Lord said, It is not good
that the man should be alone." Eve was created

from one of Adam's ribs (cf. line 6).
6. Papaya tree.

25   Adam had learned the jolly deed of kind:
    He took her in his arms and there and then,
    Like the clean beasts, embracing from behind,
    Began in joy to found the breed of men.

    Then from the spurt of seed within her broke
30   Her terrible and triumphant female cry,
    Split upward by the sexual lightning stroke.
    It was the beasts now who stood watching by:

    The gravid elephant, the calving hind,
    The breeding bitch, the she-ape big with young
35   Were the first gentle midwives of mankind;
    The teeming lioness rasped her with her tongue;

    The proud vicuña[7] nuzzled her as she slept
    Lax on the grass; and Adam watching too
    Saw how her dumb breasts at their ripening wept,
40   The great pod of her belly swelled and grew,

    And saw its water break, and saw, in fear,
    Its quaking muscles in the act of birth,
    Between her legs a pigmy face appear,
    And the first murderer[8] lay upon the earth.

1955

Advice to Young Ladies

    A.U.C.[9] 334: about this date
    For a sexual misdemeanour, which she denied,
    The vestal virgin[1] Postumia was tried.
    Livy records it among affairs of state.

5   They let her off: it seems she was perfectly pure;
    The charge arose because some thought her talk
    Too witty for a young girl, her eyes, her walk
    Too lively, her clothes too smart to be demure.

    The Pontifex Maximus, summing up the case,
10   Warned her in future to abstain from jokes,
    To wear less modish and more pious frocks.
    She left the court reprieved, but in disgrace.

---

7. Species of wild llama, a camel-like animal.
8. Cf. Genesis 4: "And Adam knew Eve his wife; and she conceived, and bare Cain . . . and it came to pass . . . that Cain rose up against Abel his brother, and slew him."
9. *Ab urbe Condita*, "from the founding of the city" (Latin); the city is Rome, traditionally founded in 753 B.C.E. In his *History of Rome from*

its Foundation, the Roman historian Livy (59 B.C.E.–17 C.E.) records the incident narrated in the first three stanzas.
1. One of the young, female priests who tended the shrine of Vesta, goddess of the hearth. They were governed by the Pontifex Maximus (line 9), chief priest of the Roman religion.

What then? With her the annalist° is less   *historian*
Concerned than what the men achieved that year:
15   Plots, quarrels, crimes, with oratory to spare!
I see Postumia with her dowdy dress,

Stiff mouth and listless step; I see her strive
To give dull answers. She had to knuckle down.
A vestal virgin who scandalized that town
20   Had fair trial, then they buried her alive.[2]

Alive, bricked up in suffocating dark,
A ration of bread, a pitcher if she was dry,
Preserved the body they did not wish to die
Until her mind was quenched to the last spark.

25   How many the black maw has swallowed in its time!
Spirited girls who would not know their place;
Talented girls who found that the disgrace
Of being a woman made genius a crime;

How many others, who would not kiss the rod[3]
30   Domestic bullying broke or public shame?
Pagan or Christian, it was much the same:
Husbands, St. Paul declared,[4] rank next to God.

Livy and Paul, it may be, never knew
That Rome was doomed; each spoke of her with pride.
35   Tacitus,[5] writing after both had died,
Showed that whole fabric rotten through and through.

Historians spend their lives and lavish ink
Explaining how great commonwealths collapse
From great defects of policy—perhaps
40   The cause is sometimes simpler than they think.

It may not seem so grave an act to break
Postumia's spirit as Galileo's,[6] to gag
Hypatia as crush Socrates,[7] or drag
Joan as Giordano Bruno[8] to the stake.

45   Can we be sure? Have more states perished, then,
For having shackled the inquiring mind,

2. As punishment for breaking her vows of chastity.
3. As the symbol of obedience and chastisement.
4. In Ephesians 5.22: "Wives, submit yourselves unto your own husbands, as unto the Lord."
5. Roman historian (ca. 77–117), whose *Histories* criticize the degeneracy of the times as exemplified by three Roman emperors who ruled and were successively deposed in 68–69.
6. In 1633, the Italian astronomer Galileo Galilei was forced by the Roman Catholic Church to condemn his own scientific conclusions and was for a time imprisoned.
7. In 415, Hypatia, a beautiful and learned Egyptian woman, was murdered, allegedly by order of an archbishop. In 399 B.C.E., Socrates was sentenced to die by poison because of his supposedly subversive teachings.
8. Both were burned at the stake, Joan of Arc in 1431 for heresy and sorcery, Bruno in 1600 for theological and scientific heresies.

Than whose who, in their folly not less blind,
Trusted the servile womb to breed free men?

1966

Inscription for a War

Stranger, go tell the Spartans
we died here obedient to their commands.
—Inscription at Thermopylae[9]

Linger not, stranger; shed no tear;
Go back to those who sent us here.

We are the young they drafted out
To wars their folly brought about.

5   Go tell those old men, safe in bed,
We took their orders and are dead.

1981

LOUIS MacNEICE
1907–1963

The Sunlight on the Garden[1]

The sunlight on the garden
Hardens and grows cold,
We cannot cage the minute
Within its nets of gold,
5   When all is told
We cannot beg for pardon.

Our freedom as free lances
Advances towards its end;
The earth compels, upon it
10 Sonnets and birds descend;
And soon, my friend,
We shall have no time for dances.

The sky was good for flying
Defying the church bells

9. Thermopylae takes its name from hot baths near the pass, twenty-five feet wide at its narrowest, between Thessaly and Locris in Greece. This place was defended by Leonides and three hundred Spartans (with seven hundred Thespians) against a huge Persian army led by Xerxes. The Persians infiltrated the Greek line by treachery, and the Spartans were wiped out.
1. MacNeice's farewell to his first wife, Mary (née Ezra), once the best dancer in Oxford (see line 12).

15　And every evil iron
　　Siren and what it tells:
　　The earth compels,
　　We are dying, Egypt, dying[2]

　　And not expecting pardon,
20　Hardened in heart anew,
　　But glad to have sat under
　　Thunder and rain with you,
　　And grateful too
　　For sunlight on the garden.

1938

Bagpipe Music[3]

It's no go the merrygoround, it's no go the rickshaw,
All we want is a limousine and a ticket for the peepshow.
Their knickers[4] are made of crêpe-de-chine, their shoes are made of
　　python,
Their halls are lined with tiger rugs and their walls with heads of bison.

5　John MacDonald found a corpse, put it under the sofa,
　Waited till it came to life and hit it with a poker,
　Sold its eyes for souvenirs, sold its blood for whiskey,
　Kept its bones for dumbbells to use when he was fifty.

　It's no go the Yogi-man, it's no go Blavatsky[5]
10　All we want is a bank balance and a bit of skirt in a taxi.

　Annie MacDougall went to milk, caught her foot in the heather,
　Woke to hear a dance record playing of Old Vienna.
　It's no go your maidenheads, it's no go your culture,
　All we want is a Dunlop tyre and the devil mend the puncture.

15　The Laird o' Phelps spent Hogmanay[6] declaring he was sober,
　Counted his feet to prove the fact and found he had one foot over.
　Mrs. Carmichael had her fifth, looked at the job with repulsion,
　Said to the midwife "Take it away; I'm through with overproduction."

　It's no go the gossip column, it's no go the Ceilidh,[7]
20　All we want is a mother's help and a sugar-stick for the baby.

---

2. From Shakespeare, *Antony and Cleopatra* 4.16.43, Antony's speech to Cleopatra: "I am dying, Egypt, dying."
3. The poem is set in Scotland in the 1930s, the years of the Depression, years that led up to the Munich crisis of 1938 and to the outbreak of World War II in 1939.
4. Women's panties.

5. Madame Helena Petrovna Blavatsky (1831–1891), Russian occultist and theosophist, in whose writings there was renewed interest in the 1930s.
6. New Year's Eve (Scottish).
7. Pronounced *kaley*; Gaelic term for a social gathering with traditional music, storytelling, or dancing.

Willie Murray cut his thumb, couldn't count the damage,
Took the hide of an Ayrshire cow and used it for a bandage.
His brother caught three hundred cran[8] when the seas were lavish,
Threw the bleeders back in the sea and went upon the parish.[9]

25   It's no go the Herring Board, it's no go the Bible,
       All we want is a packet of fags° when our hands are idle.   *cigarettes*

       It's no go the picture palace, it's no go the stadium,
       It's no go the country cot° with a pot of pink geraniums,   *cottage*
       It's no go the Government grants, it's no go the elections,
30   Sit on your arse for fifty years and hang your hat on a pension.

       It's no go my honey love, it's no go my poppet;
       Work your hands from day to day, the winds will blow the profit.
       The glass° is falling hour by hour, the glass will fall forever,   *barometer*
       But if you break the bloody glass you won't hold up the weather.

1937   1938

From Autumn Journal[1]

IV

       September has come and I wake
           And I think with joy how whatever, now or in future, the system
       Nothing whatever can take
           The people away, there will always be people
5   For friends or for lovers though perhaps
           The conditions of love will be changed and its vices diminished
       And affection not lapse
           To narrow possessiveness, jealousy founded on vanity.
       September has come, it is *hers*
10   Whose vitality leaps in the autumn,
       Whose nature prefers
           Trees without leaves and a fire in the fire-place;
       So I give her this month and the next
           Though the whole of my year should be hers who has rendered
               already
15   So many of its days intolerable or perplexed
           But so many more so happy;
       Who has left a scent on my life and left my walls
           Dancing over and over with her shadow,
       Whose hair is twined in all my waterfalls
20   And all of London littered with remembered kisses.
       So I am glad
           That life contains her with her moods and moments
       More shifting and more transient than I had

8. A measure of just-caught herrings (about 750).
9. I.e., went on relief.
1. A book-length "documentary" poem covering events (public and, as here, private) in autumn 1938.

Yet thought of as being integral to beauty;
25   Whose mind is like the wind on a sea of wheat,
    Whose eyes are candour,
And assurance in her feet
    Like a homing pigeon never by doubt diverted.
To whom I send my thanks
30   That the air has become shot silk, the streets are music,
And that the ranks
    Of men are ranks of men, no more of cyphers.°   *zeros*
So that if now alone
    I must pursue this life, it will not be only
35 A drag from numbered stone to numbered stone
    But a ladder of angels, river turning tidal.
Off-hand, at times hysterical, abrupt,
    You are one I always shall remember,
Whom cant can never corrupt
40   Nor argument disinherit.
Frivolous, always in a hurry, forgetting the address,
    Frowning too often, taking enormous notice
Of hats and backchat—how could I assess
    The thing that makes you different?
45 You whom I remember glad or tired,
    Smiling in drink or scintillating anger,
Inopportunely desired
    On boats, on trains, on roads when walking.
Sometimes untidy, often elegant,
50   So easily hurt, so readily responsive,
To whom a trifle could be an irritant
    Or could be balm and manna.°   *food (from heaven)*
Whose words would tumble over each other and pelt
    From pure excitement,
55 Whose fingers curl and melt
    When you were friendly.
I shall remember you in bed with bright
    Eyes or in a café stirring coffee
Abstractedly and on your plate the white
60   Smoking stub your lips had touched with crimson.
And I shall remember how your words could hurt
    Because they were so honest
And even your lies were able to assert
    Integrity of purpose.
65 And it is on the strength of knowing you
    I reckon generous feeling more important
Than the mere deliberating what to do
    When neither the pros nor cons affect the pulses.
And though I have suffered from your special strength
70   Who never flatter for points nor fake responses
I should be proud if I could evolve at length
    An equal thrust and pattern.

1938

London Rain

The rain of London pimples
The ebony street with white
And the neon-lamps of London
Stain the canals of night
5 And the park becomes a jungle
In the alchemy of night.

My wishes turn to violent
Horses black as coal—
The randy mares of fancy,
10 The stallions of the soul—
Eager to take the fences
That fence about my soul.

Across the countless chimneys
The horses ride and across
15 The country to the channel
Where warning beacons toss,
To a place where God and No-God
Play at pitch and toss.

Whichever wins I am happy
20 For God will give me bliss
But No-God will absolve me
From all I do amiss
And I need not suffer conscience
If the world was made amiss.

25 Under God we can reckon
On pardon when we fall
But if we are under No-God
Nothing will matter at all,
Adultery and murder
30 Will count for nothing at all.

So reinforced by logic
As having nothing to lose
My lust goes riding horseback
To ravish where I choose,
35 To burgle all the turrets
Of beauty as I choose.

But now the rain gives over
Its dance upon the town,
Logic and lust together
40 Come dimly tumbling down,
And neither God nor No-God
Is either up or down.

The argument was wilful,
The alternatives untrue,
45 We need no metaphysics
To sanction what we do
Or to muffle us in comfort
From what we did not do.

Whether the living river
50 Began in bog or lake,
The world is what was given,
The world is what we make.
And we only can discover
Life in the life we make.

55 So let the water sizzle
Upon the gleaming slates,
There will be sunshine after
When the rain abates
And rain returning duly
60 When the sun abates.

My wishes now come homeward,
Their gallopings in vain,
Logic and lust are quiet
And again it starts to rain;
65 Falling asleep I listen
To the falling London rain.

1941

Star-gazer

Forty-two years ago (to me if to no one else
The number is of some interest) it was a brilliant starry night
And the westward train was empty and had no corridors
So darting from side to side I could catch the
      unwonted° sight   *unaccustomed*
5 Of those almost intolerably bright
Holes, punched in the sky, which excited me partly because
Of their Latin names and partly because I had read in the textbooks
How very far off they were, it seemed their light
Had left them (some at least) long years before I was.

10 And this remembering now I mark that what
Light was leaving some of them at least then,
Forty-two years ago, will never arrive
In time for me to catch it, which light when
It does get here may find that there is not
15 Anyone left alive

To run from side to side in a late night train
Admiring it and adding noughts in vain.

January 1963   1967

JOSEPHINE JACOBSEN
1908–2003

The Primer

I said in my youth
"they lie to children"
but it is not so.
Mother my goose[1] I know
5   told me the truth.

I remember that treetop minute.
That was a baby is a woman now;
in a rough wind, it was a broken bough
brought down the cradle with the baby in it.

10   I had a dumpy friend (you would not know his name,
though he indeed had several), after his fall
lay in live pieces by my garden wall
in a vain tide of epaulets and manes.

I had another friend (and you would know her name),
15   took up her candle on her way to bed.
She had a steady hand and a yellow head
up the tall stairwell, but the chopper came.

So small they meant to run away, from sightless eyes
three mice ran toward my mind instead;
20   I seized the shapely knife. They fled
in scarlet haste, the blind and tailless mice.

Cock robin was three birds of a single feather.
Three times cock robin fell when a breeze blew;
eye of fly watched; arrow of sparrow flew:
25   three times cock robin died in the same weather.

Sheep, cows, meander in the corn and meadow;
soundless the horn, fine, fine my seam;
nothing I feed, but rosy grows my cream.
My blue boy sleeps under the stack's huge shadow.

1974

1. As in the Mother Goose nursery rhymes. Each stanza of the poem rewrites one of these rhymes.

Bush

It is the sound of lions lapping.
They drink themselves
from the gold shapes that waver
and grow shallower.

5 Blue peels itself in the water-
hole; it is the sun coming.
Crouched, the lions meet
their matches at the surface.

The foxy jackals are far off
10 but the vultures cloud the flat treetop;
the drum of the zebra's body
is lined with red sunrise.

The jackals and vultures are waiting
for what happened under the moon.
15 The lions are through with it; they
lift their dripping chins and look ahead.

It is six o'clock on Christmas morning.
Now the lions have stopped lapping
the bush makes no sound
20 the vultures shift, but without sound.

The day is perfectly seamless.
Slowly the lions move like pistons past the dry grasses;
the jackals do not move yet;
the vultures show patience.

25 The lions pass a thornbush and melt.
Though the whole day is unbroken
the passage of the sun will represent heaven;
the bones will represent time.

1974

Hourglass

"Flawless" is the word, no doubt, for this third of May
that has landed on the grounds of Mayfair,
the Retirement Community par excellence.

Right behind the wheels of the mower, grass
5 explodes again, the bare trees most tenderly
push out their chartreuse tips.

Bottle bees are back. Feckless, reckless,
stingless, they probably have a function.
Above the cardinal, scarlet on the rim

10   of the birdbath, twinning himself,
they hover, cruise the flowers, mate.
The tiny water catches the sky.

On the circular inner road, the lady
untangles the poodle's leash from her cane.
15   He is wild to chase the splendid smells.

The small man with the small smile,
rapidly steering his Amigo,[2]
bowls past. She would wave, but can't.

All around, birds and sexual flowers
20   are intent on color, flight, fragrance.
The gardener sweeps his sweaty face

with a khaki sleeve. His tulips are shined
black at their centers. They have come along nicely.
He is young and will be gone before dark.

25   The man in the Amigo has in mind a May
a mirror of this, but unobtainable
as the touch of the woman in that glass.

The sun's force chills him. But the lady
with the curly poodle could melt her cane
30   in the very heat of her precious pleasure.

She perfectly understands the calendar
and the sun's passage. But she grips the leash
and leans on the air that is hers and here.

1995

THEODORE ROETHKE
1908–1963

Root Cellar

Nothing would sleep in that cellar, dank as a ditch,
Bulbs broke out of boxes hunting for chinks in the dark,
Shoots dangled and drooped,
Lolling obscenely from mildewed crates,

---

2. Brand of sport utility vehicle.

5   Hung down long yellow evil necks, like tropical snakes.
And what a congress of stinks!
Roots ripe as old bait,
Pulpy stems, rank, silo-rich,
Leaf-mold, manure, lime, piled against slippery planks.
10 Nothing would give up life:
Even the dirt kept breathing a small breath.

1948

Child on Top of a Greenhouse[1]

The wind billowing out the seat of my britches,
My feet crackling splinters of glass and dried putty,
The half-grown chrysanthemums staring up like accusers,
Up through the streaked glass, flashing with sunlight,
5 A few white clouds all rushing eastward,
A line of elms plunging and tossing like horses,
And everyone, everyone pointing up and shouting!

1948

My Papa's Waltz

The whiskey on your breath
Could make a small boy dizzy;
But I hung on like death:
Such waltzing was not easy.

5 We romped until the pans
Slid from the kitchen shelf;
My mother's countenance
Could not unfrown itself.

The hand that held my wrist
10 Was battered on one knuckle;
At every step you missed
My right ear scraped a buckle.

You beat time on my head
With a palm caked hard by dirt,
15 Then waltzed me off to bed
Still clinging to your shirt.

1948

---

1. Roethke, author of a series of "greenhouse poems," called the greenhouse "my symbol for the whole of life, a womb, a heaven-on-earth." His father, a florist, owned a greenhouse in Saginaw, Michigan.

The Lost Son

1. The Flight

At Woodlawn[2] I heard the dead cry:
I was lulled by the slamming of iron,
A slow drip over stones,
Toads brooding wells.
5   All the leaves stuck out their tongues;
I shook the softening chalk of my bones,
Saying,
Snail, snail, glister me forward,
Bird, soft-sigh me home,
10 Worm, be with me.
This is my hard time.

Fished in an old wound,
The soft pond of repose;
Nothing nibbled my line,
15 Not even the minnows came.

Sat in an empty house
Watching shadows crawl,
Scratching.
There was one fly.

20 Voice, come out of the silence.
Say something.
Appear in the form of a spider
Or a moth beating the curtain.

Tell me:
25 Which is the way I take;
Out of what door do I go,
Where and to whom?

Dark hollows said, lee° to the wind,   *shelter*
The moon said, back of an eel,
30 The salt said, look by the sea,
Your tears are not enough praise,
You will find no comfort here,
In the kingdom of bang and blab.

Running lightly over spongy ground,
35 Past the pasture of flat stones,
The three elms,
The sheep strewn on a field,
Over a rickety bridge
Toward the quick-water, wrinkling and rippling.

---

2. The New York City cemetery where Roethke's father was buried.

40   Hunting along the river,
    Down among the rubbish, the bug-riddled foliage,
    By the muddy pond-edge, by the bog-holes,
    By the shrunken lake, hunting, in the heat of summer.

   The shape of a rat?
45   It's bigger than that.
     It's less than a leg
     And more than a nose,
     Just under the water
     It usually goes.

50   Is it soft like a mouse?
    Can it wrinkle its nose?
    Could it come in the house
    On the tips of its toes?

    Take the skin of a cat
55   And the back of an eel,
    Then roll them in grease,—
    That's the way it would feel.

    It's sleek as an otter
    With wide webby toes
60   Just under the water
    It usually goes.

2. *The Pit*

  Where do the roots go?
    Look down under the leaves.
  Who put the moss there?
65   These stones have been here too long.
  Who stunned the dirt into noise?
    Ask the mole, he knows.[3]
  I feel the slime of a wet nest.
    Beware Mother Mildew.
70 Nibble again, fish nerves.

3. *The Gibber*[4]

  At the wood's mouth,
  By the cave's door,
  I listened to something
  I had heard before.

75 Dogs of the groin
  Barked and howled,
  The sun was against me,
  The moon would not have me.

3. Cf. William Blake, *The Book of Thel*, lines 1–2: "Does the Eagle know what is in the pit? / Or wilt thou go ask the Mole?" (p. 737).

4. A possible triple pun: meaningless utterance, the pouch at the base of a flower's calyx, and working-class slang for a key.

The weeds whined,
80 The snakes cried,
The cows and briars
Said to me: Die.

What a small song. What slow clouds. What dark water.
Hath the rain a father?[5] All the caves are ice. Only the snow's here.
85 I'm cold. I'm cold all over. Rub me in father and mother.
Fear was my father, Father Fear.
His look drained the stones.

        What gliding shape
        Beckoning through halls,
90   Stood poised on the stair,
        Fell dreamily down?

        From the mouths of jugs
        Perched on many shelves,
        I saw substance flowing
95   That cold morning.

        Like a slither of eels
        That watery cheek
        As my own tongue kissed
        My lips awake.

100 Is this the storm's heart? The ground is unstilling itself.
My veins are running nowhere. Do the bones cast out their fire?
Is the seed leaving the old bed? These buds are live as birds.
Where, where are the tears of the world?
Let the kisses resound, flat like a butcher's palm;
105 Let the gestures freeze; our doom is already decided.
All the windows are burning! What's left of my life?
I want the old rage, the lash of primordial milk!
Goodbye, goodbye, old stones, the time-order is going,
I have married my hands to perpetual agitation,
110 I run, I run to the whistle of money.

        Money money money
        Water water water

        How cool the grass is.
        Has the bird left?
115   The stalk still sways.
        Has the worm a shadow?
        What do the clouds say?

        These sweeps of light undo me.
        Look, look, the ditch is running white!
120   I've more veins than a tree!
        Kiss me, ashes, I'm falling through a dark swirl.

5. Quoted from Job 38.28.

4. *The Return*

The way to the boiler was dark,
Dark all the way,
Over slippery cinders
125   Through the long greenhouse.

The roses kept breathing in the dark.
They had many mouths to breathe with.
My knees made little winds underneath
Where the weeds slept.

130   There was always a single light
Swinging by the fire-pit,
Where the fireman pulled out roses,
The big roses, the big bloody clinkers.[6]

Once I stayed all night.
135   The light in the morning came slowly over the white
Snow.
There were many kinds of cool
Air.
Then came steam.

140   Pipe-knock.

Scurry of warm over small plants.
Ordnung![7] ordnung!
Papa is coming!

A fine haze moved off the leaves;
145   Frost melted on far panes;
The rose, the chrysanthemum turned toward the light.
Even the hushed forms, the bent yellowy weeds
Moved in a slow up-sway.

5. *"It was beginning winter"*

It was beginning winter,
150   An in-between time,
The landscape still partly brown:
The bones of weeds kept swinging in the wind,
Above the blue snow.

It was beginning winter,
155   The light moved slowly over the frozen field,
Over the dry seed-crowns,
The beautiful surviving bones
Swinging in the wind.

---

6. Large cinders, the remains of burned coal.   7. Order! (German).

Light traveled over the wide field;
160 Stayed.
The weeds stopped swinging.
The mind moved, not alone,
Through the clear air, in the silence.

Was it light?
165 Was it light within?
Was it light within light?
Stillness becoming alive,
Yet still?

A lively understandable spirit
170 Once entertained you.
It will come again.
Be still.
Wait.

1948

Elegy for Jane

My Student, Thrown by a Horse

I remember the neckcurls, limp and damp as tendrils;
And her quick look, a sidelong pickerel smile;
And how, once startled into talk, the light syllables leaped for her,
And she balanced in the delight of her thought,
5 A wren, happy, tail into the wind,
Her song trembling the twigs and small branches.
The shade sang with her;
The leaves, their whispers turned to kissing;
And the mold sang in the bleached valleys under the rose.

10 Oh, when she was sad, she cast herself down into such a pure depth,
Even a father could not find her:
Scraping her cheek against straw;
Stirring the clearest water.
My sparrow, you are not here,
15 Waiting like a fern, making a spiny shadow.
The sides of wet stones cannot console me,
Nor the moss, wound with the last light.

If only I could nudge you from this sleep,
My maimed darling, my skittery pigeon.
20 Over this damp grave I speak the words of my love:
I, with no rights in this matter,
Neither father nor lover.

1953

The Waking

I wake to sleep, and take my waking slow.
I feel my fate in what I cannot fear.
I learn by going where I have to go.

We think by feeling. What is there to know?
5 I hear my being dance from ear to ear.
I wake to sleep, and take my waking slow.

Of those so close beside me, which are you?
God bless the Ground! I shall walk softly there,
And learn by going where I have to go.

10 Light takes the Tree; but who can tell us how?
The lowly worm climbs up a winding stair;
I wake to sleep, and take my waking slow.

Great Nature has another thing to do
To you and me; so take the lively air,
15 And, lovely, learn by going where to go.

This shaking keeps me steady. I should know.
What falls away is always. And is near.
I wake to sleep, and take my waking slow.
I learn by going where I have to go.

1953

I Knew a Woman

I knew a woman, lovely in her bones,
When small birds sighed, she would sigh back at them;
Ah, when she moved, she moved more ways than one:
The shapes a bright container can contain!
5 Of her choice virtues only gods should speak,
Or English poets who grew up on Greek
(I'd have them sing in chorus, cheek to cheek).

How well her wishes went! She stroked my chin,
She taught me Turn, and Counter-turn, and Stand;[8]
10 She taught me Touch, that undulant white skin;
I nibbled meekly from her proffered hand;
She was the sickle; I, poor I, the rake,
Coming behind her for her pretty sake
(But what prodigious mowing we did make).

---

8. Translations of the Greek literary terms *strophe, antistrophe,* and *epode* (more properly, "the song that follows"), which are the three parts of the Pindaric ode.

15 Love likes a gander, and adores a goose:
Her full lips pursed, the errant note to seize;
She played it quick, she played it light and loose,
My eyes, they dazzled at her flowing knees;
Her several parts could keep a pure repose,
20 Or one hip quiver with a mobile nose
(She moved in circles, and those circles moved).

Let seed be grass, and grass turn into hay:
I'm martyr to a motion not my own;
What's freedom for? To know eternity.
25 I swear she cast a shadow white as stone.
But who would count eternity in days?
These old bones live to learn her wanton ways:
(I measure time by how a body sways).

1958

Wish for a Young Wife

My lizard, my lively writher,
May your limbs never wither,
May the eyes in your face
Survive the green ice
5 Of envy's mean gaze;
May you live out your life
Without hate, without grief,
And your hair ever blaze,
In the sun, in the sun,
10 When I am undone,
When I am no one.

1964

In a Dark Time

In a dark time, the eye begins to see,
I meet my shadow in the deepening shade;
I hear my echo in the echoing wood—
A lord of nature weeping to a tree.
5 I live between the heron and the wren,[9]
Beasts of the hill and serpents of the den.

What's madness but nobility of soul
At odds with circumstance? The day's on fire!
I know the purity of pure despair,
10 My shadow pinned against a sweating wall.

9. The heron is a large, solitary wading bird, the wren a small, sociable songbird.

That place among the rocks—is it a cave,
Or winding path? The edge is what I have.

A steady storm of correspondences!
A night flowing with birds, a ragged moon,
15 And in broad day the midnight come again!
A man goes far to find out what he is—
Death of the self in a long, tearless night,
All natural shapes blazing unnatural light.

Dark, dark my light, and darker my desire.
20 My soul, like some heat-maddened summer fly,
Keeps buzzing at the sill. Which I is *I*?
A fallen man, I climb out of my fear.
The mind enters itself, and God the mind,
And one is One, free in the tearing[1] wind.

1964

RICHARD WRIGHT
1908–1960

FROM HAIKU: THIS OTHER WORLD

21

On winter mornings
The candle shows faint markings
Of the teeth of rats.

31

In the falling snow
A laughing boy holds out his palms
Until they are white.

120

Crying and crying,
Melodious strings of geese
Passing a graveyard.

---

1. With a pun on "tearless" (line 17), according to a note of Roethke's.

490

Waking from a nap
And hearing summer rain falling,—
What else has happened?

762

Droning autumn rain:
A boy lines up toy soldiers
For a big battle.

783

I cannot find it,
That very first violet
Seen from my window.

ca. 1960   2000

MALCOLM LOWRY
1909–1957

Delirium in Vera Cruz[1]

Where has tenderness gone, he asked the mirror
Of the Biltmore Hotel, cuarto° 216. Alas,   *room*
Can its reflection lean against the glass
Too, wondering where I have gone, into what horror?
5 Is that it staring at me now with terror
Behind your frail tilted barrier? Tenderness
Was here, in this very bedroom, in this
Place, its form seen, cries heard, by you. What error
Is here? Am I that rashed image?
10 Is this the ghost of the love you reflected?
Now with a background of tequila, stubs, dirty collars,
Sodium perborate,[2] and a scrawled page

---

1. The chief seaport of Mexico; now Veracruz.
Canadian-born Lowry spent nineteen months in
Mexico, where his most celebrated work, the novel
Under the Volcano (1947), was set. The state of
Lowry's poem texts is extraordinarily complicated,
and the versions here are chosen from among several, offered either by his first editor, Earle Birney

(whose 1962 selected edition included some questionable changes), or the editor of the 1992 *Collected Poetry of Malcolm Lowry*, Kathleen Sherf.
This poem is a Birney version.
2. A water-soluble solid used as a bleach and as
an antiseptic.

To the dead, telephone off the hook? In rage
He smashed all the glass in the room. (Bill: $50.)

1936   1962

The Wild Cherry[3]

    We put a prop beneath the sagging bough
    That yearned over the beach, setting four stones
    Cairn-like against it, but we thought our groans
    Were the wild cherry's, for it was as though
5   Utterly set with broken seams on doom
    It listed wilfully down like a mast,
    Stubborn as some smashed recalcitrant boom
    That will neither be cut loose nor made fast.
    Going—going—it was yet no bidder
10 For life, whether for such sober healing
    We left its dead branches to consider
    Until its sunward pulse renewed, feeling
    The passionate hatred of that tree
    Whose longing was to wash away to sea.

1940–47   1962, 1992

Eye-Opener[4]

    How like a man, is Man, who rises late
    And gazes on his unwashed dinner plate
    And gazes on the bottles, empty too,
    All gulphed in last night's loud long how-do-you-do,
5   —Although one glass yet holds a gruesome bait—
    How like to Man is this man and his fate—
    Still drunk and stumbling through the rusty trees
    To breakfast on stale rum sardines and peas.

1953   1962, 1992

Strange Type[5]

    I wrote: in the dark cavern of our birth.
    The printer had it tavern, which seems better:
    But herein lies the subject of our mirth,
    Since on the next page death appears as dearth.

3. Sherf version.
4. Sherf version.
5. The title is Birney's; Lowry left the poem untitled. Though Sherf's punctuation is probably more accurate, Birney's version is given here for its reading of the last word, "bitter," which seems more likely than Sherf's "better."

5 So it may be that God's word was distraction,
   Which to our strange type appears destruction,
   Which is bitter.

1946–54   1962

STEPHEN SPENDER
1909–1995

I Think Continually of Those Who Were Truly Great

I think continually of those who were truly great.
Who, from the womb, remembered the soul's history
Through corridors of light where the hours are suns
Endless and singing. Whose lovely ambition
5 Was that their lips, still touched with fire,
Should tell of the Spirit clothed from head to foot in song.
And who hoarded from the Spring branches
The desires falling across their bodies like blossoms.

What is precious is never to forget
10 The essential delight of the blood drawn from ageless springs
Breaking through rocks in worlds before our earth.
Never to deny its pleasure in the morning simple light
Nor its grave evening demand for love.
Never to allow gradually the traffic to smother
15 With noise and fog the flowering of the spirit.

Near the snow, near the sun, in the highest fields
See how these names are fêted° by the waving grass   honored
And by the streamers of white cloud
And whispers of wind in the listening sky.
20 The names of those who in their lives fought for life
Who wore at their hearts the fire's centre.
Born of the sun they travelled a short while towards the sun,
And left the vivid air signed with their honour.

                                                                            1933

Ultima Ratio Regum[1]

The guns spell money's ultimate reason
In letters of lead on the Spring hillside.
But the boy lying dead under the olive trees
Was too young and too silly

---

1. Kings' ultimate reason, i.e., for taking action (Latin).

5 To have been notable to their important eye.
    He was a better target for a kiss.

    When he lived, tall factory hooters° never summoned him   *sirens*
    Nor did restaurant plate-glass doors revolve to wave him in.
    His name never appeared in the papers.
10 The world maintained its traditional wall
    Round the dead with their gold sunk deep as a well,
    Whilst his life, intangible as a Stock Exchange rumour, drifted outside.

    O too lightly he threw down his cap
    One day when the breeze threw petals from the trees.
15 The unflowering wall sprouted with guns,
    Machine-gun anger quickly scythed the grasses;
    Flags and leaves fell from hands and branches;
    The tweed cap rotted in the nettles.

    Consider his life which was valueless
20 In terms of employment, hotel ledgers, news files.
    Consider. One bullet in ten thousand kills a man.
    Ask. Was so much expenditure justified
    On the death of one so young, and so silly
    Lying under the olive trees, O world, O death?

                                     1939

Seascape

(In Memoriam, M.A.S.)

    There are some days the happy ocean lies
    Like an unfingered harp, below the land.
    Afternoon gilds all the silent wires
    Into a burning music for the eyes.
5 On mirrors flashing between fine-strung fires
    The shore, heaped up with roses, horses, spires,
    Wanders on water, walking above ribbed sand.

    The motionlessness of the hot sky tires
    And a sigh, like a woman's, from inland
10 Brushes the instrument with shadowing hand
    Drawing across its wires some gull's sharp cries
    Or bell, or shout, from distant, hedged-in shires;°   *counties*
    These, deep as anchors, the hushing wave buries.

    Then from the shore, two zig-zag butterflies,
15 Like errant dog-roses, cross the bright strand
    Spiraling over sea in foolish gyres°   *spiral turnings*
    Until they fall into reflected skies.
    They drown. Fishermen understand
    Such wings sunk in such ritual sacrifice,

20 Recalling legends of undersea, drowned cities.
What voyagers, oh what heroes, flamed like pyres
With helmets plumed, have set forth from some island
And them the sea engulfed. Their eyes,
Contorted by the cruel waves' desires
25 Glitter with coins through the tide scarcely scanned,
While, above them, that harp assumes their sighs.

1947

ROBERT FITZGERALD
1910–1985

Figlio Maggiore[1]

Benedict Robert Campion Fitzgerald

Twitched in her belly, or he raised a fist,
and came and cried. O red and meager baby,
umbilical, priapic,° knobby,   *phallic*
mashed and wrinkled as an old pugilist.

5 A lyric name he got and a saint's name,
a third stout name from Pa, *cioè Roberto*.[2]
Think of this Christian if you care to
filling his giant napkin° without shame.   *diaper*

And soon for happy trilled at goldy leaves
10 by a summer air. What hours our boy would warble.
You find my doting lines intolerable?
Never was infant such under such eaves.

Behave. "I'm being hayve." With Harpo's[3] grin.
At three he shook his cap and bells, our jester,
15 or tented him in a souwester°   *rain hat*
and fragrant slicker to stay in the rain in.

Never (ah!) to inherit that dripping grove,
in a DC–6 he peered at cumulo-cirrus
"trees" on ocean. (Graciously hear us,
20 lord of that aircraft gaily named I LOVE)

Ligurian fry[4] inquired, "Why is your old man
home all day? What *mestiere*[5] has he?"

---

1. Eldest son (Italian).
2. That is, Robert (Fitzgerald) (Italian). *Lyric name*: from Thomas Campion (1567–1620; see pp. 278–82), English poet and composer. *Saint's name*: Benedict.

3. Harpo Marx (1893–1964), one member of the Marx Brothers comedy team.
4. Children in Liguria, Italy.
5. Job, profession (Italian).

"*Da notte va fuori a rubare case.*"[6]
A penman's alibi. Tie it if you can.

25 Off iodine-scented rock pure undersea,
fronded, astir, awaited our explorer.
Noon. With a tentacled small horror
draped on his tines[7] he swam ashore in glee.

Daemonic lightning, ire of rebellious powers
30 could rend this patient hunter of the polyp.[8]
Bone-ache from one corrective wallop
disabled the parental hand for hours.

Child of my own rage, rippling in Tuscan speech
through five hard winters' *compiti,* my Benny,
35 *temi, storie, disegni!*[9]
What will the next years teach?

1971

NORMAN MacCAIG
1910–1996

Summer Farm

Straws like tame lightnings lie about the grass
And hang zigzag on hedges. Green as glass
The water in the horse-trough shines.
Nine ducks go wobbling by in two straight lines.

5 A hen stares at nothing with one eye,
Then picks it up. Out of an empty sky
A swallow falls and, flickering through
The barn, dives up again into the dizzy blue.

I lie, not thinking, in the cool, soft grass,
10 Afraid of where a thought might take me—as
This grasshopper with plated° face   armor-plated
Unfolds his legs and finds himself in space.

Self under self, a pile of selves I stand
Threaded on time, and with metaphysic hand
15 Lift the farm like a lid and see
Farm within farm, and in the centre, me.

1955

---

6. At night he goes out to burgle houses (Italian).
7. Meant to suggest the tines of the triton of Neptune, Roman god of the sea.

8. Tentacled sea creature.
9. Themes, stories, drawings! (Italian). *Compiti:* homework (Italian).

Return to Scalpay[1]

The ferry wades across the kyle. I drive
The car ashore
On to a trim tarred road. A car on Scalpay?
Yes, and a road where never was one before.
5 The ferrymen's Gaelic wonders who I am
(Not knowing I know it), this man back from the dead,
Who takes the blue-black road (no traffic jam)
From by Craig Lexie over to Bay Head.

A man bows in the North wind, shaping up
10 His lazybeds,[2]
And through the salt air vagrant peat smells waver
From houses where no house should be. The sheds
At the curing station[3] have been newly tarred.
Aunt Julia's[4] house has vanished. The Red Well
15 Has been bulldozed away. But sharp and hard
The church still stands, barring the road to Hell.

A chugging prawn boat slides round Cuddy Point
Where in a gale
I spread my batwing jacket and jumped farther
20 Than I've jumped since. There's where I used to sail
Boats looped from rushes. On the jetty there
I caught eels, cut their heads off and watched them slew
Slow through the water. Ah—Cape Finisterre[5]
I called that point, to show how much I knew.

25 While Hamish sketches, a crofter° tells me that   *tenant farmer*
The Scalpay folk,
Though very intelligent, are not Spinozas . . .[6]
We walk the Out End road (no need to invoke
That troublemaker, Memory, she's everywhere)
30 To Laggandoan, greeted all the way—
My city eyeballs prickle; it's hard to bear
With such affection and such gaiety.

Scalpay revisited?—more than Scalpay. I
Have no defence,
35 For half my thought and half my blood is Scalpay,
Against that pure, hardheaded innocence

1. Island in the Scottish Outer Hebrides, to the east of Harris and separated from it by a kyle, or narrow channel.
2. Earthen beds, about six feet wide, on which potatoes are grown.
3. Place where fish are salted and dried.
4. The subject of a well-known poem by MacCaig: "Aunt Julia spoke Gaelic / very loud and fast."
5. Promontory—the name meaning "world's end" (Latin)—on the Atlantic coast of northern Spain.
6. I.e., not as smart as the Dutch philosopher Benedict de (Baruch) Spinoza (1632–1677).

That shows love without shame, weeps without shame,
Whose every thought is hospitality—
Edinburgh, Edinburgh, you're dark years away.

40 Scuttering snowflakes riddling the hard wind
Are almost spent
When we reach Johann's[7] house. She fills the doorway,
Sixty years of size and astonishment,
Then laughs and cries and laughs, as she always did
45 And will (Easy glum, easy glow, a friend would say) . . .
Scones, oatcakes, herrings from under a bubbling lid.
Then she comes with us to put us on our way.

Hugging my arm in her stronger one, she says,
Fancy me
50 *Walking this road beside my darling Norman!*
And what is there to say? . . . We look back and see
Her monumental against the flying sky
And I am filled with love and praise and shame
Knowing that I have been, and knowing why,
55 Diminished and enlarged. Are they the same?

1974

Kingfisher

That kingfisher jewelling upstream
seems to leave a streak of itself behind it
in the bright air. The trees
are all the better for its passing.

5 It's not a mineral eater, though it looks it:
It doesn't nip nicks out of the edges
of rainbows.—It dives
into the burly water, then, perched
on a Japanese bough, gulps
10 into its own incandescence
a wisp of minnow, a warrior stickleback.
—Or it vanishes into its burrow, resplendent
Samurai, returning home
to his stinking slum.

1977

7. Johann Macleod, a native of Scalpay.

CHARLES OLSON
1910–1970

Merce[1] of Egypt

1

I sing the tree is a heron
I praise long grass[2]
I wear the lion skin
over the long skirt
5   to the ankle. The ankle
is a heron
I look straightly backward. Or I bend to the side straightly
to raise the sheaf
up the stick of the leg
10 as the bittern's leg, raised
as slow as
his neck grows
as the wheat. The presentation,
the representation,
15 is flat,

I am followed by women and a small boy in white carrying a duck,
all have flat feet and, foot before foot, the women with black wigs
And I intent
upon idlers,
20 and flowers

2

      the sedge
as tall as I am, the rushes
as I am
     as far as I am animal, antelope
25 with such's attendant carnivores
               and rows of beaters
drive the game to the hunter, or into nets,
where it is thick-wooded or there are open spaces
with low shrubs

3

30 I speak downfall, the ball of my foot
on the neck of the earth, the hardsong
of the rise of all trees, the jay
who uses the air. I am the recovered sickle

1. Merce Cunningham (b. 1919), American dancer and choreographer. While head of Black Mountain College, an experimental school in North Carolina, Olson brought him there to teach and even participated in some of his dance classes.

2. Olson's references to song and grass recall "Song of Myself," part of Leaves of Grass, by the American poet Walt Whitman (1819–1892; see pp. 1060–86).

with the grass-stains still on the flint of its teeth.
35 I am the six-rowed barley
they cut down.

I am tree. The boy of the back of my legs
is roots. I am water fowl
when motion is the season of my river, and the wild boar
40 casts me. But my time
is hawkweed,

4

I hold what the wind blows, and silt.
I hide in the swamps of the valley to escape civil war,
and marauding soldiers. In the new procession
45 I am first, and carry wine
made of dandelions. The new rites
are my bones

I built my first settlement
in groves

5

50   as they would flail crops
when the spring comes, and flood, the tassels
rise, as my head

1953

Variations Done for Gerald Van De Wiele³

I. Le Bonheur⁴

dogwood flakes
what is green

the petals
from the apple
5   blow on the road

mourning doves
mark the sway
of the afternoon, bees
dig the plum blossoms

3. A student at Black Mountain College during Olson's time as head there (see note 1 above).
4. The "Variations" allude repeatedly, and in complex, subtle ways, to a poem by the French poet Arthur Rimbaud (1854–1891), "Le Bonheur" ("Happiness"), the last of the poems that occur throughout Rimbaud's poem-prose complex Une

Saison en enfer (A Season in Hell, 1873). Sometimes Olson cites a word or a phrase from the poem in French, sometimes he translates a word by the English word it resembles (trépas as "trespass"), then later by the word that translates it correctly ("death").

10   the morning
stands up straight, the night
is blue from the full of the April moon

iris and lilac, birds
birds, yellow flowers
15   white flowers, the Diesel
does not let up dragging
the plow
          as the whippoorwill,
the night's tractor, grinds
20   his song

      and no other birds but us
are as busy (O saisons, o châteaux!

Délires![5]

      What soul
25   is without fault?

Nobody studies
happiness

Every time the cock crows
I salute him

30   I have no longer any excuse
for envy. My life

has been given its orders: the seasons
seize

the soul and the body, and make mock
35   of any dispersed effort. The hour of death

is the only trespass

II. *The Charge*

dogwood flakes
the green

the petals from the apple-trees
40   fall for the feet to walk on

the birds are so many they are
loud, in the afternoon

---

5. Two sections of *Une Saison en enfer* are entitled "Délires" ("Deliriums," "Frenzies"), and "Le Bonheur" occurs in "Délires II." "O saisons, o châteaux!" ("O seasons! o castles!") is the first line and refrain of "Le Bonheur."

they distract, as so many bees do
suddenly all over the place

45   With spring one knows today to see
that in the morning each thing

is separate but by noon
they have melted into each other

and by night only crazy things
50   like the full moon and the whippoorwill

and us, are busy. We are busy
if we can get by that whiskered bird,

that nightjar,° and get across, the moon   *a nocturnal bird*
is our conversation, she will say

55   what soul
isn't in default?

can you afford not to make
the magical study

which happiness is? do you hear
60   the cock when he crows? do you know the charge,

that you shall have no envy, that your life
has its orders, that the seasons

seize you too, that no body and soul are one
if they are not wrought

65   in this retort? that otherwise efforts
are efforts? And that the hour of your flight

will be the hour of your death?

III. Spring

The dogwood
lights up the day.

70   The April moon
flakes the night.

Birds, suddenly,
are a multitude

The flowers are ravined°   *hollowed out*
75   by bees, the fruit blossoms

are thrown to the ground, the wind
the rain forces everything. Noise—

even the night is drummed
by whippoorwills, and we get

80   as busy, we plow, we move,
we break out, we love. The secret

which got lost neither hides
nor reveals itself, it shows forth

tokens. And we rush
85   to catch up. The body

whips the soul. In its great desire
it demands the elixir

In the roar of spring,
transmutations. Envy

90   drags herself off. The fault of the body and the soul
—that they are not one—

the matutinal° cock clangs   *morning*
and singleness: we salute you

season of no bungling

1960

ELIZABETH BISHOP
1911–1979

Casabianca[1]

Love's the boy stood on the burning deck
trying to recite "The boy stood on
the burning deck." Love's the son
stood stammering elocution
5   while the poor ship in flames went down.

Love's the obstinate boy, the ship,
even the swimming sailors, who
would like a schoolroom platform, too,

1. Cf. Felicia Dorothea Hemans, "Casabianca" (p. 899), line 1 of which is "The boy stood on the burning deck." The boy had remained on the burn- ing ship during the 1798 Battle of the Nile (a deci- sive defeat for Napoleon), thinking that his father, the admiral, had not released him from duty.

or an excuse to stay
10   on deck. And love's the burning boy.

1946

The Fish

I caught a tremendous fish
and held him beside the boat
half out of water, with my hook
fast in a corner of his mouth.
5   He didn't fight.
He hadn't fought at all.
He hung a grunting weight,
battered and venerable
and homely. Here and there
10   his brown skin hung in strips
like ancient wallpaper,
and its pattern of darker brown
was like wallpaper:
shapes like full-blown roses
15   stained and lost through age.
He was speckled with barnacles,
fine rosettes of lime,
and infested
with tiny white sea-lice,
20   and underneath two or three
rags of green weed hung down.
While his gills were breathing in
the terrible oxygen
—the frightening gills,
25   fresh and crisp with blood,
that can cut so badly—
I thought of the coarse white flesh
packed in like feathers,
the big bones and the little bones,
30   the dramatic reds and blacks
of his shiny entrails,
and the pink swim-bladder
like a big peony.
I looked into his eyes
35   which were far larger than mine
but shallower, and yellowed,
the irises backed and packed
with tarnished tinfoil
seen through the lenses
40   of old scratched isinglass.[2]
They shifted a little, but not
to return my stare.

2. Mica in thin, transparent sheets; originally prepared from the air bladders of certain fish.

—It was more like the tipping
of an object toward the light.
45 I admired his sullen face,
the mechanism of his jaw,
and then I saw
that from his lower lip
—if you could call it a lip—
50 grim, wet, and weaponlike,
hung five old pieces of fish-line,
or four and a wire leader
with the swivel still attached,
with all their five big hooks
55 grown firmly in his mouth.
A green line, frayed at the end
where he broke it, two heavier lines,
and a fine black thread
still crimped from the strain and snap
60 when it broke and he got away.
Like medals with their ribbons
frayed and wavering,
a five-haired beard of wisdom
trailing from his aching jaw.
65 I stared and stared
and victory filled up
the little rented boat,
from the pool of bilge
where oil had spread a rainbow
70 around the rusted engine
to the bailer rusted orange,
the sun-cracked thwarts,
the oarlocks on their strings,
the gunnels—until everything
75 was rainbow, rainbow, rainbow!
And I let the fish go.

1946

Filling Station

Oh, but it is dirty!
—this little filling station,
oil-soaked, oil-permeated
to a disturbing, over-all
5 black translucency.
Be careful with that match!

Father wears a dirty,
oil-soaked monkey suit
that cuts him under the arms,
10 and several quick and saucy

and greasy sons assist him
(it's a family filling station),
all quite thoroughly dirty.

Do they live in the station?
15   It has a cement porch
behind the pumps, and on it
a set of crushed and grease-
impregnated wickerwork;
on the wicker sofa
20   a dirty dog, quite comfy.

Some comic books provide
the only note of color—
of certain color. They lie
upon a big dim doily
25   draping a taboret°   *drum-shaped table*
(part of the set), beside
a big hirsute begonia.

Why the extraneous plant?
Why the taboret?
30   Why, oh why, the doily?
(Embroidered in daisy stitch
with marguerites,° I think,   *small daisies*
and heavy with gray crochet.)

Somebody embroidered the doily.
35   Somebody waters the plant,
or oils it, maybe. Somebody
arranges the rows of cans
so that they softly say:
ESSO—SO—SO—SO[3]
40   to high-strung automobiles.
Somebody loves us all.

1965

Sandpiper

The roaring alongside he takes for granted,
and that every so often the world is bound to shake.
He runs, he runs to the south, finical, awkward,
in a state of controlled panic, a student of Blake.[4]

5   The beach hisses like fat. On his left, a sheet
of interrupting water comes and goes

---

3. The company name Esso, later changed to Exxon.
4. William Blake (1757–1827; see pp. 732–47), English poet, whose 1803 poem "Auguries of Inno-cence" begins, "To see a World in a Grain of Sand / And a Heaven in a Wild Flower, / Hold Infinity in the palm of your hand / And Eternity in an hour."

and glazes over his dark and brittle feet.
He runs, he runs straight through it, watching his toes.

—Watching, rather, the spaces of sand between them,
10 where (no detail too small) the Atlantic drains
rapidly backwards and downwards. As he runs,
he stares at the dragging grains.

The world is a mist. And then the world is
minute and vast and clear. The tide
15 is higher or lower. He couldn't tell you which.
His beak is focussed; he is preoccupied,

looking for something, something, something.
Poor bird, he is obsessed!
The millions of grains are black, white, tan, and gray,
20 mixed with quartz grains, rose and amethyst.

1965

The Armadillo[5]

For Robert Lowell

This is the time of year
when almost every night
the frail, illegal fire balloons appear.
Climbing the mountain height,

5 rising toward a saint
still honored in these parts,
the paper chambers flush and fill with light
that comes and goes, like hearts.

Once up against the sky it's hard
10 to tell them from the stars—
planets, that is—the tinted ones:
Venus going down, or Mars,

or the pale green one. With a wind,
they flare and falter, wobble and toss;
15 but if it's still they steer between
the kite sticks of the Southern Cross,[6]

receding, dwindling, solemnly
and steadily forsaking us,
or, in the downdraft from a peak,
20 suddenly turning dangerous.

5. Cf. Robert Lowell, "Skunk Hour" (p. 1601),   6. Bright constellation.
which is modeled on Bishop's poem.

Last night another big one fell.
It splattered like an egg of fire
against the cliff behind the house.
The flame ran down. We saw the pair
25   of owls who nest there flying up
and up, their whirling black-and-white
stained bright pink underneath, until
they shrieked up out of sight.

The ancient owls' nest must have burned.
30   Hastily, all alone,
a glistening armadillo left the scene,
rose-flecked, head down, tail down,

and then a baby rabbit jumped out,
short-eared, to our surprise.
35   So soft!—a handful of intangible ash
with fixed, ignited eyes.

Too pretty, dreamlike mimicry!
O falling fire and piercing cry
and panic, and a weak mailed fist
40   *clenched ignorant against the sky!*

1965

Sestina[7]

September rain falls on the house.
In the failing light, the old grandmother
sits in the kitchen with the child
beside the Little Marvel Stove,[8]
5   reading the jokes from the almanac,
laughing and talking to hide her tears.

She thinks that her equinoctial tears
and the rain that beats on the roof of the house
were both foretold by the almanac,
10   but only known to a grandmother.
The iron kettle sings on the stove.
She cuts some bread and says to the child,

It's time for tea now; but the child
is watching the teakettle's small hard tears
15   dance like mad on the hot black stove,
the way the rain must dance on the house.
Tidying up, the old grandmother
hangs up the clever almanac

7. On this verse form, see "Versification," p. 2045.   8. Brand of wood- or coal-burning stove.

on its string. Birdlike, the almanac
20   hovers half open above the child,
hovers above the old grandmother
and her teacup full of dark brown tears.
She shivers and says she thinks the house
feels chilly, and puts more wood in the stove.

25   *It was to be,* says the Marvel Stove.
I know what I know, says the almanac.
With crayons the child draws a rigid house
and a winding pathway. Then the child
puts in a man with buttons like tears
30   and shows it proudly to the grandmother.

But secretly, while the grandmother
busies herself about the stove,
the little moons fall down like tears
from between the pages of the almanac
35   into the flower bed the child
has carefully placed in the front of the house.

Time to plant tears, says the almanac.
The grandmother sings to the marvelous stove
and the child draws another inscrutable house.

1965

In the Waiting Room

In Worcester, Massachusetts,
I went with Aunt Consuelo
to keep her dentist's appointment
and sat and waited for her
5   in the dentist's waiting room.
It was winter. It got dark
early. The waiting room
was full of grown-up people,
arctics and overcoats,
10   lamps and magazines.
My aunt was inside
what seemed like a long time
and while I waited I read
the *National Geographic*
15   (I could read) and carefully
studied the photographs:
the inside of a volcano,
black, and full of ashes;
then it was spilling over
20   in rivulets of fire.
Osa and Martin Johnson[9]

9. Famous husband-and-wife explorers and writers.

dressed in riding breeches,
laced boots, and pith helmets.
A dead man slung on a pole
25   —"Long Pig,"[1] the caption said.
Babies with pointed heads
wound round and round with string;
black, naked women with necks
wound round and round with wire
30   like the necks of light bulbs.
Their breasts were horrifying.
I read it right straight through.
I was too shy to stop.
And then I looked at the cover:
35   the yellow margins, the date.

Suddenly, from inside,
came an *oh!* of pain
—Aunt Consuelo's voice—
not very loud or long.
40   I wasn't at all surprised;
even then I knew she was
a foolish, timid woman.
I might have been embarrassed,
but wasn't. What took me
45   completely by surprise
was that it was *me:*
my voice, in my mouth.
Without thinking at all
I was my foolish aunt,
50   I—we—were falling, falling,
our eyes glued to the cover
of the *National Geographic,*
February, 1918.

I said to myself: three days
55   and you'll be seven years old.
I was saying it to stop
the sensation of falling off
the round, turning world
into cold, blue-black space.
60   But I felt: you are an *I,*
you are an *Elizabeth,*
you are one of *them.*
Why should you be one, too?
I scarcely dared to look
65   to see what it was I was.
I gave a sidelong glance
—I couldn't look any higher—
at shadowy gray knees,
trousers and skirts and boots
70   and different pairs of hands

1. Polynesian cannibals' name for the human body as food.

lying under the lamps.
I knew that nothing stranger
had ever happened, that nothing
stranger could ever happen.
75 Why should I be my aunt,
or me, or anyone?
What similarities—
boots, hands, the family voice
I felt in my throat, or even
80 the *National Geographic*
and those awful hanging breasts—
held us all together
or made us all just one?
How—I didn't know any
85 word for it—how "unlikely" . . .
How had I come to be here,
like them, and overhear
a cry of pain that could have
got loud and worse but hadn't?

90 The waiting room was bright
and too hot. It was sliding
beneath a big black wave,
another, and another.

Then I was back in it.
95 The War[2] was on. Outside,
in Worcester, Massachusetts,
were night and slush and cold,
and it was still the fifth
of February, 1918.

                                        1976

The Moose

For Grace Bulmer Bowers

From narrow provinces[3]
of fish and bread and tea,
home of the long tides
where the bay leaves the sea
5 twice a day and takes
the herrings long rides,

where if the river
enters or retreats
in a wall of brown foam
10 depends on if it meets

2. World War I.
3. The maritime provinces of Canada, including   Nova Scotia, where Bishop was born, and New Brunswick.

the bay coming in,
the bay not at home;

where, silted red,
sometimes the sun sets
15 facing a red sea,
and others, veins the flats'
lavender, rich mud
in burning rivulets;

on red, gravelly roads,
20 down rows of sugar maples,
past clapboard farmhouses
and neat, clapboard churches,
bleached, ridged as clamshells,
past twin silver birches,

25 through late afternoon
a bus journeys west,
the windshield flashing pink,
pink glancing off of metal,
brushing the dented flank
30 of blue, beat-up enamel;

down hollows, up rises,
and waits, patient, while
a lone traveller gives
kisses and embraces
35 to seven relatives
and a collie supervises.

Goodbye to the elms,
to the farm, to the dog.
The bus starts. The light
40 grows richer; the fog,
shifting, salty, thin,
comes closing in.

Its cold, round crystals
form and slide and settle
45 in the white hens' feathers,
in gray glazed cabbages,
on the cabbage roses
and lupins like apostles;

the sweet peas cling
50 to their wet white string
on the whitewashed fences;
bumblebees creep
inside the foxgloves,
and evening commences.

55 One stop at Bass River.
    Then the Economies—
    Lower, Middle, Upper;
    Five Islands, Five Houses,⁴
    where a woman shakes a tablecloth
60 out after supper.

    A pale flickering. Gone.
    The Tantramar marshes⁵
    and the smell of salt hay.
    An iron bridge trembles
65 and a loose plank rattles
    but doesn't give way.

    On the left, a red light
    swims through the dark:
    a ship's port lantern.
70 Two rubber boots show,
    illuminated, solemn.
    A dog gives one bark.

    A woman climbs in
    with two market bags,
75 brisk, freckled, elderly.
    "A grand night. Yes, sir,
    all the way to Boston."
    She regards us amicably.

    Moonlight as we enter
80 the New Brunswick woods,
    hairy, scratchy, splintery;
    moonlight and mist
    caught in them like lamb's wool
    on bushes in a pasture.

85 The passengers lie back.
    Snores. Some long sighs.
    A dreamy divagation
    begins in the night,
    a gentle, auditory,
90 slow hallucination. . . .

    In the creakings and noises,
    an old conversation
    —not concerning us,
    but recognizable, somewhere,
95 back in the bus:
    Grandparents' voices

4. Towns in Nova Scotia.
5. Marshes of the Tantramar River, which empties into the Bay of Fundy.

uninterruptedly
talking, in Eternity:
names being mentioned,
100   things cleared up finally;
what he said, what she said,
who got pensioned;

deaths, deaths and sicknesses;
the year he remarried;
105   the year (something) happened.
She died in childbirth.
That was the son lost
when the schooner foundered.

He took to drink. Yes.
110   She went to the bad.
When Amos began to pray
even in the store and
finally the family had
to put him away.

115   "Yes . . ." that peculiar
affirmative. "Yes . . ."
A sharp, indrawn breath,
half groan, half acceptance,
that means "Life's like that.
120   We know *it* (also death)."

Talking the way they talked
in the old featherbed,
peacefully, on and on,
dim lamplight in the hall,
125   down in the kitchen, the dog
tucked in her shawl.

Now, it's all right now
even to fall asleep
just as on all those nights.
130   —Suddenly the bus driver
stops with a jolt,
turns off his lights.

A moose has come out of
the impenetrable wood
135   and stands there, looms, rather,
in the middle of the road.
It approaches; it sniffs at
the bus's hot hood.

Towering, antlerless,
140   high as a church,
homely as a house

(or, safe as houses).
A man's voice assures us
"Perfectly harmless. . . ."

145   Some of the passengers
exclaim in whispers,
childishly, softly,
"Sure are big creatures."
"It's awful plain."
150   "Look! It's a she!"

Taking her time,
she looks the bus over,
grand, otherworldly.
Why, why do we feel
155   (we all feel) this sweet
sensation of joy?

"Curious creatures,"
says our quiet driver,
rolling his *r*'s.
160   "Look at that, would you."
Then he shifts gears.
For a moment longer,

by craning backward,
the moose can be seen
165   on the moonlit macadam;
then there's a dim
smell of moose, an acrid
smell of gasoline.

1976

One Art

The art of losing isn't hard to master;
so many things seem filled with the intent
to be lost that their loss is no disaster.

Lose something every day. Accept the fluster
5   of lost door keys, the hour badly spent.
The art of losing isn't hard to master.

Then practice losing farther, losing faster:
places, and names, and where it was you meant
to travel. None of these will bring disaster.

10   I lost my mother's watch. And look! my last, or
next-to-last, of three loved houses went.
The art of losing isn't hard to master.

I lost two cities, lovely ones. And, vaster,
some realms I owned, two rivers, a continent.
15 I miss them, but it wasn't a disaster.

—Even losing you (the joking voice, a gesture
I love) I shan't have lied. It's evident
the art of losing's not too hard to master
though it may look like (*Write* it!) like disaster.

1976

ALLEN CURNOW
1911–2001

Landfall in Unknown Seas[1]

The 300th Anniversary of the Discovery of New Zealand by
Abel Tasman, 13 December 1642

I

Simply by sailing in a new direction
You could enlarge the world
                    You picked your captain,
Keen on discoveries, tough enough to make them,
5   Whatever vessels could be spared from other
More urgent service for a year's adventure;
Took stock of the more probable conjectures
About the Unknown to be traversed, all
Guesses at golden coasts and tales of monsters
10 To be digested into plain instructions
For likely and unlikely situations.

All this resolved and done, you launched the whole
On a fine morning, the best time of year,
Skies widening and the oceanic furies
15 Subdued by summer illumination; time
To go and to be gazed at going
On a fine morning, in the Name of God
Into the nameless waters of the world.

O you had estimated all the chances
20 Of business in those waters, the world's waters
Yet unexploited.
                    But more than the sea-empire's
Cannon, the dogs of bronze and iron barking
From Timor to the Straits, backed up the challenge.
25 Between you and the South an older enmity
Lodged in the searching mind, that would not tolerate

---

1. Written as part of New Zealand's tercentenary celebrations.

So huge a hegemony of ignorance.
There, where your Indies had already sprinkled
Their tribes like ocean rains, you aimed your voyage;
30   Like them invoked your God, gave seas to history
And islands to new hazardous tomorrows.

II

Suddenly exhilaration
Went off like a gun, the whole
Horizon, the long chase done,
35   Hove to.[2] There was the seascape
Crammed with coast, surprising
As new lands will, the sailor
Moving on the face of the waters,
Watching the earth take shape
40   Round the unearthly summits, brighter
Than its emerging colour.

Yet this, no far fool's errand,
Was less than the heart desired,
In its old Indian dream
45   The glittering gulfs ascending
Past palaces and mountains
Making one architecture.
Here the uplifted structure,
Peak and pillar of cloud—
50   O splendour of desolation—reared
Tall from the pit of the swell,
With a shadow, a finger of wind, forbade
Hopes of a lucky landing.

Always to islanders danger
55   Is what comes over the sea;
Over the yellow sands and the clear
Shallows, the dull filament
Flickers, the blood of strangers:
Death discovered the Sailor
60   O in a flash, in a flat calm,
A clash of boats in the bay
And the day marred with murder.
The dead required no further
Warning to keep their distance;
65   The rest, noting the failure,
Pushed on with a reconnaissance
To the north; and sailed away.

III

Well, home is the Sailor,[3] and that is a chapter
In a schoolbook, a relevant yesterday

2. Dropped anchor.
3. From line 7 of "Requiem," by the Scottish   writer Robert Louis Stevenson (1850–1894): "Home is the sailor, home from sea."

70 We thought we knew all about, being much apter
        To profit, sure of our ground,
    No murderers mooring in our Golden Bay.

    But now there are no more islands to be found
    And the eye scans risky horizons of its own
75 In unsettled weather, and murmurs of the drowned
        Haunt their familiar beaches—
    Who navigates us towards what unknown

    But not improbable provinces? Who teaches
    A future down for us from the high shelf
80 Of spiritual daring? Not those speeches
        Pinning on the Past like a decoration
    For merit that congratulates itself,

    O not the self-important celebration
    Or most painstaking history, can release
85 The current of a discoverer's elation
        And silence the voices saying,
    "Here is the world's end where wonders cease."

    Only by a more faithful memory, laying
    On him the half-light of a diffident glory,
90 The Sailor lives, and stands beside us, paying
        Out into our time's wave
    The stain of blood that writes an island story.

1942   1943

IRVING LAYTON
b. 1912

The Birth of Tragedy[1]

    And me happiest when I compose poems.
        Love, power, the huzza of battle
        are something, are much;
    yet a poem includes them like a pool
5   water and reflection.
    In me, nature's divided things—
        tree, mold on tree—
        have their fruition;
    I am their core. Let them swap,
10 bandy, like a flame swerve
    I am their mouth; as a mouth I serve.

1. The first book (1872) by the German philosopher Friedrich Nietzsche (1844–1900), *The Birth of Tragedy* argued for the importance of Dionysian emotionalism as well as Apollonian rationalism in the creation of tragedy.

And I observe how the sensual moths
         big with odor and sunshine
         dart into the perilous shrubbery;
15 or drop their visiting shadows
         upon the garden I one year made
of flowering stone to be a footstool
         for the perfect gods:
         who, friends to the ascending orders,
20 sustain all passionate meditations
and call down pardons
for the insurgent blood.

A quiet madman, never far from tears,
         I lie like a slain thing
25   under the green air the trees
inhabit, or rest upon a chair
         towards which the inflammable air
tumbles on many robins' wings;
         noting how seasonably
30   leaf and blossom uncurl
and living things arrange their death,
while someone from afar off
blows birthday candles for the world.

                                                 1954

The Cold Green Element

At the end of the garden walk
the wind and its satellite wait for me;
their meaning I will not know
         until I go there,
5 but the black-hatted undertaker

who, passing, saw my heart beating in the grass,
is also going there. Hi, I tell him,
a great squall in the Pacific blew a dead poet
         out of the water,
10 Who now hangs from the city's gates.

Crowds depart daily to see it, and return
with grimaces and incomprehension;
if its limbs twitched in the air
         they would sit at its feet
15 peeling their oranges.

And turning over I embrace like a lover
the trunk of a tree, one of those
for whom the lightning was too much
         and grew a brilliant
20 hunchback with a crown of leaves.

The ailments escaped from the labels
of medicine bottles are all fled to the wind;
I've seen myself lately in the eyes
    of old women,
25 spent streams mourning my manhood,

in whose old pupils the sun became
a bloodsmear on broad catalpa leaves
and hanging from ancient twigs,
    my murdered selves
30 sparked the air like the muted collisions

of fruit. A black dog howls down my blood,
a black dog with yellow eyes;
he too by someone's inadvertence
    saw the bloodsmear
35 on the broad catalpa leaves.

But the furies[2] clear a path for me to the worm
who sang for an hour in the throat of a robin,
and misled by the cries of young boys
    I am again
40 a breathless swimmer in that cold green element.

                                             1955

Berry Picking

Silently my wife walks on the still wet furze
Now darkgreen the leaves are full of metaphors
Now lit up is each tiny lamp of blueberry.
The white nails of rain have dropped and the sun is free.

5 And whether she bends or straightens to each bush
To find the children's laughter among the leaves
Her quiet hands seem to make the quiet summer hush—
Berries or children, patient she is with these.

I only vex and perplex her; madness, rage
10 Are endearing perhaps put down upon the page;
Even silence daylong and sullen can then
Enamor as restraint or classic discipline.

So I envy the berries she puts in her mouth,
The red and succulent juice that stains her lips;
15 I shall never taste that good to her, nor will they
Displease her with a thousand barbarous jests.

---

2. In classical mythology, goddesses who punished the doers of unavenged wrongs.

How they lie easily for her hand to take,
Part of the unoffending world that is hers;
Here beyond complexity she stands and stares
20   And leans her marvelous head as if for answers.

No more the easy soul my childish craft deceives
Nor the simpler one for whom yes is always yes;
No, now her voice comes to me from a far way off
Though her lips are redder than the raspberries.

1958

ROBERT HAYDEN
1913–1980

Those Winter Sundays

Sundays too my father got up early
and put his clothes on in the blueblack cold,
then with cracked hands that ached
from labor in the weekday weather made
5   banked fires blaze. No one ever thanked him.

I'd wake and hear the cold splintering, breaking.
When the rooms were warm, he'd call,
and slowly I would rise and dress,
fearing the chronic angers of that house,

10   Speaking indifferently to him,
who had driven out the cold
and polished my good shoes as well.
What did I know, what did I know
of love's austere and lonely offices?

1962

Mourning Poem for the Queen of Sunday

Lord's lost Him His mockingbird,
His fancy warbler;
Satan sweet-talked her,
four bullets hushed her.
5   Who would have thought
she'd end that way?

Four bullets hushed her. And the world a-clang with evil.
Who's going to make old hardened sinner men tremble now
and the righteous rock?

10   Oh who and oh who will sing Jesus down
to help with struggling and doing without and being colored
all through blue Monday?
Till way next Sunday?

15   All those angels
in their cretonne[1] clouds and finery
the true believer saw
when she rared back her head and sang,
all those angels are surely weeping.
Who would have thought
20   she'd end that way?

Four holes in her heart. The gold works wrecked.
But she looks so natural in her big bronze coffin
among the Broken Hearts and Gates-Ajar,
it's as if any moment she'd lift her head
25 from its pillow of chill gardenias
and turn this quiet into shouting Sunday
and make folks forget what she did on Monday.

      Oh, Satan sweet-talked her,
and four bullets hushed her.
30 Lord's lost Him His diva,
His fancy warbler's gone.
Who would have thought,
who would have thought she'd end that way?

                                  1966

Night, Death, Mississippi[2]

I

A quavering cry. Screech-owl?
Or one of them?
The old man in his reek
and gauntness laughs—

5 One of them, I bet—
and turns out the kitchen lamp,
limping to the porch to listen
in the windowless night.

     Be there with Boy and the rest
10 if I was well again.
Time was. Time was.
White robes like moonlight

---

1. Cotton or linen cloth.
2. In Philadelphia, Mississippi, in 1964, Ku Klux Klansmen and police deputies murdered Michael Schwerner, Andrew Goodman, and James Chaney, civil rights activists known as Freedom Fighters, who were challenging segregationist laws in the South.

In the sweetgum[3] dark.
Unbucked that one then
15 and him squealing bloody Jesus
as we cut it off.

Time was. A cry?
A cry all right.
He hawks and spits,
20 fevered as by groinfire.

Have us a bottle,
Boy and me—
he's earned him a bottle—
when he gets home.

II

25 Then we beat them, he said,
beat them till our arms was tired
and the big old chains
messy and red.

O Jesus burning on the lily cross

30 Christ, it was better
than hunting bear
which don't know why
you want him dead.

O night, rawhead and bloodybones night

35 You kids fetch Paw
some water now so's he
can wash that blood
off him, she said.

O night betrayed by darkness not its own

1966

" 'Mystery Boy' Looks for Kin in Nashville"

Puzzle faces in the dying elms
promise him treats if he will stay.
Sometimes they hiss and spit at him
like varmints caught
5 in a thicket of butterflies.

---

3. The dark woods of the sweet gum, a North American tree of a deep reddish brown grain.

A black doll,
one disremembered time,
came floating down to him
through mimosa's fancywork leaves and blooms
10 to be his hidden bride.

From the road beyond the creepered walls
they call to him now and then,
and he'll take off in spite of the angry trees,
hearing like the loudening of his heart
15 the name he never can he never can repeat.

And when he gets to where the voices were—
Don't cry, his dollbaby wife implores;
I know where they are, don't cry.
We'll go and find them, we'll go
20 and ask them for your name again.

1977

Paul Laurence Dunbar[4]

For Herbert Martin

We lay red roses on his grave,
speak sorrowfully of him
as if he were but newly dead

And so it seems to us
5 this raw spring day, though years
before we two were born he was
a young poet dead.

Poet of our youth—
his "cri du coeur"[5] our own,
10 his verses "in a broken tongue"

beguiling as an elder
brother's antic lore.
Their sad blackface lilt and croon
survive him like

15 The happy look (subliminal
of victim, dying man)
a summer's tintypes[6] hold.

---

4. African American poet (1872–1906; see pp. 1222–24).
5. Passionate appeal or protest (French; literally,
cry from the heart). The next line is probably a reference to Dunbar's poems in dialect (blackface).
6. I.e., old photographs.

> The roses flutter in the wind;
> we weight their stems
> 20 with stones, then drive away.

1978

MURIEL RUKEYSER
1913–1980

Boy with His Hair Cut Short

Sunday shuts down on this twentieth-century evening.
The El° passes. Twilight and bulb define   *elevated train*
the brown room, the overstuffed plum sofa,
the boy, and the girl's thin hands above his head.
5   A neighbor radio sings stocks, news, serenade.

He sits at the table, head down, the young clear neck exposed,
watching the drugstore sign from the tail of his eye;
tattoo, neon, until the eye blears, while his
solicitous tall sister, simple in blue, bending
10   behind him, cuts his hair with her cheap shears.

The arrow's electric red always reaches its mark,
successful neon! He coughs, impressed by that precision.
His child's forehead, forever protected by his cap,
is bleached against the lamplight as he turns head
15   and steadies to let the snippets drop.

Erasing the failure of weeks with level fingers,
she sleeks the fine hair, combing: "You'll look fine tomorrow!
You'll surely find something, they can't keep turning you down;
the finest gentleman's not so trim as you!" Smiling, he raises
20   the adolescent forehead wrinkling ironic now.

He sees his decent suit laid out, new-pressed,
his carfare on the shelf. He lets his head fall, meeting
her earnest hopeless look, seeing the sharp blades splitting,
the darkened room, the impersonal sign, her motion,
25   the blue vein, bright on her temple, pitifully beating.

1938

Night Feeding

Deeper than sleep but not so deep as death
I lay there sleeping and my magic head

remembered and forgot.   On first cry I
remembered and forgot and did believe.
5 I knew love and I knew evil:
woke to the burning song and the tree burning blind,
despair of our days and the calm milk-giver who
knows sleep, knows growth, the sex of fire and grass,
and the black snake with gold bones.

10 Black sleeps, gold burns;   on second cry I woke
fully and gave to feed and fed on feeding.
Cold seed, green pain, my wizards in the earth
walked through the house, black in the morning dark.
Shadows grew in my veins, my bright belief,
15 my head of dreams deeper than night and sleep.
Voices of all black animals crying to drink,
cries of all birth arise, simple as we,
found in the leaves, in clouds and dark, in dream,
deep as this hour, ready again to sleep.

1951

Rondel[1]

Now that I am fifty-six
Come and celebrate with me—

What happens to song and sex
Now that I am fifty-six?

5 They dance, but differently,
Death and distance in the mix;
Now that I'm fifty-six
Come and celebrate with me.

1973

Ballad of Orange and Grape

After you finish your work
after you do your day
after you've read your reading
after you've written your say—
5 you go down the street to the hot dog stand,
one block down and across the way.
On a blistering afternoon in East Harlem in the twentieth century.

---

1. Based loosely on the French syllabic verse form, a thirteen-line poem that turns on two rhymes, with a refrain.

Most of the windows are boarded up,
the rats run out of a sack—
10 sticking out of the crummy garage
one shiny long Cadillac;
at the glass door of the drug-addiction center,
a man who'd like to break your back.
But here's a brown woman with a little girl dressed in rose and pink,
    too.

15 Frankfurters frankfurters sizzle on the steel
where the hot-dog-man leans—
nothing else on the counter
but the usual two machines,
the grape one, empty, and the orange one, empty,
20 I face him in between.
A black boy comes along, looks at the hot dogs, goes on walking.

I watch the man as he stands and pours
in the familiar shape
bright purple in the one marked ORANGE
25 orange in the one marked GRAPE,
the grape drink in the machine marked ORANGE
and orange drink in the GRAPE.
Just the one word large and clear, unmistakable, on each machine.

I ask him :   How can we go on reading
30 and make sense out of what we read?—
How can they write and believe what they're writing,
the young ones across the street,
while you go on pouring grape into ORANGE
and orange into the one marked GRAPE—?
35 (How are we going to believe what we read and we write and we hear
    and we say and we do?)

He looks at the two machines and he smiles
and he shrugs and smiles and pours again.
It could be violence and nonviolence
it could be white and black   women and men
40 it could be war and peace or any
binary system, love and hate, enemy, friend.
Yes and no, be and not-be, what we do and what we don't do.

On a corner in East Harlem
garbage, reading, a deep smile, rape,
45 forgetfulness, a hot street of murder,
misery, withered hope,
a man keeps pouring grape into ORANGE
and orange into the one marked GRAPE,
pouring orange into GRAPE and grape into ORANGE forever.

1973

MAY SWENSON
1913–1989

Motherhood

She sat on a shelf,
her breasts two bellies
on her poked-out belly,
on which the navel looked
5   like a sucked in mouth
her knees bent and apart,
her long left arm raised,
with the large hand knuckled
to a bar in the ceiling—
10   her right hand clamping
the skinny infant to her chest—
its round, pale, new,
soft muzzle hunting
in the brown hair for a nipple,
15   its splayed, tiny hand picking
at her naked, dirty ear.
Twisting its little neck,
with tortured, ecstatic eyes
the size of lentils, it looked
20   into her severe, close-set,
solemn eyes, that beneath bald
eyelids glared—dull lights
in sockets of leather.

She twitched some chin-hairs,
25   with pain or pleasure,
as the baby-mouth found and
yanked at her nipple;
its pink-nailed, jointless
fingers, wandering her face,
30   tangled in the tufts
of her cliffy brows.
She brought her big
hand down from the bar—
with pretended exasperation
35   unfastened the little hand,
and locked it within her palm—
while her right hand,
with snag-nailed forefinger
and short, sharp thumb, raked
40   the new orange hair
of the infant's skinny flank—
and found a louse,
which she lipped, and
thoughtfully crisped
45   between broad teeth.

She wrinkled appreciative
nostrils which, without a nose,
stood open—damp holes
above the poke of her mouth.

50 She licked her lips, flicked
her leather eyelids—
then, suddenly flung
up both arms and grabbed
the bars overhead.
55 The baby's scrabbly fingers
instantly caught the hair—
as if there were metal rings there—
in her long, stretched armpits.
And, as she stately swung,
60 and then proudly, more swiftly
slung herself from corner
to corner of her cell—
arms longer than her round
body, short knees bent—
65 her little wild-haired,
poke-mouthed infant hung,
like some sort of trophy,
or decoration, or shaggy medal—
shaped like herself—but new,
70 clean, soft and shining
on her chest.

1967

Cardinal Ideograms[1]

0 A mouth. Can blow or breathe,
be funnel, or Hello.

1 A grass blade or a cut.

2 A question seated. And a proud
bird's neck.

3 Shallow mitten for two-fingered hand.

4 Three-cornered hut
on one stilt. Sometimes built
so the roof gapes.

1. Counting numbers interpreted as if they were pictures.

5
A policeman. Polite.
Wearing visored cap.

6
O unrolling,
tape of ambiguous length
on which is written the mystery
of everything curly.

7
A step,
detached from its stair.

8
The universe in diagram:
A cosmic hourglass.
(Note enigmatic shape,
absence of any valve of origin,
how end overlaps beginning.)
Unknotted like a shoelace
and whipped back and forth,
can serve as a model of time.

9
Lorgnette for the right eye.
In England or if you are Alice[2]
the stem is on the left.

10
A grass blade or a cut
companioned by a mouth.
Open? Open. Shut? Shut.

1967

Waterbird

Part otter, part snake, part bird the bird Anhinga,[3]
jalousie° wings, draped open, dry. When slack-   *shutterlike*
hinged, the wind flips them shut. Her cry,
a slatted clatter, inflates her chin-
5   pouch; it's like a fish's swim-
bladder. Anhinga's body, otter-
furry, floats, under water-
mosses, neck a snake with white-
rimmed blue round roving eyes. Those long feet stilt-
10 paddle the only bird of the marsh that flies
submerged. Otter-
quick over bream° that hover in water-   *fish*
shade, she feeds, finds fillets among the water-
weeds. Her beak, ferrule° of a folded black   *metal tip*

2. Alice, who sees the mirror images of things in the book *Through the Looking-Glass*, by the English mathematician and writer Lewis Carroll (1832–1898; see pp. 1135–39). *Lorgnette:* eye-glasses or opera glasses with a handle.
3. Also known as snake-bird or water-turkey. With a long fantail and thin neck, it swims submerged up to the neck, thus resembling a snake.

15 umbrella, with neat thrust impales her prey.
She flaps up to dry on the crooked, look-
dead-limb of the Gumbo Limbo,[4] her tan-
tipped wing fans spread, tail a shut fan dangled.

1987

Goodbye, Goldeneye[5]

Rag of black plastic, shred of a kite
caught on the telephone cable above the bay
has twisted in the wind all winter, summer, fall.

Leaves of birch and maple, brown paws of the oak
5 have all let go but this. Shiny black Mylar[6]
on stem strong as fishline, the busted kite string

whipped around the wire and knotted—how long
will it cling there? Through another spring?
Long barge nudged up channel by a snorting tug,

10 its blunt front aproned with rot-black tires—
what is being hauled in slime-green drums?
The herring gulls that used to feed their young

on the shore—puffy, wide-beaked babies standing
spraddle-legged and crying—are not here this year.
15 Instead, steam shovel, bulldozer, cement mixer

rumble over sand, beginning the big new beach house.
There'll be a hotdog stand, flush toilets, trash—
plastic and glass, greasy cartons, crushed beercans,

barrels of garbage for water rats to pick through.
20 So, goodbye, goldeneye, and grebe and scaup and loon.
Goodbye, morning walks beside the tide tinkling

among clean pebbles, blue mussel shells and snail
shells that look like staring eyeballs. Goodbye,
kingfisher, little green, black crowned heron,

25 snowy egret. And, goodbye, oh faithful pair of
swans that used to glide—god and goddess
shapes of purity—over the wide water.

1987

---

4. Tropical American tree with a smooth, coppery
bark.
5. The goldeneye, like the grebe, scaup, and loon

mentioned in line 20, is a freshwater diving duck.
6. Brand of strong, thin polyester film, here used
in string.

R. S. THOMAS
1913–2000

Welsh Landscape

> To live in Wales is to be conscious
> At dusk of the spilled blood
> That went to the making of the wild sky,
> Dyeing the immaculate rivers
> 5   In all their courses.
> It is to be aware,
> Above the noisy tractor
> And hum of the machine
> Of strife in the strung woods,
> 10   Vibrant with sped arrows.
> You cannot live in the present,
> At least not in Wales.
> There is the language for instance,
> The soft consonants
> 15   Strange to the ear.
> There are cries in the dark at night
> As owls answer the moon,
> And thick ambush of shadows,
> Hushed at the fields' corners.
> 20   There is no present in Wales,
> And no future;
> There is only the past,
> Brittle with relics,
> Wind-bitten towers and castles
> 25   With sham ghosts;
> Mouldering quarries and mines;
> And an impotent people,
> Sick with inbreeding,
> Worrying the carcase of an old song.

1955

The View from the Window

> Like a painting it is set before one,
> But less brittle, ageless; these colours
> Are renewed daily with variations
> Of light and distance that no painter
> 5   Achieves or suggests. Then there is movement,
> Change, as slowly the cloud bruises
> Are healed by sunlight, or snow caps
> A black mood; but gold at evening
> To cheer the heart. All through history
> 10   The great brush has not rested,

Nor the paint dried; yet what eye,
Looking coolly, or, as we now,
Through the tears' lenses, ever saw
This work and it was not finished?

                                                                1958

On the Farm

There was Dai Puw. He was no good.
They put him in the fields to dock° swedes,°   cut / turnips
And took the knife from him, when he came home
At late evening with a grin
5   Like the slash of a knife on his face.

There was Llew Puw, and he was no good.
Every evening after the ploughing
With the big tractor he would sit in his chair,
And stare into the tangled fire garden,
10 Opening his slow lips like a snail.

There was Huw Puw, too. What shall I say?
I have heard him whistling in the hedges
On and on, as though winter
Would never again leave those fields,
15 And all the trees were deformed.

And lastly there was the girl:
Beauty under some spell of the beast.
Her pale face was the lantern
By which they read in life's dark book
20 The shrill sentence: God is love.

                                                                1963

Lore

Job Davies, eighty-five
Winters old, and still alive
After the slow poison
And treachery of the seasons.

5   Miserable? Kick my arse!
It needs more than the rain's hearse,
Wind-drawn, to pull me off
The great perch of my laugh.

What's living but courage?
10   Paunch full of hot porridge,
Nerves strengthened with tea,
Peat-black, dawn found me

Mowing where the grass grew,
Bearded with golden dew.
15   Rhythm of the long scythe
Kept this tall frame lithe.

What to do? Stay green.
Never mind the machine,
Whose fuel is human souls.
20   Live large, man, and dream small.

1964

JOHN BERRYMAN
1914–1972

From Homage to Mistress Bradstreet[1]

[17]

The winters close, Springs open, no child stirs
130   under my withering heart, O seasoned heart
God grudged his aid.
All things else soil like a shirt.
Simon is much away. My executive[2] stales.
The town came through for the cartway by the pales,[3]
135   but my patience is short.
I revolt from, I am like, these savage foresters

[18]

whose passionless dicker in the shade, whose glance
impassive & scant, belie their murderous cries
when quarry seems to show.
140   Again I must have been wrong, twice.[4]
Unwell in a new way. Can that begin?
God brandishes. O love, O I love. Kin,
gather. My world is strange
and merciful, ingrown months, blessing a swelling trance.

1. Berryman's book-length poem about, and mostly in the voice of, the early American poet Anne Bradstreet (ca. 1612–1672; see pp. 458–67). Bradstreet speaks here of her struggle in childbirth. For a discussion of the complex stanza form Berryman invented for this poem (modeled partly on W. B. Yeats's "In Memory of Major Gregory"), as well as the form of the "dream song," see the introduction to Berryman's Collected Poems 1937– 1971 (1989), by Charles Thornbury, xl–xliii.
2. Power to act. Simon: her husband.
3. Stockade fence.
4. I.e., she twice failed to conceive.

[19]

145 So squeezed, wince you I scream? I love you & hate
off with you. Ages! *Useless*. Below my waist
he has me in Hell's vise.
Stalling. He let go. Come back: brace
me somewhere. No. No. Yes! everything down
150 hardens I press with horrible joy down
my back cracks like a wrist
shame I am voiding oh behind it is too late

[20]

hide me forever I work thrust I must free
now I all muscles & bones concentrate
155 what is living from dying?
Simon I must leave you so untidy
Monster you are killing me Be sure
I'll have you later Women do endure
I can *can* no longer
160 and it passes the wretched trap whelming and I am me

[21]

drencht & powerful, I did it with my body!
One proud tug greens Heaven. Marvellous,
unforbidding Majesty.
Swell, imperious bells. I fly.
165 Mountainous, woman not breaks and will bend:
sways God nearby: anguish comes to an end.
Blossomed Sarah,[5] and I
blossom. Is that thing alive? I hear a famisht howl.

1948–53   1956

A Sympathy, A Welcome

Feel for your bad fall how could I fail,
poor Paul, who had it so good.
I can offer you only: this world like a knife.
Yet you'll get to know your mother
5 and humourless as you do look you will laugh
and all the others
will NOT be fierce to you, and loverhood
will swing your soul like a broken bell
deep in a forsaken wood, poor Paul,
10 whose wild bad father loves you well.

1958

5. Wife of Abraham, who after long barrenness gave birth to Isaac (Genesis 17.19).

From The Dream Songs[6]

1

Huffy Henry hid   the day,
unappeasable Henry sulked.
I see his point,—a trying to put things over.
It was the thought that they thought
5   they could *do* it made Henry wicked & away.
But he should have come out and talked.

All the world like a woolen lover
once did seem on Henry's side.
Then came a departure.
10   Thereafter nothing fell out as it might or ought.
I don't see how Henry, pried
open for all the world to see, survived.

What he has now to say is a long
wonder the world can bear & be.
15   Once in a sycamore I was glad
all at the top, and I sang.
Hard on the land wears the strong sea
and empty grows every bed.

1964

4

Filling her compact & delicious body
with chicken páprika, she glanced at me
twice.
Fainting with interest, I hungered back
5   and only the fact of her husband & four other people
kept me from springing on her

or falling at her little feet and crying
"You are the hottest one for years of night
Henry's dazed eyes
10   have enjoyed, Brilliance." I advanced upon
(despairing) my spumoni.—Sir Bones: is stuffed,
de world, wif feeding girls.

—Black hair, complexion Latin, jeweled eyes
downcast . . . The slob beside her   feasts . . . What wonders is
15   she sitting on, over there?
The restaurant buzzes. She might as well be on Mars.

---

6. "[The Dream Songs are] essentially about an imaginary character (not the poet, not me) named Henry, a white American in early middle age sometimes in blackface, who has suffered an irreversible loss and talks about himself sometimes in the first person, sometimes in the third, sometimes even in the second; he has a friend, never named, who addresses him as Mr. Bones and variants thereof" [Berryman's note]. These poems were written over a period of thirteen years.

Where did it all go wrong? There ought to be a law against Henry.
—Mr. Bones: there is.

1964

14

Life, friends, is boring. We must not say so.
After all, the sky flashes, the great sea yearns,
we ourselves flash and yearn,
and moreover my mother told me as a boy
5   (repeatedly) "Ever to confess you're bored
means you have no

Inner Resources." I conclude now I have no
inner resources, because I am heavy bored.
Peoples bore me,
10 literature bores me, especially great literature,
Henry bores me, with his plights & gripes
as bad as achilles,[7]

who loves people and valiant art, which bores me.
And the tranquil hills, & gin, look like a drag
15 and somehow a dog
has taken itself & its tail considerably away
into mountains or sea or sky, leaving
behind: me, wag.

1964

29

There sat down, once, a thing on Henry's heart
só heavy, if he had a hundred years
& more, & weeping, sleepless, in all them time
Henry could not make good.
5 Starts again always in Henry's ears
the little cough somewhere, an odor, a chime.

And there is another thing he has in mind
like a grave Sienese face[8] a thousand years
would fail to blur the still profiled reproach of. Ghastly,
10 with open eyes, he attends, blind.
All the bells say: too late. This is not for tears;
thinking.

But never did Henry, as he thought he did,
end anyone and hacks her body up

---

7. The Greek hero of Homer's *Iliad,* who withdrew from battle because of a slight from Agamemnon. Berryman claimed that some of the structure of *The Dream Songs* could be traced to parallel scenes in the *Iliad.* "The chief enemy, in Achilles' case, was Hector, whom Berryman explicitly equated with Henry's father" [John Haffenden, *John Berryman: A Critical Commentary,* 1980, 55].
8. The painters of thirteenth- and fourteenth-century Siena, Italy, were known for their austere religious portraits.

15   and hide the pieces, where they may be found.
He knows: he went over everyone, & nobody's missing.
Often he reckons, in the dawn, them up.
Nobody is ever missing.

1964

40

I'm scared a lonely. Never see my son,
easy be not to see anyone,
combers out to sea
know they're goin somewhere but not me.
5 Got a little poison, got a little gun,
I'm scared a lonely.

I'm scared a only one thing, which is me,
from othering I don't take nothin, see,
for any hound dog's sake.
10 But this is where I livin, where I rake
my leaves and cop my promise,[9] this' where we
cry oursel's awake.

Wishin was dyin but I gotta make
it all this way to that bed on these feet
15 where peoples said to meet.
Maybe but even if I see my son
forever never, get back on the take,
free, black & forty-one.[1]

1964

145

Also I love him: me he's done no wrong
for going on forty years—forgiveness time—
I touch now his despair,
he felt as bad as Whitman[2] on his tower
5 but he did not swim out with me or my brother
as he threatened—

a powerful swimmer, to   take one of us along
as company in the defeat sublime,
freezing my helpless mother:
10 he only, very early in the morning,
rose with his gun and went outdoors by my window
and did what was needed.

---

9. Build my potential.
1. A play on the phrase *free, white and twenty-one*, connoting independence.
2. Charles Whitman, a sniper who, from a tower at the University of Texas at Austin, sprayed the campus with bullets for eighty minutes on August 1, 1966. Whitman wrote of fear and violent impulses before his mass killing. "He" here refers to Berryman's father, John Smith, who committed suicide when the poet was twelve years old.

I cannot read that wretched mind, so strong
& so undone. I've always tried. I—I'm
15   trying to forgive
whose frantic passage, when he could not live
an instant longer, in the summer dawn
left Henry to live on.

1968

324. *An Elegy for W.C.W.,*[3] *The Lovely Man*

Henry in Ireland to Bill underground:
Rest well, who worked so hard, who made a good sound
constantly, for so many years:
your high-jinks delighted the continents & our ears:
5   you had so many girls your life was a triumph
and you loved your one wife.

At dawn you rose & wrote—the books poured forth—
you delivered infinite babies,[4] in one great birth—
and your generosity
10   to juniors made you deeply loved, deeply:
if envy was a Henry trademark, he would envy you,
especially the being through.

Too many journeys lie for him ahead,
too many galleys & page-proofs to be read,
15   he would like to lie down
in your sweet silence, to whom was not denied
the mysterious late excellence which is the crown
of our trials & our last bride.

1968

382

At Henry's bier let some thing fall out well:
enter there none who somewhat has to sell,
the music ancient & gradual,
the voices solemn but the grief subdued,
5   no hairy jokes but everybody's mood
subdued, subdued,

until the Dancer comes, in a short short dress
hair black & long & loose, dark dark glasses,
uptilted face,
10   pallor & strangeness, the music changes
to "Give!" & "Ow!" and how! the music changes,
she kicks a backward limb

---

3. The American poet William Carlos Williams (1883–1963; see pp. 1272–83).

4. Williams was a physician and specialized in pediatrics.

on tiptoe, pirouettes, & she is free
to the knocking music, sails, dips, & suddenly
15 returns to the terrible gay
occasion hopeless & mad, she weaves, it's hell,
she flings to her head a leg, bobs, all is well,
she dances Henry away.

1968

RANDALL JARRELL
1914–1965

90 North[1]

At home, in my flannel gown, like a bear to its floe,
I clambered to bed; up the globe's impossible sides
I sailed all night—till at last, with my black beard,
My furs and my dogs, I stood at the northern pole.

5 There in the childish night my companions lay frozen,
The stiff furs knocked at my starveling throat,
And I gave my great sigh: the flakes came huddling,
Were they really my end? In the darkness I turned to my rest.

—Here, the flag snaps in the glare and silence
10 Of the unbroken ice. I stand here,
The dogs bark, my beard is black, and I stare
At the North Pole . . .
                            And now what? Why, go back.

Turn as I please, my step is to the south.
The world—my world spins on this final point
15 Of cold and wretchedness: all lines, all winds
End in this whirlpool I at last discover.

And it is meaningless. In the child's bed
After the night's voyage, in that warm world
Where people work and suffer for the end
20 That crowns the pain—in that Cloud-Cuckoo-Land[2]

I reached my North and it had meaning.
Here at the actual pole of my existence,
Where all that I have done is meaningless,
Where I die or live by accident alone—

25 Where, living or dying, I am still alone;
Here where North, the night, the berg of death

1. Ninety degrees north latitude; the North Pole.
2. In the comedy *The Birds,* by the Greek drama-
tist Aristophanes (ca. 450–ca. 388 B.C.E.), an imag-
inary city the cuckoos build in the clouds.

Crowd me out of the ignorant darkness,
I see at last that all the knowledge

I wrung from the darkness—that the darkness flung me—
30   Is worthless as ignorance: nothing comes from nothing,[3]
The darkness from the darkness. Pain comes from the darkness
And we call it wisdom. It is pain.

                                                                    1942

The Death of the Ball Turret Gunner[4]

From my mother's sleep I fell into the State,
And I hunched in its belly till my wet fur froze.
Six miles from earth, loosed from its dream of life,
I woke to black flak and the nightmare fighters.
5   When I died they washed me out of the turret with a hose.

                                                                    1945

Eighth Air Force[5]

If, in an odd angle of the hutment,°   *encampment*
A puppy laps the water from a can
Of flowers, and the drunk sergeant shaving
Whistles O *Paradiso!*[6]—shall I say that man
5   Is not as men have said: a wolf to man?

The other murderers troop in yawning;
Three of them play Pitch,° one sleeps, and one   *a card game*
Lies counting missions, lies there sweating
Till even his heart beats: One; One; One.
10   O *murderers!* . . . Still, this is how it's done:

This is a war. . . . But since these play, before they die,
Like puppies with their puppy; since, a man,
I did as these have done, but did not die—
I will content the people as I can
15   And give up these to them: Behold the man![7]

---

3. Cf. Shakespeare, *King Lear* 1.1.89: "Nothing will come of nothing"; also a statement in Aristotle, *Physics* 1.
4. "A ball turret was a plexiglass sphere set into the belly of a B-17 or B-24, and inhabited by two .50 caliber machine-guns and one man, a short small man. When this gunner tracked with his machine-guns a fighter attacking his bomber from below, he revolved with the turret; hunched upside-down in his little sphere, he looked like the foetus in the womb. The fighters which attacked him were armed with cannon firing explosive shells. The hose was a steam hose" [Jarrell's note].
5. "A poem about the air force which bombed the Continent from England. The man who lies counting missions has one to go before being sent home. The phrases from the Gospels compare such criminals and scapegoats as these with that earlier criminal and scapegoat about whom the Gospels were written" [Jarrell's note].
6. A popular operatic aria.
7. Quoting John 19.5: these are Pilate's words as he presents Jesus, scourged and wearing a crown of thorns, to the crowd.

I have suffered, in a dream, because of him,
Many things;[8] for this last saviour, man,
I have lied as I lie now. But what is lying?
Men wash their hands, in blood, as best they can:
20   I find no fault in this just man.[9]

1945

A Front[1]

Fog over the base: the beams ranging
From the five towers pull home from the night
The crews cold in fur, the bombers banging
Like lost trucks down the levels of the ice.
5   A glow drifts in like mist (how many tons of it?),
Bounces to a roll, turns suddenly to steel
And tires and turrets, huge in the trembling light.
The next is high, and pulls up with a wail,
Comes round again—no use. And no use for the rest
10   In drifting circles out along the range;
Holding no longer, changed to a kinder course,
The flights drone southward through the steady rain.
The base is closed. . . . But one voice keeps on calling,
The lowering pattern of the engines grows;
15   The roar gropes downward in its shaky orbit
For the lives the season quenches. Here below
They beg, order, are not heard; and hear the darker
Voice rising: *Can't you hear me? Over. Over—*
All the air quivers, and the east sky glows.

1945

A Field Hospital

He stirs, beginning to awake.
A kind of ache
Of knowing troubles his blind warmth; he moans,
And the high hammering drone
5   Of the first crossing fighters shakes
His sleep to pieces, rakes
The darkness with its skidding bursts, is done.
All that he has known

---

8. Pilate's wife wrote to him about Jesus: "Have nothing to do with that just man: for I have suffered many things this day in a dream because of him" (Matthew 27.19).
9. After the crowd had called on him to free the robber Barabbas and execute Jesus, Pilate had Jesus brought forth, "that you may know that I find no fault in him" (John 19.4–5). Pilate washed his hands to symbolize his freedom from responsibility for Christ's death.
1. "A front is closing in over a bomber base; the bombers, guided in by signals from the five towers of the radio range, are landing. Only one lands before the base is closed; the rest fly south to fields that are still open. One plane's radio has gone bad—it still transmits, but doesn't receive—and this plane tries to land and crashes" [Jarrell's note].

Floods in upon him; but he dreads
10 The crooked thread
Of fire upon the darkness: "The great drake
Flutters to the icy lake—
The shotguns stammer in my head.
I lie in my own bed,"
15 He whispers, "dreaming"; and he thinks to wake.
The old mistake.

A cot creaks; and he hears the groan
He thinks his own—
And groans, and turns his stitched, blind, bandaged head
20 Up to the tent-flap, red
With dawn. A voice says, "Yes, this one";
His arm stings; then, alone,
He neither knows, remembers—but instead
Sleeps, comforted.

1948

Next Day

Moving from Cheer to Joy, from Joy to All,
I take a box
And add it to my wild rice, my Cornish game hens.
The slacked or shorted, basketed, identical
5 Food-gathering flocks
Are selves I overlook. Wisdom, said William James,

Is learning what to overlook.[2] And I am wise
If that is wisdom.
Yet somehow, as I buy All from these shelves
10 And the boy takes it to my station wagon,
What I've become
Troubles me even if I shut my eyes.

When I was young and miserable and pretty
And poor, I'd wish
15 What all girls wish: to have a husband,
A house and children. Now that I'm old, my wish
Is womanish:
That the boy putting groceries in my car

See me. It bewilders me he doesn't see me.
20 For so many years
I was good enough to eat: the world looked at me
And its mouth watered. How often they have undressed me,
The eyes of strangers!
And, holding their flesh within my flesh, their vile

2. From *Principles of Psychology*, by the American philosopher William James (1842–1910).

25   Imaginings within my imagining,
      I too have taken
      The chance of life. Now the boy pats my dog
      And we start home. Now I am good.
      The last mistaken,
30   Ecstatic, accidental bliss, the blind

      Happiness that, bursting, leaves upon the palm
      Some soap and water—
      It was so long ago, back in some Gay
      Twenties, Nineties, I don't know . . . Today I miss
35   My lovely daughter
      Away at school, my sons away at school,

      My husband away at work—I wish for them.
      The dog, the maid,
      And I go through the sure unvarying days
40   At home in them. As I look at my life,
      I am afraid
      Only that it will change, as I am changing:

      I am afraid, this morning, of my face.
      It looks at me
45   From the rear-view mirror, with the eyes I hate,
      The smile I hate. Its plain, lined look
      Of gray discovery
      Repeats to me: "You're old." That's all, I'm old.

      And yet I'm afraid, as I was at the funeral
50   I went to yesterday.
      My friend's cold made-up face, granite among its flowers,
      Her undressed, operated-on, dressed body
      Were my face and body.
      As I think of her I hear her telling me

55   How young I seem; I *am* exceptional;
      I think of all I have.
      But really no one is exceptional,
      No one has anything, I'm anybody,
      I stand beside my grave
60   Confused with my life, that is commonplace and solitary.

1965

A Man Meets a Woman in the Street

Under the separated leaves of shade
Of the gingko, that old tree
That has existed essentially unchanged
Longer than any other living tree,

5   I walk behind a woman. Her hair's coarse gold
     Is spun from the sunlight that it rides upon.
     Women were paid to knit from sweet champagne
     Her second skin: it winds and unwinds, winds
     Up her long legs, delectable haunches,
10 As she sways, in sunlight, up the gazing aisle.
     The shade of the tree that is called maidenhair,
     That is not positively known
     To exist in a wild state, spots her fair or almost fair
     Hair twisted in a French twist; tall or almost tall,
15 She walks through the air the rain has washed, a clear thing
     Moving easily on its high heels, seeming to men
     Miraculous . . . Since I can call her, as Swann[3] couldn't,
     A woman who is my type, I follow with the warmth
     Of familiarity, of novelty, this new
20 Example of the type,
     Reminded of how Lorenz's[4] just-hatched goslings
     Shook off the last remnants of the egg
     And, looking at Lorenz, realized that Lorenz
     Was their mother. Quacking, his little family
25 Followed him everywhere; and when they met a goose,
     Their mother, they ran to him afraid.

     Imprinted upon me
     Is the shape I run to, the sweet strange
     Breath-taking contours that breathe to me: "I am yours,
30 Be mine!"
                Following this new
     Body, somehow familiar, this young shape, somehow old,
     For a moment I'm younger, the century is younger.
     The living Strauss,[5] his moustache just getting gray,
35 Is shouting to the players: "Louder!
     Louder! I can still hear Madame Schumann-Heink—"[6]
     Or else, white, bald, the old man's joyfully
     Telling conductors they must play *Elektra*
     Like *A Midsummer Night's Dream*[7]—like fairy music;
40 Proust, dying, is swallowing his iced beer
     And changing in proof the death of Bergotte[8]
     According to his own experience; Garbo,[9]
     A commissar in Paris, is listening attentively
     To the voice telling how McGillicuddy met McGillivray,
45 And McGillivray said to McGillicuddy—no, McGillicuddy

3. Charles Swann, a protagonist of the first book in the seven-volume novel *À la recherche du temps perdu* (*In Search of Lost Time*), by the French writer Marcel Proust (1871–1922). After Swann's infatuation with his lover Odette ceases, he remarks that she was never his type.
4. Konrad Lorenz (1903–1989), Austrian ethologist who in a 1935 study described the process of "imprinting." Just-hatched goslings preferred Lorenz to their natural mother after having received certain stimuli.
5. Richard Strauss (1864–1949), German composer, wrote the opera *Electra*.

6. Ernestine Schumann-Heink (1861–1936), American (Bohemian-born) contralto.
7. Incidental music, based on Shakespeare's play, by Felix Mendelssohn (1809–1847), German composer.
8. Character in Proust's novel, a distinguished writer.
9. Greta Garbo (1905–1990), American (Swedish-born) film actor, famous for her unsmiling demeanor. Here quoted from the film *Ninotchka* (1939), before she finally laughs for the first time on screen.

Said to McGillivray—that is, McGillivray . . . Garbo
Says seriously: "I vish dey'd never met."

As I walk behind this woman I remember
That before I flew here—waked in the forest
50 At dawn, by the piece called *Birds Beginning Day*
That, each day, birds play to begin the day—
I wished as men wish: "May this day be different!"
The birds were wishing, as birds wish—over and over,
With a last firmness, intensity, reality—
55 "May this day be the same!"
                        Ah, turn to me
And look into my eyes, say: "I am yours,
Be mine!"
                My wish will have come true. And yet
60 When your eyes meet my eyes, they'll bring into
The weightlessness of my pure wish the weight
Of a human being: someone to help or hurt,
Someone to be good to me, to be good to,
Someone to cry when I am angry
65 That she doesn't like *Elektra,* someone to start out on
        Proust with.
A wish, come true, is life. I have my life.
When you turn just slide your eyes across my eyes
And show in a look flickering across your face
As lightly as a leaf's shade, a bird's wing,
70 That there is no one in the world quite like me,
That if only . . . If only . . .
                        That will be enough.

But I've pretended long enough: I walk faster
And come close, touch with the tip of my finger
75 The nape of her neck, just where the gold
Hair stops, and the champagne-colored dress begins.
My finger touches her as the gingko's shadow
Touches her.
                Because, after all, it *is* my wife
80 In a new dress from Bergdorf's, walking toward the park.
She cries out, we kiss each other, and walk arm in arm
Through the sunlight that's much too good for New York,
The sunlight of our own house in the forest.
Still, though, the poor things need it . . . We've no need
85 To start out on Proust, to ask each other about Strauss.
We first helped each other, hurt each other, years ago.
After so many changes made and joys repeated,
Our first bewildered, transcending recognition
Is pure acceptance. We can't tell our life
90 From our wish. Really I began the day
Not with a man's wish: "May this day be different,"
But with the birds' wish: "May this day
Be the same day, the day of my life."

1967

WELDON KEES
1914–1955

What the Spider Heard

Will there be time for eggnogs and eclogues
In the place where we're going?
Said the spider to the fly.[1]

    I think not, said the fly.
5   I think not, sang the chorus.
    I think not, said a stranger
    Who mysteriously happened by.

Will they beat me and treat me the way they did here,
In the place where we're going?
10 Asked the spider of the fly.

    It is likely, said the fly.
    Very likely, sang the chorus.
    Extremely likely, said the stranger,
    With an eager gleam in his eye.

15 O, why go there when we know there is nothing there but fear
At this place where we're going?
Said the spider to the fly.

    What a question! said the fly.
    What a question! sang the chorus.
20   What a question! said the stranger,
    Leering slightly at the spider,
    Winking slyly at the fly.

1943

For H. V. (1901–1927)

I remember the clumsy surgery: the face
Scarred out of recognition, ruined and not his own.
Wax hands fattened among pink silk and pinker roses.
The minister was in fine form that afternoon.

5 I remember the ferns, the organ faintly out of tune,
The gray light, the two extended prayers,
Rain falling on stained glass; the pallbearers,
Selected by the family, and none of them his friends.

1943

1. Allusion to the children's poem "The Spider and the Fly," by the English writer Mary Howitt (1799–1888), which begins, " 'Will you walk into my parlor?' said the spider to the fly.' " The spider seduces the fly "up his winding stair" and kills her.

When the Lease Is Up

Walk the horses down the hill
Through the darkening groves;
Pat their rumps and leave the stall;
Even the eyeless cat perceives
5   Things are not going well.

Fasten the lock on the drawingroom door,
Cover the tables with sheets:
This is the end of the swollen year
When even the sound of the rain repeats:
10   *The lease is up, the time is near.*

Pull the curtains to the sill,
Darken the rooms, cut all the wires.
Crush the embers as they fall
From the dying fires:
15   Things are not going well.

1943

Robinson[2]

The dog stops barking after Robinson has gone.
His act is over. The world is a gray world,
Not without violence, and he kicks under the grand piano,
The nightmare chase well under way.

5   The mirror from Mexico, stuck to the wall,
Reflects nothing at all. The glass is black.
Robinson alone provides the image Robinsonian.

Which is all of the room—walls, curtains,
Shelves, bed, the tinted photograph of Robinson's first wife,
10   Rugs, vases, panatellas° in a humidor.   cigars
They would fill the room if Robinson came in.

The pages in the books are blank,
The books that Robinson has read. That is his favorite chair,
Or where the chair would be if Robinson were here.

15   All day the phone rings. It could be Robinson
Calling. It never rings when he is here.

Outside, white buildings yellow in the sun.
Outside, the birds circle continuously
Where trees are actual and take no holiday.

1947

2. A fictional everyman who appears in a number of Kees's poems.

NORMAN NICHOLSON
1914–1987

To the River Duddon[1]

I wonder, Duddon, if you still remember
An oldish man with a nose like a pony's nose,
Broad bones, legs long and lean but strong enough
To carry him over Hardknott at seventy years of age.
5   He came to you first as a boy with a fishing-rod
And a hunk of Ann Tyson's bread and cheese in his pocket,
Walking from Hawkshead across Walna Scar;[2]
Then as a middle-aged Rydal[3] landlord,
With a doting sister and a pension on the civil list,
10 Who left his verses gummed to your rocks like lichen,
The dry and yellow edges of a once-green spring.
He made a guide-book for you, from your source
There where you bubble through the moss on Wrynose
(Among the ribs of bald and bony fells°   *upland tracts*
15 With screes[4] scratched in the turf like grey scabs),
And twist and slither under humpbacked bridges—
Built like a child's house from odds and ends
Of stones that lie about the mountain side—
Past Cockley Beck Farm and on to Birk's Bridge,
20 Where the rocks stride about like legs in armour,
And the steel birches buckle and bounce in the wind
With a crinkle of silver foil in the crisp of the leaves;
On then to Seathwaite, where like a steam-navvy[5]
You shovel and slash your way through the gorge
25 By Wallabarrow Crag, broader now
From becks that flow out of black upland tarns°   *small lakes*
Or ooze through golden saxifrage and the roots of rowans;
Next Ulpha, where a stone dropped from the bridge
Swims like a tadpole down thirty feet of water
30 Between steep skirting-boards of rock; and thence
You dribble into lower Dunnerdale
Through wet woods and wood-soil and woodland flowers,
Tutson, the St. John's-wort with a single yellow bead,
Marsh marigold, creeping jenny and daffodils;
35 Here from hazel islands in the late spring
The catkins° fall and ride along the stream   *spiky flowerings*
Like little yellow weasels, and the soil is loosed
From bulbs of the white lily that smells of garlic,
And dippers rock up and down on rubber legs,
40 And long-tailed tits° are flung through the air like darts;   *birds*

---

1. In England's southwest Lake District, flowing down Dunnerdale from Wrynose and Hardknott passes. This poem recalls *The River Duddon: A Series of Sonnets* (1820), by William Wordsworth (1770–1850; see pp. 763–805), the "oldish man" in line 2.
2. A rocky eminence in England's Lake District.
Wordsworth lodged with Hugh and Ann Tyson while attending Hawshead Grammar School, Cumbria.
3. Lake District village where Wordsworth later lived with his sister, Dorothy (1771–1855).
4. Masses of debris at the foot of a cliff.
5. Steam-powered excavator (*navvy:* laborer).

By Foxfield now you taste the salt in your mouth,
And thrift mingles with the turf, and the heron stands
Watching the wagtails. Wordsworth wrote:
"Remote from every taint of sordid industry".[6]
45   But you and I know better, Duddon lass.
For I, who've lived for nearly thirty years
Upon your shore, have seen the slagbanks[7] slant
Like screes sheer into the sand, and seen the tide
Purple with ore back up the muddy gullies
50   And wiped the sinter dust from the farmyard damsons.[8]
A hundred years of floods and rain and wind
Have washed your rocks clear of his words again,
Many of them half-forgotten, brimming the Irish Sea,
But that which Wordsworth knew, even the old man
55   When poetry had failed like desire, was something
I have yet to learn, and you, Duddon,
Have learned and re-learned to forget and forget again.
Not the radical, the poet and heretic,
To whom the water-forces shouted and the fells
60   Were like a blackboard for the scrawls of God,
But the old man, inarticulate and humble,
Knew that eternity flows in a mountain beck°—   creek
The long cord of the water, the shepherd's numerals
That run upstream, through the singing decades of dialect.
65   He knew, beneath mutation of year and season,
Flood and drought, frost and fire and thunder,
The frothy blossom on the rowan and the reddening of the berries,
The silt, the sand, the slagbanks and the shingle,[9]
And the wild catastrophes of the breaking mountains,
70   There stands the base and root of the living rock,
Thirty thousand feet of solid Cumberland.

1944

Halley's Comet

My father saw it back in 1910,
The year King Edward died.
Above dark telegraph poles, above the high
Spiked steeple of the Liberal Club, the white
5   Gas-lit dials of the Market Clock,
Beyond the wide
Sunset-glow cirrus of blast-furnace smoke,
My father saw it fly
Its thirty-seven-million-mile-long kite
10   Across Black Combe's[1] black sky.

---

6. From *The River Duddon*, sonnet II, lines 1–2.
7. Accumulations of volcanic rock.
8. Plum trees. *Sinter:* cinder (i.e., from slag).

9. Round, water-worn gravel and pebbles.
1. Place-name meaning dark, armchair-shaped rock formation.

And what of me,
Born four years too late?
Will I have breath to wait
Till the long-circuiting commercial traveller
15   Turns up at his due?
In 1986, aged seventy-two,
Watery in the eyes and phlegmy in the flue
And a bit bad tempered at so delayed a date,
Will I look out above whatever is left of the town—
20   The Liberal Club long closed and the clock stopped,
And the chimneys smokeless above damped-down
Furnace fires? And then will I
At last have chance to see it
With my own as well as my father's eyes,
25   And share his long-ago Edwardian surprise
At that high, silent jet, laying its bright trail
Across Black Combe's black sky?

                                                              1981

HENRY REED
1914–1986

Chard Whitlow

(Mr Eliot's Sunday Evening Postscript)[1]

As we get older we do not get any younger.
Seasons return, and today I am fifty-five,
And this time last year I was fifty-four,
And this time next year I shall be sixty-two.
5   And I cannot say I should care (to speak for myself)
To see my time over again—if you can call it time,
Fidgeting uneasily under a draughty stair,
Or counting sleepless nights in the crowded Tube.[2]

There are certain precautions—though none of them very reliable—
10   Against the blast from bombs, or the flying splinter,
But not against the blast from Heaven, *vento dei venti*,[3]
The wind within a wind, unable to speak for wind;
And the frigid burnings of purgatory will not be touched
By any emollient.
15   I think you will find this put,
Far better than I could ever hope to express it,
In the words of Kharma:[4] "It is, we believe,

1. Mr. Eliot is the British (American-born) poet T. S. Eliot (1888–1965; see pp. 1340–66). Reed's title and subtitle evoke three of Eliot's titles: *Burnt Norton*, "Mr. Eliot's Sunday Morning Service," and "The *Boston Evening Transcript*." *Whitlow*: inflammatory sore on the finger.
2. Colloquial term for the London subway, in which thousands of Londoners were sheltering during the firebombing of London (known as the Blitz) of World War II, when this poem was written.
3. Wind of winds (Italian).
4. A concept common to Hinduism, Buddhism, and Jainism, the doctrine of Karma asserts that

Idle to hope that the simple stirrup-pump[5]
Can extinguish hell."

20   Oh, listeners,
And you especially who have switched off the wireless,[6]
And sit in Stoke or Basingstoke, listening appreciatively to the
      silence
(Which is also the silence of hell), pray not for yourselves but your
      souls.

And pray for me also under the draughty stair.
25 As we get older we do not get any younger.

And pray for Kharma under the holy mountain.

1941   1946

Lessons of the War

TO ALAN MICHELL

Vixi duellis nuper idoneus
Et militavi non sine gloria[7]

1. Naming of Parts

Today we have naming of parts. Yesterday,
We had daily cleaning. And tomorrow morning,
We shall have what to do after firing. But today,
Today we have naming of parts. Japonica[8]
5 Glistens like coral in all of the neighbouring gardens,
      And today we have naming of parts.

This is the lower sling swivel. And this
Is the upper sling swivel, whose use you will see,
When you are given your slings. And this is the piling swivel,
10 Which in your case you have not got. The branches
Hold in the gardens their silent, eloquent gestures,
      Which in our case we have not got.

This is the safety-catch, which is always released
With an easy flick of the thumb. And please do not let me
15 See anyone using his finger. You can do it quite easy

---

one's state in this life is a result of actions in past incarnations, and that action in this life can determine one's destiny in future incarnations. Reed deliberately misspells Karma and confuses it with Buddha.
5. A portable foot pump used to combat fires during the Blitz.
6. I.e., radio.

7. The opening lines of a Latin poem by Horace (3.26), but with Horace's word *puellis* (girls) changed to *duellis* (war, battles): "Lately I have lived in the midst of battles, creditably enough, / And have soldiered, not without glory."
8. The flowering quince (*Cydonia japonica*), a shrub with brilliant scarlet flowers.

If you have any strength in your thumb. The blossoms
Are fragile and motionless, never letting anyone see
     Any of them using their finger.

And this you can see is the bolt. The purpose of this
20 Is to open the breech, as you see. We can slide it
Rapidly backwards and forwards: we call this
Easing the spring.[9] And rapidly backwards and forwards
The early bees are assaulting and fumbling the flowers:
     They call it easing the Spring.

25 They call it easing the Spring: it is perfectly easy
If you have any strength in your thumb: like the bolt,
And the breech, and the cocking-piece, and the point of balance,
Which in our case we have not got; and the almond-blossom
Silent in all of the gardens and the bees going backwards and forwards,
30   For today we have naming of parts.

1942   1946

2. Judging Distances

Not only how far away, but the way that you say it
Is very important. Perhaps you may never get
The knack of judging a distance, but at least you know
How to report on a landscape: the central sector,
5 The right of arc and that, which we had last Tuesday,
     And at least you know

That maps are of time,[1] not place, so far as the army
Happens to be concerned—the reason being,
Is one which need not delay us. Again, you know
10 There are three kinds of tree, three only, the fir and the poplar,
And those which have bushy tops to; and lastly
     That things only seem to be things.

A barn is not called a barn, to put it more plainly,
Or a field in the distance, where sheep may be safely grazing.
15 You must never be over-sure. You must say, when reporting:
At five o'clock in the central sector is a dozen
Of what appear to be animals; whatever you do,
     Don't call the bleeders *sheep*.

I am sure that's quite clear; and suppose, for the sake of example,
20 The one at the end, asleep, endeavours to tell us
What he sees over there to the west, and how far away,
After first having come to attention. There to the west,
On the fields of summer the sun and the shadows bestow
     Vestments of purple and gold.

9. Moving the bolt of a rifle "rapidly backwards and forwards," thereby ejecting any bullets remaining in the magazine and taking pressure off the spring.

1. I.e., they convey the locations of targets through an imaginary clock with a topographical feature at its center.

25 The still white dwellings are like a mirage in the heat,
And under the swaying elms a man and a woman
Lie gently together. Which is, perhaps, only to say
That there is a row of houses to the left of arc,
And that under some poplars a pair of what appear to be humans
30   Appear to be loving.

Well that, for an answer, is what we might rightly call
Moderately satisfactory only, the reason being,
Is that two things have been omitted, and those are important.
The human beings, now, in what direction are they,
35 And how far away, would you say? And do not forget
There may be dead ground[2] in between.

There may be dead ground in between; and I may not have got
The knack of judging a distance; I will only venture
A guess that perhaps between me and the apparent lovers
40 (Who, incidentally, appear by now to have finished)
At seven o'clock from the houses, is roughly a distance
Of about one year and a half.

1943   1946

DYLAN THOMAS
1914–1953

The Force That Through the Green Fuse Drives the Flower

The force that through the green fuse drives the flower
Drives my green age; that blasts the roots of trees
Is my destroyer.
And I am dumb to tell the crooked rose
5 My youth is bent by the same wintry fever.

The force that drives the water through the rocks
Drives my red blood; that dries the mouthing streams
Turns mine to wax.
And I am dumb to mouth unto my veins
10 How at the mountain spring the same mouth sucks.

The hand that whirls the water in the pool[1]
Stirs the quicksand; that ropes the blowing wind
Hauls my shroud sail.
And I am dumb to tell the hanging man
15 How of my clay is made the hangman's lime.[2]

---

2. Military term for space that cannot be reached
by fire from a given weapon or a given point.
1. In John 5.1–4, an angel stirs the pool Bethesda,
making the water curative.
2. Quicklime poured into the graves of people
publically hanged, to hasten decomposition.

The lips of time leech to the fountain head;
Love drips and gathers, but the fallen blood
Shall calm her sores.
And I am dumb to tell a weather's wind
20   How time has ticked a heaven round the stars.

And I am dumb to tell the lover's tomb
How at my sheet[3] goes the same crooked worm.

1934

The Hand That Signed the Paper

The hand that signed the paper felled a city;
Five sovereign fingers taxed the breath,
Doubled the globe of dead and halved a country;
These five kings did a king to death.

5   The mighty hand leads to a sloping shoulder,
The finger joints are cramped with chalk;
A goose's quill has put an end to murder
That put an end to talk.

The hand that signed the treaty bred a fever,
10   And famine grew, and locusts came;
Great is the hand that holds dominion over
Man by a scribbled name.

The five kings count the dead but do not soften
The crusted wound nor stroke the brow;
15   A hand rules pity as a hand rules heaven;
Hands have no tears to flow.

1936

After the Funeral

(In Memory of Ann Jones)[4]

After the funeral, mule praises, brays,
Windshake of sailshaped ears, muffle-toed tap
Tap happily of one peg in the thick
Grave's foot, blinds down the lids, the teeth in black,
5   The spittled eyes, the salt ponds in the sleeves,
Morning smack of the spade that wakes up sleep,
Shakes a desolate boy who slits his throat

---

3. Corpse's winding-sheet.
4. Ann [Williams] Jones (d. 1933), Dylan Thomas's maternal aunt, married a tenant farmer; their rented farm, in the Welsh countryside, was Fern Hill (see p. 1571).

In the dark of the coffin and sheds dry leaves,
That breaks one bone to light with a judgment clout,
10 After the feast of tear-stuffed time and thistles
In a room with a stuffed fox and a stale fern,
I stand, for this memorial's sake, alone
In the snivelling hours with dead, humped Ann
Whose hooded, fountain heart once fell in puddles
15 Round the parched worlds of Wales and drowned each sun
(Though this for her is a monstrous image blindly
Magnified out of praise; her death was a still drop;
She would not have me sinking in the holy
Flood of her heart's fame; she would lie dumb and deep
20 And need no druid[5] of her broken body).
But I, Ann's bard on a raised hearth, call all
The seas to service that her wood-tongued virtue
Babble like a bellbuoy over the hymning heads,
Bow down the walls of the ferned and foxy woods
25 That her love sing and swing through a brown chapel,
Bless her bent spirit with four, crossing birds.
Her flesh was meek as milk, but this skyward statue
With the wild breast and blessed and giant skull
Is carved from her in a room with a wet window
30 In a fiercely mourning house in a crooked year.
I know her scrubbed and sour humble hands
Lie with religion in their cramp, her threadbare
Whisper in a damp word, her wits drilled hollow,
Her fist of a face died clenched on a round pain;
35 And sculptured Ann is seventy years of stone.
These cloud-sopped, marble hands, this monumental
Argument of the hewn voice, gesture and psalm,
Storm me forever over her grave until
The stuffed lung of the fox twitch and cry Love
40 And the strutting fern lay seeds on the black sill.

1939

The Hunchback in the Park

The hunchback in the park
A solitary mister
Propped between trees and water
From the opening of the garden lock
5 That lets the trees and water enter
Until the Sunday sombre bell at dark[6]

Eating bread from a newspaper
Drinking water from the chained cup
That the children filled with gravel

---

5. Priest, among ancient Celts of Gaul or Britain; also, magician or soothsayer.

6. The bell that warns visitors that the park gates are about to be closed for the night.

10 In the fountain basin where I sailed my ship
Slept at night in a dog kennel
But nobody chained him up.

Like the park birds he came early
Like the water he sat down
15 And Mister they called Hey mister
The truant boys from the town
Running when he had heard them clearly
On out of sound

Past lake and rockery
20 Laughing when he shook his paper
Hunchbacked in mockery
Through the loud zoo of the willow groves
Dodging the park keeper
With his stick that picked up leaves.

25 And the old dog sleeper
Alone between nurses and swans
While the boys among willows
Made the tigers jump out of their eyes
To roar on the rockery stones
30 And the groves were blue with sailors

Made all day until bell time
A woman figure without fault
Straight as a young elm
Straight and tall from his crooked bones
35 That she might stand in the night
After the locks and chains

All night in the unmade park
After the railings and shrubberies
The birds the grass the trees the lake
40 And the wild boys innocent as strawberries
Had followed the hunchback
To his kennel in the dark.

1942

A Refusal to Mourn the Death, by Fire,[7] of a Child in London

Never until the mankind making
Bird beast and flower
Fathering and all humbling darkness
Tells with silence the last light breaking
5 And the still hour
Is come of the sea tumbling in harness

---

7. During the firebombing of London, known as the Blitz, in World War II.

And I must enter again the round
Zion[8] of the water bead
And the synagogue of the ear of corn
10   Shall I let pray the shadow of a sound
Or sow my salt seed
In the least valley of sackcloth to mourn

The majesty and burning of the child's death.
I shall not murder
15   The mankind of her going with a grave truth
Nor blaspheme down the stations of the breath
With any further
Elegy of innocence and youth.

Deep with the first dead lies London's daughter,
20   Robed in the long friends,
The grains beyond age, the dark veins of her mother,
Secret by the unmourning water
Of the riding Thames.[9]
After the first death, there is no other.

                                                    1946

The Conversation of Prayer

The conversation of prayers about to be said
By the child going to bed and the man on the stairs
Who climbs to his dying love in her high room,
The one not caring to whom in his sleep he will move
5   And the other full of tears that she will be dead,

Turns in the dark on the sound they know will arise
Into the answering skies from the green ground,
From the man on the stairs and the child by his bed.
The sound about to be said in the two prayers
10   For the sleep in a safe land and the love who dies

Will be the same grief flying. Whom shall they calm?
Shall the child sleep unharmed or the man be crying?
The conversation of prayers about to be said
Turns on the quick and the dead, and the man on the stairs
15   Tonight shall find no dying but alive and warm

In the fire of his care his love in the high room.
And the child not caring to whom he climbs his prayer
Shall drown in a grief as deep as his true grave,
And mark the dark eyed wave, through the eyes of sleep,
20   Dragging him up the stairs to one who lies dead.

                                                    1946

8. Biblical term for Jerusalem and (meta-   9. River that flows through London.
phorically) City of God or heaven.

Fern Hill[1]

Now as I was young and easy under the apple boughs
About the lilting house and happy as the grass was green,
    The night above the dingle[2] starry,
      Time let me hail and climb
5   Golden in the heydays of his eyes,
And honoured among wagons I was prince of the apple towns
And once below a time I lordly had the trees and leaves
      Trail with daisies and barley
    Down the rivers of the windfall light.

10 And as I was green and carefree, famous among the barns
About the happy yard and singing as the farm was home,
    In the sun that is young once only,
      Time let me play and be
      Golden in the mercy of his means,
15 And green and golden I was huntsman and herdsman, the calves
Sang to my horn, the foxes on the hills barked clear and cold,
      And the sabbath rang slowly
    In the pebbles of the holy streams.

All the sun long it was running, it was lovely, the hay
20 Fields high as the house, the tunes from the chimneys, it was air
      And playing, lovely and watery
        And fire green as grass.
    And nightly under the simple stars
As I rode to sleep the owls were bearing the farm away,
25 All the moon long I heard, blessed among stables, the night-jars
      Flying with the ricks,[3] and the horses
      Flashing into the dark.

And then to awake, and the farm, like a wanderer white
With the dew, come back, the cock on his shoulder: it was all
30   Shining, it was Adam and maiden,[4]
      The sky gathered again
    And the sun grew round that very day.
So it must have been after the birth of the simple light
In the first, spinning place, the spellbound horses walking warm
35   Out of the whinnying green stable
      On to the fields of praise.

And honoured among foxes and pheasants by the gay house
Under the new made clouds and happy as the heart was long,
    In the sun born over and over,
40   I ran my heedless ways,
      My wishes raced through the house high hay
And nothing I cared, at my sky blue trades, that time allows
In all his tuneful turning so few and such morning songs

1. Welsh farm, rented by Thomas's aunt and uncle, in which he spent summer holidays as a boy.
2. Small wooded valley.
3. Haystacks. *Night-jars*: nocturnal birds.
4. Adam and Eve (Genesis 1).

Before the children green and golden
45   Follow him out of grace,

Nothing I cared, in the lamb white days, that time would take me
Up to the swallow thronged loft by the shadow of my hand,
In the moon that is always rising,
Nor that riding to sleep
50   I should hear him fly with the high fields
And wake to the farm forever fled from the childless land.
Oh as I was young and easy in the mercy of his means,
Time held me green and dying
Though I sang in my chains like the sea.

1946

In My Craft or Sullen Art

In my craft or sullen art
Exercised in the still night
When only the moon rages
And the lovers lie abed
5   With all their griefs in their arms,
I labour by singing light
Not for ambition or bread
Or the strut and trade of charms
On the ivory stages
10   But for the common wages
Of their most secret heart.

Not for the proud man apart
From the raging moon I write
On these spindrift⁵ pages
15   Nor for the towering dead
With their nightingales and psalms
But for the lovers, their arms
Round the griefs of the ages,
Who pay no praise or wages
20   Nor heed my craft or art.

1946

Do Not Go Gentle into That Good Night⁶

Do not go gentle into that good night,
Old age should burn and rave at close of day;
Rage, rage against the dying of the light.

5. Driven by the wind, like sea spray.
6. This villanelle was written in May 1951, during the final, prolonged illness of Thomas's father.

Though wise men at their end know dark is right,
Because their words had forked no lightning they
Do not go gentle into that good night.

Good men, the last wave by, crying how bright
Their frail deeds might have danced in a green bay,
Rage, rage against the dying of the light.

Wild men who caught and sang the sun in flight,
And learn, too late, they grieved it on its way,
Do not go gentle into that good night.

Grave men, near death, who see with blinding sight
Blind eyes could blaze like meteors and be gay,
Rage, rage against the dying of the light.

And you, my father, there on the sad height,
Curse, bless, me now with your fierce tears, I pray.
Do not go gentle into that good night.
Rage, rage against the dying of the light.

1952

ALUN LEWIS
1915–1944

All Day It Has Rained

All day it has rained, and we on the edge of the moors
Have sprawled in our bell-tents,[1] moody and dull as boors,
Groundsheets and blankets spread on the muddy ground
And from the first grey wakening we have found
No refuge from the skirmishing fine rain
And the wind that made the canvas heave and flap
And the taut wet guy-ropes ravel out and snap.
All day the rain has glided, wave and mist and dream,
Drenching the gorse and heather, a gossamer stream
Too light to stir the acorns that suddenly
Snatched from their cups by the wild south-westerly
Pattered against the tent and our upturned dreaming faces.
And we stretched out, unbuttoning our braces,
Smoking a Woodbine,[2] darning dirty socks,
Reading the Sunday papers—I saw a fox
And mentioned it in the note I scribbled home;—
And we talked of girls, and dropping bombs on Rome,
And thought of the quiet dead and the loud celebrities
Exhorting us to slaughter, and the herded refugees;

1. Conical tents with a central pole.　　2. Brand of cheap cigarette.

20 —Yet thought softly, morosely of them, and as indifferently
    As of ourselves or those whom we
    For years have loved, and will again
    Tomorrow maybe love; but now it is the rain
    Possesses us entirely, the twilight and the rain.

25 And I can remember nothing dearer or more to my heart
    Than the children I watched in the woods on Saturday
    Shaking down burning chestnuts for the schoolyard's merry play,
    Or the shaggy patient dog who followed me
    By Sheet and Steep and up the wooded scree[3]
30 To the Shoulder o' Mutton where Edward Thomas brooded long
    On death and beauty—till a bullet stopped his song.[4]

1940   1941, 1942

Song

(On seeing dead bodies floating off the Cape[5])

    The first month of his absence
    I was numb and sick
    And where he'd left his promise
    Life did not turn or kick.
5   The seed, the seed of love was sick.

    The second month my eyes were sunk
    In the darkness of despair,
    And my bed was like a grave
    And his ghost was lying there.
10 And my heart was sick with care.

    The third month of his going
    I thought I heard him say
    "Our course deflected slightly
    On the thirty-second day—"
15 The tempest blew his words away.

    And he was lost among the waves,
    His ship rolled helpless in the sea,
    The fourth month of his voyage
    He shouted grievously
20 "Beloved, do not think of me."

    The flying fish like kingfishers
    Skim the sea's bewildered crests,

---

3. Mass of debris at the foot of a cliff. *Sheet and Steep*: villages.
4. The English poet Edward Thomas (1878–1917; see pp. 1253–56) was killed in World War I. In the issue of the magazine *Horizon* in which this poem first appeared, Lewis reviewed Thomas's *The Trumpet and Other Poems*: "I have been garrisoned for six months in Edward Thomas country and walked his walks. I have sheltered from the rain in the beautiful house he built but did not inhabit." *Shoulder o' Mutton*: a hill in Hampshire.
5. The Cape of Good Hope, South Africa.

The whales blow steaming fountains,
The seagulls have no nests
25 Where my lover sways and rests.

We never thought to buy and sell
This life that blooms or withers in the leaf,
And I'll not stir, so he sleeps well,
Though cell by cell the coral reef
30 Builds an eternity of grief.

But oh! the drag and dullness of my Self;
The turning seasons wither in my head;
All this slowness, all this hardness,
The nearness that is waiting in my bed,
35 The gradual self-effacement of the dead.

1944

Goodbye

So we must say Goodbye, my darling,
And go, as lovers go, for ever;
Tonight remains, to pack and fix on labels
And make an end of lying down together.

5 I put a final shilling in the gas,[6]
And watch you slip your dress below your knees
And lie so still I hear your rustling comb
Modulate the autumn in the trees.

And all the countless things I shall remember
10 Lay mummy-cloths[7] of silence round my head;
I fill the carafe with a drink of water;
You say "We paid a guinea[8] for this bed,"

And then, "We'll leave some gas, a little warmth
For the next resident, and these dry flowers,"
15 And turn your face away, afraid to speak
The big word, that Eternity is ours.

Your kisses close my eyes and yet you stare
As though God struck a child with nameless fears;
Perhaps the water glitters and discloses
20 Time's chalice and its limpid useless tears.

Everything we renounce except our selves;
Selfishness is the last of all to go;

6. Gas fire, the fuel supply of which is controlled
by a meter that must be fed with shilling coins.
7. Bandages wrapped around an Egyptian
mummy.
8. Old British currency: one pound and one shil-
ling (105p.).

Our sighs are exhalations of the earth,
Our footprints leave a track across the snow.

25 We made the universe to be our home,
Our nostrils took the wind to be our breath,
Our hearts are massive towers of delight,
We stride across the seven seas of death.

Yet when all's done you'll keep the emerald
30 I placed upon your finger in the street;
And I will keep the patches⁹ that you sewed
On my old battledress tonight, my sweet.

1945

MARGARET WALKER
1915–1998

Since 1619¹

How many years since 1619 have I been singing Spirituals?
How long have I been praising God and shouting hallelujahs?
How long have I been hated and hating?
How long have I been living in hell for heaven?

5 When will I see my brother's face wearing another color?
When will I be ready to die in a honest fight?
When will I be conscious of the struggle—now to do or die?
When will these scales fall away from my eyes?²

What will I say when days of wrath³ descend:
10 When the money-gods take all my life away;
When the death knell sounds
And peace is a flag of far-flung blood and filth?

When will I understand the cheated and the cheaters;
Their paltry pittances and cold concessions to my pride?
15 When will I burst from my kennel an angry mongrel,
Lean and hungry and tired of my dry bones and years?

1942

9. Cloth badges of rank attached to a soldier's uniform.
1. The year that the first African slaves arrived in Jamestown, Virginia, aboard a Dutch frigate.
2. Cf. the account of Saul's conversion in Acts

9.18: "And immediately there fell from his eyes as it had been scales: and he received sight forthwith, and arose, and was baptized."
3. According to the Bible (e.g., Zephaniah 1.1.15), days of God's judgment.

Childhood

When I was a child I knew red miners
dressed raggedly and wearing carbide lamps.
I saw them come down red hills to their camps
dyed with red dust from old Ishkooda[4] mines.
5   Night after night I met them on the roads,
or on the streets in town I caught their glance;
the swing of dinner buckets in their hands,
and grumbling undermining all their words.

I also lived in low cotton country
10   where moonlight hovered over ripe haystacks,
or stumps of trees, and croppers' rotting shacks
with famine, terror, flood, and plague near by;
where sentiment and hatred still held sway
and only bitter land was washed away.

1942

JUDITH WRIGHT
1915–2000

Woman to Man

The eyeless labourer in the night,
the selfless, shapeless seed I hold,
builds for its resurrection day—
silent and swift and deep from sight
5   foresees the unimagined light.

This is no child with a child's face;
this has no name to name it by:
yet you and I have known it well.
This is our hunter and our chase,
10   the third who lay in our embrace.

This is the strength that your arm knows,
the arc of flesh that is my breast,
the precise crystals of our eyes.
This is the blood's wild tree that grows
15   the intricate and folded rose.

This is the maker and the made;
this is the question and reply;

---

4. South of Birmingham, Alabama, where Walker's family lived until she was five. The sestet of this sonnet shifts to her second childhood home, near New Orleans.

the blind head butting at the dark,
the blaze of light along the blade.
20   Oh hold me, for I am afraid.

1949

Train Journey

Glassed with cold sleep and dazzled by the moon,
out of the confused hammering dark of the train
I looked and saw under the moon's cold sheet
your delicate dry breasts, country that built my heart;

5 and the small trees on their uncoloured slope
like poetry moved, articulate and sharp
and purposeful under the great dry flight of air,
under the crosswise currents of wind and star.

Clench down your strength, box-tree and ironbark.[1]
10 Break with your violent root the virgin rock.
Draw from the flying dark its breath of dew
till the unliving come to life in you.

Be over the blind rock a skin of sense,
under the barren height a slender dance . . .

15 I woke and saw the dark small trees that burn
suddenly into flowers more lovely than the white moon.

1953

Request to a Year

If the year is meditating a suitable gift,
I should like it to be the attitude
of my great-great-grandmother,
legendary devotee of the arts,

5 who, having had eight children
and little opportunity for painting pictures,
sat one day on a high rock
beside a river in Switzerland

and from a difficult distance viewed
10 her second son, balanced on a small ice-floe,
drift down the current towards a waterfall
that struck rock-bottom eighty feet below,

---

1. Australian eucalyptus tree.

while her second daughter, impeded,
no doubt, by the petticoats of the day,
15 stretched out a last-hope alpenstock[2]
(which luckily later caught him on his way).

Nothing, it was evident, could be done;
and with the artist's isolating eye
my great-great-grandmother hastily sketched the scene.
20 The sketch survives to prove the story by.

Year, if you have no Mother's day present planned;
reach back and bring me the firmness of her hand.

1953

Eve[3] to Her Daughters

It was not I who began it.
Turned out into draughty caves,
hungry so often, having to work for our bread,
hearing the children whining,
5 I was nevertheless not unhappy.
Where Adam went I was fairly contented to go.
I adapted myself to the punishment: it was my life.

But Adam, you know . . . !
He kept on brooding over the insult,
10 over the trick They had played on us, over the scolding.
He had discovered a flaw in himself
and he had to make up for it.

Outside Eden the earth was imperfect,
the seasons changed, the game was fleet-footed,
15 he had to work for our living, and he didn't like it.
He even complained of my cooking
(it was hard to compete with Heaven).

So he set to work.
The earth must be made a new Eden
20 with central heating, domesticated animals,
mechanical harvesters, combustion engines,
escalators, refrigerators,
and modern means of communication
and multiplied opportunities for safe investment
25 and higher education for Abel and Cain
and the rest of the family.
You can see how his pride had been hurt.

2. Staff used in mountain climbing.
3. According to Genesis, the first woman, wife of Adam.

In the process he had to unravel everything,
because he believed that mechanism
30 was the whole secret—he was always mechanical-minded.
He got to the very inside of the whole machine
exclaiming as he went, So this is how it works!
And now that I know how it works, why, I must have invented it.
As for God and the Other, they cannot be demonstrated,
35 and what cannot be demonstrated
doesn't exist.
You see, he had always been jealous.

Yes, he got to the centre
where nothing at all can be demonstrated.
40 And clearly he doesn't exist; but he refuses
to accept the conclusion.
You see, he was always an egotist.

It was warmer than this in the cave;
there was none of this fall-out.
45 I would suggest, for the sake of the children,
that it's time you took over.

But you are my daughters, you inherit my own faults of character;
you are submissive, following Adam
even beyond existence.
50 Faults of character have their own logic
and it always works out.
I observed this with Abel and Cain.

Perhaps the whole elaborate fable
right from the beginning
55 is meant to demonstrate this; perhaps it's the whole secret.
Perhaps nothing exists but our faults?
At least they can be demonstrated.

But it's useless to make
such a suggestion to Adam.
60 He has turned himself into God,
who is faultless, and doesn't exist.

1966

DAVID GASCOYNE
1916–2001

Yves Tanguy[1]

The worlds are breaking in my head
Blown by the brainless wind

1. American (French-born) Surrealist painter (1900–1955).

That comes from afar
Swollen with dusk and dust
5   And hysterical rain

The fading cries of the light
Awaken the endless desert
Engrossed in its tropical slumber
Enclosed by the dead grey oceans
10   Enclasped by the arms of the night

The worlds are breaking in my head
Their fragments are crumbs of despair
The food of the solitary damned
Who await the gross tumult of turbulent
15   Days bringing change without end.

The worlds are breaking in my head
The fuming future sleeps no more
For their seeds are beginning to grow
To creep and to cry midst the
20   Rocks of the deserts to come

Planetary seed
Sown by the grotesque wind
Whose head is so swollen with rumours
Whose hands are so urgent with tumours
25   Whose feet are so deep in the sand.

1936

Ecce Homo[2]

Whose is this horrifying face,
This putrid flesh, discoloured, flayed,
Fed on by flies, scorched by the sun?
Whose are these hollow red-filmed eyes
5   And thorn-spiked head and spear-stuck side?
Behold the Man: He is Man's Son.

Forget the legend, tear the decent veil
That cowardice or interest devised
To make their mortal enemy a friend,
10   To hide the bitter truth all His wounds tell,
Lest the great scandal be no more disguised:
He is in agony till the world's end,

---

2. Behold the man (Latin); Pilate's words when presenting Christ, beaten and crowned with thorns before his Crucifixion, to the people (John 19.5).

And we must never sleep during that time!
He is suspended on the cross-tree now
15 And we are onlookers at the crime,
Callous contemporaries of the slow
Torture of God. Here is the hill
Made ghastly by His spattered blood

Whereon He hangs and suffers still:
20 See, the centurions wear riding-boots,
Black shirts and badges and peaked caps,
Greet one another with raised-arm salutes,
They have cold eyes, unsmiling lips;
Yet these His brothers know not what they do.[3]

25 And on his either side hang dead
A labourer and a factory hand,
Or one is maybe a lynched Jew
And one a Negro or a Red,
Coolie or Ethiopian, Irishman,
30 Spaniard or German democrat.

Behind His lolling head the sky
Glares like a fiery cataract
Red with the murders of two thousand years
Committed in His name and by
35 Crusaders, Christian warriors
Defending faith and property.

Amid the plain beneath His transfixed hands,
Exuding darkness as indelible
As guilty stains, fanned by funereal
40 And lurid airs, besieged by drifting sands
And clefted° landslides our about-to-be   cloven, split
Bombed and abandoned cities stand.

He who wept for Jerusalem
Now sees His prophecy extend
45 Across the greatest cities of the world,
A guilty panic reason cannot stem
Rising to raze° them all as He foretold;   knock down
And He must watch this drama to the end.

Though often named, He is unknown
50 To the dark kingdoms at His feet
Where everything disparages His words,
And each man bears the common guilt alone
And goes blindfolded to his fate,
And fear and greed are sovereign lords.

3. "Then said Jesus, Father, forgive them; for they know not what they do" (Luke 23.34).

55　The turning point of history
　　Must come. Yet the complacent and the proud
　　And who exploit and kill, may be denied—
　　Christ of Revolution and of Poetry—
　　The resurrection and the life[4]
60　Wrought by your spirit's blood.

　　Involved in their own sophistry
　　The black priest and the upright man
　　Faced by subversive truth shall be struck dumb,
　　Christ of Revolution and of Poetry,
65　While the rejected and condemned become
　　Agents of the divine.

　　Not from a monstrance[5] silver-wrought
　　But from the tree of human pain
　　Redeem our sterile misery,
70　Christ of Revolution and of Poetry,
　　That man's long journey through the night
　　May not have been in vain.

1943

P. K. PAGE
b. 1916

Stories of Snow

　　Those in the vegetable rain retain
　　an area behind their sprouting eyes
　　held soft and rounded with the dream of snow
　　precious and reminiscent as those globes—
5　souvenir of some never-nether land—
　　which hold their snow-storms circular, complete,
　　high in a tall and teakwood cabinet.

　　In countries where the leaves are large as hands
　　where flowers protrude their fleshy chins
10　and call their colors,
　　an imaginary snow-storm sometimes falls
　　among the lilies.
　　And in the early morning one will waken
　　to think the glowing linen of his pillow
15　a northern drift, will find himself mistaken
　　and lie back weeping.

4. "Jesus said unto her, I am the resurrection, and
the life" (John 11.25).
5. Open or transparent box in which the Host

(sanctified bread or wafer) is carried in the Roman
Catholic service known as the Mass.

And there the story shifts from head to head,
of how in Holland, from their feather beds
hunters arise and part the flakes and go
20   forth to the frozen lakes in search of swans—
the snow-light falling white along their guns,
their breath in plumes.
While tethered in the wind like sleeping gulls
ice-boats wait the raising of their wings
25   to skim the electric ice at such a speed
they leap jet strips of naked water,
and how these flying, sailing hunters feel
air in their mouths as terrible as ether.
And on the story runs that even drinks
30   in that white landscape dare to be no color;
how flasked and water clear, the liquor slips
silver against the hunters' moving hips.
And of the swan in death these dreamers tell
of its last flight and how it falls, a plummet,
35   pierced by the freezing bullet
and how three feathers, loosened by the shot,
descend like snow upon it.
While hunters plunge their fingers in its down
deep as a drift, and dive their hands
40   up to the neck of the wrist
in that warm metamorphosis of snow
as gentle as the sort that woodsmen know
who, lost in the white circle, fall at last
and dream their way to death.

45   And stories of this kind are often told
in countries where great flowers bar the roads
with reds and blues which seal the route to snow—
as if, in telling, raconteurs unlock
the color with its complement and go
50   through to the area behind the eyes
where silent, unrefractive whiteness lies.

1946

Deaf-Mute in the Pear Tree

His clumsy body is a golden fruit
pendulous in the pear tree

Blunt fingers among the multitudinous buds

Adriatic[1] blue the sky above and through
5   the forking twigs

---

1. Adriatic Sea, part of the Mediterranean Sea.

Sun ruddying tree's trunk, his trunk
his massive head thick-nobbed with burnished curls
tight-clenched in bud

(Painting by Generalić.[2] Primitive.)

10 I watch him prune with silent secateurs°   *pruning shears*

Boots in the crotch of branches shift their weight
heavily as oxen in a stall

Hear small inarticulate mews from his locked mouth
a kitten in a box

15 Pear clippings fall
                    soundlessly on the ground
Spring finches sing
                    soundlessly in the leaves

A stone. A stone in ears and on his tongue

20 Through palm and fingertip he knows the tree's
quick springtime pulse

Smells in its sap the sweet incipient pears

Pale sunlight's choppy water glistens on
his mutely snipping blades

25 and flags and scraps of blue
above him make regatta° of the day   *boat race*

But when he sees his wife's foreshortened shape
sudden and silent in the grass below
uptilt its face to him

30 then air is kisses, kisses

stone dissolves

his locked throat finds a little door

and through it feathered joy
flies screaming like a jay

1985

2. Ivan Generalić (1914–1992), Croatian painter in a "naive," or "primitive," style.

GWENDOLYN BROOKS
1917–2000

kitchenette building

We are things of dry hours and the involuntary plan,
Grayed in, and gray. "Dream" makes a giddy sound, not strong
Like "rent," "feeding a wife," "satisfying a man."

But could a dream send up through onion fumes
5   Its white and violet, fight with fried potatoes
And yesterday's garbage ripening in the hall,
Flutter, or sing an aria down these rooms

Even if we were willing to let it in,
Had time to warm it, keep it very clean,
10   Anticipate a message, let it begin?

We wonder. But not well! not for a minute!
Since Number Five is out of the bathroom now,
We think of lukewarm water, hope to get in it.

                                                1945

my dreams, my works, must wait till after hell

I hold my honey and I store my bread
In little jars and cabinets of my will.
I label clearly, and each latch and lid
I bid, Be firm till I return from hell.
5   I am very hungry. I am incomplete.
And none can tell when I may dine again.
No man can give me any word but Wait,
The puny light. I keep eyes pointed in;
Hoping that, when the devil days of my hurt
10   Drag out to their last dregs and I resume
On such legs as are left me, in such heart
As I can manage, remember to go home,
My taste will not have turned insensitive
To honey and bread old purity could love.

                                                1945

the birth in a narrow room

Weeps out of western country something new.
Blurred and stupendous. Wanted and unplanned.

Winks. Twines, and weakly winks
Upon the milk-glass fruit bowl, iron pot,
5   The bashful china child tipping forever
Yellow apron and spilling pretty cherries.

Now, weeks and years will go before she thinks
"How pinchy is my room! how can I breathe!
I am not anything and I have got
10   Not anything, or anything to do!"—
But prances nevertheless with gods and fairies
Blithely about the pump and then beneath
The elms and grapevines, then in darling endeavor
By privy foyer, where the screenings stand
15   And where the bugs buzz by in private cars
Across old peach cans and old jelly jars.

                                   1949

the rites for Cousin Vit

Carried her unprotesting out the door.
Kicked back the casket-stand. But it can't hold her,
That stuff and satin aiming to enfold her,
The lid's contrition nor the bolts before.
5   Oh oh. Too much. Too much. Even now, surmise,
She rises in the sunshine. There she goes,
Back to the bars she knew and the repose
In love-rooms and the things in people's eyes.
Too vital and too squeaking. Must emerge.
10   Even now she does the snake-hips with a hiss,
Slops the bad wine across her shantung,[1] talks
Of pregnancy, guitars and bridgework, walks
In parks or alleys, comes haply on the verge
Of happiness, haply hysterics. Is.

                                   1949

The Bean Eaters

They eat beans mostly, this old yellow pair.
Dinner is a casual affair.
Plain chipware on a plain and creaking wood,
Tin flatware.

5   Two who are Mostly Good.
Two who have lived their day,

---

1. Silk of an uneven texture.

But keep on putting on their clothes
And putting things away.

And remembering . . .
10 Remembering, with twinklings and twinges,
As they lean over the beans in their rented back room that is full of
    beads and receipts and dolls and clothes, tobacco crumbs, vases
    and fringes.

1960

We Real Cool

THE POOL PLAYERS. SEVEN AT THE GOLDEN SHOVEL.

We real cool. We
Left school. We

Lurk late. We
Strike straight. We

5 Sing sin. We
Thin gin. We

Jazz June. We
Die soon.

1960

Medgar Evers[2]

For Charles Evers

The man whose height his fear improved he
arranged to fear no further. The raw
intoxicated time was time for better birth or
a final death.

5 Old styles, old tempos, all the engagement of
the day—the sedate, the regulated fray—
the antique light, the Moral rose, old gusts,
tight whistlings from the past, the mothballs
in the Love at last our man forswore.

10 Medgar Evers annoyed confetti and assorted
brands of businessmen's eyes.

2. Prominent black civil rights activist (1925–1963). The first field secretary of the NAACP (National Association for the Advancement of Col-ored People) in Mississippi, he was murdered by a white supremacist.

The shows came down: to maxims and surprise.
And palsy.

Roaring no rapt arise-ye to the dead, he
15   leaned across tomorrow. People said that
he was holding clean globes in his hands.

                                         1968

Boy Breaking Glass

To Marc Crawford From Whom the Commission

Whose broken window is a cry of art
(success, that winks aware
as elegance, as a treasonable faith)
is raw: is sonic: is old-eyed première.
5   Our beautiful flaw and terrible ornament.
Our barbarous and metal little man.

"I shall create! If not a note, a hole.
If not an overture, a desecration."

Full of pepper and light
10   and Salt and night and cargoes.

"Don't go down the plank
if you see there's no extension.
Each to his grief, each to
his loneliness and fidgety revenge.

15   Nobody knew where I was and now I am no longer there."

The only sanity is a cup of tea.
The music is in minors.

Each one other
is having different weather.

20   "It was you, it was you who threw away my name!
And this is everything I have for me."

Who has not Congress, lobster, love, luau,
the Regency Room, the Statue of Liberty,
runs. A sloppy amalgamation.
25   A mistake.
A cliff.
A hymn, a snare, and an exceeding sun.

                                         1968

CHARLES CAUSLEY
1917–2003

Armistice Day[1]

I stood with three comrades in Parliament Square
November her freights of grey fire unloading,
No sound from the city upon the pale air,
Above us the sea-bell eleven exploding.

5   Down by the bands and the burning memorial
Beats all the brass in a royal array,
But at our end we are not so sartorial:
Out of (as usual) the rig of the day.

Starry is wearing a split pusser's flannel[2]
10   Rubbed, as he is, by the regular tide;
Oxo the ducks[3] that he ditched in the Channel
In June, 1940 (when he was inside).

Kitty recalls his abandon-ship station,
Running below at the Old Man's salute
15   And (with a deck-watch) going down for duration
Wearing his oppo's pneumonia-suit.[4]

Comrades, for you the black captain of carracks
Writes in Whitehall[5] his appalling decisions,
But as was often the case in the Barracks
20   Several ratings are not at Divisions.[6]

Into my eyes the stiff sea-horses stare,
Over my head sweeps the sun like a swan.
As I stand alone in Parliament Square
A cold bugle calls, and the city moves on.

1957

At the British War Cemetery, Bayeux[7]

I walked where in their talking graves
And shirts of earth five thousand lay,

---

1. November 11, when, at the eleventh hour (of the eleventh day of the eleventh month), church services throughout Britain commemorate the dead of the two world wars. A "Remembrance Day" service held at London's Parliament Square includes two minutes of silence.
2. A torn naval-issue shirt.
3. Suit made of white duck (a canvaslike material).
4. Canvas suit worn while painting the ship.

Oppo's: friend, comrade (from *opposite number*).
5. London street on which navy headquarters is located. *Carracks:* large merchant ships equipped for warfare.
6. I.e., noncommissioned sailors have skipped the parade (religious service) of the ship's company.
7. Town in northern France where many British soldiers killed in Normandy and Flanders during World War II are buried.

When history with ten feasts of fire
Had eaten the red air away.

5   "I am Christ's boy," I cried. "I bear
In iron hands the bread, the fishes.[8]
I hang with honey and with rose
This tidy wreck of all your wishes.

"On your geometry of sleep
10 The chestnut and the fir-tree fly,
And lavender and marguerite
Forge with their flowers an English sky.

"Turn now towards the belling town
Your jigsaws of impossible bone,
15 And rising read your rank of snow
Accurate as death upon the stone."

About your easy heads my prayers
I said with syllables of clay.
"What gift," I asked, "shall I bring now
20 Before I weep and walk away?"

Take, they replied, *the oak and laurel.*
Take our fortune of tears and live
Like a spendthrift lover. All we ask
Is the one gift you cannot give.

1957

Eden Rock

They are waiting for me somewhere beyond Eden Rock:
My father, twenty-five, in the same suit
Of Genuine Irish Tweed, his terrier Jack
Still two years old and trembling at his feet.

5 My mother, twenty-three, in a sprigged° dress   *floral*
Drawn at the waist, ribbon in her straw hat,
Has spread the stiff white cloth over the grass.
Her hair, the colour of wheat, takes on the light.

She pours tea from a Thermos, the milk straight
10 From an old H.P. sauce[9] bottle, a screw
Of paper for a cork; slowly sets out
The same three plates, the tin cups painted blue.

---

8. Allusion to Christ's feeding of the five thousand (John 6, Matthew 14).

9. A brand of steak sauce.

The sky whitens as if lit by three suns.
My mother shades her eyes and looks my way
15   Over the drifted stream. My father spins
A stone along the water. Leisurely,

They beckon to me from the other bank.
I hear them call, "See where the stream-path is!
Crossing is not as hard as you might think."

20   I had not thought that it would be like this.

1988

ROBERT LOWELL
1917–1977

The Quaker Graveyard in Nantucket

(FOR WARREN WINSLOW,[1] DEAD AT SEA)

Let man have dominion over the fishes of the sea and the fowls of
the air and the beasts and the whole earth, and every creeping crea-
ture that moveth upon the earth.[2]

1

A brackish reach of shoal off Madaket[3]
The sea was still breaking violently and night
Had steamed into our North Atlantic Fleet,
When the drowned sailor clutched the drag-net. Light
5   Flashed from his matted head and marble feet,
He grappled at the net
With the coiled, hurdling muscles of his thighs:
The corpse was bloodless, a botch of reds and whites,
Its open, staring eyes
10   Were lusterless dead-lights°   *porthole covers*
Or cabin-windows on a stranded hulk
Heavy with sand.[4] We weight the body, close
Its eyes and heave it seaward whence it came,
Where the heel-headed dogfish barks its nose
15   On Ahab's[5] void and forehead; and the name
Is blocked in yellow chalk.
Sailors, who pitch this portent at the sea
Where dreadnaughts° shall confess   *battleships*

1. Lowell's cousin, who died when his naval vessel
was sunk during World War II.
2. Cf. Genesis 1.26.
3. Small settlement on Nantucket Island, Massa-
chusetts. Nantucket was a center of the American
whaling industry.
4. Lines 1–12 are based on the opening chapter
of *Cape Cod*, by the American writer Henry David
Thoreau (1817–1862; see pp. 1045–46).
5. Captain Ahab, protagonist of the novel *Moby-
Dick*, by the American writer Herman Melville
(1819–1891; see pp. 1054–57), and a recurring
presence in this sequence of poems, sailed from
Nantucket on the *Pequod* in obsessive pursuit of
the white whale.

Its hell-bent deity,
20 When you are powerless
To sand-bag this Atlantic bulwark, faced
By the earth-shaker, green, unwearied, chaste
In his steel scales: ask for no Orphean lute
To pluck life back.[6] The guns of the steeled fleet
25 Recoil and then repeat
The hoarse salute.

2

Whenever winds are moving and their breath
Heaves at the roped-in bulwarks of this pier,
The terns and sea-gulls tremble at your death
30 In these home waters. Sailor, can you hear
The Pequod's sea wings, beating landward, fall
Headlong and break on our Atlantic wall
Off 'Sconset, where the yawing S-boats[7] splash
The bellbuoy, with ballooning spinnakers,°   sails
35 As the entangled, screeching mainsheet clears
The blocks: off Madaket, where lubbers° lash   landlubbers
The heavy surf and throw their long lead squids
For blue-fish? Sea-gulls blink their heavy lids
Seaward. The winds' wings beat upon the stones,
40 Cousin, and scream for you and the claws rush
At the sea's throat and wring it in the slush
Of this old Quaker graveyard where the bones
Cry out in the long night for the hurt beast
Bobbing by Ahab's whaleboats in the East.

3

45 All you recovered from Poseidon died
With you, my cousin, and the harrowed brine
Is fruitless on the blue beard of the god,
Stretching beyond us to the castles in Spain,
Nantucket's westward haven. To Cape Cod
50 Guns, cradled on the tide,
Blast the eelgrass about a waterclock
Of bilge and backwash, roil the salt and sand
Lashing earth's scaffold, rock
Our warships in the hand
55 Of the great God, where time's contrition blues
Whatever it was these Quaker sailors lost
In the mad scramble of their lives. They died
When time was open-eyed,
Wooden and childish; only bones abide
60 There, in the nowhere, where their boats were tossed

6. In Greek mythology, the musician Orpheus
used song to win his wife, Eurydice, back from the
underworld (though he lost her again before he
reached the surface). *Earth-shaker*: Poseidon,

Greek god of the sea.
7. Racing sailboats. *'Sconset*: Siasconset, a town
on Nantucket. *Yawing*: moving from side to side in
a heavy sea.

Sky-high, where mariners had fabled news
Of IS,[8] the whited monster. What it cost
Them is their secret. In the sperm-whale's slick
I see the Quakers drown and hear their cry:
65 "If God himself had not been on our side,
If God himself had not been on our side,
When the Atlantic rose against us, why,
Then it had swallowed us up quick."

4

This is the end of the whaleroad[9] and the whale
70 Who spewed Nantucket bones on the thrashed swell
And stirred the troubled waters to whirlpools
To send the Pequod packing off to hell:
This is the end of them, three-quarters fools,
Snatching at straws to sail
75 Seaward and seaward on the turntail whale,
Spouting out blood and water as it rolls,
Sick as a dog to these Atlantic shoals:
Clamavimus, O depths.[1] Let the sea-gulls wail

For water, for the deep where the high tide
80 Mutters to its hurt self, mutters and ebbs.
Waves wallow in their wash, go out and out,
Leave only the death-rattle of the crabs,
The beach increasing, its enormous snout
Sucking the ocean's side.
85 This is the end of running on the waves;
We are poured out like water. Who will dance
The mast-lashed master of Leviathans[2]
Up from this field of Quakers in their unstoned graves?

5

When the whale's viscera go and the roll
90 Of its corruption overruns this world
Beyond tree-swept Nantucket and Wood's Hole[3]
And Martha's Vineyard, Sailor, will your sword
Whistle and fall and sink into the fat?
In the great ash-pit of Jehoshaphat[4]
95 The bones cry for the blood of the white whale,
The fat flukes arch and whack about its ears,
The death-lance churns into the sanctuary, tears
The gun-blue swingle,[5] heaving like a flail,
And hacks the coiling life out: it works and drags

8. Cf. God's naming of himself to Moses as "I AM"
(Exodus 3.14).
9. An Anglo-Saxon epithet for the sea.
1. Adaptation of the Vulgate opening of Psalm
130: "Out of the depths have I cried unto thee, O
Lord" (here, "we have cried").
2. In various biblical accounts, Leviathan is a sea
monster defeated by God.
3. On the coast of Massachusetts, near the island

of Martha's Vineyard, which lies to the west of
Nantucket.
4. "The valley of judgment. The world, according
to some prophets, and scientists, will end in fire"
[Lowell's note to the American scholars Kimon
Friar and John Malcolm Brinnin]. Ahab, king of
Israel, persuaded Jehoshaphat, king of Judah, to go
to war (Joel 3.12).
5. Rod for beating flax.

100   And rips the sperm-whale's midriff into rags,
      Gobbets of blubber spill to wind and weather,
      Sailor, and gulls go round the stoven timbers
      Where the morning stars sing out together
      And thunder shakes the white surf and dismembers
105   The red flag hammered in the mast-head.[6] Hide,
      Our steel, Jonas Messias,[7] in Thy side.

6. *Our Lady of Walsingham*[8]

      There once the penitents took off their shoes
      And then walked barefoot the remaining mile;
      And the small trees, a stream and hedgerows file
110   Slowly along the munching English lane,
      Like cows to the old shrine, until you lose
      Track of your dragging pain.
      The stream flows down under the druid tree,[9]
      Shiloah's[1] whirlpools gurgle and make glad
115   The castle of God. Sailor, you were glad
      And whistled Sion by that stream. But see:

      Our Lady, too small for her canopy,
      Sits near the altar. There's no comeliness
      At all or charm in that expressionless
120   Face with its heavy eyelids. As before,
      This face, for centuries a memory,
      Non est species, neque decor,[2]
      Expressionless, expresses God: it goes
      Past castled Sion. She knows what God knows,
125   Not Calvary's Cross nor crib at Bethlehem
      Now, and the world shall come to Walsingham.

7

      The empty winds are creaking and the oak
      Splatters and splatters on the cenotaph,[3]
      The boughs are trembling and a gaff°   *spar*
130   Bobs on the untimely stroke
      Of the greased wash exploding on a shoal-bell°   *bell buoy*
      In the old mouth of the Atlantic. It's well;
      Atlantic, you are fouled with the blue sailors,
      Sea-monsters, upward angel, downward fish:[4]

---

6. As was the flag in the concluding chapter of *Moby-Dick*.
7. The prophet Jonah (also called Jonas), who emerged alive from the whale, is often linked with the Messiah as a figure of salvation. Here he is pierced by a harpoon as Jesus was pierced by a Roman soldier's spear (cf. Matthew 12.39–41).
8. Walsingham is a small town in Norfolk, England; a shrine to the Virgin Mary, built in the eleventh century, was an object of pilgrimage until it was destroyed during the Reformation. Lowell adapted this section from the description in E. I. Watkin's *Catholic Art and Culture* (1942).
9. The Druids were an order of ancient Celts of Gaul and Britain who served as priests, teachers, and magicians; their beliefs and practices are associated with trees.
1. According to Isaiah 8.6, the stream that flows past God's Temple on Mt. Sion. In Isaiah 51.11, the redeemed come "singing into Zion," the heavenly city.
2. There is no beauty or charm (Latin); quoted from Watkin.
3. An empty tomb or monument erected to the dead but not containing their remains.
4. Cf. Milton, *Paradise Lost* 1.462–63: "Dagon his name, sea monster, upward man / And downward fish."

135   Unmarried and corroding, spare of flesh
     Mart° once of supercilious, wing'd clippers,   *market*
     Atlantic, where your bell-trap guts its spoil
     You could cut the brackish winds with a knife
     Here in Nantucket, and cast up the time
140   When the Lord God formed man from the sea's slime
     And breathed into his face the breath of life,
     And blue-lung'd combers lumbered to the kill.
     The Lord survives the rainbow of His will.[5]

1946

Mr. Edwards[6] and the Spider

     I saw the spiders marching through the air,
     Swimming from tree to tree that mildewed day
       In latter August when the hay
       Came creaking to the barn. But where
5   The wind is westerly,
     Where gnarled November makes the spiders fly
     Into the apparitions of the sky,
     They purpose nothing but their ease and die
Urgently beating east to sunrise and the sea;

10   What are we in the hands of the great God?
     It was in vain you set up thorn and briar
       In battle array against the fire
       And treason crackling in your blood;
        For the wild thorns grow tame
15   And will do nothing to oppose the flame;
     Your lacerations tell the losing game
     You play against a sickness past your cure.
How will the hands be strong? How will the heart endure?[7]

     A very little thing, a little worm,
20   Or hourglass-blazoned spider,[8] it is said,
       Can kill a tiger. Will the dead
       Hold up his mirror and affirm
        To the four winds the smell
     And flash of his authority? It's well
25   If God who holds you to the pit of hell,

5. The rainbow symbolizes God's covenant with Noah never again to destroy the earth by flood (see Genesis 9.11–17).
6. Jonathan Edwards (1703–1758), Puritan theologian and preacher whose works are alluded to throughout. The first stanza draws upon a paper, "On Insects," probably written ca. 1719–20, in which Edwards records his observations of the behavior of spiders. The poem is also heavily indebted to Edwards's most famous sermon, "Sinners in the Hands of an Angry God," which compares humans to spiders: "The God that holds you over the pit of Hell, much as one holds a spider or some loathsome insect, over the fire, abhors you, and is dreadfully provoked; his wrath towards you burns like fire."
7. Cf. Ezekiel 22.14 (the point of departure of "Sinners in the Hands of an Angry God"): "Can thine heart endure, or can thine hands be strong, in the days that I shall be strong, in the days that I shall deal with thee?"
8. The black widow spider, common in North America, is marked with a red hourglass pattern on its abdomen.

Much as one holds a spider, will destroy,
Baffle and dissipate your soul. As a small boy

On Windsor Marsh,[9] I saw the spider die
When thrown into the bowels of fierce fire:
30   There's no long struggle, no desire
        To get up on its feet and fly—
            It stretches out its feet
        And dies. This is the sinner's last retreat;
        Yes, and no strength exerted on the heat
35   Then sinews the abolished will, when sick
        And full of burning, it will whistle on a brick.

        But who can plumb the sinking of that soul?
        Josiah Hawley,[1] picture yourself cast
            Into a brick-kiln where the blast
40   Fans your quick vitals to a coal—
                If measured by a glass,
        How long would it seem burning! Let there pass
        A minute, ten, ten trillion; but the blaze
        Is infinite, eternal: this is death,
45 To die and know it. This is the Black Widow, death.

                                                    1946

My Last Afternoon with Uncle Devereux Winslow

1922: THE STONE PORCH OF MY GRANDFATHER'S SUMMER HOUSE

1

"I won't go with you. I want to stay with Grandpa!"
That's how I threw cold water
on my Mother and Father's
watery martini pipe dreams at Sunday dinner.
5   . . . Fontainebleau, Mattapoisett, Puget Sound. . . .[2]
Nowhere was anywhere after a summer
at my Grandfather's farm.
Diamond-pointed, athirst and Norman,[3]
its alley of poplars
10 paraded from Grandmother's rose garden
to a scary stand of virgin pine,
scrub, and paths forever pioneering.

One afternoon in 1922,
I sat on the stone porch, looking through
15 screens as black-grained as drifting coal.

9. Near East Windsor, Connecticut, Edwards's
childhood home.
1. Edwards's uncle, Joseph Hawley, who killed
himself in 1735.
2. Desirable places to visit (in France, Massachu-

setts, and Washington State, respectively).
3. A version of Romanesque architecture devel-
oped in the French province of Normandy in the
tenth century.

Tockytock, tockytock
clumped our Alpine, Edwardian cuckoo clock,
slung with strangled, wooden game.
Our farmer was cementing a root-house[4] under the hill.
20 One of my hands was cool on a pile
of black earth, the other warm
on a pile of lime. All about me
were the works of my Grandfather's hands:
snapshots of his *Liberty Bell* silver mine;
25 his high school at *Stuttgart am Neckar*;[5]
stogie-brown beams; fools'-gold nuggets;
octagonal red tiles,
sweaty with a secret dank, crummy with ant-stale;
a Rocky Mountain chaise longue,
30 its legs, shellacked saplings.
A pastel-pale Huckleberry Finn[6]
fished with a broom straw in a basin
hollowed out of a millstone.
Like my Grandfather, the décor
35 was manly, comfortable,
overbearing, disproportioned.

What were those sunflowers? Pumpkins floating shoulder-high?
It was sunset, Sadie and Nellie
bearing pitchers of ice-tea,
40 oranges, lemons, mint, and peppermints,
and the jug of shandygaff,
which Grandpa made by blending half and half
yeasty, wheezing homemade sarsaparilla with beer.
The farm, entitled *Char-de-sa*
45 in the Social Register,
was named for my Grandfather's children:
Charlotte, Devereux, and Sarah.
No one had died there in my lifetime . . .
Only Cinder, our Scottie puppy
50 paralyzed from gobbling toads.
I sat mixing black earth and lime.

2

I was five and a half.
My formal pearl gray shorts
had been worn for three minutes.
55 My perfection was the Olympian
poise of my models in the imperishable autumn
display windows
of Rogers Peet's boys' store below the State House
in Boston. Distorting drops of water
60 pinpricked my face in the basin's mirror.

---

4. Small building, partly underground, used for storing root vegetables, bulbs, etc.
5. German city on the Neckar River.

6. Boy hero of the novel *The Adventures of Huckleberry Finn*, by the American writer Mark Twain (1835–1910).

I was a stuffed toucan
with a bibulous, multicolored beak.

3

Up in the air
by the lakeview window in the billiards-room,
65 lurid in the doldrums of the sunset hour,
my Great Aunt Sarah
was learning *Samson and Delilah*.[7]
She thundered on the keyboard of her dummy piano,
with gauze curtains like a boudoir table,
70 accordionlike yet soundless.
It had been bought to spare the nerves
of my Grandmother,
tone-deaf, quick as a cricket,
now needing a fourth for "Auction,"°   *auction bridge*
75 and casting a thirsty eye
on Aunt Sarah, risen like the phoenix[8]
from her bed of troublesome snacks and Tauchnitz[9] classics.

Forty years earlier,
twenty, auburn headed,
80 grasshopper notes of genius!
Family gossip says Aunt Sarah
tilted her archaic Athenian nose
and jilted an Astor.[1]
Each morning she practiced
85 on the grand piano at Symphony Hall,
deathlike in the off-season summer—
its naked Greek statues draped with purple
like the saints in Holy Week. . . .
On the recital day, she failed to appear.

4

90 I picked with a clean finger nail at the blue anchor
on my sailor blouse washed white as a spinnaker.
What in the world was I wishing?
. . . A sail-colored horse browsing in the bullrushes . . .
A fluff of the west wind puffing
95 my blouse, kiting me over our seven chimneys,
troubling the waters. . . .
As small as sapphires were the ponds: *Quittacus, Snippituit,*
and *Assawompset,* halved by "the Island,"
where my Uncle's duck blind
100 floated in a barrage of smoke-clouds.

7. Piano arrangement of an opera by the French
composer Camille Saint-Saëns (1835–1921).
8. A long-lived mythological bird that consumed
itself in flames and was then reborn from its ashes.
Aunt Sarah: Sarah Stark Winslow, Robert Lowell's
mother's aunt.

9. German publisher of inexpensive paperbacks,
including many English and American works in
English.
1. In the nineteenth century, three generations of
Astors in New York accumulated one of the largest
fortunes in the world.

Double-barreled shotguns
stuck out like bundles of baby crow-bars.
A single sculler° in a camouflaged kayak   rower
was quacking to the decoys. . . .

105   At the cabin between the waters,
       the nearest windows were already boarded.
       Uncle Devereux was closing camp for the winter.
       As if posed for "the engagement photograph,"
       he was wearing his severe
110   war-uniform of a volunteer Canadian officer.
       Daylight from the doorway riddled his student posters,
       tacked helter-skelter on walls as raw as a boardwalk.
       Mr. Punch,[2] a water melon in hockey tights,
       was tossing off a decanter of Scotch.
115   *La Belle France* in a red, white and blue toga
       was accepting the arm of her "protector,"
       the ingenu and porcine Edward VII.[3]
       The pre-war music hall belles
       had goose necks, glorious signatures, beauty-moles,
120   and coils of hair like rooster tails.
       The finest poster was two or three young men in khaki kilts
       being bushwhacked on the veldt[4]—
       They were almost life-size. . . .

       My Uncle was dying at twenty-nine.
125   "You are behaving like children,"
       said my Grandfather,
       when my Uncle and Aunt left their three baby daughters,
       and sailed for Europe on a last honeymoon . . .
       I cowered in terror.
130   I wasn't a child at all—
       unseen and all-seeing, I was Agrippina[5]
       in the Golden House of Nero. . . .
       Near me was the white measuring-door
       my Grandfather had penciled with my Uncle's heights.
135   In 1911, he had stopped growing at just six feet.
       While I sat on the tiles,
       and dug at the anchor on my sailor blouse,
       Uncle Devereux stood behind me.
       He was as brushed as Bayard, our riding horse.
140   His face was putty.
       His blue coat and white trousers
       grew sharper and straighter.
       His coat was a blue jay's tail,
       his trousers were solid cream from the top of the bottle.

2. A cartoon figure used as emblem for the English humor magazine *Punch*.
3. Edward VII, king of England from 1901 to 1910, helped initiate the era of good feeling between England and France known as "L'Entente Cordiale." On a poster, he is pictured with an arm around the waist of Marianne, "La Belle France,"
the traditional emblem for France.
4. Open country in South Africa. The Boer War (1899–1902) was fought by the British against the descendants of Dutch settlers in South Africa.
5. Mother of Nero (first century); her scheming helped make him Roman emperor. He later had her murdered.

145   He was animated, hierarchical,
       like a ginger snap man in a clothes-press.
       He was dying of the incurable Hodgkin's disease. . . .
       My hands were warm, then cool, on the piles
       of earth and lime,
150   a black pile and a white pile. . . .
       Come winter,
       Uncle Devereux would blend to the one color.

1959

Skunk Hour

(FOR ELIZABETH BISHOP)[6]

    Nautilus Island's[7] hermit
    heiress still lives through winter in her Spartan cottage;
    her sheep still graze above the sea.
    Her son's a bishop. Her farmer
5   is first selectman[8] in our village;
    she's in her dotage.

    Thirsting for
    the hierarchic privacy
    of Queen Victoria's century,
10 she buys up all
    the eyesores facing her shore,
    and lets them fall.

    The season's ill—
    we've lost our summer millionaire,
15 who seemed to leap from an L. L. Bean[9]
    catalogue. His nine-knot yawl
    was auctioned off to lobstermen.
    A red fox stain covers Blue Hill.

    And now our fairy
20 decorator brightens his shop for fall;
    his fishnet's filled with orange cork,
    orange, his cobbler's bench and awl;
    there is no money in his work,
    he'd rather marry.

25 One dark night,
    my Tudor Ford climbed the hill's skull;
    I watched for love-cars. Lights turned down,
    they lay together, hull to hull,

6. Lowell said that he modeled this poem on Bishop's "The Armadillo" (see p. 1519).
7. In Castine, Maine, where Lowell had a summer house.
8. Many New England towns are administered by an elected board of selectmen.
9. A mail-order company in Maine, originally specializing in hunting, fishing, and camping gear.

where the graveyard shelves on the town. . . .
30   My mind's not right.

A car radio bleats,
"Love, O careless Love. . . ."[1] I hear
my ill-spirit sob in each blood cell,
as if my hand were at its throat. . . .
35   I myself am hell;[2]
nobody's here—

only skunks, that search
in the moonlight for a bite to eat.
They march on their soles up Main Street:
40   white stripes, moonstruck eyes' red fire
under the chalk-dry and spar° spire   mastlike
of the Trinitarian Church.

I stand on top
of our back steps and breathe the rich air—
45   a mother skunk with her column of kittens swills the garbage pail.
She jabs her wedge-head in a cup
of sour cream, drops her ostrich tail,
and will not scare.

1957   1959

Water

It was a Maine lobster town—
each morning boatloads of hands
pushed off for granite
quarries on the islands,

5   and left dozens of bleak
white frame houses stuck
like oyster shells
on a hill of rock,

and below us, the sea lapped
10   the raw little match-stick
mazes of a weir,
where the fish for bait were trapped.

Remember? We sat on a slab of rock.
From this dance in time,
15   it seems the color
of iris, rotting and turning purpler,

---

1. From a popular song of the time, "Careless
Love," which includes the lines "Now you see what
careless love will do . . . / Make you kill yourself
and your sweetheart too."
2. Cf. Satan in Milton's *Paradise Lost* 4.75:
"Which way I fly is Hell; myself am Hell."

but it was only
the usual gray rock
turning the usual green
20   when drenched by the sea.

The sea drenched the rock
at our feet all day,
and kept tearing away
flake after flake.

25   One night you dreamed
you were a mermaid clinging to a wharf-pile,
and trying to pull
off the barnacles with your hands.

We wished our two souls
30   might return like gulls
to the rock. In the end,
the water was too cold for us.

1964

For the Union Dead[3]

"Relinquunt Omnia Servare Rem Publicam."

The old South Boston Aquarium stands
in a Sahara of snow now. Its broken windows are boarded.
The bronze weathervane cod has lost half its scales.
The airy tanks are dry.

5   Once my nose crawled like a snail on the glass;
my hand tingled
to burst the bubbles
drifting from the noses of the cowed, compliant fish.

My hand draws back. I often sigh still
10   for the dark downward and vegetating kingdom
of the fish and reptile. One morning last March,
I pressed against the new barbed and galvanized

fence on the Boston Common. Behind their cage,
yellow dinosaur steamshovels were grunting
15   as they cropped up tons of mush and grass
to gouge their underworld garage.

3. At the edge of Boston Common, across from the Massachusetts State House, stands a monument to Colonel Robert Gould Shaw (1837–1863) and the first all-black Civil War regiment, the 54th Massachusetts; Shaw and many of his troops were killed in the assault on Fort Wagner, South Carolina. The bronze relief, by the American (Irish-born) sculptor Augustus Saint-Gaudens (1848–1907), was dedicated in 1897. In the upper right it bears the Latin motto of the Society of the Cincinnati, *Omnia relinquit servare rem publicam* ("He gives up everything to serve the republic"). Lowell's epigraph changes "he gives" to "they give."

Parking spaces luxuriate like civic
sandpiles in the heart of Boston.
A girdle of orange, Puritan-pumpkin colored girders
20   braces the tingling Statehouse,

shaking over the excavations, as it faces Colonel Shaw
and his bell-cheeked Negro infantry
on St. Gaudens' shaking Civil War relief,
propped by a plank splint against the garage's earthquake.

25   Two months after marching through Boston,
half the regiment was dead;
at the dedication,
William James[4] could almost hear the bronze Negroes breathe.

Their monument sticks like a fishbone
30   in the city's throat.
Its Colonel is as lean
as a compass-needle.

He has an angry wrenlike vigilance,
a greyhound's gentle tautness;
35   he seems to wince at pleasure,
and suffocate for privacy.

He is out of bounds now. He rejoices in man's lovely,
peculiar power to choose life and die—
when he leads his black soldiers to death,
40   he cannot bend his back.

On a thousand small town New England greens,
the old white churches hold their air
of sparse, sincere rebellion; frayed flags
quilt the graveyards of the Grand Army of the Republic.

45   The stone statues of the abstract Union Soldier
grow slimmer and younger each year—
wasp-waisted, they doze over muskets
and muse through their sideburns . . .

Shaw's father wanted no monument
50   except the ditch,
where his son's body was thrown
and lost with his "niggers."

The ditch is nearer.
There are no statues for the last war here;
55   on Boylston Street,[5] a commercial photograph
shows Hiroshima boiling

---

4. Philosopher and psychologist (1842–1910), who taught at Harvard University.

5. A major street in Boston. *Last war*: World War II.

over a Mosler Safe, the "Rock of Ages"
that survived the blast. Space is nearer.
When I crouch to my television set,
60   the drained faces of Negro school-children rise like balloons.[6]

    Colonel Shaw
is riding on his bubble,
he waits
for the blessèd break.

65   The Aquarium is gone. Everywhere,
giant finned cars nose forward like fish;
a savage servility
slides by on grease.

    1964

Harriet[7]

    A repeating fly, blueback, thumbthick—so gross,
it seems apocalyptic in our house—
whams back and forth across the nursery bed
manned by a madhouse of stuffed animals,
5   not one a fighter. It is like a plane
dusting apple orchards or Arabs on the screen—
one of the mighty . . . one of the helpless. It
bumbles and bumps its brow on this and that,
making a short, unhealthy life the shorter.
10   I kill it, and another instant's added
to the horrifying mortmain[8] of
ephemera: keys, drift, sea-urchin shells,
you packrat off with joy . . . a dead fly swept
under the carpet, wrinkling to fulfillment.

1970   1973

Epilogue

    Those blessèd structures, plot and rhyme—
why are they no help to me now
I want to make
something imagined, not recalled?
5   I hear the noise of my own voice:
The painter's vision is not a lens,
it trembles to caress the light.

6. The struggles to integrate public schools (first
in the South, and later in the North) were fre-
quently featured in television newscasts.
7. The poet's daughter, born January 4, 1945.

8. A legal term ("dead hand") referring to perpet-
ual ownership; more generally, the influence of the
past on the present.

But sometimes everything I write
with the threadbare art of my eye
10   seems a snapshot,
lurid, rapid, garish, grouped,
heightened from life,
yet paralyzed by fact.
All's misalliance.
15   Yet why not say what happened?
Pray for the grace of accuracy
Vermeer[9] gave to the sun's illumination
stealing like the tide across a map
to his girl solid with yearning.
20   We are poor passing facts,
warned by that to give
each figure in the photograph
his living name.

1977

LAWRENCE FERLINGHETTI
b. 1919

Sometime During Eternity . . .

Sometime during eternity
                    some guys show up
and one of them
           who shows up real late
5   is a kind of carpenter[1]
from some square-type place
                like Galilee[2]
and he starts wailing
                  and claiming he is hip
10   to who made heaven
               and earth
                      and that the cat
         who really laid it on us
              is his Dad

15   And moreover
        he adds
          It's all writ down
                on some scroll-type parchments
which some henchmen
20   leave lying around the Dead Sea[3] somewheres

---

9. Jan Vermeer (1632–1675), Dutch painter known for his treatment of light.
1. Jesus was a carpenter.
2. Region in northern Israel, home of Jesus.

3. Sea between the West Bank and Jordan, where the Dead Sea Scrolls, fragments of the Jewish Essene order's library dating back to 130 B.C.E., were found in 1947.

a long time ago
                    and which you won't even find
      for a coupla thousand years or so
                    or at least for
25   nineteen hundred and fortyseven
                              of them
                 to be exact
                    and even then
      nobody really believes them
30   or me
                        for that matter

      You're hot
             they tell him

      And they cool him

35   They stretch him on the Tree to cool

         And everybody after that
                         is always making models
             of this Tree
                    with Him hung up
40   and always crooning His name
                    and calling Him to come down
             and sit in
                         on their combo
             as if he is *the* king cat
45   who's got to blow[4]
      or they can't quite make it

         Only he don't come down
                         from His Tree

      Him just hang there
50   on His Tree
      looking real Petered out[5]
                    and real cool
                         and also
             according to a roundup
55   of late world news
      from the usual unreliable sources
                              real dead

                                             1958

4. Play. *King cat*: slang for leader (Jesus was also called king of the Jews). *Combo*: group of musicians, particularly jazz players.
5. Pun referring both to a sense of defeat or exhaustion and to St. Peter, who denied being a disciple three times after Jesus' arrest (John 18.17–27).

WILLIAM MEREDITH
b. 1919

The Illiterate

Touching your goodness, I am like a man
Who turns a letter over in his hand
And you might think this was because the hand
Was unfamiliar but, truth is, the man
5   Has never had a letter from anyone;
And now he is both afraid of what it means
And ashamed because he has no other means
To find out what it says than to ask someone.

His uncle could have left the farm to him,
10   Or his parents died before he sent them word,
Or the dark girl changed and want him for beloved.
Afraid and letter-proud, he keeps it with him.
What would you call his feeling for the words
That keep him rich and orphaned and beloved?

                                                1958

Rhode Island

Here at the seashore they use the clouds over & over
again, like the rented animals in *Aïda*.[1]
In the late morning the land breeze
turns and now the extras are driving
5   all the white elephants the other way.
What language are the children shouting in?
He[2] is lying on the beach listening.

The sand knocks like glass, struck by bare heels.
He tries to remember snow noise.
10   Would powder snow ping like that?
But you don't lie with your ear to powder snow.
Why doesn't the girl who takes care
of the children, a Yale girl without flaw,
know the difference between *lay* and *lie*?

15   He tries to remember snow, his season.
The mind is in charge of things then.
Summer is for animals, the ocean is erotic,
all that openness and swaying.

---

1. During a triumphal procession in this opera by
the Italian composer Giuseppe Verdi (1813–
1901), the victorious Egyptian forces return to
Memphis with their captives; major companies
often hire horses and elephants to augment the
spectacle.
2. Hazard, the Painter (title character of the vol-
ume from which this poem comes); cf. line 25.

No matter how often you make love
20 in August you're always aware of genitalia,
your own and the half-naked others'.
Even with the gracefulest bathers
you're aware of their kinship with porpoises,
mammals disporting themselves in a blue element,
25 smelling slightly of fish. Porpoise Hazard
watches himself awhile, like a blue movie.

In the other hemisphere now people
are standing up, at work at their easels.
There they think about love at night
30 when they take off their serious clothes
and go to bed sandlessly, under blankets.

Today the children, his own among them,
are apparently shouting fluently in Portuguese,
using the colonial dialect of Brazil.
35 It is just as well, they have all been changed
into small shrill marginal animals,
he would not want to understand them again
until after Labor Day. He just lays there.

                                      1975

AMY CLAMPITT
1920–1994

Beach Glass

While you walk the water's edge,
turning over concepts
I can't envision, the honking buoy
serves notice that at any time
5 the wind may change,
the reef-bell clatters
its treble monotone, deaf as Cassandra[1]
to any note but warning. The ocean,
cumbered by no business more urgent
10 than keeping open old accounts
that never balanced,
goes on shuffling its millenniums
of quartz, granite, and basalt.
                       It behaves
15 toward the permutations of novelty—
driftwood and shipwreck, last night's
beer cans, spilt oil, the coughed-up

---

1. In Greek mythology, the daughter of Priam (last king of Troy), and a prophetess who predicted the fall of Troy. Her gift of prophecy was marred by the curse of never being believed.

residue of plastic—with random
impartiality, playing catch or tag
20   or touch-last like a terrier,
turning the same thing over and over,
over and over. For the ocean, nothing
is beneath consideration.
                    The houses
25   of so many mussels and periwinkles°   *mollusks, snails*
have been abandoned here, it's hopeless
to know which to salvage. Instead
I keep a lookout for beach glass —
amber of Budweiser, chrysoprase[2]
30   of Almadén and Gallo, lapis[3]
by way of (no getting around it,
I'm afraid) Phillips'
Milk of Magnesia, with now and then a rare
translucent turquoise or blurred amethyst
35   of no known origin.
                   The process
goes on forever: they came from sand,
they go back to gravel,
along with the treasuries
40   of Murano,[4] the buttressed
astonishments of Chartres,[5]
which even now are readying
for being turned over and over as gravely
and gradually as an intellect
45   engaged in the hazardous
redefinition of structures
no one has yet looked at.

                                         1983

Beethoven, Opus 111[6]

FOR NORMAN CAREY

There are epochs . . . when mankind, not content with the present,
longing for time's deeper layers, like the plowman, thirsts for the
virgin soil of time.

                                —OSIP MANDELSTAM[7]

—Or, conversely, hungers
for the levitations of the concert hall:
the hands like rafts of *putti*[8]

2. The green color of chalcedony quartz.
3. The deep-blue color of lapis lazuli, a mineral.
4. An island near Venice, famous for manufacturing fine glass.
5. The cathedral of Notre Dame de Chartres, in France, celebrated for its stained-glass windows.
6. *Piano Sonata No. 32 in C Minor*, Opus 111, the last work in the form, as Clampitt's note remarks, by the German composer Ludwig van Beethoven

(1770–1827). An exemplar of Romanticism and revolution, Beethoven had become deaf by the time he wrote this piece, in 1821–22.
7. Russian poet and critic (1891–1938), who was arrested for a poem on Joseph Stalin and later died in a transit camp.
8. "The stylized infant cherubs that appear to soar, plunge or hover in some Italian and Spanish paintings on Christian themes" [Clampitt's note].

out of a region where the dolorous stars
5   are fixed in glassy cerements of Art;
the *ancien régime*'s diaphanous plash[9]
athwart the mounting throb of hobnails—
shod squadrons of vibration
mining the air, its struck ores hardening
10   into a plowshare, a downward wandering
disrupting every formal symmetry:
from the supine harp-case, the strung-foot
tendons under the mahogany, the bulldozer
in the bass unearths a Piranesian[1]
15   catacomb: Beethoven ventilating,
with a sound he cannot hear, the cave-in
of recurring rage.
               In the tornado country
of mid-America, my father
20   might have been his twin—a farmer
hacking at sourdock, at the strangle-
roots of thistles and wild morning glories,
setting out rashly, one October,
to rid the fencerows of poison ivy:
25   livid seed-globs turreted
in trinities of glitter, ripe
with the malefic glee no farmer doubts
lives deep down things.[2] My father
was naïve enough—by nature
30   revolutionary, though he'd have
disowned the label—to suppose he might
in some way, minor but radical, disrupt
the givens of existence: set
his neighbors' thinking straight, undo
35   the stranglehold of reasons nations
send their boys off to war. That fall,
after the oily fireworks had cooled down
to trellises of hairy wicks,
he dug them up, rootstocks and all,
40   and burned them. Do-gooder!
The well-meant holocaust became
a mist of venom, sowing itself along
the sculptured hollows of his overalls,
braceleting wrists and collarbone—
45   a mesh of blisters spreading to a shirt
worn like a curse. For weeks
he writhed inside it. Awful.
               High art
with a stiff neck: an upright Steinway[3]
50   bought in Chicago; a chromo of a Hobbema

---

9. I.e., the extremely delicate splash of France's political and social system before the revolution in 1789. *Cerements*: shrouds for the dead.
1. As in the work of Giambattista Piranesi (1720–1778), Italian architect, painter, and engraver.
2. An allusion to Gerard Manley Hopkins, "God's Grandeur" (p. 1166), in which "There lives the dearest freshness deep down things." *Malefic*: malignant, malicious.
3. Meindert Hobbema (1638–1709), Dutch painter. *Chromo*: chromolithograph, print. *Steinway*: one of the best brands of pianos.

tree-avenue, or of Millet's imagined peasant,
the lark she listens to invisible,[4] perhaps
irrelevant: harpstrings and fripperies of air
congealed into an object nailed against the wall,
55   its sole ironic function (if it has any)
to demonstrate that one, though he may
grunt and sweat at work, is not a clod.
Beethoven might declare the air
his domicile, the winds kin,[5] the tornado
60   a kind of second cousin; here,
his labor merely shimmers—a deracinated
album leaf, a bagatelle, the "Moonlight"
rendered with a dying fall[6] (the chords
subside, disintegrate, regroup
65   in climbing sequences *con brio*);[7] there's
no dwelling on the sweet past here,
there being no past to speak of
other than the setbacks: typhoid
in the wells, half the first settlers
70   dead of it before a year was out;
diphtheria and scarlet fever
every winter; drought, the Depression,
a mortgage on the mortgage. High art
as a susurrus,° the silk and perfume   *whisper*
75   of unsullied hands. Those hands!—
driving the impressionable wild with anguish
for another life entirely: the Lyceum[8] circuit,
the doomed diving bell of Art.
                                             Beethoven
80   in his workroom: ear trumpet,
conversation book and pencil, candlestick,
broken crockery, the Graf piano
wrecked by repeated efforts to hear himself—
out of a humdrum squalor the levitations,
85   the shakes and triplets, the *Adagio
molto semplice e cantabile*,[9] the Arietta°   *little air*
a disintegrating surf of blossom
opening along the keyboard, along the fencerows
the astonishment of sweetness. My father,
90   driving somewhere in Kansas or Colorado,
in dustbowl country, stopped the car
to dig up by the roots a flower
he'd never seen before—a kind
of prickly poppy most likely, its luminousness
95   wounding the blank plains like desire.

4. Because the European skylark sings in flight, often too high to be seen, as in the famous painting of the listening peasant, by the French painter Jean-François Millet (1814–1875).
5. "In a letter to Count Brunswick dated February 13, 1814, Beethoven wrote: 'As regards me, great heavens! my dominion is in the air; the tones whirl like the wind, and often there is a whirl in my soul' " [Clampitt's note].

6. Cf. Shakespeare, *Twelfth Night* 1.1.1–4: ". . . that strain again! It had a dying fall." "*Moonlight*": Beethoven's *Piano Sonata in C Sharp Minor (Moonlight)*, Opus 27, No. 2.
7. With vigor (Italian); musical direction.
8. A building used for cultural activities, such as concerts.
9. A slow movement, played very simply and in a songlike manner (Italian).

He mentioned in a letter the disappointment
of his having hoped it might transplant—
an episode that brings me near tears,
still, as even his dying does not—
100   that awful dying, months-long, hunkered,
irascible. From a clod no plowshare
could deliver, a groan for someone
(because he didn't want to look
at anything) to take away the flowers,
105   a bawling as of slaughterhouses, slogans
of a general uprising: *Freiheit!*[1]
Beethoven, shut up with the four walls
of his deafness, rehearsing the unhearable
semplice e cantabile, somehow reconstituting
110   the blister shirt of the intolerable
into these shakes and triplets, a hurrying
into flowering along the fencerows: dying,
for my father, came to be like that
finally—in its messages the levitation
115   of serenity, as though the spirit might
aspire, in its last act,
                              to walk on air.

1983

The Sun Underfoot Among the Sundews[2]

An ingenuity too astonishing
to be quite fortuitous is
this bog full of sundews, sphagnum-°   *moss-*
lined and shaped like a teacup.
5   A step
down and you're into it; a
wilderness swallows you up:
ankle-, then knee-, then midriff-
to-shoulder-deep in wetfooted
10   understory, an overhead
spruce-tamarack horizon hinting
you'll never get out of here.
                              But the sun
among the sundews, down there,
15   is so bright, an underfoot
webwork of carnivorous rubies,
a star-swarm thick as the gnats
they're set to catch, delectable
double-faced cockleburs, each
20   hair-tip a sticky mirror
afire with sunlight, a million
of them and again a million,

---

1. Freedom! (German).   2. Carnivorous bog plants.

each mirror a trap set to
unhand unbelieving,
25   that either
a First Cause said once, "Let there
be sundews,"[3] and there were, or they've
made their way here unaided
other than by that backhand, round-
30 about refusal to assume responsibility
known as Natural Selection.[4]
                  But the sun
underfoot is so dazzling
down there among the sundews,
35 there is so much light
in the cup that, looking,
you start to fall upward.

1983

The Cormorant in Its Element

That bony potbellied arrow, wing-pumping along
implacably, with a ramrod's rigid adherence,
airborne, to the horizontal, discloses talents
one would never have guessed at. Plummeting

5 waterward, big black feet splayed for a landing
gear, slim head turning and turning, vermilion-
strapped, this way and that, with a lightning glance
over the shoulder, the cormorant astounding-

ly, in one sleek involuted arabesque, a vertical
10 turn on a dime, goes into that inimitable
vanishing-and-emerging-from-under-the-briny-

deep act which, unlike the works of Homo Houdini,[5]
is performed for reasons having nothing at all
to do with ego, guilt, ambition, or even money.

1983

Syrinx[6]

Like the foghorn that's all lung,
the wind chime that's all percussion,

---

3. See Genesis 1.14: "And God said, Let there be lights in the firmament of the heaven."
4. The theory of evolution as formulated by the English naturalist Charles Darwin (1809–1882).
5. An invented term conflating the Latin *Homo sapiens*, or humankind, with the American magician Harry Houdini (1874–1926).

6. The vocal organ of birds, named after the Arcadian mountain nymph in Greek mythology who, to protect her chastity from the god Pan, was transformed into a reed. From that reed Pan made the pan-pipe, also called the syrinx. Pastoral poets considered Pan a patron of their art.

like the wind itself, that's merely air
in a terrible fret,[7] without so much
5   as a finger to articulate
what ails it, the aeolian[8]
syrinx, that reed
in the throat of a bird,
when it comes to the shaping of
10   what we call consonants, is
too imprecise for consensus
about what it even seems to
be saying: is it *o-ka-lee*
or *con-ka-ree,* is it really *jug jug,*
15   is it *cuckoo* for that matter?—
much less whether a bird's call
means anything in
particular, or at all.

Syntax comes last, there can be
20   no doubt of it: came last,
can be thought of (is
thought of by some) as a
higher form of expression:
is, in extremity, first to
25   be jettisoned: as the diva
onstage, all soaring
pectoral breathwork,
takes off, pure vowel
breaking free of the dry,
30   the merely fricative
husk of the particular, rises
past saying anything, any
more than the wind in
the trees, waves breaking,
35   or Homer's gibbering
Thespesiae iachē:[9]

those last-chance vestiges
above the threshold, the all-
but dispossessed of breath.

1994

---

7. In the double sense of 1) worried agitation, and 2) a ridge set across the fingerboard of a stringed instrument to help the fingers stop the strings correctly.
8. Producing a windlike moaning or sighing sound.
9. Clampitt's oblique commentary, in a note, is a quotation from Homer's *Odyssey* 10.34–43, as translated by A. T. Murray: "Then there gathered from out of Erebus the spirits of those that are dead, brides, and unwedded youths, and toil-worn old men, and tender maidens with hearts yet new to sorrow, and many, too, that had been wounded with bronze-tipped spears, men slain in fight, wearing their blood-stained armour. These came thronging in crowds about the pit from every side, with a wondrous cry . . ."

BARBARA GUEST
b. 1920

Roses

"painting has no air . . ."
—GERTRUDE STEIN[1]

That there should never be air
in a picture surprises me.
It would seem to be only a picture
of a certain kind, a portrait in paper
5   or glued, somewhere a stickiness
as opposed to a stick-to-it-ness
of another genre. It might be
quite new to do without
that air, or to find oxygen
10   on the landscape line
like a boat which is an object
or a shoe which never floats
and is stationary.

                  Still there
15   are certain illnesses that require
air, lots of it. And there are nervous
people who cannot manufacture
enough air and must seek
for it when they don't have plants,
20   in pictures. There is the mysterious
traveling that one does outside
the cube and this takes place
in air.

              It is why one develops
25   an attitude toward roses picked
in the morning air, even roses
without sun shining on them.
The roses of Juan Gris[2] from which
we learn the selflessness of roses
30   existing perpetually without air,
the lid being down, so to speak,
a 1912 fragrance sifting
to the left corner where we read
"The Marvelous" and escape.

                                    1973

1. American writer (1874–1946; see pp. 1248–50), whose Paris home was a salon for leading artists and writers between the two world wars.
2. Spanish Cubist painter (1887–1927).

Twilight Polka Dots

The lake was filled with distinguished fish purchased
at much expense in their prime. It was a curious lake, half salt,
wishing to set a tone of solitude edged with poetry.
This was a conscious body aware of shelves and wandering
5   rootlings, duty suggested it provide a scenic atmosphere
of content, a solicitude for the brooding emotions.

It despised the fish who enriched the waters. Fish with
their lithesome bodies, and their disagreeable concern
with feeding. They disturbed the water which preferred
10   the cultivated echoes of a hunting horn. Inside a
mercantile heart the lake dwelt on boning and deboning,
skin and sharpened eyes, a ritual search through
dependable deposits for slimier luxuries. The surface
presented an appeal to meditation and surcease.

15   Situated below the mountain, surrounded by aged trees,
the lake offered a picture appealing both to young and
mature romance. At last it was the visual choice of two
figures who in the fixity of their shared glance were
admired by the lake. Tactfully they ignored the lacustrine[3]
20   fish, their gaze faltered lightly on the lapping
margins, their thoughts flew elsewhere, even beyond the
loop of her twisted hair and the accent of his poised tie-pin.

The scene supplied them with theatre, it was an evening
performance and the water understood and strained its
25   source for bugling echoes and silvered laments. The
couple referred to the lake without speech, by the turn
of a head, a hand waved, they placed a dignity upon the lake
brow causing an undercurrent of physical pleasure to
shake the water.

30   Until the letter fell. Torn into fragments the man tossed
it on the water, and the wind spilled the paper forward,
the cypress bent, the mountain sent a glacial flake.
Fish leapt. Polka dots now stippled the
twilight water and a superannuated gleam like a browned
35   autumnal stalk followed the couple where they shied in
the lake marsh grass like two eels who were caught.

1989

---

3. Of or pertaining to a lake.

EDWIN MORGAN
b. 1920

Strawberries

There were never strawberries
like the ones we had
that sultry afternoon
sitting on the step
5   of the open french window
facing each other
your knees held in mine
the blue plates in our laps
the strawberries glistening
10   in the hot sunlight
we dipped them in sugar
looking at each other
not hurrying the feast
for one to come
15   the empty plates
laid on the stone together
with the two forks crossed
and I bent towards you
sweet in that air
20   in my arms
abandoned like a child
from your eager mouth
the taste of strawberries
in my memory
25   lean back again
let me love you

let the sun beat
on our forgetfulness
one hour of all
30   the heat intense
and summer lightning
on the Kilpatrick hills[1]

let the storm wash the plates

1965

King Billy

Grey over Riddrie[2] the clouds piled up,
dragged their rain through the cemetery trees.
The gates shone cold. Wind rose

---

1. Upland plateau in the county of West Dunbar-
tonshire, Scotland.

2. A district of Glasgow.

flaring the hissing leaves, the branches
5 swung, heavy, across the lamps.
Gravestones huddled in drizzling shadow,
flickering streetlight scanned the requiescats,[3]
a name and an urn, a date, a dove
picked out, lost, half regained.
10 What is this dripping wreath, blown from its grave
red, white, blue, and gold
"To Our Leader of Thirty years Ago"—

Bareheaded, in dark suits, with flutes
and drums, they brought him here, in procession
15 seriously, King Billy of Brigton, dead,
from Bridgeton Cross: a memory of violence,
brooding days of empty bellies,
billiard smoke[4] and a sour pint,
boots or fists, famous sherrickings,[5]
20 the word, the scuffle, the flash, the shout,
bloody crumpling in the close,
bricks for papish° windows, get   *Roman Catholic*
the Conks[6] next time, the Conks ambush
the Billy Boys, the Billy Boys the Conks till
25 Sillitoe scuffs the razors down the stank°—   *drain*
No, but it isn't the violence they remember
but the legend of a violent man
born poor, gang-leader in the bad times
of idleness and boredom, lost in better days,
30 a bouncer in a betting club,
quiet man at last, dying
alone in Bridgeton in a box bed.
So a thousand people stopped the traffic
for the hearse of a folk hero and the flutes
35 threw "Onward Christian Soldiers" to the winds
from unironic lips, the mourners kept
in step, and there were some who wept.

Go from the grave. The shrill flutes
are silent, the march dispersed.
40 Deplore what is to be deplored,
and then find out the rest.

1968

The Dowser[7]

With my forked branch of Lebanese cedar
I quarter the dunes like downs and guide

3. *Requiescat in pace* is Latin for "Rest in peace"
(often shortened to R.I.P. on gravestones).
4. Cigarette smoke from a billiard saloon.
5. Fusses over nothing (Scottish slang).
6. Name of a Roman Catholic gang.

7. Someone who searches for underground
streams by holding a forked branch of cedar or
hazel, which twitches when it is above water. A
"water-table" (line 10) is the level to which under-
ground water rises.

an invisible plough far over the sand.
But how to quarter such shifting acres
5   when the wind melts their shapes, and shadows
mass where all was bright before,
and landmarks walk like wraiths° at noon?   ghosts
All I know is that underneath,
how many miles no one can say,
10   an unbroken water-table waits
like a lake; it has seen no bird or sail
in its long darkness, and no man;
not even pharaohs dug so far
for all their thirst, or thirst of glory,
15   or thrust-power of ten thousand slaves.
I tell you I can smell it though,
that water. I am old and black
and I know the manners of the sun
which makes me bend, not break. I lose
20   my ghostly footprints without complaint.
I put every mirage in its place.
I watch the lizard make its lace.
Like one not quite blind I go
feeling for the sunken face.
25   So hot the days, the nights so cold,
I gather my white rags and sigh
but sighing step so steadily
that any vibrance in so deep
a lake would never fail to rise
30   towards the snowy cedar's bait.
Great desert, let your sweetness wake.

1986   1988

KEITH DOUGLAS
1920–1944

Vergissmeinnicht[1]

Three weeks gone and the combatants gone
returning over the nightmare ground
we found the place again, and found
the soldier sprawling in the sun.

5   The frowning barrel of his gun
overshadowing. As we came on
that day, he hit my tank with one
like the entry of a demon.

---

1. Forget me not (German).

Look. Here in the gunpit spoil
10 the dishonoured picture of his girl
who has put: *Steffi. Vergissmeinnicht*
in a copybook gothic script.

We see him almost with content,
abased, and seeming to have paid
15 and mocked at by his own equipment
that's hard and good when he's decayed.

But she would weep to see today
how on his skin the swart° flies move;   *black*
the dust upon the paper eye
20 and the burst stomach like a cave.

For here the lover and killer are mingled
who had one body and one heart.
And death who had the soldier singled
has done the lover mortal hurt.

1943   1944

Aristocrats

The noble horse with courage in his eye,
clean in the bone, looks up at a shellburst:
away fly the images of the shires[2]
but he puts the pipe back in his mouth.

5 Peter was unfortunately killed by an 88:[3]
it took his leg away, he died in the ambulance.
I saw him crawling on the sand; he said
It's most unfair, they've shot my foot off.

How can I live among this gentle
10 obsolescent breed of heroes, and not weep?
Unicorns, almost,
for they are falling into two legends
in which their stupidity and chivalry
are celebrated. Each, fool and hero, will be an immortal.

15 The plains were their cricket pitch[4]
and in the mountains the tremendous drop fences[5]
brought down some of the runners. Here then
under the stones and earth they dispose themselves,
I think with their famous unconcern.
20 It is not gunfire I hear, but a hunting horn.[6]

Tunisia, 1943   1946

2. Counties. Cf. Wilfred Owen, "Anthem for
Doomed Youth," line 8 (p. 1386).
3. A German tank fitted with an eighty-eight-
millimeter gun.

4. Field on which the game of cricket is played.
5. Fences in the course of a steeplechase horse
race.
6. See note 7 below.

Gallantry

The Colonel[7] in a casual voice
spoke into the microphone a joke
Which through a hundred earphones broke
into the ears of a doomed race.[8]

5 Into the ears of the doomed boy, the fool
whose perfectly mannered flesh fell
in opening the door for a shell
as he had learnt to do at school.

Conrad luckily survived the winter:
10 he wrote a letter to welcome
the auspicious spring: only his silken
intentions severed with a single splinter.

Was George fond of little boys?
We always suspected it,
15 but who will say: since George was hit
we never mention our surmise.

It was a brave thing the Colonel said,
but the whole sky turned too hot
and the three heroes never heard what
20 it was, gone deaf with steel and lead.

But the bullets cried with laughter,
the shells were overcome with mirth,
plunging their heads in steel and earth—
(the air commented in a whisper).

April 1943   1949

On a Return from Egypt

To stand here in the wings of Europe
disheartened, I have come away
from the sick land where in the sun lay
the gentle sloe-eyed[9] murderers
5 of themselves, exquisites under a curse;
here to exercise my depleted fury.

---

7. "Lt. Col. J. D. Player, killed in Tunisia, Enfidaville, February 1943, left £3,000 to the Beaufort Hunt, and directed that the incumbent of the living in his gift [i.e., the church whose vicar he was entitled to appoint] should be a 'man who approves of hunting, shooting, and all manly sports, which are the backbone of the nation' " [Douglas's note on one of the manuscripts of "Aristocrats"; Player was in fact killed in April].
8. Cf. Wilfred Owen, "Anthem for Doomed Youth" (p. 1386).
9. Dark-eyed: a sloe is the dark fruit of the blackthorn.

For the heart is a coal, growing colder
when jewelled cerulean[1] seas change
into grey rocks, grey water-fringe,
10 sea and sky altering like a cloth
till colour and sheen are gone both:
cold is an opiate of the soldier.

And all my endeavours are unlucky explorers
come back, abandoning the expedition;
15 the specimens, the lilies of ambition
still spring in their climate, still unpicked:
but time, time is all I lacked
to find them, as the great collectors before me.

The next month, then, is a window
20 and with a crash I'll split the glass.
Behind it stands one I must kiss,
person of love or death
a person or a wraith,
I fear what I shall find.

March–April 1944?   1944

HOWARD NEMEROV
1920–1991

The Goose Fish

On the long shore, lit by the moon
To show them properly alone,
Two lovers suddenly embraced
So that their shadows were as one.
5 The ordinary night was graced
For them by the swift tide of blood
That silently they took at flood,
And for a little time they prized
    Themselves emparadised.

10 Then, as if shaken by stage-fright
Beneath the hard moon's bony light,
They stood together on the sand
Embarrassed in each other's sight
But still conspiring hand in hand,
15 Until they saw, there underfoot,
As though the world had found them out,
The goose fish turning up, though dead,
    His hugely grinning head.

---

1. Dark blue or green.

There in the china light he lay,
20 Most ancient and corrupt and gray
They hesitated at his smile,
Wondering what it seemed to say
To lovers who a little while
Before had thought to understand,
25 By violence upon the sand,
   The only way that could be known
      To make a world their own.

It was a wide and moony grin
Together peaceful and obscene;
30 They knew not what he would express,
So finished a comedian
He might mean failure or success,
But took it for an emblem of
Their sudden, new and guilty love
35 To be observed by, when they kissed,
      That rigid optimist.

So he became their patriarch,
Dreadfully mild in the half-dark.
His throat that the sand seemed to choke,
40 His picket teeth, these left their mark
But never did explain the joke
That so amused him, lying there
While the moon went down to disappear
Along the still and tilted track
45   That bears the zodiac.

                              1955

A Primer of the Daily Round

A peels an apple, while B kneels to God,
C telephones to D, who has a hand
On E's knee, F coughs, G turns up the sod
For H's grave, I do not understand
5 But J is bringing one clay pigeon down
While K brings down a nightstick on L's head,
And M takes mustard, N drives into town,
O goes to bed with P, and Q drops dead,
R lies to S, but happens to be heard
10 By T, who tells U not to fire V
For having to give W the word
That X is now deceiving Y with Z,
    Who happens just now to remember A
    Peeling an apple somewhere far away.

                              1958

The Blue Swallows

Across the millstream below the bridge
Seven blue swallows divide the air
In shapes invisible and evanescent,
Kaleidoscopic beyond the mind's
5   Or memory's power to keep them there.

"History is where tensions were,"
"Form is the diagram of forces."
Thus, helplessly, there on the bridge,
While gazing down upon those birds—
10   How strange, to be above the birds!—
Thus helplessly the mind in its brain
Weaves up relation's spindrift web,
Seeing the swallows' tails as nibs
Dipped in invisible ink, writing . . .

15   Poor mind, what would you have them write?
Some cabalistic° history   occult
Whose authorship you might ascribe
To God? to Nature? Ah, poor ghost,
You've capitalized your Self enough.
20   That villainous William of Occam[1]
Cut out the feet from under that dream
Some seven centuries ago.
It's taken that long for the mind
To waken, yawn and stretch, to see
25   With opened eyes emptied of speech
The real world where the spelling mind
Imposes with its grammar book
Unreal relations on the blue
Swallows. Perhaps when you will have
30   Fully awakened, I shall show you
A new thing: even the water
Flowing away beneath those birds
Will fail to reflect their flying forms,
And the eyes that see become as stones
35   Whence never tears shall fall again.

O swallows, swallows,[2] poems are not
The point. Finding again the world,
That is the point, where loveliness
Adorns intelligible things
40   Because the mind's eye lit the sun.

1967

---

1. Fourteenth-century scholastic philosopher; his central principle ("Occam's razor") was that the simplest, most economical explanation is always preferable over one that introduces unnecessary complications.
2. Cf. T. S. Eliot, *The Waste Land*, line 429 (p. 1356).

Boy with Book of Knowledge[3]

He holds a volume open in his hands:
Sepia portraits of the hairy great,
The presidents and poets in their beards
Alike, simplified histories of the wars,
Conundrums, quizzes, riddles, games and poems,

"Immortal Poems"; at least he can't forget them,
Barbara Fritchie and the Battle Hymn,
And best of all America the Beautiful,[4]
Whose platitudinous splendors ended with
"From sea to shining sea," and made him cry

And wish to be a poet, only to say such things,
From sea to shining sea. Could that have been
Where it began? the vast pudding of knowledge,
With poetry rare as raisins in the midst
Of those gold-lettered volumes black and green?

Mere piety to think so. But being now
As near his deathday as his birthday then,
He would acknowledge all he will not know,
The silent library brooding through the night
With all its lights continuing to burn

Insomniac, a luxury liner on what sea
Unfathomable of ignorance who could say?
And poetry, as steady, still, and rare
As the lighthouses now unmanned and obsolete
That used to mark America's dangerous shores.

1975

Strange Metamorphosis of Poets

From epigram to epic is the course
For riders of the American wingéd horse.[5]
They change both size and sex over the years,
The voice grows deeper and the beard appears;
Running for greatness they sweat away their salt,
They start out Emily and wind up Walt.[6]

1975

---

3. A type of reference book once used in schools.
4. "America the Beautiful" was often, and sometimes still is, sung in classrooms. "Barbara Frietchie" (Nemerov misspelled it), by the American abolitionist John Greenleaf Whittier (1807–1892; see pp. 957–60), and the "Battle-Hymn of the Republic," by the American suffragist Julia Ward Howe (1819–1910; see p. 1054), were pop-

ular patriotic poems of the Civil War.
5. Pegasus, the winged horse of Greek mythology, bore poets in flights of genius.
6. Emily Dickinson (1830–1886; see pp. 1110–27) and Walt Whitman (1819–1892; see pp. 1060–86), American poets known for their epigrammatic and epic styles, respectively.

A Cabinet of Seeds Displayed

These are the original monies of the earth,
In which invested, as the spark in fire,
They will produce a green wealth toppling tall,
A trick they do by dying, by decay,
In burial becoming each his kind
To rise in glory and be magnified
A million times above the obscure grave.

Reader, these samples are exhibited
For contemplation, locked in potency
And kept from act for reverence's sake.
May they remind us while we live on earth
That all economies are primitive;
And by their reservations may they teach
Our governors, who speak of husbandry
And think the hurricane, where power lies.

1975

GEORGE MACKAY BROWN
1921–1996

The Old Women

Go sad or sweet or riotous with beer
Past the old women gossiping by the hour,
They'll fix on you from every close and pier
An acid look to make your veins run sour.

"No help," they say, "his grandfather that's dead
Was troubled with the same dry-throated curse,
And many a night he made the ditch his bed.
This blood comes welling from the same cracked source."

On every kind of merriment they frown.
But I have known a gray-eyed sober boy
Sail to the lobsters in a storm, and drown.
Over his body dripping on the stones
Those same old hags would weave into their moans
An undersong of terrible holy joy.

1959

Haddock Fishermen

Midnight. The wind yawing nor-east.
A low blunt moon.
Unquiet beside quiet wives we rest.

A spit of rain and a gull
5   In the open door
The lit fire. A quick mouthful of ale.

We push the *Merle* at a sea of cold flame.
The oars drip honey.
Hook by hook uncoils under The Kame.

10 Our line breaks the trek of sudden thousands.
Twelve nobbled[1] jaws,
Gray cowls, gape in our hands.

Twelve cold mouths scream without sound.
The sea is empty again.
15 Like tinkers° the bright ones endlessly shift their ground.   gypsies

We probe emptiness all the afternoon,
Then pause and fill our teeth
With dependable food, beef and barley scone.

Sunset drags its butcher blade
20 From the day's throat.
We turn through an ebb salt and sticky as blood.

More stars than fish. Women, cats, a gull
Mewl at the rock.
The valley divides the meagre miracle.

1959

Shroud

Seven threads make the shroud,
The white thread,
A green corn thread,
A blue fish thread,
5   A red stitch, rut and rieving and wrath,[2]
A gray thread
(All winter failing hand falleth on wheel)
The black thread,
And a thread too bright for the eye.

1971

---

1. With knobs (lumps).   2. I.e., sexual intercourse and robbery and rage.

MONA VAN DUYN
1921–2004

Letters from a Father

I

Ulcerated tooth keeps me awake, there is
such pain, would have to go to the hospital to have
it pulled or would bleed to death from the blood thinners,
but can't leave Mother, she falls and forgets her salve
5   and her tranquilizers, her ankles swell so and her bowels
are so bad, she almost had a stoppage and sometimes
what she passes is green as grass. There are big holes
in my thigh where my leg brace buckles the size of dimes.
My head pounds from the high pressure. It is awful
10   not to be able to get out, and I fell in the bathroom
and the girl could hardly get me up at all.
Sure thought my back was broken, it will be next time.
Prostate is bad and heart has given out,
feel bloated after supper. Have made my peace
15   because am just plain done for and have no doubt
that the Lord will come any day with my release.
You say you enjoy your feeder, I don't see why
you want to spend good money on grain for birds
and you say you have a hundred sparrows, I'd buy
20   poison and get rid of their diseases and turds.

II

We enjoyed your visit, it was nice of you to bring
the feeder but a terrible waste of your money
for that big bag of feed since we won't be living
more than a few weeks longer. We can see
25   them good from where we sit, big ones and little ones
but you know when I farmed I used to like to hunt
and we had many a good meal from pigeons
and quail and pheasant but these birds won't
be good for nothing and are dirty to have so near
30   the house. Mother likes the redbirds though.
My bad knee is so sore and I can't hardly hear
and Mother says she is hoarse from yelling but I know
it's too late for a hearing aid. I belch up all the time
and have a sour mouth and of course with my heart
35   it's no use to go to a doctor. Mother is the same.
Has a scab she thinks is going to turn to a wart.

III

The birds are eating and fighting, Ha! Ha! All shapes
and colors and sizes coming out of our woods
but we don't know what they are. Your Mother hopes

40   you can send us a kind of book that tells about birds.
There is one the folks called snowbirds, they eat on the ground,
we had the girl sprinkle extra there, but say,
they eat something awful. I sent the girl to town
to buy some more feed, she had to go anyway.

IV

45   Almost called you on the telophone
but it costs so much to call thought better write.
Say, the funniest thing is happening, one
day we had so many birds and they fight
and get excited at their feed you know
50   and it's really something to watch and two or three
flew right at us and crashed into our window
and bang, poor little things knocked themselves silly.
They come to after awhile on the ground and flew away.
And they been doing that. We felt awful
55   and didn't know what to do but the other day
a lady from our Church drove out to call
and a little bird knocked itself out while she sat
and she brought it in her hands right into the house,
it looked like dead. It had a kind of hat
60   of feathers sticking up on its head, kind of rose
or pinky color, don't know what it was,
and I petted it and it come to life right there
in her hands and she took it out and it flew. She says
they think the window is the sky on a fair
65   day, she feeds birds too but hasn't got
so many. She says to hang strips of aluminum foil
in the window so we'll do that. She raved about
our birds. P.S. The book just come in the mail.

V

    Say, that book is sure good, I study
70   in it every day and enjoy our birds.
Some of them I can't identify
for sure, I guess they're females, the Latin words
I just skip over. Bet you'd never guess
the sparrows I've got here, House Sparrows you wrote,
75   but I have Fox Sparrows, Song Sparrows, Vesper Sparrows,
Pine Woods and Tree and Chipping and White Throat
and White Crowned Sparrows. I have six Cardinals,
three pairs, they come at early morning and night,
the males at the feeder and on the ground the females.
80   Juncos, maybe 25, they fight
for the ground, that's what they used to call snowbirds. I miss
the Bluebirds since the weather warmed. Their breast
is the color of a good ripe muskmelon. Tufted Titmouse
is sort of blue with a little tiny crest.
85   And I have Flicker and Red-Bellied and Red-

Headed Woodpeckers, you would die laughing
to see Red-Bellied, he hangs on with his head
flat on the board, his tail braced up under,
wing out. And Dickcissel and Ruby Crowned Ringlet
90   and Nuthatch stands on his head and Veery on top
the color of a bird dog and Hermit Thrush with spot
on breast, Blue Jay so funny, he will hop
right on the backs of the other birds to get the grain.
We bought some sunflower seeds just for him.
95   And Purple Finch I bet you never seen,
color of a watermelon, sits on the rim
of the feeder with his streaky wife, and the squirrels,
you know, they are cute too, they sit tall
and eat with their little hands, they eat bucketfuls.
100   I pulled my own tooth, it didn't bleed at all.

VI

It's sure a surprise how well Mother is doing,
she forgets her laxative but bowels move fine.
Now that windows are open she says our birds sing
all day. The girl took a Book of Knowledge[1] on loan
105   from the library and I am reading up
on the habits of birds, did you know some males have three
wives, some migrate some don't. I am going to keep
feeding all spring, maybe summer, you can see
they expect it. Will need thistle seed for Goldfinch and Pine
110   Siskin next winter. Some folks are going to come see us
from Church, some bird watchers, pretty soon.
They have birds in town but nothing to equal this.

So the world woos its children back for an evening kiss.

1982

Falling in Love at Sixty-Five

It is like the first and last time I tried a Coleman°   *lamp*
for reading in bed in Maine. Too early the camp
went dark for fossil habits, no longer could candleflame
convince my eyes, and I lit that scary lamp.
5   Instant outcry came from the savage white light
of the mantles,[2] as if a star had been brought down
out of space and trapped by the unchinked logs of the bedroom,
roaring its threat to explode the walls and be gone,
or as if the lamp could tell time and knew that one tongue
10   was no longer enough to speak with, it must double its blare,
overwhelm two senses at once, that the jaded heart
might burst into ravished applause for its *son et lumière*.[3]

1. A general reference book.   3. Sound and light show (French).
2. Incandescent cloth hoods of gaslight jets.

Perched on a pile of books on the seat of a chair
drawn to the head of the bed, the lamp called out

15   the guilty years and shamed them for cracks and shrivels
that bent the patient, scabbed logs of the walls and ceiling.
Then I opened a book whose every radiant page
was illuminated in colors of lightning and thunder
by the quick-witted lamp in its artistry of rage.

20   The book and the lamp fused to one voice, whose sense
became mine, strokes of a slow, rhythmic broom
swept a dusty pith that seemed to lie still until
some other sense told me that there were wings in the room.

In one much earlier year I had fallen asleep

25   in the meadow, head near bright heights of fireweed, fireweed
strewn on my chest from a hand that let go its bouquet,
and had wakened at eyelash touches, the delicate need
of five blue butterflies that found me in bloom.
Now, striking my neck and cheeks, came the first

30   wave of this late invasion, three flying bugs
that hit me, lit, flew again, hit, an outburst
the lamp had called for through log-gaps and screenholes, then
more entered the air, winged in gray, brown, dun,
and more, as I tried to read on, in the muted shades

35   brushed on by sundown's dimming imagination.

Beetle-bodied or light as moths they came
and, big and small, bombed the lit skin of face,
arms, shoulders, rested, crawled, unfurled, and sent
the blind wanting that stuffed full each one's carapace

40   in a clicking crash at the lampglass, then crazily flew
back to me, the bared part of me becoming a plan
for plates of an insect book whose specimens
rearranged themselves fiercely over and over again.
For as long as the lantern lasted they would have kept coming,

45   as if the grave darkness had smiled at that tiny dawn
and had hurled them in fistfuls straight at the speaking light
in answer to what was being insisted upon.

1990

RICHARD WILBUR
b. 1921

First Snow in Alsace[1]

The snow came down last night like moths
Burned on the moon; it fell till dawn,
Covered the town with simple cloths.

---

1. Region of northern France.

Absolute snow lies rumpled on
5   What shellbursts scattered and deranged,
Entangled railings, crevassed lawn.

As if it did not know they'd changed,
Snow smoothly clasps the roofs of homes
Fear-gutted, trustless and estranged.

10   The ration stacks are milky domes;
Across the ammunition pile
The snow has climbed in sparkling combs.

You think: beyond the town a mile
Or two, this snowfall fills the eyes
15   Of soldiers dead a little while.

Persons and persons in disguise,
Walking the new air white and fine,
Trade glances quick with shared surprise.

At children's windows, heaped, benign,
20   As always, winter shines the most,
And frost makes marvelous designs.

The night guard coming from his post,
Ten first-snows back in thought, walks slow
And warms him with a boyish boast:

25   He was the first to see the snow.

1947

Love Calls Us to the Things of This World[2]

The eyes open to a cry of pulleys,
And spirited from sleep, the astounded soul
Hangs for a moment bodiless and simple
As false dawn.
                    Outside the open window
5   The morning air is all awash with angels.

Some are in bed-sheets, some are in blouses,
Some are in smocks: but truly there they are.
Now they are rising together in calm swells
Of halcyon feeling, filling whatever they wear
10   With the deep joy of their impersonal breathing;

Now they are flying in place, conveying
The terrible speed of their omnipresence, moving

---

2. A quotation from St. Augustine (354–430), author of works such as the *Confessions*.

And staying like white water; and now of a sudden
They swoon down into so rapt a quiet
15 That nobody seems to be there.
                                    The soul shrinks

     From all that it is about to remember,
From the punctual rape of every blessèd day,
And cries,
          "Oh, let there be nothing on earth but laundry,
Nothing but rosy hands in the rising steam
20 And clear dances done in the sight of heaven."

     Yet, as the sun acknowledges
With a warm look the world's hunks and colors,
The soul descends once more in bitter love
To accept the waking body, saying now
25 In a changed voice as the man yawns and rises,

     "Bring them down from their ruddy gallows;
Let there be clean linen for the backs of thieves;
Let lovers go fresh and sweet to be undone,
And the heaviest nuns walk in a pure floating
30 Of dark habits,
                    keeping their difficult balance."

                                                    1956

Piazza di Spagna,[3] Early Morning

     I can't forget
How she stood at the top of that long marble stair
Amazed, and then with a sleepy pirouette
Went dancing slowly down to the fountain-quieted square;

5   Nothing upon her face
But some impersonal loneliness,—not then a girl,
     But as it were a reverie of the place,
        A called-for falling glide and whirl;

     As when a leaf, petal, or thin chip
10 Is drawn to the falls of a pool and, circling a moment above it,
        Rides on over the lip—
     Perfectly beautiful, perfectly ignorant of it.

                                                    1956

---

3. Plaza in Rome, famous for its long, curved stairway.

A Plain Song for Comadre[4]

Though the unseen may vanish, though insight fails
And doubter and downcast saint
Join in the same complaint,
What holy things were ever frightened off
5   By a fly's buzz, or itches, or a cough?
Harder than nails

They are, more warmly constant than the sun,
At whose continual sign
The dimly prompted vine
10   Upbraids itself to a green excellence.
What evening, when the slow and forced expense
Of sweat is done,

Does not the dark come flooding the straight furrow
Or filling the well-made bowl?
15   What night will not the whole
Sky with its clear studs and steady spheres
Turn on a sound chimney? It is seventeen years
Come tomorrow

That Bruna Sandoval has kept the church
20   Of San Ysidro,[5] sweeping
And scrubbing the aisles, keeping
The candlesticks and the plaster faces bright,
And seen no visions but the thing done right
From the clay porch

25   To the white altar. For love and in all weathers
This is what she has done.
Sometimes the early sun
Shines as she flings the scrubwater out, with a crash
Of grimy rainbows, and the stained suds flash
30   Like angel-feathers.

1956

A Baroque Wall-Fountain in the Villa Sciarra[6]

For Dore and Adja

Under the bronze crown
Too big for the head of the stone cherub whose feet

---

4. Peasant woman (Spanish); also, midwife, god-mother, neighbor. *Plain song:* or plainsong; the unisonous vocal music of the early Christian Church; also, any simple melody.

5. Village in San Diego County, near the Mexican border.
6. A large public park in Rome.

A serpent has begun to eat,
Sweet water brims a cockle[7] and braids down

5   Past spattered mosses, breaks
On the tipped edge of a second shell, and fills
      The massive third below. It spills
In threads then from the scalloped rim, and makes

      A scrim or summery tent
10 For a faun-ménage[8] and their familiar goose.
      Happy in all that ragged, loose
Collapse of water, its effortless descent

      And flatteries of spray,
The stocky god upholds the shell with ease,
15   Watching, about his shaggy knees,
The goatish innocence of his babes at play;

      His fauness all the while
Leans forward, slightly, into a clambering mesh
      Of water-lights, her sparkling flesh
20 In a saecular[9] ecstasy, her blinded smile

      Bent on the sand floor
Of the trefoil° pool, where ripple-shadows come   three-leaved
      And go in swift reticulum,°   netlike form
More addling to the eye than wine, and more

25   Interminable to thought
Than pleasure's calculus. Yet since this all
      Is pleasure, flash, and waterfall,
Must it not be too simple? Are we not

      More intricately expressed
30 In the plain fountains that Maderna[1] set
      Before St. Peter's—the main jet
Struggling aloft until it seems at rest

      In the act of rising, until
The very wish of water is reversed,
35   That heaviness borne up to burst
In a clear, high, cavorting head, to fill

      With blaze, and then in gauze
Delays, in a gnatlike shimmering, in a fine
      Illumined version of itself, decline,
40 And patter on the stones its own applause?

---

7. Shell-shaped basin, part of the fountain.
8. Group surrounding the faun, in classical mythology a lusty rural god usually pictured with a goat's legs and tail.
9. Lasting for ages (punning on *secular*, worldly).

1. Carlo Maderno (1556–1629), Italian architect and designer responsible for giving St. Peter's Basilica, in Rome, the shape of a cross and for completing the facade.

If that is what men are
Or should be, if those water-saints display
   The pattern of our areté,[2]
What of these showered fauns in their bizarre,

45   Spangled, and plunging house?
They are at rest in fulness of desire
   For what is given, they do not tire
Of the smart of the sun, the pleasant water-douse

      And riddled pool below,
50   Reproving our disgust and our ennui
   With humble insatiety.
Francis,[3] perhaps, who lay in sister snow

      Before the wealthy gate
Freezing and praising, might have seen in this
55   No trifle, but a shade of bliss—
That land of tolerable flowers, that state

      As near and far as grass
Where eyes become the sunlight, and the hand
   Is worthy of water: the dreamt land
60   Toward which all hungers leap, all pleasures pass.

1956

Advice to a Prophet

When you come, as you soon must, to the streets of our city,
Mad-eyed from stating the obvious,
Not proclaiming our fall but begging us
In God's name to have self-pity,

5   Spare us all word of the weapons, their force and range,
The long numbers that rocket the mind;
Our slow, unreckoning hearts will be left behind,
Unable to fear what is too strange.

Nor shall you scare us with talk of the death of the race.
10 How should we dream of this place without us?—
The sun mere fire, the leaves untroubled about us,
A stone look on the stone's face?

Speak of the world's own change. Though we cannot conceive
Of an undreamt thing, we know to our cost
15 How the dreamt cloud crumbles, the vines are blackened by frost,
How the view alters. We could believe,

---

2. "A Greek word meaning roughly 'virtue' " [Wilbur's note].

3. I.e., St. Francis of Assisi (1182–1226), known for his vow of poverty and love of nature.

If you told us so, that the white-tailed deer will slip
Into perfect shade, grown perfectly shy,
The lark avoid the reaches of our eye,
20 The jack-pine lose its knuckled grip

On the cold ledge, and every torrent burn
As Xanthus⁴ once, its gliding trout
Stunned in a twinkling. What should we be without
The dolphin's arc, the dove's return,

25 These things in which we have seen ourselves and spoken?
Ask us, prophet, how we shall call
Our natures forth when that live tongue is all
Dispelled, that glass obscured or broken

In which we have said the rose of our love and the clean
30 Horse of our courage, in which beheld
The singing locust of the soul unshelled,
And all we mean or wish to mean.

Ask us, ask us whether with the worldless rose
Our hearts shall fail us; come demanding
35 Whether there shall be lofty or long standing
When the bronze annals of the oak-tree close.

1961

Junk

Huru Welandes
                                worc ne geswiceð
        monna ænigum
                                ðara ðe Mimming can
        heardne gehealdan.
                                —Waldere⁵

An axe angles
                    from my neighbor's ashcan;
    It is hell's handiwork,
                    the wood not hickory,
5   The flow of the grain
                    not faithfully followed.
    The shivered shaft
                    rises from a shellheap
    Of plastic playthings,
10   paper plates,
    And the sheer shards
                    of shattered tumblers

4. "Haphaestus, invoked by Achilles, scalded the river Xanthus (Scamander) in *Iliad, xxi*" [Wilbur's note].
5. "The epigraph, taken from a fragmentary Anglo-Saxon poem, concerns the legendary smith Wayland, and may roughly be translated: 'Truly, Wayland's handiwork—the sword Mimming which he made—will never fail any man who knows how to use it bravely'" [Wilbur's note].

That were not annealed
for the time needful.

15   At the same curbside,
a cast-off cabinet
Of wavily-warped
unseasoned wood
Waits to be trundled
20   in the trash-man's truck.
Haul them off! Hide them!
The heart winces
For junk and gimcrack,
for jerrybuilt things
25   And the men who make them
for a little money,
Bartering pride
like the bought boxer
Who pulls his punches,
30   or the paid-off jockey
Who in the home stretch
holds in his horse.
Yet the things themselves
in thoughtless honor
35   Have kept composure,
like captives who would not
Talk under torture.
Tossed from a tailgate
Where the dump displays
40   its random dolmens,[6]
Its black barrows
and blazing valleys,
They shall waste in the weather
toward what they were.
45   The sun shall glory
in the glitter of glass-chips,
Foreseeing the salvage
of the prisoned sand,
And the blistering paint
50   peel off in patches,
That the good grain
be discovered again.
Then burnt, bulldozed,
they shall all be buried
55   To the depth of diamonds,
in the making dark
Where halt Hephaestus[7]
keeps his hammer
And Wayland's work
60   is worn away.

1961

---

6. Prehistoric monuments of horizontal stone slabs supported by upright stones; believed to be tombs.

7. Greek god of fire and the forge.

Cottage Street, 1953

Framed in her phoenix fire-screen, Edna Ward[8]
Bends to the tray of Canton,[9] pouring tea
For frightened Mrs. Plath;[1] then, turning toward
The pale, slumped daughter, and my wife, and me,

5   Asks if we would prefer it weak or strong.
Will we have milk or lemon, she enquires?
The visit seems already strained and long.
Each in his turn, we tell her our desires.

It is my office to exemplify
10 The published poet in his happiness,
Thus cheering Sylvia, who has wished to die;
But half-ashamed, and impotent to bless,

I am a stupid life-guard who has found,
Swept to his shallows by the tide, a girl
15 Who, far from shore, has been immensely drowned,
And stares through water now with eyes of pearl.

How large is her refusal; and how slight
The genteel chat whereby we recommend
Life, of a summer afternoon, despite
20 The brewing dusk which hints that it may end.

And Edna Ward shall die in fifteen years,
After her eight-and-eighty summers of
Such grace and courage as permit no tears,
The thin hand reaching out, the last word *love*,

25 Outliving Sylvia who, condemned to live,
Shall study for a decade, as she must,
To state at last her brilliant negative
In poems free and helpless and unjust.

1976

Zea[2]

Once their fruit is picked,
The cornstalks lighten, and though
Keeping to their strict

---

8. Wilbur's mother-in-law.
9. Porcelain named after the city in China.
1. Mother of Sylvia Plath, the American poet (1932–1963; see pp. 1836–45), who by 1953 had already attempted suicide and eventually took her own life.
2. Indian corn.

Rows, begin to be
5   The tall grasses that they are—
Lissom, now, and free

As canes that clatter
In island wind, or plumed reeds
Rocked by lake water.

10   Soon, if not cut down,
Their ranks grow whistling-dry, and
Blanch to lightest brown,

So that, one day, all
Their ribbon-like, down-arcing
15   Leaves rise up and fall

In tossed companies,
Like goose-wings beating southward
Over the changed trees.

Later, there are days
20   Full of bare expectancy,
Downcast hues, and haze,

Days of an utter
Calm, in which one white corn-leaf,
Oddly aflutter,

25   Its fabric sheathing
A gaunt stem, can seem to be
The sole thing breathing.

                                                                    2000

DONALD DAVIE
1922–1995

Remembering the 'Thirties

I

Hearing one saga, we enact the next.
We please our elders when we sit enthralled;
But then they're puzzled; and at last they're vexed
To have their youth so avidly recalled.

5   It dawns upon the veterans after all
That what for them were agonies, for us
Are high-brow thrillers, though historical;
And all their feats quite strictly fabulous.

This novel written fifteen years ago,
10 Set in my boyhood and my boyhood home,
These poems about "abandoned workings", show
Worlds more remote than Ithaca[1] or Rome.

The Anschluss, Guernica[2]—all the names
At which those poets thrilled or were afraid
15 For me mean schools and schoolmasters and games;
And in the process some-one is betrayed.

Ourselves perhaps. The Devil for a joke
Might carve his own initials on our desk,
And yet we'd miss the point because he spoke
20 An idiom too dated, Audenesque.[3]

Ralegh's Guiana also killed his son.[4]
A pretty pickle if we came to see
The tallest story really packed a gun,
The Telemachiad[5] an Odyssey.

II

25 Even to them the tales were not so true
As not to be ridiculous as well;
The ironmaster met his Waterloo,
But Rider Haggard[6] rode along the fell.

"Leave for Cape Wrath tonight!" They lounged away
30 On Fleming's trek or Isherwood's ascent.[7]
England expected every man that day
To show his motives were ambivalent.

They played the fool, not to appear as fools
In time's long glass. A deprecating air
35 Disarmed, they thought, the jeers of later schools;
Yet irony itself is doctrinaire,

And curiously, nothing now betrays
Their type to time's derision like this coy
Insistence on the quizzical, their craze
40 For showing Hector[8] was a mother's boy.

1. Greek island; home of Odysseus, the story of whose wandering and eventual return to his wife, Penelope, and son, Telemachus, is told in Homer's *Odyssey*.
2. Spanish town bombed by German aircraft in the Spanish Civil War, an event commemorated by the Spanish expatriate artist Pablo Picasso's painting *Guernica* (1937). *Anschluss*: union (German); name given to the German seizure of Austria in March 1938.
3. In the style of the American (English-born) poet W. H. Auden (1907–1973; see pp. 1465–81).
4. In search of gold, the English courtier-poet Sir Walter Ralegh (ca. 1552–1618; see pp. 151–58) led a military expedition to Guiana, in South America, on which his son was killed in 1617.
5. The first four books of the *Odyssey*, which center on Telemachus.
6. English writer (1856–1925), famous for boys' adventure stories and novels such as *King Solomon's Mines* (1885). *Waterloo*: battle of 1815, in Belgium, in which Napoleon was finally defeated.
7. Reference to the play *The Ascent of F6* (1936), by W. H. Auden and the American (English-born) writer Christopher Isherwood (1904–1986), both of whom met the English explorer and travel writer Peter Fleming (1907–1971) on a trip to China. The quoted line, from Auden's 1929 poem "Missing," refers to the northernmost point of mainland Scotland.
8. In Homer's *Iliad*, leader of the Trojans at the siege of Troy.

A neutral tone is nowadays preferred.
And yet it may be better, if we must,
To praise a stance impressive and absurd
Than not to see the hero for the dust.

45 For courage is the vegetable king,
The sprig of all ontologies, the weed
That beards the slag-heap with his hectoring,
Whose green adventure is to run to seed.

1955

The Fountain

Feathers up fast, and steeples; then in clods
Thuds into its first basin; thence as surf
Smokes up and hangs; irregularly slops
Into its second, tattered like a shawl;
5 There, chill as rain, stipples a danker green,
Where urgent tritons[9] lob their heavy jets.

For Berkeley[1] this was human thought, that mounts
From bland assumptions to inquiring skies,
There glints with wit, fumes into fancies, plays
10 With its negations, and at last descends,
As by a law of nature, to its bowl
Of thus enlightened but still common sense.

We who have no such confidence must gaze
With all the more affection on these forms,
15 These spires, these plumes, these calm reflections, these
Similitudes of surf and turf and shawl,
Graceful returns upon acceptances.
We ask of fountains only that they play,

Though that was not what Berkeley meant at all.

1957

Time Passing, Beloved

Time passing, and the memories of love
Coming back to me, carissima,[2] no more mockingly
Than ever before; time passing, unslackening,
Unhastening, steadily; and no more

---

9. I.e., statues depicting the Greek demigod of the sea, Triton, whose lower body was that of a fish.
1. George Berkeley (1685–1753), Irish bishop and philosopher, who maintained that the world is not an independent entity of which our minds may be an effect, but, rather, depends on our sensory perception for its existence.
2. Darling (Italian).

5   Bitterly, beloved, the memories of love
    Coming into the shore.

    How will it end? Time passing and our passages of love
    As ever, beloved, blind
    As ever before; time binding, unbinding
10 About us; and yet to remember
    Never less chastening, nor the flame of love
    Less like an ember.

    What will become of us? Time
    Passing, beloved, and we in a sealed
15 Assurance unassailed
    By memory. How can it end,
    This siege of a shore that no misgivings have steeled,
    No doubts defend?

                                                        1957

SIDNEY KEYES
1922–1943

Elegy

(*In memoriam S. K. K.*)[1]

    April again, and it is a year again
    Since you walked out and slammed the door
    Leaving us tangled in your words. Your brain
    Lives in the bank-book, and your eyes look up
5   Laughing from the carpet on the floor:
    And we still drink from your silver cup.

    It is a year again since they poured
    The dumb ground into your mouth:
    And yet we know, by some recurring word
10 Or look caught unawares, that you still drive
    Our thoughts like the smart cobs[2] of your youth—
    When you and the world were alive.

    A year again, and we have fallen on bad times
    Since they gave you to the worms.
15 I am ashamed to take delight in these rhymes
    Without grief; but you need no tears.
    We shall never forget nor escape you, nor make terms
    With your enemies, the swift departing years.

1938   1945

---

1. Keyes was sixteen when he wrote this elegy for   2. Stocky, short-legged riding horses.
his grandfather.

From The Foreign Gate

The moon is a poor woman.
The moon returns to weep with us. The crosses
Burn raw and white upon the night's stiff banners.
The wooden crosses and the marble trees
5   Shrink from the foreign moon.
The iron gate glitters. Here the soldiers lie.
Fold up the flags, muffle the soldier's drum;
Silence the calling fife.° O drape   *small flute*
The soldier's drum with heavy crêpe;
10 With mourning weeds muffle the soldier's girl.
It's a long way and a long march
To the returning moon and to the soil
No time at all.
               O call
15 The soldier's glory by another name:
Shroud up the soldier's common shame
And drape the soldier's drum, but spare
The steel-caged brain, the feet that walk to war.

Once striding under a horsehair plume
20 Once beating the taut drums for war
The sunlight rang from brass and iron;
History was an angry play—
The boy grew tall and rode away;
The door hung slack; the pale girl wept
25 And cursed the company he kept.
And dumb men spoke
Through the glib mouths of smoke;
The servile learned to strike
The proud to shriek;
30 And strangled in their lovers' lips
The young fell short of glory in the sand
Raking for graves among the scattered sand;
The tattered flags strained at the wind
Scaring the thrifty kite, mocking the dead.
35 But muffle the soldier's drum, hide his pale head,
His face a spider's web of blood. O fold
The hands that grip a splintered gun.
         The glittering gate
Baffles him still, his starvecrow[3] soul. O drape
40 The soldier's drum and cry, who never dare
Defy the ironbound brain, the feet that walk to war.

The cold hand clenches. The stupid mouth
Writhes like a ripple. Now the field is full
Of noises and dead voices . . .
45   "My rags flap

---

3. Cursed (from the Australian slang *Gawd starve the crows!*).

Though the great flags are trampled . . ."
                                        "My mouth speaks
Terror and truth, instead of hard command."
"Remember the torn lace, the fine coats slashed
50   With steel instead of velvet. Künersdorf[4]
Fought in the shallow sand was my relief."
"I rode to Naseby" . . . "And the barren land
Of Tannenberg drank me. Remember now
The grey and jointed corpses in the snow,
55   The struggle in the drift, the numb hands freezing
Into the bitter iron . . ."
                            "At Dunkirk I
Rolled in the shallows, and the living trod
Across me for a bridge . . ."
60   "Let me speak out
Against this sham of policy, for pain
Alone is true. I was a general
Who fought the cunning Africans, returned
Crowned with harsh laurel,[5] frantically cheered
65   Through Roman streets. I spoke of fame and glory.
Women grabbed at my robe. Great poets praised me.
I died of cancer, screaming, in a year."
"I fell on a black Spanish hillside
Under the thorn-hedge, fighting for a dream
70   That troubled me in Paris; vomited
My faith and courage out among the stones . . ."
"I was a barb of light, a burning cross
Of wood and canvas, falling through the night."
"I was shot down at morning, in a yard."

75   The moon regards them without shame. The wind
Rises and twitters through the wreck of bone . . .
                              "It is so hard to be alone
Continually, watching the great stars march
Their circular unending route; sharp sand
80   Straying about the eyes, blinding the quick-eyed spirit."
A soldier's death is hard;
There's no prescribed or easy word
For dissolution in the Army books.
The uniform of pain with pain put on is straiter
85   Than any lover's garment; yet the death
Of these is different, and their glory greater.
Once men, then moving figures on a map,
Patiently giving time and strength and vision
Even identity
90   Into the future's keeping;
Nourished on wounds and weeping
Faces and laughing flags and pointed laurels,
Their pain cries down the noise of poetry.

---

4. Lines 50–57 refer to famous battles from different periods of history.

5. In ancient Greece and Rome, crowns of laurel leaves were awarded as honors.

So muffle the soldier's drum, forget the battles;
95 Remember only fame's a way of living:
The writing may be greater than the speaking
And every death for something different
From time's compulsion, is a written word.
Whatever gift, it is the giving
100 Remains significant: whatever death
It is the dying matters.
                         Emblematic
Bronze eagle or bright banner or carved name
Of fighting ancestor; these never pardon
105 The pain and sorrow. It is the dying pardons,
For something different from man or emblem.
Then drape the soldier's drum
And carry him down
Beyond the moon's inspection, and the noise
110 Of bands and banners and the striking sun.
Scatter the soldier's emblems and his fame:
Shroud up the shattered face, the empty name;
Speak out the word and drape the drum and spare
The captive brain, the feet that walk to war
115 The ironbound brain, the hand unskilled in war
The shrinking brain, sick of an inner war.

1942   1942

War Poet

I am the man who looked for peace and found
My own eyes barbed.
I am the man who groped for words and found
An arrow in my hand.
5 I am the builder whose firm walls surround
A slipping land.
When I grow sick or mad
Mock me not nor chain me:
When I reach for the wind
10 Cast me not down:
Though my face is a burnt book
And a wasted town.

1942   1943

PHILIP LARKIN
1922–1985

For Sidney Bechet[1]

That note you hold, narrowing and rising, shakes
Like New Orleans reflected on the water,
And in all ears appropriate falsehood wakes,

Building for some a legendary Quarter
5   Of balconies, flower-baskets and quadrilles,[2]
Everyone making love and going shares—

Oh, play that thing! Mute glorious Storyvilles[3]
Others may license, grouping round their chairs
Sporting-house girls like circus tigers (priced

10   Far above rubies)[4] to pretend their fads,
While scholars *manqués*[5] nod around unnoticed
Wrapped up in personnels° like old plaids.   *band members*

On me your voice falls as they say love should,
Like an enormous yes. My Crescent City
15   Is where your speech alone is understood,

And greeted as the natural noise of good,
Scattering long-haired grief and scored pity.

1954   1964

Born Yesterday
for Sally Amis[6]

Tightly-folded bud,
I have wished you something
None of the others would:
Not the usual stuff
5   About being beautiful,
Or running off a spring
Of innocence and love—
They will all wish you that,
And should it prove possible,
10   Well, you're a lucky girl.

---

1. American jazz clarinetist and saxophonist (1897–1959), born in New Orleans ("Crescent City," line 14), where he spent his teenage years playing in the dance halls and brothels of the Storyville (line 7) Quarter (line 4), or district.
2. Square dance for couples.
3. Cf. Thomas Gray, "Elegy Written in a Country Churchyard," line 59: "Some mute inglorious Milton here may rest" (p. 671).
4. Cf. Proverbs 31.10: "Who can find a virtuous woman? For her price is far above rubies."
5. Would-be scholars.
6. Daughter (1954–2000) of Larkin's friend the English novelist Kingsley Amis and Amis's wife, Hilary. Cf. W. B. Yeats, "A Prayer for my Daughter" (p. 1196).

But if it shouldn't, then
May you be ordinary;
Have, like other women,
An average of talents:
15 Not ugly, not good-looking,
Nothing uncustomary
To pull you off your balance,
That, unworkable itself,
Stops all the rest from working.
20 In fact, may you be dull—
If that is what a skilled,
Vigilant, flexible,
Unemphasised, enthralled
Catching of happiness is called.

1954   1955

Church Going

Once I am sure there's nothing going on
I step inside, letting the door thud shut.
Another church: matting, seats, and stone,
And little books; sprawlings of flowers, cut
5 For Sunday, brownish now; some brass and stuff
Up at the holy end; the small neat organ;
And a tense, musty unignorable silence,
Brewed God knows how long. Hatless, I take off
My cycle-clips[7] in awkward reverence,

10 Move forward, run my hand around the font.
From where I stand, the roof looks almost new—
Cleaned, or restored? Someone would know: I don't.
Mounting the lectern, I peruse a few
Hectoring large-scale verses,[8] and pronounce
15 "Here endeth" much more loudly than I'd meant.
The echoes snigger briefly. Back at the door
I sign the book, donate an Irish sixpence,[9]
Reflect the place was not worth stopping for.

Yet stop I did: in fact I often do,
20 And always end much at a loss like this,
Wondering what to look for; wondering, too,
When churches fall completely out of use
What we shall turn them into, if we shall keep
A few cathedrals chronically on show,
25 Their parchment, plate and pyx[1] in locked cases,
And let the rest rent-free to rain and sheep.
Shall we avoid them as unlucky places?

---

7. Devices worn below the knee to keep trouser legs from getting caught in a bicycle chain.
8. I.e., biblical verses printed in large type for reading aloud.

9. An Irish sixpence has no value in England.
1. Box, often made of gold or silver, in which communion wafers are kept.

Or, after dark, will dubious women come
To make their children touch a particular stone;
30 Pick simples° for a cancer; or on some   *medicinal herbs*
Advised night see walking a dead one?
Power of some sort or other will go on
In games, in riddles, seemingly at random;
But superstition, like belief, must die,
35 And what remains when disbelief has gone?
Grass, weedy pavement, brambles, buttress, sky,

A shape less recognisable each week,
A purpose more obscure. I wonder who
Will be the last, the very last, to seek
40 This place for what it was; one of the crew
That tap and jot and know what rood-lofts[2] were?
Some ruin-bibber, randy for antique,
Or Christmas-addict, counting on a whiff
Of gown-and-bands and organ-pipes and myrrh?[3]
45 Or will he be my representative,

Bored, uninformed, knowing the ghostly silt
Dispersed, yet tending to this cross of ground
Through suburb scrub because it held unspilt
So long and equably what since is found
50 Only in separation—marriage, and birth,
And death, and thoughts of these—for which was built
This special shell? For, though I've no idea
What this accoutred frowsty barn is worth,
It pleases me to stand in silence here;

55 A serious house on serious earth it is,
In whose blent air all our compulsions meet,
Are recognized, and robed as destinies.
And that much never can be obsolete,
Since someone will forever be surprising
60 A hunger in himself to be more serious,
And gravitating with it to this ground,
Which, he once heard, was proper to grow wise in,
If only that so many dead lie round.

1954   1955

An Arundel Tomb[4]

Side by side, their faces blurred,
The earl and countess lie in stone,

2. In churches, galleries on top of carved screens separating the naves, or main halls, from the choirs, or areas where services are performed (*rood*: cross).
3. Gum resin, from trees of eastern Africa and Arabia, used to make incense; one of three pres-

ents given to the infant Jesus (Matthew 2, Luke 2). *Gown-and-bands*: gown and decorative collar worn by clergymen.
4. Fourteenth-century table tomb of Richard Fitzalan III, thirteenth earl of Arundel, and his wife, Eleanor, in Chichester Cathedral, Sussex.

Their proper habits° vaguely shown   *clothing*
As jointed armour, stiffened pleat,
5   And that faint hint of the absurd—
The little dogs under their feet.

Such plainness of the pre-baroque
Hardly involves the eye, until
It meets his left-hand gauntlet, still
10 Clasped empty in the other; and
One sees, with a sharp tender shock
His hand withdrawn, holding her hand.

They would not think to lie so long.
Such faithfulness in effigy
15 Was just a detail friends would see:
A sculptor's sweet commissioned grace
Thrown off in helping to prolong
The Latin names around the base.

They would not guess how early in
20 Their supine stationary voyage
The air would change to soundless damage,
Turn the old tenantry away;
How soon succeeding eyes begin
To look, not read. Rigidly they

25 Persisted, linked, through lengths and breadths
Of time. Snow fell, undated. Light
Each summer thronged the glass. A bright
Litter of birdcalls strewed the same
Bone-riddled ground. And up the paths
30 The endless altered people came,

Washing at their identity.
Now, helpless in the hollow of
An unarmorial age, a trough
Of smoke in slow suspended skeins
35 Above their scrap of history,
Only an attitude remains:

Time has transfigured them into
Untruth. The stone fidelity
They hardly meant has come to be
40 Their final blazon,° and to prove   *record of virtue*
Our almost-instinct almost true:
What will survive of us is love.

1956   1964

The Whitsun[5] Weddings

That Whitsun, I was late getting away:
   Not till about
One-twenty on the sunlit Saturday
Did my three-quarters-empty train pull out,
5   All windows down, all cushions hot, all sense
Of being in a hurry gone. We ran
Behind the backs of houses, crossed a street
Of blinding windscreens, smelt the fish-dock; thence
The river's level drifting breadth began,
10 Where sky and Lincolnshire and water meet.

All afternoon, through the tall heat that slept
   For miles inland,
A slow and stopping curve southwards we kept.
Wide farms went by, short-shadowed cattle, and
15 Canals with floatings of industrial froth;
A hothouse flashed uniquely: hedges dipped
And rose: and now and then a smell of grass
Displaced the reek of buttoned carriage-cloth
Until the next town, new and nondescript,
20 Approached with acres of dismantled cars.

At first, I didn't notice what a noise
   The weddings made
Each station that we stopped at: sun destroys
The interest of what's happening in the shade,
25 And down the long cool platforms whoops and skirls°   *shrill cries*
I took for porters larking with the mails,
And went on reading. Once we started, though,
We passed them, grinning and pomaded, girls
In parodies of fashion, heels and veils,
30 All posed irresolutely, watching us go,

As if out on the end of an event
   Waving goodbye
To something that survived it. Struck, I leant
More promptly out next time, more curiously,
35 And saw it all again in different terms:
The fathers with broad belts under their suits
And seamy foreheads; mothers loud and fat;
An uncle shouting smut; and then the perms,
The nylon gloves and jewellery-substitutes,
40 The lemons, mauves, and olive-ochres that

Marked off the girls unreally from the rest.
   Yes, from cafés
And banquet-halls up yards, and bunting-dressed

5. Or Whitsunday, the seventh Sunday after Easter, commemorating the day of Pentecost, when converts to the early Christian Church wore white robes. In the 1950s, British tax law made the Whitsun weekend a financially advantageous time to be married.

Coach-party annexes, the wedding-days
45 Were coming to an end. All down the line
Fresh couples climbed aboard: the rest stood round;
The last confetti and advice were thrown,
And, as we moved, each face seemed to define
Just what it saw departing: children frowned
50 At something dull; fathers had never known

Success so huge and wholly farcical;
    The women shared
The secret like a happy funeral;
While girls, gripping their handbags tighter, stared
55 At a religious wounding. Free at last,
And loaded with the sum of all they saw,
We hurried towards London, shuffling gouts of steam.
Now fields were building-plots, and poplars cast
Long shadows over major roads, and for
60 Some fifty minutes, that in time would seem

Just long enough to settle hats and say
    I nearly died,
A dozen marriages got under way.
They watched the landscape, sitting side by side
65 —An Odeon went past, a cooling tower,[6]
And someone running up to bowl[7]—and none
Thought of the others they would never meet
Or how their lives would all contain this hour.
I thought of London spread out in the sun,
70 Its postal districts packed like squares of wheat:

There we were aimed. And as we raced across
    Bright knots of rail
Past standing Pullmans,[8] walls of blackened moss
Came close, and it was nearly done, this frail
75 Travelling coincidence; and what it held
Stood ready to be loosed with all the power
That being changed can give. We slowed again,
And as the tightened brakes took hold, there swelled
A sense of falling, like an arrow-shower
80 Sent out of sight, somewhere becoming rain.

1958   1964

MCMXIV[9]

Those long uneven lines
Standing as patiently
As if they were stretched outside

6. Industrial structure for cooling hot water before reuse. *Odeon:* one in a chain of movie theaters.
7. In the sport of cricket, to pitch the ball to the batsman.
8. Railway saloons or sleeping cars first made in the United States by George M. Pullman.
9. 1914, in roman numerals, as incised on stone memorials to the dead of World War I.

The Oval or Villa Park,[1]
5   The crowns of hats, the sun
On moustached archaic faces
Grinning as if it were all
An August Bank Holiday lark;

And the shut shops, the bleached,
10 Established names on the sunblinds,
The farthings and sovereigns,[2]
And dark-clothed children at play
Called after kings and queens,
The tin advertisements
15 For cocoa and twist,° and the pubs   tobacco
Wide open all day;[3]

And the countryside not caring:
The place-names all hazed over
With flowering grasses, and fields
20 Shadowing Domesday lines[4]
Under wheat's restless silence;
The differently-dressed servants
With tiny rooms in huge houses,
The dust behind limousines;

25 Never such innocence,
Never before or since,
As changed itself to past
Without a word—the men
Leaving the gardens tidy,
30 The thousands of marriages
Lasting a little while longer:
Never such innocence again.

1960   1964

Talking in Bed

Talking in bed ought to be easiest,
Lying together there goes back so far,
An emblem of two people being honest.

Yet more and more time passes silently.
5   Outside, the wind's incomplete unrest
Builds and disperses clouds about the sky,

---

1. I.e., outside a (London) cricket ground or a
(Birmingham) soccer field. The lines consist of
men waiting to enlist.
2. At that time, the least valuable and the most
valuable British coins, respectively.
3. A 1915 law restricted the business hours of

public houses ("pubs").
4. The still-visible boundaries of medieval farmers'
long and narrow plots, ownership of which is
recorded in William the Conqueror's Domesday
Book (1085–86).

And dark towns heap up on the horizon.
None of this cares for us. Nothing shows why
At this unique distance from isolation

10   It becomes still more difficult to find
Words at once true and kind,
Or not untrue and not unkind.

1960   1964

Ambulances

Closed like confessionals,[5] they thread
Loud noons of cities, giving back
None of the glances they absorb.
Light glossy grey, arms on a plaque,
5   They come to rest at any kerb:
All streets in time are visited.

Then children strewn on steps or road,
Or women coming from the shops
Past smells of different dinners, see
10   A wild white face that overtops
Red stretcher-blankets momently
As it is carried in and stowed,

And sense the solving emptiness
That lies just under all we do,
15   And for a second get it whole,
So permanent and blank and true.
The fastened doors recede. *Poor soul,*
They whisper at their own distress;

For borne away in deadened air
20   May go the sudden shut of loss
Round something nearly at an end,
And what cohered in it across
The years, the unique random blend
Of families and fashions, there

25   At last begin to loosen. Far
From the exchange of love to lie
Unreachable inside a room
The traffic parts to let go by
Brings closer what is left to come,
30   And dulls to distance all we are.

1961   1964

5. Enclosed stalls in Roman Catholic churches, in which priests hear confession.

The Trees

The trees are coming into leaf
Like something almost being said;
The recent buds relax and spread,
Their greenness is a kind of grief.

5   Is it that they are born again
And we grow old? No, they die too.
Their yearly trick of looking new
Is written down in rings of grain.

Yet still the unresting castles thresh
10   In fullgrown thickness every May.
Last year is dead, they seem to say,
Begin afresh, afresh, afresh.

1967   1974

Sad Steps[6]

Groping back to bed after a piss
I part thick curtains, and am startled by
The rapid clouds, the moon's cleanliness.

Four o'clock: wedge-shadowed gardens lie
5   Under a cavernous, a wind-picked sky.
There's something laughable about this,

The way the moon dashes through clouds that blow
Loosely as cannon-smoke to stand apart
(Stone-coloured light sharpening the roofs below)

10   High and preposterous and separate—
Lozenge of love! Medallion of art!
O wolves of memory! Immensements! No,

One shivers slightly, looking up there.
The hardness and the brightness and the plain
15   Far-reaching singleness of that wide stare

Is a reminder of the strength and pain
Of being young; that it can't come again,
But is for others undiminished somewhere.

1968   1974

6. Cf. Sir Philip Sidney, *Astrophil and Stella* 31.1: "With how sad steps, O Moon, thou climb'st the skies"
(p. 214).

The Explosion

On the day of the explosion
Shadows pointed towards the pithead.
In the sun the slagheap[7] slept.

Down the lane came men in pitboots
5   Coughing oath-edged talk and pipe-smoke,
Shouldering off the freshened silence.

One chased after rabbits; lost them;
Came back with a nest of lark's eggs;
Showed them; lodged them in the grasses.

10   So they passed in beards and moleskins,[8]
Fathers, brothers, nicknames, laughter,
Through the tall gates standing open.

At noon, there came a tremor; cows
Stopped chewing for a second; sun,
15   Scarfed as in a heat-haze, dimmed.

The dead go on before us, they
Are sitting in God's house in comfort,
We shall see them face to face—

Plain as lettering in the chapels
20   It was said, and for a second
Wives saw men of the explosion

Larger than in life they managed—
Gold as on a coin, or walking
Somehow from the sun towards them,

25   One showing the eggs unbroken.

1970   1974

This Be The Verse[9]

They fuck you up, your mum and dad.
   They may not mean to, but they do.
They fill you with the faults they had
   And add some extra, just for you.

---

7. Pile of debris. *Pithead*: entrance to a coal mine.
8. Clothes made of heavy, durable cotton fabric.

9. Cf. Robert Louis Stevenson, "Requiem," esp. line 5: "This be the verse you grave for me."

5 But they were fucked up in their turn
By fools in old-style hats and coats,
Who half the time were soppy-stern
And half at one another's throats.

Man hands on misery to man.
10 It deepens like a coastal shelf.
Get out as early as you can,
And don't have any kids yourself.

1971   1974

Aubade[1]

I work all day, and get half-drunk at night.
Waking at four to soundless dark, I stare.
In time the curtain-edges will grow light.
Till then I see what's really always there:
5 Unresting death, a whole day nearer now,
Making all thought impossible but how
And where and when I shall myself die.
Arid interrogation: yet the dread
Of dying, and being dead,
10 Flashes afresh to hold and horrify.

The mind blanks at the glare. Not in remorse
—The good not done, the love not given, time
Torn off unused—nor wretchedly because
An only life can take so long to climb
15 Clear of its wrong beginnings, and may never;
But at the total emptiness for ever,
The sure extinction that we travel to
And shall be lost in always. Not to be here,
Not to be anywhere,
20 And soon; nothing more terrible, nothing more true.

This is a special way of being afraid
No trick dispels. Religion used to try,
That vast moth-eaten musical brocade
Created to pretend we never die,
25 And specious stuff that says *No rational being
Can fear a thing it will not feel,* not seeing
That this is what we fear—no sight, no sound,
No touch or taste or smell, nothing to think with,
Nothing to love or link with,
30 The anaesthetic from which none come round.

---

1. Music or poem announcing dawn.

And so it stays just on the edge of vision,
A small unfocused blur, a standing chill
That slows each impulse down to indecision.
Most things may never happen: this one will,
35 And realisation of it rages out
In furnace-fear when we are caught without
People or drink. Courage is no good:
It means not scaring others. Being brave
Lets no one off the grave.
40 Death is no different whined at than withstood.

Slowly light strengthens, and the room takes shape.
It stands plain as a wardrobe, what we know,
Have always known, know that we can't escape,
Yet can't accept. One side will have to go.
45 Meanwhile telephones crouch, getting ready to ring
In locked-up offices, and all the uncaring
Intricate rented world begins to rouse.
The sky is white as clay, with no sun.
Work has to be done.
50 Postmen like doctors go from house to house.

                                                            1977

HOWARD MOSS
1922–1987

The Persistence of Song

Although it is not yet evening,
The secretaries have changed their frocks
As if it were time for dancing,
And locked up in the scholars' books
5 There is a kind of rejoicing,
There is a kind of singing
That even the dark stone canyon makes
As though all fountains were going
At once, and the color flowed from bricks
10 In one wild, lit upsurging.

What is the weather doing?
And who arrived on a scallop shell
With the smell of the sea this morning?[1]
—Creating a small upheaval
15 High above the scaffolding
By saying, "All will be well.
There is a kind of rejoicing."

---

1. Venus, Roman goddess of love and beauty, was said to have been born from a shell in the sea.

Is there a kind of rejoicing
In saying, "All will be well"?
20 High above the scaffolding,
Creating a small upheaval,
The smell of the sea this morning
Arrived on a scallop shell.
What was the weather doing

25 In one wild, lit upsurging?
At once, the color flowed from bricks
As though all fountains were going,
And even the dark stone canyon makes
Here a kind of singing,
30 And there a kind of rejoicing,
And locked up in the scholars' books
There is a time for dancing
When the secretaries have changed their frocks,
And though it is not yet evening,

35 There is the persistence of song.

1968

Tourists

Cramped like sardines on the Queens,[2] and sedated,
The sittings all first, the roommates mismated,

Three nuns at the table, the waiter a barber,
Then dumped with their luggage at some frumpish harbor,

5 Veering through rapids in a vapid *rapido*
To view the new moon from a ruin on the Lido,[3]

Or a sundown in London from a rundown Mercedes,
Then high-borne to Glyndebourne for Orfeo in Hades,[4]

Embarrassed in Paris in Harris tweed, dying to
10 Get to the next museum piece that they're flying to,

Finding, in Frankfurt, that one indigestible
Comestible makes them too ill for the Festival,

Footloose in Lucerne, or taking a pub in in
Stratford or Glasgow, or maudlin in Dublin, in-

2. Ocean liner.
3. A chain of islands between the Lagoon of Ven-
ice and the Adriatic Sea. *Rapido*: Italian term for
an express passenger boat in Venice.

4. Reference to the opera *Orphée aux Enfers*, by
the French composer Jacques Offenbach (1819–
1880).

15 sensitive, garrulous, querulous, audible,
Drunk in the Dolomites, tuning a portable,

Homesick in Stockholm, or dressed to toboggan
At the wrong time of year in too dear° Copenhagen,   *expensive*

Generally being too genial or hostile—
20 Too grand at the Grand, too old at the Hostel—

Humdrum conundrums, what's to become of them?
Most will come home, but there will be some of them

Subsiding like Lawrence in Florence,[5] or crazily
Ending up tending shop up in Fiesole.[6]

1976

JAMES DICKEY
1923–1997

The Lifeguard

In a stable of boats I lie still,
From all sleeping children hidden.
The leap of a fish from its shadow
Makes the whole lake instantly tremble.
5 With my foot on the water, I feel
The moon outside

Take on the utmost of its power.
I rise and go out through the boats.
I set my broad sole upon silver,
10 On the skin of the sky, on the moonlight,
Stepping outward from earth onto water
In quest of the miracle

This village of children believed
That I could perform as I dived
15 For one who had sunk from my sight.
I saw his cropped haircut go under.
I leapt, and my steep body flashed
Once, in the sun.

Dark drew all the light from my eyes.
20 Like a man who explores his death

---

5. The English writer D. H. Lawrence (1885–1930; see pp. 1284–95) lived in Italy several times.   6. Town in Italy, near Florence.

By the pull of his slow-moving shoulders,
I hung head down in the cold,
Wide-eyed, contained, and alone
Among the weeds,

25 And my fingertips turned into stone
From clutching immovable blackness.
Time after time I leapt upward
Exploding in breath, and fell back
From the change in the children's faces
30 At my defeat.

Beneath them I swam to the boathouse
With only my life in my arms
To wait for the lake to shine back
At the risen moon with such power
35 That my steps on the light of the ripples
Might be sustained.

Beneath me is nothing but brightness
Like the ghost of a snowfield in summer.
As I move toward the center of the lake,
40 Which is also the center of the moon,
I am thinking of how I may be
The savior of one

Who has already died in my care.
The dark trees fade from around me.
45 The moon's dust hovers together.
I call softly out, and the child's
Voice answers through blinding water.
Patiently, slowly,

He rises, dilating to break
50 The surface of stone with his forehead.
He is one I do not remember
Having ever seen in his life.
The ground I stand on is trembling
Upon his smile.

55 I wash the black mud from my hands.
On a light given off by the grave
I kneel in the quick of the moon
At the heart of a distant forest
And hold in my arms a child
60 Of water, water, water.

1962

Buckdancer's[1] Choice

So I would hear out those lungs,
The air split into nine levels,
Some gift of tongues of the whistler

In the invalid's bed: my mother,
5   Warbling all day to herself
The thousand variations of one song;

It is called Buckdancer's Choice.
For years, they have all been dying
Out, the classic buck-and-wing men

10   Of traveling minstrel shows;
With them also an old woman
Was dying of breathless angina,

Yet still found breath enough
To whistle up in my head
15   A sight like a one-man band,

Freed black, with cymbals at heel,
An ex-slave who thrivingly danced
To the ring of his own clashing light

Through the thousand variations of one song
20   All day to my mother's prone music,
The invalid's warbler's note,

While I crept close to the wall
Sock-footed, to hear the sounds alter,
Her tongue like a mockingbird's break

25   Through stratum after stratum of a tone
Proclaiming what choices there are
For the last dancers of their kind,

For ill women and for all slaves
Of death, and children enchanted at walls
30   With a brass-beating glow underfoot,

Not dancing but nearly risen
Through barnlike, theaterlike houses
On the wings of the buck and wing.

1965

---

1. Performer of the buck-and-wing, a solo tap dance invented by black entertainers.

Sled Burial, Dream Ceremony

While the south rains, the north
Is snowing, and the dead southerner
Is taken there. He lies with the top of his casket
Open, his hair combed, the particles in the air
5   Changing to other things. The train stops

In a small furry village, and men in flap-eared caps
And others with women's scarves tied around their heads
And business hats over those, unload him,
And one of them reaches inside the coffin and places
10   The southerner's hand at the center

Of his dead breast. They load him onto a sled,
An old-fashioned sled with high-curled runners,
Drawn by horses with bells, and begin
To walk out of town, past dull red barns
15   Inching closer to the road as it snows

Harder, past an army of gunny-sacked bushes,
Past horses with flakes in the hollows of their sway-backs,
Past round faces drawn by children
On kitchen windows, all shedding basic-shaped tears.
20   The coffin top still is wide open;

His dead eyes stare through his lids,
Not fooled that the snow is cotton. The woods fall
Slowly off all of them, until they are walking
Between rigid little houses of ice-fishers
25   On a plain which is a great plain of water

Until the last rabbit track fails, and they are
At the center. They take axes, shovels, mattocks,
Dig the snow away, and saw the ice in the form
Of his coffin, lifting the slab like a door
30   Without hinges. The snow creaks under the sled

As they unload him like hay, holding his weight by ropes.
Sensing an unwanted freedom, a fish
Slides by, under the hole leading up through the snow
To nothing, and is gone. The coffin's shadow
35   Is white, and they stand there, gunny-sacked bushes,

Summoned from village sleep into someone else's dream
Of death, and let him down, still seeing the flakes in the air
At the place they are born of pure shadow
Like his dead eyelids, rocking for a moment like a boat
40   On utter foreignness, before he fills and sails down.

1965

PETER KANE DUFAULT
b. 1923

A Letter for All-Hallows[1] (1949)

I am still hurt, Plin,
by your desertion. Now and again,
between rains, or among
sagged syllables on a page,
5   I am stopped suddenly by your grinning
lantern-jawed, monkey-eared beautiful face—
and I am hurt because you went to war
and died right in the middle of your letters
and never said goodbye.

10   And then your father followed you,
at a respectful distance,
and the high house on the hill went
for a Trappist monkery.[2] . . . . I hope those monks
have veneration for the juniper
15   and the blackberries and the frogpond
and the dust of toy-soldiers in the attic
where we warred long November afternoons.—
Above all, for the black road that,
if I listen on All-Souls' Eve,[3] will clatter
20   to the gait of you riding home
from the white woods on Diamond, your horse.

The glue is long since dry
they made of him. Yet we mark well:
He was the last of the historic horses.
25   Revere rode him, and Sheridan,
and Sitting Bull.[4] . . .

I hope those monks treat you gently, shades
galloping alongside the emptying meadows,
from Concord and Lexington,
30   from the fords of the Shenandoah,
the forks of the Little Bighorn.[5]

Surely they would not be unmerciful
and frighten away with signs and bells and torches

1. Or All Saints' Day, a church festival celebrated
November 1 in honor of all saints.
2. The Trappist monks are members of a branch
of the austere Cistercian order.
3. Evening of November 1, before All Souls' Day
(a day of prayer for all the dead).
4. Native American warrior, victor at the Battle of
the Little Big Horn (1876). Paul Revere (1735–

1818), American patriot famous for a horseback
ride on the evening of April 18, 1775, in which he
warned Massachusetts colonists of the arrival of
British troops. Philip Henry Sheridan (1831–
1888), Union general in the American Civil War.
5. Scenes of the battles associated with Revere,
Sheridan, and Sitting Bull.

so young an old-soldier and his friend
35   who, one way or another, were made ghosts
in all their country's wars.

1949   1978

A First Night

It's the first night, I suppose,
in more than eighty year
Hattie has slept alone. . . .
And outdoors, in the falling
5   snow, without bedclothes
or night light and none near
but the deaf sunken stone
were one to awake calling.

What could old Hattie have done
10   wrong, anyway?—Made raw-
milk cheese, rubbed eggs, admired
her rose-red Christmas cactus, and
rocked, looking out at one
more mid-February thaw,
15   drifts melting and dungwagon mired—
that now like a reprimand

she might have heard sixty-eight
or seventy years ago,
(such as "Hattie thinks she is clever,
20   but will go to bed with boxed ears
and no supper") she is told: "Tonight
you'll sleep with shoes on in the snow
in the cemetery and never
never wake up in a million years."

1978

Burden

I called you because I could not stand alone
looking north to that skyline-
tree globed with its yellow apples
balancing like a fountain of planets
5   in the bright light and the blue air.

And because on the way there
I looked at a smooth cirque°   circle
the brook had worn in a stone;

and nothing as soft as water
10 could, by taking care,
have so pestled° and polished   *pounded*
that granite mortar; only
by a thousand years of indifference,
of aiming elsewhere.

15 I wish we might do—or no,
look back and find we had done—
some un-advertized thing,
overwhelming and un-self-aware
as water streamlining a stone, or a tree's
20 kindling in an empty meadow
its casual Hesperides.[6]

1976   1978

ANTHONY HECHT
1923–2004

A Hill

In Italy, where this sort of thing can occur,
I had a vision once—though you understand
It was nothing at all like Dante's,[1] or the visions of saints,
And perhaps not a vision at all. I was with some friends,
5 Picking my way through a warm sunlit piazza
In the early morning. A clear fretwork of shadows
From huge umbrellas littered the pavement and made
A sort of lucent shallows in which was moored
A small navy of carts. Books, coins, old maps,
10 Cheap landscapes and ugly religious prints
Were all on sale. The colors and noise
Like the flying hands were gestures of exultation,
So that even the bargaining
Rose to the ear like a voluble godliness.
15 And then, when it happened, the noises suddenly stopped,
And it got darker; pushcarts and people dissolved
And even the great Farnese Palace[2] itself
Was gone, for all its marble; in its place
Was a hill, mole-colored and bare. It was very cold,
20 Close to freezing, with a promise of snow.
The trees were like old ironwork gathered for scrap
Outside a factory wall. There was no wind,
And the only sound for a while was the little click
Of ice as it broke in the mud under my feet.
25 I saw a piece of ribbon snagged on a hedge,

6. In Greek mythology, a garden where golden apples were grown.
1. As in the Italian poet's *Divine Comedy*.
2. Palace in Rome.

But no other sign of life. And then I heard
What seemed the crack of a rifle. A hunter, I guessed;
At least I was not alone. But just after that
Came the soft and papery crash
30   Of a great branch somewhere unseen falling to earth.

And that was all, except for the cold and silence
That promised to last forever, like the hill.

Then prices came through, and fingers, and I was restored
To the sunlight and my friends. But for more than a week
35   I was scared by the plain bitterness of what I had seen.
All this happened about ten years ago,
And it hasn't troubled me since, but at last, today,
I remembered that hill; it lies just to the left
Of the road north of Poughkeepsie;[3] and as a boy
40   I stood before it for hours in wintertime.

1967

The Dover Bitch

A Criticism of Life

FOR ANDREWS WANNING

So there stood Matthew Arnold[4] and this girl
With the cliffs of England crumbling away behind them,
And he said to her, "Try to be true to me,
And I'll do the same for you, for things are bad
5   All over, etc., etc."[5]
Well now, I knew this girl. It's true she had read
Sophocles in a fairly good translation
And caught that bitter allusion to the sea,[6]
But all the time he was talking she had in mind
10   The notion of what his whiskers would feel like
On the back of her neck. She told me later on
That after a while she got to looking out
At the lights across the channel, and really felt sad,
Thinking of all the wine and enormous beds
15   And blandishments in French and the perfumes.
And then she got really angry. To have been brought
All the way down from London, and then be addressed
As a sort of mournful cosmic last resort
Is really tough on a girl, and she was pretty.
20   Anyway, she watched him pace the room
And finger his watch-chain and seem to sweat a bit,
And then she said one or two unprintable things.

3. Town in upstate New York.
4. English poet (1822–1888; see pp. 1087–1101),
whose most famous poem, "Dover Beach"
(p. 1101), is set on the southern coast of England.

5. Cf. "Dover Beach," lines 29–37: "Ah, love, let
us be true / To one another! . . ."
6. Cf. "Dover Beach," lines 15–18 and note 9
there.

But you mustn't judge her by that. What I mean to say is,
She's really all right. I still see her once in a while
25 And she always treats me right. We have a drink
And I give her a good time, and perhaps it's a year
Before I see her again, but there she is,
Running to fat, but dependable as they come.
And sometimes I bring her a bottle of *Nuit d'Amour*.[7]

1968

The Ghost in the Martini[8]

Over the rim of the glass
Containing a good martini with a twist
    I eye her bosom and consider a pass,
      Certain we'd not be missed

5   In the general hubbub.
Her lips, which I forgot to say, are superb,
    Never stop babbling once (Aye, there's the rub)[9]
      But who would want to curb

      Such delicious, artful flattery?
10 It seems she adores my work, the distinguished grey
    Of my hair. I muse on the salt and battery[1]
      Of the sexual clinch, and say

      Something terse and gruff
About the marked disparity in our ages.
15 She looks like twenty-three, though eager enough.
      As for the famous wages

      Of sin,[2] she can't have attained
Even to union scale, though you never can tell.
Her waist is slender and suggestively chained,
20   And things are going well.

      The martini does its job,
God bless it, seeping down to the dark old id.
    ("Is there no cradle, Sir, you would not rob?")
      Says ego, but the lid

25   Is off. The word is Strike
While the iron's hot.) And now, ingenuous and gay,
She is asking me about what I was like
      At twenty. (Twenty, eh?)

7. Night of love (French).
8. Alludes to the expression *the ghost in the machine*, a way of describing the mind/body opposition.
9. Cf. *Hamlet* 3.1.64, where the phrase refers to

a quite different double bind of the speaker, Prince Hamlet, who is considering suicide.
1. A play on *assault and battery*.
2. Cf. Romans 6.23: "For the wages of sin is death."

You wouldn't have liked me then,
30 I answer, looking carefully into her eyes.
I was shy, withdrawn, awkward, one of those men
    That girls seemed to despise,

    Moody and self-obsessed,
Unhappy, defiant, with guilty dreams galore,
35 Full of ill-natured pride, an unconfessed
    Snob and a thorough bore.

    Her smile is meant to convey
How changed or modest I am, I can't tell which,
When I suddenly hear someone close to me say,
40   "You lousy son-of-a-bitch!"

    A young man's voice, by the sound,
Coming, it seems, from the twist in the martini.
"You arrogant, elderly letch, you broken-down
    Brother of Apeneck Sweeney![3]

45   Thought I was buried for good
Under six thick feet of mindless self-regard?
Dance on my grave, would you, you galliard° stud,   *lively*
    Silenus[4] in leotard?

    Well, summon me you did,
50 And I come unwillingly, like Samuel's ghost.[5]
'All things shall be revealed that have been hid.'[6]
    There's something for you to toast!

    You only got where you are
By standing upon my ectoplasmic° shoulders,   *ghostly*
55 And wherever that is may not be so high or far
    In the eyes of some beholders.

    Take, for example, me.
I have sat alone in the dark, accomplishing little,
And worth no more to myself, in pride and fee,
60   Than a cup of luke-warm spittle.

    But honest about it, withal . . ."
("Withal," forsooth!) "Please not to interrupt.
And the lovelies went by, 'the long and the short and the tall,'[7]
    Hankered for, but untupped.[8]

---

3. Cf. T. S. Eliot, "Sweeney Among the Nightingales": "Apeneck Sweeney spreads his knees / Letting his arms hang down to laugh."
4. In Greek mythology, foster father and companion of the wine god, Dionysus; of human form, with a horse's ears and tail. Generally old, bald, and bearded. A famous legend relates that Midas made Silenus drunk to learn his secrets.
5. Saul, fearful of the army of the Philistines,

found his prayers for guidance unanswered, and so consulted a medium to raise the unwilling Samuel from the dead (1 Samuel 28).
6. A rewriting of a recurrent theme in the Gospels, as in Luke 12.2 or Matthew 10.26.
7. As in the 1940 popular song by Jimmy Hughes and Frank Lake, "Bless 'Em All."
8. Not copulated with (as a ewe is tupped by a ram).

65   Bloody monastic it was.
A neurotic mixture of self-denial and fear;
The verse halting, the cataleptic pause,
            No sensible pain, no tear,

        But an interior drip
70   As from an ulcer, where, in the humid deep
Center of myself, I would scratch and grip
            The wet walls of the keep,

        Or lie on my back and smell
From the corners the sharp, ammoniac, urine stink.
75   'No light, but rather darkness visible.'⁹
            And plenty of time to think.

        In that thick, fetid air
I talked to myself in giddy recitative:
'I have been studying how I may compare
80   This prison where I live

        Unto the world . . .'¹ I learned
Little, and was awarded no degrees.
Yet all that sunken hideousness earned
            Your negligence and ease.

85   Nor was it wholly sick,
Having procured you a certain modest fame;
A devotion, rather, a grim device to stick
            To something I could not name."

        Meanwhile, she babbles on
90   About men, or whatever, and the juniper juice
Shuts up at last, having sung, I trust, like a swan.²
            Still given to self-abuse!

        Better get out of here;
If he opens his trap again it could get much worse.
95   I touch her elbow, and, leaning toward her ear,
            Tell her to find her purse.

                                                    1977

Still Life

        Sleep-walking vapor, like a visitant ghost,
                Hovers above a lake
        Of Tennysonian³ calm just before dawn.

9. Cf. Milton, *Paradise Lost* 1.61–63, where Satan
views hell: "A Dungeon horrible, on all sides round
/ As one great Furnace flam'd, yet from those
flames / No light, but rather darkness visible."
1. Cf. Shakespeare, *Richard II* 5.5.1 ff. (the
poetic, self-absorbed King Richard's soliloquy in
prison).
2. A swan is said to sing before it dies. Juniper
juice is an ingredient used in flavoring gin.
3. As in the work of the English poet Alfred, Lord
Tennyson (1809–1892; see pp. 982–1009).

Inverted trees and boulders waver and coast
5 In polished darkness. Glints of silver break
Among the liquid leafage, and then are gone.

Everything's doused and diamonded with wet.
    A cobweb, woven taut
On bending stanchion° frames of tentpole grass,   *upright prop*
10 Sags like a trampoline or firemen's net
With all the glitter and riches it has caught,
Each drop a paperweight of Steuben glass.[4]

No birdsong yet, no cricket, nor does the trout
    Explode in water-scrolls
15 For a skimming fly. All that is yet to come.
Things are as still and motionless throughout
The universe as ancient Chinese bowls,
And nature is magnificently dumb.

Why does this so much stir me, like a code
20   Or muffled intimation
Of purposes and preordained events?
It knows me, and I recognize its mode
Of cautionary, spring-tight hesitation,
This silence so impacted and intense.

25 As in a water-surface I behold
    The first, soft, peach decree
Of light, its pale, inaudible commands.
I stand beneath a pine-tree in the cold,
Just before dawn, somewhere in Germany,
30 A cold, wet, Garand rifle in my hands.

                                            1979

The Book of Yolek

Wir haben ein Gesetz,
Und nach dem Gesetz soll er sterben.[5]

The dowsed coals fume and hiss after your meal
Of grilled brook trout, and you saunter off for a walk
Down the fern trail, it doesn't matter where to,
Just so you're weeks and worlds away from home,
5 And among midsummer hills have set up camp
In the deep bronze glories of declining day.

---

4. Brand of handmade, heavy lead crystal.
5. From the German translation of John 19.7 ("We have a law, and by that law he ought to die") by the theologian Martin Luther (1483–1546), leader in Germany of the Protestant Reformation. Hecht's poem is inspired by "Yanosz Korezak's Last Walk," by the Polish poet Hannah Mortkowicz-Olczakowa (1905–1968)—in Jacob Glatstein and Israel Knox, eds., *Anthology of Holocaust Literature* (1973), 134–37—which recounts a historical event in Germany.

You remember, peacefully, an earlier day
In childhood, remember a quite specific meal:
A corn roast and bonfire in summer camp.
10 That summer you got lost on a Nature Walk;
More than you dared admit, you thought of home;
No one else knows where the mind wanders to.

The fifth of August, 1942.
It was morning and very hot. It was the day
15 They came at dawn with rifles to The Home
For Jewish Children, cutting short the meal
Of bread and soup, lining them up to walk
In close formation off to a special camp.

How often you have thought about that camp,
20 As though in some strange way you were driven to,
And about the children, and how they were made to walk,
Yolek who had bad lungs, who wasn't a day
Over five years old, commanded to leave his meal
And shamble between armed guards to his long home.

25 We're approaching August again. It will drive home
The regulation torments of that camp
Yolek was sent to, his small, unfinished meal,
The electric fences, the numeral tattoo,
The quite extraordinary heat of the day
30 They all were forced to take that terrible walk.

Whether on a silent, solitary walk
Or among crowds, far off or safe at home,
You will remember, helplessly, that day,
And the smell of smoke, and the loudspeakers of the camp.
35 Wherever you are, Yolek will be there, too.
His unuttered name will interrupt your meal.

Prepare to receive him in your home some day.
Though they killed him in the camp they sent him to,
He will walk in as you're sitting down to a meal.

1990

Death the Painter[6]

Snub-nosed, bone-fingered, deft with engraving tools,
        I have alone been given
The powers of Joshua, who stayed the sun
        In its traverse of heaven.[7]

6. From *The Presumptions of Death*, a series of twenty-two poems written from the perspective of Death, to accompany woodcuts by the American artist Leonard Baskin (1922–2000).

7. Cf. Joshua 10.12–13; when Joshua asked the sun and the moon to stand still, "the sun stood still, and the moon stayed, until the people had avenged themselves upon their enemies."

5   Here in this Gotham[8] of unnumbered fools
I have sought out and arrested everyone.

Under my watchful eye all human creatures
    Convert to a *still life,*
As with unique precision I apply
10   White lead and palette knife.
A model student of remodelled features,
The final barber, the last beautician, I.

You lordlings, what is Man, his blood and vitals,[9]
    When all is said and done?
15   A poor forked animal,[1] a nest of flies.
    Tell us, what is this one
Once shorn of all his dignities and titles,
Divested of his testicles and eyes?

1995

RICHARD HUGO
1923–1982

The Way a Ghost Dissolves

Where she lived the close remained the best.
The nearest music and the static cloud,
sun and dirt were all she understood.
She planted corn and left the rest
5   to elements, convinced that God
with giant faucets regulates the rain
and saves the crops from frost or foreign wind.

Fate assisted her with special cures.
Rub a half potato on your wart
10   and wrap it in a damp cloth. Close
your eyes and whirl three times and throw.
Then bury rag and spud exactly where
they fall. The only warts that I have now
are memories or comic on my nose.

---

8. Proverbial town (in England) known for its foolish inhabitants.
9. Cf. Psalm 8.4: "What is man, that thou art mindful of him?"
1. Cf. *King Lear* 3.4.101 ff., where Lear encounters Edgar, disguised in rags as a madman, laments, "Is man no more than this?" and says, "unaccommodated man is no more but such a poor, bare, fork'd animal as thou art."

15 Up at dawn. The earth provided food
    if worked and watered, planted green
    with rye grass every fall. Or driven wild
    by snakes that kept the carrots clean,
    she butchered snakes and carrots with a hoe.
20 Her screams were sea birds in the wind,
    her chopping—nothing like it now.

    I will garden on the double run,
    my rhythm obvious in ringing rakes,
    and trust in fate to keep me poor and kind
25 and work until my heart is short,
    then go out slowly with a feeble grin,
    my fingers flexing but my eyes gone gray
    from cramps and the lack of oxygen.

    Forget the tone. Call the neighbor's trumpet
30 golden as it grates. Exalt the weeds.
    Say the local animals have class
    or help me say that ghost has gone to seed.
    And why attempt to see the cloud again—
    the screaming face it was before it cracked
35 in wind from Asia and a wanton rain.

                                      1961

The Lady in Kicking Horse Reservoir[1]

    Not my hands but green across you now.
    Green tons hold you down, and ten bass curve
    teasing in your hair. Summer slime
    will pile deep on your breast. Four months of ice
5 will keep you firm. I hope each spring
    to find you tangled in those pads
    pulled not quite loose by the spillway pour,
    stars in dead reflection off your teeth.

    Lie there lily still. The spillway's closed.
10 Two feet down most lakes are common gray.
    This lake is dark from the black blue Mission range
    climbing sky like music dying Indians once wailed.
    On ocean beaches, mystery fish
    are offered to the moon. Your jaws go blue.
15 Your hands start waving every wind.
    Wave to the ocean where we crushed a mile of foam.

1. Both Kicking Horse Reservoir and the Mission mountain range (line 11) are on the Flathead Indian
Reservation, in Montana.

We still love there in thundering foam
and love. Whales fall in love with gulls
and tide reclaims the Dolly skeletons[2]
20   gone with a blast of aching horns to China.
Landlocked in Montana here
the end is limited by light, the final note
will trail off at the farthest point we see,
already faded, lover, where you bloat.

25   All girls should be nicer. Arrows rain
above us in the Indian wind. My future
should be full of windy gems, my past
will stop this roaring in my dreams.
Sorry. Sorry. Sorry. But the arrows sing:
30   no way to float her up. The dead sink
from dead weight. The Mission range
turns this water black late afternoons.

One boy slapped the other. Hard.
The slapped boy talked until his dignity
35   dissolved, screamed a single "stop"
and went down sobbing in the company pond.
I swam for him all night. My only suit
got wet and factory hands went home.
No one cared the coward disappeared.
40   Morning then: cold music I had never heard.

Loners like work best on second shift.
No one liked our product and the factory closed.
Off south, the bison multiply so fast
a slaughter's mandatory every spring
45   and every spring the creeks get fat
and Kicking Horse fills up. My hope is vague.
The far blur of your bones in May
may be nourished by the snow.

The spillway's open and you spill out
50   into weather, lover down the bright canal
and mother, irrigating crops
dead Indians forgot to plant.
I'm sailing west with arrows to dissolving foam
where waves strand naked Dollys.
55   Their eyes are white as oriental mountains
and their tongues are teasing oil from whales.

1973

---

2. Specifically, here, skeletons of the Dolly Varden trout (but see also line 54).

DENISE LEVERTOV
1923–1997

Scenes from the Life of the Peppertrees

1

The peppertrees, the peppertrees!

Cats are stretching in the doorways,
sure of everything. It is morning.
     But the peppertrees
5 stand aside in diffidence, with berries
of modest red.
          Branch above branch, an air
of lightness; of shadows
scattered lightly.
10   A cat
closes upon its shadow.
Up and up goes the sun,
sure of everything.
     The peppertrees
15   shiver a little.
Robust
and soot-black, the cat
leaps to a low branch. Leaves
close about him.

2

20 The yellow moon dreamily
tipping buttons of light
down among the leaves. Marimba,
marimba—from beyond the
black street.
25   Somebody dancing,
somebody
      getting the hell
outta here. Shadows of cats
weave round the tree trunks,
30 the exposed knotty roots.

3

The man on the bed sleeping
defenseless. Look—
his bare long feet together
sideways, keeping each other
35 warm. And the foreshortened shoulders,
the head
barely visible.   He is good.

let him sleep.
              But the third peppertree
40   is restless, twitching
thin leaves in the light
of afternoon. After a while
it walks over and taps
on the upstairs window with a bunch
45   of red berries.   Will he wake?

                                                      1958

Triple Feature

Innocent decision: to enjoy.
And the pathos
of hopefulness, of his solicitude:

—he in mended serape,
5   she having plaited carefully
magenta ribbons into her hair,
the baby a round half-hidden shape
slung in her rebozo,° and the young son steadfastly   *shawl*
gripping a fold of her skirt,
10   pale and severe under a
handed-down sombrero—

                        all regarding
the stills with full attention, preparing
to pay and go in—

15   to worlds of shadow-violence, half-
familiar, warm with popcorn, icy
with strange motives, barbarous splendors!

                                                      1959

O Taste and See

The world is
not with us enough.[1]
O taste and see

the subway Bible poster said,
5   meaning The Lord,[2] meaning
if anything all that lives
to the imagination's tongue,

---

1. Cf. William Wordsworth's sonnet "The World Is Too Much with Us" (p. 802).   2. "O taste and see that the Lord is good" (Psalms 34.8).

grief, mercy, language,
tangerine, weather, to
10   breathe them, bite,
savor, chew, swallow, transform

into our flesh our
deaths, crossing the street, plum, quince,
living in the orchard and being

15   hungry, and plucking
the fruit.

1964

Tenebrae[3]

(Fall of 1967)[4]

Heavy, heavy, heavy, hand and heart.
We are at war,
bitterly, bitterly at war.

And the buying and selling
5   buzzes at our heads, a swarm
of busy flies, a kind of innocence.

Gowns of gold sequins are fitted,
sharp-glinting. What harsh rustlings
of silver moiré° there are,   *watered silk*
10   to remind me of shrapnel splinters.

And weddings are held in full solemnity
not of desire but of etiquette,
the nuptial pomp of starched lace;
a grim innocence.

15   And picnic parties return from the beaches
burning with stored sun in the dusk;
children promised a TV show when they get home
fall asleep in the backs of a million station wagons,
sand in their hair, the sound of waves
20   quietly persistent at their ears.
They are not listening.

Their parents at night
dream and forget their dreams.
They wake in the dark
25   and make plans. Their sequin plans

3. Darkness (Latin); church service observed during the final part of Holy Week to commemorate the sufferings and death of Christ.

4. Time of a march on the Pentagon to protest the continuing presence of American troops in Vietnam.

glitter into tomorrow.
They buy, they sell.

They fill freezers with food.
Neon signs flash their intentions
30   into the years ahead.

And at their ears the sound
of the war. They are
not listening, not listening.

1972

Caedmon[5]

All others talked as if
talk were a dance.
Clodhopper I, with clumsy feet
would break the gliding ring.
5   Early I learned to
hunch myself
close by the door:
then when the talk began
I'd wipe my
10   mouth and wend
unnoticed back to the barn
to be with the warm beasts,
dumb among body sounds
of the simple ones.
15   I'd see by a twist
of lit rush[6] the motes
of gold moving
from shadow to shadow
slow in the wake
20   of deep untroubled sighs.
The cows
munched or stirred or were still. I
was at home and lonely,
both in good measure. Until
25   the sudden angel affrighted me—light effacing
my feeble beam,
a forest of torches, feathers of flame, sparks upflying:
but the cows as before
were calm, and nothing was burning,

---

5. The earliest known English Christian poet (fl. 658–680), an unlettered cowherd who, the legend goes, received a divine call to praise in verse. (Cf. Cædmon's "Hymn," p. 1.) "The story comes, of course, from the Venerable Bede's *History of the* *English Church and People,* but I first read it as a child in John Richard Green's *History of the English People,* 1855" [Levertov's note].
6. Rush plants were lit to serve as candlewicks.

30   nothing but I, as that hand of fire
touched my lips and scorched my tongue
and pulled my voice
                    into the ring of the dance.

1987

JOHN ORMOND
1923–1990

Cathedral Builders

They climbed on sketchy ladders towards God,
With winch and pulley hoisted hewn rock into heaven,
Inhabited sky with hammers, defied gravity,
Deified stone, took up God's house to meet Him,

5   And came down to their suppers and small beer;
Every night slept, lay with their smelly wives,
Quarrelled and cuffed[1] the children, lied,
Spat, sang, were happy or unhappy,

And every day took to the ladders again;
10 Impeded the rights of way of another summer's
Swallows, grew greyer, shakier, became less inclined
To fix a neighbour's roof of a fine evening,

Saw naves sprout arches, clerestories[2] soar,
Cursed the loud fancy glaziers° for their luck,   *glass cutters*
15 Somehow escaped the plague, got rheumatism,
Decided it was time to give it up,

To leave the spire to others; stood in the crowd
Well back from the vestments at the consecration,
Envied the fat bishop his warm boots,
20 Cocked up a squint eye and said, "I bloody did that."

1969

Lament for a Leg

*Near the yew tree under which the body of Dafydd ap Gwilym[3] is buried
in Strata Florida, Cardiganshire, there stands a stone with the following
inscription: "The left leg and part of the thigh of Henry Hughes, Cooper,
was cut off and interr'd here, June 18, 1756". Later the rest of Henry
Hughes set off across the Atlantic in search of better fortune.*

1. Struck, especially with the palm of the hand.   main sections of churches.
2. Upper stories with their own windows. *Naves:*   3. Fourteenth-century Welsh poet.

A short service, to be sure,
With scarcely half a hymn they held,
Over my lost limb, suitable curtailment.
Out-of-tune notes a crow cawed
5   By the yew tree, and me,
My stump still tourniqued,
Awkward on my new crutch,
Being snatched towards the snack
Of a funeral feast they made.
10   With seldom a dry eye, for laughter,
They jostled me over the ale
I'd cut the casks for, and the mead.
"Catch me falling under a coach",
Every voice jested, save mine,
15   Henry Hughes, cooper. A tasteless caper!
Soon with my only, my best, foot forward
I fled, quiet, to far America:

Where, with my two tried hands, I plied
My trade and, true, in time made good
20   Though grieving for Pontrhydfendigaid.[4]
Sometimes, all at once, in my tall cups,
I'd cry in *hiraeth*[5] for my remembered thigh
Left by the grand yew in Ystrad Fflur's
Bare ground, near the good bard.
25   Strangers, astonished at my high
Beer-flush, would stare, not guessing,
Above the bar-board, that I, of the starry eye,
Had one foot in the grave; thinking me,
No doubt, a drunken dolt in whom a whim
30   Warmed to madness, not knowing a tease
Of a Welsh worm was tickling my distant toes.

"So I bequeath my leg", I'd say and sigh,
Baffling them, "my unexiled part, to Dafydd
The pure poet who, whole, lies near and far
35   From me, still pining for Morfudd's heart",[6]
Giving him, generous to a fault
With what was no more mine to give,
Out of that curt plot, my quarter grave,
Good help, I hope. What will the great God say
40   At Dafydd's wild-kicking-climbing extra leg,
Jammed hard in heaven's white doorway
(I'll limp unnimble round the narrow back)
Come the quick trumpet of the Judgement Day?

1973

---

4. Welsh place-name, as is Ystrad Fflur (line 23).   very drunk.
5. Longing, nostalgia (Welsh). *In my tall cups:*   6. The love of Morfudd.

JAMES SCHUYLER
1923–1991

Freely Espousing

a commingling sky

      a semi-tropic night
      that cast the blackest shadow
      of the easily torn, untrembling banana leaf

5   or Quebec! what a horrible city
so Steubenville[1] is better?
              the sinking sensation
when someone drowns thinking, "This can't be happening to me!"
the profit of excavating the battlefield where Hannibal whomped the
      Romans[2]
10   the sinuous beauty of words like allergy
the tonic resonance of
pill when used as in
"she is a pill"
on the other hand I am not going to espouse any short stories in
      which lawn mowers clack.
15   No, it is absolutely forbidden
for words to echo the act described; or try to. Except very directly
as in
bong. And tickle. Oh it is inescapable kiss.
Marriages of the atmosphere
20   are worth celebrating
              where Tudor City[3]
catches the sky or the glass side
of a building lit up at night in fog
"What is that gold green tetrahedron down the river?"
25   "You are experiencing a new sensation."

          if the touch-me-nots
          are not in bloom
          neither are the chrysanthemums

      the bales of pink cotton candy
30   in the slanting light
          are ornamental cherry trees.
          The greens around them, and
          the browns, the grays, are the park.
    It's. Hmm. No.
35   Their scallop shell of quiet
       is the S.S. *United States.*
       It is not so quiet and they

1. Town in Ohio.
2. In 217–216 B.C.E., the Carthaginian general Hannibal crossed the Alps and defeated Roman armies, using brilliant military tactics.
3. Large apartment complex on the east side of Manhattan.

are a medium-size couple who
when they fold each other up
40   well, thrill. That's their story.

1979

Shimmer

The pear tree that last year
was heavy laden this year
bears little fruit. Was
it that wet spring we had?
5   All the pear tree leaves
go shimmer, all at once. The
August sun blasts down
into the coolness from the
ocean. The New York Times
10 is on strike. My daily
fare! I'll starve! Not
quite. On my sill, balls
of twine wrapped up in
cellophane glitter. The
15 brown, the white, and one
I think you'd call écru.°   *beige*
The sunlight falls partly
in a cup: it has a blue
transfer of two boys, a
20 dog and a duck and says,
"Come Away Pompey." I
like that cup, half
full of sunlight. Today
you could take up the
25 tattered shadows off
the grass. Roll them
and stow them. And collect
the shimmerings in a
cup, like the coffee
30 here at my right hand.

1974

DONALD JUSTICE
1925–2004

Counting the Mad[1]

This one was put in a jacket,
This one was sent home,

---

1. This poem plays on the nursery rhyme that begins "this little pig went to market."

This one was given bread and meat
But would eat none,
5 And this one cried No No No No
All day long.

This one looked at the window
As though it were a wall,
This one saw things that were not there,
10 This one things that were,
And this one cried No No No No
All day long.

This one thought himself a bird,
This one a dog,
15 And this one thought himself a man,
An ordinary man,
And cried and cried No No No No
All day long.

1960

Men at Forty

Men at forty
Learn to close softly
The doors to rooms they will not be
Coming back to.

5 At rest on a stair landing,
They feel it moving
Beneath them now like the deck of a ship,
Though the swell is gentle.

And deep in mirrors
10 They rediscover
The face of the boy as he practices tying
His father's tie there in secret,

And the face of that father,
Still warm with the mystery of lather.
15 They are more fathers than sons themselves now.
Something is filling them, something

That is like the twilight sound
Of the crickets, immense,
Filling the woods at the foot of the slope
20 Behind their mortgaged houses.

1967

Nostalgia of the Lakefronts

Cities burn behind us; the lake glitters.
A tall loudspeaker is announcing prizes;
Another, by the lake, the times of cruises.
Childhood, once vast with terrors and surprises,
5   Is fading to a landscape deep with distance—
And always the sad piano in the distance,

Faintly in the distance, a ghostly tinkling
(O indecipherable blurred harmonies)
Or some far horn repeating over water
10   Its high lost note, cut loose from all harmonies.
At such times, wakeful, a child will dream the world,
And this is the world we run to from the world.

Or the two worlds come together and are one
On dark, sweet afternoons of storm and of rain,
15   And stereopticons° brought out and dusted,   *slide projectors*
Stacks of old *Geographics*,[2] or, through the rain,
A mad wet dash to the local movie palace
And the shriek, perhaps, of Kane's[3] white cockatoo.
(Would this have been summer, 1942?)

20   By June the city always seems neurotic.
But lakes are good all summer for reflection,
And ours is famed among painters for its blues,
Yet not entirely sad, upon reflection.
Why sad at all? Is their wish so unique—
25   To anthropomorphize the inanimate
With a love that masquerades as pure technique?

O art and the child were innocent together!
But landscapes grow abstract, like aging parents.
Soon now the war will shutter the grand hotels,
30   And we, when we come back, will come as parents.
There are no lanterns now strung between pines—
Only, like history, the stark bare northern pines.

And after a time the lakefront disappears
Into the stubborn verses of its exiles
35   Or a few gifted sketches of old piers.
It rains perhaps on the other side of the heart;
Then we remember, whether we would or no.
—Nostalgia comes with the smell of rain, you know.

1987

---

2. Issues of *National Geographic*.
3. Charles Foster Kane, the fictional newspaper
magnate in Orson Welles's 1941 film, *Citizen Kane.*

Pantoum[4] of the Great Depression

Our lives avoided tragedy
Simply by going on and on,
Without end and with little apparent meaning.
Oh, there were storms and small catastrophes.

5 Simply by going on and on
We managed. No need for the heroic.
Oh, there were storms and small catastrophes.
I don't remember all the particulars.

We managed. No need for the heroic.
10 There were the usual celebrations, the usual sorrows.
I don't remember all the particulars.
Across the fence, the neighbors were our chorus.

There were the usual celebrations, the usual sorrows
Thank god no one said anything in verse.
15 The neighbors were our only chorus,
And if we suffered we kept quiet about it.

At no time did anyone say anything in verse.
It was the ordinary pities and fears consumed us,
And if we suffered we kept quiet about it.
20 No audience would ever know our story.

It was the ordinary pities and fears consumed us.
We gathered on porches; the moon rose; we were poor.
What audience would ever know our story?
Beyond our windows shone the actual world.

25 We gathered on porches; the moon rose; we were poor.
And time went by, drawn by slow horses.
Somewhere beyond our windows shone the world.
The Great Depression had entered our souls like fog.

And time went by, drawn by slow horses.
30 We did not ourselves know what the end was.
The Great Depression had entered our souls like fog.
We had our flaws, perhaps a few private virtues.

But we did not ourselves know what the end was.
People like us simply go on.
35 We have our flaws, perhaps a few private virtues,
But it is by blind chance only that we escape tragedy.

And there is no plot in that; it is devoid of poetry.

1995

4. Verse form in which alternating lines repeat in the following stanza (see "Versification," p. 2046).

CAROLYN KIZER
b. 1925

The Erotic Philosophers

Part Five of "Pro Femina"[1]

It's a spring morning; sun pours in the window
As I sit here drinking coffee, reading Augustine.[2]
And finding him, as always, newly minted
From when I first encountered him in school.
5 Today I'm overcome with astonishment
At the way we girls denied all that was mean
In those revered philosophers we studied;
Who found us loathsome, loathsomely seductive;
Irrelevant, at best, to noble discourse
10 Among the sex, the only sex that counted.
Wounded, we pretended not to mind it
And wore tight sweaters to tease our shy professor.

We sat in autumn sunshine "as the clouds arose
From slimy desires of the flesh, and from
15 Youth's seething spring." Thank you, Augustine.
Attempting to seem blasé, our cheeks on fire,
It didn't occur to us to rush from the room.
Instead we brushed aside "the briars of unclean desire"
And struggled on through mires of misogyny
20 Till we arrived at Kierkegaard,[3] and began to see
That though Saint A. and Søren had much in common
Including fear and trembling before women,
The Saint scared himself, while Søren was scared of *us*.
Had we, poor girls, been flattered by their thralldom?

25 Yes, it was always us, the rejected feminine
From whom temptation came. It was our flesh
With its deadly sweetness that led them on.
Yet how could we not treasure Augustine,
"Stuck fast in the bird-lime of pleasure"?
30 That roomful of adolescent poets manqué°   *unsuccessful*
Assuaged, bemused by music, let the meaning go.
Swept by those psalmic cadences, we were seduced!
Some of us tried for a while to be well-trained souls
And pious seekers, enmeshed in the Saint's dialectic:
35 *Responsible for our actions, yet utterly helpless.*
A sensible girl would have barked like a dog before God.

1. A five-part poem, dealing variously with the lives of women, written over several decades.
2. St. Augustine (354–430), author of works such as the *Confessions*.
3. Søren Kierkegaard (1813–1855), Danish philosopher. His works include *Fear and Trembling* and *Either/Or* (both 1843), in the latter of which

he sets out two ways of life, the ethical and the aesthetic. In the aesthetic, the lowest and most purely sensory figure is the legendary libertine Don Juan, also known as Don Giovanni in the opera by the Austrian composer Wolfgang Amadeus Mozart (1756–1791) discussed later in Kizer's poem.

We students, children still, were shocked to learn
The children these men desired were younger than we!
Augustine fancied a girl about eleven,
40   The age of Adeodatus, Augustine's son.
Søren, like Poe,[4] eyed his girl before she was sixteen,
To impose his will on a malleable child, when
She was not equipped to withstand or understand him.
Ah, the Pygmalion[5] instinct! Mold the clay!
45   Create the compliant doll that can only obey,
Expecting to be abandoned, minute by minute.
It was then I abandoned philosophy,
A minor loss, although I majored in it.

But we were a group of sunny innocents.
50   I don't believe we knew what evil meant.
Now I live with a well-trained soul who deals with evil,
Including error, material or spiritual,
Easily, like changing a lock on the kitchen door.
He prays at set times and in chosen places
55   (At meals, in church), while I
Pray without thinking how or when to pray,
In a low mumble, several times a day,
Like running a continuous low fever;
The sexual impulse for the most part being over.
60   Believing I believe. Not banking on it ever.

It's afternoon. I sit here drinking kir°   *cocktail*
And reading Kierkegaard: "All sin begins with fear."
(True. We lie first from terror of our parents.)
In, I believe, an oblique crack at Augustine,
65   Søren said by denying the erotic
It was brought to the attention of the world.
The rainbow curtain rises on the sensual:
Christians must admit it before they can deny it.
He reflected on his father's fierce repression
70   Of the sexual, which had bent him out of shape;
Yet he had to pay obeisance to that power:
He chose his father when he broke with his Regina.[6]

Søren said by denying the erotic
It is brought to the attention of the world.
75   *You must admit it before you can deny it.*
So much for "Repetition"—another theory[7]
Which some assume evolved from his belief
He could replay his courtship of Regina
With a happy ending. Meanwhile she'd wait for him,

4. Edgar Allan Poe (1809–1849; see pp. 975–81), American writer.
5. In Greek mythology, a sculptor who fell in love with his own creation, the beautiful Galatea.
6. Regine Olsen (1822–1904), to whom Kierkegaard became engaged in 1840, though he later decided that he could "become happier in my unhappiness without her than with her." Kierkegaard's obsession with sacrificing Regine is in the background of *Fear and Trembling*, which discusses the faith of Abraham in offering to sacrifice his son Isaac to God.
7. The theory appears in Kierkegaard's book *Repetition* (1843).

80　Eternally faithful, eternally seventeen.
　　Instead, within two years, the bitch got married.
　　In truth, he couldn't wait till he got rid of her,
　　To create from recollection, not from living;
　　To use the material, not the material girl.

85　I sip my kir, thinking of *Either / Or,*
　　Especially *Either,* starring poor Elvira.[8]
　　He must have seen *Giovanni* a score of times,
　　And Søren knew the score.
　　He took Regina to the opera only once,
90　And as soon as Mozart's overture was over,
　　Kierkegaard stood up and said, "Now we are leaving.
　　You have heard the best: the expectation of pleasure."
　　In his interminable aria on the subject
　　S.K. insisted the performance *was* the play.
95　Was the overture then the foreplay? Poor Regina
　　Should have known she'd be left waiting in the lurch.

　　Though he chose a disguise in which to rhapsodize,
　　It was his voice too: Elvira's beauty
　　Would perish soon; the deflowered quickly fade:
100　A night-blooming cereus° after Juan's one-night stand.　　　*cactus*
　　Søren, eyes clouded by romantic mist,
　　Portrayed Elvira always sweet sixteen.
　　S.K.'s interpretation seems naive.
　　He didn't seem to realize that innocent sopranos
105　Who are ready to sing Elvira, don't exist.
　　His diva may have had it off with Leporello[9]
　　Just before curtain time, believing it freed her voice
　　(So backstage legend has it), and weakened his.

　　I saw La Stupenda[1] sing Elvira once.
110　Her cloak was larger than an army tent.
　　Would Giovanni be engulfed when she inhaled?
　　Would the boards shiver when she stamped her foot?
　　Her voice of course was great. Innocent it was not.
　　Søren, long since, would have fallen in a faint.
115　When he, or his doppelgänger,° wrote　　　　　　　　　*double*
　　That best-seller, "The Diary of a Seducer,"[2]
　　He showed how little he knew of true Don Juans:
　　Those turgid letters, machinations, and excursions,
　　Those tedious conversations with dull aunts,
120　Those convoluted efforts to get the girl!

　　Think of the worldly European readers
　　Who took Søren seriously, did not see
　　His was the cynicism of the timid virgin.

8. Donna Elvira in *Don Giovanni,* one of the women the dissolute seducer has betrayed.
9. Don Giovanni's servant.
1. The stupendous one (Italian); nickname for the Australian soprano Joan Sutherland (b. 1926).
2. A famous section of *Either/Or,* it presents one man's romantic exploits as "an attempt to realize the task of living poetically."

Once in my youth I knew a real Don Juan
125   Or he knew me. He didn't need to try,
The characteristic of a true seducer.
He seems vulnerable, shy; he hardly speaks.
Somehow, you know he will never speak of you.
You trust him—and you thrust yourself at him.
130   He responds with an almost absentminded grace.
Even before the consummation he's looking past you
For the next bright yearning pretty face.

Relieved at last of anxieties and tensions
When your terrible efforts to capture him are over,
135   You overflow with happy/unhappy languor.
But S.K.'s alter-ego believes the truly terrible
Is for you to be consoled by the love of another.
We women, deserted to a woman, have a duty
To rapidly lose our looks, decline, and die,
140   Our only chance of achieving romantic beauty.
So Augustine was sure, when Monica, his mother,[3]
Made him put aside his nameless concubine
She'd get her to a nunnery, and pine.[4]
He chose his mother when he broke with his beloved.

145   In Søren's long replay of his wrecked romance,
"Guilty/Not Guilty,"[5] he says he must tear himself away
From earthly love, and suffer to love God.
Augustine thought better: love, human therefore flawed,
Is the way to the love of God. To deny this truth
150   Is to be "left outside, breathing into the dust,
Filling the eyes with earth." We women,
Outside, breathing dust, are still the Other.
The evening sun goes down; time to fix dinner.
"You women have no major philosophers." We know.
155   But we remain philosophic, and say with the Saint,
"Let me enter my chamber and sing my songs of love."

2001

KENNETH KOCH
1925–2002

Permanently

One day the Nouns were clustered in the street.
An Adjective walked by, with her dark beauty.

---

3. St. Monica (322–387), credited with helping convert her son from a wayward life.
4. Allusion to *Hamlet* 3.1.122, in which Hamlet rejects Ophelia: "Get thee to a nunnery."
5. A section of his book *Stages on Life's Way* (1845).

The Nouns were struck, moved, changed.
The next day a Verb drove up, and created the Sentence.

5   Each Sentence says one thing—for example. "Although it was a dark
        rainy day when the Adjective walked by, I shall remember the
        pure and sweet expression on her face until the day I perish from
        the green, effective earth."
    Or, "Will you please close the window, Andrew?"
    Or, for example, "Thank you, the pink pot of flowers on the window
        sill has changed color recently to a light yellow, due to the heat
        from the boiler factory which exists nearby."

    In the springtime the Sentences and the Nouns lay silently on the
        grass.
    A lonely Conjunction here and there would call, "And! But!"
10   But the Adjective did not emerge.

    As the adjective is lost in the sentence,
    So I am lost in your eyes, ears, nose, and throat—
    You have enchanted me with a single kiss
    Which can never be undone
15   Until the destruction of language.

                                                    1962

You Were Wearing

You were wearing your Edgar Allan Poe printed cotton blouse.
In each divided up square of the blouse was a picture of Edgar Allan
    Poe.
Your hair was blonde and you were cute. You asked me, "Do most
    boys think that most girls are bad?"
I smelled the mould of your seaside resort hotel bedroom on your hair
    held in place by a John Greenleaf Whittier clip.
5   "No," I said, "it's girls who think that boys are bad." Then we read
    Snowbound together.
And ran around in an attic, so that a little of the blue enamel was
    scraped off my George Washington, Father of His Country,
    shoes.

Mother was walking in the living room, her Strauss Waltzes comb in
    her hair.
We waited for a time and then joined her, only to be served tea in
    cups painted with pictures of Herman Melville
As well as with illustrations from his book Moby Dick and from his
    novella, Benito Cereno.
10   Father came in wearing his Dick Tracy necktie: "How about a drink,
    everyone?"
I said, "Let's go outside a while." Then we went onto the porch and
    sat on the Abraham Lincoln swing.

You sat on the eyes, mouth, and beard part, and I sat on the knees.
In the yard across the street we saw a snowman holding a garbage can
    lid smashed into a likeness of the mad English king, George the
    Third.

1962

Variations on a Theme by William Carlos Williams[1]

1

I chopped down the house that you had been saving to live in next
    summer.
I am sorry, but it was morning, and I had nothing to do
and its wooden beams were so inviting.

2

We laughed at the hollyhocks together
5   and then I sprayed them with lye.
Forgive me. I simply do not know what I am doing.

3

I gave away the money that you had been saving to live on for the
    next ten years.
The man who asked for it was shabby
and the firm March wind on the porch was so juicy and cold.

4

10 Last evening we went dancing and I broke your leg.
Forgive me. I was clumsy, and
I wanted you here in the wards, where I am the doctor!

1962

Energy in Sweden

Those were the days
When there was so much energy in and around me
I could take it off and put it back on, like clothes
That one has bought only for a ski trip
5 But then finds that one is using every day
Because every day is like a ski trip—
I think that's how I was at twenty-three.

Seeing those six young women in a boat I was on a ski trip.
They said, We are all from Minneapolis. This was in Stockholm.

1. American poet (1883–1963; see pp. 1272–83) and physician (see line 12). This poem parodies Williams's "This Is Just to Say" (p. 1274).

10   The melding of American and Swedish-American female looks was a
        ski trip
      Although I had no particular reason at that time to put all my energy
        on
      Yet there it was, I had it, the way a giant has the hegemony of his
        nerves
      In case he needs it, or the way a fisherman has all his poles and
        lines and lures, and a scholar all his books
      The way a water heater has all its gas
15   Whether it is being used or not, I had all that energy.
      Really, are you all from Minneapolis? I said, almost bursting with
        force.
      And yes, one of them, about the second prettiest, replied. We are here
        for several days.

      I thought about this moment from time to time
      For eight or ten years. It seemed to me I should have done something
        at the time,
20   To have used all that energy. Lovemaking is one way to use it and
        writing is another.
      Both maybe are overestimated, because the relation is so clear.
      But that is probably human destiny and I'm not going to go against
        it here.
      Sometimes there are the persons and not the energy, sometimes the
        energy and not the persons.
      When the gods give both, a man shouldn't complain.

                                          1994

To My Twenties

      How lucky that I ran into you
      When everything was possible
      For my legs and arms, and with hope in my heart
      And so happy to see any woman—
5   O woman! O my twentieth year!
      Basking in you, you
      Oasis from both growing and decay
      Fantastic unheard of nine- or ten-year oasis
      A palm tree, hey! And then another
10   And another—and water!
      I'm still very impressed by you. Whither,
      Midst falling decades, have you gone? Oh in what lucky fellow,
      Unsure of himself, upset, and unemployable
      For the moment in any case, do you live now?
15   From my window I drop a nickel
      By mistake. With
      You I race down to get it
      But I find there on
      The street instead, a good friend,

20 X—— N——, who says to me
  Kenneth do you have a minute?
  And I say yes! I am in my twenties!
  I have plenty of time! In you I marry,
  In you I first go to France; I make my best friends
25 In you, and a few enemies. I
  Write a lot and am living all the time
  And thinking about living. I loved to frequent you
  After my teens and before my thirties.
  You three together in a bar
30 I always preferred you because you were midmost
  Most lustrous apparently strongest
  Although now that I look back on you
  What part have you played?
  You never, ever, were stingy.
35 What you gave me you gave whole
  But as for telling
  Me how best to use it
  You weren't a genius at that.
  Twenties, my soul
40 Is yours for the asking
  You know that, if you ever come back.

2000

A. R. AMMONS
1926–2001

Corsons Inlet[1]

I went for a walk over the dunes again this morning
to the sea,
then turned right along
 the surf
5   rounded a naked headland
   and returned

 along the inlet shore:

it was muggy sunny, the wind from the sea steady and high,
crisp in the running sand,
10 some breakthroughs of sun
 but after a bit
continuous overcast:

the walk liberating, I was released from forms,
from the perpendiculars,

---

1. Located on the southern New Jersey shore.

15   straight lines, blocks, boxes, binds
of thought
into the hues, shadings, rises, flowing bends and blends
        of sight:

                I allow myself eddies of meaning:
20 yield to a direction of significance
running
like a stream through the geography of my work:
    you can find
in my sayings
25   swerves of action
            like the inlet's cutting edge:
        there are dunes of motion,
organizations of grass, white sandy paths of remembrance
in the overall wandering of mirroring mind:

30 but Overall is beyond me: is the sum of these events
I cannot draw, the ledger I cannot keep, the accounting
beyond the account:

in nature there are few sharp lines: there are areas of
primrose
35   more or less dispersed;
disorderly orders of bayberry; between the rows
of dunes,
irregular swamps of reeds,
though not reeds alone, but grass, bayberry, yarrow, all . . .
40 predominantly reeds:

I have reached no conclusions, have erected no boundaries,
shutting out and shutting in, separating inside
        from outside: I have
        drawn no lines:
45   as

manifold events of sand
change the dune's shape that will not be the same shape
tomorrow,

so I am willing to go along, to accept
50 the becoming
thought, to stake off no beginnings or ends, establish
        no walls:

by transitions the land falls from grassy dunes to creek
to undercreek: but there are no lines, though
55   change in that transition is clear
        as any sharpness: but "sharpness" spread out,
allowed to occur over a wider range
than mental lines can keep:

the moon was full last night: today, low tide was low:
60 black shoals of mussels exposed to the risk
of air
and, earlier, of sun,
waved in and out with the waterline, waterline inexact,
caught always in the event of change:
65   a young mottled gull stood free on the shoals
and ate
to vomiting: another gull, squawking possession, cracked a crab,
picked out the entrails, swallowed the soft-shelled legs, a ruddy
turnstone° running in to snatch leftover bits: *a shorebird*

70 risk is full: every living thing in
siege: the demand is life, to keep life: the small
white blacklegged egret, how beautiful, quietly stalks and spears
the shallows, darts to shore
to stab—what? I couldn't
75   see against the black mudflats—a frightened
fiddler crab?

the news to my left over the dunes and
reeds and bayberry clumps was
fall: thousands of tree swallows
80   gathering for flight:
an order held
in constant change: a congregation
rich with entropy: nevertheless, separable, noticeable
as one event,
85   not chaos: preparations for
flight from winter,
cheet, cheet, cheet, cheet, wings rifling the green clumps,
beaks
at the bayberries
90   a perception full of wind, flight, curve,
sound:
the possibility of rule as the sum of rulelessness:
the "field" of action
with moving, incalculable center:

95 in the smaller view, order tight with shape:
blue tiny flowers on a leafless weed: carapace of crab:
snail shell:
pulsations of order
in the bellies of minnows: orders swallowed,
100 broken down, transferred through membranes
to strengthen larger orders: but in the large view, no
lines or changeless shapes: the working in and out, together
and against, of millions of events: this,
so that I make
105   no form
formlessness:

orders as summaries, as outcomes of actions override
or in some way result, not predictably (seeing me gain
the top of a dune,
110 the swallows
could take flight—some other fields of bayberry
could enter fall
berryless) and there is serenity:

no arranged terror: no forcing of image, plan,
115 or thought:
no propaganda, no humbling of reality to precept:

terror pervades but is not arranged, all possibilities
of escape open: no route shut, except in
the sudden loss of all routes:

120 I see narrow orders, limited tightness, but will
not run to that easy victory:
still around the looser, wider forces work:
I will try
to fasten into order enlarging grasps of disorder, widening
125 scope, but enjoying the freedom that
Scope eludes my grasp, that there is no finality of vision,
that I have perceived nothing completely,
that tomorrow a new walk is a new walk.

1965

The City Limits

When you consider the radiance, that it does not withhold
itself but pours its abundance without selection into every
nook and cranny not overhung or hidden; when you consider

that birds' bones make no awful noise against the light but
5 lie low in the light as in a high testimony; when you consider
the radiance, that it will look into the guiltiest

swervings of the weaving heart and bear itself upon them,
not flinching into disguise or darkening; when you consider
the abundance of such resource as illuminates the glow-blue

10 bodies and gold-skeined wings of flies swarming the dumped
guts of a natural slaughter or the coil of shit and in no
way winces from its storms of generosity; when you consider

that air or vacuum, snow or shale, squid or wolf, rose or lichen,
each is accepted into as much light as it will take, then
15 the heart moves roomier, the man stands and looks about, the

leaf does not increase itself above the grass, and the dark
work of the deepest cells is of a tune with May bushes
and fear lit by the breadth of such calmly turns to praise.

1971

The Arc Inside and Out

For Harold Bloom

If, whittler and dumper, gross carver
into the shadiest curvings, I took branch
and meat from the stalk of life, threw

away the monies of the treasured,
5   treasurable mind, cleaved memory free
of the instant, if I got right down

shucking off periphery after periphery
to the glassy vague gray parabolas
and swoops of unnailable perception,

10   would I begin to improve the purity,
would I essentialize out the distilled
form, the glitter-stone that whether

the world comes or goes clicks gleams
and chinks of truth self-making, never
15   to be shuttered, the face-brilliant core

stone: or if I, amasser, heap shoveler,
depth pumper, took in all springs and
oceans, paramoecia and moons, massive

buttes and summit slants, rooted trunks
20   and leafages, anthologies of wise words,
schemata, all grasses (including the

tidal Spartinas,² marginal, salty
broadsweeps) would I finally come on a
suasion, large, fully-informed, restful

25   scape, turning back in on itself, its
periphery enclosing our system with
its bright dot and allowing in nonparlant

quantities at the edge void, void, and
void, would I then feel plenitude
30   brought to center and extent, a sweet

2. Genus of various swamp grasses.

easing away of all edge, evil, and surprise:
these two ways to dream! dreaming them's
the bumfuzzlement—the impoverished

diamond, the heterogeneous abundance
35   starved into oneness: ultimately, either
way, which is our peace, the little

arc-line appears, inside which is nothing,
outside which is nothing—however big,
nothing beyond: however small, nothing

40   within: neither way to go's to stay, stay
here, the apple an apple with its own hue
or streak, the drink of water, the drink,

the falling into sleep, restfully ever the
falling into sleep, dream, dream, and
45   every morning the sun comes, the sun.

1972

Pet Panther

My attention is a wild
animal: it will if idle
make trouble where there
was no harm: it will

5   sniff and scratch at the
breath's sills:
it will wind itself tight
around the pulse

or, undistracted by
10   verbal toys, pommel the
heart frantic: it will
pounce on a stalled riddle

and wrestle the mind numb:
attention, fierce animal
15   I cry, as it coughs in my
face, dislodges boulders

in my belly, lie down, be
still, have mercy, here
is song, coils of song, play
20   it out, run with it.

1983

All's All

A construed entity too
lessened to syllabify;
a mite or more
dimpling
5   domy° generalization;   *domelike*
a vague locus
(the flow of air

through prisons)
a puff of
10   the whiff of
a snail falling asleep;
stringy recollections of
fruitflies cruising
rosy bowlsful of

15   mangoes ripening mild:
ghostly leavings leaving
ghosts leave: retinal
worms empurpling
light scars
20   behind today's views:
bits of

retrenched nothings:
so much so,
little and all
25   alternately disappear:
the tiniest kiss
at the world's end
ends the world.

1996

JAMES K. BAXTER
1926–1972

Wild Bees

Often in summer, on a tarred bridge plank standing,
Or downstream between willows, a safe Ophelia drifting[1]
In a rented boat—I had seen them come and go,
Those wild bees swift as tigers, their gauze wings a-glitter

---

1. Ophelia, the young heroine of Shakespeare's *Hamlet,* goes mad, then drowns while drifting down a river (*Hamlet* 4.7.137–55).

5 In passionless industry, clustering black at the crevice
   Of a rotten cabbage tree, where their hive was hidden low.

   But never strolled too near. Till one half-cloudy evening
   Of ripe January, my friends and I
   Came, gloved and masked to the eyes like plundering desperadoes,
10 To smoke them out. Quiet beside the stagnant river
   We trod wet grasses down, hearing the crickets chitter
   And waiting for light to drain from the wounded sky.

   Before we reached the hive their sentries saw us
   And sprang invisible through the darkening air,
15 Stabbed, and died in stinging. The hive woke. Poisonous fuming
   Of sulphur filled the hollow trunk, and crawling
   Blue flame sputtered—yet still their suicidal
   Live raiders dived and clung to our hands and hair.

   O it was Carthage under the Roman torches,
20 Or loud with flames and falling timber, Troy![2]
   A job well botched. Half of the honey melted
   And half the rest young grubs. Through earth-black smoldering
       ashes
   And maimed bees groaning, we drew out our plunder.
   Little enough their gold, and slight our joy.

25 Fallen then the city of instinctive wisdom.
   Tragedy is written distinct and small:
   A hive burned on a cool night in summer.
   But loss is a precious stone to me, a nectar
   Distilled in time, preaching the truth of winter
30 To the fallen heart that does not cease to fall.

                                                    1953

East Coast Journey

   About twilight we came to the whitewashed pub
   On a knuckle of land above the bay

   Where a log was riding and the slow
   Bird-winged breakers cast up spray.

5 One of the drinkers round packing cases had
   The worn face of a kumara[3] god,

---

2. References to the destruction by fire of two great cities of classical times—Carthage by the Romans in 146 B.C.E. and Troy by the Greeks at the end of the Trojan War.
3. Sweet potato (Maori); a staple food of the Maori, the Polynesian natives of New Zealand.

Or so it struck me. Later on
Lying awake in the veranda bedroom

In great dryness of mind I heard the voice of the sea
10 Reverberating, and thought: As a man

Grows older he does not want beer, bread, or the prancing flesh,
But the arms of the eater of life, Hine-nui-te-po,[4]

With teeth of obsidian and hair like kelp
Flashing and glimmering at the edge of the horizon.

1966

New Zealand

(For Monte Holcroft)

These unshaped islands, on the sawyer's[5] bench,
Wait for the chisel of the mind,
Green canyons to the south, immense and passive,
Penetrated rarely, seeded only
5 By the deer-culler's[6] shot, or else in the north
Tribes of the shark and the octopus,
Mangroves, black hair on a boxer's hand.

The founding fathers with their guns and bibles,
Botanist, whaler, added bones and names
10 To the land, to us a bridle
As if the id were a horse: the swampy towns
Like dreamers that struggle to wake,

Longing for the poet's truth
And the lover's pride. Something new and old
15 Explores its own pain, hearing
The rain's choir on curtains of gray moss
Or fingers of the Tasman[7] pressing
On breasts of hardening sand, as actors
Find their own solitude in mirrors,

20 As one who has buried his dead,
Able at last to give with an open hand.

1969

---

4. Maori goddess of death.
5. One who saws.
6. A kind of game warden, an agent of the govern-

ment who controls the herds of deer.
7. The Tasman Sea, to the west of New Zealand.

ROBERT BLY
b. 1926

Waking from Sleep

Inside the veins there are navies setting forth,
Tiny explosions at the water lines,
And seagulls weaving in the wind of the salty blood.

It is the morning. The country has slept the whole winter.
5   Window seats were covered with fur skins, the yard was full
Of stiff dogs, and hands that clumsily held heavy books.

Now we wake, and rise from bed, and eat breakfast!—
Shouts rise from the harbor of the blood,
Mist, and masts rising, the knock of wooden tackle in the sunlight.

10 Now we sing, and do tiny dances on the kitchen floor.
Our whole body is like a harbor at dawn;
We know that our master has left us for the day.

1962

Johnson's Cabinet[1] Watched by Ants

1

It is a clearing deep in a forest: overhanging boughs
Make a low place. Here the citizens we know during the day,
The ministers, the department heads,
Appear changed: the stockholders of large steel companies
5   In small wooden shoes: here are the generals dressed as gamboling
        lambs.

2

Tonight they burn the rice-supplies; tomorrow
They lecture on Thoreau;[2] tonight they move around the trees,
Tomorrow they pick the twigs from their clothes;
Tonight they throw the fire-bombs, tomorrow
10 They read the Declaration of Independence; tomorrow they are in
        church.

3

Ants are gathered around an old tree.
In a choir they sing, in harsh and gravelly voices,
Old Etruscan[3] songs on tyranny.

1. Advisors of U.S. President Lyndon B. Johnson (1908–1973), whose term was dominated by the Vietnam War and by protests against it.
2. Henry David Thoreau (1817–1862; see pp. 1045–46), American Transcendentalist philosopher, essayist, and poet.
3. An early Italian people and culture, originating in Etruria; one of its city-states became Rome.

Toads nearby clap their small hands, and join
15 The fiery songs, their five long toes trembling in the soaked earth.

1967

ROBERT CREELEY
1926–2005

Heroes

In all those stories the hero
is beyond himself into the next
thing, be it those labors
of Hercules, or Aeneas[1] going into death.

5   I thought the instant of the one humanness
in Virgil's plan of it
was that it was of course human enough to die,
yet to come back, as he said, *hoc opus, hic labor est.*[2]

That was the Cumaean Sibyl speaking.
10 This is Robert Creeley, and Virgil
is dead now two thousand years, yet Hercules
and the *Aeneid,* yet all that industrious wis-

dom lives in the way the mountains
and the desert are waiting
15 for the heroes, and death also
can still propose the old labors.

1959

I Know a Man

As I sd to my
friend, because I am
always talking,—John, I

sd, which was not his
5   name, the darkness sur-
rounds us, what

---

1. Trojan hero whose adventures and travails are recorded in Virgil's epic poem, the *Aeneid*. *Hercules:* legendary Greek hero of superhuman strength, best-known for his twelve labors.
2. *Aeneid* 6.129. When Aeneas asks the Sibyl, a priestess and prophet, how he might visit his dead father in the underworld, she answers that the descent is easy, but to return—"That is the task, that is the labor."

can we do against
it, or else, shall we &
why not, buy a goddamn big car,

10   drive, he sd, for
christ's sake, look
out where yr going,

1962

The World

I wanted so ably
to reassure you, I wanted
the man you took to be me,

to comfort you, and got
5   up, and went to the window,
pushed back, as you asked me to,

the curtain, to see
the outline of the trees
in the night outside.

10   The light, love,
the light we felt then,
grayly, was it, that

came in, on us, not
merely my hands or yours,
15   or a wetness so comfortable,

but in the dark then
as you slept, the gray
figure came so close

and leaned over,
20   between us, as you
slept, restless, and

my own face had to
see it, and be seen by it,
the man it was, your

25   gray lost tired bewildered
brother, unused, untaken—
hated by love, and dead,

but not dead, for an
instant, saw me, myself
30   the intruder, as he was not.

I tried to say, it is
all right, she is
happy, you are no longer

needed. I said,
35   he is dead, and he
went as you shifted

and woke, at first afraid,
then knew by my own knowing
what had happened—

40   and the light then
of the sun coming
for another morning
in the world.

1969

Bresson's[3] Movies

A movie of Robert
Bresson's showed a yacht,
at evening on the Seine,[4]
all its lights on, watched

5   by two young, seemingly
poor people, on a bridge adjacent,
the classic boy and girl
of the story, any one

one cares to tell. So
10   years pass, of course, but
I identified with the young,
embittered Frenchman,

knew his almost complacent
anguish and the distance
15   he felt from his girl.
Yet another film

of Bresson's has the
aging Lancelot[5] with his
awkward armor standing
20   in a woods, of small trees,

---

3. Robert Bresson (1907–1999), French director and screenwriter, known for his austere style.
4. River in northern France. The movie is *Quatre*

Nuits d'Un Rêveur (Four Nights of a Dreamer), 1971.
5. *Lancelot du Lac (Lancelot of the Lake)*, 1974.

dazed, bleeding, both he
and his horse are,
trying to get back to
the castle, itself of

25 no great size. It
moved me, that
life was after all
like that. You are

in love. You stand
30 in the woods, with
a horse, bleeding.
The story is true.

1982

ALLEN GINSBERG
1926–1997

From Howl

For Carl Solomon[1]

I

I saw the best minds of my generation destroyed by madness, starving
hysterical naked,
dragging themselves through the negro streets at dawn looking for an
angry fix,
angelheaded hipsters burning for the ancient heavenly connection to
the starry dynamo in the machinery of night,
who poverty and tatters and hollow-eyed and high sat up smoking in
the supernatural darkness of cold-water flats floating across the
tops of cities contemplating jazz,
5 who bared their brains to Heaven under the El[2] and saw Mohammedan
angels staggering on tenement roofs illuminated
who passed through universities with radiant cool eyes hallucinating
Arkansas and Blake-light[3] tragedy among the scholars of war,
who were expelled from the academies for crazy & publishing obscene
odes on the windows of the skull,
who cowered in unshaven rooms in underwear, burning their money
in wastebaskets and listening to the Terror through the wall,
who got busted in their pubic beards returning through Laredo[4] with a
belt of marijuana for New York,

1. Ginsberg met Solomon (b. 1928) while both
were patients in the Columbia Psychiatric Institute
in 1949. Many details in *Howl* come from the
"apocryphal history" that Solomon then told him,
while other details refer to experiences of Ginsberg
and his fellow Beat writers of the 1950s.

2. Elevated railway in New York City; also,
Hebrew for God.
3. In 1948, Ginsberg had a vision/hallucination of
the English poet and artist William Blake (1757–
1827; see pp. 732–47).
4. City in Texas, on the Mexican border.

10   who ate fire in paint hotels or drank turpentine in Paradise Alley,[5]
            death, or purgatoried their torsos night after night
       with dreams, with drugs, with waking nightmares, alcohol and cock
            and endless balls,
       incomparable blind streets of shuddering cloud and lightning in the
            mind leaping toward poles of Canada & Paterson,[6] illuminating
            all the motionless world of Time between,
       Peyote solidities of halls, backyard green tree cemetery dawns, wine
            drunkenness over the rooftops, storefront boroughs of teahead
            joyride neon blinking traffic light, sun and moon and tree
            vibrations in the roaring winter dusks of Brooklyn, ashcan
            rantings and kind king light of mind,
       who chained themselves to subways for the endless ride from Battery
            to holy Bronx[7] on benzedrine until the noise of wheels and
            children brought them down shuddering mouth-wracked and
            battered bleak of brain all drained of brilliance in the drear light
            of Zoo,
15   who sank all night in submarine light of Bickford's floated out and sat
            through the stale beer afternoon in desolate Fugazzi's,[8] listening
            to the crack of doom on the hydrogen jukebox,
       who talked continuously seventy hours from park to pad to bar to
            Bellevue[9] to museum to the Brooklyn Bridge,
       a lost battalion of platonic conversationalists jumping down the stoops
            off fire escapes off windowsills off Empire State out of the moon,
       yacketayakking screaming vomiting whispering facts and memories
            and anecdotes and eyeball kicks and shocks of hospitals and jails
            and wars,
       whole intellects disgorged in total recall for seven days and nights with
            brilliant eyes, meat for the Synagogue cast on the pavement,
20   who vanished into nowhere Zen New Jersey leaving a trail of
            ambiguous picture postcards of Atlantic City Hall,
       suffering Eastern sweats and Tangerian bone-grindings and migraines
            of China under junk-withdrawal in Newark's bleak furnished
            room,
       who wandered around and around at midnight in the railroad yard
            wondering where to go, and went, leaving no broken hearts,
       who lit cigarettes in boxcars boxcars boxcars racketing through snow
            toward lonesome farms in grandfather night,
       who studied Plotinus Poe St. John of the Cross[1] telepathy and bop
            kaballa[2] because the cosmos instinctively vibrated at their feet in
            Kansas,
25   who loned it through the streets of Idaho seeking visionary indian
            angels, who were visionary indian angels,

---

5. Then a tenement courtyard in New York's Lower East Side; the setting of *The Subterraneans*, a 1958 novel by the American writer Jack Kerouac (1922–1969).
6. City in New Jersey where Ginsberg was born.
7. The south and north extremes of one set of New York subway lines; the zoo is in the Bronx.
8. A bar near Greenwich Village, then New York's bohemian center. *Bickford's*: one of a chain of cafeterias open twenty-four hours a day.
9. A public hospital in New York serving as a receiving center for mental patients.
1. Spanish poet and mystic (1542–1591), who wrote *The Dark Night of the Soul*. Plotinus (205–270), Roman mystic philosopher. Edgar Allan Poe (1809–1894; see pp. 975–81), American poet and author of supernatural tales as well as the cosmological *Eureka*.
2. A tradition of mystical interpretation of the Hebrew Scriptures. *Bop*: jazz style especially influential in the 1940s and 1950s.

who thought they were only mad when Baltimore gleamed in
   supernatural ecstasy,
who jumped in limousines with the Chinaman of Oklahoma on the
   impulse of winter midnight streetlight smalltown rain,
who lounged hungry and lonesome through Houston seeking jazz or
   sex or soup, and followed the brilliant Spaniard to converse about
   America and Eternity, a hopeless task, and so took ship to Africa,
who disappeared into the volcanoes of Mexico leaving behind nothing
   but the shadow of dungarees and the lava and ash of poetry
   scattered in fireplace Chicago,
30 who reappeared on the West Coast investigating the F.B.I. in beards
   and shorts with big pacifist eyes sexy in their dark skin passing
   out incomprehensible leaflets,
who burned cigarette holes in their arms protesting the narcotic
   tobacco haze of Capitalism,
who distributed Supercommunist pamphlets in Union Square weeping
   and undressing while the sirens of Los Alamos[3] wailed them
   down, and wailed down Wall,[4] and the Staten Island ferry also
   wailed,
who broke down crying in white gymnasiums naked and trembling
   before the machinery of other skeletons,
who bit detectives in the neck and shrieked with delight in policecars
   for committing no crime but their own wild cooking pederasty
   and intoxication,
35 who howled on their knees in the subway and were dragged off the
   roof waving genitals and manuscripts,
who let themselves be fucked in the ass by saintly motorcyclists, and
   screamed with joy,
who blew and were blown by those human seraphim,[5] the sailors,
   caresses of Atlantic and Caribbean love,
who balled in the morning in the evenings in rosegardens and the
   grass of public parks and cemeteries scattering their semen freely
   to whomever come who may,
who hiccupped endlessly trying to giggle but wound up with a sob
   behind a partition in a Turkish Bath when the blonde & naked
   angel came to pierce them with a sword,[6]
40 who lost their loveboys to the three old shrews of fate[7] the one eyed
   shrew of the heterosexual dollar the one eyed shrew that winks
   out of the womb and the one eyed shrew that does nothing but
   sit on her ass and snip the intellectual golden threads of the
   craftsman's loom,
who copulated ecstatic and insatiate with a bottle of beer a sweetheart
   a package of cigarettes a candle and fell off the bed, and continued
   along the floor and down the hall and ended fainting on the wall
   with a vision of ultimate cunt and come eluding the last gyzym of
   consciousness,

---

3. Laboratory in New Mexico where the develop-
ment of the atomic bomb was completed. *Union
Square*: site of radical demonstrations in New York
in the 1930s.
4. Wall Street, the center of New York's financial
district; but also, Jerusalem's Wailing Wall, a place
of prayer and lamentation.

5. The highest order of angels.
6. An allusion to *The Ecstasy of St. Teresa*, a sculp-
ture by Lorenzo Bernini (1598–1680) based on St.
Teresa's (1515–1582) distinctly erotic description
of a religious vision.
7. In Greek mythology, the three Fates spun,
wove, and finally cut the thread of every mortal life.

who sweetened the snatches of a million girls trembling in the sunset,
and were red eyed in the morning but prepared to sweeten the
snatch of the sunrise, flashing buttocks under barns and naked in
the lake,

who went out whoring through Colorado in myriad stolen night-cars,
N.C.,[8] secret hero of these poems, cocksman and Adonis of
Denver—joy to the memory of his innumerable lays of girls in
empty lots & diner backyards, moviehouses' rickety rows, on
mountaintops in caves or with gaunt waitresses in familiar
roadside lonely petticoat upliftings & especially secret gas-station
solipsisms of johns, & hometown alleys too,

who faded out in vast sordid movies, were shifted in dreams, woke on
a sudden Manhattan, and picked themselves up out of basements
hungover with heartless Tokay and horrors of Third Avenue[9] iron
dreams & stumbled to unemployment offices,

45   who walked all night with their shoes full of blood on the snowbank
docks waiting for a door in the East River to open to a room full
of steamheat and opium,

who created great suicidal dramas on the apartment cliff-banks of the
Hudson under the wartime blue floodlight of the moon & their
heads shall be crowned with laurel[1] in oblivion,

who ate the lamb stew of the imagination or digested the crab at the
muddy bottom of the rivers of Bowery,[2]

who wept at the romance of the streets with their pushcarts full of
onions and bad music,

who sat in boxes breathing in the darkness under the bridge, and rose
up to build harpsichords in their lofts,

50   who coughed on the sixth floor of Harlem crowned with flame under
the tubercular sky surrounded by orange crates of theology,

who scribbled all night rocking and rolling over lofty incantations
which in the yellow morning were stanzas of gibberish,

who cooked rotten animals lung heart feet tail borsht & tortillas
dreaming of the pure vegetable kingdom,

who plunged themselves under meat trucks looking for an egg,

who threw their watches off the roof to cast their ballot for Eternity
outside of Time, & alarm clocks fell on their heads every day for
the next decade,

55   who cut their wrists three times successively unsuccessfully, gave up
and were forced to open antique stores where they thought they
were growing old and cried,

who were burned alive in their innocent flannel suits on Madison
Avenue[3] amid blasts of leaden verse & the tanked-up clatter of
the iron regiments of fashion & the nitroglycerine shrieks of the
fairies of advertising & the mustard gas of sinister intelligent
editors, or were run down by the drunken taxicabs of Absolute
Reality,

---

8. Neal Cassady (1926–1968), a friend and lover
of Ginsberg. Also a friend of Jack Kerouac, he is
the hero of Kerouac's novel *On the Road* (1957).
9. In Manhattan. *Tokay:* a Hungarian wine.
1. In classical Greece, victors in the Pythian
games were crowned with laurel. *Hudson:* the
Hudson River, between Manhattan and New Jer-

sey.
2. Lower end of Third Avenue; traditional haunt
of alcoholics and derelicts.
3. The center of New York's advertising industry.
Cf. *The Man in the Gray Flannel Suit,* a best-
selling 1955 novel by the American writer Sloan
Wilson (b. 1920).

who jumped off the Brooklyn Bridge this actually happened and
walked away unknown and forgotten into the ghostly daze of
Chinatown soup alleyways & firetrucks, not even one free beer,
who sang out of their windows in despair, fell out of the subway
window, jumped in the filthy Passaic,[4] leaped on negroes, cried
all over the street, danced on broken wineglasses barefoot
smashed phonograph records of nostalgic European 1930's
German jazz finished the whiskey and threw up groaning into the
bloody toilet, moans in their ears and the blast of colossal
steamwhistles,
who barreled down the highways of the past journeying to each other's
hotrod-Golgotha jail-solitude watch or Birmingham[5] jazz
incarnation,
60   who drove crosscountry seventytwo hours to find out if I had a vision
or you had a vision or he had a vision to find out Eternity,
who journeyed to Denver, who died in Denver, who came back to
Denver & waited in vain, who watched over Denver & brooded &
loned in Denver and finally went away to find out the Time, &
now Denver is lonesome for her heroes,
who fell on their knees in hopeless cathedrals praying for each other's
salvation and light and breasts, until the soul illuminated its hair
for a second,
who crashed through their minds in jail waiting for impossible
criminals with golden heads and the charm of reality in their
hearts who sang sweet blues to Alcatraz,
who retired to Mexico to cultivate a habit, or Rocky Mount to tender
Buddha or Tangiers to boys or Southern Pacific to the black
locomotive or Harvard to Narcissus to Woodlawn[6] to the
daisychain or grave,
65   who demanded sanity trials accusing the radio of hypnotism & were
left with their insanity & their hands & a hung jury,
who threw potato salad at CCNY lecturers on Dadaism[7] and
subsequently presented themselves on the granite steps of the
madhouse with shaven heads and harlequin speech of suicide,
demanding instantaneous lobotomy,
and who were given instead the concrete void of insulin metrasol
electricity hydrotherapy psychotherapy occupational therapy
pingpong & amnesia,
who in humorless protest overturned only one symbolic pingpong
table, resting briefly in catatonia,
returning years later truly bald except for a wig of blood, and tears and
fingers, to the visible madman doom of the wards of the
madtowns of the East,
70   Pilgrim State's Rockland's and Greystone's[8] foetid halls, bickering with
the echoes of the soul, rocking and rolling in the midnight
solitude-bench dolmen-realms[9] of love, dream of life a nightmare,
bodies turned to stone as heavy as the moon,

---

4. The river that flows through Paterson.
5. In Alabama. *Golgotha*: hill near Jerusalem where Jesus was crucified.
6. Cemetery in the Bronx. Kerouac was then living in Rocky Mount, North Carolina. Ginsberg and the American writer William Burroughs (1914–1997) had lived in Tangiers. Cassady worked as a brakeman for the Southern Pacific Railroad.

7. An artistic movement based on absurdity and accident; it flourished during World War I. CCNY: City College of New York.
8. Three mental hospitals near New York. Carl Solomon was an inmate at Pilgrim State and Rockland, and Ginsberg's mother was institutionalized at Greystone.
9. Dolmens are prehistoric monuments of hori-

with mother finally * * * * * *, and the last fantastic book flung out of
the tenement window, and the last door closed at 4 AM and the
last telephone slammed at the wall in reply and the last furnished
room emptied down to the last piece of mental furniture, a yellow
paper rose twisted on a wire hanger in the closet, and even that
imaginary, nothing but a hopeful little bit of hallucination—
ah, Carl, while you are not safe I am not safe, and now you're really in
the total animal soup of time—
and who therefore ran through the icy streets obsessed with a sudden
flash of the alchemy of the use of the ellipse the catalog the
meter & the vibrating plane,
who dreamt and made incarnate gaps in Time & Space through
images juxtaposed, and trapped the archangel of the soul between
2 visual images and joined the elemental verbs and set the noun
and dash of consciousness together jumping with sensation of
Pater Omnipotens Aeterna Deus[1]

75 to recreate the syntax and measure of poor human prose and stand
before you speechless and intelligent and shaking with shame,
rejected yet confessing out the soul to conform to the rhythm of
thought in his naked and endless head,
the madman bum and angel beat in Time, unknown, yet putting down
here what might be left to say in time come after death,
and rose reincarnate in the ghostly clothes of jazz in the goldhorn
shadow of the band and blew the suffering of America's naked
mind for love into an eli eli lamma lamma sabacthani[2] saxophone
cry that shivered the cities down to the last radio
with the absolute heart of the poem of life butchered out of their own
bodies good to eat a thousand years.

San Francisco 1955   1956

A Supermarket in California

What thoughts I have of you tonight, Walt Whitman,[3] for I
walked down the sidestreets under the trees with a headache self-
conscious looking at the full moon.
    In my hungry fatigue, and shopping for images, I went into the
neon fruit supermarket, dreaming of your enumerations!
    What peaches and what penumbras!° Whole families   *shadows*
shopping at night! Aisles full of husbands! Wives in the avocados,
babies in the tomatoes!—and you, García Lorca,[4] what were you doing
down by the watermelons?

---

zontal stone slabs supported by upright stones,
found in Britain and France and believed to be
tombs.
1. All-powerful Father, Eternal God (Latin;
"Aeterna" is feminine, the nouns are masculine).
Paul Cézanne (1839–1906), the French Impres-
sionist painter, used this phrase to describe the
effects of nature on him.

2. My God, my God, why have you forsaken me?
(Hebrew). These are Jesus' last words from the
cross (Matthew 27.46, Mark 15.34, Psalm 22.1).
3. American poet (1819–1892; see pp. 1060–86),
of great influence on Ginsberg.
4. Federico García Lorca (1898–1936), Spanish
poet and dramatist.

I saw you, Walt Whitman, childless, lonely old grubber, poking
among the meats in the refrigerator and eyeing the grocery boys.
5   I heard you asking questions of each: Who killed the pork
chops? What price bananas? Are you my Angel?
I wandered in and out of the brilliant stacks of cans following
you, and followed in my imagination by the store detective.
We strode down the open corridors together in our solitary fancy
tasting artichokes, possessing every frozen delicacy, and never passing
the cashier.

Where are we going, Walt Whitman? The doors close in an
hour. Which way does your beard point tonight?
(I touch your book and dream of our odyssey in the supermarket
and feel absurd.)
10   Will we walk all night through solitary streets? The trees add
shade to shade, lights out in the houses, we'll both be lonely.
Will we stroll dreaming of the lost America of love past blue
automobiles in driveways, home to our silent cottage?
Ah, dear father, graybeard, lonely old courage-teacher, what
America did you have when Charon quit poling his ferry and you got
out on a smoking bank and stood watching the boat disappear on the
black waters of Lethe?[5]

1956

To Aunt Rose

Aunt Rose—now—might I see you
with your thin face and buck tooth smile and pain
of rheumatism—and a long black heavy shoe
for your bony left leg
5   limping down the long hall in Newark on the running carpet
past the black grand piano
in the day room
where the parties were
and I sang Spanish loyalist songs[6]
10   in a high squeaky voice
(hysterical) the committee listening
while you limped around the room
collected the money—
Aunt Honey, Uncle Sam, a stranger with a cloth arm
15   in his pocket
and huge young bald head
of Abraham Lincoln Brigade[7]

---

5. In Greek mythology, a river of Hades, signifying
forgetfulness; Charon ferried the dead across it.
6. During the Spanish Civil War (1936–39),
Spanish loyalists fought against the Fascists,
whose eventual triumph led to the dictatorship of
Francisco Franco (1892–1975). Ginsberg's rela-
tives in Newark, New Jersey, were among the many
left-wing Americans who supported the loyalists.
7. A group of American volunteers in the Spanish
Civil War.

—your long sad face
        your tears of sexual frustration
20   (what smothered sobs and bony hips
                    under the pillows of Osborne Terrace)
        —the time I stood on the toilet seat naked
        and you powdered my thighs with Calomine
            against the poison ivy—my tender
25   and shamed first black curled hairs
        what were you thinking in secret heart then
            knowing me a man already—
        and I an ignorant girl of family silence on the thin pedestal
            of my legs in the bathroom—Museum of Newark.
30   Aunt Rose
        Hitler is dead, Hitler is in Eternity; Hitler is with
            Tamburlane and Emily Brontë[8]

        Though I see you walking still, a ghost on Osborne Terrace
            down the long dark hall to the front door
35   limping a little with a pinched smile
                in what must have been a silken
                    flower dress
        welcoming my father, the Poet, on his visit to Newark
                —see you arriving in the living room
40   dancing on your crippled leg
            and clapping hands his book
                had been accepted by Liveright[9]

        Hitler is dead and Liveright's gone out of business
        The Attic of the Past and *Everlasting Minute* are out of print
45   Uncle Harry sold his last silk stocking
            Claire quit interpretive dancing school
                Buba[1] sits a wrinkled monument in Old
                    Ladies Home blinking at new babies

        last time I saw you was the hospital
50   pale skull protruding under ashen skin
                blue veined unconscious girl
                    in an oxygen tent
            the war in Spain has ended long ago
                    Aunt Rose

Paris 1958   1961

---

8. English poet and novelist (1818–1848), whose
novel *Wuthering Heights* is in part a ghost story.
Tamburlane: E. Timur (1336–1405), Turkic con-
queror; the bloodthirsty hero of Christopher
Marlowe's tragedy *Tambulaine the Great* (1587).
9. Company (now a subsidiary of W. W. Norton)
that published *The Everlasting Minute,* a 1937
book of poems by Ginsberg's father, Louis, whose
first book, *The Attic of the Past,* was published in
1920.
1. Grandmother (Yiddish).

JAMES MERRILL
1926–1995

The Broken Home[1]

Crossing the street,
I saw the parents and the child
At their window, gleaming like fruit
With evening's mild gold leaf.

5   In a room on the floor below,
Sunless, cooler—a brimming
Saucer of wax, marbly and dim—
I have lit what's left of my life.

I have thrown out yesterday's milk
10   And opened a book of maxims.
The flame quickens. The word stirs.

Tell me, tongue of fire,
That you and I are as real
At least as the people upstairs.

15   My father, who had flown in World War I,
Might have continued to invest his life
In cloud banks well above Wall Street and wife.[2]
But the race was run below, and the point was to win.

Too late now, I make out in his blue gaze
20   (Through the smoked glass of being thirty-six)
The soul eclipsed by twin black pupils, sex
And business; time was money in those days.

Each thirteenth year he married. When he died
There were already several chilled wives
25   In sable orbit—rings, cars, permanent waves.
We'd felt him warming up for a green bride.

He could afford it. He was "in his prime"
At three score ten. But money was not time.

When my parents were younger this was a popular act:
30   A veiled woman would leap from an electric, wine-dark car

---

1. This poem is composed of sonnets, some "broken" into unconventional proportions and rhyme schemes.
2. Charles Merrill, the poet's father, was a co-founder of the investment firm Merrill Lynch. Wall Street is the hub of the financial industry in New York City.

To the steps of no matter what—the Senate or the Ritz Bar—
And bodily, at newsreel speed, attack

No matter whom—Al Smith or José Maria Sert
Or Clemenceau[3]—veins standing out on her throat
35 As she yelled *War mongerer! Pig! Give us the vote!*,
And would have to be hauled away in her hobble skirt.[4]

What had the man done? Oh, made history.
Her business (he had implied) was giving birth,
Tending the house, mending the socks.

40 Always that same old story—
Father Time and Mother Earth,[5]
A marriage on the rocks.

One afternoon, red, satyr-thighed[6]
Michael, the Irish setter, head
45 Passionately lowered, led
The child I was to a shut door. Inside,

Blinds beat sun from the bed.
The green-gold room throbbed like a bruise.
Under a sheet, clad in taboos
50 Lay whom we sought, her hair undone, outspread,

And of a blackness found, if ever now, in old
Engravings where the acid bit.
I must have needed to touch it
Or the whiteness—was she dead?
55 Her eyes flew open, startled strange and cold.
The dog slumped to the floor. She reached for me. I fled.

Tonight they have stepped out onto the gravel.
The party is over. It's the fall
Of 1931. They love each other still.

60 She: Charlie, I can't stand the pace.
He: Come on, honey—why, you'll bury us all!

A lead soldier guards my windowsill:
Khaki rifle, uniform, and face.
Something in me grows heavy, silvery, pliable.

3. Georges Clemenceau (1841–1929), premier of
France during World War I, visitor to the United
States in 1922. Alfred Smith (1873–1944), gov-
ernor of New York and 1928 candidate for the U.S.
presidency. José Maria Sert y Badia (1876–1945),
Spanish painter and muralist, who decorated New
York's Waldorf-Astoria Hotel in 1930.
4. Long, straight skirt.

5. A reference to the Greek mythological figures
Cronus (ruler of the Titans; his name means
"Time") and Rhea (his wife; an Earth deity known
as Mother of the Gods).
6. In Greek mythology, the satyrs were minor
nature deities, their upper halves resembling men,
their lower halves resembling goats or horses.

65 How intensely people used to feel!
Like metal poured at the close of a proletarian novel,[7]
Refined and glowing from the crucible,
I see those two hearts, I'm afraid,
Still. Cool here in the graveyard of good and evil,
70 They are even so to be honored and obeyed.

. . . Obeyed, at least, inversely. Thus
I rarely buy a newspaper, or vote.
To do so, I have learned, is to invite
The tread of a stone guest[8] within my house.

75 Shooting this rusted bolt, though, against him,
I trust I am no less time's child than some
Who on the heath impersonate Poor Tom[9]
Or on the barricades risk life and limb.

Nor do I try to keep a garden, only
80 An avocado in a glass of water—
Roots pallid, gemmed with air. And later,
When the small gilt leaves have grown
Fleshy and green, I let them die, yes, yes,
And start another. I am earth's no less.

85 A child, a red dog roam the corridors,
Still, of the broken home. No sound. The brilliant
Rag runners halt before wide-open doors.
My old room! Its wallpaper—cream, medallioned
With pink and brown—brings back the first nightmares,
90 Long summer colds, and Emma, sepia-faced,
Perspiring over broth carried upstairs
Aswim with golden fats I could not taste.

The real house became a boarding school.
Under the ballroom ceiling's allegory
95 Someone at last may actually be allowed
To learn something; or, from my window, cool
With the unstiflement of the entire story,
Watch a red setter stretch and sink in cloud.

1966

---

7. Type of socialist novel that romanticized work-
ers and sometimes, as here, industry.
8. In the play *The Stone Feast,* by the French
dramatist Jean-Baptiste Molière (1622–1673), a
stone statue of the commander of Seville drags his
murderer, Don Juan, down to hell. A version of this
story appears in the opera *Don Giovanni,* by the
Austrian composer Wolfgang Amadeus Mozart
(1756–1791).
9. The nickname that Edgar, the disowned son of
Gloucester in Shakespeare's *King Lear,* gives to
himself when he wanders the heath in disguise as
a disheveled madman.

The Victor Dog[1]

For Elizabeth Bishop

Bix to Buxtehude to Boulez,
The little white dog on the Victor label
Listens long and hard as he is able.
It's all in a day's work, whatever plays.

5 From judgment, it would seem, he has refrained.
He even listens earnestly to Bloch,
Then builds a church upon our acid rock.[2]
He's man's—no—he's the Leiermann's best friend,[3]

Or would be if hearing and listening were the same.
10 *Does* he hear? I fancy he rather smells
Those lemon-gold arpeggios in Ravel's
"Les jets d'eau du palais de ceux qui s'aiment."[4]

He ponders the Schumann Concerto's tall willow hit
By lightning, and stays put. When he surmises
15 Through one of Bach's eternal boxwood mazes[5]
The oboe pungent as a bitch in heat,

Or when the calypso decants its raw bay rum
Or the moon in *Wozzeck*[6] reddens ripe for murder,
He doesn't sneeze or howl; just listens harder.
20 Adamant° needles bear down on him from   diamond

Whirling of outer space, too black, too near—
But he was taught as a puppy not to flinch,
Much less to imitate his bête noire Blanche
Who barked, fat foolish creature, at King Lear.[7]

25 Still others fought in the road's filth over Jezebel,[8]
Slavered° on hearths of horned and pelted barons.   drooled
His forebears lacked, to say the least, forbearance.
Can nature change in him? Nothing's impossible.

1. Long a trademark of RCA, the dog "Nipper"—here, called "Victor" (line 38)—was on the label of RCA Victor records, listening intently to a gramophone, with the caption "His master's voice." In the poem, passing reference is made to the jazz trumpeter Bix Beiderbecke (1903–1931), to the classical composers Dietrich Buxtehude (1637–1707), Johann Sebastian Bach (1685–1750), George Frederick Handel (1685–1759), Franz Schubert (1797–1828), and Robert Schumann (1810–1856), and to the modernists Pierre Boulez (b. 1925), Ernest Bloch (1880–1959), Maurice Ravel (1875–1937), and Alban Berg (1885–1935).
2. Cf. Matthew 16.18: ". . . upon this rock I will build my church . . ."
3. In Schubert's song "Der Leiermann" ("The Organ-Grinder"), an old man cranks his barrel-organ in the winter cold to an audience of snarling dogs.
4. The palace fountains of those who are in love with each other (French).
5. The composer's works are compared to labyrinths executed in living boxwood plants, popular in eighteenth-century formal gardens.
6. An opera by Berg in which the protagonist murders his unfaithful wife beneath a rising moon.
7. In *King Lear*, the mad king says, "The little dogs and all. / Tray, Blanch, and Sweet-heart, see, they bark at me" (3.6.57–58). *Bête noire*: a person or thing detested or avoided; in French, its literal meaning is "black beast," whereas *blanche* means "white."
8. The proverbial wicked woman, she was killed in the street; when the body was recovered for burial, dogs had eaten most of it, as had been prophesied earlier by Elijah (1 Kings 21, 2 Kings 9.30–37).

The last chord fades. The night is cold and fine.
His master's voice rasps through the grooves' bare groves.
Obediently, in silence like the grave's
He sleeps there on the still-warm gramophone

Only to dream he is at the première of a Handel
Opera long thought lost—*Il Cane Minore*.[9]
Its allegorical subject is his story!
A little dog revolving round a spindle

Gives rise to harmonies beyond belief,
A cast of stars. . . . Is there in Victor's heart
No honey for the vanquished? Art is art.
The life it asks of us is a dog's life.

1972

Lost in Translation

for Richard Howard

Diese Tage, die leer dir scheinen
und wertlos für das All,
haben Wurzeln zwischen den Steinen
und trinken dort überall.[1]

A card table in the library stands ready
To receive the puzzle which keeps never coming.
Daylight shines in or lamplight down
Upon the tense oasis of green felt.
Full of unfulfillment, life goes on,
Mirage arisen from time's trickling sands
Or fallen piecemeal into place:
German lesson, picnic, see-saw, walk
With the collie who "did everything but talk"—
Sour windfalls of the orchard back of us.
A summer without parents is the puzzle,
Or should be. But the boy, day after day,
Writes in his Line-a-Day° *No puzzle.*   diary

He's in love, at least. His French Mademoiselle,
In real life a widow since Verdun,[2]
Is stout, plain, carrot-haired, devout.
She prays for him, as does a curé in Alsace,[3]

---

9. The little dog (Italian).
1. These days which seem empty and entirely fruitless to you have roots between the stones and drink from everywhere (German). From the translation by the Austrian poet Rainer Maria Rilke (1875–1926) of "Palme," by the French poet Paul Valéry (1871–1945). Ironically, the epigraph provides the very translation Merrill claims, within the poem, to be "lost"—or difficult to find. Though the expression *lost in translation* is in common use,

Merrill may have meant to refer also to Robert Frost's definition of poetry as that which is lost in translation. The American poet Richard Howard (b. 1929; see pp. 1778–83) is also well known as a translator.
2. His French-speaking governess, called Mademoiselle, widowed since the battle of Verdun in World War I.
3. Region of France on the border of Germany. *Curé:* priest (French).

Sews costumes for his marionettes,
Helps him to keep behind the scene
20   Whose sidelit goosegirl, speaking with his voice,
Plays Guinevere as well as Gunmoll Jean.[4]
Or else at bedtime in his tight embrace
Tells him her own French hopes, her German fears,
Her—but what more is there to tell?
25   Having known grief and hardship, Mademoiselle
Knows little more. Her languages. Her place.
Noon coffee. Mail. The watch that also waited
Pinned to her heart, poor gold, throws up its hands—
No puzzle! Steaming bitterness
30   Her sugars draw pops back into his mouth, translated:
"Patience, chéri. Geduld, mein Shatz."[5]
(Thus, reading Valéry the other evening
And seeming to recall a Rilke version of "Palme,"
That sunlit paradigm° whereby the tree   *pattern*
35   Taps a sweet wellspring of authority,
The hour came back. Patience dans l'azur.
Geduld im . . . Himmelblau? Mademoiselle.)

Out of the blue, as promised, of a New York
Puzzle-rental shop the puzzle comes—
40   A superior one, containing a thousand hand-sawn,
Sandal°-scented pieces. Many take   *sandalwood*
Shapes known already—the craftsman's repertoire
Nice in its limitation—from other puzzles:
Witch on broomstick, ostrich, hourglass,
45   Even (surely not just in retrospect)
An inchling, innocently branching palm.
These can be put aside, made stories of
While Mademoiselle spreads out the rest face-up,
Herself excited as a child; or questioned
50   Like incoherent faces in a crowd,
Each with its scrap of highly colored
Evidence the Law must piece together.
Sky-blue ostrich? Likely story.
Mauve of the witch's cloak white, severed fingers
55   Pluck? Detain her. The plot thickens
As all at once two pieces interlock.

Mademoiselle does borders—(Not so fast.
A London dusk, December last.
Chatter silenced in the library
60   This grown man reenters, wearing grey.
A medium. All except him have seen
Panel slid back, recess explored,
An object at once unique and common

4. Term for a gangster's female accomplice. *Goose-girl:* as in the fairy tale "The Goosegirl"; i.e., an impersonating voice. *Guinevere:* in English legend, wife of King Arthur.
5. Patience, my dear (French and German). Mer-

rill is reminded, in the lines to follow, of Valéry's "Palme" and Rilke's translation, "Patience in the Blue," which refers to the palm tree's patience in growth. The "blue" of the German "Himmelblau" provides Merrill with his own "Out of the blue."

Displayed, planted in a plain tole°   *coated-metal*
65   Casket the subject now considers
Through shut eyes, saying in effect:
"Even as voices reach me vaguely
A dry saw-shriek drowns them out,
Some loud machinery—a lumber mill?
70   Far uphill in the fir forest
Trees tower, tense with shock,
Groaning and cracking as they crash groundward.
But hidden here is a freak fragment
Of a pattern complex in appearance only.
75   What it seems to show is superficial
Next to that long-term lamination
Of hazard and craft, the karma that has
Made it matter in the first place.
Plywood, Piece of a puzzle." Applause
80   Acknowledged by an opening of lids
Upon the thing itself. A sudden dread—
But to go back. All this lay years ahead.)

Mademoiselle does borders. Straight-edge pieces
Align themselves with earth or sky
85   In twos and threes, naive cosmogonists[6]
Whose views clash. Nomad inlanders meanwhile
Begin to cluster where the totem
Of a certain vibrant egg-yolk yellow
Or pelt of what emerging animal
90   Acts on the straggler like a trumpet call
To form a more sophisticated unit.
By suppertime two ragged wooden clouds
Have formed. In one, a Sheik with beard
And flashing sword hilt (he is all but finished)
95   Steps forward on a tiger skin. A piece
Snaps shut, and fangs gnash out at us!
In the second cloud—they gaze from cloud to cloud
With marked if undecipherable feeling—
Most of a dark-eyed woman veiled in mauve
100   Is being helped down from her camel (kneeling)
By a small backward-looking slave or page-boy
(Her son, thinks Mademoiselle mistakenly)
Whose feet have not been found. But lucky finds
In the last minutes before bed
105   Anchor both factions to the scene's limits
And, by so doing, orient
Them eye to eye across the green abyss.
The yellow promises, oh bliss,
To be in time a sumptuous tent.

110   *Puzzle begun* I write in the day's space,
Then, while she bathes, peek at Mademoiselle's
Page to the curé: ". . . cette innocente mère,

---

6. Theorists about the universe's origin.

Ce pauvre enfant, que deviendront-ils?"[7]
Her azure script is curlicued like pieces
115   Of the puzzle she will be telling him about.
(Fearful incuriosity of childhood!
"Tu as l'accent allemand,"[8] said Dominique.
Indeed. Mademoiselle was only French by marriage.
Child of an English mother, a remote
120   Descendant of the great explorer Speke,[9]
And Prussian father. No one knew. I heard it
Long afterwards from her nephew, a UN
Interpreter. His matter-of-fact account
Touched old strings. My poor Mademoiselle,
125   With 1939[1] about to shake
This world where "each was the enemy, each the friend"
To its foundations, kept, though signed in blood,
Her peace a shameful secret to the end.)
"Schlaf wohl, chéri."[2] Her kiss. Her thumb
130   Crossing my brow against the dreams to come.

This World that shifts like sand, its unforeseen
Consolidations and elate routine,
Whose Potentate had lacked a retinue?
Lo! it assembles on the shrinking Green.

135   Gunmetal-skinned or pale, all plumes and scars,
Of Vassalage the noblest avatars—[3]
The very coffee-bearer in his vair°   fur-trimmed
Vest is a swart Highness, next to ours.

Kef[4] easing Boredom, and iced syrups, thirst,
140   In guessed-at glooms old wives who know the worst
Outsweat that virile fiction of the New:
"Insh'Allah,[5] he will tire—" "—or kill her first!"

(Hardly a proper subject for the Home,
Work of—dear Richard, I shall let *you* comb
145   Archives and learned journals for his name—
A minor lion attending on Gérôme.[6])

While, thick as Thebes[7] whose presently complete
Gates close behind them, Houri and Afreet[8]
Both claim the Page.[9] He wonders whom to serve,
150   And what his duties are, and where his feet,

7. This innocent mother, this poor child, what will become of them? (French).
8. You have a German accent (French).
9. John Hanning Speke (1827–1864), English explorer; possible pun on *speak*.
1. When World War II began.
2. Sleep well, darling (German, French).
3. The noblest incarnations of slavery.
4. Narcotic made from hemp.
5. As Allah wills (Arabic).
6. Jean Léon Gérôme (1824–1940), French

painter; also, an allusion to Saint Jerome, who, the legend goes, pulled a thorn from the paw of a lion, which then befriended him.
7. Capital of ancient Upper Egypt; pun on *thick as thieves*.
8. Evil demon in Arabian mythology. *Houri:* one of the beautiful virgins who live with the blessed in the Islamic paradise.
9. The servant, with a suggestion too of the printed page.

And if we'll find, as some before us did,
That piece of Distance deep in which lies hid
Your tiny apex sugary with sun,
Eternal Triangle, Great Pyramid!

155 Then Sky alone is left, a hundred blue
Fragments in revolution, with no clue
To where a Niche will open. Quite a task,
Putting together Heaven, yet we do.

It's done. Here under the table all along
160 Were those missing feet. It's done.

The dog's tail thumping. Mademoiselle sketching
Costumes for a coming harem drama
To star the goosegirl. All too soon the swift
Dismantling. Lifted by two corners,
165 The puzzle hung together—and did not.
Irresistibly a populace
Unstitched of its attachments, rattled down.
Power went to pieces as the witch
Slithered easily from Virtue's gown.
170 The blue held out for time, but crumbled, too.
The city had long fallen, and the tent,
A separating sauce mousseline,[1]
Been swept away. Remained the green
On which the grown-ups gambled. A green dusk.
175 First lightning bugs. Last glow of west
Green in the false eyes of (coincidence)
Our mangy tiger safe on his bared hearth.

Before the puzzle was boxed and readdressed
To the puzzle shop in the mid-Sixties,[2]
180 Something tells me that one piece contrived
To stay in the boy's pocket. How do I know?
I know because so many later puzzles
Had missing pieces—Maggie Teyte's[3] high notes
Gone at the war's end, end of the vogue for collies,
185 A house torn down; and hadn't Mademoiselle
Kept back her pitiful bit of truth as well?
I've spent the last days, furthermore,
Ransacking Athens for that translation of "Palme."
Neither the Goethehaus[4] nor the National Library
190 Seems able to unearth it. Yet I can't
Just be imagining. I've seen it. Know
How much of the sun-ripe original
Felicity Rilke made himself forego
(Who loved French words—verger, mûr, parfumer[5])
195 In order to render its underlying sense.
Know already in that tongue of his

---

1. A white, creamy sauce.
2. The streets numbered in the mid-Sixties in Manhattan.
3. English soprano (1888–1976), known for her

repertoire in French.
4. A German library.
5. Orchard, ripe, to scent (French).

What Pains, what monolithic Truths
Shadow stanza to stanza's symmetrical
Rhyme-rutted pavement. Know that ground plan left
200 Sublime and barren, where the warm Romance
Stone by stone faded, cooled; the fluted nouns
Made taller, lonelier than life
By leaf-carved capitals in the afterglow.
The owlet umlaut[6] peeps and hoots
205 Above the open vowel. And after rain
A deep reverberation fills with stars.

Lost, is it, buried? One more missing piece?

But nothing's lost. Or else: all is translation
And every bit of us is lost in it
210 (Or found—I wander through the ruin of S[7]
Now and then, wondering at the peacefulness)
And in that loss a self-effacing tree,
Color of context, imperceptibly
Rustling with its angel,[8] turns the waste
215 To shade and fiber, milk and memory.

1976

From The Book of Ephraim[9]

Correct but cautious, that first night, we asked
Our visitor's name, era, habitat.
EPHRAIM came the answer. A Greek Jew
Born AD 8 at XANTHOS Where was that?
5 In Greece WHEN WOLVES & RAVENS WERE IN ROME
(Next day the classical dictionary yielded
A Xanthos on the Asia Minor Coast.)
NOW WHO ARE U We told him. ARE U XTIANS
We guessed so. WHAT A COZY CATACOMB
10 Christ had WROUGHT HAVOC in *his* family,
ENTICED MY FATHER FROM MY MOTHERS BED
(I too had issued from a broken home[1]—
The first of several facts to coincide.)
Later a favorite of TIBERIUS[2] Died

6. German accent mark ("), the two high dots of which resemble an owl's eyes.
7. Initial of a former lover.
8. Pun on *wrestling with its angel*. Jacob wrestled with an angel, saying, "I will not let thee go, except thou bless me" (Genesis 32.26).
9. The first part of an epic trilogy, *The Changing Light at Sandover,* which also includes *Mirabell: Books of Number* and *Scripts for the Pageant. The Book of Ephraim* originally appeared in the volume *Divine Comedies,* which made explicit Merrill's debt to Dante's tripartite *Divine Comedy.* Merrill (JM) records encounters through the Ouija board that he and his companion, David Jackson (DJ),

have with spirits from the other world, who illuminate a system of reincarnation and purification as well as suggest theories about the creation and future of the universe. Merrill models the structure of each part of the trilogy on the design of the Ouija board; thus *Ephraim* is in twenty-six parts, one for each letter of the alphabet. In "C" (identified by the large initial letter), the spirit guide Ephraim introduces himself; uppercase letters indicate the "speech" of the Ouija board.
1. Cf. Merrill's poem "The Broken Home" (p. 1716).
2. Roman emperor (42 B.C.E.–37 C.E.)

15   AD 36 on CAPRI throttled
      By the imperial guard for having LOVED
      THE MONSTERS NEPHEW (sic) CALIGULA³
      Rapidly he went on—changing the subject?
      A long incriminating manuscript
20   Boxed in bronze lay UNDER PORPHYRY°   *rock*
      Beneath the deepest excavations. He
      Would help us find it, but we must please make haste
      Because Tiberius wanted it destroyed.
      Oh? And where, we wondered of the void,
25   *Was* Tiberius these days? STAGE THREE

      Why was he telling *us*? He'd overheard us
      Talking to SIMPSON   Simpson? His LINK WITH EARTH
      His REPRESENTATIVE   A feeble nature
      All but bestial, given to violent
30   Short lives—one ending lately among flames
      In an Army warehouse. Slated for rebirth
      But not in time, said Ephraim, to prevent
      The brat from wasting, just now at our cup,⁴
      Precious long distance minutes—don't hang up!

35   So much facetiousness—well, we were young
      And these were matters of life and death—dismayed us.
      Was he a devil? His reply MY POOR
      INNOCENTS left the issue hanging fire.
      As it flowed on, his stream-of-consciousness
40   Deepened. There was a buried room, a BED
      WROUGHT IN SILVER   I CAN LEAD U THERE
      IF If ? U GIVE ME   What? HA HA YR SOULS
      (Another time he'll say that he misread
      Our innocence for insolence that night,
45   And meant to scare us.) Our eyes met. What if . . .
      The blood's least vessel hoisted jet-black sails.
      Five whole minutes we were frightened stiff
      —But after all, we weren't *that* innocent.
      The Rover Boys⁵ at thirty, still red-blooded
50   Enough not to pass up an armchair revel
      And pure enough at heart to beat the devil,
      Entered into the spirit, so to speak,
      And said they'd leave for Capri⁶ that same week.

      Pause. Then, as though we'd passed a test,
55   Ephraim's whole manner changed. He brushed aside
      Tiberius and settled to the task
      Of answering, like an experienced guide,
      Those questions we had lacked the wit to ask.

      Here on Earth—huge tracts of information
60   Have gone into these capsules flavorless

---

3. Roman emperor (12–41 C.E.).
4. JM and DJ place hands on a teacup to "read"
the Ouija board.

5. Heroes of a popular series of children's books.
6. Italian island, in the Bay of Naples.

And rhymed for easy swallowing—on Earth
We're each the REPRESENTATIVE of a PATRON
—Are there that many patrons? YES O YES
These secular guardian angels fume and fuss
65 For what must seem eternity over us.
It is forbidden them to INTERVENE
Save, as it were, in the entr'acte° between   *intermission*
One incarnation and another. Back
To school from the disastrously long vac°   *summer vacation*
70 Goes the soul its patron crams yet once
Again with savoir vivre.[7] Will the dunce
Never—by rote, the hundredth time round—learn
What ropes make fast that point of no return,
A footing on the lowest of NINE STAGES
75 Among the curates and the minor mages?°   *priests, magicians*
Patrons at last ourselves, an upward notch
Our old ones move   THEYVE BORNE IT ALL FOR THIS
And take delivery from the Abyss
Of brand-new little savage souls to watch.
80 One difference: with every rise in station
Comes a degree of PEACE FROM REPRESENTATION
—Odd phrase, more like a motto for abstract
Art—or for Autocracy—In fact
Our heads are spinning—From the East a light—
85 BUT U ARE TIRED MES CHERS[8]   SWEET DREAMS   TOMORROW NIGHT

1976

Arabian Night[9]

Features unseen embers and tongs once worried
bright as brass, cool, trim, of a depth to light his
way at least who, trusting mirages, finds in
them the oasis,

5   what went wrong? You there in the mirror, did our
freshest page get sent to the Hall of Cobwebs?
Or had Rime's Emir[1] all along been merely
after your body?

No reply. Then ("there" of course, also) insight's
10 dazzle snaps at gloom, like a wick when first lit.
Look! on one quick heartstring glissando,[2] stranger
kindles to father

---

7. Knowledge of how to live (French).
8. My dears (French).
9. *The Arabian Nights,* also known as *One Thousand and One Nights,* is a collection of tales of unknown date (but referred to by the tenth century) and of mixed origins, including Indian, Persian, and Arabic. Compiled in its "original" form in Egypt by the fifteenth century, it is united by a framework in which the newly married Scheherazade preserves her life by telling tales.
1. An Arab prince, provincial governor, or military commander. Also, the word is a mirror image of *rime,* rare spelling for *rhyme,* which here is synonymous with poetry. The "page" of the previous line thus connotes not only the emir's servant but a page of poetry.
2. Italian term for a rapid series of consecutive notes played by sliding fingers over keys or a string.

thirty years a shade, yet whose traits (plus others
not so staring—loyalty, cynicism,
15   neophyte's pure heart in erotic mufti[3]
straight out of Baghdad)

solve the lifelong riddle: a face no longer
sought in dreams but worn as my own. Aladdin[4]
rubs his lamp—youth? age?—and the rival two beam
20   forth in one likeness.

                                                            1988

FRANK O'HARA
1926–1966

The Day Lady[1] Died

It is 12:20 in New York a Friday
three days after Bastille day,[2] yes
it is 1959 and I go get a shoeshine
because I will get off the 4:19 in Easthampton[3]
5   npat 7:15 and then go straight to dinner
and I don't know the people who will feed me

I walk up the muggy street beginning to sun
and have a hamburger and a malted and buy
an ugly NEW WORLD WRITING to see what the poets
10   in Ghana are doing these days
                                    I go on to the bank
and Miss Stillwagon (first name Linda I once heard)
doesn't even look up my balance for once in her life
and in the GOLDEN GRIFFIN[4] I get a little Verlaine
15   for Patsy with drawings by Bonnard although I do
think of Hesiod, trans. Richmond Lattimore or
Brendan Behan's new play or Le Balcon or Les Nègres
of Genet, but I don't, I stick with Verlaine
after practically going to sleep with quandariness

20   and for Mike I just stroll into the PARK LANE
Liquor Store and ask for a bottle of Strega and
then I go back where I came from to 6th Avenue
and the tobacconist in the Ziegfeld Theatre and
casually ask for a carton of Gauloises and a carton
25   of Picayunes, and a NEW YORK POST with her face on it

3. Civilian clothes worn by someone usually in
military uniform.
4. Boy in "The Story of Aladdin and the Magic
Lamp," popularly believed to be collected in the
original Arabian Nights but actually an eighteenth-
century addition. In it, Aladdin has a magic lamp
whose genie promises to grant any wish.
1. Billie Holiday (1915–1959), American jazz and

blues singer, called Lady Day.
2. July 14, the French national holiday that cele-
brates the storming of the Bastille prison in 1789.
3. One of "the Hamptons," towns on eastern Long
Island, popular, especially in the summer, with
New York City artists and writers.
4. An avant-garde bookshop near the Museum of
Modern Art, where O'Hara was a curator.

and I am sweating a lot by now and thinking of
leaning on the john door in the 5 SPOT
while she whispered a song along the keyboard
to Mal Waldron[5] and everyone and I stopped breathing

1959   1964

How to Get There

White the October air, no snow, easy to breathe
beneath the sky, lies, lies everywhere writhing and gasping
clutching and tangling, it is not easy to breathe
lies building their tendrils into dim figures
5   who disappear down corridors in west-side[6] apartments
into childhood's proof of being wanted, not abandoned, kidnaped
betrayal staving off loneliness, I see the fog lunge in
and hide it
            where are you?
10   here I am on the sidewalk
under the moonlike lamplight thinking how precious moss is
so unique and greenly crushable if you can find it
on the north side of the tree where the fog binds you
and then, tearing apart into soft white lies, spreads its disease
15   through the primal night of an everlasting winter
which nevertheless has heat in tubes, west-side and east-side
and its intricate individual pathways of white accompanied
by the ringing of telephone bells beside which someone sits in
silence denying their own number, never given out! nameless
20   like the sound of troika[7] bells rushing past suffering
in the first storm, it is snowing now, it is already too late
the snow will go away, but nobody will be there

police cordons for lying political dignitaries ringing too
the world becomes a jangle
25   from the index finger
to the vast empty houses filled with people, their echoes
of lies and the tendrils of fog trailing softly around their throats
now the phone can be answered, nobody calling, only an echo
all can confess to be home and waiting, all is the same
30   and we drift into the clear sky enthralled by our disappointment
            never to be alone again
                                 never to be loved
sailing through space: didn't I have you once for my self? West Side?
      for a couple of hours, but I am not that person

1960   1964

5. Billie Holiday's accompanist (1926–2002).
6. "West-side" and "east-side" in the poem refer to
areas in Manhattan (west or east of Fifth Avenue).

7. A Russian vehicle drawn by three horses
abreast.

Ave Maria[8]

Mothers of America
            let your kids go to the movies!
get them out of the house so they won't know what you're up to
it's true that fresh air is good for the body
5   but what about the soul
that grows in darkness, embossed by silvery images
and when you grow old as grow old you must
                              they won't hate you
they won't criticize you they won't know
10   they'll be in some glamorous country
they first saw on a Saturday afternoon or playing hookey
they may even be grateful to you
                      for their first sexual experience
which only cost you a quarter
15   and didn't upset the peaceful home
they will know where candy bars come from
                        and gratuitous bags of popcorn
as gratuitous as leaving the movie before it's over
with a pleasant stranger whose apartment is in the Heaven on Earth
    Bldg
20 near the Williamsburg Bridge[9]
                    oh mothers you will have made the little tykes
so happy because if nobody does pick them up in the movies
they won't know the difference
                  and if somebody does it'll be sheer gravy
25 and they'll have been truly entertained either way
instead of hanging around the yard
                  or up in their room
                         hating you
prematurely since you won't have done anything horribly mean yet
30 except keeping them from the darker joys
                      it's unforgivable the latter
so don't blame me if you won't take this advice
                    and the family breaks up
and your children grow old and blind in front of a TV set
35   seeing
movies you wouldn't let them see when they were young

1960   1964

Why I Am Not a Painter

I am not a painter, I am a poet.
Why? I think I would rather be
a painter, but I am not. Well,

8. Hail Mary (Latin); the Catholic prayer addressed to the Virgin Mary, mother of Jesus.

9. Bridge connecting lower Manhattan with the Williamsburg section of Brooklyn.

for instance, Mike Goldberg[1]
5 is starting a painting. I drop in.
"Sit down and have a drink" he
says. I drink; we drink. I look
up. "You have SARDINES in it."
"Yes, it needed something there."
10 "Oh." I go and the days go by
and I drop in again. The painting
is going on, and I go, and the days
go by. I drop in. The painting is
finished. "Where's SARDINES?"
15 All that's left is just
letters, "It was too much," Mike says.

But me? One day I am thinking of
a color: orange. I write a line
about orange. Pretty soon it is a
20 whole page of words, not lines.
Then another page. There should be
so much more, not of orange, of
words, of how terrible orange is
and life. Days go by. It is even in
25 prose, I am a real poet. My poem
is finished and I haven't mentioned
orange yet. It's twelve poems, I call
it ORANGES. And one day in a gallery
I see Mike's painting, called SARDINES.

1971

W. D. SNODGRASS
b. 1926

From Heart's Needle[1]

For Cynthia

" 'Your father is dead.' 'That grieves me,' said he. 'Your mother is
dead,' said the lad. 'Now all pity for me is at an end,' said he. 'Your
brother is dead,' said Loingsechan. 'I am sorely wounded by that,'
said Suibne. 'Your daughter is dead,' said Loingsechan. 'And an only
daughter is the needle of the heart,' said Suibne. 'Dear is your son
who used to call you "Father," ' said Loingsechan. 'Indeed,' said he,
'that is the drop that brings a man to the ground.' "

FROM AN OLD IRISH STORY,
The Frenzy of Suibne,
AS TRANSLATED BY MYLES DILLON

---

1. New York painter (b. 1924), whose silk-screen
prints appear in O'Hara's *Odes* (1960).

1. Snodgrass's long poem for his daughter, after a
divorce, is written in ten sections.

2

Late April and you are three; today
We dug your garden in the yard.
To curb the damage of your play,
Strange dogs at night and the moles tunneling,
5   Four slender sticks of lath° stand guard   *wood*
Uplifting their thin string.

So you were the first to tramp it down
And after the earth was sifted close
You brought your watering can to drown
10 All earth *and* us. But these mixed seeds are pressed
With light loam in their steadfast rows.
Child, we've done our best.

Someone will have to weed and spread
The young sprouts. Sprinkle them in the hour
15 When shadow falls across their bed.
You should try to look at them every day
Because when they come to full flower
I will be away.

3

The child between them on the street
Comes to a puddle, lifts his feet
And hangs on their hands. They start
At the live weight and lurch together,
5   Recoil to swing him through the weather,
Stiffen and pull apart.

We read of cold war² soldiers that
Never gained ground, gave none, but sat
Tight in their chill trenches.
10 Pain seeps up from some cavity
Through the ranked teeth in sympathy;
The whole jaw grinds and clenches

Till something somewhere has to give.
It's better the poor soldiers live
15 In someone else's hands
Than drop where helpless powers fall
On crops and barns, on towns where all
Will burn. And no man stands.

---

2. The post–World War II rivalry between the Soviet Union and the United States.

7

Here in the scuffled dust
    is our ground of play.
I lift you on your swing and must
    shove you away,
5   see you return again,
        drive you off again, then

stand quiet till you come.
    You, though you climb
higher, farther from me, longer,
10   will fall back to me stronger.
Bad penny, pendulum,
    you keep my constant time

to bob in blue July
    where fat goldfinches fly
15 over the glittering, fecund
        reach of our growing lands.
Once more now, this second,
    I hold you in my hands.

10

The vicious winter finally yields
    the green winter wheat;
the farmer, tired in the tired fields
    he dare not leave will eat.

5   Once more the runs come fresh; prevailing
        piglets, stout as jugs,
harry their old sow to the railing
        to ease her swollen dugs

and game colts trail the herded mares
10   that circle the pasture courses;
our seasons bring us back once more
    like merry-go-round horses.

With crocus mouths, perennial hungers,
    into the park Spring comes;
15 we roast hot dogs on old coat hangers
        and feed the swan bread crumbs,

pay our respects to the peacocks, rabbits,
    and leathery Canada goose
who took, last Fall, our tame white habits
20   and now will not turn loose.

In full regalia, the pheasant cocks
    march past their dubious hens;

the porcupine and the lean, red fox
   trot around bachelor pens

25 and the miniature painted train
   wails on its oval track:
you said, I'm going to Pennsylvania!
   and waved. And you've come back.

If I loved you, they said, I'd leave
30   and find my own affairs.
Well, once again this April, we've
   come around to the bears;

punished and cared for, behind bars,
   the coons° on bread and water   *raccoons*
35 stretch thin black fingers after ours.
   And you are still my daughter.

1959

Mementos, 1

Sorting out letters and piles of my old
   Canceled checks, old clippings, and yellow note cards
That meant something once, I happened to find
   Your picture. *That* picture. I stopped there cold,
5 Like a man raking piles of dead leaves in his yard
   Who has turned up a severed hand.

Still, that first second, I was glad: you stand
   Just as you stood—shy, delicate, slender,
In that long gown of green lace netting and daisies
10   That you wore to our first dance. The sight of you stunned
Us all. Well, our needs were different, then,
   And our ideals came easy.

Then through the war³ and those two long years
   Overseas, the Japanese dead in their shacks
15 Among dishes, dolls, and lost shoes; I carried
   This glimpse of you, there, to choke down my fear,
Prove it had been, that it might come back.
   That was before we got married.

—Before we drained out one another's force
20   With lies, self-denial, unspoken regret
And the sick eyes that blame; before the divorce
   And the treachery. Say it: before we met. Still,
I put back your picture. Someday, in due course,
   I will find that it's still there.

1968

---

3. World War II.

ELIZABETH JENNINGS
1926–2001

My Grandmother

She kept an antique shop—or it kept her.
Among Apostle spoons and Bristol glass,[1]
The faded silks, the heavy furniture,
She watched her own reflection in the brass
5   Salvers° and silver bowls, as if to prove   *round trays*
Polish was all, there was no need of love.

And I remember how I once refused
To go out with her, since I was afraid.
It was perhaps a wish not to be used
10 Like antique objects. Though she never said
That she was hurt, I still could feel the guilt
Of that refusal, guessing how she felt.

Later, too frail to keep a shop, she put
All her best things in one long narrow room.
15 The place smelt old, of things too long kept shut,
The smell of absences where shadows come
That can't be polished. There was nothing then
To give her own reflection back again.

And when she died I felt no grief at all,
20 Only the guilt of what I once refused.
I walked into her room among the tall
Sideboards and cupboards—things she never used
But needed: and no finger-marks were there,
Only the new dust falling through the air.

1961

One Flesh

Lying apart now, each in a separate bed,
He with a book, keeping the light on late,
She like a girl dreaming of childhood,
All men elsewhere—it is as if they wait
5 Some new event: the book he holds unread,
Her eyes fixed on the shadows overhead.

Tossed up like flotsam from a former passion,
How cool they lie. They hardly ever touch,
Or if they do it is like a confession

---

1. Prized glassware of a deep blue color. *Apostle spoons:* set of teaspoons, the handles of which are in the form of male figures, supposedly the Apostles.

10   Of having little feeling—or too much.
      Chastity faces them, a destination
      For which their whole lives were a preparation.

      Strangely apart, yet strangely close together,
      Silence between them like a thread to hold
15   And not wind in. And time itself's a feather
      Touching them gently. Do they know they're old,
      These two who are my father and my mother
      Whose fire from which I came, has now grown cold?

                                                    1966

JOHN ASHBERY
b. 1927

The Painter

      Sitting between the sea and the buildings
      He enjoyed painting the sea's portrait.
      But just as children imagine a prayer
      Is merely silence, he expected his subject
5   To rush up the sand, and, seizing a brush,
      Plaster its own portrait on the canvas.

      So there was never any paint on his canvas
      Until the people who lived in the buildings
      Put him to work: "Try using the brush
10   As a means to an end. Select, for a portrait,
      Something less angry and large, and more subject
      To a painter's moods, or, perhaps, to a prayer."

      How could he explain to them his prayer
      That nature, not art, might usurp the canvas?
15   He chose his wife for a new subject,
      Making her vast, like ruined buildings,
      As if, forgetting itself, the portrait
      Had expressed itself without a brush.

      Slightly encouraged, he dipped his brush
20   In the sea, murmuring a heartfelt prayer:
      "My soul, when I paint this next portrait
      Let it be you who wrecks the canvas."
      The news spread like wildfire through the buildings:
      He had gone back to the sea for his subject.

25   Imagine a painter crucified by his subject!
      Too exhausted even to lift his brush,
      He provoked some artists leaning from the buildings

To malicious mirth: "We haven't a prayer
Now, of putting ourselves on canvas,
30 Or getting the sea to sit for a portrait!"

Others declared it a self-portrait.
Finally all indications of a subject
Began to fade, leaving the canvas
Perfectly white. He put down the brush.
35 At once a howl, that was also a prayer,
Arose from the overcrowded buildings.

They tossed him, the portrait, from the tallest of the buildings;
And the sea devoured the canvas and the brush
As though his subject had decided to remain a prayer.

1956

Soonest Mended[1]

Barely tolerated, living on the margin
In our technological society, we were always having to be rescued
On the brink of destruction, like heroines in *Orlando Furioso*[2]
Before it was time to start all over again.
5 There would be thunder in the bushes, a rustling of coils,
And Angelica, in the Ingres painting,[3] was considering
The colorful but small monster near her toe, as though wondering
    whether forgetting
The whole thing might not, in the end, be the only solution.
And then there always came a time when
10 Happy Hooligan[4] in his rusted green automobile
Came plowing down the course, just to make sure everything was
    O.K.,
Only by that time we were in another chapter and confused
About how to receive this latest piece of information.
Was it information? Weren't we rather acting this out
15 For someone else's benefit, thoughts in a mind
With room enough and to spare for our little problems (so they began
    to seem),
Our daily quandary about food and the rent and bills to be paid?
To reduce all this to a small variant,
To step free at last, minuscule on the gigantic plateau—
20 This was our ambition: to be small and clear and free.
Alas, the summer's energy wanes quickly,
A moment and it is gone. And no longer
May we make the necessary arrangements, simple as they are.
Our star was brighter perhaps when it had water in it.

1. Allusion to the expression *Least said, soonest mended*.
2. Epic by the Italian poet Ludovico Ariosto (1474–1533); his much-rescued heroine is Angelica.
3. *Roger Delivering Angelica* (1819), painting depicting Ariosto's heroine by the French artist Jean-Auguste-Dominique Ingres (1780–1867).
4. Character in a comic strip of the 1920s and 1930s.

25 Now there is no question even of that, but only
Of holding on to the hard earth so as not to get thrown off,
With an occasional dream, a vision: a robin flies across
The upper corner of the window, you brush your hair away
And cannot quite see, or a wound will flash
30 Against the sweet faces of the others, something like:
This is what you wanted to hear, so why
Did you think of listening to something else? We are all talkers
It is true, but underneath the talk lies
The moving and not wanting to be moved, the loose
35 Meaning, untidy and simple like a threshing floor.[5]

These then were some hazards of the course,
Yet though we knew the course *was* hazards and nothing else
It was still a shock when, almost a quarter of a century later,
The clarity of the rules dawned on you for the first time.
40 *They* were the players, and we who had struggled at the game
Were merely spectators, though subject to its vicissitudes
And moving with it out of the tearful stadium, borne on shoulders, at
        last.
Night after night this message returns, repeated
In the flickering bulbs of the sky, raised past us, taken away from us,
45 Yet ours over and over until the end that is past truth,
The being of our sentences, in the climate that fostered them,
Not ours to own, like a book, but to be with, and sometimes
To be without, alone and desperate.
But the fantasy makes it ours, a kind of fence-sitting
50 Raised to the level of an esthetic ideal. These were moments, years,
Solid with reality, faces, namable events, kisses, heroic acts,
But like the friendly beginning of a geometrical progression
Not too reassuring, as though meaning could be cast aside some day
When it had been outgrown. Better, you said, to stay cowering
55 Like this in the early lessons, since the promise of learning
Is a delusion, and I agreed, adding that
Tomorrow would alter the sense of what had already been learned,
That the learning process is extended in this way, so that from this
        standpoint
None of us ever graduates from college,
60 For time is an emulsion, and probably thinking not to grow up
Is the brightest kind of maturity for us, right now at any rate.
And you see, both of us were right, though nothing
Has somehow come to nothing; the avatars°   incarnations
Of our conforming to the rules and living
65 Around the home have made—well, in a sense, "good citizens" of us,
Brushing the teeth and all that, and learning to accept
The charity of the hard moments as they are doled out,
For this is action, this not being sure, this careless
Preparing, sowing the seeds crooked in the furrow,
70 Making ready to forget, and always coming back
To the mooring of starting out, that day so long ago.

                                                                    1970

5. On which, at harvest time, wheat is separated from chaff (debris).

Ode to Bill

Some things we do take up a lot more time
And are considered a fruitful, natural thing to do.
I am coming out of one way to behave
Into a plowed cornfield. On my left, gulls,
5   On an inland vacation. They seem to mind the way I write.

Or, to take another example: last month
I vowed to write more. What is writing?
Well, in my case, it's getting down on paper
Not thoughts, exactly, but ideas, maybe:
10   Ideas about thoughts. Thoughts is too grand a word.
Ideas is better, though not precisely what I mean.
Someday I'll explain. Not today though.

I feel as though someone had made me a vest
Which I was wearing out of doors into the countryside
15   Out of loyalty to the person, although
There is no one to see, except me
With my inner vision of what I look like.
The wearing is both a duty and a pleasure
Because it absorbs me, absorbs me too much.

20   One horse stands out irregularly against
The land over there. And am I receiving
This vision? Is it mine, or do I already owe it
For other visions, unnoticed and unrecorded
On the great, relaxed curve of time,
25   All the forgotten springs, dropped pebbles,
Songs once heard that then passed out of light
Into everyday oblivion? He moves away slowly,
Looks up and pumps the sky, a lingering
Question. Him too we can sacrifice
30   To the end progress, for we must, we must be moving on.

1975

Paradoxes and Oxymorons

This poem is concerned with language on a very plain level.
Look at it talking to you. You look out a window
Or pretend to fidget. You have it but you don't have it.
You miss it, it misses you. You miss each other.

5   The poem is sad because it wants to be yours, and cannot.
What's a plain level? It is that and other things,
Bringing a system of them into play. Play?
Well, actually, yes, but I consider play to be

A deeper outside thing, a dreamed role-pattern,
10 As in the division of grace these long August days
Without proof. Open-ended. And before you know
It gets lost in the steam and chatter of typewriters.

It has been played once more. I think you exist only
To tease me into doing it, on your level, and then you aren't there
15 Or have adopted a different attitude. And the poem
Has set me softly down beside you. The poem is you.

                                                    1981

Brute Image

It's a question of altitude, or latitude,
Probably. I see them leaving their offices.
By seven they are turning smartly into the drive
To spend the evening with small patterns and odd,
5 Oblique fixtures. Authentic what? Did I say,
Or more likely did you ask is there any
Deliverance from any of this? Why yes,
One boy says, one can step for a moment
Out into the hall. Spells bring some relief
10 And antique shrieking into the night
That was not here before, not like this.
This is only a stand-in for the more formal,
More serious side of it. There is partial symmetry here.
Later one protests: How did we get here
15 This way, unable to stop communicating?
And is it all right for the children to listen,
For the weeds slanting inward, for the cold mice
Until dawn? Now every yard has its tree,
Every heart its valentine, and only we
20 Don't know how to occupy the tent of night
So that what must come to pass shall pass.

                                                    1992

GALWAY KINNELL
b. 1927

First Song

Then it was dusk in Illinois, the small boy
After an afternoon of carting dung
Hung on the rail fence, a sapped thing
Weary to crying. Dark was growing tall

5   And he began to hear the pond frogs all
    Calling on his ear with what seemed their joy.

    Soon their sound was pleasant for a boy
    Listening in the smoky dusk and the nightfall
    Of Illinois, and from the fields two small
10 Boys came bearing cornstalk violins
    And they rubbed the cornstalk bows with resins
    And the three sat there scraping of their joy.

    It was now fine music the frogs and the boys
    Did in the towering Illinois twilight make
15 And into dark in spite of a shoulder's ache
    A boy's hunched body loved out of a stalk
    The first song of his happiness, and the song woke
    His heart to the darkness and into the sadness of joy.

                                                    1960

The Correspondence School Instructor Says Goodbye to His Poetry Students

    Goodbye, lady in Bangor, who sent me
    snapshots of yourself, after definitely hinting
    you were beautiful; goodbye,
    Miami Beach urologist, who enclosed plain
5   brown envelopes for the return of your *very*
    "Clinical Sonnets"; goodbye, manufacturer
    of brassieres on the Coast, whose eclogues
    give the fullest treatment in literature yet
    to the sagging breast motif; goodbye, you in San Quentin,[1]
10 who wrote, "Being German my hero is Hitler,"
    instead of "Sincerely yours," at the end of long,
    neat-scripted letters demolishing
    the pre-Raphaelites:[2]

    I swear to you, it was just my way
15 of cheering myself up, as I licked
    the stamped, self-addressed envelopes,
    the game I had
    of trying to guess which one of you, this time,
    had poisoned his glue. I did care.
20 I did read each poem entire.

---

1. Prison in California.
2. A group of nineteenth-century English painters and poets, who wished to restore the methods and spirit of the arts before the Italian painter Raphael (1483–1520).

I did say what I thought was the truth
in the mildest words I knew. And now,
in this poem, or chopped prose, not any better,
I realize, than those troubled lines
I kept sending back to you,
I have to say I am relieved it is over:
at the end I could feel only pity
for that urge toward more life
your poems kept smothering in words, the smell
of which, days later, would tingle
in your nostrils as new, God-given impulses
to write.

Goodbye,
you who are, for me, the postmarks again
of shattered towns—Xenia, Burnt Cabins, Hornell—
their loneliness
given away in poems, only their solitude kept.

1968

After Making Love We Hear Footsteps

For I can snore like a bullhorn
or play loud music
or sit up talking with any reasonably sober Irishman
and Fergus will only sink deeper
into his dreamless sleep, which goes by all in one flash,
but let there be that heavy breathing
or a stifled come-cry anywhere in the house
and he will wrench himself awake
and make for it on the run—as now, we lie together,
after making love, quiet, touching along the length of our bodies,
familiar touch of the long-married,
and he appears—in his baseball pajamas, it happens,
the neck opening so small he has to screw them on—
and flops down between us and hugs us and snuggles himself to sleep,
his face gleaming with satisfaction at being this very child.

In the half darkness we look at each other
and smile
and touch arms across this little, startlingly muscled body—
this one whom habit of memory propels to the ground of his making,
sleeper only the mortal sounds can sing awake,
this blessing love gives again into our arms.

1980, 1993

W. S. MERWIN
b. 1927

The Drunk in the Furnace

For a good decade
The furnace stood in the naked gully, fireless
And vacant as any hat. Then when it was
No more to them than a hulking black fossil
5   To erode unnoticed with the rest of the junk-hill
By the poisonous creek, and rapidly to be added
      To their ignorance.

      They were afterwards astonished
To confirm, one morning, a twist of smoke like a pale
10   Resurrection, staggering out of its chewed hole,
And to remark then other tokens that someone,
Cozily bolted behind the eye-holed iron
Door of the drafty burner, had there established
      His bad castle.

15   Where he gets his spirits
It's a mystery. But the stuff keeps him musical:
Hammer-and-anviling with poker and bottle
To his jugged bellowings, till the last groaning clang
As he collapses onto the rioting
20   Springs of a litter of car-seats ranged on the grates,
      To sleep like an iron pig.[1]

      In their tar-paper church
On a text about stoke-holes[2] that are sated never
Their Reverend lingers. They nod and hate trespassers.
25   When the furnace wakes, though, all afternoon
Their witless offspring flock like piped rats[3] to its siren
Crescendo, and agape on the crumbling ridge
      Stand in a row and learn.

1960

Odysseus[4]

For George Kirstein

Always the setting forth was the same,
Same sea, same dangers waiting for him
As though he had got nowhere but older.

1. A crude block poured from a smelting furnace.
2. Furnace mouths.
3. As in the German folktale about the Pied Piper of Hamelin, whose playing lured first the rats and then the children out of town.
4. Hero of Homer's *Odyssey*, in which, after the Trojan War, he wanders for ten years, attempting to return to his home island, Ithaca.

Behind him on the receding shore
5   The identical reproaches, and somewhere
Out before him, the unraveling patience
He was wedded to. There were the islands
Each with its woman and twining welcome
To be navigated, and one to call "home."[5]
10   The knowledge of all that he betrayed
Grew till it was the same whether he stayed
Or went. Therefore he went. And what wonder
If sometimes he could not remember
Which was the one who wished on his departure
15   Perils that he could never sail through,
And which, improbable, remote, and true,
Was the one he kept sailing home to?

1960

Separation

Your absence has gone through me
Like thread through a needle.
Everything I do is stitched with its color.

1973

Losing a Language

A breath leaves the sentences and does not come back
yet the old still remember something that they could say

but they know now that such things are no longer believed
and the young have fewer words

5   many of the things the words were about
no longer exist

the noun for standing in mist by a haunted tree
the verb for I

the children will not repeat
10 the phrases their parents speak

somebody has persuaded them
that it is better to say everything differently

so that they can be admired somewhere
farther and farther away

---

5. Alluding to Odysseus's encounters with the sorceress Circe and the nymph Calypso, and to his wife,
Penelope, waiting for him on Ithaca.

15   where nothing that is here is known
      we have little to say to each other

      we are wrong and dark
      in the eyes of the new owners

      the radio is incomprehensible
20   the day is glass

      when there is a voice at the door it is foreign
      everywhere instead of a name there is a lie

      nobody has seen it happening
      nobody remembers

25   this is what the words were made
      to prophesy

      here are the extinct feathers
      here is the rain we saw

                                                      1988

Whoever You Are

      By now when you say *I stop somewhere waiting for you*[6]
      who is the I and who come to that is you

      there are those words that were written a long time ago
      by someone I have read about who they assure me is you

5   the handwriting is still running over the pages
      but the one who has disappeared from the script is you

      I wonder what age you were when those words came to you
      though I think it is not any age at all that is you

      stopping and waiting under the soles of my feet
10   this morning this waking this looking up is you

      but nothing has stopped in fact and I do not know
      what is waiting and surely that also is you

      every time you say it you seem to be speaking
      through me to some me not yet there who I suppose is you

15   you said you were stopping and waiting before I was here
      maybe the one I heard say it then is you

                                                      1999

---

6. Final line of Walt Whitman's "Song of Myself" (see p. 1066).

CHARLES TOMLINSON
b. 1927

Farewell to Van Gogh[1]

The quiet deepens. You will not persuade
    One leaf of the accomplished, steady, darkening
Chestnut-tower to displace itself
    With more of violence than the air supplies
5   When, gathering dusk, the pond brims evenly
    And we must be content with stillness.

Unhastening, daylight withdraws from us its shapes
    Into their central calm. Stone by stone
Your rhetoric is dispersed until the earth
10   Becomes once more the earth, the leaves
A sharp partition against cooling blue.

Farewell, and for your instructive frenzy
    Gratitude. The world does not end tonight
And the fruit that we shall pick tomorrow
15   Await us, weighing the unstripped bough.

1960

The Picture of J.T. in a Prospect of Stone[2]

     What should one
       wish a child
         and that, one's own
     emerging
5   from between
        the stone lips
    of a sheep-stile[3]
       that divides
         village graves
10 and village green?
      —Wish her
        the constancy of stone.
     —But stone
      is hard.
15   —Say, rather
    it resists
       the slow corrosives
       and the flight

1. Vincent Van Gogh (1853–1890), Dutch Post-impressionist painter, who suffered bouts of insanity and finally killed himself.
2. Cf. Andrew Marvell, "The Picture of Little T. C. in a Prospect of Flowers" (p. 481).
3. Steps that enable a person to climb over a fence or wall.

of time
20   and yet it takes
          the play, the fluency
from light.
          —How would you know
          the gift you'd give
25 was the gift
          she'd wish to have?
              —Gift is giving,
gift is meaning:
      first
30   I'd give
then let her
      live with it
          to prove
its quality the better and
35   thus learn
          to love
what (to begin with)
      she might spurn.
          —You'd
40 moralize a gift?
          —I'd have her
              understand
the gift I gave her.
          —And so she shall
45   but let her play
her innocence away
      emerging
          as she does
between
50   her doom (unknown),
          her unmown green.

                                    1963

Mr. Brodsky

I had heard
before, of an
American who would have preferred
to be an Indian;
5   but not
until Mr. Brodsky, of one
whose professed and long
pondered-on passion
was to become a Scot,
10 who even sent for haggis⁴ and oatcakes

---

4. Traditional Scottish dish, consisting of minced heart, lungs, and liver of a sheep or calf, boiled in an artificial bag (or the animal's stomach) with oatmeal.

across continent.
Having read him
in Cambridge English
a verse or two
15 from MacDiarmid,[5]
I was invited
to repeat the reading
before a Burns Night Gathering[6]
where the Balmoral Pipers
20 of Albuquerque would
play in the haggis
out of its New York tin.
Of course, I said
No. No. I could *not* go
25 and then
half-regretted I had not been.
But to console
and cure the wish, came
Mr. Brodsky, bringing
30 his pipes and played
until the immense, distended
bladder of leather seemed
it could barely contain its water—
tears (idle
35 tears) for the bridal of Annie Laurie[7]
and Morton J. Brodsky.
A bagpipe in a dwelling is
a resonant instrument
and there he stood
40 lost in the gorse
the heather or whatever
six thousand
miles and more
from the infection's source,
45 in our neo–New Mexican parlour
where I had heard
before of an
American who would have preferred
to be merely an Indian.

1966

Ararat[8]

We shall sleep-out together through the dark
The earth's slow voyage across centuries

---

5. Hugh MacDiarmid, pen name of the Scottish poet Christopher Murray Grieve (1892–1978; see pp. 1376–80).
6. Meeting devoted to Scottish culture, on the evening of January 25, birthday of the Scottish poet Robert Burns (1759–1796; see pp. 747–60).

7. Subject of an anonymous Scottish folk song. "Tears, idle tears" are the first words of a song in Alfred, Lord Tennyson's narrative poem *The Princess* (see p. 995).
8. The mountain on which Noah's ark came to rest (Genesis 6–10).

Towards whatever Ararat its ark
Is steering for. Our atoms then will feel
5   The jarring and arrival of that keel
In timelessness, and rise through galaxies,
Motes starred by the first and final light to show
Whether those shores are habitable or no.

1987

JAMES WRIGHT
1927–1980

A Note Left in Jimmy Leonard's Shack

Near the dry river's water-mark we found
      Your brother Minnegan,
Flopped like a fish against the muddy ground.
Beany, the kid whose yellow hair turns green,
5   Told me to find you, even in the rain,
      And tell you he was drowned.

I hid behind the chassis on the bank,
      The wreck of someone's Ford:
I was afraid to come and wake you drunk:
10 You told me once the waking up was hard,
The daylight beating at you like a board.
      Blood in my stomach sank.

Besides, you told him never to go out
      Along the river-side
15 Drinking and singing, clattering about.
You might have thrown a rock at me and cried
I was to blame, I let him fall in the road
      And pitch down on his side.

Well, I'll get hell enough when I get home
20   For coming up this far,
Leaving the note, and running as I came.
I'll go and tell my father where you are.
You'd better go find Minnegan before
      Policemen hear and come.

25 Beany went home, and I got sick and ran,
      You old son of a bitch.
You better hurry down to Minnegan;
He's drunk or dying now, I don't know which,
Rolled in the roots and garbage like a fish.
30   The poor old man.

1959

A Blessing

Just off the highway to Rochester, Minnesota,
Twilight bounds softly forth on the grass.
And the eyes of those two Indian ponies
Darken with kindness.
5   They have come gladly out of the willows
To welcome my friend and me.
We step over the barbed wire into the pasture
Where they have been grazing all day, alone.
They ripple tensely, they can hardly contain their happiness
10   That we have come.
They bow shyly as wet swans. They love each other.
There is no loneliness like theirs.
At home once more,
They begin munching the young tufts of spring in the darkness.
15   I would like to hold the slenderer one in my arms,
For she has walked over to me
And nuzzled my left hand.
She is black and white,
Her mane falls wild on her forehead,
20   And the light breeze moves me to caress her long ear
That is delicate as the skin over a girl's wrist.
Suddenly I realize
That if I stepped out of my body I would break
Into blossom.

1963

Speak

To speak in a flat voice
Is all that I can do.
I have gone every place
Asking for you.
5   Wondering where to turn
And how the search would end
And the last streetlight spin
Above me blind.

Then I returned rebuffed
10   And saw under the sun
The race not to the swift
Nor the battle won.[1]
Liston[2] dives in the tank,
Lord, in Lewiston, Maine,

---

1. As in Ecclesiastes 9.11: "I returned, and saw under the sun, that the race is not to the swift, nor the battle to the strong. . . ."

2. In a controversial bout for the heavyweight boxing title in 1965, Cassius Clay knocked out Sonny Liston in one minute.

15   And Ernie Doty's drunk
    In hell again.

    And Jenny, oh my Jenny
    Whom I love, rhyme be damned,
    Has broken her spare beauty
20   In a whorehouse old.
    She left her new baby
    In a bus-station can,
    And sprightly danced away
    Through Jacksontown.[3]

25   Which is a place I know,
    One where I got picked up
    A few shrunk years ago
    By a good cop.
    Believe it, Lord, or not.
30   Don't ask me who he was.
    I speak of flat defeat
    In a flat voice.

    I have gone forward with
    Some, few lonely some.
35   They have fallen to death.
    I die with them.
    Lord, I have loved Thy cursed,
    The beauty of Thy house:
    Come down. Come down. Why dost
40   Thou hide thy face?[4]

1968

PETER DAVISON
b. 1928

Equinox 1980

    In the stillness after dawn we two
        paddled a noiseless boat
    before wakefall across
        a bay smooth as a mirror,
5   changeless as its glass.
        Not a whisper of passage.
    Hardly a single stir
        inside the horizon
    except for the rippling
10   wrinkles pushed by our prow

3. Town in central Ohio.
4. As in Job 13.24: "Wherefore hidest thou thy face, and holdest me for thine enemy?"

and the faraway swoop and flurry
    of a squadron of terns.
The tide at its landward edge
    ignited a smudge of commotion,
15 skittering sandpipers
    along the farther shore.
In all the days of our marriage
    we had never seen
so unruffled a morning:
20   never had any event
shimmered with so costly a light
    as we ascended the meandering
creek in our sweet boat,
    surprising no one except
25 a bright-eyed otter.
     Pushed by mere hints
from our paddles,
    we rode up the thickening tide
among heavy wands
30   of ripe marsh grass
that wagged seed-bundles
    high above our heads.

Neither one speaking,
    we rose to go ashore
35 and lugged away
    our featherweight kayak
to winter quarters,
    knowing as we stowed it
that this would be the last time,
40   that we would never set out to sea
together again.

1989

Peaches

A mouthful of language to swallow:
stretches of beach, sweet clinches,
breaches in walls, pleached° branches;   *plaited*
britches hauled over haunches;
5 hunched leeches, wrenched teachers.
What English can do: ransack
the warmth that chuckles beneath
fuzzed surfaces, smooth velvet
richness, plashy° juices.   *splashy*
10 I beseech you, peach,
clench me into the sweetness
of your reaches.

1989

DONALD HALL
b. 1928

Exile[1]

A boy who played and talked and read with me
Fell from a maple tree.

I loved her, but I told her I did not,
And wept, and then forgot.

5   I walked the streets where I was born and grew,
And all the streets were new.

1951–55   1969

From The One Day[2]

Prophecy

I will strike down wooden houses; I will burn aluminum
clapboard skin; I will strike down garages
where crimson Toyotas sleep side by side; I will explode
palaces of gold, silver, and alabaster: — the summer
5   great house and its folly together. Where shopping malls
spread plywood and plaster out, and roadhouses
serve steak and potatoskins beside Alaska king crab;
where triangular flags proclaim tribes of identical campers;
where airplanes nose to tail exhale kerosene,
10   weeds and ashes will drowse in continual twilight.

I reject the old house and the new car; I reject
Tory and Whig[3] together; I reject the argument
that modesty of ambition is sensible because the bigger
they are the harder they fall; I reject Waterford;[4]
15   I reject the five and dime; I reject Romulus and Remus;[5]
I reject Martha's Vineyard and the slamdunk contest;
I reject leaded panes; I reject the appointment made

1. Many versions of this poem exist; cf. a much longer one, written earlier but published later (in Hall's 1990 *Old and New Poems*).
2. A three-part, book-length poem written over several decades. "Prophecy" is the first of the "Four Classic Texts" within the poem's central section, which is introduced with two epigraphs: "Of the opposites that which tends to birth or creation is called war or strife. That which tends to destruction by fire is called concord or peace" (Heraclitus) and "Poetry is preparation for death" (Nadezhda Mandelstam). The two principal voices of the poem, a female sculptor and the author, are set aside here for a "general consciousness that narrates. . . . There are many borrowings and allu-

sions" [Hall's note]. The tone of "Prophecy" suggests particularly an indebtedness to Heraclitus (ca. 540–ca. 480 B.C.E.), the Greek philosopher who argued that the essential stuff of the universe is pure fire, and to the first part of the book of Isaiah, who in a vision saw the vain and the wicked destroyed by fire. Nadezhda Mandelstam (1899–1980), memoirist, was married to the Russian poet Osip Mandelstam (1891–1938).
3. Historically, opposing parties in British politics.
4. Brand of crystal made in Waterford, Ireland.
5. In Roman mythology, twin sons of the god Mars and the mortal Rhea Silvia; descendants of the hero Aeneas; founders of the city of Rome.

at the tennis net or on the seventeenth green; I reject
the Professional Bowlers Tour; I reject matchboxes;
20 I reject purple bathrooms with purple soap in them.

Men who lie awake worrying about taxes, vomiting
at dawn, whose hands shake as they administer Valium, —
skin will peel from the meat of their thighs.
Armies that march all day with elephants past pyramids
25 and roll pulling missiles past generals weary of saluting
and past president-emperors splendid in cloth-of-gold, —
soft rumps of armies will dissipate in rain. Where square
miles of corn waver in Minnesota, where tobacco ripens
in Carolina and apples in New Hampshire, where wheat
30 turns Kansas green, where pulpmills stink in Oregon, —

dust will blow in the darkness and cactus die
before it flowers. Where skiers wait for chairlifts,
wearing money, low raspberries will part rib bones.
Where the drive-in church raises a chromium cross,
35 dandelions and milkweed will straggle through blacktop.
I will strike from the ocean with waves afire;
I will strike from the hill with rainclouds of lava;
I will strike from darkened air
with melanoma in the shape of decorative hexagonals.
40 I will strike down embezzlers and eaters of snails.

I reject Japanese smoked oysters, potted chrysanthemums
allowed to die, Tupperware parties, Ronald McDonald,
Kaposi's sarcoma, the Taj Mahal, Holsteins wearing
electronic necklaces, the Algonquin, Tunisian aqueducts,
45 Phi Beta Kappa keys, the Hyatt Embarcadero, carpenters
jogging on the median, and betrayal that engorges
the corrupt heart longing for criminal surrender.
I reject shadows in the corner of the atrium
where Phyllis or Phoebe speaks with Billy or Marc
50 who says that afternoons are best although not reliable.

Your children will wander looting the shopping malls
for forty years, suffering for your idleness,
until the last dwarf body rots in a parking lot.
I will strike down lobbies and restaurants in motels
55 carpeted with shaggy petrochemicals
from Maine to Hilton Head, from the Skagit[6] to Tucson.
I will strike down hang gliders, wiry adventurous boys;

6. A bay and county in Washington State. *Hilton Head:* resort in South Carolina.

their thigh bones will snap, their brains
slide from their skulls. I will strike down
60   families cooking wildboar in New Mexico backyards.

Then landscape will clutter with incapable machinery,
acres of vacant airplanes and schoolbuses, ploughs
with seedlings sprouting and turning brown through colters.[7]
Unlettered dwarves will burrow for warmth and shelter
65   in the caves of dynamos and Plymouths, dying
of old age at seventeen. Tribes wandering
in the wilderness of their ignorant desolation,
who suffer from your idleness, will burn your illuminated
missals to warm their rickety bodies.
70   Terrorists assemble plutonium because you are idle

and industrious. The whip-poor-will shrivels
and the pickerel chokes under the government of self-love.
Vacancy burns air so that you strangle without oxygen
like rats in a biologist's bell jar. The living god sharpens
75   the scythe of my prophecy to strike down red poppies
and blue cornflowers. When priests and policemen
strike my body's match, Jehovah will flame out;
Jehovah will suck air from the vents of bombshelters.
Therefore let the Buick swell until it explodes;
80   therefore let anorexia starve and bulimia engorge.

When Elzira leaves the house wearing her tennis dress
and drives her black Porsche to meet Abraham,
quarrels, returns to husband and children, and sobs
asleep, drunk, unable to choose among them, —
85   lawns and carpets will turn into tar together
with lovers, husbands, and children.
Fat will boil in the sacs of children's clear skin.
I will strike down the nations astronauts and judges;
I will strike down Babylon,[8] I will strike acrobats,
90   I will strike algae and the white birches.

Because professors of law teach ethics in dumbshow,
let the colonel become president; because chief executive
officers and commissars collect down for pillows,
let the injustice of cities burn city and suburb;
95   let the countryside burn; let the pineforests of Maine
explode like a kitchenmatch and the Book of Kells[9] turn

7. Cutting tools attached to plows.
8. The city to which the Jews were carried in cap-
tivity (2 Kings 24–25); also, a great but fallen city,
epitomizing sinfulness (Revelation 18).
9. An ornately illustrated manuscript of the Gos-
pels of the Christian Scriptures, produced by Scot-

ash in a microsecond; let oxen and athletes
flash into grease:—I return to Appalachian rocks;
I shall eat bread; I shall prophesy through millennia
100   of Jehovah's day until the sky reddens over cities:

Then houses will burn, even houses of alabaster;
the sky will disappear like a scroll rolled up
and hidden in a cave from the industries of idleness.
Mountains will erupt and vanish, becoming deserts,
105   and the sea wash over the sea's lost islands
and the earth split open like a corpse's gassy
stomach and the sun turn as black as a widow's skirt
and the full moon grow red with blood swollen inside it
and stars fall from the sky like wind-blown apples, —
110   while Babylon's managers burn in the rage of the Lamb.[1]

1988

Independence Day Letter

Five A.M., the Fourth of July.
I walk by Eagle Pond[2] with the dog,
wearing my leather coat
against the clear early chill,
5   looking at water lilies that clutch
cool yellow fists together,
as I undertake another day
twelve weeks after the Tuesday
we learned that you would die.

10   This afternoon I'll pay bills
and write a friend about her book
and watch Red Sox baseball.
I'll walk Gussie again.
I'll microwave some Stouffer's.[3]
15   A woman will drive from Bristol
to examine your mother's Ford
parked beside your Saab
in the dead women's used car lot.

Tonight the Andover fireworks
20   will have to go on without me
as I go to bed early, reading
The Man Without Qualities[4]
with insufficient attention

---

tish and Irish monks and completed in Kells, Ireland, in the ninth century.
1. The Lamb of God; i.e., Jesus. This stanza is a freely reconceived paraphrase of Revelation 6.12–16.

2. Pond near Hall's home in New Hampshire. Bristol and Andover are nearby towns.
3. Brand of frozen meals.
4. Unfinished, massive novel by the Austrian author Robert Musil (1880–1942).

because I keep watching you die.
25 Tomorrow I will wake at five
to the tenth Wednesday
after the Wednesday we buried you.

1998

THOMAS KINSELLA
b. 1928

Another September

Dreams fled away, this country bedroom, raw
With the touch of the dawn, wrapped in a minor peace,
Hears through an open window the garden draw
Long pitch black breaths, lay bare its apple trees,
5 Ripe pear trees, brambles, windfall-sweetened soil,
Exhale rough sweetness against the starry slates.
Nearer the river sleeps St. John's,[1] all toil
Locked fast inside a dream with iron gates.

Domestic Autumn, like an animal
10 Long used to handling by those countrymen,
Rubs her kind hide against the bedroom wall
Sensing a fragrant child come back again
—Not this half-tolerated consciousness,
Its own cold season never done,
15 But that unspeaking daughter, growing less
Familiar where we fell asleep as one.

Wakeful moth-wings blunder near a chair,
Toss their light shell at the glass, and go
To inhabit the living starlight. Stranded hair
20 Stirs on the still linen. It is as though
The black breathing that billows her sleep, her name,
Drugged under judgment, waned and—bearing daggers
And balances—down the lampless darkness they came,
Moving like women: Justice, Truth, such figures.

1958

Ancestor

I was going up to say something,
and stopped. Her profile against the curtains
was old, and dark like a hunting bird's.

---

1. Church dedicated to St. John the Evangelist.

It was the way she perched on the high stool,
5   staring into herself, with one fist
gripping the side of the barrier around her desk
—or her head held by something, from inside.
And not caring for anything around her
or anyone there by the shelves.
10   I caught a faint smell, musky and queer.

I may have made some sound—she stopped rocking
and pressed her fist in her lap; then she stood up
and shut down the lid of the desk, and turned the key.
She shoved a small bottle under her aprons
15   and came toward me, darkening the passageway.

Ancestor . . . among sweet- and fruit-boxes.
Her black heart . . .
                Was that a sigh?
—brushing by me in the shadows,
20   with her heaped aprons, through the red hangings
to the scullery, and down to the back room.

                                                  1973

Tear

I was sent in to see her.
A fringe of jet drops
chattered at my ear
as I went in through the hangings.

5   I was swallowed in chambery dusk.
My heart shrank
at the smell of disused
organs and sour kidney.

The black aprons I used to
10   bury my face in
were folded at the foot of the bed
in the last watery light from the window

(Go in and say goodbye to her)
and I was carried off
15   to unfathomable depths.
I turned to look at her.

She stared at the ceiling
and puffed her cheek, distracted,
propped high in the bed
20   resting for the next attack.

The covers were gathered close
up to her mouth,
that the lines of ill-temper still
marked. Her grey hair

25 was loosened out like
a young woman's all over
the pillow, mixed with the shadows
criss-crossing her forehead

and at her mouth and eyes,
30 like a web of strands tying down her head
and tangling down toward the shadow
eating away the floor at my feet.

I couldn't stir at first, nor wished to,
for fear she might turn and tempt me
35 (my own father's mother)
with open mouth

—with some fierce wheedling whisper—
to hide myself one last time
against her, and bury my
40 self in her drying mud.

Was I to kiss her? As soon
kiss the damp that crept
in the flowered walls
of this pit.

45 Yet I had to kiss.
I knelt by the bulk of the death bed
and sank my face in the chill
and smell of her black aprons.

Snuff and musk, the folds against my eyelids,
50 carried me into a derelict place
smelling of ash: unseen walls and roofs
rustled like breathing.

I found myself disturbing
dead ashes for any trace
55 of warmth, when far off
in the vaults a single drop

splashed. And I found
what I was looking for
—not heat nor fire,
60 not any comfort,

but her voice, soft, talking to someone
about my father: "God help him, he cried
big tears over there by the machine
for the poor little thing." Bright

65 drops on the wooden lid for
my infant sister. My own
wail of child-animal grief
was soon done, with any early guess

at sad dullness and tedious pain
70 and lives bitter with hard bondage.
How I tasted it now—
her heart beating in my mouth!

She drew an uncertain breath
and pushed at the clothes
75 and shuddered tiredly.
I broke free

and left the room
promising myself
when she was really dead
80 I would really kiss.

My grandfather half looked up
from the fireplace as I came out,
and shrugged and turned back
with a deaf stare to the heat.

85 I fidgeted beside him for a minute
and went out to the shop.
It was still bright there
and I felt better able to breathe.

Old age can digest
90 anything: the commotion
at Heaven's gate—the struggle
in store for you all your life.

How long and hard it is
before you get to Heaven,
95 unless like little Agnes
you vanish with early tears.

1973

PHILIP LEVINE
b. 1928

They Feed They Lion

Out of burlap sacks, out of bearing butter,
Out of black bean and wet slate bread,
Out of the acids of rage, the candor of tar,
Out of creosote, gasoline, drive shafts, wooden dollies,
5   They Lion grow.
             Out of the gray hills
Of industrial barns, out of rain, out of bus ride,
West Virginia to Kiss My Ass, out of buried aunties,
Mothers hardening like pounded stumps, out of stumps,
10   Out of the bones' need to sharpen and the muscles' to stretch,
They Lion grow.
             Earth is eating trees, fence posts,
Gutted cars, earth is calling in her little ones,
"Come home, Come home!" From pig balls,
15   From the ferocity of pig driven to holiness,
From the furred ear and the full jowl come
The repose of the hung belly, from the purpose
They Lion grow.
             From the sweet glues of the trotters[1]
20   Come the sweet kinks of the fist, from the full flower
Of the hams the thorax[2] of caves,
From "Bow Down" come "Rise Up,"
Come they Lion from the reeds of shovels,
The grained arm that pulls the hands,
25   They Lion grow.
             From my five arms and all my hands,
From all my white sins forgiven, they feed,
From my car passing under the stars,
They Lion, from my children inherit,
30   From the oak turned to a wall, they Lion,
From they sack and they belly opened
And all that was hidden burning on the oil-stained earth
They feed they Lion and he comes.

                          1972

You Can Have It

My brother comes home from work
and climbs the stairs to our room.
I can hear the bed groan and his shoes drop
one by one. You can have it, he says.

---

1. Cooked pigs' feet.   2. Chest cavity.

5   The moonlight streams in the window
and his unshaven face is whitened
like the face of the moon. He will sleep
long after noon and waken to find me gone.

Thirty years will pass before I remember
10   that moment when suddenly I knew each man
has one brother who dies when he sleeps
and sleeps when he rises to face this life,

and that together they are only one man
sharing a heart that always labors, hands
15   yellowed and cracked, a mouth that gasps
for breath and asks, Am I gonna make it?

All night at the ice plant he had fed
the chute its silvery blocks, and then I
stacked cases of orange soda for the children
20   of Kentucky, one gray boxcar at a time

with always two more waiting. We were twenty
for such a short time and always in
the wrong clothes, crusted with dirt
and sweat. I think now we were never twenty.

25   In 1948 in the city of Detroit, founded
by de la Mothe Cadillac for the distant purposes
of Henry Ford,[3] no one wakened or died,
no one walked the streets or stoked a furnace,

for there was no such year, and now
30   that year has fallen off all the old newspapers,
calendars, doctors' appointments, bonds,
wedding certificates, drivers licenses.

The city slept. The snow turned to ice.
The ice to standing pools or rivers
35   racing in the gutters. Then bright grass rose
between the thousands of cracked squares,

and that grass died. I give you back 1948.
I give you all the years from then
to the coming one. Give me back the moon
40   with its frail light falling across a face.

---

3. American automobile manufacturer (1863–1947), associated with Detroit. Antoine Laumet de la Mothe Cadillac (1658–1730), born in France, established a fur-trade post, later the city of Detroit; Cadillac cars are named for him.

Give me back my young brother, hard
and furious, with wide shoulders and a curse
for God and burning eyes that look upon
all creation and say, You can have it.

1979

The Simple Truth

I bought a dollar and a half's worth of small red potatoes,
took them home, boiled them in their jackets
and ate them for dinner with a little butter and salt.
Then I walked through the dried fields
5   on the edge of town. In middle June the light
hung on in the dark furrows at my feet,
and in the mountain oaks overhead the birds
were gathering for the night, the jays and mockers
squawking back and forth, the finches still darting
10   into the dusty light. The woman who sold me
the potatoes was from Poland; she was someone
out of my childhood in a pink spangled sweater and sunglasses
praising the perfection of all her fruits and vegetables
at the road-side stand and urging me to taste
15   even the pale, raw sweet corn trucked all the way,
she swore, from New Jersey. "Eat, eat," she said,
"Even if you don't I'll say you did."
                                    Some things
you know all your life. They are so simple and true
20   they must be said without elegance, meter and rhyme,
they must be laid on the table beside the salt shaker,
the glass of water, the absence of light gathering
in the shadows of picture frames, they must be
naked and alone, they must stand for themselves.
25   My friend Henri and I arrived at this together in 1965
before I went away, before he began to kill himself,
and the two of us to betray our love. Can you taste
what I'm saying? It is onions or potatoes, a pinch
of simple salt, the wealth of melting butter, it is obvious,
30   it stays in the back of your throat like a truth
you never uttered because the time was always wrong,
it stays there for the rest of your life, unspoken,
made of that dirt we call earth, the metal we call salt,
in a form we have no words for, and you live on it.

1994

ANNE SEXTON
1928–1974

The Truth the Dead Know

For my mother, born March 1902, died March 1959,
and my father, born February 1900, died June 1959

Gone, I say and walk from church,
refusing the stiff procession to the grave,
letting the dead ride alone in the hearse.
It is June. I am tired of being brave.

5   We drive to the Cape. I cultivate
myself where the sun gutters from the sky,
where the sea swings in like an iron gate
and we touch. In another country people die.

My darling, the wind falls in like stones
10   from the whitehearted water and when we touch
we enter touch entirely. No one's alone.
Men kill for this, or for as much.

And what of the dead? They lie without shoes
in their stone boats. They are more like stone
15   than the sea would be if it stopped. They refuse
to be blessed, throat, eye and knucklebone.

1962

And One for My Dame[1]

A born salesman,
my father made all his dough
by selling wool to Fieldcrest, Woolrich and Faribo.

A born talker,
5   he could sell one hundred wet-down bales
of that white stuff. He could clock the miles and sales

and make it pay.
At home each sentence he would utter
had first pleased the buyer who'd paid him off in butter.

10   Each word
had been tried over and over, at any rate,
on the man who was sold by the man who filled my plate.

1. Allusion to the nursery rhyme "Baa Baa Black Sheep," which ends "One for the master / And one for the dame, / And one for the little boy / Who lives down the lane."

My father hovered
over the Yorkshire pudding and the beef:
15   a peddler, a hawker, a merchant and an Indian chief.

Roosevelt! Willkie! and war![2]
How suddenly gauche I was
with my old-maid heart and my funny teenage applause.

Each night at home
20   my father was in love with maps
while the radio fought its battles with Nazis and Japs.

Except when he hid
in his bedroom on a three-day drunk,
he typed out complex itineraries, packed his trunk,

25   his matched luggage
and pocketed a confirmed reservation,
his heart already pushing over the red routes of the nation.

I sit at my desk
each night with no place to go,
30   opening the wrinkled maps of Milwaukee and Buffalo,

the whole U.S.,
its cemeteries, its arbitrary time zones,
through routes like small veins, capitals like small stones.

He died on the road,
35   his heart pushed from neck to back,
his white hanky signaling from the window of the Cadillac.

My husband,
as blue-eyed as a picture book, sells wool:
boxes of card waste, laps and rovings he can pull

40   to the thread
and say *Leicester, Rambouillet, Merino,*[3]
a half-blood, it's greasy and thick, yellow as old snow.

And when you drive off, my darling,
Yes, sir! Yes, sir! It's one for my dame,
45   your sample cases branded with my father's name,

your itinerary open,
its tolls ticking and greedy,
its highways built up like new loves, raw and speedy.

1966

2. Franklin Delano Roosevelt (1882–1945), U.S. president during World War II, was opposed by Wendell Lewis Willkie (1892–1944).
3. Types of wool.

L. E. SISSMAN
1928–1976

From Dying: An Introduction[1]

IV. Path. Report

Bruisingly cradled in a Harvard chair
Whose orange arms cramp my pink ones, and whose black
Back stamps my back with splat marks, I receive
The brunt of the pathology report,
5   Bitingly couched in critical terms of my
Tissue of fabrications, which is bad.
That Tyrian° specimen on the limelit stage   *purplish*
Surveyed by Dr. Cyclops,[2] magnified
Countless diameters on its thick slide,
10 Turns out to end in -oma.[3] "But be glad
These things are treatable today," I'm told.
"Why, fifteen years ago—" a dark and grave-
Shaped pause. "But now, a course of radiation, and—"
Sun rays break through. "And if you want X-ray,
15 You've come to the right place." A history,
A half-life of the hospital. Marie
Curie must have endowed it. Cyclotrons,[4]
Like missile silos, lurk within its walls.
It's reassuring, anyway. But bland
20 And middle-classic as these environs are,
And sanguine as his measured words may be,
And soft his handshake, the webbed, inky hand
Locked on the sill, and the unshaven face
Biding outside the window still appall
25 Me as I leave the assignation place.

V. Outbound

Outside, although November by the clock,
Has a thick smell of spring,
And everything—
The low clouds lit
5   Fluorescent green by city lights;
The molten, hissing stream
Of white car lights, cooling
To red and vanishing;
The leaves,
10 Still running from last summer, chattering
Across the pocked concrete;
The wind in trees;
The ones and twos,

---

1. A long poem in five parts.
2. Title character of a 1940 science fiction/horror movie, a "mad scientist" who shrinks people; named for the one-eyed giants of Greek myth.
3. I.e., a cancer.

4. Accelerators in which particles are propelled in spiral paths. *Half-life:* time required for half the atoms of a radioactive substance to disintegrate. Marie Curie (1867–1934), Polish physicist in France, codiscoverer of radium.

The twos and threes
15 Of college girls,
Each shining in the dark,
Each carrying
A book or books,
Each laughing to her friend
20 At such a night in fall;
The two-and-twos
Of boys and girls who lean
Together in an A and softly walk
Slowly from lamp to lamp,
25 Alternatively lit
And nighted; Autumn Street,
Astonishingly named, a rivulet
Of asphalt twisting up and back
To some spring out of sight—and everything
30 Recalls one fall
Twenty-one years ago, when I,
A freshman, opening
A green door just across the river,
Found the source
35 Of spring in that warm night,
Surprised the force
That sent me on my way
And set me down
Today. Tonight. Through my
40 Invisible new veil
Of finity, I see
November's world—
Low scud, slick street, three giggling girls—
As, oddly, not as sombre
45 As December,
But as green
As anything:
As spring.

1968

A Deathplace

Very few people know where they will die,
But I do: in a brick-faced hospital,
Divided, not unlike Caesarean Gaul,[5]
Into three parts: the Dean Memorial
5 Wing, in the classic cast of 1910,
Green-grated in unglazed, Aeolian
Embrasures:[6] the Maud Wiggin Building, which
Commemorates a dog-jawed Boston bitch
Who fought the brass[7] down to their whipcord knees

5. Roman emperor Julius Caesar (100–44 B.C.E.) conquered Gaul and divided it into three parts.
6. Recesses of doors or windows in the shape of an Aeolian harp.
7. High-ranking military officers.

10 In World War I, and won enlisted men
    Some decent hospitals, and, being rich,
    Donated her own granite monument;
    The Mandeville Pavilion, pink-brick tent
    With marble piping, flying snapping flags
15 Above the entry where our bloody rags
    Are rolled in to be sponged and sewn again.
    Today is fair; tomorrow, scourging rain
    (If only my own tears) will see me in
    Those jaundiced and distempered corridors
20 Off which the five-foot-wide doors slowly close.
    White as my skimpy chiton,° I will cringe   gown
    Before the pinpoint of the least syringe;
    Before the buttered catheter goes in;
    Before the I.V.'s lisp and drip begins
25 Inside my skin; before the rubber hand
    Upon the lancet takes aim and descends
    To lay me open, and upon its thumb
    Retracts the trouble, a malignant plum;
    And finally, I'll quail before the hour
30 When the authorities shut off the power
    In that vast hospital, and in my bed
    I'll feel my blood go thin, go white, the red,
    The rose all leached away, and I'll go dead.
    Then will the business of life resume:
35 The muffled trolley wheeled into my room,
    The off-white blanket blanking off my face,
    The stealing, secret, private, *largo*° race   slow
    Down halls and elevators to the place
    I'll be consigned to for transshipment, cased
40 In artificial air and light: the ward
    That's underground; the terminal; the morgue.
    Then one fine day when all the smart flags flap,
    A booted man in black with a peaked cap
    Will call for me and troll me down the hall
45 And slot me into his black car. That's all.

                                                                1969

THOM GUNN
1929–2004

On the Move

"Man, you gotta Go."

The blue jay scuffling in the bushes follows
Some hidden purpose, and the gust of birds
That spurts across the field, the wheeling swallows,

Have nested in the trees and undergrowth.
5   Seeking their instinct, or their poise, or both,
One moves with an uncertain violence
Under the dust thrown by a baffled sense
Or the dull thunder of approximate words.

On motorcycles, up the road, they come:
10   Small, black, as flies hanging in heat, the Boys,
Until the distance throws them forth, their hum
Bulges to thunder held by calf and thigh.
In goggles, donned impersonality,
In gleaming jackets trophied with the dust,
15   They strap in doubt—by hiding it, robust—
And almost hear a meaning in their noise.

Exact conclusion of their hardiness
Has no shape yet, but from known whereabouts
They ride, direction where the tyres press.
20   They scare a flight of birds across the field:
Much that is natural, to the will must yield.
Men manufacture both machine and soul,
And use what they imperfectly control
To dare a future from the taken routes.

25   It is a part solution, after all.
One is not necessarily discord
On earth; or damned because, half animal,
One lacks direct instinct, because one wakes
Afloat on movement that divides and breaks.
30   One joins the movement in a valueless world,
Choosing it, till, both hurler and the hurled,
One moves as well, always toward, toward.

A minute holds them, who have come to go:
The self-defined, astride the created will
35   They burst away; the towns they travel through
Are home for neither bird nor holiness,
For birds and saints complete their purposes.
At worst, one is in motion; and at best,
Reaching no absolute, in which to rest,
40   One is always nearer by not keeping still.

California   1957

A Map of the City

I stand upon a hill and see
A luminous country under me,
Through which at two the drunk must weave;
The transient's pause, the sailor's leave.

5   I notice, looking down the hill,
     Arms braced upon a window sill;
     And on the web of fire escapes
     Move the potential, the grey shapes.

     I hold the city here, complete:
10   And every shape defined by light
     Is mine, or corresponds to mine,
     Some flickering or some steady shine.

     This map is ground of my delight.
     Between the limits, night by night,
15   I watch a malady's advance,
     I recognize my love of chance.

     By the recurrent lights I see
     Endless potentiality,
     The crowded, broken, and unfinished!
20   I would not have the risk diminished.

                                                    1961

Black Jackets

     In the silence that prolongs the span
     Rawly of music when the record ends,
       The red-haired boy who drove a van
     In weekday overalls but, like his friends,

5   Wore cycle boots and jacket here
     To suit the Sunday hangout he was in,
       Heard, as he stretched back from his beer,
     Leather creak softly round his neck and chin.

         Before him, on a coal-black sleeve
10   Remote exertion had lined, scratched, and burned
         Insignia that could not revive
     The heroic fall or climb where they were earned.

         On the other drinkers bent together,
     Concocting selves for their impervious kit,
15   He saw it as no more than leather
     Which, taut across the shoulders grown to it,

         Sent through the dimness of a bar
     As sudden and anonymous hints of light
         As those that shipping give, that are
20   Now flickers in the Bay,[1] now lost in night.

---

1. San Francisco Bay.

He stretched out like a cat, and rolled
The bitterish taste of beer upon his tongue,
   And listened to a joke being told:
The present was the things he stayed among.

25   If it was only loss he wore,
He wore it to assert, with fierce devotion,
   Complicity and nothing more.
He recollected his initiation,

   And one especially of the rites.
30 For on his shoulders they had put tattoos:
   The group's name on the left, The Knights,
And on the right the slogan Born To Lose.

1961

My Sad Captains

One by one they appear in
the darkness: a few friends, and
a few with historical
names. How late they start to shine!
5 but before they fade they stand
perfectly embodied, all

the past lapping them like a
cloak of chaos. They were men
who, I thought, lived only to
10 renew the wasteful force they
spent with each hot convulsion.
They remind me, distant now.

True, they are not at rest yet,
but now that they are indeed
15 apart, winnowed° from failures,   *separated*
they withdraw to an orbit
and turn with disinterested
hard energy, like the stars.

1961

From the Wave

It mounts at sea, a concave wall
  Down-ribbed with shine,
And pushes forward, building tall
  Its steep incline.

Then from their hiding rise to sight
    Black shapes on boards
Bearing before the fringe of white
    It mottles towards.

Their pale feet curl, they poise their weight
10   With a learn'd skill.
It is the wave they imitate
    Keeps them so still.

The marbling bodies have become
    Half wave, half men,
15 Grafted it seems by feet of foam
    Some seconds, then,

Late as they can, they slice the face
    In timed procession:
Balance is triumph in this place,
20   Triumph possession.

The mindless heave of which they rode
    A fluid shelf
Breaks as they leave it, falls and, slowed,
    Loses itself.

25 Clear, the sheathed bodies slick as seals
    Loosen and tingle;
And by the board the bare foot feels
    The suck of shingle.[2]

They paddle in the shallows still;
30   Two splash each other;
Then all swim out to wait until
    The right waves gather.

1971

"All Do Not All Things Well"[3]

Implies that some therefore
Do well, for its own sake,
One thing they undertake,
Because it has enthralled them.

5 I used to like the two
Auto freaks as I called them
Who laboured in their driveway,

---

2. Coarse, rounded pebbles and stones at the seashore.

3. Thomas Campion, "Now Winter Nights Enlarge," line 17 (see p. 281).

Its concrete black with oil,
In the next block that year.

10 One, hurt in jungle war,
Had a false leg, the other
Raised a huge beard above
A huge Hell's Angel belly.

They seemed to live on beer
15 And corn chips from the deli.

Always with friends, they sprawled
Beneath a ruined car
In that inert but live way
Of scrutinizing innards.
20 And one week they extracted
An engine to examine,
Transplant shining like tar
Fished out into the sun.

"It's all that I enjoy,"
25 Said the stiff-legged boy.
That was when the officious
Realtor had threatened them
For brashly operating
A business on the street
30 —An outsider, that woman
Who wanted them evicted,
Wanted the neighbourhood neat
To sell it. That was when
The boy from Viet Nam told me
35 That he'd firebomb her car.
He didn't of course, she won.

I am sorry that they went.
Quick with a friendly greeting,
They were gentle joky men
40 —Certainly not ambitious,
Perhaps not intelligent
Unless about a car,
Their work one thing they knew
They could for certain do
45 With a disinterest
And passionate expertise
To which they gave their best
Desires and energies.
Such oily-handed zest
50 By-passed the self like love.
I thought that they were good
For any neighbourhood.

1992

The Missing

Now as I watch the progress of the plague,[4]
The friends surrounding me fall sick, grow thin,
And drop away. Bared, is my shape less vague
—Sharply exposed and with a sculpted skin?

5   I do not like the statue's chill contour,
Not nowadays. The warmth investing me
Let outward through mind, limb, feeling, and more
In an involved increasing family.

Contact of friend led to another friend,
10 Supple entwinement through the living mass
Which for all that I knew might have no end,
Image of an unlimited embrace.

I did not just feel ease, though comfortable:
Aggressive as in some ideal of sport,
15 With ceaseless movement thrilling through the whole,
Their push kept me as firm as their support.

But death—Their deaths have left me less defined:
It was their pulsing presence made me clear.
I borrowed from it, I was unconfined,
20 Who tonight balance unsupported here,

Eyes glaring from raw marble, in a pose
Languorously part-buried in the block,
Shins perfect and no calves, as if I froze
Between potential and a finished work.

25 —Abandoned incomplete, shape of a shape,
In which exact detail shows the more strange,
Trapped in unwholeness, I find no escape
Back to the play of constant give and change.

1987   1992

4. AIDS.

JOHN HOLLANDER
b. 1929

Swan and Shadow

```
                    Dusk
                Above  the
        water   hang   the
                     loud
                     flies
                     Here
                     O so
                     gray
                     then
                What            A pale signal will appear
                When            Soon before its shadow fades
                Where           Here in this pool of opened eye
                In us      No Upon us As at the very edges
                of where we take shape in the dark air
                this object bares its image awakening
                ripples of  recognition  that  will
                brush darkness up into light
even after this bird this hour both drift by atop the perfect sad instant now
                already passing out of sight
                toward yet-untroubled reflection
                this image bears its object darkening
                into memorial shades Scattered bits of
                light      No of water Or something across
                water          Breaking up No Being regathered
                soon           Yet by then a swan will have
                gone                Yes out of mind into what
                vast
                pale
                hush
                of a
                place
                past
        sudden  dark  as
            if  a  swan
                sang
```

Adam's Task

"And Adam gave names to all cattle, and to the fowl of the air, and
to every beast of the field . . ."

—*Gen.* 2:20

Thou, paw-paw-paw; thou, glurd; thou, spotted
    Glurd; thou, whitestap, lurching through
The high-grown brush; thou, pliant-footed,
    Implex; thou, awagabu.

5 Every burrower, each flier
    Came for the name he had to give:
Gay, first work, ever to be prior,
    Not yet sunk to primitive.

Thou, verdle; thou, McFleery's pomma;
10   Thou; thou; thou—three types of grawl;
Thou, flisket; thou, kabasch; thou, comma-
    Eared mashawk; thou, all; thou, all.

Were, in a fire of becoming,
    Laboring to be burned away,
15 Then work, half-measuring, half-humming,
    Would be as serious as play.

Thou, pambler; thou, rivarn; thou, greater
    Wherret, and thou, lesser one;
Thou, sproal; thou, zant; thou, lily-eater.
20   Naming's over. Day is done.

1971

An Old-Fashioned Song

(Nous n'irons plus au bois)[1]

No more walks in the wood:
The trees have all been cut
Down, and where once they stood
Not even a wagon rut
5 Appears along the path
Low brush is taking over.

No more walks in the wood;
This is the aftermath
Of afternoons in the clover
10 Fields where we once made love

---

1. " '*Nous n'irons plus au bois / Les lauriers sont coupés*' (We'll go no more to the woods / The laurels have
been cut down)—from a French children's round dance" [Hollander's note].

Then wandered home together
Where the trees arched above,
Where we made our own weather
When branches were the sky.
15   Now they are gone for good,
And you, for ill, and I
Am only a passer-by.

We and the trees and the way
Back from the fields of play
20   Lasted as long as we could.
No more walks in the wood.

1993

Variations on a Fragment by Trumbull Stickney[2]

I hear a river thro' the valley wander
Whose water runs, the song alone remaining.
A rainbow stands and summer passes under,

Flowing like silence in the light of wonder.
5   In the near distances it is still raining
Where now the valley fills again with thunder,

Where now the river in her wide meander,
Losing at each loop what she had been gaining,
Moves into what one might as well call yonder.

10   The way of the dark water is to ponder
The way the light sings as of something waning.
The far-off waterfall can sound asunder

Stillness of distances, as if in blunder,
Tumbling over the rim of all explaining.
15   Water proves nothing, but can only maunder.[3]

Shadows show nothing, but can only launder
The lovely land that sunset had been staining,
Long fields of which the falling light grows fonder.

Here summer stands while all its songs pass under,
20   A riverbank still time runs by, remaining.
I will remember rainbows as I wander.

1993

2. Cf. Stickney's "Fragments," IX (p. 1252). The   3. Move aimlessly; also, mutter.
three-line poem provides Hollander's first stanza.

RICHARD HOWARD
b. 1929

Nikolaus Mardruz to his Master Ferdinand, Count of Tyrol, 1565[1]

A tribute to Robert Browning and in celebration of the 65th birthday of Harold Bloom,[2] who made such tribute only natural.

My Lord recalls Ferrara?[3] How walls
rise out of water yet appear to recede
   identically
   into it, as if
5 built in both directions: soaring and sinking . . .
   Such mirroring was my first dismay—
             my next, having crossed
           the moat, was making
  out that, for all its grandeur, the great
10 pile, observed close to, is close to a ruin!
   (Even My Lord's most
   unstinting dowry
  may not restore these wasted precincts to what
   their deteriorating state demands.)
15   Queasy it made me,
           glancing first down there
   at swans in the moat apparently
  feeding on their own doubled image, then up
   at the citadel,
20 so high—or so deep,
  and *everywhere* those carved effigies of
   men and women, monsters among them
            crowding the ramparts
            and seeming at home
25   in the dingy water that somehow
  held them up as if for our surveillance—ours?
   anyone's who looked!
   All that pretension
  of marble display, the whole improbable
30   menagerie with but one purpose:
            having to be seen.
           Such was the matter
  of Ferrara, and such the manner,
  when at last we met, of the Duke in greeting
35 My Lordship's Envoy:
  life in fallen stone!

1. This poem is in the voice of the envoy of the Count of Tyrol, upon returning home to Austria from the visit to the Duke of Ferrara portrayed in "My Last Duchess," by the English poet Robert Browning (1812–1899). Browning's poem implies that the Duke ordered his first wife's death; the possibility of marriage between himself and the Count's niece closes the poem and provides the occasion for Howard's poem. Cf. footnote 4 to "My Last Duchess" (p. 1012) for Browning's blending of fact and fiction.
2. American literary critic (b. 1930).
3. City in northern Italy.

Several hours were to elapse, in the keeping
of his lackeys, before the Envoy
of My Lord the Count
40   of Tyrol might see
or even be seen to by His Grace
the Duke of Ferrara, though from such neglect
no *deliberate*
slight need be inferred:
45 now that I have had an opportunity
—have had, indeed, the obligation—
to fix on His Grace
that perlustration°   *thorough inspection*
or power of scrutiny for which
50 (I believe) My Lord holds his Envoy's service
in some favor still,
I see that the Duke,
by his own lights or, perhaps, more properly
said, by his own *tenebrosity,*°   *obscurity*
55   could offer some excuse
for such cunctation° . . .   *tardiness*
Appraising a set of cameos
just brought from Cairo by a Jew in his trust,
His Grace had been rapt
60 in connoisseurship,
that study which alone can distract him
from his wonted courtesy; he was
affability
itself, once his mind
65 could be deflected from mere *objects.*

At last I presented (with those documents
which in some detail
describe and define
the duties of both signators) the portrait
70   of your daughter the Countess,
observing the while
his countenance. No
fault was found with our contract, of which
each article had been so correctly framed
75 (if I may say so)
as to ascertain
a pre-nuptial alliance which must persuade
and please the most punctilious (and
impecunious)
80   of future husbands.
Principally, or (if I may be
allowed the amendment) perhaps Ducally,
His Grace acknowledged
himself *beguiled* by
85 Cranach's[4] portrait of our young Countess, praising
the design, the hues, the glaze—the frame!

---

4. Lucas Cranach the Younger (1515–1586), German painter and graphic artist.

and appeared averse,
for a while, even
to letting the panel leave his hands!
90   Examining those same hands, I was convinced
that no matter what
the result of our
(at this point, promising) negotiations,
your daughter's likeness must now remain
95   "for good," as we say,
among Ferrara's
treasures, already one more trophy
in His Grace's multifarious *holdings,*
like those marble busts
100   lining the drawbridge,
like those weed-stained statues grinning up at us
from the still moat, and—inside as well
as out—those grotesque
figures and faces
105   fastened to the walls. So be it!

                                    Real
bother (after all, one painting, for Cranach
—*and* My Lord—need be
no great forfeiture)
110   commenced only when the Duke himself led me
out of the audience-chamber and
laboriously
(he is no longer
a young man) to a secret penthouse
115   high on the battlements where he can indulge
those despotic tastes
he denominates,
half smiling over the heartless words,
"the relative consolations of semblance."
120   "Sir, suppose you draw
that curtain," smiling
in earnest now, and so I sought—
but what appeared a piece of drapery proved
a painted deceit!
125   My embarrassment
afforded a cue for audible laughter,
and only then His Grace, visibly
relishing his trick,
turned the thing around,
130   whereupon appeared, on the reverse,
the late Duchess of Ferrara to the life!
Instanter the Duke
praised the portrait
so readily provided by one Pandolf[5]—
135   a monk by some profane article
attached to the court,

---

5. Fra (i.e., Brother) Pandolph, an artist invented by Browning.

                                hence answerable
                    for taking likenesses *as required*
            in but a day's diligence, so it was claimed . . .
140   Myself I find it
            but a mountebank's°   *charlatan's*
        proficiency—another chicane, like that
                illusive curtain, a waxwork sort
                            of nature called forth:
145   cold legerdemain!°   *sleight of hand*
            Though *extranea* such as the hares
        (copulating!), the doves, and a full-blown rose
                were showily limned,
                I could not discern
150   aught to be loved in that countenance itself,
            likely to rival, much less to excel
                        the life illumined
                    in Cranach's image
                of *our* Countess, which His Grace had set
155   beside the dead woman's presentment . . . And took,
            so evident was
            the supremacy,
        no further pains to assert Fra Pandolf's skill.
                One last hard look, whereupon the Duke
160   resumed his discourse
                        in an altered tone,
            now some unintelligible rant
        of *stooping*—His Grace chooses "never to stoop"
            when he makes reproof . . .
165   My Lord will take this
        as but a figure: not only is the Duke
            no longer young, his body is so
                            queerly misshapen
                            that even to *speak*
170   of "not stooping" seems absurdity:
        the creature *is* stooped, whether by cruel or
            impartial cause—say
            Time or the Tempter°—   *Devil*
        I shall not venture to hypothecate. Cause
175   or no cause, it would appear he marked
                        some motive for his
                        "reproof," a mortal
                chastisement in fact inflicted on
        his poor Duchess, *put away* (I take it so)
180   for smiling—at whom?
            Brother Pandolf? or
        some visitor to court during the sitting?
            —too generally, if I construe
                    the Duke's clue rightly,
185   to survive the terms
                of his . . . severe protocol. My Lord,
        at the time it was delivered to me thus,
            the admonition

if indeed it was
190   any such thing, seemed no more of a menace
than the rest of his rodomontade;°   *boasting*
item, he pointed,
as we toiled downstairs,
to that bronze *Neptune* by our old Claus
195   (there must be at least six of them cluttering
the Summer Palace
at Innsbruck), claiming
it was "cast in bronze for me."[6] Nonsense, of course.

But upon reflection, I suppose
200   we had better take
the old reprobate
at his unspeakable word . . . Why, even
assuming his boasts should be as plausible
as his avarice,
205   no "cause" for dismay:
once ensconced here as the Duchess, your daughter
need no more apprehend the Duke's
murderous temper
than his matchless taste.
210   For I have devised a means whereby
the dowry so flagrantly pursued by our
insolvent Duke ("no
just pretense of mine
be disallowed"[7] indeed!), instead of being
215   paid as he pleads in one globose° sum,   *globe-shaped*
should drip into his
coffers by degrees—
say, one fifth each year—then after five
such years, the dowry itself to be doubled,
220   always assuming
that Her Grace enjoys
her usual smiling health. The years are her
ally in such an arbitrament,
and with confidence
225   My Lord can assure
the new Duchess (assuming her Duke
abides by these stipulations and his own
propensity for
accumulating
230   "semblances") the long devotion (so long as
he lasts) of her last Duke . . . Or more likely,
if I guess aright
your daughter's intent,
of that young lordling I might make so
235   bold as to designate her next Duke, as well . . .

---

6. Cf. "My Last Duchess," lines 54–56. Claus of   7. Cf. "My Last Duchess," lines 50–51.
Innsbruck is also fictional.

Ever determined in
My Lordship's service,
I remain his Envoy
to Ferrara as to the world.
240   Nikolaus Mardruz.

1995

JOHN MONTAGUE
b. 1929

Like Dolmens[1] Round My Childhood, the Old People

Like dolmens round my childhood, the old people.

Jamie MacCrystal sang to himself,
A broken song without tune, without words;
He tipped me a penny every pension day.
5   Fed kindly crusts to winter birds.
When he died, his cottage was robbed,
Mattress and money box torn and searched.
Only the corpse they didn't disturb.

Maggie Owens was surrounded by animals,
10   A mongrel bitch and shivering pups,
Even in her bedroom a she-goat cried.
She was a well of gossip defiled,[2]
Fanged chronicler of a whole countryside;
Reputed a witch, all I could find
15   Was her lonely need to deride.

The Nialls lived along a mountain lane
Where heather bells bloomed, clumps of foxglove.
All were blind, with Blind Pension and Wireless,[3]
Dead eyes serpent-flicked as one entered
20   To shelter from a downpour of mountain rain.
Crickets chirped under the rocking hearthstone
Until the muddy sun shone out again.

Mary Moore lived in a crumbling gatehouse,
Famous as Pisa[4] for its leaning gable.
25   Bag-apron and boots, she tramped the fields
Driving lean cattle from a miry stable.
A by-word for fierceness, she fell asleep
Over love stories, Red Star and Red Circle,[5]
Dreamed of gypsy love rites, by firelight sealed.

1. Ancient standing stones.
2. Cf. Edmund Spenser, *Faerie Queene* 4.2.32: "Dan [i.e., 'Sir'] Chaucer," well of English undefiled."
3. Radio. *Blind Pension:* state-provided income for sightless people.
4. The Leaning Tower of Pisa.
5. Cheap-magazine romances.

30   Wild Billy Eagleson married a Catholic servant girl
  When all his Loyal[6] family passed on:
  We danced round him shouting "To Hell with King Billy",[7]
  And dodged from the arc of his flailing blackthorn.°   *knobbed cane*
  Forsaken by both creeds, he showed little concern
35   Until the Orange° drums banged past in the summer   *Protestant*
  And bowler and sash aggressively shone.

  Curate and doctor trudged to attend them,
  Through knee-deep snow, through summer heat,
  From main road to lane to broken path,
40   Gulping the mountain air with painful breath.
  Sometimes they were found by neighbours,
  Silent keepers of a smokeless hearth,
  Suddenly cast in the mould of death.

  Ancient Ireland, indeed! I was reared by her bedside,
45   The rune and the chant, evil eye and averted head,
  Fomorian[8] fierceness of family and local feud.
  Gaunt figures of fear and of friendliness,
  For years they trespassed on my dreams,
  Until once, in a standing circle of stones,[9]
50   I felt their shadows pass

  Into that dark permanence of ancient forms.

                                     1959

Old Mythologies

  And now, at last, all proud deeds done,
  Mouths dust-stopped, dark they embrace
  Suitably disposed, as urns, underground.
  Cattle munching soft spring grass
5   —Epicures of shamrock and the four-leaved clover—
  Hear a whimper of ancient weapons,
  As a whole dormitory of heroes turn over,
  Regretting their butchers' days.
  This valley cradles their archaic madness
10   As once, on an impossibly epic morning,
  It upheld their savage stride:
  To bagpiped battle marching,
  Wolfhounds, lean as models,
  At their urgent heels.

                                       1961

6. Loyalist, Protestant.
7. A Roman Catholic taunt to Protestant coreligionists of King William III of England, who at the Battle of the Boyne (1690) defeated his predecessor, the Roman Catholic King James II, thereby establishing the Protestant domination of Ireland.
8. The Fomorians were demons or evil gods in Irish pagan mythology.
9. Prehistoric ring of large blocks of stone set upright in the ground.

The Trout

Flat on the bank I parted
Rushes to ease my hands
In the water without a ripple
And tilt them slowly downstream
5   To where he lay, light as a leaf,
In his fluid sensual dream.

Bodiless lord of creation
I hung briefly above him
Savouring my own absence
10   Senses expanding in the slow
Motion, the photographic calm
That grows before action.

As the curve of my hands
Swung under his body
15   He surged, with visible pleasure.
I was so preternaturally close
I could count every stipple
But still cast no shadow, until

The two palms crossed in a cage
20   Under the lightly pulsing gills.
Then (entering my own enlarged
Shape, which rode on the water)
I gripped. To this day I can
Taste his terror on my hands.

1966

All Legendary Obstacles

All legendary obstacles lay between
Us, the long imaginary plain,
The monstrous ruck of mountains
And, swinging across the night,
5   Flooding the Sacramento, San Joaquin,[1]
The hissing drift of winter rain.

All day I waited, shifting
Nervously from station to bar
As I saw another train sail
10   By, the San Francisco Chief or
Golden Gate, water dripping
From great flanged° wheels.   *ribbed*

---

1. River in central California that flows northwest into the Sacramento River.

At midnight you came, pale
Above the negro porter's lamp.
15 I was too blind with rain
And doubt to speak, but
Reached from the platform
Until our chilled hands met.

You had been travelling for days
20 With an old lady, who marked
A neat circle on the glass
With her glove, to watch us
Move into the wet darkness
Kissing, still unable to speak.

1966

PETER PORTER
b. 1929

A Consumer's Report

The name of the product I tested is *Life,*
I have completed the form you sent me
and understand that my answers are confidential.

I had it as a gift,
5 I didn't feel much while using it,
in fact I think I'd have liked to be more excited.
It seemed gentle on the hands
but left an embarrassing deposit behind.
It was not economical
10 and I have used much more than I thought
(I suppose I have about half left
but it's difficult to tell)—
although the instructions are fairly large
there are so many of them
15 I don't know which to follow, especially
as they seem to contradict each other.
I'm not sure such a thing
should be put in the way of children—
It's difficult to think of a purpose
20 for it. One of my friends says
it's just to keep its maker in a job.
Also the price is much too high.
Things are piling up so fast,
after all, the world got by
25 for a thousand million years
without this, do we need it now?
(Incidentally, please ask your man

to stop calling me "the respondent",
I don't like the sound of it.)
30   There seems to be a lot of different labels,
sizes and colours should be uniform,
the shape is awkward, it's waterproof
but not heat resistant, it doesn't keep
yet it's very difficult to get rid of:
35   whenever they make it cheaper they seem
to put less in—if you say you don't
want it, then it's delivered anyway.
I'd agree it's a popular product,
it's got into the language; people
40   even say they're on the side of it.
Personally I think it's overdone,
a small thing people are ready
to behave badly about. I think
we should take it for granted. If its
45   experts are called philosophers or market
researchers or historians, we shouldn't
care. We are the consumers and the last
law makers. So finally, I'd buy it.
But the question of a "best buy"
50   I'd like to leave until I get
the competitive product you said you'd send.

1970

An Angel in Blythburgh Church[1]

Shot down from its enskied formation,
This stern-faced plummet rests against the wall;
Cromwell's soldiers peppered it[2] and now the death-
  watch beetle has it in thrall.[3]

5   If you make fortunes from wool, along
The weeping winter foreshores of the tide,
You build big churches with clerestories[4]
  And place angels high inside.

Their painted faces guard and guide. Now or
10   Tomorrow or whenever is the promise—
The resurrection comes: fix your eyes halfway
  Between Heaven and Diss.[5]

1. Medieval statue in Blythburgh, a small village in northeast Suffolk, England.
2. The English general and statesman Oliver Cromwell (1599–1658) led the anti-Royalist "Roundheads," who defeated the "Cavaliers" loyal to King Charles I in the English Civil War. Largely Puritan, they defaced many church decorations that they considered idolatrous.
3. Cf. Keats, "La Belle Dame sans Merci," lines 39–40 (p. 918). *Death-watch beetle:* a bug that eats wood.
4. Upper stories with their own windows.
5. A town in Norfolk, near Blythburgh; also, as Dis, the Roman god of the underworld.

The face is crudely carved, simplified by wind;
It looks straight at God and waits for orders,
15 Buffeted by the organ militant, and blasted
        By choristers and recorders.

Faith would have our eyes as wooden and as certain.
It might be worth it, to start the New Year's hymn
Allowing for death as a mere calculation,
20   A depreciation, entered in.

Or so I fancy looking at the roof beams
Where the dangerous beetle sails. What is it
Turns an atheist's mind to prayer in almost
        Any church on a country visit?

25 Greed for love or certainty or forgiveness?
High security rising with the sea birds?
A theology of self looking for precedents?
        A chance to speak old words?

Rather, I think of a woman lying on her bed[6]
30 Staring for hours up to the ceiling where
Nothing is projected—death the only angel
        To shield her from despair.

                                    1978

An Exequy[7]

In wet May, in the months of change,
In a country you wouldn't visit, strange
Dreams pursue me in my sleep,
Black creatures of the upper deep—
5   Though you are five months dead, I see
You in guilt's iconography,
Dear Wife, lost beast, beleaguered child,
The stranded monster with the mild
Appearance, whom small waves tease,
10 (Andromeda[8] upon her knees
In orthodox deliverance)
And you alone of pure substance,
The unformed form of life, the earth
Which Piero's[9] brushes brought to birth
15 For all to greet as myth, a thing
Out of the box of imagining.

6. Porter's wife, who committed suicide in 1974.
7. Funeral rite. See note 6 above.
8. In Greek mythology, an Ethiopian princess. Her mother, Cassiopeia, claimed to be more beautiful than the Nereids, sea nymphs who then persuaded the god Neptune to send a sea monster to her homeland. An oracle demanded that Andromeda be sacrificed to the monster in expiation, but she was saved by Perseus. After her death, she was placed among the stars.
9. Piero della Francesca (ca. 1420–1492), Italian painter.

This introduction serves to sing
Your mortal death as Bishop King[1]
Once hymned in tetrametric rhyme
20 His young wife, lost before her time;
Though he lived on for many years
His poem each day fed new tears
To that unreaching spot, her grave,
His lines a baroque architrave[2]
25 The Sunday poor with bottled flowers
Would by-pass in their mourning hours,
Esteeming ragged natural life
("Most dearly loved, most gentle wife"),
Yet, looking back when at the gate
30 And seeing grief in formal state
Upon a sculpted angel group,
Were glad that men of god could stoop
To give the dead a public stance
And freeze them in their mortal dance.

35 The words and faces proper to
My misery are private—you
Would never share your heart with those
Whose only talent's to suppose,
Nor from your final childish bed
40 Raise a remote confessing head—
The channels of our lives are blocked,
The hand is stopped upon the clock,
No one can say why hearts will break
And marriages are all opaque:
45 A map of loss, some posted cards,
The living house reduced to shards,
The abstract hell of memory,
The pointlessness of poetry—
These are the instances which tell
50 Of something which I know full well,
I owe a death to you—one day
The time will come for me to pay
When your slim shape from photographs
Stands at my door and gently asks
55 If I have any work to do
Or will I come to bed with you.
O scala enigmatica,[3]
I'll climb up to that attic where
The curtain of your life was drawn
60 Some time between despair and dawn—
I'll never know with what halt steps
You mounted to this plain eclipse
But each stair now will station me

---

1. Bishop Henry King (1592–1669), English poet, author of "An Exequy to His Matchless, Never-to-Be-Forgotten Friend" (see p. 363).
2. Lintel or other molding around a door.

3. O enigmatic stairs (Latin); an allusion to the stairs leading to the attic in which Porter's wife died.

A black responsibility
65 And point me to that shut-down room,
"This be your due appointed tomb."

I think of us in Italy:
Gin-and-chianti-fuelled, we
Move in a trance through Paradise,
70 Feeding at last our starving eyes,
Two people of the English blindness
Doing each masterpiece the kindness
Of discovering it—from Baldovinetti[4]
To Venice's most obscure jetty.
75 A true unfortunate traveller, I
Depend upon your nurse's eye
To pick the altars where no Grinner°   grotesque fiend
Puts us off our tourists' dinner
And in hotels to bandy words
80 With Genevan girls and talking birds,
To wear your feet out following me
To night's end and true amity,
And call my rational fear of flying
A paradigm of Holy Dying—
85 And, oh my love, I wish you were
Once more with me, at night somewhere
In narrow streets applauding wines,
The moon above the Apennines°   mountain chain
As large as logic and the stars,
90 Most middle-aged of avatars,
As bright as when they shone for truth
Upon untried and avid youth.

The rooms and days we wandered through
Shrink in my mind to one—there you
95 Lie quite absorbed by peace—the calm
Which life could not provide is balm
In death. Unseen by me, you look
Past bed and stairs and half-read book
Eternally upon your home,
100 The end of pain, the left alone.
I have no friend, or intercessor,
No psychopomp[5] or true confessor
But only you who know my heart
In every cramped and devious part—
105 Then take my hand and lead me out,
The sky is overcast by doubt,
The time has come, I listen for
Your words of comfort at the door,
O guide me through the shoals of fear—
110 "Fürchte dich nicht, ich bin bei dir."[6]

1978

4. Alessio Baldovinetti (1425–1499), Italian
painter.
5. Someone who acts as a guide of the soul; also,
a conductor of souls to the place of the dead.
6. Fear not, I am with you (German); opening lyrics of Bach's motet BMV 228.

ADRIENNE RICH
b. 1929

Aunt Jennifer's Tigers

Aunt Jennifer's tigers prance across a screen,
Bright topaz denizens of a world of green.
They do not fear the men beneath the tree;
They pace in sleek chivalric certainty.

5   Aunt Jennifer's fingers fluttering through her wool
Find even the ivory needle hard to pull.
The massive weight of Uncle's wedding band
Sits heavily upon Aunt Jennifer's hand.

When Aunt is dead, her terrified hands will lie
10 Still ringed with ordeals she was mastered by.
The tigers in the panel that she made
Will go on prancing, proud and unafraid.

1951

Snapshots of a Daughter-in-Law

1

You, once a belle in Shreveport,[1]
with henna-colored hair, skin like a peachbud,
still have your dresses copied from that time,
and play a Chopin prelude
5   called by Cortot: *"Delicious recollections
float like perfume through the memory."*[2]

Your mind now, moldering like wedding-cake,
heavy with useless experience, rich
with suspicion, rumor, fantasy,
10 crumbling to pieces under the knife-edge
of mere fact. In the prime of your life.

Nervy, glowering, your daughter
wipes the teaspoons, grows another way.

2

Banging the coffee-pot into the sink
15 she hears the angels chiding, and looks out

---

1. City in Louisiana.
2. A remark made by the French pianist Alfred Cortot (1877–1962) in his book *Chopin: 24 Preludes* (1930); he is referring specifically to Prelude

No. 7, Andantino, A Major, by Frederic Chopin (1810–1849), Polish composer and piano virtuoso, who settled in Paris in 1831.

past the raked gardens to the sloppy sky.
Only a week since They said: *Have no patience.*

The next time it was: *Be insatiable.*
Then: *Save yourself; others you cannot save.*
20 Sometimes she's let the tapstream scald her arm,
a match burn to her thumbnail,

or held her hand above the kettle's snout
right in the woolly steam. They are probably angels,
since nothing hurts her anymore, except
25 each morning's grit blowing into her eyes.

3

A thinking woman sleeps with monsters.
The beak that grips her, she becomes.[3] And Nature,
that sprung-lidded, still commodious
steamer-trunk of *tempora* and *mores*[4]
30 gets stuffed with it all: the mildewed orange-flowers,
the female pills,[5] the terrible breasts
of Boadicea[6] beneath flat foxes' heads and orchids.

Two handsome women, gripped in argument,
each proud, acute, subtle, I hear scream
35 across the cut glass and majolica
like Furies[7] cornered from their prey:
The argument *ad feminam*,[8] all the old knives
that have rusted in my back, I drive in yours,
ma semblable, ma soeur![9]

4

40 Knowing themselves too well in one another:
their gifts no pure fruition, but a thorn,
the prick filed sharp against a hint of scorn . . .
Reading while waiting
for the iron to heat,
45 writing, *My Life had stood—a Loaded Gun—*[1]
in that Amherst pantry while the jellies boil and scum,
or, more often,

---

3. A reference to W. B. Yeats's "Leda and the Swan" (p. 1200), in which Zeus in the shape of a swan rapes Leda and then lets her drop from "the indifferent beak."
4. Literally, times and customs—from the ancient Roman orator Cicero's famous phrase, "O tempora! O mores!"
5. Remedies for menstrual pain.
6. British queen (d. 60 C.E.), who led her people in a large though ultimately unsuccessful revolt against Roman rule.
7. Greek goddesses of vengeance. *Majolica:* a glazed earthenware.
8. Feminine version of the Latin phrase *ad hominem* (to the man), referring to an argument

directed not to reason but to personal prejudices and emotions.
9. The last line of "Au lecteur" ("To the Reader"), by the French poet Charles Baudelaire (1821–1867), addresses *"Hypocrite lecteur!—mon semblable—mon frère!"* ("Hypocrite reader!—my likeness!—my brother!"); Rich here instead addresses *"ma soeur"* (my sister). See also T. S. Eliot, *The Waste Land*, line 76 (p. 1346).
1. *"Emily Dickinson, Complete Poems,* ed. T. H. Johnson, 1960, p. 369" [Rich's note]; see p. 1115. Amherst, referred to in the next line, is the town in Massachusetts where Dickinson lived her entire life (1830–1886).

iron-eyed and beaked and purposed as a bird,
dusting everything on the whatnot every day of life.

5

50 *Dulce ridens, dulce loquens,*[2]
she shaves her legs until they gleam
like petrified mammoth-tusk.

6

When to her lute Corinna sings[3]
neither words nor music are her own;
55 only the long hair dipping
over her cheek, only the song
of silk against her knees
and these
adjusted in reflections of an eye.

60 Poised, trembling and unsatisfied, before
an unlocked door, that cage of cages,
tell us, you bird, you tragical machine—
is this *fertilisante douleur?*[4] Pinned down
by love, for you the only natural action,
65 are you edged more keen
to prise the secrets of the vault? has Nature shown
her household books to you, daughter-in-law,
that her sons never saw?

7

"To have in this uncertain world some stay
70 *which cannot be undermined, is*
of the utmost consequence."[5]
                Thus wrote
a woman, partly brave and partly good,
who fought with what she partly understood.
75 Few men about her would or could do more,
hence she was labeled harpy, shrew and whore.

8

"You all die at fifteen," said Diderot,[6]
and turn part legend, part convention.
Still, eyes inaccurately dream

---

2. Sweetly laughing, sweetly speaking (Latin); from Horace, *Odes* 22.23–24.
3. First line of a lyric by Thomas Campion (see p. 280).
4. Fertilizing (i.e., life-giving) sorrow (French).
5. "From Mary Wollstonecraft, *Thoughts on the Education of Daughters,* London, 1787" [Rich's note]. Wollstonecraft (1759–1797), one of the first

feminist thinkers, is best-known for her *Vindication of the Rights of Woman* (1792).
6. Denis Diderot (1713–1784), French philosopher, encyclopedist, playwright, and critic. " 'You all die at fifteen': 'Vous mourez toutes a quinze ans,' from the *Lettres à Sophie Volland,* quoted by Simone de Beauvoir in *Le Deuxième Sexe,* Vol. II, pp. 123–24" [Rich's note].

80 behind closed windows blankening with steam.
Deliciously, all that we might have been,
all that we were—fire, tears,
wit, taste, martyred ambition—
stirs like the memory of refused adultery
85 the drained and flagging bosom of our middle years.

9

Not that it is done well, but
that it is done at all?[7] Yes, think
of the odds! or shrug them off forever.
This luxury of the precocious child,
90 Time's precious chronic invalid,—
would we, darlings, resign it if we could?
Our blight has been our sinecure:
mere talent was enough for us—
glitter in fragments and rough drafts.

95 Sigh no more, ladies.
                    Time is male
and in his cups[8] drinks to the fair.
Bemused by gallantry, we hear
our mediocrities over-praised,
100 indolence read as abnegation,
slattern thought styled intuition,
every lapse forgiven, our crime
only to cast too bold a shadow
or smash the mold straight off.

105 For that, solitary confinement,
tear gas, attrition shelling.
Few applicants for that honor.

10

                    Well,
she's long about her coming, who must be
110 more merciless to herself than history.
Her mind full to the wind, I see her plunge
breasted and glancing through the currents,
taking the light upon her
at least as beautiful as any boy
115 or helicopter,[9]

---

7. "Sir, a woman's preaching is like a dog's walking on his hinder legs. It is not done well; but you are surprised to find it done at all": the English writer Samuel Johnson (1709–1784), to his friend and biographer, James Boswell (1740–1795).
8. While drinking. "Sigh no more, ladies, sigh no more, / Men were deceivers ever": Shakespeare, *Much Ado About Nothing* 2.3.56–57.
9. "She comes down from the remoteness of ages, from Thebes, from Crete, from Chichén-Itzá; and she is also the totem set deep in the African jungle; she is a helicopter and she is a bird; and there is this, the greatest wonder of all: under her tinted hair the forest murmur becomes a thought, and words issue from her breasts" (Simone de Beauvoir, *The Second Sex*, trans. H. M. Parshley [1953], p. 729). (A translation of the passage from *Le Deuxième Sexe*, Vol. II, p. 574, cited in French by Rich.)

                poised, still coming,
    her fine blades making the air wince

       but her cargo
       no promise then:
120   delivered
       palpable
       ours.

1958–60   1963

Orion[1]

       Far back when I went zig-zagging
       through tamarack pastures
       you were my genius,° you   *attendant spirit*
       my cast-iron Viking, my helmed
5   lion-heart king in prison.[2]
       Years later now you're young

       my fierce half-brother, staring
       down from that simplified west
       your breast open, your belt dragged down
10   by an oldfashioned thing, a sword
       the last bravado you won't give over
       though it weighs you down as you stride

       and the stars in it are dim
       and maybe have stopped burning.
15   But you burn, and I know it;
       as I throw back my head to take you in
       an old transfusion happens again:
       divine astronomy is nothing to it.

       Indoors I bruise and blunder,
20   break faith, leave ill enough
       alone, a dead child born in the dark.
       Night cracks up over the chimney,
       pieces of time, frozen geodes[3]
       come showering down in the grate.

25   A man reaches behind my eyes
       and finds them empty
       a woman's head turns away
       from my head in the mirror
       children are dying my death
30   and eating crumbs of my life.

1. Constellation of the winter sky that appears as a warrior with belt and sword; named after a giant hunter in Greek mythology.
2. Alluding to the English king Richard the Lion-Hearted (1157–1199), imprisoned in Austria on his return from the Crusades.
3. Small, spheroid stones, with a cavity often lined with crystals.

Pity is not your forte.
Calmly you ache up there
pinned aloft in your crow's nest,[4]
my speechless pirate!
35 You take it all for granted
and when I look you back

it's with a starlike eye
shooting its cold and egotistical[5] spear
where it can do least damage.
40 Breathe deep! No hurt, no pardon
out here in the cold with you
you with your back to the wall.

1965   1969

A Valediction Forbidding Mourning[6]

My swirling wants. Your frozen lips.
The grammar turned and attacked me.
Themes, written under duress.
Emptiness of the notations.

5 They gave me a drug that slowed the healing of wounds.

I want you to see this before I leave:
the experience of repetition as death
the failure of criticism to locate the pain
the poster in the bus that said:
10 *my bleeding is under control.*

A red plant in a cemetery of plastic wreaths.

A last attempt: the language is a dialect called metaphor.
These images go unglossed: hair, glacier, flashlight.
When I think of a landscape I am thinking of a time.
15 When I talk of taking a trip I mean forever.
I could say: those mountains have a meaning
but further than that I could not say.

To do something very common, in my own way.

1970   1971

---

4. Lookout post on the masts of old ships.
5. "One of two phrases suggested by Gottfried Benn's essay, *Artists and Old Age* in *Primal Vision*, edited by E. B. Ashton, New Directions" [Rich's note]. Benn (1886–1956), German poet and critic, advises the modern artist: "Don't lose sight of the cold and egotistical element in your mission. . . .

With your back to the wall, careworn and weary, in the gray light of the void, read Job and Jeremiah and keep going."
6. The title of a poem by John Donne (see p. 306), in which he forbids his wife to lament his departure on a trip to the Continent.

Diving into the Wreck

First having read the book of myths,
and loaded the camera,
and checked the edge of the knife-blade,
I put on
5   the body-armor of black rubber
the absurd flippers
the grave and awkward mask.
I am having to do this
not like Cousteau[7] with his
10 assiduous team
aboard the sun-flooded schooner
but here alone.

There is a ladder.
The ladder is always there
15 hanging innocently
close to the side of the schooner.
We know what it is for,
we who have used it.
Otherwise
20 it is a piece of maritime floss
some sundry equipment.

I go down.
Rung after rung and still
the oxygen immerses me
25 the blue light
the clear atoms
of our human air.
I go down.
My flippers cripple me,
30 I crawl like an insect down the ladder
and there is no one
to tell me when the ocean
will begin.

First the air is blue and then
35 it is bluer and then green and then
black I am blacking out and yet
my mask is powerful
it pumps my blood with power
the sea is another story
40 the sea is not a question of power
I have to learn alone
to turn my body without force
in the deep element.

7. Jacques-Yves Cousteau (1910–1997), French underwater explorer, photographer, and author.

And now: it is easy to forget
45   what I came for
among so many who have always
lived here
swaying their crenellated[8] fans
between the reefs
50   and besides
you breathe differently down here.

I came to explore the wreck.
The words are purposes.
The words are maps.
55   I came to see the damage that was done
and the treasures that prevail.
I stroke the beam of my lamp
slowly along the flank
of something more permanent
60   than fish or weed

the thing I came for:
the wreck and not the story of the wreck
the thing itself and not the myth
the drowned face[9] always staring
65   toward the sun
the evidence of damage
worn by salt and sway into this threadbare beauty
the ribs of the disaster
curving their assertion
70   among the tentative haunters.

This is the place.
And I am here, the mermaid whose dark hair
streams black, the merman in his armored body
We circle silently
75   about the wreck
we dive into the hold.
I am she: I am he

whose drowned face sleeps with open eyes
whose breasts still bear the stress
80   whose silver, copper, vermeil[1] cargo lies
obscurely inside barrels
half-wedged and left to rot
we are the half-destroyed instruments
that once held to a course
85   the water-eaten log
the fouled compass

We are, I am, you are
by cowardice or courage
the one who find our way

---

8. With repeated indentations.
9. I.e., one of the female figureheads that orna-

mented old sailing ships' bows.
1. Gilded silver or bronze.

90 back to this scene
    carrying a knife, a camera
    a book of myths
    in which
    our names do not appear.

1973

From Eastern War Time[2]

1

Memory lifts her smoky mirror: 1943,
single isinglass window   kerosene
stove in the streetcar barn   halfset moon
8:15 a.m. Eastern War Time dark
5   Number 29 clanging in and turning
    looseleaf notebook   *Latin for Americans*
    Breasted's *History of the Ancient World*
    on the girl's lap
    money for lunch and war-stamps in her pocket
10 darkblue wool wet acrid on her hands
    three pools of light   weak ceiling bulbs
    a schoolgirl's hope-spilt terrified
    sensations wired to smells
    of kerosene wool and snow
15 and the sound of the dead language
    praised as key   torchlight of the great dead
    Grey spreading   behind still-flying snow
    the lean and sway of the streetcar she must ride
    to become one   of a hundred girls
20 rising white-cuffed and collared in a study hall
    to sing *For those in peril on the sea*[3]
    under plaster casts of the classic frescoes
    chariots horses draperies certitudes.

8

A woman wired in memories
stands by a house   collapsed in dust
her son beaten in prison   grandson
shot in the stomach   daughter
5   organizing the camps   an aunt's unpublished poems
    grandparents' photographs   a bridal veil
    phased into smoke   up the obliterate air
    With whom shall she let down and tell her story
    Who shall hear her to the end
10 standing if need be for hours   in wind

---

2. Rich's invented term conflating Eastern Standard Time, the time zone in which she grew up (in Baltimore), with the time of World War II. The poem, in ten parts, juxtaposes Rich's childhood memories, as an American Jew, with facts of the Holocaust, in Europe.
3. A hymn, also known as "Eternal Father, Strong to Save" and the "Navy Hymn."

that swirls the levelled dust
in sun that beats through their scarfed hair
at the lost gate by the shattered prickly pear
Who must hear her to the end
15 but the woman   forbidden to forget
the blunt groats° freezing in the wooden ladle   *hulled grain*
old winds   dusting the ovens with light snow?

1995

Modotti[4]

Your footprints of light on sensitive paper
that typewriter you made famous
my footsteps following you up stair-
wells of scarred oak and shredded newsprint
5 these windowpanes smeared with stifled breaths
corridors of tile and jaundiced plaster
if this is where I must look for you
then this is where I'll find you

From a streetlamp's wet lozenge bent
10 on a curb plastered with newsprint
the headlines aiming straight at your eyes
to a room's dark breath-smeared light
these footsteps I'm following you with
down tiles of a red corridor
15 if this is a way to find you
of course this is how I'll find you

Your negatives pegged to dry in a darkroom
rigged up over a bathtub's lozenge
your footprints of light on sensitive paper
20 stacked curling under blackened panes
the always upstairs of your hideout
the stern exposure of your brows
—these footsteps I'm following you with
aren't to arrest you

25 The bristling hairs of your eyeflash
that typewriter you made famous
your enormous will to arrest and frame
what was, what is, still liquid, flowing
your exposure of manifestos, your
30 lightbulb in a scarred ceiling
well if this is how I find you
Modotti so I find you

---

4. "Tina Modotti (1896–1942): photographer, political activist, revolutionary. Her most significant work was done in Mexico in the 1920s, including a study of the typewriter belonging to her lover, the Cuban revolutionary Julio Antonio Mella. Framed for his murder by the fascists in 1929, she was expelled from Mexico in 1930. After some years of political activity in Berlin, she returned incognito to Mexico, where she died in 1942" [Rich's note].

In the red wash of your darkroom
from your neighborhood of volcanoes
35 to the geranium nailed in a can
on the wall of your upstairs hideout
in the rush of breath a window
of revolution allowed you
on this jaundiced stair in this huge lashed eye
                                                 these
40 footsteps I'm following you with

1996   1999

A. K. RAMANUJAN
1929–1993

Snakes

No, it does not happen
when I walk through the woods.
But, walking in museums of quartz
or the aisles of bookstacks,
5   looking at their geometry
without curves
and the layers of transparency
that make them opaque,
dwelling on the yellower vein
10 in the yellow amber
or touching a book that has gold
on its spine,
                    I think of snakes.

The twirls of their hisses
15 rise like the tiny dust-cones on slow-noon roads
winding through the farmers' feet.
Black lorgnettes[1] are etched on their hoods,
ridiculous, alien, like some terrible aunt,
a crest among tiles and scales
20 that moult with the darkening half
of every moon.

A basketful of ritual cobras
comes into the tame little house,
their brown-wheat glisten ringed with ripples.
25 They lick the room with their bodies, curves
uncurling, writing a sibilant[2] alphabet of panic
on my floor. Mother gives them milk
in saucers. She watches them suck
and bare the black-line design
30 etched on the brass of the saucer.

---

1. Eyeglasses or opera glasses with a handle.   2. Having or producing the sound of *s* or *sh*.

The snakeman wreathes their writhing
round his neck
for father's smiling
money. But I scream.

35 Sister ties her braids
with a knot of tassel.
But the weave of her knee-long braid has scales,
their gleaming held by a score of clean new pins.
I look till I see her hair again,
40 My night full of ghosts from a sadness
in a play, my left foot listens to my right footfall,
a clockwork clicking in the silence
within my walking.
                    The clickshod heel suddenly strikes
45 and slushes on a snake: I see him turn,
the green white of his belly
measured by bluish nodes, a water-bleached lotus stalk
plucked by a landsman hand. Yet panic rushes
my body to my feet, my spasms wring
50 and drain his fear and mine. I leave him sealed,
a flat-head whiteness on a stain.
                              Now
frogs can hop upon this sausage rope,
flies in the sun will mob the look in his eyes,

55 and I can walk through the woods.

                                        1966

Breaded Fish

Specially for me, she had some breaded
fish; even thrust a blunt-headed
smelt into my mouth;

and looked hurt when I could
5 neither sit nor eat, as a hood
of memory like a coil on a heath

opened in my eyes: a dark half-naked
length of woman, dead
on the beach in a yard of cloth,

10 dry, rolled by the ebb, breaded
by the grained indifference of sand. I headed
for the shore, my heart beating in my mouth.

                                        1966

Self-Portrait

I resemble everyone
but myself, and sometimes see
in shop-windows,
    despite the well-known laws
5   of optics,
the portrait of a stranger,
date unknown,
often signed in a corner
by my father.

1966

EDWARD KAMAU BRATHWAITE
b. 1930

FROM THE ARRIVANTS: A NEW WORLD TRILOGY

New World A-Comin'

1

Helpless like this
leader-
less like this,
heroless,
5   we met you: lover,
warrior, hater,
coming through the files
of the forest
soft foot
10 to soft soil
of silence:
we met in the soiled
tunnel of leaves.

Click lock
15 your fire-
lock fore-
arm fire-
arm flashed
fire and our firm
20 fleshed, flame
warm, fly
bitten warriors
fell.

How long
25   how long
O Lord
O devil
O fire
O flame
30   have we walked
have we journeyed
to this place
to this meeting
this shock
35   and shame
in the soiled
silence.

How long have we
travelled down
40   valleys down
slopes, silica
glinted, stones
dry as water,
to this flash
45   of flame in the forest.
O who now will help
us, help-
less, horse-
less, leader-
50   less, no
hope, no
Hawkins, no
Cortez[1] to come.
Prempeh imprisoned,
55   Tawiah dead,
Asantewa[2] bridled
and hung.
O who now can help
us: Geronimo, Tackie,
60   Montezuma[3] to come.

And the fire, our
fire, fashioning locks,
rocks darker than iron;

1. Hernando Cortez (1485–1547), the Spanish conqueror of Mexico. *Hawkins:* Sir John Hawkins (1532–1595), the first Englishman to traffic in slaves.
2. Yaa Asentewaa (1850–1921), the queen mother who, in Ghana, led Ashanti opposition against the British. Captured in 1901, she was exiled to the Seychelles. *Prempeh:* last king of the Ashanti (1888–1931). He reigned from 1894 until 1896, when he was deposed by the British and exiled to the Seychelles. *Tawiah:* probably Nii Takie Tawiah (1862–1902), king of Accra, Ghana.
3. Montezuma II (1480?–1520), the last Mexican emperor, was killed in the resistance against Cortez's conquest of Mexico. *Geronimo:* a chief of the Chiricahwa group of Apache Indians (ca. 1829–1909). His forces terrorized New Mexico and Arizona from 1875 until 1885, but surrendered to General George Cook in 1886. *Tackie:* Tacky, a Caribbean priest/leader. The 1760 Tacky Rebellion in Jamaica was fomented and in places led by obeah men (spiritual leaders).

fire betrayed us once
65   in our village; now
in the forest, fire falls
us like birds, hot pods
in our belly. Fire
falls walls, fashions
70   these fire-
locks darker than iron,
and we filed down the path
linked in a new
clinked silence of iron.

2

75   It will be a long long time before we see
this land again, these trees
again, drifting inland with the sound
of surf, smoke rising

It will be a long long time before we see
80   these farms again, soft wet slow green
again: Aburi, Akwamu,[4]
mist rising

Watch now these hard men, cold
clear eye'd like the water we ride,
85   skilful with sail and the rope and the tackle

Watch now these cold men, bold
as the water banging the bow in a sudden wild tide,
indifferent, it seems, to the battle

of wind in the water;
90   for our blood, mixed
soon with their passion in sport,

in indifference, in anger,
will create new soils, new souls, new
ancestors; will flow like this tide fixed

95   to the star by which this ship floats
to new worlds, new waters, new
harbours, the pride of our ancestors mixed

with the wind and the water
the flesh and the flies, the whips and the fixed
100   fear of pain in this chained and welcoming port.

1967

4. Towns in the Akan-speaking area of Ghana.

Ancestors

1

Every Friday morning my grandfather
left his farm of canefields, chickens, cows,
and rattled in his trap down to the harbour town
to sell his meat He was a butcher.
5   Six-foot-three and very neat: high collar,
winged, a grey cravat,° a waistcoat, watch-   *scarf*
chain just above the belt, thin narrow-
bottomed trousers, and the shoes his wife
would polish every night. He drove the trap
10   himself: slap of the leather reins
along the horse's back and he'd be off
with a top-hearted homburg[5] on his head:
black English country gentleman.

Now he is dead. The meat shop burned,
15   his property divided. A doctor bought
the horse. His mad alsatians killed it.
The wooden trap was chipped and chopped
by friends and neighbours and used to stop-
gap fences and for firewood. One yellow
20   wheel was rolled across the former cowpen gate.
Only his hat is left. I "borrowed" it.
I used to try it on and hear the night wind
man go battering through the canes, cocks waking up and thinking
it was dawn throughout the clinking country night.
25   Great caterpillar tractors clatter down
the broken highway now; a diesel engine grunts
where pigs once hunted garbage.
A thin asthmatic cow shares the untrashed garage.

2

All that I can remember of his wife,
30   my father's mother, is that she sang us songs
("Great Tom Is Cast"[6] was one), that frightened me.
And she would go chug chugging with a jar
of milk until its white pap turned to yellow
butter. And in the basket underneath the stairs
35   she kept the polish for grandfather's shoes.

All that I have of her is voices:
laughing me out of fear because a crappaud°   *toad*
jumped and splashed the dark where I was huddled
in the galvanized tin bath; telling us stories
40   round her fat white lamp. It was her Queen
Victoria lamp, she said; although the stamp

---

5. Old-fashioned, tall, felt hat.   6. Song about the making (or "casting") of a bell.

read Ever Ready. And in the night, I listened to her singing
in a Vicks and Vapour Rub-like voice what you would call the blues

3

Come-a look
45 come-a look
see wha' happen

come-a look
come-a look
see wha' happen

50 Sookey dead
Sookey dead
Sookey dead-o

Sookey dead
Sookey dead
55 Sookey dead-o.

Him a-wuk
him a-wuk
till 'e bleed-o

him a-wuk
60 him a-wuk
till 'e bleed-o

Sookey dead
Sookey dead
Sookey dead-o

65 Sookey dead
Sookey dead
Sookey dead-o . . .

1969

GREGORY CORSO
1930–2001

Marriage

Should I get married? Should I be good?
Astound the girl next door with my velvet suit and faustus hood?[1]
Don't take her to movies but to cemeteries

---

1. The legendary Faust, a medieval alchemist, sold his soul to the Devil. He gained not only knowledge
and power but renewed youth and attractiveness to young women.

tell all about werewolf bathtubs and forked clarinets
5   then desire her and kiss her and all the preliminaries
and she going just so far and I understanding why
not getting angry saying You must feel! It's beautiful to feel!
Instead take her in my arms lean against an old crooked tombstone
and woo her the entire night the constellations in the sky—

10   When she introduces me to her parents
back straightened, hair finally combed, strangled by a tie,
should I sit knees together on their 3rd degree sofa
and not ask Where's the bathroom?
How else to feel other than I am,
15   often thinking Flash Gordon² soap—
O how terrible it must be for a young man
seated before a family and the family thinking
We never saw him before! He wants our Mary Lou!
After tea and homemade cookies they ask What do you do for a living?

20   Should I tell them? Would they like me then?
Say All right get married, we're losing a daughter
but we're gaining a son—
And should I then ask Where's the bathroom?

O God, and the wedding! All her family and her friends
25   and only a handful of mine all scroungy and bearded
just wait to get at the drinks and food—
And the priest! he looking at me as if I masturbated
asking me Do you take this woman for your lawful wedded wife?
And I trembling what to say say Pie Glue!
30   I kiss the bride all those corny men slapping me on the back
She's all yours, boy! Ha-ha-ha!
And in their eyes you could see some obscene honeymoon going on—
Then all that absurd rice and clanky cans and shoes
Niagara Falls! Hordes of us! Husbands! Wives! Flowers! Chocolates!
35   All streaming into cozy hotels
All going to do the same thing tonight
The indifferent clerk he knowing what was going to happen
The lobby zombies they knowing what
The whistling elevator man he knowing
40   The winking bellboy knowing
Everybody knowing! I'd be almost inclined not to do anything!
Stay up all night! Stare that hotel clerk in the eye!
Screaming: I deny honeymoon! I deny honeymoon!
running rampant into those almost climactic suites
45   yelling Radio belly! Cat shovel!
O I'd live in Niagara forever! in a dark cave beneath the Falls
I'd sit there the Mad Honeymooner
devising ways to break marriages, a scourge of bigamy
a saint of divorce—

---

2. A 1930s science fiction "space opera" that first appeared as a comic strip, then as popular radio and
movie serials.

50 But I should get married I should be good
    How nice it'd be to come home to her
    and sit by the fireplace and she in the kitchen
    aproned young and lovely wanting my baby
    and so happy about me she burns the roast beef
55 and comes crying to me and I get up from my big papa chair
    saying Christmas teeth! Radiant brains! Apple deaf!
    God what a husband I'd make! Yes, I should get married!
    So much to do! like sneaking into Mr Jones' house late at night
    and cover his golf clubs with 1920 Norwegian books
60 Like hanging a picture of Rimbaud[3] on the lawnmower
    like pasting Tannu Tuva postage stamps[4] all over the picket fence
    like when Mrs Kindhead comes to collect for the Community Chest
    grab her and tell her There are unfavorable omens in the sky!
    And when the mayor comes to get my vote tell him
65 When are you going to stop people killing whales!
    And when the milkman comes leave him a note in the bottle
    Penguin dust, bring me penguin dust, I want penguin dust—

    Yet if I should get married and it's Connecticut and snow
    and she gives birth to a child and I am sleepless, worn,
70 up for nights, head bowed against a quiet window, the past behind
        me,
    finding myself in the most common of situations a trembling man
    knowledged with responsibility not twig-smear nor Roman coin soup—
    O what would that be like!
    Surely I'd give it for a nipple a rubber Tacitus[5]
75 For a rattle a bag of broken Bach records
    Tack Della Francesca[6] all over its crib
    Sew the Greek alphabet on its bib
    And build for its playpen a roofless Parthenon

    No, I doubt I'd be that kind of father
80 Not rural not snow no quiet window
    but hot smelly tight New York City
    seven flights up, roaches and rats in the walls
    a fat Reichian[7] wife screeching over potatoes Get a job!
    And five nose running brats in love with Batman
85 And the neighbors all toothless and dry haired
    like those hag masses of the 18th century
    all wanting to come in and watch TV
    The landlord wants his rent
    Grocery store Blue Cross Gas & Electric Knights of Columbus
90 Impossible to lie back and dream Telephone snow, ghost parking—
    No! I should not get married I should never get married!
    But—imagine If I were married to a beautiful sophisticated woman

3. Arthur Rimbaud (1854–1891), French Symbolist poet.
4. Collector's items issued by this Siberian republic located on the border between Russia and Mongolia.
5. Cornelius Tacitus (ca. 56–120), Roman historian; punning on *tacitus,* Latin for "silent."

6. Piero della Francesca (ca. 1420–1492), Italian painter. Johann Sebastian Bach (1685–1750), German composer.
7. Wilhelm Reich (1897–1957) founded a controversial school of psychiatry that emphasized love and sexual pleasure as the basis of mental health.

tall and pale wearing an elegant black dress and long black gloves
holding a cigarette holder in one hand and a highball in the other
95 and we lived high up in a penthouse with a huge window
from which we could see all of New York and ever farther on clearer
        days
No, can't imagine myself married to that pleasant prison dream—

O but what about love? I forget love
not that I am incapable of love
100 it's just that I see love as odd as wearing shoes—
I never wanted to marry a girl who was like my mother
And Ingrid Bergman[8] was always impossible
And there's maybe a girl now but she's already married
And I don't like men and—
105 but there's got to be somebody!
Because what if I'm 60 years old and not married,
all alone in a furnished room with pee stains on my underwear
and everybody else is married! All the universe married but me!

Ah, yet well I know that were a woman possible as I am possible
110 then marriage would be possible—
Like SHE in her lonely alien gaud[9] waiting her Egyptian lover
so I wait—bereft of 2,000 years and the bath of life.

                                                        1960

TED HUGHES
1930–1998

The Thought-Fox

I imagine this midnight moment's forest:
Something else is alive
Beside the clock's loneliness
And this blank page where my fingers move.

5 Through the window I see no star:
Something more near
Though deeper within darkness
Is entering the loneliness:

Cold, delicately as the dark snow,
10 A fox's nose touches twig, leaf;
Two eyes serve a movement, that now
And again now, and now, and now

---

8. Swedish actor (1915–1982) in American films, known for her beauty.
9. Showy clothing. In H. Rider Haggard's 1887 novel of this title, "She" gains eternal youth by bathing in a pillar of flame and waits thousands of years for the return of her lover.

Sets neat prints into the snow
Between trees, and warily a lame
15 Shadow lags by stump and in hollow
Of a body that is bold to come

Across clearings, an eye,
A widening deepening greenness,
Brilliantly, concentratedly,
20 Coming about its own business

Till, with a sudden sharp hot stink of fox
It enters the dark hole of the head.
The window is starless still; the clock ticks,
The page is printed.

1957

Wind

This house has been far out at sea all night,
The woods crashing through darkness, the booming hills,
Winds stampeding the fields under the window
Floundering black astride and blinding wet

5 Till day rose; then under an orange sky
The hills had new places, and wind wielded
Blade-light, luminous and emerald,
Flexing like the lens of a mad eye.

At noon I scaled along the house-side as far as
10 The coal-house door. I dared once to look up—
Through the brunt wind that dented the balls of my eyes
The tent of the hills drummed and strained its guyrope,

The fields quivering, the skyline a grimace,
At any second to bang and vanish with a flap:
15 The wind flung a magpie away and a black-
Back gull bent like an iron bar slowly. The house

Rang like some fine green goblet in the note
That any second would shatter it. Now deep
In chairs, in front of the great fire, we grip
20 Our hearts and cannot entertain book, thought,

Or each other. We watch the fire blazing,
And feel the roots of the house move, but sit on,
Seeing the window tremble to come in,
Hearing the stones cry out under the horizons.

1957

Pike

Pike, three inches long, perfect
Pike in all parts, green tigering the gold.
Killers from the egg: the malevolent aged grin.
They dance on the surface among the flies.

5   Or move, stunned by their own grandeur,
Over a bed of emerald, silhouette
Of submarine delicacy and horror.
A hundred feet long in their world.

In ponds, under the heat-struck lily pads—
10   Gloom of their stillness:
Logged on last year's black leaves, watching upwards.
Or hung in an amber cavern of weeds

The jaws' hooked clamp and fangs
Not to be changed at this date;
15   A life subdued to its instrument;
The gills kneading quietly, and the pectorals.

Three we kept behind glass,
Jungled in weed: three inches, four,
And four and a half: fed fry° to them—   *young fish*
20   Suddenly there were two. Finally one

With a sag belly and the grin it was born with.
And indeed they spare nobody.
Two, six pounds each, over two feet long,
High and dry and dead in the willow-herb—

25   One jammed past its gills down the other's gullet:
The outside eye stared: as a vice locks—
The same iron in this eye
Though its film shrank in death.

A pond I fished, fifty yards across,
30   Whose lilies and muscular tench[1]
Had outlasted every visible stone
Of the monastery that planted them—

Stilled legendary depth:
It was as deep as England. It held
35   Pike too immense to stir, so immense and old
That past nightfall I dared not cast

---

1. Variety of freshwater fish.

But silently cast and fished
With the hair frozen on my head
For what might move, for what eye might move.
40 The still splashes on the dark pond,

Owls hushing the floating woods
Frail on my ear against the dream
Darkness beneath night's darkness had freed,
That rose slowly towards me, watching.

1959, 1960

Theology

No, the serpent did not
Seduce Eve to the apple.[2]
All that's simply
Corruption of the facts.

5 Adam ate the apple.
Eve ate Adam.
The serpent ate Eve.
This is the dark intestine.

The serpent, meanwhile,
10 Sleeps his meal off in Paradise—
Smiling to hear
God's querulous calling.

1967

Examination at the Womb-Door[3]

Who owns these scrawny little feet? *Death.*
Who owns this bristly scorched-looking face? *Death.*
Who owns these still-working lungs? *Death.*
Who owns this utility coat of muscles? *Death.*
5 Who owns these unspeakable guts? *Death.*
Who owns these questionable brains? *Death.*
All this messy blood? *Death.*
These minimum-efficiency eyes? *Death.*
This wicked little tongue? *Death.*
10 This occasional wakefulness? *Death.*

Given, stolen, or held pending trial?
Held.

2. Cf. Genesis 3.
3. The demonic hero of the Crow myth is interrogated by an unidentified questioner.

Who owns the whole rainy, stony earth? *Death*.
Who owns all of space? *Death*.

15   Who is stronger than hope? *Death*.
Who is stronger than the will? *Death*.
Stronger than love? *Death*.
Stronger than life? *Death*.

But who is stronger than death?
                        Me, evidently.
20   Pass, Crow.

                                        1970

Daffodils

Remember how we[4] picked the daffodils?
Nobody else remembers, but I remember.
Your daughter came with her armfuls, eager and happy.
Helping the harvest. She has forgotten.
5   She cannot even remember you. And we sold them.
It sounds like sacrilege, but we sold them.
Were we so poor? Old Stoneman, the grocer,
Boss-eyed, his blood-pressure purpling to beetroot[5]
(It was his last chance,
10   He would die in the same great freeze as you),
He persuaded us. Every Spring
He always bought them, sevenpence a dozen,
"A custom of the house".

Besides, we still weren't sure we wanted to own
15   Anything. Mainly we were hungry
To convert everything to profit.
Still nomads—still strangers
To our whole possession. The daffodils
Were incidental gilding of the deeds.[6]
20   Treasure trove. They simply came,
And they kept on coming.
As if not from the sod but falling from heaven.
Our lives were still a raid on our own good luck.
We knew we'd live for ever. We had not learned
25   What a fleeting glance of the everlasting
Daffodils are. Never identified
The nuptial flight of the rarest ephemera[7]—
Our own days!
                        We thought they were a windfall.
30   Never guessed they were a last blessing.
So we sold them. We worked at selling them

---

4. Hughes is addressing his first wife, the American poet Sylvia Plath (1932–1963; see pp. 1836–45), who committed suicide during London's coldest winter in the twentieth century.

5. A beet with edible, purplish-red roots.
6. Documents establishing legal possession of a house.
7. Insect that lives only a few days.

As if employed on somebody else's
Flower-farm. You bent at it
In the rain of that April—your last April.
35 We bent there together, among the soft shrieks
Of their jostled stems, the wet shocks shaken
Of their girlish dance-frocks—
Fresh-opened dragonflies, wet and flimsy,
Opened too early.

40 We piled their frailty lights on a carpenter's bench,
Distributed leaves among the dozens—
Buckling blade-leaves, limber, groping for air, zinc-silvered—
Propped their raw butts in bucket water,
Their oval, meaty butts,
45 And sold them, sevenpence a bunch—

Wind-wounds, spasms from the dark earth,
With their odourless metals,
A flamy purification of the deep grave's stony cold
As if ice had a breath—

50 We sold them, to wither.
The crop thickened faster than we could thin it.
Finally, we were overwhelmed
And we lost our wedding-present scissors.

Every March since they have lifted again
55 Out of the same bulbs, the same
Baby-cries from the thaw,
Ballerinas too early for music, shiverers
In the draughty wings of the year.
On that same groundswell of memory, fluttering
60 They return to forget you stooping there
Behind the rainy curtains of a dark April,
Snipping their stems.

But somewhere your scissors remember. Wherever they are.
Here somewhere, blades wide open,
65 April by April
Sinking deeper
Through the sod—an anchor, a cross of rust.

1998

Platform One[8]

Holiday squeals, as if all were scrambling for their lives,
Panting aboard the "Cornish Riviera".[9]

8. On platform number one of London's Padding-ton Station, Charles Sargeant Jagger's larger-than-life-size bronze statue of the soldier described in this poem stands as a memorial to the "Men and Women of the Great Western Railway who gave their Lives for King and Country" in the World Wars of 1914–18 and 1939–45.
9. Coastal resort of south Cornwall. Here, the name of a steam locomotive.

Then overflow of relief and luggage and children,
Then ducking to smile out as the station moves.

5   Out there on the platform, under the rain,
Under his rain-cape, helmet and full pack,
Somebody, head bowed reading something,
Doesn't know he's missing his train.

He's completely buried in that book.
10 He's forgotten utterly where he is.
He's forgotten Paddington, forgotten
Timetables, forgotten the long, rocking

Cradle of a journey into the golden West,
The coach's soft wingbeat—as light
15 And straight as a dove's flight.
Like a graveyard statue sentry cast

In blackened old bronze. Is he reading poems?
A letter? The burial service? The raindrops
Beaded along his helmet rim are bronze.
20 The words on his page are bronze. Their meanings bronze.

Sunk in his bronze world he stands, enchanted.
His bronze mind is deep among the dead.
Sunk so deep among the dead that, much
As he would like to remember us all, he cannot.

1996

GARY SNYDER
b. 1930

Above Pate Valley[1]

We finished clearing the last
Section of trail by noon,
High on the ridge-side
Two thousand feet above the creek
5   Reached the pass, went on
Beyond the white pine groves,
Granite shoulders, to a small
Green meadow watered by the snow,
Edged with Aspen—sun
10 Straight high and blazing
But the air was cool.

---

1. In Yosemite National Park.

Ate a cold fried trout in the
Trembling shadows. I spied
A glitter, and found a flake
15   Black volcanic glass-obsidian—
By a flower. Hands and knees
Pushing the Bear grass, thousands
Of arrowhead leavings over a
Hundred yards. Not one good
20   Head, just razor flakes
On a hill snowed all but summer,
A land of fat summer deer,
They came to camp. On their
Own trails. I followed my own
25   Trail here. Picked up the cold-drill,
Pick, singlejack,[2] and sack
Of dynamite.
Ten thousand years.

1959

Four Poems for Robin

Siwashing it out once in Siuslaw Forest[3]

I slept under   rhododendron
All night   blossoms fell
Shivering on   a sheet of cardboard
Feet stuck   in my pack
5   Hands deep   in my pockets
Barely   able   to   sleep.
I remembered   when we were in school
Sleeping together   in a big warm bed
We were   the youngest lovers
10   When we broke up   we were still nineteen.
Now our   friends are married
You teach   school back east
I dont mind   living this way
Green hills   the long blue beach
15   But sometimes   sleeping in the open
I think back   when I had you.

A spring night in Shokoku-ji[4]

Eight years ago this May
We walked under cherry blossoms
At night in an orchard in Oregon.

---

2. Short-handled hammer used, with the other tools, to cut holes in solid rock for dynamite.
3. West of Eugene, Oregon. *Siwashing:* camping with light equipment, roughing it.
4. Fourteenth-century Zen monastery in Kyoto (once the capital of Japan).

20 All that I wanted then
Is forgotten now, but you.
Here in the night
In a garden of the old capital
I feel the trembling ghost of Yugao[5]
25 I remember your cool body
Naked under a summer cotton dress.

An autumn morning in Shokoku-ji

Last night watching the Pleiades,[6]
Breath smoking in the moonlight,
Bitter memory like vomit
30 Choked my throat.
I unrolled a sleeping bag
On mats on the porch
Under thick autumn stars.
In dream you appeared
35 (Three times in nine years)
Wild, cold, and accusing.
I woke shamed and angry:
The pointless wars of the heart.
Almost dawn. Venus and Jupiter.[7]
40 The first time I have
Ever seen them close.

December at Yase[8]

You said, that October,
In the tall dry grass by the orchard
When you chose to be free,
45 "Again someday, maybe ten years."
After college I saw you
One time. You were strange.
And I was obsessed with a plan.

Now ten years and more have
50 Gone by: I've always known
          where you were—
I might have gone to you
Hoping to win your love back.
You still are single.

---

5. In the Japanese novel *Genji monogatori* (*The Tale of Genji*), written between 1001 and 1006, Murasaki-no-Shikibu (Lady Murasaki) recounts the amorous exploits of the young Prince Genji. Genji has a brief liaison with a young woman, Yugao, who dies suddenly and mysteriously. After happening upon a dress of hers, he writes a poem.

6. A cluster of stars in the constellation Taurus; named after the seven daughters of Atlas, in Greek mythology.
7. Snyder both names the plants and alludes to the Roman gods (Venus, goddess of love and beauty; Jupiter, ruler of all the gods).
8. Near northeast Kyoto.

55 I didn't.
I thought I must make it alone. I
Have done that.

Only in dream, like this dawn,
Does the grave, awed intensity
60 Of our young love
Return to my mind, to my flesh.

We had what the others
All crave and seek for;
We left it behind at nineteen.

65 I feel ancient, as though I had
Lived many lives.

And may never now know
If I am a fool
Or have done what my
70   karma demands.

                                          1968

Instructions

Fuel filler cap
     —haven't I seen this before? The
     sunlight under the eaves, mottled
     shadow, on the knurled° rim of   *milled*
5   dull silver metal.

Oil filler cap
     bright yellow,
     horns like a snail
     —the oil's down there—
10   amber, clean, it
     falls back to its pit.

Oil drain plug
     so short, from in to out. Best
     let it drain when it is hot.

15 Engine switch
     off, on. Off, on. Just
     two places. Forever,

     or, not even one.

                                          1996

DEREK WALCOTT
b. 1930

A Far Cry from Africa

A wind is ruffling the tawny pelt
Of Africa. Kikuyu,¹ quick as flies,
Batten upon the bloodstreams of the veldt.²
Corpses are scattered through a paradise.
5   Only the worm, colonel of carrion, cries:
"Waste no compassion on these separate dead!"
Statistics justify and scholars seize
The salients of colonial policy.
What is that to the white child hacked in bed?
10   To savages, expendable as Jews?

Threshed out by beaters,³ the long rushes break
In a white dust of ibises whose cries
Have wheeled since civilization's dawn
From the parched river or beast-teeming plain.
15   The violence of beast on beast is read
As natural law, but upright man
Seeks his divinity by inflicting pain.
Delirious as these worried beasts, his wars
Dance to the tightened carcass of a drum,
20   While he calls courage still that native dread
Of the white peace contracted by the dead.

Again brutish necessity wipes its hands
Upon the napkin of a dirty cause, again
A waste of our compassion, as with Spain,⁴
25   The gorilla wrestles with the superman.
I who am poisoned with the blood of both,
Where shall I turn, divided to the vein?
I who have cursed
The drunken officer of British rule, how choose
30   Between this Africa and the English tongue I love?
Betray them both, or give back what they give?
How can I face such slaughter and be cool?
How can I turn from Africa and live?

1962

---

1. An east African tribe whose members, as Mau
Mau fighters, conducted an eight-year campaign
of violent resistance against British colonial set-
tlers in Kenya.
2. Grassland, usually with some trees and shrubs.

Batten: feed gluttonously.
3. In big-game hunting, people are hired to beat
the brush, driving birds—such as ibises (line 12)—
and other animals into the open.
4. The Spanish Civil War (1936–39).

Nights in the Gardens of Port of Spain⁵

Night, the black summer, simplifies her smells
into a village; she assumes the impenetrable

musk of the negro, grows secret as sweat,
her alleys odorous with shucked oyster shells,

5   coals of gold oranges, braziers of melon.
Commerce and tambourines increase her heat.

Hellfire or the whorehouse: crossing Park Street,
a surf of sailors' faces crests, is gone

with the sea's phosphoresence; the boites-de-nuit⁶
10   tinkle like fireflies in her thick hair.

Blinded by headlamps, deaf to taxi klaxons,°   *horns*
she lifts her face from the cheap, pitch oil flare

towards white stars, like cities, flashing neon,
burning to be the bitch she must become.

15   As daylight breaks the coolie turns his tumbril⁷
of hacked, beheaded coconuts towards home.

                                    1964

The Glory Trumpeter

Old Eddie's face, wrinkled with river lights,
Looked like a Mississippi man's. The eyes,
Derisive and avuncular at once,
Swivelling, fixed me. They'd seen
5   Too many wakes, too many cathouse nights.
The bony, idle fingers on the valves
Of his knee-cradled horn could tear
Through "Georgia on My Mind" or "Jesus Saves"
With the same fury of indifference,
10   If what propelled such frenzy was despair.

Now, as the eyes sealed in the ashen flesh,
And Eddie, like a deacon at his prayer,
Rose, tilting the bright horn, I saw a flash
Of gulls and pigeons from the dunes of coal

5. Capital of Trinidad, British West Indies.
6. Nightclubs (French).

7. Open cart used during the French Revolution to carry condemned people to the guillotine.

15 Near my grandmother's barracks on the wharves,
I saw the sallow faces of those men
Who sighed as if they spoke into their graves
About the Negro in America. That was when
The Sunday comics sprawled out on her floor,
20 Sent from the States, had a particular odour,
A smell of money mingled with man's sweat.

And yet, if Eddie's features held our fate,
Secure in childhood I did not know then
A jesus-ragtime or gut-bucket blues
25 To the bowed heads of lean, compliant men
Back from the States in their funereal serge,
Black, rusty Homburgs[8] and limp waiters' ties
With honey accents and lard-coloured eyes
Was Joshua's ram's horn wailing for the Jews
30 Of patient bitterness or bitter siege.[9]

Now it was that as Eddie turned his back
On our young crowd out fêteing, swilling liquor,
And blew, eyes closed, one foot up, out to sea,
His horn aimed at those cities of the Gulf,
35 Mobile and Galveston and sweetly meted
The horn of plenty through a bitter cup,
In lonely exaltation blaming me
For all whom race and exile have defeated,
For my own uncle in America,
40 That living there I never could look up.

1964

The Gulf

[FOR JACK AND BARBARA HARRISON]

I

The airport coffee tastes less of America.
Sour, unshaven, dreading the exertion
of tightening, racked nerves fuelled with liquor,

some smoky, resinous Bourbon,
5 the body, buckling at its casket hole,
a roar like last night's blast racing its engines,

watches the fumes of the exhausted soul
as the trans-Texas jet, screeching, begins
its flight and friends diminish. So, to be aware

---

8. Old-fashioned, felt hats. *Funereal serge:* cheap,
dark suits.

9. At the fall of the city of Jericho (Joshua 6.1–
21).

10 of the divine union the soul detaches
    itself from created things.[1] "We're in the air,"
    the Texan near me grins. All things: these matches

    from LBJ's[2] campaign hotel, this rose
    given me at dawn in Austin by a child,
15 this book of fables by Borges,[3] its prose

    a stalking, moonlit tiger. What was willed
    on innocent, sun-streaked Dallas,[4] the beast's claw
    curled round that hairspring rifle is revealed

    on every page as lunacy or feral law;
20 circling that wound we leave Love Field.[5]
    Fondled, these objects conjure hotels,

    quarrels, new friendships, brown limbs
    nakedly moulded as these autumn hills
    memory penetrates as the jet climbs

25 the new clouds over Texas; their home means
    an island suburb, forest, mountain water;
    they are the simple properties for scenes

    whose joy exhausts like grief, scenes where we learn,
    exchanging the least gifts, this rose, this napkin,
30 that those we love are objects we return,

    that this lens on the desert's wrinkled skin
    has priced our flesh, all that we love in pawn
    to that brass ball, that the gifts, multiplying

    clutter and choke the heart, and that I shall
35 watch love reclaim its things as I lie dying.
    My very flesh and blood! Each seems a petal

    shrivelling from its core. I watch them burn,
    by the nerves' flare I catch their skeletal
    candour! Best never to be born

40 the great dead cry.[6] Their works shine on our shelves,
    by twilight tour their gilded gravestone spines,
    and read until the lamplit page revolves

---

1. With reference to the Neoplatonic doctrine that earthly relationships and attachments contaminate the striving for spiritual union with God; in contrast to the teaching that divine love is manifested in the created world and in human relationships.
2. Lyndon Baines Johnson (1906–1973), thirty-sixth president of the United States.
3. Jorge Luis Borges (1899–1986), Argentinian man of letters, best-known for his short stories.
4. With an allusion to the assassination there of President John F. Kennedy, November 22, 1963.
5. The Dallas airport.
6. E.g., in Sophocles, *Oedipus at Colonus:* "Not to be born surpasses thought and speech. / The second best is to have seen the light / And then to go back quickly whence we came."

to a white stasis° whose detachment shines   *stillness*
like a propeller's rainbowed radiance.
45 Circling like us; no comfort for their loves!

II

The cold glass darkens. Elizabeth wrote once
that we make glass the image of our pain;
I watch clouds boil past the cold, sweating pane

above the Gulf. All styles yearn to be plain
50 as life. The face of the loved object under glass
is plainer still. Yet, somehow, at this height,

above this cauldron boiling with its wars,
our old earth, breaking to familiar light,
that cloud-bound mummy with self-healing scars

55 peeled of her cerements° again looks new;   *grave clothes*
some cratered valley heals itself with sage,
through that grey, fading massacre a blue

light-hearted creek flutes of some seige
to the amnesia of drumming water.
60 Their cause is crystalline: the divine union

of these detached, divided States, whose slaughter
darkens each summer now, as one by one,
the smoke of bursting ghettos clouds the glass

down every coast where filling-station signs
65 proclaim the Gulf, an air, heavy with gas,
sickens the state, from Newark to New Orleans.

III

Yet the South felt like home. Wrought balconies,
the sluggish river with its tidal drawl,
the tropic air charged with the extremities

70 of patience, a heat heavy with oil,
canebrakes, that legendary jazz. But fear
thickened my voice, that strange, familiar soil

prickled and barbed the texture of my hair,
my status as a secondary soul.
75 The Gulf, your gulf, is daily widening,

each blood-red rose warns of that coming night
when there's no rock cleft to go hidin' in[7]
and all the rocks catch fire, when that black might,

---

7. A reference to the hymn that begins "Rock of Ages, cleft for me, / Let me hide myself in thee." The "rock" signifies Christ, "cleft" in his Crucifixion.

their stalking, moonless panthers turn from Him
80   whose voice they can no more believe, when the black X's[8]
mark their passover with slain seraphim.[9]

IV

The Gulf shines, dull as lead. The coast of Texas
glints like a metal rim. I have no home
as long as summer bubbling to its head

85   boils for that day when in the Lord God's name
the coals of fire are heaped upon the head
of all whose gospel is the whip and flame,

age after age, the uninstructing dead.

                                                                    1969

From The Schooner *Flight*

1 *Adios, Carenage*[1]

In idle August, while the sea soft,
and leaves of brown islands stick to the rim
of this Caribbean, I blow out the light
by the dreamless face of Maria Concepcion
5   to ship as a seaman on the schooner *Flight*.
Out in the yard turning grey in the dawn,
I stood like a stone and nothing else move
but the cold sea rippling like galvanize
and the nail holes of stars in the sky roof,
10   till a wind start to interfere with the trees.
I pass me dry neighbour sweeping she yard
as I went downhill, and I nearly said:
"Sweep soft, you witch, 'cause she don't sleep hard,"
but the bitch look through me like I was dead.
15   A route taxi pull up, park-lights still on.
The driver size up my bags with a grin:
"This time, Shabine, like you really gone!"
I ain't answer the ass, I simply pile in
the back seat and watch the sky burn
20   above Laventille[2] pink as the gown
in which the woman I left was sleeping,
and I look in the rearview and see a man
exactly like me, and the man was weeping
for the houses, the streets, the whole fucking island.
25   Christ have mercy on all sleeping things!
From that dog rotting down Wrightson Road

8. Such as Malcolm X, the Black Muslim leader, assassinated February 21, 1965, and the Black Panthers, a militant black organization.
9. Angels of the highest order.
1. Careening (French), or the pulling of a ship onto land, especially for cleaning or repairing; the name of a port in Trinidad, west of Port of Spain. *Adios:* goodbye (Spanish).
2. Hilly, low-income suburb east of Port of Spain.

to when I was a dog on these streets;
if loving these islands must be my load,
out of corruption my soul takes wings,
30 But they had started to poison my soul
with their big house, big car, big-time bohbohl,³
coolie, nigger, Syrian, and French Creole,
so I leave it for them and their carnival—
I taking a sea-bath, I gone down the road.
35 I know these islands from Monos to Nassau,
a rusty head sailor with sea-green eyes
that they nickname Shabine, the patois° for   *spoken dialect*
any red nigger, and I, Shabine, saw
when these slums of empire was paradise.
40 I'm just a red nigger who love the sea,
I had a sound colonial education,
I have Dutch, nigger, and English in me,
and either I'm nobody, or I'm a nation.

But Maria Concepcion was all my thought
45 watching the sea heaving up and down
as the port side of dories, schooners, and yachts
was painted afresh by the strokes of the sun
signing her name with every reflection;
I knew when dark-haired evening put on
50 her bright silk at sunset, and, folding the sea,
sidled under the sheet with her starry laugh,
that there'd be no rest, there'd be no forgetting.
Is like telling mourners round the graveside
about resurrection, they want the dead back,
55 so I smile to myself as the bow rope untied
and the *Flight* swing seaward: "Is no use repeating
that the sea have more fish. I ain't want her
dressed in the sexless light of a seraph,°   *angel*
I want those round brown eyes like a marmoset,⁴ and
60 till the day when I can lean back and laugh,
those claws that tickled my back on sweating
Sunday afternoons, like a crab on wet sand."
As I worked, watching the rotting waves come
past the bow that scissor the sea like silk,
65 I swear to you all, by my mother's milk,
by the stars that shall fly from tonight's furnace,
that I loved them, my children, my wife, my home;
I loved them as poets love the poetry
that kills them, as drowned sailors the sea.

70 You ever look up from some lonely beach
and see a far schooner? Well, when I write
this poem, each phrase go be soaked in salt;
I go draw and knot every line as tight
as ropes in this rigging; in simple speech

---

3. Or *bobol*: corruption by highly placed people
(Eastern Caribbean English).   4. South American monkey.

75   my common language go be the wind,
      my pages the sails of the schooner *Flight*.

1979

Midsummer

    Certain things here[5] are quietly American—
    that chain-link fence dividing the absent roars
    of the beach from the empty ball park, its holes
    muttering the word umpire instead of empire;
5   the gray, metal light where an early pelican
    coasts, with its engine off, over the pink fire
    of a sea whose surface is as cold as Maine's.
    The light warms up the sides of white, eager Cessnas[6]
    parked at the airstrip under the freckling hills
10 of St. Thomas. The sheds, the brown, functional hangar,
    are like those of the Occupation in the last war.
    The night left a rank smell under the casuarinas,[7]
    the villas have fenced-off beaches where the natives walk,
    illegal immigrants from unlucky islands
15 who envy the smallest polyp its right to work.
    Here the wetback crab and the mollusc are citizens,
    and the leaves have green cards. Bulldozers jerk
    and gouge out a hill, but we all know that the dust
    is industrial and must be suffered. Soon—
20 the sea's corrugations are sheets of zinc
    soldered by the sun's steady acetylene. This
    drizzle that falls now is American rain,
    stitching stars in the sand. My own corpuscles
    are changing as fast. I fear what the migrant envies:
25 the starry pattern they make—the flag on the post office—
    the quality of the dirt, the fealty changing under my foot.

1984

From Omeros[8]

Chapter XXXVIII

III

    Who decrees a great epoch? The meridian of Greenwich.[9]
    Who doles out our zeal, and in which way lies our
    hope? In the cobbles of sinister Shoreditch,[1]

5. I.e., in Trinidad.
6. Make of small aircraft.
7. Trees with jointed branches.
8. *Omeros* (the Greek name for Homer) is a book-length epic poem that transposes elements of Homer's *Iliad* and *Odyssey* from the Aegean to the Caribbean. Walcott's principal subject—like Homer's—is the history of his people, and in this chapter the poem's narrator questions British claims for the "great epoch" of their empire, bitterly juxtaposing "our" Caribbean experience of exploitation with the experience of the exploiting imperialists.
9. The system of geographic longitude was worked out in London's Royal Observatory, beside the river Thames at Greenwich. The prime meridian, or longitude 0°, passes through the Observatory.
1. District, for many centuries a slum, in London's

in the widening rings of Big Ben's iron flower,[2]
5   in the barges chained like our islands to the Thames.
Where is the alchemical corn and the light it yields?

Where, in which stones of the Abbey, are incised our names?[3]
Who defines our delight? St. Martin-in-the-Fields.[4]
After every Michaelmas,[5] its piercing soprano steeple

10 defines our delight. Within whose palatable vault
will echo the Saints' litany of our island people?
St. Paul's salt shaker,[6] when we are worth their salt.

Stand by the tilted crosses of well-quiet Glen-da-Lough.[7]
Follow the rook's crook'd finger to the ivied grange.[8]
15 As black as the rook is, it comes from a higher stock.

Who screams out our price? The crows of the Corn Exchange.[9]
Where are the pleasant pastures? A green baize-table.[1]
Who invests in our happiness? The Chartered Tour.

Who will teach us a history of which we too are capable?
20 The red double-decker's view of the Bloody Tower.[2]
When are our brood, like the sparrows, a public nuisance?

When they screech at the sinuous swans on the Serpentine.[3]
The swans are royally protected,[4] but in whose hands
are the black crusts of our children? In the pointing sign

25 under the harps of the willows, to the litter of Margate Sands.[5]
What has all this to do with the price of fish, our salary
tidally scanned with the bank-rate by waxworks tellers?[6]

Where is the light of the world?[7] In the National Gallery.
In Palladian Wren. In the City[8] that can buy and sell us
30 the packets of tea stirred with our crystals of sweat.

East End.
2. Famous bell in the Clock Tower of London's Houses of Parliament.
3. Many British poets are commemorated in the Poets' Corner of Westminster Abbey.
4. Church, famous for its music, at the edge of London's Trafalgar Square.
5. The feast of St. Michael, September 29.
6. The great dome of London's St. Paul's Cathedral may be said to resemble a salt shaker (or an onion, as in line 32).
7. Celtic crosses of the monastic community, founded in the seventh century, in the Wicklow Hills of southern Ireland.
8. Country house with attached farm buildings.
9. Handsome building in London's Mark Lane, erected in 1828 to be the center of the city's wholesale corn trade.
1. Imitation-felt-covered table for playing bridge, craps, roulette, etc.

2. From the upper deck of a London bus one can see the Bloody Tower (reputedly the site of the murder of the little princes, Edward V and Richard, duke of York) in the larger complex of the Tower of London.
3. Lake in London's Hyde Park.
4. Swans in England are, by tradition, owned by the Crown.
5. Popular seaside resort on the Thames Estuary, or lower end, where it meets the North Sea.
6. I.e, bank clerks working mechanically.
7. Reference to the Pre-Raphaelite painter William Holman Hunt's famous picture of Christ, *The Light of the World.*
8. London's financial district. *Palladian Wren:* Sir Christopher Wren (1632–1723), architect of St. Paul's Cathedral and many lesser London churches, was a leading exponent of the neoclassical style inaugurated by the Italian architect Andrea Palladio (1508–1580).

Where is our sublunar[9] peace? In that sickle sovereign
peeling the gilt from St. Paul's onion silhouette.
There is our lunar peace: in the glittering grain

of the coined estuary, our moonlit, immortal wheat,[1]
35   its white sail cresting the gradual swell of the Downs,[2]
startling the hare from the pillars on Salisbury Plain,[3]

sharpening the grimaces of thin-lipped market towns,
whitewashing the walls of Brixton,[4] darkening the grain
when coal-shadows cross it. Dark future down darker street.

1990

ALAN BROWNJOHN
b. 1931

Common Sense[1]

An agricultural labourer, who has
A wife and four children, receives 20s[2] a week.
¾ buys food, and the members of the family
Have three meals a day.
5   How much is that per person per meal?
        —From Pitman's Common Sense Arithmetic, 1917

A gardener, paid 24s a week, is
Fined ⅓ if he comes to work late.
At the end of 26 weeks, he receives
10   £30.5.3. How
Often was he late?
        —From Pitman's Common Sense Arithmetic, 1917

A milk dealer buys milk at 3d a quart. He
Dilutes it with 3% water and sells
15   124 gallons of the mixture at
4d per quart. How much of his profit is made by
Adulterating the milk?
        —From Pitman's Common Sense Arithmetic, 1917

9. Of the terrestrial world.
1. Cf. Thomas Treherne, Centuries of Meditations
3.3: "The corn was orient and immortal wheat."
2. The South Downs, an area of rolling upland on
the English south coast.
3. Stonehenge, prehistoric circle of gigantic
standing stones set in the middle of Salisbury
Plain, on the Downs.
4. District of south London.
1. Brownjohn writes of this "found poem" (see

"Versification," p. 2050): "The book and its date
are real, and so are the 'sum' stanzas, but I short-
ened, adapted the phrasing to make manageable
lines. Occasionally, the math doesn't make sense
as a result of my adaptation."
2. s: abbreviation of shilling, coin worth 12d—
abbreviation of denarii (Latin), pennies—of former
British currency. £30.5.3 (line 10) = 30 pounds,
5 shillings, and 3 pennies.

The table printed below gives the number
20   Of paupers in the United Kingdom, and
The total cost of poor relief.[3]
Find the average number
Of paupers per ten thousand people.
            —*From Pitman's Common Sense Arithmetic, 1917*

25   An army had to march to the relief of
A besieged town, 500 miles away, which
Had telegraphed that it could hold out for 18 days.
The army made forced marches at the rate of 18
Miles a day. Would it be there in time?
30   —*From Pitman's Common Sense Arithmetic, 1917*

Out of an army of 28,000 men,
15% were
Killed, 25% were
Wounded. Calculate
35   How many men there were left to fight.
            —*From Pitman's Common Sense Arithmetic, 1917*

These sums are offered to
That host of young people in our Elementary Schools, who
Are so ardently desirous of setting
40   Foot upon the first rung of the
Educational ladder . . .
            —*From Pitman's Common Sense Arithmetic, 1917*

                                                                    1989

JAY MacPHERSON
b. 1931

The Swan

White-habited, the mystic Swan
Walks her rank° cloister as the night draws down,   *overgrown*
In sweet communion with her sister shade,
Matchless and unassayed.

5   The tower of ivory sways,
Gaze bends to mirrored gaze:
This perfect arc embraces all her days.
And when she comes to die,
The treasures of her silence patent lie:
10   "I am all that is and was and shall be,
My garment may no man put by."

                                                                    1957

3. Welfare payments.

A Lost Soul

Some are plain lucky—we ourselves among them:
Houses with books, with gardens, all we wanted,
Work we enjoy, with colleagues we feel close to—
    Love we have, even:

5   True love and candid, faithful, strong as gospel,
Patient, untiring, fond when we are fretful.
Having so much, how is it that we ache for
    Those darker others?

Some days for them we could let slip the whole damn
10   Soft bed we've made ourselves, our friends in Heaven
Let slip away, buy back with blood our ancient
    Vampires and demons.

First loves and oldest, what names shall I call you?
Older to me than language, old as breathing,
15   Born with me, in this flesh: by now I know you're
    Greed, pride and envy.

Too long I've shut you out, denied acquaintance,
Favoured less barefaced vices, hoped to pass for
Reasonable, rate with those who more inclined to
20   Self-hurt than murder.

You were my soul: in arrogance I banned you.
Now I recant—return, possess me, take my
Hands, bind my eyes, infallibly restore my
    Share in perdition.

1981

GEOFFREY HILL
b. 1932

The Distant Fury of Battle

Grass resurrects to mask, to strangle
Words glossed on stone, lopped stone-angel;
But the dead maintain their ground—
That there's no getting round—

5   Who in places vitally rest,
Named, anonymous; who test
Alike the endurance of yews
Laurels, moonshine, stone, all tissues;

With whom, under licence and duress,
10   There are pacts made, if not peace.
Union with the stone-wearing dead
Claims the born leader, the prepared

Leader, the devourers and all lean men.
Some, finally, learn to begin.
15   Some keep to the arrangement of love
(Or similar trust) under whose auspices move

Most subjects, toward the profits of this
Combine of doves and witnesses.
Some, dug out of hot-beds, are brought bare,
20   Not past conceiving but past care.

1955   1959

The Guardians

The young, having risen early, had gone,
Some with excursions beyond the bay-mouth,
Some toward lakes, a fragile reflected sun.
Thunder-heads drift, awkwardly, from the south;

5   The old watch them. They have watched the safe
Packed harbours topple under sudden gales,
Great tides irrupt, yachts burn at the wharf
That on clean seas pitched their effective sails.

There are silences. These, too, they endure:
10   Soft comings-on; soft aftershocks of calm.
Quietly they wade the disturbed shore;
Gather the dead as the first dead scrape home.

1956   1959

September Song

Born 19.6.32—Deported 24.9.42[1]

Undesirable you may have been, untouchable
you were not. Not forgotten
or passed over at the proper time.

As estimated, you died. Things marched,
10   sufficient, to that end.

---

1. Hill was born on June 18, 1932, one day before the birthdate given here.

Just so much Zyklon[2] and leather, patented
terror, so many routine cries.

      (I have made
      an elegy for myself it
10   is true)

September fattens on vines. Roses
flake from the wall. The smoke
of harmless fires drifts to my eyes.

This is plenty. This is more than enough.

1968

From Mercian Hymns[3]

VI

The princes of Mercia were badger and raven. Thrall[4]
    to their freedom, I dug and hoarded. Orchards
    fruited above clefts. I drank from honeycombs of
    chill sandstone.

5   "A boy at odds in the house, lonely among brothers."
    But I, who had none, fostered a strangeness; gave
    myself to unattainable toys.

Candles of gnarled resin, apple-branches, the tacky
    mistletoe. "Look," they said and again "look." But
10   I ran slowly; the landscape flowed away, back to
    its source.

In the schoolyard, in the cloakrooms, the children
    boasted their scars of dried snot; wrists and
    knees garnished with impetigo.[5]

VII

Gasholders, russet among fields. Milldams, marlpools[6]
    that lay unstirring. Eel-swarms. Coagulations of
    frogs; once, with branches and half-bricks, he
    battered a ditchful; then sidled away from the
5   stillness and silence.

2. Hydrocyanic acid, used in fumigation; also
(Zyklon-B) used in the gas chambers of the Nazi
concentration camps.
3. "The historical Offa reigned over Mercia (and
the greater part of England south of the Humber)
in the years A.D. 757–796. During early medieval
times he was already becoming a creature of leg-
end. The Offa who figures in this sequence might
perhaps most usefully be regarded as the presiding
genius of the West Midlands, his dominion endur-
ing from the middle of the eighth century until the
middle of the twentieth (and possibly beyond). The
indication of such a timespan will, I trust, explain
and to some extent justify a number of anachro-
nisms" [Hill's note].
4. Slave.
5. Skin disease.
6. Pools in deposits of crumbling clay and chalk.
Gasholders: or gasometers, large metal receptacles
for gas.

Ceolred[7] was his friend and remained so, even after
the day of the lost fighter: a biplane, already
obsolete and irreplaceable, two inches of heavy
snub silver. Ceolred let it spin through a hole
10   in the classroom-floorboards, softly, into the
rat droppings and coins.

After school he lured Ceolred, who was sniggering
with fright, down to the old quarries, and flayed
him. Then, leaving Ceolred, he journeyed for hours,
15   calm and alone, in his private derelict sandlorry
named *Albion*.[8]

VIII

The mad are predators. Too often lately they harbour
against us. A novel heresy exculpates all maimed
souls. Abjure it! I am the King of Mercia, and
I know.

5   Threatened by phone-calls at midnight, venomous letters,
forewarned I have thwarted their imminent devices.

Today I name them; tomorrow I shall express the new
law. I dedicate my awakening to this matter.

1971

From Lachrimae[9]

OR

SEVEN TEARS FIGURED IN SEVEN PASSIONATE PAVANS

> Passions I allow, and loves I approve, onely
> I would wish that men would alter their
> object and better their intent.
> —ST. ROBERT SOUTHWELL,[1] *Mary Magdalen's
> Funeral Tears*, 1591

1. Lachrimae Verae

Crucified Lord, you swim upon your cross
and never move. Sometimes in dreams of hell
the body moves but moves to no avail
and is at one with that eternal loss.

---

7. A ninth-century bishop of Leicester, but the name is here used as a characteristic Anglo-Saxon Mercian name.
8. An old Celtic name for England; also, the name of a famous make of British truck. *Sandlorry*: sand truck.
9. Tears (Latin). Hill takes his title from the

sixteenth-century composer John Dowland's piece for viols and lutes. Dowland's "Lachrimae" is divided into seven parts: "Antiquae," "Novae," "Genentes," "Tristes," "Coactae," "Amantis," and "Verae" ("true"). A pavan is a stately dance or the music for this.
1. English Jesuit priest and poet (1561–1595).

5 You are the castaway of drowned remorse,
you are the world's atonement on the hill.
This is your body twisted by our skill
into a patience proper for redress.

I cannot turn aside from what I do;
10 you cannot turn away from what I am.
You do not dwell in me nor I in you
however much I pander to your name
or answer to your lords of revenue,
surrendering the joys that they condemn.

1978

From An Apology for the Revival of Christian Architecture in England

the spiritual, Platonic old England . . . [2]
—STC, *Anima Poetae*

"Your situation," said Coningsby, looking up
the green and silent valley, "is absolutely
poetic."
"I try sometimes to fancy," said Mr. Millbank,
with a rather fierce smile, "that I am in the
New World."
—BENJAMIN DISRAELI,[3] *Coningsby*

9. *The Laurel Axe*

Autumn resumes the land, ruffles the woods
with smoky wings, entangles them. Trees shine
out from their leaves, rocks mildew to moss-green;
the avenues are spread with brittle floods.

5 Platonic England, house of solitudes,
rests in its laurels and its injured stone,
replete with complex fortunes that are gone,
beset by dynasties of moods and clouds.

It stands, as though at ease with its own world,
10 the mannerly extortions, languid praise,
all that devotion long since bought and sold,

the rooms of cedar and soft-thudding baize,[4]
tremulous boudoirs where the crystals kissed
in cabinets of amethyst and frost.

1978

---

2. I.e., an idealized orderly rural England. STC: the English poet and philosopher Samuel Taylor Coleridge (1772–1834; see pp. 805–31).
3. British novelist and statesman (1804–1881); the "New World" referred to is that of an idealized rural America.

4. I.e., billiard rooms in great old British homes; the "soft-thudding baize" refers to the soft green cloth covering billiard tables as well as to the "green-baize door" traditionally dividing the family quarters in a grand house from the servants' quarters.

Veni Coronaberis[5]

A *Garland for Helen Waddell*[6]

The crocus armies from the dead
rise up; the realm of love renews
the battle it was born to lose,
though for a time the snows have fled

5   and old stones blossom in the south
with sculpted vine and psaltery[7]
and half-effaced adultery
the bird-dung dribbling from its mouth;

and abstinence crowns all our care
10 with martyr-laurels[8] for this day.
Towers and steeples rise away
into the towering gulfs of air.

1978

SYLVIA PLATH

1932–1963

The Colossus[1]

I shall never get you put together entirely,
Pieced, glued, and properly jointed.
Mule-bray, pig-grunt and bawdy cackles
Proceed from your great lips.
5   It's worse than a barnyard.

Perhaps you consider yourself an oracle,
Mouthpiece of the dead, or of some god or other.
Thirty years now I have labored
To dredge the silt from your throat.
10 I am none the wiser.

Scaling little ladders with gluepots and pails of lysol
I crawl like an ant in mourning
Over the weedy acres of your brow
To mend the immense skull plates and clear
15 The bald, white tumuli[2] of your eyes.

---

5. Come and you will be crowned (Latin).
6. British scholar (1889–1965), who translated several volumes of Latin poems, most notably *Medieval Latin Lyrics*.
7. Ancient and medieval stringed instrument.
8. Laurels were a classical symbol of victory,

achievement.
1. Alluding to the gigantic statue of this name that stood at the entrance of the harbor to Rhodes, Greece, in the third century B.C.E.
2. I.e., grave mounds.

A blue sky out of the Oresteia[3]
Arches above us. O father, all by yourself
You are pithy and historical as the Roman Forum.
I open my lunch on a hill of black cypress.
20 Your fluted bones and acanthine[4] hair are littered

In their old anarchy to the horizon-line.
It would take more than a lightning-stroke
To create such a ruin.
Nights, I squat in the cornucopia
25 Of your left ear, out of the wind,

Counting the red stars and those of plum-color.
The sun rises under the pillar of your tongue.
My hours are married to shadow.
No longer do I listen for the scrape of a keel
30 On the blank stones of the landing.

1959   1960

Morning Song

Love set you going like a fat gold watch.
The midwife slapped your footsoles, and your bald cry
Took its place among the elements.

Our voices echo, magnifying your arrival. New statue.
5 In a drafty museum, your nakedness
Shadows our safety. We stand round blankly as walls.

I'm no more your mother
Than the cloud that distills a mirror to reflect its own slow
Effacement at the wind's hand.

10 All night your moth-breath
Flickers among the flat pink roses. I wake to listen:
A far sea moves in my ear.

One cry, and I stumble from bed, cow-heavy and floral
In my Victorian nightgown.
15 Your mouth opens clean as a cat's. The window square

Whitens and swallows its dull stars. And now you try
Your handful of notes;
The clear vowels rise like balloons.

1961   1965

---

3. Trilogy of plays by the Greek dramatist Aeschylus (525–456 B.C.E.) that recounts Orestes' and Electra's efforts to avenge the murder of their father, Agamemnon, by their mother, Clytemnestra.
4. I.e., curved like the acanthus leaves depicted atop some Greek columns.

Tulips

The tulips are too excitable, it is winter here.
Look how white everything is, how quiet, how snowed-in.
I am learning peacefulness, lying by myself quietly
As the light lies on these white walls, this bed, these hands.
5   I am nobody; I have nothing to do with explosions.
I have given my name and my day-clothes up to the nurses
And my history to the anaesthetist and my body to surgeons.

They have propped my head between the pillow and the sheet-cuff
Like an eye between two white lids that will not shut.
10   Stupid pupil, it has to take everything in.
The nurses pass and pass, they are no trouble,
They pass the way gulls pass inland in their white caps,
Doing things with their hands, one just the same as another,
So it is impossible to tell how many there are.

15   My body is a pebble to them, they tend it as water
Tends to the pebbles it must run over, smoothing them gently.
They bring me numbness in their bright needles, they bring me sleep.
Now I have lost myself I am sick of baggage—
My patent leather overnight case like a black pillbox,
20   My husband and child smiling out of the family photo;
Their smiles catch onto my skin, little smiling hooks.

I have let things slip, a thirty-year-old cargo boat
Stubbornly hanging on to my name and address.
They have swabbed me clear of my loving associations.
25   Scared and bare on the green plastic-pillowed trolley
I watched my tea-set, my bureaus of linen, my books
Sink out of sight, and the water went over my head.
I am a nun now, I have never been so pure.

I didn't want any flowers, I only wanted
30   To lie with my hands turned up and be utterly empty.
How free it is, you have no idea how free—
The peacefulness is so big it dazes you,
And it asks nothing, a name tag, a few trinkets.
It is what the dead close on, finally; I imagine them
35   Shutting their mouths on it, like a Communion tablet.

The tulips are too red in the first place, they hurt me.
Even through the gift paper I could hear them breathe
Lightly, through their white swaddlings, like an awful baby.
Their redness talks to my wound, it corresponds.
40   They are subtle: they seem to float, though they weigh me down,
Upsetting me with their sudden tongues and their color,
A dozen red lead sinkers round my neck.

Nobody watched me before, now I am watched.
The tulips turn to me, and the window behind me

45   Where once a day the light slowly widens and slowly thins,
     And I see myself, flat, ridiculous, a cut-paper shadow
     Between the eye of the sun and the eyes of the tulips,
     And I have no face, I have wanted to efface myself.
     The vivid tulips eat my oxygen.

50   Before they came the air was calm enough,
     Coming and going, breath by breath, without any fuss.
     Then the tulips filled it up like a loud noise.
     Now the air snags and eddies round them the way a river
     Snags and eddies round a sunken rust-red engine.
55   They concentrate my attention, that was happy
     Playing and resting without committing itself.

     The walls, also, seem to be warming themselves.
     The tulips should be behind bars like dangerous animals;
     They are opening like the mouth of some great African cat,
60   And I am aware of my heart: it opens and closes
     Its bowl of red blooms out of sheer love of me.
     The water I taste is warm and salt, like the sea,
     And comes from a country far away as health.

1961   1965

Elm

For Ruth Fainlight

    I know the bottom, she says. I know it with my great tap root:
    It is what you fear.
    I do not fear it: I have been there.

    Is it the sea you hear in me,
5   Its dissatisfactions?
    Or the voice of nothing, that was your madness?

    Love is a shadow.
    How you lie and cry after it.
    Listen: these are its hooves: it has gone off, like a horse.

10   All night I shall gallop thus, impetuously,
    Till your head is a stone, your pillow a little turf,
    Echoing, echoing.

    Or shall I bring you the sound of poisons?
    This is rain now, this big hush.
15   And this is the fruit of it: tin-white, like arsenic.

    I have suffered the atrocity of sunsets.
    Scorched to the root
    My red filaments burn and stand, a hand of wires.

Now I break up in pieces that fly about like clubs.
20 A wind of such violence
Will tolerate no bystanding: I must shriek.

The moon, also, is merciless: she would drag me
Cruelly, being barren.
Her radiance scathes me. Or perhaps I have caught her.

25 I let her go. I let her go
Diminished and flat, as after radical surgery.
How your bad dreams possess and endow me.

I am inhabited by a cry.
Nightly it flaps out
30 Looking, with its hooks, for something to love.

I am terrified by this dark thing
That sleeps in me;
All day I feel its soft, feathery turnings, its malignity.

Clouds pass and disperse.
35 Are those the faces of love, those pale irretrievables?
Is it for such I agitate my heart?

I am incapable of more knowledge.
What is this, this face
So murderous in its strangle of branches?——

40 Its snaky acids kiss.
It petrifies the will. These are the isolate, slow faults
That kill, that kill, that kill.

1962   1965

Daddy

You do not do, you do not do
Any more, black shoe
In which I have lived like a foot
For thirty years, poor and white,
5 Barely daring to breathe or Achoo.

Daddy, I have had to kill you.
You died before I had time——
Marble-heavy, a bag full of God,
Ghastly statue with one grey toe[5]
10 Big as a Frisco seal

5. Plath's father's toe turned black from gangrene.

And a head in the freakish Atlantic
Where it pours bean green over blue
In the waters off beautiful Nauset.
I used to pray to recover you.
15 Ach, du.[6]

In the German tongue, in the Polish town[7]
Scraped flat by the roller
Of wars, wars, wars.
But the name of the town is common.
20 My Polack friend

Says there are a dozen or two.
So I never could tell where you
Put your foot, your root,
I never could talk to you.
25 The tongue stuck in my jaw.

It stuck in a barb wire snare.
Ich, ich, ich, ich,[8]
I could hardly speak.
I thought every German was you.
30 And the language obscene

An engine, an engine
Chuffing me off like a Jew.
A Jew to Dachau, Auschwitz, Belsen.[9]
I began to talk like a Jew.
35 I think I may well be a Jew.

The snows of the Tyrol,[1] the clear beer of Vienna
Are not very pure or true.
With my gypsy ancestress and my weird luck
And my Taroc pack and my Taroc pack[2]
40 I may be a bit of a Jew.

I have always been scared of *you*,
With your Luftwaffe,[3] your gobbledygoo.
And your neat moustache
And your Aryan eye, bright blue.
45 Panzer[4]-man, panzer-man, O You——

Not God but a swastika
So black no sky could squeak through.
Every woman adores a Fascist,
The boot in the face, the brute
50 Brute heart of a brute like you.

6. Ah, you (German).
7. Grabów, Poland, Otto Plath's birthplace.
8. I, I, I, I (German).
9. German concentration camps, where millions of Jews were murdered during World War II.

1. Austrian Alpine region.
2. Tarot cards, used for fortune-telling.
3. The German air force.
4. Armor (German), especially, during World War II, referring to the German armored tank corps.

You stand at the blackboard, daddy,
In the picture I have of you,
A cleft in your chin instead of your foot
But no less a devil for that, no not
55 Any less the black man who

Bit my pretty red heart in two.
I was ten when they buried you.
At twenty I tried to die
And get back, back, back to you,
60 I thought even the bones would do.

But they pulled me out of the sack,
And they stuck me together with glue,[5]
And then I knew what to do.
I made a model of you,
65 A man in black with a Meinkampf[6] look

And a love of the rack and the screw.
And I said I do, I do.
So daddy, I'm finally through.
The black telephone's off at the root,
70 The voices just can't worm through.

If I've killed one man, I've killed two——
The vampire who said he was you
And drank my blood for a year,
Seven years, if you want to know.
75 Daddy, you can lie back now.

There's a stake in your fat black heart
And the villagers never liked you.
They are dancing and stamping on you.
They always *knew* it was you.
80 Daddy, daddy, you bastard, I'm through.

1962   1965

Ariel[7]

Stasis in darkness.
Then the substanceless blue
Pour of tor° and distances.   *craggy hill*

God's lioness,
5   How one we grow,
Pivot of heels and knees!—The furrow

---

5. An allusion to Plath's first suicide attempt.
6. *Mein Kampf* (*My Struggle*) is Hitler's political autobiography and Nazi polemic, published before his rise to power.

7. Lion of God (Hebrew); the name of a horse Plath often rode; also, the airy spirit in Shakespeare's *Tempest*.

Splits and passes, sister to
The brown arc
Of the neck I cannot catch,

10 Nigger-eye
Berries cast dark
Hooks—

Black sweet blood mouthfuls,
Shadows.
15 Something else

Hauls me through air—
Thighs, hair;
Flakes from my heels.

White
20 Godiva,[8] I unpeel—
Dead hands, dead stringencies.

And now I
Foam to wheat, a glitter of seas.
The child's cry

25 Melts in the wall.
And I
Am the arrow,

The dew that flies
Suicidal, at one with the drive
30 Into the red

Eye, the cauldron of morning.

1962   1965

Lady Lazarus[9]

I have done it again.
One year in every ten
I manage it—

A sort of walking miracle, my skin
5 Bright as a Nazi lampshade,[1]
My right foot

---

8. According to legend, Lady Godiva (ca. 1010–
1067) rode naked through the streets of Coventry,
England, to persuade her husband, the local lord,
to lower taxes.
9. Lazarus was raised from the dead by Jesus (John

11.1–44).
1. In the Nazi death camps, the skins of victims
were sometimes used to make lampshades and the
bodies to make soap.

A paperweight,
My face a featureless, fine
Jew linen.

10   Peel off the napkin
O my enemy.
Do I terrify?—

The nose, the eye pits, the full set of teeth?
The sour breath
15   Will vanish in a day.

Soon, soon the flesh
The grave cave ate will be
At home on me

And I a smiling woman.
20   I am only thirty.
And like the cat I have nine times to die.

This is Number Three.
What a trash
To annihilate each decade.

25   What a million filaments.
The peanut-crunching crowd
Shoves in to see

Them unwrap me hand and foot—
The big strip tease.
30   Gentleman, ladies,

These are my hands,
My knees.
I may be skin and bone,

Nevertheless, I am the same, identical woman.
35   The first time it happened I was ten.
It was an accident.

The second time I meant
To last it out and not come back at all.
I rocked shut

40   As a seashell.
They had to call and call
And pick the worms off me like sticky pearls.

Dying
Is an art, like everything else.
45   I do it exceptionally well.

I do it so it feels like hell.
I do it so it feels real.
I guess you could say I've a call.

It's easy enough to do it in a cell.
50   It's easy enough to do it and stay put.
It's the theatrical

Comeback in broad day
To the same place, the same face, the same brute
Amused shout:

55   "A miracle!"
That knocks me out.
There is a charge

For the eyeing of my scars, there is a charge
For the hearing of my heart—
60   It really goes.

And there is a charge, very large charge,
For a word or a touch
Or a bit of blood

Or a piece of my hair or my clothes.
65   So, so, Herr Doktor.
So, Herr Enemy.

I am your opus,
I am your valuable,
The pure gold baby

70   That melts to a shriek.
I turn and burn.
Do not think I underestimate your great concern.

Ash, ash—
You poke and stir.
75   Flesh, bone, there is nothing there—

A cake of soap,
A wedding ring,
A gold filling.

Herr God, Herr Lucifer,
80   Beware
Beware.

Out of the ash²
I rise with my red hair
And I eat men like air.

1962   1965

2. An allusion to the phoenix, the mythical bird that dies in flames and is reborn from its own ashes.
Beware / Beware: cf. Samuel Taylor Coleridge, "Kubla Khan," line 49 (p. 810).

JOHN UPDIKE
b. 1932

V. B. Nimble, V. B. Quick

Science, Pure and Applied, by V. B. Wigglesworth, F.R.S.,[1] Quick
Professor of Biology in the University of Cambridge.
                    —a talk listed in the B.B.C.'s *Radio Times*

> V. B. Wigglesworth wakes at noon,
> Washes, shaves, and very soon
> Is at the lab; he reads his mail,
> Tweaks a tadpole by the tail,
> 5 Undoes his coat, removes his hat,
> Dips a spider in a vat
> Of alkaline, phones the press,
> Tells them he is F.R.S.,
> Subdivides six protocells,
> 10 Kills a rat by ringing bells,
> Writes a treatise, edits two
> Symposia on "Will Man Do?,"
> Gives a lecture, audits three,
> Has the Sperm Club in for tea,
> 15 Pensions off an aging spore,
> Cracks a test tube, takes some pure
> Science and applies it, finds
> His hat, adjusts it, pulls the blinds,
> Instructs the jellyfish to spawn,
> 20 And, by one o'clock, is gone.

1954

I Missed His Book, but I Read His Name

"The Silver Pilgrimage," by M. Anantanarayanan . . . 160 pages.
Criterion. $3.95.
                    —*The New York Times*

> Though authors are a dreadful clan
> To be avoided if you can,
> I'd like to meet the Indian,
> M. Anantanarayanan.
>
> 5 I picture him as short and tan.
> We'd meet, perhaps, in Hindustan.[2]
> I'd say, with admirable *élan,*°   zest
> "Ah, Anantanarayanan—

---

1. Fellow of the Royal Society.   2. Predominantly Hindu area of India.

I've heard of you. The *Times* once ran
10   A notice on your novel, an
Unusual tale of God and Man."
And Anantanarayanan

Would seat me on a lush divan
And read his name—that sumptuous span
15   Of "a"s and "n"s more lovely than
"In Xanadu did Kubla Khan"³—

Aloud to me all day. I plan
Henceforth to be an ardent fan
Of Anantanarayanan—
20   M. Anantanarayanan.

1963

ANNE STEVENSON
b. 1933

Temporarily in Oxford

Where they will bury me
I don't know.
Many places might not be
sorry to store me.

5   The Midwest has right of origin.
Already it has welcomed my mother
to its flat sheets.

The English fens that bore me
have been close curiously often.
10   It seems I can't get away from
dampness and learning.

If I stay where I am
I could sleep in this educated earth.

But if they are kind
15   they'll burn me and
send me to Vermont.

I'd be an education for the trees
and would relish, really,
flaring into maple each October—
20   my scarlet letter to you.

---

3. First line of Samuel Taylor Coleridge's "Kubla Khan" (p. 809).

Your stormy north is possible.
You will be there, engrossed in its peat.

It would be handy not to have to
cross the whole Atlantic
25   each time I wanted to
lift up the turf
and slip in beside you.

1977

Arioso Dolente[1]

(for my grandchildren when they become grandparents)

Mother, who read and thought and poured herself into me;
she was the jug and I was the two-eared cup.
How she would scorn today's "show-biz inanity,
democracy twisted, its high ideals sold up!"
5   Cancer filched her voice, then cut her throat.
Why is it
none of the faces in this family snapshot
looks upset?

Father, who ran downstairs as I practised the piano;
10   barefooted, buttoning his shirt, he shouted "G,
D-natural, *C-flat! Dolente, arioso.*
Put all the griefs of the world in that change of key."
Who then could lay a finger on his sleeve
to distress him with
15   "One day, Steve, two of your well-taught daughters
will be deaf."

Mother must be sitting, left, on the porch-set,
you can just see her. My sister's on her lap.
And that's Steve confiding to his cigarette
20   something my mother's mother has to laugh at.
The screened door twangs, slamming
on its sprung hinge.
Paint blisters on the steps; iced tea, grasscuttings,
elm flowers, mock orange . . .

25   A grand June evening, like this one, not too buggy,
unselfquestioning midwestern, maybe 1951.
And, of course, there in my grandmother's memory
lives just such another summer—1890 or 91.
Though it's not on her mind now/then.
30   No, she's thinking of
the yeast-ring rising, in the oven. Or how *any* shoes
irritate her bunion.

---

1. A sorrowful melodic passage (Italian); here, "from Beethoven's piano sonata, opus 110, third movement; introduction to the fugue" [Stevenson's note].

Paper gestures, pictures, newsprint laughter.
And after the camera winks and makes its catch,
35   the decibels drain away *for ever and ever*.
No need to say "Look!" to these smilers on the porch,
      "Grandmother will have her stroke,
      and you, mother, will nurse her."
Or to myself, this woman died paralysed-dumb, and that one
40   dumb from cancer.

Sufficient unto the day . . . [2] Grandmother, poor and liturgical,
whose days were duties, stitches in the tea-brown blanket
she for years crocheted, its zigzag of yellow wool,
her grateful offering, her proof of goodness to present,
45   gift-wrapped, to Our Father in Heaven. "Accept,
     O Lord, this best-I-can-make-it soul."
And He: "Thou good and faithful sevant, lose thyself
          and be whole."

Consciousness walks on tiptoe through what happens.
50 So much is felt, so little of it said.
But ours is the breath on which the past depends.
"What happened" is what the living teach the dead,
     who, smilingly lost to their lost concerns,
         in grey on grey,
55   are all of them deaf, blind, unburdened
         by today.

As if our recording selves, our mortal identities,
could be cupped in a concave universe or lens,
ageless at all ages, cleansed of memories,
60 not minding that meaningful genealogy extends
     no further than mind's flash images reach back.
       As for what happens next,
       let all the griefs of the world
       find keys for that.

                             2000

FLEUR ADCOCK
b. 1934

The Ex-Queen Among the Astronomers

They serve revolving saucer eyes,
dishes of stars; they wait upon
huge lenses hung aloft to frame
the slow procession of the skies.

---

2. Matthew 6.34: "Sufficient unto the day is the evil thereof."

5 They calculate, adjust, record,
    watch transits, measure distances.
    They carry pocket telescopes
    to spy through when they walk abroad.

    Spectra[1] possess their eyes; they face
10 upwards, alert for meteorites,
    cherishing little glassy worlds:
    receptacles for outer space.

    But she, exile, expelled, ex-queen,
    swishes among the men of science
15 waiting for cloudy skies, for nights
    when constellations can't be seen.

    She wears the rings he let her keep;
    she walks as she was taught to walk
    for his approval, years ago.
20 His bitter features taunt her sleep.

    And so when these have laid aside
    their telescopes, when lids are closed
    between machine and sky, she seeks
    terrestrial bodies to bestride.

25 She plucks this one or that among
    the astronomers, and is become
    his canopy, his occultation;[2]
    she sucks at earlobe, penis, tongue

    mouthing the tubes of flesh; her hair
30 crackles, her eyes are comet-sparks.
    She brings the distant briefly close
    above his dreamy abstract stare.

1979

Poem Ended by a Death

    They will wash all my kisses and fingerprints off you
    and my tearstains—I was more inclined to weep
    in those wild-garlicky days—and our happier stains,
    thin scales of papery silk . . . Fuck that for a cheap
5 opener; and false too—any such traces
    you pumiced away yourself, those years ago
    when you sent my letters back, in the week I married
    that anecdotal ape. So start again. So:

1. Images retained for a time on the retina of the eye when it is turned away after gazing fixedly at bright objects.

2. Concealment of a heavenly body behind the body of Earth.

They will remove the tubes and drips and dressings
10 which I censor from my dreams. They will, it is true,
wash you; and they will put you into a box.
After which whatever else they may do
won't matter. This is my laconic° style.   *terse*
You praised it, as I praised your intricate pearled
15 embroideries; these links laced us together,
plain and purl³ across the ribs of the world . . .

1979

The Soho Hospital for Women

1

Strange room, from this angle:
white door open before me,
strange bed, mechanical hum, white lights.
There will be stranger rooms to come.

5   As I almost slept I saw the deep flower opening
and leaned over into it, gratefully.
It swimmingly closed in my face. I was not ready.
It was not death, it was acceptance.

*

Our thin patient cat died purring,
10 her small triangular head tilted back,
the nurse's fingers caressing her throat,
my hand on her shrunken spine; the quick needle.

That was the second death by cancer.
The first is not for me to speak of.
15 It was telephone calls and brave letters
and a friend's hand bleeding under the coffin.

*

Doctor, I am not afraid of a word.
But neither do I wish to embrace that visitor,
to engulf it as Hine-Nui-te-Po
20 engulfed Maui;⁴ that would be the way of it.

And she was the winner there: her womb crushed him.
Goddesses can do these things.
But I have admitted the gloved hands and the speculum⁵
and must part my ordinary legs to the surgeon's knife.

3. Stitch in knitting with needle moved in opposite
to normal (plain) direction.
4. Supernatural hero in Polynesian mythology,
Maui the sun-snarer, fire-stealer, monster-slayer,
entered the womb of Hine, sleeping goddess of the
underworld, in search of immortality. He intended
to depart through her mouth, but when his bird
companion laughed at the sight, Hine awoke and
crushed Maui to death.
5. Surgical instrument for dilating orifices of the
body to facilitate examination or operation.

2

25 Nellie has only one breast
    ample enough to make several.
    Her quilted dressing-gown softens
    to semi-doubtful this imbalance
    and there's no starched vanity
30 in our abundant ward-mother:
    her silvery hair's in braids, her slippers
    loll, her weathered smile holds true.
    When she dresses up in her black
    with her glittering marcasite brooch[6] on
35 to go for the weekly radium treatment
    she's the bright star of the taxi-party—
    whatever may be growing under her ribs.

                              *

    Doris hardly smokes in the ward—
    and hardly eats more than a dreamy spoonful—
40 but the corridors and bathrooms
    reek of her Players Number 10,[7]
    and the drug-trolley pauses
    for long minutes by her bed.
    Each week for the taxi-outing
45 she puts on her skirt again
    and has to pin the slack waistband
    more tightly over her scarlet sweater.
    Her face, a white shadow through smoked glass,
    lets Soho display itself unregarded.

                              *

50 Third in the car is Mrs Golding
    who never smiles. And why should she?

3

    The senior consultant on his rounds
    murmurs in so subdued a voice
    to the students marshalled behind
55 that they gather in, forming a cell,
    a cluster, a rosette around him
    as he stands at the foot of my bed
    going through my notes with them,
    half-audibly instructive, grave.

60 The slight ache as I strain forward
    to listen still seems imagined.

    Then he turns his practised smile on me:
    "How are you this morning?" "Fine,
    very well, thank you." I smile too.

6. Cheap brooch made of crystallized iron pyrites.   7. Brand and type of cigarette.

65   And possibly all that murmurs within me
      is the slow dissolving of stitches.

4

      I am out in the supermarket choosing—
      this very afternoon, this day—
      picking up tomatoes, cheese, bread,

70   things I want and shall be using
      to make myself a meal, while they
      eat their stodgy suppers in bed:

      Janet with her big freckled breasts,
      her prim Scots voice, her one friend,
75   and never in hospital before,

      who came in to have a few tests
      and now can't see where they'll end;
      and Coral in the bed by the door

      who whimpered and gasped behind a screen
80   with nurses to and fro all night
      and far too much of the day;

      pallid, bewildered, nineteen.
      And Mary, who will be all right
      but gradually. And Alice, who may.

85   Whereas I stand almost intact,
      giddy with freedom, not with pain.
      I lift my light basket, observing

      how little I needed in fact;
      and move to the checkout, to the rain,
90   to the lights and the long street curving.

                                                        1979

POPULAR BALLADS OF THE
TWENTIETH CENTURY

Pete Seeger (b. 1919) • Where Have All the Flowers Gone?[1]

Where have all the flowers gone?—long time passing
Where have all the flowers gone?—long time ago

---

1. With additional verse by Joe Hickerson. Cf. Jean Elliot, "The Flowers of the Forest" (p. 677).

Where have all the flowers gone?—girls have picked them every one
When will they ever learn? When will they ever learn?

5   Where have all the young girls gone?—long time passing
Where have all the young girls gone?—long time ago
Where have all the young girls gone?—they've taken husbands every one
When will they ever learn? When will they ever learn?

Where have all the young men gone?—long time passing
10 Where have all the young men gone?—long time ago
Where have all the young men gone?—gone for soldiers every one
When will they ever learn? When will they ever learn?

Where have all the soldiers gone?—long time passing
Where have all the soldiers gone?—long time ago
15 Where have all the soldiers gone?—gone to graveyards everyone
When will they ever learn? When will they ever learn?

Where have all the graveyards gone?—long time passing
Where have all the graveyards gone?—long time ago
Where have all the graveyards gone?—gone to flowers everyone
20 When will they ever learn? When will they ever learn?

1961

Bob Dylan (b. 1941) • Boots of Spanish Leather

Oh, I'm sailin' away my own true love,
I'm sailin' away in the morning.
Is there something I can send you from across the sea,
From the place that I'll be landing?

5   No, there's nothin' you can send me, my own true love,
There's nothin' I wish to be ownin'.
Just carry yourself back to me unspoiled,
From across that lonesome ocean.

Oh, but I just thought you might want something fine
10 Made of silver or of golden,
Either from the mountains of Madrid
Or from the coast of Barcelona.

Oh, but if I had the stars from the darkest night
And the diamonds from the deepest ocean,
15 I'd forsake them all for your sweet kiss
For that's all I'm wishin' to be ownin'.

That I might be gone a long time
And it's only that I'm askin',
Is there something I can send you to remember me by,
20 To make your time more easy passin'.

Oh, how can, how can you ask me again,
It only brings me sorrow.
The same thing I want from you today,
I would want again tomorrow.

25 I got a letter on a lonesome day,
It was from her ship a-sailin',
Saying I don't know when I'll be comin' back again,
It depends on how I'm a-feelin'.

Well, if you, my love, must think that-a-way,
30 I'm sure your mind is roamin'.
I'm sure your heart is not with me,
But with the country to where you're goin'.

So take heed, take heed of the western wind,
Take heed of the stormy weather.
35 And yes, there's something you can send back to me,
Spanish boots of Spanish leather.

                                                                    1963

Dudley Randall (b. 1914) • Ballad of Birmingham

(On the bombing of a church in Birmingham, Alabama, 1963)[2]

"Mother dear, may I go downtown
Instead of out to play,
And march the streets of Birmingham
In a Freedom March today?"

5 "No, baby, no, you may not go,
For the dogs are fierce and wild,
And clubs and hoses, guns and jails
Aren't good for a little child."

"But, mother, I won't be alone.
10 Other children will go with me,
And march the streets of Birmingham
To make our country free."

"No, baby, no, you may not go,
For I fear those guns will fire.
15 But you may go to church instead
And sing in the children's choir."

---

2. Two weeks after Martin Luther King's August 23rd March on Washington; in Birmingham, King had led nonviolent civil rights demonstrations that were met with attack dogs, tear gas, cattle prods, and firehoses.

She has combed and brushed her night-dark hair,
And bathed rose petal sweet,
And drawn white gloves on her small brown hands,
20   And white shoes on her feet.

The mother smiled to know her child
Was in the sacred place,
But that smile was the last smile
To come upon her face.

25   For when she heard the explosion,
Her eyes grew wet and wild.
She raced through the streets of Birmingham
Calling for her child.

She clawed through bits of glass and brick,
30   Then lifted out a shoe.
"O, here's the shoe my baby wore,
But, baby, where are you?"

1969

AMIRI BARAKA (LEROI JONES)
b. 1934

In Memory of Radio

Who has ever stopped to think of the divinity of Lamont Cranston?[1]
(Only Jack Kerouac,[2] that I know of: & me.
The rest of you probably had on WCBS and Kate Smith,
Or something equally unattractive.)

5   What can I say?
It is better to have loved and lost
Than to put linoleum in your living rooms?[3]

Am I a sage or something?
Mandrake's hypnotic gesture of the week?
10   (Remember, I do not have the healing powers of Oral Roberts . . .
I cannot, like F. J. Sheen, tell you how to get saved & *rich*!
I cannot even order you to gaschamber satori[4] like Hitler or Goody
        Knight

---

1. The hero's alter ego on the 1930–50s radio
serial "The Shadow." The poem refers to promi-
nent characters (Mandrake) and personalities that
Jones would have heard on the radio as a boy: Kate
Smith (1907–1986), a popular American singer,
best-known for her frequent performances of "God
Bless America"; Oral Roberts (b. 1918), evangelist;
Fulton J. Sheen (1895–1979), Roman Catholic
popularizer of religion; Goodwin Knight (1896–
1970), one of the first politicians to exploit radio
and television—as governor of California in the
1950s, he wanted University of California teachers
to sign a loyalty oath as a condition of employment.
2. American writer (1922–1969), affiliated, as was
Baraka (loosely), with the Beat movement.
3. Cf. Alfred, Lord Tennyson, "In Memoriam
A. H. H.," 28.15–16, 85.3–4: "Tis better to have
loved and lost / than never to have loved at all."
4. The state of spiritual enlightenment sought in
Zen Buddhism.

& Love is an evil word.
Turn it backwards / see, what I mean?
15 An evol word. & besides
Who understands it?
I certainly wouldn't like to go out on that kind of limb.

Saturday mornings we listened to *Red Lantern* & his undersea folk.
At 11, *Let's Pretend* / & we did / & I, the poet, still do, Thank God!

20 What was it he used to say (after the transformation, when he was
        safe
& invisible & the unbelievers couldn't throw stones?) "Heh, heh, heh,
Who knows what evil lurks in the hearts of men? The Shadow knows."

O, yes he does
O, yes he does.
25 An evil word it is,
This Love.

1961

An Agony. As Now.

I am inside someone
who hates me. I look
out from his eyes. Smell
what fouled tunes come in
5 to his breath. Love his
wretched women.

Slits in the metal, for sun. Where
my eyes sit turning, at the cool air
the glance of light, or hard flesh
10 rubbed against me, a woman, a man,
without shadow, or voice, or meaning.

This is the enclosure (flesh,
where innocence is a weapon. An
abstraction. Touch. (Not mine.
15 Or yours, if you are the soul I had
and abandoned when I was blind and had
my enemies carry me as a dead man
(if he is beautiful, or pitied.

It can be pain. (As now, as all his
20 flesh hurts me.) It can be that. Or
pain. As when she ran from me into
that forest.
        Or pain, the mind
silver spiraled whirled against the
25 sun, higher than even old men thought

God would be. Or pain. And the other. The
yes. (Inside his books, his fingers. They
are withered yellow flowers and were never
beautiful.) The yes. You will, lost soul, say
30   "beauty." Beauty, practiced, as the tree. The
slow river. A white sun in its wet sentences.

Or, the cold men in their gale. Ecstasy. Flesh
or soul. The yes. (Their robes blown. Their bowls
empty. They chant at my heels, not at yours.) Flesh
35   or soul, as corrupt. Where the answer moves too quickly.
Where the God is a self, after all.)

Cold air blown through narrow blind eyes. Flesh,
white hot metal. Glows as the day with its sun.
It is a human love. I live inside. A bony skeleton
40   you recognize as words or simple feeling.

But it has no feeling. As the metal, is hot, it is not,
given to love.

It burns the thing
inside it. And that thing
45   screams.

                                            1964

AUDRE LORDE
1934–1992

Coal

I
is the total black, being spoken
from the earth's inside.
There are many kinds of open
5   how a diamond comes into a knot of flame
how sound comes into a word, colored
by who pays what for speaking.

Some words are open like a diamond
on glass windows
10   singing out within the passing crash of sun
Then there are words like stapled wagers
in a perforated book—buy and sign and tear apart—
and come whatever wills all chances
the stub remains
15   an ill-pulled tooth with a ragged edge.
Some words live in my throat

breeding like adders. Others know sun
seeking like gypsies over my tongue
to explode through my lips
20　like young sparrows bursting from shell.
Some words
bedevil me.

Love is a word, another kind of open.
As the diamond comes into a knot of flame
25　I am Black because I come from the earth's inside
now take my word for jewel in the open light.

1968, 1976

From the House of Yemanjá[1]

My mother had two faces and a frying pot
where she cooked up her daughters
into girls
before she fixed our dinner.
5　My mother had two faces
and a broken pot
where she hid out a perfect daughter
who was not me
I am the sun and moon and forever hungry
10　for her eyes.

I bear two women upon my back
one dark and rich and hidden
in the ivory hungers of the other
mother
15　pale as a witch
yet steady and familiar
brings me bread and terror
in my sleep
her breasts are huge exciting anchors
20　in the midnight storm.

All this has been
before
in my mother's bed
time has no sense
25　I have no brothers
and my sisters are cruel.

---

1. "Mother of the other *Orisha* [the goddesses and gods . . . of the Yoruba peoples of Western Nigeria], Yemanjá is also the goddess of oceans. Rivers are said to flow from her breasts. One legend has it that a son tried to rape her. She fled until she collapsed, and from her breasts, the rivers flowed. Another legend says that a husband insulted Yemanjá's long breasts, and when she fled with her pots he knocked her down. From her breasts flowed the rivers, and from her body then sprang forth all the other *Orisha*. River-smooth stones are Yemanjá's symbol, and the sea is sacred to her followers. Those who please her are blessed with many children" [Lorde's note].

Mother I need
mother I need
mother I need your blackness now
30   as the august earth needs rain.

I am
the sun and moon and forever hungry
the sharpened edge
where day and night shall meet
35   and not be
one.

                                          1978

Echoes

There is a timbre of voice
that comes from not being heard
and knowing   you are not being
heard   noticed only
5   by others   not heard
for the same reason.

The flavor of midnight fruit   tongue
calling your body through dark light
piercing the allure of safety
10   ripping the glitter of silence
around you
         dazzle me with color
         and perhaps I won't notice
till after you're gone
15   your hot grain smell tattooed
into each new poem   resonant
beyond escape   I am listening
in that fine space
between desire and always
20   the grave stillness
before choice.

As my tongue unravels
in what pitch
will the scream hang unsung
25   or shiver like lace on the borders
of never   recording
which dreams heal   which
dream can kill
stabbing a man and burning his body
30   for cover   being caught
making love to a woman
I do not know.

                                          1993

N. SCOTT MOMADAY
b. 1934

Headwaters

Noon in the intermountain plain:
There is scant telling of the marsh—
A log, hollow and weather-stained.
An insect at the mouth, and moss—
5   Yet waters rise against the roots,
Stand brimming to the stalks. What moves?
What moves on this archaic force
Was wild and welling at the source.

1976

The Eagle-Feather Fan

The eagle is my power,
And my fan is an eagle.
It is strong and beautiful
In my hand. And it is real.
5   My fingers hold upon it
As if the beaded handle
Were the twist of bristlecone.
The bones of my hand are fine
And hollow; the fan bears them.
10 My hand veers in the thin air
Of the summits. All morning
It scuds on the cold currents;
All afternoon it circles
To the singing, to the drums.

1976

The Gift

For Bobby Jack Nelson

Older, more generous,
We give each other hope.
The gift is ominous:
Enough praise, enough rope.

1976

Two Figures

These figures moving in my rhyme,
Who are they? Death and Death's dog, Time.

1976

WOLE SOYINKA
b. 1934

Telephone Conversation

The price seemed reasonable, location
Indifferent. The landlady swore she lived
Off premises. Nothing remained
But self-confession. "Madam," I warned,
5   "I hate a wasted journey—I am African."
Silence. Silenced transmission of
Pressurized good-breeding. Voice, when it came,
Lipstick coated, long gold-rolled
Cigarette-holder pipped. Caught I was, foully.
10   "HOW DARK?" . . . I had not misheard . . . "ARE YOU LIGHT
OR VERY DARK?" Button B. Button A.[1] Stench
Of rancid breath of public hide-and-speak.
Red booth. Red pillar-box.° Red double-tiered   mailbox
Omnibus squelching tar. It *was* real! Shamed
15   By ill-mannered silence, surrender
Pushed dumbfoundment to beg simplification.
Considerate she was, varying the emphasis—
"ARE YOU DARK? OR VERY LIGHT?" Revelation came.
"You mean—like plain or milk chocolate?"
20   Her assent was clinical, crushing in its light
Impersonality. Rapidly, wave-length adjusted,
I chose. "West African sepia"[2]—and as afterthought,
"Down in my passport." Silence for spectroscopic[3]
Flight of fancy, till truthfulness clanged her accent
25   Hard on the mouthpiece. "WHAT'S THAT?" conceding
"DON'T KNOW WHAT THAT IS." "Like brunette."
"THAT'S DARK, ISN'T IT?" "Not altogether.
Facially, I am brunette, but, madam, you should see
The rest of me. Palm of my hand, soles of my feet
30   Are a peroxide blond. Friction, caused—
Foolishly, madam—by sitting down, has turned
My bottom raven black—One moment, madam!"—sensing
Her receiver rearing on the thunderclap

---

1. Buttons to be pressed by caller who has inserted
a coin into an old type of British public pay phone.

2. Reddish brown.
3. Related to study of the color spectrum.

About my ears—"Madam," I pleaded, "wouldn't you rather
35 See for yourself?"

1962

MARK STRAND
b. 1934

The Prediction

That night the moon drifted over the pond,
turning the water to milk, and under
the boughs of the trees, the blue trees,
a young woman walked, and for an instant

5 the future came to her:
rain falling on her husband's grave, rain falling
on the lawns of her children, her own mouth
filling with cold air, strangers moving into her house,

a man in her room writing a poem, the moon drifting into it,
10 a woman strolling under its trees, thinking of death,
thinking of him thinking of her, and the wind rising
and taking the moon and leaving the paper dark.

1970

Always

for Charles Simic

Always so late in the day
In their rumpled clothes, sitting
Around a table lit by a single bulb,
The great forgetters were hard at work.
5 They tilted their heads to one side, closing their eyes.
Then a house disappeared, and a man in his yard
With all his flowers in a row.
The great forgetters wrinkled their brows.
Then Florida went and San Francisco
10 Where tugs and barges leave
Small gleaming scars across the Bay.
One of the great forgetters struck a match.
Gone were the harps of beaded lights
That vault the rivers of New York.
15 Another filled his glass
And that was it for crowds at evening
Under sulphur yellow streetlamps coming on.

And afterwards Bulgaria was gone, and then Japan.
"Where will it stop?" one of them said.
20 "Such difficult work, pursuing the fate
Of everything known," said another.
"Down to the last stone," said a third,
"And only the cold zero of perfection
Left for the imagination." And gone
25 Were North and South America,
And gone as well the moon.
Another yawned, another gazed at the window.
No grass, no trees . . .
The blaze of promise everywhere.

1990

FROM DARK HARBOR[1]

XVI

It is true, as someone has said, that in
A world without heaven all is farewell.[2]
Whether you wave your hand or not,

It is farewell, and if no tears come to your eyes
5   It is still farewell, and if you pretend not to notice,
Hating what passes, it is still farewell.

Farewell no matter what. And the palms as they lean
Over the green, bright lagoon, and the pelicans
Diving, and the glistening bodies of bathers resting,

10 Are stages in an ultimate stillness, and the movement
Of sand, and of wind, and the secret moves of the body
Are part of the same, a simplicity that turns being

Into an occasion for mourning, or into an occasion
Worth celebrating, for what else does one do,
15 Feeling the weight of the pelicans' wings,

The density of the palms' shadows, the cells that darken
The backs of bathers? These are beyond the distortions
Of chance, beyond the evasions of music. The end

Is enacted again and again. And we feel it
20 In the temptations of sleep, in the moon's ripening,
In the wine as it waits in the glass.

---

1. A forty-five-section, book-length poem in which Strand recounts a spiritual quest while paying homage to several guiding influences in poetry. Among the most important are Dante (whose three-line stanzas he borrows, though not Dante's terza rima rhyme scheme) and William Wordsworth (1770–1850; see pp. 763–805).
2. Cf. Wallace Stevens, "Waving Adieu, Adieu, Adieu," lines 5–8 (p. 1266).

XX

Is it you standing among the olive trees
Beyond the courtyard? You in the sunlight
Waving me closer with one hand while the other

Shields your eyes from the brightness that turns
5   All that is not you dead white? Is it you
Around whom the leaves scatter like foam?

You in the murmuring night that is scented
With mint and lit by the distant wilderness
Of stars? Is it you? Is it really you

10   Rising from the script of waves, the length
Of your body casting a sudden shadow over my hand
So that I feel how cold it is as it moves

Over the page? You leaning down and putting
Your mouth against mine so I should know
15   That a kiss is only the beginning

Of what until now we could only imagine?
Is it you or the long compassionate wind
That whispers in my ear: alas, alas?

1993

CHARLES WRIGHT
b. 1935

Homage to Claude Lorraine[1]

I had a picture by him—a print, I think—on my bedroom wall
In Verona in 1959,
             via Anzani n. 3.[2]
Or maybe a drawing, a rigged ship in a huge sea,
5   Storm waves like flames above my bed.
It's lost between there and here now,
                      and has been for years,
Trapped in the past's foliage, as so much else is
In spite of our constancy, or how
10   We rattle the branches and keep our lights on the right place.

The room had a vaulted ceiling and faced east.
The living room was a tower with skylights on four sides.

1. Or Claude Lorrain, pseudonym of Claude Gel-   2. Address in Verona, Italy.
lée (1600–1682), French painter.

A third room sloped with the roof
               until it was two feet high at the far wall,
15   All of this part of a reconstructed attic, and washed white.

I lived there for two years,
               one block from the Adige[3]
Where seagulls, like little loaves of fresh bread,
Drifted and turned on its grey coils.
20   Between the sea fires of Claude Lorraine
               and the curled sheets of the river,
I burned on my swivel stool
Night after night,
               looking into the future, its charred edges
25   Holding my life like a frame
I'd hope to fit into one day, unsigned and rigged for the deeps.

                                                1984

Chinese Journal

In 1935, the year I was born,
               Giorgio Morandi[4]
Penciled these bottles in by leaving them out, letting
The presence of what surrounds them increase the presence
5   Of what is missing,
               keeping its distance and measure.

———

The purple-and-white spike plants
               stand upright and spine-laced,
As though poised to fight by keeping still.
10   Inside their bristly circle,
The dwarf boxwood
               flashes its tiny shields at the sun.

———

Under the skylight, the Pothos° plant   *climbing shrub*
Dangles its fourteen arms
15   into the absence of its desire.
Like a medusa in the two-ply, celadon[5] air,
Its longing is what it grows on,
               heart-leaves in the nothingness.

———

3. River that runs through Verona.
4. Italian painter (1890–1964).
5. Grayish yellow-green. *Medusa:* in Greek myth- ology, one of three snake-haired Gorgons who turned those who looked at them into stone; also, a kind of jellyfish.

To shine but not to dazzle.
20 Falling leaves, falling water,
                              everything comes to rest.

———————

What can anyone know of the sure machine that makes all things
        work?
To find one word and use it correctly,
                                    providing it is the right word,
25 Is more than enough:
An inch of music is an inch and a half of dust.

                                                        1988

As Our Bodies Rise, Our Names Turn into Light

The sky unrolls like a rug,
                        unwelcoming, gun-grey,
Over the Blue Ridge.[6]
Mothers are calling their children in,
5   mellifluous syllables, floating sounds.
The traffic shimmies and settles back.

The doctor has filled his truck with leaves
Next door, and a pair of logs.
                        Salt stones litter the street.
10 The snow falls and the wind drops.
How strange to have a name, any name, on this poor earth.

January hunkers down,
                    the icicle deep in her throat—
The days become longer, the nights ground bitter and cold,
15 Single grain by single grain
Everything flows toward structure,
                        last ache in the ache for God.

                                                        1995

Quotations

Renoir,[7] whose paintings I don't much like,
Says what survives of the artist is the feeling he gives by means of
        objects.

---

6. Eastern ridge of the Appalachian Mountains, ranging from Pennsylvania into Georgia.

7. Pierre-Auguste Renoir (1841–1919), French painter.

I do like that, however,
The feeling put in as much as the feeling received
5   To make a work distinctive,
Though I'm not sure it's true,
                                    or even it's workable.

When Chekhov[8] died, he died at dawn,
                                    a large moth circling the lamp,
10   Beating its pressed wings.
Placed in a zinc casket, the corpse, labeled *Fresh Oysters*,
Was sent to Moscow in a freight car from Germany.
His last words were, *Has the sailor left?*
I am dying, Ich sterbe.[9]

———

15   *My breath is corrupt, my days are extinct, the graves are ready for me,*
Job[1] *says. They change the night into day—*
The light is short because of darkness . . .
I have said to corruption,
                                    thou art my father, to the worm,
20   *Thou art my mother and my sister—*
They shall go down to the bars of the pit,
                                    when our rest together is in the dust.

———

That's all. There's nothing left after that.
As Meng Chiao[2] says,
25   *For a while the dust weighs lightly on my cloak.*

                                                                        1998

DARYL HINE

b. 1936

Letting Go

I loved you first the time I saw you last,
I knew you best before I let you go.
All the misapprehensions of the past
Dissipated in an hour or so,

---

8. Anton Chekhov (1860–1904), Russian fiction
writer and playwright.
9. I am dying (German).
1. In the Hebrew Scriptures, a virtuous man

tested by God with many forms of suffering. These
quotations are taken from Job 17.
2. Chinese poet (751–814).

⁵ Naked to the human eye you lay
Candid as a cadaver on the couch
I could have slept on, but I went away
Ashamed to stay, afraid almost to touch.

Lost, you seemed the only vivid thing
¹⁰ In a world made moribund and flat
By worldliness. Renunciations bring
Their own reward, apparently, like that
Last look of yours, ironical or tender,
A valediction and a benediction,
¹⁵ Which endless reruns will not soon surrender,
The indispensable, improper fiction
Of your unforgettable perfection.

1990

Riddle

Invisible, chimerical
Revolution of the air,
Fickle, hyperactive, fair,
Impulsive, unpredictable
⁵ Flibbertigibbet capable
Of never settling anywhere;
Fortuitously musical
Condition of the atmosphere,
Zephyr, monsoon, hurricane,
¹⁰ Tempest, typhoon, gust or gale—
When will inspiration fail?—
Accomplice of the hail and rain,
Blind but palpable as braille

Wind answers the Weathervane.

1990

C. K. WILLIAMS
b. 1936

Repression

More and more lately, as, not even minding the slippages yet, the
    aches and sad softenings,
I settle into my other years, I notice how many of what I once thought
    were evidences of repression,

sexual or otherwise, now seem, in other people anyway, to be varieties
of dignity, withholding, tact,
and sometimes even in myself, certain patiences I would have once
called lassitude, indifference,
5 now seem possibly to be if not the rewards then at least the
unsuspected, undreamed-of conclusions
to many of the even-then-preposterous self-evolved disciplines, rigors,
almost mortifications
I inflicted on myself in my starting-out days, improvement days, days
when the idea alone of psychic peace,
of intellectual, of emotional quiet, the merest hint, would have meant
inconceivable capitulation.

1987

Snow: II

It's very cold, Catherine is bundled in a coat, a poncho on top of that,
high boots, gloves,
a long scarf around her neck, and she's sauntering up the middle of
the snowed-in street,
eating, of all things, an apple, the blazing redness of which shocks
against the world of white.
No traffic yet, the *crisp crisp* of her footsteps keeps reaching me until
she turns the corner.
5 I write it down years later, and the picture still holds perfectly, precise,
unwanting,
and so too does the sense of being suddenly bereft as she passes
abruptly from my sight,
the quick wash of desolation, the release again into the memory of
affection, and then affection,
as the first trucks blundered past, chains pounding, the first delighted
children rushed out with sleds.

1987

The Question

The middle of the night, she's wide awake, carefully lying as far away
as she can from him.
He turns in his sleep and she can sense him realizing she's not in the
place she usually is,
then his sleep begins to change, he pulls himself closer, his arm
comes comfortably around her.
"Are you awake?" she says, then, afraid that he might think she's
asking him for sex,
5 she hurries on, "I want to know something; last summer, in Cleveland,
did you have someone else?"

She'd almost said—she was going to say—"Did you have a *lover*?" but she'd caught herself;

she'd been frightened by the word, she realized; it was much too definite, at least for now.

Even so, it's only after pausing that he answers, "No," with what feeling she can't tell.

He moves his hand on her, then with a smile in his voice asks, "Did you have somebody in Cleveland?"

10   "That's not what I was asking you," she says crossly. "But that's what I asked *you*," he answers.

She's supposed to be content now, the old story, she knows that she's supposed to be relieved,

but she's not relieved, her tension hasn't eased the slightest bit, which doesn't surprise her.

She's so confused that she can't really even say now if she wants to believe him or not.

Anyway, what about that pause? Was it because in the middle of the night and six months later

15   he wouldn't have even known what she was talking about, or was it because he needed that moment

to frame an answer which would neutralize what might after all have been a shocking thrust

with a reasonable deflection, in this case, his humor: a laugh that's like a lie and is.

"When would I have found the time?" he might have said, or, "Who in Cleveland could I love?"

Or, in that so brief instant, might he have been finding a way to stay in the realm of truth,

20   as she knew he'd surely want to, given how self-righteously he esteemed his ethical integrities?

It comes to her with a start that what she most deeply and painfully suspects him of is a *renunciation*.

She knows that he has no one now; she thinks she knows there's been no contact from Cleveland,

but she still believes that there'd been something then, and if it was as important as she thinks,

it wouldn't be so easily forgotten, it would still be with him somewhere as a sad regret,

25   perhaps a precious memory, but with that word, renunciation, hooked to it like a price tag.

Maybe that was what so rankled her, that she might have been the object of his charity, his *goodness*.

That would be too much; that he would have wronged her, then sacrificed himself for her.

Yes, "Lover," she should have said it, "Lover, lover," should have made him try to disavow it.

She listens to his breathing; he's asleep again, or has he taught himself to feign that, too?

30   "No, last summer in Cleveland I didn't have a lover, I have never been to Cleveland, I love you.

There is no Cleveland, I adore you, and, as you'll remember, there was no last summer:

the world last summer didn't yet exist, last summer still was universal
  darkness, chaos, pain."

1992

TONY HARRISON
b. 1937

On Not Being Milton

for Sergio Vieira & Armando Guebuza (Frelimo)[1]

Read and committed to the flames, I call
these sixteen lines that go back to my roots
my *Cahier d'un retour au pays natal*,[2]
my growing black enough to fit my boots.

5   The stutter of the scold out of the branks[3]
of condescension, class and counter-class
thickens with glottals to a lumpen[4] mass
of Ludding morphemes[5] closing up their ranks.
Each swung cast-iron Enoch of Leeds stress[6]
10   clangs a forged music on the frames of Art,
the looms of owned language smashed apart!

Three cheers for mute ingloriousness![7]

Articulation is the tongue-tied's fighting.
In the silence round all poetry we quote
15   Tidd the Cato Street conspirator[8] who wrote:

Sir, I Ham a very Bad Hand at Righting.

1978

---

1. Mozambique freedom-fighters.
2. Notebook of a return to one's land of birth
(French). The title of a poem by the Martinican
poet, historian, and politician Aimé Césaire (b.
1913). Published in 1939, *Cahier d'un retour au
pays natal* is a seminal work in the literature of
négritude, describing the condition of colonized
black (in Césaire's case West Indian) people, and
charting a literal and physical journey back from
exile to the homeland.
3. "Bridles," or gagging devices put over the
mouths of "scolds," people who habitually com-
plain and nag. As the old northern word for poet
is *scald*, the line could refer to poets who speak out
in defiance of the society that silences them, as
well as to political agitators and revolutionaries.
4. Lower-class. *Glottals*: sounds made by opening
and closing the larynx. The Leeds dialect uses glot-
tal stops, the sound made when the word *butter* is
pronounced as two syllables without an interven-
ing *t*.
5. Smallest meaningful language units. *Ludding*:
Luddites were reactionary groups opposed to the
mechanization of mills and factories, a change that
led to unemployment and starvation.
6. Forceful or prominent syllable or sound. "An
'Enoch' is an iron sledge-hammer used by the Lud-
dites to smash the frames which were also made
by the same Enoch Taylor of Marsden. The cry
was: 'Enoch made them, Enoch shall break
them!' " [Harrison's note].
7. A reference to Thomas Gray, "Elegy Written in
a Country Churchyard," line 59: "Some mute
inglorious Milton here may rest" (p. 671).
8. Participant in a failed early nineteenth-century
plot to assassinate the British cabinet. The con-
spirators met in a loft on Cato Street, near
London's Edgware Road.

Classics Society

(Leeds Grammar School 1552–1952)[9]

The grace of Tullies eloquence doth excell
any Englishmans tongue . . . my barbarous stile . . . [1]

The tongue our leaders use to cast their spell
was once denounced as "rude", "gross", "base" and "vile".

5   How fortunate we are who've come so far!

We boys can take old Hansards[2] and translate
the British Empire into SPQR[3]
but nothing demotic° or too up-to-date,   *slangy*
and *not* the English that I speak at home,
10 not Hansard standards, and if Antoninus[4]
spoke like delinquent Latin back in Rome
he'd probably get gamma double minus.[5]

And so the lad who gets the alphas works
the hardest in his class at his translation
15 and finds good Ciceronian for Burke's:

a dreadful schism in the British nation.[6]

1978

Them & [uz]

for Professors Richard Hoggart & Leon Cortez[7]

I

αἰαῖ, ay, ay! . . . stutterer Demosthenes[8]
gob° full of pebbles outshouting seas—   *mouth*

9. Harrison won a scholarship to Leeds Grammar School, a highly academic school for pupils aged eleven to eighteen, otherwise for fee-paying students.
1. A quotation from Robert Recorde's preface to his *Ground of Arts* (1543), a textbook that expresses the ethos of Leeds Grammar School in preferring the (now defunct) language of "Tully," the Roman statesman, orator, and writer Marcus Tullius Cicero (106–43 B.C.E.), to contemporary English.
2. Printed reports of debates in the British Houses of Parliament.
3. *Senatus Populusque Romanus:* the senate and people of Rome (Latin).
4. A third-century Roman emperor. As Harrison's first name, Tony, has been wrongly taken to be a diminutive of Anthony (see "Them & [uz]," below), this could be a humorous reference to an imaginary self in ancient Rome.
5. Marking in British schools and universities is often based on the Greek alphabet. Thus alpha would be A, beta B, and gamma double minus C−−, or fail.
6. Edmund Burke (1729–1797), an Irishman, became one of Britain's foremost political thinkers. His writings advocated a sound constitutional statesmanship in a time of misgovernment and corruption. Though he was against the concept of inalienable human rights, he supported the notion of the "social contract." He warned that the "dreadful schism" in British society could lead to revolution and regicide as in France, and he called for the suppression of free opinions.
7. Richard Hoggart (b. 1918) is an academic and, like Tony Harrison, from a working-class, north-of-England background. "Professor" Leon Cortez (1898–1970) was a music-hall comedian, whose act included recitations of Shakespeare's *Macbeth* in Cockney (working-class London) English.
8. Athenian orator (385?–322 B.C.E.)

4 words only of *mi 'art aches*[9] and . . . "Mine's broken,
you barbarian, T.W.!"[1] *He* was nicely spoken.
5   "Can't have our glorious heritage done to death!"

I played the Drunken Porter in *Macbeth*.

"Poetry's the speech of kings. You're one of those
Shakespeare gives the comic bits to: prose!
All poetry (even Cockney Keats?) you see
10 's been dubbed by [vs][2] into RP,
Received Pronunciation, please believe [vs]
your speech is in the hands of the Receivers."

"We say [vs] not [uz], T.W.!" That shut my trap.
I doffed my flat a's (as in "flat cap")
15 my mouth all stuffed with glottals,[3] great
lumps to hawk up and spit out . . . *E-nun-ci-ate!*

II

So right, yer buggers, then! We'll occupy
your lousy leasehold Poetry.

I chewed up Littererchewer and spat the bones
20 into the lap of dozing Daniel Jones,[4]
dropped the initials I'd been harried as
and used my *name* and own voice: [uz] [uz] [uz],
ended sentences with by, with, from,
and spoke the language that I spoke at home.
25 RIP RP, RIP T.W.
I'm *Tony* Harrison no longer you!

You can tell the Receivers where to go
(and not aspirate it) once you know
Wordsworth's *matter* / *water* are full rhymes,
30 [uz] can be loving as well as funny.

My first mention in the *Times*[5]
automatically made Tony Anthony!

1978

---

9. Cf. John Keats, "Ode to a Nightingale," line 1 (p. 935). To the despair of his teacher, the young Harrison, speaking the Leeds dialect, says "mi 'art" instead of "my heart."
1. Harrison's first names are Tony William. His first work was published under the name T. W. Harrison.
2. Phonetic transcription representing the Received Pronunciation form of *us*. The northern dialect form is *uz*.

3. Sounds made by opening and closing the larynx. The Leeds dialect uses glottal stops, the sound made when the word *butter* is pronounced as two syllables without an intervening *t*.
4. English phonetician (1881–1967), whose *Outline of English Phonetics* (1918) is considered the first comprehensive description of Received Pronunciation.
5. A London "quality" newspaper.

A Kumquat for John Keats

Today I found the right fruit for my prime,
not orange, not tangelo, and not lime,
nor moon-like globes of grapefruit that now hang
outside our bedroom, nor tart lemon's tang
5   (though last year full of bile and self-defeat
I wanted to believe no life was sweet)
nor the tangible sunshine of the tangerine,
and no incongruous citrus ever seen
at greengrocers' in Newcastle or Leeds
10 mis-spelt by the spuds° and mud-caked swedes,°   *potatoes / Swedish turnips*
a fruit an older poet might substitute
for the grape John Keats thought fit to be Joy's fruit,
when, two years before he died, he tried to write
how Melancholy dwelled inside Delight,[6]
15 and if he'd known the citrus that I mean
that's not orange, lemon, lime or tangerine,
I'm pretty sure that Keats, though he had heard
"of candied apple, quince and plum and gourd"[7]
instead of "grape against the palate fine"[8]
20 would have, if he'd known it, plumped for mine,
this Eastern citrus scarcely cherry size
he'd bite just once and then apostrophize
and pen one stanza how the fruit had all
the qualities of fruit before the Fall,[9]
25 but in the next few lines be forced to write
how Eve's apple tasted at the second bite,
and if John Keats had only lived to be,
because of extra years, in need like me,
at 42 he'd help me celebrate
30 that Micanopy[1] kumquat that I ate
whole, straight off the tree, sweet pulp and sour skin—
or was it sweet outside, and sour within?
For however many kumquats that I eat
I'm not sure if it's flesh or rind that's sweet,
35 and being a man of doubt at life's mid-way
I'd offer Keats some kumquats and I'd say:
You'll find that one part's sweet and one part's tart:
say where the sweetness or the sourness start.

I find I can't, as if one couldn't say
40 exactly where the night became the day,
which makes for me the kumquat taken whole
best fruit, and metaphor, to fit the soul
of one in Florida at 42 with Keats
crunching kumquats, thinking, as he eats

---

6. Cf. John Keats, "Ode on Melancholy," lines 25–26 (p. 938).
7. Cf. Keats, "The Eve of St. Agnes," line 265 (p. 913).
8. Cf. Keats, "Ode on Melancholy," line 28 (p. 938).
9. Cf. Genesis 2–3.
1. Place in southern Florida.

45   the flesh, the juice, the pith, the pips,° the peel,   seeds
       that this is how a full life ought to feel,
       its perishable relish prick the tongue,
       when the man who savours life 's no longer young,
       the fruits that were his futures far behind.
50   Then it's the kumquat fruit expresses best
       how days have darkness round them like a rind,
       life has a skin of death that keeps its zest.

       History, a life, the heart, the brain
       flow to the taste buds and flow back again.
55   That decade or more past Keats's span
       makes me an older not a wiser man,
       who knows that it's too late for dying young,
       but since youth leaves some sweetnesses unsung,
       he's granted days and kumquats to express
60   Man's Being ripened by his Nothingness.
       And it isn't just the gap of sixteen years,
       a bigger crop of terrors, hopes and fears,
       but a century of history on this earth
       between John Keats's death and my own birth—
65   years like an open crater, gory, grim,
       with bloody bubbles leering at the rim;[2]
       a thing no bigger than an urn explodes
       and ravishes all silence, and all odes,
       Flora° asphyxiated by foul air   Roman goddess of flowers
70   unknown to either Keats or Lemprière,[3]
       dehydrated Naiads, Dryad amputees[4]
       dragging themselves through slagscapes with no trees,
       a shirt of Nessus fire that gnaws and eats[5]
       children half the age of dying Keats . . .

75   Now were you twenty five or six years old
       when that fevered brow at last grew cold?
       I've got no books to hand to check the dates.
       My grudging but glad spirit celebrates
       that all I've got to hand 's the kumquats, John,
80   the fruit I'd love to have your verdict on,
       but dead men don't eat kumquats, or drink wine,
       they shiver in the arms of Proserpine,[6]
       not warm in bed beside their Fanny Brawne,[7]
       nor watch her pick ripe grapefruit in the dawn
85   as I did, waking, when I saw her twist,
       with one deft movement of a sunburnt wrist,
       the moon, that feebly lit our last night's walk
       past alligator swampland, off its stalk.
       I thought of moon-juice juleps[8] when I saw,

2. Cf. Keats, "Ode to a Nightingale," line 17
(p. 935).
3. John Lemprière (ca. 1765–1824), English clas-
sical scholar and author of The Classical Dic-
tionary—for many years a standard work.
4. Landscapes dominated by heaps of rubble,
refuse from mines. Dryad: wood nymph. Naiads:

water nymphs.
5. A magical shirt, named for the centaur Nessus
in Greek mythology, that once donned cannot be
removed and that consumes the wearer in flames.
6. In Greek mythology, queen of the underworld.
7. A young woman loved by Keats.
8. Drinks made from spirits, sugar, ice, and mint.

90   as if I'd never seen the moon before,
the planet glow among the fruit, and its pale light
make each citrus on the tree its satellite.

Each evening when I reach to draw the blind
stars seem the light zest squeezed through night's black rind;
95   the night's peeled fruit the sun, juiced of its rays,
first stains, then streaks, then floods the world with days,
days, when the very sunlight made me weep,
days, spent like the nights in deep, drugged sleep,
days in Newcastle by my daughter's bed,
100   wondering if she, or I, weren't better dead,
days in Leeds, grey days, my first dark suit,
my mother's wreaths stacked next to Christmas fruit,
and days, like this in Micanopy. Days!

As strong sun burns away the dawn's grey haze
105   I pick a kumquat and the branches spray
cold dew in my face to start the day.
The dawn's molasses make the citrus gleam
still in the orchards of the groves of dream.

The limes, like Galway after weeks of rain,
110   glow with a greenness that is close to pain,
the dew-cooled surfaces of fruit that spent
all last night flaming in the firmament.
The new day dawns. O days! My spirit greets
the kumquat with the spirit of John Keats.
115   O kumquat, comfort for not dying young,
both sweet and bitter, bless the poet's tongue!
I burst the whole fruit chilled by morning dew
against my palate. Fine, for 42!

I search for buzzards as the air grows clear
120   and see them ride fresh thermals overhead.
Their bleak cries were the first sound I could hear
when I stepped at the start of sunrise out of doors,
and a noise like last night's bedsprings on our bed
from Mr Fowler sharpening farmers' saws.

1981

The Heartless Art

in memoriam *S.T., died 4 April 1985*

Death is in your house, but I'm out here
sackclothing kumquats against the forecast freeze,
filling the hole you took two days to clear
of briars, beercans, and bleached, barkless trees,
5   with hackberry leaves, pine needles, stuff like that.

Next spring, when you're no longer here
we'll have the land grassed over and quite flat.

When the Southern sun starts setting it sets fast.
I've time to tip one more load if I run.
10   Because I know this light could be your last
I drain the day of every drop of sun.
The barrow wheel spins round with a clock's tick.
I hear, three fields away, a hunter's gun,
you, in the silence after, being sick.

15   I watched you, very weak, negotiate
the childproof pill jar, panting to draw breath,
and when you managed it you poured your hate
more on the poured-out contents than on death,
and, like Baptists uttering Beelzebub°   the Devil
20   syllable by syllable, spat *Meth-*
a-done,[9] and there's also the poetic rub!

I've often heard my fellow poets (or those
who write in metres something like my own
with rhyme and rhythm, not in chopped-up prose
25   and brood on man's mortality) bemoan
the insufficiency of rhymes for death—
hence my syllabifying *Methadone*
instead of just saying that you fought for breath.

Maybe the main but not the only cause;
30   a piece of engineering I'll explain.
Each syllable *was* followed by a pause
for breathlessness, and scorn of drugs for pain.
Another reason, though, was to delay
the use of one more rhyme stored in my brain
35   that, alas, I'll have a use for any day.

I'd stored away this rhyme when we first met.
Knowing you crawled on hands and knees to prime
our water pump, I'll expiate one debt
by finally revealing that stored rhyme
40   that has the same relentlessness as death
and comes to every one of us in time
and comes to you this April full moon, SETH!

In return for all those oily working parts
you took the time and trouble to explain,
45   the pump that coughs, the saw that never starts,
I'll show you to distract you from the pain
you feel, except when napping, all the time
because you won't take drugs that dull the brain,
a bit about my metre, line and rhyme.

9. Drug used as substitute for morphine or heroin.

50 In Arthur Symons' *St Teresa*[1] Nazaréth
    is stressed on the last against its spoken flow
    to engineer the contrast Jesus/Death.
    Do I endorse that contrast? I don't, no!
    To have a life on Earth and then want Heaven
55 seems like that all-night bar sign down below
    that says that *Happy Hour*'s from 4 to 7.

    Package lounges[2] are like ambulances:
    the Bourbon-bibber° stares at us and glowers   -drinker
    at what he thinks are pained or pitying glances.
60 We don't see his face but he sees ours.
    The non-dying don't see you but you see them
    passing by to other rooms with flowers
    as you fill the shining kidney with red phlegm.

    I've left some spaces (   )[3]
65 benumbed by morphia° and *Methadone*   painkilling drug
    until the (   )[4] of April, (   )[5]
    When I began these lines could I have known
    that the nurse's registration of the time
    you let your spirit go with one last groan
70 would help complete the first and third line rhyme?

    Those bits I added later. Them apart
    I wrote this *in memoriam* for Seth,
    meant to show him something of my art,
    almost a whole week before his death.
75 The last thing the dying want to read,
    I thought, 's a poem, and didn't show it,
    and you, not dying yet, why should you need
    to know the final failure of the poet?

                                                              1985

ELEANOR WILNER

b. 1937

Reading the Bible Backwards[1]

All around the altar, huge lianas
curled, unfurled the dark green
of their leaves to complement the red

---

1. The poetry of the Spanish nun and mystic St. Teresa of Ávila (1515–1582), translated by the English poet and critic Arthur Symons (1865–1945).
2. Bars (Floridian colloquialism).
3. "how you stayed alive" [Harrison's note].
4. "4th" [Harrison's note].

5. "10.05" [Harrison's note].
1. Or from the Apocalypse in Revelation, the final book of the Christian Scriptures, to the Creation in Genesis, the first book of the Hebrew Scriptures. Wilner fuses details from both Christian and Hebrew Scriptures throughout the poem.

of blood spilled there—a kind of Christmas
5   decoration, overhung with heavy vines
and over them, the stars.
When the angels came, messengers like birds
but with the oiled flesh of men, they hung
over the scene with smoldering swords,[2]
10   splashing the world when they beat
their rain-soaked wings against the turning sky.

The child was bright in his basket[3]
as a lemon, with a bitter smell from his wet
swaddling clothes. His mother bent
15   above him, singing a lullaby
in the liquid tongue invented
for the very young—short syllables
like dripping from an eave
mixed with the first big drops of rain
20   that fell, like tiny silver pears, from
the glistening fronds of palm. The three
who gathered there—old kings uncrowned:
the cockroach, condor and the leopard, lords
of the cracks below the ground, the mountain
25   pass and the grass-grown plain, were not
adorned, did not bear gifts, had not
come to adore; they were simply drawn
to gawk at this recurrent, awkward son
whom the wind had said would spell
30   the end of earth as it had been.

Somewhere north of this familiar scene
the polar caps were melting, the water was
advancing in its slow, relentless
lines, swallowing the old
35   landmarks, swelling the seas that pulled
the flowers and the great steel cities down.
The dolphins sport in the rising sea,
anemones wave their many arms like hair
on a drowned gorgon's head,[4] her features
40   softened by the sea beyond all recognition.

On the desert's edge where the oasis dies
in a wash of sand, the sphinx[5] seems to shift
on her haunches of stone, and the rain, as it runs down,
completes the ruin of her face. The Nile
45   merges with the sea, the waters rise
and drown the noise of earth. At the forest's

---

2. Suggests the flaming sword of the cherubim
stationed east of the Garden of Eden (Genesis
3.24).
3. Moses' mother hid him in a covered wicker bas-
ket, which she set in reeds by the Nile, to protect
him from Pharoah's command to cast all sons into
the river (Exodus 2.2–3). The lines following
return to Christ's nativity and the gifts brought to
him by the wise men (Matthew 2.1–12).

4. The water imagery suggests both the flood from
which Noah escaped in the ark (Genesis 7) and
the end of the Ice Age. In Greek mythology, the
Gorgons were three sisters who had snakes for
hair.
5. Wilner's sphinx evokes not the Egyptian but the
Greek model, a winged creature with a woman's
head and lion's body.

edge, where the child sleeps, the waters gather—
as if a hand were reaching for the curtain
to drop across the glowing, lit tableau.

50 When the waves closed over, completing the green
sweep of ocean, there was no time for mourning.
No final trump,[6] no thunder to announce
the silent steal of waters; how soundlessly
it all went under: the little family
55 and the scene so easily mistaken
for an adoration. Above, more clouds poured in
and closed their ranks across the skies;
the angels, who had seemed so solid, turned
quicksilver in the rain.
60   Now, nothing but the wind
moves on the rain-pocked face
of the swollen waters, though far below
where giant squid lie hidden in shy tangles,
the whales, heavy-bodied as the angels,
65 their fins like vestiges of wings,
sing some mighty epic of their own—
a great day when the ships would all withdraw,
the harpoons fail of their aim, the land
dissolve into the waters, and they would swim
70 among the peaks of mountains, like eagles
of the deep, while far below them, the old
nightmares of earth would settle
into silt among the broken cities, the empty
basket of the child would float
75 abandoned in the seaweed until the work of water
unraveled it in filaments of straw,
till even that straw rotted
in the planetary thaw the whales prayed for,
sending their jets of water skyward
80 in the clear conviction they'd spill back
to ocean with their will accomplished
in the miracle of rain: *And the earth*
was without form and void, and darkness
was upon the face of the deep. And
85 *the Spirit moved upon the face of the waters.*[7]

1989

High Noon at Los Alamos[8]

To turn a stone
with its white squirming
underneath, to pry the disc

6. The final trumpet; image of the Last Judgment.
7. As in Genesis 1.2.
8. Los Alamos, New Mexico; a major site of the

Manhattan Project to develop an atomic bomb
(1942–45).

from the sun's eclipse—white heat
5   coiling in the blinded eye: to these malign
necessities we come
from the dim time of dinosaurs
who crawled like breathing lava
from the earth's cracked crust, and swung
10 their tiny heads above the lumbering tons
of flesh, brains no bigger than a fist
clenched to resist the white flash
in the sky the day the sun-flares
pared them down to relics for museums,
15 turned glaciers back, seared Sinai's
meadows[9] black—the ferns withered, the swamps
were melted down to molten mud, the cells
uncoupled, recombined, and madly
multiplied, huge trees toppled to the ground,
20 the slow life there abandoned hope,
a caterpillar stiffened in the grass.
Two apes, caught in the act of coupling,
made a mutant child
who woke to sunlight wondering, his mother
25 torn by the huge new head
that forced the narrow birth canal.[1]

As if compelled to repetition
and to unearth again
white fire at the heart of matter—fire
30 we sought and fire we spoke,
our thoughts, however elegant, were fire
from first to last—like sentries set to watch
at Argos for the signal fire
passed peak to peak from Troy
35 to Nagasaki,[2] triumphant echo of the burning
city walls and prologue to the murders
yet to come—we scan the sky
for that bright flash,
our eyes stared white from watching
40 for the signal fire that ends
the epic—a cursèd line
with its caesura, a pause
to signal peace, or a rehearsal
for the silence.

1989

9. In the Sinai Peninsula, a triangular region linking Africa with Asia.
1. The effects of extreme radiation can include gene mutation.
2. Japanese city, site of the second atomic bomb explosion in 1945. Lines 32–34 refer to the beginning of *Agamemnon*, the first play in the *Oresteia* trilogy by the Greek dramatist Aeschylus (525–456 B.C.E.). The play opens with a watchman in Argos— a city on the lower peninsula of Greece, and the home of Agamemnon—looking for "the light, the signal-fire / breaking out of Troy" (i.e., signalling Greek victory in the Trojan War).

DOM MORAES
b. 1938

Kanheri Caves

Over these blunted, these tormented hills,
Hawks hail and wheel, glissading° down the sky: *gliding*
It seems this green ambiguous landscape tilts
And teeters the perspective of the eye.
5   Only two centuries after Christ, this cliff
Was colonized by a mild antique race,
Who left us, like a faded photograph,
Their memories that dry up in this place.

They left no ghosts. The rock alone endures.
10   Their drains and cisterns work: storms wrecked the stairs:
Blocks are fallen: sunlight cracks those floors
And fidgets in a courtyard where a pair
Of giant Buddhas smile and wait their crash;
Then temples, audience-halls, a lonely tomb.
15   I touch its side. The stone's worn smooth as flesh.
A stranger dangles peaceful in that womb.

Worm he will be, if born: blink in the sun.
I'll crawl into his dark: perhaps he'll climb
Beyond the trippers to the final stone
20   Flat of the hillock, there to grow in Time.
Dry pubic ferns prickle the bitter sand.
Hawks in a hot concentric ecstasy
Of flight and shriek will wake his vision. And,
When the clouds lift, he'll glimpse the miles-off sea.

1957

Snow on a Mountain

That dream, her eyes like rocks studded the high
Mountain of her body that I was to climb.
     One moment past my hands had swum
     The chanting streams of her thighs:
5   Then I was lost, breathless among the pines.

Alone, alone with the nervous noise of water,
Climbing, I hoped to emerge on a path, but I knew
     When the spurred trees were past
     I should go on no farther
10   But fall there, dazzled by the miles of snow.

My dream was broken by the knock of day.
Yet, within my mind, these pictures linger:

I touch her with my clumsy words of love
And sense snow in her eye,
15 Mists, and the winds that warn, Stranger, O stranger!

                                                              1957

From Two from Israel

Rendezvous

(FOR NATHAN ALTERMANN)[1]

Altermann, sipping wine, reads with a look
Of infinite patience and slight suffering.
When I approach him, he puts down his book,

Waves to the chair beside him like a king,
5   Then claps his hands, and an awed waiter fetches
Bread, kosher sausage, cake, a chicken's wing,

More wine, some English cigarettes, and matches.
"Eat, eat," Altermann says, "this is good food."
Through the awning over us the sunlight catches

10 His aquiline° sad head, till it seems hewed   *eaglelike*
From tombstone marble. I accept some bread.
I've lunched already, but would not seem rude.

When I refuse more, he feeds me instead,
Heaping my plate, clapping for wine, his eyes
15 —Expressionless inside the marble head—

Appearing not to notice how the flies
Form a black, sticky icing on the cake.
Thinking of my health now, I visualise

The Aryan snow floating, flake upon flake,
20 Over the ghetto wall where only fleas
Fed well, and they and hunger kept awake

Under sharp stars, those waiting for release.
Birds had their nests, but Jews nowhere to hide
When visited by vans and black police.

25 The shekinah° rose where a people died,   *divine presence*
A pillar of flame by night, of smoke by day.
From Europe then the starved and terrified

Flew. Now their mourner sits in this café,
Telling me how to scan a Hebrew line.
30 Though my attention has moved far away

1. Israeli poet (1910–1970).

His features stay marble and aquiline.
But the eternal gesture of his race
Flowing through the hands that offer bread and wine

Reveals the deep love sealed in the still face.

1965

LES MURRAY

b. 1938

Noonday Axeman

Axe-fall, echo and silence. Noonday silence.
Two miles from here, it is the twentieth century:
cars on the bitumen,[1] powerlines vaulting the farms.
Here, with my axe, I am chopping into the stillness.

5   Axe-fall, echo and silence. I pause, roll tobacco,
twist a cigarette, lick it. All is still.
I lean on my axe. A cloud of fragrant leaves
hangs over me moveless, pierced everywhere by sky.

Here, I remember all of a hundred years:
10   candleflame, still night, frost and cattle bells,
the draywheels'[2] silence final in our ears,
and the first red cattle spreading through the hills

and my great-great-grandfather here with his first sons,
who would grow old, still speaking with his Scots accent,
15   having never seen those highlands that they sang of.
A hundred years. I stand and smoke in the silence.

A hundred years of clearing, splitting, sawing,
a hundred years of timbermen, ringbarkers, fencers
and women in kitchens, stoking loud iron stoves
20   year in, year out, and singing old songs to their children

have made this silence human and familiar
no farther than where the farms rise into foothills,
and, in that time, how many have sought their graves
or fled to the cities, maddened by this stillness?

25   Things are so wordless. These two opposing scarves°   *incisions*
I have cut in my red-gum squeeze out jewels of sap

---

1. Name given to various inflammable mineral   2. Wheels of a long, heavy cart.
substances, here probably asphalt.

and stare. And soon, with a few more axe-strokes,
the tree will grow troubled, tremble, shift its crown

and, leaning slowly, gather speed and colossally
30 crash down and lie between the standing trunks.
And then, I know, of the knowledge that led my forebears
to drink and black rage and wordlessness, there will be silence.

After the tree falls, there will reign the same silence
as stuns and spurs us, enraptures and defeats us,
35 as seems to some a challenge, and seems to others
to be waiting here for something beyond imagining.

Axe-fall, echo and silence. Unhuman silence.
A stone cracks in the heat. Through the still twigs, radiance
stings at my eyes. I rub a damp brow with a handkerchief
40 and chop on into the stillness. Axe-fall and echo.

The great mast murmurs now. The scarves in its trunk
crackle and squeak now, crack and increase as the hushing
weight of high branches heels outward, and commences
tearing and falling, and the collapse is tremendous.

45 Twigs fly, leaves puff and subside. The severed trunk
slips off its stump and drops along its shadow.
And then there is no more. The stillness is there
as ever. And I fall to lopping branches.

Axe-fall, echo and silence. It will be centuries
50 before many men are truly at home in this country,
and yet, there have always been some, in each generation,
there have always been some who could live in the presence of
    silence.

And some, I have known them, men with gentle broad hands,
who would die if removed from these unpeopled places,
55 some again I have seen, bemused and shy in the cities,
you have built against silence, dumbly trudging through noise

past the railway stations, looking up through the traffic
at the smoky halls, dreaming of journeys, of stepping
down from the train at some upland stop to recover
60 the crush of dry grass underfoot, the silence of trees.

Axe-fall, echo and silence. Dreaming silence.
Though I myself run to the cities, I will forever
be coming back here to walk, knee-deep in ferns,
up and away from this metropolitan century,

65 to remember my ancestors, axemen, dairymen, horse-breakers,
now coffined in silence, down with their beards and dreams,
who, unwilling or rapt, despairing or very patient,
made what amounts to a human breach in the silence,

made of their lives the rough foundation of legends—
70   men must have legends, else they will die of strangeness—
then died in their turn, each, after his own fashion,
resigned or agonized, from silence into great silence.

Axe-fall, echo and axe-fall. Noonday silence.
Though I go to the cities, turning my back on these hills,
75   for the talk and dazzle of cities, for the sake of belonging
for months and years at a time to the twentieth century,

the city will never quite hold me. I will be always
coming back here on the up-train, peering, leaning
out of the window to see, on far-off ridges,
80   the sky between the trees, and over the racket
of the rails to hear the echo and the silence.

I shoulder my axe and set off home through the stillness.

                                                  1965

Once in a Lifetime, Snow

For Chris and Mary Sharah

Winters at home brought wind,
black frost and raw
grey rain in barbed-wire fields,
but never more

5   until the day my uncle
rose at dawn
and stepped outside—to find
his paddocks gone,

his cattle to their hocks
10   in ghostly ground
and unaccustomed light
for miles around.

And he stopped short, and gazed
lit from below,
15   and half his wrinkles vanished
murmuring *Snow*.

A man of farm and fact
he stared to see
the facts of weather raised
20   to a mystery

white on the world he knew
and all he owned.

Snow? Here? he mused. I see.
High time I learned.

25 Here, guessing what he meant
had much to do
with that black earth dread old men
are given to,

he stooped to break the sheer
30 crust with delight
at finding the cold unknown
so deeply bright,

at feeling it take his prints
so softly deep,
35 as if it thought he knew
enough to sleep,

or else so little he
might seek to shift
its weight of wintry light
40 by a single drift,

perceiving this much, he scuffed
his slippered feet
and scooped a handful up
to taste, and eat

45 in memory of the fact
that even he
might not have seen the end
of reality . . .

Then, turning, he tiptoed in
50 to a bedroom, smiled,
and wakened a murmuring child
and another child.

1969

The Quality of Sprawl

Sprawl is the quality
of the man who cut down his Rolls-Royce
into a farm utility truck, and sprawl
is what the company lacked when it made repeated efforts
5 to buy the vehicle back and repair its image.

Sprawl is doing your farming by aeroplane, roughly,
or driving a hitchhiker that extra hundred miles home.

It is the rococo[3] of being your own still centre.
It is never lighting cigars with ten-dollar notes:
10 that's idiot ostentation and murder of starving people.
Nor can it be bought with the ash of million-dollar deeds.

Sprawl lengthens the legs; it trains greyhounds on liver and beer.
Sprawl almost never says Why not? with palms comically raised
nor can it be dressed for, not even in running shoes worn
15 with mink and a nose ring. That is Society. That's Style.
Sprawl is more like the thirteenth banana in a dozen
or anyway the fourteenth.

Sprawl is Hank Stamper in *Never Give an Inch*[4]
bisecting an obstructive official's desk with a chainsaw.
20 Not harming the official. Sprawl is never brutal
though it's often intransigent. Sprawl is never Simon de Montfort[5]
at a town-storming: Kill them all! God will know his own.
Knowing the man's name this was said to might be sprawl.

Sprawl occurs in art. The fifteenth to twenty-first
25 lines in a sonnet, for example. And in certain paintings;
I have sprawl enough to have forgotten which paintings.
Turner's glorious *Burning of the Houses of Parliament*[6]
comes to mind, a doubling bannered triumph of sprawl—
except, he didn't fire them.

30 Sprawl gets up the nose of many kinds of people
(every kind that comes in kinds) whose futures don't include it.
Some decry it as criminal presumption, silken-robed Pope Alexander[7]
dividing the new world between Spain and Portugal.
If he smiled *in petto*[8] afterwards, perhaps the thing did have sprawl.

35 Sprawl is really classless, though. It's John Christopher Frederick
      Murray
asleep in his neighbours' best bed in spurs and oilskins
but not having thrown up:
sprawl is never Calum who, drunk, along the hallways of our house,
reinvented the Festoon.[9] Rather
40 it's Beatrice Miles going twelve hundred ditto in a taxi,[1]

---

3. Style of architecture, decoration, and furniture prevalent in Louis XV's France. Characteristically asymmetrical, overornamented, and florid.
4. U.K. title of Paul Newman's movie *Sometimes a Great Notion* (1971), an adaptation of the Ken Kesey novel about Oregon logger Hank Stamper and his family.
5. Thirteenth-century earl of Leicester; leader of the barons in disaffection against Henry III, and so an archetypal "overmighty subject."
6. Famous landscape by the English artist Joseph Mallord William Turner (1775–1851), whose painting, in watercolor and, later, oil, foreshadowed Impressionism.

7. Eight popes took the name Alexander. Possibly Alexander VI, Rodrigo Borgia (1431–1503), father of Caesar, Lucretia, and other children. He secured the papal throne through blatant bribery.
8. To himself (Italian).
9. Chain of flowers, leaves, etc., hung in a curve between two points.
1. The Australian bohemian Beatrice Miles (1902–1973) was famous for, among other things, riding in taxis and taking public transport but refusing to pay the fares, for making a nineteen-day taxi journey from Sydney to Perth and paying the fare, and for reciting Shakespeare (line 42) from memory. *Ditto*: i.e., miles.

No Lewd Advances, No Hitting Animals, No Speeding,
on the proceeds of her two-bob-a-sonnet Shakespeare readings.
An image of my country. And would that it were more so.

No, sprawl is full-gloss murals on a council-house° wall.   *town hall*
45 Sprawl leans on things. It is loose-limbed in its mind.
Reprimanded and dismissed
it listens with a grin and one boot up on the rail
of possibility. It may have to leave the Earth.
Being roughly Christian, it scratches the other cheek
50 and thinks it unlikely. Though people have been shot for sprawl.

1983

Morse

Tuckett. Bill Tuckett. Telegraph operator, Hall's Creek,
which is way out back of the Outback, but he stuck it,
quite likely liked it, despite heat, glare, dust and the lack
of diversion or doctors. Come disaster you trusted to luck,
5 ingenuity and pluck. This was back when nice people said pluck,
the sleevelink and green eyeshade epoch.[2]
                                    Faced, though, like Bill Tuckett
with a man needing surgery right on the spot, a lot
would have done their dashes. It looked hopeless (dot dot dot)
10 Lift him up on the table, said Tuckett, running the key hot
till Head Office turned up a doctor who coolly instructed
up a thousand miles of wire, as Tuckett advanced slit by slit
with a safety razor blade, pioneering on into the wet,
copper-wiring the rivers off, in the first operation conducted
15 along dotted lines, with rum drinkers gripping the patient:
d-d-dash it, take care, Tuck!
                          And the vital spark stayed unshorted.
Yallah![3] breathed the camelmen. Tuckett, you did it, you did it!
cried the spattered la-de-dah jodhpur[4]-wearing Inspector of Stock.
20 We imagine, some weeks later, a properly laconic
convalescent averring Without you, I'd have kicked the bucket . . .

From Chungking to Burrenjuck,[5] morse keys have mostly gone silent
and only old men meet now to chit-chat in their electric
bygone dialect. The last letter many will forget
25 is dit-dit-dit-dah, V for Victory. The coders' hero had speed,
resource and a touch. So ditditdit daah for Bill Tuckett.

1983

---

2. I.e., the nineteenth century. *Sleevelink*: cuff
link.
3. God be praised! (Arabic).
4. Long breeches for riding, close-fitting from
knee to ankle.
5. I.e., from southwest China to southeast Austra-
lia.

CHARLES SIMIC
b. 1938

Watch Repair

A small wheel
Incandescent,
Shivering like
A pinned butterfly.

5   Hands thrown up
In all directions:
The crossroads
One arrives at
In a nightmare.

10   Higher than that
Number 12 presides
Like a beekeeper
Over the swarming honeycomb
Of the open watch.

15   Other wheels
That could fit
Inside a raindrop.

Tools
That must be splinters
20   Of arctic starlight.

Tiny golden mills
Grinding invisible
Coffee beans.

When the coffee's boiling
25   Cautiously,
So it doesn't burn us,
We raise it
To the lips
Of the nearest
30   Ear.

1974

Prodigy[1]

I grew up bent over
a chessboard.

I loved the word *endgame*.

All my cousins looked worried.

5   It was a small house
near a Roman graveyard.
Planes and tanks
shook its windowpanes.

A retired professor of astronomy
10 taught me how to play.

That must have been in 1944.

In the set we were using,
the paint had almost chipped off
the black pieces.

15 The white King was missing
and had to be substituted for.

I'm told but do not believe
that that summer I witnessed
men hung from telephone poles.

20 I remember my mother
blindfolding me a lot.
She had a way of tucking my head
suddenly under her overcoat.

In chess, too, the professor told me,
25 the masters play blindfolded,
the great ones on several boards
at the same time.

1980

A Book Full of Pictures

Father studied theology through the mail
And this was exam time.
Mother knitted. I sat quietly with a book
Full of pictures. Night fell.

1. This poem and "Cameo Appearance" (p. 1893) allude to the Nazi bombing of Belgrade, where Simic was born, in World War II.

5 My hands grew cold touching the faces
Of dead kings and queens.

There was a black raincoat
    in the upstairs bedroom
Swaying from the ceiling,
10 But what was it doing there?
Mother's long needles made quick crosses.
They were black
Like the inside of my head just then.

The pages I turned sounded like wings.
15 "The soul is a bird," he once said.
In my book full of pictures
A battle raged: lances and swords
Made a kind of wintry forest
With my heart spiked and bleeding in its branches.

                                                    1992

Cameo Appearance

I had a small, nonspeaking part
In a bloody epic. I was one of the
Bombed and fleeing humanity.
In the distance our great leader
5 Crowed like a rooster from a balcony,
Or was it a great actor
Impersonating our great leader?

That's me there, I said to the kiddies.
I'm squeezed between the man
10 With two bandaged hands raised
And the old woman with her mouth open
As if she were showing us a tooth

That hurts badly. The hundred times
I rewound the tape, not once
15 Could they catch sight of me
In that huge gray crowd,
That was like any other gray crowd.

Trot off to bed, I said finally.
I know I was there. One take
20 Is all they had time for.
We ran, and the planes grazed our hair,
And then they were no more
As we stood dazed in the burning city,
But, of course, they didn't film that.

                                                    1997

MARGARET ATWOOD
b. 1939

This Is a Photograph of Me

It was taken some time ago.
At first it seems to be
a smeared
print: blurred lines and gray flecks
5 blended with the paper;

then, as you scan
it, you see in the left-hand corner
a thing that is like a branch: part of a tree
(balsam or spruce) emerging
10 and, to the right, halfway up
what ought to be a gentle
slope, a small frame house.

In the background there is a lake,
and beyond that, some low hills.

15 (The photograph was taken
the day after I drowned.

I am in the lake, in the center
of the picture, just under the surface.

It is difficult to say where
20 precisely, or to say
how large or small I am:

the effect of water
on light is a distortion

but if you look long enough,
25 eventually
you will be able to see me.)

1966

At the Tourist Center in Boston

There is my country under glass,
a white relief-
map with red dots for the cities,
reduced to the size of a wall

5   and beside it 10 blownup snapshots
one for each province,
in purple-browns and odd reds,
the green of the trees dulled;
all blues however

10   of an assertive purity.

Mountains and lakes and more lakes
(though Quebec is a restaurant and Ontario the empty
interior of the parliament buildings),
with nobody climbing the trails and hauling out

15   the fish and splashing in the water

but arrangements of grinning tourists—
look here, Saskatchewan
is a flat lake, some convenient rocks
where two children pose with a father

20   and the mother is cooking something
in immaculate slacks by a smokeless fire,
her teeth white as detergent.

Whose dream is this, I would like to know:
is this a manufactured

25   hallucination, a cynical fiction, a lure
for export only?

I seem to remember people,
at least in the cities, also slush,
machines and assorted garbage. Perhaps

30   that was my private mirage

which will just evaporate
when I go back. Or the citizens will be gone,
run off to the peculiarly-
green forests

35   to wait among the brownish mountains
for the platoons of tourists
and plan their odd red massacres.

Unsuspecting
window lady, I ask you:

40   Do you see nothing
watching you from under the water?

Was the sky ever that blue?

Who really lives there?

1968

You Begin

You begin this way:
this is your hand,
this is your eye,
that is a fish, blue and flat
5   on the paper, almost
the shape of an eye.
This is your mouth, this is an O
or a moon, whichever
you like. This is yellow.

10 Outside the window
is the rain, green
because it is summer, and beyond that
the trees and then the world,
which is round and has only
15 the colors of these nine crayons.

This is the world, which is fuller
and more difficult to learn than I have said.
You are right to smudge it that way
with the red and then
20 the orange: the world burns.

Once you have learned these words
you will learn that there are more
words than you can ever learn.
The word *hand* floats above your hand
25 like a small cloud over a lake.
The word *hand* anchors
your hand to this table,
your hand is a warm stone
I hold between two words.

30 This is your hand, these are my hands, this is the world,
which is round but not flat and has more colors
than we can see.

It begins, it has an end,
this is what you will
35 come back to, this is your hand.

1978

Flowers

Right now I am the flower girl.
I bring fresh flowers,

dump out the old ones, the greenish water
that smells like dirty teeth
5   into the bathroom sink, snip off the stem ends
with surgical scissors I borrowed
from the nursing station,
put them into a jar
I brought from home, because they don't have vases
10 in this hotel for the ill,
place them on the table beside my father
where he can't see them
because he won't open his eyes.

He lies flattened under the white sheet.
15 He says he is on a ship,
and I can see it—
the functional white walls, the minimal windows,
the little bells, the rubbery footsteps of strangers,
the whispering all around
20 of the air-conditioner, or else the ocean,
and he is on a ship;
he's giving us up, giving up everything
but the breath going in
and out of his diminished body;
25 minute by minute he's sailing slowly away,
away from us and our waving hands
that do not wave.

The women come in, two of them, in blue;
it's no use being kind, in here,
30 if you don't have hands like theirs—
large and capable, the hands
of plump muscular angels,
the ones that blow trumpets and lift swords.
They shift him carefully, tuck in the corners.
35 It hurts, but as little as possible.
Pain is their lore. The rest of us
are helpless amateurs.

A suffering you can neither cure nor enter—
there are worse things, but not many.
40 After a while it makes us impatient.
Can't we do anything but feel sorry?

I sit there, watching the flowers
in their pickle jar. He is asleep, or not.
I think: He looks like a turtle.
45 Or: He looks erased.
But somewhere in there, at the far end of the tunnel
of pain and forgetting he's trapped in
is the same father I knew before,
the one who carried the green canoe
50 over the portage, the painter trailing,

myself with the fishing rods, slipping
on the wet boulders and slapping flies.
That was the last time we went there.

There will be a last time for this also,
55 bringing cut flowers to this white room.
Sooner or later I too
will have to give everything up,
even the sorrow that comes with these flowers,
even the anger,
60 even the memory of how I brought them
from a garden I will no longer have by then,
and put them beside my dying father,
hoping I could still save him.

                                                      1995

Up

You wake up filled with dread.
There seems no reason for it.
Morning light sifts through the window,
there is birdsong,
5 you can't get out of bed.

It's something about the crumpled sheets
hanging over the edge like jungle
foliage, the terry slippers gaping
their dark pink mouths for your feet,
10 the unseen breakfast—some of it
in the refrigerator you do not dare
to open—you will not dare to eat.

What prevents you? The future. The future tense,
immense as outer space.
15 You could get lost there.
No. Nothing so simple. The past, its density
and drowned events pressing you down,
like sea water, like gelatin
filling your lungs instead of air.

20 Forget all that and let's get up.
Try moving your arm.
Try moving your head.
Pretend the house is on fire
and you must run or burn.
25 No, that one's useless.
It's never worked before.

Where is it coming from, this echo,
this huge No that surrounds you,

silent as the folds of the yellow
30 curtains, mute as the cheerful

Mexican bowl with its cargo
of mummified flowers?
(You chose the colours of the sun,
not the dried neutrals of shadow.
35 God knows you've tried.)

Now here's a good one:
you're lying on your deathbed.
You have one hour to live.
Who is it, exactly, you have needed
40 all these years to forgive?

1995

SEAMUS HEANEY
b. 1939

Digging

Between my finger and my thumb
The squat pen rests; snug as a gun.

Under my window, a clean rasping sound
When the spade sinks into gravelly ground:
5 My father, digging. I look down

Till his straining rump among the flowerbeds
Bends low, comes up twenty years away
Stooping in rhythm through potato drills[1]
Where he was digging.

10 The coarse boot nestled on the lug, the shaft
Against the inside knee was levered firmly.
He rooted out tall tops, buried the bright edge deep
To scatter new potatoes that we picked
Loving their cool hardness in our hands.

15 By god, the old man could handle a spade.
Just like his old man.

My grandfather cut more turf[2] in a day
Than any other man on Toner's bog.
Once I carried him milk in a bottle
20 Corked sloppily with paper. He straightened up

---

1. Small furrows in which seeds are sown.
2. Slabs of peat that, when dried, are a common domestic fuel in Ireland.

To drink it, then fell to right away
Nicking and slicing neatly, heaving sods
Over his shoulder, going down and down
For the good turf. Digging.

25 The cold smell of potato mould, the squelch and slap
Of soggy peat, the curt cuts of an edge
Through living roots awaken in my head.
But I've no spade to follow men like them.

Between my finger and my thumb
30 The squat pen rests.
I'll dig with it.

1966

The Forge

All I know is a door into the dark.
Outside, old axles and iron hoops rusting;
Inside, the hammered anvil's short-pitched ring,
The unpredictable fantail of sparks
5 Or hiss when a new shoe toughens in water.
The anvil must be somewhere in the centre,
Horned as a unicorn, at one end square,
Set there immoveable: an altar
Where he expends himself in shape and music.
10 Sometimes, leather-aproned, hairs in his nose,
He leans out on the jamb, recalls a clatter
Of hoofs where traffic is flashing in rows;
Then grunts and goes in, with a slam and flick
To beat real iron out, to work the bellows.

1969

Punishment[3]

I can feel the tug
of the halter at the nape

3. In 1951, the peat-stained body of a young girl who lived in the late first century was recovered from a bog in Windeby, Germany. As P. V. Glob describes her in *The Bog People* (1969), she "lay naked in the hole in the peat, a bandage over the eyes and a collar round the neck. The band across the eyes was drawn tight and had cut into the neck and the base of the nose. We may feel sure that it had been used to close her eyes to this world. There was no mark of strangulation on the neck, so that it had not been used for that purpose." Her hair "had been shaved off with a razor on the left side of the head. . . . When the brain was removed the convolutions and folds of the surface could be clearly seen [Glob reproduces a photograph of her brain]. . . . This girl of only fourteen had had an inadequate winter diet. . . . To keep the young body under, some birch branches and a big stone were laid upon her." According to the Roman historian Tacitus (ca. 56–ca. 120), the Germanic peoples punished adulterous women by shaving off their hair and then scourging them out of the village or killing them. In more recent times, her "betraying sisters" (line 38) have sometimes been shaved, stripped, tarred, and handcuffed by the Irish Republican Army to the railings of Belfast in punishment for keeping company with British soldiers.

of her neck, the wind
on her naked front.

5 It blows her nipples
to amber beads,
it shakes the frail rigging
of her ribs.

I can see her drowned
10 body in the bog,
the weighing stone,
the floating rods and boughs.

Under which at first
she was a barked sapling
15 that is dug up
oak-bone, brain-firkin:°   *-small cask*

her shaved head
like a stubble of black corn,
her blindfold a soiled bandage,
20 her noose a ring

to store
the memories of love.
Little adulteress,
before they punished you

25 you were flaxen-haired,
undernourished, and your
tar-black face was beautiful.
My poor scapegoat,

I almost love you
30 but would have cast, I know,
the stones of silence.
I am the artful voyeur

of your brain's exposed
and darkened combs,[4]
35 your muscles' webbing
and all your numbered bones:

I who have stood dumb
when your betraying sisters,
cauled[5] in tar,
40 wept by the railings,

who would connive
in civilized outrage

---

4. Cellular structure, as in honeycomb.
5. Wrapped or enclosed. A caul is the inner fetal membrane that at birth, when it is unruptured, sometimes covers the infant's head.

yet understand the exact
and tribal, intimate revenge.

1975

The Skunk

Up, black, striped and damasked like the chasuble[6]
At a funeral mass, the skunk's tail
Paraded the skunk. Night after night
I expected her like a visitor.

5   The refrigerator whinnied into silence.
My desk light softened beyond the verandah.
Small oranges loomed in the orange tree.
I began to be tense as a voyeur.

After eleven years I was composing
10   Love-letters again, broaching the word "wife"
Like a stored cask, as if its slender vowel
Had mutated into the night earth and air

Of California. The beautiful, useless
Tang of eucalyptus spelt your absence.
15   The aftermath of a mouthful of wine
Was like inhaling you off a cold pillow.

And there she was, the intent and glamorous,
Ordinary, mysterious skunk,
Mythologized, demythologized,
20   Snuffing the boards five feet beyond me.

It all came back to me last night, stirred
By the sootfall of your things at bedtime,
Your head-down, tail-up hunt in a bottom drawer
For the black plunge-line nightdress.

1979

A Dream of Jealousy

Walking with you and another lady
In wooded parkland, the whispering grass
Ran its fingers through our guessing silence
And the trees opened into a shady
5   Unexpected clearing where we sat down.
I think the candour of the light dismayed us.

6. Sleeveless vestment worn by the priest celebrating Mass, its color regulated by the feast of the day.

We talked about desire and being jealous,
Our conversation a loose single gown
Or a white picnic tablecloth spread out
10   Like a book of manners in the wilderness.
"Show me," I said to our companion, "what
I have much coveted, your breast's mauve star."
And she consented. O neither these verses
Nor my prudence, love, can heal your wounded stare.

1979

From Station Island[7]

12

Like a convalescent, I took the hand
stretched down from the jetty, sensed again
an alien comfort as I stepped on ground

to find the helping hand still gripping mine,
5   fish-cold and bony, but whether to guide
or to be guided I could not be certain

for the tall man in step at my side
seemed blind, though he walked straight as a rush
upon his ash plant,[8] his eyes fixed straight ahead.

10   Then I knew him in the flesh
out there on the tarmac among the cars,
wintered hard and sharp as a blackthorn bush.

His voice eddying with the vowels of all rivers[9]
came back to me, though he did not speak yet,
15   a voice like a prosecutor's or a singer's,

cunning,[1] narcotic, mimic, definite
as a steel nib's downstroke, quick and clean,
and suddenly he hit a litter basket

with his stick, saying, "Your obligation
20   is not discharged by any common rite.
What you must do must be done on your own

---

7. "*Station Island* is a sequence of dream encounters with familiar ghosts, set on Station Island on Lough Derg in Co. Donegal. The island is also known as St. Patrick's Purgatory because of a tradition that Patrick was the first to establish the penitential vigil of fasting and praying which still constitutes the basis of the three-day pilgrimage. Each unit of the contemporary pilgrim's exercises is called a 'station,' and a large part of each station involves walking barefoot and praying round the 'beds,' stone circles which are said to be the remains of early medieval monastic cells" [Heaney's note]. In this last section of the poem, the familiar ghost is that of the Irish novelist James Joyce (1882–1941).

8. Walking stick made of ash. Joyce was almost blind.

9. The Anna Livia Plurabelle episode of Joyce's *Finnegans Wake* (1939) resounds with the names of many rivers.

1. "The only arms I allow myself to use—silence, exile, and cunning" (Joyce, *Portrait of the Artist as a Young Man*, 1916).

so get back in harness. The main thing is to write
for the joy of it. Cultivate a work-lust
that imagines its haven like your hands at night

25   dreaming the sun in the sunspot of a breast.
You are fasted now, light-headed, dangerous.
Take off from here. And don't be so earnest,

let others wear the sackcloth and the ashes.[2]
Let go, let fly, forget.
30   You've listened long enough. Now strike your note."

It was as if I had stepped free into space
alone with nothing that I had not known
already. Raindrops blew in my face

as I came to. "Old father, mother's son,
35   there is a moment in Stephen's[3] diary
for April the thirteenth, a revelation

set among my stars—that one entry
has been a sort of password in my ears,
the collect of a new epiphany,[4]

40   the Feast of the Holy Tundish."[5] "Who cares,"
he jeered, "any more? The English language
belongs to us. You are raking at dead fires,

a waste of time for somebody your age.
That subject° people stuff is a cod's° game,   *colonized / fool's*
45   infantile, like your peasant pilgrimage.

You lose more of yourself than you redeem
doing the decent thing. Keep at a tangent.
When they make the circle wide, it's time to swim

out on your own and fill the element
50   with signatures on your own frequency,
echo soundings, searches, probes, allurements,

elver-gleams[6] in the dark of the whole sea."
The shower broke in a cloudburst, the tarmac
fumed and sizzled. As he moved off quickly

55   the downpour loosed its screens round his straight walk.

1984

2. As worn by penitents in biblical times and later.
3. Stephen Dedalus: protagonist in *Portrait of the Artist*, major character in Joyce's *Ulysses* (1922), and Joyce's alter ego.
4. Manifestation of a superhuman being, as of the infant Jesus to the Magi (Matthew 2). In the Christian calendar, the Feast of the Epiphany is January 6. *Collect*: short prayer assigned to a particular day.
5. "See the end of James Joyce's *Portrait of the*

Artist as a Young Man" [Heaney's note]: "*13 April:* That tundish [funnel] has been on my mind for a long time. I looked it up and find it English and good old blunt English too. Damn the dean of studies and his funnel! What did he come here for to teach us his own language or to learn it from us? Damn him one way or the other!"
6. Gleams as of young eels.

From Clearances[7]

IN MEMORIAM M.K.H.,[8] 1911–1984

She taught me what her uncle once taught her:
How easily the biggest coal block split
If you got the grain and hammer angled right.

The sound of that relaxed alluring blow,
5 *Its co-opted and obliterated echo,*
Taught me to hit, taught me to loosen,

Taught me between the hammer and the block
To face the music. Teach me now to listen,
To strike it rich behind the linear black.

III

When all the others were away at Mass
I was all hers as we peeled potatoes.
They broke the silence, let fall one by one
Like solder weeping off the soldering iron:
5 Cold comforts set between us, things to share
Gleaming in a bucket of clean water.
And again let fall. Little pleasant splashes
From each other's work would bring us to our senses.

So while the parish priest at her bedside
10 Went hammer and tongs at the prayers for the dying
And some were responding and some crying
I remembered her head bent towards my head,
Her breath in mine, our fluent dipping knives—
Never closer the whole rest of our lives.

VII

In the last minutes he said more to her
Almost than in all their life together.
"You'll be in New Row on Monday night
And I'll come up for you and you'll be glad
5 When I walk in the door . . . Isn't that right?"
His head was bent down to her propped-up head.
She could not hear but we were overjoyed.
He called her good and girl. Then she was dead,
The searching for a pulsebeat was abandoned
10 And we all knew one thing by being there.
The space we stood around had been emptied
Into us to keep, it penetrated
Clearances that suddenly stood open.
High cries were felled and a pure change happened.

7. Enforced depopulation (as of the Scottish   8. Margaret Kathleen Heaney, the poet's mother.
Highlands).

VIII

I thought of walking round and round a space
Utterly empty, utterly a source
Where the decked chestnut tree had lost its place
In our front hedge above the wallflowers.
5   The white chips jumped and jumped and skited° high.   *shot*
I heard the hatchet's differentiated
Accurate cut, the crack, the sigh
And collapse of what luxuriated
Through the shocked tips and wreckage of it all,
10   Deep-planted and long gone, my coeval°   *equally old*
Chestnut from a jam jar in a hole,
Its heft and hush become a bright nowhere,
A soul ramifying and forever
Silent, beyond silence listened for.

1987

Casting and Gathering

FOR TED HUGHES[9]

Years and years ago, these sounds took sides:

On the left bank, a green silk tapered cast
Went whispering through the air, saying *hush*
And *lush,* entirely free, no matter whether
5   It swished above the hayfield or the river.

On the right bank, like a speeded-up corncrake,[1]
A sharp ratcheting went on and on
Cutting across the stillness as another
Fisherman gathered line-lengths off his reel.

10   I am still standing there, awake and dreamy,
I have grown older and can see them both
Moving their arms and rods, working away,
Each one absorbed, proofed by the sounds he's making.

One sound is saying. "You are not worth tuppence,
15   But neither is anybody. Watch it! Be severe."
The other says, "Go with it! Give and swerve.
You are everything you feel beside the river."

I love hushed air. I trust contrariness.
Years and years go past and I do not move

---

9. English poet (1930–1998; see pp. 1810–16).   1. Bird with a distinctive cry.

20 For I see that when one man casts, the other gathers
    And then *vice versa*, without changing sides.

                                                    1991

The Settle Bed[2]

Willed down,[3] waited for, in place at last and for good.
Trunk-hasped, cart-heavy, painted an ignorant brown.
And pew-strait, bin-deep, standing four-square as an ark.

If I lie in it, I am cribbed° in seasoned deal°   *confined / pine or fir wood*
5   Dry as the unkindled boards of a funeral ship.
    My measure has been taken, my ear shuttered up.

Yet I hear an old sombre tide awash in the headboard:
Unpathetic *och ochs* and *och hohs*,[4] the long bedtime
Sigh-life of Ulster,[5] unwilling, unbeaten,

10 Protestant, Catholic, the Bible, the beads,°   *rosary*
    Late talks at gables by moonlight, boots on the hearth,
    The small hours chimed sweetly away so next thing it was

The cock on the ridge-tiles.[6]
                          And now this is "an inheritance"—
Upright, rudimentary, unshiftably planked
15 In the long long ago, yet willable forward

Again and again and again, cargoed with
Its own dumb, tongue-and-groove[7] worthiness
And un-get-roundable weight. But to conquer that weight,

Imagine a dower[8] of settle beds tumbled from heaven
20 Like some nonsensical vengeance come on the people,
    Then learn from that harmless barrage that whatever is given

Can always be reimagined, however four-square,
Plank-thick, hull-stupid and out of its time
It happens to be. You are free as the lookout,

25 That far-seeing joker posted high over the fog,
    Who declared by the time that he had got himself down
    The actual ship had stolen away from beneath him.

                                                    1991

---

2. A bed like a large wooden chest with a hinged
("hasped," line 2) lid that, when closed, can be
used as a bench.
3. Inherited.
4. Expressions of mild regret (Irish).

5. The northernmost of Ireland's four provinces.
6. I.e., the rooster crows on the roof.
7. Carpenters' term for the interlocked joining of
parallel planks.
8. Dowry, inheritance.

From Glanmore Revisited

6 *Bedside Reading*

The whole place airier. Big summer trees
Stirring at eye level when we waken
And little shoots of ivy creeping in
Unless they've been trained out—like memories
5 You've trained so long now they can show their face
And keep their distance. White-mouthed depression
Swims out from its shadow like a dolphin
With wet, unreadable, unfurtive eyes.

I swim in Homer.[9] In Book Twenty-three.
10 At last Odysseus and Penelope
Waken together. One bedpost of the bed
Is the living trunk of an old olive tree
And is their secret. As ours could have been ivy,
Evergreen, atremble and unsaid.

7 *The Skylight*

You were the one for skylights. I opposed
Cutting into the seasoned tongue-and-groove[1]
Of pitch pine. I liked it low and closed,
Its claustrophobic, nest-up-in-the-roof
5 Effect. I liked the snuff-dry feeling,
The perfect, trunk-lid fit of the old ceiling.
Under there, it was all hutch and hatch.
The blue slates kept the heat like midnight thatch.[2]

But when the slates came off, extravagant
10 Sky entered and held surprise wide open.
For days I felt like an inhabitant
Of that house where the man sick of the palsy
Was lowered through the roof, had his sins forgiven,
Was healed, took up his bed and walked away.[3]

1991

Fosterling[4]

"That heavy greenness fostered by water"
John Montague[5]

At school I loved one picture's heavy greenness—
Horizons rigged with windmills' arms and sails.
The millhouses' still outlines. Their in-placeness

---

9. Homer's epic poem the *Odyssey*.
1. See note 7 above.
2. The roof tiles kept the house as warm at night as thatch famously does.

3. See Christ's miraculous cure, in John 5.8.
4. Foster child.
5. Irish (American-born) poet (b. 1929).

Still more in place when mirrored in canals.
5 I can't remember not ever having known
The immanent hydraulics of a land
Of glar° and glit° and floods at   *mud / oozing water*
       dailigone.°   *dusk*
My silting hope. My lowlands of the mind.

Heaviness of being. And poetry
10 Sluggish in the doldrums of what happens.
Me waiting until I was nearly fifty
To credit marvels. Like the tree-clock of tin cans
The tinkers made. So long for air to brighten,
Time to be dazzled and the heart to lighten.

                                                          1991

From Squarings

Lightenings

VIII

The annals° say: when the monks of Clonmacnoise[6]   *histories*
Were all at prayers inside the oratory
A ship appeared above them in the air.

The anchor dragged along behind so deep
5 It hooked itself into the altar rails
And then, as the big hull rocked to a standstill,

A crewman shinned and grappled down the rope
And struggled to release it. But in vain.
"This man can't bear our life here and will drown,"

10 The abbot said, "unless we help him." So
They did, the freed ship sailed, and the man climbed back
Out of the marvellous as he had known it.

                                                          1991

Two Lorries[7]

It's raining on black coal and warm wet ashes.
There are tyre-marks in the yard, Agnew's old lorry
Has all its cribs[8] down and Agnew the coalman
With his Belfast accent's sweet-talking my mother.
5 Would she ever go to a film in Magherafelt?[9]
But it's raining and he still has half the load

---

6. Famous monastic settlement beside the river
Shannon, near Athlone, Ireland.
7. Trucks.

8. Hinged, wooden side-flaps.
9. Small town in County Tyrone, Northern Ireland.

To deliver farther on. This time the lode
Our coal came from was silk-black, so the ashes
Will be the silkiest white. The Magherafelt
10   (Via Toomebridge) bus goes by. The half-stripped lorry
With its emptied, folded coal-bags moves my mother:
The tasty ways of a leather-aproned coalman!

And films no less! The conceit of a coalman . . .
She goes back in and gets out the black lead
15   And emery paper,¹ this nineteen-forties mother,
All business round her stove, half wiping ashes
With a backhand from her cheek as the bolted² lorry
Gets revved and turned and heads for Magherafelt

And the last delivery. Oh, Magherafelt!
20   Oh, dream of red plush and a city coalman
As time fastforwards and a different lorry
Groans into shot,° up Broad Street, with a payload   *view*
That will blow the bus station to dust and ashes . . .
After that happened, I'd a vision of my mother,

25   A revenant° on the bench where I would meet her   *ghost*
In that cold-floored waiting-room in Magherafelt,
Her shopping bags full up with shovelled ashes.
Death walked out past her like a dust-faced coalman
Refolding body-bags, plying his load
30   Empty upon empty, in a flurry

Of motes° and engine-revs, but which lorry   *dust*
Was it now? Young Agnew's or that other,
Heavier, deadlier one, set to explode
In a time beyond her time in Magherafelt . . .
35   So tally° bags and sweet-talk darkness, coalman.   *keep a record of*
Listen to the rain spit in new ashes

As you heft a load of dust that was Magherafelt,
Then reappear from your lorry as my mother's
Dreamboat coalman filmed in silk-white ashes.

1996

MICHAEL LONGLEY
b. 1939

The Linen Industry

Pulling up flax¹ after the blue flowers have fallen
And laying our handfuls in the peaty water

---

1. Abrasive-coated paper, here used with a prep-
aration of "black lead" to polish the stove.
2. With the sides folded up and locked in place.

1. Blue-flowered plant grown for its textile fiber
and treated in water from the Irish peat bog.

To rot those grasses to the bone, or building stooks[2]
That recall the skirts of an invisible dancer,

5   We become a part of the linen industry
And follow its processes to the grubby town
Where fields are compacted into window-boxes
And there is little room among the big machines.

But even in our attic under the skylight
10   We make love on a bleach green, the whole meadow
Draped with material turning white in the sun
As though snow reluctant to melt were our attire.

What's passion but a battering of stubborn stalks,
Then a gentle combing out of fibres like hair
15   And a weaving of these into christening robes,
Into garments for a marriage or funeral?

Since it's like a bereavement once the labour's done
To find ourselves last workers in a dying trade,
Let flax be our matchmaker, our undertaker,
20   The provider of sheets for whatever the bed—

And be shy of your breasts in the presence of death,
Say that you look more beautiful in linen
Wearing white petticoats, the bow on your bodice
A butterfly attending the embroidered flowers.

1979

Gorse Fires

Cattle out of their byres° are dungy still, lambs   *cowsheds*
Have stepped from last year as from an enclosure.
Five or six men stand gazing at a rusty tractor
Before carrying implements to separate fields.

5   I am travelling from one April to another.
It is the same train between the same embankments.
Gorse fires are smoking, but primroses burn
And celandines and white may and gorse flowers.

1991

Ghetto

I

Because you will suffer soon and die, your choices
Are neither right nor wrong: a spoon will feed you,

2. Sheaves standing together.

A flannel keep you clean, a toothbrush bring you back
To your bathroom's view of chimney-pots and gardens.
5 With so little time for inventory or leavetaking,
You are packing now for the rest of your life
Photographs, medicines, a change of underwear, a book,
A candlestick, a loaf, sardines, needle and thread.
These are your heirlooms, perishables, worldly goods.
10 What you bring is the same as what you leave behind,
Your last belonging a list of your belongings.

II

As though it were against the law to sleep on pillows
They have filled a cathedral with confiscated feathers:
Silence irrefrangible,° no room for angels' wings,   *unbreakable*
15 Tons of feathers suffocating cherubim and seraphim.[3]

III

The little girl without a mother behaves like a mother
With her rag doll to whom she explains fear and anguish,
The meagreness of the bread ration, how to make it last,
How to get back to the doll's house and lift up the roof
20 And, before the flame-throwers and dynamiters destroy it,
How to rescue from their separate rooms love and sorrow,
Masterpieces the size of a postage stamp, small fortunes.

IV

From among the hundreds of thousands I can imagine one
Behind the barbed-wire fences as my train crosses Poland.
25 I see him for long enough to catch the sprinkle of snowflakes
On his hair and schoolbag, and then I am transported
Away from that world of broken hobby-horses and silent toys.
He turns into a little snowman and refuses to melt.

V

For street-singers in the marketplace, weavers, warp[4]-makers,
30 Those who suffer in sewing-machine repair shops, excrement-
Removal workers, there are not enough root vegetables,
Beetroots, turnips, swedes,[5] nor for the leather-stitchers
Who are boiling leather so that their children may eat;
Who are turning like a thick slice of potato-bread
35 This page, which is everything I know about potatoes,
My delivery of Irish Peace, Beauty of Hebron, Home
Guard, Arran Banners, Kerr's Pinks,[6] resistant to eelworm,
Resignation, common scab, terror, frost, potato-blight.

---

3. Types of angels.
4. Thread stretched lengthwise in a weaver's loom.
5. Rutabagas.
6. Varieties of potatoes (lines 36–37).

VI

There will be performances in the waiting room, and time
40 To jump over a skipping rope, and time to adjust
As though for a dancing class the ribbons in your hair.[7]
This string quartet is the most natural thing in the world.

VII

Fingers leave shadows on a violin, harmonics,[8]
A blackbird fluttering between electrified fences.

VIII

45 Lessons were forbidden in that terrible school.
Punishable by death were reading and writing
And arithmetic, so that even the junior infants
Grew old and wise in lofts studying these subjects.
There were drawing lessons, and drawings of kitchens
50 And farms, farm animals, butterflies, mothers, fathers
Who survived in crayon until in pen and ink
They turned into guards at executions and funerals
Torturing and hanging even these stick figures.
There were drawings of barracks and latrines as well
55 And the only windows were the windows they drew.

                                                        1991

ROBERT PINSKY
b. 1940

From Essay on Psychiatrists

IV. A Lakeside Identification

Yes, crazy to suppose one could describe them—
And yet, there was this incident: at the local beach
Clouds of professors and the husbands of professors

Swam, dabbled or stood to talk with arms folded
5   Gazing at the lake . . . and one of the few townsfolk there,
With no faculty status—a matter-of-fact, competent,

Catholic woman of twenty-seven with five children
And a first-rate body—pointed her finger
At the back of one certain man and asked me,

---

7. Cf. T. S. Eliot, "The Love Song of J. Alfred   8. Tones produced by touching vibrating strings.
Prufrock" (p. 1340).

10   "Is that guy a psychiatrist?" and by god he was! "Yes,"
    She said, "He *looks* like a psychiatrist."
    Grown quiet, I looked at his pink back, and thought.

V. *Physical Comparison With Professors And Others*

    Pink and a bit soft-bodied, with a somewhat jazzy
    Middle-class bathing suit and sandy sideburns, to me
    He looked from the back like one more professor.

    And from the front, too—the boyish, unformed carriage
5   Which foreigners always note in American men, combined
    As in a professor with that liberal, quizzical,

    Articulate gaze so unlike the more focused, more
    Tolerant expression worn by a man of action (surgeon,
    Salesman, athlete). On closer inspection was there,

10   Perhaps, a self-satisfied or benign air, a studied
    Gentleness toward the child whose hand he held loosely?
    Absurd to speculate; but then—the woman saw *something*.

1975

A Long Branch[1] Song

    Some days in May, little stars
    Winked all over the ocean. The blue
    Barely changed all morning and afternoon:

    The chimes of the bank's bronze clock;
5   The hoarse voice of Cookie, hawking
    The Daily Record for thirty-five years.

1984

The Street

    Streaked and fretted with effort, the thick
    Vine of the world, red nervelets
    Coiled at its tips.

    All roads lead from it.[2] All night
5   Wainwrights and upholsterers work finishing
    The wheeled coffin

---

1. Long Branch, New Jersey, where Pinsky was
born.
    2. A twist on the expression *All roads lead to Rome.*

Of the dead favorite of the Emperor,
The child's corpse propped seated
On brocade, with yellow

10   Oiled curls, kohl on the stiff lids.
Slaves throw petals on the roadway
For the cortege, white

Languid flowers shooting from dark
Blisters on the vine, ramifying
15   Into streets. On mine,

Rockwell Avenue, it was embarrassing:
Trouble—fights, the police, sickness—
Seemed never to come

For anyone when they were fully dressed.
20   It was always underwear or dirty pyjamas,
Unseemly stretches

Of skin showing through a torn housecoat.
Once a stranger drove off in a car
With somebody's wife,

25   And he ran after them in his undershirt
And threw his shoe at the car. It bounced
Into the street

Harmlessly, and we carried it back to him;
But the man had too much dignity
30   To put it back on,

So he held it and stood crying in the street:
"He's breaking up my home," he said,
"The son of a bitch

Bastard is breaking up my home." The street
35   Rose undulant in pavement-breaking coils
And the man rode it,

Still holding his shoe and stiffly upright
Like a trick rider in the circus parade
That came down the street

40   Each August. As the powerful dragonlike
Hump swelled he rose cursing and ready
To throw his shoe—woven

Angular as a twig into the fabulous
Rug or brocade with crowns and camels,
45   Leopards and rosettes,

All riding the vegetable wave of the street
From the John Flock Mortuary Home
Down to the river.

It was a small place, and off the center,
50   But so much a place to itself, I felt
Like a young prince

Or aspirant squire. I knew that *Ivanhoe*[3]
Was about race. The Saxons[4] were Jews,
Or even Coloreds,

55   With their low-ceilinged, unbelievably
Sour-smelling houses down by the docks.
Everything was written

Or woven, ivory and pink and emerald—
Nothing was too ugly or petty or terrible
60   To be weighed in the immense

Silver scales of the dead: the looming
Balances set right onto the live, dangerous
Gray bark of the street.

                                                            1984

ABC

Any body can die, evidently. Few
Go happily, irradiating joy,

Knowledge, love. Many
Need oblivion, painkillers,
5   Quickest respite.

Sweet time unafflicted,
Various world:

X = your zenith.

                                                            2000

---

3. Historical novel by the Scottish writer Sir Walter Scott (1771–1832), considered the inventor of the form.
4. The Germanic peoples in ancient times, some of whom invaded Britain in the fifth and sixth centuries; here, used to mean an English person or Anglo-Saxon. In the first pages of *Ivanhoe*, Scott reflects on the social effects of the Norman Conquest of England in 1066: "Four generations had not sufficed to blend the hostile blood of the Normans and Anglo-Saxons, or to unite, by common language and mutual interests, two hostile races." The Saxons were dispossessed of both land and status.

BILLY COLLINS
b. 1941

Japan

Today I pass the time reading
a favorite haiku,
saying the few words over and over.

It feels like eating
5   the same small, perfect grape
again and again.

I walk through the house reciting it
and leave its letters falling
through the air of every room.

10   I stand by the big silence of the piano and say it.
I say it in front of a painting of the sea.
I tap out its rhythm on an empty shelf.

I listen to myself saying it,
then I say it without listening,
15   then I hear it without saying it.

And when the dog looks up at me,
I kneel down on the floor
and whisper it into each of his long white ears.

It's the one about the one-ton
20   temple bell
with the moth sleeping on its surface,[1]

and every time I say it, I feel the excruciating
pressure of the moth
on the surface of the iron bell.

25   When I say it at the window,
the bell is the world
and I am the moth resting there.

When I say it into the mirror,
I am the heavy bell
30   and the moth is life with its papery wings.

And later, when I say it to you in the dark,
you are the bell,
and I am the tongue of the bell, ringing you,

---

1. Haiku by the Japanese poet and painter Taniguchi Buson (1715–1783): "On the one-ton temple bell / a moon-moth, folded into sleep, / sits still" (trans. X. J. Kennedy).

and the moth has flown
35   from its line
and moves like a hinge in the air above our bed.

1998

Litany

You are the bread and the knife,
The crystal goblet and the wine.
JACQUES CRICKILLON[2]

You are the bread and the knife,
the crystal goblet and the wine.
You are the dew on the morning grass,
and the burning wheel of the sun.
5   You are the white apron of the baker
and the marsh birds suddenly in flight.

However, you are not the wind in the orchard,
the plums on the counter,
or the house of cards.
10   And you are certainly not the pine-scented air.
There is no way you are the pine-scented air.

It is possible that you are the fish under the bridge,
maybe even the pigeon on the general's head,
but you are not even close
15   to being the field of cornflowers at dusk.

And a quick look in the mirror will show
that you are neither the boots in the corner
nor the boat asleep in its boathouse.

It might interest you to know,
20   speaking of the plentiful imagery of the world,
that I am the sound of rain on the roof.

I also happen to be the shooting star,
the evening paper blowing down an alley,
and the basket of chestnuts on the kitchen table.

25   I am also the moon in the trees
and the blind woman's teacup.
But don't worry, I am not the bread and the knife.
You are still the bread and the knife.
You will always be the bread and the knife,
30   not to mention the crystal goblet and—somehow—the wine.

2002

2. Belgian poet (b. 1940).

ROBERT HASS
b. 1941

Meditation at Lagunitas[1]

All the new thinking is about loss.
In this it resembles all the old thinking.
The idea, for example, that each particular erases
the luminous clarity of a general idea. That the clown-
5   faced woodpecker probing the dead sculpted trunk
of that black birch is, by his presence,
some tragic falling off from a first world
of undivided light. Or the other notion that,
because there is in this world no one thing
10   to which the bramble of *blackberry* corresponds,
a word is elegy to what it signifies.
We talked about it late last night and in the voice
of my friend, there was a thin wire of grief, a tone
almost querulous. After a while I understood that,
15   talking this way, everything dissolves: *justice,*
pine, hair, woman, you and I. There was a woman
I made love to and I remembered how, holding
her small shoulders in my hands sometimes,
I felt a violent wonder at her presence
20   like a thirst for salt, for my childhood river
with its island willows, silly music from the pleasure boat,
muddy places where we caught the little orange-silver fish
called *pumpkinseed.* It hardly had to do with her.
Longing, we say, because desire is full
25   of endless distances. I must have been the same to her.
But I remember so much, the way her hands dismantled bread,
the thing her father said that hurt her, what
she dreamed. There are moments when the body is as numinous[2]
as words, days that are the good flesh continuing.
30   Such tenderness, those afternoons and evenings,
saying *blackberry, blackberry, blackberry.*

1979

Tahoe[3] in August

What summer proposes is simply happiness:
heat early in the morning, jays
raucous in the pines. Frank and Ellen have a tennis game
at nine, Bill and Cheryl sleep on the deck

---

1. Little lake (Spanish); a small town in Califor-
nia, near San Francisco.
2. Filled with a sense of divinity.

3. A lake in the Sierra Nevada Mountains, in both
eastern California and western Nevada.

5   to watch a shower of summer stars. Nick and Sharon
     stayed in, sat and talked the dark on,
     drinking tea, and Jeanne walked into the meadow
     in a white smock to write in her journal
     by a grazing horse who seemed to want the company.
10   Some of them will swim in the afternoon.
     Someone will drive to the hardware store to fetch
     new latches for the kitchen door. Four o'clock;
     the joggers jogging—it is one of them who sees
     down the flowering slope the woman with her notebook
15   In her hand beside the white horse, gesturing, her hair
     from a distance the copper color of the hummingbirds
     the slant light catches on the slope; the hikers
     switchback down the canyon from the waterfall;
     the readers are reading, Anna is about to meet Vronsky,[4]
20   that nice M. Swann is dining in Combray.
     with the aunts, and Carrie has come to Chicago.[5]
     What they want is happiness: someone to love them,
     children, a summer by the lake. The woman who sets aside
     her book blinks against the fuzzy dark,
25   re-entering the house. Her daughter drifts downstairs;
     out late the night before, she has been napping,
     and she's cross. Her mother tells her David telephoned.
     "He's such a dear," the mother says, "I think
     I made him nervous." The girl tosses her head as the horse
30   had done in the meadow while Jeanne read it her dream.
     "You can call him now, if you want," the mother says,
     "I've got to get the chicken started,
     I won't listen." "Did I say you would?"
     the girl says quickly. The mother who has been slapped
35   this way before and done the same herself another summer
     on a different lake says, "Ouch." The girl shrugs
     sulkily. "I'm sorry." Looking down: "Something
     about the way you said that pissed me off."
     "Hannibal has wandered off," the mother says,
40   wryness in her voice, she is thinking it is August,
     "why don't you see if he's at the Finleys' house
     again." The girl says, "God." The mother: "He loves
     small children. It's livelier for him there."
     The daughter, awake now, flounces out the door,
45   which slams. It is for all of them the sound of summer.
     The mother she looks like stands at the counter snapping beans.

1989

4. The lover of Anna Karenina, in the novel of the same name by the Russian novelist Leo Tolstoy (1828–1910).
5. In *Sister Carrie*, by the American novelist Theodore Dreiser (1871–1945), the heroine, Carrie Meeber, moves to Chicago. *M. Swann*: Charles Swann, a protagonist of *Swann's Way*, the first book in the seven-volume *A la recherche du temps perdu* (*In Search of Lost Time*), by the French novelist Marcel Proust (1871–1922). Swann visits the aunts of the narrator, Marcel, at Combray, a town based on Illiers, near Chartres.

DEREK MAHON
b. 1941

In Carrowdore Churchyard

(at the grave of Louis MacNeice)[1]

Your ashes will not stir, even on this high ground,
However the wind tugs, the headstones shake.
This plot is consecrated, for your sake,
To what lies in the future tense. You lie
5   Past tension now, and spring is coming round
Igniting flowers on the peninsula.

Your ashes will not fly, however the rough winds burst
Through the wild brambles and the reticent trees.
All we may ask of you we have; the rest
10 Is not for publication, will not be heard.
Maguire, I believe, suggested a blackbird
And over your grave a phrase from Euripides.[2]

Which suits you down to the ground, like this churchyard
With its play of shadow, its humane perspective.
15 Locked in the winter's fist, these hills are hard
As nails, yet soft and feminine in their turn
When fingers open and the hedges burn.
This, you implied, is how we ought to live—

The ironical, loving crush of roses against snow,
20 Each fragile, solving ambiguity. So
From the pneumonia of the ditch, from the ague°   fever
Of the blind poet and the bombed-out town you bring
The all-clear to the empty holes of spring,
Rinsing the choked mud, keeping the colours new.

1968

A Disused Shed in Co. Wexford[3]

Let them not forget us, the weak souls among the asphodels.
—SEFERIS,[4] *Mythistorema*, tr. Keeley and Sherrard

(for J. G. Farrell)

Even now there are places where a thought might grow—
Peruvian mines, worked out and abandoned

---

1. Irish poet (1907–1963; see pp. 1485–91), buried in Carrowdore Churchyard, County Down, Northern Ireland.
2. Maguire is the name MacNeice gives his old friend the Belfast artist George McCann in his book-length poem *Autumn Sequel* (1954). The suggested phrase from the Greek dramatist Eurip-ides (ca. 484–406 B.C.E.) was not carved on Mac-Neice's gravestone.
3. County in southeast Ireland.
4. George Seferis (1900–1971), Greek poet. Below, James Gordon Farrell (1935–1979), Anglo-Irish novelist.

To a slow clock of condensation,
An echo trapped for ever, and a flutter
5 Of wild-flowers in the lift-shaft,
Indian compounds where the wind dances
And a door bangs with diminished confidence,
Lime crevices behind rippling rain-barrels,
Dog corners for bone burials;
10 And in a disused shed in Co. Wexford,

Deep in the grounds of a burnt-out hotel,
Among the bathtubs and the washbasins
A thousand mushrooms crowd to a keyhole.
This is the one star in their firmament
15 Or frames a star within a star.
What should they do there but desire?
So many days beyond the rhododendrons
With the world waltzing in its bowl of cloud,
They have learnt patience and silence
20 Listening to the rooks querulous in the high wood.

They have been waiting for us in a foetor°   *fetid aura*
Of vegetable sweat since civil war days,
Since the gravel-crunching, interminable departure
Of the expropriated mycologist.[5]
25 He never came back, and light since then
Is a keyhole rusting gently after rain.
Spiders have spun, flies dusted to mildew
And once a day, perhaps, they have heard something—
A trickle of masonry, a shout from the blue
30 Or a lorry° changing gear at the end of the lane.   *truck*

There have been deaths, the pale flesh flaking
Into the earth that nourished it;
And nightmares, born of these and the grim
Dominion of stale air and rank moisture.
35 Those nearest the door grow strong—
"Elbow room! Elbow room!"
The rest, dim in a twilight of crumbling
Utensils and broken pitchers, groaning
For their deliverance, have been so long
40 Expectant that there is left only the posture.

A half century, without visitors, in the dark—
Poor preparation for the cracking lock
And creak of hinges. Magi,° moonmen,   *wise men*
Powdery prisoners of the old regime,
45 Web-throated, stalked like triffids,[6] racked by drought
And insomnia, only the ghost of a scream

---

5. Someone who studies mushrooms.
6. Mobile, flesh-eating plants in John Wyndham's
science fiction novel *The Day of the Triffids* (1951)
and the 1962 movie based on it.

At the flash-bulb firing-squad we wake them with
Shows there is life yet in their feverish forms.
Grown beyond nature now, soft food for worms,
50   They lift frail heads in gravity and good faith.

They are begging us, you see, in their wordless way,
To do something, to speak on their behalf
Or at least not to close the door again.
Lost people of Treblinka and Pompeii![7]
55   "Save us, save us," they seem to say,
"Let the god not abandon us
Who have come so far in darkness and in pain.
We too had our lives to live.
You with your light meter and relaxed itinerary,
60   Let not our naive labours have been in vain!"

1975

The Window

```
            woodwoodwoodwoodwoodwoodwoodwood
            io                            oo
            n o                          o w
            d  d                         w  i
            o  w                         o  n
            w  o                         o  d
            i  o                         d  o
            n  d                         w  w
            d  w                         o  i
            o  o                         o  n
            w  o                         d  d
            i  d                         w  o
            n  w          wind           o  w
            d  o                         o  i
            o  o                         d  n
            w  d                         w  d
            i  w                         o  o
            n  d                         w  w
            d o                          o  i
            oo                            on
            woodwoodwoodwoodwoodwoodwoodwood
            dwoodwoodwoodwoodwoodwoodwoodwoodw
            odwoodwoodwoodwoodwoodwoodwoodwoodwo
```

1979

7. Roman city preserved under ash and lava after a volcanic eruption that killed most of its inhabitants. *Treblinka:* site, in northern Poland, of a principal Nazi concentration camp.

Girls on the Bridge

—*Pykene na Brukken*, Munch, 1900[8]

Audible trout,
Notional° midges.° Beds,   *imaginary / tiny flies*
Lamplight and crisp linen wait
In the house there for the sedate
5   Limbs and averted heads
Of the girls out

Late on the bridge.
The dusty road that slopes
Past is perhaps the high road south,
10   A symbol of world-wondering youth,
Of adolescent hopes
And privileges;

But stops to find
The girls content to gaze
15   At the unplumbed, reflective lake,
Their plangent° conversational quack   *plaintive*
Expressive of calm days
And peace of mind.

Grave daughters
20   Of time, you lightly toss
Your hair as the long shadows grow
And night begins to fall. Although
Your laughter calls across
The dark waters,

25   A ghastly sun
Watches in pale dismay.
Oh, you may laugh, being as you are
Fair sisters of the evening star,
But wait—if not today
30   A day will dawn

When the bad dreams
You scarcely know will scatter
The punctual increment of your lives.
The road resumes, and where it curves,
35   A mile from where you chatter,
Somebody screams.

8. *Girls on a Bridge*, title of a painting in Expressionist style by the Norwegian artist Edvard Munch (1863–1944), whose best-known painting is *The Scream* (lines 36 and 40).

The girls are dead,
The house and pond have gone.
Steel bridge and concrete highway gleam
40   And sing in the arctic dark; the scream
We started at is grown
The serenade

Of an insane
And monstrous age. We live
45   These days as on a different planet,
One without trout or midges on it,
Under the arc-lights of
A mineral heaven;

And we have come,
50   Despite ourselves, to no
True notion of our proper work,
But wander in the dazzling dark
Amid the drifting snow
Dreaming of some

55   Lost evening when
Our grandmothers, if grand
Mothers we had, stood at the edge
Of womanhood on a country bridge
And gazed at a still pond
60   And knew no pain.

1982

ERIC ORMSBY
b. 1941

Starfish

The stellar sea crawler, maw
Concealed beneath, with offerings of
Prismed crimson now darkened, now like
The smile of slag,° a thing made rosy   *volcanic rock*
5   As poured ingots, or suddenly dimmed—

I appreciate the studious labour
Of your rednesses, the scholarly fragrance
Of your sex. To mirror tidal drifts
The light ripples across or to enhance darkness
10   With palpable tinctures, dense as salt.

You crumple like a puppet's fist
Or erect, bristling, your tender luring barbs.
Casual abandon, like a dropped fawn glove.
Tensile symmetries, like a hawk's claw.

15 You clutch the seafloor.

You taste what has fallen.

1990

Skunk Cabbage

The skunk cabbage with its smug and opulent smell
Opens in plump magnificence near the edge
Of garbage-strewn canals, or you see its shape
Arise near the wet roots of the marsh.
5   How vigilant it looks with its glossy leaves
Parted to disclose its bruised insides,
That troubled purple of its blossom!
It always seemed so squat, dumpy and rank,
A noxious efflorescence of the swamp,
10 Until I got down low and looked at it.
Now I search out its blunt totemic shape
And bow when I see its outer stalks
Drawn aside, like the frilly curtains of the ark,
For the foul magenta of its gorgeous heart.

1990

Origins

I wanted to go down to where the roots begin,
to find words nested in their almond-skin,
the seed-curls of their birth, their sprigs of origin.

At night the dead set words upon my tongue,
5   drew back their coverings, laid bare the long
sheaths of their roots where the earth still clung.

I wanted to draw their words from the mouths of the dead,
I wanted to strip the coins from their heavy eyes,
I wanted the rosy breath to gladden their skins.

10 At night the dead remembered their origins,
at night they nested in the curve of my eyes,
and I tasted the savour of their seed-bed.

1993   1997

DOUGLAS DUNN
b. 1942

A Removal from Terry Street[1]

On a squeaking cart, they push the usual stuff,
A mattress, bed ends, cups, carpets, chairs,
Four paperback westerns. Two whistling youths
In surplus U.S. Army battle-jackets
5   Remove their sister's goods. Her husband
Follows, carrying on his shoulders the son
Whose mischief we are glad to see removed,
And pushing, of all things, a lawnmower.
There is no grass in Terry Street. The worms
10 Come up cracks in concrete yards in moonlight.
That man, I wish him well. I wish him grass.

1969

In the Grounds

Yorkshire, 1975

Barbarians in a garden, softness does
Approve of who we are as it does those
Who when we speak proclaim us barbarous
And say we have no business with the rose.

5   Gently the grass waves, and its green applauds
The justice, not of progress, but of growth.
We walk as people on the paths of gods
And in our minds we harmonize them both.

Disclosures of these grounds—a river view,
10 Two Irish wolfhounds watching on a lawn;
A spinster with her sewing stares at you,
And begs you leave her pretty world alone.

More books than prejudice in our young minds . . .
We could not harm her, would not, would prefer
15 A noise less military and more kind
Than our boots make across her wide *parterre*.[2]

We are intransigent, at odds with them.
They see our rabble-dreams as new contempt
For England's art of house and leaf. Condemn
20 Our clumsiness—you do not know, how, unkempt

---

1. In Hull, England.
2. French landscaping term for an arrangement of flower beds.

And coarse, we hurt a truth with truth, still true
To who we are: barbarians, whose chins
Drool with ale-stinking hair, whose horses chew
Turf owned by watching, frightened mandarins,°   bureaucrats

25 Their surly nephews lounging at each gate,
Afraid we'll steal their family's treasured things,
Then hawk them—pictures, furniture and plate—
Round the encampments of our saddle-kings.

1979

From Elegies

Thirteen Steps and the Thirteenth of March

She sat up on her pillows, receiving guests.
I brought them tea or sherry like a butler,
Up and down the thirteen steps from my pantry.
I was running out of vases.

5   More than one visitor came down, and said,
"Her room's so cheerful. She isn't afraid."
Even the cyclamen and lilies were listening,
Their trusty tributes holding off the real.

Doorbells, shopping, laundry, post and callers,
10 And twenty-six steps up the stairs
From door to bed, two times thirteen's
Unlucky numeral in my high house.

And visitors, three, four, five times a day;
My wept exhaustions over plates and cups
15 Drained my self-pity in these days of grief
Before the grief. Flowers, and no vases left.

Tea, sherry, biscuits, cake, and whisky for the weak . . .
She fought death with an understated mischief—
"I suppose I'll have to make an effort"—
20 Turning down painkillers for lucidity.

Some sat downstairs with a hankie
Nursing a little cry before going up to her.
They came back with their fears of dying amended.
"Her room's so cheerful. She isn't afraid."

25 Each day was duty round the clock.
Our kissing conversations kept me going,
Those times together with the phone switched off,
Remembering our lives by candlelight.

John and Stuart brought their pictures round,
30   A travelling exhibition. Dying,
She thumbed down some, nodded at others,
An artist and curator to the last,

Honesty at all costs. She drew up lists,
Bequests, gave things away. It tore my heart out.
35   Her friends assisted at this tidying
In a conspiracy of women.

At night, I lay beside her in the unique hours.
There were mysteries in candle-shadows,
Birds, aeroplanes, the rabbits of our fingers,
40   The lovely, erotic flame of the candlelight.

Sad? Yes. But it was beautiful also.
There was a stillness in the world. Time was out
Walking his dog by the low walls and privet.°   *hedge*
There was anonymity in words and music.

45   She wanted me to wear her wedding ring.
It wouldn't fit even my little finger.
It jammed on the knuckle. I knew why.
Her fingers dwindled and her rings slipped off.

After the funeral, I had them to tea and sherry
50   At the Newland Park. They said it was thoughtful.
I thought it was ironic—one last time—
A mad reprisal for their loyalty.

                                              1985

ALFRED CORN
b. 1943

Navidad, St. Nicholas Ave.[1]

An infant quirk of a pine
with aerosol frosting, spangles,
and bulbs that blink red-blue-gold.
Manolito, three days home, they've put

5   in his picket-fence crib,
paper diaper cinched tight,
eyes squinted in a mask
that looks Chinese or in pain.

1. Street in the Harlem section of Manhattan; here, the name alludes to St. Nick, or Santa Claus. *Navidad*: nativity (Spanish).

Asleep. Trailing sighs and smiles
10   they tiptoe out to where the Magnavox
screen extolls some *producto*[2]
whose logo's a crystal star.

She glances up at the window
brimming with sodium light.
15   And, *mira,* snow begins to fall
like manna[3] in the warming air

as from down the avenue a taxi
beeps a brass triad. Then an offended
wail summons mother, father,
20   *todo el mundo*[4] back to his side.

1988

A Conch from Sicily[5]

The
Attic[6] once
My nursery is like
An early language no longer
5   Spoken, a babble too small ever
Again to house adults. Yet the spiral
Stair remains, Maestro Fibonacci[7] the builder,
Who made it pirouette downward like a clockwork
Calla.° In the Southern Hemisphere it would run   *lily*
10   Counterclockwise, yet I as well as the conchs
Down under have a silhouette like South
America, and we all smooth the path
That clothes our foot with orange
Coral enamel paneling and floor,
15   As far down as this loosely
Furled calyx, one concave
Rondo's[8] calm finale—or,
If not the last, then
The next-to-last
20   Summing up, a
Single word:
Il tempo[9]—
Weather,
Speed,
25   Time.

1997

2. Product (Spanish). *Magnavox:* brand of televi-
sion.
3. The food that miraculously fell to the Israelites
in the wilderness (Exodus 16.14–36). *Mira:* look
(Spanish).
4. All the world, everybody (Spanish).
5. Island off the southern coast of Italy.
6. Dialect of ancient Athens, or Attica, as well as
the upper floor of a house.
7. Leonardo Pisano Fibonacci (1170–1250), Ital-
ian mathematician, known for discovering a
sequence of numbers that can be used in describ-
ing many forms in nature, including the spiral of a
seashell.
8. Musical form with a recurring theme.
9. Weather, speed, time (Italian).

LOUISE GLÜCK
b. 1943

Gretel[1] in Darkness

This is the world we wanted.
All who would have seen us dead
are dead. I hear the witch's cry
break in the moonlight through a sheet
5   of sugar: God rewards.
Her tongue shrivels into gas. . . .

           Now, far from women's arms
and memory of women, in our father's hut
we sleep, are never hungry.
10 Why do I not forget?
My father bars the door, bars harm
from this house, and it is years.

No one remembers. Even you, my brother,
summer afternoons you look at me as though
15 you meant to leave,
as though it never happened.
But I killed for you. I see armed firs,
the spires of that gleaming kiln—

Nights I turn to you to hold me
20 but you are not there.
Am I alone? Spies
hiss in the stillness, Hansel,
we are there still and it is real, real,
that black forest and the fire in earnest.

                         1975

The Garden

I couldn't do it again,
I can hardly bear to look at it—

in the garden, in light rain
the young couple planting
5 a row of peas, as though
no one has ever done this before,
the great difficulties have never as yet
been faced and solved—

They cannot see themselves,
10 in fresh dirt, starting up

1. As in the fairy tale of Hansel and Gretel.

without perspective,
the hills behind them pale green, clouded with flowers—

She wants to stop;
he wants to get to the end,
15   to stay with the thing—

Look at her, touching his cheek
to make a truce, her fingers
cool with spring rain;
in thin grass, bursts of purple crocus—

20   even here, even at the beginning of love,
her hand leaving his face makes
an image of departure

and they think
they are free to overlook
25   this sadness.

                                 1992

Vita Nova[2]

You saved me, you should remember me.

The spring of the year; young men buying tickets for the ferryboats.
Laughter, because the air is full of apple blossoms.

When I woke up, I realized I was capable of the same feeling.

5   I remember sounds like that from my childhood,
laughter for no cause, simply because the world is beautiful,
something like that.

Lugano.[3] Tables under the apple trees.
Deckhands raising and lowering the colored flags.
10   And by the lake's edge, a young man throws his hat into the water;
perhaps his sweetheart has accepted him.

Crucial
sounds or gestures like
a track laid down before the larger themes

15   and then unused, buried.

Islands in the distance. My mother
holding out a plate of little cakes—

2. New life (Latin). Glück takes for her book *Vita Nova*, and for two poems within it, the title of Dante's first major poem (ca. 1292).

3. Lake on the border between Switzerland and Italy.

as far as I remember, changed
in no detail, the moment
20   vivid, intact, having never been
exposed to light, so that I woke elated, at my age
hungry for life, utterly confident—

By the tables, patches of new grass, the pale green
pieced into the dark existing ground.

25   Surely spring has been returned to me, this time
not as a lover but a messenger of death, yet
it is still spring, it is still meant tenderly.

1999

MICHAEL ONDAATJE
b. 1943

Letters & Other Worlds

"for there was no more darkness for him and, no doubt like Adam
before the fall, he could see in the dark"

My father's body was a globe of fear
His body was a town we never knew
He hid that he had been where we were going
His letters were a room he seldom lived in
5   In them the logic of his love could grow

My father's body was a town of fear
He was the only witness to its fear dance
He hid where he had been that we might lose him
His letters were a room his body scared

10   He came to death with his mind drowning.
On the last day he enclosed himself
in a room with two bottles of gin, later
fell the length of his body
so that brain blood moved
15   to new compartments
that never knew the wash of fluid
and he died in minutes of a new equilibrium.

His early life was a terrifying comedy
and my mother divorced him again and again.
20   He would rush into tunnels magnetized
by the white eye of trains
and once, gaining instant fame,
managed to stop a Perahara[1] in Ceylon

1. Or Anuradhapura Perahera, an annual religious festival of Sri Lanka (formerly Ceylon) commem-

—the whole procession of elephants dancers
25 local dignitaries—by falling
dead drunk onto the street.

As a semi-official, and semi-white at that,
the act was seen as a crucial
turning point in the Home Rule Movement
30 and led to Ceylon's independence in 1948.

(My mother had done her share too—
her driving so bad
she was stoned by villagers
whenever her car was recognized)

35 For 14 years of marriage
each of them claimed he or she
was the injured party.
Once on the Colombo[2] docks
saying goodbye to a recently married couple
40 my father, jealous
at my mother's articulate emotion,
dove into the waters of the harbour
and swam after the ship waving farewell.
My mother pretending no affiliation
45 mingled with the crowd back to the hotel.

Once again he made the papers
though this time my mother
with a note to the editor
corrected the report—saying he was drunk
50 rather than broken hearted at the parting of friends.
The married couple received both editions
of *The Ceylon Times* when their ship reached Aden.[3]

And then in his last years
he was the silent drinker,
55 the man who once a week
disappeared into his room with bottles
and stayed there until he was drunk
and until he was sober.

There speeches, head dreams, apologies,
60 the gentle letters, were composed.
With the clarity of architects
he would write of the row of blue flowers
his new wife had planted,
the plans for electricity in the house,
65 how my half-sister fell near a snake
and it had awakened and not touched her.

---

orating the birth of Vishnu, one of the three pri-
mary Hindu gods. On its fifth and final day, the
festival culminates in nocturnal processions such
as that described here, the elephants bearing

shrines and relics.
2. Port city, capital of Sri Lanka.
3. City and port in South Yemen.

Letters in a clear hand of the most complete empathy
his heart widening and widening and widening
to all manner of change in his children and friends
70   while he himself edged
into the terrible acute hatred
of his own privacy
till he balanced and fell
the length of his body
75   the blood entering
the empty reservoir of bones
the blood searching in his head without metaphor.

                                                        1979

Driving with Dominic in the Southern Province We See Hints of the Circus

The tattered Hungarian tent

A man washing a trumpet
at a roadside tap

Children in the trees,

5   one falling
into the grip of another

                                                        2000

House on a Red Cliff

There is no mirror in Mirissa[4]

the sea is in the leaves
the waves are in the palms

old languages in the arms
5   of the casuarina pine[5]
parampara

parampara,[6] from
generation to generation

The flamboyant[7] a grandfather planted
10   having lived through fire
lifts itself over the roof

---

4. Town on the southern coast of Sri Lanka.
5. Indigenous tree of Sri Lanka with jointed, tree-less branches.
6. One following the other, succession (Sanskrit);
the Hindu method of transmitting knowledge through a guru's answering a disciple's questions.
7. Plant with flame-colored flowers.

unframed

the house an open net

where the night concentrates
15   on a breath
        on a step
a thing or gesture
we cannot be attached to

The long, the short, the difficult minutes
20   of night

where even in darkness
there is no horizon without a tree

just a boat's light in the leaves

Last footstep before formlessness

                             2000

MICHAEL PALMER
b. 1943

Of this cloth doll which[1]

(Sarah's fourth)

Of this cloth doll which
says Oh yes
and then its face changes
to Once upon a time
5   to Wooden but alive
to Like the real
to Late into the night
to There lived an old
to Running across ice
10   (but shadows followed)
to Finally it sneezed
to The boat tipped over
to Flesh and blood
to Out of the whale's mouth

                             1984

1. The fractured sentence of this poem borrows phrases from fairy tales, and especially from the children's story *The Adventures of Pinocchio,* by the Italian writer Carlo Collodi (1826–1890).

I Do Not

"Je ne sais pas l'anglais."
GEORGES HUGNET[2]

I do not know English

I do not know English, and therefore I can have nothing to say about
   this latest war, flowering through a night scope in the evening
   sky.

I do not know English and therefore, when hungry, can do no more
   than point repeatedly to my mouth.

Yet such a gesture might be taken to mean any number of things.

5   I do not know English and therefore cannot seek the requisite
   permissions, as outlined in the recent protocol.

Such as: May I utter a term of endearment; may I now proceed to put
   my arm or arms around you and apply gentle pressure; may I now
   kiss you directly on the lips; now on the left tendon of the neck;
   now on the nipple of each breast? And so on.

Would not in any case be able to decipher her response.

I do not know English. Therefore I have no way of communicating
   that I prefer this painting of nothing to that one of something.

No way to speak of my past or hopes for the future, of my glasses mys-
   teriously shattered in Rotterdam,[3] the statue of Eros and Psyche[4]
   in the Summer Garden, the sudden, shrill cries in the streets of
   São Paulo,[5] a watch abruptly stopping in Paris.

10   No way to tell the joke about the rabbi and the parrot, the bartender
   and the duck, the Pope and the porte-cochère.[6]

You will understand why you have received no letters from me and
   why yours have gone unread.

Those, that is, where you write so precisely of the confluence of the
   visible universe with the invisible, and of the lens of dark matter.[7]

No way to differentiate the hall of mirrors from the meadow of mul-
   lein, the beetlebung from the pinkletink, the kettlehole from the
   ventifact.

2. I do not know English (French). Hugnet
(1906–1974), French poet, essayist, and pub-
lisher.
3. Dutch city bombed by the Allies during World
War II.
4. Figures from Greek mythology: Psyche was so
beautiful that envious Aphrodite, the goddess of

love and beauty, sent Eros, the god of erotic love,
to make her fall in love with an ugly creature;
instead, Eros became her lover.
5. Capital city of Brazil.
6. Gateway for carriages, leading into a courtyard.
7. Matter indirectly detected by astronomers, who
believe it accounts for gravitational effects.

Nor can I utter the words science, seance, silence, language and
    languish.

15   Nor can I tell of the arboreal shadows elongated and shifting along the
    wall as the sun's angle approaches maximum hibernal declination.

Cannot tell of the almond-eyed face that peered from the well, the
    ship of stone whose sail was a tongue.

And I cannot report that this rose has twenty-four petals, one slightly
    cancred.

Cannot tell how I dismantled it myself at this desk.

Cannot ask the name of this rose.[8]

20   I cannot repeat the words of the Recording Angel[9] or those of the
    Angle of Erasure.

Can speak neither of things abounding[1] nor of things disappearing.

Still the games continue. A muscular man waves a stick at a ball. A
    woman in white, arms outstretched, carves a true circle in space.
    A village turns to dust in the chalk hills.

Because I do not know English I have been variously called Mr.
    Twisted, The One Undone, The Nonrespondent, The Truly Lost
    Boy, and Laughed-At-By-Horses.

The war is declared ended, almost before it has begun.

25   They have named it The Ultimate Combat between Nearness and
    Distance.

I do not know English.

2000

EAVAN BOLAND
b. 1944

That the Science of Cartography[1] Is Limited

—and not simply by the fact that this shading of
forest cannot show the fragrance of balsam,

8. Allusion to *The Name of the Rose*, by the Italian novelist Umberto Eco (b. 1932).
9. In Christian doctrine, the angel receiving the soul in heaven.
1. Cf. St. John Chrysostom, homily 4 on 1 Thessalonians 3.5–8: "If the fire of the Sun of Right-

eousness has touched our souls, it will leave nothing frozen, nothing hard, nothing burning, nothing unfruitful. It will bring out all things ripe, all things sweet, all things abounding with much pleasure."
1. Mapmaking.

the gloom of cypresses
is what I wish to prove.

5   When you and I were first in love we drove
to the borders of Connacht[2]
and entered a wood there.

Look down you said: this was once a famine road.

I looked down at ivy and the scutch grass
10 rough-cast stone had
disappeared into as you told me
in the second winter of their ordeal, in

1847, when the crop[3] had failed twice,
Relief Committees gave
15 the starving Irish such roads to build.

Where they died, there the road ended

and ends still and when I take down
the map of this island, it is never so
I can say here is
20 the masterful, the apt rendering of

the spherical as flat, nor
an ingenious design which persuades a curve
into a plane,
but to tell myself again that

25 the line which says woodland and cries hunger
and gives out among sweet pine and cypress,
and finds no horizon

will not be there.

1994

The Dolls Museum in Dublin

The wounds are terrible. The paint is old.
The cracks along the lips and on the cheeks
cannot be fixed. The cotton lawn[4] is soiled.
The arms are ivory dissolved to wax.

5   Recall the Quadrille. Hum the waltz.
Promenade on the yacht-club terraces.
Put back the lamps in their copper holders,
the carriage wheels on the cobbled quays.

2. Western province of Ireland.
3. Of potatoes, staple diet of Irish peasants in the
nineteenth century.
4. Usually fine linen, but also, as here, fine cotton.

And recreate Easter in Dublin.[5]
10 Booted officers. Their mistresses.
Sunlight criss-crossing College Green.
Steam hissing from the flanks of horses.

Here they are. Cradled and cleaned,
held close in the arms of their owners.
15 Their cold hands clasped by warm hands,
their faces memorized like perfect manners.

The altars are mannerly with linen.
The lilies are whiter than surplices.[6]
The candles are burning and warning:
20 Rejoice, they whisper. After sacrifice.

Horse-chestnuts hold up their candles.
The Green is vivid with parasols.
Sunlight is pastel and windless.
The bar of the Shelbourne[7] is full.

25 Laughter and gossip on the terraces.
Rumour and alarm at the barracks.
The Empire is summoning its officers.
The carriages are turning: they are turning back.

Past children walking with governesses,
30 Looking down, cossetting° their dolls,   pampering
then looking up as the carriage passes,
the shadow chilling them. Twilight falls.

It is twilight in the dolls' museum. Shadows
remain on the parchment-coloured waists,
35 are bruises on the stitched cotton clothes,
are hidden in the dimples on the wrists.

The eyes are wide. They cannot address
the helplessness which has lingered in
the airless peace of each glass case:
40 to have survived. To have been stronger than

a moment. To be the hostages ignorance
takes from time and ornament from destiny. Both.
To be the present of the past. To infer the difference
with a terrible stare. But not feel it. And not know it.

1994

---

5. What became known as the "Easter Rising" began on Easter Monday, 1916, when fifteen hundred Irish Nationalists seized key points in Dublin and an Irish Republic was proclaimed from the General Post Office. See W. B. Yeats, "Easter 1916" (p. 1194).
6. White linen vestments worn over cassocks.
7. Large Dublin hotel.

The Pomegranate

The only legend I have ever loved is
the story of a daughter lost in hell.
And found and rescued there.
Love and blackmail are the gist of it.
5 Ceres and Persephone the names.[8]
And the best thing about the legend is
I can enter it anywhere. And have.
As a child in exile in
a city of fogs and strange consonants,
10 I read it first and at first I was
an exiled child in the crackling dusk of
the underworld, the stars blighted. Later
I walked out in a summer twilight
searching for my daughter at bed-time.
15 When she came running I was ready
to make any bargain to keep her.
I carried her back past whitebeams°   *trees*
and wasps and honey-scented buddleias.°   *bushes*
But I was Ceres then and I knew
20 winter was in store for every leaf
on every tree on that road.
Was inescapable for each one we passed.
And for me.
                    It is winter
25 and the stars are hidden.
I climb the stairs and stand where I can see
my child asleep beside her teen magazines,
her can of Coke, her plate of uncut fruit.
The pomegranate! How did I forget it?
30 She could have come home and been safe
and ended the story and all
our heart-broken searching but she reached
out a hand and plucked a pomegranate.
She put out her hand and pulled down
35 the French sound for apple and
the noise of stone and the proof
that even in the place of death,
at the heart of legend, in the midst
of rocks full of unshed tears
40 ready to be diamonds by the time
the story was told, a child can be
hungry. I could warn her. There is still a chance.
The rain is cold. The road is flint-coloured.
The suburb has cars and cable television.
45 The veiled stars are above ground.

8. In Roman mythology, Ceres (Greek Demeter) was the goddess of agriculture. Her daughter, Proserpina (Greek Persephone), was carried off to Orcus (Greek Hades), the underworld, by its king. Ceres found her, but by then Proserpina had eaten six pomegranate seeds and was condemned to spend six months of each year in the underworld (when Earth mourns) and six aboveground (when Earth rejoices and fertility returns).

It is another world. But what else
can a mother give her daughter but such
beautiful rifts in time?
If I defer the grief I will diminish the gift.
50   The legend will be hers as well as mine.
She will enter it. As I have.
She will wake up. She will hold
the papery flushed skin in her hand.
And to her lips. I will say nothing.

1994

CRAIG RAINE
b. 1944

The Onion, Memory

Divorced, but friends again at last,
we walk old ground together
in bright blue uncomplicated weather.
We laugh and pause
5   to hack to bits these tiny dinosaurs,
prehistoric, crenellated,° cast   *having battlements*
between the tractor ruts in mud.

On the green, a junior Douglas Fairbanks,[1]
swinging on the chestnut's unlit chandelier,
10   defies the corporation spears[2]—
a single rank° around the bole,°   *row / tree trunk*
rusty with blood.
Green, tacky phalluses curve up, romance.
A gust—the old flag blazes on its pole.

15   In the village bakery
the pasty babies pass
from milky slump to crusty cadaver,
from crib to coffin—without palaver.°   *idle talk*
All's over in a flash,
20   too silently . . .

Tonight the arum lilies fold
back napkins monogrammed in gold,
crisp and laundered fresh.
Those crustaceous gladioli, on the sly,
25   reveal the crimson flower-flesh
inside their emerald armour plate.

1. American actor (1883–1939) famous for his
swashbuckling daredevil exploits in movies of the
1920s and 1930s.

2. I.e., spiked fence put up by the town corpora-
tion.

The uncooked herrings blink a tearful eye.
The candles palpitate.
The Oistrakhs bow and scrape
30 in evening dress, on Emi-tape.[3]

Outside the trees are bending over backwards
to please the wind : the shining sword
grass flattens on its belly.
The white-thorn's frillies[4] offer no resistance.
35 In the fridge, a heart-shaped jelly
strives to keep a sense of balance.

I slice up the onions. You sew up a dress.
This is the quiet echo—flesh—
white muscle on white muscle,
40 intimately folded skin,
finished with a satin rustle.
One button only to undo, sewn up with shabby thread.
It is the onion, memory,
that makes me cry.

45 Because there's everything and nothing to be said,
the clock with hands held up before its face,
stammers softly on, trying to complete a phrase—
while we, together and apart,
repeat unfinished gestures got by heart.

50 And afterwards, I blunder with the washing on the line—
headless torsos, faceless lovers, friends of mine.

1978

A Martian Sends a Postcard Home

Caxtons[5] are mechanical birds with many wings
and some are treasured for their markings—

they cause the eyes to melt
or the body to shriek without pain.

5 I have never seen one fly, but
sometimes they perch on the hand.

Mist is when the sky is tired of flight
and rests its soft machine on ground:

---

3. A popular British brand of audiotape. David Oistrakh (1908–1974) and his son Igor (b. 1931), celebrated Russian violinists.
4. British colloquialism for frilled undergarments.
5. I.e., books, which William Caxton (ca. 1422– 1491) was the first to print in English; in the next couplet, the Martian observes the effects of books on their readers, but does not know the words for *cry* or *laugh*.

then the world is dim and bookish
10 like engravings under tissue paper.

Rain is when the earth is television.
It has the property of making colours darker.

Model T[6] is a room with the lock inside—
a key is turned to free the world

15 for movement, so quick there is a film
to watch for anything missed.

But time is tied to the wrist
or kept in a box, ticking with impatience.

In homes, a haunted apparatus sleeps,
20 that snores when you pick it up.

If the ghost cries, they carry it
to their lips and soothe it to sleep

with sounds. And yet, they wake it up
deliberately, by tickling with a finger.

25 Only the young are allowed to suffer
openly. Adults go to a punishment room

with water but nothing to eat.
They lock the door and suffer the noises

alone. No one is exempt
30 and everyone's pain has a different smell.

At night, when all the colours die,
they hide in pairs

and read about themselves—
in colour, with their eyelids shut.

1979

For Hans Keller[7]

There will be more of this,
more of this than I had realised
of finding our friends

---

6. I.e., automobiles; the "key" (next line) is the
ignition key.

7. English (Austrian-born) musicologist (1919–
1985).

irrevocably changed,

5   skewed like Guy Fawkes[8] in a chair
because all the muscles have gone
and talking as if nothing has happened

when nothing has happened.

There will be more of this,
10   more of coming to crematoria
to learn that a life can come to an end

like a Haydn quartet,[9] without a repeat.

There will be too much and then more of this,
of hearing instruments negotiate with silence,
15   stating the case with gravitas°   *moral earnestness*

and anxious insect antennae.

We stand for the coffin at a word from the usher.
The speaker's hand feels for his pocket,
as his nerves die down

20   and the nerves take over.

That hand is alive and my feet are alive,
feeling the pinch of expensive new shoes,
and I am moved by being moved

as the coffin crawls to the fire.

25   Hans, there is still more of this,
more of undertakers locking the hearse
and seeing the plastic safety bolts

slide, like suppositories, slowly away,

as we re-enter the sunshine alive
30   with eyes to see by Camden Lock[1]
a bedstead, sleeping rough,

like dead beloved bodies everywhere.

1996

8. Conspirator (1570–1606) in the so-called Gun-
powder Plot to blow up the British Parliament.
When this failed, in 1605, Fawkes was arrested,
tortured, and executed. Annually on November 5
ever since, his effigy has been burnt on bonfires
across the U.K.
9. Composition for four instrumentalists by the
Austrian composer Joseph Haydn (1732–1809).
1. London market.

KIT WRIGHT
b. 1944

Mantles[1]

White as the sacrament, in my grandmother's house the mantles
Were taught to flower in the dusk. On their soft weighbridge°   platform
They balanced the light, on their milkmaid's yoke they carried it
Over mahogany mountains,
5 Till the room was breathing its secret to the ghost of the wind in the
     bay.

That radiant patience made a lake of the stern piano
Where she sang *The Isle of Capri*.[2] Such
Beauty in the frail old voice, so long a river of widowhood
The light went running with through the banks of shadow . . .

10 It caught the little pointed breasts of brass
Nubian goddesses on the mantelpiece. It put in the shade
A mysterious cavern under the table
Where African butterflies, in the pinned tomb of their wooden boxes,
Spread their gorgeous wings that reeked of camphor.

15 In my grandmother's house there existed a borrowed shrimping net
And a maiden aunt, your best friend ever.
A peacock feather. An ostrich egg. A time
When the breathing of time was audible in gas mantles,
Conspiratorial and benign.

2000

A Love Song of Tooting[3]

In Tooting, the tomato
    Hangs heavy on the vine
The blackbird's *obbligato*[4]
    Fulfils its liquid line
5 On summertime allotments°   vegetable plots
    By lenient design.

Nine beanrows will I have there,[5]
    Not ten, not eight, but nine,
And I shall build a pav° there,   pavillion, hut

1. Incandescent cloth hoods of gaslight jets.
2. Hit song written in 1934.
3. District of south London.
4. In a musical composition, a necessary, gener-
ally melodic line accompanying a solo.
5. Cf. W. B. Yeats, "The Lake Isle of Innisfree,"
lines 2–3 (p. 1190).

10   Or shed of weathered pine,
     And all shall be contentment
          Down by the railway line.

     My shed, beside a toolbox,
          A coolbox° shall confine   *cooler*
15   And we from out the coolbox
          Shall quaff the rare white wine.
     The dove shall plight its truelove
          And I shall sing to mine.

                                        2000

My Version

     I hear that since you left me
     Things go from bad to worse,
     That the Good Lord, quite rightly,
     Has set a signal curse

5   On you, your house and lover.
     (I learn, moreover, he
     Proves twice as screwed-up, selfish
     And sodden, dear, as me.)

     They say your days are tasteless,
10   Flattened, disjointed, thinned.
     Across the waste my absence,
     Love's skeleton, has grinned.

     Perfect. I trust my sources
     Of information are sound?
15   Or is it just some worthless rumour
     I've been spreading round?

                                        2000

WENDY COPE
b. 1945

Bloody Men

Bloody men are like bloody buses—
You wait for about a year
And as soon as one approaches your stop
Two or three others appear.

5 You look at them flashing their indicators,
Offering you a ride.
You're trying to read the destinations,
You haven't much time to decide.

If you make a mistake, there is no turning back.
10 Jump off, and you'll stand there and gaze
While the cars and the taxis and lorries° go by   *trucks*
And the minutes, the hours, the days.

1992

Flowers

Some men never think of it.
You did. You'd come along
And say you'd nearly brought me flowers
But something had gone wrong.

5 The shop was closed. Or you had doubts—
The sort that minds like ours
Dream up incessantly. You thought
I might not want your flowers.

It made me smile and hug you then.
10 Now I can only smile.
But, look, the flowers you nearly brought
Have lasted all this while.

1992

Valentine

My heart has made its mind up
And I'm afraid it's you.
Whatever you've got lined up,
My heart has made its mind up
5 And if you can't be signed up
This year, next year will do.
My heart has made its mind up
And I'm afraid it's you.

1992

Serious Concerns

"She is witty and unpretentious, which is both her strength and her limitation."

(ROBERT O'BRIEN in the *Spectator*,[1] 25.10.86)

I'm going to try and overcome my limitation—
Away with sloth!
Now should I work at being less witty? Or more pretentious?
Or both?

"They (Roger McGough and Brian Patten)[2] have something in common with her, in that they all write to amuse."

(IBID.)

5 Write to amuse? What an appalling suggestion!
I write to make people anxious and miserable and to worsen their
    indigestion.

1992

YUSEF KOMUNYAKAA

b. 1947

Facing It

My black face fades,
hiding inside the black granite.
I said I wouldn't
dammit: No tears.
5 I'm stone. I'm flesh.
My clouded reflection eyes me
like a bird of prey, the profile of night
slanted against morning. I turn
this way—the stone lets me go.
10 I turn that way—I'm inside
the Vietnam Veterans Memorial[1]
again, depending on the light
to make a difference.
I go down the 58,022 names,
15 half-expecting to find
my own in letters like smoke.
I touch the name Andrew Johnson;
I see the booby trap's white flash.
Names shimmer on a woman's blouse
20 but when she walks away

1. English magazine, in which O'Brien was writing about Cope.
2. Two of the so-called Liverpool poets, popular in the late 1960s and early 1970s.

1. In Washington, D.C.

the names stay on the wall.
Brushstrokes flash, a red bird's
wings cutting across my stare.
The sky. A plane in the sky.
25 A white vet's image floats
closer to me, then his pale eyes
look through mine. I'm a window.
He's lost his right arm
inside the stone. In the black mirror
30 a woman's trying to erase names:
No, she's brushing a boy's hair.

1988

Banking Potatoes

Daddy would drop purple-veined vines
Along rows of dark loam
& I'd march behind him
Like a peg-legged soldier,
5 Pushing down the stick
With a V cut into its tip.

Three weeks before the first frost
I'd follow his horse-drawn plow
That opened up the soil & left
10 Sweet potatoes sticky with sap,
Like flesh-colored stones along a riverbed
Or diminished souls beside a mass grave.

They lay all day under the sun's
Invisible weight, & by twilight
15 We'd bury them under pine needles
& then shovel in two feet of dirt.
Nighthawks scalloped the sweaty air,
Their wings spread wide

As plowshares. But soon the wind
20 Knocked on doors & windows
Like a frightened stranger,
& by mid-winter we had tunneled
Back into the tomb of straw,
Unable to divide love from hunger.

1992

The Smokehouse

In the hickory scent
Among slabs of pork

Glistening with salt,
I played Indian
5   In a headdress of redbird feathers
& brass buttons
Off my mother's winter coat.
Smoke wove
A thread of fire through meat, into December
10   & January. The dead weight
Of the place hung around me,
Strung up with sweetgrass.
The hog had been sectioned,
A map scored into skin;
15   Opened like love,
From snout to tail,
The goodness
No longer true to each bone.
I was a wizard
20   In that hazy world,
& knew I could cut
Slivers of meat till my heart
Grew more human & flawed.

1992

Sunday Afternoons

They'd latch the screendoors
& pull venetian blinds,
Telling us not to leave the yard.
But we always got lost
5   Among mayhaw° & crabapple.   *berry tree*

Juice spilled from our mouths,
& soon we were drunk & brave
As birds diving through saw° vines.   *saw palmetto*
Each nest held three or four
10   Speckled eggs, blue as rage.

Where did we learn to be unkind,
There in the power of holding each egg
While watching dogs in June
Dust & heat, or when we followed
15   The hawk's slow, deliberate arc?

In the yard, we heard cries
Fused with gospel on the radio,
Loud as shattered glass
In a Saturday-night argument
20   About trust & money.

We were born between Oh Yeah
& Goddammit. I knew life

Began where I stood in the dark,
Looking out into the light,
25 & that sometimes I could see

Everything through nothing.
The backyard trees breathed
Like a man running from himself
As my brothers backed away
30 From the screendoor. I knew

If I held my right hand above my eyes
Like a gambler's visor, I could see
How their bedroom door halved
The dresser mirror like a moon
35 Held prisoner in the house.

1992

JANE SHORE
b. 1947

High Holy Days[1]

It was hot. A size too large,
my wool winter suit scratched.
Indian summer flaring up through fall.
The shul's[2] broken window
5 bled sunlight on the congregation; the Red Sea
of the scarlet carpet parted the women from the men.[3]
Mother next to daughter, father next to son
flipped through prayerbooks in unison
trying to keep the place. Across the aisle,
10 my father wore a borrowed prayershawl.
A black yarmulke[4] covered his bald spot.

The rabbi unlocked the ark[5]
and slid the curtain open. Propped inside,
two scrolls of the Torah[6] dressed like matching dolls,
15 each, a king and a queen. Ribbons hung down
from their alabaster satin jackets;

1. Also called Days of Awe, combining Rosh Ha-shanah, the Jewish New Year, with Yom Kippur, the Day of Atonement, ten days later; generally in September and October.
2. Synagogue's (Yiddish).
3. Men and women are seated separately in Orthodox Jewish congregations. Shore's "Red Sea" of carpet, acting as a divider, reverses the image in Exodus 14.21–22, where Moses parts the Red Sea, allowing the nation of Israel to escape pursuit by the Egyptians.

4. Skullcap worn, like the "prayershawl" (a garment), by Jewish men during services.
5. A large cabinet on the altar, in which the locked Torahs are kept; the Jewish equivalent of the ark of the Covenant (Exodus 25.10–22).
6. The five books of Moses (Genesis, Exodus, Leviticus, Numbers, and Deuteronomy), written in Hebrew. The scrolls, on two wooden rollers, are decorated with sterling-silver crowns and wrapped in fabric; called the "king's possessions" because of their centrality to Jewish religious life.

each one wore two silver crowns.
I wondered, could the ancient kings
have been so small? So small,
20 and still have vanquished our enemies?

The cantor's voice rose
like smoke over a sacrificial altar,
and lambs,[7] we rose to echo the refrain.
Each time we sat down
25 my mother rearranged her skirt.
Each time we stood up
my head hurt from the heat, dizzy
from tripping over the alphabet's
black spikes and lyres,
30 stick-figure batallions marching to defend
the Second Temple of Jerusalem.[8]

Rocking on their heels, boats
anchored in the harbor of devotion,
the temple elders davenned Kaddish,[9] mourning the dead.
35 Our neighbor who owned the laundry down the street
covered his left wrist out of habit—
numbers indelible as those
he inked on my father's shirt collars.[1]
Once, I saw that whole arm disappear
40 into a tub of soapy shirts,
rainbowed, buoyant as the pastel clouds
in *The Illustrated Children's Bible*,
where God's enormous hand reached down
and stopped a heathen army in its tracks.[2]
45 But on the white-hot desert of the page
I was reading, it was noon,
the marching letters swam, the regiments
wavered in the heat,
a red rain falling on their ranks.
50 I watched it fall one drop at a time.
I felt faint. And breathed out sharply,
my nose spattering blood across the page.[3]

I watched it fall, and thought,
you are a Chosen One,[4]
55 *the child to lead your tribe.*
I looked around the swaying room.
Why would God choose me

7. Under a system instituted by Moses, sins were atoned for by the sacrificing of a lamb (or ox, goat, or bird) as a burnt offering to God. *Cantor*: religious official who sings or chants prayers.
8. Temple built after the Jews returned from captivity in Babylon in the sixth century B.C.E.; destroyed by the Romans in 70 C.E.
9. Recited prayers in memory of the dead.
1. Reference to the Nazi practice of tattooing registration numbers on the left arms of some prisoners before they were sent to concentration camps.
2. God's hand is commonly said to bring Israel deliverance from its enemies (e.g., 1 Samuel 7.13).
3. One of the three readings required on the morning of Yom Kippur (Leviticus 16.1–34) details how the priest is to consecrate the ark of the Covenant by sprinkling the blood of a sacrificed bull and goat on the cover.
4. Moses underscored the special role of the descendants of Abraham, Isaac, and Jacob as God's chosen people.

to lead this congregation of mostly strangers,
defend them against the broken windows,
60   the spray-painted writing on the walls?[5]

Overhead, the red bulb of the everlasting light[6]
was burning. As if God held me in His fist,
I stumbled down the synagogue stairs
just in time to hear
65   a cyclone of breath twist through
the shofar,[7] a battle cry so powerful
it blasted city walls to rubble.
And I reeled home through the dazed traffic
of the business day—
70   past shoppers, past my school,
in session as usual,
spat like Jonah from the whale[8]
back into the Jew-hating world.

1987

RICHARD KENNEY
b. 1948

Aubade

Cold snap. Five o'clock.
Outside, a heavy frost—dark
footprints in the brittle
grass; a cat's. Quick coffee,
5   jacket, watch-cap, keys.
Stars blaze across the black
gap between horizons;
pickup somehow strikes
its own dim spark—an arc—
10   starts. Inside, familiar
metal cab, an icebox
full of lightless air,
limns green with dash-light. Vinyl
seat cracks, cold and brittle;
15   horn ring gleams, and chrome
cuts hard across the wrist

5. Reference to *Kristallnacht* (Night of the Broken Glass), November 9 and 10, 1938, when, in a pogrom throughout Germany and Austria, the Nazis committed violent acts such as breaking the windows of Jewish stores.
6. A red electric light, symbolic of God's eternal presence, is kept burning continuously in the ceiling of an Orthodox synagogue.
7. Trumpet made of ram's horn; blown in syna-gogues on the High Holy Days. In Joshua 6.20, when the people hear the priests blow a shofar, they raise such a great shout that the walls of Jericho fall.
8. After Jonah had been swallowed by a great fish, God spoke to it and it spew Jonah out (Jonah 2.10). The Book of Jonah is read in its entirety on Yom Kippur.

where the sleeve falls off the glove,
as moon-track curves its cool tiara
somewhere underneath your sleep
20   this very moment, love—

1985

Apples on Champlain[1]

Oil-slick, slack shocks, ancient engine
smoking like a burning tire,
Augustus' old truck yaws and slews,[2]
its leaf-springs limp these centuries
5   suspending apples, somehow pulls
the last hill past the bridge at Isle
La Motte.[3] I hear the iron arches
groaning. Why not? Whole orchards
rattling, empty racks behind us,
10   emptied into grain sacks, piled
behind us—home ahead, we broach
the mile-long causeway cross from Grande Isle[4]
back.
        A blue heron's motionless
15   in marsh grass to my right, and pole
and icepack at my left—one line,
two lanes, a roostertail of blue
exhaust, we part the cooling waters
of Champlain.
20   The moon's a pool
of mercury. It's zero. Ice soon.
Steaming like a teacup, losing
heat, the lake is tossing clouds up
all around the truck; and tucked
25   so in its fragile ribcage creel,
the cold heart *thump* accordions
to keep alive, and fills, as apples
interrupt this landscape's black-
on-grey like heartbeats full of blood,
30   strung beads, a life of little suns
gone rolling down the press and sump
of memory and changing form
as *thump,* horizon groans and ladles
light, and the real sun comes up,
35   sudden, weightless, warm.

1985

---

1. Lake Champlain, which divides New York State and Vermont near the Canadian border.
2. Pivots, skids. *Yaws:* moves side to side, like a ship in a heavy sea.
3. Vermont town on one of the islands in Lake Champlain.
4. Group of four islands in Lake Champlain.

Sawmill

Snap tempered tooth chips
sawyer shouts *steel in sawlog*
lock engine off slack
line carriage back echo
5   like a gunshot ricochets
off galvanized tin roof the great
blade ringing like a gong
and every man down low:
look, along the log's sheer face,
10   the bright metal shows itself:
a tap, a nail, a bit of buried
wire, some wrong coordinate
or undetected intercept
exactly *there*—count the rings—
15   just forty years ago.

1985

ROBYN SARAH

b. 1949

Courtney, Mentioned in Passing, Years After

"The most beautiful girl in the college,
and she had to go move to Thailand!"
                              Then
he says her name, and it turns out
5   you knew her, years ago:

you remember her from when she was small,
decked out as Pharaoh's daughter
in the Grade Two play, in an amazing dress
her mother cut for her, designed
10   with the help of colour plates
from the school encyclopaedia, Volume E.

You remember how she,
who lived to ride horses, who drew
(in ink) horses on every surface of her
15   fuchsia and mauve and turquoise and pink
vinyl ring-binders, used
to punish herself at recess
when her team lost
at murder-ball°—   *dodge ball*

20   how
(almost weeping in her fury)
she would cry, "Oh—
I *hate* the horses now!"

For a moment, then, in Montreal,
25 in February slush, shifting from foot to foot
in the bus-stop line, you think
of Courtney in Thailand, hating the horses.
You see her there,
grown up, but still
30 in her Egyptian sleeves. Her sudden
wake of colours.

                                              1998

Relics

    Digging a new
    cellar access
    you unearth

    a cat's skull. Then
5   a metal stencil, rust-
    encrusted. Then

    the small bottle
    in which ink
    has dried black

10   with the cap
    rusted on. And
    other bottles—small

    vials, of coloured
    pharmacist's glass,
15   and—intact—

    filled with packed dirt,
    its surface glazed
    with rainbow patina—

    the wide-lipped, plain
20   round thick-glassed pint
    of childhood gone,

    that held—again
    and again—fresh
    cream (thick too)

25 waiting, capped,
each morning
on the stoop.

1998

AGHA SHAHID ALI
1949–2001

The Dacca Gauzes[1]

. . . for a whole year he sought to accumulate the most exquisite
Dacca gauzes.
—OSCAR WILDE / *The Picture of Dorian Gray*

Those transparent Dacca gauzes
known as woven air, running
water, evening dew:

a dead art now, dead over
5   a hundred years. "No one
now knows," my grandmother says,

"what it was to wear
or touch that cloth." She wore
it once, an heirloom sari from

10   her mother's dowry, proved
genuine when it was pulled, all
six yards, through a ring.

Years later when it tore,
many handkerchiefs embroidered
15   with gold-thread paisleys

were distributed among
the nieces and daughters-in-law.
Those too now lost.

In history we learned: the hands
20   of weavers were amputated,
the looms of Bengal silenced,

and the cotton shipped raw
by the British to England.
History of little use to her,

1. Thin, finely woven muslins once made in the Bangladeshi city of Dacca.

25 my grandmother just says
how the muslins of today
seem so coarse and that only

in autumn, should one wake up
at dawn to pray, can one
30 feel that same texture again.

One morning, she says, the air
was dew-starched: she pulled
it absently through her ring.

1987

Lenox Hill[2]

*(In Lenox Hill Hospital, after surgery, my mother said the sirens sounded
like the elephants of Mihiragula when his men drove them off cliffs in the
Pir Panjal Range.)*[3]

The Hun so loved the cry, one falling elephant's,
he wished to hear it again. At dawn, my mother
heard, in her hospital-dream of elephants,
sirens wail through Manhattan like elephants
5 forced off Pir Panjal's rock cliffs in Kashmir:
the soldiers, so ruled, had rushed the elephant,
The greatest of all footprints is the elephant's,
said the Buddha.[4] But not lifted from the universe,
those prints vanished forever into the universe,
10 though nomads still break news of those elephants
as if it were just yesterday the air spread the dye
("War's annals will fade into night / Ere their story die"),[5]

the punishing khaki whereby the world sees us die
out, mourning you, O massacred elephants!
15 Months later, in Amherst,[6] she dreamt: She was, with dia-
monds, being stoned to death. I prayed: If she must die,
let it only be some dream. But there were times, Mother,
while you slept, that I prayed, "Saints, let her die."
Not, I swear by you, that I wished you to die
20 but to save you as you were, young, in song in Kashmir,
and I, one festival, crowned Krishna[7] by you, Kashmir
listening to my flute. You never let gods die.

2. On the structure of this poem, which is a can-
zone, see "Versification," p. 2046. Ali's mother was
treated for brain cancer at Lenox Hill Hospital,
New York City, but died in a hospital in North-
ampton, Massachusetts, on April 27, 1997.
3. Himalayan mountains. Mihiragula, the early
sixth-century White Hun invader of Kashmir, is
said to have been so entranced by the scream of
one of his elephants falling from a cliff that he
ordered a hundred more to be driven over.
4. Sanskrit name, meaning Enlightened One, of
Siddhartha Gautama (ca. 563–483 B.C.E.),
founder of Buddhism.
5. Cf. Thomas Hardy, "In Time of 'The Breaking
of Nations,' " lines 11–12 (p. 1161).
6. Town in Massachusetts, near Northampton.
7. Widely revered Indian deity.

Thus I swear, here and now, not to forgive the universe
that would let me get used to a universe

25 without you. She, she alone, was the universe
as she earned, like a galaxy, her right not to die,
defying the Merciful of the Universe,
Master of Disease, "in the circle of her traverse"[8]
of drug-bound time. And where was the god of elephants,[9]
30 plump with Fate, when tusk to tusk, the universe,
dyed green, became ivory? Then let the universe,
like Paradise, be considered a tomb. Mother,
they asked me, *So how's the writing?* I answered *My mother
is my poem.* What did they expect? For no verse
35 sufficed except the promise, fading, of Kashmir
and the cries that reached you from the cliffs of Kashmir

(across fifteen centuries) in the hospital. *Kashmir,
she's dying!* How her breathing drowns out the universe
as she sleeps in Amherst. Windows open on Kashmir:
40 *There,* the fragile wood-shrines—so far away—of Kashmir!
O Destroyer,[1] let her return there, if just to die.
Save the right she gave its earth to cover her, Kashmir
has no rights. When the windows close on Kashmir,
I see the blizzard-fall of ghost-elephants.
45 I hold back—she couldn't bear it—one elephant's
story: his return (in a country far from Kashmir)
to the jungle where each year, on the day his mother
died, he touches with his trunk the bones of his mother.

"As you sit here by me, you're just like my mother,"
50 she tells me. I imagine her: a bride in Kashmir,
she's watching, at the Regal,[2] her first film with Father.
If only I could gather you in my arms, Mother,
I'd save you—now my daughter—from God. The universe
opens its ledger. I write: How helpless was God's mother!
55 Each page is turned to enter grief's accounts. Mother,
I see a hand. *Tell me it's not God's.* Let it die.
I see it. It's filling with diamonds. Please let it die.
Are you somewhere alive, somewhere alive, Mother?
Do you hear what I once held back: in one elephant's
60 cry, by his mother's bones, the cries of those elephants

that stunned the abyss? Ivory blots out the elephants.
I enter this: *The Belovéd leaves one behind to die.*
For compared to my grief for you, what are those of Kashmir,
and what (I close the ledger) are the griefs of the universe
65 when I remember you—beyond all accounting—O my mother?

2002

---

8. Cf. Wallace Stevens, "The Paltry Nude Starts
on a Spring Voyage," lines 15–16: "She touches
the clouds, where she goes / In the circle of her
traverse of the sea."
9. I.e., Ganesh, Hindu god with the head of an
elephant, able to answer prayers and bring good
fortune.
1. I.e., Shiva, Hindu god of, among other things,
destruction and the Himalayan mountains.
2. Name of a movie theater.

JAMES FENTON
b. 1949

Dead Soldiers

When His Excellency Prince Norodom Chantaraingsey[1]
Invited me to lunch on the battlefield
I was glad of my white suit for the first time that day.
They lived well, the mad Norodoms, they had style.
5 The brandy and the soda arrived in crates.
Bricks of ice, tied around with raffia,°   *palm fibers*
Dripped from the orderlies' handlebars.

And I remember the dazzling tablecloth
As the APCs[2] fanned out along the road,
10 The dishes piled high with frogs' legs,
Pregnant turtles, their eggs boiled in the carapace,°   *shell*
Marsh irises in fish sauce
And inflorescence[3] of a banana salad.

On every bottle, Napoleon Bonaparte
15 Pleaded for the authenticity of the spirit.[4]
They called the empties Dead Soldiers
And rejoiced to see them pile up at our feet.

Each diner was attended by one of the other ranks[5]
Whirling a table-napkin to keep off the flies.
20 It was like eating between rows of morris dancers[6]—
Only they didn't kick.

On my left sat the prince;
On my right, his drunken aide.
The frogs' thighs leapt into the sad purple face
25 Like fish to the sound of a Chinese flute.
I wanted to talk to the prince. I wish now
I had collared his aide, who was Saloth Sar's brother.
We treated him as the club bore. He was always
Boasting of his connections, boasting with a head-shake
30 Or by pronouncing of some doubtful phrase.
And well might he boast. Saloth Sar, for instance,
Was Pol Pot's[7] real name. The APCs
Fired into the sugar palms but met no resistance.

---

1. Military governor of Cambodia, uncle of King
Norodom Sihanouk (b. 1922). Fenton was a war
correspondent in Cambodia and Vietnam.
2. Armored personnel carriers: trucks for trans-
porting troops.
3. Arrangement of flowers on an axis; blossoming.
4. Napoleon brandy (i.e., of high quality).
5. General infantrymen.
6. Performers of British folk dances, which
include the waving of scarves, handkerchiefs, and
sometimes wooden staves.
7. Kampuchean politician (1925–1998). Part of
the anti-French resistance in the 1940s, he
became leader of the pro-French Communist
Party, and prime minister in 1976. His government
was overthrown after the Vietnamese invasion of
1979.

In a diary, I refer to Pol Pot's brother as the Jockey Cap.
35 A few weeks later, I find him "in good form
And very skeptical about Chantaraingsey."
"But one eats well there," I remark.
"So one should," says the Jockey Cap:
"The tiger always eats well,
40 It eats the raw flesh of the deer,
And Chantaraingsey was born in the year of the tiger.
So, did they show you the things they do
With the young refugee girls?"

And he tells me how he will one day give me the
      gen.°   *inside information*
45 He will tell me how the prince financed the casino
And how the casino brought Lon Nol[8] to power.
He will tell me this.
He will tell me all these things.
All I must do is drink and listen.

50 In those days, I thought that when the game was up
The prince would be far, far away—
In a limestone faubourg,° on the promenade at Nice,[9]   *suburb*
Reduced in circumstances but well enough provided for.
In Paris, he would hardly require his private army.
55 The Jockey Cap might suffice for café warfare,
And matchboxes for APCs.

But we were always wrong in these predictions.
It was a family war. Whatever happened,
The principals were obliged to attend its issue.
60 A few were cajoled into leaving, a few were expelled,
And there were villains enough, but none of them
Slipped away with the swag.°   *loot*

For the prince was fighting Sihanouk,[1] his nephew,
And the Jockey Cap was ranged against his brother
65 Of whom I remember nothing more
Than an obscure reputation for virtue.
I have been told that the prince is still fighting
Somewhere in the Cardamoms or the Elephant Mountains.
But I doubt that the Jockey Cap would have survived his good
      connections.
70 I think the lunches would have done for him—
Either the lunches or the dead soldiers.

1981

---

8. General (1913–1985) and right-wing politi-
cian, who became president of Cambodia in 1970
after his faction overthrew Sihanouk (see note 1
below). He was overthrown by Pol Pot.

9. Resort city on the French Riviera.
1. Norodom Sihanouk was made king of Cambo-
dia by the French in 1941. Overthrown by Lon
Nol, he was reinstated in 1993.

A German Requiem[2]

(To T. J. G.-A.)

For as at a great distance of place, that which wee look at, appears
dimme, and without distinction of the smaller parts; and as Voyces
grow weak, and inarticulate: so also after great distance of time,
our imagination of the Past is weak; and wee lose (for example) of
Cities wee have seen, many particular Streets; and of Actions, many
particular circumstances. This *decaying sense,* when wee would
express the thing it self, (I mean *fancy* it selfe,) wee call *Imagination,*
as I said before: But when we would express the *decay,* and signifie
that the Sense is fading, old, and past, it is called Memory. So that
Imagination and *Memory* are but one thing . . .

—HOBBES,[3] *Leviathan*

It is not what they built. It is what they knocked down.
It is not the houses. It is the spaces between the houses.
It is not the streets that exist. It is the streets that no longer exist.
It is not your memories which haunt you.
5   It is not what you have written down.
It is what you have forgotten, what you must forget.
What you must go on forgetting all your life.
And with any luck oblivion should discover a ritual.
You will find out that you are not alone in the enterprise.
10 Yesterday the very furniture seemed to reproach you.
Today you take your place in the Widow's Shuttle.[4]

*

The bus is waiting at the southern gate
To take you to the city of your ancestors
Which stands on the hill opposite, with gleaming pediments,[5]
15 As vivid as this charming square, your home.
Are you shy? You should be. It is almost like a wedding,
The way you clasp your flowers and give a little tug at your veil. Oh,
The hideous bridesmaids, it is natural that you should resent them
Just a little, on this first day.
20 But that will pass, and the cemetery is not far.
Here comes the driver, flicking a toothpick into the gutter,
His tongue still searching between his teeth.
See, he has not noticed you. No one has noticed you.
It will pass, young lady, it will pass.

*

25 How comforting it is, once or twice a year,
To get together and forget the old times.
As on those special days, ladies and gentlemen,
When the boiled shirts[6] gather at the graveside
And a leering waistcoat approaches the rostrum.

2. Mass or chant for the dead. Also, title of a piece
by the German composer Johannes Brahms
(1833–1897).
3. Thomas Hobbes (1588–1679), English philosopher.
4. Popular name for bus going to the cemetery.
5. Triangular structures crowning the fronts of
buildings.
6. (Men wearing) dress shirts with starched fronts.

30   It is like a solemn pact between the survivors.
     The mayor has signed it on behalf of the freemasonry.[7]
     The priest has sealed it on behalf of all the rest.
     Nothing more need be said, and it is better that way—

                              *

     The better for the widow, that she should not live in fear of surprise,
35   The better for the young man, that he should move at liberty between
          the armchairs,
     The better that these bent figures who flutter among the graves
     Tending the nightlights and replacing the chrysanthemums
     Are not ghosts,
     That they shall go home.
40   The bus is waiting, and on the upper terraces
     The workmen are dismantling the houses of the dead.

                              *

     But when so many had died, so many and at such speed,
     There were no cities waiting for the victims.
     They unscrewed the name-plates from the shattered doorways
45   And carried them away with the coffins.
     So the squares and parks were filled with the eloquence of young
          cemeteries:
     The smell of fresh earth, the improvised crosses
     And all the impossible directions in brass and enamel.

                              *

     "Doctor Gliedschirm, skin specialist, surgeries 14–16 hours or by
          appointment."
50   Professor Sargnagel was buried with four degrees, two associate
          memberships
     And instructions to tradesmen to use the back entrance.
     Your uncle's grave informed you that he lived on the third floor, left.
     You were asked please to ring, and he would come down in the lift[8]
     To which one needed a key . . .

                              *

55   Would come down, would ever come down
     With a smile like thin gruel, and never too much to say.
     How he shrank through the years.
     How you towered over him in the narrow cage.[9]
     How he shrinks now . . .

                              *

60   But come. Grief must have its term? Guilt too, then.
     And it seems there is no limit to the resourcefulness of recollection.
     So that a man might say and think:
     When the world was at its darkest,

7. Fraternity for mutual help, called "Free and   8. Elevator.
Accepted Masons" and having elaborate secret   9. Of the wire-screened elevator.
rituals.

When the black wings passed over the rooftops[1]
65 (And who can divine His purposes?) even then
There was always, always a fire in this hearth.
You see this cupboard? A priest-hole![2]
And in that lumber-room whole generations have been housed and fed.
Oh, if I were to begin, if I were to begin to tell you
70 The half, the quarter, a mere smattering of what we went through!

*

His wife nods, and a secret smile,
Like a breeze with enough strength to carry one dry leaf
Over two pavingstones, passes from chair to chair.
Even the enquirer is charmed.
75 He forgets to pursue the point.
It is not what he wants to know.
It is what he wants not to know.
It is not what they say.
It is what they do not say.

1982

God, A Poem

A nasty surprise in a sandwich,
A drawing-pin caught in your sock,
The limpest of shakes from a hand which
You'd thought would be firm as a rock,

5 A serious mistake in a nightie,
A grave disappointment all round
Is all that you'll get from th'Almighty,
Is all that you'll get underground.

Oh he *said*: "If you lay off the crumpet°   *women*
10 I'll see you alright in the end.
Just hang on until the last trumpet.
Have faith in me, chum—I'm your friend."

But if you remind him, he'll tell you:
"I'm sorry, I must have been pissed°—   *drunk*
15 Though your name rings a sort of a bell. You
Should have guessed that I do not exist.

"I didn't exist at Creation,
I didn't exist at the Flood,
And I won't be around for Salvation
20 To sort out the sheep from the cud—

---

1. Cf. Exodus 12.27: "It is the sacrifice of the Lord's passover, who passed over the houses of the children of Israel in Egypt, when he smote the Egyptians, and delivered our houses."

2. One of the hiding places, for Roman Catholic priests, built in sixteenth-century England after the banning of Catholicism.

"Or whatever the phrase is. The fact is
In soteriological° terms   *salvational*
I'm a crude existential malpractice
And you are a diet° of° worms.   *food / for*

25   "You're a nasty surprise in a sandwich.
You're a drawing-pin caught in my sock.
You're the limpest of shakes from a hand which
I'd have thought would be firm as a rock,

"You're a serious mistake in a nightie,
30   You're a grave disappointment all round—
That's all that you are," says th'Almighty,
"And that's all that you'll be underground."

                                                              1983

In Paris with You

Don't talk to me of love. I've had an earful
And I get tearful when I've downed a drink or two.
I'm one of your talking wounded.
I'm a hostage. I'm maroonded.
5   But I'm in Paris with you.

Yes I'm angry at the way I've been bamboozled
And resentful at the mess that I've been through.
I admit I'm on the rebound
And I don't care where are *we* bound.
10   I'm in Paris with you.

Do you mind if we do *not* go to the Louvre,
If we say sod³ off to sodding Notre Dame,
If we skip the Champs Elysées
And remain here in this sleazy

15   Old hotel room
Doing this and that
To what and whom
Learning who you are,
Learning what I am.

20   Don't talk to me of love. Let's talk of Paris,
The little bit of Paris in our view.
There's that crack across the ceiling
And the hotel walls are peeling
And I'm in Paris with you.

25   Don't talk to me of love. Let's talk of Paris.
I'm in Paris with the slightest thing you do.

---

3. English slang, similar to but milder than *bugger*.

I'm in Paris with your eyes, your mouth,
I'm in Paris with . . . all points south.
Am I embarrassing you?
30   I'm in Paris with you.

1993

CHARLES BERNSTEIN
b. 1950

Of Time and the Line

George Burns[1] likes to insist that he always
takes the straight lines; the cigar in his mouth
is a way of leaving space between the
lines for a laugh. He weaves lines together
5   by means of a picaresque narrative;
not so Hennie Youngman, whose lines are strict-
ly paratactic.[2] My father pushed a
line of ladies' dresses—not down the street
in a pushcart but upstairs in a fact'ry
10   office. My mother has been more concerned
with her hemline. Chairman Mao[3] put forward
Maoist lines, but that's been abandoned (most-
ly) for the East-West line of malarkey
so popular in these parts. The prestige
15   of the iambic line has recently
suffered decline, since it's no longer so
clear who "I" am, much less who *you* are. When
making a line, better be double sure
what you're lining in & what you're lining
20   out & which side of the line you're on; the
world is made up so (Adam didn't so much
name as delineate).[4] Every poem's got
a prosodic° lining, some of which will   *metrical*
unzip for summer wear. The lines of an
25   imaginary are inscribed on the
social flesh by the knifepoint of history.
Nowadays, you can often spot a work
of poetry by whether it's in lines
or no; if it's in prose, there's a good chance
30   it's a poem. While there is no lesson in
the line more useful than that of the pick-
et line, the line that has caused the most ad-
versity is the bloodline. In Russia

1. American comedian and actor (1896–1996),
always seen with a cigar.
2. Placed one after another without connectives,
as in "Take my wife. Please"—the most famous
one-liner delivered by Henry "Henny" Youngman
(1906–1998), American comedian.

3. Mao Tse-tung (1893–1976), Communist
leader of the People's Republic of China.
4. Cf. Genesis 1.19–20: ". . . and whatsoever
Adam called every living creature, that was the
name thereof."

everyone is worried about long lines;
35   back in the USA, it's strictly soup-
lines. "Take a chisel to write," but for an
actor a line's got to be cued. Or, as
they say in math, it takes two lines to make
an angle but only one lime to make
40   a Margarita.

1991

frequently unasked questions

I've a pile of memories on my other
drive, just give me the word and I'll
configure them for you. I've got
the pearl blue organizer and the banquette
5   with double lacerators, but nothing
floral like those diphthong transducers.
Was a time I'd arrive decked to the,
well that's no way to establish
contagious proximity. It poured several
10   days in a row so that when the blimp
finally appeared we were focussed
elsewise. Later, much later, got
to cash in my gold for those new
chits—look so shiny over there.

2001

why we ask you not to touch

Human emotions and cognition

leave a projective film over the poems

making them difficult to perceive.

Careful readers maintain a measured

5   distance from the works in order

to allow distortion-free comprehension

and to avoid damaging the meaning.

2001

this poem intentionally left blank

2001

ANNE CARSON
b. 1950

New Rule

A New Year's white morning of hard new ice.
High on the frozen branches I saw a squirrel jump and skid.
Is this scary? he seemed to say and glanced

    down at me, clutching his branch as it bobbed
5 in stiff recoil—or is it just that everything sounds wrong today?
    The branches

clinked.
He wiped his small cold lips with one hand.
Do you fear the same things as

10 I fear? I countered, looking up.
His empire of branches slid against the air.
The night of hooks?

The man blade left open on the stair?
Not enough spin on it, said my true love
15 when he left in our fifth year.

The squirrel bounced down a branch
and caught a peg of tears.
The way to hold on is

afterwords
20 so
clear.

2000

Sumptuous Destitution[1]

"Sumptuous destitution"
*Your opinion gives me a serious feeling: I would like to be what you
    deem me.*
           (Emily Dickinson letter 319 to Thomas Higginson)[2]
is a phrase
5 *You see my position is benighted.*
           (Emily Dickinson letter 268 to Thomas Higginson)

---

1. Phrase from poem (Franklin number 1404, Johnson number 1382) by the American poet Emily Dickinson (1830–1886; see pp. 1110–27), in which she remarks that joy "leaves a sumptuous Destitution- / Without a name."
2. All of the italicized quotations, except the last (line 23), are from letters written by Dickinson.

The mentor she addresses explicitly in many letters is the American literary critic Thomas Wentworth Higginson (1823–1911). Carson makes evident her belief that some of the letters here, whose undisclosed recipient Dickinson called "Master," were to Higginson. "Master" 's identity continues to be disputed by scholars.

scholars use
She was much too enigmatical a being for me to solve in an hour's
interview.
> (Thomas Higginson letter 342a to Emily Dickinson)

10 of female
God made me [Sir] Master—I didn't be—myself.
> (Emily Dickinson letter 233 to Thomas Higginson)

silence.
Rushing among my small heart—and pushing aside the blood—
15 > (Emily Dickinson letter 248 to Thomas Higginson)

Save what you can, Emily.
And when I try to organize—my little Force explodes—and leaves me
bare and charred.
> (Emily Dickinson letter 271 to Thomas Higginson)

Save every bit of thread.
20 *Have you a little chest to put the Alive in?*
> (Emily Dickinson letter 233 to Thomas Higginson)

One of them may be
By Cock, said Ophelia.[3]
> (Emily Dickinson letter 268 to Thomas Higginson)

25 the way out of here.

2000

The Beauty of the Husband

IV. HE SHE WE THEY YOU YOU YOU I HER SO PRONOUNS BEGIN THE DANCE CALLED WASHING WHOSE NAME DERIVES FROM AN ALCHEMICAL FACT THAT AFTER A SMALL STILLNESS THERE IS A SMALL STIR AFTER GREAT STILLNESS A GREAT STIR[4]

Rotate the husband and expose a hidden side. A letter he wrote from
Rio de Janeiro.[5]
Why Rio de Janeiro? is not a question worth asking.
We had been separated three years but not yet divorced.
He turned up anywhere.

5 Could be counted upon to lie if asked why. Otherwise could not be
counted upon.
When I say hidden
I mean funny.
A husband's tears are never hidden.

---

3. Allusion to Shakespeare, *Hamlet* 4.5.59–60, where the mad Ophelia, spurned by Hamlet, implies he has "tumbled" her: "Young men will do't if they come to't, / By Cock, they are to blame."

4. Section of Carson's book-length poem *The Beauty of the Husband: A Fictional Essay in 29 Tangos.*
5. Former capital city of Brazil.

Rio, April 23
10   *I don't understand this business of linguistics.*
Make me cry.
Don't make me cry.
I cry. You cry. We make ourselves cry.

Travelling foolish work spending money is what I make myself do.
15   *Carioca.*[6]
I'm in an apartment in Rio with some Brazilians arguing over
how to make a washing machine work.
In half an hour they'll forget about it and go out for dinner
leaving the machine on fire.
20   *They will come back from dinner to find their clothes burned up,*
slap each other on the head
and decide they in fact bought
a dryer which they don't know how to operate.
I have just gone to look at this machine. It is indeed a washer on
        fire.
25   *So now what happens. You and I.*

We have this deep sadness between us and its spells so habitual I
    can't
tell it from love.
You want a clean life I live a dirty one old story. Well.

30   *Not much use to you without you am I.*
I still love you.
You make me cry.
There are three things to notice about this letter.

First
35   its symmetry:
Make me cry. . . . You make me cry.
Second
its casuistry:
cosmological[7] motifs, fire and water, placed right before talk of love
40   to ground it in associations of primordial eros and strife.
Third no return address.
I cannot answer. He wants no answer. What does he want.
Four things.
But from the fourth I flee
45   chaste and craftily.

2001

---

6. Spanish term for resident of Rio de Janeiro.
7. Related to metaphysical speculation about the
nature of the universe. *Casuistry:* plausible but
invalid reasoning.

DANA GIOIA
b. 1950

Prayer

Echo of the clocktower, footstep
in the alleyway, sweep
of the wind sifting the leaves.

Jeweller of the spiderweb, connoisseur
5   of autumn's opulence, blade of lightning
harvesting the sky.

Keeper of the small gate, choreographer
of entrances and exits, midnight
whisper travelling the wires.

10   Seducer, healer, deity or thief,
I will see you soon enough—
in the shadow of the rainfall,

in the brief violet darkening a sunset—
but until then I pray watch over him
15   as a mountain guards its covert ore

and the harsh falcon its flightless young.

1991

The Next Poem

How much better it seems now
than when it is finally done—
the unforgettable first line,
the cunning way the stanzas run.

5   The rhymes soft-spoken and suggestive
are barely audible at first,
an appetite not yet acknowledged
like the inkling of a thirst.

While gradually the form appears
10 as each line is coaxed aloud—
the architecture of a room
seen from the middle of a crowd.

The music that of common speech
but slanted so that each detail
15 sounds unexpected as a sharp
inserted in a simple scale.

No jumble box of imagery
dumped glumly in the reader's lap
or elegantly packaged junk
20   the unsuspecting must unwrap.

But words that could direct a friend
precisely to an unknown place,
those few unshakeable details
that no confusion can erase.

25   And the real subject left unspoken
but unmistakable to those
who don't expect a jungle parrot
in the black and white of prose.

How much better it seems now
30   than when it is finally written.
How hungrily one waits to feel
the bright lure seized, the old hook bitten.

1991

NICHOLAS CHRISTOPHER
b. 1951

The Palm Reader

In her storefront living room—
overstuffed couch, oversized TV, a bowl of mints
on the Plexiglas coffee table—
she watches *Edge of Night*[1] and files her nails.
5   The paraphernalia pertaining to her trade
crowd a shelf beneath the large green hand
painted onto the window: a Tarot deck,
coins and obelisks, a chalky bust with numbered
phrenological divisions on the skull.
10   Through the beaded curtain in the rear
some clues emerge as to *her* life:
two children trading insults,
a man calling out, "Eggs!"
as a frying pan clatters into a sink,
15   a dog running by with a wig in his mouth.
She herself is plump, heavily made up,
wearing a red dress and a shawl imprinted
with the signs of the zodiac.
A gold pyramid hangs from her throat

---

1. A soap opera.

20   and she has combed glittering
        silver stars through her black hair.
        From a plush rocker she beckons you,
        at the window, to a straight-back chair
        in which she will divine (according to the sign
25   on the door) "the roads into your future,
        and helpful information from the Beyond."
        Though the latter, especially, tempts
        you powerfully, you decline,
        and she shrugs with a rueful smile.
30   And because it is close to noon,
        and the sidewalk is empty, as you cross
        the street she closes up for lunch.
        Her living room in which matters of life
        and death—of human destiny laid bare—
35   suddenly reverts to its other function:
        husband slumped on the couch clutching a beer,
        children sopping bread across paper plates,
        the dog sprawled under the table.
        All of them watching *Edge of Night* now.
40   The fate of whose characters, which keeps
        a faithful public tuning in day after day,
        year after year, is presumably known
        to this woman, lighting a cigarette
        and surveying that room, open to all passersby
45   yet utterly remote, as inescapable
        as the future itself, that jumps out
        at her from every stranger's hand.

                                                1995

Far from Home

        A broken-down hotel on an inhospitable sea,
        and behind it, a field of thorns in which
        a man wearing white gloves is digging a hole
        with the exact proportions of a grave.

5   Down the hall, the young chambermaid
        is staring into a basin full of red water.
        Her hair is white and her hands are wrinkled.
        A shark tooth dangles from her ear.

        In the evening she leaves a tray by my door:
10   a glass, a carafe of water, and a bottle
        containing liquor that swirls like mist.
        Mornings she brings bitter tea and a map.

        Always the same map—not of the island
        we're on, but of one I left long ago.

15 (If it were this island, I wouldn't know,
    having never ventured from the hotel.)

    There is a bowl of black seashells by my bed.
    The maps—thirteen of them—are stacked
    between the lamp that flickers like a star
20 and the quartz lions veined with light.

    The clerk at the front desk could be a statue.
    His dark glasses reflect the bare lobby,
    its leafless plants and shuttered windows.
    At his fingertips is a tumbler filled with dust.

25 The day I check out, the other guests line
    the balcony, wrapped in sheets, speaking
    a language I've never heard—sibilant as
    the sea, but with no two words sounding alike.

    The man in white gloves appears, to carry
30 my suitcase, and pauses before a mirror
    in which I see, not his image, but towering
    iron waves, rising to mesh with an iron sky.

                                                    1995

JORIE GRAHAM
b. 1951

The Geese

Today as I hang out the wash I see them again, a code
as urgent as elegant,
tapering with goals.
For days they have been crossing. We live beneath these geese

5   as if beneath the passage of time, or a most perfect heading.
    Sometimes I fear their relevance.
    Closest at hand,
    between the lines,

    the spiders imitate the paths the geese won't stray from,
10 imitate them endlessly to no avail:
    things will not remain connected,
    will not heal,

    and the world thickens with texture instead of history,
    texture instead of place.
15 Yet the small fear of the spiders
    binds and binds

the pins to the lines, the lines to the eaves, to the pincushion bush,
as if, at any time, things could fall further apart[1]
and nothing could help them
20   recover their meaning. And if these spiders had their way,

chainlink over the visible world,
would we be in or out? I turn to go back in.
There is a feeling the body gives the mind
of having missed something, a bedrock poverty, like falling

25   without the sense that you are passing through one world,
that you could reach another
anytime. Instead the real
is crossing you,

your body an arrival
30   you know is false but can't outrun. And somewhere in between
these geese forever entering and
these spiders turning back,

this astonishing delay, the everyday, takes place.

1980

At Luca Signorelli's[2] Resurrection of the Body

See how they hurry
        to enter
their bodies,
        these spirits.
5   Is it better, flesh,
        that they

should hurry so?
        From above
the green-winged angels
10   blare down
trumpets and light. But
        they don't care,

they hurry to congregate,
        they hurry
15   into speech, until
        it's a marketplace,
it is humanity. But still
        we wonder

---

1. Cf. W. B. Yeats, "The Second Coming," line 3: "Things fall apart; the centre cannot hold" (p. 1196).   2. Italian painter (ca. 1450–1523), whose series on the Last Judgment is displayed in the gothic cathedral of Orvieto, Italy.

in the chancel[3]
20   of the dark cathedral,
is it better, back?
    The artist
has tried to make it so: each tendon
    they press

25 to re-enter
    is perfect. But is it
perfection
    they're after,
pulling themselves up
30   through the soil

into the weightedness, the color,
    into the eye
of the painter? Outside
    it is 1500,
35 all round the cathedral
    streets hurry to open

through the wild
    silver grasses. . . .
The men and women
40   on the cathedral wall
do not know how,
    having come this far,

to stop their
    hurrying. They amble off
45 in groups, in
    couples. Soon
some are clothed, there is
    distance, there is

perspective. Standing below them
50   in the church
in Orvieto, how can we
    tell them
to be stern and brazen
    and slow,

55 that there is no
    entrance,
only entering. They keep on
    arriving.
wanting names,
60   wanting

happiness. In his studio
    Luca Signorelli

3. Part of a church containing the altar.

in the name of God
and Science
65   and the believable
broke into the body

studying arrival.
But the wall
of the flesh
70   opens endlessly,
its vanishing point so deep
and receding

we have yet to find it,
to have it
75   stop us. So he cut
deeper,
graduating slowly
from the symbolic

to the beautiful. How far
80   is true?
When his one son
died violently,
he had the body brought to him
and laid it

85   on the drawing-table,
and stood
at a certain distance
awaiting the best
possible light, the best depth
90   of day,

then with beauty and care
and technique
and judgment, cut into
shadow, cut
95   into bone and sinew and every
pocket

in which the cold light
pooled.
It took him days,
100   that deep
caress, cutting,
unfastening,

until his mind
could climb into
105 the open flesh and
mend itself.

1993

The Surface

It has a hole in it. Not only where I
                  concentrate.
The river still ribboning, twisting up,
               into its re-
5   arrangements, chill enlightenments, tight-knotted
                           quickenings
and loosenings—whispered messages dissolving
                      the messengers—
the river still glinting-up into its handfuls, heapings,
10   glassy
forgettings under the river of
my attention—
and the river of my attention laying itself down—
                      bending,
15   reassembling—over the quick leaving-offs and windy
                      obstacles—
and the surface rippling under the wind's attention—
rippling over the accumulations, the slowed-down drifting
                      permanences
20   of the cold
bed.
I say *iridescent* and I look down.
The leaves very still as they are carried.

                                          1993

PAUL MULDOON
b. 1951

Why Brownlee Left

Why Brownlee left, and where he went,
Is a mystery even now.
For if a man should have been content
It was him; two acres of barley,
5   One of potatoes, four bullocks,
A milker, a slated farmhouse.
He was last seen going out to plough
On a March morning, bright and early.

By noon Brownlee was famous;
10   They had found all abandoned, with
The last rig[1] unbroken, his pair of black

---

1. Ridge between a pair of plow furrows.

Horses, like man and wife,
Shifting their weight from foot to
Foot, and gazing into the future.

1980

Meeting the British[2]

We met the British in the dead of winter.
The sky was lavender

and the snow lavender-blue.
I could hear, far below,

5   the sound of two streams coming together
(both were frozen over)

and, no less strange,
myself calling out in French

across that forest-
10   clearing. Neither General Jeffrey Amherst

nor Colonel Henry Bouquet[3]
could stomach our willow-tobacco.

As for the unusual
scent when the Colonel shook out his hand-

15   kerchief: *C'est la lavande,*
une fleur mauve comme le ciel.[4]

They gave us six fishhooks
and two blankets embroidered with smallpox.

1987

Milkweed and Monarch

As he knelt by the grave of his mother and father
the taste of dill, or tarragon—
he could barely tell one from the other—

---

2. I.e., the British forces, met by Native Americans who were allied with France during the French and Indian War (1754–63).
3. British officer (1719–1766), who with the commander-in-chief, Amherst (1717–1797), devised

and apparently executed a plan to spread smallpox among the Native Americans through infected blankets.
4. It is lavender, a flower as mauve as the sky (French).

filled his mouth. It seemed as if he might smother.
5   Why should he be stricken
with grief, not for his mother and father,

but a woman slinking from the fur of a sea-otter
in Portland, Maine, or, yes, Portland, Oregon—
he could barely tell one from the other—

10   and why should he now savour
the tang of her, her little pickled gherkin,
as he knelt by the grave of his mother and father?

*

He looked about. He remembered her palaver°   *idle talk*
on how both earth and sky would darken—
15   "You could barely tell one from the other—"

while the Monarch butterflies passed over
in their milkweed-hunger: "A wing-beat, some reckon,
may trigger off the mother and father

of all storms, striking your Irish Cliffs of Moher
20   with the force of a hurricane."
Then: "Milkweed and Monarch 'invented' each other."

*

He looked about. Cow's-parsley in a samovar.[5]
He'd mistaken his mother's name, "Regan", for "Anger":

as he knelt by the grave of his mother and father
25   he could barely tell one from the other.

1994

Third Epistle to Timothy[6]

You made some mistake when you intended to favor me with some
of the new valuable grass seed . . . for what you gave me . . . proves
mere timothy.

A letter from Benjamin Franklin to Jared Eliot,[7]
July 16th, 1747

I

Midnight. June, 1923. Not a stir except for the brough and brouhaha[8]
surrounding the taper or link[9]

---

5. Russian tea urn.
6. St. Paul writes two epistles to Timothy (Christian Scriptures books 1 Timothy and 2 Timothy). With a poem that often quotes St. Paul, Muldoon provides a third.
7. Early American minister, physician, and scientist (1685–1763). *Timothy:* a native British grass, introduced during the eighteenth century into North America.
8. Commotion. *Brough:* luminous ring around the moon.
9. A torch made of flax fiber and pitch (a resinous substance).

in which a louse
flares up and a shadow, my da's,
5   clatters against a wall of the six-by-eight-by-six-foot room
he sleeps in, eleven years old, a servant-boy at Hardy's of Carnteel.[1]
There's a boot-polish lid filled with turps or
paraffin oil
under each cast-iron bed-leg, a little barrier
10   against bed-bugs under each bed-foot.

II

That knocking's the knocking against their stalls of a team
of six black Clydesdales[2] mined in Coalisland
he's only just helped to unhitch from the cumbersome
star of a hay-rake. Decently and in order[3]
15   he brought each whitewashed nose
to its nosebag of corn, to its galvanized bucket.
One of the six black Clydesdale mares
he helped all day to hitch and unhitch
was showing, on the near hock, what might be a bud of farcy[4]
20   picked up, no doubt, while on loan to Wesley Cummins.

III

"Decently and in order," Cummins would proclaim, "let all
      Inniskillings[5]
be done." A week ago my da helped him limber° up   hook
the team to a mowing machine as if to a gun carriage. "For no
      Dragoon°   cavalry member
can function without his measure of char."°   tea
25   He patted his belly-band. "A measure, that is, against dysentery."
This was my da's signal to rush
into the deep shade of the hedge to fetch such little tea as might
      remain
in the tea urn. "Man does not live," Cummins would snort, "only by
      scraps
of wheaten farls and tea dregs.[6]
30   You watch your step or I'll see you're shipped back to Killeter."[7]

IV

"Killeeshill," my da says, "I'm from Killeeshill." Along the cast-iron
rainbow of his bed-end
comes a line
of chafers° or cheeselips° that have scaled   beetles / cockchafers, wood lice
      the bed-legs

---

1. Parish in County Tyrone, Northern Ireland, as is Coalisland (line 12).
2. A breed of horse used on farms.
3. Cf. St. Paul's First Epistle to the Corinthians (1 Corinthians) 14.40: "Let all things be done decently and in order."
4. A disease that causes small tumors known as farcy buds. *Hock:* the joint between the knee and the fetlock on a horse.
5. Named after the town in County Fermanagh that it was established to defend, the Royal Inniskilling Fusiliers was a regiment of the British Army. Cummins rephrases St. Paul's "Let all things be done."
6. Cf. Deuteronomy 8.3: "man doth not live by bread only." *Farls:* small Scottish cakes or biscuits.
7. Village in County Tyrone, as is Killeeshill (line 31).

35 despite the boot-polish lids. Eleven years of age. A servant-boy
on the point of falling asleep. The reek of paraffin
or the pinewoods reek
of turpentine
good against roundworm in horses. That knocking against their stalls
40 of six Clydesdales, each standing at sixteen hands.

V

Building hay even now, even now drawing level with the team's
    headbrass,[8]
buoyed up by nothing more than the ballast
of hay—meadow cat's-tail, lucerne,[9] the leaf upon trodden leaf
of white clover and red—
45 drawing level now with the taper-blooms of a horse chestnut.
Already light in the head.
"Though you speak, young Muldoon . . ." Cummins calls up from
    trimming the skirt
of the haycock,° "though you speak with the tongue   *small pile of hay*
of an angel,[1] I see you for what you are . . . Malevolent.
50 Not only a member of the church malignant[2] but a *malevolent* spirit."

VI

Even now borne aloft by bearing down on lap-cocks and shake-cocks[3]
from under one of which a ruddy face
suddenly twists and turns upwards as if itself carried
on a pitchfork and, meeting its gaze,
55 he sees himself, a servant-boy still, still ten or eleven,
breathing upon a Clydesdale's near hock and finding a farcy-bud
like a tiny glow in a strut° of charcoal.   *stick*
"I see you," Cummins points at him with the pitchfork, "you little
    by-blow,°   *bastard*
I see you casting your spells, your sorceries,
60 I see you coming as a thief in the night[4] to stab us in the back."

VII

A year since they kidnapped Anketell Moutray from his home at
    Favour Royal,[5]
dragging him, blindfolded, the length of his own gravel path,
eighty years old, the Orange county grand master.[6] Four A-Specials[7]
    shot on a train

8. A team of horses pulling a plow, the head brass being the ornamental brass plaque attached to their bridle. Cf. Edward Thomas, "As the team's head brass" (p. 1255).
9. Plant resembling clover and cultivated for fodder. *Meadow cat's-tail:* another name for timothy grass in Britain and Ireland.
1. Cf. St. Paul's First Epistle to the Corinthians 13.1: "Though I speak with the tongues of men and of angels, and have not charity, I am become as sounding brass, or a tinkling cymbal."
2. Cummins attacks the servant boy's Roman Catholicism, thereby adding the "church malignant" to Catholicism's distinction between the church triumphant (souls in heaven), the church

suffering (souls in purgatory), and the church militant (faithful on Earth).
3. Like lap-cocks, elaborate shapes made of hay.
4. Cf. St. Paul's First Epistle to the Thessalonians 5.2: "For yourselves know perfectly that the day of the Lord so cometh as a thief in the night."
5. Demesne (estate) in County Tyrone.
6. The Orange order is a Protestant fraternity founded in 1795. Often accused of sectarian bigotry, the order and its members have been the target of violent attacks.
7. As a response to sectarian violence, the British government established the Ulster Special Constabulary in 1920. Overwhelmingly Protestant, this new force was divided into three sections: the

in Clones. The Clogher valley[8]
65   a blaze of flax-mills and hay-sheds. Memories of the Land League.
      Davitt and Biggar.[9]
      Breaking the boycott at Lough Mask.[1]
      The Land Leaguers beaten
      at the second battle of Saintfield.[2] It shall be revealed . . . [3]
      A year since they cut out the clapper° of a collabor . . . a   *tongue*
      collabor . . .
70   a collaborator from Maguiresbridge.[4]

VIII

      That knocking's the team's near-distant knocking on wood
      while my da breathes upon
      the blue-yellow flame on a fetlock, on a deep-feathered pastern[5]
      of one of six black Shires° . . . "Because it shall be   *large farm horses*
      revealed by fire,"
75   Cummins's last pitchfork is laden
      with thistles, "as the sparks fly upward
      man is born unto trouble.[6] For the tongue may yet be cut
      from an angel." The line of cheeselips and chafers
      along the bed-end. "Just wait till you come back down and I get a
      hold
80   of you, young Muldoon . . . We'll see what spells you'll cast."

IX

      For an instant it seems no one else might scale
      such a parapet of meadow cat's-tail, lucerne, red and white clovers,
      not even the line of chafers and cheeselips
      that overthrow as they undermine
85   when, light in the head, unsteady on his pegs as Anketell Moutray,
      he squints through a blindfold of clegs°   *horseflies*
      from his grass-capped, thistle-strewn vantage point,
      the point where two hay-ropes cross,

A-Specials were full-time and paid as if regular policemen; the B-Specials were part-time and unpaid; and the C-Specials were a reserve force, also unpaid.

8. Rural area in County Tyrone, the scene of agrarian unrest. *Clones:* town in County Monaghan, Northern Ireland.

9. Michael Davitt (1846–1906) helped found the Land League, an organization of Irish tenant farmers founded in 1879 to resist the cruelties of landlords. Its campaign prompted the passing, in 1881, of a Land Act that provided a commission to fix fair rents. Joseph Biggar (1828–1890) was the Land League's treasurer.

1. In 1880, at Lough Mask in County Mayo, now part of the Irish Republic, Captain Charles Boycott, acting as agent for the landowner Lord Erne, so angered the tenant farmers that he was ostracized by all his employees (hence the modern term *boycott*). English soldiers were sent in to perform the household and agricultural tasks, but after poor treatment by Boycott they eventually sided with the tenants.

2. Saintfield in County Down, Northern Ireland, was the site of a battle in 1798 between the British Army and a group of United Irishmen fighting for independence. In 1880, Michael Davitt addressed an audience at Saintfield on the subject of land reform, calling for tenants to become proprietors.

3. Cf. St. Paul's First Epistle to the Corinthians 3.13: "Every man's work shall be made manifest: for the day shall declare it, because it shall be revealed by fire; and the fire shall try every man's work what it is."

4. Parish in County Fermanagh, Northern Ireland. *Collabor:* Muldoon plays on the Irish *clabaire*, meaning an open-mouthed person.

5. Part of a horse's foot. *Fetlock:* part of a horse's leg.

6. Cf. Job 5.7: "Yet man is born unto trouble, as the sparks fly upward."

where Cummins and his crew have left him, in a straw hat with a
    fraying brim,
90 while they've moved on to mark out the next haycock.

X

That next haycock already summoning itself from windrow[7] after
    wind-weary windrow
while yet another brings itself to mind in the acrid stink
of turpentine. There the image of Lizzie,
Hardy's last servant-girl, reaches out from her dais°   *platform*
95 of salt hay, stretches out an unsunburned arm
half in bestowal, half beseechingly, then turns away to appeal
to all that spirit-troop
of hay-treaders as far as the eye can see, the coil on coil
of hay from which, in the taper's mild uproar,
100 they float out across the dark face of the earth, an earth without
    form, and void.[8]

1998

RITA DOVE
b. 1952

Parsley[1]

1. The Cane[2] Fields

    There is a parrot imitating spring
    in the palace, its feathers parsley green.
    Out of the swamp the cane appears

    to haunt us, and we cut it down. El General
5   searches for a word; he is all the world
    there is. Like a parrot imitating spring,

    we lie down screaming as rain punches through
    and we come up green. We cannot speak an R—
    out of the swamp, the cane appears

10   and then the mountain we call in whispers *Katalina*.[3]
    The children gnaw their teeth to arrowheads.
    There is a parrot imitating spring.

7. A row in which mown grass or hay is laid, to be dried by the wind before being made into heaps or cocks.
8. Cf. Genesis 1.1–2: "In the beginning God created the heaven and the earth. And the earth was without form, and void; and darkness was upon the face of the deep."
1. "On October 2, 1937, Rafael Trujillo (1891–

1961), dictator of the Dominican Republic, ordered 20,000 blacks killed because they could not pronounce the letter r in *perejil*, the Spanish word for parsley" [Dove's note].
2. Sugar cane.
3. I.e., Katarina (since the people "cannot speak an R").

El General has found his word: *perejil.*
Who says it, lives. He laughs, teeth shining
15   out of the swamp. The cane appears

in our dreams, lashed by wind and streaming.
And we lie down. For every drop of blood
there is a parrot imitating spring.
Out of the swamp the cane appears.

2. *The Palace*

20   The word the general's chosen is parsley.
It is fall, when thoughts turn
to love and death; the general thinks
of his mother, how she died in the fall
and he planted her walking cane at the grave
25   and it flowered, each spring stolidly forming
four-star blossoms. The general

pulls on his boots, he stomps to
her room in the palace, the one without
curtains, the one with a parrot
30   in a brass ring. As he paces he wonders
Who can I kill today. And for a moment
the little knot of screams
is still. The parrot, who has traveled

all the way from Australia in an ivory
35   cage, is, coy as a widow, practising
spring. Ever since the morning
his mother collapsed in the kitchen
while baking skull-shaped candies
for the Day of the Dead,[4] the general
40   has hated sweets. He orders pastries
brought up for the bird; they arrive

dusted with sugar on a bed of lace.
The knot in his throat starts to twitch;
he sees his boots the first day in battle
45   splashed with mud and urine
as a soldier falls at his feet amazed—
how stupid he looked!—at the sound
of artillery. *I never thought it would sing*
the soldier said, and died. Now

50   the general sees the fields of sugar
cane, lashed by rain and streaming.
He sees his mother's smile, the teeth

---

4. All Souls' Day, November 2. An Aztec festival
for the spirits of the dead that coincides with the
Catholic calendar. In Latin America and the Carib-
bean, friends and relatives of the dead process into
cemeteries, bearing candles, flowers, and food, all
of which may be shaped to resemble symbols of
death, such as skulls or coffins.

gnawed to arrowheads. He hears
the Haitians sing without R's
55   as they swing the great machetes:
Katalina, they sing, *Katalina,*

mi madle, mi amol en muelte.[5] God knows
his mother was no stupid woman; she
could roll an R like a queen. Even
60   a parrot can roll an R! In the bare room
the bright feathers arch in a parody
of greenery, as the last pale crumbs
disappear under the blackened tongue. Someone

calls out his name in a voice
65   so like his mother's, a startled tear
splashes the tip of his right boot.
My mother, my love in death.
The general remembers the tiny green sprigs
men of his village wore in their capes
70   to honor the birth of a son. He will
order many, this time, to be killed

for a single, beautiful word.

1983

Dusting[6]

Every day a wilderness—no
shade in sight. Beulah
patient among knicknacks,
the solarium a rage
5   of light, a grainstorm
as her gray cloth brings
dark wood to life.

Under her hand scrolls
and crests gleam
10   darker still. What
was his name, that
silly boy at the fair with
the rifle booth? And his kiss and
the clear bowl with one bright
15   fish, rippling
wound!

Not Michael—
something finer. Each dust
stroke a deep breath and
20   the canary in bloom.
Wavery memory: home
from a dance, the front door
blown open and the parlor
in snow, she rushed
25   the bowl to the stove, watched
as the locket of ice
dissolved and he
swam free.

That was years before
30   Father gave her up
with her name, years before
her name grew to mean
Promise, then
Desert-in-Peace.[7]
35   Long before the shadow and
sun's accomplice, the tree.

Maurice.

1986

The Bistro Styx[8]

She was thinner, with a mannered gauntness
as she paused just inside the double
glass doors to survey the room, silvery cape
billowing dramatically behind her. *What's this,*

5   I thought, lifting a hand until
she nodded and started across the parquet;
that's when I saw she was dressed all in gray,
from a kittenish cashmere skirt and cowl

down to the graphite signature of her shoes.
10   "Sorry I'm late," she panted, though
she wasn't, sliding into the chair, her cape

7. *Beulah* means "married, possessed" in Hebrew. In the Bible, it refers to the promised land.
8. Part of a sonnet sequence in *Mother Love,* a book-length modernization of the Greek myth of Persephone, the girl who is abducted to the underworld by Hades, and whose mother, Demeter, goddess of agriculture, is so grief-stricken she allows the crops to wither. "Before returning to the surface, the girl eats a few pomegranate seeds, not realizing that anyone who partakes of the food of the dead cannot be wholly restored to the living" [Dove's note]. Persephone spends half of each year with Hades thereafter, and her return to Earth heralds spring. In Dove's version, she resurfaces in modern Paris, in a restaurant named for the Styx, the river in the underworld over which dead souls were ferried.

tossed off in a shudder of brushed steel.
We kissed. Then I leaned back to peruse
my blighted child, this wary aristocratic mole.

15 "How's business?" I asked, and hazarded
a motherly smile to keep from crying out:
Are you content to conduct your life
as a cliché and, what's worse,

an anachronism, the brooding artist's demimonde?
20 Near the rue Princesse[9] they had opened
a gallery *cum*° souvenir shop which featured   *with*
fuzzy off-color Monets[1] next to his acrylics, no doubt,

plus bearded African drums and the occasional miniature
gargoyle from Notre Dame[2] the Great Artist had
25 carved at breakfast with a pocket knife.

"Tourists love us. The Parisians, of course"—
she blushed—"are amused, though not without
a certain admiration . . ."
                    The Chateaubriand[3]

arrived on a bone-white plate, smug and absolute
30 in its fragrant crust, a black plug steaming
like the heart plucked from the chest of a worthy enemy;
one touch with her fork sent pink juices streaming.

"Admiration for what?" Wine, a bloody
Pinot Noir, brought color to her cheeks. "Why,
35 the aplomb with which we've managed
to support our Art"—meaning he'd convinced

her to pose nude for his appalling canvases,
faintly futuristic landscapes strewn
with carwrecks and bodies being chewed

40 by rabid cocker spaniels. "I'd like to come by
the studio," I ventured, "and see the new stuff."
"Yes, if you wish . . ." A delicate rebuff

before the warning: "He dresses all
in black now. Me, he drapes in blues and carmine—
45 and even though I think it's kinda cute,
in company I tend toward more muted shades."

She paused and had the grace
to drop her eyes. She did look ravishing,
spookily insubstantial, a lipstick ghost on tissue,
50 or as if one stood on a fifth-floor terrace

9. Street in Paris.
1. Reproductions of work by the French painter
Claude Monet (1840–1926).

2. Notre Dame de Paris, the cathedral.
3. Elegant beef dish.

peering through a fringe of rain at Paris'
dreaming chimney pots, each sooty issue
wobbling skyward in an ecstatic oracular spiral.

"And he never thinks of food. I wish
55 I didn't have to plead with him to eat. . . ." Fruit
and cheese appeared, arrayed on leaf-green dishes.

I stuck with café crème. "This Camembert's
so ripe," she joked, "it's practically grown hair,"
mucking a golden glob complete with parsley sprig
60 onto a heel of bread. Nothing seemed to fill

her up: She swallowed, sliced into a pear,
speared each tear-shaped lavaliere⁴
and popped the dripping mess into her pretty mouth.
Nowhere the bright tufted fields, weighted

65 vines and sun poured down out of the south.
"But are you happy?" Fearing, I whispered it
quickly. "What? You know, Mother"—

she bit into the starry rose of a fig—
"one really should try the fruit here."
70 *I've lost her,* I thought, and called for the bill.

1995

DANIEL HALL
b. 1952

Love-Letter-Burning

The archivist in us shudders at such cold-
blooded destruction of the word, but since
we're only human, we commit our sins
to the flames. Sauve qui peut;¹ fear makes us bold.

5 Tanka² was bolder: when the weather turned
from fair to frigid, he saw his way clear
to build a sacrificial fire
in which a priceless temple Buddha burned.

---

4. Jeweled pendant necklace; here, the jewel itself.
1. Save (yourself) if you can (French); also, a panic or stampede.
2. The Zen master Tan-hsai, or Tanka (738–824). "It was so cold at the temple . . . that he took one of the three images from the altar and burned it for firewood. When the horrified chief monk asked him . . . how he dared profane the sacred image of the Buddha, he replied that he was burning it to obtain its *sarira* (an indestructible substance believed to reside in the ashes of holy men)" [M. Conrad Hyers, *Zen and the Comic Spirit*]. Not finding *sarira* in one wooden Buddha, Tanka proposed burning the other two as well.

(The pretext? Simple: what he sought
10   was legendary Essence in the ash.
But if it shows up only in the flesh—?
He grinned and said, Let's burn the lot!)

Believers in the afterlife perform
this purifying rite. At last
15   a match is struck: it's done. The past
will shed some light, but never keep us warm.

1990

Mangosteens

These are the absolute top of the line,
I was telling him, they even surpass
the Jiangsu peach and the McIntosh°   *apple*
for lusciousness and subtlety. . . . (He frowned:
5   McIntosh. How spelling.) We were eating
our way through another kilogram
of mangosteens, for which we'd both fallen
hard. I'd read that Queen Victoria[3]
(no voluptuary) once offered a reward
10   for an edible mangosteen: I don't know
how much, or whether it was ever claimed.
(But not enough, I'd guess, and no, I hope.)
Each thick skin yields to a counter-twist,
splits like rotted leather. Inside, snug
15   as a brain in its cranium, half a dozen
plump white segments, all but dry, part
to the tip of the tongue like lips—they *taste*
like lips, before they're bitten, a saltiness
washed utterly away; crushed, they release
20   a flood of unfathomable sweetness,
gone in a trice. He lay
near sleep, sunk back against a slope
of heaped-up bedding, stroked slantwise by fingers
of afternoon sun. McIntosh, he said again,
25   still chewing. I'd also been reading *The Spoils
of Poynton*,[4] so slowly the plot seemed to unfold
in real-time. " 'Things' were of course
the sum of the world," James tosses out
in that mock-assertive, contradiction-baffling
30   way he has, quotation marks gripped like a tweezers

3. Queen of Great Britain from 1837 to 1901.
4. Novel by the British (American-born) writer Henry James (1843–1916). Mrs. Gereth, a recently widowed collector of beautiful things, is faced with giving up her house, Poynton, to her son, who has inherited it. She attempts unsuccessfully to make a match between him and an intense young woman friend. When Poynton is destroyed by fire, the cause is not given; here, Hall suspects Mrs. Gereth.

lest he soil his hands on *things,*
as if the only things that mattered
were that homage be paid to English widowhood,
or whether another of his young virgins
35 would ever marry. (She wouldn't, but she would,
before the novel closed, endure one shattering
embrace, a consummation.) I spent the day
sleepwalking the halls of museums, a vessel
trembling at the lip. Lunch was a packet
40 of rice cakes and an apple in a garden
famed for its beauty, and deemed beautiful
for what had been taken away. I can still hear it,
still *taste* it, his quick gasp of astonishment
caught in my own mouth. I can feel that house
45 going up with a shudder, a clockwise funnel
howling to the heavens, while the things of her world
explode or melt or shrivel to ash
in the ecstatic emptying. The old woman set the fire
herself, she must have, she had to. His letter,
50 tattooed with postmarks, was waiting for me
back at the ryokan,[5] had overtaken me
at last, half in Chinese, half in hard-won
English, purer than I will ever write—

    Please don't give up me in tomorrow

55 The skin was bitter. It stained the tongue.

    I want with you more time

1993   1996

SEAN O'BRIEN
b. 1952

Cousin Coat

You are my secret coat. You're never dry.
You wear the weight and stink of black canals.
Malodorous companion, we know why
It's taken me so long to see we're pals,
5 To learn why my acquaintance never sniff
Or send me notes to say I stink of stiff.°   *the dead*

But you don't talk, historical bespoke.°   *made-to-order*
You must be worn, be intimate as skin,
And though I never lived what you invoke,

5. Inn (Japanese).

10   At birth I was already buttoned in.
      Your clammy itch became my atmosphere,
      An air made half of anger, half of fear.

      And what you are is what I tried to shed
      In libraries with Donne and Henry James.[1]
15   You're here to bear a message from the dead
      Whose history's dishonoured with their names.
      You mean the North, the poor, and troopers sent
      To shoot down those who showed their discontent.[2]

      No comfort there for comfy meliorists[3]
20   Grown weepy over Jarrow[4] photographs.
      No comfort when the poor the state enlists
      Parade before their fathers' cenotaphs.°   *war memorials*
      No comfort when the strikers all go back
      To see which twenty thousand get the sack.

25   Be with me when they cauterize° the facts.   *deaden*
      Be with me to the bottom of the page,
      Insisting on what history exacts.
      Be memory, be conscience, will and rage,
      And keep me cold and honest, cousin coat,
30   So if I lie, I'll know you're at my throat.

                                                    1987

Welcome, Major Poet!

      We have sat here in too many poetry readings
      Wearing the liberal rictus° and cursing our folly,   *gaping mouth*
      Watching the lightbulbs die and the curtains rot
      And the last flies departing for Scunthorpe.[5]
5   Forgive us. We know all about you.
      Autumn gives way to midwinter once more,
      As states collapse, as hemlines rise, as we miss both,
      And just as our teeth fall discreetly into our handkerchiefs,
      Slowly the bones of our co-tormentees will emerge
10   Through their skins. QED and *hic jacent*.[6]
      Except we are seated bolt upright on customized
      "Chairs" of the torturers' school. Here it comes,
      Any century now, the dread declaration:
      And next I shall read something longer. Please
15   Rip out our nails and accept your applause!

1. English (American-born) novelist (1843–
1916). John Donne (1572–1631; see pp. 293–
322), English poet.
2. Possibly an allusion to the Peterloo Massacre
(1819); see note 8, p. 872.
3. Those who believe the world may be made bet-
ter by human effort.
4. Seaport in southeast England, from which, in
the economic depression and high unemployment
of the 1930s, a famous series of "hunger marches"
headed for London.
5. Industrial town in northeast England. *Flies:*
stagecoach.
6. Here lies (Latin); first words of an epitaph.
QED: quod erat demonstrandum; as has been dem-
onstrated (Latin).

Stretch-limo back to the Ritz and ring home:
Bore the arse off your nearest and dearest instead,
Supposing they haven't divorced you already
Or selfishly put themselves under a train.
20 Please call them, at length and at public expense.
Send flunkies for cold Stolichnaya,° an ox   *brand of vodka*
Or an acre of coke and a thousand-quid°   *costing a thousand pounds*
    hooker.
Why not make it three, in a chariot
Flown to your penthouse by eunuchs° on leopards?   *harem attendants*
25 Whatever you like, only spare us the details of when
You were struck by your kinship with Dante and Vergil.[7]
And don't feel obliged to remind us just now
What it was Robert Lowell[8] appeared to be saying—
You'd read him the poem you mean to read us—
30 When the doors of the lift he was in and you weren't
Began closing. Just leave us the screams
You could hear as the vehicle descended: *Poor Cal.*
Up to then he'd been perfectly normal. Ah, well.

2001

VIKRAM SETH
b. 1952

From The Golden Gate[1]

5.1

A week ago, when I had finished
Writing the chapter you've just read
And with avidity undiminished
Was charting out the course ahead,
5 An editor—at a plush party
(Well-wined, -provisioned, speechy, hearty)
Hosted by (long live!) Thomas Cook
Where my Tibetan travel book[2]
Was honored—seized my arm: "Dear fellow,
10 What's your next work?" "A novel . . ." "Great!
We hope that you, dear Mr. Seth—"
". . . In verse," I added. He turned yellow.

---

7. The greatest Roman poet (70–19 B.C.E.), as Dante (1265–1321) is the greatest Italian poet.
8. American poet (1917–1977; see pp. 1592–1606), known to close friends as Cal (line 32).
1. Strait in western California that connects San Francisco Bay with the Pacific Ocean. Set in San Francisco in the 1980s, this satirical romance consists of 690 sonnets written in the tetrameter verse (see "Versification," p. 2032) and stanza form of the Russian poet Alexander Pushkin's verse novel, *Eugene Onegin* (1833), which Seth read in the English translation of Sir Charles Johnston (1977). 2. Seth's *From Heaven Lake: Travels through Sinkiang and Tibet* (1983) won the Thomas Cook Travel Book Award for 1983.

"How marvelously quaint," he said,
And subsequently cut me dead.

5.2

Professor, publisher, and critic
Each voiced his doubts. I felt misplaced.
A writer is a mere arthritic
Among these muscular Gods of Taste.
5   As for that sad blancmange,° a poet—   *opaque jelly*
The world is hard; he ought to know it.
Driveling in rhyme's all very well;
The question is, does spittle sell?
Since staggering home in deep depression,
10 My will's grown weak. My heart is sore.
My lyre is dumb. I have therefore
Convoked a morale-boosting session
With a few kind if doubtful friends
Who've asked me to explain my ends.

5.3

How do I justify this stanza?
These feminine rhymes? My wrinkled muse?°   *source of inspiration*
This whole passé extravaganza?
How can I (careless of time) use
5   The dusty bread molds of Onegin
In the brave bakery of Reagan?[3]
The loaves will surely fail to rise
Or else go stale before my eyes.
The truth is, I can't justify it.
10 But as no shroud of critical terms
Can save my corpse from boring worms,
I may as well have fun and try it.
If it works, good; and if not, well,
A theory won't postpone its knell.

5.4

Why, asks a friend, attempt tetrameter?
Because it once was noble, yet
Capers before the proud pentameter,
Tyrant of English. I regret
5   To see this marvelous swift meter
Demean its heritage, and peter
Into mere Hudibrastic tricks,[4]
Unapostolic[5] knacks and knicks.

---

3. Ronald Reagan (1911–2004), governor of California 1967–75, U.S. president 1981–89.
4. In the style of Samuel Butler's mock-heroic satirical poem, *Hudibras* (1663).
5. Unorthodox (literally, in a style of which Christ's twelve apostles would have disapproved).

But why take all this quite so badly?
10 I would not, had I world and time[6]
To wait for reason, rhythm, rhyme
To reassert themselves, but sadly
The time is not remote when I
Will not be here to wait. That's why.

5.5

Reader, enough of this apology;
But spare me if I think it best,
Before I tether my monology,°   monologue
To stake a stanza to suggest
5 You spend some unfilled day of leisure
By that original spring of pleasure:
Sweet-watered, fluent, clear, light, blithe
(This homage merely pays a tithe°   small part
Of what in joy and inspiration
10 It gave me once and does not cease
To give me)—Pushkin's masterpiece
In Johnston's luminous translation:
Eugene Onegin—like champagne
Its effervescence stirs my brain.

1986

GARY SOTO
b. 1952

The Soup

The lights off, the clock glowing 2:10,
And Molina is at the table drawing what he thinks is soup
And its carrots rising through a gray broth.

He adds meat and peppers it with pencil markings.
5 The onion has gathered the peas in its smile.
The surface is blurred with the cold oils squeezed from a lime.

He adds hominy and potato that bob
In a current of pork fat, from one rim to the other,
Crashing into the celery that has canoed such a long way.

10 *Spoon handle that is a plank an ant climbs.*
Saucer that is the slipped disk of a longhorn.
Napkin that is shredded into a cupful of snow.

1978

6. Cf. Andrew Marvell, "To His Coy Mistress," line 1 (p. 478).

Not Knowing

By then, by the time my brother
Was getting married, weeks before the old
Apartment was pulled down,
The evenings were warm and the sounds of
5   Freight trains absorbed by three oleanders,°   *evergreen shrubs*
Whipped by wind and iron clanging.
By then, by the time I was nineteen
And the crickets were hauling their armor
Into the weeds and dusty bushes,
10   I was thinking that I would have to read more.
I had to put together the meaning of our neighbors
Fighting in bed, then loving in bed from 3:30 to 4:00.
I would have to read more. My other neighbor
Had painted his porch light blue, and the first
15   Black family on our college-poor street
Were so friendly that they disturbed my views
About trust and mistrust. And I was stymied
When my brother and I tried
To remove the refrigerator
20   Down a narrow flight of steps.
Now it was stuck, lodged between
The walls, an absurd physics for the wrecking crew
To solve. The beast of machinery would start up
And the old apartment would come down
25   The weekend my brother would pin
A carnation to his lapel, the ruffle of petal
Perfuming the air as he walked down the aisle.
By then, by the time my brother was ready
And the refrigerator was leaking
30   Its gray liquids and gases,
I would sit my sorrow on a lawn,
Flattening the grass with the heel of my palm.
The grass springing back from this kind of pressure,
Another physics I couldn't figure on paper
35   Or a blackboard of low math. The spin
Of light and wind
And the residue
Of an exhausted star told me nothing.
After my brother was gone
40   I sat with a book on the lawn,
The evening blood-red in the west
And my palm pressing the balance of solitary grass,
The world of unknowable forces stirring
Every live and dead tree.

1995

BRAD LEITHAUSER
b. 1953

The Buried Graves

From the pier, at dusk, the dim
    Billowing arms of kelp
Seem the tops of trees, as though
    Not long ago
5 A summer wood stood here, before a dam
    Was built, a valley flooded.

    Such a forest would release
    Its color only slowly,
And the leafy branches sway, as they'd
10   More lightly swayed
Under a less distant sun and far less
    Even weather. Now, deeper down,

    Those glimmers of coral might
    Be the lots of some hard-luck
15 Town, or—depositing on the dead
    A second bed—
A submerged cemetery. . . . To this mute,
    Envisioned, birdless wood would

    Come a kind of autumn, a tame
20   Sea-season, with foliage tumbling
Through a weighty, trancelike fall;
    And come, as well,
Soon in the emptying fullness of time,
    A mild but an endless winter.

                                     1985

In Minako Wada's House

    In old Minako Wada's house
    Everything has its place,
    And mostly out of sight:
       Bedding folded away
5   All day, brought down
       From the shelf at night,

      Tea things underneath
    Low tea table and tablecloth—
    And sliding screen doors,
10   Landscape-painted, that hide

Her clothes inside a wash
Of mountains. Here, the floors

Are a clean-fitting mosaic,
Mats of a texture like
15 A broom's; and in a niche
    In the tearoom wall
    Is a shrine to all of her
    Ancestors, before which

    She sets each day
20 A doll-sized cup of tea,
    A doll-sized bowl of rice.
        She keeps a glass jar
        Of crickets that are fed fish
        Shavings, an eggplant slice,

25 And whose hushed chorus,
    Like the drowsy toss
    Of a baby's rattle, moves in
        On so tranquil a song
        It's soon no longer heard.
30 The walls are thin

    In Minako Wada's little house,
    Open to every lifting voice
    On the street—by day, the cries
        Of the children, at night
35 Those excited, sweet,
    Reiterated goodbyes

    Of men full of beer who now
    Must hurry home. Just to
    Wake in the night inside this nest,
40   Late, the street asleep (day done,
        Day not yet begun), is what
        Perhaps she loves best.

                                                1985

Old Bachelor Brother

Here from his prominent but thankfully
uncentral position at the head of the church—
a flanking member of the groom's large party—
he stands and waits to watch the women march

5   up the wide aisle, just the way they did
    at last night's long and leaden-joked rehearsal.

Only this time, it's all changed. There's now a crowd,
of course, and walls of lit stained glass, and Purcell[1]

ringing from the rented organist,
10   and yet the major difference, the one
that hits his throat as a sort of smoky thirst,
is how, so far away, the church's main

doors are flung back, uncovering a square
of sun that streams into the narthex,° so that   covered walkway
15   the women who materialize there
do so in blinding silhouette,

and these are not the women he has helloed
and kissed, and who have bored, ignored, or teased him,
but girls—whose high, garlanded hair goes haloed
20   by the noon-light . . . The years have dropped from them.

One by one they're bodied forth, edged with flame,
as new as flame, destined to part the sea
of faces on each side, and approaching him
in all their passionate anonymity.

1990

GJERTRUD SCHNACKENBERG
b. 1953

Darwin[1] in 1881

Sleepless as Prospero back in his bedroom
In Milan, with all his miracles
Reduced to sailors' tales,[2]
He sits up in the dark. The islands loom.
5   His seasickness upwells,
Silence creeps by in memory as it crept
By him on water,[3] while the sailors slept,
From broken eggs and vacant tortoise shells.
His voyage around the cape of middle age
10   Comes, with a feat of insight, to a close,
The same way Prospero's
Ended before he left the stage
To be led home across the blue-white sea,
When he had spoken of the clouds and globe,
15   Breaking his wand, and taking off his robe:[4]
Knowledge increases unreality.

1. Henry Purcell (ca. 1659–1695), English composer.
1. The English naturalist Charles Darwin (1809–1882), who developed a theory of evolution.
2. In Shakespeare's *The Tempest*, the magician

Prospero is the usurped and exiled duke of Milan; at the play's end, he is restored to his dukedom.
3. Cf. *The Tempest* 1.2.395: "This music crept by me upon the waters."
4. Allusion to Prospero's words: "the great globe

He quickly dresses.
Form wavers like his shadow on the stair
As he descends, in need of air
20   To cure his dizziness,
Down past the ship-sunk emptiness
Of grownup children's rooms and hallways where
The family portraits stare,
All haunted by each other's likenesses.

25   Outside, the orchard and a piece of moon
Are islands, he an island as he walks,
Brushing against weed stalks.
By hook and plume
The seeds gathering on his trouser legs
30   Are archipelagoes, like nests he sees
Shadowed in branching, ramifying trees,
Each with unique expressions in its eggs.
Different islands conjure
Different beings; different beings call
35   From different isles. And after all
His scrutiny of Nature
All he can see
Is how it will grow small, fade, disappear,
A coastline fading from a traveler
40   Aboard a survey ship. Slowly,
As coasts depart,
Nature had left behind a naturalist
Bound for a place where species don't exist,
Where no emergence has a counterpart.

45   He's heard from friends
About the other night, the banquet hall
Ringing with bravos—like a curtain call,
He thinks, when the performance ends,
Failing to summon from the wings
50   An actor who had lost his taste for verse,
Having beheld, in larger theaters,
Much greater banquet vanishings
Without the quaint device and thunderclap
Required in Act 3.[5]
55   He wrote, Let your indulgence set me free,[6]
To the Academy, and took a nap
Beneath a *London Daily* tent,
Then puttered on his hothouse walk
Watching his orchids beautifully stalk
60   Their unreturning paths, where each descendant
Is the last—
Their inner staircases

---

itself, / Yea, all which it inherit, shall dissolve; / And, like this insubstantial pageant faded, / Leave not a rack behind" (4.1.153–55) and "But this rough magic / I here abjure. . . . I'll break my staff" (5.1.50–54).

5. Prospero conjures up a banquet and then makes it disappear with thunder and (as in the stage direction) "a quaint device" (3.3.52).

6. Prospero's final speech, the last line of the play (Epilogue 20). *Academy:* The Royal Society for the Improving of Natural Knowledge.

Haunted by vanished insect faces
So tiny, so intolerably vast.
65 And, while they gave his proxy the award,
He dined in Downe[7] and stayed up rather late
For backgammon with his beloved mate,
Who reads his books and is, quite frankly, bored.

Now, done with beetle jaws and beaks of gulls
70 And bivalve hinges, now, utterly done,
One miracle remains, and only one.
An ocean swell of sickness rushes, pulls,
He leans against the fence
And lights a cigarette and deeply draws,
75 Done with fixed laws,
Done with experiments
Within his greenhouse heaven where
His offspring, Frank, for half the afternoon
Played, like an awkward angel, his bassoon
80 Into the humid air
So he could tell
If sound would make a Venus's-flytrap close.
And, done for good with scientific prose,
That raging hell
85 Of tortured grammars writhing on their stakes,
He'd turned to his memoirs, chuckling to write
About his boyhood in an upright
Home: a boy preferring gartersnakes
To schoolwork, a lazy, strutting liar
90 Who quite provoked her aggravated look,
Shushed in the drawing room behind her book,
His bossy sister itching with desire
To tattletale—yes, that was good.
But even then, much like the conjurer
95 Grown cranky with impatience to abjure
All his gigantic works and livelihood
In order to immerse
Himself in tales where he could be the man
In Once upon a time there was a man,

100 He'd quite by chance beheld the universe:
A disregarded game of chess
Between two love-dazed heirs
Who fiddle with the tiny pairs
Of statues in their hands,[8] while numberless
105 Abstract unseen
Combinings on the silent board remain
Unplayed forever when they leave the game
To turn, themselves, into a king and queen.
Now, like the coming day,
110 Inhaled smoke illuminates his nerves.

7. Darwin's home.
8. That is, playing chess, as in *The Tempest* 5.1.173 ff.

He turns, taking the sandwalk as it curves
Back to the yard, the house, the entrance way
Where, not to waken her,

He softly shuts the door,
115 And leans against it for a spell before
He climbs the stairs, holding the banister,
Up to their room: there
Emma sleeps, moored
In illusion, blown past the storm he conjured
120 With his book,[9] into a harbor
Where it all comes clear,
Where island beings leap from shape to shape
As to escape
Their terrifying turns to disappear.
125 He lies down on the quilt,
He lies down like a fabulous-headed
Fossil in a vanished riverbed,
In ocean drifts, in canyon floors, in silt,
In lime, in deepening blue ice,
130 In cliffs obscured as clouds gather and float;
He lies down in his boots and overcoat,
And shuts his eyes.

1982

Supernatural Love

My father at the dictionary-stand
Touches the page to fully understand
The lamplit answer, tilting in his hand

His slowly scanning magnifying lens,
5 A blurry, glistening circle he suspends
Above the word "Carnation." Then he bends

So near his eyes are magnified and blurred,
One finger on the miniature word,
As if he touched a single key and heard

10 A distant, plucked, infinitesimal string,
"The obligation due to every thing
That's smaller than the universe." I bring

My sewing needle close enough that I
Can watch my father through the needle's eye,
15 As through a lens ground for a butterfly

---

9. Prospero's book of magic helped him conjure a tempest. Darwin's book *On the Origin of Species by Means of Natural Selection* (1859) was equally powerful, culturally and scientifically.

Who peers down flower-hallways toward a room
Shadowed and fathomed as this study's gloom
Where, as a scholar bends above a tomb

To read what's buried there, he bends to pore
20   Over the Latin blossom. I am four,
I spill my pins and needles on the floor

Trying to stitch "Beloved" X by X.
My dangerous, bright needle's point connects
Myself illiterate to this perfect text

25   I cannot read. My father puzzles why
It is my habit to identify
Carnations as "Christ's flowers," knowing I

Can give no explanation but "Because."
Word-roots blossom in speechless messages
30   The way the thread behind my sampler does

Where following each X I awkward move
My needle through the word whose root is love.
He reads, "A pink variety of Clove,

Carnatio, the Latin, meaning flesh."
35   As if the bud's essential oils brush
Christ's fragrance through the room, the iron-fresh

Odor carnations have floats up to me,
A drifted, secret, bitter ecstasy,
The stems squeak in my scissors, *Child, it's me,*

40   He turns the page to "Clove" and reads aloud:
"The clove, a spice, dried from a flower-bud."
Then twice, as if he hasn't understood,

He reads, "From French, for *clou,* meaning a nail."
He gazes, motionless. "Meaning a nail."
45   The incarnation blossoms, flesh and nail,

I twist my threads like stems into a knot
And smooth "Beloved," but my needle caught
Within the threads, *Thy blood so dearly bought,*

The needle strikes my finger to the bone.
50   I lift my hand, it is myself I've sewn,
The flesh laid bare, the threads of blood my own,

I lift my hand in startled agony
And call upon his name, "Daddy daddy"—
My father's hand touches the injury

55 As lightly as he touched the page before,
Where incarnation bloomed from roots that bore
The flowers I called Christ's when I was four.

1985

LOUISE ERDRICH
b. 1954

The Butcher's Wife

1

Once, my braids swung heavy as ropes.
Men feared them like the gallows.
Night fell
When I combed them out.
5 No one could see me in the dark.

Then I stood still
Too long and the braids took root.
I wept, so helpless.
The braids tapped deep and flourished.

10 A man came by with an ox on his shoulders.
He yoked it to my apron
And pulled me from the ground.
From that time on I wound the braids around my head
So that my arms would be free to tend him.

2

15 He could lift a grown man by the belt with his teeth.
In a contest, he'd press a whole hog, a side of beef.
He loved his highballs, his herring, and the attentions of women.
He died pounding his chest with no last word for anyone.

The gin vessels in his face broke and darkened. I traced them
20 Far from that room into Bremen on the Sea.[1]
The narrow streets twisted down to the piers.
And far off, in the black, rocking water, the lights of trawlers
Beckoned, like the heart's uncertain signals,
Faint, and final.

1984

---

1. Germany's oldest seaport, today the second largest after Hamburg.

I Was Sleeping Where the Black Oaks Move

We watched from the house
as the river grew, helpless
and terrible in its unfamiliar body.
Wrestling everything into it,
5   the water wrapped around trees
until their life-hold was broken.
They went down, one by one,
and the river dragged off their covering.

Nests of the herons, roots washed to bones,
10   snags of soaked bark on the shoreline:
a whole forest pulled through the teeth
of the spillway. Trees surfacing
singly, where the river poured off
into arteries for fields below the reservation.

15   When at last it was over, the long removal,
they had all become the same dry wood.
We walked among them, the branches
whitening in the raw sun.
Above us drifted herons,
20   alone, hoarse-voiced, broken,
settling their beaks among the hollows.

Grandpa said, *These are the ghosts of the tree people,*
moving above us, unable to take their rest.

Sometimes now, we dream our way back to the heron dance.
25   Their long wings are bending the air
into circles through which they fall.
They rise again in shifting wheels.
How long must we live in the broken figures
their necks make, narrowing the sky.

1984

Birth

When they were wild
When they were not yet human
When they could have been anything,
I was on the other side ready with milk to lure them,
5   And their father, too, each name a net in his hands.

1989

CAROL ANN DUFFY
b. 1955

Warming Her Pearls

Next to my own skin, her pearls. My mistress
bids me wear them, warm them, until evening
when I'll brush her hair. At six, I place them
round her cool, white throat. All day I think of her,

5   resting in the Yellow Room, contemplating silk
or taffeta, which gown tonight? She fans herself
whilst I work willingly, my slow heat entering
each pearl. Slack on my neck, her rope.

She's beautiful. I dream about her
10   in my attic bed; picture her dancing
with tall men, puzzled by my faint, persistent scent
beneath her French perfume, her milky stones.

I dust her shoulders with a rabbit's foot,
watch the soft blush seep through her skin
15   like an indolent sigh. In her looking-glass
my red lips part as though I want to speak.

Full moon. Her carriage brings her home. I see
her every movement in my head. . . . Undressing,
taking off her jewels, her slim hand reaching
20   for the case, slipping naked into bed, the way

she always does. . . . And I lie here awake,
knowing the pearls are cooling even now
in the room where my mistress sleeps. All night
I feel their absence and I burn.

1993

Prayer

Some days, although we cannot pray, a prayer
utters itself. So, a woman will lift
her head from the sieve of her hands and stare
at the minims° sung by a tree, a sudden gift.   *short notes*

5   Some nights, although we are faithless, the truth
enters our hearts, that small familiar pain;
then a man will stand stock-still, hearing his youth
in the distant Latin chanting of a train.

Pray for us now. Grade I piano scales[1]
10 console the lodger looking out across
a Midlands[2] town. Then dusk, and someone calls
a child's name as though they named their loss.

Darkness outside. Inside, the radio's prayer—
Rockall. Malin. Dogger. Finisterre.[3]

1993

Anne Hathaway[4]

"Item I gyve unto my wief my second best bed . . ."
(from Shakespeare's will)

The bed we loved in was a spinning world
of forests, castles, torchlight, clifftops, seas
where he would dive for pearls. My lover's words
were shooting stars which fell to earth as kisses
5 on these lips; my body now a softer rhyme
to his, now echo, assonance; his touch
a verb dancing in the centre of a noun.
Some nights, I dreamed he'd written me, the bed
a page beneath his writer's hands. Romance
10 and drama played by touch, by scent, by taste.
In the other bed, the best, our guests dozed on,
dribbling their prose. My living laughing love—
I hold him in the casket of my widow's head
as he held me upon that next best bed.

1999

Little Red-Cap

At childhood's end, the houses petered out
into playing fields, the factory, allotments°   *vegetable plots*
kept, like mistresses, by kneeling married men,
the silent railway line, the hermit's caravan,
5 till you came at last to the edge of the woods.
It was there that I first clapped eyes on the wolf.

He stood in a clearing, reading his verse out loud
in his wolfy drawl, a paperback in his hairy paw,
red wine staining his bearded jaw. What big ears
10 he had! What big eyes he had! What teeth!
In the interval, I made quite sure he spotted me,
sweet sixteen, never been, babe, waif, and bought me a drink,

1. Musical exercises for beginners.   casts.
2. Central counties in England.   4. William Shakespeare's wife (1557?–1623).
3. Coastal regions named in British weather fore-

my first. You might ask why. Here's why. Poetry.
The wolf, I knew, would lead me deep into the woods,
15   away from home, to a dark tangled thorny place
lit by the eyes of owls. I crawled in his wake,
my stockings ripped to shreds, scraps of red from my blazer
snagged on twig and branch, murder clues. I lost both shoes

but got there, wolf's lair, better beware. Lesson one that night,
20   breath of the wolf in my ear, was the love poem.
I clung till dawn to his thrashing fur, for
what little girl doesn't dearly love a wolf?[5]
Then I slid from between his heavy matted paws
and went in search of a living bird—white dove—

25   which flew, straight, from my hands to his open mouth.
One bite, dead. How nice, breakfast in bed, he said,
licking his chops. As soon as he slept, I crept to the back
of the lair, where a whole wall was crimson, gold, aglow with books.
Words, words were truly alive on the tongue, in the head,
30   warm, beating, frantic, winged; music and blood.

But then I was young—and it took ten years
in the woods to tell that a mushroom
stoppers the mouth of a buried corpse, that birds
are the uttered thought of trees, that a greying wolf
35   howls the same old song at the moon, year in, year out,
season after season, same rhyme, same reason. I took an axe

to a willow to see how it wept. I took an axe to a salmon
to see how it leapt. I took an axe to the wolf
as he slept, one chop, scrotum to throat, and saw
40   the glistening, virgin white of my grandmother's bones.
I filled his old belly with stones. I stitched him up.
Out of the forest I come with my flowers, singing, all alone.

1999

DIONISIO D. MARTINEZ
b. 1956

In a Duplex Near the San Andreas Fault[1]

When she tells him about the lump in her breast,
he kisses her on the shoulder for the first time—a natural
reflex twenty-some years in the making. Suddenly,

---

5. Cf. Sylvia Plath, "Daddy," line 48 (p. 1841).
1. An active strike-slip fault extending from San Francisco to southern California.

their entire vocabulary revolves around *benign*
5   and *malignant*—words reserved
for these occasions—though they will say

very little now, then nothing for a long time. His hands
are just as pale and nearly as fragile as rice paper,
but she's not familiar with rice paper

10   and what she wants most desperately now
is a point of reference. Calla lilies bloom
like some glorious, abandoned music out on the lawn.

She takes one of his hands and thinks
of the spathe, which has the responsibility
15   of being leaf and petal, content and shape: without it

there would be no calla lily to remember,
nothing to see when she closes
her eyes and places his hand on her breast.

1995

From What the Men Talk About When
the Women Leave the Room

Stieglitz[2]

The room itself. The women. The absence of women
in the room. What the absence of women does
to a room. The sound of all those women getting

up and leaving; all of them at once, like wild
5   birds or hunger. How the world can be conquered
if only . . . Just don't tell the women.

What the absence of women will do to men
eventually. Fears. Men talk about fears, bad
dreams, women leaving, the room swelling with

10   the absence of women. Bad dreams have a way
of walking in the room when the women leave.
Each dream is an afterimage of a woman leaving.

1995

---

2. Alfred Stieglitz (1864–1946), American photographer; husband of the artist Georgia O'Keeffe.

LI-YOUNG LEE
b. 1957

Persimmons

In sixth grade Mrs. Walker
slapped the back of my head
and made me stand in the corner
for not knowing the difference
5   between *persimmon* and *precision*.
How to choose

persimmons. This is precision.
Ripe ones are soft and brown-spotted.
Sniff the bottoms. The sweet one
10   will be fragrant. How to eat:
put the knife away, lay down newspaper.
Peel the skin tenderly, not to tear the meat.
Chew the skin, suck it,
and swallow. Now, eat
15   the meat of the fruit,
so sweet,
all of it, to the heart.

Donna undresses, her stomach is white.
In the yard, dewy and shivering
20   with crickets, we lie naked,
face-up, face-down.
I teach her Chinese.
Crickets: *chiu chiu*. Dew: I've forgotten.
Naked: I've forgotten.
25   *Ni, wo*: you and me.
I part her legs,
remember to tell her
she is beautiful as the moon.

Other words
30   that got me into trouble were
fight and *fright, wren* and *yarn.*
Fight was what I did when I was frightened,
fright was what I felt when I was fighting.
Wrens are small, plain birds,
35   yarn is what one knits with.
Wrens are soft as yarn.
My mother made birds out of yarn.
I loved to watch her tie the stuff;
a bird, a rabbit, a wee man.

40   Mrs. Walker brought a persimmon to class
and cut it up
so everyone could taste

a *Chinese apple.* Knowing
it wasn't ripe or sweet, I didn't eat
45   but watched the other faces.

My mother said every persimmon has a sun
inside, something golden, glowing,
warm as my face.

Once, in the cellar, I found two wrapped in newspaper,
50   forgotten and not yet ripe.
I took them and set both on my bedroom windowsill,
where each morning a cardinal
sang, *The sun, the sun.*

Finally understanding
55   he was going blind,
my father sat up all one night
waiting for a song, a ghost.
I gave him the persimmons,
swelled, heavy as sadness,
60   and sweet as love.

This year, in the muddy lighting
of my parents' cellar, I rummage, looking
for something I lost.
My father sits on the tired, wooden stairs,
65   black cane between his knees,
hand over hand, gripping the handle.
He's so happy that I've come home.
I ask how his eyes are, a stupid question.
All gone, he answers.

70   Under some blankets, I find a box.
Inside the box I find three scrolls.
I sit beside him and untie
three paintings by my father:
Hibiscus leaf and a white flower.
75   Two cats preening.
Two persimmons, so full they want to drop from the cloth.

He raises both hands to touch the cloth,
asks, *Which is this?*

This is persimmons, Father.

80   *Oh, the feel of the wolftail on the silk,*
the strength, the tense
precision in the wrist.
I painted them hundreds of times
eyes closed. These I painted blind.
85   *Some things never leave a person:*
scent of the hair of one you love,

the texture of persimmons,
in your palm, the ripe weight.

1986

Out of Hiding

Someone said my name in the garden,

while I grew smaller
in the spreading shadow of the peonies,

grew larger by my absence to another,
5   grew older among the ants, ancient

under the opening heads of the flowers,
new to myself, and stranger.

When I heard my name again, it sounded far,
like the name of the child next door,
10   or a favorite cousin visiting for the summer,

while the quiet seemed my true name,
a near and inaudible singing
born of hidden ground.

Quiet to quiet, I called back.
15   And the birds declared my whereabouts all morning.

2001

CYNTHIA ZARIN
b. 1959

The Ant Hill

Sand pyramid, size of a child, each September
it was moved thirty feet back from the veranda's
longest shadow, which stopped in its daily

violet slope near the withering yew. Moved gently,
5   with a wide flat shovel. From the kitchen,
the wrecked hill was a slag heap, its mussel

color germinating in rain to brown, to velvet, to mica,
so that after a time a reflection shone from it
and scattered, and each June, Mother said aloud

10 that it seemed the house moved closer to the hill,
   even though the hill was long moved back.
     For the little girls who watched, who heard,

   each tremble-leg was a signal in their own patois,
    a wave good-bye, the whole a black bead curtain
15   like the one at Mrs. Hennessey's, where sometimes,

   of an afternoon, they were left—her doorway with its
    there, not there, its speechless partings, the
     dark italic hedge too small to read. A decade

   of exile: of school, of being sent to bed, of being
20   told to put the book down, as every year the ants
     were wrenched from their own tenacious fondness

   for the veranda pilings, for the black blossoms of old tires
    that clung to them like clematis until—a moving
     picture of transit—the ants crossed over again

25   for their mysterious attendance on the flagstones,
    the hill again grown pointed, night-colored, earth
     turned to mirror-water, a satellite by

   the fence post that was flattened, excavated, removed.
    And then the white house was a flipped coin,
30   by and by deserted, its face showing not

   the sun but the moon, and the girls who drew with a stick
    under the yew and learned their letters now
     stood under its cracked limbs to bicker, to

   divide the world between them to say what Mother
35   said, to speak too subtly, about the ant hill now
     taller than the pilings, the veranda

   turned violet as its shadow.

                           1993

Song

   My heart, my dove, my snail, my sail, my
    milktooth, shadow, sparrow, fingernail,
     flower-cat and blossom-hedge, mandrake

   root now put to bed, moonshell, sea-swell,
5   manatee, emerald shining back at me,
     nutmeg, quince, tea leaf and bone, zither,

cymbal, xylophone; paper, scissors, then
　　there's stone—Who doesn't come through the door
　　　to get home?

　　　　　　　　　　　　　　　　　　　　　　　　　　1993

LAVINIA GREENLAW
b. 1962

Skin Full

I laugh till my jaw unhinges,
we hold me in with ribboning fingers.
Moderation in moderation. Who said that?
It makes extraordinary sense to me.

5　You say that life is a three-legged race.
They show us the door and we have some difficulty,
bound like that from thigh to ankle.
The street is a blanket. We will sleep

with you on your front, me on your back.
10　The night will be endless and we will be endless,
layer on layer, infinitely warm.
I sing as we lie shoulder to shoulder

and tell you there is no such thing as anything
that is not a small circle. Now it is morning.
15　Can the bones we broke out of be mended?
My eyes . . . The sun picks over their embers.

　　　　　　　　　　　　　　　　　　　　　　　　　　1997

What's Going On

The demolition crew are petulant.
Swinging the ball, they could lay bets and lose.
We cannot help but stand in the street,
smile up at the light where half the roof
5　has fallen away and the sky comes at us
from all three sides through a couple of windows,
surprisingly large and somehow intact.

　　　　　　　　　　　　　　　　　　　　　　　　　　1997

A World Where News Travelled Slowly

It could take from Monday to Thursday
and three horses. The ink was unstable,
the characters° cramped, the paper tore where it creased.   *letters*
Stained with the leather and sweat of its journey,
5   the envelope absorbed each climatic shift,
as well as the salt and grease of the rider
who handed it over with a four-day chance
that by now things were different and while the head
had to listen, the heart could wait.

10   Semaphore[1] was invented at a time of revolution;
the judgement of swing in a vertical arm.
News travelled letter by letter, along a chain of towers,
each built within telescopic distance of the next.
The clattering mechanics of the six-shutter telegraph
15   still took three men with all their variables
added to those of light and weather,
to read, record and pass the message on.

Now words are faster, smaller, harder
    . . . *we're almost talking in one another's arms.*
20   Coded and squeezed, what chance has my voice
to reach your voice unaltered and to leave no trace?
Nets tighten across the sky and the sea bed.
When London made contact with New York,
there were such fireworks, City Hall caught light.
25   It could have burned to the ground.

1997

GLYN MAXWELL
b. 1962

From Letters to Edward Thomas[1]
for Derek Walcott[2]

*

Poem to Mr Thomas and Mr Frost,
Created by a dandelion you passed
As you in talk about a stanza crossed

1. Signaling apparatus, consisting of an upright post with a moveable arm or arms with lanterns attached, for use (especially on railways) by day or night.
1. (Philip) Edward Thomas (1878–1917; see pp. 1253–56), whose friendship with the American poet Robert Frost (1874–1963; see pp. 1227–45) was of central importance to the lives and work of both men.
2. West Indian poet (b. 1930; see pp. 1820–29).

Half Herefordshire,[3] till you sat at last
5   In silence. I'm the dandelion that saw
Two aspens shake and shed in a quick wind,
And tried to loose her own leaves to the floor
Like they did and did manage in the end,
When they were both long gone in the great storm.[4]
10 One to the west and one to the east, away
Towards the blood-commander in the dawn
And all his soldiers, pink becoming grey.
And you won't see this, if you live as long
As what you sent me: "As the team's head-brass"[5]
15 It starts but isn't titled. If I'm wrong
And your great hands one day are holding these
        Dandelion hairs,
The storm would not have come, the trees have kept
Their ground, and through the hearts of all the shires
20 Would Mr Thomas and Mr Frost have stepped
        And war like a rough sky
Been overlooked in talk, and blown on by.

                          *

Poem for Mr Edward Eastaway,[6]
Who lives here care of me, so no one knows
25 His name is Rumplestiltskin[7] and by day
He rips your verse to pieces in great prose.
By night he turns his prose to poetry
Because a poet told him to who saw
A mighty fine recruit for poverty
30 And wrote the line that opened his front door.
They have rejected Edward Eastaway
Again: the letter came this afternoon.
One knows precisely what a fool will say
Somehow. We've many stars to the one moon
35 In our night sky, but all that makes a face
Of that recurring rock is the one sun
It likes, without which it must find its place
To hide behind, or make believe it's gone.
        Edward Eastaway,
40 Whose name that isn't and whose time it ain't,
Who's living here or was just yesterday,
Or in Wales, Wiltshire, Oxfordshire or Kent,[8]
        The rumour's that you crossed
The Channel. Stanza-break, sighs Mr Frost.

                          *

3. English county on the Welsh border.
4. World War I, also known as the Great War (1914–18).
5. The opening words of one of Thomas's poems (see p. 1255).
6. Thomas published his first poems under the pseudonym Edward Eastaway.
7. Malevolent dwarf in traditional fairy tale collected and transcribed from oral sources by the brothers Jacob and Wilhelm Grimm.
8. The latter three are English counties southeast of Herefordshire—stepping-stones toward the English channel (line 44).

45   Dear Father Thomas, every Christmas Eve
      Good children of the world are quite as shy
      As I am to write *Dear* and then believe
      For twenty lines our goodness could be why
      It's worth our time. Our faith turns to this thread
50   That shuttles downward while the mischievous
      Need nothing but a coalsack by the bed,
      And wake to the same carols. Each of us
      Is writing, Edward, asking the great space
      Below us what is missing still, what gift
55   Will make us whole again. We fold and place
      Our answers in the chimney and are left
      These pink embarrassed authors by the fire.
      We all talk tommy-rot° we understand.   *nonsense*
      Somebody coughs, politely to enquire
60   Did they not kick a ball on No Man's Land
          Two years ago?[9] "That's so,"
      Smiles Peter, adding: "Not tonight, I fear."
      And I hear George's voice say: "Cricket, though,
      So Edward gets a knock."° But he's not here,   *opportunity to bat*
65   George, he's where you are,
      Restless tonight like all good children are.

                *

      One dead was sent a Valentine, so both
      Were spared their lover's blushes. What I write
      Is on its way nowhere, is less than breath,
70   So might be anything, as nothing might.
      It's that there's nothing now that doesn't seem
      As if it's where it ended. All the paths
      Beyond this word or this become the same:
      Thickets, or a handing-down of deaths
75   As by a school official, not a teacher,
      A visiting official by one gate.
      Now all the hope there is is in a picture
      Of P. E. Thomas gone, because my fate
      Is never to foresee, believed or no.
80   Is to be wrong. These words are packing up
      And going. Words I mean you not to know
      Don't see why they should move in any step
          I fix them with. So go,
      You English words,[1] while he's alive, and blow
85   Through all of him so Englishmen will know
      You loved him and who cares how long ago,
       And hide him from the light
      He'll strike and hold until his clay's° alight.   *clay pipe*

                *

9. Preparing the men of his company for their part in the Allied assault on July 1, 1916, the first day of the Battle of the Somme, Captain Neville of the 8th East Surrey Regiment gave each of his four platoons a football and offered a prize for the first platoon to reach the German trenches. *No Man's Land:* unoccupied area between opposing armies.
1. Edward Thomas, "Words," lines 10–11: "Choose me / You English words?"

Dear Edward, when the war was over, you
90　Were standing where a wood had been, and though
Nothing was left for you to name or view
You waited till new trees had hidden you.
Then you came home and in a forest called
The Times your name was found, and not among
95　The officers but in a clearing filled
With verses, yours. Then your new name was sung
With all the old. And children leafing through
And old men staring and their daughters stilled
With admiration: all this happened too,
100　Or had already by the time you pulled
The book I hide this in from your top shelf
And blew its dust away. The year is what,
1930? '40? Please yourself,
But do remember as you smile and sit
105　　　That everything's foreseen
By a good reader, as I think I am
On David's Day of 1917,
Reaching for blotting-paper.[2] Now's the time
　　To fold the work away
110　And find me on this bleak or brilliant day.

　　　　　　　　　　　*

Choose me, Sie deutsche Worte.[3] This is the first
Of all the letters you will never read,
Edward. I was shy in my own west
Always, so you never read a word
115　I sent, but this is written with as clear
A mind as has been opened like a shell.
"Greatly loved in the battery,"° writes this dear　　　*artillery unit*
Major Lushington, who says you fell
In early morning with some battle won
120　And all the soldiers dancing. You were loved
In the battery and in the morning sun
Brought out the blessed clay, when something moved
Like cloud perhaps. The Major asked us round
To tell us you knew nothing. That your book
125　Of Shakespeare's Sonnets that they knelt and found
Was strangely creased and the clay didn't break[4]
　　Which Helen[5] gave your son,
And Robert's *North of Boston*[6] in your kit
They gave to me, not needing it. And when
130　They reached you you were not marked, not hit,
　　Breeze blowing in your hair,
Chosen. What had stopped your heart was air.

2. Spongy paper for absorbing ink when writing. *David's Day:* March 1, feast day of St. David, patron saint of Wales.
3. You German words (German). See note 1 directly above.
4. Thomas was killed by the blast of a German shell on Easter Monday 1917. His body was unmarked and his clay pipe unbroken, but the vacuum created by the blast creased the pages of his book and stopped the watch in his pocket.
5. Thomas's wife (1877–1967).
6. Collection of Frost's poems (1914), favorably reviewed by Thomas.

*

Dear Edward, now there's no one at the end
There's nothing I can't say. Some eight or nine
135   I have by heart. Your farmer-poet friend[7]
Is flying around the world on a fine line
That starts in you, or grows out from the days
You passed together. England is the same,
Cheering to order, set in its new ways
140   It thinks are immemorial. The Somme[8]
Has trees beside it but some shovelwork
Will bring the dead to light. There's so much more
I want to say, because the quiet is dark,
And when the writing ends I reach a shore
145   Beyond which it's so cold and that's what changed,
Edward, on that Easter Monday.[9] You
Were land to me, where England unestranged,
Were what I thought it had amounted to,
         But look at the fields now,
150   Look eyelessly at them, like the dug men
Still nodding out of Flanders.[1] Tell them how
You walked and how you saw, and how your pen
         Did nothing more than that,
And, when it stopped, what you were gazing at.

*

155   Dear Edward Thomas, Frost died, I was born.
I am a father and you'd like the names
We gave our girl. I'm writing this at dawn
Where Robert lived, in Amherst,[2] and your poems
I keep by his, his housebrick to your tile.
160   I teach you to my students, and aloud
I wonder what you would have come to. While
I wonder they look out at a white cloud
And so we pass the time. Perhaps I'll guess
Which one will ask me what they always ask:
165   Whom do I write for? Anybody? Yes,
You. And I'll walk home in the great dusk
Of Massachusetts that extends away
Far west and north, the ways you meant to go
To save your life. A good end to the day,
170   That's going to be. It's going to be cool, though,
         I see out in the town,
And start to turn the trees to what the world
Comes flocking here to see: eight shades of brown
Men never saw, and ninety-nine of gold,
175   More shades than can have names,
Or names to bring them back when the snow comes.

1998

7. Frost.
8. French river, site of the major battle mentioned
in note 9 above.
9. See note 4, p. 2019.
1. Perhaps, "the dead" of line 142 still (at present)

coming "to light" (142) in the fields of Flanders.
2. From 1917 until 1938, Frost taught at Amherst
College (in Amherst, Massachusetts), where Max-
well teaches.

SIMON ARMITAGE
b. 1963

From Killing Time[1]

Meanwhile, somewhere in the state of Colorado, armed to the teeth
    with thousands of flowers,
two boys entered the front door of their own high school
    and for almost four hours
5 gave floral tributes to fellow students and members of staff,
    beginning with red roses
strewn amongst unsuspecting pupils during their lunch hour,
    followed by posies
of peace lilies and wild orchids. Most thought the whole show
10   was one elaborate hoax
using silk replicas of the real thing, plastic imitations,
    exquisite practical jokes,
but the flowers were no more fake than you or I,
    and were handed out
15 as compliments returned, favours repaid, in good faith,
    straight from the heart.
No would not be taken for an answer. Therefore a daffodil
    was tucked behind the ear
of a boy in a baseball hat, and marigolds and peonies
20   threaded through the hair
of those caught on the stairs or spotted along corridors,
    until every pupil
who looked up from behind a desk could expect to be met
    with at least a petal
25 or a dusting of pollen, if not an entire daisy-chain,
    or the colour-burst
of a dozen foxgloves, flowering for all their worth,
    or a buttonhole to the breast.
Upstairs in the school library, individuals were singled out
30   for special attention:
some were showered with blossom, others wore their blooms
    like brooches or medallions;
even those who turned their backs or refused point-blank
    to accept such honours
35 were decorated with buds, unseasonable fruits and rosettes
    the same as the others.
By which time a crowd had gathered outside the school,
    drawn through suburbia
by the rumour of flowers in full bloom, drawn through the air
40   like butterflies to buddleia,[2]
like honey bees to honeysuckle, like hummingbirds
    dipping their tongues in,

---

1. In what came to be known as the Columbine Massacre, two seniors of Columbine High School, Colorado, went to school on April 20, 1999, armed with guns, knives, and bombs. At the end of the day, twelve students, one teacher, and the two murderers were dead.
2. Also known as "butterfly bush."

some to soak up such over-exuberance of thought, others
    to savour the goings-on.
45   Finally, overcome by their own munificence or hay fever,
    the flower-boys pinned
the last blooms on themselves, somewhat selfishly perhaps,
    but had also planned
further surprises for those who swept through the aftermath
50   of broom and buttercup:
garlands and bouquets were planted in lockers and cupboards,
    timed to erupt
like the first day of spring into the arms of those
    who, during the first bout,
55   either by fate or chance had somehow been overlooked
    and missed out.
Experts are now trying to say how two apparently quiet kids
    from an apple-pie town
could get their hands on a veritable rain-forest of plants
60   and bring down
a whole botanical digest of one species or another onto the heads
    of classmates and teachers,
and where such fascination began, and why it should lead
    to an outpouring of this nature.
65   And even though many believe that flowers should be kept
    in expert hands
only, or left to specialists in the field such as florists,
    the law of the land
dictates that God, guts and gardening made the country
70   what it is today
and for as long as the flower industry can see to it
    things are staying that way.
What they reckon is this: deny a person the right to carry
    flowers of his own
75   and he's liable to wind up on the business end of a flower
    somebody else has grown.
As for the two boys, it's back to the same old debate:
    is it something in the mind
that grows from birth, like a seed, or is it society
80   makes a person that kind?

                                        1999

The Shout

We went out
into the school yard together, me and the boy
whose name and face

I don't remember. We were testing the range
5   of the human voice:
he had to shout for all he was worth,

I had to raise an arm
from across the divide to signal back
that the sound had carried.

10 He called from over the park—I lifted an arm.
Out of bounds,
he yelled from the end of the road,

from the foot of the hill,
from beyond the look-out post of Fretwell's Farm—
15 I lifted an arm.

He left town, went on to be twenty years dead
with a gunshot hole
in the roof of his mouth, in Western Australia.

Boy with the name and face I don't remember,
20 you can stop shouting now, I can still hear you.

2002

GREG WILLIAMSON
b. 1964

Outbound

We live life forwards and think about it backwards
Howard Nemerov[1]

We passengers ride backward on the train
And train our eyes on what has passed us by.
A cobalt blur composes
Into a woman picking roses,
5 Who is already fading in the pane
As in the failing hindsight of the eye.

A line of oaks comes into focus, fades,
Supplanted by the double-dagger poles
Of power companies,
10 Footnotes that redefine the trees.
An asterisk in glass, then window shades,
Graffiti, billboards, tattered banderoles°   *long scrolls*

Of southbound birds. . . . Whatever comes to view
Corrects the view, but never will explain
15 The random next event

1. American poet (1920–1991; see pp. 1623–27).

Or anything but where we went,
Where long ago a woman wearing blue
Began forgetting someone on a train.

1995

From Double Exposures[2]

III. Visiting Couple Kissing and Halved Onion

Unjustly I've imposed upon my friends
This? It's an onion that's been cut in half
When they're (how shall I say?) making amends
Right in the middle of the photograph,
5   **After a night of words, and here they stand**
Less like those pure, textbook transparencies
Wrapped up in one another, hand in hand,
Than layered and opaque identities,
An arm around a shoulder, face to face,
10 Developed in the dark to this full kit
And captured in this rapturous embrace.
Which has so many tears inside of it.

XXV. Group Photo with Winter Trees

These were my neighbors. It's a big group pose:
On mist-gray skies, the stark, black branches etch
Horizon, lawn, in loose haphazard rows.
As if in tin, or as in some old sketch,
5   **That's The Great Bob. And that's our good Queen Paul**
Whose lines, whose every nuance was precise,
With Champagne Anne and Rick the dog. They're all
But faded now. I've seen the trees in ice,
Decked out (Liz, too, who helped me do the plumbing),
10 But I'll be gone when their spring blooms and scatters
Even the children. And, God, they're all becoming.
Shades, as the new leaves turn to other matters.

2001

New Year's: A Short Pantoum[3]

The sunlight was falling. A part
Played out in the deep snow.
We were all there. At the start
We knew how the year would go,

---

2. The title refers to a form invented by William-son, in which three poems can be read in one: the bold type, the standard type, and the combination.
3. On this verse form, see "Versification," p. 2046.

5   Played out in the deep snow.
    The sunlight was falling apart.
    We knew how the year would go.
    We were all there at the start.

                                        2001

Versification

A poem is a composition written for performance by the human voice. What your eye sees on the page is the composer's verbal score, waiting for your voice to bring it alive as you read it aloud or hear it in your mind's ear. Unlike your reading of a newspaper, the best reading—that is to say, the most satisfying reading—of a poem involves a simultaneous engagement of eye and ear: the eye attentive not only to the meaning of words, but to their grouping and spacing as lines on a page; the ear attuned to the grouping and spacing of sounds. The more you understand of musical notation and the principles of musical composition, the more you will understand and appreciate a composer's score. Similarly, the more you understand of versification (the principles and practice of writing verse), the more you are likely to understand and appreciate poetry and, in particular, the intimate relationship between its form and its content. *What* a poem says or means is the result of *how* it is said, a fact that poets are often at pains to emphasize. "All my life," said W. H. Auden, "I have been more interested in technique than anything else." And T. S. Eliot claimed that "the conscious problems with which one is concerned in the actual writing are more those of a quasi-musical nature, in the arrangement of metric and pattern, than of a conscious exposition of ideas." Fortunately, the principles of versification are easier to explain than those of musical composition.

The oldest classification of poetry into three broad categories still holds:

1. **Epic:** a long narrative poem, frequently extending to several "books" (sections of several hundred lines), on a great and serious subject. See, for example, Spenser's *The Faerie Queene* (p. 165), Milton's *Paradise Lost* (p. 420), Wordsworth's *The Prelude* (p. 781), and Barrett Browning's *Aurora Leigh* (p. 948). With one notable exception, Merrill's *The Changing Light at Sandover* (p. 1725), the few poems of comparable length to have been written in the twentieth century—for example, Williams's *Paterson* and Pound's *Cantos* (p. 1306)—have a freer, less formal structure.

2. **Dramatic:** poetry, monologue or dialogue, written in the voice of a character assumed by the poet. Space does not permit the inclusion in this anthology of speeches from the many great verse dramas of English literature, but see such dramatic monologues as Tennyson's "Ulysses" (p. 992), Browning's "My Last Duchess" (p. 1012), and Howard's response to that poem, "Nikolaus Mardruz to his Master Ferdinand, Count of Tyrol, 1565" (p. 1778).

3. **Lyric:** originally, a song performed in ancient Greece to the accompaniment of a small harplike instrument called a lyre. The term is now used for any fairly short poem in the voice of a single speaker, although that speaker may sometimes quote others. The reader should be wary of identifying the lyric speaker with the poet, since the "I" of a poem will frequently be that of a fictional character invented by the poet. The majority of poems in this book are lyrics, and the principal types of lyric will be found set out under "Forms" (p. 2039).

Rhythm

Poetry is the most compressed form of language, and rhythm is an essential component of language. When we speak, we hear a sequence of **syllables.** These, the basic units of pronunciation, can consist of a vowel sound alone or a vowel with attendant consonants: *oh; syl-la-ble.* Sometimes *m, n,* and *l* are counted as vowel sounds, as in *riddle (rid-dl)* and *prism (pri-zm).* In words of two or more syllables, one is almost always given more emphasis or, as we say, is more heavily stressed than the others, so that what we hear in ordinary speech is a sequence of such units, variously stressed and unstressed as, for example:

> A **poem** is a **composition writ**ten for **perform**ance by the
> **human voice.**

We call such an analysis of stressed and unstressed syllables **scansion** (the action or art of **scanning** a line to determine its division into metrical feet); and a simple system of signs has been evolved to denote stressed and unstressed syllables and any significant pause between them. Adding such scansion marks will produce the following:

> Ă póĕm ĭs ă cómpŏsítĭŏn ‖ wrĭttĕn fŏr pĕrfórmănce bў
> thĕ húmăn vóĭce.

The double bar, known as a **caesura** (from the Latin word for "cut"), indicates a natural pause in the speaking voice, which may be short (as here) or long (as between sentences); the ˘ sign indicates an unstressed syllable, and the ´ sign indicates one that is stressed.

The pattern of emphasis, stress, or accent can vary from speaker to speaker and situation to situation. If someone were to contradict my definition of a poem, I might reply:

> Ă póĕm ís ă cómpŏsítĭŏn . . .

with a heavier stress on **is** than on any other syllable in the sentence. The signs ˘ and ´ make no distinction between varying levels of stress and unstress—it being left to the reader to supply such variations—but some analysts use the sign ˋ to indicate a stress falling between heavy and light.

Most people pay little or no attention to the sequence of stressed and unstressed syllables in their speaking and writing, but to a poet there may be no more important element of a poem.

Meter

If a poem's rhythm is structured into a recurrence of regular—that is, approximately equal—units, we call it meter (from the Greek word for "measure"). For many centuries after its origins were lost in the mists of antiquity, meter was the principal feature distinguishing poetry from prose. There are four metrical systems in English poetry: the accentual, the accentual-syllabic, the syllabic, and the quantitative. Of these, the second accounts for more poems in the English language—and in this anthology—than do the other three together.

Accentual meter, sometimes called *strong-stress meter,* is the oldest. The earliest recorded poem in the language—that is, the oldest of Old English or Anglo-Saxon poems, Cædmon's seventh-century "Hymn" (p. 1)—employs a line divided in two by a heavy caesura, each half dominated by the two strongly stressed syllables:

> **Hé aérĕst scĕŏp** ‖ **aéldă béarnŭm**
> [He first created⠀⠀for men's sons]
> **héofŏn tŏ hŕofĕ** ‖ **háliğ Scýppĕnd**
> [heaven as a roof⠀⠀holy creator]

Here, as in most Old English poetry, each line is organized by stress and by **alliteration** (the repetition of speech sounds—vowels or, more usually, consonants—in a sequence of nearby words). In a line structured by accentual meter, one and generally both of the stressed syllables in the first half-line alliterate with the first stressed syllable in the second half-line.

Accentual meter continued to be used into the late fourteenth century, as in Langland's *Piers Plowman* (p. 71), which begins:

> Iň ă sómĕr śesŏn, ‖ whăn sóft wăs thĕ sónnĕ,
> [In a summer season⠀⠀⠀⠀when mild was the sun,]
> Ĭ shóp mĕ iň shróuds, ‖ ăs Ĭ ă shépe wĕre . . .
> [I clad myself in clothes⠀⠀as if I'd become a sheep . . .]

However, following the Saxons' conquest by the Normans in 1066, Saxon native meter was increasingly supplanted by the metrical patterns of Old French poetry brought to England in the wake of William the Conqueror, although the nonalliterative four-stress line would have a long and lively continuing life—structuring, for example, section 2 of Eliot's "The Dry Salvages." The Old English metrical system has been occasionally revived in more recent times, as for Heaney's translation of *Beowulf* (p. 2), or the four-stress lines of Coleridge's "Christabel" and Wilbur's "Junk" (p. 1638); and many English poets from Spenser onward have used alliteration in ways that recall the character of Old and Middle English verse.

Accentual-syllabic meter provided the metrical structure of the new poetry to emerge in the fourteenth century, and its basic unit was the **foot**, a combination of two or three stressed and/or unstressed syllables. The four most common metrical feet in English poetry are:

1. **Iambic** (the noun is *iamb*): an unstressed followed by a stressed syllable, as in "New **York**." Between the Renaissance and the rise of free verse (p. 2048) in the last century, iambic meter was the dominant rhythm of English poetry, considered by many writers in English as well as classical Latin the meter closest to that of ordinary speech. For this reason, iambic meter is also to be found occasionally in the work of prose writers. Dickens's novel *A Tale of Two Cities,* for example, begins:

Ĭt wăs | thĕ **bést** | ŏf **tímes,** ‖ ĭt wăs | thĕ **wórst** | ŏf **tímes** . . .

2. **Trochaic** (the noun is *trochee*): a stressed followed by an unstressed syllable, as in the word *London* or the line from the nursery rhyme,

Lóndŏn | **brí**dge ĭs̆ | **fáll**ĭñg | **down** . . .

Here, as in many other trochaic lines, the final unstressed syllable has been dropped. This shortening, which gives prominence to the stressed syllable necessary for rhyme (p. 2036), is called a **catalectic** line end.

The word *London* may be a trochee, but it does not have to appear in a trochaic line. Provided its natural stress is preserved, it can take its place comfortably in an iambic line, like that from Eliot's *The Waste Land*:

Ă **crówd** | flow̆ed **óv** | ĕr **Lón** | dŏn **brídge** . . .

Whereas iambic meter has a certain gravity, making it a natural choice for poems on solemn subjects, the trochaic foot has a lighter, quicker, more buoyant movement. Hence, for example, its use in Milton's "L'Allegro" (lines 25–29, for example, on p. 403) and Blake's "Introduction" to *Songs of Innocence* (p. 733).

3. **Anapestic** (the noun is *anapest*): two unstressed syllables followed by a stressed syllable, as in *Tennessee* or the opening of Byron's "The Destruction of Sennacherib" (p. 834).

Thĕ **Ăssýr** | ĭăn căme **dówn** | lĭk̆e thĕ **wólf** | ŏn thĕ **fóld** . . .

The last three letters of the word *Assyrian* should be heard as one syllable, a form of contraction known as **elision**.

4. **Dactylic** (the noun is *dactyl*): a stressed syllable followed by two unstressed syllables, as in *Leningrad*. This, like the previous "triple" (three-

syllable) foot, the anapest, has a naturally energetic movement, making it suitable for poems with vigorous subjects, though not these only. See Hardy's "The Voice" (p. 1160), which begins:

Wŏmăn mŭch | mĭssed, hŏw yŏu | cáll tŏ mĕ, | cáll tŏ mĕ . . .

Iambs and anapests, which have a strong stress on the last syllable, are said to constitute a **rising meter,** whereas trochees and dactyls, ending with an unstressed syllable, constitute a **falling meter.** In addition to these four standard metrical units, there are two other (two-syllable) feet that occur only as occasional variants of the others:

5. **Spondaic** (the noun is *spondee*): two successive syllables with approximately equal strong stresses, as on the words "draw back" in the second of these lines from Arnold's "Dover Beach" (p. 1101):

Lĭstĕn! | yŏu héar | thĕ grát | ĭng róar
Ŏf péb | blĕs whĭch | thĕ waves | dráw báck, | ănd flíng . . .

6. **Pyrrhic** (the noun is also *pyrrhic*): two successive unstressed or lightly stressed syllables, as in the second foot of the second line above, where the succession of light syllables seems to mimic the rattle of light pebbles that the heavy wave slowly draws back.

Poets, who consciously or instinctively will select a meter to suit their subject, have also a variety of line lengths from which to choose:

1. **Monometer** (one foot): see the fifth and sixth lines of each stanza of Herbert's "Easter Wings" (p. 368), which reflect, in turn, the poverty and thinness of the speaker. Herrick's "Upon His Departure Hence" is a rare example of a complete poem in iambic monometer. The fact that each line is a solitary foot (˘ ´) suggests to the eye the narrow inscription of a gravestone, and to the ear the brevity and loneliness of life.

> Thus I
> Pass by
> And die,
> As one,
> Unknown,
> And gone:
> I'm made
> A shade,
> And laid
> I'th grave,
> There have
> My cave.
> Where tell
> I dwell,
> *Farewell.*

2. **Dimeter** (two feet): iambic dimeter alternates with iambic pentameter in Donne's "A Valediction of Weeping" (p. 300); and dactylic dimeter (´ �‿ ˘ | ´ ˘ ˘) gives Tennyson's "The Charge of the Light Brigade" (p. 1005) its galloping momentum:

> Cannon to right of them,
> Cannon to left of them,
> Cannon in front of them
> Volleyed and thundered;
> Stormed at with shot and shell,
> Boldly they rode and well,
> Into the jaws of Death,
> Into the mouth of hell
> Rode the six hundred.

Lines 4 and 9, each lacking a final unstressed syllable, are *catalectic,* a common feature of dactylic as of trochaic poems.

3. **Trimeter** (three feet): Ralegh's "The Lie" (p. 154) and Roethke's "My Papa's Waltz" (p. 1494) are written in iambic trimeter; and all but the last line of each stanza of Shelley's "To a Skylark" (p. 876) in trochaic trimeter.

4. **Tetrameter** (four feet): Marvell's "To His Coy Mistress" (p. 478) is written in iambic tetrameter; and Shakespeare's "Fear No More the Heat o' the Sun" (p. 276) in trochaic tetrameter.

5. **Pentameter** (five feet): the most popular metrical line in English poetry, the iambic pentameter provides the basic rhythmical framework, or **base rhythm,** of countless poems from the fourteenth century to the twenty-first, from Chaucer's "General Prologue" to *The Canterbury Tales* (p. 19) and Shakespeare's sonnets (p. 257) to Hill's "Lachrimae" (p. 1834) and Schnackenberg's "Supernatural Love" (p. 2003). It even contributes to the stately prose of the Declaration of Independence:

> Wĕ **hóld** | **thése trúths** | tŏ **bé** | **sélf-év** | ĭdeńt . . .

Anapestic pentameter is to be found in Browning's "Saul":

> Aš thў **lóve** | iš discóv | erĕd ălmíght | ў, ălmíght | ў, bĕ **próved**
> Thў **poẃer,** | thăt ĕxiśts | wĭth ańd **fór** | ĭt, ŏf **bé** | iňg bĕlóved!

A missing syllable in the first foot of the second line gives emphasis to the important word "power," which Browning (like many nineteenth-century Englishmen, but unlike most twenty-first-century Americans) probably pronounced as a single syllable.

6. **Hexameter** (six feet): The opening sonnet of Sidney's "Astrophil and Stella" (p. 213) and Dowson's "Non sum qualis eram bonae sub regno Cynarae" (p. 1211) are written in iambic hexameter, a line sometimes known as an **alexandrine** (probably after a twelfth-century French poem, the *Roman*

d'Alexandre). A single alexandrine is often used to provide a resonant termination to a stanza of shorter lines, as, for example, the Spenserian stanza (p. 2042) or Hardy's "The Convergence of the Twain" (p. 1156), in which the shape of the stanza suggests the iceberg that is the poem's subject. Swinburne's "The Last Oracle" is written in trochaic hexameter:

> Dáy bў | dáy thў | shádŏw | shínes iň | heávén bĕ | hóldĕn . . .

7. **Heptameter** (seven feet): Kipling's "Tommy" (p. 1181) is written in iambic heptameter (or **fourteeners,** as they are often called, from the number of their syllables), with an added initial syllable in three of the four lines that make up the second half of each stanza.

8. **Octameter** (eight feet): Browning's "A Toccata of Galuppi's" (p. 1017) is the most famous example of the rare trochaic octameter.

Poets who write in strict conformity to a single metrical pattern will achieve the music of a metronome and soon drive their listeners away. Variation, surprise, is the very essence of every artist's trade; and one of the most important sources of metrical power and pleasure is the perpetual tension between the regular and the irregular, between the expected and the unexpected, the base rhythm and the variation.

John Hollander has spoken of the "metrical contract" that poets enter into with their readers from the first few words of a poem. When Frost begins "The Gift Outright"—

> Thĕ lánd | wăs oúrs | bĕfóre | wé wĕre | thĕ lánd's

—we expect what follows to have an iambic base meter, but the irregularity or variation in the fourth foot tells us that we are hearing not robot speech but human speech. The stress on "we" makes it, appropriately, one of the two most important words in the line, "we" being the most important presence in the "land."

Frost's poem will serve as an example of ways in which skillful poets will vary their base meter:

1. Thĕ lánd | wăs oúrs | bĕfóre | wé wĕre | thĕ lánd's.
2. Shé wăs | oúr lánd ‖ móre thăn | ă hún | drĕd yéars
3. Bĕfóre | wé wĕre | hér péo | plĕ. | Shé | wăs oúrs
4. Iň Máss | ăchú | sĕtts, ‖ iň | Vírgĭn | ĭa,
5. Bŭt wé | wĕre Eng | lănd's, ‖ stíll | cŏlón | ĭăls,
6. Pŏsséss | ĭng whát | wĕ stíll | wĕre ún | pŏsséssed | bў.
7. Pŏsséssed | bў whát | wĕ nów | nó móre | pŏsséssed.
8. Sómethĭng | wé wĕre | wĭthhóld | ĭng máde | ŭs wéak
9. Uňtíl | wĕ foúnd | oút thăt | ĭt wăs | oŭrsélves
10. Wé wĕre | wĭthhóld | ĭng frŏm | oŭr lánd | ŏf lív | ĭng,
11. Aňd fórth | wĭth foúnd | săĺva | tiŏn iň | sŭrrén | dĕr.
12. Súch ăs | wĕ wére | wĕ gáve | oŭrsélves | oútríght

13. (Thĕ déed | ŏf gíft | wăs mán | ў deéds | ŏf wár)
14. Tŏ thĕ lánd | váguelў | reăl | ĭzĭñg | wéstwărd,
15. Bŭt stíll | uñstór | iĕd, ‖ art | lĕss, ‖ ún | ĕnhañced,
16. Súch ăs | shĕ wás, ‖ súch ăs | shĕ woúld | bĕcóme.

The iambic pentameter gives the poem a stately movement appropriate to the unfolding history of the United States. In the trochaic "reversed feet" at the start of lines 2, 10, 12, and 16, the stress is advanced to lend emphasis to a key word or, in the case of line 8, an important syllable. Spondees in lines 2 ("our land") and 3 ("her people") bring into equal balance the two partners whose union is the theme of the poem. Such additional heavy stresses are counterbalanced by the light pyrrhic feet at the end of lines 4 and 5, in the middle of line 10, and toward the end of line 14. The multiple irregularities of that line give a wonderful impression of the land stretching westward into space, just as the variations of line 16 give a sense of the nation surging toward its destiny in time.

Frost's reading of this poem at President Kennedy's inauguration differed at a number of points from the above scansion, in that it was more colloquial, less emphatic, but authors cannot control others' reading of their work as they control its writing. Scansion is to some extent a matter of interpretation, in which the rhetorical emphasis a particular reader prefers alters the stress pattern. Other readers of "The Gift Outright" might—no less correctly— prefer the following rhetorical variations of the base meter:

7. . . . wé nŏw . . .
9. Uñtíl | wé foŭnd . . .

An important factor in varying the pattern of a poem is the placing of its pauses, or caesurae. One falling in the middle of a line—as in line 4 above— is known as a medial caesura; one falling near the start of a line, an initial caesura; and one falling near or at the end of a line, a terminal caesura. When a caesura occurs as in lines 13 and 14 above, those lines are said to be **end-stopped.** Lines 3 and 9, however, are called **run-on lines** (or, to use a French term, they exhibit **enjambment**—"a striding over"), because the thrust of the incomplete sentence carries on over the end of the verse line. Such transitions tend to increase the pace of the poem, as the end-stopping of lines 10 through 16 slows it down.

A strikingly original and influential blending of the Old English accentual and more modern accentual-syllabic metrical systems was **sprung rhythm,** conceived and pioneered by Gerard Manley Hopkins.

Finding the cadences of his Victorian contemporaries—what he called their "common rhythm"—too measured and mellifluous for his liking, he sought a stronger, more muscular verse movement. Strength he equated with stress, arguing that "even one stressed syllable may make a foot, and consequently two or more stresses may come running [one after the other], which in common rhythm can, regularly speaking, never happen." In his system of sprung rhythm, each foot began with a stress and could consist of a single stressed syllable (ˊ), a trochee (ˊ ˘), a dactyl (ˊ ˘ ˘), or what he called a **first paeon** (´ ˘ ˘ ˘). His lines will, on occasion, admit other unstressed syllables, as in the sonnet "Felix Randal" (p. 1168):

> Félĭx | Rándăl, ‖ thĕ | fárriĕr, ‖ Ŏ ĭs hĕ | deád thĕn? ‖ my |
>   dútў ăll | éndĕd,
> Who hăve | watchĕd hĭs | mould ŏf măn, ‖ bĭg- | bonĕd
>   ănd | hárdў-| hándsŏme
> Pínĭng, ‖ pínĭng, ‖ tĭll | tíme whĕn | réasŏn | rámblĕd ĭn ĭt |
>   ănd sŏme
> Fátăl | fóur dĭs | órdĕrs, ‖ fléshed thĕre, ‖ áll cŏn | téndĕd?

A poetry structured on the principle that strength is stress is particularly well suited to stressful subjects, and the sprung rhythm of what Hopkins called his "terrible sonnets" (pp. 1167–72), for example, gives them a dramatic urgency, a sense of anguished struggle that few poets have equalled in accentual-syllabic meter.

A number of other poets have experimented with two other metrical systems.

Syllabic meter measures only the number of syllables in a line, without regard to their stress. Being an inescapable feature of the English language, stress will of course appear in lines composed on syllabic principles, but will fall variously, and usually for rhetorical emphasis, rather than in any formal metrical pattern. When Marianne Moore wished to attack the pretentiousness of much formal "Poetry" (p. 1329), she shrewdly chose to do so in **syllabics**, as lines in syllabic meter are called. The effect is carefully informal and prosaic, and few unalerted readers will notice that there are 19 syllables in the first line of each stanza; 22 in the second; 11 in the third (except for the third line of the third stanza, which has 7); 5 in the fourth; 8 in the fifth; and 13 in the sixth. That the poem succeeds in deflating Poetry (with a capital P) while at once celebrating poetry and creating it is not to be explained by Moore's talent for arithmetic so much as by her unobtrusive skill in modulating the stresses and pauses of colloquial speech. The result is a music like that of good free verse (p. 2048).

Because stress plays virtually no role in Romance languages such as French and Italian and in Japanese, their poetry tends to be syllabic in construction. One Japanese form that has taken root in English poetry on both sides of the Atlantic and beyond is the **haiku,** a three-line poem of seventeen syllables (divided 5, 7, 5). The haiku traditionally offers an image from the natural world—a flower, a branch of cherry blossom—and this convention Paul Muldoon adopts and adapts in his series of 110 "Hopewell Haiku":

> Good Friday. At three,
> a swarm of bees sets its heart
> on an apple tree.

Brilliantly, the Irish Roman Catholic grafts on to a form inextricably linked with the Japanese Shinto religion an image of Christ dying on the cross at three in the afternoon on the first Good Friday. Ezra Pound adapted the Japanese form in a poem whose title is an integral part of the whole:

In a Station of the Metro

The apparition of these faces in the crowd;
Petals on a wet, black bough.

The syllable count here (8, 12, 7) bears only a token relation to that of the strict Japanese pattern, but the poem succeeds largely because its internal rhymes (p. 2037)—*Station / apparition; Metro / petals / wet; crowd / bough*—point up a series of distinct stressed syllables that suggest, in an impressionist fashion, a series of distinct white faces. Other American masters of this form are Richard Wright (p. 1502) and Richard Wilbur (p. 1632), whose poem "Zea" (p. 1640) is composed of stanzas of rhymed haiku like Muldoon's.

A number of modern poets—among them Auden, Dylan Thomas, and Gunn—have written notable poems in syllabics; their efforts to capture the spirit—if not the letter—of a foreign linguistic and poetic tradition may be compared with those of many poets since the Renaissance who have attempted to render Greek and Latin meters into English verse, using the fourth metrical system to be considered here.

Quantitative meter, which structures most Greek, Sanskrit, and later Latin poetry, is based on notions of a syllable's "quantity," its duration in time (or its *length*). This is determined by various conventions of spelling as well as by the type of vowel sound it contains. Complexities arise because Latin has more word-stress than does ancient Greek, and hence there is often an alignment of stress and quantity in foot-patterns of later Latin verse. This is ironic in light of the efforts, on the part of some Renaissance English poets, to "ennoble" the vernacular English tradition by following classical metrical models. Although poets like Spenser and Sidney devised elaborate rules for determining the "length" of English syllables according to ancient rules, the theoretical prescriptions often generated poems in which "long" syllables are in fact stressed syllables. Indeed, one defender of quantitative meter in English, Thomas Campion, explicitly recommended a metrical system aligning stress with quantity; he illustrated his theory with some highly successful poems such as "Rose-cheeked Laura" (p. 280). Although some Renaissance experiments in quantitative meter produced poems distinctly less pleasing to the ear than to the (highly educated) eye, others, such as those in Sidney's *Arcadia,* work well and remind us that experiments in cultural translation—some more successful than others—have been an enduring part of the English poetic tradition from the Anglo-Saxon era to the present.

Rhyme

Ever since the poetry of Chaucer sprang from the fortunate marriage of Old French and Old English, rhyme (the concurrence, in two or more lines, of the last stressed vowel and of all speech sounds following that vowel) has been closely associated with rhythm in English poetry. It is to be found in the early poems and songs of many languages. Most English speakers meet it first in nursery rhymes, many of which involve numbers ("One, two, /

Buckle my shoe"), a fact supporting the theory that rhyme may have had its origin in primitive religious rites and magical spells. From such beginnings, poetry has been inextricably linked with music—Cædmon's "Hymn" (p. 1) and the earliest popular ballads (p. 97) were all composed to be sung—and rhyme has been a crucial element in the music of poetry. More than any other factor it has been responsible for making poetry memorable. Its function is a good deal more complicated than may at first appear, in that by associating one rhyme-word with another, poets may introduce a remote constellation of associations that may confirm, question, or on occasion deny the literal meaning of their words. Consider, for example, the opening eight lines, or *octave* (p. 2042), of Hopkins's sonnet "God's Grandeur" (p. 1166):

1. The world is charged with the grandeur of God.
2. It will flame out, like shining from shook foil;
3. It gathers to a greatness, like the ooze of oil
4. Crushed. Why do men then now not reck his rod?
5. Generations have trod, have trod, have trod;
6. And all is seared with trade; bleared, smeared with toil;
7. And wears man's smudge and shares man's smell: the soil
8. Is bare now, nor can foot feel, being shod.

The grand statement of the first line is illustrated not by the grand examples that the opening of lines 2 and 3 seem to promise, but by the surprising similes of shaken tin foil and olive oil oozing from its press. The down-to-earthiness that these objects have in common is stressed by the *foil / oil* rhyme that will be confirmed by the *toil / soil* of lines 6 and 7. At the other end of the cosmic scale, "The grandeur of *God*" no less appropriately rhymes with "his *rod*." But what of the implicit coupling of grand God and industrial humanity in the ensuing *trod / shod* rhymes of lines 5 and 8? These rhymes remind Hopkins's reader that Christ, too, was a worker, a walker of hard roads, and that "the grandeur of God" is manifest in the world through which the weary generations tread.

Rhymes appearing like these at the end of a line are known as **end rhymes,** but poets frequently make use of **internal rhyme** such as the *then / men* of Hopkins's line 4, the *seared / bleared / smeared* of line 6, or the *wears / shares* of line 7. **Assonance** (the repetition of identical or similar vowel sounds) is present in the *not / rod* of line 4. This sonnet also contains two examples of a related sound effect, **onomatopoeia,** sometimes called *echoism,* a combination of words whose sound seems to resemble the sound it denotes. So, in lines 3 and 4, the long, slow, alliterative vowels—"ooze of oil"—seem squeezed out by the crushing pressure of the heavily stressed verb that follows. So, too, the triple repetition of "have trod" in line 5 seems to echo the thudding boots of the laboring generations.

All the rhymes so far discussed have been what is known as **masculine rhymes** in that they consist of a single stressed syllable. Rhyme words in which a stressed syllable is followed by an unstressed syllable—*chiming / rhyming*—are known as **feminine rhymes.** Single (one-syllable) and double (two-syllable) rhymes are the most common, but triple and even quadruple rhymes are also to be found, usually in a comic context like that of Gilbert's

"I Am the Very Model of a Modern Major-General" (p. 1144) or Byron's *Don Juan* (p. 837):

> But—Oh! ye lords of ladies intell*ectual,*
> Inform us truly, have they not hen-*pecked you all?*

If the correspondence of rhyming sounds is exact, it is called **perfect rhyme** or else *full* or *true rhyme.* For many centuries, almost all English writers of serious poems confined themselves to rhymes of this sort, except for an occasional **poetic license** (or violation of the rules of versification) such as **eye rhymes,** words whose endings are spelled alike, and in most instances were pronounced alike, but have in the course of time acquired a different pronunciation: *prove / love; daughter / laughter.* Since the nineteenth century, however, an increasing number of poets have felt the confident chimes of perfect rhymes inappropriate for poems of doubt, frustration, and grief, and have used various forms of **imperfect rhyme,** including:

Off-rhyme (also known as *half rhyme, near rhyme,* or *slant rhyme*) differs from perfect rhyme in changing the vowel sound and/or the concluding consonants expected of perfect rhyme. See Byron's *gone / alone* rhyme in the second stanza of "On This Day I Complete My Thirty-sixth Year" (p. 862), or Dickinson's rhyming of *Room / Storm; firm / Room*; and *be / Fly* in "I heard a Fly buzz - when I died -" (p. 1121).

Vowel rhyme goes beyond off-rhyme to the point at which rhyme words have only their vowel sound in common. See, for example, the muted but musically effective rhymes of Dylan Thomas's "Fern Hill" (p. 1571): *boughs / towns; green / leaves; starry / barley; climb / eyes / light.*

Pararhyme, in which the stressed vowel sounds differ but are flanked by identical or similar consonants, is a term coined by Edmund Blunden to describe Wilfred Owen's pioneering use of such rhymes. Although they had occurred on occasion before—see *trod / trade* in lines 5 and 6 of "God's Grandeur"—Owen was the first to employ pararhyme consistently. In a poem such as "Strange Meeting" (p. 1389), the second rhyme is usually lower in pitch (has a deeper vowel sound) than the first, producing effects of dissonance, failure, and unfulfillment that subtly reinforce Owen's theme. The last stanza of his "Miners" shows a further refinement:

> The centuries will burn rich loads
>   With which we groaned,
> Whose warmth shall lull their dreaming lids,
>   While songs are crooned.
> But they will not dream of us poor lads,
>   Left in the ground.

Here, the pitch of the pararhyme rises to reflect the dream of a happier future—*loads / lids*—before plunging to the desolate reality of *lads,* a rise and fall repeated in *groaned / crooned / ground.*

The effect of rhyming—whether the chime is loud or muted—is to a large extent dictated by one rhyme's distance from another, a factor frequently dictated by the rhyme scheme of the poet's chosen stanza form. At one extreme stands the **monorhyme,** a poem of no predetermined meter, line-length, or number of lines; the sole requirement being its one rhyme. The greater the length of a monorhyme, the greater the difficulty of achieving the conversational fluency and ease of Dick Davis's "Monorhyme for the Shower":

> Lifting her arms to soap her hair
> Her pretty breasts respond—and there
> The movement of that buoyant pair
> Is like a spell to make me swear
> Twenty odd years have turned to air;
> Now she's the girl I didn't dare
> Approach, ask out, much less declare
> My love to, mired in young despair.
>
> Childbearing, rows, domestic care—
> All the prosaic wear and tear
> That constitute the life we share—
> Slip from her beautiful and bare
> Bright body as, made half aware
> Of my quick surreptitious stare,
> She wrings the water from her hair
> And turning smiles to see me there.

At the other end of the spectrum of rhyme stands Paul Muldoon's use of the same (or virtually the same) rhymes of the ninety-line poem, "Third Epistle to Timothy" (p. 1981), in the same order, in four other ninety-line poems: "Yarrow," "Incantata," "The Mud Room," and "The Bangle (Slight Return)." Only marginally less remarkable is Dylan Thomas's "Author's Prologue," a poem of 102 lines, in which line 1 rhymes with line 102, line 2 with 101, and so on, down to the central couplet of lines 51–52. Rhyme schemes, however, are seldom so taxing for poets (or their readers) and, as with their choice of meter, are likely to be determined consciously or subconsciously by their knowledge of earlier poems written in this or that form.

Forms

Basic Forms

Having looked at—and listened to—the ways in which metrical feet combine in a poetic line, one can move on to see—and hear—how such lines combine in the larger patterns of the dance, what are known as the forms of poetry.

1. **Blank verse,** at one end of the scale, consists of unrhymed (hence "blank") iambic pentameters. Introduced to England by Surrey in his translations from the *Aeneid* (1554), it soon became the standard meter for Elizabethan poetic drama. No verse form is closer to the natural rhythms of spoken English or more adaptive to different levels of speech. Following the example

of Shakespeare, whose kings, clowns, and countryfolk have each their own voice when speaking blank verse, it has been used by dramatists from Marlowe to Eliot. Milton chose it for his religious epic *Paradise Lost* (p. 420), Wordsworth for his autobiographical epic *The Prelude* (p. 781), and Coleridge for his meditative lyric "Frost at Midnight" (p. 810). During the nineteenth century, it became a favorite form of **dramatic monologues** such as Tennyson's "Ulysses" (p. 992) and Browning's "Fra Lippo Lippi" (p. 1026), in which a single speaker (who is not the poet) addresses a dramatically defined listener in a specific situation and at a critical moment. All of these poems are divided into **verse paragraphs** of varying length, as distinct from the **stanzas** of equal length that make up Tennyson's "Tears, Idle Tears" (p. 995) or Stevens's "Sunday Morning" (p. 1257).

2. The **couplet,** two lines of verse, usually coupled by rhyme, has been a principal unit of English poetry since rhyme entered the language. The first of the anonymous thirteenth- and fourteenth-century lyrics in this anthology (p. 15) is in couplets, but the first poet to use the form consistently was Chaucer, whose "General Prologue" to *The Canterbury Tales* (p. 19) exhibits great flexibility. His narrative momentum tends to overrun line endings, and his pentameter couplets are seldom the self-contained syntactic units one finds in Jonson's "On My First Son" (p. 323). The sustained use of such **closed couplets** attained its ultimate sophistication in what came to be known as **heroic couplets** ("heroic" because of their use in epic poems or plays), pioneered by Denham in the seventeenth century and perfected by Dryden and Pope in the eighteenth. The Chaucerian energies of the iambic pentameter were reined in, and each couplet made a balanced whole within the greater balanced whole of its poem, "Mac Flecknoe" (p. 517), for example, or "The Rape of the Lock" (p. 604). As if in reaction against the elevated ("heroic" or "mock heroic") diction and syntactic formality of the heroic couplet, more-recent users of the couplet have tended to veer toward the other extreme of informality. Colloquialisms, frequent enjambment, and variable placing of the caesura mask the formal rhyming of Browning's "My Last Duchess" (p. 1012), as the speaker of that dramatic monologue seeks to mask its diabolical organization. Owen, with the pararhymes of "Strange Meeting" (p. 1389), and Yeats, with the off-rhymed tetrameters of "Under Ben Bulben" (p. 1208), achieve similarly informal effects.

3. The **tercet** is a stanza of three lines traditionally linked with a single rhyme, although the tercets of Williams's "Poem" (p. 1275) and those of some other modern poets are unrhymed. It may also be a three-line section of a larger poetic structure, as, for example, the sestet of a sonnet (p. 2042). Tercets can be composed of lines of equal length—iambic tetrameter in Herrick's "Upon Julia's Clothes" (p. 359), trochaic octameter in Browning's "A Toccata of Galuppi's" (p. 1017)—or of different length, as in Hardy's "The Convergence of the Twain" (p. 1156). An important variant of this form is the linked tercet, or **terza rima,** in which the second line of each stanza rhymes with the first and third lines of the next. A group of such stanzas is commonly concluded with a final line supplying the missing rhyme, as in Wilbur's "First Snow in Alsace" (p. 1632), although Shelley expanded the conclusion to a couplet in his "Ode to the West Wind" (p. 872). No verse form in English

poetry is more closely identified with its inventor than is terza rima with Dante, who used it for his *Divine Comedy*. Shelley invokes the inspiration of his great predecessor in choosing the form for his "Ode" written on the outskirts of Dante's Florence, and T. S. Eliot similarly calls the *Divine Comedy* to mind with the tercets—unrhymed, but aligned on the page like Dante's—of a passage in part 2 of "Little Gidding" that ends:

> "From wrong to wrong the exasperated spirit
> Proceeds, unless restored by that refining fire
> Where you must move in measure, like a dancer."
> The day was breaking. In the disfigured street
> He left me, with a kind of valediction,
> And faded on the blowing of the horn.

4. The **quatrain,** a stanza of four lines, rhymed or unrhymed, is the most common of all English stanzaic forms. And the most common type of quatrain is the **ballad stanza,** in which lines of iambic tetrameter alternate with iambic trimeter, rhyming *abcb* (lines 1 and 3 being unrhymed) or, less commonly, *abab*. This, the stanza of popular ballads such as "Sir Patrick Spens" (p. 103), Coleridge's literary ballad "The Rime of the Ancient Mariner" (p. 812), and Dickinson's "I felt a Funeral, in my Brain" (p. 1115), also occurs in many hymns and is there called **common meter.** The expansion of lines 2 and 4 to tetrameters produces a quatrain known (particularly in hymnbooks) as **long meter,** the form of Hardy's "Channel Firing" (p. 1157). When, on the other hand, the first line is shortened to a trimeter, matching lines 2 and 4, the stanza is called **short meter.** Gascoigne uses it for "And If I Did, What Then?" (p. 144) and Hardy uses it for "I Look into My Glass" (p. 1153). Stanzas of iambic pentameter rhyming *abab*, as in Gray's "Elegy Written in a Country Churchyard" (p. 669), are known as **heroic quatrains.** The pentameter stanzas of FitzGerald's "Rubáiyát of Omar Khayyám of Naishápúr" (p. 961) are rhymed *aaba*, a rhyme scheme that Frost elaborates in "Stopping by Woods on a Snowy Evening" (p. 1237), where the third line (unrhymed in the "Rubáiyát") rhymes with lines 1, 2, and 4 of the following stanza, producing an effect like that of terza rima. Quatrains can also be in **monorhyme,** as in Rossetti's "The Woodspurge" (p. 1105); composed of two couplets, as in "Now Go'th Sun under Wood" (p. 15); or rhymed *abba,* as in Tennyson's "In Memoriam A. H. H." (p. 996).

5. **Rhyme royal,** a seven-line iambic-pentameter stanza rhyming *ababbcc,* was introduced by Chaucer in *Troilus and Criseide* (p. 67), but its name is thought to come from its later use by King James I of Scotland in "The Kingis Quair." Later examples include Wyatt's "They Flee from Me" (p. 127) and those somber stanzas in Auden's "The Shield of Achilles" (p. 1479) that describe the twentieth century, as a contrast to the eight-line stanzas with a ballad rhythm that describe a mythic past.

6. **Ottava rima** is an eight-line stanza, as its Italian name indicates, and it rhymes *abababcc*. Like terza rima and the sonnet (below), it was introduced to English literature by Sir Thomas Wyatt. Byron put it to brilliant use in *Don Juan* (p. 837), frequently undercutting with a comic couplet the seem-

ing seriousness of the six preceding lines. Yeats used ottava rima more gravely in "Sailing to Byzantium" (p. 1199) and "Among School Children" (p. 1200).

7. The **Spenserian stanza** has nine lines, the first eight being iambic pentameter and the last an iambic hexameter (an **alexandrine**), rhyming ababbcbcc. Chaucer had used two such quatrains, linked by three rhymes, as the stanza form of "The Monk's Tale," but Spenser's addition of a concluding alexandrine gave the stanza he devised for *The Faerie Queene* (p. 165) an inequality in its final couplet, a variation reducing the risk of monotony that can overtake a long series of iambic pentameters. Keats and Hopkins wrote their earliest known poems in this form, and Keats went on to achieve perhaps the fullest expression of its intricate harmonies in "The Eve of St. Agnes" (p. 907). Partly, no doubt, in tribute to that poem, Shelley used the Spenserian stanza in his great elegy for Keats, "Adonais" (p. 879); later, the form was a natural choice for the narcotic narrative of Tennyson's "The Lotos-Eaters" (p. 988).

Ottava rima and the Spenserian stanza each open with a quatrain and close with a couplet. These and other of the shorter stanzaic units similarly recur as component parts of certain lyrics with a fixed form.

8. The **sonnet,** traditionally a poem of fourteen iambic pentameters linked by an intricate rhyme scheme, is one of the oldest verse forms in English. Used by almost every notable poet in the language, it is the best example of how rhyme and meter can provide the imagination not with a prison but with a theater. The sonnet originated in Italy and, since being introduced to England by Sir Thomas Wyatt (see his "Whoso List to Hunt," p. 126) in the early sixteenth century, has been the stage for the soliloquies of countless lovers and for dramatic action ranging from a dinner party (p. 1108) to the rape of Leda and the fall of Troy (p. 1200). There are two basic types of sonnet—the Italian, or Petrarchan (named after the fourteenth-century Italian poet Petrarch), and the English, or Shakespearean—and a number of variant types, of which the most important is the Spenserian. They differ in their rhyme schemes, and consequently their structure, as shown on p. 2043.

The Italian sonnet, with its distinctive division into **octave** (an eight-line unit) and **sestet** (a six-line unit), is structurally suited to a statement followed by a counterstatement, as in Milton's "When I Consider How My Light Is Spent" (p. 418). The blind poet's questioning of divine justice is checked by the voice of Patience, whose haste "to prevent That murmur" is conveyed by the accelerated **turn** (change in direction of argument or narrative) on the word "but" in the last line of the octave, rather than the first of the sestet. Shelley's "Ozymandias" (p. 870) follows the same pattern of statement and counterstatement, except that its turn comes in the traditional position. Another pattern common to the Italian sonnet—observation (octave) and amplifying conclusion (sestet)—underlies Keats's "On First Looking into Chapman's Homer" (p. 905) and Hill's "The Laurel Axe" (p. 1835). Of these, only Milton's has a sestet conforming to the conventional rhyme scheme:

The Spenserian Sonnet

First quatrain	a b a b
Second quatrain	b c b c
Third quatrain	c d c d
Couplet	e e

couplet link

couplet link

The English Sonnet

First quatrain	a b a b
Second quatrain	c d c d
Third quatrain	e f e f
Couplet	g g

Turn

The Italian Sonnet

Octave	First quatrain	a b b a
	Second quatrain	a b b a

Turn

Sestet	First tercet	c d e
	Second tercet	c d e

others, such as Donne's "Holy Sonnets" (p. 318), end with a couplet, some-
times causing them to be mistaken for sonnets of the other type.

The English sonnet falls into three quatrains, with a turn at the end of
line 12 and a concluding couplet often of a summary or epigrammatic char-
acter M H. Abrams has well described the unfolding of Drayton's "Since
there's no help, come let us kiss and part" (p. 238): "The lover brusquely
declares in the first two quatrains that he is glad the affair is cleanly broken
off, pauses in the third quatrain as though at the threshold, and in the last
two rhymed lines suddenly drops his swagger to make one last plea." Spenser,
in the variant form that bears his name, reintroduced to the English sonnet
the couplets characteristic of the Italian sonnet. This interweaving of the
quatrains, as in sonnet 75 of his "Amoretti" (p. 194), makes possible a more
musical and closely developed argument, and tends to reduce the sometimes
excessive assertiveness of the final couplet. That last feature of the English
sonnet is satirized by Brooke in his "Sonnet Reversed," which turns romantic
convention upside down by *beginning* with the couplet:

> Hand trembling towards hand; the amazing lights
> Of heart and eye. They stood on supreme heights.

The three quatrains that follow record the ensuing anticlimax of suburban
married life. Meredith in "Modern Love" (p. 1107) stretched the sonnet to
sixteen lines; Hopkins cut it short in what he termed his **curtal** (a curtailed
form of "curtailed") **sonnet** "Pied Beauty" (p. 1167); while Shakespeare con-
cealed a sonnet in *Romeo and Juliet* (1.5.90–103). Shakespeare's 154 better-
known sonnets form a carefully organized progression, or **sonnet sequence,**
following the precedent of earlier sonneteers such as Sidney with his "Astro-
phil and Stella" (p. 213) and Spenser with his "Amoretti" (p. 190). In the
nineteenth century, Elizabeth Barrett Browning's "Sonnets from the Portu-
guese" (p. 947) continued a tradition in which the author of "Berryman's
Sonnets" has since, with that title, audaciously challenged the author of
Shakespeare's sonnets.

The twentieth century saw the introduction to English poetry of a Russian
sonnet, the stanza form of Alexander Pushkin's verse novel, *Eugene Onegin*
(1823–31). This was successfully translated—preserving its original form—
by Sir Charles Johnston in 1977; but it was not until 1986 that the Push-
kinian stanza first entered English poetry, in its own right, in Vikram Seth's
verse novel, *The Golden Gate* (p. 1994). Arguably the most technically
demanding of all English poetic forms, the Pushkinian stanza is composed
of fourteen tetrameter (not pentameter) lines rhyming as follows:

a	feminine rhyme (p. 2037)
b	masculine rhyme (p. 2037)
a	feminine
b	masculine
c	feminine
c	feminine
d	masculine

d	masculine
e	feminine
f	masculine
f	masculine
e	feminine
g	masculine
g	masculine

9. The **villanelle,** a French verse form derived from an earlier Italian folk song, retains the circular pattern of a peasant dance. It consists of five tercets rhyming *aba* followed by a quatrain rhyming *abaa,* with the first line of the initial tercet recurring as the last line of the second and fourth tercets and the third line of the initial tercet recurring as the last line of the third and fifth tercets, these two **refrains** (lines of regular recurrence) being again repeated as the last two lines of the poem. If A^1 and A^2 may be said to represent the first and third lines of the initial tercet, the rhyme scheme of the villanelle will look like this:

$$
\begin{array}{rccc}
\text{tercet 1:} & A^1 & B & A^2 \\
2: & A & B & A^1 \\
3: & A & B & A^2 \\
4: & A & B & A^1 \\
5: & A & B & A^2 \\
\text{quatrain:} & A & B & A^1\ A^2
\end{array}
$$

The art of writing complicated forms like the villanelle and sestina (see below) is to give them the graceful momentum of good dancing, and the vitality of the dance informs triumphant examples such as Roethke's "The Waking" (p. 1500), Bishop's "One Art" (p. 1527), and Thomas's "Do Not Go Gentle into That Good Night" (p. 1572).

10. The **sestina,** the most complicated of the verse forms initiated by the twelfth-century wandering singers known as troubadours, is composed of six stanzas of six lines each, followed by an **envoy,** or concluding stanza, that incorporates lines or words used before: in this case the *words* (instead of *rhymes*) end each line in the following pattern:

$$
\begin{array}{rcccccc}
\text{stanza 1:} & A & B & C & D & E & F \\
2: & F & A & E & B & D & C \\
3: & C & F & D & A & B & E \\
4: & E & C & B & F & A & D \\
5: & D & E & A & C & F & B \\
6: & B & D & F & E & C & A
\end{array}
$$

envoy: E C A or A C E [these lines should contain the remaining three end words]

The earliest example in this anthology is, in fact a *double* sestina: Sidney's "Ye Goatherd Gods" (p. 208). Perhaps daunted by the intricate brilliance of this, few poets attempted the form for the next three centuries. It was reintroduced by Swinburne and Pound, who prepared the way for notable contemporary examples such as Bishop's "Sestina" (p. 1520), Hecht's "The Book of Yolek" (p. 1566), and Ashbery's "The Painter" (p. 1736).

11. The **canzone,** another verse form initiated by the twelfth-century trou-badours, has a history of varying lengths and patterns. It often consists of five twelve-line stanzas and a five-line envoy, all employing the same five line-end words. A common pattern of repetition is that followed (with minor variations) by Agha Shahid Ali's "Lenox Hill" (p. 1959): *abaacaadaee / eaeebeeccedd / deddaddbbcc / cdcceccaacbb / bcbbdbbeebaa / abcde.*

12. The **pantoum,** a Malayan form in origin, entered English poetry by way of nineteenth-century French poetry. It may consist of any number of quat-rains, lines 2 and 4 of which are repeated as lines 1 and 3 of the next quatrain. The poem rhymes *abab / bcbc,* and so on, and generally ends with a quatrain whose **repetons** (repeated lines) are lines 1 and 3 of the first stanza in reversed order, or in a **repeton couplet** consisting of lines 1 and 3 of the first stanza in reversed order. See Donald Justice's "Pantoum of the Great Depression" (p. 1687) and Greg Williamson's "New Year's: A Short Pan-toum" (p. 2024).

13. The **limerick** (to end this section on the first of two lighter notes) is a five-line stanza thought to take its name from an old custom at convivial parties whereby each person was required to sing an extemporized "nonsense verse," which was followed by a chorus containing the words "Will you come up to Limerick?" The acknowledged Old Master of the limerick is Edward Lear (p. 1041), who required that the first and fifth lines end with the same word (usually a place-name), a restriction abandoned by many Modern Mas-ters, though triumphantly retained by the anonymous author of this:

> There once was a man from Nantucket
> Who kept all his cash in a bucket;
> But his daughter named Nan
> Ran away with a man,
> And as for the bucket, Nantucket.

14. The **clerihew,** named after its inventor, Edmund Clerihew Bentley (1875–1956), is a short comic or nonsensical poem about a famous person, consisting of two rhymed couplets with lines of unequal length. Some of the best are to be found in W. H. Auden's "Academic Graffiti"—this, for exam-ple:

> John Milton
> Never stayed in a Hilton
> Hotel,
> Which was just as well.

Composite Forms

Just as good poets have always varied their base rhythm, there have always been those ready to bend, stretch, or in some way modify a fixed form to suit the demands of a particular subject. The earliest systematic and successful pioneer of such variation was John Skelton, who gave his name to what has come to be called **Skeltonic verse**. His poems typically—see, for example, the extract from "Colin Clout" (p. 92)—have short lines of anything from three to seven syllables containing two or three stresses (though more of both are common), and exploit a single rhyme until inspiration and the resources of the language run out. The breathless urgency of this form has intrigued and influenced modern poets such as Graves and Auden.

Another early composite form employed longer lines: iambic hexameter (twelve syllables) alternating with iambic heptameter (fourteen syllables). This form, known as "poulter's measure"—from the poultryman's practice of giving twelve eggs for the first dozen and fourteen for the second—was used by sixteenth-century poets such as Wyatt (p. 126), Queen Elizabeth I (p. 142), and Sidney (p. 208), but has not proved popular since.

The element of the unexpected often accounts for much of the success of poems in a composite form such as Donne's "The Sun Rising" (p. 295). His stanza might be described as a combination of two quatrains (the first rhyming *abba,* the second *cdcd*), and a couplet (*ee*). That description would be accurate but inadequate in that it takes no account of the variation in line length, which is a crucial feature of the poem's structure. It opens explosively with the outrage of the interrupted lover:

> Busy old fool, unruly sun,
> Why dost thou thus
> Through windows and through curtains call on us?

Short lines, tetrameter followed by dimeter, suggest the speaker's initial shock and give place, as he begins to recover his composure, to the steadier pentameters that complete the first quatrain. Continuing irritation propels the brisk tetrameters that form the first half of the second quatrain. This, again, is completed by calmer pentameters, and the stanza rounded off like an English sonnet, with a summary pentameter couplet:

> Love, all alike, no season knows nor clime
> Nor hours, days, months, which are the rags of time.

This variation in line length achieves a different effect in the third stanza, where the brief trimeter suggests an absence contrasting with the royal presences in the preceding tetrameter:

> She's all states, and all princes, I,
> Nothing else is.

And these lines prepare, both rhetorically and visually, for the contraction and expansion so brilliantly developed in the poem's triumphant close. Similar structural considerations account for the composite stanza forms of Arnold's "The Scholar-Gypsy" (p. 1089) and Lowell's "Skunk Hour" (p. 1601), though variations of line length and rhyme scheme between the six-line stanzas of Lowell's poem bring it close to the line that divides composite form from the next category.

Irregular Forms

A poet writing in irregular form will use rhyme and meter but follow no fixed pattern. A classic example is Milton's "Lycidas" (p. 410), which is written in iambic pentameters interspersed with an occasional trimeter, probably modeled on the occasional half-lines that intersperse the hexameters of Virgil's *Aeneid*. Milton's rhyming in this **elegy** (a formal lament for a dead person) is similarly varied, and a few lines are unrhymed. The most extensive use of irregular form is to be found in one of the three types of **ode**.

Long lyric poems of elevated style and elaborate stanzaic structure, the original odes of the Greek poet Pindar were modeled on songs sung by the chorus in Greek drama. The three-part structure of the regular **Pindaric ode** has been attempted once or twice in English, but more common and more successful has been the irregular Pindaric ode, which has no three-part structure but sections of varying length, varying line length, and varying rhyme scheme. Each of Pindar's odes was written to celebrate someone, and celebration has been the theme of many English Pindaric odes, among them Dryden's "A Song for St. Cecilia's Day" (p. 524), Tate's "Ode to the Confederate Dead" (p. 1417), and Lowell's "The Quaker Graveyard in Nantucket" (p. 1592). The desire to celebrate someone or something has also prompted most English odes of the third type, those modeled on the subject matter, tone, and form of the Roman poet Horace. More meditative and restrained than the boldly irregular Pindaric ode, the **Horatian ode** is usually written in a repeated stanza form—Marvell's "An Horatian Ode (Upon Cromwell's Return from Ireland)" (p. 486) in quatrains, for example, and Keats's "To Autumn" (p. 939) in a composite eleven-line stanza.

Open Forms or Free Verse

At the opposite end of the formal scale from the fixed forms (or, as they are sometimes called, **closed forms**) of sonnet, villanelle, and sestina, we come to what was long known as free verse, poetry that makes little or no use of traditional rhyme and meter. The term is misleading, however, suggesting to some less thoughtful champions of **open forms** (as free-verse structures are now increasingly called) a false analogy with political freedom as opposed to slavery, and suggesting to traditionalist opponents the disorder or anarchy implied by Frost's in/famous remark that "writing free verse is like playing tennis with the net down." There was much unprofitable debate in the last century over the relative merits and "relevance" of closed and open forms, unprofitable because, as will be clear to any reader of this anthology, good poems continue to be written in both. It would be foolish to wish that Larkin wrote like Whitman, or Atwood like Dickinson. Poets must find forms and rhythms appropriate to their voices. When, around 1760, Smart chose an open form for "Jubilate Agno" (p. 678), that incantatory catalog of the attributes of his cat Jeoffry proclaimed its descent from the King James translation of the Hebrew Scriptures and, specifically, such parallel cadences as those of Psalm 150:

> Praise ye the Lord. Praise God in his sanctuary:
> praise him in the firmament of his power.

Praise him for his mighty acts: praise him
   according to his excellent greatness.
Praise him with the sound of the trumpet: praise
   him with the psaltery and harp.

These rhythms and rhetorical repetitions, audible also in Blake's prophetic books, resurfaced in the work of the nineteenth-century founder of American poetry, as we know it today. Whitman's elegy for an unknown soldier, "Vigil Strange I Kept on the Field One Night" (p. 1071), may end with a traditional image of the rising sun, like Milton's "Lycidas" (p. 410), but its cadences are those of the Hebrew Scriptures he read as a boy:

And there and then and bathed by the rising sun, my son in his grave, in
   his rude-dug grave I deposited,
Ending my vigil strange with that, vigil of night and battle-field dim,
Vigil for boy of responding kisses, (never again on earth responding,)
Vigil for comrade swiftly slain, vigil I never forget, how as day
   brighten'd,
I rose from the chill ground and folded my soldier well in his blanket,
And buried him where he fell.

Whitman's breakaway from the prevailing poetic forms of his time was truly revolutionary, but certain traditional techniques he would use for special effect: the concealed *well* / *fell* rhyme that gives his elegy its closing chord, for example, or the bounding anapests of an earlier line:

Ońe lóok | Ĭ bŭt **gáve** | whĭch yŏur **déar** | eўes rĕtuŕn'd |
   with ă **lóok** | Ĭ shăll **név** | ĕr fŏrgét . . .

The poetic revolution that Whitman initiated was continued by Pound, who wrote of his predecessor:

       It was you that broke the new wood,
       Now is a time for carving.

Pound, the carver, unlike Whitman, the pioneer, came to open forms by way of closed forms, a progression reflected in the first four sections of Pound's partly autobiographical portrait of the artist, "Hugh Selwyn Mauberley" (p. 1298). Each section is less "literary," less formal than the last, quatrains with two rhymes yielding to quatrains with one rhyme and, in section 4, to Whitmanian free verse. A similar progression from the mastery of closed forms to the mastery of open forms can be seen in the development of poets such as Lawrence, Eliot, Auden, Lowell, Rich, and Plath (pp. 1284, 1340, 1465, 1592, 1791, 1836, respectively).

   Pound may have called himself a carver, but he, too, proved a pioneer, opening up terrain that has been more profitably mined by his successors than the highlands, the rolling cadences explored by Smart, Blake, and Whitman. Pound recovered for poets territory then inhabited only by novelists, the low ground of everyday speech, a private rather than a public language. He was aided by Williams, who, in a poem such as "The Red Wheelbarrow," used the simplest cadences of common speech to reveal the extraordinary nature of "ordinary" things:

> so much depends
> upon
>
> a red wheel
> barrow
>
> glazed with rain
> water
>
> beside the white
> chickens.

Each line depends upon the next to complete it, indicating the interdependence of things in the poem and, by extension, in the world. "The Red Wheelbarrow" bears out the truth of Auden's statement that in free verse "you need an infallible ear to determine where the lines should end."

Other Forms of Poetry

Probably no century of the sixty since people began writing saw more experimentation in the arts generally, and in poetry particularly, than the last. The twentieth-century pioneers of what came to be known as the Confessional, Imagist, L=A=N=G=U=A=G=E, and Objectivist "schools" of poetry defined these modes by aesthetic or philosophic criteria, rather than by any distinct formal characteristics (that would qualify them for inclusion in this essay).

By contrast, the twentieth century witnessed the development of at least five other categories of experimental poetry that *can* be defined by their formal characteristics:

1. **Prose poetry** originated in nineteenth-century France, reaching perhaps its highest point in the work of Charles Baudelaire and Arthur Rimbaud. A prose poem may have any or all of the features of the lyric, except that it is set out on the page for the eye—though not the ear—as prose. Hill's "Mercian Hymns" may look like prose, but the poet insists that his lines are to be printed exactly as they appear on pp. 1833–34; and the reader's ear will detect musical cadences no less linked and flowing than in good free verse, with which prose poetry has much in common.

2. **Found poetry,** a twentieth-century offshoot of prose poetry, converts a passage or passages of someone else's prose—from a novel, a newspaper, even an advertisement—into a poem. This may involve some modification, like that described, for example, in Brownjohn's footnote to his poem "Common Sense" (p. 1829).

3. **Shaped poetry** has a distinguished lineage, extending from ancient Greece to modern England and America. Eye and ear together are never

more dramatically engaged than in the reading of shaped poems such as Herbert's "Easter Wings" (p. 368), Hollander's "Swan and Shadow" (p. 1775), and Corn's "A Conch from Sicily" (p. 1930).

4. **Concrete poetry** is an exception to the generalization at the start of this essay: "A poem is a composition written for performance by the human voice." (All generalizations are false, as the French say, including this one.) The term *concrete poetry* was coined by a group of Brazilian poets in 1952 to cover a loose category of verbal explorations by avant-garde artists and poets around the world. These range from ingenious typographic structures that, unlike the shaped poems mentioned above, cannot be "voiced"— Mahon's "The Window" (p. 1923), for example—to Jonathan Williams's "Three ripples in Tuckasegee River," which can:

TSI	KSI	TSI
KSI	TSI	KSI
TSI	KSI	TSI

The poet's note to this says: "Tsiksitsi is a Cherokee onomatopoeia for the sound of running water."

5. **Sound poetry,** extending the latter, more abstract form of concrete poetry into a kind of music, has been called "the ultimate performance poetry." Its performative nature is engagingly demonstrated by Edwin Morgan's poem "Interview," which begins:

> —When did you start writing sound-poetry?
>
> —Vindaberry am hookshma tintöl ensa ar'er.
>   Vindashton hama haz temmi-bloozma töntek.
>
> —I see. So you were really quite precocious.
>   And did your parents encourage you?
>
> —Zivva mimtod enna parahashtom ganna,
>   spod zivva didtod quershpöt quindast volla!
>   Mindetta brooshch quarva tönch bot.
>   Spölva harabashtat su!

Suggestions for Further Reading

Poets have been making poems for as long as composers have been making music or carpenters furniture, and just as it would be unreasonable to expect to find the lore and language of music or carpentry distilled into one short essay, so there is more to be said about the making and appreciating of poems than is said here. The fullest treatment of the subject is to be found in *A History of English Prosody from the Twelfth Century to the Present Day*, by George Saintsbury (3 vols., New York, 1906–10), and the *Princeton Ency-*

clopedia of Poetry and Poetics, edited by Alex Preminger, Frank J. Warnke, and O. B. Hardison, Jr. (Princeton, 1965; enl. ed., 1974). More suitable for students are *The Making of a Poem: A Norton Anthology of Poetic Forms,* edited by Mark Strand and Eavan Boland (New York, 2000), *The Poem's Heartbeat,* by Alfred Corn (Ashland, Ore., 1997), *An Introduction to English Poetry,* by James Fenton (London and New York, 2002), *Poetic Meter and Poetic Form,* by Paul Fussell (New York, 1965; rev. ed., 1979), *The Structure of Verse,* edited by Harvey Gross (New York, 1966; rev. ed., 1979), *Rhyme's Reason: A Guide to English Verse,* by John Hollander (New Haven, 1981; enl. ed., 1989), *The Poetry Handbook: A Guide to Reading Poetry for Pleasure and Practical Criticism,* by John Lennard (Oxford and New York, 1996), and the appropriate entries in *A Glossary of Literary Terms,* by M. H. Abrams (New York, 1957; 6th ed., 1990), and *The Oxford Companion to Twentieth-Century Poetry,* edited by Ian Hamilton (Oxford and New York, 1994). Each of these has its own more detailed suggestions for further reading.

JON STALLWORTHY

Poetic Syntax

In Alexander Pope's "The Rape of the Lock" (5.47; p. 619), there is a line few native speakers of English can grasp on first reading: " 'Gainst Pallas, Mars; Latona, Hermes arms." What do we make of such a line, which is punctuated as a self-contained unit of thought? And why does it occur in the work of a poet renowned for his elegance and clarity of expression? The answer, or at least one answer, is that Pope is using *poetic syntax* to mimic the hurried confusion that soldiers experience in battle. Describing a moment when two pairs of Greek gods are arming themselves to fight each other, as related in Homer's *Iliad*, Pope adapts a classic syntactic pattern with a Greek name—*zeugma*—for his own poetic purposes. **Zeugma** occurs when a single verb governs several parallel words or clauses (verbal units, discussed below on p. 2056). Using a pattern that some but not all of his English-speaking readers would have recognized, Pope makes a densely compressed line that slows any reader down, impeding easy comprehension. But perhaps that is part of Pope's aim, as he constructs a linguistic analogue for certain aspects of the imagined battle scene. In so doing, Pope uses syntax not only to communicate ideas but also to create certain dramatic and meaningful effects by the very structure of his lines.

What Is Syntax?

Syntax has been defined in many ways; we can begin our own inquiry into the theory and various historical practices of **poetic syntax** by saying that it concerns transactions between poets and their audiences—readers and listeners—about the meanings of certain sequences of words. The meanings emerge as words unroll in time and also—if we are reading the poem—in space. But meaning is also a function of how words and groups of words hark back to earlier ones, sometimes with the effect of suspending or even contesting time's forward motion.

The word *syntax,* from the Greek words *syn* (together) and *tax* (to arrange), denotes the "orderly or systematic arrangements of parts or elements." At the most general level, these elements involve symbols, including mathematical ones, that are arranged to create propositions or statements. The symbols that matter most for poetic syntax are words and groups of words; but punctuation marks, line shapes, stanza forms, metrical schemes, and rhyme patterns are also important for understanding poetic syntax as an arrangement of words that generates meaningful statements.

When we are discussing poetry, **syntax** may refer either to actual arrangements of words or to the rules of grammar and conventions of word order that are reflected—but also sometimes challenged—in such arrangements. We usually think of rules as governing behavior, and syntactic rules do govern the behavior of statements in various languages. In the domain of poetry, however, notions about governance, obedience, and order often exist in counterpoint to notions about the aesthetic as well as the social values of certain kinds of unruliness—those traditionally discussed under the rubric *poetic license*. Poetic syntax, therefore, is a slippery and even in some ways a contradictory topic, for while we are thinking about syntax as an orderly arrangement of verbal elements according to the conventions of a particular language, we also need to be thinking about poetic syntax as the making of significant disorder within a language—and often with allusions to other languages and their rules or practices of syntax. We can highlight a paradox inherent in any attempt to define poetic syntax by comparing poetic syntax to a game with complex rules that include—under certain circumstances—the option to break the rules.

Poets have played the syntactic game for a long time, often in competition with each other as well as with real and imagined audiences. In this game, some syntactic rules have changed; but many retain signs of the close historical links between English and Latin, two very different languages that nonetheless share many words as well as many ways of defining what constitutes syntactical "correctness." For students of poetic syntax, the most important difference between English and Latin is that in English, meaning depends on certain words being neighbors to one another, whereas in Latin, proximity and distance between words matters little for understanding most written statements. In Latin, a highly inflected language, endings of words (**suffixes**) tell us a great deal about which words in a given statement go with which other words; the endings of nouns, adjectives, and verbs change (are "inflected") according to their function in a given statement. English is a much less inflected language, although certain words need to "agree" with each other, as is true in Latin and many other languages too: singular nouns take singular verbs, for instance. In English, however, the most important determinant of meaning is the order of words, individually or in groups. The contrast can be summed up this way: in Latin you can tell your friend that she has *hit the nail on the head* by saying *"rem acu tetigisti"* or *"tetigisti acu rem."* But in English, you cannot perform the same linguistic operation without severe semantic consequences: there is a considerable difference between saying that *you hit the nail* and saying that *the nail hit you.*

Poets in English play incessantly with normal patterns of word order, thus creating a multitude of interesting, witty, logically subtle, and often surprising effects requiring us to ponder parallels between words and groups of words sometimes more widely separated from each other than they would be in an ordinary prose statement. Some poets in English use syntactic arrangements in ways that challenge the reader's expectations about word order; alternatively or additionally, some poets build sentences with multiple parts more complexly related to each other than they would be in most modern English speech or writing. To participate in the syntactic games poets typically play, we need some shared terms for describing the elements that poets arrange in orderly—but also apparently disorderly—fashion.

Parts of Syntax

Sentences and Words

The first rule of the poetic game of syntax as it is represented in an anthology like this one, which includes a wide range of poems written at many times in many forms of English, is that most poets use the grammatical unit called the *sentence* as a major unit of meaning, along with—but often in counterpoint to—the unit of the *poetic line* or the unit of the *stanza* (see "Versification," p. 2040). The **sentence** is the largest meaning-bearing unit of syntax, while the **word** is the smallest. Neither unit can be easily defined. This is so because both sentences and words can be compounded and divided in various ways that become more complex the more closely we look at them across the arc of history. (Because English has changed so much over time, in other words, we can't safely assume that modern rules apply in centuries-old texts; as best we can, we need to bring history into our readings.)

Sentences are sometimes defined as units that have **subjects** and **predicates**—in the simplest cases, a noun-subject and a predicate consisting only of a verb (*Jill runs*). In the most common type of English sentence, a noun working as a subject is followed by a verb, which leads to (and conceptually affects, acts on) a noun, which may or may not be modified and which is called a **direct object**: *the bird eats the worm* or, more elaborately, Edwin Muir's "The grasses threw straight shadows far away" ("Childhood"; p. 1337).

In a second very common sentence type, the subject is followed by a predicate that **complements** (refers back to) the subject. In this kind of sentence, the verb is usually a form of *to be* (or *to seem*) and there is no direct object; instead, a predicate complement tells us something about the subject, as in the first line of Dryden's "Mac Flecknoe" (p. 517): "All human beings are subject to decay"; another example is T. S. Eliot's line "I am not Prince Hamlet, nor was meant to be" ("The Love Song of J. Alfred Prufrock"; p. 1343); yet another is A. R. Ammons's wonderful opening to "Pet Panther" (p. 1700): "My attention is a wild / animal." This type of sentence lends itself to reflections about identity and to metaphor-making.

In yet a third type of sentence, the subject is followed by a verb that takes neither a direct object nor a predicate complement. Because they neither act on a direct object nor reflect back on the subject, such verbs are called **intransitive**: *Money talks*, for example, or *Jill faints*. A more elaborate example comes again from Eliot: "The winter evening settles down / With smell of steaks in passageways" ("Preludes"). Some verbs are always intransitive, while others can be either intransitive or **transitive**. If *a duck flies overhead*, the verb is intransitive; if *I fly my plane to Reno*, the verb is transitive. (When in doubt, check the dictionary.)

Some modern poets and philosophers prefer sentences with transitive verbs to all others. Indeed, early in the last century, a philosopher named Ernest Fenellosa, who was a student of Chinese poetry and a major influence on Ezra Pound, urged poets writing in English to strive for concreteness by avoiding the verb *to be* and intransitive verbs. Arguing that the "transfer of power" is a basic truth of nature, Fenellosa maintained that the proper work of poetic syntax is to show an agent (subject) performing an act (transitive verb) on an object, as in *Farmer pounds rice* (Davie, *Articulate Energy*, 36).

Fenellosa's theory can be contested on many counts, but it has the virtue of helping us understand why even those modern English-language poets who seem to wage war on the rules of grammar and punctuation nonetheless rely on the traditional subject/verb/direct object sentence as a basic building block of their poems. This is so, paradoxically, even in cases where the poem does *not* seem to include full sentences (see "Nominal Syntax" below, p. 2060). Because poets know that competent readers of English expect sentences, poets can assume that readers will work to create a sentence even when none seems to exist at first glance. Such work (which can also be seen as play) occurs when we reread the line by Pope quoted at the beginning of this essay: " 'Gainst Pallas, Mars; Latona, Hermes arms." Why do we eventually decide that "arms" is a verb and not a noun in this poetic sentence, which is chock-full of inert proper names and which doesn't give us a verb where we would normally expect it to be? The answer, or one answer, is that Pope expects us to resolve the "confusion" of his fighting gods into a kind of peace: the sense offered by the sentence. Aided by a knowledge of syntax, we can see not only that "arms" in this line functions as a verb, but also that it functions retroactively, as it were, serving as the intransitive verb for both parts of the statement. We can translate it into prose as *Mars [arms] against Pallas; Hermes arms against Latona.* Armed with a knowledge of syntax, and willing to expend time on translating or paraphrasing Pope's impacted statement, we can win meaning from his odd arrangement of words.

Although some poets (and English teachers) share Fenellosa's preference for sentences with a subject, an active verb, and a direct object, many poets vary their sentence structures to capture different shades of thought about action and passion—and to create subtly varied rhythms. Consider, for example, the opening stanza of Kenneth Koch's "Permanently" (p. 1691), which illustrates all three basic types of English sentence structure and concludes with special praise for one of them. Can you identify each type?

> One day the Nouns were clustered in the street.
> An Adjective walked by, with her dark beauty.
> The Nouns were struck, moved, changed.
> The next day a Verb drove up, and created the Sentence.*

As Koch's lines remind us, many sentences are little narratives; in them, something happens, a story is told, time passes in a consequential way. At the end, we pause, and that pause has been signaled, in writing since the late Middle Ages, with a period. This mark is the graphic equivalent of a drop in the voice or a time for breathing between thoughts. The word *period* has many historical meanings. One denotes the sentence itself; another denotes a particular kind of sentence, in which several *subordinate clauses* build toward a *main clause.*

Clauses

A **clause** is a verbal unit that may look like, may even be, a sentence because both contain subjects and predicates. *Jill runs home* is both a clause

---

*Line 1: subject + predicate complement (Nouns / were clustered).
Line 2: subject + intransitive verb (Adjective / walked by).
Line 3: subject + predicate complement (Nouns / were struck, moved, changed).
Line 4: subject + intransitive verb (Verb / drove up) and subject + transitive verb + direct object (Verb . . . / created / the Sentence).

and a sentence. But we understand the sentence to be the larger or "containing" unit and a clause to be the smaller or "component" unit. This is because a sentence may contain more than one clause. The "periodic" sentence, mentioned above, has one **main** (or **independent**) **clause** and any number of subordinate clauses (*When she remembered the time, which she did when the bell rang, Jill ran home*). Some sentences have two (or more) main clauses, although in such cases, the term *main* (again, or *independent*) loses some of its conventional meaning. Clauses in such sentences are **coordinate** and therefore, in truth, only semi-independent. They are sometimes connected by certain punctuation marks other than the period; today, independent clauses are usually yoked by the semicolon, but in older writing, the colon often connects clauses that are independent but nonetheless closely related. Alternatively, such clauses may be connected by **coordinating conjunctions** such as *and, but, so, for*. An example of such a conjunction occurs in Denise Levertov's poem "The Closed World":

> The house-snake dwells here still
> under the threshold
> but for months I have not seen it. . . .

A **subordinate clause** has a subject and a predicate, but cannot stand alone in (or as) a sentence. Such clauses appear in various positions in complex sentences—some precede, others follow, a main clause, and some are embedded in main clauses in ways that blur the grammatical and conceptual distinction between independence and dependence. Subordinate clauses often elaborate, qualify, or even undermine an idea or image in the main clause. In many English poems, clauses are building blocks of thought that invite the reader to look back at the beginning of the sentence, to do a mental double take, in order to grasp the logical relations among a sentence's multiple parts.

Subordinate clauses play syntactic roles similar to those played by three parts of speech: the noun, the adverb, and the adjective. Modern handbooks of grammar will give you full lists of the "joining words" that typically introduce the different kinds of subordinate clauses; adverbial clauses, for instance, usually follow subordinating conjunctions such as *after, although, as, as if, because, whether, while*. Shakespeare's Sonnet 106 (p. 265) begins with such an adverbial clause: "When in the chronicle of wasted time / I see descriptions of the fairest wights. . . ." Adjectival clauses, modifying a noun or pronoun, are typically introduced by **relative pronouns** (*that, which, who, whom, whose*) or by **relative adverbs** (*when, where, why*). Shakespeare's Sonnet 116 ("Let me not to the marriage of true minds"; p. 266) uses an adjectival clause in its second main clause: "Love is not love," Shakespeare writes, "which alters when it alteration finds." Here, the subordinate clause follows and explains the contradictory proposition of the main clause (a good example, by the way, of the kind of predicate complement clause that Fenellosa thought poets should avoid).

The lines illustrate not only an adjectival clause at work but also the complex relation that can exist between main and subordinate clauses. When we read Shakespeare's lines carefully, we mentally reorder the syntactic elements to place the subordinate, or "dependent" (from the Latin *pendere*, hanging), clause between, rather than after, the subject and its predicate complement, which is of course also "love": the same word but different in syntactic function. If we visualize this main clause and its dependent one (only part of a much longer sentence in the sonnet), we could diagram the relationship this way:

Love   is not love
     \
        which alters when it alteration finds

Such diagramming, which reminds us that in Latin, *sub* means "beneath," can often be a useful tool for sorting out relations among syntactic parts of poems. (For a fine example of such diagramming, see James Winn's rendering of the opening sentence of Milton's *Paradise Lost*, which Linda Gregerson reproduces and trenchantly discusses in "Anatomizing Death," 105.)

Adjectival and adverbial clauses are fairly easy to discern because they modify a noun, pronoun, or verb in the main clause and can be diagrammed as hanging from (depending on) a word in the main clause. Noun clauses are harder to spot. They can be introduced by relative pronouns and also by other pronouns such as *whoever, whomever, what, whatever, whichever*. Moreover, noun clauses can follow many of the same subordinating conjunctions that signal adverbial clauses. The key to identifying noun clauses is to understand their syntactic functions in the poetic sentences with which we are working. Noun clauses may be subjects, direct objects, objects of prepositions, or predicate complements; but they always appear in statements that cannot stand alone. Sometimes, however, we have to excavate these clauses because the poet has omitted the joining or articulating words that would help us see the poem's syntactic skeleton clearly. If we know how the clauses are working syntactically, however, we can catch them; there are many rewards to doing so.

Let's consider Shakespeare's Sonnet 106 (p. 265) as an illustration of how a poet uses interplay among clauses to make meaning. In the version below, to clarify the poem's structure, we have put the beginnings of main clauses (introductory words followed by subjects and verbs) in **bold**; we have put the beginnings of subordinate clauses in *italic*.

> *When* in the chronicle of wasted time
> *I see* descriptions of the fairest wights,
> And beauty making beautiful old rhyme
> In praise of ladies dead and lovely knights,
> 5 **Then,** in the blazon of sweet beauty's best,
> Of hand, of foot, of lip, of eye, of brow,
> **I see** *their antique pen would have expressed*
> Even such a beauty *as you master* now.
> **So** all their **praises are** but prophecies
> 10 Of this our time, all you prefiguring;
> **And,** *for they looked but with divining eyes,*
> **They had not** skill enough your worth to sing:
> **For we,** *which now behold these present days,*
> **Have** eyes to wonder, **but lack** tongues to praise.

Finding the main clause or clauses is the first step in analyzing this or any poem. Having found the poem's head and torso, as it were, we can proceed to finding the subordinate clauses, which can be compared to the poem's limbs. Whether the body arises into (new) life depends in part on who is reading it, how. In this sonnet, we have to wait patiently for a main clause to appear ("I see," in line 7); and when it does, we may not recognize it, for its thought as well as its syntax seem, paradoxically, to depend on those of the initial dependent clause. Although the "when . . . then" structure embodies a careful balance of ideas (each clause gets exactly four lines), the second clause is the main clause: "When" sets up expectations for the thought to be completed, and it is completed, albeit in a way that the rest of the sonnet elaborates and qualifies.

We've found the main subject and verb, and we may well expect to find a direct object too. We do, momentarily, in the phrase "their antique pen." But the syntax soon asks us to correct that idea, for the image of the pen is followed by a verb phrase that makes the pen the subject of a new little story: "I see [that] their antique pen would have expressed / Even such a beauty . . ." Experienced readers will add *that* (the missing relative pronoun) automatically, but even they will have to engage in some subliminal revision, reversing the usual forward motion of reading (left to right, on the page of a text in English).

What advantage is there to recognizing the first main clause's direct object as a subordinate (noun) clause? Doing so helps us see that the "object" the poet finally sees in his main clause is not really an object, a thing, at all; instead, what the Shakespearean speaker sees (here and elsewhere in his sonnets) is an amazing blending of past and present, of certainty and supposition: a constructed object rather than a natural one. The main clause and its exfoliating direct object thus work to tell us something about the speaker's way of seeing as well as about what he sees. This may interest us as readers, because what the speaker is seeing arises from his interpretation of meanings located in old books (they are to him as he is to us) considered in relation to his present and, by implication, his future.

In line 8, we need to excavate or cocreate another subordinate clause to make sense of the sonnet. As we needed to supply *that* to see the noun clause serving as the direct object of "I see," so we also need to supply missing words to line 8 to make it work: "Even such a beauty as [the one that] you master now." This subordinate clause, functioning both to rename and to describe the "beauty" that is the direct object of the noun clause functioning as a direct object of "I see," blurs the traditional distinction between adjectival and noun clause. Thus the syntax, particularly the interplay of main and subordinate clauses, contributes to the poem's larger meditation on themes of mastery, competition, and relations of interdependence between past and present, lover and beloved, writer and reader, subject and object of seeing.

In the last six lines, we have more main clauses than in the first eight, and they come more rapidly (and briefly) in the final couplet. They are introduced by coordinating conjunctions that, when singled out, help us see the logical skeleton of the poet's thought: "So," "And," "For." Note, finally, that the embedded subordinate clause in line 11 may fool us into thinking it a main clause ("for," after all, introduces a main clause just two lines later). Upon close analysis, however, we see that the group of words introduced by the first "for" works adverbially, to modify the verb phrase that comes in the next line. "For" is therefore glossed (translated as) "because" by this anthology's editors, not because they have access to some mysterious dictionary unavailable to readers but rather because they have decoded the poem's syntax and come to the conclusion—as you can too—that line 11, after "And," both interrupts and helps explain the poet's claim that his predecessors lacked the skill to praise the speaker's beloved because they could see him or her only by "divining," or imagining, him or her.

Distinguishing between main and subordinate clauses is not always easy; but it is an important skill for players of the syntax game. Equipped with terms for describing syntactic elements precisely, we turn now to other moves poets make with sentences—and with readers' expectations about them.

Moves in the Game

Syntax operates as a kind of promise or contract of expectation between poet and reader, so the use of subordinate clauses to delay a main verb can function as a kind of tease. Milton, for instance, at the opening of *Paradise Lost* (p. 421), and William Collins, at the opening of "Ode to Evening" (p. 675), give us many lines of complexly interrelated subordinate clauses to ponder—and remember—before we reach the main verb of the first poetic sentence. In Milton's epic, the imperative verb "sing" arrives after five lines; in Collins's ode, the imperative verb phrase "now teach me" arrives only in line 15, after a many-stranded subordinate clause (beginning "If aught . . .") in which the poet seems to attempt to prove to his addressee—the "Evening" personified as "Eve"—that his own "pastoral song" has the power "to soothe thy modest ear."

Poets' relations to their readers are often figured in terms of pleas and commands addressed to a *muse,* a source of inspiration traditionally gendered female and often addressed as *thou.* In both Milton's and Collins's poems, the exquisitely delayed arrival of the main verb challenges the reader to participate in the poet's game of call-and-response over a space of time epitomized by the sentence's prolonged unfolding. Milton's opening sentence points back to Genesis and forward to Christ's Second Coming; Collins's opening sentence points back to Milton while also mimicking the gradual coming of evening in a northern, English latitude. The Romantic poet Hannah More, meanwhile, provides an interesting variant on the syntactic pattern of the Miltonic *invocation* (the poem's opening address to a muse) by addressing an ungendered and plural set of muses ("Airy spirits") in line 1 of her "Inscription in a Beautiful Retreat Called Fairy Bower" (p. 707) while delaying her main verb ("come") to line 7. In other poems, the verb doesn't come at all.

Nominal Syntax

Consider, for example, this very short poem by Ezra Pound:

In a Station of the Metro

The apparition of these faces in the crowd;
Petals on a wet, black bough.

Giving us two **noun phrases** but no verb, Pound's poem illustrates what some critics have called **nominal syntax**: the use of noun phrases in a way that asks the reader to make a conceptual or emotional connection between the poem's syntactic parts (Cureton, 322). "In a Station of the Metro" derives from Pound's appropriation of the ancient Japanese haiku for the modern Imagist movement. But if we read these three lines carefully, and with some knowledge of syntactic traditions in English-language poetry, we see that Pound not only provides us with striking images but also plays creatively with the poetic tradition of the delayed opening verb, which is itself related to the oratorical tradition of periodic sentences aimed at keeping the audience in a state of suspense. Pound's poem figuratively has us wait—in a French subway station—for a verb that never arrives. If, however, we play the poet's syntactic game by supplying some conceptual or emotional link between the poems' two major images, which seem to come from two very different worlds—on the one hand that of the bustling city, on the other hand that of nature, or (perhaps) of nature as represented in Japanese art—we will have played a role traditionally ascribed to the poet's muse: that of setting the poet's train of thoughts in motion.

As Pound's poem suggests, even modern poets who use various techniques of sentence fragmentation to challenge poetic tradition as well as conventions of ordinary language-use presuppose that the reader knows sentence rules well enough to appreciate meanings created when expectations are not fulfilled. Such poets dramatize the notion mentioned above: of syntax as a kind of contract between poet and reader. Their shared knowledge of rules, like soccer players' knowledge of the moves of their game, is often barely conscious until it is analyzed (as in a slow-speed replay). And for readers as for athletes, new knowledge often comes when we feel that rules have been bent or broken, and we stop to ask what's wrong.

In the opening stanza of "since feeling is first" (p. 1394), E. E. Cummings seems to justify the breaking of syntactic and other language-use rules:

> since feeling is first
> who pays any attention
> to the syntax of things
> will never wholly kiss you;

But what is Cummings really saying here about paying (or not paying) attention to "the syntax of things"? He is using an old and important poetic technique—what the critic William Empson calls **double syntax**—to make two quite different statements in this four-line unit ending with a semicolon, a punctuation mark that, as we've seen, typically signals the end of a main clause.

Double Syntax

This occurs when a phrase, line, or group of lines can be read in two different ways in relation to the syntax that precedes and/or follows the unit. In many examples of double syntax, the poet gives us an apparently complete thought—in a syntactic unit that appears to be an independent clause—but then goes on to revise the thought, often in a witty or paradoxical way, by showing us that the unit we thought was complete is part of a larger (and usually more conceptually challenging) syntactic structure, often a sentence.

In Cummings's "since feeling is first," the first three lines can be interpreted as a complex sentence, with a subordinate adverbial clause followed by a main one. The statement emphasizes with a **rhetorical question** a consequence of an apparently logical opening premise. We can make sense of the first three lines by adding a question mark after line 3 and paraphrasing them thus: *Because feeling comes first, that is, is most important in a scale of values, who in her or his right mind would pay any attention to the syntax (orderly or logical arrangement) of things?* The question is rhetorical because it assumes a simple answer that everyone agrees on; such questions are often used to imply that everyone consents to an idea that might well merit questioning and even dissent.

Cummings undermines his own poem's rhetorical question (and also the coercive logic of its initial clause) when, in line 4, he offers a phrase that seems, at first, a sentence fragment jarringly unrelated to the first three lines. If, however, we pay attention to Cummings's syntax, we will go back and reread the first three lines in the light of the new thought given in line 4. We can then paraphrase the unit as a whole this way: *Since feeling comes first (logically and, in this poem, temporally too), he or she who pays attention to the syntax of things will never kiss you fully or totally.* The second, fuller reading requires us to supply a pronoun subject before the word "who"; that word thus becomes a relative pronoun as the opening lines change from asking a simple (and arguably simplistic) rhetorical question into making a more syntactically complex statement.

Word Order Inversions

Many poetic ambiguities, including many of those in examples of double syntax, arise from **inversions** of the basic transitive sentence, subject/verb/object. The most common of these changes places the direct object before the subject and verb: "A curious knot God made in paradise," Edward Taylor writes, for example, at the beginning of his "Upon Wedlock, and Death of Children" (p. 537). Had Taylor used normal word order for this opening clause—"God made a curious knot in paradise"—he would have lost the opportunity to establish a meaningful and visually striking parallel between his title's first noun, "wedlock," and the word "knot" in his opening line. By putting "wedding" and "knot" into parallel positions, Taylor sets the stage for the conceptual definition of "knot" as "marriage"; but by inverting normal word order to achieve the parallelism, he also subtly introduces another meaning of "knot" developed in the poem: knot as a puzzle, as something that challenges reason and even faith in God's providential plan (note the pun on "knot" and "not"). Here, as in many poems, word order inversion allows the poet to emphasize a certain idea or image by giving it pride of place. The inversion, often accompanied by interesting rhythms and rhymes, works to provoke thought.

In many of the older poems in this anthology, lines that may seem completely obscure at first become clear, even witty, when we unscramble a word order inversion. John Donne's famous poem commanding his mistress to undress and make love to him begins, for instance, with the following independent clause: "Come, Madam, come, all rest my powers defy . . ." If we try to read this as a sentence that uses the most common English pattern, subject/verb/direct object, we will be perplexed, for how can one's "rest" "defy" one's "powers"? If we work at the syntax, however, we will see that the verb form offers a clue that an "inversion" is occurring here. "Defy" goes ("agrees") with a plural subject, not a singular one (you wouldn't say, "My cat defy my dog"). Mentally rearranging Donne's word order, we arrive at a clause that is both grammatically correct and a brilliant introduction to the poem's bawdy, boasting humor: *my powers defy all rest.* "Rest," we see, turns out to be the direct object, not the subject, of the statement. The subject (in terms of grammar but also of theme) is the speaker's "powers," which, he says, "defy" or resist "rest," either as "sleep" or as masculine "slackness." The poem goes on to develop an intricate association (a curious knot?) between a man's sexual powers and his verbal powers of persuasion.

Edmund Spenser also uses word order inversion to create witty effects that have serious metaphysical implications. Early in his epic poem *The Faerie Queene* (1.1.8–9; p. 167), he describes his young, inexperienced hero this way:

> Full jolly knight he seemd, and faire did sitt,
> As one for knightly giusts and fierce encounters fit.

The first clause, we see, is a sentence of the type we've classified as a predicate complement; using normal English word order to make the same point, we could say that *he seemed a very jolly [i.e., gallant or cheerful] knight.* Putting the sentence this way—performing the operation known as "paraphrasing"—is critical to understanding not only Spenser's syntax but also some of the larger themes of his Protestant epic. Indeed, syntax—which in this case requires us to think twice about our first impression of how the hero looks as a soldier—is one of Spenser's main tools for warning the reader not to take appearances as the truth.

In Spenser's Protestant poem, syntax often works to dramatize the value of faith in an "invisible" reality; such faith is accompanied by, indeed grows from, a distrust of sensory impressions in general and of visual images in particular. Advancing his lesson in iconoclasm or distrust of images, Spenser crafts a sentence in which we first see (the words for) "jolly knight"; then we get the sentence's grammatical subject, "he"; and then we get a verb that creates irony at the hero's expense by retroactively questioning the "fit" between the hero's appearance and his inward state of readiness for religious battle. In the narrative that follows, the hero will repeatedly fall into error by believing first impressions.

In Spenser's poem as in many others in this anthology, syntactic inversion acquires resonance when considered along with historical, philosophical, religious, and other determinants of meaning. In his elegy "Adonais" (31–34; p. 880), for example, Percy Bysshe Shelley uses word order inversion in the course of raising some broad questions about theology, history, and politics—questions that require us to move from text to context to interpret syntactically difficult lines. In them, Shelley describes the poet John Milton as

> Blind, old, and lonely, when his country's pride,
> The priest, the slave, and the liberticide,
> Trampled and mocked with many a loathed rite . . .

Which of the nouns preceding the transitive verbs is the subject of the subordinate clause beginning with "when," and which is the object? Two patterns of poetic inversion—subject/object/verb or object/subject/verb—are most common in metrical English poetry. Is the pride of the country performing the actions of trampling and mocking the priest, the slave, and the "liberticide," that is, the killer of liberty? Or are the three figures mentioned in the passage's second line trampling and mocking the kind of pride in his country that Milton felt?

We can't solve this puzzle unless we go beyond the syntax just of these lines to learn something about Milton and about Shelley's views of his precursor, who was finally on the losing side of the English Civil War and who was denounced as a *regicide* (king killer) by some of his enemies. Once we know that Shelley shared Milton's love of liberty and his scorn for the "rites" of the established English Church and state, we can see that the second paraphrase given above is distinctly preferable to the first: the priest, slave, and liberticide trampled and mocked Milton's pride in his country. We can also now see another possible reading of the lines: the phrase "when his country's pride" can describe Milton, a meaning that shifts our understanding of what is a subordinate, what a main clause here. We can, that is, also paraphrase these lines as saying that *the priest, the slave, and the liberticide trampled and mocked Milton when [he was] his country's pride, and they did so with many a loathed rite.*

Shelley's syntax is famously fluid. Indeed, some have denounced it as incoherent. Others have defended it by arguing that Shelley's poetry creates "the vocabulary and syntax" of a new vision of reality (Simpson, 82). For both philosophical and political reasons, Shelley wanted to blur traditional distinctions between subjects and objects; his syntax reflects that interest. In the case we have just examined, the syntactic obstacles to (immediate) comprehension dramatize the ongoing competition between different political views of liberty in England and challenge the reader to resolve the competition in a way that rejects one possible reading to respect others more consonant with what we can glean from many sources about Shelley's—and Milton's—views of liberty.

Because the significant ambiguities in a poem's syntax may be historically motivated, they often send us to other poems by the same author, other poems by authors we know or suspect that our poet read, and even to the larger texts of history, which include ongoing political, theological, and literary debates. Ambiguities of poetic syntax also invite us to consider other meaningful aspects of poems such as rhythm, stanza forms, line breaks, and punctuation. These phenomena are no less important to poems we hear read aloud, or sung, than they are to poems we encounter primarily through the eye. But when we read poems on the page, we necessarily confront the myriad ways in which printers and editors, in tandem with the poems' original authors, shape what we see. Our very perception of some poetic ambiguities depends on the presence or absence of judgments by other readers about, for instance, punctuation marks and spelling. With older poems in particular, punctuation marks may represent a printer's or an editor's interpretation of a line. Conventions of punctuation have changed over time, and the meaning of punctuation is always open to interpretation whether or not we possess a material text thought to represent an author's intent—which, in any case, may have changed in his or her own lifetime as a reader of his or her own poems. In any case, it is appropriate to end this introduction to poetic syntax with some brief examples of syntactic analysis linked to questions about punctuation, about the poem's mode of being as a (reproducible) material object, and about acts of interpretation—including those of editors and other readers—as moves in a game without closure.

The Game of Interpretation
Emily Dickinson

When poems exist in multiple manuscript versions, editors necessarily make interpretive decisions about syntax simply by deciding which version to print. This is strikingly the case for editors of Emily Dickinson, since Dickinson published few of her poems during her life and left almost two thousand poems—in various groupings (including more than forty hand-bound booklets called "fascicles") and in various kinds of drafts (including scrawls on the backs of envelopes)—at her death. Many poems exist in several different forms (available at www.emilydickinson.org and in the vario-rum edition by R. W. Franklin). In some Dickinson poems, the presence or absence of a certain punctuation mark contributes to rich opportunities for interpretive debate. Compare, for example, two versions of her poem "A Bird, came down the Walk" (no. 359 [328]; p. 1116). In one version, printed in R. W. Franklin's reading edition of Dickinson's poems and in this anthology, the complex relation between the bird and the poem's speaker—an "I"/eye looking at the bird as the bird is looking at the speaker—is rendered as follows in the third stanza and the beginning of the fourth:

> He glanced with rapid eyes,
> That hurried all abroad -
> They looked like frightened Beads, I thought,
> He stirred his Velvet Head. -
>
> Like one in danger, Cautious,
> I offered him a Crumb . . .

In another version of this poem, however—a version printed in many modern anthologies—the transition between the third and fourth stanzas occurs without any punctuation. This editorial choice changes the poem's syntax and, in so doing, invites debate about how we perceive the relation between two creatures, the bird and the human speaker, caught in the act of looking at each other:

> He stirred his Velvet Head
>
> Like one in danger, Cautious,
> I offered him a Crumb

The absence of punctuation between the stanzas in this version of the poem allows us initially to read the new stanza as part of the preceding clause, in which the subject is "he," the bird. Reading on, however, we see that the new stanza's opening line can also be understood as belonging to a new clause, one with "I," the speaker, as its subject. This ambiguity creates an unsettling effect, making the reader go back and forth between syntactic alternatives in a conceptual movement subtly likened—through the poet's craft—to the bird's head movements or to the dizzying exchanges of gazes, and of fears, between human and bird. Like the earlier example from Cummings's "since feeling is first," this version of Dickinson's poem gives us two readings that are equally plausible in syntactic terms; the second reading, however, which necessarily encompasses our consideration of the first, is more complex, in part because the idea of a human in danger when offering a crumb to a bird is less commonsensical than the idea of a bird feeling in danger when approaching a human. This bird, however, has been described earlier in the poem as biting a worm "in halves" and as eating "the fellow, raw," while not knowing he is being watched by the speaker. The poem as a whole creates a coolly terrifying atmosphere in which the possibility arises that the speaker is in no less danger from an unknown "watcher" than the bird is. Double syntax works to slow us down and make us aware of an unfamiliar world where some "hidden purpose," as the poet Thom Gunn calls it, causes such creatures as birds to look, by the poem's end, like butterflies leaping "off Banks of Noon" and landing without splashes in an alien element where they may live or die "as they swim."

In another poem by Dickinson, "On a Columnar Self" (no. 740 [789]; p. 1121), we have to intervene more actively to make the double syntax work; here, as is often the case in poetic interpretation, we must supply either a missing word or a punctuation mark to make sense of the lines:

> On a Columnar Self -
> How ample to rely
> In Tumult - or Extremity -
> How good the Certainty
>
> That Lever cannot pry -
> And Wedge cannot divide
> Conviction - That Granitic Base -
> Though none be on our side -

We can read the first stanza as an independent syntactic unit if we mentally supply a period after "Certainty"; then we take "That Lever" as the subject of a new sentence. Alternatively (and, as is typical for double syntax, in addition), we may take the absence of a period after "Certainty" as license to interpret "That Lever" as a relative clause modifying "Certainty": in this case, we supply the word *which* after "Certainty," conceptually bridging the stanza break and thus making the poem's first two stanzas into building blocks, it seems, for a "columnar" self that consists of yoked pieces. Read as a whole, however, the poem resists giving us a simple answer to the implied question of whether the self is divided or undivided, singular or plural. (Read on—see what you can make of the syntactic options created by the absence of a punctuation mark after "divide." Does the poem's third stanza resolve the question of what kind of "column" the "self" is? As you reread, note that the poem's variable metrical pattern of trimeter and tetrameter lines contributes to its questions about the shape and nature of a "columnar self.")

John Keats

Consider the famous opening line of John Keats's "Ode on a Grecian Urn" (p. 938): "Thou still unravished bride of quietness. . . ." Does the word "still" function as an adjective or an adverb? In other words, is the urn, here addressed as "thou" and thus given qualities of personhood, "still" in the sense of *unmoving* (the adjectival meaning), or is the urn "still unravished," with "still" in the adverbial sense of *as yet,* which, in connection with "unmoving," shades into *not yet ravished*?

To appreciate Keats's use of "still," we will need not only to recognize that ambiguous part of speech in the ode's first line but also to ponder it in relation to the rest of this ode, which goes on to explore the idea of "ravished" in two different senses: as ecstatically delighted; and as violated, raped. The poem is about an apparently timeless and inanimate painted object, which is personified as a bride and hence likened to the "maidens loath," struggling to escape pursuers, in one of the scenes painted on the urn; the urn is also likened to the heifer painted on the urn and described as "lowing," though the poet cannot hear her voice and cannot be sure whether or not she is being led to death as a victim of sacrifice. Keats's ode, like Shakespeare's Sonnet 106, uses syntactic ambiguity to slow us down as we ponder a poem about time's passing and the art that succeeds—but only partially and paradoxically—in escaping death.

Thomas Gray

Thomas Gray, who died some twenty years before Keats was born, also wrote an ode about a painted vase; and his poem too uses syntactic ambiguity to enrich a meditation on the relation between visual (unmoving) artifacts and poetry, an inherently temporal mode of art. In some versions, the "Ode (On the Death of a Favorite Cat, Drowned in a Tub of Goldfishes)" (p. 668) begins with the following lines:

> 'Twas on a lofty vase's side,
> Where China's gayest art had dyed
>   The azure flowers that blow;
> Demurest of the tabby kind,
> The pensive Selima reclined,
>   Gazed on the lake below.

Upon first reading these lines, we probably take "reclined" as an intransitive verb telling us what the cat did. As we go on to read line 6, however, we encounter a fine instance of double syntax enabled by punctuation, for we must revise our understanding of the initial five lines to comprehend the syntax of line 6. Either we mentally supply *and,* taking "reclined" and "gazed" as a compound verb phrase; or we retroactively interpret "reclined" as a **past participle**—a verb used as an adjective—describing the cat's position and thus creating a witty but melancholy joke: the cat that will, we know from the title, fall into that "lofty" painted vase and drown is here caught, through the two possible interpretations of "reclined," between life and death. A cat that can recline is alive; a cat "reclined" is perhaps already dead. In yet a third alternative, suggested by poem as a whole, the cat may exist in that strange state of suspension between life and death that is created by art. This paradoxical state, implied by the pun on "dyed" and *died,* is neatly captured in the name of a certain genre of paintings: *still life.*

The ambiguity of "reclined" adds further shades of meaning to the poem's opening description of the cat *on* the side of a vase. What does that preposition mean? We might read it as suggesting that the cat is *painted on* the vase. We may firmly reject that possibility when we get to "gazed," in line 6, and stanza 2's description of the cat's tail "declaring" her "conscious joy"; this is (or was) evidently a real, moving cat, not a painted one—and hence her *reclining* can be pictured as a lively, comic, even wildly acrobatic act of being at rest. And yet this poem is an ode that the title declares is "on the death" of a favorite cat; how does that "on" relate to the "on" of the opening line? The poem as a whole re-creates, reanimates, something long dead and still, exploring paradoxes of stillness and incipient movement similar to those in Keats's "Ode on a Grecian Urn." There, as we've seen, a scene painted on an old vase prompts the poet to reflect on the ways in which an artwork arrests time's passage while also testifying to time's power. Gray's ode also invites us to ponder the relations between artistic representations (verbal and visual), and (what counts) as reality, or life.

The tiny bit of double syntax at the end of Gray's opening stanza, which invites us to do a double take, to revise our understanding of the relation between verbs and adjectives, terms of motion and of stasis, disappears when modern editors add a comma to line 5, as many have done when reprinting Gray's poem for busy twentieth- and twenty-first-century readers. Consider the difference:

> Demurest of the tabby kind,
> The pensive Selima[,] reclined,
> Gazed on the lake below.

Does this difference matter? Many readers have chosen not to pause on this comma, or its absence, because interpretations based on the presence or absence of one mark of punctuation lead into territories where it's famously hard to be sure one is right. In many historical examples of double syntax, including, notoriously, Shakespeare's sonnets, we can never be certain whether a given punctuation mark—or the absence thereof—reflects the writer's original intention or a printer's interpretation (or error). Uncertainty about authorial intention need not bother us if we accept the idea that meanings are culturally conditioned and the game of interpretation often requires us to make informed guesses.

John Dryden

Like Gray, John Dryden exploits the syntactic ambiguities lurking in past participles. Verbs arrested to modify nouns, participles often help poets explore the relations between ideas of stillness and ideas of motion; when participles are used in such a way that they may also be interpreted as verbs in the past tense, they can help raise questions about bondage, freedom, and human agency. In lines 939–41 of his long poem *Absalom and Achitophel,* Dryden's character King David breaks a long silence with the following lines about how he plans to punish his rebellious son Absalom:

> Thus long have I by native mercy *swayed*
> My wrongs *dissembled,* my revenge *delayed;*
> So willing to forgive the offending age,
> So much the father did the king assuage. (my emphasis)

Modern editors—including those of this anthology (see p. 515)—often simplify this statement by adding explanatory commas around the phrase "by native mercy swayed," which makes it definitively into an adjectival modifier; the punctuation erases the possibility that David is saying that he has ruled for a long time in a merciful way while at the same time pretending not to see the wrongs done to him—or, in another reading allowed by the syntax, ruling in an apparently merciful way while dissembling the wrongs he does to others. In the form in which they were originally printed in 1681, the lines allow for several very different interpretations (the critic William Empson counts seven!), depending on whether the reader takes "swayed," "dissembled," or "delayed" as the main verb of the first clause. If we reread the clause aloud, trying out each possible main verb with the other two then becoming past participles, we see how subtly our perceptions of David's character change, along with our estimates of the harshness with which he is likely now to undertake the punishment of the rebel. Since Dryden's poem uses the biblical story to figure a contemporary drama of political power (David represents King Charles II of England, Absalom his illegitimate son Monmouth), syntactic ambiguity is a potentially important protective shield for the poet attempting to analyze the relations between what a ruler "shows" and what he "dissembles" as he contemplates "revenge." In removing syntactic ambiguities in some political poems of the past such as Dryden's, modern editors may, ironically, be blunting one of the weapons poets have traditionally used to avoid censorship.

William Blake

For a final example of interpretation enriched by attention to syntax and to punctuation, let's look at William Blake's "The Lamb." One of a series called *Songs of Innocence,* which Blake eventually combined with the *Songs of Experience,* this poem was originally published in an illuminated book, a form Blake devised; writing in 1793, he described his illuminated books as the result of a "method of Printing which combines the Painter and the Poet" (Prospectus, cited in Viscomi). Much has been written about Blake's beautiful books, which exist in multiple copies made during his lifetime from his etchings. For our purposes, one of these books' most interesting features is what they show about the interplay of punctuation and syntax in creating ambiguities of meaning. An illustrated poem like the one reproduced on p. 2071 allows us some access to Blake's thoughts about punctuation. The access is only partial, however, because eighteenth-century understandings of punctuation differ from modern ones and because Blake, as his great editor David Erdman observes, often uses punctuation for "rhetorical" pur-

2070 / POETIC SYNTAX

poses rather than to clarify syntax (787). In addition, different marks appear slightly differently in different copies of the illustrated poems; indeed, as Erdman also remarks, it is "impossible to copy Blake exactly" in print because the marks in the illuminated books sometimes "grade into each other" so that, for instance, a comma will be compounded with a question mark, or the difference between a comma and a period will be impossible to determine. Even trained scholars may therefore disagree about how to transcribe (rewrite, copy) a given Blake poem. Moreover, recognizing the gaps between eighteenth-century conventions of punctuation and modern ones, many modern editors feel that an attempt to follow Blake's punctuation exactly will distract readers rather than helping them appreciate the poems. One practical solution to this conundrum is to compare a "modernized" version of a poem by Blake (or by Dickinson or Shakespeare or other poets in this anthology) with a reproduction of a manuscript or early printed version of the text. Such a comparative practice, now much easier than it used to be because old versions of poems are readily viewable on the Web, allows us to see that editing, and even translating a text among different media, generates interpretations we can play with, and against which we can test our own understanding of a poem. A fascinating historical set of transcriptions and illustrations of Blake's poems is available for study at the innovative Web site of the Blake Archives (www.blakearchive.org).

In the case of "The Lamb," there are some interesting differences in punctuation among the more than twenty copies of the combined *Songs* made before Blake's death; the poem's penultimate line in Blake's version, for instance—"Little Lamb God bless thee"—is followed by a period in some transcriptions, a comma in others, and nothing—perhaps because the illustration's colors extended farther into the text—in still others. All of the illuminated copies, however, are very lightly punctuated, at least by today's standards and in striking contrast to most modern teaching editions of the poem, including the one in this anthology (p. 734). The difference is underscored by the absence of punctuation marks in the poem's opening lines as Blake printed them: "Little Lamb who made thee / Dost thou know who made thee" (see etching). Why is this significant? The presence or absence of punctuation marks in this poem gives us a glimpse into the ongoing history of reading as a process of trying to make sense of challenging poetic statements. The effort of making sense of syntax is, as we've seen, a key move in the game of interpretation. But so is the move of resisting premature submission to common sense. Blake invites us to tolerate, even relish, an experience of syntactic ambiguity abetted by the absence of punctuation and not unlike what John Keats called "negative capability," or "being in uncertainties, mysteries, doubts, without any irritable reaching after fact and reason."

When modern editors add question marks and commas to the opening of Blake's poem, they make sense of it by making it fit the type of English sentence we have so often discussed in this essay. Punctuating Blake's first line with a question mark at the end and (as is usually the case) a comma after the opening words, editors help us grasp the line as an independent (interrogative) clause beginning with an address (an **apostrophe**) to the lamb: "Little lamb, who made thee?" In this version, the speaker apostrophizes the lamb, and then the speaker poses a grammatically self-contained and immediately comprehensible question: "who" (subject) "made" (verb) "thee" (direct object, referring back to the lamb as initially addressed)?

"The Lamb": plate 8 from *Songs of Innocence and of Experience*
(copy AA), ca. 1815–26 (etching, ink, and watercolor), William
Blake (1757–1827) / Fitzwilliam Museum, University of Cam-
bridge, U.K. / www.bridgeman.co.uk

The absence of punctuation marks in Blake's first two lines—an absence
echoed, as it were, in the stanza's last two lines—makes the poem much less
easily legible than it is in modern editions. Blake's etching leaves open several
possible interpretations of the first lines, the first stanza, and the poem as a
whole. In Blake's versions, the first line need not be read as a full interrog-
ative sentence. It can also (or instead) be read as having a subject ("little
lamb") followed by a subordinate (adjectival) clause describing the lamb as
the one who made "thee." Reading the line thus, as part of a larger syntactic
unit in which the main verb has yet to appear, we suddenly see the word
"thee" in a new light: it could now refer to an addressee who is not the lamb
but rather the lamb's creation, the child or adult reader being addressed as
"thee" and "thou." But even as we consider this alternative reading, which
is an alternative syntax for the poem, supported by different punctuation (a
comma after the first line instead of a question mark, for instance), we can-

not consider the traditional interpretation of the line or the poem *wrong*. Nor can we reject yet a third possible reading of the opening line or lines: as a prayerful address to Christ in his guise of lamb. In this reading, the referent for "thou" in the second line would be Christ, and the question the speaker is posing would shift back and forth from one about who made God's human and animal creatures to one about who made the Son of God. Thus the apparently "elementary" little poem opens toward sophisticated theological debates about the relation among God's different "persons": the Christian trinity, like the three pronouns in the poem ("thee," "He," and "I"), is three-in-one, one-in-three.

Our willingness to grant theological complexity to the poem goes hand in hand with a willingness to see its multiple syntactic possibilities as mutually illuminating rather than in competition with each other. The poem's final lines, which ring an echoing change on the opening ones, leave the theological and human questions of identity and origin teasingly open even as Blake chooses (for the first time) to end two lines with periods: one after "name," the other after the final "thee." If we join in this process of cocreating poetic meaning, we could imaginatively punctuate many lines in the poem in several different ways, none of which would conflict with the light punctuation Blake left for us. The poem quietly suggests that the reader is always cocreating the poem: our choices about syntax are choices about meaning. Fortunately, with this poem, making one syntactic choice at one time does not prevent us from making another later—and from attempting to hold all the possibilities in mind at once. The poem remains circular, fluid, teasing, and the final lines continue to solicit different interpretations, signaled here by the added commas:

> Little lamb[,] God bless thee,
> Little lamb God[,] bless thee.

Scorn Not Syntax

In the nineteenth century, one meaning of *syntax* was "a class in certain English Roman Catholic schools . . . below that called *poetry*" and often just above a class devoted to the subject of "grammar" (*Oxford English Dictionary* 2.c.). For modern students and their teachers, the relations among grammar, syntax, and poetry are rarely so orderly as such a curricular sequence suggests. Indeed, for many of us, the words *syntax* and *grammar*, like *versification*, conjure up associations with dryness and discipline: with the acts of scientific analysis that William Wordsworth, in "The Tables Turned" (p. 764), denounced as the work of a "meddling intellect" that "murder[s] to dissect." In this famous poem, part of a dialogue in which Wordsworth adopts different attitudes toward the old question of the relation between reason and emotion in poetry, the speaker seems to praise nature and the mind that is open to nature's gifts as superior to all things that the mind actively produces through science *or* through art. By allying mental labor with some kind of dissection practiced on the corpses of naturally lovely things, Wordsworth's speaker articulates a feeling many have had at the moment when the work of analyzing a poem (or a picture or a feeling of love) seems to destroy something simple, vital, and whole.

But there is another way to see the work of analyzing poems and, in particular, their syntactic bones. Playing on Wordsworth's title for another poem—"Scorn Not the Sonnet" (p. 804)—and harking back to Edward Taylor's phrase "the curious knot," we could argue for the value of untying syntactic knots as an intellectual exercise that teaches us something about our own relation to language. Analyzing poems, we need not think of ourselves as murderers, or even as surgeons performing an autopsy. Instead, we can think of ourselves as readers with the power to animate poetic meanings and test our cocreations in conversations with other readers. That group includes, of course, poets themselves, both the dead and the living.

MARGARET FERGUSON

Suggestions for Further Reading

Austin, Timothy R. *Language Crafted: A Linguistic Theory of Poetic Syntax.* Bloomington: Indiana University Press, 1984.

Borck, Jim S. "Blake's 'The Lamb': The Punctuation of Innocence." *Tennessee Studies in Literature* 19 (1974): 163–75.

Boroff, Marie. *The Language and the Poet: Verbal Artistry in Frost, Stevens, and Moore.* Chicago: University of Chicago Press, 1979.

Brooke Rose, Christine. *A Grammar of Metaphor.* London: Martin, Seeker, and Warburg, 1958.

Collins, Martha. "On Syntax in Poetry." *Field* (Spring 1999): 74–84.

Cureton, Richard. "Poetic Syntax and Aesthetic Form." *Style* 14 (Fall 1980): 318–409.

Davie, Donald. *Articulate Energy.* 1955. London, Boston: Routledge and Kegan Paul, 1976.

Dillon, George L. "Inversions and Deletions in English Poetry." *Language and Style* 8.3 (1975): 220–37.

Easthope, Anthony. *Poetry as Discourse.* London: Methuen, 1983.

Empson, William. *Seven Types of Ambiguity.* New York: New Directions, 1947.

Erdman, David, ed. "The Punctuation." In *The Poetry and Prose of William Blake,* rev. ed., 786–87. New York: Doubleday, 1982.

Fairley, Gene. *E. E Cummings and Ungrammar.* Searingtown, N.Y.: Watermill Publishers, 1975.

Francis, W. Nelson. "Syntax and Literary Interpretation." In S. Chatman and S. Levin, *Essays in the Language of Literature,* 209–16. Boston: Houghton Mifflin, 1967.

Franklin, R. H., ed. *The Poems of Emily Dickinson,* variorum ed. Cambridge, Mass.: Harvard University Press (Belknap), 1998.

———. *The Poems of Emily Dickinson,* reading ed. Cambridge, Mass.: Harvard University Press (Belknap), 1999.

Gregerson, Linda. "Anatomizing Death." In *Imagining Death in Spenser and*

Milton, 95–115. Ed. Elizabeth Jane Bellamy, Patrick Cheney, and Michael Schoenfeldt. New York: Palgrave Macmillan, 2003.

Huddleston, Rodney and Geoffrey K. Pullum, et al. *Cambridge Grammar of the English Language*. Cambridge, U.K., and New York: Cambridge University Press, 2002.

Kintgen, Eugene R. "Perceiving Poetic Syntax." *College English* 40.1 (Sept. 1978): 17–27.

Lanham, Richard. *A Handlist of Rhetorical Terms*. Berkeley: University of California Press, 1991.

Miller, Cristanne. *Emily Dickinson: A Poet's Grammar*. Cambridge, Mass.: Harvard University Press, 1987.

Nowottny, Winifred. *The Language Poets Use*. London: Athlon Press, 1962.

Oberhaus, Dorothy Huff. *Emily Dickinson's Fascicles: Method and Meaning*. University Park, Pa.: Pennsylvania State University Press, 1995.

Simpson, David. *Irony and Authority in Romantic Poetry*. New Jersey: Rowan and Littlefield, 1979.

Viscomi, Joseph. "Illuminated Printing." In "About Blake" at *The Blake Archive* <www.blakearchive.org>.

Wasserman, Earl R. *The Subtler Language: Critical Readings of Neoclassic and Romantic Poems*. 1959. Westport, Conn.: Greenwood Press, 1979.

Biographical Sketches

Fleur Adcock (b. 1934), *pp. 1849–53*
Fleur Adcock was born in New Zealand, but lived in England until 1947. She was educated at Victoria University, New Zealand, and taught Classics there and at Otago University. In 1963, she moved to London to become a librarian at the Foreign and Commonwealth Office. Since 1979, she has been a freelance writer based in London, though she has spent time at universities in the north of England, as a Northern Arts Fellow. She has translated works from Romanian and from medieval Latin, and edited the *Faber Book of Twentieth-Century Women's Poetry*. She was awarded an OBE in 1996, and her *Poems 1960–2000* was published in 2000.

Conrad Aiken (1889–1973), *pp. 1370–71*
Conrad Aiken was born in Savannah, Georgia, and raised there until age eleven, when his father shot Aiken's mother and himself to death. Aiken was sent to live with relatives in Cambridge, Massachusetts. He was educated at Harvard University, where he and his classmate T. S. Eliot began a lifelong, troubled friendship. After traveling extensively in Europe, he settled into a career as a writer. During the 1920s and 1930s, he lived in New York, but he spent much time abroad, mostly in England. In his later years, he lived in Savannah and on Cape Cod, Massachusetts. An exceptionally prolific writer, Aiken published some thirty volumes of poetry, five novels, dozens of short stories, a multitude of essays and reviews, and an autobiography. His *Senlin* (1918) employs what he called the "symphony" form, where each section of the poem functions like a musical movement.

Agha Shahid Ali (1949–2001), *pp. 1958–60*
Agha Shahid Ali was born in New Delhi, India, and raised in Kashmir. He was educated at the University of Kashmir, Srinagar; the University of Delhi; Pennsylvania State University; and the University of Arizona, Tucson. He held teaching posts at various institutions, including Princeton and the University of Massachusetts, Amherst. In addition to his own poetry, Ali wrote on T. S. Eliot and translated the work of Faiz Ahmed Faiz from Urdu. One of the few Indians from an Islamic background to write poetry in English, he identified a "triple heritage" of Hindu, Muslim, and Western culture that informs his poems.

A. R. Ammons (1926–2001), *pp. 1695–1701*
A(rchie) R(andolph) Ammons was born and grew up on a small tobacco farm near Whiteville, North Carolina, and started writing poetry while on a U.S. Navy destroyer escort in the South Pacific. After World War II, he earned a B.A. from Wake Forest University and worked variously as an elementary school teacher, a real estate salesman, an editor, and a sales executive at his father's glassmaking firm. Although he published his first volume, *Ommateum* (1955), at his own expense, he became over a career that included some thirty volumes of poetry one of the most influential and respected American poets, and one of the few to embark on book-length poems, such as *Glare* and *Garbage*. He was long associated with Cornell University.

Simon Armitage (b. 1963), *pp. 2021–23*
Simon Armitage was born in Huddersfield, England. He studied geography at Portsmouth Polytechnic and took a postgraduate degree in social work at Manchester University. He worked as a probation officer before becoming a full-time writer. His first volume of poems, *Zoom!*, was published in 1989, and his popularity has grown steadily ever since. A prolific writer and presenter for television, radio, and film, he has also written two novels, *Little Green Men* and *The White Stuff*; published a collection of essays about the north of England, *All Points North*; and coedited *The Penguin Anthology of Poetry from Britain and Ireland since 1945*. He published *Selected Poems* in 2001 and *The Universal Home Doctor*, a new collection, in 2002. He has taught at the Universities of Leeds and Iowa and currently teaches at Manchester Metropolitan University.

Matthew Arnold (1822–1888), *pp. 1087–1101*
Matthew Arnold was born in Laleham-on-Thames, England, the son of Dr. Thomas Arnold, headmaster of Rugby School, and was

educated at Balliol College, Oxford, where he became a close friend of the poet Arthur Clough, whom he later eulogized in "Thyrsis" (1866). In 1851, Arnold became an inspector of schools, a position he held for thirty-five years. His writing on education advocated the study of the Bible and the humanities as the remedy for what he saw as the philistinism and insularity of the times, and he worked indefatigably to improve standards and introduce rigor into the school curriculum. After writing most of his memorable poetry between 1845 and 1867, he turned away from poetry, believing himself unable to convey "Joy." Although he was elected professor of poetry at Oxford University in 1858, other than *New Poems* (1867) he subsequently published only prose, including *Essays in Criticism* (1865, 1888) and *Culture and Anarchy* (1869).

John Ashbery (b. 1927), *pp. 1736–40*
John Ashbery was born in Rochester, New York, and raised on a farm near Lake Ontario. He was educated at Harvard University, where he wrote his thesis on W. H. Auden, who selected his first book, *Some Trees* (1956), for the Yale Series of Younger Poets. He received his M.A. from Columbia University and attended New York University before working as a copywriter in New York City. Beginning in 1955, he worked for a decade as an art reviewer in Paris. He has since served as poetry editor of the *Partisan Review* and art critic for *New York* and *Newsweek* magazines. He joined the faculty of Brooklyn College in 1974. In addition to poetry, Ashbery has written three plays and (with James Schuyler) a collaborative novel. Loosely connected to what has been called the New York school—along with Schuyler and fellow poets Frank O'Hara and Kenneth Koch—he frequently adopts and adapts the techniques of musicians as well as Abstract Expressionist and Surrealist painters. Like the work of Gertrude Stein, about whom he has written, his poems are characterized by radical disjunctions. He is one of the most prolific and influential poets of the last half-century.

Anne Askew (1521–1546), *pp. 140–41*
Anne Askew (or Ascue) was born into an old Lincolnshire, England, family that educated her well. As a young woman, she devoted herself to Bible study and engaged the local clergy in disputes about the interpretation of scripture. Forced into marriage and eventually turned out of doors by her husband, Askew went to London, where she became a friend of Joan Bocher, a Protestant of known heterodoxy. Examined in 1545 for heretical views about the sacraments, she was not found guilty but, in June 1546, was condemned by a special commission that called no jury and no witnesses. The next day, she was tortured; after four weeks, she was burned at the stake. The Protestant bishop John Bale (1495–

1563) published two accounts of her examination and death, in 1546 and 1547. John Foxe's *Acts and Monuments* (1563) contains a description of her sufferings as a Protestant martyr, and ballads about her were written in the seventeenth century.

Margaret Atwood (b. 1939), *pp. 1894–99*
Margaret Atwood was born in Ottawa, Canada, and raised there and in Toronto. As a child, she spent much time in the woods of northern Quebec, where her father conducted entomological research. Educated at the University of Toronto, Radcliffe College, and Harvard University, Atwood has taught at a number of Canadian universities and has worked as an editor for the Anansi publishing house. Though known primarily as one of Canada's premier novelists, she has also published poetry, short stories, children's books, critical essays, and a study of Canadian literature, and she has edited several collections of verse. She is an active supporter of Amnesty International and other human rights organizations. The subjects of her sometimes futuristic work include the social roles of women, the power dynamics between men and women, and the conflicts between nation and nation.

W. H. Auden (1907–1973), *pp. 1465–81*
W(ystan) H(ugh) Auden was born in York, England, and educated at Christ Church College, Oxford, where he became a friend of the "Pylon" poets Stephen Spender and Cecil Day Lewis. In the 1930s, Auden embarked on a series of formative travels: to Germany, where he was introduced to Sigmund Freud's work; Iceland, which he visited with the poet Louis MacNeice; Spain, as a Republican sympathizer during the Spanish Civil War; China, with Christopher Isherwood during the Sino-Japanese War; and the United States, to which he emigrated in 1939, taking American citizenship in 1946. He was awarded the Pulitzer Prize in 1948. With the move to America, Auden threw off the conflict between his privileged background and youthful left-wing sympathies that characterized his early poetry, and gradually returned to the Anglican faith of his mother, a change that left a strong imprint on his later work. He also published prose, drama, and (in collaboration with Chester Kallman) libretti. He taught at a number of institutions, including Oxford, where he was professor of poetry from 1956 until 1961. For the next ten years, he divided his time between New York and Europe, but in 1972 he returned to Oxford to live at Christ Church. He diagnosed his century's banalities and horrors with relentless honesty and incisive wit, but also with compassion.

Joanna Baillie (1762–1851), *pp. 760–63*
Joanna Baillie was born in Lanarkshire, Scotland, the daughter of Dorothea Hunter and

James Baillie, a Prebyterian clergyman, later professor of divinity at Glasgow University. At age ten, she was sent to a boarding school in Glasgow. Her father died in 1778. Baillie, her mother, and her sister lived in Lanarkshire until 1784, when they moved to London to keep house for her brother, who had inherited a small medical museum from his uncle, Dr. William Hunter. Baillie was introduced to London literary circles by her aunt, a minor poet, and was friends with the poet Anna Laetitia Barbauld. After her mother's death in 1806, Baillie lived with her sister (when not traveling in England and on the Continent) for the rest of her life. Her *Poems* appeared in 1790, but during her lifetime she was best-known for her verse dramas, which were published in three volumes (1798–1812) under the title *Series of Plays, in which It Is Attempted to Delineate the Stranger Passions of the Mind*. One, *De Montfort*, was staged at Drury Lane in 1800 and featured Sarah Siddons. Edmund Kean took the title role in an 1821 revival. A philanthropic woman, Baillie gave much of her earnings to charity and published *A Collection of Poems, Chiefly Manuscript, and from Living Authors* (1823) to raise funds for needy acquaintances. Her last book of poems was published only weeks before her death.

Amiri Baraka (LeRoi Jones) (b. 1934),
pp. 1856–58
Amiri Baraka was born LeRoi Jones in Newark, New Jersey. He earned a B.A. from Howard University and an M.A. from Columbia University. From 1954 until 1956, he served in the United States Air Force. Since then he has taught at, among other schools, the New School for Social Research and Columbia University and has devoted himself to various experimental artistic ventures and radical political causes. He was instrumental in the founding of several small magazines; the Black Arts Repertory Theatre, in Harlem; and Spirit House, in Newark. In the 1970s, when he became a Black Muslim and took the name Imamu Amiri Baraka (although he later dropped Imamu), he began to write polemic poetry espousing black nationalism, which he later denounced. In addition to poetry, he has written a novel, a collection of short stories, an autobiography, several plays, and numerous tracts on social issues. From 1979 to 1999, he taught at the State University of New York at Stony Brook.

Anna Laetitia Barbauld (1743–1825),
pp. 705–07
Anna Laetitia Barbauld (née Aikin) was born at Kibworth Harcourt, Leicestershire, England, and taught at home by her father, a schoolmaster who became a classical tutor at the new Warrington Academy for Dissenters, an intellectual center where Barbauld spent fifteen years. She married in 1774 and followed her husband to Palgrave, where they managed a school for which she taught and wrote textbooks, one of which, *Hymns in Prose to Children* (1781), went through thirty editions and was translated into five languages. The Barbaulds left Palgrave in 1785 and settled in London, where Anna devoted herself to writing tracts in support of causes such as dissenting politics, democratic government, public education, and the French Revolution; and to literary work, such as editing the poetry of William Collins, collecting six volumes of the correspondence of Samuel Richardson, and writing prefaces to the entries in all fifty volumes of *The British Novelists*. In 1773, she published a volume of poems containing works in a variety of genres: the ode, the hymn, the fable, and the satire. In 1808, her husband drowned, having become mentally ill and violent. Barbauld published an anthology for girls, *The Female Speaker*, in 1811, and a poem, *Eighteen Hundred and Eleven*, in 1812. The latter was so badly reviewed that she published very little during the final thirteen years of her life.

James K. Baxter (1926–1972), *pp. 1701–03*
James K. Baxter was born in Dunedin, New Zealand, and educated at Quaker schools in New Zealand and England, the University of Otago, and the University of Victoria at Wellington. He worked as a laborer, journalist, and teacher, and from 1954 until 1960 edited the Wellington magazine *Numbers*. Following a long battle against alcoholism, he became a Roman Catholic in 1958, and subsequently founded a religious commune and became active in social welfare programs. An extraordinarily prolific writer, Baxter published more than thirty collections of poetry as well as plays and literary criticism. His work shows a deep understanding of complex political and social issues and often attacks exploitation and materialism. Later poems express his appreciation of indigenous Maori culture and disdain for those who threatened it. His final work, based on his experiences in a Maori village called Jerusalem, articulates a fervent religious faith.

Aphra Behn (1640?–1689), *pp. 540–49*
Different accounts and opinions exist about Aphra Behn's date of birth, parentage, religion, given name, and marital status. Most historians agree, however, that she visited Surinam with her family in her youth, returned to England when the colony was handed over to the Dutch, and was briefly married to a merchant of Dutch extraction. While spying for King Charles II in Antwerp in 1666, she seems to have uncovered a Dutch plot to sail up the river Thames and burn the British fleet; letters survive in which she complains of the king's failure to pay her for her work, and she may have been briefly imprisoned for debt in the late 1660s. Writing plays became her main means of support, and she was

one of the most prolific playwrights of the Restoration era. Her first play, *The Forced Marriage*, was produced in 1670; she subsequently wrote seventeen plays, including many comedies that satirize the consequences of ill-suited marriages. Her one tragedy, *Abdelazar* (1676), draws on previous dramatic portraits, including Shakespeare's in *Othello* and *Titus Andronicus*, of black men who love white women. Her prose romance, *Oroonoko, or the Royal Slave* (1688), was based on her experiences in Surinam and criticized the enslavement and subsequent torture and execution of a princely black hero whom the white female narrator greatly admires. Behn also wrote occasional poems, elegies, prologues and epilogues for other dramatists, including John Dryden, and erotic pastoral poems such as "The Disappointment." Her tragicomedy set in colonial Virginia, *The Widow Ranter,* was performed and published the year after Behn died.

Charles Bernstein (b. 1950), *pp. 1967–68*
Charles Bernstein was born in New York City and educated at Harvard University, where he studied philosophy and was an activist against the Vietnam War. He worked as a commercial writer and editor in health care for twenty years. With Bruce Andrews, he cofounded *L=A=N=G=U=A=G=E* magazine in 1978, and since then has been a principal figure in the L=A=N=G=U=A=G=E poetry movement and a prominent theorist of radical poetics. He has taught at the State University of New York at Buffalo since 1990.

John Berryman (1914–1972), *pp. 1546–52*
John Berryman was born John Smith in McAlester, Oklahoma. When he was ten, his family moved to Tampa, Florida, where his father committed suicide, shooting himself outside his son's window. The family moved to Massachusetts, then resettled in New York, where Mrs. Smith married a banker named John Berryman, who adopted her sons. The younger John Berryman was educated at Columbia University and Clare College, Cambridge University, where he studied Shakespeare. A scholar, particularly of Shakespeare, and celebrated teacher, whose students included the poets Donald Justice, Philip Levine, and W. D. Snodgrass, Berryman taught at, among other schools, Harvard University, Princeton University, and the University of Minnesota. He also wrote a biography of Stephen Crane. Dogged by alcoholism and a nervous temperament, he committed suicide in 1972. His major contribution was a series of hundreds of poems in an inventive, eighteen-line form he called "dream songs."

John Betjeman (1906–1984), *pp. 1460–63*
John Betjeman was born in London and attended Madgalen College, Oxford, which he left without taking a degree. During World War II, he held several posts in the Ministry of Information. He later served as United Kingdom press attaché in Dublin. Betjeman had a lifelong avidity for architecture and devoted considerable energy to the preservation of historic landmarks and scenic views. After 1945, he worked as a freelance writer and journalist and became a celebrated television personality. His many honors included the Queen's Gold Medal for Poetry (1960) and a knighthood (1969). In 1972, he was a popular choice as poet laureate, a post he held until his death.

Earle Birney (1904–1991), *pp. 1447–48*
Earle Birney was born in Calgary, Alberta, and raised on a farm in Erickson, British Columbia. He worked as a bank clerk, a farm laborer, and a park ranger before attending the University of British Columbia, the University of Toronto, and the University of California at Berkeley, from which he earned a Ph.D. in Old and Middle English. He then taught at the Universities of Utah, Toronto, and British Columbia. During World War II, Birney served with the Canadian Army as a personnel-selection officer and as supervisor of the International Service of the Canadian Broadcasting Corporation. In addition to poetry, he published novels, radio plays, and literary essays.

Elizabeth Bishop (1911–1979), *pp. 1515–28*
Elizabeth Bishop was born in Worcester, Massachusetts. After her father's death in 1911 and her mother's permanent hospitalization for mental illness in 1917, Bishop lived with relatives in Nova Scotia and Massachusetts. She was educated at Vassar College, and while still a student met the poet Marianne Moore, who recognized her promise and became her mentor. Her literary friendship with Robert Lowell was also a sustenance for both. Bishop traveled extensively and often addressed questions of travel in her work. In 1952, she settled in Rio de Janeiro with Lota de Macedo Soares, a Brazilian architect and landscape designer; the relationship ended tragically with Soares's suicide, in 1967. Bishop returned to the United States to teach, first at the University of Washington in Seattle, then at Harvard University. In addition to poetry, she wrote short stories and essays; translated from the French, Spanish, and Portuguese; and was a fine amateur painter. During her lifetime, she won the respect of her peers, and since her death she has come to be regarded as among the major poets of the century.

William Blake (1757–1827), *pp. 732–47*
William Blake was born in London. He attended art schools, including the Royal Academy school, and at age fourteen was apprenticed to an engraver. In 1800, he secured a patron at

Felpham, in Sussex, but found the arrangement stultifying. Determined to follow his "Divine Visions," he returned to London. He published numerous collections of poetry, including *Songs of Innocence* (1789) and *Songs of Experience* (1794), which were illustrated with his own fantastic etchings. From the 1820s, he devoted himself exclusively to pictorial art. His early work reveals his dissatisfaction with the prevailing literary styles of his day; he took as his models the Elizabethan and early seventeenth-century poets, the Ossianic poems, and the work of William Collins, Thomas Chatterton, and others working outside the prevailing contemporary literary conventions. Between 1795 and 1820, Blake developed a complex mythology to explain human history and suffering and came to see himself as a visionary, prophetic figure, or Bard. His writings in this vein center around the biblical stories of the Fall, the Redemption, and the reestablishment of Eden, but Blake gave these materials his own spin. In his mythos, the Fall is seen as a psychic disintegration that results from the "original sin" of Selfhood, and the Redemption and return to Eden as a restitution of psychic wholeness, a "Resurrection to Unity." His schema centers around a "Universal Man" who incorporates God rather than around a transcendent Being distinct from humanity.

Edmund Blunden (1896–1974), *pp. 1404–06*

Edmund Blunden was born in London, raised in Yalding, Kent, and educated at Christ's Hospital School, in Sussex. In 1915, he joined the army and was sent to the front in France. Upon his return to England, he briefly attended The Queen's College, Oxford; then moved to London to work as an assistant to J. Middleton Murry at the *Athenaeum* magazine. For the next thirty years, he led a peripatetic existence, teaching at the Imperial University of Tokyo, the University of Hong Kong, and Merton College, Oxford. Blunden edited collections of poetry by John Clare, Wilfred Owen, and Ivor Gurney that brought about revivals of their flagging reputations. Unlike many poets of World War I, he did not engage in antiwar invective. In his poetry and in his prose memoir, *Undertones of War* (1928), he focused instead on the experience of the men in the trenches, recording the "agony" etched into "each grey face" but also acknowledging the moments of happiness amid the slaughter. He was one of the only poets to mourn the devastation of the European landscape, and his poems about the English countryside are considered among his finest. He settled finally in Suffolk in 1964 and was elected professor of poetry at Oxford in 1966.

Robert Bly (b. 1926), *pp. 1704–05*

Robert Bly was born in the town of Madison, in rural Minnesota, where he has lived nearly all his life. He studied as an undergraduate at St. Olaf's College and Harvard University and as a graduate student at the University of Iowa Writers' Workshop. From 1944 until 1946, he served in the navy. Bly founded and edited an influential journal named for each decade—*The Fifties, The Sixties, The Seventies, The Eighties,* and *The Nineties.* He has translated into English the work of many important poets, including Rilke, Goethe, Neruda, and Vallejo. He is associated with the mystical Deep Image school and, in recent years, has figured prominently in the men's movement.

Louise Bogan (1897–1970), *pp. 1406–09*

Louise Bogan was born in Livermore Falls, Maine. She attended Boston University for one year, then left school to marry. In 1919, newly single, Bogan moved to New York City to pursue writing. She became the poetry critic for *The New Yorker* in 1931 and held the post until she retired, in 1969. Bogan taught at several universities, including the University of Washington, the University of Chicago, the University of Arkansas, and Brandeis University. She also translated Jünger, Goethe, and Jules Renard and wrote two influential critical works. Despite her professional success, her standards for her formal, polished poems were so exacting that she published only 105 in her lifetime. Her reputation as a poet has grown posthumously, to match that in her lifetime as a critic.

Eavan Boland (b. 1944), *pp. 1938–42*

Eavan Boland, the daughter of the Irish diplomat F. H. Boland and the Postexpressionist painter Frances Kelley, was born in Dublin, educated in London, where her father was Irish ambassador, and New York, where he was a representative to the United Nations. After graduating from Trinity College, Dublin, she lectured in English there but found herself "completely unsuited to being an academic," and subsequently taught on a short-term basis at institutions in Ireland and the United States in order to devote her energies to writing. She has written essays on contemporary Irish literature, translated Irish poetry and work by Horace, Mayakovsky, and Nelly Sachs, and is a well-regarded reviewer and broadcaster. Her *Collected Poems* (1995) brought together seven collections published over twenty years. She is professor of English at Stanford University.

Anne Bradstreet (ca. 1612–1672), *pp. 458–67*

Anne Bradstreet (née Dudley) was born in Northampton, England, daughter of a gentlewoman named Dorothy Yorke and of Thomas Dudley, a nonconformist minister who managed the business interests of the earl of Lincoln. Educated by private tutors in the earl's households, she married Simon Bradstreet, a future governor of the Massachusetts Bay Colony, in 1628; in 1630, Bradstreet emigrated to America with her husband and parents. When she first came to the colonies, she "found a new world and new manners," as she later remembered. "But after I was convinced it was the way of God I submitted to it and joined to the church of Boston." While caring for her growing family (she had eight children), she continued to write. A volume of poems was published in London in 1650. Entitled *The Tenth Muse Lately Sprung Up in America,* the book was published by Bradstreet's brother-in-law without her knowledge (or so she claimed). It sold very well; a second edition, containing numerous corrections and additions, appeared six years after her death. She compiled but did not publish a collection of prose meditations on life and death for her son Simon when he was about to become minister in 1664.

Edward Kamau Brathwaite (b. 1930), *pp. 1803–07*
Edward Kamau Brathwaite was born in Bridgetown, Barbados, and educated at Harrison College; Pembroke College, Cambridge; and Sussex University. After working for the Ministry of Education in Ghana (Africa) from 1955 until 1962, he returned to his homeland to become a professor of social and cultural history at the University of the West Indies. Since the 1970s, he has taught at a variety of institutions in the United States, publishing scholarly works on West Indian history and culture and on dialect, and is now professor of comparative literature at New York University.

Emily Brontë (1818–1848), *pp. 1046–50*
Emily Brontë, sister of novelists Charlotte and Anne, was raised in the parsonage at Haworth, on the North Yorkshire moors of England. She was educated largely at home, leaving in 1838 to work as a teacher at a girls' school in Halifax. She remained there only six months. In 1842, she went to Brussels with Charlotte to study language and music, and on her return began to write feverishly. For her first published work, the joint collection *Poems* (1846) by Currer, Ellis and Acton Bell, she assumed a pseudonym to avoid being stereotyped as a "lady poet." The book was largely ignored, selling only two copies, and she is best remembered for the novel *Wuthering Heights* (1847). Many of her poems (including "The Prisoner" and "Remembrance") were originally written (with Anne) as part of the "Gondal" saga, a series of intricate and elaborate tales set in an imaginary kingdom. The meter and form of Emily Brontë's poems often derive from the Wesleyan hymns she sang as a child. Much of her imagery is Gothic, and her concern with the transience of human life and beauty, as well as her reliance on a personal inner vision, links her to the Romantics. She died at Haworth, of tuberculosis.

Rupert Brooke (1887–1915), *pp. 1324–27*
Rupert Brooke was born in Rugby, England, where his father was a housemaster of the famous public school, and educated there and at King's College, Cambridge. After graduation, he established himself in the house immortalized in "The Old Vicarage, Grantchester." Following a series of unhappy love affairs, he traveled in Europe, the United States, Canada, and the South Seas. When war broke out, he returned to England and was commissioned into the Royal Naval Division. He was at the siege of Antwerp in October 1914 and spent the following winter training in Dorset, where he composed his "war sonnets." The following year, while on a troopship bound for Gallipoli, he died after contracting dysentery and blood poisoning. Much of his early work was published in Edward Marsh's anthologies of Georgian verse and was praised for its conversational diction, vivid descriptions, and delight in the commonplace. His war sonnets, published posthumously as *1914 and Other Poems* (1915), celebrate patriotism, peace, friendship, love, and the values that galvanized the British public in the early days of the conflict—values Brooke had once derided as "Nineteenth Century grandiose thoughts, about the Destiny of Man, the Irresistibility of Fate, the Doom of Nations, the fact that Death awaits us All."

Gwendolyn Brooks (1917–2000), *pp. 1586–89*
Gwendolyn Brooks was born in Topeka, Kansas, and raised in Chicago, Illinois. She published her first poem at age thirteen and was giving poetry readings until just days before her death. A graduate of Wilson Junior College, she was active in the civil rights movement of the 1960s and after, and often wrote on political themes. Her first book, *Bronzeville* (1945), takes its title from the phrase journalists used for Chicago's black ghetto. Brooks ran poetry workshops for underprivileged youths and taught at various institutions, including City College of New York. She published more than twenty volumes of poetry and received more than fifty honorary doctorates.

George Mackay Brown (1921–1996), *pp. 1627–28*
George Mackay Brown was born in Stromness, a small fishing and shipbuilding seaport in the Orkney Islands of Scotland. Apart from the time he spent at Newbattle Abbey College and the University of Edinburgh, he remained in the Orkneys all his life. A sufferer from tuberculosis, he underwent several periods of extended treatment and convalescence in local sanatoriums. He became a Roman Catholic in 1961. Whether in poetry or in his lyrical short stories and plays, Brown wrote almost invariably on themes connected with his remote northern homeland. His work was inspired by Norse saga, Catholic lit-

urgy and ceremony, elemental rituals, ballad, myth, legend, island folklore, and local history, recorded and imagined. In addition to publishing thirty-one books of poetry, twelve collections of short stories, and five novels, including *Greenvoe* (1972), he collaborated with the composer Peter Maxwell Davies on an opera, *The Martyrdom of St. Magnus*.

Sterling A. Brown (1901–1989), *pp. 1426–29*
Sterling A. Brown was born in Washington, D.C., and educated at Williams College and at Harvard University. Upon graduation from Harvard, he embarked on a long and distinguished academic career, during which he taught at Virginia Seminary College and Lincoln, Fisk, and (for nearly fifty years) Howard Universities. From 1936 until 1939, Brown worked with the Federal Writers' Project of the Works Progress Administration (WPA). For a time, he edited *Negro Affairs* magazine, and he later worked at *Opportunity*. In addition to poetry, he published several seminal works on African American literature. Brown cited the regionalists and realists E. A. Robinson and Robert Frost as important influences. Like Jean Toomer, he set his work primarily in rural surroundings, and like Langston Hughes, to whom Brown is often compared, he derived many of his forms from the ballad, the work song, jazz, and the blues.

Elizabeth Barrett Browning (1806–1861), *pp. 947–51*
Elizabeth Barrett was raised in Herefordshire, England. She received no formal education, but studied the classics at home and was extremely well educated for a woman of her day. Her two-volume *Poems* (1844) attracted the attention of Robert Browning, and in 1846 they were secretly married and eloped to Italy. In England, she had lived the life of an invalid, but in Italy her strength and spirits revived. She developed a passion for Italian politics, supporting unification and writing energetically on behalf of the cause. Her poetry was well received, and at the time of her death, her reputation outstripped her husband's. She is best-known for *Sonnets from the Portuguese* (1850), a sequence of forty-four Petrarchan sonnets that document her burgeoning love for Browning, but she is most admired for *Aurora Leigh* (1857), a nine-book verse novel. That work shocked many of its readers, who took offense at her criticism of the stultifying social forms imposed on women, but deeply impressed contemporary writers, including John Ruskin, who called it "the greatest poem written in English."

Robert Browning (1812–1889), *pp. 1009–41*
Robert Browning was born in a suburb of London. He attended London University, but received most of his education by reading vora-

ciously in his father's eclectic library. In 1846, he eloped with the poet Elizabeth Barrett, and he lived with her in Italy until her death, in 1861. His early work, which included drama and poetry, was poorly received by the public, but brought him the respect of influential literary figures such as John Forster, Thomas Carlyle, Charles Dickens, and Alfred, Lord Tennyson. With the publication of *Dramatis Personae* in 1864, followed by the popular *The Ring and the Book*, which appeared in monthly installments between November 1868 and February 1869, Browning's reputation grew prodigious. His collected poems were published in sixteen volumes between April 1888 and July 1889. After his death, in Italy, his body was brought back to London for a funeral in Westminster Abbey and buried in its Poets' Corner.

Alan Brownjohn (b. 1931), *pp. 1829–30*
Alan Brownjohn was born in London and educated at Merton College, Oxford. A schoolteacher from 1957 to 1965, he was also a lecturer at Battersea College of Education and South Bank Polytechnic before becoming a full-time writer in 1979. The first of his eleven collections of poems, *The Railings*, was published in 1961; his most recent, *The Cat without E-mail*, in 2001; and he was the chairman of the Poetry Society from 1982 to 1988. He has been poetry critic for the *New Statesman, Encounter*, and, since 1990, the *Sunday Times*. He has also written three novels, two books for children, and a critical study of Philip Larkin. His *Collected Poems 1952–1983* was reissued in 1988.

William Cullen Bryant (1794–1878), *pp. 902–05*
William Cullen Bryant was born in Cummington, Massachusetts, a descendant of early Puritan immigrants. He spent a year at Williams College and, at his father's urging, three years reading law at Worthington and Bridgewater Colleges. Bryant's reputation as a poet was established in 1817 with the publication of "Thanatopsis" (Greek for "a view of death"), the first version of which he wrote at age sixteen. In 1825, he abandoned law for literature. He served on the editorial board of several journals, including the *New York Review*, and in 1829 he assumed the editorship of New York's *Evening Post*, a position he held for nearly fifty years. In his later years, he devoted much energy to translating the *Iliad* (1870) and the *Odyssey* (1871–72) into blank verse. He wrote essays and travel journals, and also published his speeches and orations.

Basil Bunting (1900–1985), *pp. 1421–25*
Basil Bunting was born in Newcastle, Northumberland. He attended the London School of Economics. After being imprisoned for six months as a conscientious objector during World War I, he lived a bohemian existence that

took him to France (where he met the poet Ezra Pound), Greece, Italy, Germany, and the Canary Islands. He enlisted in the Royal Air Force on the outbreak of World War II, served in a number of posts across the globe, and after the war was appointed to the British Embassy in Tehran. He returned to Northumberland in 1953 and went to work for a small newspaper. After the publication of *Briggflatts* (1966), the collection upon which his reputation largely rests, he was much in demand on the university circuit and taught at several institutions in England and the United States. Like Pound, Bunting exploited the deep connection between poetry and music, and his major poems are written in forms he identified as the "ode" and the "sonata." His *Collected Poems* was published in 1968, and *Uncollected Poems* appeared posthumously in 1991.

Robert Burns (1759–1796), *pp. 747–60*
Robert Burns was born into a farming family in Ayrshire, Scotland. He received a modest education at the "adventure" school established by his father and his neighbors, but was largely self-taught. He spent a year and a half in Edinburgh following the publication of his immensely popular first book, *Poems, Chiefly in the Scottish Dialect* (1786), but returned home the following year when he was awarded a sinecure in the Excise Office. Burns farmed and performed his official duties until 1791, when he gave up his land and moved to Dumfries. He devoted his last years to collecting Scottish folk songs as part of a project to preserve Scottish culture and the Scottish national identity. He most often wrote in Scots, a form of English spoken by the Scottish peasantry that incorporates many dialect words, and his subject matter was frequently drawn from Scottish folk tales and legends, Scottish landscapes, and local events. He has been compared to figures such as Robert Henryson, William Dunbar, and Gavin Douglas, who wrote in the fifteenth and sixteenth centuries, the golden age of Scottish literature, and spawned a revival of interest in Scottish culture.

Witter Bynner (1881–1968), *pp. 1269–70*
Witter Bynner was born in Brooklyn, New York, and raised in Norwalk, Connecticut, and Brookline, Massachusetts. He was educated at Harvard University. Until 1906, he worked as an editor, then quit to devote himself to writing. Bynner traveled extensively in the United States and in China. In addition to poetry, he published several verse dramas and numerous essays. With the assistance of Kiang Kang-hu, he undertook the twentieth century's first significant translation of Chinese poetry into English. Bynner gained fame, or infamy, for perpetuating the "Spectricism" hoax, in which he and Arthur Davidson Fincke published a well-received volume of poems intended as a spoof on Imagism.

George Gordon, Lord Byron (1788–1824), *pp. 833–63*
George Gordon, Lord Byron was born near Aberdeen, Scotland, to dissolute aristocratic parents who had fallen on hard times. Their difficulties were alleviated when Byron inherited his title at age ten. Upon graduation from Trinity College, Cambridge, he embarked on a two-year tour of Portugal, Spain, Malta, Greece, and Asia Minor, during which he gathered much of the material for his most important poems. He became a celebrity overnight in 1812 with the publication of the first two cantos of *Childe Harolde's Pilgrimage,* but notoriety supplanted fame when his affair with his half-sister, whom he had met as an adult, became public knowledge. His marriage collapsed, and he was forced to leave England in 1816. He followed the poet Percy Bysshe Shelley to Geneva and Italy, then went on to Greece, where he organized a contingent of soldiers to fight for independence from the Turks. After he fell sick in the woods during a training exercise and died, he was mourned as a national hero throughout Greece. His work was widely known in Europe and was immensely influential on the major European writers of his day. Perhaps his most significant contribution to literature was the development of the Byronic hero, a doomed but impassioned wanderer, often driven by guilt and alienated from his society, but superior to it. In *Don Juan,* his masterpiece, he uses the narrator to attack institutions such as the government, the Church, and marriage; criticize vices such as hypocrisy, greed, and lust; and subtly extol virtues such as courage, loyalty, and candor. Although many critics considered the poem a wanton celebration of the misadventures of a profligate, Byron called it "the most moral of poems."

Roy Campbell (1902–1957), *pp. 1436–37*
Roy Campbell was born in Natal, South Africa. After living briefly in England in his early twenties, he returned to South Africa and founded the literary magazine *Voorslag* ("Whiplash"), which satirized the values of the Afrikaners. Among the volumes of poetry he produced during the 1920s and 1930s were *The Georgiad,* an attack on the Bloomsbury group; *Flowering Reeds,* a return to his earlier lyricism; and *Flowering Rifle,* in which he eulogized the Spanish dictator Francisco Franco. In 1935, Campbell became a Roman Catholic, and during World War II he served in the British army. He died in a car crash in Portugal. In addition to poetry, he wrote two autobiographical works. His translations of Spanish and Portuguese fiction, and particularly of Federico García Lorca's poetry and Charles Baudelaire's *Les Fleurs du Mal,* are highly regarded.

Thomas Campion (1567–1620), *pp. 278–82*
Thomas Campion was born in London and educated at Peterhouse, Cambridge, which he left

without taking a degree but with a taste for classical literature, and at Gray's Inn, though he was never called to the bar. After receiving an M.D. from the University of Caen in 1605, he was practicing medicine in London by 1606. He considered himself to be first and foremost a classicist and a composer, however, his chief aim being to "couple my words and notes lovingly together." He fulfilled this ambition in a number of lyrics in four *Books of Airs* for lute and voice, and in his composition of court masques including *The Lord Hay's Masque*, performed in 1607, and the *Somerset Masque* and the *Lord's Masque*, both performed in 1613. Five poems by Campion were published, anonymously, in 1591, and his *Poemata*, consisting of Latin panegyrics, elegies, and epigrams, appeared in 1595. In his treatise *Observations in the Art of English Poesy* (1602), he advocated the classical or "quantitative" system of meter, prompting Samuel Daniel's *Defense of Rhyme* (1602). Though Campion dismissed his own early, mainly rhymed, verse as "superfluous blossoms of my deeper studies," his unrhymed, experimental poems have a musical quality no less impressive than that of his rhyming poems.

Thomas Carew (ca. 1595–1640), *pp. 385–90*
Thomas Carew (pronounced *Carey*) was born in West Wickham, Kent, England. Son of Sir Matthew Carew, who worked in the court of law known as the Chancery, Carew was educated at Merton College, Oxford, and the law school of the Middle Temple. He was secretary to Sir Dudley Carleton, the ambassador to Venice and later to The Hague, from 1613 to 1616, when he returned to England. He was next employed by Sir Edward Herbert, the ambassador to France, during which time he established his reputation as a poet and found favor with King Charles I, who made him a gentleman of the privy chamber in 1628. Carew is the earliest of those authors who, like his friends Sir John Suckling and Richard Lovelace, are today known as "Cavalier" poets. They were Royalist in politics, looked to the classical poets (through Ben Jonson) for their models, and composed graceful, witty, elegantly crafted verse. Carew saw his own work as "a mine of rich and pregnant fancy," and brought lucidity, directness, a frank sexuality, and urbane cynicism to amatory verse, but also wrote on other themes, most notably in his "An Elegy upon the Death of the Dean of Paul's, Dr. John Donne." Carew's masque, *Coelum Britannicum*, was performed before Charles I in 1634, and a collection, *Poems*, was published in 1640.

Lewis Carroll (Charles Lutwidge Dodgson) (1832–1898), *pp. 1135–39*
Charles Lutwidge Dodgson was born in Daresbury, Cheshire, England, and educated at Rugby and at Christ Church, Oxford, on whose grounds he was to live for the rest of his life. In 1855, he became a lecturer in mathematics, and thereafter he published several books on the subject, including a defense of Euclid. He was an inventor and a skilled photographer; although he became a clergyman in 1861, his habitual shyness caused a bad stammer that kept him from preaching often. In addition to poems, puns, pastiche, conundrums, problems of logic, and some adventurous linguistics, he wrote children's books (under the pseudonym Lewis Carroll, a Latinized form of Lutwidge Charles). *Alice's Adventures under Ground* (1865), now usually known as *Alice's Adventures in Wonderland*, like its sequel, *Through the Looking-glass and What Alice Found There* (1871), began in tales told during boating trips on the river Thames to the three daughters (one of whom was Alice) of Henry Liddell, dean of Christ Church. The stories were an instant and enduring success, perhaps because of the absence of the "improving" matter found in most children's literature of the time.

Anne Carson (b. 1950), *pp. 1969–71*
Anne Carson was born and raised in Toronto, Canada. She did both her undergraduate and graduate work at the University of Toronto. Her Ph.D. is in classical studies, and she has a distinguished reputation not only as a poet but also as a classical scholar, translator, and essayist. Her poetry collections also tend to transgress the boundaries of genre, as can be seen in titles such as *The Beauty of the Husband: A Fictional Essay in 29 Tangos*. She is a professor of classics at McGill University, in Montreal.

Charles Causley (1917–2003), *pp. 1590–92*
Charles Causley was born in Launceston, Cornwall, and lived there all his life. His father, a private soldier, returned from France after World War I a hopeless invalid, and died seven years later from the residual effects of nerve gas. Causley was educated at a local grammar school, then worked in a builder's office and later for a small electrical supply company. His service in the Royal Navy from 1940 until 1946 proved decisive to his literary career, drawing him from prose to poetry and providing him with a subject. After the war, he became a teacher, and his first book of poetry, *Hands to Dance*, was published in 1951. After retiring in 1965 to become a full-time writer, he accepted offers to teach in various colleges and universities in Australia, Canada, and the United States. He also published plays, short stories, and children's verse, and edited numerous collections of poetry. He won the Queen's Gold Medal for Poetry and was made CBE in 1986.

Margaret Cavendish (1623–1673), *pp. 499–500*
Margaret Cavendish was born in England to an aristocratic family and became a maid of honor

to Queen Henrietta Maria. At twenty-two, she married the Royalist William Cavendish, then marquis of Newcastle, later first duke. She met him in Paris, where they both lived in exile during the Commonwealth. In 1651, having returned to England to try to recover part of her husband's estate, she wrote *Fancies* (1653) and *Philosophical Fancies* (1653; revised as part of *Philosophical and Physical Opinions*, 1655). Her wide-ranging intellectual interests, among them chemistry and natural philosophy, inform these and subsequent writings in a variety of genres, including the deliberately hybrid *Worlds of Olio* of 1655 (the term *Olio* refers to a Portuguese stew with many ingredients). She explores the question of women's "secondary" status from many and sometimes contradictory perspectives in volumes of plays (1662 and 1668), in *Natures Pictures* (with autobiography; 1656), in her *Sociable Letters* (1664), and in her utopian narrative, *The New Blazing World* (1668). She visited the Royal Society, a newly instituted scientific institution, in 1667 and was viewed as an "eccentric" both in her own time and later.

Geoffrey Chaucer (ca. 1343–1400), pp. 19–70

Geoffrey Chaucer was born into a middle-class merchant family and at about age fifteen became a page to the countess of Ulster. While serving her husband, Lionel (the second son of King Edward III), during the Hundred Years War, Chaucer was captured at the siege of Reims and eventually ransomed. In 1365, he married Philippa Roet, sister-in-law of the powerful peer John of Gaunt, who was the uncle and advisor of King Richard II. In 1367, Chaucer was granted an annuity in the royal household and soon began traveling on diplomatic missions: to Spain (1366), to France (1368), and to Italy (1372 and 1378). During his travels, he encountered works by French and Italian authors such as Jean Froissart, Guillaume Machaut, Dante, Petrarch, and Boccaccio. These authors influenced Chaucer in a variety of ways; his first important original work, *The Book of the Duchess*, shows the influence of French courtly poetry; and his later *House of Fame* parodies Dante's *Divine Comedy* by depicting a poet's journey—in the talons of an eagle—to the celestial palace of the goddess of Fame. And his *Troilus and Criseide* (1385) was deeply indebted to Boccaccio's *Filostrato*. Chaucer's work also shows the influence of two texts that he translated into English from French and Latin, respectively: a thirteenth-century dream vision entitled *The Romance of the Rose* and a fourth-century philosophical dialogue by Boethius, *The Consolation of Philosophy*. At a time when many of his contemporaries were writing in French and Latin, Chaucer's use of English helped to establish the vernacular as a viable medium for serious poetry. He was an innovator

in both technique and language; a great number of words and phrases, many of French origin, appear for the first time in his writings. His *Canterbury Tales*, begun in 1386, is an unfinished group of tales told by members of a company of pilgrims. The tales draw on Chaucer's knowledge of many different social roles and events. He lived through several plagues and the Peasant's Revolt of 1381; he served as controller of the export tax on wool, sheepskins, and leather for the port of London; he was justice of the peace and a member of Parliament for the county of Kent; and he was also a deputy forester. Although he never completed his plan of writing one hundred and ten Canterbury Tales (two for each pilgrim to tell on the way to Canterbury, two for the way back), the twenty-two tales and two fragments that he did complete contain, as John Dryden said, "God's plenty."

Nicholas Christopher (b. 1951), pp. 1973–75

Nicholas Christopher was born and raised in New York City and has lived there most of his life. He was educated at Harvard University, where he studied with the poets Robert Lowell and Anthony Hecht, and has taught at New York and Columbia Universities. A prolific writer, he has published poetry and novels—as well as an amalgam of the two in his "novella in verse," *Desperate Characters* (1989)—and he has edited several collections of contemporary American poetry. He is also the author of a prose work on film noir.

Amy Clampitt (1920–1994), pp. 1609–15

Amy Clampitt was born and raised in New Providence, Iowa. She was educated at Grinnell College and, briefly, at Columbia University. After working as an editor at Oxford University Press and E. P. Dutton and as a reference librarian at the National Audubon Society, she became a freelance writer in 1982. Clampitt published her first collection of poetry at age sixty-three; *The Kingfisher* established her immediately as one of the nation's most acclaimed poets. Like John Keats, about whom she wrote a series of poems, she reveled in the sensuousness of the natural world and of language. A New Yorker most of her life, she died in Lenox, Massachusetts.

John Clare (1793–1864), pp. 893–96

John Clare was born in the small rural village of Helpstone, in Northamptonshire, England. After leaving school at age twelve, he worked on the land, as gardener, hedge-settler, lime-burner, and field hand, and published his first collection, *Poems Descriptive of Rural Life and Scenery*, in 1820. The book was a success, but as literary tastes changed, and the vogue for "ploughman poets" declined, subsequent volumes were not. Clare had a strong sense of place and was deeply attached to his native countryside. A move to a village four miles distant from his birthplace seems to have been the catalyst for chronic mental insecurity and, along with his parting from his first love, Mary Joyce, provided the theme of loss so prevalent in his writing. After manifesting signs of mental illness for many years, he was sent to an asylum in 1837 and, having been declared insane, transferred to Northampton General Lunatic Asylum, where he remained until his death. Written in his own combination of dialect and idiosyncratic grammar, his descriptions of rural landscape and elegies for a dying pastoral England are highly evocative. Clare's poetry remained in semi-obscurity until the mid-twentieth century, when his evident authenticity of feeling and complex sensibility were made available through new editions of his poems, autobiographical prose, and letters. A memorial to him in the Poets' Corner of Westminster Abbey was dedicated in 1989.

Arthur Hugh Clough (1819–1861),
pp. 1051–53
Arthur Hugh Clough (rhymes with *rough*) was born in Liverpool, England, to a cotton merchant and the daughter of a banker. His family moved to South Carolina in 1822, but Clough returned to England in 1828 to attend first Rugby School, then Balliol College, Oxford. In 1842, he earned a fellowship at Oriel College, Oxford, where he became friends with the poet Matthew Arnold. Like Arnold, he struggled with his religious beliefs, and in 1848 he resigned from his fellowship because he would not take clerical orders without sincerely believing the doctrines of the Church of England. That same year, he published his first work, *The Bothie of Tober-na-Vuolich*, a verse novel about the romance between a student and a Scottish peasant. After traveling to Rome and writing more poetry, including *Amours de Voyage*, he took an administrative position at the University of London; in 1851, however, uncertainties about his religious faith again led him to resign. During the next year, Clough returned to America with the thought of emigrating; he settled in Boston, where he tutored, wrote for magazines, and established a lasting friendship with Ralph Waldo Emerson. He returned to England in 1853, took an appointment in the Education Office, and married a cousin of Florence Nightingale. He died in Florence, Italy, while touring the Continent in the hope of improving his health, and Matthew Arnold wrote "Thyrsis" in memory of his friend. Most of Clough's work was published posthumously.

Samuel Taylor Coleridge (1772–1834),
pp. 805–31
Samuel Taylor Coleridge was born in Ottery St. Mary, a rural village in Devon. He was educated at Christ's Hospital School, London, and Jesus College, Cambridge, where he studied Classics,

but fell into a dissolute lifestyle. He fled to London and served in the 15th Light Dragoons until his brothers secured his release some months later. In 1794, he met Robert Southey, then an undergraduate at Balliol College, Oxford. Together they conceived the utopian philosophy of Pantisocracy and planned to start a commune in New England. This never came to fruition, but Coleridge and Southey continued to lecture in Bristol on political issues. Coleridge married Sara Fricker in 1794. The following year, he met William Wordsworth and Wordsworth's sister, Dorothy, in Somerset. It was one of the most creative periods of his life, inspiring the composition of poems such as "Kubla Khan," "The Rime of the Ancient Mariner," and "Christabel." With Wordsworth, he published *Lyrical Ballads* (1798), one of the most revolutionary collections of poetry in the history of English literature. From age thirty, Coleridge largely gave up poetry for philosophy and criticism. He is credited with introducing the works of the philosophers Immanuel Kant, Friedrich von Schlegel, and Friedrich von Schelling to England. At the height of his powers, he became addicted to opium, which had been prescribed to relieve physical pains that Wordsworth said were so unbearable they drove Coleridge to "throw himself down and writhe like a worm upon the ground." He had also fallen in love with Sara Hutchinson, Wordsworth's future sister-in-law, but although his relationship with Sara Fricker was deteriorating, he would not end the marriage. His despair was later channeled into "Dejection: An Ode," published in 1802. He spent his last years in the care of a London clergyman, writing and attempting to be reconciled with estranged family and friends alienated by his addiction, depression, and extreme behavior. The younger Romantics held him in great esteem, and his reputation was further enhanced by *Christabel and Other Poems*, published in 1814, and editions of his *Collected Poems*, which appeared in 1817, 1828, and 1834. In an age dominated by skepticism and empiricism, Coleridge held fast to his belief in the powers of the imagination, which he saw as capable of leading humanity to Truth—through appeals not to reason but to the senses. If Wordsworth determined the content of a century or more of English poetry, Coleridge determined its shape. His theories on "organic form" provided a basis for the development of a freer poetic and may have been the progenitor of many twentieth-century experiments in free verse.

Billy Collins (b. 1941), *pp. 1917–18*
Billy Collins was born in New York City. He attended parochial schools, graduated from Holy Cross College, and earned his Ph.D. in Romantic poetry from the University of California at Riverside. Although he published his first

book, *Pokerface,* in 1977, it was not until the 1990s that he became one of the most popular poets and poetry readers in American literary history, prized for his accessibility and humor. A professor at Lehman College, City University of New York, since the 1970s, he was the poet laureate of the United States in 2001–02. He lives in Somers, New York.

William Collins (1721–1759), *pp. 673–77*
William Collins was born in Chichester, England, where his father was twice mayor. Educated at Winchester School and Magdalen College, Oxford, he published *Persian Eclogues* as an undergraduate. Allegedly "too indolent even for the army," he went to London to earn a living from writing. His finances were always insecure, and ruin was averted only by the action of friends such as Samuel Johnson. His *Odes on Several Descriptive and Allegoric Subjects* (1747) was not esteemed at the time of publication, but a small inheritance enabled Collins to return to Chichester, where he could study and write. In 1750, he gave the Scottish playwright John Home an unfinished draft of "Ode on the Superstitions of the Highlands," in which (as the poet Robert Lowell put it) "the whole Romantic School is foreshadowed." Soon after, Collins's melancholia worsened, and after unsuccessfully seeking a cure in France he was confined to a Chelsea asylum. Released to the care of his sister, he remained with her, experiencing spells of lucidity, until his death. Though he left fewer than fifteen hundred lines of verse, he was one of the most influential poets of his time.

Wendy Cope (b. 1945), *pp. 1947–49*
Wendy Cope was born in Erith, Kent, and educated at St. Hilda's College, Oxford, and the Westminster College of Education, Oxford. She has been a primary school teacher, a music teacher, the arts and reviews editor of the Inner London Education Authority's *Contact* magazine, and television columnist for the *Spectator.* She began writing while undergoing psychoanalysis for severe depression following her father's death. In addition to her verse for adults and children, she has edited a collection of poetry by women. Cope's acerbic, witty, epigrammatic poems invite comparison with the work of Dorothy Parker and Stevie Smith. Like them, she has serious aims and proves, as she says, "a humorous poem can also be . . . deeply felt and saying something that matters."

Alfred Corn (b. 1943), *pp. 1929–30*
Alfred Corn was born and brought up in Georgia. He was educated at Emory and Columbia Universities; his graduate studies were in French literature. A reviewer, an essayist, and an art critic, he has also edited an anthology of writings on the Christian Scriptures. His narrative impulse has demonstrated itself not only

in a novel, *Part of His Story,* but also in nearly book-length poems such as *Notes from a Child of Paradise.* The author of a much-used prosody manual, *The Poem's Heartbeat,* Corn shows an attention to formal concerns in his many volumes of verse. Having taught at Columbia, Yale, and elsewhere, he now lives in Lenox, Massachusetts.

Gregory Corso (1930–2001), *pp. 1807–10*
Gregory Corso was born in New York City to Italian immigrants. During his childhood, his mother died and his father returned for a time to Italy. Corso lived in an orphanage and, eventually, four foster homes; when he was twelve, his father returned, remarried, and took custody of him. He first went to prison for stealing a radio from a boys' home. During a later prison sentence, he discovered literature through books given to him by an elderly inmate. When in 1950 he left prison, he met Allen Ginsberg, who further guided his reading and education as a poet. In 1954, he spent time in Cambridge, Massachusetts, at the invitation of Harvard and Radcliffe students, who gathered the money to publish his first book, *The Vestal Lady on Brattle* (1955). His travels with Ginsberg to San Francisco and Mexico inspired the poems in *Gasoline* (1958).

Abraham Cowley (1618–1667), *pp. 470–72*
Abraham Cowley (pronounced *Cooley*) was born after the death of his father, a wealthy London stationer, and was educated at Westminster School and Trinity College, Cambridge. At age fifteen, he published his first book of poems, containing among other works a verse romance he had written at ten. In 1638, he published a pastoral drama, *Love's Riddle,* and a Latin comedy, *Naufragium Joculare.* Given a fellowship at his college in 1640, he lost it when the civil war began, for he was a Royalist and went to France as secretary of the queen. He was imprisoned when he returned to England ten years later, because he was working as a spy and partly because he had published the satire *The Puritan and the Papist* (1643). A political epic, *The Civil War,* was not published until 1679, but he celebrated the king's return to power with an "Ode, Upon the Blessed Restoration" (1660). In his "Pindarique Odes," included in *Poems* (1656), he introduced the irregular ode form that would influence John Dryden, among others.

William Cowper (1731–1800), *pp. 695–705*
William Cowper (pronounced *Cooper*) was born in Great Berkhamstead, Herfordshire, England, and was educated at a private school and Westminster; his experience of bullying at the former lead to the attack on private schools in his "Tirocinium" (1785). He studied law at the Inner Temple and was called up to the bar, but never practiced. From his early years, he suffered from

depression, which was accelerated into mental instability both by his father's forbidding his marriage to his cousin, Theodora, and by an uncle's attempt to get him a sinecure in the House of Lords, the prospect of examination for which brought on a suicide attempt. Treated at St. Albans asylum, Cowper turned to the consolations of evangelical Christianity, and on his release became "a sort of adopted son" in the household of the Reverend Morley Unwin. After Unwin's death, Cowper, Mary Unwin, and her children set up house together in Olney, Buckinghamshire. Cowper's mental health again declined and eventually collapsed, but nursed by Mary he began to write again. They lived together until her death, in 1794, after which Cowper never fully recovered his physical and mental health.

George Crabbe (1754–1832), pp. 723–31
George Crabbe was born into poverty in Aldeburgh, Suffolk, England. Although he attended grammar schools between ages ten and fourteen, he was educated largely at home by his father. He was parish doctor of Aldeburgh before leaving for London and a literary career in 1780. With the help of his friend and admirer Edmund Burke, he published *The Library* (1781), was introduced to contemporary literary circles, and was encouraged to join the clergy to relieve his financial distress. In 1781, he became curate of Aldeburgh, and from 1782 until 1785 was chaplain to the duke of Rutland. Burke and Samuel Johnson helped him revise *The Village* (1783), a grimly realist portrait of rural poverty. After a period when he published little, in 1807 he produced a collection of earlier and new works including "The Parish Register," which established him as a narrative poet. He published several more collections during his lifetime and left a quantity of unpublished work on his death. Known for his use of the heroic couplet characteristic of the departing Augustan Age, he was, according to Lord Byron, "Nature's sternest painter yet the best."

Hart Crane (1899–1932), pp. 1410–16
Hart (Harold) Crane was born in Garrettsville, Ohio, and raised in Cleveland. He left high school in 1916 and moved to New York. From 1918 to 1923, he shuttled between New York and Cleveland and worked for advertising agencies (where he wrote copy), a munitions plant, a local newspaper, and his father's candy company. In 1923, Crane settled in New York, but in 1931 he sailed to Mexico, where he planned to write an epic about the Spanish Conquest. On a return trip to the United States, he committed suicide by leaping into shark-infested waters. Crane's long poem, *The Bridge*, which brought him fame, is his "mythical synthesis of America," following in the tradition of Walt Whitman. Its fifteen sections of varying length move westward, from New York to California;

feature historical figures, including Pocahontas and Rip Van Winkle; and celebrate natural as well as technological wonders, including the Brooklyn Bridge.

Stephen Crane (1871–1900), pp. 1220–22
Stephen Crane was born in Newark, New Jersey, and was raised in upstate New York. He attended Lafayette College and Syracuse University before moving to New York City, where he worked as a reporter and began to write fiction. His first novel, a naturalistic account of urban poverty called *Maggie: A Girl of the Streets* (1893), was poorly received, but his next book, *The Red Badge of Courage* (1894–95), earned him international fame. Although Crane had written this Civil War narrative without seeing combat, he received commissions to report on conflicts across the globe, including the Cuban Insurrection, the Turkish War, and the Spanish-American War. He died in Germany, where he had gone in search of a cure for his tuberculosis. Although he became famous for his prose, Crane preferred his poems, which are now considered pioneering examples of free verse. The poet John Berryman, his biographer, revived Crane's flagging posthumous reputation.

Richard Crashaw (1613–1649), pp. 468–70
Richard Crashaw's mother and stepmother both died before he was nine years old, and he spent most of his life rebelling against the austere religion of his father, a Puritan preacher. Crashaw was educated at Charterhouse and Pembroke Hall, Cambridge, where he was influenced by the Anglican Nicholas Ferrar, founder of the religious community at Little Gidding. After losing his fellowship at Peterhouse with the Royalists' defeat, Crashaw spent two years in exile, converting to Catholicism in 1645 and fleeing to Paris, where another friend, the writer Abraham Cowley, persuaded Queen Henrietta Maria to get Crashaw a position as an attendant to an Italian cardinal and, subsequently, as a subcanon at the Cathedral of Loretto. In 1634, Crashaw published a book of Latin poems, *Epigrammatum Sacrorum Liber*. His *Steps to the Temple, Sacred Poems with Other Delights of the Muses* (1646, revised and enlarged 1648) contains both religious and secular poems and indicates its debt to George Herbert in its title. A passionate admirer of the Spanish mystic Saint Teresa, Crashaw sought to represent the experience of religious ecstasy in words and, perhaps, in visual media. The manuscript as well as the printed volumes of his poetry contain elaborate titles in different-sized letters; and the emblematic engravings in his final (posthumously published) volume, the *Carmen Deo Nostro* (1652), may be by his own hand.

Robert Creeley (1926–2005), pp. 1705–08
Robert Creeley was born in Arlington, Massachusetts, and educated at Harvard University.

From 1944 to 1945, he interrupted his studies to drive an ambulance for the American Field Service in the India-Burma theater, then later left Harvard during his last semester to take up subsistence farming. He traveled to France and Mallorca, Spain (where he established the Divers Press), and returned to the United States in 1956. As a member of the faculty at the experimental Black Mountain College, Creeley founded its *Review*. In 1966, he began teaching at the State University of New York at Buffalo. Deeply influenced by Charles Olson, William Carlos Williams, and the Beats, all of whom composed their poems (as Allen Ginsberg put it) directly from feeling, he wrote a spare and compressed verse.

Countee Cullen (1903–1946), *pp. 1443–46*
Countee Cullen was born in Louisville, Kentucky. At age fifteen, he was adopted by an Episcopal minister from New York City. Educated at New York University and Harvard University, he worked as an assistant editor at *Opportunity* magazine, a prominent periodical of the Harlem Renaissance, from 1926 until 1928, when a fellowship enabled him to spend a year in Paris. From 1934 onward, he taught English and French in New York City public schools. In addition to writing five collections of poetry, Cullen translated Euripides, published a novel about life in Harlem, edited an influential anthology of African American poetry, and wrote two children's books. Wanting to be known foremost "as a poet and not as a Negro poet," he employed traditional forms while often exploring themes of African American life.

E. E. Cummings (1894–1962), *pp. 1392–97*
E(dward) E(stlin) Cummings was born in Cambridge, Massachusetts, and educated at Harvard University. In the early 1920s, he lived in both New York City (where he was affiliated with the *Dial* magazine group, which included the poet Marianne Moore) and Paris (where he met the poets Ezra Pound, Hart Crane, and Archibald MacLeish). In his later years, he lived primarily in New York. At the time of his death, he was one of the best-known and best-loved American poets. Like his paintings, Cummings's poems reflect the influence of the Impressionist and Cubist movements in the visual arts and Imagism, Vorticism, and Futurism in literature. Through his radical experiments with syntax, typography, and line, he defamiliarized common subjects, often with humor, whether light-hearted or satirical.

Allen Curnow (1911–2001), *pp. 1528–30*
Allen Curnow was born in Timaru, New Zealand, the son of an Anglican clergyman and author of light verse. He worked as a journalist before attending the Universities of Canterbury and Auckland and beginning studies for the ministry (which he later abandoned) at St. John's College. He taught English at Auckland University from 1950 until 1976. In addition to serious poetry, Curnow published satirical verse under the pseudonym Whim-Wham, as well as plays and literary criticism. He edited two landmark anthologies, *A Book of New Zealand Verse* and *The Penguin Book of New Zealand Verse*. In the 1930s, Curnow was involved with poets associated with the left-wing magazine *Phoenix*, and his early work reflects their shared belief in the importance of establishing a national literature for New Zealand. These poems characteristically make detailed observation of the natural world. In 1972, after a fifteen-year silence, he began writing in a new mode, exploring the relationship between self and place, the mystery of nature, and death.

Samuel Daniel (1563–1619), *pp. 230–35*
Samuel Daniel was born near Taunton, England; educated at Magdalen Hall, Oxford; and traveled widely throughout Europe, learning several languages. He enjoyed the patronage of Mary Sidney, countess of Pembroke, to whose son he was tutor; and his neoclassical tragedy *Cleopatra* (1594, revised 1607), was influenced by Mary Sidney's translation of a French play about Cleopatra and Antony (*Antonie*, 1592). Daniel wrote works in a variety of genres, from a history of the War of the Roses to tragic and pastoral dramas, to court masques. His *Defense of Rhyme* (1602?), a response to Thomas Campion's treatise alleging the superiority of classical prosody, occupies an important place in the debate on the status of the vernacular as a literary language. In 1592, Daniel published his sonnet cycle to "Delia"; a romance, *The Complaint of Rosamond*, appeared in the same volume. Another collection, *Certain Small Poems* (1605), caused Daniel to lose the favor of King James I because it contained a tragedy whose protagonist, Philotas, was identified with Queen Elizabeth I's rebellious courtier, the earl of Essex. Daniel was nonetheless patronized by James's queen, Anne, and he continued to write masques for the court, including *Tethys' Festival* (1610) and *Hymen's Triumph* (1615). Ben Jonson, with whom Daniel was "at jealousies," criticized his poetry, but others, including Samuel Taylor Coleridge, have praised his poetic language.

Donald Davie (1922–1995), *pp. 1641–44*
Donald Davie was born in Barnsley, Yorkshire, England, to Baptist parents, and brought up in "the industrially ravaged landscape" of the West Riding. He was educated at Barnsley Hogate Grammar School and at St. Catherine's College, Cambridge, where he was greatly influenced by the critic F. R. Leavis. His studies were interrupted by service in the Royal Navy, but he then

returned to Cambridge and took his B.A., M.A., and Ph.D. He taught at Trinity College, Dublin; the University of California at Santa Barbara; and Gonville and Caius College, Cambridge. He joined the newly founded University of Essex, serving on its faculty from 1964 until 1968, when he moved to Stanford University. In 1978, he moved to Vanderbilt University, from which he retired in 1988 to live in Devon. Davie's first collection of poetry, *Brides of Reason*, appeared in 1955, to be followed by many others, including his *Collected Poems* in 1990. He also published a number of influential studies of English poetry, diction, and syntax, as well as criticism of the work of Hardy, Pound, and Pasternak; translations of the work of Polish, Hungarian, and Russian writers; and a study of English hymnology. His editorial work included several collections of poetry, including the *New Oxford Book of Christian Verse* (1981). Davie's *Purity of Diction in English Verse* (1952) was virtually a manifesto for The Movement, a group of writers who eschewed the symbolism and syntactical disjunctions of Imagism and Symbolism in favor of paraphrasable logic, plain diction, straightforward syntax, and traditional forms.

Peter Davison (b. 1928), *pp. 1751–52*
Peter Davison was born in New York City and raised in Colorado. He was educated at Harvard University and St. John's College, Cambridge, and spent two years in the United States Army. Davison has had a distinguished editorial career at Harcourt, Brace; Harvard University Press; Atlantic Monthly Press; and Houghton Mifflin. As the poetry editor of *The Atlantic Monthly* since 1972, he has notably influenced poets and poetry readers. His work shows an affinity with that of his father, the English poet Edward Davison, and family friend and mentor Robert Frost. He lives in Boston and in Gloucester, Massachusetts.

Walter de la Mare (1873–1956), *pp. 1225–27*
Walter de la Mare was born in Charlton, Kent, England. In 1890, he took a job as a bookkeeper at the London offices of the Standard Oil Company, a position he held for eighteen years, until a government pension enabled him to devote himself full-time to writing. In 1902, he published his first collection of poetry, *Songs of Childhood*, under the pseudonym Walter Ramal. Over the next forty-five years, he published voluminously, producing novels, short stories, and poetry, as well as editing several influential anthologies of literature, including *Come Hither* (1923) and *Behold the Dreamer* (1939). He was made a Companion of Honour in 1948 and awarded the Order of Merit in 1953.

James Dickey (1923–1997), *pp. 1661–64*
James Dickey was born in Atlanta, Georgia. In 1942, he attended Clemson College, in South

Carolina, then left to join the air force. After serving as a fighter-bomber pilot during World War II, he attended Vanderbilt University, where he began writing poetry. He received B.A. and M.A. degrees from Vanderbilt and did further graduate work there and at Rice University, in Texas. Following another two years in the air force (this time as a training officer during the Korean War), he spent six years as a writer of advertising copy, then later taught at a number of universities. In 1960, he published his first book of poetry, and from 1966 to 1968 he served as poetry consultant to the Library of Congress. In addition to poetry, he published fiction, including the best-selling novel *Deliverance* (1970)—which he adapted into a Hollywood film—and nonfiction, including reviews and autobiographical works.

Emily Dickinson (1830–1886), *pp. 1110–27*
Emily Dickinson was born in Amherst, Massachusetts, to a prominent family. For one year, she attended Mount Holyoke Female Seminary (now College), in nearby South Hadley, then withdrew and returned to Amherst. Dickinson lived at her family home in Amherst from 1848 on, rarely received visitors, and in her mature years never went out. Suffering from agoraphobia (the fear of public places) and perhaps from an eye disorder, she became known as "the Myth" and "the character of Amherst." Fewer than a dozen of her poems were published in her lifetime. Such a solitary life hardly dulled her sensibilities, however, for Dickinson's works include nearly two thousand poems, plus voluminous correspondence. The poems reveal her intimate knowledge of the Bible, classical myth, and the works of Shakespeare; in addition, she admired the work of Transcendentalists Thoreau and Emerson. In an era marked by its evangelical fervor, Dickinson adopted skepticism, irony, ambiguity, paradox, and sardonic wit. She often wrote in the meters of hymns and made masterful use of the ballad stanza and of slant rhyme. Although her innovations initially baffled critics, the public's fascination with her life soon extended to her verse. She is, along with Walt Whitman, the most revered and influential of nineteenth-century American poets.

John Donne (1572–1631), *pp. 293–322*
John Donne was born in London, his father an ironmonger and his mother, a devout Catholic, the daughter of the dramatist John Heywood as well as a descendent of Sir Thomas More. Donne studied at Oxford without taking a degree, because to do so would have required him to swear an oath affirming that the English monarch was head of the Church. After travel in Europe, he entered the legal institution of Lincoln's Inn in 1592. In 1595, Donne participated in a naval expedition against Spain, and in

1596 he joined an expedition to the Azores. On his return, he became private secretary to Sir Thomas Egerton, lord keeper of the Great Seal, but was dismissed when his secret marriage to Lady Egerton's seventeen-year-old niece, Ann More, was discovered. The marriage effectively blocked Donne's career as a courtier; and after many years of seeking offices and patrons, he took orders in the Church of England in 1615—as King James I had been urging him to do since 1607. Two years later, his wife died. He became dean of St. Paul's Cathedral in 1621, and his sermons were very well attended. His private devotions (in prose) were published in 1624, but very few of the poems he had been writing since the 1590s were printed during his lifetime; instead, they circulated widely in manuscript, creating many textual variants and many questions about dating for future editors and readers. His poems were divided into nine generic groups in the second edition of his poetry (1635), including the *Elegies*, modeled on Ovid's erotic verse; the *Songs and Sonnets*, containing a variety of secular love poems; and the *Holy Sonnets*.

H. D. (Hilda Doolittle) (1886–1961), *pp. 1311–16*

Hilda Doolittle was born in Bethlehem, Pennsylvania. In 1901, she met the poet Ezra Pound, who encouraged her writing. Doolittle attended Bryn Mawr College, then moved to Greenwich Village, where she established her reputation as a writer. She traveled to London in 1911, intending to visit Pound, but stayed in Europe for the rest of her life. In 1912, Pound submitted three of Doolittle's poems to Harriet Monroe, editor of *Poetry* magazine, signing them "H. D. Imagiste." Although H. D. moved beyond Imagism—and Vorticism, its quick successor—fairly early, her reputation has remained closely tied to that short-lived but momentous movement. In 1933, H. D. entered psychoanalysis with Sigmund Freud. In her work, she set her own experience against the great storehouses of literature, myth, history, religion, and the occult, and her *Trilogy* included three long poems concerning World War II, most notably *The Walls Do Not Fall* (1944). In addition to poetry, she published numerous volumes of prose, worked as a translator, and wrote verse dramas.

Charles d'Orléans (1391–1465), *pp. 77–78*

Charles, duke of Orléans (brother of King Charles VI of France), married his cousin Isabella (widow of Richard II of England) in 1406. Commander of the French forces at the Battle of Agincourt, in 1415, he was captured after their defeat by the English army under Henry V. He spent the next twenty-five years in prison, and during this time composed his poems in English as well as French. He produced chansons, complaintes, and translations, as well as

poems in intricate forms such as the ballade and rondel, usually on the theme of courtly love. After payment of a huge ransom, he was released from prison and returned to France in 1440. He spent his last years at Blois, where his court became a center of music and literature.

Keith Douglas (1920–1944), *pp. 1620–23*

Keith Douglas was born in Tunbridge Wells, Kent, England, and brought up near Cranleigh. His childhood was difficult, as his father became a drifter and his mother was stricken with "sleepy sickness." At Merton College, Oxford, his tutor was Edmund Blunden, the soldier-poet of World War I. In 1940, Douglas enlisted, and a year later he was posted to Egypt; though ordered to remain in reserve, he commandeered a truck and joined his regiment at the front. He was badly injured when he stepped on a land mine, but after convalescence in Palestine was sent to the European front, and was killed during the invasion of Normandy. Before his death, Douglas had prepared a collection for publication, but it did not reach print until 1966. He also wrote a memoir, *Alamein to Zem Zem*, based on his experiences in the Middle East. In this, as in his poems, he presents himself in dual roles: victim and killer, satirist and eulogist, disinterested spectator and committed participant. His *Collected Poems* appeared, posthumously, in 1951, and an edition of his letters was published in 2001.

Rita Dove (b. 1952), *pp. 1985–90*

Rita Dove was born in Akron, Ohio. She was educated at Miami University (Ohio), the University of Tübingen (Germany), and the University of Iowa, and has taught at Arizona State University and the University of Virginia. Dove has traveled widely and has lived abroad, notably in Berlin and Jerusalem. In 1993, she became poet laureate of the United States. In addition to poetry, she has written fiction and drama. Her own mixed European and African American heritage has been a source of inspiration, as have mythology and history.

Ernest Dowson (1876–1900), *pp. 1211–12*

Ernest Dowson was born in Kent, England. He went to The Queen's College, Oxford, but left without obtaining a degree. He studied Latin poetry, and through extended stays on the Continent became familiar with French literature. With the writers Lionel Johnson, Ernest Rhys, Arthur Symons, William Butler Yeats, and others, Dowson formed the Rhymers' Club, an informal writers' group based in London, and contributed to two of the club's anthologies as well as to *The Yellow Book* and the *Savoy*. In 1891, he met Adelaide Foltinowicz, "Missie," for whom he harbored a lifelong but unrequited passion, and who became a symbol of love and innocence in his poetry. He was received into the Roman Catholic Church about 1891. From 1895 onward, Dowson lived an increasingly dissolute life, traveling between England, Ireland, and France, and supporting himself through translation. His last years were marred by poverty, ill health, and depression. He died, of tuberculosis, at the London home of a friend, R. H. Sherard, who had looked after him in the final six months of his life.

Michael Drayton (1563–1631), *pp. 235–38*
Michael Drayton was a year older than Shakespeare and born in the same county, Warwickshire, England. Drayton was brought up as a page in the house of Sir Henry Goodyere, whose daughter Anne (later Lady Rainsford) Drayton loved, perforce platonically, for many years. At age ten, he dedicated himself to a poetic career, and without benefit of a university education he became a learned and accomplished practitioner of most of the Renaissance poetic genres. He settled in London in 1590 and the next year published his first work, *The Harmony of the Church*. For reasons that remain obscure, this series of verse paraphrases of the Bible was suppressed by public order, except for forty copies (of which only one has survived) retained by the bishop of Canterbury. In 1593, he published *Idea: The Shepherd's Garland* (1593), which shows the influence of Spenser's pastoral poetry. A collection of sonnets, *Idea's Mirror*, appeared the next year (it was frequently revised and expanded); in both works Drayton honored Anne Goodyere under the name "Idea." He considered *Poly-Olbion* his greatest poem, but this thirty-thousand-line celebration of the topography of Britain (1612–22) proved less popular than most of Drayton's other works, among them *England's Heroical Epistles* (1597), modeled on Ovid's *Heroides*. Although Drayton wrote a poem of fulsome praise when King James I took the crown, he never found favor at the court after Elizabeth I's death; and his vision of the English nation as well as his most popular poetry suggest that he belonged to the Elizabethan Age even though he long outlived it.

John Dryden (1631–1700), *pp. 500–26*
John Dryden, the son of a country gentleman and his wife, was educated at Westminster School and Trinity College, Cambridge. Although he wrote his first poem, *Heroic Stanzas* (1659), to commemorate Oliver Cromwell's death, he celebrated the return of King Charles II in *Astraea Redux* (1660). A loyal Royalist for the rest of his life, he was made poet laureate in 1668. He wrote twenty-four plays for the newly reopened London theaters and numerous important songs, poems, and elegies. Many of these were written for specific occasions such as a coronation, a military victory, or a death. These poems, together with his long works of political and literary satire, such as *Absalom and Achitophel* (1681) and the mock-heroic *Mac Flecknoe* (1682), affirmed the public role of the poet and established the basic forms of verse, most notably the heroic couplet, that dominated the neoclassical period and persisted into the early nineteenth century. His introductions and essays, at once learned and commonsensical, earned him the title of "the father of English criticism" from his successor Samuel Johnson and helped shape English prose style for centuries. In his later years, after writing a poem defending the Anglican Church, Dryden converted to Catholicism. This decision, which led his enemies to charge him with opportunism (James II, a Catholic, had recently succeeded to the throne), eventually resulted in Dryden's losing his public offices and stipends, when the Protestant rulers William and Mary replaced James in 1688. Nearing sixty, Dryden supported himself by writing plays and translating classical writers, Chaucer, and Boccaccio.

Peter Kane Dufault (b. 1923), *pp. 1665–67*
Peter Kane Dufault was born in Newark, New Jersey, and attended Harvard University. During World War II, he served in the United States Army Air Force. Since then, he has worked as a news editor, a house painter, a tree surgeon, a folk singer, a fiddler, a country-dance caller, an actor, and a teacher of writing at Williams College and Berkshire Community College (Massachusetts). His work typically observes the natural world closely and carefully, sometimes imbuing its subjects with mystical qualities. He lives in Hillsdale, New York.

Carol Ann Duffy (b. 1955), *pp. 2007–09*
Carol Ann Duffy was born in Glasgow, Scotland, brought up in Staffordshire, England, and studied philosophy at the University of Liverpool. She has been a visiting professor and a writer-in-residence at a number of institutions. A regular reviewer and broadcaster, she now lectures in poetry at Manchester Metropolitan University. Her book *Mean Time* (1993) won both the Whitbread Prize for Poetry and the Forward Prize. The hallmarks of her poetry—her ability to invent plausible characters, to explore a range of points of view, and to pace her poetry so as to surprise readers—derive in large part from her experience of writing for the stage. Like Robert Browning, she favors the dramatic monologue, and like him she creates personae with complex emotions, questionable ethics, and rich fantasy lives.

Paul Laurence Dunbar (1872–1906), *pp. 1222–24*
Paul Laurence Dunbar was born in Dayton, Ohio, the son of former slaves. His father had escaped to Canada via the Underground Rail-

road, but returned to the United States to enlist in the second black regiment of the Union Army. Dunbar attended a white high school, where he showed an early talent for writing. He was unable to fund further education, however, and went to work as an elevator operator. When his reputation as a writer grew, the abolitionist Frederick Douglass secured a job for him at the Columbian Exposition, in Chicago. From 1897 to 1898, he worked as an assistant in the reading room of the Library of Congress, and he later supported himself by writing and lecturing in the United States and England. In addition to poetry, Dunbar published four novels and four volumes of short stories.

William Dunbar (ca. 1460–ca. 1525), *pp. 86–90*
William Dunbar was born to a noble Scottish family and apparently took an M.A. from St. Andrews University (near Edinburgh) in 1479. He became a Franciscan friar and traveled in England and France before leaving the order. Employed in various civil and diplomatic capacities abroad by James IV of Scotland, he went to England with the ambassadorial mission to arrange the king's marriage to Margaret Tudor, for which occasion (in 1503) he wrote *The Thrissil and the Rois,* a political allegory in which James is the thistle, Margaret the rose. This was followed by poems allegorical, satirical, visionary, and narrative, on both religious and secular themes. Influenced by Chaucer and the French poet François Villon, Dunbar wrote in a Scottish form of English, describing, in *The Flyting* (i.e., quarrel) *of Dunbar and Kennedie,* the antipathy between "Inglis"-speaking southern borderlanders and the Scots/Gaelic-speakers of the highlands and west. He received a royal pension in 1500, and some of his poems—"The Queenis Progress at Aberdeen," for instance, and perhaps his "In Prais of Wemen"—suggest that Queen Margaret was his real or desired patron.

Douglas Dunn (b. 1942), *pp. 1927–29*
Douglas Dunn was born in Inchinnan, Renfrewshire, Scotland, and was educated at the Scottish School of Librarianship and the University of Hull. He worked as a librarian in a number of places, including Akron, Ohio, and at the University of Hull, where he worked under Philip Larkin, whose influence can be seen in his early poems. Those contained in his first collection, *Terry Street* (1969), graphically describe the squalid living conditions and impoverished intellectual life of the underprivileged of Hull. From 1981 until 1982, he was a creative writing fellow at the University of Dundee. In 1984, he settled in Tayport, Fife; in 1985, he won the Whitbread Book of the Year Award for his *Elegies,* poems written for his wife, an artist and a curator, who died, of cancer, at thirty-seven. Dunn has also published short stories, written

plays for radio and television, and translated Racine's *Andromache.* He has edited a selection of Delmore Schwartz's poems, a collection of work by Hull poets, and *The Faber Book of Twentieth-Century Scottish Poetry.* He is a professor in the School of English at the University of St. Andrews.

Richard Eberhart (b. 1904), *p. 1450*
Richard Eberhart was born in Austin, Minnesota. He received his undergraduate education at the University of Minnesota and Dartmouth College. As a crew member on a tramp steamer, he made his way to England, where he undertook studies in English at St. John's College, Cambridge. Upon his return to the United States, Eberhart did graduate study at Harvard University, then taught at St. Mark's School (near Boston), where the poet Robert Lowell was one of his pupils. During World War II, Eberhart served as an aerial gunnery instructor. In the mid-1940s, he joined his father-in-law's floor-wax company, but in the 1950s he began an academic career and taught at, among other schools, the University of Washington, Princeton University, and Dartmouth College. In addition, he helped found the Poets' Theatre, in Cambridge, Massachusetts.

T. S. Eliot (1888–1965), *pp. 1340–66*
T(homas) S(tearns) Eliot was born to a distinguished New England family, raised in St. Louis, Missouri, and educated at Harvard University, the Sorbonne, and Oxford University, where he wrote his Ph.D. dissertation on the English logician and metaphysician F. H. Bradley. The critic Arthur Symons's work on the French Symbolists was a seminal influence on Eliot, as was the poet Ezra Pound, who encouraged him to stay in Europe and would eventually edit his masterpiece *The Waste Land* (1922). From 1917 until 1925, he worked in the International Department at Lloyd's Bank, after which he joined the publishing house of Faber and Faber, where he published the work of W. H. Auden, Stephen Spender, Louis MacNeice, and other young poets. He also edited the *Egoist* magazine and founded the influential *Criterion.* In 1927, Eliot took British citizenship and joined the Church of England. In his later years, he wrote compelling critical studies on literature, culture, society, and religion, and he is generally considered the most important critic of the century. In addition, he wrote several successful verse dramas. He was awarded the Nobel Prize for Literature in 1948. Although he dismissed *The Waste Land,* which he wrote largely while hospitalized for a breakdown in 1921, as "the relief of a personal and wholly insignificant grouse against life," his generation considered it a definitive explication of its distress. Eliot's later work documents his conversion to Christianity

and culminates in *Four Quartets* (1935–43), which he considered his greatest work.

Queen Elizabeth I (1533–1603), *pp. 142–43*
The daughter of Henry VIII and his second wife, Anne Boleyn, Elizabeth was declared a bastard by her father, who executed her mother in 1534 on probably spurious grounds of adultery. Questions about the legitimacy of Elizabeth's birth (at a time when Henry's first wife, Katharine of Aragon, was still living) fueled many later attacks on her, especially those by Catholics who supported the claims to the throne of Mary Tudor, Elizabeth's elder half-sister, or later, those of Mary Queen of Scots, Elizabeth's cousin. Elizabeth replaced Mary Tudor on the throne of England in 1558, supported by many of the Protestants who had welcomed her half-brother Edward VI's brief reign (1547–53). Elizabeth was, however, more adroit at religious compromise than Edward or Mary had been; the years of Elizabeth's long reign were relatively peaceful, despite the plots on her life and the criticisms made by many of her male subjects of a woman's right to rule England. Well-educated in languages and rhetoric, the youthful Elizabeth translated works by Boethius, Petrarch, and Marguerite of Navarre, among others; as a queen, Elizabeth gave eloquent speeches that were recorded by others, sometimes in several quite different versions. She wrote many letters and some lyric poems. In her speeches and writings, Elizabeth often sought to control, and sometimes to counter, the many images of her produced by her subjects. If some of the most famous Elizabethans portrayed her as a "fairy queen" (Spenser did so in his epic of that name, as did Shakespeare in his play *A Midsummer Night's Dream*), she preferred to portray herself as a woman who had the "heart and stomach of a king."

Jean Elliot (1727–1805), *p. 677*
Jean (or Jane) Elliot was born in Teviotdale, Scotland, to a judge and his wife. On her father's death, she, her mother, and her sister moved to Edinburgh, where Elliot remained until returning to Teviotdale shortly before her death. She was the author of probably the most popular version of the old ballad "The Flowers of the Forest," a haunting lament for the dead of the Battle of Flodden (Field), fought in September 1513 and a crushing defeat for Scotland. Published anonymously in 1756, Elliot's poem was greatly admired by the poets Robert Burns and Walter Scott, among others. "The manner of the ancient minstrels is so happily imitated," wrote Scott, "that it required the most positive evidence to convince me that the song was of modern date." Indeed, many readers assumed the poem was a genuine relic of the sixteenth century.

Ralph Waldo Emerson (1803–1882), *pp. 941–46*
Ralph Waldo Emerson was born and raised in Boston, the son of a Unitarian minister and his wife. He was educated at Harvard University and Harvard Divinity School. Ordained as junior pastor of Boston's Second Church, he left the church in 1832 because of deep doubts concerning organized religion. That same year, he traveled to Europe, where he met the poets William Wordsworth and Samuel Taylor Coleridge and the essayist and historian Thomas Carlyle, who became a close friend and great influence. He also was introduced to German idealism, and this philosophy, along with the writings of Plato and Swedenborg and the sacred texts of Hinduism, largely determined Emerson's interpretation of Transcendentalism. Although he never developed his beliefs into a full-fledged system, Emerson preached self-reliance and optimism and promoted instinct over reason. The Transcendental circle that formed around him included the writers Henry David Thoreau, Jones Very, Margaret Fuller, and Nathaniel Hawthorne. Although he used conventional meters and forms for his early poems, Emerson came to believe that "a thought so passionate and alive . . . has an architecture of its own," and this "organic" theory of composition informed his later works.

William Empson (1906–1984), *pp. 1463–64*
William Empson was born at Yokefleet Hall, near Howden, Yorkshire, and educated at Magdalene College, Cambridge. He took degrees in mathematics and, under the tutelage of critic I. A. Richards, English. After spending the 1930s abroad, teaching at the Tokyo University of Literature and Science and for the Southwest Associated Universities in China, Empson returned to England when World War II broke out and worked for the BBC, where he edited scripts for foreign broadcast. In 1947, he returned to China to teach at Peking National University, and there he witnessed the Chinese civil war and the subsequent rise of Communism. He returned to England in 1952 and was appointed professor of literature at Sheffield University, a position he held until his retirement (in 1971). In addition to poetry, he published several scholarly studies, including *Seven Types of Ambiguity* (1930) and *Some Versions of Pastoral* (1935). *Milton's God* (1961) was one of a series of writings that caused controversy during his tenure at Sheffield. Philip Larkin was among the poets who took Empson's work as a model for confronting the despair inherent in the modern condition with grace and stoicism.

Louise Erdrich (b. 1954), *pp. 2005–06*
Louise Erdrich was born in Little Falls, Minnesota, and raised in Wahpeton, North Dakota,

a small town near the Turtle Mountain Reservation and the Minnesota border. She was educated at Dartmouth College—where she studied with the late Michael Dorris, who would become her husband and collaborator—and at Johns Hopkins University. She has worked at a variety of jobs, including teaching poetry in prisons and editing a newspaper dedicated to Native American affairs (her mother was of French Chippewa descent). Known primarily as a novelist and short-story writer, Erdrich is a storyteller in her poetry as well. Many of her poems are dramatic monologues spoken by the inhabitants of a mythical small town in the early twentieth century.

James Fenton (b. 1949), *pp. 1961–67*
James Fenton was born in Lincoln, England, and educated at Magdalen College, Oxford, where he studied politics, philosophy, and psychology. He has worked as a literary and political journalist, and as a foreign correspondent in Germany, Cambodia, and Vietnam. His publications include collections of poetry, theater reviews, and accounts of his travels and experiences as a war reporter. He has translated Verdi's *Rigoletto* for the English National Opera and contributed to the musical version of Hugo's *Les Miserables.* He was professor of poetry at Oxford University from 1994 to 1999.

Lawrence Ferlinghetti (b. 1919), *pp. 1606–07*
Lawrence Ferlinghetti was born in Yonkers, New York. Upon graduation from the University of North Carolina at Chapel Hill, he joined the navy and served during World War II. He worked for *Time* magazine and later resumed his education at Columbia University and the Sorbonne. After moving to San Francisco, he started the City Lights Bookstore and the City Lights Press, which launched the careers of a generation of American poets. He was associated with the San Francisco Group, started by the poet Kenneth Rexroth, and with the Beats, whose prominent members included Jack Kerouac, William Burroughs, Gregory Corso, and Allen Ginsberg, whose popular but controversial *Howl and Other Poems* he published and defended when it was charged in court as indecent. His own *A Coney Island of the Mind* (1958), hip and satirical, was a huge success.

Anne Finch, Countess of Winchilsea (1661–1720), *pp. 556–66*
Anne Finch was born in Sydmonton, Berkshire, England. After the deaths of her parents, Sir William Kingsmill and Anne Haslewood, she was raised and educated by an uncle. In 1683, with the poet Anne Killigrew, Finch became a maid of honor to Mary Modena, the duchess of York and future wife of King James II, and at court met Colonel Heneage Finch, future earl of Winchilsea, who became her husband. Col-

onel Finch was arrested while attempting to follow James to France after the king was deposed in 1688; following his release, he and his wife retired to their estate in Eastwell, Kent. Encouraged by her husband, Anne Finch began to write in the 1680s, and her long poem "The Spleen" was anthologized in 1701. In 1709, Jonathan Swift addressed a poem, "Apollo Outwitted," to her, and she exchanged poems with Alexander Pope about the representation of "female wits" in his *The Rape of the Lock* (1714). In 1713, she published her *Miscellany Poems on Several Occasions,* which included a tragedy, *Aristomenes,* but many of her poems remained in manuscript at her death. William Wordsworth praised her nature poems, especially "A Nocturnal Reverie," and included seventeen of her poems in an anthology he compiled for Lady Mary Lowther in 1819. Only recently, however, have Finch's satiric poems and meditations on the problems of women writers achieved their due recognition.

Edward FitzGerald (1809–1883), *pp. 961–73*
Edward FitzGerald was born in Bredfield, Suffolk, England, and educated at Trinity College, Cambridge, where he met the writers William Thackeray and Alfred, Lord Tennyson. He never adopted a trade, but lived a retired and abstemious life occupied with study and translation. In the 1850s, he took up oriental studies, a prevalent interest of mid-nineteenth-century intellectuals, and in 1856 he produced his first translation. The work for which he is best known is his free translation of *The Rubáiyát of Omar Khayyám of Naishápúr,* which he published anonymously in 1859, expanded in 1868, and revised further in 1872 and 1879. FitzGerald maintained the structure of Omar Khayyám's epigrammatic *ruba'i,* or quatrains, including their *aaba* rhyme scheme and mounting tension, but deviated significantly from the twelfth-century Persian manuscript. Imposing unity on the work by introducing a time frame and dramatic situation, he stripped it to its essential themes, including the evanescence of life and the consequent necessity to "seize the day" (carpe diem). Initially ignored, the work rapidly gained in popularity when it was discovered by the painter and poet Dante Gabriel Rossetti and his Victorian coterie, the Pre-Raphaelites, who found its themes and tone strikingly contemporary.

Robert Fitzgerald (1910–1985), *pp. 1507–08*
Robert Fitzgerald was born in Geneva, New York, and grew up in Springfield, Illinois. He was educated at Harvard University and also did informal studies at Trinity College, Cambridge. After working as a reporter for the *New York Herald Tribune* and later for *Time* magazine, he served in the navy during World War II. Begin-

ning in 1949, Fitzgerald divided his time between the United States and Italy. He served as poetry editor of *The New Republic* and taught at, among other schools, Sarah Lawrence College and Princeton, Harvard, and Yale Universities. Renowned primarily for his translations of Homer and Virgil, he (with Dudley Fitts) also translated Euripides and Sophocles.

John Fletcher (1579–1625), *p. 345*
John Fletcher was born in Rye, Sussex, England, and was educated at Benet College, Cambridge. After the death of his father, bishop of London, Fletcher was left to make his own way. In London, he befriended Francis Beaumont, with whom he cowrote a number of plays for the fashionable boys' companies. Along with Shakespeare, Fletcher and Beaumont became leading playwrights of the King's Men, the most prominent theatrical company of the day. Their joint works include *Philaster* (ca. 1609), *The Maid's Tragedy* (ca. 1610), and *A King and No King* (1611). Following Beaumont's early retirement and death, Fletcher collaborated with other playwrights, most notably Philip Massinger, with whom he wrote *Sir John van Olden Barnavelt* (ca. 1619) and *The Beggar's Bush* (ca. 1622), among other plays, and Shakespeare, with whom he probably wrote *Henry VIII* (1613) and *The Two Noble Kinsmen* (1613). Fletcher is credited with sole authorship of a number of plays, including *The Faithful Shepherdess* (ca. 1609), *The Chances* (ca. 1617), *The Wild-Goose Chase* (ca. 1621), and *Rule a Wife and Have a Wife* (1624). His success reflected his alertness to changing tastes as well as his deft handling of tragicomedy and the comedy of manners. Like many dramatists of his day, he included lyrics and songs in his plays.

Philip Freneau (1752–1832), *pp. 716–18*
Philip Freneau was born and raised in New York City. He was educated at the College of New Jersey (now Princeton University). From 1776 until nearly 1779, he worked as a secretary to a plantation owner in the West Indies. Upon a second trip to the West Indies, in 1780, he was captured by the British and held as a prisoner of war. In 1790, he became a clerk of foreign languages for the State Department, and he later worked for a number of journals. He spent his last years on his family's plantation in New Jersey, fell into poverty and obscurity, and died of exposure when he lost his way home during a snowstorm. Best known for his satires (many of which were anti-British), his polemics, and his lyrics, Freneau was called "the poet of the American Revolution," and many consider him the first major American poet.

Robert Frost (1874–1963), *pp. 1227–45*
Robert Frost was born and raised (until age eleven) in San Francisco. He attended Dartmouth and Harvard Colleges. For a decade, around the turn of the century, he worked as a farmer in New Hampshire. From 1912 until 1915, he, his wife, and their four children lived in England, where he published his first book, *A Boy's Will* (1913), and met the poets Ezra Pound and Edward Thomas, both of whose shrewd reviews helped establish his reputation. Upon his return to America, Frost held a number of teaching appointments, his most enduring association being with Amherst College. From the publication of his second book, *North of Boston* (1914), onward, Frost became one of the best-known and most celebrated American poets. In 1961, he read his poem "The Gift Outright" at President John F. Kennedy's inauguration, an honor indicating his unique status for the American people. His poems, often rooted in New England and phrased in common language, also showed a classical influence. Not only the poems but also his theories about prosody continue to mark the work of living poets.

George Gascoigne (ca. 1534–1577), *pp. 144–46*
George Gascoigne was probably educated at Trinity College, Cambridge, and entered Gray's Inn in 1555. Seeking a career as a courtier, he sold his patrimony to cover his debts. In 1561, he wed the already married Elizabeth Boyes; nine years later, he was imprisoned for debt. Having served twice in Parliament in the late 1550s, he was refused his seat in 1572 on the grounds of his bad reputation. From 1572 until 1573, he served as a soldier in the Netherlands, during which time an unauthorized edition of his play and poems, *A Hundred Sundry Flowers Bound Up in One Small Posy*, appeared, which he corrected and extended as *The Posies of George Gascoigne*. Acknowledging Chaucer as his poetic master, Gascoigne translated from the Italian Ariosto's *The Supposes* and wrote the first original poem in English, *The Steel Glass*, a satire. His *The Adventures of Master F. J.* is a pioneering work of novelistic prose. He divided his poems into three categories: "flowers," or "pleasant" poems written on "light occasions"; "herbs," or "profitable" poems on moral subjects; and "weeds," or poems "neither delightful nor yet profitable" on his own follies. His *Certain Notes of Instruction Concerning the Making of Verse or Rhyme in English*, the first important work on English prosody, is a pithy and practical handbook showing a wide knowledge of poetic forms.

David Gascoyne (1916–2001), *pp. 1580–83*
David Gascoyne was born in Harrow, Middlesex, England, and educated at Regent Street Polytechnic, London. He published his first collection of poems at age sixteen. In 1933, he traveled to Paris to investigate the Surrealist movement (and wrote the first English study of it when he was nineteen), and he lived in France from 1937 to 1939 and 1954 to 1965. He joined the Communist Party in 1936 and made a brief

sojourn in Spain, but his support for the Party proved ephemeral, though his interest in social and political issues endured. In the late years of World War II, he became an actor. Psychological problems following his war experiences culminated in several nervous breakdowns. In addition to his poems, he published a semi-autobiographical novel and translated the work of several European poets, including Jean Jouve. He was made *Chevalier dans l'Ordre des Arts et Lettres* by the French Ministry of Culture in 1996.

John Gay (1685–1732), *pp. 594–96*

John Gay was born in Barnstaple, Devon, England. Educated at a Devon school, he was apprenticed to a London silk dealer, but was released from service due to poor health and began to haunt London literary society. He soon gained the attention of Alexander Pope, Jonathan Swift, and John Arbuthnot, with whom he founded the "Scriblerus Club." With their help, he obtained posts with influential figures, including the duchess of Monmouth, widow of the duke figured in Dryden's *Absalom and Achitophel*; Lord Clarendon, whom he followed to the court of Hanover; and the duke and duchess of Queensberry, who housed him at their estate and managed his financial affairs. He was eventually awarded a modest sinecure as lottery commissioner. Gay achieved fame with *The Beggar's Opera* (1728), a satire on Italian opera and English politics. This work's evocative lyrics and pleasing tunes established Gay's reputation as the premiere lyricist of his day.

W. S. Gilbert (1836–1911), *pp. 1144–46*

W(illiam) S(chwenck) Gilbert was born in London. Educated at King's College, University of London, he studied law at the Inner Temple, though his career as a barrister was unsatisfying and, therefore, brief. In 1857, he joined the militia, in which he served for twenty years. He began writing comic verse and operatic burlesques during the 1860s, and in 1869 met the eminent composer Arthur Sullivan, with whom he wrote a series of exceptionally popular operettas, including *Trial by Jury*, which satirizes the English legal system; *H.M.S. Pinafore*, which parodies the Royal Navy; *Patience*, a wry satire on aesthetes such as Oscar Wilde, Dante Gabriel Rossetti, and James McNeill Whistler; *The Pirates of Penzance;* and *The Mikado*. Gilbert and Sullivan's collaboration ended in 1896 due to differences in temperament. The public adored Gilbert's poems and libretti, but he referred to himself disparagingly as "a doggerel bard." Satiric verse was his forte. His wit was so biting and incisive that some thought he exhibited bad taste and others that he bordered on the seditious. Queen Victoria, for instance, snubbed Gilbert by leaving his name off the program at a public performance of his work and by

knighting him only in 1907, twenty-five years after Sullivan was knighted.

Allen Ginsberg (1926–1997), *pp. 1708–15*

Allen Ginsberg was born in Newark, New Jersey, and was educated at Columbia University. After spending much time in New York City with William Burroughs, Jack Kerouac, and other Beat writers, he moved to San Francisco, where Lawrence Ferlinghetti's City Lights Press published *Howl and Other Poems* (1956). The title poem—a condemnation of bourgeois culture, a celebration of sexuality, and a manifesto for the Beat movement—has been published in many languages and remains the source of Ginsberg's worldwide reputation. Before dropping out of the workaday world, Ginsberg had held a variety of jobs. He subsequently traveled across England, the Far East, and the United States; was active in radical politics; and taught at a variety of schools. He closely studied Tibetan Buddhism and Western mystics such as William Blake. Long before his death, in New York, his countercultural poetry had been widely embraced by the literary establishment.

Dana Gioia (b. 1950), *pp. 1972–73*

(Michael) Dana Gioia was born in Los Angeles. After receiving a B.A. at Stanford University, he studied at Harvard University and at the Stanford University Business School. From 1977 until 1992, he worked as an executive at General Foods, in New York City. He subsequently left the business world to devote himself to writing, and settled in Santa Rosa, California. Author of controversial essays such as "Notes on the New Formalism" and "Can Poetry Matter?," he is also known as a translator, a librettist, and an anthologist. In 2004, he became chairman of the National Endowment for the Arts.

Louise Glück (b. 1943), *pp. 1931–33*

Louise Glück was born in New York City, raised on Long Island, and educated at Sarah Lawrence College and Columbia University, where she studied with the poet Stanley Kunitz. She lives in Vermont and has taught at Williams College since 1984. Her poems combine autobiography and myth, strong feeling and cool abstraction, in spare language. In addition to poetry, she has written one volume of criticism. She was poet laureate of the United States in 2003–04.

Oliver Goldsmith (ca. 1730–1774), *pp. 686–95*

Oliver Goldsmith was born at Pallas, County Longford, Ireland, the son of an Anglo-Irish clergyman and his wife. He was brought up in rural parishes including Lissoy, which may be one source for his poem "The Deserted Village" (1770). After graduation from Trinity College, Dublin, his worldly career began with a series of misstarts: rejected for the ministry, he considered reading law, decided on medicine, and enrolled at the University of Edinburgh, withdrew to study in Leyden, wandered the Continent, and on his return failed the surgeon's exam. Through a series of essays, poems, plays, histories, and biographies, he attracted the attention of Samuel Johnson and Sir Joshua Reynolds. The former saved him from prosecution for debt by arranging the sale (for £60) of *The Vicar of Wakefield* (1766), the novel for which Goldsmith is chiefly remembered. His great comedy, *She Stoops to Conquer* (1773), was an immediate success.

Jorie Graham (b. 1951), *pp. 1975–79*
Jorie Graham was born in Italy, to religious historian Curtis B. Pepper and sculptor Beverly Pepper, and raised in Italy and France. She attended both the Sorbonne and New York University before earning her M.F.A. at the University of Iowa. She was associated with Iowa and several other universities before being appointed Boylston Professor of Rhetoric and Oratory at Harvard University. Greatly influential on a generation of poets, she writes allusive, far-ranging poems that often explore the nature of consciousness.

Robert Graves (1895–1985), *pp. 1400–1404*
Robert Graves was born in Wimbledon, England. The end of his school days coincided with the start of World War I, and in the summer of 1914 he took a commission with the Royal Welch Fusiliers. Sent to the front in France, where he met the poet Siegfried Sassoon, he was gravely injured at the Battle of the Somme (1916) and sent home. After demobilization in 1919, he attended St. John's College, Oxford, and in 1926 he taught English at the University of Cairo, Egypt. That same year, he began a relationship with the American poet Laura Riding, with whom he founded the Seizin Press (London). From 1929, he lived mainly in Majorca, Spain. He wrote prolifically in a number of genres, including poetry, fiction, biography, autobiography, criticism, and translation, and his career can be divided into several distinct phases. When a young man, he was published in Edward Marsh's anthologies of Georgian poetry. As a result of the pressures of war, however, which shattered his faith in the values with which he had been raised, he began writing bald transcriptions of life on the battlefield, though he later suppressed this work, believing it inferior to the war poetry of Sassoon and Wilfred Owen. His memoir, *Goodbye to All That* (1929), remains Graves's best-known contribution to the literature of World War I. Under Riding's influence, he experimented with modernism. While doing research for a novel, he constructed the mythological system that lay behind his late work, centering around a figure he called the White Goddess. His novels *I, Clau-*

dius and *Claudius the God* (both 1934) were adapted for television in 1976. His reputation as a poet reached its zenith in the 1950s and '60s as he embarked on lecture tours, published his *Collected Poems* (1959), and was accorded honors such as the Queen's Gold Medal for Poetry (1968). He was professor of poetry at Oxford from 1961 to 1966.

Thomas Gray (1716–1771), *pp. 666–73*
Thomas Gray was born in Cornhill, London, the son of a scrivener and his wife, and the only child of twelve to survive infancy. Educated at Eton and Peterhouse College, Cambridge, he divided his time between London and Stoke Poges before settling into a fellowship at Cambridge, where he pursued his studies in Classics, early English poetry, and ancient Welsh and Norse literatures. Other than brief stays in London and tours of the Lake District and Scotland in search of the picturesque, Gray rarely left the university. He embarked on a tour of France and Italy with the writer Horace Walpole in 1739, but after a quarrel returned alone. He began to write English poetry in about 1741. Little of his work was published in his lifetime, but his poems circulated in manuscript among friends. In Gray's "Elegy Written in a Country Churchyard," Samuel Johnson found "sentiments to which every bosom returns an echo" and "images which find a mirror in every mind."

Matthew Green (1696–1737), *pp. 645–48*
Little is known about Matthew Green's life, except that he was born into a Quaker family and employed at the London Customs House. He published nothing during his lifetime, but left his manuscripts to his friend Richard Glover, who brought some of the poems to press after Green's death. Green's reputation rests solely on "The Spleen"; indeed, its author came to be known as "Spleen-Green."

Lavinia Greenlaw (b. 1962), *pp. 2015–16*
Lavinia Greenlaw was born in London and educated at Kingston Polytechnic, the London College of Printing, and the Courtauld Institute. She worked as a book editor and an arts administrator before becoming a freelance writer and broadcaster. *Night Photograph,* her first collection, was published in 1993. A recipient of numerous awards, including the Forward Prize for best poem of the year (1997), she has written dramas and adaptations for BBC radio, and her first novel, *Mary George of Allnorthover,* was published in 2001. She reviews regularly for both U.K. and U.S. journals and teaches in the Creative Writing M.A. Programme at Goldsmith's College, University of London.

Fulke Greville, Lord Brooke (1554–1628), *pp. 206–07*
Fulke Greville was born into a family of Warwickshire, England, landowners and was sent to Shrewsbury School in the same year as Sir

Philip Sidney, who became his close friend. After attending Jesus College, Cambridge, Greville went to court, where he was introduced to the "Areopagus" club, an association of courtiers and poets named after the meeting place of the Athenian aristocratic council. Knighted in 1597, he served as treasurer to the navy from 1589 to 1604. Although he fell from favor in the early years of James I's reign, he served as chancellor of the exchequer from 1614 to 1622 and was made first baron Brooke in 1621. Warwick Castle, granted to him on his elevation to the peerage, was the scene of his murder by a servant, who stabbed first Greville and then himself. Greville is perhaps best known for *The Life of the Renowned Sir Philip Sidney* (1652), which expresses Greville's political disillusionment after Queen Elizabeth's death, and which helped to establish Sidney's reputation as the greatest of the Renaissance chivalric courtier-poets. Greville also wrote *Caelica,* a sequence of songs and sonnets; the neo-Stoic *Letter to an Honorable Lady;* a verse *Treatise of Monarchy;* and two tragedies, *Alaham* and *Mustapha,* which deal with political and religious themes.

Barbara Guest (b. 1920), *pp. 1616–17*
Barbara Guest was born in Wilmington, North Carolina, and raised in California and Florida. She was educated at the University of North Carolina, the University of California at Los Angeles, and the University of California at Berkeley. From 1951 to 1954, Guest served as an associate editor at *ARTnews.* In addition to poetry, she has written plays, fiction, and a biography of H. D. Often associated with the poets of the so-called New York school and the L=A=N=G=U=A=G=E poets who descended from them, Guest has identified her concerns as "what happens every day, . . . memory, . . . conscience, . . . the brevity of ideas, . . . time, disorder, flux, etc."

Thom Gunn (1929–2004), *pp. 1768–74*
Thom Gunn was born in Gravesend, Kent, England, but moved frequently as a child in the wake of his father, a journalist. After school, Gunn served in the army for two years, then went to Paris, where he worked on the Métro by day and attempted to write a novel by night, and to Rome. He then went up to Trinity College, Cambridge, where he attended lectures by the critic F. R. Leavis and published his first collection of poems, *Fighting Terms* (1954). He did graduate work at Stanford University under the poet Yvor Winters. Except for a year in San Antonio, Texas, Gunn lived in San Francisco for the rest of his life. He taught at the University of California at Berkeley from 1958 until 1966, but gave up full-time teaching to devote himself to writing. His collection *The Man with Night Sweats* won the 1992 Forward Prize, and his *Collected Poems* was published in 1993. In addition to writing poetry and essays, he edited collections of verse by Ben Jonson and Fulke Greville.

Ivor Gurney (1890–1937), *pp. 1371–73*
Ivor Gurney was born in Gloucester, England. He attended the Royal College of Music, London, until 1915, when he enlisted in the army. (He was initially rejected in 1914 because of poor eyesight.) Sent to the front in France, he was gassed at Ypres in 1917 and sent home; he suffered a breakdown the following year. He returned briefly to his studies at the Royal College, where the composer Ralph Vaughan Williams became his tutor. From 1919 to 1922, he lived restlessly, continuing to compose music and to write but also working at a number of odd jobs, ranging from organist to cinema pianist to tax clerk. In 1922, suffering from schizophrenia, he was committed to the City of London Mental Hospital, where he died fifteen years later. Two volumes of poems appeared in his lifetime, *Severn and Somme* (1917) and *War's Embers* (1919), and his songs were regularly published during the 1920s. Critical appreciation of Gurney's artistry continued after his death with editions of his songs, letters, and poetry.

Daniel Hall (b. 1952), *pp. 1990–92*
Daniel Hall was born in Pittsfield, Massachusetts. He has traveled extensively throughout the British Isles and Asia. His first book, *Hermit with Landscape* (1990), was selected for the Yale Series of Younger Poets by James Merrill. He is writer-in-residence and director of the Creative Writing Center at Amherst College.

Donald Hall (b. 1928), *pp. 1753–57*
Donald Hall was born in New Haven, Connecticut. Educated at Harvard and Oxford Universities, he has served as poetry editor at *The Paris Review,* as a member of the editorial board for poetry at Wesleyan University Press, and as a poetry consultant for Harper & Row. After teaching at Stanford University, Harvard, and the University of Michigan, he retired in 1975 and moved back to his family home in Danbury, New Hampshire, to work full-time as a writer. In addition to poetry, Hall has published literary criticism, personal reminiscences, and children's books, and has edited a number of widely used anthologies and textbooks. Among his most praised works are his poems addressing the final illness and death of his wife, the poet Jane Kenyon (1947–1995).

Thomas Hardy (1840–1928), *pp. 1152–62*
Thomas Hardy was born in Dorset, England, the area he made famous as "Wessex" in his novels. He left school at age sixteen to work as an apprentice to an architect in Dorchester who specialized in church restoration. He went to London in 1861 to continue work as an archi-

tect, but after several years returned to Dorset, where he lived for the rest of his life. Though he seriously considered taking holy orders, he lost his faith, in part because of the writings of prominent agnostics of the day, such as Charles Darwin. He published his first novel, *Desperate Remedies*, in 1871, but made his reputation as a novelist with *Far from the Madding Crowd*, in 1874. He published no poetry until 1897, after the publication of his final novel, *The Well-Beloved*, but then dedicated the last thirty years of his life to poetry, which he claimed to love more than prose. Hardy was a versatile poet, writing lyrics, ballads, sonnets, dramatic monologues, and a series of moving love poems composed upon the death of his wife, Emma. *Wessex Poems* (1898) brought together his poetry from over thirty years. It was followed in 1901 by *Poems of the Past and Present*, and in 1909 by *Time's Laughingstocks*. His verse epic about the Napoleonic Wars, *The Dynasts*, was published in three parts between 1904 and 1908, and his *Satires of Circumstance* in 1914. His reputation as a poet has grown steadily ever since Philip Larkin included more of Hardy's poems than those of Yeats and Eliot in his 1973 *Oxford Book of Twentieth-Century English Verse*.

Tony Harrison (b. 1937), *pp. 1872–79*
Tony Harrison was born in Leeds, England, and was educated at Leeds University, where he read Classics and linguistics and published his first poems. He lectured in Nigeria from 1962 until 1966, and in Prague from 1966 until 1967. Upon his return to England, he became the first Northern Arts Fellow at the Universities of Newcastle-upon-Tyne and Durham. In addition to a number of original verse plays, many of which he also directed, he has written films and adaptations of works by Molière, Racine, and others, including acclaimed versions of the *Oresteia* and the medieval Mystery plays. His volume *The Gaze of the Gorgon* won the 1992 Whitbread Prize for Poetry, and in 1995 he was commissioned by *The Guardian* newspaper to write poems on the war in Bosnia.

Robert Hass (b. 1941), *pp. 1919–20*
Robert Hass was born in San Francisco, California. He was educated at St. Mary's College and at Stanford University, where he studied under the poet Yvor Winters. He has taught at the State University of New York at Buffalo, St. Mary's College, and the University of California at Berkeley. In addition to poetry, he has written essays and criticism and translated much European poetry, most notably that of Czeslaw Milosz. He was poet laureate of the United States in 1995–96.

Robert Hayden (1913–1980), *pp. 1533–37*
Robert Hayden was born Asa Bundy Sheffey in a poor neighborhood of Detroit, Michigan, and raised by foster parents. He was educated at Detroit City College (now Wayne State University) and the University of Michigan at Ann Arbor, where he studied with W. H. Auden. In 1936, Hayden joined the Writers' Project of the Works Progress Administration, and the research he did on local folklore and the history of Michigan's Underground Railroad later made its way into many of his poems. Hayden taught at Fisk University, in Nashville, Tennessee, from 1946 until 1969, and at the University of Michigan from then until his death. He professed the Baha'i faith and, beginning in 1967, served a long tenure as editor of its *World Order* journal. In addition, he wrote a play on Malcolm X, published a collection of prose, and edited several anthologies.

Seamus Heaney (b. 1939), *pp. 1899–1910*
Seamus Heaney was born in Mossbawn, County Derry, Northern Ireland, to a Catholic farmer and his wife. He was educated at Queen's University, Belfast, where he later lectured in English. His first volume of poetry, *Digging*, established his reputation as the most gifted poet of his generation, a reputation confirmed by the ten major collections that have followed. Robert Lowell dubbed him "the best Irish poet since W. B. Yeats." Not wanting to be constrained as a "political poet" in the north of Ireland, Heaney moved to the Irish Republic. He now lives in Dublin, having taught at the University of California at Berkeley, Harvard University, and, from 1989 to 1994, as professor of poetry at Oxford University. A distinguished critic and accomplished translator, he won the Whitbread Book of the Year Award for his version of *Beowulf*. In 1995, he was awarded the Nobel Prize for Literature. "Crediting Poetry," his acceptance speech, was published in *Open Ground*, which collected thirty years of his poems.

Anthony Hecht (1923–2004), *pp. 1667–74*
Anthony Hecht was born in New York City. After graduation from Bard College, he joined the army and was stationed in Europe and Japan. He later taught at Kenyon College, where he studied informally with fellow faculty member John Crowe Ransom, then returned to New York and did graduate work at Columbia University. In the years following, he taught at, among other schools, Smith College, the University of Rochester, and Georgetown University. He published books of criticism—including a study of W. H. Auden (a key influence)—and undertook translation, most notably of Aeschylus and Joseph Brodsky. He also collaborated with artist Leonard Baskin on several sequences of poems. A gifted writer of light verse, he co-invented (with John Hollander) the comic "double dactyl," and even his graver poems often register a dark humor. He lived in Washington,

D.C., where in 1982–84 he served as consultant in poetry to the Library of Congress.

Felicia Dorothea Hemans (1793–1835), pp. 897–901

Felicia Dorothea Hemans was born in Liverpool, England, and raised in Wales. She was educated at home by her mother, who recognized her writing talent. Hemans was exceptionally prolific, publishing her first two volumes of poetry at age fifteen, and publishing a volume almost every year during the last two decades of her life. She was immensely popular in her day and is thought to be England's first professional female poet. In 1812, she married Captain Alfred Hemans; the couple produced five sons, but separated in 1818. From 1827 until 1831, she lived in the Liverpool suburb of Wavertree, where she had gone to secure an education for her boys, and from 1831 until her death she lived in Dublin. She carried on an active correspondence with many eminent writers of her day, and published poems and articles in periodicals such as the *Edinburgh Annual Register, Blackwood's Edinburgh Magazine,* and the *New Monthly Magazine.* Her most successful book was *Records of Woman: With Other Poems* (1828). She was included in Oxford University Press's Standard Authors series until 1914 but neglected in the wake of modernism. The upsurge of Women's Studies in the 1980s rekindled an appreciation of her writing.

Edward Herbert (1582–1648), p. 346

Edward Herbert was born at Eyton, in Shropshire, England. He was the eldest son of Richard Herbert and the elder brother of the poet George Herbert. Educated at University College, Oxford, he lived in Oxford until moving to London with his wife in 1600. He was knighted soon after the accession of King James I. From 1608 to 1618, he traveled widely on the Continent as a soldier of fortune; in 1619, he became ambassador to France. After his recall in 1624, James awarded him an Irish peerage and made him Lord Herbert of Cherbury. In that same year, he published his most important work, *De Veritate,* a Latin philosophical treatise on knowledge, psychology, truth, and religion. His poems and his autobiography were published posthumously.

George Herbert (1593–1633), pp. 367–85

George Herbert was the fifth son of Richard Herbert, who died when the poet was three, and the younger brother of Edward, Lord Herbert of Cherbury, also a writer. He was educated at Westminster School and King's Scholar of Trinity College, Cambridge. At age sixteen, he sent his mother, Magdalen, two accomplished and devout sonnets with a letter announcing his dedication of his poetic powers to God, though this did not preclude his harboring worldly ambition. His fellowship at Trinity required him to join the clergy within seven years, but after being elected public orator (a springboard into higher positions at court), he left his university duties to proxies while he pursued a secular career. Two terms as a member of Parliament evidently disillusioned him. He was ordained deacon, installed as canon of Lincoln Cathedral, and, in 1630, having been ordained priest, received a living as rector of Bemerton, near Salisbury. In 1629, he married his stepfather's cousin, Jane Danvers, and they adopted his two orphaned nieces. In addition to a prose treatise, *A Priest to the Temple: Or the Country Parson, his Character and Rule of Life* (1652), he wrote many poems in both English and Latin. Shortly before his death, he sent his English poems to his friend the Anglican clergyman Nicholas Ferrar, asking him to publish them if he believed that they could "turn to the advantage of any dejected soul"; otherwise, Ferrar was to burn them. The poems collected in *The Temple* (1633) represented, Herbert wrote, "a picture of the many spiritual conflicts that have passed betwixt God and my soul, before I could subject mine to the will of Jesus my master."

Robert Herrick (1591–1674), pp. 354–63

Robert Herrick was born into a family of wealthy London goldsmiths. Apprenticed to his uncle at age sixteen, he did not go up to Cambridge until 1613. After taking his M.A. in 1620, Herrick returned to London, where he became an admirer and friend of Ben Jonson. He joined the clergy in 1623, acted as a chaplain on the duke of Buckingham's disastrous expedition to the Isle of Rhé, and as a reward was given the living of dean priory, in Devon, a position he took up in 1630. The rural tranquility of the parish, though at first alien to the urbane and social Herrick, made possible his prolific writing career; he produced over twenty-five hundred compositions, many written to imaginary mistresses, others about his maid, his dog, his cat, and rural customs and pleasures. He also wrote on religious themes. Dispossessed of his living by the Puritans, he returned to London and published in 1648 a volume containing his secular poems, the *Hesperides,* and his religious poems, the *Noble Numbers.* Among the former were his imitations of the classical poets Catullus and Horace. After the restoration of the monarchy in 1660, Herrick returned to Devon and spent his last years quietly, apparently without composing further poems.

Geoffrey Hill (b. 1932), pp. 1831–36

Geoffrey Hill was born in Bromsgrove, Worcestershire, England. He was educated at Keble College, Oxford, and has since taught at the University of Leeds; Emmanuel and Trinity Colleges, Cambridge; and, since 1988, Boston University; as well as being a visiting lecturer at several institutions in England, Nigeria, and the United States. His first collection of poems, *For the Unfallen,* appeared in 1959. Distinctively resonant as is the voice of those early poems, they remain consistently impersonal. Even when the poet's boyhood self is conflated with that of Offa in *Mercian Hymns* (1971), subjectivity dissolves in the objective projection of a historical imagination of great range and power. Where that book had been concerned on one level with "the matter of Britain," a later collection, *Canaan* (1996), attempts to diagnose the matter with Britain (identifying the U.K. with "Canaan, the land of the Philistines," excoriated in the Bible). That and his more recent books, *The Triumph of Love* (1998) and *Speech! Speech!* (2001), examine more searchingly and more savagely the themes that have long preoccupied him, but these works have a new and powerful personal dimension. Hill's critical writings include *The Lords of Limit: Essays on Literature and Ideas* and *The Enemy's Country: Words, Conjecture and Other Circumstances of Language.* He has also produced a verse translation of Ibsen's *Brand* for the London stage. A winner of the Whitbread and Hawthornden Prizes, he is a fellow of the American Academy of the Arts and Sciences.

Daryl Hine (b. 1936), *pp. 1868–69*
Daryl Hine was born in Vancouver, British Columbia, and was educated at McGill University and the University of Chicago. He taught at Chicago until 1968, when he became editor of *Poetry* magazine. After serving in this post for a decade, he returned to teaching, mostly in the Chicago area. In addition to poetry, he has published a novel, a travel book, and several plays. He also has coedited an anthology of verse and has translated Homer and Theocritus.

John Hollander (b. 1929), *pp. 1775–77*
John Hollander was born in New York City. He was educated at Columbia University and Indiana University at Bloomington, from which he received a Ph.D. Upon graduation, he embarked on an academic career, during which he has taught at Harvard University, Connecticut College, Hunter College, and Yale University. In addition to poetry, Hollander has written plays, children's verse, and several works on prosody. Respected as much for his scholarship as for his poetry, he has edited numerous anthologies of essays and poems, including a comprehensive edition of nineteenth-century American verse. He is also coinventor (with Anthony Hecht) of the "double dactyl" verse form.

Oliver Wendell Holmes (1809–1894), *p. 974*
Oliver Wendell Holmes was born in Cambridge, Massachusetts. He studied law at Harvard Uni-

versity, underwent two years of medical training in Europe, and returned to Harvard to complete his M.D. A dedicated Unitarian, he served as professor of anatomy at Dartmouth College and at Harvard, and later as dean of Harvard Medical School. He established his reputation in medicine by discovering that puerperal fever, commonly associated with childbirth and often fatal, was contagious; his work helped to stem its spread. He began writing in earnest shortly after earning his medical degree, and he was a popular lecturer on the New England lyceum circuit. *The Autocrat of the Breakfast-Table* (1858), a series of witty essays first published in *The Atlantic Monthly,* is generally considered his best work. Although his best-known poem is perhaps "Old Ironsides" (a stirring *vers d'occasion* that rescued the U.S.S. Constitution from the salvage yard), "The Chambered Nautilus" was his favorite.

A. D. Hope (1907–2000), *pp. 1481–85*
A(lec) D(erwent) Hope was born in Cooma, New South Wales, Australia. He was educated at Sydney University and University College, Oxford. Upon graduation, he taught English in the New South Wales school system, and in 1937 became a lecturer in education at Sydney Teachers' College. He taught English at the University of Melbourne from 1945 to 1965 and at Canberra University College from 1965 to 1968, when he retired to devote himself to writing. Although his work is rich in literary, biblical, and mythological allusions, he recrafted traditional myths to fit the times in which he lived. Locating himself in the tradition of poets from Chaucer to Browning—earlier masters of narrative, argument, and exposition—he valued general statement over local or particular detail and individual expression. In a voice ferociously witty and authoritative, often sardonic and satiric, he typically approached modern life with disdain, although he softened this stance in his later work.

Gerard Manley Hopkins (1844–1889), *pp. 1166–72*
Gerard Manley Hopkins was born in Stratford, Essex, England, and was educated at Balliol College, Oxford. Under the influence of Cardinal John Henry Newman, he converted to Catholicism in 1866, became a novitiate of the Society of Jesuits two years later, and was ordained in 1877. Hopkins served as a parish priest and teacher of Classics, his lengthiest appointment being with University College, Dublin. He stopped writing poetry in 1868, believing it interfered with his priestly vocation. Encouraged by Church authorities, he resumed writing in 1875, with "The Wreck of the Deutschland," a poem commemorating the death of several Franciscan nuns, exiled from Germany by the Falck Laws, in a shipwreck at the mouth of the

river Thames. In his subsequent poems, Hopkins explored his relationship to God. Central to his complex theories on prosody are the terms *inscape, instress,* and, most important to future poets, *sprung rhythm.* Little of his poetry was published during his lifetime, but the poet Robert Bridges, Hopkins's friend since Oxford, brought out an edition in 1918.

A. E. Housman (1859–1936), *pp. 1173–80*

A. E. Housman was born in Fockbury, Worcestershire, England, and was educated at St. John's College, Oxford. For a decade, he worked for the Patent Office in London, while continuing his studies and publishing scholarly essays in literary journals. He held appointments at University College, London, and Trinity College, Cambridge. While he published extensively on the classics (in particular Propertius, Juvenal, Lucan, and Manilius), he came to poetry relatively late and had to publish his first collection, *A Shropshire Lad* (1896), at his own expense. It gradually gained wide public recognition and made Housman famous. His Shropshire is less a geographic locale than an emotional one and depicts an English pastoral world that was rapidly disappearing. He eventually responded to demands for a sequel by publishing *Last Poems* in 1922, but resolutely declined honorary degrees and an Order of Merit. In 1996, a plaque was dedicated to him in Westminster Abbey's Poets' Corner.

Henry Howard, Earl of Surrey (ca. 1517–1547), *pp. 137–40*

Henry Howard, also known as "Surrey," was the eldest son of an old aristocratic family. His father, who became third duke of Norfolk, had royal ancestors, as did his mother. Two of his nieces, Anne Boleyn and Catherine Howard, were wives of Henry VIII, and the king's illegitimate son, Henry Fitzroy, was a childhood friend. Surrey fought ably in campaigns against the French and was imprisoned in 1537 on suspicion of sympathizing with the "Pilgrimage of Grace" rebellion against the dissolution of the monasteries. During his brief life (he was executed on a frivolous charge of treason), Surrey wrote courtly poems and circulated them in manuscript. He followed Wyatt in translating sonnets from Petrarch's Italian and wrote his first English poem in blank verse, a translation of books 2 and 4 of Virgil's *Aeneid*. His work in this "strange meter," as the publisher called it, appeared in print in 1554 (book 4) and 1557 (book 2). Many of his lyrics were included, along with Wyatt's, in Tottel's *Songs and Sonnets* (1557). His (probably fictional) love for "Geraldine" is dramatized in Thomas Nashe's *The Unfortunate Traveller,* where Surrey appears as the traveler's "master."

Richard Howard (b. 1929), *pp. 1778–83*

Richard Howard was born in Cleveland, Ohio, and educated at Columbia University and the Sorbonne. In Cleveland and New York City, he worked as a lexicographer for the World Publishing Company, then turned to translation and has since brought into English more than 150 French texts, including works by Daudelaire, Barthes, de Beauvoir, Breton, Camus, and Gide. In addition, he has worked as a poetry editor for journals such as *The New Republic, The Paris Review,* and *Shenandoah,* and has taught at, among other schools, Columbia University, Johns Hopkins University, and the universities of Houston and Cincinnati. He lives in New York City. A prolific writer in several modes, he is known especially for his mastery of the dramatic monologue.

Julia Ward Howe (1819–1910), *p. 1054*

Julia Ward was born in New York City, to a prominent family, and was educated at home. In 1843, she married Samuel Gridley Howe, the social activist and reformer who founded the Perkins Institute for the Blind. The couple settled in Boston, where the poet gave birth to six children. She devoted herself not only to motherhood and writing but also to the abolition and women's suffrage movements. In addition to poetry, Howe published two plays and much prose, including a well-received biography of Margaret Fuller. She is best remembered for the apocalyptic "Battle-Hymn of the Republic" (1862).

Langston Hughes (1902–1967), *pp. 1429–35*

Langston Hughes was born in Joplin, Missouri, and raised in Missouri, Kansas, Illinois, and Ohio. He attended Columbia University from 1921 until 1922, then traveled extensively in South America and Europe before moving to Washington, D.C., in 1925. The next year, Hughes published his first collection of poems, *The Weary Blues,* to great acclaim. In 1929, he received a B.A. from Lincoln University, in Pennsylvania, but from 1928 until 1930 he lived in New York City and was an important figure in the Harlem Renaissance. In addition to poetry, he wrote fiction, drama, screenplays, essays, and autobiography. Because of his journalistic work in support of the Republican side during the Spanish Civil War and his sympathies for the American Communists, in 1953 he was called to testify before Senator Joseph McCarthy's committee on subversive activities, and for many years following he worked to restore his reputation. Always concerned "largely . . . with the depicting of Negro life in America," Hughes documented it in poems that drew meters and moods from street language, jazz, and the blues.

Ted Hughes (1930–1998), pp. 1810–16
Ted Hughes was born in Mytholmroyd, South Yorkshire, England, and was raised in Mexborough, a coal-mining town in South Yorkshire. He won a scholarship to Pembroke College, Cambridge, but served two years in the Royal Air Force before matriculating. He studied English, archaeology, and anthropology, specializing in mythological systems (an interest that informed much of his poetry). He later worked as a gardener, night watchman, zookeeper, scriptwriter, and teacher. In 1956, he married the American poet Sylvia Plath, and the couple spent a year in the United States before moving to England in 1959. Plath committed suicide in 1963. In 1970, Hughes settled on a farm in Devon. In addition to poetry, he wrote plays, short stories, and books for children. He also edited numerous collections of verse and prose, and was a founding editor of *Modern Poetry in Translation* magazine. He was poet laureate of England from 1984 until his death. His poems vividly describe the beauty of the natural world, but celebrate its raw, elemental energies. He often embodies the primal forces of nature as mythic animals such as the pike, the hawk, and "Crow," a central character in a long cycle of poems. His translation and recasting of *Tales from Ovid* was published to critical acclaim in 1997, and less than a year later he broke his silence on his relationship with Plath with the publication of *Birthday Letters*. He received the Order of Merit from Queen Elizabeth II only twelve days before his death, from cancer.

Richard Hugo (1923–1982), pp. 1674–76
Richard Hugo was born in Seattle and educated at the University of Washington, where he studied with the poet Theodore Roethke. A bombardier in the United States Army Air Corps during World War II, he subsequently worked for the Boeing Corporation, then began an academic career, during which he taught at the University of Washington, the University of Iowa Writers' Workshop, and (from 1964 until 1982) the University of Montana at Missoula. From 1977 until 1982, he served as editor of the Yale Series of Younger Poets, and he helped to launch the careers of many poets. His poems typically are set in desolate landscapes of the American West.

Laura (Riding) Jackson (1901–1991), pp. 1425–26
Laura Riding was born in New York City and attended Cornell University. For a short time, she was affiliated with the Fugitives, a prominent group of southern writers. In the 1930s, Riding was associated with the poet and critic Robert Graves, with whom she wrote *A Survey of Modernist Poetry* (1927), an influential study that advocated close textual reading. Riding and Graves also founded the Seizin Press, in Lon-don. In 1939, she stopped writing verse, returned to the United States, and with Schuyler Jackson, her second husband, embarked on a series of lexicographic and linguistic studies. In conformity with the late author's wish, her Board of Literary Management asks us to record that, in 1940, Laura (Riding) Jackson renounced, on grounds of linguistic principle, the writing of poetry: she had come to hold that "poetry obstructs general attainment of something better in our linguistic way-of-life than we have."

Josephine Jacobsen (1908–2003), pp. 1491–93
Josephine Jacobsen was born in Cobourg, Ontario, to American parents. She was educated by private tutors at Roland Park Country School, in Baltimore, where she resided for much of her life, although she was an extensive traveler. Active in the public service of poetry, and the author of numerous collections, she served as poetry consultant to the Library of Congress and in other capacities for the Poetry Society of America, the Folger Library, and the National Endowment for the Arts. She published her first poem at age eleven and began writing short stories at age sixty. She also published literary and dramatic criticism.

Randall Jarrell (1914–1965), pp. 1552–58
Randall Jarrell was born in Nashville, Tennessee, but spent some of his early years in California. He was educated at Vanderbilt University, where he studied psychology and English (with the poet John Crowe Ransom) and wrote his M.A. thesis on A. E. Housman. He taught at several schools, including Kenyon College, where he roomed with the novelist Peter Taylor and the poet Robert Lowell; the University of Texas at Austin; and Women's College, University of North Carolina at Greensboro. In World War II, he was stationed stateside, working with B-29 crews, and, based partly on their reports, wrote some of the most prized poems to come out of the war. He also earned a reputation as an astute, acerbic, and influential critic of poetry. Williams, Frost, Bishop, and Lowell were among those he favored. In addition to poetry, he wrote a novel and children's stories, as well as translations of Goethe, Chekhov, and several of Grimm's fairy tales. After being hospitalized for depression early in 1965, he died some months later when struck by a car.

Robinson Jeffers (1887–1962), pp. 1320–24
(John) Robinson Jeffers was born in Pittsburgh, Pennsylvania, to a Classics professor in a theological seminary and his wife. He was educated at Occidental College. Before turning to writing, he studied medicine and forestry at the graduate level. In 1914, he moved to Carmel, California,

where he lived in relative isolation—in a home overlooking the dramatic Pacific coastline that figures prominently in his work. He also built with his own hands a structure he called Hawk Tower. Jeffers dubbed his philosophical stance "inhumanism" and defined it as "a shifting emphasis and significance from man to not-man." He challenged humanity's overreliance on the flawed social structures of its own making and urged its return to a more primal relation with the natural world. He achieved his greatest fame with his 1946 translation of Euripides' *Medea*, which was performed on Broadway.

Elizabeth Jennings (1926–2001), pp. 1735–36
Elizabeth Jennings was born in Boston, Lincolnshire, England, and educated at St. Anne's College, Oxford. Her poems were first published in the 1948 edition of *Oxford Poetry,* edited by Kingsley Amis and James Michie. She worked at various professions—including advertising, librarianship, and publishing—before devoting herself exclusively to writing. In the 1960s, she suffered recurrent mental breakdowns, which resulted in hospitalization. Her later work documents her illness and subsequent recovery. She also published critical essays, children's verse, and a translation of Michelangelo's sonnets. Her last volume of poems, *Timely Issues,* appeared shortly before her death.

Samuel Johnson (1709–1784), pp. 655–65
Samuel Johnson was born in Lichfield, England, to a bookseller and his wife. As a child, he contracted scrofula (tuberculosis of the lymphatic system) and smallpox, a combination that left him badly scarred, with impaired sight and hearing, and prone to involuntary gesticulation. He went to Pembroke College, Oxford, but financial difficulties forced him to leave after fourteen months. After a period spent teaching in Birmingham, in 1737 he settled in London, where he worked on *The Gentleman's Magazine,* and the next year published "London," an imitation of Juvenal's satires that was an immediate success, as was his second satire, "The Vanity of Human Wishes" (1749). Johnson's contribution to literary scholarship, criticism, and lexicography is incalculable. In addition to his many reviews and essays, he published the ambitious *Lives of the Poets* (1779–81), founded and edited *The Rambler* magazine, collected the works of Shakespeare, and produced his monumental, if idiosyncratic, *A Dictionary of the English Language* (1755).

Ben Jonson (1572–1637), pp. 323–45
Ben(jamin) Jonson was born in London after the death of his father, a clergyman. Educated at Westminster School, he was working for his stepfather as a bricklayer by the early 1590s. He volunteered for military service in the Low Countries and after returning to England began a career in the theater, first as an actor, then as a playwright. In 1598, he killed a fellow actor in a duel but escaped hanging by claiming "benefit of clergy," that is, by demonstrating his ability to read a verse from the Bible. His conversion to Catholicism in that same year no doubt contributed to the charges of "popery" and treason leveled against him after he published his neoclassical tragedy *Sejanus* (1606), which dramatized conspiracy and assassination. Jonson had also incurred the wrath of authorities by coauthoring *The Isle of Dogs* (1597) and *Eastward Ho* (1605); the former, considered a "lewd play, containing very seditious and slanderous matter," caused its authors to be briefly imprisoned and was so effectively censored that no copies now exist; the latter, which also led to Jonson's imprisonment, contained a passage about the Scots that offended the court and the Scottish king, James I. Jonson soon gained the king's favor, however, with the series of court masques he began to create—with the designer Inigo Jones—in 1605; in 1616, after he had published his *Works* and had returned (in 1610) to the Church of England, he received a substantial pension from the king and effectively occupied the position of poet laureate. Learned in the classics and skilled in a variety of poetic and dramatic forms, Jonson first acquired fame as the author of "comedies of humors" satirizing the eccentricities and "ruling passions" of his characters. In addition to his many successful plays—*Volpone* (1605), *The Alchemist* (1610), and *Bartholomew Fair* (1614), for instance—Jonson wrote poetry in a variety of forms, including witty epigrams, epitaphs, songs (both freestanding and designed for plays and masques), and "occasional" poems celebrating events and people. In contrast to his contemporary Shakespeare, whose plays were collected only posthumously, Jonson was concerned with constructing an imposing authorial persona. Modeling himself in part on classical writers such as Martial and Horace, he was the first English poet to inspire a "school": the Sons, or Tribes, of Ben, which included poets such as Robert Herrick and Thomas Carew.

Donald Justice (1925–2004), pp. 1684–87
Donald Justice was born and raised in Miami, Florida. He earned a B.A. from the University of Miami, an M.A. from the University of North Carolina at Chapel Hill, and a Ph.D. from the University of Iowa, where his teachers included the poets John Berryman, Robert Lowell, and Karl Shapiro. He also studied with the poet Yvor Winters at Stanford University. He taught at, among other schools, the University of Iowa Writers' Workshop and the University of Florida at Gainesville and counted among his students Mark Strand, Charles Wright, and Jorie Graham. An accomplished painter as well, he

became known for understated, sometimes darkly humorous poems.

Patrick Kavanagh (1904–1967), *pp. 1450–54*
Patrick Kavanagh was born in Inniskeen, County Monaghan, Ireland. He left school at age thirteen to go to work. During the 1930s, he became active on the Dublin literary scene, writing reviews for local publications while supporting himself by farming. His first collection, *"Ploughman" and Other Poems,* was published in 1936. In 1949, he sold his land and devoted himself entirely to literature. He made a precarious living over the next two decades; despite the critical success of *The Great Hunger* (1942), sales were sluggish and he had difficulty finding a publisher for subsequent work. His difficulties brought him close to despair, but his autobiographical novel, *Tarry Flynn,* was issued in 1948, and in 1955 he experienced a powerful spiritual rebirth and his work enjoyed a brief revival. Kavanagh has been credited with maintaining public interest in Irish peasant culture in the period following the Celtic Twilight.

John Keats (1795–1821), *pp. 905–41*
John Keats was born in London, the son of a livery stableman and his wife. At age fifteen, he was apprenticed to an apothecary-surgeon, and on completion of his apprenticeship did further training at Guy's Hospital, London. Having qualified, Keats abandoned medicine for poetry. In 1818, he fell in love with Fanny Brawne, but was prevented from marrying her by financial difficulties. In 1819, his annus mirabilis, he produced all of his great odes, a number of fine sonnets, and several other masterpieces. The following year, he developed tuberculosis, the disease that had killed his mother and younger brother, Tom. Hoping to prolong his life, he traveled to Italy, but died in Rome—in lodgings in the Piazza di Spagna (now a museum)—the following spring. At the time of his death, he had published only fifty-four poems, and it was not until the publication of Richard Monkton Milne's *Life, Letters and Literary Remains of John Keats* in 1848 that his reputation as a great poet was established. In his poetry, he struggled to make sense of a world riddled with "misery, heartache and pain, sickness and oppression." Rather than take solace in religious or philosophical creeds, as did Wordsworth and Coleridge, he looked to sensation, passion, and imagination to guide him. "I am certain of nothing," he wrote to a friend, "but of the holiness of the Heart's affections and the truth of Imagination—What the imagination seizes as Beauty must be truth."

Weldon Kees (1914–1955), *pp. 1559–60*
Weldon Kees was born in Beatrice, Nebraska, and educated at Doane College and the University of Missouri before graduating from the University of Nebraska. Initially a fiction writer, Kees moved to New York City, where he painted, wrote art criticism, and published his first book of poems, *The Last Man* (1943). In 1950, he moved to the West Coast and worked as a photographer, film producer, radio broadcaster, and jazz pianist. When his car was found parked near the Golden Gate Bridge in July 1955, he was presumed a suicide. His best-known work is a series of wistful, ironic poems about an urban everyman he called Robinson.

Richard Kenney (b. 1948), *pp. 1954–56*
Richard Kenney was born in Glens Falls, New York. He attended Dartmouth College and studied Celtic lore in Ireland and Scotland. He teaches English at the University of Washington in Seattle and for some years has led its summer seminars in creative writing, in Rome. The first of his three volumes of poetry, *The Evolution of the Flightless Bird* (1984), was selected by James Merrill for the Yale Series of Younger Poets. He lives in Port Townsend, Washington.

Sidney Keyes (1922–1943), *pp. 1644–47*
Sidney Keyes was born in Dartford, England. He was educated at Tonbridge School, where he began to write poetry, and at The Queen's College, Oxford, where he became friends with John Heath-Stubbs and Michael Meyer, coeditors of *Eight Oxford Poets,* which includes some of Keyes's work. His first collection, *The Iron Laurel,* appeared in 1942, shortly before he was commissioned into his father's regiment, the Queen's Own Royal West Kent. After only two weeks of active service in Tunisia, he was killed near Sidi Abdullah. A second volume of poems, *The Cruel Solstice,* was posthumously published in 1943, and a collected poems appeared in 1945. In his war poems, he portrays death as a real presence to which the good soldier must submit courageously and with a measure of detachment. Confronted with the reality of death, he changed his stance, advocating active resistance against the forces of extinction.

Anne Killigrew (1660–1685), *pp. 554–56*
Anne Killigrew was born in London; she died of smallpox. Her father, an amateur dramatist and chaplain to the duke of York, encouraged Anne's literary talents and oversaw the posthumous publication (in 1685–86) of her poems. In an ode composed for this memorial volume, John Dryden praises her accomplishments in the "sister arts" of poetry and painting (two of her poems describe her own paintings), but also presents her as an entirely "artless" poet whose gifts were from "nature." Killigrew worked at her craft, however, by writing in a variety of poetic genres—among her poems is a heroic tribute to Alexander the Great. Recognizing that a female writer's desire to create "deathless numbers"

might be viewed as overly ambitious by some readers, Killigrew drew inspiration from her near-contemporary Katherine Philips: "Nor did sex at all obstruct her fame," Killigrew wrote about Philips, in a poem addressed to those who impugned Killigrew's status as an author by saying that her verses "Were Made by Another."

Henry King (1592–1669), *pp. 363–66*
Henry King was the son of a bishop of London and his wife. Educated at Westminster and Christ Church, Oxford, he entered the Church of England and rose steadily through its ranks, becoming the bishop of Chichester in 1642. A staunch opponent of Puritanism, he was ejected from his position by Parliamentarians in 1643. After seventeen years in retirement with friends, he was reinstated as bishop in 1660, following the return of the monarchy. He published a verse translation of the Psalms in 1651 and composed both sacred and secular poems— including elegies on his friend John Donne, Ben Jonson, and Sir Walter Ralegh—that were published anonymously in an unauthorized edition called *Poems, Elegies, Paradoxes and Sonnets* (1657). He was known as an impressive preacher, and a number of his sermons have been published. His best-known work, however, is "An Exequy to His Matchless, Never-to-Be-Forgotten Friend," a moving lament for his wife, Anne Berkeley, who died in 1624, at age twenty-four.

Galway Kinnell (b. 1927), *pp. 1740–42*
Galway Kinnell was born in Providence, Rhode Island. He was educated at Princeton University and the University of Rochester. From 1945 until 1946, he served in the navy, and he then did field work for the Congress on Racial Equality. He has traveled widely in the Middle East and Europe and has taught at more than twenty institutions, including the University of California at Irvine, the University of Pittsburgh, Sarah Lawrence College, and New York University. He has edited several other poets and feels a particular affinity for Whitman. He lives in Vermont.

Thomas Kinsella (b. 1928), *pp. 1757–60*
Thomas Kinsella was born in Dublin, Ireland. He studied science at University College, Dublin, but left to work for the Irish Civil Service. After retiring from the Department of Finance in 1965, he taught in the United States. In 1972, in Dublin, he founded the Peppercanister Press, which published much of his own work. He has translated Gaelic poetry, notably *The Tain* (1969), and has edited the *New Oxford Book of Irish Verse.* His *Collected Poems* was published in 1996.

Rudyard Kipling (1865–1936), *pp. 1181–88*
Rudyard Kipling was born in Bombay, India, to British parents. He was educated in England, but in 1882 returned to India to work as a journalist. When he moved back to England, in 1889, he enjoyed celebrity status for books such as *Plain Tales from the Hills* (1888), *The Jungle Book* (1894), and *Kim* (1901). He was awarded the Nobel Prize for Literature in 1907, but by the time of his death his reputation had declined, due largely to the jingoism that pervaded his writings during the Boer War and World War I. Following the death of his only son at the Battle of Loos, Kipling became a prominent member of the Imperial War Graves Commission and wrote a history of the Irish Guards (1923). The rousing rhythms that propel many of his poems are derived from music-hall songs and Protestant hymns, leading T. S. Eliot to call his work "the poetry of oratory." Although, as child of empire, Kipling held in high regard what he considered the glories of civilization, in a moving series of monologues from the mouths of common soldiers he explores and acknowledges the cost of attaining values such as justice, patriotism, and sacrifice of self to a larger ideal.

Carolyn Kizer (b. 1925), *pp. 1688–91*
Carolyn Kizer was born in Spokane, Washington, and was educated at Sarah Lawrence College, Columbia University, and the University of Washington. From 1959 to 1965, she was an editor of *Poetry Northwest.* She taught at a woman's college in Pakistan for the U.S. State Department before resigning in protest against the Vietnam War; later, she served as director of literary programs for the National Endowment for the Arts. An essayist as well as poet, she lives in Paris and in Sonoma, California. Her best-known work is a career-spanning, five-part poem, *Pro Femina.*

Kenneth Koch (1925–2002), *pp. 1691–95*
Kenneth Koch was born in Cincinnati, Ohio. He served as a rifleman in the Pacific during World War II, before attending Harvard University and earning his Ph.D. from Columbia University. With the exception of brief periods abroad, especially in France and Italy, Koch lived in New York City from 1950 on, and was a key figure, with his friends John Ashbery, Frank O'Hara, James Schuyler, and others, in what became known as the New York school of poetry. Writing poems closely linked with Abstract Expressionists and Surrealists, he sometimes exhibited his poems alongside these artists' works. Gifted with an offbeat sense of humor, Koch was known also for his fiction, his plays, and his work in teaching children to write poetry. He was a professor at Columbia University until his death.

Yusef Komunyakaa (b. 1947), *pp. 1949–52*
Yusef Komunyakaa was born in Bogalusa, Louisiana. He served in Vietnam as a war correspondent and for a time edited the *Southern*

Cross. Decorated with a Bronze Star, he later wrote poems deriving from his Vietnam experience, first collected in *Dien Cai Dau* (1988). Following his years in the military, Komunyakaa studied at the University of Colorado, Colorado State, and the University of California at Irvine. He has also lived in Australia, Saint Thomas, Puerto Rico, and Japan. He teaches at Princeton University. Many of his poems harken back to his childhood in a poor, rural, and largely black Southern community. They grapple with hard realities, including race and social class, and take some of their rhythms and melodic effects from jazz and the blues.

Stanley Kunitz (b. 1905), *pp. 1454–56*
Stanley Kunitz was born and raised in Worcester, Massachusetts. After graduation from Harvard University, he worked as an editor in New York City. During World War II, he served in the army, and during the academic career that followed he taught at, among other schools, Columbia University. He has been an influential teacher to many poets, including Louise Glück and Robert Hass. In addition to writing poetry, he has assembled (in collaboration with Howard Haycraft) biographical dictionaries of literary figures; edited a collection of William Blake's work; and translated the work of Anna Akhmatova and Andrei Voznesenksy from the Russian. He cofounded the Fine Arts Work Center, in Provincetown, Massachusetts, and Poet's House, in New York City. In 2000–01, he served as poet laureate of the United States.

Walter Savage Landor (1775–1864), *pp. 831–33*
Walter Savage Landor was born in Warwick, England, and educated at Rugby School and at Trinity College, Oxford. A short-lived marriage, with its interludes of domestic tranquility, provided the basis for several of his most interesting poems. He lived in Italy from 1815 until 1835 and from 1857 until his death. Fluent in French, Italian, and Greek and possessing a prodigious knowledge of history, Landor was steeped in classicism. His most enduring works, in particular his *Imaginary Conversations* (1824), based on his studies, made him an important figure to poets such as Robert Browning and Ezra Pound. He died in Florence and was buried in the Protestant cemetery there.

William Langland (ca. 1330–ca. 1400), *pp. 71–74*
A note found in the margins of an early manuscript of *Piers Plowman* in a fifteenth-century hand is the single piece of evidence that ascribes this poem to a man named William Langland. The note, which many scholars accept as reliable, states that William Langland was the son of Stacy de Rokayle, a man of gentle birth who lived in Shipton-under-Wychwood and was tenant of Lord Spenser in the county of Oxfordshire. The note concludes: "this aforesaid William made the book that is called Piers Plowman." Texts of the poem both support and elaborate on the note's information. In line 52 of Passus 15 of the B-text, the narrator seems to offer a cryptogram of the name Langland: " 'I have lyved in londe,' quod I, 'my name is Longe Wille.' " At the beginning of the poem, the narrator depicts himself awakening from his dream in the "Malvern Hills," in the West Midland region of England; elsewhere, he presents himself as a man who has moved from the country to the city and is at the time of the poem's composition living in Cornhill, in London, making a living as a cleric who chants prayers for the souls of the dead. The poem further presents the narrator as elderly, as learned in the Bible and in Latin, and as the husband of Kit and the father of Calotte; from these details, we may infer that the author had received a clerical education, but had never been ordained a priest. Passus 5 of the C-text states that the narrator comes from "franklins," or free men, and from married parents. This latter detail may serve to counter suspicions about the legitimacy of the poet's birth.

Sidney Lanier (1842–1881), *pp. 1162–65*
Sidney Lanier was born in Macon, Georgia, and educated at Oglethorpe College. In 1861, he enlisted in the Confederate Army, and in 1864 he was captured by Union forces and imprisoned for four months at Point Lookout, Maryland, where he probably contracted the tuberculosis from which he later died. After the war, Lanier played in the Peabody Symphony as a flutist and, in 1879, became lecturer in literature at Johns Hopkins University. In addition to poetry, he wrote novels—including *Tiger-Lilies* (1867), which documents his war experience—and critical studies, including *The Science of English Verse* (1880), in which he argues that the same laws govern music and poetry.

Aemilia Lanyer (1569–1645), *pp. 284–92*
Aemilia Lanyer was the daughter of Baptist Bassano, an Italian court musician, and his wife, Margaret Johnson. She was probably educated in the noble household of Susan Wingfield, countess of Kent. As the mistress of Henry Cary, Lord Hunsdun, a wealthy courtier forty-five years her senior, she enjoyed a luxurious and privileged life until she became pregnant; she then married Captain Alfonso Lanyer, another court musician, in 1592. In 1617, she set up a school in the fashionable St. Giles in the Fields for the children of the nobility and gentlemen, but it failed in 1619. Lanyer was the first Englishwoman to publish a substantial collection of original poems in her own name, as well as actively to seek patronage from a host of noble ladies addressed in the prefatory poems affixed

to her collection, *Salve Deus Rex Judaeorum* (1611).

Philip Larkin (1922–1985), *pp. 1648–59*
Philip Larkin was born in Coventry, England, and educated at King Henry VIII School and St. John's College, Oxford. He worked as a librarian for the rest of his life, starting in the small town of Wellington and moving through the university libraries of Leicester and Belfast before settling at Hull. Although he tried to achieve recognition as a novelist, with *Jill* in 1946 and *A Girl in Winter* in 1947, he made his reputation in poetry. Along with Donald Davie, Thom Gunn, and his college friend Kingsley Amis, Larkin came to be known as a writer of The Movement, a group of postwar poets anthologized in Robert Conquest's *New Lines* (1956). Although he produced only four volumes of poetry in his lifetime—*The North Ship* (1945), *The Less Deceived* (1955), *The Whitsun Weddings* (1965), and *High Windows* (1974)—Larkin was a highly influential presence in the second half of the twentieth century, editing the *Oxford Book of Twentieth-Century English Verse* (1973) and serving on various arts councils and library committees. He turned down the poet laureateship, which was offered to him on the death of John Betjeman. His *Collected Poems* was published in 1988, followed by *Selected Letters, 1940–1985* in 1992, the latter collection arousing controversy and even outrage at some of his racist and xenophobic opinions.

D. H. Lawrence (1885–1930), *pp. 1284–95*
D(avid) H(erbert) Lawrence was born in Eastwood, Nottinghamshire, England, and attended University College, Nottingham. His first published work, a group of poems, appeared in 1909; his first short story and his first novel, *The White Peacock,* the following year. From 1908 to 1912, he taught in a London school, but he gave this up after falling in love with the German wife of a professor at Nottingham. They went to Germany together and married in 1914, after she had been divorced by her first husband. Living abroad, Lawrence finished *Sons and Lovers,* the autobiographical novel at which he had been working off and on for years. The war brought the couple back to England, where his wife's German origins and Lawrence's fierce objection to the war gave him trouble with the authorities. More and more—especially after the banning of his next novel, *The Rainbow,* in 1915—he came to feel that the forces of modern civilization were arrayed against him. As soon as he could leave England after the war, he sought refuge in Italy, Australia, Mexico, then again Italy, and finally in the south of France, often desperately ill, restlessly searching for an ideal, or at least a tolerable, community. He died in France, of tuberculosis.

Irving Layton (b. 1912), *pp. 1530–33*
Irving Layton was born in Romania to Jewish parents who emigrated to Montreal, Canada, the year after his birth. He was educated at Macdonald College, served briefly in the Canadian Army, then attended McGill University. Layton taught English in secondary schools and colleges until 1970, when he joined the faculty of York University (Toronto). He retired from teaching in 1978. One of the most prolific poets of the twentieth century, he has published some fifty volumes of poetry. He also has written political essays and a memoir and has edited numerous collections of verse.

Emma Lazarus (1849–1887), *pp. 1172–73*
Emma Lazarus was born in New York City, to a prominent Sephardic (Spanish Jewish) family. She was educated at home. In 1868, she met the writer Ralph Waldo Emerson, who became her literary mentor. Lazarus developed a passionate interest in Semitism. She translated medieval Hebrew poets from the German and wrote impassioned essays on behalf of the wave of Jewish immigrants seeking refuge from persecution in Europe after the assassination of Russian Czar Alexander II, in 1881. Lazarus was appalled by the squalid conditions in which many of these refugees were forced to live and sympathetic to their difficulty in finding employment. The last five lines of "The New Colossus," the poem for which she is best-remembered, are engraved on the pedestal of the Statue of Liberty, which was dedicated in 1886.

Edward Lear (1812–1888), *pp. 1041–44*
Edward Lear was born in Holloway, London. Educated mainly at home by his elder sisters, he began to work as an illustrator at age fifteen. In 1846, he published *A Book of Nonsense,* which he had written and illustrated to amuse the grandchildren of his patron, the earl of Derby. It went through twenty-four editions in Lear's lifetime. In the 1830s, he became a wanderer, supporting himself by painting landscapes across Europe—he became known for his watercolors—and writing travel journals. He popularized the limerick (see "Versification," p. 2046), and, following his example, poets as diverse as Dante Gabriel Rossetti, Algernon Swinburne, Rudyard Kipling, and Alfred, Lord Tennyson, in the nineteenth century, and Ogden Nash, in the twentieth, employed the form.

Li-Young Lee (b. 1957), *pp. 2011–13*
Li-Young Lee was born in Jakarta, Indonesia, to Chinese parents; his father had been a personal physician to Mao Zedong before becoming a political prisoner. Upon fleeing Indonesia, the family lived in Hong Kong, Macau, and Japan before settling in the United States. Some of the family's story is recounted in Lee's memoir, *The Winged Seed: A Remembrance,* as well as in his

three volumes of poems. An American citizen with degrees from several U.S. universities, he has taught at Northwestern University and the State University of New York at Brockport. He lives in Chicago.

Brad Leithauser (b. 1953), *pp. 1998–2000*
Brad Leithauser was born and grew up in Detroit, Michigan. He was educated at Harvard College and Harvard Law School. The author of four volumes of poetry and five novels, he also edited *The Norton Book of Ghost Stories* and is a frequent reviewer and essayist. Among his recent books are collaborations with his brother, the artist Mark Leithauser, who illustrated his verse novel, *Darlington's Fall,* and an alphabet verse book, *Lettered Creatures.* He teaches at Mount Holyoke College and lives in Amherst, Massachusetts.

Denise Levertov (1923–1997), *pp. 1677–81*
Denise Levertov was born in Ilford, Essex, England, and educated at home. After working as a nurse in London during World War II, she immigrated to the United States in 1948. She became a U.S. citizen in 1955, but from 1956 to 1959 she lived in Mexico. She then taught at a number of schools, including Stanford University from 1981 on. In addition to poetry, she published two collections of prose. Her early work was written in a predominantly English vein, but as a result of her associations with the Imagists William Carlos Williams, Ezra Pound, and H. D., and the Black Mountain poets Robert Creeley, Cid Corman, and Robert Duncan, she remade herself into a notably American poet. Her poetry often took on difficult social issues, such as the effects of the Vietnam War.

Philip Levine (b. 1928), *pp. 1761–63*
Philip Levine was born in Detroit, Michigan, to Russian Jewish immigrant parents. After graduation from Wayne State University, he worked at, as he put it, "a succession of stupid jobs," then left Detroit "for good." In 1957, he earned an M.F.A. from the University of Iowa, where his teachers included John Berryman. From 1958 until his retirement, he taught at California State University in Fresno. In addition to poetry, he has written criticism and autobiography, and he has translated from the Spanish. Spanish and Latin American poets figure largely in his imagination. Levine also identifies strongly with the working class and its struggles, setting many of his poems in the decimated industrial landscape of Detroit.

Alun Lewis (1915–1944), *pp. 1573–76*
Alun Lewis was born in Cwmaman, a depressed mining town in South Wales. His parents were both schoolteachers, and he excelled in his years at Aberystwyth College, coming first in history and writing for the college magazine. He earned his M.A. at Manchester University and returned to Aberystwyth for a teacher's training course. Although he wavered at the thought of participating in World War II, he enlisted in the army in 1940. In 1941, he married Gweno Ellis. Both his collection of short stories, *The Last Inspection,* and his first collection of poetry, *Raider's Dawn,* were published in 1942 and focused on the experiences of English soldiers. Lewis traveled with his battalion to India and finally to Burma to face the Japanese, but under the influences of the war, a love affair, Eastern religions, and culture shock, he began to feel he was losing his grasp on his own fate. He committed suicide by shooting himself. A collection of the poems he had written while overseas, *Ha! Ha! Among the Trumpets,* was published posthumously in 1945, followed by *In the Green Tree,* a collection of short stories and letters, in 1948.

C. Day Lewis (1904–1972), *pp. 1448–50*
C(ecil) Day Lewis was born in Ballintubber, Ireland, and raised in England. He was educated at Wadham College, Oxford, where he came to know the poets W. H. Auden, Louis MacNeice, and Stephen Spender. In the 1930s, Day Lewis became active in left-wing politics and was a member of the Communist Party for three years, but grew disillusioned when the movement fell short of its ideals. His *Collected Poems* was published in 1954, and he also wrote a series of successful detective stories under the pseudonym Nicholas Blake, and several novels under his own name. He translated Virgil, whose influence can be detected in his later poems. Like his fellow "Pylon" poets, as the Oxford group was sometimes called, Day Lewis introduced modern diction into his poems and made broad reference to the issues of the day. He was poet laureate from 1968 until his death.

Thomas Lodge (1558–1625), *p. 222*
Thomas Lodge, the son of a lord mayor of London and his wife, was educated at Merchant Taylors' School and Trinity College, Oxford. He entered Lincoln's Inn to study law in 1578, but soon turned to writing; in 1580, he wrote a "Defence" of plays in response to Stephen Gosson's attack on the theater in *The School of Abuse* (1579). Gosson answered Lodge in another pamphlet, and in 1584 Lodge retorted with a lively attack on the usurers; in this work, he depicted the dangers that moneylenders presented for young spendthrifts. Short of funds, he joined several voyages to the New World. During one, he wrote *Rosalynde, Euphues Golden Legacy* (1590), a prose romance with verse interludes that is the source for Shakespeare's *As You Like It.* Lodge returned from a later voyage with another prose romance interspersed with many lyrics, *A Margarite of America.* He translated many French love lyrics (for instance, from Pierre Ronsard's *Amours*), and after his conver-

sion to Catholicism in 1600 translated prose works by ancient authors such as Seneca and the Jewish historian Josephus. Having turned away from secular poetry after his conversion, Lodge became a noted physician in London.

Henry Wadsworth Longfellow (1807–1882), *pp. 931–37*

Henry Wadsworth Longfellow was born in Portland, Maine (then part of Massachusetts). He was educated at Bowdoin College, where Nathaniel Hawthorne was a classmate and where he delivered a commencement speech calling for a national literature. He spent three years in Europe studying foreign languages and, upon his return, was appointed professor of modern languages at his alma mater. In 1835, he accepted a similar position at Harvard University, where he remained until 1854. He had already attained fame before the publication of his first book (1839), and later works such as *Evangeline* (1847) and *The Song of Hiawatha* (1855) were hugely popular. In 1843, he became partially blind, and in 1861 he was badly injured as he tried to extinguish the flames that, when her dress caught fire, burned his second wife to death. Longfellow translated Dante, as well as many poets he collected in his anthology *The Poets and Poetry of Europe* (1845). He also wrote fiction and verse drama. Greatly beloved in his day, though his reputation later declined, Longfellow has been credited with popularizing American themes abroad and bringing European themes home.

Michael Longley (b. 1939), *pp. 1910–13*

Michael Longley was born in Belfast, Northern Ireland, and educated at Trinity College, Dublin, where he read Classics. He worked as a schoolteacher until 1970, when he joined the Arts Council of Northern Ireland as combined arts director, a post he held until 1991. He has written scripts for BBC radio and is a frequent commentator on the arts in Northern Ireland. A fellow of the Royal Society of Literature, he was awarded the Queen's Gold Medal for Poetry in 2001.

Audre Lorde (1934–1992), *pp. 1858–60*

Audre Lorde was born in New York City to West Indian parents. She was educated at Hunter College and Columbia University, where she earned a master's degree in library science. In addition to working as a librarian, she taught at Tougaloo College and throughout the City University of New York system. She published numerous collections of poetry and two prose memoirs, one about her struggle with cancer and the other about her emergent lesbian identity. Although she once described herself as a "black lesbian feminist warrior poet," her contemporary Adrienne Rich added the appellations "mother," "daughter," and "visionary."

Richard Lovelace (1618–1658), *pp. 472–75*

Richard Lovelace was born in Kent, England, to a wealthy family and was educated at the Charterhouse School and Gloucester Hall, Oxford. He lived the life of a cultured courtier before taking arms for the king in the Scottish expeditions of 1639–40. He was imprisoned by Parliament in 1642 for presenting a Royalist petition, and he was jailed again in 1648 after returning to England from battles where he had fought with the French against the Spanish. Although he was released from prison after the king's execution in 1649, Lovelace spent his final years in poverty. One of the group of Royalist writers now known as "Cavalier" poets, he was strongly influenced by Ben Jonson. Lovelace is best-known for occasional poems and lyrics that were written mostly during his periods of imprisonment; his "To Althea, from Prison" regained popularity after its inclusion in Percy's *Reliques of Ancient English Poetry* (1765), as did his "To Lucasta, Going to the Wars." The name Lucasta (from *Lux casta*, Latin for "pure light") probably refers to Lucy Sacheverell, Lovelace's fiancée, who married another man after receiving a false report of Lovelace's death. She is honored in the title of Lovelace's one volume of poems published during his lifetime (*Lucasta*, 1649) and again in the posthumous collection published by Lovelace's brother (*Lucasta Poems Posthume*, 1659).

Amy Lowell (1874–1925), *pp. 1245–48*

Amy Lowell was born in Brookline, Massachusetts, into one of Boston's most prominent families; the poet James Russell Lowell was a distant uncle, and the poet Robert Lowell a distant nephew. She was educated at home and mainly self-taught. From 1914 on, she lived with the actress Ada Dwyer Russell, who inspired many of her poems. In addition to poetry, Lowell wrote a biography of John Keats and much influential criticism. Flamboyant and eccentric, a celebrity on the lecture circuit, she generously supported many struggling artists. Lowell is best-remembered for her association with Imagism, of which she edited three collections.

Robert Lowell (1917–1977), *pp. 1592–1606*

Robert Lowell was born in Boston, Massachusetts, to a distinguished family; his ancestors include the poets James Russell Lowell and Amy Lowell. Following his family's expectations, he attended Harvard University, but under the advice of the psychiatrist who treated him for the first of many breakdowns and manic episodes, transferred to Kenyon College. There he studied with the poets John Crowe Ransom and Allen Tate, and met lifelong friends and literary mentors Peter Taylor and Randall Jarrell, in addition to his first wife, the fiction writer Jean Stafford. After graduation from Kenyon, Lowell moved to Louisiana State University, where he worked with the New Critics Robert Penn Warren and Cleanth Brooks. He was imprisoned as a conscientious objector during World War II, and his fiercely held Catholicism was central in his early, densely patterned poetry. In the late 1950s, he began writing in an autobiographical strain. The publication of *Life Studies* (1959) heralded what would be called the Confessional school of poetry. Later, Lowell wrote loose sonnet sequences in which he explored the events of his first fifty years. Lowell also was a controversially freehanded translator of poetry, a critical essayist, and the adaptor of several classic works for the stage. He held teaching appointments at a number of universities, including Harvard, Oxford, and Essex. He is often considered the most important American poet of the mid-twentieth century. At the time of his sudden death, he was returning to his second wife, the writer Elizabeth Hardwick, after breaking with his third, Lady Caroline Blackwood.

Malcolm Lowry (1909–1957), *pp. 1503–05*
Malcolm Lowry was born in Birkenhead, Cheshire, just outside of Liverpool, England. Before attending St. Catherine's College, Cambridge (from which he received a B.A.), he worked as a crew member on a freighter bound for China and on a ship sailing to Oslo. He lived in London and then Paris until 1935, when he moved to Hollywood, and then to Cuernevaca, Mexico, which became the setting of his most famous novel, *Under the Volcano* (1947). From 1940 until 1954, he lived in a primitive cabin in Dollarton, British Columbia, and from 1954 until his death he lived in Italy and then England. Best-known as a novelist, he wrote plays, film scripts, and hundreds of poems, only a handful of which were published during his lifetime.

John Lyly (1554–1606), *pp. 207–08*
John Lyly was born in Kent, England, the grandson of William Lyly, the humanist author of a famous Latin grammar book. Educated at Magdalen College, Oxford, and later at Cambridge, Lyly was employed for a time by Queen Elizabeth I's treasurer, Lord Burghley, and was appointed vice-master of the St. Paul's choristers. He served several terms as a Member of Parliament and possibly hoped to obtain a place at court. He had gained fame as the author of a romance in two parts, *Euphues, or the Anatomie of Wit* (1578) and *Euphues and His England* (1580). Lyly also wrote several plays that combined classical and traditional English dramatic forms. The striking style of these works, which has given us the term *euphuism*, entails an elaborate sentence structure marked by balance, antithesis, and alliteration, among other rhetorical effects, as well as fulsome use of imagery drawn mainly from the works of the ancient naturalist Pliny.

Norman MacCaig (1910–1996), *pp. 1508–10*
Norman MacCaig was born in Edinburgh, Scotland. He was educated at the University of Edinburgh, where he took a degree in Classics. During World War II, he served time in prison as a conscientious objector. MacCaig was a primary school teacher until 1970, when he was appointed a lecturer in poetry at the University of Stirling. His early work was heavily influenced by the New Apocalypse movement, in which he was a central figure, and which concerned itself with the relationship between art and the unconscious. He later repudiated his work in this mode and began what he called "the long haul back to lucidity." He was awarded the Queen's Gold Medal for Poetry in 1986 and published his *Collected Poems* in 1990.

Hugh MacDiarmid (Christopher Murray Grieve) (1892–1978), *pp. 1376–80*
Hugh MacDiarmid was born in Langholm, Dumfriesshire, in the Scottish Borders. He worked on several local newspapers before joining the Royal Army Medical Corps in 1915. After serving in the Balkans and France, he resumed his career in journalism and became active in Communist and Scottish nationalist politics, involvement in each movement bringing him difficulty with the other. MacDiarmid was a central figure of the Scottish Renaissance, a loose collection of artists, writers, and musicians dedicated to reinvigorating Scottish culture and countering the sentimentality and insipidity that had crept into the arts since the time of Robert Burns. His magazine *Scottish Chapbook* and his collections *Sangschaw* (1925) and *Penny Wheep* (1926) were highly influential contributions to the movement. *A Drunk Man Looks at the Thistle* (1926), an extended dramatic monologue in Scots, though not enthusiastically received at the time, is now considered MacDiarmid's masterpiece. He wrote many of his early poems in "Lallans," a synthesized language culled from the dialects of several regions of Scotland. His linguistic experiments influenced those of, among others, James Joyce. In the 1930s, he wrote politically committed poetry; from the 1940s on, he increasingly drew on philosophy, linguistics, and science. *Hugh MacDiarmid: Complete Poems 1920–1976* was published in 1978 and revised in 1993.

Archibald MacLeish (1892–1982), *pp. 1381–82*
Archibald MacLeish was born and raised in Illinois. He was educated at Yale University and Harvard Law School. During World War I, he volunteered to serve at the front. In the early 1920s, he lived in Paris, and throughout the 1930s he served on the editorial board of *Fortune* magazine. MacLeish was influential in the upper echelons of American government under

Franklin Delano Roosevelt and held the posts of librarian of Congress and assistant secretary of state, among others. After leaving government, he taught at Harvard University. In addition to poetry, he wrote prose; verse plays, most famously *J.B.* (1957); radio plays; and the Oscar-winning screenplay for *The Eleanor Roosevelt Story* (1965). In his later work, MacLeish attempted to reconcile the conflict between his famous dictum "A poem should not mean / but be" and his political commitment.

Louis MacNeice (1907–1963), *pp. 1485–91*
(Frederick) Louis MacNeice was born in Belfast, Ireland, and raised in Carrickfergus. Educated at Marlborough College and Merton College, Oxford, he became a lecturer in Classics at Birmingham University and, later, at Bedford College, London. Following the breakup of his first marriage, he traveled to Iceland with his friend W. H. Auden, then to Spain on the eve of—and again during—the Spanish Civil War, and to the United States at the beginning of World War II. After returning to England in 1940, he joined the BBC as a feature writer and producer, and, except for a year and a half spent in Athens as director of the British Institute, he remained with the BBC for the rest of his life. He was a pioneer of radio drama, a notable playwright, a translator (of Aeschylus's *Agamemnon* and Goethe's *Faust*), and a literary critic. Best-known as a poet, however, he was early and somewhat carelessly identified with the other Oxford poets—Auden, Stephen Spender, and C. Day Lewis; but just as he never, as they did, sympathized with Communism, he never moved, as they did, to the political right. The consistency and integrity of the man characterizes his work. He delights in the surface of the world his senses apprehend and celebrates "the drunkenness of things being various," often with wit and a wild gaiety. An "unfinished autobiography" called *The Strings Are False* and his *Collected Poems* were published in 1965 and 1966.

Jay MacPherson (b. 1931), *pp. 1830–31*
Jay (Jean) MacPherson was born in London. When she was nine, her family emigrated to Canada and settled in Newfoundland. MacPherson was educated at Carleton College, McGill University, University College (London), and the University of Toronto, where she studied with the literary critic Northrop Frye. She taught at Toronto from 1957 until 1996. MacPherson's first collection of poems, issued when she was twenty-one, was published by Robert Graves's Seizen Press; her next collection bore the imprint of her own press, Emblem Books. *The Boatman* (1957) won her national acclaim and established her reputation as a poet. She has also published literary criticism and a textbook on mythology.

Derek Mahon (b. 1941), *pp. 1921–25*
Derek Mahon was born in Belfast, Northern Ireland, and read French at Trinity College, Dublin. After graduation, he traveled in France, Canada, and the United States, supporting himself through teaching and odd jobs. He has worked as a scriptwriter for the BBC, a freelance writer and reviewer, drama critic of the *Listener*, features editor of *Vogue*, and poetry and fiction editor of the *New Statesman*. His first collection, *Twelve Poems*, was published in 1965, while a collected edition spanning 1962 to 1975 appeared in 1979. A new edition of *Selected Poems* was published in 2000. Mahon has also published translations of French writers including Molière and Philippe Jaccottet.

Christopher Marlowe (1564–1593), *pp. 238–56*
Christopher Marlowe was born in Canterbury, England, to an artisan family (his father was a successful shoemaker) and attended Corpus Christi College, Cambridge, on a fellowship designated for students preparing to become ministers. Marlowe, however, spent his university years writing plays (his tragedy, *Dido Queen of Carthage,* perhaps written with Thomas Nashe, apparently dates from the 1580s) and working as a spy abroad; when university officials wanted to deny Marlowe his M.A. in 1587, the Privy Council intervened, citing his service to the queen in "matters touching the benefit of his country." His contacts at court also seem to have intervened on his behalf in 1589, when he was involved in a murderous brawl but only briefly imprisoned; in 1592, when he was arrested for counterfeiting coins in the Netherlands but spared imprisonment; and again in 1593, when he was arrested on suspicion of dangerous religious views, having been denounced by his one-time friend Thomas Kyd for atheism and treason. In the same year that he received his Cambridge M.A., his enormously popular play *Tamburlaine* was produced on the London stage; a sequel soon followed. His other plays include *The Jew of Malta, Doctor Faustus,* and the chronicle history *Edward II.* In addition, Marlowe translated from the Latin Ovid's *Amores* and Lucan's *Pharsalia* (about the Roman civil wars) and wrote the erotic mythological poem *Hero and Leander,* which was entered in the Stationers' Register in September 1593, just a few months after the poet's mysterious death, from a knife wound in a barroom brawl.

Dionisio D. Martinez (b. 1956), *pp. 2009–10*
Dionisio D. Martinez was born in Cuba. Following his family's exile from their homeland in 1965, he lived in northern Spain and southern California. He settled in Tampa, Florida, in 1972 and has worked as a poet in the schools, an affiliate writer at the University of Tampa,

and a collaborating artist with the YMCA National Writer's Voice Project. Author of three volumes of poetry, he is also a reviewer and an essayist.

Andrew Marvell (1621–1678), *pp. 475–89*
Andrew Marvell was born in Yorkshire, England, the son of a Calvinist minister and his wife; moved to Hull on his father's appointment as lecturer at Holy Trinity Church, and was educated at Hull Grammar School and Trinity College, Cambridge. He spent the civil war years touring Europe, finding "the Cause too good to have been fought for," and on his return moved in London literary circles, befriending, among others, John Milton and Richard Lovelace. From 1650 until 1652, he tutored the daughter of the Parliamentarian general Fairfax; at Fairfax's house, Nun Appleton, in Yorkshire, Marvell wrote a number of poems about gardens and rural life, including the famous "country house" poem "Upon Appleton." He became Oliver Cromwell's unofficial laureate, and in 1657 replaced Milton as secretary to the Council of State. In 1659, he became a member of Parliament for Hull and adroitly managed to retain that seat after the Restoration. He fought for toleration of religious dissenters in verse and prose satires, many published anonymously, and some attacking the king's corrupt ministers and even the king. Most of Marvell's poems were not published until after his death, the lyrics in 1681, the satires in 1689.

The Massachusetts Bay Psalm Book (1640), *pp. 391–93*
The Bay Psalm Book, also known as *The Whole Book of Psalms Faithfully Translated into English Metre,* was the authoritative hymnal of the Massachusetts Bay Colony and the first book published in America. Translated by Richard Mather, John Eliot, and Thomas Weld, this work replaced a version produced in England that the Bay Puritans felt to be corrupted by the translators' willingness to employ poetic license in their renderings. The Puritan translators, by contrast, took scrupulous pains to render the poems as they appeared in the original, devoid of added ornamentation. "God's Altar needs not our Polishings," John Cotton declared in his preface to the work. The book enjoyed a wide circulation for nearly a century and was reprinted numerous times.

Glyn Maxwell (b. 1962), *pp. 2016–20*
Glyn Maxwell was born in Welwyn Garden City, England, and educated at Worcester College, Oxford, and Boston University. *Tale of the Mayor's Son,* his first volume of poems, was published in 1990 and was followed by other well-received collections. He has also written plays for radio and the stage, a novel, and, with Simon Armitage, *Moon Country* (1996), a travel book

that traces the journey to Iceland taken by W. H. Auden and Louis MacNeice. Since 1996, he has lived in the U.S. and has taught at Amherst College, Massachusetts; Columbia University; and New School University, New York City. He is poetry editor of *The New Republic* and a Fellow of the Royal Society of Literature.

John McCrae (1872–1918), *p. 1225*
John McCrae was born in Guelph, Ontario, and educated at the University of Toronto. An accomplished physician and researcher, he practiced medicine at several hospitals in the United States and Canada. McCrae served as a medical officer in the Canadian Army during the Boer War and World War I. In the latter, he was initially stationed at the front in France, then transferred to a military hospital in Boulogne, where he contracted a fatal case of double pneumonia. He published only a handful of poems in his lifetime and is best remembered for "In Flanders Field," which he composed during the Second Battle of Ypres.

Herman Melville (1819–1891), *pp. 1054–57*
Herman Melvill (the *e* was added in the 1830s) was born and raised in New York City. The son of a well-connected merchant who lost his fortune, he was taken out of school at age twelve when his father died. In 1839, he sailed to Liverpool, England, as a cabin boy, and this voyage inculcated in him an enduring love for the sea. In 1841, he sailed on a whaler, but jumped ship in the Marquesas Islands. Captured by cannibalistic natives, he escaped and went to Tahiti, where he worked as a field laborer, and to Honolulu, where he enlisted as a seaman. In 1843, he returned home and began writing romantic novels based on his exotic adventures. His early work sold well and won him a wide following, but he thought little of it. His masterpieces, including the novel *Moby-Dick* (1851), were critical and commercial failures, and his poems were largely ignored. His 1866 volume of poems, *Battle-Pieces,* is now considered some of the greatest verse inspired by the Civil War. An epic poem, *Clarel,* followed in 1876. Melville worked from 1866 on as a customs inspector in New York City, and he died in near obscurity and dire poverty. At his death, the novella *Billy Budd, Sailor* was left not quite finished.

George Meredith (1828–1909), *pp. 1107–10*
George Meredith was born in Portsmouth, England. He received little education except for two years at a Moravian academy at Neuweid, in Germany. In 1845, he was apprenticed to a lawyer, but found the work uncongenial. He published his first poem in 1849 and was the model for Henry Wallis's painting *The Death of Thomas Chatterton* (1851). Needing money, he

turned to journalism, then to publishing; he was a reader for Chapman and Hall from 1860 until 1895. In 1864, Meredith settled in Flint Cottage at Box Hill, Surrey. Like his admirer Thomas Hardy, he was better-known for his novels—such as *The Egoist* (1879) and *Diana of the Crossways* (1885)—than for his poetry, but preferred the latter to the former. His most enduring work of verse is *Modern Love* (1862), a cycle of fifty sonnets about the breakup of a marriage. Its inception was autobiographical—Meredith's marriage to the widowed daughter of Thomas Love Peacock collapsed in 1857 when she left him for Wallis—but he significantly changed real events and drafted protagonists distinct from himself and his wife for the work. In his later years, he was a much-respected man of letters, and he was awarded the Order of Merit in 1905.

William Meredith (b. 1919), *pp. 1608–09*
William Meredith was born in New York City and was educated at Princeton University. After working as a reporter for *The New York Times* in the early 1940s, he spent five years in the armed forces, mainly as a naval aviator in the Pacific theater of World War II. He reenlisted to fly missions in the Korean War. His academic career included teaching posts at, among other schools, Princeton, the University of Hawaii, and Connecticut College. He has been an opera critic for the *Hudson Review,* poetry consultant to the Library of Congress, and a chancellor of the Academy of American Poets. In addition to poetry, he has published criticism and a libretto; he has edited several collections of poetry; and he has translated the poetry of Guillaume Apollinaire.

James Merrill (1926–1995), *pp. 1716–28*
James Merrill was born and raised in New York City, a son of Charles Merrill, founding partner of the Merrill Lynch investment firm, and his wife. He was educated at Amherst College. Near the end of World War II, he interrupted his studies to serve a year with the United States Army. In 1954, he settled in Stonington, Connecticut, and eventually divided his time between Connecticut and Florida, although he spent long periods in Greece. In addition to poetry, he published novels, plays, a collection of criticism, and a memoir. Widely admired from the outset of his career, Merrill developed a poetic that was autobiographical without being "confessional." His elegant, witty, highly wrought style reflected the influence of Marcel Proust and Henry James. His epic, *The Changing Light at Sandover* (1977–1982), a seventeen-thousand-line trilogy that draws from communications he received on a Ouija board with his partner, David Jackson, is considered one of the major achievements of twentieth-century poetry.

W. S. Merwin (b. 1927), *pp. 1743–45*
W(illiam) S(tanley) Merwin was born in New York City and raised in Union City, New Jersey, and Scranton, Pennsylvania. He was educated at Princeton University, where he studied with the poets John Berryman and R. P. Blackmur. He later traveled through Europe, and in Mallorca, Spain, was a tutor to the poet Robert Graves's son. For several years, he worked as a translator at the BBC in London, and from 1951 until 1953 he was poetry editor at *The Nation.* He has since lived in, among other places, Mexico and France, and currently resides in Hawaii. In addition to lyric poetry, Merwin has written book-length poems and several plays, and has translated Latin, Greek, French, Spanish, Italian, Chinese, and Japanese poetry into English. In addition to a version of *Sir Gawain and the Green Knight,* he has published essays and memoirs. He continues to be one of America's most prolific poets.

Charlotte Mew (1869–1928), *pp. 1216–19*
Charlotte Mew was born in London and attended Gower Street School. In her thirties, she wrote short stories; in her forties, she turned to poetry. Her first collection, *The Farmer's Bride,* was published in 1916. Her work was much admired by poets such as John Masefield, Walter de la Mare, and Thomas Hardy, who became a close friend and once called her "far and away the best living woman poet." Her life was punctuated by difficulty and sadness. She watched two siblings succumb to insanity; looked after her demanding, widowed mother; nursed her sister, who had developed inoperable cancer; and suffered unrequited love for Ella D'Arcy, assistant editor of the *Yellow Book,* and for the novelist May Sinclair. She entered a nursing home in 1927, but committed suicide a short time later.

Edna St. Vincent Millay (1892–1950), *pp. 1382–86*
Edna St. Vincent Millay was born in Rockland, Maine. In 1912, she gained national attention when her precocious poem "Renascence" was published in *The Lyric Year,* an anthology of contemporary poetry. After her graduation from Vassar College, Millay moved to Greenwich Village, where her literary reputation quickly flourished. She associated with many of the prominent artists, writers, and political radicals of her day, including the poets Hart Crane and Wallace Stevens, the playwright Eugene O'Neill, the editor Max Eastman, and the critic Edmund Wilson. In 1925, she settled with her husband in Austerlitz, New York, where she lived for the rest of her life. Witty, sometimes cynical, always polished, she is unusual in having produced some of the most traditional as well as most modern verse of her day.

John Milton (1608–1674), *pp. 394–451*
John Milton was born in London, the son of Sara and John Milton. The latter earned his living by composing music and working as a "scrivener," that is, drawing up contracts and performing other business tasks requiring writing. The young Milton was educated at St. Paul's School and Christ's College, Cambridge, where he received his B.A. in 1629 and his M.A. in 1632, and where his "niceness of nature" and "honest haughtiness" (and, perhaps, his flowing locks), earned him the nickname "the lady of Christ's." According to his own testimony in the volume of the early poems he published (and carefully arranged) in 1645, his earliest poetic endeavors were two paraphrases of Psalms done when he was fifteen. During his university years, Milton wrote various poems in both English and Latin, and his 1645 book opens with "On the Morning of Christ's Nativity," written in 1629, while he was still at Cambridge. From 1632 until 1638, he lived at his parents' house, studying and writing, supported by his father. During this period, he wrote his masque, *Comus*, in collaboration with the musician Henry Lawes; performed in 1634, it was not published under Milton's name until 1645. His first published poem was "On Shakespeare," an epitaph printed in the Second Folio (1632) of Shakespeare's plays. In November of 1637, the year his mother died, Milton published his pastoral elegy "Lycidas" in a volume memorializing Edward King, a Cambridge student who had drowned. In 1638, Milton traveled to France and then to Italy, where he met, among others, the astronomer and physicist Galileo. Upon returning to an England entering the era of political and religious conflict known as the civil wars, he began the career as political writer that led him to advocate freedom of divorce (in pamphlets published soon after Milton's own hasty marriage, to Mary Powell, had failed in 1642); freedom from censorship of the press (*Areopagitica*, 1644); and freedom from what he and others considered tyranny. An ardent supporter of Oliver Cromwell's republican regime, Milton supported the execution of King Charles in 1649 and became Cromwell's "secretary for foreign tongues" that same year. As an official defender of the new regime, Milton wrote many prose tracts during the 1650s, despite having become completely blind by 1652, the same year that Mary (who had returned to him in 1645, and with whom he had three daughters) died. He remarried in 1655, to Katherine Woodstock, but she died in childbirth in 1658. With the restoration of the monarchy in 1660, Milton was in danger of execution; friends, including the writer Andrew Marvell, intervened, and Milton was able to return to writing poetry during his final years. In 1663, he married a third time, in 1667 he published *Paradise Lost*, and in 1671 he published a volume containing his "brief epic," *Paradise Regained*, and his closet drama, *Samson Agonistes*.

N. Scott Momaday (b. 1934), *pp. 1861–62*
N. Scott Momaday was born in Lawton, Oklahoma, a member of the Kiowa Native American tribe. He was educated at the University of New Mexico and Stanford University. Since then, he has taught at Stanford, the University of California at Santa Barbara, the University of California at Berkeley, and the University of Arizona at Tucson. Known primarily as a novelist, he is also a landscape artist. Although his work is rooted in the Native American literary tradition, it reveals broader influences.

Lady Mary Wortley Montagu (1689–1762), *pp. 639–45*
Lady Mary Wortley Montagu was born Lady Mary Pierrepont, daughter of a wealthy Whig peer who became duke of Kingston in 1715 and of Lady Mary Fielding, who died when her daughter was thirteen. Educated at home, Lady Mary taught herself Latin. In 1712, she eloped with Edward Wortley Montagu, whom she followed to Turkey when he was appointed ambassador to Constantinople in 1716. Her letters from her travels were witty and immensely popular. On her return to England in 1718, she popularized the practice of inoculation against smallpox. She left England again in 1739, largely to escape her by then loveless marriage, and lived in Europe, mostly Italy, for the rest of her life, returning home only to die. She was connected to most of contemporary literary London: the novelist Henry Fielding was her second cousin; the poet Alexander Pope was initially a friend, but after she spurned a declaration of love, he bitterly mocked her in *The Dunciad* and "Epistle to a Lady." Joseph Addison and Sir Richard Steele, founders of the *Spectator*, were her first publishers, and the writers William Congreve and John Gay were acquaintances. In "Epistle from Mrs. Yonge to Her Husband," she critiques sexual inequality and advises women trapped in loveless marriages to take lovers, as she had in her later years.

John Montague (b. 1929), *pp. 1783–86*
John Montague was born in Brooklyn, New York, where his Irish parents had fled in 1920 to avoid prosecution for Republican activities (his father had reputedly burned the homes of absentee landlords), and was brought up by his aunts on a farm in Garvaghey, County Tyrone, Northern Ireland. He was educated at University College, Dublin; Yale University; and the Universities of Iowa and California at Berkeley. He worked as a journalist before becoming a lecturer in poetry at University College, Cork, and he has been a visiting lecturer at several institutions in the United States, Europe, and Britain. While literary director of Claddagh Records (from 1962 until 1975), he organized recordings of poets such as Robert Graves, Seamus Heaney, Thomas Kavanagh, Thomas Kinsella, and

Hugh MacDiarmid. His own poetry is to be found in collections such as *Forms of Exile* (1958), *A Chosen Light* (1967), and *New Selected Poems* (1990). He has also published short stories, a play, and a novella, and has translated Gaelic writing and edited collections of Irish verse.

Marianne Moore (1887–1972), *pp. 1328–36*

Marianne Moore was born in Kirkwood, Missouri, and was raised in Carlisle, Pennsylvania. After receiving a degree in biology from Bryn Mawr College, she took business courses at Carlisle Commercial College; taught business skills and commercial law at the U.S. Industrial Indian School, in Carlisle; and traveled to Europe. Moore lived all her adult life with her mother, first in New Jersey, then in Greenwich Village, then in Brooklyn. Her first collection of poetry, *Poems* (1921), was brought out by the writers H. D., whom she had befriended at Bryn Mawr, and Bryher (Winifred Ellerman). Although she devoted most of her energies to writing poetry and criticism, Moore worked variously as a teacher, a secretary, and a librarian, and she edited the influential magazine *Dial* from 1925 until 1929, when it ceased publication. In her poetry, sometimes written in syllabics, she united precise observation, and deliberately prosaic speech that was nonetheless highly inventive, with ornate diction and elaborate patterns. Her friend Elizabeth Bishop was among the many poets on whom she had a profound influence. She is considered one of the major modernists.

Dom Moraes (b. 1938), *pp. 1883–85*

Dom(inic) Moraes was born in Bombay, India. He moved to England in 1954 and matriculated at Jesus College, Oxford, then published his first collection of poetry at nineteen. With that book, *A Beginning* (1957), he became the youngest poet to win the Hawthornden Prize. He has since been a journalist, a scriptwriter, and an editor; has worked for the United Nations Fund for Populations; and has served as an honorary colonel with the United States Army, in Vietnam. He eventually returned to India, where he married the actress Leela Naidu. In addition to poetry, Moraes has published an acclaimed prose autobiography called *My Father's Son* (1968) and collections of essays on writing and on life in India and Pakistan.

Hannah More (1745–1833), *pp. 707–11*

Hannah More was born in Stapleton, Gloucestershire, England, the daughter of Jacob More, a master of a Free School, and his wife, Mary Grace, a farmer's child. Sent to the boarding school opened in Bristol by her two older sisters, she there learned French, Italian, Spanish, and Latin, and eventually joined the staff. She wrote her first play, *The Search after Happiness*, a drama for schoolgirls, at age eighteen. Originally published in Bristol in 1762, it was republished in London in 1773 and became hugely popular. Her tragedy *The Inflexible Captive* was printed with a postscript by the famous actor David Garrick, who staged the play at Bath in 1775. Another play, *Percy*, was performed at Covent Garden in 1777 to great acclaim. In addition to Garrick, More met Samuel Johnson; Johnson's biographer, James Boswell; Sir Joshua Reynolds; and other distinguished London men of letters. She was also introduced to the "Bluestockings," a circle of women centered on Elizabeth Montagu. Although More became a popular and respected dramatist, she gradually moved from secular to religious and didactic writing, advocating social reform and poverty relief. With her sisters, she promoted Sunday schools to instruct poor children in reading the Bible, but she was against "overeducating" the lower classes. She wrote forty-nine pamphlets for the Cheap Repository Tracts series and published her important work *Strictures on the Modern System of Female Education* in 1799. At her death, she left £30,000 to more than seventy charities.

Edwin Morgan (b. 1920), *pp. 1618–20*

Edwin Morgan was born in Glasgow, Scotland, and educated at the University of Glasgow, interrupting his studies to serve in the Royal Army Medical Corps, but returning in 1947 as a lecturer. His first collection, *A Vision of Cathkin Braes* (1952), was followed by many others, including *Sonnets from Scotland* (1985) and *From the Video Box* (1986). He is best-known for his ingenious experimental and "concrete" poems. He was a visiting professor at Strathclyde University from 1987 until 1990. He has translated *Beowulf* as well as the work of numerous poets, including several Latin Americans whose magical-realist mode has influenced his own work. He has also published many essays and reviews and has edited several collections of poetry, prose, and drama.

William Morris (1834–1896), *pp. 1139–44*

William Morris was born in Walthamstow, England, and educated at Exeter College, Oxford, where he became lifelong friends with the painter and designer Edward Burne-Jones. Their circle was strongly influenced by the Pre-Raphaelite school, which they encountered in about 1854. After graduation from Oxford, Morris joined an architectural firm, but left to paint and to design the furnishings sold by his company Morris, Marshall, Faulkner and Co. (later Morris and Co.). Producing his own furniture out of frustration at not being able to find anything suitable for the striking Red House designed for him by Philip Webb, Morris started a revival of the decorative arts and a revolution in Victorian taste. He founded the Society for the Preservation of Ancient Buildings, joined the Social Democratic Federation, on its dissolution assumed the leadership of the Socialist League, and wrote and lectured for the cause of Socialism with unflagging enthusiasm. As a poet (and a translator), he drew on the traditions of Icelandic, Anglo-Saxon, and classical literature. He combined the two strands of his talent in 1891, when he founded the Kelmscott Press, producing books designed for beauty rather than for economy.

Howard Moss (1922–1987), *pp. 1659–61*
Howard Moss was born in New York City. He received his undergraduate education at the University of Michigan and Wisconsin University and did postgraduate work at Harvard and Columbia Universities. During World War II, he served in the War Information Office, and between 1945 and 1948 he was an editor at *Time* magazine and the *Junior Bazaar*. In 1948, he joined the staff of *The New Yorker*, where he served as poetry editor for nearly forty years and helped establish the reputations of a wide range of poets, from Theodore Roethke to Mark Strand. He published poetry, light verse, plays, and criticism, and he edited several anthologies of poetry. He also taught at, among other schools, Barnard College and Columbia University.

Edwin Muir (1887–1959), *pp. 1336–40*
Edwin Muir was born in the Orkney Islands. In 1901, his family moved to Glasgow in search of work, but within five years both of his parents and two of his brothers had died due to the harsh conditions in the city's slums and sweatshops. Muir left school at age eleven and worked in a beer-bottling factory, several law offices, and a factory that burned bones to charcoal. In 1919, he moved to London and began a literary career. He was assistant to A. R. Orage on the *New Age* and reviewed for the *Athenaeum* and *The Scotsman*. From 1921 until 1956, he and his wife, Willa, moved between Europe, England, and Scotland, eventually settling in Cambridgeshire, England. Muir's *First Poems* was published in 1925. He was a prolific reviewer and critic, and collections of his writings include *Latitudes* (1924) and *Essays on Literature and Society* (1949). He worked for the British Council from 1942 to 1950 in Edinburgh, Prague, and Rome, and he was Charles Eliot Norton Professor at Harvard University from 1955 to 1956. *The Complete Poems of Edwin Muir* was published in 1991.

Paul Muldoon (b. 1951), *pp. 1979–85*
Paul Muldoon was born in Portadown, County Armagh, Northern Ireland, and was raised in The Moy, a small village featured prominently in many of his poems. He was educated at Queen's University, Belfast, where he met Sea-

mus Heaney, Michael Longley, and other poets of the Belfast "Group." Muldoon worked for the BBC in Belfast until the mid-1980s, when he became a freelance writer and moved to the United States, where he has taught at a number of institutions. He was professor of poetry at Oxford from 1999 to 2004, and is now professor of humanities and creative writing at Princeton. He has written a children's book, translated Gaelic verse, and collaborated on the opera *Shining Brow*.

Les Murray (b. 1938), *pp. 1885–90*
Les Murray was born in the Nabiac, New South Wales, Australia, and raised on a dairy farm in nearby Bunyah. After studying arts and modern languages at the University of Sydney, he worked as a translator of foreign scholarly and technical materials at the Australian National University before embarking on a career as a freelance writer. He has been writer-in-residence at various institutions. In 1975, he repurchased part of the family farm in Bunyah, and in 1985 he returned there to live. An exceptionally prolific writer, he has published, in addition to poetry, several collections of critical essays and an acclaimed verse novel. He has been coeditor of *Poetry Australia*; poetry editor at Angus & Robertson; and, since 1991, literary editor of *Quadrant*. He compiled *The New Oxford Book of Australian Verse* and *The Anthology of Australian Religious Verse*. His *Collected Poems* was published in 1999.

Ogden Nash (1902–1971), *pp. 1437–38*
Ogden Nash was born in Rye, New York. He attended Harvard University for one year, then taught French, sold bonds, and wrote copy for streetcar advertisements, before embarking on a literary career. In 1929, he joined the staff of the fledgling *New Yorker* magazine. In addition to writing poetry, Nash wrote children's books, collaborated on several musicals, the most successful of which was the Broadway hit *One Touch of Venus* (1943), and lectured across the country. He was one of America's funniest and most popular poets.

Thomas Nashe (1567–1601), *pp. 282–84*
Thomas Nashe, the son of a poor curate and his wife, became a fellowship student at St. John's College, Cambridge, and was graduated in 1586. After touring France and Italy, he joined the circle of London writers that included Robert Greene. His first published work, a preface to Greene's *Menaphon* (1589), was an indictment of contemporary drama and poetry; his second, *The Anatomy of Absurdity* (1589), attacked the artificiality of recent romances. When Richard Harvey accused Nashe of presumption in writing the preface to *Menaphon*, Nashe replied with a tract called *Pierce Penniless, His Supplication to the Devil* (1592). When

Gabriel Harvey wrote a contentious description of the end of Robert Greene's life in *Four Letters* (1592), Nashe replied in *Four Letters Confuted* (1593). The exchange was finally ended, in 1599, by Episcopal decree and confiscation of the adversaries' publications. Nashe's other works include *The Unfortunate Traveler* (1594), which has been called the first "picaresque" novel in English, and the plays *Summer's Last Will* (1592) and (with Ben Jonson) *The Isle of Dogs* (1597), which was suppressed for its allegedly lewd and seditious content. Though his reputation was based on his stinging wit and his rhetorical skills (he coined many new words in his prose works), Nashe also wrote fine lyrics.

Howard Nemerov (1920–1991), *pp. 1623–27*

Howard Nemerov was born and raised in New York City. He was the brother of the photographer Diane Arbus. Upon graduation from Harvard University, he entered the Canadian Air Force to fight in World War II and later transferred to the United States Air Force. After the war, he returned to New York and worked as an editor at *Furioso* magazine for one year. During the academic career that followed, he taught at, among other schools, Hamilton College, Bennington College, Brandeis University, and (from 1969 on) Washington University. From 1963 until 1964, he served as consultant in poetry to the Library of Congress. Influenced by Yeats, Eliot, and Auden, Nemerov was known for his wit, his use of irony and paradox, and his mastery of form. Both his serious and his more humorous poems asked thorny questions. In addition to poetry, he wrote fiction. He was named poet laureate of the United States in 1988.

Norman Nicholson (1914–1987), *pp. 1561–63*

Norman Nicholson was born in Millom, Cumberland, in the Lake District of England. Except for the years 1930–32, which he spent in a Hampshire sanitorium undergoing treatment for tuberculosis, he lived in Millom all his life, in a small apartment above the tailor shop where his father had worked. His *Collected Poems*—incorporating seven volumes published between 1944 and 1984 and some unpublished work—appeared in 1994. He also wrote an autobiography and several prose works about the Lake District. Nicholson identified his main theme as the "sense of community, of organic relationship between man and his environment"; continuity and change are other important themes in his work, the imagery of which is drawn predominantly from the Bible—at age twenty-three he "reconverted" to Christianity—and the natural world.

Sean O'Brien (b. 1952), *pp. 1992–94*

Sean O'Brien was born in London and raised in Hull. Educated at Selwyn College, Cambridge, and the Universities of Birmingham, Hull, and Leeds, he has taught at Sussex University and Sheffield Hallam University. He was Northern Arts Literary Fellow from 1992 to 1994 and was a visiting writer at the University of Odense, Denmark, and at Hokudai University, Sapporo, Japan. His collection *Ghost Train* won the Forward Prize for Poetry. He was cofounder and editor of the literary magazine *The Printer's Devil* and reviews regularly for *The Times Literary Supplement* and other periodicals. He has been commissioned by the BBC to produce a radio dramatization of Yevgeny Zamayatin's novel *We*, and his verse version of Aristophanes' *The Birds* was staged at the National Theatre in 2002. His critical work, *The Deregulated Muse*, brings together his essays on contemporary British and Irish poetry.

Frank O'Hara (1926–1966), *pp. 1728–31*

Frank O'Hara was born in Baltimore, Maryland, and raised in Grafton, Massachusetts. From 1944 until 1946, he served in the navy in the South Pacific. He was educated at Harvard University and the University of Michigan, and in 1951 he settled in New York. A fringe member of the Beats and a central figure in the so-called New York school of poets, whose practitioners included John Ashbery, Kenneth Koch, and James Schuyler, he enjoyed a long association with the Museum of Modern Art (where he served for a time as associate curator) and was friends with Abstract Expressionist artists such as Willem De Kooning, Jackson Pollock, and Franz Kline. He also edited *Art News* from 1953 until 1955. Like the painters he admired, O'Hara stressed the process of composition. His poems are filled with the bric-a-brac of contemporary life and pay tribute to popular figures such as Billie Holiday. His exuberant tone continues to make his work very popular.

Charles Olson (1910–1970), *pp. 1511–15*

Charles Olson was born in Worcester, Massachusetts, and educated at Wesleyan, Harvard, and Yale Universities. In 1948, he began his association with the experimental Black Mountain College, which he directed from 1951 until it closed, in 1956. During Olson's tenure, the composer John Cage, the choreographer Merce Cunningham, and the artist Franz Kline taught at the school; poets Robert Creeley, Robert Duncan, and Denise Levertov studied there; and writers Allen Ginsberg, Jack Kerouac, and Louis Zukofsky published early work in its influential magazine, *The Black Mountain Review*. In 1957, Olson settled in Gloucester, Massachusetts, and began work on the "Maximus" poems, which occupied him for the rest of his life. In a 1950 essay, Olson dubbed his poetry "Projective

Verse." Believing that art "does not seek to describe but to enact," he attempted to convey in his work a sense of immediacy and energy.

Michael Ondaatje (b. 1943), *pp. 1933–36*
Michael Ondaatje was born in Colombo, Ceylon (now Sri Lanka), to parents of Sinhalese, Tamil, and Dutch origin, and was raised in England from age nine. In 1962, he moved to Canada, where he studied at Bishop's University, the University of Toronto, and Queen's University. Ondaatje has taught at the University of Western Ontario and York University, has worked as an editor at Coach House Press, and has directed several films. In addition to poetry, he has written memoirs, plays, literary criticism, and highly acclaimed fiction, including the novel *The English Patient*. He also has edited a collection of long poems and several volumes of short stories. Much of his recent poetry is set in his native Sri Lanka.

John Ormond (1923–1990), *pp. 1681–82*
John Ormond (Thomas) was born at Dunvant near Swansea, Glamorgan, Wales. He was educated at the University College, Swansea, and studied drawing at the Swansea School of Art. After graduation, he worked as a journalist from 1945 until 1955, then joined the BBC as a television news assistant. He worked as a documentary filmmaker from 1957 until his retirement, and is best-remembered for the series of films he produced on Welsh poets and writers. Ormond was first published in 1943, but grew increasingly dissatisfied with his poems and largely stopped writing until the 1960s, when new work showed that he had found a new voice. He subsequently established himself as one of the foremost Welsh poets of his generation.

Eric Ormsby (b. 1941), *pp. 1925–26*
Eric Ormsby was born in Atlanta, Georgia, raised in Florida, and later moved to Canada. Educated at Columbia, Rutgers, and Princeton Universities, as well as the University of Pennsylvania, he is a specialist in Islamic theology and classical Arabic language and literature. The author of scholarly works and five volumes of poetry, among them *Daybreak at the Straits* (2004), he lives in Montreal, where he is a professor at McGill University's Institute of Islamic Studies.

Wilfred Owen (1893–1918), *pp. 1386–91*
Wilfred Owen was born in Oswestry, Shropshire, England. He left school in 1911, served as assistant to a vicar in Oxfordshire, and taught English in Bordeaux. In 1915, he returned to England to enlist in the army and was sent to the front in France. Two years later, having been invalided to the Craiglockhart War Hospital with shellshock, he met Siegfried Sassoon, who encouraged his work. After returning to combat

in 1918 and winning the Military Cross, he was killed in action one week before the signing of the armistice. Only five of his poems were published in his lifetime, but his posthumous reputation as a "poet's poet" grew with successive editions of his work by four poets—Sassoon (1920), Edmund Blunden (1931), Cecil Day Lewis (1963), and Jon Stallworthy (1983)—culminating with Benjamin Britten's setting of some of his poems in the composer's *War Requiem* (1962).

P. K. Page (b. 1916), *pp. 1583–85*
P. K. Page was born in Swanage, Dorset, England. Her family emigrated to Canada when she was three years old and settled in Red Deer, Alberta. After high school, Page worked as a shop assistant, a radio actress, a filing clerk, a researcher, and a scriptwriter. She then taught poetry at the Writers' Workshop in Toronto and at the University of Victoria. From 1942 until 1945, she worked on the editorial board of *Preview* magazine. From 1953 until 1964, she accompanied her husband, an ambassador, to Australia, Brazil, and Mexico, and while living abroad she resumed her earlier studies in painting. In addition to poetry, Page has written essays, short stories, a romance, and a memoir of her days in Brazil.

Michael Palmer (b. 1943), *pp. 1936–38*
Michael Palmer was born and raised in New York City and educated at Harvard University. He has taught at several schools, such as the New College of California, and has lived most of his life in the San Francisco area. In addition to writing poetry, Palmer has translated French literature and literary theory and has collaborated on books with painters and dancers. Like the artists and theorists he admires—including Gertrude Stein, Louis Zukofsky, Robert Creeley, and the Surrealists—Palmer in his work frequently examines the ways in which words signify meaning. As a L=A=N=G=U=A=G=E poet, he regards the reader as a cocreator of the text.

Dorothy Parker (1893–1967), *pp. 1391–92*
Dorothy Parker was born and raised in New York City. Early in her career, she worked for a number of prominent magazines, including *Vogue* and *Vanity Fair,* where she developed her reputation as an acerbic wit, and *The New Yorker,* for which she wrote the popular "Constant Reader" column and many short stories. In the 1930s, she and her second husband, Alan Campbell, moved to Hollywood and wrote screenplays; with Lillian Hellman and Dashiell Hammett, Parker helped found the Screen Writers' Guild. In the 1920s and 1930s, she became active in leftist politics, and she was blacklisted during the McCarthy era. Considered one of the foremost wits of her day, she belonged to a

famous literary lunch group that called itself the Algonquin Club. Parker was as celebrated for her short stories as for her poetry, but she spent her later years in isolation in New York.

George Peele (1557–1596), p. 221
George Peele was the son of James Peele, a clerk of Christ's Hospital who wrote pageants as well as a book on accounting, and his wife. After taking a B.A. and an M.A. from Oxford, Peele moved to London and made a bare living from writing pageants, plays, and poems. He is portrayed as a dissolute man-about-town in the anonymous book *Merry Conceited Jests of George Peele* (1607), but the portrait seems to bear little relation to Peele's actual life. While still at university, he translated Euripides' *Iphigenia*, and he later may have worked as an actor in London. His first play, *The Arraignment of Paris* (ca. 1584), was performed before Queen Elizabeth I and combines pastoral and debate, with songs interspersed. In this and other plays (including a historical one on Edward II that may predate Christopher Marlowe's play on the same tragic king), Peele uses blank-verse lines and lyric interludes in ways that anticipate Shakespeare. Peele also used blank verse effectively in nondramatic poems, many of them published in *Polyhymnia* (1590) and *The Honor of the Garter* (1593).

Katherine Philips (1632–1664), pp. 526–30
Katherine Philips, the daughter of a London merchant and his wife, first attended school in Hackney, England, then moved to Pembrokeshire when her widowed mother remarried, in 1646. Katherine was married to James Philips, thirty-eight years her senior, when she was sixteen, and spent twelve quiet years in Wales—the culture of which she celebrated in her poems on the Welsh language—while her husband served as a member of Oliver Cromwell's Parliament. Philips claimed that she "never writ a line in my life with intention to have it printed," but her poetry was being circulated before 1651, when Henry Vaughan eulogized her in his *Olor Iscanus* (1651). In 1655, her son Hector was born; when he died two weeks later, she lamented his death in an epitaph. Known as "the matchless Orinda" in her circle of friends and in the wider literary world, she named her schoolmate Mary Aubrey "Rosania" in several poems and addressed her friend Anne Owen as "Lucasia" in others. Despite being born, and having married, a Puritan, Philips had Royalist sympathies and contributed panegyrics to the returning monarchy, although her husband's fortunes declined after the Restoration. On a visit to Ireland in 1662, Philips translated Pierre Corneille's *La Morte de Pompée*, which was staged and printed in Dublin the next year. Though only her initials appeared on the title

page, Philips gained fame, eventually becoming the best-known female poet of her age. An unauthorized edition of her poems (*By the Incomparable Mrs. K. P.*) appeared in 1664; suppressed four days later, it closely resembles the authorized edition, published in 1667.

Robert Pinsky (b. 1940), pp. 1913–16
Robert Pinsky was born in Long Branch, New Jersey. He was educated at Rutgers University and Stanford University, where he studied under the poet Yvor Winters. He has taught at Wellesley College, the University of California at Berkeley, and Boston University, and served as poetry editor of *The New Republic* and *Slate*. In addition to his own poetry, Pinsky has published volumes of criticism, a translation of Dante's *Inferno*, and translations (with Robert Hass) of the writings of Polish poet Czeslaw Milosz. Poet laureate of the United States from 1997 to 2000, he had during his tenure an especially important role in popularizing the genre through his "Favorite Poems" project and other programs.

Sylvia Plath (1932–1963), pp. 1836–45
Sylvia Plath was born in Boston, Massachusetts. She was educated at Smith College and Newnham College, Cambridge, where she met her husband, the poet Ted Hughes. In 1953, Plath suffered a bout of depression, attempted suicide, and was hospitalized for six months; these events form the gist of her novel, *The Bell Jar* (1963). In 1958, she attended Robert Lowell's verse-writing seminar at Boston University, where the poet Anne Sexton was a fellow student. In 1963, following the dissolution of her marriage, she suffered another bout of depression and committed suicide. Like Lowell and Sexton, Plath is generally considered a "Confessional" poet. As Robert Lowell writes in his preface to *Ariel*, the posthumously published collection that established her reputation, in her poems "Sylvia Plath becomes . . . one of those super-real, hypnotic, great classical heroines."

Edgar Allan Poe (1809–1849), pp. 975–81
Edgar Poe was born in Boston to itinerant actors, orphaned in 1811, and then raised by John Allan, a Richmond merchant. He attended the University of Virginia for one year. When he ran up gambling debts, his adoptive father withdrew support, and Poe enlisted in the army. Although he received an appointment to West Point, he failed at military life. He then embarked on a literary career, which took him to Baltimore, Richmond, Philadelphia, and New York. A brilliant storyteller whose 1839 collection *Tales of the Grotesque and Arabesque,* a publishing failure, gave way to internationally successful poems, especially "The Raven," in the 1840s, he won numerous prizes and published in respected journals, but earned too little

money to survive. He and his young wife nearly starved, and she died of tuberculosis in 1845. Poe, who had struggled long with mental instability, tried in 1849 to stop drinking, but his death was probably of alcohol poisoning. He considered poems "written solely for the poem's sake" superior to those written to convey, for instance, "the precepts of Duty." His poems were greatly appreciated by the French Symbolists and other adherents of "pure poetry," such as Dante Gabriel Rossetti, Algernon Swinburne, and Ernest Dowson.

Alexander Pope (1688–1744), *pp. 596–638*
Alexander Pope was born in London, to a Catholic linen-draper and his wife. Debarred from university by his religion, he learned Greek, Latin, Italian, and French with the help of a local priest. At age twelve, he contracted a form of tuberculosis, probably Pott's Disease, which left his spine weakened, his growth stunted, and his health permanently damaged. His family moved to Binfield, in Windsor Forest, where at age sixteen Pope composed his "Pastorals" (published 1709). His friend the playwright William Wycherley introduced him to London literary society, and his *Essay on Criticism* (1711) attracted the attention of Joseph Addison, though Pope was to leave Addison's circle for the "Scriblerus Club," which included John Gay, Jonathan Swift, and other writers. *The Rape of the Lock* appeared in 1712, and the first volume of his translation of the *Iliad* into heroic couplets followed in 1715. This, together with his translation of the *Odyssey* (1725–26), brought him financial security, and he moved to Twickenham, the Jacobite rebellion having made Catholics no longer welcome in the city center. There he wrote *The Dunciad* (1728–42, revised 1743), a satire on the alleged dullness of contemporary culture; the wittily and wickedly satirical "Epistle to Dr. Arbuthnot" (1735); and the *Essay on Man,* the first volume of a projected work in four books, reflecting Pope's interest in philosophical and intellectual speculation.

Peter Porter (b. 1929), *pp. 1786–90*
Peter Porter was born in Brisbane, Australia, and educated at local grammar schools. He worked as a journalist and in the clothing industry before, in 1951, moving to London, where he worked as a clerk, a bookseller, and an advertising copywriter; he later served as a visiting lecturer at several English and Australian universities. During the 1950s, he was associated with the Group, a circle of poets who critiqued one another's work with the aim of achieving accessible verse. A prolific reviewer and broadcaster, he has published many volumes of poetry, including *The Last of England* (1970), *The Cost of Seriousness* (1978), and *The Automatic Oracle* (1987), and a collection of

translations, *After Martial* (1972). A two-volume *Collected Poems* was published in 1999.

Ezra Pound (1885–1972), *pp. 1295–1310*
Ezra Pound was born in Hailey, Idaho, and raised in a suburb of Philadelphia. He was educated at Hamilton College and at the University of Pennsylvania, where he studied languages and became lifelong friends with the poet William Carlos Williams. In 1908, Pound moved to London, where he met prominent artists and writers, including W. B. Yeats, for whom he worked as secretary. He also championed the careers of promising writers such as Robert Frost, T. S. Eliot, and James Joyce. Pound moved to Paris in 1920, and to Rapallo, Italy, in 1924. During World War II, he made a series of pro-Fascist and anti-Semitic radio broadcasts that culminated in an indictment for treason. He was adjudged mentally unfit and sentenced to St. Elizabeth's Hospital for the Criminally Insane, in Washington, D.C., where he remained until 1958. Upon his release, he returned to Italy. In 1912, Pound, H. D., and Richard Aldington had launched Imagism, and later, influenced by visual artists such as Wyndham Lewis, Pound moved on to Vorticism, whose practitioners strove to depict dynamic energies rather than represent static images. In 1920, Pound's attempts to modernize his work, to "make it new," while preserving the best history had to offer, resulted in *Hugh Selwyn Mauberley,* a work that anticipated Eliot's *The Waste Land* (1922), which Pound edited masterfully. The crowning achievement of his career is his epic, *The Cantos,* which he began to write in earnest in 1924 but never finished to his satisfaction. It is one of the principal texts of modernism.

E. J. Pratt (1883–1964), *pp. 1270–72*
E(dwin) J(ohn) Pratt was born in Western Bay, Newfoundland, Canada. An ordained Methodist minister, he taught and preached in several remote communities. Pratt held degrees in philosophy and theology from Victoria College, University of Toronto. He was a staff psychologist at the college until 1919, when he joined the English Department, where he taught until his retirement, in 1953. In 1936, he helped found, and until 1942 was an editor of, the *Canadian Poetry Magazine,* which launched the careers of many important Canadian poets.

Matthew Prior (1664–1721), *pp. 566–68*
Matthew Prior was born in Wimborne, Dorset, England, the son of a joiner and his wife. Through the patronage of Lord Dorset he was educated at Westminster School, and with a scholarship from the duchess of Somerset went to St. John's College, Cambridge. He was secretary to the ambassador at The Hague, but turned Tory in Queen Anne's reign, acted as a

secret agent, and was instrumental in bringing about the Treaty of Utrecht (1713), for which he was imprisoned for two years after the queen's death. He never held public office again, but Tory friends prevented his ruin by subscribing to a deluxe folio edition of Prior's work (1719). A gift of £4,000 from Lord Harley enabled him to buy Down Hall, in Essex. Prior wrote in a variety of forms, including "Public Panegyrics, Amorous Odes, Serious Reflections, [and] Idle Tales," and defended his enjoyment of a range of verse forms thus: "He that writes in Rhimes, dances in Fetters: And as his Chain is more extended, he may certainly take larger steps."

Craig Raine (b. 1944), *pp. 1942–45*
Craig Raine was born in Bishop Aukland, Durham, England, and was educated at Exeter College, Oxford, where he became a lecturer. He has worked for a number of journals and for ten years was poetry editor at Faber and Faber. A fellow of New College, Oxford, Raine has written the libretto for the opera *The Electrification of the Soviet Union*, which was adapted from Boris Pasternak's novella *The Last Summer*, and has adapted Racine's *Andromaque* for the stage. His work is characterized by arresting, inventive metaphors that defamiliarize the commonplace, and the poet James Fenton has dubbed him and his followers "The Martian School," because poems such as "A Martian Sends a Postcard Home" have "taught us to become strangers in our familiar world, to release the faculty of perception."

Sir Walter Ralegh (ca. 1552–1618), *pp. 151–58*
Sir Walter Ralegh was born in Devonshire, England, to a "gentle" but not wealthy family, and was educated at Oriel College, Oxford. He became a favorite of Queen Elizabeth I, whom he praised in many poems. He was renowned for his courage as a sailor, soldier, and explorer as well as for his eloquence and courtly wit. Though he lost the queen's favor when he seduced and married one of her maids of honor in 1592, she nonetheless gave him a royal patent to pursue an ill-fated search for gold in Guiana in 1595. Earlier, he had directed the colonization of Virginia, which he had named after his queen; he introduced tobacco from the colony to England. After Elizabeth died, the new king, James, had Ralegh imprisoned in the Tower of London on a questionable charge of treason. There he began his history of the world—which was to have been dedicated to his supporter, Henry, the prince of Wales. But Henry died in 1612 and Ralegh never finished the *History*. Although he was briefly released to pursue a second (and equally unsuccessful) search for gold in Guiana, he spent most of his later years in prison until he was executed on the old charge of treason.

A. K. Ramanujan (1929–1993), *pp. 1801–03*
A(ttipat) K(rishnaswami) Ramanujan was born in Mysore, Karnataka, India, and educated at Mysore University, Deccan College, and Indiana University. From 1950 until 1958, he taught English at various colleges and universities in India, and from 1962 until his death he taught at the University of Chicago. He was a respected scholar of Dravidian languages, linguistics, culture, and folklore; a gifted translator of works in classical Tamil and medieval and modern Kannada; and an engaging poet in both English and Kannada. In addition to poetry, he published plays, a novel, short stories, and an autobiography (this last in Kannada).

John Crowe Ransom (1888–1974), *pp. 1367–69*
John Crowe Ransom was born in Pulaski, Tennessee. He was educated at Vanderbilt University and Christ Church College, Oxford. After enlisting in the army during World War I, he served on the front in France. A member of the Vanderbilt faculty from 1914 until 1937, he spearheaded the Agrarian movement, whose members included the poet and novelist Robert Penn Warren and the poets Allen Tate and Donald Davidson. The group championed a vision of an agrarian economy based on old Southern values—which they saw as a corrective for an urban, Northern economy. Ransom later joined the faculty of Kenyon College, where he founded the influential *Kenyon Review* and helped spur the New Criticism, a critical school that emphasized close textual scrutiny and would dominate the American literary scene for several decades.

Henry Reed (1914–1986), *pp. 1563–66*
Henry Reed was born in Birmingham, England, and educated at Birmingham University. From 1937 to 1941, he worked as a teacher and as a journalist. During World War II, he served one year in the Royal Army Ordnance Corps and three as a cryptographer in the department of Naval Intelligence. In 1945, he went to work as a broadcaster, journalist, and playwright for the BBC, where his coworkers included the poets W. H. Auden, Louis MacNeice, and Dylan Thomas. He later taught at the University of Washington in Seattle. His reputation as a poet rests almost exclusively on the five-part "Lessons of the War," which may be the most anthologized poem of World War II. He also wrote some famously funny radio plays.

Adrienne Rich (b. 1929), *pp. 1791–1801*
Adrienne Rich was born in Baltimore, Maryland, and educated at Radcliffe College. Her

first book of poems, *A Change of World* (1951), was selected by W. H. Auden for the Yale Series of Younger Poets. She has taught at, among other schools, Rutgers University and Stanford University, and now lives in California. A prolific writer, Rich has published numerous collections of poetry (including *Collected Early Poems 1950–1970*, *The Fact of a Doorframe: Selected Poems 1950–2001*, and *The School among the Ruins: Poems 2000–2004*), in which her work has evolved from closed forms to a poetics of change, rooted in a radical imagination and politics. In prose works such as *What Is Found There: Notebooks on Poetry and Politics* (1993, new edition 2003) and *Arts of the Possible: Essays and Conversations* (2001), she combines autobiography, history, and politics. In 2004, she edited Muriel Rukeyser's *Selected Poems* for the Library of America.

Edwin Arlington Robinson (1869–1935), *pp. 1212–16*
Edwin Arlington Robinson was born in Head Tide, Maine, and raised in Gardiner, Maine, the model for "Tilbury Town," the setting of many of his poems. He attended Harvard University, but was able to afford only two years. In 1896, Robinson moved to New York City, where he worked as a subway-construction inspector and in the Customs House. In 1910, despite financial difficulties, he devoted himself full-time to writing poetry. Robinson's early work received little recognition; fame came to him late, with the publication of *The Town Down the River* (1910) and *The Man against the Sky* (1916). By the time of his death, he was one of the most acclaimed poets in America, having won the Pulitzer Prize three times. Although he wrote lyric poems, dramatic monologues, and, later, long blank-verse narratives (such as his trilogy of verse novels based on Arthurian legend), he is best-remembered for his wry poems on fictional New England characters.

Theodore Roethke (1908–1963), *pp. 1493–1502*
Theodore Roethke was born and raised in Saginaw, Michigan, where his German grandfather, his uncle, and his father operated greenhouses, which would figure prominently in Roethke's work. Roethke was educated at the University of Michigan and, briefly, Harvard University. In 1935, he was hospitalized for the first of several mental breakdowns. From 1947 until his death, he taught at the University of Washington, where his students included the poets Richard Hugo and James Wright. His early work was typically comprised of short, tightly structured lyrics; a shift to more open form occurred with *The Lost Son and Other Poems* (1948). According to Roethke, these poems trace the spiritual and personal history "of a protagonist (not 'I' personally but of all haunted and harried men)."

Although he is considered a precursor of the "Confessional" poets, his work is also visionary and imbued with nature.

Isaac Rosenberg (1890–1918), *pp. 1373–76*
Isaac Rosenberg was born in Bristol, England, and raised in the East End of London. He attended elementary schools until age fourteen, when he became apprenticed as an engraver in a firm of art publishers and attended evening classes in the Art School of Birkbeck College. His first ambition was to be a painter, and in 1911, when his apprenticeship ended, a group of three Jewish women provided the means for him to study at the Slade School of Art. His interest in writing poetry developed steadily, and with the encouragement of his married sister he circulated copies of his poems among members of London's literary set and gained a certain reputation, though neither his poetry nor his painting won him material success. In 1914, Rosenberg went to South Africa for his health and lived there with another of his sisters. He returned to England in 1915, enlisted in the army, and was killed in action on April 1, 1918. Initially buried in an unmarked grave, his remains were discovered in 1926 and reinterred in a Flanders cemetery.

Christina Rossetti (1830–1894), *pp. 1128–34*
Christina Rossetti, sister of the poet and Pre-Raphaelite painter Dante Gabriel Rossetti, was born in London. Except for two brief trips abroad, she lived with her mother (who educated her) all her life. A committed High Anglican, she was deeply influenced by the Tractarian, or Oxford, movement. Her first poems were published pseudonymously in the first issue of *The Germ*, in 1850, and her first major collection, *Goblin Market and Other Poems*, was published in 1866. The last collection published during her lifetime was the devout *The Face of the Deep: A Devotional Commentary on the Apocalypse* (1892).

Dante Gabriel Rossetti (1828–1882), *pp. 1102–07*
Dante Gabriel Rossetti, brother of the poet Christina Rossetti, was born in London. As a promising painter, he attended various art schools, including the Royal Academy School. In 1848, along with several painters, poets, and critics, among them J. E. Millais and W. Holman Hunt, he formed the short-lived but influential Pre-Raphaelite Brotherhood. During the 1850s, Rossetti moved away from the naturalism of the Pre-Raphaelites toward aestheticism. He joined a coterie of unconventional thinkers—including the designer and poet William Morris, the painter and designer Edward Burne-Jones, and the poet Algernon Swinburne—whose work

set a new standard of taste and thinking and influenced the Aesthetes and Decadents of the next generation, including the writers Walter Pater and Oscar Wilde.

Muriel Rukeyser (1913–1980), pp. 1537–39

Muriel Rukeyser was born in New York City. She attended Vassar College—where she, the poet Elizabeth Bishop, and the novelist Mary McCarthy founded the *Student Review*—and Columbia University. Her first book of poems, *Theory of Flight* (1935), used imagery from her studies at Roosevelt Aviation School. She taught writing at the California Labor School in Berkeley, California, and later at Sarah Lawrence College. In addition to poetry, Rukeyser published biographies of the mathematicians Willard Gibbs and Thomas Hariot and Republican presidential candidate Wendell Willkie, collections of literary criticism, and children's books. She also translated the work of Gunnar Ekelof, Bertolt Brecht, and Octavio Paz. Social and political issues were her primary concern, and her phrase "no more masks!" became a rallying cry for feminists, including the poets Adrienne Rich and Anne Sexton.

Carl Sandburg (1878–1967), pp. 1252–53

Carl Sandburg was born in Galesburg, Illinois. He left school after the eighth grade, but later attended Lombard College. His first collection of poetry, *Chicago Poems*, was published in 1914 and was followed by several highly acclaimed and immensely popular volumes, including *Cornhuskers* (1918), which documents Sandburg's war experience, *Smoke and Steel* (1920), and the book-length poem *The People, Yes* (1936). Sandburg was a leading figure in the Chicago Renaissance, along with the architect Frank Lloyd Wright, the novelist Theodore Dreiser, and the poets Vachel Lindsay and Edgar Lee Masters. In the 1930s, Sandburg became active in the Socialist movement. He devoted thirty years to the study of Abraham Lincoln and traveled the country in search of folk songs and ballads, which he collected as *The American Songbag* (1927). He also wrote novels and children's stories.

Robyn Sarah (b. 1949), pp. 1956–58

Robyn Sarah was born in New York City, to Canadian parents, and grew up in Montreal. She has a degree in music from the Conservatoire de Musique et d'Art Dramatique du Québec and in philosophy from McGill University. Cofounder, with Fred Louder, of the literary press Villeneuve Publications, she has taught English at Champlain Regional College for over twenty years. An essayist and reviewer, she has published several collections of short stories as well as of poetry. She lives in Montreal.

Siegfried Sassoon (1886–1967), pp. 1317–20

Siegfried Sassoon was born in Kent, England, and attended Clare College, Cambridge. For several years, he divided his time between London, where he moved in fashionable literary circles, and his family's country estate, where he lived as a leisured Edwardian gentleman. At the outbreak of World War I, he enlisted and went to the front with the Royal Welch Fusiliers. Known as "Mad Jack" for his acts of reckless courage, he was awarded the Military Cross, but in 1917 he publicly protested that the war was being "deliberately prolonged by those who have the power to end it." His actions landed him in the Craiglockhart War Hospital (authorities claimed he was suffering from "shell shock"), where he befriended the poet Wilfred Owen. Although Edward Marsh included some of Sassoon's early work in his anthologies of Georgian poetry, these poems bear little resemblance to the fierce war poems of *The Old Huntsman* (1917) and *Counter Attack* (1918). A prolific diarist, he wrote seven volumes of (sometimes fictionalized) autobiography. He was received into the Roman Catholic Church in 1957 and regarded himself at the end of his life as above all a religious poet.

Gjertrud Schnackenberg (b. 1953), pp. 2000–2005

Gjertrud Schnackenberg was born in Tacoma, Washington. She attended Mount Holyoke College and earned early admiration for her writing. She has traveled extensively, has lived in Rome, and currently resides in Boston. A highly allusive poet, Schnackenberg fuses her personal history with that of Dante in her book *A Gilded Lapse of Time* (1992) and revisits the myth of Oedipus in her book-length poem *The Throne of Labdacus* (2000).

James Schuyler (1923–1991), pp. 1683–84

James Schuyler was born in Chicago and raised in Washington, D.C., and western New York State. He was educated at Bethany College. After living in Italy during the 1950s, he settled in New York City. Like the poet Frank O'Hara, Schuyler worked at the Museum of Modern Art, served on the editorial board of *Art News*, and was deeply influenced by the practices of avant-garde artists. In addition to poetry, he wrote three novels, all of them comedies of manners.

Vikram Seth (b. 1952), pp. 1994–96

Vikram Seth was born in Calcutta, India, and educated at Corpus Christi College, Oxford; Stanford University; and Nanjing University. His first volume of poems, *Mappings*, appeared in 1980, and his 1985 collection, *The Humble Administrator's Garden*, won the Commonwealth Poetry Prize (Asia). He published his first novel, *The Golden Gate*, in 1986, but it was his epic, award-winning *A Suitable Boy* (1993) that brought him international fame. That was followed by *An Equal Music* in 1999. A prolific reviewer, he has also written a travel book, *From Heaven Lake: Travels through Sinkiang and Tibet;* a series of animal stories in verse for children, *Beastly Tales from Here and There;* and an opera libretto, *Arion and the Dolphin,* which was performed at the English National Opera in 1994.

Anne Sexton (1928–1974), *pp. 1764–65*
Anne Sexton was born in Newton, Massachusetts, and attended Garland Junior College. Following the birth of her first child, in 1951, she suffered the first in a series of mental breakdowns, which culminated in her suicide, in 1974. Sexton began writing poetry in earnest in 1957. She studied under Robert Lowell and W. D. Snodgrass, whose *Heart's Needle* (1959) influenced her profoundly, and developed important friendships with Sylvia Plath and Maxine Kumin. Along with teaching poetry in high schools, at mental institutions, and at colleges and universities (including Harvard, Oberlin, and Boston), she coauthored three children's books with Kumin. Sexton is often considered a prime example of what came to be called the Confessional school of poetry, although she also wrote nonautobiographical poems, based on legend and fairy tale.

William Shakespeare (1564–1616), *pp. 257–77*
We know less about Shakespeare's life than we know about that of almost any other major English writer. He was born the third of eight children in Stratford-on-Avon. His father, John, was a maker of gloves who became an alderman and a bailiff before suffering financial troubles. Shakespeare's mother, Mary Arden, was the daughter of a rich farmer and brought land to the marriage. Shakespeare probably attended the Stratford grammar school, but received no university education and was referred to as an "upstart crow" by one of the better-educated "university wits" when he arrived in London, in the early 1590s. The first record of him after his christening dates from 1582, when he married Anne Hathaway; they had a daughter in 1583 and twins, Judith and Hamnet, in 1585. For most of his career, he was an actor and shareholder in, and principal playwright of, the most successful theatrical company of his time. He quickly gained a reputation as "the most excellent" English dramatist in both comedy and tragedy and was well known for his history plays, narrative poems, and the "sugared Sonnets" that were circulated "among his private friends." After the turn of the century, he composed in rapid succession his tragic masterpieces *Hamlet, Othello, King Lear, Macbeth,* and *Antony and Cleopatra.* He apparently retired to Stratford

around 1610, and during his later years he worked mainly in the genres of romance and tragicomedy. When he died, no collected edition of his works had been published; the First Folio, a collection of his plays (but not his narrative poems or sonnets), appeared in 1623.

Percy Bysshe Shelley (1792–1822), *pp. 863–93*
Percy Bysshe Shelley was born near Horsham, Sussex, to a well-to-do, conservative family. In 1810, he went to University College, Oxford, but was expelled in his first year for refusing to recant an atheistic pamphlet he had published with a classmate. He married a schoolgirl the following year. In 1813, he moved to London, where he worked for a number of social causes and came under the influence of the radical social philosopher William Godwin. Shelley fell in love with Godwin's daughter, Mary Wollstonecraft Godwin (author of the novel *Frankenstein*), and eloped to Europe with her. Byron joined them in Switzerland in 1816 and followed them to Italy in 1818. Shelley was drowned when his small boat was caught in a squall on the Gulf of Spezia. Lord Byron eulogized him as "without exception, the best and least selfish man I ever knew." The superlative opinion of friends did not reflect public opinion at large, however. Due to his radical social, political, and philosophical ideas and his unorthodox lifestyle, Shelley had few admirers in his lifetime. An avid student of Hume and Plato, he was deeply influenced by skeptical empiricism and idealism; he distrusted all claims to certainty—he never confessed a religious or philosophical creed—but held fast to his faith in the redeeming powers of love and the imagination.

James Shirley (1596–1666), *pp. 390–91*
James Shirley was born in London and was educated at Merchant Taylors' School. He went on to St. John's College, Oxford, and St. Catherine's Hall, Cambridge. After joining the Anglican clergy, he served in St. Alban's and taught at the town's grammar school from 1623 until 1625, but lost his position there when he converted to Catholicism in 1624–25. Returning to London, he began a career as a dramatist with *The School of Compliment* (later, *Love Tricks;* 1625). This was the first of thirty-six plays he wrote, many for the Cockpit Theatre, until 1640, when he succeeded Phillip Massinger as principle dramatist for the King's Men. Shirley's plays were largely comedies and tragicomedies in the style of (Francis) Beaumont and (John) Fletcher, and dramatized patriotic debates such as *The Contention of Ajax and Ulysses for the Armour of Achilles* (1658), but Shirley also composed masques such as *The Triumph of Peace,* commissioned by the Inns of Court in 1634, and poetry. As a Royalist and Catholic, Shirley was fortunate in finding employment as a school-

teacher during Oliver Cromwell's Commonwealth, but his luck did not long outlast it; he died of exposure during the Great Fire of London.

Jane Shore (b. 1947), pp. 1952–54

Jane Shore was born in Newark, New Jersey, and educated at Goddard College and the University of Iowa. She was fellow in poetry at the Radcliffe Institute from 1971 until 1973. During the mid-1970s, she taught at Harvard University—where one of her colleagues was the poet Elizabeth Bishop, a clear influence on Shore—and she now teaches at George Washington University. The author of four volumes of poetry, among them *Happy Family* (1999), she lives in Washington, D.C., and in Vermont.

Mary Sidney (1561–1621), pp. 225–30

Mary Sidney was the third of eleven children born to Sir Henry Sidney and his wife, Mary. Well-educated at home, Mary became proficient in Latin as well as in French and Italian; between 1575 and 1577, she acquired a courtly education by serving, as her mother had before her, as a lady-in-waiting to Queen Elizabeth I. In 1577, she married Henry Herbert, the second earl of Pembroke. As a patron of letters and inspiration to poets ranging from Edmund Spenser to Isabella Whitney, Mary Sidney Herbert made her country estate, Wilton, into an intellectual center. In the early 1580s, Mary's eldest brother, Philip, probably wrote his *Defense of Poesy* there along with portions of his *Arcadia*, the second version of which was unfinished when he died, in 1586. He had dedicated the first version to his sister, and in 1590 she published a composite version of the two texts, an enormously influential work known as *The Countess of Pembroke's Arcadia*. Sharing with her brother a hope that England would become a defender of Protestantism in Europe, Mary worked after his death to complete a series of verse translations of the Psalms that he had begun; having revised the forty-three psalms that he had finished, she composed another 107 in a wide variety of meters and forms. Mary articulated some of her own religious beliefs not only in her versions of the Psalms but also in her translation of Du Plessis Mornay's *Discourse of Life and Death* and in her rendering, in terza rima, of Petrarch's *Triumph of Death*. In 1591, she published her *Antonie*, a translation of a French play by Robert Garnier. Her original verse often appears under the "handmaidenly" cloak of translation and even, perhaps, under others' names: some critics have argued for her authorship of the "Lay of Clorinda" long attributed to Spenser and published in *Astrophil*, the elegy for Philip Sidney that Spenser dedicated to Mary.

Sir Philip Sidney (1554–1586), pp. 208–20

Philip Sidney was born at Penshurst, in Kent, England, to an aristocratic family that included among its poets Sidney's brother Robert, his sister Mary, and his niece, Mary Wroth. His mother, also Mary, was the sister of Queen Elizabeth I's sometime favorite, Robert Dudley, earl of Leicester, and his father, Sir Henry, had served the queen as lord deputy of Ireland. After attending Shrewsbury School with his friend (and later, biographer) Fulke Greville, Sidney spent time at Oxford and Cambridge. From 1572 until 1575, he traveled in Europe, during which time he established a firm friendship with Hubert Languet, who encouraged his zealous Protestantism. When in 1580 Queen Elizabeth considered marrying a French Catholic, Sidney criticized the idea in a letter and was consequently banished from court. He spent his enforced "idleness" composing poetry; his famous work of literary criticism, the *Defense of Poesy*; and two versions of his pastoral romance, the *Arcadia*, which was dedicated to his sister Mary and which she published after his death in a widely read version that conflates his first text, the *Old Arcadia*, with his unfinished revision, the *New Arcadia*. Legendary in life and death as the quintessential Elizabethan gentleman, Sidney was in reality more marked by the "great expectation" he mentions in one of his sonnets than by political or romantic success. His *Astrophil and Stella*, the first great sonnet sequence in English—like his other poetic works, circulated in manuscript but not published until after his death—uses (and revises) Petrarchan conventions to record various experiences of unfulfilled desire. These include, but are not exhausted by, the erotic frustration caused by his failure to win Penelope Devereux, the historical model for Stella, as his wife. Although she was briefly engaged to Sidney, in 1581 she married Lord Robert Rich; Sidney was married to Frances, daughter of the powerful courtier Sir Francis Walsingham, in 1583, the same year he was knighted. Sidney was granted a chance to fight for Protestantism in the Low Countries after being made governor of Flushing (an English possession in the Low Countries) in 1586. He died of gangrene from a wound in the leg.

Charles Simic (b. 1938), pp. 1891–93

Charles Simic was born in the former Yugoslavia and raised there during the Nazi occupation. At age eleven, he emigrated to the United States with his family. Simic was educated at the University of Chicago and New York University. Besides serving in the United States Army, he has worked as a bookkeeper, an accountant, a house painter, and a salesman. Since then, he has taught at California State College and the University of New Hampshire. In addition to many volumes of poetry, he has published several collections of essays and has translated a number of European poets into English. His poems' mystery and sense of danger derive in large part from folklore and fairy tale as well as from the tragic events of the past century, especially World War II.

L. E. Sissman (1928–1976), *pp. 1766–68*
L(ouis) E(dward) Sissman was raised in Detroit, Michigan. After graduation from Harvard University, he held a series of odd jobs: shelving books in a library, editing copy in a New York publishing house, working on John F. Kennedy's first Senate campaign, and selling vacuum cleaners and Fuller brushes. In 1956, he began a successful career in advertising. In 1958, after a ten-year hiatus, he began to write poetry in earnest, and he published prolifically from that time until his death, from Hodgkins' disease. In addition, he wrote regularly for *The Atlantic Monthly.* He lived in Boston nearly all his adult life. Although his illness was a primary subject, Sissman treated personal material with irony, urbanity, wit, and grim cheer.

John Skelton (1460–1529), *pp. 90–97*
Skelton often referred to himself as "poet laureate," a title conferred on him by the universities of Oxford and Cambridge in 1490 and 1493, respectively. Trained in Latin and in rhetoric, he was ordained a priest and subsequently served as a tutor for the future king Henry VIII. After writing a satire on court life, *The Bowge of Court,* in 1498, he became rector of the parish church of Diss, a town in Norfolk. While at Diss (from approximately 1502 until 1511), Skelton apparently kept a mistress and fathered children; he also wrote his comic lament "Phillip Sparow" and "Ware the Hawk," which denounces the actions of a neighboring priest who pursued his quarry, a hawk, into the sanctified space of Skelton's church. Both in its (highly original) form and in some of its content, this poem anticipates Skelton's later attacks on Henry VIII's chancellor, Cardinal Wolsey; Wolsey's desecration of monastic spaces are the object of Skelton's comic invective in long poems such as *Speak Parrot, Why Come Ye Not to Court,* and *Colin Clout,* all from the early 1520s, when Skelton was living at the Abbey of Westminster, protected by the laws of sanctuary from Wolsey's (and perhaps also the king's) anger. Skelton also wrote *The Turning of Eleanor Rumming,* a satiric portrait of an alewife; a morality play, *Magnificence;* and a number of short lyrics including the ironic song "Mannerly Margery Milk and Ale." The "Skeltonic" style that he invented typically blends high and low diction in short rhymed lines containing from two to five beats.

Christopher Smart (1722–1771), *pp. 678–86*
Christopher Smart was born in Kent, England, and educated in Durham and at Pembroke College, Cambridge, where he became a fellow. He was a brilliant classical scholar, but began to exhibit symptoms of obsessive behavior, including a compulsion to public prayer. After moving to London in 1749, he won prizes for poetry, but his illness worsened, and he was several times committed to the lunatics' ward at St. Luke's Hospital, where he divided his time between writing, gardening, and his cat, Jeoffry. In 1758, he was transferred to a private institution at Bethnal Green. Released in 1763, he declined into poverty, and in 1770 was remanded to the King's Bench debtor's prison, where he died. William Butler Yeats regarded Smart's *A Song to David* as the inaugural poem of the Romantic period. Smart's other well-known work, *Jubilate Agno,* which he referred to as his "Magnificat," was, like *A Song to David,* composed during Smart's confinement, but was unpublished until 1939.

Charlotte Smith (1749–1806), *pp. 711–15*
Charlotte Smith (née Turner) was born in London and brought up on her family's estates: Bignor Park, Sussex, and Stoke Place, Surrey. Raised by her maternal aunt after the death of her mother in childbirth in 1753, she began writing poems at age six. Educated at schools in Sussex and London, she married, at age fifteen, Benjamin Smith, the son of a wealthy merchant in the West Indies trade. They had twelve children, one of whom died in infancy and two of whom died in childhood. Benjamin was imprisoned for debt in 1783, and Charlotte shared some of the eight-month sentence with him. On his release, the family fled to France to escape creditors. Charlotte's first collection, *Elegiac Sonnets and Other Essays,* was published in 1784, went through numerous editions, and was translated into French and Italian. While in France, she translated Antoine-François Prévost's *Manon Lescaut,* which she published in 1785 but subsequently withdrew over accusations of plagiarism. The Smiths separated when they returned to England, and Charlotte become a prolific writer, publishing three collections of poetry, six children's books, and ten novels, including *The Old Manor House* (1793), which was admired by Sir Walter Scott. Continual litigation over her father-in-law's estate as well as family sorrow and misfortune plagued her all her life. Benjamin Smith predeceased Charlotte by eight months, dying in a Scottish debtors' prison. A posthumous collection of her work, *Beachy Head; with Other Poems,* was published in 1807.

Stevie Smith (1902–1971), *pp. 1439–43*
Stevie Smith was born Florence Margaret Smith in Yorkshire, England. She was raised by an aunt

in the north London suburb of Palmers Green and lived there for the rest of her life. A secretary in the magazine publishing house of Newnes, Pearson, Ltd for thirty years, she retired in 1953 following a severe breakdown and devoted the rest of her life to writing. Her first volume of poetry, *A Good Time Was Had by All,* was published in 1937 and was accompanied by her own comic illustrations. This was followed by six more collections and three novels. She was awarded the Queen's Gold Medal for Poetry in 1969.

W. D. Snodgrass (b. 1926), *pp. 1731–34*
W(illiam) D(eWitt) Snodgrass was born in Wilkinsburg, Pennsylvania, and raised in Beaver Falls, Pennsylvania, where he began undergraduate studies at Geneva College before entering the navy. He served in the Pacific during the last months of World War II. He later studied at the University of Iowa, where he attended Robert Lowell's poetry workshops. Snodgrass has held teaching appointments at a number of universities, including Cornell, Rochester, Wayne State, Syracuse, Old Dominion, and Delaware. In 1959, he published *Heart's Needle,* a revolutionary work credited, along with Robert Lowell's *Life Studies* (published the same year), with spawning the so-called Confessional school of poetry. Snodgrass often takes up complex moral issues; in *The Führer Bunker* (1977), he presents a series of dramatic monologues spoken by prominent figures in the Third Reich during the final days of the Nazi regime.

Gary Snyder (b. 1930), *pp. 1816–19*
Gary Snyder was born in San Francisco and raised on a farm near Seattle. He was educated at Reed College. In the early 1950s, he worked as a logger, forest-fire lookout, trail-crew worker, carpenter, proofreader, seaman, and teacher. He subsequently studied Asian languages at the University of California at Berkeley, where he was a member of the Beat movement, and spent a dozen years in Japan, where he studied Zen Buddhism. Upon his return to the United States, he settled in a remote community in the Sierra Nevadas. He taught at the University of California at Davis from 1986 until his retirement, in 2002. Influenced by "five-and-seven-character line Chinese poems . . . which work like sharp blows on the mind," he arranges "tough, simple, short words" into abbreviated lines. He has translated from ancient and modern Japanese and wrote a memoir in the Japanese form of a poetry-and-prose travel journal.

Gary Soto (b. 1952), *pp. 1996–97*
Gary Soto was born in Fresno, California. He has worked as a field hand and in a tire factory, and he often writes about working-class Mexican Americans. Educated at California State University, Fresno (where he studied with Philip Levine), and the University of California at

Irvine (from which he earned an M.F.A.), he taught at San Diego State University and the University of Cincinnati before settling at the University of California at Berkeley from 1979 to 1996. In addition to poetry, he has published a memoir, books for children, and a collection of essays on poetry, and he has edited a book of recollections and stories about California.

Robert Southwell (ca. 1561–1595), *pp. 223–24*
Robert Southwell was born in Harsham, Norwich, England, to a Roman Catholic family, and was educated at the Jesuit School in Douai, France, accepted for the Jesuit novitiate in Rome, and ordained in 1585. Despite the law of 1584 forbidding English-born subjects who had taken Catholic orders since the queen's accession to remain in England longer than forty days, on pain of death, Southwell returned to England to minister to Catholics in 1586. In 1589, he became chaplain to Ann Howard, countess of Arundel, whose husband had been imprisoned, and to whom Southwell addressed his *Epistle of Comfort.* In 1592, Southwell was arrested while saying Mass, tortured, imprisoned in the Tower, and finally executed. He was beatified as a martyr in 1929 and canonized in 1970. He wrote religious prose and verse in both Latin and English. His narrative poem, "St. Peter's Complaint," and his best-known lyric, "The Burning Babe," were both published in 1595. The latter is an unusually fine example of a poem in "fourteeners," or fourteen-syllable lines, a form that Sir Philip Sidney had parodied in "What Length of Verse?" Southwell's work became popular soon after his death, and Ben Jonson told a friend that he would willingly have destroyed many of his own poems if he could have written "The Burning Babe."

Wole Soyinka (b. 1934), *pp. 1862–63*
Wole Soyinka was born in Ijebut Isara, Nigeria, and spent his early years in Abeokuta. Educated at University College, Ibadan, and Leeds University, he has taught at the Universities of Lagos, Ibadan, and Ife, and lectured all over the world. In the late 1950s, he worked as a reporter for the BBC. From August 1967 to October 1969, he was imprisoned as a political prisoner by the Federal Military Government of Nigeria. An exceptionally prolific writer, Soyinka has published poetry, novels, autobiography, critical essays, an anthology of African poetry, and numerous plays for radio, television, and the stage. He was founding director of Masks Theatre, the Orison Theatre, and the Guerrilla Theatre Unit of the University of Ife. He was awarded the 1986 Nobel Prize for Literature.

Stephen Spender (1909–1995), *pp. 1505–07*
Stephen Spender was born in London and attended University College, Oxford, where he

became friends with the writers W. H. Auden, Christopher Isherwood, and Louis MacNeice, with whom he shared an interest in left-wing politics. In 1937, he joined the British Communist Party and traveled to Spain to write propaganda for the Spanish Republicans' fight against Fascism, but soon grew to feel that Communism was intolerant of individual vision and freedom of expression. In the 1930s, he, Auden, MacNeice, and Cecil Day Lewis were dubbed by critics the "Pylon" school, after Spender's poem "The Pylons," for their conspicuous use of industrial imagery. During World War II, he served with the Fire Service and in the Foreign Office. From 1945 to 1947, he was literary counselor to UNESCO, and for the next twenty-five years he traveled and lectured in the United States. He was coeditor of the journals *Horizon* and *Encounter*. In addition to writing his own poetry, he translated from Spanish, German, and Greek. He was knighted in 1983.

Edmund Spenser (1552–1599), *pp. 159–205*
Edmund Spenser was born in London, to a family of modest circumstances, and educated at the Merchant Taylors' School. After studying as a "poor scholar" at Cambridge, Spenser served as secretary to several prominent men, including the powerful earl of Leicester, uncle of Spenser's friend Sir Philip Sidney. In 1580, he was appointed secretary to the lord governor of Ireland, whose job it was to defend the English settlement there against the Irish "rebels" who objected to English rule of their land. Spenser remained in Ireland, as civil servant, settler, and landholder, for the rest of his life, and in 1596 wrote *A View of the Present State of Ireland*, a political treatise detailing his views on the "Irish problem." He wanted nothing less than to be the national poet of England, and he consciously modeled his career on that of Virgil, the great poet of imperial Rome. Like Virgil, Spenser initially wrote in the mode of pastoral, publishing in 1591 his *Shepheardes Calender*. Chaucer was another of Spenser's main sources of inspiration, as were Italian writers such as Ludovico Ariosto and Torquato Tasso. Ariosto's *Orlando Furioso* (1516) provided, in its blending of epic and romance narrative structures, a particularly important model for Spenser's *The Faerie Queene*. That poem's first three books, published in 1590, were well received, and in 1596 Spenser republished the poem with three additional completed books and a portion of a seventh. He thus completed only a little over half of the poem he described, in a prefatory letter to Walter Ralegh, as designed to fashion a gentleman by illustrating twelve moral virtues in twelve books. He received a modest royal pension after the first three books of *The Faerie Queene* were published, but he never received a post at court nor the royal recognition he had hoped for. His disappointed expectations and his

belief that the queen was mismanaging affairs in Ireland may have contributed to the sometimes critical ways in which he represented her in *The Faerie Queene*. Elizabeth was the name not only of the queen whom he "shadowed," but also of his wife; she is figured in his sonnet sequence *Amoretti* and also in his two marriage poems, *Epithalamion* and *Prothalamion*.

Gertrude Stein (1874–1946), *pp. 1248–50*
Gertrude Stein was born in Allegheny, Pennsylvania, and raised in Oakland, California. She was educated at Radcliffe College, where she studied with the psychologist and philosopher William James (whose theories about consciousness influenced her deeply) and at Johns Hopkins University, where she studied medicine. In 1902, she and her brother, Leo, moved to Paris and established a salon that attracted the most prominent avant-garde artists of the day, including Pablo Picasso, Georges Braque, and Henri Matisse. In 1907, she began a relationship with Alice B. Toklas (which led to Stein's wryly titled and popular *Autobiography of Alice B. Toklas*), and, apart from Stein's very successful lecture tour of the United States in 1934, they resided permanently in France. Stein's work—in prose, poetry, drama, and autobiography—was highly experimental (she was called "the Mama of Dada"). Her reputation as a stylist and arbiter of taste, great in her day, has continued to grow.

Wallace Stevens (1879–1955), *pp. 1256–69*
Wallace Stevens was born and raised in Reading, Pennsylvania. After attending Harvard University for three years, Stevens moved to New York City, where he went to law school, worked in a number of law firms, and associated with prominent artists, including the poets William Carlos Williams and Marianne Moore. In 1916, he went to work for the Hartford Accident and Indemnity Company, and he stayed with the firm for the rest of his life, having become a vice president in 1934. His quiet life, in an upper-class neighborhood in Hartford, Connecticut, seemed in sharp contrast with the cosmopolitanism and vitality of his poems. Both sensuous and philosophical, Stevens's work continues to be hugely influential. His first book, *Harmonium* (1923), is considered one of the major debuts in American poetry. His work of the 1930s and after, plainer in diction and more abstract, included the long poem "Notes toward a Supreme Fiction." Poetry was the supreme fiction, as he also wrote in his important prose work *The Necessary Angel* (1951).

Anne Stevenson (b. 1933), *pp. 1847–49*
Anne Stevenson was born in Cambridge, England, to American parents, and raised in the United States, primarily in Cambridge, Massachusetts, and New Haven, Connecticut. She was educated at the University of Michigan, where she studied with the poet Donald Hall. In

the early 1950s, she worked as a schoolteacher, and in 1956 settled in England, where she taught at a number of institutions and held several fellowships. She was the founder of the Poetry Bookshop at Hay-on-Wye, Wales. Her publications include a study of Elizabeth Bishop, a biography of Sylvia Plath, and several radio plays. Her best-known collection, *Correspondences,* is a sequence of epistolary poems interspersed with journal entries recounting her family history.

Trumbull Stickney (1874–1904), *pp. 1250–52*
Trumbull Stickney was born in Geneva, Switzerland, and spent his early years abroad. He was educated by his father, a Classics scholar, until he entered Harvard University, and he later became the first American to earn a Ph.D. at the Sorbonne. He taught Greek at Harvard University for one year, then died suddenly, of a brain tumor. Although during his lifetime he published only one book, *Dramatic Verses* (1902), he left much work in manuscript, and the poet William Vaughn Moody, a friend of Stickney from Harvard, helped assemble a posthumous collection.

Mark Strand (b. 1934), *pp. 1863–65*
Mark Strand was born on Prince Edward Island, Canada, and raised in various cities across the United States. He was educated at Antioch College, Yale University, the University of Florence, and the University of Iowa, where he studied with the poet Donald Justice. Strand has taught at the University of Utah, Johns Hopkins University, and the University of Chicago, and has served as the poetry editor of *The New Republic.* A noted anthologist, a translator of several European and Latin American poets, he also has written short stories, books for children, and art criticism, including a study of Edward Hopper. He is also a painter. Among many notable collections is his book-length poem *Dark Harbor* (1993), which obliquely recounts a journey of the mind through memory and into the afterlife. In 1990–91, he was poet laureate of the United States.

Sir John Suckling (1609–1642), *pp. 452–58*
John Suckling was born into an old Norfolk, England, family, through which he inherited great estates. Educated at Trinity College, Cambridge, he traveled in Holland and was knighted on his return in 1630. He was part of the 1631 embassy to Germany, returning the next year to court and a life of dissipation. In 1639, he fought on the (losing) Royalist side against the Scots, and in 1641 levied a force to free the imprisoned earl of Strafford. The conspiracy, named the "Army Plot," was uncovered, and Suckling fled to France, where he might have

committed suicide by drinking poison. Like other "Cavalier" poets who supported the cause of Charles Stuart, Suckling embodied the courtly quality of *sprezzatura,* in which the most highly refined and polished style is disguised as effortless effusion. His literary reputation was established by 1637, when his satirical mock-ballad *The Wits (or Sessions of the Poets)* was sung before King Charles I. The next year, his tragedy *Aglaura* proved a theatrical success. Poems such as "Song" ("Why so pale and wan, fond lover?") and "A Ballad upon a Wedding" are collected in *Fragmenta Aurea* (1646).

May Swenson (1913–1989), *pp. 1540–43*
May Swenson was born in Logan, Utah, to a Mormon family. After graduation from Utah State University, she moved to New York and worked with the Writers' Project of the Works Progress Administration. From 1956 until 1966, she was an editor at New Directions Press. In addition, she was a visiting professor at many colleges and universities. She translated from the Swedish, most notably the poems of Tomas Tranströmer. Her high-spirited poetry, like that of her friend Elizabeth Bishop, is marked by a keen interest in the natural world.

Jonathan Swift (1667–1745), *pp. 568–89*
Jonathan Swift was born in Dublin, Ireland, to English parents, but after his mother's return to England he lived in the care of his uncle. He was educated at Trinity College, Dublin. From 1689 until 1699, he was secretary to his kinsman Sir William Temple and tutor to "Stella," Ester Johnson (daughter of the companion to Temple's sister), to whom "Stella's Birthday" is addressed, and for whom Swift developed a lasting passion. Swift frequented London, where he became active in Tory politics and met the leading literary figures of the day. In 1694, he returned to Ireland to join the clergy, and he later served in several parishes and was appointed dean of St. Patrick's Cathedral in 1713. Despite his staunch conservatism, he became an ardent champion of Irish resistance to English oppression. Best-known for *Gulliver's Travels* (1726), the only piece of writing for which he was paid, he was a prolific author of poetry, prose, pamphlets, letters, dialogues, and satires.

Algernon Charles Swinburne (1837–1909), *pp. 1146–52*
Algernon Charles Swinburne was born in London and attended Balliol College, Oxford, where he became a friend of the poet and Pre-Raphaelite painter Dante Gabriel Rossetti, the painter and designer Edward Burne-Jones, and the designer and poet William Morris. Swinburne introduced the phrase *art for art's sake* into the English aesthetic lexicon in an 1862 review of the French poet Charles Baudelaire's

Les Fleurs du Mal. He became an adherent of Baudelaire's aesthetic, until, in 1867, he met Giuseppe Mazzini, whose fervor for Italian independence from Austrian rule caused Swinburne to repudiate *art for art's sake* and turn to politically motivated poetry. He wrote prolifically, and his work, which characteristically explores the relationship between pleasure and pain, love and death, shows the influence of sources as diverse as the Marquis de Sade, the Bible, Greek drama, and the Border Ballads.

Allen Tate (1899–1979), *pp. 1417–21*
Allen Tate was born in Winchester, Kentucky. He was educated at Vanderbilt University, where he roomed with the poet Robert Penn Warren and was affiliated with the Fugitive movement. Along with Warren, and Vanderbilt professors John Crowe Ransom and Donald Davidson, Tate later joined the Agrarians, who called for an agriculturally based Southern economy and championed traditional Southern values. In 1924, he moved to New York to embark on a literary career; the poet Hart Crane lived in his household for a time. In 1928–29, Tate lived in England and France, and spent time with fiction writers Ford Madox Ford, Ernest Hemingway, and F. Scott Fitzgerald. He later taught at, among other schools, Princeton University, New York University, and the University of Minnesota. In addition to poetry, he published biographies, a novel, and several collections of criticism.

Edward Taylor (ca. 1642–1729), *pp. 536–40*
Edward Taylor was born in Leicestershire, England, but migrated to Massachusetts in 1668. After graduation from Harvard University in 1671, he served as the minister of Westfield, Massachusetts, then a frontier town. Taylor published some poems in his lifetime, but most of his writings remained in manuscript when he died; the poems were preserved by Ezra Stiles, Taylor's grandson and the president of Yale. Only in 1937 was a selection of Taylor's poems published, with a more complete edition following in 1960. A Puritan who believed in salvation by grace alone, Taylor adhered to tradition (specifically, the Old New England Way) in matters of church practice. In addition to occasional pieces, he composed *Preparatory Meditations*, whose starting points are images from biblical texts, and the series *God's Determinations Touching His Elect; and the Elect's Combat in Their Conversion, and Coming up to God in Christ: Together with the Comfortable Effects Thereof.*

Alfred, Lord Tennyson (1809–1892), *pp. 982–1009*
Alfred, Lord Tennyson was born in Somersby, England. He was educated at Trinity College, Cambridge, where he met Arthur Henry Hallam, whom he later immortalized in *In Memoriam* (1850). Tennyson began to write when a child, largely to escape the oppressiveness of his home life, made miserable by his father's drinking and violence. He published some of his best-known poems, such as "Mariana" and "The Kraken," when he was only twenty; in "Mariana," he displays his early, and enduring, gift for using objects and landscapes to convey states of mind and particular emotions. Between 1833, the date of Hallam's death, and 1843, when Tennyson received an annual government pension to support his writing, he was especially hard-hit by the melancholia that would plague him all his life and so dominate his poetry. In the wake of Hallam's death, his work assumed a decidedly darker note. He expressed his grief abstrusely in poems such as "Ulysses" and "Break, Break, Break" and directly in *In Memoriam,* a series of 131 quatrain stanzas, which Tennyson began within days of Hallam's death and continued to write over a period of seventeen years. With the publication of this great elegy, he finally attained the public recognition long denied him and earned sufficient money to marry Emily Sellwood after a ten-year on-again, off-again courtship. In 1850, he succeeded William Wordsworth as poet laureate, and nine years later published the first four (of an eventual twelve) parts of *Idylls of the King,* a project that had occupied him for nearly fifty years.

Dylan Thomas (1914–1953), *pp. 1566–73*
Dylan Thomas was born in the Welsh seaport of Swansea. Ignoring his father's advice to attend university, he left school in 1931 to embark on a literary career. After working at the local newspaper, he headed for London in 1934. His first volume, *18 Poems,* appeared that year. He worked as a broadcaster, prose writer, poet, and lecturer, and this varied career necessitated his traveling through the United Kingdom, Europe, and the United States. He died in New York City during a reading tour, his excessive drinking and generally riotous lifestyle hastening his early death but also responsible, in part, for the burning intensity of his poems, whose exuberant rhetoric sometimes masks his careful crafting. His most famous work, *Under Milk Wood,* was recorded in New York before his death and rerecorded a year later in Britain by Richard Burton. Greatly admired and imitated, Thomas's work was also greatly despised. The New Apocalypse writers took him as a model; the Movement writers, including Philip Larkin, were said to have formed in reaction to the excesses, personal and poetic, of Dylan Thomas and his admirers.

Edward Thomas (1878–1917), *pp. 1253–56*
Edward Thomas was born in the London suburb of Lambeth and educated at Lincoln College, Oxford. His arduous biographical, critical, and

review work often left him drained and depressed, but he was forced to be prolific in order to support a growing family. He began to write poetry in 1914 with the encouragement of the poet Robert Frost, whom he greatly admired. After joining the army in 1915, he was killed in battle at Arras on Easter Monday 1917. Thomas's *Poems* (1917) was published under his pseudonym, Edward Eastaway. It was followed by *Last Poems* (1918) and *Collected Poems* (1920), which appeared in his own name. His wife, Helen, published two evocative memoirs of their life together.

R. S. Thomas (1913–2000), *pp. 1544–46*
R(obert) S(tuart) Thomas was born in Cardiff, Wales, and raised in Anglesey. He studied Classics at the University College of North Wales, Bangor, and theology at St. Michael's Theological College, in Llandaff. Ordained in the Anglican Church, he served at Chirk, Denbighshire, and a number of rural parishes before retiring from the Church in 1978. He learned to speak Welsh in college to communicate with his parishioners and to gain a deeper understanding of Welsh culture. Throughout a long life, he published a new volume of poetry every two or three years and edited anthologies such as *The Penguin Book of Religious Verse*. He was awarded the Queen's Gold Medal for Poetry in 1964.

James Thomson (1700–1748), *pp. 649–51*
James Thomson was born in Ednam Manse, Kelso, Scotland, and educated at Jedburgh School and Edinburgh University, preparing for the ministry. After abandoning his studies, he tried to make a living as a writer in London, where he became friendly with the leading writers of the day, including John Arbuthnot, Thomas Gay, and Alexander Pope. "Winter," a short, blank-verse poem, appeared in 1726, and "Summer" and "Spring" in 1727 and 1728, respectively. *The Seasons,* which collected all three with "Autumn," was published in 1730. In 1731, Thomson accompanied Charles Talbot, son of the solicitor-general, on the Grand Tour, which provided the inspiration for his patriotic poem *Liberty* (1735–36), dedicated to the prince of Wales, who awarded him a pension. Further patronage came through the poem *Britannia* (1729), together with sinecures such as the surveyor-generalship of the Leeward Islands. Thomson's *Alfred, a Masque* (1740) includes the famous song "Rule Britannia," also attributed to his friend David Mallet. His *Seasons* was one of the most popular and influential poems of the century, heralding the shift of poetic attention from humanity (the center of the Augustan universe) to nature, and ushering in the period of topographical poetry and the "cult of the picturesque."

Henry David Thoreau (1817–1862), *pp. 1045–46*
Henry David Thoreau was born and lived nearly all his life in Concord, Massachusetts. He was educated at Harvard University, where the poet Jones Very was his tutor. After graduation, he worked briefly as a schoolteacher. He lived in the household of Ralph Waldo Emerson, his chief literary champion, for a time and became active in Emerson's Transcendentalist club. From 1845 until 1847, Thoreau lived in a wooden hut at Walden Pond, an experience he documented in the celebrated prose work *Walden* (1854). A rugged individualist and observer of nature, he regarded moral law more highly than civil law, as demonstrated in his refusal to pay poll and church taxes and in his early support for the as yet unpopular abolition movement. His most famous essay, "Resistance to Civil Government" (known posthumously as "Civil Disobedience"), was like several other works published anonymously, and his full-length book *Cape Cod* was not published in its entirety until after his death. Most of his poetry was written before 1840, but it achieved prominence in *The Atlantic Monthly* and elsewhere in the years immediately following his death. He is especially prized today for his environmentalist approach to nature.

Chidiock Tichborne (d. 1586), *p. 151*
The Tichbornes were an old, probably pre-Conquest family of Hampshire, England, and were pious Catholics. Chidiock Tichborne was interrogated on several occasions on suspicion of "popish practices" (i.e., attending Mass) and in 1586 was involved in a plot led by Anthony Babington against the life of Queen Elizabeth I. Tichborne was arrested and sentenced to be hanged and disemboweled. Imprisoned in the Tower of London, he is said to have written his "Elegy" on the eve of his execution. Tichborne's speech from the scaffold and his poem of farewell became widely known in the Elizabethan and Jacobean periods.

Charles Tomlinson (b. 1927), *pp. 1746–49*
Charles Tomlinson was born in Stoke-on-Trent, England, and educated at Queens' College, Cambridge, where he studied with the poet Donald Davie, and the University of London. He taught at a London school for a number of years and worked as a private secretary in Italy before joining the faculty of the University of Bristol in 1957. He has also taught at various institutions in the United States. From the start, Tomlinson identified more strongly with the American poetic and artistic tradition (he is also an accomplished artist) than with the British. *Some Americans* (1981) offers a vivid personal record of his debt to American modernism and of his efforts to unite its discoveries with English traditions. The translator (with the late Henry Gifford) of

Versions from Fyodor Tyutchev (1960) and *Castilian Ilexes: Versions from Antonio Machado* (1963), Tomlinson has edited *The Oxford Book of Verse in English Translation.*

Jean Toomer (1894–1967), *pp. 1398–1400*
Jean Toomer was born in Washington, D.C. He was raised by his mother and maternal grandfather, P. B. S. Pinchback, who had served as acting governor of Louisiana during Reconstruction. Toomer attended several colleges, but never received a degree. He spent much of his early adulthood in New York City; his work was both influenced by and influential on the Harlem Renaissance. In 1921, he taught in Sparta, Georgia, where he gathered material for *Cane* (1923), a mosaic of poetry, prose, and drama on black themes, and the work on which his reputation stands. In his later years, Toomer wrote extensively on religion and philosophy—he had studied the work of the Russian mystic Gurdjieff and had become a Quaker—but was unable to find a publisher for his work. He also left unpublished fiction, plays, and an autobiography.

Thomas Traherne (1637–1674), *pp. 531–36*
Thomas Traherne was the son of a Hereford, England, shoemaker and his wife—who, it is thought, died when Thomas and his brother were young, leaving them to be brought up by Philip Traherne, a wealthy innkeeper who was twice mayor of the city. Thomas was educated at Brasenose College, Oxford, and became rector of Credenhill, Herefordshire, in 1657. He was ordained in 1660, the year before taking his M.A. In 1669, he was made B.D., probably in recognition of his *Roman Forgeries* (which exposed ecclesiastical forgery of documents), and appointed chaplain to Sir Orlando Bridgeman, lord keeper of the Great Seal, after which he lived in London. His *Christian Ethics* appeared a year after his death, but his poems and prose meditations remained unknown until the early twentieth century, when manuscript volumes began to be discovered and published. His *Centuries of Meditation* was probably written during his time at Credenhill, when he was part of a religious circle led by Susanna Hopton, a High Anglican who converted for a time to Catholicism and to whom Traherne dedicated the *Centuries.*

Frederick Goddard Tuckerman (1821–1873), *pp. 1086–87*
Frederick Goddard Tuckerman was born in Boston, Massachusetts, to a distinguished New England family. He was educated at Harvard University (where the poet Jones Very was one of his tutors) and Harvard Law School. In the late 1840s, Tuckerman gave up the law to study his first loves: astronomy, botany, and poetry. He lived a retired and scholarly life at his family home in Greenfield, Massachusetts. Tuckerman's one published volume of poems was well received by the best poets of his day, including Emerson, Longfellow, and Tennyson, yet his name fell into obscurity until the twentieth century, when his work was rediscovered by the poet Witter Bynner. Among the poems not published during Tuckerman's lifetime are three sonnet sequences.

John Updike (b. 1932), *pp. 1846–47*
John Updike was born in Reading, Pennsylvania, and raised in nearby Shillington. He was educated at Harvard University and studied drawing at the Ruskin School of Drawing and Fine Arts, in Oxford, England. Upon his return to the United States, he joined the staff of *The New Yorker*, where he continues to publish fiction and reviews. In 1957, he and his family moved from New York City to Ipswich, Massachusetts, where he concentrated wholly on writing. One of the most versatile, prolific, and highly acclaimed contemporary American writers, Updike has published many novels (most notably his series about the character Harry "Rabbit" Angstrom), short stories, plays, poems, essays, and reviews of both literature and art.

Mona Van Duyn (1921–2004), *pp. 1629–32*
Mona Van Duyn was born in Waterloo, Iowa, and was educated at the University of Northern Iowa and the University of Iowa at Iowa City. She taught at, among other schools, the University of Iowa, the University of Louisville, and Washington University. From 1974 to 1978, Van Duyn and her husband, Jarvis Thurston, edited *Perspective: A Quarterly of Literature.* Generally writing about ordinary people and the realities of their lives, she also found inspiration in current events, literature, and philosophy. She was poet laureate of the United States in 1992–93.

Henry Vaughan (1621–1695), *pp. 490–98*
Henry Vaughan was born in Newton-upon-Usk, Breconshire, the son of a Welsh gentleman and his wife, and the twin of Thomas, who became a natural physician, or alchemist. Henry attended Jesus College, Oxford, and went on to London to study law, but was deflected by the civil war. He may have fought for the Royalists before returning to Breconshire, where he seems to have taken up medicine, perhaps in the 1640s. A poem in his first collection (1646), "Upon the Priory Grove," records his courtship of Catherine Wise, whom he was to marry and whose younger sister, Elizabeth, became his second wife. The collection is almost entirely secular, as was his second, *Olor Iscanus* (1651), but his third, *Silex Scintillans* (1655), and his subsequent work, is of religious and devotional nature. An interest in Hermeticism appears in several poems, which allude to theories found in

his brother's treatises on the subject. Vaughan acknowledged George Herbert as a significant influence, writing that Herbert's "holy life and verse gained many pious Converts (of whom I am the least)."

Jones Very (1813–1880), *pp. 1044–45*
Jones Very was born in Salem, Massachusetts. He was educated at Harvard College, then became a tutor in Greek while he pursued a degree at the Divinity School. In 1838, after a conversion experience, Very repudiated Unitarianism for a rigorous mysticism and felt compelled to surrender himself completely to the will of God. Remanded to an asylum for evaluation at the request of his colleagues, he was declared sane and released, after which he retired to his parental home, in Salem, where he lived a scholarly and reclusive life. In the eighteen months following his release, Very wrote some three hundred poems, including a mystical sonnet sequence. His one published collection, *Essays and Poems* (1839), was edited by Ralph Waldo Emerson. Very's work fell into obscurity until the twentieth century, when it was rediscovered by the poet and critic Yvor Winters.

Derek Walcott (b. 1930), *pp. 1820–29*
Derek Walcott was born on the island of St. Lucia, in the British West Indies, and educated there at St. Mary's College and at the University of the West Indies, in Jamaica. He then moved to Trinidad, where he has worked as a book reviewer, an art critic, a playwright, and the artistic director of a theater workshop. He has also been poet-in-residence at a number of American colleges and universities and has received a MacArthur Award. At once flamboyant and disciplined, poems such as his wittily titled *A Far Cry from Africa* proclaim his divided roots, as a black poet writing from within both the English literary tradition and the history of a subject people. He has since proved the truth of Yeats's statement that "out of the quarrel with ourselves we make poetry." Isolation is Walcott's theme; and as with Yeats, the writing and producing of plays has increased the emotional and dramatic range of his poetry. The movement of *Another Life* (1973) and *Midsummer* (1984) is freer, more flexible than that of earlier work, but Walcott's language still has the accuracy and energy that proclaim him—more than any of his American contemporaries—the natural heir of his friend Robert Lowell. In 1992, following the publication of his verse epic *Omeros,* which transposes elements of Homeric epic from the Aegean to the Caribbean, Walcott was awarded the Nobel Prize for Literature.

Margaret Walker (1915–1998), *pp. 1576–77*
Margaret Walker was born in Birmingham, Alabama. She received her B.A. from Northwestern University and M.A. and Ph.D. from the University of Iowa. From 1936 until 1939, she was employed by the Writer's Project of the Works Progress Administration in Iowa, where she struck up a mutually beneficial association with her coworker the novelist and, later, poet Richard Wright. She subsequently worked as a social worker, reporter, and magazine editor and taught at Livingston College, West Virginia State College, and Jackson State College (now University). In addition to poetry, she published a biography of Wright and a collection of autobiographical essays. Her poems, set in a Southern landscape, sometimes call upon African Americans to take action against oppressive social conditions.

Edmund Waller (1606–1687), *pp. 393–94*
Edmund Waller was the eldest son of a wealthy landowner in Hertfordshire, England, and his wife. Educated at Eton and King's College, Cambridge, he became a Member of Parliament at age sixteen and swiftly gained a reputation as a brilliant orator. In his thirties, he courted Dorothy Sidney, granddaughter of Robert Sidney and grandniece of Philip and Mary Sidney; he addressed her under the poetic name "Saccharissa" (Sweetness). After participating in the philosophical circle around Lucius Cary at Great Tew, Oxfordshire, he changed his political stance from Parliamentarian to Royalist. His part in a plot to secure London for the king was discovered in 1643, but he avoided execution by a confession and an eloquent plea for clemency. Exiled, he traveled in France, Italy, and Switzerland with his friend John Evelyn until 1651, when he was allowed to return to England; although he wrote in praise of Oliver Cromwell, he regained a place in Parliament after the Restoration and advocated religious toleration. Waller's first known poem, commemorating Prince Charles's escape from shipwreck (ca. 1625), is an early example of the use of heroic couplets in English. His *Instructions to a Painter* appeared in 1666. John Dryden was among his admirers, praising the "sweetness" of Waller's style.

Robert Penn Warren (1905–1989), *pp. 1456–60*
Robert Penn Warren was born in Guthrie, Kentucky. He was educated at Vanderbilt University, the University of California at Berkeley, Yale University, and Oxford University. At Vanderbilt, Warren associated with the Fugitives, a literary group whose members included professors John Crowe Ransom and Donald Davidson and fellow student Allen Tate. He later became a member of the Agrarian movement. Warren taught at, among other schools, Vanderbilt; Louisiana State University, where with Cleanth Brooks he cofounded the influential *Southern Review;* the University of Minnesota; and Yale.

In addition to poetry, he wrote *Brother to Dragons* (1953), a verse drama; fiction (his novel *All the King's Men* won the Pulitzer Prize in 1946); and criticism. A textbook he cowrote with Cleanth Brooks, *Understanding Poetry,* influenced generations of students. In 1986, he was named the first poet laureate of the United States.

Isaac Watts (1674–1748), *pp.* 589–94
Isaac Watts was born in Southampton, England, and educated in the city's grammar school and the Nonconformist academy at Stoke Newington. His father was a clothier who later became a Nonconformist schoolmaster. Watts became minister of Mark Lane Chapel, London, in 1702; when overwork led to illness in 1712, he moved into the household of Sir Thomas and Lady Abney, where he remained the rest of his life. Although he wrote theological and educational works, Pindaric odes, blank verse, and experimental poems such as "The Day of Judgment," which is in English Sapphics, he is chiefly remembered for his *Divine Songs for Children* (1715) and four collections of hymns. The volume *The Psalms of David Imitated in the Language of the New Testament* (1719) contains some of the most famous hymns in English. Watts wanted his poems to "elevate" readers "to the most delightful and divine Sensations" and to provide models of appropriate Christian responses to trial and difficulty.

Charles Wesley (1707–1788), *pp.* 652–55
Charles Wesley was born at Epworth Rectory, Lincolnshire, England. Like his older brother John Wesley, the founder of Methodism, he was educated at Christ Church, Oxford. Ordained in the Anglican Church, he accompanied John to Georgia in 1735 to act as secretary to James Edward Oglethorpe, governor of the colony, but returned to England the following year. When the established Church charged him with "irregularity," he became an itinerant minister. For seventeen years, he traveled the countryside, preaching and helping groups of believers to found churches. He retired in 1756 due to poor health and lived out his last years in Bath and London. An accomplished poet who wrote on a variety of subjects—including love, marriage, and family life—he is best-known as an extraordinarily prolific hymn writer, publishing some sixty-five hundred hymns in his lifetime, many of which remain popular today.

Phillis Wheatley (ca. 1753–1784), *pp.* 719–23
Phillis Wheatley was born in Africa, sold into slavery, and in 1761 shipped to the slave market in Boston. She was bought by John Wheatley, a prosperous tailor, for his wife, Susannah. The family gave Wheatley a good education and encouraged her writing talent, and she published a poem in a Boston newspaper in 1767. In 1773, they sent her to London with their son, in the hope of strengthening her frail constitution. She published a collection of poems during her stay, but returned after a few months when her mistress fell ill. Freed on her return, she married John Peters, a free black man, in 1778; after bearing and burying three children, she died in poverty and obscurity. Influenced by John Milton and Alexander Pope, she characteristically wrote in rhymed iambic-pentameter couplets or the ballad form, often using highly artificial diction. Like other Puritan colonial writers, however, she employed an emotionally restrained, highly accessible, "plain" style for poems on religious subjects.

Walt Whitman (1819–1892), *pp. 1060–86*
Walt Whitman was born on Long Island, New York, and raised in Brooklyn. He left school at age eleven and worked as an office boy, a printer's apprentice, and a teacher before establishing himself as a journalist affiliated with several prominent New York newspapers. In 1862, moved by the scenes he witnessed while staying with his brother (a wounded Union soldier) in Washington, D.C., he spent several months visiting and nursing Civil War veterans. This work found its way into his 1865 poetry volume, *Drum-Taps*. After the war, Whitman worked briefly at the Department of the Interior—he was fired for being the author of the "scandalous" *Leaves of Grass* (1855)—and for several years at the office of the attorney general. After suffering a debilitating stroke in 1873, he moved to his brother's home in Camden, New Jersey, where he remained until his death. In *Leaves of Grass*, the masterpiece that he revised for several decades, Whitman assumed the mantle of the public poet; his preface to the 1855 edition calls "the United States themselves" his subject. Poetry that celebrated the body and sexuality, however, opened him up to charges of obscenity. His prosody proved as controversial and ultimately as influential as his subject matter. He is usually considered, along with Emily Dickinson, the most important of nineteenth-century American poets.

Isabella Whitney (fl. 1567–1573), *pp.* 146–50
Isabella Whitney was born into a middle-class, Reformist family and apparently had two brothers (one of whom published a collection of poetry) and several sisters. Almost nothing is known of her personal life, although it is thought that by 1600 she had married and begun raising two children. Of the three books of poetry published by English women during the sixteenth century, two are hers. *Copy of a Letter Lately Written in Meter, by a Young Gentlewoman: to Her Unconstant Lover. With an Admonition to All Young Gentlewomen, and to*

All Other Maids in General to Beware of Men's Flattery (1567) contains both the letter described and the gentleman's reply; *A Sweet Nosegay or Pleasant Posy, Containing a Hundred and Ten Philosophical Flowers* (1573) was the first book of poems ever published by an Englishwoman. The "flowers," which render folk and Christian wisdom in ballad-stanza form, have not yet been republished in their entirety.

John Greenleaf Whittier (1807–1892),
pp. 957–60
John Greenleaf Whittier was born into a Quaker family on a farm near Haverhill, Massachusetts. Except for a year's study at Haverhill Academy, he received little formal education. With the help of literary-minded friends, Whittier found a number of jobs with small newspapers. In the 1830s, he became an early, ardent abolitionist; in the late 1860s, following the Civil War, he turned his full attention to writing, often on behalf of the causes he espoused. Fame came in 1866 with the publication of *Snow-Bound*, a recollective idyll on his childhood. Several of his religious poems were set to music and became popular hymns, but his reputation rests on the poems that capture the essence of preindustrial life in the villages of New England.

Richard Wilbur (b. 1921), *pp. 1632–41*
Richard Wilbur was born in New York City and educated at Amherst College and Harvard University. He enlisted in the army in 1942 and served as a cryptographer. His first volume of poems, *The Beautiful Changes,* was published in 1947; since that early success, he has become known as one of America's major formalist poets. An acclaimed writer for children and literary essayist, he is also a translator, and his rhymed versions of Molière, in particular, have won him international esteem. He was poet laureate of the United States in 1987–88 and has taught at many institutions, including Harvard, Wellesley College, Wesleyan University, and Smith College. He lives in western Massachusetts and in Key West, Florida.

C. K. Williams (b. 1936), *pp. 1869–72*
C(harles) K(enneth) Williams was born in Newark, New Jersey. He was educated at Bucknell College and the University of Pennsylvania. He established a poetry-therapy program for emotionally disturbed adolescents, served as a contributing editor to *American Poetry Review,* and ghostwrote articles on psychiatry and architecture, before beginning an academic career. Having taught at a number of colleges and universities, he now teaches at Princeton University and lives part of each year in Paris. In addition to poetry, he has published translations, including Sophocles' *Women of Trachis* and Euripides' *The Bacchae.* Williams writes almost exclusively in long and discursive lines

and has a particular facility for depicting dramatic situations.

William Carlos Williams (1883–1963),
pp. 1272–83
William Carlos Williams was born in Rutherford, New Jersey. In 1906, he earned an M.D. from the University of Pennsylvania, where he met the poets Ezra Pound and H. D. In 1910, he opened a pediatrics practice in Rutherford, where, except for a year's "sabbatical" in Europe, he lived and practiced medicine for the rest of his life. Although strongly established in Rutherford, Williams was hardly provincial. He moved in New York's avant-garde circles—along with the poets Marianne Moore and Wallace Stevens—and was affiliated with several short-lived but influential journals. In addition to poetry, he wrote fiction, drama, and essays. Williams was an early proponent of Imagism, a movement he valued for its stripping away of conventions. Later, he declared himself an Objectivist. Williams called on his contemporaries to create a distinctly American art, firmly rooted in particulars: "No ideas but in things," he insisted. His epic, *Paterson* (1946–58), is a five-volume poem that recounts the history of Rutherford and nearby Paterson and transforms it into the locus of modern humanity.

Greg Williamson (b. 1964), *pp. 2023–25*
Greg Williamson was born in Columbia, Ohio, and raised in Nashville, Tennessee. He holds degrees from Vanderbilt University and the University of Wisconsin at Madison, as well as from Johns Hopkins University, where he now teaches in the Writing Seminars. The author of two volumes of poetry, he is an ingenious inventor of forms, most notably of the "double exposure."

**John Wilmot, Earl of Rochester
(1647–1680),** *pp. 549–53*
John Wilmot was born at Ditchley, Oxfordshire, England, to a Cavalier hero and a devout Puritanical mother. After attending Wadham College, Oxford, he toured Europe, returning in 1664. He quickly became a favorite of King Charles II and a leading member of the court "wits." At age eighteen, he abducted the heiress Elizabeth Malet and was consequently imprisoned in the Tower of London. He married her eighteen months later, having regained his position by serving courageously in the second Dutch War (1665). His time was then divided between family life in the country and life in London with a number of mistresses, including Elizabeth Barry, a popular actress. According to Samuel Johnson, Rochester "blazed out his youth and health in lavish voluptuousness" (he claimed that he went five years without being sober); and by his early thirties, drink and venereal disease were exacting a price. He consulted a number of theologians, including the royal

chaplain, Gilbert Burnet, who wrote a highly popular pamphlet describing Rochester's renunciation of skepticism and conversion to Christianity. A friend of many poets including John Dryden and Aphra Behn, Rochester was renowned both as a satirist and as the author of erotic, sometimes pornographic, poetry, much of which was meant to be circulated in manuscript. He also wrote dramatic prologues and epilogues, imitations and adaptations of classical authors, and dramatic poems of self-analysis both comic and grim.

Eleanor Wilner (b. 1937), *pp. 1879–82*
Eleanor Wilner was born in Cleveland, Ohio. She was educated at Goucher College and Johns Hopkins University, from which she received a Ph.D. A lifelong civil rights and peace activist, she worked as a newspaper reporter, as a feature writer at a radio station, and as a consultant to the Maryland State Commission on the Aging before beginning an academic career. She has taught at many institutions, including the University of Chicago, Northwestern University, and Smith College. She currently teaches at Warren Wilson College and lives in Philadelphia.

William Wordsworth (1770–1850), *pp. 763–805*
William Wordsworth was born in Cockermouth, Cumberland, in the north of England's Lake District, and was educated at St. John's College, Cambridge. A walking tour of Europe in his early twenties brought him into contact with the first throes of the French Revolution, whose ideals he supported until the onset of the Terror. Upon his return to England, he settled with his sister, Dorothy, in the Lake District, where, apart from some few brief travels, he remained for the rest of his life. In 1795, he met the poet Samuel Taylor Coleridge, with whom he published *Lyrical Ballads* (1798), one of the most important and innovative works in the history of English literature. In his later years, he grew increasingly conservative, and many former devotees accused him of apostasy, but his poetry remained both popular and influential—so influential and so formative of modern ideas about poetry that the scope of his achievement is easily overlooked. In his preface to the second edition (1800) of the *Lyrical Ballads,* Wordsworth attacks the poetic diction and elaborate figures of speech characteristic of eighteenth-century poetry, asserting that he had "taken as much pains to avoid it as others take to produce it," and advocating the "language really used by men." He succeeded Robert Southey as poet laureate in 1843 and completed a fully revised, six-volume edition of his work before his death.

Charles Wright (b. 1935), *pp. 1865–68*
Charles Wright was born in Pickwick Dam, Tennessee. After his graduation from Davidson College, he served in the Intelligence Corps of the U.S. Army, in Italy. Having further studied at the University of Iowa (under Donald Justice) and in Rome, he published his first book, *Six Poems,* in 1965. He has taught widely, at several institutions in Italy and at the University of California at Irvine. He now lives in Charlottesville, Virginia, where he has been on the faculty of the University of Virginia since 1983. He is known both for his erudition (Italian and East Asian literature are among the influences in his poems) and for his attachment to rural life and landscape, especially that of Appalachia.

James Wright (1927–1980), *pp. 1749–51*
James Wright was born and raised in Martin's Ferry, Ohio. Upon graduation from high school, he joined the army and was stationed in occupied Japan. After his military service, he attended Kenyon College, where he studied with the poet John Crowe Ransom, and the University of Washington, where he studied with the poet Theodore Roethke. He later taught at the University of Minnesota and Hunter College. Influenced by the psychologist Carl Jung, the Expressionist poet Georg Trakl, and South American Surrealists Pablo Neruda and Caesar Vallejo, he developed a style of juxtaposing disparate images and relying on the subconscious mind to intuit connections between them. He was also a poet of social concerns, often writing of the working class.

Judith Wright (1915–2000), *pp. 1577–80*
Judith Wright was born in Armidale, New South Wales, Australia, and was educated at the Universities of Sydney and Queensland. Active in the antiwar movement of the 1960s, she later became a conservationist, and she ascribed her interest in the environment to working the land at her family's estate at Willamumbi during World War II. Wright made her home at Mount Tambourine, Queensland, for many years, but moved to an animal preserve near Braidwood, New South Wales. She wrote prolifically in a number of genres, including poetry, criticism, fiction, and children's fiction. She was awarded the Queen's Gold Medal for Poetry in 1992, and her *Collected Poems, 1942–1985* was published in 1994.

Kit Wright (b. 1944), *pp. 1946–47*
Kit Wright was born in Kent, England, and educated at New College, Oxford. He was a lecturer in Canada before becoming, in 1970, education officer at the Poetry Society in London, a post he held for five years. From 1977 to 1979, he was Fellow Commoner in Creative Art at Trinity College, Cambridge. His first volume of poems, *The Bear Looked over the Mountain* (1977) won the Geoffrey Faber Memorial Prize. His collection *Hoping It Might Be So* (2000) brings together poems spanning nearly thirty years. He

is also a prolific writer for children and a broadcaster.

Richard Wright (1908–1960), *pp. 1502–03*
Richard Wright was born in Rucker's Plantation, Mississippi, the child of a sharecropper and the grandchild of slaves. He was raised by various relatives across the South before moving to Chicago, where he wrote for the Federal Writers' Project. He became a member of the Communist Party and an editor of *The Daily Worker*. Fame came to him on the publication of his best-selling novel, *Native Son* (1940). In 1942, he left the Communist Party and moved with his family to Paris, where he became active in African nationalism. Widely regarded for his novels but living in illness and poverty, he turned, in his final year, to an early love, poetry, and wrote thousands of haiku.

Mary Wroth (1587–1651?), *pp. 347–53*
Lady Mary Wroth was born into an aristocratic family. Her mother, Barbara Gamage, a first cousin of Sir Walter Ralegh, was praised by Ben Jonson for ensuring that her children were "well taught." Wroth's father, Robert Sidney, her uncle, Philip Sidney, and her aunt, Mary Sidney, were all poets. Her arranged marriage to Sir Robert Wroth was unhappy; after his death in 1614, she had two children by her lover and cousin, William Herbert, third earl of Pembroke and Montgomery. In 1621, she boldly published *The Countess of Montgomery's Urania*, addressed to her lover's wife. Like Philip Sidney's *Arcadia*, on which it is modeled, this long prose romance is interspersed with poems in a variety of forms and meters. Appended to the romance is a sonnet sequence, *Pamphilia to Amphilanthus*, similarly modeled on Sidney's sonnet sequence, *Astrophil and Stella*, but with a male love-object and narrated from the perspective of a woman. The *Urania* caused a scandal because it contained thinly veiled satire of well-known court figures, and Wroth's continuation of the work, like her pastoral verse play, *Love's Victory*, was not published. Ben Jonson dedicated *The Alchemist* to Wroth and, in a sonnet addressed to her, praised her poems for making him a "better lover, and much better poet."

Thomas Wyatt (1503–1542), *pp. 126–36*
Thomas Wyatt was born at Allingham Castle, Kent, England, and educated at St. John's College, Cambridge. He held various positions at court and served on diplomatic missions to France, Spain, and Italy. Although he was knighted in 1535, his position as a courtier was never secure. Imprisoned in 1534 for brawling and perhaps for sexual misconduct (he had separated from his wife), he was again imprisoned, after a quarrel with the duke of Suffolk, in 1536. Some have linked this imprisonment also with the fall of Henry VIII's second wife, Anne Bol-

eyn. Said to have been Wyatt's mistress, Boleyn is almost certainly an allegorical referent of Wyatt's poem "Whoso List to Hunt" and perhaps of other poems. Released soon after her execution—which he witnessed through a grate from his own cell in Bell Tower of the Tower of London—Wyatt fell from royal favor again in 1541, when he was accused of treason; and in 1554, during the reign of Queen Mary, his son, Thomas Wyatt "the younger," was hanged for treason. It was probably to avoid any associations to Wyatt's son that Richard Tottel left Wyatt "the elder's" name off the title page of the famous anthology of "songs and sonnets" that he published in 1557, the last year of Mary's reign. Although Tottel praises the "weightiness of the deepwitted Sir Thomas Wyatt the Elder's verse" in the preface and includes ninety-seven of Wyatt's poems in the first edition of the anthology, the title page mentions only Wyatt's younger poetic imitator, Henry Howard, "late earl of Surrey." Tottel regularized the meter of many of Wyatt's poems and added titles to them, but most also survive in manuscript versions, some written and corrected in Wyatt's hand; they exhibit a great variety of tones, forms, and rhythms. As a translator of Petrarch, Wyatt introduced the sonnet form to English; he also enriched English literature with satiric verse epistles modeled on classical and Italian poems.

Elinor Wylie (1885–1928), *pp. 1310–11*
Elinor Wylie (née Hoyt) was born in Somerville, New Jersey, to a prominent family. Apart from a college preparatory course, she was educated at home, learning French, German, and drawing. A socialite who courted scandal when she left her husband and child, she lived at various times in England, New York City, and Washington, D.C., and counted the writers Dorothy Parker, Ernest Hemingway, Edmund Wilson, and Edna St. Vincent Millay among her friends. In addition, her work brought her the respect of prominent writers such as W. B. Yeats, who admired her poems, and William Faulkner, Max Beerbohm, and Aldous Huxley, who praised her fiction.

William Butler Yeats (1865–1939),
pp. 1188–1211
W. B. Yeats was born in Sandymount, Dublin, to a lawyer turned portrait-painter and his wife, both of English Protestant stock, though both families had lived in Ireland for several generations. He studied painting at the Dublin Metropolitan School of Art before turning his full attention to literature. Yeats's childhood and early manhood were spent in Sligo, London, and Dublin, and each contributed something to his development. In Sligo, he acquired a knowledge of the peasantry's life and vigorous folklore. In London in the 1890s, he met the important poets of the day. In Dublin, he was influenced

by the currents of Irish nationalism and, although often disagreeing with those who wished to use literature for crude political ends, nevertheless learned to see his poetry as contributing to a rejuvenated Irish culture. His work falls into three main periods. In the first, he wrote dreamy poems and plays, laden with poetic diction, many of them expressing his love for Maud Gonne, a beautiful actress and violent nationalist, who persistently refused to marry him. His reading of the German philosopher Friedrich Nietzsche in 1902 prompted him to abandon the subservient posture of the courtly lover, as his work in the theater was making his writing less ornate and more colloquial. The second period saw him involved—with Lady Gregory and J. M. Synge—in the 1904 founding of the Abbey Theatre and its subsequent rise and decline. He was becoming a national figure. Three public controversies moved him to anger and to poetry: the first was over the hounding of "the uncrowned king of Ireland," Charles Stewart Parnell; the second, over Synge's play *The Playboy of the Western World*, in 1907; the third, over the Lane pictures, a collection of modern French paintings not housed in Dublin due to lack of funding, in 1913. In each, the cause for which he fought was defeated by representatives of the Roman Catholic middle class; at last, bitterly turning his back on Ireland, Yeats moved to England. Then came the 1916 Easter Rising, mounted by members of the class and religion that had so long opposed him. Persuaded by

Gonne (whose estranged husband had been executed as a leader of the Rising) that "tragic dignity had returned to Ireland," Yeats returned. To mark his new commitment, he refurbished and occupied the Norman tower, on Lady Gregory's land, that was to become one of the central symbols of his later poetry. In 1917, he married a woman who, over the next twenty years, would prove so sympathetic to his imaginative needs that the automatic writing she produced for several years (believed by Yeats to have been dictated by spirits) gave him the elements of a symbolic system that he later worked out in his book *A Vision* (1925, 1937). This system prompted the later and greater poems of his third period, those of *The Tower* (1928) and *The Winding Stair* (1933). In 1922, Yeats was appointed a senator of the recently established Irish Free State, and the following year he was awarded the Nobel Prize for Literature.

Cynthia Zarin (b. 1959), *pp. 2013–15*
Cynthia Zarin was born in New York City and raised on Long Island. She was educated at Harvard College and Columbia University. Artist-in-residence at the Cathedral of St. John the Divine, in New York City, she is a versatile writer of nonfiction and has published several children's books as well as three volumes of poetry. She has taught at the Columbia School of Journalism and Princeton University, and is a staff writer for *The New Yorker*.

PERMISSIONS ACKNOWLEDGMENTS

Adcock, Fleur: "The Ex-Queen Among the Astronomers," "Poem Ended by a Death," and "The Soho Hospital for Women" from POEMS 1960–2000. Copyright © 2000 by Fleur Adcock. Reprinted by permission of the publisher, Bloodaxe Books Ltd.

Ali, Agha Shahid: "The Dacca Gauzes" from THE HALF-INCH HIMALAYAS. Copyright © 1987 by Agha Shahid Ali. Reprinted with permission of Wesleyan University Press. "Lenox Hill" from ROOMS ARE NEVER FINISHED by Agha Shahid Ali. Copyright © 2002 by Agha Shahid Ali. Used by permission of W. W. Norton & Co., Inc.

Ammons, A. R.: "The Arc Inside and Out," copyright © 1971 by A. R. Ammons. "The City Limits," copyright © 1971 by A. R. Ammons. "Corsons Inlet," copyright © 1963 by A. R. Ammons. From THE SELECTED POEMS: EXPANDED EDITION by A. R. Ammons. "Pet Panther," copyright © 1983 by A. R. Ammons. From LAKE EFFECT COUNTRY by A. R. Ammons. "All's All," copyright © 1996 by A. R. Ammons. From BRINK ROAD by A. R. Ammons. Used by permission of W. W. Norton & Co., Inc.

Armitage, Simon: "The Shout" from THE UNIVERSAL HOME DOCTOR. "The Two of Us" and excerpt from "Killing Time" from SELECTED POEMS. Reprinted by permission of David Godwin Associates for the author and Faber & Faber Ltd.

Ashbery, John: "Brute Image" from HOTEL LAUTREAMONT. Copyright © 1992 by John Ashbery. "Soonest Mended" from A DOUBLE DREAM OF SPRING. Copyright © 1970, 1969, 1968, 1967, 1966 by John Ashbery. "The Painter" from SOME TREES. Copyright © 1956 by John Ashbery. "Paradoxes and Oxymorons" from SHADOW TRAIN. Copyright © 1980, 1981 by John Ashbery. Reprinted by permission of Georges Borchardt, Inc. for the author. "Ode to Bill" from SELF-PORTRAIT IN A CONVEX MIRROR by John Ashbery, copyright © 1974 by John Ashbery. Used by permission of Viking Penguin, a division of Penguin Group (USA), Inc. All poems published in Great Britain by Carcanet Press, Ltd. and reprinted by the publisher's permission.

Atwood, Margaret: "At the Tourist Center in Boston" from SELECTED POEMS 1966–1984 by Margaret Atwood. Copyright © 1990 by Margaret Atwood. Reprinted by permission of Oxford University Press Canada. "You Begin" from SELECTED POEMS II: POEMS SELECTED AND NEW, 1976–1986 by Margaret Atwood, copyright © 1987 by Margaret Atwood. Also published in SELECTED POEMS 1966–1984, copyright © 1990 by Margaret Atwood. Reprinted by permission of Houghton Mifflin Co., Oxford University Press Canada, and Time Warner Books UK. All rights reserved. "Up" and "Flowers" from MORNING IN THE BURNED HOUSE by Margaret Atwood. Copyright © 1995 by Margaret Atwood. Reprinted by permission of Houghton Mifflin Co., McClelland & Stewart Ltd. The Canadian Publishers, and Curtis Brown Group Ltd., London on behalf of the author. All rights reserved. "This Is a Photograph of Me" from THE CIRCLE GAME by Margaret Atwood, copyright © 1968, 1998 by Margaret Atwood. Reprinted with the permission of House of Anansi Press, Toronto.

Auden, W. H.: "As I Walked Out One Evening," copyright © 1940 and renewed 1968 by W. H. Auden. "Twelve Songs, IX, Funeral Blues," copyright © 1940 and renewed 1968 by W. H. Auden. "Twelve Songs XII, O Tell Me the Truth about Love," copyright © 1940 and renewed 1968 by W. H. Auden. "Lullaby (Lay Your Sleeping Head, My Love)," copyright © 1972 by W. H. Auden. "Spain 1937," copyright © 1940 and renewed 1968 by W. H. Auden. "Musée des Beaux Arts," copyright © 1940 and renewed 1968 by W. H. Auden. "In Memory of W. B. Yeats," copyright © 1940 and renewed 1968 by W. H. Auden. "In Praise of Limestone," copyright © 1951 by W. H. Auden. "The Shield of Achilles," copyright © 1952 by W. H. Auden. "September 1, 1939," copyright © 1940 and renewed 1968 by W. H. Auden. "Their Lonely Betters," copyright © 1951 by W. H. Auden. From COLLECTED POEMS by W. H. Auden. Used by permission of Random House, Inc. and Faber & Faber Ltd.

Baraka, Amiri: "An Agony, As Now" from THE DEAD LECTURER by Amiri Baraka. Copyright © by Amiri Baraka. "In Memory of Radio" from THE AMIRI BARAKA READER. Copyright © by Amiri Baraka. Reprinted by permission of SLL/ Sterling Lord Literistic, Inc.

Baxter, James K.: "Wild Bees," "East Coast Journey," and "New Zealand" published in COLLECTED POEMS OF JAMES K. BAXTER, ed. J. R. Weir, Oxford University Press, Australia and New Zealand, 1979. Reproduced by permission of J. C. Baxter.

Bernstein, Charles: "frequently unasked questions," "why we ask you not to touch," and "this poem intentionally left blank" from WITH STRINGS (Chicago: Univ. of Chicago Press, 2001). Used by permission of the author. "Of Time and the Line" from ROUGH TRADES (Los Angeles: Green Integer Books, 1991), pp. 42–43. Copyright © 1991 by Charles Bernstein. Reprinted with the permission of the publisher.

Berryman, John: From "Homage to Mistress Bradstreet" and "A Sympathy, A Welcome" from COLLECTED POEMS 1937–1971 by John Berryman. Copyright © 1989 by Kate Donahue Berryman. Dream Songs #1, #4, #14, #29, #40, #145, #324, #382 from THE DREAM SONGS by John Berryman. Copyright © 1969 by John Berryman. Copyright renewed 1997 by Kate Donahue Berryman. Reprinted by permission of Farrar, Straus, & Giroux, LLC and Faber & Faber Ltd.

Betjeman, John: "Death in Leamington," "The Arrest of Oscar Wilde at the Cadogan Hotel," "East Anglian Bathe," and "False Security" from COLLECTED POEMS by John Betjeman. Copyright © 1958, 1962, 1970, 1979 by John Betjeman. Reproduced by permission of John Murray Publishers.

Birney, Earle: "Bushed" and "The Bear on the Delhi Road" from THE COLLECTED POEMS OF EARLE BIRNEY. Used by permission, McClelland & Stewart Ltd. The Canadian Publishers.

Bishop, Elizabeth: "The Armadillo," "Casabianca," "Filling Station," "The Fish," "In the Waiting Room," "The Moose," "One Art," "Sandpiper," and "Sestina" from THE COMPLETE POEMS 1927–1979 by Elizabeth Bishop. Copyright © 1979, 1983 by Alice Helen Methfessel. Reprinted by permission of Farrar, Straus and Giroux, LLC.

Blunden, Edmund: "Forefathers" and "1916 seen from 1921" from SELECTED POEMS, ed. by Robyn Marsack (1982). Reprinted by permission of Carcanet Press Ltd.

Bly, Robert: "Waking from Sleep" from SILENCE IN THE SNOWY FIELDS by Robert Bly, Wesleyan University Press,

1962. Copyright © 1962 by Robert Bly. Reprinted with his permission. "Johnson's Cabinet Watched by Ants" from THE LIGHT AROUND THE BODY by Robert Bly. Copyright © 1967 by Robert Bly. Copyright renewed 1995 by Robert Bly. Reprinted by permission of HarperCollins Publishers Inc.

Bogan, Louise: "Juan's Song," "Man Alone," "Medusa," "Night," "Roman Fountain," and "Song for the Last Act" from THE BLUE ESTUARIES by Louise Bogan. Copyright © 1968 by Louise Bogan. Copyright renewed 1996 by Ruth Limmer. Reprinted by permission of Farrar, Straus & Giroux, LLC.

Boland, Eavan: "That the Science of Cartography Is Limited," "The Dolls Museum in Dublin," and "The Pomegranate"from IN A TIME OF VIOLENCE, copyright © 1994 by Eavan Boland. Reprinted by permission of W. W. Norton & Co., Inc. and Carcanet Press Ltd.

Brathwaite, Edward Kamau: "New World A-Comin', 1, 2" and "Ancestors 1, 2, 3" from ARRIVANTS: A NEW WORLD TRILOGY (1973) by Edward Kamau Brathwaite. Reprinted by permission of Oxford University Press (UK).

Brooks, Gwendolyn: "kitchenette building," "my dreams, my works, must wait till after hell," "the birth in a narrow room," "the rites for Cousin Vit," "The Bean Eaters," "We Real Cool," "Medgar Evers," and "Boy Breaking Glass" from BLACKS (Chicago: Third World Press, 1987). Reprinted with permission of the author.

Brown, George MacKay: "The Old Women," "Haddock Fisherman," and "Shroud" from SELECTED POEMS 1954–1983 by George MacKay Brown. Copyright © 1959, 1965, 1971 by George MacKay Brown. Reproduced by permission of John Murray Publishers.

Brown, Sterling A.: "Slim in Atlanta," copyright © 1932 by Harcourt Brace & Co. Copyright renewed 1960 by Sterling A. Brown. "Chillen Get Shoes," "Conjured," and "Bitter Fruit of the Tree," copyright © 1980 by Sterling A. Brown. From THE COLLECTED POEMS OF STERLING A. BROWN, ed. by Michael S. Harper. Reprinted by permission of HarperCollins Publishers, Inc.

Brownjohn, Alan: "Common Sense" from COLLECTED POEMS 1952–83 by Alan Brownjohn. Copyright © 1983 by Alan Brownjohn. Reprinted by permission of Rosica Colin Ltd.

Bunting, Basil: Excerpt from "Briggflatts: An Autobiography" from COMPLETE POEMS of Basil Bunting (2000). Reprinted by permission of Bloodaxe Books Ltd.

Bynner, Witter: "Chinese Drawings: A Philosopher," "Haskell," "More Lovely than Antiquity," and "The Wintry Mind" from SELECTED POEMS by Witter Bynner. Copyright © 1978 by The Witter Bynner Foundation. Reprinted by permission of Farrar, Straus & Giroux, LLC.

Campbell, Roy: "The Zulu Girl" and "The Sisters" from THE COLLECTED POEMS OF ROY CAMPBELL. Reprinted by permission of Francisco Campbell Custodio and Jonathan Ball Publishers/A. D. Donker Publishers.

Carson, Anne: "IV" from THE BEAUTY OF THE HUSBAND by Anne Carson, copyright © 2001 by Anne Carson. "New Rule" and "Sumptuous Destitution" from MEN IN THE OFF HOURS by Anne Carson, copyright © 2000 by Anne Carson. Used by permission of the publishers, Alfred A. Knopf, a division of Random House, Inc. and Jonathan Cape, a division of The Random House Group Limited.

Causley, Charles: "Armistice Day," "At the British War Cemetery, Bayeux," and "Eden Rock" from COLLECTED POEMS 1951–1975 (Macmillan). Reprinted by permission of David Higham Associates.

Christopher, Nicholas: "The Palm Reader" and "Far from Home" from 5° AND OTHER POEMS by Nicholas Christopher. Reprinted by permission of the author.

Clampitt, Amy: "Beach Glass," "Beethoven, Opus 111," "The Sun Underfoot among the Sundews," and "The Cormorant in Its Element" from THE KINGFISHER by Amy Clampitt, copyright © 1983 by Amy Clampitt. "Syrinx" from THE COLLECTED POEMS OF AMY CLAMPITT by Amy Clampitt, copyright © 1997 by the Estate of Amy Clampitt. Used by permission of Alfred A. Knopf, a division of Random House, Inc. and Faber & Faber Ltd.

Collins, Billy: "Litany," copyright © 2002 by Billy Collins, from NINE HORSES by Billy Collins. Used by permission of Random House, Inc. and SLL/Sterling Lord Literistic, Inc. "Japan" from PICNIC, LIGHTNING by Billy Collins, copyright © 1998. Reprinted by permission of the University of Pittsburgh Press.

Cope, Wendy: "Bloody Men," "Flowers," "Valentine," and "Serious Concerns" from SERIOUS CONCERNS. Copyright © 1992 by Wendy Cope. Reprinted by permission of Faber & Faber Ltd.

Corn, Alfred: "Navidad, St. Nicholas Ave." from THE WEST DOOR by Alfred Corn. Copyright © 1988 by Alfred Corn. Reprinted by permission of the author. "A Conch from Sicily" from PRESENT by Alfred Corn. Copyright © 1997 by Alfred Corn. Reprinted by permission of Counterpoint Press, a member of Perseus Books, LLC.

Corso, Gregory: "Marriage" from THE HAPPY BIRTHDAY OF DEATH, copyright © 1960 by New Directions Publishing Corp. Reprinted by permission of New Directions Publishing Corp.

Crane, Hart: "At Melville's Tomb," "My Grandmother's Love Letters," "Proem: To Brooklyn Bridge," "To Emily Dickinson," "Voyages I, II, III, IV, V, VI" from COMPLETE POEMS OF HART CRANE by Hart Crane, ed. by Marc Simon. Copyright © 1933, 1958, 1966 by Liveright Publishing Corp. Copyright © 1986 by Marc Simon. Used by permission of Liveright Publishing Corp.

Creeley, Robert: "Bresson's Movies" from MIRRORS, copyright © 1983 by Robert Creeley. Reprinted by permission of New Directions Publishing Corp. and Marion Boyars Publishers. "I Know a Man," "Heroes," and "The World" from THE COLLECTED POEMS OF ROBERT CREELEY, 1945–1975. Copyright © 1983 by The Regents of the University of California. Reprinted with the permission of the University of California Press.

Cullen, Countee: "Heritage," "Incident," and "Yet Do I Marvel" are from the Countee Cullen Collection, Amistad Research Center at Tulane University. Reprinted by permission.

Cummings, E. E.: "All in green went my love riding," "the Cambridge ladies who live in furnished souls," "Spring is like a perhaps hand," 'next to of course god america i," "since feeling is first," "somewhere i have never travelled,gladly beyond," "anyone lived in a pretty how town," "may i feel said he," "who are you,little i" from COMPLETE POEMS: 1904–1962 by E. E. Cummings, ed. by George J. Firmage. Copyright © 1923, 1925, 1926, 1931, 1935, 1938, 1939, 1940, 1944, 1945, 1946, 1947, 1948, 1949, 1950, 1951, 1952, 1953, 1954, © 1955, 1956, 1957, 1958, 1959, 1960, 1961, 1962, 1963, 1966, 1967, 1968, 1972, 1973, 1974, 1975, 1976, 1977, 1978, 1979, 1980, 1981, 1982, 1983, 1984, 1985, 1986, 1987, 1988, 1989, 1990, 1991 by the Trustees for the E. E. Cummings Trust. Copyright © 1973, 1976, 1978, 1979, 1981, 1983, 1985, 1991 by George James Firmage. Used by permission of Liveright Publishing Corp.

1923, 1928, 1947, 1969 by Henry Holt and Co. Published in Great Britain by Jonathan Cape. Used by permission of Henry Holt and Co., LLC and the Estate of Robert Frost and The Random House Group Ltd.

Gascoyne, David: "Yves Tanguy" and "Ecce Homo" from COLLECTED POEMS (1970) by David Gascoyne. Used by permission of Oxford University Press (UK).

Ginsberg, Allen: Part 1 from "Howl," copyright © 1955 by Allen Ginsberg, "To Aunt Rose," copyright © 1958 by Allen Ginsberg, "A Supermarket in California," copyright © 1955 by Allen Ginsberg. From COLLECTED POEMS 1947–1980 by Allen Ginsberg. Copyright © 1984 by Allen Ginsberg. Reprinted by permission of HarperCollins Publishers, Inc. and Penguin Books Ltd.

Gioia, Dana: "Prayer" and "The Next Poem" from THE GODS OF WINTER by Dana Gioia. Copyright © 1991 by Dana Gioia. Reprinted with the permission of Graywolf Press, St. Paul, MN 55114.

Glück, Louise: "Gretel in Darkness" from THE HOUSE ON THE MARSHLAND from THE FIRST FOUR BOOKS OF POEMS by Louise Glück. Copyright © 1968, 1971, 1973, 1974, 1975, 1976, 1977, 1978, 1979, 1980, 1985, 1995 by Louise Glück. "Vita Nova" from VITA NOVA by Louise Glück. Copyright © 1999 by Louise Glück. "The Garden," p. 16 from THE WILD IRIS by Louise Glück. Copyright © 1993 by Louise Glück. Reprinted by permission of HarperCollins Publishers, Inc. and Carcanet Press Ltd.

Graham, Jorie: "The Geese," "At Luca Signorelli's Resurrection of the Body," and "The Surface" from THE DREAM OF THE UNIFIED FIELD: POEMS 1974–1994 by Jorie Graham. Copyright © 1995 by Jorie Graham. Reprinted by permission of HarperCollins Publishers, Inc. and Carcanet Press Ltd.

Graves, Robert: "Love Without Hope," "In Broken Images," "Warning to Children," "The Persian Version," "To Juan at the Winter Solstice," and "The White Goddess" from COMPLETE POEMS (2000), by Robert Graves. Reprinted with the permission of Carcanet Press Ltd.

Greenlaw, Lavinia: "Skin Full," "What's Going On," and "A World Where News Travelled Slowly" from A WORLD WHERE NEWS TRAVELLED SLOWLY. Reprinted by permission of Faber & Faber Ltd.

Guest, Barbara: "Twilight Polka Dots" from FAIR REALISM (Los Angeles: Green Integer Books, 1989), pp. 55–56. Copyright © 1989 by Barbara Guest. Reprinted with the permission of the author and publisher. "Roses" from SELECTED POEMS. Copyright © 1995, 1993, 1989, 1976, 1973, 1968, 1962 by Barbara Guest. Reprinted with the permission of the author.

Gunn, Thom: " 'All Do Not All Things Well,' " "Black Jackets," "From the Wave," "A Map of the City," "The Missing," "My Sad Captains," and "On the Move" from COLLECTED POEMS by Thom Gunn. Copyright © 1994 by Thom Gunn. Reprinted by permission of Farrar, Straus and Giroux, LLC and Faber & Faber Ltd.

Gurney, Ivor: "To His Love," "The Silent One," and "First Time" from COLLECTED POEMS OF IVOR GURNEY (1982), ed. by P. J. Kavanagh. Reprinted with the permission of Carcanet Press Ltd.

Hall, Daniel: "Mangosteens" by Daniel Hall first appeared in THE NEW REPUBLIC, Dec. 6, 1993. Copyright © 1993 by Daniel Hall. Reprinted by permission of the author. "Love-Letter-Burning" from HERMIT WITH LANDSCAPE, copyright © 1990 by Daniel Hall. Reprinted by permission of Yale University Press.

Hall, Donald: "Exile" from THE ALLIGATOR BRIDE: POEMS NEW AND SELECTED by Donald Hall. Copyright © 1983 by Donald Hall. Reprinted by permission of the author. "Independence Day Letter" from WITHOUT: POEMS by Donald Hall. Copyright © 1998 by Donald Hall. "Prophecy" from THE ONE DAY by Donald Hall. Copyright © 1988 by Donald Hall. Reprinted by permission of Houghton Mifflin Co. All rights reserved.

Hamer, Richard, tr.: "Riddles 1, 2, 3," "The Wife's Lament," and excerpt from "The Seafarer" from A CHOICE OF ANGLO-SAXON VERSE. Copyright © 1970 by Richard Hamer. Reprinted with the permission of Faber & Faber Ltd.

Harrison, Tony: "On Not Being Milton," "Classics Society," "Them & [uz] I & II," "A Kumquat for John Keats," and "The Heartless Art" from SELECTED POEMS, 2nd ed. Copyright © 1984, 1987 by Tony Harrison. Reprinted with the permission of Gordon Dickerson.

Hass, Robert: "Tahoe in August" from HUMAN WISHES by Robert Hass. Copyright © 1989 by Robert Hass. Reprinted by permission of HarperCollins Publishers, Inc. "Meditation at Lagunitas" from PRAISE by Robert Hass. Copyright © 1974, 1975, 1976, 1977, 1978, 1979 by Robert Hass. First published by The Ecco Press in 1979. Reprinted by permission.

Hayden, Robert: " 'Mystery Boy' Looks for Kin in Nashville," "Night, Death, Mississippi," copyright © 1962, 1966 by Robert Hayden. "Mourning Poem for the Queen of Sunday," copyright © 1966 by Robert Hayden. "Paul Laurence Dunbar," copyright © 1978 by Robert Hayden. "Those Winter Sundays," copyright © 1966 by Robert Hayden. From COLLECTED POEMS OF ROBERT HAYDEN by Robert Hayden, ed. by Frederick Glaysher. Copyright © 1985 by Emma Hayden. Used by permission of Liveright Publishing Corp.

Heaney, Seamus: From BEOWULF, tr. by Seamus Heaney. Copyright © 2000 by Seamus Heaney. Used by permission of W. W. Norton & Co., Inc. and Faber & Faber Ltd. Excerpt from "Clearances," "Digging," "A Dream of Jealousy," "The Forge," "Fosterling," "Punishment," "The Settle Bed," "The Skunk," "The Skylight," excerpt from "Squarings," excerpt from "Station Island," and "Two Lorries" from OPENED GROUND: SELECTED POEMS 1966–1996 by Seamus Heaney. Copyright © 1998 by Seamus Heaney. "Casting and Gathering" from SEEING THINGS by Seamus Heaney. Copyright © 1991 by Seamus Heaney. Reprinted by permission of Farrar, Straus & Giroux, LLC and Faber & Faber Ltd.

Hecht, Anthony: "Death the Painter," copyright © 1995 by Anthony Hecht. Reprinted by permission of the author. "A Hill," "The Ghost in the Martini," "Still Life," and "The Dover Bitch" from COLLECTED EARLIER POEMS by Anthony Hecht, copyright © 1990 by Anthony E. Hecht. Used by permission of Alfred A. Knopf, a division of Random House, Inc. and the author. "The Book of Yolek" from THE TRANSPARENT MAN by Anthony Hecht, copyright © 1990 by Anthony E. Hecht. Used by permission of Alfred A. Knopf, a division of Random House, Inc.

Hill, Geoffrey: "The Laurel Axe" and "Lachrimae Verae" first published in TENEBRAE (1978), copyright © 1978, 1985 by Geoffrey Hill. "Veni Coronaberis," "The Distant Fury of Battle," and "The Guardians" first published in FOR THE UNFALLEN (1959), copyright © 1959, 1985 by Geoffrey Hill. "September Song" first published in KING LOG (1968), copyright © 1968, 1985 by Geoffrey Hill. VI, VII, VIII first published in MERCIAN HYMNS (1971), copyright © 1971, 1985 by Geoffrey Hill. From NEW AND COLLECTED POEMS, 1952–1992 by Geoffrey Hill. Copyright © 1994 by Geoffrey Hill. Published in Great Britain in COLLECTED POEMS by Geoffrey Hill. Reprinted by permission of Houghton Mifflin Co. and Penguin Books Ltd. All rights reserved.

Hine, Daryl: "Letting Go" and "Riddle" from POSTSCRIPTS by Daryl Hine, copyright © 1990 by Daryl Hine. Used by permission of Alfred A. Knopf, a division of Random House, Inc.

Hollander, John: "Swan and Shadow" from TYPES OF SHAPE (New Haven: Yale Univ. Press, 1991). Reprinted by permission of the author. "Adam's Task" from SELECTED POETRY by John Hollander, copyright © 1993 by John Hollander. "An Old-Fashioned Song" and "Variations on a Fragment by Trumbull Stickney" from TESSARAE AND OTHER POEMS by John Hollander, copyright © 1993 by John Hollander. Used by permission of Alfred A. Knopf, a division of Random House, Inc.

Hope, A. D.: "Imperial Adam," "Australia," "Advice to Young Ladies," and "Inscription for War" by A. D. Hope from COLLECTED POEMS 1930–1970. Reprinted by permission of Curtis Brown Pty Ltd.

Housman, A. E.: "Crossing Alone the Nighted Ferry" and "Here Dead Lie We Because We Did Not Choose" from THE COLLECTED POEMS OF A. E. HOUSMAN. Copyright © 1936 by Barclays Bank Ltd., © 1964 by Robert E. Symons, © 1965 by Henry Holt and Co. Reprinted by permission of Henry Holt and Co., LLC and The Society of Authors as the Literary Representative of the Estate of A. E. Housman. "Loveliest of Trees, the Cherry Now," "Reveille," "When I Watch the Living Meet," "To an Athlete Dying Young," "Is My Team Ploughing," "On Wenlock Edge the Wood's in Trouble," "From Far, from Eve and Morning," "With Rue My Heart Is Laden," " 'Terence, This Is Stupid Stuff . . . ,' " "Astronomy," "Epitaph on an Army of Mercenaries," "Crossing Alone the Nighted Ferry," and "Here Dead Lie We Because We Did Not Choose." Reprinted by permission of The Society of Authors as the Literary Representative of the Estate of A. E. Housman.

Howard, Richard: "Nikolaus Mardruz to his Master Ferdinand, Count of Tyrol, 1565" first appeared in THE YALE REVIEW, 83, #3 (July 1995). Copyright © 1995 by Richard Howard. Reprinted by permission of the author.

Hughes, Langston: From THE COLLECTED POEMS OF LANGSTON HUGHES by Langston Hughes, copyright © 1994 by The Estate of Langston Hughes. Used by permission of Alfred A. Knopf, a division of Random House, Inc. and Harold Ober Associates, Inc.

Hughes, Ted: "The Thought-Fox," "Wind," "Pike," "Theology," Examination at the Womb Door," "Daffodils," and "Platform One" from COLLECTED POEMS by Ted Hughes. Copyright © 2003 by The Estate of Ted Hughes. Reprinted by permission of Farrar, Straus, & Giroux, LLC and Faber & Faber Ltd.

Hugo, Richard: "The Lady in Kicking Horse Reservoir," copyright © 1973 by Richard Hugo. "The Way a Ghost Dissolves," from MAKING CERTAIN IT GOES ON: COLLECTED POEMS OF RICHARD HUGO by Richard Hugo. Copyright © 1984 by The Estate of Richard Hugo. Used by permission of W. W. Norton & Co., Inc.

Jackson, Laura Riding: FROM THE POEMS OF LAURA RIDING. Copyright © 2001 by the Board of Literary Management of the late Laura (Riding) Jackson. Reprinted by permission of Persea Books, Inc. (New York).

Jacobsen, Josephine: "Bus," "The Primer," and "Hourglass" from NEW AND SELECTED POEMS by Josephine Jacobsen. Copyright © 1974 by Josephine Jacobsen. Reprinted with the permission of the author.

Jarrell, Randall: "The Death of the Ball Turret Gunner," "Eighth Air Force," "A Field Hospital," "A Front," "A Man Meets a Woman in the Street," "Next Day," and "90 North" from THE COMPLETE POEMS by Randall Jarrell. Copyright © 1969, renewed 1997 by Mary von S. Jarrell. Reprinted by permission of Farrar, Straus & Giroux, LLC and Faber & Faber Ltd.

Jeffers, Robinson: "Hurt Hawks" from SELECTED POEMS, copyright © 1927 by R. Jeffers, renewed © 1955 by Robinson Jeffers. "Shine, Perishing Republic," "Boats in a Fog," "The Purse-Seine," and "Birds and Fishes" from THE SELECTED POETRY OF ROBINSON JEFFERS. Copyright © 1924, 1925, 1928, 1937, 1954 and renewed 1949, 1953, 1956 by Robinson Jeffers. Copyright © 1963 by Steuben Glass. Reprinted with the permission of Jeffers Literary Properties.

Jennings, Elizabeth: "One Flesh" and "My Grandmother" from COLLECTED POEMS 1953–1985 (Carcanet Press Ltd.). Reprinted by permission of David Higham Associates.

Justice, Donald: From NEW AND SELECTED POEMS by Donald Justice, copyright © 1995 by Donald Justice. Used by permission of Alfred A. Knopf, a division of Random House, Inc.

Kavanagh, Patrick: "Sanctity," excerpt from "The Great Hunger," "Epic," and "Canal Bank Walk" from COLLECTED POEMS (N.Y.: W. W. Norton & Co, Inc., 1964). Copyright © 1964 by Patrick Kavanagh. Reprinted with the permission of Devin-Adair Publishers, Inc., Old Greenwich, CT 06830.

Kees, Weldon: "What the Spider Heard," "Robinson," "When the Lease Is Up," and "For H. V." reprinted from THE COLLECTED POEMS OF WELDON KEES, ed. by Donald Justice, by permission of the University of Nebraska Press. Copyright © 1975 by the University of Nebraska Press. Copyright © renewed by the University of Nebraska Press.

Kenney, Richard: "Aubade," "Apples on Champlain," and "Sawmill" from ORRERY. Copyright © 1985 by Richard Kenney. Reprinted by permission of the author.

Keyes, Sidney: "War Poet," "Elegy," and excerpt from "The Foreign Gate" from COLLECTED POEMS OF SIDNEY KEYES, ed. by Michael Meyer (Routledge, 1988). Reprinted by permission of David Higham Associates.

Kinnell, Galway: "First Song" from WHAT A KINGDOM IT WAS by Galway Kinnell. Copyright © 1960, renewed 1988 by Galway Kinnell. "The Correspondence School Instructor Says Goodbye to His Poetry Students" and "After Making Love, We Hear Footsteps" from THREE BOOKS by Galway Kinnell. Copyright © 1993 by Galway Kinnell. Reprinted by permission of Houghton Mifflin Co. All rights reserved.

Kinsella, Thomas: "Ancestor," "Tear," and "Another September" from POEMS 1956–1973. Copyright © 1956, 1968, 1979 by Thomas Kinsella. Reprinted with the permission of Wake Forest University Press.

Kipling, Rudyard: "Tommy," "Recessional," and "Epitaphs of the War" from RUDYARD KIPLING'S VERSE: DEFINITIVE EDITION. Reprinted with the permission of A. P. Watt Ltd. on behalf of the National Trust for Places of Historic Interest of Natural Beauty.

Kizer, Carolyn: "The Erotic Philosophers" from COOL, CALM & COLLECTED: POEMS 1960–2000. Copyright © 2001 by Carolyn Kizer. Reprinted with the permission of Copper Canyon Press, P.O. Box 271, Port Townsend, WA 98368–0271.

Koch, Kenneth: "To My Twenties" from NEW ADDRESSES by Kenneth Koch. Reprinted by permission of the Kenneth Koch Literary Estate. "Energy in Sweden" from ONE TRAIN by Kenneth Koch (N.Y.: Alfred A. Knopf, 1994). Copyright © 1994 by Kenneth Koch. "Permanently," "You Were Wearing," and "Variations on a Theme by William Carlos Williams" from THANK YOU AND OTHER POEMS (N.Y.: Grove Press, 1962). Copyright © 1962 and renewed 1990 by Kenneth Koch. Reprinted by permission of the author.

Komunyakaa, Yusef: "Banking Potatoes," "The Smokehouse," and "Sunday Afternoons" from MAGIC CITY. Copyright © 1992 by Yusef Komunyakaa. "Facing It" from PLEASURE DOME. Copyright © 2001 by Yusef Komunyakaa. Reprinted with the permission of Wesleyan University Press.

Kunitz, Stanley: "He," "Robin Redbreast," and "Touch Me" from THE COLLECTED POEMS by Stanley Kunitz. Copyright © 2000 by Stanley Kunitz. Used by permission of W. W. Norton & Co., Inc.

Larkin, Philip: "Church Going" and "Born Yesterday" from THE LESS DECEIVED by Philip Larkin by permission of The Marvell Press, England and Australia. "Ambulances," "Aubade," "An Arundel Tomb," "The Explosion," "For Sidney Bechet," "MCMXIV," "Sad Steps," "Talking in Bed," "This Be The Verse," "The Trees," and "The Whitsun Weddings" from COLLECTED POEMS by Philip Larkin. Copyright © 1988, 1989 by the Estate of Philip Larkin. Reprinted by permission of Farrar, Straus & Giroux, LLC and Faber & Faber Ltd.

Lawrence, D. H.: "Snake," "Elemental," "Self-Protection," "Trees in the Garden," "The English Are So Nice!" "Andraitx—Pomegranate Flowers," "Bavarian Gentians," and "The Ship of Death" from THE COMPLETE POEMS OF D. H. LAWRENCE by D. H. Lawrence, ed. by V. de Sola Pinto and F. W. Roberts, copyright © 1964, 1971 by Angelo Ravagli and C. M. Weekley, Executors of the Estate of Frieda Lawrence Ravagli. Used by permission of Viking Penguin, a division of Penguin Group (USA), Inc.

Layton, Irving: "The Birth of Tragedy," "Berry Picking," and "The Cold Green Element" from THE COLLECTED POEMS OF IRVING LAYTON. Used by permission of McClelland & Stewart Ltd. The Canadian Publishers.

Lee, Li-Young: "Persimmons" from ROSE. Copyright © 1986 by Li-Young Lee. "Out of Hiding" from BOOK OF MY NIGHTS. Copyright © 2001 by Li-Young Lee. Reprinted with the permission of BOA Editions Ltd.

Leithauser, Brad: "Old Bachelor Brother" from THE MAIL FROM ANYWHERE by Brad Leithauser, copyright © 1990 by Brad Leithauser. "The Buried Graves" and "In Minako Wada's House" from CATS OF THE TEMPLE by Brad Leithauser, copyright © 1986 by Brad Leithauser. Used by permission of Alfred A. Knopf, a division of Random House, Inc.

Levertov, Denise: "Caedmon" from BREATHING THE WATER, copyright © 1987 by Denise Levertov. "Scenes from the Life of the Peppertrees" and "Triple Feature" from COLLECTED EARLIER POEMS 1940–1960, copyright © 1957, 1958, 1959, 1960, 1961, 1979 by Denise Levertov. "O Taste and See" from POEMS 1960–1967, copyright © 1964 by Denise Levertov. "Tenebrae" from POEMS 1968–1972, copyright © 1968 by Denise Levertov. Reprinted by permission of New Directions Publishing Corp. and Pollinger Ltd.

Levine, Philip: "They Feed They Lion" and "You Can Have It" from NEW SELECTED POEMS by Philip Levine, copyright © 1991 by Philip Levine. "The Simple Truth" from THE SIMPLE TRUTH by Philip Levine, copyright © 1994 by Philip Levine. Used by permission of Alfred A. Knopf, a division of Random House, Inc.

Lewis, Alun: "All Day It Has Rained" from RAIDER'S DAWN by Alun Lewis. Copyright © 1941 by Alun Lewis. "Song" and "Goodbye" from HA! HA! AMONG THE TRUMPETS by Alun Lewis. Copyright © 1945 by Alun Lewis. Reprinted by permission of HarperCollins Publishers Ltd.

Lewis, C. Day: "Two Songs" and "Where are the War Poets" from THE COMPLETE POEMS OF C. DAY LEWIS, published by Sinclair-Stevenson (1992), copyright © 1992 in this edition, and the Estate of C. Day Lewis. Reprinted by permission of Random House Group Ltd.

Longley, Michael: "Gorse Fires" and "Ghetto" from GORSE FIRES. Copyright © 1991 by Michael Longley. "The Linen Industry" from POEMS 1963–1983. Copyright © 1983 by Michael Longley. Reprinted with the permission of the author and Wake Forest University Press.

Lorde, Audre: "Coal" from UNDERSONG: CHOSEN POEMS OLD AND NEW by Audre Lorde. Copyright © 1973, 1970, 1968 by Audre Lorde. Used by permission of W. W. Norton & Co., Inc. and Abner Stein Ltd. "Echoes" from THE MARVELOUS ARITHMETICS OF DISTANCE: POEMS 1987–1992 by Audre Lorde. Copyright © 1993 by Audre Lorde. Used by permission of W. W. Norton & Co., Inc. and Abner Stein Ltd. "From the House of Yemanjá" from THE BLACK UNICORN by Audre Lorde. Copyright © 1978 by Audre Lorde. Used by permission of W. W. Norton & Co., Inc.

Lowell, Robert: "The Quaker Graveyard in Nantucket" and "Mr. Edwards and the Spider" from LORD WEARY'S CASTLE, copyright © 1946 and renewed 1974 by Robert Lowell, reprinted by permission of Harcourt, Inc. and Faber & Faber Ltd. "Epilogue," "For the Union Dead," "Harriet" (p. 607), "My Last Afternoon with Uncle Devereux Winslow," "Skunk Hour," and "Water" from COLLECTED POEMS by Robert Lowell. Copyright © 2003 by Harriet Lowell and Sheridan Lowell. Reprinted by permission of Farrar, Straus & Giroux, LLC and Faber & Faber Ltd.

Lowry, Malcolm: "Delirium in Vera Cruz" and "Strange Type" from SELECTED POEMS OF MALCOLM LOWRY, ed. by Earle Birney with the assistance of Margerie Lowry. Copyright © 1962 by Margerie Lowry. Reprinted by permission of City Lights Books. "The Wild Cherry" and "Eye-Opener" from THE COLLECTED POETRY OF MALCOLM LOWRY, ed. by Kathleen Scherf. Copyright by The Estate of Malcolm Lowry. Reprinted by permission of SLL/Sterling Lord Literistic, Inc.

MacCaig, Norman: "Kingfisher," "Summer Farm," and "Return to Scalpay" from COLLECTED POEMS by Norman MacCaig, published by Chatto & Windus. Used by permission of The Random House Group Ltd.

MacDiarmid, Hugh: "Another Epitaph on an Army of Mercenaries," from SELECTED POETRY, ed. by Alan Riach and Michael Grieve. Copyright © 1992 by Michael Grieve. Reprinted by permission of New Directions Publishing Corp. and Carcanet Press Ltd. Excerpt from "Lament for the Great Music" and excerpt from "In Memoriam James Joyce" from COMPLETE POEMS, ed. by Michael Grieve and W. R. Aitken (1993). Copyright © 1993 by Michael Grieve. Reprinted by permission of Carcanet Press Ltd.

MacLeish, Archibald: "Ars Poetica" and "The Snowflake Which Is Now and Hence Forever" from COLLECTED POEMS 1917–1982 by Archibald MacLeish. Copyright © 1985 by The Estate of Archibald MacLeish. Reprinted by permission of Houghton Mifflin Co. All rights reserved.

MacNeice, Louis: Excerpt from "Autumn Journal," "The Sunlight on the Garden," "Bagpipe Music," "London Rain," and "Star-Gazer" from THE COLLECTED POEMS OF LOUIS MACNEICE, ed. by E. R. Dodds. Published by Faber & Faber Ltd. Reprinted with the permission of David Higham Associates Ltd.

O'Brien, Sean: "Cousin Coat" from COUSIN COAT: SELECTED POEMS, 1976–2001 by Sean O'Brien and "Welcome, Major Poet!" from DOWNRIVER by Sean O'Brien. Reprinted by permission of the publisher Pan Macmillan, London, UK.

O'Hara, Frank: "Why I Am Not a Painter," from COLLECTED POEMS by Frank O'Hara, copyright © 1971 by Maureen Granville-Smith, Administratrix of the Estate of Frank O'Hara. Used by permission of Alfred A. Knopf, a division of Random House, Inc. "The Day Lady Died," "How to Get There," and "Ave Maria" from LUNCH POEMS by Frank O'Hara. Copyright © 1964 by Frank O'Hara. Reprinted by permission of City Lights Books.

Olson, Charles: "Merce of Egypt" and "Variations Done for Gerald Van de Wiele" from COLLECTED POETRY OF CHARLES OLSON, tr. and ed. by George Butterick. Copyright © 1987 Estate of Charles Olson (previously published poetry), © 1987 University of Connecticut (previously unpublished poetry). Reprinted with the permission of the University of California Press.

Ondaatje, Michael: "Driving with Dominic in the Southern Province We See Hints of the Circus" and "House on a Red Cliff" from HANDWRITING by Michael Ondaatje, copyright © 1987 by Michael Ondaatje. Used by permission of Ellen Levine Literary Agency/Trident Media Group and Bloomsbury Publishing PLC. "Letters and Other Worlds" from THE CINNAMON PEELER, copyright © 1979, 1989 by Michael Ondaatje. Reprinted by permission of Alfred A. Knopf, a division of Random House, Inc. and Ellen Levine Literary Agency/Trident Media Group.

Ormond, John: "Cathedral Builders" and "Lament for a Leg" from CATHEDRAL BUILDERS AND OTHER POEMS by John Ormond (1991). Reprinted by permission of Glenys Ormond Thomas.

Ormsby, Eric: "Starfish" and "Skunk Cabbage" from COASTLINES by Eric Ormsby. Copyright © 1992 by Eric Ormsby. Reprinted by permission of ECW Press, Toronto, Canada. "Origins" from FOR A MODEST GOD by Eric Ormsby. Copyright © 1997 by Eric Ormsby. Used by permission of Grove/Atlantic, Inc.

Page, P. K.: "Stories of Snow" and "Deaf-Mute in the Pear Tree" from THE HIDDEN ROOM (in 2 vols.) by P. K. Page (Erin, Ontario: The Porcupine's Quill, 1997). Reprinted by permission of the publisher.

Palmer, Michael: "I Do Not" from THE PROMISES OF GLASS, copyright © 1999 by Michael Palmer. Reprinted by permission of New Directions Publishing Corp. "Of this cloth doll which" from FIRST FIGURE, copyright © 1984 by Michael Palmer. Reprinted by permission of the author.

Parker, Dorothy: "Unfortunate Coincidence," "Résumé," and "One Perfect Rose" from DOROTHY PARKER: COMPLETE POEMS, published in Great Britain in THE COLLECTED DOROTHY PARKER. Copyright © 1999 by The National Association for the Advancement of Colored People. Reprinted by permission of Penguin, a division of Penguin Group (USA), Inc. and Gerald Duckworth & Co. Ltd.

"Pearl": Excerpt from PEARL, by anonymous, ed. and tr. by Sara de Ford and others. Copyright © 1967 by Harlan Davidson, Inc. Reprinted by permission.

Pinsky, Robert: "Essay on Psychiatrists, IV and V" from SADNESS AND HAPPINESS, copyright © 1975 by Princeton University Press. Reprinted with the permission of the author and the publisher. "ABC" from JERSEY RAIN by Robert Pinsky. Copyright © 2000 by Robert Pinsky. "A Long Branch Song" and "The Street" from THE FIGURED WHEEL: NEW AND COLLECTED POEMS 1966–1996 by Robert Pinsky. Copyright © 1996 by Robert Pinsky. Reprinted by permission of Farrar, Straus & Giroux, LLC.

Plath, Sylvia: "Ariel," "Elm," "Tulips," "Morning Song," "Lady Lazarus," and "Daddy" from ARIEL by Sylvia Plath. Copyright © 1961, 1962, 1963, 1965 by Ted Hughes. Copyright renewed. From ARIEL by Sylvia Plath. Reprinted by permission of HarperCollins Publishers, Inc. and Faber & Faber Ltd. "Colossus" from THE COLOSSUS AND OTHER POEMS by Sylvia Plath, copyright © 1962 by Sylvia Plath. Used by permission of Alfred A. Knopf, a division of Random House, Inc. and Faber & Faber Ltd.

Porter, Peter: "A Consumer's Report," "An Angel in Blythburgh Church," and "An Exequy" from COLLECTED POEMS. Copyright © 1983 by Peter Porter. Reprinted with permission of the author.

Pound, Ezra: "Portrait d'une Femme," "The Garden," "A Pact," "Ts'ai Chi'h," "In a Station of the Metro," "The River-Merchant's Wife: a Letter," "Hugh Selwyn Mauberley: Life and Contacts," "Medallion," and "The Seafarer" from PERSONAE, copyright © 1926 by Ezra Pound. Canto I and Canto XLV from THE CANTOS OF EZRA POUND, copyright © 1934, 1937, 1940, 1948, 1956, 1959, 1962, 1963, 1966, and 1968 by Ezra Pound. Reprinted by permission of New Directions Publishing Corp. and Faber & Faber Ltd.

Pratt, E. J.: "Come Not the Seasons Here" and "From Stone to Steel" from E. J. Pratt, COMPLETE POEMS, ed. by Sandra Djwa and R. G. Mayles. Copyright © 1989 by University of Toronto Press. Reprinted with permission of the publisher.

Raine, Craig: "The Onion Memory," "A Martian Sends a Postcard Home," and "For Hans Keller" from COLLECTED POEMS, 1978–1999 by Craig Raine. Reprinted by permission of David Godwin Associates on behalf of the author.

Ralegh, Sir Walter: "Fortune Hath Taken Thee Away, My Love" from "A Lost Poem by Queen Elizabeth 1" by L. G. Black, TIMES LITERARY SUPPLEMENT, May 23, 1968, 535. Reprinted by permission.

Ramanujan, A. K.: "Snakes," "Breaded Fish," and "Self-Portrait" from THE STRIDERS by A. K. Ramanujan (1966). Reprinted with the permission of the Estate of A. K. Ramanujan.

Randall, Dudley: "Ballad of Birmingham" from POEM COUNTERPOEM by Margaret Danner and Dudley Randall (Detroit: Broadside Press, 1969). Copyright © 1966 by Margaret Danner and Dudley Randall. Reprinted with the permission of Dudley Randall.

Ransom, John Crowe: From SELECTED POEMS, 3rd ed., revised and enlarged by John Crowe Ransom, copyright © 1924, 1927 by Alfred A. Knopf, Inc. and renewed 1952, 1955 by John Crowe Ransom. Used by permission of Alfred A. Knopf, a division of Random House, Inc. and Carcanet Press Ltd.

Reed, Henry: "Chard Whitlow" and "Lessons of War 1, 2" from COLLECTED POEMS of Henry Reed (1991), ed. by Jon Stallworthy. Reprinted by permission of Oxford University Press (UK).

Rich, Adrienne: Parts 1 and 8 of "Eastern War Time" from AN ATLAS OF THE DIFFICULT WORLD: POEMS 1988–1991 by Adrienne Rich. Copyright © 1991 by Adrienne Rich. "Modotti" from MIDNIGHT SALVAGE: POEMS 1995–1998 by Adrienne Rich. Copyright © 1999 by Adrienne Rich. "Aunt Jennifer's Tigers," copyright © 2002, 1951 by Adrienne Rich. "Snapshots of a Daughter-in-Law," copyright © 2002, 1967, 1963 by Adrienne Rich. "Orion," copyright © 2002 by Adrienne Rich. Copyright © 1969 by W. W. Norton & Co., Inc. "A Valediction Forbidding Mourning," copyright © 2002

by Stephen Spender. "Seascape," copyright © 1947 by Stephen Spender, from POEMS OF DEDICATION by Stephen Spender. Used by permission of Random House, Inc. and Ed Victor Ltd.

Stein, Gertrude: From "Stanzas in Meditation" from STANZAS IN MEDITATION AND OTHER POEMS. Used by permission of the Estate of Gertrude Stein, through its Literary Executor, Mr. Stanford Gann, Jr. of Levin & Gann, P.A.

Stevens, Wallace: From THE COLLECTED POEMS OF WALLACE STEVENS by Wallace Stevens, copyright © 1954 by Wallace Stevens and renewed 1982 by Holly Stevens. Used by permission of Alfred A. Knopf, a division of Random House, Inc. and Faber & Faber Ltd.

Stevenson, Anne: "Temporarily in Oxford" from THE COLLECTED POEMS 1955–1995 (Bloodaxe Books, 2000) and "Arioso Dolente" from GRANNY SCARECROW (Bloodaxe Books, 2000). Reprinted by permission of the publisher.

Strand, Mark: "Always" from THE CONTINUOUS LIFE by Mark Strand, copyright © 1990 by Mark Strand. Part XVI and XX from THE DARK HARBOR by Mark Strand, copyright © 1993 by Mark Strand. "The Prediction" from SELECTED POEMS by Mark Strand, copyright © 1979, 1980 by Mark Strand. Used by permission of Alfred A. Knopf, a division of Random House, Inc.

Swenson, May: "Motherhood" from NATURE by May Swenson. Copyright © 1994 by The Literary Estate of May Swenson. Reprinted by permission of Houghton Mifflin Co. All rights reserved. "Cardinal Ideograms" from THE COMPLETE POEMS TO SOLVE by May Swenson. "Waterbird" and "Goodbye, Goldeneye" from IN OTHER WORDS by May Swenson. Used with permission of The Literary Estate of May Swenson.

Tate, Allen: "Ode to the Confederate Dead" and "The Swimmers" from COLLECTED POEMS 1919–1976 by Allen Tate. Copyright © 1977 by Allen Tate. Reprinted by permission of Farrar, Straus & Giroux, LLC.

Thomas, Dylan: "The Force That Through the Green Fuse Drives the Flower," "The Hand That Signed the Paper," copyright © 1939 by New Directions Publishing Corp., "After the Funeral," copyright © 1938 by New Directions Publishing Corp., "The Hunchback in the Park," copyright © 1943 by New Directions Publishing Corp., "A Refusal to Mourn the Death, by Fire, of a Child in London," "Fern Hill," copyright © 1945 by The Trustees for the Copyrights of Dylan Thomas, "In My Craft or Sullen Art," copyright © 1946 by New Directions Publishing Corp., "Do Not Go Gentle into That Good Night," copyright © 1952 by Dylan Thomas, and "The Conversation of Prayer," copyright © 1967 by The Trustees for the Copyrights of Dylan Thomas, from THE POEMS OF DYLAN THOMAS. Reprinted by permission of New Directions Publishing Corp. and David Higham Associates.

Thomas, R. S.: "Welsh Language," "The View from the Window," "On the Farm," and "Lore" from COLLECTED POEMS, reprinted by permission of J. M. Dent, a division of The Orion Publishing Group, as the publisher.

Tomlinson, Charles: "Farewell to Van Gogh," "The Picture of J.T. in a Prospect of Stone," "Mr. Brodsky" from COLLECTED POEMS (1987) and "Ararat" from THE RETURN (1987). Reprinted by permission of Carcanet Press Ltd.

Toomer, Jean: "Face," "Georgia Dusk," "Harvest Song," "Portrait in Georgia," "Reapers" from CANE by Jean Toomer. Copyright © 1923 by Boni & Liveright, renewed 1951 by Jean Toomer. Used by permission of Liveright Publishing Corp.

Updike, John: "V.B. Nimble, V.B. Quick" from COLLECTED POEMS 1953–1993 by John Updike, copyright © 1993 by John Updike. Published in Great Britain in HOPING FOR A HOOPOE by John Updike. Used by permission of Alfred A. Knopf, a division of Random House, Inc. and Victor Gollancz, a division of The Orion Publishing Group, as the publishers. "I Missed His Book, But I Read His Name" from COLLECTED POEMS 1953–1993 by John Updike, copyright © 1993 by John Updike. First published in TELEPHONE POLES AND OTHER POEMS by Deutsch 1963, Hamish Hamilton 1993, copyright © 1961, 1993 by John Updike. Used by permission of Alfred A. Knopf, a division of Random House, Inc. and Penguin Books Ltd.

Van Duyn, Mona: "Letters from a Father" and "Falling in Love at Sixty-Five" from IF IT NOT BE I by Mona Van Duyn, copyright © 1959 by Mona Van Duyn. Used by permission of Alfred A. Knopf, a division of Random House, Inc.

Walcott, Derek: "The Gulf" from THE GULF AND OTHER POEMS by Derek Walcott. Copyright © 1970, renewed 1998 by Derek Walcott. Used by permission of Farrar, Straus & Giroux, LLC and Jonathan Cape c/o The Random House Group Ltd. "XXVII" from Midsummer, "A Far Cry from Africa," "The Glory Trumpeter," "Nights in the Gardens of Port of Spain," and "Adios, Carenage" from "The Schooner Flight" from COLLECTED POEMS 1948–1984 by Derek Walcott. Copyright © 1986 by Derek Walcott. Reprinted by permission of Farrar, Straus & Giroux, LLC and Faber and Faber Ltd. Excerpt from OMEROS by Derek Walcott. Copyright © 1990 by Derek Walcott. Reprinted by permission of Farrar, Straus & Giroux, LLC and Faber & Faber Ltd.

Walker, Margaret: "Since 1619" and "Childhood" from THIS IS MY CENTURY: NEW AND COLLECTED POEMS by Margaret Walker. Copyright © 1987 by Margaret Walker. Reprinted by permission of The University of Georgia Press.

Warren, Robert Penn: "Bearded Oaks," "Masts at Dawn," "Evening Hawk," and "There's a Grandfather Clock in the Hall" from THE COLLECTED POEMS OF ROBERT PENN WARREN. Copyright © 1998 by Estate of Robert Penn Warren. Reprinted by permission of William Morris Agency, Inc. on behalf of the Estate of Robert Penn Warren.

Wilbur, Richard: "Piazza di Spagna, Early Morning," "A Baroque Wall-Fountain in the Villa Sciarra," "Love Calls Us to the Things of This World," and "A Plain Song for Comadre" from THINGS OF THIS WORLD, copyright © 1956 and renewed 1984 by Richard Wilbur, reprinted by permission of Harcourt, Inc. "Advice to a Prophet," copyright © 1959 and renewed 1987 by Richard Wilbur, and "Junk," copyright © 1961 and renewed 1989 by Richard Wilbur, from ADVICE TO A PROPHET AND OTHER POEMS, reprinted by permission of Harcourt, Inc. "First Snow in Alsace" from THE BEAUTIFUL CHANGES AND OTHER POEMS, copyright © 1947 and renewed 1975 by Richard Wilbur, reprinted by permission of Harcourt, Inc. "Cottage Street, 1953" from THE MIND-READER, copyright © 1972 by Richard Wilbur, reprinted by permission of Harcourt, Inc. and Faber & Faber Ltd. "Zea" from MAYFLIES: NEW POEMS AND TRANSLATIONS, copyright © 2000 by Richard Wilbur, reprinted by permission of Harcourt, Inc.

Williams, C. K.: "Repression" and Snow: II" from FLESH AND BLOOD. Copyright © 1987 by C. K. Williams. "The Question" from DREAM OF MIND. Copyright © 1992 by C. K. Williams. These poems were published in SELECTED POEMS by C. K. Williams. Copyright © 1994 by C. K. Williams. Reprinted by permission of Farrar, Straus & Giroux, LLC and Bloodaxe Books Ltd.

Williams, William Carlos: "Danse Russe," "Portrait of a Lady," "The Red Wheelbarrow," "Queen-Anne's-Lace," "This Is Just to Say," "Poem," "The Yachts" from COLLECTED POEMS: 1909–1939, vol. 1, copyright © 1938 by New Directions

Publishing Corp. "A Sort of a Song," and "Asphodel, That Greeny Flower, Book I" from COLLECTED POEMS 1939–1962, vol. 2, copyright © 1944 by William Carlos Williams, "Landscape with the Fall of Icarus" from COLLECTED POEMS 1939–1962, vol. 2, copyright © 1953 by William Carlos Williams. Reprinted by permission of New Directions Publishing Corp. and Carcanet Press Ltd.

Williamson, Greg: "Double Exposures, III and XXV" and "New Year's: A Short Pantoum" from ERRORS IN THE SCRIPT, copyright © 2001 by Greg Williamson. Reprinted with the permission of The Overlook Press. "Outbound" from THE SILENT PARTNER by Greg Williamson. Reprinted with permission of the author and Story Line Press (www. storylinepress.com).

Wilner, Eleanor: "Reading the Bible Backwards" and "High Noon at Los Alamos" from SARAH'S CHOICE (Chicago: University of Chicago Press, 1989). Reprinted by permission of the author.

Wright, Charles: "Quotations" from APPALACHIA by Charles Wright. Copyright © 1998 by Charles Wright. "As Our Bodies Rise, Our Names Turn into Light" from CHICKAMAUGA by Charles Wright. Copyright © 1995 by Charles Wright. "Chinese Journal" and "Homage to Claude Lorrain" from THE WORLD OF TEN THOUSAND THINGS: POEMS 1980–1990 by Charles Wright. Copyright © 1990 by Charles Wright. Reprinted by permission of Farrar, Straus & Giroux, LLC.

Wright, James: "A Note Left in Jimmy Leonard's Shack," "A Blessing," and "Speak" from ST. JUDAS. Copyright © 1959 by James Wright. Reprinted by permission of Wesleyan University Press.

Wright, Judith: "Woman to Man," "Train Journey," "Eve to Her Daughters," and "Request to a Year" from A HUMAN PATTERN: SELECTED POEMS (ETT Imprint, Sydney, 1996). Reprinted by permission of the publisher.

Wright, Kit: "A Love Song of Tooting," "Mantles," "My Version" from HOPING IT MIGHT BE SO by Kit Wright (Leviathan, 2000). Reprinted by permission of the author.

Wright, Richard: Reprinted from HAIKU: THIS OTHER WORLD by Richard Wright, published by Arcade Publishing, New York, N.Y. Copyright © 1998 by Ellen Wright. Reprinted by permission of the publisher and John Hawkins & Associates, Inc.

Yeats, W. B.: "Sailing to Byzantium," "Leda and the Swan," "Among School Children," copyright © 1928 by The Macmillan Company; copyright renewed 1956 by Georgie Yeats. "Byzantium," "Crazy Jane Talks with the Bishop," copyright © 1933 by The Macmillan Company, copyright renewed 1961 by Bertha Georgie Yeats. "Lapis Lazuli," "Long-Legged Fly," "The Circus Animals' Desertion," "Under Ben Bulben," copyright © 1940 by Georgie Yeats, copyright renewed 1968 by Bertha Georgie Yeats, Michael Butler Yeats, and Anne Yeats. Reprinted with the permission of Scribner, an imprint of Simon & Schuster Adult Publishing Group, from THE COLLECTED WORKS OF W. B. YEATS, VOLUME 1: THE POEMS, Revised, edited by Richard J. Finneran. Rights in the British Commonwealth excluding Canada were granted by A. P. Watt Ltd. on behalf of Michael B. Yeats.

Zarin, Cynthia: "The Ant Hill" and "Song" from FIRE LYRIC by Cynthia Zarin, copyright © 1993 by Cynthia Zarin. Used by permission of Alfred A. Knopf, a division of Random House, Inc.

Every effort has been made to contact the copyright holders of each selection. Rights holders of any selection not credited should contact W. W. Norton & Co., Inc., 500 Fifth Avenue, New York, NY 10110, for a correction to be made in the next reprinting of our work.

Index